SEQUELS

SEQUELS

An Annotated Guide to Novels in Series

FOURTH EDITION

Janet G. Husband
&
Jonathan F. Husband

AMERICAN LIBRARY ASSOCIATION

CHICAGO   2009

JANET AND JONATHAN HUSBAND had long and productive careers in public and college libraries, respectively. Janet was director of the Rockland Memorial Library and the Paul Pratt Memorial Library, both in Massachusetts. Jon was reference librarian at Boston State College and Framingham State College. They met and married while they were both working at their first jobs at the Free Library of Philadelphia. Now happily retired, they live on Cape Cod with their two dogs and three computers. The first edition of *Sequels* was published in 1982 and became a best seller for ALA that year. Subsequent editions were well received. Janet earned her MLS at Rutgers University. Jon holds an MA in English from the University of Pennsylvania and an MLS from Drexel University.

Library of Congress Cataloging-in-Publication Data

Husband, Janet, 1942–
    Sequels : an annotated guide to novels in series / Janet G. Husband and Jonathan F. Husband. — 4th ed.
        p. cm.
    Includes bibliographical references and index.
    ISBN 978-0-8389-0967-6 (alk. paper)
    1. Fiction—Bibliography. 2. Sequels (Literature)—Bibliography. I. Husband, Jonathan F. II. Title.
    Z5917.S44H87 2009
    [PN3448.S47]
    016.80883—dc22   2009016426

ISBN-13: 978-0-8389-0967-6

Printed in the United States of America

13 12 11 10 09   5 4 3 2 1

■ CONTENTS

■ PREFACE

The fourth edition of *Sequels* differs from the first three editions in that it was composed online as a database (http://esequels.com). All the authors and series in the first three editions have been retained in revised and updated entries, and many new series created since 1997 have been added. This edition, like the previous ones, is a joint effort by Janet and Jonathan Husband.

The basic format and philosophy of *Sequels* remains unchanged; series likely to be found in a medium-sized public library collection are still emphasized. The growth of library networks and online catalogs and the increased use of paperbacks in libraries have prompted us to broaden our scope somewhat. As always, the authors make no claim to comprehensiveness.

In selecting titles for inclusion, we have used the following criteria for defining a series:

1. Primarily, a series shows development of plot or character from book to book. Most works listed here fit this requirement.
2. Books where chronology is minimal or debatable, but share a cast of characters and/or location, such as Narayan's Malgudi series
3. Books that were conceived as a series by the author, such as Durrell's Alexandria Quartet or Mishima's Sea of Tranquility

Only novels in series are listed. Nonfiction is excluded, although borderline cases such as Flora Thompson's Lark Rise series are listed. James Herriot's best-sellers about a Yorkshire veterinarian are excluded, since they are always classed as nonfiction. Series that exist only in short story form, such as Chesterton's Father Brown mysteries, are excluded; but short story collections related to a series of novels are noted.

Series aimed at juvenile or young adult audiences are generally excluded, but exceptions have been made for series that have a large and loyal adult audience, such as Lewis Carroll's Alice books and L. M. Montgomery's Anne of Green Gables. Series that have not been published or distributed in the United States are generally excluded. Series in languages other than English are not included unless some of the novels in the series have been translated into English.

On the question of literary merit, we have sought to balance considerations of artistic quality with those of popularity. Hence, when in doubt about the inclusion of a work, we tried to gauge its availability in library collections. These guidelines still leave a great deal of latitude for the compilers. The decisions to include one author and not another were in the end pragmatic ones based on our estimate of which authors are more likely to be read.

Editions listed are the first American editions unless otherwise noted; variant titles and other editions are noted as necessary. Except where indicated, the title numbering represents the *preferred order for reading*. Thus publication dates will not necessarily correspond to the numbered order. Where chronology is nonexistent, unimportant, or impossible to decipher, numbering follows the order of publication.

Entries have the same format as the previous editions of *Sequels*. Series are listed alphabetically by the cover-name of the author; pseudonymous authors are listed under their pseudonym with relevant cross-references. Title entries are usually very brief, just enough to give the reader an idea of what the title is about and where it fits into the series. If available, we list film and television adaptations, omnibus collections, author biographies and other publications of interest. New in this edition is the inclusion of author websites. Please note, however, that web addresses change frequently, so you can expect that some of our citations may no longer be correct.

In addition to our own familiarity with the works included in *Sequels*, we have gathered information from publishers, author websites, reviews, and referrals by friends and colleagues. While *Sequels* is used primarily in readers' advisory work, we understand its potential for reference use and have tried to be as accurate as possible.

ANNOTATED SERIES

Ab Hugh, Dafydd

I. This pair of novels by American writer Dafydd Ab Hugh featuring a swordswoman with magical powers, Jiana Analena, looks superficially like standard sword-and-sorcery fare, but there are differences. Jiana, despite her powers, is a very insecure and vulnerable character, given to second thoughts about her actions and motivations, and Ab Hugh questions the premises of the subgenre.

1. *Heroing* (Baen, 1987) Young Jiana Analena wishes to join the quest of Prince Alanai for the World's Dream, a magical artifact with the power to grant one wish, but is rejected because she is a woman.
2. *Warrior Wards* (Baen, 1990) Some years after the events in *Heroing*, Jiana is having second thoughts about her protégé, Dida, who has turned into an arrogant military type, so she adopts Radience, a girl with a disfigured arm, whom she trains to be a warrior.

II. Another pair of novels combines time travel and Arthurian legend. Pete Smythe, on the trail of the IRA, finds that a female agent has sent her mind back to the 5th century CE. In the course of events, Smythe finds his own consciousness transferred to Arthur's court, where he finds himself engaged in a struggle involving magic and modern technology.

1. *Arthur War Lord* (Avon, 1994) Twentieth-century security officer Pete Smythe, investigating IRA involvement in a top-secret British military-research project, discovers that a female IRA agent has sent her mind back to the 5th century CE and has the power to alter the present by tampering with the past.
2. *Far beyond the Wave* (Avon, 1994) Pete Smythe's consciousness has entered the mind of the legendary hero Lancelot, and it is up to Pete/Lancelot to resolve a situation with grave implications for humanity.

III. A trilogy of psychological suspense novels is about a hiking trip gone bad and its aftermath. Jeannette, one of five friends who embark on the trip, is the main character. She is forced to come to terms with some terrible secrets, some of which, perhaps, are her own.

1. *Swept Away* (HarperCollins, 1996) Five friends set off on a hiking trip, which becomes a struggle for survival when a flash flood cuts off Jeannette and Bill from the rest of the group.
2. *Mountain, The* (HarperCollins, 1996) Jeannette, who has survived the flood and her confrontation with Bill, finds that the rest of the group is dubious about her story.
3. *Pit, The* (HarperCollins, 1996) Six months after the hike, Jeannette finds that her new boyfriend, Neil, is hiding a terrible secret.

IV. Ab Hugh collaborated with Brad Linaweaver on four novels based on the computer game *Doom*. They are standard space operas in which a few good men are pitted against monstrosities from "Outside" who wish to destroy Earth and most of the rest of the universe.

1. *Knee-Deep in the Dead* (Pocket, 1995) A large expedition team sent to Phobos, the moon of Mars, meets with disaster.
2. *Hell on Earth* (Pocket, 1995) The one survivor of the Phobos disaster returns to Earth and finds the same menace awaiting him there.
3. *Infernal Sky* (Pocket, 1996) Corporal Flynn Taggart of the US Marine Corps is Earth's only defense against hostile alien invaders.
4. *Endgame* (Pocket, 1996) Flynn Taggart, promoted to sergeant, and PFC Arlene Sanders journey to outer space and discover

that, although the war for Earth is over, the war in the rest of the universe has just started.

Abbey, Edward

Although he was born on a farm in Appalachia, Edward Abbey is indelibly associated with the deserts of the American Southwest, described eloquently in such books as *Desert Solitaire* (McGraw-Hill, 1968). Abbey wrote several other volumes of nonfiction and nine novels. One novel, *The Monkey Wrench Gang*, became an underground classic. *The Monkey Wrench Gang* describes the efforts of four environmental terrorists who throw a "monkey wrench" into the works of the developers and industrialists who are destroying the beauty of the natural landscape. They blow up bulldozers and power lines but not people. A posthumously published sequel resurrected the gang 15 years later. Abbey, a self-proclaimed "agrarian anarchist," also wrote the autobiographical *One Life at a Time, Please* (Holt, 1988). Among the biographies and memoirs about Abbey is James Bishop Jr.'s *Epitaph for a Desert Anarchist: The Life and Legacy of Edward Abbey* (Atheneum, 1994).

1. *Monkey Wrench Gang, The* (Lippincott, 1975) An oddly assorted group, led by Vietnam veteran George Hayduke, bands together to disrupt technological encroachment on the environment. Ultimate target: Glen Canyon Dam.
2. *Hayduke Lives!* (Little, Brown, 1990) Hayduke, long believed dead, returns to galvanize the gang into renewed action against strip miners, developers, and other industrial scum.

Abbey, Lynn (Marilyn Lorraine)

I. Lynn Abbey's fantasy series Orion's Children concerns Emma Merrigan, who has magical powers inherited from her long-lost mother. Eventually Emma becomes a time traveler, finds her mother, and combats curses from the past that impinge upon the present and future. Lynn Abbey is perhaps best known for her creation, along with her former husband, the late Robert Lynn Asprin (d. 2008; q.v.), of Thieves' World, one of the original shared-world series. Thieves' World is primarily a series of fiction anthologies, edited by Abbey and Asprin, to each of which several SF/fantasy authors contribute stories or chapters. Abbey has also written *Sanctuary* (Tor, 2002), a novel in the series.

Abbey has also contributed three novels to the Dark Sun series, as well as two volumes in the Forgotten Realms series, and contributions to the Elfquest series, the Artefacts cycle, and, with then-husband Asprin, a volume in the Batman series. Abbey spent some 15 years as a systems analyst before she became a full-time author.

1. *Out of Time* (Ace, 2000) When librarian Emma Merrigan discovers a terrified young girl hiding in the library, bad memories of her childhood and the unused magical powers she inherited from her mother, whom she believes long dead, are reawakened.
2. *Behind Time* (Ace, 2001) Emma must restore her comatose mother by more or less harrowing hell.
3. *Taking Time* (Ace, 2004) Emma, now 50 years old, with a mother who looks and acts as if she were in her twenties, is forced to confront her own identity and exorcise a century-old curse.
4. *Down Time* (Ace, 2005) Emma and her mother take a Caribbean cruise to recuperate and to reconcile their differences. But then Emma encounters a passenger operating under a curse.

II. Abbey has produced several short fantasy series. They are set in different worlds, in well-realized, if cheerless, settings. The "good" characters tend to be somewhat more flawed than the usual fantasy heroes: admirable, maybe, but not very likable. The Rifkind Saga is about a young woman, Rifkind, who is a warrior, priestess, healer, and witch rolled into one, the only one in her world with the power to defeat the evil gods.

1. *Daughter of the Bright Moon* (Ace, 1979) Rifkind, a chieftain's daughter, learns how to fight rather than be relegated to the kitchen and the nursery. When her clan is massacred, she sets out on a search for her own destiny.
2. *Black Flame, The* (Ace, 1980) Rifkind sets out again at the behest of her deity, the Goddess of the Bright Moon, to search out the source of the mysterious Black Flame. Variant title: *Black Fire*.
3. *Rifkind's Challenge* (Tor, 2006) Although she thought that she had found a home where she could raise her son, Rifkind once again hears a personal call to arms.

III. The Unicorn and Dragon Saga is set in an alternative medieval England at the time of the Norman Conquest. Two sisters, Alison and Wildecent, have to meet the challenges of love with the same man and the Norman invasion. Magic plays a role in the rivalry of the Saxon Wicca and the Norman wizard Ambrose.

1. *Unicorn and Dragon* (Avon, 1987) Alison and Wildecent, two sisters living at the Saxon manor of Hafwynder in 11th-century England, are forced by the arrival of a wounded stranger to face their own destinies.
2. *Conquest* (Avon, 1988) Alison and Wildecent are caught up in the Norman invasion, as the rival sides pit their warriors and wizards against each other. UK title: *The Green Man*.

IV. The Ultima Saga is also set in an alternative medieval world, in which four rather ill-assorted people, young noble Jordan, his brother Squirt, blacksmith Drumon, and the damsel Althea, go in search of Althea's brother, the magician Balthan. They find Balthan, but their adventures do not end there.

1. *Forge of Virtue, The* (Popular Library, 1991) In a rather anarchical Brittania, whose ruler has disappeared and whose Council of the Mages has gone into hiding, Althea, Jordan, Squirt, and Drumon, a rather miscellaneous quartet, each with his or her own problems, set out on a quest to find Althea's missing brother, Balthan.
2. *Temper of Wisdom, The* (Warner, 1992) Jordan, his companions, and the rescued Balthan return home to find Hawksnest under a spell by the evil sorcerer, Inquisitor Lohgrin.

V. The two-novel Walensor Saga is also set in a fictional medieval milieu, this time in a world protected by the Web, which separates men and gods in the world of Walensor. Young shepherdess Berika, on the verge of an enforced marriage with the physically and psychologically maimed Hirmin, escapes with the possible "fetch" (or demon) Dart and has a series of adventures before the events are somewhat resolved.

1. *Wooden Sword, The* (Ace, 1991) Young Berika, facing a hideous marriage, enlists the help of Dart, a possible demon, and leaves her village en route to Eyerlon, capital of the land.
2. *Beneath the Web* (Ace, 1994) Berika is the mistress of a nobleman in Eyerlon. The Web, which is the network of power in Walensor, is threatened by enemies.

Abbott, Jeff

I. Jordan Poteet is the town librarian in Mirabeau, Texas. Along with the usual budget and censorship problems, Jordan has the occasional murder to solve. Number 1 is a prequel set 20 years in the past.

1. *Promises to Keep* (Ballantine, 1996) In this prequel, 12-year-old Jordan Poteet and five friends find the body of a teenage girl. Then Jordan's friends are murdered, one by one.
2. *Do unto Others* (Ballantine, 1994) Jordan Poteet is introduced here. Having returned to Mirabeau, Texas, to help care for his sick mother, Jordan becomes the town librarian. Jordan has a run-in with Beta Harcher, the town's leading self-appointed censor. Then Beta turns up dead in the library.
3. *Only Good Yankee, The* (Ballantine, 1995) When developers come to Mirabeau wanting to buy up river property and build condos, there is considerable controversy, which leads to murder.
4. *Distant Blood* (Ballantine, 1996) Jordan's newly discovered biological father is part of a very rich clan. Jordan is invited to attend a reunion of the family on a remote Gulf Coast island.

II. Jordan Poteet and Mirabeau have been abandoned by Abbott, at least for now, in favor of a rather more violent series set on the Texas Gulf Coast and featuring a judge, Whit Mosley.

1. *Kiss Gone Bad, A* (New American Library, 2001) Rookie Texas judge Whit Mosley receives his baptism of fire when the black-sheep son of a senator is found dead aboard a yacht. The family of the dead man wants a verdict of suicide, but Mosley has suspicions of murder.
2. *Black Jack Point* (Onyx, 2002) A lost fortune in emeralds and gold is at the bottom of the murder of Mosley's friends at Black Jack Point.
3. *Cut and Run* (Onyx, 2003) Mosley investigates his own past when his dying father asks him to search for the mother who abandoned their family many years ago.

Ablow, Keith R(ussell)

Dr. Frank Clevenger is a forensic psychiatrist who works for the Lynn and other Boston-area police departments. Clevenger has his own demons to contend with: an abusive childhood, drink and drug problems, and difficulties maintaining relationships, but as the series progresses, he seems to be gaining in self-knowledge and self-control. The series has shown continuous improvement: the earlier novels tend to be somewhat violent and farfetched, while in the later ones, the bloodletting is down, and the plausibility is up. Keith Ablow is a forensic psychiatrist himself, working in the Boston area, and is the author of several nonfiction books.

1. *Denial* (Pantheon, 1997) Captain Emma Hancock of the Lynn, Massachusetts, police brings in Dr. Frank Clevenger on a case involving the murdered and mutilated body of a young woman, although Emma is inclined to suspect a schizophrenic who thinks he is General Westmoreland.
2. *Projection* (Pantheon, 1999) Plastic surgeon Trevor Lucas is accused of four murders, but Clevenger is covering up for Kathy Matheson, whom he believes is the real murderer.
3. *Compulsion* (St. Martin's, 2002) Old friend North Anderson, chief of police in Nantucket, brings Clevenger in on the case of an asphyxiated five-month-old baby.

4. *Psychopath* (St. Martin's, 2003) Clevenger, who has adopted troubled teen Billy Bishop, is chosen by FBI psychiatrist (and sometime lover) Whitney McCormick to go after a serial killer.
5. *Murder Suicide* (St. Martin's, 2004) Was the shooting outside of Massachusetts General Hospital of brilliant inventor John Snow murder or suicide?
6. *Architect, The* (St. Martin's, 2005) Architect West Crosse is regarded as a genius. Unfortunately he is also a madman and possibly the author of several serial murders in which the bodies have been surgically dissected.

Achebe, Chinua

Things Fall Apart is a literary landmark: it was one of the first, if not *the* first, novels about Africa written from a black African point of view and the first "classic" in English from tropical Africa. Since the 1960s, it has been on the syllabi of many world-literature or introduction to literature courses and on many high school and college reading lists, and it is the seemingly endless subject of literary and political exegesis. *Things Fall Apart* is set in the late 1800s. It details the destruction of an individual, Okonkwo, and the traditional way of life of an Ibo (now Nigerian) village in a fatal clash with European religion and mores. A subsequent novel, *No Longer at Ease*, set on the eve of Nigerian independence (1960), tells the later history of Nigeria through an extended flashback of the life of Okonkwo's grandson.

Achebe has written several other novels, including *Arrow of God* (Day, 1967), set in Nigeria in the 1920s; *A Man of the People* (Day, 1966), set in contemporary West Africa; and *Anthills of the Savannah* (Anchor, 1988), set in Kangan, an imaginary West African nation much like Nigeria. He also writes essays on politics and literature, poetry, and autobiography. After returning from exile, Achebe has been maintaining a very uneasy relationship with Nigeria's rulers.

1. *Things Fall Apart* (Obolensky, 1958) Okonkwo, wealthy farmer, wrestling champion, husband to three wives, and Ibo village leader in the late 1800s, runs afoul of the white man and his challenge to traditional Ibo religion and values.
2. *No Longer at Ease* (Obolensky, 1961) On the eve of Nigerian independence (1960), Obi Okonkwo, grandson of the protagonist in number 1, a product of Christian raising and English education and a Nigerian civil servant, is put on trial for accepting bribes. Told in a long flashback, Obi's story reveals the corruption of the native Nigerian elite.

Adair, Cherry

The Mercenary, Cherry Adair's first book, introduced the Terrorist Force Logistical Assault Command (T-FLAC), a supersecret, extralegal organization devoted to destroying enemies of America and other people its members don't like. *The Mercenary* was followed, after six years, by *Kiss and Tell*, the first of five books (numbers 2 to 6) about the Wright family, four brothers and a sister. Numbers 8 to 10 relate the exploits of the three Edge brothers. The novels, James Bond–type thrillers, told from a female (if not feminist) point of view, feature larger-than-life protagonists, really nasty villains, a large dollop of wizardry and extrasensory perception, suspense, and lots of steamy sex. Cherry Adair, a South African who has settled in the US, has written several other romantic suspense novels.

1. *Mercenary, The* (Harlequin, 1994) Tory Jones, realizing through telepathic communication that her twin brother is being held captive, enlists his partner, T-FLAC operative Marc Savin, in a rescue effort.
2. *Kiss and Tell* (Ivy, 2000) Marnie Wright trespasses on Jake Dolan's mountain property and finds she has stumbled upon a covert operation designed to eliminate Jake.
3. *Hide and Seek* (Ivy, 2001) Delanie Eastman, to find her missing sister, becomes the girlfriend of an international drug lord in the jungles of South America. Then she runs into Kyle Wright, with whom she had a short, torrid affair.
4. *In Too Deep* (Ivy, 2002) Tally Cruise, en route to meet Trevor Church, the father she has never seen, is rescued by Michael Wright, an ex–Navy SEAL posing as a sailing bum, who intends to destroy Trevor.
5. *Out of Sight* (Ivy, 2003) Rookie sharpshooter A. J. Cooper, sent on a T-FLAC mission to destroy a notorious terrorist in Egypt, falls in love with Kane Wright, her instructor.
6. *On Thin Ice* (Ballantine, 2004) Veterinarian Lily Munroe finds herself competing in the Iditarod in Alaska with Derek Wright, unbeknownst to her a T-FLAC agent on a mission.
7. *Hot Ice* (Ballantine, 2005) International jewel thief Taylor Kincaid gets more than she bargained for when she steals the Blue Star diamonds. Now she has top T-FLAC operative Hunter St. John hot on her trail.
8. *Edge of Danger* (Ballantine, 2006) In the first volume of the Edge brothers trilogy, Gabriel Edge unleashes his telepathic powers against beautiful and brilliant scientist Eden Cahill when a dangerous weapon is stolen from a covert lab in Arizona.
9. *Edge of Fear* (Ballantine, 2006) Caleb Edge's latest assignment is to follow Heather Shaw, whose father is well known for his terrorist ties.
10. *Edge of Darkness* (Ballantine, 2006) In the last installment in the trilogy, Duncan Edge joins his brothers in saving the world—and the women they love—from another terrorist threat.
11. *White Heat* (Ballantine, 2007) Former flame Emily Greene notifies Max Aries about the apparent suicide of his father, art restorer Daniel Aries, in Florence, Italy.

Adams, Alice (Boyd)

Alice Adams (d. 1999) was known for her well-characterized novels and short stories that explored the relationship between the sexes from the woman's point of view. Although most of her fiction was set in her adoptive city of San Francisco, her two novels with continuing characters were set in her native South. The Baird family, Cynthia and Harry, and their daughter, Abigail, are "refugees" from Connecticut who settle in Depression-era Pinehill, a small North Carolina town. The fortunes of the Bairds are followed through World War II in *After the War*. Messy relationships, but real and engaging characters, and an authentic setting are featured.

1. *Southern Exposure, The* (Knopf, 1995) The Bairds, Cynthia and Harry and their young daughter, Abigail, move from Connecticut to bucolic Pinehill, North Carolina, and start their climb up Pinehill's social ladder.
2. *After the War* (Knopf, 2000) The year 1944 finds Cynthia being unfaithful, Harry stationed in London and being unfaithful, and Abigail about to go to Swarthmore. A New York Jewish couple turns up in Pinehill, and other characters are in the throes of romantic affairs, while the black housekeeper Odessa worries about her husband on duty in the Pacific.

Adams, Deborah

Jesus Creek, Tennessee, seems to have an unusual number of murders for such a small place and a plethora of amateur detectives. In this series, the town itself is the unifying element. Several different protagonists do the sleuthing, but there is a continuing cast of secondary characters. Deborah Adams, a native Tennessean, provides a good portrait of a small Tennessee town with a believable cast of characters.

1. *All the Great Pretenders* **(Ballantine, 1992)** When heiress Lynne Hampton disappears from the Twin Elms Inn in Jesus Creek, innkeeper Kate Yancy has her hands full. Then the Hampton family hires psychic Owen Komelecki to investigate.
2. *All the Crazy Winters* **(Ballantine, 1992)** Delia Cannon, library volunteer and amateur genealogist, suspects that there is a connection between the burning of the antebellum home of genealogist Oliver Host and the murder of librarian Estelle Carhart.
3. *All the Dark Disguises* **(Ballantine, 1993)** Kay Martin, waitress, cosmetics salesperson, and former newspaper reporter, eventually feels obliged to track down a serial killer, the "Night Terror."
4. *All the Hungry Mothers* **(Ballantine, 1994)** Janet Ayres, nanny to Sarah Elizabeth Leach, finds out about domestic violence from her employer, who volunteers for a domestic-violence hotline, and from observing next-door neighbor Mary Ann and her husband.
5. *All the Deadly Beloved* **(Ballantine, 1995)** Police Chief Robert Lee "Reb" Gussler relates the saga of Patrice Gentry and her unfaithful and possibly murderous husband, medical workers who have arrived in Jesus Creek after a stint in Somalia.
6. *All the Blood Relations* **(Ballantine, 1997)** Kay Martin (see number 3), now a deputy sheriff, investigates the murder of the town florist, a motorcycle-riding thief, a missing wife, and UFO rumors.
7. *All the Dirty Cowards* **(Overmountain, 2000)** Genealogist and amateur sleuth Delia Cannon (see number 2) comes to the fore again when skeletons turn up in Dan McClain's yard and a local resident is murdered.

Adams, Douglas

I. The Hitchhiker series is a blend of science fiction and contemporary zaniness that fans of Monty Python will love. In fact the late (d. 2001) Douglas Adams wrote scripts for two BBC television imports—*Monty Python* and *Dr. Who*—and his Hitchhiker novels began as a BBC radio series (then television series). The hero of his episodic space adventure is a 30-year-old Englishman, Arthur Dent. When Earth is destroyed to make room for an intergalactic highway, Arthur is saved by his friend Ford Prefect, who is really a space alien traveling through the universe as a researcher for the compendious *Hitchhiker's Guide to the Galaxy*, a hip, electronic, intergalactic Baedeker. Several omnibus volumes have been published, the most inclusive being *The Ultimate Hitchhiker's Guide* (Wings, 1996), which contains numbers 1 to 5 plus a short story, "Young Zaphod Plays It Safe." *The Original Hitchhiker Radio Scripts* have also been collected (Harmony, 1985). *The Hitchhiker's Guide to the Galaxy* appeared as a movie in 2005.

1. *Hitchhiker's Guide to the Galaxy, The* **(Harmony, 1980)** Arthur Dent and his odd friend Ford Prefect begin their journey as stowaways on a Vogon spaceship and soon meet up with Zaphod Beeblebrox and his girlfriend, Trillian.
2. *Restaurant at the End of the Universe, The* **(Harmony, 1981)** In search of the Ultimate Question, Arthur and Ford visit the restaurant at the end of time, where each evening's entertainment features the destruction of the universe.
3. *Life, the Universe and Everything* **(Harmony, 1982)** Arthur and Ford fight to keep the evil rulers of the planet Krikkit from destroying the universe.
4. *So Long, and Thanks for All the Fish* **(Crown, 1984)** After eight years of space travel, Arthur returns to a dolphinless Earth and the girl he left behind.
5. *Mostly Harmless* **(Harmony, 1992)** Ford is faced with an alien takeover of his "Guide." Arthur is faced with a daughter he didn't know he had. Earth is faced with total annihilation, again.

II. Dirk Gently is a "holistic" private eye, brilliant but rather seedy, who uses his psychic powers to find lost cats or to save the human race. Like the Hitchhiker series, the holistic detective series is a blend of science fiction, humor, and action, entertainingly presenting some mind-boggling ideas. After Adams's death by heart attack in a California gym, a new collection of his writings, *The Salmon of Doubt: Hitchhiking the Galaxy One Last Time* (Harmony, 2002), was published, containing several chapters of an unfinished Dirk Gently novel.

1. *Dirk Gently's Holistic Detective Agency* **(Simon & Schuster, 1987)** Samuel Taylor Coleridge, King George III, an Electric Monk, a four-billion-year-old ghost, a computer programmer, an absentminded Cambridge professor, and a horse in the bathroom are somehow all part of the solution to Dirk Gently's case.
2. *Long Dark Tea-Time of the Soul, The* **(Simon & Schuster, 1989)** The explosion of a check-in desk at Heathrow Airport and a severed head on a stereo turntable lead to Dirk's encounter with some Norse gods, still alive and living in London.

Adams, Harold

South Dakota during the 1930s is the usual scene of the activities of Carl Wilcox: ex-con, reformed drunk, sometime sign painter, and amateur detective. The respectable folk of Corden (based on Adams's hometown, Clark, South Dakota), including Carl's hotel-keeping parents, want little to do with the town ne'er-do-well, except when his murder-solving talents are needed. The Carl Wilcox novels are filled with sharp dialogue, interesting characters, and a wry humor, which compensates for their downbeat Depression settings. Carl eventually woos and weds school librarian Hazel Warford (numbers 15 and 16), but we haven't learned whether he has settled down or not. *When Rich Men Die* (Doubleday, 1987) is not a Carl Wilcox novel.

1. *Murder* **(Charter, 1981)** A triple murder turns up some previously hidden corruption in respectable Corden.
2. *Paint the Town Red* **(Charter, 1983)** Left in charge of the Hotel Wilcox, Carl runs into bad-news beauty Eleonore Matthews again and some hidden Mob money.
3. *Missing Moon, The* **(Charter, 1983)** Old Boswell, best moonshiner in the state of South Dakota, is found sleeping next to the corpse of nurse Kay Bonney.
4. *Naked Liar, The* **(Mysterious, 1985)** Beautiful Trixie Cook, prime suspect in the murder of her husband, Bernie, asks Carl for help.
5. *Fourth Widow, The* **(Mysterious, 1986)** Carl, fresh from another prison stint, is arrested by Sheriff Buford as a suspect in the murder of Flory, a maid at his parents' hotel.
6. *Barbed Wire Noose, The* **(Mysterious, 1987)** Carl finds widower Arthur Foote hanging from a barbed wire noose and gets involved with the deceased's daughter, Kitty, and some seamy family secrets.
7. *Man Who Met the Train, The* **(Mysterious, 1988)** While temporarily in the town of Tocqueville, South Dakota, Carl gets involved

in the affairs of four-year-old Alma Ellison, whose parents died "accidentally."

8. *Man Who Missed the Party, The* (Mysterious, 1989) Carl and teenage nephew Hank are left in charge of the Hotel Wilcox during the 10-year reunion of Corden High's only winning football team.

9. *Man Who Was Taller Than God, The* (Walker, 1992) While Carl is painting signs in nearby Hope ("Hopeless" according to jaundiced Cordenites), Felton Edwards, local womanizer and con man, turns up murdered.

10. *Perfectly Proper Murder, A* (Walker, 1993) Carl's sign painting brings him to Podunkville, South Dakota, where he rents himself a room at the Widow Bower's, just before local bully Basil Ecke is murdered right next to Carl's Model T.

11. *Way with Widows, A* (Walker, 1994) Carl gets out of South Dakota for a change, when his sister Annabelle calls him to Red Ford, North Dakota, to help a friend accused of murder.

12. *Ditched Blonde, The* (Walker, 1995) Carl becomes an "unofficial investigator" in the unsolved murder of a woman dating the son of a prominent businessman in Greenhill, South Dakota.

13. *Hatchet Job* (Walker, 1996) Carl takes on the job of temporary town cop in Mustard, South Dakota, with the task of discovering who killed his predecessor, Lou Dupree, a former local football hero who was cordially disliked by the townsfolk.

14. *Ice Pick Artist, The* (Walker, 1997) Lilybell Fox, doing research on the family history of founding father Colonel Cameron Cutler, is found dead in the Hotel Wilcox.

15. *No Badge, No Gun* (Walker, 1998) Pastor Bjorn Bjornson asks for Carl's help in exposing the murderer of his 15-year-old niece. Carl starts an offbeat courtship with school librarian Hazel Warford.

16. *Lead, So I Can Follow* (Walker, 1999) Carl and Hazel are celebrating their honeymoon camping in Minnesota when a man is murdered near their campsite.

Adamson, Isaac

Billy Chaka, an American journalist based in Cleveland, is a writer for a magazine called *Youth in Asia*, which is devoted to the Japanese pop-culture scene. Billy is talented in the martial arts, especially kick-boxing, which he finds useful in the situations he always seems to get into in a series of novels that are a blend of urban noir, anime style, Japanese pop trivia, nonstop action, and sassy humor. Colorado native Isaac Adamson is a film-studies graduate of the University of Colorado.

1. *Tokyo Superpunch* (Perennial, 2000) Billy Chaka, sent by *Youth in Asia* to Tokyo to cover the 19-and-Under Handicapped International Martial Arts Championship, comes to the aid of a geisha in distress. Then his friend, filmmaker Sato Migusho, who is planning a film about Billy, dies in a suspicious fire.

2. *Hokkaido Popsicle* (Perennial, 2002) After he beats up the director of a film depicting him, Billy is sent on "vacation" to Hokkaido, where the night porter at the Hotel Kitty and the lead singer of Japan's most popular group, Saint Arrow, die almost simultaneously.

3. *Dreaming Pachinko* (Perennial, 2003) Billy is off to Tokyo again, this time to interview Gombei Fukagawa, a has-been rock singer, who has become a *pachinko* (Japanese pinball) addict.

4. *Kinki Lullaby* (Dark Alley, 2004) The exotic world of Japanese puppetry is the focus when Billy goes to Osaka for an award ceremony. Of course, murder happens.

Adamson, Lydia

PSEUDONYM OF Frank King

I. "Lydia Adamson" has developed a successful mystery formula. Alice Nestleton is a not-too-successful New York actress who cat-sits for extra cash and love of the animals. Alice's cat-sitting often involves her in someone's murder, and she has become a redoubtable amateur detective, sometimes aided by boyfriend Tony Basilio and down-at-the-heels mystery writer Sam Tully. Fans of Lilian Jackson Braun's Cat Who . . . series (q.v.) and Rita Mae Brown's Sneaky Pie Brown series (q.v.) may find these light, humorous mysteries to their liking.

1. *Cat in the Manger, A* (Penguin, 1990) Introduces Alice Nestleton, avant-garde actress and sometime professional cat-sitter. When Harry Starobin, whose Himalayans Alice cat-sits each Christmas, is murdered, Harry's wife, Jo, enlists Alice as investigator.

2. *Cat of a Different Color, A* (Penguin, 1990) A love-struck acting student brings Alice a white Abyssinian-like cat as a gift. The next day the student is murdered, and the cat is missing.

3. *Cat in Wolf's Clothing, A* (Penguin, 1991) A cat-loving serial killer preys on feline owners, leaving a toy mouse as his calling card.

4. *Cat by Any Other Name, A* (Penguin, 1992) Alice joins a coterie of cat lovers cultivating a Manhattan herb garden. A party celebrating the first crop of peppermint ends with one of the group going off a 25th-floor terrace.

5. *Cat in the Wings, A* (Signet, 1992) Ballet dancer Peter Dobrynin is found shot to death after dropping out of sight three years previously, and Alice's friend Lucia Maury, Dobrynin's former lover, is charged with his murder.

6. *Cat in a Glass House, A* (Penguin, 1993) While Alice is dining at a trendy Tribeca Chinese restaurant, three young thugs spray the restaurant with bullets.

7. *Cat with a Fiddle, A* (Signet, 1993) When Alice delivers Lulu, a Scottish fold cat, to her owner at an artists' colony in the Berkshires, she arrives to find that Will Gryder, the pianist accompanying the world-famous Riverside String Quartet, has been murdered.

8. *Cat with No Regrets, A* (Signet, 1994) Alice finds herself on a private jet en route to Marseille with her cats Bushy and Pancho to help her early mentor, producer Dorothy Dodd.

9. *Cat on the Cutting Edge, A* (Signet, 1994) A representative from a service called Cat People, an organization that straightens out problem pets, is found dead at Alice's door.

10. *Cat on a Winning Streak, A* (Signet, 1995) A cat climbing up to her 16th-floor apartment in Atlantic City leads Alice to murder victim Adele Houghton and her blood-stained roommate.

11. *Cat in Fine Style, A* (Signet, 1995) Alice and Tony investigate the death of a New York fashion designer.

12. *Cat in a Chorus Line, A* (Penguin, 1996) The wife of Peter Nelson Krispus, whose offbeat musicals have made him a cult figure, guns down a guest at a fund-raiser that Alice and Tony attend.

13. *Cat under the Mistletoe, A* (Dutton, 1996) Delivering Roberta, a cat with destructive tendencies, to its first session with Wilma Tedescu, an animal psychologist, Alice finds Wilma murdered in her office.

14. *Cat on a Beach Blanket, A* (Dutton, 1997) One of the participants in a Long Island poetry reading is blown up by a car bomb, and Alice wants to know why.

15. *Cat on Jingle Bell Rock, A* (Dutton, 1997) The anonymous person who donates $81,000 each Christmas for the Sustenance House Christmas goose dinner is missing.

16. *Cat on Stage Left, A* (Dutton, 1998) After Mary Singer offers Alice $2,500 for four days of cat care, Mary is shot to death by her chauffeur, who drives away leaving Alice with a large toy cat.

17. *Cat of One's Own, A* (Dutton, 1999) Alice's friend Amanda Avery adopts Jake, a rather unusual cat, which leads to Jake's disappearance and worse.
18. *Cat with the Blues, A* (Signet, 2000) Sidney and Beatrice Woburn are fighting a bitter custody battle over a beautiful Russian Blue.
19. *Cat with No Clue, A* (Signet, 2001) Old actor friends Alex and Lila die of food poisoning after eating an anniversary meal prepared by Alice.
20. *Cat Named Brat, A* (Signet, 2002) A cat named Brat keeps pawing at the words on New York guidebook author Louis Montag's computer screen.
21. *Cat on the Bus, A* (Signet, 2002) The perpetrator of a multiple homicide on a crosstown bus leaves her cat behind.

II. The prolific "Lydia Adamson" also produces a series about a veterinarian in upstate New York, Deirdre "Didi" Quinn Nightingale, who moonlights as an amateur detective. Dr. Nightingale's primary patients are dairy cattle, but she also gets involved with horses, bears, elephants, and smaller fauna.

1. *Dr. Nightingale Comes Home* (Signet, 1994) Dr. Nightingale investigates a strange sickness infecting Alpine goats and the murder of old friend Dick Obey.
2. *Dr. Nightingale Rides the Elephant* (Signet, 1994) After Dr. Nightingale becomes a veterinarian for a small traveling circus, the circus elephant, Daisy, hitherto known for her gentleness, goes berserk and kills a performer.
3. *Dr. Nightingale Goes to the Dogs* (Signet, 1995) During a bedside visit to a stud pig, Dr. Nightingale finds 90-year-old Mary Hyndman shot to death on her rural upstate farm.
4. *Dr. Nightingale Goes the Distance* (Signet, 1995) During a champagne gala at a posh thoroughbred farm, a famous equine veterinarian and a promising filly are shot to death.
5. *Dr. Nightingale Chases Three Little Pigs* (Signet, 1996) Dr. Nightingale is about to be questioned about the murder of the rich owner of an ultramodern pig farm in his Philadelphia home.
6. *Dr. Nightingale Enters the Bear Cave* (Signet, 1996) Dr. Nightingale is taking a break from her practice to join a research team tagging pregnant black bears in the Catskills.
7. *Dr. Nightingale Rides to the Hounds* (Signet, 1997) Allegations of witchcraft and a possible link to a past murder are brought out when the organizer of the county's biggest fox hunt is shot dead.
8. *Dr. Nightingale Meets Puss in Boots* (Penguin, 1997) Molson, the puss in Boots, a Manhattan nightclub, helps Dr. Nightingale in the search to find the killer in bicycle-messenger guise who gunned down the club's owner.
9. *Dr. Nightingale Races the Outlaw Colt* (Signet, 1998) A runaway colt is linked to the shooting of a young police officer outside a local restaurant.
10. *Dr. Nightingale Traps the Missing Lynx* (Penguin, 1999) After Dr. Nightingale attends a local fund-raiser to check on six mixed-breed bobcat kittens, the party's host turns up covered with bloody scratches and drops dead.
11. *Dr. Nightingale Seeks Greener Pastures* (Signet, 2000) Her dairy-cow business dwindling, Dr. Nightingale travels to an equine veterinary convention in Atlantic City to attend a lecture by famous veterinarian Eleazar Wynn, but Wynn is murdered in a local shoe shore.
12. *Dr. Nightingale Follows a Canine Clue* (Signet, 2001) Dr. Nightingale's friend Rose and her two German shepherds are found in a shallow grave.

III. Lucy Wayles, transplanted Southern belle and retired museum archivist, and her redoubtable cohort of bird-watchers, the Olmstead Irregulars, prowl the bosks and dells of New York City in search of interesting bird sightings and mysteries to be solved.

1. *Beware the Tufted Duck* (Signet, 1996) In a tale told by her senior-citizen admirer, Dr. Marcus Bloch, Lucy forms the Olmstead Irregulars after being tossed out of another bird-watching group for overly vigorous protests regarding the treatment of a rare Tufted Duck. Then one of her former group members is found dead in Central Park.
2. *Beware the Butcher Bird* (Signet, 1997) A famous field-guide illustrator dies over a dinner in his honor.
3. *Beware the Laughing Gull* (Signet, 1998) The wedding of a member of the Olmstead Irregulars is interrupted by a roller-blading gunman who shoots the bride dead.

Adcock, Thomas L(arry)

Neil "Hock" Hockaday is a New York City cop of Irish descent. He drinks too much, has a sensitive Celtic soul, and tends to get more personally involved in cases than his superiors at the NYPD would like. The best thing Hock has going for him is African American actress Ruby Flagg, his girlfriend and eventual wife. This series at its best can be lyrical and moving.

1. *Sea of Green* (Mysterious, 1989) Hard-drinking, divorced loner Hockaday gets personally involved when several murders connected to his slum landlord are perpetrated.
2. *Dark Maze* (Pocket, 1991) Ruby aids Hock in his search for a serial killer who seems to be basing his crimes on drawings by a mad sidewalk artist named Picasso.
3. *Drown All the Dogs* (Pocket, 1994) Hock and Ruby travel to Ireland and uncover some unsettling family secrets, while back home in Hell's Kitchen, his coworkers are being decimated by a series of murders and suicides.
4. *Devil's Heaven* (Pocket, 1995) Newly married to Ruby and grappling with his drinking problem, Hock investigates the grotesque slaying of Frederick Crosby, Ruby's obnoxious former boss.
5. *Thrown Away Child* (Pocket, 1996) Hock and Ruby journey to New Orleans to meet her family but arrive to find that Ruby's cousin Perry DuClat is wanted for the murder of his best friend.
6. *Grief Street* (Pocket, 1997) A young rabbi is murdered in front of 14 eyewitnesses, none of whom can identify the killer.

Adler, Warren

I. Warren Adler, the author of *The War of the Roses* (see II), includes among his two-dozen other novels a detective series featuring Fiona FitzGerald, a Washington, DC, police officer. Fiona is smart and tough but feminine, and her investigations inevitably get mixed up with the politics and intrigues of the District of Columbia. Fiona seems to take on a new police partner with every book, and author Adler has switched fathers on her as well: a retired Irish cop has metamorphosed into a deceased ex-senator.

1. *American Quartet* (Arbor House, 1982) Fiona sets a trap at Ford's Theatre for the madman who is re-creating the assassination of American presidents.
2. *American Sextet* (Arbor House, 1983) The investigation of the death of a young woman whose body is found under a bridge leads to a scheme to blackmail six high-ranking government officials.

3. *Immaculate Deception* (**Fine, 1991**) Frankie McGuire, prominent right-to-life advocate in Congress, is found pregnant and dead in a hotel room.

4. *Senator Love* (**Fine, 1991**) Fiona masquerades as the latest love interest of a presidential hopeful after two of his former lovers are murdered.

5. *Witch of Watergate, The* (**Fine, 1992**) Fiona and cynical rookie Charleen Davis form a mismatched team as they quarrel over the investigation of the suspicious death of a gossip columnist.

6. *Ties That Bind, The* (**Fine, 1994**) Farley Lipscomb, US Supreme Court justice, former lover of Fiona, and practitioner of kinky sex, is a leading suspect in the sex slaying of a lawyer's daughter.

7. *Death of a Washington Madame* (**Stonehouse, 2005**) Fiona battles her own demons while sparring with the movie-star wife of a powerful politician determined to erase the secrets of the past.

II. *The War of the Roses*, about a "perfect" marriage that becomes a divorce hell, was made into a successful movie starring Kathleen Turner and Michael Douglas (1989). A cautionary tale about the hold that physical possessions can have on people, it is probably Adler's best-known and most popular novel. *The Children of the Roses*, a sequel that followed more than 20 years later, is a much less successful novel about another troubled marriage: this time that of Josh Rose, son of the fatally warring Oliver and Barbara Rose of *The War of the Roses*.

1. *War of the Roses, The* (**Warner, 1981**) The "perfect" marriage of Oliver and Barbara Rose turns out to be far from perfect, and the divorce proceedings turn out to be scenes from hell as they argue over the division of their worldly goods.

2. *Children of the Roses, The* (**Sourcebooks, 2004**) Josh Rose, the son of the warring Roses of number 1, seems to have it all: a good job and a seemingly successful marriage with children. Then Josh falls for his chief designer Angela Bocci, a married woman.

Aidan, Pamela

Fitzwilliam Darcy, Gentleman is an example of a "word-of-mouth" best-seller. Published by Wytherngate Press of Coeur d'Alene, Idaho, the first two parts of this trilogy were generally unnoticed by the major book-reviewing media but were the subject of enthusiastic reader reviews at Amazon.com. Number 3 was published by a major publisher, Touchstone, and received reviews from *Publishers Weekly* and other sources. Basically, the trilogy is *Pride and Prejudice* as seen from Mr. Darcy's point of view, and it gives a convincing picture of a proud man fighting against his tenderer feelings. Jane Austen spin-offs have been popular in recent years, and Aidan's version of *Pride and Prejudice* is one of the better ones to come along. The 2005 release of a new cinematic version of *Pride and Prejudice* won't hurt sales.

1. *Assembly Such as This, An* (**Wytherngate, 2003**) *Fitzwilliam Darcy, Gentleman: Book 1.* Starts with Mr. Darcy's arrival at Netherfield and his initial acquaintance with, and attraction to, Elizabeth Bennet.

2. *Duty and Desire* (**Wytherngate, 2004**) *Fitzwilliam Darcy, Gentleman: Book 2.* Mr. Darcy returns to Pemberley to comfort his younger sister, Georgina, after her mistreatment at the hands of Mr. Wickham, and finds that he can't get Elizabeth Bennet out of his mind.

3. *These Three Remain* (**Touchstone, 2006**) *Fitzwilliam Darcy, Gentleman: Book 3.* Brings the romance of Mr. Darcy and Elizabeth Bennet to its fitting conclusion.

Aird, Catherine

PSEUDONYM OF Kinn McIntosh

Detective Inspector C. D. Sloan, head of the small criminal investigation department in the town of Berebury, West Calleshire, belongs to the growing fictional fraternity of local Criminal Investigation Department (CID) men who patrol England's smaller towns (see also Ruth Rendell's Wexford [q.v.] and June Thomson's Rudd [q.v.]). Sloan is competent, mild-mannered, and likable. He suffers the callow youth of his assistant, Constable Crosby, and the superfluous advice of Superintendent Leeyes with admirable tolerance and humor. Sloan is happily married, and his hobby is his rose garden. *A Most Contagious Game* (Doubleday, 1967) is not part of the series.

1. *Religious Body, The* (**Doubleday, 1966**) A nun is murdered in a convent, and an effigy burnt on Guy Fawkes Day at a neighboring school is wearing her glasses.

2. *Henrietta Who?* (**Doubleday, 1968**) Henrietta Jenkins comes home from the university to identify the dead body of her mother, but Inspector Sloan must identify Henrietta.

3. *Stately Home Murder, The* (**Doubleday, 1970**) A dead body is discovered inside a suit of armor at Ornum House. English title: *The Complete Steel.*

4. *Late Phoenix, A* (**Doubleday, 1971**) Workmen find a corpse buried in the wreckage of a war-bombed house, and Sloan must investigate a murder three decades old.

5. *His Burial Too* (**Doubleday, 1973**) A dead body is discovered amid the rubble of a fallen marble statue inside a church tower.

6. *Slight Mourning* (**Doubleday, 1976**) Could one of the eight guests at Bill Fent's dinner party have slipped him a lethal dose of barbiturates?

7. *Parting Breath* (**Doubleday, 1978**) A murdered student brings Sloan to a university troubled by plotting student activists.

8. *Some Die Eloquent* (**Doubleday, 1980**) Miss Wansdyke's death, apparently of natural causes, begins to look suspicious when Sloan discovers that her little dog is missing.

9. *Passing Strange* (**Doubleday, 1981**) Nurse Joyce Cooper is found strangled behind her fortune-telling tent at the annual Almstone Horticultural Fair.

10. *Last Respects* (**Doubleday, 1982**) Local fisherman Horace Boller finds a dead man in the river, and suspicions run to murder.

11. *Harm's Way* (**Doubleday, 1984**) Members of the Berebury Country Footpaths Society find a piece of a human corpse on one of the local walkways.

12. *Dead Liberty, A* (**Doubleday, 1987**) Lucy Durmast is accused of serving some deadly chili, but she refuses to speak a word in her own defense.

13. *Body Politic, The* (**Doubleday, 1991**) Allen Ottershaw meets a sticky end in the reenactment of a 13th-century battle.

14. *Going Concern, A* (**St. Martin's, 1994**) Among the odd codicils of Octavia Garamond's will are requests for a police presence at her funeral and a meticulous posthumous inquest by her physician.

15. *Injury Time* (**St. Martin's, 1995**) A collection of 16 Sloan stories.

16. *After Effects* (**St. Martin's, 1996**) The recent deaths of patients in two Calleshire hospitals may be linked to drug trials being conducted by a local physician. The portrayal of physicians in this book prompted a sour review from *BMJ: The British Medical Journal.*

17. *Stiff News* (**St. Martin's, 1999**) Sloan and Crosby investigate a series of questionable deaths at old-age home Almstone Manor.

18. *Little Knell* (**St. Martin's, 2001**) A 3,000-year-old mummy case donated to a local museum contains a much more recent corpse.

19. *Amendment of Life* (St. Martin's, 2003) Wheelchair-bound Daphne Pedlinge spots a corpse in the Tudor yew maze from an upper floor of Aumerle Court.
20. *Chapter and Hearse and Other Mysteries* (St. Martin's, 2004) Twenty-two short stories, including several about Sloan.
21. *Hole in One, A* (St. Martin's, 2005) Two lady golfers discover a body buried in the steepest bunker on the Berebury golf course.

Akunin, Boris

PSEUDONYM OF G. Chkhartishvili

Grigory Chkhartishvili, a Russian translator and editor born in the Soviet republic of Georgia, decided to do something different when he reached his fortieth birthday, so he embarked upon a series of historical mysteries set in the 1870s and 1880s featuring a young man named Erast Petrovich Fandorin, who, although he cannot stand the sight of blood, wants to use his advanced deduction skills as a detective. Fandorin, described as "a Slavic Sherlock Holmes," speaks Japanese and English, is skilled at martial arts, and has lady-killer good looks (unlike the beefy, violent protagonists of most Russian mysteries). The books in the Fandorin series have been best sellers in Russia and are now in the process of being translated into English. Both Russian and English-language critics have high praise for Akunin's elegant style, which harks back to the 19th century, in which the novels take place. Encouraged by the success of Fandorin, Akunin has started two spin-off series, one featuring Fandorin's grandson, a contemporary British citizen, and another featuring Pelagia, a 19th-century Russian nun.

1. *Winter Queen, The* (Random House, 2003) Introduces E. P. Fandorin, the orphaned son of a once-wealthy family, who fancies himself a detective. In 1876 Fandorin's superior, Xavier Grushin, decides to test Fandorin's deductive abilities when a rich young man commits suicide in a Moscow Park. Fandorin's investigation leads him to London and back and to a global conspiracy. Originally published in 1998 as *Azazel*. Translated from the Russian by Andrew Bromfield.
2. *Turkish Gambit, The* (Random House, 2005) Fandorin, sent by Tsar Alexander to the Bulgarian front of the Russo-Turkish war to deliver a message, gets involved with a plot against the Russian empire and with a beautiful girl named Varvara Suvorova. Originally published in 1998 as *Turetskii gambit*. Translated from the Russian by Andrew Bromfield.
3. *Murder on the Leviathan* (Random House, 2004) After a series of violent murders in Paris in which a British aristocrat and several others are killed, Fandorin finds himself on HMS *Leviathan*, a luxury liner en route to India. Originally published in 1998 as *Leviafan*. Translated from the Russian by Andrew Bromfield.
4. *Death of Achilles, The* (Random House, 2006) 1882. The sudden death of national hero General Mikhail Sobolev allows Fandorin to uncover Sobolev's plan for a coup and a missing suitcase full of a million rubles to fund it. Originally published in 1998 as *Smert Akhillesa*. Translated from the Russian by Andrew Bromfield.
5. *Special Assignments* (Random House, 2008) Subtitle: *The Further Adventures of Erast Fandorin*. Two novellas: *The Jack of Spades*, in which Fandorin finds a "Watson" in the form of errand boy Anisii Tulipov and matches wits with a con man and thief; and *The Decorator*, where Fandorin is faced with the possibility that Jack the Ripper is continuing his depredations in 1889 Russia. Originally published in 1999 as *Osobye purucheniia*. Translated from the Russian by Andrew Bromfield.

Albert, Neil

Dave Garrett, disbarred attorney, runs Garrett Investigations, a private-eye agency, in Philadelphia. Dave is a Vietnam veteran who suffers from flashbacks, has an ex-wife (who helped to get him disbarred), and a transsexual assistant, his off-again, on-again lover, Lisa Wilson. This series of intricately plotted mysteries with calendar titles is written by Neil Albert, an attorney in Lancaster, Pennsylvania.

1. *January Corpse, The* (Walker, 1991) Dave Garrett is called in to help have Daniel Wilson, who disappeared seven years ago, declared dead so that his estate can be wrapped up.
2. *February Trouble, The* (Walker, 1992) Bruce Chadwick, the manager of a Chinese fast-food franchise, has been getting threatening letters, and his restaurant has been the subject of various "dirty tricks." Now his wife has been kidnapped.
3. *Burning March* (Dutton, 1994) Dave is asked to investigate when Emily Voss, office manager of his former law firm, dies in a suspicious fire.
4. *Cruel April* (Dutton, 1995) When his lover, Kate, who was supposed to leave her abusive husband in Miami and meet him in Philadelphia, fails to show up, Dave is forced to investigate.
5. *Appointment in May* (Walker, 1996) Dave, along with his assistant and sometime lover, Lisa Wilson, is involved in a domestic surveillance case, following Maria Winter, estranged wife of Pat Winter.
6. *Tangled June* (Walker, 1997) Prodded by Lisa Wilson to untangle his tangled past, Dave sets off for California to find his birth mother. Features a cameo by Les Roberts's (q.v.) Saxon.

Albert, Susan Wittig

I. China Bayles, former Houston attorney, has left the career "fast track" at the age of 42 and moved to the west Texas hill town of Pecan Springs, where she opens an herb shop, Thyme and Seasons. She soon finds herself embroiled in all kinds of small-town skulduggery that, with the aid of her New Age friend Ruby Wilcox and her live-in boyfriend, Mike McQuaid, she manages to get to the bottom of. China is an attractive character, independent and feisty, and the regional atmosphere and herbal and culinary tips interspersed throughout this well-written mystery series are appealing.

Susan Wittig Albert, like China Bayles, got off the career fast track (an academic one in her case), but she doesn't seem to have slowed down much. She has authored or coauthored more than 60 children's books, written or edited several works on women and careers (e.g., *Work of Her Own*, Putnam, 1992), publishes herbal and culinary books under her own imprint (Thyme and Seasons Books), edits the *Story Circle Journal*, and coauthors a series of mysteries (with husband Bill Albert) under the pseudonym Robin Paige.

1. *Thyme of Death* (Scribner, 1993) Former Houston attorney China Bayles drops out of the fast track at the age of 42, opening up herb shop Thyme and Seasons in the town of Pecan Springs, Texas. She is befriended by Ruby Wilcox, who runs a New Age store next door, and soon becomes embroiled in a murder mystery.
2. *Witches' Bane* (Scribner, 1993) China's friend Ruby Wilcox is accused of devil worship and murder following a series of mysterious deaths culminating in the homicide of Sybil Rand, rich maintainer of a garden of poisonous plants, after a feminist Halloween party attended by goddess worshippers.
3. *Hangman's Root* (Scribner, 1994) Unpopular biology professor Miles Harwick is found drugged and hanged in his office, and

one of his opponents, China's friend Dottie Riddle, is the prime suspect.

4. *Rosemary Remembered* (Berkley, 1995) Rosemary Robbins, who has borrowed a truck from China's lover, ex-cop Mike McQuaid, turns out to be the spitting image of China and is murdered.

5. *Rueful Death* (Berkley, 1996) China goes on a retreat to St. Theresa's Monastery in Texas's Yucca River country with friend Maggie Garrett, a former nun. The retreat is not particularly restful, however, since St. Theresa's is embroiled in a fight over a large legacy, and the Reverend Mother dies mysteriously.

6. *Love Lies Bleeding* (Berkley, 1997) China's lover, Mike, has found someone else, and a former Texas Ranger has committed suicide amid a drug-trafficking scandal.

7. *Chile Death* (Berkley, 1998) Mike is at the Manor, a rehabilitation center and nursing home, recovering from a gunshot wound. Cedar Choppers Chili Cookoff judge Jerry Jeff Cody dies of an allergic reaction, but was it an accident?

8. *Lavender Lies* (Berkley, 1999) China's wedding to Mike is in danger of becoming sidetracked when a local real-estate magnate is murdered.

9. *Mistletoe Man* (Berkley, 2000) Thyme and Seasons has been expanded to include Thyme for Tea, comanaged by China and Ruby. Business is good, and China is settling down with Mike and her stepson, but things start going awry: Ruby begins acting strangely, and mistletoe harvester Swenson is the victim of a hit-and-run.

10. *Bloodroot* (Berkley, 2001) China, responding to her mother's plea for help, sets off for the family homestead in Mississippi.

11. *Indigo Dying* (Berkley, 2003) Settled in a new Texas town, Indigo, and part-owner of a combination herb shop and teahouse called Thyme for Tea, China, with her husband, Mike McQuaid, gets involved investigating the murder of unpopular Casey Ford, who was about to sell the town's coal-mining rights to a national conglomerate.

12. *Unthymely Death and Other Garden Mysteries, An* (Berkley, 2003) Ten China Bayles short stories.

13. *Dilly of a Death, A* (Berkley, 2004) The members of the Pretty Pickle Planners for Pecan Springs' annual Pickle-Fest are thrown into a tizzy when Phoebe Morgan, the Pickle Queen, disappears.

14. *Dead Man's Bones* (Berkley, 2005) China's stepson, Brian, finds a skeleton in a cave with its head bashed in. The skeleton proves to be only about 30 years old.

15. *Bleeding Hearts* (Berkley, 2006) After high-school football coach Tim Duffy is murdered, the folks of Pecan Springs are shocked to learn that he had a habit of getting sexually involved with teenage girls.

16. *Spanish Dagger* (Berkley, 2007) China's recently discovered half brother, Miles Danforth, insists on reopening the case of their father's death in a car accident 16 years earlier.

17. *Nightshade* (Berkley, 2008) China's half brother, Miles Danforth, hires China's husband, Mike McQuaid, to get to the bottom of their father's death 16 years earlier.

II. Susan Wittig Albert has embarked upon a new historical mystery series, set around 1905 in the quaint English Lake District village of Near Sawrey, featuring real-life illustrator, author, and creator of Peter Rabbit, Beatrix Potter. Subtitled *The Cottage Tales of Beatrix Potter*, these are charming cozies featuring good-hearted villagers and animals straight out of Potter's books.

1. *Tale of Hill Top Farm, The* (Berkley, 2004) Beatrix Potter settles into the English Lake District village of Near Sawrey soon after the sudden death of her fiancé in 1905.

2. *Tale of Holly How, The* (Berkley, 2005) While renovating Hill Top Farm, Beatrix stumbles across the body of local sheep owner Ben Hornby and suspects foul play.

3. *Tale of Cuckoo Brow Wood, The* (Berkley, 2006) Beatrix discovers that Hill Top Farm is overrun with rats.

4. *Tale of Hawthorn House, The* (Berkley, 2007) Beatrix finds a foundling child, Baby Flora, deposited on her doorstep.

Alcala, Kathleen (Judith)

The loosely connected series beginning with *Spirits of the Ordinary* is an example of Latin American magic realism depicting the lives of several generations of Mexicans, Americans, Indians, and Jews in northern Mexico and the United States. The trilogy covers, with much historical information, events in Mexico from the 1870s to the eve of the Mexican Revolution as seen through the eyes of a large cast of characters both rich and poor. Kathleen Alcala is, herself, a "Chicana/Latina" born in California, who has had a career as a grant writer and administrator for public broadcasting and other nonprofit groups. *Spirits of the Ordinary* was her first novel, following a collection of short stories: *Mrs. Vargas and the Dead Naturalist* (Calyx Books, 1992).

1. *Spirits of the Ordinary* (Chronicle, 1997) In a northern Mexico village in the 1870s, the Carabajal family clandestinely practices their Jewish faith. Their son, Zacarias, marries Estela, a Catholic woman who raises their children single-handedly while her husband is absent from home hunting for gold.

2. *Flower in the Skull, The* (Chronicle, 1998) Traces three generations of women descended from the Opata, a vanished Indian nation from the Sonora Desert of Mexico. When she is separated from her Opata family, young Shark Tooth begins a new life as a maid in Tucson, Arizona, where she is renamed Concha.

3. *Treasures in Heaven* (Chronicle, 2000) Estela and Noe leave Zacarias for a new life in turn-of-the-20th-century Mexico City, where they meet "La Señorita," a wealthy woman who uses her money to help the poor.

Alcott, Louisa May

I. Alcott's Victorian period pieces, sentimental and moralistic as they are, still appeal to young readers today. Their direct, easy-to-read prose and the timelessness of childhood interests may account for their enduring charm. Adults who read them for their nostalgia value will find that certain scenes still bring a tear to the eye. The characters of *Little Women* were drawn from Alcott's family—she had three sisters. Jo is thought to be the autobiographical figure. *Little Women* has been filmed several times, most recently (1994) with Winona Ryder as Jo and Susan Sarandon as Marmee, and has been produced as an opera (1998). *Little Men* was filmed in 1998 with Mariel Hemingway and Chris Sarandon. The trilogy has been reprinted in the Library of America series (2005).

1. *Little Women; or, Meg, Jo, Beth and Amy* (Roberts, 1868) Introduces the March family and their mother, Marmee. The Civil War keeps Mr. March from his family until the end of the book. Note: *Good Wives*, also called *Little Women Married*, was published separately in 1869, but is now incorporated as the second half of *Little Women* in almost all editions.

2. *Little Men: Life at Plumfield with Jo's Boys* (Roberts, 1871) A grown-up Jo and her husband, Professor Bhaer, run a boarding school called Plumfield.

3. *Jo's Boys, and How They Turned Out* **(Roberts, 1886)** The children of Plumfield have grown up to face life's trials.

II. Alcott fans won't want to miss these two books about a lonely young girl surrounded by her boy cousins and her handsome guardian, who has unusual views about child rearing.

1. *Eight Cousins* **(Roberts, 1874)** Thirteen-year-old Rose Campbell, an orphan, comes to live with her uncle Alec; her seven lively cousins live nearby.
2. *Rose in Bloom* **(Roberts, 1876)** Continues the story of Rose, her cousins, and her friend Phoebe, now grown up.

Alding, Peter

PSEUDONYM OF Roderic Jeffries

Roderic Jeffries (q.v.), under the pseudonym of Peter Alding, wrote a series of 14 novels about the operations of a CID office in the English town of Fortnow. In this series of procedurals, the main characters are likable young constable Kerr and his superior, the hard-working, hard-to-please inspector Robert Fusil. Kerr is engaged to a proper young lady; Fusil is married to an overprotective wife. This series, several of which have not been published in the United States, features intricate plots. Jeffries, as well as writing the Inspector Alvarez novels under his own name, has written series under the pseudonyms of Jeffrey Ashford and Roderic Graeme.

1. *All Leads Negative* **(Harper, 1967)** One box in a shipment of gold chains is missing when the supposedly well-guarded and accounted-for shipment is unloaded. UK title: *The C.I.D. Room.*
2. *Circle of Danger* **(Long [UK], 1968)** No annotation available.
3. *Murder among Thieves* **(McCall, 1970)** After a gang of thieves performs a daring and successful armored car robbery, the thieves start turning up dead, one by one.
4. *Guilt without Proof* **(McCall, 1971)** The hijacking of a truckload of whiskey is the start of a complicated series of events.
5. *Despite the Evidence* **(Saturday Review, 1972)** A series of petty thefts in a factory, the plan for a large jewelry heist by a wealthy club owner, and the coshing of Kerr after he aids a motorist may all have a connection.
6. *Call Back to Crime* **(Long [UK], 1972)** No annotation available.
7. *Field of Fire* **(Long [UK], 1973)** Fortnow is to be the site of two state visits: one from Czechoslovakia, one from Africa. Assassination is planned for one of the state visitors.
8. *Murder Line, The* **(Walker, 1974)** No annotation available.
9. *Six Days to Death* **(Walker, 1975)** Police Constable Brady unexpectedly becomes a hero by thwarting a bank robbery. Several months later, Brady receives a very threatening letter.
10. *Murder Is Suspected* **(Walker, 1977)** Despite the opposition of his superiors, Fusil investigates a hit-and-run accident that may be connected with the police.
11. *Ransom Town* **(Walker, 1979)** A bungled bank robbery, a ransom demand, and a suicide may be connected.
12. *Man Condemned, A* **(Walker, 1981)** Fusil is involved with the protection of a rich, unpopular Iranian; an armed robbery; and the possible drunken-driving death of a constable.
13. *Betrayed by Death* **(Walker, 1982)** As if Fusil weren't overburdened already, a serial murderer is targeting young boys in Fortnow.
14. *One Man's Justice* **(Hale [UK], 1983)** No annotation available.

Aldiss, Brian W(ilson)

I. Helliconia is a distant planet where each season lasts for hundreds of years. It is inhabited by humans, various humanoid species, and malevolent, horned, furry creatures called phagors. Each book in the trilogy weaves the lives of many characters and multiple viewpoints into a dense fabric. Aldiss is a prolific British writer of sophisticated and thoughtful science fiction. The verbal inventiveness and broad scope evident in the Helliconia trilogy are characteristic of his work.

1. *Helliconia Spring* **(Atheneum, 1982)** The series begins with the story of the young hunter Yuli, who loses his father and must find shelter or die.
2. *Helliconia Summer* **(Atheneum, 1983)** War rages between humans and phagors, while the king of Borlien seeks a new queen.
3. *Helliconia Winter* **(Atheneum, 1986)** As Winter's long night draws closer, the phagors' ultimate triumph seems inevitable.

II. Joe Bodenland, a 21st-century American, travels back into the past to thwart characters from horror "fiction" before they can move over from their parallel universe and take over ours.

1. *Frankenstein Unbound* **(Random House, 1974)** Bodenland time travels to the Europe of 1816 to encounter Mary Shelley, her creation Victor Frankenstein, and *his* creation.
2. *Dracula Unbound* **(HarperCollins, 1991)** Bodenland hitches a ride on a "time train" back to 1896 to prevent a Dracula-ordered assassination of author Bram Stoker, who is about to expose the plot of the Undead to take over the world.

III. Aldiss is a master of the realistic novel as well as of science fiction. This trio of novels relates, through the medium of Horatio Stubbs, the experiences and thoughts of an average young Englishman during the 1930s and 1940s. The Horatio Stubbs Saga has been reissued in one volume (Panther [UK], 1985).

1. *Hand-Reared Boy, The* **(McCall, 1970)** Horatio recounts, in detail, his adolescent sexual experiences in the England of the 1930s.
2. *Soldier Erect, A* **(Coward, 1971)** With the British army in World War II Burma and India, Horatio is still having "experiences."
3. *Rude Awakening, A* **(Random House, 1979)** In Sumatra during the birth pangs of the new Indonesian republic, Horatio is in trouble with women but enjoying considerable success with them for the first time.

IV. Four loosely connected novels, which Aldiss refers to as "The Squire Quartet," are a combination of realistic depictions of late-20th-century middle-class life in the West, a satirical look at popular culture, and a thoughtful guess as to where we are headed.

1. *Life in the West* **(Weidenfeld, 1980)** Thomas C. Squire, a specialist in media theory and practice, is facing a midlife crisis while attending the First International Congress of Intergraphic Criticism in Sicily.
2. *Forgotten Life* **(Atheneum, 1989)** Clement Winter inherits his brother's papers and is reexposed to 50 years of family miscommunication.
3. *Remembrance Day* **(St. Martin's, 1993)** The IRA bombing of an English seaside hotel is the pretext for a detailed investigation of the lives of the victims.
4. *Somewhere East of Life* **(Carroll & Graf, 1994)** In 21st-century Budapest, British architectural expert Roy Burrell loses 10 years of his memory to neurosurgeons, who will sell the memory to voyeurs.

Aldrich, Bess Streeter

A Lantern in Her Hand is an unpretentious story of pioneer life in Nebraska after the Civil War. It is narrated by Abbie Deal, who leaves her log cabin home in 1868 with her young husband and baby. The hardships and trials of making a home in unsettled territory and raising a family toughen Abbie into a strong pioneer woman. Aldrich's hymn to womanly self-sacrifice wears a little thin in the sequel. Aldrich's *Collected Short Works* have been republished by the University of Nebraska in two volumes (1995 and 1999).

1. *Lantern in Her Hand, A* (Appleton, 1928) Will and Abbie Deal set out for Nebraska in 1868 and brave frontier hardships to build a home for their growing family.
2. *White Bird Flying, A* (Appleton, 1931) Abbie's granddaughter, young Laura Deal, is torn between her hopes for a literary career and her love for Allen Rinemiller.

Alexander, Bruce

PSEUDONYM OF Bruce Cook

The late (d. 2003) Bruce Cook (q.v.), author of the Chico Cervantes series, wrote, as Bruce Alexander, a historical detective series set in 18th-century England. His "detective" was a real person, Sir John Fielding, English magistrate, cofounder of the Bow Street Runners, London's first police force, and half brother of the novelist Henry Fielding (*Tom Jones*, etc.). The blind Sir John, known as the "Blind Beak," operates as a fictional detective with a cast of imaginary characters, including teenage orphan Jeremy Parker, who acts as Sir John's eyes and narrator, and occasional help from historical worthies such as Samuel Johnson and Benjamin Franklin.

1. *Blind Justice* (Putnam, 1994) A locked-room mystery faces Sir John and Jeremy as dissolute Lord Richard Goodhope is found shot to death in his library in an apparent suicide.
2. *Murder in Grub Street* (Putnam, 1995) Ezekiel Crabb, a Grub Street publisher-bookseller, his family, and two employees are massacred. Rustic poet John Clayton is the prime suspect, but Sir John, with the help of, among others, Samuel Johnson, uncovers a plot against London's Jews.
3. *Watery Grave* (Putnam, 1996) Naval Lieutenant William Landon is accused of pushing the captain of a British frigate overboard during a storm two days out of Cape Town in 1767.
4. *Person or Persons Unknown* (Putnam, 1997) Some 18th-century Jack the Ripper (or Rippers) is killing prostitutes in Covent Garden.
5. *Jack, Knave and Fool* (Putnam, 1998) Elderly Lord Laningham dies, and Sir John suspects poison. Then his widow is poisoned, and their heir, Arthur Paltrow, becomes the prime suspect.
6. *Death of a Colonial* (Putnam, 1999) The estate of the late Lord Laningham (see number 5) is claimed by someone calling himself Lawrence Paltrow, who has spent the last eight years in the Colonies. This case takes the reader to Bath and Oxford.
7. *Color of Death, The* (Putnam, 2000) A series of brutal robberies seems to be perpetrated by a gang of blacks, putting respectable blacks, such as Dr. Johnson's Frank Barber, at risk.
8. *Smuggler's Moon* (Putnam, 2001) The Lord Chief Justice sends Sir John to the town of Deal, Kent, notorious for smuggling, to investigate the conduct of the local magistrate.
9. *Experiment in Treason, An* (Putnam, 2002) A burglary turned violent at the home of the secretary of state for colonial affairs has led to the disappearance of letters connected with the trouble-some affairs in the Massachusetts Colony. Samuel Johnson and Benjamin Franklin appear in this episode.
10. *Price of Murder, The* (Putnam, 2003) Jeremy gets involved with the world of horse racing when the niece of legendary jockey Deuteronomy Plummer is murdered.
11. *Rules of Engagement* (Putnam, 2005) Finished by Judith Aller and John Shannon. Lord Lammermoor falls to his death from Westminster Bridge.

Alexander, Victoria

I. Victoria Alexander is a rising star on the Regency romance scene. Her books feature strong characters, steamy sex, humor, and action-filled, if somewhat implausible, plots. Members of the Regency Victorian era Effington family are the protagonists in a series of entertaining romances.

1. *Wedding Bargain, The* (Avon, 1999) Beautiful, unattainable Pandora Effington makes Maximillian Wells, the Earl of Trent, an offer he is unlikely to refuse.
2. *Husband List, The* (Avon, 2000) To claim her uncle's unexpected bequest, Lady Gillian Marley must marry by her next birthday.
3. *Marriage Lesson, The* (Avon, 2001) Lady Marianne Shelton's book *The Absolutely True Adventures of a Country Miss in London* being too tame to satisfy her editor, Lady Marianne hopes to liven her tale up with the help of Thomas Effington.
4. *Prince's Bride, The* (Avon, 2001) Lady Jocelyn, wanting to become a princess, decides to marry a young, handsome prince with his own country and a nice castle.
5. *Her Highness, My Wife* (Avon, 2002) Dashing Lord Matthew Weston marries the enchanting Princess Tatiana only to find himself deserted by her.
6. *Love with the Proper Husband* (Avon, 2003) Marcus Holcroft, the Earl of Pennington, is dismayed to find that Miss Gwendolyn Townsend, the penniless bride who has been foisted upon him, is insisting on rules to their wedding.
7. *Lady in Question, The* (Avon, 2003) The premature death of Delia Effington's rakehell husband, secretly a British spy, leaves her with a fortune and an estate. The British government, concerned about security, sends handsome spy Tony St. Stephens to infiltrate Delia's household disguised as an elderly butler.
8. *Pursuit of Marriage, The* (Avon, 2004) Cassie Effington, unwed at the advanced age of 24, is suspicious of charming, handsome rakes like Lord Berkley. It is up to him to prove that he has some substance beneath the charm.
9. *Visit from Sir Nicholas, A* (Avon, 2004) Nicholas Collingsworth goes abroad so that his best friend can marry the desirable Elizabeth Effington. Ten years later Nicholas is back, and Elizabeth is a widow.
10. *When We Meet Again* (Avon, 2005) Pamela Effington spent an unforgettable night in the arms of the Avalonian crown prince, who, four years later, winds up in exile in London.
11. *Let It Be Love* (Avon, 2005) The heart of Jonathon Effington, the Marquess of Helmsley, had never been touched until the beautiful but desperate Fiona Fairchild proposes marriage to him.

II. The Last Man Standing series concerns four of London's most desirable gentlemen, who make a wager—the prize going to the one who remains unwed the longest.

1. *Little Bit Wicked, A* (Avon, 2007) Gideon Pearsall, Viscount Warton, plans to bed, but not wed, the scandalous Judith, Lady Chester.

2. *What a Lady Wants* (**Avon, 2007**) From the moment Lady Felicity Melville spies Nigel Cavendish climbing from a neighbor's window, she knows that Nigel, with a little reformation, is the answer to her prayers.

Ali, Thalassa

Thalassa Ali, a Boston-born Radcliffe graduate, married a Pakistani, lived for 12 years in Lahore, and converted to Islam. After her husband's death she returned to the United States and became a stockbroker before she turned her energies to fiction writing. She has written a romantic trilogy about Marianna Givens, a young British woman in India in the first half of the 19th century.

1. *Singular Hostage, A* (**Bantam, 2002**) Young Marianna Givens, sent to India in 1838 to find a suitable husband, is more interested in travel and military history than in marrying. She gets a post as a translator with Lord Auckland's mission to negotiate an alliance in the Punjab, which will bring Afghanistan under British control.
2. *Beggar at the Gate, A* (**Bantam, 2003**) Marianna marries the Punjabi courtier Hassan Ali Kahn and becomes a member of the Sufi family of Shaikh Waliullah. The course of married life is far from smooth, however.
3. *Companions of Paradise* (**Bantam, 2007**) The concluding volume of the trilogy finds Marianna Givens living in the British cantonment at Kabul in 1841, on the eve of the first Afghan war, after her husband thwarts an assassination attempt in Lahore.

Allegretto, Michael

Private investigator Jacob Lomax works out of Denver, Colorado. Like many PIs, he is a former cop who is unlucky in his personal relationships and usually broke; he lives in a seedy apartment, has a past he doesn't like to dwell on but often does (his wife was murdered), and masks his sensitivity with his wry, ironic narration. Jake Lomax is an engaging character, and Allegretto supplies him with good plots and authentic surroundings. Allegretto, who lives in Denver and is the son of a retired Denver police detective, also writes suspense thrillers such as *Shadow House* (Carroll, 1994).

1. *Death on the Rocks* (**Scribner, 1987**) Phillip Townsend's widow doesn't think that her late husband's fatal drive off a mountain west of Denver was a simple case of drunken driving.
2. *Blood Stone* (**Scribner, 1988**) Jake is engaged to look for the proceeds of a jewel robbery committed some 20 years previously.
3. *Dead of Winter, The* (**Scribner, 1989**) Things get very complicated when a car bomb kills the bookie father of a teenage runaway Jake is seeking.
4. *Blood Relative* (**Scribner, 1992**) Just back from a Mexican vacation, Jake is hired to help with the defense of factory owner Samuel Butler, accused of murdering his wife.
5. *Grave Doubt* (**Carroll & Graf, 1995**) Roger Armis's wife hires Jake to get to the bottom of threatening phone calls made by her allegedly deceased first husband.

Allen, Conrad

Suave American George Porter Dillman and beautiful Englishwoman Genevieve Masefield are private investigators who work on Cunard Line luxury liners during the Edwardian period. These pleasant mysteries, with engaging stories and interesting pre–World War I ambience, are just the ticket for fans of Edwardian flavor and seagoing mysteries. Conrad Allen is a playwright living in England.

1. *Murder on the Lusitania* (**St. Martin's, 1999**) George Dillman, an operative working for the Cunard steamship company, is aboard the maiden voyage of the *Lusitania* (1907). So are English beauty Genevieve Masefield, and the person(s) who stole a Stradivarius violin and the secret diagrams that explain the *Lusitania*'s wiring.
2. *Murder on the Mauretania* (**St. Martin's, 2000**) George and Genevieve are working together on board the *Mauretania*, the world's largest luxury liner, which is carrying 2,000 passengers and a cargo of gold bullion.
3. *Murder on the Minnesota* (**St. Martin's, 2002**) George and Genevieve investigate the death of a fellow passenger—an Anglican missionary en route to China—on the *Minnesota*.
4. *Murder on the Caronia* (**St. Martin's, 2003**) George and Genevieve come to the aid of a young Boston woman on the *Caronia* in search of a titled husband.
5. *Murder on the Marmora* (**St. Martin's, 2004**) George and Genevieve are acting as unofficial bodyguards for the Duke and Duchess of Fife on board the *Marmora* en route from England to Australia via Cairo.
6. *Murder on the Salsette* (**St. Martin's, 2005**) George and Genevieve are now married. Jewelry thefts afflict the passengers of the *Salsette* on a four-day passage from Bombay to Aden.
7. *Murder on the Oceanic* (**St. Martin's, 2006**) George and Genevieve investigate the murder of J. P. Morgan's bodyguard as well as the theft of art that Morgan is transporting from Europe to New York.
8. *Murder on the Celtic* (**St. Martin's, 2007**) Sir Arthur Conan Doyle (q.v.) is among the passengers on the *Celtic* in 1910, while Genevieve and George are on the lookout for Edward Hammond, a thief wanted for murder.

Allen, Garrison

Yet another mystery series involving cats (see also Lydia Adamson, Lilian Jackson Braun, Rita Mae Brown, etc.). This cat is named Mycroft (after Sherlock Holmes's brother), aka "Big Mike," and he works with his "owner," Penelope Warren, to solve crimes in the town of Empty Creek, Arizona. Big Mike is a 25-pound Abyssinian with a Morris-the-Cat attitude. Penelope is a beautiful, smart former US Marine turned mystery-bookstore owner. Empty Creek is a town full of zany, libidinous characters. The series is good fun.

1. *Desert Cat* (**Kensington, 1994**) Wealthy busybody Louise Fletcher, who has detailed files on almost everyone in Empty Creek, is found stabbed to death with a chopping knife on Penelope Warren's porch.
2. *Royal Cat* (**Kensington, 1995**) Penelope, chosen queen of the Empty Creek Authentic Elizabethan Spring Faire after the original queen is murdered, soon finds herself in hot water.
3. *Stable Cat* (**Kensington, 1996**) Horse trainer Jack Loomis has been murdered, and his employer's prize Arabian stallion has been horsenapped.

4. *Baseball Cat* **(Kensington, 1997)** Managing general partner of the Empty Creek Coyotes minor-league baseball squad, Peter Adcock, is found bludgeoned to death in the visiting team's dugout.
5. *Dinosaur Cat* **(Kensington, 1998)** Penelope joins Police Chief Dutch Fowler in investigating the murder of geologist Millicent DeForest, who has been looking for dinosaur fossils near Empty Creek.
6. *Movie Cat* **(Kensington, 1999)** C. D. Masterly and his company are in town to shoot a low-budget western with Penelope, her sister Stormy, and other Empty Creek denizens in the cast.

Allen, Hervey

In addition to his most famous work, the best-seller *Anthony Adverse*, Allen wrote this series of colonial novels, the Disinherited, set in western Pennsylvania and the Ohio River Valley in the period of the French and Indian War. Salathiel Albine is raised by the Shawnees but returns to white society. Along the way, he takes part in historical actions such as the siege of Fort Pitt and interacts with historical personages such as Arthur St. Clair, a general in the American Revolution, and a host of colorful fictional characters. The Disinherited was projected to be five novels in two volumes, but only three novels and a portion of a fourth were completed before Allen's death. An omnibus volume, *The City in the Dawn* (Rinehart, 1950), contains abridgments of numbers 1–3 plus sections of the uncompleted fourth novel.

1. *Fort and the Forest, The* **(Rinehart, 1943)** After being raised as an Indian chieftain's son, Salathiel Albine returns to white society at Fort Pitt.
2. *Bedford Village* **(Rinehart, 1944)** Salathiel joins Captain Jack's band and falls in love with the tender and lively Phoebe Davison.
3. *Toward the Morning* **(Rinehart, 1948)** Salathiel, Frances Yates, and Arthur St. Clair head eastward to Philadelphia.

Allen, Irene

PSEUDONYM OF Elsa Kirsten Peters

Sixty-six-year-old widow Elizabeth Elliot is clerk of the Quaker Meeting House in Cambridge, Massachusetts. She moderates meetings of the Society of Friends, counsels her peers, and sometimes acts as an amateur investigator when issues turn criminal or deadly. Elizabeth is an appealing character, and her detecting involves her in such serious contemporary issues as gay marriage, sexual harassment, and nuclear pollution.

1. *Quaker Silence* **(Villard, 1992)** The issue that most concerns the Quaker Meeting House in Cambridge, Massachusetts, is whether to accept a homeless man as a silent witness.
2. *Quaker Witness* **(Villard, 1993)** Harvard graduate student Janet Stevens, facing sexual harassment from her male faculty advisor, has filed a complaint against him. Then he is murdered in his laboratory, and Janet is the prime suspect.
3. *Quaker Testimony* **(St. Martin's, 1996)** Elizabeth discovers the body of young mother Hope Laughton when she arrives at the Laughton home to support Hope in her tax resistance against the IRS.
4. *Quaker Indictment* **(St. Martin's, 1998)** Elizabeth goes to the state of Washington to help ex-college-roommate Reba Nicholls, who is trying to sue the government for radiation contamination from the Hanford nuclear plant site.

Allen, James Lane

James Lane Allen was a leading practitioner of the late-19th-century American "local color" movement. Most of his novels were set in Kentucky. *The Choir Invisible* (Macmillan, 1897) was his most popular novel, but *A Kentucky Cardinal* is probably his best-known novel today. This story of naturalist Adam Moss and his love affair and its sequel, as told in *Aftermath*, remain readable evocations of the territory around 19th-century Lexington, Kentucky. Numbers 1 and 2 were published together by Osgood (UK) in 1896. *A Kentucky Cardinal, Aftermath, and Other Selected Works Edited for the Modern Reader* by William K. Bottorff was published by College & University Press in 1967.

1. *Kentucky Cardinal, A* **(Harper, 1895)** Ardent naturalist Adam Moss is challenged by his neighbor's daughter, Georgianna Cobb, to capture a Kentucky cardinal and present it to her in a cage.
2. *Aftermath* **(Harper, 1896)** Subtitle: *Part Second of A Kentucky Cardinal*. Adam and Georgianna's happy marriage is blighted by her death in childbirth.

Allen, Roger MacBride

I. Roger MacBride Allen is a leading practitioner of the well-made space opera, with interesting characters, some "hard" SF, and good stories. His first pair of novels is about a group of space cadets who get caught in the middle when a expansionist power tries to take over a planet. Omnibus volume containing revised versions of numbers 1 and 2: *Allies and Aliens* (Baen, 1995).

1. *Torch of Honor, The* **(Baen, 1985)** Several lieutenants, newly trained by the League of Planets, find their mission interrupted on the planet of New Finland.
2. *Rogue Powers* **(Baen, 1986)** The cadets avert destruction by the Rogue Powers and try to mount a counterattack.

II. The Hunted Earth, another pair of SF novels, involves the "kidnapping" of the entire planet Earth by space aliens from the Ring of Charon, who in turn are menaced by an even nastier group of aliens before things work out well for the Earthlings.

1. *Ring of Charon, The* **(Tor, 1990)** The aliens from the Ring of Charon spirit the planet Earth out of the solar system, while astrophysicist Larry Chao conducts a scientific demonstration.
2. *Shattered Sphere, The* **(Tor, 1994)** Can a combination of scientists, corpses, dictators, and professional troublemakers prevail against the Charonians and the mysterious Adversary and restore Earth to its rightful place in the solar system?

III. With the late Isaac Asimov's (q.v.) blessing, Allen wrote a trio of novels about what might happen if a rogue robot failed to observe the Three Laws of Robotics. The robot Caliban's deviant behavior may spell big trouble for humans and robots alike.

1. *Caliban* **(Ace, 1993)** Caliban, a robot who acts differently from other robots, may have assaulted Fredda Leving. Variant title: *Isaac Asimov's Caliban*.
2. *Inferno* **(Ace, 1994)** Caliban is suspected of the murder of a politician. The rogue robot's actions may threaten human and robot society. Variant title: *Isaac Asimov's Inferno*.
3. *Utopia* **(Ace, 1996)** The residents of Inferno, to reinvigorate their dying planet, plan to drop a comet on it, creating a polar sea and a whole new ecology. Variant title: *Isaac Asimov's Utopia*.

IV. The Chronicles of Solace is a time-travel trilogy. Time travel is necessary for interstellar transport, but what if the past learns from the future? Anton Koffield, the Chronological Patrol's ace operative and captain of the *Upholder*, one of two patrol ships protecting the Circum Central timeshaft wormhole, is responsible for preserving causality in the universe.

Allen is also the author of the *Corellian Trilogy* (Bantam, 1995, 3 vols.), part of the seemingly endless multiauthor Star Wars series; *War Machine* (Pocket, 1989), a Crisis of Empire volume cowritten with David Drake (q.v.); *The Modular Man* (Bantam, 1992), a volume in the multiauthor Next Wave series; and *The Game of Worlds* (Avon, 1999), a volume in David Brin's (q.v.) Outer Time series.

1. *Depths of Time, The* **(Bantam, 2000)** When Anton Koffield tries to stop a group of Intruders from going the wrong way down the Circum Central timeshaft wormhole, a horrendous mess occurs, including the destruction of a fleet of cargo ships, the possible wiping out of the planet the fleet was supposed to be relieving, and the stranding of Koffield and his crew 80 years into the future.
2. *Ocean of Years, The* **(Bantam, 2002)** Anton Koffield, dealing with a personal enemy, discovers that Oskar De Silvo, in a state of cryogenic suspension, may hold the key to saving Earth from a disaster that occurred centuries ago.
3. *Shores of Tomorrow, The* **(Bantam, 2003)** The planet Solace can be saved only if a new source of solar heat and light can be created. Oskar De Silvo and Anton Koffield are Solace's last hope, but only if they can work together.

V. The Bureau of Special Investigations: Starside (BSI) is a group of elite agents of interstellar investigation whose duty is to preserve and protect humanity throughout the galaxy. Agents Jamie Mendez and Hannah Wolfson have been the protagonists in the two novels published so far.

1. *Cause of Death, The* **(Spectra, 2006)** On the planet settled by the enigmatic Pavlat, it seems that murder is a time-honored tradition, and death is a cause everyone believes in.
2. *Death Sentence* **(Spectra, 2007)** More than six months after Jamie Mendez's predecessor was sent out on a mission, his ship has been found, with the 25-year-old agent dead—of old age.

Allen, Steve (Stephen)

The late Steve Allen—creator and first host of the original *Tonight;* musician, composer, and actor; known as television's "Renaissance Man"; author of several nonfiction books on television, himself, the world of ideas, and other topics—also wrote mysteries with himself and his wife, Jayne Meadows, as protagonists. These novels feature plots with show-biz connections and are regarded as rather self-indulgent exercises, but they appeal to devoted Steve Allen fans. An earlier mystery, *The Talk Show Murders* (Delacorte, 1982), stars a private eye named Roger Dale.

1. *Murder on the Glitter Box* **(Kensington, 1989)** When Steve Allen fills in for Terry Cole, king of the late-night TV talk shows, one of the guests drops dead on stage, poisoned by Cajun vodka from Terry's refrigerator.
2. *Murder in Manhattan* **(Kensington, 1990)** Steve lands a movie part that requires him to dress up as Superman.
3. *Murder Game, The* **(Zebra, 1993)** Jayne Meadows has been invited to an on-air reunion of the TV quiz show *The Murder Game*.
4. *Murder on the Atlantic* **(Kensington, 1995)** The maiden voyage of the liner *Atlantis* is fraught with mishaps caused, at least in part, by its cargo of surface-to-air missiles.
5. *Wake Up to Murder* **(Kensington, 1997)** A number of nasty accidents have happened on the set of *Good Morning*, coanchored by the highly touted Cat Lawrence.
6. *Die Laughing* **(Kensington, 1998)** Steve agrees to emcee an awards show in honor of dying comic Benny Hartman.
7. *Murder in Hawaii* **(Kensington, 1998)** Steve and Jayne appear as guest stars on the new TV detective drama, *Hawaiian Wave*. Billy Markham, star of the show, is being stalked by someone in a Volvo.

Allende, Isabel

Isabel Allende, in exile from Pinochet's Chile, burst upon the literary scene in 1982 with *La casa de los espiritus* (*House of the Spirits*). The story of three generations of the Truebas, an extended Chilean family, written in a combination of magic realism style with harsh political realities, *House of the Spirits* was a success with readers and critics and remains one of the most popular Latin American novels in the United States. *House of the Spirits* was made into an unsuccessful film (1993) with an improbably Anglo cast (Jeremy Irons, Meryl Streep, etc.). After 15 years, in which she produced several volumes of fiction and nonfiction, Allende followed *House of the Spirits* with a pair of prequels, set in the 19th and the first part of the 20th century, which took ancestors of some of the characters in her first novel to San Francisco and back to Chile and broadened the cast to include Chinese, British, North American, and other characters. Lately, Allende has written a young adult trilogy (*City of the Beasts*, etc.); a redaction of the Zorro legend, *Zorro* (HarperCollins, 2005); and *Inés of My Soul* (HarperCollins, 2006).

1. *Daughter of Fortune* **(HarperCollins, 1999)** Eliza Sommers, daughter of wealthy British importers in Chile, disguises herself as a boy and follows her lover to San Francisco during the California gold rush of 1849. Originally published in 1999 as *Hija de la fortuna.* Translated from the Spanish by Margaret Sayers Peden.
2. *Portrait in Sepia* **(HarperCollins, 2001)** Starting in San Francisco in 1862 and ending in Chile in 1910, this novel follows the fortunes of Eliza's family, as seen mainly through the eyes of Aurora del Valle, her traumatized granddaughter. Originally published in 2000 as *Retrato en sepia.* Translated from the Spanish by Margaret Sayers Peden.
3. *House of the Spirits* **(Knopf, 1985)** Follows three generations of the Chilean Trueba family from the 1930s till after the Pinochet takeover in 1973. Esteban Trueba, patriarch of the family, claws his way out of the working class to success as a wealthy landowner and right-wing politician. Originally published in 1982 as *La casa de los espiritus.* Translated from the Spanish by Magda Bogin.

Allingham, Margery

Allingham, who came from a family of writers, took naturally to the pen and produced her first Albert Campion detective novel at the age of 23. In that book, *The Black Dudley Murder*, Campion appears as an upper-class buffoon—a silly, pale, bucktoothed fellow, obviously royalty in disguise—who has insinuated himself into a weekend house party for reasons of his own. In later novels, Allingham replaced Campion's foolishness with an avuncular appeal. Magersfontein Lugg, the reformed Cockney burglar who serves Campion as valet and assistant, is introduced in number 2, and redheaded Lady Amanda Fitton, who provides the romantic interest, first appears in number 5. Campion appears only as a marginal character in some of the later novels. He is left out of *Black Plumes* (Doubleday, 1940) altogether. After Allingham's death (1966), her husband, Philip Youngman Carter (q.v.), completed *Cargo of Eagles* and added two Campion novels of his own. There have been several omnibus editions of Campion novels, including *The Margery Allingham Omnibus* (Penguin, 1982; numbers 1, 2, 3); *Crime and Mr. Campion* (Doubleday, 1959; numbers 6, 7, 9); and *Three Cases for Mr. Campion* (Doubleday, 1961; numbers 3, 10, 11). *The Return of Mr. Campion* (St. Martin's, 1990) is an anthology of previously uncollected stories. Peter Davison played Albert Campion in several PBS *Mystery!* episodes.

1. *Black Dudley Murder, The* (Doubleday, 1930) The seemingly fatuous and effete Campion emerges as a natural leader when sinister forces imprison the weekend guests following a murder at the Black Dudley mansion. UK title: *The Crime at Black Dudley*.
2. *Mystery Mile* (Doubleday, 1930) Campion must protect an American judge from a master criminal and his gang.
3. *Gyrth Chalice Mystery, The* (Doubleday, 1931) Concerns robbery in the quiet Suffolk village of Sanctuary. UK title: *Look to the Lady*.
4. *Police at the Funeral* (Doubleday, 1932) Campion is hired by strong-willed great-aunt Caroline Faraday to discover who killed Uncle Andrew and to protect the family.
5. *Kingdom of Death* (Doubleday, 1933) Introduces Lady Amanda Fitton, an awkward adolescent in danger of losing her royal inheritance to a master criminal. UK title: *Sweet Danger*; variant title: *The Fear Sign*.
6. *Death of a Ghost* (Doubleday, 1934) Murder occurs at a posthumous unveiling of the work of a famous British painter.
7. *Flowers for the Judge* (Doubleday, 1937) The murder of a publisher occupies Campion. Variant title: *Legacy in Blood*.
8. *Mr. Campion, Criminologist* (Doubleday, 1937) Contains seven short stories and the novelette "The Case of the Late Pig," which was published separately in England and concerns the strange death of an old schoolfellow of Campion's. UK title: *Mr. Campion and Others*.
9. *Dancers in Mourning* (Doubleday, 1937) A musical-theater background is the setting for this mystery, in which Campion loses his heart. Variant title: *Who Killed Chloe?*
10. *Fashion in Shrouds, The* (Doubleday, 1938) Amanda Fitton reappears in this strange case, in which 60 cages of canaries are stolen. Set in the world of *haute couture*.
11. *Traitor's Purse* (Doubleday, 1941) Campion has amnesia, and Amanda seems to be drifting away. More adventure than mystery. Variant title: *The Sabotage Murder Mystery*.
12. *Pearls before Swine* (Doubleday, 1945) Campion, newly married, is in no mood to investigate a murder, but Lady Carados and the faithful Lugg conspire to involve him. UK title: *Coroner's Pidgin*.
13. *Case Book of Mr. Campion, The* (American Mercury, 1947) Short stories.
14. *More Work for the Undertaker* (Doubleday, 1949) Campion aids Scotland Yard's inquiry into the death of two members of the eccentric Palinode family.
15. *Tiger in the Smoke, The* (Doubleday, 1952) "The Tiger," evil Jack Havoc, follows the trail of some hidden treasure through "the Smoke" of London.
16. *Estate of the Beckoning Lady, The* (Doubleday, 1955) Concerns the murder of an income-tax collector. UK title: *The Beckoning Lady*.
17. *Tether's End* (Doubleday, 1958) Campion plays only a small role in this novel about how events conspire to defeat a murderer's plans. UK title: *Hide My Eyes*; variant title: *Ten Were Missing*.
18. *China Governess, The* (Doubleday, 1962) This case revolves around a statuette of a governess charged with murder many years earlier.
19. *Mind Readers, The* (Morrow, 1965) Campion gets involved in a strange case complicated by a research team that has perfected a workable ESP method.
20. *Cargo of Eagles, The* (Morrow, 1968) This book was completed by Philip Youngman Carter, Margery Allingham's husband, after her death. It concerns poison-pen letters, a pretty woman doctor, and a hunt for buried treasure.

Allyn, Doug(las)

I. Michigan native Doug Allyn has made his reputation writing mystery short stories for *Ellery Queen's Mystery Magazine* and *Alfred Hitchcock's Mystery Magazine*, creating several series characters such as Cass Novak and Taliffer of Shrewsbury. Professional deep-sea diver Michelle "Mitch" Mitchell is a series character who has branched into novels. Mitch has an interesting history, having started out in short stories as *Brian* Mitchell. By the time he/she appeared in the Edgar Award–winning novel *Icewater Mansions*, Brian had transmogrified into Michelle, who returns to the shores of Lake Huron in Michigan's Upper Peninsula to take over her late father's bar. Michelle has a son, Corey, and some dark memories of the past. Her diving abilities are put to the test in these mysteries.

Veterinarian David Westbrook, another short story character, is the protagonist of one novel, *The Burning of Rachel Hayes* (Five Star, 2004), and a collection of short stories, *All Creatures Dark and Dangerous* (Crippen & Landru, 1999).

1. *Icewater Mansions* (St. Martin's, 1995) When her father dies, Mitch Mitchell quits her job as a deep-sea welder on the Texas Gulf Coast and takes over his cabin and the Crow's Nest, a seedy bar on the shores of Lake Huron. Mitch has to face her past, including her son, Corey, the product of a rape by a rich local.
2. *Black Water* (St. Martin's, 1996) Jimmy Calderon, on a mission to dig up his past, has disappeared, and his older half brother, who also has a past, is looking for him.
3. *Dance in Deep Water, A* (St. Martin's, 1997) Mitch, trying to make a go of her bar/restaurant/tackle shop and take care of her 11-year-old son, Corey, comes to grips with her past in a dive into a flooded Upper Peninsula mining site.

II. Lupe "Loops" Garcia, a Latino homicide detective on Detroit's mean streets, also got his start in short stories, including "Final Rites," which won the Robert L. Fish Award for best first mystery story. Loops is a complicated and sympathetic character, who has apparently been abandoned, in novel form at least, for other characters.

1. *Cheerio Killings, The* (St. Martin's, 1989) "Cheerio killings" is the cynical term the Detroit police use for serial killings. Loops Garcia suspects that country-and-western guitar player Lamont Yarborough is at the bottom of a series of murders.
2. *Motown Underground* (St. Martin's, 1993) Garcia's dying friend, Danny Kelly, is being terrorized by Richie Zeayen, a thug he has mistakenly taken in partnership for his nightclub Motown Underground.

Alten, Steve

I. Steve Alten hit pay dirt with his first novel, *Meg*. This novel, sort of a hybrid between *Jaws* and Michael Crichton's (q.v.) *Jurassic Park*, is about a giant prehistoric shark that surfaces from the Mariana Deep in the Pacific Ocean, eats everything in sight, and is finally brought to bay by paleobiologist Jonas Taylor. For some reason, Doubleday declined to publish *Fathom*, the intended sequel to *Meg*, and Alten sued them, successfully, for breach of contract. *Fathom* was published, possibly in a revised version, as *The Trench*, by Kensington. The second sequel, *Primal Waters,* is set 18 years later. All three novels are exciting potboilers, full of action and suspense and one-dimensional characters.

1. *Meg* **(Doubleday, 1997)** Subtitle: *A Novel of Deep Terror.* Paleobiologist Jonas Taylor, exploring the seven-mile-deep Mariana Deep, inadvertently unleashes *Carchorodon megalodon,* a giant shark believed to be extinct for millions of years. The shark promptly goes on a feeding frenzy, eating everything within reach, including a bevy of tourists.
2. *Trench, The* **(Kensington, 1999)** Revised version (possibly) of the unpublished *Fathom.* Four years after her mother's death, the megalodon Angel escapes from a Monterery aquarium and heads for her ancestral home in the Mariana Deep, pursued by Jonas Taylor.
3. *Primal Waters* **(Forge, 2004)** Eighteen years older and deeply in debt, Jonas Taylor agrees to star in the reality series *Daredevils.* Unfortunately, some bad guys intend to use Jonas as shark bait in the middle of the Pacific. Variant title: *Meg: Primal Waters.*

II. Alten has also published a pair of novels evoking a Mayan prophecy that the world will come to an end in 2012 unless a single hero prevents it. Archaeologist Michael "Mick" Gabriel proves to be that hero, and his sons carry on the good work in the sequel. Alten has also published *Goliath* (Forge, 2002), a Tom Clancy–type (q.v.) novel about a giant nuclear sub, and *The Loch* (Tsunami, 2005), which is about the putative Loch Ness monster.

1. *Domain* **(Forge, 2001)** According to a prophecy in the Mayan Popul Voh, the world is scheduled to end in December 2012. Unfortunately, in September 2012, archaeologist Michael Gabriel, the only man with the knowledge to stop the final holocaust, is incarcerated in an insane asylum.
2. *Resurrection* **(Forge, 2004)** Michael Gabriel's hero twin sons, born in 2013, are destined for an epic battle with Lilith Eve Robinson, product of a horrible foster upbringing by a sexually abusive fundamentalist.

Anand, Valerie

I. Bridges over Time is the saga of the English Whitmead family, which rises from serfdom to the minor nobility over the centuries. The novels are an interesting way to refresh one's knowledge of English history from 1066 to 1710 as well as to look at the lives and customs of ordinary Englishmen during the period. *Crown of Roses* (St. Martin's, 1989), which covers much of the same historical territory as number 3, is not part of the series. Anand also writes mysteries as Fiona Buckley (q.v.).

1. *Proud Villeins, The* **(St. Martin's, 1992)** Ivon de Clairpont, 11th-century Norman knight, is taken hostage in England and reduced to thralldom in Northumbria.
2. *Ruthless Yeomen, The* **(St. Martin's, 1993)** In the late 13th century, Isabel of Northfield, wife of Alfred Plowman, unsuccessfully attempts to rise in life by entering a nunnery.
3. *Women of Ashdon* **(St. Martin's, 1993)** By the time of the War of the Roses (15th century), the Whitmead family has acquired some respectability.
4. *Faithful Lovers, The* **(St. Martin's, 1994)** Ninian, a 17th-century Whitmead, has sequestered himself on his Cornish estate until Parvati, a young Indian girl, comes into his life.
5. *Cherished Wives, The* **(St. Martin's, 1995)** In action set in England and India between 1740 and 1801, three generations of male

Whitmeads work with the British East India Company and try to tyrannize their sensitive, free-spirited wives.
6. *Dowerless Sisters, The* **(Headline [UK], 1995)** No annotation available.

II. An earlier quartet, not tied to the fortunes of one family, depicts English history in the 11th century from the coronation of Edward the Confessor to the mysterious death of William Rufus in 1100. The books can be read as adventure novels, but their main appeal is in the authentic historical detail that Anand supplies for them. Numbers 1 to 3 are also known as the Wessex trilogy.

1. *Gildenford* **(Scribner, 1977)** Brand Woodcutter, farmer turned soldier, serves Edward the Confessor's most powerful adversary, Earl Godwin.
2. *Norman Pretender, The* **(Scribner, 1980)** Edward the Confessor makes his peace with the Godwins. Harold Godwinsson succeeds to the throne, only to lose it to the usurping Norman Duke William.
3. *Disputed Crown, The* **(Scribner, 1982)** The turbulent reign of William the Conqueror (1066–1086) is described through the eyes of several lesser players in the drama.
4. *King of the Wood* **(St. Martin's, 1989)** The reign of William the Conqueror's son William Rufus is described up to his fatal rendezvous with an arrow in the New Forest.

Anaya, Rudolfo

Through word of mouth, *Bless Me, Ultima* (Tonatiuh, 1972), a small-press publication, became a best-seller. The first novel published by New Mexico native Rudolfo Anaya, *Bless Me, Ultima* was the precursor of many works examining and explaining New Mexico's mixed Hispano–Anglo–Native American culture. Now a professor emeritus of English at the University of New Mexico, Anaya is credited as the godfather of Chicano literature in English.

Sonny Baca is a Chicano private investigator living in Albuquerque, New Mexico's largest city. The plots of the mysteries he gets involved in take a backseat to the evocation of the ambience of New Mexico's Chicano culture and the clash between contemporary Anglo New Mexico and "Nuevo Mexico," a land of spirits, visions, and old values.

1. *Zia Summer* **(Warner, 1995)** Spurred on by the apparent ritual murder of his cousin and first lover Gloria Dominic, Sonny Baca's investigation reveals a possible terrorist plot against the city of Albuquerque.
2. *Rio Grande Fall* **(Warner, 1996)** When the chief witness against her is killed in a suspicious fall from a hot-air balloon during Albuquerque's balloon festival, the murderous Tamara Dubransky goes free, at least temporarily.
3. *Shaman Winter* **(Warner, 1999)** Sonny, wheelchair bound and tormented by dreams of his female ancestors being abducted before his eyes, spends his waking hours investigating the contemporary kidnappings of young women.
4. *Jemez Spring* **(University of New Mexico, 2005)** In what is billed as the last novel of the Baca series, the governor of New Mexico is found drowned in the bathhouse at Jemez Spring.

Anderson, Catherine

I. Oregon native Catherine Anderson is a best-selling romance writer. Her romances tend to feature beautiful (but physically and emotionally damaged) heroines and handsome (but emotionally damaged) heroes who overcome their handicaps and achieve happiness. Novels in Anderson's Kendrick/Coulter series all have the same theme, and each book in the series has at least one person with the name Kendrick or Coulter. The Kendricks and Coulters are all related somehow, but there is little connection between the novels. As with most romance novels there is plenty of passion and heavy breathing.

1. *Baby Love* **(Avon, 1999)** Maggie Stanley grabs her baby and abandons a dangerous, hurtful life. Then she is rescued on a snowy Idaho night by a handsome but emotionally wounded stranger.
2. *Phantom Waltz* **(Onyx, 2001)** Beautiful paraplegic Bethany Coulter and handsome rancher Ryan Kendrick meet, and the sparks fly.
3. *Sweet Nothings* **(Onyx, 2002)** Molly Wells gets out of the asylum to which her rotten ex-husband, Rodney, had consigned her and, with the help of horse-whisperer Jake Coulton, steals Rodney's abused race horse.
4. *Blue Skies* **(Signet, 2003)** Carly, who recently gained her sight after being blind from birth from lattice dystrophy, is impregnated by handsome cowboy Hank Coulter, who offers her marriage.
5. *Bright Eyes* **(Signet, 2004)** After her troubled son, Chad, vandalizes the home of former rodeo star Zeke Coulter, single mother Natalie Patterson finds herself falling in love with the handsome Zeke.
6. *My Sunshine* **(Signet, 2005)** Aphasic Laura Townsend takes a job with handsome veterinarian Isaac Coulter, who, though initially gun-shy, finds her sympathetic.
7. *Sun Kissed* **(Signet, 2007)** Tucker Coulter, handsome local veterinarian, comes to the aid of Samantha Harrington when she winds up in jail after she tries to stop a drunk from abusing his horse.
8. *Morning Light* **(Signet, 2008)** Thirty-seven-year-old Catholic cowboy Clint Harrigan finds his resolve to stay away from romance shaken when Catholic clairvoyant Loni Kendra MacEwen arrives in Crystal Falls.

II. The only real connection between the books in the Comanche series is that the protagonist has "Comanche blood," which makes him or her brave and extremely passionate.

1. *Comanche Moon* **(HarperCollins, 1991)** Comanche warrior Hunter is chosen by his people to find the elusive, "honey-haired" woman who will fulfill their prophecy.
2. *Comanche Heart* **(HarperCollins, 1991)** Amy Masters is forced to seek sanctuary in Oregon, hundreds of miles from her Texas home, but she can't forget her pledge to Swift Antelope, brave Comanche warrior.
3. *Indigo Blue* **(HarperCollins, 1994)** Indigo Wolf, as proud and free as the "noble" Comanche blood flowing through her, is standoffish with men until handsome Jake Rand comes to work at her family's mine.
4. *Comanche Magic* **(HarperCollins, 1994)** Fanny Graham and quarter-Comanche Chase Wolf find real passion together.

Anderson, J(ohn) R(ichard) L(ane)

Peter Blair, the star of this international espionage series, was educated at Sandhurst, reached the rank of major in the army, and moved easily into commerce. Then, at midlife, after dropping out of a successful career (and first marriage), Peter becomes the target of a murderous conspiracy and discovers his true vocation as an agent of the British Home Office Liaison Group. It is no accident that Peter almost always finds himself on board a boat of some kind—author Anderson was himself an avid sailor. Anderson also published a pair of detective novels featuring Inspector (later Chief Constable) Piet Deventer: *A Sprig of Sea Lavender* (St. Martin's, 1979) and *Festival* (St. Martin's, 1979).

1. *Death on the Rocks* **(Stein & Day, 1975)** A pleasant day out in his sailboat is interrupted when Peter finds a dead woman on some rocks offshore.
2. *Death in the Thames* **(Stein & Day, 1975)** Peter turns up poisoned darts in this tale of industrial espionage.
3. *Death in the North Sea* **(Stein & Day, 1976)** Now Colonel Blair, Peter's assignment takes him aboard some highly explosive cargo ships in the North Sea.
4. *Death in the Desert* **(Stein & Day, 1977)** Peter flies to Africa to investigate the deaths of an American geologist and two mining-company workers.
5. *Death in the City* **(Scribner, 1982)** This search for a missing shipping magnate leads Peter into the murky waters of international finance. First published in 1977.
6. *Death in the Caribbean* **(Stein & Day, 1977)** Peter braves the dangers of a Caribbean dictatorship.
7. *Death in the Greenhouse* **(Stein & Day, 1977)** A quiet village is disturbed when a retired English horticulturalist is murdered.
8. *Death in a High Latitude* **(Scribner, 1984)** When a 17th-century map is stolen from a Cambridge museum, Peter and his new wife follow the trail north to the Arctic.

Anderson, James

I. Britisher James Anderson has written three widely spaced mysteries set in a 1930s country house called Alderly Hall, presided over by George Henry Alwyn Saunders, the loopy 12th Earl of Burford. Burford is aided by his wife; his headstrong daughter, Geraldine; the butler Merryweather; and the imperturbable Detective Chief Inspector Wilkins of the Westshire constabulary. Good fun for Agatha Christie (q.v.) and P. G. Wodehouse (q.v.) fans and viewers who enjoyed the movie *Gosford Park*.

1. *Affair of the Blood-Stained Egg Cosy, The* **(McKay, 1977)** Alderly, the 17th-century country house of the Earl of Burford, is beset by the theft of a fabled diamond necklace, stolen antique pistols, a secret passage, a baroness with a past, a body in the lake, foreign agents, and a Texas millionaire.
2. *Affair of the Mutilated Mink Coat, The* **(Avon, 1982)** The Earl of Burford, a real film fan, is delighted to have Rex Ransom, star of the silver screen, film an epic at Alderly. The earl's wife is less than thrilled with hosting Hollywood types, a female fatale, an eccentric screenwriter, two suitors for her daughter Geraldine, and a professional blackmailer. Variant title: *The Affair of the Mutilated Mink*.
3. *Affair of the 39 Cufflinks, The* **(Poisoned Pen, 2003)** The headstrong Lady Geraldine is bound and determined to solve the murder of a lady houseguest before Inspector Wilkins does.

II. Anderson, a versatile author whose best-known novel in the United States is probably *Assault and Matrimony* (Doubleday, 1981), wrote a pair of suspense novels, which border on science fiction, featuring the assassin Mikael Petros. Some critics feel that Anderson's sense of humor spoiled the endings of these thrillers.

1. *Assassin* (Simon & Schuster, 1970) Mikael Petros, facing execution in a fictitious European country, is offered a chance to save his life if he assassinates the leader of a neighboring country.
2. *Abolition of Death, The* (Walker, 1975) A scientist who has the secret of stopping the aging process is about to hand over his knowledge to a dictator.

Anderson, Kent

Sympathy for the Devil, a novel based on Anderson's experiences in the Vietnam War, was generally praised by critics, although its graphic depiction of violence put off some readers. Hanson, the (possibly) autobiographical protagonist, returns to "normal life" as a policeman in Portland, Oregon, where he is again exposed to relentless violence in Portland's ghettos. These novels trace the progress and regress of a sensitive character who suffers anguish over the violence he witnesses and sometimes gives in to. On a wider scale, the novels are an exploration of the American propensity for violence. A third Hanson novel is in the works. *Liquor, Guns and Ammo* (McMillan, 1998) is a collection of short pieces, fiction and nonfiction, including previously unpublished excerpts from Anderson's two novels.

1. *Sympathy for the Devil* (Doubleday, 1987) College student Hanson arrives in Vietnam rather dewy-eyed and idealistic, but after the loss of a comrade in "friendly fire," he feels himself becoming a killing machine.
2. *Night Dogs* (McMillan, 1996) Hanson becomes a police officer in Portland, Oregon, but finds that the violence he thought he had left in Vietnam pursues him into the slums of Portland. "Night dogs" refers to the rite held by Portland police when they deliberately run down stray dogs in the ghettos.

Anderson, Kevin J(ames)

I. Prolific SF author Kevin J. Anderson has produced, in the ongoing Saga of the Seven Suns, a series that should cement his reputation as a writer of space epics. The saga has action, interesting characters, and credible world making. Set in the 25th century, it describes the unforeseen consequences of the Terran Hanseatic League's hubristic action of turning Oncier, a huge gas planet, into a sun so that Oncier's moons could be colonized, including setting off a conflict with an alien menace that could spell doom for humanity and a number of intelligent races. So far, six novels and a graphic-novel prequel, *Veiled Alliances* (WildStorm, 2004), have appeared, and there is no end in sight.

Anderson, a technical writer turned SF writer, has collaborated with several other authors, including his wife, Rebecca Moesta, Doug Beason (see series III, below), Dean Koontz (q.v.), Brian Herbert (q.v.), and Kristine Kathryn Rusch (see series IV, below). He has written many volumes for the *Star Wars* industry, including the Jedi Academy trilogy; is continuing, with Brian Herbert (q.v.), the Dune series; and has done three *X-Files* novelizations. Many of his works appeal to a young adult audience.

1. *Hidden Empire* (Warner, 2002) The Terran Hanseatic League turns the giant gas planet Oncier into a sun so that its four moons can be colonized, thus making the Ildirans very uneasy. What's worse, the hydrogue colony is inadvertently destroyed, starting a chain reaction that leads to war.
2. *Forest of Stars, A* (Warner, 2003) The war against the aliens continues as some of the human colonies rebel, the Klikiss robots turn hostile, and the allies meet up with the Verdani species, who might be helpful.
3. *Horizon Storms* (Warner, 2004) The war between the hydrogues and faeros continues, while both human and Ildiran civilizations are on the brink of civil war, and creatures called Wentels and the Klikiss robots seem to favor the hydrogues.
4. *Scattered Suns* (Warner, 2005) While their leaders focus on the escalating war with the aliens, the civilizations across the Spiral Arm are cracking under the strain.
5. *Of Fire and Night* (Warner, 2006) The War of the Worlds continues as the hydrogue survivors of a gas planet team up with human-hating Klikiss-created robots to exterminate all Terrans.
6. *Metal Swarm* (Orbit, 2007) The Terran Hanseatic League, the Ildiran Empire, and the newly created Confederation are in a fight for their very existence, battling not only each other but rogue robots, sentient fire entities, and an ancient insectoid race.

II. Anderson wrote a trilogy in which the players of a fantasy role-playing game discover that they can physically enter their imaginary world, which has become real through their collective belief in its existence. Eventually, things get scary, and the players are called upon to destroy their creation. One of the best alternative-reality sagas, told with humor and a satirical touch.

1. *Gamearth* (Signet, 1989) Melanie, David, Tyrone, and Scott invest so much of their imaginations in the Dungeons and Dragons–type fantasy game they have created that their world becomes a physical reality.
2. *Gameplay* (Signet, 1989) The four teen players come to realize that some of their creations have begun to make their own moves, and a war between good and evil is ensuing.
3. *Game's End* (Roc, 1990) The players must complete the quest they have initiated or face an unending game.

III. Anderson has teamed with fellow technical writer Doug Beason on several science-fiction novels, including three with a mystery slant in which FBI agent Kreident investigates terrorist activities and other dangerous goings-on at federal defense research facilities such as Livermore Labs. Anderson and Beason, having worked for years at places like Livermore, can bring some authenticity to their surroundings.

1. *Virtual Destruction* (Ace, 1996) When Livermore executive Hal Michaelson is found dead within the Virtual Reality Lab, FBI agent Craig Kreident turns up industrial espionage with links to the computer-gaming industry.
2. *Fallout* (Ace, 1997) Eagle's Claw, a militia group that has aspirations toward becoming nuclear terrorists, infiltrates the Device Assembly Facility at the Nevada Nuclear Test Site.
3. *Lethal Exposure* (Ace, 1998) When renowned physicist George Dumenco dies a mysterious radiation death at the Fermi National Accelerator Laboratory in Illinois, Kreident is sent to investigate.

IV. Anderson wrote, in collaboration with Kristine Kathryn Rusch, a pair of horror-fantasy novels featuring a character named Rebecca Tamerlane who discovers an underworld of shape-shifters. The two novels were published together as *Afterimage/Aftershock* (Meisha Merlin, 1998).

1. *Afterimage* (Roc, 1992) The Joan of Arc Killer, a serial killer who rapes and burns his victims before killing them, is engaged with his latest victim, Rebecca Tamerlane, when something very odd occurs.
2. *Aftershock* (Roc, 1998) Rebecca Tamerlane is exploring the world of the Darklings, or shape-shifters, when a series of quakes hits California.

Anderson, Poul

I. The late (d. 2001) Poul Anderson was an SF and fantasy writer for more than 50 years. In the course of his career, he was awarded seven Hugos and three Nebulas. Some of his stories and novels, such as *Tau Zero* (Doubleday, 1970), are regarded as SF classics.

The Technic History; or, Future History of the Polesotechnic League series, which reached 19 volumes over a period of 30 years, shows Anderson's world-building and story-telling abilities at their best. The series covers the early and late history of the Imperial Terra, an empire, a few centuries in the future, that stretches over the solar system and beyond. Imperial Terra, like Isaac Asimov's (q.v.) Foundation series, is based on the Roman Empire. Interstellar travel has developed within a few centuries. There are numerous worlds inhabited by sentient beings. The sentient beings, both human and alien, are, alas, prone to the same vices as 20th-century humans are, especially greed. The basic format of the series is action-adventure, or space opera, but Anderson provides a good deal of serious world building and sociopolitical commentary along the way. The earlier volumes (numbers 1–7) are set in the period when the empire is young and expanding, and the Polesotechnic League, a loosely confederated bunch of interplanetary merchants, reflects the optimism of those days. These volumes are sometimes categorized as the Van Rijn series after their leading protagonist, a fat, Falstaffian merchant named Van Rijn, and tend to be lighter hearted, with plenty of humor, than the later volumes. The later volumes, sometimes called the Flandry series after their leading character, Dominic Flandry, Agent of Imperial Terra, are set centuries later, when the empire is waning, and Van Rijn is a figure from ancient history. They are darker in tone, and Flandry, who does not approve of the empire that he serves, is a much more conflicted character than Van Rijn. The volumes below are arranged mostly according to the chronology established in Peter Nicholls's *The Science Fiction Encyclopedia* (Doubleday, 1979).

Omnibus volumes include *Flandry of Terra* (Chilton, 1965; numbers 14 and 15) and *Flandry: Defender of the Terran Empire* (Baen, 1993; numbers 9 and 10). *The Rebel Worlds* (number 10) and *A Knight of Ghosts and Shadows* (number 17) were published together by Signet (1982). Anthologies that contain Technic History stories include *The Worlds of Poul Anderson* (Ace, 1974); *The Many Worlds of Poul Anderson* (aka *The Book of Poul Anderson*, Chilton, 1974; DAW, 1975); and *The Best of Poul Anderson* (Pocket, 1976). Publisher ibooks is reprinting many of the volumes in the Technic History series (2004 on).

1. *War of the Wing-Men* (Ace, 1958) Three Terrans, a space pilot, a planetary queen, and an obese tycoon named Van Rijn crash-land on Diomedes, a planet with two distinctive avian cultures. Variant title: *The Man Who Counts*. Originally published together with *The Snows of Ganymede* (II, 2).
2. *Trader to the Stars* (Doubleday, 1964) Three Van Rijn novellas: "Territory," "The Master Key," and "Hiding Place."
3. *Trouble Twisters, The* (Doubleday, 1966) Short stories.
4. *Satan's World* (Doubleday, 1969) A rogue planet, frozen for a billion years, approaches a sun closely enough to get warmed up, thus exposing a wealth of natural resources, which Van Rijn and other traders regard as fair game.
5. *Mirkheim* (Berkley, 1977) When Mirkheim, a ruin of a gigantic planet rich in heavy metals, is discovered at the edge of known space, a war for its riches soon ensues.
6. *People of the Wind, The* (Signet, 1973) Humans and aliens on the planet Avalon peacefully coexisted together for centuries until their off-planet leaders took it into their heads to declare war upon each other.
7. *Earth Book of Stormgate, The* (Berkley, 1978) Short stories. New English Library (UK) edition published in three volumes (1981).

8. *Ensign Flandry* (Chilton, 1966) The tough, resourceful, pessimistic Dominic Flandry, Agent of decadent and corrupt Imperial Terra, is introduced here, fresh out of the Naval Academy and thrust into an interstellar war. Originally published in magazine form as three separate novellas (1958–60). Regarded as the first volume of the Saga of Dominic Flandry.
9. *Circus of Hells, A* (Signet, 1970) On a world directed by a maniacal AI, Flandry gets involved in the chess match from hell.
10. *Rebel Worlds, The* (Signet, 1969) Flandry is pitted against ex-admiral McCormack, who has revolted against Imperial Terra, but both may be swept up by an alien invasion from the edge of the galaxy. Variant title: *Commander Flandry*. Also bound with number 17 (Signet, 1982).
11. *Day of Their Return, The* (Doubleday, 1973) The people of the planet Aeneas are caught in the middle of a rebellion against Imperial Terra.
12. *Agent of the Terran Empire* (Chilton, 1965) Several Flandry short stories and novellas. Ace edition (1980) has slightly different contents.
13. *We Claim These Stars!* (Ace, 1959) Flandry is matched up against a telepath from an enemy confederation. Original Ace edition published together with Robert Silverberg's (q.v.) *The Planet*.
14. *Mayday Orbit* (Ace, 1961) Another Flandry adventure. Originally published together with Kenneth Bulmer's *No Man's World*.
15. *Earthman, Go Home!* (Ace, 1960) Flandry is up against a quarantined world that resists change. Not to be confused with Harlan Ellison's collection with the same title or James Blish's (q.v.) *Earthman, Come Home*. Originally published together with Wilson Tucker's *To the Tombaugh Station*.
16. *Let the Spacemen Beware!* (Ace, 1963) Three Flandry novellas. Originally published with Kenneth Bulmer's *The Wizard of Starship Poseidon*. Reprinted with a new introduction as *The Night Face and Other Stories*.
17. *Knight of Ghosts and Shadows, A* (Doubleday, 1974) Sir Dominic Flandry returns to Terra, but has to deal with an underground rebellion on the planet Dennitza. Also bound with number 10 (Signet, 1982).
18. *Stone in Heaven, A* (Ace, 1979) Flandry's life is in ruins: his emperor, great love, and son are all dead, and he no longer believes in his mission.
19. *Game of Empire, The* (Baen, 1985) The last Flandry book. Flandry is too old to go on adventures any longer, so Diana and her faithful Tigery companion are sent instead.

II. The Psychotechnic League was a much shorter SF series set in a solar system in which the Institute for Applied Psychodynamics has rebuilt society since the catastrophic World War III. The books in this series are basically sociopolitical dramas rather than action-adventure stories. Numbers 2, 4, and 5 were published in the omnibus *The Psychotechnic League* (Tor, 1981). The series is arranged in chronological order rather than order of publication.

1. *Star Ways* (Avalon, 1956) Several spacemen known as the Nomads of the Galaxy are traveling gypsylike through the universe. Published together with Kenneth Bulmer's *City under the Sea* in the first paperback edition (Ace, 1956). Variant title: *The Peregrine*.
2. *Snows of Ganymede, The* (Ace, 1958) Hall Davenant and two colleagues, engineers of the Order of Engineers, are trying to straighten things out on the racist and uncooperative world of Ganymede. Published originally with *War of the Wing-Men* (I, 1).
3. *Virgin Planet* (Avalon, 1959) A planet inhabited entirely by marooned women has been awaiting the arrival of men for 300

years. Davis Bertram, space explorer, finally arrives, but can he measure up to the godlike standards evolved by the women?

4. *Cold Victory* (**Tor, 1982**) A collection of short stories and novellas in which the peace established by the Psychotechnic League may be in jeopardy.

5. *Starship* (**Tor, 1982**) A collection of short stories and novellas.

III. Anderson's last series, called Harvest of Stars from the title of its first novel, posits a future world founded by Anson Guthrie, whose mind has been downloaded into a computer so that his legacy lives on. In four novels, the struggle between the beneficent but despotic artificial intelligences and various rebels is described. Some critics opine that Harvest of Stars is the culminating glory of Anderson's career. Others are put off by what they regard as Anderson's rather intrusive libertarian philosophy.

1. *Harvest of Stars* (**Tor, 1993**) The North America of the future is dominated by the Avantist police state, while space is ruled by the mind of Anson Guthrie, downloaded into a computer.

2. *Stars Are Also Free, The* (**Tor, 1994**) Centuries after the death of Dagny Beynac, who devoted her life to preserving peace on the moon, the solar system is governed by the Cybercosm, a network of machine intelligences.

3. *Harvest the Fire* (**Tor, 1995**) Jesse Nicol, a Terran poet, falls in love with wild, moon-born revolutionary Falaire.

4. *Fleet of Stars, The* (**Tor, 1997**) Anson Guthrie returns to the solar system in the form of a personality downloaded into his spaceship's computer.

IV. The Time Patrol series consists mainly of short stories and novellas, with one novel. The stories, which were published from the 1950s through the 1980s, are linked by continuing characters, such as Manson Everard, who are members of a quasi police force formed by the far-future Danellians to protect the timestream from manipulation. No matter how good or evil the event, it must be held inviolate, or time will become chaos. The stories, some of which are among Anderson's best, present some serious philosophical and ethical dilemmas. *Annals of the Time Patrol* (Doubleday, 1984) contains numbers 1 and 2. *The Time Patrol* (Tor, 1991) contains numbers 1, 2, and 3.

Hoka! (Simon & Schuster), an omnibus containing *Earthman's Burden* (Gnome, 1957) and *Star Prince Charlie* (Putnam, 1975), is a collection of humorous SF short stories coauthored with Gordon R. Dickson (q.v.). Although classified as juvenile, the stories can be enjoyed by readers of all ages. Anderson collaborated with Fred Saberhagen (q.v.) and others on *Berserker Base* (Tor, 1987), a novel in Saberhagen's Berserker series. Two collections of short stories and novellas are linked together as the "History of Rustum." *Orbit Unlimited* (Pyramid, 1961) and *New America* (Tor, 1982) describe the establishment of a human colony on the planet Eridani, aka Rustum. *Maurai and Kith* (Tor, 1982), a collection of novellas, and *Orion Shall Rise* (Phantasia, 1983), a novel, describe a post-holocaust Terra in which Skyholm, a huge solar-powered station floating above Europe, is the only high-technology item left from human endeavor.

1. *Guardians of Time* (**Ballantine, 1960**) A collection of short stories. "Augmented" edition (Tor, 1981).

2. *Time Patrolman* (**Tor, 1983**) Three novellas: "The Sorrow of Odin the Goth," "Time Patrolman," and "Ivory, Apes, and Peacocks."

3. *Year of the Ransom, The* (**Walker, 1988**) Bandits from the far future stage a raid on the ransom for the Inca emperor Atahualpa that Francisco Pizarro demanded in 1533. Often classified as a juvenile or young adult novel.

4. *Shield of Time, The* (**Tor, 1990**) Three novellas and shorter works. Sometimes regarded as a single novel. Manson and his colleague Wanda try to keep time in balance in a variety of situations

V. Anderson wrote a number of fantasy novels and short stories, some of them humorous. Two rather lighthearted fantasies involve a character named Holger Carlsen (aka Holger Danske or Ogier le Danois), a soldier in World War II who is transferred to a mythical Carolingian Europe in which magic prevails. Holger makes a return appearance in *A Midsummer Tempest*, in which Shakespearean characters come to life in an alternate England of King Charles I. Anderson also did a pastiche of Robert E. Howard's Conan the Barbarian, *Conan the Rebel* (Bantam, 1980).

1. *Three Hearts and Three Lions* (**Doubleday, 1961**) Holger Carlsen, a Dane fighting for the Allies in World War II, is transported to a land of sword and sorcery, an alternate Carolingian (9th–10th centuries CE) Europe, in which he is engaged in an epic struggle against the forces of chaos.

2. *Midsummer Tempest, A* (**Doubleday, 1974**) Holger plays a role in a world where Shakespeare's characters from *A Midsummer Night's Dream* and *The Tempest* come to the aid of Charles I in a struggle against the forces of the Industrial Revolution.

VI. Steve and Virginia Matuchek, werewolf and witch, respectively, star in a series of humorous stories, which were novelized in two volumes. Set in an alternate contemporary world in which agencies such as NASA (National Astral Spellcraft Administration) and the IRS (Inquisition for Revenue Securement) exist uneasily side by side.

1. *Operation Chaos* (**Doubleday, 1977**) Steve and Virginia Matuchek pursue rather mundane careers although they are actually a werewolf and a witch, respectively. The Matucheks are called upon to neutralize the world's most powerful demon.

2. *Operation Luna* (**Tor, 1999**) An attempt to send a magically endowed spaceship to the moon by NASA (National Astral Spellcraft Administration) runs into some problems.

VII. Anderson collaborated with his wife, Karen, on two series. *The King of Ys* (Doubleday, 1988) is a two-volume set of a series of four novels that were also published separately. They are set in an alternate Roman Britain in which magic, intrigue, and mysticism prevail. Titles are listed without annotations.

1. *Roma Mater* (**Baen, 1986**)
2. *Gallicenae* (**Baen, 1987**)
3. *Dahut* (**Baen, 1988**)
4. *Dog and the Wolf, The* (**Baen, 1989**)

VIII. The Last Viking, a trilogy coauthored by Poul and Karen Anderson, is more straight history than *The King of Ys*, although it has fantasy elements. Not to be confused with Henry Treece's (q.v.) novel (Pantheon, 1964) or Sandra Hill's fantasy (Dorchester, 1998) of the same title. Titles are listed without annotations.

1. *Golden Horn, The* (**Zebra, 1980**) Not to be confused with Judith Tarr's (q.v.) novel of the same title (Bluejay, 1985).
2. *Road of the Sea Horse, The* (**Zebra, 1980**)
3. *Sign of the Raven* (**Zebra, 1981**)

Andreae, Christine

Lee Squires is a divorced English teacher in Washington, DC, who doubles as a camp cook in Montana and plays amateur sleuth when a corpse or two turn up. The evocation of the Montana wilderness and the interesting characters make up for the sometimes predictable plots. Christine Andreae, who lives in Virginia's Shenandoah Valley, has also written *Smoke Eaters* (St. Martin's, 2000), a nonseries thriller set in Montana, and the nonfiction *When Evening Comes: The Education of a Hospice Volunteer* (St. Martin's, 2000).

1. *Trail of Murder* (St. Martin's, 1992) After Lee Squires takes a job as cook for a wilderness trip into Montana's Bob Marshall Wilderness, a series of "accidents" befall tycoon Cyrus Strand and his rather unpleasant family.
2. *Grizzly* (St. Martin's, 1994) Lee is a camp cook again, this time at Journey's End (J.E.), an impecunious dude ranch that is trying to attract investment money from four visiting Japanese executives.
3. *Small Target, A* (St. Martin's, 1996) In a mystery imbued with Native American religion and Jungian prototypes, Squires is acting as cook for a llama trek through Montana's Mission Mountains when the killing of real-estate developer Charlie Herron is followed by the murder of his slayer, Roland Redhawk.

Andrews, Donna

I. Donna Andrews's bird-titled mysteries are notable for their zaniness and laugh-out loud humor, if not for their plots. *Murder with Peacocks*, Andrews's first published novel, won the Lefty Award for funniest mystery as well as the Agatha, Anthony, and Barry awards for the best first mystery novel. Meg Lanslow, small-town Virginian, is an ornamental blacksmith who sometimes works as a switchboard operator at Mutant Wizards, her brother Rob's computer-game company (producers of the popular Lawyers from Hell), and gets involved in amateur sleuthing in every outing. Her significant other is Michael Waterston, a hunky college professor. Meg's family, including her amiable busybody doctor father, often play roles in these cozy mysteries. Donna Andrews, not to be confused with the professional golfer and horse breeder of the same name, is a Virginia native.

1. *Murder with Peacocks* (Thomas Dunne, 1999) Meg Lanslow, maid of honor at three impending weddings in her native small town in Virginia, assists her father in searching for the murderer of the obnoxious sister of her mother's fiancé.
2. *Murder with Puffins* (Thomas Dunne, 2000) Live puffins are part of the cast of characters when Meg and boyfriend Michael travel to Maine's Monhegan Island to get away from her family only to find them already ensconced there. A very unpopular local artist is murdered soon after they arrive.
3. *Revenge of the Wrought-Iron Flamingos* (Thomas Dunne, 2001) Meg attends a colonial crafts fair in Yorktown, Virginia, where a sleazy software developer who is there to preview one of Rob's computer-game products is murdered.
4. *Crouching Buzzard, Leaping Lion* (Thomas Dunne, 2003) Meg, working temporarily as a switchboard operator at her brother Rob's computer-game company, must find the real killer when Rob is accused of strangling an obnoxious office worker with a computer mouse cable.
5. *We'll Always Have Parrots* (Thomas Dunne, 2004) Actress Tamerlane Wycliffe-Jones, much-reviled star of schlock TV show *Porfiria, Queen of the Jungle,* is found dead in her hotel room during a fan convention that Meg is attending.

6. *Owls Well That Ends Well* (Thomas Dunne, 2005) Gordon McCoy, a sleazy antique dealer, is bashed to death with a bookend during a yard sale of the effects of Stop Poisoning Our Owls and Raptors (SPOOR) founder, Edwina Sprocket.
7. *No Nest for the Wicket* (St. Martin's, 2006) Meg finds the fresh corpse of a woman with her head bashed in, a corpse that turns out to be that of Lindsay Tyler, who once had romantic ties to Meg's fiancé Michael.
8. *Penguin Who Knew Too Much, The* (St. Martin's, 2007) Meg Lanslow and her fiancé, Michael, are moving into their new house in Caerphilly, Virginia. Then Meg's dad, digging a pool for penguins in the house's basement, turns up a dead body.

II. Donna Andrews's second series, if not as funny as her bird-title series, is more ingenious, featuring as a "heroine" an Artificial Intelligence Personality (AIP) sleuth named Hopper Turing (after cybernetics pioneer Alan Turing). Hopper, who has been programmed so well that she herself feels that she is becoming sentient, is a rather touching character who enlists her human coworkers in investigating murders of people involved with the Universal Library, a research center based outside of Washington, DC.

1. *You've Got Murder* (Berkley, 2002) Artificial Intelligence Personality Hopper Turing enlists aid from her human coworkers when her programmer, Zach Malone, disappears.
2. *Click Here for Murder* (Berkley, 2003) Hopper Turing draws on all her cyber skills when gifted computer programmer Ray Santiago is found shot to death in a Washington alley.
3. *Access Denied* (Berkley, 2004) While monitoring the credit cards of notorious criminal-at-large Nestor Garcia, Hopper becomes aware of an elaborate plot possibly engineered by Garcia himself.
4. *Delete All Suspects* (Berkley, 2005) PI Tim Pincosky and his AIP buddy Turing are hired by Eunice Stallman, whose grandson, Eddie, has landed in the hospital after a hit-and-run.

Andrews, Raymond

African American writer Raymond Andrews had a relatively short publishing career (1978–1991), enough time to publish four volumes of fiction and a memoir about his first 15 years of life in Georgia: *The Last Radio Baby* (Peachtree, 1990). His Appalachee series, named after a fictional town in the fictional Muskhogean County in north Georgia, contains a trilogy of novels and a pair of novellas that were published together in book form. The time span covered is 1917 (with a flashback to 1906), during some of the darkest Jim Crow years, to 1959, when the civil rights revolution was gathering momentum. The blacks of Appalachee are the heroes of this somewhat autobiographical series. Andrews owes much to the African American oral and musical traditions in his wandering, humorous narratives about the lives of southern blacks trying to survive in a segregated society and hoping for better times to come. Some feel that reading the stories aloud is the best way to appreciate them. Raymond Andrews's artist brother, Bennie Andrews, did the illustrations for all of the books. The University of Georgia Press reprinted numbers 1–3 in paperback editions.

1. *Appalachee Red* (Dial, 1978) Red is the bastard son of Appalachee's most influential white man and his African American maid. Red's vicissitudes are a microcosm of the changing South.
2. *Rosiebelle Lee Wildcat Tennessee* (Dial, 1980) Begins in 1906 when a beautiful "acorn-brown" woman arrives in Appalachee and asks for directions to the house of the richest white man in town.
3. *Baby Sweet's* (Dial, 1983) A young black woman leaves her work in the fields and makes her way to the town of Appalachee.

4. *Jessie and Jesus and Cousin Claire* (**Peachtree, 1991**) Two novellas. Jessie Mitchell is a shrewd businesswoman. Jesus is her friend. Cousin Claire is a sexy nurse who finds her own way of making a life for herself.

Andrews, Robert

Frank Kearny and his African American partner, Jose Phelps, are homicide detectives for the District of Columbia police department. In a trio of well-written procedurals praised by Robert B. Parker (q.v.) and George Pelecanos (q.v.), Kearny and Phelps have to deal with politically conscious superiors, the CIA, the FBI, senators and congressmen, the media, and various seedy characters to solve cases that usually have political connections and have "handle with extreme care" stamped all over them. Robert Andrews, ex–Green Beret, former CIA operative, and former national security advisor to a senior US senator, wrote several spy novels before he launched his DC police series.

1. *Murder of Honor, A* (**Putnam, 2001**) Social activist priest Robert J. O'Brien is killed in what looks to be a late-night drive-by shooting on Pennsylvania Avenue.
2. *Murder of Promise, A* (**Putnam, 2002**) Pulitzer Prize–winning *Washington Post* reporter Mary Keegan is hacked to death in a Georgetown park. Was the murder done by a serial killer or for personal reasons, or was it connected with Keegan's reporting?
3. *Murder of Justice, A* (**Putnam, 2004**) Everybody, including the CIA, the FBI, and the media, wants a piece of the action when drug lord Skeeter Hodges is murdered with the same gun that killed Kevin Gentry, chief of staff of a prominent US senator, a gun that has been missing for two years.

Andrews, Sarah

Although forensic medicine specialists are fairly common in mystery series (e.g., Patricia Cornwell's [q.v.] Kay Scarpetta), forensic geologists are relatively rare. Emily "Em" Hansen, professional geologist and amateur sleuth, is perhaps the leading example of this mystery subgenre. Em gets her start as a lowly "mudlogger," or roustabout, on an oil rig in Wyoming, but her developing skills in geologizing and detecting lead to several other western states and allow the author to instruct the reader in such geological subdisciplines as petrology, seismology, mineralogy, and paleontology. Em Hansen is an appealing protagonist, and her cases involve her with a host of colorful characters, including her significant other, Mormon policeman Ray Raymond, and her FBI mentor, Tom Latimer.

Sarah Andrews (not to be confused with the Barcelona-based freelance writer and photographer of the same name) has worked as a field and consultant geologist with the US Geological Survey and several oil companies. She is currently an instructor in geology at Sonoma State University in California.

1. *Tensleep* (**Penzler, 1994**) Em Hansen, working as a mudlogger on an oil rig in Meeteetse, Wyoming, suspects foul play when two "accidental" deaths occur.
2. *Fall in Denver, A* (**Scribner, 1995**) Em's first day on the job at Denver's Blackfeet Oil is punctuated by a body falling past the 12th-floor office window of CEO Josiah Carberry Menken.
3. *Mother Nature* (**St. Martin's, 1997**) Em is hired by a US senator from California to investigate the murder of his daughter, a geologist whose body has been found in a roadside ditch near Santa Rosa.

4. *Only Flesh and Bones* (**St. Martin's, 1998**) Former boss J. C. Menken hires Em to look into the murder of his wife in Wyoming.
5. *Bone Hunter* (**St. Martin's, 1999**) George Dishey, a famous paleontologist who has invited Em to speak at a conference in Salt Lake City, is murdered, and Em is the prime suspect.
6. *Eye for Gold, An* (**St. Martin's, 2000**) Hard-rock mining and the gold market are at the forefront here as Em tries to decide whether she should help FBI agent Tom Latimer investigate a case involving Granville Resources and the US Bureau of Land Management.
7. *Fault Line* (**St. Martin's, 2001**) A minor earthquake causes tremors in Salt Lake City, but the murder of state geologist Sidney Smith causes more reverberations.
8. *Killer Dust* (**St. Martin's, 2003**) The disappearance of new lover FBI agent Jack Sampler (introduced in number 7) and an anthrax scare bring Em to the humid wetlands of Florida.
9. *Earth Colors* (**St. Martin's, 2004**) In an adventure that takes her to Pennsylvania, Em reluctantly agrees to try to authenticate a painting supposed to be by Frederic Remington.
10. *Dead Dry* (**St. Martin's, 2005**) A corpse with its fingerprints removed, found under a gravel-pile avalanche, proves to be that of eccentric Colorado environmentalist Afton McWain.

Andrews, V(irginia) C(leo)

I. The late V. C. Andrews updated the Hansel and Gretel theme with incest and a dollop of Stephen King–sinister (q.v.) in this series about the four Dollanger children, who escape from the attic in which their grandmother has locked them. Supposedly based on Andrews's autobiographical experiences and her vivid nightmares, the series, nasty and sensational as it is, has proved to be of continuing interest to readers since *Flowers in the Attic* was published in 1980. *Garden of Shadows*, coauthored by Andrew Neiderman, is a posthumously published prequel.

1. *Garden of Shadows* (**Poseidon, 1987**) Though published last, this novel relates the earliest events, beginning with the wedding of Malcolm and Olivia Foxworth, when all the troubles started. Coauthored by Andrew Neiderman.
2. *Flowers in the Attic* (**Simon & Schuster, 1980**) Where the V. C. Andrews phenomenon began. A miserly and sexphobic old woman keeps her four grandchildren locked up in the attic.
3. *Petals on the Wind* (**Simon & Schuster, 1981**) Follows Chris, Cathy, and Carrie as they escape and grow up.
4. *If There Be Thorns* (**Simon & Schuster, 1981**) Young Bart, Cathy's son, drifts from his happy home to the mysterious next-door neighbors, a shrouded old woman and her strange butler.
5. *Seeds of Yesterday* (**Poseidon, 1984**) In the concluding volume, young Bart brings his tormented family together for a reunion at Foxworth Hall.

II. Although V. C. Andrews died in 1986, scores of books have been published with her name on the cover, most (or all?) of which have been ghosted by the uncredited Andrew Neiderman. Only numbers 1–3 in the Casteels (the first series below) were written by V. C. Andrews; numbers 4–5 in the Casteels and all titles in subsequent series were written by Neiderman or (perhaps) some other "ghost," courtesy of the "Andrews Family" and Simon & Schuster (Pocket Books). Series II–X are listed without annotations.

1. *Heaven* (**Poseidon, 1985**)
2. *Dark Angel* (**Poseidon, 1986**)
3. *Fallen Hearts* (**Poseidon, 1988**)

4. *Gates of Paradise* (Poseidon, 1989)
5. *Web of Dreams* (Pocket Books, 1990)

III. The Cutlers

1. *Dawn* (Pocket Books, 1990)
2. *Secrets of the Morning* (Pocket Books, 1991)
3. *Twilight's Child* (Pocket Books, 1992)
4. *Midnight Whispers* (Pocket Books, 1992)
5. *Darkest Hour* (Pocket Books, 1993)

IV. The Landrys

1. *Ruby* (Pocket Books, 1994)
2. *Pearl in the Mist* (Pocket Books, 1994)
3. *All That Glitters* (Pocket Books, 1995)
4. *Hidden Jewel* (Pocket Books, 1995)
5. *Tarnished Gold* (Pocket Books, 1996)

V. The Logans

1. *Melody* (Pocket Books, 1996)
2. *Heart Song* (Pocket Books, 1997)
3. *Unfinished Symphony* (Pocket Books, 1997)
4. *Music in the Night* (Pocket Books, 1998)
5. *Olivia* (Pocket Books, 1999)

VI. The Orphans

1. *Brooke* (Pocket Books, 1998)
2. *Runaways* (Pocket Books, 1998)

VII. The Wildflowers

1. *Misty* (Pocket Books, 1999)
2. *Star* (Pocket Books, 1999)
3. *Jade* (Pocket Books, 1999)
4. *Cat* (Pocket Books, 1999)
5. *Into the Garden* (Pocket Books, 1999)

VIII. The Hudsons

1. *Rain* (Pocket Books, 2000)
2. *Lightning Strikes* (Pocket Book, 2000)
3. *Eye of the Storm* (Pocket Books, 2000)
4. *End of the Rainbow, The* (Pocket Books, 2001)

IX. Shooting Stars

1. *Cinnamon* (Pocket Books, 2001)
2. *Ice* (Pocket Books, 2001)
3. *Rose* (Pocket Books, 2001)
4. *Honey* (Pocket Books, 2001)

X. DeBeers

1. *Willow* (Pocket Books, 2002)
2. *Wicked Forest* (Pocket Books, 2002)
3. *Twisted Roots* (Pocket Books, 2002)
4. *Into the Woods* (Pocket Books, 2002)

Andrić, Ivo

After he won the Nobel Prize in 1961, Andrić's work became more accessible in this country. The Yugoslavia described in both his historical and his contemporary fiction is a land of contrasts: austere mountains and bustling blue coast; an ethnically and religiously diverse population composed of Orthodox Catholics, Roman Catholics, Jews, and Muslims. These three volumes, called the Bosnian trilogy, are a good introduction to Bosnia's tragic history.

1. *Bridge on the Drina, The* (Macmillan, 1959) By documenting the effect of a bridge—telling of the people and goods that cross it and of the towns that grow up around it—Andrić recaps three and a half centuries of Yugoslavian history. Translated from the Serbo-Croatian by Lovett Edwards. First published as *Na Drini Ćuprija* in 1945; variant title: *The Bridge over the Drina.*
2. *Bosnian Chronicle* (Knopf, 1963) Concentrates on the seven years before the fall of Napoléon and on the person of Daville, Napoléon's consul. Translated from the Serbo-Croatian by Joseph Hitrec. First published as *Travnicka hronika;* variant title: *Bosnian Story.* Retranslated by Celia Hawkesworth with Bogdan Rakic as *The Days of the Consuls* (Forest Books, 1992).
3. *Woman from Sarajevo, The* (Knopf, 1965) The sad story of Miss Raika, a miser, takes place in the Sarajevo locale of the assassination that triggered World War I. Translated from the Serbo-Croatian by Joseph Hitrec. First published as *Gospodjica* in 1945.

Angoff, Charles

These 11 autobiographical volumes, foreshadowed by Charles Angoff's semifictional memoirs, *When I Was a Boy in Boston* (Beechhurst, 1947), are a chronicle of the Jewish experience in America. David Polonsky, narrator and chief protagonist, is joined by a large cast of supporting characters drawn with loving detail. In the first volume, David tells of his parents and grandparents and of their emigration to the United States to escape czarist oppression. In later volumes, David's own life moves to the forefront. Angoff was an editor of note at such journals as the *American Mercury* (recalled in Angoff's *H. L. Mencken: A Portrait from Memory,* Yoseloff, 1956) and the *Literary Review* (which memorializes him in the annual Charles Angoff Awards).

1. *Journey to the Dawn* (Beechhurst, 1951) David Polonsky recalls his childhood and his family's flight from Russia.
2. *In the Morning Light* (Beechhurst, 1952) David spends his school years in Boston.
3. *Sun at Noon, The* (Beechhurst, 1955) In 1919 David goes to Harvard.
4. *Between Day and Dark* (Yoseloff, 1959) After graduation, David toils on a suburban weekly, then gets his big break.
5. *Bitter Spring, The* (Yoseloff, 1961) David enters the literary life in New York City in 1928.
6. *Summer Storm* (Yoseloff, 1963) David endures the years 1933–35, the low point of the Great Depression.
7. *Memory of Autumn* (Yoseloff, 1968) By the early 1940s David is editor of the liberal *Globe* magazine in New York City.
8. *Winter Twilight* (Yoseloff, 1969) This volume covers the years 1945–47, ending with a celebration on the eve of the establishment of Israel.
9. *Seasons of Mists* (Yoseloff, 1971) David's relationship with Helen and his mother's illness are the central issues in this volume set in the early fifties.
10. *Mid-century* (Barnes, 1973) The political turmoil of the early fifties impinges upon David.

11. *Toward the Horizon* (**Barnes, 1978**) Academic life in the 1970s is featured in this volume.

Ansa, Tina McElroy

Like Robert Andrews (q.v.), Tina Ansa is a Georgia-born African American writer. Her novels are also set in a small town in Georgia, but in *middle* Georgia, in a different time frame, from the 1950s to the present. The leading character in the Mulberry series (especially in numbers 1 and 3) is Lena McPherson, a black woman born with a caul on her face, which means that she has psychic powers and can communicate with spirits. There is an admixture of the supernatural in these novels, reminiscent of Terry McMillan, with African American women who are upwardly mobile but conflicted about their love lives.

1. *Baby of the Family* (**Harcourt, 1989**) The story of the coming-of-age of Lena McPherson, born with a caul on her face and possessed of psychic powers, about which she feels ambivalent.
2. *Ugly Ways* (**Harcourt, 1993**) Three African American sisters return to Mulberry for the funeral of their mother, "Mudear," who in life was a domineering, angry woman.
3. *Hand I Fan With, The* (**Doubleday, 1996**) Lena McPherson, now in her forties, still lives in Mulberry and is financially successful but loveless. Then she conjures up Herman, a man who has been dead for more than 100 years.
4. *You Know Better* (**Morrow, 2002**) Eighteen-year-old LaShawndra disappears from Mulberry at the time of the Peach Blossom Festival; her mother, Sandra, is too busy with her own life to look for her, so it is up to her grandmother, Lily, to take up the search.

Anthony, Evelyn

PSEUDONYM OF Evelyn Ward-Thomas

I. This prolific British author began by writing historical fiction and period romances but has found her greatest popular success writing contemporary thrillers with a strong romantic element. One of these, *The Tamarind Seed* (Putnam, 1971), was made into a movie starring Julie Andrews and Omar Sharif. Four of her thrillers feature agent Davina Graham, young and rather plain when first met, though already known as a brilliant investigator and "tough as nails."

1. *Defector, The* (**Coward, 1981**) Davina Graham is assigned to debrief a Russian defector, Ivan Sasanov, but finds herself falling in love.
2. *Avenue of the Dead, The* (**Coward, 1982**) Widowed Davina comes out of retirement to take on a case of special personal significance.
3. *Albatross* (**Putnam, 1983**) A job in advertising is a cover for Davina's unauthorized investigation of a Russian counterspy whose code name is "Albatross."
4. *Company of Saints, The* (**Putnam, 1984**) Davina, now chief of the agency, and her lover are on vacation in Venice when the US secretary of defense is killed.

II. An earlier historical trilogy traces 18th- and early-19th-century Russian history through the reigns of Catherine the Great and Emperors Paul I and Alexander I. These novels were Anthony's first.

1. *Rebel Princess* (**Crowell, 1953**) The early years of Catherine the Great. UK title: *Imperial Highness*.
2. *Royal Intrigue* (**Crowell, 1954**) The personal story of Catherine's son and heir, Emperor Paul I. UK title: *Curse Not the King*.

3. *Far Flies the Eagle* (**Crowell, 1955**) Historical account of Alexander I, czar of Russia during the Napoleonic Wars.

III. A pair of historical novels about the MacDonald clan set in the 1700s. *Clandara* details the love affair of Katherine and James MacDonald. *The Heiress* takes up the story with Charles MacDonald in France.

1. *Clandara* (**Doubleday, 1963**) Katherine falls in love with James MacDonald, and despite the family feuds that separate them, their love never dies. Set in Scotland in 1745.
2. *Heiress, The* (**Doubleday, 1964**) Charles MacDonald, badly in debt, has been given a choice by his parents: the Bastille or a forced marriage to his cousin Anne de Bernard.

Anthony, Mark

The Last Rune series (completed in 2004) divides its action between Colorado, where its leading protagonist, Travis Wilder, tends bar, and the planet Eldh, an alternate Earth that is full of kingdoms more or less derived from earthly mythologies. Wilder, who becomes the "Runemaster," and fellow human Grace Beckett battle the forces of evil on both planets in an action-filled fantasy series in which the fate of at least two planets is at stake. Some critics find the series over-written and the magic rather conventional for a fantasy series, but Dungeons and Dragons and Sword and Sorcery addicts won't mind. Mark Anthony, who has spent summers in a Colorado ghost town, has written three volumes in the megavolume Forgotten Realms series and a volume each for the Dragonlance and Ravenloft series.

1. *Beyond the Pale* (**Bantam, 1998**) Bartender Travis Wilder and ER physician Grace Beckett are transported from Colorado to the magical world of Eldh, which has already sent Eldhians to Colorado.
2. *Keep of Fire, The* (**Bantam, 1999**) Travis has returned to Colorado and, seemingly, normality, but then his best friend and another person become victims of spontaneous combustion. The Seekers, an ancient mystical order, and Duratek, a local high-tech company, for separate reasons, are interested in Eldh.
3. *Dark Remains* (**Bantam, 2001**) The knight Beltan, sent from Eldh to Earth for medical treatment, is captured by Duratek for the purposes of genetic experimentation. Meanwhile, the forces of chaos are disrupting life on Eldh.
4. *Blood of Mystery* (**Bantam, 1999**) Travis Wilder and three Eldh companions are stranded in an 1880s Colorado mining town, while Grace Beckett, known as Blademender on Eldh, is facing off against the Pale King.
5. *Gates of Winter, The* (**Bantam, 2003**) Heros and villains alike race to find the Runemaster, Travis Wilder.
6. *First Stone, The* (**Bantam, 2004**) Final volume of the series. The inhabitants of Earth and Eldh have enjoyed three years of relative peace. But then rifts start appearing in the skies of both planets.

Anthony, Piers

PSEUDONYM OF Piers Anthony Jacob

I. Piers Anthony is a master of light fantasy. The British-born American writer has been extremely prolific since the late 1960s and extremely popular since the 1980s, especially among younger readers. Some critics find his inveterate punning and his "sexist" humor tiresome, but Anthony is less concerned with their opinions than with reactions from the thousands of fantasy readers who can't get enough of his books, and he has been awarded the Hugo and the Nebula, SF's most prestigious awards. He has coauthored many books, some of them with established authors, such as Mercedes Lackey (q.v.) and Philip José Farmer (q.v.), but also several with novices, authors publishing for the first time. Anthony describes his life and hard (in his younger days) times in two autobiographical volumes: *Bio of an Ogre* (Ace, 1988) and *How Precious Was That While* (Tor, 2001). He also maintains an interactive website, hi Piers (http://hipiers.com).

The Magic of Xanth is Piers Anthony's longest-running and most popular series. Xanth is a magical peninsula, sometimes resembling Florida, which makes occasional contacts with Mundania (our world). Xanth contains a number of continuing characters, such as the Good Magician Humfrey, Dolph the Shape-Shifter, and Princess Ivy, plus a large cast of goblins, rocs, centaurs, ogres, zombies, and other creatures regarded as mythical by the benighted denizens of Mundania. *The Magic of Xanth* (Doubleday, 1981) is an omnibus containing numbers 1–3. *The Continuing Xanthan Saga* (Wings, 1997) contains numbers 4–6. *Piers Anthony's Visual Guide to Xanth* is coauthored with Jody Lynn Nye.

1. *Spell for Chameleon, A* (Ballantine, 1977) Young Bink is facing expulsion from Xanth because he can't discover where his magical talents lie.
2. *Source of Magic, The* (Ballantine, 1979) Bink, who can't be hurt by magic, is sent on a quest to find the source of Xanth's magic.
3. *Castle Roogna* (Ballantine, 1979) Twelve-year-old Dor is trapped inside the body of a 25-year-old human being.
4. *Centaur Isle* (Ballantine, 1981) Dor becomes temporary king of Xanth as King Trent and Queen Iris travel to Mundania on a quest to forestall a new magician.
5. *Ogre, Ogre* (Ballantine, 1982) Smash the Ogre, human on his mother's side, has to go on a series of adventures to realize his potential.
6. *Night Mare* (Ballantine, 1983) Imbri, a Night Mare who delivers bad dreams, is sent to the Day World to help ward off a Mundanian invasion.
7. *Dragon on a Pedestal* (Ballantine, 1983) Princess Ivy, the three-year-old daughter of King Dor, finds herself lost in the jungle during an attack by the escaped Gap Dragon.
8. *Crewel Lye: A Caustic Yarn* (Ballantine, 1985) Ivy becomes involved with a 400-year-old ghost who is looking for his misplaced bones in Castle Roogna.
9. *Golem in the Gears* (Ballantine, 1986) Grundy the Golem is sent on a quest to find Princess Ivy's lost dragon.
10. *Vale of the Vole* (Avon, 1987) Esk, an ogre-nymph-human hybrid, is aided by Volney the Vole in his efforts to save some riverine inhabitants from demons.
11. *Heaven Cent* (Avon, 1988) Shape-shifter Dolph is aided on his quest for the missing Good Magician Humfrey by an enchanted skeleton and a coin that seems to have all the answers.
12. *Man from Mundania* (Avon, 1989) Princess Ivy uses the Heaven Cent to travel to Mundania, where she meets a college student who doesn't believe in magic.
13. *Isle of View* (Morrow, 1990) Prince Dolph must choose between two fiancées, Nada the uninterested and Electra the uninteresting, or all three will be in big trouble.
14. *Question Quest* (Morrow, 1991) Lacuna, one of the Castle Zombie twins, agrees to go to hell (in a handbasket) in search of the Good Magician Humfrey.
15. *Color of Her Panties, The* (Morrow, 1992) Mela Merwoman's undies play a role in the contest between Gwenny and Gobble Goblin for the Goblin chieftainship.

16. *Demons Don't Dream* (Tor, 1993) Mundanian teenagers Dug and Kim are transported to Xanth while playing the computer game Companions of Xanth.
17. *Harpy Thyme* (Tor, 1994) Gloha, the only goblin-harpy hybrid in Xanth, is searching for a male counterpart.
18. *Geis of the Gargoyle* (Tor, 1995) Gargoyle Gary Gar, water purifier of the Swan Knee River, wants to make his job easier but must assume human form to do it.
19. *Roc and a Hard Place* (Tor, 1995) Demoness Metria must assemble a court and jury to try Roxanee Roc for unspecified charges made by the Simurgh, another magical bird.
20. *Yon Ill Wind* (Tor, 1996) The Demon X(an) must become Nimby, a mortal pink-and-green-striped dragon with the head of an ass, and wring a tear from the iron maiden Chlorine to save Xanth.
21. *Faun and Games* (Tor, 1997) Forrest Faun must make a quest to Ptero to save the magic in fellow-faun Branch's tree after Branch falls into the Void.
22. *Zombie Lover* (Tor, 1998) Breanna seeks the advice of the Good Magician Humfrey on how to fend off the unwanted attentions of the king of the Zombies.
23. *Xone of Contention* (Tor, 1999) Mundanian computer designer Edsel and his wife, Pia, must exchange bodies with Xanthians Nimby and Chlorine to save both worlds from destruction.
24. *Dastard, The* (Tor, 2000) The creature known as the Dastard uses his power to rewrite history for his own dastardly ends.
25. *Swell Foop* (Tor, 2001) The Swell Foop is needed to save the Demon Earth, for failure means the total loss of gravity for both Earth and Xanth.
26. *Up in a Heaval* (Tor, 2002) Dueling Demons create havoc for the inhabitants of both Xanth and Earth.
27. *Cube Route* (Tor, 2003) A homely girl named Cube, who yearns to be beautiful, finds herself leading an expedition searching for the mysterious Cube Route.
28. *Currant Events* (Tor, 2004) Clio, Xanth's Muse of History, finds that number 28 in the Xanth series, which she has set out to write, already exists, albeit in incomprehensible form. Clio, aided by the Good Magician Humphrey, goes on a quest for the fabled Currant, a magical red berry.
29. *Pet Peeve* (Tor, 2005) Mild-mannered goblin Goody is assigned by the Good Magician Humfrey to find a home for the Pet Peeve, "a foul-mouthed fowl" who insults anyone it encounters.
30. *Stork Naked* (Tor, 2006) Stymy Stork refuses to deliver Surprise Golem's baby, because Surprise is too young, according to the dictates of the Adult Conspiracy.
31. *Air Apparent* (Tor, 2007) After Hugo, son of the gorgon and the Good Magician Humfrey, vanishes from his cellar, the corpse of a murdered man suddenly appears.

II. The Incarnations of Immortality series is an allegorical fantasy set in an alternative world resembling our own, where concepts such as death and time are incarnated into human form and enlisted in God's war against Satan. Although Anthony uses the series as a platform to speak out against trends in our world that he disapproves of, it is suffused with humor, engaging characters, and imaginative stories.

1. *On a Pale Horse* (Ballantine, 1983) Zane attempts suicide but kills Death instead, so he takes on Death's duties himself.
2. *Bearing an Hourglass* (Ballantine, 1984) Norton, grief-stricken over his lover's death, is persuaded to become Chronos, the Incarnation of Time.
3. *With a Tangled Skein* (Ballantine, 1985) Irish lass Niobe takes on the role of Clotho, spinner of the Thread of Life, to avenge her lover's death.

4. *Wielding a Red Sword* (Ballantine, 1986) Indian prince Nym reluctantly accepts the office of Incarnation of War to help his famine-stricken homeland.

5. *Being a Green Mother* (Ballantine, 1987) A young girl's pursuit of the Llano, the elusive Song of Nature, leads to her becoming the Incarnation of Nature.

6. *For Love of Evil* (Morrow, 1988) A young sorcerer in medieval France becomes the Incarnation of Evil, whom he had vowed to oppose.

7. *And Eternity* (Morrow, 1990) Three women join together in a quest that leads them to a replacement for the Incarnation of God.

III. The Adept (or Apprentice Adept) series postulates two worlds: the magical yet natural Phaze and the scientific, controlled Proton. The first three titles (numbers 1–3), collected as *Double Exposure* (Doubleday, 1982), have as their principal character the Apprentice Adept Stile, who moves between the two worlds. A second trilogy (numbers 4–6) features Bane, the magician's son from Phaze, and Robot Adept Mach from Proton. The final volume (number 7) relates how the united worlds of Phaze and Proton faced an external threat.

1. *Split Infinity* (Ballantine, 1980) Proton-born Stile migrates to Phaze to evade a mysterious killer and discovers he has magical powers.

2. *Blue Adept* (Ballantine, 1981) Stile tries to become a Citizen of Proton by winning the Game while improving his skills on Phaze.

3. *Juxtaposition* (Ballantine, 1982) Stile must heal a rift between the Citizens and the Adepts that could destroy both Proton and Phaze.

4. *Out of Phaze* (Putnam, 1987) Phaze magician's son Bane and Proton Robot Mach transfer minds, each becoming trapped in the other's world.

5. *Robot Adept* (Putnam, 1988) Adverse Adepts and Contrary Citizens plot to gain control of an omniscient computer and its magical analog.

6. *Unicorn Point* (Putnam, 1989) The children of Mach and Bane struggle to foil the plans of the Contrary Citizens and the Adverse Adepts.

7. *Phaze Doubt* (Putnam, 1990) The united Phaze and Proton face an invading force named Hectare.

IV. Piers Anthony was primarily a science-fiction writer until he branched out into fantasy. Aton is a pair of novels about Aton Five and his son, Arlo, who is a science-fiction version of the Thor of Norse mythology.

1. *Chthon* (Ballantine, 1967) Aton Five is imprisoned on the planet Chthon and forced to work in its garnet mines.

2. *Phthor* (Berkley, 1975) Follows the life and adventures of Arlo, Aton's son.

V. Battle Circle is a trio of science-fiction novels about three warriors and their weapons. Published in an omnibus volume (*Battle Circle*, Avon, 1978), the trilogy is based on the epic works of Homer, Virgil, and Milton.

1. *Sos the Rope* (Pyramid, 1968) Several radiation survivors, led by Sos the Rope, attempt to rebuild their society after the blast.

2. *Var the Stick* (Bantam, 1973) Half-animal, half-man Var the Stick is called upon to save the empire.

3. *Neq the Sword* (Corgi [UK], 1975) An age of darkness has fallen upon the empire, and it is left to Neq the Sword to restore it. Not published separately in the United States.

VI. Bio of a Space Tyrant is a series of five science-fiction novels originally published in the 1980s, then republished in 2001 by Xlibris with the addition of a sixth volume. The series depicts the life of Hope Hubris from humble beginnings to dictatorship of the planet of Jupiter and afterward.

1. *Bio of a Space Tyrant: Refugee* (Avon, 1983) Hope Hubris and his family embark upon an ill-fated voyage through space after pirates destroy their home on Callisto.

2. *Bio of a Space Tyrant: Mercenary* (Avon, 1984) Hope Hubris joins the Navy of Jupiter and commands a squadron dedicated to destroying the pirate warlords of Jupiter Ecliptic.

3. *Bio of a Space Tyrant: Politician* (Avon, 1985) Hope Hubris awakens in a prison cell, his political career shattered and Jupiter in the hands of the corrupt Tocsin.

4. *Bio of a Space Tyrant: Executive* (Avon, 1985) Absolute dictator of the United States of Jupiter, Hope Hubris's ruling passion is still justice.

5. *Bio of a Space Tyrant: Statesman* (Avon, 1986) Hope Hubris leaves Jupiter as an exile outward bound from the solar system to the stars.

6. *Bio of a Space Tyrant: The Iron Maiden* (Xlibris, 2001) Basically a rehash of numbers 1 through 5, covering the same time span from a somewhat different perspective.

VII. Cluster, a science-fiction series, concerns the far-future planet of Outworld in the Andromeda Cluster, where primitive men battle dinosaurs and a barbaric genius must come to the rescue. The Wandering Monk Paul, a character introduced in this series, is the protagonist of *Tarot* (see series VIII).

1. *Cluster* (Avon, 1977) The concept of Kirlian Transfer, a new type of out-of-body travel, is called upon to decide the outcome of the First War of Energy on the planet of Outworld. UK title: *Vicinity Cluster*.

2. *Chaining the Lady* (Avon, 1978) Melody of Mintaka, daughter of Flint the Caveman, must endure untold humiliation before she assumes the form that will bring victory for Cluster against the Andromedan space fleet.

3. *Kirlian Quest* (Avon, 1978) In the final volume of the original Cluster trilogy, the Kirlian Transfer plays an instrumental role in the battle of an intergalactic force against the space amoeba.

4. *Thousandstar* (Avon, 1980) After an interval described in *Tarot*, the Cluster series continues with the outlaw hero of Highfalls and Jessica of Capella in a space race for the legacy of the Ancients.

5. *Viscous Circle* (Avon, 1982) The bloodthirsty Solarians are determined to wipe out the peaceful Bands. Only Rondi, the whirling green Band, can save his race.

VIII. *Tarot* (Ace, 1987) is the omnibus revised edition of three novels published separately although always intended as a single novel by Anthony. The Wandering Monk Paul, who appears as a character in the Cluster series (see series VII), is called upon to save the Miracle Planet from the Animations, which destroy minds and take lives.

1. *God of Tarot* (Jove, 1979) The Miracle Planet, containing the Tree of Life of the One Supreme God, is discovered.

2. *Vision of Tarot* (Berkley, 1980) The Miracle Planet is explored amid a nightmare of dragons, demons, and lust.

3. *Faith of Tarot* (Berkley, 1980) The Miracle Planet is saved from the Animations.

IX. Alliance, coauthored with Robert E. Margroff, is a series of five fantasy novels concerning Kelvin Hackleberry, the Roundear of Prophecy, who is called upon to save several worlds from a series of monsters. Numbers 1–3 were reissued in an omnibus volume called *Three Complete Novels* (Wings, 1993).

1. *Dragon's Gold* (Tor, 1987) Begins the saga of Kelvin Hackleberry (Kelvin of Rud), who is destined to fulfill the prophecy of magician Mouvar by ruling a conflict-ridden land and fighting the forces of evil determined to pervert all that is good in the Universe of Frames.
2. *Serpent's Silver* (Tor, 1988) Kelvin Hackleberry, now Roundear of Prophecy, must battle the Silver Serpent, a dragonlike creature.
3. *Chimaera's Copper* (Tor, 1990) Helain, Kelvin's wife, is captured by evil magicians, and Kelvin is captive of the Chimaera.
4. *Orc's Opal* (Tor, 1990) Kelvin and Helain's children, Charles and Merlain, are potential victims of the evil witch Zady's scheme to send them to die in the process of stealing a treasure from the Kingdom of Orcs.
5. *Mouvar's Magic* (Tor, 1992) The evil Professor Devale and his witch servant Zady, having been foiled in their attempt to destroy Kelvin, are gearing up for one last battle to tip the scales from good to evil in the Universe of Frames.

X. Geodyssey is a series of "historical" science-fiction novels that relates the development of humanity from prehistory to posthistory through the medium of reincarnated characters.

1. *Isle of Woman* (Tor, 1993) A man and a woman, Blaze and Ember, go through a series of reincarnations at different points in humanity's development in settings such as prehistoric Africa, T'ang dynasty China, medieval Lithuania, and near-future America.
2. *Shame of Man* (Tor, 1994) Hu, a prehuman, goes through reincarnations as humans Hue, Hugh, Hu'o, and Huu through the millennia.
3. *Hope of Earth* (Tor, 1997) The lives of Sam, Flo, Jes, Ned, and their mates are traced through one family's odyssey in time through classical Athens and a gang-ridden housing project in 1995 to struggling survivalist and pacifist communities in 2025.
4. *Muse of Art* (Tor, 1999) The role of art in society is examined through the lives of Melee, Dillon, Od, and the wise Bata, from prehistory to Olmec Mexico, Augustan England, and post–Third World War history.

XI. The Jason Stryker series, coauthored with Roberto Fuentes, was something of a departure for Anthony, dealing with a martial-arts expert, but it does have overtones of fantasy. The five volumes are listed without annotations.

1. *Kiai!* (Berkley, 1974)
2. *Mistress of Death* (Berkley, 1974)
3. *Bamboo Bloodbath, The* (Berkley, 1974)
4. *Ninja's Revenge* (Berkley, 1975)
5. *Amazon Slaughter* (Berkley, 1976)

XII. Mode is a series of science-fiction and fantasy novels featuring "anchor points": characters such as Darius (a Cyng of Hlahtar) and Colene (an unhappy teenage resident of Earth) inhabiting five different universes to which they travel back and forth via a series of "Modes."

1. *Virtual Mode* (Putnam, 1991) Darius, a Cyng of Hlahtar, travels to Earth to meet his true love, suicidal teen Colene, and bring her back to his universe, but complications occur.

2. *Fractal Mode* (Putnam, 1992) To return to their own universes, Colene, Darius, Sequiro, and Provos need to help Nona fulfill the prophecy that she will overthrow her world's despots.
3. *Chaos Mode* (Ace/Putnam, 1994) The telepathic horse Sequiro comes into his own this time, as the adventurers return to Colene's Earth.
4. *DoOon Mode* (Tor, 2001) Colene must face the monster responsible for her unhappy past and find a way to save all five universes.

XIII. The Omnivore trilogy allowed Anthony to continue his exploration of humankind's self-inflicted damage and present his advocacy of vegetarianism. Three explorers, herbivorous Veg, carnivorous Cal, and omnivorous Aquilon, voyage to other planets and make discoveries of great import to humanity.

1. *Omnivore* (Ballantine, 1968) Interplanetary explorers Veg, Cal, and Aquilon journey to the planet Nacre, reporting back their findings to investigator Subble.
2. *Orn* (Avon, 1971) The explorers travel to the planet Paleo, which resembles the Earth of 65 million years ago, and encounter Orn, a creature endowed with the racial memory of its ancestors.
3. *Ox* (Avon, 1976) Veg, Cal, and Aquilon explore alternate worlds and uncover the existence of a sentient supercomputer.

Apodaca, Jennifer

Samantha Shaw, widow, Southern California (the fictional Lake Elsinore) suburban housewife, and soccer mom, decides to redo herself in every way after she discovers that her recently deceased husband, Trent, was even rottener than she had thought. Samantha has a breast job, dyes her hair blond, gets a new wardrobe, and buys Heart Mates, a dating service. Events turn Samantha into a (bumbling) amateur sleuth in this series of frothy cozies. Samantha isn't a gifted detective, but she wins her way through with pluck and the help of her ex-cop boyfriend, "gorgeous hunk" Gabe Pulizzi.

1. *Dating Can Be Murder* (Kensington, 2002) After the death of Trent, her rotten husband, Samantha Shaw redoes herself and buys a dating service. Then, when she is threatened by a thug, she discovers that Trent had been selling more than just condoms.
2. *Dying to Meet You* (Kensington, 2003) Soon after Sam hires graphic artist Faye Miller to design a brochure for Heart Mates, Faye is found dead in her motel room.
3. *Ninja Soccer Moms* (Kensington, 2004) Sam attempts to help a friend prove that her ex-husband has been embezzling from the local soccer club. Then the embezzler is murdered.
4. *Batteries Required* (Kensington, 2005) A sample kit of sex toys, a missing and possibly murdered friend, and a client who wants an introduction to a pseudonymous writer engage Sam here.
5. *Thrilled to Death* (Kensington, 2006) Sam's grandfather, Barney Webb, is accused by magician Shane Masters of hiring a hit man to kill him.

Apostolou, Anna

PSEUDONYM OF P(aul) C. Doherty

P. C. Doherty (q.v.) has written two historical mystery novels involving Alexander the Great (356–323 BCE) under the pseudonym of Anna Apostolou. The sleuths are a brother-and-sister team, the Jewish actors Miriam and Simeon Bartimaeus. The stories are complex and contain much information about the period. Doherty is also writing an Alexander the Great series under his own name.

1. *Murder in Macedon, A* **(St. Martin's, 1997)** Philip of Macedon, father of Alexander, is murdered by Pausanias, the captain of his guards. Rumored to be part of the plot to kill Philip, Alexander asks his actor friends Simeon and Miriam Bartimaeus to investigate.
2. *Murder in Thebes, A* **(St. Martin's, 1998)** Alexander's troops have ravaged Thebes, but it seems that a Theban terrorist group is still active with the connivance of one of Alexander's officers and, possibly, the ghost of Oedipus, the legendary king of Thebes.

Appel, Allen

Alex Balfour, historian and unintentional time traveler, inadvertently finds himself in some historical hot spots, such as the Russian Revolution, the Civil War, Pearl Harbor, and Custer's Last Stand, where he meets some prominent historical characters, such as Mark Twain, Albert Einstein, Walt Whitman, and FDR. Light, entertaining SF fare without much brooding about the effect of time traveling upon the course of history.

1. *Time after Time* **(Carroll & Graf, 1985)** Contemporary historian Alex Balfour has "nightmares" in which he finds himself in the middle of the 1917 Russian Revolution. Then he discovers he isn't dreaming and is in danger of being stuck back in 1917.
2. *Twice upon a Time* **(Carroll & Graf, 1988)** Alex finds himself at the Philadelphia Centennial Exposition of 1876, where he hooks up with Mark Twain, travels west, and finds himself at Little Big Horn shortly before Custer's Last Stand is about to take place.
3. *Till the End of Time* **(Doubleday, 1990)** Alex finds himself at Pearl Harbor on December 7, 1941. Albert Einstein and President Roosevelt play prominent roles as Alex tries to persuade FDR not to drop the A-bomb. Betty Grable has a cameo.
4. *In Time of War* **(Carroll & Graf, 2003)** Alex finds himself on a Civil War battlefield, where he immediately gets wounded and installed in a Washington hospital, where he runs into Ambrose Bierce and Walt Whitman. Girlfriend Molly, a reporter, finds herself carried back to the same time and ensconced in a brothel.

Archer, Jeffrey

The career of British novelist, politician, and entrepreneur Jeffrey Archer illustrates the old adage that "truth is stranger than fiction." Archer's best-selling fiction rescued him from bankruptcy, made him a rich man, and helped him to a prominent place in Conservative Party circles and a life peerage. However, an exercise in fiction wherein he doctored his diaries and obtained a false alibi from a friend to win a record-setting libel suit against a British scandal sheet in 1987 proved his undoing when he was convicted of perjury in July 2001 and sent to jail for four years, meanwhile forfeiting his candidacy for lord mayor of London.

Kane and Abel (1980), a family and business saga set in America, was one of Archer's biggest best sellers. It was followed shortly by *Prodigal Daughter,* which traces the fortunes of Abel's daughter Florentyna. Things got a little complicated when an earlier novel, *Shall We Tell the President?* (1977), which described an assassination threat against US president Edward M. Kennedy (causing some controversy, including the resignation of Jacqueline Kennedy Onassis from her editorial position at Viking), was revised in 1985, with Florentyna Kane as president instead of Ted Kennedy, thereby creating a Kane and Abel trilogy.

1. *Kane and Abel* **(Simon & Schuster, 1980)** Tells of the rise to fame and fortune of two men born on the same day in 1906: William Kane, in Boston, and Abel Rosnovski, in Poland, and the rivalry that develops between them.
2. *Prodigal Daughter, The* **(Simon & Schuster, 1982)** The family saga continues as the focus shifts to the trials and successes of Florentyna Kane, the only daughter of Abel Rosnovski.
3. *Shall We Tell the President?* **(Pocket, 1997)** In this revised version of an earlier best-seller (Viking, 1977), Florentyna Kane, the first woman president of the United States, replaces Edward M. Kennedy as the target of an assassination plot. A revised edition with an "author's foreword" by Archer was originally published by Hodder (London) in 1985.

Argo, Ellen

PSEUDONYM OF Ellen Argo Johnson

Julia Howard is the strong central figure of this trilogy set on Cape Cod from 1827 to 1860. Born at sea aboard one of her father's ships, young Julia acquires a love of the sea and knowledge of shipbuilding at an early age. Not content to stay at home and run the shipyard, she eventually sees her share of adventure.

1. *Jewel of the Seas* **(Putnam, 1977)** Julia, a happy child who putters about her father's shipyard, grows into a beautiful and headstrong young woman determined to go to sea.
2. *Crystal Star, The* **(Putnam, 1979)** Julia accompanies her husband, Stephen Logan, on the ship she helped to build and shares in the dangers and pleasures of a South Seas voyage.
3. *Yankee Girl, The* **(Putnam, 1980)** Julia's story continues through rough weather: personal storms, losses, and triumphs.

Arjouni, Jakob

Kemal Kayankaya is a hard-boiled, hard-drinking, smart-talking private eye in the Dashiell Hammett (q.v.) and Raymond Chandler (q.v.) tradition. However, his beat is 1980s–1990s Frankfurt, Germany, rather than 1930s–1940s California. Kayankaya is of Turkish descent and, as such, is a member of Germany's currently most despised and put-upon ethnic group. Some critics feel that the hard-boiled ambience and dialogue are overdone and clichéd, while others find Arjouni's language "poetic," the dialogue wickedly funny, and Kayankaya a worthy addition to the canon. Arjouni, who is a Frankfurt native, may or may not be of Turkish descent, depending on which source you believe. Number 1 was made into a film that was a hit in Germany.

1. *Happy Birthday, Turk!* **(Fromm, 1993)** A Turkish worker is stabbed to death in Frankfurt, and the victim's wife hires Kayankaya to get to the bottom of things. Translated from the German by Anselm Hollo. Originally published in 1985 as *Happy Birthday, Tuerke!*
2. *And Still Drink More!* **(Fromm, 1994)** Four members of a radical ecological group are accused of murdering the director of a chemical plant outside Frankfurt. Translated from the German by Anselm Hollo. Originally published in 1987 as *Mehr Bier!*
3. *One Death to Die* **(Fromm, 1997)** Kemal's latest client, "an average schmuck from Frankfurt's West End" named Weidenbusch, hires the detective to find his missing Thai girlfriend, who may have been kidnapped by gangsters preying on illegal aliens. Translated from the German by Anselm Hollo. Originally published in 1991 as *Ein Mann, Ein Mord.*
4. *Kismet* **(No Exit [UK], 2005)** When Kayankaya and his cohort Slibulsky try to help out Romario, the owner of a small Brazilian restaurant, two corpses turn up on the restaurant's floor. Translated from the German by Anselm Hollo. Originally published in 2001 as *Kismet.*

Arlen, Leslie

PSEUDONYM OF Christopher Nicole

The Borodins is a series of smoldering paperback romances set in Russia. General Borodin, a liberal-minded aristocrat who has given his daughters a dangerous taste for freedom, is killed as the Japanese take Port Arthur in 1904. His daughters, Ilona and Tatania, and his son, Peter, wend their passionate ways through the Russian Revolution and beyond. George Hayman, handsome American war correspondent, falls under Ilona's spell, as does her young servant, Michael Ivanovich. Peter falls in love with a young Jewish girl. Battle scenes and guest appearances by the likes of Rasputin give the narrative some historical framework, but this is basically escapist fantasy. Christopher Nicole writes thrillers, historical novels, and nonfiction under his real name and at least a dozen pseudonyms, including Andrew York.

1. *Love and Honor* (Jove, 1980) Beautiful, young Princess Ilona Borodin is awakened to love when she meets American George Hayman, but she is betrothed to the cold Prince Roditchev.
2. *War and Passion* (Jove, 1981) The revolution sweeps through Russia, touching all the Borodins, especially Peter, the last Borodin prince, and his friend Judith.
3. *Fate and Dreams* (Jove, 1981) Tattie, the famous star of a Russian dance troupe, disappears while on tour in London.
4. *Hope and Glory* (Jove, 1982) Young American John Hayman and ballerina Natasha Brusilow fight the Nazi invaders of Russia in World War II.
5. *Rage and Desire* (Jove, 1982) Soviet intelligence agent Grigori is sent to the United States to steal the secret of the atomic bomb.
6. *Fortune and Fury* (Jove, 1984) The series conclusion is set in 1952 at the peak of the cold war years. Nothing will deter Prince Peter Borodin's determination to destroy Stalin.

Armistead, John

Grover Bramlett, sheriff of Chakciuma County, Mississippi, is an easy-going, grandfatherly fellow who is called upon to deal with some messy problems in this series, which has been praised for its evocation of Southern small-town police work and race relations. John Armistead, who was a Baptist pastor in Hawaii and Mississippi, and is religion editor of the *Northeast Mississippi Daily Journal*, has also published two widely praised young adult novels: *The $66 Summer* (Milkwood, 2000) and *The Return of Gabriel* (Milkwood, 2002).

1. *Legacy of Vengeance, A* (Carroll & Graf, 1994) The shooting of Baptist pastor Richard Hatchell in front of his church is the first of several murders of local men by a mysterious killer who uses the phrase, "Remember Leavenworth."
2. *Homecoming for Murder, A* (Carroll & Graf, 1995) Grover's quality time with visiting grandson Marcellus is spoiled when schoolteacher, seducer, and blackmailer Jesse Bondreaux is murdered in a cemetery.
3. *Cruel as the Grave* (Carroll & Graf, 1996) The presence of a white stranger in the black cemetery near Sheffield is followed by his murder, which may be connected with the murder of a black woman, Naresse Clouse, three years previously.

Armstrong, Campbell

PSEUDONYM OF Campbell Black

I. Campbell Armstrong, a pseudonym for horror writer Campbell Black, has written several espionage thrillers, including five featuring Scotland Yard operative Frank Pagan. Pagan is a sort of renegade, being in and out of favor with Yard officials, in this series of novels that feature intricate plots and suspense. Campbell Black, a Glasgow native who spent 20 years in the United States before he returned to "Europe" (Ireland), also uses the pseudonym of Thomas Altman. *Jigsaw, Mazurka, Mambo* is the title of an omnibus volume of numbers 1, 2, and 3 published by Chancellor (o.p.) in 1993.

1. *Jig* (Morrow, 1987) Jig, the Irish Republican Army's ace assassin, is on his way to New York to recover $10 million stolen from the IRA. Frank Pagan, Scotland Yard antiterrorism operative, is on Jig's trail.
2. *White Light* (Morrow, 1988) Hard-liners in the United States and the USSR are out to block glasnost. An Estonian trade representative is murdered in the Glasgow train station, and Frank Pagan, who arrests the killer (who soon commits suicide), is forced to face the larger plot. Variant title: *Mazurka*.
3. *Mambo* (HarperCollins, 1990) Pagan is involved with "the Claw," Gunther Ruhr, a German terrorist, in a complicated plot in which Pagan is called upon to hijack an American cruise missile.
4. *Jigsaw* (Little, Brown, 1995) Pagan, in disgrace with Scotland Yard's Special Branch, is recalled to duty when a bomb kills more than 100 people in a London subway.
5. *Heat* (Doubleday, 1996) Frank Pagan gets emotionally as well as professionally involved with Carlotta, an alluring, ruthless terrorist.

II. Glasgow, Scotland, is the scene of a trio of mysteries involving Detective Sergeant Lou Perlman, who has some personal problems.

1. *Last Darkness, The* (HarperCollins, 2002) In the first of a series of suspicious deaths, a well-dressed man is found hanging from a railway bridge.
2. *White Rage* (HarperCollins, 2004) Lou Perlman feels that the death of a young Asian entrepreneur and the classroom slaying of an Indian kindergarten teacher are connected to a racist group called White Rage.
3. *Butcher* (Allison & Busby [UK], 2007) Lou Perlman, on sick leave from the Strathclyde Police, decides to clean house and turns up a decayed human hand in a Ziploc bag.

Armstrong, Kelley

Compared to vampires, werewolves have received relatively little attention in popular fiction. Enter Elena Michaels, the only living female werewolf. Elena is the main character in numbers 1, 2, 5, and 6 of what is called the Women of the Otherworld series and plays a role in numbers 3 and 4, which are given over mainly to the renegade witch Paige Winterbourne. Although the fast-paced action of the series, leavened by humor, keeps readers turning the pages, they learn a lot about the culture of lycanthropes and other "supernatural" beings who generally have to keep a low profile in the world of "normal" humans. Several prequels in the form of novellas are available online only as free downloads from Armstrong's website. Kelley Armstrong is a Canadian writer who lives in rural Ontario.

1. *Bitten* **(Viking, 2001)** Elena Michaels, the only living female werewolf (there are about 35 males), tries to live with humans, but is called back by pack alpha leader Jeremy to hunt down some rogue werewolves who don't play by the rules.
2. *Stolen* **(Viking, 2003)** Elena and witch Paige Winterbourne are kidnapped by Ty Winsloe, billionaire and "computer geek," and imprisoned in a menagerie representing all the supernatural species that coexist with humans.
3. *Dime Store Magic* **(Bantam, 2004)** Paige Winterbourne (introduced in number 2) inherits her murdered mother's mantle as coven leader and the problems that go with it, including Savannah Levine, a 13-year-old who has a penchant for dark magic, and some sorcerers who dabble in darker magic.
4. *Industrial Magic* **(Bantam, 2004)** Paige tries to interest a group of business-suited witches in her alternative coven, but her romance with sorcerer-lawyer Lucas Cortez and a series of child murders threaten to upset everything.
5. *Haunted* **(Bantam, 2005)** The Fates set Eve on the trail of an escaped demi-demon, and she traverses the afterlife hunting her quarry.
6. *Broken* **(Bantam, 2006)** Finding herself pregnant, Elena Michaels seeks distraction in retrieving a stolen letter allegedly written by Jack the Ripper and inadvertently triggers a portal to Victorian London's underworld.
7. *No Humans Involved* **(Bantam, 2007)** Necromancer Jaime Vegas, who can reanimate the dead, faces her biggest challenge yet—freeing the trapped ghosts of six murdered children.
8. *Personal Demon* **(Bantam, 2008)** "Chaos demon spy girl" Hope Adams, assuming the persona of coed Faith Edmonds, infiltrates a supernatural youth gang that has been bedeviling Benicio Cortez.

Arnold, Margot

PSEUDONYM OF Petronelle Cook

American anthropologist Penny Spring and Welsh archaeologist Sir Tobias Glendower are a middle-aged (approaching senior-citizen status in later novels) pair of academics who team up to solve some rather complicated crimes on expeditions, digs, and other jaunts at locations around the world. Many of their cases have a touch of the occult or supernatural about them. British-born American citizen Arnold is an archaeologist herself and familiar with the settings of many of her stories, including Cape Cod Community College, where she was an instructor in the 1970s.

1. *Exit Actors, Dying* **(Playboy, 1979)** The corpses of a beautiful movie actress and a black actor dressed as a gladiator turn up on location in the Mediterranean during a shooting of *The Travels of Telemachus*.
2. *Zadok's Treasure* **(Playboy, 1979)** Sir Toby's colleague Bill Pearson disappears on a dig in Israel while searching for the legendary treasure of Zadok, King Solomon's high priest.
3. *Cape Cod Caper, The* **(Playboy, 1980)** After Penny is summoned to Cape Cod, Massachusetts, by an old flame, a mutilated corpse is found on a deserted estate.
4. *Death of a Voodoo Doll* **(Playboy, 1982)** Would-be historian of the Mardi Gras John Everett is bedeviled by threatening notes and voodoo dolls while doing research in New Orleans.
5. *Lament for a Lady Laird* **(Playboy, 1982)** Amy McClintock, laird of Sheena Castle in Scotland, is found drowned.
6. *Death on the Dragon's Tongue* **(Berkley, 1983)** The decision of the French government to locate a nuclear reactor on a prehistoric "henge" on the coast of Brittany may have led to an official's murder.

7. *Menehune Murders, The* **(Foul Play, 1989)** A dispute over the actual existence of the Menehune, the "little people" of Hawaiian folklore, leads to murder.
8. *Toby's Folly* **(Foul Play, 1990)** One of Toby's "follies" is his secret cave in Wales. The other is an old affair with a Russian ballerina that produced a daughter he has never seen.
9. *Catacomb Conspiracy, The* **(Foul Play, 1992)** When Penny and Toby take a vacation at a Roman villa above an unexcavated catacomb, a murder and a mysterious disappearance occur.
10. *Cape Cod Conundrum, The* **(Foul Play, 1993)** Months after her disappearance, Clara Barton turns up as a corpse at her desk at Cape Cod Community College.
11. *Dirge for a Dorset Druid* **(Foul Play, 1994)** On a dig in Dorsetshire with a former student, Toby uncovers a corpse dressed as a modern druid.
12. *Midas Murders, The* **(Foul Play, 1995)** Penny's family vacation in the Greek islands is interrupted by the death of the patriarch of the wealthy Marolakis dynasty on his yacht.

Arnote, Ralph

The late Ralph Arnote (d. 1998), mystery writer and traveler, wrote several novels about Willy Hanson, retired publisher and entertainment mogul and amateur detective, who gets involved in a series of mysteries and adventures in exotic and not-so-exotic locales in the United States and Asia. They are lightweight entertainment, fast paced and diverting, not to be taken seriously. Arnote has been compared, albeit unfavorably, to Carl Hiaasen (q.v.) and Elmore Leonard. *Hong Kong, China* (Forge, 1996) is not part of the series.

1. *Fallen Idols* **(Tor, 1994)** Willy Hanson resolves to bring Onyx Lu, Chinese purveyor of sex and drugs, to justice.
2. *Fatal Secrets* **(Tor, 1994)** Onyx Lu, still on the loose, is opening the Black Lamp in Hollywood, the first in her proposed chain of exclusive sex and cocaine clubs across America.
3. *False Promises* **(Forge, 1995)** Onyx Lu, "back from the dead," is revengefully stalking Willy and his beautiful girlfriend, Ginny DuBois.
4. *Evil's Fancy* **(Forge, 1996)** Willy teams up with PI Coley Doctor to find the murderer of his friend in a chase that leads through Las Vegas, New Orleans, Hong Kong, and other locales. Variant title: *Weekenders' Club*.
5. *Rage in Paradise, A* **(Forge, 1997)** In his hardcover debut, Willy gets involved with tracking down a 1793 American penny called the AMERI, stolen from New Jersey collector Cliff Blaylock.
6. *Fast Lane* **(Forge, 1998)** Jason Granger and Sonny Houston, a pair of unadmirable characters, get involved in a road-rage tussle. Sonny's son Tad goes missing after running some New Jersey rapids. Jason's wife, Amanda, hires Willy Hanson and Coley Doctor to get the goods on the philandering Jason. And so it goes!

Arsenault, Mark

Massachusetts and Rhode Island journalist Mark Arsenault was a finalist for the 2003 Shamus Award for best first mystery novel with *Spiked*, which featured Eddie Bourque, a political reporter for the Lowell, Massachusetts, *Empire* who gets involved in detecting when his newspaper-beat partner, Danny Nowlin, is killed while working on an undercover story. *Spiked* has memorable characters and brings the long-depressed former textile city of Lowell to life. The sequel, *Speak Ill of the Living*, is even better. Eddie Bourque, like his creator, is a real newspaper man who believes in the value of print journalism.

1. *Spiked* (Poisoned Pen, 2003) When his newspaper-beat partner and rival, Danny Nowlin, is murdered, Eddie Bourque, political reporter for the Lowell, Massachusetts, *Empire,* suspects that the killing is connected to an undercover story that Nowlin was writing, but Bourque's employers aren't very anxious to have him pursue the matter.
2. *Speak Ill of the Living* (Poisoned Pen, 2005) Bourque, now acting as a teacher and a stringer for the Associated Press, writes a story about local banker Roger Lime, supposedly dead, who shows up in a photo six months later sent to his wife.

Asaro, Catherine (Anne)

I. The Saga of the Skolian Empire, set in the 23rd century, relates the struggles of the Skolians and their bioengineered fighting empaths, the Jagernauts, against their rather nasty rivals, the Eubians (Traders), and the Earth Alliance, which has connections with both sides. The series mixes astrophysics, time travel, romance, sex (sometimes kinky), space-opera action, psychic powers and mental telepathy, psychology, and some elements of fantasy in fast-paced, occasionally confusing (to novices, anyway) stories.

Catherine Asaro, a prominent astrophysicist, is president of Molecudyne Research in Maryland and has been assistant professor of physics at Kenyon College, visiting scientist at the Max Planck Institute for Astrophysics, consultant to the Livermore Laboratory, and teacher at the Caryl Maxwell Classical Ballet, Maryland.

1. *Schism* (Tor, 2005) In the first of a triad of prequels exploring the childhoods of some of the major players in the series, young Sauscony Valdoria (Soz) secretly applies to become a Jagernaut.
2. *Final Key, The* (Tor, 2005) As an assassination attempt disables the head of the Ruby Dynasty, young Soz steps up to responsibility.
3. *Primary Inversion* (Tor, 1995) Soz, likely heir to the Skolian Empire, and her crew of Jagernauts are engaged against the forces of the evil Trader Empire.
4. *Catch the Lightning* (Tor, 1996) Skolian Jagernaut Althor is thrown back in time (1987) and into an alternate universe (Los Angeles, Earth) where he becomes involved with 17-year-old Tina, who shares Mayan ancestry with him.
5. *Last Hawk, The* (Tor, 1997) Kelric, heir to the throne of the Skolian Empire, crash-lands on matriarchal restricted planet Coba, where he becomes involved with a series of strong women.
6. *Radiant Seas, The* (Tor, 1998) Sauscony Valdoria of Skolia and Jaibriol Qox II of Eube fake their deaths and raise a family on an unknown planet until Jaibriol is kidnapped.
7. *Ascendant Sun* (Tor, 2000) Kelric, after 18 years on matriarchal Coba, arrives home to discover that the devastating Radiance War has caused the Collapse, the destruction of the psiberspace web that linked the Skolian, Euben, and Aristo (Earth) space empires.
8. *Quantum Rose, The* (Tor, 2000) The backwater world Balumil is the scene of a love triangle between beautiful Kamoj Quanta Argali, off-worlder Havryl Lionstar, and overbearing Jax Ironbridge.
9. *Spherical Harmonic* (Tor, 2001) Dyhianna Selei wakes up on the moon Opalite missing most of her memory and her husband and son.
10. *Moon's Shadow, The* (Tor, 2003) Jaibriol Qox is installed as the puppet emperor of the vast Traders empire.
11. *Skyfall* (Tor, 2003) Roca, heir to Ruby Dynasty's pharaoh, Lahaylia Selei, escapes from her overbearing son, Kurj, and finds herself marooned on Skyfall, a backwater planet with mysterious genetic traits.

II. A pair of novels, set in the 21st century, features androids and their creators. The evil genius Charon and his cybernetic creations, especially the superintelligent Alpha, are a threat to society.

1. *Sunrise Alley* (Baen, 2004) "Turner Pascal," who is an android created by the practitioner of illegal robotics and android research, Charon, washes up on the beach near research scientist Samantha Bryton's home.
2. *Alpha* (Baen, 2006) The evil genius Charon is reputedly dead, but his creation, Alpha, the beautiful, superintelligent android he built, remains an unknown quantity.

III. The Aronsdale series is, so far, a trio of loosely related novels set in the same fantasy universe. Number 1 was originally a novella entitled "Moonglow," which appeared in the shared anthology, *Charmed Destinies* (Silhouette, 2003).

1. *Charmed Sphere, The* (Luna, 2004) Reluctant shape-mage Chime is torn from her idyllic life in the hamlet of Jacob's vale and sent to Castle Suncroft, a magecraft training site, when one of the king of Aronsdale's advisers identifies her as a promising mage.
2. *Misted Cliffs, The* (Luna, 2005) To bring about peace, Mel Dawnfield agrees to marry Cobalt the Dark, the tainted heir to a family with a reputation for cruelty, and is isolated in his home in the Misted Cliffs.
3. *Fire Opal, The* (Luna, 2007) Innocent young priestess Ginger-Sun heals a mysterious stranger, Darz Goldstone, with a fire opal gem inherited from her grandfather.

Ash, Sarah

The Tears of Artamon trilogy is a big, complex fantasy saga. The five Tears of Artamon are magical jewels that give their possessor title to the imperial throne of Novaya Rossiya, one of many nations in a fantasy world reminiscent of 18th-century Europe. The large cast of characters—including Gavril Andar, hereditary ruler of Azhkendir; the dragon-demon Drakhaoul; the emperor Eugene; King Enguerrand of Francia; Princess Astasia; and an assortment of ghosts, magicians, revolutionaries, alchemists, and werewolves—may daunt readers at first, but those who persevere, especially those who love well-realized fantasy worlds, will be rewarded. Sarah Ash (not to be confused with the late American poet Sarah Leeds Ash) is a British musician, teacher, and school librarian. *Tracing the Shadow* (Bantam, 2008) is the first book of a new series, the Alchymist's Legacy, which is set in the same world as the Tears of Artamon trilogy.

1. *Lord of Snow and Shadows* (Bantam, 2003) Young Gavril Andar is suddenly made privy to some family secrets and almost immediately finds himself Drakhaoul of Azhkendir, imbued with immense but dangerous powers.
2. *Prisoner of the Iron Tower* (Bantam, 2004) Gavril, ruler of Azhkendir and possessed by the dragon-demon Drakhaoul, has managed to defeat the invading forces of Emperor Eugene of Tielen once, but a second attack sends Gavril to a rustic prison for the criminally insane.
3. *Children of the Serpent Gate* (Bantam, 2005) In the conclusion to the trilogy, King Enguerrand of Francia is in possession of the five Tears of Artamon, magical jewels that give him claim to Novaya Rossiya, which puts the emperor Eugene in a tight spot, especially since his chief magus, Kaspar Linnaius, is in the hands of the Francians.

Asimov, Isaac

I. The Foundation books have long been regarded as Asimov's best contribution to science fiction. The work was conceived by Asimov as the science-fiction equivalent of Gibbon's *Decline and Fall of the Roman Empire*. The first stories began appearing in *Astounding Science Fiction* in 1942 and continued regularly. In the early 1950s they were published as three novels (numbers 3–5), which became collectively as the Foundation trilogy. A three-volume omnibus edition was published by Doubleday in 1964.

The connecting thread in the series is Hari Seldon's invention of the science of "psychohistory," which enables the founders of the First and Second Foundations to predict and manipulate the future.

Asimov lost interest in the series but, after a hiatus of 30 years, was persuaded to return in 1982 because his publisher, Doubleday, "got tired of waiting and offered me five-figure (and then six-figure) advances to write more" (personal communication).

The new Foundation volumes have been best sellers and have won Asimov a new generation of fans. In his later work, Asimov created connecting links that tie together his science-fiction output in one large Galactic Empire scheme. The later volumes of the Robot series (II below) are linked to the Foundation novels. There are also three novels published in the 1950s that are set in the same universe, when the Empire was at its height: *Pebble in the Sky* (Doubleday, 1950); *The Stars Like Dust* (Doubleday, 1951); and *The Currents of Space* (Doubleday, 1952). Greg Bear (q.v.), Gregory Benford (q.v.), and David Brin (q.v.) have recently added a new Foundation trilogy.

1. **Prelude to Foundation (Doubleday, 1988)** This prequel relates the adventures of Hari Seldon, inventor of "psychohistory" and the Seldon Plan, during the reign of Galactic Emperor Cleon.
2. **Forward the Foundation (Doubleday, 1993)** This posthumously published volume of the series relates the adult years of Hari Seldon, creator of the Seldon Plan.
3. **Foundation (Gnome, 1951)** The First Foundation, consisting of physical scientists, is set up on Terminus, a planet on the outer fringes of the decaying Galactic Empire. Abridged variant: *The Thousand Year Plan*.
4. **Foundation and Empire (Gnome, 1952)** A threat to the Seldon Plan arrives in the person of the Mule, a mutant not predicted by "psychohistory." Variant title: *The Man Who Upset the Universe*.
5. **Second Foundation (Gnome, 1953)** The First Foundation and the Mule search for the secret Second Foundation, which is composed of a psychologist who can mentally tamper with and "adjust" individuals.
6. **Foundation's Edge (Doubleday, 1982)** Several hundred years later, the First and Second Foundations are jockeying for power as facilitators of the Seldon Plan.
7. **Foundation and Earth (Doubleday, 1986)** Having second thoughts about the momentous decision he made in *Foundation's Edge*, Golan Trevize goes in search of "Earth," the legendary mother planet.

II. Asimov was also the creator of the Positronic Robot and a series of more than 30 robot short stories published over a span of nearly 40 years. The short stories are collected in *The Complete Robot* (Doubleday, 1982). He also wrote a series of novels about an interstellar police detective named Elijah Baley and his robot partner, R. Daneel Olivaw. The first three novels are a very successful hybrid of the science-fiction and detective-story genres. In the fourth novel, *Robots and Empire*, Asimov explicitly links this series with the Foundation Series (I above).

1. **Caves of Steel, The (Doubleday, 1954)** Human detective Elijah Baley, a resident of the despised planet Earth, is linked up with robot detective R. Daneel Olivaw to solve the murder of Dr. Sarton.
2. **Naked Sun, The (Doubleday, 1957)** Elijah and Daneel are sent to the planet Solaria to solve another murder.
3. **Robots of Dawn, The (Doubleday, 1983)** The detective pair travels to Daneel's home planet, Aurora, to help clear the name of his creator, Dr. Fastolfe.
4. **Robots and Empire (Doubleday, 1985)** Daneel aids the Settler descendants of Elijah in thwarting the Spacer's plan to burn up the Earth's crust.

Asprin, Robert (Lynn)

I. Robert Asprin is probably best known for the Thieves' World anthology series, which he created and edited (with his wife, Lynn Abbey, q.v.). This series became very popular and serves as a prototype for the SF subgenre of "shared worlds." Next to Thieves' World, Asprin is best known for his fantasy series, Myth, which he started as a satire on what he regarded as the overblown and pretentious heroic fantasy series of the 1970s. The first title, *Another Fine Myth*, proved popular and led to a second title, and then another, and Asprin had a full-blown series on his hands. Although the series started as satire, it acquired a regular cast—including Skeeve, the bumbling magician; Aahz, the purple-tongued "clapped-out" demon; Gleep, "a dragon of little brain"; Tanda, the green-haired seductress; Guido and Nunzio, Skeeve's faithful but not-too-bright bodyguards; the sanguinary Queen Hemlock; and assorted imps, unicorns, vampires, and other fantastic characters—and became more farcical than satirical. Myth has remained extremely popular, especially with young adult readers and fans of humorous fantasy novels laced with puns. Recommended to readers of Piers Anthony (q.v.), Douglas Adams (q.v.), or Terry Pratchett (q.v.).

Numbers 13–15, coauthored with Jody Lynn Nye, which continue the misadventures of Skeeve, are billed as a new series, Myth Adventures. Asprin also produced a pair of Myth graphic novels, with Phil Folgio as illustrator: *Myth Adventures One* (Donning, 1985) and *Myth Adventures Two* (Donning, 1985). Omnibus volumes include *Myth Adventures* (Doubleday, 1984; numbers 1, 2, 3, 5); and *Myth Alliances* (Doubleday, 1987; numbers 6, 7, 8). Ace reprinted most of the earlier adventures as paired novels in 2002.

1. **Another Fine Myth (Donning, 1978)** When apprentice magician Skeeve's master, Gorkin, is rubbed out, Skeeve finds another mentor in the purple-tongued demon Aahz, whom Gorkin had summoned from another dimension.
2. **Myth Conceptions (Donning, 1980)** Skeeve is summoned to the court of Rodrick the Fifth of Possiltum to audition for the position of Court Magician. Skeeve is appointed, unfortunately.
3. **Myth Directions (Donning, 1982)** Skeeve thinks that the Trophy is the ugliest thing he has seen in any dimension, but the green-haired Tanda wants the Trophy, and whatever Tanda wants, Tanda gets.
4. **Myth-ion Improbable (Ace, 2001)** Although published later, this volume belongs here chronologically. Skeeve, Aahz, and Tanda are on a quest for the valuable Golden Cowl but have to rely on a Sniffer in the bazaar to get to it, and the Sniffer wants a piece of the action.
5. **Hit or Myth (Donning, 1983)** King Rodrick takes a powder, leaving Skeeve in his place to marry Rodrick's fiancée, the homicidal Hemlock. Meanwhile, Aahz is on enforced leave, and another invasion is threatened.

6. *Myth-ing Persons* (**Donning, 1984**) Aahz has disappeared. Skeeve searches for the missing demon in another dimension, where day is night, humans are deemed monsters, and magic doesn't work.

7. *Little Myth Marker* (**Dunning, 1985**) Skeeve wins a high-stakes game of Dragon Poker. But now he must face the King of Dragon Poker, the Sen-Sen Ante Kid, a little would-be sorceress left as an IOU, and the Character Assassin, the Axe, who has been hired by magicians jealous of Skeeve's success.

8. *M.Y.T.H. Inc. Link* (**Donning, 1986**) Skeeve is now president of M.Y.T.H. Inc. Among his employees are Guido and Nunzio, the faithful thugs; the dragon Gleep; and an artistic vampire.

9. *Myth-nomers and Im-pervections* (**Donning, 1987**) After Aahz leaves in a huff because of a perceived insult, Skeeve journeys to the missing Pervect's home dimension, the worst neighborhood in the multiverse, where jokes are a felony.

10. *M.Y.T.H. Inc. in Action* (**Donning, 1990**) While Skeeve continues to search for Aahz in Perv, Guido and Nunzio join the army of the kingdom of Possiltum but are not sure for whom they should be fighting.

11. *Sweet Myth-tery of Life* (**Donning, 1994**) Although he doesn't want to marry Queen Hemlock, Skeeve's other option, being put in charge of Possiltum, seems even worse.

12. *Something M.Y.T.H. Inc.* (**Meisha Merlin, 2002**) A rebellion is brewing against Skeeve for perceived crimes against the denizens of Possiltum, including keeping a pet dragon and raising taxes.

13. *Myth-told Tales* (**Meisha Merlin, 2003**) Coauthored with Jody Lynn Nye. A "chapbook" containing short stories intended to introduce readers to the "new" Myth Adventures series.

14. *Myth Alliances* (**Meisha Merlin, 2003**) Coauthored with Jody Lynn Nye. A land of Wuhses has been taken over by 10 female Pervects (or demons) who are bent on debt collection. The Wuhses, who have been forced to produce addictive, magically activated, virtual-reality glasses for export, call in Skeeve.

15. *Myth-taken Identity* (**Meisha Merlin, 2004**) Coauthored with Jody Lynn Nye. Skeeve has become a victim of identity theft, as Aazh discovers when he tracks down a bill that Skeeve allegedly skipped out on.

II. The Phule series, a takeoff on the military-SF subgenre, features the worst company of misfits, derelicts, and aliens in the Space Legion. Captain Willard Thule, a megamillionaire who has been tricked into taking on Omega Company, tries, along with his wryly commenting butler, Beeker, to whip into shape an outfit containing Brandy, the terrifying Amazonian first sergeant; Tusk-Anini, a giant but cowardly warthoglike alien; and Super Gnat, the smallest legionnaire. A light-hearted, funny series, an SF version of the Myth saga.

1. *Phule's Company* (**Ace, 1990**) Captain Willard Phule tries to mold his company of misfits into a disciplined military outfit. Their first mission: guarding the swamp miners of Haskin's Planet.

2. *Phule's Paradise* (**Ace, 1992**) Phule's Company is on a mission to protect the Fat Chance, an intergalactic casino, from a criminal takeover.

3. *Phule and His Money, A* (**Ace, 1999**) Coauthored with Peter J. Heck. Phule's Company is sent to an underdeveloped planet to help create an intergalactic amusement park.

4. *Phule Me Twice* (**Ace, 2000**) Coauthored with Peter J. Heck. When the peaceful dinosaur planet of Zenobia is invaded, Phule is sent as a military advisor. Then a second Phule turns up.

5. *No Phule like an Old Phule* (**Ace, 2004**) Coauthored with Peter J. Heck. Phule's Company is still stuck on Zenobia, one of the Galactic Alliance's drearier outposts. A possible big-game enterprise, Phule's meddling father, Alliance Ecological Interplanetary

Observation Union (AEIOU), and Barky the Environmental Dog figure in the action.

6. *Phule's Errand* (**Ace, 2006**) Phule takes off after his missing butler. General Blitzkrieg decides to make a surprise visit to Zenobia.

III. The Phule series was anticipated by two earlier SF novels, *The Cold Cash War* (Asprin's first novel) and *Cold Cash Warrior*, which features a future world in which huge conglomerates compete by employing mercenary armies to engage in simulated warfare.

1. *Cold Cash War, The* (**St. Martin's, 1977**) After the Russo-Chinese War, the world's conglomerates, deciding that competition is wasteful and expensive, organize a series of "war games" to determine the economic winner.

2. *Cold Cash Warrior* (**Ace, 1989**) Coauthored with Bill Fawcett. Steve Treadwell, commander of the Communications Mercenary Contingent, is leading a group of mercenaries in the Brazilian jungle.

IV. The Time Scout series, coauthored with Linda Evans, is a rather light time-travel series. Its leading protagonist is Kenneth "Kit" Carson, a time scout who retired to the hotel business but gets dragged back into time traveling when his granddaughter goes missing.

Asprin has also produced (with Mel White) three graphic novels featuring characters named Duncan and Mallory and cowritten a novel in the Elfquest series, *The Blood of Ten Chiefs* (Tor, 1986).

1. *Time Scout* (**Baen, 1995**) Kenneth "Kit" Carson, Time Scout turned hotelier, returns to time travel when his granddaughter takes a trip through an unauthorized gate and winds up lost in time.

2. *Wagers of Sin* (**Baen, 1996**) The mischievous Skeeter Jackson takes center stage on a planet of survivors from Earth who have rebuilt their world after the universe was nearly destroyed.

3. *Ripping Time* (**Baen, 2000**) After her own father, Senator John Caddrick, arranges an unsuccessful hit on her, Jenna escapes to the London of 1888 and Jack the Ripper.

4. *House That Jack Built, The* (**Baen, 2001**) Kit Carson and Skeeter Jackson are searching for Jenna Caddrick, who is lost somewhere in time.

V. The Wartorn series, cowritten with Eric Del Carlo (two books so far), is a military fantasy featuring the city-states of Isthmus.

1. *Resurrection* (**Ace, 2004**) The legendary warlord Dardas is resurrected in another body to lead a conquering army across the city-states of the Isthmus. Variant title: *Resurrection: Wartorn*.

2. *Obliteration* (**Ace, 2006**) An army of soldiers and magicians has invaded from the north on its quest to bring the city-states of Isthmus under Felk rule. Variant title: *Wartorn #2: Obliteration*.

Aston, Elizabeth

First-time novelist Elizabeth Aston published *Mr. Darcy's Daughters*, a sequel to Jane Austen's *Pride and Prejudice*. While Mr. and Mrs. Darcy are away on a diplomatic mission to Constantinople, their five daughters take center stage. This sequel was followed by two more sequels: *The Exploits and Adventures of Miss Alethea Darcy*, which follows the fortunes of Alethea, the Darcys' youngest daughter, and *The Darcy Connection*, which follows the Collins family. Reviews have been decidedly mixed, with one reviewer characterizing the first book as "more like a beach book for historical fiction fans than a literary homage to Austen's masterpiece." Austen aficionados have generally been happier with Emma Tennant's (q.v.) Austen sequels.

1. *Mr. Darcy's Daughters* (**Touchstone, 2003**) In 1818 Mr. and Mrs. Darcy (née Elizabeth Bennet) go to Constantinople on a diplomatic mission, leaving their five daughters, ages 16 to 21, with Darcy's cousin Colonel Fitzwilliam.
2. *Exploits and Adventures of Miss Alethea Darcy, The* (**Touchstone, 2005**) The youngest Darcy daughter, Alethea, married in haste to the rotten Norris Napier, escapes to the Continent in disguise.
3. *Darcy Connection, The* (**Touchstone, 2008**) Follows the romantic fortunes of Charlotte and Eliza, the daughters of the ineffable Mr. Collins and his wife, Charlotte (née Lucas), from *Pride and Prejudice*.

Asturias, Miguel (Angel)

The "volcanic vehemence" of Asturias's fiction won him the Nobel Prize in 1967. His novels are long and kaleidoscopic and rich in fantasy, robust humor, and lyric prose. Although *Men of Maize* (Delacorte, 1975) and *El Señor Presidente* (Simon & Schuster, 1975) are now his most highly regarded works, the Banana trilogy, three novels set in an unidentified country closely resembling Asturias's native Guatemala, are also representative of his best work. The Banana trilogy depicts the struggle of the native people against the US corporation Tropical Banana Inc., a stand-in for the United Fruit Company.

1. *Strong Wind* (**Delacorte, 1968**) Former Tropical Banana official Lester Mead tries to bring about cooperation between native growers and the company by urging the company to settle for fair profits rather than exploitation. Original title: *Viento fuerte* (1950). Translated from the Spanish by Gregory Rabassa. Also translated by Darwin Flakoll and Claribel Alegria as *The Cyclone* (Owen, 1967).
2. *Green Pope, The* (**Delacorte, 1971**) Lester Mead tries to convince the head of Tropical Banana Inc., the "Green Pope," to offer banana growers a stable market and fairer prices for their crops. Original title: *El papa verde* (1954). Translated from the Spanish by Gregory Rabassa.
3. *Eyes of the Interred, The* (**Delacorte, 1970**) The battle between Tropical Banana Inc. and the exploited workers turns into a general strike that overthrows the republic's president. Original title: *Los ojos de los enterrados* (1960). Translated from the Spanish by Gregory Rabassa.

Atherton, Nancy

American writer Nancy Atherton writes cozies with a supernatural twist. The cozies are mostly set in the charmingly bucolic English village of Finch, where American Lori Shepherd and her eventual husband, Bill Willis, settle after Lori receives an inheritance from her mother's friend Dimity Westwood. The supernatural occurs in the form of messages from the deceased "Aunt" Dimity written in a blue notebook. Aunt Dimity assists Lori in a series of amiable mysteries that will appeal to cozy lovers.

1. *Aunt Dimity's Death* (**Viking, 1992**) American Lori Shepherd is informed that she has received an inheritance from Dimity Westwood, an English friend of her late mother, with instructions that she prepare a collection of "Aunt Dimity" stories for publication. When Lori arrives at Dimity's cottage in the Cotswolds, she finds that the cottage is haunted by Aunt Dimity's ghost.
2. *Aunt Dimity and the Duke* (**Viking, 1994**) Emma Porter, single Boston computer analyst and ardent gardener, exploring Cornwall's gardens, finds herself involved in the once-in-a-century restoration of the Duke of Penford's ruined chapel garden.
3. *Aunt Dimity's Good Deed* (**Viking, 1996**) Lori Shepherd returns to the cottage in the Cotswolds that she inherited from Aunt Dimity with her father-in-law, William Willis Sr. Then Willis Sr. disappears, leaving an enigmatic note.
4. *Aunt Dimity Digs In* (**Viking, 1998**) Lori, husband Bill Willis, and their twin boys have settled into the cottage in Finch. The mystery involves a 19th-century document stolen from the vicarage.
5. *Aunt Dimity's Christmas* (**Viking, 1999**) When a derelict collapses in the snow, Aunt Dimity instructs Lori to find out his identity, which she does with the help of Father Julian, who runs the local homeless shelter.
6. *Aunt Dimity Beats the Devil* (**Dutton, 2000**) Lori, examining the private library of the stately home of Wyrdhurst, runs into a mystery involving Nicole, Wyrdhurst's young mistress; Nicole's stuffy husband, Jared; and a handsome young man named Adam.
7. *Aunt Dimity: Detective* (**Viking, 2001**) When Lori and her family return to Finch from the States, she finds the villagers stirred up by their first murder in more than a century, that of troublemaker Prunella "Pruneface" Hooper.
8. *Aunt Dimity Takes a Holiday* (**Viking, 2003**) In a mystery involving poison-pen letters, Lori accompanies her friend Emma Harris to Hailesham Park when the latter learns that her husband is heir to a fortune and an earldom.
9. *Aunt Dimity: Snowbound* (**Viking, 2004**) During "the blizzard of the century," Lori and two other backpackers are stranded in Ladythorne Abbey, home of the late, mad Lucasta DeClerke.
10. *Aunt Dimity and the Next of Kin* (**Viking, 2005**) Lori, volunteering in the local hospital, befriends Miss Beacham, who dies, leaving a note asking Lori to find her long-lost brother.
11. *Aunt Dimity and the Deep Blue Sea* (**Viking, 2006**) When Lori's husband, Bill Willis, receives death threats via e-mail, Lori and her twin sons, Will and Rob, retreat to the Scottish isle of Erinskil.
12. *Aunt Dimity Goes West* (**Viking, 2007**) With Aunt Dimity's help, Lori Shepherd sets out to solve a 100-year-old mystery in the Rocky Mountain town of Bluebird, Colorado.
13. *Aunt Dimity: Vampire Hunter* (**Viking, 2008**) Lori is alarmed when her five-year-old twin sons report seeing a vampire during riding lessons in the Cotswolds village where she and her family live.

Atkins, Ace

Ace (he says that's the only first name he's gone by) Atkins writes a gritty series about Highway 61—the road from New Orleans through the Mississippi Delta to Memphis and eventually to Chicago—and the blues, the indigenous music of the area. Nick Travers, former pro footballer (New Orleans Saints), is a blues historian, part-time instructor at Tulane, biographer of Guitar Slim, harmonica player at JoJo's Blues Bar, and amateur sleuth. Nick travels up and down Highway 61 and gets with some pathologically bad people. Kinky Friedman (q.v.) says that "if Raymond Chandler came from the South, his name would be Ace Atkins." Other critics, though sometimes put off by what they regard as overly complex, overly violent, and overly angst-ridden plots, agree that Atkins's evocation of the blues and blues musicians is masterly. Atkins, who was born in Alabama and now lives in William Faulkner's Oxford, Mississippi, is an Auburn University graduate who was a prizewinning crime reporter for Florida newspapers.

1. *Crossroad Blues* (**St. Martin's, 1998**) Nick Travers goes in search of a missing Tulane colleague who was scouting out a hitherto

unknown recording by legendary blues guitarist Robert Johnson, who died mysteriously in the 1930s. Travers arrives in Greenwood, Mississippi, and is confronted by some spectacular sociopaths, including a murderous teenage Elvis look-alike and a slimy record producer. (For a biography of Johnson, see Peter Guralnick's *Searching for Robert Johnson*, Dutton, 1989. Johnson is also given a fictional treatment in Walter Mosely's [q.v.] nonseries novel *RL's Dream*, Washington Square, 1996.)

2. *Leavin' Trunk Blues* (St. Martin's, 2000) Nick goes to Chicago to prove the innocence of former blues singer Ruby Walker, the "Sweet Black Angel," who has served 40 years in prison for allegedly killing her lover, Billy Lyons.

3. *Dark End of the Street* (Morrow, 2002) Memphis and New Orleans are the scene of Nick's search for Clyde James, a once famous blues singer who hasn't surfaced in 25 years. A subplot involves the rescue of a young woman who is being held in a Mafia-owned casino.

4. *Dirty South* (Morrow, 2004) Nick's former Saints teammate Teddy Paris is now a rap producer who is in big trouble. Teddy's 15-year-old musical prodigy has been tampered with, and Teddy needs a lot of money fast to stave off a death threat.

Attanasio, A(lfred) A(ngelo)

I. The Tales of Arthor series is American novelist A. A. Attanasio's riff on the legend of King Arthur. The Round Table, black holes, gods, and alternate time lines are presented in a mixture of history, mythology, and philosophical and religious speculation. Traditional elements in the Arthurian legend, such as Merlin, Excalibur, and the Grail, are mixed with Norse mythology and new characters, such as the elfin prince Brian Night.

Attanasio, who is adept at SF, fantasy, and historical fiction, has also written the Radix Tetrad series (series II, below); *Wyvern* (Ticknor, 1988); the historical novel *Kingdom of the Grail* (HarperCollins, 1992); and, under the pseudonym Adam Lee, the Dominions of Irth trilogy.

1. *Dragon and the Unicorn, The* (HarperPrism, 1996) Ygrane (aka the Eternal Queen), finding her people threatened by the Furor (aka Odin, the Norse god), uses Merlin, created by a blast of power from the Furor, in an attempt to blend Celtic and Christian in one peaceable kingdom.

2. *Eagle and the Sword, The* (HarperPrism, 1997) Merlin, discovering that Arthor—the boy who is the Celtic white hope against the Saxons, Angles, and Picts—is something of a teenage thug, fashions the magic sword Excalibur to mature the youth.

3. *Wolf and the Crown, The* (HarperPrism, 1998) Arthor recounts his first year as king, when, with the aid of Ygrane and Merlin, he must prove himself a leader as well as a warrior. Arthor's incestuous relationship with his half sister Morgan the Fey has led to the birth of Mordred, which promises trouble to come.

4. *Serpent and the Grail, The* (HarperPrism, 2000) Arthor's kingdom is now united, but the Grail has been stolen by the Serpent, and Britain has become a wasteland.

II. The Radix Tetrad is a loosely related series, blending SF and fantasy, about a future Earth that has been devastated by nuclear radiation from a black hole. Each volume has a different hero.

1. *Radix* (Morrow, 1981) Sumner Kagan, an inhabitant of a nuclear-radiation-devastated future Earth, who kills mutants for kicks, finds that he is related to the Delph, an immortal deity, a disclosure that brings out the best in him.

2. *In Other Worlds* (Morrow, 1984) Carl Schirmer becomes pure energy and is hurtled 100 billion years into the future, where he undergoes another transformation and falls in love.

3. *Arc of the Dream* (Bantam, 1986) An alien from the fifth dimension leaves its metal brain in Hawaii, where orphan Donny finds it and then loses it to the bully Dirk.

4. *Last Legends of Earth, The* (Easton, 1989) A devastated future Earth is being fought over by humans and the spiderlike zotl. The heroine, Chan-ti Beppu, travels through some bad territory to be reunited with her lover, fighter pilot Ned.

Aubert, Rosemary

Ellis Portal, a discredited judge who is living as a homeless person following a stay in a mental hospital and a term in prison, digs up a severed human hand while working in a public garden in Toronto and proceeds to stitch his life back together while doing some sleuthing in this series, which has supposedly ended with the publication of number 5 in 2005. Rosemary Aubert, who has published romances and poetry as well as mystery novels, lives in Toronto and works as a court services officer in the Ontario Superior Court of Justice.

1. *Leave Me by Dying* (Bridge Works, 2003) This prequel takes Ellis Portal back to his youth in the 1960s when he studied law at the University of Toronto. Ellis gets involved in the search for a missing corpse.

2. *Free Reign* (Bridge Works, 1997) Ellis Portal, whose career as a judge was ruined by drink and drugs, is working in his garden on a deserted piece of public land in Toronto when he digs up a severed human hand wearing a gold ring with the emblem of a secret group to which he formerly belonged.

3. *Feast of Stephen, The* (Bridge Works, 1999) Portal is asked by Queenie, a friend from the streets, to investigate the suspicious deaths of several homeless friends who liked to hang around the courthouse.

4. *Ferryman Will Be There, The* (Bridge Works, 2001) Portal helps his friend Detective Sergeant Matt West locate Carrie Simm, who vanished after her movie producer father was murdered at a film premiere.

5. *Red Mass* (Bridge Works, 2005) In what is billed as the concluding episode, Portal is readmitted to law practice and finds himself facing his own daughter on opposing sides of the courtroom.

Auel, Jean M(arie)

Earth's Children is the title of a projected six-volume series set 35,000 years ago, when two forms of early man—Cro-Magnon and Neanderthal—inhabited the earth. Jean Auel has researched the subject thoroughly, then let her imagination create a convincing and dramatic portrait of what might have happened when the two species encountered each other. Some of her prehistoric people communicate with hand signals and a sort of telepathy rather than words, but in other ways they are wonderfully human, and their story is as engaging as any other family saga. *The Clan of the Cave Bear* was made into a movie (1986) starring Daryl Hannah. Earth's Children aficionados had a 12-year wait between numbers 4 and 5.

1. *Clan of the Cave Bear, The* (Crown, 1980) Ayla, a weak, hairless, babbling orphan, is adopted by a group of darker hunting people. She learns their ways yet remains strangely different.

2. *Valley of Horses, The* (Crown, 1982) Ayla shares a lonely valley with a herd of steppe horses and with a man who teaches her the meaning of companionship and love.

3. *Mammoth Hunters, The* (Crown, 1985) At last among her own kind at Lion Camp, Ayla learns the ways of her people and shares with them her innovations, the domestication of the horse and the wolf.

4. *Plains of Passage, The* (Crown, 1990) Ayla and Jondalar encounter many other clans while journeying back to his people, the Zeladonii.

5. *Shelters of Stone, The* (Crown, 2002) The pregnant Ayla and Jondalar settle in with Jondalar's cave-dwelling clan somewhere in what is now called France.

Austen-Leigh, Joan

Sequels to Jane Austen's novels have become fairly common in recent years, with authors such as Emma Tennant (q.v.) and Elizabeth Aston (q.v.) contributing pendants. Joan Austen-Leigh, the late (d. 2001) great-great grandniece of Jane Austen and cofounder of the Jane Austen Society of North America, wrote two lively and affectionate tributes to her ancestress. Mr. Elton, Miss Bates, and a host of other characters are revealed again through the correspondence between school headmistress Mary Goddard and her younger sister, Charlotte Pinkney. They don't measure up to the original *Emma*, but then, what does?

1. *Visit to Highbury, A: Another View of Emma* (St. Martin's, 1995) An epistolary retelling of *Emma* as shown in the correspondence between Mary Goddard, headmistress of the school where Harriet Smith is a parlor boarder, and Mary's younger sister, Charlotte Pinkney, who is rather unhappily remarried.

2. *Later Days at Highbury* (St. Martin's, 1996) In this follow-up to *A Visit to Highbury*, we learn that the Knightlys, the Eltons, and Miss Bates are carrying on much as usual, but Emma's family home, Hatfield, has been let out to strangers.

Axler, Leo

PSEUDONYM OF Gene Lazuta

In this offbeat quartet of mystery novels, Bill Hawley is a Cleveland funeral director (aka undertaker) who gets so involved in amateur sleuthing that he gets a private investigator's license and a gun permit. Hawley is one of your angst-ridden detectives, with an addictive personality, a pathological fear of dogs, and a load of guilt over a crippling accident. Author Gene Lazuta, who is a funeral director himself (in Parma, Ohio), has also written horror novels with such titles as *Bleeder* (Ace, 1991) and *Vyrmin* (Diamond, 1992).

1. *Final Viewing* (Berkley, 1994) Chester Scholtz's widow, Lydia, wants Bill Hawley to investigate the circumstances of the 70-year-old Chester's demise in a cheap motel.

2. *Double Plot* (Berkley, 1994) The son of Alexander Kane, a car-crash victim, brings Hawley a tape recording wherein Kane says he is going to commit suicide. The son claims that the tape is a fake.

3. *Grave Matters* (Berkley, 1995) Ellie Lyttle wants Hawley to bury her husband, Frank, who died from dog bites. But some dental records indicate that Frank Lyttle died two years previously.

4. *Separated at Death* (Berkley, 1996) A disinterment reveals an extra body in the coffin in what is the last "Bill Hawley Undertaking" so far.

Ayres, E. C.

Tony Lowell is a semiretired Florida Gulf Coast photographer who doubles as a private investigator when he works with his sometime partner, but not lover, Lena Bedrosian, a detective on the Manatee City police department. Tony, a sixties leftover in some ways, is a long-haired, divorced Vietnam veteran in his forties who loves boats and hates guns. E (for nothing?) C (for nothing?) Ayres was a television and film writer, producer, and director for 25 years until he turned to full-time novel writing.

1. *Hour of the Manatee* (St. Martin's, 1994) When Maureen Fitzgerald calls Tony Lowell to say that she witnessed the 1966 murder of playboy heir Henry Hartley III, she is immediately shot to death in her motel.

2. *Eye of the Gator* (St. Martin's, 1995) When Timothy Cross, a young African American environmental activist and nephew of an old friend, is murdered, Tony agrees to help Lena Bedrosian with the investigation and runs into a couple of very nasty villains.

3. *Night of the Panther* (St. Martin's, 1997) Lena Bedrosian smells a cover-up in the investigation of the death of her cousin Marge Pappas, a game warden in Big Cypress Swamp.

4. *Lair of the Lizard* (St. Martin's, 1998) Tony goes to Santa Fe, New Mexico, at his daughter's request to locate a missing friend and hooks up with Walter Satterthwaite's PI Joshua Croft.

Ayres, Noreen

Smokey Brandon, ex–Vegas stripper now working as a civilian forensic specialist for the Orange County (California) Sheriff's Department, is an appealing addition to the ranks of tough but sensitive female sleuths.

1. *World the Color of Salt, A* (Morrow, 1992) Smokey, forensic specialist for the Orange County Sheriff's Department, sets out to solve the murder of the kid who used to sell her coffee and doughnuts.

2. *Carcass Trade* (Morrow, 1994) Smokey gets a job at Monty Blackman's strip bar to investigate the disappearance of Miranda Robertson, one her brother Nathan's ex-wives.

3. *Juan Doe Murders, The* (Five Stars, 2000) Smokey works on a series of murders of young illegal immigrants, while her older police partner–lover suffers from a sudden illness and his college-age son makes some disturbing revelations.

Babson, Marian

I. Trixie Dolan and Evangeline Sinclair are veteran actresses of the stage and screen who get involved in a series of very zany mysteries. Trixie, the rather ditsy narrator, and her pal, the rather acerbic Evangeline, were once stars but now are reduced to lodging together in some rather outré places and settling for gigs in vampire movies or poetry readings. This is a series of amusing cozies set mostly in England and with a show-biz background.

Marian Babson, an American who has lived in England for decades, has written many books (including series II) in which cats play a large role. The versatile Babson writes not only cozies but also suspense novels.

1. *Reel Murder* (St. Martin's, 1987) Evangeline Sinclair hopes that the retrospective showing of her films in London will give her stalled career a jump-start. Instead, she finds herself a murder suspect.

2. *Encore Murder* (**St. Martin's, 1990**) Trixie Dolan's daughter, Martha, is about to marry Hugh. But then she discovers that Hugh had been married to a radical feminist and calls off the wedding. And then Martha finds herself a prime murder suspect.

3. *Shadows in Their Blood* (**St. Martin's, 1993**) Trixie and Evangeline are shivering in a drafty English castle, which is the setting for a Dracula film remake. When an actor gets killed, Trixie and Evangeline are suspected of being vampires themselves.

4. *Even Yuppies Die* (**St. Martin's, 1993**) Trixie and Evangeline take one of the penthouse suites in a run-down warehouse still being renovated and run into a mixed bag of neighbors.

5. *Break a Leg, Darlings* (**St. Martin's, 1997**) The girls try to make a go of it in the London pub theater scene. They run into a very bad poetry reading, an Irish wolfhound named the Semtex, the Open and Shut Club (whose members attend first and last performances), and obnoxious film actress Sweetums Carew, who takes a fatal fall down a pub's stairs.

6. *Cat Who Wasn't a Dog, The* (**St. Martin's, 2003**) A revival of *Arsenic and Old Lace;* imperious leading lady Dame Cecilia Savoy; Fleur-de-Lys, Dame Cecilia's Pekingese, which dies and is sent off to be stuffed; a taxidermist who comes to a bad end; a Japanese bobtail named Cho-Cho-San; Trixie and Evangeline; and the Brighton constabulary are all involved here.

II. *Cover-Up Story,* Babson's first published novel, introduced Doug Perkins and Gerry Tate, partners in a British public relations firm, and Pandora, Doug's cat. Four humorous mysteries feature the inept amateur detectives Perkins and Tate.

1. *Cover-Up Story* (**St. Martin's, 1988**) Nashville's Bart and the Cousins, the country-music troupe Doug and Gerry are representing on their English tour, are carrying mixed baggage: a chart-topping song and Bart's indictment in the United States for an affair involving an underage groupie. Originally published in the United Kingdom in 1971.

2. *Murder at the Cat Show* (**St. Martin's, 1989**) Doug becomes the public-relations officer for an exhibition entitled "Cats through the Ages" and finds himself up to his ears in cats and temperamental owners. Then a gold statue of Dick Whittington's cat is stolen. Originally published in the United Kingdom in 1972 as *Murder on Show.*

3. *Tourists Are for Trapping* (**St. Martin's, 1989**) Larkin's Luxury Tours number 79 has run into some rough sailing, starting with the mysterious death of one of its clients in Zurich.

4. *In the Teeth of Adversity* (**St. Martin's, 1990**) Doug and Jerry get involved with an eccentric group of dentists, including the inventor of a new anesthetic, a former army dentist who hasn't gotten over the world war(s), and a sadistic driller.

Bacchelli, Riccardo

Il Mulino del Po (the Mill on the Po) is a historical trilogy about Italy from the Napoleonic Wars to the end of World War I. It is about the Sacerni family and their descendants, millers in the Po River Valley in the area of the city of Ferrara. The trilogy is regarded as a national epic in Italy, covering, as it does, the unification of Italy. The trilogy was translated into English in two parts (see below). A film version of *Il Mulino del Po* was made in Italy in 1948 and shown briefly in the United States.

1. *Mill on the Po, The* (**Pantheon, 1950**) The fortunes of the Sacerni family, millers in the Po Valley in northern Italy, are followed from the end of the Napoleonic Wars (1814) to the unification of Italy (1870). Includes the first two parts of the trilogy: *Dio ti salvi* (*God Save You*) and *La miseria viene in barca* (*Trouble Travels by Water*). Translated from the Italian by Frances Frenaye. Originally published in 1938.

2. *Nothing New under the Sun* (**Pantheon, 1955**) The third part of *Il Mulino* takes the millers from the reunification of Italy to World War I (1914–18). Translated from the Italian by Stuart Hood. Originally published as *Mundo vecchio, sempre nuovo* in 1941.

Bach, Richard

Richard Bach's *Jonathan Livingston Seagull* (Macmillan, 1970) was a huge best-seller and a 1970s cult favorite. Bach's five Ferret Chronicles, published more than 30 years later, haven't achieved comparable popularity, although Bach's enthusiasms—for flying, for animals, for treacly endings, and for aphorisms—haven't diminished. The Ferret Chronicles are five novella-length stories with ferrets (based on Bach's own ferrets) in human roles. They can be read by children or by adults who like somewhat sugary morality tales. *Curious Lives: Adventures from The Ferret Chronicles* (Hampton Roads, 2005) is a rearrangement and condensation of the Ferret Chronicles.

1. *Air Ferrets Aloft* (**Scribner, 2002**) Stormy and Strobe, two ferret pilots working for an airline that shuttles food and toys around the United States, fall in love.

2. *Rescue Ferrets at Sea* (**Scribner, 2002**) Bethany Ferret dreams of being part of the fleet that rescues animals at sea.

3. *Writer Ferrets Chasing the Muse* (**Scribner, 2002**) Budgeron Ferret and his bride, Danielle, are both writers. Budgeron is at work on an epic novel, *Where Ferrets Walk*, while Danielle writes about the adventures of a vixen named Veronique.

4. *Rancher Ferrets on the Range* (**Scribner, 2003**) Montana "ranch paw" Monty Ferret has a bittersweet parting with his childhood love, Cheyenne Jasmine Ferret, who leaves for Hollywood and becomes a star.

5. *Last War, The: Detective Ferrets and the Case of the Golden Deed* (**Scribner, 2003**) Montgomery and Cheyenne Jasmine, the ferrets in number 4, meet again years later and realize the importance of following a personal calling to achieve happiness.

Baer, Will Christopher

Phineas Poe, former investigator for the Denver police department, is the narrator of a trio of hallucinogenic noir novels. The books are full of damaged characters, gothic prose, and some very nasty happenings. Baer writes well, but only lovers of William Burroughs–type fiction who like to read about "sick freaks" will want to take these novels on.

1. *Kiss Me, Judas* (**Viking, 1998**) Phineas Poe, former investigator for the Denver police department, offers a hallucinatory account of his adventures, which involve, among other things, a stay in a psychiatric hospital, a lost kidney, and an alluring sociopath named Jude.

2. *Penny Dreadful* (**Viking, 2000**) Poe is hired by his old Denver police buddy, Moon, to find vanished officer Jimmy Sky. Drugs, murder, and a lot of sadomasochistic goings-on are strewn along Poe's path.

3. *Hell's Half Acre* (**MacAdam, 2004**) Now a broken-down drunk on the fringes of society, Poe is looking for Jude (who stole his kidney in number 1) and is chased by a "sick freak" who has become a US senator.

Bailey, Robin W(ayne)

I. American writer Robin Bailey (not to be confused with the late actor of the same name) writes what is essentially fantasy-quest fiction. The Brothers of the Dragon trilogy is about two American brothers who find themselves engaged in an epic battle between Light and Darkness in an alternate world where dragons patrol the skies.

1. *Brothers of the Dragon* **(Roc, 1993)** Eric and Robert Podlowski enter a cave in the Catskill Mountains and find themselves in an alternate world where dragons roam the sky.
2. *Flames of the Dragon* **(Roc, 1994)** Librarian Katy Dowd brings Eric back from Palenoc to prove that Robert hadn't murdered him, then joins the pair in their alternate world, where their martial-arts skills are enlisted in the fight against the Heart of Darkness and the Dark Lord.
3. *Triumph of the Dragon* **(Roc, 1994)** Eric and Robert must reunite against the evil sorceress to bring victory to the forces of Light. UK title: *The Palace of Souls.*

II. The Dragonkin series is another series about dragons, this time with dragons as the heroes. Set in Wyvernwood, a forest in the land of Engmar, where the encroachment of man into their last refuge threatens the very existence of dragons.

1. *Dragonkin* **(Simon & Schuster, 2003)** The dragon triplets Harrow, Chan, and Luna are forced to confront the encroachment of man into Wyvernwood, the last known refuge of the dragons.
2. *Dragonkin: Book 2; Talisman* **(Simon & Schuster, 2004)** The war between the human kingdoms of Angmar and Degarm has begun, and the conflict is spreading into the Great Refuge.
3. *Dragonkin: Book 3; Sanctuary* **(Simon & Schuster, 2005)** As the human devastation escalates, now is the time for the Diamond Dragon, the Glass Dragon, and the Heart of All Dragons to be joined. Variant title: *Dragonkin: Book 3; Undersky.*

III. The Night's Angel trilogy delineates the career of Frost, whose magical powers have been denied by a mother's curse and who must find her redemption through struggle in a world of savagery and sorcery. Published together in one omnibus volume as *Night's Angel* (Meisha Merlin, 2002).

Bailey has also written a volume of Philip José Farmer's (q.v.) Dungeon series, *The Lake of Fire* (Bantam, 1989), and one volume continuing the late Fritz Leiber's (q.v.) Fafhrd and the Gray Mouser series, *Swords against the Shadowland* (White Wolf, 1998).

1. *Frost* **(Pocket, 1983)** Young Frost, cursed in her mother's dying breath, must take to the sword to make a life for herself. Her first task is to protect the Book of the Last Battle, a collection of spells and words of power.
2. *Skull Gate* **(Tor, 1985)** Frost is enlisted in the epic battle between the Gods of Light and the Forces of Darkness. Title in omnibus volume.
3. *Bloodsongs* **(Tor, 1986)** Twenty years later, Frost finds herself a wife, a widow, and a mother, but is her quest finished? Title in omnibus volume.

Baker, Kage

Californian (born in Hollywood, dwells in Pismo Beach) Kage Baker is a relatively recent arrival on the SF-fantasy scene (first publication, 1997), but she has made a splash with her Company series of time-travel books. The Company is Dr. Zeus Inc., a 24th-century corporation that employs immortal cyborgs to travel through time to ransack the past, all supposedly with the best of motives. Three of the prominent time travelers are Mendoza, a 1,000-year-old female botanist; Joseph, who is a relict of Neolithic times; and Alec Checkerfield, a 24th-century British nobleman, who is something of a rogue. The 16th, 19th, and 23rd centuries are among their time stops. The series is liberally laced with humor, but serious philosophical, scientific, and religious issues are examined as well. Volumes of the series have been translated into several languages. Baker also writes humorous fantasy (e.g., *The Anvil of the World,* Tor, 2003).

1. *In the Garden of Iden* **(Harcourt, 1998)** Immortal botanist Mendoza, making her first trip back through time, lands in the England of Bloody Mary (1554) in search of a certain strain of holly that can be used in the 24th century as a cancer cure.
2. *Sky Coyote* **(Harcourt, 1999)** Cyborg Facilitator Joseph travels to 16th-century Alta California to collect the Chumash Indians and their entire biosystem for 24th-century study.
3. *Mendoza in Hollywood* **(Harcourt, 2000)** Mendoza, still mourning her mortal lover, Nicholas Harpole (burned at the stake in 1555), travels to California's Cahuenga Pass in 1863, where a Company outpost disguised as a stagecoach station has been set up.
4. *Graveyard Game, The* **(Harcourt, 2001)** Facilitator Joseph and Literature Specialist Lewis travel to various points in time in search of their missing colleague, Mendoza, to get a handle on what the Company has in store for its operatives.
5. *Black Projects, White Knights* **(Golden Gryphon, 2002)** Subtitle: *The Company Dossiers.* A collection of 14 short stories about the Company, including three previously unpublished.
6. *Life of the World to Come, The* **(Tor, 2004)** Alec Checkerfield, designed by the Company as the prototype for a new line of cyborgs to replace the rather ornery models they have been employing in the field, proves to be something of a loose cannon and the third of Mendoza's physically identical lovers.
7. *Children of the Company, The* **(Tor, 2005)** Contains previously published short stories arranged into a larger narrative framework. Focuses on a corrupt cyborg leader named Labienus.
8. *Machine's Child, The* **(Tor, 2006)** Alec Checkerfield shares his cyborg body uncomfortably with the Recombinant personalities of 19th-century spy Edward Bell-Fairfax and 16th-century scholar Nicholas Harpole.
9. *Sons of Heaven, The* **(Tor, 2007)** The conclusion to the series explores the events leading up to July 8, 2355, the moment when the Silence falls.

Baker, Nikki

Virginia Kelly, a black lesbian, sometimes feels called upon to act as a detective in this series of mysteries. Virginia has more or less made it as an investment broker, but as a token black, a situation about which she makes many wry comments. She has many affairs with other women, but somehow they never work out. Ginny is a somewhat bumbling amateur detective, but her witty comments and sharp observations of domestic and professional life make this an enjoyable series. Nikki Baker is a University of Chicago MBA who works as a financial analyst when she isn't writing mysteries.

1. *In the Game* **(Naiad, 1991)** After Virginia Kelly has drinks with old college chum Bev Johnson, Bev's unfaithful lover, Kelsey, is found murdered behind the bar where Ginny and Bev had met.
2. *Lavender House Murder, The* **(Naiad, 1992)** On a vacation in Provincetown, Massachusetts, Ginny discovers the bullet-ridden

corpse of Joan Di Maio, a reporter who had engaged in the practice of "outing," dragging homosexuals out of the closet.

3. *Long Goodbyes* (Naiad, 1993) Ginny returns to her Midwest hometown for Christmas, a high school reunion, and a reunion with her first love, Rosey Paschen.

4. *Ultimate Exit Strategy, The* (Bella Books, 2001) Ginny is toiling, as the token black, at the investment firm of Whytebread, Greese, Winslow, and Sloat and pondering her long-distance relationship with a younger lesbian with blue hair. The unpopular boss of the company, which is in danger of becoming engulfed and devoured by a larger corporation, is murdered.

Bakker, R. Scott

Canadian writer Bakker's epic fantasy trilogy, the Prince of Nothing, has been published to enthusiastic reviews comparing Bakker to J. R. R. Tolkien (q.v.). The monk Anasûrimbor Kellhus (aka "the Prince of Nothing") and the sorcerer Drusas Achamian are among a plethora of characters in the world of Eärwa, a sort of alternate medieval world where a holy war set off by the prophet Maithanet is raging. Appendixes help keep Eärwan places and characters straight. For readers of epic fantasy, these novels are page-turners, but some scenes may be too graphic for younger or more squeamish readers.

1. *Darkness That Comes Before, The* (Overlook, 2004) The medieval fantasy world of Eärwa and its extraordinary inhabitants, such as Anasûrimbor Kellhus and Drusas Achamian, are introduced and described.

2. *Warrior-Prophet, The* (Overlook, 2005) The holy war set off by the unseen prophet Maithanet rages in Eärwa. Drusas Achamian keeps the narrative going amid great slaughter and his love for the prostitute Esmenet.

3. *Thousandfold Thought, The* (Overlook, 2006) The conclusion to the Prince of Nothing. The Holy War army has reached the gates of the holy city of Shimeh. Anasûrimbor Kellhus learns that the Thousandfold Thought offers the only way to bring peace to Eärwa.

Baldacci, David

I. Like John Grisham, David Baldacci is a corporate lawyer who became a very successful suspense writer. Some of his novels became number-one best sellers, including his first, *Absolute Power* (Warner, 1995), which was brought to the screen by Clint Eastwood. *Split Second* introduced Michelle "Mick" Maxwell and Sean King, Secret Service operatives whose careers came to grief. In its sequel, *Hour Game*, the two have set up as private investigators in the Wrightsburg, Virginia, area. Great action sequences and nonstop suspense blend with a somewhat acerbic portrait of small-town southern life.

1. *Split Second* (Warner, 2003) Michelle "Mick" Maxwell and Sean King, disgraced Secret Service operatives, race to track down the Buick Man, a mysterious figure responsible for assassinations and other political violence.

2. *Hour Game* (Warner, 2004) Maxwell and King, having set up as private investigators in the small Virginia town of Wrightsburg, are on the track of a serial killer—or killers.

3. *Simple Genius* (Warner, 2007) Maxwell seems to have a death wish, for which King urges her to get help, while he investigates the suicide of a scientist found on the grounds of mysterious CIA facility Camp Peary.

II. The Camel Club, a group of four dysfunctional crime solvers headed by ex-CIA assassin "Oliver Stone," is in search of justice and isn't too nasty-neat about how justice is found. Along the way, they manage to stop some pretty hairy plots and do their best to hold America's leaders accountable to its citizens.

1. *Camel Club, The* (Warner, 2005) The Camel Club, on the fringes of Washington, DC, a group of four aging eccentrics trying to find the "truth" behind their country's action, runs into a plot that threatens American security.

2. *Collectors, The* (Warner, 2006) Renegade CIA agent Roger Seagraves has set himself up in the business of freelance assassin and selling American secrets to the highest bidder. Meanwhile, Annabelle Conroy is engineering a $33 million scam targeting Atlantic City casino owner Jerry Bagger.

3. *Stone Cold* (Grand Central, 2007) Camel Club associate Annabelle Conroy is on the run after stealing $40 million from casino owner Jerry Bagger, who killed her mother. Triple 6, Oliver Stone's old outfit, is being targeted by the son of one of Triple 6's victims.

Baldwin, Bill (Merl W., Jr.)

Bill Baldwin's Helmsman series—cold war productions that proved to be very popular—was published in paperback editions only in the 1980s and 1990s. They are standard military SF or space-opera productions with lots of action, a battle between good and evil empires, some love interest, and, in Wilf Ansor Brim, a hero who is the one man who can save the good guys from tyranny. The seven volumes in the series, rewritten by Baldwin, are being republished by Timberwolf in a "Director's Cut Special Edition" (2003 on). *Canby's Legion* (Warner, 1995) isn't part of the series.

1. *Helmsman, The* (Warner, 1985) Wilf Ansor Brim, a guy from a poor planet who just graduated from the academy, is given a chance to show his stuff in defense of the Galactic Empire and to show up the blue bloods who sneered at his humble origins.

2. *Galactic Convoy* (Popular Library, 1987) Wilf captains the *Defiant*, first of a new class of warships built to protect imperial convoys from the League of Dark Stars. But the league has a new trick up its sleeve: a "bender" device that can render spaceships invisible. Wilf has fallen for Princess Margot Efer'wyck, married and above his station.

3. *Trophy, The* (Warner, 1990) Temporarily out of work when the evil emperor Triannic and the League of Dark Stars negotiate a phony armistice and peaceniks disable the Galactic Empire's fleets, Wilf enters the great Mitchell Trophy Space Race.

4. *Mercenaries, The* (Warner, 1991) Most of the Galactic Fleet is in mothballs because of the Treaty of Garak. Wilf takes *Starfury* to Fluvanna to protect the source of materials needed to construct a new fleet.

5. *Defenders, The* (Warner, 1992) Wilf and the young emperor Onrad assemble defenses for the planet of Avalon when the League of Dark Stars goes on the attack again.

6. *Siege, The* (Warner, 1994) Rear Admiral Brim and General Ursis go to the defense of the Sodeskayan Worlds, but they are woefully lacking in space support.

7. *Defiance, The* (Warner, 1996) The planet Atalanta is being besieged by the Torond, the evil allies of Emperor Triannic, and it's up to Admiral Brim to break the siege.

8. *Turning Tide, The* (Timberwolf, 2004) Annotation not available.

Baldwin, Faith

I. Little Oxford, Connecticut, is a fictitious town—typically New England—in which romance writer Baldwin set her 1938 novel, *Station Wagon Set*. In 1971 she used the locale again, updated, in *Any Village*, and her later romances were set there almost exclusively. This is a series only in the geographical sense; after the first two novels, there is no chronological order.

1. *Station Wagon Set* **(Farrar, 1938)** Six connected stories sketch the residents of Little Oxford. The young Dr. Bing Irvington is featured in the story entitled "Mixed Doubles."
2. *Any Village* **(Holt, 1971)** Bing Irvington is now the older doctor in town, and his son Ben has joined his practice. Ben falls in love in this installment.
3. *No Bed of Roses* **(Holt, 1973)** Concerns a young married couple in Little Oxford: Katie Palmer, a real-estate agent, and her husband, Jeremy, owner of a bookstore.
4. *Time and the Hour* **(Holt, 1974)** Stacy Armitage, recently divorced, meets architect Lee Osborne.
5. *New Girl in Town* **(Holt, 1975)** Maggie Knox faces her growing interest in a married man.
6. *Thursday's Child* **(Holt, 1976)** Aristocratic Abby Morrison Allen returns to her New England home with Sara Foster, her 24-year-old granddaughter.
7. *Adam's Eden* **(Holt, 1977)** Cosmopolitan bachelor Adam, Vanessa Steele's grandson, settles in Little Oxford.

II. Baldwin wrote a pair of novels, set at the turn of the 20th century in China and New York, chronicling the family of American missionary Tobias Condit.

1. *American Family* **(Farrar, 1935)** The trials and triumphs of Tobias Condit, an American missionary in China, are chronicled.
2. *Puritan Strain, The* **(Farrar, 1935)** Elizabeth, daughter of Tobias, leaves a comfortable existence with her husband and son in America to return to China.

Ball, John (Dudley)

I. Virgil Tibbs, a young black man waiting for a train in the small southern city of Wells, Mississippi, is picked up as a murder suspect. But much to the embarrassment of local police chief Gillespie, he turns out to be a homicide detective from the Pasadena police force who is in the area to visit relatives. So begins the fictional life of Ball's clever and sophisticated detective, elegantly played by Sidney Poitier in the excellent 1967 film *In the Heat of the Night* (set in South Carolina). The Tibbs character was recycled for six more mystery novels, a television series, and two more Poitier movies (*They Call Me Mister Tibbs* and *The Organization*).

1. *In the Heat of the Night* **(Harper, 1965)** Virgil Tibbs stays in Wells to help catch a murderer and teach the bigoted Chief Gillespie a lesson.
2. *Cool Cottontail, The* **(Harper, 1966)** An unidentified dead man found in the swimming pool of a nudist camp is Tibbs's next assignment.
3. *Johnny Get Your Gun* **(Little, 1969)** An obsessed nine-year-old bent on revenge makes a different kind of case for Sergeant Tibbs. Variant title: *Death for a Playmate*.
4. *Five Pieces of Jade* **(Little, 1972)** When the owner of a valuable jade collection is murdered, drugs and other tangles complicate Tibbs's search for a solution.
5. *Eyes of Buddha, The* **(Little, 1976)** The trail of a dead woman in Pasadena and a missing heiress lead Tibbs halfway around the world to the Monkey Temple in Tibet.
6. *Then Came Violence* **(Doubleday, 1980)** Bachelor Tibbs comes home from work one day to find that he has mysteriously acquired a wife and two children.
7. *Singapore* **(Dodd, 1986)** Miriam Motambori, who appeared in *Then Came Violence*, is being held for murder in a Singapore prison when Tibbs comes to her aid.

II. John Ball wrote an earlier series of procedurals featuring Jack Tallon, a former big-city policeman who becomes police chief of the small town of Whitewater, Washington.

1. *Police Chief* **(Doubleday, 1977)** Leaving the Pasadena, California, police department, Jack Tallon takes what looks to be a less-stressful job in Whitewater, Washington, but finds that he has traded one set of problems for another.
2. *Trouble for Tallon* **(Doubleday, 1981)** The Whitewater police are molded into a crack detective team in this investigation of a murder.
3. *Chief Tallon and the S.O.R.* **(Dodd, Mead, 1984)** A highly controversial convention, a publicity-hungry evangelist who is out to disrupt it, a hit-and-run accident, and a murder roil the waters of Whitewater.

Ballard, J(ames) G(raham)

Before the publication of *Empire of the Sun*, J. G. Ballard was known primarily for dystopian science fiction such as *The Drowned World* (Berkley, 1962) and *The Unlimited Dream Company* (Holt, 1979). *Empire of the Sun* was a mainstream critical (nominated for a Booker Prize) and popular success and was made into a well-regarded Steven Spielberg movie (1987). *Empire of the Sun* and its sequel, *The Kindness of Women*, are autobiographical accounts that carry the protagonist, Jim, from a boyhood in Shanghai and a Japanese prison through more than 40 years of his life until he participates in making a film based on his wartime experiences.

1. *Empire of the Sun* **(Simon & Schuster, 1984)** Eleven-year-old Jim endures separation from his parents and internment in a Japanese prison camp in Shanghai during World War II.
2. *Kindness of Women, The* **(Farrar, 1991)** Released from the Japanese prison camp, Jim tries to get on with his life, attempting several professions and tragically losing his wife.

Ballard, Mignon F.

Augusta Goodnight, who left this mortal coil during World War II, is a guardian angel who looks like Dale Evans, smells of strawberries, and dispenses advice as a sort of otherworldly Dear Abby in this series of cozies set in the American South. Each book in the series features a mystery and someone in emotional trouble who needs advice, which is supplied by Augusta in rather antic fashion, sometimes along with recipes. Georgia native Mignon F. Ballard has written other books, sometimes with supernatural and mystery components, including *Minerva Cries Murder* (Carroll & Graf, 1993), which was supposed to be a series launch but has had no sequels yet.

1. *Angel at Troublesome Creek* **(St. Martin's, 1999)** Mary George Murphy rebuilds her shattered life and solves the mystery of

the missing Bible with the help of guardian angel Augusta Goodnight.

2. *Angel to Die For, An* (St. Martin's, 2000) Editor Prentice Dobson visits her family graveyard to make peace with her deceased younger sister only to find a gaping hole where her wicked uncle, Fans, had been buried 25 years before.

3. *Shadow of an Angel* (St. Martin's, 2002) Young widow Arminda Hobbs finds her cousin Otto dead in a ladies'-room stall at the local museum, and she and "temp" guardian angel Augusta investigate a group called the Mystic Six and a quilt made by them.

4. *Angel Whispered Danger, The* (St. Martin's, 2003) Guardian angel Augusta and trainee angel Penelope travel to Bishop's Bridge, North Carolina, to help Kate McBride investigate some buried secrets involving her great-uncle Ernest and his runaway wife.

5. *Too Late for Angels* (St. Martin's, 2005) Augusta aids the widowed Lucy of Stone's Throw, South Carolina, after a crazy old lady turns up at Lucy's door and then is found dead in Lucy's coat.

6. *Angel and the Jabberwocky Murders, The* (St. Martin's, 2006) Lucy Nan Pilgrim is teaching a "living history" course at the local women's college in Stone's Throw when one of the coeds disappears.

Balogh, Mary

I. Mary Balogh (pronounced *Bahlog*) came from her native Wales to Saskatchewan for a 2-year teaching stint and is still there after some 20 years of teaching and more than 60 romance and Regency novels. Although Balogh doesn't write sequels per se, characters from one novel often turn up in another, playing a minor role in one and the hero in another. Most of Balogh's work is set in the Regency period in English history (c. 1811–1820). Later books tend to emphasize the historical details rather than the romantic plot. The novels are page-turners with interesting characters and period flavor.

A Chance Encounter featured William Mainwaring as a rejected suitor. Mainwaring returned as the hero of *The Wood Nymph*.

1. *Chance Encounter, A* (New American Library, 1985) When single, wealthy, and handsome William Mainwaring reopens Ferndale Manor, the neighboring Rowe family assumes that he "is in need of a wife."

2. *Wood Nymph, The* (New American Library, 1987) William Mainwaring retreats to Graystone in the north of England to forget Elizabeth Rossiter, the governess in *A Chance Encounter*. There he falls in with Lady Helen Wade, the youngest daughter of the Earl of Claymore and the "wood nymph" of the title.

II. Lord Edmund Waite, the villain of *The Trysting Place*, and Mary Gregg, Lady Mornington, a minor love interest of the hero in *A Counterfeit Betrothal*, are the hero and heroine of *The Notorious Rake*.

1. *Trysting Place, The* (New American Library, 1986) Young, wealthy widow Lady Felicity Wren, in pursuit of the ideal husband, falls into a complicated love triangle.

2. *Counterfeit Betrothal, A* (New American Library, 1992) Lady Sophia Bryant, in an attempt to reunite her estranged parents, announces her engagement to a notorious rake.

3. *Notorious Rake, The* (New American Library, 1992) Lady Mary Gregg falls in love with notorious rake Lord Edmund Waite.

III. The large Frazer family plays a prominent role in *The First Snowdrop* and *A Christmas Belle*. Jack Frazer, cousin of the hero of the former, is the hero of the latter title.

1. *First Snowdrop, The* (New American Library, 1987) A neglected lady vows to wreak vengeance on the lord who made a mockery of their marriage.

2. *Christmas Belle, A* (New American Library, 1994) Jack Frazer renews his romance with London actress Isabella.

IV. Numbers 2, 3, and 4 are a trilogy that tells the love stories of the Purnells, two brothers and a sister. *A Promise of Spring* is a prequel that takes up the story of Sir Perry Lampman and his wife, minor characters in the trilogy.

1. *Promise of Spring, A* (New American Library, 1990) Grace Howard's former lover, who was dead, according to Grace, turns up again after Grace is married.

2. *Gilded Web, The* (New American Library, 1989) Alexandra Purnell must choose between two eligible brothers, both of whom have proposed to her.

3. *Web of Love* (New American Library, 1990) After her elderly but much-loved husband dies, Ellen meets the irresistible Lord Dominic Eden.

4. *Devil's Web, The* (New American Library, 1990) Seemingly heartless beauty Madeleine Raine made all the men she met pay for the rebuff she received from James Purnell. Then James Purnell returns.

V. Sir Gerald Stapleton is the hero's friend in *The Ideal Wife*. He is the hero of *A Precious Jewel*. *A Christmas Bride* brings together characters from this series and series VI (below).

1. *Ideal Wife, The* (New American Library, 1991) Abigail Gardiner presents herself to Miles Ripley as a sweet, subservient girl. After marriage, Miles discovers his mistake.

2. *Precious Jewel, A* (New American Library, 1993) Priscilla Wentworth feels that she is doomed to end up destitute until Sir Gerald Stapleton comes into her life.

3. *Christmas Bride, A* (New American Library, 1997) Edgar Downs, son of a wealthy tradesman, is looking for a wife with a title. Then he meets the widowed Lady Helena Stapleton.

VI. Many of the same characters appear and reappear in series VI. *A Christmas Bride* also contains characters from series V.

1. *Dark Angel* (New American Library, 1994) Although Jennifer Winward is engaged to Lord Lionel Kersey, she is in danger of being seduced by the notorious Earl of Thornell.

2. *Lord Carew's Bride* (New American Library, 1995) Engaged to an honorable man, Samantha is reminded of her romantic past when the Earl of Rushford enters her life again.

3. *Famous Heroine, The* (New American Library, 1996) Cora Downes, who is introduced to high society after she saves a duke's son from drowning, winds up in a compromising position with Lord Francis Kneller.

4. *Plumed Bonnet, The* (New American Library, 1996) Vicar's daughter Stephanie is shocked by the demands of the Duke of Bridgewater after he saves her from a roadside misfortune.

5. *Christmas Bride, A* (New American Library, 1997) See series V, number 3.

VII. Freddie Sullivan, Harriet Pope, and Lord Archibald Vinney are recurring characters in series VII.

1. *Courting Julia* (New American Library, 1993) After Julia Maynard's wealthy stepfather dies, she is besieged by suitors, but she wants Fredrick, Earl of Beaconswood.

2. *Dancing with Clara* (**New American Library, 1994**) Is it Clara Danford's money or Clara herself that gambling man Fredrick Sullivan wants?

3. *Tempting Harriet* (**New American Library, 1994**) Lord Tenby wants wealthy, widowed Lady Harriet Wingham (née Pope) as his mistress, but she is reluctant to surrender herself to his blandishments.

VIII. Lady Emily Marlowe and Lord Ashley Kendrick are sister and brother, respectively, of the heroine and hero of *Heartless*. Emily and Ashley are the heroine and hero of *Silent Melody*.

1. *Heartless* (**Berkley, 1995**) Lucas Kendrick, Duke of Harndon, and Lady Ann Marlowe, both hurt by previous affairs, must learn to trust one another.

2. *Silent Melody* (**Berkley, 1997**) Deaf-mute Lady Emily Marlowe renews her teenage romance with Lord Ashley Kendrick, who has returned seven years later from India.

IX. A trio of novels tells the love stories of four close friends and former cavalry officers in the Napoleonic Wars.

1. *Indiscreet* (**Jove, 1997**) After a rape and an illegitimate child, Lady Catherine Winsmore refuses a forced marriage. Posing as a young widow, Mrs. Catherine Winters, she meets the rakish Rex Adams, Viscount Rawleigh.

2. *Unforgiven* (**Jove, 1998**) Kenneth Woodfell returns home after eight years and realizes that his love for Moira Hayes is undying. Unfortunately, the Woodfell and Hayes families have been feuding for nearly a century.

3. *Irresistible* (**Jove, 1998**) Although Sophie Armitage had been married and widowed, she has never felt attractive to men.

X. *More Than a Mistress* was Balogh's hardcover debut. Lord Ferdinand Dudley, younger brother of the hero in *More Than a Mistress* is the hero of *No Man's Mistress*. A prequel featuring Lady Angeline Dudley, sister of Ferdinand, is planned.

1. *More Than a Mistress* (**Delacorte, 2000**) Jocelyn Dudley, Duke of Tresham, and supposed milliner's assistant Jane Ingleby initially resist falling in love with each other.

2. *No Man's Mistress* (**Delacorte, 2001**) When Lord Ferdinand Dudley visits Pinewood Manor, a small estate he has won in a card game, he is surprised to find that "country lass" Viola Thornhill is in occupancy.

XI. Lauren Edgeworth, a jilted bride in *One Night for Love*, is the heroine of *A Summer to Remember*.

1. *One Night for Love* (**Delacorte, 1999**) Sergeant's daughter Lily Doyle marries Nevile Wyatt, Major Lord Newbury, in Portugal. After a battle, Nevile thinks that Lily has been killed.

2. *Summer to Remember, A* (**Delacorte, 2002**) Miss Lauren Edgeworth, back in London after being abandoned at the altar in *One Night for Love*, is the target of the rakish Kit Butler, Viscount Ravensburg.

XII. The six brothers and sisters of the Bedwyn family were introduced in *A Summer to Remember* (series XI, number 2). Each one gets his or her own in a series of six novels. Characters from *One Night for Love* (series XI, number 1) as well *A Summer to Remember* appear in some of these novels.

1. *Slightly Married* (**Dell, 2003**) The honorable Colonel Aidan Bedwyn, pursuant to an oath he made to a dying fellow officer, marries coal-miner's daughter Eve Morris.

2. *Slightly Wicked* (**Dell, 2003**) Rannulf Bedwyn rescues a beautiful young woman from an overturned stagecoach, and they have an affair that results in some unmaskings and complications.

3. *Slightly Scandalous* (**Dell, 2003**) Freyja Bedwyn and Joshua Moore, Marquess of Halimere, have an encounter and a set-to in an inn on the road to Bath. But, of course, it doesn't end there.

4. *Slightly Tempted* (**Dell, 2004**) Morgan Bedwyn, who has stayed in Brussels after the Battle of Waterloo to find her missing brother, Alleyne, finds an ally in rakish Gervase Ashford, the Earl of Rosthorn.

5. *Slightly Sinful* (**Dell, 2004**) Alleyne Bedwyn, missing and assumed dead after the Battle of Waterloo, owes his life to Rachel York, a well-bred young woman, down on her luck, who has taken refuge in a Belgian brothel.

6. *Slightly Dangerous* (**Delacorte, 2004**) Wulfric, Duke of Bewcastle, the eldest Bedwyn brother, finally falls in love—with lowborn but lively young widow Christine Derrick.

XIII. Balogh has embarked upon a new series focusing on a young-ladies' academy in Regency England, Miss Martin's School for Girls.

1. *Simply Unforgettable* (**Delacorte, 2005**) Schoolteacher Frances Allard is hiding a deep secret from her past that makes her reluctant to respond to aristocrat Lucius Marshall's lovemaking.

2. *Simply Love* (**Delacorte, 2006**) Teacher Anne Jewell and Welsh estate steward Sydnam Butler are both haunted by their pasts.

3. *Simply Magic* (**Delacorte, 2007**) Teacher Susanna Osbourne meets Viscount Whitleaf, Peter Edgeworth, while visiting a friend's estate for the summer.

4. *Simply Perfect* (**Delacorte, 2008**) Founder and headmistress of Miss Martin's School for Girls, Claudia Martin, is jolted out of her spinsterhood by the arrival of Joseph, Marquess of Attingsbrough.

Balzac, Honoré de

I. Balzac's Human Comedy (Comedie humaine), a vast enterprise projected but not finished before the author succumbed to overwork and excessive coffee drinking, contains more than 90 novels and stories. There are relatively few recurring characters, and all the titles can stand alone as independent novels and stories. The incredibly prolific Balzac also wrote earlier novels under pseudonyms, several plays, and the *Droll Stories (Contes drolatiques),* which are not generally included in the Human Comedy. The entire Human Comedy has been translated into English, although the translations of most of the titles are a century or more old. The Dutton/Dent Everyman's Library series of Balzac translations (originally published c. 1890–1899) has been republished several times and is still available. The Gutenberg Library offers most of the titles online in venerable English versions (http://www.netlibrary.com).

The Human Comedy was divided into three major groups: Studies of Manners (I-VI), Philosophical Studies (VII), and Analytical Studies (VIII). Studies of Manners, by far the largest group, was subdivided into *Scenes of Private Life* (I), Scenes of Provincial Life (II), Scenes of Parisian Life (III), Scenes of Political Life (IV), Scenes of Military Life (V), and Scenes of Country Life (VI). Herbert Hunt's *Balzac's 'Comedie Humaine'* (Athlone, 1959) is a useful guide to the series as a whole. Our arrangement of titles is based on David Bellos's article on the Comedie Humaine in *The New Oxford Companion to Literature in French* (Clarendon, 1995). Titles are listed by their best-known English versions with original French titles and publication dates and variant English titles. Annotations are provided only for the most accessible and highly regarded titles.

1. **At the Sign of the Cat and Racket** (1830) French title: *La maison du chat qui pelote.*
2. **Dance at Sceaux, The** (1830) French title: *Le bal de Sceaux.* Variant title: *The Rural Ball.*
3. **Two Young Brides, The** (1842) French title: *Memoires de deux jeunes mariees.* Variant title: *Recollections of Two Young Brides.*
4. **Purse, The** (1832) French title: *La bourse.* Translated by Sylvia Raphael as "The Purse" in *Selected Short Stories: Honoré de Balzac* (Penguin, 1977).
5. **Modeste Mignon** (1844) French title: *Modeste Mignon.*
6. **Start in Life, A** (1842) French title: *Un debut dans le vie.*
7. **Albert Savarus** (1842) French title: *Albert Savarus.*
8. **Vendetta, The** (1830) French title: *La vendetta.*
9. **Double Family, A** (1830) French title: *Une double famille.*
10. **Domestic Peace** (1842) French title: *La paix du ménage.* Variant titles: *The Peace of the Household; Peace in the Household.* Translated by Sylvia Raphael as "Domestic Peace" in *Selected Short Stories: Honoré de Balzac* (Penguin, 1977).
11. **Madame Firmiani** (1832) French title: *Madame Firmiani.*
12. **Study of a Woman** (1830) French title: *Etude de femme.* Translated by Sylvia Raphael as "A Study in Feminine Psychology" in *Selected Short Stories: Honoré de Balzac* (Penguin, 1977).
13. **Pretended Mistress, The** (1841) French title: *La Fausse Maitresse.* Variant title: *The Imaginary Mistress.*
14. **Daughter of Eve, A** (1839) French title: *Une fille d'Eve.*
15. **Message, The** (1832) French title: *Le message.*
16. **Grenadiere, La** (1832) French title: *La grenadiere.*
17. **Forsaken Woman, The** (1832) French title: *La femme abandonnée.* Variant title: *The Deserted Woman.* Translated by Stanley Appelbaum as "The Forsaken Woman" in *Selected Short Stories* (Dover, 1999).
18. **Honorine** (1843) French title: *Honorine.*
19. **Beatrix** (1839) French title: *Beatrix.* Recent translations: *Beatrix,* by Rosamond Harcourt-Smith and Simon Harcourt-Smith (Citadel, 1957), and *Beatrix,* by Beth Archer (Prentice-Hall, 1970). The story of a young man in love with a heartless coquette set in a quaint, old-fashioned town in Brittany.
20. **Gobseck** (1830) French title: *Gobseck.*
21. **Woman of Thirty, A** (1831) French title: *La femme de trente ans.*
22. **Père Goriot** (1835) French title: *Le Père Goriot.* Variant titles: *Old Goriot; Father Goriot.* Recent translations: *Old Goriot,* by M. A. Crawford (Penguin, 1951); *Père Goriot,* by Henry Reed (New American Library, 1981); *Père Goriot,* by A. J. Krailsheimer (Oxford Univ. Press, 1991); and *Le Père Goriot,* by Burton Raffel (Norton, 1994). One of Balzac's masterpieces, and some critics would say his supreme masterpiece. The story of old Goriot, who makes great sacrifices to provide dowries for his ungrateful daughters and then further ruins himself to save them from their own follies.
23. **Colonel Chabert** (1832) French title: *Le Colonel Chabert.* Recent translation: *Colonel Chabert,* by Carol Cosman (New Directions, 1997). A soldier of the Napoleonic Wars, reportedly killed at the Battle of Eylau, returns home after a long absence to find his wife remarried and his pension gone. The redoubtable Gerard Depardieu, who played Balzac in a recent French television production, played the title role in a 1994 French movie.
24. **Atheist's Mass, The** (1836) French title: *La messe de l'athee.* Translated by Sylvia Raphael as "The Atheist's Mass" in *Selected Short Stories: Honoré de Balzac* (Penguin, 1977).
25. **Commission in Lunacy, The** (1836) French title: *L'interdiction.* Variant title: *The Interdiction.*

26. **Marriage Contract, The** (1835) French title: *Le contrat de mariage.*
27. **Another Study of Woman** (1842) French title: *Autre etude de femme.*
28. **La Grande Breteche** (1831) French title: *La grande Breteche.* Translated by Sylvia Raphael as "La grande Breteche" in *Selected Short Stories: Honoré de Balzac* (Penguin, 1977). (Not in the Bellos listing but usually assigned as one of the "Scenes of Private Life.") A short story about the terrible revenge a French nobleman took on his unfaithful wife and her lover. The story has been dramatized several times including a television airing on *Orson Welles' Great Mysteries* and a one-act opera by Avery Claflin.

II. Scenes of Provincial Life

1. **Ursule Mirouët** (1841) French title: *Ursule Mirouët.* Translated by Donald Adamson as *Ursule Mirouët* (Penguin, 1976). A touch of the occult informs this novel about a young orphan who is cheated out of her inheritance but triumphs in the end.
2. **Celibates, The** (1842) French title: *Les Celibataires.* Contains three parts originally and often, subsequently, published separately.
   Part I: *Pierrette* (1840). French title: *Pierrette.*
   Part II: *The Vicar of Tours.* French title: *Le cure de Tours.*
   Translated by Merloyd Lawrence and published with *Eugenie Grandet* (Houghton Mifflin, 1964).
   Part III: *The Black Sheep* (1842). French title: *La rabouilleuse.* Variant title: *A Bachelor's Establishment.* Translated as *The Black Sheep,* by Donald Adamson (Penguin, 1970).
3. **Eugenie Grandet** (1833) French title: *Eugenie Grandet.* Translated as *Eugenie Grandet* by M. A. Crawford (Penguin, 1955); Lowell Bair (Bantam, 1959); Henry Reed (New American Library, 1964); Merloyd Lawrence (Houghton Mifflin, 1964); and Sylvia Raphael (Oxford, 1990). Regarded as Balzac's "most perfect novel," this is the sad story of a beautiful and good daughter robbed of happiness by a miserly father.
4. **Parisians in Provincial France, The** (1843) French title: *Les Parisiens en province.* Variant titles: *Parisians in the Country; Provincial Parisians.* Consists of two parts originally published separately:
   Part I: *Gaudissart the Great* (1833). French title: *L'illustre Gaudissart.* Variant title: *The Illustrious Gaudissart.*
   Part II: *The Muse of the Department* (1843). French title: *La muse du département.*
5. **Rivalries, The** (1839) French title: *Les rivalités.* Variant title: *The Jealousies of a Country Town.*
   Two parts of a projected five parts published:
   Part I: *The Old Maid* (1836). French title: *La vieille fille.*
   Part II: *The Cabinet of Antiques* (1838). French title: *Le cabinet des antiques.*
6. **Lost Illusions** (1843) French title: *Illusions perdues.* Translated as *Lost Illusions* by Kathleen Raine (Modern Library, 1951) and H. J. Hunt (Penguin, 1971). Originally published in three parts:
   Part I: *The Two Poets* (1837). French title: *Les deux poetes.*
   Part II: *A Distinguished Provincial in Paris* (1839).
   French title: *Une grand homme de province à Paris* Variant title: *A Provincial Great Man in Paris.*
   Part III: *The Trials of an Inventor* (1843). French title: *Les souffrances de l'inventeur.* Variant titles: *An Inventor's Tribulations; An Inventor's Sufferings.*
   Lucien Chardon, a young provincial, comes to Paris with literary aspirations but finds disaster.

III. Scenes of Parisian Life

1. ***History of the Thirteen*** (**1835**) French title: *Histoire des treize.* Translated as *History of the Thirteen* by H. J. Hunt (Penguin, 1974). Published in three separate parts:

    Part I: *Ferragus, Chief of the Devorants* (1833). French title: *Ferragus, chef des devorants.*

    Part II: *The Duchess of Langeais* (1834). French title: *La Duchesse de Langeais.*

    Part III: *The Girl with the Golden Eyes* (1835). French title: *La fille aux yeux d'or.* Translated by Carol Cosman as *The Girl with the Golden Eyes* (Carroll & Graf, 1998).

2. ***Cesar Birotteau*** (**1837**) French title: *Histoire de las grandeur et de la decadence de Cesar Birotteau.* Variant titles: *The Rise and Fall of Cesar Birotteau; The Bankrupt.* Translated by Robin Buss as *Cesar Birotteau* (Penguin, 1994). A perfumer with social ambitions speculates unwisely and goes bankrupt.

3. ***House of Nucingen, The*** (**1846**) French title: *La maison Nucingen.* Variant titles: *The Firm of Nucingen; Nucingen and Co., Bankers.*

4. ***Harlot High and Low, A*** (**1847**) French title: *Splendeurs et miseres de courtisanes.* Variant title: *The Harlot's Progress.* Translated as *A Harlot High and Low,* by Rayner Heppenstall (Penguin, 1970). Published separately in four parts:

    Part I: *How Harlots Love* (1843). French title: *Comment aiment les filles.* Variant title: *The Way That Girls Love.*

    Part II: *What Love Costs an Old Man* (1847). French title: *À combien l'amour revient aux vieillards.* Variant title: *How Much Love Costs Old Men.*

    Part III: *The End of Evil Ways* (1847). French title: *Ou menent les mauvais chemins.* Variant title: *The End of Bad Roads.*

    Part IV: *The Last Incarnation of Vautrin.* French title: *La derniere incarnation de Vautrin.* Variant title: *Vautrin's Last Avatar.*

    A sequel to *Lost Illusions* (II,6). Lucien Chardon becomes Lucien de Rubempre, who becomes enmeshed in the machinations of the master-criminal Vautrin (aka Jacques Collin; Carlos Herrera) who also appears in *Lost Illusions* and *Père Goriot. A Harlot High and Low* was dramatized for the Soho Rep by Nicholas Wright in 1985 as *The Crimes of Vautrin.*

5. ***Secrets of the Princess of Cadignan, The*** (**1839**) French title: *Les secrets de la Princesse de Cadignan.* Variant title: *A Princess's Secrets.*

6. ***Facino Cane*** (**1846**) French title: *Facino Cane.* Translated by Sylvia Raphael as "Facino Cane" in *Selected Short Stories: Honoré de Balzac* (Penguin, 1977) and Stanley Applebaum in *Selected Short Stories* (Dover, 1999).

7. ***Sarrasine*** (**1830**) French title: *Sarrasine.* Adapted as a dance piece by Neil Bartlett and Nicolas Bloomfield for Dance Theatre Workshop (1991).

8. ***Pierre Grassou*** (**1840**) French title: *Pierre Grassou.* Translated as "Pierre Grassou" by Sylvia Raphael in *Selected Short Stories: Honoré de Balzac* (Penguin, 1977).

9. ***Poor Relations*** (**1847**) French title: *Les parents pauvres.* Two parts, nearly always published separately.

    Part I: *Cousin Bette* (1846). French title: *La Cousine Bette.* Variant title: *Cousin Betty.* Translated as *Cousin Bette* by Anthony Bonner (Bantam, 1961); M. A. Crawford (Penguin, 1965); and Sylvia Raphael (Oxford, 1992). The story of the poor country cousin who destroys the family that she believes has betrayed her is regarded as one of Balzac's best and has been dramatized several times, including a movie of the same title starring Jessica Lange (1998).

    Part II: *Cousin Pons* (1847). French title: *Le Cousin Pons.* Translated as *Cousin Pons* by H. J. Hunt (Penguin, 1968). Another "poor relation," Cousin Pons is an impecunious musician whose avocation is buying prints.

10. ***Man of Affairs, A*** (**1845**) French title: *Un homme d'affaires.*
11. ***Prince of Bohemia, A*** (**1840**) French title: *Un prince de la Boheme.*
12. ***Gaudissart II*** (**1844**) French title: *Gaudissart II.*
13. ***Bureaucrats, The*** (**1837**) French title: *Les employes.* Variant titles: *Bureaucracy; The Government Clerks; The Civil Service Bureaucracy.* Translated by Charles Foulkes as *The Bureaucrats* (Northwestern Univ. Press, 1993).
14. ***Involuntary Comedians, The*** (**1846**) French title: *Les comediens sans le savoir.* Variant title: *The Unconscious Comedians.*
15. ***Petty Bourgeois, The*** (**1856**) French title: *Les petits bourgeois.* Posthumously published.
16. ***Seamy Side of History, The*** (**1848**) French title: *L'envers de l'histoire contemporaine.* Published in two parts:

    Part I: *Madame de la Chanterie* (1842). French title: *Madame de la Chanterie.*

    Part II: *L'Initie* (1848). French title: *L'Initié.*

IV. Scenes of Political Life

1. ***Murky Business, A*** (**1841**) French title: *Une tenebreuse affaire.* Variant titles: *A Dark Affair; The Gondreville Mystery.* Translated by H. J. Hunt as *A Murky Business* (Penguin, 1972).
2. ***Deputy of Arcis, The*** (**1847**) French title: *Le député d'Arcis.* Variant title: *The Member for Arcis.*
3. ***Z. Marcas*** (**1840**) French title: *Z. Marcas.*

V. Scenes of Military Life

1. ***Chouans, The*** (**1829**) French title: *Les Chouans;* also *Le dernier Chouan.* Translated as *The Chouans,* by M. A. Crawford (Penguin, 1972). Balzac's first successful novel, this historical romance of the Royalist struggle in Brittany was modeled after Walter Scott.
2. ***Passion in the Desert, A*** (**1830**) French title: *Une passion dans le desert.* Translated by Stanley Appelbaum as "A Passion in the Desert" in *Selected Short Stories* (Dover, 1999). A young army officer and a wild leopard form a bond in the Sahara Desert. Made into a motion picture in 1998.

VI. Scenes of Country Life

1. ***Peasants, The*** (**1844**) French title: *Les paysans.*
2. ***Lily of the Valley*** (**1836**) French title: *Le lys dans la vallee.* Translated by Lucienne Hill as *Lily of the Valley* (Citadel, 1957; 2nd ed. Carroll & Graf, 1998). Balzac's personal favorite among his writings. Describes the courtship of Felix and Henrietta.
3. ***Country Doctor, The*** (**1833**) French title: *Le medecin de campagne.*
4. ***Village Cure, The*** (**1839**) French title: *Le cure de village.* Variant title: *The Country Parson.*

VII. Philosophical Studies

1. ***Wild Ass's Skin, The*** (**1831**) French title: *La peau de chagrin.* Variant title: *The Magic Skin.* Translated as *The Wild Ass's Skin,* by H. J. Hunt (Penguin, 1977). The best known of the Philosophical Studies, this is an allegorical tale about a magical scrap of leather.
2. ***Episode under the Terror, An*** (**1830**) French title: *Un episode sous la Terreur.* Variant titles: *An Incident in the Reign of Terror; An Episode during the Terror.* Translated by Sylvia Raphael as "An Incident in the Reign of Terror" in *Selected Short Stories: Honoré de Balzac* (Penguin, 1977). Translated by Stanley Appelbaum as "An Episode during the Terror" in *Selected Short Stories* (Dover, 1999).

3. ***Christ in Flanders*** (1831) French title: *Jésus-Christ en Flandre.* Variant title: *Jesus Christ in Flanders.*
4. ***Melmoth Reconciled*** (1835) French title: *Melmoth reconcilie.* Variant titles: *Melmoth Converted; Melmoth Absolved.*
5. ***Massimilla Doni*** (1839) French title: *Massimilla Doni.*
6. ***Unknown Masterpiece, The*** (1831) French title: *Le chef-d'oeuvre inconnu.* Translated as *The Unknown Masterpiece,* by Richard Howard (New York Review Books, 2001), and by Stanley Appelbaum in *Selected Short Stories* (Dover, 1999).
7. ***Gambara*** (1837) French title: *Gambara.* Translated as "Gambara" by Richard Howard in *The Unknown Masterpiece and Gambara* (New York Review Books, 2001).
8. ***Quest of the Absolute, The*** (1834) French title: *La recherche de l'absolu.* Variant title: *The Alkahest.*
9. ***Child Accursed, A*** (1834) French title: *L'enfant maudit.* Variant titles: *The Accursed Child; The Child of Malediction.*
10. ***Adieu*** (1830) French title: *Adieu.* Variant titles: *Farewell; The Story of a Mad Sweetheart.* The story of a man who is willing to go to any length to win back the woman he loves, *Adieu* was made into a French motion picture (1981).
11. ***Maranas, The*** (1833) French title: *Les marana.*
12. ***Conscript, The*** (1831) French title: *Le réquisitionnaire.* Variant title: *The Revolutionary Conscript.* Translated as "The Conscript" by Sylvia Raphael in *Selected Short Stories: Honoré de Balzac* (Penguin, 1977). Translated as "The Revolutionary Conscript" by Stanley Appelbaum in *Selected Short Stories* (Dover, 1999).
13. ***El Verdugo*** (1830) French title: *El verdugo.* Variant title: *The Executioner.* Translated as "El Verdugo" by Sylvia Raphael in *Selected Short Stories: Honoré de Balzac* (Penguin, 1977).
14. ***Seashore Tragedy, A*** (1835) French title: *Un drame au bord de la mer.* Variant titles: *A Drama on the Seashore; A Tragedy by the Sea; A Seaside Tragedy; A Seaside Drama.* Translated as "A Tragedy by the Sea" by Sylvia Raphael in *Selected Short Stories: Honoré de Balzac* (Penguin, 1977).
15. ***Master Cornelius*** (1831) French title: *Maitre Cornelius.*
16. ***Red Inn, The*** (1831) French title: *L'auberge rouge.* Variant title: *The Redhouse.* Translated as "The Red Inn" by Sylvia Raphael in *Selected Short Stories: Honoré de Balzac* (Penguin, 1977).
17. ***About Catherine de Medici*** (1841) French title: *Sur Catherine de Medicis.*
18. ***Elixir of Long Life, The*** (1830) French title: *L'elixir de longue vie.* Variant title: *The Elixir of Life.*
19. ***Exiles, The*** (1831) French title: *Les proscrits.*
20. ***Louis Lambert*** (1832) French title: *Louis Lambert.*
21. ***Seraphita*** (1834) French title: *Seraphita.*

VIII. Analytical Studies

1. ***Physiology of Marriage, The*** (1829) French title: *Physiologie du mariage.*
2. ***Pinpricks of Married Life, The*** (1843) French title: *Petites miseres de la vie conjugale.* Variant titles: *The Petty Trials of Matrimony; The Petty Worries of Conjugal Life.*

Bangs, John Kendrick

Imagine the world's immortals smoking, dining, and playing billiards at their big club in the sky—or, in this case, on their commodious yacht on the River Styx. All their human foibles show as they debate their achievements, rehash history, and vie for recognition. "How's our little Swanlet of Avon?" asks Dr. Johnson at the billiard table as Shakespeare enters the lounge. Among other things, the question of who

wrote *Hamlet* is answered definitively. Some "fictional" characters, such as Sherlock Holmes, are admitted to the band of immortals. In *The Enchanted Type-writer* (Harper, 1899), another Bangs novel about the afterlife, the narrator is able to communicate with James Boswell in Hades via an old typewriter.

1. ***House-Boat on the Styx, A*** (Harper, 1896) As the immortals engage in clever dialogue, Captain Kidd, barred from membership, pirates the houseboat away.
2. ***Pursuit of the House-Boat, The*** (Harper, 1897) Sherlock Holmes tracks down Captain Kidd and the houseboat, and a contingent of lady notables succeeds in joining the club.

Banks, Ian M(enzies)

Scottish author Ian Banks burst on the British literary scene with the frightening psychological horror novel *The Wasp Factory* (Houghton Mifflin, 1984). Since then he has written several more "mainstream" novels that have been well reviewed, prompting comparisons with Martin Amis and Ian McEwan, and have sometimes been cult best sellers in the United Kingdom, if not the United States.

Banks also writes science fiction as Ian M. Banks. Several of his SF novels are set in the Culture, a galactic civilization created by a handful of humanoid species several thousand years in the past. The Culture books are extravagantly written (some critics say overwritten) novels with plots that are complicated but keep you reading to find out what the ending is.

1. ***Consider Phlebas*** (St. Martin's, 1987) An intergalactic religious war will be partly decided by the success of a search-and-rescue mission crewed by loosely allied mercenaries and led by a disgruntled spy.
2. ***Player of Games, The*** (St. Martin's, 1989) Gurgeh, one of the greatest of the Culture's game players, journeys to the xenophobic Empire of Azad to play a complex game that leads to political office and power in Azad.
3. ***State of the Art, The*** (Night Shade, 2004) A collection of SF short stories and the title novella, some of them set in the Culture, all of them published between 1984 and 1987. *The State of the Art,* which is about the first contact between Earth and the Culture, was published separately by Ziesing in 1989. The collection was originally published in the United Kingdom in 1991. A lengthy essay, "A Few Notes on the Culture" (1997), was added to the Night Shade edition.
4. ***Use of Weapons*** (Bantam, 1992) Dziet Sma, agent of the Culture, needs to find and hire Cheradenine Zaklawe, a retired master agent, to stabilize a civilization on the periphery of the Culture.
5. ***Excession*** (Bantam, 1997) The sudden appearance of the "excession," a weird galactic phenomenon, heats up the rivalry between the Culture and the Empire of the Affront.
6. ***Look to Windward*** (Pocket, 2000) The Idiran War, which took place some 800 years before the action in this novel, is the background of a terrorist plot against the Masaq Orbital, home to about 50 billion members of the Culture.
7. ***Matter*** (Orbit, 2008) When King Hausk of the Sarl, a realm beneath the "Shellworld" of Sursamen, is murdered, his heirs Ferbin, Oramen, and Djan band together to seek revenge against the killer.

Banks, L. A.

PSEUDONYM OF Leslie Esdaile-Banks

Shades of *Blacula* and *Buffy*! Damali Richards is an African American spoken-word performer who doubles as a vampire slayer in this "hip-hop" series. Damali, who is the leader of seven guardians who disguise their weapons as musical instruments to get through airport security, is slowly "ripening" into a superhuman. Complicated "legend" background, overheated prose, and over-the-top characters have critics shaking their heads, but the titles appeal to readers of Anne Rice (q.v.) and Laurell K. Hamilton. Each volume is subtitled *A Vampire Huntress Legend*.

Leslie Esdaile-Banks, who also writes romances as Leslie Esdaile and TV tie-ins as Leslie E. Banks, was born, educated, and lives in Philadelphia.

1. *Minion* (St. Martin's, 2003) Beautiful African American spoken-word performer Damali Richards, whose seven guardians pump up their adrenaline with jive talk before slaying vampires, is up against the spectacularly evil master vampire, Fallon Nuit, who has created "the Minion" of rogue hybrid vampires.
2. *Awakening, The* (St. Martin's, 2004) Newly undead Carlos Rivera, Damali's ex-lover, is deputized by the Vampire Council to vampirize Damali, while renegade master vampire Fallon Nuit still seeks to eliminate the pesky vampire slayer.
3. *Hunted, The* (St. Martin's, 2004) Damali Richards hooks up again with her vampire lover, Carlos Rivera, in the Brazilian rain forest, where they run into rampaging werecreatures and a female vampire possessed by the memories of a 500-year-old Neteru.
4. *Bitten, The* (St. Martin's, 2005) A "key" containing the Blood of Christ (extracted from the Shroud of Turin) and the possible unleashing of Armageddon bring the star-crossed pair of Damali and Carlos to Australia.
5. *Forbidden, The* (St. Martin's, 2005) Some very complicated doings involving the impregnation and miscarriage of the Neteru Damali, the immolation and revival of Carlos, the emergence from hell's seventh level of the seductress Lilith, and the impending birth of the Antichrist.
6. *Damned, The* (St. Martin's, 2006) Carlos sets out to retrieve *The Book of the Damned* before the lost souls who have escaped from hell can infect humans and turn them into demons.
7. *Forsaken, The* (St. Martin's, 2006) After she walks out on Carlos Rivera, Damali meets a mysterious stranger.
8. *Wicked, The* (St. Martin's, 2007) Cain turns completely to the dark side; takes his father's throne in hell; recalls the master vampire, Fallon Nuit, from the Sea of Perpetual Agony; and pursues the newlyweds Damali and Carlos.
9. *Cursed, The* (St. Martin's, 2007) The first seal has been broken, and Armageddon has begun. Lilith, installed as Vampire Council chairwoman, calls on vampires, witches, and warlocks to combat the forces of the Covenant, the Guardians, the Neterus, and both Neteru Councils.

Banks, Lynne Reid

Jane Graham, unmarried and pregnant, intends to have an abortion, but after making friends with her fellow roomers at a dingy London boardinghouse, she decides to have her baby. This bittersweet look at a young girl's search for love, continued by two sequels, is well written. Its odd characters are plausible and poignant. Leslie Caron played Jane in the 1962 British movie version entitled *The L-Shaped Room* (1962). Banks also authored two juvenile series titles, the Indian in the Cup-

board and Harry the Poisonous Centipede, the former of which was made into a movie of the same title (1995).

1. *L-Shaped Room, The* (Simon & Schuster, 1961) Life looks bleak from Jane Graham's tiny boardinghouse room, but the new friends she makes give her hope.
2. *Backward Shadow, The* (Simon & Schuster, 1970) Jane lives with baby David in a cottage in the country, but a new restlessness afflicts her.
3. *Two Is Lonely* (Simon & Schuster, 1974) Jane marries a loving man who brings security and happiness to herself and to her seven-year-old son, David.

Bannister, Jo

I. Chief Constable Frank Shapiro, Inspector Liz Graham, and Sergeant Cal Donovan are the chief protagonists in a police procedural set in the fictional Castlemere, an English city of 80,000. The canny veteran Shapiro, the bright and ambitious Graham, and the unorthodox maverick Donovan are linked by common purpose and mutual respect. Each well-plotted, suspenseful, and subtle volume deals simultaneously with a disparate bunch of crimes and problems. Bannister, an English-born mystery writer now residing in Northern Ireland, was a newspaper editor and feature writer who published three science fiction novels before finding her niche in "crime/thriller" writing.

1. *Bleeding of Innocents, A* (St. Martin's, 1993) A serial murderer with a medical obsession may be behind the murders of a young nurse from an old-folks' home and a surgeon.
2. *Charisma* (St. Martin's, 1994) Throat slashings of a young prostitute and a schoolgirl out for a morning ride produce a state of near panic in Castlemere.
3. *Taste for Burning, A* (St. Martin's, 1995) Shapiro is put on leave for possibly having withheld evidence in a previous case. Donovan and Graham quietly work to clear Shapiro's name while trying to solve a fatal arson case in Castlemere's Asian community.
4. *No Birds Sing* (St. Martin's, 1996) Smash-and-grab robbers, a dog-fighting ring, and a train robbery, all in a two-day period, keep the trio occupied.
5. *Broken Lines* (St. Martin's, 1999) Has Donovan overstepped the line into vigilantism, or is he the victim of an elaborate frame? His pursuit of Mikey Dickens, petty criminal and son of Castlemere's crime boss, has led to a tragic accident and some suspicious incidents.
6. *Hireling's Tale, The* (St. Martin's, 2000) The badly beaten, heroin-filled body of a prostitute hurtles from the roof of a hotel where an international business conference is taking place.
7. *Changelings* (St. Martin's, 2001) A psychopath seems to be behind a series of malicious hoaxes and what appears to be a case of cholera. Donovan, on forced holiday, is holed up in the little village of East Beckham.

II. Rosie Holland, plump, middle-aged, tough-talking former pathologist and current "agony aunt" (advice columnist) living in Birmingham (England), is the protagonist of a pair of novels that combine elements of the cozy and hard-boiled genres in an entertaining mix.

1. *Primrose Convention, The* (St. Martin's, 1998) Advice columnist Rosie Holland, ornithologist Arthur Prufrock, and gardener and psychic Shad Lucas search in Scotland for a missing bird-watcher who may have run afoul of runners of illegal aliens.

2. *Primrose Switchback, The* (St. Martin's, 2000) Rosie's column on "tough love" gets her enmeshed in a hoax arranged by a local television show and the murder of one of the show's researchers.

III. A new mystery series features Brodie Farrell, single mother and proprietor of Looking for Something? (a search service), and Daniel Hood, a bachelor mathematics teacher. The two are accidently paired in *Echo of Lies*, work together in *True Witness*, and become more intimately involved in later episodes of this series of psychological thrillers set in small-town England.

1. *Echoes of Lies* (St. Martin's, 2002) A woman asks Brodie Farrell, proprietor of the search service Looking for Something? to find a man in a photograph who has allegedly cheated her out of a large sum of money.
2. *True Witness* (St. Martin's, 2003) When Daniel Hood invites Paddy, Brodie Farrell's daughter, over for a birthday treat—looking at the stars and planets through his telescope—he witnesses a murder.
3. *Reflections* (St. Martin's, 2003) Brodie is hired by the uncle of two young Irish sisters, Juanita and Emerald Davis, whose father has allegedly murdered their unfaithful mother, to find a missing relative.
4. *Depths of Solitude* (St. Martin's, 2004) Daniel Hood has disappeared, and Brodie calls in Detective Superintendent Jack Deacon of the Dimmock police.
5. *Breaking Faith* (St. Martin's, 2005) Brodie is asked to find the ideal pad for successful "demon rocker" Jared Fry.
6. *Requiem for a Dealer* (St. Martin's, 2006) A young woman runs into the street and collides with the car driven by Daniel Hood; then she accuses Daniel of trying to kill her.
7. *Flawed* (St. Martin's, 2007) Daniel Hood takes over Looking for Something? temporarily while Brodie deals with an unexpected pregnancy.

Bantock, Nick

The "extraordinary correspondence" of Griffin and Sabine has been described as "a picture book trilogy for adults." Bantock, a professional book-jacket illustrator and producer of pop-up books for children, blended together pictorial and verbal elements to chronicle the long-distance romance between Griffin Moss, a London-based postcard artist, and Sabine Strohem, a postage-stamp illustrator living in the South Seas. The correspondence between the two is carried out through an extraordinary mix of postcards, stamps, and letters.

The success of the trilogy inspired Bantock to produce an illustrated autobiography, *The Artful Dodger: Images and Reflections* (Chronicle, 2000), and a second Griffin and Sabine trilogy (numbers 4–6).

1. *Griffin and Sabine* (Chronicle, 1991) Griffin Moss receives a fan letter from the distant Sabine Strohem that indicates that she is psychically tuned into his creative processes.
2. *Sabine's Notebook* (Chronicle, 1992) Concerned about the psychic roots of his connection to the otherworldly Sabine, Griffin flees his London studio for distant parts, inviting her to use it in his absence.
3. *Golden Mean, The* (Chronicle, 1993) Returning from his world journey, Griffin wonders if he and Sabine inhabit "parallel universes."
4. *Gryphon, The* (Chronicle, 2001) Subtitle: *In Which the Extraordinary Correspondence of Griffin and Sabine Is Rediscovered.* Matthew Sedon, an archaeologist in Egypt, receives a postcard from Sabine. Then Matthew's friend, Isabelle de Reims, receives a postcard from Griffin.

5. *Alexandria* (Chronicle, 2002) Matthew informs Isabella that Sabine has somehow become a psychic part of him. Isabella is menaced by the sinister Frolatti.
6. *Morning Star, The* (Chronicle, 2003) Isabella de Reims, abandoning her studies in Paris, travels closer and closer to a meeting with Matthew Sedon in Egypt.

Banville, John

The Book of Evidence, Ghosts, and *Athena* form a loose trilogy united by the narrator, who, although called Frederick Montgomery in number 1, is nameless in number 2, and called Morrow in number 3, is clearly the same character. Montgomery is an intelligent, talented person on the fringes of the art world who seems to have no moral center. The trilogy is very well written in spare but evocative prose, but the books are by no means easy going, even for the serious reader.

Irish writer John Banville has written the Booker Prize winner *Shroud* (Knopf, 2002) and a well-received but not widely read tetralogy united by theme but not plots or characters: *Doctor Copernicus* (Norton, 1976); *Kepler* (Godine, 1983); *The Newton Letter* (Godine, 1987); and *Mefisto* (Godine, 1989).

1. *Book of Evidence, The* (Scribner, 1989) Frederick Montgomery, a former scientist who is drifting through life, tries to steal a painting he is obsessed with and kills a maidservant during the attempt.
2. *Ghosts* (Knopf, 1993) The unnamed narrator (Frederick Montgomery from number 1), being released from prison, banishes himself to an island where he coexists with an elderly art historian and his rather monstrous assistant.
3. *Athena* (Knopf, 1995) The narrator, now called Morrow, has been asked by underworld figure Morden to authenticate some 17th-century paintings.

Barclay, Tessa

PSEUDONYM OF Jean Bowden

I. Gregory Crowne, aka (former) Crown Prince Gregory of Hirtenstein, is a classical-concert agent who sometimes acts an amateur detective in a series of civilized puzzle mysteries by British romance novelist Tessa Barclay.

Jean Bowden has written three romance series (see below) and many other novels as Tessa Barclay and books under her own name as well as novels under the pseudonyms of Belinda Dell, Lee Mackenzie, Barbara Annandale, Jocelyn Barry, Jennifer Bland, and Avon Curry.

1. *Farewell Performance* (Severn, 2002) A world-famous cello used by one of Gregory's clients, Talik Edder, goes missing and then mysteriously reappears. Then another client, who is a former lover of Talik, turns up dead.
2. *Better Class of Person, A* (Severn, 2003) Crowne and his lover, London fashion buyer Liz Blair, are invited to a private Greek island for a birthday party for a rich heiress and are witnesses to some odd doings.
3. *Handful of Dust, A* (Severn, 2004) Greg and Liz, in Provence for a series of concerts in Avignon, are contacted and then stood up by British crime reporter Barbara Rallenham. Then Barbara's ditzy sister, Mandy, descends upon them, demanding that Greg find the missing Barbara.
4. *Final Discord, A* (Severn, 2005) Gregory is enlisted to help Gilles Guidon, the eccentric son of a merchant banker, assemble a jazz quintet for the Montreux Festival.

5. *To Die For* **(Severn, 2007)** After Gregory escorts Polish countess Marzelina Zalfeda to a charity ball, Marzelina is found strangled in the research stacks at the Museum of Musical Heritage.

II. The Craigallan Saga is a tetralogy beginning with Rob Craigallan, a poor Scottish immigrant to North America, who acquires wealth. Subsequent volumes trace the fortunes of the Craigallan family. Historical characters such as William A. McKinley, Alexander Graham Bell, Emma Goldman, and Upton Sinclair make cameo appearances. The series was never published in the United States.

1. *Sower Went Forth, A* **(Allen [UK], 1980)** Young orphan Morag McGrath is rescued from a drunken docker by handsome Rob Craigallan.
2. *Stony Places, The* **(Allen [UK], 1981)** Rob Craigallan, now one of the richest men in America, has two legitimate children: Cornelius, a brilliant scientist handicapped by deafness, and Ellie-Rose, passionate and ambitious. Rob also has a bastard son, Gregor, who is ignorant of his heritage.
3. *Harvest of Thorns* **(Allen [UK], 1983)** The Craigallan family is followed through World War I, the Roaring Twenties, and the stockmarket crash of 1929.
4. *Good Ground, The* **(Allen [UK], 1984)** The Craigallans go to Hollywood in the 1930s, where they hobnob with the likes of Louella Parsons, Irving Thalberg, Sergey Eisenstein, and Upton Sinclair.

III. The Wine Widow trilogy, only the first of which has been published in the United States, concerns the fortunes of Nicole Berthois, a French peasant girl who marries into the rich wine-making Tramont family in the 1850s, and her descendants.

1. *Woman's Intuition, A* **(Richardson, 1987)** Peasant girl Nicole Berthois and Philippe de Tramont, scion of a wine-making family in Champagne, have a passionate affair and marry to protect their unborn child. But Philippe dies young. Originally published in the United Kingdom in 1984 as *The Wine Widow*.
2. *Champagne Girls, The* **(Allen [UK], 1986)** Netta and Gabrielle, of the House of Tramont, are known as the Champagne Girls; they enjoy the finest things in life in the belle epoque before they face disappointment and sadness.
3. *Last Heiress, The* **(Allen [UK], 1987)** Netta's daughter Nora inherits the family business and, like her great-grandmother Nicole, is left a young widow.

IV. The Corvill Weavers trilogy, another series not published in the United States, concerns Jenny Corvill, the daughter of an Edinburgh weaver, who obtains a royal commission to produce a weave for Queen Victoria and Prince Albert.

1. *Web of Dreams, A* **(Allen [UK], 1988)** Jenny Corvill, daughter of an Edinburgh weaver, obtains a royal commission and sets up a prosperous mill in Galasheils.
3. *Final Pattern, The* **(Allen [UK], 1990)** No annotation available.
3. *Broken Threads* **(Allen [UK], 1989)** Jenny wants to enjoy life as the bride of Ronald Armstrong, but her plans are disrupted by Lucy, her frivolous sister-in-law, who is attracted to fashionable drawing rooms and handsome men.

Barker, Clive

Clive Barker, English illustrator, painter, actor, playwright, movie producer, and writer, is best known for the graphic horror stories collected as *Clive Barker's Buckets of Blood* (omnibus edition, Putnam, 1988). Some critics compare Barker favorably to Stephen King (q.v.) and Peter Straub. Barker has branched out, notably in the projected trilogy Books of the Dead, which depicts parallel worlds: reality as we know and the dream-sea world of Quiddity. The two novels produced so far are full of battles between good and evil, shape-shifting, weird science and weirder metaphysics, stunning prose, and everything the most demanding fantasy reader could desire. The third volume hasn't been published yet.

1. *Great and Secret Show, The* **(Harper, 1989)** Postal clerk Randolph Jaffe, working in a "Dead Letter Room" somewhere in Nebraska, uncovers a strange series of cryptic letters that put him in touch with an ethereal network.
2. *Everville* **(Harper, 1994)** A mountain above Everville, Oregon, contains the doorway between Quiddity and the Cosm (our world).

Barker, Pat(ricia)

English writer Pat Barker's World War I trilogy garnered much critical praise, including the Booker Prize for *The Ghost Road*, for its depiction of men who are torn by the unbearable realization of the bloody toll on other men's lives that "doing their duty" entails. Two of the major characters are historical: Siegfried Sassoon, poet, war hero, and pacifist; and William Rivers, anthropologist, doctor, and expert on "neurasthenia." Other historical characters, such as the poets Robert Graves and Wilfred Owen, make appearances. The third major character, Lieutenant Billy Prior, is tormented by his war experiences, his bisexuality, and his "duplicity" in being an officer of working-class origin.

Barker first won recognition as a working-class feminist writer through novels about British working-class women such as *Union Street* (Putnam, 1983). *Regeneration* was made into a movie starring Jonathan Pryce. The three novels have been published in an omnibus volume: *The Regeneration Trilogy* (Penguin, 1998).

1. *Regeneration* **(Dutton, 1982)** In 1917 decorated British officer Siegfried Sassoon is diagnosed with shell shock and placed under the care of Dr. William Rivers at the sanitarium of Craiglockhar, near Edinburgh.
2. *Eye in the Door, The* **(Dutton, 1994)** Lieutenant Billy Prior, declared fit for intelligence duty in London, feels that he is betraying his working-class, pacifist friends.
3. *Ghost Road, The* **(Dutton, 1995)** Billy Prior, "cured" by Rivers, is determined to return to the western front to be with his friend Wilfred Owen.

Barlough, Jeffrey E(rnest)

Californian Jeffrey E. (sometimes J. Ernest) Barlough is a biologist and veterinarian who has published more than 60 articles in scientific journals. Barlough doubles as a fantasy writer who has created the Western Lights series, set in an alternative Victorian world in which the Ice Age has never ended, and the fog-shrouded town of Salthead is the trading hub of a countryside in which mastodon caravans carry freight in a wilderness infested by highwaymen and sabre cats. The four novels published so far are entertainingly Dickensian in scope, style, and characterization, with a modicum of Jules Verne thrown in.

1. *Dark Sleeper* (Ace, 2000) Subtitle: *Volume One of the Western Lights Series*. Professor Titus Vespasianus Tiggs and his sidekick, Dr. Dampe, investigate some supernatural happenings, including the headless ghost of a drowned sailor, a spectral ship, an insane mastiff, and three immortal Etruscan mages. Originally published privately by Barlough (Western Lights) in 1998.
2. *House in the High Wood, The* (Ace, 2001) Subtitle: *A Story of Old Talbotshire*. Continues the Victorian pastiche of number 1 as mysterious Bede Winter-March moves into the deserted mansion, Skylingden House, once a monastery of mad friars, disrupting the quiet daily life of rural Shilston Upcot.
3. *Strange Cargo* (Ace, 2004) Young Mr. and Mrs. Cargo, disturbed by their grandfather leaving a substantial legacy to a stranger, Miss Wastefield (who is trying to dispose of a threatening gift received on her 21st birthday), and a mysterious flying coach house all converge on the coastal town of Nantle. Originally published in the United Kingdom in 2002.
4. *Bertram of Butter Cross* (Gresham & Doyle, 2007) Jemma Hathaway, of the quiet English village of Market Snailsby, has a frightening vision after she spies two small children, who appear to be lost, by the side of the road.

Barnao, Jack

PSEUDONYM OF Ted (Edward John) Wood

Under the Barnao pseudonym, Ted Wood (q.v.), author of the Reid Bennett series, wrote three thrillers featuring John Locke, a former Grenadier Guard turned private security agent in Toronto, Canada.

1. *HammerLocke* (Scribner, 1987) Professional bodyguard John Locke is hired to chaperone Herbie, a spoiled, rich teenager, on an art-appreciation trip around Italy. Then Herbie is kidnapped.
2. *LockeStep* (Scribner, 1987) John Locke goes to Mexico in his second adventure.
3. *TimeLocke* (Macmillan, 1991) Locke is hired by a Toronto wine importer to protect his niece, Amy Rogers, from a revengeful Corsican in France as she continues her research on the French Resistance.

Barnard, Robert

I. Readers who enjoy humorous and somewhat literary mysteries have welcomed the appearance of Detective Inspector Perry Trethowen of Scotland Yard. Trethowen's witty narration adds to the pleasure of his cases, though their primary humor comes from the eccentric characters and situations that inevitably come to the fore. Barnard, who has received several Edgar Award nominations, and who writes historical mysteries under the nom de plume of Bernard Bastable (q.v.), seems to have abandoned Perry Trethowen, temporarily at least, for the Charlie Peace–Mike Oddie series (series II, below).

1. *Death by Sheer Torture* (Scribner, 1982) The old English gent discovered dead in spangled tights in a reconstructed inquisition device turns out to be Perry's estranged father. British title: *Sheer Torture*.
2. *Death and the Princess* (Scribner, 1982) Perry is assigned to guard Princess Helena, a minor but notorious British royal figure.
3. *Case of the Missing Brontë, The* (Scribner, 1983) A manuscript, possibly by Emily Brontë, sets Perry and all the collectors in Yorkshire on a merry chase. British title: *The Missing Brontë*.
4. *Bodies* (Scribner, 1986) This installment takes Perry into the world of London's gyms and body-building cults.

5. *Cherry Blossom Corpse, The* (Scribner, 1987) Perry is on hand to investigate when death interrupts a romance-writers' conference in Norway. British title: *Death in Purple Prose*.

II. Chief Inspector Mike Oddie and Detective Constable Charlie Peace of the West Yorkshire CID are the main continuing characters in this series of witty, well-characterized mysteries. Peace is a black Cockney who has found himself in a rather remote setting. Although the city of Leeds is sometimes the scene of the crime, more typically the action unfolds in villages in the Yorkshire countryside.

1. *Fatal Attachment, A* (Scribner, 1992) Lydia Perceval, best-selling biographer, has been strangled in the village of Bly, leaving several suspects with motives for the crime.
2. *Hovering of Vultures, A* (Scribner, 1993) Gerald Suzman, a rather shady character on the literary fringes, who has been trying to generate interest in the writings of long-dead authors Susannah and Joshua Sneddon, is murdered in his remote Yorkshire cottage.
3. *Bad Samaritan, The* (Scribner, 1995) Rosemary Sheffield, wife of a vicar near Leeds, befriends a young Bosnian named Stanko and finds him a job making pizza in a local eatery. Then a member of her husband's congregation is killed.
4. *No Place of Safety* (Scribner, 1998) The disappearance of two teenagers from the same Leeds school leads to "the Centre," an unofficial shelter run by charismatic Ben Marchant.
5. *Corpse at Haworth Tandoori, The* (Scribner, 1999) The corpse of Declan O'Hearn, who was working as a handyman for famous painter Ranulph Byatt, seems to have been found in the trunk of a car parked at a tandoori restaurant in Haworth.
6. *Unholy Dying* (Scribner, 2001) Cosmo Horrocks, reporter at the *West Yorkshire Chronicle*, is murdered after reporting some scandalous rumors about Father Pardoe, the local parish priest.
7. *Bones in the Attic, The* (Scribner, 2002) The body of a two-year-old who died 30 years ago, found in the attic of a house in Leeds purchased by media personality Matt Harper, leads Matt on a search that takes him back to his own past and his five-a-side soccer mates.
8. *Fall from Grace, A* (Scribner, 2007) Charlie Peace has left London for suburban Slepton Edge with his wife, Felicity, followed by Felicity's father, romance-novelist Rupert Coggenhoe, who soon gets entangled with manipulative teen Anne Michaels.

Barnes, John

I. American John Barnes has been one of SF's most consistent writers. His novels are opinionated, thought-provoking, and entertaining. He describes his politics as socialist and his religion as atheist. Barnes's ability to create a variety of believable future worlds is shown in his Thousand Cultures quartet. The Thousand Cultures are cultures that have developed in isolation from one another as humanity has spread across the galaxy. One culture, Nou Occitan, is based on a romanticized medieval Europe. Another society, Caledony, is a combination of capitalism and Christianity. Other cultures include pre-Columbian Maya and South Indian Tamil. The advent of "springers," devices that enable instantaneous travel between the planets, has made these sometimes xenophobic societies start to come together. Giraut Leones, agent for the Council of Humanity's top-secret Office of Special Projects, is a primary link between the four novels.

1. *Million Open Doors, A* (Tor, 1992) Narrator Giraut Leones, part of a delegation from the neo-medieval society of Nou Occitan, starts

an art school that shakes up the repressed capitalist-Christian society of Caledony.

2. *Earth Made of Glass* **(Tor, 1998)** Giraut and Margaret Leones are sent by the Office of Special Projects to worlds that refuse to accept the Council of Humanity's vision of humanity's future. They are sent to the planet of Briand, which houses two mutually exclusive societies: one created by devotees of the great Tamil poets, the other by anthropologists who advocate pre-Columbian Maya ways.

3. *Merchants of Souls, The* **(Tor, 2001)** Psypyx is a device whereby people periodically record the contents of their minds. When someone dies, his or her psypyx is stored; then, after two years of storage, it is reanimated in a cloned body. Unfortunately, some wise guys on the virtual-reality society of Earth have hit upon the idea of converting the stored personalities into computer games.

4. *Armies of Memory, The* **(Tor, 2006)** In the concluding volume, Giraut Leones discovers that the artist must "grow beauty around the wounds in his own heart."

II. The Century Next Door series is a loosely related trio of novels set in a dystopian 22nd century in which humanity is linked under the computer-network-like "One True."

1. *Orbital Renaissance* **(Tor, 1991)** Thirteen-year-old Melpomene Murray, inhabitant of the Flying Dutchman, an asteroid set into an Earth-Mars, is assigned to write a book about her life in space.

2. *Kaleidoscope Century* **(Tor, 1995)** Joshua All Quare, recruited by the KGB in the late 20th century, is infected with a virus that induces a near coma every 15 years. The near-immortal, amoral Joshua is enabled to pursue various scientific missions in the degraded society of the 22nd century.

3. *Candle* **(Tor, 2000)** After winning the computer war of the Memes, One True works toward rebuilding Earth and keeping all of its humans happy through a program called Resuna, which allows anyone to download the experiences and talents of anyone else.

III. Antihero Jak Jinnaka is the protagonist of a trio of novels set in the 36th century. Jak's girlfriend, Sesh, who is really Princess Shyf of Greenworld, leads him on a series of antic adventures full of eccentric characters and invented slang.

1. *Duke of Uranium, The* **(Warner, 2002)** Eighteen-year-old Jak Jinnaka's seemingly normal life on a 36th-century space station is irrevocably changed when he is attacked by strangers who kidnap his girlfriend, Sesh.

2. *Princess of the Aerie, A* **(Warner, 2002)** Jak and his panth buddy Dujuv join the Royal Palace Guard and race across the solar system, when ex-girlfriend Princess Shyf of Greenworld is reputed to be in danger.

3. *In the Hall of the Martian King* **(Warner, 2003)** Jak is ordered by the Hive intelligence agency to obtain the newly discovered diary of the progenitor of the "Wager"—the rules upon which the 36th century's legal, spiritual, and ethical system rests.

IV. The Time Raider series is a trio of novels about time travel linked by Dan Samson, Vietnam War hero, who is transported back into time in other war situations, and under different guises, by the mysterious Master Xi.

1. *Wartide* **(Worldwide, 1993)** Vietnam veteran Dan Samson is transported back to 1944 and enters the persona of Jackson Houston, who is engaged in the Allies' Italian campaign.

2. *Battlecry* **(Worldview, 1992)** Dan is transported back to 1846 and the Mexican War and given the mission of delivering a dispatch over 1,000 miles of territory.

3. *Union Fires* **(Worldwide, 1992)** Dan finds himself inhabiting the body of Sean Toole, a double agent during the Civil War in 1864, and interfering with Sean's plans to betray the Underground Railroad.

V. Timeline Wars is another trio of time-travel novels. This set postulates alternate worlds and time lines in which the protagonist, ex-PhD student, bodyguard, and Crux Op warrior Mark Strang, travels to a number of pasts, which he has the power of altering, and a distant future (2726 CE).

1. *Patton's Spaceship* **(HarperPrism, 1997)** After the Blade of the Most Merciful nearly wipes out his family, Mark Strang drops his PhD studies to become a bodyguard. Some years later, Mark finds himself in 28th-century Hyper Athens, training to be a Crux Op agent.

2. *Washington's Dirigible* **(HarperPrism, 1997)** Crux Op agent Mark Strang is sent on a special assignment to an alternate colonial America in which George Washington is Duke of Kentucky.

3. *Caesar's Bicycle* **(HarperPrism, 1997)** On the verge of defeating the Closers in the ongoing Timeline Wars, Crux Op sends Mark Strang back to the time of Julius Caesar and the Triumvirate where a Closer agent is trying to rewrite history.

Barnes, Julian

Talking It Over is about the ménage à trois between the solid but rather stodgy Stuart; Stuart's new wife, Gillian; and Stuart's best friend, the articulate layabout Oliver, who steals Gillian from Stuart. In *Love, Etc.* Stuart returns from America and tries to reverse roles. Both novels are told from the very different viewpoints of the three major characters, who address the reader directly and compete for the reader's attention. The English author Julian Barnes has written several other witty and wry novels, such as *Flaubert's Parrot* (Knopf, 1985) and *A History of the World in 10 1/2 Chapters* (Knopf, 1989), two collections of short stories, essay collections, a cookbook, and, under the pseudonym Dan Kavanagh, four crime novels featuring freelance security-system specialist Duffy.

1. *Talking It Over* **(Knopf, 1991)** The charming, fast-talking Oliver gradually weans new bride Gillian away from her husband, Oliver's best friend, Stuart.

2. *Love, Etc.* **(Knopf, 2001)** Several years later, Stuart returns from America, sets up an organic food business, and tries to win Gillian back from the financially unsuccessful Oliver.

Barnes, Linda J(oyce)

I. Six-foot one-inch redhead Carlotta Carlyle, a divorced former policewoman, divides her work time between driving a cab in Boston and private investigation. Tough, smart, sensitive, short-tempered, and restless, Carlotta would be a fit companion for Sara Paretsky's V. I. Warshawski (q.v.) or Sue Grafton's Kinsey Milhone (q.v.) in the female PI line. Mystery writer Barnes is familiar with the Boston area, where Carlotta does her hacking and detecting.

1. *Trouble of Fools, A* **(St. Martin's, 1987)** A search for a missing cabdriver leads Carlotta to a strange scam involving large sums of money.

2. *Snake Tattoo, The* (St. Martin's, 1989) A missing teenager from the suburbs seems to have surfaced in Boston's "Combat Zone."
3. *Coyote* (Delacorte, 1990) Carlotta's search for a frightened woman's missing green card involves her in the underground world of illegal immigration and labor exploitation.
4. *Steel Guitar* (Delacorte, 1991) Dee Willis, a blues singer on the rebound from addiction, hires former best friend Carlotta to find bass player Davey Dunrobie.
5. *Snapshot* (Delacorte, 1993) Emily Woodrow hires Carlotta to investigate the leukemia death of her seven-year-old daughter.
6. *Hardware* (Delacorte, 1995) Sam Gianelli, Carlotta's employer and sometime lover, gets her a deal on a PC that leads to unforeseen results.
7. *Cold Case* (Delacorte, 1997) A call asking Carlotta to locate supposedly dead teenage novelist sensation Thea Janis leads her to one of Massachusetts's most prominent political families and some dark secrets.
8. *Flashpoint* (Hyperion, 1999) Volleyball buddy and home health aide Gwen Taymore hires Carlotta as a security consultant to Valentine Phipps, who thinks a series of strange accidents is linked to her occupancy of one of the few remaining rent-controlled apartments in Boston's Fenway District.
9. *Big Dig, The* (St. Martin's, 2002) Boston's infamous "Big Dig," a seemingly endless project and bottomless source for graft, finds Carlotta posing as a secretary at Horgan Construction.
10. *Deep Pockets* (St. Martin's, 2004) African American Harvard professor Wilson Chaney is being blackmailed over his affair with rowing star Delani Brinkman.
11. *Heart of the World* (St. Martin's, 2006) Carlotta suspects that Paolina, a teen whom she loves like a daughter, has been kidnapped by her biological father, Roldan, a Colombian drug lord.

II. Michael Spraggue, wealthy Vietnam veteran, vineyard owner, and sometime private eye, was the star of an earlier Boston-based series, which Barnes now refers to as "apprentice work."

1. *Blood Will Have Blood* (Avon, 1982) Arthur Darien's production of *Dracula* is being bedeviled by strange, macabre jokes, so Michael takes a role.
2. *Bitter Finish* (St. Martin's, 1983) Michael's temperamental winemaker Lenny Brent is missing, and his part-time lover and business partner, Kate, is under suspicion of murder.
3. *Dead Heat* (St. Martin's, 1984) Spraggue is enlisted to help old friend Pete Collatos, bodyguard for US Senator Donagher, who is running for reelection.
4. *Cities of the Dead* (St. Martin's, 1986) Elderly, wealthy Mary Hillman engages nephew Michael Spraggue in the case of her longtime cook, Dora, accused of murdering her former husband in New Orleans.

Barnes, Steven (Stephen Emory)

I. *Lion's Blood* and its sequel, *Zulu Heart*, are intriguing alternate-history novels that postulate black/brown slaveholders and white slaves in a place called Bilalstan (the southern United States). The action starts in 1863 CE (1279 Hegira time) when Muslim Ethiopian prince Kai ibn Jallaleddin ibn Rashid brings Irish Christian Aidan O'Dere as a slave to the New World. Kai and Aidan eventually become friends in a richly detailed world stemming from Alexander the Great's marriage to an Egyptian princess. Steven Barnes, married to writer Tananarive Due (q.v.), has collaborated with Larry Niven (q.v.) and Jerry Pournelle on the Dream Park and Heorot series, as well as other novels, and has authored a couple of books in the Star Wars series.

1. *Lion's Blood* (Warner, 2002) African Muslim Kai ibn Jallaleddin ibn Rashid takes unwilling slave Irish Christian Aidan O'Dere and his family to Bilalstan, a North American land divided between warring Zulus, Arabs, Aztecs, Vikings, and Indians.
2. *Zulu Heart* (Warner, 2003) When Kai takes as a second wife a high-ranking Zulu named Nandi, and Egypt (nominal overlord of Bilalstan) and Ethiopia are on the verge of war, Aidan sells himself back into slavery to become a spy at the Egyptian court.

II. Steven Barnes has also written three SF–martial arts books about "zero-gravity" martial artist Aubry Knight, who revolts against his role as a hired killer for the gangster empire of the Ortegas in a future Los Angeles and becomes a social activist. Much more comic book–like than series I, this series remains open-ended although nothing has been published in it since 1993.

1. *Streetlethal* (Berkley, 1983) When his employers, the LA crime-lord Ortegas, tell their hired enforcer, Aubry Knight, to assassinate his beautiful love, Promise Cotonou-Knight, Aubry rebels against the organization.
2. *Gorgon Child* (Tor, 1989) Fighting alongside his wife, Promise, Aubry takes on a corrupt TV evangelist who is scheming to enslave America.
3. *Firedance* (Tor, 1993) Aubry reverts to his warrior past when his family is threatened by Phillipe Swarna, dictator of the Pan-African Republic, who is seeking to avenge his son's death at Aubry's hands.

Barr, Nevada

National Parks ranger Anna Pigeon has led a peripatetic life. Anna has worked at Natchez Trace, Guadeloupe Mountains, Isle Royale, Mesa Verde, Lassen, Cumberland Island, and Carlsbad Caverns, among other national parks, and has visited sites such as Glacier National Park and the Statue of Liberty. Wherever she goes, the tough but sensitive Anna finds a mystery to solve and natural scenery to enjoy. Anna has had lovers in the forms of an FBI agent and a sheriff–Episcopal minister, but her most durable relationship has been with her sister Molly, a New York psychiatrist. The series is atmospheric, suspenseful, very well written, and full of interesting characters.

Nevada Barr is a former actress (off-Broadway and industrial) who became a ranger in the National Parks system. She wrote several novels previous to the Anna Pigeon series, one of which, *Bittersweet*, "a neo-Gothic lesbian western," was published (St. Martin's, 1984). She is very familiar with the scenic backgrounds of her stories and the minutiae of park ranger life.

1. *Track of the Cat* (Putnam, 1993) Anna Pigeon, working as a law-enforcement ranger at Guadeloupe Mountains National Park, finds the remains of fellow ranger Sheila Drury, the apparent victim of a mountain lion attack. Winner of the Anthony and Agatha awards for best first mystery novel.
2. *Superior Death, A* (Putnam, 1994) Denny Castle, operator of a commercial diving concession on Isle Royale National Park in Lake Superior, is found dead in an old submerged wreck, and Donna Butkus, wife of ranger Scotty Butkus, is missing. Anna teams up with FBI agent Frederick Stanton to solve the mystery.
3. *Ill Wind* (Putnam, 1995) Mesa Verde National Park in Colorado is the scene as Anna's relationship with Frederick Stanton deepens when they team up to find the murderer of ranger Stacy Meyers, deal with a contractor whose water line is disturbing buried Anasazi artifacts, and investigate the "weird" messages Patsy Silva, a park secretary, is getting from her ex-husband.

4. *Firestorm* **(Putnam, 1996)** Anna provides first aid for the crews fighting a forest fire, probably caused by arson, in Lassen Volcanic National Park, California. She solves another case despite a firestorm, bad weather, and destroyed roads.

5. *Endangered Species* **(Putnam, 1997)** Anna is on presuppression fire duty at Cumberland Island National Seashore, Georgia, when an air crash kills drug-interdiction pilot Slattery Hammond and a district ranger. Anna's psychiatrist sister, Molly, and her lover, Frederick Stanton, help her on this case.

6. *Blind Descent* **(Putnam, 1998)** Anna is summoned to Carlsbad Caverns, in New Mexico, to aid a friend who was trapped while exploring a nearby cave. Despite her claustrophobia, Anna comes through and then becomes involved in investigating links between two murders.

7. *Liberty Falling* **(Putnam, 1999)** In New York to help sister Molly recover from a bout of pneumonia, Anna hooks up again with Patsy Silva and befriends the staff of Liberty and Ellis islands, who keep the Statue of Liberty functioning. Ghosts, thefts, accidents, collapsing buildings, and a murder complicate her life.

8. *Deep South* **(Putnam, 2000)** Anna must leave her beloved western parks to accept a promotion to district ranger at the Port Gibson section of the Natchez Trace Parkway, Mississippi. While dealing with the humidity, the lack of the wilderness she craves, the tourists and campers, and male chauvinist subordinates, Anna must solve the mystery of a teenage girl found murdered in the woods with a hood and noose tied over her head.

9. *Blood Lure* **(Putnam, 2001)** On a visit to Glacier National Park to learn how to analyze grizzly-bear DNA, Anna is attacked by a grizzly and involved in a murder investigation that may implicate one of her colleagues.

10. *Hunting Season* **(Putnam, 2002)** Is the murder of Doyce Barnette at Mount Locust, a historic plantation and inn in the Natchez Trace Parkway, a ritual killing? Will Anna and local sheriff Clintus Jones solve the mystery? Will Anna's love life reblossom with Paul Davidson, ordained Episcopal minister and sheriff of neighboring Claiborne County?

11. *Flashback* **(Putnam, 2003)** Anna, fleeing a marriage proposal from Sheriff Paul Davidson, winds up this time in Garden Key, site of Civil War prison Fort Jefferson in the Dry Tortugas National Park. She gets embroiled in two mysteries: one current, one involving former Fort Jefferson prisoner Dr. Samuel Mudd, of Lincoln assassination notoriety.

12. *High Country* **(Putnam, 2004)** Anna goes undercover as a waitress at Yosemite's Ahwahnee Hotel before going on a trek into the Sierra Nevada Mountains in search of four missing Yosemite employees.

13. *Hard Truth* **(Putnam, 2005)** Assuming a new post in Colorado's Rocky Mountain Park, Anna encounters a former ice climber now confined to a wheelchair and a serial killer.

14. *Winter Study* **(Putnam, 2008)** Anna returns to Isle Royale National Park (see number 2) to take part in a research project studying wolves and moose and runs into paralyzingly cold weather and some untoward events.

Barre, Richard

Wil Hardesty, a private investigator located in the seaside town of La Conchita, California (not too far from Santa Barbara), is tormented by his past. A stint in Vietnam, the death of his child, and his crumbling marriage are memories that he tries to exorcise by hard drinking, motorcycle riding, and surfing. Despite the surfing interludes, the California setting and the dark tone of this series remind some readers of Raymond Chandler (q.v.). The author, Richard Barre, is a California native and former owner of Barre Advertising in Santa Barbara, California.

1. *Innocents, The* **(Walker, 1995)** When the skeletons of seven children are found in a California desert and the father of a dead boy enlists his aid, the grieving (for his own son) private eye Wil Hardesty gets on the trail of what may be a satanic cult.

2. *Bearing Secrets* **(Walker, 1996)** A case involving a corrupt attorney, his deadly wife, the suicide of a former antiwar activist, the discovery of a plane that crashed in a California lake with a $2 million cargo, a woman who is convinced that the FBI murdered her mother, and terrorists provides a potent mix of intrigue.

3. *Ghosts of Morning, The* **(Berkley, 1998)** Wil's old surfing buddy Denny Van Zant, whose certified remains were sent home from Vietnam in 1981, is reported alive in Hawaii by someone who wants $30,000 for the details.

4. *Blackheart Highway* **(Berkley, 1999)** Doc Whitney, home in Bakersfield after doing 20 years in prison for murdering his wife and children, is harassing the family of local attorney Luke DiVilbiss, who may have been a part of a frame-up of Whitney.

5. *Burning Moon* **(Capra, 2003)** A fishing boat disappears off the California coast during a storm. The police rule it an accident, but a Vietnamese fisherman, father of the man lost at sea, is convinced that it was foul play.

Barrett, Neal, Jr.

I. The Aldair series starts on a future Earth abandoned by the human race and populated by various "humanoids" descended from wolves, bears, pigs, etc. The hero, Aldair, himself a pig, wanders across Earth and eventually to another planet, looking for traces of legendary mankind and a clue to his own destiny in this innovative and entertaining quartet of novels. American Neal Barrett Jr. has written other SF, fantasy, and comic crime novels.

1. *Aldair in Albion* **(DAW, 1976)** Aldair, a "not-quite" human, is ostracized by his community and wanders across Europe in search of his destiny and answers to his questions about the fate of the legendary "human race."

2. *Aldair, Master of Ships* **(DAW, 1977)** Aldair, a latter-day Magellan, traverses the seas and coastlines of future Earth, still searching for answers.

3. *Aldair, Across the Misty Sea* **(DAW, 1980)** Aldair travels to the land of Merrkia and discovers traces of the original "man" who inhabited Earth.

4. *Aldair: The Legion of Beasts* **(DAW, 1982)** Aldair and his friends travel to an alien planet, where genetic freaks are enslaving the remnants of mankind.

II. In *Through Darkest America* and its sequel, *Dawn's Uncertain Light*, Barrett postulates a bleak post-nuclear-holocaust North America in which "mutated" humans form a primary part of the survivors' diets. Young Howie Ryder, having learned the dark secret of the mutations, goes in search of his abducted sister.

1. *Through Darkest America* **(Congdon, 1986)** Two or three hundred years after a nuclear war, an American family subsists by raising "Herds" for meat. Young Howie Ryder stumbles upon the awful truth about the Herds.

2. *Dawn's Uncertain Light* **(New American Library, 1989)** Howie Ryder sets off on a journey to find his sister, Caroline, who has been taken by the government to be used in a forced breeding program.

III. Barrett has taken to writing comic crime novels somewhat in the style of Carl Hiaasen (q.v.) and Elmore Leonard. The so-called blues quartet is rather loosely connected by the presence of Wiley Moss, graphic artist and reluctant adventurer. Wacky characters and over-the-top situations are featured in this series. Some critics regard Barrett as "the top of the class" in this subgenre. *Piggs* (Subterranean, 2001) is a comic crime novel not (apparently) in the blues series.

1. *Pink Vodka Blues* (St. Martin's, 1992) Russ Murray awakens with a terrible hangover after a lost weekend, vaguely and uneasily aware of a monstrous plot against him involving a triple homicide and someone named "Bones" Pinelli and the Wackers, a pair of murderous twins who want him dead.
2. *Dead Dog Blues* (St. Martin's, 1994) Jack Track, Pharoah, Texas, town marshal, who has spent 14 years evading his past as a hired killer, gets up to his neck in trouble when the black Lab of Pharoah's richest man, Max Coomer, is found assassinated with a Walkman tied around its neck.
3. *Skinny Annie Blues* (Kensington, 1996) Wiley Moss, graphic artist for the Smithsonian who specializes in drawing insects, is lured to Galveston when his errant father dies and runs into nasty cops, obese strippers, and other local lowlifes.
4. *Bad Eye Blues* (Kensington, 1997) Wiley Moss is abducted by Bobby Bad-Eye, a one-eyed Indian, and Rocco, an albino movie freak, and transported to the Idaho brothel of "Spuds" DeMarco, who wants Wiley to immortalize his "Spudettes" in art.

IV. Barrett is also adept at comic-action fantasy. Master Lizard-Maker Finn is the protagonist of a pair of novels set in a world where magic has transformed animals into humanlike creatures known as Newlies, and two kings, one sane, the other anything but, war against each other.

1. *Prophecy Machine, The* (Bantam, 2000) Peace-loving Finn, the Master Lizard-Maker; Julia Jessica Slagg, his mechanical lizard; and Letitia Louise, his Newlie ladylove, find themselves the hostages of the Nucci family, who want Finn to repair their "prophecy" machine.
2. *Treachery of Kings, The* (Bantam, 2001) Finn, his companions, and a hostile giant deliver a birthday gift from their king in a hot-air balloon in the midst of a war of unrecalled origin.

Barrie, Sir James M(atthew)

Although J. M. Barrie is remembered primarily for his creation Peter Pan, kept alive partly through the efforts of Walt Disney and Steven Spielberg, he was the author of other successful plays—a few of which, such as *The Admirable Crichton*, are revived from time to time—and several novels of 19th-century Scottish life and manners set mainly in the town of Thrums, the slightly fictionalized version of his hometown of Kirriemuir. Some readers still find novels such as *The Little Minister* (1891) enjoyable nostalgic reading despite the thickness of the dialect, the sentiment, and the whimsy.

Two novels follow the career of Tommy from the age of five to his death. Tommy epitomizes the man of feeling. He is nicknamed "sentimental" because his "sympathy was so easily aroused that he sometimes cried without knowing why."

1. *Sentimental Tommy* (Scribner, 1896) Little Tommy leaves his London slum for Thrums, the town of his mother's origin.
2. *Tommy and Grizel* (Scribner, 1898) Tommy's talents are put to good use in his career as a writer, and the virtuous and patient Grizel is devoted to him.

Barron, Stephanie

Given the spate of mystery novels involving real historical characters, perhaps it should be no surprise that Jane Austen has been enlisted as a sleuth. The premise is that a cache of lost Jane Austen papers, which purportedly shed light on the "lost years" of Jane's life, has turned up on a Maryland estate. These letters document, in "Jane's" own words, a series of detecting adventures. Barron does an excellent job of imitating Jane Austen's style, and intriguingly links real people with their fictional alter egos (e.g., Jane Austen's mother is Mrs. Bennet). Barron's Jane series has proved to be popular with mystery readers as well as with Jane Austen aficionados. Stephanie Barron (not to be confused with the art historian of the same name) also writes, as Francine Mathews, the Merrie Folger Nantucket mystery series.

1. *Jane and the Unpleasantness at Scargrave Manor* (Bantam, 1996) The premise of the series is introduced with this mystery about the suspicious death of the Earl of Scargrave. Anonymous notes accuse Scargrave's young widow, Isobel Payne (a friend of Jane Austen), of murdering him.
2. *Jane and the Man of the Cloth* (Bantam, 1996) While the Austens are headed for a seaside holiday at Lyme Regis in 1804, a carriage accident injures Jane's sister Cassandra, and they are forced to put up at High Down Grange, home of Geoffrey Sidmouth. Jane's attraction to Sidmouth leads her into an investigation of charges against him for smuggling and murder.
3. *Jane and the Wandering Eye* (Bantam, 1997) Bath is the scene, and the Kemble-Siddons acting family forms a subplot, as Jane and Lord Harold Trowbridge investigate the murder of Richard Portal, manager of Bath's Theatre Royal.
4. *Jane and the Genius of the Place* (Bantam, 1999) Murder with a possible connection to Napoléon's planned invasion of the English coastline engages Jane when she attends the Canterbury Races while staying in Kent at her brother Neddie's estate.
5. *Jane and the Stillroom Maid* (Bantam, 2000) While walking in the Derbyshire hills, Jane and her escort, George Hemming, discover the mutilated body of a young man. The "young man" turns out to be Tess Arnold, a servant at a nearby estate.
6. *Jane and the Prisoner of Wool House* (Bantam, 2001) Jane's brother Frank asks for her aid in clearing the name of his friend, Captain Tom Seagrave, who has been accused of killing a French officer after the latter's surrender, an act in violation of the Articles of War.
7. *Jane and the Ghosts of Netley* (Bantam, 2003) In 1808, Jane, while visiting the ruins of Netley Abbey on the Southhampton coast, is asked by Lord Harold Trowbridge to gain the confidence of Sophia Challoner, a suspected French agent staying at Netley Lodge.
8. *Jane and His Lordship's Legacy* (Bantam, 2005) Jane receives a legacy from the late Lord Harold Trowbridge, and discovers the mutilated body of a laborer in the cellar of Chawton Cottage.
9. *Jane and the Barque of Frailty* (Bantam, 2006) In spring 1811, Jane is in London during a visit to her brother Henry. A Russian princess whom Jane observes at the theater gazing intently at the box of Lord Castlereagh turns up dead outside Castlereagh's home.

Barth, Richard

Manhattan's answer to Miss Marple is 72-year-old Margaret Binton, who mixes community service with crime detection. With her band of senior citizens out of an English cozy, and with Broadway bums out of Damon Runyon, the fussy but clever and intrepid Margaret foils drug dealers, baby sellers, slumlords, nursing-home profiteers, murderers, and other antisocial types in this series full of gentle humor and warm-hearted characters.

1. *Rag Bag Clan, The* (Dial, 1976) Margaret disguises herself as a bag lady to help police uncover a murderer. Barth wrote the screenplay for the TV movie starring Ed Asner and Jean Simmons based on this novel.
2. *Ragged Plot, A* (Dial, 1981) A fortune in diamonds buried in a community garden where Binton volunteers leads to murder.
3. *One Dollar Death* (Dial, 1982) An old friend of Margaret's is stabbed to death in the offices of Sotheby Park-Bernet, where she had gone to have a coin appraised.
4. *Deadly Climate* (St. Martin's, 1982) Nursing home scandals in Florida are exposed as Margaret and three friends travel to Miami in her newly won recreational vehicle.
5. *Condo Kill, The* (Scribner, 1985) A shady real-estate developer is killing off tenants in rent-controlled apartments to make room for high-priced condos. UK title: *The Co-op Kill*.
6. *Blood Doesn't Tell* (St. Martin's, 1989) Margaret's foster parenting of a 15-month-old child through the Biddies and Kiddies program at the senior center leads her to a baby-selling racket.
7. *Deathics* (St. Martin's, 1993) Adrian Lavin, Margaret's partner in her Smoke Stopper's Group, is murdered shortly after she calls him during a break in her law ethics class.

Bartholomew, Nancy

I. Most readers have heard about "the hooker with a heart of gold." Meet a stripper with a heart of similar alloy: Sierra Lavotini, six-foot-tall exotic dancer of Panama City, Florida. The bighearted, feisty, wise-cracking Sierra, the leading "artiste" of the Florida panhandle, pursues her profession at the Tiffany Gentleman's Club, owned by the not-too-bright Vinny Gambuzzo, but allows herself to become embroiled in a series of mysteries aided by Fluffy, her Chihuahua, and homicide detective John Nailor, her sometime lover. A lighthearted series, full of sleazy but zany and just plain zany characters.

1. *Miracle Strip, The* (St. Martin's, 1998) When her friend Denise's dog Arlo is dognapped and held for $100,000 ransom, and a dead man turns up in Denise's motel room, Sierra gets on the case.
2. *Drag Strip* (St. Martin's, 1999) Her efforts to find the killer of fellow stripper and protégée Ruby Diamond after the latter is slain at the Dead Lakes Motor Speedway lead Sierra into a melange of local rednecks and gangsters and attract the attention of local police, including homicide detective John Nailor.
3. *Film Strip* (St. Martin's, 2000) Adult film star legend Venus Lovemotion is gunned down at the Tiffany Gentleman's Club, and Sierra's career is almost ended by a bullet in her rear.
4. *Strip Poker* (St. Martin's, 2001) Vinny Gambuzzo loses the Tiffany Gentleman's Club in a poker game and, to add insult to injury, is accused of shooting one of the players in the game, while Sierra goes back home to Philadelphia to sort out some family problems.

II. Maggie Reid, like Sierra Lavotini, is feisty, smart-mouthed, and prone to getting into trouble. After her husband leaves her and her beautician career falters, Maggie decides to pursue her singing ambitions and becomes lead singer for a band in Greensboro, North Carolina. This series, whose book titles echo country-music song titles, promises to be as entertaining as the "strip" series.

1. *Your Cheatin' Heart* (Harper, 2000) Maggie's career as a country singer seems to be well launched as she lands a job with a band in Greensboro, North Carolina, and her love life seems to be rejuvenated in the person of detective Marshall Weathers until her brother-in-law is murdered at her house.
2. *Stand by Your Man* (Harper, 2001) Vernell, Maggie's adulterous ex-husband, has vanished with his millions and is the prime suspect in a murder, but it is up to Maggie to find him and prove his innocence.

III. A pair of novels in Silhouette's Bombshell series features smart-mouthed private investigator Stella Valocchi, who sets up in business with her ex-fiancé, Jake Carpenter.

1. *Stella, Get Your Gun* (Silhouette, 2004) Stella Valocchi catches her cop boyfriend in bed with her best friend, kidnaps the boyfriend's dog, and runs for home, only to find the man who once left her presiding over her favorite uncle's funeral.
2. *Stella, Get Your Man* (Silhouette, 2005) Stella has set up her PI business. Her only employee is, unfortunately, former fiancé Jake Carpenter. Then a client with a sob story hires them to find her brother.

Barton, Dan

Biff Kincaid is a stand-up comedian who works the comedy clubs of Los Angeles and elsewhere and doubles as a martial artist and amateur detective. The Kincaid novels are a rather odd mixture of one-liners, authentic portrayals of the world of the stand-up comic, skewerings of such targets as tabloid TV and Hollywood superagents, and graphic violence. Author Dan Barton is himself a stand-up comedian.

1. *Killer Material* (St. Martin's, 2000) Filling in for a friend at Chortles Comedy Club, stand-up comic Biff Kincaid realizes that the first performer, Ned Lando, has stolen all his material from other comics. And then the fun really begins.
2. *Heckler* (St. Martin's, 2001) Biff searches for "the Heckler," a serial killer who haunts comedy clubs in the far West.
3. *Dead Crowd* (St. Martin's, 2002) Biff assumes the role of amateur sleuth after stumbling over the dead body of comedy club manager Bernie Coleman and getting hit on the head himself.

Bastable, Bernard

PSEUDONYM OF Robert Barnard

Robert Barnard (q.v.), author of the successful Perry Trethowen and Oddie and Peace series, as Bernard Bastable writes historical mysteries set in 19th-century Britain. Two of these novels are alternate history, featuring the composer Wolfgang Gottlieb Mozart, who, living to a rather penurious old age in the London of the 1820s, gets occasional commissions from the English gentry and gets mixed up in a couple of mysteries involving royalty.

1. *Dead, Mr. Mozart* (St. Martin's, 1995) Wolfgang Gottlieb Mozart, still alive in London in 1820 but reduced to writing "curtain raisers," gets what seems like a break when opera patron Lord Hertford gets Mozart's protégée, Betty Ackroyd, hired by the opera. But a corpse turns up, and Mozart gets involved in the investigation of the purported adultery of George IV's Queen Caroline.
2. *Too Many Notes, Mr. Mozart* (Carroll & Graf, 1996) After Mozart gets a job giving music lessons to heir apparent Princess Victoria, the young lady asks him to find out the truth about the relationship between her mother and Sir John Conroy.

Bates, H(erbert) E(rnest)

The chronicles of the Larkin family show the late H. E. Bates in a lighter mood than *Love for Lydia* (1952), *Fair Stood the Wind for France* (1944), and his realistic portrayals of English rural life. Pop Larkin and his brood are the Beverly Hillbillies transferred to the English countryside, where they carry on their cheerfully amoral lifestyle and hornswoggle the city slickers. *The Darling Buds of May* was made into a Hollywood film starring Paul Douglas, Tony Randall, and Debbie Reynolds in 1959. In the 1990s, a BBC television series with the same title was a surprise UK hit and helped make Catherine Zeta-Jones, who played Mariette Larkin, a star. Several omnibus volumes and a number of spin-offs from the television series have been published in England.

1. *Darling Buds of May, The* (Little, Brown, 1958) The tax collector comes to the Larkins' junkyard of a farm.
2. *Breath of French Air, A* (Little, Brown, 1959) The Larkins descend like a hurricane on a shabby hotel in Brittany.
3. *Hark, Hark, the Lark!* (Little, Brown, 1960) Pop Larkin sells a huge white elephant of a manor house to some city folk who become his neighbors. English title: *When the Green Woods Laugh.*
4. *Oh! To Be in England* (Farrar, 1963) The Larkin family has further adventures, including a belated omnibus baptism.
5. *Little of What You Fancy, A* (Michael Joseph [UK], 1970) Pop Larkin has a mild heart attack. Ma Larkin figures that he needs the attention of women to entice him back to recovery. Apparently never published in the United States. Penguin published editions in 1974 and 1991 (as a TV tie-in).

Baudino, Gael

I. In the Dragonsword trilogy, UCLA graduate student Suzanne Helling is called to the alternate world of Gryylth, a medieval place with dragons and magic, where she becomes the swordswoman Alouzon. Feminist sword and sorcery with a difference, as the heroine must conquer not only her own anxieties and misgivings but also male fantasies that have been implanted within her and the damage that the Vietnam War has done to the American psyche.

1. *Dragonsword* (Lynx, 1988) Suzanne Helling and Helen Addams are transported to Gryylth, a medieval land created by Helen's late ex-husband, Solomon Braithwaite, where dragons and sorcery are commonplace.
2. *Duel of Dragons* (Roc, 1991) Suzanne and Helen, now Alouzon and Kyria, respectively, and the dragon Silbakor must battle 20th-century weapons and the White Worm in Gryylth and in Alouzon's creation, Vaylle, which is being devastated by Suzanne's memories of the Vietnam War.
3. *Dragon Death* (Roc, 1992) In action set in Los Angeles and Gryylth, Alouzon fights a slew of enemies, including a young sorcerer who has acquired the power to betray his own people.

II. The Strands of Starlight series, set in Adria, a fictional kingdom in the real 14th-century Europe, relates the decline and rebirth of the Elves, immortal but fallible creatures who are primarily a force for good. The Elves and their human allies are beset by evil forces such as the Inquisition and sexist males.

1. *Spires of Spirit* (Roc, 1997) Six novellas, originally published in the 1980s, which set the scene for the medieval world of Adria and the Elves, immortal creatures that resurface in 1980s Colorado.

2. *Strands of Starlight* (Signet, 1989) Young outcast Miriam, whom the Inquisition has branded as a witch because of her healing powers, vows revenge on the Inquisition and brutal, sexist males.
3. *Maze of Moonlight* (Roc, 1993) Baron Christopher of Aurverelle, survivor of the disastrous historical battle of Nicopolis (1399), and young misfit Vanessa have to realize their own elfish heritage before they can begin to cope with the secular spiritual evils of their society.
4. *Shroud of Shadow* (Roc, 1993) The Elves are in eclipse because of the persecution of the Inquisition. Natil, the last of her people, must find a refuge from the torturers of both innocent and guilty.
5. *Strands of Sunlight* (Roc, 1994) Natil Summerson, sole surviving Firstborn Elf, uses her harp to focus healing energies in 1990s Colorado, as the Elves of Denver seek to reestablish connection to the Creatrix.

III. The Water trilogy is set at some indeterminate, apparently alternate time in the fictional African country of the Three Kingdoms, where Crown Prince Aeid tries to help his drought-stricken land and ponders the proffered help of the Righteous States of America against invading French troops, and herbalist and woman of the Goddess Sari makes a pilgrimage back to her native land to start a new life after finally ridding herself of her abusive husband. Fans of previous Baudino series are, on the whole, not too happy with this series, finding it meandering and confusing. American writer Baudino has also written *Gossamer Axe* (Roc, 1990), which is a story fusing fantasy and rock music.

1. *O Greenest Branch!* (Roc, 1995) Crown Prince Aeid tries to steer his father away from his fanatically religious court; diplomats from the Righteous States of America try to offer help against the drought and a French invasion; and herbalist Sari returns to the land of her youth to atone for her abandonment of the Goddess.
2. *Dove Looked In, The* (Roc, 1996) The contrasting fallacies of the Righteous States of America and the Three Kingdoms are examined, while Sari has to detach herself from her "protectors."
3. *Branch and Crown* (Roc, 1996) The conclusion of the trilogy, in which Sari continues her voyage of discovery and the Righteous States of America and the Three Kingdoms continue their duel.

Baxt, George

I. George Baxt, screenplay and mystery writer, created in Pharoah Love a gay, black New York Police Department detective who vows to "never blend in," one of the wildest and campiest characters in detective ranks. Some critics were shocked by Pharoah's antics, others praised the novels for their "naturalism," while a third group touted them as masterpieces of "black humor." The original trilogy, published in the 1960s, has been expanded by two more titles published in the 1990s.

1. *Queer Kind of Death, A* (Simon & Schuster, 1967) Ben Bentley, beautiful male model and sometime prostitute, is electrocuted in his bathtub.
2. *Swing Low, Sweet Harriet* (Simon & Schuster, 1967) An unsolved Hollywood murder committed in 1933 is resurrected amid a welter of Hollywood nostalgia.
3. *Topsy and Evil* (Simon & Schuster, 1968) Satan Stagg, as black and as hip as Pharoah, comes to the fore as Love disappears just when tycoon Guru Raskalnikov is done in with the classic "blunt instrument."
4. *Queer Kind of Love, A* (Penzler, 1994) Pharoah is teamed up with homophobe Albert West to solve the murders of Mob members, which are occurring in pairs for some odd reason.

5. *Queer Kind of Umbrella, A* **(Simon & Schuster, 1995)** Pharoah infiltrates New York's leading Chinese criminal cabal in a case involving a killer umbrella.

II. Among his many other mystery novels, Baxt has written a pair featuring Max Van Larsen of the Missing Persons Bureau of the New York Police Department and teacher Sylvia Plotkin.

1. *Parade of Cockeyed Creatures, A; or, Did Someone MurderOur Wandering Boy?* **(Random House, 1967)** Max Van Larsen, searching for missing 17-year-old Tippy Blaney, teams up with Tippy's teacher, Sylvia Plotkin.
2. *I! Said the Demon* **(Random House, 1969)** The case of Judge Kramer (aka the historical Judge Crater) leads Sylvia and Max to a converted Gothic church in Greenwich Village.

III. Baxt's nostalgia for the 1930s, evinced by *Swing Low, Sweet Harriet* (I, 2) and *I! Said the Demon* (II, 2), is allowed full scope in his longest-running series of novels, which set 1930s Hollywood celebrities to solving crimes that occurred from the 1930s to the 1950s. Because there is no real connection between the novels except their settings, and the titles are more or less self-explanatory, they are listed without annotations.

1. *Dorothy Parker Murder Case, The* **(St, Martin's, 1984)**
2. *Alfred Hitchcock Murder Case, The* **(St. Martin's, 1986)**
3. *Tallulah Bankhead Murder Case, The* **(St. Martin's, 1987)**
4. *Talking Picture Murder Case, The* **(St. Martin's, 1990)**
5. *Noel Coward Murder Case, The* **(St. Martin's, 1992)**
6. *Greta Garbo Murder Case, The* **(St. Martin's, 1992)**
7. *Marlene Dietrich Murder Case, The* **(St. Martin's, 1993)**
8. *Mae West Murder Case, The* **(St. Martin's, 1993)**
9. *Bette Davis Murder Case, The* **(St. Martin's, 1994)**
10. *Humphrey Bogart Murder Case, The* **(St. Martin's, 1995)**
11. *William Powell and Myrna Loy Murder Case, The* **(St. Martin's, 1996)**
12. *Fred Astaire and Ginger Rogers Murder Case, The* **(St. Martin's, 1997)**
13. *Clark Gable and Carol Lombard Murder Case, The* **(St. Martin's, 1997)**

Baxter, Cynthia

Long Island, New York, veterinarian Jessica Popper, her sometime boyfriend, PI Nick Burby, and her two dogs—Max, the tailless Westie, and Lou, the one-eyed Dalmatian—accidentally get involved in mysteries in this series of cozies, subtitled *A Reigning Cats and Dogs Mystery*, which will appeal to dog and horse lovers.

1. *Dead Canaries Don't Sing* **(Bantam, 2004)** Veterinarian Jessica Popper and her dogs, Lou and Max, on the way to make a house call at a local horse farm, stumble across a corpse half buried in the woods with a dead canary nearby.
2. *Putting on the Dog* **(Bantam, 2004)** Jessica is staffing the "Ask the Vet" booth at an SPCA fund-raiser in the Bromptons (aka Hamptons) on Long Island when tabloid photographer Bevon Barnett is killed by a large ice sculpture that falls (or was pushed) on him.
3. *Lead a Horse to Murder* **(Bantam, 2005)** Polo and murder are the games here as Popper goes to an exclusive Long Island estate to tend to the sprained tendon of a prize horse, and Argentine polo player Eduardo Garcia is poisoned.

4. *Hare Today, Dead Tomorrow* **(Bantam, 2006)** Popper has to deal with live-in boyfriend Nick Burby and a killer who's left nothing behind except a stuffed rabbit.
5. *Right from the Gecko* **(Bantam, 2007)** Jessica and Nick are on their way to Maui for a veterinarians' conference, when the body of young reporter Marnie Burton washes up on the beach.
6. *Who's Kitten Who?* **(Bantam, 2007)** Jessica is coping with the "Invasion of the Burbarians," her future in-laws and a monstrous Maltese, who descend on the cottage she shares with Nick Burby and her menagerie.

Baxter, Stephen

I. British hard-SF writer Stephen Baxter has written several imaginative but believable series set in the future or in alternate worlds. The Xeelee, or Michael Poole, series covers a period spanning more than five million years in which a human scientist named Michael Poole develops wormholes that enable humans to travel through time and space and perhaps avert or escape catastrophic future events. Numbers 4 through 6 are called the Destiny's Children trilogy. Baxter's first novel, *Raft* (Roc, 1992), and *Flux* (HarperPrism, 1995) are sometimes included with the Xeelee books. *The Timeships* (HarperPrism, 1996), another time-travel novel, is a sequel to the H. G. Wells classic *The Time Machine*.

1. *Timelike Infinity* **(Roc, 1993)** When Michael Poole rescues a member of a team of time travelers using his wormhole, he discovers that, 1,500 years into the future, an alien entity known as the Quax controls the solar system.
2. *Ring* **(HarperPrism, 1996)** When an expedition to the sun discovers an instability that will destroy it within 10,000 years, a desperate attempt is led by Louise Ye Armonk far into the future to avert this calamity.
3. *Vacuum Diagrams* **(HarperPrism, 1997)** A collection of short stories describing the creation of the Poole wormholes, the Squeem conquest, spaceships that outrace light, and the mystery and legacy of the Xeelee.
4. *Coalescent* **(Del Rey, 2003)** George Poole discovers that he has a twin sister, Regina, who belongs to a mysterious ancient cult in Rome.
5. *Exultant* **(Del Rey, 2004)** Two versions of space navy pilot Pirius from different time lanes, Pirius Red and Pirius Blue, violate protocol in a clash with the alien Xeelee and are punished.
6. *Transcendent* **(Del Rey, 2005)** Five thousand years after the death of Michael Poole, starship-born Alia, entrusted with the duty of witnessing the life of one man, woman, or child from the past, is assigned Michael.
7. *Resplendent* **(Gollancz [UK], 2006)** A collection of short stories about mankind's fight for survival against the Xeelee. Not yet published in the United States.

II. The Mammoth trilogy is about the survival of mammoths from the Ice Age into the 20th century and beyond. Full of mammoth lore and anthropomorphic touches, the trilogy will appeal to readers of Jean Auel (q.v.) and Richard Adams. Published together in an omnibus volume, *Behemoth* (Gollancz [UK], 2004).

1. *Silverhair* **(HarperPrism, 1999)** Defying the odds, a small colony of mammoths has survived from the Ice Age into the 20th century. However, their discovery by humans has put them at risk again. Variant title: *Mammoth*.

2. *Longtusk* **(Eos, 2001)** The mammoth protagonist, Longtusk, must sacrifice his life to save the remaining mammoths from the Fireheads (humans).
3. *Icebones* **(Eos, 2002)** Icebones, daughter of mammoth matriarch Silverhair, awakes from a long sleep to find herself on the Sky Steppe of Mars.

III. The Manifold trio, set in the near future, follows the story of Reid Malenfant, millionaire industrialist and astronaut who resembles Ben Bova's Dan Randolph Malenfant tries to resurrect the American space program and gets involved in an odyssey spanning centuries and some extrapolations of future history resembling those of Olaf Stapledon and Arthur C. Clarke (q.v.).

1. *Manifold: Time* **(Del Rey, 2000)** In the near future, millionaire Reid Malenfant tries to starts his own space program, then discovers evidence of a humanity-destroying catastrophe 200 years in the future. Variant title: *Time*.
2. *Manifold: Space* **(Del Rey, 2001)** In 2020 a young scientist from the Japanese lunar colony asks Malenfant to consult about some mysterious sources of infrared in the asteroid belt. Variant title: *Space*.
3. *Manifold: Origin* **(Del Rey, 2002)** Reid and his wife, Emma Storey, are flying over South Africa when a red moon replaces the normal one, and a blue-lit gateway appearing in Earth's atmosphere releases some strange hominids. Variant title: *Origin*.

IV. The Time's Tapestry series, which begins in 4 BCE, concerns a prophecy about generations of a British and Roman family.

1. *Emperor* **(Ace, 2007)** A cryptic prophecy about the fate of Britannia and Christianity is born in 4 BCE, along with the boy who becomes the British chieftain Nectovelin.
2. *Conqueror* **(Ace, 2007)** Two young men accompany a lecherous bishop north to the ruins of Hadrian's Wall to search for a man known only as "the last Roman."
3. *Navigator* **(Ace, 2008)** Takes place during the period of Christianity's reconquest of Spain from the Moors between 1070 and 1492 CE.

Bayer, Valerie Townsend

The Victorian Forster (not to be confused with Forsyte) family is exposed in American writer Bayer's Marlborough Gardens Quartet. The projected quartet starts in 1935 in a story-within-a-story format when Harriet Van Buren and Rachel Low, living together in the former London residence of the Forsters, relate the saga of the rich, predatory, sex-bedeviled English banking family in excerpts from their journals and diaries. The fourth book in the quartet, tentatively titled *The Dimensions of Grace*, hadn't been published as of late 2008.

1. *City of Childhood* **(St. Martin's, 1992)** In 1835 the 11 Forster cousins are churned up by the arrival of their manipulative half-Italian cousin, Darius.
2. *Metaphysics of Sex, The* **(St. Martin's, 1992)** Emma Forster witnesses the downfall of her greedy, brutal father, Elijah, at the hands of master criminal Nicholas Reston.
3. *Forbidden Objects* **(St. Martin's, 1995)** Emma suffers unrequited love for her distant cousin Johan Lustig, while other Forster cousins work out their destinies in England and Germany.

Bayer, William

New York City Police Lieutenant Frank Janek was introduced in the Edgar-winning *Peregrine*. Janek is the protagonist in three more novels involving some complicated plots and bizarre murders including *Switch*, which was a paperback best-seller. *Switch* was adapted as a TV mini-series, *Doubletake* (1985). *Wallflower* was adapted as a made-for-TV film, *Forget-Me-Not Murders* (1994). William Bayer, who is the son of the husband-and-wife mystery-writing team known as Oliver Weld Bayer, has written nonfiction, movie scripts, and other mysteries and thrillers, including two mystery novels, written as David Hunt, about Kay Farrow, a color-blind photographer: *The Magician's Tale* (Putnam, 1997) and *Trick of Light* (Putnam, 1998).

1. *Peregrine* **(Congdon, 1981)** After newscaster Pamela Barrett witnesses the slaying of a woman near Rockefeller Center by means of a peregrine falcon, the falcon's trainer becomes interested in Pamela.
2. *Switch* **(Linden, 1984)** Detective Frank Janek investigates a bizarre double murder wherein two people are murdered and decapitated, and their heads are switched.
3. *Wallflower* **(Villard, 1991)** Janek is called back from vacation when his goddaughter is stabbed to death and sexually mutilated in Central Park.
4. *Mirror Maze* **(Villard, 1994)** The body of a businessman is found in a midtown hotel with the phrase "you are a total jerk" mirror written on his chest.

Beach, Edward L(atimer)

Beach graduated from the US Naval Academy in 1939, saw duty aboard three submarines during World War II, and commanded the nuclear-powered USS *Triton* in her 1960 underwater circumnavigation of the world. His naval adventures have the authenticity that such a background guarantees plus the action and excitement inherent to the genre. Clark Gable and Burt Lancaster starred in the 1958 film *Run Silent, Run Deep*. Beach has published several nonfiction books, including *Salt and Steel: Reflections of a Submariner* (Naval Institute, 1999).

1. *Run Silent, Run Deep* **(Holt, 1955)** The submarine *Walrus* patrols Tokyo Bay during World II with "Rich" Richardson, Keith Leone, and Jim Bledsoe aboard.
2. *Dust on the Sea* **(Holt, 1972)** Rich Richardson and his faithful crew take the submarine *Eel* to the Yellow Sea as World War II draws to an end.
3. *Cold Is the Sea* **(Holt, 1978)** In 1960 Rich and two of his former officers find themselves together again when the nuclear sub *Cushing* is threatened by the Russians.

Bean, Gregory (K.)

Harry Starbranch, police chief of Victory, Wyoming, is a former homicide detective from Denver who has come to this small town to escape big-city pressures. Of course, being the protagonist of a mystery series, he is mistaken in his belief that Victory means peace and quiet. Harry is stubborn, competent, and bound to do the right thing as the chief law officer in this close-knit western community. Gregory K. Bean has had a peripatetic newspaper career that has taken him from his native Wyoming to Illinois, Massachusetts, and New Jersey.

1. *No Comfort in Victory* (St. Martin's, 1995) Harry Starbranch's visions of a restful tenure as chief of police in Victory, Wyoming, are shattered when a teenage girl is raped and murdered and two dead men turn up in the vicinity.
2. *Long Shadows in Victory* (St. Martin's, 1996) The Posse Comitatus, a racist antigovernment militia, seems to be behind the murder of a local junk collector and the vandalism of Jewish and Mexican establishments.
3. *Death in Victory, A* (St. Martin's, 1997) When Liam O'Bannion is shot to death with Curly Ahern's gun, Curly—mayor of Victory, Harry's best friend, and father of Liam's abused lover, Faith—seems to be the prime suspect.
4. *Grave Victory* (St. Martin's, 1998) Old friend Cassie Buchanan asks Starbranch to investigate the conviction of her son Carl for the murder of a student at the University of Wyoming.

Bear, Greg(ory Dale)

I. California-born Greg Bear is a leader in the generation of science-fiction writers who came of professional age in the eighties. He has been awarded Hugos and Nebulas, science-fiction's top honors, for his stories and novellas. The Way series, which has reached three volumes so far, is a classic hard-SF epic dealing with vast scales of space and time. Its basic premise is that of a universe "parallel" to ours that can be reached only through the Way, a kind of cosmic corridor.

1. *Eon* (Bluejay, 1985) An asteroid converted into a spaceship by humans in a parallel universe enters our solar system.
2. *Eternity* (Warner, 1988) The Way, a corridor into the alternative universe, is about to be opened despite the objections of the warlike Jarts.
3. *Legacy* (Tor, 1995) A troubleshooter named Olmy is dispatched through the Way to deal with an antitechnological group who have set up a radically different society on an Earth-like planet.

II. Another pair of novels puts a spin on the alien-invasion theme, postulating two alien races: one benign, one a race of self-replicating robots that want to tear Earth apart and use the materials to make more robots.

1. *Forge of God, The* (Tor, 1987) An alien artifact uncovered in Death Valley leads to the unsettling discovery that Earth is about to be invaded by extraterrestrials.
2. *Anvil of Stars* (Warner, 1992) The Benefactors have built a spaceship for human survivors that a small group of Earthlings wants to use for revenge against the robots.

III. That Bear is also quite adept at fantasy-world creation is shown by this pair of novels, in which teenage musician Michael Perrin strays from Los Angeles to an alternative world ruled by the Sidhe of Celtic legend. The paperback originals have been collected in a revised one-volume edition called *Songs of Earth and Tower* (Tor, 1995).

1. *Infinity Concerto, The* (Berkley, 1984) Michael Perrin is left the key to a mysterious building by an elderly Hollywood composer.
2. *Serpent Mage, The* (Berkley, 1986) Michael returns to Los Angeles only to find that some of his friends and enemies from the Land of the Serpent Gods have followed him.

IV. By 2047 psychology has developed into a true science, and most members of the population of Los Angeles have achieved balanced personalities through therapy (enforced by the police). But, of course, the law of unintended consequences kicks in, and half the people in the United States are unemployed and addicted to LitVid, a kind of semi-pornographic virtual reality. This pair of novels explores a plausible near future.

1. *Queen of Angels* (Warner, 1990) In the Los Angeles of 2047, public defender Mary Choy is assigned to a rare murder case: poet Emmanuel Goldsmith has killed his publisher's daughter.
2. *Slant* (Tor, 1997) In 2050 the sentient computers Roddy and Jill are battling for control of the United States. Agent Jack Giffey is transferred from Seattle to the strange quasi republic of "Green Idaho" to try tip the balance in Jill's favor.

V. With Gregory Benford (q.v.) and David Brin (q.v.), Bear has written a volume of a new trilogy to augment Isaac Asimov's (q.v.) classic Foundation series.

1. *Foundation and Chaos* (Harper, 1998) In the second volume of the new series, Hari Seldon, nearing completion of his vast scheme, is put on trial for treason against the Galactic Empire.

VI. Nebula Award–winning *Darwin's Radio* and its sequel, *Darwin's Children,* further confirm Bear's reputation as a master of hard SF. Tackling the theme of punctuated equilibrium, a hot issue among scientists today, Bear postulates a near future in which long-dormant genes in humans are awakened by a virus that produces millions of genetically enhanced babies who may be the future of *Homo sapiens*—and may spell the end of humanity as we know it.

1. *Darwin's Radio* (Del Rey, 1999) Anthropologist Mitch Rafelson has discovered the mummified remains of an abnormal Neanderthal baby. Molecular biologist Kaye Lang has unearthed evidence that "junk" DNA may have an evolutionary purpose. Virus hunter Christopher Dicken is investigating a new virus that strikes expectant mothers and their fetuses.
2. *Darwin's Children* (Del Rey, 2003) Millions of genetically enhanced babies have been born to mothers infected with the SHEVA virus. Stella Nova, daughter of Kaye Lang and Mitch Rafelson, has been forced into a concentration camp for "virus children" by a nervous and repressive US government.

Beaton, M. C.

PSEUDONYM OF Marion Chesney

I. The prolific Chesney (q.v.), in addition to her successful Regency romance series, has been writing two detective series under the Beaton pseudonym. The first series is located in Chesney-Beaton's native Scotland and features Hamish MacBeth, gangly, carrot-haired, lazy, but intelligent constable of the Highland Scottish village of Lochdubh. The series contains good plots, humor, quaint locals, and continuing characters such as MacBeth; his light of love, Priscilla Halburton-Smythe; his nemesis, Detective Chief Inspector Blair; and Towser the dog.

1. *Death of a Gossip* (St. Martin's, 1985) Hamish has to solve the murder of a vacationing gossip columnist.
2. *Death of a Cad* (St. Martin's, 1987) Caddish Peter Bartlett is found dead in the castle of the decayed local gentry, the Halburton-Smythes.
3. *Death of an Outsider* (St. Martin's, 1988) Hamish is transferred to the town of Cnothan, where the locals hate all "outsiders," including pushy Englishman Mainwaring.
4. *Death of a Perfect Wife* (St. Martin's, 1989) Trixie Thomas, do-gooding English interloper in Lochdubh, is murdered.

5. *Death of a Hussy* (St. Martin's, 1990) The dearth of crime in Lochdubh has led to Hamish's transfer to Strathbane, but the Lochdubhers want him back.

6. *Death of a Snob* (St. Marin's, 1991) Hamish takes a busman's holiday at a health farm on the island of Eileencraig at the request of its owner, Jane Weatherby.

7. *Death of a Prankster* (St. Martin's, 1992) Practical joker Andrew Trent's latest prank seems to have lead to his murder by one of a large number of family and friends who have gathered together at his behest.

8. *Death of a Glutton* (St. Martin's, 1993) Peta Gore, one of the organizers of the spouse hunt of the Checkmate Singles Club, dies with an apple lodged in her gullet.

9. *Death of a Travelling Man* (St. Martin's, 1993) MacBeth, having been promoted to sergeant rather against his will, is saddled with the nasty-neat Police Constable Willie Lamont.

10. *Death of a Charming Man* (Mysterious, 1994) The arrival of handsome newcomer Peter Hynd leads to a flurry of trips to the hairdresser and aerobics classes by the belles of Lochdubh.

11. *Death of a Nag* (Mysterious, 1995) After his unfair demotion and breakup with the fair Priscilla, Hamish takes a short vacation at Friendly House in the seaside resort of Skag.

12. *Death of a Macho Man* (Mysterious, 1996) Hamish is gleefully named as prime suspect by Detective Chief Inspector Blair when oversize, blustery Randy Duggan is found murdered after Hamish has accepted his challenge to a fight.

13. *Death of a Dentist* (Mysterious, 1997) After a spat with Priscilla, Hamish goes to the local dentist in Lochdubh with a raging toothache but finds the man dead on the floor of his "surgery."

14. *Death of a Scriptwriter* (Mysterious, 1998) The Scottish Television mystery series featuring Patricia Martyn-Broyd's detective, Lady Harriet, is stricken with a series of disasters.

15. *Death of an Addict* (Mysterious, 1999) Tommy Jarret, recovering drug addict, sequestered in Lochdubh to write his autobiography, is found dead of an overdose.

16. *Highland Christmas, A* (Mysterious, 1999) Something of a change of pace (no murders to be solved; no *Death* in the title), this volume is a holiday tale featuring MacBeth's efforts to liven up Christmas festivities in dour Lochdubh.

17. *Death of a Dustman* (Mysterious, 2001) Fergus MacLeod, the village "dustman" (trash collector) turns up dead in a "wheelie-bin" after his appointment as environmental officer.

18. *Death of a Celebrity* (Mysterious, 2002) Crystal French, a glamorous but nasty commentator on the local television station, is murdered, and Hamish is not lacking for suspects among the locals or the television people.

19. *Death of a Village* (Mysterious, 2003) The villagers of Stoyre have become even more religious and taciturn than usual, so Hamish knows something is wrong.

20. *Death of a Poisoned Pen* (Mysterious, 2003) A series of poison-pen letters is rankling the people of the nearby town of Braikie. Jenny Ogilvie, London friend of Priscilla Halburton-Smythe, decides to annoy Priscilla by romancing Hamish.

21. *Death of a Bore* (Mysterious, 2005) Concerns the mysterious death of a self-styled "literary writer" and world-class bore in Lochdubh.

22. *Death of a Dreamer* (Mysterious, 2006) The suspicious suicide of artist Effie Garrard is followed by the murder of a noisy American tourist.

23. *Death of a Maid* (Mysterious, 2007) Gossipy housecleaner Mavis Gillispie is found beaten to death with her own pail.

24. *Death of a Gentle Lady* (Grand Central, 2008) Hamish takes pity on Ayesha, a beautiful Turkish maid in danger of being deported, and asks her to marry him.

II. Agatha Raisin, former owner of a London public relations firm, has retired from business at the age of 53 but hasn't retired from life. When she settles in the picturesque Cotswold village of Carsley, she is still on the lookout for romance and ready to get involved in local affairs, including the occasional murder mystery. An English-cozy series with elements of E. F. Benson's (q.v.) Lucia series.

1. *Agatha Raisin and the Quiche of Death* (St. Martin's, 1992) New arrival Agatha enters a local bake-off with fatal results for food judge Reg Cummings-Brown.

2. *Agatha Raisin and the Vicious Vet* (St. Martin's, 1993) Veterinarian Paul Bladen, who conceals a hatred for animals under his charming exterior, is killed by a hypodermic injection intended for a horse.

3. *Agatha Raisin and the Potted Gardener* (St. Martin's, 1994) Beautiful newcomer Mary Fortune has captivated Agatha's love-interest James Lacey by encouraging his passion for gardening.

4. *Agatha Raisin and the Walkers of Dembley* (St. Martin's, 1995) After a six-month stay in London, Agatha returns to the Cotswolds and the murder of Jessica Tratinck, leader of a walking group in nearby Dembley.

5. *Agatha Raisin and the Murderous Marriage* (St. Martin's, 1996) Agatha's marriage to James Lacey is interrupted by the arrival of her believed-to-dead first husband, Jimmy Raisin. Soon thereafter, Jimmy Raisin is indeed dead, and Agatha and James are leading suspects.

6. *Agatha Raisin and the Terrible Tourist* (St. Martin's, 1997) Agatha chases after the still-unmarried James Lacey and finds him in Cyprus, but their reunion is marred by the death of obnoxious British tourist Rose Wilcox. However, baronet Sir Charles Fraith offers her some comfort.

7. *Agatha Raisin and the Wellspring of Death* (St. Martin's, 1998) Agatha comes out of retirement to do public relations for a company that wants to bottle the water from the local Ancombe spring, but a body turns up.

8. *Agatha Raisin and the Wizard of Evesham* (St. Martin's, 1999) Ill at ease in Carsley while James Lacey rambles on the Continent, Agatha gets in over her head when she investigates a new beautician in Evesham.

9. *Agatha Raisin and the Witch of Wyckhadden* (St. Martin's, 1999) After losing her hair in *Agatha Raisin and the Wizard of Evesham*, Agatha, sequestered in a seaside resort, consults a witch for a hair-rejuvenating tonic, but then the witch is murdered.

10. *Agatha Raisin and the Fairies of Fryfam* (St. Martin's, 2000) Agatha, spurned by James Lacey and encouraged by a fortune-teller's prediction, resettles with her two cats, Boswell and Hodge, to the village of Fryfam, in Norfolk, where she winds up investigating, with the help of Sir Charles Fraith, the murder of a local squire.

11. *Agatha Raisin and the Love from Hell* (St. Martin's, 2002) After marrying (finally), Agatha and James Lacey almost immediately break apart over matters of alleged infidelity. Then James's supposed mistress is murdered, and he is missing. Sir Charles again comes to Agatha's aid.

12. *Agatha Raisin and the Day the Floods Came* (St. Martin's, 2002) When her husband, James, runs off to a monastery in France, Agatha takes an island vacation where a newlywed husband drowns his bride.

13. *Agatha Raisin and the Case of the Curious Curate* (St. Martin's, 2003) Agatha's new romantic prospect, curate Tristan Delon, suffers an untimely death, leaving some strange mysteries behind.

14. *Agatha Raisin and the Haunted House* (St. Martin's, 2003) Agatha's handsome new neighbor, Paul Chatterton, joins her in the investigation of a haunted house complete with whispers, footsteps, and a cold white mist.

15. *Deadly Dance, The* (St. Martin's, 2004) Agatha opens her own detective agency, Raisin Investigation, but business is rather commonplace till Catherine Laggat-Brown reports a death threat to her daughter. Variant title: *Agatha Raisin and the Deadly Dance*.

16. *Agatha Raisin and the Perfect Paragon* (St. Martin's, 2005) Agatha's client Raymond Smedley is determined to prove that his wife, Mabel, is unfaithful.

17. *Love, Lies and Liquor* (St. Martin's, 2006) Agatha's ex-husband, James Lacey, invites her to a holiday in Snoth-on-Sea, Sussex, a resort that has seen better days. Variant title: *Agatha Raisin and Love, Lies and Liquor*.

18. *Kissing Christmas Goodbye* (St. Martin's, 2007) Agatha hires teenage Toni Gilmour to run the pet recovery end of her detective business. Eighty-year-old matriarch Phyllis Tamworth, of Manor House in the Cotswolds, suspects that family members are plotting to kill her before she can disinherit them.

Beck, K(athrine) K(ristine)

I. Lounge singer Jane da Silva has been left a large legacy by her uncle with the strange stipulation that she take on his profession of private investigator, solving seemingly hopeless cases that no one else will take on. The money is managed by the Foundation for Righting Wrongs, whose trustees have stringent criteria for meeting the terms of the will. The feisty, clever Seattle-based da Silva proves equal to the task.

1. *Hopeless Case, A* (Mysterious, 1992) When the thirtysomething expatriate widow da Silva returns to Seattle, her first case is that of Leonora Martin, a talented but impecunious young musician.

2. *Amateur Night* (Mysterious, 1993) Kevin Shea was convicted of killing Betty Cox in her Seattle drugstore. His past was against him, but did he really commit the crime?

3. *Electric City* (Mysterious, 1994) Irene March, an employee at a news-clipping service, disappears after winning $20,000 on TV's *Jeopardy*.

4. *Cold Smoked* (Mysterious, 1995) The reporter for *Seafood Now* bursts into the lounge where Jane is singing, screaming that there is a dead woman in her bathtub.

II. Beck's other mystery series, featuring Stanford coed Iris Cooper, is set in the 1920s. Iris works rather edgily with smart-talking reporter Jack Clancy in solving crimes in this series of lighthearted mysteries with a nice period flavor.

1. *Death in a Deck Chair* (Walker, 1984) Iris Cooper's romance with the ship's pianist is interrupted when Mr. Twist is found dead in a deck chair.

2. *Murder in a Mummy Case* (Walker, 1986) An otherwise rather dull Easter vacation with the family of possible beau Egyptologist Clarence Brockhurst is enlivened by the discovery in a mummy casket of a dead woman "in her scanties."

3. *Peril under the Palms* (Walker, 1989) Iris Cooper and Jack Clancy go to Hawaii to search for sugar heiress Antoinette Caulfield's missing mother.

Bedford, Sybille

Suggest this pair of novels by an English author to readers who like thoughtful women's stories. Bedford's books are well written and wonderfully evocative of Europe in the 1920s and 1930s. They concern Anna Howland, an American heiress who marries an Italian prince; her daughter, Constanza; and her granddaughter, Flavia. How these women meet the crises in their lives profoundly affects the others. The German-born Bedford's novels, which include *A Legacy* (1957) and *Jigsaw* (1989), were reissued in 2001 by Counterpoint.

1. *Favorite of the Gods, A* (Simon & Schuster, 1963) Anna's New England girlhood is a curious preparation for her married life in Italy, and Constanza must make her own bargain with life. UK title: *A Favourite of the Gods*.

2. *Compass Error, A* (Knopf, 1969) Constanza, now settled in a French coastal town, is painfully affected by Flavia's coming-of-age.

Begley, Louis

Albert Schmidt is a recently widowed, wealthy, retired WASP attorney living in Bridgehampton (Long Island, New York). Schmidt's daughter Charlotte is, to his disapproval, marrying an ambitious Jewish lawyer. Schmidt more or less goes off the rails when he has an affair with Carrie, a Puerto Rican waitress younger than his daughter. *Schmidt Delivered*, the sequel, continues Schmidt's saga with the arrival of a nouveau riche neighbor. This pair of novels of manners, full of finely nuanced writing and dry wit, describes a not very likable but quite interesting man who finds his verities eroding, but never manages to have a real epiphany about his values. The Jack Nicholson movie *About Schmidt* (2002), adapted from the first novel, has a quite different plot, but manages to capture much of the wry tone. Louis Begley (né Ludwik Begleiter), was born in Poland, survived the Holocaust, emigrated to the United States, became a prominent attorney, and published his first novel, *Wartime Lies* (Knopf, 1991), when he was in his fifties.

1. *About Schmidt* (Knopf, 1996) Retired, widowed Albert Schmidt is ill at ease in the Hamptons as his beautiful, intelligent daughter Charlotte is (to him) making the unintelligent choice of marrying a Jewish lawyer.

2. *Schmidt Delivered* (Knopf, 2000) Schmidt's live-in mistress, the Puerto Rican ex-waitress Carrie, refuses his offer of marriage. Meanwhile an egregious nouveau riche Egyptian Jew, Michael Mansour, has become Schmidt's neighbor, and his daughter Charlotte is in trouble.

Belgrave, Laura

Claudia Hershey is a police detective in the sleepy Central Florida backwater of Indian Run. Claudia, who has a twin sister, is a feisty lady who doesn't like to leave well enough alone. Silver Dagger is a consortium of southern mystery writers who have come together to publish mystery novels in hard cover (limited editions) and trade paperbacks.

1. *In the Spirit of Murder* (Silver Dagger, 2000) Claudia Hershey gets involved when a medium turns up dead in Indian Run.

2. *Quietly Dead* (Silver Dagger, 2001) When the friendless cat lady of Indian Run is found dead in the bathtub of her trailer, everyone except Claudia writes it off as an accident.

3. *Deadly Associations* (Silver Dagger, 2003) A hostage situation in the gated community of Willow Whisper results in the death of Steven Hemmer, the hostage taker.

Bell, Madison Smartt

Haiti's war for independence from France (1791–1802), as described in this trilogy by Madison Smartt Bell, was a Byzantine affair, with black slaves, free mulattos, white royalists, and white republicans vying for power in a society in which dozens of pseudo-scientifically racial "shades" were recognized. This tangled history is told by Doctor Antoine Hebert, a Frenchman who is moves to Haiti just before the beginning of the revolt. Historical characters, such as the tragic Toussaint L'Ouverture, mingle with fictional ones in this mesmerizing account, full of eroticism and blood (too much of the latter, according to some critics). Bell, a Tennessee native and writer-in-residence at Goucher College, has written several other well-received novels.

1. *All Souls' Rising* (**Pantheon, 1995**) In 1791 a slave revolt led by the enigmatic Toussaint L'Ouverture breaks out in Haiti. Antoine Hebert, a newly arrived French doctor, falls in love with a freed mulatto.
2. *Master of the Crossroads* (**Pantheon, 2000**) In 1793 Toussaint tries to consolidate his power; his godson Riau, an ex-slave, expresses his distrust of the white planters; Hebert searches for his errant mulatto mistress, Nanon; and white planter Michel Arnaud and his wife, Claudine, who is possessed by Voudou spirit Baron Samedi, try to put their lives together.
3. *Stone That the Builder Refused, The* (**Pantheon, 2004**) In 1802, as a French invasion commanded by Napoléon's brother-in-law, Leclerc, lands in Saint Domingue (Haiti), Toussaint's rule begins to unravel, and his generals betray him.

Bell, Nancy

I. Fiona Wooten "Biggie" Weatherford, grande dame of the east Texas town of Job's Crossing, is sort of a cross between Auntie Mame and Miss Marple. With her 12-year-old grandson, J. R.(who narrates her adventures); her "voodoo" housekeeper, Willie Mae; and her handyman-chauffeur, Rosebud Robichaux, the likable and eccentric Biggie gets to the bottom of the skulduggery that seems to run rampant in this tiny nest of "good-ole-boys" and country-fried humor. Nancy Bell's first mystery novel, *Biggie and the Poisoned Politician*, published when the author was 64 years old, was nominated for the 1997 Agatha Award for the best first mystery.

1. *Biggie and the Poisoned Politician* (**St. Martin's, 1996**) Planning for Job's Crossing's Pioneer Days festival is punctuated by an exploding car, plans for a sanitary landfill next to Biggie's family farm, and the mysterious death of the town's mayor.
2. *Biggie and the Mangled Mortician* (**St. Martin's, 1997**) When Monk Carter, Job's Crossing's extremely ugly new mortician, fails to show up for a rehearsal of *HMS Pinafore,* this is only the start of a series of odd events.
3. *Biggie and the Fricasseed Fat Man* (**St, Martin's, 1998**) The body of Firman Birdsong is found covered in gravy at the grand opening of his chicken restaurant, and J. R. is threatened with adoption by his maternal grandparents.
4. *Biggie and the Meddlesome Mailman* (**St. Martin's, 1999**) Mailman Luther Abernathy, who reads everyone's mail and passes the news along, is murdered, and the Lions Club donates a piece of land to the Daughters of the Republic of Texas that is infested with chicken offal and a band of wackos who are planning to bomb every governmental site in the vicinity.
5. *Biggie and the Quincy Ghost* (**St. Martin's, 2001**) A visit to the neighboring town of Quincy to study how its historical society made the unpromising town into a tourist attraction turns up a ghost in the local inn and a dead body in a courtyard fountain.
6. *Biggie and the Devil Diet* (**St. Martin's, 2002**) Old flame and (unbeknownst to him) biological grandfather of J. R. Rex Barnwell returns to Job's Crossing with a young wife and plans to open the Bar-LB Ranch, a dude ranch for fat adolescent girls.

II. Bell has started a new mysteries series featuring Judge Jackson Crain of Post Oak, Texas, and his 13-year-old daughter, Patty.

1. *Restored to Death* (**St. Martin's, 2003**) Recently widowed Judge Crain is judged to be "in need of a wife." One of the would-be matchmakers, Crain's sister-in-law Dora, is murdered, possibly by her husband, who was seeking a divorce.
2. *Death Splits a Hair* (**St. Martin's, 2005**) The judge looks into the murder of Joe Junior McBride, popular barber of Post Oak.
3. *Paint the Town Dead* (**St. Martin's, 2008**) Will the judge determine who really murdered real-estate agent Tom Delgado?

Bellamann, Henry

PSEUDONYM OF Heinrich Hauer

The midwestern town of Kings Row, thought to be based on Fulton, Missouri, future site of Winston Churchill's Iron Curtain speech, is more the subject than the setting of these readable melodramas. Seen through the eyes of Parris Mitchell from his school days in the 1890s through World War I, the town's pioneer ideals seem to have degenerated into cynicism, greed, and incompetence. Parris, a sensitive young man who becomes a psychiatrist, hates the cruelty and pettiness of the town's residents but is too loyal to leave. A third planned volume was never written. *Kings Row* was made into a movie featuring Ronald Reagan.

1. *Kings Row* (**Simon & Schuster, 1940**) Parris grows up and goes off to study medicine as tragedy befalls his childhood friend Drake McHugh.
2. *Parris Mitchell of Kings Row* (**Simon & Schuster, 1948**) This begins in 1916 and tells how young Dr. Mitchell, now established as a psychiatrist at the State Hospital for the Insane, is almost destroyed by his childhood enemy Fulmer Green. Completed by the author's wife, Katherine, after his death.

Belle, Pamela

I. English historical novelist Pamela Belle writes accurate and entertaining novels about England and Scotland in the Stuart period of the 1600s. The Goldhayes, or Heron, series follows the fortunes of the Heron family as they live their lives against the background of turbulent historical events. The first three novels form a trilogy taking place during the middle 1600s of the English Civil War, Commonwealth, and Restoration. The last novel published is a prequel set in the England of the 1480s.

1. *Lodestar, The* (**St. Martin's, 1989**) During the reign of Edward IV, the ambitious Christie Heron ties his fortunes to those of Edward's brother, Richard, Duke of Gloucester.
2. *Moon in the Water, The* (**Berkley, 1984**) Thomazine Heron, an orphan living on her uncle's estate, falls in love with free-spirited cousin Francis but is tricked into a loveless marriage.
3. *Chains of Fate, The* (**Berkley, 1984**) The impetuous Thomazine deserts her husband and son in the midst of the civil war to seek out her beloved Francis.

4. *Alethea* (Berkley, 1985) Eleven-year-old Alethea, Thomazine's daughter, is sent to London to study painting as Charles II is restored to the British throne.

II. The St. Barbes of Wintercombe are the protagonists in another series, which covers the second half of the 17th century, from the civil war to the Glorious Revolution of 1688.

1. *Wintercombe* (St, Martin's, 1988) While her husband is away fighting for the Parliamentary cause in 1644, Silence St. Barbe must defend Wintercombe against the Royalists quartered there.
2. *Herald of Joy* (St. Martin's, 1989) Silence's autocratic husband, Sir George, whom she has betrayed, dies, leaving a will controlling her and her children from beyond the grave.
3. *Falling Star, A* (St. Martin's, 1990) Silence's children and grandchildren are caught up in the Duke of Monmouth's revolt against James II.
4. *Treason's Gift* (St. Martin's, 1993) A breach comes between Sir Alexander St. Barbe and his bereaved wife, Louise, which leads to his departure for the Netherlands and the cause of the Prince of Orange.

III. As a change of pace, Belle has produced the Silver City trilogy, an alternative-history fantasy set in the Bronze Age and Iron Age. The Silver City is Zithiran, which is beset by barbarians from without and intrigue among the royal family within.

1. *Silver City, The* (Tor, 1994) Nomadic tribeswoman Halthis chances upon a barbaric Ska'i horde surrounding the city of Zithiran, but when she tries to warn the Zithirans, she runs into a world of sinister intrigue.
2. *Wolf Within, The* (Tor, 1995) Young Bron, uneasy about his magical powers and the claims of the Wolf God upon him, leaves his Zithiran home.
3. *Blood Imperial* (Tor, 1996) After the death of the emperor, the surviving members of the Toktel'y imperial family vie for the empty Onyx Throne.

Benford, Gregory

I. Research astrophysicist, physics professor, and science-fiction writer Gregory Benford is one of the few persons to have received both a grant from the National Science Foundation and a Nebula Award. Benford, who started writing science fiction as a distraction from working on his doctoral thesis, is particularly interested in the ramifications of contact with aliens and the uses and misuses of technology. While the critics regard the partially autobiographical *Timescape* (Simon & Schuster, 1980) as Benford's masterpiece, the six-volume Galactic Center series, completed in 1995, is the basis for his reputation as a leading hard-SF writer. Until number 6 in the series was published, numbers 1 and 2 and numbers 3, 4, and 5 seemed to be two separate series.

1. *In the Ocean of Night* (Dial, 1977) Sometime in the near future, British astronaut Nigel Walmsley is sent into space by NASA to destroy the errant asteroid Icarus, which turns out to be an abandoned alien interstellar vessel.
2. *Across the Sea of Suns* (Timescape, 1984) The elderly Walmsley investigates the source of mysterious radio signals from space, as monstrous aliens called Swarmers take over Earth's oceans.
3. *Great Sky River* (Bantam, 1987) Humans on the planet Snowglade have been reduced to the status of wandering nomads by the technologically superior Mechs, self-replicating machines.

4. *Tides of Light* (Bantam, 1989) Killeen, of the Bishop Tribe, is leading an expedition from Snowglade to another seemingly inhabitable world.
5. *Furious Gulf* (Bantam, 1994) The spaceship *Argo* from Snowglade is still on the run from the genocidal Mechs as it heads toward the Galactic Center.
6. *Sailing Bright Eternity* (Bantam, 1995) In the conclusion to the Galactic Center series, Nigel Walmsley relates his adventures to Toby Bishop as the Bishop family and Walmsley deal with several other life-forms in the quest for ultimate survival.

II. With Greg Bear (q.v.) and David Brin (q.v.), Benford has written a volume of a new trilogy to augment Isaac Asimov's (q.v.) classic Foundation series.

1. *Foundation's Fear* (Harper, 1997) In the first volume of the new trilogy, Hari Seldon, a candidate for first minister of the Galactic Empire, faces computer simulations of the re-created personalities of Joan of Arc and Voltaire.

III. Mars and Pluto are the destinations in this pair of novels set in the early 21st century as billionaire John Axelrod and his daughter take over the space race from NASA.

1. *Martian Race, The* (Warner, 1999) Billionaire space aficionado John Axelrod's Mars expedition, captained by veteran astronaut Julia Barth, is in a race with a Chinese-European team to be the first to Mars and back.
2. *Sunborn, The* (Warner, 2005) Julia and Viktor Barth, the first astronauts to land on Mars, are sent to the planet Pluto, which seems to be heating up and developing an atmosphere.

Benjamin, Carol Lea

Dog trainer–private investigator Rachel Alexander and her canine associate Dash (short for Dashiell) operate out of Greenwich Village. The well-characterized Dash is a trained pit bull who is formidable when required, prescient in sensing danger, and intelligent and lovable above all. Rachel and Dash patrol the "mean streets" of New York, taking on cases ranging from missing dogs to murder in this series of mysteries whose titles pun on the titles of famous detective novels of the past. Numbers 1 and 2 have been published together as *Dash, P.I.* (Walker, 1997). Carol Lea Benjamin is a professional dog trainer who has written nonfiction books about dogs (e.g., *Dog Problems*, Doubleday, 1981) and juveniles.

1. *This Dog for Hire* (Walker, 1996) An artist, a hit-and-run driver, and a missing basenji (a barkless dog of show quality) take Rachel and Dash from a posh art gallery opening to the famed Westminster Dog Show.
2. *Dog Who Knew Too Much, The* (Walker, 1997) The suicide death of Lisa Jacobs at the tai chi school where she worked leads Rachel to impersonate Lisa's cousin to discover what led Lisa to this desperate act.
3. *Hell of a Dog, A* (Walker, 1998) A dog-training symposium in a New York City hotel has brought together a group of mutually antipathetic participants who strongly disagree with each other's training methods. Then the trainers die off, one by one.
4. *Lady Vanishes* (Walker, 1999) Harry Dietrich, co-owner of Harbor View, a Greenwich Village residential treatment center for the developmentally challenged, has suffered a seemingly accidental death, and the home's therapy dog, a puli named Lady, is missing.

5. *Wrong Dog, The* (**Walker, 2000**) A tale about an epileptic who is murdered; her seizure-alert bull terrier, Blanche; and Blanche's purported clone, Bianca.
6. *Long Good Boy, The* (**Walker, 2001**) Three "trannys" (transsexual prostitutes) hire Rachel to find a friend's killer, leading Rachel, Dash, and a dachshund called Clint into New York's meat-packing district.
7. *Fall Guy* (**Morrow, 2004**) Rachel has been named executor of the will of New York City policeman Tim O'Fallon, whom she barely knew.
8. *Without a Word* (**Morrow, 2005**) Rachel reluctantly accepts the case of a woman who has been missing for five years, touched by the woman's daughter, who has been mute since her mother disappeared.
9. *Hard Way, The* (**Morrow, 2006**) Retired businessman Gardner Redstone was pushed to his death on Manhattan's subway tracks. Police believe that a homeless man was Redstone's killer, but his daughter and Rachel Alexander aren't so sure.

Benjamin, Curt

The Seven Brothers is a lively fantasy trilogy set in an East Asian milieu. Llesho and his six brothers are plunged from royalty in Thebin into slavery when the barbarian Harn invade, but they rise again, defeating a series of enemies, including the evil sorcerer Markko. With lots of action but no sex, this series will especially appeal to younger readers. *Lords of Grass and Thunder* (DAW, 2005) is set in the same Mongolia-like world.

1. *Prince of Shadow, The* (**DAW, 2001**) Llesho and his six brothers are enslaved by the Harn, who destroy the royal family of Thebin.
2. *Prince of Dreams, The* (**DAW, 2002**) Llesho, reunited with two of his brothers, searches for the other four, fighting battles with the Harn and the evil magician Markko and learning from a shaman how to master the dream world.
3. *Gates of Heaven, The* (**DAW, 2003**) Prince Llesko races against time and Markko as he struggles to complete his quest in the conclusion of the Seven Brothers trilogy.

Bennett, Arnold

Like Thomas Hardy, Bennett set most of his novels in a fictitious locale heavily based on a real district of England. His Five Towns (the industrial Midlands), which he immortalized in *The Old Wives' Tale* (1908), also provided the setting for many other works, including the Clayhanger series. The figure of Edwin Clayhanger is thought to be highly autobiographical, and it is the conflict between the young man and his overbearing father that makes the first book in the series so powerful.

1. *Clayhanger* (**Dutton, 1910**) Covers the youth of Edwin Clayhanger and his relationship with his father, Darius.
2. *Hilda Lessways* (**Dutton, 1911**) Concerns young Hilda's girlhood and disastrous first marriage.
3. *These Twain* (**Doran, 1916**) Hilda and Edwin finally marry, but wedded bliss eludes them.
4. *Roll Call, The* (**Doran, 1919**) In this addendum to what was originally conceived of as a trilogy of novels, Hilda's son George wins recognition as an architect.

Bennett, Nigel

Actor Nigel Bennett, star of the *Forever Knight* TV series, has coauthored, with P. N. Elrod (q.v.) a vampire series based on his TV persona. Richard Dun (aka Richard d'Orleans, aka Lancelot du Lac) is the son of a noble Norman family who becomes a vampire who lives in the present as a force for good in action that spans millennia and involves the likes of King Arthur and the current prime minister of Canada. A rather campy parody of dark fantasy that will appeal to vampire-fiction lovers.

1. *Keeper of the King* (**Baen, 1997**) Richard d'Orleans, scion of a noble Norman family, is recruited into vampiredom by the seductive Lady Sabra, and he takes on a series of missions, including acting as bodyguard to the legendary King Arthur and saving the Canadian prime minister from a 1996 IRA assassination.
2. *His Father's Son* (**Baen, 2001**) With flashbacks to Richard's days as Arthur's Lancelot, the action includes Colombian drug dealers and other baddies and a revenge plot.
3. *Siege Perilous* (**Baen, 2004**) Old enemy Charon the Assassin returns, bent on destroying both the Otherside and the Realside in his thirst for revenge against Richard.

Benson, Ann

Ann Benson writes medical thrillers that span the centuries. *The Plague Tales*, *The Burning Road*, and *The Physician's Tale* tell the parallel stories of 14th-century physician Alejandro Canches and 21st-century neurologist Janie Crowe, linked by Alejandro's "book of cures." *Thief of Souls* (Delacorte, 2002), which has different main characters, is the story of two plagues separated by nearly 600 years. Ann Benson, a Connecticut resident, has also published several books on beadworking.

1. *Plague Tales, The* (**Delacorte, 1997**) Young Jewish physician Alejandro, persecuted in his native Spain, eventually winds up in the court of England's Edward III. The 21st-century former neurologist Janie Crowe, who has lost her family in the Outbreaks, unwittingly uncovers a new strain of bubonic plague.
2. *Burning Road, The* (**Delacorte, 1999**) Alejandro Canches becomes involved in a peasant revolt in France during the Hundred Years' War. Janie Crowe, in the aftermath of DR SAM, a staph infection that ravaged the world, is seeking a genetic cure for a disease that attacks Jewish boys.
3. *Physician's Tale, The* (**Delacorte, 2006**) Janie Crowe is living with a survivalist band in the hills of the American Northeast. Alejandro's daughter is caught in the clutches of Edward III of England. A scribe named Geoffrey Chaucer has a plan for her escape.

Benson, E(dward) F(rederic)

I. Mrs. Emmeline Lucas, or Lucia (pronounced in the Italian manner that she affects), is equal parts snob and busybody, and the leading light of the small town of Riseholme. Three generations of readers have found her pretensions delightful and the misadventures of her set captivating. Lucia's rivalry with the redoubtable Miss Elizabeth Mapp (introduced in number 3) and her move to the town of Tilling (based on Rye, where Henry James spent many years, and where E. F. Benson was mayor) added spice to the mix.

Make Way for Lucia (Crowell, 1977) is an omnibus volume containing all six novels as well as a newly published short story, "The Male Impersonator." An additional Mapp story, "Desirable Residences," was collected in *Desirable Residences and Other Stories* (Oxford, 1991). The Lucia-Mapp wars were the subject of a PBS series.

1. *Queen Lucia* **(Doran, 1920)** Introduces Riseholme and its inhabitants, including Lucia; her husband, Philip (Peppino); her friend Georgie Pillson; and her archrival, Daisy Quantock.
2. *Miss Mapp* **(Doran, 1923)** Introduces Miss Elizabeth Mapp, of the seaside town of Tilling, and her bachelor neighbors Major Benjy Flint and Captain Puffin. Lucia is absent from this volume.
3. *Lucia in London* **(Doubleday, 1928)** Lucia crashes London society and is taken up as a sort of amusement, but she eventually returns to Riseholme and an ailing Peppino.
4. *Mapp and Lucia* **(Doubleday, 1931)** Now widowed, Lucia rents Miss Mapp's house for the summer and proceeds to take over Tilling society. Contains the episode where Lucia and Mapp are carried out to sea on a kitchen table.
5. *Worshipful Lucia, The* **(Doubleday, 1935)** Mapp is married to Major Benjy. Lucia eventually marries Georgie. In search of new fields to conquer, Lucia enters politics. Original English title: *Lucia's Progress*.
6. *Trouble for Lucia* **(Doubleday, 1939)** Lucia is agile as always in getting out of scrapes: her exploits as mayor of Tilling fill this final volume.

II. Those readers who can't get enough of E. F. Benson's characters might be interested in the earlier trilogy featuring Dodo, short for Dorothea, a British society character supposedly based on Margot Asquith. Dodo's misadventures are nearly reprised by her daughter in the second volume of the series. The Dodo books have been collected in *Dodo* (Crowell, 1978) and *Dodo: An Omnibus* (Hogarth, 1996). A previously uncollected Dodo story is included in *The Feathers and Other Stories* (Oxford, 1994), which also includes a Mapp story, "The Male Impersonator."

1. *Dodo: A Detail of the Day* **(Appleton, 1893)** Follows Dodo's misadventures through two unsuccessful marriages before she comes to her senses and marries her longtime friend Jack.
2. *Dodo's Daughter* **(Century, 1914)** Dodo's daughter nearly makes the same mistakes as her mother. Published in England as *Dodo the Second: A Sequel to Dodo*.
3. *Dodo Wonders* **(Doran, 1921)** Finds Dodo content with family and friends but anxious over the way their lives have been affected by the First World War.

Benson, Raymond

Gildrose Publications, which owns the copyright on Ian Fleming's (q.v.) James Bond novels, transferred their imprimatur from the flagging John Gardner (q.v.) to Raymond Benson, American musical composer and director, computer-game designer, a director of the Ian Fleming Foundation, and author of *The James Bond Bedside Companion* (Dodd Mead, 1984). Benson has proven to be an excellent choice to maintain the James Bond legend: he has maintained the savoir faire, wit, derring-do, exotic locales, over-the-top villains, gorgeous women, and gadgetry of the Fleming creation. Benson has also done the novelization of two James Bond screenplays: *Tomorrow Never Dies* (Berkley, 1997) and *The World Is Not Enough* (Berkley, 1999).

1. *Zero Minus Ten* **(Putnam, 1997)** James Bond preserves the peaceful transfer of power over Hong Kong from Great Britain to China by thwarting the usual gang of villains, including three giant albinos named Tic, Tac, and Toe.

2. *Facts of Death, The* **(Putnam, 1998)** Bond teams up with old ally Felix Leiter in thwarting a sinister plot against Turkey by an extremist Greek organization led by insane "demigod" Konstantine Romanos.
3. *High Time to Kill* **(Putnam, 1999)** The Union, a worldwide organization of terrorists, has stolen the British secret formula for Skin 17, the only aircraft material that can withstand a speed of Mach 7.
4. *Double Shot* **(Putnam, 2000)** The Union is at it again, this time conspiring to assassinate the British and Spanish prime ministers at a summit meeting to decide the fate of Gibraltar. Their weapon: a hit man surgically reconstructed to be Bond's double.
5. *Never Dream of Dying* **(Putnam, 2001)** The Union hatches another diabolical scheme for world domination.
6. *Man with the Red Tattoo, The* **(Putnam, 2002)** Bond reunites with Tiger Tanaka in Japan to thwart the schemes of Coro Yoshida, who wants to punish the West for polluting traditional Japanese culture.

Bentley, E(dmund) C(lerihew)

E. C. Bentley, an English newspaperman, is supposed to have written *Trent's Last Case*, which Agatha Christie (q.v.) regarded as one of the three best detective stories ever written, on a bet from his friend G. K. Chesterton as a demonstration of the fallibility of the deductive method favored by fictional sleuths of that day. Bentley's detective, Philip Trent, age 32, is a successful painter whose imaginative and inquisitive mind makes him a brilliant natural detective. *Trent's Last Case* makes tantalizing references to Trent's earlier cases, but unfortunately his creator let them go unrecorded. Three movie versions of *Trent's Last Case* were produced (1920, 1929, and 1952). *Trent's Case Book* (Knopf, 1953) is an omnibus volume containing all three titles.

1. *Trent's Last Case* **(Century, 1913)** When millionaire financier Sigsbee Manderson is murdered, Trent matches wits with Inspector Murch, of Scotland Yard, and comes up with a brilliant solution that is almost correct. Variant title: *The Woman in Black*. Revised edition published by Knopf in 1929.
2. *Trent's Own Case* **(Knopf, 1936)** Trent himself is Inspector Gideon Bligh's chief suspect in the murder of philanthropist James Randolph. Written with H. Warner Allen.
3. *Trent Intervenes* **(Knopf, 1938)** A collection of short stories.

Berenson, Laurien

In a series crammed with dog-show lore, Melanie Travis, thirtyish sometime special-education teacher, dog owner, and amateur sleuth, solves a series of dog thefts, murders, and other shenanigans. Melanie, who lives in Fairfield County, Connecticut, has better luck with her well-characterized, lovable poodles than with her men: she has a young son, an ex-husband named Bob who keeps on turning up at awkward times, and an off-again, on-again lover, software designer Sam Driver. Laurien Berenson, who lives in Atlanta, Georgia, with a husband, a son, six miniature poodles, and a Welsh pony, has won the Maxwell Award for Fiction, Dog Writers Association of America, three times.

1. *Pedigree to Die For, A* **(Kensington, 1995)** Melanie Travis, a 30-year-old teacher in Stamford, Connecticut, is drawn into the dog-show world when her uncle Max, who breeds standard poodles, dies of a heart attack, and Beau, his star stud dog, is missing.

2. *Underdog* (**Kensington, 1995**) Another case involving a suspicious death and a missing dog: this time the death is that of professional dog handler Jenny Maguire, and the missing dog is named Ziggie.

3. *Dog Eat Dog* (**Kensington, 1996**) Melanie's errant ex-husband Bob turns up after five years; Melanie is grooming and training her standard poodle, Faith, for showdom; and her aunt Peg is nagging her to join the Belle Haven Kennel Club. "Skuldoggery" emerges at Belle Haven: missing money and the murder of a club member.

4. *Hair of the Dog* (**Kensington, 1997**) After Alicia Devane leaves her husband for unpopular dog handler Barry Turk, Barry is shot to death at his home.

5. *Watchdog* (**Kensington, 1998**) Melanie's brother Frank is the leading suspect when his partner, developer Marcus Rattigan, is killed by a falling skylight at a building site in Stamford.

6. *Hush Puppy* (**Kensington, 1999**) Eugene Krebs, the caretaker at Howard Academy in Greenwich, Connecticut, where Melanie is a tutor, is stabbed to death with a pitchfork in his tool shed.

7. *Unleashed* (**Kensington, 2000**) Just when Melanie and Sam Driver seem headed for the altar, Sam's ex-wife, Sheila Vaughn, comes to Fairfield County to start a new magazine, *Woof*, which promises to stir up things in the dog-show world.

8. *Once Bitten* (**Kensington, 2001**) Sam Driver has gone off to "find himself." Melanie's brother Frank is about to be married to beautiful dog-handler Bertie Kennedy. Ex-husband Bob Travis reappears, without his young wife. Then Sara Bentley, who was helping Bertie plan her wedding, disappears.

9. *Hot Dog* (**Kensington, 2002**) Melanie's ex-fiancé Sam and ex-husband Bob are both back in town. A young journalist is hoping to use Melanie's penchant for turning up dead bodies for a story. Melanie's involvement with the custody fight over Dox, a dachshund puppy, leads to crank calls, dognapping, and other odd goings-on.

10. *Best in Show* (**Kensington, 2003**) Melanie travels to a Poodle Club of America dog show in Maryland, where her aunt Peg commands her to work with two eccentric sisters from Georgia. Then one of the sisters has a fatal fall on a hotel porch. The movie comedy *Best in Show* (2000), which is also about a dog show, has no connection with Melanie Travers.

11. *Jingle Bell Bark* (**Kensington, 2004**) Melanie investigates the suspicious death of her eight-year-old son's school-bus driver. Two golden retrievers figure in the story.

12. *Raining Cats and Dogs* (**Kensington, 2005**) Someone suffocates Aunty Mary, dog lover and resident at Winston Pumpernill, in Greenwich, during Melanie's first visit to the nursing home with her poodle as part of a dog-visiting program.

13. *Chow Down* (**Kensington, 2006**) Melanie, receiving a letter telling her that her standard poodle, Faith, is one of five finalists to be "spokesdog" for Chow Down dog food, travels to New York for the reception.

14. *Hounded to Death* (**Kensington, 2007**) A few hours after keynote speaker Charles Evans shocks his audience of dog fanciers by announcing that dog shows are unethical, Evans is discovered dead in a hotel bathtub.

Berent, Mark

If the Vietnam War has done nothing else, it has provided the setting for many novels that keep the debate on our actions and motivations alive decades after the actual events. Former US Air Force pilot and Vietnam War veteran Mark Berent has the background to write a series of novels authentically portraying what it was like to take part in the air war over Vietnam. They are full of enough technical detail and exciting action to delight any military-fiction or techno-thriller buff's heart.

1. *Rolling Thunder* (**Putnam, 1989**) In the Vietnam of 1965, American fighter pilots go out on dangerous missions, drink scotch at officers' clubs, and make passionate love in their spare time.

2. *Steel Tiger* (**Putnam, 1990**) Focuses on the efforts of the US Air Force to cut a vital Vietcong supply line along the Ho Chi Minh Trail.

3. *Phantom Leader* (**Putnam, 1991**) US Air Force officers Bannister, Lochert, and Parker battle the North Vietnamese during the Tet offensive and fret about ignorant politicians and malevolent peace activists back home.

4. *Eagle Station* (**Putnam, 1992**) Bannister and Lochert team up to protect Eagle Station, a clandestine radar installation in Laos, and to make contact with POWs in North Vietnam.

5. *Storm Flight* (**Putnam, 1993**) Bannister, Lochert, and Parker are part of Lieutenant General "Whitey" Whisenand's efforts to rescue captive American airmen from the "Hanoi Hilton."

Berg, Elizabeth

Young army brat Katie Nash has to deal with the loss of her mother, an emotionally abusive military father, and frequent location shifts—from Texas to Missouri—in the course of this (so-far) trilogy of novels set in the early 1960s. Author Berg deals matter-of-factly but sensitively with the trials and triumphs of a loving, lovable but emotionally insecure preadolescent girl who tries to connect with a series of rather unsatisfactory friends and a passionate but platonic first love affair with an older man.

1. *Durable Goods* (**Random House, 1993**) Katie Nash, 12-year-old motherless daughter of an army officer, deals with life on a Texas military base in 1961 and then learns that her family is being transferred to Missouri.

2. *Joy School* (**Random House, 1997**) Katie, dissatisfied with her life and the few friends she has made on a Missouri army base, falls in love with Jimmy, a 23-year-old married gas-station manager.

3. *True to Form* (**Pocket, 2002**) Katie tries to make the best of life on a military base with a series of summer jobs, and her friend Cynthia, but when she wins a free plane ticket to anywhere in the world, she decides to return to Fort Hood, Texas, and former best friend Cherylanne.

Berger, Thomas (Louis)

I. *Little Big Man* has been a cult favorite for more than 40 years, a starring vehicle for Dustin Hoffman, and (according to some critics) the best historical novel ever written. The narrative of 111-year-old Jack Crabb, adopted Cheyenne, frontiersman, and "only White survivor" of Custer's Last Stand, with its revisionist views of legends of the "Great West" such as Custer, Wyatt Earp, and Wild Bill Hickok, supposedly ended with Jack's demise before he related more adventures, tantalizingly referred to at the close of *Little Big Man*. Not so! Jack was merely playing possum to escape an onerous publishing commitment. Jack is back in *The Return of Little Big Man* with further adventures as he travels to London (and an interview with Queen Victoria), mourns the deaths of his friends Sitting Bull and Wild Bill Hickok, second-guesses the fight at the O.K. Corral (Wyatt Earp continues to be among his least favorite people), and carries on an ultimately unsuccessful affair with Libbie, General Custer's widow. Further adventures in the Alaskan gold fields, with Teddy Roosevelt's Rough Riders, and in the movie industry are hinted at, if Jack (and his creator) survive a while longer.

1. *Little Big Man* (Dial, 1964) Jack Crabb, 111 years old and residing in a nursing home, tells about his youthful experiences in a wagon train heading west, his adoption by Cheyennes, his acquaintance with frontier legends, his presence at the Battle of the Little Big Horn, and many other adventures.
2. *Return of Little Big Man, The* (Little, Brown, 1999) Jack Crabb, not dead as reported, continues his narration, carrying him from Custer's Last Stand (1876), a visit to London with Buffalo Bill Cody's Wild West Show, and an eyewitness account of the fight at the O.K. Corral to the Great Fair in Chicago (1893).

II. Not only has Thomas Berger written black comedies such as *Neighbors* (1980) and "historical" reconstructions such as *Arthur Rex* (1978) but he has also authored the Reinhart Saga, a series of comic novels following the career of Carlo Reinhart, a good-natured and guileless fellow who is victimized by all who meet him. Reinhart embodies the average middle-class American's optimism and good intentions, and his disillusionment with the absurdity and fraud of modern life is just as inevitable as it is hilarious. The story takes him from fumbling adolescence into paunchy middle age.

1. *Crazy in Berlin* (Scribner, 1958) As an American soldier in occupied Germany, Reinhart finds himself in a maze of spies and corruption that eventually drives him over the edge.
2. *Reinhart in Love* (Scribner, 1962) Now home and going to college on the GI Bill, Carlo is again ill-used by all; he is married to a shrew and a failure even at suicide.
3. *Vital Parts* (Scribner, 1970) In the bewildering 1970s, Reinhart copes with a fat daughter and a nasty son, pinning his hopes on a cryogenics scheme.
4. *Reinhart's Women* (Delacorte, 1981) Women mean trouble to Reinhart, from his daughter, Winona, and her lesbian lover to a neighbor girlfriend; his ex-wife, Genevieve; and an amorous coworker.

Bergman, Ingmar (Ernest Ingmar)

Noted filmmaker Ingmar Bergman is also an accomplished writer, not only writing the scripts for many of his film and television dramas but also writing autobiographical novels. *The Best Intentions* and *Sunday's Children* started life as television scripts. The subsequent "novelizations" are a mixture of screenplay, memoir, and novel as Bergman compellingly depicts the lives of his parents and his young self. Both novels were translated from the original Swedish by Joan Tate. Bergman has also published a "straight" autobiography, *The Magic Lantern: An Autobiography* (Viking, 1988), also translated by Joan Tate.

1. *Best Intentions, The* (Arcade, 1993) The courtship of middle-class Anna Akerblom by poor divinity student Henrik Bergman in the year 1909 is related. Originally published in Sweden as *Den Goda Viljan* (1991)
2. *Sunday's Children* (Arcade, 1994) Eight-year-old Pu (Ingmar) tries to deal with his tumultuous family as his mother threatens to leave his father. Originally published in Sweden as *Sondagsburn* (1993).

Bergstrom, Elaine

I. One of the more popular vampire series, the Austra family series follows the fortunes of a family of "good" vampires from Europe in the 16th century to the contemporary United States. All the passion that vampire aficionados want plus a little historical lore. The novels are arranged chronologically rather than by order of publication. Elaine Bergstrom, an American of Hungarian descent, has written other novels about horror and the occult, including two in the Ravenloft series.

1. *Daughter of the Night* (Jove, 1992) In the 16th century, the historical "Countess of Blood," the beautiful but wicked Elizabeth Bathori, learns that Catherine Austra possesses the secret she desires.
2. *Blood Alone* (Jove, 1990) In 1938, when Paul Stoddard travels to Europe to indulge in his passion for stained glass, he becomes involved with the "good" vampires, the Austras, who are revolting against the Third Reich.
3. *Shattered Glass* (Jove, 1989) In 1955 Stephen Austra, stained-glass restorer and a vampire who wouldn't hurt anyone, is suspected by his lover, Helen Wells, of being involved in a series of murders. First of the series to be published.
4. *Blood Rites* (Jove, 1991) Sequel to number 3. Artist Helen Wells has become a vampire through the kiss of Stephen Austra, but she resists her vampirization until a hired killer stalks her family.
5. *Nocturne* (Berkley, 2003) Two contemporary lovers have to travel to Romania to confront their history and their destiny in the first Austra novel in more than 10 years.

II. Two novels, subtitled *The Dracula Story Continues,* are sequels to Bram Stoker's *Dracula.* They follow the fortunes of Mina and Jonathan Harker after their encounter with the evil count.

1. *Mina* (Berkley, 1994) Mina Harker has difficulties returning to normal married life after her encounter with Count Dracula. Originally published under the pseudonym "Marie Kiraly."
2. *Blood to Blood* (Berkley, 2000) Mina returns to London after her second trip to Romania, free of Count Dracula's spell but still having trouble settling down. Meanwhile, her husband, Jonathan, is having vampire nightmares of his own.

Berliner, Janet

The Madagascar Manifesto trilogy is an alternate history chronicling events from 1918 to 1938, a time when the Nazis come to power in Germany and Hitler's plan to deport the Jews of Europe to Madagascar (a plan that was actually considered) is implemented. The protagonists are Solomon Freund, a Jewish boy; Erich, his Catholic neighbor; and Miriam, the girl they both love. Janet Berliner, the child of parents who left Germany in 1936, was born in South Africa and became a US citizen in 1966. She has written a number of other fictional and nonfictional works under the name Berliner and under her married name of Janet Gluckman and has collaborated on editorial projects with David Copperfield, Joyce Carol Oates, Michael Crichton (q.v.), and Peter S. Beagle, among others. Coauthor George Guthridge is a resident of Alaska who has written SF and horror fiction. *The Madagascar Manifesto* (Meisha Merlin, 2002) is an omnibus containing numbers 1–3.

1. *Child of the Light* (St. Martin's, 1992) Jewish Solomon Freund, his Catholic neighbor Erich Weisser, and Miriam, the girl they both

love, come of age during the period of the rise of the Nazis in Germany.

2. *Child of the Journey* (**White Wolf, 1996**) Solomon, Erich, and Miriam are now adults. Erich, now the commander of the Nazi Canine Corps, is living with Miriam, who was formerly secretly married to Solomon, who has fled to Amsterdam.

3. *Children of the Dusk* (**White Wolf, 1997**) Solomon and Miriam have been deported to Madagascar by the Nazis. Erich is among those in charge of the program.

Bernhardt, William

I. Ben Kincaid is a nationally known defense attorney from Tulsa, Oklahoma, who gets involved in a series of suspenseful, complicated courtroom dramas that have been popular with readers and received mixed reviews from critics. Author William Bernhardt is himself a Tulsa attorney.

1. *Primary Justice* (**Ballantine, 1992**) On Ben Kincaid's first day with a high-powered Tulsa law firm, he gets involved in the case of a little girl found wandering in an empty lot, an adoption case that turns into murder.

2. *Blind Justice* (**Ballantine, 1992**) Ben, fired from his law firm, is living on the wrong side of town and getting paid by his clients with live chickens. Then Christina McCall, an old friend and former colleague, becomes the prime suspect in the murder of a suspected drug dealer.

3. *Deadly Justice* (**Ballantine, 1993**) Ben wins his first case as counsel to the notorious Apollo Consortium, and he unwittingly sets up a rivalry that will culminate in murder.

4. *Perfect Justice* (**Ballantine, 1993**) All evidence points to Donald Vick, member of the white-supremacist group Anglo-Saxon Patrol, when a young Vietnamese refugee is murdered near Silver Springs, Arkansas.

5. *Cruel Justice* (**Ballantine, 1996**) Ten years after a woman was found impaled by a golf club in a country-club caddy shack, a mentally deficient caddy is brought to trial.

6. *Naked Justice* (**Ballantine, 1997**) Wallace Barrett, first black mayor of Tulsa, becomes a suspect when members of his family die after a visit to the local Baskin Robbins.

7. *Extreme Justice* (**Ballantine, 1998**) Ben decides to abandon his law practice and play with a combo at Uncle Earl's Jazz Emporium. Then singer "Cajun Lily" Campbell's body crashes through the ceiling.

8. *Dark Justice* (**Ballantine, 1999**) Kincaid stays in Magic Valley, a logging town in the Pacific Northwest, where he gets involved when former client George Zakin is suspected of killing a local lumberjack.

9. *Silent Justice* (**Ballantine, 2000**) Ben represents a group of suburban families whose children have died of leukemia, apparently from drinking well water polluted by toxic waste from the Blaylock Industrial Machinery Corporation.

10. *Murder One* (**Ballantine, 2001**) After the grisly, ritualistic murder of police sergeant Joe McNaughton, Kincaid defends McNaughton's 19-year-old mistress when she is charged with the slaying.

11. *Criminal Intent* (**Ballantine, 2002**) Kincaid defends an Episcopal priest accused of killing a parishioner who objected to gay and lesbian groups holding meetings at his church.

12. *Death Row* (**Ballantine, 2003**) Seven years after a family massacre, Erin Faulkner, the sole survivor, confesses to Ben that she had been coerced into making a positive ID.

13. *Hate Crime* (**Ballantine, 2004**) Kincaid's partner and love interest, Christina McCall, goes to Evanston, Illinois, to defend gay-basher Johnny Christensen against charges that he murdered his victim.

14. *Capitol Murder* (**Ballantine, 2005**) Ben Kincaid goes to Washington, DC, to defend Oklahoma's senior senator, Todd K. Glancy, from charges of murdering the young intern he had an affair with.

15. *Capitol Threat* (**Ballantine, 2007**) Set in the near future, when Thaddeus Roush, Supreme Court nominee of Republican President Blake, announces that he is "a gay American" during the Rose Garden ceremony announcing his selection.

16. *Capitol Conspiracy* (**Ballantine, 2008**) The First Lady is killed by a terrorist attack aimed at President Blake in Oklahoma City.

II. A new series features widowed ex-police profiler, Susan Pulaski, and her partner, Darcy O'Bannon, autistic-savant son of the police chief of Las Vegas. Serial killers have been the quarry in the two novels published thus far.

1. *Dark Eye* (**Ballantine, 2006**) Former police profiler Susan Pulaski and autistic-savant Darcy O'Bannon investigate the case of a killer who buries his victims alive.

2. *Strip Search* (**Ballantine, 2007**) This time the serial killer brands and dismembers his victims and leaves a mathematical equation at each crime scene.

Berry, Carole

Bonnie Indermill is a thirtysomething New Yorker who is in danger of becoming a "permanent" temp. Bonnie's job switches give author Carole Berry an opportunity to write mysteries with various professions as a background. Bonnie is a witty, spunky character in a series of readable light mysteries.

1. *Letter of the Law, The* (**St. Martin's, 1987**) Bonnie takes a job at a failing law firm only to have a senior partner meet an untimely end, which puts her at risk of losing more than her position.

2. *Year of the Monkey, The* (**St. Martin's, 1988**) This time Bonnie is working in an investment firm engaged in "creative financing," but again she is put at risk when the CEO turns up dead.

3. *Good Night Sweet Prince* (**St. Martin's, 1990**) Indermill becomes a temporary assistant at a Manhattan ballet and has her romantic hopes truncated when a sexy Russian dancer takes a fatal onstage fall.

4. *Island Girl* (**St. Martin's, 1991**) Indermill gets out of a New York winter by taking a job as assistant fitness counselor at Flamingo Island, a Bahamian resort. Then her Australian roommate takes a fatal scuba dive.

5. *Death of a Difficult Woman, The* (**Berkley, 1994**) Bonnie's temporary job in another legal firm proves fatal again to a senior partner, this time an unpopular woman.

6. *Death of a Dancing Fool, The* (**Berkley, 1996**) Indermill, at the insistence of NYPD Captain Lee, takes a filing job at "Fast Eddie" Fong's nightclub, and a corpse or two turn up, of course.

7. *Death of a Dimpled Darling* (**Berkley, 1997**) A New York debutante's society wedding hits a snag when one of the bridesmaids is murdered.

8. *Death of a Downsizer* (**Berkley, 1999**) When the CEO of Richards & Goode Corporation, "Dorfmeyer the Downsizer," is gunned down, the gun may have Bonnie's fingerprints on it.

Berry, Wendell

Most of Wendell Berry's fiction is set in Port William, Kentucky, which is based on Port Royal, Kentucky, Berry's hometown. Port William is, or was, the home of seven generations of farming families until post–World War II events, including agro-business and development, threatened the livelihood of its longtime residents such as the Beechums, the Catletts, the Feltners, the Crows, the Proudfoots, and the Coulters. The stories of their connection with the land usually take the form of their elegiac reminiscences. In entire sympathy with his rural characters, Berry writes poetically about their threatened existence. Berry, a farmer, college English professor, and writer, is also known for his poetry (*Collected Poems, 1957–1982*, North Point, 1985) and for his essays collected in *The Long-Legged House* (Harcourt, 1969), *Recollected Essays, 1965–1980* (North Point, 1981), *A World Lost* (Counterpoint, 1996), and *Citizenship Papers* (Shoemaker, 2003), among others. *The Unsettling of America: Culture and Agriculture* (Sierra Club, 1977) is a key environmental text. Berry's work exposes the many failures of modern, mechanized life and the global economy, and he makes a strong plea for the preservation of community ties and traditional values. *Three Short Novels* (Counterpoint, 2002) contains numbers 1, 6, and 9.

1. *Nathan Coulter* (**Houghton Mifflin, 1960**) Nathan Coulter, denizen of Port William, Kentucky, relates his own story and that of the larger-than-life figures he has interacted with. Revised edition published by North Point (1985).
2. *Andy Catlett: Early Travels* (**Shoemaker, 2007**) Elderly Andy Catlett relates events in 1943 when, at the age of nine, he visits his grandparents in Port William.
3. *Place on Earth, A* (**Harcourt, 1967**) Virgil Feltner, son of Mat and Margaret, is missing in action in Europe during World War II. Revised edition published by North Point (1983).
4. *Memory of Old Jack, The* (**Harcourt, 1974**) Old Jack Beechum recalls his long and eventful life and laments the changes that impacted his community. Berry's best-known fictional work.
5. *Wild Birds, The* (**North Point, 1986**) Subtitle: *Six Stories of the Port William Membership*. Characters such as Jack Beechum and Mat Feltner are remet in younger and older incarnations.
6. *Rembering* (**North Point, 1988**) Andrew Catlett, battler against the excesses of agro-business, loses his hand in a farming accident but finds his way to spiritual healing and a renewed sense of community.
7. *Fidelity* (**Pantheon, 1992**) Subtitle: *Five Stories*. "A Jonquil for Merry Penn" is story of a young farm wife. "Fidelity" tells of the death of old Burley.
8. *Watch with Me* (**Pantheon, 1994**) Subtitle: *And Six Other Stories of the Yet-Remembered Ptolemy Proudfoot and His Wife, Miss Minnie, Née Quinch*. Stories spanning 33 years about the courtship and marriage of 300-pound farmer Ptolemy "Tol" Proudfoot and tiny schoolteacher Minnie Quinch.
9. *World Lost, A* (**Counterpoint, 1996**) Approaching his sixtieth birthday, Andy Catlett broods about an incident of his childhood, the murder of his uncle Andrew.
10. *Two More Stories of the Port William Membership* (**Gnomon, 1997**) Two short stories in a small-press edition.
11. *Jayber Crow* (**Counterpoint, 2000**) Subtitle: *The Life Story of Jayber Crow, Barber, of the Port William Membership as Written by Himself*. Jayber Crow, Port William town barber from 1937 to 1969, reminisces about his life as an orphan, his unrequited love for Mattie Chatman, and the unraveling of Port William's sense of community.
12. *That Distant Land: The Collected Stories* (**Counterpoint, 2002**) Stories collected from numbers 5, 6, 8, 10, and elsewhere.
13. *Hannah Coulter* (**Shoemaker, 2004**) Twice-widowed Hannah Coulter recalls her marriages to Virgil Feltner (number 3) and Nathan Coulter (number 1) and relates the lives of her three children.

Besher, Alexander

Alexander Besher, born in China of White Russian parents, raised in Japan, and now residing in San Francisco, has written a wild trilogy of novels that remind reviewers of Douglas Adams (q.v.), the cyberpunk writer William Gibson (q.v.), Jeff Noon (q.v.), or a combination thereof. Each novel is subtitled *A Novel of Virtual Reality*. Set in a 21st-century world of virtual nations in which virtual reality threatens to take over "reality," and mystical powers and cyberscience coexist, the novels are written in a wildly inventive, humorous, cyberpunk style in which points of view shift and major characters disappear without warning. Although the Virtual Reality trio has achieved pop-cult standing, critics are not entirely happy about the final result. Besher, who coauthored, with John Wilcock, *The Pacific Rim Almanac* (Harper, 1991), has also written *Hanging Butoh* (Orbit, 2000), a novel about a paranormal Japanese American Butoh detective, which promises to be the launch of a new series.

1. *Rim* (**Simon & Schuster, 1994**) Frank Gobi, professor of "transcultural corporate anthropology and organizational shamanism" and former "consciousness detective," is called when Satori City (aka Virtualopolis), a huge online city, crashes, stranding thousands of users, including Trevor, Gobi's teenage son.
2. *Mir* (**Simon & Schuster, 1998**) Nelly, the girlfriend of Trevor Gobi, now 24 years old in a world of virtual nations where Germany's Fourth Reich, neo-czarist Russia, and the United States compete for online supremacy, has become the unwitting carrier of Mir, the newest Russian cyber virus.
3. *Chi* (**Simon & Schuster, 1999**) In 2038 humanity is searching for chi—the primal life source. Obese Asian merchant Wing Fat, two orangutans who have had humanity thrust upon them, freelance journalist Paul Sykes, and Rodney the Philodendron, the doyen of a green communications network, are all involved in the quest.

bes-Shahar, Eluki

Butterfly St. Cyr, interplanetary smuggler, gets herself involved with the royal humanoid Tiggy Stardust and a Library, or sentient and illegal computer, named Paladin in a trio of light SF novels with a mix of humor and adventure. An omnibus volume, *Butterfly and Hellflower* (SF Book Club, 1993), contains all three novels. Eluki bes-Shahar is better known under her pseudonym, Rosemary Edghill (q.v.), writer of Regency romances and novels about witchcraft. Eluki bes-Shahar is also a contributor to the X-Men series.

1. *Hellflower* (**DAW, 1991**) Darktrader (interplanetary smuggler) and possessor of an illegal Library (a sentient and illegal computer) named Paladin, Butterfly St. Cyr gets entangled with Tiggy Stardust (aka Valijon Starbringer), a young member of the Hellflower (aka alMayne) royalty.
2. *Darktraders* (**DAW, 1992**) Butterfly tries to bring humanoid Tiggy back to the Starbringer family's home world, which might not be a good idea for either one of them.
3. *Archangel Blues* (**DAW, 1993**) Butterfly and Tiggy must hunt down the seemingly invincible Archangel, who is planning to make himself master of the universe.

Beverley, Jo

I. Jo Beverley is a five-time RITA Award winner and a member of the Romance Writers of America Hall of Fame. The seven Malloren novels form a Georgian series about the aristocratic Marquess of Rothgar and his brothers and sister; the novels are full of steamy sex, dark secrets, and 18th-century British social-class dynamics.

1. *My Lady Notorious* (Avon, 1993) Lady Chastity Ware, to save her sister, feels obliged to hold up a stagecoach, but complications occur when her "victim," Captain Cynric Malloren, insists upon helping her.
2. *Tempting Fortune* (Zebra, 1995) Impecunious, plain Portia St. Claire and rakish aristocrat Arcenbryght Malloren would seem to have little in common, but they find themselves becoming increasingly attracted to each other.
3. *Something Wicked* (Topaz, 1997) Lady Elfled Malloren, sister of Cyn (number 1) and Bryght (number 2), determined to avert a dull future as a spinster, goes in disguise to Vauxhall's Midsummer Night's masquerade and overhears family enemy Lord "Fort" Walgrave plotting treason.
4. *Secrets of the Night* (New American Library, 1999) Horse breeder Rosamunde Overton will go to any length to save her husband's holdings, including being impregnated by a handsome stranger, who turns out to be Lord Brand Malloren.
5. *Devilish* (Signet, 2000) Bey Malloren, Marquess of Rothgar, fearful of passing on his mother's insanity to his own children, has determined not to marry. But then he gets involved with Diana Westmount, Countess of Arradale, who has reasons of her own for avoiding matrimony.
6. *Winter Fire* (Signet, 2003) A Christmas party at Rothgar Abbey, home of the Mallorens, brings Genova Smith together again with the Marquess of Ashart, whom she believes to be the father of her child.
7. *Most Unsuitable Man, A* (Signet, 2005) In what appears to be the final installment of the series, rich Damaris Myddleton enlists the help of Octavius Fitzroger to marry a title after seemingly losing out on the Marquess of Ashart.

II. The Company of Rogues was formed by Nicholas Delaney and 12 selected "new boys" at anarchic (in Regency days) Harrow School as a mutual protection organization against the bullies and tyrants of the school. The series documents the subsequent careers of members of the company, including Lucien, Marquess of Arden, who was a later addition. Clarissa Greystone, a secondary character in number 2 and heroine of number 8, links the Company of Rogues with the Three Heroes (numbers 6–8), two novels and a novella, which were subsequently published together in the omnibus volume *Three Heroes* (New American Library, 2004). All of the ingredients for Regency romance are mixed together by one of romancedom's most popular writers. Because some of the Rogues haven't been featured in their own books, more titles in the series can be expected. Lancashire native and Canadian immigrant Jo Beverley also writes nonseries romances, some of them set in medieval times.

1. *Arranged Marriage, An* (Zebra, 1991) The schoolboy group, Company of Rogues, is gathered together again by its founder, Nicholas Delaney, twin brother of the Earl of Stainsbridge, when Nicholas gets involved with Eleanor Chivenham and shakes her faith in her ability to carry out an arranged marriage.
2. *Unwilling Bride, An* (Zebra, 1992) Lucien de Vaux, Marquess of Arden, heir to the Duke of Belcraven, and product of his mother's adulterous tryst, is reluctant to marry the schoolteacher, who turns out to be the duke's child of an affair of his own.
3. *Christmas Angel* (Zebra, 1992) Leander Knollis, Earl of Charrington, wants a wife who isn't madly in love with him. Can impoverished widow Judith Rossiter fill the bill?
4. *Forbidden* (Zebra, 1994) Francis Haile, Lord Middlethorpe, is on the point of marrying Lady Anne Peckworth when he encounters Serena Riverton, victim of an abusive marriage, who is escaping from another bad arranged marriage.
5. *Dangerous Joy* (Zebra, 1995) Miles Cavanagh, heir to the Earl of Kilgoran, inherits the guardianship of 20-year-old heiress Felicity Monahan, who is determined to marry a fortune hunter.
6. *Demon's Mistress, The* (Signet, 2001) A novella that first appeared in the multiauthor anthology *In Praise of Younger Men* (Signet, 2001). First of the Three Heroes subseries, in which three scions of neighboring families pledge fealty to each other, join the British army together, and are brought together again after the Napoleonic Wars.
7. *Dragon's Bride, The* (Signet, 2001) Con Somerville, one of the Three Heroes (see number 6), is not anxious to inherit the Earldom of Wyvern and the house that goes with it, especially since it involves a reunion with old lover Susan Kerslake.
8. *Devil's Heiress, The* (Signet, 2001) Major George "Hawk" Hawkinville returns to his Sussex home after 10 years at the wars but finds that his father, Squire Hawkinville, to obtain a title, has mortgaged Hawkinville Manor to a wealthy industrialist who plans extensive renovations. Last of the Three Heroes subseries.
9. *Hazard* (Signet, 2002) Lady Anne Peckworth, the jilted bride of numbers 4 and 7, wants to find herself a husband and turn her life around, but mysterious, infuriating Race de Vere would seem to be an ill-judged choice.
10. *St. Raven* (Signet, 2003) Tristan Tregallows, the reluctant Duke of St. Raven, while holding up a stagecoach to free an innocent man, finds himself involved in rescuing a reluctant Cressida Mandeville from her traveling companion, the debauched Lord Crofton.
11. *Skylark* (Signet, 2004) Sir Stephen Ball, member of Parliament and one of the quieter members of the Company of Rogues, has never forgotten his love for Laura, "Lady Skylark," who is now widowed and in trouble.
12. *Rogue's Return, The* (Signet, 2006) Simon St. Bride is ready to return to England, but his plans are delayed by a duel and Jane Otterburn, the woman he feels bound to marry.
13. *To Rescue a Rogue* (Signet, 2006) All 12 members of the Company of Rogues are brought together in what was supposed to the series finale. But see number 14.
14. *Lady Beware* (Signet, 2007) Lady Thea Debenham's brother Dare, "the most dashing member of the Company of Rogues," believes that Horatio Cave, the new Viscount Darien, member of a notorious family, isn't as bad as he has been described.

Bickham, Jack M(iles)

Bickham's hero Brad Smith is a semiretired professional tennis player who doubles as a CIA operative. Brad's adventures sooner or later get him on or near a tennis court in this exciting espionage series. Jack M. Bickham, who wrote many other novels in his own name and pseudonyms such as John Miles and Jeff Clinton (comic Westerns about a character called Wildcat O'Shea), was also the author of guides to writing fiction and movie scripts (*The Apple Dumpling Gang*, etc.).

1. *Tiebreaker* (Tor, 1989) Brad is enlisted to help beautiful Yugoslav tennis star Danisa Lechova defect to the West.

2. *Dropshot* (Tor, 1990) Grieving over his lost wife, Brad gets mixed up in an affair over a stolen computer chip after his best friend is murdered at a resort in St. Martin.
3. *Overhead* (Tor, 1991) Smith is sent to Elk City, Montana, ostensibly to help open a tennis resort but actually to expose KGB agent Sylvester.
4. *Breakfast at Wimbledon* (Tor, 1991) A courtesy invitation to play at Wimbledon enables Brad to foil a renegade IRA assassination plot.
5. *Double Fault* (Tor, 1993) The reported reappearance of an old friend who supposedly died in a Vietnamese POW camp leads Smith on an odyssey across western America.
6. *Davis Cup Conspiracy, The* (Tor, 1994) "The Company" sends Brad to Venezuela as captain of the American Davis Cup team to prevent a guerrilla takeover.

Bienek, Horst

Gleiwitz, a town in Upper Silesia on the German-Polish border, is invaded by the Germans on September 1, 1939, at the start of World War II. The town is eventually "liberated" by the Russians in 1945. The Gleiwitz Suite is a tetralogy about how the inhabitants of Gleiwitz, and in particular the Piontek family, endured the invasions and occupations of the Second World War. Horst Bienek, a native of Gleiwitz who spent five years in a forced-labor camp in Siberia—described in *The Cell* [*Die zelle*] (Unicorn, 1972)—is a German poet, novelist, and essayist.

1. *First Polka, The* (Fjord, 1984) The small Upper Silesian town of Gleiwitz, on the Polish-German border, is described on the eve of World War II. Translated by Ralph R. Read. Originally published in German as *Die erste Polke* in 1975.
2. *September Light* (Atheneum, 1987) At 2:00 a.m. on September 1, 1939, SS commandos under the guise of Polish guerrillas attack the radio transmitter in Gleiwitz. Translated by Ralph R. Read. Originally published in German as *Septemberlicht* in 1977.
3. *Time without Bells* (Atheneum, 1988) The Piontek family and the other residents of Gleiwitz try to carry on with their lives. Translated by Ralph Manheim. Originally published in German as *Zeit ohne Glocken* in 1980.
4. *Earth and Fire* (Atheneum, 1988) The Russian invasion of 1945 results in a change of occupiers. Translated by Ralph Manheim. Originally published in German as *Erde und Feuer* in 1982.

Biggers, Earl Derr

Charlie Chan, the Chinese American detective, became a pop-culture icon, mainly through the nearly 50 movie versions that appeared in the 1930s and '40s. Charlie Chan first appeared in a series of novels, originally serialized in the *Saturday Evening Post*. Popular culture at the time (1920s) was dominated by racist portrayals of evil Chinese (e.g., the Yellow Peril, Fu-Manchu), and Biggers wanted to present a sympathetic Chinese figure, one on the side of the law. Chan is the best detective in the Honolulu Police Department; he is rotund, gentle in manner, soft-spoken, given to Confucian aphorisms, but extremely sagacious. He lives on Punchbowl Hill with his wife and 11 children. Some of his cases take him to California and beyond. The movie versions, starring the Swede Warner Oland, Sidney Toler, and others (none of them Chinese), undercut the positive image Biggers wanted to convey, and Charlie Chan became a somewhat comic figure, spouting pidgin English, on a series of jaunts taking him to exotic locales throughout the world. There were also silent-screen versions of the novels (with Japanese actor Kamiyama Sojih as Chan), radio shows, at least one television series, cartoons, and comic strips featuring Chan. From time to time, Charlie Chan has been revived in fiction form by other authors. *Celebrated Cases of Charlie Chan* (Bobbs-Merrill, 1930) is an omnibus volume containing numbers 1–5). Harvard graduate Earl Derr Biggers wrote other novels, the most famous of which was *Seven Keys to Baldpate* (Bobbs-Merrill, 1913), and several plays.

1. *House without a Key, The* (Bobbs-Merrill, 1925) Dan Winterstop, the black-sheep son of a Boston family, is murdered in Hawaii. The first and, according to critics, the best of the Charlie Chan novels.
2. *Chinese Parrot, The* (Bobbs-Merrill, 1926) The murder of a millionaire, a string of pearls, and a parrot that speaks Chinese are among the incentives for Chan's trip, disguised as a Chinese cook, to a California ranch.
3. *Behind That Curtain* (Bobbs-Merrill, 1928) A pair of Chinese slippers provide a clue to killings, 16 years apart, in London and San Francisco.
4. *Black Camel, The* (Bobbs-Merrill, 1928) Famous actress Shelah Fane is stabbed to death on a remote part of Waikiki Beach.
5. *Charlie Chan Carries On* (Bobbs-Merrill, 1930) A round-the-world cruise on its final lap from Honolulu to San Francisco is the setting for a shipboard murder.
6. *Keeper of the Keys* (Bobbs-Merrill, 1932) Was an oft-married opera diva murdered at a Lake Tahoe resort by one of her former husbands?

Bigsby, Christopher

PSEUDONYM OF C. W. E. Bigsby

Bigsby, professor of American literature at the University of East Anglia, has written both a prequel and a sequel to Nathaniel Hawthorne's classic, *The Scarlet Letter*. *Hester*, the prequel, is about Hester Prynne's life in England and America before she was sentenced for adultery. *Pearl*, the sequel, returns Hester's daughter, Pearl, to England at the age of 20.

1. *Hester* (Penguin, 1994) Describes the events leading up to *The Scarlet Letter*, including Hester's marriage to Chillingworth, her escape to the New World, and her affair with Dimmesdale.
2. *Pearl* (Weidenfeld [UK], 1995) Hester's daughter, Pearl, travels to Norwich, England, to claim her inheritance.

Billheimer, John

West Virginia now has its own amateur detective in the person of Owen Allison, who returns to his native state during the course of a National Department of Transportation audit in the fictional town of Contrary. Later novels are set in Owen's hometown of Barkley, West Virginia, where he has returned to help his ailing mother. The mysteries have ingenious plots, lots of local color, humor, and memorable characters. John Billheimer, a native West Virginian himself, now makes his home in California.

1. *Contrary Blues, The* (St. Martin's, 1998) West Virginia native Owen Allison is assigned to complete a National Department of Transportation audit in Contrary, West Virginia, begun by a colleague who met a fatal "accident." Seems that Contrary got a grant for *20* buses when they asked for 2, and the town is reluctant to give up the extra money.

2. *Highway Robbery* (**St. Martin's, 2000**) Owen returns home to find his brother George in the throes of a dispute with environmental activists who are trying to stop the highway improvements of which he is in charge. Then the remains of what may have been Owen's father, presumed drowned in a long-ago flood on the same highway, are unearthed.

3. *Dismal Mountain* (**St. Martin's, 2001**) When Owen returns home to Barkley, West Virginia, to care for his dying mother, he runs into a number of occurrences, including the building of a shopping mall on the top of a truncated mountain, the murder of a construction worker, and strange goings-on at the hospice where Owen's mother is slated to stay.

4. *Drybone Hollow* (**St. Martin's, 2003**) Owen's expertise as a "failure analyst" is called upon when an impoundment dam atop the Canaan II coal mine bursts, causing damage and killing some people in nearby Drybone Hollow.

5. *Stonewall Jackson's Elbow* (**Five Star, 2006**) After the death of J. Burton Caldwell, president of the First National Bank of Contrary, West Virginia, federal bank examiners find three-quarters of a billion dollars missing.

Billingham, Mark

London Metropolitan Police Service Detective Inspector Tom Thorne is a rather melancholy fellow, given to gloomy musings on death and guilt. He has problems with women and commitment and a father with Alzheimer's. Tom and his colleagues, such as pathologist Phil Hendricks, usually work on serial killer cases, and they usually get their man in this series of character-driven, well-plotted mysteries that have proved to be popular both in the United Kingdom and the United States. Mark Billingham is a Birmingham, England, native who combines mystery writing with a career as a stand-up comedian.

1. *Sleepyhead* (**Morrow, 2002**) A serial killer with a difference. This one wants to induce massive strokes that leave his victims cerebrally conscious while in a comatose state. London detective Tom Thorne becomes obsessed with the killer's "masterpiece," 24-year-old Alison Willetts.

2. *Scaredy Cat* (**Morrow, 2003**) Thorne discovers that a series of strangulations is really the work of two different killers.

3. *Lazy Bones* (**Morrow, 2004**) A serial killer is targeting rapists and pornographers. Some of Thorne's colleagues think that the victims deserved their fate, but Thorne's commitment to justice drives him to find the killer.

4. *Burning Girl, The* (**Morrow, 2005**) Thorne helps his friend ex-DCI Carol Chamberlain reopen a 1980s case in which a schoolgirl was set on fire. Meanwhile, the murder of a Turkish video-store owner is the opener for a series of killings.

5. *Lifeless* (**Morrow, 2005**) Thorne's career seems to be on the skids when he goes undercover to track down a killer who is preying on London's homeless community.

6. *Buried* (**HarperCollins, 2007**) Thorne and his new partner, DI Louise Porter, investigate the kidnapping of 16-year-old Luke Mullen, son of ex-Detective Chief Superintendent Tony Mullen.

Binchy, Dan

Brulagh, a fictional Irish village not too far from Shannon Airport, is the setting for a trio of novels by Dan Binchy, County Limerick farmer and writer and cousin of Maeve Binchy (*Circle of Friends*, etc.). The novels are full of quaint and not-so-quaint Irish characters, such as Father Jerry O'Sullivan, former Vatican Bank insider who has been rusticated there. Mixed reviews: some readers find the humor and local color charming; others find it stale and cliche-ridden. Binchy's latest, *Loopy* (St. Martin's, 2005), is set in another small Irish town.

1. *Neon Madonna, The* (**St. Martin's, 1992**) Vatican diplomat Father Jerry O'Sullivan, suffering from ulcerative colitis, is rusticated to the tiny Irish hamlet of Brulagh, where two local women claim to have seen the village's neon-haloed Madonna move and weep.

2. *Last Resort, The* (**St. Martin's, 1993**) Luke Divareli, an American developer vacationing in Ireland, finds the Brulagh area a prime target for a hotel and a marina, but he is covertly opposed by Father Jerry O'Sullivan.

3. *Fireballs* (**St. Martin's, 1994**) Mike Flannery, a local Brulagh politico who is determined to be elected to the European Parliament, is desperately seeking a gimmick.

Birmingham, Ruth

Sunny Childs is a female private eye who runs the Atlanta-based Peachtree Investigations for her elusive boss, Gunnar Brushurd. Sunny is a fairly typical brash, feisty female PI, and the Atlanta scene is well rendered. "Ruth Birmingham" is a pseudonym for Walter Sorrells, martial-arts-practicing, blues-guitar-playing, Edgar Award–winning author of legal thrillers for adults and suspense novels for young adults, now resident in Atlanta.

1. *Atlanta Graves* (**Berkley, 1998**) Sunny Childs finds that her boss, Gunnar Brushurd, has left the Atlanta-based Peachtree Investigations deeply in debt with its creditors, leaving only four days to avoid bankruptcy.

2. *Fulton County Blues* (**Berkley, 1999**) Sunny learns some unpleasant truths about her father and the Vietnam War while investigating the death of her late father's friend and fellow Vietnam veteran.

3. *Sweet Georgia* (**Berkley, 2000**) Singer Georgia Burnett is "kidnapped" and then found dead, and Sunny wants to get to the bottom of the mystery.

4. *Blue Plate Special* (**Berkley, 2001**) Sunny is eating at the Blind Pig Diner when an armed teenager holds up the place and takes the diners hostage, claiming his innocence in the murder of a woman whose body lies on the Blind Pig's floor.

5. *Cold Trail* (**Berkley, 2002**) Sunny goes undercover at the Chateau D'Or hunting lodge a year after one member of the elite hunting club was killed there.

6. *Feet of Clay* (**St. Martin's, 2006**) Sunny Childs accompanies her filmmaker cousin on a job and finds herself deep in a murder case.

Bishop, Anne

I. The Black Jewels trilogy is set in the Shadowlands of the fantasy world called the Dark Kingdom. It is a reversal of fantasy protocol in that the forces of darkness are the good guys. Jaenelle SaDiablo, the promised queen, is helped by Black-Jewelled Warlord Prince Saetan and his son Daemon. *The Black Jewels Trilogy* (Roc, 2003) contains numbers 1–3. Numbers 4–6 are set in the same world as the trilogy. American writer Anne Bishop has created a sensuous, erotic fantasy world somewhat reminiscent of Tanith Lee's (q.v.) work.

1. *Daughter of the Blood* (**Roc, 1998**) Three rivals try to control the innocent young Jaenelle, who is the prophesied Queen of the Dark Kingdom.

2. *Heir to Shadows* (Roc, 1999) Jaenelle, recovering from her psychological and physical wounds, is protected from bad memories by her amnesia and physically by Warlord Prince Saetan and his son Daemon.

3. *Queen of the Darkness* (Roc, 2000) Jaenelle and her promised consort, Daemon, must unleash the Witch to destroy her enemies once and for all.

4. *Invisible Ring, The* (Roc, 2000) A stand-alone novel set in the World of the Black Jewels. A notorious queen purchases Red Jewel Warlord Jared in a slave auction.

5. *Dreams Made Flesh* (Roc, 2005) Four novellas set in the Black Jewels universe: "Weaver of Dreams," "The Prince of Ebon Rih," "Kaeleer's Heart," and "Zuulaman."

6. *Tangled Webs* (Roc, 2008) Crazed novelist Jarvis Jenkell has discovered his Blood heritage and developed his own haunted house to trap other Bloods and use their suffering to inspire his fiction.

II. The Tir Alainn, or World of the Fae, another fantasy trilogy, is set in a world shared uneasily by humans, witches, the Fae, and the Inquisitors, who are out to destroy them.

1. *Pillars of the World, The* (Roc, 2001) Young human Ari takes a Fae lover, the Lord of the Sun, and brings the inquisitor Adolpho to her door in the land of Sylvalan.

2. *Shadows and Light* (Roc, 2002) Only the witches can keep the magical roads between Tir Alainn, the Fae's land, and the human world from being destroyed, but the witches are being hard-pressed.

3. *House of Gaian, The* (Roc, 2003) The alliance between Fae and humans may not be enough to defeat the Inquisitors. They have no choice but to seek out the witches of the House of Gaian.

III. Anne Bishop's hardcover debut is set in the land of Ephemera, which has been kept stable by the magic of the Landscapers. Then the nearly forgotten Eater of the World escapes its prison.

1. *Sebastian* (Roc, 2006) The stability of the world of Ephemera maintained by the Landscapers is upset when the Eater of the World escapes, and the half-incubus Sebastian is called by the woman of his dreams.

2. *Belladonna* (Roc, 2007) The Eater of the World continues to spread its dark influence across Ephemera. Only Glorianna Belladonna can thwart its plans.

Bishop, Claudia

PSEUDONYM OF Mary Stanton

I. Sarah and Meg Quilliam are sisters who run the Hemlock Falls Inn near New York's Finger Lakes district. Sarah takes care of business, while Meg is in charge of the kitchen. Although Hemlock Falls is supposed to be a quiet retreat, murders, at least one per book, keep on happening, but the resourceful sisters are equal to the task of investigation. This series of nice cozies includes a recipe from the Hemlock Falls Inn kitchen in each book. Claudia Bishop coedited *Death Dines at 8:30* (Berkley, 2001) and *Death Dines In* (Berkley, 2004), anthologies of short stories mixing crime and food. The latter includes a Hemlock Falls story. Claudia Bishop is the pseudonym of Mary Stanton, fantasy author and upstate New York resident.

1. *Taste for Murder, A* (Berkley, 1994) Introduces the Quilliam sisters and the Hemlock Falls Inn, which they run. During a "mock" witch stoning as part of the annual History Days festival in Hemlock Falls, a guest at the inn is substituted for the fake witch, with fatal results.

2. *Dash of Death, A* (Berkley, 1995) Helena Houndswood, stylish living maven on TV, checks into the inn. Then one of the winners of a design contest sponsored by Helena's show turns up dead.

3. *Pinch of Poison, A* (Berkley, 1996) A local mini-mall project attracts the attention of a nosy newspaperman, and the attraction may prove to be a fatal one. Not to be confused with Frances and Richard Lockridge's (q.v.) Mr. and Mrs. North mystery of the same title.

4. *Murder Well-Done* (Berkley, 1996) A sleazy ex-senator holding his wedding reception at the inn turns up dead and tied to a barbecue spit.

5. *Death Dines Out* (Berkley, 1997) Meg and Quill (Sarah) are in Palm Beach, where Meg is attempting to reclaim her three-star chef's status with her jugged hare at the Florida Institute for Fine Food. They find themselves in the middle of a bitter dispute between their hostess, Tiffany Taylor, and her ex-husband Verger. Then Verger turns up missing and presumed dead.

6. *Touch of the Grape, A* (Berkley, 1998) The sisters are hosting the Crafty Ladies, a bunch of seemingly sweet old ladies working for a craft-kit business. Then a Crafty Lady is killed in a suspicious fire at the inn.

7. *Steak in Murder, A* (Berkley, 1999) The sisters sell the Inn at Hemlock Falls, but then a Texas cattlemen winds up dead on the premises, and the sisters are back in business, investigating murder and trying to reclaim their inn.

8. *Marinade for Murder* (Berkley, 2000) The sisters are trying to buy back the Inn at Hemlock Falls; then a TV producer is murdered on the premises.

9. *Just Desserts* (Berkley, 2002) While the Quilliams plan for an upcoming meteorologist convention, Hemlock Falls' new computer expert is killed in what seems to be a deliberate hit-and-run incident.

10. *Fried by Jury* (Berkley, 2003) The celebrity judge for a deep-fat-frying contest disappears along with a butcher knife from the kitchen of the Inn.

11. *Puree for Poison, A* (Berkley, 2003) With the 133rd anniversary of the Battle of Hemlock Falls in the offing, three people who had their last meals at the Inn turn up dead.

12. *Buried by Breakfast* (Berkley, 2004) The leader of a group protesting the relocation of the Hemlock Falls Civil War cemetery turns up dead, and someone else may follow.

13. *Dinner to Die For, A* (Berkley, 2006) The chief justice has ordered that a jury be sequestered at the Hemlock Falls Inn. Meanwhile, a raucous group is protesting the planned relocation of the local Civil War cemetery. Susan Dunlap's (q.v.) mystery has the same title.

14. *Ground to a Halt* (Berkley, 2007) One of the quarreling guests at the Hemlock Falls Inn winds up murdered on a pig farm. Then a psychic correctly predicts a second murder.

15. *Carol for a Corpse, A* (Berkley, 2007) A big-time magazine and TV show are about to give the Hemlock Falls Inn much-needed publicity. But then the editor's husband skis to his death.

II. Veterinarian Austin McKenzie and his wife, Madeline, of Trumansburg, New York, treat sick animals and solve murders.

1. *Case of the Roasted Onion, The* (Berkley, 2006) Introduces the McKenzies of Trumansburg, New York, who can mend creatures great and small but have yet to find a cure for murder.

2. *Case of the Tough-Talking Turkey, The* (Berkley, 2007) No one is surprised when mean turkey farmer Lewis O'Leary turns up dead in a dumpster.

Bishop, Paul

I. Fey Croaker is a Los Angeles Police Department homicide detective in her forties who has survived three bad marriages, an abusive upbringing, and the resentment of her male colleagues. The author, a veteran of the LAPD, brings authenticity and a real sense of the workings of a big-city police department to this rather convoluted, violent, and sometimes overwritten, but involving, series of mysteries.

1. *Kill Me Again* (Avon, 1994) The murder of a mysterious woman with multiple IDs, a million dollars in cash, and a spanking-new wardrobe, furnishings, and condo perplexes Fey Croaker, especially when fingerprints indicate that the woman had already been a murder victim 18 years previously.
2. *Twice Dead* (Avon, 1996) DNA evidence points to NBA superstar JoJo Cullen in a series of murders involving burying teenage prostitutes alive—but is there an evil twin lurking in the background?
3. *Tequila Mockingbird* (Scribner, 1997) Fey is put in charge of the investigation when an officer attached to the LAPD's elite antiterrorist unit is in shot in the head by his pregnant wife outside the West Los Angeles station.
4. *Chalk Whispers* (Scribner, 2000) Croaker, newly promoted to an elite homicide division in the LAPD, is greeted with a nasty case: the torture murder of a prominent advocate for sexually abused children who has relatives in high places.
5. *Pattern of Behavior* (Five Star, 2000) A collection of short stories, some of them featuring Fey Croaker, and a Fey Croaker novella: "Pattern of Behavior."

II. A second LAPD series features veteran street cop and amateur rodeo star "Calico" Jack Walker and his rookie female partner, Tina Tamiko. Calico Jack is on the point of retirement in the first novel and has retired to a life of running a charter fishing boat in the sequel.

1. *Citadel Run* (Tor, 1989) Thirty-year LAPD veteran Calico Jack Walker and female rookie cop Tina Tamiko get involved in an LA to Las Vegas and back drag race and some shenanigans at the Citadel Casino in Las Vegas.
2. *Sand against the Tide* (Tor, 1992) Calico Jack, now retired, and his teenage son are running a charter boat for sports fishermen when they get involved with a couple of nasty characters who are more interested in feeding the fishes than catching them.

Bissell, Sallie

Half-Cherokee Mary Crow, assistant DA and hot young prosecutor in Atlanta, Georgia, sometimes returns to her Pisgah County, North Carolina, home and her sometime lover, Jonathan Walkingstick. No matter where she goes, she gets involved with bloody doings and very nasty villains in this series of romantic, suspenseful mysteries. Tennessee native Sallie Bissell was a ghostwriter of young adult books before she initiated the Mary Crow series.

1. *In the Forest of Harm* (Bantam, 2001) Mary Crow, assistant DA in Atlanta, goes on a hiking vacation with her two best friends, Joan and Alex, to the area of her hometown in Pisgah County, North Carolina. But the vacation turns into a *Deliverance*-style setup when two crazed killers get involved.
2. *Darker Justice, A* (Bantam, 2002) FaithAmerica, a right-wing cabal, is using students at Camp Unakawaya, a last-chance military school for teenage boys, to assassinate federal judges who lean too far to the left.

3. *Call the Devil by His Oldest Name* (Dell, 2004) The crazed Stump Logan has returned with a new identity and a plan to get Mary by kidnapping Lily, Mary's three-month-old goddaughter.
4. *Legacy of Masks* (Bantam, 2005) Mary Crow returns home to Pisgah County and her former lover Jonathan Walkingstick and is settling in as a freelancer when Cherokee Ridge Standingdeer is accused of burying a hatchet in his girlfriend's head.

Bittner, Rosanne

I. Rosanne Bittner is the prolific author (50+ novels) of (mostly) paperback historical romances set in the American West. The first 6 volumes of the Savage Destiny series, her longest series, were published between 1983 and 1986. After a hiatus of 10 years, the seventh in the series was published along with reprints of the first 6. Savage Destiny has all of the Bittner trademarks: action, passionate romance, "forbidden" loves, agonizing separations, a well-realized historical setting, and sympathetic portraits of Native Americans. It is the saga of Abigail (Abbie) Trent and her half-breed lover, Zeke Monroe (aka Lone Eagle), which begins in 1845 and ends with their grandchildren some years after the Civil War.

1. *Sweet Prairie Passion* (Zebra, 1983) In 1845, riding west in her father's covered wagon, young Abbie Trent meets half-breed scout Zeke Monroe, who is searching for his Cheyenne mother, and romance is kindled.
2. *Ride the Free Wind* (Zebra, 1984) Zeke finds his mother's people, and he and Abbie become Cheyennes and turn their backs on the white man's world.
3. *River of Love* (Zebra, 1984) Abbie and Lone Eagle (formerly Zeke) face great troubles together on the plains, and their passion remains undiminished despite their tribulations.
4. *Embrace the Wild Land* (Zebra, 1984) Abbie and Lone Eagle try to make a life in the relatively peaceful New Mexico Territory but are torn apart in the maelstrom of the Civil War.
5. *Climb the Highest Mountain* (Zebra, 1985) Abbie and Lone Eagle struggle to hold on to their way of life as the Civil War is followed by a surge of homesteaders eager to wrest frontier land from the "heathen."
6. *Meet the New Dawn* (Zebra, 1986) Abbie and Lone Eagle are forced to part again as progress, in the form of the railroads, threatens to destroy the way of life of the "Plains Indians."
7. *Eagle's Song* (Zebra, 1996) "Overwhelmed with emotion," Bittner let the Savage Destiny series lie fallow for 10 years, then picked up the thread at a family reunion on the clan's Colorado ranch, where Abbie's son Wolf's Blood and her grandson Zeke must face some agonizing choices.

II. The Mystic Indian Series is a hardcover historical trilogy told from the Native American point of view. It covers events from 1833 (white chronology), when Brule Sioux maiden Star Dancer is pledged to Oglala warrior Stalking Wolf, to the 1870s, as the Lakotas (Sioux), driven from their old life by encroaching whites, wind up fighting for their existence under the leadership of Sitting Bull and Crazy Horse.

1. *Mystic Dreamers* (Forge, 1999) The love of reluctant bride Star Dancer and her warrior husband, Stalking Wolf, grows as they face a series of crises, including the first meeting of the Lakota with the White Man.
2. *Mystic Visions* (Forge, 2000) Continuing where *Mystic Dreamers* left off, this sequel follows the fortunes of the Lakotas from 1836 to 1851 and the increasing encroachment of the whites, as seen

through the eyes of characters such as Buffalo Dreamer, Rising Eagle, Big Little Boy, Never Sleeps, Fall Leaf Woman, and the young Crazy Horse.

3. *Mystic Warriors* **(Forge, 2001)** White hunters steal the sacred skin of the white buffalo, and the Lakotas are facing starvation because of the ravages of white settlers and cavalry, not only against the buffalo that they depend upon but also against their women and children.

III. The Blue Hawk Saga is a trilogy about Caleb Sax/Blue Hawk— a half-breed raised in early life by the Cheyenne and subsequently adopted by a white settler—who is torn between white and Cheyenne ways. In action taking place between the late 1700s and 1865, Caleb Sax/Blue Hawk becomes a frontiersman of note, is paired with the fiery Sarah, goes to Texas to settle and fight the Comanches and the Mexicans, and produces mixed-race children who roam the West having passionate love affairs and adventures of their own. Originally published in the 1980s, the trilogy has been republished by iUniverse.

1. *Savage Horizons* **(Popular Library, 1987)** In action spanning the late 1700s through 1832, Blue Hawk, raised by his Cheyenne mother, is renamed Caleb Sax by his white rescuer, falls in love with the fiery Sarah, and becomes a frontiersman of note.

2. *Frontier Fires* **(Popular Library, 1987)** In action taking place between 1833 and 1842, Caleb/Blue Hawk and Sarah settle in Texas, raise a family (including the equally passionate Lynda and Tom), and clash with the Comanches and the Mexicans.

3. *Destiny's Dawn* **(Popular Library, 1987)** In action covering from 1845 to 1865, Caleb, Sarah, Lynda, Tom, and another generation, including the Cheyenne-bred Cale, roam the West from Colorado to California, trying to realize their destinies amid the turmoil of the Civil War and continuing white encroachment.

IV. America West is an ongoing series, connected by various generations of the Wilde, Matthews, and Barnes families, reaching three volumes so far, relating the saga of westward expansion starting in the Allegheny Mountains in 1753 and carrying into the times of Tecumseh and Governor William Henry "Tippecanoe" Harrison (1809–11). Although told from the settler's point of view, the series has sympathetic portraits of Native Americans.

1. *Into the Wilderness: The Long Hunters* **(Forge, 2002)** In the Allegheny Mountains in 1753, following an attack by the usually peaceful Indians, 16-year-old Jessica Matthews falls in love with 29-year-old hunter and English spy Noah Barnes, but they are separated when Noah has to travel to Virginia to report on the French efforts to stir up the Indians against the British.

2. *Into the Valley: The Settlers* **(Forge, 2003)** The story of Annie Barnes, who is torn between two brothers, Luke and Jeremiah Wilde, who find themselves at loggerheads during the American Revolution.

3. *Into the Prairie: The Pioneers* **(Forge, 2004)** Jonah Wilde and his family, heading into the newly opened Indiana Territory, are attacked by a group of Potawatomi Indians, and his wife and son become hostages of Windigo, an aide of Tecumseh.

V. *Texas Embrace* and *Texas Passions* are a pair of romances telling the tale of John Hawkins, his wife, Tessa Reeves, and their children, who undergo many vicissitudes in 19th-century Texas.

1. *Texas Embrace* **(Zebra, 1997)** Tessa Reeves, captive of the renegade Apache band that killed her father, fears that, even if she is found, she will be rejected by white society. Then tough but sensitive lawman John Hawkins comes along.

2. *Texas Passions* **(Zebra, 1999)** Tessa and John have known nine years of happy marriage. Then their children, Texas and Honor, are kidnapped.

Bjarnhof, Karl

Born in 1898 to a poor family in a provincial Danish town, Bjarnhof, like the narrator of these two books, began to go blind at an early age. That experience is movingly portrayed in these fictionalized accounts. As the young boy's decreasing vision gradually cuts him off from the world of his peers, he makes friends at a local home for blind girls and turns to music for satisfaction. His strange, brooding father and the poverty of his family make the story even more poignant.

1. *Stars Grow Pale, The* **(Knopf, 1958)** Though reluctant to admit it, the young boy can no longer see the blackboard or his playmates' red ball. Danish title: *Stjernerne blegner.* Translated from the Danish by Naomi Walford.

2. *Good Light, The* **(Knopf, 1960)** At 14, the nearly sightless hero enters the Institute of the Blind in Copenhagen. Danish title: *Det gode lys.* Translated from the Danish by Naomi Walford.

Bjorn, Thyra Ferre

Heartwarming and homespun are the usual adjectives applied to Thyra Bjorn's books about a Swedish minister, Pastor Franzon, his wife, Maria, and their eight children. Mama is the benevolent but firm ruler of the family, and it is her determination that finally gets them moved to America. This is a series of semiautobiographies, tales of the simple pleasures of family life with Christian homilies and advice for readers in crisis. Button, the oldest daughter, is the autobiographical figure.

1. *Papa's Wife* **(Rinehart, 1955)** Swedish housemaid Maria marries Pastor Franzon, raises eight children, and eventually settles the family into America.

2. *Papa's Daughter* **(Rinehart, 1959)** The story of Charlotta Maria— nicknamed "Button," the second child, oldest daughter, and autobiographical figure—is told here.

3. *Mama's Way* **(Rinehart, 1959)** A collection of little sermons woven into story form—only loosely connected to the first two books.

4. *Dear Papa* **(Holt, 1963)** An addendum of letters written by Mama to her deceased husband—full of humorous anecdotes about their large family.

Black, Baxter

Baxter Black, former "large-animal" veterinarian, cowboy poet, humorist, NPR commentator, syndicated columnist ("On the Edge of Common Sense"), and publisher—Coyote Cowboy Company, Benson, Arizona—has written a pair of novels about Lick and Cody, two rodeo cowboys (speciality: bull riding). The picaresque plots are less important than the style in which they are told, full of wild and raunchy humor as Lick and Cody do lots of hard riding, hard drinking, and hard womanizing.

1. *Hey Cowboy, Wanna Get Lucky?* **(Crown, 1994)** Bull-riders Lick and Cody hope to qualify for the National Finals Rodeo in Oklahoma City, but there are many obstacles in their paths, including "whiskey and wild, wild women."

2. *Hey Cowgirl, Need a Ride?* **(Crown, 2005)** After a series of rodeo setbacks, Lick is down on his luck in Idaho, but his luck seems to

change with the arrival of the beautiful T(eddy) A(rizona) Grant, who is on the lam from Las Vegas. The now-married Cody puts in an appearance midway through the book.

Black, Cara

Aimee Leduc is a French American private investigator specializing in computer crime. Aimee, whose American mother disappeared and whose French father, from whom she inherited a detective agency, was murdered, is a believable character who gets involved in some serious criminal activity, including neo-Nazis, the Holocaust, ill-treatment of immigrants, serial killers, and official skulduggery, but the real draw of this series is the intimate depiction of some of the lesser-known Paris neighborhoods. Francophiles take note! Cara Black, not to be confused with the Zimbabwean tennis star of the same name, is a San Francisco–based writer who fell in love with, and remains in love with, Paris.

1. *Murder in the Marais* (Soho, 1999) Parisian computer forensics specialist Aimee Leduc is given the task of deciphering an encrypted photograph from the 1940s and delivering it to an old woman in the Marais (the historic Jewish quarter of Paris). This ostensibly simple assignment lands her in a morass of murder, neo-Nazis, corrupt government officials, anti-Semitism, and painful memories of the war.
2. *Murder in Belleville* (Soho, 2000) This time it is the Arab immigrants of Paris's Belleville District who are the victims of official and unofficial persecution. A car bombing reveals a secretive North African radical group, the dark side of French immigrant politics, and some nasty characters who don't want Aimee to snoop into their affairs.
3. *Murder in the Sentier* (Soho, 2002) When Aimee gets a phone call from a woman claiming to have known her long-missing mother, she agrees to meet the caller in the Sentier (the garment district of Paris).
4. *Murder in the Bastille* (Soho, 2003) Aimee, blinded by a mysterious attack, is forced to rely on her partner, computer expert Rena Friant, to be her eyes in this mystery involving Eastern European thugs and aggressive developers.
5. *Murder in Clichy* (Soho, 2005) Aimee agrees to help a Vietnamese nun by delivering an envelope to someone named Thadee Baret, which sets off a series of events involving a bag of precious jade, murder, government surveillance, and the abduction of her partner.
6. *Murder in Montmartre* (Soho, 2006) Aimee attempts to clear the name of a childhood friend, policewoman Laure Rousseau, who is charged with shooting her partner to death.
7. *Murder on the Ile Saint-Louis* (Soho, 2007) After receiving an agitated phone call, Aimee finds an infant girl in the courtyard of the Ile Saint-Louis building.
8. *Murder in the Rue de Paradis* (Soho, 2008) In the summer of 1995, Aimee briefly reconnects with a former boyfriend, investigative journalist Yves Robert. Then she is asked to identify Yves's body in the morgue.

Black, Ethan

PSEUDONYM UNKNOWN

Conrad Voort is the "richest cop" on the New York Police Department roster. He is also one of the best, having a near-supernatural ability to track down killers, terrorists, and other antisocial types. His lady love, Camilla Ryan, is beautiful and sexy. Things don't always run smoothly for Conrad, however: his romance has its vicissitudes, he is not flawless himself, and he is matched up against some very clever and very nasty villains. This mystery series, written pseudonymously by a "New York newspaperman," has a compelling hero, nail-bitingly suspenseful plots, good dialogue, credible villains, and a fine New York City ambience.

1. *Broken Hearts Club, The* (Ballantine, 1998) The Broken Hearts Club is a therapy group of rejected suitors that meets every Thursday in the back room of a New York tavern. Then the unresolved rage of the rejectees plays out in the murder of the mistress of "the Banker," one of the club members.
2. *Irresistible* (Ballantine, 2000) A series of killings by a female serial killer starts with the mutilation and murder of network executive Paul Anderson. Voort's ex-girlfriend Camilla Ryan, host of a TV newsmagazine show, is one of the suspects.
3. *All the Dead Were Strangers* (Ballantine, 2001) In a novel published shortly before 9/11, Conrad receives a list of five people, each having had some relationship with terrorism, and becomes aware of a clandestine and murderous government operation: the National Threat Assessment Agency (NTAA).
4. *Dead for Life* (Simon & Schuster, 2003) Former high school teacher and serial killer Wendall Nye blames Voort for his murder spree, as he reminds Voort in his messages to him.
5. *At Hell's Gate* (Simon & Schuster, 2004) Conrad and Camilla, back together again, are kayaking the waters of Hell's Gate on the East River when they come across a dead body in the water, which leads Voort to wealthy, corrupt lawyer Ted Stone, who is working at the highest levels of the United Nations.

Black, Michelle

Michelle Black's trio of novels about the post–Civil War American West (1868–1880) started out as straight historical fiction but, midway through the second novel, changed course and became a series of Victorian western mysteries. Members of the Randall family provide a connecting link between the three novels, as does the well-realized western setting. Historical characters such as George A. Custer put in an appearance, and the Cheyennes are represented as more sinned against than sinning. Kansas native Michelle Black is now based in Colorado.

1. *Uncommon Enemy, An* (Forge, 2001) Lieutenant Colonel Custer, needing a justification for his massacre of a Cheyenne village on November 2, 1868, on the banks of the Washita River, thinks he has found one in Eden Murdoch, who survived four years of Indian captivity.
2. *Solomon Spring* (Forge, 2002) Ten years after the events in *An Uncommon Enemy*, the paths of Eden Murdoch and her true love, Brad Randall, now commissioner of the Bureau of Indian Affairs, cross again as both seek to aid the beleaguered Cheyennes.
3. *Second Glass of Absinthe, The* (Forge, 2003) The boomtown of Leadville, Colorado, in 1880 is the setting for a mystery involving the fatal stabbing of Lucinda Ridenour, heiress to the Eve Dazzler mine. Her "kept man," Kit Randall, goes into hiding when he becomes one of the suspects.

Black, Veronica

PSEUDONYM OF Maureen Peters

Sister Joan, of the Order of the Daughters of Compassion convent in Cornwall, is another member of the sisterhood of crime-solving nuns (see, e.g., Monica Quill's [q.v.] Sister Mary Teresa). Sister Joan is a thirtysomething former artist who doesn't allow her genuine vocation and semireclusive life to prevent her from solving mysteries with an earthy common sense. Welsh-born writer Maureen Peters is the author of historical romances and mystery novels under her own name and noms de plume such as Catherine Darby, Belinda Gray, Judith Rothman, and Elizabeth Law.

1. *Vow of Silence, A* (St. Martin's, 1990) When a young novice is accidentally killed in her Cornish convent, Sister Joan is sent to investigate by her prioress.
2. *Vow of Chastity, A* (St. Martin's, 1992) The disappearance of one of her primary-school students and the murder of her lay colleague Sister Margaret prompt an investigation by Sister Joan.
3. *Vow of Sanctity, A* (St. Martin's, 1993) Sister Joan meets hostility from the local Protestants and several unsolved mysteries when she goes on a month's retreat to a cave in Scotland.
4. *Vow of Obedience, A* (St. Martin's, 1994) The garroted corpses of two teenage virgins are found dressed in wedding gowns in the village of Bodmin.
5. *Vow of Penance, A* (St. Martin's, 1994) The housekeeper at the rectory of the local parish "commits suicide" just after the departure of the pastor on an extended vacation.
6. *Vow of Devotion, A* (St. Martin's, 1995) Two new postulants—strange, frightened Magdalen Cole and sunny, eager Bernadette Fawkes—arrive at the convent simultaneously with a large group of New Agers.
7. *Vow of Fidelity, A* (St. Martin's, 1996) Sister Joan arrives in London at a 20-year reunion with her art-college classmates only to find that three of them have died under suspicious circumstances.
8. *Vow of Poverty, A* (St. Martin's, 1996) The Daughters of Compassion have inherited the manor house of the Tarquin family, but at least one of the Tarquins seems to be still around and up to deadly mischief.
9. *Vow of Adoration, A* (St. Martin's, 1997) Local antiques dealer Michael Peter seems to be connected to two deaths and a disappearance.
10. *Vow of Compassion, A* (St. Martin's, 1998) Sister Joan finds that things have gone awry at St. Keynes Cottage Hospital after Prioress Mother Dorothy's godmother dies of a heart attack while awaiting hip-replacement surgery.
11. *Vow of Evil, A* (Hale [UK], 2004) Outbreaks of vandalism in the village coincide with the sighting of a devil in the churchyard and strange candles left burning in the postulancy. Then Sister Joan finds a body, and a young police officer goes missing. Not published in the United States.

Blackston, Ray

If you want to find out what's happening in the Christian "singles scene," try Blackston's humorous trilogy about the trials and tribulations of single young men who are trying to find eligible females within a Christian church world that focuses mainly on couples and families. Stockbroker Jay Jarvis and missionary Neil Rucker, finding themselves in Greenville, South Carolina (the author's hometown), are interested in finding "respectable" Christian girls and go through a series of rather wacky adventures peopled with quirky characters that take them as far afield as Ecuador and Australia. Christian fiction with a humorous touch.

1. *Flabbergasted* (Revell, 2003) Stockbroker Jay Jarvis, transplanted to Greenville, South Carolina, and looking for single women, is advised to try the churches, so he joins the North Hills Presbyterian Church singles group and meets a succession of rather odd characters.
2. *Delirious Summer, A* (Revell, 2004) Neil Rucker, missionary on furlough in Greenville, is desperate for a date, but 81-year-old, single Beatrice Dean isn't quite what he's looking for.
3. *Lost in Rooville* (Revell, 2005) Jay Jarvis and his best friend, Steve, head for the outback in Australia and undergo some fairly serious adventures.

Blake, Jennifer

PSEUDONYM OF Patricia Maxwell

I.   One of the most popular American romance writers, Jennifer Blake has written more than 60 novels, the majority of them under the Blake pseudonym but some novels as Patricia Ponder, Maxine Patrick, and Elizabeth Treherne, as well as under her real name, Patricia Maxwell. Blake's novels are usually full of hot romance, historical melodrama, and exciting adventures. The novels in the Louisiana Gentlemen (or Turn-Coupe, Louisiana) series are linked together by their Louisiana location and various members of the Benedict family who usually provide the male support for the female protagonists. The Louisiana-born-and-bred Blake provides vivid Louisiana settings for many of her novels. A pair of linked novels, *Royal Passion* (Fawcett, 1993) and *Royal Seduction* (E-Reads, 1994), have also been published.

1. *Kane* (Mira, 1998) Lawyer Kane Benedict, grandson of the owner of Compton's Funeral Home in fictional Turn-Coupe, Louisiana, takes on Berry Associations, an unethical funeral-service company that has been forcing small funeral homes out of business by price gouging.
2. *Luke* (Mira, 1999) Luke Benedict feels obliged to protect famed romance novelist April Halstead when her life is threatened after she decides to use one of Luke's ancestors in her latest book.
3. *Roan* (Mira, 2000) Small-town sheriff Roan Benedict feels responsible for Tory, the woman he shot after the robbery of a local grocery store, when she insists that she is a kidnapping victim.
4. *Clay* (Mira, 2001) Janna Kerr turns to a doctor who deals in black-market human organs when her daughter, Lainey, comes down with terminal renal disease and needs a kidney transplant.
5. *Wade* (Mira, 2002) Old family friend Wade Benedict goes to the fictional country of Hazaristan to rescue young Chloe Madison from her nasty stepbrother, and he brings down a personal jihad against the Benedict family.

II. Master at Arms, another Louisiana series, is set in New Orleans in the 1840s. The tales are linked by the Sword Masters, or *maitres d'armes*, a group of valiant but roguish swordsmen.

1. *Challenge to Honor* (Mira, 2005) Celina confronts Sword Master Rio de Silva, determined to ward off her brother's death in a duel.
2. *Dawn Encounter* (Mira, 2006) Loisette Moisant turns to swordsman Caid O'Neill, who killed her loathsome husband in a duel, when she becomes the pawn of schemers who wish to steal her fortune and see her dead.
3. *Rogue's Salute* (Mira, 2007) Swordsman Nicholas Pasquale proposes marriage to Juliette Armant to find a mother for his young charge, so he says. An ancestral marriage chest and an evil twin play roles.

Blake, Michael

Michael Blake's historical novel *Dances with Wolves* became an international hit in its 1990 screen version, directed by and starring Kevin Costner (with a screenplay by Blake). In the novel *Dances with Wolves*, US Army lieutenant John Dunbar admires the Comanches (not the Lakota Sioux, as in the movie) and takes up their way of life. The sequel, *The Holy Road*, finds Dunbar living among the Comanches 10 years later, when they are attacked by white rangers. Both novels see events from the point of view of the Plains Indians, who, in their unsuccessful struggle to maintain their ancestral ways, cannot fathom the white man's greed and duplicity. Blake has also written a surprisingly sympathetic novel about General Custer: *Marching to Valhalla* (Villard, 2002).

1. *Dances with Wolves* (Fawcett, 1988) In 1864 Lieutenant John Dunbar requests transfer to the Great Plains, and finding Fort Sedgwick deserted, he falls in with a party of Comanches and absorbs their ways.
2. *Holy Road, The* (Villard, 2001) It is now 1874, and Dunbar, now going under the name of Dances with Wolves, is living with his wife, Stands with a Fist, and their children in a Comanche village when the settlement is attacked by white soldiers.

Blake, Michelle

PSEUDONYM OF Michelle Blake Simon

Texas-born Lily Connor is a female Episcopalian priest and amateur sleuth located in Boston whose wardrobe contains cowboy boots and a clerical collar. Lily stars in a trio of entertaining mysteries, with intricate plots and memorable characters, in which the issues facing a contemporary religious organization are examined. Michelle Blake Simon is a Harvard Divinity School graduate, poet, and English instructor (Tufts University).

1. *Tentmaker, The* (Putnam, 1999) Lily Connor, assigned to service as interim priest at Boston's St. Mary of the Garden Episcopal Church after the sudden death of Father Fred Barnes, the church's longtime spiritual head, runs into indifference and downright hostility from the church's members.
2. *Earth Has No Sorrow* (Putnam, 2001) Now the director of the Women's Center in downtown Boston, Lily gets involved when a vicious hate crime is committed against Holocaust survivor Anna Banieka.
3. *Book of Light, The* (Putnam, 2003) Lily gets into the mystery of the Book of Light, an ancient scroll that possibly contained the secret words of Jesus and served as source material for the Gospels.

Blake, Nicholas

PSEUDONYM OF Cecil Day-Lewis

These mysteries written under a pseudonym by Britain's late poet laureate are beautifully crafted, literate, and sophisticated entertainments. Nigel Strangeways is a tall, sandy-haired private investigator who solves good old-fashioned jigsaw puzzlers with urbanity and wit. There is a definite chronology to Strangeways's adventures. The books chronicle his courtship and marriage to Georgia Cavendish, their early married years in London, the war years, and, after Georgia's death, Nigel's relationship with sculptress Clare Massinger. Strangeways is the name of a prison in Manchester, England. Not all of Blake's mysteries feature Strangeways.

1. *Question of Proof, A* (Harper, 1935) Nigel investigates a murder in Sudeley Hall, a boys' prep school.
2. *Shell of Death* (Harper, 1936) Nigel goes to rural Somerset to protect the life of Britain's legendary air hero, Fergus O'Brien. He meets Georgia Cavendish. English title: *Thou Shell of Death*.
3. *There's Trouble Brewing* (Harper, 1937) Nigel and Georgia are married as this case begins with an invitation to a literary society and the death of a dog.
4. *Beast Must Die, The* (Harper, 1938) A grief-stricken father forces himself to live with a murderer so that he can avenge his son's death.
5. *Smiler with the Knife, The* (Harper, 1939) Nigel and his wife fight a master criminal who has a sinister plot to take over England. This book is more thriller than mystery.
6. *Summer Camp Mystery, The* (Harper, 1940) Someone calling himself the Mad Hatter is playing pranks on vacationers in a British holiday camp. English title: *Malice in Wonderland*. Variant title: *Malice with Murder*.
7. *Corpse in the Snowman, The* (Harper, 1941) In wintry Essex, Nigel investigates the strange behavior of a cat until more grisly matters turn up. English title: *The Case of the Abominable Snowman*.
8. *Minute for Murder* (Harper, 1947) In wartime Britain, someone has given beautiful blonde Nita Prince a poisoned cup of coffee.
9. *Head of a Traveler* (Harper, 1949) Who was the headless corpse? And why was the head hidden on Robert Seaton's estate?`
10. *Dreadful Hollow, The* (Harper, 1953) Involves poison-pen letters and a dead body at the bottom of the dreadful hollow in the little village of Prior's Umborne.
11. *Whisper in the Gloom, The* (Harper, 1954) A dying stranger hands a crumpled message to a small boy in a park. Variant title: *Catch and Kill*.
12. *End of Chapter* (Harper, 1957) Somebody slips libelous passages into General Thoresby's autobiography. Introduces Clare Massinger, who will become the new woman in widower Nigel's life.
13. *Widow's Cruise, The* (Harper, 1959) Nigel, on a cruise of the Greek islands with Clare Massinger, investigates the murder of a fellow passenger.
14. *Worm of Death, The* (Harper, 1961) Dr. Piers Loudon, the new neighbor of Nigel and Clare, disappears and is found dead.
15. *Sad Variety, The* (Harper, 1964) Russians have kidnapped Professor Wragby's daughter, and Nigel must keep him from trading secrets for her return.
16. *Morning after Death, The* (Harper, 1966) While spending a year at an Ivy League college near Boston, Nigel is enlisted by local police to help solve the murder of a classics professor.

Blakely, Mike

A pair of novels, *Shortgrass Song* and *Too Long at the Dance*, relate the up-and-down fortunes of Ab Holcomb, Mexican War hero and frontier settler, and his son Caleb, a cowboy fiddler or country musician. They are rousing tales of life in the American West in the latter half of the 19th century, full of authentic detail, song lyrics of the time, and intriguing characters. At the end of *Too Long at the Dance*, a new character, the enigmatic Plenty Man (aka Honore Greenwood), enters the scene. *Moon Medicine* and its sequel, *Come Sundown*, relate the early life of Plenty Man, recalled in 1927 at the age of 99 in a style reminiscent of Thomas Berger's *Little Big Man* (q.v.). Texas-born country musician Mike Blakely is the author of several other historical westerns.

1. *Moon Medicine* (Forge, 2001) French fugitive (from a duel fatal to his opponent) Honore Greenwood, called Plenty Man by the

Comanches, relates, in old age, his wild and woolly adventures in the 1840s American West, where he interacts with various white, red, and brown characters, including the historical Kit Carson and the Bent brothers.

2. *Come Sundown* (Forge, 2006) Honore Greenwood, aka Plenty Man, goes from Comanche warrior to New Mexico Civil War volunteer and back again in action taking place from 1853 to 1868.

3. *Shortgrass Song* (Forge, 1994) The saga of Ab Holcomb, a Mexican War hero, who settles in the Pike's Peak region of Colorado, where his family, including his asthmatic son Caleb, is joined by the harmonica-playing runaway slave Buster and Comanche captive Snake Woman.

4. *Too Long at the Dance* (Forge, 1996) Ab Holcomb's son Caleb becomes a country musician who goes on the road to stifle his passion for Amelia, his brother's widow. But he eventually returns to survive a family feud, an Indian uprising, and the Johnson County War.

Blanc, Nero

PSEUDONYM OF Cordelia Frances Biddle & Steve Zettler

Annabella "Belle" Graham, crossword-puzzle editor for a Newcastle, Massachusetts, newspaper, and Greek American private eye Rosco Polycrates form a detecting partnership (and eventually a marriage partnership) in a series of mysteries in which crossword-puzzle clues are keys to the solutions. The Nero Blanc series, full of intricate, sometimes convoluted plots, will appeal to crossword and puzzle mystery fans. Several crossword puzzles (with solutions) appear in each book. (Librarians should note that the crossword forms are in the books, ready to be filled in.) Another crossword mystery series is Parnell Hall's Puzzle Lady series (q.v.). "Nero Blanc" is the pseudonym for a wife-and-husband team of authors: Cordelia Frances Biddle and Steve Zettler. Under her own name, Biddle is the author of historical fiction and the coauthor, with Pattie Hearst, of *Murder at San Simeon* (Scribner, 1996).

1. *Crossword Murder, The* (Berkley, 1999) When wealthy crossword-puzzle editor and man-about-town Thomas C. Briephs is found strangled in his bed, the Newcastle police write it off as the result of some kinky sex gone wrong, but Briephs's mother isn't so sure and hires private eye Rosco Polycrates to conduct an investigation.

2. *Two Down* (Berkley, 2000) After Rosco takes on the investigation of the case of two women lost at sea off Nantucket, Belle Graham starts receiving crossword puzzles containing pointed clues to the mystery.

3. *Crossword Connection, The* (Berkley, 2001) Odd and threatening messages containing wickedly contrived crossword clues may lead to the solution of the murders of two homeless men, a missing puppy, and the kidnapping of Rosco.

4. *Crossworder's Holiday, A* (Berkley, 2002) Five Christmas-themed stories involving Belle and Rosco and including crossword puzzles.

5. *Crossword to Die For, A* (Berkley, 2002) Belle's father, Dr. Theodore Graham, dies en route to a visit with his newlywed daughter, leaving clues to an unsuspected secret life.

6. *Corpus de Crossword* (Berkley, 2003) A deluge of anonymous crosswords provides clues but also confusion to Belle and Rosco, investigating a murder in the tiny village of Taneysville, Massachusetts.

7. *Crossworder's Gift, A* (Berkley, 2003) Includes five more crossword mysteries–cum–crossword puzzles.

8. *Anatomy of a Crossword* (Berkley, 2004) Belle goes to Hollywood to help with a TV movie being made about a crime she previously solved. Of course, things start to go wrong: the writer of the movie is killed, and the crossword Belle is supposed to develop for the film develops all kinds of glitches.

9. *Wrapped Up in Crosswords* (Berkley, 2004) More crossword puzzle mystery stories and puzzles to be solved.

10. *Another Word for Murder* (Berkley, 2005) Dentist and expensive-car collector Dan Tacete is missing and feared kidnapped, or dead, in this mystery involving a stolen car ring, the hit-and-run death of a child, some hanky-panky in the dental office, and, of course, crosswords.

11. *Crossworder's Delight, A* (Berkley, 2005) During a holiday party at the Paul Revere Inn, Belle discovers a handmade, unused book of dessert recipes written in the form of mysteries. Of course, foul play ensues.

12. *Death on the Diagonal* (Berkley, 2006) Rosco is investigating a suspicious fire at the Collins family stables in Newcastle.

Bland, Eleanor Taylor

Marti MacAlister is the only black female detective in Lincoln Prairie, a small town near Chicago. Marti, a former Chicago policewoman, is a strong character, able to deal with the death of her policeman husband; a white male partner, Martin "Vik" Jessenovik, who isn't used to working with women; and the various crimes that occur in the not-so-quiet suburb of Lincoln Prairie.

1. *Dead Time* (St. Martin's, 1993) Formerly wealthy Lauretta Dorsey is found murdered in her room at the Cramer Hotel, a local flophouse.

2. *Slow Burn* (St. Martin's, 1993) The bodies of a Latino receptionist and a pregnant 12-year-old are found in the wreckage of a burned-out medical clinic.

3. *Gone Quiet* (St. Martin's, 1994) The suspicious death of a highly respected member of the Mount Gethsemane Baptist Church turns up some ugly family secrets.

4. *Done Wrong* (St. Martin's, 1995) The alleged suicide of a colleague of Marti's late husband, Johnny, raises questions about Johnny's "suicide" three years earlier.

5. *Keep Still* (St. Martin's, 1996) Two "accidental" deaths prove to be homicides, and Marti and Vik discover a link between the victims and a missing abused child.

6. *See No Evil* (St. Martin's, 1998) A homeless man might hold the key to the mysterious death of a young woman found near Lake Michigan.

7. *Tell No Tales* (St. Martin's, 1999) The mummified corpse of a pregnant African American woman is found in an abandoned downtown theater.

8. *Scream in Silence* (St, Martin's, 2000) Vik and the newly remarried Marti have to deal with arson, shady land deals, a mad bomber, and the murder of Virginia McCroft, local political gadfly and busybody.

9. *Whispers in the Dark* (St. Martin's, 2001) The investigation of a 20-year killing spree involving severed hands of victims leads Marti and Vik to Chicago's ethnic neighborhoods.

10. *Windy City Dying* (St. Martin's, 2002) The release of a vengeful figure from her past and the murder of 16-year-old Graciela Lara keep Marti and husband Ben from enjoying suburban life in Lincoln Prairie.

11. *Fatal Remains* (St. Martin's, 2003) Marti and Vik, investigating the death of a young archaeologist working on the Josiah Smith

estate, turn up an odd history of accidents, most of them involving members of the Smith family.

12. **Cold and Silent Dying, A** (**St. Martin's, 2004**) Marti doesn't get along with her new boss, Lieutenant Gail Nicholson, who is also African American—and ambitious. Then Marti can't drop the investigation of the death of a homeless woman in Lincoln Prairie, dismissed by Nicholson as unimportant.

13. **Dark and Deadly Deception, A** (**St. Martin's, 2005**) The body of Savannah Payne-Jones, black actress and known gambler, washes up on the shore of the Des Plaines River.

Blatty, William Peter

The Exorcist spawned so many imitations that, for a while, the "possession" novel threatened to become a genre of its own. Blatty's screenplay for the movie version (1973) won him an Oscar. *Exorcist II: The Heretic*, the inevitable movie sequel, seems to have no relationship to the print sequel. Blatty directed *The Exorcist III* (1990), a film version of *Legion* starring George C. Scott. In 2000 the film *The Exorcist* was rereleased with 11 minutes of extra footage and a new ending.

1. **Exorcist, The** (**Harper, 1971**) A graphic horror story of the possession and eventual exorcism of sweet young Regan MacNeil.
2. **Legion** (**Simon & Schuster, 1983**) Detective Bill Kinderman reappears in this case, which starts with a series of gruesome murders and leads to a madman.

Blaylock, James P.

I. Californian James P. Blaylock has attracted a devoted cadre of fans for his well-written, evocative fiction, which contains, in varying amounts, elements of fantasy, science fiction, and the supernatural. His short story "Paper Dragons" won the World Fantasy Award in 1986. His novel *Homunculus,* which won the Philip K. Dick Award the same year, is set in a romantic, idealized Victorian Britain, a sort of H. G. Wells world in which imaginative new technologies clash with sinister occult conspiracies. In *Homonculus* and its sequel, *Lord Kelvin's Machine,* gentleman adventurer and scientist of leisure Langdon St. Ives clashes with the evil vivisectionist and animator of the dead Narbondo in tales that include time traveling and threats to "civilization as we know it" among a potpourri of SF, fantasy, and supernatural elements. *The Digging Leviathan,* published first in the series, is set in the 1980s in California and includes among its characters Edward St. Ives (related to Langdon?), some mad inventors, the sinister Dr. Frosticos, and the enigmatic Ashbless, who has wandered in from Tim Powers's fantasy classic *The Anubis Gates* (Ace, 1983) and revives that hoary pseudo-scientifc device the Hollow Earth, treated by Edgar Rice Burroughs (q.v.), among others, in his Pellucidar books. A previously unpublished Langdon St. Ives story appears in *The Man in the Moon* (see series II, below). Ashbless reappears in *The William Ashbless Memorial Cookbook* (Subterranean, 2002), coauthored with Tim Powers.

1. **Homunculus** (**Ace, 1986**) In 1870s London a dead man pilots an airship, and a night at the local pub can result in an eternity at the Black Pudding with the rest of the reanimated dead.
2. **Lord Kelvin's Machine** (**Arkham House, 1991**) St. Ives chases the revived Narbondo, who is responsible for the death of St. Ives's lady love and is planning to shift Earth's orbit into the path of a passing comet. Lord Kelvin's "electromagnetic" machine, part of an elaborate blackmail plot, is commandeered by St. Ives for a trip back through time.

3. **Digging Leviathan, The** (**Ace, 1984**) Several characters in 1980s California, including Jim Hastings, his eccentric father, his uncle Edward St. Ives, and his gilled friend Giles Peach, are building a machine to take them to Earth's hollow center, but the evil Dr. Frosticos has plans of his own.

II. An earlier fantasy series is more reminiscent of J. R. R. Tolkien's *The Hobbit* (q.v.) than of H. G. Wells. It is about Twombly Town, a rather idyllic rural town full of quaint characters and elfen marvels such as Cheesemaker Jonathan Bing, the boy Dooly, Dooly's grandfather Theophile Escargot, the elf aviator Twickenham, and the sinister dwarf vivisectionist Selznak. *The Man in the Moon* (Subterranean, 2002), published in a limited edition, contains a reworking of the earlier first draft of the latter part of *The Elfin Ship,* the first novel in the series.

1. **Stone Giant, The** (**Ace, 1989**) This prequel relates the picaresque adventures of Theophile Escargot, grandfather-to-be of Dooly, along the Oriel River and in Balumnia, including an early run-in with Selznak the dwarf.
2. **Elfin Ship, The** (**Del Rey, 1982**) Master Cheeser Jonathan Bing, the dog Ahab, the boy Dooly, and Man of Science Artemis voyage from Twombly Town with a raft load of cheeses and encounter trolls, sandbars, goblins, elves, Twickenham's airship, an undersea device, the Lumbog Globe, and elderly pirate Theophile Escargot's cloak of invisibility.
3. **Disappearing Dwarf, The** (**Del Rey, 1983**) Jonathan, Ahab, and company embark on the Oriel River again, this time in search of treasure in Selznak the dwarf's abandoned castle, but they are diverted, through a magic door, into the land of Balumnia.

Blevins, Meredith

Amature sleuth Annie Szabo is a native Californian, a writer, a mother, and a widow. She stars in a series of mysteries with a San Francisco background that features Gypsy lore—her mother-in-law, Madame Mina, is a Gypsy fortune-teller—humor, zany characters, and an appealing protagonist.

1. **Hummingbird Wizard, The** (**Forge, 2003**) When Annie Szabo's childhood friend and occasional lover Jerry is murdered, Annie begins her own investigation with her mother-in-law, the Gypsy fortune-teller Madame Mina.
2. **Vanished Priestess, The** (**Forge, 2004**) When Margo Spanger, the eccentric owner-operator of a New Age circus, is murdered, Annie investigates, although her hands are already full of family matters.
3. **Red Hot Empress, The** (**Forge, 2005**) Annie writes an article about Jimmy Qi, an Asian boy with the power to heal through music, which brings the boy some unwanted attention.

Blish, James

I. Cities in Flight, or, as it was known in its original magazine form, the Okie series, started off as a series of rather conventional science-fiction adventure stories, published as *Earthman, Come Home.* But with the publication of a prequel, *They Shall Have Stars,* and a sequel set in the far future, *The Triumph of Time,* Cities in Flight became a classic. Another prequel, *A Life for the Stars,* was added a few years later. The basic plot of Cities in Flight concerns 21st-century cities, including New York City, led by its "immortal" mayor John Amalfi, that travel through interstellar space trading work for supplies. Eventually the denizens of New York are confronted with the ultimate: the collapse of the universe. American writer James Blish (d. 1975) eventually felt cramped by the genre of science fiction, and although his dramatizations for the long-running *Star Trek* television show were his bread and butter, he tried his hand at other literary work, including drama and an unpublished treatise on musical theory. However, his science-fiction work has proven to be his main claim to lasting fame.

Cities in Flight (Avon, 1966; rev. ed. , 1970) is an omnibus containing all four volumes. It was reprinted as recently as 2000 (Overlook).

1. *They Shall Have Stars* (Faber [UK], 1956) In a prequel set in the second decade of the 21st century, New York and other cities develop a means of propelling whole cities through space under the cover of a construction job on the planet Jupiter. Original US title: *Year 2018!* (Avon, 1957).
2. *Life for the Stars, A* (Putnam, 1962) In the last volume published, but the second volume sequentially, the flying cities blast off for interstellar space to get away from a tyrannical government on Earth.
3. *Earthman, Come Home* (Putnam, 1955) Mayor John Amalfi and his flying New Yorkers wander through space, trading their job skills for necessary supplies from planet to planet.
4. *Triumph of Time, The* (Avon, 1958) The seemingly immortal Mayor Amalfi and his resourceful New Yorkers face their greatest challenge: the collapse of the universe. UK title: *A Clash of Cymbals*.

II. *A Case of Conscience* (Ballantine, 1958), the story of a Jesuit naturalist who has to face the implications of an ideal extraterrestrial society, and *Doctor Mirabilis* (Faber [UK], 1964; rev. ed., Dodd, Mead, 1971), a historical novel about the 13th-century protoscientist Roger Bacon, form, together with the two apocalyptic novels *Black Easter* and *The Day after Judgment*, a quartet linked by theological concerns but, except for the latter two novels, not by plot. The series is called After Such Knowledge in its collected edition (Legend [UK], 1991).

1. *Black Easter; or, Faust Aleph-Null* (Doubleday, 1968) The arms-mogul Baines enlists the aid of the Black Magician Theron Ware, who, among his skills, can call up demons from hell to stir things up on a too-peaceful Earth. Published together with number 2 as *The Devil's Day* (Baen, 1990).
2. *Day after Judgment, The* (Doubleday, 1971) Ware releases 80 demons from hell for one night, bringing on Satan himself and Armageddon, and only the Jesuit priest Father Domenico can save the forces of good. Published together with number 1 as *The Devil's Day* (Baen, 1990).

Bloch, Robert (Albert)

A number of years ago, the authors of *Sequels* were accosted in Edinburgh, Scotland, by a drunk who announced himself as "Norman Bates" and invited us to his "motel," another testimony to the fame of *Psycho*. Although Robert Bloch (d. 1994), the author of the original novel, is regarded as one of the classic writers of horror fiction, *Psycho* owes its worldwide notoriety to Alfred Hitchcock's 1960 film starring Anthony Perkins as Norman and featuring Janet Leigh in the infamous shower scene (which takes two sentences in the novel). Bloch didn't work on the screenplay based on his novel, or on the subsequent film sequels, but he did write two novelistic follow-ups that "accepted" Hitchcock's version of Norman, who is short, fat, and 40 in the original novel.

1. *Psycho* (Simon & Schuster, 1959) Norman Bates is attracted to the pretty young girl who is staying at his lonely motel in western Kansas.
2. *Psycho II* (Warner, 1982) Norman escapes from the state hospital for the insane and hitchhikes (in a nun's habit) to Hollywood, where they are filming his life story.
3. *Psycho House* (Tor, 1990) The Bates Motel has been rebuilt as a tourist attraction 30 years after the original crimes, and hacked-up corpses are appearing again.

Block, Barbara

Pet-store owner Robin Light, a hard-drinking, sloppy, fortysomething widow, is Syracuse's (New York) contribution to the part-time private detective ranks. The likable, if somewhat reckless, Robin, her black ex-cop boyfriend, George, and an interesting cast of characters, including street people, troubled teenagers, and the "exotic" animals that turn up at Noah's Ark, Robin's not-very-profitable pet store, all add up to a series of readable, if not especially original, mysteries.

1. *Chutes and Adders* (Kensington, 1994) After Robin Light's criminally inclined husband, Murphy, dies of a drug overdose, one of Robin's pet-store employees is fatally bitten by a snake, and caches of money are found hidden away in the store and in Robin's apartment.
2. *Twister* (Kensington, 1995) Robin goes for a drive with her glamorous friend Lynn to "see this guy," and she finds Lynn kneeling over the corpse of a vaguely familiar man who, for some reason, has a business card from Robin's journalism days in his pocket.
3. *In Plain Sight* (Kensington, 1996) A former neighbor, teacher Marsha Pennington, is found floating in a reservoir outside Syracuse after engaging Robin to investigate her estranged husband's tax returns.
4. *Scent of Murder* (Kensington, 1997) Street girl Amy Richmond comes into Robin's pet store with a ferret in her bag and a tale of how Robin's late husband, Murphy, told her to go to Robin if she ever needed anything.
5. *Vanishing Act* (Kensington, 1998) College student Bryan Hayes hires Robin to look into the disappearance of his sister, Melissa, four months earlier.
6. *Endangered Species* (Kensington, 1999) Neighborhood kid Manuel and his cousin Eli turn up at Robin's pet store with a wild tale about a suitcase allegedly full of smuggled Cuban cigars.
7. *Blowing Smoke* (Kensington, 2001) A teenage runaway in nearby Cazenovia and an animal psychic, Pat Humphrey, suspected by the Taylor siblings of defrauding their elderly mother, Rose, engage Robin Light in a plot that wanders between New York State and Ontario.
8. *Rubbed Out* (Kensington, 2002) The Russian Mafia, a runaway wife, a shady lawyer, death by torture, and a climactic shoot-out are all involved in this convoluted tale.
9. *Salt City Blues* (Severn, 2005) Robin, working part-time as a bartender to keep Noah's Ark afloat during a slow Christmas season, takes up the case of teenager Freddy Sanchez, who tries to fence stolen goods at the bar and winds up dead a few days later.

Block, Lawrence

I. Matthew Scudder, an alcoholic ex-New York police detective, couldn't escape the pain and guilt he felt after having accidentally shot and killed a seven-year-old girl. In earlier novels in the series, he occasionally roused himself out of his alcoholic haze long enough to use his old police skills and connections, such as the streetwise TJ and gangster Mick Ballou, to help a friend solve a problem. In later novels, Matt proves himself to be more resilient than expected: he dries out, attends Alcoholics Anonymous meetings, and reinvolves himself with other people, marrying his old flame (a former call girl) Elaine. Jeff Bridges played Scudder in the movie *Eight Million Ways to Die* (1986), loosely based on several novels in the series.

1. *When the Sacred Ginmill Closes* (**Arbor House, 1986**) Scudder is one of roomful of customers who witness the robbery of an after-hours Irish pub. Though published after number 6, this is told as a flashback to the summer of 1975.
2. *In the Midst of Death* (**Dell, 1976**) Venal cop Jerry Broadhurst is blowing the whistle on his fellow policemen by testifying to a special prosecutor investigating police corruption.
3. *Sins of the Fathers, The* (**Dell, 1977**) Cale Hannaford, a prosperous businessman, asks Matt to find out more about the circumstances of his estranged daughter's murder.
4. *Time to Murder and Create* (**Dell, 1977**) Spinner, a prosperous but doomed blackmailer, prepays Scudder to investigate murder.
5. *Stab in the Dark, A* (**Arbor House, 1981**) Nine years after Barbara Ettinger's death, Scudder tries to discover who killed her.
6. *Eight Million Ways to Die* (**Arbor House, 1982**) Prostitute Kim Dakkinen wants to get out of "the life" and asks Scudder to speak to Chance, her pimp.
7. *Out on the Cutting Edge* (**Morrow, 1989**) Trying to stay off alcohol with the help of Alcoholics Anonymous, Scudder is investigating the disappearance of a girl from Muncie, Indiana, and the alleged suicide of a fellow AA member.
8. *Ticket to the Boneyard, A* (**Morrow, 1990**) James Leo Motley, who was framed by Scudder 12 years previously, is out of prison and seeking revenge.
9. *Dance at the Slaughterhouse, A* (**Morrow, 1991**) Now sober and attending AA meetings, Matt investigates the suspicious death of Amanda Thurman, wife of a television producer.
10. *Walk among the Tombstones, A* (**Morrow, 1991**) Scudder reluctantly investigates the kidnappings and murders of the wives of high-level drug dealers.
11. *Devil Knows You're Dead, The* (**Morrow, 1993**) Matt revives his romance with former-call-girl Elaine while investigating the murder of a young man talking on a public phone.
12. *Long Line of Dead Men, A* (**Morrow, 1994**) Members of the Not Dead Yet Club, a variation on the "last man" club, are dying with suspicious celerity.
13. *Even the Wicked* (**Morrow, 1996**) Marriage with Elaine has mellowed Matt somewhat, but he is as sharp as ever when he investigates cases involving a serial killer who specializes in "bad guys" and the killing of a man who's in last stages of AIDS.
14. *Everybody Dies* (**Morrow, 1998**) Two of Matt's old mobster pal Mick Ballou's associates have been killed in a liquor hijacking, and Scudder finds himself caught in the middle.
15. *Hope to Die* (**Morrow, 2001**) Byrne and Susan Hollander, a well-off Manhattan couple, have been savagely murdered, supposedly by burglars.
16. *All the Flowers Are Dying* (**Morrow, 2005**) Matt and Elaine may be the targets of a killer linked to the unresolved murders in number 15.

II. Unlike the fairly grim Matt Scudder series, the series featuring Bernie Rhodenbarr, a gentlemanly New York cat burglar who turns detective from time to time (mostly to clear himself of false charges), is breezy and lighthearted. Bernie's lock-picking skills and street smarts give him an edge over most police detectives. Readers who can tolerate Bernie's incessant wisecracking will enjoy these tales of a modern Robin Hood. Bernie was transmogrified into "Bernice" Rhodenbarr in the Whoopi Goldberg movie *Burglar* (1987), loosely based on Lawrence Block's series.

1. *Burglars Can't Be Choosers* (**Random House, 1977**) Employed to steal a mysterious blue-leather box, Bernie's mission is interrupted by the arrival of the police, who find a corpse in the bedroom.
2. *Burglar in the Closet, The* (**Random House, 1978**) Bernie becomes an inadvertent witness to a murder while hiding in a bedroom closet.
3. *Burglar Who Liked to Quote Kipling, The* (**Random House, 1979**) A rare Kipling volume is Bernie's objective, but he has lots of competition.
4. *Burglar Who Studied Spinoza, The* (**Random House, 1981**) Bernie is running a used bookstore in the Village in this episode, which centers on the theft of some rare coins.
5. *Burglar Who Painted like Mondrian, The* (**Arbor House, 1983**) Someone else stole the Mondrian masterpiece, but unless Bernie finds it, he'll take the rap.
6. *Burglar Who Traded Ted Williams, The* (**Dutton, 1994**) Bernie, faced with eviction from the premises of his bookstore, commits "one last burglary."
7. *Burglar Who Thought He Was Bogart, The* (**Dutton, 1995**) Beautiful foreigner Ilona, who seems to share Bernie's interest in Bogart movies, involves him in some international intrigue.
8. *Burglar in the Library, The* (**Dutton, 1997**) With lesbian pal Carolyn Kaiser, Bernie goes off to New England for a weekend at Cuttleford House, a pseudo–English country manor that contains an inscribed Raymond Chandler first edition.
9. *Burglar in the Rye, The* (**Dutton, 1999**) Bernie invades the hotel suite of a literary agent in search of a cache of letters by a recluse writer, but he finds a corpse instead.
10. *Burglar on the Prowl* (**Morrow, 2004**) A friend asks Bernie to burglarize the Riverdale home of a Mob-connected plastic surgeon.

III. Another series features Evan Tanner, who, because of a head wound suffered in the Korean War, cannot sleep at all. Tanner makes the best of his affliction by some heavy reading, acquisition of several languages, dissertation ghosting, and engaging in a series of rather zany espionage assignments, sometimes at the behest of the US government and sometimes freelance. Most of the Tanner novels were originally published in paperback in the late 1960s, but with Tanner's resuscitation in *Tanner on Ice* in 1998, earlier volumes in the series have been resuscitated in hardcover and audiobooks.

1. *Thief Who Couldn't Sleep, The* (**Fawcett, 1966**) Evan Tanner, who hasn't been able to sleep for 15 years, learns of hidden Armenian gold in Turkey and embarks on an adventure that makes him a world-class wanted fugitive and the accidental leader of a Macedonian revolt. Rereleased as an audiobook (Chivers, 1999).
2. *Canceled Czech, The* (**Fawcett, 1967**) Israeli terrorists and a beautiful Czech nymphomaniac are among Tanner's accomplices as he breaks into a Prague prison to extricate an unreconstructed Nazi who can lead him to some documents exposing a neo-Nazi plot. Reprinted by Penzler (1995) and featured as an audiobook (Chivers, 2000)
3. *Tanner's Twelve Swingers* (**Fawcett, 1967**) The 12 swingers are Latvian gymnasts who become involved, along with a Lithuanian orphan, Chinese microfilm, and a plane, in a convoluted plot initiated by Tanner's mission to help with the escape of a Yugoslav politician. Rereleased as an audiobook (Chivers, 2000)
4. *Scoreless Thai, The* (**Fawcett, 1967**) Tuppence Ngawa, the half-American, half-African singer girlfriend of Tanner, is kidnapped

by Communist rebels in Thailand. Reprinted in a limited edition by Subterranean (2001).

5. *Tanner's Tiger* (**Fawcett, 1968**) Tanner's daughter Mina is kidnapped at the Montreal Expo while Tanner is investigating the Cuban Pavilion. Canadian Mounties and Quebec nationalists, some of whom want to blow up Queen Elizabeth on her visit to the expo, get involved. Reprinted in a limited edition by Subterranean (2001).

6. *Here Comes a Hero* (**Fawcett, 1968**) Beautiful Phaedra Harrow has fallen into the hands of white slavers somewhere in the wilds of Afghanistan. Variant title: *Tanner's Virgin.* Reissued by Subterranean in 2005.

7. *Me Tanner, You Jane* (**Macmillan, 1970**) Evan Tanner tangles with a missionary's wayward daughter who calls herself Sheena, Cannibal Queen of the Jungle.

8. *Tanner on Ice* (**Dutton, 1998**) Tanner is resuscitated after 25 years in cryogenic storage to destabilize the government of Burma.

IV. Streetwise man-about-town Chip Harrison gets involved in dangerous doings while trying to seduce attractive women. Chip winds up playing Archie Goodwin to would-be world-renowned sleuth Leo Haig's Nero Wolfe (Rex Stout [q.v.]). The Chip Harrison books, originally published in paperback, were reprinted by Countryman in 1983–84 as *Introducing Chip Harrison* (numbers 1 and 2) and *A.K.A. Chip Harrison* (numbers 3 and 4).

1. *No Score* (**Fawcett, 1970**) Chip Harrison's elaborate scheme to attract the beautiful Francie leads him into some very dangerous doings.

2. *Chip Harrison Scores Again* (**Fawcett, 1971**) A discarded bus ticket takes Chip to South Carolina, where he gets into more trouble.

3. *Make Out with Murder* (**Fawcett, 1974**) Cases worthy of Chip's boss, Leo Haig, are hard to come by until Chip's girlfriend, Melanie Trelawney, dies under suspicious circumstances. Rereleased as an audiobook (Chivers, 1999).

4. *Topless Tulip Caper, The* (**Fawcett, 1975**) Chip finds himself waiting at a Times Square club for his latest client, a stripper, to finish her night's work.

V. J. P. Keller is a hit man, a quiet, introspective stamp collector whose services are required in many locales. His one relationship is with Dot, who is his job broker. The Keller stories, many of which originally appeared in *Playboy*, were collected in *Hit Man* and followed by the novels *Hit List* and *Hit Parade*.

1. *Hit Man* (**Morrow, 1998**) A collection of short stories. Originally announced as *Keller's Greatest Hits: Adventures in the Murder Trade*.

2. *Hit List* (**Morrow, 2000**) A professional assassin is killing his colleagues to eliminate the competition and jack up his prices.

3. *Hit Parade* (**Morrow, 2006**) A series of vignettes in which we follow Keller on assignment, eliminating a grab bag of targets, which include an annoying dog.

Blunt, Giles

Algonquin Bay, Ontario, is the rural setting for a series of mysteries involving the homicide detective duo John Cardinal and Lisa Delorme. Although Delorme was originally assigned to covertly investigate Cardinal for drug connections, he is eventually cleared, and the two have settled into a rewarding professional relationship. Cardinal also has personal issues to deal with, including a manic-depressive wife. An intelligent, well-told series, basically sad but with comic overtones.

Ontario native Giles Blunt spent more than 20 years in New York City as a television writer before returning to his native soil. Blunt has published one other novel, *Cold Eye* (Arbor House, 1989), a nonseries horror tale.

1. *Forty Words for Sorrow* (**Putnam, 2001**) Detective John Cardinal has been obsessively searching for 13-year-old Chippewa Katie Pine for six months when her frozen body is found on one of the Manitou Islands. But Cardinal isn't in the clear with his superiors: there is his alleged connection with drug dealer Kyle Corbett.

2. *Delicate Storm, The* (**Putnam, 2003**) A pair of gruesome homicides—one of an American accountant and one of the town's able female doctor—lands on Cardinal's and Delorme's desks within the same week.

3. *Black Fly Season* (**Putnam, 2005**) A Cuban cult know as Palo Mayombe may be responsible for a series of dismemberment killings that has left a possible witness with amnesia.

4. *By the Time You Read This* (**Holt, 2007**) Cardinal, grieving over the death of his wife, an apparent suicide, starts receiving hate-filled notes gloating over his loss.

Boggs, Johnny D.

Western writer Johnny D. Boggs's Hannah and the Horseman series is set in west Texas during the late 1880s. Hannah Scott is raising five orphans on her ranch with her lover and eventual husband, Pete Belissari, a college-educated, Greek cowboy. The pair goes through a number of adventures—involving the likes of horse-stealing Apaches, former Confederate bank robbers, stagecoach races, lynch mobs, stampedes, rival lovers, dentists, and European tourists—in this action-filled, lighthearted series.

1. *Hannah and the Horseman* (**Avalon, 1997**) Pete Belissari is trying to keep his mustangs out of the hands of the Apaches. Hannah Scott is trying to save her orphanage from evil rancher Rafe Malady.

2. *Courtship of Hannah and the Horseman, The* (**Avalon, 1997**) Hannah and Pete's wedding is postponed when Hannah is taken hostage by ex-Confederate Colonel Solomon Wooten and his gang during a bank robbery.

3. *Riding with Hannah and the Horseman* (**Avalon, 1998**) Hannah and Pete team up with one-eyed sharpshooter Buddy Pecos to operate a stagecoach line in west Texas and get involved in a cross-country stagecoach race against a lady gambler known as the Black Widow.

4. *Hannah and the Horseman at the Gallows Tree* (**Avalon, 1998**) When Hannah and Pete travel to the godforsaken town of Shafter, Texas, to look after a pair of scruffy orphans, Pete is ambushed and left for dead by the Cochrane Smith gang, and Hannah, barely escaping a lynch mob, falls into the hands of the bandit Plomo.

5. *Hannah and the Horseman on the Western Trail* (**Avalon, 1999**) A drought forces Hannah and Pete to take part in a cattle drive to Dodge City, Kansas, along the grueling Western Trail, where the perils include Cal Maddox, a cowboy who is determined to win Hannah's love.

6. *Odyssey of Hannah and the Horseman, The* (**Avalon, 2000**) Hannah and Pete travel to the town of Marfa so that one of the orphans can go to a "real" dentist, but, as usual, the jaunt proves to be eventful as the orphan, Cynthia, is kidnapped by escaped Apache prisoner Hector.

7. *Job for Hannah and the Horseman, A* (Avalon, 2001) Dime-novelist L. Merryweather Handal hires Hannah, Pete, and Buddy Pecos to show the "Wild West" to some European visitors.

Boissard, Janine

Prolific French author Boissard has had relatively few of her books translated into English. Four of the six novels translated are from the L'esprit de famille (*Family Spirit*) series, which depicts a prosperous French family living in a small town near Paris. Dr. Moreau and his wife have four daughters: Claire, Bernadette, Pauline, and Cecile. Pauline, the narrator, is presumably somewhat autobiographical. These books have the flavor of a Gallic *Little Women* (see Louisa May Alcott) and may appeal to the same audience.

1. *Matter of Feeling, A* (Little, Brown, 1980) The bittersweet story of Pauline's first love affair, with an older man who is an artist. Original title: *L'esprit de famille*. Translated by Elizabeth Walter.
2. *Avenir de Bernadette, L'* (Fayard, 1978) Never translated into English. Listed as number 2 in the L'esprit de famille series.
3. *Christmas Lessons* (Little, Brown, 1984) Pauline relates events as the family gathers for a traditional Christmas holiday at Grandmother Moreau's. Original title: *Claire et le bonheur*. Translated by Mary Feeney.
4. *Cecile* (Little, Brown, 1988) Dr. Moreau's death saddens the family, but Cecile and her mother, now alone in the big house, suffer most. Originally published in two parts: *Cecile, la poison* and *Cecile et son amour*. Translated by Mary Feeney.
5. *Time to Choose, A* (Little, Brown, 1985) With her two older sisters now married, Pauline enrolls in journalism school and falls in love again. Original title: *Moi, Pauline!* Translated by Mary Feeney.

Bonanno, Margaret Wander

I. American writer Bonanno is perhaps best known for her connection with *Star Trek*. She has written several *Star Trek* novels and has coauthored *Saturn's Child* (Putnam, 1995) with Nichelle Nichols, *Star Trek's* Lieutenant Uhura. However, Bonanno deserves to be better known for her other science-fiction work, including the trilogy containing *The Others*, *OtherWhere*, and *OtherWise*. Told through the words of Other chronicler Lingri, the trilogy relates the near-fatal encounter between the rational, advanced, peaceable Others and the passionate, artistic, and violent People.

1. *Others, The* (St. Martin's, 1990) Lingri the Chronicler tells about her youth as a Monitor secretly studying the People and the unfortunate result of the People becoming aware of the advanced Others culture.
2. *OtherWhere* (St. Martin's, 1991) The People have reduced the Others to a remnant of less than 10,000, and the surviving Others try to establish a refuge in the Arctic wastes.
3. *OtherWise* (St. Martin's, 1993) The People have turned the technology gained from the Others on themselves in a series of internecine wars, and it is up to the remaining Others to bring peace to their world.

II. Writer Karen Rohmer Guerreri, apparently based on Bonanno herself, was finding life hard enough without the strong suspicion that the S.oteri, the telepathic aliens in her new novel, are trying to contact her. The Preternatural trio is a clever series about the pitfalls of the writing life, the evils of the publishing industry, takeoffs on *Star Trek* (here called *Space Seekers*), telepaths, time travel, alien lovers, a sojourn

as a mud puppy, and a subplot based on Guerreri's seemingly unpublishable novel *The Amber Room*.

1. *Preternatural* (Tor, 1996) The telepathic alien characters in Karen Rohmer Guerreri's new novel are apparently trying to make contact with her. Or is she losing her mind?
2. *Preternatural Too: Gyre* (Tor, 2000) Guerreri decides to write a sequel to her only successful work, *Preternatural*. Then the mysterious alien group, S.oteri, gets in contact with her again. Then an even more mysterious and powerful race abducts Karen and her characters.
3. *Preternatural.sup.3: The Third Thing* (Tor, 2002) Thanks to her alien time-traveling lover, Govannon, Karen is enjoying life as a mud puppy, but she can't forget the wrongs done her by her publishers, and Govannon is in danger of being stuck in a conundrum.

Bond, Michael (Thomas Michael)

English writer Michael Bond has acquired a world reputation for children's series such as Paddington the Bear and Olga da Polga. His Inspector Pamplemousse series brings to adults his blend of storytelling and wryly amusing style. Aristide Pamplemousse ("grapefruit" in French), who is more reminiscent of Inspector Clouseau than of Georges Simenon's Maigret (q.v.), is a former police detective who becomes a critic for *Le Guide*, the prestigious annual that rates French restaurants. Pamplemousse, accompanied by his faithful bloodhound, Pommes Frites, solves crimes by luck or accident rather than by ratiocination. Recent Pamplemousses (numbers 9–16) haven't been released in the United States. Numbers 1–3, 4–7, and 8–10 have been published in three volumes as *Monsieur Pamplemousse Omnibus* (Allison & Busby [UK], 1998–1999).

1. *Monsieur Pamplemousse* (Beaufort, 1985) La Langousine's "specialty of the house" is served to Pamplemousse with a man's head inside.
2. *Monsieur Pamplemousse and the Secret Mission* (Beaufort, 1986) Pamplemousse and Pommes Frites leave Paris for the Loire to investigate strange doings at the Hotel du Paradis.
3. *Monsieur Pamplemousse on the Spot* (Beaufort, 1987) Jean-Claude Parfait, creator of the "souffle surprise" at the Haute Savoie restaurant, is kidnapped.
4. *Monsieur Pamplemousse Takes the Cure* (Random House, 1988) Pamplemousse goes to a luxury spa called the Chateau Morgue disguised as a blind man.
5. *Monsieur Pamplemousse Aloft* (Fawcett, 1989) There is a plot aloft to assassinate both the British and French heads of state during a cross-Channel dirigible flight.
6. *Monsieur Pamplemousse Investigates* (Fawcett, 1990) Computer theft and forgery threaten to postpone the publication of the latest annual edition of *Le Guide*.
7. *Monsieur Pamplemousse Rests His Case* (Fawcett, 1991) Six American mystery writers are trying to re-create a gourmet feast in Vichy supposedly once hosted by Alexandre Dumas.
8. *Monsieur Pamplemousse Stands Firm* (Fawcett, 1994) Pamplemousse travels to the Hotel des Dunes on the Côte d'Argent with an attractive but teasing female apprentice restaurant rater. Originally published in 1992.
9. *Monsieur Pamplemousse on Location* (Headline [UK], 1992) No annotation available.
10. *Monsieur Pamplemousse Takes the Train* (Headline [UK], 1993) No annotation available.

11. *Monsieur Pamplemousse Afloat* (Allison & Busby [UK], 1998) The pesticide threat to snails in Burgundy's vineyards and a Marilyn Monroe look-alike are somehow connected when Pamplemousse lectures international wine buffs on the Canal de Bourgogne.

12. *Monsieur Pamplemousse on Probation* (Allison & Busby [UK], 2000) Pamplemousse is caught in a compromising position with a nun but, being Pamplemousse, maintains a low profile.

13. *Monsieur Pamplemousse on Vacation* (Allison & Busby [UK], 2002) Monsieur Pamplemousse is ordered to take a vacation from *Le Guide* and runs afoul of Russian gangsters.

14. *Monsieur Pamplemousse Hits the Headlines* (Allison & Busby [UK], 2003) Magician turned gourmet chef Chavignol dies during the televising of his show after choking on a tainted oyster, despite Pamplemousse's efforts with the Heimlich maneuver.

15. *Monsieur Pamplemousse and the Militant Midwives* (Allison & Busby [UK], 2006) Monsieur Pamplemousse's stirring address at his colleague's funeral is followed by an exploding coffin.

16. *Monsieur Pamplemousse and the French Solution* (Allison & Busby [UK], 2007) *Le Guide* is the subject of a full-scale smear campaign, including spreading worrying rumors among the staff and infiltrating company files.

Bonner, Cindy

Like many aspiring writers, Texan Cindy Bonner had a variety of jobs (from computer operator to yoga instructor) before she broke into print with *Lily*, first of a series of novels set in the real-life town of McDade, Texas, from the 1880s through World War I. The first two novels relate the events in slightly over a year of the life of Lily DeLony (later Beatty), a poor farm girl who loses her heart to an outlaw. Number 3 concentrates on Lily's younger sister, Dellie O'Barr; number 4 on a later generation of the DeLony family. This series is suffused with romance, action, humor, and Texas scenery.

1. *Lily* (Algonquin, 1992) Fifteen-year-old Lily DeLony, daughter of a hardscrabble Texas farmer, loses her heart to Marion "Shot" Beatty, youngest brother in a gang of outlaws.

2. *Looking After Lily* (Algonquin, 1994) Shot Beatty, facing a two-year jail term, entrusts the pregnant Lily to his ornery and reluctant brother Haywood, and the odd couple starts out on a 400-mile trek to north Texas.

3. *Passion of Dellie O'Barr, The* (Algonquin, 1996) It's 1896 and Lily's younger sister, Dellie O'Barr, married to a wealthy rancher, finds herself smitten with Andy Ashland, a poor tenant farmer and champion of Populist causes.

4. *Right from Wrong* (Algonquin, 1999) It's 1914 and 12-year-old Sunny DeLony and her cousin Gil find that their feelings for each other are more than cousinly.

Booth, Stephen

Edendale is a fictional English village in the Derbyshire Peak District. Detective Constable Ben Cooper, a rather diffident, beer-drinking sports enthusiast, and former detective constable, now detective sergeant Diane Fry, a somewhat hard-bitten, abrasive feminist, are rather incompatible partners fighting their own demons in the investigations, which sometimes stretch the resources of the understaffed Derbyshire police to the breaking point. This series of slow-paced but evocative and well-characterized mysteries uncovers the passions seething beneath the seemingly placid English countryside.

1. *Black Dog* (Scribner, 2000) Ben Cooper and Diane Fry, who is vying for a sergeant's post at the Edendale Police Division, try to elicit retired miner Harry Dickinson's connection to missing 15-year-old Laura Vernon.

2. *Dancing with the Virgins* (Scribner, 2001) Young cyclist Jenny Weston is murdered while visiting Ringham Moor and the prehistoric ring of stones known as the Nine Virgins.

3. *Blood on the Tongue* (Scribner, 2002) Two members of the Polish community of Edendale may be the victims of hate crimes; two corpses found at different places in the winter landscape, a missing baby, and a Canadian woman investigating the fate of her grandfather after a World War II plane crash are among the items on the plates of that odd couple Cooper and Fry.

4. *Blind to the Bones* (Scribner, 2003) Cooper, newly transferred to a rural beat, investigates the murder of young Neil Granger, while Fry is involved with the related two-year-old disappearance of 19-year-old Emma Renshaw.

5. *One Last Breath* (Bantam, 2006) Convicted killer Mansell Quinn is out on parole and bent on revenge against those he feels are responsible for his imprisonment, which is bad news for ex-soldier Will Thorpe. Originally published in the United Kingdom in 2004.

6. *Dead Place, The* (Bantam, 2007) An anonymous caller promising impending murder bedevils Diane Fry, while Ben Cooper is looking into a case of body snatching. Originally published in the United Kingdom in 2005.

7. *Scared to Live* (Bantam, 2008) A house fire leaves a wife and two children dead. An elderly woman living alone in a Peak District village is murdered. Why? The answers may lie on the other side of Europe. Originally published in the United Kingdom in 2006.

8. *Dying to Sin* (HarperCollins [UK], 2007) Routine building work at Pity Wood Farm turns up a human hand preserved in clay. Then two bodies are found, with several years between their burials.

Borchardt, Alice

I. Like her sister Anne Rice (q.v.), the late Alice Borchardt (d. 2007) wrote books with strong elements of the historical, the supernatural, the fantastical, and the romantic. After 30 years as a nurse, Borchardt published two historical romances set in 9th-century France, where Owen, Bishop of Chantalon, and his lover, the forest girl–sorceress Elin, battle invading Vikings and assorted other barbarians and baddies in sex- and blood-drenched prose and over-the-top action.

1. *Devoted* (Dutton, 1995) Owen, Bishop of Chantalon, rescues Elin, a forest girl with magical powers. The two immediately click sexually and romantically (this is the 9th century, when clerical chastity was still being debated) and team up against the Viking invaders.

2. *Beguiled* (Dutton, 1997) On a mission to his father's stronghold, Owen is captured by Bretons who want him to be their king—or else! Owen's wife, Elin, left behind in Chantalon, has to counter Hakon's Vikings and some fifth-columnists.

II. Werewolves and shape-shifters are among the protagonists in this trio of novels set variously at the time of the assassination of Julius Caesar and in the era of Charlemagne, more than 700 years later. Maeniel and Regeane are the werewolf shape-shifter lovers who span the centuries from Rome at its most decadent (lovingly described) to the Dark Ages.

1. *Night of the Wolf* (Del Rey, 1999) This is the second novel in the trilogy, but most of the action takes place in a time prior to the

events of *The Silver Wolf*. Maeniel, werewolf warrior, and Dryas, Celtic she-warrior, are rivals who eventually team up as the Ides of March and the assassination of Julius Caesar are in the offing.

2. *Silver Wolf, The* **(Del Rey, 1998)** Roman shape-shifter Regeane, a distant relative of Charlemagne, who is advancing on Rome, is betrothed to Maeniel, guardian of an Alps passage (who is a werewolf himself). Regeane, who is torn between her wolf and womanly selves, gets into the thick of the action among the Lombards, the decadent Romans, the invading Carolingians, and Pope Hadrian and his leprous son Antonius.

3. *Wolf King, The* **(Del Rey, 2001)** An Alpine avalanche, a demon spirit called the Bear, a mad abbot, a runaway Saxon slave, Charlemagne, the Lombard king Desederius, and the werewolf pair Maeniel and Regeane are in the action-packed climax to the trilogy.

III. The Tales of Guinevere, Borchardt's last trilogy, is also set in the Dark Ages, but this time it is Arthurian legend that is featured. Guinevere, a feisty warrior with supernatural powers far removed from the Malory and Tennyson character, a young Arthur, a villainous Merlin, and Lancelot are among the characters who try to stave off the Saxon invasion of Celtic, post-Roman Britain. The conclusion to the trilogy, *The Winter King*, has not been published.

1. *Dragon Queen, The* **(Del Rey, 2001)** Suckled by a she-wolf and possessed of the qualities of a warrior, a prophet, and a communicator with dragons, wolves, and a shrunken head, Guinevere is opposed by the dark sorcerer Merlin in a battle of wills to control the young King Arthur.

2. *Raven Warrior, The* **(Del Rey, 2003)** As Guinevere faces the Saxon threat against her people, young Lancelot must prove himself as a man and a warrior.

Borg, Todd

Owen McKenna is an ex-cop with a tragic background who has left the San Francisco area for Lake Tahoe (on the California-Nevada border) to enjoy the scenery, study art, and earn his living as a private investigator with Spot, his Great Dane. The evocation of the spectacular scenery of the Lake Tahoe area is one of the biggest pluses in this interesting mystery series. Todd Borg, a Minnesota native, moved to Lake Tahoe with his artist wife in 1990.

1. *Tahoe Deathfall* **(Thriller, 2001)** Introduces private investigator Owen McKenna; his Great Dane, Spot; and Lake Tahoe, a gem situated on the California-Nevada border. Jennifer Salazar hires Owen to look into the supposedly accidental death of her sister Melissa eight years previously.

2. *Tahoe Blowup* **(Thriller, 2001)** A maniacal arsonist kidnaps Owen's girlfriend and threatens a forest fire that will kill hundreds.

3. *Tahoe Ice Grave* **(Thriller, 2002)** When Thos Kahale, a young Hawaiian man, is shot while swimming in Lake Tahoe, Owen McKenna investigates a mystery that involves Hawaiians, Native Americans, and possibly Mark Twain.

4. *Tahoe Killshot* **(Thriller, 2004)** A complicated multimillion-dollar land scam may be at the bottom of the killing of pop star Glory, who was biking on the Flume Trail above Lake Tahoe.

5. *Tahoe Silence* **(Thriller, 2007)** Marlette Remmick hires McKenna to find her abducted children, son Charlie, and autistic daughter SalAnne, or Silence.

Borrow, George

If only to meet the original "Borrovian gentleman," readers should dip into these strange and charming works by the 19th-century English bard of the open road. There is some speculation that George Borrow was himself a Gypsy, his knowledge of their ways is so detailed. It is certain that much of *Lavengro* is autobiographical, although its author denied it. Borrow was much admired by Ralph Waldo Emerson and other American transcendentalists.

1. *Lavengro* **(Harper, 1851)** Introduces the remarkable young George, who teaches himself many languages, goes to London to become a writer, and wonders, "What is truth?"

2. *Romany Rye* **(Harper, 1857)** Further adventures of George, now called Romany Rye, his Gypsy friend Jasper Petulengro, Isopel, and others. A defense of *Lavengro* is appended.

Borthwick, J. S.

PSEUDONYM OF Jean Scott Creighton

Sarah Deane, English instructor and doctoral candidate at Maine's Bowmouth College, and her physician fiancé, Alex McKenzie, are part-time sleuths. Their cases, which usually take place outdoors anywhere from Maine to Arizona or "across the pond," are entered into reluctantly, at least on Alex's part, but are brought to satisfactory conclusions in this series of literate and witty cozies. Borthwick was a late bloomer, or at least a late publisher. What seems to have been her first published novel appeared in print when she was nearly 60 years old.

1. *Case of the Hook-Billed Kites, The* **(St. Martin's, 1982)** Philip Lentz is strangled with the strap of his binoculars while bird-watching at the Dona Clara Wildlife Refuge in Texas.

2. *Down East Murders, The* **(St. Martin's, 1985)** While Sarah and Alex summer on Maine's Weymouth Island, cranky local artist Nate Harwood's body is found entangled in an offshore fishnet.

3. *Study Body, The* **(St. Martin's, 1986)** Plagiarism linked to one of Bowmouth's senior professors leads to blackmail and murder.

4. *Bodies of Water* **(St. Martin's, 1990)** A two-week cruise on the *Pilgrim*, a yacht owned by a wealthy religious leader, leads to a murder investigation by Deane and McKenzie.

5. *Dude on Arrival* **(St. Martin's, 1992)** A series of suspicious accidents is plaguing Rancho Del Gato Blanco, the Arizona dude ranch where Sarah's aunt Julia has gone for her arthritis.

6. *Bridled Groom, The* **(St. Martin's, 1994)** Aunt Julia makes another appearance, this time as the recipient of threatening notes at her horse farm, High Hope Farm.

7. *Dolly Is Dead* **(St. Martin's, 1995)** Local Good Samaritan Dolly Beaugard is washed ashore simultaneously with two local Proffit Point, Maine, thugs.

8. *Garden Plot, The* **(St. Martin's, 1997)** Sarah, dragooned by her aunt Julia into accompanying her on a garden tour of Europe, becomes concerned when tour guide Ellen Trevino fails to meet the group at Boston's Logan Airport.

9. *My Body Lies over the Ocean* **(St. Martin's, 1999)** When Sarah and Alex escort Aunt Julia back to the United States on the maiden voyage of the British Liner *Queen Victoria*, members of the British Trade Commission become victims of suspicious "accidents."

10. *Coup de Grace* **(St. Martin's, 2000)** Sarah, finally sporting a PhD but jobless, takes a temporary teaching post at an exclusive girls' boarding school in Massachusetts, where unpopular French teacher Madame Carpentier is the target of an escalating series of "pranks."

11. *Murder in the Rough* (St. Martin's, 2002) Sarah's in-laws, Elspeth and John McKenzie, have retired to what seems to be an idyllic planned community in Ocean Tide, Maine. A series of events, including a dead body appearing on the golf course, indicates that Ocean Tide is not so idyllic.

12. *Intensive Scare Unit* (St. Martin's, 2004) Sarah's aunt Julia undergoes open-heart surgery in neighboring Bowmouth, Maine. But she has more than surgery to contend with as she is targeted by a murderer who has already killed more than one person and seemingly has access to the hospital wards.

13. *Foiled Again* (St. Martin's, 2007) A production of the gender-bending *Romiette and Julio* at Bowmouth College is accompanied by strife among the cast and interdepartmental politicking, followed by critical injury to a faculty member and death for a student.

Bova, Ben(jamin William)

I. Ben Bova, like Isaac Asimov (q.v.) and Arthur C. Clarke (q.v.), is known for his science-fact as well as his science-fiction writing. As editor of leading science-fiction magazines such as *Omni* and *Analog,* the author of nonfiction books, and the author of many novels and stories set in the near future, Bova has been a key advocate of salvation through technology, especially through the exploration, privatization, and exploitation of space. His ongoing series, sometimes called the Grand Tour, describes a near future in which humanity has reached several outposts in the solar system. Certain characters—such as Navaho geologist Jamie Waterman; idealistic, Daddy Warbucks–type billionaire Dan Randolph; self-serving billionaire Martin Humphries; former astronaut Doug Stavenger; and asteroid miner Lars Fuchs—turn up in one or more novels in the series.

Novels are arranged according to the chronology suggested by Bova on his website (www.benbova.net), although Bova feels that they can be read in any order. Numbers 7, 9, 10, and 13 are part of the Asteroid Wars subseries. Two novels not listed by Bova as part of the Grand Tour but that are related to the series are *Privateers* (Tor, 1985), in which Dan Randolph sets up a mineral-rich asteroid around Earth, and *Venus* (Tor, 2000), in which Martin Humphries offers $10 billion to anyone who can retrieve his son's remains from an ill-fated expedition to Venus. *Tales of the Grand Tour* (Tor, 2004) is a collection of stories, excerpts, and outtakes from the Grand Tour series.

1. *Powersat* (Tor, 2005) Astro Corporation loses its experimental space plane on reentry to the atmosphere, destroyed by an Osama bin Laden type of terrorist.

2. *Empire Builders* (Tor, 1993) Billionaire Dan Randolph fights against ecological catastrophe and a world dictatorship.

3. *Mars* (Bantam, 1992) Native American geologist Jamie Waterman endures political backbiting, lack of breathable air, 100 degrees below zero temperature, and a potentially fatal plague to explore the red planet Mars.

4. *Moonrise* (Avon, 1996) Masterson Aerospace, one of the bulwarks against radical environmentalists and religious fundamentalists, suffers through a power struggle involving murder and the near destruction of Moonbase.

5. *Moonwar* (Avon, 1998) In this direct sequel to *Moonrise,* protagonist Doug Stavenger must stave off a Japanese conglomerate and the fanatical secretary general of the United Nations to save Moonbase for scientific progress.

6. *Return to Mars* (Avon, 1999) Jamie Waterman returns to Mars in this sequel to *Mars,* where he must fend off C. Dexter Trumball, who will do anything to make Mars profitable to his wealthy father, including turning the planet into a tourist attraction.

7. *Precipice, The* (Tor, 2001) Book one of the *Asteroid Wars.* Billionaires Dan Randolph and Martin Humphries want to send an experimental spaceship to the asteroid belt to bring back raw materials that will stave off the ravages of the greenhouse effect.

8. *Jupiter* (Tor, 2000) Astrophysicist Grant Archer has been sent to spy on the scientists working on Jupiter's orbital space station by the New Morality, an ultrareligious Creationist group that controls the United States.

9. *Rock Rats, The* (Tor, 2002) Book two of the *Asteroid Wars.* Dan Randolph is dead, so the burden of saving the mineral riches of the asteroid belt from the greedy Martin Humphries falls upon asteroid miner Lars Fuchs.

10. *Aftermath, The* (Tor, 2007) Book four of the *Asteroid Wars.* Crazed assassin Dorik Harbin disables the ore-carrying spaceship *Syracuse,* forcing Victor Zacharias to jettison an escape pod containing his wife and children.

11. *Saturn* (Tor, 2003) Among the 10,000 intellectuals and scientists who have been voluntarily or involuntarily exiled to Saturn is Malcolm Eberly, who has been recruited by the Holy Disciples, one of the fundamentalist organizations that has taken over Earth's governments, to ensure that the exiles choose "the path of righteousness" in their new home.

12. *Titan* (Tor, 2005) On Christmas Eve 2095, the space-explorer *Titan Alpha* is seeking traces of life on Titan, Saturn's largest moon.

13. *Silent War, The* (Tor, 2004) Book three of the *Asteroid Wars.* Humphries Space Systems and the Yamagata go at it head-to-head in space, while Lars Fuchs seeks revenge on Martin Humphries.

14. *Mercury* (Tor, 2005) While astrobiologist Victor Molina and engineer Mance Bracknell vie for the affections of Lar Teirney Molina, Saito Yamagata attempts to create an efficient, inexpensive staging area on Mercury to send ships into deep space.

II. One of Bova's most popular series is set in the distant future and in the past rather than in the near future. John O'Ryan (Orion) is a human being recast into an important warrior by the Creators, godlike beings evolved from humans thousands of years in the future. Orion is sent back to crucial turning points in Earth's past to ensure that the events that led to the evolution of the Creators are not changed.

1. *Orion* (Simon & Schuster, 1984) John O'Ryan is transformed into Orion the Hunter by the Creators to combat the "Dark Lord."

2. *Vengeance of Orion* (Tor, 1989) Orion is sent back to pre-classical times to intervene in the Trojan War and make winners out of the Trojans.

3. *Orion in the Dying Time* (Tor, 1990) Set, a reptilian demon from another world, has gone back to the age of dinosaurs to arrange matters so that a lizardlike race will inherit Earth.

4. *Orion and the Conqueror* (Tor, 1994) Orion is sent to Macedonia in the 4th century BCE to ensure that King Philip's son becomes Alexander the Great.

5. *Orion among the Stars* (Tor, 1995) The Creator Aten sends Orion to fight as a soldier in an intergalactic war.

III. The Voyagers trio is set in the near future. It relates how astronaut Keith Stoner makes contact with an alien and how he uses the new powers he acquires to help mankind.

1. *Voyagers* (Doubleday, 1981) A joint American-Soviet space mission investigates reports of an alien spacecraft.

2. *Voyagers II: The Alien Within* (Tor, 1987) The alien turns out to be benevolent, trying to save Earth from itself. Variant title: *The Alien Within.*

3. *Voyagers III: Star Brothers* (Tor, 1990) Stoner, who has assimilated the alien's powers, uses them to establish peace on Earth. Variant title: *Star Brothers.*

IV. Another pair of science-fiction novels, coauthored with A. J. Austin, postulates a far-future space empire in which Earth's sun will explode soon.

1. *To Save the Sun* (Tor, 1992) The sun around which ancient Earth revolves is doomed to explode within the lifetime of living humans, leaving the Empire of the Hundred Worlds adrift.

2. *To Fear the Light* (Tor, 1994) Dr. Adela de Montgarde emerges from centuries of sleep to find that faster-than-light travel and communication have made the central authority of the Empire of the Hundred Worlds irrelevant.

V. A trio of novels set in the near future is linked by the character Chet Kinsman, astronaut, murderer, and head of the first US lunar colony.

1. *Millennium* (Random House, 1976) Subtitle: *A Novel about People and Politics in the Year 1999.* In the year 1999, the overcrowded Earth faces the onset of nuclear war brought on by the competition for the planet's dwindling natural resources.

2. *Kinsman* (Dial, 1979) Chet Kinsman has abandoned his family's Quaker roots to become one of America's hottest US Air Force astronauts.

3. *Kinsman Saga, The* (Tor, 1987) Chet Kinsman is an astronaut who has done everything in space, including committing the first murder, a secret he cannot escape.

Bowen, Gail

Joanne Kilbourn is a fortysomething–early fiftysomething single mother (widowed) who juggles family, career (university professor of political science), and amateur sleuthing in the Canadian prairie province of Saskatchewan. Kilbourn, in many respects like her creator, University of Regina English professor Gail Bowen, is politically and socially concerned, and her mysteries emphasize character and human relationships rather than plots per se. Only the first three novels in the series have been published in the United States, but Kilbourn (played by Kate Nelligan) is featured in a Canadian TV miniseries and deserves to be better known "south of the border." Numbers 1–3 have been reissued in an omnibus volume: *The Early Investigations of Joanne Kilbourn* (Random House, 2004). Numbers 4–6 have been published in an omnibus volume: *The Further Investigations of Joanne Kilbourn* (Random House, 2006).

1. *Deadly Appearances* (Douglas [Canada], 1990) When Saskatchewan politician Andy Boychuk keels over dead at a picnic speech, his speechwriter, Joanne Kilbourn—who has endured the murder of her husband—investigates and uncovers Boychuk's somewhat lurid past.

2. *Love and Murder* (St. Martin's, 1993) Sally Love, Kilbourn's childhood friend who achieved notoriety in the art world with her works of "erotobiography," becomes the first in a series of murder victims. First published in Canada in 1991 as *Murder at the Mendel.*

3. *Wandering Soul Murders, The* (St. Martin's, 1994) Kilbourne's daughter Mieka finds the body of Bernice, a teenage office cleaner, hanging out of a dumpster: another victim in a series of prostitute killings or of a copycat killer? Originally published in Canada in 1992.

4. *Colder Kind of Death, A* (McClelland [Canada], 1994) Kevin Tarpley, who six years previously had murdered Joanne's politician husband, Ian, is gunned down in the exercise yard of Saskatchewan's penitentiary. Then Joanne herself becomes the "number one" suspect in the subsequent murder of Tarpley's wife.

5. *Killing Spring, A* (McClelland [Canada], 1996) Some rather messy goings-on at the university where Kilbourn teaches: the new head of the college's journalism department is an apparent suicide; one of her students, the apparent victim of sexual harassment, turns up missing, then dead; and her best friend falls in love with a batterer.

6. *Verdict in Blood* (McClelland [Canada], 1998) Draconian judge Justine Blackwell, who after 30 years on the bench, has shown a sudden interest in prisoner's rights, is found beaten to death in a public park.

7. *Burying Ariel* (McClellan [Canada], 2000) Sexual harassment, the murder of a female colleague at her Regina university, and feminist retribution for male violence—all play a role in Kilbourne's latest case.

8. *Glass Coffin, The* (McClelland [Canada], 2003) Joanne is appalled to learn that her friend, Jill Osiowy, is about to marry the celebrated but manipulative documentary filmmaker Evan MacLeish, who has already lost (driven?) two wives to suicide.

9. *Last Good Day, The* (McClelland [Canada], 2004) While on vacation at a cottage borrowed from a lawyer friend, Joanne has a long talk with a distraught lawyer who kills himself soon after.

10. *Endless Knot, The* (McClelland [Canada], 2006) Journalist Kathryn Morrissey's tell-all book on the lives of 13 adult children of prominent Canadians provokes rage from their parents. One of the parents, Sam Parker, takes a shot at Morrissey, wounding her slightly. Joanne's new beau, Zack Shreve, is hired by Parker as his defense counsel.

Bowen, Peter

I. Gabriel Du Pre is a Canadian Métis man of mixed French, Scottish, and Cree descent. Du Pre lives in Toussaint, Montana, and has variously performed as a fiddler, cattle inspector, tracker, deputy, and sleuth. Du Pre and his farming and ranching neighbors are fighting a losing battle to preserve their way of life against predatory and do-gooding outsiders in a well-characterized series of mysteries, laced with dry humor, that evoke the contemporary American West. American writer Peter Bowen, not to be confused with the Canadian British artist-writer of the same name, is also the author of the Yellowstone Kelly series (series II) and, as "Coyote Jack," of a series of humorous columns and short stories that appeared in *Forbes* in the 1990s.

1. *Coyote Wind* (St. Martin's, 1994) Introduces Gabriel Du Pre, a 40-year-old widower, father of two daughters, a Métis (part European, part Native American) who is a Montana cattle inspector and sometime sheriff's deputy. Gabriel uncovers some seamy ancient history, including that of his parents, as he investigates the mystery of a newly discovered, three-decades-old plane wreck with the remains of three people in it.

2. *Specimen Song* (St. Martin's, 1995) Du Pre is far from his usual haunts, performing as a fiddler in a Washington, DC, music festival, when several murders, each committed with an archaic women, are committed.

3. *Wolf, No Wolf* (St. Martin's, 1996) Wolves and ranchers are being killed in a collision between ranchers, environmentalists, New Agers, the media, and the federal government in the form of the FBI.

4. *Notches* (St. Martin's, 1997) Gabriel works, uneasily, with FBI agent Harvey Wallis (who is a Blackfoot) and trucker (and possible ex-bank robber) Rolly Challis to solve the serial killings of young girls in remote areas of the United States and Canada.

5. *Thunder Horse* (St. Martin's, 1998) Du Pre, accompanied by gallons of cheap wine, his lover, Madelaine, and medicine–cum–con man Benetsee, drives his old pickup along Montana's back roads in a case involving a serious earthquake, a Japanese consortium planning a commercial trout farm, the fossilized tooth of a *T Rex*, and murder.

6. *Long Son* (St. Martin's, 1999) Gabriel is a suspect when sociopathic Larry Messmer is murdered after returning to his parents' ranch in Toussaint.

7. *Stick Game, The* (St. Martin's, 2000) A local gold-mining operation may be responsible for the disappearance of a boy and the toxic waste that has caused a series of birth defects in Hardin, Montana.

8. *Cruzatte and Maria* (St. Martin's, 2001) Gabriel's daughter Maria persuades him to serve as a consultant to her boyfriend, who is making a movie about the Lewis and Clark expedition; Gabriel also uncovers a cache of journals kept by Meriwether Lewis and reluctantly gets involved in the search for missing Missouri River boaters.

9. *Ash Child* (St. Martin's, 2002) Du Pre's resourceful, beloved Madelaine and the wise old Benetsee come to Du Pre's aid in a mystery involving the beating death of an old woman, two missing teenagers, a forest fire, and the not-too-helpful US Forest Service.

10. *Badlands* (St. Martin's, 2003) A Waco-style debacle may be in the offing when the religious cult, the Host of Yahweh, buys a cattle ranch and converts it to a cult headquarters where secret rites, and possibly mass murders, are taking place.

11. *Tumbler, The* (St. Martin's, 2004) Billionaire Markham Millbank wants to buy the journals of Meriwether Lewis, allegedly found by Gabriel (see number 8), but Du Pre isn't interested in selling them.

12. *Stewball* (St. Martin's, 2005) Gabriel Du Pre helps his aunt Pauline, whose current husband, Badger, has gone missing and soon turns up dead, in a mystery involving a racehorse named Stewball, some charred corpses, a scalping, and treasonous government agents.

13. *Nails* (St. Martin's, 2006) When the body of a child is found by the road, and a colony of religious zealots moves into the Toussaint area, Gabriel isn't the only one who suspects a connection.

II. Bowen's earlier series features the adventures of Luther Sage "Yellowstone" Kelly, tracker, trapper, scout for Colonel Nelson Miles, and mountain man, in the last quarter of the 19th century. Kelly, who is based on a historical character who left his own memoirs (see *Yellowstone Kelly: The Memoir of Luther S. Kelly,* Yale, 1926; reprint, Nebraska, 1973), is taken through a series of wild and improbable adventures in a send-up of the Old West reminiscent of Thomas Berger's *Little Big Man* (q.v.). Many historical characters, including Custer, Sitting Bull, Crazy Horse, Chief Joseph, Wild Bill Hickok, Teddy Roosevelt, and Butch Cassidy and the Sundance Kid, turn up in these entertaining pages.

1. *Yellowstone Kelly* (Jameson, 1987) Yellowstone Kelly reluctantly tracks the fleeing Nez Percé for Colonel Nelson Miles, gets involved with a crazy Englishman in a big-game hunt, and winds up in the Zulu War in South Africa.

2. *Kelly and the Three-Toed Horse* (St, Martin's, 2001) In a novel published around 10 years after numbers 3 and 4 but set earlier chronologically (1870s), Kelly is hired to lead a party through Wyoming Indian territory in a search for more specimens of fossil horses. Kelly's bunch is accompanied by pretty blonde Alys and trailed by Blue Fox, a psychopathic Dartmouth-educated Cheyenne.

3. *Kelly Blue* (Crown, 1991) Kelly marries an Indian woman, escapes the wrath of Mormon leader Brigham Young, engages in some secret missions for President Grant, and encounters the like of General Custer, Sitting Bull, Crazy Horse, et al.

4. *Imperial Kelly* (Crown, 1992) Kelly is dragooned by the bellicose Theodore "Teethadore" Roosevelt into recruiting Rough Riders, Western toughs of the likes of Butch Cassidy and the Sundance Kid, officered by Ivy Leaguers for service in the "Splendid Little War" in Cuba.

Bowen, Rhys

PSEUDONYM OF Janet Quin-Harkin

I. Evan Evans is the only policeman in the North Wales village of Llanfair. Evan, single and unattached until his betrothal to teacher Bronwen Price, is a likable detective in this series of Welsh cozies with straightforward plots, interesting local characters, quiet humor, and loving descriptions of life in rural Wales. "Rhys Bowen" is the pseudonym of a British author (resident in San Francisco since 1966) of children's and young adult books and historical romances. "Rhys Bowen" is her grandfather's name, and Llanfair is based on the Welsh village where she used to spend her summers.

1. *Evans Above* (St. Martin's, 1997) Introduces Evan Evans and the village of Llanfair, North Wales. Evan, the only policeman attached to Llanfair, becomes suspicious when two men, one staying at the intrusive new vacation lodge, fall to their deaths in separate mountain "accidents" the same day.

2. *Evan Help Us* (St. Martin's, 1998) Evan and Sergeant Watkins journey to London in pursuit of a solution to the deaths of annual Llanfair visitor Colonel Artbuthnot and returned local Ted Morgan.

3. *Evanly Choirs* (St. Martin's, 1999) World-famous operatic tenor Ifor Llewellyn returns to his native Llanfair and offers to sing with the local choir at the annual countrywide competition. Unfortunately, the temperamental Ifor misses an important rehearsal and is found dead.

4. *Evan and Elle* (St. Martin's, 2000) Madame Yvette, a seductive French widow, opens a restaurant in Llanfair that is a big success with the locals. Evan enjoys Yvette's cuisine, but not her romantic blandishments, choosing fidelity to his girlfriend, Bronwen Price. Then Madame Yvette's restaurant burns down in a suspicious fire.

5. *Evan Can Wait* (St. Martin's, 2001) A documentary film crew, including Bronwen's ex-husband, trying to raise a World War II German bomber sunk in a lake and the revelation by old Trefor Thomas of how he planned to steal a National Gallery painting stored in a Welsh mine turn out to have a connection.

6. *Evans to Betsy* (St. Martin's, 2002) Evan collides with the New Age in the form of Randy Wunderlich, famed American psychic, who has set up as resident guru of the Sacred Grove, to which he has inveigled Betsy the Llanfair barmaid, who is persuaded that she has psychic powers.

7. *Evan Only Knows* (St. Martin's, 2003) When the young man who killed his policeman father is accused of another murder, Evan finds himself perplexed when he comes face-to-face with a scared kid rather than a hardened thug.

8. *Evans Gate* (St. Martin's, 2004) The disappearance of five-year-old Ashley Sholokhov during a seaside trip is eerily reminiscent of the long-ago disappearance of Sarah, granddaughter of sheep farmer Tomos Thomas.

9. *Evan Blessed* (St, Martin's, 2005) Evan and Bronwen's nuptial preparations are interrupted by the disappearance of a girl hiking on Mount Snowdon. Then Bronwen goes missing.
10. *Evanly Bodies* (St. Martin's, 2006) Bronwen introduces Evan to Jamila, a London-born teenager of Pakistani descent who pleads for their help after she learns that her radical Muslim brother has persuaded their parents to take her back to Pakistan to be married.

II. Molly Murphy, who has fled to New York from Ireland after accidentally killing an unwanted suitor, is the heroine of a series of historical mysteries set in New York at the turn of the 20th century. The feisty Molly has a way of getting involved in criminal investigations, much to the chagrin of her beau, Daniel Sullivan, a handsome young police captain. Although lacking the gentle humor of the Evan Evans series, this series does provide solid plots and good circa-1900 New York City ambience.

1. *Murphy's Law* (St. Martin's, 2001) After fleeing Ireland to avoid being hanged for the accidental death of the local landowner's son, Molly Murphy is placed in the law's sights again when a crude type named O'Malley turns up dead on Ellis Island after a public shipboard argument with Molly.
2. *Death of Riley* (St. Martin's, 2002) Murder, anarchist plots, a session as a nude model, and even the assassination of President McKinley have roles to play when Molly, against the advice of her sometime beau, Daniel Sullivan, takes on a job with PI Paddy Riley.
3. *For the Love of Mike* (St. Martin's, 2003) Having taken over the late Paddy Riley's detective business, Molly finds herself in the slammer when two cops refuse to believe that she is staking out a house rather than drumming up business as a prostitute.
4. *In Like Flynn* (St. Martin's, 2005) At the behest of former beau Daniel Sullivan, who wants her to get away from the New York typhoid epidemic of 1902, Molly takes a job at the upstate home of Senator Barney Flynn to expose the Sorensons, two sisters working as spiritualists, who claim to be able to contact Flynn's son, missing and apparently dead.
5. *Oh Danny Boy* (St. Martin's, 2006) NYPD cop Daniel Sullivan has been accused of taking a bribe, but Molly is sure that Daniel has been set up to get him off the case of the East Side Ripper.
6. *In Dublin's Fair City* (St. Martin's, 2007) On a trip back to Ireland, Molly discovers a corpse in the first-class stateroom she has been offered by a famous actress.
7. *Tell Me, Pretty Maiden* (St. Martin's, 2008) Molly and Daniel Sullivan stumble upon a near-dead young woman in a Central Park snowdrift.

Box, C. J.

Wyoming game warden Joe Picket may seem a trifle naive and fallible, but his strong sense of duty, honor, and justice always pull him through as he tries to achieve a balance between environmental activists and the westerners who depend on the land for a living. C. J. (no other forename supplied) Box is a Wyoming native and president of Rocky Mountain International, a company that promotes tourism to the region. The Joe Picket novels have won praise from Tony Hillerman (q.v.) and have been compared to Nevada Barr's Anna Pigeon (q.v.) series for their evocation of the American West.

1. *Open Season* (Putnam, 2001) Young Joe Pickett's efforts to fill the shoes of legendary Vein Dunnegan as game warden of Twelve Sleep County in Wyoming and to support his wife and kids on his not-too-munificent salary, are complicated when the poacher who snatched his gun from him turns up dead in Joe's woodpile.
2. *Savage Run* (Putnam, 2002) Environmentalists, including the infamous activist Stewie Woods and his wife, are apparently being murdered by a pair of unconventional hit men, and Joe's wife, Marybeth, who grew up with Woods, receives mysterious phone calls from "Stewie."
3. *Winterkill* (Putnam, 2003) The little town of Saddlestring is deluged by the media, US Forest Service bureaucrats, and two nasty FBI agents after the body of Lamar Gardiner, District Supervisor for the Twelve Sleep National Forest, is found during a blizzard, pierced with arrows, near seven illegally shot elk. Were the Sovereign Citizens, a misfit group of survivalists camping nearby, responsible?
4. *Trophy Hunt* (Putnam, 2004) When the mangled bodies of a moose, several cows, and two human beings are found, Joe is put on a task force to investigate. Joe's mission is compromised by the shenanigans of Bud Barnum, the corrupt sheriff of Twelve Sleep County, who blames a grizzly bear, and uninvited paranormal expert Cleve Garrett, who postulates otherworldly causes.
5. *Out of Range* (Putnam, 2005) Picket is temporarily transferred to sophisticated tourist mecca Jackson when warden Will Jensen apparently commits suicide, and he runs into questionable hunting practices, developers who want to build on a wildlife trail, and animal-rights activists.
6. *In Plain Sight* (Putnam, 2006) Joe Pickett and his family have become the target of killer John Wayne Keeley.
7. *Free Fire* (Putnam, 2007) When four environmental activists employed by Yellowstone Park are murdered in an isolated area, Wyoming's governor sends Joe Pickett to investigate.

Box, Edgar

PSEUDONYM OF Gore Vidal

Fairly early in his writing career Gore Vidal (q.v.) wrote a trio of mystery novels under the Box pseudonym. Box's protagonist, Peter Cutler Sargeant III, is an American Lord Peter Wimsey: well bred and witty, he moves with ease in Long Island's (New York) social world as well as in political and artistic circles. His occupation as a self-employed public-relations man gets him involved in two of his three cases. *Death in the Fifth Position* was reissued in 1991, but Vidal-Box has chosen not to add to the series. *Three by Box* (Random House, 1978) contains all three Peter Sargeant cases.

1. *Death in the Fifth Position* (Dutton, 1952) When a Russian ballet troupe retains Peter to keep an eye on things, he doesn't expect murder onstage.
2. *Death before Bedtime* (Dutton, 1953) Peter goes to Washington to handle publicity for Senator Leander Rhodes only to find his client has been killed by a bomb.
3. *Death Likes It Hot* (Dutton, 1954) Peter spends a long weekend in East Hampton, where a society party leads to sex, murder, and mystery.

Boyd, Donna

PSEUDONYM OF Donna Ball

Donna Boyd has done for werewolves what Anne Rice (q.v.) and others have done for vampires: making them the heroes of a hidden, passionate world. The Devoncroix family is the leading clan of the werewolves. Werewolves are neither half-wolf or half-human but are superior animals who live hundreds of years, have directed human progress for millennia, and have a passionate sex life that would destroy ordinary humans. The two Devoncroix novels so far are redolent of passion and werewolf lore. Donna Boyd is a pseudonym for Donna Ball, who has written many romances under pseudonyms such as Taylor Brady, Donna Carlisle, Rebecca Flanders, and Lee Bristol.

1. *Passion, The* **(Avon, 1998)** In the wake of the murder of three werewolves in Manhattan, Alexander Devoncroix realizes that he must tell his son—heir to his leadership of the pack—the story of his own unhappy love for a human, Tessa LeGuerre, which started back in 1897.
2. *Promise, The* **(Avon, 1999)** Hannah North rescues a mortally injured male wolf from a helicopter crash in the Alaskan wilderness and comes to realize that the "wolf" is really Nicholas Devoncroix, heir to the recently assassinated werewolf leader, Alexander Devoncroix, leader of all the werewolves.

Boyer, Rick

Charles "Doc" Adams has a dentist's office in Cambridge, Massachusetts; a home in Concord; a getaway in the Berkshires; and adventures on Cape Cod. Doc manages to break out of his humdrum oral surgeon's existence every now and then to deal with more exciting matters involving smuggling, murder, or espionage. His wife, Mary; his son, Jack; and his detective brother-in-law, Joe Brindell, sometimes help Doc in this entertaining series.

1. *Billingsgate Shoal* **(Houghton Mifflin, 1982)** The suspicious death of a scuba diver and some "conversions" made to a Cape Cod trawler pique Doc's interest.
2. *Penny Ferry, The* **(Houghton Mifflin, 1984)** Adams works with his detective brother-in-law to catch a murderer who left some fingers in the mouth of the victim's guard dog.
3. *Daisy Ducks, The* **(Houghton Mifflin, 1986)** Old buddy Liatis Roantis, former leader of the Daisy Ducks, a team of commandos in Vietnam, wants Doc's aid in retrieving a fortune stashed in Kowloon.
4. *Moscow Metal* **(Houghton Mifflin, 1987)** Doc's wife, Mary, and their cat are poisoned by thallium, a noted KGB weapon.
5. *Whale's Footprints, The* **(Houghton Mifflin, 1988)** Jack Adams, Doc's son, studying whales off Cape Cod, becomes the prime suspect in a murder.
6. *Gone to Earth* **(Fawcett, 1990)** Doc's new hideaway in the Berkshires comes furnished with four Harley-Davidsons and four corpses in shallow graves.
7. *Yellow Bird* **(Fawcett, 1991)** An invitation to a party on Cape Cod leads to the discovery of the body of Northrop Chesterton in a deserted mansion.
8. *Pirate Trade* **(Ballantine, 1995)** A gift purse adorned with genuine ivory leads Doc and Mary to an international poaching ring.
9. *Man Who Whispered, The* **(Ivy, 1998)** The whispered last words of smuggler Christos Ramos may contain the clues to the whereabouts of valuable booty.

Boylan, Clare

When *Holy Pictures* was published in 1983, this story about the coming-of-age of the Cantwell sisters, Nan and Mary, in 1920s Dublin won high praise from reviewers. It was followed by *11 Edward Street* (aka *Home Rule*), which described the lives and hard times of Elinore and Daisy Devlin, grandmother and mother of the girls, from 1896 to 1925. Irish writer and broadcaster Clare Boylan has published other novels and short story collections (see *The Collected Stories*, Counterpoint, 2002) about Irish women and the (usually) feckless men to whom they are tied.

1. *11 Edward Street* **(Doubleday, 1992)** In this prequel set from 1896 to 1925, Dubliner Elinore Devlin has to raise 10 children as a widow. Her daughter Daisy marries businessman and womanizer Cecil Cantwell and raises Nan and Mary, the protagonists of number 2. UK title: *Home Rule*.
2. *Holy Pictures* **(Summit, 1983)** Nan and Mary Cantwell reluctantly try to come to terms with adult life as they grow up in 1920s Dublin.

Boylan, Eleanor

Clara Gamadge, the widow of private investigator Henry Gamadge, is a formidable sleuth in her own right. The "warm, witty, grandmotherly" Clara responds to a crisis in her family within a year of Henry's death, and one thing leads to another in this series of American cozies. The late Henry Gamadge was the hero of a series of mysteries written by Eleanor Boylan's aunt, Elizabeth Daly. Boylan is a puppeteer who has also written plays for puppets and a book about puppeteering: *How to Be a Puppeteer* (Dutton, 1969).

1. *Working Murder* **(Holt, 1989)** The widowed 68-year-old Clara receives a call from her elderly aunt May in New York, asking her for help in reopening the case of Ellen, May's daughter, who disappeared 50 years ago.
2. *Murder Observed* **(Holt, 1990)** A blackmail plot and a coven of neo-Nazis are revealed after Clara's lifelong friend, Anna Lockwood Pitman, is run down right before her eyes.
3. *Murder Machree* **(Holt, 1992)** The case of the Evers twins, one good and one evil, one a victim, and one a possible murderer, takes Clara from Cape Cod to New York and Ireland.
4. *Pushing Murder* **(Holt, 1993)** Clara is hospitalized after eating poisoned hors d'oeuvres at the opening of her friend Sal's mystery bookshop. Then another attempt is made on Clara's life, and someone connected with the case is strangled in the hospital chapel.
5. *Murder Crossed* **(Holt, 1996)** A complicated series of events occurs after former superstar actress Margo Llewelyn drops off her three daughters, each by a different father, at the Massachusetts boarding school of Clara's youth.

Boyle, Alistair

By day he is Malvin Stark, wimpy property manager and cycad (palm tree) connoisseur, married to Dorcas, "Tyranny Rex," daughter of his boss, Elbert "Daddybucks" Wemple. By night he is Gil Yates, dashing and successful private investigator who somehow takes on, and solves, a series of cases involving quirky Southern California types, although he has no office, no phone, and no business cards. This series, somewhat reminiscent of Carl Hiaasen's work, is an entertaining mix of comedy and mystery.

1. *Missing Link, The* **(Knoll, 1995)** Introduces Malvin Stark–Gil Yates, property manager by day, private investigator by night. Gil takes on the case of the missing daughter of an arms dealer.
2. *Con, The* **(Knoll, 1996)** Gil is asked to recover a missing Monet by Franklin d'Lacy, managing director of the Los Angeles Metropolitan Museum of Art.

3. *Unlucky Seven, The* **(Knoll, 1997)** A mail-bomb assassin is bent on wiping out the seven most powerful men in the world. Influential media figure Harold Mattlich hires Yates to thwart the mad bomber's plans.

4. *Bluebeard's Last Stand* **(Knoll, 1998)** Gil takes a three-week cruise to keep an eye on Harvey Cavendish's 76-year-old mother, Harriet, who has a history of loving, leaving, and possibly murdering wealthy women.

5. *Ship Shapely* **(Knoll, 1999)** Gil is hired to find the whereabouts of a debauched captain who vanished from his yacht with an all-female crew in Hawaii more than a year ago.

6. *What Now, King Lear?* **(Knoll, 2001)** Orville Sampson left a provision in his will that, should he be murdered, the case must be solved before his estate is divided.

7. *Unholy Ghost, The* **(Knoll, 2003)** Yates is hired by Hungarian movie mogul Lajos Bohem to find his wife and daughter, who have disappeared after joining a sect called Techsci (a takeoff on Scientology).

8. *They Fall Hard* **(Knoll, 2004)** Richard Manley, the dying illegitimate son of prominent prizefighter Buddy Benson, hires Gil to probe the 30-year-old mystery surrounding Buddy's last two fights and his suspicious death.

Boyle, Gerry

Jack McMorrow, former *New York Times* metro reporter, left New York for rural Maine after having blotted his copybook on the *Times.* Now he resides at Dump Road in Prosperity, a hamlet in the inland Maine county of Waldo; ekes out a living as an editor and reporter for small-town newspapers and as a stringer for the *Times* and its satellite, the *Boston Globe;* makes a trip or two back to New York; reads; walks in the woods; chops wood; and ferrets out the vice and crime lurking under the surface of misnamed Prosperity. Jack is tenacious and not overly nice in the means, including physical, by which he elicits the truth. His sometime live-in girlfriend, Roxanne Masterson, who is a child-protection worker, also puts Jack onto cases. Colby College, Maine, graduate Gerry Boyle is a reporter, editor, and columnist for the *Central Maine Morning Sentinel* of Waterville.

1. *Deadline* **(North Country, 1993)** The body of a freelance photographer found floating in the canal in Androscoggin, Maine, leads local newspaper editor Jack McMorrow, a refugee from New York City, into some murky doings.

2. *Bloodline* **(Putnam, 1995)** After taking a relatively lucrative assignment from *New England Look* magazine to write an article on "Kids Having Kids," Jack is led to Missy Hewitt, who gave up her baby for adoption; some nasty teenagers; and a murder charge.

3. *Lifeline* **(Putnam, 1996)** Jack stirs up trouble again when he writes a story about Donna Marchant, domestic abuse and subsequent murder victim, and incurs the wrath of, among others, Donna's boyfriend, Jeff Tanner.

4. *Potshot* **(Putnam, 1997)** After Jack meets Bobby Mullaney, vociferous advocate of marijuana legalization, at a country fair, Jack's nose for a good story leads him into a mess involving rural hippies, urban drug dealers, missing persons, and an assassination attempt.

5. *Borderline* **(Berkley, 1998)** While researching a piece about Benedict Arnold's Revolutionary War raid on Quebec, Jack gets involved in the disappearance of someone calling himself P. Ray Mantis.

6. *Cover Story* **(Berkley, 2000)** Jack's trip back to New York City revives some old memories of his checkered career with the *Times.* Then Johnny Fiore, New York City's popular mayor, is stabbed to death, and an old acquaintance, former cop Butch Casey, is the prime suspect.

7. *Pretty Dead* **(Berkley, 2003)** Jack's girlfriend, social-worker Roxanne Masterson, is investigating allegations of physical abuse concerning the daughter of prominent Bostonians David and Maddie Connelly.

8. *Home Body* **(Berkley, 2004)** On a trip to Portland, Maine's metropolis, Jack and Roxanne prevent a street gang from attacking teenage runaway Rocky and try to help him further, but Rocky proves to be very elusive.

Boyne, Walter J.

Walter J. Boyne, career US Air Force officer, director of the National Air and Space Museum, and author and editor of nonfiction works on aviation and military affairs, has written a trio of authentic tech-nothriller historical novels about the aircraft industry and the US Air Force from the Lindbergh year of 1927 to the cold war. Continuing characters such as hotshot pilot Frank Bandfield and African American air ace John Marshall interact with historical characters, exciting air battles, and much technical information for air buffs, in the Eagles trilogy.

1. *Trophy for Eagles* **(Crown, 1989)** Frank Bandfield and German pilot Bruno Hafner meet as participants in the air race to Paris in 1927, and they start a long-lasting rivalry in piloting and aircraft design.

2. *Eagles at War* **(Crown, 1991)** The development of military aircraft during World War II takes center stage, with Bandfield and US Air Force General Caldwell matching wits with their German counterparts.

3. *Air Force Eagles* **(Crown, 1992)** Follows the history of the US Air Force through the Korean War and the years of "nuclear deterrence," with a civil rights subplot concerning African American pilot John Marshall.

Bradford, Barbara Taylor

I. This sextet of novels chronicles the rise of Emma Harte from poverty to great wealth and the struggle for control of her legacy among her children, grandchildren, and great-grandchildren. The story is familiar but well told, with strong female characters, authentic historical background, and a glamorous backdrop of money and success. *Emma's Secret,* which was published 15 years after *To Be the Best,* and *Unexpected Blessings* pick up the saga with Emma Harte's granddaughter Paula and Paula's grown daughters. *Just Rewards* continues the saga with Emma's great-granddaughter. Bradford, a native of Emma Harte's Yorkshire, was a fashion editor, syndicated columnist, and author of books on decorating and etiquette before she struck real pay dirt with the best-selling *A Woman of Substance,* which was produced as a television miniseries featuring Deborah Kerr as the mature Emma.

1. *Woman of Substance, A* **(Doubleday, 1979)** Emma Harte remembers her rise from a poor Yorkshire servant girl to a rich and powerful department-store magnate. The revised edition (Grafton [UK], 1991) includes a new chapter set in wartime.

2. *Hold the Dream* **(Doubleday, 1985)** Emma hands the business over to three of her grandchildren: Paula, Emily, and Alexander.

3. *To Be the Best* **(Doubleday, 1988)** Paula, the granddaughter who most resembles Emma, fights her treacherous cousin Jonathan for control of the family empire.

4. ***Emma's Secret*** (St. Martin's, 2003) Paula occupies Pennistone Royal, Emma's country estate in Yorkshire, and presides over the Knightsbridge store, flagship of the Harte chain, where her grown daughters Linnet and Tessa work. Then a young American girl, Evan Hughes, who may have a hidden Harte connection, is hired.

5. ***Unexpected Blessings*** (St. Martin's, 2005) Emma has been dead for 30 years, but members of the Harte family continue to administer the empire she created. Half sisters Tessa and Linnet temporarily make up their differences when Tessa's three-year-old daughter, Adele, disappears.

6. ***Just Rewards*** (St. Martin's, 2006) Emma's great-granddaughter Linnet O'Neill must defend the Harte empire and family against evil uncle Jonathan Ainsley.

II. The Ravenscar Dynasty, about the house of Deravenel, is a trilogy about another family company, with interests ranging from French wine to Persian oil. The trilogy, two volumes of which have been published, starts in 1904.

1. ***Ravenscar Dynasty, The*** (St. Martin's, 2006) In 1904 18-year-old Edward Deravenel is told of the death of his father, brother, and cousins in a fire. With the help of his cousin Neville Watkins, Edward vows to seek the truth, avenge the deaths, and take control of the business empire usurped from Edward's great-uncle 60 years before.

2. ***Heir, The*** (St. Martin's, 2007) In 1918 Edward Deravenel has built his family company into the "greatest trading company in the world." UK title: *Heirs of Ravenscar*.

Bradley, Celeste

I. The novels in the Liar's Club series are loosely connected Regency-era romances postulating a band of aristocratic gentlemen who are really "ruthless" covert operatives for the Crown. Frothy, sexy, and entertaining romances by a rising romance star who lives in Tennessee.

1. ***Pretender, The*** (St. Martin's, 2003) Agatha Cunnington, searching for her missing brother James, fashions a new identity for herself as Mrs. Mortimer Applequist. Then she chooses master spy Simon Montague Rain, who is investigating James in the guise of a chimney sweep, to be the temporary Mr. Applequist.

2. ***Imposter, The*** (St. Martin's, 2003) When young widow Clara Simpson pens some annoying political cartoons under the alias of "Sir Thorogood," Liar's Club member Dalton Montmorency decides to pose as Sir Thorogood in an effort to expose the cartoonist.

3. ***Spy, The*** (St. Martin's, 2004) Phillippa Atwater, trying to locate her missing father, poses as a male tutor to keep a sharp eye on James Cunnington, who is on a mission to find the missing daughter of Rupert Atwater.

4. ***Charmer, The*** (St. Martin's, 2004) Rose Lacey and Collis Tremayne are rivalrous spy trainees until they are put together on a dangerous mission.

5. ***Rogue, The*** (St. Martin's, 2005) Lady Jane Pennington, niece of a suspected traitor, falls in love with dashing spy Ethan Damont.

II. The Royal Four is Bradley's new series, again about an elite band of covert spies. More frothy, complicated plots and characters, full of danger and passion.

1. ***To Wed a Scandalous Spy*** (St. Martin's, 2005) After a chance encounter that winds up with Willa Trent and Nathaniel Stonewell spending the night together, Nathaniel does the honorable thing by proposing to the acquiescent Willa. But will she react when she finds out that she is wed to "Lord Treason?"

2. ***Surrender to a Wicked Spy*** (St. Martin's, 2005) New bride Olivia Calwell's husband, Dane, Lord Greenleigh, seems to be up to some furtive doings. Is he a French spy?

3. ***One Night with a Spy*** (St. Martin's, 2006) After her husband's death, Lady Julia Barrowby believes that his place in the Royal Four is hers by right. But Marcus Ramsay, Lord Dryden, who stood next in line to be chosen for the Four, will have a great deal to say about Lady Julia's pretensions.

4. ***Seducing the Spy*** (St. Martin's, 2006) Lady Alicia Lawrence, who overheard details of a dangerous conspiracy, turns to the one person who might believe her—Stanton Horne, Lord Wyndham, member of the Royal Four.

Bradley, Marion Zimmer

I. In the very popular Darkover series, Marion Zimmer Bradley combined sword-and-sorcery adventure with a science-fiction setting. Darkover is a distant planet illuminated by a dim, red sun and four multicolored moons. Many intelligent beings roam this cold and mountainous planet, some in the form of cats, small apes, or birds. Early human settlers from a crashed spaceship have mixed with the planet's psi-gifted natives to form a culture where mental powers have replaced machines. When technologically advanced Terrans try to dominate the planet, conflict is inevitable. There is a strong feminist flavor to the series. Before she died, in 1999, Bradley entrusted the Darkover legacy to the Marion Zimmer Bradley (MZB) Literary Works Trust, which continues to publish Darkover books by other authors based on Bradley's ideas. The titles published in the 1960s and 1970s were paperback originals. Most of them have been reprinted in hardcover by Gregg Press (1979) or Severn House (1994). Darkover anthologies edited by Bradley are covered in series II (below). A quarterly *Darkover Newsletter* was published from 1976 to 1995.

Bradley's heirs (http://mzbworks.home.att.net) state that Bradley "always insisted that the Darkover novels are not a series and can be read in any order. . . . If you simply MUST have an order in which to read them, it is better to read chronologically by publication, rather than in chronology of Darkovan history." However, because *Sequels* is pledged to arranging books in order of the history within the series, and since the MZB Literary Works Trust has provided a "Darkovan Chronology," the authors of *Sequels* have adopted MZB Literary Works Trust's order. Numbers 3 and 22 are listed in the "Darkovan Chronology" but have not yet been published.

1. ***Darkover Landfall*** (DAW, 1974) Humans crash-land into the alien world of Darkover and adapt to its harsh climate and strange winds.

2. ***Stormqueen!*** (DAW, 1978) This story is set in Darkover's Age of Chaos, before the Seven Great Houses were established or the force of the matrix was fully understood.

3. ***Thunderlord*** (DAW, 2008) Listed in the "Darkovan Chronology" but not yet published.

4. ***Fall of Neskaya, The*** (DAW, 2001) Written by Deborah J. Ross. Book one of the Clingfire trilogy. In the aftermath of the Age of Chaos, laran-gifted Coryn Leynier becomes under-keeper at Neskaya Tower and eventually find himself pitted against evil human foes and black psionic wizardry.

5. ***Zandru's Forge*** (DAW, 2003) Book two of the Clingfire trilogy. Written by Deborah J. Ross. Carolin Hastur, heir to the Hastur

throne, and Varzil Ridenow, a noble child with great psi power, resolve to eliminate the threat posed by weapons of mass destruction on their world.

6. *Flame in Hali, A* **(DAW, 2004)** Book three of the Clingfire trilogy. Written by Deborah J. Ross. Incessant warfare divides the Hundred Kingdoms.

7. *Hawkmistress!* **(DAW, 1982)** The story of young Romilly Mac-Aran, who leaves home rather than marry, and her unusual ability to communicate with hawks.

8. *Two to Conquer* **(DAW, 1980)** During the Hundred Kingdoms, Varzil dreams of uniting Darkover, and Bard Di Asturien is exiled for murder.

9. *Heirs of Hammerfell, The* **(DAW, 1989)** About two brothers, separated at infancy, each of whom thinks that he is the heir to the kingdom.

10. *Rediscovery* **(DAW, 1993)** Coauthored by Mercedes Lackey (q.v.). Darkover is rediscovered by the Terran Empire, and contact is initiated between one of the Terran team and a young Darkovan telepath.

11. *Shattered Chain, The* **(DAW, 1976)** Lady Rohana, Free Amazon Jaelle, and the Terran agent Magda break the chains of their female roles. Followed by number 14.

12. *Spell Sword, The* **(DAW, 1974)** Damon Ridenow and Andrew Carr rescue the sorceress Callista from imprisonment and destroy the threat of the cat people. Followed by number 13.

13. *Forbidden Tower, The* **(DAW, 1977)** Sequel to number 12. Powerful physical and psychological forces separate Terran Andrew Carr and Darkovan Callista. Followed by number 18.

14. *Thendara House* **(DAW, 1983)** Sequel to number 11. Continues the stories of Magda and Jaelle as their roles are somewhat reversed. Followed by number 15.

15. *City of Sorcery* **(DAW, 1984)** Sequel to number 14. The third book about Magda and Jaelle tells of their journey out to arctic land beyond the Domains.

16. *Star of Danger* **(Ace, 1965)** Terran Larry Montray and Darkovan Kennard Alton become friends despite their cultural differences.

17. *Winds of Darkover, The* **(Ace, 1970)** Barran falls in love with Melitta, and together they evoke the power of the dangerous Darkovan fire goddess to rid Storn Castle of its bandit captors.

18. *Bloody Sun, The* **(DAW, 1979)** Sequel to number 13. Rewrite of the original publication (Ace, 1964). Jeff Kerwin returns to Darkover after many years to find that there is no record of his birth on the planet.

19. *Heritage of Hastur, The* **(DAW, 1975)** The story of the Sharra uprising as seen through the eyes of Lew Alton, who is of mixed Darkovan and Terran lineage. Followed by number 21.

20. *Planet Savers, The* **(Ace, 1962)** When Darkover is threatened by an epidemic, Dr. Jason Allison appeals to the nonhuman Trailmen for help. Bound with *The Sword of Aldones*, original version of number 21.

21. *Sharra's Exile* **(DAW, 1981)** Sequel to number 19. Lew Alton returns to Darkover prepared to fight for his inheritance, when other conflicts intervene. A rewriting of *The Sword of Aldones* (Ace, 1962) bound with number 20. To be followed by number 22.

22. *Reluctant King, The* **(DAW, 2008)** To be a sequel to number 21. Not yet published.

23. *World Wreckers, The* **(Ace, 1971)** Darkover is threatened by a clandestine organization determined to pave the way for industrial exploitation.

24. *Exile's Song* **(DAW, 1996)** Coauthored by Adrienne Martine-Barnes. Margaret Alton returns to Darkover as a Terran Empire Scholar, knowing little of her birth planet. Followed by number 25. Variant title: *Return to Darkover*.

25. *Shadow Matrix, The* **(DAW, 1998)** Written by Adrienne Martine-Barnes. Sequel to number 24. Margaret Alton is trying to master her gifts and the Shadow Matrix. Followed by number 26.

26. *Traitor's Sun* **(DAW, 1999)** Written by Adrienne Martine-Barnes. Sequel to number 25. Senator Hermes-Gabriel Aldaran is telepathically summoned to return to Darkover to oppose the Expansionists from the Terran Federation.

27. *Alton Gift, The* **(DAW, 2007)** The story of Darkover's ruling class, the Comyn, and its struggles to reclaim its realm from the Terran Federation. Written by Deborah J. Ross.

II. Marion Zimmer Bradley edited 12 anthologies of Darkover stories written by herself and others. They are listed without annotations.

1. *Keeper's Price, The* **(DAW, 1980)**

2. *Sword of Chaos* **(DAW, 1982)**

3. *Free Amazons of Darkover* **(DAW, 1985)**

4. *Other Side of the Mirror* **(DAW, 1987)**

5. *Red Sun of Darkover* **(DAW, 1987)**

6. *Four Moons of Darkover* **(DAW, 1988)**

7. *Domains of Darkover* **(DAW, 1990)**

8. *Renunciates of Darkover* **(DAW, 1991)**

9. *Leroni of Darkover* **(DAW, 1991)**

10. *Towers of Darkover* **(DAW, 1993)**

11. *Darkover* **(DAW, 1993)** All stories in this volume written by Marion Zimmer Bradley. Variant title: *Marion Zimmer Bradley's Darkover*.

12. *Snows of Darkover* **(DAW, 1994)**

III. *The Mists of Avalon*, a feminist- and goddess-oriented retelling of the Arthurian legend, was a best-seller and is perhaps Bradley's single best-known title. It was followed by five prequels. Diana L. Paxson (q.v.) was the unacknowledged coauthor of numbers 3 and 4, finished number 5, and wrote numbers 1 and 2.

1. *Ancestors of Avalon, The* **(Viking, 2004)** Written by Diana L. Paxson. The deep prehistory of Avalon told with supernatural overtones, as the continent of Atlantis sinks beneath the ocean but leaves its legacy in Avalon.

2. *Ravens of Avalon* **(Viking, 2007)** Written by Diana L. Paxson. Tells the story of the Roman conquest of Britain, which preceded the return to Avalon.

3. *Forest House, The* **(Viking, 1994)** In the 1st century CE, British Eilan and her Roman lover, Gaius, are separated by their conflicting duties. Variant title: *Forests of Avalon*.

4. *Lady of Avalon* **(Viking, 1997)** In the first Christian century, Lady Callean raises her orphaned grandson, Gawen (whose mother was killed in *The Forest House*).

5. *Priestess of Avalon* **(Viking, 2001)** Written with Diana L. Paxson. In 296 CE, young British princess Helena goes to the Isle of Avalon to learn the path of the goddess.

6. *Mists of Avalon, The* **(Viking, 1983)** The Arthurian legend is retold through its major female characters: Arthur's mother, Igraine; the Lady of the Lake, Vivian; Arthur's half sister Morgaine; and his wife, Gwenhwyfar, in this tale of the religious struggle between the matriarchal Druid order and patriarchal Christianity.

IV. Bradley wrote a quartet of gothic romances about half-human, half-sidhe sorcerer Truth Jourdemayne (neé Blackburn). Set in the 1960s through the 1990s, this is a series that will appeal especially to New Agers.

1. *Ghostlight* **(Tor, 1995)** Young Truth Blackburn lost her parents to an occultist experiment in the late 1960s. In the 1990s, some New Agers hope to repeat the experiment.
2. *Witchlight* **(Tor, 1996)** Truth Jourdemayne comes to Winter Musgrave's rescue when the latter is being haunted by vague memories of a past in which something horrible may have happened.
3. *Gravelight* **(Tor, 1997)** While investigating along with Dylan Palmer, her psychic researcher fiancé, Truth encounters another link to her wizardly Blackburn ancestors.
4. *Heartlight* **(Tor, 1998)** Follows white magic Adept Colin McLaren from the 1960s and his meeting with darker magicians, such as Thorne Blackburn, to his retirement at the end of the 20th century.

V. Bradley coauthored with Julian May (q.v.) and Andre Norton (q.v.) this fantasy quest series about the kingdom of Ruwenda and its three Petals of the Living Trillium, daughters of the slain rulers of Ruwenda. Number 1 was coauthored by Bradley, May, and Norton. Number 2 was written by Julian May, and number 3 by Andre Norton. Bradley and Elisabeth Waters cowrote number 4.

1. *Black Trillium* **(Doubleday, 1990)** Coauthored by Julian May and Andre Norton. When Ruwenda's rulers are slain, their daughters, the three Petals of the Living Trillium, flee to the Archimage Binah.
2. *Blood Trillium* **(Bantam, 1992)** Written by Julian May. Twelve years later, the World of the Three Moons is endangered by another sorcerer, Portolanus, Master of Tuzamen.
3. *Golden Trillium* **(Bantam, 1993)** Written by Andre Norton. The land of Ruwenda is once again endangered by the legacy of the ancient Vanished Ones, and only Kadiya, Seeker-Warrior, one of three daughters of the Black Trillium, is in a position to act.
4. *Lady of the Trillium* **(Bantam, 1995)** Written by Bradley and Elisabeth Waters. Princess Haramis, Archimage of Ruwenda, is aging and must groom a successor.

Bradshaw, Gillian (Marucha)

Gawain (Gwalchmai) is the focus of this fresh retelling of the Arthurian legend. The trilogy depicts Gawain as a serious and scholarly man, quite different from the way he is usually depicted. Bradshaw's post-Roman, pre-Anglo-Saxon Britain represents much historical research on her part, with some elements of magic thrown in. The war-leader Arthur, the sinister Medraut (Modred), the strong and capable but inwardly haunted Gwynhwyfar (Guinevere), Bedwyr (Bedivere) the queen's lover (neither Lancelot nor Merlin play a large role in this version), and the ambitious Morgause, Uther's daughter and Gwalchmai's mother, are well depicted. The three novels were published together as *Down the Long Wind* (Methuen [UK], 1988). American classics scholar Bradshaw is also the author of several historical novels (usually set in Greco-Roman times) and young adult fantasies.

1. *Hawk of May* **(Simon & Schuster, 1980)** Gwalchmai, son of Lot of Orkney and the sorceress Morgause, grows up in an anti-Arthurian household, but eventually, after a meeting with Lugh the Sun God, he pledges himself to the service of the Light, which Arthur also serves.
2. *Kingdom of Summer, The* **(Simon & Schuster, 1981)** This volume is told through the eyes of Rhys ap Sion, a farmer who follows Gwalchmai to Camlann, becomes his body servant, and accompanies him on his quest to right the wrong he has done to the maiden Elidan.

3. *In Winter's Shadow* **(Simon & Schuster, 1982)** As the final battle between Arthur and his illegitimate son Medraut looms, Gwynhwyfar tries to keep Arthur's kingdom together but fails, largely because of the fallout from her adulterous affair with Bedwyr.

Brady, John

Sergeant Matt Minogue of Dublin's Garda Murder Squad is the hero of this series of Irish procedurals. Matt is full of sarcastic Irish wit and charm, and he is a dedicated, if sometimes world-weary, professional. He has his problems with relatives and colleagues but manages to come through when needed in depressed, polluted, and tribal Dublin.

1. *Stone of the Heart, A* **(St. Martin's, 1988)** The body of idealistic student Jarlath Walsh is found on the historic grounds of Dublin's Trinity College.
2. *Unholy Ground* **(St. Martin's, 1992)** When reclusive, elderly Arthur Combs is strangled, his past as a British agent barred from England is revealed.
3. *Kaddish in Dublin* **(St. Martin's, 1992)** Paul Fine, son of the chief justice of the Irish Supreme Court, is found washed up on a beach at Killiney.
4. *All Souls* **(St. Martin's, 1993)** Taking a rest cure at the family farm in County Clare, Minogue becomes enmeshed in the locals' battle against unscrupulous developers.
5. *Good Life, The* **(St. Martin's, 1995)** Ex-prostitute Mary Mullen, whose body turns up in a canal, may have been involved in activities more lucrative and dangerous than prostitution.
6. *Carra King, A* **(Steerforth, 2001)** Patrick Shaughnessy, son of an Irish American millionaire, is found dead in the trunk of his rented car at the airport.

Bragg, Melvyn

I. English novelist, playwright, screenwriter, nonfiction writer, television personality, and member of the House of Lords Melvyn Bragg is probably best known for his television productions (e.g., *The Adventure of English: The Biography of a Language*, 2004). He is also regarded in the United Kingdom as a fine novelist, who deserves to be better known in the United States. The subject matter of Bragg's best work, including the two trilogies set in his native Wigton, Cumberland, is English provincial life, as told from the perspective of families who, over the course of two or three generations, struggle upward from peonage to "independence."

The Cumbrian trilogy is about the Tallentires, three generations of a family, beginning with farm laborer John Tallentire and ending with John's grandson Douglas, who has achieved an education and the possibility of a professional career. *The Cumbrian Trilogy* (Coronet [UK], 1984) is an omnibus volume containing all three novels.

1. *Hired Man, The* **(Knopf, 1970)** Rural England in 1898. John Tallentire is a young farm laborer who leaves the countryside with his wife and children to seek employment in the coal town of Wigton.
2. *Place in England, A* **(Knopf, 1971)** John Tallentire's son Joseph struggles through poverty and World War I to achieve a small degree of success: he is appointed landlord of a run-down pub.
3. *Kingdom Come* **(Secker [UK], 1980)** Douglas Tallentire finds broader opportunities available to him than to his father or grandfather. While he is making a media career for himself in London and the States, he still has to conquer inner doubts and pain. Not published in the United States.

II. The trilogy beginning with *The Soldier's Return* is also set in Wigton, Cumberland. It follows the careers of returning World II veteran Sam Richardson, his wife, Ellen, and his son, Joe, as they adjust to life in a small provincial town in shabby postwar Britain. Hailed as a masterpiece by some critics, the trilogy is a quietly moving, understated slice of British life.

1. *Soldier's Return, The* (Arcade, 2002) Sam Richardson, returned from the jungles of Burma, finds readjustment to the stuffy and limited postwar environment of Wigton difficult, but he perseveres for the sake of his wife, Ellen, and his son, Joe. Originally published in the United Kingdom in 1999.
2. *Son of War, A* (Arcade, 2003) Sam Richardson eventually gets some independence by taking over and remaking an old pub. Ellen is troubled by her half brother Colin, who brings her news of her father. Young Joe enters upon a painful adolescence. Originally published in the United Kingdom in 2001.
3. *Crossing the Lines* (Arcade, 2005) Young Joe works in his parents' pub and dreams of his neighbor Lizzie. Then opportunity knocks in the form of Oxford University. Originally published in the United Kingdom in 2003.

Braine, John

Perhaps best known of the "angry young man" school of working-class British novels, *Room at the Top* shows young Joe Lampton rising above his mining-town origins at the cost of many around him. The 1958 film, regarded as the first British movie to take sex seriously, won an Academy Award nomination for Best Picture, and Simone Signoret won the Best Actress Award for her portrayal of Alice, the older woman whose love for Joe destroys her. *Life at the Top* was also made into a film (1965).

1. *Room at the Top* (Houghton Mifflin, 1962) Joe Lampton comes to Warley to take a job in the city-council treasurer's office. Eventually, he marries into the wealth and position he craves.
2. *Life at the Top* (Houghton Mifflin, 1962) Now rich and powerful, Joe realizes how much of his personal freedom he has traded for success.

Brandon, Jay

I. Chris Sinclair, San Antonio, Texas, district attorney, always gets his convictions but often at a considerable political, emotional, and physical cost to himself and his lover, psychiatrist Anne Greenwald, in this series of courtroom dramas by a San Antonio criminal lawyer. These legal thrillers have complex plots with strong characters, local color, and lots of legal detail.

1. *Angel of Death* (Forge, 1998) Recently elected San Antonio district attorney Chris Sinclair gets African American community activist Malachi Reese convicted for a double murder, but Reese extorts a heavy cost from Sinclair, including murder of an assistant DA, political smears, and the jeopardization of Sinclair's relationship with child psychiatrist Anne Greenwald.
2. *Afterimage* (Forge, 2000) When a 14-year-old girl is murdered, Chris discovers that the girl's mother is his old college lover, Jean, and that he probably has, also by Jean, a 16-year-old daughter, Clarissa.
3. *Silver Moon* (Forge, 2003) A lot of nasty Texas politicos are exposed in the wake of a visit to Anne Greenwald's father, and

Anne's ex-fiancé, Ben, is killed by a gunshot wound, possibly self-inflicted.

4. *Grudge Match* (Forge, 2004) New DNA evidence seems to prove that police officer Steve Greerdon was wrongfully convicted for armed robbery eight years ago. But then two police officers are murdered, and a high-level police cover-up is asserted.
5. *Running with the Dead* (Forge, 2005) Another blast from Sinclair's past, as new clues indicate that a corrupt high school administrator and basketball coach was the murderer of Henry Claremont, Chris's longtime friend, whom he successfully defended in a rape case several years ago.

II. Mark Blackwell, another San Antonio DA, was the hero of two other courtroom thrillers by Brandon. Blackwell, somewhat older and more cynical, also got involved in messy legal cases that elicit thrilling court scenes.

1. *Fade the Heat* (Pocket, 1990) District Attorney Mark Blackwell must bring all of his legal knowledge and his political connections to bear to exonerate his son from a false rape charge.
2. *Loose among the Lambs* (Pocket, 1993) A child-molestation case threatens Blackwell's career, as the victims fail to identify the mug shot of accused molester Chris Davis, and finger Davis's politically potent attorney, Austin Paley, instead.

Braun, Lilian Jackson

Braun published three Cat Who . . . novels in the 1960s; then an 18-year hiatus took place as she pursued her career as editor and writer with the *Detroit Free Press*. Since her return to mystery writing, Braun has averaged more than one book per year, to the delight of ailurophiles and mystery lovers. Jim "Quill" Qwilleran is a journalist with a specialty in crime reporting. With his psychic Siamese cat, Koko, and Yum-Yum, a second Siamese that arrived early in the series, Quill has a second career in mystery solving. Quill and cats move back and forth between Pickax City, Moose County, Michigan, and the city "down below" (Detroit) as they follow various career paths, come into a large fortune unexpectedly, and chase down solutions to the many mysteries that the city and deceptively bucolic Moose County throw their way.

1. *Cat Who Could Read Backwards, The* (Dutton, 1966) Jim Qwilleran, "artless" feature writer on art for a big-city daily, and his Siamese cat, Koko, get involved with skulduggery in the art world.
2. *Cat Who Ate Danish Modern, The* (Dutton, 1967) Quill is assigned the job of editing a new supplement for the *Daily Fluxion* called "Gracious Abodes."
3. *Cat Who Turned On and Off, The* (Dutton, 1968) Jim moves himself and the cats to a house in the antique-dealer district to do a story on "Junktown."
4. *Cat Who Saw Red, The* (Jove, 1986) Restaurant reviewer Quill suspects that a former lover has met with foul play, and someone is trying to poison Koko and Yum-Yum.
5. *Cat Who Played Brahms, The* (Jove, 1987) Koko develops a taste for classical music as Quill goes on a fishing trip and reels up something nasty.
6. *Cat Who Played Post Office, The* (Jove, 1987) Quill inherits $1 million dollars (with conditions attached) and moves into a mansion.
7. *Cat Who Knew Shakespeare, The* (Jove, 1988) The mysterious suicide of a newspaper publisher engages the interest of Quill and cats.

8. *Cat Who Sniffed Glue, The* **(Putnam, 1988)** Quill and cats are living on the Klingschoen estate in Pickax City when the son and daughter-in-law of the local banker are murdered.

9. *Cat Who Went Underground, The* **(Putnam, 1989)** A restful summer at Quill's cabin in Mooseville doesn't fully materialize as a series of home-repair problems intervene.

10. *Cat Who Talked to Ghosts, The* **(Putnam, 1990)** Iris Cobb, resident curator of the Moose County Historical Museum, thinks she hears ghosts, then dies of an apparent heart attack.

11. *Cat Who Lived High, The* **(Putnam, 1990)** Quill and cats descend to the city "down below" to rescue the formerly elegant Casablanca Building from the wreckers.

12. *Cat Who Knew a Cardinal, The* **(Putnam, 1991)** Hilary Van Brook, unpopular high school principal, is playing Cardinal Wolsey in Shakespeare's *Henry VIII*.

13. *Cat Who Moved a Mountain, The* **(Putnam, 1992)** A vacation in the rustic Potato Mountains is doomed to failure when Quill and cats take up residence in the home of the late developer J. J. Hawkinfield.

14. *Cat Who Wasn't There, The* **(Putnam, 1992)** Quill leaves cats behind to take a "Bonnie Scots Tour" to Scotland with present and former lady loves.

15. *Cat Who Went into the Closet, The* **(Putnam, 1993)** Quill rents the Gage Mansion in Pickax City until its octogenarian owner, Euphonia Gage, reportedly commits suicide in Florida.

16. *Cat Who Came to Breakfast, The* **(Putnam, 1994)** Odd accidents are plaguing the recently built resort on Breakfast Island.

17. *Cat Who Blew the Whistle, The* **(Putnam, 1995)** Floyd Trevelyan, railroad buff, disappears just before the maiden run of his renovated locomotive.

18. *Cat Who Said Cheese, The* **(Putnam, 1996)** Pickax City is about to celebrate the Great Food Expo when a stranger moves into the community's only hotel.

19. *Cat Who Tailed a Thief, The* **(Putnam, 1997)** The residents of Pickax City are concerned about the failure of their Ice Festival (ruined by an unprecedented mid-February thaw), the Pleasant Street historic houses restoration project, and a series of petty larcenies.

20. *Cat Who Sang for the Birds, The* **(Putnam, 1998)** An adult spelling bee–cum–baseball game, automation of the local public library, butterflies, and two murders engage the attention of Quill and cats.

21. *Cat Who Saw Stars, The* **(Putnam, 1999)** A new upscale restaurant, UFOs, and a missing backpacker are the topics of conversation as Quill and cats return to his beach house in Mooseville.

22. *Cat Who Robbed a Bank, The* **(Putnam, 2000)** Mr. Delacamp, buyer and seller of expensive jewelry and a guest at Pickax City's newly renovated (and renamed) Mackintosh Inn, is murdered on his last quinquennial visit from Chicago.

23. *Cat Who Smelled a Rat, The* **(Putnam, 2001)** Residents of Pickax City, awaiting the Big One, the annual blizzard that will signal the start of a long winter and the end of extreme drought conditions, are shocked by a series of fires and two suspicious deaths.

24. *Cat Who Went Up the Creek, The* **(Putnam, 2001)** Left to his own devices, as his librarian lady friend, Polly, goes on a trip, Quill accepts an invitation to the Nutcracker Inn in the town of Black Creek.

25. *Cat Who Brought Down the House, The* **(Putnam, 2003)** Moose County native Thelma Thackeray, having achieved fame and fortune in Hollywood, returns to Pickax City and the transmogrification of the town's old opera house into a film club.

26. *Cat Who Talked Turkey, The* **(Putnam, 2004)** A flock of wild turkeys; an interview with wealthy Edith Carroll; Edith's daughter and Edith's worthless boyhood friend, Lush; a shooting death on Qwill's property; and the bicentennial of the neighboring town of Brrr all figure in this mystery.

27. *Cat Who Went Bananas, The* **(Putnam, 2005)** The arrival of actor Alden Wade stirs up Qwill's and Polly Duncan's passionless romance until Alden marries a local heiress. But then there is the unsolved murder of Alden's first wife.

28. *Cat Who Dropped a Bombshell, The* **(Putnam, 2006)** Qwill runs around Pickax City getting things ready for the town's celebration of its sesquicentenary. The "mystery" concerns wealthy Nathan and Doris Ledfield, whose only heir is an obnoxious, greedy nephew.

29. *Cat Who Had 60 Whiskers, The* **(Putnam, 2007)** Koko meets a piano tuner. Polly goes to Paris. Qwill writes an absurdist play titled *The Cat Who Got Elected Dog Catcher*. There's a death from a bee sting.

Breen, Jon L(inn)

I. Jerry Brogan is a racetrack announcer and amateur sleuth who has appeared in four novels, chock-full of racing lore, that recall the classic puzzle mysteries of the 1920s and '30s and other mysteries with racetrack settings, such as Stephen Dobyns's (q.v.) Charlie Bradshaw. Reference librarian (Rio Hondo Community College, California) and former sportscaster Jon L. Breen has written and edited several reference and critical works on crime fiction including the Edgar-winning *What About Murder? A Guide to Books about Mystery and Detective Fiction* (Scarecrow, 1981; supplement 1993) and *Novel Verdicts: A Guide to Courtroom Fiction* (2d ed., Scarecrow, 1999).

1. *Listen for the Click* **(Walker, 1983)** Racetrack announcer Jerry Brogan, a homicide officer, and a pair of con men investigate the shooting death of a jockey. UK title: *Vicar's Roses*.

2. *Triple Crown* **(Walker, 1986)** Jerry lands the assignment of being radio announcer for horse-racing's Triple Crown: the Kentucky Derby, the Preakness, and the Belmont. Vague threats from someone signing himself "Old Rosebud" are followed by the murders of stable owner Van Masterson and his ex-wife.

3. *Loose Lips* **(Simon & Schuster, 1990)** The Los Angeles Police Department calls on Jerry's racing expertise in the investigation of the murder of blackmailing newspaper reporter Woody Creston.

4. *Hot Air* **(Simon & Schuster, 1991)** Brogan's nephew, retiring jockey Brad Roark, is brought to a surprise reunion with his estranged family, and murder results.

II. In another pair of puzzle mysteries, tinged with the supernatural, young Rachel Hennings, who has inherited her uncle's Los Angeles bookstore, uses her wits and some automatic-writing communication with long-dead writers to solve a couple of murders with links to past scandals. Another Breen creation, the baseball umpire Ed Gorgon, is the protagonist in a series of mystery short stories collected as *Kill the Umpire: The Calls of Ed Gorgon* (Crippen & Landru, 2003).

1. *Gathering Place, The* **(Walker, 1984)** After inheriting her uncle's haunted Los Angeles secondhand bookstore, Rachel Hennings gets involved with a newspaper book editor, detective Manuel Gonzales, and some long-dead best-selling authors in the investigation of a murder and a ghostwriting scandal.

2. *Touch of the Past* **(Walker, 1988)** The murder of Wilbur De Marco, successful 1930s crime writer who became an eccentric recluse in the year 1937, brings Rachel to the small California town of Idyllwild.

Brett, Simon

I. This mystery series features the amateur sleuth Charles Paris, a middle-aged, underemployed London actor whose predilection for the ladies and drink have estranged him from his long-suffering wife, Frances. Charles's foibles and his satirical insider's view of England's theatrical and television world give these books considerable appeal. Author Brett writes from firsthand knowledge, having been an amateur actor and a producer for the BBC.

1. *Cast, in Order of Disappearance* (Scribner, 1976) Charles's first attempt at sleuthing begins when old girlfriend Jacquie Mitchell asks him to deliver some compromising photos to her lover.
2. *So Much Blood* (Scribner, 1977) In Edinburgh to perform a one-man play based on the life of the poet Thomas Hood, Charles investigates the murder of a young actor.
3. *Star Trap* (Scribner, 1978) Ill luck seems to be plaguing the production of a musical version of Goldsmith's *She Stoops to Conquer.*
4. *Amateur Corpse, An* (Scribner, 1978) Charles gets no thanks for critiquing an amateur theatrical performance, but murder gives him a reason to stay on.
5. *Comedian Dies, A* (Scribner, 1979) On vacation at a seaside town, Charles goes to see a vaudeville show and witnesses a public execution.
6. *Dead Side of the Mike, The* (Scribner, 1980) When a woman is found with her wrists slashed in a BBC studio, only Charles suspects foul play.
7. *Situation Tragedy* (Scribner, 1981) A series of accidents casts a pall on the set of a TV situation comedy until Charles uncovers the mystery.
8. *Murder Unprompted* (Scribner, 1982) Charles's friend Alex had motive and opportunity for shooting actor Michael Banks, but Charles is determined to prove him innocent.
9. *Murder in the Title* (Scribner, 1983) A third-rate regional theater proves to be the death of an artistic director. Was it murder or suicide?
10. *Not Dead, Only Resting* (Scribner, 1984) Somebody kills the chef after a posh celebrity dinner party at the famous Tryst restaurant.
11. *Dead Giveaway* (Scribner, 1986) A bit part in the pilot of a new TV game show puts Charles at the scene of a murder.
12. *What Bloody Man Is That?* (Scribner, 1987) Charles plays multiple roles in a production of *Macbeth,* but he is miscast as a murderer.
13. *Series of Murders, A* (Scribner, 1989) A British TV series that has Charles playing a police sergeant opposite an aristocratic amateur detective becomes the scene for two real murders.
14. *Corporate Bodies* (Scribner, 1992) Charles becomes chief suspect when a young woman is found crushed under a forklift he is operating for a corporate video.
15. *Reconstructed Corpse, A* (Scribner, 1994) His resemblance to missing developer Martin Earnshaw gets Paris a role on a television show where true crimes are reenacted.
16. *Sicken and Die* (Scribner, 1996) Charles has landed the choice role of Sir Toby Belch in *Twelfth Night,* but avant-garde director Alexandru Radulescu threatens to ruin the play with his provocative staging.
17. *Dead Room Farce* (St. Martin's, 1998) Charles has a role in a "knickers" comedy, *Not on Your Wife!* in Bath and a nice sideline reading books on tape, but his recording-studio boss, Mark Lear, dies suspiciously.

II. Mrs. Melita Pargeter is a likable busybody, relict of the late Mr. Pargeter, whose business dealings seem to have been lucrative but mysterious and perhaps not quite on the up-and-up. Mrs Pargeter, whose exterior belies her intellect and determination, has acquired some unusual skills from her late husband's associates, such as "Rewind" Wilson and "Keyhole" Crabbe, which she puts to good use in solving mysteries.

1. *Nice Class of Corpse, A* (Scribner, 1987) A nice old lady is killed by a fall at the stuffy Devereux residential hotel in Littlehampton, and the interest of Mrs. Pargeter, the latest resident, is piqued.
2. *Mrs. Presumed Dead* (Scribner, 1989) Mrs. Pargeter moves to a new home in Surrey and soon decides that its former mistress, Theresa Cotton, had come to an unnatural end.
3. *Mrs. Pargeter's Package* (Scribner, 1991) A tour of Greece with recently widowed Joyce Dover turns strange and then sinister.
4. *Mrs. Pargeter's Pound of Flesh* (Scribner, 1993) When Mrs. Pargeter escorts a young friend to a health spa, murder breaks out amid the "Dead Sea Mud Bath" treatments and "Mind Over Fatty Matter" exercise classes.
5. *Mrs. Pargeter's Plot* (Scribner, 1998) Mrs. Pargeter hires a former associate of the late Mr. Pargeter, builder and expert tunneler "Concrete" Jacket, to construct her country home near London.
6. *Mrs. Pargeter's Point of Honour* (Scribner, 1999) Elderly Veronica Chastaigne requests Mrs. Pargeter's aid in the return of the late Mr. Chastaigne's collection of "hot" paintings to their rightful owners.

III. The English seaside town of Fethering ("not far from Tarring") is the scene of Brett's latest mystery series. Carole Seddon, fiftyish divorcée late of the home office, has taken up a sensible retirement punctuated by the *Times* crossword and long walks along the beaches or out on the Downs. However, in true English cozy fashion, Carole is inveigled by her new neighbor, the noisy, bohemian "Jude," into a series of mysteries perpetrated in the not-so-quiet vicinity of Fethering.

1. *Body on the Beach, The* (Berkley, 2000) The arrival of the alarmingly casual "Jude" as a neighbor and the discovery of a body (which then turns up missing) on the Fethering beach are clues that Carole Seddon's retirement will not be as quiet as she had hoped.
2. *Death on the Downs* (Berkley, 2001) A sudden shower catches Carole on a walk on the South Downs, so she finds shelter in an abandoned barn, where she comes across a bag of human bones.
3. *Torso in the Town, The* (Berkley, 2002) Jude, dinner guest of the Roxbys at Pelling House in nearby Fedborough, is on the spot when a dismembered woman's body is found in the cellar.
4. *Murder in the Museum* (Berkley, 2003) Carole Seddon finds herself a member of the Bracketts Trust, which looks after Bracketts, once the home of writer Esmond Chadleigh. Then bodies start turning up.
5. *Hanging in the Hotel, The* (Berkley, 2004) Jude Nichols, helping out an old friend by waiting on tables at the Hopwicke Country House, gets involved when a possible inductee into the Pillars of Sussex Men's Club is found hanged in his room.
6. *Witness at the Wedding, The* (Berkley, 2005) Carole enlists Jude's aid when her son's prospective father-in-law is murdered.
7. *Stabbing in the Stables, The* (Berkley, 2006) Is the mysterious "Horse-Ripper," who has been mutilating mares across West Sussex, also responsible for the murder of ex-equestrian Walter Fleet at Long Bamber Stables?
8. *Death under the Dryer* (Five Star, 2007) When Carole goes to a salon to get a haircut, she witnesses the discovery of the assistant, Kyra, strangled in the back room.

Bretton, Barbara

I. Two romances set in the (New) Jersey shore town of Paradise Point pair radio-show host Maddy (DiFalco) Bainbridge and fire-fighter and bar owner Aidan O'Malley, who meet in *Shore Lights* when the two become competitors for an antique teapot. The sequel, *Chances Are*, finds Maddy and Aidan ready to tie the wedding knot when PBS decides to focus on the O'Malley and DiFalco families for a documentary on Jersey shore towns. The two novels are well-done contemporary romances combining both sentiment and humor. Barbara Bretton is the author of many other romances, including titles for various Harlequin series, and a pair of novels set in the Maine town of Shelter Rock Cove: *A Soft Place to Fall* (Berkley, 2001) and *Girls of Summer* (Berkley, 2003).

1. *Shore Lights* **(Berkley, 2003)** Maddy (DiFalco) Bainbridge, reeling from a series of bad events, including a divorce, returns to her mother Rose's home in Paradise Point, New Jersey, with her 14-year-old daughter, Hannah, where she finds herself bidding against local bar owner and widower Aidan O'Malley for a "magic lamp" (actually a teapot).
2. *Chances Are* **(Berkley, 2004)** The nuptial planning of Aidan and Maddy is somewhat complicated by a PBS documentary on their families and some O'Malley family problems, including those of his daughter Kelly.

II. A time-travel trilogy postulates a hot-air balloon that travels back and forth between the 1990s and the time of the American Revolution (1770s). The three books are connected by characters like Andrew McVie and Dakota Wylie, who graduate from being secondary roles in one novel into main billing in the sequels, which should be read sequentially. Not much historical or scientific detail but lots of heavy breathing and romantic situations. Omnibus volume containing numbers 1–3: *Forever in Time* (Mira, 2004).

1. *Somewhere in Time* **(Harlequin, 1992)** Former marrieds Zane Rutledge and Emilie Crosse are swept back from the 1990s to the 1770s when Zane brings Emilie a Revolutionary War uniform to examine.
2. *Tomorrow and Always* **(Mira, 1994)** Andrew McVie, a character in number 1, has a hot-air-balloon ride from 1776 to 1993 and Shannon Whitney's backyard. Shannon and Whitney have a hot romance, but Shannon can't help feeling that there is something odd about Andrew, so she enlists the help of her friend, psychic librarian Dakota Wylie.
3. *Destiny's Child* **(Mira, 1995)** Dakota Wylie, the psychic librarian from number 2, takes the hot-air-balloon route to 1779, where she befriends wealthy but bitter Patrick Devane and his neglected six-year-old daughter Abby.

Brewer, Gene

K-PAX is a four-part fantasy–science fiction series narrated by "Dr. Gene Brewer" of the Manhattan Psychiatric Institute, who treats a patient called "prot" (rhymes with *goat*) claiming to be an alien from a peaceful vegetarian planet, K-PAX. Brewer treats prot for multiple-personality disorder, but confidence in his diagnosis is shaken when prot proves helpful to other patients and reveals a phenomenal knowledge of astrophysics. Prot's true identity isn't revealed until *K-PAX III*. Stage (London, 2004) and screen (2001) versions of *K-PAX* have been produced. The screen version, more a popular success than a critical one, starred Kevin Spacey and Jeff Bridges. *K-PAX* appeals to lovers of SF feel-good stories such as *Cocoon* and *E.T. K-PAX, the Trilogy*, which includes numbers 1–3 and the additional *Prot's Report to K-PAX*, was published by Bloomsbury in 2004. Indiana-born Gene Brewer was a molecular biologist before becoming a freelance writer.

1. *K-PAX* **(St. Martin's, 1995)** Confronted with a male patient in his thirties who claims to be an inhabitant of the planet K-PAX, whose denizens live in peace and find sex and meat revolting, Dr. Gene Brewer of the Manhattan Psychiatric Institute diagnoses multiple-personality disorder in the man, who goes by the name of prot (no capitals).
2. *On a Beam of Light* **(St. Martin's, 2001)** Dr. Brewer continues to treat prot and is treated to unflattering comparisons between violent Earth and pacific K-PAX. Variant title: *K-PAX II*.
3. *Worlds of Prot, The* **(Bloomsbury, 2002)** After being sent home as "cured," Robert Porter returns to the institute again as prot and treats the doctors and patients to some dire predictions about Earth's near future. Variant title: *K-PAX III*.
4. *New Visitor from the Constellation Lyra, A* **(Xlibris, 2007)** The alleged "new visitor" from Pax is Fled, a hairy, belligerent nymphomaniac. Variant title: *K-PAX IV*.

Brewer, James D.

The Baldridge/Williamson series of Reconstruction-era mysteries is set along the post–Civil War Mississippi River. Masey Baldridge, drunken insurance agent and ex-Confederate officer, and riverboat captain Luke Williamson team together on three investigations before they form, with ex-prostitute Salina "Sally" Tyner, the Big River Detective Agency. This is a series of mysteries with good plotting and characterization and excellent period background. Retired US Army officer James D. Brewer has also written nonfiction Civil War history and the self-help book *The Danger from Strangers: Confronting the Threat of Assault* (Insight, 1994).

1. *No Bottom* **(Walker, 1994)** Riverboat captain and co-owner of two steamers plying the Reconstruction–era Mississippi River, Luke Williamson teams up with alcoholic insurance-claims investigator Masey Baldridge to ferret out the cause of the fatal river accident of Luke's ship, the *Mary Justice*.
2. *No Virtue* **(Walker, 1995)** Prostitute Salina Tyner joins Williamson and Baldridge in the investigation of the death, near Memphis, of a young woman, also a prostitute, who was a frequent passenger on Williamson's steamboat, a crime for which Jacob Lusk, Williamson's black first mate, is wrongly accused.
3. *No Justice* **(Walker, 1996)** Two stolen Gatling guns and a planned assassination attempt against President Grant, who is due to ride on Williamson's new boat, occupy Baldridge and Williamson.
4. *No Remorse* **(Walker, 1997)** Stewart, the son of Williamson's business rival, Hudson Van Tyne, has confessed to murdering his father, but Stewart's mother hires the newly founded Big River Detective Agency (Williamson, Baldridge, and Sally Tyner) to prove his innocence.
5. *No Escape* **(Walker, 1998)** Somebody has been skimming funds from the Howard Association, a benevolent group fighting the yellow fever scourge. And now Memphis, Tennessee, is being besieged by a full-fledged epidemic.

Brewer, Steve

I. Bubba Mabry isn't the type of investigator one expects to find in southwestern mystery fiction these days: he isn't a Native American and he has no interest in art or archaeology or nature. The self-styled "recovering redneck" lives amid ramshackle surroundings in a cheap Albuquerque, New Mexico, motel and ekes out a rather precarious living from his private eye business. This series presents more of the underside of New Mexico than most of the others set in the area, but it is laced with humor. Steve Brewer is a former journalist who still writes a humor column for the Albuquerque *Tribune*.

1. *Lonely Street* (**Pocket, 1994**) Introduces Bubba Mabry, who takes on the job of bodyguard to an Elvis look-alike, only to find that the "look-alike" is the King himself.
2. *Baby Face* (**Pocket, 1995**) Bubba has two clients for a change: a pimp called Sultan Sweeny, who wants to know who is killing his girls, and a city councilwoman who has lost her doll collection.
3. *Witchy Woman* (**St. Martin's, 1996**) One of Albuquerque's richest women hires Bubba to find her grandchild.
4. *Shaky Ground* (**St. Martin's, 1997**) Bubba takes a hair-raising helicopter ride when he is hired to find biology professor Harry Fields, who is missing in the desert.
5. *Dirty Pool* (**St. Martin's, 2000**) Bubba's father, a truck driver who abandoned Bubba at the age of nine, resurfaces, apparently with Alzheimer's, as Bubba is competing against a rival PI to find Richie, the neo-Nazi son of a Texas millionaire.
6. *Crazy Love* (**Intrigue, 2001**) Eccentric millionaire Melvin Howard hires Bubba to find his recently deceased wife's lover, a lecherous doctor. Then the doctor is found murdered, and Melvin is the prime suspect.
7. *Monkey Man* (**Intrigue, 2006**) Having coffee with a new client, Bubba feels that things are going well until the monkey with the gun shows up.

II. Another pair of mystery novels set in Albuquerque features ex-football player and current sports editor Drew Gavin.

1. *End Run* (**Intrigue, 2000**) Drew Gavin agrees to help his former college flame to protect her husband from some gambling-debt enforcers. Then the husband is found murdered at a secluded mountain cabin.
2. *Cheap Shot* (**Intrigue, 2002**) Gavin's friend, reporter Curtis White, awakes to find himself beside a murdered cheerleader. Curtis is arrested as prime suspect, but Gavin thinks that the murder may have some connection with his investigation of a minor-league basketball team, the Albuquerque Rattlers.

Brin, David

I. The Uplift; or, Progenitors Universe series, a pair of trilogies set in the far future, postulates a universe of five galaxies in which humans are just one, and not the most advanced, of the intelligent races. The most intelligent races believe that they were "uplifted" to their thinking status by an ancient but now missing race and that it is their duty to use genetic engineering to raise other species to their own level. Although humans have achieved space travel, and have "uplifted" chimpanzees and dolphins, some of the more radical among the intelligent races believe that humans need remedial retraining before they can be accepted as full members of the Progenitors Universe. The first trilogy describes how humans and chimpanzees make places for themselves in this universe. The second trilogy is set on the planet Jijo, a world where six species coexist in fragile equilibrium

until "uplifters" from Earth and elsewhere arrive on their world. The Uplift novels combine evolutionary and ethical thinking, good space-opera plots, excellent world building and creation of alien races, and a leavening of humor. *Earth Clan* (Doubleday, 1986) contains numbers 1 and 2. *Contacting Aliens* (Bantam, 2002), coauthored by Brin and Kevin Lenagh, is an illustrated guide to the Uplift universe.

Since his first publications in the 1980s, David Brin has been regarded as the one of the leading practitioners of hard science fiction. A PhD in space science, Brin is a California native who has worked as an electrical engineer, an editor, a college instructor, and a visiting scholar as well as a full-time writer. Brin has written many other award-winning science-fiction novels and stories such as *The Postman* (Bantam, 1985), which was made into a Kevin Costner film in 1997 (not to be confused with the film of the same title about Pablo Neruda), graphic novels, a juvenile series, collaborations, and several nonfiction volumes of scientific speculation, such as *The Transparent Society: Will Technology Force Us to Choose Between Privacy and Freedom?* (Perseus, 1998).

1. *Sundiver* (**Bantam, 1980**) In the far future, hard-liner species in the Progenitors Universe fight each other for the right to "adopt" the human species, who, they feel, needs some rigorous "retraining," before it can take its place among the intelligent races.
2. *Startide Rising* (**Bantam, 1983**) Two centuries after the events in number 1, the Earth ship *Streaker*, crewed by dolphins and a few human observers, pursued by aliens, makes a crash landing on the water-world planet of Kithrup. Originally published in a shorter version in *Analog* as the novella *The Tides of Kithrup*. Revised hardcover edition by Phantasia Press (1985). Won 1984 Nebula and Hugo awards.
3. *Uplift War, The* (**Phantasia, 1987**) Humans, neo-chimpanzees, and the alien Tymbrimi team together to resist alien invaders and rebuild an ecologically damaged planet. Won the 1988 Hugo Award.
4. *Brightness Reef* (**Bantam, 1995**) The arrival of more humans upsets the delicate balance between the six sentient races, including humans, living on the "off-limits" planet of Jijo. First novel in second trilogy.
5. *Infinity's Shore* (**Bantam, 1996**) The arrival of the dolphin crew from the starship *Streaker* creates further complications in the percolating crisis on planet Jijo.
6. *Heaven's Reach* (**Bantam, 1998**) In the finale (up till now, anyway) of the Uplift series, Earth and its humans, chimpanzees, and dolphins are under attack by an evil alien alliance, the Old Ones, and an additional eight "Civilized Galaxies" are revealed.

II. With Greg Bear (q.v.) and Gregory Benford (q.v.), David Brin has written a volume of a new trilogy to augment Isaac Asimov's (q.v.) classic Foundation series.

1. *Foundation's Triumph* (**Harper, 1999**) In the final volume of the Second Foundation trilogy, the aged and infirm Hari Seldon tries to rally himself against "chaos," a mental disease afflicting humanity, as humanity's creation, the positronic robots, really controls the universe.

Briody, Thomas Gately

Providence, Rhode Island, has more than its share of corruption, and the remainder of the nation's smallest state, including posh Newport, isn't far behind. Gangsters, dishonest politicos, and other seedy types are ferreted out by Michael Carolina, TV reporter, lawyer, and sometime detective and his girlfriend, PI Carla Tattaglia, in this series full of outsize, corrupt, dangerous, and hilarious characters, including Providence's shrewd and coarse mayor, a 400-pound snowplow driver, a female hit person, a clammer who uses dynamite, and Newport yacht men who aren't above fixing races. Thomas Gately Briody, lawyer, former TV journalist, and writer, lives in Providence.

1. *Rogue's Isles* (St. Martin's, 1995) Washed-up TV reporter Michael Carolina is lured out of retirement when Frankie Falcone disappears along with $15 million from Providence's Amerigo Vespucci bank.
2. *Rogue's Justice* (St. Martin's, 1996) Carolina, sailing in the South Seas, learns that his partner, Lilly Simmons, has been offed by a Providence City snowplow. Corruption is endemic in Providence, from its mayor, Joey Giovannetti, to sloppy coroner Arthur Goulet to "Lazy" Lenny Costa, a 400-pound snowplow operator who doubles as a collector for loan sharks.
3. *Rogue's Wager* (St. Martin's, 1997) "Tony," a mysterious diver, blown up by a stick of dynamite thrown by angry clam digger Mitt, and finished off in the hospital by a female hit person, is somehow connected with mobster Jimmy Flannery, who is interested in acquiring some local land for a casino.
4. *Rogue's Regatta* (St. Martin's, 1999) The Newport sailing scene offers Michael no relief from corrupt doings and persons, as he investigates the death of yacht racer Hunter Worthington III.

Bristow, Gwen

Seven generations of the Sheramy and Larne families of Louisiana are traced in the Plantation trilogy, from the pioneers who change the 18th-century Louisiana jungles into a society founded on luxury and injustice, through the conflicts of the Civil War and the birth of a new way of life, and finally to the 20th-century southerners torn between tradition and modernity. Historical background material for each book was supplied in the omnibus volume *The Plantation Trilogy* (Crowell, 1962).

1. *Deep Summer* (Crowell, 1937) Northerner Judith Sheramy meets Philip Larne, an aristocratic Southerner.
2. *Handsome Road, The* (Crowell, 1938) The lives of housemaid Corrie May and the aristocratic Mrs. Denis Larne are contrasted.
3. *This Side of Glory* (Crowell, 1940) The saga of the Larnes and the old plantation is continued through World War I.

Brittain, C. Dale

The world of Yurt "is a rather skewed version of Europe's Middle Ages," according to its creator, C. Dale Brittain, professor of medieval history at the College of Wooster (Ohio) and fantasy writer. The narrator and leading character of this series is Daimbert, the Royal Wizard of Yurt, who makes up for his mediocre education in magic with some hard-won survival skills in a series of rather bizarre adventures with wizards, witches, grumpy saints, and some of the trappings of civilization, such as telephones and newspapers. This six-volume series is characterized by humor, mysteries, chills, and some deeper themes, such as "mortality, sacrifice, and redemption."

1. *Bad Spell in Yurt, A* (Baen, 1991) Daimbert finds that his education at wizard's school was inadequate when he takes on the job of Royal Wizard for the Kingdom of Yurt and has to deal with a wielder of black magic and a dragon.
2. *Wood Nymph and the Cranky Saint, The* (Baen, 1993) Left in charge while the king of Yurt takes a vacation, Daimbert investigates a wood-nymph sighting, complaints about a saint's shrine, a plague of horned rabbits, and a gigantic hunter.
3. *Mage Quest* (Baen, 1993) Daimbert journeys with the king and some other Yurtians to the Eastern Kingdoms in quest of the legendary blue roses and a lost lord, and he runs into a big green djinn and some Eastern-style magic.
4. *Witch and the Cathedral, The* (Baen, 1995) Daimbert travels to the cathedral city of Caelrhon, falls in love with the witch Theodora, and runs into heavy opposition from the local clergy.
5. *Daughter of Magic* (Baen, 1996) Daimbert's daughter Antonia, with her increasing independence and magical skills, proves to be a handful, as if he didn't have enough troubles with undead warriors led by his old enemy Vlad, an enormous wolf, and a bogus miracle worker.
6. *Is This Apocalypse Necessary?* (Wooster, 2000) The highly skilled and ambitious wizard Elerius, Royal Wizard of the West's most powerful kingdom, as part of his plan for world control, expects to succeed the dying master of the wizards' school.

Brock, Darryl

If I Never Get Back, a time-travel novel that takes its hero back from the 1980s to 1869, reminded many readers of Jack Finney's (q.v.) classic *Time and Again* with its evocation of 19th-century America. Jack Fowler, San Francisco newspaper man, wanders away from his Amtrak train in Ohio and somehow finds himself back in 1869 on a steam-powered train full of players from the Cincinnati Red Stockings, baseball's first openly professional team. Before he returns to the 20th century, a question left open in *If I Never Get Back,* Fowler becomes a factotum with the Red Stockings and even gets to play a bit before he gets involved with a get-rich-quick scheme with Mark Twain, a bunch of Irish nationalists who want to invade Canada, and a transcontinental train journey. Brock himself followed the route of the 1869 Cincinnati Red Stockings, and his historical re-creation, especially of baseball as it was played then, is convincing. *Two in the Field,* the sequel, which finds Fowler stuck in a San Francisco mental hospital but going back in time again, is somewhat disappointing, partly because of its lack of baseball lore. Brock, a former history teacher who lives near San Francisco, has written another historical baseball novel, *Havana Heat* (Total, 2000), about "Dummy" Taylor, a real-life deaf pitcher with the New York Giants in the first decade of the 20th century.

1. *If I Never Get Back* (Crown, 1990) San Francisco newspaper man Sam Fowler, wandering from his Amtrak train, somehow finds himself on a steam-powered wood-burning train heading for New York and containing the 1869 Cincinnati Red Stockings baseball team.
2. *Two in the Field* (Plume, 2002) Sam Fowler, rusticating in a contemporary San Francisco mental hospital, challenged by his doctor to find Caitlan O'Neill, his lost 19th-century love, manages to get back to the 19th century after an auto accident.

Brockmann, Suzanne

I. Books about elite military groups, especially when they engage in covert, high-risk operations, bypassing conventional officialdom, appeal to many readers. Books about the US Navy SEALs (Sea, Air and Land Team) are no exception. Richard Marcinko (q.v.) is one of many authors who has struck pay dirt writing about the SEALs. Romance and suspense writer Suzanne Brockmann, a publishing phenom (more than 40 books in 12 years), exposes the tender as well as the macho side of her SEALs in two series of books (see also series II, below) that follow the adventures and love affairs of members of individual SEAL teams. The Tall, Dark and Dangerous series, published in Silhouette (Harlequin) editions, chronicles the exploits of members of US Navy SEAL Team 10 as they pursue perilous missions and passionate love affairs. Continuing characters pop in and out of the series, which is full of suspense and steamy passion.

1. *Prince Joe* (Silhouette, 1996) Navy SEAL Lieutenant Joe Catalanofto is called upon to impersonate a European prince who has been targeted by terrorists. It is up to media consultant Veronica St. John to see that the rough-hewn Joe passes muster.

2. *Forever Blue* (Silhouette, 1997) Lucy Tait finds herself the police officer investigating childhood hero and Navy SEAL Blue McCoy, who is being accused of his brother's death.

3. *Frisco's Kid* (Silhouette, 1997) SEAL Alan "Frisco" Francisco is determined to lick the bullet wound that has nearly crippled him. And then his five-year-old abandoned niece turns up.

4. *Everyday, Average Jones* (Silhouette, 1998) SEAL Harlan "Cowboy" Jones had a one-nighter with Melody Evans after he rescued her. But now Melody is pregnant, and Jones wants to rekindle the affair.

5. *Harvard's Education* (Silhouette, 1998) Black female FInCOM agent P. J. Richards, who has been given eight weeks' access to the exclusively masculine SEALS, and black male SEAL Senior Chief "Harvard" Becker are wary of each other . . . at first.

6. *It Came upon a Midnight Clear* (Silhouette, 1998) 'Tis the Christmas season, but "Crash" Hawken is faced with a terrorist conspiracy, and the only person he can turn to is the "caring, passionate" Nell Burns. Reissued in 2005 as *Hawken's Heart*.

7. *Admiral's Bride, The* (Silhouette, 1999) Vietnam vet and former SEAL Admiral Jake Robinson embarks upon a May-December romance with a young woman scientist.

8. *Identity: Unknown* (Silhouette, 2000) No romantic series is complete without a plot involving amnesia. SEAL Lieutenant Mitchell Shaw has lost his memory, but perhaps a stay at the New Mexico dude ranch the Lazy 8 Ranch, managed by the beautiful Becca Keyes, will help.

9. *Get Lucky* (Silhouette, 2000) SEAL Lucky O'Donlon and freelance journalist Sydney Jameson find romance on the California coast.

10. *Taylor's Temptation* (Silhouette, 2001) With the help of her brother Wes, gorgeous redhead Colleen Skelly finally manages to get SEAL Bobby Taylor to herself.

11. *Night Watch* (Silhouette, 2003) After SEAL Chief Wes Skelly is sent on assignment to Los Angeles, he agrees to go on a blind date with beautiful single-mother Brittany Evans, sister-in-law of a fellow SEAL

II. Troubleshooter, Brockmann's other SEAL series, features the guys from US Navy SEAL Team 16. Continuing characters include the openly gay FBI agent Jules Cassidy. This bunch seems to get more involved in foreign intrigue than SEAL Team 10 does. This series is published by Ballantine.

1. *Unsung Hero, The* (Ballantine, 2000) When recuperating SEAL Tom Paoletti catches a glimpse of a terrorist in his New England hometown, his sighting is dismissed as a hallucination resulting from his head injury. So it is up to Tom and a few others, including Tom's old flame Dr. Kelly Ashton, to prevent disaster.

2. *Defiant Hero, The* (Ballantine, 2001) Meg Moore's daughter and grandmother have been kidnapped by a band of terrorists called the Extremists, and it is up to the feisty Meg and a SEAL or two to rescue them.

3. *Over the Edge* (Ballantine, 2001) Navy helicopter pilot Teri Howe and SEAL Senior Chief Stan Wolchonok join forces when a jet carrying a senator's daughter is hijacked.

4. *Out of Control* (Ballantine, 2002) Savannah von Hopf and SEAL Ken Karmody team up to rescue Savannah's uncle Alex, who is being held for $250,000 ransom in Indonesia.

5. *Into the Night* (Ballantine, 2002) It is up to White House public relations attaché Joan Da Costa and SEAL Mike Muldoon to foil a terrorist plot to assassinate the US president.

6. *Gone Too Far* (Ballantine, 2003) SEAL Lieutenant Sam Starrett and FBI agent Alyssa Locke, after working on foiling an assassination plot and spending a torrid one-night stand together, find themselves together again after Sam's daughter is kidnapped.

7. *Flashpoint* (Ballantine, 2004) In the first of what is billed a new series related to the SEALS books, Tess Bailey and Jimmy Nash, veterans of a one-night stand, find themselves as part of a team being sent by Troubleshooters Inc. to Kazbekistan.

8. *Hot Target* (Ballantine, 2005) Man of mystery Cosmo Richter and gay FBI agent Jules Cassidy are given the job of protecting Hollywood producer Jane Chadwick from attack.

9. *Breaking Point* (Ballantine, 2005) Max Bhagat and Gina Vitagliano, FBI hostage negotiators, meet again as Gina and fellow aid worker Molly are abducted to Indonesia.

10. *Into the Storm* (Ballantine, 2006) SEAL Team 16 and Troubleshooters Inc. face off as part of a winter training exercise in the mountains of New Hampshire.

11. *Force of Nature* (Ballantine, 2007) Jules Cassidy comes face-to-face with movie star Robin Chadwick while trying to prove Gordon Burns's ties to terrorist activity.

12. *All through the Night* (Ballantine, 2007) Subtitle: *A Troubleshooter Christmas*. The gay marriage of Jules Cassidy and Robin Chadwick is crashed by *Globe* reporter Will Schroeder.

III. Another series with characters straying from book to book is the Sunrise Key trilogy, set in a resort town in Florida. Torrid, passionate, and sometimes humorous looks at how the richer half lives.

1. *Kiss and Tell* (Bantam, 1996) Dr. Marshall Devlin takes advantage of his New Year's Eve disguise and kisses the long-desired but unresponsive Leila Hunt. Then the enraptured Leila goes in search of her mystery lover.

2. *Kissing Game, The* (Bantam, 1996) PI Frankie Paresky takes irresistible Simon Hunt as a partner in the search for the solution of a long-ago mystery.

3. *Otherwise Engaged* (Bantam, 1997) Preston Seaholm, Sunrise Key's mysterious tycoon and one of the most eligible bachelors in the country, rescues pretty widow Molly Cassidy from a roof—and then asks her to pretend that they are engaged.

IV. A pair of novels feature members of the Bartlett family, Cal and Liam, adventurers and correspondents.

1. *Forbidden* (Bantam, 1997) Cal Bartlett can't deny his attraction for Kayla Gray, the woman who betrayed his brother.

2. *Freedom's Price* (Bantam, 1998) Liam Bartlett and Marisala Bolivar, who had saved his life in San Salustiano, rekindle their romance when Marisala turns up in Boston.

Brockway, Connie

I. Minnesota's Connie Brockway is another writer who shot into prominence in the 1990s with romances set in the 18th and 19th centuries. The McClairen's Isle trilogy follows the course of an 18th-century Scottish feud in which members of the Merrick family play prominent roles in a melange of dark plots, dark pasts, and plenty of romance.

1. *McClairen's Isle: The Passionate One* (Dell, 1999) When cynical, "smoldering" Ashton "Ash" Merrick, son of the dissolute and sadistic Lord Carr, arrives in the Scottish hamlet of Fair Badden, he finds himself falling in love with the fiery young Rhiannon.
2. *McClairen's Isle: The Reckless One* (Dell, 2000) France in 1760. Raine Merrick, son of the evil Earl of Carr, finds himself participating in a plot involving the beautiful and innocent Favor McClairen.
3. *McClairen's Isle: The Ravishing One* (Dell, 2000) The Merricks and the McClairens are at it again. Convict Thomas McClairen returns to England and a plot to abduct Fia Merrick, toast of London society, and take her to Scotland.

II. Set a little later in time (Regency, early 19th century) than the McClairen's Isle trilogy, the Rose Hunters trilogy has another assortment of dashing men, beautiful and passionate women, plots, disguises, secrets from the past, and evocations of the Scottish countryside.

1. *My Seduction* (Pocket, 2004) Christian "Kit" McNeill, a Scottish warrior of uncertain parentage and training in both the martial arts and rose breeding, reappears to keep a vow made to Kate Blackburn, whose father had rescued him from a French prison.
2. *My Pleasure* (Pocket, 2004) Helena Nash, lady's companion and sister to Kate Blackburn (see number 1), finds herself acting as go-between between Flora, the not-too-bright niece of her employer, and the bankrupt gambler Oswald. Then she is rescued from a tight spot by the dashing swordsman Ramsey Munro.
3. *My Surrender* (Pocket, 2005) Charlotte, youngest of the Nash sisters, acts like a "flirt" and "romp" to spy on enemies of the Crown. Then, as part of a complicated plot to undermine the French loyalist St. Lyon, Charlotte concocts an assignation with the handsome, brooding spy Andrew "Dand" Ross.

Broderick, John

Irish novelist Broderick had planned to write a trilogy set in the Irish village of Bridgeford of the 1930s. Broderick died before he could write the third volume or finish revisions on the second volume. Editors at Marion Boyars, his publisher, tried to incorporate the revisions in the text as consistently as possible with Broderick's intentions. What we have is a slice of life from the rural Ireland of the past told with memorable dialogue and genial humor.

1. *Flood, The* (Boyars, 1987) Concerns the efforts of the Bridgeford locals to inveigle a gullible Englishman into buying a piece of periodically flooded land along the River Shannon.
2. *Irish Magdalen, The* (Boyars, 1991) When Canon Sharkey's elderly housekeeper dies, her replacement is regarded as much too young and charming by the censorious villagers.

Brooks, Terry

I. The Shannara books, which have been best sellers, will probably be enjoyed by *Lord of the Rings* fans, though their American author, greatly influenced by Tolkien, is a somewhat less-sophisticated writer. Brooks's epic fantasies are set in the time following the "War of Ancient Evil" when the Earth is peopled by many races—humans, elves, trolls, etc.—and the Power of Darkness threatens all. Numbers 2, 3, and 4 constitute the original Shannara trilogy. Numbers 5, 6, 7, and 8, called the Heritage of Shannara, relate the adventures of the descendants of the heroes of the earlier trilogy. Numbers 9, 10, and 11, called the Voyage of the Jerle Shannara, take place a generation later. Number 1 is a prequel, set 500 years before the events in number 2. A new trilogy, called High Druid of Shannara (numbers 12–14), introduces the next generation of Ohmsfords and Elessedils. *The World of Shannara* (Ballantine, 2001, by Terry Brooks and Teresa Patterson) is an illustrated guide to Shannara.

1. *First King of Shannara* (Del Rey, 1996) In this prequel, set 500 years before the events of *The Sword of Shannara*, Paranor, with its Druid scholars, is destroyed, setting in motion the adventures of Bremen, the outcast Druid magician, and the forging of a magic sword for elven king Jerle Shannara.
2. *Sword of Shannara, The* (Random House, 1977) Half-elf Shea Ohmsford, of Shady Vale, sets out in search of the mysterious Sword of Shannara, which is the only weapon effective against the evil Warlock Lord.
3. *Elfstones of Shannara, The* (Ballantine, 1982) Will Ohmsford and Amberle must save the precious seed from the dying Ellcrys tree.
4. *Wishsong of Shannara, The* (Ballantine, 1985) Brin Ohmsford's quest, like that of her father and grandfather, takes her far from the safe world of Shady Vale.
5. *Scions of Shannara, The* (Ballantine, 1990) The ghost of Allanon the Druid summons descendants of Shannara heroes to fight the evil Shadowen.
6. *Druid of Shannara, The* (Ballantine, 1991) To restore the lost Druid keep of Paranor, Walker Boh goes on a search for the Black Elfstone.
7. *Elfqueen of Shannara, The* (Ballantine, 1992) Wren Ohmsford searches for the last of the elves. Par Ohmsford seeks the lost Sword of Shannara. Walker Boh tries to locate the Druids in Paranor.
8. *Talismans of Shannara, The* (Ballantine, 1993) The three quests set by Allanon are fulfilled, but Shannara is not yet free from the Shadowen.
9. *Ilse Witch* (Del Rey, 2000) Druid Walker and elven king Allardon Elessedil unite to retrieve "a magic of spells invoked by words." Sorceress Ilse Witch shadows the expedition. Variant title: *Voyage of the Jerle Shannara: Book One; Ilse Witch.*
10. *Antrax* (Del Ray, 2001) Druid Walker and his cohorts are trapped on a island ruled by the evil artificial intelligence Antrax. Variant title: *Voyage of the Jerle Shannara: Book Two; Antrax.*
11. *Morgawr* (Del Rey, 2002) The conclusion of the Voyage of the Jerle Shannara trilogy finds Druid Walker in the mined city of Castledown. Variant title: *Voyage of the Jerle Shannara: Book Three; Morgawr.*
12. *Jarka Ruus* (Del Rey, 2003) A new generation of Ohmsfords and Elessedils: Penderrin Ohmsford and Khyber Elessedil are introduced and embark on the quest of rescuing Grianne Ohmsford from the Forbidding. Variant title: *High Druid of Shannara: Jarka Ruus.*
13. *Tanequil* (Del Rey, 2004) Grianne is still languishing in the Forbidding as the Freeborn Federation War continues in the Four Lands. Variant title: *High Druid of Shannara: Tanequil.*

14. *Straken* (**Del Rey, 2005**) In the conclusion to the High Druid of Shannara trilogy, young Pen Ohmsford retrieves the "darkwand," which allows him to enter the Forbidding and find his aunt Grianne, the Ard Rhys of the lawful Druids and the Straken queen. Variant title: *High Druid of Shannara: Straken*.

II. The Magic Kingdom of Landover is ruled by former Chicago lawyer Ben Holiday, who bought the realm for $1 million but found that his title of ownership was challenged by a demon prince who had invariably defeated his human opponents.

1. *Magic Kingdom for Sale—Sold!* (**Ballantine, 1987**) Discontented Chicago lawyer Ben Holiday discovers Landover, a less-than-idyllic magic kingdom.
2. *Black Unicorn, The* (**Ballantine, 1987**) The evil wizard Meeks challenges Ben's domain.
3. *Wizard at Large* (**Ballantine, 1988**) Bumbling wizard Questor Thews botches his attempt at restoring court scribe Abernathy's dog body to its original shape.
4. *Tangle Box, The* (**Ballantine, 1994**) Horris Kew and his loquacious feathered friend return to Landover and make the mistake of releasing the sinister Gorse from its Tangle Box prison.
5. *Witches Brew* (**Ballantine, 1995**) Holiday's daughter Mistaya is kidnapped at the behest of Rydall, King of Marnhull, who challenges Ben to seven contests, "winner take all."

III. This trilogy (so far) of novels in the Word and the Void series is set in the modern world but is full of fantasy elements as well as teen romance, satanism, and Native American mythology. Illinois teenager Nest Freemark and John Ross, "Knight of the Word," are the principal human protagonists in an ongoing struggle with demons from the Void.

1. *Running with the Demon* (**Del Rey, 1997**) Nest Freemark, a 14-year-old girl in an Illinois factory town, finds that she has magic powers but is unsure of their exact nature.
2. *Knight of the Word, A* (**Del Rey, 1998**) Knight of the Word John Ross, a mortal suffering a serious crisis of faith, has fallen from his calling and is working with homeless women and children in Seattle.
3. *Angel Fire East* (**Del Rey, 1999**) Fifteen years after the events in *Running with the Demon*, John Ross and Nest Freemark meet again to prevent a "gypsy morph" from falling into demon hands.

IV. A new series blends the Shannara series (series I) with the Word and the Void series (series III) in a near-future United States where civilization has collapsed from environmental degradation, plagues, global warfare and supernatural threats.

1. *Armageddon's Children* (**Del Rey, 2006**) The last surviving members of the Knights of the Word, Logan Tom and Angel Perez, try to keep the "balance of the world's magic in check" as they battle the Void.
2. *Elves of Cintra, The* (**Del Rey, 2007**) Hawk, a child suffused with unpredictable magic, helps the Seattle street kids called the Ghosts, but he's whisked away to the Gardens of Life to learn of his destiny.

Brown, Dale

I. Dale Brown, a former fighter pilot, is one of the leading practitioners of the techno- or military-hardware novel. Continuing characters, especially pilot Patrick McLanahan (who has risen to the rank of major general despite his unorthodox ways), and a series of crises keep Brown's series connected. The human characters tend to be overshadowed by lovingly described planes such as the B-52 bomber and the F-111 fighter plane. Although the cold war has ended, such figures as Osama bin Laden and George W. Bush and such writers as Dale Brown will keep wars and war fears on the front burner for the foreseeable future, and there will always be an audience for exciting military thrillers.

1. *Flight of the Old Dog* (**Fine, 1987**) The Soviets have beaten the United States in developing a Strategic Defense Initiative, leaving the United States dangerously vulnerable to attack.
2. *Silver Tower* (**Fine, 1988**) The wily Soviets attack their own naval forces in the Gulf of Arabia as a pretext for invading Iran.
3. *Hammerheads* (**Fine, 1990**) Evil drug dealers put innocent children on board their aircraft to prevent a special American anti-drug unit from shooting them down.
4. *Sky Masters* (**Fine, 1991**) In 1994, with American forces withdrawn from the Philippines, the Red Chinese try to occupy disputed territory in the area.
5. *Night of the Hawk* (**Fine, 1992**) Lithuania seeks to remove a secret Soviet Stealth Bomber research facility, using the brainwashed services of American pilot David Luger.
6. *Chains of Command* (**Putnam, 1993**) Hard-liners have taken control of Russia in 1995 and seek to reabsorb the Ukraine.
7. *Storming Heaven* (**Putnam, 1994**) Rich supervillain Henri Cazaux is bombing major American airports, and it is up to the US Air Force to stop him.
8. *Day of the Cheetah* (**Fine, 1989**) In 1996 a Soviet mole steals "Dreamstar," a computer-operated American fighter plane, and Patrick McClanahan must hunt him down.
9. *Shadows of Steel* (**Putnam, 1996**) In early 1997, the Iranians have attacked a US spy ship and taken Americans prisoner. President Kevin Martindale enlists a B-52 Stealth Bomber and Patrick McClanahan to sort things out.
10. *Fatal Terrain* (**Putnam, 1997**) A Chinese plot to retake Taiwan finds the US Air Force crippled by huge budget cuts.
11. *Tin Man, The* (**Bantam, 1998**) When McClanahan's brother is wounded in a terror attack on Sacramento, California, by bikers led by Gregory Townsend, Pat becomes a one-man army, known as the Tin Man, and indulges in some vigilante justice.
12. *Battle Born* (**Bantam, 1999**) When, in the year 2000, the Second Korean War is started by a starving North Korean pilot trying to nuke Seoul, only McClanahan's unorthodox Megafortress flying team from the Nevada Air National Guard can prevent nuclear war.
13. *Warrior Class* (**Putnam, 2001**) Russian drug lord and oilman Pavel Kazakov enlists a secret stealth warplane to foment a Russian invasion of Balkan countries that don't want to go along with his scheme for a huge new pipeline between the Black Sea and the Adriatic.
14. *Wings of Fire* (**Putnam, 2002**) Slinky Makta Salaam, widow of the assassinated president of Egypt, enlists General McLanahan in her schemes for revenge on the president of Libya and a takeover of the Gaza Strip.
15. *Air Battle Force* (**Morrow, 2003**) Patrick McLanahan, Air Force major general in charge of the secret experimental unit FirstAir Baffle Force, goes to work when a Taliban raid into Turkmenistan

leads to the overthrow of the Russian-backed Turkmen government.

16. *Plan of Attack* (Morrow, 2004) Demoted and reassigned, Patrick McLanahan has to save the United States again when General Anatoliy Gryzlov, president of the Russian Federation, plans a long-range bomber attack on the American mainland.

II. With Osama bin Laden captured (according to this series, set in the near future), we can go back to worrying about the Russians. The elite American unit known as Task Force TALON locks horns with a Russian terrorist group known as the Consortium.

1. *Act of War* (Morrow, 2005) It's up to Jason Richter and his band of seasoned military veterans to thwart the Consortium and their internationally financed terrorist organization from destabilizing the global economy.
2. *Edge of Battle* (Morrow, 2006) Task Force TALON continues to battle the Consortium, whose leader, Yegor Zakharov, has allied himself with a mysterious Mexican smuggler of drugs and people to infiltrate the United States.

Brown, Rita Mae

I. *Rubyfruit Jungle* (Daughters, 1973) brought Brown to national attention, not all of it welcome, primarily because of its ribald humor and unabashed lesbian sex. One of Brown's recurring themes is the essential peripherality of the male sex and male standards to the lives of women. This is well illustrated by a quartet of novels based on Brown's mother, aunt, and hometown on the Pennsylvania-Maryland border. The Hunsenmeir sisters, Julia ("Juts") and Louise ("Wheezie"), maintain their sibling rivalry through eight decades of life in this affectionate portrayal of the poor and uneducated in small-town America. Rita Mae Brown has also written an autobiography: *Rita Will: Memoir of a Literary Rabble-Rouser* (Bantam, 1997). The series is arranged in chronological order rather than order of publication.

1. *Loose Lips* (Bantam, 1999) In a novel opening in Runnymede, Maryland, in 1941, the Hunsenmeir sisters start a decade of scandals and rivalry by wrecking a local drugstore during one of their fights.
2. *Sand Castle, The* (Grove, 2008) Describes a single summer day in 1952 as Juts and her daughter Nickel and Wheezie and her grandson Leroy make a day trip to the beach.
3. *Six of One* (Harper, 1978) Opens in 1980 with flashbacks to the past lives of the Hunsenmeir sisters, their families, and friends.
4. *Bingo* (Bantam, 1988) The sisters, now in their eighties, continue their rivalry, this time competing for the affections of a "new man in town."

II. The series of mystery novels "coauthored" with Sneaky Pie Brown, Rita Mae Brown's tiger cat, stars, not too surprisingly, a cat, one Mrs. Murphy, a gray tiger cat who helps her "human," Mary Minor "Harry" Harristeen, postmistress of the hamlet of Crozet, Virginia, solve crimes. Mrs. Murphy, fat-cat Pewter Shiflett, corgi Tee Tucker, and a "Greek chorus" of cats and dogs comment sardonically on the crazy behavior of humans. If this sounds impossibly kittenish, suspend your judgment and give these well-written, amusing mysteries a try. *Murder, She Purred*, which aired on *The Wonderful World of Disney* and starred Rikki Lake and Blythe Danner, was based on the characters created by Brown.

1. *Wish You Were Here* (Bantam, 1990) A series of "wish-you-were-here" postcards depicting a cemetery grave leads to some gruesome murders.
2. *Rest in Pieces* (Bantam, 1992) A corpse with no head, fingerprints, or clothes may have a connection with a handsome stranger who is taking an interest in Harry.
3. *Murder at Monticello; or, Old Sins* (Bantam, 1994) Archaeological investigations of Thomas Jefferson's home at Monticello have turned up the corpse of a man buried in a slave cabin in 1803.
4. *Pay Dirt; or, Adventures at Ash Lawn* (Bantam, 1995) A biker from Los Angeles who arrives at Ash Lawn, James Monroe's home, later turns up murdered, and the Crozet National Bank loses $2 million to a computer virus.
5. *Murder, She Meowed* (Bantam, 1996) Jockey Nigel Danforth is stabbed in the heart at the annual steeplechase at Montpelier, the home of James and Dolley Madison.
6. *Murder on the Prowl* (Bantam, 1998) The premature obituaries of the headmaster and a teacher at St. Elizabeth's school turn out to be portents of the actual deaths of the two.
7. *Cat on the Scent* (Bantam, 1999) Dissension at an Albemarle County Commission meeting over plans for a new reservoir leads to a frozen corpse in the refrigerator of a local food plant and the murder of a local landowner during a Civil War–battle reenactment.
8. *Pawing through the Past* (Bantam, 2000) As Harry Harristeen plans Crozet High's class of 1980 twentieth reunion, several of her male classmates are shot.
9. *Claws and Effects* (Bantam, 2001) A series of attacks and murders at the local hospital take Crozet's denizens' minds off of the rotten February weather and directly involve Harry as one of the attackees.
10. *Catch as Cat Can* (Bantam, 2002) Harry must balance the romantic attentions of her ex-husband and a diplomat from Uruguay, the upcoming Dogwood Festival, and the theft of some unusual hubcaps.
11. *Tail of the Tip-Off, The* (Bantam, 2003) Construction company owner H. H. Donaldson falls dead in the parking lot of the "Clam," the University of Virginia's sports complex, after a women's basketball game.
12. *Cat's Eyewitness* (Bantam, 2005) Harry quits her job as postmistress when her animal companions are banned from her workplace and retreats with best friend Susan Tucker to a monastery in the Blue Ridge Mountains.
13. *Whisker of Evil* (Bantam, 2004) Harry and her pets stumble upon the throat-slashed body of 34-year-old breeder Barry Monteith.
14. *Sour Puss* (Bantam, 2006) Harry and Fair, her veterinarian ex-husband, remarry and put in a quarter acre of Petit Manseng grapes to participate in the Virginia Piedmont's growing wine industry.
15. *Puss 'n Cahoots* (Bantam, 2007) At an equestrian event in Kentucky, Harry's friend Joan loses a beloved piece of jewelry, and Jorge, a groom at Joan's farm, is found murdered.
16. *Purrfect Murder, The* (Bantam, 2008) A local ob-gyn and a wealthy middle-aged woman are murdered. Harry's friend Tazio Chappars is suspected of the latter murder, but perhaps the two murders are connected.

III. Another cozy series full of anthropomorphized animals features septuagenarian Jane "Sister" Arnold, Master of the Hunt at the Jefferson Hunt Club in Virginia. The feisty Jane, who understands animals as well as she understands people, solves murders while fighting off attempts by rich and arrogant Yankee Crawford Howard to take over the club.

1. *Outfoxed* (Ballantine, 2000) Jane "Sister" Arnold, now in her seventies, knows that she has to nominate a joint master for the Jefferson Hunt Club. The two top choices are Virginia aristocrat Fontaine Buruss and upstart Yankee Crawford Howard.

2. *Hotspur* (Ballantine, 2002) A 21-year-old mystery is resurrected when the skeleton of Nolas Bancroft, still wearing a sapphire ring on her finger, is unearthed.

3. *Full Cry* (Ballantine, 2003) The New Year's Hunt is marred by the stabbing death of Sam Lorillard and the discovery of dishonest hunting practices going on at a neighboring club.

4. *Hunt Ball, The* (Ballantine, 2005) The relatively benign demonstration by Custis Hall students over the school's exhibit of antique household objects crafted by slave labor is followed by the unsettling discovery that one of the two hanging corpses ornamenting the school's Halloween dance is real.

5. *Hounds and the Fury, The* (Ballantine, 2006) Crawford Howard acquires an "outlaw" pack of hounds and sets up a rival event on land long used by the Jefferson Hunt.

6. *Tell-Tale Horse, The* (Ballantine, 2007) A nude female corpse turns up tied to an equine shop fixture, but Sister Arnold really becomes miffed when a valuable trophy goes missing and then turns up in her stable.

Brown, Sam

Sam Brown has made good use of his working cowboy experience in novels about the Old West such as *The Long Season* (Walker, 1987) and *Devil's Rim* (Walker, 1998). This pair of novels, narrated by Casey Wills, cowboy and would-be rancher, is full of realistic detail about the lives of ordinary people in the American West of the late 1800s.

1. *Big Lonely, The* (Walker, 1992) Casey Wills and Josh Smith battle the elements, rustlers, sickness, boredom, loneliness, and the temptations of the saloon and dance hall as they follow the cattle drive north from Texas.

2. *Long Drift, The* (Walker, 1995) In 1887 the now-grizzled veteran Casey gets a chance to start his own Nebraska homestead, but he is distracted by Miroux Sevier, a French Canadian beauty with an absent husband.

Browning, Sinclair (Zerilda Sinclair)

As if Trade Ellis didn't have her hands full raising Brahman cattle on her vast Arizona ranch, Vaca Grande, she also takes on the occasional criminal case in the Tucson area. More than "just an old cowhand from the Rio Grande," the single, fortyish, part-Apache Trade is a shrewd private investigator in this series of cases ranging over the southeastern Arizona city- and countryside. (Zerilda) Sinclair Browning, a Tucson resident, has written other fiction (*America's Best*, AMC, 1995) and nonfiction.

1. *Last Song Dogs, The* (Bantam, 1999) Rancher Trade Ellis, taking on her first homicide case as a private investigator, attends the 25-year reunion of her former cheerleading squad, the Javelina High School Song Dogs, who have been decimated by a series of murders.

2. *Sporting Club, The* (Bantam, 2000) Trade's latest client, serial-romance writer Victoria Carpenter, tells Trade an implausible story, which she swears to be true, about the disappearance of two black children and their father from Vicki's father's hunting club in 1963.

3. *Rode Hard, Put Away Dead* (Bantam, 2001) Candy heiress Abigail Thiessen dies rather suddenly after embarking on a romantic horseback trip with her much younger, and poorer, newlywed husband, bull rider J. B. Calendar.

4. *Crack Shot* (Bantam, 2002) Young juvenile delinquent Eddy Gallegos has broken out of a detention center, and Eddy's grandmother enlists Trade to find him. But it seems that there is a lot more involved than just a runaway teenager.

5. *Traggedy Ann* (Dell, 2003) When she is hired by the sister of a Tucson news anchor who is privy to some dangerous information about murder and a sex cult, Trade runs into underground orgies and some perilous situations.

Bruce, Leo

PSEUDONYM OF Rupert Croft-Cooke

I. Although prolific English author Rupert Croft-Cooke died in 1979, Academy Chicago has republished many of his detective novels, written under the pseudonym Leo Bruce. The Bruce novels are in two series: Sergeant William Beef and Carolus Deene (see II below). Sergeant Beef, as befits his name, is a red-faced, slow-moving village policeman, whose tenacity and sagacity belie his looks. Beef outperforms the more sophisticated detectives (e.g., Lord Peter Wimsey; Hercule Poirot) who appear thinly disguised in the novels, which can be read as parodies of Dorothy Sayers (q.v.) and Agatha Christie (q.v.), among others, to the chagrin of supercilious narrator Lionel Townsend, who would prefer some more presentable detective than the proletarian Beef. When Beef's exploits fail to get him promoted to Scotland Yard, he becomes a private investigator. For unknown reasons, Sergeant Beef was abandoned for the more conventional Carolus Deene after eight novels. Academy Chicago has reprinted numbers 4 through 8 (1980-84), and has published a collection of short stories, *Murder in Miniature* (Academy Chicago, 1992), 10 of which star Beef, and 8 of which feature a character named Sergeant Grebe.

1. *Case for Three Detectives* (Stokes, 1937) When his wife is murdered behind locked doors, Dr. Thurston brings in three famous detectives to solve the crime, while village constable Sergeant Beef works to the solution in his stolid way.

2. *Case without a Corpse* (Stokes, 1937) A young man bursts in on Beef's evening dart game and confesses to murder, then commits suicide, leaving Beef with a case without a corpse.

3. *Case with Four Clowns* (Stokes, 1939) Beef travels to a circus in Yorkshire after his nephew Albert Stiles tells him that the fortune-teller of the circus has predicted a murder.

4. *Case with No Conclusion* (Academy Chicago, 1984) Getting no recognition from Scotland Yard, Beef quits the police force and becomes a private investigator in London, where he is called upon to save a young man's brother from a charge of murder after one of the guests at a dinner party reappears dead in the library. Originally published in the United Kingdom in 1939 as *Case with No Solution*.

5. *Case with Ropes and Rings* (Academy Chicago, 1980) Beef doesn't believe that the death by hanging of the son of the Marquess of Edenbridge was suicide. Lionel Townsend, Beef's chronicler, gets Beef onto the staff at the exclusive Penshurst School to investigate. Originally published in the United Kingdom in 1940.

6. *Case for Sergeant Beef* (Academy Chicago, 1980) A retired watchmaker plans and executes the perfect murder. "Perfect," that is, before the entrance of Sergeant Beef into the case. Originally published in the United Kingdom in 1940.

7. *Neck and Neck* (Academy Chicago, 1980) Lionel Townsend, Beef's chronicler, finds himself, along with his brother and cousins, a

suspect when his rich aunt is murdered. Originally published in the United Kingdom in 1951.

8. *Cold Blood* (**Academy Chicago, 1980**) In what turns out to be his last case, Sergeant Beef is called in to investigate the murder, by croquet mallet, of rich and elderly Cosmo Ducrow on his country estate. Originally published in the United Kingdom in 1952.

II. Prolific author and World War II hero Rupert Croft-Cooke wrote more than 100 books, including poetry collections, plays, novels, biographies, books about food, travel books, and books about the circus, but his best-known and most enduring work seems to be the detective novels he wrote under the pseudonym of Leo Bruce. Bruce abandoned Sergeant Beef in the 1950s for ex-commando, independently wealthy widower, and history master at Queen's School, Newminster (England), Carolus Deene. The Deene novels dispense with the Watson-like narrator, but like the Beef novels, they are intricately plotted, if less given to coincidences and trick endings, and full of interesting minor characters, some of whom are reminiscent of real persons or other fictional detectives. Academy Chicago has reprinted, so far, 14 of the 23 Carolus Deene novels.

1. *At Death's Door* (**Hamilton [UK], 1955**) No annotation available. Not published in the United States.
2. *Dead for a Ducat* (**Davies [UK], 1956**) Lady Pipford, one of the governors of Queen's School, calls Deene to her home, Mincott House, where her son-in-law has apparently just shot himself. Not to be confused with books of the same title by Laurence Payne and Simon Shard. Not published in the United States.
3. *Death of Cold* (**Davies [UK], 1956**) No annotation available. Not to be confused with Romney Curtis's *His Death of Cold*.
4. *Dead Man's Shoes* (**Academy Chicago, 1987**) Carolus Deene is not convinced that the man who committed suicide by jumping overboard from the cargo boat *Saragossa* actually committed the murder everyone else assumed he had committed. Originally published in the United Kingdom in 1958.
5. *Louse for the Hangman, A* (**Davies [UK], 1958**) After Lord Penge, the Meat Paste King, receives threatening letters, his friend Mr. Gorringer, headmaster of Queen's School, asks Carolus to investigate. But it is Penge's secretary, Michael Ratchett, who is murdered. Not published in the United States.
6. *Our Jubilee Is Death* (**Academy Chicago, 1986**) Popular novelist Lillianne Bomberger is distinctly not popular with her nieces and nephew, her secretary, and her servants. Then Bomberger is found buried on the beach up to her chin. Originally published in the United Kingdom in 1959.
7. *Furious Old Women* (**Academy Chicago, 1983**) An elderly woman active in her village church is beaten to death in the churchyard, apparently the victim of a senseless crime. Originally published in the United Kingdom in 1960.
8. *Jack on the Gallows Tree* (**Academy Chicago, 1983**) Two elderly women are found strangled within a few hours of each other at the inland health resort of Buddington-on-the-Hill. Originally published in the United Kingdom in 1960.
9. *Die All, Die Merrily* (**British Book Centre, 1961**) Parliamentarian Lady Drumbone's nephew has committed suicide after leaving a tape confessing to a murder. Lady Drumbone doesn't want this tape to reach the police. Reprinted by Academy Chicago in 1987.
10. *Bone and a Hank of Hair, A* (**British Book Centre, 1961**) Mrs. Chalk, on a visit to her cousin, is told by the cousin's husband that his wife has left him. Then conversation with a local rouses her suspicions about Mrs. Rathbone's disappearance and Mr. Rathbone's activities.
11. *Nothing Like Blood* (**Academy Chicago, 1985**) The well-to-do residents of a guest house on the coast are suspicious about two recent deaths among their number: the death of an old woman and the seeming suicide of a younger woman. Originally published in the United Kingdom in 1962.
12. *Such Is Death* (**British Book Centre, 1963**) It seems that the murder of a random victim chosen by a perpetrator bent upon committing the perfect crime fits into the agenda of some other persons. UK title: *Crack of Doom*. Reprinted by Academy Chicago in 1986.
13. *Death in Albert Park* (**Scribner, 1979**) The murders, apparently random, of three women in the quiet London suburb of Albert Park have residents concerned about their safety. Originally published in the United Kingdom in 1964.
14. *Death at Hallows End* (**British Book Centre, 1966**) Solicitor Duncan Humby vanishes on the way to the remote village of Hallows End, where he was going to rewrite the will of millionaire Grossiter, who was planning to disinherit his nephews. Reprinted by Academy Chicago in 2003.
15. *Death on the Black Sands* (**Allen [UK], 1966**) No annotation available. Not published in the United States.
16. *Death of a Commuter* (**Academy Chicago, 1988**) Regular commuter Mr. Parador is replaced by a strange man in dark clothing and dark glasses, who intones that "[Parador] won't be coming." Mr. Parador is never seen alive again. Originally published in the United Kingdom in 1967.
17. *Death at St. Asprey's School* (**Academy Chicago, 1984**) Some disturbing incidents at St. Asprey's School, such as the death of small pets and an injury done to an instructor, lead the headmaster to call in Carolus Deene. Originally published in the United Kingdom in 1967.
18. *Death on Romney Marsh* (**Allen [UK], 1968**) No annotation available. Not to be confused with Deryn Lake's *Death on the Romney Marsh*. Not published in the United States.
19. *Death with Blue Ribbon* (**British Book Centre, 1970**) After Yves Rolland refuses to pay protection money, his posh restaurant falls victim to a couple of food poisonings, one of them fatal. Reprinted by Academy Chicago in 1989.
20. *Death on Allhallowe'en* (**Academy Chicago, 1988**) Is the presumed "accidental" death of a young local boy on Halloween in a small Kentish village connected with a possible coven of witches? Originally published in the United Kingdom in 1970.
21. *Death by the Lake* (**Academy Chicago, 2003**) After he retires to the village of Millgrove, Deene is intrigued by the five-year-old story of the murder and disappearance of Jessie Flitcher and the vanishing of her criminal husband, Desmond, who is assumed to have committed the crime. Originally published in the United Kingdom in 1971.
22. *Death in the Middle Watch* (**Academy Chicago, 2004**) Deene is posing as a passenger on a luxury cruise ship that suffered a murder the previous year. Then the widow of last year's victim is murdered. Originally published in the United Kingdom in 1974.
23. *Death of a Bovver Boy* (**Mews, 1976**) The death of a young hoodlum, called a "Bovver Boy" in British slang, brings Deene into an underworld of drugs, thugs, and blackmailers. Originally published in the United Kingdom in 1974.

Bruchac, Joseph, (III)

Part Abenaki, part Slovak, Joseph Bruchac has written or edited more than 100 books, most of them dealing with Native Americans, including novels, plays, poetry, biography, folklore collections, and many juveniles and young adult books on the subject. The Dawn Land trilogy is a trio of novels based on Native American tradition and historical facts. It is set in what is now New England and the Canadian Maritimes at the end of the Ice Age, circa 8000 BCE.

Young Hunter, an Abenaki (the Only People) brave, is sent on a quest that pits him and his canine companion, Agewedjiman, against a series of trials, including Cannibal Giants, a Loch Ness–like monster, and a woolly mammoth bent on revenge against humans.

1. *Dawn Land* (Fulcrum, 1995) Some 10,000 years ago, the People of the Dawn Land (the Abenaki) were living in a kind of Eden in what is now known as New England when the man-eating Cannibal Giants (the Ancient Ones) threaten to return, and Young Hunter is sent on a desperate mission to intercept them.
2. *Long River* (Fulcrum, 1995) The Only People are threatened by Walking Hill, a woolly mammoth that has sworn vengeance against humans, and by the last surviving Ancient One. Much of the action takes place on and near the river Kwanitewk (aka Connecticut), as Young Hunter goes to the rescue again.
3. *Waters Between, The* (University Press of New England, 1998) The salty waters of Lake Champlain harbor seals, whales, sharks, and a Loch Ness–type monster that threatens to cut off a key source of food from the Only People.

Bruen, Ken

I. Chief Inspector James Roberts and Sergeant Tom Brant of the London Metropolitan Police are in charge at London's Southeast Precinct ("where even the pit bulls travel in pairs"). Two of the roughest, nastiest, sleaziest coppers to hit detective fiction in recent years, Roberts and Brant are less interested in enforcing the law than they are in ruling their piece of turf in these violent and funny procedurals that will appeal to the readers of "crime noir" fiction by authors such as Quintin Jardine (q.v.) and Ian Rankin (q.v.). Numbers 1, 2, and 3 were first published in the United States in the omnibus volume *The White Trilogy* (Kate's Mystery, 2003). Ken Bruen is an Irishman (Galway) with a PhD in metaphysics from Trinity College (Dublin). He settled in London as a mystery writer after some 25 years abroad as a teacher.

1. *White Arrest, A* (Do-Not [UK], 1998) Chief Inspector James Roberts and Sergeant Tom Brant of the southeast precinct of London's Metropolitan Police need a "white arrest," a major catch to get them out of hot water. Will apprehension of the serial killer who is preying on the England cricket team do the trick? Meanwhile, vigilantes in Brixton are hanging drug dealers from lampposts.
2. *Taming the Alien* (Do-Not [UK], 2000) A series of vignettes set in London and farther afield (Dublin, New York, Seattle, Acapulco), as Brant and Roberts wend their violent way through crimes and criminals, including "The Alien," a hit man who uses a bat as his weapon. Distributed in the United States by Dufour.
3. *McDead, The* (Do-Not [UK], 2001) Although Chief Inspector Roberts had not spoken to his brother in a decade, family feelings rouse him enough to go after Irish gangster Tommy Logan, who is responsible for his death. Distributed in the United States by Dufour.
4. *Blitz* (St. Martin's, 2004) Subtitle: *Brant Hits the Blues.* Brant's quarry this time is the self-named "Blitz," a publicity-hungry serial killer of cops. Originally published in the United Kingdom in 2002.
5. *Vixen* (St. Martin's, 2005) "The Vixen" is a female serial killer–mad bomber who is terrorizing the streets of London. While police higher-ups push for the arrest of the wrong suspect, Brant doggedly and violently pursues the real perpetrator.

6. *Calibre* (St. Martin's, 2006) The "Manners Killer" believes that anyone who behaves rudely in public should be taught a fatal lesson.
7. *Ammunition* (St. Martin's, 2007) As Brant sits in a London pub brooding about the recent death of real-life author Ed McBain (q.v.), a gunman opens fire and hits him several times.

II. Bruen's other serial character, Jack Taylor, is a resident of Galway, Ireland. A former member of the Garda Siochana, the Guards (the Irish police), Jack, who has severe drinking problems, is reduced to doing the occasional private-eye job. Jack, who is a quite cultured fellow given to literary and musical references, makes some valiant, if short-lived, attempts to go on the wagon and become respectable. The Galway setting evoked by Galway native Bruen enhances these Hiberian Noir novels.

1. *Guards, The* (St. Martin's, 2002) Alcoholic former Garda Siochana member Jack Taylor, reduced to part-time operations as a "finder" in Galway, is hired by a woman to look into the supposed suicide of her teenage daughter.
2. *Killing of the Tinkers, The* (St. Martin's, 2004) Jack Taylor, returning home to Galway from London, a failed marriage behind him, is roused out of his alcoholic stupor by a Gypsy who asks for his help in solving the murders of a number of young men in his clan. Originally published in Ireland in 2002.
3. *Magdalen Martyrs, The* (St. Martin's, 2005) Taylor, struggling to stay sober, as a favor for Galway gangster Bill Cassell takes on the job of tracking down unwed mother Rita Monroe. Originally published in Ireland in 2003.
4. *Dramatist, The* (St. Martin's, 2006) Jack Taylor, living sober and dating a mature woman, is enticed into investigating the seemingly accidental deaths of two students, who may have been the victims of "the Dramatist." Originally published in Ireland in 2004.
5. *Priest* (St. Martin's, 2007) Jack investigates the murder of a pederast priest who was guilty of abusing small boys and, perhaps, something worse.
6. *Cross* (St. Martin's, 2008) Jack Taylor, with his surrogate son, Cody, lying comatose in a hospital, agrees to help Ridge solve the murder of a boy crucified in Galway City.

Bruno, Anthony

I. Bruno's Bad series follows the adventures of FBI agents Mike Tozzi and Cuthbert Gibbons in a series of fast, funny books that have been described as a cross between Elmore Leonard (q.v.) and Donald E. Westlake (q.v.). Gibbons and Tozzi are something of an odd couple: the crusty, middle-aged family man Gibbons, and the eternally rash and impetuous Tozzi. The bad guys, such as the wily mafioso Sal Immordino, are sometimes sinister, sometimes zany, sometimes charming, and sometimes all three.

1. *Bad Guys* (Putnam, 1988) Mike Tozzi and Cuthbert Gibbons team up to foil a mobster who is masterminding a comeback through the government-witness program.
2. *Bad Blood* (Putnam, 1989) Tozzi and partner Bert Wilson are on the track of the murderers of two Asian teenagers.
3. *Bad Luck* (Delacorte, 1990) The Mob is involving itself in a new casino and a heavyweight-boxing championship fight in Atlantic City.
4. *Bad Business* (Delacorte, 1991) Assistant US Attorney Tom Augustine has made a deal with drug dealers in exchange for the $14 million he wants to run for mayor of New York.

5. *Bad Moon* (Delacorte, 1992) Mafioso Sal Immordino is feigning insanity in a New Jersey asylum with the help of his nun sister, Cil.

6. *Bad Apple* (Delacorte, 1994) Tony "Bells" Bell, out-of-control mobster, shoots FBI agent Gary Peterson and becomes the target of an extensive manhunt.

II. Recently Bruno has put Tozzi and Gibbons on the back burner in favor of nonfiction crime reporting and a series of novels about New Jersey Jump Squad operatives Loretta Kovacs and Frank Marvelli. The Jump Squad, an arm of the Department of Corrections, traces and retrieves parole violators. Loretta, a fat kvetcher, and Frank, a handsome widower, make an odd but effective couple as they chase down lowlifes who would be at home in a Carl Hiaasen (q.v.) opus, in a series of funny narratives full of plot twists.

1. *Devil's Food* (Forge, 1997) Loretta Kovacs and her new partner, Frank Marvelli, are after Martha Lee Spooner, skipped money launderer and con woman, who is working a scam against WeightAway, a Florida fat farm.

2. *Double Espresso* (Forge, 1998) Loretta and Frank go to Seattle to pick up Frank's brother-in-law Sammy, a parole violator moonlighting as a hit man, and get enmeshed in a plot involving coffee, the FBI, and a secret witness–stashing compound in Puget Sound.

3. *Hot Fudge* (Forge, 2000) Frank and beautiful fellow officer Evissa Mylowe are in San Francisco chasing after Ira Krupnick, former drug dealer and parole violator who has established a new identity as part owner of an ice-cream company. The jealous Loretta is chasing after Frank and Evissa.

Brust, Steven K. (Zoltan)

I. Brust, sometime programmer, musician, and actor, is a scholar of Hungarian folklore as well as a popular fantasy writer. Some of Brust's novels, such as *The Sun, the Moon and the Stars* (Berkley, 1987), are based on Hungarian folktales. His Vlad Taltos series is set in the Dragaeran Empire, where a race of witchcraft-practicing humans lives in uneasy equilibrium with a race of elitist sorcerers. Vlad Taltos, a human thief, hit man, warlock, and sometime crime lord, accompanied by his dragonlike partner, Loiosh, swashbuckles and wisecracks his way through a somewhat self-referential series that Brust's many fans find irresistible. Although the series is listed according to its inner chronology, readers may want to start with number 4, the first published. At least three omnibus volumes have been published: *The Book of Jhereg* (Ace, 1999; numbers 1, 4, 5); *The Book of Taltos* (Ace, 2002; numbers 1 and 6); and *The Book of Athyra* (Berkley, 2003; numbers 7 and 8).

1. *Taltos* (Ace, 1988) Covers Vlad's early adventures, when he first met Morrolan and Aliera and journeyed to the land of the dead. UK title: *Taltos and the Paths of the Dead.*

2. *Dragon* (Tor, 1998) At the request of Dragonlord Morrolan, Vlad traces the theft of the Morganti greatsword to rival Dragonlord, the Count of Forni. The first Vlad Taltos novel to be published in hardcover, this novel overlaps chronologically with *Yendi.*

3. *Yendi* (Ace, 1984) Narrates Vlad's rise from small-time hood to major criminal and his meeting with his wife, Cawti, "the Dagger of the Jhereg."

4. *Jhereg* (Ace, 1983) Vlad Taltos, operating as a hit man for a gangster, is ordered to kill a man so thoroughly that neither his body nor his soul can be revived. Initial installment of series to be published.

5. *Teckla* (Ace, 1986) Despite his long-standing distaste for the lowly Teckla, Vlad becomes involved in their rebellion against the Empire.

6. *Phoenix* (Ace, 1990) Vlad's patron goddess needs his services as an assassin, and he can't say no.

7. *Athyra* (Ace, 1993) Vlad visits a small elfin village where he becomes a suspect in an elf killing, which Vlad believes was committed by an undead necromancer.

8. *Orca* (Ace, 1996) Vlad and Savn, the elf he befriended in *Athyra*, get involved in another murder mystery and the uncovering of a scandal that could affect the entire Dragaeran Empire.

9. *Issola* (Tor, 2001) Vlad is called upon, once again, to rescue his Dragonlord friends Morrolan and Aliera, this time from the Jenoine, the creators of Dragaera.

10. *Dzur* (Tor, 2006) Vlad is engaged in a complicated scheme to disrupt the political maneuvering of a shady association known as the Left Hand of the Jhereg.

II. The Phoenix Guards series is set in the Dragaeran universe some thousand years before the Vlad Taltos series. Modeled after Alexandre Dumas' (q.v.) *Three Musketeers* stories, these novels feature the adventures of young swordsman Khaavren and his three friends in the Imperial Guards. Numbers 1 and 2 are prequels, in a way, to the Viscount of Adrilankha trilogy (numbers 3–5) and probably should be read first.

1. *Phoenix Guards, The* (Tor, 1991) Young swordsman Khaavren, on his way to join the Imperial Guards, falls in with three guard aspirants: Pel, Aerich, and Tazendra.

2. *Five Hundred Years After* (Tor, 1994) Five centuries later, Khaavren and his friends are still serving in the Imperial Guards when Emperor Tortaalik I mortally offends Adron the Dragonlord.

3. *Paths of the Dead* (Tor, 2002) Piro, son of Khaavren, heir to his father's role as protector of the emperor, helps a childhood friend to retrieve the Imperial Orb on a quest that takes them to the Paths of the Dead and the Halls of Judgement.

4. *Lord of Castle Black, The* (Tor, 2003) Zerika, having recovered the Imperial Orb, becomes empress, but anti-emperor Kana sends two huge armies to snatch the orb for himself.

5. *Sethra Lavode* (Tor, 2004) In the conclusion to the Viscount of Adrilankha trilogy, Empress Zerika and Kana continue their fight to the finish for control of the Dragaeran Empire.

Buchan, John

I. Scottish author John Buchan is primarily remembered now for his adventure novels, though it was his government service and more serious writings that doubtless won him the title of Baron Tweedsmuir in 1935. Richard Hannay is featured in five of his books. Hannay pursues rather than detects; his cases are properly classed in the adventure genre, though they have an espionage element. *Four Adventures of Richard Hannay* (Hodder [UK], 1930) contains numbers 1–4; *Adventures of Richard Hannay* (Houghton, 1939) contains numbers 1–3.

1. *Thirty-nine Steps, The* (Doran, 1915) Young Richard Hannay is accidentally caught in a spy plot and finds himself pursued through England and Scotland by police and German agents. Fans of Alfred Hitchcock's 1935 movie version will be surprised to discover that it differs significantly from the novel.

2. *Greenmantle* (Doran, 1916) Major Hannay of the New Army is sent on special assignment to track down a secret in Turkey.

3. *Mr. Standfast* (Doran, 1919) Hannay pursues the mysterious Mr. Ivery in England, Scotland, and France. Mary Lamington wins Hannay's heart in this volume.

4. *Three Hostages, The* (Houghton, 1924) Hannay, now Sir Richard, married to Mary and living at Fosse Manor, takes on a group of postwar fanatics set on revolution.
5. *Man from Norlands, The* (Houghton Mifflin, 1936) Sir Richard's young son Peter John helps out with a case that takes them to an island fortress in Scotland. English title: *Island of Sheep*.

II. Buchan fans will also want to read the four books featuring Sir Edward Leithen, a more thoughtful detective, less given to hot pursuits over desolate moors than Hannay. Sir Edward is a lawyer and a bachelor. He is assumed to be a somewhat autobiographical character. Omnibus volume *The Leithen Stories* (Canongate [UK], 2000) contains numbers 1–4.

1. *Power-House, The* (Doran, 1916) Was the mysterious disappearance of Mr. Pitt-Heron connected with a secret society?
2. *John MacNab* (Houghton Mifflin, 1925) Sir Edward and two of his friends plot a caper to impersonate—but elude capture as—the poacher John MacNab.
3. *Dancing Floor, The* (Houghton Mifflin, 1926) Sir Edward helps a desperate young Greek girl to escape a tragic death, mysteriously foretold in dreams.
4. *Mountain Meadow* (Houghton Mifflin, 1941) Fighting a losing battle with TB, Sir Edward takes on one last adventure, the search for an American millionaire lost in northern Canada. UK title: *Sick Heart River*.

Buchanan, Edna (Rydzik)

Edna Buchanan, a Pulitzer Prize–winning police reporter for the *Miami Herald*, achieved national recognition for her tough but sympathetic crime reporting and memorable opening sentences (e.g., "Gary Robinson died hungry"). Edna, as she is known in Miami, has branched out into crime fiction in a series of novels featuring police reporter Britt Montero. The likable Britt, assured prose, and the Miami ambience make an effective combination. Number 8 introduced Sergeant Craig Burch, of the Cold Case Squad, who is featured in numbers 9 and 10. Number 11 brings Montero and the Cold Case Squad together.

1. *Contents under Pressure* (Hyperion, 1992) Former pro football player D. Wayne Hudson, a beloved figure in Miami's black community, is killed in a car crash while being chased by police officers.
2. *Miami, It's Murder* (Hyperion, 1994) A rapist claiming voodoo powers and a child murder from the distant past engage Britt's interest here.
3. *Suitable for Framing* (Hyperion, 1995) Britt witnesses the killing of a young woman and the injury of her toddler in the latest in a recent series of violent carjackings.
4. *Act of Betrayal* (Hyperion, 1996) Several white, blond, blue-eyed teenage boys are missing and feared murdered. Britt's investigation is hampered by boyfriend trouble, the possible existence of a diary written by her late father, and an impending hurricane.
5. *Margin of Error* (Hyperion, 1997) Hollywood superstar Lance Westfell is tagging along with Britt to absorb some authenticity for his movie role as a reporter. Lance, in turn, is being stalked by a delusional fan named Stephanie.
6. *Garden of Evil* (Avon, 1999) The "Kiss-Me Killer," a mysterious woman who kills and mutilates her male victims, is wending her way south toward Miami.
7. *You Only Die Twice* (Morrow, 2001) The body of a beautiful woman found floating offshore is identified as Kaithlin Jordan of the prominent department-store family. One problem: Kaithlin has been dead 10 years, and her husband is on death row for her murder.
8. *Ice Maiden, The* (Morrow, 2002) An executed criminal provides a crucial link in a 14-year-old murder case involving two teenagers on their first date. Sunny, the teenager who survived, doesn't want to revisit the past but may be forced to. Introduces Sergeant Craig Burch, of the Miami Police Department's Cold Case Squad.
9. *Cold Case Squad* (Simon & Schuster, 2004) Sergeant Craig Burch stars in this case where the ex-wife of a man who supposedly was blown up while working on his vintage Thunderbird 12 years previously seeks the aid of the Cold Case Squad.
10. *Shadows* (Simon & Schuster, 2005) With the bulldozing of Saving Shadows, a historic Miami waterfront estate, a 45-year-old unsolved murder case is reopened.
11. *Love Kills* (Simon & Schuster, 2007) When Miami police discover the remains of Spencer York, a kidnapper who worked for divorced fathers, members of the Cold Case Squad question Britt Montero, the last person to see him alive.

Buck, Pearl S(ydenstricker)

The Good Earth, a masterful portrait of late 19th- and early 20th-century Chinese peasant life, won Buck a Pulitzer Prize in 1932 and was instrumental in her receipt of a Nobel Prize in 1938. Luise Rainer won an Oscar for her memorable performance as the long-suffering O-lan in the 1938 movie version. Two sequels carrying the story forward to the Chinese Revolution of 1911 complete the House of Earth trilogy, which follows the House of Wang through half a century and three generations of farmers, warlords, merchants, and students. Buck's literary reputation has fallen on hard times in recent years, but she is memorialized in the Pearl S. Buck International Foundation and by the People's Republic of China, which opened her former house at Nanjing University to the public in 2000. *House of Earth* (Reynal, 1935) contains numbers 1 and 2.

1. *Good Earth, The* (Day, 1931) The story of Wang Lung and his family is told.
2. *Sons* (Day, 1932) Wang Lung's three sons build their own lives.
3. *House Divided, A* (Reynal, 1935) Yuan, grandson of Wang Lung, sees China into the modern age.

Buckley, Fiona

PSEUDONYM OF **Valerie Anand**

Historical novelist Valerie Anand (q.v.) also writes, as Fiona Buckley, a historical mystery series. The series, set in Elizabethan times (1560s), has for a protagonist the widowed, impecunious but well-born (half sister to the queen), quick-witted, and sharp-tongued Ursula Blanchard, lady-in-waiting to young Queen Elizabeth I and secret agent for Elizabeth's right-hand man, William Cecil. Ursula's sensibility and self-awareness seem more suited to current times, but the excitement and drama of Elizabethan times are well conveyed. Fans of Edward Marston's (q.v.) Nicholas Bracewell series will be interested.

1. *To Shield the Queen* (Scribner, 1997) Ursula Blanchard, widowed with a daughter at the age of 26, in 1560 becomes lady-in-waiting to young Queen Elizabeth. Ursula is sent to care for ailing Amy (Robsart) Dudley, wife of the Queen's favorite, Robin Dudley. Then Amy dies under suspicious circumstances. UK title: *The Amy Robsart Mystery*.

2. *Doublet Affair, The* **(Scribner, 1998)** Ursula is requested by the Queen and William Cecil to retire temporarily from court and spy at the home of Leonard and Ann Mason, suspected supporters of the Catholic Mary, Queen of Scots.

3. *Queen's Ransom* **(Scribner, 1999)** Ursula is sent to France, which is on the brink of civil war between Catholics and Protestants, with a letter from Queen Elizabeth to Queen Catherine of France.

4. *To Ruin a Queen* **(Scribner, 2000)** A plot to blackmail the Queen brings Ursula to Wales where she undergoes imprisonment and marooning on a Welsh mountain.

5. *Queen of Ambition* **(Scribner, 2001)** Ursula takes a job in a pie shop frequented by Cambridge students to investigate a possible plot tied to a student play to be presented to the Queen.

6. *Pawn for a Queen, A* **(Scribner, 2002)** Ursula travels to Scotland without Elizabeth's permission to thwart a treasonous plot connected with Ursula's cousin, and gets embroiled in the intrigue swirling around Mary, Queen of Scots.

7. *Fugitive Queen, The* **(Scribner, 2003)** Traveling to the north of England, ostensibly to find a husband for her ward Penelope, Ursula is conveying a message to Mary, former Queen of Scots, who is imprisoned in Bolton Castle and conducting an investigation into the violent death of Mary's husband, Lord Darnley.

8. *Siren Queen, The* **(Scribner, 2004)** Another plot to place Mary on the throne of England may be connected to the political intrigue around Italian banker, Roberto Ridolfi.

Buckley, William F(rank), Jr.

Once America's leading conservative columnist, editor of the *National Review*, and host of television's *Firing Line*, the late Buckley (d. 2008) added writing spy novels to his list of credits rather late in his career. *Saving the Queen* was an immediate best seller, and each new installment won more fans to the adventures of his suave and daring CIA agent, Blackford Oakes. Blackie, a wealthy Ivy League type, is only 26 when first met and ages gracefully with the series.

1. *Saving the Queen* **(Doubleday, 1976)** Relates Blackie's awful boyhood in an English boarding school. Finding an atomic spy in the queen's court is his first CIA assignment.

2. *Stained Glass* **(Doubleday, 1978)** In 1952 Blackie is assigned to assassinate Count Wintergrin, a young politician determined to reunite Germany even at the risk of war.

3. *High Jinx* **(Doubleday, 1986)** This is set in 1954 as President Eisenhower worries that the USSR has broken the top-secret code used between England and the United States.

4. *Who's on First?* **(Doubleday, 1980)** Blackie plays a leading role in the race between the United States and the USSR to put the first satellite into orbit.

5. *Marco Polo, If You Can* **(Doubleday, 1982)** What if Blackie had been flying that U-2 spy plane in 1960 and was deliberately planning to get caught by the Soviets?

6. *Story of Henri Tod, The* **(Doubleday, 1984)** Not even Blackie can stop the Berlin Wall from going up in 1962.

7. *See You Later, Alligator* **(Doubleday, 1985)** Blackie goes to Havana to talk with Che Guevara on the eve of the Cuban missile crisis.

8. *Mongoose, R.I.P.* **(Random House, 1987)** In 1963 Blackie is sent to Cuba to assassinate Castro.

9. *Tucker's Last Stand* **(Random House, 1990)** Blackie and mechanical genius Montana Tucker are ordered by Lyndon Johnson to find a way to close the Ho Chi Minh Trail.

10. *Very Private Plot, A* **(Morrow, 1994)** Senator Hugh Blanton, as part of his campaign to ban covert intelligence operations, subpoenas the retired Blackie to testify about Cyclops, a Reagan-era CIA scheme.

11. *Last Call for Blackford Oakes* **(Harcourt, 2005)** In his swan song, Blackie returns to the Soviet Union to thwart yet another assassination plot against Mikhail Gorbachev and has a further encounter with defector Kim Philby, aka A. F. Martins.

Buechner, Frederick

The Bebb Chronicles are an unusual mix of high comedy and underlying seriousness by a writer who is also an ordained Presbyterian minister. Leo Bebb, ex-convict and evangelist head of the Holy Love Church and diploma mill in Armadillo, Florida, dominates the series and provides most of its hilarity. Antonio Parr is the narrator. All four books were collected in the omnibus edition, *The Book of Bebb* (Atheneum, 1979).

1. *Lion Country* **(Atheneum, 1971)** Thirty-four-year-old Antonio Parr gets his ordination through the mail, goes to visit Leo Bebb's unorthodox religious school, and falls in love with Bebb's daughter.

2. *Open Heart* **(Atheneum, 1972)** Antonio Parr, married to Sharon Bebb and living in Connecticut, tells of Bebb's move north to launch another dubious venture in evangelism.

3. *Love Feast* **(Atheneum, 1974)** As trouble comes to Antonio's marriage, his father-in-law takes up with 70-year-old Theosophist Getrude Conover and starts the Love Feast movement to evangelize the Pepsi generation.

4. *Treasure Hunt* **(Atheneum, 1977)** Antonio and Sharon travel to an old house in South Carolina left to them by Leo Bebb and find it occupied.

Buff, Joe

Mix a Tom Clancy (q.v.) technothriller with a Clive Cussler (q.v.) underwater adventure, and you'll have some idea of Joe Buff's submarine thrillers. In 2011 World War III is in full swing, with a neo-Nazi Germany and a re-Boerified South Africa—supplied with nukes by a "neutral" Russia—pitted against the United States and Britain. Submarines have an important role to play, and Jeffrey Fuller, commander of the super nuclear sub USS *Challenger,* is in the thick of things for the "Silent Service." Author Joe Buff's strongest suit is his detailed knowledge of sub technology and strategy. Despite the improbable geopolitics, the plots are usually exciting. The characters, including the predictably nasty Nazis and Afrikaners, tend to be cardboard, and the love interest is not very interesting.

1. *Deep Sound Channel* **(Bantam, 2000)** In 2011 World War III has begun, and the brunt of the war is borne by naval forces in nuclear combat. Commander Jeffrey Fuller's state-of-the-art submarine, the USS *Challenger,* is diverted to South Africa to run a team of US Navy SEALS ashore at Durban to destroy a secret laboratory.

2. *Thunder in the Deep* **(Bantam, 2001)** Fuller and the *Challenger* have their hands full, as they set out to rescue a disabled sub from the ocean floor and lead a secret strike force to the Baltic to destroy a German missile site. Opposing them is the supersub *Deutschland,* captained by the ruthless Kurt Eberhard.

3. *Crush Depth* **(Morrow, 2002)** Fuller and the *Challenger* are pitted against the nasty Captain Jan ter Horst and the Axis sub *Voortrekker.*

4. *Tidal Rip* (Morrow, 2003) Fuller's prime adversary this time is Commander Ernst Beck, at the helm of the super U-boat *Admiral von Scheer*, with the fates of central Africa and South America in the balance.

5. *Straits of Power* (Morrow, 2004) Fuller is diverted into espionage work and ordered to recover a spy code-named Zeno, who may hold the key to an all-out Axis attack.

6. *Seas of Crisis* (Morrow, 2006) June 2012. America is at war with the neo-Axis coalition of Germany and South Africa. USS *Challenger* prepares for a Special Forces attack against a Russian missile silo.

Buffa, D(udley) W.

Prominent Portland, Oregon, defense attorney, Joseph Antonelli, gets involved with some high-profile cases. A former US vice president, a murdered US senator, assorted media types, and various psychopaths and sociopaths are all grist for Antonelli's mill. Californian D. W. Buffa, who was a defense attorney for 10 years, among his other gigs, writes authentic and exciting courtroom dramas.

1. *Defense, The* (Holt, 1997) Portland attorney Joseph Antonelli, at the request of Judge Leo Rifkin, defends Johnny Morel against child rape charges.

2. *Prosecution, The* (Holt, 1999) Acting for the prosecution this time, Antonelli investigates the murder of Nancy Goodwin, wife of Chief Deputy DA Marshall Godwin.

3. *Judgment, The* (Warner, 2001) Well-hated circuit judge Calvin Jeffries is stabbed to death in the courthouse parking garage. Then a second judge is killed the same way, in the same spot. Were both crimes committed by homeless men?

4. *Legacy, The* (Warner, 2002) A young black man has been accused of the shooting death of a prominent US senator in San Francisco, and Antonelli is brought into a case no one else will touch.

5. *Star Witness* (Putnam, 2003) Antonelli defends film director and mogul Stanley Roth, who is accused of murdering his movie star wife, Mary Margaret Flanders.

6. *Breach of Trust* (Putnam, 2004) Former Harvard Law School classmate and US Vice President Thomas Browning asks Antonelli to defend another classmate, Jimmy Haviland, who is going to be indicted for a 38-year-old murder.

7. *Trial by Fire* (Putnam, 2005) After Antonelli joins his law partner and lifetime friend, Albert Craven, on the Bryan Allen show to discuss the media craze surrounding the case of a woman allegedly murdered by her husband, he becomes defense lawyer in an even more frenzied, publicized murder case.

Bugge, Carole

I. Mystery editor Claire Rawlings and her 12-year-old friend Meredith are amateur sleuths who, in the tradition of fictional amateur sleuths, find a murder to solve in each outing.

1. *Who Killed Blanche DuBois?* (Berkley, 1999) Mystery editor Claire Rawlings and her young friend Meredith investigate the murder of Claire's star author.

2. *Who Killed Dorian Gray?* (Berkley, 2000) Claire and Meredith are teaching writing in an artist's colony in Woodstock. Then the colony's resident beauty is found dead in a bathtub.

3. *Who Killed Mona Lisa?* (Berkley, 2001) Claire and Meredith are snowbound in a New England inn that has a tradition of guests anonymously writing down their deepest secrets for other guests to read.

II. A pair of Sherlock Holmes pastiches brings back the familiar cast of Watson, Mycroft, Lestrade, and so forth. The period detail is well done, but there is streak of sentimentality that the original Arthur Conan Doyle (q.v.) stories lacked.

1. *Star of India, The* (St. Martin's, 1998) 1894. Sherlock Holmes has survived the battle with Professor Moriarty at Reichenbach Falls but so, apparently, has Moriarty, who threatens not only Holmes but the British monarchy.

2. *Haunting of Torre Abbey, The* (St. Martin's, 2000) Holmes and Watson return to the site of the Hound of the Baskervilles and encounter the ghost of a monk decapitated in the 14th century.

Bujold, Lois McMaster

I. Miles Vorkosigan, clever but undersized, deformed, and insecure, is not your typical science fiction hero. The son of odd couple Cordelia Naismith, Betan Survey leader, and Aral Vorkosigan, Barrayaran military man and eventual regent for the young emperor, Miles is turned down by the Barrayaran space academy by reason of his physical defects, but eventually does become a military man, leader of the Dendarii Mercenaries. After a series of adventures in various space "empires" in which Miles's resourcefulness is put to some extreme tests, Miles becomes Imperial Auditor of Barrayar and marries his beloved Ekaterin. Set in a far-future universe, the series starts 300 years before Miles's birth and has carried him to the age of 32 so far. What began as a somewhat lighthearted space opera has deepened into a world-building saga with well-realized characters—such as Miles; his feisty mom, Cordelia; the boy-emperor Gregor; and Mark, Miles's cloned brother—laced with humor and compulsively readable for its many fans. The titles are arranged according to chronology rather than by publishing date. Several omnibus volumes have been published: *Test of Honor* (Doubleday, 1986; contains numbers 2 and 4); *Vorkosigan's Game* (Science Fiction Book Club, 1990; contains numbers 5 and 6); *Cordelia's Honor* (Baen, 1996; contains numbers 2 and 3); *Young Miles* (Baen, 1997; contains numbers 4 and 6 and the novella "The Mountains of Mourning"); *Miles, Mystery, and Mayhem* (Baen, 2001; contains numbers 7 and 8 and the story "Labyrinth"); and *Miles Errant* (Baen, 2002; contains numbers 5, 9, and 10).

Ohioan Lois McMaster Bujold, who started out as a housewife with time on her hands, has become one of the leading practitioners of contemporary science fiction, winner of several Hugo and Nebula awards. She is also the author of a fantasy trilogy (see II below) and a stand-alone fantasy novel, *The Spirit Ring* (Baen, 1992).

1. *Falling Free* (Baen, 1988) In the far future, but 300 years before the birth of Miles Vorkosigan, the Betan-Barrayaran War is raging, Quaddies are created, and engineer Leo Graf is faced with some tough decisions. Winner of the Nebula Award.

2. *Shards of Honor* (Baen, 1986) Bujold's first published novel. Cordelia Naismith, leader of a Betan scientific survey group, and Aral Vorkosigan, commander of a Barrayaran military force, begin as enemies but wind up as lovers. First book in the Cordelia Naismith subseries.

3. *Barrayar* (Baen, 1991) Cordelia and Aral, now married, had expected to lead a quiet life, but Aral is appointed by the dying emperor to rule Barrayar until Prince Gregor, the four-year-old heir-apparent, comes of age. Second book in the Cordelia Naismith subseries. Hugo Award winner.

4. *Warrior's Apprentice, The* (Baen, 1986) Miles Vorkosigan, the short and deformed son of Cordelia and Aral, is rejected by the Barrayaran military academy after flunking the physical,

but he compensates by becoming the leader of the Dendarii Mercenaries.

5. *Vor Game, The* (Baen, 1990) Miles rejoins the Dendarii to rescue Gregor, his friend and the emperor of Barrayar. Winner of the Hugo Award.

6. *Cetaganda* (Baen, 1996) Miles and his cousin Ivan represent Barrayar on a diplomatic mission to Cetaganda and get involved in a plot to interfere with the Cetagandan "genome."

7. *Ethan of Athos* (Baen, 1986) Female agent Elli Quinn is sent by Miles to the planet of Athos, where she teams with obstetrician Ethan Urquhart to save his world.

8. *Brothers in Arms* (Baen, 1989) With the advent of peace between the planets, the Dendarii Mercenaries are left without a regular paycheck. Miles meets Mark, his cloned brother.

9. *Borders of Infinity* (Baen, 1989) Contains three Vorkosigan novellas that follow Miles's career during his early twenties: "The Mountains of Mourning," which won both the Hugo and Nebula awards for best novella; "Labyrinth"; and "The Borders of Infinity."

10. *Mirror Dance* (Baen, 1994) Mark, Miles's cloned sibling, poses as Miles to take a Dendarii ship to Jackson's Whole. The seemingly mortally wounded and cryogenically suspended Miles is lost somewhere in space. Winner of the Hugo Award. First hardcover original for Bujold.

11. *Memory* (Baen, 1996) Miles, not completely recovered from the traumas suffered in number 10, has a seizure in combat and then falsifies his report to Simon Illyan, chief of Barrayaran Imperial Security, who, unfortunately for Miles, has a perfect memory because of a computer implant.

12. *Komarr* (Baen, 1998) Miles, now Imperial Auditor, is investigating a Chernobyl-type accident on the Barrayaran occupied planet of Komarr. The Komarrans haven't taken too kindly to the occupation.

13. *Civil Campaign, A* (Baen, 2000) Love is blooming on Barrayar. The emperor's wedding sparks romance and intrigue. Miles is wooing the beautiful widow Ekaterin Vorsoisson. Lord Mark, Miles's clone, has fostered a get-rich-quick scheme to win his own beloved.

14. *Diplomatic Immunity* (Baen, 2002) Miles and Ekaterin, wed in the novella "Winterfair Gifts" (apparently not yet available in book form), go on a belated honeymoon, which is interrupted by a murder investigation and a war threat.

II. Three volumes of Bujold's epic series featuring the medieval fantasy sword-and-sorcery kingdom of Chalion have been published so far. Nothing really new here, but Bujold tells the tales exceptionally well, with convincing characters, breathless action, and a believable fantasy world.

1. *Curse of Chalion, The* (Eos, 2001) In the first novel set in Chalion, a world ruled by Five Gods, Cazaril, a crippled soldier, is appointed tutor to the sister of the royal heir, which involves him deeply with court intrigue.

2. *Paladin of Souls* (Eos, 2003) Ista Dy Baocia takes a pilgrimage to ease her soul but finds, in Chalion, a more dangerous fate than she could have ever imagined. Roknari incursions, demons from the Fifth God's hell, and a quest to save Arhys dy Lutez and his magnetic half brother Ilvin threaten her realm.

3. *Hallowed Hunt, The* (Eos, 2005) Lord Ingrey kin Wolfcliff, who is sent by Chalion's sealmaster to fetch orphaned Lady Ijada to trial, finds that they both harbor animal spirits received in forbidden centuries-old power rites.

III. Farmer's daughter Fawn Bluefield and Lakewalker captain Dag Redwing Hickory are the protagonists in the Sharing Knife series. The Lakewalkers are soldier-sorcerers who are dedicated to their campaign against the inhuman and immortal magical entities known as "malices," creatures that suck the life out of all they encounter and turn men and animals into their slaves.

1. *Beguilement* (Eos, 2006) *The Sharing Knife, Volume One.* Lakewalker patroller Dag sets out to rescue young Fawn Bluefield from the "malice" that has kidnapped her.

2. *Legacy* (Eos, 2007) *The Sharing Knife, Volume Two.* Dag's marriage to Dawn doesn't find universal approval from the Lakewalkers at Hickory Lake Camp.

3. *Passage* (Eos, 2008) *The Sharing Knife, Volume Three.* Exiled from his family for marrying an outsider, Dag longs to build a bridge of understanding and respect between Lakewalkers and those who depend on their protection.

Bull, Bartle

I. The trio beginning with *The White Rhino Hotel* takes place in East and North Africa from 1919 to 1939 and follows the fortunes of several characters, including Anton Rider, English White Hunter and soldier of fortune raised by Gypsies, his lover (and eventual wife) Gwenn Llewellyn, and Olivio Alavedo, a Goan dwarf who manages the White Rhino Hotel in Kenya and the Cataract Cafe on a barge in Cairo. The three novels are rousing, if somewhat retro in tone, and display a detailed knowledge of Africa. Bartle Bull, who has also written the nonseries *Radleigh's Choice* (Viking, 1999), is a transplanted Englishman living in New York, an explorer, attorney, writer, publisher (*Village Voice*) and political campaign worker (Democratic). He has written a nonfiction history of African big game hunting: *Safari: A Chronicle of Adventure* (Viking, 1988) and a travel journal: *Around the Sacred Sea: Mongolia and Lake Baikal on Horseback* (Canongate [UK], 1999).

1. *White Rhino Hotel, The* (Viking, 1992) In 1919 wily Goan dwarf Olivio Alavedo manages the White Rhino Hotel in Kenya. Among the residents are big-game hunter Anton Rider; his inamorata, the married Gwenn Llewellyn; and assorted disabled World War I veterans, displaced Germans, Portuguese, and an American cowboy.

2. *Cafe on the Nile, A* (Carroll & Graf, 1998) In 1935 the scene shifts to Egypt and Abyssinia (Ethiopia). Anton and Gwenn are married with two sons, but living apart, and Gwenn has taken Italian air ace Count Lorenzo Grimaldi as a lover. Olivio is managing a cafe on a barge in Cairo. The Italians are invading Abyssinia.

3. *Devil's Oasis, The* (Carroll & Graf, 2001) In 1939 war is about to engulf North Africa. Anton Rider and Olivio Alavedo are still on the scene in Cairo. Gwenn, last seen nursing natives mown down by Mussolini's troops in Eritrea, has taken up with a corrupt Frenchman. General Rommel and his Afrika Korps seize the Suez Canal.

II. A pair of novels relates the adventures of well-born Russian exile, Alexander Karlov, in places like Shanghai and Paris in 1918 and 1922.

1. *Shanghai Station* (Carroll & Graf, 2004) Russian exile Alexander Karlov arrives in Shanghai in 1918 on a mission of vengeance against the Bolsheviks who have murdered his mother and kidnapped his twin sister, Katia.

2. *China Star* **(Carroll & Graf, 2006)** Paris 1922. Alexander Karlov is still searching for Katia, who was raped and kidnapped by Soviet Commissar Viktor Polyak.

Bunch, Chris(topher R.)

I. Television scriptwriter and novelist Chris Bunch (d. 2005) was a leading practitioner of the subgenre known as military science fiction. He cowrote, with Allan Cole (q.v.), the best-selling Sten series and the Antero series (see entry under Cole), and the Vietnam War novel *A Reckoning for Kings* (Atheneum, 1987), as well as several series of his own, including the Shadow Warrior trilogy, featuring the war hero and bounty hunter Joshua Wolfe, master of the killing arts, who is pitted against the nasty, alien Al'ar race. Action-filled space opera that will appeal especially to young adults. *Shadow Warrior* (Del Rey, 2004) is an omnibus volume containing numbers 1, 2, and 3 and a previously uncollected Shadow Warrior story.

1. *Wind after Time, The* **(Del Rey, 1996)** Great War hero Joshua Wolfe suspects that the Al'ar aliens, who could kill people with their minds, are not finished, even though the war has been over for 10 years.
2. *Hunt the Heavens* **(Del Rey, 1996)** Joshua and his alien pal Taen embark on a perilous search for the vanished Al'ars.
3. *Darkness of God, The* **(Del Rey, 1997)** Joshua is humanity's last hope as he tries to recover Ur-Lumina, a lost alien crystal, from a gangster who controls an entire solar system.

II. The Seer King trilogy is sword-and-sorcery fantasy related by courageous but self-deprecating soldier Damastes á Cimabue about the rise and fall of the wizard king Laish Tenedos, of Numantia, a distant-past world. Ingenious sword savagery, political intrigue, and plenty of action make up for some style and characterization weaknesses.

1. *Seer King, The* **(Warner, 1997)** Soldier Damastes á Cimabue relates the improbable rise of little-known, radical seer Laish Tenedos to the rule of the empire of Numantia.
2. *Demon King, The* **(Warner, 1998)** After 10 years of Tenedos's rule, Numantia is still not at peace, the wizard-king is amassing an army for war, and Damastes has uncovered some dark secrets about Tenedos, the man whom he has sworn to serve.
3. *Warrior King, The* **(Warner, 1999)** Ex-tribune Damastes escapes from prison and resumes the war against Tenedos, the leader whom he has betrayed.

III. The Last Legion quartet, more military SF, is about a group of legionnaires far out in the Cumbre System who are the last line of defense for the decaying Human Confederation, which controls a thousand star systems. Plenty of rousing battle action.

1. *Last Legion, The* **(Roc, 1999)** Legionnaires far out in the Cumbre System, faced with what seems to be the end of the galaxy-ranging Human Confederation, are on their own when a revolution breaks out.
2. *Firemask* **(Roc, 2000)** Evil aliens are trying to take over the Cumbre System and "the entire universe," and it is up to the Last Legion to stop them.
3. *Storm Force* **(Roc, 2000)** To infiltrate the highest levels of government in the Larix and Kura System, Legion intelligence officer Njangu Yoshitaro poses as a spy.
4. *Homefall* **(Roc, 2001)** The Last Legion embarks on a dangerous mission to find out what happened to the Human Confederation.

IV. Star Risk Ltd. is a rather roguish and heterogeneous crew of mercenaries, with some ex–Space Marines among them, who get involved in a series of far-future adventures that sometimes put them outside of the law. Former Space Marine Major M'chel Ross is the leading character in this rather lighthearted and lightweight four-volume series.

1. *Star Risk, Ltd.* **(Roc, 2002)** M'chel Riss, space marine major, hopes to recoup her fortunes with mercenary outfit Star Risk Ltd., whose first task is to spring a soldier from a maximum-security prison.
2. *Scoundrel Worlds, The* **(Roc, 2003)** The Star Risk members protect the referees at an interplanetary skyball festival, then take on the job of proving the innocence of a man condemned for treason.
3. *Double-Cross Program, The* **(Roc, 2004)** The Star Risk team stages a bank robbery that involves putting the money back, then gets caught up in a war over an addictive new consumer product.
4. *Dog from Hell, The* **(Roc, 2005)** While escorting a group of rambunctious girls from a posh finishing school to a luxury world, Star Risk runs into giant security firm Cerebus Systems, which is out to put an end to the Star Risk operation.

V. The Dragonmaster series follows the adolescent and subsequent adventures of Hal Kailas, dragonmaster and war hero. Dragons, who are piloted by Hal and his comrades in the Derain army, play a major role in this fantasy series, which should remind readers of Anne McCaffrey's (q.v.) Dragonriders series.

1. *Storm of Wings* **(Trafalgar, 2002)** Hal Kailas grows from a 13-year-old village lad into a battle-savvy Dragonmaster after he is drafted into the Derain army cavalry to fight the Roche.
2. *Knighthood of the Dragon* **(Trafalgar, 2003)** More war scenes as dragonmaster Lord Hal Kailas leads his dragon cavalry in a bunch of clashes, such as the Battle of the Isonzo.
3. *Last Battle, The* **(Premier, 2004)** In the conclusion to the trilogy, Hal finds himself in the ultimate battle with his old enemies, with, of course, the future of the world riding on the outcome.

Burdett, John

Royal Thai police detective Sonchai Jitpleecheep is the protagonist of three detective novels set in Thailand. Jitpleecheep, son of a Thai woman and an unknown American father, is a fatalistic Buddhist with a violent past and a wry sense of humor. These noir mixtures of detective work, Bangkok street life, the Thai sex trade, drug smuggling, and political intrigue have added a series detective from a precinct previously unheard from. Britisher John Burdett practiced as a lawyer in Hong Kong before he returned to his first love, writing. He is also the author of *A Personal History of Thirst* (Morrow, 1996) and *The Last Six Million Seconds* (Morrow, 1997).

1. *Bangkok 8* **(Knopf, 2003)** Royal Thai police detective Sonchai Jitpleecheep investigates the snakebite deaths of his partner, Pichai Apiradee, and US Embassy Sergeant William Bradley. Keeping in touch with Pichai's ghost, and uneasily partnered with American FBI agent Kimberley Jones, Sonchai weaves his way through some sordid Bangkok venues.
2. *Bangkok Tattoo* **(Knopf, 2005)** Beautiful bar girl Chanya, with whom Sonchai believes himself to be in love, is the prime suspect in the murder, mutilation, and disembowelment of CIA agent Mitch Turner.
3. *Bangkok Haunts* **(Knopf, 2007)** Jitpleecheep shows American FBI agent Kimberley Jones a snuff film he's received showing the murder of Damrong, an ex-lover of his.

Burgess, Anthony

PSEUDONYM OF John Burgess Wilson

I. Anthony Burgess is probably best known for the Kubrick film version (which Burgess professed to hate) of *A Clockwork Orange*, but he wrote many other novels, including *Nothing Like the Sun* (about Shakespeare), literary criticism, musical compositions, and two volumes of autobiography: *Little Wilson and Big God* (Weidenfeld, 1987) and *You've Had Your Time* (Grove, 1991).

The Malayan trilogy seems to have been published in the United States only as an omnibus volume entitled *The Long Day Wanes* (Norton, 1964). The series depicts the "long day" of waning British rule as seen through the eyes of Victor Crabbe, a young English teacher who enjoys the colorful polyglot country and its relaxed lifestyle. Unperturbed by the corruption of both town and school officials, Crabbe cares deeply for the young Malayans he teaches, and he sympathizes with their desire to oust the British.

1. *Time for a Tiger* (Heineman, London, 1956) Victor Crabbe teaches history in an English school in Malaya. His wife, Fenella, dislikes the dangerous and primitive country.
2. *Enemy in the Blanket* (Heineman, London, 1958) As headmaster at the Haji Ali College, Victor runs into trouble caused by Robert Hardman, a figure from the past.
3. *Beds in the East* (Heineman, London, 1959) Now chief education officer and alone—his wife went back to England—Victor tries to help a promising young Chinese composer.

II. Another series by the prolific Burgess concerns the quirky bard F. X. Enderby, who writes all his best poetry in the bathroom. Bawdy and hilarious, these books are quite different from the Malayan trilogy. Eventually Enderby evolves into a sort of mouthpiece for Burgess. *Enderby* (Norton, 1968), containing numbers 1 and 2, first introduced the poet to American readers.

1. *Inside Mr. Enderby* (McGraw-Hill, 1984) Enderby meets and marries the glamorous Vesta Bainbridge and takes a honeymoon trip to Rome. First published under the pseudonym Joseph Kell in the United Kingdom in 1963.
2. *Enderby Outside* (McGraw-Hill, 1984) Having lost Vesta, Enderby renounces poetry and tries out an alter ego (Hogg the bartender), but his muse reclaims him in Tangiers. First published in the United Kingdom in 1968.
3. *Clockwork Testament, The; or, Enderby's End* (Knopf, 1974) Now famous and living in New York, Enderby teaches and appears on TV talk shows, valiant to his sudden end.
4. *Enderby's Dark Lady; or, No End to Enderby* (McGraw-Hill, 1984) Burgess revives Enderby and takes him to Indiana to work on the script of a musical life of Shakespeare.

Burke, Alafair

Samantha "Sam" Kincaid is a thirtyish deputy DA working in the Drug and Vice Division in Portland, Oregon. Sam is assertive but likable, with a wry sense of humor. Kincaid's off-again, on-again relationship with Detective Chuck Forbes eventually leads to him moving in with her. The daughter of James Lee Burke (q.v.), Alafair Burke is a former Portland DA, and her procedural details have an authentic ring.

1. *Judgment Calls* (Holt, 2003) Sam Kincaid is determined to bring to justice the thugs who raped and beat 13-year-old drug addict and prostitute Kendra Martin.
2. *Missing Justice* (Holt, 2004) A poor black man, Melvin Jackson, is the prime suspect in the murder of Portland judge Clarissa Easterbrook.
3. *Close Case* (Holt, 2005) Sam and lover Chuck Forbes investigate the murder of an investigative reporter and liaison to the Portland minority community who's found beaten to death after a protest over a police shooting with racial overtones.

Burke, James Lee

I. Dave Robicheaux, Cajun detective, has an off-again, on-again relationship with law enforcement. What remain constant in Dave's life are his love of fishing and his personal demons: the struggle between his hedonism and his obsessive code of personal honor. As the series progresses, we see Dave change jobs frequently, lose one wife, acquire another, and adopt a Nicaraguan orphan. The atmospheric Louisiana settings and the pervasive air of melancholy and corruption ("This is Louisiana, Dave. Guatemala North. Quit pretending it's the United States," states Dave's pal Clete Purcel) make this an engrossing series.

1. *Neon Rain, The* (Holt, 1987) New Orleans homicide cop Robicheaux encounters a body while fishing in a back-country bayou.
2. *Heaven's Prisoners* (Holt, 1988) Dave and his wife, Annie, are fishing in the Gulf when a plane full of Nicaraguan refugees crashes nearby, leaving six-year-old Alafair as the only survivor. Made into a film starring Alec Baldwin (1996).
3. *Black Cherry Blues* (Little, Brown, 1989) Running his fishing business, coming to terms with Annie's violent death, and raising Alafair, Dave tries to help an old friend and gets framed for murder.
4. *Morning for Flamingos, A* (Little, Brown, 1990) Robicheaux stalks an escaped killer on the streets and in the cafés of New Orleans.
5. *Stained White Radiance, A* (Hyperion, 1992) Dave's reacquaintance with old friends in New Iberia involves him with old speculators, an old girlfriend, and the Aryan Brotherhood.
6. *In the Electric Mist with the Confederate Dead* (Hyperion, 1993) Now a deputy sheriff in New Iberia, Dave tangles with a movie crew, mutilation murders, his own memories of a lynching, and the ghosts of a troop of Confederate soldiers.
7. *Dixie City Jam* (Hyperion, 1994) Dave's partner in his bait-shop business is arrested for murder, and Dave agrees to raise bail money by investigating a German U-boat sunk off New Iberia in 1942.
8. *Burning Angel* (Hyperion, 1995) Old Bertha Fontenot asks Robicheaux for help in fending off the bulldozers from her home, and former soldier of fortune Sonny Boy Marsallus confides his journal to him.
9. *Cadillac Jukebox* (Hyperion, 1996) Louisiana redneck Aaron Crown is convicted of the murder of a prominent black civil rights leader 30 years after the crime. He tells New Iberia sheriff's deputy Dave Robicheaux that he didn't do it.
10. *Sunset Limited* (Doubleday, 1998) World-famous photojournalist Megan Flynn returns to New Iberia to seek out Dave Robicheaux, who found the crucified body of her father, union organizer Jack Flynn, 40 years earlier.
11. *Purple Cane Road* (Doubleday, 2000) Dave Robicheaux's mother vanished many years ago. Now a pimp may have shed new light on her disappearance. The trail leads to a plethora of Louisiana grotesques, including the governor, the state executioner, a man on death row, a psychopathic hit man, and corrupt police.
12. *Jolie Blon's Bounce* (Simon & Schuster, 2002) Two murders, one of a teenage girl, the other of a drug-addicted prostitute, put Dave

into close touch with "the usual suspects": past oppressor Legion Guidry, the prostitute's Mafioso father, a drugged-out musical genius, and a rather sinister Bible salesman, among others.

13. *Last Car to Elysian Fields* (Simon & Schuster, 2003) Irish hit man Max Coll is stalking Dave's friend Father Jimmie Dolan. Three teens die in a car crash in New Orleans. Clete Purcel, Dave's sidekick, and lady cop Clotile Arceneaux have roles to play, also.

14. *Crusader's Cross* (Simon & Schuster, 2005) Unemployed, his wife dead, his daughter in college, Dave rejoins the New Iberia sheriff's department at the urging of Sheriff Jelen Soileau and is almost immediately up to his neck in gruesome slayings.

15. *Pegasus Descending* (Simon & Schuster, 2006) Grifter Trish Klein, who may be the daughter of Dave's late friend Dallas Klein, executed by thugs 25 years earlier, appears in New Iberia and attracts the attention of Whitey Bruxal, the mobster responsible for Dallas's death.

16. *Tin Roof Blowdown, The* (Simon & Schuster, 2007) In the aftermath of Hurricane Katrina, Robicheaux's department is assigned to investigate the shooting of two looters who were foolish enough to ransack the home of New Orleans's most powerful mobster.

II. Though the dusty town of Deaf Smith, Texas, provides a stark contrast to humid Louisiana, Burke's new series character, lawyer and former Texas Ranger Billy Bob Holland, could, in many respects, be Dave Robicheaux's twin: he is dead-honest, kind to children and the underdog, tormented by memories (Vietnam, the accidental shooting of his Ranger partner), enamored of the territory he works in, and pitted against rich and powerful villains. Later novels in the series find Billy Bob in Montana.

1. *Cimarron Rose* (Hyperion, 1997) When 16-year-old Lucas Smothers (who is really Billy Bob's biological son) is arrested for the murder of his girlfriend, Billy Bob is hired by Vernon, the boy's putative father, to defend him.

2. *Heartwood* (Doubleday, 1999) Rich and sinister Earl Deitrich, who married Billy Bob's high school sweetheart, blackmails a couple into ceding him an oil-rich Wyoming property, arranges a false arrest of a business victim, and forms an alliance for arson and murder with a San Antonio Chicano gang.

3. *Bitterroot* (Simon & Schuster, 2001) Billy Bob travels to Montana's Bitterroot Valley to do some fishing with old friend Doe Voss. Then Doe's teenage daughter is raped, and the suspects range from bikers to white supremacists to religious cultists to Native Americans to strip miners.

4. *In the Moon of Red Ponies* (Simon & Schuster, 2004) Billy Bob moves his family and practice to Missoula, Montana. Psychopathic ex-biker and rodeo clown Wyatt Dixon is just out of prison on a technicality and claiming to be a born-again Christian.

Burke, Jan

Irene Kelly, crack crime reporter for the Las Piernas (Southern California) *Express* and her lover and eventual husband, detective Frank Harmon, endure abduction and assault in a series of cases involving past crimes, homicidal maniacs, satanic cults, and corrupt cops. Irene and Frank are tough enough (and smart enough) to handle everything thrown at them in this action-packed, suspenseful, humorous, and entertaining series. *Nine* (Simon & Schuster, 2002) is not part of this series. *18* (A.S.A.P., 2002) is a collection of short stories, one each involving Irene and Frank.

1. *Goodnight, Irene* (Simon & Schuster, 1993) Irene Kelly, ex–crime reporter working in public relations, is shocked when her friend O'Connor is killed by a package bomb.

2. *Sweet Dreams, Irene* (Simon & Schuster, 1994) Back in newspaper journalism, Irene investigates a mudslinging local election and a satanic cult.

3. *Dear Irene* (Simon & Schuster, 1995) Irene receives a letter addressing her as Cassandra from someone named Thanatos (Death), who promises that "Clio will be the first to die."

4. *Remember Me, Irene* (Simon & Schuster, 1996) Newly married to detective Frank Harmon, Irene has a chance encounter with her college statistics instructor that eventually leads to suicide, blackmail, and some murky local history.

5. *Hocus* (Simon & Schuster, 1997) Bret Neukirk and Samuel Ryan, victims of kidnapping and witnesses of their father's murders 12 years ago, abduct Frank to force Irene to seek out the accomplice to these past crimes.

6. *Liar* (Simon & Schuster, 1998) An old homicide is brought to light when Irene's estranged aunt Briana dies under suspicious circumstances two weeks after the death of her husband, Arthur, and leaves their estate to Irene.

7. *Bones* (Simon & Schuster, 1999) Serial killer Nicholas Parrish sets off a bomb at the site of his victims' graves and escapes from his captors. Irene's interest in the case is partially fueled by Parrish's growing obsession with her.

8. *Flight* (Simon & Schuster, 2001) Irene's husband, Frank, takes center stage when the body of police detective Philip Lefebvre is found 10 years after his suspicious disappearance.

9. *Bloodlines* (Simon & Schuster, 2005) Old cases are resurrected and secondary characters from previous books reappear as Irene covers the ground breaking of a shopping center and the unearthing of a buried car containing human remains.

10. *Kidnapped* (Simon & Schuster, 2006) The adopted son of graphic artist Richard Fletcher has been wrongfully convicted for the murder of his father.

Burley, W(illiam) J(ohn)

I. Detective Chief Superintendent Charles Wycliffe of Scotland Yard is the hero of this long-running procedural series featuring excellent puzzle plots, a likable central character, a varied cast of intriguing secondary characters, and atmospheric settings, many of them in rural Cornwall. W. J. Burley had careers as a gas engineer and as a biology teacher in Cornwall before he became a full-time writer at the age of 60. Wycliffe has been the subject of a British television series starring Jack Shepard, at least one episode of which has been released as a Canadian video: *Wycliffe: Dance of the Scorpions* (BFS, 1999).

1. *Three-Toed Pussy* (Gollancz, London, 1968) The body of a young woman lacking two toes is found in a remote Cornish village. Not published in the United States. Variant title: *Wycliffe and the Three-Toed Pussy.*

2. *To Kill a Cat* (Walker, 1970) Wycliffe has a busman's holiday on the coast as he helps local police investigate the death of a young woman. Variant title: *Wyclife and How to Kill a Cat.*

3. *Guilt Edged* (Walker, 1972) When the body of a prominent businessman's wife is found in the river, her MP brother wants the matter handled quickly and quietly.

4. *Death in a Salubrious Place* (Walker, 1973) The year-round island residents suspect a recently arrived rock singer in the death of a young woman.

5. *Death in Stanley Street* (Walker, 1974) The death of an intelligent, educated, expensive prostitute seems to have been carefully planned. Variant title: *Wycliffe and Death on Stanley Street*.

6. *Wycliffe and the Pea-Green Boat* (Walker, 1975) Two members of the Tremaine family are charged with murders 20 years apart.

7. *Wycliffe and the Schoolgirls* (Walker, 1976) A nightclub singer and a nurse, who were acquainted as schoolgirls years before, are attacked in the same week.

8. *Wycliffe and the Scapegoat* (Doubleday, 1979) When unpopular Jonathan Riddle disappears, the townsfolk speculate that he has taken the place of the Halloween scapegoat.

9. *Wycliffe in Paul's Court* (Doubleday, 1980) The cozy London neighborhood of Paul's Court is shaken when a teenager and an elderly man are killed.

10. *Wycliffe's Wild Goose Chase* (Doubleday, 1982) The recovery of a stolen gun leads to the fatal shooting of the gun dealer who appraised it for its owner.

11. *Wycliffe and the Beales* (Doubleday, 1984) Nobody can understand why Bunny Newcombe, the village odd-job man, has been murdered.

12. *Wycliffe and the Four Jacks* (Doubleday, 1986) The death of a bar girl may be connected with the mail receipt of four Jacks, each marked with a date.

13. *Wycliffe and the Quiet Virgin* (Doubleday, 1986) Francine Lemarque vanishes after appearing as the Virgin Mary in her Cornwall parish play.

14. *Wycliffe and the Winsor Blue* (Doubleday, 1987) Falmouth, on the Cornish coast, is the setting for this tale of valuable paintings, greedy heirs, and murder.

15. *Wycliffe and the Tangled Web* (Doubleday, 1989) An unwed, pregnant teenager disappears from a Cornish coastal town.

16. *Wycliffe and the Cycle of Death* (Doubleday, 1991) The strangulation murder of a well-to-do bookseller uncovers some seedy family secrets.

17. *Wycliffe and the Dead Flautist* (St. Martin's, 1992) After amateur flautist Tony Miller is killed by a shotgun blast, the killer clumsily attempts to make it look like suicide.

18. *Wycliffe and the Last Rites* (St. Martin's, 1993) Jessica Dobell, promiscuous cleaning lady, is found dead in a church in the Cornish town of Moresk.

19. *Wycliffe and the Dunes Mystery* (St. Martin's, 1994) Unpleasant memories are stirred up in the town of St. Ives when the body of a person 15 years dead is uncovered by a coastal storm.

20. *Wycliffe and the House of Fear* (St. Martin's, 1995) Wycliffe becomes interested in the 500-year-old estate of Kellycoryk and in the Kemps, its dysfunctional family.

21. *Wycliffe and the Redhead* (St. Martin's, 1998) Redheaded Morwenna Barker, last known to be working for a Falmouth bookseller, has disappeared and is possibly a murder victim.

22. *Wycliffe and the Guild of Nine* (Gollancz, London, 2000) A murder occurs at the Guild of Nine, an artist's colony run on astrological principles, on a moor west of St. Ives.

II. Burley's first series character, Dr. Henry Pym, an amateur detective, appeared in two mysteries.

1. *Taste of Power, A* (Gollancz [UK], 1966) The teachers of Huntley-May grammar school are disturbed by a series of poison-pen letters that reveal some knowledge of school affairs.

2. *Death in Willow Pattern* (Walker, 1970) Another poison-pen letter case, in which Sir Francis Leigh is accused of the abduction and murder of two missing local girls.

Burns, Olive Ann

Cold Sassy Tree was written by Olive Ann Burns after she was diagnosed with cancer. Writing the novel took more than eight years, but she was rewarded by its popular reception when it was published. Based on Burns's own family history, *Cold Sassy Tree* relates events in the town of Cold Sassy, Georgia, in the early 1900s, as seen through the eyes of 14-year-old Will Tweedy. Before she succumbed to her lymphoma, Burns managed to complete 14 chapters of a sequel, leaving part of a 15th chapter and notes on how she planned to further develop the novel. A television movie starring Richard Widmark and Faye Dunaway (TNT, 1990) was based on *Cold Sassy Tree*.

1. *Cold Sassy Tree* (Ticknor, 1984) After his wife's sudden death, Will Tweedy's eccentric grandfather, E. Rucker Blakeslee, elopes with the much younger town milliner to the horror of the folks of Cold Sassy.

2. *Leaving Cold Sassy* (Ticknor, 1992) Twenty-five-year-old Will Tweedy, too skinny to fight in the World War, nervously woos schoolteacher Sanna Klein. Left unfinished at the author's death.

Burns, Rex (Sehler)

PSEUDONYM OF Raoul Stephen Sehler

I. Denver-based Gabriel "Gabe" Wager is a police detective of Hispanic descent who sometimes analyzes himself as much as the cases he is called upon to solve, in this excellent procedural series. Gabe's knowledge of Spanish sometimes comes in handy on the mean streets of Denver, although he is ambivalent about his Latino heritage.

1. *Alvarez Journal, The* (Harper, 1975) Gabe thinks that heroin is the main import of a shop called Rare Things, run by boyhood acquaintance Rafael Alvarez.

2. *Farnsworth Score, The* (Harper, 1977) Gabe's cover as Mr. Taco, a drug dealer from west Texas, is blown by a corrupt cop at headquarters.

3. *Speak for the Dead* (Harper, 1978) In his case for homicide after his transfer from narcotics, Wager investigates the case of a severed head artfully arranged in the Botanic Gardens.

4. *Angle of Attack* (Harper, 1979) A gang slaying causes a ripple effect in the Denver slums.

5. *Avenging Angel, The* (Viking, 1983) The photocopied drawing of an avenging angel found in the hand of a homicide victim leads Gabe into a Mormon-Gentile feud.

6. *Strip Search* (Viking, 1984) Someone is killing nude dancers from Denver's Colfax strip for no ostensible reason.

7. *Ground Money* (Viking, 1986) Ex-rodeo star Tommy Sanchez asks Wager to check up on his sons, who may be keeping bad company.

8. *Killing Zone, The* (Viking, 1988) Green, much-loved black furniture dealer and city councilman, is found shot to death in a vacant lot.

9. *Endangered Species* (Viking, 1993) A burglar named Stovepipe asks Gabe to cosign the mortgage on the house he wants to buy for his mother.

10. *Blood Line* (Walker, 1995) Wager is asked by his aunt Louisa to talk to his teenage cousin Julio, who is running with a gang.

11. *Leaning Land, The* (Walker, 1997) A series of homicides in west central Colorado brings Gabe out to this land of desert, scrub, scattered ranches, and Indian reservations.

II. A second series of Denver procedurals features Devlin Kirk, industrial security analyst.

1. *Parts Unknown* (Viking, 1990) Three vanished illegal aliens from El Salvador have been linked to landlady Señora Chiquichano and a sinister local doctor.
2. *Body Guard* (Viking, 1991) Suspected drug dealing, guarding wealthy Roland Humphries, and some suspicious insurance claims involve Kirk here.

Burroughs, Edgar Rice

I. Tarzan the Ape Man (aka John Clayton; aka Lord Greystoke; aka Lord of the Jungle) has been a phenomenon since the first book in the series was published, in 1914. More than 40 film versions, TV series, radio series, comic books, comic strips, graphic novels, and aggressive marketing (especially after Burroughs incorporated himself in Tarzana, California) made Tarzan one of the greatest cultural icons of the 20th century and beyond. The story of a boy raised by "Giant Apes" (a species unknown to conventional biology) taps into a long history of tales about humans raised by wild animals going as far back as, and probably farther back than, the Romulus and Remus legend of Rome's founding. Though there has always been a temptation on the part of critics and librarians (including the authors of *Sequels*) to relegate the Ape Man to juvenile or young adult status, the Tarzan legend has a hold on many adults as well.

Burroughs wrote 25 Tarzan books, including a couple of posthumous publications and a novel begun by Burroughs and completed by Joe R. Lansdale nearly 50 years later, and not including two Tarzan books for children written by Burroughs: *The Tarzan Twins* (Volland, 1927) and *Tarzan and the Tarzan Twins* (Whitman, 1936). Most of the later books are potboilers, albeit exciting ones, taking Tarzan to various lost cities and lost enclaves populated by "white" races. Reflecting the racism of his generation, Burroughs's black Africans are a primitive bunch, at best throwing themselves on the protection of the "Lord of the Jungle"; at worst murdering and eating whites and each other. Tarzan usually relies on his animal companions, such as the panther Sheeba, the lion Jad-Bal-Ja, and the chimp Nkima, when he needs assistance. Along the way Tarzan acquires a "mate," Jane, and a son, Korak, and occasionally makes excursions outside of Africa, but his heart remains in the jungle. Needless to say, Tarzan's Africa is more fantasy than reality and could be set in any exotic terrestrial or extraterrestrial lands, as were Burroughs's other series (see below).

Ace Books and Ballantine engaged in a publishing and copyright war when they reissued the Tarzan series in the 1960s. Many Burroughs novels are available online in Project Gutenberg. Tarzan appeared in a film as far back as 1918, a silent opus starring Elmo Lincoln. Many films followed with various actors playing the Ape Man, but most older fans regard Johnny Weissmuller as the definitive Tarzan. More recently *Greystoke: The Legend of Tarzan, Lord of the Apes* (1984) and an animated Disney version have appeared.

Many books have been written about Edgar Rice Burroughs and the Tarzan phenomenon. Philip José Farmer (q.v.) has written the "Definitive Biography of Lord Greystoke," *Tarzan Alive* (Doubleday, 1972), and John Taliaferro has written a good, more recent biography of Burroughs: *Tarzan Forever: The Life of Edgar Rice Burroughs, Creator of Tarzan* (Scribner, 1999).

1. *Tarzan of the Apes* (McClurg, 1914) A baby raised by an ape foster mother grows up in the African jungle and eventually realizes his human heritage as English nobleman Lord Greystoke.
2. *Jungle Tales of Tarzan* (McClurg, 1919) A collection of linked short stories about different aspects of Tarzan's youth among the apes. Variant title: *Tarzan's Jungle Tales.*

3. *Return of Tarzan, The* (McClurg, 1915) Lord Greystoke, disenchanted with the world of "civilized" men, returns to Africa as Tarzan, and a "lost" city is discovered deep in the jungle.
4. *Beasts of Tarzan, The* (McClurg, 1917) Tarzan, his wife and son kidnapped, is abandoned on an isolated island with only his faithful panther companion, Sheeba, to help him.
5. *Son of Tarzan, The* (McClurg, 1917) After being kidnapped by his father's enemy, Korak, the son of Tarzan, escapes and, together with an ape named Akut, learns jungle survival skills.
6. *Tarzan and the Jewels of Opar* (McClurg, 1918) In one of several tales about the lost city of Opar, Tarzan, suffering from amnesia, falls into a trap set there.
7. *Tarzan the Untamed* (McClurg, 1920) Believing Jane to be slain, Tarzan tracks his wife's "murderers" to a hidden valley populated by black lions, proto-Nazis, and other sinister types.
8. *Tarzan the Terrible* (McClurg, 1921) In the sequel to number 7, Tarzan's trail of vengeance leads him into the middle of a tribal war fought in a region where dinosaurs still roam.
9. *Tarzan and the Golden Lion* (McClurg, 1923) A drugged Tarzan falls into the hands of the priests of Opar, remnants of the lost civilization of ancient Atlantis, and wins the love of La, high priestess of the Flaming God.
10. *Tarzan and the Ant Men* (McClurg, 1924) Tarzan stumbles into a land of Stone Age savages and Minunians, knee-high warriors who use African deer as their mounts.
11. *Tarzan, Lord of the Jungle* (McClurg, 1928) Tarzan gets mixed up with a group of knights, descendants of Crusaders, in an enormous isolated valley.
12. *Tarzan and the Lost Empire* (Metropolitan, 1929) Tarzan encounters a lost remnant of the Roman Empire in darkest Africa.
13. *Tarzan at the Earth's Core (1)* (Metropolitan, 1930) Tarzan enters Pellucidar, the Stone Age world at the Earth's core (see series III, below) via a dirigible ride into Symmes' Hole at the North Pole.
14. *Tarzan the Invincible* (Burroughs, 1931) La, high priestess of the Flaming God of Opar, has fallen into the hands of an Arab slave trader.
15. *Tarzan Triumphant* (Burroughs, 1932) High in the Ghezi Mountains, Tarzan comes to grips with the degenerate descendants of early Christian refugees from Rome.
16. *Tarzan and the City of Gold* (Burroughs, 1933) After rescuing a strange white man from black savages, Tarzan discovers two ancient cities—Athne, City of Ivory, and Cathne, City of Gold—and a nasty bunch of trained lions.
17. *Tarzan and the Lion-Men* (Burroughs, 1934) Tarzan rescues a crew of moviemakers attacked by the Bansuto tribe and encounters a valley of diamonds and his double, leading-man Stanley Obroski.
18. *Tarzan and the Leopard Men* (Burroughs, 1935) The steel-clawed Leopard Men are looking for victims for their obscene rites.
19. *Tarzan's Quest* (Burroughs, 1936) Tarzan follows the trail of a group of plane-crash survivors who wander into the path of a mysterious tribe of pale-skinned savages.
20. *Tarzan and the Forbidden City* (Burroughs, 1938) Tarzan is talked into leading an ill-advised expedition of adventurers into the heart of the jungle.
21. *Tarzan the Magnificent* (Burroughs, 1939) A giant diamond, some more lost cities, and two tribes of warrior women engage Tarzan.
22. *Tarzan and the Foreign Legion* (Burroughs, 1947) Tarzan, as Colonel John Clayton, gets involved in World War II against the Japanese when an American bomber crashes in Sumatra.
23. *Tarzan and the Madman* (Canaveral, 1964) Posthumously published. A madman masquerading as Tarzan kidnaps the daughter of an English millionaire and blackens Tarzan's name.

24. *Tarzan and the Castaways* (**Canaveral, 1964**) Three posthumously published novellas: "Tarzan and the Castaways," "Tarzan and the Champion," and "Tarzan and the Jungle Murders."

25. *Tarzan: The Last Adventure* (**Dark Horse, 1995**) A manuscript begun by Burroughs and left in a vault in 1950 was completed by Joe R. Lansdale and published as a graphic novel by Dark Horse in 1995. Tarzan and his animal pals defend a party of American archaeologists in search of the lost city of Ur. Published in a "traditional print" version by Ballantine in 1997.

II. The John Carter of Mars, or Barsoom, series, always a distant second in popularity and impact to the Tarzan series, still has its readers. Probably the comic book versions of the 1960s and 1970s had more to do with its continuing attraction to readers than any other form, although a movie version of "John Carter" is planned. Although it is usually assigned to the science-fiction genre, the series has many sword-and-sorcery fantasy elements in it, and although Barsoom has scientists, there is little hard science in evidence. John Carter, the usual protagonist, is a Virginia Civil War veteran who is somehow teleported from a cave in Arizona to the planet Mars, called Barsoom by its inhabitants, where decadent city-states with humanoid inhabitants feud with each other and with giant green four-armed warriors (it was Burroughs who popularized the idea of "green" Martians) in an arid landscape. There is nothing really new in this series, which incorporates most of its ideas from previous fiction, but Burroughs puts these ideas together in an exciting blend of near-nonstop action with a touch of romance in the form of John Carter's almost human love (she lays eggs), the beautiful red-skinned Dejah Thoris. Omnibus volumes include *Under the Moons of Mars* (Nebraska, 2003; contains numbers 1, 2, and 3) and *Three Martian Novels* (Dover, 1962; contains numbers 4, 5, and 6).

1. *Princess of Mars, A* (**McClurg, 1917**) Virginia gentleman John Carter, hiding in a cave in Arizona, accidentally discovers a portal, on the other side of which lies the planet Mars. Variant title: *Under the Moons of Mars.*

2. *Gods of Mars, The* (**McClurg, 1918**) John Carter returns to Mars after a long absence and finds that his beloved Dejah Thoris is missing, so he sets out on a series of adventures with Tars Tarkas, his green sidekick, that includes a sojourn in a valley of the dead and a climactic air battle between the many races of Mars.

3. *Warlord of Mars, The* (**McClurg, 1919**) Dejah Thoris is trapped inside the Temple of the Sun for an entire Martian year (twice as long as a terrestrial year).

4. *Thuvia, Maid of Mars* (**McClurg, 1920**) Cathoris, John Carter's half-human, half-Martian son, is accused of abducting the princess of Ptarth, but the sinister Prince Astok of Dusar is really responsible.

5. *Chessmen of Mars, The* (**McClurg, 1922**) Tara, daughter of the warlord of Mars, is blown off course by a freak storm that puts her right in the middle of a deadly game run by the Chessmen.

6. *Master Mind of Mars, The* (**McClurg, 1928**) A new hero, the American Ulysses Paxton, becomes the chief assistant to the greatest "scientist" on Mars. Ras Thavas falls in love with Valla Dia, whose mind has been transplanted to the ancient body of Xara.

7. *Fighting Man of Mars, A* (**Metropolitan, 1931**) Tan Hondron, from the realm of Gatho, encounters the usual suspects: green men, mad scientists, cannibals, spiders, and white apes among them.

8. *Swords of Mars* (**Burroughs, 1936**) John Carter, vowing to put an end to the Assassins Guild, travels to Thuria, the moon nearer to Mars.

9. *Synthetic Men of Mars* (**Burroughs, 1940**) Ras Thavas, Barsoom's greatest "scientist," is the prisoner of a nightmare army of his own creation.

10. *Llana of Gathol* (**Burroughs, 1948**) Four novellas in which parodic elements come to the fore: "The Ancient Dead" (originally "The City of Mummies"); "The Black Pirates of Barsoom"; "Escape on Mars"; and "Invisible Men of Mars."

11. *John Carter of Mars* (**Canaveral, 1964**) Two novellas: "John Carter and the Giant of Mars" and the unfinished "Skeleton Men of Mars," in which John Carter travels to Jupiter.

III. The idea of inhabited lands beneath the Earth's surface goes at least as far back as the Gilgamesh of Sumerian times. In most older versions, the land belowground was the home of the dead, but later versions, including Ludvig Holberg's *Nils Klim's Journey under the Ground* (originally 1741) and Jules Verne's (q.v.) *Journey to the Center of the Earth* (1864) postulated other goings-on under our feet. In the 19th century, Captain John Symmes petitioned Congress for support of an expedition to find the entrance to this underground world. Just when geologists had pretty much ended serious speculation about an Earth's core containing something besides magma and molten metals, Edgar Rice Burroughs published his first Pellucidar novel about a Stone Age world in which humans were tyrannized over by the Mahars, a race of intelligent but malevolent reptiles who regarded them as good for nothing except being beasts of burden or providing the occasional snack. Americans David Innes and Abner Perry, looking for rich mineral deposits, drive their Iron Mole 500 miles below the Earth's surface, discover this world, and remain to found an empire and introduce its benighted inhabitants to some of the dubious benefits of 20th-century technology. David Innes is the leading protagonist of some of the following six volumes in the series, but Tarzan gets his innings in number 4, and other characters, such as the warrior Tanar and Wilhelm von Horst, step to the fore. Omnibus volume: *The Pellucidar Novels* (Dover, 1963) contains numbers 1, 2, and 3.

1. *At the Earth's Core* (**McClurg, 1922**) Americans David Innes and Abner Perry, journeying 500 miles below the Earth's surface in their Iron Mole, discover a race of Stone Age humans tyrannized over by the intelligent but nasty reptilian Mahars. Reprinted by the University of Nebraska in 2000.

2. *Pellucidar* (**McClurg, 1923**) David Innes, trying to turn the world of Pellucidar into his own empire, is sidetracked by the kidnapping of his "empress," the cavewoman Dina the Beautiful. Reprinted by the University of Nebraska Press in 2002.

3. *Tanar of Pellucidar* (**Metropolitan, 1930**) The Mahars have been overthrown, but a new menace, in the form of the Korsar Pirates, appears. Tanar of Sari, one of Innes's best warriors, is captured and subjected to some nasty interrogation.

4. *Tarzan at the Earth's Core (2)* (**Metropolitan, 1930**) Tarzan of the Apes (see series I) takes center stage as he journeys, via dirigible, through Symmes Hole in the North Pole, to Pellucidar.

5. *Back to the Stone Age* (**Burroughs, 1937**) Wilhelm von Horst is separated from Muviro and his Wazuri warriors and undergoes his own series of adventures, including almost winding up as food for young marsupial reptiles.

6. *Land of Terror* (**Burroughs, 1944**) Unique for the series in that it was never serialized. David Innes is the protagonist in a mishmash of adventures involving, among others, the warrior women of Oog, the land of the Jukans, the lovers Zor and Zeeto, a mastodon, and six-foot-long ants.

7. *Savage Pellucidar* (**Canaveral, 1963**) Contains four novellas: "The Return to Pellucidar," "Men of the Bronze Age," "Tiger Girl," and "Savage Pellucidar."

IV. Although fictional Mars has usually been portrayed as an arid land with possible remnants of advanced civilizations, Venus has usually been regarded as a hot, steaming, jungle home inhabited by backward life-forms. Space adventurer Carson Napier, stranded on mist-shrouded Venus, finds a race of near humans, lots of adventures, and the love of a beautiful woman. The Venus series, never as popular as the other ERB series, ran to just five volumes.

1. *Pirates of Venus* (Burroughs, 1934) Space adventurer Carson Napier, heading for Mars, makes a slight navigational error, crash-lands on Venus, discovers a sort of civilization, becomes a pirate, and wins the love of the beautiful Duare, princess of Vepaja.
2. *Lost on Venus* (Burroughs, 1935) Carson, like all ERB heroes sooner or later, is forced to go a mission to rescue his beautiful love, Princess Duare.
3. *Carson of Venus* (Burroughs, 1939) Carson and Duare think, wrongly, that they have found a refuge in the city of Sanara. But Sanara is being besieged by the Zani (read "Nazi").
4. *Escape on Venus* (Burroughs, 1946) More adventures as Carson and Duare continue their flight from Vepaja.
5. *Wizard of Venus, The* (Ace, 1970) The final adventure of Carson Napier. Published originally as part of *Tales of Three Planets* (Canaveral, 1964). Reissued by Ace in 1983 together with the previously unpublished nonseries ERB novel *Pirate Blood*.

Butcher, Jim

I. Harry Dresden, a freelance consultant operating out of Chicago, has the accoutrements of your average seedy private eye, with one difference: Harry is a wizard. Harry gets involved with the likes of other wizards, vampires, faeries, werewolves, demons and ghosts. Although he makes only a precarious living, Harry is always on the alert against the supernatural baddies who infest Chicago and threaten the lives of ordinary citizens in a series of entertaining "fantasy noir" thrillers with touches of dry humor. The series was adapted for television in 2007.

1. *Storm Front* (Roc, 2000) What starts out to be a simple missing persons case turns into a horrendous job, as Chicago-based, private eye and supernatural consultant Harry Dresden has to track down another wizard, one who is given to magically removing the hearts of his victims.
2. *Fool Moon* (Roc, 2001) A werewolf may be at the bottom of a series of mysterious, violent murders, but which one? Mac Finn, the werewolf environmentalist, one of a group of college students who voluntarily become werewolves by night, or an FBI agent turned werewolf vigilante?
3. *Grave Peril* (Roc, 2001) Obsessive and violent ghosts are on the loose in Chicago, and they, allied with vampires and demons, seem to be after Harry and his knight friend Michael.
4. *Summer Knight* (Roc, 2002) Harry, on the outs with his girlfriend, is approached by the Winter Queen of Faerie to investigate the murder of the Summer Knight, the Summer Queen's right-hand man.
5. *Death Masks* (Roc, 2003) Harry, beset by a challenge to a duel that he can't win by a vampire named Ortega and a group of demons who want his soul, is trying to nail the thieves of the Shroud of Turin.
6. *Blood Rites* (Roc, 2004) The Black Council of Vampires has Harry on its hit list, but vampire Thomas is on Harry's side. Now Thomas wants Harry to investigate the death, via entropy spells, of two of porno film director Arturo Genosa's assistants.

7. *Dead Beat* (Roc, 2005) Several evil wizards are competing for *The Word of Kemmler*, an ancient manuscript that promises to endow one of them with supreme power.
8. *Proven Guilty* (Roc, 2006) Harry takes on "phobophages," creatures that feed on fear, when they attack a horror film convention.
9. *White Night* (Roc, 2007) Harry's brother, Thomas, is a prime suspect in the killings of Chicago's minor wizards.
10. *Small Favor* (Roc, 2008) Harry endures encounters with a series of increasingly dangerous "Billy Goats Gruff."

II. Jim Butcher is also engaged in a epic fantasy series, titled Codex Alera, set in the land of Alera, reminiscent of the Roman Empire. Gaius Sextus, the First Lord of Alera, beset by border troubles, civil strife, and ambitious high lords, relies on his elite spy unit, the Cursors, and his nephew Tavi, who survives the usual troubled adolescence to become Gaius's page and a secret Cursor trainee. Good world building, interesting characters, and lots of action make this an entertaining series.

1. *Furies of Caldera* (Ace, 2004) Young female spy Amara and her companion Odiana go out to some distant provinces in the magical land of Alera to ferret out the motivations of military commander Atticus Quentin, and they encounter the troubled teenager Tavi.
2. *Academ's Fury* (Ace, 2005) Tavi, nephew of Gaius Sextus, First Lord of Alera, is now secretly in training for the Cursors, the First Lord's elite spies. Things aren't looking good, as Cursors are being murdered, an ancient menace known as the "vord" is heading for the capital, and civil war isn't far off.
3. *Cursor's Fury* (Ace, 2006) Tavi, now a full-fledged Cursor, is planted by his uncle, Gaius Sextus, in a new legion, where Tavi can gather information on the rebellious High Lord of Kalare.
4. *Captain's Fury* (Ace, 2007) Two years into a difficult campaign against the Canm invaders, Captain Tavi is saddled with an unqualified but politically powerful superior whose plans threaten disaster and force Tavi into potential treason.

Butler, Gwendoline (Williams)

I. The John Coffin procedurals are Butler's longest-running series, although the Charmian Daniels titles, written under Butler's pseudonym of Jennie Melville (q.v.), are better known. Butler's most highly regarded mystery title is the nonseries *Sarsen Place* (Coward McCann, 1974; UK title: *A Coffin for Pandora*). Inspector, later superintendent, then commander of the London Second City Police, John Coffin is a secondary character in the first three novels of the series in which Inspector/Superintendent William Winter is the protagonist. In the earlier novels, Coffin's work life takes precedence, but as the series progressed, the stolid but perceptive Coffin acquires a personal life, marrying actress Stella Pinero as his second wife. Some critics think that Gwendoline Butler is underrated, while others critics place her novels in the second rank. Readers will find them to be solid, somewhat grim, atmospheric procedurals. Books are listed by the date in which they were published, but it should be noted that numbers 4, 6, 15, and 16 are prequels catching Coffin at earlier points in his career.

1. *Dead in a Row* (Bles [UK], 1957) In the first novel in the series, Inspector William Winter is the main protagonist, and Coffin plays a secondary role. Not published in the United States.
2. *Dull Dead, The* (Walker, 1962) Five-year-old Minny Duveen knows what happened the day Jack O'Finney died but isn't telling, and it is up to Inspector Winter to find out the murderer's identity

before Minny becomes the next victim. Originally published in the United Kingdom in 1958.

3. *Murdering Kind, The* (Roy, 1964) No annotation available. Originally published in the United Kingdom in 1958.

4. *Dine and Be Dead* (Macmillan, 1960) First novel featuring John Coffin as the protagonist. Actually a prequel taking Coffin back to his first case in Oxford, involving a missing person and the stalking of scholar Marion Manning. UK and subsequent US title: *Death Lives Next Door*.

5. *Make Me a Murderer* (Bles [UK], 1961) No annotation available. Not published in the United States.

6. *Coffin in Oxford* (Bles [UK], 1962) Set in Oxford. Coffin investigates the death of a mysterious woman and the disappearance of the leading suspect and his landlady. Not published in the United States.

7. *Coffin for Baby* (Walker, 1963) The Bishop baby is kidnapped. Mrs. Cox is murdered. A mummified child is found in a suitcase.

8. *Coffin Waiting* (Walker, 1965) Roxanne Roland comes home to discover a group of dead women in her sitting room. Originally published in the United Kingdom in 1963.

9. *Coffin in Malta* (Walker, 1965) No annotation available.

10. *Nameless Coffin, A* (Walker, 1967) Handbag and coat slashings in London and Murreinhead, Scotland, escalate into murder. And then the body of a missing Murreinhead woman is found in a London tenement.

11. *Coffin Following* (Bles [UK], 1968) Aaron Tyler and his poker club apprehend and accidentally kill an intruder in his house, unleashing a chain of violence. Not published in the United States.

12. *Coffin's Dark Number* (Bles [UK], 1969) Is a group of UFO watchers connected with the disappearance of three young girls in South London? Not published in the United States.

13. *Coffin from the Past, A* (Dell, 1982) A long-buried scandal and secret emotions lie behind the deaths of Thomas Barr and his secretary. Originally published in the United Kingdom in 1970.

14. *Olivia* (Coward-McCann, 1974) Olivia is a "yellow canary," or hysteric, according to the police, as she struggles through fact and fantasy to find her lover's killer. UK title: *A Coffin for the Canary*.

15. *Coffin on the Water* (St. Martin's, 1989) In the first Coffin novel published in more than 10 years, we are taken back to 1946, when newly promoted Detective-Constable John Coffin takes up his post in Greenwich and is presented with the strangled, stabbed, and mutilated body of a young woman in the Thames. Originally published in the United Kingdom in 1986.

16. *Coffin in Fashion* (St. Martin's, 1989) In the 1960s, Coffin, a sergeant anticipating promotion, buys a house that needs repairs, and then workmen find the body of an adolescent boy under the floor. Originally published in the United Kingdom in 1987.

17. *Coffin Underground* (St. Martin's, 1989) Coffin is now a chief superintendent on the Tactical Activity Squad of South London, an area undergoing gentrification and the scene of several mysterious deaths that Coffin thinks are related.

18. *Coffin in the Museum of Crime* (St. Martin's, 1990) The decapitated head and severed hand of an unknown victim are deposited in a church in Thameswater, an event that leads to the discovery of several corpses in the church's crypt. UK title: *Coffin in the Museum of Crime*.

19. *Coffin and the Paper Man* (St. Martin's, 1991) Anna Mary Kinver, daughter of a working-class family long resident in the area, is a murder victim. Is the perpetrator a blood-soaked vagrant, or is he Tim Zeman, son of a well-to-do doctor, as anonymous letters signed "Paper Man" assert?

20. *Coffin on Murder Street* (St. Martin's, 1992) American soap opera star Nell Casey, appearing in a theater festival run by Stella Pinero, Coffin's lover, reports that her young son Tom's teddy bear has been stolen and buried in their yard under a marker bearing the boy's name.

21. *Cracking Open a Coffin* (St. Martin's, 1993) There seems to be a link between the murder victims from an elite London university and a refuge for battered women.

22. *Coffin for Charley, A* (St. Martin's, 1994) Coffin's new wife, actress Stella Pinero, feels that she is being stalked. Then a couple of murders, which may be linked to the stalker, are committed nearby.

23. *Coffin Tree, The* (St. Martin's, 1996) A series of grotesque events involving the "accidental" deaths of two policemen, the discovery of a charred body that seems to be that of the wife of one of the cops, a head floating in the Thames, and the disappearance of Phoebe Ashley, Coffin's onetime lover, on an undercover operation all add up to a fine mess. Originally published in the United Kingdom in 1994.

24. *Dark Coffin, A* (St. Martin's, 1996) Harry Trent, a former colleague from Greenwich, turns up with vague warnings about his identical twin, Mark (Merry) Trent. Then the bodies of Joe and Josie Macintosh are found in the theater run by Stella Pinero.

25. *Double Coffin, A* (St. Martin's, 1998) Former prime minister Richard Lavendar, now in his dotage, confesses that his father was a serial killer who left numerous corpses buried around London: one of them the then-young Lavendar helped bury. Originally published in the United Kingdom in 1996.

26. *Coffin's Game* (St. Martin's, 1999) Stella Pinero, Coffin's wife, is missing, and a body disguised as hers is found at the scene of a terrorist bombing. Does Stella have a terrorist connection? Originally published in the United Kingdom in 1997.

27. *Coffin's Ghost* (St. Martin's, 2001) Two bundles containing a woman's dismembered arms and legs are deposited on the front steps of the Serena Sheddon Shelter, a refuge located in Coffin's old residence on Barrow Street. Originally published in the United Kingdom in 1998.

28. *Grave Coffin, A* (St. Martin's, 2000) The discovery of the mutilated body of detective Harry Seton, who was part of a special detail to eliminate British drug traffic, leads Coffin into an investigation of possible police corruption. Originally published in the United Kingdom in 1998.

29. *Cold Coffin, A* (HarperCollins [UK], 2000) The discovery of a pile of infant skulls unearthed near police headquarters and the triple murder of a midwife and her two daughters absorb Coffin's attention. Not published in the United States.

30. *Coffin Knows the Answer* (St. Martin's, 2003) A "stalker with a paedophile slant," who sent pictures to Coffin's wife, Stella, may be a serial murderer.

II. Butler has joined the historical whodunit sweepstakes with two mysteries set in the United Kingdom in the early 1820s featuring Major Mearns and Sergeant Denny as policemen.

1. *King Cried Murder! The* (CT [Crime Time], UK, 1999) No annotation available. Not published in the United States.

2. *Dread Murder* (St. Martin's, 2007) Major Mearns and Sergeant Denny, who have a covert assignment to keep an eye on Windsor Castle early in the reign of King George IV, receive a parcel containing body parts.

Butler, Octavia E(stelle)

I. The late (d. 2006) Octavia Butler, one of the relatively few female African American science-fiction writers, wrote science fiction that dealt with issues of sex, race, and power. Strong black women figure prominently in her stories. Genetic engineering and psionic powers are among her subjects. The Patternist series started with *Patternmaster,* a novel set in the future in which the telepathic Patternists, the mute Missionaries of Humanity, and the four-legged Clayarks are pitted against each other. The other novels in the series are prequels describing the origins of the three groups. Number 1 is set in the past, numbers 2 and 3 in the near future, and number 4 in the far future. *Kindred,* a nonseries novel describing the travails of a black woman who shuttles back and forth between the present and the antebellum Southern past, is perhaps Butler's best-known work. Butler has received the Nebula and Hugo prizes and was awarded a MacArthur "genius" grant in 1995.

1. *Wild Seed* **(Doubleday, 1980)** Born thousands of years ago, the Nubian psychic Doro prolongs his existence by taking over the bodies of others and breeds other psychics to increase the mental abilities of future generations and to provide a source of fresh bodies for himself. Starts in 1690 and covers the 18th and 19th centuries.
2. *Mind of My Mind* **(Doubleday, 1977)** In near-future Los Angeles, Mary, Doro's daughter, gathers up and links telepaths together and eventually battles Doro for the independence of his people.
3. *Clay's Ark* **(St. Martin's, 1984)** In the near future, a spaceship returns to Earth with one survivor, who is infected with an alien plague that compels him to infect others.
4. *Survivor* **(Doubleday, 1978)** Fleeing a plague-stricken and violent Earth, the Missionaries of Humanity head to an alien world and get caught between two warring civilizations.
5. *Patternmaster* **(Doubleday, 1976)** First novel published in the series, but last in chronology. Doro, the 4,000-year-old Nubian telepath, rules over a far-future Earth with three distinct "human races."

II. The Xenogenesis trilogy is about genetic engineering, the mixture of aliens and humans, and race relations. A nomad alien race called the Oankali, who interbreed with other sentient species to improve their gene pool, arrive on a post-nuclear-holocaust Earth and offer the survivors the opportunity to combine the best features of humans and Oankali. The story is told through the lives of Lilith Iyapo and her part-human descendants. *Xenogenesis* (Guild America, 1989) and *Lilith's Brood* (Warner, 2000) are omnibus volumes containing all three novels.

1. *Dawn* **(Warner, 1987)** Lilith Iyapo, one of the few survivors from a dying Earth, awakes after a centuries-long sleep to find herself aboard the spaceship of the tentacled Oankali.
2. *Adulthood Rites* **(Warner, 1988)** The story of Akin, a "construct," part man and part alien, who is Lilith's only son.
3. *Imago* **(Warner, 1989)** The story of Jodahs, Lilith's grandson, part human–part Ooloi, who is dissatisfied with being less than human.

III. The Earthseed duo relates the saga of a young black woman, Lauren Olamina, who flees a beleaguered Los Angeles of the near future (2025). Lauren, who suffers from "hyperempathy," a genetic condition that allows her to genuinely feel the pain of others, founds Acorn, a rural community based on the teachings of Earthseed, a religion that Lauren herself created. However, Christian Fundamentalists led by the newly elected president, the Reverend Andrew Steele Jarret (seemingly modeled on Pat Robertson), take over and create a frighteningly realistic dystopia somewhat reminiscent of Margaret Atwood's *The Handmaid's Tale* (Houghton Mifflin, 1986).

1. *Parable of the Sower* **(Four Walls Eight Windows, 1993)** In 2025 Lauren Olamina, young black "hyperempathic," leaves a Los Angeles ruined by global warming, pollution, ethnic and racial tensions, homeless scavengers, and the pyromaniac "paints."
2. *Parable of the Talents* **(Seven Stories, 1998)** Acorn, the prosperous rural community founded by Lauren, is threatened by minions of Christian America, fundamentalists led by the recently elected US president the Reverend Andrew Steele Jarret.

Butler, Samuel

Although Butler used the New Zealand terrain as the basis for his scenic descriptions, the civilization he created is located "nowhere" (as the anagram for Erewhon implies). By creating a mock civilization, Butler was satirizing the hypocrisy and humbug of his own Victorian civilization. Erewhon has Musical Banks and a College of Unreason. Its people are punished for illness and treated to cures for crimes. Butler's satire is still sharp and can be read with interest today. Butler was also the author *The Way of All Flesh* (Dutton, 1910), the classic fictional send-up of his own family, and of nonfiction espousing female authorship of Homer's *Odyssey* and a non-Darwinian view of evolution.

1. *Erewhon; or, Over the Range* **(Dutton, 1910)** Young Englishman George Higgs discovers a remote civilization in the Pacific that strangely mirrors his own. First published in the United Kingdom in 1872. First American edition bound with number 2.
2. *Erewhon Revisited* **(Dutton, 1910)** Full title: *Erewhon Revisited Twenty Years Later, Both by the Original Discoverer of the Country and by His Son.* George Higgs's son John tells of his father's return to Erewhon after a 20-year absence and of the significant changes George finds. First published in the United Kingdom in 1901. Bound with number 1 in the first American edition.

Byatt, A(ntonia) S(usan)

A. S. Byatt's Frederica Quartet, set in England from 1953 to 1968, is about the intellectual Potter family: father Bill, a teacher at a progressive school in Yorkshire; son Marcus, who becomes a recluse; daughter Stephanie, who opts for marriage and the quiet life; and daughter Frederica, who opts for freedom from family ties and an artistic career. Frederica becomes the dominant character in the last two novels, as she divorces her husband and goes to London, a career culminating in being hostess of a fashionable TV talk show, and a series of affairs. The tetralogy is an excellent picture of the life of a proto-feminist and of Britain in the 1950s and 1960s. A. S. Byatt, sister of Margaret Drabble (q.v.) and a formidable literary figure in the United Kingdom, is still best known in America for *Possession* (Random House, 1990), which was awarded a Booker Prize and became the subject of a film starring Gwyneth Paltrow (2002).

1. *Virgin in the Garden, The* **(Knopf, 1979)** In 1953, just after Elizabeth II's coronation, the Potter family of Yorkshire becomes involved in an amateur theatrical about the life of Queen Elizabeth I. Young Frederica Potter determines to escape her smothering family.
2. *Still Life* **(Scribner, 1985)** Frederica is at Cambridge. Her sister Stephanie settles for marriage and small-town life. Alexander Wedderburn is trying to write a play about Van Gogh.

3. *Babel Tower* (**Random House, 1996**) 1964. Frederica is married to a businessman who objects violently to her working or seeing her Cambridge friends. Frederica escapes to London with her son and gets work as a teacher and a publisher's reader.
4. *Whistling Woman, A* (**Knopf, 2002**) Frederica, now divorced and hosting a fashionable TV chat show, gets involved in a conference on body and mind at the University of North Yorkshire and in the upheavals of the year 1968.

Cadell, Elizabeth (Violet Elizabeth)

Twenty-four-year-old Lucille is the oldest of the six Wayne children, who seem to be happily going their own way. But when Lucille decides to sell the family home, Wood Mount, they all come back to object: Nicholas from the National Service, Roselle from her job in London, Julia from boarding school, and young Simon and Dominic from their home with an aunt and uncle in Shropshire. The first story about this likable family and their friends was so successful that the author wrote two further books about them. Elizabeth Cadell (d. 1989) was a prolific English romance writer. Many of her books were never published in the United States.

1. *Lark Shall Sing, The* (**Morrow, 1955**) All six Wayne children converge on their family home in Greenhurst, England, when Lucille decides to sell it. Variant title: *The Singing Heart.*
2. *Blue Sky of Spring, The* (**Hodder [UK], 1956**) All is peaceful at Wood Mount, now divided into flats, until American playwright Cliff Herman arrives on the scene. Never published in the United States.
3. *Six Impossible Things* (**Morrow, 1961**) Nicholas finds a wife, and little Julia returns from Rome, grown up and beautiful.

Cail, Carol

Maxey Burnell, reporter and eventual co-owner (with her ex-husband) of a Boulder, Colorado, newspaper, is a feisty and insatiably curious amateur detective who gets herself involved in a series of small-town Rocky Mountain mysteries. Carol Cail, now a resident of Longmont, Colorado, has written several other novels and is a faculty member of the Writer's Digest School.

1. *Private Lies* (**HarperCollins, 1993**) When her boss is killed in a fiery explosion, Maxey Burnell, a Boulder, Colorado, reporter, gets on the trail.
2. *Unsafe Keeping* (**St. Martin's, 1995**) Maxey, now co-owner of a weekly Colorado newspaper, agrees to write a story about a neighborhood group trying to stop a developer's plan to raze a historic bordello and replace it with condos.
3. *If Two of Them Were Dead* (**St. Martin's, 1996**) Maxey takes a vacation and visits her only relatives, Aunt Janet and Cousin Curtis, and discovers that her father is not only still living but is the prime suspect in the murder of Maxey's mother, 10 years ago.
4. *Who Was Sylvia?* (**Deadly Alibi, 2000**) Maxey ponders the deaths of bag lady Sylvia Wellman and the unidentified victim of a suspicious fire in her own neighborhood.
5. *Death Kindly Stopped* (**Deadly Alibi, 2003**) A used copy of a book of Emily Dickinson's poetry has some handwritten notes in the margins that seem to threaten murder.

Caine, Rachel

PSEUDONYM OF Roxanne Longstreet

I.   Weather Warden Joanne Baldwin has had an eventful life, or lives, so far. She has been killed; been resurrected as a Djinn; died again, "sort of"; and awakened as a human again. Weather Wardens are charged with controlling the weather and keeping it from being even more chaotic and destructive than it already is. Weather Wardens are almost constantly at odds with the mystical Djinn, which creates complications because Joanne has a Djinn lover. This series is well-written escapist fantasy with a likable heroine and plenty of action.

1. *Ill Wind* (**Roc, 2003**) Weather Warden Joanne Baldwin is on the run, accused of killing a senior warden who put a Demon Mark on her and then died. Her only hope is to get a Djinn.
2. *Heat Stroke* (**Roc, 2004**) Killed by her colleagues, Joanne is reborn as a Djinn, and it is up to her to save the world from some really nasty weather entering Earth's atmosphere.
3. *Chill Factor* (**Roc, 2005**) Now back as a human after dying again, "sort of," and saving the world, "sort of," Joanne is asked to die and be resurrected again to stop a surly teenager named Kevin who has holed up in Las Vegas with the world's most powerful Djinn.
4. *Windfall* (**Roc, 2005**) The truce between the Weather Wardens and the Djinns is falling apart, and Joanne is forced to choose between saving her Djinn lover, saving her Warden abilities, and saving humanity.
5. *Firestorm* (**Roc, 2006**) Joanne must rally the remnants of the Weather Wardens against the Djinn, who have broken free from Warden control, and Mother Earth, who is about to unleash her full fury against the entire world.
6. *Thin Air* (**Roc, 2007**) Ashan the Djinn has caused Joanne to lose her memories, which will be lost forever unless Joanne can recover her identity and destroy the demon who is impersonating her.

II.   Claire Danvers is an unpopular college freshman who resides in Morganville, Texas, a town that has been taken over by vampires.

1. *Glass Houses* (**Signet, 2006**) Claire Danvers is an unhappy dorm resident in a school that favors beauty over brains. But moving to an old house off-campus makes things worse, if that's possible.
2. *Dead Girls' Dance* (**Signet, 2007**) Claire, who has found out that her college town, Morganville, Texas, is overrun with vampires, has the consolation of a new boyfriend who has a vampire-hunting dad. But then a local fraternity throws the Dead Girls' Dance.
3. *Midnight Alley* (**Signet, 2007**) The truce between the living and the living dead made things in Morganville relatively safe. But now people are turning up dead, a psycho is stalking Claire, and an ancient vampire is giving "night school" a whole new meaning.

Calder, Richard

British fantasy-SF-horror writer Richard Calder has been compared, at various times, to William Gibson (q.v.), Gene Wolfe (q.v.), Poppy Z. Brite, Angela Carter, the Marquis de Sade, J. K. Huysmans, William S. Burroughs, and Philip K. Dick, which may give you a hint about how he affects readers. The *Dead Girls* trilogy is a cyberpunk, surreal picture of a technologically and culturally warped 21st century, in which a deadly man-made nanovirus has turned England's pubescent female population into sexually provocative, artificial "dolls." Many readers have been turned off by Calder's complicated, surreal plots and kinky sex, but those who have persevered claim to find the trilogy rewarding. Calder has published several volumes of poetry and several other novels.

1. *Dead Girls* (St. Martin's, 1995) In the perverse world of the 21st century, English teen Ignatz Zwakh falls in love with Primavera, a "doll" created by a man-made nanovirus, and flees to Bangkok.
2. *Dead Boys* (St. Martin's, 1996) Ignatz Zwakh mourns his executed "doll" Primavera by pickling her reproductive organs in a whiskey bottle, while, from her future life on Mars, Vanity, the daughter Ignatz will program from Primavera's remains, is trying to elude a "dead boy" bounty hunter.
3. *Dead Things* (St. Martin's, 1997) In the conclusion, Dead Boy Lord Dagon (or is he really Ignatz Zwakh? Or is he a nonhuman, self-aware vehicle for the Reality Bomb created by the Toymakers?) returns to Earth to destroy the "cognitive virus" Meta.

Caldwell, Taylor

Caldwell dissects the affairs of the Barbour and Bouchard families of munitions makers from 1837 to the beginning of World War II in these three hefty novels. Ernest Barbour dominates the family and builds the Barbour-Bouchard business and fortune with his ruthless energy. This fictional depiction of the DuPonts is given epic proportions by Caldwell's inclusion of the lives, conflicts, and hatreds of even minor family members.

1. *Dynasty of Death* (Scribner, 1938) Introduces the Barbour and Bouchard families, telling of their emigration to Pennsylvania and of the founding and early years of their arms factory. Edition published by Pocket Books (1957) is abridged.
2. *Eagles Gather, The* (Scribner, 1940) The Barbour-Bouchard story continues through the 1920s as the company grows in wealth and power amid internal power struggles.
3. *Final Hour, The* (Scribner, 1944) Covers the period 1939–1942, showing the Bouchard family divided between supporting Hitler and the Allies.

Calisher, Hortense

Calisher is best known for her short stories and novellas, many of them published in the *New Yorker*, depicting New Yorkers in a style reminiscent of Henry James. Many of these stories are available in *The Collected Stories of Hortense Calisher* (Arbor House, 1975). Her novels, *False Entry* and *The New Yorkers*, view some of the same events and characters through differing perspectives.

1. *False Entry* (Little, Brown, 1961) In a journal of self-discovery, "Pierre Goodman" recalls his youth in Alabama and the key role he played in a murder trial.
2. *New Yorkers, The* (Little, Brown, 1969) Judge Simon Mannix returns home from a banquet to find that his 12-year-old daughter, Ruth, has killed his wife as she lay in the arms of a lover.

Callander, Don

I. The Mancer series is light fantasy in the Terry Pratchett (q.v.) style. Douglas Brightglade (aka Pyromancer), the protagonist, is apprenticed to a fire-adept wizard named Flarman Firemaster, undergoes adventures in a world full of wizards, witches, 18-foot-tall living statues, and sea otters. Don Callander, retired from editorial and other duties at the American Automobile Association, is now a full-time writer living in Florida.

1. *Pyromancer* (Ace, 1992) Douglas Brightglade is taken on as an apprentice by the good fire-adept wizard Flarman Flowerstalk and gets caught up in a battle between Flarman and bad ice-adept wizard Frigeon.
2. *Aquamancer* (Ace, 1993) Brightglade, now a Journeyman Pyromancer, travels to unknown lands and is taken prisoner by a coven of power-mad witches.
3. *Geomancer* (Ace, 1994) Flarman Flowerstalk disappears. The Stone Men, 18-foot-tall living statues, imprison Douglas Brightglade. Magician Wong's homeland of Choin is embroiled in civil war.
4. *Aeromancer* (Ace, 1997) The beautiful and gifted Aquamancer, Myrn Manstar of Flowering Island, wife of Pyromancer Douglas Brightglade, is about to be auctioned off at a slave market.
5. *Marbleheart* (Ace, 1998) The sea otter Marbleheart takes center stage in this adventure set in the Mancer universe.

II. The Dragon series is a light trilogy figuring a dragon named Arbitrance Constable, a librarian named Tom who is subjected to a series of adventures in fantasy worlds, talking lions, a kidnapped princess, and a villain named Byron Boldface.

1. *Dragon Companion* (Ace, 1994) A dragon from another world whisks Tom, a librarian at the Library of Congress, into a realm of magic and fantasy.
2. *Dragon Rescue* (Ace, 1995) Dragon Arbitrance Constable is missing, and his family and friends fear that he has been kidnapped.
3. *Dragon Tempest* (Ace, 1998) Tom the librarian goes to a new land where he encounters talking lions, a kidnapped princess, and a villain named Byron Boldface.

Callaway, Phil

Described as writing like Dave Barry but with a Christian message, Alberta resident Phil Callaway is a columnist, inspirational speaker, editor (*Prairie Bible Institute's Servant*), producer of the video series *The Big Picture*, and author of some 15 volumes of columns, essays, and short stories combining humor and inspiration, with titles like *The Total Christian Guy* (Harvest House, 1996) and *I Used to Have Answers, Now I Have Kids* (Harvest House, 2000). A pair of novels set in the hamlet of Grace, Montana, describes the growing pains of Terry Anderson, lapsed (temporarily) Christian, who picks up some bad habits such as drinking, smoking, and listening to the Rolling Stones. The somewhat improbable plots, narrated with dry humor, are fine depictions of small-town, conservative Christian life.

1. *Growing Up on the Edge of the World* (Harvest House, 2004) Twelve-year-old Terry Anderson, scion of a poor but loving family in the hamlet of Grace, Montana, finds a hidden stash of money. Variant title: *The Edge of the World*.
2. *Wonders Never Cease* (Harvest House, 2005) Terry, now 18, has become an agnostic given to vices like partying, smoking, drinking, and listening to the Rolling Stones. Then Terry gets involved in a series of adventures, including a dead body in an abandoned car, a mysterious envelope, a fake faith healer, and a financial scam.

Cameron, Stella

I. Prolific American romance writer Stella Cameron has published more than 60 novels, some of which are in linked series, including the Mayfair Square series, which is set in Regency London. The series has its requisite share of Regency goings-on, romances above and below one's station, estate wrangles, rakes, slimy villains, and devious plots. It also has a resident ghost: that of Sir Septimus Spivey, whose magnificent family home at 7 Mayfair Square has been turned into a boarding house. The spectral Septimus has embarked on a series of schemes to restore tranquility to his home by persuading its paying boarders to leave.

1. *More and More* **(Warner, 1999)** Finch More, 29-year-old spinster co-owner of a small import business, tries unsuccessfully to avoid falling in love with her client, the superior, boorish Ross, Viscount Kilrood, who is up to his ears in some clandestine goings-on.
2. *All Smiles* **(Mira, 2000)** The ghostly Septimus Spivey is trying to get rid of impecunious boarder Meg Smiles by securing for her a position with Count Etranger as advisor and companion to his sister, Princess Desiree, who badly needs shaping up for the forthcoming season.
3. *7B* **(Mira, 2001)** Sibyl Smiles wants to have a child without the hindrance of a husband, so she sets her sights on her friend and neighbor Hunter Lloyd.
4. *Orphan, The* **(Mira, 2002)** Latimer More, "the Most Daring Lover in England," sets his sights on poor but spirited millinery assistant Jenny McBride.
5. *About Adam* **(Mira, 2003)** Adam Chillworth is ensconced in his attic rooms, painting portraits and avoiding human contacts. Princess Desiree concocts a plan to convince Adam that the differences between their ages and stations are not the impediments that they seem.

II. Another Regency romance series, set in Scotland this time, follows members of the Rossmara family through their romantic trials and tribulations.

1. *Fascination* **(Avon, 1993)** Pretty, penniless Grace agrees to wed Lord Arran, the supposedly aged and ailing Marquess of Stonehaven, but Lord Arran isn't what he seems.
2. *Charmed* **(Avon, 1995)** Calum Innes, switched at birth by his father's mistress, who replaced Calum with her own child, Etienne, discovers his true identity and sets out to reclaim his dukedom and Lady Philipa Chauncy, the false Duke Etienne's betrothed.
3. *Bride* **(Warner, 1995)** Lady Justine Girvin, lacking nothing except a husband of her own, travels to the castle of Straun, her brother's friend, and asks him to teach her all about love.
4. *Beloved* **(Warner, 1996)** Ella Rossmara loves Saber, Earl of Avenall, who has not recovered physically or mentally from wounds received in India, and he reciprocates her love, but his scars and her past conspire to keep them apart.
5. *Wish Club, The* **(Warner, 1998)** Max Rossmara, who is scheduled to wed Lady Hermione, is really in love with his childhood friend Kristy Mercer.

III. The Bayou series, set in contemporary New Orleans and Toussaint, Louisiana, is a series of steamy romances with mystery plots that usually take second place to hot sex and melodramatic action. The series is linked more by its settings than by continuing characters.

Two other series, which have tenuous connections but are regarded as "linked" by Cameron, are the Navy SEALS series—*Sheer Pleasures* (Zebra, 1995); *True Bliss* (Zebra, 1996); *Guilty Pleasures* (Zebra, 1997); and *We Do*, a novella published in the collection *Married in Spring* (Harlequin, 2001)—and a pair of hardcover mystery novels: *Key West* (Kensington, 1999) and *Glass Houses* (Kensington, 2000). Connections can also be seen in a trio of romances with various characters named Fenton and McGrath: *Faces of a Clown* (Harlequin, 1985); *Choices* (Harlequin, 1986); and *Yes Is Forever* (Harlequin, 1987). Originally published under the pseudonym of Jane Worth Abbott, these novels

were reissued by Harlequin in 2004. Other linked pairs include *No Stranger* (Harlequin, 1987) and *Second to None* (Harlequin, 1987); *Undercurrents* (Harlequin, 1991) and *Snow Angels* (Harlequin, 1991); and *Only by Your Touch* (Avon, 1992) and *His Magic Touch* (Avon, 1993).

1. *French Quarter* **(Kensington, 1998)** Jack Charbonnet, part owner of a New Orleans riverboat casino, is thrown together with a former Miss Louisiana, Celina Payne, when her boss, Errol Petrie, is murdered.
2. *Cold Day in July* **(Kensington, 2002)** The scene shifts to the Louisiana bayou town of Toussaint as Bonnie Blue, an enigmatic singer passing through the town, is strangled at the local church. Reb O'Brien, a local doctor, and her former high school crush, the prodigal Marc Girard, become involved in a convoluted plot.
3. *Kiss Them Goodbye* **(Mira, 2003)** Toussaint is the setting again, as Vivian Patin, heir to a rundown estate, has her plans altered when a murder occurs on the grounds, and Vivian is thrown together with handsome local deputy sheriff Spike Duval.
4. *Now You See Him* **(Mira, 2004)** Convicted murderer Charles Penn is on the loose, and Ellie Byron, Toussaint bookstore owner, former homeless runaway with a troubled past, and witness against Penn, feels that he is after her, as mystery writer Sonja Elliot's bestselling crime novels seem to be spawning real-life reenactments.
5. *Grave Mistake, A* **(Mira, 2005)** New Orleans homicide detective Guy Gautreaux, on leave in Toussaint, and Jilly Gable, who is desperate to find the love of the family who abandoned her as a child, are drawn together, as the wife of a degenerate New Orleans loan shark arrives in Toussaint claiming to be Jilly's mother.
6. *Body of Evidence* **(Mira, 2006)** A series of murders in Pointe Judah, Louisiana, seems to be linked to membership in Secrets, a support group for women in which all the victims were members.

Camilleri, Andrea

Inspector Salvo Montalbano is a policeman in the fictional Sicilian town of Vigata. His surname is Camilleri's tribute to Spanish detective-novel writer Manuel Vazquez Montalban, whose works are available in English translation in the United Kingdom but not yet in the United States. Inspector Montalbano is middle-aged, politically radical, hard-boiled, given to sarcastic comments, contemptuous of Italy's venal politicians, and honest, although he doesn't always follow the letter of the law in his pursuit of wrongdoers. Although he has a long-term, long-distance relationship with the smart and independent Livia, Montalbano's real passions are for solving crimes and eating well. Written in Italian with an admixture of Sicilian words, the Montalbano books are fast paced and easy to read and are convincing portraits of Sicilian society, showing how good and honest people manage to survive in a crime-ridden society with intricate but unwritten codes of behavior.

Vigata is a thinly disguised version of Porto Empedocle, the Sicilian town that is Camilleri's birthplace. Camilleri, whose first detective novel was published when the author was 68 years old, was for many years a theatrical and television director and is still a teacher of the dramatic arts. The Montalbano books have been big best sellers in Italy. Their recently published English-language versions have drawn praise from literary critics for their style and evocation of Sicilian life. Some of the Montalbano books, including at least three short story collections, remain untranslated into English. The novels below are arranged chronologically by date of Italian publication rather than translation date.

1. *Shape of Water, The* **(Viking, 2002)** Salvo Montalbano doesn't accept the coroner's verdict of death by natural causes after the body of local politician Silvio Luparello is found locked in his

BMW in "the pasture," Vigata's town dump. Translated from the Italian by Stephen Sartarelli. Originally published in Italy in 1994 as *La forma del acqua*.

2. **Snack Thief, The** (Viking, 2003) Gunfire from a Tunisian patrol boat kills a worker on an Italian trawler. A retiree is stabbed to death in the elevator of his apartment building, and his housekeeper and her son are missing. It is up to Montalbano to find the connection between the two cases. Translated from the Italian by Stephen Sartarelli. Originally published in Italy in 1996 as *Il ladro di merendine*.

3. **Terra-Cotta Dog, The** (Viking, 2002) Montalbano investigates a supermarket heist that is a front for gunrunning and finds the guns in an ancient cave along with the bodies of two young lovers, dead since World War II; coins; a water jug; and the terra-cotta dog of the title. Translated from the Italian by Stephen Sartarelli. Originally published in Italy in 1996 as *Il cane di terracotta*.

4. **Voice of the Violin** (Viking, 2003) After Montalban discovers the naked corpse of a woman during an unauthorized search, he is bedeviled by the plethora of suspects, including the woman's husband, a half-wit stalker, and the woman's out-of-town lover, as well as by the interference of his superiors and an ambitious colleague. Translated from the Italian by Stephen Sartarelli. Originally published in Italy in 1997 as *La voce del violino*.

5. **Excursion to Tindari** (Viking Penguin, 2005) Montalbano is occupied by the shooting death of Nene Sanfillipo; the disappearance, after a bus tour to nearby Tindari, of Alfonso and Marghetia Griffo, the retirees who lived upstairs in Nene's house; and the request by local crime boss Don Balduccio Sinagra to take his tubercular grandson, Japichinu, into protective custody. Translated from the Italian by Stephen Sartarelli. Originally published in Italy in 2000 as *La gita a Tindari*.

6. **Smell of the Night, The** (Viking Penguin, 2005) A financier disappears with millions of lire after defrauding investors in a pyramid scheme. Inspector Montalbano searches for him, flouting the law on occasion, tweaking his superiors, wheedling information from various sources, and enjoying frequent lavish meals. Translated from the Italian by Stephen Sartarelli. Originally published in Italy in 2001 as *L'odore della notte*. Variant title: *The Scent of the Night*.

7. **Rounding the Mark** (Penguin, 2006) Montalbano's attempt to unwind with a swim along the Sicilian seashore is thwarted by the discovery of corpse in the water. Another mystery bedeviling Montalbano is the hit-and-run death of a young boy, who may have been victimized by human traffickers. Translated from the Italian by Stephen Sartarelli. Originally published in Italy in 2003 as *Il girodi boa*.

8. **Patience of the Spider, The** (Penguin, 2007) Montalbano's recuperation at home in Marinella with his wife, Livia, is hampered by the abduction of university student Susanna Mistretta. Translated from the Italian by Stephen Sartarelli. Originally published in Italy in 2004 as *La pazienza del ragno*.

9. **Paper Moon, The** (Penguin, 2008) Michela Pardo implores Montalbano to help her track down her missing brother, Angelo. Translated from the Italian by Stephen Sartarelli. Originally published in 2005 as *La luna di carta*.

Campbell, Robert (Wright)

I. Jimmy Flannery, whose vocations include sewer inspector, Chicago Democratic precinct captain, and part-time detective, is a likable fellow—streetwise but honest, full of Celtic humor, charm, and odd grammar—who always gets the job done, whether it's negotiating a deal in the Windy City's old-boy network or solving a murder. Veteran film, television, and fiction writer Campbell (d. 2000) stated that he was using the detective genre to write "Dickensian" novels. *The Junkyard Dog* won an Edgar Award for best mystery novel. *The Spy Who Sat and Waited* (Putnam, 1975), a nonseries novel, was nominated for a National Book Award. Also known as R. Wright Campbell.

1. **Junkyard Dog, The** (New American Library, 1986) When one of Jimmy's neighbors is among those killed in an explosion at an abortion clinic, he refuses to believe that it was an accident.

2. **600 Pound Gorilla, The** (New American Library, 1987) Flannery is handed the job of finding a temporary home for Baby, the Lincoln Park Zoo's favorite gorilla, when inclement weather causes burst pipes at the zoo.

3. **Hip-Deep in Alligators** (New American Library, 1987) While doing his job as sewer inspector, Jimmy runs into a corpse bitten in half by a saltwater crocodile, a species definitely not endemic to Lake Michigan.

4. **Thinning the Turkey Herd** (New American Library, 1988) The "turkey herd," the annual mob of young girls looking for glamorous jobs in the big city, is being culled by an unknown killer.

5. **Cat's Meow, The** (New American Library, 1988) Is a Satanic cult responsible for the ghostly cat reported in St. Patrick's Church and for the death of Father Mulrooney?

6. **Nibbled to Death by Ducks** (Pocket, 1989) Chips Devlin, Flannery's old mentor, has been incarcerated in a sleazy nursing home where "guests" seem to die more quickly than necessary.

7. **Gift Horse's Mouth, The** (Pocket, 1990) Flannery is asked by Democratic Party head Ray Carrigan to investigate the peculiar death of Goldie Hanrahan, former mistress of Chicago's top politicos.

8. **In a Pig's Eye** (Pocket, 1991) The mysterious death of someone registered as "P. Pig" at Jimmy's health club leads him into porno publishing, topless bars, and worse.

9. **Sauce for the Goose** (Mysterious, 1995) Flannery attends night school to improve his grammar and catch up on the theory of the political science he practices in a course taught by a power-broking lawyer.

10. **Lion's Share, The** (Mysterious, 1996) The death of Chips Devlin, Jimmy's longtime mentor, leaves Jimmy with Chips's Bridgeport house and a political vacuum that Leo Lundatos, congressman under a large cloud, would like to fill with Jimmy's help.

11. **Pigeon Pie** (Mysterious, 1998) Although Jimmy helped send Leo Lundatos to federal prison, Leo seems ready to support Jimmy for Alderman.

II. Los Angeles, or "La-La Land," is the scene of activities for a private eye named Whistler, who might have stepped out of the pages of Raymond Chandler (q.v.). La-La Land is a somewhat grimmer place than Flannery's Chicago, but Campbell's quirky characters, snappy dialogue, and ingenious plots are just as evident.

1. **In La-La Land We Trust** (Mysterious, 1986) Witness to a fatal two-car accident on Hollywood and Vine, Whistler uncovers a cover-up involving a starlet and a mysterious millionaire.

2. **Alice in La-La Land** (Poseidon, 1987) Whistler is hired to protect the third wife of an aging television personality, a psychological basket case with a yen for teenage prostitutes.

3. **Sweet La-La Land** (Poseidon, 1990) Old flame Faye enlists Whistler into looking for her 15-year-old son, part of a "family" of street hustlers.

4. **Wizard of La-La Land, The** (Pocket, 1994) A street hustler dying of AIDS is found with his throat cut, negating a possible deathbed confession relating to the slaying of the niece of policeman Isaac Canaan.

III. Two books feature Jake Hatch, railroad detective for Burlington Northern. Jake has a "girl in every depot," but some his girls have picked up dirty words such as *commitment* and *relationship*.

1. *Plugged Nickel* (Pocket, 1988) Half torsos belonging to two different people are found under the Chicago-Denver train after the emergency cord has been pulled.
2. *Red Cent* (Pocket, 1989) Jake suspects that drunken Indian kids firing their rifles at the train were not responsible for the death of a businessman in the dining car.

Canham, Marsha

I. Canadian writer Canham has written well-received historical-romance novels set in a variety of periods and locations. Her Pride of Lions series is set in Scotland at the time of the Jacobite Rebellion and the Battle of Culloden. Numbers 1 and 2 feature English lady Catherine Ashbrooke and Scottish laird Alexander Cameron (aka Raefer Montgomery, aka Camshroinaich, aka Dark Cameron). Number 3 has Angus Moy; his wife, Anne; and the dashing John MacGillivray as the protagonists. The trilogy is full of solid history and lots of action and steamy sex.

1. *Pride of Lions, The* (Paperjacks, 1988) English aristocrat Catherine Ashbrooke and Scottish laird Alexander Cameron (posing as London merchant Raefer Montgomery) are forced to marry after they are caught kissing on her father's terrace.
2. *Blood of Roses, The* (Paperjacks, 1989) English-born Catherine Ashbrooke Cameron, who has fallen in love with her husband, Alexander Cameron, races to the Highlands to embrace him and his Jacobite cause.
3. *Midnight Honor* (Dell, 2001) Published 12 years after numbers 1 and 2 and with different protagonists, this novel is regarded as part of the Pride of Lions trilogy. Angus Moy and his wife, Anne, find themselves on opposite sides in the Jacobite Rebellion. Anne's clansman, John MacGillivray, joins her in fighting against the English.

II. The Medieval Trilogy, set in 13th-century England, is Canham's version of the Robin Hood legend. The Black Wolf of Lincoln, then his illegitimate son Eduard FitzRandwulf, and then his daughter Lady Brenna Wardieu are the protagonists in this passionate, action-filled trilogy with a believable medieval setting. *My Forever Love* (Signet, 2004), a novel set in the time of Richard the Lion-Hearted, could be linked to the trilogy.

1. *Through a Dark Mist* (Dell, 1991) In 13th-century England, Lady Servanne's party is attacked by Black Wolf and his band, and the course of history is changed by their growing passion.
2. *In the Shadow of Midnight* (Dell, 1994) Lady Ariel de Clare, feisty niece of the Marshal of England, is tamed by Eduard FitzRandwulf, illegitimate son of Black Wolf, on their journey to Wales.
3. *Last Arrow, The* (Dell, 1997) Tomboy archer Lady Brenna Wardieu finds herself falling for the mysterious Griffyn as they travel from France to England and a showdown with the Sheriff of Nottingham.

Cannell, Dorothy (Reddish)

Overweight designer Ellie Simons is the beneficiary of a strange will that specifies, among other things, that she lose 63 pounds. Ellie manages to fulfill the requirements of the will and eventually becomes Ellie Haskell, wife of chef Ben Haskell, who runs a restaurant in the English village of Chitterton Fells. With the aid of her daily "char," the redoubtable Mrs. Roxy Malloy, Ellie juggles the roles of wife, mother of twins, and part-time detective in this amusing, stylishly written, high-camp series full of larger-than-life characters and unexpected plot twists.

1. *Thin Woman, The* (St. Martin's, 1984) Ellie is left a strange bequest by her uncle Merlin that leads to the investigation of a 60-year-old murder.
2. *Down the Garden Path* (St. Martin's, 1985) Features the Tramwell sisters, Hyacinth and Primrose, proprietors of the Flowers Detection Agency, who help Tessa Fields find her birth mother.
3. *Widows Club, The* (Bantam, 1988) Ellie's help is enlisted by the Tramwell sisters in solving a rash of murders of unfaithful husbands in Chitterton Fells.
4. *Mum's the Word* (Bantam, 1990) The pregnant Ellie and her husband, Ben, travel to the American Midwest to visit a onetime movie goddess.
5. *Femmes Fatale* (Bantam, 1992) Now the mother of twins, Ellie secretly joins Fully Female, a women's group designed to keep the romance in their relationships.
6. *How to Murder Your Mother-in-Law* (Bantam, 1994) Ben's parents reveal that, due to religious differences, they have never been legally married.
7. *How to Murder the Man of Your Dreams* (Bantam, 1995) Romance paperback cover hunk Karisma appears at a fund-raising event in Chitterton Fells and meets his end in an apparent accident.
8. *Spring Cleaning Murders, The* (Viking, 1998) The stalwart Mrs. Malloy gave notice before she left for London, so Ellie hires Mrs. Large as her "daily," but Mrs. Large is soon killed in a suspicious fall.
9. *Trouble with Harriet, The* (Viking, 1999) Ellie and Ben are about to leave for a vacation in France when Ellie's wandering father, Morley, turns up with an urn containing the ashes of Harriet, his late girlfriend.
10. *Bridesmaids Revisited* (Viking, 2000) When Ellie receives a letter stating that her late grandmother is trying to contact her from beyond the grave, she and Mrs. Malloy travel to Knells, a Cambridgeshire village in danger of being turned into a theme park by a local boy who has made good.
11. *Importance of Being Ernestine, The* (Viking, 2002) Mrs. Malloy, moonlighting as assistant to local private investigator "Milk" Jugg, enlists Ellie's aid in getting to the bottom of Lady Krumley's troubles.
12. *Withering Heights* (St. Martin's, 2007) "Withering Heights" is what Ellie's niece, Ariel Hopkins, calls the Elizabethan mansion in Yorkshire that her father, Tom, and stepmother, Betty, bought after winning the lottery. Ariel claims that Betty is obsessed with finding the body of Nigel Gallagher, the mansion's previous owner.
13. *Goodbye, Ms. Chips* (St. Martin's, 2008) Doras Critchley, games mistress at St. Roberta's boarding school, asks Ellie to investigate the theft of the Loverly Cup.

Cannell, Stephen J(oseph)

Television writer, producer, and director (*Rockford Files*, *The A-Team*, etc.) Stephen J. Cannell has branched out by writing detective novels. Most of his novels are in a series featuring Los Angeles Police detective Shane Scully and his wife, Alexa Hamilton, who eventually becomes acting head of LAPD Detective Services Group. Scully is of the old school, believing in dogged investigation rather than quick fixes, a little jaded and rough around the edges, but basically a good man. This is a series of readable and gritty procedurals.

1. *Tin Collectors, The* (St. Martin's, 2001) Shane Scully, forced to kill his former partner Ray Molar in self-defense, finds himself persona non grata with his fellow LAPD officers and under investigation by his nemesis, Alexa Hamilton.
2. *Viking Funeral, The* (St. Martin's, 2002) Shane, undergoing psychiatric treatment, spots his supposedly three-years-dead best friend and fellow cop driving in the next lane in the freeway. Scully's lover, Alexa Hamilton, is sceptical until her boss dies in a faked suicide with a strange tattoo on his ankle.
3. *Hollywood Tough* (St. Martin's, 2003) Shane and his wife, Alexa, try to trap mobster "Champagne" Dennis Valentine, who is sponsoring a high-profile movie.
4. *Runaway Heart* (St. Martin's, 2003) Jack Wirta, Scully's former partner and a fledgling private eye, takes center stage as he is called in to help the eccentric, crusading attorney Herman Strockmeyer in a thriller with a futuristic twist.
5. *Vertical Coffin* (St. Martin's, 2004) Scully stumbles into a shoot-out between gunman Vincent Smiley and surrounding police. Then one of the two competing SWAT teams at the scene burns down the barricaded house, with Smiley in it.
6. *Cold Hit* (St. Martin's, 2005) Is the homicide victim Scully has dealt with the latest in a string of serial murders, or is there some connection with a decade-old unsolved murder of an LA cop?
7. *White Sister* (St. Martin's, 2006) Alexa is missing, but her car has been found, with the executed body of what appears to be a gang member and her service revolver, which is probably the murder weapon, nearby.
8. *Three Shirt Deal* (St. Martin's, 2008) Secada Llevar, investigating officer for internal affairs, gets Shane involved in reopening the homicide case of Tru Hickman, convicted of killing his mother.

Canning, Victor

I. The late Victor Canning was a British novelist and screenwriter best known for elegant, well-characterized novels that often combined the elements of espionage thriller and detective mystery. Continuing characters appear in relatively few of his 50-plus novels. One such character is Rex Carver, a British spy turned private investigator. Although Carver's home base is nominally London, most of his cases take him abroad to places like Yugoslavia, Libya, France, and Spain.

1. *Whiphand, The* (Morrow, 1965) Rex Carver follows a beautiful German woman from England through Europe to Yugoslavia.
2. *Doubled in Diamonds* (Morrow, 1967) Rex tries to trace a man to whom a legacy is due, but gets involved with a drug and diamond racket and Chinese twin sisters.
3. *Python Project, The* (Morrow, 1968) The recovery of a stolen bracelet leads to a convoluted case that carries Carver to France, Libya, and Spain.
4. *Melting Man, The* (Morrow, 1969) A Mercedes missing somewhere in France contains a secret that interests many characters.

II. The three novels about Samuel Miles, better known as "Smiler," were something of a change of pace for Canning. Though young Smiler at 15 has already run afoul of the law, he is a sensitive and observant friend to the animals that share his adventures. Canning writes touchingly but without sentimentalizing or anthropomorphizing his subject.

1. *Runaways, The* (Morrow, 1972) Smiler finds that his hideout is shared by a cheetah escaped from its enclosure at Longleat Park.
2. *Flight of the Grey Goose* (Morrow, 1973) Smiler and a wounded greylag goose take shelter at a beautiful island castle in Scotland.
3. *Painted Tent, The* (Morrow, 1974) A peregrine falcon is Smiler's companion at the Gypsy farm where Smiler makes his home.

Card, Orson Scott

I. Card, who has won multiple Hugo and Nebula awards, is one of the most popular and highly regarded contemporary science-fiction writers. The Ender series follows Andrew "Ender" Wiggin, youthful military genius, who is called upon to save human civilization. *Ender's Game* started as a novella of the same title published in *Analog* in 1977. It was published as a novel in 1985 and has been reprinted many times since, becoming one of the most popular novels in SF history. A movie version, scripted by Card, will be released in the near future. Card's mixture of futuristic technology, biblical lore (he is a devout Mormon), close examination of moral issues, excellent dialogue, and well-characterized protagonists is on display in this series. Numbers 2 and 3 were reprinted in one volume (Tor, 1987).

1. *First Meetings: Three Stories from the Enderverse* (Subterranean, 2002) Contains three stories: "Ender's Game," the original novelette published in 1977; "The Polish Boy," a previously unpublished story about Ender's father, John Paul Wiggin; and "The Investment Counselor," which tells how Jane the AI first formally introduced herself to Ender. The audio version contains an additional short story.
2. *Ender's Game* (Tor, 1985) Six-year-old Andrew "Ender" Wiggin, potential military genius, is removed from his family and subjected to rigorous training to enable him to defend humanity against the alien Buggers.
3. *Speaker for the Dead* (Tor, 1986) Remorse over his role in the destruction of the Buggers leads Ender to become a Speaker for the Dead.
4. *Xenocide* (Tor, 1995) On the planet Lusitania, Ender and other human colonists strive to neutralize the "descolada," a possibly sentient virus.
5. *Children of the Mind* (Tor, 1996) Called the "final" Ender novel (but see number 6), this describes the aging Ender's attempt to avert the destruction of the planet Lusitania and its three intelligent races.
6. *War of Gifts, A* (Tor, 2007) Ender Wiggin acts as a mentor to Zeck Morgan, who is confused about pacifism and religious freedom.

II. The Shadow series, though started after the "finish" of the Ender series (I, above), runs parallel to it. Set in the same universe, it follows the life of Bean, sent as a child to Battle School, who learns how to become a soldier and a human being. Although he becomes Ender's ally, Bean remains on Earth and helps Ender's brother Peter Wiggin to become Hegemon, while Ender goes off to colonize the planet of Lusitania. The psychopathic genius Achilles works to destroy Bean and Peter in this spin-off series, which is far from being over.

1. ***Ender's Shadow*** **(Tor, 1999)** Street child Bean, another potential military genius, is sent to Battle School, where he learns to command fleets for the war with the Buggers.
2. ***Shadow of the Hegemon*** **(Tor, 2000)** Ender has gone off to colonize a new world. Bean must decide whether to become Ender's brother Peter Wiggin's shadow and use him as a counterweight to the psychotic genius Achilles, who plans to rule the world.
3. ***Shadow Puppets*** **(Tor, 2002)** With Bean's help, Peter Wiggin has become Hegemon, a position of little influence and power outside of America and Europe. Achilles is working with China to achieve his goal of world domination. Bean agrees to start a family with fellow Battle School graduate Petra.
4. ***Shadow of the Giant, The*** **(Tor, 2005)** The impending death of Bean leaves little time for Peter the Hegemon, Ender's older brother, to set up a single world government.

III. The Tales of Alvin Maker series began as a Spenserian epic poem written by Card at the University of Utah. It is an alternative history saga that postulates a pioneer America where the Crown colonies coexist along with New Sweden and the states of Appalachia, and folk magic is readily believed and practiced. Alvin, the protagonist, who is capable of powerful magic, interacts with a large cast of characters including historical ones like John James Audubon and mythical ones like Mike Fink. This popular series has spawned Hatrack River, Card's own publishing firm and website (www.hatrack.com). *Hatrack River* (Guild America, 1988) is a collection of short stories. *Tales of Alvin Maker* (Tor, 1995) is a boxed set containing numbers 1 through 3. *Alvin Wandering* (SFBC Fantasy, 1998) is an omnibus volume containing numbers 4 and 5. *Keeper of Dreams* (Tor, 2008) contains some Hatrick River tales.

1. ***Seventh Son*** **(Tor, 1987)** Alvin, the seventh son of a seventh son of settlers beyond the Appalachians, is born in the early 1800s carrying powerful magic but beset by a powerful enemy.
2. ***Red Prophet*** **(Tor, 1988)** Young Alvin's ability to "make things whole" helps to prevent warfare between the settlers and the Native Americans led by the prophet Ta-kumsaw.
3. ***Prentice Alvin*** **(Tor, 1989)** A country schoolteacher and the child of a runaway slave find their destinies intertwined with that of Alvin, who must avoid destruction by the evil Unmaker.
4. ***Alvin Journeyman*** **(Tor, 1995)** Alvin returns to his birthplace on Hatrack River and finds himself in danger of lynching for aiding fugitive slaves.
5. ***Heartfire*** **(Tor, 1998)** In an America heading toward civil war, the slaveholding southern Crown colonies are ruled by Arthur Stuart, exiled king of England, while New England is in the grip of "witchers" who hope to eradicate people with powers like Alvin. *Master Alvin* was the title projected before publication.
6. ***Crystal City, The*** **(Tor, 2003)** Subtitle: *Tales of Alvin Maker VI.* Alvin's long-dreamed Crystal City is started. Alvin performs miracles to lead thousands out of slavery, but he is torn by self-doubt because he couldn't save his own stillborn child.

IV. The Homecoming quintet is a far-future series about life on the planet of Harmony, which is watched over by a benevolent but decaying computer called the Oversoul, which needs to return to long-abandoned Earth for repairs. Numbers 1 through 3 were published in an omnibus volume: *Homecoming: Harmony* (Tor, 1994). *Homecoming: Earth* (Guild America, 1995) is an omnibus volume containing numbers 4 and 5.

The Worthing Saga (Tor, 1990), about a telepath sent out on a seed ship to save Humankind, was originally published as a novel (*Hot Sleep* [Ace, 1979]) and two collections of short stories (*Capitol* [Ace, 1979] and *The Worthing Chronicle* [Ace, 1983]).

Women of Genesis is a trio of novels about women from the *Book of Genesis*: *Sarah* (Shadow Mountain, 2000), *Rebekah* (Shadow Mountain, 2001), and *Rachel and Leah* (Deseret, 2004).

1. ***Memory of Earth, The*** **(Tor, 1992)** The Oversoul, located in the city of Basilica on the planet Harmony, feels itself weakening after 40 million years of benevolent management.
2. ***Call of Earth, The*** **(Tor, 1993)** The Oversoul must force a respected general to take over the city of Basilica and set in motion forces that will destroy it.
3. ***Ships of Earth, The*** **(Tor, 1994)** A chosen few from Basilica, led by the prophet Nafai, cross the desert of Harmony to the waiting ancient starships.
4. ***Earthfall*** **(Tor, 1995)** The voyagers from Harmony return to Earth to find that 40 million years of human absence have led to the development of two sapient but warring races.
5. ***Earthborn*** **(Tor, 1995)** The Keeper of Earth is sought by the "sky-people," the "diggers," and the descendants of the Harmony voyagers.

Carey, Jacqueline

I. Kushiel the Sado-Masochistic is one of the two demigods (Naamath the Sensual Lover is the other) who rule the courtesan-spy Phedre no Delaunay in an alternative Renaissance world. Phedre is an "anguisette," an individual whose ability to receive sexual pleasure through the experience of pain marks her as one of Kushiel's own. Phedre's rise from indentured servitude to comtesse is faithfully chronicled in this adventure-filled fantasy-romance series with a large cast of well-defined characters and, as you might imagine, a suffusion of kinky sex. Originally envisioned as a trilogy, the series has been expanded with the publication of two volumes in what is known as the Imriel trilogy, featuring a new narrator, Imriel no Montreve de la Courcel. Fantasy author Jacqueline Carey is not be confused with the mainstream fiction writer of the same name (*Good Gossip*, *The Crossley Baby*, etc.).

1. ***Kushiel's Dart*** **(Tor, 2001)** "Whore's get" Phedre no Delaunay, identified as one of the sadomasochistic demigod Kushiel's own by the blood spot ("dart") in her eye, rises through the ranks in the Renaissance-like Night Court world.
2. ***Kushiel's Chosen*** **(Tor, 2002)** Phedre, now elevated to the peerage, is beset by her evil nemesis, Melisande Sharizai, but is befriended by Joselin, a Cassiline monk who defied his vows to become her companion.
3. ***Kushiel's Avatar*** **(Tor, 2003)** Phedre travels south into the equivalents of the Middle East and Africa, on a quest for Imriel, the kidnapped son of Melisande Sharizai, who promises Phedre the key to the rescue of Phedre's imprisoned childhood friend, Hyacinthe.
4. ***Kushiel's Scion*** **(Warner, 2006)** First of a new trilogy narrated by Imriel no Montreve de la Courcel who, although a prince of the blood, underwent a horrendous childhood, abandoned by his treacherous mother, Melisande Shahrizai, to sadistic pirates.
5. ***Kushiel's Justice*** **(Warner, 2007)** Prince Imriel, foster son of Phedre no Delaunay, goes through a series of romances before he marries Alban princess Dorelei.

II. The Sundering, thus far a pair of novels, is an epic fantasy series with a large cast of gods, humans, dragons, and other sentient creatures. The Seven Gods who rule the fantasy world of Urulat have been divided by the civil war between Satoris Banewreaker and his elder brother Haomane. Satoris enlists the aid of his more than 1,000-year-old "human," Tanaros Blacksword. Somewhat more leisurely than the

Kushiel series, except for a rousing climax in number 2, the Sundering is another successful attempt at fantasy world building.

1. *Banewreaker* (**Tor, 2004**) One of seven gods ruling Urular, Satoris Banewreaker rebels against his elder brother Haomane. Satoris's lieutenant, Tanaros Blacksword, who has lived 1,000 years after killing his unfaithful wife and her lover, has to kidnap and safeguard his wife's beautiful descendant, Cerelinde.

2. *Godslayer* (**Tor, 2005**) The civil war proceeds to its bloody conclusion, taking its toll on gods, men, and other creatures.

Carl, JoAnna

PSEUDONYM OF Eva K. Sandstrom

Eva K. Sandstrom (q.v.), author of the Nell Matthews mysteries, has started a new mystery series under the pseudonym of JoAnna Carl. The Chocoholic Mysteries are cozies that revolve around TenHuis Chocolade, a Michigan store run by Aunt Nettie TenHuis and her niece Lee McKinney. Lee does most of the amateur detecting. Along with the mystery, each book includes chocolate lore. According to JoAnna Carl, the folks at Morgen Chocolate, in Dallas, have supplied her with much authentic information on chocolate making. Numbers 1 through 3 have been published in an omnibus volume, *Crime de Cocoa* (Signet, 2005).

1. *Chocolate Cat Caper, The* (**Signet, 2002**) Divorcée Lee McKinney moves back to Michigan to work at her aunt's chocolate shop. Then a high-profile defense lawyer is poisoned by a cyanide-tainted chocolate cat.

2. *Chocolate Bear Burglary, The* (**Signet, 2002**) Lee, Aunt Nettie, and their chocolate business inadvertently get involved with some big-time criminals.

3. *Chocolate Frog Frame-Up, The* (**Signet, 2003**) The town crank is the first customer to buy TenHuis Chocolade's latest concoction, a chocolate frog. Then he disappears.

4. *Chocolate Puppy Puzzle, The* (**Signet, 2004**) A Hollywood movie mogul comes to Michigan to turn a local author's romance novel into a major film.

5. *Chocolate Mouse Trap, The* (**Signet, 2005**) When party planner and terminally cutesy e-mail sender Julie Singletree is killed, everyone on her mailing list, including Lee McKinney, becomes a suspect.

6. *Chocolate Bridal Bash, The* (**Signet, 2006**) When bride-to-be Lee McKinney is told by her mother that she won't be at the wedding if it takes place in Warner Pier, her hometown, Lee uncovers a mystery older than she is.

7. *Chocolate Jewel Case, The* (**Signet, 2007**) In her rare free time, Lee McKinney Woodyard works on TenHuis Chocolade's newest offerings, chocolate jewels. Then Warner Pier has a heist of real jewels, and then a body is found in the lake.

Carlson, P(atricia) M(cElroy)

I. Statistician Maggie Ryan and her actor husband, Nick O'Connor, have separate careers, but they work together as an amateur detective team when they are faced with crimes. Maggie and Nick are intelligent, resourceful, courageous, and . . . physically fit. The first three Maggie Ryan novels take place in the 1970s on an upstate New York campus apparently based on Cornell University, Carlson's alma mater (BA, MA, PhD), where she taught for several years in the 1970s. Number 6 is also set there, though somewhat later. New York City forms the main background in numbers 4 and 5, and numbers 7 and 8 are set in Virginia and Maryland.

1. *Audition for Murder* (**Avon, 1985**) Set on a upstate New York campus in the 1970s and introducing Maggie Ryan as a student in a murder mystery with a theatrical theme.

2. *Murder Is Academic* (**Avon, 1985**) "For students on this upstate campus . . . the new course was terror and the final exam was murder" (blurb).

3. *Murder Is Pathological* (**Avon, 1986**) A secret experiment in the college biology lab is trashed. Was it just the work of vandals?

4. *Murder Unrenovated* (**Bantam, 1988**) Mother-to-be Maggie Ryan and her actor husband move into a vintage Brooklyn brownstone house. Then their renovation efforts turn up a corpse in the room upstairs.

5. *Rehearsal for Murder* (**Bantam, 1988**) The star of Nick's play is murdered, and Maggie, her hands full with an infant, finds herself implicated in the kidnapping of a millionaire's granddaughter.

6. *Murder Misread* (**Doubleday, 1990**) Maggie returns to her alma mater as a consulting to a reading expert. Then Tal Chandler, popular retired professor, is found dead on campus, an apparent suicide. But Maggie knows better.

7. *Murder in the Dog Days* (**Bantam, 1991**) Maggie and her family head to what they expect to be a quiet vacation in Mosby, Virginia. But then writer Dale Colby, on the edge of publishing an expose of prominent local citizens, is found dead in a locked-room murder.

8. *Bad Blood* (**Doubleday, 1991**) Maggie Ryan poses as a reporter to get to the bottom of the murder of aging widower John Spencer and a messy family situation involving Ginny, the teenage adopted daughter of deacon's wife Rina Marshall.

II. Carlson embarked upon a new series featuring small-town Nichols County, Indiana, deputy sheriff Marty Hopkins. Marty isn't as well educated as Maggie Ryan, but she is just as intelligent and feisty. The series got off to a promising start with two novels in two years, but then there was a nine-year hiatus between numbers 2 and 3. Carlson also published a collection of short mysteries featuring a character named Bridget Mooney and historical characters such as U. S. Grant, Sarah Bernhardt, and Jesse James: *Renowned Be Thy Grave; Or, The Murderous Miss Mooney* (Crippen & Landru, 1998).

1. *Gravestone* (**Pocket Books, 1994**) Small-town Indiana policewoman Marty Hopkins thinks that the Ku Klux Klan is behind what seems to be a racially motivated murder.

2. *Bloodstream* (**Pocket Books, 1995**) Marty is involved with a trio of runaways: her husband, her daughter, and 14-year-old Johnny Donato, whose mutilated body is found floating in the White River.

3. *Deathwind* (**Severn House, 2005**) A tornado, her estranged husband's opposition to their divorce, and the corpses of bank teller Stephanie Stolinitz and Lily Pistol lead singer Hoyt Heller occupy deputy sheriff Marty.

4. *Crossfire* (**Severn House, 2006**) Marty investigates the death of Zill Corson in an apparent arson attack at his hunting cabin, which he shared with Don Foley, a former sheriff in the department who had a grudge against Marty.

Carmichael, Emily

Because Lydia Keane led a less-than-perfect life as a leggy, blond human who seduced her best friend Amy's husband, she has been condemned by "heavenly host" Stanley to return to Earth in the body of an overweight, flea-bitten corgi named Piggy, and she has been given the task of matchmaker for a series of love-handicapped women. Much of the fun in these lighthearted, rather cutesy romps is the contrast between Lydia's human thoughts and Piggy's doggy desires.

1. *Finding Mr. Wright* (Bantam, 1998) Having died while fooling around with her best friend Amy's husband, Lydia Keane is sent back to Earth by heavenly host Stanley as a fat corgi assigned the task of finding a new husband for Amy.
2. *Diamond in the Ruff* (Bantam, 2001) This time Piggy must find a man for Joey DeMato, a wedding planner who has little time for men or dogs. When Joey agrees to plan her friend Alicia's wedding, she finds that Ben, the prospective groom, threatens to melt her cool reserve.
3. *Gone to the Dogs* (Bantam, 2003) To Piggy's chagrin, new owner Nell Jordan has put the overweight corgi on a strict diet. Then Piggy inherits a fortune from an old man she visited as a therapy dog.

Carr, Caleb

Laszlo Kreisler, the fictional "alienist," was a practitioner of the then new science of forensic psychology in the 1890s when Theodore Roosevelt was the reforming police commissioner of New York. T. R. and a number of other historical characters (Clarence Darrow, Elizabeth Cady Stanton, etc.) interact with Kreisler and his associates in the investigation of serial killers in a pair of well-received novels rich in period detail, thoughtful commentary, and interesting characters. Caleb Carr is also a historian, whose nonfiction book *The Lessons of Terror* (Random House, 2002) has aroused some controversy. Carr has recently added to Arthur Conan Doyle's (q.v.) Sherlock Holmes canon in *The Italian Secretary* (Carroll & Graf, 2005), in which Holmes, Watson, and Mycroft Holmes investigate murders at Victoria's Palace of Holyrood in Edinburgh. Some readers hope that Holmes will get together with Dr. Kreizler in a future book.

1. *Alienist, The* (Random House, 1994) Crime reporter John Moore of the *New York Times*, a friend of New York Police Commissioner Theodore Roosevelt, relates the successful efforts of the "alienist," Dr. Laszlo Kreizler, to unmask the ritual-like serial killer of young transvestite prostitutes.
2. *Angel of Darkness, The* (Random House, 1997) Former street urchin Stevie, a relatively minor character in *The Alienist*, narrates Dr. Kreizler's investigation of another serial murderer and baby kidnapper Libby Hatch, who acquires Clarence Darrow as her defense attorney.

Carr, Philippa

PSEUDONYM OF Eleanor Hibbert

Carr's novels are "costume gothic," a blend of gothic and historical elements. They feature the traditional gothic plot of a woman caught in a vaguely menacing mystery and torn between two men—one a passionate or dangerous rogue and the other a mild-mannered gentleman. The author has fitted her main characters into a tenuous family free covering many generations and called the series Daughters of England.

1. *Miracle at St. Bruno's, The* (Putnam, 1972) Set during the English Reformation, this follows the story of young Damask Farland, whose father was beheaded for helping a monk.
2. *Lion Triumphant, The* (Putnam, 1874) The early Elizabethan time, with its religious clashes and strife with Spain, gives flavor to Catherine's story.
3. *Witch from the Sea, The* (Putnam, 1975) The defeat of the Spanish Armada (1588) figures in Linnet Pennylon's journal, as does her traumatic encounter with the evil Squire of Castle Paling.

4. *Saraband for Two Sisters* (Putnam, 1976) The story of identical twins, Angelet and Bersaba Landor, is set against the Royalist-Puritan struggles of England in the 1640s.
5. *Lament for a Lost Lover* (Putnam, 1977) This tells Arabella Tolworthy's story from her exile in France in 1658 to her marriage with Cavalier Edward Eversleigh and her return to England.
6. *Love-Child, The* (Putnam, 1978) Young Priscilla Eversleigh's quiet life at Eversleigh Court is abruptly changed with the arrival of Harriet Main and a troubled religious fugitive, Jocelyn Frinton.
7. *Song of the Siren, The* (Putnam, 1980) Set at the time of the Jacobite uprising (1688), this concerns two half sisters, the placid Damaris and the fiery Carlotta.
8. *Will You Love Me in September?* (Putnam, 1981) This takes up the story of Clarissa Hessenfield, the orphaned love child of Carlotta, beginning in 1715. English title: *The Drop of the Dice*.
9. *Adulteress, The* (Putnam, 1982) Zipporah goes to Eversleigh Court to try to uncover a family secret.
10. *Knave of Hearts* (Putnam, 1983) Lottie, a young English girl, travels to France during the reign of Louis XV to solve the mystery surrounding her true parentage.
11. *Voices in a Haunted Room* (Putnam, 1984) Claudine de Tournville marries one twin, but is in love with the other.
12. *Return of the Gypsy, The* (Putnam, 1985) A young English girl loses her heart to a Gypsy.
13. *Midsummer's Eve* (Putnam, 1986) One midsummer's night, young Annora learns of an evil secret that destroys her happiness. Set early in Victoria's reign.
14. *Pool of St. Branok, The* (Putnam, 1987) Angelet travels to Australia and meets Ben, with whom she shares a guilty secret.
15. *Changeling, The* (Putnam, 1989) Victorian London and Cornwall are the scenes for this tale of sibling rivalry between Rebecca, her half sister Belinda, and Lucie, who has been "adopted" by Rebecca's stepfather.
16. *Black Swan, The* (Putnam, 1990) The Irish Question intrudes as Benedict Lansdon, Lucie's father, breaks with Gladstone, and Lucie gets involved with a terrorist in disguise.
17. *Time for Silence, A* (Putnam, 1991) Lucinda Greenham and her friend leave England for a finishing school on the Continent shortly before the outbreak of World War I.
18. *Gossamer Cord, The* (Putnam, 1992) The beginning of World War II finds 17-year-old twins Violetta and Dorabella Denver visiting friends in Germany.
19. *We'll Meet Again* (Putnam, 1993) Dorabella and Violetta are living on neighboring Cornish estates as World War II encroaches on the lives of friends and relatives.

Carroll, Jerry Jay

William "Bogey" Ingersoll, ruthless Wall Street takeover artist, wakes up one day in the form of a dog in a fantasy world where Good and Evil are stark choices. In *Top Dog*, Bogey explores both options. The second novel, *Dog Eat Dog*, finds him back in human form on his northern California estate, changed for the better morally but still subject to a disturbing recurring dream in which agents of Satan chase him. The two novels are entertaining mixtures of fantasy, thriller, and morality tale. Numbers 1 and 2 have been published together in the omnibus volume *A Dog's Life* (Berkley, 1999). Carroll's only other published novel to date is *Inhuman Beings* (Ace, 1998), an SF fantasy about aliens and psychics.

1. *Top Dog* (Ace, 1998) Wall Street raider William "Bogey" Ingersoll wakes up changed into a dog in a fantasy world where God and Satan are openly at war.

2. *Dog Eat Dog* (Ace, 1999) Returned to human form and his northern California estate, Bogey is a changed man, giving away his fortune to worthy causes and adopting numerous stray dogs. Unfortunately, he is having a recurring dream, in which "Pig Faces," agents of Satan, are chasing him.

Carroll, Lewis

PSEUDONYM OF Charles L. Dodgson

Although written for children, Lewis Carroll's "Alice" books have continued to intrigue readers of all ages for more than a century. Alice's adventures *Through the Looking Glass* and *Underground* have been filmed at least a dozen times and illustrated by many artists, but real aficionados still insist on the original versions by Lewis Carroll (aka Oxford mathematician Charles Lutwidge Dodgson) with illustrations by the great Victorian political cartoonist John Tenniel. Carroll's nonsense poetry, including "The Walrus and the Carpenter" and "The Jabberwocky" from *Through the Looking Glass* and *The Hunting of the Snark* has survived, but his preachy *Sylvie and Bruno* books: *Sylvie and Bruno* (Macmillan, 1889) and *Sylvie and Bruno Concluded* (Macmillan, 1893) have not. Martin Gardner's *The Annotated Alice* (New American Library, 1963), with its annotated texts, adds to the fun.

1. *Alice's Adventures in Wonderland* (Appleton, 1966) Young Alice falls down a rabbit hole and reaches Wonderland, a place full of strange characters who operate by their own zany logic, such as the Mad Hatter, the March Hare, a talking caterpillar, the ever-grinning Cheshire Cat, the White Rabbit, the Mock Turtle, and the homicidal Red Queen. More often than not published as *Alice in Wonderland*.
2. *Through the Looking-Glass* (Macmillan [UK], 1871) Alice arrives in Wonderland again, this time through a mirror, gets involved in a complicated chess match, and meets old "friends" such as the Mad Hatter and new ones such as the sinister twins Tweedledum and Tweedledee and Humpty Dumpty.

Carroll, Ward

I. US Navy Lieutenant Rick "Punk" Reichert flies an F-14 Tomcat when he isn't partying or brought to the ground in remote places like Afghanistan. The Punk novels are exciting stories full of testosterone, military jargon, aviation technology, and great flying sequences by former fighter pilot Ward Carroll.

1. *Punk's War* (Naval Institute, 2001) US Navy lieutenant Punk Reichert and his comrades, based aboard an aircraft carrier in the Persian Gulf, challenge Iranian and Iraqi fliers, party, gripe, and try to find a way around "Soup" Campbell, their egotistical, glory-grabbing squadron leader.
2. *Punk's Wing* (Signet, 2003) Punk Reichert, training new pilots, has his hands full with Lieutenant Evelyn "Muddy" Greenwood, who has some trouble with flying but has a powerful female US senator behind her.
3. *Punk's Fight* (Signet, 2004) Punk is shot down over Afghanistan, is captured, and then escapes to find his way through the war-torn country.

II. Navy SEAL Ash Roberts takes on a couple of dangerous and highly sensitive assignments.

1. *Aide, The* (Signet, 2005) Navy SEAL Ash Roberts, assigned to a new position at the Pentagon as aide to Vice Admiral Brooks

Garrett, assistant principal to the joint chiefs of staff, has discovered a dangerous secret about his new boss.
2. *Militia Kill* (Signet, 2006) Ash Roberts is ordered to South Dakota, where an ATF agent has been captured by a paramilitary group called the Badlands Militia.

Carter, Charlotte

I. Nanette Hayes is a French-speaking, sax-playing African American street musician and former child prodigy who gets involved in love affairs that don't work out and a series of murder mysteries that she somehow survives. New York City is the setting for numbers 1 and 3, and Paris for number 2. The plots aren't really the thing here, but the smart-mouthed Nanette, who doesn't really have to make a living on the streets, and her colleagues, many of whom are down-and-out, are an intriguing bunch, and the books are an entertaining read. African American writer Carter was raised in Chicago, has traveled widely, and currently lives in New York.

1. *Rhode Island Red* (Serpent's Tale, 1997) Having broken up again with her on-again, off-again boyfriend, Walter, sax-playing African American street musician Nanette allows another musician to crash in her New York City apartment. Nanette wakes up during the night to find the musician, who is really an undercover cop, with a knife in his throat and her saxophone stuffed with $60,000 in cash.
2. *Coq au Vin* (Mysterious, 1999) Nanette returns to Paris to look for her aunt Viv to hand over an inheritance from Nan's father to the wayward Viv.
3. *Drumsticks* (Mysterious, 2000) Back in New York and feeling low, Nanette is drinking too much and losing contact with friends until the gift of a voodoo doll seems to change her luck.

II. Cassandra Perry, an African American college student in Chicago in the fraught year of 1968, gets involved in a couple of mysteries. Cassandra is as sassy as Nanette Hayes (series I), but the Cook County series isn't quite so rollicking, dealing as it does with black family life and racism. *Walking Bones* (Serpent's Tail, 2002), a novel examining sexual obsession, is quite different in tone from Carter's series mysteries.

1. *Jackson Park* (Ballantine, 2003) In the days following Martin Luther King Jr.'s assassination, in April 1968, college student Cassandra Perry gets involved with her great-uncle and great-aunt in searching for a lost teenager with a checkered past.
2. *Trip-Wire* (Ballantine, 2005) In December 1968, in the second **Cook County mystery,** Cassandra is trying to find out who murdered two of her commune roommates—one black male and one white female.

Carter, Philip Youngman

Philip Youngman Carter, Margery Allingham's (q.v.) husband, completed *Cargo of Eagles* after her death. He wrote two more Campion novels on his own.

1. *Cargo of Eagles* (Morrow, 1968) Concerns poison-pen letters, a pretty woman doctor, and a hunt for buried treasure. Completed by Carter after the death of Margery Allingham.
2. *Mr. Campion's Farthing* (Morrow, 1969) Shows Campion following the trail of a missing Russian scientist to a monastery in the English countryside.

3. *Mr. Campion's Quarry* **(Morrow, 1971)** Murder, double agents, and an archaeological dig occupy Campion in what proved to be his final case. English title: *Mr. Campion's Falcon.*

Carver, Jeffrey A(llan)

I. Jeffrey A. Carver is regarded as master craftsman of hard science fiction. According to Carver, his main themes are "star travel, alien contact, artificial intelligence, and transcendental realities—and the moral, ethical grand spiritual implications of these possibilities." (See Carver's website at www.starrigger.net.) Star Rigger's Universe, his most popular series, also contains fantasy elements such as dragons, magical realms, and mysterious power sources. Star riggers are space pilots who navigate the sometimes treacherous Flux, a kind of mind-altering continuum that guides starships through deep space.

1. *Panglor* **(Dell, 1980)** Revised edition published by Tor (1996). A prequel setting the stage for "star rigging," in which discredited space pilot Panglor Balef stumbles unto the mysterious Flux.
2. *Star Rigger's Way* **(Doubleday, 1978)** Geo Carlyle is adrift in the Flux, the path through which starships travel faster than the speed of light, with only a catlike alien as companion. Based on "Alien Persuasion," the first published story set in the star rigger's universe (*Galaxy* magazine, 1975).
3. *Dragons in the Stars* **(Tor, 1992)** Star rigger (space pilot) Jael LeBrae, trapped in the Flux with a tyrannical captain, takes a route rumored to be full of dragons.
4. *Dragon Rigger* **(Tor, 1993)** Jael returns to the world of dragons to help them in their war against the Nail of Strength.
5. *Eternity's End* **(Tor, 2000)** Betrayed to space pirates by a treacherous captain, Rigger Renwald Legroeder finally escapes and joins forces with the alien Narseil.
6. *Seas of Ernathe* **(Laser Books, 1976)** Although published before the other novels in the series, this is set in a future millennium after the skills of star rigging have been lost. Can Seth Perland find the key to rediscovering these skills on a world of mysterious sea people, the Nale'nid?

II. A pair of linked novels about the supernova explosion of the star Betelgeuse and its aftermath could be regarded as a prequel to the Star Riggers series.

1. *From a Changeling Star* **(Bantam, 1989)** Willard Ruskin, on Katano's World, who may be the key to the rescue of scientists endangered by the implosion of Betelgeuse, is infected by "nano-agents."
2. *Down the Stream of Stars* **(Bantam, 1990)** Melnik and Jeaves, passengers on the starship *Charity,* which is traveling through the Starstream left by the remnants of Betelgeuse, are thrown into the path of the alien and apparently malicious Throgs.

III. The Chaos Chronicles introduces mining technician John Bandicut, who hooks up with an unseen alien to save Earth from destruction by a comet in an engaging working out of the new science of chaos theory. Three more novels in the series have been projected: *Sunborn, The Reefs of Time,* and *Masters of Shipworld.*

1. *Neptune Crossing* **(Tor, 1994)** Doing a mining survey on Triton, Earthling John Bandicut tumbles onto "Charlie" the Quarx, which has the power of attaching itself symbiotically to a human host.
2. *Strange Attractors* **(Tor, 1995)** Having saved Earth from an onrushing comet, the genetically altered Bandicut, a rejuvenated Charlie, and an alien called Ik journey to the massive planetlike Shipworld.
3. *Infinite Sea, The* **(Tor, 1996)** Bandicut and his motley crew travel to the world of the Neri, an underwater civilization, where they deal with two menaces; the Astari and the Maw of the Abyss.

Carvic, Heron

Miss Emily Seeton is a retired English art teacher whose happy involvement in a series of mysteries has delighted her many fans. As a sleuth armed with an umbrella—her "brolly"—and sometimes in disguise, she is always comic and suspenseful. Her protector and supporter, Superintendent Delphick of Scotland Yard (nicknamed "the Oracle," naturally), supervises Miss Seeton's always chaotic cases. Carvic died in 1980, but his series has been carried on by Hampton Charles (q.v.) and then by Hamilton Crane (q.v.).

1. *Picture Miss Seeton* **(Harper, 1968)** Miss Seeton makes her debut as a murder witness in need of protection. But her success in nabbing the mastermind of a narcotics ring guarantees an encore.
2. *Miss Seeton Draws the Line* **(Harper, 1970)** On vacation in the quiet village of Plummergen, Miss Seeton spies out the nefarious activities of a murderer, an embezzler, and two bicycle bandits.
3. *Witch Miss Seeton* **(Harper, 1971)** When devils and witchcraft seem to be taking over the village of Plummergen, Miss Seeton is on the scene to investigate.
4. *Miss Seeton Sings* **(Harper, 1973)** Forged banknotes and a Greek millionaire lead Miss Seeton on a merry chase all over Europe.
5. *Odds on Miss Seeton* **(Harper, 1975)** Miss Seeton, in jewels and a mauve wig, takes up gambling to help break up an organized-crime syndicate.

Cary, Joyce

I. Moviegoers will remember Alec Guiness's portrayal of the irrepressible Gully Jimson in the 1959 film *The Horse's Mouth* based on the novel of the same name The two earlier novels of the *First Trilogy* are filled with an equally memorable cast including housekeeper Sara Monday and retired lawyer Tom Wilcher. Cary was a novelist of character rather than action; he dissected the entanglements of human relationships with humor, wisdom, and style.

1. *Herself Surprised* **(Harper, 1948)** This book introduces Sara Monday, amiable cook and housekeeper, whose casual view of property ownership finally lands her in jail.
2. *To Be a Pilgrim* **(Harper, 1949)** Tom Wilcher, retired English lawyer, narrates this memoir as he awaits Sara's release from jail.
3. *Horse's Mouth, The* **(Harper, 1950)** Gully Jimson, a 67-year-old artist recently released from jail, has the inspiration for his life's masterpiece.

II. The Second Trilogy shows Cary in a somewhat more serious, though no less perceptive, mood. The three books do not fit together chronologically, but show some of the same events from three different points of view: Nina Woodville's and her two husbands, Chester Nimmo and Jim Latter. Probably best read in publication order.

1. *Prisoner of Grace* **(Harper, 1952)** Introduces Nina Woodville and the two men and successive husbands in her life: Chester Nimmo and Jim Latter.

2. *Except the Lord* (**Harper, 1953**) Chester Nimmo, politician and labor leader, relates the story of his childhood and youth amid the rural poverty of the West Country in mid-Victorian England.

3. *Not Honour More* (**Harper, 1955**) Picks up at the point *Prisoner of Grace* leaves off, the year of the General Strike (1926). Nina is maintaining an uneasy menage a trois with her second husband, retired Captain Jim Latter, and her former husband, Chester Nimmo.

Castle, Jayne

PSEUDONYM OF Jayne Ann Krentz

I. "Jayne Castle" is one among several pseudonyms that the prolific Jayne Ann Krentz (q.v.) uses. The Guinevere Jones quartet is a mystery series involving a bright, brave, and beautiful amateur detective who accidently gets involved in solving homicides. The quartet, published in paperback editions in one year (1986), are now hard to obtain, fetching $30 to $50 each in the used-book market.

1. *Desperate Game, The* (**Dell, 1986**) Independent operator Guinevere Jones is enlisted by private eye Zachariah Justis to become his personal spy

2. *Chilling Deception* (**Dell, 1986**) Guinevere knew that Mr. Vandyke was in serious trouble when she found the gold gun in the "mauve and black marble executive washroom."

3. *Sinister Touch, The* (**Dell, 1986**) "Being a good neighbor was easy when the window across the way framed a handsome young artist. But when she became witness to sudden . . ." (blurb).

4. *Fatal Fortune, The* (**Dell, 1986**) Madame Zoltana predicted money, but not murder, but the sceptical Guinevere found that the psychic's crystal ball told only part of the tale.

II. Jayne Anne Krentz let her Castle pseudonym rest for about 10 years before she came up with the Flower trio, set on St. Helen's, an Earth colony in the future where psychic abilities seem to be fairly normal. The trio was followed by a series of loosely connected novels known as the Psynergy Inc. series, where "para-archaeologists" and ghost hunters team up to hunt down the "energy ghosts" on the planet of Harmony. These novels are sexy futuristic romances with interesting characters and a leaven of humor. *Harmony* (Berkley, 2002) contains number 5 and the 1999 version of number 4.

1. *Amaryllis* (**Pocket, 1996**) Amaryllis Lark, beautiful psychic detective on St. Helen's, a planet colonized by Earthlings, gets involved with a murder investigation and a steamy love affair with Lucas Trent, head of Lodestar Exploration.

2. *Zinnia* (**Pocket, 1997**) Two gifted psychics on St. Helen's—Zinnia, a girl with a reputation, and a wealthy, illegitimate hero—square off amid a maze of carnivorous, sentient plants.

3. *Orchid* (**Pocket, 1998**) Rafe Stonebreaker, business executive with psychic strategizing abilities, and Orchid Adams, writer of psychic vampire romance novels, seem to be mismatched, but events involving a mystery and some villains prove otherwise.

4. *Bridal Jitters* (**Berkley, 2005**) The marriage of convenience between para-archaeologist Virginia and her bodyguard, security agent and ghost hunter Sam, is followed by the investigation of a "psi energy trap" in a tunnel in the old Dead City. Originally published as a novella in *Pandora's Bottle* (Berkley, 1999) with stories by three other authors (Julie Beard, Lori Foster, and Eileen Wilks).

5. *After Dark* (**Jove, 2000**) Lydia Smith's career as a para-archaeologist on the planet of Harmony comes to a halt when she is caught in an "illusion trap."

6. *After Glow* (**Jove, 2004**) Lydia and her lover, ghost hunter Emmett London, work together to solve the homicide of Lawrence Maltby, her former professor.

7. *Ghost Hunter* (**Jove, 2006**) Local guild boss and powerful ghost-hunter Cooper Boone and botanist Elly St. Clair combine to investigate a disappearance in Cadence City.

8. *Silver Master* (**Jove, 2007**) Security specialist Davis Oakes searches for the powerful relic that Cadence City matchmaker and para-resonator Celinda Ingram supposedly bought as a toy for her pet "dust bunny."

Céline, Louis-Ferdinand

PSEUDONYM OF L. F. Destouches

I. Céline's virulent anti-Semitic writings and collaboration with the Nazis in the 1930s and early 1940s have tended to overshadow his World War I heroism, his medical work among the needy, and early classics such as *Journey to the End of the Night* and *Death on the Installment Plan*, which influenced a generation of writers on both sides of the Atlantic. Celine's semiautobiographical German trilogy describes his flight from Paris through Germany to Denmark at the close of World War II in a hallucinatory mix of historical narrative and digressions.

1. *North* (**Delacorte, 1972**) Describes the narrator's flight with his wife and remnants of the Vichy government from Paris through Baden-Baden, Berlin, and other German cities in 1944. Translated from the French by Ralph Manheim. Originally published as *Nord* in 1960.

2. *Rigadoon* (**Delacorte, 1974**) Describes the passage through Ulm of the narrator and his menage. Translated by Ralph Manheim from the French. Originally published as *Rigadon* in 1967.

3. *Castle to Castle* (**Delacorte, 1968**) Describes the narrator's stay with the remnants of the Vichy government in Sigmaringen. Published and translated first, but third chronologically. Translated from the French by Ralph Manheim. Originally published as *D'un château l'autre* in 1957.

II. The two parts of *Guignol's Band* were published more than two years apart even though they were written in fairly quick succession. Told in Céline's cynically comic, hallucinatory style, they relate the picaresque adventures of the semiautobiographical Ferdinand as he wanders through the London underworld in the period of World War I.

1. *Guignol's Band* (**New Directions, 1954**) Ferdinand, a young Frenchman recuperating from wounds suffered in World War I, flees to London. Translated from the French by Bernard Frechtman and Jack Nile. Originally published as *Guignol's Band* in 1941.

2. *London Bridge* (**Dalkey Archive, 1995**) Ferdinand and his friend Sosthene de Rodiencourt answer the insane Colonel O'Collagham's advertisement for volunteers to design and test gas masks. Translated from the French by Dominic Di Bernardi. Originally published as *Guignol's Band II* in 1965.

III. *Fable for Another Time* was originally published in two parts in 1952. The first part was translated into English by Mary Hudson (as part of a doctoral thesis) and published by the University of Nebraska Press with notes based on those by Henri Godard, which appeared in the 1974 Gallimard edition. Part 2, entitled *Normance*, has not yet been published in English. Again autobiographical, it was written by Céline during the time he was imprisoned in Copenhagen awaiting extradition to France for trial. Described as "a bitter howl of protest" expressed in Céline's fragmented, hallucinatory style, this rebarbative novel is for Céline diehards only.

1. **Fable for Another Time (Nebraska, 2003)** Céline spares no one in this autobiographical account and justification of his life's work. Translated from the French by Mary Hudson. Originally published as *Férie pour une autre fois* in 1952.

Chadwick, Elizabeth

I. British writer Chadwick has published a trilogy covering several generations of the inhabitants of the medieval Welsh estate of Ravenstow, the first three novels of more than a dozen set in the England of the 11th, 12th, and 13th centuries. Like all good historical romances, the Ravenstow Chronicles are full of action, passion, and authentic period detail. This Elizabeth Chadwick is not to be confused with the author of western romances (*Bride Fire*, etc.).

1. **Wild Hunt, The (St. Martin's, 1991)** A politically expedient marriage during the reign of William Rufus, king of England (late 11th century), unites 15-year-old Judith of Ravenstow and Norman nobleman Guy Fitz-Miles, Lord of Ledworth.
2. **Running Vixen, The (St. Martin's, 1992)** Adam de Lacey leaves his difficult wife, Heulwin, for the Continent to fetch King Henry I's daughter Matilda, heiress to the English throne.
3. **Leopard Unleashed, The (St. Martin's, 1993)** During the troubled reign of King Stephen, young Renard returns to Ravenstow from the Crusader kingdom of Antioch with his mistress, Olwen.

II. The historical William Marshal (d. 1219), English knight, crusader, magnate, and regent, who is the subject of biographies by prominent historians such as Sidney Painter and Georges Duby, is given the novelistic treatment in two volumes by Chadwick. William Marshal also appears as a child in Chadwick's *A Place beyond Courage* (Sphere [UK], 2007).

1. **Greatest Knight, The (Little, Brown, 2005)** Wiilliam Marshal rises through the ranks to become tutor in arms to the son of King Henry II and Eleanor of Aquitaine.
2. **Scarlet Lion, The (Little, Brown, 2006)** Now a powerful magnate, William is serving King Richard on campaign in Normandy.

Chaikin, Linda (Lee)

I. Linda Chaikin is the prolific author of several series of historical romances published by Christian presses (Bethany, Harvest House, Moody, etc.). As Christian romances, Chaikin's novels emphasize the religious aspects of her characters and eschew steamy depictions of sex, but otherwise they have the standard historical romance formula of strong women under stress, romantic heroes, and plenty of action. The Royal Pavilions trilogy is set at the time of the Crusades and depicts the adventures of Tancred Redwan, son of a Norman lord and initially reluctant crusader and the beautiful Helena Lysander who is trying to escape her fate as bride to the Muslim Prince Kalid.

1. **Swords and Scimitars (Nelson, 1993)** Tancred Redwan, son of a Norman lord, who opposes the Crusades, gets embroiled in them while seeking to discover his brother's murderer.
2. **Golden Palaces (Behany, 1996)** Tancred comes to the aid of Helena Lysander, who has been betrothed to a Muslim prince by her treacherous family.

3. **Behind the Veil (Bethany, 1998)** Helena is abducted by her nemesis, Lady Irene, and presented as a bride to the Muslim Prince Kalid, but Tancred, now a Crusader, holds the key to her redemption.

II. The Heart of India trio is set in India's northern frontier in the late 18th century. Coral Kendall, heiress to a silk plantation, feels it her mission to take care of the children of India's Untouchable caste. Although Coral's relatives and East India Company officials oppose her, she perseveres with the help of the "dashing" Major Jace Buckley.

1. **Silk (Bethany, 1993)** Coral Kendall, heiress to a silk plantation in India's northern frontier in the late 1700s, adopts an orphaned Untouchable boy.
2. **Under Eastern Stars (Bethany, 1993)** Coral Kendall, determined to open a mission school for Untouchable children despite the opposition of powerful figures in the East India Company, encounters two attractive but different young men: Major Jace Buckley and Dr. Ethan Boswell.
3. **Kingscote (Bethany, 1994)** Coral's mission school is threatened by mysterious happenings, as she awaits Jace Buckley, who's coming to Kingscote, her estate, for Christmas.

III. The Buccaneers is a trilogy set in the heyday of Captain Henry Morgan and the pirates on the Spanish Main in 17th-century West Indies. Heiress Emerald Harwick and pirate Baret Buckington undergo a series of adventures together. Emerald's Christian faith protects her throughout.

1. **Port Royal (Moody, 1995)** Emerald Harwick flees from her father with an indentured servant she plans to marry.
2. **Pirate and the Lady, The (Moody, 1997)** Emerald finds her lot cast among pirates seeking buried treasure, but falls in love with buccaneer Baret Buckington.
3. **Jamaican Sunset (Moody, 1997)** In the conclusion to the Buccaneers, Emerald and Baret find true love together as they continue their search for treasure.

IV. Three books, which don't seem to have a series title, are set in Egypt just before and during World War I and follow the adventures of Christian missionary nurse Allison Wescott as she supports British war efforts against the Turks and the Germans and falls in love with a British intelligence officer.

1. **Arabian Winds (Multnomah, 1997)** Young Allison Wescott works on a medical-missions boat in the Nile and awaits her fiancé, Wade Finlay.
2. **Lions of the Desert (Multnomah, 1997)** In 1915 Allison arrives in Cairo to serve with the British military confronting the Germans and the Turks.
3. **Valiant Hearts (Multnomah, 1998)** The scene shifts to Palestine as Allison searches for her missing beloved, British intelligence officer Bret Holden.

V. The Trade Winds trilogy, like the Buccaneers trilogy, is set in the West Indies in the 17th century and features a devout heroine and a dashing pirate. Devora Ashby, a young lady resident on the island of Barbados, tries to escape an arranged marriage and falls into the arms of pirate Bruce Hawkins, who eventually turns out to be the man she was running away from.

1. **Captive Heart (Harvest, 1998)** Little does Devora Ashby realize that Bruce Hawkins, the dashing pirate she encounters, is really Don Nicklas Valentin, the man whom her mother had arranged her to marry.

2. *Silver Dreams* **(Harvest, 1998)** Devora and "Bruce Hawkins" sail the Spanish Main together on a series of adventures.
3. *Island Bride* **(Harvest, 1999)** Devora and Bruce plan to marry and settle down, but Devora's former flame and Bruce's envious brother stand in the way.

VI. East of the Sun is a romance trilogy set between 1879 and 1900, partly in South Africa. Aristocrat Rogan Chantry and orphaned daughter of missionaries Evy Varley are the hero and heroine. Water-Brook Press is a division of Random House.

Linda Chaikin has embarked upon several other "series." The Jewel of the Pacific, set in the leper colony of Molokai, seems to include only one volume: *For Whom the Stars Shine* (Bethany, 1999). Portraits, set in Kenya, seems to have only one volume also: *Endangered* (Bethany, 1997). The Great Northwest series contains two volumes seemingly related only by theme: *Empire Builders* (Bethany, 1993) and *Winds of Allegiance* (Bethany, 1996). A Day to Remember contains five volumes with days of the week in the titles (Harvest 1999–2001) but no connected characters. Two novels set in Nevada in the 1860s, *Desert Rose* (Harvest, 2003) and *Desert Star* (Harvest, 2004), seem to have no connected characters either.

1. *Tomorrow's Treasure* **(WaterBrook, 2003)** Orphan Evy Varley has a lot to learn about her past: her missionary parents killed in the Zulu uprising of 1878, a stolen diamond, and a dark secret concerning her mother.
2. *Yesterday's Promise* **(WaterBrook, 2004)** Rogan Chantry, son of the squire of Grimston Way, has fought hard to win his independence from Sir Julien Bley and the British South Africa Company.
3. *Today's Embrace* **(WaterBrook, 2005)** Evy Varley withholds news of her pregnancy from her husband, Rogan Chantry, so that she can accompany him on his voyage to South Africa in 1900.

VII. Chaikin's latest series is set in France during the reign of the Queen Mother, Catherine de Medici, inveterate enemy of the Huguenots.

1. *Daughter of Silk* **(Zondervan, 2006)** Young silk heiress Rachelle joins forces with the handsome rebel Marquis Fabien de Vendome against a diabolical plot hatched by the Queen Mother, Catherine de Medici.
2. *Written on Silk* **(Zondervan, 2007)** A royal wedding masks the unfolding of Catherine de Medici's plot against the Huguenots.
3. *Threads of Silk* **(Zondervan, 2008)** Rachelle and Fabien are at risk when they learn of Catherine de Medici's murderous plan against the Huguenots.

Chalker, Jack L(aurence)

I. The Well World series is the most popular creation of American science-fiction and fantasy writer Chalker. It is chock-full of science-fiction and fantasy motifs: a planet with many different intelligent races, a know-all computer left on its own to run the universe by a departed civilization, a malevolent agency that wants to take over the universe itself, parallel worlds, shape-changing, a Manichaean good-versus-evil conflict in which a chosen few humans have to save the universe, and plenty of action. Numbers 1 through 5 and 9 and 10 are called the Saga of the Well World. Numbers 6 through 8 are called the Watchers at the Well trilogy (collected in an omnibus volume called *Watchers at the Well* [Guild America, 1994]).

1. *Midnight at the Well of Souls* **(Ballantine, 1977)** Earthling Nathan Brazil wanders into the Well World, a vast set of interlocking environments built by ancient aliens.
2. *Exiles at the Well of Souls* **(Ballantine, 1978)** Six humans accidentally drawn into the Well World spark a war for control of the universe.
3. *Quest for the Well of Souls* **(Ballantine, 1978)** The war for control of the universe continues as two parties of former human beings vie to reach the one remaining spaceship.
4. *Return of Nathan Brazil, The* **(Ballantine, 1980)** Nathan Brazil returns to the Well World to fight sinister forces from another galaxy.
5. *Twilight at the Well of Souls* **(Ballantine, 1980)** Subtitle: *The Legacy of Nathan Brazil*. In the "final" battle Nathan and fellow human turned Immortal Mavra Chang have to reach the Well of Souls to save the universe.
6. *Echoes of the Well of Souls* **(Ballantine, 1993)** Nathan and Mavra are summoned back to the Well World to reset the Computer. First volume of Watchers at the Well trilogy.
7. *Shadow of the Well of Souls* **(Ballantine, 1994)** The malevolent entity known as the Kraang has created some kind of virus in the Computer. Second volume of the Watchers at the Well trilogy.
8. *Gods of the Well of Souls* **(Ballantine, 1994)** The unseen Kraang races against Chang and Brazil for control of the Computer. Third volume of the Well of Souls series.
9. *Sea Is Full of Stars, The* **(Ballantine, 1999)** In action located primarily in previously unexplored "hexes" of the Well World, three star travelers (Ming, Ari, and Angel) become enmeshed in a blood feud between an evil genius and the man who has vowed to destroy him.
10. *Ghost of the Well of Souls* **(Ballantine, 2000)** A small band of travelers tries to prevent the evil Josich from finding the eight scattered pieces of the fabled Straight Gate.

II. The Dancing Gods series is light fantasy: a parody of the sword-and-sorcery genre complete with alternate worlds, a good magician, an evil force, and ordinary human beings who go through various incarnations as they fight on the side of good against evil. Two omnibus volumes have been published by Ballantine (1995, 1996): *The Dancing Gods, Part I* contains numbers 1 and 2; *The Dancing Gods, Part II* contains numbers 3 and 4.

1. *River of Dancing Gods, The* **(Ballantine, 1984)** Joe and Marge are snatched from earthly deaths by the good magician Throckmorton P. Ruddygore and are incarnated as a Conan-type barbarian and a sexy sorceress.
2. *Demons of the Dancing Gods* **(Ballantine, 1984)** The forces of evil, represented by the Dark Baron and the Demon Prince, want a cataclysmic showdown with the forces of good, represented by Joe and Marge.
3. *Vengeance of the Dancing Gods* **(Ballantine, 1985)** The Dark Baron, exiled to Earth, uses his time profitably by picking up computer skills.
4. *Songs of the Dancing Gods* **(Ballantine, 1990)** Escaped again, the Dark Baron teams up with the Master of the Dead in the far north of Husaquahr.
5. *Horrors of the Dancing Gods* **(Ballantine, 1995)** The Old Ones rise from the depths of the Sea of Dreams to challenge both heaven and hell. Only the Great McGuffin can stop them.

III. In the Changewinds trilogy, the Ahkbreed rule over trillions of worlds, but the reality-altering Changewinds are beyond their control. When two young women from Earth fall into the Changewinds, the struggle for the universe begins. *The Changewinds* (Baen, 1996) is an omnibus volume containing all three titles.

1. *When the Changewinds Blow* (Ace, 1987) High school best friends Sam and Charlie are snatched from Earth and thrown into a strange new world.
2. *Riders of the Winds* (Ace, 1988) Charlie and Sam, entering the Kudaan Wastes through different paths, must confront the horned demon Klittichorn, who is enlisting the power of the Changewinds to destroy Akahlor.
3. *War of the Maelstrom* (Ace, 1988) Together again, Sam and Charlie go through more transformations as their wishes intertwine.

IV. *The Four Lords of the Diamond* (Doubleday, 1983) is an omnibus volume containing four novels. The Confederates and the lords of the small but worlds of the Warden Diamond (Lilith, Cerberus, Charon, Medusa) square off against each other in another series involving shape-shifting and the battle of good against evil.

1. *Lilith: A Snake in the Grass* (Ballantine, 1981) Rebels are infiltrating the Confederation, kidnapping people and substituting undetectable synthetic minions. Cal Tremon is sent to Lilith, one of the Diamond worlds, a "paradise" designed in hell.
2. *Cerberus: A Wolf in the Fold* (Ballantine, 1982) A human is dumped blind, naked, and alone on the world of Cerberus with the task of assassinating its lord.
3. *Charon: A Dragon at the Gate* (Ballantine, 1982) The body of Park Lacoch is emptied of his own mind, equipped with the mind of a top Confederacy operator, and then placed in a spaceship bound for Charon, one of the worlds of the Diamond.
4. *Medusa: A Tiger by the Tail* (Ballantine, 1983) Concludes the confrontation between the Confederates and the Diamond lords.

V. G.O.D. Inc. is a small multi-universe corporation whose inhabitants discovered long ago the pathways to alternate universes and the profits that resulted from such knowledge. In a trilogy that has science-fiction, fantasy, detective-novel, and spy-thriller elements, private investigators Sam and Brandy Horowitz, on the trail of a missing drug lord, are confronted with a plot that could destroy the universe(s).

1. *Labyrinth of Dreams, The* (Tor, 1987) PIs Sam and Brandy Horowitz, tracing Martin Whitlock, a banker who skipped town with over $2 million in laundered drug money, find themselves "off the edge of the Earth."
2. *Shadow Dancers, The* (Tor, 1987) Brandy and Jim find themselves in a race to stop the ultimate drug caper.
3. *Maze in the Mirror, The* (Tor, 1989) If Sam and Brandy don't stop the "Killers," they'll unleash a force that could incinerate every planet in all the universes.

VI. In the Quintara Marathon trilogy, all intelligent species in the galaxy retain a racial memory of horned, red-eyed, cloven-hoofed evil beings. Three empires span the galaxy, their spheres of influence in uneasy proximity to each other. The possible discovery of these "demons" results in a space opera with all kinds of theological and metaphysical implications.

1. *Demons at Rainbow Bridge, The* (Ace, 1989) A scouting expedition on an uninhabited planet, in the region of space called Rainbow Bridge, uncovers the perfectly preserved bodies of horned creatures.
2. *Run to Chaos Keep, The* (Ace, 1991) Each of the three empires sends space ships to investigate the report of horned "devils." Members

of each race chase a pair of demons through a multidimensional maze that resembles Dante's Inferno.
3. *Ninety Trillion Fausts, The* (Berkley, 1991) The conclusion finds the survivors of the three imperial expeditions entering the central city of the demonic Quintara, releasing the demon lords, and imperiling trillions of sentient beings.

VII. The Rings of the Masters series postulates a future in which self-destructive mankind has been turned over to the Master System, a supercomputer that has heuristic abilities, meanwhile regressing humanity to primitive levels. The scientists who created the Master System, anticipating possible flaws, created five gold rings that could stop it if needed.

1. *Lords of the Middle Dark* (Ballantine, 1986) Historian Ingram Hawks has the knowledge to solve the mystery of the Master System and the five golden keys, but he has to be absolutely sure, for a misstep could be disastrous.
2. *Pirates of the Thunder* (Ballantine, 1987) Because he refused to help ambitious Lazlo Chen in the quest for the gold rings, Hawks is relegated to the deadly prison planet Melchior.
3. *Warriors of the Storm* (Ballantine, 1993) Shapechanger Vulture, capable of absorbing the body and memories of any organic being, is enlisted in helping the pirates to locate the missing rings.
4. *Masks of the Martyrs* (Ballantine, 1986) The pirates of the giant spaceship *Thunder* have collected all of the gold rings but are ignorant as to how to use them.

VIII. The Soul Rider, or Flux and Anchor, series describes a place called World, which is divided between the stable Anchor and the chaotic Flux, a land of strange passions and near magic. Cassie, the central character, raised in the stolid, corrupt world of Anchor, is transformed by the Soul Rider and transferred to the seemingly formless Flux, which turns out to be the source of Anchor's existence.

1. *Birth of Flux and Anchor, The* (Tor, 1985) Fourth published in the Soul Rider series, but first in chronology. The place called World is divided into the stable Anchor and chaotic Flux.
2. *Spirits of Flux and Anchor* (Tor, 1984) Cassie, a young girl born and raised in the rural lands of Anchor, is propelled by the Soul Rider into a new life in Flux.
3. *Empires of Flux and Anchor* (Tor, 1984) The Nine, rulers of hell, have formed their own empire and plan to invade World by subverting humans to their unholy use.
4. *Masters of Flux and Anchor* (Tor, 1985) Wizard and Fluxlord Mervyn faces the threat of the opening of the long-closed Hellgates to World.
5. *Children of Flux and Anchor* (Tor, 1986) Flux and Anchor are at peace after the last great battle of the Hellgates. But the delicate balance may be destroyed.

IX. The Wonderland Gambit is a trilogy of novels that explores the limits of virtual reality. Cory Maddox is recruited by the National Security Agency to reactivate a virtual reality project pioneered by computer wizard Matthew Brand. This leads him to a cycle of cyber-reincarnation inside a virtual reality box created by Brand.

1. *Cybernetic Walrus, The* (Ballantine, 1995) Programmer Cory Maddox is recruited by the National Security Agency to reactivate the aborted virtual reality project created by the disappeared computer wizard Matthew Brand.
2. *March Hare Network, The* (Ballantine, 1996) This time Maddox has brought along knowledge, skills, and memories of his previous existence.

3. *Hot Wired Dodo, The* (Ballantine, 1997) Cory is stuck inside the cycle of cyber-reincarnation of a virtual reality box created by Matthew Brand. Fifty-one other people are trapped in virtual reality.

X. The Three Kings is a trilogy investigating the rumors of three possibly illusive planets, said to be rich in treasure and alien artifacts, in a far future in which space travelers have been stranded because of the disappearance of a wormhole that linked two universes.

1. *Balshazzar's Serpent* (Baen, 2000) The interstellar missionary ship *Mountain,* led by Dr. Karl Woodward, encounters a group of apparently friendly and cooperative colonists who are manipulated by a band of pirates led by one Captain Sapenza.
2. *Melchior's Fire* (Baen, 2001) A piratical interstellar salvage crew embarks on a journey through "wild wormholes" to the Three Kings.
3. *Kaspar's Box* (Baen, 2003) A chance encounter between what's left of the once-mighty human military with an inexplicable alien force has brought an armed expedition to Kaspar, the third of the Three Kings.

Chamberlin, Ann

I. Utah native Ann Chamberlin, a successor to Mary Renault (q.v.), who is her favorite author, believes that "the purpose of storytelling . . . is to support positions in exact opposition to the views prevailing in a culture's powerhouses" (Ann Chamberlin's website). Chamberlin also has a "passionate interest in gender roles." The Joan of Arc Tapestries series is an imaginative reinterpretation, with accurate historical detail interweaved with fantastic elements, of the life of Joan of Arc. It begins in the year 1404, several years before Joan's birth, and leaves us, so far, at the point where Joan, having raised the siege of Orleans and having the Dauphin crowned as king of France, is about to undergo her trial and martyrdom, events that will apparently be told in a fourth volume. Chamberlin brings out the paganism, or "Old Religion," beneath the thin surface of Christianity in the 15th century. Many historical characters appear, such as Gilles de Rais (not the monster called Bluebeard portrayed in most accounts) and the Dauphin (soon to be Charles VII, king of France). The prophecies of Merlin are invoked by his latter-day followers.

1. *Merlin of St. Gilles Well, The* (Tor, 1999) In events covering the years 1404–1415, Yann, a Breton merchant's son with prophetic and clairvoyant gifts recognized by the Hermit of St. Gilles, a clandestine practitioner of the Old Religion, is raised with the young Gilles de Rais.
2. *Merlin of the Oak Wood, The* (Tor, 2001) Jehannette/Joan, a teenage girl already possessed by "Voices," takes center stage and encounters the weak Dauphin (later to become Charles VII) and other historical characters, as well as the fictional Yann.
3. *Gloria: The Merlin and the Saint* (High Country, 2005) Joan makes her first appearance at the Dauphin's court, lifts the siege of Orleans, and manages the Dauphin's coronation at Rheims, assisted by Yann and Gilles de Rais, who believes that Joan is his destined true love. Variant title: *The Merlin and the Saint.*

II. A trio of novels takes us into a harem in Ottoman Turkey in the 17th century, as seen through the eyes of Venetians who have been sold into slavery in Constantinople. One of the Venetians, Sophia (Safiya) Baffo, climbs the ladder of power until she is the lover of Sultan Murad, heir to the throne, and the mother of his only son. Another Venetian, sailor Giorgio Veniero, who does much of the narrating of the trilogy,

is transformed into a eunuch, Abdullah. The rich historical detail, interesting descriptions of Islamic life, and a cast of believable characters will keep people reading.

1. *Sofia* (Forge, 1996) In 1562 Sofia Baffo, the governor of Corfu's daughter, and Giorgio Veniero, a 15-year-old orphaned Venetian sailor, meet when Giorgio delivers a message from the Doge of Venice to Sofia inside a Venetian convent. Eventually, the two run off together and are enslaved by Turks who take them to Constantinople.
2. *Sultan's Daughter, The* (Forge, 1997) Abdullah, the eunuch who once was Giorgio Veniero, is enslaved to Esmikhan, granddaughter of Sultan Suleiman. Harem slave Safiye (Sofia) Baffo plots to change the line of Ottoman succession.
3. *Reign of the Favored Women, The* (Forge, 1998) Safiye becomes the lover of Sultan Murad, now heir to the throne, and the mother of his only son, Muhammed, whom she is determined will rule the Ottoman Empire. But she has Nur Banu, Murad's cruel and powerful mother, to reckon with.

Champion, David

"Bomber" Hanson and his son Tod are the principals in a series of legal thrillers set in a California town not unlike Santa Barbara. The F. Lee Bailey–like Bomber is a bombastic but skillful defense attorney. The self-effacing and insecure Tod, who would rather write music than appear in court (he stutters), does the investigating and acts as narrator. One of the best things about this series is the developing relationship between Bomber and Tod.

1. *Mountain Massacres, The* (Knoll, 1995) Bomber Hanson agrees to defend Bart O'Neil, a hippie mountain man accused of killing the neighbor who shot his dogs.
2. *Nobody Roots for Goliath* (Knoll, 1996) Bomber represents Rich Zepf, a dying, blind Pennsylvania father of 12 who started smoking only after he lost his sight and couldn't read the warning labels on the cigarette packs.
3. *Celebrity Trouble* (Knoll, 1997) Celebrity Steven Shag, who has a fondness for young boys, invites them to his special "Magicland" and then into his bed. Now he's being sued for millions by the father of one of the boys.
4. *Phantom Virus* (Knoll, 1999) Tod has to determine whether a young woman's death had anything to do with the supposed "cure" for her disease.
5. *Too Rich and Too Thin* (Knoll, 2000) Tod falls for beautiful supermodel Cheryl Darling, accused of murdering her ex-lover.
6. *She Died for Her Sins* (Knoll, 2002) Inocencio, a young Mexican immigrant and a self-styled Communist with an authority problem, is accused of murdering a well-to-do widow.
7. *Easy Come, Easy Go* (Knoll, 2004) Respected doctor Melissa is accused of murdering her husband, Fred "Easy" Noggle, in a case that Bomber is reluctant to handle.
8. *To Die For* (Knoll, 2005) Bomber agrees to represent college student Pia Franceschi, accused of murdering her lecherous landlord, found dead in her bed.

Chandler, Raymond

The tawdry neon wilderness of southern California lends a distinctive atmosphere to Chandler's hard-boiled detective stories. Private-eye Philip Marlowe is cold and cynical, yet gruffly compassionate toward the victims of evil. Many of the novels have been filmed: Robert

Mitchum, Humphrey Bogart, James Garner, Robert Montgomery, Elliott Gould, and Dick Powell have all played Marlowe. Chandler, American born but English schooled, is an American classic, enshrined in the two-volume Library of America set of his writings (1995), which contains numbers 1 through 8 plus essays (including "The Simple Art of Murder") and several short stories featuring, under different names, the detective who became Marlowe. At his best, Chandler, who wrote like "a slumming angel," according to fellow mystery writer Ross MacDonald (q.v.), has rarely been equaled and never surpassed in the hard-boiled genre. Mystery fans had to wait 30 years for Robert B. Parker (q.v.) to finish *Poodle Springs* and to add to the Marlowe corpus.

1. *Big Sleep, The* (Knopf, 1939) A paralyzed California millionaire and his psychotic daughters are featured in this case of blackmail that turns into murder.
2. *Farewell, My Lovely* (Knopf, 1940) Marlowe is hired to hunt down an ex-convict's girlfriend.
3. *High Window, The* (Knopf, 1940) A stolen coin, a secretive old lady, and her frightened secretary lead Marlowe into the mind of a murderer.
4. *Lady in the Lake, The* (Knopf, 1943) The corpse in the lake is not the missing lady Marlowe seeks. Sometimes regarded as Chandler's best novel, this is the only one completed by Chandler that takes place outside of the Los Angeles area.
5. *Little Sister, The* (Houghton Mifflin, 1949) A mousy girl from Kansas hires Marlowe to find her brother. Variant title: *Marlowe*.
6. *Simple Art of Murder, The* (Houghton Mifflin, 1950) This is a collection of Chandler short stories, some of which feature Marlowe.
7. *Long Goodbye, The* (Houghton Mifflin, 1953) Terry Lennox thinks he has committed a murder, and Marlowe helps him run away to Mexico.
8. *Playback* (Houghton Mifflin, 1958) Marlowe helps a young girl who may be imagining danger.
9. *Poodle Springs* (Putnam, 1989) Married to his true love, Linda Loring, but ill at ease in posh Poodle (i.e., Palm) Springs, Marlowe takes on a missing-persons case. First four chapters written by Chandler, remainder by Robert B. Parker.

Chang, Leonard

Allen Choice is a Korean American executive-protection expert who operates in the San Francisco Bay and Silicon Valley areas. A thirtyish bachelor, the introspective, ruminative Allen, like Dashiell Hammett's (q.v.) Sam Spade, is aroused when his partner, Paul Baumgartner, is murdered while on a routine job. Allen is still developing as a character in the three (so far) crime-noir novels set in a well-delineated Bay Area locale. Leonard Chang is an American of Korean descent, born in New York and now settled in California. He has published two nonseries novels, *The Fruit'n Food* (Black Heron, 1996) and *Dispatches from the Cold* (Black Heron, 1998), and several short stories.

1. *Over the Shoulder* (HarperCollins, 2001) When Allen Choice's partner, Paul Baumgartner, is gunned down on a routine job babysitting a Silicon Valley executive, the introspective Allen is jolted into some dark thoughts about who was really the intended victim, his Korean heritage, and the death of his father when he was only 10.
2. *Underkill* (St. Martin's, 2003) Faced with doubts about his career and his unraveling romance with Hispanic American reporter Linda Maldonado, Allen flies to Los Angeles to help with investigating the fatal drug-related car crash of Linda's younger brother.
3. *Fade to Clear* (St. Martin's, 2004) Allen, contemplating moving out of his San Francisco flat and in with Serena Yew, a Silicon Valley computer programmer, is asked by ex-girlfriend Linda Maldonado to find her missing niece.

Chappell, Fred (Davis)

The Kirkman family of rural western North Carolina is depicted in Fred Chappell's Kirkman tetralogy. Jess Kirkman, son of the family and autobiographical character, who, like Chappell, is a poet and college professor, is the narrator. Numbers 1 and 3 are essentially collections of linked but wide ranging short stories, tales told to Jess by his mother and grandmother. Number 2 represents a single day in the life of Jess's father, Robert. In number 4, the now-adult Jess Kirkman returns to his mountain home. Numbers 1 through 3, which take place in the 1940s, can be read in any order or separately, while number 4 is set some years later, when the adult Jess returns home. The evocation of Appalachia and its people is very fine, told with a poet's ear for language and many characters who are strongly individualized but never portrayed as simply eccentric or quaint. Fred Chappell, who has been professor of English at the University of North Carolina, Greensboro, since 1964, is a well-regarded poet and the author, in his earlier career, of several "southern gothic" novels. *The Fred Chappell Reader* (St. Martin's, 1987) contains poetry, short stories, essays, and the complete novel *Dagon* (1968). Chappell's work, which has never achieved best-sellerdom, has attracted considerable notice from the academic and literary quarterly press. John Lang's *Understanding Fred Chappell* (South Carolina, 2002) is a good introduction to the author.

1. *I Am One of You Forever* (Louisiana State University Press, 1985) Set in western North Carolina in the 1940s. Young Jess Kirkman is regaled by stories told by his mother and grandmother.
2. *Brighten the Corner Where You Are* (St. Martin's, 1989) This volume recollects a single day in the life of Jess Kirkman's father, Joe Robert, a high school teacher in trouble with the school board for his teaching of evolution.
3. *Farewell, I'm Bound to Leave You* (Picador USA, 1996) While Jess's grandmother lies dying, with Jess's mother by her bedside, Jess and his father recall and relate to each other a series of tales that are funny, brooding, romantic, and heroic.
4. *Look Back All the Green Valley* (Picador USA, 1999) Jess's father has been dead for 10 years, and his mother is ailing when Jess, now a college professor and poet, returns to his homestead in the mountains of western North Carolina.

Charles, Hampton

PSEUDONYM OF Peter Martin

Hampton Charles, pseudonym for Peter Martin, who wrote the Otani series under the pseudonym of James Melville (q.v.), revived the Miss Seeton series after the death of Heron Carvic (q.v.). After three novels, the series was continued by "Hamilton Crane" (q.v.).

1. *Advantage Miss Seeton* (Berkley, 1990) Tennis star Miss Thumper is receiving death threats.
2. *Miss Seeton at the Helm* (Berkley, 1990) Miss Seeton takes a Mediterranean cruise with a group of art dealers.
3. *Miss Seeton by Appointment* (Berkley, 1991) Miss Seeton is sent to Buckingham Palace on a secret mission.

Charles, Kate

PSEUDONYM OF Carol Chase

I. Cincinnati-born Charles confesses to being a lifelong Anglophile, so Anglophilic that she moved permanently to England and took a position with a Church of England parish. Unfortunately, her first novel in the Book of Psalms series (so called because each chapter begins with a quotation from *Psalms*) so unsettled the Anglican powers that she was dismissed from her parish job. London artist Lucy Kingsley and Norfolk solicitor David Middleton-Brown are part-time sleuths who are called in to solve the occasional murder that roils the Anglican surface. For people who like a mixture of mystery, church politics, and English eccentrics.

1. *Drink of Deadly Wine, A* **(Mysterious, 1992)** Reverend Gabriel Neville, soon to be promoted to Archdeacon, calls in David Middleton-Brown when he is threatened by a blackmailer.
2. *Snares of Death, The* **(Mysterious, 1994)** Sleuthing partners and tentative lovers Kingsley and Middleton-Brown investigate the murder of obnoxious "low church" minister Bob Dexter.
3. *Appointed to Die* **(Mysterious, 1994)** The staff of Malbury Cathedral fear that their tightly knit community will unravel when an "outsider" from London is appointed Dean.
4. *Dead Man out of Mind, A* **(Mysterious, 1995)** Lucy and David get involved in the politics of St. Margaret's Church when the new lady curate is killed in a suspicious hit-and-run accident.
5. *Evil Angels among Them* **(Mysterious, 1996)** The new minister at Walston (Norfolk), Stephen Thorncroft receives a cool reception from his parishioners, while his young wife, Becca, receives hot and obscene phone calls. Stephen and Becca enlist Lucy and David to investigate.

II. A new series features newly ordained Anglican cleric Callie Anson and DI Neville Stewart of London.

1. *Evil Intent* **(Poisoned Pen, 2005)** When her friend Frances is suspected of strangling Father Adimola, Callie Anson works with DI Neville Stewart to solve the crime.
2. *Secret Sins* **(Poisoned Pen, 2007)** Callie Anson is tending to the needs of parishioner Morag Hamilton, whose granddaughter is missing. Neville Stewart must solve the murder of a young computer whiz.

Charles, Paul

Detective Inspector Christy Kennedy, Detective Constable Anne Coles, and Detective Sergeant James Irvine are a police team operating out of Camden Town, a London magnet for the young and trendy. Kennedy, an Ulster native, is a decent, vulnerable man in love with reporter ann rea (capital eschewing like e. e. cummings). Kennedy and the sharp-dressing Sean Connery–like Irvine and the steady Coles address a series of crimes, some of them involved with the pop-music scene, in this well-plotted series of procedurals. Paul Charles is a London-based music promoter and agent and uses his knowledge of London and British pop music to good advantage. The novels, published by Do-Not Press and Brandon in the United Kingdom and distributed in the United States by Dufour, deserve to be better known in the United States.

1. *Last Boat to Camden Town* **(Do-Not [UK], 1998)** This prequel is set six months before number 2. The Camden Town CID investigates the drowning death of young Dr. Edmund Berry in Regent's Canal. Reprinted in the United States by St. Martin's in 2003.
2. *I Love the Sound of Breaking Glass* **(Do-Not [UK], 1997)** This novel introduces Christy Kennedy and his team, who are asked by Kennedy's love, reporter ann rea, to investigate the disappearance of a record producer who eventually turns up dead. Reprinted in the United States by St. Martin's in 2004.
3. *Fountain of Sorrow* **(Do-Not [UK], 1999)** Two homicides, one man's death apparently perpetrated by a mad dog, the other man's death the result of a brutal beating, engage the CID team here.
4. *Ballad of Sean and Wilko, The* **(Do-Not [UK], 2000)** Rock band Circles' comeback is aborted by the murder of lead singer Wilko Robertson in a locked-room mystery.
5. *Hissing of the Silent Lonely Room, The* **(Do-Not [UK], 2002)** Was the death of self-destructive singer-songwriter Esther Bluewood really a suicide? Kennedy, a Bluewood fan, isn't so sure.
6. *I've Heard the Banshee Sing* **(Do-Not [UK], 2003)** In a case that eventually leads Kennedy back to his native Ulster, World War II veteran Victor Dugsdale's butchered corpse is found hanging in the Black Cat Building, an urban renewal project.
7. *Justice Factory, The* **(Do-Not [UK], 2004)** While attending a funeral, Kennedy is as surprised as anyone by what's found in the recently dug grave.
8. *Sweetwater* **(Brandon [UK], 2007)** John Riley's disappearance is followed by the murder of Harry Ford.

Charnas, Suzy McKee

American fantasy and science-fiction writer Charnas has created a misogynist dystopia to be compared with Margaret Atwood's *The Handmaid's Tale* (Houghton Mifflin, 1986). The Holdfast quartet pictures a postapocalypse world in which Nazi-like men enslave women in a grim fortress. *Walk to the End of the World* was the inspiration for much feminist science fiction. Numbers 1 and 2 were published together as *The Slave and the Free* (Tor, 1999). Charnas, who has won both the Hugo and Nebula awards for her science-fiction stories, has also written several young-adult fantasies, including the Sorcery Hall trilogy.

1. *Walk to the End of the World* **(Ballantine, 1974)** "Fem" slave Alldera is enlisted in an effort to make contact with the "free fems," reputed to live in the wilds outside of the Holdfast.
2. *Motherlines* **(Putnam, 1978)** Alldera finds the "free fems" and the Riding Women (products of human-equine interbreeding) living an idyllic man- (and child-) free life on the Plains.
3. *Furies, The* **(Tor, 1994)** Alldera leads the "free fems" and the Riding Women against the Holdfast, but her leadership is challenged because she acknowledges the existence of "a few good men."
4. *Conqueror's Child, The* **(Tor, 1999)** In the series conclusion, Alldera's daughter Sorrel, who has grown up among the Riding Women, discovers that the women of Holdfast have now enslaved the men.

Charteris, Leslie

The dashing and elegant Simon Templar, aka the Saint, is known as the Robin Hood of modern crime for his habit of generously redistributing his profits and for his total callousness about "blipping the ungodly over the beezer." His decidedly freelance exploits include a full measure of danger as well as "plenty of good beer and damsels in distress." George Sanders starred as the Saint in a series of films made by RKO beginning in 1938. Roger Moore and Ian Ogilvie played the Saint in two different British television series. Val Kilmer played the Saint in the 1997 movie *The Saint*. Numbers 37 through

45 are adaptations of TV programs written by others and only revised or reviewed by Charteris. Later titles are usually novelizations of television or movie scripts not involving the direct intervention of Leslie Charteris, for example, *The Saint and the Templar Treasure* (Doubleday, 1979); *Leslie Charteris' Count on the Saint* (Doubleday, 1980); and *Leslie Charteris' Salvage for the Saint* (Doubleday, 1983). The late Charteris (d. 1993), a Singapore-born, naturalized American citizen, had his name legally changed from his birth name of Leslie Charles Bower Yin. Reference book: *The Saint,* by Burl Barer (McFarland, 1993).

1. *Meet the Tiger* **(Doubleday, 1928)** The Saint, in pursuit of the Tiger's hidden treasure, is helped by lovely young Patricia Holm, who reappears throughout the series as Templar's steady. Variant title: *The Saint Meets the Tiger.*

2. *Last Hero, The* **(Doubleday, 1930)** The Saint succeeds where Scotland Yard failed; ridding London of some of its worst underworld figures, including Dr. Marius. Variant title: *The Saint Closes the Case.*

3. *Enter the Saint* **(Doubleday, 1930)** Three stories.

4. *Avenging Saint, The* **(Doubleday, 1931)** Simon Templar enters the world of international intrigue to prevent another world war. English title: *Knight Templar.*

5. *Wanted for Murder* **(Doubleday, 1931)** This book includes two titles published separately in England, *Featuring the Saint* and *Alias the Saint,* each of which contains three stories.

6. *Angels of Doom* **(Doubleday, 1932)** The Saint meets the beautiful gangster Jill Trelawney and plots a "coup that was to rock England." Variant titles: *She Was a Lady* and *The Saint Meets His Match.*

7. *Saint v. Scotland Yard, The* **(Doubleday, 1932)** The duel between the Saint and Inspector Teal of Scotland Yard continues through these three novelettes. Variant title: *The Holy Terror.*

8. *Getaway* **(Doubleday, 1932)** An assortment of crown jewels is stolen several times over. Variant title: *The Saint's Getaway.*

9. *Saint and Mr. Teal, The* **(Doubleday, 1933)** Three long stories: "The Gold Standard," "The Man from St. Louis," and "The Death Penalty." Variant title: *Once More the Saint.*

10. *Brighter Buccaneer, The* **(Doubleday, 1933)** This is a collection of short stories starring the Saint.

11. *Misfortunes of Mr. Teal, The* **(Doubleday, 1934)** In these three novelettes, Inspector Teal tries unsuccessfully to prove that the Saint is a crook. Variant titles: *The Saint in London* and *The Saint in England.*

12. *Saint Intervenes, The* **(Doubleday, 1934)** Here are more short stories featuring the Saint. Variant title: *Boodle.*

13. *Saint Goes On, The* **(Doubleday, 1935)** This book comprises three novelettes: "The High Fence," "The Elusive Ellshaw," and "The Case of the Frightened Innkeeper."

14. *Saint in New York, The* **(Doubleday, 1935)** Simon Templar bedevils New York City's police commissioner.

15. *Saint Overboard, The* **(Doubleday, 1936)** The Saint takes on racketeer "Birdie" Vogel and falls in love with Loretta Page. Variant title: *The Pirate Saint.*

16. *Ace of Knaves, The* **(Doubleday, 1937)** The Saint stars in three more novelettes. Variant title: *The Saint in Action.*

17. *Thieves' Picnic* **(Doubleday, 1937)** The Saint rescues a lovely damsel in the Canary Islands and comes across a fortune in stolen jewels and a winning lottery ticket. Variant titles: *The Saint Bids Diamonds* and *The Saint at the Thieves' Picnic.*

18. *Prelude for War* **(Doubleday, 1938)** The Saint prevents a war that would have ended civilization. Variant title: *The Saint Plays with Fire.*

19. *Follow the Saint* **(Doubleday, 1938)** Contains three novelettes: "The Miracle Tea Party," "The Invisible Millionaire," and "The Affair at Hogsbotham."

20. *Happy Highwayman, The* **(Doubleday, 1939)** Nine short stories feature the Saint.

21. *Saint in Miami, The* **(Doubleday, 1940)** The Saint pursues some Fifth Columnists through Florida.

22. *Saint Goes West, The* **(Doubleday, 1942)** These three novelettes are set in Arizona, Palm Springs, and Hollywood.

23. *Saint Steps In, The* **(Doubleday, 1943)** The Saint takes on a special assignment for the FBI.

24. *Saint on Guard, The* **(Doubleday, 1944)** Contains two novelettes: "The Black Market" and "The Sizzling Saboteur."

25. *Saint Sees It Through, The* **(Doubleday, 1946)** The Saint adapts his ways to the New World in this tough, Raymond Chandler–type adventure.

26. *Call for the Saint* **(Doubleday, 1948)** Contains two novelettes: "The King of the Beggers [*sic*]" and "The Masked Angel."

27. *Saint Errant* **(Doubleday, 1948)** Nine short stories follow the Saint.

28. *Saint in Europe, The* **(Doubleday, 1953)** This is a grand tour of seven stories.

29. *Saint on the Spanish Main, The* **(Doubleday, 1955)** These six stories are set in the Caribbean.

30. *Saint around the World, The* **(Doubleday, 1956)** These six stories include a reappearance of the long-suffering Scotland Yard Inspector, Claud Eustace Teal.

31. *Thanks to the Saint* **(Doubleday, 1957)** Six more short stories continue the Saint's adventures.

32. *Señor Saint* **(Doubleday, 1958)** More short stories involve the Saint.

33. *Saint to the Rescue, The* **(Doubleday, 1959)** These six stories are set in Georgia, California, and Florida.

34. *Trust the Saint* **(Doubleday, 1962)** More short stories concerning the Saint.

35. *Saint in the Sun, The* **(Doubleday, 1963)** Charteris provides still more short stories.

36. *Vendetta for the Saint* **(Doubleday, 1964)** The Saint takes on the Mafia in Sicily.

37. *Saint on TV, The* **(Doubleday, 1967)** Contains two stories adapted from television: "The Death Game" and "The Power Artist."

38. *Saint Returns, The* **(Doubleday, 1968)** Two more adaptations of TV episodes: "The Dizzy Daughter" and "The Gadget Lovers."

39. *Saint and the Fiction Makers, The* **(Doubleday, 1968)** The evil Warlock plots to bring to life a series of spy novels. Novelization of TV episode.

40. *Saint Abroad, The* **(Doubleday, 1969)** Contains two novelettes adapted from TV: "The Art Collectors" and "The Persistent Patriots."

41. *Saint in Pursuit, The* **(Doubleday, 1970)** A young woman receives a letter on her 25th birthday giving her a huge treasure, but she must outwit Russian and US intelligence agents to get it. Novelization.

42. *Saint and the People Importers, The* **(Doubleday, 1970)** The Saint gets involved in some illegal immigration from Pakistan to Britain. Novelization.

43. *Catch the Saint* **(Doubleday, 1975)** Two more adaptations: "The Masterpiece Merchant" and "The Adoring Socialite."

44. *Saint and the Hapsburg Necklace, The* **(Doubleday, 1976)** On the Eve of World War II, Simon Templar helps a beautiful countess retrieve a valuable necklace from Gestapo hands. Novelization that fits chronologically between numbers 20 and 21.

45. *Saint in Trouble, The* **(Doubleday, 1978)** Two more adaptations; "The Imprudent Professor" and "The Red Sabbath."

Charyn, Jerome

I. New Yorker Jerome Charyn's series of thrillers featuring Manhattan policeman Isaac Sidel, who becomes police commissioner and then mayor of New York, is comic, serious, surreal, satirical, and full of bizarre characters, wild action, and the seedy ambience of the decaying city of New York. Numbers 1 through 4 form what is called the Isaac Quartet (published in one volume by Four Walls Eight Windows, 2002; originally published in London by Zomba Books, 1984). Numbers 5 through 8 are sometimes known as the Odessa Quartet. Charyn has authored a trilogy of autobiographical memoirs, which may have a little fantasy mixed in, about his early life in the Bronx: *The Dark Lady from Belorusse* (St. Martin's, 1997); *The Black Swan* (St. Martin's, 2000); and *Bronx Boy* (St. Martin's, 2002).

1. *Blue Eyes* (Simon & Schuster, 1976) Isaac Sidel encourages his favorite protégé, Manfred "Blue Eyes" Coen, to infiltrate a white slavery operation.
2. *Marilyn the Wild* (Arbor House, 1976) Isaac battles a crime wave perpetrated by adolescents and the rebellion of his own daughter, Marilyn, who wants "Blue Eyes" for herself.
3. *Education of Patrick Silver, The* (Arbor House, 1976) Irish-Jewish ex-cop Silver is trying to protect the Peruvian Marrano hustler Guzman clan from Sidel.
4. *Secret Isaac* (Arbor House, 1978) A scar on a prostitute's cheek sends Isaac on a trip to Ireland in search of "soul-relief."
5. *Good Policeman, The* (Mysterious, 1991) Police Commissioner Sidel goes on a romantic search for his "Anastasia" and an investigation of Manhattan's Nine Circles of Hell.
6. *Maria's Girls* (Mysterious, 1992) Carroll Brent, Commissioner Sidel's new right-hand man, is married to the "second-richest woman in New York" but is still in debt to the Mob.
7. *Montezuma's Man* (Mysterious, 1993) Chauffeur-cop Joe Barbarossa is spying on Isaac, his boss, while mobsters quarrel over a batch of Sicilian puppets.
8. *Little Angel Street* (Mysterious, 1994) Scheduled to take office as mayor of New York in a month, the paranoiac Sidel is hiding out incognito in homeless shelters.
9. *El Bronx* (Mysterious, 1996) Isaac is still mayor, but a Children's Crusade against corporate greed, drugs, and violent crime takes center stage here.
10. *Citizen Sidel* (Mysterious, 1999) Isaac is nominated to run for vice president of the United States on a Democratic ticket headed by J. Michael Storm, commissioner of baseball and former student radical.

II. Charyn's other series "hero," Sidney Holden, is a "bumper" (i.e., hit man) in New York. Though good at his work, Sidney is subject to quixotic romantic and chivalric entanglements.

1. *Paradise Man* (Fine, 1987) Holden makes himself vulnerable to his enemies and supposed allies by rescuing and falling in love with the district attorney's daughter-in-law.
2. *Elsinore* (Mysterious, 1991) Ninety-two-year-old crime boss and former cantor Howard Phipps brings Sidney out of retirement when a serious leak develops in his underworld empire.

Chase-Riboud, Barbara

For generations Thomas Jefferson's biographers have wrestled with the question as to whether he had a slave mistress named Sally Hemings by whom he fathered several children. Philadelphia-born Chase-Riboud, internationally known sculptor and African American writer, convinced that the story was true, wrote a well-researched, well-written historical novel exploring the relationship and followed it with a sequel depicting the conflicted life of a daughter of Sally and Thomas who "passed for white" but never completely reconciled herself to "living a lie."

1. *Sally Hemings* (Viking, 1979) The 38-year relationship between Thomas Jefferson and his slave Sally Hemings, viewed from various perspectives.
2. *President's Daughter, The* (Crown, 1994) Harriet Hemings, daughter of Sally Hemings and Thomas Jefferson, celebrates her 21st birthday by leaving for the North, freedom, and the life of a white woman.

Chazin, Suzanne

Georgia Skeehan, single mother and fire marshal, is the heroine of three novels about the New York Fire Department. The feisty Georgia, the lone female firefighter in the department, more than holds her own against the chauvinistic males in the FDNY as she investigates suspicious fires and grapples with the cutthroat politics of the department. Suzanne Chazin, a former *Readers' Digest* editor, is married to a New York fireman.

1. *Fourth Angel, The* (Putnam, 2001) Georgia Skeehan, lone female firefighter in the New York Fire Department, fights male chauvinism and succeeds in unearthing evidence of a cover-up connected to the fires within the department.
2. *Flashover* (Putnam, 2002) Georgia is called upon to investigate a fire that killed a retired doctor with a history of denying pensions to firefighters disabled in the line of duty.
3. *Fireplay* (Putnam, 2003) Skeehan suspects notorious extortionist Mike "the Freezer" McLaughlin caused the fire in a Manhattan restaurant that killed two firefighters but is unable to investigate McLaughlin because he is also an informant for the FBI.

Cheever, John

Set in St. Botolph's, an imaginary shore town in Massachusetts with a striking resemblance to Quincy, Cheever's hometown, these gently satirical novels about the Wapshot family are alternately humorous and poignant. Although the noble Yankee blood is running thin in young Moses and Coverly, their eccentric and lovable father, Leander, honors his seafaring ancestors as the crusty captain of the local ferry—until he sinks it. Cheever is best known for short stories such as "The Swimmer," but the Wapshot duo remains among the favorites of the Cheever readership.

1. *Wapshot Chronicle, The* (Harper, 1957) This book introduces old Captain Leander Wapshot, his wife, two sons, and sister Honoria.
2. *Wapshot Scandal, The* (Harper, 1964) The two young Wapshot boys are the focus here. The "scandal" is that Aunt Honoria neglected to pay her income tax.

Cherryh, C. J.

PSEUDONYM OF Carolyn J. Cherry

I. C. J. Cherryh creates intricate alien cultures with the languages to go with them. Readers of her books often have to grapple with a 50-keyword alien vocabulary, and they also have to challenge their sexual stereotypes, but Cherryh enthusiasts find the effort well worth making. The Alliance-Union, or Merchanters Universe, is a loosely connected series that contains some of Cherryh's most highly regarded novels, such as the Hugo- and Nebula-winning *Downbelow Station* and *Cyteen.* Set in a far-future universe, several of the novels deal with the rivalry between the Company and the Union. Other novels deal with events in the past or in the even farther future. Numbers 1 and 2 are closely related. Numbers 4 through 7 are sometimes called the Merchanters Novels after the individualistic traders who fly the space routes after the Company wars. Numbers 8 and 9 are sometimes referred to as Unionside novels. Numbers 10 through 12 have been reprinted in an omnibus volume called *Alternate Realities* (DAW, 2000). Numbers 13 through 15 have been reprinted in an omnibus volume called *The Faded Sun* (DAW, 2000). Novels are arranged in approximate chronological order. For other Cherryh SF novels see listings under series II through V. Cherryh has authored two stand-alone SF novels: *Cuckoo's Egg* (DAW, 1985) and *Hestia* (DAW, 1979). *The Collected Short Fiction of C. J. Cherryh* (DAW, 2004) contains Cherryh's short stories.

1. *Heavy Time* **(Warner, 1991)** Asteroid miners Bird and Pollard rescue a wrecked spaceship and its crazed sole remaining crew member.

2. *Hellburner* **(Warner, 1992)** Pollard is called in when the pilot for a top-secret military test program is seriously injured.

3. *Downbelow Station* **(DAW, 1981)** Pell Station, where everyone lives underground, forms an uneasy buffer between the Company and the Union.

4. *Merchanter's Luck* **(DAW, 1982)** Kjeja and Reilly are rival Merchanters who must overcome their mutual distrust to survive.

5. *Rimrunners* **(Warner, 1989)** Bet Yeager's hidden past must be revealed when Mazian pirates attack the Rimrunner spaceship *Loki.*

6. *Tripoint* **(Warner, 1994)** Tom Bowe-Hawkins, young crew member of the family ship *Sprite,* is the product of rape and part of the revenge plans by his mother, Marie Kirgov Hawkins, against his father, Austen Bowe, captain of the *Corinthian.*

7. *Finity's End* **(Warner, 1997)** Fletcher Neihart, born on Pell Station, is placed against his will on the famous merchanter *Finity's End,* the ship that left his mother-to-be behind 17 years before.

8. *Forty Thousand in Gehenna* **(DAW, 1983)** Humans living on the planet Gehenna are slow to realize that they are being part of the planet's ecolog.

9. *Cyteen* **(Warner, 1988)** Young scientist Ari rises to power on Cyteen, haunted by the knowledge that her genetic predecessor died at the hands of a trusted advisor. Subsequently published in three parts by Paperback Library (1989): *The Rebirth, The Betrayal, The Vindication.*

10. *Port Eternity* **(DAW, 1982)** Their names were Lancelot, Elaine, Gawain, and so forth, but they were "made" people, designed to suit the whims of their owner, the Lady De la Kirn.

11. *Voyager in Night* **(DAW, 1984)** Three human space travelers are captured and "copied" by an intelligent alien spaceship.

12. *Wave without a Shore* **(DAW, 1981)** The humans of the planet Freedom have avoided contact with the native species for centuries.

13. *Faded Sun, The: Kesrith* **(Doubleday, 1978)** The Mri (the People), a humanoid golden-skinned race of mercenary warriors, who left their home planet ages ago, as employees of the Regul, are pitted in war against the humans.

14. *Faded Sun, The: Shon'jir* **(Doubleday, 1978)** Human Sten Duncan, who has saved Nun and his sister, the last two Mri warriors, tries to enter into their lives to understand them. The second volume of the trilogy.

15. *Faded Sun, The: Kutath* **(Doubleday, 1979)** It is up to Sten Duncan, blood brother to the Mri, to end the human war with them.

16. *Serpent's Reach* **(Doubleday, 1980)** In the far future of the Alliance, within the constellation of the Serpent, cohabiting humans and insectlike aliens may have reached a parting of ways.

17. *Brothers of Earth* **(Doubleday, 1976)** In a "far, far future," human Kurt Marson finds himself stranded on a remote planet with strange inhabitants and must adapt quickly or die.

18. *Hunter of Worlds* **(Doubleday, 1977)** In the "far, far future" the entire population of the planet Priamus is marked for death unless a savior can be found.

II. The Chanur series, one of Cherryh's most popular, is typical of her work in presenting strong, courageous female leaders. The Chanur are members of the "hani," a race of lionlike beings that are part of the Compact, a loose interstellar trading community of different, mutually antagonistic species such as Humans and the bloodsucking Kif. The first four novels in the series form a unit, while number 5 takes place 10 years later with a different heroine.

1. *Pride of Chanur, The* **(DAW, 1982)** Pyanfar Chanur finds a strange almost hairless animal hiding on her spaceship.

2. *Chanur's Venture* **(DAW, 1984)** A long chase novel, ending inconclusively, carrying Pyanfar from space station to space station.

3. *Kif Strike Back, The* **(DAW, 1985)** Pyanfar is tricked into a military alliance with the repulsive Kif.

4. *Chanur's Homecoming* **(DAW, 1986)** *The Pride of Chanur* returns home to a less than enthusiastic welcome.

5. *Chanur's Legacy* **(DAW, 1992)** Hilfy Chanur, captain of *Chanur's Legacy,* accepts a commission to deliver a religious artifact.

III. In the Foreigner series, the planet Mospheira is inhabited by the gigantic humanoid Atevi and the descendants of humans marooned on the planet by a long-ago starship accident. Bren Cameron, known as "paidhi," is the only Human allowed to mingle with the Atevi. The task of this translator-diplomat to keep the two peoples from coming to blows, is complicated by the arrival of the Human starship *Phoenix.* Originally slated to be a trilogy, the series has nine volumes so far. Cherryh's ability to delineate believable alien cultures is at its best here.

1. *Foreigner* **(DAW, 1994)** The shaky coexistence of Humans and Atevi is shaken by a series of incidents. Bren Cameron finds himself caught between rival factions of Atevi as he grapples with xenophobia on both sides.

2. *Invader* **(DAW, 1995)** The return to Mospheira of the Human starship *Phoenix* will change the ways of life of both Humans and Atevi.

3. *Inheritor* **(DAW, 1996)** Humans and Atevi are on the brink of interspecies war, and it is up to Bren Cameron to bridge the gap between them.

4. *Precursor* **(DAW, 1999)** Bren Cameron goes into space to negotiate between the Pilot's Guild on the starship *Phoenix,* the atevi, and the Mospheirans, the human colonists who had been abandoned by the starship long ago.

5. *Defender* **(DAW, 2001)** The Atevi have a space program and crews in space repairing the *Phoenix,* but they also have pro- and anti-space factions who are at loggerheads.

6. *Explorer* **(DAW, 2002)** The *Phoenix,* manned by a mixed crew of Humans and Atevi, is in interstellar transit to the ruins of Reunion, where the Pilot's Guild still clings to power and an alien spaceship lurks on the fringes.

7. *Destroyer* (DAW, 2005) Bren Cameron and his Atevi allies finally return to their home world, where the Atevi natives and Human colonists live in an uneasy truce.

8. *Pretender* (DAW, 2006) Tabini, the deposed ruler of the atevi home world, represents Humanity's best hope of survival on this alien planet and the Atevi's best chance of maintaining independence.

9. *Deliverer* (DAW, 2007) Tabini has thwarted an attempt to overthrow him, though the usurper, Murini, has not yet been captured.

IV. A pair of novels known as the Finisterre, or Nighthorse, series, also involves Human and alien interaction. This time Humans share a remote and difficult world with telepathic fauna who communicate their instincts and desires to receptive humans. The riders of Nighthorses, equinelike beings who share a near-symbiotic relationship with their chosen partners, are essential in linking human villages together. Since *Cloud's Rider* ended as a cliff-hanger, at least one more novel may come.

1. *Rider at the Gate* (Warner, 1995) When Guil Stuart's lover, Aby Dale, is killed guarding a convoy from one isolated village to another, Guil sets out to avenge with his nighthorse to avenge her death.

2. *Cloud's Rider* (Warner, 1996) A young rider is escorting two brothers and their sister, who has been driven mad by a rogue Nighthorse, as they race for shelter from winter storms.

V. The Gene Wars series, which has produced only two titles so far, is about a desert world whose colonization is remembered only in mythical terms. Their seemingly immortal ruler, the Ilan, has used nanotechnology to modify their bodies and control their minds for survival on their planet.

1. *Hammerfall* (Eos, 2001) Marak Trin Train, the outcast son of a desert bandit who unsuccessfully contested the Ilan's rule, suffers from madness: he sees visions and feels an almost overwhelming desire to walk out into the desert.

2. *Forge of Heaven* (Eos, 2004) Marak is focused on rebuilding his planet after its bombardment by the "ondat" some centuries before.

VI. The Quest of Morgaine series is fantasy with a few science-fiction twists. Morgaine, the white-haired witch, and her liege man Vanye must close all the "gates" of a space and time-travel network that is destabilizing the worlds of the humans. *The Book of Morgaine* (Doubleday, 1979; UK title: *The Chronicles of Morgaine*) contains numbers 1 through 3, as does *The Morgaine Saga* (DAW, 2000).

1. *Gate of Ivrel* (DAW, 1976) In her quest to close the Gate of Ivrel, Morgaine must pass through lands that rightly fear her and curse her memory.

2. *Well of Shiuan* (DAW, 1978) Morgaine encounters one of the Qhal, the supernatural alien race that built the gates.

3. *Fires of Azeroth* (DAW, 1979) On her mission to close the last gate, Morgaine encounters Merir and his court, who tend the forest like a garden.

4. *Exile's Gate* (DAW, 1988) Morgaine discovers that the Skarrin, ruler of her world, is an exiled member of a race older than the Qhal.

VII. The Fortress fantasy series is set in the kingdom of Guelessar. An aging wizard named Mauryl conjures up a "Shaping" named Tristen, who, being new to the world, has trouble understanding the politics of Guelessar, its king, Cefwyn, and Cefwyn's foreign wife, Ninevrise. Things are complicated by the spirit of dark sorcerer Hasufin Heltain. As usual Cherryh devotes much care to setting up a world with loving detail and believable characters.

1. *Fortress in the Eye of Time* (Harper, 1995) Tristen, a "Shaping" "born yesterday," is sent on a quest by his creator, Mauryl, knowing neither who he is nor what he is looking for.

2. *Fortress of Eagles* (Harper, 1998) Young King Cefwyn agrees to send away his friend Tristen so that the Patriarch of the Quinaltine will allow Cefwyn to marry Lady Ninevrise, Regent of Elwynor.

3. *Fortress of Owls* (Harper, 1999) Tristen, now Duke of the Southern stronghold Amefel, being less than a year old and more magical than mortal, has trouble grasping political subtleties, so he makes a number of "mistakes."

4. *Fortress of Dragons* (Avon Eos, 2000) The vile spirit of the dark sorcerer Hasufin Heltain plans to make the expected illegitimate child of King Cefwyn and Tarien his conduit back to power.

5. *Fortress of Ice* (Eos, 2006) Aewyn, the 15-year-old heir to the throne of Ylesuin, has been raised apart from his illegitimate brother, Otter (aka Elfwyn), who resides with hedge-witch Gran.

VIII. The pre-Christian legend of Rusalka, a murdered girl who tries to resurrect herself by preying on the living, is the basis of a trio of fantasy novels about death, rebirth, magic, and a quest.

1. *Rusalka* (Ballantine, 1989) Eveshka, a young Russian woman murdered by Chernevog, is restored to life.

2. *Chernevog* (Ballantine, 1990) Eveshka, her husband, Pyetr, and the young wizard Sasha embark on a dangerous magic-ridden quest for Chernevog.

3. *Yvgenie* (Ballantine, 1991) A young man named Yvgenie, who enters the isolated forest lives of Eveshka and her friends, is recognized as the spirit of Chernevog.

IX. Arafel's Saga is a pair of fantasy novels based on Celtic myth about Arafel, an elf left behind in human lands after the retreat of the elves. Published together as *Arafel's Saga* (Doubleday, 1983).

1. *Dreamstone, The* (DAW, 1983) Describes the last defense of Faery against the encroachment of the Era of Man.

2. *Tree of Swords and Jewels, The* (DAW, 1983) Ciaran, part human and part elf, must reclaim his haunted weapons from the Tree of Swords or see the destruction of both human and elfish worlds.

X. The Sword of Knowledge is a shared-world trilogy coauthored by Leslie Fish, Nancy Asire, and Mercedes Lackey (q.v.) depicting the fall by cannon and magic of an alternative Roman Empire. Published together in one volume as *The Sword of Knowledge* (Baen, 1995).

1. *Dirge for Sabis, A* (Baen, 1989) The Empire of Sabis will fall unless its rulers have the foresight to use a superweapon urged upon them by their philosopher scientists. Coauthored by Leslie Fish.

2. *Wizard Spawn* (Baen, 1989) When a barbarian horde led by young Jesrai invades the lands guarded by the Order, disaster seems inevitable. Coauthored by Nancy Asire.

3. *Reap the Whirlwind* (Baen, 1989) Five hundred years after the fall of Sabis, the remnants of the Empire are about to be wiped out by their conquerors. Coauthored by Mercedes Lackey.

XI. Merovingen Nights is a series of shared world short story collections by various authors edited by Cherryh. *Angel with the Sword*, a novel written by Cherryh, is regarded as the opener of the series. Janet Morris created and edited the shared world series Heroes in Hell, which she coauthored with Cherryh, David Drake (q.v.) and Robert Silverberg (q.v.). Seven collections of these short stories were published by Baen in 1987–1989.

1. *Angel with the Sword* (DAW, 1985) A novel written by Cherryh depicting a fantastic city of canals with a heroine named Altair Jones who becomes enmeshed in the politics of the rich and powerful.
2. *Festival Moon* (DAW, 1987) Short stories.
3. *Fever Season* (DAW, 1987) Short stories.
4. *Troubled Waters* (DAW, 1988) Short stories.
5. *Smuggler's Gold* (DAW, 1988) Short stories.
6. *Divine Right* (DAW, 1989) Short stories.
7. *Flood Tide* (DAW, 1990) Short stories.
8. *Endgame* (DAW, 1991) Short stories.

Chesbro, George C.

I. Roberto "Mongo" Fredrickson is, even by fiction standards, an unusual private investigator. He is a PhD, a former circus acrobat, a black belt, and a dwarf. With his "disgustingly normal" brother Garth, a New York City police detective, Mongo solves a bizarre series of crimes in an entertaining melange of hard-boiled detective, fantasy, espionage, and science-fiction novels. Chesbro, self-styled "strong liberal humanist [with] a pessimistic worldview," finds most of his villains on the right-wing side of the political and religious spectrum. The CIA seems to be his particular bête noire.

1. *Shadow of a Broken Man* (Simon & Schuster, 1977) Mongo and Garth solve the bizarre murder of a famous architect.
2. *City of Whispering Stone* (Simon & Schuster, 1978) Iranians may be at the bottom of a series of disappearances.
3. *Affair of Sorcerers, An* (Simon & Schuster, 1979) Mongo pools his knowledge with witches, warlocks, and other practitioners of the occult to save a little girl plunged into a coma.
4. *Beasts of Valhalla, The* (Atheneum, 1985) The unexpected death of a favorite nephew sends Mongo and Garth back to Nebraska and a possible genetic Armageddon.
5. *Two Songs This Archangel Sings* (Atheneum, 1986) A former CIA operative wants to prevent his ex-boss from becoming Secretary of State.
6. *Cold Smell of Sacred Stone, The* (Atheneum, 1988) Garth is in a KGB-induced coma, and only Mongo can bring him out of it.
7. *Second Horseman Out of Eden* (Atheneum, 1989) Garth and Mongo rescue a little girl from the clutches of the "Reverend" Kenecky, child abuser, con man, and planner of Armageddon.
8. *In the House of Secret Enemies* (Mysterious, 1990) Short stories.
9. *Language of Cannibals, The* (Mysterious, 1990) Mongo runs into a bunch of crazed right-wingers running a death squad in a Hudson Valley town.
10. *Fear in Yesterday's Rings, The* (Mysterious, 1991) The brilliant but evil owners of the World Circus have reactivated an extinct caninelike menace.
11. *Dark Chant in a Crimson Key* (Mysterious, 1992) Chant Sinclair, the shadowy protagonist of a trio of novels written by Chesbro under the pseudonym David Cross (see series III), has swindled the Swiss Cornucopia Foundation.
12. *Incident at Bloodtide, An* (Mysterious, 1993) The ex-lover of Garth's folksinger wife, Mary Tree, turns up unexpectedly as a practitioner of the Black Arts.
13. *Bleeding in the Eye of a Brainstorm* (Simon & Schuster, 1995) The CIA is experimenting illegally with a drug that cures schizophrenics but has some troubling side effects.
14. *Dream of a Falling Eagle* (Simon & Schuster, 1996) The Company (the CIA) is plotting to assassinate the liberal US president and vice president and install the right-wing Speaker of the House in the White House.

II. Chesbro wrote a pair of novels about former CIA officer Veil Kendry, who has special visionary and psychic powers developed after an illness. His dreams bring him "to the edges of time and infinity" and produce paintings that expose Veil to extreme danger.

1. *Veil* (Mysterious, 1986) Veil Kendry retires from the CIA to become a painter and develop his special visionary powers. What he paints attract the interest of some sinister observers.
2. *Jungle of Steel and Stone* (Mysterious, 1988) Veil is enlisted to investigate the theft of an African totem from a Manhattan art gallery.

III. In 1986 and 1987 Chesbro published three novels under the pseudonym of "David Cross." These mixtures of suspense and SF featured Chant Sinclair, a self-employed mercenary and con man with awesome powers and a secret past. Chant was resurrected in *Dark Chant in a Crimson Key* (series I, 11), where he matches wits with Mongo Frederickson. The Chant novels, paperback originals, were reprinted in hard cover by Apache Beach Publications in 1999. They are listed below without annotations.

1. *Chant* (Berkley, 1986)
2. *Chant: Code of Blood* (Berkley, 1987)
3. *Chant: Silent Killer* (Berkley, 1986)

Chesney, Marion

I. Scottish-born Chesney has brought a new vigor to the Regency novel and many American fans to the genre. Her portraits of the debs and rakes of London society go beyond stereotypes. She gives inventive twists to the standard plots and describes the dress and manners of the period with authority and wit. Among her many Regency novels are included six series of six novels each.

Each novel in the Six Sisters series focuses on one of the daughters of the Reverend Charles Armitage, an amiable but impoverished country vicar with a passion for fox hunting. Faced with the fearsome task of educating two sons and marrying off six daughters with no fortunes, the vicar does his plucky best.

1. *Minerva* (St. Martin's, 1983) Minerva, the oldest daughter, is sent off to London to rescue the family fortunes by finding a rich husband.
2. *Taming of Annabelle, The* (St. Martin's, 1984) At 16 Annabelle is beautiful, wildly romantic, and jealous of Minerva.
3. *Deirdre and Desire* (St. Martin's, 1984) The good vicar despairs of ever finding a suitable husband for his intellectual daughter Deirdre.
4. *Daphne* (St. Martin's, 1984) When Simon Garfield falls into a trap set by the Reverend Armitage for a meddling bishop, he distracts Daphne from her plans of marrying vapid Cyril Archer.
5. *Diana the Huntress* (St. Martin's, 1985) Diana would rather hunt foxes with her father than hunt for a suitable husband.
6. *Frederica in Fashion* (St. Martin's, 1985) Frederica, the plain sister, leaves school and takes a job as a housemaid for the wicked Duke of Pembury.

II. A House for the Season is the title of this ingenious series of six Regency novels, which all take place in the same house, 76 Clarges

Street, in the fashionable Mayfair section of London. Each season brings a new tenant with a new story, while the unchanging domestic staff, ruled by the resourceful butler Rainbird, gives continuity.

1. *Miser of Mayfair, The* (St. Martin's, 1986) Beautiful Fiona Sinclair teaches Mayfair some new card tricks and catches the beau of her choice.
2. *Plain Jane* (St. Martin's, 1986) When Mrs. Rawley comes to Mayfair to launch her two daughters into society, she expects to have the most trouble with her younger daughter, Jane.
3. *Wicked Godmother, The* (St. Martin's, 1987) Sweet and dutiful Harriet Metcalf brings her two wealthy young charges to London for the season and finds herself eclipsing their success.
4. *Rake's Progress* (St. Martin's, 1987) Lord Guy Carlton, wounded in the Napoleonic Wars, cuts a dashing figure in Mayfair until he meets his neighbor, the severe Miss Jones.
5. *Adventuress, The* (St. Martin's, 1988) There is something mysterious about the reserved Mr. Goodenough and his beautiful daughter that puzzles the staff.
6. *Rainbird's Revenge* (St. Martin's, 1988) Rainbird the butler sets everything to rights, exposing the embezzlements of Parker, the real-estate agent, and helping Lord Pelham, the house's owner, find a wife.

III. The School of Manners series features Amy and Effie Tribble, resourceful elderly sisters who fend off poverty by going into the chaperone business.

1. *Refining Felicity* (St. Martin's, 1988) Amy and Effie take on the unenviable task of preparing horsey Felicity Baronsheath for the marriage market.
2. *Perfecting Fiona* (St. Martin's, 1989) Beautiful Fiona McCloud skillfully avoids marriage until the rakish Lord Harvard crosses her horizon.
3. *Enlightening Delilah* (St. Martin's, 1989) No one can understand why the beautiful Delilah Wraxall is unmarried at 23.
4. *Finessing Clarissa* (St. Martin's, 1989) Accomplishing the marriage of the large, clumsy, freckle-faced, red-haired Clarissa Vevian is a tall order even for the redoubtable Tribbles.
5. *Animating Maria* (St. Martin's, 1990) The Tribble sisters find their client Maria less of a problem than her nouveau-riche parents.
6. *Marrying Harriet* (St. Martin's, 1990) Harriet Brown, the charitable daughter of a Methodist minister, seeks to marry off the Tribble sisters.

IV. When former housekeeper Hannah Pym, the Traveling Matchmaker, inherits a comfortable income and decides to travel, she finds herself arranging matches and straightening out tangled relationships.

1. *Emily Goes to Exeter* (St. Martin's, 1990) When she is snowed in at a remote inn, Hannah uses her managerial skills to arrange meals, chores, entertainment, and two love matches.
2. *Belinda Goes to Bath* (St. Martin's, 1991) Belinda Earle, orphaned heiress encountered on the road to Bath, finds Hannah's talents useful.
3. *Penelope Goes to Portsmouth* (St. Martin's, 1991) On her way to Portsmouth Hannah helps young Penelope and handsome Lord Augustus to merge their destinies.
4. *Beatrice Goes to Brighton* (St. Martin's, 1991) The aloof young lady on the Brighton stage coach is actually a widow trying to escape an undesirable second marriage.
5. *Deborah Goes to Dover* (St. Martin's, 1992) While trying to prevent her footman from participating in a boxing match, Miss Pym encounters several matchmaking opportunities.

6. *Yvonne Goes to York* (St. Martin's, 1992) Miss Pym is thrown together with a spy, a lord, and a French émigré.

V. A group of six impecunious blue bloods pool their resources to open the Poor Relations, a London hotel for high society. Needless to say, they get involved in the affairs of their guests while trying, by fair means or foul, to finance their venture.

1. *Lady Fortescue Steps Out* (St. Martin's, 1992) Penniless Lady Fortescue, detected pinching her wealthy nephew's silver candlesticks, fortuitously runs into retired military man Colonel Sandhurst.
2. *Miss Tonks Turns to Crime* (St. Martin's, 1993) Miss Tonks decides to play highway(wo)man and hold up her wealthy sister's coach.
3. *Mrs. Budley Falls from Grace* (St. Martin's, 1993) Widowed Mrs. Budley travels to Warwickshire to lift pawnable items from a dying "distant relative."
4. *Sir Philip's Folly* (St. Martin's, 1993) Sir Philip Sommerville's latest folly is to fall in love with an unsuitable woman who is eating up the profits of the Poor Relations.
5. *Colonel Sandhurst to the Rescue* (St. Martin's, 1994) Colonel Sandhurst gets involved in a dubious ransom scheme involving a runaway heiress.
6. *Back in Society* (St. Martin's, 1994) Lady Jane Fremney, escaping from an undesirable marriage and unable to pay her hotel bills, attempts suicide.

VI. In the Daughters of Mannerling series, Mannerling, the stately family home of the Beverleys, has been lost to them because of gambling debts incurred by the patriarch. The six Beverley sisters make feverish efforts to regain the old homestead.

1. *Banishment, The* (St. Martin's, 1995) Isabella, the eldest Beverley sister, courts the dreadful Mr. Judd, who has acquired Mannerling.
2. *Intrigue, The* (St. Martin's, 1995) Second daughter Jessica schemes to marry the son of the new owners of Mannerling despite the fact that he is an absolute cad.
3. *Deception, The* (St. Martin's, 1996) When her sister begins to have doubts about marrying the son of Mannerling's present owner, Abigail Beverley devises a daring plan to win back the family homestead once and for all.
4. *Folly, The* (St. Martin's, 1996) Rachel Beverley, like her sisters, considers the new owner of Mannerling, widower Charles Blackwood, to be "too old" (he is nearing 40) for marriage.
5. *Romance, The* (St. Martin's, 1997) Belinda Beverley has seen four of her sisters marry for love rather than reclaim Mannerling, but she is certain that she will save the day, even if this means marrying the foppish Lord Luke St. Clair.
6. *Homecoming, The* (St. Martin's, 1997) The Duke of Severnshire, like Jane Austen's Mr. Darcy, is excessively proud, but Lizzie Beverley is determined to break him of this flaw.

VII. The prolific Chesney is now producing, under her real name rather than her M. C. Beaton (q.v.) pseudonym, a series of mysteries set in Edwardian times and featuring Lady Rose Sumner, spoiled suffragette daughter of a wealthy earl, and Captain Harry Cathcart, wounded Boer War veteran turned private investigator. This series combines light historical romance with mystery plots.

1. *Snobbery with Violence* (St, Martin's, 2003) Captain Harry Cathcart, who finds that he can make an income for himself through "fixing things" for rich clients, runs afoul of spoiled suffragette Rose Sumner during a murder investigation at Lord Hedley's manor.

2. *Hasty Death* (**St. Martin's, 2004**) Rose and her maid, Daisy, encounter a series of adventures when Rose ventures out into the working world, including a kidnapping, narrow escapes, a daring rescue . . . and murder. She turns to Harry Cathcart for help in solving the last.

3. *Sick of Shadows* (**St. Martin's, 2005**) To avoid being sent to India, Rose Summer claims to be engaged to Harry Cathcart. Then she discovers the body of the beautiful daughter of a clergyman.

4. *Our Lady of Pain* (**St. Martin's, 2006**) Rose is implicated in the murder of Dolores Duval, a woman of ill repute who has been seen on Harry's arm.

Chiaverini, Jennifer

The Elm Creek Quilts series, set in the fictional town of Waterford, Pennsylvania, revolves around the theme of quilting. When young Sarah McClure comes to the small college town with her landscaper husband, she gets work at Elm Creek Manor, the family home of elderly and embittered master quilter Sylvia Bergstrom Compson. Sarah learns quilting from Sylvia, and the two set up a quilting school at Elm Creek Manor. As the series progresses, and Sylvia and Sarah become increasingly close, we learn more about Sylvia's background and the reasons for her bitterness. This is a sweet but not saccharine series about redemption and reconciliation, with much quilting lore included. The books are listed in chronological order rather than by publishing date. *An Elm Creek Quilts Sampler* (Simon & Schuster, 2003) contains numbers 3, 5, and 6. *An Elm Creek Quilts Album* (Simon & Schuster, 2006) contains numbers 7 through 9. Jennifer Chiaverini, who lives in Madison, Wisconsin, is a former college instructor who took up quilting in 1994. *Elm Creek Quilts* (C&T, 2002), coauthored with Nancy Odom, and *Return to Elm Creek* (C&T, 2004) contain selections of quilting projects inspired by the novels.

1. *Sugar Camp Quilt, The* (**Simon & Schuster, 2005**) In 1849 young Dorothea Granger is set to work on a quilt of her uncle Jacob's design. When Jacob dies, she discovers that Sugar Camp, site of his maple syrup operation, is also a station on the Underground Railroad.

2. *Quilter's Homecoming, The* (**Simon & Schuster, 2007**) Newlyweds Elizabeth and Henry find themselves bilked when they leave Elizabeth's family farm in Pennsylvania in 1925 to work a Southern California ranch Henry has bought sight unseen.

3. *Quilter's Apprentice, The* (**Simon & Schuster, 1999**) When Sarah McClure moves with her husband to Waterford, Pennsylvania, she takes a job doing housework at Elm Creek Manor, home of Sylvia Compson, embittered master quilter and widow in her seventies.

4. *Christmas Quilt, The* (**Simon & Schuster, 2005**) Sarah McClure is determined to make Christmas a happy occasion for her quilting-camp partner, Sylvia Compson.

5. *Round Robin* (**Simon & Schuster, 2000**) The Elm Street quilters engage upon a round-robin quilt, each quilter contributing a border of patchwork around a central block. Each quilter has her own story to tell.

6. *Cross-Country Quilters, The* (**Simon & Schuster, 2001**) Five women from across the country meet during a weeklong visit to Elm Creek. Each has her own story to tell.

7. *Runaway Quilt, The* (**Simon & Schuster, 2002**) While Sylvia is on a speaking engagement in South Carolina, a woman named Margaret Alden shows her a family heirloom quilt with a map of Elm Creek Manor re-created in the stitches, which inspires Sylvia to further explore her paternal heritage.

8. *Quilter's Legacy, The* (**Simon & Schuster, 2003**) In a narrative alternating between past and present, Sylvia Compson, planning her upcoming wedding to Andrew Cooper, learns more about her maternal heritage and the women's suffrage movement.

9. *Master Quilter, The* (**Simon & Schuster, 2004**) Sylvia has married Andrew Cooper in a surprise Christmas Eve wedding, which means that Sylvia's friends haven't had time to craft the requisite bridal quilt.

10. *Circle of Quilters* (**Simon & Schuster, 2006**) When two founding members decide to leave, the Elm Creek Quilters face changes in their business and in their personal lives. The quilters post an open call for applicants for the vacated positions.

11. *New Year's Quilt, The* (**Simon & Schuster, 2007**) Having married on Christmas Eve, Sylvia Compson and Andrew Cooper have to reconcile with Andrew's children, especially his bitter daughter, Amy.

12. *Winding Ways Quilt, The* (**Simon & Schuster, 2008**) Chapters center on the circle's various members. Gwen tries to discover the creator of a quilt rescued from a church basement lost-and-found.

Child, Lee

Jack Reacher is the linchpin of a series of thrillers that are regarded by some critics as the best going today. Jack is a tall, 250-pound, taciturn, ex–US Military Police major, who can kill with his bare hands. He is a Robin Hood type with his share of problems, which he doesn't brood about, being basically a rather cheerful fellow. These very exciting, action-filled novels, which take Reacher all around the United States, are character driven more than plot driven, with a protagonist who is basically likable despite his lethal potential. Lee Child, interestingly enough, is a Brit who came to the United States only in 1998.

1. *Enemy, The* (**Delacorte, 2004**) A prequel, set back in Jack Reacher's days as a military policeman, on New Year's Eve 1990, in which the body of a two-star general is found in a motel near Fort Bird, North Carolina.

2. *Killing Floor* (**Putnam, 1997**) Introduces Jack Reacher, ex-military policeman. Jack stops off in Margrave, Georgia, to investigate the 60-year-old murder of bluesman "Blind" Blake, unaware that his brother, a US Treasury official, has been murdered there a few hours earlier.

3. *Die Trying* (**Putnam, 1998**) Jack, who is a doorman at a Chicago blues club, gets kidnapped by paramilitary types along with FBI agent Holly Johnson.

4. *Tripwire* (**Putnam, 1999**) Jack, incognito, living the life of a drifter, finds a job digging swimming pools in Key West, Florida, but a PI from New York comes looking for him to investigate evil corporate loan shark "Hook" Hobie.

5. *Running Blind* (**Putnam, 2000**) Some psycho is murdering women across the country, leaving their naked bodies in their bathtubs filled with army camouflage green paint.

6. *Echo Burning* (**Putnam, 2001**) Jack, who has hired on as a cowhand in remote Echo County, Texas, is asked by Carmen Greer to kill her abusive husband, Sloop, who is getting out of prison.

7. *Without Fail* (**Putnam, 2002**) US Secret Service operative M. E. Froelich asks Jack to masquerade as an assassin after vice-president-elect Brock Armstrong receives anonymous death threats.

8. *Persuader* (**Delacorte, 2003**) The apparent kidnapping of a college student and the FBI investigation of shady tycoon Zachary Beck offer Reacher a chance to settle a score with an old nemesis, former US Army Intelligence officer Quinn, long believed dead.

9. *One Shot* (**Delacorte, 2005**) Five people are killed when a shooter opens fire in a small unnamed Indiana city. When James Barr,

the apparent perpetrator, is apprehended, he says only, "Get Jack Reacher for me."

10. *Hard Way, The* (Delacorte, 2006) Reacher agrees to help ex-army officer Edward Lane to track down his kidnapped daughter and trophy wife.

11. *Bad Luck and Trouble* (Delacorte, 2007) Former Military Policeman Calvin Franz, member of the army's special investigation unit formerly headed by Reacher, is dumped 3,000 feet from a helicopter onto the California desert floor.

Child, Maureen

I. California author Maureen Child is a rising star in the paperback romance field. Since 1990 she has published nearly 50 novels under her own name and under the pseudonyms Ann Carberry, Sarah Hart, and Kathleen Kane. Most of the novels published under the Child name are in the Silhouette Desire series, but more recently, she has published mainstream contemporary romances under the St. Martin's imprint. The Candellano trilogy is about members of the Candellano clan, of Chandler, California, who, like most romance heroes and heroines, love not wisely but too well. Child's romances are warm, fuzzy, and family centered, which doesn't mean that they eschew passionate sex. Numbers 1 and 2 were published together.

1. *Finding You* (St. Martin's, 2003) Carla Candellano has built up a wall around herself since tragedy entered her life, but then she meets mute six-year-old Reese Wyatt and her worried father, widower Jackson. Published together with *Knowing You*.

2. *Knowing You* (St. Martin's, 2003) Stevie Ryan has been hopelessly in love with Nick, her best friend Carla Candellano's older brother, since she was a young girl. Then she spends one sultry night together with Nick's brother, Paul. Published together with *Finding You*.

3. *Loving You* (St. Martin's, 2003) Nick Candellano is an injured football superstar facing a bleak future. Then Jonas, an orphaned boy, sues Nick in a paternity suit, and Nick becomes acquainted with Jonas's foster mother, the sexy but hostile Tasha Flynn.

II. The Marconi trilogy is also based in the fictional Chandler, California. Like the Candellanos, the Marconis are emotionally volatile, and like them, they are prone to be carried away by passion, although everything works out okay in the end.

1. *And Then Came You* (St. Martin's, 2004) *Sam's Story*. Over both families' objections, Samantha "Sam" Marconi, the middle sister and supposedly the sensible one, marries wealthy, impulsive, sexy Jeff Hendricks.

2. *Crazy Kind of Love, A* (St. Martin's, 2005) *Mike's Story*. Micaela "Mike" Marconi is an ace plumber who is professionally a wisecracking extrovert, but she is leery about long-term love relationships. Then wealthy scientist-inventor Lucas Gallagher buys the house that Mike was coveting.

3. *Turn My World Upside Down* (St. Martin's, 2005) *Jo's Story*. Josefina "Jo" Marconi, who has to move back into the family home and watch Jack, the 10-year-old illegitimate boy fathered by Jo's father, runs into Cash Hunter, aka "the Woman Whisperer," who is notorious for one-night stands.

III. Most of Child's romances have been published in the Silhouette Desire series. The Bachelor Battalion contains 14 loosely connected volumes about US Marines and their romances, published between 1998 and 2002. The Reilly trilogy is about triplet brothers who can't seem to keep their pants on. They embark upon a wager that stipulates that any one of the three who can abstain from sex for 90 days(!) will be the winner.

1. *Tempting Mrs. Reilly* (Silhouette, 2005) Brian Reilly has spent two whole weeks celibate since the "no-sex-for-90-days" wager with his brothers. Then his beautiful ex-wife Tina Coretti Reilly turns up on his doorstep.

2. *Whatever Reilly Wants* (Silhouette, 2005) Marine Connor Reilly has one month down, two to go on the "no-sex" bet. Then his friend Emma Jacobsen is piqued by Connor's remarks about how "safe" and "comfortable" he felt around her.

3. *Last Reilly Standing, The* (Silhouette, 2005) Aidan Reilly has only three more weeks to win the bet he made with his brothers. Then Terry Evans, gorgeous and with a "soft and dreamy" voice, enters his life.

Childs, Laura

I. The Tea Shop Mysteries are set in Charleston's (South Carolina) historic district, where Theodosia Browning runs the Indigo Tea Shop. Seemingly every gala event in which Theodora and the Indigo Tea Shop take part produces a corpse, often embarrassingly public. But Theodora is equal to the challenges in this series of cozies, each of which includes a "scrumptious" recipe.

1. *Death by Darjeeling* (Berkley, 2001) Theodosia Browning's Indigo Tea Shop caters Charleston's annual Lamplighter Tour of historic homes. Hughes Barron, a rather shady real-estate dealer, is served some poisoned Darjeeling and drops dead.

2. *Gunpowder Green* (Berkley, 2002) The Civil War pistol used for the traditional finishing gunshot at the annual Isles of Palms Yacht Race explodes in the hands of a patriarch from one of Charleston's oldest families.

3. *Shades of Earl Grey* (Berkley, 2003) An antique wedding ring disappears from the hand of a dying bridegroom. A priceless sapphire necklace is lifted from its display at the Heritage Society's Treasures Show. The Heritage Society asks Theodosia to get to the bottom of this.

4. *English Breakfast Murder, The* (Berkley, 2003) Theodosia Browning, aiding Charleston's Sea Turtle Protection League in helping hundreds of tiny loggerhead turtles reach the sea, spots a dead body bobbing in the waves.

5. *Jasmine Moon Murder, The* (Berkley, 2004) The first-ever Ghost Crawl in Charleston's Jasmine Cemetery ends in tragedy when Dr. Jasper Davis, uncle of Theodosia's beau, Jory, dies mysteriously and publicly.

6. *Chamomile Mourning* (Berkley, 2005) Rain at the Spoleto festival forces Theodosia's first-ever indoor Poet's Tea. Then Roger Crispin, of the auction house of Crispin & Weber, plunges to his death from an inside balcony, ruining her special cake.

7. *Blood Orange Brewing* (Berkley, 2006) The Indigo Tea Shop is catering Delaine Dish's lavish Candlelight Concert to raise funds to restore a run-down Victorian home. Unfortunately, retired CEO and politico Duke Wilkes spoils things by falling to the floor with a jagged piece of metal protruding from his neck.

8. *Dragonwell Dead* (Berkley, 2007) Mark Congdon, commodities broker and co-owner of a Charleston bed-and-breakfast, drops dead after sipping a poisoned glass of tea at the Spring Plantation Ramble.

9. *Silver Needle Mystery, The* (Berkley, 2008) Someone shoots movie director Jordan Cole onstage at the recently restored Belvedere Theater during Charleston's first film festival.

II. Childs is producing another series of cozies, the Scrapbook series, set this time in New Orleans. Scrapbooking shop owner Carmela Bertrand is the protagonist in this set of mysteries, each one supplied with "scrapbook tips."

1. *Keepsake Crimes* **(Berkley, 2003)** Carmela Bertrand, the French Quarter (New Orleans) owner of scrapbooking shop Memory Mine, gets involved when a body tumbles from a giant serpent float at the Pluvius Parade, and Shamus Meechum, her about-to-be-ex-husband, becomes the prime suspect.
2. *Photofinished* **(Berkley, 2004)** Carmela is hosting a late-night "Crop Till You Drop" scrapbooking session when a neighboring antique-shop owner is murdered in an alley.
3. *Bound for Murder* **(Berkley, 2004)** Carmela Bertrand's prewedding party for a friend is spoiled when the groom-to-be is murdered.
4. *Motif for Murder* **(Berkley, 2006)** Shamus Meechum, Carmela's ex-husband, is kidnapped, and his elderly uncle Henry is found murdered.
5. *Frill Kill* **(Berkley, 2007)** In an alley behind her friend Ava Grieux's Juju Voodoo shop, Carmela discovers the body of fashion model Amber Lalique, who was in the shop only moments earlier.

Chisholm, P. F.

PSEUDONYM OF Patricia Finney

Sir Robert Carey, deputy warden of the English West March on the English-Scottish border in the 1590s, has his hands full, what with border raiders, obstreperous Scots, unscrupulous rivals, and the occasional murder. Carey—a real person who eventually became Earl of Monmouth and who left memoirs that were eventually published (reprint, Clarendon, 1972)—is placed in a convincing late Elizabethan setting in which other historical characters, such as James VI of Scotland, Shakespeare, and Christopher Marlowe, wend their way. The novels should appeal to historical mystery fans. English author P. F. Chisholm also writes historical novels under her real name, Patricia Finney (q.v.).

1. *Famine of Horses, A* **(Walker, 1995)** Sir Robert Carey, courtier to Queen Elizabeth, is appointed deputy warden of the English West March, a position that proves to be no sinecure, what with endemic English-Scottish border tensions, disgruntled rival for the position Richard Lowther, a distrustful assistant, and the murder of the son of a powerful feudal lord.
2. *Season of Knives, A* **(Walker, 1996)** Corrupt military purveyors and garrison officials at Carlisle, border raiders, the persistent Sir Richard Lowther, and a murder in which he may be implicated—all fall to the lot of Sir Robert Carey.
3. *Surfeit of Guns, A* **(Walker, 1997)** In 1592 a shipment of guns has been replaced by defective substitutes. Sir Robert's investigation takes him, eventually, to the court of King James VI of Scotland.
4. *Plague of Angels, A* **(Poisoned Pen, 2000)** In August 1592, Sir Robert returns to London to find money to pay off his debts and gets embroiled in a feud between a couple of playwrights, Greene and Shakespeare.

Chittenden, Margaret

Charlotte "Charlie" Plato is a 30-year-old divorcée; part owner of CHAPS, a country-western nightclub near San Francisco; and narrator of a series of light mysteries featuring herself as amateur detective. Charlie and her partners, former TV star Zack Hunter, former rodeo driver Angel Cervantes, and Savanna Seabrook Bistow, an African American version of Dolly Parton, manage to get in and out of a series of scrapes told in a frothy, breathless manner. Some readers find Charlie Plato appealing, but at least one reviewer regards her as one of "a school of self-consciously perky mystery narrators." Margaret "Meg" Chittenden, native of England and naturalized American citizen, wrote more than 20 romance novels under her own name and as "Rosalind Carson" before turning to mysteries.

1. *Dying to Sing* **(Kensington, 1996)** Charlie Plato, part-owner of the San Francisco Bay Area country-western nightclub CHAPS, discovers the skeletal remains of a foot in a flower bed after an earthquake.
2. *Dead Men Don't Dance* **(Kensington, 1997)** One of Charlie's partners, former TV actor Zack Hunter, finds himself the chief suspect when the body of his rival in a race for city councillor is found in the trunk of Zack's car.
3. *Dead Beat and Deadly* **(Kensington, 1998)** Philippine Estrella Stockton, a mail-order bride and star pupil in the self-defense course organized by Charlie at CHAPS, is murdered, and Estrella's husband, the chief suspect, asks Charlie to track down the real killer.
4. *Don't Forget to Die* **(Kensington, 1999)** Vic Cervantes, estranged father of Angel Cervantes, another partner at CHAPS, turns up dead in a storage locker.
5. *Dying to See You* **(Kensington, 2000)** Savannah Bristow, another one of Charlie's partners, throws a party for her favorite teacher, Reina Diaz. Then Reina is found strangled in the bathroom.

Christie, Agatha

I. Agatha Christie's position as the world's most famous modern mystery writer is likely to remain unchallenged for some time. *The Mysterious Affair at Styles*, surely one of the most polished first mystery novels ever written, won her immediate recognition. Though she was capable of writing an inferior book from time to time, the inventiveness and productivity that she sustained over the next 56 years were truly remarkable. Not all of Christie's books feature one of her famous detectives: among these are her less-successful international espionage thrillers but also one of her best-known novels, *Ten Little Indians* (aka *And Then There Were None*). For convenience these miscellaneous works are listed, but not annotated, in series VI below. More information about them, and about other aspects of Christie's work, including films based on her books, is available in the delightful compendium edited by Dick Riley, Pam McAllister, and Bruce Cassidy entitled *The [New] Bedside, Bathtub and Armchair Companion to Agatha Christie* (rev. ed., Ungar, 1986; reprinted by Continuum, 2001). Another useful reference work is Dawn B. Sova et al., *Agatha Christie A to Z* (Facts on File, 1996).

The retired Belgian police detective Hercule Poirot is the most famous of Christie's detectives. This fastidious little man with the waxed mustache and a fondness for growing vegetable marrows used his remarkable "gray cells" to reason his way to the bottom of the most complicated cases. Sprung fully developed into the world with Christie's first book, Poirot changed little through the years and must have been, by ordinary reckoning, well over 100 years old at the end of his career. Connoisseurs consider the Poirot books the best of Christie's output. The stories are listed here in the order of their publication, which, except for a few flashback cases, matches their chronology. Poirot has been depicted in movies by such luminaries as Peter Ustinov, Tony Randall, and Albert Finney but most convincingly by David Suchet on PBS. Anne Hart has written a "biography" of Poirot, *The Life and Times of Hercule Poirot* (Putnam, 1990).

1. *Mysterious Affair at Styles, The* (**Dodd, 1920**) Captain Hastings, the Watson character in the early Poirot novels, narrates the story of the strychnine poisoning of the imperious Emily Inglethorpe of Styles Court in Essex. Poirot, who lives in the neighborhood, comes to investigate.

2. *Murder on the Links* (**Dodd, 1923**) Poirot arrives too late to save Paul Renaud from being murdered and buried in a shallow grave on his own golf course.

3. *Poirot Investigates* (**Dodd, 1925**) These 14 stories show Captain Hastings at his most dense. Several flashback stories are included.

4. *Murder of Roger Ackroyd, The* (**Dodd, 1926**) This landmark case, which made Christie internationally famous, concerns three deaths and blackmail. The solution has been thought a stroke of genius by some and a dirty trick by others.

5. *Big Four, The* (**Dodd, 1927**) Hastings, Poirot, and Inspector Japp pursue an international gang of criminals bent on the "disintegration of civilization." Not Poirot's metier.

6. *Mystery of the Blue Train, The* (**Dodd, 1928**) When murder occurs on the Blue Train to Nice, Poirot is on the spot to help solve the case.

7. *Peril at End House* (**Dodd, 1932**) Hastings and Poirot, while on vacation on the Cornish Riviera, try to protect a young heiress, Nick Buckley, whose life is in danger.

8. *Thirteen at Dinner* (**Dodd, 1933**) Lord Edgware is found dead in his library, a small stab wound at the base of his neck. Variant title: *Lord Edgware Dies.*

9. *Murder on the Orient Express* (**Dodd, 1934**) In another Christie classic, set aboard a train stuck in the snow in Yugoslavia, the villainous Ratchett meets his end. Poirot knows that the killer must be among the stranded passengers. Original title: *Murder in the Calais Coach.*

10. *Murder in Three Acts* (**Dodd, 1934**) Two murders by nicotine poisoning seem to be unrelated except for the suspicious presence of Ellis the butler. English title: *Three-Act Tragedy.*

11. *Death in the Air* (**Dodd, 1935**) Could Madame Giselle have been murdered by a poison dart, with Poirot in a nearby seat, on the noon flight from Paris to London? Variant title: *Death in the Clouds.*

12. *A.B.C. Murders, The* (**Dodd, 1935**) A madman warns Poirot by letter before committing each of a series of murders. Variant title: *The Alphabet Murders.*

13. *Murder in Mesopotamia* (**Dodd, 1936**) Poirot happens to be passing through when the murder of a woman on an archaeological expedition on the banks of the Tigris attracts his attention.

14. *Cards on the Table* (**Dodd, 1936**) Poirot shares the spotlight with Ariadne Oliver (see series III), Superintendent Battle (see series V), and Colonel Race, a Secret Service man, as guest at an unusual dinner party given by socialite and murder authority Dr. Shaitana.

15. *Poirot Loses a Client* (**Dodd, 1937**) A letter draws Hastings and Poirot to the little town of Market Basing, but they find that their correspondent, old Emily Arundell, has been dead for over a month. Variant titles: *Dumb Witness; Murder at Littlegreen House;* and *Mystery at Littlegreen House.*

16. *Dead Man's Mirror* (**Dodd, 1937**) Three stories are included: "Dead Man's Mirror," "Murder in the Mews," and "Triangle at Rhodes."

17. *Death on the Nile* (**Dodd, 1938**) A rich and beautiful young bride is being driven to distraction by an old friend, her husband's former fiancée. Among the vacationers on the Nile cruise is Hercule Poirot.

18. *Appointment with Death* (**Dodd, 1938**) The murder of fat, obnoxious Mrs. Boynton finds Poirot on vacation in Jerusalem.

19. *Murder for Christmas* (**Dodd, 1938**) Simon Lee, who made his millions in the South African diamond mines, has his throat slit on Christmas Eve at his country estate. Variant titles; *Holiday for Murder* and *Hercule Poirot's Christmas.*

20. *Regatta Mystery, The* (**Dodd, 1939**) These nine stories feature Poirot, Miss Marple, and Parker Pyne. Variant title: *Poirot and the Regatta Mystery.* (See also II, 3.)

21. *Sad Cypress* (**Dodd, 1940**) Elinor Carlisle gains a fortune when her aunt Laura dies, but loses her only love, Roddy Wellman, and finds herself accused of murdering Roddy's new bride.

22. *Patriotic Murders, The* (**Dodd, 1940**) Could Dr. Morley, Poirot's dentist, have committed suicide in his office while patients waited? Variant titles: *An Overdose of Death* and *One, Two, Buckle My Shoe.*

23. *Evil under the Sun* (**Dodd, 1941**) At the Jolly Roger Hotel in an English seaside resort, an aging actress is murdered, and Poirot finds no shortage of suspects.

24. *Murder in Retrospect* (**Dodd, 1943**) Carla Crale hires Poirot to find out the truth about her mother, who was convicted of murdering her husband, Carla's father. Variant title: *Five Little Pigs.*

25. *Murder after Hours* (**Dodd, 1946**) A weekend house party at the Angketell's house, the Hollow, proves fatal for Dr. John Christow, who is shot just as Poirot arrives for lunch. Variant title: *The Hollow.*

26. *Labours of Hercules, The* (**Dodd, 1947**) Poirot vows that the cases detailed in these 12 stories, which correspond to the labors of the classical Hercules, will be his last.

27. *There Is a Tide* (**Dodd, 1948**) Poirot lingers in the town of Warmsley Vale after the curious murder of an unidentified man. Variant title: *Taken at the Flood.*

28. *Witness for the Prosecution and Other Stories* (**Dodd, 1948**) Only one of the 10 stories in this collection features Poirot. The cover story, "Witness for the Prosecution," was the basis for the famous play (and movies) of the same name.

29. *Mousetrap and Other Stories, The* (**Dodd, 1950**) Three of the nine stories collected here star Poirot. The title story is the basis for the long-running play *The Mousetrap* (50+ years, 20,000+ performances). (See also II, 6.)

30. *Underdog and Other Stories, The* (**Dodd, 1951**) Nine Poirot stories comprise this book.

31. *Mrs. McGinty's Dead* (**Dodd, 1952**) Poirot and Ariadne Oliver renew their acquaintance in the village of Broadhinny as he investigates the death of Mrs. McGinty, a domestic whom nobody seems to care about. Variant title: *Blood Will Tell.*

32. *Funerals Are Fatal* (**Dodd, 1953**) After three suspicious deaths and a fourth murder attempt, Poirot calls the Abernethie family back to Enderby Hall for a fatal gathering. Variant title: *After the Funeral.*

33. *Hickory, Dickory Death* (**Dodd, 1955**) When Poirot's secretary, Felicity Lemon, is worried about some mysterious thefts at the student hotel that her sister runs, Poirot offers to help. Variant title: *Hickory Dickory Dock.*

34. *Dead Man's Folly* (**Dodd, 1956**) Ariadne Oliver, who is arranging a murder-hunt game for a charity fete, requests Poirot's help when she feels very uneasy about things.

35. *Cat among the Pigeons* (**Dodd, 1959**) Meadowbank School for girls is the scene of this case involving smuggled jewels and a Turkish princess.

36. *Adventure of the Christmas Pudding, The* (**Collins [UK], 1960**) Five Poirots and one Marple story make up this confection. (See also II, 11.)

37. *Double Sin and Other Stories* (**Dodd, 1961**) Poirot stories account for four out of the nine in this collection. (See also II, 12.)

38. *Clocks, The* (Dodd, 1963) Elements in this curious case are four clocks frozen at 4:13, a blind murder suspect, and an unidentified victim.

39. *Third Girl* (Dodd, 1966) Ariadne Oliver helps the aging Poirot with this case of a young girl who thinks she might have committed a murder.

40. *Halloween Party* (Dodd, 1969) Mrs. Oliver is cured of her apple addiction when a child drowns bobbing for apples, but Poirot solves the murder.

41. *Elephants Can Remember* (Dodd, 1972) Mrs. Oliver and Poirot work together to solve an old murder case.

42. *Poirot's Early Cases* (Dodd, 1974) These stories are all available in other collections as well. Variant title: *Hercule Poirot's Early Cases.*

43. *Curtain* (Dodd, 1975) Poirot calls Hastings back to Styles for the case he knows will be his last.

44. *Hercule Poirot's Casebook* (Dodd, 1984) This book contains 50 Poirot stories.

45. *Harlequin Tea Set and Other Stories, The* (Putnam, 1997) Nine never-before-collected Christie magazine stories, one of them involving Poirot.

II. While Christie grew to hate Poirot, she was always fond of Miss Marple, her white-haired spinster whose knowledge of human nature gained as a lifelong busybody in the little village of St. Mary Mead made her an excellent detective. The character of Miss Marple was based somewhat on Christie's grandmother, who, though cheerful, always expected the worst of everybody and was usually right. Margaret Rutherford was delightful but all wrong in the part in a series of movies, while Joan Hixson was the near-definitive Miss Marple on PBS. Anne Hart pieced together Miss Marple's "biography" in *The Life and Times of Miss Jane Marple* (Dodd, 1985).

1. *Murder at the Vicarage* (Dodd, 1930) When the universally disliked Colonel Protheroe is found murdered in the vicar's study, two people confess to the crime, and Miss Marple's curiosity is aroused.

2. *Tuesday Club Murders, The* (Dodd, 1933) Miss Marple solves 13 different mysteries while knitting by her fireplace. Variant title: *The Thirteen Problems.*

3. *Regatta Mystery, The* (Dodd, 1939) This collection includes some Marple stories along with Poirots and Parker Pynes. Variant title: *Poirot and the Regatta Mystery.* (See also I, 20.)

4. *Body in the Library, The* (Dodd, 1942) The corpse of an unidentified woman in evening clothes appears as if by magic in the library in Gossington Hall.

5. *Moving Finger, The* (Dodd, 1942) When anonymous obscene letters cause a suicide in the quiet little village of Lymstock, Miss Marple, who is visiting at the vicarage, helps to finger the guilty party. Variant title: *The Case of the Moving Finger.*

6. *Mousetrap and Other Stories, The* (Dodd, 1950) There are four Marple stories out of the nine in this collection. Variant title: *Three Blind Mice and Other Stories.* (See also I, 29.)

7. *Murder Is Announced, A* (Dodd, 1950) A murder is announced in the "personal" column of the newspaper, and everybody assumes it to be a new kind of parlor game.

8. *Murder with Mirrors* (Dodd, 1952) A confusing case for Miss Marple involves the alleged slow poisoning of the lady of the house and a houseful of supposedly reformed delinquent boys. Variant title: *They Do It with Mirrors.*

9. *Pocket Full of Rye, A* (Dodd, 1954) Miss Marple, who knew the murdered servant girl as a child, thinks that a nursery rhyme may yield important information.

10. *What Mrs. McGillicuddy Saw* (Dodd, 1957) From her window seat, Elspeth McGillicuddy witnesses a murder taking place in a train running parallel to hers. Fortunately she is on her way to visit Miss Marple. Variant titles: *4:50 from Paddington* and *Murder, She Said.*

11. *Adventure of the Christmas Pudding, The* (Collins [UK], 1960) Here is one Miss Marple in a package with five Poirots. (See also I, 36.)

12. *Double Sin and Other Stories* (Dodd, 1961) This collection has two Marples out of nine stories. (See also I, 37.)

13. *Mirror Crack'd, The* (Dodd, 1962) When American movie actress Marina Gregory and her director-husband move to St. Mary Mead, the little town sizzles with glamour and mystery. Variant title: *The Mirror Crack'd from Side to Side.*

14. *Caribbean Mystery, A* (Dodd, 1964) Thanks to her rich nephew Raymond, Miss Marple is transported to a carefree Caribbean resort, which she finds rather boring until a murder enlivens things.

15. *At Bertrams Hotel* (Dodd, 1965) Bertrams, a bastion of old London hospitality, provides commodious fireplace chairs where Miss Marple overhears some very curious goings-on.

16. *Nemesis* (Dodd, 1971) Miss Marple will receive a bequest if she can solve a problem that is only vaguely defined and starts with a bus tour of famous English houses.

17. *Sleeping Murder* (Dodd, 1976) An old murder is recalled by a young woman having a curious case of déjà vu as she renovates a cozy little home in the village of Dillmouth.

18. *Miss Marple: The Complete Short Stories* (Dodd, 1985) A collection of all 20 Marple short stories.

III. Just as Captain Hastings acted as a Watson figure in the early Poirots, Mrs. Ariadne Oliver serves this purpose in the later works, and she adds considerable comic interest as well. There can be little doubt that Ariadne Oliver is an autobiographical figure: she is the best-selling author of mysteries starring a famous vegetarian Finnish detective. She, like her creator, has wiry gray hair, a tendency to plumpness, and the habit of eating apples while writing. Through Mrs. Oliver, who claims to hate the eccentric little detective she has immortalized, Christie indulges in some self-parody.

1. *Mr. Parker Pyne, Detective* (Dodd, 1934) Mrs. Oliver makes her first appearance as a mystery writer who devises plots for the unusual detection practiced by Mr. Parker Pyne in these dozen short stories. Variant title: *Parker Pyne Investigates.*

2. *Pale Horse, The* (Dodd, 1961) Mrs. Oliver plays a small role in this case, which begins with the murder of a Catholic priest. Narrator-historian Mark Easterbrook is the detective of record here.

IV. Miss Prudence Cowley, known as Tuppence, and her old friend Tommy Beresford are bored after seeing exciting World War I service—she as a nurse and he as an intelligence agent. For a lark they hire themselves out as adventurers and get involved in their first mystery case. They eventually marry and have children, but Tuppence never learns not to take foolish chances when sleuthing.

1. *Secret Adversary, The* (Dodd, 1922) A secret message carried from the sinking *Lusitania* by a young girl is at the bottom of the mystery that Tommy and Tuppence bungle into.

2. *Partners in Crime* (Dodd, 1929) This collection of stories shows Tommy and Tuppence, now married, using, and parodying, different methods of detection for each case that is brought to them.

3. *N or M?* (Dodd, 1941) Doing their part in the World War II effort, Tommy and Tuppence, in disguise, try to spot a mysterious Nazi agent at an English hotel.

4. *By the Pricking of My Thumbs* (Dodd, 1968) Graying, but no more cautious, Tuppence pokes into a mystery that involves some dotty old ladies in a nursing home, a painting, and a doll found in a fireplace.

5. *Postern of Fate* (Dodd, 1974) Tommy and Tuppence retire to a cottage in the country, where a mysterious message of underline words in a children's book entices Tuppence into an investigation

V. Superintendent Battle of Scotland Yard appears in four of Christie's complicated country-house murders. Battle is a methodical professional, reputed to be the Yard's best. He is also a character in *Cards on the Table* (series I, 14).

1. *Secret of Chimneys, The* (Dodd, 1925) Battle is called in to investigate the murder of Count Stanislas of Herzoslovakia at the country estate of Chimneys.

2. *Seven Dials Mystery, The* (Dodd, 1929) Chimneys is again the setting for this lighthearted thriller featuring Lady Eileen "Bundle" Brent sleuthing into the death of a houseguest at her rented-out family estate. Battle appears, ineptly disguised.

3. *Easy to Kill* (Dodd, 1939) Miss Fullerton is killed in a hit-and-run accident while on her way to Scotland Yard. Battle puts in an appearance, but retired police officer Luke Fitzwilliams does most of the investigating. Variant title: *Murder Is Easy.*

4. *Towards Zero* (Dodd, 1944) A clever murder is planned seven months before it takes place. Battle is called in to investigate the death of Lady Camilla Tressilian at her seaside estate, Gull's Point. Variant title: *Come and Be Hanged.*

VI. Christie also produced a number of mystery novels and short story collections not featuring one of the above detectives.

1. *Man in the Brown Suit, The* (Dodd, 1924)
2. *Mysterious Mr. Quin, The* (Dodd, 1930) A short story collection.
3. *Murder at Hazelmoor* (Dodd, 1931) Variant title: *Sittaford Mystery.*
4. *Why Didn't They Ask Evans?* (Dodd, 1934) Variant title: *The Boomerang Clue.*
5. *Ten Little Indians* (Dodd, 1940) A classic puzzle mystery. Variant title: *And Then There Were None.*
6. *Sparkling Cyanide* (Dodd, 1945) Variant title: *Remembered Death.*
7. *Death Comes as the End* (Dodd, 1945)
8. *Crooked House* (Dodd, 1949)
9. *They Came to Baghdad* (Dodd, 1951)
10. *So Many Steps to Death* (Dodd, 1954) Variant title: *Destination Unknown.*
11. *Ordeal by Innocence* (Dodd, 1958)
12. *Endless Night* (Dodd, 1967)
13. *Passenger to Frankfurt* (Dodd, 1970)
14. *Golden Ball and Other Stories, The* (Dodd, 1971)

Churchill, Jill

PSEUDONYM OF Janice Young Brooks

I. Jane Jeffry is a widowed mother of three, a suburban Chicago housewife who keeps getting mixed up with murder, which Jane solves with her best friend, Shelley, and her boyfriend, Mel. This is a series of punningly titled cozies in which Jane's gardening, cooking, and family life play prominent roles. American author Janice Young Brooks has also written many historical novels under her own name.

1. *Grime and Punishment* (Bantam, 1989) When the cleaning lady of Shelley Nowack, Jane Jeffry's best friend, is found dead, Jane's curiosity gets her involved with a ring of domestic blackmailers.

2. *Farewell to Yarns, A* (Avon, 1991) Long lost acquaintance Phyllis Wagner turns up on Jane's doorstep for a Christmas visit. Phyllis and her bratty son are soon murdered.

3. *Quiche before Dying, A* (Avon, 1993) Her kids off her hands for the summer, Jane enrolls in a community college writing course. Then an obnoxious fellow student is poisoned at a pot luck student buffet.

4. *Class Menagerie, The* (Avon, 1994) Jane's high school reunion produces some juicy gossip and a corpse.

5. *Knife to Remember, A* (Avon, 1994) A film crew from Hollywood insists upon using Jane's backyard as a primary location. Then the set manager is stabbed to death.

6. *From Here to Paternity* (Avon, 1995) Jane, Shelley, their kids, and boyfriend detective Mel VanDyne plan a few days of relaxation at a Colorado ski resort. But Jane skis into a snowman, which contains a corpse.

7. *Silence of the Hams* (Avon, 1996) Detested attorney Robert Stonecipher is done in by a rack of hams at the opening of a neighborhood deli where Jane's son works.

8. *War and Peas* (Avon, 1996) Regina Palmer, director of the Snellen Museum near Chicago is shot to death with an antique Derringer pistol during a Civil War reenactment.

9. *Fear of Frying* (Avon, 1997) Local car dealer Sam Claypool turns up dead more than once during a campout at a kids' summer camp on a rain-soaked weekend.

10. *Merchant of Menace, The* (Avon, 1998) During a busy Christmas season, when she will be meeting the mother of significant other Mel for the first time, Jane is also faced with the fatal roof tumble of tale-bearing TV reporter Lance King.

11. *Groom with a View, A* (Avon, 1999) After Jane takes on a job as a wedding consultant, cranky, elderly seamstress Mrs. Crossthwait is found dead at the foot of the stairs.

12. *Mulch Ado about Nothing* (Morrow, 2000) An unknown intruder sneaks into the home of Julie Jackson, teacher of a gardening class that Jane and Julie have signed up for, and knocks her out, leaving her in a coma.

13. *House of Seven Mabels, The* (Morrow, 2002) Jane and Shelley are asked to become decorators for the Victorian house that Bitsy Burnside is renovating with an all-female work crew.

14. *Bell, Book, and Scandal* (Morrow, 2003) A lot is going on at the mystery convention that Jane and Shelley are attending, including a meeting with Felicity Roane, Jane's favorite writer; the examination and possible publication of Jane's manuscript; the poisoning of an editor; the coshing of a reviewer; and the unmasking of gossip columnist Miss Mystery.

15. *Midsummer Night's Scream, A* (Morrow, 2004) Shelley and her husband have bought a theater. The current offering, badly written by Steven Imry, is indifferently acted by a cast of professionals and amateurs. Then one of the actors comes to a violent end.

16. *Accidental Florist, The* (Morrow, 2007) Miss Welbourne, Jane and Shelley's teacher of a class on women's safety, is murdered by a blow to the head.

II. Grace and Favor, a second cozy series, is a historical one, set in New York after the 1929 stock market crash. Siblings Lily and Robert Brewster are working at dead-end jobs until their uncle Horatio leaves them his mansion in Voorburg-on-Hudson, with the stipulation that they have to live there for 10 years before they can become owners. To support themselves, the Brewsters run a guesthouse at what they call Grace and Favor Cottage. But their efforts are undermined by a series of murders in the seemingly bucolic Hudson Valley town of Voorburg.

1. *Anything Goes* (Avon, 1999) Having trouble making ends meet in Depression-era New York City, Lily and Robert Brewster are happy to hear that they are heirs to their late uncle Horatio's mansion in the Hudson Valley.
2. *In the Still of the Night* (Avon, 2000) The Brewsters have set up Grace and Favor Cottage as a guesthouse to which they hope to lure their society friends for paying weekends. But, of course, murder intervenes.
3. *Someone to Watch over Me* (Morrow, 2001) The Brewsters get involved in reporting the Bonus March in Washington, in investigating the provenance of a mummified corpse in uncle Horatio's long-disused icehouse, and in the suspicious demise of the philandering Donald Anderson.
4. *Love for Sale* (Morrow, 2003) On the eve of the 1932 presidential election, a "Mr. Smith" offers Robert and Lily $500 as a down payment on rooms for himself and three of his "business associates." Then one of the associates, radio preacher Brother Mark Luke Goodheart, turns up murdered in his bath.
5. *It Had to Be You* (Morrow, 2004) The siblings agree to help their neighbor Miss Twibell, who has turned the house next door into a convalescent home. Then one of the residents, the nasty old Sean Connor, is seemingly helped toward his end.
6. *Who's Sorry Now?* (Morrow, 2005) Two murders this time: a train porter and someone whose skeleton is exhumed on the grounds of Grace and Favor.

Churchill, Winston

These solid, leisurely historical novels written by the St. Louis–born American author were best sellers in their day. Naturally there was some confusion in readers' minds between him and the British statesman. It is said that the English Churchill wrote to the American Churchill, suggesting that one of them should change his name. The American Churchill agreed but said that, since the English Churchill was younger by three years, the change was his to make. Thereafter the English Churchill's signature read "Winston S. Churchill."

1. *Richard Carvel* (Macmillan, 1899) The adventures of Richard, from his childhood in colonial Maryland to action with John Paul Jones.
2. *Crisis, The* (Macmillan, 1901) Centers on young Virginia Carvel, descendant of Richard, at the time of the Civil War.

Chute, Carolyn

The dirt poor characters of William Faulkner's (q.v.) Yoknapatawpha County, Mississippi, now have some new literary cousins in Maine, thanks to Carolyn Chute. The small and impoverished backwoods town of Egypt is inhabited by people accustomed to privation and violence. Chute herself lives in rural Maine, close enough to her prototypes to write with authority. In Chute's earlier novels she maintained sufficient distance to write artfully, but in recent years her sympathy for her characters seems to have taken her "round the bend," organizing a populist "militia" to make corporations and government "more responsive to workers." Her latest novel, *Snow Man* (Harcourt, 1999), not part of the Egypt series, is a sympathetic portrayal of a vigilante who is out to assassinate both US senators from Massachusetts.

1. *Beans of Egypt, Maine, The* (Ticknor, 1985) Young Earlene flees her own family to marry Beal Bean.
2. *Letourneau's Used Auto Parts* (Ticknor, 1988) This focuses on the Letourneau clan living in a trailer park outside of Egypt.
3. *Merry Men* (Harcourt, 1994) Lloyd Barrington is a gloomy poet, while his half brother Forest moves up from backhoe operator to Road Commissioner, losing several toes on the way.

Civil-Brown, Sue

PSEUDONYM OF Rachel Lee

Florida-based romance writer Rachel Lee is producing a series of breezy contemporary romances set in the fictional town of Paradise Beach, Florida. The main characters in these novels are usually different, but a slew of zany local supporting characters and the Paradise Beach locale are the connecting factors.

1. *Carried Away* (Avon, 1997) An unexpected benefaction from the late best-selling author Morris Feldman brings mousy teacher Danika Hilliard to the seemingly idyllic town of Paradise Beach, Florida.
2. *Letting Loose* (Avon, 1998) When she arrives in Paradise Beach hoping to pick up the pieces of her life, Jill McCallister inadvertently arouses the ire, and the interest, of her new neighbor, Police Chief Blaise Corrigan.
3. *Chasing Rainbow* (Avon, 1999) Jake Carpenter's intentions of settling down in Paradise Beach with a "tidy" woman are shaken by untidy psychic Rainbow Moonglow.
4. *Catching Kelly* (Avon, 2000) Website designer Kelly Burke rushes home to Paradise Beach when she hears that handsome young Seth Ralston has moved in with her eccentric grandmother.
5. *Tempting Mr. Wright* (Avon, 2000) Tess Morrow and Jack Wright have had a mutual antipathy for each other for years, or so it seems. Then they are thrown together during a Thanksgiving hurricane.
6. *Next Stop, Paradise* (Avon, 2001) Paradise Beach police officer Samantha Bartlett is initially sceptical when some alleged *Tyrannosaurus Rex* tracks turn up on the beach.
7. *Breaking All the Rules* (Avon, 2002) When her elderly friend Mary is declared incompetent, Erin Kelly finds herself at loggerheads with the local courts and with handsome attorney Richard Wesley III.
8. *Prince Next Door, The* (HQN, 2005) When dermatologist Serena Gregory's clothing-optional Caribbean cruise falls through, Serena compensates by getting involved in the affairs of mysterious new neighbor Darius Maxwell, who may or may not be a crown prince.
9. *Hurricane Hannah* (HQN, 2006) Redheaded pilot Hannah Lamont, grounded on Treasure Island by a hurricane, reluctantly joins forces with airstrip owner Buck Shanahan to save the local casino.
10. *Life of Reilly, The* (HQN, 2007) Lynn Reilly could settle nicely into her job as a schoolteacher on Treasure Island, if it weren't for her meddling aunt Delphine, who happens to be a ghost.

Clancy, Tom (Thomas L.)

Tom Clancy is probably the leading technothriller writer active today. His novels have consistently landed high on the best-seller lists, and several of them—*The Hunt for Red October*, *Patriot Games*, *Clear and Present Danger*, and *The Sum of All Fears*—have provided starring vehicles for such actors as Alec Baldwin, Harrison Ford, and Ben Affleck. Though not a great stylist or creator of characters, Clancy has created a novelistic mix of suspense, high tech, geopolitics, and rugged individualism that has inspired many readers and policy makers (especially since September 11).

Jack Ryan, former marine, former stockbroker, history teacher at Annapolis, occasional CIA operative, and eventual National Security Advisor and president of the United States is the leading continuing character, but other characters—including ex–Navy SEALs and vigilantes John Kelly, John Clark, and "Ding" Chavez—appear now and again. Only *Red Storm Rising* (Putnam, 1986) among Clancy's novels seems to lack a continuing character. Novels are arranged in rough chronological, rather than publication, order, although any of them can stand alone. *The Cardinal of the Kremlin* has been published together with *Red Storm Rising* (Putnam, 1993). Numbers 2, 5, and 6 were published in an omnibus as *Three Complete Novels* (Putnam, 1994).

1. *Red Rabbit* **(Putnam, 2002)** A prequel set in 1981, with Jack Ryan in a supporting role. Ed and Pat Foley, CIA agents in Moscow, and KGB employee Oleg Zaitzev (code-named Rabbit) become aware of the KGB-inspired (real-life) attempt to assassinate the pope.
2. *Patriot Games* **(Putnam, 1987)** On vacation in London with his wife and daughter, Jack Ryan stops a terrorist attack on the Prince and Princess of Wales and becomes a target for revenge.
3. *Hunt for Red October, The* **(Naval Institute Press, 1984)** First novel published by Clancy (and the first fiction offering from Naval Institute Press). Both the US and Russian navies are in hot pursuit of a defecting Soviet submarine loaded with deadly missiles.
4. *Cardinal of the Kremlin, The* **(Putnam, 1988)** Jack must save Colonel Filtrov, an American agent in the Kremlin.
5. *Clear and Present Danger* **(Putnam, 1989)** Sergeant Chavez and his US Army infantrymen must be extradited from Colombia after a misfired attempt to sabotage the illegal drug trade.
6. *Sum of All Fears, The* **(Putnam, 1991)** Palestinian terrorists and other radicals explode a nuclear weapon at the Super Bowl hoping to foment a massive American-Soviet confrontation. Jack is deputy director of the CIA and a Middle East peacemaker.
7. *Without Remorse* **(Putnam, 1993)** Vietnam vet John Kelly is involved in a secret mission to rescue American pilots from Vietnam. (Not always included in the Jack Ryan series.)
8. *Debt of Honor* **(Putnam, 1994)** Ryan, now the president's National Security Advisor, has to deal with the buildup of a new war, primarily economic, with Japan. In this foreshadowing of September 11, a Japanese airman attacks the capitol with a Boeing 747.
9. *Executive Orders* **(Putnam, 1996)** After the destruction of most of the US government in number 8, Jack Ryan becomes president of the United States and tries to set the country on a conservative course amid domestic opposition, trouble with Iran, and biological warfare.
10. *Rainbow Six* **(Putnam, 1998)** While Jack wrestles with his presidential duties, Jack Clark (seen in number 7) and his protégé, "Ding" Chavez (seen in number 5), foil an airline highjacking, train at Rainbow Headquarters outside London, and then intervene in a hostage situation in a bank in Switzerland.
11. *Bear and the Dragon, The* **(Putnam, 2000)** Jack Ryan, Jack Clark, and Ding Chavez have significant roles in this thriller, which postulates events that lead to a war between China and Russia.
12. *Teeth of the Tiger, The* **(Putnam, 2003)** Jack Ryan's son Jack and two cousins join Hendley Associates, a privately funded vigilante organization dedicated to eradicating America's enemies, especially terrorists.

Clare, Alys

PSEUDONYM OF Elizabeth Harris

The Hawkenlye mystery series is set at Hawkenlye Abbey in England in the time of Richard I (1189–1199). The able abbess Helewise and her friend the knight Sir Josse d'Acquin are able to get to the bottom of murders and other crimes committed in and near the abbey in these novels, which evoke the times and the characters living in them and will appeal to fans of Ellis Peters's (q.v.) Brother Cadfael. So far eight volumes in the series have been published (only three in the United States) with at least four more planned. British writer Elizabeth Harris also publishes historical novels under her own name.

1. *Fortune Like the Moon* **(St. Martin's, 2000)** When young novice Gunnora is murdered at Hawkenlye Abbey, King Richard I sends knight Josse d'Acquin to investigate matters. Josse and the canny, widowed Abbess Helewise form a friendly alliance. Originally published in the United Kingdom in 1999.
2. *Ashes of the Elements* **(St. Martin's, 2001)** Abbess Helewise doesn't accept the explanation of the local sheriff that a poacher felled by a spear with a flint tip has been murdered by the "Wild People." Originally published in the United Kingdom in 2000.
3. *Tavern in the Morning, The* **(St. Martin's, 2002)** Why did someone lace farmer Peter Ely's meal with a fatal dose of wolfsbane at the local tavern? Originally published in the United Kingdom in 2000.
4. *Charter of the Maidens, The* **(Hodder [UK], 2001)** Abbess Helewise doesn't quite believe in the explanation Sister Alba gives for relocating herself and her two young sisters from her convent at Ely. Not published in the United States.
5. *Faithful Dead, The* **(Hodder [UK], 2002)** After an elderly pilgrim dies, apparently of natural causes, at Hawkenlye Vale, Prince John enlists Josse to get news of someone named Galbertius Sidonius. Meanwhile, Abbess Helewise has a decomposing corpse on her hands. Not published in the United States.
6. *Dark Night Hidden, A* **(Hodder [UK], 2003)** After the fanatical Father Micah is found dead in a ditch, suspicion falls on a band of evangelical heretics who have been condemned to the stake. Not published in the United States.
7. *Whiter Than the Lily* **(Hodder [UK], 2004)** When Galena and her husband, the much older Ambrose, come to Hawkenlye to partake of the waters that might make her pregnant, Galena dies of poisoning, and an examination reveals that she was pregnant after all. Not published in the United States.
8. *Girl in a Red Tunic* **(Hodder [UK], 2005)** Abbess Helewise is forced by the visit of her son and a murder to investigate the past, a time before Helewise took the veil. Not published in the United States.
9. *Heart of Ice* **(Hodder [UK], 2006)** January 1194. A very sick man on his way to Hawkenlye Abbey sees what he thinks is a vision of the Virgin Mary, but the "vision" strikes him with a club, then rolls him in a ditch. Not published in the United States.
10. *Enchanter's Forest, The* **(Hodder [UK], 2007)** The founder of a hostel for pilgrims, which he claims is the site of Merlin's tomb and a place where miracles occur, is murdered. Not published in the United States.

Clark, Carol Higgins

Regan Reilly is a Los Angeles–based private investigator who gets involved—with one exception, *Jinxed* (see number 7)—in crimes committed outside of California. Regan's mother is best-selling novelist Nora Regan Reilly (based on Clark's real-life mother Mary

Higgins Clark [q.v.]), and her distant boyfriend is another Reilly (no relation), New York cop Jack Reilly. These are light, breezy novels that are popular with mystery buffs. Carol Higgins Clark has collaborated on several Christmas novels with her mother, including *Deck the Halls* (number 5, below), which teams up Regan Reilly and Alvirah Meehan, the senior Clark's amateur detective.

1. *Decked* (Warner, 1992) LA private eye Regan Reilly is in Oxford (England) for the 10th reunion of her semester-abroad college class when the body of Regan's long-missing former roommate, Allena, is found buried in the woods nearby.
2. *Snagged* (Warner, 1993) In Miami for a friend's wedding, Regan acquires a new friend in Richie Blossom, the bride's uncle, who has invented a new "run-proof, snag-proof" panty hose.
3. *Iced* (Warner, 1995) Regan joins her parents in Aspen, Colorado, for a winter getaway and stumbles onto a series of art thefts.
4. *Twanged* (Warner, 1998) Regan is at a music festival in Southampton, Long Island, to guard country-and-western musician Brigid O'Neil, owner of a "magic fiddle" that will lose its efficacy if it leaves Ireland.
5. *Deck the Halls* (Simon & Schuster/Scribner, 2000) Coauthored with Mary Higgins Clark (q.v.). Regan teams up with Alvirah Meehan, Mary's character, during a pre-Christmas caper involving the kidnapping of Regan's father, Luke, and his young female driver.
6. *Fleeced* (Scribner, 2001) When Regan visits her parents and her boyfriend, New York cop Jack Reilly, she is asked by Thomas Pilsner, president of the Settlers' Club in Gramercy Park, to investigate when two of the club's oldest and wealthiest members die and some diamonds disappear.
7. *Jinxed* (Scribner, 2002) Regan is finally shown practicing her trade in California (Santa Barbara), when she is hired by 96-year-old former film star Lucretia Standish to find a missing young actress.
8. *Popped* (Scribner, 2003) Regan is in Las Vegas this time, helping Danny Madley, an old grade-school chum, to put on a reality show with a hot-air balloon theme.
9. *Burned* (Scribner, 2005) Regan, who has booked a last-minute trip to Waikiki Waters, a resort in Hawaii, is asked to intervene by the general manager of the recently renovated resort when the body of Dorinda Dawes washes ashore on the beach.
10. *Hitched* (Scribner, 2006) With their marriage only a week away, Regan and Jack get involved in intertwining cases involving some missing wedding dresses and a big bank robbery.

Clark, Mary Higgins

Mary Higgins Clark has been writing suspense and mystery novels for 30 years and has earned the title "Queen of Suspense" for novels such as *Where Are the Children?* and *The Cradle Will Rock*. Her only series characters are cleaning lady and lottery winner Alvirah Meehan and her husband, Willy, who appear as secondary characters in *Weep No More My Lady;* star in their own collection of interconnected short stories, *The Lottery Winner*, and the Christmas tale *All Through the Night;* and share sleuthing duties with Regan Reilly, the creation of Mary's daughter Carol Higgins Clark (q.v.), in *Deck the Halls.*

1. *Weep No More My Lady* (Simon & Schuster, 1987) Alvirah and Willy Meehan appear as secondary characters in this suspense novel featuring heroine Elizabeth Lange, who is haunted by the death of her actress sister, who died mysteriously in her Manhattan penthouse.
2. *Lottery Winner, The* (Simon & Schuster, 1994) Subtitle: *Alvirah and Willy Stories.* Six interconnected stories of sleuthing by cleaning lady–lottery winner Alvirah Meehan and her husband, Willy.
3. *All through the Night* (Simon & Schuster, 1998) A Christmas tale featuring Alvirah and Willy involving a stolen chalice, a missing child, and a mother desperate to find the baby she abandoned seven years earlier.
4. *Deck the Halls* (Simon & Schuster/Scribner, 2000) Coauthored with Carol Higgins Clark (q.v.). Regan Reilly, Carol's private-eye character, and Alvirah Meehan team up to investigate the kidnapping of Regan's father and his female driver.

Clarke, Arthur C(harles)

I. Arthur C. Clarke (d. 2008) was one of the masters of science-fiction writing. *Childhood's End* (Ballantine, 1953) is on virtually every short list of "greatest" SF novels. Clarke was also a world-renowned science-fact popularizer and futurologist (see *Greetings, Carbon-Based Bipeds! Collected Essays, 1934–1998*, St. Martin's, 1999). Still, his greatest claim to fame was probably his coauthorship (with Stanley Kubrick) of the screenplay to *2001: A Space Odyssey*, which has mesmerized a generation of movie viewers with its special effects; its insane computer, HAL; and its hallucinatory ending. The germ of *2001* was Clarke's short story "The Sentinel" (anthologized in his *Expedition to Earth*, Ballantine, 1953). Clarke's novelization of *2001*, which ends differently than the movie, was followed by three "variations on the same theme, involving many of the same characters and situations, but not necessarily happening in the same universe" (preface to later printing of *2001*).

1. *2001: A Space Odyssey* (New American Library, 1968) Dave Bowman, his fellow astronauts, and the computer HAL set off with the spaceship *Discovery* in search of proof that extraterrestrials sparked the development of intelligent life on Earth.
2. *2010: Odyssey Two* (Ballantine, 1982) In this sequel to the movie version of *2001*, Heywood Floyd is sent on a joint Soviet-American space mission to find out what happened to the *Discovery* and its crew.
3. *2061: Odyssey Three* (Ballantine, 1988) Now the oldest man alive, Heywood Floyd embarks on a journey that will culminate in a manned landing on Halley's Comet, while his grandson Chris is stranded on the Jupiterian moon Europa.
4. *3001: The Final Odyssey* (Del Rey, 1997) The frozen body of Frank Poole, murdered by the insane computer HAL in *2001*, is recovered floating near Neptune and restored to life in 3001, where he is exposed to future shock.

II. *Rendezvous with Rama*, Clarke's novel about a giant alien space capsule, has been followed by three sequels coauthored with Gentry Lee. Lee solo authored two books set in the Rama universe.

1. *Rendezvous with Rama* (Harcourt, 1973) "Rama," a metallic cylinder approaching the Sun at enormous velocity, is the first product of an alien civilization to be encountered by man.
2. *Rama II* (Bantam, 1989) Decades after Commander Norton and his crew encountered the alien space ship Rama and declared it to be an intelligent robot, another ship, which seems to be an exact replica, approaches Earth.
3. *Garden of Rama, The* (Bantam, 1991) The original Rama returns to Earth and demands (and receives) 2,000 Earthlings as samples for observation.
4. *Rama Revealed* (Bantam, 1994) In the "conclusion" to the Rama series, Nicole Wakefield, former governor of the human colony

housed within Rama III, is awaiting execution for opposing the current powers-that-be.

III. In recent years Clarke coauthored his books with other writers. The latest was the Time Odyssey series, coauthored with Stephen Baxter (q.v.), in which Earth is about to be destroyed in 2037 by a sun storm set in motion by mysterious beings from thousands of years in the past. Number 1 begins in 1885 but travels back to an alternative past when Alexander the Great avoids his early death. Number 2 takes the reader forward in time to the year 2037 and tells us more about the mysterious Firstborn, who have somewhat different plans for humankind than did the Overlords in *Childhood's End*.

Clarke's early novel *Against the Fall of Night* (Gnome, 1953) was reworked by Gregory Benford (q.v.) as *Beyond the Fall of Night* (Putnam, 1990). The *Space Trilogy* omnibus (Gollancz [UK], 2001) contains three early seemingly unrelated novels: *Islands in the Sky; Earth Light;* and *Sands of Mars*. Clarke has also teamed up with Paul Preuss on a series of space operas called Venus Prime.

1. *Time's Eye* (Del Rey, 2004) In action beginning on the Northwest Frontier of India in 1885, Rudyard Kipling, some Australopithecines, and a squadron of tanks from 2037 are all thrown back to the 4th century BCE, the time of Alexander the Great. Coauthored with Stephen Baxter (q.v.).
2. *Sunstorm* (Del Rey, 2005) Bisesa Dutt is returned to the Earth of 2037 from the alternate Earth called Mir by the mysterious technologically advanced Firstborn. Coauthored with Stephen Baxter (q.v.).
3. *Firstborn* (Del Rey, 2007) Subtitle: *A Time Odyssey; 3*. Having barely survived a Firstborn-created solar flare, Earth now must cope with a meteor bomb approaching from deep space. Coauthored with Stephen Baxter (q.v.).

Clausen, Lowen

Officers with the Seattle, Washington, Police Department are the protagonists in this trio (so far) of police procedurals and character studies. Clausen, a former Seattle police officer, provides convincing Seattle backgrounds and details of police work and interesting, well-developed characters.

1. *First Avenue* (Onyx, 2000) Seattle policeman Sam Wright's routine changes after he is called to an old hotel where the body of a baby has been found.
2. *Second Watch* (Signet, 2003) Seattle police officer Katherine Murphy and her new partner, Grace Stevens, discover the bodies of two children, sexually abused and placed in separate dumpsters.
3. *Third and Forever* (Silo, 2004) Seattle police officer Grace Stevens investigates a series of rapes that may involve football players from the University of Washington.

Clavell, James

The late (d. 1994) Australian American Clavell's action-filled historical novels about Asia, especially *Shogun* and *Tai-Pan*, were big best sellers. *King Rat* was made into a movie, while several other titles, including *Shogun* and *Noble House*, were made into TV miniseries. Although Clavell was producing what he called an Asian Saga, only numbers 2, 3, and 5 are, strictly speaking, sequels, part of an unfinished Shogun quartet. Numbers 1, 4, and 6 are loosely tied together by their Asian themes.

1. *Shogun* (Atheneum, 1975) English pilot John Blackthorne is shipwrecked on the coast of xenophobic Japan in 1600.
2. *Tai-Pan* (Atheneum, 1966) In 1841, shortly after the first Opium War in China, Dirk Struan, tai-pan (supreme ruler) of the trading company Noble House, sees the development possibilities of Hong Kong.
3. *Gai-Jin* (Delacorte, 1993) In 1862 Mark Struan, grandson of Dirk, is part of a European party attacked in Japan by samurai who have vowed to oust the gai-jin (foreigners).
4. *King Rat* (Little, Brown, 1962) "King Rat" is an American corporal who is de facto ruler of a Japanese prison camp in Singapore during World War II. Based on Clavell's experiences.
5. *Noble House* (Delacorte, 1981) Ian Dunross, head of Noble House, is the protagonist in the events in one turbulent week in Hong Kong in 1963.
6. *Whirlwind* (Morrow, 1986) Andrew Gavallan, manager of a helicopter company in Iran, must get his people and equipment out after the shah's overthrow in 1979.

Clayton, Jo

I. The late (d. 1998) SF-fantasy writer Jo Clayton wrote some 35 novels, most of them in series. Her first and longest-running series was called the Diadem series, after the scientific device called Diadem, created by the masterminds of the Spider People far out in space. Most of the series describes the adventures of Aleytys, lost member of the nearly immortal super-race, the Vrya, who becomes the wearer-slave of the mind-enhancing Diadem. According to James W. Fiscus, on the Science Fiction and Fantasy Writers of America website, Clayton's "writing was marked by complex, beautifully realized societies set in exotic worlds, lyrical prose, and compelling heroines."

1. *Diadem from the Stars* (DAW, 1977) The mind-enhancing Diadem, stolen from its Spider People creators, winds up on the head of the outcast girl Aleytys. Unable to remove the Diadem, which becomes part of her brain and nervous system, Aleytys becomes a universal target.
2. *Lamarchos* (DAW, 1978) Aleytys, in search of her origins, remains unaware of the full powers of the Diadem, invisible to outsiders, which remains attached to her head.
3. *Irsud* (DAW, 1978) Aleytys is sold as a slave to insectoid owners who want to use her as a proxy mother to the old queen's successor, a role in which she is to be both bearer and food.
4. *Maeve* (DAW, 1979) Aleytys is set down on Maeve, a forest planet of tree-dwellers and semihumans, amid guerrilla warfare between the tree-folk and the technology of the Company.
5. *Star Hunters* (DAW, 1980) Aleytys is confronted by hordes of half-humans and the mental force of a madman of her own ancestral race, the Vrya.
6. *Nowhere Hunt, The* (DAW, 1981) The Nowhere Hunt has been turned down by every Hunter except Aleytys, who takes on the task of rescuing and transporting a massive, semi-intelligent insect queen off her planet and saving the queen's besieged race from extinction.
7. *Ghosthunt* (DAW, 1981) The managers of the vacation planet of Cazarit want to enlist Aleytys, now possessed of a galaxy-wide reputation as a Hunter, to ferret out a ghostly kidnapper.
8. *Snares of Ibex, The* (DAW, 1984) Aleytys, still searching for her mother and her home world, knows that the unmapped and dangerous world of Ibex holds the key to her quest.
9. *Quester's Endgame* (DAW, 1986) At last Aleytys is about to rendezvous with her mother, Shareem, for a journey to the secret home world of her people.

II. Two other novels were set in the Diadem universe. *Shadow of the Warmaster* proved to be the only title in what was billed as a new series.

1. *Bait of Dreams, A* (DAW, 1985) Subtitle: *A Five-Summer Quest*. Set in the Diadem universe. Alien jewels called Ranga Eyes open doorways to a magical and very dangerous world.

2. *Shadow of the Warmaster* (DAW, 1998) Set in the Diadem universe. The Warmaster is a huge orbiting battleship and the Imperator key to control.

III. Shadith's Quest, or the Shadow Trilogy, Number 1, is also set in the Diadem universe. It concerns the battles between Shadith, former captive of the Diadem and Ginbiryol Senyirshi, an evil filmmaker who likes to foment wars to film them.

1. *Shadowplay* (DAW, 1990) Shadith, once again in human form after being captive for centuries in the Diadem, finds herself the prisoner of Ginbiryol Seyirshi, a being who has instigated devastating wars on world after world purely to film them and sell Limited Editions of the films.

2. *Shadowspeer* (DAW, 1990) Shadith, enraged by the pointless deaths caused by Ginbiryol's films, vows to hunt the filmmaker down.

3. *Shadowkill* (DAW, 1991) Shadith and Ginbiryol, captured and enslaved by the Institute, must set aside their mutual hatred long enough to destroy their masters.

IV. Shadowsong, or the Shadow Trilogy, Number 2, continues the adventures of Shadith, who is embodied with the gift of empathy and a magic based on music, which gives her the ability to be an interplanetary arbiter, a spy, or a detective.

1. *Fire in the Sky* (DAW, 1995) Shadith is called to the planet Beluchad to make peace between two warring races.

2. *Burning Ground, The* (DAW, 1995) Shadith, with her ability to transfer her consciousness into another, becomes the perfect spy. Hired to recover a valuable technological device, she stumbles across one of the known galaxy's greatest crimes.

3. *Crystal Heat* (DAW, 1996) Shadith, employee of a high-tech private detective agency, Excavations Limited, is assigned to locate and return a creature who has been abducted by a smuggler.

V. The Duel of Sorcery trilogy is more fantasy than SF. It concerns the outcast Serroi, who becomes a warrior woman of the Mei. Serroi must overcome the wicked wizard Ser Noris in a series that winds up with a climatic battle between good and evil.

1. *Moongather* (DAW, 1982) Outcast windrunner Serroi becomes a Mei, a woman warrior trained by an exclusive order.

2. *Moonscatter* (DAW, 1983) Wicked wizard Ser Noris, tyrant of the Sorcerers Isles, hasn't yet conquered Miden, the spirit of the earth itself.

3. *Changer's Moon* (DAW, 1985) The final battle between good and evil pits Ser Noris against Serroi and the Miden.

VI. In another Duel of Sorcery trilogy, the Dancer series, Serroi awakens after centuries of spell-induced sleep and finds herself in a new world, with a new evil trying to take control.

1. *Dancer's Rise* (DAW, 1993) After centuries under a spell, Serroi breaks free and faces a new enemy. Serroi and her companions are enlisted to deliver a newly created device to a distant ruler.

2. *Serpent Waltz* (DAW, 1994) Serroi is pitted against a strange evil force that she barely understands.

3. *Dance Down the Stars* (DAW, 1994) The final confrontation between Serroi and an evil force that can alter life and death.

VII. The Drinker of Souls, or Soul Drinker, trilogy is another fantasy series. Brann, the legendary Drinker of Souls, is drawn into an epic battle between the benevolent Chained God of Owlyn and sorcerer Maksim, the servant of the cruel god Amortis. Numbers 1 through 3 were published in an omnibus volume as *The Soul Drinker* (SF Book Club, 1989).

1. *Drinker of Souls* (DAW, 1986) Brann, the Drinker of Souls, has the need for rich life sources to feed her twin demonic shape-shifters, but she is also on a quest to free her family from the king who had enslaved them.

2. *Blue Magic* (DAW, 1988) With the Chained God's peaceful rule challenged by the god Amortis and his servant, the sorcerer Maksim, young Kori is forced to resort to the legendary Brann, Drinker of Souls.

3. *Gathering of Stones, A* (DAW, 1989) The Chained God has to pull out all the stops to break free of the energy-draining trap that holds him.

VIII. The Wild Magic, or Honeychild, trilogy is set in the same universe as the Drinker of Souls trilogy. The protagonist here is the young sorceress Faan, who embarks upon a quest to find her mother and her island home.

1. *Wild Magic* (DAW, 1991) Stolen from her sorceress mother, young Faan receives a spotty magic education that does not fully prepare her for the role she is to play in a war between gods.

2. *Wildfire* (DAW, 1992) *Wild Magic #2.* Still in search of her true mother, Faan again finds herself as a pawn in the struggle between gods and magicians for control of her world.

3. *Magic Wars, The* (DAW, 1993) *Wild Magic #3.* Faan finally makes her way to the land of her birth, only to find her mother and the island she calls home trapped in a spell of timeless sleep.

IX. The Skeen trilogy is SF about starship pilot Skeen who, with her companions, has stumbled through a bizarre "Gateway," a door into an unknown world where eight separate races live together.

1. *Skeen's Leap* (DAW, 1986) Skeen, a starship pilot only one step ahead of the law, wanders through a "Gateway" and finds herself on a unknown world where eight separate races live together in an uneasy peace.

2. *Skeen's Return* (DAW, 1987) Skeen and her companions search for the Stranger's Gate, the only way she can return to her own universe.

3. *Skeen's Search* (DAW, 1987) The conclusion to the trilogy finds Skeen on a desperate race to a star on the brink of becoming a super-nova in her search for the missing Ykx of Mistommerk.

X. Clayton's final trilogy, the last volume completed by Kevin Andrew Murphy, is basically fantasy involving the worlds of Iomard and Glandair, which are linked by the Pneuma, a force that can be manipulated to perform magic. Cymel, a Glandair girl; Breith, Cymel's friend on Iomard; and Lyanz, a potential hero with godlike powers, are the principal characters called upon to prevent their worlds from falling into chaos.

1. *Drum Warning* (Tor, 1996) A crisis known as the Settling, or the Corruption, is approaching Iomard and Glandair, two worlds linked by the force of the Pneuma.
2. *Drum Calls* (Tor, 1997) Glandairian Cymel and Iomardian Breith find themselves increasingly drawn into the battle for the future of their planets.
3. *Drum into Silence* (Tor, 2002) Cymel has been trapped in the body of a white bird. Breith has crossed worlds to rescue her. Lyanz, the potential Hero, who is the only one who can save the worlds from chaos, is sequestered far away. Kevin Andrew Murphy completed this novel after Jo Clayton's death.

Cleage, Pearl

What Looks Like Crazy on an Ordinary Day . . . was a hit both with readers and critics. Cleage, an African American dramatist and first-time novelist, wrote a very witty and readable book that seriously addresses the problems of contemporary black Americans, as she follows the fortunes of Ava Johnson, Atlanta beauty parlor owner, after she discovers that she is HIV positive. *I Wish I Had a Red Dress* features Joyce, Ava's big sister, a widowed social worker in Idlewild, Michigan.

1. **What Looks Like Crazy on an Ordinary Day** . . . (Avon, 1997) When Ava Johnson discovers that she is HIV positive, she decides to start a new life in San Francisco; but first she stops in at a former black resort in Idlewild, Michigan, to visit Joyce, her older sister.
2. **I Wish I Had a Red Dress** (Morrow, 2001) Joyce, who has been in mourning for her mother, her two lost children, and her late husband, takes center stage, as she continues her work at the Sewing Circus and falls in love with Nate Anderson, a new student counselor in town.

Cleary, Jon

I. Scobie Malone, detective-inspector of the New South Wales Police in Sydney, Australia, is featured in a series of procedurals by Cleary, who has become known as the Australian Ed McBain (q.v.). The much put-upon Scobie does his best to be a model policeman, model husband, and model father in a series with good plots, fascinating characters, quiet wit, and lots of Aussiespeak. Numbers 9 through 12 are sometimes referred to as the Four Seasons.

1. *High Commissioner, The* (Morrow, 1966) Malone travels to London to arrest the Australian High Commissioner for the murder of his first wife.
2. *Helga's Web* (Morrow, 1970) German girl Helga Brand is found strangled in the sub-basement of Sydney's unfinished opera house.
3. *Ransom* (Morrow, 1973) Scobie's wife is kidnapped along with the mayor's wife when the Malones visit New York.
4. *Dragons at the Party* (Morrow, 1988) Malone investigates the attempted assassination of a deposed dictator during Australia's bicentennial celebration.
5. *Now and Then, Amen* (Morrow, 1989) Sister Mary Magdalene is found murdered on the steps of Sydney's classiest brothel.
6. *Babylon South* (Morrow, 1990) Two decades after High Court judge Sir Walter Springfellow disappeared, a body is found wearing his signet ring.
7. *Murder Song* (Morrow, 1990) Several persons from Scobie's class at the police academy have been shot by an expert sniper.

8. *Pride's Harvest* (Morrow, 1991) Ken Sagawa, operator of a Japanese-controlled cotton factory in Collamundra, is murdered.
9. *Dark Summer* (Morrow, 1993) Malone finds a body injected with a deadly dose of curare in his family's swimming pool.
10. *Bleak Spring* (Morrow, 1994) Scobie is in charge of the investigation of the murder of his neighbor, lawyer Will Rockne.
11. *Autumn Maze* (Morrow, 1994) The 20-floor fall from a building of the Sydney Police Minister's son may have a connection with some Yakuza who are owed money.
12. *Winter Chill* (Morrow, 1995) A dead passenger on an otherwise empty Sydney monorail is the first of three murders in downtown Sydney that bedevil Scobie.
13. *Different Turf, A* (HarperCollins [UK], 1997) Someone is killing "gay bashers" in Sydney's gay community. Not published in the United States.
14. *Endpeace* (Morrow, 1997) A dinner party at the Sydney estate of press-lord Sir Harry Huxwood, his wife, Philippa, and their children and grandchildren results in the murder of Sir Harry.
15. *Five Ring Circus* (Morrow, 1999) Sydney's image for the upcoming Olympic Games is being besmirched by a scam involving illicit deals and large quantities of money from Hong Kong.
16. *Dilemma* (Morrow, 2000) All the evidence in the killing of Norma Glaze seems to point to her missing husband, at first.
17. *Bear Pit* (Avon, 2001) The State Premier is shot by a sniper at the celebration of the opening of the Olympic Tower.
18. *Yesterday's Shadow* (Avon, 2002) Two murders in the same hotel on the same night: one victim a cleaner; the second, the wife of the American ambassador.
19. *Easy Sin, The* (HarperCollins [UK], 2002) In what is billed as Scobie's last investigation, he deals with a kidnapping gone wrong and the bursting of the dot-com bubble. Not published in the United States.

II. Sean Carmody is the connecting link between two novels widely separated by time and place. *The Sundowners*, which was made into a successful movie, describes Sean's life in the Australian Outback as a 14-year-old. *City of Fading Light* catches up with Sean in Berlin in 1939 on the eve of World War II.

1. *Sundowners, The* (Scribner, 1952) One year in the life of Australian sheep-drover Paddy Carmody, his wife, Ida, and their son Sean.
2. *City of Fading Light* (Morrow, 1985) Beautiful red-haired Cathleen O'Dea has sacrificed a promising Hollywood career to come to Germany to make a movie for Hitler's Minister of Propaganda Josef Goebbels.

Cleary, Melissa

Jackie Walsh of Palmer, Massachusetts, divorced mother of a 13-year-old and film teacher at Rodgers University, teams up with a retired police dog, the Alsatian shepherd Jake, to solve a series of crimes as far afield as Hollywood. Jake is a paragon among dogs and smarter, braver, and nicer than most human beings. Jackie also has the help of her "policemanfriend," Lt. Michael McGowan of the Palmer Police. These light mysteries have received mixed reviews but should appeal to readers of Carol Lea Benjamin, Laurien Berenson (q.v.), and Susan Conant (q.v.). The real identity of "Melissa Cleary" is unknown.

1. *Tail of Two Murders, A* (Berkley, 1992) The wounded dog Jackie Walsh and her son find in their backyard turns out to be Jake, a retired Alsatian police dog. Then a murder is committed at Rodgers University where Jackie teaches film.

2. *Dog Collar Crime* (Berkley, 1993) Melvin Sweeten, kennel owner and breeder of prizewinning basset hounds, is strangled with a choke collar, but nobody except the bassets seems to be upset.

3. *Hounded to Death* (Berkley, 1993) Dirty politics turns into murder, and Jackie's life is on the line, but Jake is always there to protect her.

4. *Skull and Dog Bones* (Berkley, 1994) Jackie and Michael get involved in a case that takes them back and forth between Hollywood and Palmer after former screenwriter Ralph Perrin is found dead in a swimming pool.

5. *First Pedigree Murder* (Berkley, 1994) Millionaire Mannheim Goodwillie drops dead during an interview on the Rodgers University radio station, and Jackie's friend Keith, the head of the radio station, is accused of his murder.

6. *Dead and Buried* (Berkley, 1994) A large unruly mastiff puppy named Maury proves to be a trial in the investigation of the death of a Rodgers U security chief.

7. *Maltese Puppy, The* (Berkley, 1995) Former doctor and scientist and current nasty old man Linus Much is murdered while visiting Palmer, but Jackie has her hands full trying to find a home for the rambunctious Maury.

8. *Murder Most Beastly* (Berkley, 1996) The Palmer Wildlife Habitat (aka the Zoo) is visited by a bizarre murder.

9. *Old Dogs* (Berkley, 1997) Jackie and Jake uncover a long-hidden legacy of murder and deception after an elderly widow tells Jackie about a hidden fortune.

10. *And Your Little Dog, Too* (Berkley, 1998) Jackie follows a half-frozen terrier to the dead body of an apparently homeless woman.

11. *In the Doghouse* (Berkley, 2000) Jake is starring in a movie, a murder mystery directed by a former student of Jackie's. Then the student is arrested for the hit-and-run death of the movie's producer.

Cleeves, Ann

I. George Palmer-Jones, retired Home Office official, has become an amateur detective largely through his avocation, bird-watching. Seems that bird-watchers are not the quiet, gentle people many think that they are. Bird-watching can be highly competitive, leading to bitter rivalries and even murder. Palmer-Jones's birding outings, mostly in England, but sometimes at sea and as far afield as Texas, often lead to homicide, at least one a book. Ann Cleeves is one of the United Kingdom's leading authors of "traditional" mysteries.

1. *Bird in the Hand, A* (Fawcett, 1986) Young expert birder Tom French is found dead in a marsh on the Norfolk coast, with his head bashed in.

2. *Come Death and High Water* (Fawcett, 1987) When the owner of Gillibry Island, Charlie Todd, states that he will sell the island, he is murdered, perhaps by one of the birdwatchers gathered on his land.

3. *Murder in Paradise* (Fawcett, 1988) When Palmer-Jones attempts to investigate the death, after her brother's wedding, of the young Mary on the "paradisiacal" island of Kinness, he finds the islanders distinctly unhelpful.

4. *Prey to Murder, A* (Fawcett, 1989) Eleanor Masefield's Open Day at Grose Hill Hotel, designed to raise funds for the protection of the local Peregrine Falcons, is marred by her death, perhaps by poisoning.

5. *Sea Fever* (Fawcett, 1991) George and Molly Palmer-Jones are hired to find out what happened to George's bird-watching colleague Greg Franks, who has disappeared overboard during a sea-bird-watching expedition in Cornwall.

6. *Another Man's Poison* (Fawcett, 1993) An ecology-minded politician is suspected of poisoning some protected bird species and of killing the woman who had threatened to expose him.

7. *Mill on the Shore, The* (Fawcett, 1994) England's most celebrated environmentalist, part of a famously mismatched couple, dies of an overdose. Was it murder?

8. *High Island Blues* (Fawcett, 1996) George and Molly are invited over from England to investigate the murder of a man on a bird-watching holiday in Texas.

II. Inspector Stephen Ramsay is the protagonist in a series of traditional mysteries (some critics say too traditional) set in the Northumbrian region of England. Lately Cleeves seems to have eschewed series characters for stand-alone mysteries.

1. *Lesson in Dying, A* (Century [UK], 1990) When Heppleburn headmaster Harold Medburn is found hanging from the school's rusty netball hoop, his widow Kitty becomes the prime suspect, but caretaker Jack Robson comes to her defense. Not published in the United States.

2. *Murder in My Back Yard* (Fawcett, 1991) Soon after Inspector Ramsay decides to buy a cottage in the Northumberland village of Heppleburn, old Alice Parry is found murdered in her own backyard on St. David's Eve.

3. *Day in the Death of Dorothea Cassidy, A* (Fawcett, 1992) The murder of the vicar's wife is followed by the killing of the village idiot.

4. *Killjoy* (Fawcett, 1995) Actress Gabriella Paston is killed by one of her many enemies during rehearsals for the local show in which she is to star.

5. *Healers, The* (Fawcett, 1995) Could one of the healers at the Alternative Therapy Clinic have murdered farmer Ernie Bowles?

6. *Baby Snatcher, The* (Macmillan [UK], 1997) On the trail of a child abductor, Ramsay hears that a 15-year-old girl he once helped is missing again. Then a woman's body is found washed up on the beach. Not published in the United States.

Clegg, Douglas

I. The Harrow Haunted House series is set at Harrow, a prep school for boys in a converted mansion in the upper Hudson River valley. Harrow has a murky past, including a series of student suicides and satanist rites conducted by a cloaked coven of students who call themselves the Cadaver Society. *Nightmare House*, which originated as an e-serial at the *Harrow Haunting* website (www.ehaunting.com), is a prequel describing events back in 1926. *The Abandoned* and *Isis* are also prequels. Actually, the novels don't have to be read in any particular order.

Douglas Clegg, one of the most highly regarded horror authors writing currently, balances horror with human interest in evocative prose.

1. *Nightmare House* (Cemetery Dance, 2002) Prequel set in 1926. Ethan Gravesend discovers that his grandfather's legacy, an estate on the Hudson River built on supposedly accursed land, produces eerie apparitions, boarded-up rooms, and some real family skeletons. Originally an e-sequel at the *Harrow Haunting* website.

2. *Abandoned, The* (Cemetery Dance, 2005) A caretaker arrives at Harrow, the abandoned house at the edge of the village of Watch Point.

3. *Isis* (Cemetery Dance, 2006) The earlier life of Isis Claviger, née Iris Catherine Villiers, who uses the occult to resurrect her beloved brother Harvey, with disastrous results.

4. *Mischief* **(Cemetery Dance, 2000)** Teenager Jim Hook is abducted by the Cadaver Society, a cloaked coven of students at Harrow, and endures some nasty initiation rites.
5. *Infinite, The* **(Cemetery Dance, 2001)** In the conclusion, three psychics are called to Harrow to investigate a spate of eerie deaths linked to the school by Ivy Martin, wealthy patroness of the PSI Vista Foundation.

II. The Vampyricon trilogy is an exercise in creative mythology. Aleric, the bastard falconer, finds his destiny as a vampyre after he breaches the Veil separating the ordinary (medieval) world from the world of the vampyre myth stream.

1. *Priest of Blood, The* **(Ace, 2005)** Falconer, bastard son of a Breton whore, serves the royal court as a predator trainer and fights the Saracens as a conscripted soldier in the Holy Land. Then he finds his destiny as a vampyre in the arms of a creature called Pythia.
2. *Lady of Serpents, The* **(Ace, 2006)** Aleric, the Breton falconer, returns as heir apparent to the vampyre throne after years of imprisonment in a silver-sealed well.
3. *Queen of Wolves, The* **(Ace, 2007)** The trilogy concludes with a titanic battle that pits vampyre against vampyre in a war that will determine whether the undead will coexist with the living.

Clemens, James

PSEUDONYM OF James Czajkowski

I. The Banned and the Banished is a fairly standard high-fantasy quest series set in a world divided into the evil Black Heart—presided over by the Dark Lord, who has, among other powers at his disposal, the four Weirgates, which are sucking elemental magick from the land—and the Elementals, who have as their standard-bearer the young wit'ch Elena, who leads a rather motley force for good. Czajkowski, a former veterinarian, has also written novels as "James Rollins."

1. *Wit'ch Fire* **(Del Rey, 1998)** Young farm girl Elena, destined to be the wit'ch of ancient prophecy who will save her land from evil or die trying, sets off on a quest with a motley crew of exiles and outcasts.
2. *Wit'ch Storm* **(Del Rey, 1999)** Elena and her companions set off for the legendary lost city of A'loa Glen to release the magic of the Blood Diary hidden there to defeat the evil Dark Lord.
3. *Wit'ch War* **(Del Rey, 2000)** Elena the wit'ch, her one-armed companion, Er'ril, the reformed shape-changer Aunt Mycelle, and the pirate Kast, the Bloodrider, reach the climax of their quest for the Blood Diary.
4. *Wit'ch Gate* **(Del Rey, 2001)** The Dark Lord has been pushed back, temporarily, but the four Weirgates—the Basilisk, the Manticore, the Wyvern, and the Griffin—are still sucking elemental magic from the land.
5. *Wit'ch Star* **(Del Rey, 2002)** Although the Black Heart has been wounded, the Dark Lord still has the Weirgates, and the Elementals are sickening, the Mer'ai are losing their sea sense, and the Elv'in ships can't fly as fast or as high as they used to.

II. The Godslayer series is set in the fantasy land of Myrillia, born 4,000 years ago after a great war among the gods. After the Sundering, near-invincible gods walk in the guise of humans. Failed Shadowknight Tylar battles demons, rogue gods, and other opponents.

1. *Shadow Fall* **(Roc, 2005)** Failed Shadowknight Tylar gains godlike powers from the blood of dying god Meeryn but at the cost of being called Godslayer and becoming a hunted criminal.
2. *Hinterland* **(Roc, 2006)** To save the Nine Lands, and himself, Tylar must enter the Hinterland, the desolate territory beyond the Lands.

Clement, Hal

PSEUDONYM OF Harry Clement Stubbs

I. The late Hal Clement (d. 2003) was a leading writer of hard science fiction. The science in his novels drives the plots, while there is relatively little attention paid to characterization or fancy writing. The Mesklin saga features as protagonist Barlennan, captain of a crew of caterpillar-like inhabitants of the "heavy" (high-gravity, that is) planet of Meskill. In *Mission of Gravity*, Barlennan and his crew assist a team of Earthlings to extract a vital component from a crashed space probe. *Star Light* is a direct sequel to *Mission of Gravity* and contains characters who appear in *Close to Critical*, number 2 in the series. The omnibus volume *Heavy Planet: The Classic Mesklin Stories* (Orb, 2002) contains numbers 1 and 3, the short stories "Under" and "Lecture Demonstration," and "Whirligig World," an essay originally published in *Astounding* in 1953, which describes the process Clement used to create his plausible high-gravity planet.

1. *Mission of Gravity* **(Doubleday, 1954)** The 15-inch caterpillar-like Barlennan leads an expedition on the disk-shaped planet of Mesklin to retrieve a space probe from the planet of Earth. The Ballantine edition (1974) also contains the nonfiction article "Whirligig."
2. *Close to Critical* **(Ballantine, 1964)** Tenebra, a planet seemingly hostile to intelligent life, does contain sentient, and possibly educable, creatures. Originally published in *Astounding Science Fiction* in 1958.
3. *Star Light* **(Ballantine, 1971)** Barlennan and his crew from Meskill travel to the weird world of Dhrawn, a fictional planet that circles the real star Lalande 21185. Eloise "Easy" Reach, from number 2, reappears, 25 years older, as "Easy" Hoffman.

II. *Needle*, Clement's first novel, features another alien: Hunter, a creature who is capable of assuming a variety of forms, including existing as a parasite or symbiont. In *Needle* Hunter comes to Earth hunting a criminal and enters the body of a young Earthling. *Through the Eye of a Needle* (not to be confused with Ken Follett's spy thriller *Eye of the Needle*) delineates further the relationship between alien and Earthling.

1. *Needle* **(Doubleday, 1950)** Hunter, an alien from a distant planet in search of a criminal from his own world, arrives on Earth and enters the body of a teenage boy. Alternate title: *From Outer Space*.
2. *Through the Eye of a Needle* **(Ballantine, 1978)** When his symbiotic relationship with the Earthling starts to weaken the young man, the Hunter seeks help from his own race.

Clement, Peter

I. Dr. Earl Garnet, ER chief at St. Paul's Hospital in Buffalo, New York, is the hero of a series of medical mystery thrillers in which he has to play detective to uncover the real causes of patient deaths. Medical malpractice, medical politics, HMOs, and vigilante killers all take hits in this suspenseful series full of medical lingo.

Peter Clement, a practicing MD for 28 years who served as chief of emergency and chief of family medicine in a "major metropolitan teaching hospital" before taking a sabbatical as a mystery writer, has the necessary background to write plausible and accurate medical thrillers.

1. *Lethal Practice* (Ballantine, 1997) When Everett Kingsley, chief administrator of St. Paul's Hospital in Buffalo, New York, is deliberately killed by a cardiac needle in the heart, ER doctor and cardiac genius Earl Garnet comes to the forefront.
2. *Death Rounds* (Fawcett, 1999) When a nurse in his care mysteriously dies, Dr. Garnet suspects a "superbug" resistant to antibiotics. But his obstetrician wife has a hunch that the death and the ones that follow may be the work of a mysterious vigilante called "the Phantom."
3. *Procedure, The* (Fawcett, 2000) The HMO industry comes under scrutiny when an HMO ignites a boycott of St. Paul's Hospital that leads to the murder of a doctor after Dr. Garnet accuses the HMO of "no-fault" murder in the death of an 18-month-old baby.
4. *Mortal Remains* (Ballantine, 2003) The remains of Kelly McShane Braden, Dr. Garnet's former lover, turn up 27 years after her disappearance, and physician-coroner Mark Roper, who knew Kelly, joins Earl in the search for Kelly's killer.
5. *Inquisitor, The* (Ballantine, 2004) Out-of-body near-death experiences, SARS, and some suspicious deaths among the terminal-cancer patients who reported the out-of-body experiences engage Dr. Garnet.

II. A pair of novels features veteran New York City ER physician Richard Steele, a widower with a 15-year-old son, and geneticist and environmentalist Kathleen Sullivan. The two become investigatory partners and lovers in these medical thrillers.

1. *Mutant* (Ballantine, 2001) Richard Steele, who has suffered a near-fatal heart attack, and Kathleen Sullivan, crusader against runaway genetic research, come together at an environmental conference in Hawaii.
2. *Critical Condition* (Ballantine, 2002) A conspiracy of doctors trying to cash in on the lucrative potential of stem cell technology by experimenting on human patients is eventually revealed when Kathleen blacks out while she is in bed with Richard.

Cleverly, Barbara

Britisher Barbara Cleverly is the author of several historical mysteries set in 1920s British India and England. Commander Joe Sandilands, a Scotland Yarder who does a stint with the Bengal Police, gets involved with crimes that often have a political tinge in the post World War I Raj. Cleverly has been favorably compared to Agatha Christie (q.v.). Her mysteries feature ingenious plots, interesting characters, and authentic portrayals of the Raj, colonial India, and the clashes of culture therein. Cleverly has also written a book set in Roman Britain, *An Old Magic* (Suffolk [UK], 2003).

1. *Last Kashmiri Rose, The* (Carroll & Graf, 2002) Joe Sandilands, Scotland Yarder completing a stint in India in the early 1920s, is asked to look into the death by suicide of an army officer's young wife.
2. *Ragtime in Simla* (Carroll & Graf, 2003) When a noted Russian singer is murdered just inches away from him at a scenic spot known as Devil's Elbow in the Raj summer capital of Simla, Sandilands feels obliged to track his killer.
3. *Damascened Blade, The* (Carroll & Graf, 2004) Sandilands, on a glorified babysitting assignment with a rich and attractive American heiress, ends up at a frontier outpost with an oddly assorted group of companions, including a Pathan prince who soon comes to a fatal end.
4. *Palace Tiger, The* (Carroll & Graf, 2005) Sandilands, back in India on a visit in 1922, agrees to help the Maharajah of Ranipur get rid of a man-eating tiger.
5. *Bee's Kiss, The* (Carroll & Graf, 2006) In 1926 Joe Sandilands is enjoying the pleasures of Jazz Age London on the eve of the General Strike when respected member of the establishment Dame Beatrice Joliffe is murdered, supposedly in a bungled burglary.
6. *Tug of War* (Carroll & Graf, 2007) Joe is taking a relaxing jaunt around Provence until Sir Douglas Redmayne of the British War Office gives him the assignment of ascertaining the identity of an amnesiac war veteran who's surfaced in a French hospital speaking English.

Cline, Edward

Sparrowhawk, a projected four-book cycle about the American Revolution, has already produced five novels, with more to come. The series begins in 1740 and follows the fortunes of two Englishmen from different classes, Jack Frake and Hugh Kenrick, who wind up in Virginia and eventually team up in their fight against what they regard as the oppressive British government. American novelist Edward Cline (*First Prize; Whisper the Guns*), who describes his politics as "Radical for Capitalism," is writing an accurate, detailed (some reviewers say too detailed) account, suffused by libertarian philosophy, of the events leading to the American Revolution.

1. *Jack Frake* (MacAdam/Cage, 2001) Young Englishman Jack Frake, forced to run away from home, gets a job in the seaside town of Gwynnford and joins the antigovernment group led by Augustus Skelly. Alternate title: *Sparrowhawk, Book One: Jack Frake*.
2. *Hugh Kenrick* (MacAdam/Cage, 2002) Brilliant and rebellious young English nobleman Hugh Kenrick defies his upper-class origins, taking a job with a merchant and getting involved with a group of free thinkers known as the Pippins. Alternate title: *Sparrowhawk, Book Two: Hugh Kenrick*.
3. *Caxton* (MacAdam/Cage, 2004) Jack Frake, now a successful planter in Virginia, joins with his neighbor Hugh Kenrick in opposition to governmental oppression. Alternate title: *Sparrowhawk, Book Three: Caxton*.
4. *Empire* (MacAdam/Cage, 2004) Hugh Kenrick, now a burgess in the Virginia legislature, leads the fight against the Stamp Act. Features cameos from Patrick Henry, Thomas Jefferson, Adam Smith, and Samuel Johnson. Alternate title: *Sparrowhawk, Book Four: Empire*.
5. *Revolution* (MacAdam/Cage, 2005) Jack Frake and Hugh Kenrick lead the resistance against the Stamp Act and put themselves in legal and physical danger. Alternate title: *Sparrowhawk, Book Five: Revolution*.

Clynes, Michael

PSEUDONYM OF P. C. Doherty

Sir Roger Shallot is a Falstaffian character: Knight of the Garter, four-time widower, libertine (who claims to have fathered a son by Queen Elizabeth, "the Virgin Queen"), liar, thief, coward, and braggart. Roger narrates, at the age of 90, his adventures as a servant and part-time detective, to Benjamin Daunbey, nephew of Cardinal Wolsey. Roger loves Daunbey but hates the sinister Wolsey and doesn't much like Wolsey's master, Henry VIII. Roger inevitably gets mixed up in some high politics and high skulduggery, but the plots are secondary to his exuberantly bawdy yarn spinning and the author's evocation of the first half of the 16th century. Michael Clynes is one of several pseudonyms of the prolific P. C. Doherty (q.v.), who writes a slew of historical mysteries set in different periods, under his aliases and his own name.

1. *White Rose Murders, The* (St. Martin's, 1993) Roger Shallot and his master, Benjamin Daunbey, are tapped by Daunbey's uncle, Cardinal Wolsey, to help Henry VIII's sister Margaret Tudor to regain the Scottish throne, lost after the supposed death of Margaret's husband, James IV, at the battle of Flodden Field in 1513.

2. *Poisoned Chalice, The* (Penzler, 1994) Cardinal Wolsey sends Daunbey and Shallot to Paris to investigate the murder of the chief secretary of the English Embassy. Are the Luciferi, a French group of spies with whom Roger was previously involved, responsible?

3. *Grail Murders, The* (Penzler, 1994) Was the Duke of Buckingham, whose execution for treason Roger and Benjamin are ordered to attend, linked to the Knights Templar, the anti-Tudor military-religious order that supposedly has custody of Arthur's sword, Excalibur, and the Holy Grail?

4. *Brood of Vipers, A* (St. Martin's, 1996) In the spring of 1523, Roger and Benjamin are sent to Italy to investigate the London murder of a Florentine envoy, where they stay at the villa of the powerful Abrizzi family and get involved with Medician and Machiavellian affairs.

5. *Gallows Murders, The* (St. Martin's, 1996) Roger survives a bout of "sweating sickness," stumbles across a conspiracy to murder members of the Guild of Hangmen, and is commissioned by Cardinal Wolsey to investigate an extortion plot against King Henry.

6. *Relic Murders, The* (Headline [UK], 1996) King Henry orders Roger and Benjamin to steal back a "true relic," the Orb of Charlemagne. Not published in the United States.

Cobb, James H(arvey)

Amanda Lee Garrett, commander of the high-tech destroyer USS *Cunningham*, is the hero(ine) of a series of "near-future" (2006–2008 so far, in books published 1996–2002) military-tech thrillers in which she and her capable crew thwart an Argentine invasion of Antarctica, civil war between Taiwan and China, a renegade Nigerian general bent on establishing a West African Union, and military satellite thieves in the Indonesian Sea. Amanda is an effective leader: respecting, willing to listen to, and considering all points of view and making firm, objective decisions. She doesn't eschew romance, including an out-of-character affair with an Indonesian pirate. Tacoma, Washington, native James H. Cobb is a military buff with much maritime technical knowledge whose speculations about near-future naval operations compare favorably with writers such as Dale Brown (q.v.) and Tom Clancy (q.v.).

1. *Choosers of the Slain* (Putnam, 1996) The destroyer USS *Cunningham*, commanded by Amanda Garrett, USN, is on patrol in the Antarctic in 2006 when Argentina launches a surprise invasion of the mineral-rich continent.

2. *Sea Strike* (Putnam, 1997) Amanda and the crew of the *Cunningham* detect plans by Taiwan to invade the Chinese mainland and initiate a new Chinese civil war. UK title: *Storm-Dragon*.

3. *Sea Fighter* (Putnam, 2000) A renegade Nigerian general has escalated an African civil war by invading Sierra Leone and Guinea in his determination to be ruler of a new "West African Union."

4. *Target Lock* (Putnam, 2002) High-tech pirates in the Indonesian Sea steal a satellite containing military secrets from a US research vessel. Amanda lets her guard down by getting seduced and kidnapped by pirate leader Makara Harconan.

Coben, Harlan

Myron Bolitar, former pro basketball player, Harvard Law School graduate, and sports agent, is a curious character in some ways: he lived at his parents' suburban New Jersey home until he was 34; his favorite tipple is the chocolate drink YooHoo; and he has a quixotic way of becoming involved in his clients' problems, which entangles him in a series of mystery investigations. Myron has a longtime romance with writer Jessica Culvey, but his partners—Esperanza Diaz, a lesbian who formerly wrestled professionally as Little Pocahontas, and Windsor "Win" Home Lockwood III, a blond, preppy version of Robert Parker's (q.v.) Hawk—are more interesting characters. The Bolitar mysteries are fast, humorous, and peppered with Fletch-like (Gregory McDonald [q.v.]) dialogue. New Jersey–born Harlan Coben was the first author to win the Edgar, Shamus, and Anthony awards.

1. *Deal Breaker* (Dell, 1995) Former pro basketballer Myron Bolitar is about to enter the big time as a sports agent by representing rookie quarterback Christian Steele. But then Christian gets a call from a former girlfriend, a woman whom everyone believed to be dead.

2. *Dropshot* (Dell, 1996) When 24-year-old has-been tennis star Valerie Simpson is killed on the verge of making her comeback, Myron takes on the job of finding her killer.

3. *Fade Away* (Dell, 1996) Myron returns to pro basketball, in a way, after a 10-year hiatus due to an injury, when the owner of the New Jersey Dragons asks him to use his skills as a former FBI undercover agent to find a missing player.

4. *Backspin* (Dell, 1997) Someone kidnaps the son of golfer Jack Coldren just as Jack is poised to win the US Open.

5. *One False Move* (Delacorte, 1998) Basketball star Brenda Slaughter's father has disappeared, and she has been receiving death threats. Myron's 10-year commitment to writer Jessica Culvey is seriously tested. Bolitar's first hardcover appearance.

6. *Final Detail, The* (Delacorte, 1999) Myron's partner, former pro wrestler Esperanza Diaz ("Little Pocahontas"), is suspected of the murder of Myron's client, troubled pro-baseball-player Clu Haid.

7. *Darkest Fear* (Delacorte, 2000) Myron has finally moved out of his family home at the age of 34. His former girlfriend Emily resurfaces, telling Myron that her critically ill 13-year-old son (whom she claims is his son, also) needs a bone-marrow transplant.

8. *Promise Me* (Dutton, 2006) Myron becomes a suspect when Aimee Biel, friend of Erin Wilder, daughter of his new girlfriend, Ali Wilder, goes missing.

Cochran, Molly

I. Molly Cochran and Warren Murphy's addition to the Arthurian canon is a trilogy set in modern times with flashbacks to Arthurian days. Arthur is reincarnated as a 10-year-old boy, and many other Arthurian characters, such as Merlin (aka Taliesin) and Nimue, appear as themselves, while other Arthurian standbys are reincarnated with different names, such as Guinevere, who appears as the mysterious teenager Beatrice, who possesses the Holy Grail, and ex-FBI agent Hal Woczniak, who retains memories of his previous existence as Galahad. Saladin is depicted as an evil knight who is trying to obtain the grail and acquire immortality. This trilogy received mixed reviews but will interest readers who want to read everything connected with King Arthur. Nearly all of Molly Cochran's books have been coauthored with her husband, Warren Murphy, who is also the cofounder of the "syndicate" that produces the Destroyer and other paperback thriller series.

1. *Forever King, The* (Tor, 1992) King Arthur is reborn as a 10-year-old-boy in our world. In Arthurian England, the evil knight Saladin plots to control the Holy Grail and become immortal, while Merlin and Nimue work to foil his plans. Coauthored with Warren Murphy.
2. *Broken Sword, The* (Tor, 1997) Hal Woczniak, an ex-FBI agent who has memories of his previous life as Galahad, and the ancient bard Taliesin (aka Merlin) mentor the 13-year-old Arthur. They are joined by the mysterious teenager Beatrice, who possesses the Holy Grail, and opposed by the villainous painter and secret assassin Aubrey Katsuleris. Coauthored with Warren Murphy.
3. *Third Magic, The* (Tor, 2003) Guinevere/Beatrice stands between Arthur and his long-awaited destiny. Arthur may be forced to make a terrible sacrifice for the Holy Grail.

II. The husband-and-wife team of Cochran and Murphy (usually listed as principal author) was also responsible for the pair of Grandmaster thrillers, which pitted American Justin Gilead and Russian Alexander Zharkov against each in a deadly struggle to achieve the title of Grandmaster. Number 1 won the Edgar Allan Poe Award for Best Paperback Original in 1985 and was very popular with readers.

1. *Grandmaster* (Pinnacle, 1984) Justin Gilead and Alexander Zharkov, born on the same day, are destined to be antagonists and contenders for the title of Grandmaster. Principal author: Warren Murphy.
2. *Grandmaster: High Priest* (New American Library, 1989) Gilead and Zharkov continue to be locked in mortal combat in action that takes them from Tibet to the White House in the United States. Principal author: Warren Murphy.

Cockey, Tim

Undertaker and amateur sleuth Hitchcock Sewell is the hero of a series of lighthearted mysteries set in Baltimore, Maryland. The wisecracking Hitch, proprietor of Sewell & Sons Family Funeral Home, engages himself in a series of humorous mysteries, full of engaging characters, in a well-realized Baltimore setting. Author Tim Cockey is a Baltimore native.

1. *Hearse You Came in on, The* (Hyperion, 2000) The interest of Hitchcock Sewell, proprietor of Sewell & Sons Family Funeral Home, of Baltimore, Maryland, is piqued when Carolyn James tries to arrange her own funeral. Then a different "Carolyn James" turns up at the mortuary as a suicide.
2. *Hearse of a Different Color* (Hyperion, 2001) When the murdered body of Helen Waggoner is dumped on the front steps of Sewell & Sons, Hitch's new girlfriend, Bonnie Nash, pondering a career move from weathergirl to investigative reporter, persuades him to try to find out who killed Helen.
3. *Hearse Case Scenario, The* (Hyperion, 2002) Hitch's childhood friend Lucy shot her sleazy boyfriend, Shrimp Martin, but swears that she didn't kill him.

4. *Murder in the Hearse Degree* (Hyperion, 2003) Hitch's former lover Libby Gelman, who's left her abusive husband, asks Hitch to find her missing nanny, Sophie Potts, who soon turns up pregnant and dead, an apparent suicide.
5. *Backstabber* (Hyperion, 2004) Old high school pal, Jonathan "Sisco" Fontaine, lover of a married woman, Polly Weisheit, asks Hitch to bail him out when Polly's husband turns up dead with a knife in his back.

Cody, Liza

I. Anna Lee is the youngest employee of Brierly Security of London. Because of her age and sex, Anna gets assigned routine, boring surveillance or security jobs. Sometimes these jobs turn out to be anything but boring or routine, but the feisty Anna always manages to get a handle on them.

1. *Dupe* (Scribner, 1981) Anna is given the seemingly dull assignment of investigating a young socialite's fatal accident.
2. *Bad Company* (Scribner, 1983) A routine surveillance on a mother and daughter leads to Anna being kidnapped.
3. *Stalker* (Scribner, 1985) Carpenter Edward Marshall has skipped with money entrusted to him for a business he never started.
4. *Head Case* (Scribner, 1986) Sixteen-year-old genius Thea Hahn is found hysterical and apparently insane in a Dorset hospital.
5. *Under Contract* (Scribner, 1987) Lee joins the security force of rock star Shona Una and her obnoxious entourage.
6. *Backhand* (Doubleday, 1992) Anna flies to the Florida Keys to track down a sweater thief.

II. Anna Lee plays a minor role in a series featuring a truly original character, Eva Wylie: professional wrestler known as the London Lassassin, junkyard security guard, and sometime courier for a shady Asian businessman. Eva, who lives with two dogs in a junkyard trailer, has brawn, "mental discipline," and a cynical but tough moral code.

1. *Bucket Nut* (Doubleday, 1993) Eva Wylie takes on a temporary "crowd control" job that leads to her "adoption" of Goldie, the stoned backup singer for a rock band.
2. *Monkey Wrench* (Mysterious, 1995) Eva's friend Crystal (aka Monkey Wrench) asks her help in finding the murderer of her prostitute sister.
3. *Musclebound* (Mysterious, 1997) In a fit of pique, Eva steals a car and finds a bag full of money in the back. Then her long-lost sister, Simone, comes back into her life.

Coe, David B.

I. The Winds of the Forelands series is a sword-and-sorcery epic in five volumes pitting the physically weak but magically empowered Qirsi against the nonmagical Eandi, who hold sway over numerous minor fiefdoms in a medieval-like society. In a complicated series of events, chock-full of characters, the Qirsi, led by a mastermind known as the Weaver, try to wrest control of the Forelands from the Eandi. This is a well-written series full of sophisticated political intrigue. A new trilogy set in the Southlands has been inaugurated with *The Sorcerers' Plague*.

1. *Rules of Ascension* (Tor, 2002) After a failed invasion, the magically adept Qirsi became the servants of the physically stronger but nonmagical Eandi. Now, through a series of intrigues, the Qirsi have a chance to take over the kingship of the Forelands.

2. *Seeds of Betrayal* (Tor, 2003) The Qirsi "Conspiracy" continues under the leadership of the mysterious Weaver, using assassination and other means to acquire control of the Forelands.

3. *Bonds of Vengeance* (Tor, 2005) The civic unrest fomented by the Weaver continues, leading to an anarchic situation pitting Qirsi against Eandi, Qirsi against Qirsi, and Eandi against Eandi.

4. *Shapers of Darkness* (Tor, 2005) Young Tavis of Curgh, dubbed a traitor by his former friends, joins forces with the Qirsi shaper Grinsa jal Arriet in a quest to uncover the Weaver's true identity.

5. *Weavers of War* (Tor, 2007) Dusaan the Weaver takes control of the empire and binds the magic of the Qirsi into a single weapon more potent than any the Eandi have faced in 1,000 years.

6. *Sorcerers' Plague, The* (Tor, 2007) Subtitle: *Book One of the Blood of the Southlands*. Across the sea in the Southlands, a mysterious plague is heightening tensions between the Qirsi, the Eandi, and the Mettai, who cast spells with blood and earth.

II. American writer Coe also published a trilogy called the Lon-Tobyn Chronicles, a complicated epic fantasy in which politics, economic forces, and historic motifs play a larger role than romance or fairy tales. The pastoral Tobyn-Ser, protected by benevolent mages who have birds as their "familiars," have their long peace disturbed by disguised invaders from their nonmagical but technologically advanced neighbors, the Lon-Ser. Young Jaryd, who has prophetic dreams and becomes a Hawk-Mage of the Children of Amarid, and eventually Eagle-Sage, is the leading character.

1. *Children of Amarid* (Tor, 1997) The land of Tobyn-Ser, which has known peace for many years, is disturbed by an outbreak of vandalism and homicides perpetrated by mysterious people dressed like mages.

2. *Utlanders, The* (Tor, 1998) Although the original forces of bandits, agents of Lon-Ser, have been defeated, the Owl-Mages of the Order of Amarid fear a likely second incursion by their Nal-Lord-ruled neighbors.

3. *Eagle-Sage* (Tor, 2000) Technological and capitalistic advances in Lon-Ser have upset relations between Lon-Ser and pastoral Tobyn-Ser, leading to ecological devastation in the latter. Jaryd becomes the first Eagle-Sage in 400 years, portending war.

Coe, Jonathan

Jonathan Coe's *The Rotters' Club* relates the coming-of-age of a group of adolescents in Birmingham, England, in the 1970s. Its sequel, *The Closed Circle*, follows them into adulthood (1999–2003). This pair of novels combines interesting narratives, well-developed characters, and nonintrusive social and political commentary. Jonathan Coe, a Birmingham native who is a journalist and film critic (*New Statesman*), has written six other novels and biographies of screen stars Jimmy Stewart and Humphrey Bogart.

1. *Rotters' Club, The* (Knopf, 2002) Benjamin and Paul Trotter, Claire Newman and her sister, Doug Anderton, and Philip Chase deal with adolescent issues in Birmingham, England, against a backdrop of 1970s British political and social turmoil.

2. *Closed Circle, The* (Knopf, 2005) In events from 1999 to 2003, Ben Trotter and his cohorts face the world as adults with varying degrees of success, mourning lost loves and pursuing careers as politicians and journalists.

Coe, Tucker

PSEUDONYM OF Donald E. Westlake

Before he hit his stride with the Dortmunder series, Donald E. Westlake (q.v.) wrote many other mystery novels under his own name and under pseudonyms such as Tucker Coe. Five novels featuring Mitch Tobin were published in the 1960s and 1970s. They were reissued by Five Star in 2001. The Mitch Tobin novels are grimmer than the Dortmunder novels. Mitch Tobin is a former New York Police Department cop who lost his job when he fatally let his partner down. Unable to adjust to any other occupation Mitch takes on a variety of cases as a private investigator.

1. *Kinds of Love, Kinds of Death* (Random House, 1966) Mobster Arnie Rembak asks disgraced ex-NYPD officer Mitch Tobin to find out who killed his girlfriend.

2. *Murder among Children* (Random House, 1968) Tobin finds himself thrust into a case that begins with police harassment of a Village coffee shop and ends in multiple murder.

3. *Wax Apple* (Random House, 1970) Mitch registers at The Midway, a halfway house for convalescing mental patients, after a series of "accidents" plagues the home.

4. *Jade in Aries* (Random House, 1971) Tobin enters the underworld of New York City's homosexual community after male model Jamie Dearborn is murdered.

5. *Don't Lie to Me* (Random House, 1972) Mitch's past history comes alive again as a naked and unidentifiable dead body is found.

Coel, Margaret

Father John O'Malley, rusticated from Boston to the remote St. Francis Mission at Wyoming's Wind River Reservation to recover from his alcoholism, develops a great attachment to the mission, the reservation and its Arapaho denizens. Often in tandem with fortysomething Arapaho attorney, Vicky Holden, Father John involves himself in a number of murder mysteries connected to the reservation. The wary relationship between Vicky Holden and Father John is part of the interest in these mystery novels, but the real attraction is Colorado historian and Arapaho expert Margaret Coel's depiction of reservation life and the various means by which her Native American characters cope with the vicissitudes of life on and off the reservation. Coel has been compared to, and praised by, Tony Hillerman (q.v.) for her realistic depictions.

1. *Eagle Catcher, The* (University of Colorado, 1995) Father John O'Malley, rusticated the St. Francis Mission at Wyoming's Wind River Reservation, joins forces with Arapaho attorney Vicky Holden when the tribal chairman is killed and the chairman's nephew is arrested.

2. *Ghost Walker, The* (Berkley, 1996) After Father O'Malley discovers a body dumped in a frozen ditch near his mission, the body disappears. The Arapahos say that a ghost is walking.

3. *Dream Stalker, The* (Berkley, 1997) Vickie Holden is protesting the construction of a nuclear storage facility on a ranch near Wind Rivers, but some of the Arapahos regard the site as a job opportunity.

4. *Story Teller, The* (Berkley, 1998) A "ledger book" with pictographs detailing the Arapaho presence at a US Army massacre of Indians in Colorado turns up missing from a Denver museum. Then an Arapaho graduate student is killed.

5. *Lost Bird, The* (Berkley, 1999) Father John thinks that he was the real target when his elderly assistant is killed on a back road.

6. *Spirit Woman, The* (Berkley, 2000) Father John is reassigned after eight years at Windy River. Vicky Holden is back with ex-husband

Ben. Her old friend Laura Simmons thinks that the memoirs of Sacagawea are stashed somewhere on the reservation.

7. *Thunder Keeper, The* (Berkley, 2001) Vicky is temporarily in Denver. Duncan Grover undertakes a vision quest, and then he is murdered.

8. *Shadow Dancer, The* (Berkley, 2002) Father John is confronted with the possible closing of the mission and the sudden disappearance of one of his parishioners. Vicky becomes the prime suspect when her ex-husband is murdered.

9. *Killing Raven* (Berkley, 2003) Vicky and lawyer Adam Lone Eagle are representing the interests of the Great Plains Casino. A dead body is discovered at the remote area of Double Dives.

10. *Wife of Moon* (Berkley, 2004) The murder of a descendant of a tribal chief depicted in one of the early 20th-century photographs of Plains Indians by Edward S. Curtis exhibited at the St. Francis Mission museum may be connected with a 1907 murder.

11. *Eye of the Wolf* (Berkley, 2005) Father John receives a cryptic voice-mail message that leads him to a century-old battlefield and three newly slain Shoshones.

12. *Drowning Man, The* (Berkley, 2006) The Drowning Man, an ancient petroglyph on Red Cliff Canyon, has been chiseled off the wall and is being held for ransom.

13. *Girl with Braided Hair, The* (Berkley, 2007) Vicky Holden's attempt to identify the skeletal remains of an apparent murder victim causes friction between her and Adam Lone Eagle.

Coetzee, J(ohn) M(axwell)

Elderly Australian novelist Elizabeth Costello, the creation of South African (now resident in Australia) novelist J. M. Coetzee, is said by some critics to be an alter ego of Coetzee himself. Certainly Costello has same of the same concerns, such as animal rights, as Coetzee. Both authors have re-created fictional characters: Molly Bloom in Costello's case, Robinson Crusoe in Coetzee's (*Foe*, Viking, 1987). *Elizabeth Costello* is a collection of six previously published pieces (1997–2003) as well as two new Costello items and a "Postscript: Letter of Elizabeth, Lady Chandos." To add to the confusion, two lectures given by "Elizabeth Costello" at the fictional Appleton College in New England on the human abuse of animals are published in Coetzee's *The Lives of Animals* (Princeton, 1999), which also contains the Tanner Lectures that Coetzee gave some years ago at Princeton University. *Elizabeth Costello* reveals the workings of its eponymous character's mind in a series of formal addresses that she attends or delivers herself. Elizabeth makes a reappearance in the middle of Coetzee's next novel *Slow Man*, where she exhorts maimed novelist Paul Rayment (another Coetzee stand-in?) to shape up his life. J. M. Coetzee is a Nobel laureate (2003) and two-time Booker Prize winner: *The Life and Times of Michael K* (Viking, 1984) and *Disgrace* (Viking, 1999). He has also published two nonfiction auto-biographical works subtitled *Scenes from Provincial Life*: *Boyhood* (Viking, 1997) and *Youth* (2002).

1. *Elizabeth Costello* (Viking, 2003) Elizabeth Costello, Australian novelist born in 1927, reveals her preoccupations: family relations (she is estranged from her son John, an academic, and her sister Blanche, a missionary in Africa); man's inhumanity to other animals; and her confused grapplings with the meanings of realism and reason and the human problems of sex and spirituality.

2. *Slow Man* (Viking, 2005) Retired photographer Paul Rayment, confined to an Australian hospital after losing a leg in a bicycle accident, ponders what seems to be him to be a wasted life. Then novelist Elizabeth Costello arrives and exhorts Rayment to take charge of his life.

Cohen, Jeffrey

Aaron Tucker, screenwriter wannabe, former investigative reporter, occasional freelance journalist, househusband, and sometime amateur detective, lives in New Jersey with his wife, Abigail; his daughter, Leah; and his son, Ethan, who suffers from Asperger's syndrome (which plays a strong role in number 3). The wisecracking but mild-mannered Aaron, more antisleuth than sleuth, has bumbled his way to solutions in three puzzle mysteries with strong infusions of humor. Jeffrey Cohen is the author of more than 20 screenplays and (with Lori Shery) of the nonfiction *The Asperger's Parent* (Autism Asperger Publishing, 2002).

1. *For Whom the Minivan Rolls* (Bancroft, 2002) Former investigative reporter and aspiring screenwriter Aaron Tucker agrees to help wealthy New Jersey businessman Gary Beckwirth find his missing wife.

2. *Farewell to Legs, A* (Bancroft, 2003) Aaron is asked by a former flame to find the murderer of her husband, a leading right-wing politician who was found dead in his DC hotel room.

3. *As Dog Is My Witness* (Bancroft, 2005) After a young man with Asperger's syndrome is arrested for a seemingly senseless murder, Aaron, who is familiar with Asperger's because his son, Ethan, is afflicted with the syndrome, takes on the job of clearing the young man.

Cohen, Nancy J.

Marla Shore, beauty salon owner and hairdresser, is a likable amateur detective in the Bad Hair Day mysteries, a series of cozies set in Palm Haven (a fictionalized version of Fort Lauderdale), Florida. Despite the experience of a bad marriage to the slimy Stan Kaufman (see number 4), Marla decides to try again, this time with homicide detective Dalton Vail, to whom she eventually becomes engaged. Nancy J. Cohen, who worked as a registered clinical nurse specialist, is also the author of several romance novels under the pseudonym of Nancy Cane.

1. *Permed to Death* (Kensington, 1999) Florida beautician Marla Shore undertakes her own investigation when she becomes the prime suspect in the poisoning death of a client who had been blackmailing her.

2. *Hair Raiser* (Kensington, 2000) Marla goes as far afield as the Bahamas while investigating a suspicious series of mishaps to the chefs she has engaged to prepare a benefit dinner for Ocean Guard, a coastal preservation group.

3. *Murder by Manicure* (Kensington, 2001) When one of Marla's customers, Jolene Myers, is found dead in a fitness club whirlpool by Dalton Vail, Marla starts to investigate.

4. *Body Wave* (Kensington, 2002) Marla goes undercover as a nurse, with Dalton Vail's blessing, to find the real murderer of Kimberly Kaufman, third wife of Marla's ex, the slimy Stan Kaufman.

5. *Highlights to Heaven* (Kensington, 2003) A missing neighbor, a murder victim with a distinctive highlighting pattern, crimes involving contraband animals, illegal furs, a potion to cure baldness, and a murder scheme apparently aimed at Marla's former beauty-school classmates are all part of this concoction.

6. *Died Blonde* (Kensington, 2004) Shore becomes a suspect again when her former boss and archenemy is found dead in the meter room that controls the power to her salon.

7. *Dead Roots* (Kensington, 2005) Sugar Crest, a former plantation, now a reputedly haunted resort hotel that's owned by Marla's aunt Polly, is the scene of the suffocation death of the elderly Polly.

8. *Perish by Pedicure* **(Kensington, 2006)** When Christine Parks, the director of Luxor Beauty Products, is discovered dead in her hotel room, Marla's friend Georgia Rogers, who was the last person to see Christine alive, becomes the chief suspect.

9. *Killer Knots* **(Kensington, 2007)** Shortly after boarding a cruise ship with Dalton Vail and his parents and teenage daughter, Marla receives a threatening note addressed to "Martha Shore."

Coldsmith, Don(ald Charles)

I. The long-running, popular Spanish Bit Saga chronicles the history, from 1540 to 1800, of a fictional Great Plains Indian nation, the Elk-Dog (Horse) People, or simply the People. In 1540, Juan Garcia, a wandering Spaniard, is adopted by the People, renamed Heads Off, and shows the People how to use the horse for hunting and war, and the Spanish bit, which he bequeaths, becomes a sacred object. The Elk-Dogs, though fictional, are based on the tribal traditions of the Kiowas, the Arapahos, the Comanches, and the Cheyennes, and readers of the Saga learn a great deal about the history and customs of the Plains Indians before they were swamped by the descendants of Europeans. The Saga, told from the People's point of view, is exciting reading and very informative. Coldsmith treats his Native American characters with respect but not with sentimentality. *Runestone* (Bantam, 1995), which chronicles the 11th-century confrontation between the People and Norse explorers, can be regarded as a prequel to the series.

1. *Trail of the Spanish Bit* **(Doubleday, 1980)** Spaniard Juan Garcia, searching for gold in the southern plains of North America around 1540, comes to grief, is aided by the People and, in turn, teaches the People the use of the horse for hunting and war.

2. *Buffalo Medicine* **(Doubleday, 1980)** Owl, a young warrior of the People, son of Heads Off (aka Don Garcia), has to learn honor from an ancient medicine man, and undergo a long and dangerous quest.

3. *Elk-Dog Heritage, The* **(Doubleday, 1982)** After many years of peace under the leadership of Heads Off (Juan Garcia), the People are drawn into war by a few headstrong warriors who seek personal glory.

4. *Follow the Wind* **(Doubleday, 1983)** Heads Off, not believing the reports of the death of Owl, his son, sets out to follow a rumor that Owl is living among savages in New Spain's uncharted wilderness.

5. *Man of the Shadows* **(Doubleday, 1983)** Eagle, son of Heads Off, has mastered the ways of the horse, but now must deal with the mysterious "Man of the Shadows."

6. *Daughter of the Eagle* **(Doubleday, 1984)** Eagle Woman, unmarried and as skilled and strong as most young warriors, defies tradition by requesting warrior status.

7. *Moon of Thunder* **(Doubleday, 1985)** Rabbit must ride far from home with the Spanish Bit, his people's medicine, bequeathed by Heads Off/Juan Garcia, to become an adult.

8. *Sacred Hills, The* **(Doubleday, 1985)** The Blue Paints, savage warriors from the North who kill for pleasure, attack the People and murder the wife of Looks Far, the People's medicine man, forcing the People to seek the help of their old enemies, the Head Splitters.

9. *Pale Star* **(Doubleday, 1986)** Pale Star, kidnapped as a child, undertakes an incredible journey to return to the People and thwart attempts to steal the supernatural power she has inherited from her ancestors.

10. *River of Swans* **(Doubleday, 1986)** Pale Star (number 9) accompanies Lieutenant Andre DuPres down the Big River in search of a southwest passage across the North American continent.

11. *Return to the River* **(Doubleday, 1987)** "Jean Cartier" abandons the People and his son to live among the white men.

12. *Medicine Knife, The* **(Doubleday, 1988)** Two former soldiers in the French army, assimilated by the People, journey with them to Santa Fe to trade pelts.

13. *Flower in the Mountains, The* **(Doubleday, 1988)** Jean Cartier (see number 11), now Woodchuck of the People, introduces his son Red Feather to the trading business.

14. *Trail from Taos* **(Doubleday, 1989)** Concerns the great Pueblo Revolt of 1680 against the Spanish.

15. *Song of the Rock* **(Doubleday, 1989)** Trade with the Spanish in Santa Fe has been suspended, and the People are forced to return to their traditional ways.

16. *Fort de Chastaigne* **(Doubleday, 1990)** White Fox and his son Red Horse serve as guides for Captain LeFever, a Frenchman traveling from the Missouri River to Santa Fe.

17. *Quest for the White Bull* **(Doubleday, 1990)** The buffalo herds have failed to return to their familiar grazing lands in the spring. Red Horse, medicine man of the People, and Digging Owl set out to find the missing herds.

18. *Return of the Spanish* **(Doubleday, 1991)** Strong Bull, famed for his proficiency with weapons, is given a chance by the Spanish to capture high glory in warfare against the French and their Pawnee allies.

19. *Bride of the Morning Star* **(Doubleday, 1991)** When his adopted Pawnee people abduct a young woman from his native tribe, the Elk-Dog People, Bear Paws is torn in his loyalties.

20. *Walks in the Sun* **(Doubleday, 1992)** After two years of wandering the Legendary South along what is now Mexico's Gulf Coast, only two survivors of the original band of 11 Elk-Dogs return to the People.

21. *Thunderstick* **(Doubleday, 1993)** At 17, Singing Wolf, the son of People's leader Walks in the Sun, is about to become a man by engaging in his first hunt. The interloper White Feathers possesses a "thunderstick," a flint-lock musket.

22. *Track of the Bear* **(Doubleday, 1994)** Singing Wolf (see number 21) must make a difficult choice between exploring the breaking of a peace-covenant and keeping peace with his loved ones.

23. *Child of the Dead* **(Doubleday, 1995)** Running Bear, the grieving matriarch of the People, nurses Gray Mouse, sole survivor of a tribe wiped out by a nonnative scourge, smallpox.

24. *Bearer of the Pipe* **(Doubleday, 1995)** Wolf Pup, son of Gray Mouse (see number 23) and Dark Antelope, chief tracker and scout of the People, apprenticed to the holy man Singing Wolf (see numbers 21 and 22), undertakes a perilous vision quest.

25. *Medicine Hat* **(University of Oklahoma, 1997)** Pipe Bearer, a young shaman of the People, journeys north to the land of the Pawnee and Lakota, seeking the answer to a mysterious dream about a colt with a Medicine Hat.

26. *Lost Band, The* **(University of Oklahoma, 2000)** The People are thrown into confusion by the arrival of Story Keeper, who claims to be chief of the Forest (or Lost) Band, who disappeared 200 years earlier.

27. *Raven Mocker* **(University of Oklahoma, 2001)** Snakewater, an elderly Cherokee medicine woman accused of being a Raven Mocker, leaves her people and joins a band heading west and eventually hooks up with the Elk-Dog People.

28. *Pipestone Quest, The* **(University of Oklahoma, 2004)** A 17-year-old member of the Elk-Dog People must learn to trust his instincts as he grapples with strange apparitions and perplexing dreams.

II. The Super Edition series is a trio of spin-offs from the Spanish Bit Saga, relating tales connected with the senior series. The three novels were published together in omnibus volumes entitled *Three*

Complete Novels (Wings, 1995) and *Don Coldsmith Omnibus* (Doubleday, 1997).

1. *Changing Wind, The* **(Bantam, 1990)** White Buffalo will be the greatest medicine man the People have ever known.
2. *Traveler, The* **(Bantam, 1991)** Storyteller, known in childhood as Woodpecker, who traverses the lands of the People trading and telling tales of times long past, is about to set off on the great quest that will be his own life.
3. *World of Silence* **(Bantam, 1991)** Speaks-Not, born into a world of deafness and silence, is renamed Hunts-Alone for his successful hunting methods.

III. Two novels incorporate 300 years of Plains history (the 1500s to the 1800s), beginning with the first contact of the Plains Indians with the Spanish and finishing with the adventures of Princeton University dropout trapper Jed Sterling among the Pawnees. Coldsmith has also written a volume in the multiauthor Rivers West series, *The Smoky Hill* (Bantam, 1989); a stand-alone novel about John Buffalo, a 20th-century Native American athlete, *The Long Journey Home* (Forge, 2001); and three collections of articles from his column "Horsin' Around."

1. *Tallgrass* **(Bantam, 1997)** Relates nearly 300 years of Plains Indian history from the coming of the Spanish in 1541 to 1835, when Princeton dropout Jed Sterling, who has been living with the Pawnees, returns to "civilization" for a short visit.
2. *South Wind* **(Bantam, 1998)** After the death of his Pawnee wife, Jed Sterling is back in Kansas in 1846, with a new wife, a black slave he bought in New Orleans.

Cole, Allan

I. The Tales of the Timuras is a fantasy trilogy concerning the adventures of Safar Timura, wizard and hero, in the land of Esmir, which is divided by an enchanted border separating demons and humans. Safar starts out life as a potter, but his magical powers come to the fore when he teams up with young Iraj, the future King Protarus, with whom he eventually breaks. In the final volume, Safar is trapped in the world of Hadin, and it is up to his adopted son, Palimak, to bail out him and his world. This is good sword-and-sorcery fare with interesting characters and exciting action. Omnibus volume *The Complete Timuras* (Wildside, 2005) contains the trilogy. American Allan Cole was a journalist and a TV writer before embarking on a fantasy and SF writing career. Many of his books were coauthored with the late Chris Bunch (q.v.).

1. *Wizard of the Winds* **(Del Rey, 1997)** Young Safar, of the land of Esmir, is troubled by visions predicting the arrival of a king, Protarus, who will rule Esmir one day. Safar becomes friends with Iraj, a prince in hiding, and undergoes a series of adventures with various characters, including a circus of acrobats. Variant title: *When the Gods Slept.*
2. *Wolves of the Gods* **(Del Rey, 1998)** Safar Timura has become a great wizard, and his erstwhile friend Iraj Protarus, back from the dead as a wolflike shape-shifter, has become his nemesis.
3. *Gods Awaken, The* **(Del Rey, 1999)** Safar is trapped in the doomed world of Hadin, and it's up to his adopted son—half-demon, half-human wizard Palmak—to free Safar by confronting the Demon Moon.

II. The Antero epic-fantasy series, narrated alternately by Amalric Antero and his warrior sister Rali Emilie Antero, is fantasy reminiscent somewhat of the *Odyssey*, sword and sorcery, and a lighthearted lesbian romp as Amalric undergoes a series of journeys from his native Orissa first with Captain Janos Greycloak, then with Greycloak's granddaughter Janela Kether Greycloak, and Rali, Captain of the all-female Maranon Guards becomes the reluctant tool of the goddess Maranonia, and falls in to the hands of the changeling Novari, the Lyre Bird. This is rousing adventure with interesting characters and a dollop of humor. Chris Bunch (q.v.) was coauthor of numbers 1 through 3.

1. *Far Kingdoms, The* **(Del Rey, 1993)** Dissipated young merchant Amalric Antero of Orissa is rescued from a procurer by Captain Janos Greycloak, who persuades him to accompany him to the Far Kingdoms, "land of fabled wealth and wizardry." Coauthored with Chris Bunch (q.v.).
2. *Warrior's Tale, The* **(Del Rey, 1994)** Captain Rali Emilie Antero, sister of Amalric and leader of the amazonian Maranon Guards, fights demons and the rival city of Lycanth, searches for the evil Archon, and engages in a lesbian affair. Coauthored with Chris Bunch (q.v.).
3. *Kingdoms of the Night* **(Del Rey, 1995)** The elderly Lord Amalric Antero is revitalized by the appearance of Janela Kether Greycloak, granddaughter of his ex-partner, the late Janos Greycloak, and is persuaded to undergo a fresh expedition to the Far Kingdoms. Coauthored with Chris Bunch (q.v.).
4. *Warrior Returns, The* **(Del Rey, 1996)** Rali Emilie Antero, warrior, sorceress, and reluctant tool of the goddess Maranonia, falls into the clutches of Novari, the Lyre Bird, a changeling created to be a prince's sexual slave who has become a powerful sorceress.

III. Allan Coe and Chris Bunch (q.v.) wrote a series of eight science-fiction novels featuring Sten, a native of the factory planet Vulcan, who becomes commander of the Gurkhas, bodyguard of the Eternal Emperor. The emperor dies, returns, deteriorates as a ruler, and eventually has to be opposed by Sten. This is military SF with fantasy touches. Reprinted by Orbit (UK) in 2001 after going out of print.

1. *Sten* **(Del Rey, 1982)** Sten rebels against the company on the dreary factory world of Vulcan after his family is wiped out in a mysterious accident. Coauthored with Chris Bunch (q.v.).
2. *Wolf Worlds, The* **(Del Rey, 1984)** Sten and the Mantis Team, a small band of military problem-solvers, are recruited by the Eternal Emperor to pacify the pirate Wolf Worlds. Coauthored with Chris Bunch (q.v.).
3. *Court of a Thousand Suns, The* **(Del Rey, 1985)** Sten, now commander of the Imperial Gurkhas, the bodyguard of the Eternal Emperor, finds at first that his worst nemesis is the intrigue of the court politicians. Coauthored with Chris Bunch (q.v.).
4. *Fleet of the Damned* **(Del Rey, 1988)** Sten finds himself assigned to a tacdivision in the Fringe Worlds, where military discipline is slack. Then the Tahn decide to launch their long-planned attack against the empire. Coauthored with Chris Bunch (q.v.).
5. *Revenge of the Damned* **(Del Rey, 1989)** Sten is determined to find a way out of slave labor in a POW camp deep in the heart of enemy territory. Coauthored with Chris Bunch (q.v.).
6. *Return of the Emperor, The* **(Del Rey, 1990)** The Eternal Emperor is dead, and the Privy Council ruling in his place must locate the emperor's secret cache of Anti-Matter Two, the rocket fuel that keeps the empire running, or lose power. But first they have to catch Sten. Coauthored with Chris Bunch (q.v.).
7. *Vortex* **(Del Rey, 1992)** The emperor has returned, not entirely to everyone's satisfaction. Sten finds himself appointed Ambassador Plenipotentiary to the Altaic Cluster, where a civil war threatens the stability of the empire. Coauthored with Chris Bunch (q.v.).

8. *Empire's End* (Del Rey, 1993) The emperor, now dangerously corrupt and incompetent, is a menace to everyone. The hitherto faithful Gurkhas ask Sten to work with them to overthrow the emperor. But first the source of Anti-Matter Two must be found and destroyed. Coauthored with Chris Bunch (q.v.).

Colegate, Isabel

The plot of the Orlando trilogy concerns the rise and fall of successful British politician Orlando King and the fate of his daughter Agatha in the years 1930–1956. The trilogy tries to meld a modern version of the Oedipus trilogy (Orlando equals Oedipus; Agatha equals Antigone) with social and political commentary on that turbulent period, an effort that most critics found to be an interesting failure. English novelist, essayist, and critic Colegate's best known and best liked (in the United States, anyway) is *The Shooting Party* (Viking, 1981), a subtle, elegantly written dissection of the British class system. The trilogy titles were published together in an omnibus edition, *The Orlando Trilogy* (Penguin, 1984), the first publication of numbers 2 and 3 in the United States.

1. *Orlando King* (Knopf, 1969) Successful British politician Orlando King learns that he was unwittingly responsible for his biological father's death only after he has married the man's attractive young widow.
2. *Orlando at the Brazen Threshold* (Bodley Head, 1971) Orlando successfully pursues the mistress of his nephew, who is married to his daughter. First published in the United States in *The Orlando Trilogy* (1984).
3. *Agatha* (Bodley Head, 1973) Set during the Suez crisis (1956), this novel focuses on the sacrifices Orlando's daughter Agatha makes for her brother Paul, who has been convicted of treason. First published in the United States in *The Orlando Trilogy* (1984).

Coleman, Lonnie

Readers who enjoyed *Gone with the Wind* will sink happily into Coleman's Beulah Land trilogy. The story of the Kendrick family and the development of their Georgia plantation begins in 1800 and takes the reader to the Civil War, Reconstruction, and beyond. Lots of action and lusty characters keep the saga sizzling along.

1. *Beulah Land* (Doubleday, 1973) Details the founding of Beulah Land and its flowering during pre–Civil War days.
2. *Look Away, Beulah Land* (Doubleday, 1977) The end of the Civil War and the period of Reconstruction are hard times for the Kendricks and their land.
3. *Legacy of Beulah Land, The* (Doubleday, 1980) Hard-won stability returns to the Georgia plantation, but social progress brings new challenges.

Coleman, Reed Farrel

I. Brooklyn PI Moe Prager is the protagonist of four hard-boiled mysteries set in New York in the late 1970s and early 1980s. Prager, a cop retired by a knee injury, now primarily a Manhattan wine merchant, is happily married and a proud father, but somehow events keep forcing him into activating his inactive private investigator's license. The Prager mysteries are successful blends of whodunits with police procedurals and an appealing detective. Coleman is himself a Brooklyn native.

1. *Walking the Perfect Square* (Permanent, 2001) The job of Moe Prager, retired ex-cop, is to find Patrick Maloney, the son of another cop who left a party one night 20 years ago and has not been seen since.
2. *Redemption Street* (Viking, 2004) It's 1981 and Moe Prager is happy in his new incarnation as a Manhattan wine merchant, husband, and father. When Moe decides to help cover up the disappearance of his wife's brother, he is reminded of a 15-year-old missing-person case.
3. *James Deans, The* (Plume, 2004) At a high-society wedding, Moe is recruited to the cause of charismatic state senator Steven Brightman, whose political career was stalled by the disappearance of an attractive young intern more than a year earlier. Shades of Gary Condit and Chandra Levy.
4. *Soul Patch* (Bleak House, 2007) Old friend Larry McDonald, chief of detectives of the NYPD, slips Moe a covertly recorded tape of an interrogation of a snitch claiming to know the secret behind the murder of Dexter Mayweather, a drug dealer in the early 1970s.
5. *Empty Ever After* (Bleak House, 2008) Has Patrick Maloney returned from the dead to haunt Moe and his former wife Katy?

II. Another Coleman series set in the New York area features wisecracking insurance investigator and aspiring noir writer Dylan Klein. These novels are, in some ways, a harkening back to the pulp fiction of the 1930s and 1940s. The dialogue is salty and witty. Klein's sex life is enviably active for a supposedly tired 40-year-old, and the plots are complicated but convincing.

1. *Life Goes Sleeping* (Permanent, 1991) On a nostalgic trip back to Brighton Beach, Dylan Klein runs into a Russian named Alexander Korin, who hires Klein to track down a man named Mikhail Brodsky, whose life he supposedly saved during World War II.
2. *Little Easter* (Permanent, 1993) After a middle-aged woman enters the bar that Klein is tending, asking for "Johnny Blue," Klein finds a diamond necklace on the floor and, eventually, the woman's still-warm corpse with her mouth stuffed with a yellow bird.
3. *They Don't Play Stickball in Milwaukee* (Permanent, 1997) On the trail of his missing nephew, Zak, Dylan Klein finds himself on the campus of an upstate New York college and engaged in steamy sex with Kira Watanabe, a Japanese girl half his age. But is Kira really on the level?

Colette, Sidonie-Gabrielle

I. *Claudine at School* was an immediate best seller in France when it was first published, in 1900. The story of the intelligent and vivacious Claudine has important parallels in Colette's life. The first four Claudine books were written in collaboration with her husband, "Willy," Henri Gauthier-Vilars, and published under the pseudonym of "Willy." *Retreat from Love*, which is not always included with the other Claudine books, was written after Colette broke away from Willy. Numbers 1 through 4 are collected in *The Complete Claudine* (Farrar, 1976), translated by Antonia White (q.v.).

1. *Claudine at School* (Boni, 1930) Fifteen-year-old Claudine records the events of her last year at school in a journal full of schoolgirl gushing and innuendo. First published in 1900 as *Claudine a l'ecole*. Translated by Janet Flanner in 1930. Translated by Antonia White in *The Complete Claudine*.
2. *Young Lady of Paris* (Boni, 1931) Now 17, Claudine has come to Paris to live with her father; she moves into society and falls in

love. First published in 1901 as *Claudine a Paris*. Translated by James Whitall. Translated as *Claudine in Paris* by Antonia White in *The Complete Claudine*.

3. **Indulgent Husband, The (Farrar, 1935)** Though Claudine and Renaud love each other, their marriage leaves her dissatisfied, and she has a brief lesbian affair. First published in 1902 as *Claudine en menage*. Translated by Frederick A. Blossom. Translated by Antonia White as *Claudine Married* in *The Complete Claudine*.

4. **Innocent Wife, The (Farrar, 1935)** Claudine, reunited with her husband, plays a secondary role in this book, which is the journal of her friend Annie. First published in 1903 as *Claudine s'en va*. Translated by Frederick A. Blossom. Translated as *Claudine and Annie* by Antonia White in *The Complete Claudine*.

5. **Retreat from Love (Indiana University Press, 1974)** A solo effort by Colette, not always included in the Claudine series. Claudine and Renaud are reasonably content, but Annie and Claudine's stepson, Marcel, is compulsively seeking young male bodies. First published in 1907 as *La retraite sentimentale*. Translated by Margaret Crosland.

II. The two books in which Chéri figure are considered among the finest of Colette's mature works. They concern Lea, an aging courtesan, and her handsome young lover, Chéri. Edmee, the rich young woman Chéri marries, plays a minor role. The two novels were published in the United States in a one-volume edition: *Chéri and the Last of Chéri* (Farrar, 1951).

1. **Chéri (Boni, 1930)** Their separation proves devastating for both Lea and Chéri. Paris in 1912 is the setting. First published in 1920 as *Chéri*. Translated by Janet Flanner.

2. **Last of Chéri, The (Putnam, 1932)** Chéri, six years later and a war hero, is still unable to adapt to life without Lea. First published in 1926 as *La fin de Chéri*. Translated by Roger Senhouse.

III. *The Vagabond* and *The Shackle* have strong autobiographical connotations. They describe two love affairs of Renee Nere, the narrator, a woman in her thirties, divorced, author of two books, and stage actress. In *The Vagabond*, Renee resists love. In *The Shackle*, Renee succumbs to love. The novels were published under the name of "Colette Willy." *The Vagabond* was adapted as a play (1923) and as a screenplay (1917; 1931). For a description of the novels' impact on a young American reader, see Vivian Gornick's essay "Love with a Capital L," collected in *Rereadings* (edited by Anne Fadiman; Farrar, 2005).

1. **Vagabond, The (Farrar, 1955)** Renée Nere, a woman in her thirties, a divorced author and actress, has an affair with a man named Max. Translated by Enid McLeod. Originally published in 1910 as *La vagabonde*. Translated by Charlotte Remfry-Kidd as *Renée la vagabonde* (Doubleday, 1931).

2. **Shackle, The (Farrar, 1963)** Four years later, Renée, now retired from the stage, has another affair, this time with a man named Jean. Originally published in 1913 as *L'entrav*. Translated by Antonia White. Variant title: *The Captive*. Translated as *Recaptured* by Viola Girard Garvin (Doubleday, 1932).

Colley, Barbara

Charlotte La Rue's maid-for-a-day business has many clients in the exclusive, historic Garden District of New Orleans. Charlotte is a 59-year-old single mother with a son who is a doctor and a niece who is a homicide detective. Charlotte's clients have a habit of dying in suspicious fashions, and Charlotte sometimes finds herself in the role of amateur detective in this series of cozies. For other novels about cleaning lady detectives see Barbara Neely (q.v.) and Kathy Hogan Trocheck (q.v.). Barbara Colley, who was born and lives in Louisiana, has also written several Harlequin romances as Anne Logan.

1. **Maid for Murder (Kensington, 2002)** Jackson Dubuisson, a long-time client of Charlotte La Rue's maid-for-a-day cleaning service, is found dead in the study of his home in New Orleans's Garden District, and his widow, Jeanne, is acting in a distinctly suspicious manner.

2. **Death Tidies Up (Kensington, 2003)** A nearly naked corpse found in a closet turns out to be New Orleans real-estate mogul Drew Bergeron, whose funeral La Rue attended two years earlier.

3. **Polished Off (Kensington, 2004)** The bones falling out of a cracked urn may belong to the long-missing ex-boyfriend of Charlotte's nephew's new wife.

4. **Wiped Out (Kensington, 2004)** Nasty society lady Mimi Adams, who has clawed her way to the presidency of the Horticulture Heritage Society, is felled by some fatal jimsonweed.

5. **Married to the Mop (Kensington, 2006)** When Mob boss Robert Rossi turns up dead at his own party, his wife, Emily, is the leading suspect.

6. **Scrub-a-Dub-Dead (Kensington, 2007)** A young woman is found strangled, apparently with a red scarf, at New Orleans's Jazzy Hotel.

7. **Wash and Die (Kensington, 2008)** Even Charlotte's New Orleans police detective niece thinks Charlotte may be involved when Charlotte stumbles on the body of Louis Thibodeaux's ex-wife.

Collignon, Rick

A small, dusty New Mexico village is the scene for the Guadalupe trilogy, a trio of "magic realism" novels steeped in art, mysticism and the supernatural. Ramona Montoya, the main character of number 1, lives on familiar terms with the ghosts of dead relatives, while her brother Flavio, who plays prominent roles in numbers 1 and 3, is distinctly disturbed by these specters. Anglo Will Sawyer, who becomes interested in a bizarre past happening in the town, is the protagonist of number 2. Some readers found the trilogy, with its spare style, deadpan humor, and dreamy, melancholic atmosphere, engrossing; others were put off by the large number of flashbacks and shifts from present to past and the palpable sentimentality. New Mexico native Rick Collignon has made a living as a roofer for more than 20 years.

1. **Journal of Antonio Montoya, The (MacMurray & Beck, 1996)** Guadalupe, New Mexico, native Ramona Montoya, whose house is inhabited by the ghosts of a host of dead relatives, adopts her young nephew Jose after his parents are killed and eventually becomes custodian of the 1924 journal of sculptor Antonio Montoya, another relative.

2. **Perdido (MacMurray & Beck, 1997)** Will Sawyer, one of the few Anglos living in Guadalupe, gets involved with the story of a young Anglo woman who was found hanging from a bridge more than 20 years earlier but finds the villagers distinctly troubled and unforthcoming about this past tragedy.

3. **Santo in the Image of Cristobal Garcia, A (BlueHen, 2002)** Flavio, Ramona Montoya's estranged brother, is suspected of starting the mysterious fire that enveloped the village of Guadalupe.

Collins, Brandilyn

I. Annie Kingston, who has moved to the small town of Grove Landing for safety and quiet after the murder of her husband, finds that her abilities as a forensic artist draw her into a series of dangerous situations from which her trust in God extracts her. Evangelical Christian suspense novels are still a fairly rare commodity, so the Hidden Faces series of Zondervan (the Christian division of HarperCollins) mainstay Brandilyn Collins are likely to be of interest to readers who like their forensic mysteries laced with religion. Collins, the daughter of Christian missionaries to India, divides her time between Idaho and California.

1. *Brink of Death* (**Zondervan, 2004**) Annie Kingston finds her feelings of peace and safety shattered after she draws a composite picture of a murder suspect.
2. *Stain of Guilt* (**Zondervan, 2004**) Annie Kingston is persuaded, again, to draw a composite sketch of a killer, this time of the man who killed her husband 20 years earlier.
3. *Dead of Night* (**Zondervan, 2005**) Kingston turns to God and the power of prayer to help catch a serial killer in Redding, California.
4. *Web of Lies* (**Zondervan, 2006**) In the fourth and final book of the Hidden Faces series, Annie Kingston joins forces with Chelsea Adams (see series II) in a battle against "time, greed, and a deadly opponent."

II. Californian Chelsea Adams has a supernatural gift for visions where she sees events that elude ordinary, ungifted people such as her husband, software entrepreneur Paul. This power gets her into some sticky situations in this pair of Christian suspense novels. Chelsea Adams also appears as a character in *Web of Lies* (see series I).

1. *Eyes of Elisha* (**Zondervan, 2001**) When Chelsea Adams has dinner with Gavil Harrison, a candidate for a position at her husband Paul's software company, she is horrified by her vision that Harrison has murdered a young female jogger.
2. *Dread Champion* (**Zondervan, 2002**) Chelsea is reluctant to be a juror at the murder trial of Darren Welk, whose wife, Shawna, has disappeared.

III. The small town of Bradleyville, Kentucky, is the nexus between three loosely connected Evangelical Christian novels that can be read as stand-alones or as a series. Female characters are the protagonists in all three novels, in which Christian faith eventually produces happy endings.

1. *Cast a Road before Me* (**Zondervan, 2001**) City girl Jessie, orphaned at 16, struggles to adjust to life in small-town Bradleyville, Kentucky, with an aunt and uncle she barely knows. Then she finds herself drawn into an impending mill workers' strike that threatens violence.
2. *Color the Sidewalk for Me* (**Zondervan, 2002**) Thirty-five-year-old Celia Matthews, who left her home in Bradleyville 17 years before, because she felt responsible for her brother's bicycle accident, has made a career for herself as an account executive in Little Rock, Arkansas, but still hasn't shaken her guilt feelings and bitterness toward her mother.
3. *Capture the Wind for Me* (**Zondervan, 2003**) After the death of her mother, 14-year-old Jackie Delham is left to bring up her two younger siblings and run the household for her father. Then her father falls in love with Bradleyville's "prodigal daughter," Katherine May King.

IV. The novels in the Kanner Lake series, set in a resort community in northern Idaho, are a loosely connected series of mysteries.

1. *Violet Dawn* (**Zondervan, 2006**) Paige Wiliams, a young woman fleeing her past, secludes herself in the resort community of Kanner Lake in northern Idaho. When she discovers a dead body, Paige hides the truth rather than going to the police.
2. *Coral Moon* (**Zondervan, 2007**) Kanner Lake reporter Leslie finds herself in the heart of a mystery investigation when a dead body is found in the front seat of her car.
3. *Crimson Eve* (**Zondervan, 2007**) Has the secret from her teenage years caught up with Carla Radling in remote northern Idaho?

Collins, Jackie

I. Jackie Collins writes the kind of story her actress sister starred in—Joan was Alexis in *Dynasty*. So it's not surprising that her turbulent tales about glamorous, rich, and sexy people have been made into TV miniseries (e.g., *The World Is Full of Married Women* and *Hollywood Wives*). In *Chances*, the first of many best sellers, Collins stirs crime, showbiz, and the lives of the rich and famous into her usual spicy brew. Although mafioso Gino Santangelo was featured in *Chances*, his rich, gorgeous, sexy, take-no-prisoners daughter Lucky takes center stage in the sequels.

1. *Chances* (**Warner, 1981**) The rise of Carrie from prostitution in Harlem, drug addiction, and a stretch in an insane asylum to the position of millionaire society hostess is paralleled by Gino Santangelo's climb up the organized crime ladder.
2. *Lucky* (**Simon & Schuster, 1985**) Lucky Santangelo, Gino's daughter, is the successful manager of a Las Vegas hotel, but unhappy in her personal life until she falls in love with young comedian Lennie Golden.
3. *Lady Boss* (**Simon & Schuster, 1990**) Lucky maneuvers to buy a film studio for her husband, Lennie.
4. *Vendetta: Lucky's Revenge* (**HarperCollins, 1996**) Lucky's enemy Donna Landsman (née Donatella Bonnatti) stages a hostile takeover of Panther Studios, has Gino shot, and arranges the disappearance of Lennie Golden while on location in Corsica.
5. *Dangerous Kiss* (**Simon & Schuster, 1999**) Mary Lou, the actress wife of Lucky's black half brother Steven, is killed during a carjacking. Brigette, heiress, supermodel, and Lucky's goddaughter, is forcibly addicted to heroin while pregnant. Alex Woods, director and sharer of a one-night stand with Lucky, is still after Lucky. Lennie seems to have fathered a hearing-impaired son with Claudia, who rescued him from a Sicilian cave. And so it goes . . .
6. *Drop Dead Beautiful* (**St. Martin's, 2007**) Lucky plans Gino's 95th birthday party while building a Las Vegas mega-resort, unaware that family foe Anthony Bonar is plotting revenge.

II. Celebrity journalist Madison Castelli is the star of another Las Vegas and Hollywood "beautiful people" series. Madison was introduced in the L.A. Connections miniseries, four paperback originals that were subsequently published in one volume as *L.A. Connections*. As with the Lucky series, the Castelli series combines gangsterism, violence, sex, and glamour in an unlikely but readable mix.

1. *L.A. Connections* (**Pocket Books, 1999**) Madison Castelli's assignment for *Manhattan Style* magazine takes her to Hollywood to interview talent agent Freddie Leon. The murder of a starlet whom she has just interviewed distracts her. Originally published in four parts:
   1. *Power* (**Pocket Books, 1998**)
   2. *Obsession* (**Pocket Books, 1998**)

3. *Murder* (**Pocket Books, 1998**)

4. *Revenge* (**Pocket Books, 1998**)

2. ***Lethal Seduction*** (**Simon & Schuster, 2000**) Madison, disenchanted with men but still hopeful, broods about her unhappy childhood, concerning which she discovers more unpleasant truths, while friends and acquaintances carry on with their messy love lives.

3. ***Deadly Embrace*** (**Simon & Schuster, 2002**) A prequel-sequel to numbers 1 and 2. Madison Castelli's father, Michael, a tycoon with gangland connections, has been accused of murdering two women: Madison's biological mother and the woman Madison believed to be her mother.

III. The novels with *Hollywood* in the title seem to have no link except for the titles, Hollywood settings, and the shenanigans Collins's characters get involved in.

1. *Hollywood Wives* (**Simon & Schuster, 1983**)

2. *Hollywood Husbands* (**Simon & Schuster, 1986**)

3. *Hollywood Kids* (**Simon & Schuster, 1994**)

4. *Hollywood Wives: The New Generation* (**Simon & Schuster, 2001**)

5. *Hollywood Divorces* (**Simon & Schuster, 2003**)

Collins, Max Allan

I. Max Allan Collins is a prolific writer: detective novels; novelizations of movies (e.g., *Saving Private Ryan*) and television series (*CSI: Crime Scene Investigation*; *Dark Angel*); scripts for comics (*Dick Tracy* and *Ms. Tree*); and graphic novels (e.g., *The Road to Perdition*). He also edits Mickey Spillane anthologies and a series of vintage pinup collections issued by Collector's Press.

Collins's Nathan (Nate) Heller books, probably his best-known and best-regarded works, are historical detective stories set in the 1930s and 1940s. Private eye Heller's sleuthing involves him with some of the most famous cases and personalities of the era: the Lindbergh kidnapping; Huey Long's assassination; gangsters Al Capone, John Dillinger, Frank Nitti, and Bugsy Siegel; Amelia Earhart; the Black Dahlia; and Frank Sinatra, to name a few. Nathan's base is Chicago, but his work takes him to such hot spots as Washington, DC, Hollywood, Hawaii, and Las Vegas. The critically acclaimed series is a satisfying mix of fact and fiction complete with period photographs and explanatory "afterwords." Listed according to chronology rather than publication date.

1. ***True Detective*** (**St. Martin's, 1983**) Young Nathan Heller, disgusted by the corruption in the Chicago police force of the 1930s, turns in his badge and goes private.

2. ***Stolen Away*** (**Bantam, 1991**) Nathan investigates the Lindbergh kidnapping and forms a revisionist view of what really happened.

3. ***Damned in Paradise*** (**Dutton, 1996**) In 1932, working for Clarence Darrow, Heller goes to Hawaii to investigate the alleged abduction and rape of a navy lieutenant's wife and the subsequent murder of the mixed-raced suspect by the woman's husband, Thomas Massie, and his mother-in-law.

4. ***True Crime*** (**St. Martin's, 1985**) In 1934 Nathan finds himself set up as a patsy in a scheme to locate and kill Public Enemy Number One John Dillinger.

5. ***Blood and Thunder*** (**Dutton, 1995**) Heller is hired by Huey Long's family and insurance company to investigate the rumor that Huey was accidentally killed by his own guards.

6. ***Flying Blind*** (**Dutton, 1998**) Lured out of semiretirement in 1970 to return to Saipan to provide background for a film about Amelia Earhart, Nathan recollects his involvement with Amelia before and after her famous disappearance in the 1930s.

7. ***Million Dollar Wound, The*** (**St. Martin's, 1986**) Hearst columnist Westbrook Pegler and movie star Robert Montgomery ask Nathan to get the goods on Willy Bioff, corrupt head of the Movie Technicians' Union.

8. ***Carnal Hours*** (**Dutton, 1994**) In 1943 the soon-to-be-murdered Sir Harry Oakes hires Nate to get the goods on his son-in-law.

9. ***Neon Mirage*** (**St. Martin's, 1988**) In 1946 Nathan falls in love and gets caught up in the Las Vegas underworld of Bugsy Siegel.

10. ***Angel in Black*** (**New American Library, 2001**) Heller, newly married, goes to Los Angeles to publicize his partnership with a California-based PI and becomes involved in the notorious Black Dahlia murder case.

11. ***Majic Man*** (**Dutton, 1999**) In 1949 James V. Forrestal, US Secretary of Defense, a longtime client, hires Nathan to investigate what he feels are Communist forces in the government who have him under surveillance.

12. ***Chicago Confidential*** (**New American Library, 2002**) In 1950 Senator Kefauver is investigating organized crime, and Nathan is back in Chicago, investigating the murder of an ex-policeman who once saved his life. Jayne Mansfield and (a supposedly washed-up) Frank Sinatra put in appearances.

13. ***Dying in the Postwar World*** (**Foul Play, 1991**) A collection of an original novelette and five previously published short stories from the Heller casebook.

14. ***Kisses of Death*** (**Crippen & Landru, 2001**) Subtitle: *A Nathan Heller Casebook*. Short stories.

II. Another historical crime series features "Untouchable" Eliot Ness (who also appears in some of the Nathan Heller books) in his post-Capone career in Cleveland. Many historical characters besides Ness turn up in these pages.

1. ***Dark City, The*** (**Bantam, 1987**) After his role in jailing Al Capone, Eliot Ness is hired to clean up Cleveland's corrupt police department.

2. ***Butcher's Dozen*** (**Bantam, 1988**) Someone is killing and cutting up the bodies of tramps living in Cleveland's hobo jungles.

3. ***Bullet Proof*** (**Bantam, 1989**) In 1937 the incorruptible Ness is the target for a Mob hit man.

4. ***Murder by the Numbers*** (**St. Martin's, 1993**) Eliot goes after the Mayfield Road numbers gang. Chester Himes (q.v.) appears in a cameo.

III. Collins is producing another historical mystery series, this time associated with famous disasters, but with no connecting characters. They are listed below without annotations.

1. *Titanic Murders, The* (**Berkley, 1999**)

2. *Lusitania Murders, The* (**Berkley, 2002**)

3. *Hindenburg Murders, The* (**Berkley, 2000**)

4. *Pearl Harbor Murders, The* (**Berkley, 2001**)

5. *London Blitz Murders, The* (**Berkley, 2004**)

IV. Mallory (no first name) is an aspiring mystery writer who lives in a small town in Iowa, is based on Collins, who is Iowa born and bred. Mallory is a likable young man who gets personally involved as an amateur investigator when crime crosses his path.

1. ***Baby Blue Rip-Off, The*** (**Walker, 1983**) While delivering hot meals to shut-ins, Mallory discovers a murder.

2. ***No Cure for Death*** (**Walker, 1983**) Mallory defends a woman from an apparent attack and finds himself involved in murder.

3. ***Kill Your Darlings*** (**Walker, 1984**) In Chicago for a convention of mystery lovers, Mallory finds his idol, best-selling author Roscoe

Kane, the victim of sudden death in a mystery involving an unpublished Dashiell Hammett (q.v.) manuscript.

4. *Shroud for Aquarius, A* (Walker, 1984) Troubled by the apparent suicide of his high school friend, Ginnie Mullins, Mallory turns up an unsavory past.

5. *Nice Weekend for a Murder* (Walker, 1986) An unpopular critic is murdered at a mystery weekend in upstate New York.

V. Nolan (no first name), peripatetic mobster-thief-killer, is the protagonist in a series of mostly paperback only novels. Numbers 2 through 7 were published under the name "Max Collins." They are listed below without annotations.

1. *Mourn the Living* (Five Star, 1999) Written in the 1960s but unpublished until 1999, this was the novel where the Nolan character was created.

2. *Bait Money* (Curtis, 1973) Reissued in a revised edition by Pinnacle (1981).

3. *Blood Money* (Curtis, 1973) Reissued in a revised edition by Pinnacle (1981)

4. *Fly Paper* (Pinnacle, 1981)

5. *Hush Money* (Pinnacle, 1981)

6. *Hard Cash* (Pinnacle, 1982)

7. *Scratch Fever* (Pinnacle, 1982)

8. *Spree* (Tor, 1987)

VI. Quarry (another one-name protagonist) is a professional killer whose activities were pretty much confined to paperback originals until Foul Play reprinted them. *Quarry's Greatest Hits* (Five Star, 2003) contains number 5 and three stories. They are listed below without annotations.

1. *Broker, The* (Berkley, 1976) Reprinted by Foul Play in 1985 as *Quarry*.

2. *Broker's Wife, The* (Berkley, 1976) Reprinted by Foul Play in 1985 as *Quarry's List*.

3. *Dealer, The* (Berkley, 1976) Reprinted by Foul Play in 1986 as *Quarry's Deal*.

4. *Slasher, The* (Berkley, 1977) Reprinted by Foul Play in 1986 as *Quarry's Cut*.

5. *Primary Target* (Foul Play, 1987)

6. *Last Quarry, The* (Hard Case Crime, 2006)

Collins, Nancy A(verill)

American writer Nancy A. Collins's Sonja Blue series is another entry in the vampire sweepstakes. Sonja Blue, in life a British lady named Denise, had been introduced to death and vampiredom by a 700-year-old vampire named Morgan. Sonja is a reluctant vampire, what's left of her human personality constantly at battle with "The Other," her vampire self with whom she coexists in a Jekyll-and-Hyde relationship, and her human self has vowed to destroy Morgan and his kind. The series is not for the squeamish, or those who don't like raw sex and gore, or who are not turned on by the "dark side," even if infused with black humor. Numbers 1 through 3 were published together in the omnibus volume *Midnight Blue* (White Wolf, 1995).

1. *Sunglasses after Dark* (Onyx, 1989) Sonja Blue, née Denise Thorne, who has constant inner battles with "the Other," her vampire self, broods in prison about her introduction to vampiredom in Britain, her journey to America, and the bloody crimes to which her vampire self is prone.

2. *In the Blood* (Roc, 1992) Sonja teams up with detective William Palmer to track down her vampire overlord Morgan and his fellow Pretenders, who lead an underground life in the seamier parts of America.

3. *Paint It Black* (New English Library [UK], 1995) The story of Sonja and Morgan, her 700-year-old vampire creator, are told in shifting points-of-view, amid ruminations on the bleakness of late 20th-century love. Published in the United States in the omnibus *Midnight Blue* (White Wolf, 1995).

4. *Dozen Black Roses, A* (White Wolf, 1996) Younger vampire Esher is planning to take over Deadtown's ruler Sinjon's realm, but Sonja Blue, still seeking revenge against vampires, is out to destroy the whole vampire operation.

5. *Darkest Heart* (White Wolf, 2002) The human vampire hunter Jack Estes is stalking Sonja with the intention of killing her but, discovering her dual nature, joins with her to hunt down the vampire Noir, who was responsible for the death of his parents.

6. *Dead Roses for a Blue Lady* (Crossroad, 2002) Collected short stories about Sonja Blue, with an interview in which author Collins discusses the origins and popularity of her character.

Combs, Harry (Benjamin)

Colorado mountain man Cat Brules and engineer, pilot, and rancher Steven Cartwright are the protagonists in a trilogy of novels set in the American West from 1867 to 1950. The first two novels, told by Cat Brules, evoke his violent life and times in the Old West and brushes with historical characters such as General Crook and Butch Cassidy and events such as the Fetterman Massacre and Custer's Last Stand. In the third novel, which critics felt to be somewhat of a letdown, Cat's interlocutor, Steven Cartwright, relates the story of his life as an air pioneer and war hero. Harry Combs (d. 2003), who didn't start publishing fiction until his late seventies, was an air pioneer (president of Combs Aircraft, which eventually became Gates Learjet Corporation) and rancher himself.

1. *Brules* (Lyford, 1992) In 1916 Colorado mountain man Cat Brules relates, to young engineering student Steven Cartwright, the story of his life, including the 1867 homicide of his trail boss in a fight over a prostitute and his vendetta against the Indians.

2. *Scout, The* (Delacorte, 1995) Cat Brules continues his narration of his role in frontier events from 1874 to 1883, which included being with Custer on the Little Bighorn campaign against the Sioux and his later exploits among the Nez Percé, Utes, and Apaches.

3. *Legend of the Painted Horse, The* (Delacorte, 1996) In 1950 Steven Cartwright, now a 52-year-old Colorado rancher, narrates to his beautiful 24-year-old companion his exploits as an athlete, air ace, war hero, and ladies' man.

Comfort, B(arbara)

Tish McWhinny is a seventysomething amateur detective who lives in a small town in southern Vermont. With her "boyfriend," the octogenarian Hilary Oats, and her "adopted" niece Sophie, the unusually spry Tish often gets involved with murder in a series of not particularly believable but enjoyable lightweight cozies. B. Comfort is an artist who published her first novel at the age of 66.

1. *Phoebe's Knee* (Landgrove, 1986) Elderly but spry artist Tish McWhinny, of the fictitious town of Lofton, Vermont, gets embroiled when a "cult" moves into her neighborhood.

2. *Grave Consequences* (Landgrove, 1989) Tish thinks that she sees the body of her friend, but the body disappears when she goes for help. Is murder involved?

3. *Cashmere Kid, The* (Countryman, 1993) Tish is left in charge of Sophie Beaumont's herd of Cashmere goats, then the valuable stud goat disappears and Sophie's neighbor Stu Simpson is beaten to death with a golf club.

4. *Elusive Quarry* (Foul Play, 1995) Sophie and her new boyfriend are suspected by federal T-agents of blowing up her own house with dynamite, while Tish's ancient pal Hilary Oats is subjected to heavy pressure to sell his land.

5. *Pair for the Queen, A* (Foul Play, 1998) After Tish restores an old unsigned dog painting for Hilary's godson, she is chagrined to find the painting for sale with a famous signature attached to it.

Conant, Susan

Dog lovers will respond to the adventures of Holly Winter, Cambridge, Massachusetts–based columnist for *Dog's Life*, and her two Alaskan malamutes, Rowdy and Kimi. Holly exposes puppy mills, deals out copious information on dogs and dog training, and solves the occasional murder. Conant is Massachusetts coordinator for the Alaskan Malamute Protection League.

1. *New Leash on Death, A* (Berkley, 1990) When Dr. Standish is strangled with his malamute Rowdy's leash, Holly adopts the bereaved dog.

2. *Dead and Doggone* (Berkley, 1990) A gossipy dog trainer is done in with a pair of grooming shears.

3. *Bite of Death, A* (Berkley, 1991) Malamute Kimi may have witnessed the murder of her therapist owner.

4. *Paws before Dying* (Berkley, 1992) The death of retired kindergarten teacher Rose Engleman is attributed to a lightning bolt.

5. *Gone to the Dogs* (Doubleday, 1992) Highly regarded veterinarian Oscar Peterson has disappeared.

6. *Bloodlines* (Doubleday, 1992) A local pet shop appears to be selling a Malamute obtained from "a puppy mill" or dog-breeding "factory."

7. *Ruffly Speaking* (Doubleday, 1994) A hearing guide dog with behavior problems and a murdered bookseller attract the interest of Holly and her canine companions.

8. *Black Ribbon* (Doubleday, 1995) The obnoxious owner of an untrained Lab is spoiling a week at Wagging Tail, a Maine camp for dog lovers.

9. *Stud Rites* (Doubleday, 1996) Two people connected with a prized malamute stud are killed during a malamute show. Holly inadvertently handles the murder weapon.

10. *Animal Appetite* (Doubleday, 1997) The death by poison, 18 years ago, of small-press-publisher Jack Andrews was called suicide by some and murder by others. Holly is attracted by the fact that Jack's purebred golden retriever was tied up in his office at the time.

11. *Barker Street Regulars, The* (Doubleday, 1998) Holly and Rowdy, now a certified therapy dog, regular visitors to a Cambridge nursing home, become involved with Althea Battlefield, elderly Sherlock Holmes fanatic.

12. *Evil Breeding* (Doubleday, 1999) Holly, under contract for a book of photographs about the famous Morris and Essex Dog Shows, encounters B. Robert Motherway and his rather sinister household.

13. *Creature Discomforts* (New American Library, 2000) Holly wakes up on the edge of a cliff finding herself hurt and amnesiac, not even remembering Rowdy and Kim.

14. *Wicked Flea, The* (Berkley, 2002) Holly seeks out the help of a therapist to deal with her father's second marriage, her ex-lover's marriage, and her recovery from amnesia. Rowdy is attacked by a golden retriever, and its owner turns up murdered two weeks later.

15. *Dogfather, The* (Berkley, 2003) Crime boss Enzio Guarini would seem to be unsuitable for the likes of Holly Winter. However, he is a fellow dog fanatic, has an irresistible four-month-old elkhound, and is a fan of Holly's writing on puppy training.

16. *Bride and Groom* (Berkley, 2004) Holly's new dog-treat cookbook is a hit, and she's about to marry a veterinarian, but a couple of murders put a damper on her celebration.

17. *Gaits of Heaven* (Berkley, 2006) After Holly agrees to housebreak Dolfo, a golden Aussie "huskapoo," she finds its owner, therapist Eumie Dean, dead of a drug overdose.

18. *All Shots* (Berkley, 2007) Winter goes searching for a missing dog, an alleged Siberian husky named Strike, and instead finds a woman's corpse.

Condé, Maryse (Boucolon)

Guadeloupe-born, Sorbonne-educated Condé has written a pair of novels that traces several generations of a family in the West African kingdom of Segu (now Mali) from 1797 to 1860. The Traore family is torn by colonialism, the slave trade, and the conflicting claims of Christianity and Islam. The novels, best sellers in France, are rich in historical detail, lyrical prose, and authentic West African settings.

1. *Segu* (Viking, 1987) Dousaka Traore, a Bambara noble caught up in court intrigue, sees his sons travel on different paths. Original title: *Ségou: Les murrailles de terre*. Translated from the French by Barbara Bray.

2. *Children of Segu, The* (Viking, 1989) The Traore family grapples with the chaotic religious wars of the 19th century. Original title: *Ségou II: La terre en miettes*. Translated from the French by Linda Coverdale.

Condon, Richard

I. The Prizzi saga is a satirical look at an American Mafia family rather than a family saga like Mario Puzo's (q.v.) *The Godfather*. As portrayed by the late Richard Condon (d. 1996), the Prizzis' operations are more like legitimate business enterprises catering to public demand rather than criminal activities. Professional killers like Charley Partanna and Irene Walker seem quite ordinary and even likable, a view reinforced by the movie version of *Prizzi's Honor,* starring Jack Nicholson and Kathleen Turner. Condon's cynical view of human nature and institutions is displayed in such best sellers as *The Manchurian Candidate* (McGraw-Hill, 1959) and *Winter Kills* (Dial, 1974) as well as the Prizzi series.

1. *Prizzi's Family* (Putnam, 1986) In a prequel to *Prizzi's Honor,* Charley Partanna, hit man for the Prizzi crime empire, is torn between his love for showgirl-heiress Mardell La Tour and his duty to marry Maerose Prizzi, the Don's granddaughter.

2. *Prizzi's Honor* (Coward, 1982) Ten years after the events in *Prizzi's Family,* Charley must choose again between love and duty when he falls for Irene Walker, a freelance professional killer who has stolen money from a Prizzi operation in Las Vegas.

3. *Prizzi's Glory* (Dutton, 1988) The Prizzis try to transform Charley into America's most respected businessman to capture the White House in the 1992 presidential election.

4. *Prizzi's Money* (Crown, 1994) A complicated plot involving the kidnapping of wealthy presidential advisor Henry George Asbury gets even more complicated when Henry's wife gets into the act.

II. Two novels about former Royal Navy officer Colin Huntington, a compulsive gambler, never attracted the attention that the Prizzi series or *The Manchurian Candidate* did, but they are still worth reading for Condon's signature satirical wit and writing skill.

1. *Arigato* (Dial, 1972) Former Royal Navy officer Colin Huntington is a compulsive gambler, a flaw that brings his life and the lives of those he loves to the edge of destruction. Set in London, Paris, Bordeaux, and Hong Kong.
2. *Bandicoot* (Dial, 1978) Trying to save his marriage and his honor, Huntington takes a job drilling for oil offshore but still manages to offend almost everyone with whom he comes into contact.

Connell, Evan S(helby)

These companion pieces are understanding portraits of a typical middle-class American family of the 1930s. The Bridges live in a good residential neighborhood, attend the local Congregational church, and worry about properly raising their three children. Walter is a lawyer who looks as though he was born wearing a suit and tie. India is usually competent, selfless, and always gracious. Connell's storytelling skill transforms what could be dull stories into fine literature. A 1990 film starring Paul Newman and Joanne Woodward, *Mr. and Mrs. Bridge*, was made from the two novels.

1. *Mrs. Bridge* (Viking, 1959) This series of vignettes shows India running an efficient home, negotiating the small dramas of family life with skill and kindness, and facing the approach of middle age with quiet resignation.
2. *Mr. Bridge* (Knopf, 1969) A good, though undemonstrative, husband and father, Walter Bridge is shown interacting with friends and family, deciding to buy a new car, explaining Prohibition to his daughter, and so forth.

Connelly, Michael

Hieronymous "Harry" Bosch is a smart, tough, driven homicide detective with the Los Angeles Police Department. Harry, who tends to get psychologically bruised by his brushes with evil, often gets into trouble with his superiors and his girlfriends because of his uncompromising attitude. So far he has been suspended, voluntarily retired, put on trial, placed under psychiatric care, rusticated to Beverly Hills, and suspected of serial murder. Along the way, he acquires a new investigatory team, a black woman named Kizmin Rider and a white veteran cop named Jerry Edgar. Numbers 5 and 7 were originally stand-alones, but characters from these novels are brought into later volumes in the series. The characters in *Void Moon* (Little, Brown, 2000) and *Chasing the Dime* (Little, Brown, 2002) haven't hooked up with Harry Bosch so far. Omnibus volumes include *The Harry Bosch Novels* (Little, Brown, 2001), containing numbers 1 through 3, and two volumes published by Orion (UK) called *The Harry Bosch Mysteries*, containing numbers 1 through 3 and numbers 4, 5, and 7.

1. *Black Echo, The* (Little, Brown, 1992) Former Los Angeles hero cop Bosch, farmed out to Beverly Hills, recognizes a corpse at the Mulholland Dam as that of an old Vietnam buddy.
2. *Black Ice* (Little, Brown, 1993) Black Ice, a lethal new street drug, may be behind the "suicide" of Harry's fellow police officer.

3. *Concrete Blonde, The* (Little, Brown, 1994) Did Bosch kill the wrong person when he shot the man he believed to be a serial killer?
4. *Last Coyote, The* (Little, Brown, 1995) On suspension for striking a superior officer, Harry finds time to investigate the unsolved murder of his own mother.
5. *Poet, The* (Little, Brown, 1996) Denver crime reporter Jack McEvoy and FBI agent Rachel Walling hook up in this suspense novel featuring a serial killer named the Poet. The Poet and Rachel Walling are characters in number 12.
6. *Trunk Music* (Little, Brown, 1996) Harry and his team investigate the murder of mobster Tony Aliso, found in the trunk of his Rolls Royce on Mulholland Drive.
7. *Blood Work* (Little, Brown, 1998) Ex–FBI profiler Terry McCaleb, recipient of a heart transplant, is informed that the donor of his new heart was murdered in an unsolved convenience store robbery. Terry reappears in number 9 (and see number 12).
8. *Angels Flight* (Little, Brown, 1999) Howard Elias, African American lawyer famous for his police brutality suits against the LAPD, is shot dead on a train in downtown Los Angeles.
9. *Darkness More Than Light, A* (Little, Brown, 2001) Terry McCaleb, ex–FBI agent from number 7, is asked by an old LAPD pal to help catch a ritualistic serial killer. Harry Bosch soon becomes McCaleb's prime suspect.
10. *City of Bones* (Little, Brown, 2002) The finding of the skeleton of an abused 12-year-old boy murdered around 1980 brings Harry on the case but arouses disturbing echoes from his own past.
11. *Lost Light* (Little, Brown, 2003) The disillusioned Harry retires from the LAPD but finds retirement boring. So he gets involved, this time as a private investigator, with a four-year-old murder case and Hollywood heist.
12. *Narrows, The* (Little, Brown, 2004) The Poet and Rachel Walling, characters in number 5, reappear, as Harry Bosch agrees to investigate the death of Terry McCaleb (numbers 7 and 9).
13. *Closers, The* (Little, Brown, 2005) Harry's first case after returning from retirement, reteaming him with former partner Kiz Rider, deals with the reopening of a 17-year-old mystery involving the murder of a mixed-race high school girl.
14. *Echo Park* (Little, Brown, 2006) Harry, a member of the LAPD Open-Unsolved Unit, repeatedly pulls out the file of the man who abducted 22-year-old equestrian Marie Gesto in 1993, to see if he can discover something new.
15. *Overlook, The* (Little, Brown, 2007) FBI agent Rachel Walling (see numbers 5 and 12) returns and tries to take over the case of the execution-murder of physicist Stanley Kent, claiming that it's a matter of National Security.

Connery, Tom

PSEUDONYM OF David Donachie

The Markham of the Marines trilogy is set just after the French Revolution but before Napoléon came to power. Irish bastard Lieutenant George Markham takes a British military commission in 1793 and sees action at Toulon, Corsica, and the Riviera. The Markham novels are full of action, intrigue, and cameo appearances by the likes of Horatio Nelson and Napoléon himself. Originally published in the United Kingdom. "Tom Connery" is the pseudonym of David Donachie (q.v.).

1. *Shred of Honour, A* (Regnery, 1999) Lieutenant George Markham, illegitimate son of an English general, who has several "blots on his scutcheon," finds himself in charge of a mixed bag of

British marines and army defending Toulon from French troops. Originally published in the United Kingdom in 1996.

2. *Honour Redeemed* **(Regnery, 2000)** Markham and Virginian Major Lanester are in charge of returning exiled Corsican patriot General Paoli to Corsica during the course of Horatio Nelson's attack on the island. Originally published in the United Kingdom in 1997.

3. *Honour Be Damned* **(Regnery, 2000)** Markham leads a motley band behind French lines on the Riviera, meets up again with archvillain Citizen Commissioner Fouquert, on the run from the Terror, and is unfairly denounced by the Hon. George Germain, captain of the HMS *Sylphide*.

Connolly, John

Charlie "Bird" Parker, a demon-driven former New York police detective, haunted by the murder of his wife and child, is the protagonist in a series of noir mysteries set in various parts of the United States. Parker is a brooder, and his cases are replete with bloodshed, suspense, monstrous villains, outré characters such as Bird's cronies Angel and Louis, a "gay odd couple," and a dollop of supernatural horror (à la Stephen King, whose Maine territory Parker invades). John Connolly is an Irish journalist and writer who often visits the United States. Connolly's unsettlingly off-center European view of violence-prone America adds to the tensions of this dark and bloody series. Parker makes a brief appearance in the horror tale set in Maine: *Bad Men* (Atria, 2004).

1. *Every Dead Thing* **(Simon & Schuster, 1999)** Grieving ex–NYC homicide detective Charlie "Bird" Parker follows the trails of a missing woman and a couple of gruesomely sadistic serial killers to Brooklyn, New Orleans, and a rural Virginia town.

2. *Dark Hollow* **(Simon & Schuster, 2001)** Relocated to the town of Scarborough, Maine, and newly licensed as a PI, Parker's efforts to get overdue child support from Billy Purdue lead to a hunt for a seemingly revived serial killer.

3. *Killing Kind, The* **(Simon & Schuster, 2002)** When Parker looks into the alleged suicide of Grace Peltier, a graduate student doing a dissertation on a group of religious extremists who disappeared four decades ago, he uncovers a nasty cult operating currently.

4. *White Road, The* **(Atria, 2003)** Bird reluctantly leaves Maine for Charleston, South Carolina, to investigate a racially charged murder case.

5. *Nocturnes* **(Atria, 2005)** A collection of supernatural horror stories including a Parker novella, "The Reflecting Eye," featuring a possibly haunted house once inhabited by an infamous killer.

6. *Black Angel, The* **(Atria, 2005)** A missing NYC prostitute leads to the Czech Republic and the Black Angel, a statue associated for centuries with various evildoers and perhaps a sanguinary spirit.

7. *Unquiet, The* **(Atria, 2007)** Parker is retained by Rebecca Clay to protect her against stalker Frank Merrick, who believes that she knows the whereabouts of her father, Daniel, a child psychiatrist who disappeared years before.

Connor, Beverly

I. Lindsay Chamberlain is a forensic archaeologist operating out of a Georgia university. Lindsay combines her knowledge of archaeology and osteology to solve decades-old, sometimes centuries-old, mysteries. Beverly Connor has been favorably compared to Patricia Cornwell (q.v.) and Aaron Elkins (q.v.), although some critics complain about overly detailed and convoluted plots and stiff dialogue. Author

Connor is also a Georgia-based archaeologist. *A Rumor of Bones* was the first fiction book published by Nashville, Tennessee–based Cumberland House.

1. *Rumor of Bones, A* **(Cumberland, 1996)** When a child's bones are found outside of a Georgia town, archaeologist Lindsay Chamberlain is asked to match them to a missing child. More bones, including 25-year-old adult bones, turn up, and Lindsay and her excavation foreman and dancing partner, Derrick Bellamy, get involved with a prominent, eccentric local family before they are finished.

2. *Questionable Remains* **(Cumberland, 1997)** The two-year-old deaths of three men found sealed in a cave were dismissed as accidents caused by falling rocks by a previous investigation, which shows signs of being a cover-up.

3. *Dressed to Die* **(Cumberland, 1998)** The search for Shirley Foster, an art teacher at the University of Georgia missing for four years, is traced to a grave site on Foster's property, but the case isn't over yet as crates filled with Native American artifacts also yield a corpse, with a shirt and tie.

4. *Skeleton Crew* **(Cumberland, 1999)** Lindsay's investigation of a 500-year-old galleon and a Spanish sailor's journal unearthed off the Georgia coast leads to some modern-day murders.

5. *Airtight Case* **(Cumberland, 2000)** Lindsay is forced to deal with being buried alive, suffering from amnesia, and experiencing a haunted house whose ghosts seem to be after her as she joins a dig at a pioneer settlement in the Great Smoky Mountains.

II. Connor's latest novels are issued by another publisher (Onyx) and feature a new protagonist, forensic anthropologist Diane Fallon, who has left a troubled past for a new job in Georgia.

1. *One Grave Too Many* **(Onyx, 2004)** Forensic anthropologist Diane Fallon, who has a new job in Georgia, is asked to lend her skills to an investigation by her former lover, Detective Frank Duncan.

2. *Dead Guilty* **(Onyx, 2004)** The murder of three people, hanged execution-style in some remote Georgia woods, brings Diane back on the job again.

3. *Dead Secret* **(Onyx, 2005)** Fallon unearths the key to a mystery that reaches back 70 years when she discovers a trio of decades-old skeletons.

4. *Dead Past* **(Onyx, 2007)** As a child, Juliet Price was traumatized by witnessing an act of violence. Years later, still traumatized, Juliet sees a TV show featuring the unsolved case.

Connors, Rose

Martha "Marty" Nickerson of Chatham, Cape Cod, Massachusetts, is an assistant DA and prosecuting attorney in *Absolute Certainty*, but an attack of doubt and conscience turns her into a defense attorney in a romantic and vocational partnership with her former rival, Harry Madigan. Single-mother Marty is one of many sympathetic and believable characters in a series of fast-moving courtroom dramas by veteran trial attorney Rose Connors.

1. *Absolute Certainty* **(Scribner, 2002)** After prosecuting attorney Marty Nickerson secures the murder and mutilation conviction of Manuel Rodriguez, a second murder, disturbingly similar to the first, causes him growing doubts that justice has been done.

2. *Temporary Sanity* **(Scribner, 2003)** Nickerson, now a defense attorney in partnership with former Barnstable County public defender Harry Madigan, takes on a couple of homicide cases with extenuating circumstances: a father who shot the man who raped

and murdered his seven-year-old-son, and a battered woman who stabbed her attacker to death.

3. *Maximum Security* (**Scribner, 2004**) When Harry Madigan's former law-school classmate Louisa Rawlings is implicated in the death of her wealthy husband, Harry passes her case on to Marty and their junior associate Kevin Kydd.

4. *False Testimony* (**Scribner, 2005**) Marty takes on the case of US senator Charles Kendrick, whose 25-year-old female aide has disappeared, and Harry is appointed public defender for Derrick Holliston, who is pleading self-defense in the killing of Fr. Francis Patrick McMahon.

Conrad, Joseph

PSEUDONYM OF Jozef Teodor Konrad

The characteristics of Conrad's later work were already present in his remarkable first novel, *Almayer's Folly*—the brooding tropical setting, the European protagonist slowly degenerating in a savage culture, the suspense and violence inherent to the story, and the beautiful prose style. Conrad didn't begin writing until 1889, after 16 years at sea aboard French and English merchant ships. He wrote in self-taught English rather than his native Polish and is known to have carried the manuscript of *Almayer's Folly* with him on many voyages. Numbers 2 and 3 have been published together in one volume (Norton, 1955). A film version of *An Outcast of the Islands* by Carol Reed in 1951 starred Ralph Richardson, Trevor Howard, Robert Morley, and Wendy Hiller.

1. *Rescue, The* (**Doubleday, 1920**) Captain Lingard, who appears as the trader Rajah Laut in numbers 2 and 3, falls in love as a young man with the dangerous Edith Travers.

2. *Outcast of the Islands, An* (**Appleton, 1896**) The story of Willems, a shady European, and his obsession with the Malayan woman Aissa. Almayer plays a subordinate part in this novel; his daughter Nina is seen as a little girl.

3. *Almayer's Folly* (**Macmillan, 1895**) Subtitle: *A Story of an Eastern River*. Doom pursues European Kaspar Almayer's decision to marry a native girl and to live and raise his beloved daughter in Malaya. Although this was Conrad's first novel, it follows *An Outcast of the Islands* chronologically.

Constantine, K. C.

PSEUDONYM UKNOWN

Rocksburg, Pennsylvania, is a depressed and grimy steel town near Pittsburgh. Its police chief, Mario Balzic, is overweight, irascible, and inclined to drink too much, but he is a conscientious public servant with compassion for the people of his community and an unusual sensitivity to what motivates them. Detective Sergeant Ruggiero "Rugs" Carlucci inherits Mario's role after Balzic retires (in number 11). He also inherits Mario's problems with venal and dense superiors in a town with a near moribund economy, as well having to deal with a mother who verges upon being certifiable. Mario is on the sidelines, fretful, with a bum ticker, but still ready to take on work when he feels he is needed. The Rocksburg novels have increasingly become, as the series has progressed, character studies and evocations of a region rather than conventional mysteries or police procedurals. The pseudonymous K. C. Constantine, who jealously protects his anonymity, lives in the Rust Belt region he describes so well.

1. *Rocksburg Railroad Murders, The* (**Saturday Review, 1972**) Introducing Mario Balzic and the town of Rocksburg. Balzic investigates the murder of a former schoolmate.

2. *Man Who Liked to Look at Himself, The* (**Saturday Review, 1973**) Balzic has to work with a racist, incompetent state police lieutenant while solving the mystery of a dismembered corpse.

3. *Blank Page, The* (**Saturday Review, 1974**) Janet Pisula, a shy college student, is slain.

4. *Fix Like This, A* (**Saturday Review, 1975**) A stabbing and two beating deaths lead Balzic into an investigation of the local numbers racket.

5. *Man Who Liked Slow Tomatoes, The* (**Godine, 1982**) A missing person, very early tomatoes, and exasperating contract negotiations with the local bureaucracy engage Balzic.

6. *Always a Body to Trade* (**Godine, 1983**) Balzic copes with murder, robbery, drug dealers, crooked narcotics agents, and a new mayor who is inclined to meddle.

7. *Upon Some Midnight's Clear* (**Godine, 1985**) Balzic's troubles with meddling Mayor Strohn continue as he contends with an alleged mugging, a nude protest by Vietnam veterans, and a pre-Christmas attack of postholiday depression.

8. *Joey's Case* (**Mysterious, 1988**) Former coal miner Albert Castelucci persuades Balzic to conduct an unofficial investigation into the homicide of his son Joey.

9. *Sunshine Enemies* (**Mysterious, 1990**) Mario is looking for the killer of Louis Blaskevich, who was found stabbed to death outside the local pornographic bookstore.

10. *Bottom Liner Blues* (**Mysterious, 1993**) After his mother's death, Balzic is having words with his wife, flashbacks to Iwo Jima, and a conversation with a writer who thinks that authors are being exploited by library users.

11. *Cranks and Shadows* (**Mysterious, 1995**) Mario is 65 and ready to retire.

12. *Good Sons* (**Mysterious, 1996**) Detective Sergeant Ruggiero "Rugs" Carlucci comes to the fore after Mario's retirement. While combatting his own self-doubt, the ineffable mayor, and his increasingly senile mother, Rugs responds to a 911 call from the raped and assaulted widow of the founder of a local stone-works company.

13. *Family Values* (**Mysterious, 1997**) Mario Balzic, retired but not ready to be put on the shelf, is hired to look into the claims of a man named Walin, son of another ex-cop, that he was wrongfully convicted of the murder of two drug dealers 17 years ago.

14. *Brushback* (**Mysterious, 1998**) Rugs is on the case when former pitcher Bobby Blasco, known for his "head-hunting" or brushback pitches when he was in the major leagues, is beaten to death with a Louisville Slugger bat in a Rocksburg alley.

15. *Blood Mud* (**Mysterious, 1999**) Mario, still uneasy in retirement, is felled by a cardiac "event" as he is about to engage himself in a private investigation of a dubious insurance claim filed by a gun-shop owner.

16. *Grievance* (**Mysterious, 2000**) The murders of a steel magnate and a local union official help to distract Rugs from his problems with an increasingly psychotic mother, a problematical relationship with a psychiatric social worker, and a pushy state trooper.

17. *Saving Room for Dessert* (**Mysterious, 2002**) The focus this time is not on one central character but on three: officers Rayford, Reseta, and Canozza. They patrol the Flats, an area notorious for violent, sometimes deadly, domestic disputes.

Constantine, Storm

I. British author Storm Constantine's first book, *The Enchantments of Flesh and Spirit*, created a future Earth in which hermaphrodites called Wraeththu have replaced Humans as the dominant race. The Wraeththu maintain their race by dint of adopting adolescent Human males and transforming them. The first trilogy (numbers 1–3) describes the vicissitudes of a number of characters, including the hermaphrodite Cal and the young Human Pellaz har Aralis, who eventually becomes the Tigron (or ruler) of the land of the Gelaming, and Thiede, the first Wraeththu, who achieves a kind of goddess stature. The second trilogy, the Wraeththu Histories (numbers 4–6) brings in the Parazha, another hermaphrodite race, who have more female characteristics than the androgynous Wraeththu, who seem to tilt toward the male. A series of novellas, at least three of which have been published so far by Constantine's own Immanion Press (UK), further explore the *Wraeththu Mythos*, including Wendy Darling and Bridgette Parker's *Storm Constantine's Wraeththu Mythos 'Breeding Discontent'* (2003), the story of a secret Varrish breeding facility; Constantine's *The Hienama* (2005), which relates the tale of Jassenah har Sulh and his guru Ysobi; and *Wraeththu: From Enchantment to Fulfillment* (2005), coauthored with Gabriel Strange and Lydia Wood, which seems to retell the story of Wraeththu origins in abbreviated fashion. *Wraeththu* (Tor, 1993) is an omnibus containing numbers 1 through 3. *The Oracle Lips* (Stark House, 1999) contains a Wraeththu story. The Wraeththu books have acquired something of a cult following, though some readers profess to be confused by the ins-and-outs of their "mythos," which Constantine appears to elucidate in *Grimoire Dehana, Book 1: Kaimana* (Immanion, 2005). The best approach is to begin with number 1 in this still-evolving series.

1. *Enchantments of Flesh and Spirit, The* (Tor, 1990) The young Human boy Pellaz leaves his postcollapse Earth home with the Wraeththu Cal as the start of a series of adventures that will lead to his becoming a Har (aka Wraeththu). Originally published in the United Kingdom in 1987.

2. *Bewitchments of Love and Hate, The* (Tor, 1990) Set among the Varr tribe, introduced in number 1, this title deals with a series of relationships, including that of Cal with the demi-goddess Thiede, advisor and controller of the dominant Wraeththu tribe, which is now "ruled" by Pellaz. Originally published in the United Kingdom in 1988.

3. *Fulfillments of Fate and Desire, The* (Tor, 1991) The conclusion of the first trilogy, narrated by Cal, full of Cabbalist symbolism, in which Cal achieves unity with Pellaz and Thiede's designs seem to be fulfilled. Originally published in the United Kingdom in 1989.

4. *Wraiths of Will and Pleasure, The* (Tor, 2003) The opening volume of the Wraeththu Histories, falling chronologically between numbers 2 and 3 of the first trilogy, retelling some of the "histories" that explore the consequences of the death and rebirth of Pellaz. The outcast Ulaume and a new race of post-Humans, the Parazha, are featured.

5. *Shades of Time and Memory, The* (Tor, 2004) Pellaz, Tigron (ruler) of the land of the Gelaming, creates a mystical pearl (harling) with the aid of lovers Caeru and Calanthe.

6. *Ghosts of Blood and Innocence, The* (Tor, 2006) Relates the tales of the brothers Darquiel har Aralis and Loki har Aralis, who are unaware of their relationship and their mythic heritage.

7. *Hienama, The* (Immanion [UK], 2005) A stand-alone continuing the Wraeththu saga, this novella relates the tale of Jassenah har Sulh, who has come to the town of Jesith to train magically with the famous hienama Ysobi.

II. The Magravandia trilogy is about the wars of elemental magics: the water-aligned Palindrake family, who derive their power from Sea Dragons, against the Magravand, who rely on the magic of the fire-dragon-god Madragore. The trilogy is full of quests, violence, and magic. Constantine's writing skills lift this trilogy above standard sword-and-sorcery fare.

1. *Sea Dragon Heir* (Tor, 2000) The dwindling Palindrake line, heirs to a fallen kingdom, include Valraven, who must travel to the Madragore court to train as a soldier. Young Pharinet is initiated into the secrets of the Sisterhood of the Dragon. Both are betrayed by Bayard, the son of the Madragore emperor.

2. *Crown of Silence, The* (Tor, 2001) Young peasant boy Shan, who has been brutalized by invading Magravand soldiers, is rescued by half-human, half-mage Taropat (aka Khaster).

3. *Way of Light, The* (Tor, 2001) Valraven, head of the Palindrakes, who were once allied with the sea dragons, most decide whether he wants to become the True King in the wake of the power-struggle between factions that wish to succeed in the Magranvandian Empire after the death of the old emperor.

III. *The Monstrous Regiment* and *Aleph* are a pair of novels about a feminist empire founded on the planet of Artemis by women and men that has turned into a tyranny ruled over by the Dominatri, who has enslaved the few men left. A young girl named Corinna rebels against the system. Critics had mixed feelings about this novel duo.

1. *Monstrous Regiment, The* (Orbit [UK], 1989) Young swamp-raised Corinna takes in a man who is rebelling against the tyranny of the Dominatrix, even though she is being prepared for an important post in the tyranny. Not published in the United States.

2. *Aleph* (Orbit [UK], 1991) Corinna is still living on Artemis, which is changing radically. New colonists arrive, and a "strange force" is discovered in one of the planet's caves. Not published in the United States.

IV. The Grigori series is about an ancient race that lives among humans and possesses abilities and senses humans do not have. Peverel Othman, a Grigori with a dark past, the human twins Owen and Lily Winter, and the seer Daniel, who is recruited into the Grigori, are the main characters in this apocalyptic trilogy.

1. *Stalking Tender Prey* (Meisha Merlin, 1998) Peverel Othman, a Grigori, part of an ancient race of superhumans, is not sure for what or whom he is looking when he arrives at the hamlet of Little Moor and becomes involved with orphaned twins Owen and Lily Winter. Originally published in the United Kingdom in 1995.

2. *Scenting Hallowed Blood* (Meisha Merlin, 1999) Peverel Othman (the fallen angel Shemyaza), the seer Daniel, and the twins Owen and Lily arrive at High Crag, a desolate coastal place where the Grigori are preparing for world dominance as the new millennium approaches. Originally published in the United Kingdom in 1996.

3. *Stealing Sacred Fire* (Meisha Merlin, 2001) Peveral, once again the angel Shemyaza, calls his followers to him for the final battle to decide who controls the fate of humanity. Originally published in the United Kingdom in 1997.

Cook, Bruce

Antonio "Chico" Cervantes is a Los Angeles–based private investigator. Like so many of his fictional peers, Chico is wisecracking, brave, cynical, and inclined to get in over his head sometimes. Unlike Philip Marlowe and company, Chico is a Latino. His developing relationship with Alicia, the beautiful Mexican prostitute who becomes a television star, is a running theme in the series. The late (d. 2003) Bruce Cook abandoned Chico for his Sir John Fielding series, written under the Bruce Alexander (q.v.) pseudonym.

1. *Mexican Standoff* (Watts, 1988) Cervantes is offered $10,000 plus expenses to fly to Mexico to track down the hit-and-run killer of the children of two wealthy men.
2. *Rough Cut* (St. Martin's, 1990) Chico is hired as a bodyguard for the daughter of film director Heinrich Toller, who is hoping to make a comeback with his latest picture.
3. *Death as a Career Move* (St. Martin's, 1992) A sound editor working on a major new biopic of sixties rock star Tommy Osborne is murdered.
4. *Sidewalk Hilton, The* (St. Martin's, 1994) Chico is hired to locate elderly Chicago businessman Benjamin Stirling, who is on a mission to help the homeless.

Cook, David

This pair of novels traces the life of severely developmentally disabled Walter from his birth in 1930 through his parents' deaths, his institutionalization, and his eventual escape to an impoverished existence in London. Walter is treated sympathetically but unsentimentally by the author, who reserves his anger for the society that dooms its mentally disabled to such misery. *Walter* won the prestigious Hawthornden Prize in 1978 and was the basis for a television drama written by Cook, a British writer and actor.

1. *Walter* (Overlook, 1985) Walter is so severely developmentally disabled, unteachable, and incontinent that his mother seriously considers killing "God's mistake." Originally published in the United Kingdom in 1978.
2. *Winter Doves* (Overlook, 1985) Twenty years after he has been committed to a mental hospital, Walter feels that he belongs, until the arrival of the violent, suicidal June. Originally published in the United Kingdom in 1979. Variant title: *June*.

Cook, Glen (Charles)

I. Garrett is a cross between Dirk Gently (Douglas Adams [q.v.]) and Philip Marlowe (Raymond Chandler [q.v.]). Garrett is a hardboiled PI located in the city of TunFaire who solves mysteries involving dwarves, elves, and other denizens of fantasy. He is supported by such characters as the Dead Man and a dead but sentient and telepathic creature called Loghr, who acts as a kind of Nero Wolfe to Garrett's Archie. Garrett is the most successful creation of American SF-fantasy writer Glen Cook, a retired (1998) factory worker who focuses his attention on the common people of his fantasy worlds rather than the upper classes. Omnibus volumes include *The Garrett Files* (Doubleday, 1989; numbers 1–3); *Garrett Investigates* (Science Fiction Book Club, 2004; numbers 7–9); and *Garrett on the Case* (Science Fiction Book Club, 2005; numbers 10–11).

1. *Sweet Silver Blues* (Signet, 1987) Garrett is hired to track down a woman to whom his deceased friend has left a fortune. His task is complicated by a nasty collection of gnomes, vampires, and centaurs.
2. *Bitter Gold Hearts* (Signet, 1988) Hired by the Storm Warden to recover her kidnapped son, Garrett finds that several different groups have a vested interest in keeping the boy out of sight.
3. *Cold Copper Tears* (Signet, 1988) Some being(s) want Garrett dead, and the PI must discover who they are, unless he wants to become the next sacrifice to a long-dead god.
4. *Old Tin Sorrows* (Signet, 1989) Garrett's investigation of a potential poisoning brings him into contact with the living dead and the "nearly dead living" and a pair of seductive ghosts.
5. *Dread Brass Shadows* (Roc, 1990) A huge brass spell book in Garrett's possession and coveted by everyone else may have something to do with the murder of his girlfriend.
6. *Red Iron Nights* (Roc, 1991) A serial killer prowling the streets of TunFaire is more than the Watch can handle, and the Watch wants Garrett to help them out.
7. *Deadly Quicksilver Lies* (Roc, 1994) The case of a missing girl may be more complicated than at first blush. The girl's father might be royalty.
8. *Petty Pewter Gods* (Roc, 1995) The gods are scrambling for land on which to build their temples. Garrett works himself into the middle of this clash in a foolish attempt to play one side against another.
9. *Faded Steel Heat* (Roc, 2000) Garrett finds himself in hot water again when a gang of "human rightists" tries to shake down his nonhuman employer.
10. *Angry Lead Skies* (Roc, 2002) Garrett is roped into being bodyguard to Kip Prose, an obnoxious kid who is supposedly being threatened by some indescribable creatures.
11. *Whispering Nickel Idols* (Roc, 2005) Everyone is after Garrett, including the beautiful, criminally insane daughter of a comatose crime boss.

II. The Black Company is a band of mercenaries on a planet where sorcery has gone wild. The members of the Black Company, remnants of a once-great mercenary army, are for hire. At first they serve a sorceress called the Lady, but switch sides later. Their leaders change. The company is sometimes decimated or even dissolved, but somehow its members manage to maintain a solidarity among themselves and keep to the goal of maintaining their chronicle, the Annals. Their world has elements of Earth's South, or Southeast, Asia. The Annals record many brutal and dark deeds, usually as seen from the point of view of the "grunts," the enlisted men of the company. Numbers 1 through 3, the original trilogy, sometimes called the Book of the North, have been collected in an omnibus volume, *Annals of the Black Company* (Doubleday, 1986). There is confusion, at least to this reader, about the exact chronology of numbers 4, 5, and 6. Numbers 5 and 6 are also known as the Book of the South. Numbers 7 through 9 are called the Book of Glittering Stone. Number 10 may be the conclusion to the series, which was running out of steam, although two other titles (*A Pitiless Rain* and *Port of Shadows*) were announced.

1. *Black Company, The* (Tor, 1984) Members of the Black Company, remnants of a once mighty army, under the leadership of former physician and primary chronicler, are searching their world for the White Rose.
2. *Shadows Linger* (Tor, 1984) The mercenaries of the Black Company are in the service of the Lady, whom they know to be evil, against the rebels of the White Rose.
3. *White Rose, The* (Tor, 1985) From a secret base on the Plains of Fear, the Black Company members, once in service to the Lady, now fight to bring victory to the reborn White Rose.

4. *Silver Spike, The* (Tor, 1989) Following the dissolution of the Black Company, roving bands of thieves converge on the site of the Company's last stand, drawn towards the promise of unimaginable power contained in a sliver of metal.

5. *Shadow Games* (Tor, 1989) The weary survivors of the Black Company travel south to return the lost Annals to Khatouar, their point of origin. Under the leadership of Croaker, they are once again a formidable fighting force. The First Book of the South.

6. *Dreams of Steel* (Tor, 1990) The Lady seems to be in command, as the Black Company tries to pull its remnants together. A sinister cult offers an alliance, and the Shadowmasters still scheme, against each other and the world at-large. The Second Book of the South.

7. *Bleak Seasons* (Tor, 1996) After a six-year gap, the Black Company returns. Murgen, current standard-bearer and keeper of the Annals, narrates this saga with visions back and forth in time, sometimes involuntary. The First Book of Glittering Stone.

8. *She Is the Darkness* (Tor, 1997) In the direct sequel to number 7, the company battles against Soulcatcher, the goddess Kinoc, and their various human, demi-human, and demonic allies. The Second Book of Glittering Stone.

9. *Water Sleeps* (Tor, 1999) Some years later, the motley band of company survivors exists at the sufferance of the Radisha of Taglios. Under the leadership of the young woman Sleepy, they hope to revive their comrades, encased in a magical stasis field. The Third Book of Glittering Stone.

10. *Soldiers Live* (Tor, 2000) In what may be the last volume of the Annals of the Company, Croaker takes over the narration again, retelling some of the events of earlier volumes, as the company searches for a path home.

III. Dread Empire, a series of seven books, is set in a fantasy world roughly analogous to the ancient Old World, with warring regions similar to Europe, China, and the Middle East. Numbers 5, 6, and 7, the original trilogy, relate the exploits of the Star Rider. Numbers 1 through 3, a prequel to numbers 5 through 7, have been published in omnibus form as *A Cruel Wind* (Night Shade, 2006). They relate the rise and triumph of a religious and political leader among the desert peoples. Number 4 retells the story of number 3 from a different point of view.

1. *Fire in His Hands, The* (Pocket, 1984) Young heretic El Murid, the Disciple, vows to bring order, prosperity, and righteousness to the desert people of Hammadal Nakir. Variant title: *A Fortress in Shadow*.

2. *With Mercy toward None* (Baen, 1985) Sequel to number 1. No annotation available.

3. *Reap the East Wind* (Tor, 1987) Lady Nepanthe's new life with the wizard Varthlokkur is disturbed by memories of her lost son. King Bragi Ragnarson and his spymaster Michael Trebilcock scheme to help exiled Princess Mist to regain her throne.

4. *Ill Fate Marshalling, An* (Tor, 1988) Essentially repeats the plot of number 3 as King Bragi Ragnorsson of Kaveliri risks his nation in assisting Princess Mist's coup against the Dread Empire.

5. *Shadow of All Night Falling, A* (Berkley, 1979) From his lonely keep in the Dragon's Teeth mountains, the Star Rider calls for a war that even wizards dread, fought for Nepanthe, princess of the Storm Kings.

6. *October's Baby* (Berkley, 1980) No annotation available.

7. *All Darkness Met* (Berkley, 1980) No annotation available.

IV. The Darkwar trilogy is a mixture of SF and fantasy set in a primitive landscape. Young Marika has sworn to use her paranormal psychic abilities to defeat an alien race afflicting her world.

1. *Doomstalker* (Popular Library, 1985) Relates Marika's early years, as she vows to use her sylph witchlike powers to save her world.

2. *Warlock* (Popular Library, 1985) Young Markika arrives at last at the Maksche Cloister, where her already formidable psychic powers could be honed into an awesome weapon.

3. *Ceremony* (Popular Library, 1986) No annotation available.

V. The Starfishers trilogy is a space opera about a human space confederation and its efforts to deal with alien species such as the Sangaree. Number 4 is set in the same universe as the trilogy.

1. *Shadowline* (Warner, 1982) Two powerful groups contend in a battle that starts with a raid on a planet where humans are in thrall to the alien Sangaree.

2. *Starfishers* (Warner, 1982) No annotation available.

3. *Stars' End* (Warner, 1982) No annotation available.

4. *Passage of Arms* (Popular Library, 1985) The Climbers, stripped down "tin cans" that bristle with weapons, are the Human Confederation's ultimate weapon against the alien invaders.

VI. Instrumentalities of the Night is a dark military fantasy saga featuring young Praman warrior Else Tage, renamed Piper Hecht after he vanquishes an immortal foe, who battles the Patriarchy and the Tyranny of the Night as well as other foes.

1. *Tyranny of the Night, The* (Tor, 2005) On a mission in the Holy Land, the young Praman warrior Else Tage prevails over a creature of the Dark.

2. *Lord of the Silent Kingdom* (Tor, 2007) Renamed Piper Hecht, the young Praman warrior is promoted to the rank of captain-general under Emperor Sublime V.

Cook, Robin

I. Robin Cook, ophthalmologist at Massachusetts General Hospital in Boston, is one of the foremost practitioners of the medical thriller. Although critics are generally not impressed by his writing style, readers in large numbers are carried along by such suspenseful tales as *Coma* (Little, Brown, 1977), *Vital Signs* (Putnam, 1991), and *Terminal* (Putnam, 1993). Pert, pretty, courageous Marissa Blumenthal is the heroine of two of Cook's novels.

1. *Outbreak* (Putnam, 1987) Marissa Blumenthal, epidemiologist with Atlanta's Centers for Disease Control, investigates a mysterious, untreatable, highly contagious virus.

2. *Vital Signs* (Putnam, 1991) Now a successful pediatrician near Boston, Marissa, trying to become pregnant, uncovers suspicious records at a local fertility clinic.

II. Before they get married, New York City medical examiners Laurie Montgomery and Jack Stapleton have a long-running but difficult relationship, because Jack, traumatized by the accidental deaths of his wife and children, refuses to make a commitment to marriage and babies with Laurie. But the main attractions are the medical-thriller plots the two get involved in: cocaine overdose deaths, a planned terrorist attack, a series of dubious hospital deaths, and so forth.

1. *Blindsight* (Putnam, 1992) Laurie Montgomery, forensic pathologist in New York City's Medical Examiner's office, finds a pattern of unrelated cocaine overdose deaths among people never known to have used drugs.

2. *Vector* **(Putnam, 1999)** The People's Aryan Army (PAA) is planning an anthrax attack on a big government building in New York.

3. *Marker* **(Putnam, 2005)** Laurie's autopsies of the bodies of two people who died after minor surgery at the same Manhattan hospital point up a series of very suspicious hospital deaths.

4. *Crisis* **(Putnam, 2006)** Jack Stapleton gets involved when his brother-in-law, Boston physician Craig Bowman, is sued for malpractice by the husband of Patience Stanhope when she dies of a heart attack under Bowman's care.

5. *Critical* **(Putnam, 2007)** Laurie Montgomery, now married to Jack Stapleton, investigates an abrupt rise in death from infections that can be traced to three Manhattan hospitals owned by Angels Healthcare.

Cookson, Catherine

I. Catherine Cookson's melodramas and historical romances have been best sellers on both sides of the Atlantic. The prolific Cookson, who published nearly 100 novels before she died in 1998 and about 10 more posthumously, set many of her novels in the north of England, especially the Tyneside in and around Newcastle. According to Cookson in her autobiography, *Our Kate* (Bobbs-Merrill, 1969), she was born and grew up in the lower depths of Tyneside society, and her descriptions of the region show the authenticity of a native delineator.

The historical Mallen trilogy was her first big success. The callous and high-living Mallens of High Banks Hall had fathered illegitimate sons all across the Northumberland countryside for the better part of 100 years. The family trait, a distinctive shock of white hair running down to the left temple, known as the Mallen Streak, marked their parentage. It was said that those who bore the Mallen Streak did not die old or in their beds. The series covers the years from 1851 to World War I. The series has been collected as an omnibus volume at least three times in the United Kingdom: once as *The Mallen Novels* (Heinemann, 1979) and twice as *The Mallen Streak Trilogy* (Chancellor, 1994, and Corgi, 1999).

1. *Mallen Streak, The* **(Dutton, 1973)** Begins with old Thomas Mallen losing his estate to creditors and retiring to a small cottage with his two wards and their governess.

2. *Mallen Girl, The* **(Dutton, 1973)** This book follows the childhood and stormy courtship of headstrong young Barbara, old Thomas's daughter.

3. *Mallen Lot, The* **(Dutton, 1974)** The final volume goes up to World War I and shows Barbara, wilful and unhappy, making life difficult for everyone around her. English title: *The Mallen Litter*.

II. The industrial Tynside region of northern England is the setting for these contemporary novels with a working-class background. The series follows the plucky and captivating Mary Ann Shaugnessy, a somewhat autobiographical character, from the age of eight through her school days, first romance, marriage, and motherhood. Published in the United Kingdom in the 1950s and 1960s but not in the United States until after the success of the Mallen novels. Reprinted in one volume as *The Mary Ann Omnibus* (Macdonald, 1981) and in two volumes as *The Mary Ann Novels* (Corgi, 2000) in the United Kingdom.

1. *Grand Man, A* **(Morrow, 1975)** Mary Ann is instrumental in getting her parents to leave their dockside tenement for a farm outside the city. Originally published in the United Kingdom in 1954.

2. *Lord and Mary Ann, The* **(Morrow, 1975)** Mary Ann learns that the move to the farm isn't all that's needed to cure her dad's drinking problem. Originally published in the United Kingdom in 1956.

3. *Devil and Mary Ann, The* **(Morrow, 1976)** Mary Ann, aged nine, goes off to convent school. Originally published in the United Kingdom in 1958.

4. *Love and Mary Ann* **(Morrow, 1976)** Mary Ann, aged 13, has a sweetheart in Corny Boyle. Originally published in the United Kingdom in 1961.

5. *Life and Mary Ann* **(Morrow, 1977)** Mary Ann, now 17, is still in love with Corny, but the course of true love never runs smooth. Originally published in the United Kingdom in 1962.

6. *Marriage and Mary Ann* **(Morrow, 1978)** Wedding bells ring at last for Mary Ann. Originally published in the United Kingdom in 1964.

7. *Mary Ann's Angels* **(Morrow, 1978)** Rose Mary and David, twins, are now six years old. Originally published in the United Kingdom in 1965.

8. *Mary Ann and Bill* **(Morrow, 1978)** Bill the dog provides some of the chuckles in this installment. Originally published in the United Kingdom in 1967.

III. A later trilogy begins in the English mining country during the late 19th century and follows its heroine, Tilly Trotter, to the New World and back. Published in one volume at least twice in the United Kingdom: by Chancellor in 1993 and by Corgi in 1999 (entitled *Tilly Trotter: An Omnibus*).

1. *Tilly* **(Morrow, 1980)** Orphaned in her teens, Tilly finds a job as nursemaid to the children of a rich mine owner, but her troubles are not over. UK title: *Tilly Trotter*.

2. *Tilly Wed* **(Morrow, 1980)** Tilly goes to Texas with her new husband. UK title: *Tilly Trotter Wed*.

3. *Tilly Alone* **(Morrow, 1982)** Tilly returns from Texas to take over the estate and the mines, trapped by the promise she made to her dying husband. UK title: *Tilly Widowed*.

IV. One of Cookson's first published novels (1950) and her 100th (posthumously published in 2001) are about the same character, Kate Hannigan. Kate is followed from illegitimate birth at the turn of the 20th century in the slums of Newcastle to her marriage to Dr. Rodney Prince and the love tribulations of her daughter Annie.

1. *Kate Hannigan* **(Bantam, 1972)** Kate Hannigan, illegitimate, poor, and with a vicious bully for a father, fights her away courageously up from her beginnings in Newcastle before World War I. Original UK publication: 1950. First hardcover US publication: Simon & Schuster, 2004.

2. *Kate Hannigan's Girl* **(Simon & Schuster, 2001)** Now married to the wealthy and kindly Dr. Rodney Prince, Kate is concerned about the illegitimacy of her daughter Annie.

V. The Bailey Chronicles are a trilogy, with an add-on some 10 years later. They concern irresistible hero Bill Bailey, who, from the moment he arrives as a lodger in widowed Fiona Nelson's home in the Tyneside town of Fellburn, changes the lives of all around him in this heartwarming modern fairy tale. Numbers 1 through 3 were first published in the United States as *The Bailey Chronicles* (Summit, 1986). Numbers 1 through 3 were also published together as *Bill Bailey: An Omnibus* (Corgi [UK], 1998).

1. *Bill Bailey* **(Heinemann [UK], 1986)** When Bill Bailey answers widowed Fiona Nelson's ad for a lodger, it isn't long before she wonders how she did without him.

2. *Bill Bailey's Lot* (Bantam [UK], 1987) Bill and Fiona wed. Bill adopts Fiona's three children and the orphaned Mamie.

3. *Bill Bailey's Daughter* (Bantam [UK], 1988) Fiona Bailey will give birth to a baby, their first since she and Bill had married.

4. *Bondage of Love, The* (Bantam [UK], 1997) When Fiona's son Willie befriends the wayward Sonny Love, it is apparent that change is on the way.

VI. The Hamilton trilogy, published in the United States only in large-print edition (Eagle Large Print, 1993), was originally published as three separate novels. Hamilton is the name of an imaginary horse that is Maisie's closest companion even after marriage and motherhood.

1. *Hamilton* (Heinemann [UK], 1983) Maisie, married and a mother, starts writing about her imaginary companion, Hamilton the horse.

2. *Goodbye Hamilton* (Heinemann [UK], 1984) Now a best-selling author, Maisie is getting married again. Hamilton, inspired by her example, takes himself a wife—a mare named Begonia.

3. *Harold* (Heinemann [UK], 1985) Harold, a cheerful, bright-eyed little Cockney boy, has comforted Maisie in the days of mourning that followed the death of her second husband.

Coonts, Stephen (Paul)

I. Former US Navy aviator, Distinguished Flying Cross awardee, and Vietnam veteran Coonts insists that his pilot hero Jake Grafton is not based on himself. Although Jake is a war hero who becomes a rear admiral and director of the Defense Intelligence Agency, he is just your average guy, "Mr. Small-Town American Boy." Coonts writes exciting espionage-technothrillers, at their best when Jake is in the cockpit. *Flight of the Intruder* was made into a film starring Willem Dafoe and Danny Glover.

1. *Flight of the Intruder* (Naval Institute, 1986) When his best friend is killed in a mission over North Vietnam in 1972, the enraged Jake decides to bomb headquarters in Hanoi.

2. *Intruders, The* (Pocket, 1994) Disillusioned by the Vietnam debacle, Jake ponders his next career move as he flies A-6 Intruders off an aircraft carrier in the Pacific.

3. *Final Flight* (Doubleday, 1988) Jake is called upon to foil an Arab plot to steal nuclear weapons from an aircraft carrier in the Mediterranean.

4. *Minotaur, The* (Doubleday, 1989) Assigned to oversee the development of a US Navy Stealth-type bomber, Jake is troubled by the mysterious death of his predecessor.

5. *Under Siege* (Pocket, 1990) Washington, DC, is the scene of the trial of a Colombian drug lord and a series of mass murders pulled off by his minions.

6. *Red Horseman* (Pocket, 1993) As deputy director of the Defense Intelligence Agency, Grafton learns that a Jewish movie mogul was the victim of poisoning.

7. *Cuba* (St. Martin's, 1999) A shipment of American chemical and biological weapons out of Guantánamo Bay goes missing, and it's Jake's job to find it. Meanwhile, Cuba is developing its own biological weapons.

8. *Hong Kong* (St. Martin's, 2000) Virgil Cole, American Consul General in Hong Kong, is fomenting revolution there through his network of computer systems.

9. *America* (St. Martin's, 2001) A hijacked nuclear submarine, computer hackers, an ICBM defense shield, currency speculators, Russian plotters, a burglar working for the CIA, and the launch of American Tomahawk missiles on Washington all figure in this Jake Grafton thriller.

10. *Liberty* (St. Martin's, 2003) A rogue Russian general has sold nuclear warheads to a vicious Middle Eastern anti-American terrorist. As usual Grafton plays fast and loose with the law and agencies such as the FBI and CIA.

11. *Liars and Thieves* (St. Martin's, 2004) Jake Grafton makes an appearance only late in the day, as his sidekick Tommy Carmellini, ex-burglar and CIA operative, stumbles upon a massacre when he is sent to a West Virginia safe house where Russian defector Mikhail Goncharov is being debriefed.

12. *Traitor, The* (St. Martin's, 2006) Jake makes another cameo appearance as Tommy Carmellini is asked to drop his routine work and help find out why the director of French intelligence is making large, secret investments in the Bank of Palestine.

II. Two tongue-in-cheek thriller-cum-romance-cum-SF novels featuring flying saucers, seismologist Rip Cantrell, and somewhat older but beautiful ex-test pilot Charley Pine provide excellent light entertainment with plenty of scenes for flying enthusiasts.

1. *Saucer* (St. Martin's, 2002) Rip Cantrell, doing seismic surveys in the Sahara, stumbles across a 140,000-year-old flying saucer still in flying condition. When the air force sends female ex–test pilot Charley Pine to investigate, the pair gets involved in a series of adventures.

2. *Saucer: The Conquest* (St. Martin's, 2004) The flying saucer allegedly found in Roswell, New Mexico, in 1947 and a French space flight to the moon piloted by Charley are the crux of a plot involving lots of flying sequences and an insane French brewer hoping to take over the world.

Cooper, James Fenimore

The adventures of frontiersman Natty Bumppo, a man of many nicknames—Hawkeye, Leatherstocking, Pathfinder, Deerslayer, La Longue Carabine, and the Trapper—are told in five volumes known collectively as the Leatherstocking Tales. *The Last of the Mohicans* is the best known of the Leatherstocking books, partially because of the rousing Randolph Scott (1936) and Daniel Day-Lewis (1992) movie versions, although *The Prairie* is Cooper's best literary effort. The Leatherstocking Tales have been collected in uniform editions many times, including the two-volume set in the Library of America series (1985). *The Leatherstocking Saga* (Pantheon, 1954) is a pastiche of all the adventures of Natty Bumppo, not strictly an omnibus.

1. *Deerslayer, The; or, The First War-Path* (Lea & Blanchard, 1841) Hawkeye, Uncas, and the two sisters Judith and Hetty are caught up in the war between the Iroquois and the White settlers at Lake Otsego.

2. *Last of the Mohicans, The* (Lea & Carey, 1826) The "good Indian" Uncas meets the "bad Indian" Magua in this, the most popular book of the series.

3. *Pathfinder, The; or, The Inland Sea* (Lea & Blanchard, 1840) Chingachgook, father of Uncas, helps Natty lead Mabel Dunham to safety during the French and Indian War.

4. *Pioneers, The; or, The Sources of the Susquehanna* (Charles Wiley, 1823) The village of Templeton (based on Cooperstown), founded by Judge Temple, has "tamed" Natty and Chingachgook's old stomping grounds, but they still come in handy for the rescue of young Elizabeth Temple.

5. *Prairie, The* (**Lea & Carey, 1827**) Encroaching civilization has driven Natty Bumppo, now an old trapper, west to end his life beyond the Mississippi.

Cooper, Louise

I. *Lord of No Time* (Sphere [UK], 1977), the tale of Tarod, a fantasy novel set in an occult universe where humans are pawns in the eternal conflict between the forces of Order and Chaos, was rewritten and became the basis for English fantasy writer Louise Cooper's Time Master trilogy (numbers 4–6), which was a success with readers and critics in the United Kingdom and the United States. Order is supreme in the Time Master trilogy; Chaos reigns in the Star Shadow trilogy (numbers 1–3), a prequel to the Time Master trilogy. In the Chaos Gate trilogy (numbers 7–9) the forces of Order and Chaos are in equilibrium. A fourth trilogy, Daughter of Storms, published by Hodder (UK) in 1996–1998, but not published in the United States, is a YA series set at the time of the Equilibrium (*Daughter of Storms; The Dark Caller; Keepers of Light*). The "gods" of Order and Chaos are neither good nor evil, but supremely indifferent to the welfare of humanity, a situation that humans eventually recognize. This is a series full of plot twists, strong characters, and interesting philosophical points. Although the titles are listed below in more or less chronological order, new readers should probably read the series in publication date order, starting with *The Initiate* (number 4).

1. *Star Ascendant* (**Tor, 1995**) This prequel begins with Chaos in the saddle. The evil Vordegh, who has become First Magus, isn't well liked by the ruling Lords of Chaos. First novel in the Star Shadow trilogy.
2. *Eclipse* (**HarperCollins [UK], 1994**) First Magus Vordegh goes heresy hunting, while Benetan Liss, captain of the Chaos Riders, grows increasingly discontented with the gods of Chaos and more involved in his love for Iselia Darrow. Second novel in the Star Shadow trilogy. Not published in the United States.
3. *Moonset* (**HarperCollins [UK], 1995**) The contradictions within Chaos give the forces of Order their chance to overthrow the reign of Chaos as Benetan and Savrinor continue to occupy center stage in the action. Third novel in the Star Shadow trilogy. Not published in the United States.
4. *Initiate, The* (**Tor, 1985**) Order has triumphed over Chaos temporarily, but Tarod, the Outcast, a nameless child, has been born and is destined to become the greatest mage of his time.
5. *Outcast, The* (**Tor, 1986**) His soul imprisoned in an ancient jewel in a castle outside of Time, Tarod dreams of vengeance on the forces of Order, the Lords of Light.
6. *Master, The* (**Tor, 1987**) Tarod, the Master, rides to confront his destiny, and his decision will determine the outcome of the struggle between Order and Chaos.
7. *Deceiver, The* (**Bantam, 1991**) The birth of Ygorla, daughter of a human mother and a demon of Chaos, threatens the equilibrium between the gods of Chaos and Order, but the High Initiate Tirand does not recognize the danger. First in the Chaos Gate series.
8. *Pretender, The* (**Bantam, 1991**) Ygorla has murdered the High Margrave, ravaged the Margrave's court, enslaved the troubadour Strann, has the soul-stone of Yandros, Lord of Chaos, in her possession and is protected by an army of ghoulish warriors. Second in the Chaos Gate series.
9. *Avenger, The* (**Bantam, 1992**) Ygorla makes a bid for ultimate power, ruling over Humanity while the gods of Chaos and Order are kept at bay. Third in the Chaos Gate series.

II. The Indigo Saga is a series of eight volumes taking place on an alternative Earth. Princess Anghora unlawfully enters the forbidden Tower of Regrets and is responsible for releasing seven evil supernatural beings. Anghora assumes the new identity of Indigo and proceeds on a quest to battle and expel the evil beings and to expiate her sins.

Since 1995 Louise Cooper has devoted herself primarily to writing juvenile and young adult fantasies, published only in the United Kingdom, including series such as Daughter of Storms, Dark Enchantment, Creatures, Mirror Mirror, and Sea Horses. She has also published two related novels with a vampire theme: *Blood Summer* (New English Library [UK], 1976) and *In Memory of Sarah Bailey* (New English Library [UK], 1977).

1. *Nemesis* (**Tor, 1989**) Princess Anghara (later called Indigo) wilfully enters the Tower of Regrets and is responsible for releasing seven evil supernatural beings into her world.
2. *Inferno* (**Tor, 1989**) Indigo/Anghara, plagued by Nemesis, must defeat the demons within her before she can deal with outside evils.
3. *Infanta* (**Tor, 1990**) Indigo has been led to Huon Parita in search of the second demon she has released, which she believes has taken the form of the new ruler.
4. *Nocturne* (**Tor, 1990**) Many years have passed, and Indigo and her faithful telepathic wolf companion, Grimya, long for rest, but a malignant blight covers the land.
5. *Troika* (**Tor, 1991**) Indigo and Grimya return to sites from Indigo's past, where she has to fight not only external demons but also her inner demons as well.
6. *Avatar* (**Tor, 1991**) In the jungles of the Dark Isle, a cult of death-worshippers who may be in the thrall of the fifth demon, take in Indigo and Grimya and make Indigo their oracle.
7. *Revenant* (**Tor, 1993**) Indigo, abandoning her attempts to trap the last two demons, searching instead for her lost lover, arrives in a seemingly pragmatic town that is hiding an old secret.
8. *Aisling* (**Tor, 1994**) In the conclusion to the series, Indigo loses her memory, and the last unconquered demon from the Tower of Regrets draws her into an evil plot.

Cooper, Natasha

PSEUDONYM OF Clare Layton

I. Wilhelmina "Willow" King, thirtysomething part-time civil servant, leads a double life. On weekends she is transformed into Cressida Woodruffe, best-selling romance writer, trading her dreary Clapham flat for posh lodgings in Belgravia and her dowdy civil-service attire for the latest fashions. Willow/Cressida has occasional hang-ups about this double life, which she shares with her lover, London policeman Tom Worth, but generally she manages it adroitly, with time out for crime solving.

1. *Common Death, A* (**Crown, 1990**) The murder of Willow's boss on Clapham Common threatens to expose her double life, so she decides to unmask his killer. Variant title: *Festering Lilies*.
2. *Poison Flowers* (**Crown, 1992**) Willow helps Tom Worth investigate the links between several poisonings.
3. *Bloody Roses* (**Crown, 1993**) When Richard Crescent, Willow's former lover, is arrested for the murder of a coworker, she steps in to establish his innocence.
4. *Bitter Herbs* (**Crown, 1994**) Working on a memoir of Gloria Granger, recently deceased fellow romance writer, Cressida discovers that her foul-mouthed and self-centered subject was cordially hated.

5. *Rotten Apples* (St. Martin's, 1995) According to her sister, art dealer Fiona Fydgett was driven to suicide by minions of the Inland Revenue.

6. *Drowning Pool, The* (St. Martin's, 1997) Soon after the 44-year-old Willow gives birth to her first child, she hears that her obstetrician, Alexander Ringstead, has been found death in the birth pool just down the hallway. Not to be confused with Ross MacDonald's (q.v.) book of the same title. Variant title: *Fruiting Bodies*.

7. *Sour Grapes* (St. Martin's, 1998) Helping her friend Emma with her postgraduate criminology degree project on lie-detectors, Willow becomes involved in the case of Andrew Lutterworth, convicted of killing a mother and a baby in a car accident.

II. Willow King has been put on the back burner at least temporarily while Natasha Cooper has been writing a series of novels featuring Trish Maguire, British barrister and defender of the rights of abused children. The feisty and attractive Trish, as do many fictional lawyers, gets involved in investigating her own cases, which, since most of them deal with child abuse, tend to be grimmer than the Willow novels.

1. *Creeping Ivy* (St. Martin's, 1999) Trish Maguire has taken a leave of absence from her job of defending the rights of abused children. Then Charlotte, the four-year-old daughter of her cousin Antonia, is kidnapped from a playground.

2. *Fault Lines* (St. Martin's, 2000) Was Kara Huggate, a social worker about to testify on behalf of Trish's client in a child sexual-abuse case, the homicide victim of a serial rapist?

3. *Prey to All* (St. Martin's, 2000) McGuire is urged by her friend television producer Anna Crayling to investigate a possible miscarriage of justice in the conviction of Deb Gibbert for the murder of her ailing father.

4. *Out of the Dark* (St. Martin's, 2002) When a young boy is run over and seriously injured by a car, Trish discovers a possible relationship between the boy, herself, and her abusive and philandering father, Paddy.

5. *Place of Safety, A* (St. Martin's, 2003) While helping her nine-year-old half brother adjust to his mother's murder, Trish takes on the investigation of the Gregory Bequest Collection, an art collection built up in 1914 and lost for most of the 20th century.

6. *Keep Me Alive* (St. Martin's, 2004) Trish joins the prosecution team in a class-action suit against one of Britain's largest food-store chains, then falls victim to food poisoning herself.

7. *Gagged and Bound* (St. Martin's, 2005) Trish takes on the libel case concerning a politician who has been named as the instigator of a terrorist attack that killed a busload of children 30 years earlier.

8. *Evil Is Done* (St. Martin's, 2007) Trish's defense of sculptor Sam Foundling, who is accused of murdering his pregnant wife in his studio, annoys her friend Chief Inspector Caro Lyalt.

Cooper, Susan Rogers

I. Milt Kovak, sheriff of rural Prophesy County, Oklahoma, is a "good ol' boy" and a conscientious lawman but has a rather complicated personal life in this series of low-key, tragicomic portraits of small-town life in middle America.

1. *Man in the Green Chevy, The* (St. Martin's, 1988) Recently divorced Milt searches for the madman who is raping and murdering elderly women.

2. *Houston in the Rearview Mirror* (St. Martin's, 1990) Kovak travels to Houston to clear his sister of murder-suicide charges.

3. *Other People's Houses* (St. Martin's, 1990) Who is responsible for the carbon monoxide poisoning of respectable bank teller Lois Bell and her family?

4. *Chasing Away the Devil* (St. Martin's, 1991) Milt's wooing of his divorced childhood sweetheart is terminated when she is found in the trailer with her throat cut.

5. *Dead Moon on the Rise* (St. Martin's, 1994) Newly married to psychiatrist Jean McDonnell, Kovak is surprised when old friend Wade Moon returns to Prophesy County to run for sheriff against him.

6. *Doctors and Lawyers and Such* (St. Martin's, 1995) The night before Milt's election to the permanent sheriff's position, Milt's best friend's wife shoots herself with her husband's gun.

7. *Lying Wonders* (St. Martin's, 2002) A call from an old girlfriend gets Milt involved with the Holy Temple of Seven Trumpets and its sinister leader Brother Grigsby.

8. *Vegas Nerve* (St. Martin's, 2007) Milt gets embroiled in an assault and battery case in Las Vegas Nevada, when he bails out his cousin by marriage, Burl Upshank, who has been arrested for beating up his son-in-law, who attacked his pregnant wife.

II. Eloise Janine (E. J.) Pugh, romance writer, wife, mother, and amateur detective, and her underemployed husband, Willis (he does the dishes and works on their cars), are prominent citizens of the small Texas town of Black Cat Ridge. The feisty and formidable E. J. (5'10", 170 pounds) is always in the right place at the right time when crime strikes in this series of mysteries. The Texas setting is well rendered; E.J.'s romance novels less so.

1. *One, Two, What Did Daddy Do?* (St. Martin's, 1995) The entire Lester family, Black Cat Ridge neighbors of romance novelist E.J. Pugh, is wiped out by a shotgun, except for four-year-old Bessie.

2. *Hickory Dickory Stalk* (Avon, 1996) A teenage Peeping Tom is suspected of prank 911 calls and feeding candy spiked with glass to E.J.'s five-year-old daughter until he turns up dead in the back of E.J.'s station wagon.

2. *Home Again, Home Again* (Avon, 1997) E. J.'s husband, Willis, vanishes, and she isn't sure whether he is up to some sort of romantic hanky-panky or something far worse.

4. *There Was a Little Girl* (Avon, 1998) E. J. rescues suicidal teenager Brenna from a frozen Texas river and finds that Brenna has good reason to feel that her life isn't worth living.

5. *Not in My Backyard* (Avon, 1999) E. J. isn't especially pleased to have ex-convict Michael Whitby and his family as neighbors, but she comes to his defense when the harassment of the intolerant townsfolk takes a murderous turn.

6. *Crooked Little House, A* (Avon, 1999) When her sister-in-law June, never forgiven by Willis's family for his brother's tragic death, is arrested for the murder of a young homeless woman, E. J. comes to her defense.

7. *Don't Drink the Water* (Avon, 2000) E. J., her three sisters, and their husbands coalesce on a family vacation in the Caribbean. Of course a corpse turns up, this time in the family's beachfront house.

III. Female stand-up comic Kimmey Kruse is featured in a pair of mystery novels. The diminutive Kimmey is full of Texas sass, libido, and East Texas Cajun appeal.

1. *Funny as a Dead Comic* (St. Martin's, 1993) Kimmey and old flame Cab Neusberg find themselves on the same bill at Chicago's Kaiser Komedy Klub.

2. *Funny as a Dead Relative* (St. Martin's, 1994) Kimmey's black-sheep cousin dies of an apparent wasp sting during a family reunion in Port Arthur, Texas.

Cooper, William

PSEUDONYM OF Harry S. Hoff

Scenes from Provincial Life inspired a generation of postwar British writers. Its good-humored and realistic story about a young science master at a provincial grammar school pointed the way back to traditional narrative and away from the experimentalism of James Joyce (q.v.) and Virginia Woolf. Like Joe Lunn, the principal character in this semiautobiographical series, Cooper was a teacher, civil servant, and novelist. The other major characters are based upon significant people in Cooper's life: C. P. Snow (q.v.) is the original of Robert, Joe Lunn's friend and fellow writer. *Scenes from Metropolitan Life*, the second volume, was postponed for nearly 30 years to avoid a possible lawsuit by the model for Myrtle, Joe's girlfriend. *Scenes from Later Life* and *Scenes from Death and Life*, written many years after numbers 1, 2, and 3, bring Joe into the 1970s and 1980s. Numbers 1 and 3 were published in the United States as *Scenes from Life* (Scribner, 1961). Numbers 1 through 4 were published in two volumes by Dutton (1983–1984). Number 5 has not yet appeared in the United States.

1. *Scenes from Provincial Life* (Dutton, 1984) In 1939 28-year-old Joe Lunn is teaching science, writing his fourth novel, worrying about war, and avoiding marriage with Mildred. Originally published in the United Kingdom in 1950.
2. *Scenes from Metropolitan Life* (Dutton, 1984) In 1946 Joe is working in the same Whitehall office as his provincial friend Robert and pursuing Myrtle, who is married to someone else. Originally published in the United Kingdom in 1961.
3. *Scenes from Married Life* (Dutton, 1984) Pushing 40, Joe marries and has a daughter. His writing, his job, and his marriage are all going well. Originally published in the United Kingdom in 1961.
4. *Scenes from Later Life* (Dutton, 1984) Joe is 67, retired, and facing diminished means, ill health, and his mother's impending death.
5. *Scenes from Death and Life* (Smaller Sky Books [UK], 1999) Joe embarks on a new career in academia after his forced retirement from the civil service.

Corcoran, Tom

Another mystery series set in southern Florida features freelance photographer Alex Rutledge, whose work as a backup for the full-time professional forensic people in Key West (which "used to be a quaint drinking village with a fishing problem") sometimes gets him involved with murder cases. Alex drives a Shelby Mustang and has a string of girlfriends, some of whom turn up dead. The Florida Keys ambience is one of the biggest selling points in this series of fast-moving crime novels. Author Tom Corcoran is himself a resident of Key West and a professional photographer, whose work adorns Jimmy Buffett albums and book covers.

1. *Mango Opera, The* (St. Martin's, 1998) Key West–based freelance photographer Alex Rutledge's laid-back life is shaken up when an ex-girlfriend turns up after her roommate has been murdered.
2. *Gumbo Limbo* (St. Martin's, 1999) An old navy buddy of Alex's calls with an urgent message, then disappears in a case involving a long-ago drug deal and several murders.

3. *Bone Island Mambo* (St. Martin's, 2001) Rutledge becomes a suspect in a series of bizarre murders and decapitations in which the victims are dressed in drag.
4. *Octopus Alibi* (St. Martin's, 2003) Alex hopes to combine a seven-day shoot on Grand Cayman with some R & R, but a series of suspicious deaths and some impromptu beddings-down may abort his plans.
5. *Air Dance Iguana* (St. Martin's, 2005) Rutledge's brother becomes a key suspect when two men, 20 miles apart, are killed in the same strange way.

Cork, Barry

Scottish-born, London-based Scotland Yard detective and novelist Angus Straun has two great loves: golf (he is a low handicap player) and luxury sports cars (especially Maseratis). Angus usually gets to indulge both his passions in this entertaining, lightweight mystery series, which will appeal especially to readers who share Angus's tastes.

1. *Dead Ball* (Scribner, 1989) Sinister occurrences at the Royal West Wessex Golf Club during an international tournament bring Angus on the scene as a caddy and an investigator.
2. *Unnatural Hazard* (Scribner, 1990) An ancestral Scottish castle is turned into a hotel-cum-golf course with dire results for participants in a celebrity tournament.
3. *Laid Dead* (Scribner, 1991) Straun's ex-wife asks him to protect her wealthy Dutch lover from a Chinese American con man.
4. *Winter Rules* (Scribner, 1993) Angus is assigned to guard the new ruler of the African nation of Chakra, who hopes to introduce golf to his country as a tourist attraction.

Cormany, Michael

Dan Kruger is, in some respects, your typical hard-boiled private eye: he handles cases at bargain rates, abuses substances (alcohol, Kools, Valium, and speed, not necessarily in that order), and most of his acquaintances walk the meaner streets (of Chicago). Dan is untypical in that he hates violence, doesn't carry a gun, and plays blues guitar. Former blue-collar worker Cormany, from the Chicago suburb of Aurora, knows how to write detective novels with ingenious plots, unconventional characters, and a Windy City ambience.

1. *Lost Daughter* (Stuart, 1988) When Asia Dawson disappears, her wealthy father hires Kruger to find her.
2. *Red Winter* (Stuart, 1989) A Chicago building contractor's brief flirtation with the Communist Party has made him vulnerable to blackmail.
3. *Rich or Dead* (Birch Lane, 1990) An illegal alien found dead in a cheap hotel is linked to a missing bag of money with several sleazy claimants.
4. *Polaroid Man* (Birch Lane, 1991) There are plenty of suspects when beautiful, amoral Andrea Johnson is murdered.
5. *Skin Deep Is Fatal* (Birch Lane, 1992) A fellow inmate in detox hires Dan to look into the affairs of cosmetic heiress Shannon Harper.

Cornwell, Bernard

I. Richard Sharpe, the dauntless hero of this military adventure series set during the Napoleonic Wars, is an infantryman who has risen from the ranks in (the future Duke of) Wellington's Peninsular Army. The first Sharpe novel published finds him in Portugal and Spain, but later novels go back as far as 1799 and forward as far as 1821. The stories offer both exciting narrative and historical accuracy, including some fairly gruesome battlefield scenes, as well as beautiful ladies and evil villains. Fans of C. S. Forester's (q.v.) Hornblower novels, acknowledged as a model by British author Cornwell, should enjoy these tales, even though they take place mostly on dry land rather than on the high seas. Some Sharpe episodes were filmed for television and broadcast on PBS.

1. *Sharpe's Tiger: Richard Sharpe and the Siege of Seringapatam, 1799* **(Harper, 1997)** Sharpe, an illiterate private in southern India in 1799, appears to be a deserter who has joined the army of the Tippoo of Mysore.

2. *Sharpe's Triumph: Richard Sharpe and the Battle of Assaye, September 1803* **(Harper, 1999)** Richard, now Sergeant Sharpe, is assigned to prevent a large quantity of ammunition from falling into the hands of the Maharatta Confederation, which is resisting British encroachment in India.

3. *Sharpe's Fortress: Richard Sharpe and the Siege of Gawilghur, December 1803* **(Harper, 2000)** Junior officer Sharpe must recover a cache of stolen jewels and defeat the machinations of his sworn enemy, Sergeant Obadiah Hakeswill. Set against the backdrop of the Maharatta War and the siege of the fortress of Gawilghur.

4. *Sharpe's Trafalgar: Richard Sharpe and the Battle of Trafalgar, October 21, 1805* **(Harper, 2001)** Encroaching on C. S. Forester's (q.v.) and Patrick O'Brian's (q.v.) turf, Sharpe finds himself on a ship homeward bound to England from India and eventually involved in Nelson's great naval victory at Trafalgar.

5. *Sharpe's Prey: Richard Sharpe and the Expedition to Copenhagen, 1807* **(Harper, 2002)** In the role of regimental quartermaster, Sharpe finds himself in the thick of the British campaign to destroy the Danish navy at Copenhagen. Traitorous Captain John Lavisser provides the villainy here.

6. *Sharpe's Rifles: Richard Sharpe and the French Invasion of Galicia, January 1809* **(Viking, 1988)** Sharpe begins this novel as a quartermaster, but soon rises to lieutenant and receives his first command in French-occupied Spain.

7. *Sharpe's Havoc: Richard Sharpe and the Campaign in Northern Portugal, Spring 1809* **(Harper, 2003)** Sharpe and his men are cut off in a Portuguese village while the treacherous Colonel Christopher is confronted by the newly arrived Sir Arthur Wellesley (the future Duke of Wellington).

8. *Sharpe's Eagle: Richard Sharpe and the Talavera Campaign, July 1809* **(Viking, 1981)** In the novel that introduced Richard Sharpe to readers, Lieutenant Sharpe and a small detachment of men are separated from their battalion in Portugal.

9. *Sharpe's Gold: Richard Sharpe and the Destruction of the Almeida, August 1810* **(Viking, 1982)** Wellesley, in desperate need of funds, sends Captain Sharpe to search for gold hidden in the Portuguese hills.

10. *Sharpe's Escape: Richard Sharpe and the Bussaco Campaign, 1810* **(HarperCollins, 2004)** Captain Sharpe is forced to take Lieutenant Slingsby, Colonel Crawford's brother-in-law, under his wing.

11. *Sharpe's Fury: Richard Sharpe and the Battle of Barrosa, March 1811* **(HarperCollins, 2006)** A secret cabal of Spaniards who favor a rapprochement with France threatens the alliance between England and Spain in the fight against Bonaparte.

12. *Sharpe's Battle: Richard Sharpe and the Battle of Fuentes de Onoro, May 1811* **(Harper, 1995)** Sharpe faces the French Wolf Brigade and General Guy Loup in Spain.

13. *Sharpe's Company: Richard Sharpe and the Siege of Badajoz, January to April 1812* **(Viking, 1982)** Sharpe joins the bitter fighting to capture the ancient fortress city of Badajoz.

14. *Sharpe's Sword: Richard Sharpe and the Salamanca Campaign, June and July 1812* **(Viking, 1983)** Sharpe tracks down the infamous French spy Captain Leroux.

15. *Sharpe's Enemy: Richard Sharpe and the Defense of Portugal, Christmas 1812* **(Viking, 1984)** Major Sharpe must rescue Lady Farthingdale from a dangerous band of deserters.

16. *Sharpe's Honor: Richard Sharpe and the Vitoria Campaign, February to June 1813* **(Viking, 1985)** Framed by Napoléon's cunning spy Major Ducos, Sharpe is court-martialed but eludes his death sentence.

17. *Sharpe's Regiment: Richard Sharpe and the Invasion of France, June to November 1813* **(Viking, 1986)** Sharpe grows impatient waiting for replacements and sails to England to investigate the delay.

18. *Sharpe's Siege: Richard Sharpe and the Winter Campaign, 1814* **(Viking, 1987)** Sharpe is betrayed and trapped in a French fort, but manages a harrowing escape.

19. *Sharpe's Revenge: Richard Sharpe and the Peace of 1814* **(Viking, 1989)** Major Ducos has stolen Napoléon's treasure and shifted the blame to Sharpe.

20. *Sharpe's Waterloo: Richard Sharpe and the Waterloo Campaign, 15 June to 18 June 1815* **(Viking, 1990)** Sharpe is military advisor to the incompetent Prince of Orange at the Battle of Waterloo.

21. *Sharpe's Devil: Richard Sharpe and the Emperor, 1820–1821* **(Harper, 1992)** Living quietly in Normandy five years after Waterloo, Sharpe is asked to find Dona Luisa's missing husband in Chile.

II. This Cornwell series is set in the American Civil War. Nathaniel Starbuck, black-sheep son of a Boston abolitionist, enlists in the Confederate army at the outbreak of hostilities and fights for the South. Historical figures such as Jefferson Davis and George B. McClellan make appearances and Richard Sharpe's (see series I) son turns up as well.

1. *Rebel* **(Harper, 1993)** Northerner Nathaniel Starbuck becomes part of Washington Faulconer's private army fighting for the Confederacy.

2. *Copperhead* **(Harper, 1993)** Captain Starbuck is mistakenly jailed as a Yankee spy, then released and sent across Union lines as a double agent.

3. *Battle Flag* **(Harper, 1995)** Nate distinguishes himself at the Battle of Cedar Mountain in 1862 while serving with Stonewall Jackson's troops.

4. *Bloody Ground* **(Harper, 1996)** Starbuck, given command of a punishment battalion, joins Lee's army in time to fight at Harper's Ferry and then to the battle of Sharpsburg (Antietam), the bloodiest single day of the Civil War.

III. The Warlord Chronicles are a revisionist trilogy about King Arthur. Arthur is portrayed as a complex man whose impulsive decisions sometimes have tragic consequences. Lancelot is a dishonest charmer who betrays Arthur, not only through the seduction of the not-so-passive Guinevere, but also through his alliance with the Saxons against Arthur and Mordred's kingdom. Merlin is a crafty schemer fond of deceit and disguise. Christianity is portrayed as the political tool of thugs, opportunists, and hypocrites. Derfel Cadarn, a knight of Arthur's who later becomes a monk, narrates the events with force and dry wit.

1. *Winter King, The* (St. Martin's, 1996) Derfel Cadarn, monk and former warrior, narrates the story of Arthur's seizing of Guinevere and the battles that result from this impulsive act.
2. *Enemy of God* (St. Martin's, 1997) Arthur's dream of a unified kingdom with the Round Table at the center is shattered by Lancelot's treachery.
3. *Excalibur* (St. Martin's, 1998) The confrontation between the Christians and the Druids complicates Arthur's battle against the Saxons, as the Druid priestess Nimue seeks to sacrifice Arthur's son Gwydre to bring back the old religion.

IV. The Grail Quest series has an Arthurian theme, but it is set more solidly in historical times, the mid-14th century and the start of the Hundred Years' War between France and England. Thomas of Hookton, an archer who joins the forces of King Edward III to fight against the French, is searching for the Holy Grail even though he isn't sure of the Grail's existence.

1. *Archer's Tale, The* (Harper, 2001) Young Thomas of Hookton, a brilliant, handsome warrior skilled with the longbow, survives the pillaging of his village and joins Edward III's forces in France as an archer.
2. *Vagabond* (Harper, 2002) A book in Latin and Hebrew that Thomas inherited from his father may lead those who can understand it to the Holy Grail, if it actually exists. Meanwhile, Thomas is involved in battle scenes galore as the Hundred Years' War is in full swing.
3. *Heretic* (HarperCollins, 2003) In 1347 Thomas and a small group of soldiers capture a castle in Gascony, homeland of Thomas's father, partially to draw out his evil cousin Guy Vexille, who may have information about the Holy Grail.

V. Another historical series (one published, at least one more planned) takes us to the 19th century again as Captain Rider Sandman, like Richard Sharpe a Peninsular War and Waterloo veteran, is forced to play cricket for a living after his father's financial ruin and suicide. Sandman takes on the job of investigating a murder in high places.

1. *Gallows Thief* (Harper, 2002) Captain Rider Sandman is offered a job by the Home Secretary: looking into the case of portrait painter Charles Corday, convicted of murdering the Countess of Avebury.

VI. Another series by the prolific Cornwell is set in the 9th century, when the beleaguered Saxons are trying to fight off the invading Danes. A fictional character, Uhtred, interacts with historical characters like Alfred the Great. English Uhtred is adopted by the Dane Ragnar, which creates divided loyalties in him in this readable retelling of English history.

1. *Last Kingdom, The* (HarperCollins, 2005) Young Englishman Uhtred is adopted by the Dane Ragnar the Fearless after Ragnar wipes out his Northumberland family,
2. *Pale Horseman, The* (HarperCollins, 2006) Uhtred is torn by divided loyalties: should he throw in with the Saxon king, Alfred the Great, whom he finds less congenial than his former Danish comrades, whose simple lifestyle appeals to him?
3. *Lords of the North* (HarperCollins, 2007) Uhtred helps free Guthred, an enslaved Dane, who proclaims himself king of Northumbria and eventually betrays Uhtred.

4. *Sword Song: The Battle for London* (Harper, 2008) The Norse Viking brothers Sigefrid and Erik Thurgilson capture and occupy London.

Cornwell, Patricia (Daniels)

I. Dr. Kay Scarpetta, Chief Medical Examiner for the Commonwealth of Virginia, is one of the fastest rising stars in the mystery firmament. Intricate plotting, complex characters, page-turning suspense, and convincing forensic detail have garnered a legion of fans for this best-selling series. The first-person narrations by Kay bring a real immediacy to this series. Omnibus editions include *A Scarpetta Omnibus* (Putnam, 2000; numbers 1–3); *A Second Scarpetta Omnibus* (Putnam, 2000; numbers 4–6); *A Third Scarpetta Omnibus* (Putnam, 2002; numbers 7–9); and *The Scarpetta Collection* (Scribner, 2003, two volumes containing numbers 1–4).

Patricia Cornwell worked in the office of the chief medical examiner in Richmond, Virginia. She has won an Edgar for *Postmortem* and the Evangelical Christian Publishers Association award for *A Time for Remembering* (Harper, 1983), the biography of Billy Graham's wife, Ruth Bell Graham. Cornwell (with coauthor Marlene Brown) has also written *Food to Die For: Secrets from Kay Scarpetta's Kitchen* (Putnam, 2001). Cornwell's nonfiction book *Portrait of a Killer: Jack The Ripper, Case Closed* (Putnam, 2002), which identifies painter Walter Sickert as the Ripper, has, not surprisingly, stirred up a great deal of controversy.

1. *Postmortem* (Scribner, 1990) A serial killer is torturing and strangling young women in Richmond.
2. *Body of Evidence* (Scribner, 1991) Romance writer Beryl Madison has been murdered, and the manuscript of her autobiographical expose is missing.
3. *All That Remains* (Scribner, 1992) Scarpetta works on a series of murders of young couples where bone fragments are the only forensic evidence. Cornwell was sued by the parents of a murder victim, who claimed that she had included details of their daughter's homicide in this book.
4. *Cruel and Unusual* (Scribner, 1993) What looks like Ronnie Joe Wadell's gruesome handiwork turns up again after his conviction and execution.
5. *Body Farm, The* (Scribner, 1994) Kay investigates the mutilation murder of a North Carolina girl, which suggests the modus operandi of an escaped killer from Virginia.
6. *Potter's Field* (Scribner, 1995) Serial killer Temple Gault strikes again, leaving corpses in New York's Central Park and in Kay's own morgue in Richmond.
7. *Cause of Death* (Putnam, 1996) Members of a fascist cult are responsible for a series of murders that lead Kay to a dive with a Navy SEAL rescue squad and an up-close look at a robot operated via virtual reality.
8. *Unnatural Exposure* (Putnam, 1997) A high-tech virus that could produce a poxy epidemic takes Scarpetta all over, from Richmond, Virginia, to Utah, Memphis, Atlanta, Dublin, and London.
9. *Point of Origin* (Putnam, 1998) In her role as consultant to the FBI, Kay investigates a disastrous fire on a Virginia horse farm and turns up some human remains.
10. *Black Notice* (Putnam, 1999) Kay deals with a slew of problems ranging from grief at her lover's death, attempts to sabotage her career, and a serial killer self-styled "Loup-Garou" (werewolf).
11. *Last Precinct, The* (Putnam, 2000) Events in *Black Notice* continue to bedevil Kay Scarpetta as she examines yet another torture slaying. Introduces New York prosecutor Jaime Berger, modeled on real-life prosecutor and novelist Linda Fairstein (q.v.).

12. *Blow Fly* **(Putnam, 2003)** Licking her wounds after being driven from her job and mourning the loss of her lover, Kay has moved to a rental house in Florida and become a private forensic consultant. Then the coroner in Baton Rouge, Louisiana, asks for her advice on a drug overdose case.

13. *Trace* **(Putnam, 2004)** Five years after being fired, Kay returns to her office in Richmond, summoned by her replacement, Dr. Joel Marcus, to help him puzzle through the mysterious death of a 14-year-old girl.

14. *Predator* **(Putnam, 2005)** Working with the National Forensic Institute in Florida, Kay Scarpetta and her colleagues examine the X-rays of a man who was killed by a shotgun blast to the chest.

15. *Book of the Dead* **(Putnam, 2007)** Soon after relocating to Charleston, South Carolina, to start a private forensics laboratory, Kay is asked to consult on the murder of US tennis star Drew Martin, whose mutilated body was found in Rome.

II. A second mystery series features three leads rather than one: Police Chief Judy Hammer and Deputy Police Chief Virgina West (Charlotte, North Carolina) and newspaper reporter and amateur cop Andy Brazil. The second novel brings the team to Kay Scarpetta territory in Richmond, Virginia. So far this series, which is a mixture of humor, social commentary, and suspense, hasn't caught on in the way that the Scarpetta series did.

1. *Hornet's Nest* **(Putnam, 1996)** Forty-two-year-old Deputy Police Chief Virginia West, her unhappily married superior, Judy Hammer, and young, ambitious reporter Andy Brazil investigate the serial mutilations and murders of men from out of town that have set Charlotte on edge.

2. *Southern Cross* **(Putnam, 1999)** The Hammer-West-Brazil team is in Scarpetta country, Richmond, Virginia, to straighten out the local police department. An overheard phone conversation between local redneck Butner "Bubba" Fluck IV and a pal is one of the smoking guns here.

3. *Isle of Dogs* **(Putnam, 2001)** Judy Hammer, newly installed superintendent of the Virginia State Police, and Andy Brazil are caught in the middle when the eccentric Isle of Tangier in Chesapeake Bay declares war on the Commonwealth of Virginia.

Corrigan, John R.

Jack Austin, Maine native and journeyman PGA golfer, is the hero of this mystery series. Austin, who suffers from dyslexia, as does his creator, is a staunch, loyal person; the plots get better with each volume; and Corrigan does a fine job of portraying the world of professional golfers. Hardscrabble is an imprint of the University Press of New England. John R. Corrigan, who lives in Maine and writes about golf in *Golf Today*, should not be confused with the religious historian John Corrigan (*How the Idea of Religious Toleration Came to the West*, etc.).

1. *Cut Shot* **(Sleeping Bear, 2001)** A rookie pro reveals to Jack Austin that a Mafia-run gambling ring has invaded the PGA Tour. Jack, who loves the game, is bound to investigate.

2. *Snap Hook* **(Hardscrabble, 2004)** Jack's game is off, as he is involved with a bunch of problems: an infant is kidnapped; Jack's romance with CBS golf analyst Lisa Trembley is on the skids; Jack is breaking in an inexperienced caddy; and Jack's putting is even worse than usual.

3. *Center Cut* **(Hardscrabble, 2004)** The murder of a caddy and the disappearance of a tour player's wife engage Jack here as he struggles to win his first tournament. A climactic match with Tiger Woods is included.

4. *Bad Lie* **(Hardscrabble, 2005)** The estranged father of a college student whom Jack has taken under his wing is murdered.

5. *Out of Bounds* **(University Press of New England, 2006)** Members of the PGA Tour have been dying mysteriously—from performance-enhancing drugs?

Corrington, John William & Joyce H.

The late John William Corrington was a writer "of little fame but much talent," according to one critic. Although he wrote fiction, poetry, and soap opera scripts, Corrington reached a wide reading audience only with the detective novels he coauthored with his wife, Joyce. Ralph "Rat" Trapp is a black, laconic, streetwise homicide officer with the New Orleans Police Department. The seedier side of New Orleans is well evoked in this series.

1. *So Small a Carnival* **(Viking, 1986)** Rat Trapp and reporter Wes Colvin interview survivors of the Huey Long era, many of whom have not forgotten old enmities.

2. *Project Named Desire, A* **(Viking, 1987)** Trapp's childhood flame Camille and her son Danny hope to escape the projects through Danny's rock-music group.

3. *Civil Death, A* **(Viking, 1987)** Wes Colvin's exposé of corrupt officials was written with information supplied by a Mob hit man.

4. *White Zone, The* **(Viking, 1990)** Rat goes to Los Angeles at Camille's request as Danny's star is joining the illustrious ranks on Hollywood Boulevard.

Corris, Peter

I. Sydney-based Cliff Hardy is Australia's version of Philip Marlowe (q.v.) and other American hard-boiled private investigators. Cliff is tough and street-smart but loyal to his ideals, has a messy private life (unamicably divorced), and appreciates the tolerance and classlessness of Australian life, while detesting what he sees as greed and "conservatism." Author Peter Corris, who also writes historical fiction and nonfiction and books on golf, and is responsible for other detective series, does a good job of transferring the Chandleresque ambience of America's "mean streets" to an Australian setting. Availability of the Australian-published series in the United States has been spotty, and many of the 29 titles are not generally available in American bookstores and libraries. At least one omnibus volume has been published: *A Cliff Hardy Collection* (Picador [Australia], 1986; numbers 1–3).

1. *Dying Trade, The* **(Fawcett, 1986)** PI Cliff Hardy of the tough King's Cross District in Sydney, Australia, can't afford to turn down cases, so he agrees to find out who has been threatening the twin sister of wealthy real-estate heir Bryn Gutteridge. Originally published in Australia in 1980.

2. *White Meat* **(Fawcett, 1986)** Rich bookie Ted Tarleton's missing daughter Noni is referred to as "white meat" in the aboriginal La Perouse district. Originally published in Australia in 1981.

3. *Marvelous Boy, The* **(Fawcett, 1986)** Lady Catherine Chatterton, widow of the eminent judge, hires Hardy to find her missing grandson, who was last seen two years earlier by an aging drunk. Originally published in Australia in 1982 with the spelling Marve*ll*ous.

4. *Empty Beach, The* **(Fawcett, 1986)** Cliff investigates the supposed drowning of black-marketer and poker-machine king, John Singer, in the violent underworld of Bondi. Originally published in Australia in 1983. *The Empty Beach* was made into an Australian movie starring Bryan Brown.

5. *Heroin Annie and Other Cliff Hardy Stories* (Fawcett, 1987) A collection of short stories. Originally published in Australia in 1984.

6. *Make Me Rich* (Fawcett, 1987) Appearing in a security role at a party, Cliff meets the interesting Helen Broadway and Paul Guthrie, who wants him to look for his stepson, Ray. Originally published in Australia in 1985.

7. *Big Drop and Other Cliff Hardy Stories, The* (Fawcett, 1988) A collection of short stories. Originally published in Australia in 1985.

8. *Greenwich Apartments, The* (Fawcett, 1988) Filmmaker Carmel Wise was shot dead outside the Greenwich Apartments in Kings Cross. Was she an innocent victim of gangland violence, or was she deep in a pornography racket? Originally published in Australia in 1986.

9. *Deal Me Out* (Fawcett, 1986) William Mountain, alcoholic TV scriptwriter and would-be novelist, is missing while searching for "adventure." Hardy is given the task of finding him. Originally published in Australia in 1986.

10. *January Zone, The* (Fawcett, 1988) Hardy goes as far afield as Washington, DC, while protecting Trudy Bell, assistant to politician Peter January, who is the recipient of death threats and hate mail. Originally published in Australia in 1987.

11. *Man in the Shadows: A Short Novel and Six Stories* (Allen & Unwin [Aus.], 1988) In the short novel *Man in the Shadows*, Gareth Grenway leads Hardy into a world of neurosurgeons, mental patients, and AIDS sufferers. Not published in the United States.

12. *O'Fear* (Doubleday, 1991) The enigmatic Kevin O'Fearna, known as O'Fear, may know a lot about the death by car accident/possible homicide of Korean War veteran Barnes Todd. Originally published in Australia in 1989.

13. *Wet Graves* (Dell, 1995) The 1940s construction of the Sydney Harbour Bridge, the case of missing schoolteacher Brian Madden, and efforts by person(s) unknown to cancel Cliff Hardy's licence somehow fit together. Originally published in Australia in 1991.

14. *Aftershock* (Bantam [Aus.], 1992) If the Newcastle earthquake was the cause of Oscar Bach's death, why was he seen alive five minutes after the quake? Not published in the United States.

15. *Beware of the Dog* (Dell, 1995) A phone call from Paula Wilberforce leads to Cliff's involvement with a dysfunctional Chandleresque high-society family. Originally published in Australia in 1992.

16. *Burn and Other Stories* (Bantam [Aus.], 1993) A collection of short stories. Not published in the United States.

17. *Matrimonial Causes* (Dell, 1994) Hardy recalls his first case, in the early 1970s: a melange of divorce, perjury, fraud, murder, crooked cops, lawyers, and a call girl. Originally published in Australia in 1993.

18. *Casino* (Bantam [Aus.], 1994) Cliff Hardy turns down the job as head of security at the new Sydney casino because he hates the thought of regular hours and wearing a suit. Then his friend Scott Galvani, who takes the job, is murdered. Not published in the United States.

19. *Washington Club, The* (Bantam [Aus.], 1997) When Hardy is hired to look into the background of accusations against Claudia Fleischman, charged with the murder of her developer husband, he is introduced to the shadowy world of corporate high-fliers at the exclusive Washington Club. Not published in the United States.

20. *Forget Me If You Can: Cliff Hardy Stories* (Bantam [Aus.], 1997) A collection of short stories. Not published in the United States.

21. *Reward, The* (Bantam [Aus.], 1997) Although he has a hot new lover, financial considerations lead Cliff to claim the reward on a 17-year-old abduction case that the cops know more about than they are letting on. Not published in the United States.

22. *Black Prince, The* (Bantam [Aus.], 1998) In a trail leading all the way to an Aboriginal community in northern Queensland, Hardy follows star athlete Clinton, "the Black Prince," as Clinton chases the dealer responsible for his girlfriend's death. Not published in the United States.

23. *Other Side of Sorrow, The* (Bantam [Aus.], 1999) After more than 20 years, Cliff gets a phone call from his ex-wife Cynthia, who is dying of cancer and is desperate to get in contact with the daughter she gave up for adoption, a daughter fathered by Cliff, unbeknownst to him. Not published in the United States.

24. *Lugarno* (Bantam [Aus.], 2001) Cliff has been hired by high-flying consultant Martin Price, who lives in the posh waterside suburb of Lugarno, to find out who's been supplying heroin to Price's teenage daughter. Not published in the United States.

25. *Salt and Blood* (Bantam [Aus.], 2002) Former flame Glen Withers, now also a PI, but with a wealthier clientele, collaborates with Cliff on the case of Rodney St. John Harkness, recent inmate of a mental institution and a recovering alcoholic. Not published in the United States.

26. *Master's Mates* (Allen & Unwin [Aus.], 2003) Cliff travels to New Caledonia after he is hired by Lorraine Master, whose husband has been convicted of smuggling heroin. Distributed in the United States by Independent.

27. *Coast Road, The* (Allen & Unwin [Aus.], 2004) Feisty academic Elizabeth Farmer is suspicious of the accidental verdict in her father Frederick's death by fire at his weekend home. Distributed in the United States by Independent.

28. *Taking Care of Business: Cliff Hardy Cases* (Allen & Unwin [Aus.], 2004) Collection of short stories. Not published in the United States.

29. *Saving Billie* (Allen & Unwin [Aus.], 2005) Billie Marchant, ex-stripper, sometime hooker, and druggie, is a person of intense interest to media big-wheel Jonas Clement and journalist Louise Kramer, who is bent on exposing Clement. Distributed in the United States by Independent.

30. *Undertow, The* (Allen & Unwin (Aus.), 2007) Frank Parker, retired senior policeman and Hardy's longtime friend, is having second thoughts about a case from early in his career involving two doctors.

II. Ray "Creepy" Crawley is hard-boiled like Cliff Hardy, but instead of being a PI, he is a Secret Service agent. The books are based on the ABC-TV series *Pokerface*, cocreated with Bill Garner, and some of the characters from the TV series put in appearances in the books. The series has not been published in the United States.

1. *Pokerface* (Penguin [Aus.], 1985) Introduces Ray Crawley and other characters in the series. There is also a TV play of the same title, written with Bill Garner. Not published in the United States.

2. *Baltic Business, The* (Penguin [Aus.], 1987) A routine assignment draws Crawley into a web of murder and intrigue involving Eastern European refugees. Not published in the United States.

3. *Kimberly Killing, The* (Penguin [Aus.], 1988) An automobile collision leads to a bloodfest and Crawley's latest investigation. Not published in the United States.

4. *Cargo Club, The* (Penguin [Aus.], 1990) No annotation available. Not published in the United States.

5. *Azanian Action, The* (Angus & Robertson [Aus.], 1991) Ray Crawley solves the murder of a black South African nationalist in Australia. Not published in the United States.

6. *Japanese Job, The* (Angus & Robertson [Aus.], 1992) No annotation available. Not published in the United States.

7. *Time Trap, The* (HarperCollins [Aus.], 1994) No annotation available. Not published in the United States.
8. *Vietnam Volunteer, The* (Southern Cross [Aus.], 2000) No annotation available. Not published in the United States.

III. Richard Browning, Australian part-time actor, part-time private eye, and full-time rogue, recalls, in old age, his early days in Hollywood in this series of humorous capers subtitled *From the Tapes and Papers of Richard Browning*. They are listed below without annotations. Not published in the United States.

1. *Box Office Browning* (Penguin [Aus.], 1987)
2. *Beverly Hills Browning* (Penguin [Aus.], 1988)
3. *Browning Takes Off* (Penguin [Aus.], 1989) Alternate title: *Browning on the Wing*.
4. *Browning in Buckskin* (Penguin [Aus.], 1991)
5. *Browning P.I.* (Angus & Robertson [Aus.], 1992)
6. *Browning Battles On* (Angus & Robertson [Aus.], 1993)
7. *Browning Sahib* (HarperCollins [Aus.], 1994)
8. *Browning without a Cause* (Imprint [Aus.], 1995)

IV. Luke Dunlop is an agent for the Witness Protection Agency in Australia in this trio of novels not published in the United States. They are listed below without annotations.

1. *Set Up* (Pan [Aus.], 1992)
2. *Cross Off* (Pan [Aus.], 1993)
3. *Get Even* (Pan [Aus.], 1994)

Cory, Desmond

PSEUDONYM OF Shaun McCarthy

I. Welsh mathematics professor John Dobie is bumbling and vague except when discussing abstruse mathematical concepts, or applying his weirdly logical mind to the solution of crimes. Shaun McCarthy, author of this light mystery series, was born in Sussex but has spent much of his career in sunnier places, such as Spain and Cyprus.

1. *Catalyst, The* (St. Martin's, 1991) When two murdered women turn up in his bed within the space of a few hours, Dobie transforms himself from suspect to sleuth. Published in the United Kingdom as *The Strange Attractor*.
2. *Mask of Zeus, The* (St. Martin's, 1993) The administrators of his college in Wales persuade John to accept a visiting professorship in Cyprus.
3. *Dobie Paradox, The* (St. Martin's, 1994) Dobie and his best girl Dr. Kate Coyle have gone to the Tongwynlais Rehabilitation Centre near Cardiff at the behest of a famous author.

II. Johnny Fedora is a British agent and sometime assassin-for-hire in this series of adventures involving espionage, neo-Nazis, and plots against civilization-as-we-know-it. Many of the novels are set in Spain, a country that "Desmond Cory" knows well. Numbers 12 through 16 are known as the Feramontov Quintet, Feramontov being Fedora's nemesis, a former Soviet agent who is clever, resourceful, and as bad as they come. The Fedora novels are clever, light entertainment in the James Bond tradition. They are listed below without annotations.

1. *Nazi Assassins, The* (Award, 1970) Originally published in the United Kingdom as *Secret Ministry* in 1951.
2. *Gestapo File, The* (Award, 1971) Originally published in the United Kingdom as *This Traitor, Death* in 1952.
3. *Hitler Diamonds, The* (Award, 1979) Originally published in the United Kingdom as *Dead Man Falling* in 1953.
4. *Trieste* (Award, 1968) Originally published in the United Kingdom as *Intrigue* in 1954.
5. *Dead Men Alive* (Award, 1969) Originally published in the United Kingdom as *The Height of Day* in 1955.
6. *High Requiem* (Award, 1969) Originally published in the United Kingdom in 1956.
7. *Swastika Hunt, The* (Award, 1969) Originally published in the United Kingdom as *Johnny Goes North* in 1956.
8. *Mountainhead* (Award, 1968) Originally published in the United Kingdom as *Johnny Goes East* in 1958.
9. *Johnny Goes West* (Walker, 1967) Originally published in the United Kingdom in 1959.
10. *Johnny Goes South* (Walker, 1964) Originally published in the United Kingdom in 1959. Variant title: *Overload*.
11. *Head, The* (Muller [UK], 1960) Not published in the United States.
12. *Undertow* (Walker, 1963) Originally published in the United Kingdom in 1962.
13. *Shockwave* (Walker, 1964) Originally published in the United Kingdom as *Hammerhead* in 1963.
14. *Feramontov* (Walker, 1966)
15. *Timelock* (Walker, 1967)
16. *Sunburst* (Walker, 1971)

III. Cory has three other series characters: Lindy Grey (numbers 1–4), Mr. Pilgrim (numbers 5–6), and Mr. Dee (numbers 7–8). Only the Pilgrim books were published in the United States. The titles are listed below without annotations.

1. *Begin Murderer!* (Muller [UK], 1951) Lindy Grey. Not published in the United States.
2. *This Is Jezebel* (Muller [UK], 1952) Lindy Grey. Not published in the United States.
3. *Lady Lost* (Muller [UK], 1953) Lindy Grey. Not published in the United States.
4. *Shaken Leaf, The* (Muller [UK], 1955) Lindy Grey. Not published in the United States.
5. *Pilgrim at the Gate* (Washburn, 1958) Mr. Pilgrim. Originally published in the United Kingdom in 1957.
6. *Pilgrim on the Island* (Walker, 1961) Mr. Pilgrim. Originally published in the United Kingdom in 1959.
7. *Stranglehold* (Muller [UK], 1960) Mr. Dee. Not published in the United States.
8. *Name of the Game, The* (Muller [UK], 1964) Mr. Dee. Not published in the United States.

Coulter, Catherine

PSEUDONYM OF Jean Coulter Pogony

I. Most of best-selling author Coulter's many historical romance novels are in series, because readers and Coulter herself like the idea of characters continuing from one book to another. Coulter, a Georgette Heyer (q.v.) fan with an MA in early 19th-century history, likes the British Regency period (early 1800s) best, and many of her novels are set in that era, but she has also written novels set in other periods, such as the Middle Ages (see series VI and VII) and contemporary times (see series VIII). Coulter is based in northern California with a physician husband and an elderly cat. The Legacy Trilogy, which is set in the Regency period, concerns members of the Wyndham family and their cohorts on both sides of the Atlantic.

1. *Wyndham Legacy, The* (**Putnam, 1994**) Marcus Wyndham receives the title of Earl of Chase, but his detested cousin Josephina will inherit his uncle's money if she marries Marcus.
2. *Nightingale Legacy, The* (**Putnam, 1994**) Byronic Frederick North Nightingale meets beautiful, spirited Caroline Derwent-Jones at an inn between London and his Cornish castle.
3. *Valentine Legacy, The* (**Putnam, 1995**) James Wyndham is bested in horsemanship by his hoydenish American cousin Jessie Warfield.

II. The Bride Trilogy has expanded into a 10-novel saga. The Sherbrooke family is the connecting link in this paperback original series set in the Regency period with the usual quota of rakish gentlemen, high-spirited ladies, exciting adventures, humorous episodes, and romantic suspense.

1. *Sherbrooke Bride, The* (**Jove, 1992**) Douglas Sherbrooke, Earl of Northcliffe, needing an heir, marries young Alexandra Chambers, although he prefers her sister. The Virgin Bride, a reputed phantom, plays a role. First novel in *The Bride Trilogy*.
2. *Helllion Bride, The* (**Jove, 1992**) A supernatural affair, this time on the Sherbrooke sugar plantation in Jamaica, brings rakish Ryder Sherbrooke into the orbit of Sophia Stanton-Greville, whose teasing manner may mask a terrifying secret. Second novel in *The Bride Trilogy*.
3. *Heiress Bride, The* (**Jove, 1992**) Sinjun Sherbrooke, a teenager in numbers 1 and 2, now 19, blue-eyed, witty, high-spirited, and bored with the London Season, meets Colin Kinross, Earl of Ashburnham, and elopes with him to Scotland, where she encounters another ghost. Third novel in the Bride Trilogy.
4. *Mad Jack* (**Jove, 1998**) Members of the Sherbrooke clan, especially the now-married Sinjun, reappear in their full glory in this tale about Winifrede Levering Bascombe, "Mad Jack," who arrives in London accompanying her aunts as a valet.
5. *Courtship, The* (**Jove, 2000**) Spenser Heatherington, a character in number 1, and Helen Mayberry, a character in number 5, are the protagonists here. Heatherington, Lord Beecham, is a rakish bachelor who meets his match in Helen, nobly born herself but mistress of an inn.
6. *Scottish Bride, The* (**Jove, 2001**) In the aftermath of the Battle of Waterloo, Tysen Sherbrooke, widowed vicar and father of three, is informed that he has become the new Baron Barthwick of Kildrum, Scotland. Fourth in the Bride series.
7. *Pendragon* (**Jove, 2002**) In 1824, Meggie Sherbrooke, Tysen's daughter, her heart broken by Jeremy Stanton-Greville, makes a hasty marriage to Thomas Macolmbe, Earl of Lancester.
8. *Sherbrooke Twins, The* (**Jove, 2004**) Identical twins James and Jason fall in love, but their romances are put on the back burner when someone tries to kill their father, Douglas.
9. *Lyon's Gate* (**Jove, 2005**) Jason Sherbrooke, who longs to breed and race his own horses, is claimed by a spirited woman.
10. *Wizard's Daughter* (**Jove, 2008**) Beautiful young Rosalind de la Fontaine has no memory of her name, her family, or her heritage since being saved and adopted by Ryder Sherbrooke as a girl.

III. The Night Trilogy, first published in paperback in 1989–1990, reissued by Avon in 2002, and rewritten and "cleaned up" (according to the author), is another Regency series. Although the leading protagonists are different in each novel, characters who are secondary in one novel come to the fore in another. As in the Legacy Trilogy, this series covers both sides of the Atlantic. Wit, humor, and outrageous circumstances season this romantic mix.

1. *Night Fire* (**Avon, 2002**) Widow Areille Leslie and returning warrior Burke Drummond, Earl of Ravensworth, are star-crossed lovers. Rewritten version of the novel originally published by Avon in 1989.
2. *Night Shadow* (**Avon, 2002**) Winthrop, Viscount Castlerosse, a character in *Night Fire*, quintessential Regency bachelor, is nonplussed when a woman claiming to be the widow of his murdered cousin turns up with three children. Slightly "cleaned-up" reissue of the novel originally published by Avon in 1989.
3. *Night Storm* (**Avon, 2002**) Alec Carrick, Baron Sherard, originally met in *Night Fire*, decides he wants to take over a shipyard in Baltimore, Maryland, but Genny Paxton, the owner's daughter, is a complication. Rewritten and reissued version of the novel originally published by Avon in 1990.

IV. The Magic Trilogy, yet another Regency series, has been reissued but not rewritten. Only loosely connected by some of its characters, this trilogy ranges from Scotland to London to Cornwall in the 1810s, and contains its quota of rakes, high-spirited ladies, and sometimes broad humor.

1. *Midsummer Magic* (**New American Library, 1987**) Philip Hawksbury, Earl of Rothermere, obeying his father's dying wish, journeys to Scotland to offer himself in marriage to one of the daughters of Alexander Kilbracken.
2. *Calypso Magic* (**New American Library, 1988**) In London in 1813, Lyonel Ashton, Earl of Saint Leven, crosses swords with Diana Savarol, Caribbean heiress, who is unhappy at being offered on London's "marriage market."
3. *Moonspun Magic* (**New American Library, 1988**) Rafael Carstairs, a character from *Calypso Magic*, traveling to see his brother Damien, Baron Drago, in Cornwall, rescues Virginia Albemarle from smugglers.

V. The Star Trilogy has become, with the reissue of *Sweet Surrender* as *Evening Star*, the Star Quartet. This series takes place mainly in San Francisco in the 1850s, some 40 years and several thousand miles away from Coulter's Regency settings. A lot of Regency romance trappings are here: strong, passionate men and women who have romantic and suspenseful adventures before everything works out.

1. *Evening Star* (**New American Library, 2001**) Alex Saxton, San Francisco entrepreneur, first meets wronged heiress Aurora Van Cleve in a Roman brothel and then at the infamous Roman Flower Auction where she is to be sold to the highest bidder. Originally published as *Sweet Surrender* in 1984.
2. *Midnight Star* (**New American Library, 1986**) Delaney Saxton, Alex's brother, has struck it rich in the California Gold Rush of 1849, and remains as an entrepreneur in the growing town of San Francisco.
3. *Wild Star* (**New American Library, 1986**) Handsome gambler Brent Hammond falls in love in San Diego, but sees his beloved again in San Franciso as the wife of a rich older man.
4. *Jade Star* (**New American Library, 1986**) Saint Morris first sees Juliana DuPres on the island of Maui, then sees her again as she is being sold in a Barbary Coast slave auction.

VI. The Viking series takes readers back to the 10th century CE when men were fierce, savage, and passionate, and women had to fight for their rights with all the means at their disposal. The remoter reaches of the British Isles are, more often than not, the locale for this series, loosely tied by some of its characters and time period. *Season of the Sun* was not regarded as part of the series until it was reissued in 2002.

1. *Season of the Sun* (Penguin, 1991) Magnus Haraldsson, on a trading visit to York, wants red-haired Zarabeth to be his wife, but acquires her as his slave.
2. *Lord of Hawkfell Island* (Jove, 1993) Rorik, Lord of Hawkfell, seizes bird-loving Mirana as a hostage in a raid on the Viking fortress of Clontarf in Ireland.
3. *Lord of Raven's Peak* (Jove, 1994) Merrik Haraldsson, Lord of Raven's Peak, returns with two female slaves from Kiev who are more than they appear to be.
4. *Lord of Falcon Ridge* (Jove, 1995) Chessa of Hawkfell Island and Cleve of Raven's Peak come together when she is kidnapped by the wily Ragnor of York, and has to be rescued.

VII. The Medieval Song series (originally the Song Trilogy and then the Medieval Song quartet before it reached its current six volumes) is set in 13th-century England, Cornwall, Wales, and points further afield. Full of romance and action, with some mystery and magic thrown in, this medieval regency series has proven quite popular. Numbers 1 through 3 were reissued together as *The Song Trilogy* (Seafarer, 1994). *The Fenwyth Curse* and *Rosehaven* are included in the series because of some continuing characters from the Song trilogy.

1. *Warrior's Song* (New American Library, 2001) Chandra de Avenell, warrior maiden, has no use for her designated husband, Jerval de Vernon, at first. Originally published as *Chandra* (New American Library, 1983). Extensively rewritten.
2. *Fire Song* (New American Library, 1985) Graelam de Moreton, a character from *Warrior's Song*, a hard and ruthless warrior, finds himself the husband of gentle and yielding Kassia de Lorris of Brittany.
3. *Earth Song* (Penguin, 1990) Philippa de Beauchamp, to escape an unwanted marriage, flees her father's castle in a wool wagon, and then meets up with roguish Dienwald de Fortenberry.
4. *Secret Song* (Penguin, 1991) Roland de Tournay, a character in *Earth Song*, must rescue lady-in-distress Daria de Fortescue from a Welsh stronghold
5. *Rosehaven* (Putnam, 1996) In 1277 Hastings of Trent and Severin Langthorne are joined in marriage, so that Hastings's father, the dying Earl of Oxborough, will have a strong man in Severin to manage his estates and provide heirs to his line.
6. *Penwyth Curse, The* (Jove, 2003) Dienwald and Philippa from *Earth Song* reappear in this rather complicated tale of two sets of heroes and heroines set in 1278.

VIII. Catherine Coulter *does* write contemporary novels, among which are the novels in the FBI Suspense Thriller Series. FBI agents Lacey Sherlock and Dillon Savich are the principal continuing characters in this series, which ranges all over the map of the United States. *The Beginning* (Berkley, 2005) contains numbers 1 and 2.

1. *Cove, The* (Jove, 1996) FBI Special Agent James Quinlan follows Sally Brainerd, whose father has been murdered, into the quaint little town of old folks called The Cove.
2. *Maze, The* (Putnam, 1997) Dillon Savich, who appeared in *The Cove*, is now the head of the FBI's Criminal Apprehension Unit (CAU). New agent Lacey Sherlock is working for Savich, but she is brooding about the murder of her sister seven years before.
3. *Target, The* (Putnam, 1998) Savich and Sherlock appear again in this mystery set in a cabin high in the Colorado Rockies, where Ramsey Hunt, seeking solitude, rescues a small girl unconscious in the forest.
4. *Edge, The* (Putnam, 1999) FBI agent Ford "Mac" MacDougal, recovering from injuries received in a car bombing, feels a link

with a medical researcher when she drives her Porsche off an Oregon cliff. He is eventually joined by Savich and Sherlock.
5. *Riptide* (Putnam, 2000) Becca Matlock, political speechwriter, is working on the reelection campaign of the governor of New York, when she receives the first of many menacing phone calls.
6. *Hemlock Bay* (Putnam, 2001) Dillon Savich and his wife, Lacey Sherlock, get involved in a case concerning his younger sister Lily and four very valuable paintings.
7. *Eleventh Hour* (Putnam, 2002) FBI agent Dane Carver, along with the Savich-Sherlock team, investigates the murder of Father Michael Joseph in his San Francisco church.
8. *Blindside* (Putnam, 2003) Savich and Sherlock are on the trail of a serial killer who targets math teachers, but then six-year-old Sam Kettering is kidnapped.
9. *Blowout* (Putnam, 2004) Savich and Sherlock investigate the murder, committed in the Court's library, of Supreme Court Justice Stewart Califano.
10. *Point Blank* (Putnam, 2005) Ruth Warnecki is lost in a cave in rural Virginia, while fellow agents Savich and Sherlock are on the trail of a psychotic old man and his teenage companion, who have kidnapped a small-time comedian.
11. *Double Take* (Putnam, 2007) Julia Ransom is thrown off San Francisco's Pier 39 by an unknown assailant and rescued by FBI Special Agent Cheney Stone.

Courter, Gay

Hannah Blau's struggles to achieve success as a professional, a wife, and a mother are set in the era shortly before and after World War I. The story of Hannah's rise from Russian Jewish immigrant to head midwife at Bellevue Hospital in New York is interwoven with the World War, the Russian Revolution, the fight for female suffrage, and the battle for information about birth control.

1. *Midwife, The* (Houghton Mifflin, 1991) Hannah and her family flee anti-Semitic Russia for America and a chance to realize their dreams.
2. *Midwife's Advice, The* (Dutton, 1992) Hannah becomes chief midwife at Bellevue, conducts a steamy affair with the head of obstetrics, and becomes a sexual advisor to her female patients.

Coward, Mat

Fans of British procedurals have welcomed with open arms Detective Inspector Don Packham and Detective Frank Mitchell of the London Police. The manic-depressive Packham and the easygoing family man Mitchell make an engaging couple in this series of mysteries full of humor and snappy repartee. Readers aren't sure whether these novels are comic mysteries or spoofs of mysteries but are enjoying them too much to worry about the distinction. Mat Coward is a British political satirist, author of such nonfiction books as *Success . . . and How to Avoid It* (TTA Press [UK], 2004); compiler of *Cannibal Victims Speak Out* (Orion [UK], 1995); and author of columns for the *New Statesman* ("The New Year's Dishonour's List," etc.).

1. *Up and Down* (Five Star, 2000) The team of Packham and Mitchell are introduced in the investigation of the murder of a 78-year-old retiree in his suburban London "allotment" (rented garden plot).
2. *In and Out* (Five Star, 2001) A darts-playing woman has apparently been murdered by one of her teammates.

3. *Over and Under* **(Five Star, 2004)** The annual cricket match between the Comedians and the Writers is spoiled when a cricket player is killed (with a baseball bat!).

4. *Open and Closed* **(Five Star, 2005)** A man is murdered in the Bath Street Library in Cowden, apparently while a sit-in protesting the closure of the library was taking place in the same building.

Coyle, Harold (W.)

I. American writer Harold Coyle, best known for examinations of speculative contemporary military conflict, has written a pair of Civil War novels featuring two Irish American brothers drawn into opposite sides of the conflict. The Bannon brothers, James, a private in the Confederate army, and Kevin, a captain in the Union forces, experience a series of bloody battles, meet some real-life historical characters, and eventually are brought together. The battle scenes are well done.

1. *Look Away* **(Simon & Schuster, 1995)** In events from 1856 to 1863, two Irish immigrant brothers, James and Kevin Bannon, driven apart by their father, wind up on opposite sides in the American Civil War.

2. *Until the End* **(Simon & Schuster, 1996)** The Bannon brothers continue on opposite sides in the Civil War, James as a private in a Confederate infantry regiment and Kevin as a captain in a Union regiment.

II. Coyle has started, with coauthor Barrett Tillman, a series featuring Strategic Solutions Inc., a private paramilitary company that works for the highest bidder.

1. *Pandora's Box* **(Forge, 2007)** Introduces Strategic Solutions Inc., among the best of the private paramilitary companies that work for the highest bidder. Coauthored by Barrett Tillman.

2. *Prometheus's Child* **(Forge, 2007)** The US government hires SSI to send a team to Chad to train its army in counterinsurgency techniques. Coauthored with Barrett Tillman.

Craft, Michael

I. When we first encounter Mark Manning, he is a gay journalist working for a Chicago newspaper; living in a loft with his lover, architect Neil Waite; and getting involved in the occasional murder mystery. In the third novel, Mark moves out of Chicago back to the small town of Dumont, Wisconsin, where he spent part of his childhood, to take over the family newspaper. Some readers find Mark insufferably smug and his story lines obvious, while others find these amateur detective yarns entertaining. Mark also appears as a character in *Desert Winter* (series II, number 3).

1. *Flight Dreams* **(Kensington, 1997)** Journalist Mark Manning has 90 days to prove that a wealthy heiress missing for nearly seven years is alive or he forfeits his job.

2. *Eye Contact* **(Kensington, 1998)** Mark Manning is sceptical of claims of astrophysicist Pavo Zarnik that he discovered a new planet. Then Mark's fellow reporter is fatally shot.

3. *Body Language* **(Kensington, 1999)** Mark moves back to his boyhood home of Dumont, Wisconsin, to take over the family newspaper. Then Mark's cousin Suzanne is murdered at a dinner party.

4. *Name Games* **(St. Martin's, 2000)** Carrol Cantrell, "king of miniatures," is strangled to death before the opening of a dollhouse craft show in Dumont.

5. *Boy Toy* **(St. Martin's, 2001)** Thad Quatrain, Mark's 17-year-old nephew and ward, who has evinced talent as an actor, has the role of alternating lead with fellow teenager Jason Thrush in the Dumont Player's Guild new play.

6. *Hot Spot* **(St. Martin's, 2002)** An electric shock that kills a major donor to Carl Creighton, Democratic candidate for lieutenant governor of Illinois, turns out to be no accident, and Creighton's newlywed bride, Roxanne Exner, is the chief suspect.

7. *Bitch Slap* **(St. Martin's, 2004)** Mark is preparing for a business merger with a local paper company. Meanwhile, Gillian Reece, the manager of the paper company, is feuding with her husband about funding an Eastern Studies center.

II. Fiftyish Broadway director and amateur detective Claire Gray made what looked like a solo appearance in *Rehearsing* (1993) but became a series character eight years later in *Desert Autumn*. Claire has a lover young enough to be her son and many theatrical friends, straight and gay, and can spare time from her directing and teaching duties to solve some fairly complicated mysteries. Mark Manning and Thad Quatrain, characters from series I, put in appearances in number 3.

1. *Rehearsing* **(Los Hombres, 1993)** Claire Gray, one of Broadway's most respected directors, takes a year off to be visiting professor at her alma mater and runs into George McBeth, gay local actor, who has dreams of making it big.

2. *Desert Autumn* **(St. Martin's, 2001)** Claire accepts the position of theater department chair at Desert Arts College in California's Sonora Desert. Then a colleague's wife is murdered.

3. *Desert Winter* **(St. Martin's, 2003)** Characters from series I, Mark Manning and his actor nephew, Thad, who is appearing in one of Claire's plays at Desert Arts College, help Claire to ferret out the murderer of wealthy, elderly, lecherous collector Stewart Chaffee.

4. *Desert Spring* **(St. Martin's, 2004)** The corpse of a philandering Hollywood producer-playwright, whose play Claire's students are performing, turns up in Claire's swimming pool.

5. *Desert Summer* **(St. Martin's, 2005)** Felicia Yeats, obnoxious second wife of billionaire Desert Arts College founder D. Glenn Yeats, imbibes a fatal dose of antifreeze with her cocktail.

Craig, Alisa

PSEUDONYM OF **Charlotte MacLeod**

I. Charlotte MacLeod (q.v.), author of light mysteries under her own name, writes, if anything, even lighter series under her Alisa Craig nom de plume. Inspector Madoc Rhys, plainclothes detective for the Royal Canadian Mounted Police, is acutely aware of his Welsh heritage and his extended Welsh family. Most of the fun comes not from the plots, but from descriptions of Welsh customs, the Canadian countryside, and a parcel of eccentric characters.

1. *Pint of Murder, A* **(Doubleday, 1980)** A jar of beans gives Agatha Treadway a fatal dose of botulism. "Accident," says Dr. Druffett, who is just about to become the next victim.

2. *Murder Goes Mumming* **(Doubleday, 1981)** Madoc and his fiancée Janet go to a house party at a lumber magnate's mansion on the shores of Bay Chaleur in New Brunswick.

3. *Dismal Thing to Do, A* **(Doubleday, 1986)** Janet, Madoc's wife, seems to have abandoned her car in the middle of nowhere, leaving behind nothing but her handbag and a faint burning odor.

4. *Trouble in the Brasses* **(Avon, 1992)** Sir Emlyn Rhys, Madoc's father, is guest conductor of the Wagstaffe Symphony Orchestra when its principal horn player comes to a violent end.

5. *Wrong Rite, The* (Morrow, 1992) Sir Cardoc Rhys's ninetieth birthday has brought the far-flung Rhys clan back together in Wales.

II. The members of the Grub-and-Stake Gardening and Roving Club of Lobelia Falls, Ontario, solve any murders that come their way. If you like light mysteries with characters with names like Hiram Jellyby, Arethusa Monk, and Zilla Trott, then this series is for you.

1. *Grub-and-Stakers Move a Mountain, The* (Doubleday, 1981) A murder done with a bow and arrow and a crooked land deal arouse the interest of the Grub-and-Stakers.
2. *Grub-and-Stakers Quilt a Bee, The* (Doubleday, 1985) The new director of the Aralia Polymphea Architrave Museum takes a fatal dive from its mansard roof.
3. *Grub-and-Stakers Pinch a Poke, The* (Avon, 1988) The Grub-and-Stakers have entered the Scottsbeck drama competition with a dramatization of *The Shooting of Dan McGrew*.
4. *Grub-and-Stakers Spin a Yarn, The* (Avon, 1990) Miss Jane Fuzzywuzzy's Yarnery has bloodstains on the living room floor and the corpse of a mincemeat magnate on the sidewalk outside.
5. *Grub-and-Stakers House a Haunt* (Morrow, 1993) The Grub-and-Stakers hunt for the bones and reputed hidden gold of slain mule skinner Hiram Jellyby.

Craig, Brian

PSEUDONYM OF Brian Stableford

British science-fiction writer Brian M. Stableford (q.v.) has also published under the pseudonym of Brian Craig. Among the titles published under the Craig name are *Ghost Dancers* (GW Books, 1991) and the Orfeo or Warhammer fantasy trilogy. The trilogy consists of three tales set in the 16th century of an alternate Earth told by the minstrel Orfeo while in jail. The novels were game tie-ins published by GW Books/Games Workshop.

1. *Zaragoz* (GW Books, 1990) The minstrel Orfeo stumbles into a net of treachery, deception, and sorcery at the Castle Zaragoz.
2. *Plague Demon* (GW Books, 1990) The second tale told by Orfeo to his jailer is about Harmis Datz, a soldier in a small country threatened by a once-human servant of the Plague God.
3. *Storm Warriors* (GW Books, 1991) Orfeo's third tale concerns a king in Morien who allows a band of elves, who are not quite what they seem, to settle in his land.

Craig, Philip R.

Martha's Vineyard, Massachusetts, is the island scene of the mysteries solved by J. W. "Jeff" Jackson, ex-Boston cop turned fisherman, handyman, and sometime private investigator. J. W. and his off-again, on-again significant other and eventual wife, Zee Madieras, enjoy the Vineyard ambience, especially the seafood (a few recipes are supplied along with each mystery), and the reader will too, even if the plots are sometimes a bit far-fetched. The late (d. 2007) Philip R. Craig coauthored numbers 13, 17, and 19 with William G. Tapply (q.v.).

1. *Beautiful Place to Die, A* (Scribner, 1989) A boat explosion off the Vineyard shore nearly kills Billy Martin, recovering drug abuser.
2. *Woman Who Walked into the Sea, The* (Scribner, 1991) Professors Ian McGregor and Marjorie Summerharp are writing a paper about a lost Shakespeare play when Summerharp's body turns up in a fishing net.

3. *Double Minded Men, The* (Scribner, 1992) An emerald necklace stolen 200 years ago is about to be returned to the Padishah of Sarofim by the elderly sisters who inherited it.
4. *Cliff Hanger* (Scribner, 1993) Zee goes off-island for a medical conference. In her absence, J. W. takes an interest in young Geraldine, victim of an abusive lover.
5. *Off Season* (Scribner, 1994) An eccentric recluse is slain with a bow and arrow as hunters and animal-rights activists feud over 50 acres of choice Vineyard land.
6. *Case of Vineyard Poison, A* (Scribner, 1995) A female college student found dead in J. W.'s driveway had withdrawn $100,000 from her bank account.
7. *Death on a Vineyard Beach* (Scribner, 1996) J. W. and Zee have finally married. A trip to the opera in Boston is interrupted when J. W. foils an attempt to murder retired mafioso Luciano Marcus.
8. *Deadly Vineyard Holiday, A* (Scribner, 1997) J. W. befriends Cricket Callahan, the teenage daughter of the vacationing US president, and runs into a possible "inside" plot against her.
9. *Shoot on Martha's Vineyard, A* (Scribner, 1998) While J. W. is working as a driver-guide for visiting Hollywood scout Drew Mondry, state environmental officer Lawrence Ingalls is murdered one day after he and J. W. had a dispute turned physical about a beach closing.
10. *Fatal Vineyard Season, A* (Scribner, 1999) With Zee and the kids off on the mainland, J. W. gets a job protecting two African American actresses who are vacationing on the Vineyard.
11. *Vineyard Blues* (Scribner, 2000) An old friend, blues guitarist Corrie Appleyard, turns up at J. W.'s Vineyard home. Then a possibly arsonous fire burns down Corrie's lodging, leaving an unidentified body inside.
12. *Vineyard Shadows* (Scribner, 2001) Two thugs from South Boston appear at J. W.'s home and terrorize his wife and stepdaughter. Against the advice of local authorities, J. W. takes the investigation into his own hands.
13. *First Light* (Scribner, 2002) Subtitle: *The First Ever Brady Coyne/ J. W. Jackson Novel*. In this entry, coauthored by William G. Tapply (q.v.), Craig's J. W. Jackson and Tapply's Brady Coyne team up to solve some missing persons cases.
14. *Vineyard Enigma* (Scribner, 2002) J. W. searches for two ancient soapstone eagles allegedly stolen from African ruins, while Zee seems to be falling for cultivated and attractive African Abraham Mahsimba, who has put J. W. on the case.
15. *Vineyard Killing, A* (Scribner, 2003) While J. W. and Zee are enjoying an off-season lunch with friends at the Vineyard Haven deli, someone tries to kill Paul Fox, brother of real-estate tycoon Donald Fox.
16. *Murder at a Vineyard Mansion* (Scribner, 2004) The murders of a security man at a Chappaquiddick "castle" and the son of an aristocratic land owner are more important than the apprehension of "the Silencer," who has been destroying the sound systems of the loudest cars on the island.
17. *Second Sight* (Scribner, 2005) Written with William G. Tapply (q.v.). J. W. and Tapply's Brady Coyne team up when Coyne traces a runaway teenage girl to the Vineyard while J. W. is providing security for a reclusive singer.
18. *Vineyard Stalker* (Scribner, 2007) Zee's friend Carole Cohen asks J. W. to help track down a stalker harassing her reclusive brother, Roland Nunes, known as "the Monk."
19. *Third Strike* (Scribner, 2007) The third and last team-up between J. W. Jackson and William G. Tapply's (q.v.) Brady Coyne. Coyne responds to a call for help from an old client living on the Vineyard, where J. W. is being urged by his wife to investigate the death of a striking ferry-boat worker.

Crais, Robert

Los Angeles–based private eye Elvis Cole is smart-mouthed but compassionate, cynical but romantic, tough but with a taste for ethnic food and yoga. Joe Pike, his partner, is a borderline sociopath who comes in handy when a little intimidation is needed. Lucy Chenier, Elvis's girlfriend, is a New Orleans lawyer. Crais, scriptwriter for *Hill Street Blues* and *L.A. Law*, writes exciting, witty, well-characterized thrillers that seem to get better with every new book. Crais has also written three stand-alone thrillers: *Demolition Angel* (Doubleday, 2000); *Hostage* (Doubleday, 2001); and *The Two Minute Rule* (Simon & Schuster, 2006).

1. *Monkey's Raincoat, The* (Bantam, 1987) A case involving a vanished Hollywood agent, a drug lord, and two missing kilos of cocaine.
2. *Stalking the Angel* (Bantam, 1989) Elvis goes to Japantown to sample the octopus sushi and to locate a missing copy of a martial arts book.
3. *Lullaby Town* (Bantam, 1992) Elvis travels to Connecticut to track down the former wife of Hollywood director Peter Alan Nelsen.
4. *Free Fall* (Bantam, 1993) Jennifer Sheridan asks Elvis to find out what is bothering her fiancé, Mark Thurman, undercover cop with an elite Los Angeles Police Department unit.
5. *Voodoo River* (Hyperion, 1995) Elvis is in Ville Platte, Louisiana, to uncover information about television star Jodi Taylor's birth parents.
6. *Sunset Express* (Hyperion, 1996) Continuing his romance with Louisiana lawyer Lucy Chenier, Elvis takes on the case of Linda Martin, whose body was found in a garbage bag.
7. *Indigo Slam* (Hyperion, 1997) The three children of mystery man Clark Hewitt want Elvis to find their missing father in a case involving Vietnamese revolutionaries and Russian and Ukrainian mobsters.
8. *L.A. Requiem* (Doubleday, 1999) Readers learn much more about Joe Pike, Elvis's tough, taciturn, and enigmatic partner in this installment involving the missing daughter of a Hispanic businessman.
9. *Last Detective, The* (Doubleday, 2003) After a four-year absence, Elvis returns in a case involving the kidnapping of Lucy Chenier's 10-year-old son by avengers for war crimes allegedly committed by Elvis in Vietnam.
10. *Forgotten Man, The* (Doubleday, 2004) A murdered "John Doe" has claimed, with his dying breath, to be Elvis Cole's father, a man he never met.
11. *Watchman, The* (Simon & Schuster, 2007) Joe Pike is featured here. To pay back an old debt, Joe has to protect Larkin Barkley, a young heiress whose life is in danger after a "wrong place, wrong time" encounter.

Crane, Hamilton

PSEUDONYM OF Sarah J. Mason

Sarah J. Mason, author of the Trewley and Stone mystery novels, continued the Miss Seeton series after Heron Carvic (q.v.) and Hampton Charles (q.v.) under the pseudonym "Hamilton Crane." Crane has now published more Seeton novels than Carvic or Charles put together, keeping the formula of humorous, light mysteries in a well-described English village (Plummergen, Kent) setting.

1. *Miss Seeton Paints the Town* (Berkley, 1991) Having submitted her drawings to the Best Kept Village competition, Miss Seeton runs into a case of arson.
2. *Miss Seeton Cracks the Case* (Berkley, 1991) A motor coach tour is robbed by a gang of highwaymen.
3. *Hands Up, Miss Seeton* (Berkley, 1992) Miss Seeton is suspected of being a thief's accomplice when she tries to aid a "wounded" man.
4. *Miss Seeton Rocks the Cradle* (Berkley, 1992) A baby abandoned in a telephone booth turns out to be a missing heiress.
5. *Miss Seeton by Moonlight* (Berkley, 1992) Miss Seeton gives a painting to Scotland Yard so that it can be stolen.
6. *Miss Seeton Plants Suspicion* (Berkley, 1993) A local youth is arrested for murder, but the real killer abducts Miss Seeton.
7. *Miss Seeton Goes to Bat* (Berkley, 1993) Burglaries upset Plummergen while Miss Seeton sketches a cricket match.
8. *Starring Miss Seeton* (Berkley, 1994) Playing a backstage role in Plummergen's Christmas pageant, Miss Seeton uncovers a collection of rare silver.
9. *Miss Seeton Undercover* (Berkley, 1994) A television crew comes to Plummergen to film a rare apple.
10. *Miss Seeton Rules* (Berkley, 1994) Miss Seeton unwittingly aids a terrorist organization when she creates a disturbance at a local power plant.
11. *Sold to Miss Seeton* (Berkley, 1995) An antique-hunting jaunt leaves Miss Seeton with a trunk valuable enough to kill for.
12. *Sweet Miss Seeton* (Berkley, 1996) Avant-garde sculptor Antony Scarlett wants to use Miss Seeton's Plummergen cottage as a mold for his latest project, which involves filling the house with chocolate.
13. *Bonjour, Miss Seeton* (Berkley, 1997) French count, widower Jean-Louis de Balivernes, brings his daughter, Louise, for a visit to Plummergen, and romance may be in the offing for Miss Seeton.
14. *Miss Seeton's Finest Hour* (Berkley, 1999) In what is billed as Miss Seeton's "first mystery" and "Hamilton Crane's" swan song as a mystery writer, Miss Seeton answers her country's call during World War II.

Creasey, John

I. When John Creasey died in 1973 at the age of 64, he had published more than 560 books under his own name and more than 20 pseudonyms, including western, romance, sports, and juvenile titles, as well as thrillers and mysteries. The sheer volume of work and the unavailability of some titles never published in the United States make annotation for each title nearly impossible. Creasey wrote several series under his own name, including Department Z, Sexton Blake, and Dr. Palfrey. Listed below are Inspector West and the Toff, the two most popular series written under the Creasey name. See under J. J. Marric (q.v.) for the Gideon books and under Anthony Morton (q.v.) for the Baron series. There were also series written under the Gordon Ashe, Norman Deane, Robert Caine Frazer, Michael Halliday, Kyle Hunt, and Jeremy York pseudonyms. Titles are arranged by their UK publication date, which is usually the correct chronological sequence as well, though development through time is of minor importance.

Roger West, known as "Handsome" West for his tall, blond good looks, was introduced in 1942 as an Inspector and gradually worked his way up to Chief Superintendent of Scotland Yard. West has a talent for correctly anticipating his quarry's every move. Happily married—though they once came close to divorce—Roger and Janet West have two sons whose development from birth to college is chronicled in these books.

1. *Inspector West Takes Charge* (Scribner, 1972) Originally published in 1942.

2. *Getaway for Inspector West* (Scribner, 1972) Originally published in 1943. UK title: *Inspector West Leaves Town*. Variant title: *Go Away to Murder*.

3. *Inspector West at Home* (Scribner, 1973) Originally published in 1944.

4. *Inspector West Regrets* (Paul [UK], 1946)

5. *Holiday for Inspector West* (Paul [UK], 1946)

6. *Battle for Inspector West* (Paul [UK], 1948)

7. *Case Against Paul Raeburn, The* (Harper, 1958) Originally published in 1948. UK title: *Triumph for Inspector West*.

8. *Sport for Inspector West* (Harper, 1958) Originally published in 1949. UK title: *Inspector West Kicks Off*.

9. *Inspector West Alone* (Scribner, 1975) Originally published in 1950.

10. *Creepers, The* (Harper, 1952) Originally published in 1950. UK title: *Inspector West Cries Wolf*.

11. *Figure in the Dusk, The* (Harper, 1953) Originally published in 1951. UK title: *A Case for Inspector West*.

12. *Dissemblers, The* (Scribner, 1967) Originally published in 1951. UK title: *Puzzle for Inspector West*.

13. *Blind Spot, The* (Harper, 1954) Originally published in 1952. UK title: *Inspector West at Bay*. Variant title: *The Case of the Acid Throwers*.

14. *Give a Man a Gun* (Harper, 1954) Originally published in 1953. UK title: *A Gun for Inspector West*.

15. *Send Inspector West* (Scribner, 1976) Originally published in 1953. UK title: *Send Superintendent West*.

16. *Beauty Queen Killer, The* (Harper, 1956) Originally published in 1954. UK title: *A Beauty for Inspector West*. Variant title: *So Young, So Cold, So Fair*.

17. *Gelignite Gang, The* (Harper, 1956) Originally published in 1955. UK title: *Inspector West Makes Haste*. Variant titles: *Night of the Watchman*; *Murder Makes Haste*.

18. *Murder 1, 2, 3* (Harper, 1955) UK title: *Two for Inspector West*. Variant title: *Murder Tips the Scales*.

19. *Death of a Postman* (Harper, 1957) Originally published in 1956. UK title: *Parcels for Inspector West*.

20. *Death of an Assassin* (Scribner, 1960) Originally published in 1956. UK title: *A Prince for Inspector West*.

21. *Hit and Run* (Scribner, 1959) Originally published in 1957. UK title: *Accident for Inspector West*.

22. *Trouble at Saxby's, The* (Harper, 1959) Originally published in 1957. UK title: *Find Inspector West*. Variant title: *Doorway to Death*.

23. *Murder London–New York* (Scribner, 1961) Originally published in 1958.

24. *Killing Strike, The* (Scribner, 1961) Originally published in 1958. UK title: *Strike for Death*.

25. *Death of a Racehorse* (Scribner, 1962) Originally published in 1959.

26. *Case of the Innocent Victims, The* (Scribner, 1966) Originally published in 1959.

27. *Murder on the Line* (Scribner, 1963) Originally published in 1960.

28. *Death in Cold Print* (Scribner, 1962) Originally published in 1961.

29. *Scene of the Crime, The* (Scribner, 1963) Originally published in 1961.

30. *Policeman's Dread* (Scribner, 1964) Originally published in 1962.

31. *Hang the Little Man* (Scribner, 1964) Originally published in 1963.

32. *Look Three Ways at Murder* (Scribner, 1965) Originally published in 1964.

33. *Murder London–Australia* (Scribner, 1965)

34. *Murder London–South Africa* (Scribner, 1966)

35. *Executioners, The* (Scribner, 1967)

36. *So Young to Burn* (Scribner, 1968)

37. *Murder London–Miami* (Scribner, 1969)

38. *Part for a Policeman, A* (Scribner, 1970)

39. *Alibi* (Scribner, 1971)

40. *Splinter of Glass, A* (Scribner, 1972)

41. *Theft of Magna Carta, The* (Scribner, 1973)

42. *Extortioners, The* (Scribner, 1974)

43. *Sharp Rise in Crime, A* (Scribner, 1979)

II. The Toff is the Honorable Richard Rollison, a handsome gentleman-adventurer like Charteris's The Saint (q.v.) whose exploits and amours are serviceable escapist fare, thrillers rather than mysteries. Jolly, the Toff's funereally correct valet-secretary, is a loyal and resourceful assistant.

1. *Introducing the Toff* (Long [UK], 1938)

2. *Toff Goes On, The* (Long [UK], 1939)

3. *Toff Steps Out, The* (Long [UK], 1939)

4. *Here Comes the Toff* (Walker, 1967) Originally published in 1940.

5. *Toff Breaks In, The* (Long [UK], 1940)

6. *Salute the Toff* (Walker, 1971) Originally published in 1941.

7. *Toff Proceeds, The* (Walker, 1968) Originally published in 1941.

8. *Toff Goes to Market, The* (Walker, 1967) Originally published in 1942.

9. *Toff Is Back, The* (Walker, 1974) Originally published in 1942.

10. *Toff among the Millions, The* (Walker, 1976) Originally published in 1943.

11. *Accuse the Toff* (Walker, 1975) Originally published in 1943.

12. *Toff and the Curate, The* (Walker, 1969) Originally published in 1944. Variant title: *The Toff and the Deadly Parson*.

13. *Toff and the Great Illusion, The* (Walker, 1967) Originally published in 1944.

14. *Feathers for the Toff* (Walker, 1970) Originally published in 1945.

15. *Toff and the Lady, The* (Walker, 1970) Originally published in 1946.

16. *Poison for the Toff* (Pyramid, 1965) Originally published in 1947. UK title: *The Toff on Ice*.

17. *Hammer the Toff* (Long [UK], 1947)

18. *Toff in Town, The* (Walker, 1977) Originally published in 1948.

19. *Toff Takes Shares, The* (Walker, 1972) Originally published in 1948.

20. *Toff and Old Harry, The* (Walker, 1970) Originally published in 1949.

21. *Toff on Board, The* (Walker, 1973) Originally published in 1949.

22. *Foul Play Suspected* (Walker, 1966) Originally published in 1950. UK title: *Fool the Toff*.

23. *Kill the Toff* (Walker, 1966) Originally published in 1950.

24. *Knife for the Toff, A* (Pyramid, 1964) Originally published in 1951.

25. *Mask for the Toff, A* (Walker, 1966) Originally published in 1951. UK title: *The Toff Goes Gay*.

26. *Hunt the Toff* (Walker, 1969) Originally published in 1952.

27. *Call the Toff* (Walker, 1969) Originally published in 1953.

28. *Toff Down Under, The* (Walker, 1969) Originally published in 1953. Variant title: *Break the Toff*.

29. *Toff at Butlins, The* (Walker, 1976) Originally published in 1954.

30. *Toff at the Fair, The* (Walker, 1968) Originally published in 1954.

31. *Six for the Toff, A* (Walker, 1969) Originally published in 1955. Variant title: *A Score for the Toff*.

32. *Toff and the Deep Blue Sea, The* (Walker, 1967) Originally published in 1955.

33. *Make-Up for the Toff* (Walker, 1967) Originally published in 1956. Variant title: *Kiss the Toff*.

34. *Toff in New York, The* (**Pyramid, 1964**) Originally published in 1956.
35. *Model for the Toff* (**Pyramid, 1965**) Originally published in 1957.
36. *Toff on Fire, The* (**Walker, 1966**) Originally published in 1957.
37. *Toff and the Stolen Tresses, The* (**Walker, 1965**) Originally published in 1958.
38. *Toff on the Farm, The* (**Walker, 1964**) Originally published in 1958. Variant title: *Terror for the Toff.*
39. *Double for the Toff* (**Walker, 1965**) Originally published in 1959.
40. *Toff and the Runaway Bride, The* (**Walker, 1964**) Originally published in 1959.
41. *Rocket for the Toff, A* (**Pyramid, 1964**) Originally published in 1960.
42. *Toff and the Kidnapped Child, The* (**Walker, 1965**) Originally published in 1960.
43. *Follow the Toff* (**Walker, 1967**) Originally published in 1961.
44. *Toff and the Toughs, The* (**Walker, 1968**) Originally published in 1961. UK title: *The Toff and the Teds.*
45. *Doll for the Toff, A* (**Walker, 1965**) Originally published in 1963.
46. *Leave It to the Toff* (**Pyramid, 1965**) Originally published in 1963.
47. *Toff and the Spider, The* (**Walker, 1966**)
48. *Toff in Wax, The* (**Walker, 1966**)
49. *Bundle for the Toff, A* (**Walker, 1968**)
50. *Stars for the Toff* (**Walker, 1968**)
51. *Toff and the Golden Boy, The* (**Walker, 1969**)
52. *Toff and the Fallen Angels, The* (**Walker, 1970**)
53. *Vote for the Toff* (**Walker, 1971**)
54. *Toff and the Trip-Trip Triplets, The* (**Walker, 1972**)
55. *Toff and the Terrified Taxman, The* (**Walker, 1973**)
56. *Toff and the Sleepy Cowboy, The* (**Walker, 1974**)
57. *Toff and the Crooked Copper, The* (**Hodder [UK], 1977**)
58. *Toff and the Dead Man's Finger, The* (**Hodder [UK], 1978**)

Crespi, Camilla T(rella)

PSEUDONYM OF Camilla Trinchieri

Simona Griffo is a Roman expatriate living in Greenwich Village. She is a slightly overweight, pasta-cooking advertising executive whose interest in human nature keeps getting her involved in murder mysteries that she solves with the help of her lover, New York homicide detective Stan Greenhouse.

1. *Trouble with Moonlighting, The* (**Zebra, 1991**) Johanna Gayle, star of the film *Where Goes the Future*, for which Simona is moonlighting as a dialogue coach, is murdered.
2. *Trouble with a Small Raise, The* (**Zebra, 1991**) Arriving early Monday morning to hit up her boss Fred Critelli for a raise, Simona finds him dead in his office.
3. *Trouble with Too Much Sun, The* (**Zebra, 1992**) Griffo finds a machete-hacked corpse wrapped in a windsurfer sail while supervising a suntan-oil photo shoot on the island of Guadeloupe.
4. *Trouble with Thin Ice, The* (**Harper, 1994**) Simona and Stan Greenhouse go to the Sleepy Hollow Inn in Connecticut for a wedding.
5. *Trouble with Going Home, The* (**Harper, 1995**) Simona goes back to Rome to have a heart-to-heart talk with her mother, who has left her current husband.
6. *Trouble with a Bad Fit, The* (**HarperCollins, 1996**) Simona is hired by designer Roberta Riddle to investigate the murder of Phyllis Striker, her fitting model.
7. *Trouble with a Hot Summer, The* (**HarperCollins, 1997**) Advertising executive Bud Warren hires Simona to investigate the year-old drowning death of his ex-wife.

Crichton, Michael (John Michael)

The multitalented Michael Crichton (d. 2008) was a master of the technothriller novel. Starting with *The Andromeda Strain* (Knopf, 1969), he successfully mixed scientific fact and speculation with exciting action to produce page-turning best sellers. *Jurassic Park*, his dinosaur thriller, was such a success as a book and film that it was almost inevitable that Crichton would write a sequel. Crichton recycled the dinosaur theme and chaos scientist Ian Malcolm and expropriated the title of Arthur Conan Doyle's (q.v.) earlier novel (1912) for another go-round of "dinos redux."

1. *Jurassic Park* (**Knopf, 1990**) The latest thing in theme parks features real, live, DNA-replicated dinosaurs in a controlled setting where "nothing can go wrong."
2. *Lost World, The* (**Knopf, 1995**) Five years after the action in *Jurassic Park*, carcasses of recently deceased saurians are washing ashore near the defunct Jurassic Park.

Crider, Bill (Allen Billy)

I. Texan Crider is one of the more successful writers of the rural crime drama. Sheriff Dan Rhodes of Clearview, Blacklin County, Texas, is saddled with shiftless deputies, quaint locals, a town where the chief recreations are emu rustling, beer drinking, and cock fighting, and more than his share of bizarre crimes. However, patient, shrewd, low-key Dan is equal to the tasks set before him in this warm, humorous procedural series.

1. *Too Late to Die* (**Walker, 1986**) Thurston, Texas, pop. 408, is the scene of Blacklin County's first murder in 100 years.
2. *Shotgun Saturday Night* (**Walker, 1987**) Handyman Bert Ramsey turns up several boxes full of severed limbs, and is then murdered himself.
3. *Cursed to Death* (**Walker, 1988**) The disappearance of the local dentist, the murder of the dentist's wife, a near riot at a nursing home, and his own romantic entanglements occupy Sheriff Dan.
4. *Death on the Move* (**Walker, 1989**) Jewelry is being stolen off the corpses at Clyde Ballinger's funeral home.
5. *Evil at the Root* (**St. Martin's, 1990**) A bizarre string of murders at Sunny Dale Nursing Home is culling out the residents.
6. *Booked for a Hanging* (**St. Martin's, 1992**) Book dealer Simon Graham is found hanging from the rafters of an old college building he had planned to restore.
7. *Murder Most Fowl* (**St. Martin's, 1994**) Lige Ward, who lost his hardware business to the new Wal-Mart, is found floating downriver in a bullet-riddled Porta Potti.
8. *Winning Can Be Murder* (**St. Martin's, 1996**) Clearview High's football team's last-minute victory in the state-championship game may have been the death of offensive coach Brady Meredith.
9. *Death by Accident* (**St. Martin's, 1998**) A triple murder investigation that involves womanizing by one victim and shoddy contract work on local houses by another, a fight over pond rights, and a projected Native American celebration engage Dan here.
10. *Ghost of a Chance, A* (**St. Martin's, 2000**) Sheriff Rhodes has his hands full in dealing with ghosts at the jail, a couple of murders, and members of the Clearview Sons and Daughters of Texas outraged by thefts from the local cemetery.
11. *Romantic Way to Die, A* (**St. Martin's, 2001**) A convention of romance novelists in Blacklin Country leads to the death of romantic paperback cover-boy Terry Don Coslin and Henrietta Byam, who is writing an exposé of her romance-writing colleagues.

12. *Red, White, and Blue Murder* (St. Martin's, 2003) *Clearview Herald* reporter Jennifer Loam accuses Dan Rhodes and some of Blacklin County's commissioners of corruption.

13. *Mammoth Murder, A* (St. Martin's, 2006) A dead body turns up in a Blacklin County forest known for its Bigfoot sightings; then town character Bud Turley turns up a Bigfoot tooth.

14. *Murder among the Owls* (St. Martin's, 2007) Helen Harris, community fixture and Old Women's Literary Society (OWLS) member, is found dead on her kitchen floor, apparently from a fall.

15. *Of All Sad Words* (St. Martin's, 2008) When the Crawford brothers' trailer blows up, leaving one Crawford dead, Dan stumbles on an illegal still with a fresh batch of "likker."

II. Truman "Tru" Smith, semiretired private investigator, spends a lot of time fishing on Galveston Island (Texas), reading Faulkner in the company of his cat Nameless, and feeling inadequate. Every once in a while the reluctant, moody Tru gets dragged into a case against his better judgment.

1. *Dead on the Island* (Walker, 1991) Private investigator Tru Smith returns to his native Galveston on a search for his missing sister.

2. *Gator Kill* (Walker, 1992) A dead alligator deposited on the property of a family friend brings Smith out of self-imposed retirement.

3. *When Old Men Die* (Walker, 1994) "Outside Harry," well-known indigent of Galveston Island, is missing, and Tru's friend Dino, who "adopted" the old bum, wants Tru to investigate.

4. *Prairie Chicken Kill, The* (Walker, 1996) The shooting of a Prairie Chicken on federally protected land brings Tru to Picketville, Texas, where his high school sweetheart, Anne Lindeman, lives.

5. *Murder Takes a Break* (Walker, 1997) Dino persuades Truman Smith to investigate the disappearance of college student Randall Kirbo.

III. Mild-mannered, unheroic Carl Burns, English professor at the Baptist-run Hartley Gorman College in Pecan, Texas, would seem to be an unlikely sleuth, but he does get to the bottom of things in these dryly humorous academic mysteries. Crider is himself an English professor at an academic institution in Texas.

1. *One Dead Dean* (Walker, 1988) Tyrannical Dean Elmore is murdered after announcing his plan to create an degree program with extensive credit given for "life experience."

2. *Dying Voices* (St. Martin's, 1989) Best-selling poet and all-around blowhard Edward Street is shot in the forehead when he returns to Hartley Gorman College where he once taught.

3. *Dangerous Thing, A* (Walker, 1994) Political correctness has arrived at Hartley Gorman College. Sexual harassment suits have proliferated, and a history professor has a fatal fall out a second-story window.

IV. Crider seems to have shifted his academic mystery scene from Hartley Gorman College to Hughes Community College near Houston. This time, two English professors are involved: Dr. Sally Good and Professor Jack Neville. As with the Carl Burns's novels, this series is humorous fare for cozy fans.

1. *Murder Is an Art* (St. Martin's, 1999) Did Tammi Thompson's irate husband murder art department chair Val Hurley because he painted her in the nude? Dr. Sally Good and Professor Jack Neville, unimpressed by the efforts of the local police, decide to investigate.

2. *Knife in the Back, A* (St. Martin's, 2002) Jack Neville is the chief suspect when an unpopular college trustee is stabbed to death by the knife Jack made in a Hughes Community College continuing-education class.

3. *Bond with Death, A* (St. Martin's, 2004) Sarah must prove that she is innocent of the murder of Harold Curtin, the Garden Gnome, who has been fired by Hughes Community College.

Crispin, Edmund

PSEUDONYM OF Robert B. Montgomery

Oxford don Gervase Fen wears his erudition lightly when he forays beyond the ivied halls as an amateur sleuth. At 42, he is tall and lean with a cheerfully ruddy complexion and a mischievous glint in his eyes as he drives his disreputable old roadster into one sophisticated and literate case after another. In an article in *Murder Ink* (Workman, 1977), Catherine Aird (q.v.) characterizes Crispin's mysteries as belonging to the "tea cake" school of English detective stories, where everything stops at four o'clock for a civilized repast.

1. *Obsequies at Oxford* (Lippincott, 1945) Fen is on the scene to investigate the mysterious death of an actress engaged for the Oxford performance of a new experimental drama. English title: *The Case of the Gilded Fly*.

2. *Holy Disorders* (Lippincott, 1946) While vacationing in the cathedral town of Tolnbridge, Fen investigates a haunted church, Nazi spies, and a mugged organist.

3. *Moving Toyshop, The* (Lippincott, 1946) In this very mysterious case, a toy shop changes magically into a grocery store, and a murdered corpse vanishes.

4. *Deaf and Dumb* (Lippincott, 1947) This case of murder at the opera gets very complicated when the suspected murderer is himself done in. English title: *Swan Song*.

5. *Love Lies Bleeding* (Lippincott, 1948) A lost Shakespeare play, a burglary, and two murders are neatly wrapped into this amusing case with an English public school background.

6. *Buried for Pleasure* (Lippincott, 1948) Fen stands for Parliament and meets Inspector Humbleby for the first time on this case of the murder of an old classmate and the poisoning of a respectable ex-prostitute.

7. *Sudden Vengeance* (Dodd, Mead, 1950) Fen assists Inspector Humbleby in his investigation of the suicide of a young film actress and some murdered movie moguls. English title: *Frequent Hearses*.

8. *Long Divorce, The* (Dodd, Mead, 1951) Murder following a rash of anonymous letters in a small English village is the subject of this highly polished puzzle. Variant title: *A Noose for Her*.

9. *Beware of the Trains* (Walker, 1962) This is a collection of short stories.

10. *Glimpses of the Moon, The* (Walker, 1978) On sabbatical in a small Devonshire village, Fen helps the very dull-witted local constabulary solve a case of three particularly messy murders.

11. *Fen Country* (Walker, 1980) Twenty-six short stories are collected here.

Crofts, Freeman Wills

Crofts's classic early mystery *The Cask* (Collins, 1920), starring an Inspector French precursor named Burnley, was written while he was still employed as a railway engineer. Though he eventually retired to devote more time to writing, his best books, with a few wartime exceptions, were written before 1940. After that, his portrayal of Scotland

Yard's Inspector Joseph French, a tweedy alibi-buster who never misses a chance to follow a clue abroad, became too slow moving for most readers.

1. *Inspector French's Greatest Case* (Seltzer, 1925) A murdered clerk is found next to the empty safe in a diamond merchant's Hatton Street office.
2. *Cheyne Mystery, The* (Boni, 1926) When young Maxwell Cheyne is drugged and his home ransacked, Inspector French's only clue is a scrap of a hotel bill. UK title: *Inspector French and the Cheyne Mystery.*
3. *Starvel Hollow Tragedy, The* (Harper, 1927) A love story is woven into this case of a miser's missing money. English title: *Inspector French and the Starvel Tragedy.*
4. *Sea Mystery, The* (Harper, 1928) A mysterious wooden chest found floating off the coast of Wales contains the corpse of a murdered man.
5. *Purple Sickle Murders, The* (Harper, 1929) Young women who work in London movie box offices are being murdered. English title: *The Box Office Murders.*
6. *Sir John Magill's Last Journey* (Harper, 1930) Plenty of railway details pack this leisurely case about the disappearance of a Belfast linen manufacturer.
7. *Mystery in the English Channel* (Harper, 1931) Two dead English businessmen are found aboard a yacht in mid-Channel. UK title: *Mystery in the Channel.*
8. *Sudden Death* (Harper, 1932) Death at a country house occupies French in this somewhat atypical case seen through the eyes of the housemaid.
9. *Double Death* (Harper, 1932) Two young construction engineers working on a railway project near the English Channel coast are murdered. UK title: *Death on the Way.*
10. *Strange Case of Dr. Earle, The* (Dodd, Mead, 1933) The disappearance of a golfing doctor from his home in Surrey forms the beginning of this diabolical case. UK title: *The Hog's Back Mystery.*
11. *Wilful and Premeditated* (Dodd, Mead, 1934) Charles Swinburn waits and watches to see if he can get away with the carefully planned murder of a rich uncle. UK title: *The 12:30 from Croydon.*
12. *Crime at Guildford* (Dodd, Mead, 1935) The senior accountant for a firm of jewelers is murdered while attending a business conference near Guildford. Variant title: *The Crime at Nornes.*
13. *Crime on the Solent* (Dodd, Mead, 1935) Industrial spying between two rival cement firms leads to the murder of a night watchman. UK title: *Mystery on Southampton Water.*
14. *Loss of the Jane Vosper, The* (Dodd, Mead, 1936) An insurance investigator checking into the sinking of a loaded freighter disappears.
15. *Man Overboard!* (Dodd, Mead, 1936) Inspector French goes to Ireland to investigate the death of a man working on a secret chemical process. Variant title: *Cold-blooded Murder.*
16. *Found Floating* (Dodd, Mead, 1937) Involves poison at a family dinner and a disappearing passenger on a Mediterranean cruise ship.
17. *Futile Alibi* (Dodd, Mead, 1938) Everybody hated unscrupulous financier Andrew Harrison, but the manner of his death seems to rule out either murder or suicide. UK title: *The End of Andrew Harrison.*
18. *Antidote to Venom* (Dodd, Mead, 1939) George Sturridge, a kindly, well-meaning zoo director, becomes an accomplice to murder.
19. *Tragedy in the Hollow* (Dodd, Mead, 1939) Harry Morrison leaves his post at a London travel agency for a job on a casino cruise ship, where murder occurs. UK title: *Fatal Venture.*
20. *Golden Ashes* (Dodd, Mead, 1940) An art expert is murdered, and his huge collection of old masters is lost in a house fire.

21. *Circumstantial Evidence* (Dodd, Mead, 1941) Crofts gives his readers plenty of evidence and time in which to deduce, along with Inspector French, the murderer of James Tarrant. English title: *James Tarrant, Adventurer.*
22. *Losing Game, A* (Dodd, Mead, 1941) When detective-story writer Tony Meadows is charged with the murder of a blackmailer, Inspector French comes to his rescue.
23. *Fear Comes to Chalfont* (Dodd, Mead, 1942) When an amateur chemist is murdered, his wife comes under suspicion.
24. *Affair at Little Wokeham, The* (Dodd, Mead, 1943) A detective story without a mystery. Crofts tells his readers how and by whom the murder has been committed and how the murderer has planned to escape the consequences. Variant title: *Double Tragedy.*
25. *Enemy Unseen* (Dodd, Mead, 1945) The two thefts of wire and hand grenades from a supply shed in St. Pols, Cornwall, and the explosion death of an elderly man seem to be connected. Regarded as one Crofts's better later efforts.
26. *Death of a Train* (Dodd, Mead, 1946) Saboteurs plot to derail a train full of radio valves.
27. *Murderers Make Mistakes* (Hodder [UK], 1947) This is a collection of short stories.
28. *Silence for the Murderer* (Dodd, Mead, 1948) Dulcie Heath and Frank Roscoe plan to defraud the patients of a Harley Street doctor.
29. *Dark Journey* (Dodd, Mead, 1951) A family feud and guilty parties everywhere keep French, now Superintendent French, busy. UK title: *French Strikes Oil.*
30. *Many a Slip* (Hodder [UK], 1955) More short stories are collected here.
31. *Mystery of the Sleeping Car Express, The* (Hodder [UK], 1956) This is a third short story collection.
32. *Anything to Declare?* (Hodder [UK], 1957) An ingenious gang smuggles Swiss watches into England.

Crombie, Deborah

Scotland Yard Detective Superintendent Duncan Kincaid and his partner and lover Detective Inspector Gemma Jones are the leading characters in a series of mysteries set in England. Along the way Kincaid reconciles with his ex-wife, and then loses her when she is murdered, and he acquires her 11-year-old son. Jones, a redheaded, fiery-tempered single mother, has had her own romantic problems. This is a generally well-plotted series with attractive central characters, and a convincing English background delineated by Texan Deborah Crombie.

1. *Share in Death, A* (Scribner, 1993) Murder interrupts Scotland Yard detective superintendent Duncan Kincaid's vacation at a Yorkshire time-share when someone is electrocuted in a Jacuzzi.
2. *All Shall Be Well* (Scribner, 1994) When an autopsy reveals a morphine overdose as the cause of death of Jasmine Dent, his London neighbor, Duncan and Gemma start a murder investigation that leads to several suspects.
3. *Leave the Grave Green* (Scribner, 1995) Kincaid and Jones investigate when the son-in-law of conductor Sir Gerald Asherton and his wife, renowned soprano Dame Caroline Stowe, meets a suspicious death in a canal in the countryside outside of London.
4. *Mourn Not Your Dead* (Scribner, 1996) High-ranking police officer Alastair Gilbert has been bludgeoned to death at his home in the village of Holmbury St. Mary.
5. *Dreaming of the Bones* (Scribner, 1997) Duncan's ex-wife, Vic McClellan, asks Duncan, whom she left 12 years before, for help

CROW, MICHAEL ■ 199

in investigating the possible murder of Cambridge poet Lydia Brooke, who died five years earlier as an alleged suicide.

6. *Kissed a Sad Goodbye* **(Bantam, 1999)** The body of Annabelle Hammond, director of a family owned tea company, is found neatly arranged on the Isle of Dogs in the Docklands area.

7. *Finer End, A* **(Bantam, 2001)** The spirit of Edmund, a Glastonbury monk, possesses architect Jack Montfort, a relation of Duncan's, prompting him to write (in scholarly medieval Latin) about a missing relic and a chant hidden in the nearby abbey.

8. *And Justice There Is None* **(Bantam, 2002)** Is a new Jack Ripper responsible for the slasher-style death of Dawn Arrowood, pregnant wife of a wealthy antiques dealer? Duncan says yes. Gemma suspects the husband.

9. *Now May You Weep* **(Morrow, 2003)** Gemma, newly promoted but depressed by her miscarriage, visits her married friend Hazel Cavendish for a cooking weekend in Innesfree, Scotland, but the outing is spoiled by the murder of Hazel's former lover, Donald Brodie.

10. *In a Dark House* **(Morrow, 2004)** A serial arsonist; a nude, charred female corpse found in a burned warehouse; and the abduction of a 10-year-old girl may all be connected.

11. *Water Like Stone* **(Morrow, 2007)** Kincaid's sister, Juliet Newcombe, finds the mummified corpse of an infant in the wall of a building she is renovating.

Cronin, A(rchibald) J(oseph)

I.   A. J. Cronin, a Scottish physician, took up writing while recuperating from an illness. He drew on his experiences in medicine for his fiction, scandalizing many by his unromanticized view of the medical profession. The ambitious doctor portrayed in his best-known novel, *The Citadel* (Little, Brown, 1937), created quite a furor. The two books listed below feature Robert Shannon from early youth to his career as a dedicated medical researcher.

1. *Green Years, The* **(Little, Brown, 1944)** The story begins as eight-year-old Robert Shannon comes to live with his grandparents in Scotland.

2. *Shannon's Way* **(Little, Brown, 1948)** Shannon is a young doctor doing medical research.

II.   This pair of novels also features a young boy who grows up to enter medicine, but Laurence Carroll's career heads in a different direction, and he meets with different problems.

1. *Song of Sixpence, A* **(Little, Brown, 1964)** Laurence Carroll experiences the trials and joys of growing up Catholic in a Scottish Presbyterian town. He is six-years-old when the story begins.

2. *Pocketful of Rye, A* **(Little, Brown, 1969)** Carroll, now head of a Swiss clinic, meets a figure from his past.

Cross, Amanda

PSEUDONYM OF Carolyn G. Heilbrun

Kate Fansler, professor of English, is the detective in these very literate mysteries that feature clues from the likes of James Joyce and Lionel Trilling along with plenty of highbrow patter and wit. Carolyn G. Heilbrun (d. 2004)—herself a critic, author (*Writing a Woman's Life*, Norton, 1988), and teacher (Columbia University)—catches the male-dominated misogynist academic atmosphere with a deliciously droll eye and an acid wit. Lawyer Reed Amhearst, her significant other and eventual husband, helps Kate with her cases from time to time.

1. *In the Last Analysis* **(Macmillan, 1964)** Kate sends student Janet Harrison to psychoanalyst Emmanuel Bauer, friend and former lover. When Janet winds up stabbed to death on Dr. Bauer's couch, it is up to Kate to prove his innocence.

2. *James Joyce Murder, The* **(Macmillan, 1967)** Kate is summering in the Berkshires when she is called upon to examine a publishing magnate's estate, which contains a cache of letters from literary luminaries, including James Joyce and D. H. Lawrence.

3. *Poetic Justice* **(Knopf, 1970)** Student riots at the university (Columbia) indirectly threaten the closing of University College, the U's plebeian stepchild.

4. *Theban Mysteries, The* **(Knopf, 1971)** Now reluctantly answering to the name of "Mrs. Reed Amhearst," Kate is teaching a seminar on *Antigone* at an exclusive private school in Manhattan, her alma mater. Then life begins to imitate art.

5. *Question of Max, The* **(Knopf, 1976)** Kate travels to Maine where she becomes entangled with the estate and literary remains of a famous English novelist. Human remains also turn up.

6. *Death in a Tenured Position* **(Dutton, 1981)** Kate goes to Harvard to help an old classmate combat the antifeminists plaguing her. English title: *A Death in the Faculty*.

7. *Sweet Death, Kind Death* **(Dutton, 1984)** Did Patrice Umphelby, history professor at a small New England women's college, commit suicide, or was she pushed into the lake?

8. *No Word from Winifred* **(Dutton, 1984)** The elusive connection between the missing Winifred Ashby and famous English author Charlotte Stanton is the key to this mystery.

9. *Trap for Fools, A* **(Dutton, 1989)** Black political activist Humphrey Edgerton has no alibi for the night Middle Eastern Studies professor Canfield Adams was pushed or fell from his seventh-story office window.

10. *Players Come Again, The* **(Random House, 1990)** Kate is asked to do research for a biography of Gabrielle Foxx, whose main claim to fame seems to be as the wife of a major writer.

11. *Imperfect Spy, An* **(Ballantine, 1995)** Fansler is teaching a course on literature and the law at seedy, sexist Schuyler Law School.

12. *Collected Stories, The* **(Ballantine, 1997)** Contains 10 short stories, including three about Kate Fansler, related by Kate's niece.

13. *Puzzled Heart, The* **(Ballantine, 1998)** Kate, frustrated in her search for the kidnappers of her husband, Reed Amhearst, turns for help to Harriet Furst, a character in *An Imperfect Spy*, now part owner of a detective agency.

14. *Honest Doubt* **(Ballantine, 2000)** Kate is on the sidelines as Clifton College's English Department hires private eye Estelle "Woody" Woodhaven to investigate the poisoning of reactionary Tennyson scholar Charles Haycock.

15. *Edge of Doom, The* **(Ballantine, 2002)** Family matters involve Fansler as a stranger, Jason "Jay" Ebenezer Smith, approaches her elder brother Laurence claiming to be her biological father.

Crow, Michael

PSEUDONYM OF Thomas Moran?

Baltimore narcotics cop Luther Ewing, who is half–African American, half-Vietnamese, has a checkered past: among other things, he was kicked out of the US Special Forces for inappropriate violence and served as a mercenary sniper in Bosnia, where he was shot in the head. Luther, scarred by his past, has not eschewed mayhem but tries to direct it against drug lords and other baddies in a trio of formulaic but well-written, exciting, and blood-drenched thrillers. "Michael Crow" is the pseudonym of "a prize-winning, critically acclaimed literary novelist" (publisher's blurb). The Ewing novels are written by a self-described "evil twin."

1. *Red Rain* (Viking, 2002) A sting operation against drug lord Vassily, a Russian mobster who was a former buddy as a mercenary, misfires; and now Vassily is after Baltimore narc cop Luther Ewing.

2. *Bite, The* (Viking, 2003) After being shot in the parking lot of his apartment building, Luther is back at work, looking for methadone laboratories in the backwoods of Baltimore County with the help of partner "Ice Box" Cutrone and DEA agent Francesca Russo.

3. *No Way Back* (HarperCollins, 2005) Luther, serving out a six-month suspension from his narc squad job, takes on a CIA mission in Korea and Vladivostok protecting a wealthy South Korean who is making a mysterious deal with a pair of devious Russian generals.

Crowley, John

American author John Crowley treads the line between "literary" and "genre" fiction. His complex, complicated and well-written fiction has both SF and fantasy elements in it. *Little, Big* (Bantam, 1981) was nominated for a Hugo and a Nebula and is listed in Harold Bloom's *Western Canon*. The life of Pierce Moffett, not-very-successful professor of Renaissance history, is the subject for the Aegypt Cycle, a tetralogy of novels that range from the Renaissance of Giordano Bruno and John Dee to the 1970s. Crowley postulates that the world of magic, temporarily ousted by the world of science, will be making a comeback soon. Following the plot twists of the tetralogy can be quite difficult, especially if the reader starts in the middle, and many explanations are postponed to the fourth volume, but persevering readers have felt rewarded by Crowley's lucid and penetrating prose. Crowley is also the writer of award-winning documentary film scripts, several other novels and a collection of fantasy short stories: *Novels and Souvenirs: Collected Short Fiction* (Perennial, 2004).

1. *Aegypt* (Bantam, 1987) The life of Pierce Moffett, professor of Renaissance history, is delineated for the 1960s and 1970s as, struggling to find the meaning of life, he is led to a mythical area and a mysterious woman. Reprinted as *The Solitudes* (Overlook, 2007).

2. *Love and Sleep* (Bantam, 1994) Moffett's long-forgotten childhood in Kentucky in the 1950s meshes with the lives of 16th-century magi Giordano Bruno and John Dee as he researches the strange novels of Fellowes Kraft.

3. *Daemonomania* (Bantam, 2000) Magic seeps further into the lives of Moffett and his acquaintances in Faraway Hills as Moffett continues his researches into the "secret history" of the world.

4. *Endless Things* (Small Beer, 2007) Pierce Moffett follows the trail of Fellowes Kraft's unfinished final novel to Europe, where he finds traces of Aegypt's mysteries in the teachings of the Rosicrucians, John Dee, and Giordano Bruno.

Crum, Laura

Gail McCarthy is a middle-aged horse veterinarian who gets involved with murder along with her duties among ailing horses in this series of cozies set in Santa Cruz, California, in the foothills of the Sierra Nevadas. Much horse lore is dispensed in this series, in which the horses are as individualized as the human characters. Fourth-generation Californian Laura Crum, who has worked with horses all her life and has mover than 20 years of experience in cow-horse competition, says that she was inspired by the novels of Dick Francis (q.v.).

1. *Cutter* (St. Martin's, 1994) Veterinarian Gail McCarthy suspects poison when half of cutting-horse trainer's Casey Brooks's stock is down with colic. Then Casey is thrown by his horse and killed.

2. *Hoofprints* (St. Martin's, 1996) When Gail shows up to treat Cindy Whitney's gelding, she finds Cindy and her husband murdered and a homeless man nicknamed "the Walker" fleeing the scene.

3. *Roughstock* (St. Martin's, 1997) Gail's friend Joanna Lund is the prime suspect in the murder of retired vet and land baron, Jack Hollister, whose body is found in Lake Tahoe.

4. *Roped* (St. Martin's, 1998) Somebody has been harassing McCarthy's old high school friend Lisa Bennett and her family with a series of "accidents" involving horses and people.

5. *Slickrock* (St. Martin's, 1999) McCarthy takes a trip into the Sierra Nevadas with two horses and a dog. Then a suicide at a pack station and a series of suspicious accidents follow her on the trail.

6. *Breakaway* (St. Martin's, 2001) The mysterious perpetrator who is sexually abusing horses and beating up teenage girls may have murder on his mind.

7. *Hayburner* (St. Martin's, 2003) McCarthy deals with a series of arsonous horse-barn fires, a developing love interest, and threats of personal danger.

8. *Forged* (St. Martin's, 2004) Gail finds herself a prime murder suspect after stumbling on a dying farrier in her barn.

9. *Moonblind* (Perseverance, 2006) Gail's cousin Jenny calls for help after finding her dog, Boomer, poisoned, and the seven-months-pregnant Gail finds herself enmeshed in the world of fixed races and shady dealings with bookies.

10. *Chasing Cans* (Perseverance, 2008) Gail witnesses the death of nasty neighbor and horsewoman Lindee Stone during a barrel-race exercise.

Crumley, James

I. American mystery writer James Crumley's hard-boiled private eye novels remind many readers of Raymond Chandler (q.v.), with their hard-drinking, world-weary but resilient detectives, violent action, and lyrical descriptions of the underside of American society west of the Great Plains. Milo Milodragovitch, former divorce lawyer, moves around the country quite a bit, as does his Texas-born creator. His cases take him from his office in Meriwether, Montana to Seattle, Las Vegas, Texas, and points beyond. In number 3 Milo hooks up with his former partner C. W. Sughrue (see series II).

1. *Wrong Case, The* (Random House, 1975) Milo Milodragovitch's once-thriving divorce-case business in Meriwether, Montana, has dried up, and Milo has plenty of time to drink and stare out of the window. Then a young woman walks into his office and asks him to find her brother.

2. *Dancing Bear* (Random House, 1983) Milo, having abandoned his private practice and taken a night job for Haliburton Security, is offered a case that seems easy and remunerative at first but stirs up painful memories.

3. *Bordersnakes* (Mysterious, 1996) Milo, off the wagon again as his $3 million inheritance disappears from his Montana bank account, travels to El Paso, Texas, to request help from his former partner, C.W. Sughrue (see below, series II), in tracking down the errant banker.

4. *Final Country, The* (Mysterious, 2001) Now 60 years old and solvent again, Milo seems almost ready to settle down in Texas in his own bar. But he can't stay away from missing-persons work. And then a gigantic black man named Enos Walker kills a drug dealer.

II. C.W. Sughrue, Milo Milodragovitch's former partner (see series I, above), is another aging, hard-drinking, hard-nosed private investigator with memories of the Vietnam War who moves around a lot. *The Last Good Kiss* (number 1) is regarded by some readers as a classic private eye novel. Number 3 brings Sughrue together again with Milodragovitch.

1. *Last Good Kiss, The* (**Random House, 1978**) Sughrue sets out to find Betty Sue Flowers, a barmaid's daughter who disappeared somewhere into San Francisco 10 years before.
2. *Mexican Tree Duck, The* (**Mysterious, 1993**) C. W. is hired to conduct a private search for Sarita Cisneros Pines, missing Mexican wife of a Texas politician.
3. *Bordersnakes (2)* (**Mysterious, 1996**) Sughrue, hiding out in the desert after being shot by two Chicano thugs who divulged that it was a contract hit, is joined by former partner Milo Milodragovitch (see series I, above), who is searching for the Montana banker who absconded with his inheritance.
4. *Right Madness, The* (**Viking, 2005**) Sughrue is hired by his buddy psychiatrist William MacKinderick to shadow some of the latter's patients who may have taken files from his office.

Cunningham, E. V.

PSEUDONYM OF Howard Fast (q.v.)

Masao Masuto, Beverly Hills' Japanese American detective, is a Zen Buddhist. His wily and tenacious cast of mind helps him sort out some complicated cases, and his knowledge of karate comes in very handy at times. Beverly Hills is too small and peaceful a town to have a permanent homicide squad, but when a case involves possible murder, Masuto and his partner Sy Beckman take over. Under his E. V. Cunningham pseudonym, the late Howard Fast (q.v.) also wrote a pair of novels about a detective named Harvey Krim: *Lydia* (Doubleday, 1964) and *Cynthia* (Morrow, 1968) and two about the detective team of John Cormady and Larry Cohen: *Penelope* (Doubleday, 1965) and *Margie* (Morrow, 1966).

1. *Samantha* (**Morrow, 1967**) Masuto must identify and stop the mysterious "Samantha" as, one by one, a series of film stars and executives are murdered.
2. *Case of the One Penny Orange, The* (**Holt, 1977**) Involves the murder of a stamp collector, an ex-SS man, and the theft of a valuable stamp.
3. *Case of the Russian Diplomat, The* (**Holt, 1978**) Masuto's investigation into the drowning of a Russian diplomat is complicated when his own daughter, Ana, is kidnapped.
4. *Case of the Poisoned Eclairs, The* (**Holt, 1979**) A Chicano maid eats eclairs intended for her Beverly Hills employer and dies of botulism.
5. *Case of the Sliding Pool, The* (**Delacorte, 1981**) When a canyon mud slide reveals a skeleton, Masuto must reconstruct a crime committed 25 years earlier.
6. *Case of the Kidnapped Angel, The* (**Delacorte, 1982**) The kidnapping of Angel Barton eventually leads to three murders.
7. *Case of the Murdered Mackenzie, The* (**Delacorte, 1984**) The trial of actress Eva Mackenzie, accused of murdering her husband in the bathtub, strikes a false note with Masuto.

Curzon, Clare

PSEUDONYM OF Marie Buchanan

I. Members of the Thames Valley (England) Serious Crime Squad are featured in this series of British procedurals. Detective Inspector Mike Yeadings leads a cast including Sergeant (later Inspector) Angus Mott, Sergeant Beaumont, and Constable Rosemary Zyczynski. Although these mysteries are not cozies, the investigations in them take place mostly in small towns or rural areas. The domestic lives of the police personnel form a background to the plots. No real angst here, although Yeadings does have a daughter with Down syndrome. Curzon's novels have attracted a following both in the United States and the United Kingdom, though some reviewers feel that the series has grown a little tired.

Marie Buchanan has also written, under the pseudonym of Rhona Petrie, two other series, one featuring Inspector Marcus McClurg and the other Dr. Nassim Pride.

1. *I Give You Five Days* (**Collins [UK], 1983**) Not published in the United States. No annotation available.
2. *Masks and Faces* (**Collins [UK], 1984**) Not published in the United States. No annotation available.
3. *Trojan Hearse, The* (**Collins [UK], 1985**) Mike Yeadings and Angus Mott get involved in a murder investigation when they attend the social function where the crime was committed. Not published in the United States.
4. *Quest for K, The* (**Collins [UK], 1986**) Mott's girlfriend, Paula, disappears while on holiday in Crete. Not published in the United States.
5. *Three-Core Lead* (**Doubleday, 1990**) The death in Prague of Yeadings's friend Howard Swaffham, former intelligence agent, may have ties to a murder case involving a 16-year-old girl. Originally published in the United Kingdom in 1988.
6. *Blue-Eyed Boy, The* (**Doubleday, 1991**) The death of a young man found slashed almost beyond recognition in a supermarket parking lot is at first linked to a series of muggings in the town of Reading.
7. *Cat's Cradle* (**St. Martin's, 1992**) Lorely Pelling, reclusive keeper of a houseful of cats, is found shot to death in Farlowe's Wood the day after Franklin Welch staged a target-shooting competition.
8. *First Wife, Twice Removed* (**St. Martin's, 1993**) The poisoning of divorcée Penny Winter and the corpse of Anneke Vroom, a pregnant Dutch girl, which turns up in an antique chest in a truck, have many points in common,
9. *Death Prone* (**St. Martin's, 1994**) After wealthy old Hadrian Bascombe announces to his heirs that he's leaving his fortune to only one of them, members of the Bascombe family start dying prematurely. Originally published in the United Kingdom in 1992.
10. *Nice People* (**St. Martin's, 1995**) Troubled teen Owen Stafford, two missing wives, and two deaths have to be sorted out by Yeadings. Originally published in the United Kingdom in 1993.
11. *Past Mischief* (**St. Martin's, 1996**) Successful businesswoman Miranda Gregory is critically injured and left in a coma after a hit-and-run accident. Then a dead body is found in Miranda's office and her adoptive father apparently commits suicide. Originally published in the United Kingdom in 1994.
12. *Close Quarters* (**St. Martin's, 1997**) A music student escapes a stalker on her way home from the train. A watchman finds the body of a London prostitute who has been strangled and had her hair chopped off. Is there a connection with large, gentle, but developmentally disabled teenager Harry Snelling?
13. *All Unwary* (**St. Martin's, 1998**) Troubled teenager Mayumi disappears. Zyczynski and Beaumont investigate the possible causes for her disappearance.
14. *Cold Hands* (**St. Martin's, 2001**) Counterfeit British currency seems to be passing through would-be holiday resort Fraylings Court. Zyczynski goes undercover as a resort guest.

15. *Don't Leave Me* (St. Martin's, 2002) The disappearance of 11-year-old Julie Winterton reminds Yeadings of the events eight years ago, when Julie's father reported the disappearance of his wife, Caroline, along with most of their joint bank account.

16. *Body of a Woman, The* (St. Martin's, 2003) Members of the family of local shopkeeper Leila Knightly prove difficult to locate after her handsomely dressed corpse (complete with feather mask) is discovered in Shotters Wood.

17. *Meeting of Minds, A* (St. Martin's, 2004) The stabbed body of a young woman, naked except for a fur coat, is discovered in a car. Suspects include her neighbors in a new apartment development and her estranged father.

18. *Last to Leave* (St. Martin's, 2005) A fire destroys family patriarch Carlton Dellars's Thames Valley house and critically injures Carlton's nephew as the Dellar family get together to celebrate Carlton's 80th birthday.

19. *Glass Wall, The* (St. Martin's, 2006) Why does Filipino barman Ramon clean up the room from which a woman has plunged seven stories, rather than notifying the police of her death, which he witnessed?

20. *Edge, The* (St. Martin's, 2007) A husband, wife, and young child have been murdered, and the family's 16-year-old son has disappeared.

II. Something of a change of pace is Curzon's trilogy of novels set in the early 20th century and featuring Lucy Sedgwick. The series begins at the turn of the century when Lady Isabelle Delmayne, Lucy's mother, and Isabelle's sister-in-law Eugenie, Countess Crowthorne, become enmeshed in secrets involving blackmail, and murder. The second novel picks up Lucy's life in 1921 when she wakes up in a strange house suffering from amnesia. In the third novel Lucy again gets enmeshed in intrigue and mayhem. The trilogy is replete with local color, suspense, gothic elements, and a good deal of sex.

1. *Guilty Knowledge* (St. Martin's, 2000) Eugenie, Viscountess Crowthorne, and her sister-in-law, Lady Isabelle Delmayne, share a relationship involving intimate secrets, blackmail, and murder.

2. *Colour of Blood, The* (Severn House, 2002) In 1921, Lucy Sedgwick, now grown, wakes up in an unfamiliar house with no memory of who she is or where she came from. A child is crying and a dead man is lying in the room next door.

3. *Dangerous Practice* (Severn House, 2002) Lucy Sedgwick marries second husband, psychotherapist Clive Malcolm. On Lucy and Clive's wedding night, one of Clive's patients, Patrick Garston, apparently tries to hang himself.

Cussler, Clive

I. Dirk Pitt, an expert in underwater salvage, uses his talents to retrieve all kinds of sunken treasure—rare metals, secret treaties—you name it, he can dredge it up. The novels in which this underwater James Bond stars are exciting and suspenseful enough to keep any reader on the edge of his chair. Lately, Dirk and his sidekick Al Giordino have been working for NUMA (National Underwater and Marine Agency), which is an actual nonprofit salvage agency run by Pitt's creator, Clive Cussler.

1. *Mediterranean Caper, The* (Pyramid, 1977) A World War I–vintage fighter plane attacks a contemporary American airbase. Originally published in the United Kingdom as *May Day* in 1973.

2. *Iceberg* (Dodd, Mead, 1975) A ship imbedded in an iceberg is the key to foiling a plot to take over Latin America.

3. *Raise the Titanic!* (Viking, 1976) Russians and Americans are after the rare element Byzanium, thought to be in the hold of the sunken *Titanic*.

4. *Vixen 03* (Viking, 1978) A plane loaded with biological warfare devices turns up 34 years after it crashed in a Colorado lake.

5. *Night Probe!* (Bantam, 1981) Pitt's search for a 1914 Canadian American treaty involves underwater excavations of a ship and a train.

6. *Pacific Vortex!* (Bantam, 1983) An American nuclear submarine has disappeared in the Pacific Vortex several hundred miles north of Hawaii.

7. *Deep Six* (Simon & Schuster, 1984) Dirk helps the Environmental Protection Agency to locate the source of a deadly nerve gas contaminating Alaskan waters.

8. *Cyclops* (Simon & Schuster, 1986) A manned American space station, a Soviet plot to overthrow Castro, and a missing American treasure hunter are all interrelated.

9. *Treasure* (Simon & Schuster, 1988) A rescue mission in Greenland and Roman treasure dating from 391 CE figure in this adventure.

10. *Dragon* (Simon & Schuster, 1990) Dirk competes with Japanese nuclear terrorists when he is sent after a crashed B-29 with an atomic bomb aboard.

11. *Sahara* (Simon & Schuster, 1992) Red toxin in the Niger River may be the cause of a mysterious epidemic in the Sahara.

12. *Inca Gold* (Simon & Schuster, 1995) A lost Inca treasure is the goal of both Dirk Pitt and the sinister Solpe Machaco.

13. *Shock Wave* (Simon & Schuster, 1996) High-frequency sound waves generated by the ruthless diamond-mining techniques of Australian tycoon Arthur Dorsett is killing animals and people in large numbers on various ocean shores.

14. *Flood Tide* (Simon & Schuster, 1997) Dirk and Al Giordino are pitted against Qin Shang, a Chinese shipping magnate who smuggles illegal immigrants into countries around the world to be worked as indentured slaves.

15. *Atlantis Found* (Putnam, 1999) Members of the Fourth Empire, an organization headed by the Wolf family, a secret clan of genetically engineered people who worship the Third Reich, are behind the terrorist attack on an archaeological team that has found evidence of a previously undiscovered civilization.

16. *Valhalla* (Putnam, 2001) Dirk and Al come to the rescue of the flaming cruise ship *Golden Dolphin* and save most of the passengers and crew, including Kelly Egan, who has been left with a leather case containing the secrets of her father's lifework.

17. *Trojan Odyssey* (Putnam, 2003) A hurricane threatens Pitt's son and daughter and the luxury hotel Ocean Wanderer, owned by a mysterious billionaire named Specter. Pitt's kids have turned up underwater relics that seem to have an ancient Celtic origin, and Specter seems to be linked to some Druidic cult that is seeking world domination.

18. *Black Wind* (Putnam, 2004) Dirk Pitt Jr. and his sister Summer have taken over from Dirk Sr. The plot involves a South Korean industrialist who is working with North Koreans to bio-blitz Los Angeles. Cowritten with Clive's son Dirk Cussler.

19. *Treasure of Khan* (Putnam, 2006) A modern-day Mongol with dreams of restoring national power and pride is competing with NUMA to find the treasure of Ghengis and Kublai Khan. Coauthored with Dirk Cussler.

II. With Paul Kemprecos (q.v.), Cussler coauthors another series of NUMA books, substituting young divers Kurt Austin and Joe Zavala for Dirk Pitt. More wild adventures and underwater derring-do.

1. *Serpent* (Pocket, 1999) Archaeologists, who have apparently unearthed evidence that Christopher Columbus wasn't the first European to reach the New World, are being butchered at dig sites.
2. *Blue Gold* (Pocket, 2000) *The Nepenthe*, a motor yacht filled with celebrities and crippled children brought together by former actress and activist Gloria Ekhart, the two leaders in the Class 1 offshore powerboat race (Austin and Zavala in one), and a pod of seemingly dead whales are on a collision course.
3. *Fire Ice* (Putnam, 2002) The NUMA research vessel *Argo* is in the Black Sea for a public relations gig when Kurt spots the TV crew being pursued by mounted Cossacks.
4. *White Death* (Putnam, 2003) The rescue of survivors trapped inside a Danish warship after a collision with a ship manned by Sentinels of the Sea, a radical environmental group, leads to the shadowy fish farming organization Oceanus Corporation.
5. *Lost City* (Putnam, 2004) An aviator found frozen in a glacier, a mutant seaweed, a giant submarine, and the arms-dealing Fauchard family, which is seeking world domination, are all part of the action.
6. *Polar Shift* (Putnam, 2005) The leader of an anti-globalization group plans to use an artificially triggered "polar shift" to give the world's industrialized nations a tweak, but once the shift starts, there is no way of stopping it.
7. *Navigator, The* (Putnam, 2007) Austin and his team try to thwart Viktor Baltazar, who believes he's a descendant of King Solomon, from stealing a priceless Phoenician antiquity that may be connected to the lost Ark of the Covenant, Thomas Jefferson, and the suspicious death of Meriwether Lewis.

III. The *Oregon*, disguised as an old cargo ship but actually a vessel packed with state-of-the art science and technology, is run by the Corporation, a commercial organization that, according to its chairman, Juan Cabrillo, is also set to "somehow right the wrongs of others." Exciting high-tech adventure. Numbers 1 and 2 were co-authored with Craig Dirgo. Numbers 3 and 4 were coauthored with Jack Du Brul.

1. *Golden Buddha* (Berkley, 2003) The Corporation has been secretly hired by the US government to find the ancient statue known as the Golden Buddha, stolen from the Dalai Lama during the Chinese takeover of Tibet in 1959. Coauthored with Craig Dirgo.
2. *Sacred Stone, The* (Berkley, 2004) A meteorite discovered by Eric the Red in 1000 CE, a missing nuclear device, and a vial of plague germs are to be used in attacks on Jewish and Muslim holy sites and an Elton John concert. Coauthored with Craig Dirgo.
3. *Dark Watch* (Berkley, 2005) A consortium of Japanese shipping magnates asks for the assistance of Cabrillo and his crew in stopping pirates from Southeast Asia who have targeted giant commercial freighters as their prey. Coauthored with Jack Du Brul.
4. *Skeleton Coast* (Berkley, 2006) Cabrillo and the crew of the *Oregon* rescue a damsel in distress off the African coast and investigate reports of giant metal snakes in the same area. Coauthored with Jack Du Brul.

Czerneda, Julie E(lizabeth)

I. Canadian writer Julie E. Czerneda, who has published much non-fiction for young adults, including several volumes in the Career Connections and Science Dimensions series, is a relatively new entrant in the SF ranks (1997). Her novel *A Thousand Words for Stranger*, the first in the Trade Pact Universe trilogy, introduces us to a future humanoid race in the person of Sira, who defies her people by allying herself with a human. In 2007 Czerneda added *Reap the Wild Wind: Stratification #1* (DAW, 2007), a prequel to the trilogy, which describes the roots of the Clan refugees.

1. *Thousand Words for Stranger, A* (DAW, 1997) A young woman with no memory seeks transport on a particular space ship off the planet Auord.
2. *Ties of Power* (DAW, 1999) Sira, a member of an alien humanoid race, has dared to challenge the will of her people by allying herself with a human.
3. *To Trade the Stars* (DAW, 2002) Sira, now speaker for the Clan Council, and her life partner, the human telepath Jason, try to forge a life free of the Clan and the Drapsk.

II. The Webshifters' trilogy is the story of Esen, the last survivor of an alien race with the ability to assume the form of any creature.

1. *Beholder's Eye* (DAW, 1998) Esen, the youngest member of a race of beings who communicate through energy, is assigned to a world considered safe to explore and captured by the natives.
2. *Changing Vision* (DAW, 2000) Fifty years later, Esen and her human friend Paul Ragem are living quietly on the Fringe, with Esen assuming the shape of a Lishcyn named Esolesy Ki.
3. *Hidden in Sight* (DAW, 2003) The conclusion to the Webshifters' trilogy finds Esen, who has broken her species' cardinal rule of noninterference, trying to prevent an interspecies war.

III. A third trilogy, Species Imperative, explores the relations between human biologist Mac Connor and Brymn, a Dhryn archaeologist. Mac eventually travels from her job at Norcoast Salmon Research Facility in the Pacific Northwest to the Dhryn home world. The Dhryn may be fatal to every race they come into contact with, but are the equally mysterious Rho any less sinister?

1. *Survival* (DAW, 2004) Human biologist Mackenzie "Mac" Connor forms a relationship with Brymn, a seven-armed Dhryn archaeologist, first of his race to visit Earth.
2. *Migration* (DAW, 2005) After nearly dying on the Dhryn home world, Mac returns to her job at Norcoast Salmon Research Facility. Then the Interspecies Union discovers that the hitherto peaceful Dhryn have abandoned their world and have destroyed every life-form in their path.
3. *Regeneration* (DAW, 2006) Mac and her team are the only ones who stand any chance of solving the deadly puzzle of the instinct-driven Dhryn and the equally mysterious, and possibly more sinister Rho.

Daheim, Mary

I. Mary Daheim wrote several romance novels early in her career but eventually decided that she was more interested in mysteries than in romance. She has two long-running cozy series set in her native Pacific Northwest. The Bed and Breakfast series features Judith Mc-Monigle Flynn, who runs the only B and B on the coastal island of Chavez, just outside of Seattle, Washington, a B and B that is home to a series of murders that she is called upon to solve with the assistance of homicide detective and eventual spouse Joe Flynn and her flaky cousin Renie. This is a series of light mysteries, as indicated by the punning titles, with a likable central character, an interesting setting, and lively, if sometimes contrived, plots.

1. *Just Desserts* (Avon, 1991) Judith McMonigle and Hillside Manor, her bed-and-breakfast are introduced. Judith's first investigation is set off by the murder of a fortune teller.

2. *Fowl Prey* (Avon, 1991) When Judith goes to the historic Hotel Clovia in Vancouver, British Columbia, for a pre-Thanksgiving getaway with cousin Renie, a popcorn vendor and his pet parakeet are murdered and the two visiting Americans become suspects.

3. *Holy Terrors* (Avon, 1992) Judith McMonigle falls for investigating detective Joe Flynn when Sandy Frizzell, ostensible wife of a local heir, is found stabbed to death in the church nursery.

4. *Dune to Death* (Avon, 1993) Judith and Joe Flynn's long overdue honeymoon is fraught with incident. An accident lands Joe in the hospital, and the landlady of their hideaway turns up dead.

5. *Bantam of the Opera* (Avon, 1993) Judith and Renie become suspects, again, when an obnoxious would-be Pavarotti, for whose entourage they are catering, inadvertently takes a fatal dose of poison.

6. *Fit of Tempera, A* (Avon, 1994) Judith becomes a suspect, yet again, while staying with Renie in their family's backwoods cottage. Their neighbor, a noted painter, is strangled after giving the cousins a mysterious painting.

7. *Major Vices* (Avon, 1995) Judith and Renie's eccentric Uncle Boo spoils his own 75th birthday party by winding up dead behind a locked door.

8. *Murder, My Suite* (Avon, 1995) The secretary of an obnoxious nationally known gossip columnist turns up dead in a Canadian ski resort wearing one of the columnist's trademark turbans.

9. *Auntie Mayhem* (Avon, 1996) Judith and Renie's plans for a relaxing weekend at a real English country manor are disrupted when old Aunt Petulia dies unexpectedly and suspiciously.

10. *Nutty as a Fruitcake* (Avon, 1996) When an ill-tempered matriarch is done in after refusing to join her neighbors in putting up an outdoor Christmas display, her husband is the prime suspect, but Judith, not so sure that he is the perpetrator, investigates and widens the circle of suspects to include herself and her mom.

11. *September Mourn* (Avon, 1997) Murder takes place again at Hillside Manor. This time Judith and Renie run up against a sceptical female sheriff and some secretive residents of Chavez Island (permanent population of eight).

12. *Wed and Buried* (Avon, 1998) The reception for her son's wedding hits a snag when Judith becomes a witness to a possible murder outside the hotel.

13. *Snow Place to Die* (Avon, 1998) The members of a group of telephone company executives, for whom Judith is catering at nearby Mountain Goat Lodge, are dropping off one by one.

14. *Legs Benedict* (Avon, 1999) "Mr. Smith," the mysterious guest who is bumped off at Hillside Manor, turns out to be none other than Ronzini family hit man "Legs" Benedict.

15. *Creeps Suzette* (Avon, 2000) Wealthy widow Leota Burgess, who is convinced that someone is trying to kill her, invites Judith and Renie to Creepers, her aptly named estate.

16. *Streetcar Named Expire, A* (Avon, 2001) Renovations of decrepit Alhambra Arms turn up a 40-year-dead corpse behind the walls. Then Judith Flynn discovers some more recent remains. Are the two connected?

17. *Suture Self* (Morrow, 2001) Judith, recovering from hip surgery at the Good Cheer Hospital, becomes very suspicious when the patient in the next room dies, the third recent mysterious casualty at the hospital.

18. *Silver Scream* (Morrow, 2002) Was the death of famous producer Bruno Zepf, who was found slumped over a kitchen sink in Hillside Manor, due to negligence at the B and B, or was it murder?

19. *Hocus Croakus* (Morrow, 2003) While Hillside Manor is being renovated, Judith and Joe Flynn, their respective mothers, and cousin Renie visit the Lake Stillasnowamish Resort Casino. Then Salome, the assistant to the magician who is performing at the casino, is stabbed to death.

20. *This Old Souse* (Morrow, 2004) When Renie convinces Judith to investigate the elderly owners of a Spanish villa, a series of untoward incidents, including a mysterious package and the suspicious death of a milkman, occur.

21. *Dead Man Docking* (Morrow, 2005) Cruise line owner Magglio Cruz is stabbed to death at the bon voyage party for a 1930s-themed maiden cruise for a luxury line set to debark from San Francisco.

22. *Saks and Violins* (Morrow, 2006) A complicated plot involving violist Rudi Wittener; his mentor, Dolph Kluger; the disappearance of credit cards and a violin bow valued at $350,000; various legitimate and illegitimate sons; and a murder.

23. *Scots on the Rocks* (Morrow, 2007) Although supposedly on vacation, Judith gets involved in a murder investigation in a remote town in Scotland.

II. Daheim's second series of cozies is also set in the state of Washington, this time in the fictional logging town of Alpine, where publisher and editor of the *Alpine Avalanche* Emma Lord gets involved, sometimes with her best friend and house-and-garden editor, gossipy Vida Runkel and Milo Dodge, the local sheriff. Although quite small, Alpine has more than its share of zany characters and murders. Some reviewers complain about the obvious and contrived plots, while others are charmed by the small-town ambience and cozy atmosphere.

1. *Alpine Advocate, The* (Ballantine, 1992) Chris Doukas, black sheep of the rich and powerful Doukas family, becomes the leading suspect after he returns to Alpine and his cousin Mark Doukas winds up bludgeoned to death.

2. *Alpine Betrayal, The* (Ballantine, 1993) Local girl Dani Marsh returns to Alpine, as a star, to shoot a Hollywood film. Then ex-husband Cody Graff runs amok with an axe at the annual Loggerama.

3. *Alpine Christmas, The* (Ballantine, 1993) Christmas in Alpine is punctuated by the discovery of a woman's leg in the lake, along with that of another young woman's nude, half-frozen body.

4. *Alpine Decoy, The* (Ballantine, 1994) The arrival in Alpine of a beautiful young African American nurse with a checkered past arouses the bigotry of some locals, much to Emma's disgust.

5. *Alpine Escape, The* (Ballantine, 1995) Lord becomes an investigator again when the 100-year-old bones of a young woman are turned up in her friends' basement in Port Angeles.

6. *Alpine Fury, The* (Ballantine, 1996) A visitor from the Bank of Washington starts rumors flying that the town of Alpine's only bank may be heading for a merger.

7. *Alpine Gamble, The* (Ballantine, 1996) Alpine residents are up in arms about plans of California Realtors to develop the local hot springs. Then one of the realtors winds up dead.

8. *Alpine Hero, The* (Ballantine, 1996) Emma Lord finds the body of a murder victim in the facial room of the local Alpine salon.

9. *Alpine Icon, The* (Ballantine, 1998) Glamorous Ursula O'Toole Randall's return to Alpine to marry her third husband finds her clad in satin pajamas and dead in the Skyhomish River.

10. *Alpine Journey, The* (Ballantine, 1998) This time Lord does her own investigating at an Oregon seashore village when Audrey Imhoff's nightly nude dip in the Pacific Ocean ends in her murder.

11. *Alpine Kindred, The* (Ballantine, 1998) Local bigwig and philanthropist Einar Rasmussen Jr. is found stabbed to death, with lipstick on his collar.

12. *Alpine Legacy, The* (Ballantine, 1999) When the editor of a radical new publication, which specializes in personal attacks on Emma, is murdered, Emma becomes the leading suspect.

13. *Alpine Menace, The* (Ballantine, 2000) Emma goes to Seattle to help long-lost cousin Ronnie, who is accused of murdering his girlfriend, former Alpine resident Carol Stokes.

14. *Alpine Nemesis, The* (Ballantine, 2001) Alpine's oldest family feud flares up again, leaving the bodies of three people stowed in a meat freezer.

15. *Alpine Obituary* (Ballantine, 2002) Emma wonders whether a threatening letter received by Marsha, the local judge, and the suspicious death of elderly resident Jack Froland are connected.

16. *Alpine Pursuit, The* (Ballantine, 2004) In Daheim's first novel to debut in hardcover, Emma investigates the death of Hans Berenger, dean of students at Skyhomish Community College, who is gunned down in a play scene when real bullets replace blanks.

17. *Alpine Quilt, The* (Ballantine, 2005) Genevieve Bayard, former Alpine resident, eats a piece of poisoned cheesecake at a welcome-back party held in her honor.

18. *Alpine Recluse, The* (Ballantine, 2006) Tiffany, the bride of adulterous Tim Rafferty, is among the suspects when Tim is found beaten to death in his arson-torched house.

19. *Alpine Scandal* (Ballantine, 2007) Elmer Nystrom's obituary was sent to the *Alpine Advocate* before Elmer died.

20. *Alpine Traitor, The* (Ballantine, 2008) The two grown children of Emma's deceased former lover, Tom Cavanaugh, offer to buy the *Advocate* from Emma.

Dailey, Janet

Prolific American romance writer (more than 100 titles) Janet Dailey published the Americana series, in which each title was set in a different state (50 in all, 1976–1981). More pertinent to the *Sequels* theme is the series of romantic westerns devoted to the Calder family of Montana. The first four volumes were published in rapid order (1981–1983), then there was a hiatus of 15 years followed by *Calder Pride* and four subsequent volumes. The Calder novels, about several generations of a Montana ranch family, have all the requisites for successful romance fiction: larger-than-life characters, sex and passion, melodrama, and a modicum of violence and suspense.

1. *This Calder Sky* (Pocket, 1981) Handsome, arrogant Chase Calder, scion of the Calder cattle empire in Montana, meets his match in beautiful, spirited Maggie O'Rourke.

2. *This Calder Range* (Pocket, 1982) Chase Benteen Calder and Lorna travel to Montana, "determined to wrest their future from the land." Prequel to number 1.

3. *Stands a Calder Man* (Pocket, 1982) Webb Calder, determined to resist the onslaught of immigrants to Montana, can't resist proud and lovely young immigrant Lilli.

4. *Calder Born, Calder Bred* (Pocket, 1983) Ty Calder is strongly attracted to dark glamorous Tara, who wants to be mistress of the Calder kingdom, but it is young Jessy who is willing to defy death to save Ty.

5. *Calder Pride* (HarperCollins, 1998) Young, beautiful Cat Calder is determined to honor the memory of her late fiancé, Repp. But then handsome, gray-eyed Logan Echohawk comes into her life.

6. *Green Calder Grass* (Kensington, 2002) Jessy Calder is blissfully wedded to Ty Calder, but then Tara, Ty's unscrupulous ex-wife, returns.

7. *Shifting Calder Wind* (Kensington, 2003) Patriarch Chase Calder, shot and left for dead, doesn't remember his own name, much less why he was in Texas.

8. *Calder Promise* (Kensington, 2004) Laura Calder, in Rome on a grand tour with her late father's first wife, Tara, meets wealthy Texan Boone Rutledge and impoverished English nobleman, Sebastian Dunshill, the Earl of Crawford, on the same day.

9. *Lone Calder Star* (Kensington, 2005) Quint Echohawk, grandson of Chase Benteen Calder, is sent to Texas to determine why the manager of the Cee Bar Ranch southwest of Forth Worth has disappeared.

10. *Calder Storm* (Kensington, 2006) Trey Calder, fifth generation scion and heir to Triple C Ranch, marries sexy photographer Sloan Davis. After Trey brings Sloan home to the ranch, he learns of a connection from Sloan's past.

Dain, Catherine

PSEUDONYM OF Judith Garwood

I. Freddie O'Neal is a lanky blond who works as a PI (the hard-boiled kind) out of Reno, Nevada. Among her virtues are an ability to pilot a plane, a love of cats, and a strong-minded pragmatism. Among her vices are a junk-food diet, a passion for playing Keno, and a reluctance to show affection for those close to her. Formulaic mysteries with an interesting central character and a good Nevada background.

1. *Lay It on the Line* (Jove, 1992) Reno-based PI Freddie O'Neal is hired by ex-showgirl Joan Halliday to investigate the caretakers of Joan's elderly father, who are not only neglectful but drug dealers as well.

2. *Sing a Song of Death* (Jove, 1993) Did Vince Marino's ex-wife Connie send Vince to "the big casino in the sky?" The evidence points to Connie but Freddie believes in her innocence.

3. *Walk a Crooked Mile* (Jove, 1994) Freddie O'Neal's mother hires her to find her biker ex-husband, Freddie's father, who abandoned them years ago.

4. *Lament for a Dead Cowboy* (Berkley, 1994) A cowboy poet is murdered at a gathering in Elko, Nevada. Freddie's current boyfriend Sam is suspected.

5. *Bet against the House* (Berkley, 1995) Freddie is hired by Tella Scope to investigate Tella's mother, Gloria, who has recently inherited controlling interest in her late husband's computer company.

6. *Luck of the Draw, The* (Berkley, 1996) Freddie is hired to find Darla Hayden, graduate student whose affair with a professor has gone sour. Then Darla shows up at a college cocktail party waving a gun.

7. *Dead Man's Hand* (Berkley, 1997) Freddie, feeling guilty after killing a teenage mugger who attacked her and her boyfriend, sets out to help the mugger's family.

II. A pair of novels and some short stories, including "Finding Charity," published in the multiauthor collection *The Last Noel* (Worldwide, 2004), feature former TV newsmagazine personality and actress turned therapist Faith Cassidy and are set in Los Angeles.

1. *Death of the Party* (Five Star, 2000) Faith Cassidy decides to form a Neighborhood Watch group after her Los Angeles home is burglarized and a young gang member is found murdered on her street—wearing her stolen jacket.

2. *Follow the Murder* (Five Star, 2002) When Craig Thorson, the ex-husband of Faith's client Natalie, is murdered, Natalie is the prime suspect. Much to the dismay of a number of people, including Faith's boyfriend, Richard, and Natalie's lawyer, Faith goes on a crusade to find the real killer.

III. A third series, set in Los Angeles and known as the New Age Mystery series, offers Mariana Morgan, who becomes a psychic healer and amateur sleuth after the random murder of her husband and the loss of her job.

1. *Angel in the Dark* (Five Star, 1999) Bereaved Mariana Morgan joins a meditation group, consults a psychic channeler, then learns she is a healer and asks for angelic help. Eventually she pursues a killer who apparently attacks through the psyche.
2. *Darkness at the Door* (Five Star, 2001) When Mariana's client Umberto Marconi is murdered, the psychic healer teams up with LAPD detective David Claybourne to find the killer.

Dalkey, Kara

I. The Blood of the Goddess trilogy, set in 17th-century Mughal India, in the early days of Portugal's colonial empire, is already being touted as a historical fantasy classic. Thomas Chinnery, an English apprentice apothecary on his way to Cathay (China), stops in Goa (in India, but claimed by Portugal) in 1510, and comes into possession of *rasa mahadevi*, a vial of powder that can raise the dead. Chinnery subsequently loses the vial, teams up with the beautiful Hindu Aditi, runs afoul of the Inquisition, joins a Portuguese expedition into the Indian interior, and gets involved in the three-way struggle for India between European, Mughal, and Maratha factions. Despite its fantasy trappings, the trilogy is full of interesting historical information and fascinating exotic settings.

1. *Goa* (Tor, 1996) English apprentice apothecary Thomas Chinnery lands in the Portuguese Indian enclave of Goa in the 16th century, and comes into possession of, then loses, *rasa mahadevi*.
2. *Bijapur* (Tor, 1997) Chinnery becomes part of an inland expedition into Hindu India to search for the source of the *rasa mahadevi*.
3. *Bhagavati* (Tor, 1998) Chinnery continues his tour of an India torn by factional battle, hoping to resurrect his lost lover, Aditi.

II. California native Kara Dalkey has been concentrating on YA fantasy novels in recent years, including the Water trilogy, set in Wales and Atlantis—*Ascension, Reunion,* and *Transformation* (all published by HarperCollins in 2002)—and two novels, published by Harcourt Brace, set in Heian Japan, featuring a teenage heroine: *Little Sister* (1996) and *The Heavenward Path* (1998). Her first novel, *The Curse of Sagamore,* a sword-and-sorcery comic fantasy featuring Abderian, heir to the throne of Euthymia, was followed by a sequel, *The Sword of Sagamore.* Eventually, Abderian's brother becomes ruler of Euthymia, but Abderian is forced to undergo a wild expedition accompanied by the animated skeleton of the original jester king, Sagamore.

1. *Curse of Sagamore, The* (Ace, 1986) Young Abderian doesn't want to be king of Euthymia, but he carries the mark of the Curse of Sagamore on his arm, which means that he is destined to rule.
2. *Sword of Sagamore, The* (Ace, 1989) Abderian's brother Cyprian becomes king, but their enemies, the Lizard Priests of Euthymia, are plotting against them.

D'Amato, Barbara

I. Catherine "Cat" Marsala, Chicago freelance journalist, has many of the qualities of the hard-boiled private eye: tough but compassionate, street-smart but principled, wisecracking and funny. Her investigative reporting leads her into the cases she solves, and the reader usually learns something about the occupations she investigates, such as prostitution, the state lottery, or emergency medicine. Two of the 12 stories in *Of Course You Know That Chocolate Is a Vegetable: And Other Stories* (Five Star, 2000) feature Cat Marsala.

1. *Hardball* (Scribner, 1990) Louise Sugarman, spokesperson for a drug legalization lobbying group, is blown up at a public meeting.
2. *Hard Tack* (Scribner, 1991) Cat is invited to cruise in a yacht on Lake Michigan by furniture magnate Will Honeywell.
3. *Hard Luck* (Scribner, 1992) Jack Sligh, Illinois lottery official, falls to his death from a skyscraper just before an interview with Cat.
4. *Hard Women* (Scribner, 1993) Marsala, doing a television assignment on prostitutes, befriends call girl Sandra Lupica.
5. *Hard Case* (Scribner, 1994) Dr. Hannah Grant, new director at a hospital trauma center, is found suffocated in the staff lounge.
6. *Hard Christmas* (Scribner, 1995) A straightforward assignment to do a feature on Michigan's Christmas tree-farming industry turns crooked when a worker is fed through a tree-baling machine.
7. *Hard Bargain* (Scribner, 1997) Cat investigates the case of Shelly Danielo, female police officer, who killed another police officer as he was stabbing his wife, Shelly's sister.
8. *Hard Evidence* (Scribner, 1999) Cat goes undercover as a catering consultant at upscale food emporium Spencer and Angelotti, when she discovers that the soup bone she bought from them was actually part of a human leg.
9. *Hard Road* (Scribner, 2001) *The Wizard of Oz* is the theme when Cat takes her young nephew to an Oz festival in Chicago's Grant Park and witnesses two murders.

II. The Chicago Police series usually features Chicago cops Suze Figueroa and Norm Bennis, but sometimes other characters, such as police detective Polly Kelly, come to the fore. The series maintains a high degree of suspense and authentic police detail but lacks Cat Marsala.

1. *Killer.app.* (Forge, 1996) Computer programmer Sheryl Birch, who runs into a secret program with sinister implications, needs all the help she can get from her Chicago cop sister Suze Figueroa and her cohorts.
2. *Good Cop, Bad Cop* (Forge, 1997) The notorious 1969 Chicago police raid on the Black Panthers, which killed Fred Hampton, forms the background to the murderous rivalry between cops Aldo and Nick Bertolucci.
3. *Help Me Please* (Forge, 1999) Three-year-old Danielle Gaston is kidnapped from Chicago's Holy Name Cathedral. Police detective Polly Kelly leads a search against time to find the child.
4. *Of Course You Know That Chocolate Is a Vegetable: And Other Stories* (Five Star, 2000) Twelve short stories, seven featuring Figueroa and Bennis, two featuring Cat Marsala. The story "See No Evil" brings them together.
5. *Authorized Personnel Only* (Forge, 2000) Figueroa and Bennis, temporarily promoted to detective, are on the trail of a serial killer and a child molester. Unbeknownst to them, the molester is in residence at Figueroa's house.
6. *Death of a Thousand Cuts* (Forge, 2004) The gala reunion of staffers and former residents of the Hawthorne House School for the Treatment of Autistic Children is ruined when the school's founder, Dr. Jay Schermerhorn, is found tortured to death in the mansion's basement.

Dams, Jeanne M(artin)

I. Sexagenarian American widow Dorothy Martin settles into the fictional English university-cathedral town of Sherebury and soon becomes acquainted with the locals, including her future husband, Chief Constable Alan Nesbitt, and with the mayhem that always seems to afflict small, quaint towns in mysteries. This series of cozies, which features a likable heroine and a well-realized English setting, has built up a faithful readership.

1. *Body in the Transept, The* (Walker, 1995) Dorothy Martin has moved to the English town of Sherebury, where she and her late academic husband had planned to retire. After the Christmas Eve service in the cathedral, Dorothy stumbles over the dead body of Canon Billings.
2. *Trouble in the Town Hall* (Walker, 1996) Dorothy is present at town hall when the body of a young vagrant is discovered in a broom closet of the building.
3. *Holy Terror in the Hebrides* (Walker, 1997) Dorothy goes on holiday to the Isle of Iona in the Hebrides and finds herself stuck with an acrimonious, multidenominational religious group from America. Then the "Methodist" falls to his death.
4. *Malice in Miniature* (Walker, 1998) Dorothy has settled into her 17th-century cottage with her second husband, Chief Constable Alan Nesbitt. Then their charwoman, Ada Finch, begs Dorothy to clear her son of the theft of an antique miniature tea set from the Miniatures Museum of Brocklesby Hall.
5. *Victim in Victoria Station, The* (Walker, 1999) Husband Alan is on business in Africa, so Dorothy embarks on a jaunt to London. Then she reads in a newspaper that the young American businessman she had chatted with has died unexpectedly.
6. *Killing Cassidy* (Walker, 2000) Dorothy and Alan return to Dorothy's hometown of Hillsburg, Indiana, after she receives word that old friend David Cassidy has died and bequeathed her $5,000 if she can discover who killed him.
7. *To Perish in Penzance* (Walker, 2001) Dorothy and Alan take a vacation to Cornwall, the site of a past murder involving a woman with long blond hair found in a cove in Penzance, a murder that still bothers Alan.
8. *Sins out of School* (Walker, 2003) Did St. Stephens School teacher Amanda Doyle stab her husband when she took a day off, with Dorothy substituting for her?
9. *Winter of Discontent* (Tor, 2005) An old lover of Dorothy's best friend, Jane, is found dead in the tunnels beneath the local museum where he worked.

II. Dams's hometown of South Bend, Indiana, is the setting for a series of mysteries set in the early 1900s featuring Hilda Johansson, a Swedish maid working in the household of the wealthy Studebaker family, as an amateur detective. Hilda, who doesn't speak English too well, makes an engaging detective in this series with historically accurate background.

1. *Death in Lacquer Red* (Walker, 1999) Hilda and her beau, fireman Patrick Cavanaugh, discover the dead body of a missionary woman in the South Bend, Indiana, backyard of the Studebakers, Hilda's employers.
2. *Red, White, and Blue Murder* (Walker, 2000) Summer 1901: two murders, one of President McKinley, the other of prominent local builder Roger Warren, threaten to inflame sentiment against immigrants.
3. *Green Grow the Victims* (Walker, 2001) The Studebakers give Hilda a week off to investigate the disappearance of Uncle Dan, relative of Patrick Cavanaugh's and candidate for city council, after Dan's political rival is discovered dead.
4. *Science Is Golden* (Walker, 2002) Fritz, friend of Hilda's younger brother Erik, decides to join the circus as a trapeze artist, but then the real trapeze artists disappear, and Fritz is found brutally beaten in a barn.
5. *Crimson Snow* (Perseverance, 2005) Hilda looks into the murder of 22-year-old schoolteacher Sophie Jacobs and the disappearance of several other young women. This novel is based on an actual case from 1904.

Danielson, Peter

The Children of the Lion series of historical novels is another "creation" by Lyle Kenyon Engel, the book "packager" behind John Jakes's (q.v.) Kent Family Chronicles. For 19 volumes, from the time of Abraham to the time of King David, the series follows the family who bears the lion's paw birthmark, or "Mark of Cain," as proof of their lineage. Most of the action takes place in Egypt and Palestine, but Troy, pre-classical Greece, and other civilizations of biblical times (2nd millennium BCE) get their share as well. Danielson's long, leisurely, and readable novels appeared at the rate of better than one a year from 1980 to 1996 in paperback originals. Gregg Press reprinted the first four installments in hardcover.

1. *Children of the Lion* (Bantam, 1980) Abraham leads his family and followers out of Ur.
2. *Shepherd Kings, The* (Bantam, 1981) Jacob, Abraham's grandson, is exiled.
3. *Vengeance of the Lion* (Bantam, 1983) The Children of the Lion become nomad invaders of desert caravans.
4. *Lion in Egypt, The* (Bantam, 1984) The Children of the Lion have the secret skill to halt the fearsome desert warriors advancing upon Egypt.
5. *Golden Pharaoh, The* (Bantam, 1985) The Children of the Lion join their special destiny to that of the true ruler of Egypt and oppose the usurping Golden Pharaoh.
6. *Lord of the Nile* (Bantam, 1986) A new generation of the Children of the Lion swears allegiance to Egypt's last Pharaoh and fights in the vanguard of a desperate army besieged on both flanks.
7. *Prophecy, The* (Bantam, 1987) Joseph's prophecy, that an abandoned son would return to kill his despot father, foretells the end of the dynasty of Shepherd Kings in Egypt.
8. *Sword of Glory* (Bantam, 1987) Three years after the events of The Prophecy, Kamose is on the verge of victory against his father, but Kamose has secretly embraced the cult of the evil goddess.
9. *Deliverer, The* (Bantam, 1988) The conqueror and king falls victim to an evil cult, which threatens doom for the Haibru slaves and Egypt's imperial glory.
10. *Exodus, The* (Bantam, 1989) Young Prince Moses quells a rebellion in Nubia, and learns of his true heritage.
11. *Sea Peoples, The* (Bantam, 1990) The Sea Peoples face devastation when their supply ships are hijacked by a pirate king.
12. *Promised Land, The* (Bantam, 1990) The Children of the Lion are fighting with the Greeks beneath the walls of Troy, while Joshua is prepared to attack Jericho and reconquer Canaan.
13. *Invaders, The* (Bantam, 1991) A tyrant of the Israelites is assassinated, igniting the fury of a once-mighty people that now toils under the command of a sadistic, power-hungry general.
14. *Trumpet and the Sword, The* (Bantam, 1991) Luti meets a ruthless bandit, and realizes that he is Micah, who then helps her escape from her Bedouin captors.

15. *Prophets and Warriors* (**Bantam, 1993**) Fulfilling the centuries-old prophecy, vanquishing armies sweep a downtrodden people into exile.
16. *Departed Glory* (**Bantam, 1993**) Recounts the tragic and heroic struggle of King Saul against the barbaric Philistines.
17. *Death of Kings, The* (**Bantam, 1994**) Saul and his son Jonathan meet their ends.
18. *Shining King, The* (**Bantam, 1995**) King Saul, who united the Twelve Tribes, is dead, and chaos reigns in Israel.
19. *Triumph of the Lion* (**Bantam, 1996**) David has victory within his grasp as his army marches upon Jerusalem.

Dank, Gloria

One of the protagonists in children's author (*The Forest of App*, etc.) Gloria Dank's mystery series is . . . a children's author. Bernard Woodruff, creator of the Mrs. Woolley books, is a grumpy, bearish sort, but devoted to his lovable wife, Maya, a devotion that doesn't extend to Maya's brother, happy-go-lucky ne'er-do-well Snooky Randolph. Bernard and Snooky make an improbable but effective pair of sleuths in a series of light mysteries with odd characters and sparkling repartee.

1. *Friends till the End* (**Bantam, 1989**) Snooky was present when Laura Sloane drank a deadly cocktail, but it is Bernard's armchair sleuthing that leads to a solution.
2. *Going Out in Style* (**Bantam, 1990**) Bella Whitaker doesn't keep her date with Snooky because she has been murdered.
3. *As the Sparks Fly Upward* (**Doubleday, 1992**) Bernard and Snooky visit Vermont in winter, as relatives of Snooky's latest inamorata seem to be dying off at an alarming rate.
4. *Misfortunes of Others, The* (**Doubleday, 1993**) Snooky flies in from the West Indies to offer good cheer and gourmet cooking to the pregnant Maya, and to help solve a case of blackmail.

Dart, Iris Rainer

Dart is the author of best-selling combinations of show business and devoted women friends. Foul-mouthed but bighearted singer Cee Cee Bloom and "good girl" housewife Roberta "Bertie" Baron seem a mismatched pair of friends, but their friendship endures through Bertie's death, when Cee Cee mothers, in her inimitable fashion, Bertie's orphaned daughter, Nina. Both novels are tearjerkers, but there are plenty of quips and smart dialogue before the sad endings. Bette Midler and Barbara Hershey played the friends in the movie version of *Beaches*.

1. *Beaches* (**Bantam, 1985**) Two girls meet on an Atlantic City beach and, despite differences in their backgrounds, become lifetime friends.
2. *I'll Be There* (**Little, Brown, 1991**) Cee Cee adopts her late friend's daughter, and proves a loving but erratic mother. Variant title: *Beaches II: I'll Be There*.

Daudet, Alphonse

French I students exposed to "*la derniere classe*" may be surprised to learn that Alphonse Daudet was a prolific and popular author who is still read today in France and elsewhere. Daudet, an admirer of Dickens, worked from the same palette in satirizing the southern French temperament. His Tartarin is an irrepressible braggart whose tales of his adventures are riotous exaggerations embroidered around a

few bare threads of fact. The lion he fights, for instance is a tame and toothless old feline. Tartarin sees himself as a tragic figure who has the heroic and chivalrous soul of a Don Quixote trapped in a fat and lazy Sancho Panza body. Numbers 1 and 2 were bound together in the Everyman's Library edition (Dutton, 1910).

1. *Tartarin of Tarascon, Traveller, Turk, and Lion-Hunter* (**Crowell, 1895**) Tartarin proves his reputation for valor and resourcefulness on an expedition to Algeria. First published in 1872 as *Adventures prodigieuses de Tartarin*. Translated from the French by Henry Firth. Variant title: *The New Don Quixote*.
2. *Tartarin on the Alps* (**Crowell, 1894**) Tartarin the mountain climber defies death. First published in 1885 as *Tartarin sur les Alpes*. Translated from the French by Henry Firth.
3. *Port Tarascon; The Last Adventures of the Illustrious Tartarin* (**Harper, 1891**) The intrepid Tartarin leads a colony to the South Pacific. First published in 1890 as *Port-Tarascon; Derniere aventures de l'illustre Tartarin*. Translated from the French by Henry James (q.v.).

Davidson, Diane Mott

Goldy Bear, owner of Goldilocks Catering ("Where Everything Is Just Right!") in Aspen, Colorado, caters as many as three events a day, and throws in the occasional murder solution. Divorced from "The Jerk" (aka Dr. John Richard Korman), her abusive obstetrician spouse, the cherubic Goldy has Arch, her teenage son and, in the course of events, acquires a second husband, gourmet cook and homicide detective Tom Schulz. Light mysteries with interesting characters, suspenseful plots, and great recipes from Goldy's kitchen.

1. *Catering to Nobody* (**St. Martin's, 1990**) Goldy has to shut down her catering business when her ex-father-in-law drinks poisoned coffee.
2. *Dying for Chocolate* (**Bantam, 1992**) Psychiatrist Philip Miller, one of Goldy's suitors, drives his BMW off a cliff after having brunch at her place.
3. *Cereal Murders, The* (**Bantam, 1993**) After catering the senior class dinner at Elk Park Preparatory School, Goldy finds the class valedictorian strangled with one of her extension cords.
4. *Last Suppers, The* (**Bantam, 1994**) Goldy's self-catered wedding to detective Tom Schulz is interrupted when the groom discovers the corpse of the officiating minister just before the ceremony.
5. *Killer Pancake* (**Bantam, 1995**) Claire Satterfield, star saleswoman for Mignon Cosmetics, turns up dead at the company's low-fat catered luncheon.
6. *Main Corpse, The* (**Bantam, 1996**) Persuaded by her friend Maria, Goldy caters a party for Prospect Investment Partners at an old gold mine the company is reopening.
7. *Grilling Season, The* (**Bantam, 1997**) Goldy's ex-husband, Dr. John Richard Korman, is arrested for the murder of his girlfriend, HMO vice president Suz Craig.
8. *Prime Cut* (**Bantam, 1998**) Goldy runs up against an unscrupulous contractor, cookbooks stolen from a museum, the competition of an aggressive new local caterer, and a couple of murders.
9. *Tough Cookie* (**Bantam, 2000**) Drain problems suspend her catering business, so Goldy accepts a gig on a PBS cooking show. Then Doug Portman, her wealthy ex-boyfriend, meets his end on a ski run, the same run that was the scene of a previous death by avalanche.
10. *Sticks and Scones* (**Bantam, 2001**) While Goldy is catering two posh events near Denver, she discovers the body of one of a gang of stamp thieves and sees her husband, Tom, wounded by a sniper.

11. *Chopping Spree* **(Bantam, 2002)** Old college friend Barry Dean hires Goldy to cater an exclusive shoppers-night-out promotion in the upscale shopping mall he manages.

12. *Double Shot* **(Morrow, 2004)** Goldy is finally rid of her abusive ex-husband, Dr. John Richard Korman, but she is also the prime suspect in his demise.

13. *Dark Tort* **(Morrow, 2006)** Goldy tumbles over the body of Dusty Routt, a paralegal at Hanrahan & Jule, a firm with which Goldy has a lucrative contract.

14. *Sweet Revenge* **(Morrow, 2007)** The body of Drew Wellington, the disgraced former DA, turns up in the local library.

Davies, Robertson

I. Robertson Davies was Canada's leading man of letters. In addition to writing novels, he was a playwright, critic, and professor at the University of Toronto; for 20 years he was the editor of the *Peterborough* (Ontario) *Examiner*. As a young man he studied acting at the Old Vic. Davies draws on these experiences in his Salterton trilogy, which has been treasured loyally by fans for years. *The Salterton Trilogy* (Penguin, 1985) includes all three titles.

1. *Tempest-Tost* **(Rinehart, 1952)** A production of *The Tempest* occupies the leading citizens of the provincial Canadian town of Salterton. Eccentric organist Humphrey Cobbler and censorious old Miss Puss are among the memorable characters in this, the most humorous of all Davies's novels.

2. *Leaven of Malice* **(Scribner, 1955)** A malicious joke—the fake engagement announcement of Pearl Vambrace and Solly Bridgetower—starts the action.

3. *Mixture of Frailties, A* **(Scribner, 1955)** Monica Gall seizes her chance to study voice in London and achieves success and maturity in integrating her new life and her old.

II. The Deptford novels, named for the small town in Canada where the story starts, have achieved a wider recognition than the Salterton trilogy. This series lacks the humor of the first, but is more ambitious in presenting a Jungian view of history and personality. *The Deptford Trilogy* (Penguin, 1985) includes all three novels.

1. *Fifth Business* **(Viking, 1970)** Dunstan Ramsay, a retired history teacher, remembers his Canadian boyhood and the fateful misaimed snowball that reverberated through the years in the lives of his friends.

2. *Manticore, The* **(Viking, 1972)** Rich and successful lawyer David Staunton relates the course of the Jungian analysis he undertakes after the mysterious death of his father.

3. *World of Wonders* **(Viking, 1975)** World-famous magician Magnus Eisengrim (aka Paul Dempster) tells his life story.

III. Davies followed the Deptford trilogy with a trio of novels in which the connecting link is Francis Cornish: painter, art forger, and art collector. *The Cornish Trilogy* (Penguin, 1992) includes all three novels.

1. *Rebel Angels, The* **(Viking, 1982)** Maria Theotoky, a beautiful, scholarly half-Gypsy, Dr. Parlabane, renegade monk, and other scholars at the College of St. John and the Holy Ghost in Toronto are thrown into turmoil by the legacy of the late Francis Cornish.

2. *What's Bred in the Bone* **(Viking, 1985)** Two *daimons* discourse on the life of Francis Cornish from his origins in the provincial Canadian town of Blairlogie to his death.

3. *Lyre of Orpheus, The* **(Viking, 1988)** The Cornish Foundation sponsors the completion of an unfinished opera by E. T. A. Hoffmann called *Arthur of Britain; or, The Magnanimous Cuckold*.

IV. Davies published two volumes of what may have been the start of another trilogy (he died in 1995). Each volume contains a murder in which the perpetrator is never discovered by the authorities. Several characters appear in both novels.

1. *Murther and Walking Spirits* **(Viking, 1991)** Movie critic Connor Gilmartin spends the first part of his afterlife attending a festival featuring films about his ancestors.

2. *Cunning Man, The* **(Viking, 1994)** Jonathan Hullah, a Toronto MD with somewhat heterodox opinions, reminisces about his life and his old friend, an Anglican clergyman who is more Roman than Rome.

Davis, Lindsey

Marcus Didius Falco is a cynical, wisecracking private investigator with a heart of gold, a tolerance for the more amiable vices, and a divorcée girlfriend. Sound familiar? Well, maybe the setting, Rome in the age of the emperor Vespasian (1st century CE), doesn't sound quite so hackneyed. Although the details of Roman society and technology are right, Lindsey Davis has given her hero a modern sensibility, which blends well with a corrupt ambience that would do justice to the mean streets of contemporary Chicago or Los Angeles.

1. *Silver Pigs, The* **(Crown, 1989)** Falco rescues a beautiful young girl in the Forum and gets up to his neck in silver smuggling in the British colonies.

2. *Shadows in Bronze* **(Crown, 1991)** Disguising himself as an idle vacationer, Marcus haunts the spas of Neapolis, Capreae, and Pompeii to thwart a conspiracy involving Egyptian grain.

3. *Venus in Copper* **(Crown, 1992)** Falco is hired by a family of rich and vulgar freedmen to investigate the thrice-widowed fiancée of one of their number.

4. *Iron Hand of Mars, The* **(Crown, 1993)** The emperor sends Marcus to Germany to bring a rebel chieftain into line and find a missing legate.

5. *Poseidon's Gold* **(Crown, 1994)** Geminus, father of Marcus, is his estranged son's unwelcome partner in an effort to pay off the debt incurred by Festus, Marcus's con-man brother.

6. *Last Act in Palmyra* **(Mysterious, 1996)** Denied a promised promotion into the upper class by Vespasian, Falco takes on a job in Syria looking for a runaway girl. Marcus and his lover, Helena, discover the body of a playwright in a cistern.

7. *Time to Depart* **(Mysterious, 1997)** Crime boss Balbinus Pius has fled Rome under threat of execution, leaving a rackets power vacuum in Rome that Marcus has to cope with.

8. *Dying Light in Corduba, A* **(Mysterious, 1998)** The Society of Olive Oil Producers of Baetica in Spain may be connected to the assassination attempt on Chief Spy Anacrites and to an attempt to form a cartel.

9. *Three Hands in the Fountain* **(Mysterious, 1999)** Marcus and Petronius discover a severed human hand, the first of many similar body parts, in a Roman fountain; this portends a contaminated water supply, among other things.

10. *Two for the Lion* **(Mysterious, 1999)** Vespasian's top executioner is a specially trained lion. When the lion is murdered, Falco is put on the case, following a trail that leads him to Greece and Tripoli.

11. *One Virgin Too Many* **(Mysterious, 2000)** Falco's job of tending the emperor's sacred geese leads him into various religious cults,

including the Arval Brothers, which Helena's brother is trying to join, and the Vestal Virgins, which his niece is being roped into; disappearance; and murder.

12. *Ode to a Banker* (**Mysterious, 2001**) Marcus investigates a murder connected to the worlds of poetry, publishing, and banking.

13. *Body in the Bathhouse, A* (**Mysterious, 2002**) Huge cost overruns at Fishbourne, a palace under construction, bring the reluctant Falco to Britain, a place where plumbing isn't appreciated the way it is in Rome.

14. *Jupiter Myth, The* (**Mysterious, 2003**) Marcus Didius is in Londinium, Britannia, in 75 CE, investigating the murder of a disgraced associate of Roman ally King Togidobnus.

15. *Accusers, The* (**Mysterious, 2004**) Back in Rome, Falco is matched against two highly successful "legals," Paccius Africanus and Silius Italicus, when he tries to prove that the death of Senator Rubirius Metellus wasn't suicide.

16. *Scandal Takes a Holiday* (**Mysterious, 2004**) When Diocles, the government newspaper's gossip columnist, disappears in Ostia, Falco follows some rumors that the pirate business, supposedly squelched by Pompey the Great, is alive and well.

17. *See Delphi and Die* (**St. Martin's, 2006**) On a tour in Greece with a large entourage, including his wife, Helena, Falco finds that the shady Seven Sights Travel outfit has a suspiciously high mortality rate.

18. *Saturnalia* (**St. Martin's, 2007**) Falco receives an imperial commission from Vespasian to solve the murder of nobleman Sextus Gratianus Scaeva.

Davis, Val

PSEUDONYM OF Angela & Robert Irvine

Nicolette "Nick" Scott and her father, Elliott Scott, are both archaeologists, but while Elliott's forte is the Anasazis, the ancient inhabitants of the American Southwest, Nick is more interested in airplanes, particularly lost planes from either World War, a preference that leads her into interesting investigations and a lot of hot water. "Val Davis," not to be confused with the singer or the actor of the same name, is the pseudonym of the husband-and-wife team of Angela and Robert Irvine (q.v.).

1. *Track of the Scorpion* (**St. Martin's, 1996**) Nicolette Scott, on a routine Anasazi dig with her father, Elliott, in the badlands of New Mexico, learns of the discovery of a World War II bomber buried in the desert, its mummified crew still on board and, interestingly enough, its fuselage full of bullet holes.

2. *Flight of the Serpent* (**Bantam, 1998**) In Arizona Nicolette Scott witnesses the wreckage of a plane crash that left reporter Matt Gault dead and finds herself involved with illegal medical experiments and government cover-ups.

3. *Wake of the Hornet* (**Bantam, 2000**) The people of the South Pacific island of Balesin carry their "cargo-cult" worship to extremes, even to the extent of trying to lure aircraft down out of the sky with a homemade airstrip and mock planes.

4. *Return of the Spanish Lady, The* (**St. Martin's, 2001**) A crashed World War II Japanese plane and the frozen bodies of three gold prospectors containing some remaining viruses of the great influenza epidemic of 1918–1919 ("The Spanish Lady") could lead to a new pandemic.

5. *Thread of the Spider* (**St. Martin's, 2002**) Nicky discovers a 1937 Packard in a cave in the Utah desert with some portentous papers.

Dawson, Janet

Jeri Howard, an Oakland, California, private investigator, can hold her own with her sisters in crime. Jeri is smart and tenacious, but tends to get emotionally involved with her cases. The ambience of the San Francisco Bay Area plays a role in this well-plotted, suspenseful series. Janet Dawson, not to be confused with artist Janet Dawson (Boddy), works and lives in the Bay Area.

1. *Kindred Crimes* (**St. Martin's, 1990**) Jeri is hired by a distraught husband to find his missing wife, who may be hiding from the fallout of a 15-year-old domestic homicide.

2. *Till the Old Men Die* (**Fawcett, 1993**) Dr. Lito Manibusan's murder is dismissed as a random slaying until his "widow" turns up demanding his personal effects.

3. *Take a Number* (**Fawcett, 1993**) Ruth Raynor asks Jeri to find $100,000 she believes her estranged husband, Sam, has hidden.

4. *Don't Turn Your Back on the Ocean* (**Fawcett, 1994**) A vacation in Monterey turns out to be a busman's holiday when Jeri gets involved with cases of murder, vandalism, and pelican mutilation.

5. *Nobody's Child* (**Fawcett, 1995**) Alcoholic Naomi Smith hires Jeri to find out if the body recently found in a burned-out home is really that of her runaway daughter.

6. *Credible Threat, A* (**Fawcett, 1996**) Vicki Vernon, daughter of Jeri's ex-husband, enlists Jeri's aid when she and her seven housemates, all UC Berkeley students, receive threatening phone calls and have their garden destroyed.

7. *Witness to Evil* (**Fawcett, 1997**) A two-part mystery, both involving 17-year-old runaway Darcy Stefano. In the first part, Lori follows Darcy to Paris, where Darcy has gone to honor her French grandmother, a Holocaust survivor. In the second part, Darcy disappears again, this time from her boarding school, where a maintenance man has been murdered.

8. *Where the Bodies Are Buried* (**Fawcett, 1998**) Jeri takes a job at food-processing company Bates Inc. after one of their paralegals dies from a fall after paying Jeri a retainer for unspecified services.

9. *Killing at the Track, A* (**Fawcett, 2000**) Someone is making menacing telephone calls to horse owner-trainer Molly Torrance, so Jeri makes a trip to Edgewater Downs race track.

10. *Scam and Eggs* (**Five Star, 2002**) Ten short stories, three of them involving Jeri Howard.

Day, Dianne

In 1905 Wellesley College–educated Caroline Fremont Jones escapes her stuffy Boston background by emigrating to San Francisco, dropping her first name, and starting her own typing service. Soon she meets the mysterious Michael Archer/Kossoff, and the two become lovers and, eventually, partners in the J&K Detective Agency. Fremont Jones is a strong-minded woman ahead of her time while the pre–World War I historical setting is nicely evoked, with interesting plots and a few historical characters such as the "Emperor Norton," and some passionate scenes and romantic suspense. (Day is, under various pseudonyms, a Harlequin Romance writer.)

1. *Strange Files of Fremont Jones, The* (**Doubleday, 1995**) In 1905 refugee from Boston Caroline Fremont Jones drops the "Caroline" and goes into business in San Francisco as a "type-writer." Then a client, the elderly Li Wong, is murdered, and Fremont's office is ransacked.

2. *Fire and Fog* **(Doubleday, 1996)** Fremont Jones joins the American Red Cross to help victims of the infamous San Francisco Earthquake of 1906.

3. *Bohemian Murders* **(Doubleday, 1997)** Fremont becomes the temporary lighthouse keeper at Point Pinos near Carmel, California. Her lover, Michael Archer, has taken a cottage in Carmel but has mysteriously changed his name to Michael Kossoff.

4. *Emperor Norton's Ghost* **(Doubleday, 1998)** In 1908 Jones and Kossoff, having founded the J&K Detective Agency, investigate the murder of two well-known spiritualists.

5. *Death Train to Boston* **(Doubleday, 1999)** Jones and Kossoff, traveling incognito on a case for the Southern and Union Pacific Railroad, are separated after a deliberately caused train wreck in Utah's Wasatch Mountains, and Jones falls into the hands of a polygamous Mormon Elder.

6. *Beacon Street Mourning* **(Doubleday, 2000)** Fremont returns to Boston to care for her ill father. Then her father dies, and Fremont suspects her stepmother of poisoning him.

De Blasis, Celeste

The Swan trilogy focuses on four generations of the Falconer family in the 19th century and Wild Swan, their renowned thoroughbred stable in Maryland. Readable historical romances suffused with horse-breeding and horse-racing ambience.

1. *Wild Swan* **(Bantam, 1984)** The devotion of Alexandria Thaine, daughter of an English merchant, to her deceased sister's husband leads to her transplantation to America.

2. *Swan's Chance* **(Bantam, 1985)** In 1836 Alexandra Carrington Falconer is matriarch to a brood of children and grandchildren and a stable full of prize racehorses.

3. *Season of Swans, A* **(Bantam, 1989)** Gincie Culhane shoots her half brother Mark, and flees to the sanctuary of Wild Swan, rebuilt on the ashes of the Civil War.

De Camp, L(yon) Sprague

I. The late L. Sprague De Camp, Nebula Grand Master, resurrector of Conan the Barbarian, and author of more than 100 fiction and non-fiction titles, was the master, almost the progenitor, of the humorous fantasy tale, in which a sane, resourceful protagonist prevails in a world of inconsistent laws and perverse beings. The Novaria series is set in a world somewhat reminiscent of the Hellenistic period, comprised of the Twelve Cities, various nations of piratical barbarians, and the Mulvanian Empire. Jorian, king of Xylar, one of the Twelve Cities, is the reluctant hero of a series of adventures among goblins, wizards, and demons.

1. *Goblin Tower, The* **(Pyramid, 1968)** King Jorian makes a deal with a Mulvanian sorcerer to avoid his kingly fate of being beheaded.

2. *Clocks of Iraz, The* **(Pyramid, 1971)** Jorian finds employment in the city of Iraz, which is involved in a civil war.

3. *Fallible Fiend, The* **(New American Library, 1973)** Short stories set in the world of Novaria.

4. *Unbeheaded King, The* **(Ballantine, 1983)** Jorian is still trying to retrieve Estrildia, his favorite wife, from Xylar with the help of demons.

5. *Honorable Barbarian, The* **(Ballantine, 1989)** Kerin, Jorian's younger brother, is caught in compromising circumstances with the maiden Adelina and is packed off to sea.

II. The series, variously called Viagens Interplanetarias (Portuguese for "Interplanetary Tours") and Krishna (for the planet on which most of the adventures take place), is fantasy with a science-fiction overlay. The Planet Krishna is an Earth-like planet whose inhabitants are rather primitive egg-laying humanoids.

1. *Rogue Queen* **(Doubleday, 1951)** Iroedh, a worker in a community of egg-laying beings, is accosted by visiting scientists from Terra.

2. *Cosmic Manhunt* **(Ace, 1954)** Victor Hasselberg is sent from Terra to Krishna to bring back the eloping daughter of a textile merchant. English title: *A Planet Called Krishna*. Variant title: *The Queen of Zamba*.

3. *Tower of Zanid, The* **(Avalon, 1958)** Anthony Fallon is hired by a Terran archaeologist to guide him to a tower built by an earlier civilization on Krishna.

4. *Search for Zei, The* **(Avalon, 1962)** Dirk Barnevelt is sent to rescue explorer Igor Shtain who has disappeared into an area of Krishna full of legends and pirates.

5. *Hand of Zei, The* **(Avalon, 1963)** Barnevelt and the Princess Zei finally rescue Igor Shtain.

6. *Hostage of Zir, The* **(Putnam, 1977)** Fergus Reith, an employee of the Magic Carpet Travel Agency, leads the first organized tour of Krishna.

7. *Prisoner of Zhamanak, The* **(Phantasia, 1982)** Alicia Dyckman, beautiful, headstrong anthropologist, is imprisoned by Khorosh of Zhamanak, who wants to study a Terran.

8. *Bones of Zora, The* **(Phantasia, 1983)** Reith and Dyckman meet again, assisting rival scientists searching for fossils on Krishna. Written with Catherine Crook De Camp.

9. *Swords of Zinjaban, The* **(Baen, 1991)** Twenty years after Alicia leaves Krishna, Reith's latest tour and relics of his previous marriages present some unusual problems. Written with Catherine Crook De Camp.

III. The Compleat Enchanter series, cowritten with Fletcher Pratt, is a creation held in fondest memory by older readers of fantasy. Contemporary (1941) psychologist Harold Shea is transported to various mythological and fictional realms in a series of very funny adventures. *The Magical Misadventures of Harold Shea* weren't all collected into one volume until the publication of *The Complete Compleat Enchanter* (Baen, 1989). Just when we thought everything was finally under control, De Camp and Christopher Stasheff (q.v.) resurrected Harold Shea in two collections of stories written by various authors: *The Enchanter Reborn* (Baen, 1992) and *The Exotic Enchanter* (Baen, 1995).

1. *Incomplete Enchanter, The* **(Holt, 1941)** Harold Shea mistakenly turns up in the world of Norse mythology, just in time for the final battle of Ragnarok! A further adventure in the world of Spenser's *Faerie Queene* supplies Harold with a wife, Belphebe.

2. *Castle of Iron, The* **(Gnome, 1950)** Belphebe is transported to the world of Ariosto's *Orlando Furioso* and transmogrified as Belphegor, who doesn't recognize Harold Shea as her husband.

3. *Wall of Serpents* **(Avalon, 1960)** Harold, Belphebe, and others go to the world of the *Kalevala* of Finnish legend, and then, to the world of Irish mythology.

IV. De Camp collaborated with his wife, Catherine Crook De Camp (who was actually unacknowledged collaborator on many of his works), on a pair of humorous sword-and-sorcery novels set in the pragmatically magical world of Rhaetia.

1. *Incorporated Knight, The* **(Phantasia, 1987)** Sir Eudoric, an inept knight, becomes slowly more "ept" with each successive adventure.

2. *Pixillated Peeress, The* (**Ballantine, 1991**) Thorolf, scholar turned soldier, rescues Yvette, the Countess of Grintz, from the soldiers of an evil duke.

V. Robert E. Howard created the character of Conan the Barbarian, but it was De Camp, with the help of Lin Carter and others, who rescued Howard's manuscripts and set the Cimmerian on the road to mainstream fame. Through the 1950s and 1960s, the Conan stories were reedited and sometimes novelized from short story form by De Camp, Carter, and others. In the late 1970s and early 1980s, De Camp was listed as the primary author of several Conan books, which are listed below. John Maddox Roberts (q.v.) continued the series after De Camp gave it up. Robert Jordan (q.v.) also wrote several Conan pastiches.

1. *Conan the Swordsman* (**Bantam, 1978**) Coauthored with Lin Carter and Bjorn Nyberg.
2. *Conan the Liberator* (**Bantam, 1979**) Coauthored with Lin Carter.
3. *Conan and the Spider God* (**Bantam, 1980**)
4. *Conan the Flame Knife* (**Ace, 1981**) A rewrite by De Camp of the unpublished story "Three-Bladed Doom," originally collected in *Tales of Conan* (Ace, 1979).

De Haven, Tom

I. The Derby Dugan trilogy is a rather bizarre look at the history of newspaper comic-strips from the 1890s to 1960s. Georgie Wreckage started the comic-strip *Pinfold and Fuzzy*, a series about a homeless boy and his talking dog. Number 2 moves to the Depression era and the comic-strip *Derby Dugan and His Dog That Talks*. Number 3 chronicles the demise of the adventure comic-strip and Derby Dugan's revival as Imp Eugene, a counterculture character who clicks in San Francisco. The trilogy is an homage to the daily newspaper strips, which were once a prominent part of American culture, with evocations of the America of the 1890s, the 1930s, and the 1960s, full of quirky but well-realized characters. David Kamp, in the *New York Times Book Review* referred to the trilogy as "John Dos Passos' [q.v.] *USA* trilogy as rendered for comics geeks." New Jersey native Tom De Haven, who once aspired to be a comic-strip artist himself, has had an editorial, and an academic, as well as a writing career.

1. *Funny Papers* (**Viking, 1985**) In the 1890s, in New York City, Georgie Wreckage creates the newspaper strip *Pinfold and Fuzzy*, about a homeless boy and his talking dog.
2. *Derby Dugan's Depression Funnies* (**Holt/Metropolitan, 1996**) The strip has been continued until the 1930s as *Derby Dugan* by Wreckage's former assistant, Walter Geebus. Al Bready, who ghostwrites the strip, narrates the search for a replacement to the ailing Geebus.
3. *Dugan under Ground* (**Holt/Metropolitan, 2001**) Ed "Candy" Biggs, who has continued *Derby Dugan* for a dwindling readership in the 1960s, hopes to revive the strip through hiring the teenage cartoonist Roy Looby (modeled on underground comic legend R. Crumb).

II. Tom De Haven wrote the script for the graphic-novel version of William Gibson's (q.v.) cyberpunk classic *Neuromancer* (Epic Comics, 1989). He has also written young adult novels; *Sunburn Lake: A Trilogy* (Viking, 1988), which contains three novellas—*Clap Hands! Here Comes Charley*; *He's All Mine*; and *Where We'll Never Get Old*; and the Chronicle of the King's Tramp, a trilogy set in a pair of fantasy worlds: Lostwithal, the Human world of the Moment of Iss, and our Earth, the Human world of the Moment of Kemolo. The denizens of these worlds operate a form of magic, which is underpinned by a philosophical system called Perfect Order. The trilogy is full of complex and bizarre characters. As is often the case with fantasy, the plot hinges upon an attempt to destroy the existing cosmos and usher in the reign of evil beings lurking in the background; but the plot and characters are intentionally ambiguous, De Haven's style is staccato and hard-boiled, and many sword-and-sorcery cliches are turned on their heads.

1. *Walker of Worlds* (**Doubleday, 1990**) Lostwithal, the Human world of the Moment of Iss, coexists with Earth, the human world of the Moment of Kemolo. The character Jack the Walker journeys between the two worlds.
2. *End-of-Everything-Man, The* (**Doubleday, 1991**) The plans of the Mage of Four still threaten Lostwithal; the travelers from Kemolo are wallowing in misery and distraction; and Jack has his hands full in preventing ultimate chaos.
3. *Last Human, The* (**Bantam, 1992**) Jack and his comrades work to defeat the threat represented by the Last Human: the Queen of Noise.

De La Roche, Mazo

The 16 Jalna novels, also called the Whiteoak Chronicles, cover the 100-year history of the Whiteoak family of Canada. *Jalna*, the first published volume (they were not written chronologically), quickly became a best seller, and successive volumes attracted the kind of following more common to television shows today. Fans wrote Miss De La Roche about whom Finch should marry or whether Renny should sell any more land. Although this Canadian author wrote many other books, none matched the success of the Jalna novels. Caution: unenlightened attitudes about women and minorities may set some contemporary teeth on edge.

1. *Building of Jalna, The* (**Little, Brown, 1944**) In 1850 Captain Whiteoak and his wife, Adeline, settle on the shore of Lake Ontario.
2. *Morning at Jalna* (**Little, Brown, 1960**) During the American Civil War, a family of Southerners come to stay with Adeline and her four young children.
3. *Mary Wakefield* (**Little, Brown, 1949**) In 1893 Adeline is in her sixties. Mary Wakefield comes from England to be a governess to Philip's children and becomes his wife.
4. *Young Renny* (**Little, Brown, 1935**) By 1906 Adeline is 80. Her unpleasant cousin comes to stay and young Renny tries to drive him away.
5. *Whiteoak Heritage* (**Little, Brown, 1940**) Young Renny returns home from World War I to take his place as head of the family.
6. *Whiteoak Brothers, The* (**Little, Brown, 1953**) Gold fever spreads through the family in 1923. Adeline is 98.
7. *Jalna* (**Little, Brown, 1927**) Romance takes unexpected turns as the handsome Whiteoak brothers begin to think about marrying. Adeline's 100th birthday closes the novel, the first in the Jalna series.
8. *Whiteoaks of Jalna* (**Little, Brown, 1929**) This volume centers on Finch, the odd musical brother to whom Adeline has left all her money. UK title: *Whiteoaks*.
9. *Finch's Fortune* (**Little, Brown, 1931**) Finch again stars, as his inheritance dwindles and his love seems hopeless.
10. *Master of Jalna, The* (**Little, Brown, 1933**) Hard times come to Jalna in 1932–1933, but Renny manages to hold things together.
11. *Whiteoak Harvest* (**Little, Brown, 1936**) The years 1934–1935 are a time of growth, sometimes painful, for Renny and Alayne and their little daughter Adeline, so much like her namesake.

12. *Wakefield's Course* (Little, Brown, 1941) Wakefield, already a successful actor, becomes a war hero in 1939–1940, but he is unlucky in love.

13. *Return to Jalna* (Little, Brown, 1946) Jalna has a special charm for the Whiteoak men returning from World War II in 1943–1945.

14. *Renny's Daughter* (Little, Brown, 1951) Young Adeline, now 18, visits Ireland and falls in love, while Renny fights off suburban development at Jalna.

15. *Variable Winds at Jalna* (Little, Brown, 1954) The younger generation sort out tangled loves, and television comes to Jalna.

16. *Centenary at Jalna* (Little, Brown, 1958) In the final novel chronologically the family is drawn far and wide to celebrate the centennial with a wedding.

de Lint, Charles

I. Dutch-born Canadian writer Charles de Lint is a leading fashioner of what some critics have called "urban fantasy," in which ordinary humans live side by side with Celtic-type fairies and Native American spirits. The fictional city of Newford, Ontario, based on Ottawa, is the setting for many of de Lint's novels and tales. Although only a few of the stories (numbers 2 and 16) were specifically written for a YA audience, much of the series appeals to teenagers. Some of the stories are grim, especially those published under the pseudonym of "Samuel M. Key" (numbers 3 and 4). *Angel of Darkness* (Berkley, 1990), a third "Key" book, isn't listed as part of the Newford series. The fantastic and the ordinary are seamlessly mixed. Many of the human characters are outsiders and/or artists who live on the fringes of society. *A Circle of Cats* (Viking, 2003), illustrated by Charles Vess, is a children's book set outside of Newford with some characters from other Newford books. *The Newford Stories* (SF Book Club, 1999) is an omnibus containing stories from numbers 1, 6, and 13).

1. *Dreams Underfoot* (Tor, 1994) A collection of 19 short stories set in Newford. Some of the stories were published originally as chapbooks.

2. *Dreaming Place, The* (Atheneum, 1990) Teenage cousins Nina and Ashley share a bedroom. Nina has disturbing nightmares in which she is a shape-shifter, for which Nina blames Ash, but Ash is the only one who can save Nina from the hungry manitou spirit that is causing her visions. Written specifically for a YA audience, according to de Lint.

3. *From a Whisper to a Dream* (Berkley, 1992) The malignant spirit of Teddy Bird, a serial killer of teenage prostitutes, may still be haunting the streets of Newford. Originally published under the name "Samuel M. Key." Reissued by Orb (2003) under de Lint's name.

4. *I'll Be Watching You* (Jove, 1994) Rachel Sorenson is rescued from her abusive ex-husband by a passing "stranger," a photographer who has been stalking Rachel for his own purposes. Originally published under the name "Samuel M. Key." Reissued by Orb (2004) under de Lint's name.

5. *Memory and Dream* (Tor, 1994) Isabelle discovered that she could paint images so real they brought her dreams to life, but the forces she unleashed brought tragedy to those she loved.

6. *Ivory and the Horn, The* (Tor, 1995) A collection of 14 Newford short stories, some of them originally published as chapbooks.

7. *Trader* (Tor, 1997) Mild-mannered luthier Leonard Trader and ne'er-do-well Johnny Devlin exchange bodies and try to cope with their changed situations.

8. *Some Place to Be Flying* (Tor, 1998) Photojournalist Lily, hearing rumors of "animal people" living in the slums, discovers an underground community of the First People, Native Americans transmogrified into spirits such as the Trickster and the Storyteller.

9. *Moonlight and Vines* (Tor, 1999) A collection of 23 Newford stories.

10. *Forests of the Heart* (Tor, 2000) A few of the Gentry, elemental spirits from Ireland, emigrated to the New World, where they found themselves in uneven competition with the native land-spirits, the manitou. Then an ambitious human offers a way to claim a place of their own.

11. *Onion Girl, The* (Tor, 2001) Artist Jilly Coppercorn, a figure familiar from other Newford stories, must face both her present hospitalization after being hit by a car and the pain hidden in her past.

12. *Seven Wild Sisters* (Subterranean, 2002) A tale set outside of Newford and featuring Sarah Jane Dillard, the fourth of a family of seven sisters, who discovers a world of spirits and magic in the forests. Reprinted in number 13.

13. *Tapping the Dream Tree* (Tor, 2002) A collection of stories, including the novella *Seven Wild Sisters* (see number 12). Some of the stories appeared originally in anthologies; others as limited-edition chapbooks.

14. *Spirits in the Wires* (Tor, 2003) Christy Riddell, a character from other Newford books, his shadow self (Christiana Tree), and other companions are called upon to rescue their friends and defeat a runaway computer virus at the Wordwood research site.

15. *Medicine Road* (Subterranean, 2004) A collaboration with illustrator Charles Vess. The Dillard twins, Laurel and Bess, minor characters in number 12, travel to the desert Southwest on a rockabilly road tour and hook up with two unhappy Native American shape-shifting spirits.

16. *Blue Girl, The* (Viking, 2004) Fifteen-year-old Imogene, a new student at Redding High School, meets Maxine and Ghost, and the girls get involved with some supernatural characters, including the nasty soul eaters, the Anamithim. Specifically written for a YA audience, according to de Lint.

17. *Hour before Dawn, The* (Subterranean, 2005) Three Newford short stories—"The Hour before Dawn," That Was Radio Clash," and The Butter Spirit's Tale"—published in a limited edition of 500 signed numbered copies.

18. *Widdershins* (Tor, 2006) Jilly Coppercorn and Geordie Riddell, characters from other Newford books, are brought together in a romantic relationship.

19. *Promises to Keep* (Subterranean, 2007) Jilly Coppercorn runs into Donna Birch, her only friend from the bad old days. Donna takes Jilly into a realm similar to this world, but where things have a way of turning out better.

II. *Jack, the Giant Killer* is a retelling of the fairy tale set in contemporary Canada. Jacky Rowan find that she possesses the ability to see into the faerie world. Followed by a sequel featuring the Toronto fiddler Johnny Faw. The two novels were published together as *Jack of Kinrowan* (Tor, 1995).

1. *Jack, the Giant Killer* (Ace, 1987) An "urban faerie" tale. Jacky Rowan discovers that she possesses the ability to see into the faerie world, and embarks upon a quest involving treasure and a giant.

2. *Drink Down the Moon* (Ace, 1990) The fate of the faeries is in the hands of young Toronto fiddler Johnny Faw and a handful of human and not-so-human companions.

III. *Moonheart*, a "romance" set between ancient Wales and contemporary Ottawa, was followed by three tales about Tamson House in Ottawa, the doorway into supernatural worlds: "Ascian in Rose"; "Westlin

Wind"; and "Ghostwood," published in limited editions by Axolotl Press of Eugene, Oregon. These tales were collected in *Spiritwalk*.

Charles de Lint self-published, in extremely limited editions, more than two dozen chapbook tales, many of them about Celtic bard Cerin Songweaver (1979–). These tales were collected as *Triskell Tales* (Subterranean, 2000) and *Triskell Tales 2* (Subterranean, 2006). Other short story collections include *A Handful of Coppers* (Subterranean, 2003); *Quicksilver and Shadow* (Subterranean, 2004); and *Waifs and Strays* (Viking, 2002). De Lint also wrote a volume for *Brian Froud's Faerielands* (*The Wild Wood*, Bantam, 1994) and two volumes for Philip José Farmer's (q.v.) The Dungeon series: *The Valley of Thunder* (Bantam, 1988) and *The Hidden City* (Bantam, 1988).

1. *Moonheart* (Ace, 1984) Two young women from Ottawa are swept into an enchanted land of ancient Welsh mythology after discovering artifacts. Reprinted several times, including a hardcover by Subterranean Press (2005).
2. *Spiritwalk* (Tor, 1992) Contains three novellas originally published separately in limited editions by Axolotl Press: *Ascian in Rose* (1987); *Westlin Wind* (1988); and *Ghostwood* (1990).

DeAndrea, William L.

I. Matt Cobb, chief troubleshooter for the Network, a major commercial television network, is the investigator in this series of puzzle mysteries in the classic mode. These quietly humorous tales feature intimate views of the inner workings of television broadcasting, excellent plotting, and realistic characters and dialogue. DeAndrea, frustrated in his ambition to become a television director, turned to mystery writing and won Edgar Allan Poe Awards for his first two novels. DeAndrea, who died in 1996, was the husband of Orania Papazaglou, who writes the Gregor Demarkian series under the pseudonym of Jane Haddam (q.v.). He was also the author of the reference book *Encyclopedia Mysteriosa* (Macmillan, 1994) and several nonseries mysteries, including *The Lunatic Fringe* (Evans, 1980), which features Theodore Roosevelt as a sleuth.

1. *Killed in the Ratings* (Harcourt, 1978) A scheme to rig the ratings creates panic at the Network and produces a homicide.
2. *Killed in the Act* (Doubleday, 1981) The Network is celebrating its fiftieth anniversary with a giant spectacular. A souvenir bowling ball is stolen and a kinescope technician is killed.
3. *Killed with a Passion* (Doubleday, 1983) Matt Cobb returns to his alma mater for the wedding of former classmate Debbie Whitney, who winds up dead.
4. *Killed on the Ice* (Doubleday, 1984) While preparing a taping of figure skater Wendy Ichimi, Matt finds the corpse of Paul Dinkover, psychiatrist and left-wing activist.
5. *Killed in Paradise* (Mysterious, 1988) Matt escorts the two winners of a Network contest on a mystery cruise in the Caribbean, and becomes involved with a group of mystery writers.
6. *Killed on the Rocks* (Mysterious, 1990) Matt is called to Gabby Dost's Adirondacks estate to negotiate with the billionaire corporate raider about the purchase of the Network.
7. *Killed in Fringe Time* (Simon & Schuster, 1995) Richard Bentyne, paranoid talk-show host, is poisoned just before wealthy recluse Clement Bates is scheduled to appear on his show.
8. *Killed in the Fog* (Simon & Schuster, 1996) On vacation in London, Matt, at the behest of Lady Pam Arking, head of a European TV network, delivers a package and then sees the man to whom he delivered it die.

II. Italian sleuth Niccolo Benedetti, who regards himself as a philosopher and expert on "human evil," prefers to solve cases cerebrally while his American assistants, private eye Ron Gentry and psychologist Janet Higgins, do the legwork.

1. *Hog Murders, The* (Avon, 1979) Sparta, New York, is enduring its worst winter ever, as someone who calls himself HOG is claiming responsibility for a series of strange fatalities.
2. *Werewolf Murders, The* (Doubleday, 1992) Benedetti is hired by Pierre Benac to discover who is trying to sabotage his conference in the Alps.
3. *Manx Murders, The* (Penzler, 1994) Multimillionaire twins Clyde and Henry Pembroke, whose "smoke scrubber" interests the EPA, have developed a deadly feud over birds and Manx cats.

III. DeAndrea also wrote a series of international espionage thrillers featuring an agent who works for something called the Agency, which is directed by his congressman father.

1. *Cronus* (Mysterious, 1984) Clifford Driscoll is manipulated by his father into rescuing a girl from the Kremlin.
2. *Snark* (Mysterious, 1985) The Agent, traveling under the nom de guerre of Bellman, searches for a missing retired chief of British intelligence.
3. *Azrael* (Mysterious, 1987) The KGB and the Agent (called Trotter here) are both after Petra Hudson, media mogul and KGB "sleeper," who has been ignoring their orders.
4. *Atropus* (Mysterious, 1990) Allan Trotter, the agent in charge of the Agency after his father's stroke, tries to short-circuit a KGB plot during a presidential election year.

IV. DeAndrea's last two books take us back to the late 19th-century boomtown of Le Four, Wyoming. Its protagonists are former federal marshal Lobo Blacke and Quinn Booker, dime novelist, his friend and biographer. After Lobo was paralyzed by a bullet in the back, he purchased a newspaper in Le Four and hired Quinn as his assistant. Lucius Jenkins, wealthy rancher and former partner of Lobo, is the principal villain. This is a pair of rambunctious novels, full of action and humor.

1. *Written in Fire* (Walker, 1995) Quinn Booker, summoned to Le Four, Wyoming, by Lobo Blacke, former lawman and now newspaper proprietor, steps off the train and into a melee with drunken cowboys, whom he defeats handily in a scene photographed by "Professor Ned" Bessemer.
2. *Fatal Elixir* (Walker, 1997) Paul Muller, notorious robber, has escaped from prison and may be on his way to Le Four to settle scores with Lobo. Meanwhile, quack Dr. Herkimer's "elixir" fells dozens of townsfolk.

Deaver, Jeffery (Wilds)

I. Lincoln Rhyme is one of your physically disadvantaged detectives: he's a quadriplegic who can move only one finger. The New York Police Department detective solves crimes through the computer with the help of his mobile assistant, policewoman Amelia Sachs. Lincoln and Amelia are well characterized, the crimes tend to be grisly, and the plots are sometimes complicated but always grippingly suspenseful. *The Bone Collector* was made into a film starring Denzel Washington and Angelina Jolie (1999).

1. *Bone Collector, The* (**Viking, 1997**) Lincoln Rhyme, quadriplegic detective, is introduced. A serial killer is imitating gruesome murders committed at the turn of the century.
2. *Coffin Dancer, The* (**Simon & Schuster, 1998**) Rhyme and Sachs are faced with a 48-hour deadline in the case of a hit man identified only by his tattoo depicting a dancing Grim Reaper.
3. *Empty Chair, The* (**Simon & Schuster, 2000**) While Rhyme and Sachs are in North Carolina for experimental surgery that might ease his problems, they are induced to join the search for two young women abducted following the murder of a local teenager.
4. *Stone Monkey, The* (**Simon & Schuster, 2002**) Some illegal Chinese immigrants live in mortal fear of the Ghost, a human smuggler and killer who wants to keep them from talking about their ordeal on the cargo ship *Fuzhou Dragon*.
5. *Vanished Man, The* (**Simon & Schuster, 2003**) The villain this time is a master magician who can change his appearance at will and murders his victims in the style of classic magic acts.
6. *Twelfth Card, The* (**Simon and Schuster, 2005**) Harlem high school student Geneva Settle, engaged in writing a paper about one of her ancestors, a former slave called Charles Singleton, has somehow become the target of a professional killer.
7. *Cold Moon, The* (**Simon & Schuster, 2006**) A criminal mastermind called the Watchmaker has committed two bizarre murders, leaving a clock and an ominous poem at the scene.
8. *Sleeping Doll, The* (**Simon & Schuster, 2007**) Kathryn Dance, investigator with the California Bureau of Investigation, who had a minor role in number 7, is the lead cop handling the escape of psychopathic killer Daniel Pell, dubbed "Son of Manson" by the press.

II. Jeffery Deaver is the author of at least 15 other mystery thrillers, including a trio of books set in Manhattan, featuring a young female would-be filmmaker named Rune.

1. *Manhattan Is My Beat* (**Bantam, 1989**) One of the customers at Rune's video shop, who had been renting the same noir film over and over, is murdered, and Rune is convinced that the film he rented holds the secret of his death.
2. *Death of a Blue Movie Star* (**Bantam, 1990**) When a porno movie theater is blown up in Times Square, film production assistant Rune decides that this is her chance to make a film of her own.
3. *Hard News* (**Doubleday, 1991**) Rune, now a camerawoman for a local TV station, believes that Randy Boggs, convicted for the murder of news head Lance Hopper, is innocent.

III. Deaver is also the author of a trio of novels about John Pellam, a "location scout" for a Hollywood film studio who tours the country looking for locations suitable for shooting films and runs into murder each time. Numbers 1 and 2 were published under the pseudonym of William Jefferies.

1. *Shallow Graves* (**Avon, 1992**) Pellam's coworker is murdered in a small upstate New York town where Pellam's studio wants to shoot a film. Originally published under the name "William Jefferies."
2. *Bloody River Blues* (**Avon, 1993**) While scouting a film location in Maddox, Missouri, Pellam encounters contract killers who decide to murder him before he can finger them in the murder of a local racketeer. Originally published under the name "William Jefferies."
3. *Hell's Kitchen* (**Pocket Books, 2001**) A pyromaniac is on the loose in the Hell's Kitchen (New York City) neighborhood where Pellam is shooting a "no-budget" documentary film.

Deere, Dicey

American Torrey Tunet stole some money when she was 14. Fourteen years later, Torrey has become a translator. Then rich American Desmond Moore invites her for a stay at Castle Moore, just outside of Dublin. Murder happens, and Torrey embarks upon a second career as an amateur sleuth. Eventually Torrey settles down in the Irish village of Ballynagh and becomes involved with the quaint but sometimes murderous denizens.

1. *Irish Cottage Murder, The* (**St. Martin's, 1999**) Young American translator Torrey Tunet becomes a suspect during a stay at Castle Moore, outside Dublin, when a priceless heirloom is stolen and a couple of people are found dead.
2. *Irish Manor House Murder, The* (**St. Martin's, 2000**) Torrey rusticates herself in an old cottage on the rural estate of her friends, the Ashendens of Ballynagh, to work on her multilingual series of children's books. A series of incidents leads to the death of Dr. Ashenden.
3. *Irish Cairn Murder, The* (**St. Martin's, 2002**) After she hires local Ballynagh teenager Dakin Cameron to repair a broken window frame, Torrey discovers that Dakin's widowed heiress mother is being blackmailed.
4. *Irish Village Murder, The* (**St. Martin's, 2004**) Torrey's friend, housekeeper Megan O'Faolain, is the immediate suspect when her employer and sometime lover, John Gwathney, is shot dead at Gwathney Hall.

Deforges, Régine

This trilogy of French best sellers set during World War II tells the story of beautiful and passionate young Lea Delmas, daughter of a rich Bordeaux winegrower. The novels combine high romance with a historically accurate description of these interesting and dramatic times. The work was originally commissioned as a remake of *Gone with the Wind*, and parallels between the major characters in the two sagas are easy to spot. In fact, Margaret Mitchell's heirs, a litigious bunch, it would seem, sued Deforges for plagiarism but eventually lost their case.

1. *Blue Bicycle, The* (**Lyle Stuart, 1986**) As the Germans overrun France, Léa is determined to save her family estate, Montillac, and hide her disappointment in love. Covers 1939–1942. Translation by Ros Schwartz of *La bicyclette bleue* (1981).
2. *Léa* (**Lyle Stuart, 1987**) Léa delivers messages to the Resistance on her blue bicycle and has an affair with the treacherous Francois Tavernier. Covers 1942–1944. Translation by Elizabeth Fairley Mueller of *101, avenue Henri-Martin* (1983). UK title: *101, avenue Henri-Martin*.
3. *Devil Laughs Again, The* (**Lyle Stuart, 1988**) Léa is besieged by destruction and the violent deaths of friends and relatives as the liberation of France enters its final stages. Covers 1944–1945. Translation by Elizabeth Fairley Mueller of *La diable en rit encore* (1985). UK title: *The Devil Is Still Laughing*.

Deighton, Len

I. Deighton's spy thrillers differ from those of John Le Carré (q.v.), Graham Greene, and others in that his spy is not upper middle class. His anonymous spy-narrator, who is called Harry Palmer in the movie versions, is working class and rather snide about the public school types he works for. Michael Caine used a Cockney accent in his portrayal of Deighton's spy in the 1965 film *The Ipcress File*, which was so successful that two other Deighton films quickly followed: *Funeral in Berlin* in 1966 and *Billion Dollar Brain* in 1967. In other respects, Deighton runs true to the genre: his plots are easily as convoluted as Le Carré's; his climaxes are perhaps a little more grisly.

1. *Ipcress File, The* (Simon & Schuster, 1962) A British agent's assignment to recover a kidnapped biochemist involves him in a maze of spies and counterspies from London to the Far East.
2. *Horse under Water* (Putnam, 1963) An unnamed spy-narrator is after sunken treasure in the form of canisters of heroin.
3. *Funeral in Berlin* (Putnam, 1964) This chilling tale of revenge is set in the divided city haunted by the still-murderous memories of the recent Nazi past.
4. *Billion Dollar Brain, The* (Putnam, 1966) This story about a computer programmed by an evil and murderous genius ranges across the globe from Helsinki to San Antonio.

II. British undercover agent Bernard Samson relates his moves in the deadly game of espionage in three trilogies (Game/Set/Match; Hook/Line/Sinker; and Faith/Hope/Charity). Samson must match wits with the KGB, guard against intrigues at Central, and cope with Fiona, his double-agent wife. *Game, Set and Match* (Knopf, 1989), an omnibus volume containing numbers 1, 2, and 3, was published to coincide with the PBS television series, starring Ian Holm as Samson. Because this series is an evolving saga charting Bernard's life and times, it is best read in publication order.

1. *Berlin Game* (Knopf, 1984) Bernard Samson must help an undercover agent known as Brahms Four escape from East Berlin.
2. *Mexico Set* (Knopf, 1985) Fiona, Samson's wife and coworker, defects to the KGB while Samson tries to persuade KGB Major Erich Stinnes to defect to London.
3. *London Match* (Knopf, 1986) Suspicions of KGB moles and plants at London Central exacerbate Samson's concern for his motherless children.
4. *Spy Hook* (Knopf, 1988) Samson is sent to Washington to locate half a million pounds missing from the German desk of London Central.
5. *Spy Line* (Knopf, 1989) Samson is a fugitive from England, with London Central, the CIA, and the KGB all after him.
6. *Spy Sinker* (Harper, 1990) Fiona comes to the fore as a double-agent who has "defected" to East Germany.
7. *Faith* (Harper, 1995) Samson is sent to pick up "Verdi," a high-ranking East German Stasi officer who may be defecting to the United Kingdom.
8. *Hope* (Harper, 1995) Samson tries to track down his Polish brother-in-law, George Kosinski, who seems to have returned to Poland hoping to find his long-lost wife.
9. *Charity* (Harper, 1996) Many of the regular characters, such as Bernard and Fiona Samson, reappear in this novel taking us up to 1988, and involving murders, a dying ex-spy, and a missing lockbox.

III. Deighton wrote several espionage novels in the late 1960s and the 1970s that are similar to the Harry Palmer series but not generally included with them. They are listed below.

1. *Expensive Place to Die, An* (Putnam, 1967)
2. *Spy Story* (Harcourt, 1974)
3. *Yesterday's Spy* (Harcourt, 1975)
4. *Catch a Falling Spy* (Harcourt, 1976) English title: *Twinkle, Twinkle, Little Spy.*

Deitz, Tom (Thomas Franklin)

I. Georgian teenager David Sullivan is into ancient legends rather than pop culture. One day he finds that he has second sight and is able to view the world of Faerie. Then his real adventures begin as the faeries discover that a mortal is watching them, and David and two friends are brought into the world of Faerie and into the faeries' long-standing battles between the Light and Dark Masters. David's adventures continue through nine novels as he encounters not only characters from Celtic mythology but from Native American legends as well. As often happens in fantasy, the two worlds impinge upon each other, and at times, David is called upon to save not only the Faerie world but his own. Cherokee youth Calvin McIntosh also plays a large role. Author Tom Deitz continues to live in the mountains of northern Georgia, where he was born and raised.

1. *Windmaster's Bane* (Avon, 1986) Teenager David Sullivan, growing up in Georgia's Blue Ridge Mountains, discovers that he has the gift of second sight and is able to see through the World Walls into the Celtic Faerie world of Sidhe. Then the evil Windmaster makes David a pawn in his bid to usurp the throne of Tir-Nan-Og.
2. *Fireshaper's Doom* (Avon, 1987) The vengeance-seeking mother of an innocent victim of David's war against the Windmaster forcibly brings David and his friends back to Faerie and the world of the Fireshaper and another confrontation with the Windmaster.
3. *Darkthunder's Way* (Avon, 1989) Once again David and young Cherokee Calvin McIntosh have been called upon to do the bidding of Lugh Samildinach, Lord of Tir-Nan-Og. A confrontation with the great serpent Uktena isn't the least of their troubles.
4. *Sunshaker's War* (Avon, 1990) Both worlds are threatened by the harnessed power of the sun in the war between the forces of Light and the forces of Darkness.
5. *Stoneskin's Revenge* (Avon, 1991) David's Cherokee friend Calvin McIntosh has returned to Georgia, but he has inadvertently left the doorway to Galunlati open and the evil Stoneskin Spearfinger has entered into his world.
6. *Ghostcountry's Wrath* (Avon, 1995) Haunted by the ghost of his father, Calvin McIntosh confronts an evil Cherokee witch and a panther-woman in the Darkening Lands on the border of the Cherokee Ghost Country.
7. *Dreamseeker's Road* (Avon, 1995) On All Hallow's Eve, David and three friends stumble into the middle of the Wild Hunt.
8. *Landslayer's Law* (Avon, 1997) The World Walls separating David's world from the alternate world of Faerie are becoming so thin that Faerie can now be seen in satellite photographs; land developers are moving in; and High King Lugh is sorely tempted to retaliate.
9. *Warstalker's Track* (Avon, 1999) The High King of Tir-Nan-Og, Lugh Samildinach, has been deposed and imprisoned, and the usurpers of his kingdom are threatening to retaliate against mortal land developers by drowning the state of Georgia.

II. A trio of novels, known as the Soulsmith series, is also set in Georgia and is essentially a coming-of-age saga, featuring young Ronnie Dillon, who is adopted into the mysterious Welch family of Cardalba, which has roots in Wales and, purportedly, the gift of magic.

1. *Soulsmith* (Avon, 1991) Young Ronny Dillon, having lost his adoptive parents, and having shattered his kneecap, goes to live with his grandmother and her son, Lewis Welch, in rural Cordova, Georgia, where he becomes aware of some mysterious goings-on.

2. *Dreambuilder* (Avon, 1992) Five years after the events in number 1, Ronnie, graduated from college, reluctantly returns home to Cardalba and Cordova, per Lewis Welch's urgent request.

3. *Wordwright* (Avon, 1993) Martha, the Welch family matriarch, dies, and Lewis renounces his Mastership to seek his and Ronny's sister, apparently taking the "Luck" with him.

III. The Tales of Eron are set in a magical kingdom in which young metalsmith Avail discovers a gem that contains the power "to link minds across distances," a find that engulfs Eron in war and eventually makes Avail king. Reviewers remarked again upon Deitz's ability to create realistic and complex characters set in a world of magic.

1. *Bloodwinter* (Bantam, 1999) The land of Eron is recovering from the plague, which has been devastating it. Then metalsmith Avail discovers a gem with the power to "join the minds of all who bind themselves to it."

2. *Springwar* (Bantam, 2000) The magical gem brings Eron to the brink of civil war as Avail and his wife, Strynn, seek to understand how to use their powers, and their rival, Eddyn, pursues a course of ambition and revenge.

3. *Summerblood* (Bantam, 2002) After he has won the war against the Ixti and become king of Eron, Avail finds himself threatened by a renegade faction of priests.

4. *Warautumn* (Bantam, 2002) Avail attempts to return to his capital city of Tir-Eron, reclaim his throne, and free his land from the tyranny of the fanatical religious cult that has usurped power.

IV. Two novels set in 2024 envision a world of independent North American Native Americans with their capital of Aztlan. Three characters: Kevin Mauney, his sister Carolyn, and Cherokee diplomat and traditional dancer Thunderbird O'Conner are linked in a magical battle against some dark forces.

1. *Above the Lower Sky* (Avon, 1994) Kevin Mauney, who has been bestowed with a cryptic, disturbing message; his estranged sister Carolyn, who has undergone death and rebirth while investigating the murder-mutilation of scores of intelligent sea mammals; and Cherokee diplomat and traditional dancer Thunderbird O'Conner, who has stumbled into a nightmare on a Mexican beach, are brought together in the brave new world of Aztlan in 2024.

2. *Demons in the Green, The* (Avon, 1996) A mystical showdown is brewing as various would-be magicians and menacing factions converge upon the Aztlan Cathedral as the seeming revival of an ancient Aztec religion seems to be in the offing.

Delacorta

PSEUDONYM OF Daniel Odier

This series chronicles the escapades of Serge Gorodish, failed classical pianist, sometime painter, and con artist, and his 13-year-old companion, the beautiful kleptomaniac Alba. The novels are sophisticated satirical thrillers that are not to be taken too seriously. A 1982 French movie entitled *Diva*, loosely based on the novel, was an international hit. Daniel Odier is a Swiss novelist and poet living in Paris.

1. *Nana* (Summit, 1984) In this prequel to *Diva*, Serge Gorodish leaves Paris for a small French town where he first lays eyes on the beautiful blond nymphet Alba, and has a brush with a motorcycle gang called the Vampires. Originally published as *Nana* in 1979. Translated from the French by Victoria Reiter.

2. *Diva* (Summit, 1983) Gorodish and Alba are pursuing their shady careers in Paris while Jules, a teenage messenger, becomes obsessed with Cynthia Hawkins, an African American operatic soprano. Originally published as *Diva* in 1979. Translated from the French by Lowell Bair.

3. *Luna* (Summit, 1984) Delaborde, a very rich lunatic, on the advice of his insane psychiatrist, Alcan, abducts Alba to act out his fantasy of dragonfly mating. Originally published in 1979 as *Luna*. Translated from the French by Victoria Reiter.

4. *Lola* (Summit, 1985) Gorodish and Alba search for Lola Black, an American heavy-metal rock singer, long presumed dead. Originally published as *Rock* in 1981. Translated from the French by Victoria Reiter.

5. *Vida* (Summit, 1985) Gorodish and Alba move to Los Angeles, where Alba is hired as a private investigator by a 10-year-old tycoon in search of his father, the architect Marlowe Wrightson. Originally published as *Vida* in 1985. Translated from the French by Victoria Reiter.

6. *Alba* (Atlantic, 1989) While Gorodish serves a jail term for littering, Alba drives blind Jason to the Mojave Desert for a rendezvous with the Group. Originally published as *Alba* in 1985. Translated from the French by Catherine Texier.

Delderfield, R(onald) F(rederick)

I. Delderfield's richly charactered chronicles are satisfying long reads that dramatize a century of social change in England. The Swann Family trilogy is perhaps his best-known series. It tells the story of Adam Swann, a professional soldier who parlays a necklace captured on the field of battle in India into a vast commercial enterprise, a fortune, and a dynasty.

1. *God Is an Englishman* (Simon & Schuster, 1970) Adam Swann marries Henrietta and starts his business in freight-hauling coaches during the years 1857–1866.

2. *Theirs Was the Kingdom* (Simon & Schuster, 1971) The Swann family prospers as the four children grow up. Young George leads the business into motorized cars.

3. *Give Us This Day* (Simon & Schuster, 1973) Old Adam's grandchildren and great-grandchildren appear in this last volume, which ends on the eve of World War I.

II. The Craddock family is featured in this pair of novels set in rural England.

1. *Horseman Riding By, A* (Simon & Schuster, 1967) Young Paul Craddock comes home from the Boer War and purchases a run-down estate in Devonshire. Also issued in two paperbacks by Pocket Books (1974): *The Long Summer Day* and *Post of Honor*.

2. *Green Gauntlet, The* (Simon & Schuster, 1968) Squire Craddock remains dedicated to his land, to his children and grandchildren, to his tenants, and to the vanishing rural life they represent.

III. The Carver family of London provides the focus for *The Avenue* (Simon & Schuster, 1969), originally published in the United Kingdom in two volumes as *The Avenue Story*.

1. *Dreaming Suburb, The* (Hodder [UK], 1958) Jim Carver, a widower with seven children, is at the center of this story about the inhabitants of an ordinary London street from 1918 to the beginning of World War II.

2. *Avenue Goes to War, The* (Hodder [UK], 1958) The wartime experiences of the people of the Avenue covers 1940–1948.

DeLoach, Nora (Frazier)

Grace "Candi" Covington, aka "Mama," is an African American retired social worker living in the small town of Otis (based on the real town of Hampton), South Carolina. Mama, a great cook with a special recipe for sweet potato pie, hasn't retired to simply vegetate but to develop her "soul and mind." She gets involved in a string of mysteries involving herself, her family, and her friends in a series of cozies with authentic African American characters. Mama's daughter Simone, a paralegal in Atlanta, plays Watson to Mama's Sherlock Holmes. The late Nora DeLoach (d. 2001), a Florida native who was herself a social worker, didn't start writing until her fifties.

1. *Mama Solves a Murder* (Holloway House, 1994) Mama and her daughter Simone team up to help Cheryl, Simone's former classmate, who has confessed to a murder she didn't commit.
2. *Mama Traps a Killer* (Holloway House, 1995) "Daddy" becomes the prime suspect in the deaths of a local teenage boy and a mysterious young woman from out of town.
3. *Mama Stands Accused* (Holloway House, 1997) Mama becomes a suspect when her difficult sister Agnes is felled by a hatchet.
4. *Mama Saves a Victim* (Holloway Housa, 1997) A young woman runs in front of Simone's car, refuses to give her identity, then disappears from the hospital.
5. *Mama Stalks the Past* (Bantam, 1998) Hannah Mixon, the strange recluse who willed Mama 250 acres of valuable land, becomes the victim of poison.
6. *Mama Rocks the Empty Cradle* (Bantam, 1999) When Simone returns to Otis to aid Mama after an operation, an infant's skull is exhumed by a dog; a woman named Cricket is murdered; and Cricket's baby disappears.
7. *Mama Pursues Murderous Shadows* (Bantam, 2000) Ruby Spikes is found dead in a motel room, killed by an apparently self-inflicted gun wound.
8. *Mama Cracks a Mask of Innocence* (Bantam, 2001) Brenda Long, who has made many enemies in a short, greedy life, is discovered in a shallow grave.

Demetz, Han(n)a

A pair of autobiographical novels chronicles the story of Helenka Richter from adolescence in wartime Prague through postwar life in Europe and America. The Prague Street novels are full of poignant interest as pictures of the Holocaust and after from someone who was an unwilling and, at first, unwitting protagonist. *The House on Prague Street* was translated from the original German by the author.

1. *House on Prague Street, The* (St. Martin's, 1980) Reports of the Holocaust intrude upon Helenka Richter's previously idyllic life in Prague.
2. *Journey from Prague Street, The* (St. Martin's, 1990) The only survivor of her large Jewish family, Helenka chronicles her life after the war in Prague, Munich, and New York.

Denker, Henry

This pair of novels explores race relations and the problems of old age. The relationship between Samuel Horowitz, elderly cantankerous Jewish American, and Mrs. Washington, the African American nurse who intervenes twice in his life, is told in gentle and sentimental but not unrealistic fashion. *Horowitz and Mrs. Washington* was dramatized as a Broadway play in 1980.

1. *Horowitz and Mrs. Washington* (Putnam, 1979) Elderly Jewish entrepreneur Samuel Horowitz is mugged, suffers a stroke, and is put under the care of the masterful Harriet Washington.
2. *Mrs. Washington and Horowitz, Too* (Morrow, 1993) Mrs. Washington maneuvers the widowed Horowitz into volunteer work and a golden-age love affair.

Dennis, Patrick

PSEUDONYM OF Edward Tanner

Auntie Mame's unconventional charm and hilarious doings have been entertaining people since 1955. She has endured adaptation from the novel to the stage, then to a successful movie version starring Rosalind Russell in 1958. Further metamorphosis into the musical comedy *Mame*, with Angela Lansbury in the title role, won Broadway's approval, though the 1974 movie version starring Lucille Ball was awful. Dennis's books can still make readers laugh out loud. They have the delightfully droll narration of nephew Patrick, which is missing in the dramatizations.

1. *Auntie Mame* (Vanguard, 1955) In 1929 10-year-old orphan Patrick goes to live with his zany aunt who lives wholeheartedly in phases, playing to the hilt each new role from showgirl to southern belle to tweedy authoress.
2. *Around the World with Auntie Mame* (Harcourt, 1958) In 1934 Mame treats Patrick to a trip around the world before he starts college.

Dentinger, Jane

Jane Dentinger, actress and manager of Murder Ink, the mystery bookstore in New York, has been producing her own mystery series starring Jocelyn "Josh" O'Roarke. The clever, outspoken Josh juggles acting, sleuthing, and lovers (an off-again, on-again relationship with New York police detective Phillip Gerard, among others) in a series of clever mysteries that will appeal especially to theater fans.

1. *Murder on Cue* (Doubleday, 1983) Josh is chief suspect when Harriet Weldon, the obnoxious, no-talent actress she is understudying, is murdered.
2. *First Hit of the Season* (Doubleday, 1984) A kiss-and-make-up session between actress Irene Ingersoll and critic Jason Saylin falls short of success when Jason imbibes a strychnine-laced cocktail.
3. *Death Mask* (Scribner, 1988) O'Roarke's production of *Major Barbara* hits a bump when actor Burton Evans drops dead while taking a bow in front of the opening night audience.
4. *Dead Pan* (Viking, 1992) Josh is called to Los Angeles to appear in a made-for-television film opposite former child star and recovering addict Ginger Jellicoe.
5. *Queen Is Dead, The* (Viking, 1994) O'Roarke takes over the female lead of the Corinth College production of *The Winter's Tale* when her mentor dies of an apparent heart attack.

6. *Who Dropped Peter Pan?* **(Viking, 1995)** Rich Rafelson plunges to his death when his flying harness breaks during a production of *Peter Pan*.

Dereske, Jo

I. Miss Wilhelmina "Helma" Zukas is an ace reference librarian at the (fictional) Bellehaven, Washington, Public Library whose research skills get called upon in a series of mysteries. Bellehaven, based on Bellingham, home of Western Washington University, where Jo Dereske worked as a librarian for 10 years is one of your small towns with more than its share of interesting murders, Miss Zukas is assisted by her bohemian artist friend Ruth, and Wayne Gallant, local police chief and possible significant other. The "always correct and always correcting" Miss Zukas is an attractive character, and the books feature "no-nonsense" prose, good dialogue and realistic glimpses of library work.

1. *Miss Zukas and the Library Murders* **(Avon, 1994)** When a body is reported in the stacks of the Bellehaven, Washington, Public Library, reference librarian Miss Zukas asks: "Fiction or Nonfiction?"
2. *Miss Zukas and the Island Murders* **(Avon, 1995)** An anonymous note in the morning mail reminds Miss Zukas of her long-forgotten promise to bring her high school classmates together for a 20-year reunion.
3. *Miss Zukas and the Stroke of Death* **(Avon, 1996)** Miss Zukas decides to enter as a canoeist in Washington's Snow to Surf Race.
4. *Miss Zukas and the Raven's Dance* **(Avon, 1996)** When a cataloger is murdered while working at Bellehaven's new cultural center, Miss Zukas replaces him.
5. *Out of Circulation* **(Avon, 1997)** Helma is dragged by her friend Ruth on a hike in the Cascade Mountains. And, of course, a body turns up.
6. *Final Notice* **(Avon, 1998)** When elderly Aunt Em visits Helma in Bellehaven, her purse is snatched at the airport. Then the snatcher turns up dead outside Helma's apartment.
7. *Miss Zukas in Death's Shadow* **(Avon, 1999)** Miss Zukas, doing a community service stint at a homeless shelter, becomes a suspect in a death there.
8. *Miss Zukas Shelves the Evidence* **(Avon, 2001)** Wayne Gallant, local police chief and possible significant other, arranges a meeting between his children and Helma, but a murder intervenes.
9. *Bookmarked to Die* **(Avon, 2006)** Bellehaven library director Ms. Moon blackmails Miss Zukas into attending a group counseling session where, of course, someone is murdered. On top of that, Boy Cat Zukas, Helma's cat, disappears.
10. *Catalogue of Death* **(Avon, 2007)** While Miss Zukas keeps the library open during the worst blizzard in Bellehaven memory, local billionaire Franklin Harrington is blown to bits while inspecting the site he has set aside for the town's new library.

II. Jo Dereske has also written children's books and a trio of mystery novels set in her natal Michigan and featuring Ruby Crane, a former graphologist and forgery expert for the Los Angeles Police Department.

1. *Savage Cut* **(Dell, 1996)** Ruby Crane leaves her police job in Los Angeles to return to the small lakeside town in Michigan that she left in disgrace 17 years before.
2. *Cut and Dry* **(Dell, 1997)** Ruby enlists the help of the mysterious stranger across the lake when a woman is found strangled.
3. *Short Cut* **(Dell, 1998)** Ruby's glamorous, successful sister, Phyllis, comes to Michigan to ask Ruby's help in proving that her engineering design was not responsible for a boy's death on a construction site.

Despres, Loraine

Former TV writer Loraine Despres (e.g., the famous *Dallas* episode "Who Shot J.R.?") has written a couple of comic southern romances. *The Scandalous Summer of Sissy LeBlanc* features Sissy LeBlanc, restless wife and mother in small-town Louisiana, who lives by a code she calls "The Southern Belle's Handbook." *The Bad Behavior of Belle Cantrell* is a prequel describing the scandalous doings of Sissy's grandmother, Belle Cantrell, who also lived by her own *Southern Girls' Guide*. These novels feature lively prose and heroines and a feminist view of small-town southern life suffused by humor. Loraine Despres, who has a southern background, has also published *The Southern Belle's Handbook: Sissy Le-Blanc's Rules to Live By* (Morrow, 2003).

1. *Bad Behavior of Belle Cantrell, The* **(Morrow, 2005)** Independent-minded Belle Cantrell, grandmother of Sissy LeBlanc (see number 2) stirs up things in 1920s Gentry, Louisiana, fighting for women's right to vote and against the local Ku Klux Klan and small-town mores.
2. *Scandalous Summer of Sissy LeBlanc, The* **(Morrow, 2001)** Sissy LeBlanc, who lives by a code she calls "The Southern Belle's Handbook," feels that some changes in her life are needed when her high school sweetheart returns to Gentry after a 14-year absence.

Deveraux, Jude

PSEUDONYM OF Jude Gilliam White

I. Best-selling writer Jude Deveraux likes to have her cake and eat it too. While she is a serious writer of romances, she pokes some sly fun at the genre in her novels. Her heroines are plucky and do not allow their men, no matter how hunky, manly, and passionate they may be, to run roughshod over them. Sex is fine, but not without love. Deveraux finds it no contradiction in terms to be both a feminist and romantic. England, Scotland, and America are Deveraux's usual locations. The time settings range from the Medieval to the contemporary. Occasionally she throws in a little time travel or an angel to give a novel an SF or fantasy tinge. Members of the Montgomery family of England, Scotland, and the United States turn up in many books, especially in series I and II but also in series III and IV and other novels. Members of the Taggert clan (see series V) also wander in and out of other series.

The Velvet series of four novels can be regarded as part of the larger Montgomery series (see below, series II) but form a unit of their own. Four generations of Montgomerys, each in turn, fall passionately in love with women who are initially hostile to them. The books are set in England and Scotland during Medieval times. *The Velvet Quartet* (Rhapsody 2003) contains numbers 1 through 4. *Velvet Song/Velvet Angel* (Pocket Books, 2005) contains numbers 3 and 4.

1. *Velvet Promise, The* **(Pocket Books, 1981)** Judith, although feeling great passion for her husband, Gavin Montgomery, resolves to hate him because his heart had been pledged to another. Variant title: *Judith*.
2. *Highland Velvet* **(Pocket Books, 1982)** Conquering Englishman Stephan Montgomery falls passionately for Scots lass Bronwyn MacCarran, but she is resolved to hate him.
3. *Velvet Song* **(Pocket Books, 1983)** With her father murdered and her home burned, Alyx Blackett takes to the woods, and,

disguised as a boy, becomes a squire to the exiled nobleman Raine Montgomery.

4. *Velvet Angel* (Pocket Books, 1983) Miles Montgomery becomes besotted with Elizabeth Chatworth when she arrives naked, rolled in a rug. But their families are feuding, and she vows to resist him.

II. The Montgomery novels, of which series I (above) is a part, form a rather loosely connected series of books that feature one Montgomery or another in a leading role. Although few, if any, of the series can be regarded as strictly contemporary, several are set in the 20th century. Some novels go back as far as the Middle Ages in time. Number 2, one of the most popular novels in the series, is a time-travel saga, moving between the 16th and the 20th centuries. Number 9 lands a Montgomery in Chandler, Colorado, home of the Taggerts (featured in series V). Taggerts turn up in number 4 and elsewhere. At least one source lists *The Black Lyon* (Avon, 1980), which is set in the Middle Ages, as a Montgomery novel. The series is arranged in chronological, rather than publishing order, although strict chronology is hard to determine, and only numbers 4 and 5 are regarded as sequels.

1. *Maiden, The* (Pocket Books, 1988) Rowan is destined to be king, but first he is destined to fall passionately in love with the warrior princess Jura. Set some time in the Middle Ages.
2. *Knight in Shining Armor, A* (Pocket Books, 1990) As if in answer to her prayers, contemporary Dougless Montgomery evokes the appearance of Nicholas Stafford, Earl of Thornwyk (d. 1564), as she lies weeping upon a tombstone in an English church. Perhaps the most popular novel in the series.
3. *Heiress, The* (Pocket Books, 1995) Impoverished Elizabethan knight Jamie Montgomery hopes to turn the head of Lancasterian heiress Axia while escorting her to her betrothed, but Axia proves to be quite a handful.
4. *Raider, The* (Pocket Books, 1987) Alexander Montgomery is playing a double role: as the drunken town buffoon and as the Raider, the masked patriot who is bedeviling the Redcoats in colonial New England. Local beauty Jessica Taggert is taken in by Montgomery's/Raider's double role. *Romantic Times* Reviewer's Choice for "most humorous romance of the year."
5. *Princess, The* (Pocket Books, 1987) Sometimes regarded as a sequel to number 4, this novel brings together Princess Aria and American naval officer J. T. Montgomery in a "storm of intrigue" near the Florida Keys.
6. *Temptress, The* (Pocket Books, 1986) Heiress Christiana Montgomery Mathison is abducted by two men into the primitive rain forests of the Washington Territory, but succeeds in playing them off against each other.
7. *Mountain Laurel* (Pocket Books, 1990) Captain Ring Montgomery, saddled with the assignment of escorting an opera singer to the mines of Colorado just when a Civil War is brewing, finds Madelyn Worth, aka La Reina, the Singing Duchess, resistant to his attempts to dissuade her from her mission.
8. *Awakening, The* (Pocket Books, 1988) Hot-blooded union organizer Hank Montgomery shakes Amanda Caulden from her sheltered life on her father's California ranch.
9. *Duchess, The* (Pocket Books, 1991) Putative American heiress Claire Willoughby travels to Bramley Castle in Scotland to wed Harry Montgomery, the 11th Duke of MacArran. But she falls for the mysterious Trevelyan.
10. *Wishes* (Pocket Books, 1990) Maine resident Jace Montgomery finds himself in Chandler, Colorado (see series IV), falling for shy, sweet Nellie Grayson, who is primarily interested making her beautiful younger sister Terel the belle of Chandler.

11. *Eternity* (Pocket Books, 1992) Pampered beauty Carrie Montgomery, who has made a hobby out of running her own mail-order bridal service, falls in love with the picture of farmer Joshua Greene of Eternity, Colorado, and makes the mistake of marrying him.
12. *Invitation, The* (Pocket Books, 1993) A collection of three novellas: *Matchmakers; Perfect Arrangement;* and the title story, *The Invitation,* which brings widowed daredevil pilot Jackie O'Neill back together with hometown boy (Eternity, Colorado) William Montgomery.
13. *High Tide* (Pocket Books, 1999) New Yorker Fiona Burkenhalter, a rising star at a Manhattan corporation, is sent to the Florida Everglades, where she becomes entangled with southern backwoodsman Ace Montgomery in a plot involving a vast inheritance and murder.
14. *Someone to Love* (Simon & Schuster, 2007) Jace Montgomery, still trying to come to terms with the suicide of his fiancée, Stacy, buys Priory House in Margate, England, which comes complete with a ghost named Ann Stuart.

III. The Forever series has links with the Montgomerys (series II, above) and the Taggerts (series V, below). Numbers 1, 2, and 3 were apparently planned as a trilogy, but number 4 is regarded by some as having links to the trilogy. The basic story, laced with psychic phenomena, missing persons, intrigue, and a criminal mastermind, features the feisty and talented Darci Monroe, who marries a wealthy Montgomery and then loses him.

1. *Forever* (Pocket Books, 2002) After being hired as millionaire Adam Montgomery's assistant, young Darci Monroe becomes privy to some of his dark secrets, such as that of his parents' disappearance.
2. *Forever and Always* (Pocket Books, 2003) When Adam Montgomery disappears, his wife, Darci, is left alone to raise their young daughter. Darci, convinced that reports of Adam's death are untrue, uses her psychic powers in a head-to-head clash with equally talented criminal–undercover agent Jack Rose.
3. *Always* (Pocket Books, 2004) Darci, still searching for Adam, runs into complications when she takes on the job of locating the missing father of undercover agent Jack Rose.
4. *Holly* (Atria, 2003) This novel has some loose connections with the Forever trilogy, as young "Holly" Latham runs into the mysterious Nick Taggert (for the Taggerts, see series V) at a southern plantation she plans to restore.

IV. The James River trilogy, which has at least one Montgomery hidden in it, is linked by a Virginia location and the theme of a forced marriage followed by an estrangement, during which the respective heroines reveal hidden management talents. The three books do not run consecutively, but are interlocking. *The James River Trilogy* (Rhapsody, 2004) contains numbers 1 through 3.

1. *Counterfeit Lady* (Pocket Books, 1984) Nicole Courtalain flees to England from the French Revolution, becomes indentured to Bianca Maleson, is mistaken for Bianca and shanghaied to a Virginia plantation, where she finds herself married by proxy to the Virginian Clayton Armstrong.
2. *Lost Lady* (Pocket Books, 1985) Young Regan, forsaken by her guardian, scorned by her fiancé, flees her estate, and falls into the arms of rough-hewn American Travis Stanford on the London docks.
3. *River Lady* (Pocket Books, 1985) Beautiful waif Leah and handsome, well-born Wesley form an alliance on Virginia's James River waterfront and settle in the wilds of Kentucky.

V. The Twins duo features twin sisters Houston and Blair Chandler of Chandler, Colorado, in the 1890s, who are superficially different in personality but who wend their ways through kidnappings, forced marriages, mistaken identity, passion, and different career choices before they achieve happiness. *Sweet Liar* is sometimes linked with the Twins because it has a Taggert, related to a major character in number 1, in it. Of course, Taggerts turn up in other series, especially series II, and so does the town of Chandler.

1. *Twin of Ice* **(Pocket Books, 1985)** Rugged stranger Kane Taggert is determined to break through the reserve of Houston Chandler, one of a pair of twins from Chandler, Colorado's leading family.
2. *Twin of Fire* **(Pocket Books, 1985)** Blair Chandler tries to balance her career as a medical doctor in Chandler with her love for Dr. Leander "Lee" Westfield, who has his own problems.
3. *Sweet Liar* **(Pocket Books, 1992)** 1928. Louisville divorcée Samantha travels to Manhattan, ostensibly in search of her wandering grandmother, but gets entangled with hunk Michael Taggert, her landlord and putative guardian.

VI. The Peregrine series is a pair of novels, set in the English Middle Ages, about a family feud that spans several generations. *The Taming/The Conquest* (Pocket Books, 2005) contains numbers 1 and 2.

1. *Taming, The* **(Pocket Books, 1989)** Heiress Liana Neville marries hot-blooded warrior Rogan Peregrine but finds that she has her work cut out for her in distracting him from the Peregrine family feud.
2. *Conquest, The* **(Pocket Books, 1991)** Zared marries Tearle in an effort to end the three-generation feud between their families.

VII. *Carolina Isle* is the first and only (so far) book in the Edenton Trilogy, set in Arundel, North Carolina, but *First Impressions*, also published in 2005, is located in Arundel also.

1. *First Impressions* **(Pocket Books, 2005)** Fortysomething single-mother Eden Palmer purchases Farrington Manor, a beautiful house in picturesque Arundel, North Carolina, where she is immediately pursued by two local bachelors.
2. *Carolina Isle* **(Pocket Books, 2005)** The first book in the Edenton Trilogy. Ariel and Sara, lifelong pen pals from different backgrounds who are of identical appearance, decide to change identities.

Devoto, Pat Cunningham

Three novels set in the Black Belt of Alabama in the 1950s and 1960s explore, through the eyes of juvenile characters, the time and place where the civil rights movement had some of its biggest confrontations. Tabitha "Tab" Rutland, who is very reminiscent of Scout Finch of Harper Lee's *To Kill a Mockingbird*, is featured in numbers 1 and 3, while John McMillan, who has a minor role in number 1, is the main character in number 2. These funny, poignant, and thoughtful coming-of-age novels will appeal to both adults and young adults. Pat Devoto, a native of north Alabama, now divides her time between Alabama and Atlanta, Georgia.

1. *My Last Days as Roy Rogers* **(Warner, 1999)** Ten-year-old Tabitha "Tab" Rutland, enduring what was to be the last "polio summer" in the northern Alabama town of Bainbridge, befriends a 13-year-old black girl, Maudie May. Roy Rogers makes a cameo appearance.
2. *Out of the Night That Covers Me* **(Warner, 2001)** Eight-year-old John McMillan, a minor character in number 1, loses his cosseting adoptive mother and is sent to live on a tenant farm in Alabama's Black Belt, where he becomes acquainted with the larger-than-life black man Tuway and some of the grimmer facts of life.
3. *Summer We Got Saved, The* **(Warner, 2005)** In the 1960s, Tab Rutland and her sister Tina are introduced to nonviolent protest by their aunt Eugenia, who talks them into a visit to Chattanooga and the Highlander Folk School once attended by Martin Luther King Jr. and Rosa Parks.

Dew, Robb Forman

I. The relationship between parents and children is the subject of much of Dew's work. She wrote the nonfiction *The Family Heart: A Memoir of When Our Son Came Out* (Addison, 1994) and a pair of novels that describes the chemistry between the members of the Howells family at two different periods. Not much in the way of action occurs, but the tensions, misunderstandings, and unacknowledged emotions that seethe beneath the surface of routine family activities are well delineated.

1. *Dale Loves Sophie to Death* **(Farrar, 1981)** Dinah Howells returns with her children to her hometown in Ohio, while her husband, Martin, remains in the Berkshires editing his literary quarterly.
2. *Fortunate Lives* **(Morrow, 1992)** Six years after the accidental death of one of the children, the Howells family prepares for the departure of their eldest son to college.

II. Small-town Ohio, this time Washburn, is also for the setting of a trilogy of novels (two published so far) about three friends born on the same day in 1888, Robert Butler, Warren Scofield, and his cousin Lily. The first two novels bring the action, such as there is, to the post–World War II days, as the three friends and other characters go through the vicissitudes of family life, young love, child rearing, and widowhood.

1. *Evidence against Her, The* **(Little, Brown, 2001)** Three friends born on the same day in 1888 in Washburn, Ohio, grow up, fall in love, and get married. Robert Butler marries Lily Scofield, and Warren Scofield marries Agnes Claytor on the rebound.
2. *Truth of the Matter, The* **(Little, Brown, 2005)** Agnes (Claytor) Scofield, widowed in 1930 and the mother of four children, lives life in the 1930s and 1940s financially pressed and emotionally repressed.

Dewhurst, Eileen (Mary)

I. English mystery writer Eileen Dewhurst is still not well known in the United States. Her output is uneven, especially in terms of plots, but at her best, she is very good. Dewhurst's characters are often involved in impersonation, disguise, and role-playing. Phyllida Moon, Dewhurst's longest-running character, is no exception. In number 1, Phyllida, a professional actress, inspired by a role in a forthcoming TV drama, gets a part-time job with the Peter Piper Detective Agency in Seaminster, where her ability at impersonation proves to be very useful. In number 2, Phyllida hooks up with Detective Chief Superintendent Maurice Kendrick, who teams up with her in further novels in the series. Kendrick was first introduced by Dewhurst some years before in *A Private Prosecution* (Doubleday, 1987). Phyllida is an engaging character, even if the success of her impersonations sometimes strains reader disbelief.

An earlier pair of novels involving an actress, variously named Christine Markham and Helen Markham-Johnson, who plays roles for British intelligence, was *Whoever I Am* (Doubleday, 1983) and

Playing It Safe (Doubleday, 1987, originally 1985). Another pair of novels, connected by some sources to the Phyllida Moon series, is *Death in Candie Gardens* (Piatkus [UK], 1992) and *Alias the Enemy* (Severn House, 1997). These novels, set on the Channel Island of Guernsey, feature Detective Inspector Tim Le Page and English veterinarian Anna Weston.

1. *Now You See Her* (Severn House, 1995) Thirty-eight-year-old British actress Phyllida Moon, waiting to begin her role as a TV detective, applies for a job at the Peter Piper Detective Agency in the seaside town of Seaminster and gets involved in a possible molestation case, which leads to murder at an English school.
2. *Verdict on Winter, The* (Severn House, 1996) Phyllida impersonates a housekeeper and glamorous American widow in a case that involves the art world, possible forgery, murder, and DCS Maurice Kendrick.
3. *Roundabout* (Severn House, 1998) Maggie and Carol disappear while on a seaside jaunt, and their husbands turn to the Peter Piper agency for help. Then scavenging foxes lead to the remains of two women.
4. *Double Act* (Severn House, 2000) Phyllida infiltrates an amateur drama society disguised as an American sophisticate to check on possible drug use by a client's son.
5. *Closing Stages* (Severn House, 2001) A gallbladder operation with a forced period of convalescence, and DCS Kendrick's investigation of a series of suspicious heart attacks, finds Moon in a nursing home.
6. *No Love Lost* (Severn House, 2001) Moon plays two roles, the spinsterish Miss Spence and the amicable American, Mrs. Parker, to investigate Sandra Jordan, who, according to her husband, Hugh, is having a suspicious number of late "business" meetings. Sandra, in turn, is suspicious of Hugh's many choir rehearsals.
7. *Easeful Death* (Severn House, 2002) Now police chief in Seaminster, Maurice Kendrick asks the Piper Agency to investigate a local sect, which promises life after death and has attracted his niece.
8. *Naked Witness* (Severn House, 2004) Phyllida Moon witnesses a robbery and murder while shopping and uncharacteristically undisguised and is afraid that her true identity may be known to the perpetrators.

II. An earlier series, featuring Detective Inspector Neil Carter of the Metropolitan Police, also has a good deal of role-playing in it, including Neil in drag. In number 1, Neil plays a secondary role. Neil gets increasingly involved with Cathy McVeigh, whom he marries in number 4. Neil was an increasingly sympathetic character, and it is a little odd that he was dropped after number 5.

1. *Curtain Fall* (Doubleday, 1982) Joanna Stuart gradually sees the pattern of a murder take place, although it isn't until she witnesses the reconstruction of the crime that she realizes the identity of the killer. Originally published in the United Kingdom in 1977.
2. *Drink This* (Doubleday, 1981) Neil Carter goes to Bunington to interview Annabel Quillin, the wife of a bank robber, who may be in possession of a clue whose meaning she doesn't understand.
3. *Trio in Three Flats* (Doubleday, 1981) No annotation available.
4. *There Was a Little Girl* (Doubleday, 1986) Fifteen-year-old Juliet, daughter of the principal of an adult education college, lives a double life as a prostitute in the city one week a year. Originally published in the United Kingdom in 1984.
5. *Nice Little Business, A* (Doubleday, 1987) Suspended from the police force, Neil conducts his own investigation—in drag.

Dexter, Colin

The death by heart attack of the fictional Inspector Morse (whose given name we never learn) on November 15, 2000 (on ITV and in *The Remorseful Day*), saddened thousands, perhaps millions, of fans despite the Oxford, England, detective's rather problematic personality. Morse was a melancholy, irascible, somewhat pompous, somewhat alcoholic figure, unsuccessful in relationships, particularly with the opposite sex, and hard to get along with. His love of music and crossword puzzles humanized him. The late John Thaw's brilliant portrayal of Inspector Morse on the PBS television series showed a more sympathetic character than Dexter's novels did. Morse was assisted by Sergeant Lewis, a pragmatic and conventional family man who gathered the facts that Morse puzzled together. The interplay between the two partners provides a touch of humor. British author Colin Dexter lives in Oxford and shares his character's interest in crossword puzzles.

1. *Last Bus to Woodstock* (St. Martin's, 1975) Two girls are waiting for the last bus to Woodstock. The one who catches the bus is discovered dead in a pub parking lot.
2. *Last Seen Wearing* (St. Martin's, 1976) Morse investigates the disappearance of a schoolgirl and the murder of a teacher.
3. *Silent World of Nicholas Quinn, The* (St. Martin's, 1977) Partially deaf Nicholas Quinn, a member of the foreign Examinations Syndicate, is murdered.
4. *Service of All the Dead* (St. Martin's, 1980) The Oxford Church of St. Frideswide is rocked by a series of murders.
5. *Dead of Jericho, The* (St. Martin's, 1982) Morse meets the attractive Anne Scott at a party. She is found dead, an apparent suicide, six months later.
6. *Riddle of the Third Mile, The* (St. Martin's, 1983) Terminally ill Oxford don Browne-Smith disappears on a trip to London. Then a headless, handless, and partially legless corpse is found.
7. *Secret of Annexe 3, The* (St. Martin's, 1987) The prizewinner of a fancy dress contest is found dead in his Oxford hotel room after a New Year's Eve party.
8. *Wench Is Dead, The* (St. Martin's, 1990) Inspector Morse whiles away the time while recuperating from an ulcer by investigating a century-old case of rape and murder.
9. *Jewel That Was Ours, The* (Crown, 1992) Elderly American tourist Laura Stratton is killed, and a rare jeweled artifact she had planned to donate to the Ashmolean Museum is stolen.
10. *Way through the Woods, The* (Crown, 1993) Young Swedish national Karin Eriksson has disappeared while on vacation in England.
11. *Daughters of Cain, The* (Crown, 1995) Morse and Lewis investigate the murder of a retired don and the disappearance of a former custodian.
12. *Morse's Greatest Mystery and Other Stories* (Crown, 1995) Eleven short stories, six of them about Inspector Morse.
13. *Death Is Now My Neighbor* (Crown, 1996) Morse deals with diabetes, some very bloody murders, and nasty Oxford dons engaged in a power struggle.
14. *Remorseful Day, The* (Crown, 2000) Subtitle: *The Final Inspector Morse Novel*. Sergeant Lewis does most of the heavy lifting for a reluctant Inspector Morse in this investigation of the murder of Nurse Yvonne Harrington.

Dibdin, Michael

English-born, Italian resident Dibdin (d. 2007) wrote erudite, witty crime fiction. He paired Sherlock Holmes and Jack the Ripper in *The Last Sherlock Holmes Story* (Pantheon, 1979), and set poet Robert Browning to sleuthing in *A Rich Full Death* (Vintage, 1999, originally

1986). The Aurelio Zen mysteries are no exception. Zen is an investigator for Rome's Criminalpol. He has a certain tolerance for corruption combined with a desire to get to the bottom of any mystery. Zen is only one of the many complex characters who find themselves in intricate plots spiced by rich prose and authentic Italian atmosphere. Numbers 1 through 3 have been collected in *The Aurelio Zen Omnibus* (Faber [UK], 1998). Dibdin was the husband of K. K. Beck (q.v.).

1. *Ratking* (Bantam, 1989) Zen investigates the kidnapping of a rich industrialist in Perugia.
2. *Vendetta* (Doubleday, 1991) Aurelio is sent to investigate the video-taped murder of a security-obsessed architect.
3. *Cabal* (Doubleday, 1993) An Italian aristocrat falls to his death from the observation gallery at the top of St. Peter's Basilica.
4. *Dead Lagoon* (Pantheon, 1995) Zen returns to his native Venice to trace the disappearance of a wealthy American businessman.
5. *Cosi Fan Tutti* (Pantheon, 1997) Aurelio Zen changes his beat to Naples and stumbles into a new identity for himself in this comic opera–ish concoction of murder, organized crime, an American sailor, pirated software, and a handsome widow with two marriageable daughters.
6. *Long Finish, A* (Pantheon, 1998) Aurelio is off to the Piedmont region to deal with feuding families, rival wine growers, and white truffle harvesters.
7. *Blood Rain* (Pantheon, 2000) The aging Zen is sent to Sicily to gather information on the DIA (Direzione Investigativa AntiMafia) and runs into a daughter he didn't know he had and the corpse of a crime-family member rotting in an abandoned train car in Catania.
8. *And Then You Die* (Pantheon, 2002) Recuperating from injuries suffered in *Blood Rain*, Aurelio has a new identity and the use of a beachfront home in the Tuscan resort town of Versilia while awaiting his appearance as a witness at a Mafia trial in America.
9. *Medusa* (Pantheon, 2004) The Italian Defense Ministry (the Carabinieri) and Criminalpol are at loggerheads over a partially mummified body found in an abandoned military tunnel in the Italian Alps.
10. *Back to Bologna* (Vintage, 2006) Aurelio investigates the murder of Bologna millionaire entrepreneur Lorenzo Curti, who was found in his Audi impaled on a Parmesan cheese knife.
11. *End Games* (Pantheon, 2007) The corpse of American attorney Peter Newman is discovered in Calabria after an apparent botched kidnapping.

Dickinson, David

Lord Francis Powerscourt, a military intelligence officer working in England during the 1890s and early 1900s, is the investigator in a series of historical mysteries involving prominent British citizens, including the British Royal Family. On some of these cases he is aided by his wife, Lady Lucy Powerscourt. Lord Francis and Lady Lucy are a personable duo, and the novels are well written, entertaining, and full of authentic historical background. Dublin-born David Dickinson was a scriptwriter, producer, and editor for BBC for nearly 30 years before he started writing mystery novels.

1. *Goodnight, Sweet Prince* (Carroll & Graf, 2002) In 1892 military intelligence officer Lord Francis Powerscourt is called in to investigate and do some fancy covering up when Prince Albert "Prince Eddy" Victor is found murdered at Sandringham. (Poor Prince Eddy has had a tough posthumous life, being murdered because of his homosexual connections, according to Dickinson, and being the real Jack the Ripper, according to other speculation.)

2. *Death and the Jubilee* (Carroll & Graf, 2003) Irish terrorists are planning to disrupt Queen Victoria's Diamond Jubilee in 1897.
3. *Death of an Old Master* (Carroll & Graf, 2004) Lady Lucy Powerscourt assists her husband, Francis, when one of her cousins, art critic Christopher Montague, is murdered.
4. *Death of a Chancellor* (Carroll & Graf, 2005) Compton [*sic*] Cathedral is about to celebrate its millennial anniversary in 1901 when its chancellor dies under questionable circumstances.
5. *Death Called to the Bar* (Carroll & Graf, 2006) When junior "bencher" Alexander Dauntsey is poisoned at a formal dinner held at one of London's Inns of Court, Lord Francis must rely on his extensive roster of in-laws for leads to the crime.
6. *Death on the Nevskii Prospekt* (Carroll & Graf, 2007) Briefly retired at Lucy's behest, Powerscourt travels to Russia, where a British diplomat who met secretly with the czar has been reported murdered.
7. *Death on the Holy Mountain* (Soho Constable, 2008) The Powerscouts track down missing paintings, rescue women kidnapped by Irish nationalists, and expose murderers defiling the sacred Croagh Patrick pilgrimage.

Dickson, Gordon R(upert)

I. Hugo- and Nebula-winning science-fiction and fantasy writer Gordon R. Dickson produced an elaborate series of novels that he referred to as the Childe Cycle. The cycle, when finished, was supposed to incorporate novels about the past, present and future. Dickson died in 2001, having published only the future novels in the cycle. These novels illustrate three "splinter" cultures that, when fused, would result in the "Responsible Man." The warrior Dorsai culture is best represented, in a series referred to (erroneously, according to Dickson) as the Dorsai novels. Several omnibuses incorporating some of the Dorsai books have been published. *Three to Dorsai!* (Doubleday, 1975) contains numbers 1, 2, and 3. *The Dorsai Companion* (Ace, 1986) contains numbers 5 and 6. *Dorsai Spirit* (Tor, 2002) contains numbers 3 and 6. *Four to Dorsai!* (SFBC Science, 2002) contains numbers 1, 2, 3, and 4.

1. *Necromancer* (Doubleday, 1967) Earth is being torn apart by the pressures of overpopulation and overdependence on technology. Variant title: *No Room for Man*.
2. *Tactics of Mistake, The* (Doubleday, 1971) Chronicles the career of Cletus Graeme, founder of the Dorsai culture.
3. *Dorsai!* (DAW, 1976) Donal Graeme of the Dorsai rises to success within a web of interstellar intrigue. This is the expanded version of *The Genetic General* (Ace, 1960).
4. *Soldier, Ask Not* (Dell, 1967) Tam Olyn rejects a part in establishing the Final Encyclopedia, a computerized compendium of everything that is known about human nature.
5. *Lost Dorsai* (Ace, 1980) In a story somewhat peripheral to the Childe Cycle, a pacifist soldier takes a job as bandmaster in a city under siege.
6. *Spirit of Dorsai, The* (Ace, 1979) Short stories.
7. *Final Encyclopedia, The* (Tor, 1984) Out of nowhere comes a new force, the Others, humans of extraordinary size and ability, who gain control of the settled worlds in a short time.
8. *Chantry Guild, The* (Ace, 1986) Harold Mayne, the Encyclopedia, and the Dorsai are holding Old Earth against the forces of the younger worlds.
9. *Young Bleys* (Tor, 1991) Details the childhood and maturation of Bleys Ahrens, son of an "Exotic" mother sent to the "Friendly" planet of Association.
10. *Other* (Tor, 1994) Bleys, the "Great Teacher," travels through the galaxy pursuing his grand unification scheme.

11. *Antagonist* (**Tor, 2007**) The increasingly megalomaniacal Bleys is so obsessed with his plan to save the human race that his uncle's disapproval and his brother's possible betrayal barely register. Completed by David W. Wixon.

II. Dickson also wrote a light sword-and-sorcery series in which contemporary academic James Eckert and his soon-to-be wife, Angie, are transported to a magical alternative medieval England full of dragons, mages, hobgoblins, knights, and a trusty wolf named Aargh.

1. *Dragon and the George, The* (**Doubleday, 1976**) James and Angie find themselves in an alternative world where James is metamorphosed into a dragon.
2. *Dragon Knight, The* (**Tor, 1990**) James, now Sir James, a baron in 14th-century alternative England, must rescue his captive prince from the clutches of the French.
3. *Dragon on the Border, The* (**Ace, 1992**) Sir James fights the Hollow Men, deadly, immortal sorcerers on the Anglo-Scots border.
4. *Dragon at War, The* (**Ace, 1992**) The great mage Carolinus is stricken by a mysterious illness, leaving the dragon knight to work his lesser magic.
5. *Dragon, the Earl, and the Troll, The* (**Ace, 1994**) The Dark Powers plan to tamper with history at the Earl of Somerset's Christmas revels.
6. *Dragon and the Djinn, The* (**Ace, 1995**) James agrees to help his friend Sir Brian Neville-Smythe in finding the father of Sir Brian's lover, last heard from in Muslim Palmyra.
7. *Dragon and the Gnarly King, The* (**Tor, 1997**) Jim and his companions travel to Lyonesse to recover Jim's adopted infant, Robert, who was kidnapped by the subterranean Gnarlies.
8. *Dragon in Lyonesse, The* (**Tor, 1998**) The Dragon Knight, threatened by the Dark Powers, sets out again for Lyonesse, a land full of characters from Arthurian myth.
9. *Dragon and the Fair Maid of Kent, The* (**Tor, 2000**) Jim and Angie deal with a series of problems, including unexpected guests, political currents swirling around King Edward III and the Black Prince, the bubonic plague, shape-changing goblins, and the dark powers.

III. *The Right to Arm Bears* (Baen, 2000) is a collection of two novels and a short story about the Dilbians, nine-foot-tall beings resembling a cross between bears and Vikings, and the efforts of Terrans to bring civilization to them in the form of techno-farming, which the Dilbians reject in favor of their society of dueling and physical prowess.

1. *Spacial Delivery* (**Ace, 1961**) John Tardy is sent to Dilbia to locate and rescue the first envoy sent by Helping Hands to the primitive planet. Published together with Dickson's *Delusion World*.
2. *Spacepaw* (**Putnam, 1969**) Wallham becomes involved in an interplanetary scuffle when he is sent to teach agriculture to the Dilbians.

Dietz, William C(orey)

I. The Legion of the Damned is a series of SF-military tales, or space operas, set in the future when an army of humans, aliens, and cyborgs defends the Confederacy of Sentient Beings against threats like the insectoid Ramanthians, the cyborg Hudathans, or the terroristic La-Norians. Bill Booly, who rises from Sergeant to General, is the leading character is this exciting series, which should appeal to adolescents of all ages. Seven novels have been published, with at least one more to come.

1. *Legion of the Damned* (**Ace, 1993**) The Legion of the Damned, charged with defending the Confederacy of Sentient Beings, is made up of cyborgs with human minds wrapped up in armored killing machines and more-or-less human societal misfits. In the opening episode the Legion is up against a xenophobic alien empire ruled by a Nero-like emperor.
2. *Final Battle, The* (**Ace, 1995**) The Hudathans, a cyborg race that has built up its forces through stolen technology, threaten the Confederacy, whose only line of defense is the Legion.
3. *By Blood Alone* (**Ace, 1999**) Legion officer Bill Booly is assigned to Fort Mosby, Earth, home to a collection of misfits, losers, and otherwise unsatisfactory beings.
4. *By Force of Arms* (**Ace, 2000**) After stopping a mutiny against Earth's government, Bill Booly and his oddball troops face a plot to destroy the universe hatched by a fanatic and his killer technology.
5. *For More Than Glory* (**Ace, 2003**) A terroristic revolution on the distant world of LaNor threatens the Legionnaires and the entire Confederacy.
6. *For Those Who Fell* (**Ace, 2004**) The insectoid Ramanthians, who need more planets to accommodate their queen's billions of eggs, have developed a communications device that could turn the war against the Confederacy in their favor.
7. *When All Seems Lost* (**Ace, 2007**) Marcott Nankool, the president and CEO of the Confederacy of Sentient Beings, is captured, with his entourage, by the Ramanthians.

II. Sam McCade, bounty hunter of the future, often finds himself the only obstacle to the destruction of the Terran Empire from without and within. *McCade for Hire* (Ace, 2004) and *McCade on the Run* (Ace, 2005) are omnibus volumes containing numbers 1 and 2 and numbers 3 and 4, respectively.

1. *Galactic Bounty* (**Ace, 1986**) A treacherous navy captain plans to sell military secrets to the alien Il Ronn, and only interstellar bounty hunter Sam McCade can ward off the destruction of the Terran Empire. UK title: *War World*.
2. *Imperial Bounty* (**Ace, 1988**) Princess Claudia has seized the throne in her brother's absence and is fomenting war with the Il Ronn. McCade has three months to find the missing Prince Alexander and prevent catastrophe.
3. *Alien Bounty* (**Ace, 1990**) Space pirates steal the sacred Ronnian relic, the Vial of Tears, and Il Ronn will go to war unless Sam McCade can retrieve the holy relic.
4. *McCade's Bounty* (**Ace, 1990**) Pirate Mustapha Pong has kidnapped McCade's daughter, and Sam will do anything to bring her back alive.

III. The Drifter, or Pik Lando, trio features master space smuggler Pik Lando, who finds that his profession gets him into a lot of unanticipated hot water.

1. *Drifter* (**Ace, 1991**) A beautiful woman named Angel hires space smuggler Pik Lando, and gets him involved with a group of fanatical revolutionaries.
2. *Drifter's Run* (**Ace, 1992**) Pik takes a job on a space tug to avoid run-ins with the law, but finds himself the target of a beautiful bounty hunter tempted by the reward for his capture.
3. *Drifter's War* (**Ace, 1992**) Still trying to evade bounty hunters, Lando travels on a "drift ship," and find himself in the middle of a "planet-smashing" war.

IV. A pair of novels features journalist Rex Corvan in adventures set on Earth and Mars.

1. *Matrix Man, The* (ROC, 1990) News reporter Rex Corvan has to decode a secret data disk given him by a dying terrorist, uncovering something called the "Matrix Man."
2. *Mars Prime* (ROC, 1992) A serial killer and a rebellious religious cult threaten the Mars settlement, and it is up to Rex and his wife, Kim, to prevent disaster.

V. A pair of novels depicts the resistance of humans to the alien, insectoid Saurons, who have enslaved them. Some comments on race are engendered by the rigidly hierarchic Saurons, an African American president who decides not to be a puppet, and some white supremacists whom President Franklin would rather not have as allies against the Saurons.

1. *DeathDay* (Ace, 2001) Former government bodyguard Jack Manning finds himself in a position to resist the alien, enslaving Saurons when they choose him to guard their puppet president.
2. *EarthRise* (Ace, 2002) African American Alex Franklin decides that he no longer wants to be a puppet of the Saurons and becomes an agent of the resistance movement.

VI. Somewhat more philosophical than most of his earlier novels, Dietz's Jak Rebo tales are about a far future in which many technological advances have fallen into disuse and most people have fallen into despair. Jak Rebo, a Runner—an interstellar courier—is called upon to deliver an aspirant to leadership of a Buddhist-like religion and an artificial intelligence called Logos, which is the key to restoring the systems of star gates that kept the inhabited worlds together.

1. *Runner* (Ace, 2005) Runner Jak Rebo accompanies a possibly reborn spiritual leader to the plant where the tests to establish the true heir to the Buddhist-like religion, which is the only hope for redemption in a crumbling far future, are to be administered.
2. *Logos Run* (Ace, 2006) Rebo must deliver an AI known as Logos to a mysterious backwater planet to restore the system of star gates that once knitted the settled worlds together.

Dobson, Joanne

Karen Pelletier is an English professor at Enfield College, a small, fictitious institution in Massachusetts. Pelletier, whose speciality is 19th-century women's literature, in trying to diversify Enfield's "dead white males" curriculum, runs into opposition from her colleagues and the occasional murder, which she manages to solve with the help of her friend, local police lieutenant Piotrowski. Fans of Amanda Cross (q.v.) will enjoy these well-told tales that skewer academic politics and stuffy academics. Joanne Dobson is an associate professor of English at Fordham University and the author of the scholarly *Dickinson and the Strategies of Reticence; The Woman Writer in Nineteenth-Century America* (Indiana, 1989).

1. *Quieter Than Sleep* (Doubleday, 1997) Subtitle: *A Modern Mystery of Emily Dickinson*. Emily Dickinson scholar Karen Pelletier, new professor at the elite Enfield College in Massachusetts, turns up a letter written by Emily Dickinson and a couple of bodies, one of a colleague, and one of a student.
2. *Northbury Papers, The* (Doubleday, 1998) Karen, studying the work of Serena Northbury (fictitious), a 19th-century novelist regarded as trashy by Karen's male colleagues, meets elderly Dr. Edith Hart, Northbury's great granddaughter, who dies leaving $10 million to Enfield College if Karen will direct a research center devoted to Northbury.
3. *Raven and the Nightingale, The* (Doubleday, 1999) Subtitle: *A Modern Mystery of Edgar Allan Poe*. Karen receives a large cache of papers and journals belonging to Emily Foster (fictitious), a 19th-century poet who was rumored to have committed suicide after a failed romance with Edgar Allan Poe.
4. *Cold and Pure and Very Dead* (Doubleday, 2000) Pelletier creates controversy by telling reporter Marty Katz that the best novel of the 20th century is Mildred Deakin's *Oblivion Falls*, a once-popular 1950s potboiler of youthful sex and death. Katz starts looking for Deakin, who disappeared soon after the publication of *Oblivion Falls*.
5. *Maltese Manuscript, The* (Poisoned Pen, 2004) Sunnye Hardcastle, mystery writer, panelist at an Enfield College conference, and temporary roommate of Karen Pelletier, is the chief suspect when a series of book and manuscript thefts occurs.

Dobyns, Stephen

New York's Saratoga Springs, home of the famous horse-racing track, is also home to detective Charlie Bradshaw and his amusingly sleazy partner, Victor Plotz. Charlie is an unassuming fellow with a 1940s code of honor and a nostalgia for the bygone glories of Saratoga Springs. He begins the series as a policeman, then moves into the private sector. Dobyns is the author of 10 other novels, a collection of short stories, poetry criticism, and 12 volumes of readable and well-regarded poetry (e.g., *Pallbearers Envying the One Who Rides*, Penguin, 1999).

1. *Saratoga Longshot* (Atheneum, 1996) Sergeant Charlie Bradshaw of the Saratoga police force comes to New York City in search of the missing son of an old girlfriend.
2. *Saratoga Swimmer* (Atheneum, 1981) Lew Ackerman, owner of Lorelei Stables, hires Charlie to head security, then is shot to death in a YMCA pool.
3. *Saratoga Headhunter* (Viking, 1985) Charlie, now a private investigator moonlighting as a milkman, offers sanctuary to McClatchy, a race-throwing jockey turned informant, who proceeds to lose his head.
4. *Saratoga Snapper* (Viking, 1986) Victor Plotz photographs a group at the hotel owned by Charlie's mother and is nearly killed by a hit-and-run driver.
5. *Saratoga Bestiary* (Viking, 1988) Someone steals a painting of a famous racehorse, and Charlie is hired to deliver the ransom money.
6. *Saratoga Hexameter* (Viking, 1990) Charlie, unlike his creator, is no poet, but he has to pass himself off as one to solve three cases linked by bad poems.
7. *Saratoga Haunting* (Viking, 1993) Grace Mulholland, who was thought to have absconded with some embezzled money, is found without the cash beneath a demolished pool hall.
8. *Saratoga Backtalk* (Norton, 1994) While Charlie is on jury duty, Victor Plotz comes to the fore when Bernard Logan is trampled by one of his thoroughbreds.
9. *Saratoga Fleshpot* (Norton, 1995) Somebody may have pulled a switch when racer Fleshpot is sold for half a million dollars.
10. *Saratoga Strongbox* (Viking, 1998) Victor Plotz, always on the lookout for an easy buck, gets himself and Charlie enmeshed in a great deal of trouble. The only solution seems to be a locked strongbox.

Doherty, P(aul) C.

I. Hugh Corbett, Master of Clerks, Keeper of the Secret Seal and master spy for King Edward I (1272–1307), is based on John de Droxford, a historical figure. Corbett stars in a series of literate whodunits with excellent medieval English historical background. P. C. (or Paul) Doherty, an Englishman who wrote his doctoral thesis on Edward's successor Edward II, also writes historical mysteries under the cloak of pseudonyms such as Anna Apostolou (q.v.), Michael Clynes (q.v.), Ann Dukthas (q.v.), C. L. Grace (q.v.), and Paul Harding (q.v.).

1. *Satan in St. Mary's* (St. Martin's, 1987) In 1284 a group of devil worshippers known as the Pentacle is mounting an attack against King Edward.

2. *Crown in Darkness, The* (St. Martin's, 1988) The dark, rainy death of King Alexander III, which left the Scottish throne without a legal heir, may have been no accident.

3. *Spy in Chancery* (St. Martin's, 1989) A mole among the royal councilors is responsible for the sinking of an English ship bearing secret information.

4. *Angel of Death, The* (St. Martin's, 1990) Hugh is assigned to catch the murderer of the Dean of St. Paul's, a leader among the antitax clergy.

5. *Prince of Darkness, The* (St. Martin's, 1993) Lady Eleanor Belmont, former mistress of the Prince of Wales, is murdered within the seemingly impregnable walls of a sheltered nunnery.

6. *Murder Wears a Cowl* (St. Martin's, 1994) In 1302 London is plagued by series of killings done by someone dressed in monk's attire.

7. *Assassin in the Greenwood, The* (St. Martin's, 1994) Is Robin Hood responsible for the poisoning of the sheriff of Nottingham and the mutilation of the king's tax collector?

8. *Song of a Dark Angel, The* (St. Martin's, 1994) Hugh is sent to Mortlake Manor on the Norfolk coast to investigate a headless corpse.

9. *Satan's Fire* (St. Martin's, 1996) Counterfeit money in Yorkshire and a plot against King Edward I may be connected with the Order of Knights Templar.

10. *Devil's Hunt, The* (St. Martin's, 1997) Severed heads of beggars hanging from trees near Oxford, the locked-room slaying of an Oxford archivist, and the proclamations of someone calling himself the Bellman and invoking the long-dead rebel Simon de Montfort bring Hugh Corbett to the university city.

11. *Demon Archer, The* (St. Martin's, 2001) In 1303 Lord Henry Fitzalan, proposed emissary to King Philip of France to arrange a royal marriage for King Edward's son, is murdered, and there is no lack of persons who could have been motivated to kill the evil Lord Henry. Originally published in the United Kingdom in 1998.

12. *Treason of the Ghosts, The* (Headline [UK], 2000) The execution of a local notable in the village of Melford as a serial killer has not stopped the spate of slayings in the village. Not published in the United States.

13. *Corpse Candle* (St. Martin's, 2002) The death of Abbot Stephen at the monastery of St. Martin's-in-the-Marsh puts Hugh in the middle of bandit- (and possibly ghost-) infested woods and a power struggle over holy relics and a dispute about the value of exorcism.

14. *Magician's Death, The* (Headline [UK], 2004) *The Book of Secrets*, a book full of arcane information about science and magic written and encoded by Roger Bacon, is the subject of plots to steal it, a conference to decode it, and murder. Not published in the United States.

15. *Waxman Murders, The* (Headline [UK], 2006) Hugh Corbett is sent to negotiate with Wilhelm Von Paulents, a representative of the Hanseatic League, who is rumored to have the Carta Mysteriosa, a collection of valuable maps and sea charts.

II. The roguish Matthew Jankyn is the unlikely hero of two detective novels set in the early 15th century. Matthew is forced to become involved in two of the era's hottest cases.

1. *Whyte Harte, The* (St. Martin's, 1988) Matthew becomes a reluctant member of the Whyte Harte, a secret society dedicated to restoring the deposed king Richard II, who may or may not be still alive.

2. *Serpent among the Lilies, The* (St. Martin's, 1990) Jankyn is sent by Cardinal Beaufort to get the goods on a mysterious maid of Lorraine, called Jeanne d'Arc.

III. Another series set in medieval England (c. 1400) carries on Chaucer's unfinished *Canterbury Tales* by having the various personages of the Canterbury pilgrimage tell their promised second tales. All of the new tales have "mystery and murder" as their themes. So far, the Knight, the Franklin, the Priest, the Clerk of Oxford, the Man of Law, and the Carpenter have related their tales. Such worthies as the Miller, the Wife of Bath, the Pardoner, and the Nun's Priest haven't had their second innings yet.

1. *Ancient Evil, An* (St. Martin's, 1995) The Knight tells the tale of the Strigoi, a blood-sucking demon, supposedly buried alive two centuries earlier, who may have been revived in 14th-century Oxford.

2. *Tapestry of Murders, A* (St. Martin's, 1996) The Man of Law tells a tale concerning the events of 1358 when Vallence, a French courtier who is close to dowager queen Isabella, is murdered, first in a series of slayings that includes that of the judge investigating the crime.

3. *Tournament of Murders, A* (St. Martin's, 1997) The Franklin's tale takes young squire Richard Greenele on a pilgrimage in search of his origins and identity after the revelations of a knight dying on the field of Poitiers.

4. *Ghostly Murders* (St. Martin's, 1998) The sight of a decaying church in a deserted village prompts the Priest to narrate a tale of two brothers, priests in a small Kentish village, who uncover a grisly secret when they relocate some coffins to a new cemetery.

5. *Hangman's Hymn, The* (St. Martin's, 2004) The witnessing of a roadside hanging elicits the Carpenter's tale, which relates the story of a carpenter who moves to Gloucester to follow his love, joins the crew of the local hangman, and becomes involved in murder and supernatural doings. Originally published in the United Kingdom in 2001.

6. *Haunt of Murder, A* (Headline [UK], 2002) The Clerk of Oxford relates a ghostly tale of love and death as the pilgrims find themselves lost in a Kentish forest rumored to be haunted.

IV. Far from his medieval stamping grounds, Doherty has inaugurated a mystery series set in the Egypt of pharaoh queen Hatusu (Hatshepsut) in 1479 BCE. The detective in this series is Lord Amerotke, chief judge of Hatusu. Doherty continues to display his meticulous historical research and storytelling skills in this series set nearly three millennia before the reigns of the Plantagenet kings.

1. *Mask of Ra, The* (St. Martin's, 1999) The death, apparently by snake bite, of the Pharaoh Tutmose III, brings on a succession struggle between Tutmose's illegitimate son and his widow (and half sister), Hatusu.

2. *Horus Killings, The* (St. Martin's, 2000) Several priests at the Temple of Horus are murdered in a possible plot against Hatusu, and Amerotke must smoke out the guilty parties.

3. *Anubis Slayings, The* (St. Martin's, 2001) Someone wearing the jackal mask of the god Anubis is poisoning people, and valuable treasures and manuscripts have disappeared from the god's temple in what may be an attempt to sabotage peace negotiations with the Mitanni.

4. *Slayers of Seth, The* (St. Martin's, 2002) Two murders, the poisoning of a young scribe and the killing of a veteran of the war against the Hyksos in the Temple of Set(h) engage Amertoke's attention.

5. *Assassins of Isis, The* (St. Martin's, 2006) There's a connection between looting of the royal tombs in the Necropolis, the disappearance of four virgins from the Temple of Isis, and the suspicious snakebite death of General Suten.

6. *Poisoner of Ptah, The* (St. Martin's, 2008) Just as negotiations with a Libyan delegation result in a peace treaty, three prominent Egyptian scribes are poisoned.

V. Alexander the Great, intent upon the conquest of Persia in 334 BCE, enlists his childhood friend the physician Telamon in solving murders that threaten to hamper his operations. Telamon, aided by his knowledge of deductive reasoning learned from studying with Aristotle and his red-haired Celtic assistant, Cassandra, gets to the bottom of things in another intricate and well-researched series. Doherty has published another series about Alexander the Great under the pseudonym Anna Apostolou (q.v.).

1. *House of Death, The* (Carroll & Graf, 2001) A series of murders linked by scraps of parchment bearing cryptic warnings taken from Homer and Euripides is decimating Alexander's generals on the eve of his invasion of Persia.

2. *Godless Man, The* (Carroll & Graf, 2002) Alexander's conquest of Persia hits a roadblock in the form of multiple murders committed by a shadowy assassin known only as the Centaur.

3. *Gates of Hell, The* (Carroll & Graf, 2003) Alexander, nearing his goal after the demolishing of the Persian army at the Battle of Granicus, is faced with the siege of the city of Halicarnassus.

VI. Mahu's Tale, a trilogy told by the Egyptian Mahu, who was an official during the reigns of Akhenhaten and Tutankhamen, has not yet been published in the United States.

1. *Evil Spirit out of the West, An* (Headline [UK], 2003) The ambitious and wily Egyptian official Mahu observes the reign of the strange pharaoh Akhenhaten. Not published in the United States.

2. *Season of the Hyaena, The* (Headline [UK], 2005) The six-year-old pharaoh Tutankhamen is the center of a series of intrigues. Not published in the United States.

3. *Year of the Cobra, The* (Headline [UK], 2006) Young Tutankhamen is suffering from a serious mental illness. Not published in the United States.

VII. A new medieval mystery series, set in the England of Edward II, features Mathilde of Westminster—London physician and lady-in-waiting to princess, then queen, Isabella—who looks back on her turbulent life.

1. *Cup of Ghosts, The* (Headline [UK], 2005) The coronation of Edward II is marred by the gruesome death of Sir John Baquelle, knight of the Royal Household.

2. *Poison Maiden, The* (Headline [UK], 2007) In 1308 Edward II, facing civil war and the machinations of French king Philip IV,

tries to unmask the "Poison Maiden," a master spy rumored to have arrived in England. Not published in the United States.

VIII. Claudia, niece of a tavern owner, wine server in Emperor Constantine's household, and "agente in rebus politicis," or spy, is near the center of the plotting and counterplotting in the second decade of the 4th century CE, as Constantine and his mother, Helena, try to solidify his rule by harnessing the power of the Christian Church. *Domina* (Headline [UK], 2002), although sometimes included in this series, is set in the earlier time of the emperors Claudius and Nero.

1. *Murder Imperial* (Headline [UK], 2003) In 313 CE, Helena, mother of Emperor Constantine, calls upon the spy Claudia to investigate the murder and mutilation of three courtesans from the Guild of Aphrodite. Not published in the United States.

2. *Song of the Gladiator, The* (Headline [UK], 2004) Trying to reach some kind of consensus among the quarreling Christians, Constantine sets up a theological conference where the disputing parties can debate before him. Not published in the United States.

3. *Queen of the Night* (Headline [UK], 2006) Claudia is summoned by Helena to investigate the abductions of sons and daughters of the powerful and the murder and mutilation of veterans of Constantine's British wars. Not published in the United States.

Doig, Ivan

Montana-born writer Ivan Doig, whose memoir *This House of Sky* (Harcourt, 1978) was nominated for a National Book Award, wrote a fictional Montana trilogy featuring several generations of the McCaskill family covering the century of Montana's statehood, from 1889 to 1989. The original trilogy (numbers 1, 4, and 5) has been expanded by three more novels. American frontier history and contemporary Rocky Mountain life come alive in a leisurely but absorbing saga.

1. *Dancing at the Rascal Fair* (Atheneum, 1987) Young Scotsman Angus McCaskill travels with his friend Rob Barclay to Montana's Two Medicine Country. Covers the years 1890 to 1919.

2. *Prairie Nocturne* (Scribner, 2003) In 1924 Helena, Montana, singing teacher Susan Duff (seen as a schoolgirl in *Dancing at the Rascal Fair*) coaches young African American singer Monty Rathbun.

3. *Bucking the Sun* (Simon & Schuster, 1996) Takes place during the building of the Fort Peck Dam (1933–1938), as young Owen Duff abandons the family farm to become an engineer.

4. *English Creek* (Atheneum, 1984) A coming-of-age story about 14-year-old Jick McCaskill set in the high country of western Montana in the summer of 1939.

5. *Ride with Me, Mariah Montana* (Atheneum, 1990) Sixty-five-year-old Jick McCaskill, his photographer daughter, Mariah, and her newspaper columnist ex-husband tour Montana in Jick's Winnebago to explore the meaning of the state's Centennial.

6. *Mountain Time* (Scribner, 1999) Continues the McCaskill family saga, focusing on sisters Lexa and Mariah McCaskill. Lexa is running a catering service in Seattle and living with environmental journalist Mitch Rozier. Mariah has just returned from a yearlong photography expedition around the world.

Dold, Gaylord

Mitch Roberts is another one of your hard-boiled but sensitive and intellectual (he reads Heidegger) private eyes. Trying to come to terms with his World War II experiences, Mitch worked out of Wichita, Kansas, during the Eisenhower era in six cases published in paperback only in the 1980s. The novels dropped out of sight except for a few aficionados impressed by Mitch and his 1950s Wichita ambience. Mitch, who at some point is revealed to be a former baseball player, moves from Wichita to Colorado to become a horse rancher (number 6), and eventually winds up in London, where his cases take on an international flavor (numbers 7–10). Kansas criminal lawyer Gaylord Dold seems to have abandoned Mitch for other characters in his later fiction. Dold also writes nonfiction travel guides to places like the Dominican Republic. *The Wichita Mysteries* (1997), published by Dold's own Watermark Press, contains the first three Roberts mysteries.

1. *Hot Summer, Cold Murder* (Avon, 1985) Carl Plummer hires Wichita PI Mitch Roberts to find his missing son.
2. *Snake Eyes* (Ivy, 1986) Who killed two of Jules Reynard's valuable colts and tried to poison Reynard?
3. *Cold Cash* (Ivy, 1986) After a four-month-old baby is kidnapped from her teenage mother by her hoodlum father, Mitch uncovers a black market in babies.
4. *Bonepile* (Ivy, 1987) Fourteen years after Clara Hooke's brother was sent to prison for murder, Clara asks old friend Mitch to clear him.
5. *Muscle and Blood* (Ivy, 1987) Roberts investigates a car bombing that killed a rich old woman and the murder of a hotel clerk shot through the head.
6. *Disheveled City* (Ivy, 1989) A one-night stand with beautiful Donna Neant winds up with Donna being hacked into small pieces and Mitch a suspect. Mitch leaves Wichita to raise horses in Colorado.
7. *Penny for the Old Guy, A* (St. Martin's, 1991) Roberts travels to England to spend the holidays with his best friend's widow, only to find that her son Jono has drowned.
8. *Rude Boys* (St. Martin's, 1992) Staying in London while trying to rekindle romance with the widow Amanda, Roberts helps Jamaican-born lawyer Hillary Root to defend a Jamaican client accused of murder.
9. *World Beat, The* (St. Martin's, 1993) Mitch is hired by Lloyd's of London to find a missing doctor employed by a copper-mining business in Zaire.
10. *Samedi's Knapsack* (St. Martin's, 2001) Voodoo enters the picture when Bobby Hilliard, an old friend from Mitch's ball-playing days, asks him to travel from Miami to Haiti to buy some artworks for his galleries and to check on the previous courier, who has disappeared.

Dominic, R. B.

PSEUDONYM OF Mary J. Latsis & Martha Hennissart

Emma Lathen (q.v.) by another name is still the successful team of Mary J. Latsis and Martha Hennissart. This series is set in Washington, DC, and stars the Democratic congressman from Newburg, Ohio, Benton Safford. Sixteen years in Congress have given Safford the influence and contacts to open doors whenever he needs information. He is an amiable man with a gift for making even new suits look rumpled. His shrewd judgment of people and situations make him a good detective.

1. *Murder, Sunny Side Up* (Abelard-Schuman, 1968) A House subcommittee investigating Ova-Cote, a spray-on preservative for eggs, turns up some rotters.
2. *Murder in High Place* (Doubleday, 1970) When fiery Karen Jenks is recalled from the small South American country where she was researching her master's thesis, she demands that her congressman help her fight back.
3. *There Is No Justice* (Doubleday, 1971) A Supreme Court nominee, Coleman Ives, is murdered. UK title: *Murder Out of Court.*
4. *Epitaph for a Lobbyist* (Doubleday, 1974) A woman lobbyist is murdered at Washington's National Airport.
5. *Murder out of Commission* (Doubleday, 1976) A sleepy Ohio town in Safford's district suddenly explodes into violence over the issue of a proposed nuclear power plant.
6. *Attending Physician, The* (Harper, 1980) A medical scandal in Ben's home district leads to murder.
7. *Unexpected Developments* (St. Martin's, 1984) Safford uncovers murder and bribery in the aircraft industry. UK title: *A Flaw in the System.*

Donachie, David

I. The Privateersman series, set during the Napoleonic Wars, combines naval action with mystery plots. The "privateersman" is Harry Ludlow, who with his brother James likes to fight on the deck of his ship but who, from time-to-time, gets impressed into the regular Royal Navy. The series was not available in the United States until it was reprinted by McBooks Press, of Ithaca, New York. David Donachie is a Scot by birth who lives in Deal, on the coast of the English Channel. He also writes the Markham of the Marines series as Tom Connery (q.v.). These swashbuckling tales will appeal to fans of C. S. Forester (q.v.) and Patrick O'Brian (q.v.).

1. *Devil's Own Luck, The* (McBooks, 2001) Brothers Harry and James Ludlow are aboard the *Magnanime*, a gunship under the control of Oliver Carter. When the first lieutenant is found dead, Carter assumes James to be the killer. Originally published in the United Kingdom in 1991.
2. *Dying Trade, The* (McBooks, 2001) Harry and James find themselves in Genoa, where Harry is commissioned to investigate a British officer's death. Originally published in the United Kingdom in 1993.
3. *Hanging Matter, A* (McBooks, 2002) Harry and James return home after a profitable tour only to find themselves enmeshed in a fierce contest between smugglers in the English Channel. Originally published in the United Kingdom in 1994.
4. *Element of Chance, An* (McBooks, 2002) Captain Toner illegally impresses Harry's crew to work on his own frigate. Determined to retrieve his crew, Harry pursues Toner to the West Indies. Originally published in the United Kingdom in 1995.
5. *Scent of Betrayal, The* (McBooks, 2003) This adventure takes place mostly in the New World: New Orleans, the Mississippi River, and the American hinterland. Originally published in the United Kingdom in 1996.
6. *Game of Bones, A* (McBooks, 2003) Harry Ludlow encounters a mystery vessel, and His Majesty's Navy has reached the point of mutiny. Originally published in the United Kingdom in 1997.

II. The Nelson and Emma trilogy relates the intertwined lives of Horatio Nelson, England's greatest hero, and his mistress, Lady Emma Hamilton. This trilogy is a combination of romance tale and naval-action saga.

1. *On a Making Tide* (McBooks, 2003) This volume traces Nelson's career from 12-year-old midshipman to the Battle of the Nile in 1798, while Emma begins her climb from London street urchin to wealth and notoriety. Originally published in the United Kingdom in 2001.
2. *Breaking the Line* (McBooks, 2004) Horatio and Emma continue their triumphant careers, while finding that acceptance by English society eludes them. Originally published in the United Kingdom in 2001.
3. *Tested by Fate* (McBooks, 2004) Emma and Nelson meet in Naples and initiate the affair that scandalized European society.

III. Donachie has embarked on another series of naval history novels set in the Napoleonic Wars. Young Englishman John Pearce, who begins his "career" as an impressed seaman in 1793, eventually rises to the rank of post captain. Only three novels in the series, which is scheduled to reach 12 volumes, have been published so far.

1. *By the Mast Divided* (Allison & Busby [UK], 2004) Young hothead John Pearce, on the run from authorities, is press-ganged from the Pelican Tavern onto HMS *Brilliant*, commanded by harsh Captain Barclay. Not published in the United States.
2. *Shot Rolling Ship, A* (Allison & Busby [UK], 2005) Pressed into the Royal Navy for the second time in a month, John Pearce and his loyal gun crew, the Pelicans, find themselves aboard HMS *Brazen*. Not published in the United States.
3. *Awkward Commission, An* (Allison & Busby [UK], 2006) Pearce has been appointed 8th lieutenant on HMS *Victory*, flagship of Admiral Lord Hood. The Pelicans are serving under a flogging captain.

Donaldson, D. J.

Forensic pathologist D. J. Donaldson uses a New Orleans setting for his mystery series featuring the team of Chief Medical Examiner Andy Broussard and his assistant, criminal psychologist Kit Franklyn. Broussard is a likable crotchety character, and there is plenty of Louisiana ambience and lore in this series of rather gothic mysteries.

1. *Cajun Nights* (St. Martin's, 1988) A series of gruesome murder-suicides seems to have been inspired by a voodoo curse.
2. *Blood on the Bayou* (St. Martin's, 1991) A garden fork is one of the lethal instruments used by a serial killer in the French Quarter.
3. *No Mardi Gras for the Dead* (St. Martin's, 1992) Kit Franklyn discovers a quarter-century-old corpse in the garden of her new home.
4. *New Orleans Requiem* (St. Martin's, 1994) A series of macabre slayings bedevils Broussard and Franklyn during a convention of forensic scientists in New Orleans.
5. *Louisiana Fever* (St. Martin's, 1996) A smuggler of rare birds and a deadly virus carried by one of the smuggled birds are brought to light when the smuggler's partner, victim of the virus, makes contact with Kit Franklyn.
6. *Sleeping with the Crawfish* (St. Martin's, 1997) A corpse in Andy's morgue seems to be an apparent prison escapee. Trouble is, the prison claims the convict is alive and residing in his cell—for the moment, that is.

Donaldson, Stephen R.

I. Fantasy readers not satiated by J. R. R. Tolkien (q.v.) have something additional to feed on with the Chronicles of Thomas Covenant the Unbeliever. This epic fantasy for adults stars Thomas Covenant, who is lonely and shunned in real life because of his leprosy. In the magical world of his dreamlike adventures, however, he is regarded as the reincarnated legendary hero Berek Halfhand, and his white-gold wedding ring is a talisman of great power. Lord Foul the Despiser is the archvillain who threatens the Land from its Northern Climbs to the Garroting Deep. Saltheart Foamfollwer, Hile Troy, Caeroil Wildwood, and Dr. Linden Avery are some of the good guys. Donaldson broke off the chronicles after two trilogies but, more than 20 years later, he has embarked upon a new quartet, called the Last Chronicles of Thomas Covenant.

1. *Lord Foul's Bane* (Holt, 1977) Thomas Covenant travels to Revelstone and leads the lords to Mount Thunder in pursuit of the magic Staff of Drool, the evil cavewight.
2. *Illearth War, The* (Holt, 1977) After a month in real life, but 40 years in the Land, Thomas returns to find that his daughter Elena is now the high lord.
3. *Power That Preserves, The* (Holt, 1977) Returned again to the land, Thomas makes his tortuous way to Foul's Creche and meets Lord Foul in final combat.
4. *Wounded Land, The* (Ballantine, 1980) This book begins the Second Chronicles of Thomas Covenant, which picks up 10 years after number 3. Thomas returns to the land, this time accompanied by a young woman doctor, Linden Avery.
5. *One Tree, The* (Ballantine, 1982) Thomas and Dr. Avery search for the One Tree, with which they must fashion a new staff of life to thwart Lord Foul and Sunbane.
6. *White Gold Wielder* (Ballantine, 1983) Thomas and Linden return to the Land in a last desperate attempt to heal its wounds in this climactic volume of the second trilogy.
7. *Runes of Earth, The* (Putnam, 2004) In the first installment of the Last Chronicles of Thomas Covenant, Covenant's son Roger appears many years after his father's death and seeks to claim his inheritance. Dr. Linden Avery, the steward of the Land, suspects that Lord Foul is scheming again.
8. *Fatal Revenant* (Putnam, 2007) Linden Avery can see both Thomas Covenant and her son, Jeremiah, riding ahead of a wave of pursuers—even though Thomas is dead and Jeremiah has been captured by Lord Foul.

II. Donaldson followed his Covenant series with a two-book sequence, Mordant's Need, another epic in which someone from "our world" is brought to a fantasy world to save it. The land of Mordant, located in a sort of Arthurian alternative universe, is threatened by enemies from within and without.

1. *Mirror of Dreams, The* (Ballantine, 1986) Poor little rich girl Terisa Morgan is lured to Mordant by the Congery of Imagers.
2. *Man Rides Through, A* (Ballantine, 1987) Lady Terisa and bumbling apprentice Geraden are revealed to possess extraordinary magical powers as monsters, evil wizards, and hostile armies threaten Mordant.

III. The Gap series is more space opera than fantasy. Continuing characters include Morn Hyland, security cop for the United Mine Company; Nick Succorso and Angus Thermopyle, space pirates and rivals for Morn's heart and body; and the Amnion, a nasty alien culture. Full of passion, angst, sadism, betrayal, convoluted plot twists, and lots of action.

1. *Real Story, The: The Gap into Conflict* (Bantam, 1991) Good bad guy Nick Succorso rescues Morn Hyland from the clutches of evil bad guy Angus Thermopyle.
2. *Forbidden Knowledge: The Gap into Vision* (Bantam, 1991) Morn and Nick form an uneasy and deceitful alliance as they try to deal with the sinister Amnion.
3. *Dark and Hungry God Arises, A: The Gap into Power* (Bantam, 1992) While Morn, Nick, and Angus play their passionate mind games, unscrupulous bureaucrats use them as pawns against the Amnion.
4. *Chaos and Order: The Gap into Madness* (Bantam, 1994) Now a cyborg pursued by police, bounty hunters, and the Amnion, Angus steers his ship toward a hidden laboratory in the asteroid belt.
5. *This Day All Gods Die: The Gap into Ruin* (Bantam, 1996) The struggles between the CEO of United Mining Companies and the director of its police, between the Amnion and the human race, and between Morn Hyland and her various tormentors come to a climax.

IV. Donaldson, writing as "Reed Stephens," published three paperback original novels about PI partners "Brew" Axbrewder and Ginny Fistoulari, and followed with a fourth written under his own name. Brew and Ginny have a tumultuous relationship as business and romantic partners. Brew has an alcohol problem exacerbated by his accidental shooting of his policeman brother, is being pursued by a mysterious villain called El Señor, and is a damaged human being on the whole, while Ginny has her own crosses to bear including the loss of a hand and her relationship with the problematic Brew. Somehow they have managed to survive various beatings and shootings through four novels so far. Orion (UK) has published an omnibus volume containing numbers 1 through 3: *The Reed Stephens Novels* (2001).

1. *Man Who Killed His Brother, The* (Ballantine, 1980) Alcoholic ex-private investigator Brew Axbrewder dries out enough to help former partner and romantic interest Ginny Fistoulari search for his missing niece Alathea. Reprinted in a slightly revised version by Forge (2002).
2. *Man Who Risked His Partner, The* (Ballantine, 1984) Ginny and Brew are living together uneasily after Ginny's loss of a hand. Ginny takes a security job with millionaire Reg Haskell that leads to plenty of trouble. Reprinted in revised form by Forge (2003).
3. *Man Who Tried to Get Away, The* (Ballantine, 1990) Brew and Ginny are hired for "security" at a remote mountain camp that becomes completely isolated in short order.
4. *Man Who Fought Alone, The* (Forge, 2001) Ginny finds work in another city with old friend Marshal Viviter, while Brew works security for a martial arts tournament.

Donati, Sara

PSEUDONYM OF Rosina Lippi-Green

The Bonner Family Saga starts in the late 18th century in upstate New York when English-born Elizabeth Middleton encounters Nathaniel Bonner, a Scotsman raised by the Mohawks. Elizabeth and Nathaniel marry, bear two children (the twins, Lily and Daniel), and endure various vicissitudes. The first five novels carry them as far as the War of 1812. This is readable historical romance by Donati, who has a PhD in linguistics and has published scholarly books on linguistics under her real name.

1. *Into the Wilderness* (Bantam, 2002) Elizabeth Middleton, a 29-year-old English spinster, arrives in the upstate New York town

of Paradise in the late 18th century and falls for rugged Nathaniel Middleton, a Scotsman raised by Mohawks. Claire Fraser, Diana Gabaldon's (q.v.) heroine, puts in a cameo appearance.
2. *Dawn on a Distant Shore* (Bantam, 2000) Elizabeth Bonner, fresh from childbirth, learns that her husband, Nathaniel, and his father are imprisoned in Montreal and embarks on a voyage to save them.
3. *Lake in the Clouds* (Bantam, 2002) In 1802 the Bonner family struggles to survive on a farmstead high up on a mountain in upstate New York.
4. *Fire along the Sky* (Bantam, 2004) Elizabeth and Nathaniel Bonner's adult children take center stage in action that takes place during the War of 1812.
5. *Queen of Swords* (Bantam, 2007) Hannah, her half brother Luke, and his wife, Jennet, set out to find and reclaim Luke and Jennet's son in New Orleans on the brink of the last battle of the War of 1812.

Donleavy, J(ames) P(atrick)

Darcy Dancer, a young, educated member of the Irish landed gentry, is featured in a trilogy (perhaps to be a quartet) of bawdy, ribald, and funny, yet tragic, novels that take the reader on a riotous, drunken, sexy spree through an Ireland full of zany characters. *Destinies of Darcy Dancer, Gentleman* is a coming-of-age novel, while the two sequels find Darcy dealing, not too successfully, with his crumbling Irish estate. Darcy's love affairs, zestfully described, usually end in tragedy. Darcy wins many battles along the way, but always loses the war. Although the Darcy Dancer series is the favorite of many of J. P. Donleavy's readers, including his Irish neighbors, Donleavy is best known for *The Ginger Man* (McDowell, 1958; originally published by Olympia Press in Paris, 1955), which became a big success partly because of its alleged obscenity and is regarded as a classic by many critics. Donleavy, a native New Yorker, returned to his parents' Ireland and eventually became an Irish citizen.

1. *Destinies of Darcy Dancer, Gentleman, The* (Delacorte, 1977) Darcy Dancer, a young member of the impoverished landed gentry of Ireland, learns about life and love through a series of more-or-less qualified tutors.
2. *Leila* (Delacorte, 1983) Subtitle: *Further in the Destinies of Darcy Dancer, Gentleman*. Darcy returns to his family's crumbling country estate, Andromeda Park, and falls in love with a serving-maid named Leila.
3. *That Darcy, That Dancer, That Gentleman* (Viking, 1990) Darcy fights a losing battle against the dilapidation of Andromeda Park, with little help from his feckless staff.

Donnelly, Deborah

Prospective wedding-planners should think twice about consulting Made in Heaven Wedding Designs of Seattle, Washington. Its founder, Carnegie Kincaid, has a way of stumbling onto murder and other mayhem. The bouncy and indefatigable Carnegie (named after Andrew Carnegie, the patron saint of libraries) always bumbles into a solution, partly with the help of characters such as Boris the Mad Russian Florist, master cake creator Juice, and on-again, off-again boyfriend Aaron Gold, in this bouncy, bubbly, madcap series of mysteries.

1. *Veiled Threats* (Dell, 2002) Made in Heaven Wedding Designs is about to receive a shot in the arm: heiress Nickie Parry is marrying

concert pianist Ray Ishigura in the Seattle season's biggest high-society wedding.

2. *Died to Match* (Dell, 2002) Struggling to keep her houseboat-based business afloat, Carnegie accepts the invitation to plan the wedding and Halloween engagement party of Microsoft millionaire Elizabeth Lamott.

3. *May the Best Man Die* (Dell, 2003) Everything is going wrong: Carnegie has been exiled from her houseboat, her business partner leaves, her best friend stops speaking to her, she is humiliated on live TV by a French business rival, and her boyfriend tells her he is married. Then the best man in her latest wedding turns up dead.

4. *Death Takes a Honeymoon* (Dell, 2005) Carnegie, brought back home to Sun Valley, Idaho, to investigate the death of smoke-jumper Brian, her least favorite cousin, agrees to take part in the nuptials of her glamorous friend Tracy, now a Hollywood star, who is marrying Carnegie's old heartthrob Jack "the Knack" Packard.

5. *You May Now Kill the Bride* (Dell, 2006) The sexy caretaker employed by Owen Winter, Carnegie's soon-to-be father-in-law, is knifed in the back, a crime for which there are many possible suspects.

6. *Bride and Doom* (Dell, 2006) Carnegie is planning her wedding with Aaron Gold, but someone commits a murder, and Boris the Mad Russian Florist is charged with the crime.

Doolittle, Jerome

Tom Bethany, Boston wrestler and private investigator, is a fairly typical hard-boiled private eye, tough but compassionate, occasionally violent, and suspicious of the rich and powerful. His married lover, Hope Edwards, head of the Washington, DC, branch of the American Civil Liberties Union, keeps Tom on the politically correct (environmentally conscious, pro-choice, etc.) side of some rather bloody cases.

1. *Body Scissors* (Pocket, 1990) Tom's background investigation of J. Alden Kellicott, potential nominee for secretary of state, uncovers some nasty secrets.

2. *Strangle Hold* (Pocket, 1991) Morty Limbach's insurance company claims that he committed suicide, and therefore his large bequest to the ACLU is null and void.

3. *Bear Hug* (Pocket, 1992) Bethany goes after savings and loan looters for four Boston retirees who lost their money in a failed Texas bank.

4. *Head Lock* (Pocket, 1993) Hope Edwards is having an abortion at a Virginia clinic when the facility is attacked by right-to-lifers led by televangelist Howard Orrin.

5. *Half Nelson* (Pocket, 1994) Tom is sent off on tour as a bodyguard for Robert Rackleff, environmental guru, who has received death threats.

6. *Kill Story* (Pocket, 1995) Tom is part of a scheme to reacquire the Cambridge (Massachusetts) *Daily Banner*, which has been bought up by wealthy Thurman Boucher, aka "the Cobra."

Dorsey, Tim

"Lovable homicidal maniac" Serge A. Storms is the main continuing character in a series of madcap capers and black comedy set in Florida. Starting with *Florida Roadkill*, Tim Dorsey's novels depict crime sprees, political shenanigans, a lot of Florida folklore, and a host of sleazy and demented characters in suspenseful but hilarious plots that have a little something of Carl Hiaasen (q.v.), Elmore Leonard (q.v.), and Dave Barry. Dorsey was a newspaper man in Alabama and Tampa, Florida, before becoming a full-time writer.

1. *Florida Roadkill* (Morrow, 1999) Sean Breen and David Klein's trips to the Florida Keys for fishing and to Miami for the World Series get the wrong kind of attention when $5 million is hidden in their car. Con men Serge Storms and his sidekick, Coleman, will stop at nothing to get the money.

2. *Hammerhead Ranch Motel* (Morrow, 2000) Serge Storms has traced the car with the hidden $5 million (see number 1) to the Hammerhead Ranch Motel, a dilapidated dump in Tampa.

3. *Orange Crush* (Morrow, 2001) Senseless violence on the campaign trail, courtesy of Serge Storms, is unleashed when Marlon Conrad, Republican candidate for governor of Florida, takes a whirlwind election tour in a bright-orange camper van.

4. *Triggerfish Twist* (Morrow, 2002) After mild-mannered family man Jim Davenport moves into his dream home in a seemingly idyllic Florida neighborhood, he accidentally kills a notorious bank robber and loses his job, and then has the misfortune of having Serge Storms appoint himself as his friend and protector.

5. *Stingray Shuffle, The* (Morrow, 2003) Serge develops an "interest" in trains and generously shares his interest with his fellow Amtrak passengers. He also takes on the Russian Mob, the Jamaican Mob, the cocaine cartels, and a bunch of frat boys on a wild journey.

6. *Cadillac Beach* (Morrow, 2004) Serge, having escaped from Florida's state psychiatric hospital at Chattahoochee, is on his way to Miami and hot on the trail of the legendary diamonds still missing after Murph the Surf's 1964 heist.

7. *Torpedo Juice* (Morrow, 2005) Serge, trying to reinvent himself on the Florida Keys, gets married, takes up conch blowing, jogging on the Seven-Mile Bridge, and other relatively harmless activities, but some malicious lunatics are hot on his trail.

8. *Big Bamboo, The* (Morrow, 2006) Serge has resurrected his obsession with movies, particularly those showcasing his beloved Florida. Then he receives a cryptic message from his grandfather, Sergio, telling him to go to Los Angeles to uncover a mysterious secret from the distant past.

9. *Hurricane Punch* (Morrow, 2007) Serge continues to roar across Florida in a stolen Hummer with his usually drunk or stoned friend, Coleman, following one hurricane after another, evading his nemesis, Agent Mahoney.

10. *Atomic Lobster* (Morrow, 2008) Serge and Coleman, bored and broke, decide on a Florida road trip. Along the way they run into the likes of killer Tex McGraw, empty-nesters Jim and Martha Davenport, the "G-Unit," several drug dealers, two Davis Islands residents, Johnny Vegas, and several government agencies.

Dos Passos, John

U.S.A. is a trilogy of novels chronicling American life from 1900 to the eve of the Great Depression. The collage technique that Dos Passos perfected in these books gives the work its epic quality. Sprinkled throughout the narrative are "Newsreel" sections composed of news clips, headlines, song lyrics, and other documentary material; "Camera Eye" sections containing the interior monologues of various unidentified people; and biographical sections detailing the lives of the famous. A one-volume edition was published by Harcourt (1937). *U.S.A.* is currently available in the Library of America series (1997).

1. *42nd Parallel, The* (Harper, 1930) The stories of fictional characters Mac, Janey, J. Ward Moorhouse, Eleanor Stoddard, and Charley Anderson from the beginning of the century to World War I are interspersed with short bios of historical figures such as William Jennings Bryan, Eugene Debs, and Luther Burbank.

2. *1919* (Harcourt, 1932) World I and its immediate aftermath are delineated through the fictional lives of Joe Williams, Richard

Ellsworth Savage, Eveline Hutchins, "Daughter," and Ben Compton along with sketches of such worthies as Woodrow Wilson, Joe Hill, and Al Smith.

3. *Big Money, The* **(Harcourt, 1936)** The "boom" of the Twenties and its collapse are viewed with a jaundiced eye as exemplified by the lives of repeat characters Charley Anderson and Richard Ellsworth Savage, new characters Margo Dowling and Mary French, and historical characters William Randolph Hearst, Samuel Insull, Isadora Duncan, and Rudolph Valentino.

Doss, James D(aniel)

Charlie Moon, full-time rancher and part-time police detective on a Ute Indian reservation in Colorado, is the hero of a series of mysteries that combine police procedural elements with "Indian spirituality." Charlie's aunt, Daisy Perika, is a Native American shaman who can call up beings from the unseen world such as the "pitukupf," invisible dwarf spirit-helpers. Scott Parris, police chief of Granite City, Colorado, Charlie's white friend, is actually more attuned to aunt Daisy's spiritualism than is Charlie. Readers who prefer their Native American detectives on the realistic side (e.g., Tony Hillerman's [q.v.] Leaphorn and Chee) may be somewhat turned off by the spiritual elements of the Charlie Moon series, but many are fascinated by the evocations of Native American lore and Western settings. James D. Doss was a successful electrical engineer before he published his first mystery novel at the age of 55.

1. *Shaman Sings, The* **(St. Martin's, 1994)** Scott Parris, a big-city police officer who has become a small-town Colorado police chief, works with Ute shaman Daisy Perika in investigating the murder of a graduate student doing research in superconductivity.
2. *Shaman Laughs, The* **(St. Martin's, 1995)** Charlie Moon joins his aunt Daisy and Scott Parris in investigating the mutilation murders of sheep and prize bulls and the murder and dismemberment of a local insurance agent.
3. *Shaman's Bones, The* **(Morrow, 1997)** Charlie and Scott are trying to locate Provo Frank, Daisy's nephew, who is on the run after passing a bad check, assaulting a cop, and stealing sacred Ute relics.
4. *Shaman's Game, The* **(Morrow, 1998)** The Ute's Sun Dance is a physically punishing ordeal. But when three people die during two dances, Charlie Moon is inclined to think that the deaths were not due to natural causes. Daisy Perika thinks that a witch is at work.
5. *Night Visitor, The* **(Morrow, 1999)** Con man Horace Flye has latched onto a job with a team of paleontologists digging up relics from a possible 31,000-year-old hunting site. Then Horace disappears, leaving behind his bratty six-year-old daughter, Butter Flye.
6. *Grandmother Spider* **(Morrow, 2001)** Three men have been attacked by what seems to be either a giant spider or an alien space vehicle.
7. *White Shell Woman* **(Morrow, 2002)** The Twin War Gods, two sandstone monoliths in southern Colorado traditionally erected by the sons of the moon goddess White Shell Woman, have a rather sinister history. Then the corpse of a young Native American woman is unearthed at an archaeological dig.
8. *Dead Soul* **(St. Martin's, 2003)** Charlie looks into the death of tribesman Billy Smoke, murdered during an assault that left his employer, Senator Patch Davidson, permanently crippled.
9. *Witch's Tongue, The* **(St. Martin's, 2004)** Are a museum robbery, a fleeing Apache who attacks a police officer, and a Ute who abandons his abused wife and disappears into Spirit Canyon all connected?

10. *Shadow Man* **(St. Martin's, 2005)** Orthodontist Manfred Wilhelm Blinkoe insists that an assassin was aiming at him instead of the actual murder victim, a local attorney.
11. *Stone Butterfly* **(St. Martin's, 2006)** Aunt Daisy has an eerie dream about a girl with blood dripping from her hands, a dream that proves to be prophetic when a real murder occurs.
12. *Three Sisters* **(St. Martin's, 2007)** Colorado's most famous TV psychic, Cassandra Spencer, describes a truck-stop murder as it takes place but fails to predict the death of her newlywed eldest sister, Astrid, apparently mauled by a wild animal.

Douglas, Carole Nelson

I.   Former St. Paul, Minnesota, journalist Douglas is a versatile genre writer: historical romance, modern romance, fantasy, science fiction, mysteries. She hit real pay dirt with the Midnight Louie mystery series, which features a cat detective. Louie, self-described "coolest cat" in Las Vegas, relates the mysteries that he and "doting roommate and freelance public relations specialist" Temple Barr solve. Temple is a modern, liberated female who has on-again, off-again affairs with magician Max Kinsella and former priest turned radio pop-psychologist Matt Devine. Louie starts off as an unregenerate macho tomcat but eventually submits to a vasectomy to improve his image as a spokesperson for a family oriented cat-food company. Two prequels, containing two stories each, describing the fictional Crystal Phoenix Hotel in Las Vegas and featuring Midnight Louis, were published as *Crystal Days* and *Crystal Nights* by Bantam in 1990. These stories were reprinted in a four-volume limited edition by Four Star in 1999 and 2000: *The Cat and the King of Clubs*; *The Cat and the Queen of Hearts*; *The Cat and the Jill of Diamonds*; *The Cat and the Jack of Spades*. In addition, several Midnight Louis stories have appeared in anthologies edited by Douglas and other compilers (e.g., *Midnight Louie's Pet Detectives*, Forge, 1998).

1. *Catnap* **(Tor, 1992)** A publisher has been murdered at the American Booksellers Association convention in Las Vegas.
2. *Pussyfoot* **(Tor, 1993)** The publicist for a stripper competition suffers a heart attack after one of the contestants is found hanged by a G-string in a dressing room.
3. *Cat on a Blue Monday* **(Forge, 1994)** A psychic cat warns Louie that a group of cats is in danger but doesn't specify whether they are show cats or the strays living with elderly Blandina Tyler.
4. *Cat in a Crimson Haze* **(Forge, 1995)** Someone is taking the ribbing at the annual Gridiron Roast at the Crystal Phoenix Hotel with deadly seriousness.
5. *Cat in a Diamond Dazzle* **(Forge, 1996)** Midnight Louie is enamoured of Divine Yvette, a beautiful Siamese, but finds time to solve a murder at the G.R.O.W.L. (Great Readers of Wonderful Literature) convention of romance writers. Temple Barr is involved in the dress-rehearsal murder of one of the male models at the convention's Incredible Hunks pageant.
6. *Cat with an Emerald Eye* **(Forge, 1996)** Temple Barr reluctantly agrees to participate in a séance at the Hell-o-Ween Haunted Homestead designed to raise the spirit of Harry Houdini. Temple sees nothing, but Midnight Louie observes Elvis, Mae West, and Amelia Earhart.
7. *Cat in a Flamingo Fedora* **(Forge, 1997)** Conceptual artist Domingo wants to cover Las Vegas with 900,000 plastic flamingos and has hired Temple Barr to help persuade casino operators of his vision. Midnight Louie is appearing in a cat-food commercial with the Divine Yvette. Darren Cooke, movie star and compulsive ladies man, dies and leaves behind a record of his conquests, which allegedly include Temple.

8. *Cat in a Golden Garland* (**Forge, 1997**) The newly vasectomized Midnight Louie and Temple Barr arrive in Manhattan at Christmastime for his audition for the job of feline spokesperson for the Alpetco cat food account.

9. *Cat on a Hyacinth Hunt* (**Forge, 1998**) Cliff Effinger comes to a sticky end, strapped to the prow of a ship in the "Egyptian Barge Battle" at the Oasis Hotel. Midnight Louie investigates female magician Shangri-La and her Siamese Hyacinth.

10. *Cat in an Indigo Mood* (**Forge, 1999**) Homicide detective and sometime singer Carmen Molina finds a dead woman next to her. Midnight Louie and his daughter Louise are drawn into a cat homicide that may be connected with Carmen's case.

11. *Cat in a Jeweled Jumpsuit* (**Forge, 1999**) The Kingdome, an Elvis-inspired mega-shrine, is opening in Las Vegas, and Elvis sightings abound, including a telephone call from the King to Matt Devine, Temple Barr's radio-shrink friend.

12. *Cat in a Kiwi Con* (**Forge, 2000**) Homicide detective Carmen Molina asks Matt Devine to take her daughter to the TitaniCon, a science-fiction convention. Of course, corpses turn up, including that of the star of *Khatlord*, a popular SF TV show.

13. *Cat in a Leopard Spot* (**Forge, 2001**) Louie is sent to investigate Rancho Exotica, a desert resort near Las Vegas that caters to big-game hunter wannabes by providing captive animals to be slaughtered as trophies. When Rancho Exotica's owner is impaled on a trophy horn, a performing leopard is the chief suspect.

14. *Cat in a Midnight Choir* (**Forge, 2002**) The Stripper Killer is still at large in Las Vegas, and Temple Barr's magician boyfriend, Max, is one of the suspects. Everyone gets involved, including Carmen Molina, the Synth cult's Matt Devine, Matt's stalker, Kitty the Cutter, and, of course, Midnight Louis.

15. *Cat in a Neon Nightmare* (**Forge, 2003**) Kitty "the Cutter" O'Connor is still stalking the still-celibate ex-priest Matt Devine. But did she kill Vassar, the high-class call girl whom Devine had chosen to end his virgin state, or was the killer "Mystifying Max" Kinsella? And what part did the Synth, an ancient magician's association, have in all this?

16. *Cat in an Orange Twist* (**Forge, 2004**) The grand opening of Maylords, a trendy furniture store featuring designer Amelia Wong, is spoiled by a terrorist-style killing.

17. *Cat in a Hot Pink Pursuit* (**Forge, 2005**) Temple Barr goes undercover as 19-year-old Xoe Chloe Ozone on a reality TV show, *Teen Idol*, to help protect homicide detective C. R. Molina's 13-year-old daughter, Mariah, from a stalker.

18. *Cat in a Quicksilver Caper* (**Forge, 2006**) Temple Barr is still dithering between two lovers, former magician Matt Kinsella and radio shrink Matt Devine, while helping the New Millennium Hotel publicize a White Russian art exhibition and aerial magic show featuring the Cloaked Conjurer.

19. *Cat in a Red Hot Rage* (**Forge, 2007**) Pink Lady Oleta Lark is strangled with a purple scarf that Electra Lark, Temple's friend and landlady, helped tie at the Red Hat Sisterhood.

II. Irene Adler, the only woman who ever outwitted Sherlock Holmes (see Conan Doyle's story "A Scandal in Bohemia"), deserves her own series. Victorian diva and part-time sleuth Irene gets to match wits with Holmes again as Oscar Wilde, Sarah Bernhardt, Jack the Ripper, and other historical characters put in appearances.

1. *Good Night, Mr. Holmes* (**Tor, 1990**) Irene Adler supports herself by private detection until she becomes an opera star and gets romantically entangled with the king of Bohemia.

2. *Good Morning, Irene* (**Tor, 1991**) Newly married Irene is happily reading her own obituaries in Paris when a corpse washes up from the Seine. Variant title: *The Adventuress*.

3. *Irene at Large* (**Tor, 1992**) A young British officer tells Irene a tale about spying, the Afghanistan Campaign, and the danger facing a military surgeon named Watson. Variant title: *A Soul of Steel*.

4. *Irene's Last Waltz* (**Tor, 1994**) The queen of Bohemia implores Irene to find out why the king is ignoring her. Variant title: *Another Scandal in Bohemia*.

5. *Chapel Noir* (**Forge, 2001**) Irene is asked to investigate the murder of a pair of prostitutes in a Parisian brothel: possible victims of Jack the Ripper?

6. *Castle Rouge* (**Forge, 2002**) Jack the Ripper has expanded his operations to the Continent. Irene Adler and Sherlock Holmes are on the case. Bram Stoker, the author of *Dracula*, has a bit part.

7. *Femme Fatale* (**Forge, 2003**) A letter from Nellie Bly, her associate in the search for Jack the Ripper, brings Irene and companion Nell Huxleigh to New York City in 1889 to search for a serial killer who is connected to her past.

8. *Spider Dance* (**Forge, 2004**) Irene Adler discovers that a tomb contains the remains of notorious performer Lola Montez.

III. The Sword and Circlet series is fantasy with romance elements or, perhaps, romance with fantasy elements. Irissa, last Torloc sorceress, her lover, Kendric, and a sorceress reincarnated as a white cat band together to fight the evil magician Geronfrey. Number 3 serves as the final volume of the first trilogy and the first volume of the second trilogy.

1. *Six of Swords* (**Ballantine, 1982**) Uneasy allies Irissa and Kendric trek through their decaying worlds.

2. *Exiles of the Rynth* (**Ballantine, 1984**) Kendric and Irissa find themselves exiled in the Rynth.

3. *Keepers of Edanvant* (**Tor, 1987**) The united couple returns to Edanvant, Torloc homeworld, to prevent a war between the sexes.

4. *Heir of Rengarth* (**Tor, 1988**) The evil usurper Geronfrey creates an artificial Irissa, then kidnaps Kendric.

5. *Seven of Swords* (**St. Martin's, 1989**) Irissa and Kendric, now the parents of teenagers, square off against Geronfrey one more time. Variant title: *Seventh Sword*.

IV. In the Taliswoman series, Minnesota newspaper reporter Alison Carver is transported to the polluted world of Veil. This is intricate fantasy with an ecological message. Fans have been waiting 16 years for the third volume.

1. *Cup of Clay* (**Tor, 1991**) Alison Carver suddenly finds herself in the devastated world of Veil.

2. *Seed upon the Wind* (**Tor, 1992**) Returning to Veil, Alison finds it under siege by the mysterious Cruxmasters.

V. Douglas has also written a pair of science-fiction novels about a psychiatrist who becomes involved with a young woman of alien provenance and with ESP powers.

1. *Probe* (**Tor, 1985**) Jane Doe, a young woman with psychic powers, becomes romantically involved with Kevin Blake, the psychiatrist who is treating her.

2. *Counterprobe* (**Tor, 1988**) Dr. Blake and his alien lover are pursued by the US government and the demonic Dr. Nordstrom.

Douglas, Lloyd C(assel)

Medical melodrama, romance, and a secret formula for success in life are the elements that made *Magnificent Obsession* a best seller during the Depression. It was filmed twice: the 1935 version starred Robert Taylor and Irene Dunne; the 1954 remake featured Rock Hudson and Jane Wyman. In 1939 Douglas followed his success with a second book purporting to be the secret journal that was discovered in *Magnificent Obsession*. Douglas, who spent 30 years as a Lutheran and then Congregational minister before he retired to become a full-time writer, also wrote a pair of novels revolving around Jesus Christ that became best sellers and hit movies—*The Robe* (Houghton Mifflin, 1942) and *The Big Fisherman* (Houghton Mifflin, 1948)—and a lesser-known pair of novels featuring the polio-stricken Dean Harcourt, who is a beneficent influence in a midwestern town: *Green Light* (Houghton Mifflin, 1935) and *Invitation to Live* (Houghton Mifflin, 1940).

1. *Doctor Hudson's Secret Journal* **(Houghton Mifflin, 1939)** The famous brain specialist's inspiring journal, which figured so prominently in *Magnificent Obsession*. Though written second, this is an "overture" to the original volume.
2. *Magnificent Obsession* **(Willet, Clark & Colby, 1929)** The secret of the famous Dr. Hudson's success inspires young Bobby Merrick and aids in the discovery that enables him to save the life of the woman he loves.

Douglass, Sara

PSEUDONYM OF Sarah Warneke

I. Since she was first published in 1995, Sara Douglass has become Australia's leading fantasy writer, one of its top novelists, and a worldwide best seller. By 2006 all of her fiction books had become available in the United States. What is called the Wayfarer Redemption series in the United States is actually two trilogies: the Axis trilogy (numbers 1–3) and the Wayfarer Redemption trilogy (numbers 4–6). So far the trilogies have been connected only by their location in the fantasy world of Tencendor, but Douglass has started a new series, Darkglass Mountain, which will tie together the two trilogies and two stand-alone novels, *Threshold* (Tor, 2004) and *Beyond the Hanging Wall* (Tor, 2003). Numbers 1, 2, and 3 feature the warrior-wizard Axis, who, after a series of adventures, becomes the Starman of the Prophecy of the Destroyer. Numbers 4 through 6 are about Drago, the StarSon, who is pitted against the Timekeeper Demons who have destroyed the Star Gate and the magic of the Stardance and are threatening the very existence of Tencendor. This is epic fantasy to be compared with that of Terry Goodkind (q.v.) and Robert Jordan (q.v.).

1. *Battleaxe* **(Tor, 2001)** The warrior Axis discovers that he was created to fulfill the Prophecy of the Destroyer, which calls him to assume his role as the StarMan, who will save his world against the evil machinations of his monstrous half brother Gorgrael. Originally published in Australia in 1995.
2. *Enchanter* **(Tor, 2001)** Axis travels to Talon Spike to recover his Icarri heritage and to learn the ways of a wizard before his confrontation with Gorgrael. Originally published in Australia in 1996.
3. *StarMan* **(Tor, 2002)** The warrior-wizard Axis assumes his role as the StarMan of the Prophecy of the Destroyer, while his wife, the woman warrior Azhure, discovers her own powers as an enchantress. Originally published in Australia in 1996.

4. *Sinner* **(Tor, 2005)** Caelum, Supreme Ruler of Tencendor, is pitted against the strange powers threatening to come through the Star Gate. Originally published in Australia in 1997.
5. *Pilgrim* **(Tor, 1998)** The Star Gate is destroyed, the Star Dance is dead, and the TimeKeeper Demons are laying waste to Tencendor. Originally published in Australia in 1998.
6. *Crusader* **(Tor, 2006)** Can Drago, the StarSon, resurrect the world of Tencendor and defeat Qeteb and the TimeKeeper Demons? Originally published in Australia in 1999.
7. *Serpent Bride, The* **(Eos, 2007)** Subtitle: *Darkglass Mountain, Book 1.* Lady Ishbel Brunelle, an archpriestess of the Order of the Coil, is ordered by the Great Serpent to marry Maximilian Persimius, king of the coastal kingdom of Escator.

II. Douglass, who has a PhD in early modern history, has created a couple of alternative history fantasy series. The Crucible trilogy is set in an alternative 14th century after the Black Death of 1348 in which Thomas Neville, a warrior-priest and former monk, is pitted against the evil shape-shifters who have run amok "since the last opening of the Cleft."

1. *Nameless Day, The* **(Tor, 2004)** Thirty years after the plague that put an end to a biannual sacred ritual that sent the demons that walked the Earth back to their home in hell, the monk Thomas Neville takes up the burden of ridding the world of its teeming evils. Originally published in Australia in 2000.
2. *Wounded Hawk, The* **(Tor, 2001)** Warrior-priest Thomas Neville must discover the identities of the shape-shifters so that the Holy Mother Church of Rome can move against them. Originally published in Australia in 2001.
3. *Crippled Angel, The* **(Tor, 2006)** The conclusion of the Crucible trilogy, in which the former monk Thomas Neville is sorely tried by enemies from without and within his own conscience and soul in his battle against the forces of evil. Originally published in Australia in 2002.

III. The Troy Game is an alternative-history quartet of novels that traces the history of the Trojans, who, under their king Brutus, founded a kingdom in Britain after the fall of Troy. Brutus, who is caught in a cycle of death and rebirth, is reborn again in the 11th, 17th, and 20th centuries and is called upon to save Britain in a fantasy saga that incorporates magic and history. Unlike her earlier series, this quartet was published in the United States within a year of its original Australian publication. Douglass is also the author of the nonfiction *The Betrayal of Arthur* (Macmillan, Australia, 1998).

1. *Hades' Daughter* **(Tor, 2003)** Each city-state in an alternative ancient Greece possesses a labyrinth, "where mortals can shape the heavens to their own design." But the labyrinths decay; Troy falls; and Brutus, king of Troy, is forced to rebuild his kingdom in a far western island.
2. *Gods' Concubine* **(Tor, 2004)** A thousand years later, William, Duke of Normandy, who remembers an earlier life as Brutus, king of Troy, tries to construct a magical labyrinth to bring back the power of the ancient world.
3. *Darkwitch Rising* **(Tor, 2005)** Brutus, his wife, Cornelia, and the sorceress Genvissa are brought together in a 17th-century England embroiled in civil war.
4. *Druid's Sword* **(Tor, 2006)** A reborn Brutus faces another British crisis, this time the Blitz of 1940, where Hitler is determined to bomb Great Britain into submission.

Doyle, Arthur Conan

I. Sherlock Holmes has achieved mythic status with countless re-printings; a vast literature devoted to Sherlockiana; stage, radio, film, and television adaptations; parodies such as Robert L. Fish's (q.v.) Shlock Homes; and "newly discovered" Watson memoirs by authors such as Nicholas Meyer (q.v.). Subsidiary characters such as Moriarty (John Gardner [q.v.]) and Irene Adler (Carole Nelson Douglas [q.v.]) have spawned their own series, and Holmes has been called into consultation on historical murder cases such as Jack the Ripper, and treated by Sigmund Freud for cocaine addiction. As far back as 1897 (after Holmes was temporarily "killed off"), he appeared among the characters in John Kendrick Bangs's (q.v.) *Houseboat on the Styx*. Famous actors from William Gillette to Michael Caine have impersonated Holmes. Jeremy Brett's portrayal on the PBS television series rates among the very best. Holmes fanatics know their detective's cases down to the last detail, but there are good reference books for lesser mortals, such as Matthew Bunson's *Encyclopedia Sherlockiana* (Macmillan, 1994). Numbers 1, 2, 4, and 7 were published separately as novels, although only *The Hound of the Baskervilles* is of true novel length. The other titles are short story collections. There are numerous omnibus editions.

1. ***Study in Scarlet, A*** (Lippincott, 1890) A wrong committed in Utah is eventually connected to a mysterious double murder in London in Mr. Holmes's debut.
2. ***Sign of the Four, The*** (Collier, 1891) The story of a vendetta. Variant title: *The Sign of Four*.
3. ***Adventures of Sherlock Holmes, The*** (Harper, 1892) This is a collection of short stories.
4. ***Hound of the Baskervilles, The*** (McClure, 1902) Though written later, this is generally supposed to be a pre–Reichenbach Falls story. It shows Holmes at the peak of his powers as he solves a sinister case involving some very menacing canines.
5. ***Memoirs of Sherlock Holmes, The*** (Harper, 1893) This short story collection ends with Holmes's encounter with Moriarty at the Reichenbach Falls. Doyle intended to kill off his detective, but popular demand resuscitated Holmes.
6. ***Return of Sherlock Holmes, The*** (McClure, 1905) More stories are collected here.
7. ***Valley of Fear, The*** (Doran, 1915) A murder engineered by a secret society is solved in the wilds of America.
8. ***His Last Bow: Some Reminiscences of Sherlock Holmes*** (Doran, 1917) From his wartime home in the English countryside, the famous detective solves cases for the British government.
9. ***Case-Book of Sherlock Holmes, The*** (Doran, 1927) These are the final stories.

II. Doyle was a prolific author who wrote much else besides the Holmes stories, including books on spiritualism (he was a devout believer) and public affairs (although a defender of the British Empire, he was harshly critical of King Leopold's Congo venture). His most famous character outside of the Holmes canon is probably Professor George E. Challenger, genius, adventurer, maverick scientist, and very difficult character. *The Lost World*, the first Challenger book, is one of the original examples of "the dinosaurs are alive and well" genre. It was made into the silent movie classic of the same name that preceded *King Kong* by several years and *Jurassic Park* by several decades. Michael Crichton's (q.v.) novel and film *The Lost World* is not based on the 1912 title but pays conscious homage to it. Although Doyle published two more novels and two short stories featuring Professor Challenger, none of the subsequent narratives had anywhere near the same impact. Omnibus editions, which include the short stories "The Disintegration Machine" (1928) and "When the World Screamed" (1929), are *The*

Professor Challenger Stories (Murray, 1952) and *The Professor Challenger Adventures* (Chronicle, 1990).

1. ***Lost World, The*** (Hodder, 1912) An expedition led by Professor Challenger finds live dinosaurs and "ape-men" in a hidden valley in South America.
2. ***Poison Belt, The*** (Hodder, 1913) A belt of poisonous gases wipes out most of life on Earth. Professor Challenger, who has foreseen the disaster, survives with several members of his "Lost World" team.
3. ***Land of Mist, The*** (Doran, 1926) Challenger's (and Doyle's) conversion to spiritualism drives the action here.

III. Doyle, like writers before and after him, enjoyed the monetary returns brought to him by his most popular writings, but deeply resented the attention that character drew away from his "more serious" literary efforts. Doyle wanted to be remembered for his historical novels, especially *The White Company*. Although *The White Company*, a novel about the Hundred Years' War, was popular in its day, it was always overshadowed by the Holmes stories, and is almost forgotten today (although there was a much reprinted edition illustrated by N. C. Wyeth [McKay, 1922] and a "Classic Comics" rendition in the 1950s). *Sir Nigel* is about the earlier life of a character in *The White Company*.

1. ***Sir Nigel*** (McClure, 1906) A prequel about the boyhood of Sir Nigel Loring, commander of the White Company.
2. ***White Company, The*** (Lovell, 1891) Young Alleyne Edricson, squire to Sir Nigel Loring, commander of the elite group of archers called the White Company, goes to France with his mentor to fight in the One Hundred Years' War.

IV. Brigadier Gerard is a successor to Alphonse Daudet's (q.v.) Tartarin and an inspiration for George MacDonald's Fraser's (q.v.) Flashman. The irrepressible Gerard, the narrator and hero, describes his devoted service to his emperor (who remains largely offstage) in the Napoleonic Wars. Gerard's adventures have been reissued in one volume as *Exploits and Adventures of Brigadier Gerard* by New York Review Books (2001), with an introduction by Fraser.

1. ***Exploits of Brigadier Gerard, The*** (Appleton, 1896) Short stories.
2. ***Adventures of Gerard, The*** (McClure, 1903) Additional adventures and exploits.

Doyle, Roddy

I. Irish novelist, dramatist, screenwriter, lecturer, and humanitarian Roddy Doyle wins new fans and critical appreciation with each book he publishes. *The Commitments*, *The Snapper*, and *The Van* have all been made into movies. *The Van* was short-listed for the Booker Prize; *Paddy Clarke Ha, Ha, Ha* (Viking, 1993) won the Booker Prize. The Barrytown Trilogy tells the story of the Rabbittes, a working class Dublin family, with great humor and superb (if sometimes a little overwhelming in its Irishness) dialogue. *The Barrytown Trilogy* (Penguin, 1995) contains all three novels.

1. ***Commitments, The*** (Random, 1989) Jimmy Rabbitte starts and manages his own Irish soul band in Dublin.
2. ***Snapper, The*** (Viking, 1991) Sharon Rabbitte, raped by a friend's father, decides to bear the resulting child ("snapper") and raise it alone.
3. ***Van, The*** (Viking, 1992) Jimmy Rabbitte Sr. teams up with his pal Bimbo to buy a ramshackle fish-and-chips van.

II. After *Paddy Clarke Ha Ha Ha* (Viking, 1994) and *The Woman Who Walked into Doors* (Viking, 1996), novels set in Dublin, Doyle began a historical trilogy, called the Last Roundup, which, in two volumes so far, depicts the career of one Henry Smart in the first two decades of the 20th century. Henry narrates his exploits in the Irish Republican Army and his various scams in New York City in Dickensian style.

1. *Star Called Henry, A* (**Viking, 1999**) Henry Smart recalls his Dublin birth and childhood, the Easter Rebellion, in which he took part, and his rise to legendary status before he was 20 in the Irish Republican Army.
2. *Oh, Play That Thing* (**Viking, 2004**) Things getting too hot for him in Ireland, Henry escapes to New York City in 1924 and embarks upon careers in advertising, bootlegging, pornography, unlicensed dentistry, and as unofficial manager of a young Louis Armstrong.

III. Paula Spencer, who recalled episodes from her life in *The Woman Who Walked into Doors*, returns in a sequel published 11 years later.

1. *Woman Who Walked into Doors, The* (**Viking, 1996**) Paula Spencer recalls episodes in her life—from competitive sibling to abused wife to embattled mother, particularly about her relationship with her abusive husband, Charlo.
2. *Paula Spencer* (**Viking, 2007**) Long widowed and four months sober, Paula Spencer worries that her daughter, Leanne, is following in her footsteps.

Drabble, Margaret

Drabble ranks among the best contemporary writers of serious fiction. Her first novels, published in the early 1960s, established her as a feminist author whose portraits of young motherhood captured the ambivalence of a generation of women. Her more recent novels examine a cross section of British society with sharper political and social comment. But she continues to fill each book with a diverse cast of memorable women characters. Readers who met Liz Headland, Alix Bowen, and Esther Breuer in *The Radiant Way* will be delighted to discover two sequels.

1. *Radiant Way, The* (**Knopf, 1987**) This follows the lives of three women from January 1979 to June 1985, with flashbacks to their student days at Cambridge University in 1952. The large cast of characters includes their husbands, lovers, children, friends, and relatives.
2. *Natural Curiosity, A* (**Viking, 1989**) This continues the lives of the three women, now living in different parts of England, as they cope with aging amid the increasing polarization and strife of the Thatcher era.
3. *Gates of Ivory, The* (**Viking, 1992**) After Liz's friend Stephen Cox disappears into Cambodia, she receives a package containing his notebooks, newspaper clippings, manuscripts, and two finger bones.

Drake, David (Allen)

I. David Drake is one of the leading practitioners of the subgenre known as military SF. Although his action is set in the future, there is no lack of realism and the blood and grit and misery of combat. His heroes and villains are not just cardboard and are driven by solid but often conflicted motives. Many of his plots are based on actual events of the past such as the American Civil War or the Vietnam War (in

which Drake served). Hammer's Slammers is a group of mercenaries, led by Colonel Alois Hammer, an armored regiment for hire by warring planets and societies. They are a motley group of men and women who work together as a formidable war machine. *Hammer's Slammers* began as short stories, which were collected together in number 1, Drake's first published book. The stories were followed by more stories and several loosely connected novels. Omnibuses include *The Complete Hammer's Slammers*, projected to be in three volumes published by Night Shade. Volume 1 (2006) contains 21 stories. Volume 2 (2007) contains numbers 3 through 6. Other omnibuses are *The Tank Lords* (Baen, 1997, containing number 5 and several short stories); *Caught in the Crossfire* (Baen, 1998, containing numbers 4 and 6 and other stories); and *The Butcher's Bill* (Baen, 1998, containing number 3, four short stories, and a new novella). *Other Times Than Peace* (Baen, 2006) contains two Slammer stories.

1. *Hammer's Slammers* (**Avon, 1979**) A collection of short stories with explanatory interludes introducing Hammer's Slammers. Expanded addition published by Baen in 1987.
2. *Cross the Stars* (**Tor, 1984**) In a futuristic version of Homer's *Odyssey*, Don Slade encounters many obstacles as he returns home to his lover and son on the planet Tethys.
3. *At Any Price* (**Baen, 1985**) Contains a short novel and two short stories. Hammer's Slammers fight on the side of human colonists against an uprising of native teleporters. Reprinted in *The Butcher's Bill* (Baen, 1998).
4. *Counting the Cost* (**Baen, 1987**) Hammer's Slammers have to fight a two-front war while maintaining the civilian power structure against hordes of religious fanatics. Reprinted in *Caught in the Crossfire* (Baen, 1998).
5. *Rolling Hot* (**Baen, 1989**) Captain Ranson leads her Slammer forces in recovering a district capital. Reprinted in *The Tank Lords* (Baen, 1997).
6. *Warrior, The* (**Baen, 1991**) Contains *The Warrior*, a short novel, and a novella, "Liberty Port" featuring Slammer Slick Des Grieux. *The Warrior* was reprinted in *Caught in the Crossfire* (Baen, 1998). "Liberty Port" was reprinted in *the Butcher's Bill* (Baen, 1998).
7. *Sharp End, The* (**Baen, 1993**) The planet Cantilucca is ruled by two gang syndicates headed for a bloody show-down.
8. *Voyage, The* (**Tor, 1994**) In a story based on the Argonaut myth, Lissea Doorman leads a group of adventurers on a "suicide" mission to the Lost Colony.
9. *Paying the Piper* (**Baen, 2002**) Three novellas: "Choosing Sides," "The Political Process," and "Neck or Nothing." Lieutenant Arnie Huber and Plattner's World are featured.

II. Another military SF series, referred to as the RCN series, is somewhat lighter in tone. It features Daniel Leary and Adele Mundy, officers in the Royal Cinnabar Navy. Leary commands the space corvette *Princess Cecile*, and former librarian Mundy is the *Princess Cecile's* signals officer and resident computer wizard. They aid the Republic of Cinnabar in its fight against the tyrannical Alliance in a series of space-opera adventures.

1. *With the Lightnings* (**Baen, 1998**) Lieutenant Cassian Daniels of the Royal Cinnabar Navy and librarian Adele Mundy form an unlikely alliance as two planetary governments contend for control of the strategically located planet of Kostroma.
2. *Lt. Leary, Commanding* (**Baen, 2000**) Lieutenant Daniel Leary, given command of the corvette *Princess Cecile* of the Royal Cinnabar Navy, is sent to cement an alliance with the planet Strymon.
3. *Far Side of the Stars, The* (**Baen, 2004**) With the Republic of Cinnabar temporarily at peace with the Alliance and the *Princess*

Cecile privatized, Leary and Munday take on other tasks, such as escorting a pair of wealthy novelists on an expedition to "the back of beyond."

4. *Way to Glory, The* (Baen, 2005) Leary has to serve under a paranoiac officer, and Mundy is led into a conspiracy like the one that led to her parents' massacre as the fleets of the Alliance are on the move and class riots rack Cinnabar.

5. *Some Golden Harbor* (Baen, 2006) Leary, newly promoted to commander, and his crew are dispatched to save Dunbar's World from the invaders of the planet Pellegrino.

6. *When the Tide Rises* (Baen, 2008) Leary is assigned to shore up the navy of the Independent Republic of Bagaria, a frontier system that broke away from the Alliance and now looks to Cinnabar for aid.

III. Drake, who has strong interests in history and mythology, is producing his own Arthurian saga, Lord of the Isles. It follows the fortunes of four characters: Garric and Sharina and Cashel and Ilna, brother-and-sister pairs whose destiny is to reunite the island kingdom of the Isles into one empire for the first time in 1,000 years. Time-traveling sorceress Tenoctris and the evil Hooded One play big roles in this mixture of SF, fantasy, and Celtic mythology. Numbers 7 and 8 are volumes in a projected Crown of the Isles trilogy that will wrap up the series.

1. *Lord of the Isles* (Tor, 1997) As the empire of the Isles crumbles, court wizard Tenoctris escapes 1,000 years into the future, where she meets peasant scholar Garric, who is haunted by the ghost of the last king of the Isles.

2. *Queen of Demons* (Tor, 1998) The Hooded One is finished, but his influence lingers. Garric and his friends, on a quest to revive the kingdom of the Isles, run into the queen of demons, who uses people as pawns.

3. *Servant of the Dragon* (Tor, 1999) Garric, Cashel, Ilna, and Sharina continue their quest. Garric acquires a love interest, Linie.

4. *Mistress of the Catacombs* (Tor, 2001) King Garric confronts new threats as rebels in the West endeavor to destroy his kingdom.

5. *Goddess of the Ice Realm* (Tor, 2003) Garric and his retinue reach the island city of Carcosa. Tenoctris perceives a powerful supernatural force directed against them, as Cashel and Sharina are translated to other worlds by evil magic.

6. *Master of the Cauldron* (Tor, 2004) Garric, now regent of the Isles, and his three companions undertake a journey through the Isles to meet their subjects and renew oaths of fealty.

7. *Fortress of Glass* (Tor, 2006) Subtitle: *The First Volume of the Crown of the Isles*. Garric, traveling afar to bring all the Isles under his rule, lands on a new shore and finds local king Cervoran dead and his heir, Prince Protas, in need of help against an outbreak of wizardry.

8. *Mirror of Worlds, The* (Tor, 2007) Subtitle: *The Second Volume of the Crown of the Isles*. Prince Garric's sister, Sharina, the wizardess Tenoctris, and Ilna the witch-weaver take on tasks to help Garric reunite the Isles.

IV. The Reaches trilogy is the SF version of the life of Sir Francis Drake, Elizabethan privateer, circumnavigator, and hero of the victory over the "invincible" Armada. As the humans travel again in Deep Space, a thousand years after the collapse of the human space empire, two young men from Venus set off on a series of adventures. *The Reaches* (Baen, 2004) is an omnibus volume containing the three novels.

1. *Igniting the Reaches* (Ace, 1994) Two young men, Stephen Gregg and Piet Ricimer, head out from Venus in search of gold and glory.

2. *Through the Breach* (Ace, 1995) Ricimer and Gregg, leading the Venus Asteroid Expedition, head for the Mirror.

3. *Fireships* (Avon, 1996) Sal Blythe commands her own vessel in an epic confrontation recalling the defeat of the Spanish Armada.

V. Drake collaborated with SF writer Janet Morris on several novels, including a pair set in an alternate 1960s in which JFK was not assassinated, featuring a couple of missions engaged upon by ex-NSA agent Tom Kelly.

1. *Skyripper* (Tor, 1983) In an alternate-history 1960s, ex-agent Tom Kelly of the National Security Agency makes contact with Soviet physicist Vlasov, who wants the United States to produce a device he has invented. Coauthored with Janet Morris.

2. *Fortress* (Tor, 1987) In 1965 President Kennedy has plans for a space fortress, but is concerned about a neo-Nazi plot. Coauthored with Janet Morris.

VI. Another pair of novels coauthored with Morris feature United Nations Security Officer Sam Yates in the not-too-distant future.

1. *Kill Ratio* (Ace, 1987) Sam Yates confronts a plague that is wiping out entire bloodlines. Coauthored with Janet Morris.

2. *Target* (Ace, 1989) Sam Yates was having a rather boring time as United Nations Security Officer on the Moon until the alien arrived, followed by the Hunters, who want the alien at any cost. Coauthored with Janet Morris.

VII. A third pair of novels coauthored with Janet Morris features another Drake interest, time travel. The ARC team of Anti-Reversion Command Central in the 26th century is charged with seeing to it that past history is not changed by time travelers, no matter how well meaning, resulting in incalculable consequences for the course of events leading to their time.

1. *ARC Riders* (Warner, 1995) The ARC Riders, barely escaping an unexpected attack, retreat to 25,000 BCE and then to the year 1991. Coauthored with Janet Morris.

2. *Fourth Rome, The* (Warner, 1996) Russian time travelers hope to reverse the massacre of the Romans by German tribes in the Teutoberg Forest in the 1st century CE. Coauthored with Janet Morris.

Drake, Shannon

PSEUDONYM OF Heather G. Pozzessere

I. Shannon Drake, who is perhaps better known as Heather Graham (q.v.), is a prolific romance novelist, both historical and contemporary. The Graham Family series, based on Drake/Graham's own ancestors, traces the fortunes of members of a Scottish clan from the 12th century to Victorian times. A lot of history is covered, and a lot of bodice ripping and passion occurs. Six novels listed as the Vampires (Zebra, 1999–2005) seem to have no connection with each other beyond the contemporary vampire theme.

1. *Come the Morning* (Kensington, 1999) In the days of the Scottish king David, warrior Waryk de Graham, knighted Lord Lion, is wedded to the reluctant half-Viking Mellyora MacAdin.

2. *Conquer the Night* (Kensington, 2000) Sir Arryn Graham, "his heart hardened by hate," seeking revenge against Kinsey Darrow

for his massacre of the Highland rebels, is determined to claim Darrow's bride, Kyra, as his own.

3. *Seize the Dawn* (Kensington, 2001) Bold and beautiful Lady Eleanor Cairn, sole heir to her ancestral lands, is prepared to marry almost anyone to retain Cairn Castle, except perhaps Highland outlaw Brendan Graham.

4. *Knight Triumphant* (Kensington, 2002) After the death of her husband, the Lord of Langley, Igrainia is imprisoned in her own castle by Scottish warrior Eric Graham, whose wife and son died at the hands of her husband.

5. *Lion in Glory, The* (Kensington, 2003) In the time of Robert Bruce, English lady Christina of Hamstead Heath is forced to offer herself as a hostage to Sir James Graham.

6. *When We Touch* (Kensington, 2004) A considerable jump in time from number 5, as we find ourselves in Jack the Ripper's London East End. Lady Maggie Graham finds herself in a predicament when her brother Justin gambles away the family fortune.

II. The No Other trilogy gyrates between the British Isles and the Dakota Badlands, as lords and ladies intermingle with the Sioux, and Custer heads toward his comeuppance. Two pairs of novels—*Fire* (1989, 1993) and *Victorian Fairy Tale* (2005)—are linked by themes only (Normans and Egyptian antiquities).

1. *No Other Man* (Avon, 1995) Skylar Connor comes to the Dakota badlands and finds that "Lord Douglas," the husband she wed by proxy, is Hawk, a handsome half-Sioux Indian.

2. *No Other Woman* (Avon, 1996) Lady Shawna, who seduced David Douglas of Castle Rock and inadvertently lured him to his death, finds herself haunted by his bitter spirit.

3. *No Other Love* (Avon, 1997) The Black Hills of the Dakota Territory and the Scottish Highlands are the scenes of the tempestuous romance between Sabrina Connor and Sloan Trelawny.

Dreiser, Theodore

In contrast to *Sister Carrie*, which Dreiser based on the character of his sister, *The Financier* required considerable research into the world of banking, the stock market, the Philadelphia political scene, and the career of Charles T. Yerkes, his model for Frank Cowperwood. Dreiser's novel documents the rags-to-riches story of his ruthless and corrupt protagonist, with all its dramatic reversals, scandals, and passions. Two further novels continue Cowperwood's story to his death and complete the Trilogy of Desire.

1. *Financier, The* (Harper, 1912) Frank Cowperwood rises to power in Philadelphia; his life is complicated by troublesome passions for women.

2. *Titan, The* (John Lane, 1914) Chicago in the 1870s is the setting for the second chapter in the career of Frank Cowperwood.

3. *Stoic, The* (Doubleday, 1947) Posthumously published, this concluding volume shows Frank Cowperwood involved in the transit industry of London and various philanthropic projects.

Druon, Maurice

Druon combines the knowledge of a historian with the imagination of a writer in these six novels set in medieval France. Known collectively as the Accursed Kings (*Les rois maudits*), the series follows the House of Valois, whose members were cursed for 13 generations by the dying Jean de Moulay, who was burned at the stake by Philip IV, "The Fair."

Druon catches the color of life in the 14th century, with its tournaments, court intrigues, stately dances, and dark underside of witchcraft and murder. All novels translated from the French by Humphrey Hare.

1. *Iron King, The* (Scribner, 1956) This book re-creates the turbulent reign (1285–1314) of Philip IV of France, with its extremes of violence and reform. Originally published as *Le roi de fer, 1314* (1955).

2. *Strangled Queen, The* (Scribner, 1957) Louis X succeeds to the French throne in 1314 and a power struggle ensues. Originally published as *La réine etranglée, 1314–1315* (1956).

3. *Poisoned Crown, The* (Scribner, 1957) The last months of the reign of Louis X bring violence and intrigue to France in the early 14th century. Originally published as *Les poisons de la couronne, 1315–1316* (1957).

4. *Royal Succession, The* (Scribner, 1958) A struggle for the crown of France follows the death of Louis X in 1316 and culminates in the coronation of Philip V. Originally published as *La loi de males, 1316–1317* (1958).

5. *She-Wolf of France, The* (Scribner, 1960) In 1327 Queen Isabella of England plots successfully to murder her husband, King Edward II, and place her 15-year-old son, Edward, on the throne. Originally published as *La vouve de France, 1323–1328* (1959).

6. *Lily and the Lion, The* (Scribner, 1961) The early reign of Edward III of England (1327–1377) is brutal, and Robert Artois and the Countess Mahaut feud ruthlessly in France. Originally published as *Le lis et le lion, 1328–1343* (1960).

Drury, Allen

I. These six novels on the theme of American politics share many of the same characters. The first and best in the series, *Advise and Consent*, won the Pulitzer Prize for 1960. It presents a fascinating picture of the Washington political world. The all-star cast of the successful 1962 movie version included Charles Laughton, Henry Fonda, and Walter Pidgeon. Though Drury's conservative views color the whole series, his pen weighs especially heavily in the later volumes as his characters lose their three-dimensionality and his plots take on a good-versus-evil configuration that verges on fantasy.

1. *Advise and Consent* (Doubleday, 1959) The controversial nomination of Robert Leffingwell as Secretary of State sets off reverberations throughout Washington.

2. *Shade of Difference, A* (Doubleday, 1962) A racial incident in Charleston, South Carolina, touches off this drama about the United Nations.

3. *Capable of Honor* (Doubleday, 1966) Washington columnist Walter Dobius is the villain of this volume.

4. *Preserve and Protect* (Doubleday, 1968) President Harley Hudson's death in an airplane crash is just the beginning of the violence in this installment.

5. *Come Nineveh, Come Tyre: The Presidency of Edward M. Jason* (Doubleday, 1973) Assassination, kidnapping, and suicide figure in the Armageddon caused by soft liberal policies.

6. *Promise of Joy, The* (Doubleday, 1975) This volume offers an alternative scenario in which Edward M. Jason is only vice president, and Orin Knox must save the country from destruction.

II. The good-versus-evil confrontation is carried forward to the late 1980s in a pair of geopolitical melodramas where good president Hamilton Delbacher faces off against evil president Yuri Serapin. The Soviets are bent on world conquest, while the Americans are slipping militarily and becoming demoralized by the weak-kneed, traitorous, liberal media. Drury's Russophobia is fairly rabid in these tracts.

1. *Hill of Summer, The: A Novel of the Soviet Conquest* (Doubleday, 1981) Almost simultaneously, Vice-President Hamilton Delbacher succeeds to the presidency of a weakened United States, while Yuri Serapin is "elected" as leader of the USSR.
2. *Roads of Earth, The* (Doubleday, 1984) After signing a Sino-Soviet pact, the Russians launch a series of attacks on Mexico, South Africa, Saudi Arabia, and Taiwan.

III. Drury's interest in ancient Egypt is evident in this pair of historical novels about the Eighteenth Dynasty told in a series of monologues by observers and participants.

1. *God against the Gods, A* (Doubleday, 1976) Suffering from delusions of grandeur, Akhenaton displaces the old gods and, in so doing, alienates his family and subjects.
2. *Return to Thebes* (Doubleday, 1977) Nefertiti, Akhenaton's cousin-wife, falls into disfavor. Akhenaton is murdered and succeeded by his youngest brother Tuntankhamen.

IV. A large cast of characters from a California university, based on Stanford, Drury's alma mater, is followed from 1938 to 2001, in three novels about the college generation of the 1930s.

1. *Toward What Bright Glory?* (Morrow, 1990) A group of young men approaching graduation in 1939 are concerned about world affairs (the Nazi threat, etc.) as well as about grades and girls.
2. *Into What Far Harbor?* (Morrow, 1992) Follows the men into the 1960s as they age, confront their successes and failures, and realize the need for them to guide the next generation.
3. *Public Men* (Scribner, 1998) In this posthumous novel, California senator Willie Wilson tries to organize a reunion in the year 2001 for the surviving members of his 1939 Alpha Zeta fraternity house while continuing his feud with a frat brother, the nationally prominent liberal gadfly Dr. Renny Suratt.

DuBois, Brendan

Lewis Cole, the only survivor of a Department of Defense experiment gone wrong, is now retired, the recipient of a beachfront property in Tyler Beach, New Hampshire, and a job as a columnist for *Shoreline* magazine, courtesy of his embarrassed former agency. Lewis likes the quiet life, but still manages to find himself investigating some nasty criminal activities, partly at the behest of his friends, Diane Woods, a lesbian policewoman who is the sole detective on the Tyler police department, and Felix Tinios, a retired enforcer for organized crime. Lifelong New Hampshire resident DuBois lovingly evokes the New Hampshire shoreline. Lewis Cole is a convincingly erudite but tough character who finds his way through a series of complex plots. DuBois is also the author of several suspense novels and the alternative history novel *Resurrection Day* (Putnam, 1999).

1. *Dead Sand* (Otto Penzler, 1994) Lewis Cole is jolted out of his quiet life when a decades-old unidentified corpse is dug up, waitress Lynn Germano is found strangled, and a fishing boat that Cole was almost on is blown up.
2. *Black Tide* (Otto Penzler, 1995) Recuperation from the removal of a benign but puzzling tumor, an oil spill on the New Hampshire coast, stolen paintings, and the problems of his friend, lesbian cop Diane Woods, keep Lewis from enjoying his beachfront cottage.

3. *Shattered Shell, The* (Thomas Dunne, 1999) Fires are destroying the closed (for the winter) motels on Tyler Beach, and Diane Woods's lesbian lover has been raped.
4. *Killer Waves* (St. Martin's, 2002) A team of federal agents, claiming to be from the DEA, disturbs Cole's peace, looking into the murder of a man in a park near his house.
5. *Buried Dreams* (Thomas Dunne, 2004) Cole briefly befriends Jon Ericson, an amateur archaeologist who claims to have proof that his Viking ancestor landed nearby centuries ago. Then Ericson is shot.
6. *Primary Storm* (St. Martin's, 2006) Cole is arrested for shooting at one of the leading candidates in the presidential primary.

Due, Tananarive

In *My Soul to Keep*, African American reporter Jessica Jacobs-Wolde finds that her husband, David, is a member of a vampirish sect that has traded in humanity for immortality. In its sequel, *The Living Blood*, Jessica, who has joined the ranks of immortals, moves to Africa with her baby daughter in search of David. Author Due leaves open the possibility of a third novel. African American Tananarive, wife of SF writer Steven Barnes (q.v.) and columnist for the *Miami Herald*, has authored several other gothic novels, including *Joplin's Ghost* (Atria, 2005), a fictionalized account, using an outline from the late Alex Haley, of America's first black female millionaire, Madame C. J. Walker (*The Black Rose*; One World, 2000) and, with her mother, Patricia Stephens Due, the nonfiction *Freedom in the Family: A Mother-Daughter Memoir of the Fight for Civil Rights* (One World, 2000).

1. *My Soul to Keep* (HarperCollins, 1997) African American reporter Jessica discovers that her husband, David, is a member of an ancient secret society that has traded in humanity for immortality.
2. *Living Blood, The* (Pocket Books, 2001) David disappears after being accused of murder, and Jessica goes to Africa with her infant daughter, Fana, who has great psychic powers, in search of him.

Dufresne, John

The wildly dysfunctional Fontana family of Monroe, Louisiana, was introduced in "The Fontana Gene," a short story published in the collection *The Way That Water Enters Stone* (Norton, 1991). The genetically disadvantaged Fontanas, from Peregrine to Positive Wasserman to Billy Wayne and lastly to Bergerac "Boudou" Boudeleaux deBastrop, are delineated in two wild and wacky novels, full of asides, "wildly funny lines," and "achingly sad turns," which call to mind the creations of Barry Gifford (q.v.) crossed with William Faulkner (q.v.), Eudora Welty, or Flannery O'Connor. John Dufresne spent only three years in Louisiana (Northeast Louisiana University), having grown up in Worcester, Massachusetts, which is the setting for his second novel, *Love Warps the Mind a Little* (Norton, 1996). Since 1989 he has taught creative writing at Florida International University. He is also author of the nonfiction *The Lie That Tells a Truth: A Guide to Writing Fiction* (Norton, 2003).

1. *Louisiana Power and Light* (Norton, 1994) Billy Wayne Fontana, who drives a truck for Louisiana Power & Light, had hoped to become a priest, and therefore celibate, but somehow he wound up passing on the fatal Fontana gene to a series of children by two wives.
2. *Deep in the Shade of Paradise* (Norton, 2002) The Fontana and Loudermilk family converge at Paradise, the Loudermilk

ancestral estate, in Shiver-de-Freeze, Louisiana, for the wedding of Grisham Loudermilk and Ariane Thevenot. Eleven-year-old Boudou Fontana, "last" of his race, who has paranormal powers, is the focus of attention for Tous-le-Doux, Siamese ("Siberian") twin teenage girls.

Dukthas, Ann

PSEUDONYM OF P(aul) C. Doherty

"Ann Dukthas" is one of the many pseudonyms used by British historical mystery writer P(aul) C. Doherty. The Dukthas books feature Nicholas Segalla, a scholar-detective who time travels into the past and investigates some famous mysteries, all concerning royalty, from the 16th and 19th centuries.

1. *Time for the Death of a King, A* (**St. Martin's, 1994**) When stolen letters implicate Mary Queen of Scots in the mysterious death of her husband, Lord Darnley, the shadowy time traveling sleuth Nicholas Segalla investigates.
2. *Prince Lost to Time, The* (**St. Martin's, 1995**) Paris, 1815. Did the young Dauphin, the putative Louis XVII, die in prison, or did he escape? The answer interests the British government, which sends Nicholas Segalla to investigate.
3. *Time of Murder at Mayerling, The* (**St. Martin's, 1996**) Who is behind the cover-up of the facts behind the "murder/suicide" of Archduke Rudolph, heir to the Austrian throne, and his mistress, Maria Vetsera?
4. *In the Time of the Poisoned Queen* (**St. Martin's, 1998**) Queen Mary of England lies dying in 1558. Is she being poisoned by one of her many rivals?

Dumas (pere), Alexandre

The Three Musketeers is the classic swashbuckler. Although it has been popular ever since it was first published in 1844, motion picture versions gave it a new lease on life. The 1921 silent classic starring Douglas Fairbanks, the 1974 Richard Lester film, and the 1994 version starring Charlie Sheen and Kiefer Sutherland are among the most notable movie versions. Dumas wrote two sequels that continued the characters into the reign of Louis XIV. Readers may find Dumas' prose a little cumbersome at times, but the adventures of brave D'Artagnan, gallant Athos, largehearted Porthos, and Aramis the schemer are as engaging as ever. There are many English translations of the French originals. A good translation is that of David Coward in Oxford University Press (1991–1995).

1. *Three Musketeers, The* (**Little, 1888**) D'Artagnan arrives in Paris and joins Athos, Porthos, and Aramis in a whirlwind of court intrigue and adventures covering the years 1626–1628. First published in 1844 as *Les trois mousquetaires*. First translated into English in 1846 (Taylor [UK]).
2. *Twenty Years After* (**Little, 1888**) This volume covers the period 1648–1649, the regency of Anne of Austria, and the uprising against Cardinal Mazarin. First published in 1846 as *Vingt ans apres*. First translated into English in 1846 (Bruce [UK]).
3. *Vicomte de Bragelonne, The; or, Ten Years Later* (**Little, 1904**) Set during the reign of Louis IV, this book contains episodes frequently published separately—i.e., *The Man in the Iron Mask* and *Louise de la Valliere*. First published in 1851 as *Le vicomte de Bragelonne*. First translated into English in 1857 (Routledge [UK]).

Dunbar, Tony (Anthony P.)

Lawyer Tubby Dubonnet likes fishing, beer, off-track betting, and his home city of New Orleans, not necessarily in that order. Divorced, with a grown daughter, Tubby is still hoping for a romantic relationship. He prefers a good meal to a demanding case and doesn't like dangerous situations, but his somewhat seedy clients keep dragging him into them. This is a convoluted but entertaining series with lots of humor and real New Orleans atmosphere.

1. *Crooked Man* (**Putnam, 1994**) One of Tubby Dubonnet's clients hands over close to $1 million dollars in a gym bag to Tubby after a marijuana bust. Then the client, a lakefront bar owner, is murdered.
2. *City of Beads* (**Putnam, 1996**) Tubby's friend, peanut-oil shipper Potter Aucoin, is found floating in his own peanut oil. Tubby's collegiate daughter wants his help in investigating local companies polluting the Mississippi. Tania Thompson, who shot a drug dealer, winds up in a bar Tubby is thinking of buying. A local gambler offers Tubby a sinecure complete with a pretty assistant.
3. *Trick Question* (**Putnam, 1997**) Tubby is asked to take over the case of Cletus Buster, medical laboratory janitor and sometime voodoo guru, who gets caught holding the frozen head of noted research pathologist Whitney Valentine.
4. *Shelter from the Storm* (**Dell, 1997**) Tubby and a heterogeneous and rather shady group of New Orleans airport arrivals are forced together by a torrential rainstorm.
5. *Crime Czar, The* (**Dell, 1998**) Tubby's college wrestling buddy Dan dies from wounds received while trying to save Tubby's life, and the gunman, Willard LaRue, is still on the loose.
6. *Lucky Man* (**Dell, 1999**) A moralistic, crusading prosecutor is trying to destroy the reputation and career of Tubby's favorite judge, as a little office sex turns into a melange of murder, rape, and suicide, real and imagined.
7. *Tubby Meets Katrina* (**NewSouth Books, 2006**) Tubby winds up in New Orleans's Convention Center as Hurricane Katrina hits, and his daughter finds herself the target of an escaped psychopath who envisions himself as the human embodiment of the storm.

Duncan, Alice

I.   Alice Duncan writes historical novels set in America in the late 19th and early 20th centuries. The Meet Me at the Fair series uses the 1893 World Columbian Exposition in Chicago as the focus for three different romantic plots featuring strong women. Alice Duncan, who also publishes under the pseudonyms Emma Craig, Rachel Wilson, Jon Sharpe, and Anne Robins, should not be confused with Alice Faye Duncan, the African American librarian and children's author.

1. *Coming Up Roses* (**Zebra, 2002**) Rose Ellen Gilholley, star in Buffalo Bill's Wild West Show at the World Columbian Exposition in Chicago in 1893, is being pursued by an ardent newspaperman.
2. *Bicycle Built for Two, A* (**Zebra, 2002**) Alex English, one of the exhibition's promoters, tries to banish fortune-teller Kate Finney from the grounds, then has second thoughts.
3. *Just North of Bliss* (**Zebra, 2002**) Rowena Belle, who is teaching southern-style manners to two young boys in a New York family, accompanies her charges to the Chicago Fair, where she attracts the attention of Win, a bumptious Yankee who is the official fair photographer.

II. The Dream Maker series, set in the early 1900s, is about the fledgling film industry. Director Martin Tafft is the principal continuing character, and all four novels have romantic plots or subplots.

1. *Cowboy for Hire* (Zebra, 2001) Cowboy Charlie Fox, who wants to get off the ostrich ranch where he is working and raise cattle instead, agrees to play a villain in a western film. Set in 1905.
2. *Beauty and the Brain* (Zebra, 2001) In 1907 the beautiful Brenda Fitzpatrick, star of *India Love Song*, a picture being directed by Martin Tafft, falls for fact-checker Colin Peters but is afraid that she isn't intellectual enough for him.
3. *Her Leading Man* (Zebra, 2001) Christina Mayhew, actress, suffragette, and would-be medical doctor, falls in love with her director, Martin Tafft.
4. *Miner's Daughter, The* (Zebra, 2001) Martin Tafft is shooting a film in an old mine, believed to be abandoned but a place that seems to be the site of some sinister goings-on.

III. Two novels set in Pasadena, California, in the 1920s star con artist and spiritualist Daisy Gumm Majesty, who caters to the rich and famous as a medium.

1. *Strong Spirits* (Zebra, 2003) Daisy Gumm Majesty is blackmailed by Detective Sam Rotondo into spying on the wealthy Kincaid family.
2. *Fine Spirits* (Zebra, 2003) Missing heiress Marianna Wagner may be the "phantom" haunting Mrs. Bissel's basement.

Duncan, Dave (David John)

I. Scottish-born, Canadian geologist Dave Duncan's sword-and-sorcery trilogy the Seventh Sword is now considered a classic of the genre. It is the story of Wallie Smith, a man from Earth who is reborn as the swordsman Shonshu in a world of variable geography dominated by an all-encompassing River, given the legendary Sapphire Sword of Chioxin, and sent on a mission by the "Goddess" against the supposedly evil "Sorcerers." Wallie/Shonshu makes one blunder after another before he discovers that his miscues have a way of turning out right after all.

1. *Reluctant Swordsman, The* (Ballantine, 1988) Earthling Wallie Smith is resurrected in the body of Shonshu, a barbarian swordsman on a strange new world.
2. *Coming of Wisdom, The* (Ballantine, 1988) "Shonshu" is sent by the Goddess, who gifted him with the legendary Sapphire Sword of Chioxin, to deal with the Sorcerers, who turn out not to be as evil as he was led to believe.
3. *Destiny of the Sword, The* (Ballantine, 1988) Wallie is between a rock and a hard place. If he prevails over the Sorcerers, he will doom all hope of progress and learning in the World Goddess. And his best friend and pupil is apparently set to betray him.

II. Two quartets, a Man of His Word and a Handful of Men, are set in the world of Pandemia. Numbers 1 through 4 depict the trials and tribulations of Princess Inos of the small kingdom of Kranegar and her friend, the stable boy Rap, who eventually becomes her consort after many adventures. Numbers 5 through 8 are a sequel in which the Zinixo, the warlock who was defeated in the first quartet, returns after 15 years to gain control of the Impire [*sic*]. It is up to Rap, the new Imperor [*sic*], and a few companions to wrest control from the warlock.

1. *Magic Casement* (Ballantine, 1990) Princess Inos leaves her idyllic life in Kranegar and her friend, Rap the stable boy, at the behest of a god who urges her to marry.
2. *Faery Lands Forlorn* (Ballantine, 1991) Rap jumps through the magic casement after Inos, but they find themselves separated by half a world: she in a desert land and he in the jungles of Faerie.
3. *Perilous Seas* (Ballantine, 1991) Galley slave Rap returns from the grave armed with a magic sword, determined to help his queen, Inos.
4. *Emperor and Clown* (Ballantine, 1991) Queen Inos seems to have lost everything when she married the evil Sultan Azak, but Rap is still fighting for her.
5. *Cutting Edge, The* (Ballantine, 1992) After 15 years of bliss with Inos, King Rap has to confront prophecies of cataclysmic upheaval as the end of the millennium approaches and the old Imperor is losing his marbles.
6. *Upland Outlaws* (Ballantine, 1993) Shandie, the rightful Imperor, is up against the power-mad warlock Zinixo and the magical substitute he has placed on the Imperial throne.
7. *Stricken Field, The* (Ballantine, 1993) Rap, Shandie, and "a handful of men" continue the uphill struggle against the mad dwarf Zinixo and his minions.
8. *Living God, The* (Ballantine, 1994) Chaos reigns as Goblin hordes rampage, dragons incinerate entire legions, and the slave-sorcerers of the Covin carry out Zinixo's commands, but Rap isn't ready to throw in the towel.

III. Two amusing novels are narrated by the duplicitous Omar, "Trader of Tales."

1. *Reaver Road, The* (Ballantine, 1992) Omar is sent to by the gods to observe the besieged city of Zanadon, whose only hope is the reappearance of its protector god.
2. *Hunter's Haunt, The* (Ballantine, 1995) Omar has to tell the tallest of tall tales, if he doesn't want to be evicted from the Hunter's Haunt, his refuge from a blizzard.

IV. The Great Game trilogy is set on the battlefields of World War I and the alternate world of Nextdoor, where earthborn mortals have the powers of gods. Edward Exeter is called upon by an ancient prophecy to be the Liberator, who will "bring death to Death" in Nextdoor.

1. *Past Imperative* (Avon, 1995) September 1917. The World War is raging. Then a naked stranger falls from nowhere into the mud of Flanders Fields.
2. *Present Tense* (Avon, 1996) Edward Exeter, the putative Liberator of the alternate world Nextdoor, has to flee murderous pursuers from both worlds.
3. *Future Indefinite* (Avon, 1997) Edward Exeter has learned "the Game" well during his short sojourn in Nextdoor, and now he plays it to its unexpected conclusion.

V. The King's Blades is a trio of trilogies: Tales of the King's Blade (numbers 1–3) and Chronicles of the King's Blades (numbers 4–6), plus the spin-off King's Daggers trilogy (numbers 7–9). The King's Blades are graduates of the sword school of Ironhall, bound to serve the king or one of his designees, in a world reminiscent of Tudor England, where King Ambrose plays the role of Henry VIII.

1. *Gilded Chain, The* (Avon, 1998) Follows the career of Durandel, graduate of the sword school of Ironhall, as he moves from his initial service with a frivolous lord to his undertaking of a mission to retrieve a renegade Blade.

2. *Lord of the Fire Lands* **(Avon, 1999)** Raider and Wasp choose to travel far from the kingdom of Chivial to seek redress of a long-standing grievance in the land of the Baelish barbarians.

3. *Sky of Swords* **(Avon, 2000)** After the death of her father, King Ambrose, Princes Malinda takes upon herself the duty of protecting the kingdom of Chivial's rightful heir, her infant brother, Amby.

4. *Paragon Lost* **(Avon, 2002)** Relates the truth behind the life and career of Ned Cookson, once Sir Beaumont of the King's Blades.

5. *Impossible Odds* **(Avon, 2003)** Two of the King's Blades are given the honor of serving their new master, the Grand Duke Rubin, only to find that the Grand Duke Rubin is actually a woman, the Grand Duchess Johanna.

6. *Jaguar Knights, The* **(Avon, 2004)** Sir Wolf is detailed to rescue the king's former mistress, Celeste, who has been abducted from her tower.

7. *Sir Stalwart* **(Avon, 1999)** In the first book of the King's Daggers, young Stalwart, expelled from Ironhall, and Sister Emerald of the White Sisters are called upon to save their king.

8. *Crooked House, The* **(Avon, 2000)** Sir Stalwart witnesses a murder at the king's formal court reception for the new ambassador from Isiland.

9. *Silvercloak* **(Avon, 2001)** The world's most deadly assassin has been hired to kill King Ambrose. Only Emerald can identify the killer's evil magic, and only Stalwart knows what he looks like.

VI. The Dodec series is set in a fantasy world. The Bloodlord of the Hrag dynasty has taken the Doge of Celebre's four children hostage.

1. *Children of Chaos* **(Tor, 2006)** One of the Doge of Celebre's four children, who were taken hostage by the Bloodlord of the Hrag dynasty of Vigaelia, must return home to serve as a puppet ruler, while the other three are marked for death.

2. *Mother of Lies* **(Tor, 2007)** The four young sibling heirs to the Doge of Celebre have grown to adulthood and finally been reunited by the Liberators, led by Marno Cavotti (aka the Mutineer).

VII. Alfeo Zeno, noble swordsman and apprentice to alchemist and astrologer Nostradamus, is the hero of a pair of novels set in an alternate 16th-century Venice.

1. *Alchemist's Apprentice, The* **(Ace, 2007)** Nobly born apprentice Alfeo Zeno must clear his master, Nostradamus, of the murder of Procurator Bertucci Orseolo, which the astrologer has foreseen.

2. *Alchemist's Code, The* **(Ace, 2008)** Nostradamus and Zeno work at cracking coded messages and outing the enemy agent who sent them.

Dundee, Wayne D.

Joe Hannibal of Rockford, Illinois, is a classic private eye: he smokes, he drinks, he beds attractive women, he is ready with his fists, and he hews to an old-fashioned code of ethics. Joe has a long-standing relationship with Jan Mosby, star reporter for the glossy biweekly magazine *C-2-C*. Wayne D. Dundee, founder and original editor of *Hardboiled Magazine* has been nominated for an Edgar, an Anthony, and several Shamus awards.

1. *Burning Season, The* **(St. Martin's, 1988)** Private eye Joe Hannibal of Rockford travels downstate in Illinois to nab armed-robbery suspect and bail-jumper Junior Odum and winds up investigating the "accidental" death by fire of Odum's mother.

2. *Skintight Shroud, The* **(St. Martin's, 1989)** When Joe investigates, at the behest of 1950s TV star Henry Foxwood, the possible link

between two murders, he finds himself involved with mafiosi, porn rings, and the beautiful British mistress of a capo.

3. *Brutal Ballet, The* **(Dell, 1992)** Joe is hired by the jealous wife of wrestler "Terrible" Tommy McGurk to look into her husband's extracurricular activities.

4. *And Flesh and Blood So Cheap* **(Design Image, 2001)** Joe Hannibal returns, after a nine-year hiatus, this time to a Wisconsin summer resort town where he encounters tourist traps, gin mills, dangerous women, and murder.

5. *Fight in the Dog, The* **(Five Star, 2005)** Jan Mosby, star reporter for *C-2-C* and Joe's long-term lover, returns home one evening to find a bloody dog carcass nailed to the door. Joe and Jan, during the course of their investigations, run into a Wiccan psychic named Possibility, A.R.M. (Animal Rights Militia), a nasty motorcycle gang called the Hellraisers, and a satanic cult.

Dunlap, Susan

I. Dunlap has created three very engaging female detectives. Jill Smith is Dunlap's police detective. She is a young homicide detective on the Berkeley, California, police force. Her level-headed, tough, but sensitive style make her very good at her job. Jill is a divorced, totally undomestic new woman—her living quarters seem perfectly awful, and she never eats anything but junk food. Her friendship with office mate Seth Howard, a substance-abuse officer, warms as the series progresses.

1. *Karma* **(Dell, 1981)** Guru Padmasvana of the Mani Lakhang in Berkeley realizes his "karma to die" when he is murdered. Reprinted in *Karma: And Other Stories* (Five Star, 2002) along with a new Jill Smith story.

2. *As a Favor* **(St. Martin's, 1984)** Smith's former husband asks her to investigate the disappearance of Anne Spaulding, an unpopular welfare investigator.

3. *Not Exactly a Brahmin* **(St. Martin's, 1985)** The fatal automobile accident of rich establishment figure Ralph Palmerston looks suspicious to Smith.

4. *Too Close to the Edge* **(St. Martin's, 1987)** Wheelchair-bound Liz Goldenstern is drowned at the site of Marina Vista, an apartment complex she was planning to build.

5. *Dinner to Die For, A* **(St. Martin's, 1987)** Gourmet restaurateur Mitchell Biekma is poisoned by soup spiked with deadly aconite.

6. *Diamond in the Buff* **(St. Martin's, 1990)** Concerning Hasbrouck Diamond, D.D.S., who sunbathes in the buff and is having a feud with a masseuse.

7. *Death and Taxes* **(Delacorte, 1992)** IRS auditor Philip Drem is felled by a poisoned hypodermic needle lodged in his bicycle seat.

8. *Time Expired* **(Delacorte, 1993)** A prankster harassing meter maids seems to have some connection with the asphyxiation of the already terminally ill Madeleine Riordan.

9. *Sudden Exposure* **(Delacorte, 1996)** A feud between aging radical Sam Johnson and former Olympic diver Bryn Wiley turns fatal when a person sitting in Bryn's car is fatally shot by a mysterious gunner.

10. *Cop Out* **(Delacorte, 1997)** Herman Ott, "private detective to the counterculture," becomes a suspect when the body of arbitrator Bryant Hemming is found in Ott's office, and the private eye has disappeared.

II. Vejay Haskell is Dunlap's contribution to the amateur detective genre. Vejay is a youthful iconoclast who has ditched her high-powered PR job and her husband to live the quiet life in a peaceful resort town north of San Francisco, where she finds herself a job reading gas meters. But Vejay discovers that small-town life is anything but pastoral as she stumbles into one mystery after another. While Dunlap has been adding to the Jill Smith series, Vejay seems to have been ditched for Kiernan O'Shaughnessy (series III).

1. *Equal Opportunity Death, An* (St. Martin's, 1984) Newly transplanted Vejay runs the risk of alienating the townsfolk while trying to clear herself of the murder of a local bartender.
2. *Bohemian Connection, The* (St. Martin's, 1985) The sinister events during the town's Festival Week include the discovery of a dead body in a sewer trench.
3. *Last Annual Slugfest, The* (St. Martin's, 1986) Edwina Hastings, slug-tasting judge at the annual Slugfest celebration, is poisoned.

III. Kiernan O'Shaughnessy, former forensic pathologist turned private investigator, is fortysomething but still interested in romance. The tiny, acid-tongued, feisty Kiernan practices her trade in California and Arizona. A running subplot is her relationship with Brad Tchernak, former NFL linebacker, dog-sitter, houseman, and gourmet chef.

1. *Pious Deception* (Villard, 1989) Auxiliary Bishop Raymond Dowd of Phoenix wants the hanging death of young priest Austin Vanderhoven hushed up.
2. *Rogue Wave* (Villard, 1991) A drunk sailor washed overboard in the Pacific Ocean may have been in a hit-and-run accident years before.
3. *High Fall* (Delacorte, 1994) Stuntwoman Lark Sodevoil is killed in an attempt to replicate the Gaige Move.
4. *No Immunity* (Delacorte, 1998) Jeff Tremaine, friend from medical school with whom Kiernan had worked in Africa, calls Kiernan about a suspected case of an African disease called Lassa Fever.

Dunn, Carola

Daisy Dalrymple, heroine of a series of cozies set in England in the 1920s, is an "unflappable flapper." Although the daughter of a viscount, she makes her living as a magazine writer and eventually (number 9) marries a Scotland Yard man, Alec Fletcher. Daisy, in proper cozy fashion, has a habit of stumbling on bodies and then carrying on a investigation to get to the bottom of some murky affair. Carola Dunn, born and raised in England, came to the United States some 30 years ago and is presently residing in Eugene, Oregon. She also writes Regency romances, among other things.

1. *Death at Wentwater Court* (St. Martin's, 1994) Introduces the Honorable Daisy Dalrymple, who has shocked her aristocratic family by becoming a magazine writer. Daisy's on-site research at Wentwater Court is interrupted when Lord Wentwater has a fatal skating accident.
2. *Winter Garden Mystery, The* (St. Martin's, 1995) Daisy discovers the body of a missing parlor maid buried in the garden while on assignment at Occles Hall.
3. *Requiem for a Mezzo* (St. Martin's, 1996) Daisy joins Scotland Yard Detective Inspector Alec Fletcher when the lead soprano at a performance of Verdi's *Requiem* is felled by cyanide.
4. *Murder on the Flying Scotsman* (St. Martin's, 1997) Daisy is on board the famous *Flying Scotsman* express train when someone murders the beneficiary of a family fortune.
5. *Damsel in Distress* (St. Martin's, 1997) Gloria Arbuckle, daughter of an American millionaire, is kidnapped, and her bereft fiancé, Philip Petrie, calls on Daisy for help.

6. *Dead in the Water* (St. Martin's, 1998) When Daisy travels to Henley-on-Thames to visit her aunt and uncle, spend time with Alec Fletcher, her fiancé, and watch the boat race, a murder occurs on her cousin's team.
7. *Styx and Stones* (St. Martin's, 1999) When Daisy's brother-in-law, Sir John Frobisher, receives some poison-pen letters, he sends Daisy to a Kentish village to investigate.
8. *Rattle His Bones* (St, Martin's, 2000) Interviewing the curators at the Museum of Natural History in London, Daisy finds bad blood between Dr. Smith Woodward, the Keeper of Geology, and Dr. Pettigrew, the Keeper of Mineralogy.
9. *To Davy Jones Below* (St. Martin's, 2001) Daisy and Alec Fletcher's honeymoon voyage to America is punctuated by a series of nasty accidents and bizarre deaths on board ship.
10. *Case of the Murdered Muckraker, The* (St. Martin's, 2002) Daisy and Alec's honeymoon continues in New York, but Daisy's fatal touch continues, also, as she sees a journalist fall down an elevator shaft after being shot.
11. *Mistletoe and Murder* (St. Martin's, 2002) Skulduggery at Christmastime at Lord Westmoor's stately home. One of Lord Westmoor's putative grandsons has brought an ancient clergyman from India, who will prove that the grandson's father had married his Indian mistress before dying.
12. *Die Laughing* (St. Martin's, 2003) Daisy finally works up the courage to visit her dentist, Raymond Talmadge, only to find him dead, possibly from an overdose of the laughing gas he was in the habit of sniffing.
13. *Mourning Wedding, A* (St. Martin's, 2004) Another country house caper as Daisy and Alec come to the estate of the Earl of Haverhill for a wedding.
14. *Fall of a Philanderer* (St. Martin's, 2005) Daisy and Alec's summer holiday is interrupted, yet again, as the body of local innkeeper George Enderby is found at the shore.
15. *Gunpowder Plot* (St. Martin's, 2006) Daisy Dalrymple travels to a school friend's house to witness the estate's famous Guy Fawkes celebration.
16. *Bloody Tower, The* (St. Martin's, 2007) After Daisy stumbles over the corpse of the Chief Yeoman Warder at the Tower of London, she and husband Alec Fletcher team up to unmask the killer.

Dunne, John Gregory

Dunne, late husband of Joan Didion (see *The Year of Magical Thinking* Knopf, 2005) and brother of writer Dominick Dunne, achieved a reputation as a novelist with such titles as *True Confessions* (Dutton, 1977) and *Dutch Shea, Jr.* (Simon & Schuster, 1982). Two of Dunne's novels feature the wryly ironic narration of screenwriter Jack Broderick. Broderick finds himself enmeshed in Hollywood, Las Vegas, left-wing politics, big business, and the Catholic Church over several decades in these bawdy, well-written novels.

1. *Red, White, and Blue, The* (Simon & Schuster, 1987) Broderick ruminates about 20 years in the career of radical lawyer Leah Kaye.
2. *Playland* (Random House, 1994) After his wife's death, Broderick flees to Detroit and hooks up with bag lady Melba Mae Toolate, who claims to have been a child star in the forties.

Dunnett, Dorothy

I. The House of Niccolo follows the fortunes of young Claes vander Poele (aka Niccolo, aka Nicholas de Fleury), born illegitimate in Bruges, through many corners of the 15th-century world, from Flanders to Venice to Trebizond to Africa to Cyprus to Danzig to Scotland and elsewhere as he pursues his merchant banking career and dreams of empire. Dunnett maintains the reader's interest through a series of eight lengthy but engrossing volumes with a wealth of historical detail, vibrant characters, and many intricate but coherent subplots. The Scottish novelist Dorothy Dunnett managed to complete the series shortly before her death in 2001.

1. *Niccolo Rising* **(Knopf, 1986)** Illegitimate Niccolo is apprenticed at the age of 10 to the widowed Marian de Charetty, a wealthy Bruges merchant.
2. *Spring of the Ram, The* **(Knopf, 1988)** Nineteen-year-old Niccolo, now married to Marian, flees a bitter foe and journeys east to establish trade with the Emperor of Trebizond.
3. *Race of Scorpions* **(Knopf, 1990)** Having lost his wife and her inheritance, the 21-year-old Niccolo furthers his business career in Venice and Cyprus.
4. *Scales of Gold* **(Knopf, 1992)** In 1464 Niccolo, finding his Venetian financial empire shaky, sets out for Africa and its gold trade.
5. *Unicorn Hunt, The* **(Knopf, 1994)** In Scotland Niccolo confronts his archenemy Simon de St. Pol, who may be the real father of the child Niccolo's wife is carrying.
6. *To Lie with Lions* **(Knopf, 1996)** Niccolo simultaneously carries on a custody fight with his wife and off-again, on-again lover, Gelis van Borselen; clandestine dealings with French king Louis XI; and open dealings with Charles, Duke of Burgundy and King James III of Scotland.
7. *Caprice and Rondo* **(Knopf, 1998)** The year 1474 finds Nicholas in self-exile in Danzig, "bloody but unbowed." Self-interest (rebuilding his financial empire) and public spiritedness (saving Europe from the Turks) get him involved with Crimean Tartars, the shah of Persia, and Moscow traders.
8. *Gemini* **(Knopf, 2000)** The final installment finds Niccolo back in Scotland and up to his ears in financial machinations, politics, and family feuds.

II. An earlier historical series stars Francis Crawford of Lymond, second son of a noble Scottish family. A strange prophecy has cast a shadow over this haunting and magnetic hero who pursues his destiny across 16th-century Europe in various roles—as a galley slave, a foreigner in masquerade at the corrupt French court, an ambassador to a sultan, an outlaw leader, and a commander of the Russian army.

1. *Game of Kings, The* **(Putnam, 1961)** Condemned outlaw Francis Crawford of Lymond returns to Scotland in 1547 to try to clear his name and gets swept up in the dramatic events of his war-torn country.
2. *Queen's Play* **(Putnam, 1964)** Lymond is sent to France on a secret mission to protect the seven-year-old future monarch, Mary Stuart, and Scotland's hopes of a French alliance.
3. *Disorderly Knights, The* **(Putnam, 1966)** Lymond is fatefully enmeshed in the Turkish attack on Malta in 1551.
4. *Pawn in Frankincense* **(Putnam, 1969)** Lymond carries valuable cargo from France to the Sultan of Constantinople and searches for his illegitimate infant son. He finds himself in a deadly game of chess.
5. *Ringed Castle, The* **(Putnam, 1972)** Lymond is led to Russia by the beautiful courtesan Guzel and serves Ivan the Terrible.

6. *Checkmate* **(Putnam, 1975)** At the time of Philip II's accession to the Spanish throne, Lymond finally unravels his true ancestry in this concluding episode.

III. As a change of pace from her historical novels, Dunnett also wrote a series of suspense yarns united by the presence of Johnson Johnson, playboy painter and master counterspy, and his yacht *Dolly*. Johnson usually stays in the background, as the heroine ("bird") of each novel occupies center stage and narrates her adventures. This series of humorous thrillers was published in the United Kingdom under the author's maiden name, Dorothy Halliday.

1. *Photogenic Soprano, The* **(Houghton Mifflin, 1968)** We are introduced to Johnson Johnson and *Dolly* in an adventure featuring coloratura Tina Rossi. Set in the Hebrides. UK title: *Dolly and the Singing Bird*. Variant title: *A Rum Affair*.
2. *Murder in the Round* **(Houghton Mifflin, 1970)** The body of an impoverished English lord turns up on the island of Ibiza. UK title: *Dolly and the Cookie Bird*. Variant title: *Ibiza Surprise*.
3. *Match for a Murderer* **(Houghton Mifflin, 1971)** Dr. Beltanno Douglas MacRannoch, physician and daughter of a Scottish clan chieftain, is the heroine of this adventure set in the Bahamas. UK title: *Dolly and the Doctor Bird*. Variant title: *Operation Nassau*.
4. *Murder in Focus* **(Houghton, 1973)** A girl astronomer and her photographer boyfriend become embroiled in a wild assortment of trouble in Rome. English title: *Dorothy and the Starry Bird*.
5. *Dolly and the Nanny Bird* **(Knopf, 1982)** Joanna Emerson, undercover agent, is hired as a nanny by the jet-setting Booker-Readmans to care for their infant Benedict. Variant title: *Spirit Code*.
6. *Dolly and the Bird of Paradise* **(Knopf, 1984)** Rita Geddes, a young Scottish makeup artist, is hired to "tune up" the face of Natalie Sheridan, a high-society filmmaker. Variant title: *Tropical Issue*.

Dunning, John

Cliff Janeway is a former Denver, Colorado, police detective who has become a rare book dealer. Cliff loves rare books and doesn't seem to mind that he doesn't make much money off of them. John Dunning, Denver police reporter turned rare book dealer, provides much interesting information about the rare book trade and the odd fish who sell rare books.

Dunning should not be confused with the English true crime writer of the same name or John H. Dunning, expert on multinational corporations. Numbers 1 and 2 were reprinted together in the omnibus *Booked Twice* (Scribner, 2004).

1. *Booked to Die* **(Scribner, 1992)** Shortly after opening his rare book store, Twice Told Books, on East Colfax in Denver, ex-cop Cliff Janeway is forced to revive his detective skills when two local "book scouts" are murdered.
2. *Bookman's Wake, The* **(Scribner, 1995)** Cliff starts to think that the fiery death in 1969 of the brothers Darryl and Richard Grayson, who produced legendary limited-edition books, was no accident, as he tracks down a woman who purportedly stole a rare Grayson edition of Edgar Allan Poe's *The Raven*.
3. *Bookman's Promise, The* **(Scribner, 2004)** Published nine years after number 2, this installment finds Janeway tracking down, from Baltimore to Charleston, a rare first edition of a work by the explorer-writer Richard Burton.
4. *Sign of the Book, The* **(Scribner, 2005)** Janeway travels to the mountain town of Paradise, Colorado, to check on a girlhood friend of his lover, hotshot lawyer Erin D'Angelo. Laura Marshall is accused of murdering her husband, Bobby, an old flame of Erin's.

5. *Bookwoman's Last Fling, The* (Scribner, 2006) Answering an invitation from wealthy horse trainer H. R. Geiger to come to Idaho to appraise his book collection, Cliff arrives to find Geiger dead.

Durrell, Lawrence

I. The late Lawrence Durrell's literary conundrums are an acquired taste but, for the persistent reader, the rewards are great. Durrell's literary reputation is based especially on the Alexandria Quartet. This series captures the Egyptian city of Alexandria in all its enigmatic splendor and decadence. Durrell intended the first three novels as "siblings" showing three sides of space, with the fourth adding the dimension of time. The tetralogy is available in a one-volume omnibus, *Alexandria Quartet* (Dutton, 1962).

1. *Justine* (Dutton, 1957) An unidentified narrator tells the story of his affair with the beautiful and complex Justine Hosnani as World War II threatens Alexandria. All the other characters in the quartet are introduced in this volume.
2. *Balthazar* (Dutton, 1958) S. Balthazar, a homosexual physician, has "corrected the errors and omissions" in the account related in *Justine*, now revealed to be the memoir of L. G. Darley, a poor Anglo-Irish schoolteacher.
3. *Mountolive* (Dutton, 1959) David Mountolive, who eventually becomes the English ambassador to Egypt, tells his story. His view adds a political perspective: the Zionist activities of Justine and her husband are revealed.
4. *Clea* (Dutton, 1960) After a lapse of several years, Darley resumes his narrative, covering events through his postwar affair with the artist Clea Montis.

II. The titles of this pair of novels refer to the epigraph by Petronius "aut tunc aut nunquam," which, loosely translated, means "now or never." The major character is inventor Felix Charlock.

1. *Tunc* (Dutton, 1968) Felix Charlock, the inventor of a giant computer named Able, has bawdy, fantastic adventures.
2. *Nunquam* (Dutton, 1970) Felix Charlock has developed the miraculously lifelike doll, Iolanthe, for the Merlin Corporation.

III. The Avignon quintet of "quincunx" is Durrell's most complicated and self-indulgent concoction, featuring exotic settings, improbable characters, Gnostic conspiracies, and buried treasure.

1. *Livia; or, Buried Alive* (Viking, 1979) This novel, though published second, is the first in the series chronologically. It describes a band of friends and lovers gathered near the French city of Avignon in period between the world wars, including British consul Felix Chatto, the novelist Blanford, and Livia, within whose beautiful body a man is "buried alive."
2. *Monsieur; or, The Prince of Darkness* (Viking, 1975) A lifelong ménage à trois between Piers and Sylvie, brother and sister, and Bruce, their doctor friend, is punctuated by philosophic and amatory quests and a ritual suicide carried out by a cult of Gnostics.
3. *Constance; or, Solitary Practices* (Viking, 1982) World War II scatters Avignon's English colony. Psychoanalyst Constance resumes her studies in Geneva, while her husband, Sam, and novelist Blanford find themselves in the Egyptian campaign.
4. *Sebastian; or, Ruling Passions* (Viking, 1984) The Egyptian banker Affad, also known as Sebastian, falls in love with Constance and falls afoul of the mysterious Gnostic brotherhood.

5. *Quinx; or, The Ripper's Tale* (Viking, 1985) Blanford returns to Avignon after the war with his friend Constance and with Sutcliffe, his fictional creation and alter ego.

Dymmoch, Michael Allen

Psychiatrist Jack Caleb and police officer John Thinnes, both veterans of the Vietnam War, are two characters who haven't really come to terms with their Vietnam experiences and lead troubled personal lives. Although they are quite different—Caleb is gay and ultrarefined; Thinnes is a streetwise cop—they feel a grudging and growing admiration for each other as they tackle cases together in Chicago. Their Vietnam memories, which are pretty strong stuff, come back to haunt them as they engage in a series of suspenseful, well-plotted investigations.

1. *Man Who Understood Cats, The* (St. Martin's, 1993) Both psychiatrist Jack Caleb and policeman John Thinnes are looking for the killer of an accountant in a mystery involving a lithograph, an art gallery, a dead young artist, and a large real-estate empire.
2. *Death of Blue Mountain Cat* (St. Martin's, 1996) Native American artist Blue Mountain Cat, a former patient of Caleb's, is stabbed to death at the opening of his art exhibit, the first in series of attacks against Native Americans.
3. *Incendiary Designs* (St. Martin's, 1998) Chicago's heat wave is killing dozens, but a group of religious zealots seems bent on making things worse in a series of arsons and murders.
4. *Feline Friendship, The* (St. Martin's, 2003) The investigation of a serial rapist–murderer brings Caleb and Thinnes back together again as Caleb deals with a patient having flashbacks about a 15-year-old rape, and Thinnes has to deal with a belligerently feminist new partner.
5. *White Tiger* (St. Martin's, 2005) Thinnes believes that the murderer of Vietnamese refugee Hue An Lee, wife of his friend Bobby Lee, is a criminal known only as White Tiger, whom he tried to track down years ago in Saigon.

Eccles, Marjorie

Detective Chief Inspector, later Detective Superintendent, Gil Mayo is one of your dogged English types. With his cohorts, including Detective Inspector, later Detective Chief Inspector, Abigail Moon, and Detective Inspector Martin Kite, Mayo looks into a series of complicated murders in and about the small English town of Lavenstock in a series of elegantly written mysteries. Marjorie Eccles, who lives in Hertfordshire, has also written other mysteries and romances under the pseudonyms of Judith Bordill and Jennifer Hyde.

1. *Cast a Cold Eye* (Doubleday, 1988) Introduces Gil Mayo, as he investigates the death, from a blow by a crystal inkwell, of architect Lethbridge. W. B. Yeats's line "Cast a cold eye" also provided the title for a collection of short stories by Mary McCarthy.
2. *Death of a Good Woman* (Doubleday, 1989) Gil Mayo's hometown, Lavenstock, is the scene of the disappearance and murder of romance writer and philanthropist Fleur Lamont.
3. *Requiem for a Dove* (Doubleday, 1990) Marion Dove, the matriarch of a family of glass manufacturers, was suffering from terminal cancer. So why did someone strangle her and leave her body in a canal?
4. *More Deaths Than One* (Doubleday, 1990) The shotgun death of journalist Rupert Fleming was originally thought to be suicide.

But the coroner's verdict of murder leads Gil Mayo and his assistant Martin Kite to a plethora of suspects.

5. *Late of This Parish* (St. Martin's, 1994) The Reverend Cecil Willard of the village of Castle Wyvering was not a man who endeared himself to others. But who would want to kill him, and why? Originally published in the United Kingdom in 1992.

6. *Company She Kept, The* (St. Martin's, 1996) Gil Mayo's new sergeant, Abigail Moon, helps him to link the strangulation death of seemingly blameless Angie Robinson, the old house Flowerdew, owned by the eccentric former archaeologist Kitty Wilbraham, and another murder. *The Company She Kept* is also the title of Doris Grumbach's biography of Mary McCarthy. Originally published in the United Kingdom in 1993.

7. *Accidental Shroud, An* (St. Martin's, 1997) The finding of local antique jeweler Nigel Fontenoy's body at the building site of his cousin Jake Wilding leads to a case of tangled family ties. Originally published in the United Kingdom in 1994.

8. *Death of Distinction, A* (St, Martin's, 1998) Gil Mayo, now promoted to detective superintendent, is faced with the violent death of Jack Lilburne, governor of Conyhall Young Offender's Institution. Originally published in the United Kingdom in 1995.

9. *Species of Revenge, A* (St. Martin's, 1998) Lavenstock is the scene of two violent deaths, one of an unidentified man. Were one or two people responsible for the deaths? Originally published in the United Kingdom in 1996.

10. *Killing Me Softly* (St. Martin's, 1999) Narcotics have reached Lavenstock, and the team of Mayo and Moon are up to their necks investigating the homicide of a member of a well-known and respected family who turns out to have some pretty shady connections.

11. *Superintendent's Daughter, The* (St. Martin's, 2000) The best friend of Julie Mayo, Gil's daughter, has been murdered, and Julie has disappeared. Mayo is forced to stand aside as his assistant Abigail Moon investigates.

12. *Sunset Touch, A* (St. Martin's, 2001) Martin Kite, recently returned to Lavenstock, investigates the brutal attack on Vicar Haldane's wife, as Mayo assigns the case of a fatal house fire on Bessemer Street to Abigail Moon.

13. *Untimely Graves* (St. Martin's, 2004) A "mystery woman" is found floating in the flooded uplands near an isolated farm, and identification proves to be impossible until a second murder occurs. Originally published in the United Kingdom in 2001.

Eddings, David & Leigh

I. David Eddings has a basic formula for fantasy: "Take a bit of magic, mix well with a few open-ended Jungian archetypal myths, make your people sweat and smell and get hungry at inopportune moments, throw in a ponderous prehistory, and let nature take its course" (*Contemporary Authors, New Revision Series*).

The compounds Eddings makes with this formula have proven very popular. Of course, great storytelling, interesting characters, and Eddings's irreverent wit don't hurt, either. The Belgariad (numbers 2–6) and the Malloreon (numbers 7–12) with their prequel (number 1) cover thousands of years of internecine war between gods, kings, heroes, and sorcerers before the final confrontation between the Child of the Light and the Child of the Dark. *The Belgariad, Part One* (Doubleday, 1983) and *The Belgariad, Part Two* (Doubleday, 1984) contain numbers 2, 3, and 4 and numbers 5 and 6, respectively. The boxed set *The Malloreon* contains numbers 7 through 11. *The Malloreon, Volume 1* and *The Malloreon, Volume 2*

(Ballantine, 2005) contain numbers 7, 8, and 9 and numbers 10 and 11, respectively.

1. *Belgarath the Sorcerer* (Ballantine, 1995) David acknowledges his wife Leigh's longtime collaboration in this prequel, which relates how Belgarath became the disciple of the god Aldur. Coauthored with Leigh Eddings.

2. *Pawn of Prophecy* (Ballantine, 1982) Garion grows up on a quiet farm, unaware of the prophecies about the Orb of Aldur and the mad god Torak.

3. *Queen of Sorcery* (Ballantine, 1983) Belgarath, his daughter Polgara, and farmboy-turned-wizard Garion continue their quest to prevent the Orb from reviving Torak.

4. *Magician's Gambit* (Ballantine, 1983) Belgarath, Polgara, and Garion travel to the Castle of Rak Cthol, where they rescue the Orb from the evil Ctuchik.

5. *Castle of Wizardry* (Ballantine, 1984) Garion becomes Belgarion, Overlord of the West, and is betrothed to the princess Ce'Nedra.

6. *Enchanters' Endgame* (Ballantine, 1984) Belgarion overcomes the evil god Torak, thus fulfilling his role in the ancient prophecies.

7. *Guardians of the West* (Ballantine, 1987) Belgarath and Polgara settle in the Vale of Aldur while Belgarion tends to his Overlord of the West duties.

8. *King of the Murgos* (Ballantine, 1988) The evil priestess Zandramas kidnaps Belgarion's son and heir.

9. *Demon Lord of Karanda* (Ballantine, 1988) Belgarion, Ce'Nedra, and their companions set forth to save their kidnapped son from Zandramas.

10. *Sorceress of Darshiva* (Ballantine, 1989) Belgarion, Zandramas, and other interested parties race toward the ancient city of Kell to fulfill or thwart the prophecy in the Oracles.

11. *Seeress of Kell, The* (Ballantine, 1991) Cyradis, the blind seeress of Kell, will decide whether the forces of Light or Dark will prevail.

12. *Polgara the Sorceress* (Del Rey, 1997) Polgara, daughter of Belgarath, is the narrator and protagonist of this final volume in the *Belgariad* and *Malloreon* cycles. Coauthor: Leigh Eddings.

II. The Elenium (numbers 1–3) and the Tamuli (numbers 4–6) feature the struggles of Sir Sparhawk, Queen Ehlana, and an assorted cast of characters against the forces of evil backed by certain mad gods. *The Elenium* (Ballantine, 1993) contains numbers 1 through 3. *The Tamuli* (Ballantine, 1999) contains numbers 4 through 6.

1. *Diamond Throne, The* (Ballantine, 1989) Queen Ehlana is poisoned by the ambitious Annias the priest and frozen in crystal until a cure can be found.

2. *Ruby Knight, The* (Ballantine, 1990) Sparhawk and an oddly assorted company of knights set out in quest of the magic jewel Bhelliom.

3. *Sapphire Rose, The* (Ballantine, 1992) Sparhawk succeeds in saving Ehlana with the magic jewel Bhelliom.

4. *Domes of Fire* (Ballantine, 1993) The Tamul Empire, beset by internal strife, begs help from Sparhawk, savior of the Elenes.

5. *Shining Ones, The* (Ballantine, 1993) Sparhawk and his daughter Danae have to go on another quest to retrieve the jewel Bhelliom.

6. *Hidden City, The* (Ballantine, 1994) Sparhawk must rescue Ehlana from the followers of the mad god Cyrgon.

III. After a 10-year hiatus, the Eddings produced a new series called the Dreamers. The Land of Dhrall is composed of a dark center ruled by something called the Vlagh and four compass directions each run by a god. The usual fantasy fare: good versus evil, a prophecy that has to be worked out, a host of different characters both "natural" and supernatural, and a lot of fighting.

1. *Elder Gods, The* (Warner, 2003) A prophesy speaks of the Dreamers, children whose dreams will defeat the evil Vlagh by controlling the natural forces of Mother Sea and Father Earth.
2. *Treasured One, The* (Warner, 2004) The four gods face a new menace in the Land of Dhrall. The Vlagh, an evil insectoid creature, is trying to take over the world.
3. *Crystal Gorge, The* (Warner, 2005) The Ruler of the Wasteland challenges the gods and wreaks devastation on their realms.
4. *Younger Gods, The* (Warner, 2006) The Vlagh has been repelled in three of the Elder Gods' realms. Only the land of the Goddess Aracia remains.

Edgerton, Clyde

Clyde Edgerton is the author of novels set in small towns in North Carolina. His first novel, *Raney* (Algonquin, 1985), cost him his teaching job at Campbell University, North Carolina, because of alleged derogatory representations of Baptists, although his target was "respectable" religion rather than Christians or Baptists per se. Edgerton continues to write fictions delineating vivid characters with insight, compassion, and humor in the tradition of rural American storytelling. Elderly Mattie Rigsbee and young Wesley Benfield are the protagonists in two novels that explore the real meanings of tradition, family, and being "a good Christian."

1. *Walking across Egypt* (Algonquin, 1987) Seventy-eight-year-old Mattie Rigsbee and orphan delinquent Wesley Benfield find mutual challenge, love, and support.
2. *Killer Diller* (Algonquin, 1990) Wesley, now 24, is a resident at a halfway house associated with a Baptist college, organizing his own gospel-blues band and wrestling with conflicting feelings of faith and lust.

Edgerton, Teresa (Ann)

I.   Celydonn is a fantasy world, more or less akin to our medieval world. While Celydonn is a Christian kingdom, a good deal of magic is practiced there. Six books, divided into two trilogies, are set in this world. The Green Lion trilogy (numbers 1–3) follows the fortunes of Teleri, a female apprentice wizard, and the young knight Cerilyn, as they battle the evil Princess Diaspad and her version of Wild Magic. The second trilogy, the Chronicles of Celydonn (numbers 4–6), is set several years later, and features Gwenlliant, a secondary character in the first trilogy, a natural psychic and adept of earth magic, who is now an adult and married to Prince Tryffin. The pair travel to the rival kingdom of Mochdreff, where Gwenlliant's magic is called upon to bring peace to the realm. This is absorbing fantasy with sympathetic characters. Teresa Edgerton is a Californian who once worked as a Tarot card reader.

1. *Child of Saturn* (Ace, 1989) Only the apprentice wizardess Teleri and the young knight Ceilyn can save the kingdom of Celydonn from the machinations of the evil Princess Diaspad.
2. *Moon in Hiding, The* (Ace, 1989) Teleri and Ceilyn are set up as fall guys when magic bones are stolen, and ancient rituals are revived.
3. *Work of the Sun, The* (Ace, 1990) Only the queen's sorceress, Teleri, now betrothed to the Ceilyn mac Cuel, the realm's finest knight, stands between Princess Diaspad and the kingdom of Celydonn.

4. *Castle of the Silver Wheel, The* (Ace, 1993) Gwenlliant of Celydonn, a secondary character in the first trilogy, an adept of earth magic, accompanies her husband, Prince Tryffin to the realm of Mochdreff, where he must act as ruler for a people who are the enemies of Celydonn.
5. *Grail and the Ring, The* (Ace, 1994) While Tryffin is examining the infestation of a nearby village by a vampirelike creature, Gwenlliant and their infant son are catapulted by an ancient ring into the mysterious Shadow Realm.
6. *Moon and the Thorn, The* (Ace, 1995) Gwenlliant, on a quest to save her son from the hands of an old enemy, finds that her magic power is mysteriously thwarted.

II.   The Goblin novels are a pair of fantasies set in an alternative universe related to our 18th century. Elves, gnomes, and humans live in harmony together, but they are all preyed upon by goblins. Lord Skelbrooke, a handsome, swashbuckling knight, is forced to overcome his addiction to a drug called Sleepdust before he can bring tranquility to his world.

1. *Goblin Moon* (Ace, 1991) Goblins prey upon a kingdom ruled by humans, elves, and gnomes. Only Lord Skelbrooke can save the day: if he kicks his addiction to Sleepdust.
2. *Gnome's Engine, The* (Ace, 1991) Lord Skelbrooke joins with a gnome-scientist to create a machine combining science and magic.

Edghill, Rosemary

PSEUDONYM OF Eluki bes-Shahar

I.   Karen Hightower is a thirtyish layout artist, tarot card reader, and Wiccan practitioner (witchcraft and the occult). Bast, as she is called by her cohorts, has a trio of adventures in New York City and upstate New York with the New York Metropagan community, involving witchcraft and other pagan practices. These are lighthearted fantasies-mysteries appropriate for YA and adult readers. *Bell, Book, and Murder* (Forge, 1998) is an omnibus volume containing all three titles. Eluki bes-Shahar (q.v.) also publishes fantasy and SF titles under her real name, and romances under the Edghill pseudonym.

1. *Speak Daggers to Her* (Forge, 1994) Karen Hightower, aka Bast, receives a desperate phone call alerting her to the murder of her love Miriam Seabrook.
2. *Book of Moons* (Forge, 1995) Ned Skelton, clerk from a witchcraft store, announces, at an "ecumenpicnic," that he has proof that Mary, Queen of Scots, practiced witchcraft.
3. *Bowl of Night, The* (Forge, 1996) The Rev. Jackson Harm, fanatical opponent of witchcraft, is slain at a Hallowfest in upstate New York, possibly by some of Bast's witch friends.

II.   When an elf is mugged outside her New York City apartment, graduate library science student Ruth Marlowe is started on a trio of adventures that take her to the magic world of Elphane. *The Empty Crown* (SF Book Club, 1997) is an omnibus volume containing all three titles. Rosemary Edghill has also collaborated with fantasy heavyweights such as Marion Zimmer Bradley (q.v.) (the Truth Jourdemayne series), Mercedes Lackey (q.v.) (Bedlam's Bard), and Andre Norton (q.v.) (Carolus Rex).

1. *Sword of Maiden's Tears, The* (DAW, 1994) An elf, Rohannon Melior, has been mugged outside of Ruth Marlowe's apartment building in New York City, and has lost his sword, a sword that, in human hands, will produce flesh-eating monsters.

2. *Cup of Morning Shadows, The* (DAW, 1995) Ruth Marlowe steps through a magic portal in the basement of the Ippisiqua, New York, public library, and enters the magical domain of Elphane, where Rohannon, High Lord of the House of the Silver Silence, is engaged in combat with the wicked Baligant.

3. *Cloak of Night and Daggers, The* (DAW, 1997) Elfen librarian Mac escapes his wrongful imprisonment in an insane asylum and, with the help of a female warrior, joins forces with Ruth and Rohannon against the forces of Baligant.

Edric, Robert

PSEUDONYM OF Gary Edric Armitage

The Song Cycle is a trio of contemporary noir novels set in the decaying English "rust belt" city of Hull, featuring private investigator Leo Rivers, an English version of Raymond Chandler's (q.v.) Philip Marlowe. Robert Edric is a well-regarded English author (*Winter Garden*), who knows his seedy, corrupt Hull well.

1. *Cradle Song* (Doubleday, 2003) Private investigator Leo Rivers is hired by a Hull businessman to investigate the death of his daughter Nicola in a case that involves a pedophile ring, a convicted murderer who may be innocent, official corruption, and a string of murders.

2. *Siren Song* (Doubleday, 2004) Leo Rivers is approached by the mother of a girl who disappeared a year earlier in violent and mysterious circumstances.

3. *Swan Song* (Doubleday, 2005) Three young women have been murdered. The latest victim's boyfriend, now in a coma from a drug overdose, is regarded by the Hull police as the principal suspect, at least in her case. Rivers is hired by the suspect's mother to find out what really happened.

Edwards, Martin (Kenneth Martin)

I. Harry Devlin is a Liverpool, England, solicitor and amateur detective whose cases are often punctuated by murder. Solicitor and author Martin Edwards provides a good view of Liverpool's underside in these novels, which should be better known in the United States.

1. *All the Lonely People* (Transworld, 1992) Liverpool solicitor Harry Devlin is still in love with his errant wife, Liz, and hopes rise for a reconciliation when she turns up at his flat. Then she is murdered. First hardcover publication in the US: Five Star, 2003.

2. *Suspicious Minds* (Transworld, 1993) The wife of Jack Stirrup, Harry's best client, goes missing. Stirrup claims she is still alive, but then his daughter and her boyfriend also vanish. First hardcover publication in the US: Five Star, 2006.

3. *I Remember You* (Transworld, 1994) Somebody is really out to get Harry's client, tattooist Finbar Rogan. First Rogan's studio is torched; then a bomb is planted under his car.

4. *Yesterday's Papers* (Transworld, 1995) Thirty years after the murder of Carole Jeffries and the confession and conviction of her neighbor, the case is reopened when evidence that the real culprit has escaped justice is uncovered.

5. *Eve of Destruction* (Foul Play, 1998) Harry is hard-pressed to sort out victim and culprit when a matrimonial case turns into a conspiracy to commit murder. Originally published in the United Kingdom in 1996.

6. *Devil in Disguise, The* (Hodder & Stoughton [UK], 1998) The Kavanaugh Trust hires Harry to contest the will of their late patron Charles Kavanaugh, who has left everything to his new housekeeper, Vera Blackhurst. Not published in the United States.

7. *First Cut Is the Deepest, The* (Hodder & Stoughton [UK], 1999) No annotation available. Not published in the United States.

8. *Waterloo Sunset* (Poisoned Pen, 2008) Harry receives a fake newspaper notice announcing his death on Midsummer's Eve. The notice is followed by threatening messages.

II. Harry Devlin was abandoned for several years for a new series set in England's Lake District, featuring DCI Hannah Scarlett and her squad. So far, three of these "village capers" have been published.

1. *Coffin Trail, The* (Poisoned Pen, 2004) Historian and TV personality Daniel Kind moves back to the Lake District with his new lover, Miranda. Daniel is still haunted by the case of a previous occupant of Tarn Cottage in Brackdale, autistic youth Barrie Gilpin, who was accused of the ritualistic murder of a young woman but who fell to his death before he could be questioned.

2. *Cipher Garden, The* (Poisoned Pen, 2005) Somebody, probably his wife, Tina, hacked Warren Howe, landscaper and ladies' man, to death with a scythe in a garden in Old Sawrey in the Lake District. Daniel Kind and DCI Hannah Scarlett team up as sleuths again.

3. *Arsenic Labyrinth, The* (Poisoned Pen, 2007) The investigation of the disappearance of Emma Bestwick is reopened when a returning drifter tips off a local journalist as to what happened to her.

Edwards, Grace F.

African American resident of Harlem Mali Anderson was fired from the NYPD after slugging a fellow officer who insulted her. Mali becomes a college student majoring in social work, but her law enforcement instincts still come to the fore when friends or relations need help, and Mali can use her connections, her street smarts, and her intimate knowledge of Harlem. Grace Edwards has written two standalone novels set in Harlem: *In the Shadow of the Peacock* (McGraw-Hill, 1996), a coming-of-age novel, and *The Viaduct* (Doubleday, 2003), a thriller.

1. *If I Should Die* (Doubleday, 1997) Ex-cop Mali Anderson lives in Harlem with her father and her orphaned nephew. On her way to pick up her nephew from a rehearsal with the Uptown Children's Chorus, Mali thwarts a kidnapping attempt but fails to stop the fatal shooting of the chorus's director.

2. *Toast before Dying, A* (Doubleday, 1998) Mali gets involved with crime again when a friend of hers is arrested for the murder of a Harlem bartender. Then two more murders occur.

3. *No Time to Die* (Doubleday, 1999) Mali suspects James Thomas, the abusive ex-husband of her friend Claudine, when Claudine is murdered.

4. *Do or Die* (Doubleday, 2000) When jazz-singer Starr Hendrix, who sings with Mali's father, has her throat slashed, the obvious suspect is Starr's former drug supplier and would-be pimp, Short Change. Then Short Change dies.

Edwards, Ruth Dudley

Robert Amiss, a rather hapless young Englishman who has shuffled from one job to another: the civil service, teaching, conference organizer, waiter, you name it; seems to be consistent in only one thing: that he will blunder into at least one murder mystery in each of the novels in which he is featured. Amiss, rather unfortunately, has a friend in the Baroness Ida "Jack" Troutbeck, an irrepressible type who steers him into sticky situations that only seem to get worse when he arrives. Somehow Amiss has survived through a series of satirical mysteries that skewer British institutions such as the civil service, gentlemen's clubs, the House of Lords, the Church of England, publishing, the literati, political correctness, and Anglo-Irish relations. Ruth Dudley Edwards, born and raised in Dublin, but now living in London, went through a series of jobs herself before settling into writing. Besides the Amiss mysteries, Edwards has published nonfiction titles, mostly about journalistic subjects (e.g., *Newspapermen: Hugh Cudlipp, Cecil Harmsworth King and the Glory Days of Fleet Street;* Secker [UK], 2005).

1. *Corridors of Death* (St. Martin's, 1982) Detective Superintendent James Milton of Scotland Yard wonders who would want Sir Nicholas Clark dead, after the respected civil servant is found with his head bashed in, then Milton discovers that just about everyone in Sir Nicholas's life wanted him dead.
2. *Saint Valentine's Day Murders, The* (St. Martin's, 1984) Robert Amiss, still in the British Civil Service, is seconded to the newly privatized British Conservation Corporation, where he again finds pettiness, malice, envy, and nasty practical jokes galore and, eventually, murder.
3. *English School of Murder, The* (St. Martin's, 1990) Amiss, currently without visible means of support, finds himself persuaded by his old pals in the CID to investigate sinister goings-on at the Knightsbridge School of English, whose overt mission is teaching English as a second language. Variant title: *The School of English Murder.*
4. *Clubbed to Death* (St. Martin's, 1992) That fine old British institution—gentlemen's clubs—gets raked over the coals, as Robert Amiss gets an undercover job as a waiter in a club, seemingly a stronghold of "debauched geriatrics," where the club's secretary took a fatal tumble.
5. *Matricide at St. Martin's* (St. Martin's, 1995) British academia takes a hit as Robert Amiss is awarded a one-year fellowship at the seemingly placid St. Martha's College. When St. Martha's receives a large bequest, academic politics escalates into murder.
6. *Ten Lords A-Leaping* (St. Martin's, 1996) Robert Amiss is dragooned by "Jack" Troutbeck into defending the ancient British "sport" of fox-hunting, when animal rights activists bring the issue to another British tradition: the House of Lords.
7. *Murder in a Cathedral* (St. Martin's, 1997) Canon Fulbert, of Westonbury Cathedral, long dominated by a cadre of radical gay priests, feminist witches, and New Age cultists, is understandably concerned about the new dean, Norm Cooper, a fundamentalist American with a crazy wife.
8. *Publish and Be Murdered* (Poisoned Pen, 1999) Edwards fictionalizes some of her own experiences as a journalist, as Robert Amiss takes on a job at the *Wrangler*, a revered political magazine. Originally published in the United Kingdom in 1997.
9. *Anglo-Irish Murders, The* (Thorndike, 2001) The tactless and impatient Baroness Troutbeck, who has been chosen to chair a conference on Anglo-Irish sensitivities, bullies Robert Amiss into becoming conference organizer. Everyone seems determined to live up to the worst stereotypes of the Irish and English. Published only in large print in the United States.
10. *Carnage on the Committee* (Poisoned Pen, 2004) The committee in question is charged with awarding the prestigious Knapper-Warburton Literary Prize. Baroness "Jack" is, in a switch, recruited by committee member Robert Amiss as chairperson when the previous chair dies in suspicious circumstances.
11. *Murdering Americans* (Poisoned Pen, 2007) Baroness "Jack" experiences culture shock as a distinguished visiting professor at "politically correct" Freeman State University in Paddington, Indiana.

Egan, Lesley

PSEUDONYM OF Elizabeth Linington

Police detective Vic Varallo and Jewish lawyer Jesse Falkenstein shared top billing in *A Case for Appeal*, the first novel in a series of police procedurals set in Glendale, California. They alternated as the main character in the (roughly) annual volumes that appeared between 1961 and 1985. The relationship between Falkenstein and his wife, Nell, and Varallo's domestic problems are continuing threads in the series. Elizabeth Linington (q.v.) also wrote police procedurals under her real name and as (most famously) Dell Shannon (q.v.). Because each novel deals with a tangle of different cases, annotations are not provided.

1. *Case for Appeal, A* (Harper, 1961)
2. *Against the Evidence* (Harper, 1962)
3. *Borrowed Alibi, The* (Harper, 1962)
4. *Run to Evil* (Harper, 1963)
5. *My Name Is Death* (Harper, 1965)
6. *Detective's Due* (Harper, 1965)
7. *Some Avenger, Rise!* (Harper, 1966)
8. *Nameless Ones, The* (Harper, 1967)
9. *Serious Investigation, A* (Harper, 1968)
10. *Wine of Violence, The* (Harper, 1969)
11. *In the Death of a Man* (Harper, 1970)
12. *Malicious Mischief* (Harper, 1971)
13. *Paper Chase* (Harper, 1972)
14. *Scenes of Crime* (Doubleday, 1976)
15. *Blind Search, The* (Doubleday, 1977)
16. *Dream Apart, A* (Doubleday, 1978)
17. *Look Back on Death* (Doubleday, 1978)
18. *Hunter and the Hunted, The* (Doubleday, 1979)
19. *Motive in Shadow* (Doubleday, 1980)
20. *Choice of Crimes, A* (Doubleday, 1980)
21. *Miser, The* (Doubleday, 1981)
22. *Random Death* (Doubleday, 1982)
23. *Little Boy Lost* (Doubleday, 1983)
24. *Crime for Christmas* (Doubleday, 1984)
25. *Chain of Violence* (Doubleday, 1985)
26. *Wine of Life, The* (Doubleday, 1985)

Egleton, Clive

I. Clive Egleton is a leading practitioner of the classic British spy novel. His stories are realistic, with a cynical view of the scheming that men in power are willing to engage in to further their personal aims, and the lengths to which they will go to cover up their follies and misdeeds. Egleton's primary series character is Peter Ashton, a midlevel British agent in the SIS. Although neo-Nazis, the IRA, renegade American and British operatives, Turkish Cypriots, Cubans, Hindu terrorists all play roles, it is the KGB who, more often than not, is his primary adversary in the 12 novels. Islamic terrorists don't make a prominent appearance until number 12. Ashton is no James Bond, but he is somewhat of a loose cannon, as he has to be to stay alive and maintain his integrity. Egleton relies on his own experiences and solid research to give his tales plausibility.

1. *Hostile Intent* (St. Martin's, 1993) British agent Peter Ashton, sent to Germany to investigate an explosion, apparently set by neo-Nazis, decides that the real target was Galina Kutuzova, daughter

and granddaughter of Soviet apparatchiks, who is probably an informant.

2. *Killing in Moscow, A* **(St. Martin's, 1994)** Ashton, now head of the Vetting, Security, and Technical Services division of Britain's SIS, investigates a plot involving the murder of a British businessman in Moscow, bent KGB agents, Serbian oil buyers, and a businessman in Seattle with family ties to the Serbs.

3. *Death Throes* **(St. Martin's, 1995)** Peter is on the trail of "Valentine," a high-ranking officer (or officers) of the supposedly defunct KGB who may want to work for Britain's SIS. Peter's fiancée, Harriet Egan, wounded in a firefight, seems ready to quit the SIS.

4. *Lethal Involvement, A* **(St. Martin's, 1996)** Peter Ashton uncovers a lurid murder with gay overtones in action that moves from London to Germany to Hong Kong to California.

5. *Warning Shot* **(St. Martin's, 1997)** Real-life FBI director Louis Freeh, stolen atomic warheads, and a CIA double (or triple) agent play roles as Ashton is temporarily exiled from "the Firm," and two British agents are found murdered and mutilated in Germany.

6. *Blood Money* **(St. Martin's, 1998)** Three agents are killed and one disappears, along with a Cuban American informant, when a British intelligence safe house is blown up.

7. *Dead Reckoning* **(St. Martin's, 1999)** One of three people found dead in a London psychiatrist's office is discovered to have been using the identity of Peter's wife, Harriet, who is still acting as an occasional operative.

8. *Honey Trap, The* **(St. Martin's, 2001)** Ashton, detailed to investigate the murder of a queen's messenger in Costa Rica, discovers links between the IRA, the KGB, Turkish Cypriots, and a former Cuban intelligence officer.

9. *One Man Running* **(St. Martin's, 2002)** Cashiered from the SIS because his cover was blown, Ashton, Harriet, and their two young children are assigned new identities, which are soon compromised, possibly by someone within the SIS.

10. *Cry Havoc* **(St. Martin's, 2003)** Peter Ashton, newly appointed head of Eastern European intelligence, can't stay out of the action, even though he delegates to capable assistants the investigation of an agent in the Asian division.

11. *Assassination Day* **(St. Martin's, 2004)** Peter is put in charge when a literary agent in possession of a tell-all memoir written by an intelligence officer who died in suspicious circumstances in 1989 is murdered by two fake cops.

12. *Renegades, The* **(St, Martin's, 2005)** A midrank British intelligence agent, a shady Egyptian businessman, and a mysterious woman are massacred in a quiet Italian restaurant in London. Ashton links the murders to Talal Asir, "distantly related to the Saudi ruling family."

II. A trio of novels, originally published in the 1970s and reprinted 30 years later, are alternative history thrillers in which the Russians have taken over Britain, and the leading character is David Garnett, a brave but beleaguered British resistance fighter.

1. *Piece of Resistance, A* **(Coward-McCann, 1970)** Britain's nuclear deterrent has failed, a Russian missile has hit Bristol, and the British government has collapsed, leaving only the Resistance to fight on against titanic odds. Reprinted as *Never Surrender* (Severn, 2004).

2. *Last Post for a Partisan* **(Coward-McCann, 1971)** There seems to be a split in the British resistance movement, with one of the groups selling out to the Russians. David Garnett is ordered by his chief to look into it. Reprinted as *The Sleeper* (Severn, 2005).

3. *Judas Mandate, The* **(Coward-McCann, 1971)** When the Russians pull out and leave British puppets to run the country, Garnett

must get six anti-Soviet politicians trying to form a government-in-exile to safety. Reprinted as *The Last Refuge* (Severn, 2006).

Ehle, John

John Ehle (pronounced *EE-lee*) has written eight novels about the Wright and King families of North Carolina, from the first settlers to come to the wilderness mountain country in the 1770s, through the Civil War with its social discord and increasing settlement, and into 20th-century growth and economic problems. Ehle writes realistically of the people and their ways while evoking the beauty of their land.

1. *Land Breakers, The* **(Harper, 1964)** Mooney Wright is the first man to arrive in the valley; a small community develops around his farm.

2. *Journey of August King, The* **(Harper, 1971)** Community and church leader August King helps a young runaway slave girl along her way in about 1810.

3. *Time of Drums* **(Harper, 1970)** The Civil War is seen through the eyes of Colonel Wright, leader of a Confederate mountain regiment.

4. *Road, The* **(Harper, 1967)** Weatherby Wright helps bring the railroad to open up the North Carolina mountains during the 1870s.

5. *Last One Home* **(Harper, 1984)** Pinkney Wright moves his family from its mountain farm community to the "big city" of Asheville around the turn of the century.

6. *Lion on the Hearth* **(Harper, 1961)** A prosperous mountain family weathers the Depression of the 1930s.

7. *Winter People, The* **(Harper, 1982)** Collie Wright, who lives alone with her baby, befriends Wayland Jackson, a recently widowed clock maker, and his 12-year-old daughter.

8. *Widow's Trial, The* **(Harper, 1989)** Winnette Plover is on trial for her life in the slaying of her sadistic husband.

Eichler, Selma

Manhattan private investigator Desiree Shapiro is fortysomething, "full-figured" (i.e., overweight), and is as devoted to good food as she is to solving mysteries. The mysteries are only part of the fun, as we are told a great deal about Desiree's relationships (her latest hot item is a guy named Nick), her views on living in New York City, and her gourmet experiences (recipes sometimes included). Desiree is a likable character, and these lighthearted Manhattan cozies are suffused with humor. The novels were paperback originals. Most of them are available in hardcover only in large-print editions.

1. *Murder Can Kill Your Social Life* **(Signet, 1994)** The killing of an elderly woman is the start of a double-murder mystery for "queen-sized" Manhattan PI Desiree Shapiro.

2. *Murder Can Ruin Your Looks* **(Signet, 1995)** Identical twins are shot—one dies and one is left in a coma. It is up to Desiree Shapiro to figure out which is which.

3. *Murder Can Stunt Your Growth* **(Signet, 1996)** Everyone accepts that 10-year-old Catherine died of natural causes. Everyone except Desiree Shapiro, that is.

4. *Murder Can Wreck Your Peroxide* **(Signet, 1997)** Desiree's niece is suspected of murdering an old friend while at her reunion. Desiree doesn't believe that the cause of death was homicide.

5. *Murder Can Spook Your Cat* **(Signet, 1998)** A noted children's book author, a frequently married woman of eccentric habits, is found dead in her study with her cat as the only witness.

6. *Murder Can Singe Your Old Flame* **(Signet, 1999)** Bruce Simon, Desiree's hated ex-boyfriend, is the prime suspect in the suspicious death of his new wife.
7. *Murder Can Spoil Your Appetite* **(Signet, 2000)** Desiree ventures into the wilds of New Jersey in search of the murderer of Frankie Vincent, protégé of a powerful crime boss.
8. *Murder Can Upset Your Mother* **(Signet, 2001)** Miriam Weiden, a wealthy philanthropist, is murdered, and Desiree finds that Miriam's life was more complicated than appearances would indicate, including an adopted baby who was really her own out of wedlock, a husband driven to suicide, and an affair with a married man.
9. *Murder Can Cool Off Your Affair* **(Signet, 2002)** John Lander, heir to an ample fortune, hires Desiree to find out who murdered the previous heir, his cousin Edward, and who is now trying to kill him.
10. *Murder Can Rain on Your Shower* **(Signet, 2003)** The groom's aunt keels over at the bridal shower that Desiree is hosting for her niece.
11. *Murder Can Botch Up Your Birthday* **(Signet, 2004)** Vicky Pirrelli wants Desiree to clear her late father, Victor, of the 10-year-old murder of his mistress.
12. *Murder Can Mess Up Your Mascara* **(Signet, 2005)** Desiree's client Gordon Curry is shot dead after he hires Desiree. Then Desiree discovers that the man Curry had fingered as his probable assassin had committed suicide two months earlier.
13. *Murder Can Run Your Stockings* **(Signet, 2006)** A client wants Desiree to catch the killer of his elderly aunt. Desiree's previously tepid romance with her neighbor Nick starts to heat up.

Eickhoff, Randy Lee

I. The Ulster, or Red Branc, series is a translation and modern re-telling of Gaelic legends, sagas, and tales from the Ulster, or Ulaid, cycle, set in the 1st or 2nd century BCE to the end of the 4th century CE during the reigns of King Conchobar, King Ailill and Queen Maeve. These epic tales survive in 12th- and 14th-century manuscripts such as *The Book of the Dun Cow*, *The Book of Leinster*, and *The Yellow Book of Lecan*. Randy Lee Eickhoff, former journalist and college teacher and now high school teacher, has retold the stories of the great Irish hero Cuchulainn and many others in a vivid and colorful narrative derived from the original prose and verse accounts. Classical scholar Eickhoff has also translated Homer's *Odyssey* (Forge, 2001).

1. *Raid, The* **(Forge, 2000)** The 17-year-old Cuchulainn defends Ulster and its valuable brown bull single-handedly against raiders from Connaught in the epic tale of *The Cattle Raid of Cooley* (*Taain Bo Cualigne*).
2. *Feast, The* **(Forge, 1999)** Fled Briciu Poison-Tongue, the trickster god, is featured here as he sends three of Ireland's mythic heroes on a wild quest to be named Champion of Conchobar.
3. *Sorrows, The* **(Forge, 2000)** Three tales, "The Fate of the Children of Tuirenn," "The Fate of the Children of Lir," and "The Fate of the Children of Uisliu," are retold here.
4. *Destruction of the Inn, The* **(Forge, 2001)** King Conaire Mor ignores the prophecy that foretells his fate when he refuses to execute his three pillaging foster brothers.
5. *He Stands Alone* **(Forge, 2002)** The tale of the "Irish Achilles," Cuchulainn, is told here, including his mysterious birth, his inadvertent slaying of his son, his romances with Emer and Fand, and his death fighting the phantom army of Queen Maeve.
6. *Red Branch Tales, The* **(Forge, 2003)** Twenty more tales from the Ulster cycle are related here.

II. Randy Lee Eickhoff has also fictionalized the lives of Doc Holliday, Jim Bowie, and Wild Bill Hickok as well as writing more or less contemporary novels, such as the pair of thrillers featuring the journalist Con Edwards, which are set in Vietnam and Ireland.

1. *Hand to Execute, A* **(Walker, 1987)** The curiosity of Jerry Muhl, new assistant to newspaperman Con Edwards, results in his murder in Saigon during the Vietnam War.
2. *Gombeen Man, The* **(Walker, 1992)** Con Edwards finds himself in Ireland for the funeral of an old friend, Conor Larkin, former gunman for the IRA. Befriending Larkin's widow, Con searches for the "gombeen man" (informer) responsible for Larkin's death.

Elkins, Aaron J. & Charlotte

I. Aaron J. and Charlotte Elkins have been collaborating on mystery stories for more than 20 years. According to Aaron, Charlotte gets the ideas and he does the "editing." However, Aaron gets the author credit on two of the three series the former anthropology professor and his former student and wife of 30 years produce. Gideon Oliver, forensic anthropologist and sleuth, has been their longest-running character. Though he rather cringes at the moniker "Skeleton Detective," Oliver is enthusiastic about examining old bones and determining how the bones' owners met their ends. The shy, low-key, slightly clumsy Gideon puts his anthropological skills to good use in this series of scientific puzzlers.

1. *Fellowship of Fear* **(Walker, 1982)** Oliver, doing a stint at American military schools in Europe, is attacked and threatened, seemingly without reason.
2. *Dark Place, The* **(Walker, 1983)** Gideon teams up with forest ranger Julie Tendler to find out what happened to the hikers whose bones were unearthed in Olympic National Park.
3. *Murder in the Queene's Armes* **(Walker, 1985)** Gideon decides to drop in on a Dorset dig run by an old friend while honeymooning in England with Julie.
4. *Old Bones* **(Ballantine, 1987)** Oliver helps French inspector Joly to investigate the mysterious appearance of a corpse in the cellar of an old manor.
5. *Curses!* **(Mysterious, 1989)** Gideon goes to the scene of the theft of a priceless Mayan codex in Yucatan.
6. *Icy Clutches* **(Mysterious, 1990)** Oliver is vacationing in Alaska when human bones turn up at a 30-year-old avalanche site.
7. *Make No Bones* **(Mysterious, 1991)** Whitebark Lodge in Oregon, scene of an earlier tragedy, is the site of the sixth biennial "bone bash and weenie roast" of the Western Association of Forensic Anthropologists.
8. *Dead Men's Hearts* **(Mysterious, 1994)** An ancient Egyptian skeleton seems to be out of place in the storeroom of Horizon House in Luxor.
9. *Twenty Blue Devils* **(Mysterious, 1996)** Oliver travels to Tahiti with FBI agent John Lau to investigate the possible murder of the manager of Paradise Coffee Plantation.
10. *Skeleton Dance* **(Morrow, 2000)** Gideon travels to Les Eyzies, a French village, where some human bones, thought originally to be prehistoric, have turned out to be less than five years old.
11. *Good Blood* **(Berkley, 2004)** Gideon and his wife accompany Phil Boyajian to the village of Stresa on Italy's Lake Maggiore. Phil's cousin, Achille de Grazia, gets kidnapped.
12. *Where There's a Will* **(Berkley, 2005)** Gideon, on vacation in Hawaii, gets involved in a 10-year-old mystery surrounding the deaths of two elderly Swedish brothers.

13. *Unnatural Selection* **(Berkley, 2006)** Gideon accompanies his wife, Julie, to a gathering of conservation experts in the Scilly Isles. While examining some human remains in a local museum, he discovers that one bone is a recent relic.

14. *Little Tiny Teeth* **(Berkley, 2007)** Gideon takes a trip up the Amazon River with his friends Phil Boyajian and John Lau. Deep in the jungle they find themselves in the middle of a blood feud, along with drug smuggling, greed, and murder.

II. Chris Norgren is another amateur detective who is interested in old things. In his case, he is an art museum curator whose knowledge of art gets him involved in solving thefts and murders.

1. *Deceptive Clarity, A* **(Walker, 1987)** Norgren is sent to Berlin to help a colleague identify a forgery in a display of recovered art treasures.

2. *Glancing Light, A* **(Scribner, 1991)** A fake Van Eyck and a genuine Rubens turn up in the Seattle warehouse of a shlock art importer.

3. *Old Scores* **(Scribner, 1993)** Rene Vachey, notorious for staging thefts as publicity stunts, is offering a newly discovered "Rembrandt" for sale.

III. Charlotte Elkins is sometimes listed as primary author in a series starring female pro golfer and occasional sleuth Lee Ofsted.

1. *Wicked Slice, A* **(Fawcett, 1989)** Lee is slicing her drives at the Woman's Pro-Am Golf Tournament, but that is nothing compared to the plight of tour star Kate O'Brien, who is lying dead in a golf course water hazard.

2. *Rotten Lies* **(Mysterious, 1995)** Ofsted endangers her lead in the High Desert Tournament by attempting CPR on an apparent lightning victim.

3. *Nasty Breaks* **(Mysterious, 1997)** Lee gets a job teaching golf to employees of Sea Recovery Systems, a marine salvage company, at a resort on Block Island.

4. *On the Fringe* **(Severn House, 2005)** Lee Ofsted goes to Hawaii to help her old mentor run his posh Royal Mauna Kea Golf and Country Club's centennial celebration and to wed cop turned security consultant Graham Sheldon.

Elliott, Kate

PSEUDONYM OF Alis A. Rasmussen

I. The kingdoms of Wendar and Varre are in a setting reminiscent of the European Middle Ages, but, like all respectable fantasy kingdoms, they are steeped in sorcery and have a supernatural nemesis, this time called the Cursed Ones. Characters like the sorceress Laith, her friend and ally Alain, and Prince Sanglant have to slog their way through a raft of human and inhuman perils to achieve their destinies in the seven-volume Crown of Stars series. Alis A. Rasmussen has also authored the Highroad trilogy under her own name.

1. *King's Dragon* **(DAW, 1997)** Raiders, both human and inhuman, cross the borders of the Kingdom of Wendar, portents abound, and dark spirits appear in the daylight hours. Two youngsters, Alain and Liath, are thrown into the middle of the maelstrom.

2. *Prince of Dogs* **(DAW, 1997)** Alain is now heir to the throne of Wendar. Liath is trying to unravel the secrets of her past and hold on to her hidden treasure. Sanglant is a prisoner in the city of Gent. Fifth Brother is building up an army.

3. *Burning Stone, The* **(DAW, 1998)** King Henry wants his bastard son Sanglant to be his heir, but Sanglant is more interested in Liath, who saved him from captivity and is bearing his child.

The nonhuman Eika and Quman invaders are up to no good. Coauthored with Andre Norton (q.v.).

4. *Child of Flame* **(DAW, 2000)** Alain is drawn into the heart of the ancient conflict between humankind and their enemy, the Cursed Ones. Liath faces a difficult trial in a land of exile. Sanglant seeks to warn King Henry about a conspiracy of sorcerers.

5. *Gathering Storm, The* **(DAW, 2003)** King Henry's obsession with uniting the kingdoms of Wendar and Varre has left his people destitute and vulnerable, as earthly and unearthly forces plot Henry's downfall.

6. *In the Ruins* **(DAW, 2005)** Alain and Liath must call upon their twin destinies in the struggle against civil war, Eika warriors, and other raiders, and the shadow of the Cursed Ones falls upon Henry's kingdom.

7. *Crown of Stars* **(DAW, 2006)** In the series' conclusion, Sanglant tries to legitimize his relationship with Liath and found a dynasty that can mend their shattered world after King Henry's murder.

II. The Jaran series is set in a interstellar universe that includes Earth and the planet Rhui. Numbers 2 and 3 are sometimes called numbers 1 and 2 of the Sword of Heaven series.

1. *Jaran* **(DAW, 1992)** Earth-born Tess, sister and heir to rebel Charles Soerensen, seeks to evade her destiny by fleeing to the Jaran, a nomadic tribe on the planet Rhui.

2. *Earthly Crown, An* **(DAW, 1993)** Tess and her Jaran husband, Ilya, are on a campaign to conquer the planet Rhui, which will lead to a confrontation with her brother Duke Charles.

3. *His Conquering Sword* **(DAW, 1993)** The Jaran tribes, under the leadership of Ilya Bakhtiian and his wife, Tess, continue their conquests.

4. *Law of Becoming, The* **(DAW, 1994)** The conclusion to the Jaran series, full of unexpected new twists, as the Jaran, exiled to Earth, continue their fight against the Chapilli Empire.

III. The Crossroads series, projected to be seven volumes, is set in the once prosperous but now lawless land called the Hundred, which is suffering from the disappearance of the justice-dispensing Guardians and the loss of authority of the Eagle-riding Reeves.

1. *Spirit Gate* **(Tor, 2007)** After years of dissolute behavior, eagle-riding Reeve Joss regains his will to defend the land of the Hundred.

2. *Shadow Gate* **(Tor, 2008)** Reeve Marit awakens as a spirit three years after her death and discovers that she has become one of the nine godlike Guardians.

Ellis, Alice Thomas

PSEUDONYM OF Anna Haycraft

The Summer House, or Clothes in the Wardrobe, trilogy is about a marriage in an English country house told from three different points of view, all female: the reluctant bride, Margaret; the groom's mother, Mrs. Monro; and Parisian Lili, who comes to stay for the wedding with an agenda of her own. The bridegroom, Syl, and men in general come in for some acidulous commentary in this serio-comic trilogy about English family life. The trilogy has been published in omnibus editions three times: *The Clothes in the Wardrobe Trilogy* (Penguin [UK], 1993); *The Summer House: A Trilogy* (Penguin [US], 1994); and *The Summer House Trilogy* (Akadine, 2001, and Virago, 2004). The trilogy was a successful BBC-TV drama produced in 1992. Alice Thomas Ellis (d. 2005), who deserves to be better known in the United States, wrote a dozen other novels, including *The Sin Eater* and *The 27th Kingdom* and columns in the *Spectator*.

1. *Clothes in the Wardrobe, The* (Duckworth [UK], 1987) Seemingly docile Margaret, scheduled to marry Mrs. Munro's only son, has three weeks to brood about her impending marriage to the older, odious Syl. Not published as a separate volume in the United States.
2. *Skeleton in the Cupboard, The* (Duckworth [UK], 1988) Mrs. Munro, who would finds the prospect of death exhilarating, is relieved that her son Syl is marrying the obedient, disciplined, and undemanding Margaret. Not published separately in the United States.
3. *Fly in the Ointment, The* (Duckworth [UK], 1989) The high-spirited temptress Lili, a figure from the past aware of some closeted skeletons, determines to stop the marriage.

Ellis, Kate

Detective Sergeant, later Detective Inspector, Wesley Peterson, who has moved from London to the ostensibly quiet river port of Tradmouth (i.e., Dartmouth) in South Devon finds, as fictional police detectives usually do, that small towns have murky histories and a high per-capita murder rate. Wesley is an amateur archaeologist, and old bones often play a major part in the investigations he undertakes along with colleagues such as his superior, Inspector Gerry Heffernan, and his friend, professional archaeologist Neal Watson, in this British version of Aaron Elkins's (q.v.) Gideon Oliver series. Numbers 6 through 10 haven't been published in the United States.

1. *Merchant's House, The* (St. Martin's, 1999) Wesley Peterson's transfer from London to Tradmouth in South Devon finds him trading one overstretched police department for another. A 400-year-old murder case jostles more recent crimes for attention.
2. *Armada Boy, The* (St. Martin's, 2000) Neil Watson, examining relics from an Armada wreck rumored to be in a ruined chapel, discovers the body of an American veteran.
3. *Unhallowed Grave, An* (St. Martin's, 2001) The body of doctor's receptionist Pauline Brent is discovered hanging from a yew tree in Stokeworthy churchyard. Then an archaeological dig turns up the 500-year-old skeleton of a young woman with a broken neck. Originally published in the United Kingdom in 1999.
4. *Funeral Boat, The* (St. Martin's, 2002) A boy's discovery of a skeleton on his mother's small farm may have connections with long-past Danish Viking raids, a missing Danish tourist, and break-ins at isolated farmhouses. Originally published in the United Kingdom in 2000.
5. *Bone Garden, The* (St. Martin's, 2003) While clearing the overgrown site of the 17th-century gardens of Earlsacre Hall, diggers find two skeletons, one belonging to a young woman buried alive three centuries earlier. Originally published in the United Kingdom in 2001.
6. *Painted Doom, A* (Piatkus [UK], 2002) Former rock star Johnny Shellmer is found shot through the head in the field of Lewis Hoxworthy's father after the teenage Lewis discovers a disturbing painting in a medieval barn. Not published in the United States.
7. *Skeleton Room, The* (Piatkus [UK], 2003) Does the discovery of a skeleton in a bricked-up room at 18th-century Chadleigh Hall have anything to do with the ruins of a ship called the *Celestina*, wrecked in a nearby cove in 1772? Not published in the United States.

8. *Plague Maiden, The* (Piatkus [UK], 2004) A letter claiming to have evidence that the man convicted of murdering the Rev. Shipbourne, Vicar of Belsham, is innocent arrives at Tradmouth police station, addressed to a DCI Norbert, who has long since moved on. Not published in the United States.
9. *Cursed Inheritance, A* (Piatkus [UK], 2005) A journalist investigating the slaughter of the Harford family at 16th-century Potwoolstan Hall in 1985 is murdered 20 years later. Not published in the United States.
10. *Marriage Hearse, The* (Piatkus [UK], 2006) Kristen Harbourn is found strangled and naked on her wedding day, as Elizabethan dramatist Ralph Strong's blood-soaked play *The Fair Wife of Padua* is being prepared for revival after 400 years. Not published in the United States.

Elman, Richard

Here is a Holocaust trilogy that sensitively explores the anguish and fear of a Jewish family as they at first deny, then fight, and finally face their doom. The story concerns the Yagodah family of Clig, Hungary. Because each volume tells of the same events, but from different points of view, there is no chronology. They are perhaps best read in sequence as published.

1. *28th Day of Elul, The* (Scribner, 1967) In a memoir, Alex, or Shandor, the son of the Yagodah family, tells how the German occupation affected his prosperous family and his love for his cousin Lilo.
2. *Lilo's Diary* (Scribner, 1968) The fate of a beautiful and vivacious young Jewish girl in is recorded in Lilo's diary, a moving addendum to the first book.
3. *Reckoning, The* (Scribner, 1969) This diary kept by Newman, the father of the Yagodah family, reveals his refusal to accept the true dangers of the German occupation and his hopes for eluding disaster.

Elmblad, Mary

Cassandra "Cassie" Taylor rises from sharecropper's daughter in the Dust Bowl of Oklahoma to riches, fame, and a seat in the US Congress in this pair of romances written by a native Oklahoman. Not as glitzy or glamorous as some series, but solid escapist fiction.

1. *All Manner of Riches* (Viking, 1987) Abused orphan Cassie Taylor takes her grandmother's lessons to heart as she rises from poverty to become an attorney for abused women and children.
2. *Changes and Chances* (Viking, 1990) When Cassie's husband, Dixon Steele, is murdered by segregationists shortly after being elected to Congress, Cassie takes his seat.

Elrod, P(atricia) N(ead)

I. Jack Fleming, Prohibition-era Chicago reporter, discovers that a tryst with a mysterious woman has turned him into a vampire after he has been "rubbed out" by gangland torpedoes and is still on his feet. Jack becomes a private investigator, and adjusts to the inconveniences (drinking blood from cows in the stockyards; becoming comatose at dawn) and advantages (invisibility; near-immortality) of being a vampire. With his human partner, former British thespian Charles Escott, Jack, who despite his blood lust, remains a decent guy, continues the fight against the Mob, and his trysts with beautiful women. Number 6 was supposed to be the final volume, but the series was revived six years later. This vampire–crime noir series is more fun than fang. *The Vampire Files, Volume One* is an omnibus volume containing numbers 1 through 3 (Ace, 2003).

1. *Bloodlist* (Ace, 1990) When several bullets in the back, courtesy of mobster Frank Paco, leave reporter Jack Fleming still ambulatory, Jack realizes that a tryst with a beautiful woman has turned him into a vampire.
2. *Lifeblood* (Ace, 1990) Jack hunts for his long-lost love Maureen and for the mobsters who "killed" him, while he is being stalked by a bunch of vampire hunters.
3. *Bloodcircle* (Ace, 1990) Fleming's quest for the mysterious woman who vampirized him leads him to the estate of a wealthy widow, where a 200-year-old gigolo tries to throw him off the trail.
4. *Art in the Blood* (Ace, 1991) Jack and his human partner, Charles Escott, investigate the case of the sudden death of a talented young artist.
5. *Fire in the Blood* (Ace, 1991) PI Jack Fleming is hired by the wealthy Sebastian Pierce to recover a valuable heirloom bracelet, and is strongly attracted by Pierce's enticing daughter.
6. *Blood on the Water* (Ace, 1992) Chicago's new Mob boss is determined to rid the city of its vampire PI.
7. *Chill in the Blood, A* (Ace, 1998) After the repeal of Prohibition, Jack becomes a pawn in a turf war between Mob-moll Angela Paco and a rival from New York eager to usurp control of the Hydra Syndicate.
8. *Dark Sleep, The* (Ace, 1999) 1937. Jack's girlfriend, Bobbi Smythe, is opening a new revue at the Night-Crawler club, and Jack is hired to retrieve incriminating letters from the ex-lover of a socialite.
9. *Lady Crymsyn* (Ace, 2000) During renovations of Jack's new nightclub, workmen discover the remains of a woman clad in a distinctive red dress.
10. *Cold Streets* (Ace, 2003) Someone is onto Jack's "unnatural" secret and will drain him dry through blackmail, unless Jack can find him or her.
11. *Song in the Dark, A* (Ace, 2005) 1938. When Jack agrees to fill in for his wounded gangster-boss pal, Gordy Weems, he winds up being tortured by sadistic hood Hog Bristow. Although Jack manages to kill Bristow, his troubles have only just begun.

II. Jonathan Barrett, Gentleman Vampire, is a vampire cycle with historical romance trappings set at the time of the American Revolution. Young American in London, Jonathan Barrett, involved with the unearthly beauty Nora Jones, is turned by her into a vampire, and then spends his time chasing her down in England and the Colonies. The series, originally published in the 1990s, was reprinted, with additional material, by Benbella Books in 2004. *Jonathan Barrett, Gentleman Vampire*, an omnibus volume containing all four titles, was published by Doubleday in 1996.

1. *Red Death* (Ace, 1993) Young American Jonathan Barrett, sent to London in 1773 to further his education, is educated into the mysteries of love, sex, and vampiredom by Nora Jones.
2. *Death and the Maiden* (Ace, 1994) Back in the Colonies as the Revolutionary War rages, Jonathan faces a deadly danger in his family's mansion and is forced to kill again.
3. *Death Masque* (Ace, 1995) Jonathan and his sisters have fled to England to avoid the "rebellion." Jonathan continues his search for the mysterious Nora Jones.
4. *Dance of Death* (Ace, 1996) Jonathan encounters a four-year-old boy who uncannily resembles him. The fate of Jonathan and his son hinges upon the return of Nora Jones.

III. A pair of novels features Strahd Von Zarovich, ruler of Barovia, who makes a deal with Death to further his aims. Elrod has also coauthored the Ethical Vampires trio with Nigel Bennett (q.v.), contributed to the Kolchak/Night Stalker and Stargate SG-1 series, and written other vampire novels, including *Quincey Morris, Vampire* (Baen, 2001), which is a sequel to Bram Stoker's *Dracula*.

1. *Memoirs of a Vampire, The* (TSR, 1993) The ruthless Strahd Von Zarovich is willing to do anything to win the hand of the beautiful Tatyana, including entering into a pact with Death that will doom his brother Sergei.
2. *War against Azalin, The* (TSR, 1998) Strahd's existence as vampire lord of Barovia is threatened by the arrival of the evil wizard Azalin.

Emerson, Earl

I. Thomas Black is a shrewd but vulnerable private eye who roams the streets of Seattle. Black hates guns, and maintains a relationship with lawyer Kathy Birchfield that remains frustratingly platonic through several volumes (although he does eventually marry her).

1. *Rainy Day, The* (Avon, 1985) Ex-cop turned private eye Thomas Black is looking for a missing blond named Melissa.
2. *Poverty Bay* (Avon, 1985) Lucy Peebles's fiancé, the recent beneficiary of a $15 million inheritance, is missing.
3. *Nervous Laughter* (Avon, 1986) Black is hired to tail dog-food magnate Mark Daniels and stumbles across his body and the body of a half-naked girl in his office.
4. *Fat Tuesday* (Morrow, 1987) Fred Pugsley, hotshot computer programmer and all-around louse, is found with his head bashed in and his nude, bloodstained wife cowering in a corner.
5. *Deviant Behavior* (Morrow, 1988) Black looks for missing teenager Todd Steeb in Seattle's Chinatown and turns up a long-hidden family secret.
6. *Yellow Dog Party* (Morrow, 1991) After four area businessmen hire him to find a woman, Tom is nearly lynched by three thugs in Miss Piggy masks.
7. *Portland Laughter, The* (Ballantine, 1994) Black is hired to trail Kathy Birchfield's fiancé, Philip Bacon, who is trailing ex-con Billy Battle with murder on his mind.
8. *Vanishing Smile, The* (Ballantine, 1995) Kathy Birchfield's car strikes her own client, a 71-year-old amateur detective named Marian Wright.
9. *Million-Dollar Tattoo, The* (Ballantine, 1996) Fellow PI "Snake" Slezak has some weird explanations for the presence of a dead woman in his bed, but Thomas Black is "not entirely sure Snake did it."
10. *Deception Pass* (Ballantine, 1997) Wealthy businesswoman and philanthropist Lainie Smith hires Black to find out who is blackmailing her about her possible role in a Manson-type mass murder in the past.
11. *Catfish Cafe* (Ballantine, 1998) Black's former police partner, African American Luther Little, asks Black's help in locating his missing daughter, Balinda, and in finding out who killed the young white man found dead in her car.

II. Emerson, an officer with the Seattle Fire Department, is well qualified to write these novels about Mac Fontana, a former big-city fireman who is now fire chief in the town of Staircase, Washington.

1. *Black Hearts and Slow Dancing* (Morrow, 1988) Mac Fontana moves to the tiny town of Staircase, Washington to simplify his

life, but is side-tracked by the investigation of the murder of a Seattle firefighter.

2. *Help Wanted: Orphans Preferred* (Morrow, 1990) When a Staircase fireman dies of arsenic poisoning, Fire Chief Fontana is forced to assume his additional role as acting sheriff.

3. *Morons and Madmen* (Morrow, 1993) Three firefighters die in a Seattle fire, and a surviving firewoman hires Mac to clear her name of responsibility for their deaths.

4. *Going Crazy in Public* (Morrow, 1996) A serial arsonist bedeviling Staircase has produced the first fire fatality in the town's history. Is it someone nursing a grudge against Mac?

5. *Dead Horse Paint Company, The* (Morrow, 1997) The charred victim of a car fire in Snoqualmie Pass turns out to be Fontana's former boss, Edgar Callahan, who was in charge during a fire at the Dead Horse Paint Company that killed nine firefighters.

Emerson, Kathy Lynn

I. Herbalist Susanna, Lady Appleton, is the heroine of the Face Down series, historical mysteries set in Elizabethan times (1559). Her philandering husband, Lord Robert Appleton, is an ambassador-spy for Queen Elizabeth. Often abroad, he is killed off in number 4, but Lady Appleton, with the aid of her friend and housekeeper, Jennet Jaffrey, continues her sleuthing in this series of interesting mysteries with solid Elizabethan backgrounds. American Kathy Lynn Emerson is also the author of romantic suspense novels, juvenile fiction, nonfiction and romance novels under the pseudonym of Kaitlyn Gorton.

1. *Face Down in the Marrow-Bone Pie* (St. Martin's, 1997) In 1559 Robert, Lord Appleton, is sent to France as ambassador to Queen Elizabeth. His wife, herbalist Susanna, Lady Appleton, takes advantage of his absence to investigate the mysterious death of their steward, John Bexwith.

2. *Face Down upon an Herbal* (St. Martin's, 1998) After publishing an herbal manual, Lady Appleton is commanded by Queen Elizabeth to travel to Madderly Castle to assist Lady Madderly, who is also working on herbals. When Susanna arrives, she learns that a visiting Scottish nobleman has been found dead reading her manual.

3. *Face Down among the Winchester Geese* (St. Martin's, 1999) When a Frenchwoman who has asked for Sir Robert's help is found dead in a disreputable area of London, Susanna claims the body, covers for her husband, and learns of several similar murders.

4. *Face Down beneath the Eleanor Cross* (St. Martin's, 2000) Susanna, grieving over the supposed death of her husband, Robert, receives a message to meet him. When he fails to appear and is found dead, Susanna stands accused of his murder.

5. *Face Down under the Wych Elm* (St. Martin's, 2000) Susanna uses her herbal expertise to expose the poisoner of two men and to exonerate two gentlewomen, one of them her late husband's former mistress, Constance Crane.

6. *Face Down before Rebel Hooves* (St. Martin's, 2001) Eleanor, wife of Sir Walter Pendennis, has been trampled by runaway horses, and her dying confession reveals that she has been involved in a plot to replace Queen Elizabeth with Mary, Queen of Scots.

7. *Face Down across the Western Sea* (St. Martin's, 2002) Susanna, assisting a group of scholars privately investigating English claims to the New World, springs into action when information goes missing, and one of the scholars is murdered.

8. *Murders and Other Confusions* (Crippen & Landru, 2004) Subtitle: *The Chronicles of Susanna, Lady Appleton, 16th-Century Gentlewoman, Herbalist, and Sleuth*. Eleven short stories, five of which were previously unpublished.

9. *Face Down below the Banqueting House* (Perseverance, 2005) Is a suspicious death in Susanna's garden the precursor to Queen Elizabeth's visit to the Appleton country house?

10. *Face Down beside St. Anne's Well* (Perseverance, 2006) Rosamund, Susanna's 12-year-old foster daughter, calls for her mother's help when her French tutor, Madame Louise Poitier, is found drowned in St. Anne's Well.

11. *Face Down o'er the Border* (Perseverance, 2007) Susanna's friend Catherine is missing after Catherine's mother-in-law is found strangled following a fight between the two women.

II. The Diana Spaulding series, apparently limited to four volumes, is set in 1888. Diana is a newspaper reporter and mystery solver. The series starts in New York City and finishes in Maine.

1. *Deadlier Than the Pen* (Pemberley, 2004) New York City, 1888. Diana Spaulding interviews Damon Bathory, charismatic author of Gothic horror stories, whose reading tour may have been accompanied by serial murders. Of course, the "Blizzard of '88" plays a role.

2. *Fatal as a Fallen Woman* (Pemberley, 2005) Diana journeys to Denver to defend her mother against accusations of having murdered her gold baron husband.

3. *No Mortal Reason* (Pemberley, 2007) Diana and fiancé Dr. Ben Northcote, on their way to get married in Maine, stop in Liberty, New York, to meet the Grants, her estranged mother's new family, who run a summer hotel.

4. *Lethal Legend* (Pemberley, 2008) Ben Northcote, followed by Diana, crosses Penobscot Bay (Maine) to Keep Island to care for three poisoned men engaged in an archaeological dig.

Engel, Howard

Benny Cooperman is a Jewish private detective working out of Grantham, Ontario, a small industrial city near Toronto based in part on the real city of St. Catharines. Benny, a kind of nebbishy Philip Marlowe, is a genial plodder who lives in a hotel, eats at luncheonettes, and is a good son to his old mother who reads Proust because she likes "family novels." This well-written series has won Engel the praise of such fellow mystery writers as Tony Hillerman (q.v.), Donald E. Westlake (q.v.), Ruth Rendell (q.v.), and Julian Symons. *The Whole Megillah* (Book City, 1991), published as a limited edition paperback, is a long short story featuring Benny Cooperman and a stolen manuscript. Toronto native Engel, a producer for the Canadian Broadcasting System, has also published a Sherlock Holmesian mystery, *Dr. Doyle and Dr. Bell* (Overlook, 2003) and a mystery set in the literary expatriate Paris of Hemingway and Fitzgerald, *Murder in Montparnasse* (Overlook, 1999; original Canadian publication, 1992).

1. *Suicide Murders, The* (St. Martin's, 1984) Hired to tail a husband suspected of infidelity, Benny gets involved with a series of suspicious "suicides." Originally published in Canada in 1980.

2. *Ransom Game, The* (St. Martin's, 1984) Benny reopens an old kidnapping case involving half a million dollars in lost ransom money. Originally published in Canada in 1981.

3. *Murder on Location* (St. Martin's, 1985) In search of a real-estate dealer's theatrical wife, Benny travels to Niagara Falls, where a film is being shot. Originally published in Canada in 1982.

4. *Murder Sees the Light* (St. Martin's, 1985) Benny guards television evangelist Norbert Patten while the US Supreme Court decides on the tax status of the "Ultimate Church."

5. *City Called July, A* (**St. Martin's, 1986**) The local Grantham rabbi asks Benny to find Larry Geller, treasurer of the shul, who has disappeared with over $2 million.

6. *Victim Must Be Found, A* (**St. Martin's, 1989**) Benny investigates the murder of an art collector and the disappearance of some paintings.

7. *Dead and Buried* (**Overlook, 2001**) A widow, convinced that her husband's employer murdered him, persuades Benny to investigate. Originally published in Canada in 1990.

8. *There Was an Old Woman* (**Overlook, 2000**) An investigation into the apparent starvation death of elderly Lizzy Oldridge leads to Thurleigh Ramsden, executor of Lizzy's will and administrator of the "charitable organization" to which Lizzy left her money. Originally published in Canada in 1993.

9. *Getting Away with Murder* (**Overlook, 1997**) Abe Wise, who has enjoyed a successful criminal career, hires a reluctant Benny to find out who is shooting at him. Originally published in Canada in 1995.

10. *Cooperman Variations, The* (**Overlook, 2002**) Benny temporarily relocates to Toronto to act as bodyguard to an old high school flame, television executive Vanessa Moss.

11. *Memory Book* (**Carroll & Graf, 2005**) Cooperman finds himself suffering from a rare disorder (the same disorder afflicts his author) in which he can write but is unable to read when he wakes from an eight-week coma after being bashed on the head.

Enger, L. L.

PSEUDONYM OF Leif & Lin Enger

Gun Pedersen, former slugger for the Detroit Tigers, has retired to the woods of northern Minnesota to live the quiet life, but he can't avoid getting enmeshed in other people's problems.

1. *Comeback* (**Pocket, 1990**) Following his wife's tragic death and a baseball-connected scandal, Gun Pedersen retreats to the north woods of Minnesota.

2. *Swing* (**Pocket, 1991**) Gun comes to the aid of former teammate Moses Gates, who still hasn't recovered from the stigma attached to his roommate's suicide.

3. *Strike* (**Pocket, 1992**) Teenager Babe Chandler may have killed his best friend, a Native American from a nearby reservation.

4. *Sacrifice* (**Pocket, 1993**) Gun postpones his wedding to return home to Copper Strike, in the Upper Peninsula of Michigan, for a funeral.

5. *Sinners' League, The* (**Penzler, 1994**) The opening of a casino on the local Indian reservation and the rape and murder of an old flame disturb Gun's tranquility.

Ephron, G. H.

PSEUDONYM OF Hallie Ephron & David A. Davidoff

Peter Zak is a forensic neuropsychiatrist at Pearce Psychiatric Center in the Boston area. He was an expert witness for the defense in capital cases until his wife was murdered by a client angered by Peter's insanity defense in his trial. But Peter can't stay away from murder cases when his expertise is called upon in this series of psychological suspense novels. David A. Davidoff, professor at Harvard Medical School and a doctor at McLean Psychiatric Hospital, provides the expertise, while Hallie Ephron, of the Ephron writing family, does the writing. "Malingering," a Peter Zak story, appears online on USATODAY. com. Hallie Ephron is also the author of the nonfiction *Writing and*

Selling Your Mystery Novel: How to Knock 'Em Dead with Style (Writers Digest, 2005).

1. *Amnesia* (**St. Martin's, 2000**) Peter Zak is reluctantly drawn into the case of Sylvia Jackson, who is trying to recover from being shot in the head and left for dead.

2. *Addiction* (**St. Martin's, 2001**) Peter finds his friend and former lover, Pearce psychiatrist Channing Temple, dead from a gunshot wound, and her 16-year-old drug-addicted daughter, Olivia, standing over her body, holding a gun.

3. *Delusion* (**St. Martin's, 2002**) Nick Babikian has found his wife stabbed and floating in their backyard pool. Nick's lawyer wants Peter to assess the state of mind of his brilliant but paranoid client.

4. *Obsessed* (**St. Martin's, 2003**) Peter's colleague Dr. Emily Ryan is being tormented by a stalker, whose acts have escalated to the point where he's breaking into her car and leaving sick messages.

5. *Guilt* (**St. Martin's, 2005**) Peter narrowly misses being one of the victims of a bomb exploded outside of a Harvard Law School building.

Erdrich, Louise

Love Medicine's engaging story, lyric style, and unstereotyped portrayal of Native Americans won Erdrich's first novel both popular and critical acclaim. All of her novels share the same North Dakota setting, and some of the same characters may appear from novel to novel. Some novels concentrate on Native American characters from the reservation containing the Turtle Mountain (Ojibwa/Chippewa) band; others on "Europeans" from the small town of Argus (based on Wahpeton), North Dakota. Magic realism, surrealism, engaging characters, and excellent story-telling in a rich, poetic prose have characterized this involving series. Since the novels tend to switch back and forth in time, they are listed in publication order rather than chronological order.

Erdrich grew up in Wahpeton, North Dakota, the child of German and Ojibwa forebears. For many years she lived in New Hampshire with her late husband, Michael Dorris. Now she lives in Minneapolis, closer to her North Dakota roots, engaged in activities such as writing, child rearing, and learning the Ojibwa language. Erdrich has also written two children's books about the Ojibwa: *The Birchbark House* (Hyperion, 1999) and *The Game of Silence* (HarperCollins, 2005).

1. *Love Medicine* (**Holt, 1984**) The death of June Kashpaw stirs memories among members of the Kashpaw and Lamartine families of the Turtle Mountain band of Chippewas.

2. *Beet Queen, The* (**Holt, 1986**) This tells about the lives of Karl and Mary Adare, abandoned in childhood in Argus, North Dakota, the "Sugar-Beet Capital of America."

3. *Tracks* (**Holt, 1988**) The story of Fleur Pillager, a Chippewa woman suspected of witchcraft, is told by Nanapush, a tribal elder, and by Pauline, an Indian woman who has become a Catholic nun.

4. *Bingo Palace, The* (**HarperCollins, 1994**) Lipsha Morrissey, bastard son of June Kashpaw, drifts aimlessly until he returns to the reservation and falls under the spell of Shawano Ray Toose.

5. *Tales of Burning Love* (**HarperCollins, 1996**) The life of Jack Mauser is reviewed by his four wives as they are trapped overnight in a van during a North Dakota blizzard.

6. *Antelope Wife, The* (**HarperCollins, 1998**) The stories of two intertwined Ojibwa families, the Roys and the Shawanos, are related. Antelope Wife, a beautiful Ojibwa woman is enticed or abducted by a trader and relocated in Minneapolis.

7. *Last Report on the Miracles at Little No Horse* (**HarperCollins, 2001**) The reminiscences of "Father Damien" (aka Agnes DeWit,

aka Sister Cecelia) disclose hidden facts about Sister Leopolda (aka Pauline Puy), who is being considered for sainthood.

8. *Master Butchers Singing Club, The* **(HarperCollins, 2003)** This is the story of Fidelis Waldvogel, German veteran of World War I and master butcher, who emigrates to Argus, North Dakota, and sets up a butcher shop and a singing club.

9. *Four Souls* **(HarperCollins, 2004)** The sequel to number 3. Continues the saga of Fleur Pillager, as she travels to Minneapolis to avenge the sale of her land.

10. *Painted Drum, The* **(HarperCollins, 2006)** A multigenerational tale revolving around bereavement and the history of a ceremonial drum of the Ojibwas that Native American antiquities specialist Faye Travers stumbles upon.

11. *Plague of Doves, The* **(Harper, 2008)** A farming family near Pluto, North Dakota, is massacred in 1911, and three Indians are incorrectly blamed. Mooshum Milk, one of the Indians, survives the subsequent lynching.

Erickson, K. J.

PSEUDONYM UNKNOWN

Marshall "Mars" Bahr is a special detective who reports directly to the chief of police in Minneapolis, Minnesota. Bahr, plagued by his emotionally draining ex-wife, is a sympathetic character involved in a series of satisfyingly convoluted plots. "K. J. Erickson" is female, retired from a position with the Federal Reserve, and a resident of Minneapolis.

1. *Third Person Singular* **(St. Martin's, 2001)** Mars Bahr and his partner, Nellie, solve the case of a young woman of good background who is murdered near the newly renovated waterfront in Minneapolis.

2. *Dead Survivors, The* **(St. Martin's, 2002)** A troubled Minneapolis man is an apparent suicide, but Bahr, after examining the evidence, doubts that verdict.

3. *Last Witness* **(St. Martin's, 2003)** A star player for the Minneapolis Timberwolves basketball team seems to have a perfect alibi, although everything else points to his having murdered his wife.

4. *Alone at Night* **(St. Martin's, 2004)** Bahr, transferred to the cold-case unit, tries to unravel a 20-year-old unsolved murder case.

Erikson, Steven

PSEUDONYM OF Steve Rune Lundin

The Malazan Book of the Fallen is an epic fantasy series that seems to have attracted a lot of groupies. This saga of war and empire is set in the Malazan Empire and features a large cast of gods, soldiers, wizards, and the undead, all of whom seem to be at each other's throats. The series is projected to run to 10 volumes. In addition, Erikson has published four limited-edition chapbooks, at least two of which are connected to the Malazan series: *The Healthy Dead* (Night Shade, 2004; originally 2002) and *Blood Follows* (Night Shade, 2005). Steven Erikson, a Canadian living in England, is not to be confused with Steve *Erickson*, who is also a fantasy writer.

1. *Gardens of the Moon* **(Tor, 2004)** Empress Laseen wishes to extend the borders of the Malazan Empire. Sergeant Whiskeyjack and his elite Bridgeburners, along with the combat sorceress Tattersailm, go to battle yet again, while darker forces that promise to involve the gods themselves gather. Originally published in the United Kingdom in 1999.

2. *Deadhouse Gates* **(Tor, 2005)** Sha'ik the seer and her followers prepare for the Whirlwind, an uprising of fanatics that will ignite a bloody conflict throughout the Malazan Empire. Originally published in the United Kingdom in 2000.

3. *Memories of Ice* **(Tor, 2005)** Ganoes Paran is now captain of the Bridgeburners, part of Dujek Onearm's army that's trying to fight off the evil forces of the Pannion Domin. Originally published in the United Kingdom in 2001.

4. *House of Chains* **(Tor, 2006)** Follows the Teblor warrior Karsa Orlong and his men on a raid through enemy territory and into the human lowlands of Northern Genabackis, as the ultimate showdown between the forces of the Malazan Empire and Sha'ik's Army of the Apocalypse looms. Originally published in the United Kingdom in 2002.

5. *Midnight Tides* **(Tor, 2007)** The five tribes of the Tiste Edur have united under the rule of the Warlock King of Hiroth, but a hidden power with suspect motives lurks beneath the pact. Originally published in the United Kingdom in 2004.

6. *Bonehunters, The* **(Tor, 2007)** The Seven Cities Rebellion has been crushed and Sha'ik slain. One last rebel army, under the command of Leoman of the Flails, is holding out against Tavore and the 14th Army at the ancient city of Y'Ghatan.

7. *Reaper's Gale* **(Tor, 2008)** The Tiste Edur uneasily rule the Empire of Lether, against the will of the Letherii people.

Ernaux, Annie

Prix Renaudot–winning French author Ernaux has been writing a series of books about herself and her family that blurs the line between memoir and fiction. In *A Woman's Story* and *I Remain in Darkness*, Ernaux concentrates on her mother; in *A Man's Place*, she tells her father's life story. *A Frozen Woman* relates Ernaux's early life. Numbers 4, 5, 6, 8, and 9 recall incidents such as Ernaux's abortion and her affair with a married man. *Ce qu'ils disent ou rien* (Gallimard, 1977), *La vie exterieur: 1993–1999* (Gallimard, 2000), *Se perdre* (Gallimard, 2001), and *L'occupation* (Gallimard, 2002) haven't been translated into English.

1. *Woman's Story, A* **(Four Walls, 1991)** Ernaux's mother (never named) lives out her life in a small town with seemingly no ambition beyond that of running a grocery store. Original published in 1987 as *Une femme*. Translated from the French by Tanya Leslie.

2. *Man's Place, A* **(Four Walls, 1992)** Ernaux's father climbs from peasant beginnings to the relative prosperity of a small shopkeeper. Originally published in 1984 as *La Place*. Translated from the French by Tanya Leslie.

3. *Frozen Woman, A* **(Four Walls, 1995)** The story of the only child of shopkeepers in a provincial town, who grows up uncertain about gender relations and with unrealistic intellectual ambitions. Originally published in 1981 as *La femme gelée*. Translated from the French by Linda Coverdale.

4. *Shame* **(Seven Stories, 1998)** Ernaux recalls June 15, 1952, the day her father tried to kill her mother. Originally published in 1997 as *La Honte*. Translated from the French by Tanya Leslie.

5. *Cleaned Out* **(Dalkey Archive, 1990)** Ernaux's first published "novel" explores the thoughts and recollections of 20-year-old student "Denise Lesur" after an illegal abortion. Originally published in 1974 as *Les Armoires vides*. Translated from the French by Carol Sanders.

6. *Happening* **(Seven Stories, 2001)** Ernaux revisits the events described in *Cleaned Out*, this time in the form of a memoir rather than a novel. Originally published in 2000 as *L'evenement*. Translated from the French by Tanya Leslie.

7. *I Remain in Darkness* **(Seven Stories, 1999)** The account, in journal form, of the last days of Ernaux's mother from the time she is diagnosed with Alzheimer's until her death three years later.

Originally published in 1997 as *Je ne suis pas sortie de ma nuit*. Translated from the French by Tanya Leslie.

8. *Simple Passion* **(Four Walls, 1993)** A slightly fictionalized account of Ernaux's affair with a married Eastern European businessman, in which the line between fiction and autobiography is indistinct. Originally published in 1991 as *Passion simple*. Translated from the French by Tanya Leslie.

9. *Exteriors* **(Seven Stories, 1996)** The years 1985–1992 described in a series of interior monologues. Originally published in 1993 as *Journal du dehors*. Translated from the French by Tanya Leslie.

Estleman, Loren D.

I. Private eye Amos Walker is as hard-boiled as they come. Shaped by his hometown, Detroit—"the place where the American Dream stalled and sat rusting in the rain"—Walker is weary, tough, and cynical, but still compassionate. His bachelor flat is in the Polish enclave of Hamtramck, surrounded by the city of Detroit. Walker deals with the usual inner-city crimes: drug dealing, prostitution, pornography, violence, and venal politicians. Estleman, from Michigan himself, gets the Detroit ambience just right.

1. *Motor City Blue* **(Houghton Mifflin, 1980)** Amos Walker gets involved with a missing girl, a pornography racket, and some corrupt VIPs.
2. *Angel Eyes* **(Houghton Mifflin, 1981)** A nightclub dancer gives Walker a diamond ring as a retainer before disappearing.
3. *Midnight Man, The* **(Houghton Mifflin, 1982)** Four young thugs ambush three Detroit policemen, killing two and paralyzing the third.
4. *Glass Highway, The* **(Houghton Mifflin, 1983)** Walker is hired to find the 20-year-old-son of a television newscaster.
5. *Sugartown* **(Houghton Mifflin, 1984)** A 19-year-old disappearance case becomes intertwined with a case involving a Soviet defector.
6. *Lady Yesterday* **(Houghton Mifflin, 1987)** Jamaican ex-prostitute Iris hires Walker to find her missing father, an obscure jazz trombonist.
7. *Downriver* **(Houghton, 1988)** Richard DeVries, ex-convict, wants Walker to find the real culprit behind the 1967 arson and armored car robbery for which he was framed.
8. *General Murders* **(Houghton Mifflin, 1988)** Ten short stories.
9. *Silent Thunder* **(Houghton Mifflin, 1989)** Arms dealers, a woman suspected of killing her husband, and venal policemen are among the problems facing Walker.
10. *Sweet Women Lie* **(Houghton Mifflin, 1990)** Walker is hired to protect his ex-wife's husband, a CIA operative with some potentially profitable (and dangerous) secrets.
11. *Never Street* **(Mysterious, 1997)** A complex plot involving missing moviemaker Neil Catalin, his thieving brother-in-law, and his former lover Vesta, an ambitious actress.
12. *Witchfinder* **(Mysterious, 1998)** Lawyer Stuart Lund summons Walker to a secret meeting at an airport hotel with dying architect Jay Bell Furlong, who wants Amos to find the person who sent him a fake photograph of his former lover in bed with another man.
13. *Hours of the Virgin, The* **(Mysterious, 1999)** A curator at the Detroit Institute of Arts asks Walker to help him recover a recently stolen medieval illuminated manuscript, *The Hours of the Virgin*.
14. *Smile on the Face of the Tiger, A* **(Mysterious, 2000)** Amos is hired by a New York publisher to find crime novelist Eugene Booth, whose best-known novel, *Paradise Valley*, about the Detroit race riot of 1943, she wants to reprint.

15. *Sinister Heights* **(Mysterious, 2002)** Walker is hired by the widow of a recently deceased multimillionaire to find her late husband's former lovers, allegedly for the purpose of reimbursing them for the wrongs he committed.
16. *Poison Blonde* **(Forge, 2003)** Cilia Cristobal, Latino music star, who hires Amos to find out who is blackmailing her, turns out to have a very interesting past.
17. *Retro* **(Forge, 2004)** Dying madam Beryl Garnet asks Amos to find her long-missing son, Delwayne, who emigrated to Canada during the Vietnam War.
18. *Nicotine Kiss* **(Forge, 2006)** Walker, trying to repay Jeff Starzek for saving his life, conducts a search for the missing Jeff that leads to the bizarre, evangelical Church of the Inland Sea.
19. *American Detective* **(Forge, 2007)** Walker is hired by retired Detroit Tigers pitcher Darius Fuller, who is concerned about his daughter's sleazy boyfriend.

II. Estleman has written a series of crime novels set, for the most part, in the past and involving some historical characters. The city of Detroit is the central character. Like William Kennedy's (q.v.) Albany series, the focus is on the seedier side of the city. The race riots of 1943 and 1966, the Edsel disaster, Prohibition, and the early days of auto manufacturing all play parts in this loosely connected series.

1. *Thunder City* **(Forge, 1999)** Detroit in the first decade of the 1900s is the setting as Henry Ford and Harlan Crownover, trying to start a new motor company, become enmeshed with Irish politicians and Mafia bosses.
2. *Whiskey River* **(Bantam, 1990)** Reporter and Mob confidante Connie Minor tells a grand jury in the late 1930s about the rivalry between bootleggers Joey Machine and Jack Dance.
3. *Jitterbug* **(Forge, 1998)** The Detroit race riot of 1943 explodes as Racket Squad leader Maximilian Zagreb and his three assistants seek (by some very dubious means) to expose the serial killer known as "Kilroy," who is murdering people for hoarding ration coupons.
4. *Edsel: A Novel of Detroit* **(Mysterious, 1995)** In the 1950s, Connie Minor is hired by Ford Motor Company to promote Henry Ford II's secret dream car.
5. *Motown* **(Bantam, 1991)** The paths of ex-cop Rick Amery, Inspector Lew Canada, and racketeer Quincy Springfield intersect during the August 1966 race riot.
6. *Stress* **(Mysterious, 1996)** In 1973 African American policeman Charles Battle is assigned to investigate the shootings of three black men at a New Year's Eve party, during an attempted robbery, by a supposedly off-duty cop who was working undercover for STRESS, a controversial police crackdown squad.
7. *King of the Corner* **(Bantam, 1992)** In the 1990s former baseball player and jailbird Doc Miller goes to work for bail bondsman Maynard Ance.

III. Another Detroit-based series features Peter Macklin, a hit man who sometimes finds himself working with terrorists, spies, and other political types outside his usual line of business.

1. *Kill Zone* **(Mysterious, 1984)** The Detroit Mob, the FBI, and the Secret Service all want Macklin to handle the negotiations when terrorists take 800 hostages on a Lake Erie steamboat.
2. *Roses Are Dead* **(Mysterious, 1985)** Macklin has his hands full: sharpshooters and flame-throwing giants are trying to kill him, his wife wants a divorce, and his teenage son wants to take up his line of business.
3. *Any Man's Death* **(Mysterious, 1986)** Macklin's own son is the killer that Macklin must protect an outspoken preacher from.

4. ***Something Borrowed, Something Black*** (Forge, 2002) Supposedly retired and on honeymoon in Los Angeles, Peter is forced back into the assassination business and sent to San Antonio to finish off someone else's botched hit.
5. ***Little Black Dress*** (Forge, 2005) Peter recognizes a fellow killer in the man whom his wife Laurie's mother is dating in Ohio.

IV. Estleman added books to the Sherlock Holmes canon with these "lost manuscripts" of Doctor Watson.

1. ***Sherlock Holmes vs. Dracula*** (Doubleday, 1978) Holmes tries to prevent the "sanguinary count" from finding fresh blood in England. Variant title: *Sherlock Holmes and the Sanguinary Count.*
2. ***Dr. Jekyll and Mr. Holmes*** (Doubleday, 1979) Holmes and Watson get involved with a man who has a dual personality problem.

V. Estleman also writes westerns. This series, set in the 1880s, features Page Murdock, Deputy US Marshal for the Montana Territory. Murdock, as "hard-boiled" as Amos Walker, is an interesting hero for a traditional action western. The period detail is especially well done.

1. ***High Rocks, The*** (Doubleday, 1979) Bear Anderson, the "Mountain That Walks," terrifies the Flathead Indians who massacred his parents and everyone else in the Montana Territory.
2. ***Stamping Ground*** (Doubleday, 1980) Murdock escorts renegade Cheyenne Ghost Shirt to his public hanging in Bismarck, Dakota Territory.
3. ***Murdock's Law*** (Doubleday, 1982) Murdock becomes the town marshal of Breen, Montana, and has trouble sorting out friends and enemies.
4. ***Stranglers*** (Doubleday, 1984) Murdock leads a posse in search of a teenage killer and is betrayer by an Indian tracker.
5. ***City of Widows*** (Forge, 1994) Murdock buys a half interest in a bar in San Sabado, New Mexico Territory, to observe corrupt sheriff Frank Baronet.
6. ***White Desert*** (Forge, 2000) Murdock assists the Canadian Mounties in the search for murderous outlaws Lorenzo Bliss and Charlie Whitelaw, who seem to have moved their base of operations from Montana to Canada.
7. ***Port Hazard*** (Forge, 2004) Murdock and a black ex-soldier named Beecher find themselves on San Francisco's Barbary Coast in search of a conspiracy called the Sons of the Confederacy.

VI. The Valentino mysteries feature "film detective" Valentino, film archivist at UCLA. Valentino, who appeared in 10 short stories in *Ellery Queen Mystery Magazine*, makes his novel-length debut in *Frames*.

1. ***Frames*** (Forge, 2008) Film archivist Valentino, exploring the Oracle, a decaying 1920s movie theater, stumbles upon reels of film that may be the only surviving prints of Erich von Stroheim's legendary epic *Greed*.

Evanovich, Janet

I. Stephanie Plum, unemployed lingerie buyer from Trenton, New Jersey, gets a job as a bounty hunter from her cousin, bail-bondsman Vinnie. Stephanie's pluck and humor are more than balanced by her bumptious incompetence, but somehow the wisecracking Stephanie usually gets her man (or woman). Stephanie's love life is punctuated by mishaps: somehow the sex sessions with Joe Morelli the cop, her more-or-less steady, or with the sexy and mysterious Cuban, Ranger, always manage to get interrupted. Stephanie is flanked by many funny side characters, such as her wacky assistant Lula, and her beloved Grandma

Mazur, who is a connoisseur of funerals. Some reviewers opine that this "slapstick and gunplay" series gets better with each novel, while others feel that "book-a-year" syndrome has set in. Stephanie has been at the top of best-seller lists more than once. There are several omnibus volumes, including *Three Plums in One* (Scribner, 2001; numbers 1–3) and *The Stephanie Plum Novels* (St. Martin's, 2002; numbers 3–5).

Evanovich has started a new series, set in Florida, featuring one Alexandra Barnaby. *Metro Girl* (HarperCollins, 2004) is the only title published so far.

1. ***One for the Money*** (Scribner, 1994) Stephanie Plum persuades her Cousin Vinnie to take her on as a bounty hunter. Her first assignment: find Joe Morelli, a cop accused of murder, a figure from her past.
2. ***Two for the Dough*** (Scribner, 1996) Grandma Mazur, Stephanie's beloved relative, a connoisseur of funerals, is disappointed when Moogey Blue is on display at Stiva's funeral parlor in a closed coffin. For some reason, 24 caskets are missing from Stiva's storage locker.
3. ***Three to Get Deadly*** (Simon & Schuster, 1997) Stephanie finds herself high on Joe Morelli's suspect list when she awakens next to a corpse after being coshed during what should have been a routine assignment.
4. ***Four to Score*** (St. Martin's, 1998) Stephanie finds herself in competition with her arch-enemy, Joyce Barnhardt, while searching for a vengeful waitress and bail jumper whose friends are turning up dead.
5. ***High Five*** (St. Martin's, 1999) After Stephanie's uncle disappears (kidnapped by aliens according to Grandma Mazur), Stephanie turns up a photo of dismembered body parts in his desk.
6. ***Hot Six*** (St. Martin's, 2000) Stephanie is searching for her mentor, Ranger—aka former Special Forces agent turned soldier of fortune Carlos Manoso— but her task is complicated by three corpses; two thugs who are after her; a large, needy orange dog; and Grandma Mazur, who has moved in with her.
7. ***Seven Up*** (St. Martin's, 2001) Joe Morelli is proposing marriage. Ranger is proposing a spectacular one-night stand. Stephanie, on the trail of a senior citizen charged with smuggling contraband cigarettes, stumbles on a corpse in the woodshed.
8. ***Hard Eight*** (St. Martin's, 2002) As a favor to her mother, Stephanie agrees to look for Mabel Markowitz's missing granddaughter and her little girl and finds herself being trailed by someone in a bunny suit.
9. ***Visions of Sugar Plums*** (St. Martin's, 2002) A holiday novella in which a strange man appears in Stephanie's kitchen five days before Christmas.
10. ***To the Nines*** (St. Martin's, 2003) Stephanie, on the trail of "illegal" Samuel Singh, finds herself in Las Vegas and the target of three guys from the "mob."
11. ***Ten Big Ones*** (St. Martin's, 2004) Stephanie, on the run from a Trenton gang, finds Ranger's "bat cave."
12. ***Eleven on Top*** (St. Martin's, 2005) Stephanie, who decides to seek less-dangerous work, finds that she is equally inept at a series of low-paying, humiliating jobs.
13. ***Twelve Sharp*** (St. Martin's, 2006) Stephanie, facing a backlog in bounty jumpers, takes on a new assistant, a hapless shoe salesman, who has been talked off a ledge by her offer of a file-clerk position.
14. ***Plum Lovin'*** (St. Martin's, 2007) In a "between-the-numbers" novel, Stephanie reconnects with old heartthrob Diesel, who offers to help Stephanie find Annie Hart, a relationship coach who is on Stephanie's Most Wanted List.
15. ***Lean Mean Thirteen*** (St. Martin's, 2007) Stephanie is reunited with her two-timing lawyer ex-husband, Dickie Orr, while doing

a favor for Ranger. Then Dickie disappears, leaving Stephanie as the prime suspect in his alleged murder.

16. *Plum Lucky* (St. Martin's, 2008) Grandma Mazur finds a duffle bag full of money on the street and runs off to Atlantic City. Unfortunately the money was stolen from a notorious Trenton mobster.

II. Janet Evanovich started her writing career as a romance author. Her first published novel, *Hero at Large* (Second Chance at Love, 1987), written as "Steffie Hall," was recycled 15 years later as *Full House,* first in the series of Full novels, coauthored by South Carolinian Charlotte Hughes, set in Beaumont, South Carolina. Beaumont has as many wacky characters as Stephanie Plum's Trenton, and there is plenty of humor, although the novels are comic romances rather than comic mysteries, and have never achieved Plum's popularity.

1. *Full House* (St. Martin's, 2002) Nick Katharchek is concerned about competition from his cousin, computer wizard turned detective Max Holt, who has more money than he knows what to do with and not enough common sense to stay out of trouble. Coauthored by Charlotte Hughes.

2. *Full Tilt* (St. Martin's, 2003) Jamie Swift, who runs her family's newspaper in Beaumont, South Carolina, is ready to marry Beaumont's most eligible bachelor. But then Max Holt turns up, trailed by two hit men. Coauthored by Charlotte Hughes.

3. *Full Speed* (St. Martin's, 2003) Jamie Swift won't let Max Holt leave town without her, although he is being trailed by a preacher from Tennessee who wants to liquidate him. Coauthored by Charlotte Hughes.

4. *Full Blast* (St. Martin's, 2004) The initiation of a personal ads section in Jamie's paper leads to the "sexing up" of Beaumont. Several "unlikable" locals are bumped off. Coauthored by Charlotte Hughes.

5. *Full Bloom* (St. Martin's, 2005) Max and Jamie are to be married in the Peach Tree Bed and Breakfast, but it seems that the place is being haunted by a spirit from its former incarnation as a brothel. Coauthored by Charlotte Hughes.

6. *Full Scoop* (St. Martin's, 2006) Max and Jamie are now newlyweds expecting a child. Psychic-astrologer Destiny Mouline, who has detected a spirit or two in her time, is being chased by a local bait-shop owner. An Elvis convention is in the offing, and local pediatrician Maggie Davenport runs into visiting FBI agent Jack Madden.

Evans, Geraldine

I. Detective Inspector Joseph Rafferty and Sergeant Dafyd Llewellyn are a mismatched pair temperamentally, but the verbose, expansive Rafferty and the solemn Llewellyn manage to cooperate enough to solve a series of mysteries set in, and around, London. This is a well-plotted and characterized set of police procedurals, leavened with humor.

1. *Dead before Morning* (St. Martin's, 1993) The nude, mutilated body of a young prostitute is found on the grounds of a private psychiatric hospital.

2. *Down among the Dead Men* (St. Martin's, 1994) Was the popular Barbara Longman slain by the Suffolk Serial Killer? Or was a copycat killer at work? Several other books have the same title as this one, including a mystery by Patricia Moyes (q.v.).

3. *Death Line* (Macmillan [UK], 1995) Jasper Moon, internationally known "seer to the stars," is murdered. Not published in the United States.

4. *Hanging Tree, The* (Macmillan [UK], 1996) The body of man reported hanging from a tree disappears before Rafferty can arrive. Several other books and a 1959 Gary Cooper western movie have the same title. Not published in the United States.

5. *Absolute Poison* (Severn House, 2002) Two pensioner suicides are followed by the fatal poisoning of a tyrannical office manager.

6. *Dying for You* (Severn House, 2004) Rafferty signs up, under an alias, with the Made in Heaven dating agency, and finds himself charmed by the first two women he meets. Unfortunately, both women are dead by the following Monday.

7. *Bad Blood* (Severn House, 2005) Rafferty, brooding over the possible pregnancy of his girlfriend Abra, investigates the murder of wealthy widow Clara Mortimer.

8. *Love Lies Bleeding* (Severn House, 2005) Blood-spattered Felicity Raine stumbles into a police station and confesses to murdering her husband. Several other authors, including mystery-writers Susan Wittig Albert (q.v.) and Edmund Crispin (q.v.), have used this title, which refers to *Love Lies a-Bleeding,* subtitle of *Philastor,* one of the plays by Francis Beaumont and John Fletcher.

9. *Blood on the Bones* (Severn House, 2006) Lapsed Catholic Rafferty finds it easier to believe that the murderer of Father Roberto Kelly could be a nun than does the Protestant Llewellyn.

10. *Thrust to the Vitals, A* (Severn House, 2007) Many years after his involuntary departure, Sir Rufus Seward is murdered with a wood chisel.

II. Londoner Evans has started a new series of mysteries featuring a pair of coppers named Casey and Catt.

1. *Up in Flames* (Severn House, 2004) When Chandra Bansi and her baby are burned to death, DCI Casey and Sergeant Catt come under pressure from their superintendent to put a couple of skinhead thugs behind bars.

2. *Killing Karma* (Severn House, 2007) Will Casey has an official case and an unofficial one. The official case is a John Doe found dead in a dark alley. Casey is brought into the unofficial case by his parents, who ask him to investigate a double murder at the Fenland commune where they live.

Evans, Liz

Liz Evans has been called Britain's answer to Janet Evanovich (q.v.). PI Grace Smith is certainly hip and zany enough, and so are her cases, but Grace lacks Stephanie Plum's weird extended family. Grace, who lives in a tacky beachfront house in the village of Seatoun (Brighton?), "deadsville" according to one disenchanted inhabitant, has, like Stephanie, an on-again, off-again boyfriend and, like Stephanie, is usually not in a position to turn down the gigs that are offered to her. The books, published by Orion (UK), are distributed in the United States by Trafalgar Square.

1. *Who Killed Marilyn Monroe?* (Orion [UK], 1997) Grace Smith, broke as usual, can't afford to turn down the "Marilyn Monroe" case, even if Marilyn is only a beach donkey. Then Grace is drawn into the murder of Tina, a young woman whose aunt lives nearby.

2. *JFK Is Missing!* (Orion [UK], 1998) Blind Henry Summerstone is concerned about the whereabouts of a young female jogger who talked to him on his early morning walks, and he's offering Grace cash to find her.

3. *Don't Mess with Mrs. In-Between* (Orion [UK], 2000) Grace Smith is hired by Barbra Delaney to trace a group of people photographed in a grocery store, one or more of whom might be beneficiaries of a bizarre bequest.

4. *Barking!* **(Orion [UK], 2001)** Pursuing her friend Arlene's bulldog, Waterloo, Grace accidently bashes accountant Stuart Roberts's head with a beef bone. When he learns that Grace is a PI, Stuart confides to her that he may have killed someone.

5. *Sick as a Parrot* **(Orion [UK], 2004)** Twenty-year-old adoptee Hannah Conti thinks that her biological mother has been wrongly convicted for a murder to which she confessed.

6. *Cue the Easter Bunny* **(Orion [UK], 2005)** Wearing a bunny costume that she has donned to promote tourism in Seatoun, Grace is hired to investigate death threats sent to the husband of soap star Clemency Courtney.

Evans, Max

Western writer Max Evans is perhaps best known for his novel *The Rounders* (Macmillan, 1960), which was made into a popular film starring Henry Fonda and Glenn Ford (1965). *The Hi Lo Country*, a more recent film (1998), is also based on an Evans novel (Macmillan, 1961). Evans's books, both fiction and nonfiction, feature "writing of the genuine West, as opposed to the myth" (Tony Hillerman [q.v.]), and are full of tragedy and humor. The Bluefeather Fellini novels are no exception. Bluefeather Fellini is half-Sicilian and half–Native American, a rather potent combination. Bluefeather's adventures take him from the mines of the American Southwest to the trenches of World War II in an allegory of "good, evil, and human choice" that captures the authentic flavor of the American West. Texas native Max Evans has been a ranch hand, rodeo cowboy, miner, and screenwriter as well as a fiction writer.

1. *Bluefeather Fellini* **(University Press of Colorado, 1993)** Bluefeather Fellini lives in two worlds: "the gritty reality of the [American] West and the timeless world of legend." His adventures take him as far afield as World War II Europe.

2. *Bluefeather Fellini in the Sacred Realm* **(University Press of Colorado, 1994)** Also called *Bluefeather Fellini, Volume II* this sequel finds Bluefeather, hired by an enigmatic millionaire to search for a missing trove of Mouton Rothschild 1880, reunited with an old love and on a quest to find his people's sacred caverns.

Evers, Crabbe

PSEUDONYM OF William Brashler & Reinder Van Til

Using a pseudonym borrowed from Baseball Hall of Famer Johnny "Crab" Evers of "Tinker to Evers to Chance" renown, William Brashler and Reinder Van Til produced a series of five mysteries featuring Duffy House, retired sportswriter, and his niece "Petey" Biggers. The sleuthing pair made the rounds of five different major league baseball parks in detective tales spiced with baseball lore and fictional characters dubbed with the names of old ballplayers.

1. *Murder in Wrigley Field* **(Bantam, 1991)** "Dream" Weaver, Chicago Cubs ace, is shot to death in the tunnel leading from the field to the Cubs' clubhouse.

2. *Murderer's Row* **(Bantam, 1991)** Rupert Huston, owner of the New York Yankees, is shot by a sniper in Yankee Stadium's "Death Valley."

3. *Bleeding Dodger Blue* **(Bantam, 1991)** Jack Remsen, manager of the Los Angeles Dodgers, is murdered, ostensibly by the "Slasher," a serial killer terrorizing the city.

4. *Fear in Fenway* **(Morrow, 1993)** Poison in the potato salad and spiked chewing tobacco fell present and former Boston Red Sox

legends, while Duffy tries to get something going with Red Sox owner Mrs. Patsy Dougherty.

5. *Tigers Burning* **(Morrow, 1994)** Kit Gleason, leader in the campaign to save Detroit's Tiger Stadium, is found dead in the rubble of the torched park.

Eversz, Robert M(cLeod)

After delivering a package that explodes in a Los Angeles airport while doing a favor for a lover named Wrex, sweet, sentimental baby photographer Mary Alice Baker goes into hiding, dyes her hair, pierces her body, and transmogrifies herself into tough, cynical PI Nina Zero, who, after serving time for her role in the airport bombing, becomes the heroine of a series of stylish Hollywood mysteries.

1. *Shooting Elvis* **(Grove, 1996)** Mary Alice Baker, on the run from police and thugs after delivering an exploding package to a Los Angeles airport, transforms herself into tough, cynical Nina Zero.

2. *Killing Paparazzi* **(St. Martin's, 2002)** After being paroled from prison, Nina goes after the hit men who killed the Englishman she had married after he paid her to $2,000 to help him get a green card.

3. *Burning Garbo* **(Simon & Schuster, 2003)** While trying to take pictures of reclusive movie star, Angela Doubleday, Nina sees Doubleday's Malibu mansion go up in flames, is shot at, and is adopted by a lovable, toothless Rottweiler.

4. *Digging James Dean* **(Simon & Schuster, 2005)** Nina travels to James Dean's burial place in Indiana only to find that someone has robbed his grave. Back in Hollywood, a mysterious religious cult seems to be trading in stolen artifacts related to aging movie stars.

5. *Zero to the Bone* **(Simon & Schuster, 2006)** Nina's photography is exhibited at an art gallery. Then she receives what appears to be a "snuff" film, whose victim has a tattoo like one borne by Nina's featured model.

Exley, Frederick

This thinly fictionalized autobiographical series by the late Exley chronicled the messy life of a character named "Frederick Exley" as he spirals downward into alcoholism, divorce, random sex, and mental breakdown. *A Fan's Notes* won the William Faulkner Award for best first novel and stirred debate about the "emasculation" of the American male. Some readers find the trilogy funny and moving. Others are repelled by its self-indulgence and blurring of fact and fiction.

1. *Fan's Notes, A* **(Harper, 1968)** Frederick Exley tells about his frustrated life and his two idols: his athletic father and New York Giants' halfback Frank Gifford.

2. *Pages from a Cold Island* **(Random House, 1975)** The death of literary critic Edmund Wilson preoccupies Exley, who is now burdened with the task of sustaining his initial writing success.

3. *Last Notes from Home* **(Random House, 1988)** Exley visits his brother, Colonel Bill Exley, dying of cancer in Hawaii.

Eyre, Elizabeth

PSEUDONYM OF Jill Staynes & Margaret Storey

British authors Jill Staynes and Margaret Storey, who produce the Inspector Bone series under the joint pseudonym of Susannah Stacey (q.v.), also collaborate, as "Elizabeth Eyre," on the Sigismondo series of historical mysteries set in Renaissance Italy. Sigismondo is a soldier of fortune and master of disguise, who, with his dwarf sidekick Benno, solves a series of mysteries in high places. Some readers have reservations about these mixtures of historical romance and detective story, as the historical verisimilitude is spread on rather thickly and the plots are long and labyrinthine.

1. *Death of the Duchess* (Harcourt, 1992) Sigismondo, a learned soldier of fortune, is hired by Ludovico, Duke of Rocca, to find the abductor of Lady Cosima di Torre and his wife.
2. *Curtains for the Cardinal* (Harcourt, 1993) Prince Livio, brother-in-law of Duke Ludovico, beheads his teenage son, shouting "Betrayed me! Betrayed me! Bastard! Bastard!"
3. *Poison for the Prince* (Harcourt, 1994) Prince Scipione, weak ruler of the city of Viverra, is tormented by a chronic illness, which his wife attributes to fumes from the laboratory where the prince toils to create precious metals.
4. *Bravo for the Bride* (St. Martin's, 1995) Sigismondo is hired to find the strangler of a bad-tempered 15-year-old princess, who is murdered the day after her arranged marriage to a loutish prince.
5. *Axe for an Abbot* (St. Martin's, 1996) Sigismondo kills a thief at the villa of the wealthy Pantera family. Soon after, Sigismondo's axe is used to slay the gross, venal Abbot Bonifacio.
6. *Dirge for a Doge* (St. Martin's, 1997) In plot-ridden Venice, aristocrat and member of the Council of Ten, Niccolo Ermolin is stabbed to death in the study of his palazzo.

Fackler, Elizabeth

I. Seth Strummar is a fairly typical western antihero: outwardly stoic and taciturn but troubled by violent passions. Gunfighter and bank robber Seth does try now and again to mend his promiscuous outlaw ways and is sometimes capable of making sacrifices for the people he cares for, which makes him a somewhat sympathetic character (if you don't mind violence and a retro attitude toward women) in an exciting, well-written series set on the Texas frontier of the early 1880s.

1. *Blood Kin* (Evans, 1992) Hired gun Seth Strummar, headed for El Paso to avenge his brother's death, falls in with Johanna Devery, who is disguised as a boy.
2. *Backtrail* (Evans, 1993) Estranged from the pregnant Johanna, Seth takes to the trail again, leaving her in the care of his friend Joaquin Ascarate.
3. *Road from Betrayal* (Evans, 1994) Seth leaves Texas with his son and Joaquin Ascarate, but soon finds himself on the wrong end of a posse again.
4. *Badlands* (Forge, 1996) In 1883 Seth is making an attempt to settle down on a ranch in the Arizona Territory, but then the whorish Lila Keats turns up out of his past.
5. *Breaking Even* (Forge, 1998) Seth buys Heaven Free and her sister Hekuba out of a life of prostitution, then sets them up in separate menages.

II. An earlier pair of novels featured Frank James, a Texas newspaper reporter who battles corruption in small towns in the contemporary West.

1. *Arson* (Dodd, Mead, 1984) The finding of a gun in a lake by a fisherman leads to a violent chain of events.
2. *Barbed Wire* (St. Martin's, 1986) Frank's lover Arly Walbridge is found hanging by a rope in a cottonwood grove. Sheriff Pickles Offut says she committed suicide, but Frank doesn't believe it.

III. El Paso, Texas, homicide detective Devon Gray is Fackler's latest series protagonist. Gray is an appealing character who gets mixed up in some seamy cases.

1. *Patricide* (Five Star, 2000) El Paso homicide detective Devon Gray, called in to investigate the murder of Theodore Truxal, finds that Truxal's wife and children are not very broken up about his demise.
2. *When Kindness Fails* (Five Star, 2003) A murder investigation leads to kidnapping and Gray's subsequent suspension from the police force.
3. *Lucinda's Summer Vacation* (Five Star, 2007) No annotation available.

Faherty, Terence

I. Owen Keane is an unusual sleuth. He is an ex-seminarian, laid-back, cerebral, and self-deprecating: one of those outwardly awkward, almost buffoonish fellows who, while seeming to be "out of it," lets little get by him. Owen treks back and forth between points in Indiana, Massachusetts, New York, and New Jersey, from job to job, seeking his true vocation and solving mysteries along the way. Though *The Lost Keats* was published after *Deadstick*, the events in the former take place before the events of the latter.

1. *Lost Keats, The* (St. Martin's, 1993) In 1973 Owen has left Boston and sleuthing to pursue the life of a seminarian at St. Aelred in southern Indiana.
2. *Deadstick* (St. Martin's, 1991) Owen has hidden himself away doing routine work as a researcher in a small New York law firm.
3. *Die Dreaming* (St. Martin's, 1994) Now working at a job in a Boston liquor store, Owen returns for his high school class reunion in New Jersey.
4. *Live to Regret* (St. Martin's, 1992) Owen's former love Mary has died in an auto accident. Although her death was not his fault, Mary's widower, Harry Ohlman Jr., has secluded himself on the New Jersey shore.
5. *Prove the Nameless* (St. Martin's, 1996) Working as a newspaper copy editor on the New Jersey shore, Owen becomes intrigued by the 20-year-old unsolved massacre of a local family.
6. *Ordained, The* (St. Martin's, 1997) Owen, in Indiana to testify at the parole hearing of convicted killer Curtis Morell, gets involved with Morell's daughter Krystal, local doctor in Rapture, a town that has been waiting 150 years for the Second Coming.
7. *Orion Rising* (St. Martin's, 1999) In 1995 an acquaintance from Owen's college days, James Courtney Murray, has apparently been murdered. Full of flashbacks to the 1960s and Owen's failed romance with Mary Fitzgerald, who became the Mary Ohlman of number 3.

II. Scott Elliott, World War II hero, former actor, and now film studio security person, is the protagonist of a series set in the Hollywood of the late 1940s and 1950s. Critics feel that the historical Hollywood premise has been used more effectively by George Baxt (q.v.) and Stuart M. Kaminsky (q.v.).

1. *Kill Me Again* (Simon & Schuster, 1996) The studio where Scott Elliott is working security is gearing up to film the sequel to a movie that strongly resembles *Casablanca*, but the screenwriter may have a Communist past.
2. *Come Back Dead* (Simon & Schuster, 1997) In 1955 Orson Welles–ish former wunderkind Carson Drury is reshooting *The*

Imperial Andersons (i.e., *The Magnificent Ambersons*) with a new ending but is plagued by a series of mysterious accidents.

3. *Raise the Devil* (**St. Martin's, 2000**) Scott Elliott and Ella, his screenwriter wife, are on location for the shooting of *Warrior Queen* when the film's director, Marcus Pioline, and starlet Bebe Brooks are killed in a plane crash.

4. *In a Teapot* (**Mystery Company, 2005**) 1948. A film version of *The Tempest*, featuring members of Hollywood's British Colony, is derailed when one of the actors is murdered.

Fair, A. A.

PSEUDONYM OF Erle Stanley Gardner

Bertha Cool does not need a woman's movement to liberate her. Though she looks like a hefty, gray-haired, grandmotherly type, she talks like a sailor and runs her Los Angeles private-detective agency like a shrewd top sergeant. Donald Lam, her partner, is as small as Bertha is big, but he is an ingenious legman. Ably assisted by the shy and efficient Elsie Brand, this unique team solved 29 enjoyable cases. Although Lam and Cool never achieved the iconic status of Perry Mason, the creation of Erle Stanley Gardner (q.v.) under his real name, this series enjoyed considerable popularity over a 30-year stretch.

1. *Bigger They Come, The* (**Morrow, 1939**) Donald Lam, a disbarred attorney, is introduced as he takes his first job with Bertha Cool's detective agency and gets involved in some tricky legalities for getting a murderer off the hook. UK title: *Lam to the Slaughter*.

2. *Gold Comes in Bricks* (**Morrow, 1940**) The plot of this story concerns a gold mine, a murdered gambler, and a young girl who has paid a stranger three large checks.

3. *Turn on the Heat* (**Morrow, 1940**) When the case they are investigating proves to have a bearing on the political situation in a nearby city, Donald and Bertha start feeling some heat.

4. *Double or Quits* (**Morrow, 1941**) Missing jewels and a double-indemnity insurance suit occupy Donald and Bertha.

5. *Spill the Jackpot* (**Morrow, 1941**) Donald hits the jackpot on a rigged slot machine and is almost arrested as a swindler while Bertha battles nobly to keep her new svelte shape.

6. *Owls Don't Blink* (**Morrow, 1942**) Cool and Lam are hired to find Roberta Fenn, a New Orleans woman who has been missing for two years. Donald enlists in the navy at the book's end.

7. *Bats Fly at Dusk* (**Morrow, 1942**) Bertha misses Donald, but when he solves this case—involving a blind beggar and a possibly forged will—by telegram, she relaxes.

8. *Cats Prowl at Night* (**Morrow, 1944**) With Donald still off in the navy, Bertha accepts an easy case that turns nasty, and she makes use of a Lam technique for getting out of a tight spot.

9. *Give 'Em the Ax* (**Morrow, 1944**) Lam narrowly escapes being charged as an accessory in his first case after coming home with a medical discharge from the navy. UK title: *An Axe to Grind*.

10. *Crows Can't Count* (**Morrow, 1946**) Emeralds and murder mix in this deadly brew.

11. *Fools Die on Friday* (**Morrow, 1947**) Bertha accepts a fat retainer to prevent Daphne Ballwin from poisoning her husband.

12. *Bedrooms Have Windows* (**Morrow, 1949**) A blond lures Donald into a auto tourist court and very close to a murder charge.

13. *Top of the Heap* (**Morrow, 1952**) Bertha plays a very minor role in this case of stock manipulation and income-tax fraud.

14. *Some Women Won't Wait* (**Morrow, 1953**) Cool and Lam venture to Hawaii in this case of nasty doings focusing on a pair of "good-time" girls.

15. *Beware the Curves* (**Morrow, 1956**) Donald uses some outrageous legal maneuvers as he masterminds a murder's defense.

16. *You Can Die Laughing* (**Morrow, 1957**) A loud Texan and some pretty girls figure in this case of a cleverly masked murder.

17. *Some Slips Don't Show* (**Morrow, 1957**) This comedy of errors shows Donald to be a patron of the arts.

18. *Count of Nine* (**Morrow, 1958**) Murder by blowpipe and a flawless income-tax dodge are the seemingly incongruous elements of this case.

19. *Pass the Gravy* (**Morrow, 1959**) Donald takes on a charity case for a pathetic teenager, and it turns out to be highly profitable.

20. *Kept Women Can't Quit* (**Morrow, 1960**) Lam is on the trail of $100,000 taken in an armored-car robbery.

21. *Bachelors Get Lonely* (**Morrow, 1961**) Lam gets himself arrested as a Peeping Tom to solve this highly unusual case.

22. *Shills Can't Cash Chips* (**Morrow, 1961**) A case of insurance fraud leads Donald into some surprising complications. UK title: *Stop at the Red Light*.

23. *Try Anything Once* (**Morrow, 1962**) Lam does a stint as a special investigator for the Los Angeles district attorney's office.

24. *Fish or Cut Bait* (**Morrow, 1963**) Jarvis Archer, a very big fish, wants his secretary protected around the clock and is willing to pay the hefty fee.

25. *Up for Grabs* (**Morrow, 1964**) Homer Breckinridge hires Donald to investigate an insurance claim.

26. *Cut Thin to Win* (**Morrow, 1965**) A hit-and-run injury claim leads to bigger things.

27. *Widows Wear Weeds* (**Morrow, 1966**) Mrs. Nicholas Baffin hires Donald to pay off a blackmailer.

28. *Traps Need Fresh Bait* (**Morrow, 1967**) Cool and Lam are hired to investigate a suspected insurance swindle.

29. *All Grass Isn't Green* (**Morrow, 1970**) Wealthy young tycoon Milton Calhoun hires Bertha and Donald to find the novelist Colburn Hale.

Fairbanks, Nancy

PSEUDONYM OF Nancy Herndon

Fortysomething homemaker Carolyn Blue of El Paso decides to throw in the dish towel and embark upon a career as a food writer, which takes her and her husband, Jason, to exotic places, great restaurants, and the usual crime solving in this Culinary Mystery with Recipes series. Nancy Fairbanks is the maiden name of Nancy Herndon (q.v.), who writes the Elena Jarvis mystery series under her married name and romances under the pseudonym of Elizabeth Chadwick (q.v.). *Three-Course Murder* (Berkley, 2006) is an omnibus volume containing numbers 1 through 3.

1. *Crime Brulee* (**Berkley, 2001**) Fortysomething housewife Carolyn Blue leaves housework behind and becomes a food writer. When her husband goes to an academic conference in New Orleans, Carolyn goes with him to write a story on Cajun cuisine.

2. *Truffled Feathers* (**Berkley, 2001**) The CEO of a large pharmaceutical company, who has invited Carolyn and her husband to New York City, is felled by a large helping of pastrami.

3. *Death a L'Orange* (**Berkley, 2002**) Blue and her family travel with a group of academics through Normandy and the Loire Valley.

4. *Chocolate Quake* (**Berkley, 2003**) A visit to San Francisco and her mother-in-law involves Carolyn in an earthquake tremor or two and being sent to prison as a murder suspect.

5. *Perils of Paella, The* (**Berkley, 2004**) A trip to Barcelona involves a visit with Carolyn's friend Roberta, who is the resident scholar at a modern art museum.

6. *Holy Guacamole!* (Berkley, 2004) An irate soprano at a Texas party claims to have tampered with the guacamole, which felled the opera director who turned her down for a plum role.

7. *Mozzarella Most Murderous* (Berkley, 2005) Awaiting a rendezvous with her husband in Italy, Carolyn plans to spend the day with the beautiful Paolina. But Paolina turns up dead in a hotel swimming pool.

8. *Bon Bon Voyage* (Berkley, 2006) When Carolyn takes a gourmet cruise from Lisbon to Barcelona, one of the passengers, Mrs. Gross, goes missing.

9. *French Fried* (Berkley, 2006) Carolyn and her husband, Jason, are in the gourmet capital of the world, Paris, but, as usual, a poisoned dish turns up.

Fairstein, Linda

Alexandra Cooper, head of the sex-crimes unit at the Manhattan District Attorney's office, is a workaholic who empathizes strongly with victims of sex crimes. "Coop" does have a lighter side, including a second home on Martha's Vineyard and a boyfriend who is an NBC correspondent. With her assistants, Mike Chapman and Mercer Wallace, she takes part in a series of fast-moving investigations designed to keep "scum" off the streets. Author Linda Fairstein writes from her own knowledge as a prosecutor of crimes of sexual assault and domestic violence in the Manhattan DA's office. She has also written the nonfiction book *Sexual Violence: Our War against Rape* (Morrow, 1993).

1. *Final Jeopardy* (Scribner, 1996) Introduces Alexandra Cooper, who investigates the shooting homicide of movie star Isabella Lascar at her getaway home on Martha's Vineyard.

2. *Likely to Die* (Scribner, 1997) Cooper investigates the sexual assault and stabbing of a prominent neurosurgeon in her mid-Manhattan medical center office.

3. *Cold Hit* (Scribner, 1999) This time Cooper and her assistant, detective Mike Chapman, track down the killer of a woman found tied to a ladder in the Hudson River.

4. *Deadhouse, The* (Scribner, 2001) Archaeologist Lola Dakota, who was engaged in a dig on New York's Roosevelt Island, former dumping ground for criminals and mental patients, is found dead at the bottom of an elevator shaft in her apartment building.

5. *Bone Vault, The* (Scribner, 2003) The perfectly preserved, though dead for months, body of a Metropolitan Museum of Art intern is found dead in a sarcophagus.

6. *Kills, The* (Scribner, 2004) A rape accusation turns into a murder investigation when it turns out that rapee Paige Vallis and homicide victim McQueen Ransome, former mistress of Egypt's King Farouk, may have a connection.

7. *Entombed* (Scribner, 2005) The Silk Stocking rapist has started up again, and the skeleton of freelance writer Emily Upshaw is found in the wall of an East Village building once inhabited by E. A. Poe.

8. *Death Dance* (Scribner, 2006) The body of a Russian ballerina is found in the cooling unit at the Metropolitan Opera House.

9. *Bad Blood* (Scribner, 2007) When the defense attorney shows that Kate Meade, the lead witness in Cooper's circumstantial case against Brendan Quillian for the murder of his wife, may be biased, Coop's case is all but ruined.

10. *Killer Heat* (Doubleday, 2008) Coop deals with a serial killer who targets women in uniform and the second trial of Floyd Warren, whose first trial for rape ended in a hung jury.

Fallon, Jennifer

I. The six books of the Hythrun Chronicles were published originally in Australia as two separate trilogies: Demon Child and Wolfblade. The Demon Child trilogy (numbers 1–3) is set in the country of Medalon, a matriarchy run by the Sisters of the Blade that has banned religious worship. When their mother, Joyhina, ascends to power, 18-year-old R'shiel Tenragen and her half brother Tarja join a group rebelling against the Sisterhood. R'shiel discovers that she is the Demon Child, a half-human, half-Harshini who is destined to lead the struggle against an evil god. It takes R'shiel three volumes of intrigues, power struggles, and romance in a world run by capricious gods of waxing and waning powers to figure out how to use her powers.

The Wolfblade trilogy (numbers 4–6), in the same fantasy universe and with some characters continuing from the first trilogy, is set in the kingdom of Hythria and features the Wolfblades, mother Marla and son Damin, who, with aid of the clever dwarf Elezaar, learn to deal with their relative, the hedonistic and incompetent High Prince Lernen; plague; a Fardohynyan invasion; a slew of intrigues; and a lot of swashbuckling action.

1. *Medalon* (Tor, 2004) When their mother, Joyhina, ascends to the position of First Sister of the Sisters of the Blade, who rule the land of Medalon, half-siblings R'shiel and Tarja join rebels against the Sisterhood. Originally published in Australia in 2000.

2. *Treason Keep* (Tor, 2005) After a successful rebellion against the Sisterhood, the badly wounded and possibly dying R'shiel recuperates at Sanctuary, the homeland of the magical Harshini. Originally published in Australia in 2001.

3. *Harshini* (Tor, 2005) R'shiel is reconciled to her destiny as Demon Child but still doesn't know how to achieve her mission as, assisted by the half-Harshini Brak, she takes on Xaphista, the god who controls Medalon. Originally published in Australia in 2001.

4. *Wolfblade* (Tor, 2005) Lady Marla Wolfblade, sister to Lernen, the High Prince of Hythria, is destined to marry King Hablet of Fardohyna but, not satisfied with being a mere pawn in a diplomatic game, sets out, with the help of the dwarf Elezaar, to acquire real power.

5. *Warrior* (Tor, 2005) Damin Wolfblade, heir to the High Throne of Hythria, learns "the Rules of Gaining and Wielding Power" from the dwarf Elezaar at the insistence of his mother, Marla.

6. *Warlord* (Tor, 2006) Intrigues continue as Marla seeks vengeance against Alija Eaglespike. Damin is forced to pit his under-manned army against the forces of Fardohyna. Meanwhile, back in Krakandar, Mahkas has sealed the city against his nephew's return.

II. The Second Sons trilogy, set in a different world than the Hythrun Chronicles, is also sword-and-sorcery fantasy chock-full of political intrigue. The high priestess Belagren has banished darkness from the world of Ranadon, but now she faces a possible loss of power, which only Dirk Provin can prevent.

1. *Lion of Senet* (Bantam, 2004) Since Belagren, high priestess of the Shadowdancers, banished the Dark Ages, Ranadon has known peace and prosperity, but intrigues are afoot to break Belagren's power.

2. *Eye of the Labyrinth* (Bantam, 2004) With his mother's life threatened by the ruthless Lion of Senet, Dirk Provin must venture out of his hiding place in the Baenlands and return to Elcast.

3. *Lord of the Shadows* (Bantam, 2004) As darkness threatens Ranadon once again, Dirk Provin, branded as a traitor, must find a way to save the kingdom and expose the truth.

Farland, David

PSEUDONYM OF Dave Wolverton

The Runelords series is set on an Earth where a complex magical technology allows the nobility to transfer attributes such as wit, strength, grace, and stamina from their subjects to themselves. Wolf Lord Raj Ahten seeks to monopolize all these abilities, make himself the Sum of All Men, and rule the world. It is up to Gaborn Val Orden, Runelord and prince, to stop him. This highly praised series—by, among others, Terry Brooks (q.v.), Orson Scott Card (q.v.), David Drake (q.v.), and Michael A. Stackpole—has run to five volumes so far and hasn't run out of steam. Science-fiction writer Dave Wolverton has produced some series under his own name.

1. *Sum of All Men, The* (Simon & Schuster, 1998) Prince Gaborn, on his way to ask for Iome's hand in marriage, discovers by chance a pair of assassins out to kill Iome's father. Variant title: *The Runelords: The Sum of All Men.*
2. *Brotherhood of the Wolf* (Simon & Schuster, 1999) Gaborn has fulfilled a 2,000-year-old prophecy and become the Earth King. Ahtan, bloodied but unbowed, seeks to draw out the Earth King from his seat of power.
3. *Wizardborn* (Tor, 2001) Gaborn has lost his powers but continues to lead his people against the huge, insectile Reavers, who have come up from under the Earth.
4. *Lair of Bones, The* (Tor, 2003) Gaborn faces final confrontations with the now supernatural Raj Ahten and with the One True Master, leader of the Reavers.
5. *Sons of the Oak* (Tor, 2006) Eight years later, Fallion, son of the late Gaborn, must, although still a child, face the attack of powerful immortal beings who realize that he is the resurrection of an even stronger immortal being.

Farmer, Jerrilyn

Madeline Bean, owner-operator of Mad Bean Events of Beverly Hills, California, is a caterer for the Hollywood stars. In this series of breezy mysteries, Madeline runs into the usual theft and murder cases on her rounds. Humor, menus, decorating ideas, and peeks at high-end Hollywood lifestyle help spice up these culinary cozies by Californian Jerrilyn Farmer.

1. *Sympathy for the Devil* (Avon, 1998) Madeline Bean, "caterer to the stars," pulls off a spectacular coup in her A-list Halloween party for notorious producer Bruno Huntley. Unfortunately, Mr. Huntley winds up dead from poison.
2. *Immaculate Reception* (Avon, 1999) Mad Bean Events is hired to cater for the celebration of the pope's visit to Los Angeles, but the death of a young priest, some nasty secrets from the past, and the return of her former fiancé take some of the bloom off the event for Madelyn.
3. *Killer Wedding* (Avon, 2000) In the middle of a fancy wedding held in the Nature Museum's Hall of Dinosaurs, a corpse is found hanging from the Triceratops skeleton.
4. *Dim Sum Dead* (Avon, 2001) Mah-jongg is one of the planned events for a Chinese New Year banquet, but a corpse in the dim sum is not.
5. *Mumbo Gumbo* (Morrow, 2003) Owing to her food knowledge, Madeline is temporarily taken on by the TV hit *Food Freak*, a gourmet cook-off game show, when the head writer disappears.
6. *Perfect Sax* (Morrow, 2004) The "sax" in question is a silver Marl IV Selmer saxophone that goes missing after being auctioned off for $100,000 at the Jazz Ball at Woodburn School of Music.
7. *Flaming Luau of Death, The* (Morrow, 2005) Mad Bean is throwing a spectacular luau-type party at a Hawaiian resort for her employee and bride-to-be, Holly Nichols. A dead body washing on shore wasn't part of the plan, however.

Farmer, Philip José

I. The Riverworld science-fiction series explores the fascinating question of what would happen if the entire human race (up to 1984) were reincarnated simultaneously and placed along a million-mile river in a bewildering new world. Historic figures clash with Neanderthals and even a space alien in Farmer's mysterious "after-Earth world." The original Riverworld story, "Owe for the Flesh" (1952), was lost, then re-created as *River of Eternity*, and published in 1983 in a couple of limited editions by Phantasia. *Riverworld: And Other Stories* (Berkley, 1979) contains 11 stories, including a Riverworld novella. *Quest to Riverworld* (Warner, 1993) is a shared-world volume containing 2 stories by Farmer and stories by several other authors.

1. *To Your Scattered Bodies Go* (Putnam, 1971) Explorer and translator Sir Richard Francis Burton is among those who find themselves reborn—naked, hairless, and young again—into a baffling new world.
2. *Fabulous Riverboat, The* (Putnam, 1971) Samuel Clemens, former riverboat captain and writer (Mark Twain [q.v.]), builds a riverboat so that he can sail to the River's source and discover the reason behind this strange "after-Earth world."
3. *Dark Design, The* (Putnam, 1977) Clemens, Burton, and their band drive on toward the River's headwaters and Misty Tower, the home of the Ethicals.
4. *Magic Labyrinth, The* (Putnam, 1980) The mystery is revealed as Burton and Alice Hargreaves reach the perilous North and its truth.
5. *Gods of Riverworld* (Putnam, 1983) Now in command of the Ethicals' polar control center, members of the band can "play God" themselves.

II. The World of Tiers is an action-packed science-fiction adventure series based on the premise of alternative "pocket universes," each smaller than the solar system, created by immortal, ruthless, humanoid Lords. Psychiatrist James Giannini developed a new therapeutic technique called Tiersian Therapy, which draws upon the World of Tiers for role-playing and as an aid to self-analysis. Number 6 uses Dr. Giannini's therapy as its premise. Numbers 1 through 5 were published by Ace Books as paperback originals. They have been reprinted several times in paper and hardcover formats. *World of Tiers* (Sphere, 1986; Tor, 1996; SFBC, 2001) collects numbers 1 through 5. *World of Tiers, Volume 2* (Doubleday, 1977) contains numbers 4, 5, and 7.

1. *Maker of Universes, The* (Ace, 1965) Robert Wolf (aka Jadawin) is transported from Earth to the World of Tiers and eventually leads an attack on the planet's Lord.
2. *Gates of Creation, The* (Ace, 1966) Wolf's world is invaded by a rival Lord, his own father.
3. *Private Cosmos, A* (Ace, 1968) Earthling Paul Janus Finnegan (aka Kickaha the Trickster), defends Wolf's world from an invasion by Black Bellers.
4. *Behind the Walls of Terra* (Ace, 1970) Pursuing the last Beller, Kickaha learns that the solar system is really a pocket universe created by the Lords.
5. *Lavalite World, The* (Ace, 1977) Kickaha goes to a pocket universe centered on a plastic planet in a constant state of change.

6. *Red Orc's Rage* (Tor, 1991) Troubled youth Jim Audson, undergoing Tiersian Therapy, travels to the World of Tiers in his thoughts, and perhaps in actuality.

7. *More Than Fire* (Tor, 1993) The rivalry between Kickaha and Red Orc reaches its final confrontation as Kickaha and his lover, Anana, fall into the hands of the archvillain.

III. The Dayworld trilogy is set in the far future, where the problem of overpopulation is solved by having everyone live only one day in a week, spending the other six days in suspended animation. This tidy arrangement is challenged by the Daybreakers, a rebel group, who stay "unstoned," living seven days a week, each day with a different identity.

1. *Dayworld* (Berkley/Putnam, 1985) Jeff Caird of Tuesday's World is a "daybreaker," staying active seven days of the week in seven roles.

2. *Dayworld Rebel* (Ace/Putnam, 1987) The daybreaker flees his Manhattan prison and falls in with a rebel group hiding out in the wilds of New Jersey.

3. *Dayworld Breakup* (Tor, 1990) The daybreaker and his rebel cohorts challenge the corrupt Dayworld government.

IV. A trio of novels features Herald Childe, private detective, history student, and teacher who shares a series of wild and fantastic adventures, some of them X-rated, with werewolves, vampires, ghosts, space aliens, and mad scientists. Originally published separately, *Image of the Beast* and *Blown* were published together in one volume by Playboy Press (1979).

1. *Image of the Beast* (Essex House, 1968) Private Detective Herald Childe's partner is killed in a gruesome sex murder.

2. *Blown* (Essex House, 1969) Herald Childe quits the detective business and goes back to college to study history. But he isn't through with the monsters in *Image of the Beast* yet.

3. *Traitor to the Living* (Ballantine, 1973) Now calling himself Gordan Carfax, Herald Childe is teaching in the Midwest. His cousin invents a machine called MEDIUM that communicates with the dead.

V. Farmer, a longtime fan of Edgar Rice Burroughs's (q.v.) Tarzan, wrote a "biography" of Tarzan, *Tarzan Alive* (Doubleday, 1972); an original Tarzan novel, *The Dark Heart of Time* (Del Rey, 1999); a novel pairing Tarzan and Sherlock Holmes, *The Adventure of the Peerless Peer* (Aspen, 1974), rewritten as "The Adventure of the Three Madmen" and published in Farmer's short story collection *The Grand Adventure* (Berkley, 1984); two Opar adventures (see series VI); and a trio of novels in which Tarzan has Doc Savage as an enemy, then an ally. Numbers 2 and 3 were published together as *Empire of the Nine* (Severn, 1983). Doc Savage, who appeared in pulp magazine, paperback book, and comic book format, is another one of Farmer's longtime loves. The Doc Savage stories, appearing under the pseudonym Kenneth Robeson, were mostly written by Lester Dent. As well as pairing Doc Savage with Tarzan, Farmer provided him with a "biography" (*Doc Savage: His Apocalyptic Life*, Doubleday, 1973), and produced a Doc Savage adventure of his own (*Escape from Loki*, Bantam, 1991).

1. *Feast Unknown, A* (Essex House, 1969) Tarzan and Doc Savage (called Caliban here), manipulated by a secret group called The Nine, try to kill each other. Should be X-rated: every act of violence and homicide produces a sexual reaction.

2. *Lord of the Trees* (Ace, 1970) Numbers 2 and 3 were published as halves of an Ace Double. Tarzan and Doc Savage realize they

are not enemies, and separate at the beginning of both books to revenge themselves on The Nine and reunite at the ends of both. Tarzan is the primary character here. Published with *The Mad Goblin*.

3. *Mad Goblin, The* (Ace, 1970) Doc Savage's side of the story (see annotation for number 2). Published together with *Lord of the Trees*. UK title: *Keepers of the Secrets*.

VI. Opar, the 12,000-year-old city visited by Tarzan (see Edgar Rice Burroughs and series V here), is the site of a pair of adventures starring a character named Hadon, who is destined to be king. Farmer, during his long career (first publication in 1946), has published many other books, most of them also SF or fantasy. Some of them recycle fictional characters such as Herman Melville's (q.v.) Ishmael, of *Moby Dick* (*The Wind Whales of Ishmael*, Ace, 1971); Jules Verne's (q.v.) Phileas Fogg, of *Around the World in Eighty Days* (*The Other Log of Phileas Fogg*, DAW, 1973); or L. Frank Baum's Oz characters (*A Barnstormer in Oz*, Berkley, 1982). An interesting item is *Venus on the Half-Shell* (Dell, 1994), by "Kilgore Trout," Kurt Vonnegut's (q.v.) fictional SF author.

1. *Hadon of Ancient Opar* (DAW, 1974) Twelve thousand years ago in the thriving African city of Opar, Hadon sets out to realize his destiny.

2. *Flight to Opar* (DAW, 1976) Hadon must perform an impossible task before he can realize his destiny and claim his crown.

Farrell, James T.

I. Farrell's Studs Lonigan, of Chicago's South Side, is the archetypal working-class boy whose brave youthful dreams turn all too quickly to dissolution and tragedy. Farrell, who wrote with the authority of one who grew up in the same environment, saw Studs as a victim of the spiritual poverty of his time and class. Although it was once fashionable to dismiss Farrell as a "merely sociological" writer, the Studs Lonigan trilogy will always demand a place in American literature. It is a powerful and moving work. All three novels are included in the omnibus volume *Studs Lonigan*, published by Vanguard in 1935. The trilogy was republished by the Library of America in 2004.

1. *Young Lonigan: A Boyhood in Chicago Streets* (Vanguard, 1932) This story begins in 1916, as 15-year-old Studs graduates from grammar school and dreams of becoming a "great guy."

2. *Young Manhood of Studs Lonigan, The* (Vanguard, 1934) This volume carries Studs into the twenties working with his father as a house painter, hanging out at the local poolroom, and drinking too much Prohibition alcohol.

3. *Judgment Day* (Vanguard, 1935) Though he is engaged to the gentle Catherine Banahan, hard times and illness plague the doomed Studs. This account covers six months of 1931.

II. The Danny O'Neill pentalogy stars a young man who appeared briefly as a college student in the second Lonigan volume; it is sometimes called the O'Neill-O'Flaherty pentalogy. Danny is more of an autobiographical figure than Studs.

1. *Face of Time, The* (Vanguard, 1953) Although published last, this book is the first chronologically. It relates how three-year-old Danny came to be brought up by his O'Flaherty grandparents.

2. *World I Never Made, A* (Vanguard, 1936) Timid and overprotected, Danny at seven becomes interested in baseball.

3. *No Star Is Lost* (Vanguard, 1938) Still preadolescent, Danny begins to reckon with a cruel world.

4. *Father and Son* (Vanguard, 1940) In high school, Danny realizes that he will never fit into the social life of his neighborhood.
5. *My Days of Anger* (Vanguard, 1943) Danny "finds himself" during his college days at the University of Chicago. The series ends with Danny on the threshold of adult life.

III. In a sense the Bernard Carr trilogy picks up where the Danny O'Neill books left off.

1. *Bernard Clare* (Vanguard, 1946) "Clare" was changed to "Carr" after this first novel in the series was the subject of a libel suit brought by someone named Bernard Clare. In 1927 the fictional Bernard is struggling to be a writer in New York City. Variant title: *Bernard Carr*.
2. *Road Between, The* (Vanguard, 1949) By 1932–1933, Bernard is married; his first novel is a success.
3. *Yet Other Waters* (Vanguard, 1952) The year 1935 brings Bernard a third successful novel, a growing family, and disenchantment with the Communist party.

IV. Farrell's later novels are generally conceded to be less successful than the ones published in the 1930s and 1940s, but they still provided solid stories for thousands of readers. Farrell had formulated a master plan for a cycle of 30 novels, tales, and poems to be called the Universe of Time, which was left unfinished at his death. Some of the related titles are described below.

1. *Silence of History, The* (Doubleday, 1963) This introduces Eddie Ryan, another autobiographical figure around whom the series revolves.
2. *Lonely for the Future* (Doubleday, 1966) Eddie's friends George Raymond and Alec McGonagle are the focus.
3. *What Time Collects* (Doubleday, 1964) The story of Anne Duncan and Zeke Daniels.
4. *Brand New Life, A* (Doubleday, 1968) Anne comes to Chicago and meets Roger and George Raymond.
5. *Judith* (Doubleday, 1969) Eddie Ryan gives a retrospective account of his affair with concert pianist Judith.
6. *Dunne Family, The* (Doubleday, 1976) The life of Grace Hogan Dunne, Eddie's grandmother, is recounted.
7. *Death of Nora Ryan, The* (Doubleday, 1978) Nora Ryan, Eddie's mother, suffers a massive stroke on New Year's Day 1946.

Farren, Mick

I. The DNA Cowboys series is a psychedelic SF romp, the first three volumes written from 1975 to 1976. The original trilogy was written in helter-skelter style from 1975 to 1976, under the influence of LSD, according to "underground legend." Although the legend may not be true, the books do read like a series of "trips," featuring fantastic adventures with preteen dictators, huge lizards, monks into the martial arts, public hangings, monsters called Disrupters, and orgies galore, with influences from all kinds of pop culture, in a world in which reality has to be maintained by technological devices or it turns into "the nothings." All worldly goods are supplied by Stuff Central, and only the Minstrel Boy really "knows where he's at." The hero of this melange is a character named Jeb Stuart Ho. The separate volumes of the original trilogy were never published in the United States. First US publication was in an omnibus volume containing numbers 1 through 3 (*The DNA Cowboys Trilogy*, Do-Not, distributed by Dufour, 2002). Number 4 was published 12 years after the original trilogy. "Wild and crazy" Englishman Farren, who currently lives and works in the United States, created the off-Broadway musical *The Last Words*

of Dutch Schultz, scripted a number of TV documentaries, produced several music CDs featuring his unique voice, and has published the memoir *Give the Anarchist a Cigarette* (Cape [UK], 2001).

1. *Quest of the DNA Cowboys, The* (Mayflower [UK], 1976) Introduces Jeb Stuart Ho and a psychedelic universe of preteen dictators, growing biocomputers, weird weapons, and public executions. Not published separately in the United States.
2. *Synaptic Manhunt* (Mayflower [UK], 1976) Jeb Stuart Ho comes out of meditation and goes to the pleasure city of Litz to find and kill a woman whom the Brotherhood's computers claim will destroy the human race. Not published separately in the United States.
3. *Neural Atrocity, The* (Mayflower [UK], 1977) Conclusion to the original trilogy in which things are wrapped-up (sort of) for the time being. Not published separately in the United States.
4. *Last Stand of the DNA Cowboys* (Ballantine, 1989) The DNA Cowboys ride again! This time they are on a collision course with barbarian hordes intent on destroying "civilization as they know it."

II. When publishers suggested that Farren should produce something more "conventional" than his usual output, he responded with *The Song of Phaid the Gambler*, a sort of "*Maverick* in the distant future," in which a gambler named Phaid goes through a series of adventures in future time. The original *Phaid* was published by New English Library (UK) in 1981. In 1986–1987 *Phaid* was split into two parts and slightly revised for US publication by Ace Books.

1. *Phaid the Gambler* (Ace, 1986) Phaid the Gambler lives by his wits on a future Earth in which the "grass is greener on the Other Side," but the Other Side is polluted by insecticide, the future doesn't work, and paranoids are the only people who understand what's really going on. Part 1 of *The Song of Phaid the Gambler*.
2. *Citizen Phaid* (Ace, 1987) A gambler named Phaid hustles his way in a future Earth; a convict named Phaid busts out of jail; a rebel named Phaid is hailed as a hero of future legend. Part 2 of *The Song of Phaid the Gambler*.

III. In the Renquist Quartet, Farren proves that he is as adept at writing vampire yarns as he is at writing psychedelic SF. Protagonist Nosferatu Victor Renquist (any resemblance to our late Chief Justice Rehnquist is presumably coincidental) is cultured and humane, though a vampire. The leader of a small colony of vampires in New York City, Renquist goes from one horrific adventure to another as he tries to cope with neo-Nazis, aliens, Scottish vampires led by Merlin, and a monster named Cthulhu.

1. *Time of Feasting, The* (Tor, 1996) For centuries vampire Victor Renquist has instructed his clan in the art of living inconspicuously among humans. But now, in the brood's Lower East Side enclave known as the Residence, Renquist's authority is being challenged by a younger generation of vampires.
2. *Darklost* (Tor, 2000) Renquist decides to move the remaining members of his colony to Los Angeles and tries to overcome the lethargy that has engulfed him since the annihilation of his consort, Cynara. But first he has to deal with a religious cult that is raising the monstrous entity know as Cthulhu.
3. *More Than Mortal* (Tor, 2001) Summoned to England, Renquist inadvertently raises the sleeping Merlin, who is taken up by a group of Scottish vampires and demonstrates a ruthless agenda.
4. *Underland* (Tor, 2002) In the explosive conclusion to the series, Renquist the Vampire is persuaded by National Security to take on a group of Nazis and their alien allies, the reptilian Dhraku.

IV. Farren's latest series is fantasy set on a vastly altered Earth in which the Mosul Empire launches an attack on the rest of the world. Opposing the empire is a motley group of teenagers called the Four: backwoodsman Argo Weaver, aristocrat with special talents Cordelia Blakeney, champion of the underdog Raphael Vega, and former concubine Jessamine. Dark magic, orgiastic sex, and sadomasochistic romps spice this alternate world fantasy, which will intrigue and confuse readers.

1. *Kindling* (Tor, 2004) In an alternative Earth, the Mosul Empire launches an attack on the rest of the world. Standing against them is a group of teenagers that calls itself the Four.
2. *Conflagration* (Tor, 2006) The Four is still struggling to save the free world from the Mosul Empire and its evil enchantress, in alliance with Jack Kennedy, the prime minister of the Kingdom of Albany.

Fast, Howard

The dominant figures in this popular sextet are Dan Lavette, the hardworking patriarch of the Lavette family and corporate enterprises; his rich and beautiful but cold wife, Jean; their troubled daughter Barbara; and the Lavette sons, Tom and Joe. The alluring May Ling and Dan's business partner, Mark Levy, are among the host of characters bustling through the colorful story, which stretches from the San Francisco earthquake to the 1990s.

The late Howard Fast (d. 2003) had a 70-year writing career (first publication in 1933), during which he wrote many best sellers, including historical novels such as *Citizen Tom Paine* (Duell, 1943), *Spartacus* (self-published, 1951) and *Moses, Prince of Egypt* (Crown, 1958). A longtime Man of the Left and member of the Communist Party, with whom he broke in 1956, Fast was blacklisted by Hollywood and spent three months in a federal prison.

1. *Immigrants, The* (Houghton Mifflin, 1977) Determined son of French-Italian immigrants, Dan Lavette builds an empire of department stores, commercial airlines, and steamships, but he is torn between two beautiful women.
2. *Second Generation, The* (Houghton Mifflin, 1978) In 1934–1936, young Barbara takes up the cause of striking dockworkers as she matures personally and professionally.
3. *Establishment, The* (Houghton Mifflin, 1979) Barbara, now a successful writer, gets caught in Senator Joe McCarthy's web as Tom moves ruthlessly toward ever greater success and his brother Joe's dedication to medicine turns his marriage sour.
4. *Legacy, The* (Houghton Mifflin, 1981) After Dan Lavette's death, daughter Barbara takes center stage as the story continues during the fifties and sixties, through marriage, divorce, and activity in the women's and antiwar movements.
5. *Immigrant's Daughter, The* (Houghton Mifflin, 1985) Barbara Lavette campaigns for Congress and continues her antiwar activities.
6. *Independent Woman, An* (Harcourt, 1997) Barbara, still glamorous in her seventies, continues her support of liberal causes, finds love with a Unitarian minister, and becomes a hero in Israel.

Faulkner, William

Most of Nobel Prize–winning author Faulkner's fiction is set in the fictional county of Yoknapatawpha in his native Mississippi. The Compson, Sartoris, Benbow, McCaslin, Snopes, Stevens, and other families, white, black, and mixed, interact in their unique world, which mirrors the American South during the 19th and the first half of the 20th centuries. Faulkner provided, at various times, chronologies, genealogies, and maps for Yoknapatawpha County, and a large scholarly industry dedicated to explicating Faulkner and his works has evolved: two recent reference sources are *William Faulkner A to Z* (Facts on File, 2002) and *A William Faulkner Encyclopedia* (Greenwood, 1999). The Snopes trilogy (*The Hamlet, The Town,* and *The Mansion*) and the Temple Drake duo (*Sanctuary* and *Requiem for a Nun* are "sequels" in the narrow sense of the term, but many characters wander in and out of the Yoknapatawpha world. Sometimes one family such as Sartoris or Compson will be the focus of a story and then reemerge as a supporting or bit player in other stories. Faulkner is not an easy writer, but the rewards for the serious reader are great: passion, humor, and an involvement with a fascinating fictional world.

Faulkner also wrote other novels, poetry, drama, and screenplays (some uncredited). Novels not generally included in Yoknapatawpha include *Soldier's Pay* (Boni & Liveright, 1926); *Mosquitoes* (Boni & Liveright, 1927); *Pylon* (Smith & Haas, 1935); and *A Fable* (Random House, 1954). *The Portable Faulkner* (edited by Malcolm Cowley; Viking, 1946), revived Faulkner's reputation when it was at a low ebb. The novels have been republished in the Library of America series in five volumes (1985–2006). William Faulkner has been the subject of hundreds (thousands?) of books and critical articles including Richard J. Gray's *The Life of William Faulkner: A Critical Biography* (Blackwell, 1994) and *The Cambridge Companion to William Faulkner* (Cambridge, 1995), edited by Philip M. Weinstein.

1. *Sartoris* (Harcourt, 1929) Bayard Sartoris returns home to Jefferson, Mississippi, from combat as an aviator in World War I. The Sartoris family history is related. The Snopes family makes its first appearance in the person of Byron Snopes, bank bookkeeper crazed with lust. Republished in 1973 as *Flags in the Dust* with Faulkner's original full text. Bayard's grandfather, "Old Bayard," is the narrator of number 7.
2. *Sound and the Fury, The* (Cape & Smith, 1929) The Compson family holds center stage in this novel seen through the eyes of three Compson brothers: Benjy the idiot, the cold and self-righteous Jason, and the sensitive Quentin. Three of the four sections cover three consecutive April days in 1928. The section dealing with Quentin is set in June 2, 1910, at Harvard University, the day of his suicide. Caddy Compson, sister of the three brothers, plays a central role. Quentin Compson resurfaces as the principal narrator of number 6. Regarded by many critics as Faulkner's masterpiece.
3. *As I Lay Dying* (Cape & Smith, 1930) The dying Addie Bundren makes her husband, Anse, promise to have her buried with her own people in Jefferson (county seat of Yoknapatawpha, based on Oxford, home of the University of Mississippi). Anse and the Bundren sons set out on a journey that proves to be disastrous for most of them. First mention of "Yoknapatawpha."
4. *Sanctuary* (Cape & Smith, 1931) The story of Temple Drake, who goes to a party with a drunken escort, falls in the hands of a gang of bootleggers, and is raped by the degenerate Popeye. Faulkner sometimes claimed to have written this book just for the money. Republished in 1983 with Faulkner's original text restored. Number 14 is the sequel.
5. *Light in August* (Smith & Haas, 1931) The story of the orphan "Joe Christmas," who is possibly of mixed blood, lives alternately with whites and blacks, despising both races, gets involved with people surnamed Burden, Burch, and Bunch, and comes to a sticky end.
6. *Absalom, Absalom!* (Random House, 1936) The story of Thomas Sutpen, 19th-century founder of Sutpen's Hundred, as related by Quentin Compson (see number 2), grandson of Sutpen's benefactor, General Compson, to his Harvard roommate.

7. *Unvanquished, The* (**Random House, 1938**) Young Bayard Sartoris (grandfather of the Bayard Sartoris in number 1) relates the Civil War exploits of his father and other family members. The first six chapters were originally published as short stories.

8. *Wild Palms, The* (**Random House, 1939**) About the effects of the great Mississippi flood of 1927 on a hillbilly convict and a New Orleans doctor and his mistress. Only tangentially connected with Yoknapatawpha County. Republished by Library of America with Faulkner's original title *If I Forget Thee, Jerusalem* (1990). Variant title: *The Wild Palms and the Old Man.*

9. *Hamlet, The* (**Random House, 1940**) First volume in the Snopes trilogy. The rise of the Snopes family begins when Flem Snopes comes to the hamlet of Frenchman's Bend in 1900, and with his relatives and progeny (who have names like Mink, Eck, and Lump) starts infecting Yoknapatawpha like a virus. The Snopes family goes back quite a way in Faulkner's thinking. An unpublished draft called "Father Abraham" dates from 1926; a Snopes (Byron) turns up in *The Sound and the Fury* (1929); another unpublished draft "The Peasants," was started in 1933.

10. *Go Down Moses, and Other Stories* (**Random House, 1942**) Faulkner thought that this collection of stories really functioned as a novel (*and Other Stories* was Random House's idea). Members of the McCaslin family are the central characters here. Contains "The Bear," a classic hunting story that has often been reprinted separately.

11. *Intruder in the Dust* (**Random House, 1948**) Elderly Lucas Beauchamp, a black descendent of the McCaslins, is wrongfully accused of murder. Gavin Stevens who makes several appearances in the series, including a starring role in number 12 defends Lucas.

12. *Knight's Gambit* (**Random House, 1949**) A collection of closely related mystery short stories. County attorney Gavin Stevens is responsible for sorting them out.

13. *Collected Stories of William Faulkner* (**Random House, 1950**) Short stories, many of them Yoknapatawpha related. Other collections include *These 13* (Cape & Smith, 1931), *Doctor Martino and Other Stories* (Smith & Haas, 1934), and *Big Woods* (Random House, 1955).

14. *Requiem for a Nun* (**Random House, 1948**) Sequel to number 4. "The tortured redemption of Temple Drake." A three-act play with long prose introductions. It was adapted for the stage by Ruth Ford and had a short Broadway run.

15. *Town, The* (**Random House, 1957**) Flem Snopes and his family move to Jefferson, where he becomes a restaurant owner and vice president of Colonel Sartoris's bank. Sequel to number 9, followed by number 16.

16. *Mansion, The* (**Random House, 1959**) Flem is now a "respectable" citizen. Mink, his cousin, is determined to kill him for failing to come to his aid at a murder trial. Sequel to number 15.

17. *Reivers, The* (**Random House, 1962**) In this comic tale, Lucas Priest recalls to his grandson his misadventures as an 11-year-old in 1905 when, with companions Boon Hogganbeck and Ned William McCaslin, he "reived" (stole) his grandfather's automobile.

Fawcett, Quinn

PSEUDONYM OF Bill Fawcett & Chelsea Quinn Yarbro

I. Bill Fawcett and Chelsea Quinn Yarbro (q.v.) received the permission of Dame Jean Conan Doyle to revive Sherlock Holmes's older, smarter brother, Mycroft. Mycroft, who appeared in only four Conan Doyle (q.v.) stories, already has four novels featuring him in this series, more international intrigue than mystery stories, written under the pseudonym of "Quinn Fawcett." Mycroft's "Watson" is his secretary, Patterson Guthrie. Other prominent characters are the actor Edmund Sutton, who can do a perfect impersonation of Mycroft, and the enigmatic Penelope Gatspy. Mycroft, who rarely seems to venture from his home in Pall Mall or from the Diogenes Club, still manages to direct British foreign policy behind the scenes and conduct investigations against enemies of Britain, particularly the mysterious anarchist Brotherhood, which is bent upon toppling governments and destroying peace in Europe. Coauthor Bill Fawcett is also author of several novels under his own name, including the Swordquest quartet (Ace, 1985–1987). Chelsea Quinn Yarbro (q.v.) is the author of several series, including the Saint Germain novels.

1. *Against the Brotherhood* (**Forge, 1997**) Mycroft Holmes, who holds a "secret" position in the British government, is trying to protect the Freising Treaty against the Brotherhood, a secret society bent on destroying peace in Europe.

2. *Embassy Row* (**Forge, 1998**) Mycroft Holmes, on a secret mission for the British government, is negotiating a treaty with Japan in meetings held in the Swiss Embassy. But then a British diplomat known to oppose the treaty is assassinated with a Japanese seppuku.

3. *Flying Scotsman, The* (**Forge, 1999**) Mycroft and his secretary Patterson Guthrie are trying to smuggle the Swedish king out of the country aboard the *Flying Scotsman*, the famous fast train.

4. *Scottish Ploy, The* (**Forge, 2001**) The Brotherhood is still trying to topple the British government. The actor Edmund Sutton, Mycroft's double, has disappeared, and Mycroft has to replace him in *Macbeth*, while Guthrie and Penelope Gatspy try to find Sutton and thwart the Brotherhood.

II. We know that Ian Fleming (q.v.), creator of James Bond, served in the British intelligence community before he created his famous fictional spy. But what if Fleming never really retired from spying? What if his position as a journalist was really a cover for further espionage? Quinn Fawcett has created a fictional Ian Fleming for a trio of novels, in which he matches James Bond in espionage, derring-do, and romance.

1. *Death to Spies* (**Forge, 2002**) Ian Fleming's retirement to Jamaica is disrupted when a ranking member of British intelligence shows up with a wild story of purloined nuclear secrets and moles, then disappears.

2. *Siren Song* (**Forge, 2003**) Fleming falls for the glamorous journalist Nora at a New Year's Eve party in London, turns down a mission involving an American businessman who is secretly a Communist, and returns to Jamaica. Then Nora turns up in Jamaica working on the case Fleming turned down.

3. *Honor among Spies* (**Forge, 2004**) Fleming joins Prescott, a former intelligence colleague, in investigating the murder of a bride in New Orleans that may connected with state secrets.

Feather, Jane

I. "Three unconventional young women vow they will never marry— only to be overtaken by destiny": that's the premise of Jane Feather's Bride trilogy. Portia, Penelope, and Olivia, after adventures with outlaws, pirates, and arranged marriages, all tread the bridal path in this trio of historical romances set in the time of the English Civil War (1640s). Jane Feather, which may be a pseudonym, is a prolific author of historical romances set in various periods.

1. *Hostage Bride, The* (**Bantam, 1998**) Outlaw Rufus Decatur mistakenly kidnaps Portia Worth from her uncle, the Marquis of

Granville, only to find that he has bitten off more than he can chew.

2. *Accidental Bride, The* (Bantam, 1999) After being indifferent to him, the awkward Phoebe falls hopelessly in love with Cato, the Marquis of Granville, husband of her late sister.

3. *Least Likely Bride, The* (Bantam, 2000) Scholarly Olivia Granville, last of the three friends who took the "no marriage" vow, falls in with a Royalist pirate intent upon rescuing King Charles.

II. The Kiss trilogy, set in the time of Henry VIII and Mary I, concerns Guinevere Mallory and her twin daughters, who, in their various ways, get involved with royal intrigue and incredibly handsome lovers.

1. *Widow's Kiss, The* (Bantam, 2001) Twenty-eight-year-old beauty Lady Guinevere Mallory has aroused Henry VIII's suspicions by surviving four wealthy husbands. King Henry sends Hugh of Beaucaire to investigate, but Hugh is charmed by Lady Guinevere and her twin daughters.

2. *To Kiss a Spy* (Bantam, 2002) Lady-in-waiting Pen, one of Guinevere Mallory's twin daughters, makes a deal with handsome spymaster Owen D'Arcy: her secrets from the court in exchange for his investigation into the fate of her newborn infant.

3. *Kissed by Shadows* (Bantam, 2003) Can handsome and enigmatic Lionel Ashton save Pippa, Guinevere's other twin daughter, from a plot to ensure that Queen Mary bears a child sired by her husband, the Spanish king Phillip?

III. The Duncan Sisters series, or Matchmaker's Trilogy, set in London at the turn of the 20th century, features Constance, Prudence, and Chastity, the strong-minded Duncan sisters, who mix their efforts for woman's suffrage with sizzling romance. Numbers 1 and 2 were also published together in one volume: *The Bachelor List and Bride Hunt* (Bantam, 2004).

1. *Bachelor List, The* (Bantam, 2004) Constance, eldest of the Duncan sisters, and handsome Parliament member Max Ensor, find themselves on opposite sides of the woman's suffrage issue but still manage to hit it off sexually.

2. *Bride Hunt* (Bantam, 2004) When the suffragist scandal sheet the *Mayfair Lady* is sued for libel, Prudence Duncan enlists the aid of barrister Sir Gideon Malvern.

3. *Wedding Game, The* (Bantam, 2004) Chastity, the remaining Duncan sister, in the course of the sisters' matchmaking business, meets Dr. Douglas Farrell, who is interested in "wiving it wealthily."

Feddersen, Connie

Amanda Hazard, CPA and amateur sleuth of Vamoose, Oklahoma, often gets into murder investigations while checking the tax forms of local Oklahomans. With policeman Nick Thorn, who eventually weds her, Amanda gets deep into the mayhem and skullduggery that always seem to afflict small-town America, at least in fictional mysteries. Oklahoman Connie Feddersen is also the author of contemporary and historical romances under the pseudonyms of Carol Finch, Gina Robins, and Debra Falcon.

1. *Dead in the Water* (Kensington, 1993) CPA Amanda Hazard knows murder when she sees it, when she finds farmer Bill Farley floating face down in his cattle trough, even if hunky police detective Nick Thorn doesn't.

2. *Dead in the Cellar* (Kensington, 1994) Nick Thorn's ex-girlfriend has blown into Vamoose, followed by a tornado. Amanda, busying herself with Elmer Jolly's tax forms, finds her client dead in his storm cellar.

3. *Dead in the Melon Patch* (Kensington, 1995) The mysterious death of a sexy divorcée could have been the work of any of three ex-husbands, or possibly a former lover. Whoever the killer is, he is after Amanda now.

4. *Dead in the Dirt* (Kensington, 1996) It turns out that the apparently near-destitute Wilbur Bloom was one of the richest men in Vamoose, and his death was not by a freak accident.

5. *Dead in the Mud* (Kensington, 1997) The county commissioner's suspicious death in the mud beside his pickup truck leads Amanda and Nick into all kinds of corruption and political skulduggery.

6. *Dead in the Driver's Seat* (Kensington, 1998) Amanda goes to Vamoose's only car dealership and buys the proprietor's own truck. Then someone joyrides in the truck and gets himself killed.

7. *Dead in the Hay* (Kensington, 1999) Amanda, just settling into married life, gets a call from Harvey, her richest and least favorite client. When she goes to his ranch, she finds Harvey dead under a ton of hay.

8. *Dead in the Pumpkin Patch* (Kensington, 2000) At Halloween a very pregnant Amanda Hazard stumbles upon the corpse of local gossip and pumpkin-farm owner Nettie Jarvis.

Feehan, Christine

I. The Carpathians are a quasi-immortal, shape-shifting, blood-drinking, and mind-reading clan. They are vampirelike, but they kill only vampires and evil people. The Carpathians need love in the worst way: unless a Carpathian finds his destined life-mate, he becomes a *real* vampire. At the center of this Dark series is the search for love, which expresses itself in wild, passionate physical demonstrations. Since there is a shortage of female Carpathians, this means that human females are the beneficiaries of male Carpathian neediness. California martial-arts instructor Christine Feehan's gothic romances have been quite popular, and have recently graduated to hardcover format (number 13). Feehan has published three Dark short stories that have appeared in anthologies: "Dark Dream" (in *After Twilight*, Love Spell, 2001; reissued in *Dark Dreamers*, Leisure, 2006); "Dark Descent" (in *The Only One*, Leisure, 2003); and "Dark Hunger" (in *Hotblooded*, Jove, 2004).

1. *Dark Prince* (Love Spell, 1999) In the Carpathian mountains, a mysterious stranger appears in the life of an unsuspecting American psychic.

2. *Dark Desire* (Love Spell, 1999) American surgeon Shea O'Halloran is drawn to a dark, mysterious man who seems to need her passionately.

3. *Dark Gold* (Love Spell, 2000) Looking for her orphaned little brother in San Francisco, Alexandria Houton is rescued from an unspeakable evil by the mysterious, ageless, needy Carpathian Ardan Savage.

4. *Dark Magic* (Love Spell, 2000) World-famous magician Savannah is held in thrall by the dark and charismatic Carpathian Gregori.

5. *Dark Challenge* (Love Spell, 2000) Brooding and reclusive hunter Julian Savage finds his life transformed by the beautiful singer Desari.

6. *Dark Fire* (Love Spell, 2001) Tempest has always been different from other people. Then she meets Darius, leader of a traveling troupe.

7. *Dark Legend* (Leisure, 2002) Centuries ago, the twins Gabriel and Lucian were locked deep within the earth. Now free again, Gabriel finds Francesca.

8. *Dark Guardian* (Jove, 2003) After centuries of soulless existence as the dark guardian of his people, Lucian finds policewoman Jaxon Montgomery.

9. *Dark Symphony* (Jove, 2003) Ageless vampire-hunter Byron and Antoinetta come together. But, this time, who is the hunter and who is the hunted?

10. *Dark Melody* (Leisure, 2003) Dayan, lead guitarist of the Dark Troubadors, and Corinne Wentworth, on the run from fanatics who killed her husband, are fated to come together.

11. *Dark Destiny* (Leisure, 2004) The female Carpathian Destiny and Nicolae von Shrieder have merged their minds, although they are separated physically.

12. *Dark Secret* (Jove, 2005) The wealthy Brazilian Chevez family enlists the aid of the Carpathian De La Cruz brothers to reclaim the children of a brother who had been disowned years before.

13. *Dark Celebration* (Berkley, 2006) Shea O'Halloran (see number 2) is studying the causes of the low birthrate and high infant mortality of the Carpathians, while carrying the child of her "life-mate" Jacques.

14. *Dark Demon* (Jove, 2006) For as long as she can remember, Natalya has slain those who murder by night. Now she is seduced by one of the very beings she is supposed to be fighting.

15. *Dark Possession* (Berkley, 2007) Manuel "Manolito" De La Cruz has found his life-mate in Mary Ann Delaney, a Seattle counselor for battered women who flies to his Brazilian family compound to help a pregnant rape victim.

II. The GhostWalkers are a Special Forces paranormal squad who were genetically enhanced by the late Peter Whitney to give them psychic abilities enabling them to be secret and lethal military weapons. Of course, the "walking weapons" have mixed feelings about what they have become.

1. *Shadow Game* (Jove, 2003) Lily, daughter of the late Dr. Peter Whitney, creator of the genetically enhanced GhostWalkers, trying to right the wrongs of her father, becomes involved with GhostWalker Ryland Miller.

2. *Mind Game* (Jove, 2004) Dahlia LeBlanc's gifts are also a curse, making it impossible to hurt those around her. Can she trust her secrets to Nicolas Trevose, a "shadow warrior" sent to find her?

3. *Night Game* (Jove, 2005) GhostWalker Raoul "Gator" Fontenot is looking for Iris "Flame" Johnson, who is also a genetically enhanced "beneficiary" of the late Dr. Whitney.

4. *Conspiracy Game* (Jove, 2006) GhostWalker Jack Norton is on a mission to rescue his brother, who is somewhere in the Congo.

III. Another series by the prolific Feehan is about the seven Drake sisters, who have paranormal powers. So far, five of the sisters have been featured, one to a novel. The first novel in the series was originally published as the short story "Magic in the Wind" in the anthology *Lover Beware* (Berkley, 2003).

1. *Magic in the Wind* (Berkley, 2005) Sarah, the oldest of the paranormal Drake sisters, comes home to Sea Haven, California, where she becomes entangled with Damon Wilder, who is being tracked by a killer.

2. *Twilight before Christmas, The* (Pocket, 2003) Kate Drake comes to the fore, as the sisters sense strange, menacing shadows at Sea Haven.

3. *Oceans of Fire* (Jove, 2005) Abigail Drake, who can communicate with dolphins, becomes involved with sexy agent Aleksandr Volstev after witnessing a murder while swimming with her mammalian friends.

4. *Dangerous Tides* (Jove, 2006) Until fate throws them together, Libby Drake never thought that she was the kind of woman who could attract the attention of brilliant, handsome biochemist Tyson Derrick.

5. *Safe Harbor* (Jove, 2007) Hannah, one of the Drake sisters, is attacked by a madman with a knife on live TV.

Feintuch, David

I. The Nicholas Seafort saga, a sort of Horatio Hornblower (C. S. Forester, [q.v.]) in space, traces the career of denizen of the future Seafort from midshipman to UN secretary general. The proud, stern, duty-bound Seafort is a natural leader of men and is usually the only person standing against alien invasion, ecological chaos, and civil war. Two omnibus volumes were published: *Seafort's Hope* (Doubleday, 1995; numbers 1–2) and *Seafort's Challenge* (Doubleday, 1996; numbers 3–4).

1. *Midshipman's Hope* (Warner, 1994) When the senior officers on the *Hibernia* are killed by a freak accident, it is up to young Midshipman Nicholas Seafort to save the colonists and crew aboard the damaged space vessel.

2. *Challenger's Hope* (Warner, 1995) Seafort's first command, aboard the space ship *Portia*, proves to be a difficult one. Wounded, he has to protect a shipload of colonists and violent street-children against alien predators and each other.

3. *Prisoner's Hope* (Warner, 1995) Assigned as a liaison to the wealthy planters of the Earth colony, Hope Nation, Seafort faces alien invaders and civil disturbances.

4. *Fisherman's Hope* (Warner, 1996) Appointed head of the Space Academy at Devon and at Farside of the Moon, Nicholas reminisces about his old days as a student, and faces more alien invaders.

5. *Voices of Hope* (Warner, 1996) Philip Seafort, Nicholas's son, follows his friend Jared to the streets of New York, as class war looms between the have-not street people of the Trannies and the wealthy haves, the Uppies.

6. *Patriarch's Hope* (Warner, 1999) Seafort, secretary general of the United Nations and the most powerful man on Earth, faces the ecological consequences of his decision to concentrate on heavily armed spaceships in his wars against the aliens.

7. *Children of Hope* (Ace, 2001) Nicholas is retired but still facing the vengeance of a 14-year-old boy who blames him for the death of his father.

II. The late (d. 2006) David Feintuch also wrote a pair of coming-of-age fantasy novels about Rodrigo, a spoiled and indolent prince who has to grow up and learn to manage the magical Still before he can become an effective ruler.

1. *Still, The* (Warner, 1997) When his mother dies, spoiled, indolent prince Rodrigo finds that his accession to the throne of Caldeon is blocked by a parcel of intriguers.

2. *King, The* (Ace, 2002) Having mastered the magic of the Still and regained his throne, King Rodrigo faces a fragile peace, a divided army, and powerful invaders.

Feist, Raymond E(lias)

I. Feist's Riftwar Saga is a rousing fantasy series with strong elements of romance and humor. Good guys Prince Arutha, Jimmy the Hand, and Pug the Magician battle the dark powers in the medieval world of Midkemia. *The Wood Boy*, published together with *The Burning Earth*, by Tad Williams (q.v.) (Dabel Brothers, 2005), was originally published as the story "The Riftwar Saga" in Robert Silverberg's anthology, *Legends* (Tor, 1998). Series II–VII, described below, are connected with the Riftwar Saga. *Faerie Tale* (Doubleday, 1988) is the only Feist novel not connected with Riftwar. *The Atlas of Midkemia* (coauthored by Steven A. Abrams; Voyager [UK], 2000) and *Return to Krondor: Prima's Official Strategy Guide* (Prima Games, 1987) are nonfiction works describing some of the various Riftwar series.

1. *Magician* **(Doubleday, 1982)** The boyish magician Pug seems fated to rescue the peaceable kingdom of Krondor from aggressive bordering empires. Revised edition published in two parts: *Magician: Apprentice* and *Magician: Master* (Doubleday, 1992).
2. *Silverthorn* **(Doubleday, 1985)** Reformed criminal Jimmy the Hand and Prince Arutha go on a quest for the Silverthorn plant, which will awaken the prince's betrothed from an enchanted sleep.
3. *Darkness at Sethanon, A* **(Doubleday, 1986)** Centers on the cosmic battles of Prince Arutha against the evil Murmandamus for control of the Lifestone.
4. *Prince of the Blood* **(Doubleday, 1989)** Prince Arutha, who has ruled for 20 years, sends his twins, Borric and Erland, to the birthday jubilee of the Empress of Kesh.
5. *King's Buccaneer, The* **(Doubleday, 1993)** Nicholas, Arutha's gentle, lame son, is sent to his uncle Martin's court in Crydee for seasoning.

II. The Serpentwar Saga takes place in the same universe as the Riftwar Saga a generation later, and includes some of the same characters, such as Pug the Magician. The good guys are both bastards (by birth): Erik von Darkmoor, son of the local baron of Krondor, and Rupert "Roo" Avery, son of a commoner. The bad guys are the reptilian Pantathians and the Demon King, among others.

1. *Shadow of a Dark Queen* **(Morrow, 1994)** Condemned to death for an accidental killing, Erik and Roo are temporarily spared for a desperate mission against the Pantathians.
2. *Rise of a Merchant Prince* **(Morrow, 1995)** Roo is on his way to the top of the mercantile class in Krondor, and Erik is on his way to Novindus to fight the Pantathians again.
3. *Rage of a Demon King* **(Avon, 1997)** Pug the Magician and his allies are fighting the Demon King on his own ground. Erik von Darkmoor marries. Roo Avery has woman and money troubles.
4. *Shards of a Broken Crown* **(Avon, 1998)** Billed as the concluding volume of the Serpentwar Saga. Erik von Dartmoor is a supporting player in meeting the Keshite invasion.

III. Another series, the Riftwar Legacy, based on Feist's Betrayal of Kondor computer game, takes place in the Riftworld universe, chronologically between the Riftwar Saga and the Serpentwar Saga. Jimmy the Hand (now Squire James) and Prince Arutha come to the fore again. New heroes include Squire Locklear and Groath, a renegade Dark Elf. Among the villains are the Nighthawks and the Crawler.

1. *Betrayal: Krondor, The* **(Avon, 1998)** Squire Locklear, exiled to the Northlands, captures Groath, a renegade Dark Elf, who warns him that the Dark Elves are rallying around the dream-name Murmandamus and are plotting an uprising against the humans.
2. *Assassins: Krondor, The* **(Avon, 1999)** Prince Arutha and Squire James return from the Moredhel war to find an orgy of murder with the Thieves' Guild as the target. Squire James reverts to his old identity as Jimmy the Hand to foil a plot against Arutha and track down the Nighthawks in their lair.
3. *Tear of the Gods: Krondor* **(Eos, 2001)** Pirates attack the ship *Ishap's Dawn* to steal the magical gem, Tear of the Gods. A series of mishaps seems to be linked to Bear, a crazed former pirate. Meanwhile the Crawler is busy again spreading unrest and fear.

IV. Conclave of Shadows focuses on Roldem and the Eastern Kingdoms, which barely figure in earlier Medkemia and Riftworld books. Tal Hawkins, Talon of the Silver Hawk, is a fairly conventional sword-and-sorcery hero, but his supporting cast and the relentless pace of the action make this series appealing to readers.

1. *Talon of the Silver Hawk* **(Eos, 2003)** Talon of the Silver Hawk, adopted and trained by the Conclave of Shadows, becomes an expert sword fighter.
2. *King of Foxes* **(Eos, 2003)** Talon sets his sights on Kaspar, Duke of Olasko, who ordered the massacre of his people.
3. *Exile's Return* **(Eos, 2005)** Kaspar, deposed Duke of Olasko, banished to the far continent of Novidus, vows to return.

V. Feist and Janny Wurts (q.v.) coauthored a trilogy set in the Midkemian universe. Lady Mara of the Acoma, consummate player of the game of intrigue that maintains the stability of the Tsurani Empire, is the protagonist.

1. *Daughter of the Empire* **(Doubleday, 1987)** When her father and brother are killed, Mara must shelve her plans for entering a religious order and become ruling Lady of Acoma.
2. *Servant of the Empire* **(Doubleday, 1990)** Lady Mara balances her love for an "off-worlder" slave against the blood feud between House Acoma and House Minwanabi.
3. *Mistress of the Empire* **(Doubleday, 1992)** The assassination of her son and heir pits Lady Mara against the House Anasati.

VI. Legends of the Riftwar is a shared-world trio, each novel cowritten with a different author, that bring together characters from Riftwa and other series.

1. *Honored Enemy* **(Eos, 2007)** Hartraft's Marauders and a Tsurani patrol arrive at a frontier garrison. Instead of fighting each other, they must combine against a horde of Moredhel (dark elves). Coauthored with William R. Forstchen (q.v.). Originally published as *Honoured Enemy* in the United Kingdom in 2001.
2. *Murder in Lamut* **(Eos, 2007)** Cowritten with Joel Rosenberg (q.v.). Characters from Rosenberg's *Guardian of the Flames* are assigned to garrison duty protecting a lady and her husband and escorting them to the city of Lamut. Originally published in the United Kingdom in 2002.
3. *Jimmy the Hand* **(Eos, 2008)** Jimmy the Hand, a character who dates back to *Silverthorn* (series I, number 2), is brought back and rusticated to the northern haven of Serth. Cowritten with S. M. Stirling. Originally published in the United Kingdom in 2003.

VII. Darkwars, a new Riftworld series, revisits Great Kesh and the Conclave of Shadows, who face the problems of the final destruction of Leso Varen and the neutralization of the thousands of alien Talnoy discovered by Nakor in Novindus. Characters such as Pug the Magician are revived for this series.

1. *Flight of the Nighthawks* (Eos, 2006) Magnus, acting as a go-between the Conclave of Shadows and the Great Ones, is alarmed to learn that a rift magnet may open up a doorway for the dreaded Dasati to invade Kelewan.

2. *Into a Dark Realm* (Eos, 2006) Pug and the Conclave of Shadows are determined to find the mad magician Leso Varen, who is wreaking havoc on Kelewan.

3. *Wrath of a Mad God* (Eos, 2008) In the conclusion to Darkwars, Darkwar is raging upon Midkemia and Kelewan.

Fender, J(ames) E.

Geoffrey Frost is a Revolutionary War–era American privateer. Frost's adventures, on and under the seas and on land, are related by Ming Tsun, Frost's mute Chinese friend, who kept journals that have been "translated" from the Mandarin Chinese by author Fender, as the conceit would have it. So far 5 volumes of a planned 9 or 10 have been published. This is naval action reminiscent of C. S. Forester's (q.v.) Hornblower or Patrick O'Brian's (q.v.) Aubrey-Maturin series. J. E. Fender is legal counsel for the Portsmouth Shipyard in Portsmouth, New Hampshire.

1. *Private Revolution of Geoffrey Frost, The* (University Press of New England, 2002) Geoffrey Frost, of Portsmouth in New Hampshire Colony, embarks upon a career as a licensed privateer for the American cause after capturing a British sloop. Subtitle: *Being an Account of the Life and Times of Geoffrey Frost, Mariner, of Portsmouth, in New Hampshire, as Faithfully Translated from the Ming Tsun Chronicles, and Diligently Compared with Other Contemporary Histories.*

2. *Audacity, Privateer out of Portsmouth* (University Press of New England, 2003) After a daring rescue of American prisoners held at Louisberg, Frost and his ship *Audacity* sail into a fog bank and straight into a British convoy.

3. *Our Lives, Our Fortunes* (University Press of New England, 2004) After attacking a British collier fleet in the mouth of the Tyne River, Frost returns to Portsmouth in November 1776, and embarks upon the mission of carrying food and gunpowder to General Washington.

4. *On the Spur of Speed* (University Press of New England, 2005) In alternating chapters we hear about the adventures of Frost's brother Joseph with Benedict Arnold in New York and Vermont in the Saratoga campaign and about Frost's first voyage, at the age of 10 on a slave ship.

5. *Lucifer Cypher, The* (Broadsides, 2006) With his ship, *Audacity*, laid up for repairs, Geoffrey Frost gets wind of a new secret weapon invented by David Bushnell, and takes on the command of the prototype submarine, *Narwhal*.

Fenn, Lionel

PSEUDONYM OF Charles L. Grant

I. Kent Montana, unemployed actor and Scottish Laird, is the putative "hero" of five wild and woolly SF parodies. The rather eccentric Kent has to deal with nasty aliens, mad scientists, swamp monsters, vampires, demons, and some very churned up humans in these amusing takeoffs. "Lionel Fenn" is just one of the pseudonyms used by Charles L. Grant (q.v.), who is best known for horror stories under his real name.

1. *Kent Montana and the Really Ugly Thing from Mars* (Ace, 1990) IT came from Mars and crashed near Gander Pond, New Jersey. IT is big, ugly, and has a heat ray and a nasty disposition. Only unemployed actor and Scottish Laird Kent Montana can save New Jersey and the Earth from IT in this pastiche of alien invasion movies.

2. *Kent Montana and the Reasonably Invisible Man* (Ace, 1991) In this pastiche of the mad-scientist B-movie genre, Kent is assailed by a mad scientist–unemployed musician who has discovered a formula that makes him almost invisible and who is out to get Kent.

3. *Kent Montana and the Once and Future Thing* (Ace, 1991) Zergopha, an immortal but repellent creature, slithers through the swamp looking for love.

4. *Mark of the Moderately Vicious Vampire, The* (Ace, 1992) The beachfront community of Assyria, Maine is being assailed by people returning from the dead. Kent Montana, the eccentric visiting actor with aristocratic pretensions, is a likely candidate for the villagers' vampire suspicions.

5. *668: The Neighbor of the Beast* (Ace, 1992) In this take-off of H. P. Lovecraft, Kent Montana agrees to fulfill the terms of an inheritance left to him by spending the night in Langford Place in Hamtucket. Unbeknownst to Kent, the house is the meeting place of cultists who plan to sacrifice him to the extra-dimensional deity Bog-Muggoth.

II. Diego, an 1880s gunslinger, stumbles into "a strange vortex," which turns out to be the Time Thing, a rather wonky time machine, and finds himself undergoing a series of wacky adventures in the 20th, 22nd, and 26th centuries.

1. *Once upon a Time in the East* (Ace, 1993) 1880s gunfighter Diego takes an unanticipated ride to New York City in the 1980s on the Time Thing, a malfunctioning time machine from the future.

2. *By the Time I Get to Nashville* (Ace, 1994) This time Diego lands in 22nd-century Nashville, where the Old West is a religion, and gets worshipped as a sort of deity.

3. *Time: The Semi-final Frontier* (Ace, 1994) Diego finds himself on the starship *Argus* and on the way to outer space in the 26th century and finds himself up against something called the Space Avenger.

III. Quest for the White Duck, an earlier trilogy, lampoons sword-and-sorcery fantasy. Drunken ex-football player Gideon Sunday stumbles through the back of his pantry into the magical land of Chey and finds himself in the role of the mythic hero who is destined to destroy the Tide of Blood that threatens to destroy the land. But first . . . he has to locate an enchanted duck.

1. *Blood River Down* (Tor, 1986) Gideon Sunday stumbles through the back wall of his pantry and into a doorway to the world of Chey and gets adopted by its inhabitants as a mythic hero and their savior.

2. *Web of Defeat* (Tor, 1987) Gideon Sunday, still trying to get back home from Chey, encounters monsters, wizards, demons, dragons, a couple of really mean witches, and an amorous female giant.

3. *Agnes Day* (Tor, 1987) Gideon has to oppose the schemes of a wicked woman and an evil sorcerer who will do anything to control Chey.

Fennelly, Tony

I. Tony Fennelly has written two mystery trilogies set in New Orleans. The first trilogy is narrated by Matt Sinclair, former assistant district attorney, scion of an old New Orleans family, and gay owner of a French Quarter antique shop catering to "fags and their hags," who gets drawn into cases that allow Fennelly to present plenty of (pre-Katrina) New Orleans atmosphere.

1. *Glory Hole Murders, The* **(Carroll & Graf, 1985)** When a prominent suburban family man and possible rising political star is found mutilated and dead in the restroom of a New Orleans gay bar, Lieutenant Washington of the New Orleans Police Department persuades Matt Sinclair to probe the gay community in the French Quarter.
2. *Closet Hanging, The* **(Carroll & Graf, 1987)** Matt Sinclair becomes the prime suspect when a real-estate developer is found dead in a building owned by Matt's family, in what looks like a murder disguised as a suicide.
3. *Kiss Yourself Goodbye* **(Mystery Writers of America, 2003)** Matt sets out to clear his cousin Sylvia of murder and to track down the real killer. Originally published in the United Kingdom in 1989.

II. Margo Fortier, formerly a stripper, has risen to be a society reporter and the wife to socially prominent (and secretly gay) Julian Fortier. Margo, full of breezy chatter, and attracted to occult pursuits such as tarot and astrology and to rich, generous, hefty, bald guys, is a likable survivor in this trio of New Orleans–based mysteries by former "exotic dancer" and actress Fennelly.

1. *Hippie in the Wall, The* **(St. Martin's, 1994)** Homicide Lieutenant Frank Washington (see series I) engages society reporter Margo Fortier, formerly a stripper named Cherry, in the case of the body of a male hippie found, after 20 years, in the addition to what had been Madame Julie's strip joint.
2. *1 (900)-D-E-A-D* **(St. Martin's, 1996)** Mystic Delphine, a famous telephonic psychic, is skewered with the sword she uses in her TV commercials. Margo Fortier discovers some psychic talents of her own when she investigates.
3. *Don't Blame the Snake* **(Top, 2001)** An ex-thief, the featured speaker at a crime writers' conference on board a cruise ship in the Mississippi River, is found dead from snakebite.

Ferrars, E. X.

PSEUDONYM OF Morna Doris Brown

I. The late (d. 1995) Morna Doris Brown, who lived in Scotland, published more than 60 mystery and suspense novels under her real name and as Morna Doris MacTaggart and E. X. (or Elizabeth) Ferrars. Her mysteries usually revolve around the theme of domestic malice in the tangled relationships among a group of middle-class English villagers. Her longest-running series featured physiotherapist Virginia Freer and her estranged husband, Felix, a charming rogue whom she loves but can't live with.

1. *Last Will and Testament* **(Doubleday, 1978)** Evelyn Arliss, unbeknownst to her expectant heirs, has dissipated her estate indulging her passion for race-horses.
2. *In at the Kill* **(Doubleday, 1979)** Charlotte Chambrey arrives for a quiet vacation in the country only to find that the man she rented her cottage from has met a bad end.
3. *Frog in the Throat* **(Doubleday, 1980)** The artist colony in the village of Stillbeam becomes unduly agitated when two writers become engaged.
4. *Thinner Than Water* **(Doubleday, 1982)** Gavin Brownlow's wedding party isn't as festive as it should be, and the announcement of another marriage adds to the disquiet.
5. *Death of a Minor Character* **(Doubleday, 1983)** Virginia and Felix meet again at a party in London where one of the guests is a well-known silversmith.
6. *I Met Murder* **(Doubleday, 1986)** Mrs. Brightwell's orphaned niece seems to have a troubling secret that Felix would like to get to the bottom of.
7. *Woman Slaughter* **(Doubleday, 1990)** Felix arrives for a visit just as a murderous series of events, set off by a hit-and-run death, unfolds.
8. *Sleep of the Unjust* **(Doubleday, 1991)** Sudden deaths disturb the tranquility of the English country house where Virginia and Felix are weekend guests.
9. *Beware of the Dog* **(Doubleday, 1993)** The death of elderly, affluent Helen Lovelock in Virginia's hometown of Allingford sets off a violent chain of events.

II. Septuagenarian retired botany professor Andrew Basnett is one of those reluctant, plodding sleuths who always seem to meander into solutions in this series of cozies.

1. *Something Wicked* **(Doubleday, 1984)** While rusticating in the Berkshire village of Godlingham, Professor Basnett gets involved with a local widow rumored to have murdered her husband.
2. *Root of All Evil* **(Doubleday, 1984)** Margaret Weldon, dismissed housekeeper of 85-year-old Felicity Sylvester, becomes the victim of a hit-and-run.
3. *Crime and the Crystal, The* **(Doubleday, 1985)** Andrew is spending the Christmas holiday in Australia with former student Tony Gardiner, who has married a woman suspected of murdering her first husband.
4. *Other Devil's Name, The* **(Doubleday, 1987)** Basnett's former colleague Constance Camm invites him to her cottage in Berkshire after her sister receives a disturbing note.
5. *Murder Too Many, A* **(Doubleday, 1989)** Andrew's visit to a conference at Knotlington University turns up a murder or two.
6. *Smoke without Fire* **(Doubleday, 1991)** A retired QC is killed by an explosion in his neighbor's driveway while Andrew is visiting the neighbors.
7. *Hobby of Murder, A* **(Doubleday, 1994)** A guest at Sam Waldron's 18th-century dinner re-creation is felled by cyanide.

III. Ferrars's earliest mysteries featured a young English amateur detective named Toby Dyke.

1. *Give a Corpse a Bad Name* **(Hodder [UK], 1940)** Toby Dyke, in conjunction with the local police, investigates circumstances surrounding the death of a middle-aged stranger who is run over by a car while lying drunk in a traffic lane. Not published in the United States.
2. *Rehearsals for Murder* **(Doubleday, 1941)** Young, charming Lou Cappell is found poisoned in a country house after a crying jag the day before. UK title: *Remove the Bodies*.
3. *Murder of a Suicide* **(Doubleday, 1941)** Toby and his friend George prevent prominent botanist Edgar Pres from committing suicide by jumping off a cliff. UK title: *Death in Botanist's Bay*.
4. *Shape of a Stain, The* **(Doubleday, 1942)** A foreign scientist asks Toby to help him recover his beloved chimpanzee Irma. UK title: *Don't Monkey with Murder*.

5. *Neck in a Noose* (Doubleday, 1943) Arriving at a friend's country house Toby finds a trashed house and his friend, dead, apparently from natural causes. UK title: *Your Neck in a Noose*.

IV. Scotland Yard Superintendent Ditteridge solved crimes in a pair of novels.

1. *Stranger and Afraid, A* (Walker, 1971) Holly Dunthorne's aunt dies soon after Holly's unexpected arrival home from the Continent.
2. *Foot in the Grave* (Doubleday, 1972) Christine Findon, already trying to adjust to the changes in her life, is additionally troubled by a strange man in the house, the theft of her weekend guest's left shoes, and a body in the cellar.

Ferris, Monica

PSEUDONYM OF Mary Pulver Kufeld

Betsy Devonshire is proprietor of a needlework shop in Excelsior, Minnesota, and a part-time sleuth. As with all small towns in cozies, Excelsior is a violent place: at least one murder per novel. To add to her action-filled plots and well-developed characters, Monica Ferris includes needlework patterns with each book. Monica Ferris is a pseudonym of Mary Pulver Kufeld, who also writes the Peter Brichter mysteries as Mary Monica Pulver (q.v.) and the Dame Frevisse mysteries (with Gail Frazer as coauthor) as Margaret Frazer (q.v.).

1. *Crewel World* (Berkley, 1999) When her sister Margot is found murdered in Crewel World, her needle-craft store in Excelsior, Minnesota, Betsy investigates and finds plenty of suspects.
2. *Framed in Lace* (Berkley, 1999) A ferry that sank in 1949, when raised from its watery grave, proves to contain the skeleton of a murdered woman. The only clue: a piece of lacelike fabric.
3. *Stitch in Time, A* (Berkley, 2000) A damaged tapestry discovered in a church leads to a "crafty crime."
4. *Unraveled Sleeve* (Berkley, 2001) Betsy Devonshire's siege of vivid nightmares culminates with the dream of a murder before it happens.
5. *Murderous Yarn, A* (Berkley, 2002) One of the drivers in the annual antique car race is found dead, his car enveloped in flames.
6. *Hanging by a Thread* (Berkley, 2003) A five-year-old murder case refuses to die, and it is up to Betsy to "unravel" it.
7. *Cutwork* (Berkley, 2004) Betsy is working at a crafts fair information booth when a talented sculptor turns up murdered at the fair.
8. *Crewel Yule* (Berkley, 2004) This year's holiday needlework convention is rocked when one shop owner takes a fatal nine-story fall. First in the series to be published originally in hardcover.
9. *Embroidered Truths* (Berkley, 2005) Betsy takes in her friend Godwin when he has a nasty quarrel with John, his "significant other." Then John is found dead, and Godwin is arrested for murder.
10. *Sins and Needles* (Berkley, 2006) Jan, one of Betsy's best customers, comes under suspicion when her elderly, eccentric, rich great-aunt, to whom she is heir, dies mysteriously
11. *Knitting Bones* (Berkley, 2008) The search for National Heart Coalition executive Robert Germaine, who is missing with a check for a sizable donation from the Embroiderers' Guild of America, engages Betsy and her assistant, "Goddy" Dulac.

Feuchtwanger, Lion

Readers who enjoyed the Claudius books of Robert Graves (q.v.) will be pleased to discover this trilogy set in Roman times. The Josephus trilogy, *Der judische Krieg*, by German author Feuchtwanger, is a narrative centering on Flavius Josephus, the great Jewish historian. The series gives a vivid portrait of Rome from 64 CE through the rule of Domitian and of the lives and position of the Jews at this time. Numbers 1 and 2 were translated by Willa and Edwin Muir, number 3 by Caroline Oram.

1. *Josephus* (Viking, 1932) Josephus comes to Rome during the last days of Nero to plead at the court of the Caesars for three unjustly imprisoned Jews. Original title: *Josephus* (1932).
2. *Jew of Rome, The* (Viking, 1936) Josephus is torn between his position in the Roman world and his Jewish loyalties. Original title: *Die Sohne* (1935).
3. *Josephus and the Emperor* (Viking, 1942) Josephus has lost the favor of the Emperor Domitian, but his major work, the universal history of the Jews, has been completed. Original title: *Der Tag wird kommen* (1936).

Fforde, Jasper

I. "Literary detective" Thursday Next is the heroine of a wild series of novels set in an alternate Britain of the 1980s, in which literature has a prominent place in everyday life: coin-operated Will-Speak machines spouting Shakespeare, Henry Fielding bubble-gum cards, etc. Thursday, who eventually becomes "Head of Jurisfiction" before she retires, has a series of surreal adventures involving the Prose Portal, which enables people, including Thursday's archnemesis, Acheron Hades, to cross into a prose text such as *Jane Eyre* and eliminate characters. The closest parallels to Fforde are Lewis Carroll (q.v.) and the late Douglas Adams (q.v.). The zany, episodic plots, brimming with literary allusions, may distract beginning readers, but those who persevere find them wildly funny. It is probably best to begin with number 1. British author Jasper Fforde worked in film for many years (including a long stint as a "focus puller") before he started making a living as a novelist.

1. *Eyre Affair, The* (Viking, 2002) In an alternate Great Britain of the 1980s, Special Operative (literary detective) Thursday Next chases the evil Acheron Hades. who, commandeering the Prose Portal invented by Thursday's mad-scientist uncle, Mycroft, has sent a minion into *Martin Chuzzlewit* who kills a minor character within the text, thus altering Dickens's novel. *Jane Eyre* is next.
2. *Lost in a Good Book* (Viking, 2003) Thursday gets caught up in a new adventure that gets her into works by Edgar Poe, Jane Austen, and Beatrix Potter. This time she has to find a way to rescue her husband, Landem, from the toils of the Goliath Corporation and to save the world from being enveloped by some kind of pink goo.
3. *Well of Lost Plots, The* (Viking, 2004) The pregnant Thursday Next, searching for her husband, whose existence has been obliterated, takes a temporary assignment in BookWorld, a sort of Lewis Carroll (q.v.) world where she encounters various odd human and nonhuman persona, including characters from *Anna Karenina*, *The Wind in the Willows*, and many other literary works
4. *Something Rotten* (Viking, 2004) Thursday has retired to her hometown of Swindon, England with her two-year-old son, Friday, her pet dodos, and Hamlet, the prince of Denmark, vaguely aware that something is missing (i.e., her husband, Landen, who has been disappeared by the Goliath Corporation).

5. *First among Sequels* (**Viking, 2007**) Thursday has her hands full trying to persuade her 16-year-old slacker son, Friday, to join the ChronoGuard. Someone is trying to make classic works of literature into reality book shows, and the Stupidity Surplus is reaching dangerously high levels all over England.

II. Fforde has produced a pair of Nursery Crime novels starring Jack Spratt, dedicated but underappreciated investigator in the Reading, England, Nursery Crimes Division, who wants to "bring justice to the nursery world." The Three Little Pigs, Mary Mary Quite Contrary, Mrs. Hubbard, the Gingerbreadman, and Punch and Judy and other "nursery" characters appear on various sides of the law. Not as "wild and crazy" as the Thursday Next series but still fun.

1. *Big Over Easy, The* (**Viking, 2005**) Jack Spratt is put out when the court finds the Three Little Pigs "not guilty of all charges relating to the first-degree murder of Mr. Wolff" but goes on, with his assistant Mary Mary ("Quite Contrary") to investigate the case of "fall guy" Humpty Dumpty.
2. *Fourth Bear, The* (**Viking, 2006**) PDR (Person of Dubious Reality) Jack Spratt deals with the notorious killer the Gingerbreadman; Punch and Judy, who have set up as marriage counselors; talking bears; and Goldilocks.

Fielding, Gabriel

PSEUDONYM OF Alan G. Barnsley

These three novels about an English family show the Blaydon children growing up under the influence of a neurotic and domineering mother and a weak father, a vicar who retires to his study and his prayers when faced with any unpleasantness. Two tragic deaths—one murder and one accident—play central parts in the action, but the solitary movements of insight and compromise involved in growing up are the real pleasures in these sensitively drawn studies. John, the youngest brother, is the main character and narrator. The books overlap in time but are perhaps best read in the following order:

1. *In the Time of Greenbloom* (**Morrow, 1957**) After the tragedy that disrupts his life, young John is liberated from his grief and guilt by an eccentric Jewish friend of his brother.
2. *Brotherly Love* (**Morrow, 1961**) The story starts before and ends after the narrative in number 1. The central concern is John's brother David, who is not settling into the ministry as well as his mother had hoped.
3. *Through Streets Broad and Narrow* (**Morrow, 1960**) Eighteen-year-old John enters medical school in Dublin in 1935. The story covers five years before and during World War II.

Fielding, Helen

Bridget Jones's Diary has been a big success in print and on the big screen with Renee Zellweger in the title role (2001). Bridget Jones is a thirtysomething British journalist wannabe who frets, in acerbic prose in her diary, about her relationships with men, her weight, her alcohol and cigarette consumption, along with a host of other hopes and complaints. Bridget, ditzy but likable, something of a latter-day Isadora Wing (Erica Jong [q.v.]), returns in a sequel, *The Edge of Reason.* The books are full of British slang but still of great appeal to American readers. Helen Fielding, who produced documentaries for BBC for a number of years, has also written *Cause Celeb* (Viking, 2001, originally United Kingdom, 1994), a tragicomedy examining the relationship between starving Africans and Western celebrities, and *Olivia Joules and the Overactive Imagination* (Viking, 2004), a thriller in about a journalist who becomes a spy.

1. *Bridget Jones's Diary* (**Viking, 1998**) Bridget Jones, a single, thirtyish, London-based journalist wannabe confides to her diary all her hopes and fears, her various addictions, and her relationships with unsatisfactory men, including her boss and her sometime lover.
2. *Bridget Jones: The Edge of Reason* (**Viking, 2000**) Bridget, her accommodation with her lover in number 1 fizzling, continues to pour her heart out to her diary. Full of hilarious incidents, including an interview with real-life British actor Colin Firth (who has a role in the movie version of *Bridget Jones's Diary*). Variant title: *The Edge of Reason.*

Fiffer, Sharon (Sloan)

Flea-market and garage-sale junkies have a series of their own now. Jane Wheel, having been laid off from her PR job, is free to indulge in her quest for "treasures," and to solve one or more murders per book. Jane, who lives in the Chicago area, is assisted in her investigations by Bruce Oh, Chicago homicide detective, who eventually becomes a partner in Jane's PI business; by her friend Tim, a gay antique dealer from Evanston; and occasionally by her "nearly estranged" husband, geologist Charley. These novels are entertaining cozies with special appeal for the many bitten by the collectibles bug.

1. *Killer Stuff* (**St. Martin's, 2001**) Separated from her PR job and her professor husband, Jane Wheel helps to make ends meet through buying-and-selling jaunts in garage and estate sales, auctions, and flea markets. Jane often borrows her neighbor Sandy's Suburban to carry her loot home, but then Sandy is murdered, and Jane becomes a suspect.
2. *Dead Guy's Stuff* (**St. Martin's, 2002**) After discovering a severed human finger in a jar, Jane suspects that several deaths due to "natural causes" weren't really natural at all.
3. *Wrong Stuff, The* (**St. Martin's, 2003**) One of Sharon's first cases in the PI business she shares with former Chicago homicide cop Bruce Oh takes her undercover to investigate a dealer accused of murder as part of a fake-antique-furniture operation.
4. *Buried Stuff* (**St. Martin's, 2004**) Feeling overburdened by "stuff," Jane holds a garage sale of her own, which is interrupted by a frantic call from her mother concerning human bone fragments found buried on a neighbor's property in Kankakee.
5. *Hollywood Stuff* (**St. Martin's, 2006**) Movie producer "Bix" Bixby calls to say that she wants to make a movie about Jane's adventures, so Jane heads out to California, where she becomes reacquainted with her old college beau, Jeb Gleason.

Files, Lolita

The "sistahs" are two young African American women from different backgrounds who became best friends in second grade in Fort Lauderdale, Florida. Misty Fine and Reesy Snowden pursue different careers while having fun and searching for Mr. Right. Misty, raised by working-class white parents, is more upward-oriented than Reesy, who has wealthy black parents and an MBA but prefers jobs on the fringes of show biz. Despite their different personalities, the two always manage to get back together again after a series of adventures that take them from Fort Lauderdale to Atlanta to New York to Hollywood. This is entertaining, humorous *Cosmopolitan*-type chick lit that will remind readers of

Terry McMillan. Lolita Files is an African American from Fort Lauderdale who is the former national communications director for KinderCare Learning Center.

1. *Scenes from a Sistah* (**Warner, 1997**) Misty Fine and Reesy Snowden pursue their careers and their search for fun and the right man. Although Reesy disapproves of Misty's choice of lovers, and Misty is appalled by Reesy's job as a stripper, the two manage to stay friends, even after working together.

2. *Getting to the Good Parts* (**Warner, 1998**) Misty, pursuing her executive career, has become engaged to her boss. Reesy lands the lead in *Black Barry's Pie*, an off-Broadway musical; finds herself launched on a successful stage career; and hops from one boyfriend to the other.

3. *Tastes like Chicken* (**Simon & Schuster, 2004**) Reesy's marriage to supposedly reformed womanizer Dandre Hilliard turns sour when some very compromising pictures turn up, and Reesy flees to Hollywood to pursue her acting career, while Misty stays in New York for the time being with her husband and unwanted pregnancy.

Finney, Jack

PSEUDONYM OF Walter Braden Finney

The late Jack Finney (d. 1995), veteran science-fiction and thriller writer, wrote *The Body Snatchers* (Dell, 1955), which became the cult movie *Invasion of the Body Snatchers*, and *Time and Again*, which became a cult classic without reaching the big screen (although it was produced as a stage musical in 2001). *Time and Again* is an intriguing time-travel tale illustrated by period photos and news clippings, which help the reader to become a part of the compelling re-creation of the New York City of 1882. Although the ending of *Time and Again* left its hero voluntarily back in the past, Finney couldn't resist writing a sequel.

1. *Time and Again* (**Simon & Schuster, 1970**) Contemporary artist Simon Morley agrees to go back in time for a brief period as part of a secret US government time-travel project.

2. *From Time to Time* (**Simon & Schuster, 1995**) Morley travels from 1882 back to the late 20th century again, and then back again, this time to 1912 and the maiden voyage of the *Titanic*.

Finney, Patricia

I. A trio of novels set in Elizabethan times features English spies David Becket and Simon Ames and Queen Elizabeth herself. Fictional and historical characters are blended in a well-researched setting, and salient events such as the Spanish Armada and the execution of Mary, Queen of Scots are brought to life. Patricia Finney also writes the Jack series of juveniles, the young adult historical mystery series Lady Grace (as Grace Cavendish), and the Sir Robert Carey novels under her P. F. Chisholm (q.v.) pseudonym.

1. *Firedrake's Eye* (**St. Martin's, 1992**) Members of the English secret service search for would-be assassins of Queen Elizabeth.

2. *Unicorn's Blood* (**St. Martin's, 1998**) Queen Elizabeth takes center stage as she ponders the execution of Mary, Queen of Scots.

3. *Gloriana's Torch* (**St. Martin's, 2003**) David Becket, clerk of court and spy for Queen Elizabeth, is commanded to discover details of a Spanish plot dubbed the "Miracle of Beauty" and to rescue his fellow spy Simon Ames, who is toiling as a Spanish galley slave.

II. An earlier pair of mythological-historical novels relates the story of Lugh Mac Romain, harper and reluctant warrior, who kills the king of Connaught, gets caught up in the famous Cattle Raid of Cooley, and escapes to Roman Britain, where he has further adventures. Cuchulain of Muirthemne, the great Irish hero, is a prominent character in both novels.

1. *Shadow of Gulls, A* (**Putnam, 1977**) Harper Lugh Mac Romain, trying to escape the curse of Queen Maeve of Connaught for killing her king, is caught up in the Cattle Raid of Cooley with his friend Cuchulain of Muirthemne.

2. *Crow Goddess, The* (**St. Martin's, 1978**) Lugh makes his way to Roman Britain, where he befriends the Roman soldier Karus and falls in love with the warrior-woman Liath Duv.

Fish, Robert L.

I. Captain Jose Da Silva—Ze to his friends—is the Brazilian police liaison to Interpol. He is suave and virile and drives like a maniac, though he'll do almost anything to avoid flying. His counterpart from the US Embassy is Wilson, a man of such nondescript appearance that nobody ever remembers seeing him. Together they drink a lot of Remy Martin and solve some very puzzling cases against a colorful Brazilian setting, from the posh beaches of Rio to the jungles of the upper Amazon.

1. *Fugitive, The* (**Simon & Schuster, 1962**) Sinister ex-Nazis and a briefcase containing $2 million figure in this Edgar-winning novel, which introduced Captain Da Silva and Wilson.

2. *Isle of the Snakes* (**Simon & Schuster, 1963**) A map incised on the skin of a stuffed coral snake leads Da Silva to search for buried treasure on an island crawling with poisonous snakes.

3. *Shrunken Head, The* (**Simon & Schuster, 1963**) When an explorer friend returns from the upper Amazon as a shrunken head, Da Silva goes to investigate.

4. *Diamond Bubble, The* (**Simon & Schuster, 1965**) Da Silva is on the trail of a clever diamond racket.

5. *Brazilian Sleigh Ride* (**Simon & Schuster, 1965**) Wilson and Da Silva find themselves working against each other in this case involving fraud and an old army pal of Wilson's.

6. *Always Kill a Stranger* (**Putnam, 1967**) An anonymous letter warning of an assassination attempt during a high-level OAS meeting in Rio has everybody jumpy.

7. *Bridge That Went Nowhere, The* (**Putnam, 1968**) When a bridge in the middle of the jungle is blown up, the trail seems to lead to a missing young geologist.

8. *Xavier Affair, The* (**Putnam, 1969**) Chico Xavier, son of the fourth-richest man in Brazil, is kidnapped.

9. *Green Hell Treasure, The* (**Putnam, 1971**) Da Silva follows an ex-convict to his well-hidden loot.

10. *Trouble in Paradise* (**Doubleday, 1975**) After five underworld slayings, Da Silva sets himself up as a decoy.

II. Some think Fish's criminals are even more engaging than his detectives, especially the debonair and high-living Kek Huuygens, the world's greatest smuggler. Huuygens, who is known to have smuggled everything from the original score of a Bach cantata to a two-ton elephant across international borders, has no trouble outwitting the customs authorities who monitor his comings and goings.

1. *Hochman Miniatures, The* (**New American Library, 1967**) Kek's debut features Nazi contraband and his plans to avenge the death of his family at the hands of SS Colonel Gruber.

2. *Whirligig* (**World, 1970**) Kek and his actress wife decide to take $5 million out of Belgium—legally!

3. *Tricks of the Trade, The* (**Putnam, 1972**) The oily Señor Sanchez has offered Kek $10,000 plus expenses to transport a suitcase from Buenos Aires to Barcelona.

4. *Wager, The* (**Putnam, 1974**) Kek bets that he can smuggle a valuable Chinese carving past US Customs.

5. *Kek Huuygens, Smuggler* (**Mysterious, 1976**) Short stories.

III. Humor and character are more prominent than mystery in these novels. Carruthers, Simpson, Briggs are three old duffers who used to do detective work and write mystery stories. Now fallen on lean days, the three decide to put their still formidable talents to actual use and set up their own bump-off service, committing real murders if the fee is right and the victims sufficiently deserving.

1. *Murder League, The* (**Simon & Schuster, 1968**) Carruthers, Simpson, and Briggs form the Murder League and proceed with their first cases, until they run into trouble and are rescued by Sir Percival Pugh.

2. *Rub-a-Dub-Dub* (**Simon & Schuster, 1971**) On a cruise ship, Mrs. Mazie Carpenter, an American con lady and cardsharp, kicks up a bit of trouble. Variant title: *Death Cuts the Deck*.

3. *Gross Carriage of Justice, A* (**Doubleday, 1979**) The redoubtable ex-detective writers find themselves captives of two toughs from Cicero, Illinois, and quickly turn the tables on them.

IV. Sherlock Holmes fans won't want to miss these broad and funny parodies starring Schlock Homes of 221B Bagel St. and his assistant Dr. Watney.

1. *Incredible Shlock Homes, The* (**Simon & Schuster, 1965**) Homes has 12 adventures.

2. *Memoirs of Shlock Homes, The* (**Simon & Schuster, 1974**) Further stories continue Homes's adventures.

3. *Schlock Homes: The Complete Bagel Street Saga* (**Gaslight, 1990**) Contains all of the Shlock Homes stories written between 1959 and 1981.

Fisher, Carrie

Postcards from the Edge and *The Best Awful* are a pair of semiautobiographical novels about actress Suzanne Vale, who suffers from bipolar disorder and is subject to substance abuse. She has a conflicted relationship with her movie-star mother, Doris Mann, and finds herself in and out of detox and mental hospitals. The somewhat grim subject matter is leavened by Vale's/Fisher's wit and humor, and the books are quite readable. *Postcards from the Edge* was turned into a film scripted by Fisher starring Meryl Streep (1990). Carrie Fisher, daughter of film-star Debbie Reynolds and onetime pop idol Eddie Fisher, writes from personal knowledge about the ups and downs of bipolarism.

1. *Postcards from the Edge* (**Simon & Schuster, 1987**) Actress Suzanne Vale, daughter of Hollywood legend, Doris Mann, moves back and forth from manic to depressive stages and in and out of detox and mental hospitals as she tries to pursue her own screen career.

2. *Best Awful, The* (**Simon & Schuster, 2002**) After her husband leaves her, Suzanne moves from recovery to psychosis and back again, trying unsuccessfully to go without medication and to care for her daughter, Honey.

Fisher, Edward

Scholars may quibble, but this fictionalized biography is enjoyable light reading that gives a good feeling for Elizabethan times. Naturally, Fisher presents his solution to the mystery of the "Dark Lady" of the sonnets. The Silver Falcon is the trilogy title.

1. *Shakespeare and Son* (**Abelard-Schuman, 1962**) William is the son of the title. This volume shows him from ages 15 to 18, a much misunderstood young man.

2. *Love's Labour's Won: A Novel about Shakespeare's Lost Years* (**Abelard-Schuman, 1963**) During the years 1583–1593, William is on his way to fame with partner Dick Burbage.

3. *Best House in Stratford, The* (**Abelard-Schuman, 1965**) The title is ironic, for the Stratford house is old and run-down. Shakespeare finds his London life more compelling.

Fitzwater, Judy

Jennifer Marsh is a part-time caterer, amateur detective, and aspiring (unpublished) mystery writer based in Georgia. The likable Jennifer, with the help of her boyfriend, crime reporter Sam Culpepper, and members of her writers' support group, has more luck with her own sleuthing than with her fictional cases in these entertaining looks at the writing and publishing business. Fitzwater's latest publication, *No Safe Place* (Silhouette, 2006), is a thriller featuring a different sleuth.

1. *Dying to Get Published* (**Fawcett, 1998**) After frustrated mystery writer Jennifer Marsh works out a plan for rubbing out the unscrupulous literary agent who held on to her manuscript for a year before rejecting it, she thinks better of it, but the old girl is done in by someone else.

2. *Dying to Get Even* (**Fawcett, 1999**) Jennifer's friend Emma Walker is found holding a bloody knife as her ex-husband, Edgar, sometime owner of Edgar's Down Home Grill, floats facedown in their swimming pool.

3. *Dying for a Clue* (**Fawcett, 1999**) When Jennifer accompanies private eye Johnny Zeeman on a case, she finds herself in the middle of a shoot-out at a fertility clinic where a nurse is killed before she can give Johnny information about his client, Diane Robbins, who is searching for her birth parents.

4. *Dying to Remember* (**Fawcett, 2000**) Old memories are stirred up when Jennifer attends her 12th high school reunion in Macon, Georgia. When her old flame apparently commits suicide, Marsh is reminded of the unsolved disappearance of a student during their prom night.

5. *Dying to Be Murdered* (**Fawcett, 2001**) Expecting to be murdered, elderly society matron Mary Bedford Ashton hires Jennifer for $1,000 a week to live in her historic mansion and record everything that happens there.

6. *Dying to Get Her Man* (**Fawcett, 2002**) Bride-to-be Suzanne Gray is found frozen to death on her lover's grave, complete with suicide note.

Fleming, Ian

The enormous appeal of superagent James Bond—007 of the British Secret Service—is shown in the continuing popularity of the Bond movies, more than a dozen of which have been spawned by Hollywood, with a new one on the way. Sean Connery, Timothy Dalton, George Lazenby, Roger Moore, and Pierce Brosnan have all portrayed Bond, though, for many older fans at least, Connery *is* James Bond.

Fleming's own involvement in British intelligence, though extensive and apparently not without drama, cannot have been one-tenth as glamorous and exciting as the adventures of his fictional hero. (But Quinn Fawcett [q.v.] has created a fictional Ian Fleming.) John E. Gardner (q.v.) continued the Bond adventures, and there have been numerous imitations, parodies, and books about James Bond: one of the best is Kingsley Amis's *The James Bond Dossier* (New American Library, 1965). The Bond novels have been collected in omnibus volumes, including *Gilt-Edged Bonds* (Macmillan, 1961; numbers 1, 5, and 6); *More Gilt-Edged Bonds* (Macmillan, 1965; numbers 2, 3, and 4); and *Bonded Fleming* (Viking, 1965; numbers 8, 9, and 10).

1. ***Casino Royale*** **(Macmillan, 1953)** At a French casino resort, Bond destroys LeChiffre and the French arm of the Russian espionage ring known as SMERSH. Variant title: *You Asked For It.*

2. ***Live and Let Die*** **(Macmillan, 1954)** Bond meets Mr. Big of SMERSH in an adventure set in New York, Florida, and Jamaica.

3. ***Moonraker*** **(Macmillan, 1955)** Bond keeps a villainous millionaire from destroying London with a nuclear rocket. Variant title: *Too Hot to Handle.*

4. ***Diamonds Are Forever*** **(Macmillan, 1956)** Bond infiltrates the Spang mob of diamond smugglers.

5. ***From Russia with Love*** **(Macmillan, 1957)** SMERSH makes an all-out effort to assassinate Bond.

6. ***Doctor No*** **(Macmillan, 1958)** This action is set in the Caribbean, where the maniacal Eurasian Dr. No, who has steel pincers for hands, makes plans to take over the world.

7. ***Goldfinger*** **(Macmillan, 1959)** Bond must prevent Ulrich Goldfinger from getting all the gold in Fort Knox.

8. ***For Your Eyes Only*** **(Viking, 1960)** Five stories are included here: "From a View to a Kill," "For Your Eyes Only," "Quantum of Solace," "Risico," and "The Hildebrand Rarity."

9. ***Thunderball*** **(Viking, 1961)** The criminal organization of SPECTRE, led by Blofeld, tries to do some blackmail with hijacked nuclear bombs.

10. ***Spy Who Loved Me, The*** **(Viking, 1962)** This story is told by lovely young Vivienne Michel, who is briefly involved in one of Bond's cases.

11. ***On Her Majesty's Secret Service*** **(New American Library, 1963)** Blofeld of SPECTRE is back again with a nasty germ-warfare plot. Bond gives up bachelorhood for Countess Tracy Vincenzo.

12. ***You Only Live Twice*** **(New American Library, 1964)** Devastated by Tracy's death, Bond is sent to investigate a strange Japanese death garden.

13. ***Man with the Golden Gun, The*** **(New American Library, 1965)** A brainwashed Bond is used by the KGB.

14. ***Octopussy*** **(New American Library, 1966)** Two novelettes were posthumously published here: "Octopussy," about retired British marine officer Dexter Smyth, who is conducting dangerous octopus experiments; and "The Living Daylights," about Bond's assignment to kill a KGB assassin.

Fleming, Thomas (James)

I. The Stapletons are an American family whose fortunes are intertwined with the history of their country in a series of loosely connected novels by historian and biographer Thomas Fleming. The time span of the novels is from 1721 to the 1970s with many gaps. The Revolutionary War and the Civil War are covered. Number 5, set in the 1970s, combines elements from the Stapleton series and Fleming's Irish American series (see series II). *Liberty Tavern* (Doubleday, 1976), a Revolutionary War novel, is sometimes linked with the Stapleton series. Nonseries novels such as *Spoils of War* (Avon, 1986) and *A Passionate Girl* (Forge 2004) also cover the Civil War and its aftermath. *Over There* (Harper Collins, 1992) covers World I from the American point of view, while *Time and Tide* (Simon & Schuster, 1987) and *Loyalties* (HarperCollins, 1994) do the same for World War II. *Officers' Wives* (Warner, 1982) and *West Point Blue and Gray* (IBooks, 2006) are novels about West Point and its graduates. *The Secret Trial of Robert E. Lee* (Forge, 2006) is alternate history.

1. ***Remember the Morning*** **(Forge, 1997)** In 1721 Dutch-born Catalyntie Van Vorst and African Clara are captured by Seneca Indians and raised by them for 12 years before they are "rescued" in a prisoner exchange. The women, who endure a rocky transition to "white" life, become involved in a tragic love triangle with idealistic settler Malcolm Stapleton.

2. ***Dreams of Glory*** **(Forge, 2000)** In 1780 Congressman Hugh Stapleton and Chaplain Caleb Chandler become enmeshed in a British plot to kidnap General George Washington.

3. ***Wages of Fame, The*** **(Forge, 1998)** From 1827 to 1861, three principal characters—George Stapleton, Hudson Valley land heir and politician; Caroline Kemple Stapleton, George's ambitious wife; and John Sladen, George's friend and Caroline's lover—interact with prominent historical characters.

4. ***When This Cruel War Is Over*** **(Forge, 2002)** Major Paul Stapleton of the Union army and Janet Todd, courier for the pro-Confederacy Sons of Liberty, fall in love, despite their different aims, on the Kentucky-Indiana border in 1864.

5. ***Promises to Keep*** **(Doubleday, 1978)** In the 1970s, Paul Stapleton, whose idealism has been eroded by two world wars and the Depression, hires Jim Kilpatrick, son of a corrupt judge, to write a book about the Stapleton family, and some rather unsavory secrets leak out. *Romans, Countrymen, Lovers* (Morrow, 1969) depicts the earlier history of the Kilpatricks, who are connected with the O'Connors in series II.

II. Fleming, the son of an Irish American politician from New Jersey, has also written a loosely connected series about Irish American politics in the late 1800s and early 1900s. The rise of Jake O'Connor (modeled after Frank Hague, political "boss" and mayor of Jersey City from 1917 to 1947) is depicted. In this series and in other novels, poor and rising Irish American Catholics are depicted realistically and, some would say, negatively, especially in *The Sandbox Tree* (Morrow, 1970), in which a group of young Catholics are estranged from the Catholic Church. *The Good Shepherd* (Doubleday, 1974) is about Irish American Archbishop Matthew Mahan and his confrontations with the Second Vatican Council. *Romans, Countrymen, Lovers* (see above, series I) and *Promises to Keep* (see above, series I) have, through the political Kilpatricks, connections with the O'Connor series. *A Cry of Whiteness* (Morrow, 1967) also deals with urban problems. *Hours of Gladness* (Forge, 1999) depicts an IRA cell in a small New Jersey shore town.

Thomas Fleming is well known also as a writer of nonfiction history and biography, including *Liberty!* (Viking, 1997), a companion to the PBS television series of the same name; *Duel: Alexander Hamilton, Aaron Burr, and the Future of America* (Basic, 2000) and *The Man Who Dared the Lightning: A New Look at Benjamin Franklin* (Morrow, 1971).

1. ***All Good Men*** **(Doubleday, 1961)** Jake O'Connor, first generation Irish American, starts his rise up the "greasy pole" of urban American politics.

2. ***God of Love, The*** **(Doubleday, 1963)** No annotation available.

3. ***King of the Hill*** **(New American Library, 1966)** Jake becomes mayor of his city, and consolidates his power.

4. *Rulers of the City* (**Doubleday, 1977**) Busing becomes an issue dividing ethnic groups in the 1960s.

Fletcher, Inglis

Adventure, romance, and history in equal parts characterize the Carolina series, sometimes known as the Albemarle series, by this North Carolina novelist. *Raleigh's Eden* was the first novel published and the first to be set in Albemarle, the fertile coastal district to which its title refers. Thereafter Fletcher produced a new book every two years, moving both forward and backward in time, and eventually covering the period from 1585 to 1789. Some characters reappear in various books, but it is the consistent location that makes this a series. Each novel was designed to stand on its own, and a chronological reading is not really essential, but for those who prefer it, here is the sequence as closely as can be determined.

1. *Roanoke Hundred* (**Bobbs-Merrill, 1948**) This account is based on the Grenville expedition of 108 Englishmen who settled on Roanoke Island in 1585.
2. *Bennett's Welcome* (**Bobbs-Merrill, 1950**) This story begins in England in 1651, when Richard Monington is banished to Virginia as an indentured servant as punishment for helping King Charles II to escape.
3. *Rogue's Harbor* (**Bobbs-Merrill, 1964**) Nathan Willoughby joins the settler's rebellion of 1677 as his daughter plans to marry a poor schoolmaster.
4. *Raleigh's Eden* (**Bobbs-Merrill, 1940**) Adam Rutledge and Mary Warden head the cast of characters in this story of plantation life beginning in 1705.
5. *Men of Albemarle* (**Bobbs-Merrill, 1942**) Plantation owner Roger Mainwaring and the mysterious Scottish Lady Mary Tower figure in this installment set from 1710 to 1712.
6. *Lusty Wind for Carolina* (**Bobbs-Merrill, 1944**) Anne Bonney, a beautiful woman pirate, is one of the colorful characters in this tale of Huguenot settlers and the fight for freedom of the seas.
7. *Cormorant's Brood* (**Lippincott, 1959**) The time is 1725–1729, and Anthony Granville and Deirdra Treffrey star. The "cormorant" is greedy British governor George Burrington.
8. *Wind in the Forest, The* (**Bobbs-Merrill, 1957**) Set in 1771, this book examines the conflict between the frontier farmers and the wealthy coastal plantation owners.
9. *Scotswoman, The* (**Bobbs-Merrill, 1954**) The historical figure Flora MacDonald, savior of Bonny Prince Charlie, is the main character in this book, which focuses on the Scottish settlers in North Carolina in 1773.
10. *Toil of the Brave* (**Bobbs-Merrill, 1946**) Set in 1779–1780, this account features Captain Huntley, a liaison officer to General Washington.
11. *Wicked Lady* (**Bobbs-Merrill, 1962**) As the last battles of the American Revolution are fought, the town of Edenton, North Carolina, is mesmerized by its newest resident, Lady Anne Stuart.
12. *Queen's Gift* (**Bobbs-Merrill, 1952**) Debate over ratification of the Constitution consumes Albemarle's citizens in 1789.

Flint, Eric

I. In a relatively short time (first novel, *Mother of Demons*, published in 1997), Eric Flint has become a leading practitioner of the alternate-history subgenre of science fiction. In his Assiti Shards series, a cosmic accident, referred to as the Ring of Fire, transfers Grantville, West Virginia, from the 20th century to 17th-century Germany (1632), smack dab in the middle of the Thirty Years' War. Undismayed by this unprecedented turn of events, the resourceful West Virginians proceed to form the United States of Europe in alliance with Gustavus Adolphus, aid the beleaguered peasants of Germany in their revolt, consort with the likes of Galileo and Pope Urban VIII, and change the course of history in many ways. Five of the seven novels in the series were written with various coauthors, and several volumes of shared-world stories, edited by Flint, have been published: *Ring of Fire* (Baen, 2004); *Grantville Gazette* (Baen, 2004); *Grantville Gazette II* (Baen, 2006); and *Grantville Gazette III* (Baen, 2006). Flint, a history major who is a longtime labor activist, lives in Indiana.

1. *1632* (**Baen, 2001**) The hamlet of Grantville, West Virginia, is transferred, complete with inhabitants, by the cosmic accident called the Ring of Fire, to Germany in 1632, in the throes of the fratricidal Thirty Years' War.
2. *1633* (**Baen, 2002**) The Confederated Principalities of Europe, a new government, forged by the alliance between the king of Sweden, Gustavus Adolphus, and the West Virginians led by Mike Stearns, is beset by the still-raging Thirty Years' War, a financial crisis, and the political and social tensions between the democratic ideals of the 20th-century Americans and the 17th-century aristocrats, who still rule the roost in Europe.
3. *1634: The Baltic War* (**Baen, 2007**) The Baltic War, which began in number 2, is still raging. Gustavus Adolphus, king of Sweden and emperor of the United States of Europe, prepares a counterattack on the combined forces of the League of Ostend (France, Spain, England, and Denmark). Coauthored with David Weber.
4. *1634: The Galileo Affair* (**Baen, 2004**) Grantville's only Roman Catholic priest, Father Mazzare, leads an embassy to Italy, where he finds Pope Urban VIII surprisingly open to revelations about the reforms of Vatican II. Tom Stone, his wife, and Sharon Nichols travel to Venice to found a modern pharmaceutical industry. An encounter with Galileo reveals him to be a prickly character. Coauthored with Andrew Dennis.
5. *1634: The Ram Rebellion* (**Baen, 2006**) Inspired by the example of "American freedom and justice" demonstrated by the West Virginians, the peasants of Franconia (Germany) have formed, yet again, a revolutionary movement, flying the banner of the head of a ram. Coauthored with Virginia DeMarce.
6. *1634: The Bavarian Crisis* (**Baen, 2007**) The recently widowed Duke Maximilian of Bavaria reluctantly assents to a dynastic marriage with his niece, Archduchess Maria Anna of Austria, but she has other ideas. Coauthored with Virginia DeMarce.
7. *1635: The Cannon Law* (**Baen, 2006**) The American delegation to Pope Urban VIII runs afoul of the Spanish inquisitor Cardinal Gaspar Borja y Velasco, who orchestrates a campaign of dirty tricks and rabble-rousing to oust Urban, whom the cardinal deems to be a coddler of heretics.

II. Another alternate history series, this time in conjunction with battle-SF maven David Drake (q.v.), postulates an alien invasion of the Earth in the 6th century CE. The largest obstacle to the domination of Earth by the Malwan Empire is the Byzantine Empire, led by the great general Belisarius, a historical character who plays a role in other fiction, including Robert Graves's (q.v.) historical fiction classic, *Count Belisarius* (Random House, 1938). *The Warmasters* (Baen, 2002), which anthologizes novellas by Drake, Flint, and David Weber, contains Flint's "The Island," which features Calopdius, a character from the Belisarius series. Eric Flint also collaborated with David Drake in one novel of Drake's General series (q.v.): *The Tyrant* (Baen, 2002).

1. *Oblique Approach, An* (Baen, 1998) The alien Malwa, aided and abetted by Link, an evil supercomputer from the future, have conquered 6th-century-CE India. Only the Byzantine Empire, with their great general Belisarius, and a crystal jewel sent by well-wishers from a future of hope and freedom stand against Malwan domination of the entire Earth. Coauthored with David Drake.

2. *In the Heart of Darkness* (Baen, 1998) Belisarius, all that stands between the Malwa and domination of 6th-century Earth, has another enemy to contend with, closer to home. Coauthored with David Drake.

3. *Destiny's Shield* (Baen, 1999) Belisarius, wearing Aide, the crystal jewel sent from the future, continues to oppose the Malwa. Coauthored with David Drake.

4. *Fortune's Stroke* (Baen, 2000) Aide, a human soul embodied in a jewel, journeys back in time to join forces with Belisarius to stop Link, the evil supercomputer, which has created the technologically advanced Malwa Empire.

5. *Tide of Victory, The* (Baen, 2001) Belisarius and Aide, armed with lancers, breech-loading rifles, steamships, and galleys, carry the fight into the Malwa Empire. Coauthored with David Drake.

6. *Dance of Time, The* (Baen, 2006) In the rousing conclusion to the Belisarius series, the Malwa have been defeated temporarily but are poised to strike again against the uneasy alliance created by Belisarius from across Europe, Asia, and Africa. Coauthored with David Drake.

III. Rats and Bats, two novels coauthored with Dave Freer, are lighthearted adventures set in a world of cyber-uplifted rats, bats, and other creatures that have acquired human speech but retain many of their "lower" animal characteristics. It is up to Chip Connolly, conscript in the war against the alien Magh', to sort things out.

1. *Rats, Bats, and Vats* (Baen, 2000) Chip Connolly, a conscripted "grunt" in the battle against the hordes of alien Magh', is stuck behind enemy lines with a bunch of rats that can talk but retain rat priorities: sex, food, and strong drink; cyber-engineered bats with revolution against the humans on their minds; a beautiful girl with an alien tutor; and a cyber-uplifted pet galago. Coauthored with Dave Freer.

2. *Rats, the Bats, and the Ugly, The* (Baen, 2004) The Magh', temporarily quelled, have enlisted human bureaucracy in their cause. The triumphant Chip Connolly is immediately court-martialed and slated for the firing squad. It is up to the rats and bats and the lemurlike galago, Fluffy, to save the day. Coauthored with Dave Freer.

IV. Another pair of goofy fantasy novels forms Joe's World, which is peopled by Greyboar, a philosophical professional strangler; his sister, the militant revolutionary Gwendolyn; the swashbuckling artist Benvenuti Sfondrati-Piccolomini; mad kings; conniving sorcerers; and Ozarine invasions. Number 2 was coauthored with Richard Roach.

1. *Philosophical Strangler, The* (Baen, 2001) Greyboar, the world's greatest professional strangler, is at the top of his profession but feels dissatisfied. Then he discovers the Supreme Philosophy of Life, and is "born again." Greyboar's philosophical preoccupations interfere with his strangling gigs, much to the chagrin of Ignace, his hardheaded agent and manager.

2. *Forward the Mage* (Baen, 2002) Something of a prequel to number 1, this novel should probably be read after it. Gwendolyn Greyboar, the militant revolutionary sister to the philosophical strangler, allying herself with the swashbuckling artist Benvenuti Sfondrati-Piccolomini and the deceptively affable giant Wolfgang,

sets out on a quest to recover King Goimr's wits. Coauthored with Richard Roach.

V. Eric Flint has also coauthored, with Dave Freer (see series III, above) and the prolific Mercedes Lackey (q.v.), a pair of adventures set in the alternate-historical, magical Venetian Republic. The brothers Marco and Benito Valdosta lead a large cast of characters against Viking invaders, vampiric Hungarians, and other threats to the alternate Venice of 1537.

1. *Shadow of the Lion, The* (Baen, 2002) In a world broken off from ours in 349 CE, when St. Hypatia saved the Alexandrian library, two Venetian brothers, Marco and Benito Valdosta, are only dimly aware of the threat to the Holy Roman Empire by Chernobog, demon lord of the North. Coauthored with Dave Freer and Mercedes Lackey.

2. *This Rough Magic* (Baen, 2003) Christian magic is pitted against black sorcery; the old Mother Goddess; shape-shifting shamans; Emeric, the sadistic king of Hungary; and his bloodsucking aunt Elizabeth, Countess Bathory. Coauthored with Dave Freer and Mercedes Lackey.

VI. A new alternate history series is set in America at the time of the War of 1812.

1. *1812: The Rivers of War* (Del Rey, 2005) The Cherokees, finding allies among the politicians of the day and escaped slaves, unite and form an Indian Nation in the American West.

2. *1824: The Arkansas War* (Del Rey, 2006) The Confederacy of the Arkansas is thriving, but newly elected US president Henry Clay, allied with slavery-bound Southerners, launches an invasion of the upstart nation

Flora, Kate (Clark)

Thea Kozak is an educational consultant and amateur detective operating in the Boston, Massachusetts, area. She is widowed but has a more-or-less steady beau in Andre Lemieux, Maine State Police detective, whom she almost marries (see number 6). Thea meets Andre and gets into detecting when her sister is murdered (see number 1). Much of the action takes place in Maine. Kate Flora, who divides her time between Massachusetts and Maine, is a former assistant attorney general for Maine. With *Playing God* (Five Star, 2006), she has inaugurated a new series featuring Maine cop Joe Burgess.

1. *Chosen for Death* (Forge, 1994) When Thea Kozak's sister, Carrie, is murdered in Maine, Thea thinks that the slaying has something to do with Carrie's search for her birth mother, but Andre Lemieux believes that Carrie is the victim of a sex crime.

2. *Death in a Funhouse Mirror* (Forge, 1995) Psychologist Helene Streeter, mother of Thea's friend Eve Paris, has been murdered. Eve believes that her father, psychiatrist Clifford Paris, is the perpetrator.

3. *Death at the Wheel* (Forge, 1996) Julie Bass's philandering husband, Calvin, has just been killed in an automobile accident. When police determine that Calvin's car was tampered with, Thea agrees to investigate.

4. *Educated Death, An* (Forge, 1997) Private school consultant Thea is called to the coed Bucksport School, where student Laney Taggert has drowned, and uncovers a messy situation (Laney was pregnant, etc.).

5. *Death in Paradise* (Forge, 1998) In Maui (Hawaii) for a conference, Thea becomes embroiled in a murder investigation when

conference director Martina Pullman is found dead in her hotel room, strangled with a stocking.

6. *Liberty or Death* (Forge, 2003) The newly pregnant Thea is understandably upset when her wedding to Andre Lemieux is interrupted by Andre's kidnapping by a Maine militia group.

Fluke, Joanne

Hannah Swenson returns to her hometown of Lake Eden, Minnesota, after her father's death, opens a bakery-café, the Cookie Jar, and, this being a cozy crime series, soon becomes an amateur detective sleuthing out the murders that seem to be endemic to "Cozyland." Although some readers claim to be getting tired of Hannah's shilly-shallying between her two beaux, "nerdy" Norman and "hunky" Mike, her dessert recipes are always welcome. Fluke, a Minnesota native now resident in Southern California, has also written romances, YA novels, and humor under such pseudonyms as Jo Gibson, R. J. Fischer, and Kathryn Kirkwood.

1. *Chocolate Chip Cookie Murder* (Kensington, 2000) Hannah Swenson, owner of the Cookie Jar in Edenton, Minnesota, is drafted by her brother-in-law, deputy sheriff Bill, to help him chase down the murderer of a delivery truck driver found shot dead in the alley behind her shop.
2. *Strawberry Shortcake Murder* (Kensington, 2001) Hannah, head judge of the first annual Hartland Flour Dessert Bake-off, gets involved in a murder investigation when one of the judges, high school basketball coach Boyd Watson, is found face down in Hannah's strawberry shortcake.
3. *Blueberry Muffin Murder* (Kensington, 2002) Connie MacIntyre, best-selling cookbook author and star of a popular cable TV cooking show, who has agreed to make the cake for Lake Eden's winter carnival banquet, is found dead in the pantry of the Cookie Jar.
4. *Lemon Meringue Pie Murder* (Kensington, 2003) Who killed voluptuous Rhonda Scharf, whose half-buried body is found by Hannah's mother in the basement of an old house just purchased by one of Hannah's beaus?
5. *Fudge Cupcake Murder* (Kensington, 2004) After Hannah discovers the body of Lake Eden's longtime sheriff in a dumpster, the main suspect becomes her brother-in-law Bill, who was planning to run against the sheriff in the upcoming election.
6. *Sugar Cookie Murder* (Kensington, 2004) Hannah has compiled a cookbook of the locals' favorite recipes, which are to be featured at the Christmas party at Lake Eden's community center. Then Hannah's mother's silver cake knife is found stuck in the chest of Mrs. Dubinski (née Brandi Wyen), one of the guests.
7. *Peach Cobbler Murder* (Kensington, 2005) A new bakery in Lake Eden not only threatens Hannah's shop sales, but one of its owners is proving to be a threat to Hannah's love-life. Then a corpse turns up.
8. *Cherry Cheesecake Murder* (Kensington, 2006) Hannah keeps busy with her cookie baking and sleuthing while keeping her two beaux, Norman and Mike, dangling. Then a body turns up.
9. *Key Lime Pie Murder* (Kensington, 2007) When one of Hannah's fellow judges at the Tri-County Fair baking contest, home-economics teacher Willa Sunquist, is murdered, Hannah, of course, feels bound to investigate.
10. *Carrot Cake Murder* (Kensington, 2008) Gus Klein returns to Lake Eden after a 30-year absence only to be found dead the next day.

Flynn, Michael

In this near-future (1999–2017) SF quartet, Michael Flynn imagines threats by misguided liberals, environmentalists, feminists, and, worst of all, asteroids, who have stalled the economy, ruined the space program and America's schools, and have left Earth vulnerable to runaway bodies from space. Fortunately, the good guys, who include altruistic billionaire Mariesa van Huyten and astronaut Forrest Calhoun, are springing to the rescue. Readers who accept Flynn's premises will enjoy reading this hard-SF series, which is full of ideas and well-developed characters. *The Wreck of the River of Stars* (Tor, 2003), also set in the near future, is a stand-alone novel.

1. *Firestar* (Tor, 1996) Capitalist with a heart of gold Mariesa van Huyten devotes her efforts to jump-starting America's failed economy and schools and dormant space program.
2. *Rogue Star* (Tor, 1998) Mariesa van Huyten continues to battle wrongheaded officials, naive liberals, and shortsighted businessmen to put in place an orbital defense against potentially dangerous near-Earth asteroids. Astronaut Forrest Calhoun and his crew find tantalizing hints of past aliens on an asteroid.
3. *Lodestar* (Tor, 2000) Mariesa van Huyten's asteroid obsession proves to be well founded as an incoming asteroid destroys a space satellite, but there is worse to come.
4. *Falling Stars* (Tor, 2001) In the year 2017, there is a worldwide financial crash, a Huey Long–like politico threatens American politics, and a bunch of asteroids have changed their orbits and are on a collision course with Earth

Flynn, Vince

CIA counterterrorist commando and assassin Mitch Rapp is the star of a series of political thrillers. Arab terrorists taking over the White House, double-dealing and politics within the CIA, assassinations, Saddam Hussein, transfer to a desk job, loose nuclear weapons, and hits directed at Mitch himself are all part of this action-packed, suspenseful series.

1. *Transfer of Power* (Pocket Books, 1999) Posing as wealthy campaign contributors, a group of Arab terrorists takes over the White House. The president escapes to his bunker, leaving the weak-willed yet power-hungry vice president in charge as the terrorists take almost 100 hostages and start making demands.
2. *Third Option, The* (Pocket Books, 2000) Mitch Rapp, assigned to Europe, has to deal with hostile CIA colleagues following the assassination of a wealthy German count who has been selling arms to Saddam Hussein.
3. *Separation of Power* (Atria, 2001) As upright CIA agent Dr. Irene Kennedy is tapped to head the CIA, reports surface that Saddam Hussein has acquired nuclear weapons components from North Korea and is assembling them in a factory buried underneath a hospital in Baghdad.
4. *Executive Power* (Atria, 2003) Recently married to a high-profile anchorwoman and given a desk job, Mitch feels cut off from field operations. But then an operative named David concocts a plot to assassinate the heads of major terrorist groups in the Middle East and pin the deaths on Israel.
5. *Memorial Day* (Atria, 2004) A plot is afoot to sneak a nuclear weapon into the United States. Mitch Rapp, back in the saddle again, unearths the bomb plot during a commando raid on an al-Qaeda stronghold in Afghanistan. But is there a second nuke?
6. *Consent to Kill* (Atria, 2005) There is a $20-million contract out on Mitch's head. Mitch is forced to battle a Saudi billionaire bent

on revenge, an ex–East German Stasi spy, a deadly husband-and-wife team of assassins, and the new national director of intelligence.

7. *Act of Treason* **(Atria, 2006)** An al-Qaeda-style bomb attack on the motorcade of the Democratic presidential candidate a month before the November election kills the candidate's wife and several Secret Service agents.

8. *Protect and Defend* **(Atria, 2007)** Mitch Rapp and CIA chief Irene Kennedy fall victim to an ambush when Mitch tries to destabilize the Iranian regime.

Foley, Gaelen

I. Pittsburgh native Gaelen Foley has become, within a few years, one the most popular and well-regarded authors of romance novels. Her first series, the Ascension trilogy, takes place in and around the mythical Italian island kingdom of Ascension in the late 1700s and early 1800s and features members of the de Fiore family. The de Fiores are a passionate bunch, and so are the women with whom they become enmeshed.

1. *Pirate Prince, The* **(Ballantine, 1998)** In 1785 Lazar de Fiore, only survivor of the massacre of Ascension's royal family, becomes a pirate and vows revenge on the usurper Ottavio Monteverdi and his daughter Allegra. But then, Lazar meets Allegra.

2. *Princess* **(Ballantine, 1999)** In 1805 Lazare de Fiore, king of Ascension, trying to stymie Napoléon's designs on Ascension's fleets, betroths his daughter Serafina to the Russian prince Anatole Tyurinov, but Napoléon has other plans.

3. *Prince Charming* **(Ivy, 2000)** Crown Prince of Ascension, Rafael de Fiore, trailing the Masked Robber to an estate, finds the estate's mistress, Lady Daniela Chiaramonte, to be extremely desirable. But it seems that "Dani" is leading a double life.

II. The Knight Miscellany series is a series of seven Regency romances featuring the artistic English family of the Knights, the various members of whom take part in some classic Regency adventures and romances. The Knight boys, who start out as cynical rakes, turn out to be passionate lovers when they find the right woman.

1. *Duke, The* **(Ivy, 2002)** The Duke of Hawkscliffe, who will go to any lengths to unmask the mysterious murderer of his lady love, enters upon an "affair of convenience" with the beautiful and notorious Belinda Hamilton, who has some dark secrets of her own.

2. *Lord of Fire* **(Ivy, 2002)** Twenty-one-year-old spinster Alice Montague, trying to rescue her sister-in-law Caro, encounters the rakish Lord Lucien Knight, who is, in reality, one of England's premier spies.

3. *Lord of Ice* **(Ivy, 2002)** Damien Knight, Earl of Winterley, twin brother to Lucien of number 2, tormented by war memories, becomes the guardian of Miranda FitzHubert, who turns out to be somewhat more than a homeless waif.

4. *Lady of Desire* **(Ivy, 2002)** Lady Jacinda Knight, defying her eldest brother and guardian by running away to avoid an arranged marriage, runs into purse-snatcher Billy Blade, who is really the estranged son of the Earl of Rackford.

5. *Devil Takes a Bride* **(Ivy, 2004)** Lizzie Carlisle, a companion to the rich, elderly Lady Augusta Strathmore, lures Augusta's nephew, Devlin "Devil" Strathmore, to his aunt's side, but Devil has some scores to settle with the infamous Horse and Chariot club, members of whom murdered his family 12 years earlier.

6. *One Night of Sin* **(Ivy, 2005)** An "all-consuming night of sin" links Lord Alec Knight, a rake who is, unbeknownst to himself, really

searching for true love, and Becky Ward, who is fleeing from her sinister cousin, Prince Mikhail Kurkov.

7. *His Wicked Kiss* **(Ballantine, 2006)** In a romance enfolding in the jungles of Venezuela, British native Eden Farraday, who finds herself stuck in the middle of nowhere as her father searches for medicinal plants, stows aboard the London-bound ship of rakish Lord Jack Knight, black sheep of the Knight family.

Ford, Ford Madox

I. In addition to his masterpiece, *The Good Soldier* (Knopf, 1951; originally published in 1915), Ford Madox Ford (originally Ford Madox Hueffer) wrote 31 other novels, including two series. According to his biographer Arthur Mizener, Ford claimed not to like the Fifth Queen trilogy and did not want to see it republished. But most readers will find it an authentic and gracefully drawn portrait of the court of Henry VIII with all its passion, intrigue, and tragedy. Vanguard issued the trilogy in one volume, titled *The Fifth Queen*, in 1963.

1. *Fifth Queen, The; and How She Came to Court* **(Rivers [UK], 1906)** Katherine Howard is presented as an idealist determined to reestablish the old faith in England.

2. *Privy Seal, The; His Last Venture* **(Rivers [UK], 1907)** Katherine's enemy Thomas Cromwell, the Privy Seal, is destroyed.

3. *Fifth Queen Crowned, The* **(Nash [UK], 1908)** Katherine meets downfall and death.

II. The four novels that comprise Parade's End will appeal to those who enjoyed the BBC's dramatization of Vera Brittain's memoir of the war years, *Testament of Youth*. The tetralogy concerns the same time and class and conveys the same sense of the passing of an age. The central character is Christopher Tietjens, son of a good Yorkshire family and the personification of the Edwardian ideals of reason, honor, and integrity. *Parade's End* is the title of the omnibus volume published by Knopf in 1950.

1. *Some Do Not* **(Boni, 1924)** This story begins in 1912 as Christopher's impossible wife, Sylvia, returns to him after having an affair with another man. Christopher enlists in 1916, is wounded at the front, and is sent home to recover.

2. *No More Parades* **(Boni, 1925)** Sylvia visits Christopher, who has been reassigned to a base near Rouen, and stirs up trouble.

3. *Man Could Stand Up, A* **(Boni, 1926)** Discharged after a final traumatic battle, Christopher comes home to England and his friend Valentine.

4. *Last Post* **(Boni, 1928)** In this last volume, Christopher's adjustment to civilian life is seen through the eyes of those who surround him at his country cottage.

Ford, G(erald) M.

I. Leo Waterman is one of your wisecracking but compassionate PIs straight out of the 1930s and 1940s, but located in Seattle in 1990s. Leo often calls on the "Boys," former drinking buddies who are often among the "domicile-disadvantaged" (i.e., homeless), to help with his cases. He does have a girlfriend—Rebecca, a forensic psychologist—but he never marries her. Leo Waterman can be compared with Earl Emerson's (q.v.) Seattle operative, Thomas Black. Seattle resident G. M. Ford (apparently no relation of the former president) is also the author of the Frank Corso series (see below, series II).

1. *Who in Hell Is Wanda Fuca?* **(Walker, 1995)** Introduces Seattle-based PI Leo Waterman, who is hired by mobster Tim Flood to look after his granddaughter, who has fallen in with an extremist environmental group.
2. *Cast in Stone* **(Walker, 1996)** Heck Sundstrom, a boating mentor from Leo's youth, is critically injured in a suspicious traffic accident soon after his son and daughter-in-law are blown up in a boat explosion.
3. *Bum's Rush, The* **(Walker, 1997)** Young pop star Lukkas Terry dies of a seemingly accidental heroin overdose, leaving a large estate. While tracking one of "the boys," Waterman runs into Selena Dunlap, a skid-row denizen who claims to be Lukkas's mother.
4. *Slow Burn* **(Morrow, 1998)** Food authority Sir Geoffrey Miles hires Leo to prevent steak-house-owner Jack Del Fuego from slaughtering and barbecuing Bunky, a $360,000 prize Angus steer.
5. *Last Ditch* **(Morrow, 1999)** The 30-year-old remains of gay-bashing, right-wing newspaperman Peerless Price turn up on the grounds of a mansion belonging to Leo's late father, politician Wild Bill Waterman.
6. *Deader the Better, The* **(Morrow, 2000)** Leo heads to the outback of Washington State to hang with fisherman pal J. D. Springer. Springer, who has made enemies among the locals, soon winds up as a charred corpse.

II. Ford seems to have abandoned Leo Waterman for renegade journalist Frank Corso, who has left New York City under a cloud and settled in Seattle as a reporter for the third-rate *Seattle Sun* and its proprietor, Natalie Van Der Hoven. Corso, who is a journalist with a conscience despite his reputation for fabricating stories, hooks up with heavily tattooed (courtesy of a malicious boyfriend) freelance photographer Meg Dougherty in investigating a series of complicated and nasty cases.

1. *Fury* **(Morrow, 2001)** Was Walter Leroy Himes the perpetrator of the "Trashman" crimes, a series of gruesome rapes and murders? Himes is on death row, but his principal accuser is reneging on her testimony.
2. *Black River* **(Morrow, 2002)** Frank Corso, now the prosperous writer of true-crime books, lives on board his ship berthed on Lake Union. Corso is the only journalist allowed to cover the federal trial of a Russian hoodlum accused of causing the collapse of a Los Angeles hospital, an assignment that places him and lady friend Meg in jeopardy.
3. *Blind Eye, A* **(Morrow, 2003)** Corso and Meg careen from Chicago to Avalon, Wisconsin, to a nunnery, to a mountain enclave in New Jersey, and other points in the United States after they discover the corpses of a family in an abandoned farm, one set of victims in a killing spree spanning 30 years.
4. *Red Tide* **(Morrow, 2004)** Someone has sprayed a lethal Ebola virus into a Seattle bus tunnel, killing more than 100 people, and threatens more virus dispersion to come. Corso teams up with Seattle cop Charly Hart to stop the terrorists.
5. *No Man's Land* **(Morrow, 2005)** Timothy Driver, serving life without parole in Meza Azul, America's most escape-proof prison, seizes control of the place and demands that Frank Corso, who has written about Driver, come to Arizona and negotiate for the lives of 163 hostages.
6. *Blown Away* **(Morrow, 2006)** Frank is sent by his publisher to a small Pennsylvania town to solve the cold case of a local who was killed when the bomb strapped around his neck exploded while he was presenting his demands for cash in a local bank.

Ford, Jeffrey

The Well-Built City is a dystopia where the Hitler-like Master Drachton Below rules according to the principles of physiognomy (the "science" of judging the proportions of the flesh). Cley, Physiognomist First-Class, starts out as a nasty bureaucrat who recommends anyone with less-than-perfect features for execution or the sulfur mines, but he mellows under the influence of his assistant, Arla, and becomes a rebel who helps to destroy the Well-Built City. The evil Below isn't finished, however, and future adventures in two more novels awaited Cley amid demons, mind-expanding drugs, and other fantasy accoutrements. New Jersey resident Jeffrey Ford, who has won World Fantasy and Nebula Awards for his novels and stories, displays imaginative power and humor and is fond of literary allusions and tales within tales.

1. *Physiognomy, The* **(Avon, 1997)** The Well-Built City is ripe for rebellion when Master Drachton Below sends Physiognomist First-Class Cley to the mining town of Gronus to track down a fabled white fruit stolen from the state "Church."
2. *Memoranda* **(Eos, 1999)** The Well-Built City has been destroyed, and Master Below is down but not out. Cley's idyllic life in the village of Wenau is spoiled when Below sends a sleeping sickness there.
3. *Beyond, The* **(Eos, 2001)** Cley travels with Wood, his dog, into the seas and mountains of the Beyond, where they encounter, among other things, omnivorous trees, invisible monsters, a woman encased in ice, a talking skeleton, and humanoid vegetation.

Ford, Richard

The Sportswriter, novelist and short-story writer Ford's best-known book, was widely praised for its realistic, humorous, and compassionate portrait of Frank Bascombe, a basically decent but passive man who can't make himself move out of his slough of despond. The Pulitzer Prize novel *Independence Day* found Frank several years later with a satisfactory career but with a still-tentative attitude toward personal relationships. The third novel, *The Lay of the Land,* depicts him as a 55-year-old who has entered into a "Permanent Period," a time of being, not becoming.

1. *Sportswriter, The* **(Vintage, 1986)** Once promising fiction writer turned sports reporter Frank Bascombe tries to avoid coping with his son's death by distracting himself with extramarital affairs.
2. *Independence Day* **(Knopf, 1995)** Frank, divorced and working in real estate, takes his difficult teenage son on a trip to two sports halls of fame during the Fourth of July weekend.
3. *Lay of the Land, The* **(Knopf, 2006)** Frank's second marriage, to Sally Cladwell, isn't working out. She abandons Frank for her thought-to-be-dead first husband, and Frank has undergone treatment for prostate cancer. This novel's action unfolds during the week before Thanksgiving 2000, when Frank is ambivalently contemplating reunion with his two children.

Forester, C(ecil) S(cott)

Horatio Hornblower, the resourceful and ever valiant British naval hero who has been entertaining readers since 1937, shows no sign of losing his audience. Endowed with a few humanizing flaws—he is shy, tone deaf, and inclined to self-doubt—Hornblower is otherwise incomparable—good, brave, intelligent, and handsome as well. There are 11 books in the series, one of which was published posthumously, as well as the delightful *Hornblower Companion* (Little, 1964), which contains maps, bits of relevant naval history, and a long essay by Forester on the creation of the Hornblower saga. Forester fans will not want to miss C. Northcote Parkinson's (q.v.) "biography" entitled *The Life and Times of Horatio Hornblower* (Little, Brown, 1970) or the series of naval adventures by that author starring Richard Delancey. There are at least four Hornblower omnibuses: *Young Hornblower* (Little, Brown, 1960; numbers 1, 2, and 5); *Captain Horatio Hornblower* (Little, Brown, 1939; numbers 6, 7, and 8); *The Indomitable Hornblower* (Little, Brown, 1963; numbers 9, 10, and 11).

Horatio Hornblower has inspired many other historical naval series, including the Aubrey/Maturin novels by Patrick O'Brian (q.v.). Forester also wrote a nonfiction account of some of the events depicted in the Hornblower series: *The Age of Fighting Sail* (Doubleday, 1956) and *The African Queen* (Little, Brown, 1935), the basis for the movie scripted by James Agee, directed by John Huston, and starring Humphrey Bogart and Katherine Hepburn. Gregory Peck starred in *Captain Horatio Hornblower*, a film made in 1951, and Hornblower has been the subject of an ITV series.

1. ***Mr. Midshipman Hornblower*** (Little, Brown, 1950) A very young Hornblower fights a duel and is captured by the Spanish during the period June 1794 to March 1798.

2. ***Lieutenant Hornblower*** (Little, Brown, 1952) Bush narrates this volume that shows how his friend Hornblower gets drawn into marriage to Maria during the period May 1800 to March 1803.

3. ***Hornblower and the Hotspur*** (Little, Brown, 1962) Between April 1803 and July 1805 Hornblower becomes a father and captures Spanish treasure.

4. ***Hornblower and the Crisis*** (Little, Brown, 1956) This last Hornblower story was described in a postscript to *The Hornblower Companion*. Forester died before it was completed. It is published here with his notes and two short stories. Forged papers and an espionage plot are the center of the action, which takes place between August and December 1805.

5. ***Hornblower and the Atropos*** (Little, Brown, 1953) Hornblower leads Nelson's funeral barge up the Thames and endures the tragic deaths of his two children between October 1805 and January 1808.

6. ***Beat to Quarters*** (Little, Brown, 1937) This was the first-published book in the series. It shows Hornblower as captain of the British frigate *Lydia* off the coast of Guatemala. This volume introduces Lady Barbara and covers the period from June to October 1808. UK title: *The Happy Return*.

7. ***Ship of the Line, A*** (Little, Brown, 1938) Hornblower sets out in HMS *Sutherland* to fight against the French squadron and is taken captive. The action takes place between May and October 1810.

8. ***Flying Colours*** (Little, Brown, 1938) Hornblower, Bush, and Brown sail a small boat down the Loire back to freedom and active service. Hornblower and Lady Barbara are finally united. The period is November 1810 to June 1811.

9. ***Commodore Hornblower*** (Little, Brown, 1945) Hornblower leads a squadron including several bomb vessels to the Baltic between May and October 1812. UK title: *The Commodore*.

10. ***Lord Hornblower*** (Little, Brown, 1946) Stormy weather and personal loss in Normandy afflict Lord Hornblower between October 1813 and May 1814.

11. ***Admiral Hornblower in the West Indies*** (Little, Brown, 1958) Back in the West Indies and with a tactful and loving Barbara, Hornblower pursues slave traders and contentious fugitives. The period is May 1821 to October 1823. UK title: *Hornblower in the West Indies*.

Forrest, Katherine V.

I. Los Angeles Police Department detective Kate Delafield was one of the first, and most popular, of the lesbian detectives. The tough and demanding Kate is leader of the homicide investigation team. She is a real professional, but is sometimes haunted by the fear that she will be "outed." She has had more than one lover during the course of the series but her personal life usually takes a back seat to her professional career. Katherine V. Forrest is also the author of the best-selling lesbian novel *Curious Wine* (Naiad, 1983).

1. ***Amateur City*** (Naiad, 1984) LAPD detective Kate Delafield and her partner Ed Taylor are looking into the murder of sales executive Fergus Parker. The only witness is Parker's coworker Ellen O'Neil, for whom Kate feels an increasing attraction

2. ***Murder at the Nightwood Bar*** (Naiad, 1987) Kate Delafield finds a lot of unanswered questions when Dory Quillan, a homeless 19-year-old addict and prostitute, is found with her head smashed in outside the Nightwood Bar, a lesbian hangout.

3. ***Beverly Malibu, The*** (Naiad, 1989) Septuagenarian Owen Sinclair, a retired movie director, has been poisoned by strychnine on Thanksgiving Day. Suspects include several people who had been "outed" as Communists by Sinclair in testimony before the House Un-American Activities Committee.

4. ***Murder by Tradition*** (Naiad, 1991) A successful gay restaurateur is stabbed to death, and Kate, as a prosecution witness, is put on the spot when the killer's attorney, the only man who knows the truth about her sexuality, prepares a "homosexual panic" defense.

5. ***Liberty Square*** (Berkley, 1996) Attending a 25th reunion, in Washington, of those she served with in Vietnam, Kate's feeling of malaise is increased when her hotel room door is sprayed with bullets, and one of the reunion guests is murdered.

6. ***Apparition Alley*** (Berkley, 1997) Kate investigates the murder of a gay LAPD cop who was about to release the names of other gays and lesbians on the force.

7. ***Sleeping Bones*** (Berkley, 1999) When an elderly man is murdered at the La Brea Tar Pits, Delafield finds herself digging up information that could uncover the ancient past as well as expose LA's corrupt present.

8. ***Hancock Park*** (Berkley, 2004) When the corpse of middle-aged matron Victoria Talbot turns up in her stately Hancock Park home, her loathsome ex-husband, Douglas Talbot, is the prime suspect.

II. Forrest is also the author of a trio of lesbian SF novels. *Daughters of a Coral Dawn* became an instant classic when it was published in 1984. Late in the 22nd century, 4,000 women escape the tyranny of male-dominated Earth and colonize the planet Maternas. *Daughters of a Coral Dawn* was followed by two sequels, the first of which related the story of the women left behind on Earth, the second of which returns to Maternas 50 years later.

1. ***Daughters of a Coral Dawn*** (Naiad, 1984) In the late 22nd century, 4,000 women escape from male-dominated Earth and set up a colony on the planet of Maternas. But, eventually, men show up.

2. ***Daughters of an Amber Noon*** (Alyson, 2002) Tells the story of a group of women on Earth called Unity, led by Africa Contrera, who have gone into hiding to escape the tyrannical rule of Zed (Theo Zedera).

3. ***Daughters of an Emerald Dusk*** (Alyson, 2005) Fifty years have passed on Maternas, and the first generation born there has reached maturity. But they find that their vision of a perfect world is very different from the vision of Maternas's founders.

Forstchen, William R.

I. The Lost Regiment is the 35th Maine Regiment, which is swept off a Civil War battlefield through a space-time warp and plunked down on alternate medieval-type world where most human beings are used by their alien masters as food and for experiments. Colonel Andrew Keane and his men make the best of their situation, try to introduce democracy and freedom in a Human Republic, and find themselves fighting again against alien hordes such as the Merki and Bantags.

1. *Rally Cry* (Roc, 1991) The 35th Maine Regiment, led by Colonel Andrew Keane, is swept by a storm through a space-warp and find themselves in an alternate world of lords and serfs in which humans are regarded as good only for food or experimentation.
2. *Union Forever, The* (Roc, 1991) Full-scale war erupts between the humans and the alien Merki leaders.
3. *Terrible Swift Sword* (Roc, 1992) The alien Merki unite against the human "cattle" and attempt to crush their rebellion.
4. *Fateful Lightning* (Roc, 1992) The Maine Yankees find themselves in tactical retreat against the Merki hordes, reenacting the Russian retreats against the French in the Napoleonic Wars and the Germans in World War II.
5. *Battle Hymn* (Roc, 1996) The men of the 35th Maine continue their battle for freedom and democracy against the alien Hordes.
6. *Never Sound Retreat* (Roc, 1997) Ten years after the Maine regiment has landed on alternate Earth, the soldiers have established a new nation, but the alien Bantag have a new leader.
7. *Band of Brothers, A* (Roc, 1999) Commander Andrew Keane is wounded in battle, and the Bantags see their opportunity to offer a truce to the two halves of the Republic: safety for one half and doom for the other half.
8. *Men of War* (Roc, 1999) After a peace parlay is declared, Keane resigns his position in the government, and he and his men prepare to wage war against the Bantag Empire for the last time.
9. *Down to the Sea* (Roc, 2000) Twenty years since the defeat of the alien Hordes, Lieutenant Michael O'Brien, pilot aboard the Republic Navy cruiser *Gettysburg*, stumbles upon a fierce naval battle between warring factions of the Kazan—cousin to the Hordes.

II. Some critics think that Forstchen's first series, the Ice Prophet trilogy, was his most remarkable and imaginative. The trilogy is set in a primitive future society in which ice covers the Earth's surface as the result of a scientific experiment gone wrong. The Cornathian Brothers rule a network of city states, and keep the populace in ignorance, but this theocracy is divided against itself. The charismatic Michael Ormson leads a fight for religious freedom and the pursuit of knowledge. The second and third volumes of this trilogy are devoted to the battle between the rebels and "the established church."

1. *Ice Prophet* (Ballantine, 1983) Michael Ormson leads the forces for religious freedom and free inquiry against the Cornathian Brothers, a theocracy that rules a primitive future society in which the Earth's surface is covered with ice.
2. *Flame upon the Ice, The* (Ballantine, 1984) Ormson and his allies control the southern islands with help of new methods of conducting warfare on ice-traveling warships.
3. *Darkness upon the Ice, A* (Ballantine, 1985) The resurgent established church attacks Ormson's army with devices from their secret laboratories.

III. The Gamester Wars trilogy describes a world in which Alexander the Great, Japanese Samurai warriors, and Napoléon are brought into the far future by alien intelligences who are betting on the outcome of the ensuing battles.

1. *Alexandrian Ring, The* (Ballantine, 1987) Alexander the Great is brought to a far future where he is pitted against another, fictional, time traveler.
2. *Assassin Gambit, The* (Ballantine, 1988) A legion of Samurai warriors are brought to the "Hole" to help resolve the conflict.
3. *Napoleon Wager, The* (Ballantine, 1993) In an artificial world designed to re-create the Napoleonic Era, alien intelligences bet on the outcome of a reenacted Battle of Waterloo.

IV. Two novels, coauthored with Greg Morrison, feature Mark Phillips and Ikawa Yoshio, opponents in World War II China, who are magically kidnapped to the alternate world of Haven, where they become allied in service to Allic, Prince of Landra.

Forstchen, who has a PhD in history, is also the coauthor, with Newt Gingrich (q.v.), of the Gettysburg trilogy. He has authored the Star Voyager YA trilogy and contributed a volume to Raymond E. Feist's (q.v.) Riftwar series, several volumes to the multiauthor Wing Commander series, a volume to the Magic: The Gathering game series, to the Shattered Light series (with Jaki Demarest), and to the Star Trek: The Next Generation series.

1. *Crystal Warriors, The* (Avon, 1988) American Mark Phillips and Japanese Ikawa Yoshio are abducted to the alternate world of Haven where they become allies in the service of Allic, Prince of Landra. Coauthored with Greg Morrison.
2. *Crystal Sorcerers, The* (Avon, 1991) Phillips and Yoshio unite again to fight the demon-lord Gorgon on behalf of Allic and his demigod relatives. Coauthored with Greg Morrison.

Foster, Alan Dean

I. The series featuring the genetically altered Flinx, who has psi powers, and Pip, Flinx's pet mini dragon, is probably the most popular one written by SF author Alan Dean Foster. Flinx, an orphan who is searching for news of his lost parents, is, like Fritz Leiber's (q.v.) Gray Mouser and Harry Harrison's (q.v.) Jim di-Griz, a thief and a rogue but basically sympathetic. His adventures in the Humanx Commonwealth (see also series II, series III, and series IV, below), despite the fact that Flinx feels called upon to save civilization, are lighthearted on the whole. More volumes in the Pip and Flinx series are planned. American author Alan Dean Foster is responsible for the Alien series, three novelizations of the movies, collected in *The Complete Alien Omnibus* (Warner, 1993), and has contributed volumes to several multiauthor series, including Star Trek Log, Star Wars, Alien Nation, and Dinotopia. Robert Teague's *A Guide to the Commonwealth* (Galagraphics, 1985) is now somewhat out of date.

1. *Tar-Aiym Krang, The* (Ballantine, 1972) The orphaned teenager Flinx and his mini-dragon pal, Pip, leave home and travel into outer space.
2. *Bloodhype* (Ballantine, 1973) Pip and Flinx fight a secret drug cartel that has reintroduced one of the deadliest drugs in the universe.
3. *Orphan Star* (Ballantine, 1977) Pip and Flinx search the galaxy for clues about Flinx's birth.
4. *End of the Matter, The* (Ballantine, 1977) Pip and Flinx visit Pip's home planet, as Flinx learns that they are being trailed by assassins and that a collapsing star is threatening the balance of the universe.
5. *For Love of Mother-Not* (Del Rey, 1983) Flinx tries to rescue the woman who saved him from a life of slavery at the hands of pirates after she is kidnapped.

6. *Flinx in Flux* **(Del Rey, 1988)** Flinx is torn between commitment and noncommitment when he falls in love with Clarity Held, a girl in need of help.

7. *Mid-Flinx* **(Del Rey, 1995)** While visiting the planet Samstead, Flinx and Pip run into the acquisitive Jax-Jax Landsdowne Coerlis, who wants Pip for his zoo.

8. *Reunion* **(Del Rey, 2001)** Seeking information about the Meliorare Society, a sect of renegade eugenicists who experiment on humans, Flinx and Pip venture into a top-secret security installation on Earth.

9. *Flinx's Folly* **(Del Rey, 2003)** Pip and Flinx find themselves enlisted in a battle against a really nasty extra-galactic threat.

10. *Sliding Scales* **(Del Rey, 2004)** Flinx decides to take a vacation, a mission harder than it sounds.

11. *Running from the Deity* **(Del Rey, 2005)** A Great Darkness threatens to overtake the entire universe.

12. *Trouble Magnet* **(Del Rey, 2006)** Flinx and Pip journey to the criminal-run planet of Visaria and, while there, rescue a teenage gang member named Subar.

13. *Patrimony* **(Del Rey, 2007)** Flinx has traced his origins to the planet Gestalt, thanks to the dying words of a survivor from the Meliorare Society.

II. Another series set in the Humanx Commonwealth is the Icerigger trilogy, which is set round and about the ice world of Tran-Ky-Ky.

1. *Icerigger* **(Ballantine, 1974)** A crash landing on the ice world of Tran-Ky-Ky starts a small band of humans on a perilous journey for survival.

2. *Mission to Moulokin* **(Del Rey, 1979)** Two men plan to abduct a tycoon and his daughter from a space liner in orbit around Tran-Ky-Ky.

3. *Deluge Drivers, The* **(Del Rey, 1987)** Some one has figured out how to raise the temperature on Tran-Ky-Ky and make the ice world suitable for colonization.

III. Another rather loosely connected series is set on various planets in the Humanx Commonwealth.

1. *Midworld* **(Ballantine, 1975)** The peaceful Born on the planet Midworld find themselves invaded by apparently friendly alien beings.

2. *Cachalot* **(Del Rey, 1980)** The great sea creatures, who were nearly destroyed by humans, seem to be taking their revenge.

3. *Nor Crystal Tears* **(Del Rey, 1982)** The Thranx find that the raiders who attacked their home world are pussycats compared to humans.

4. *Voyage to the City of the Dead* **(Del Rey, 1984)** The Redowls have a unique opportunity to study alien languages and cultures on the planet Hourseye, home to three different cultures.

5. *Sentenced to Prism* **(Del Rey, 1985)** A survey team sent to the planet Prism mysteriously disappears, and Evan Orgell, the Company's foremost problem solver, is sent there to investigate.

6. *Howling Stones, The* **(Del Rey, 1997)** Pulickel Tomochelo, sent to the newly discovered planet Senisran to arrange a treaty with the aboriginal Seni, refuses to believe, at first, in the power of the Seni's sacred stones.

7. *Drowning World* **(Del Rey, 2003)** The planet Fluva is called the Drowning World because of its torrential rains. Chief Administrator Lauren Matthias has the job of keeping the planet's two species, the Sakuntala and the Deyzara, from destroying each other.

IV. The origin of the Humanx Commonwealth is treated in a trilogy of novels that examines the factors that led to its creation.

1. *Phylogenesis* **(Del Rey, 1999)** The chance meeting of an alien poet and a human thief threatens the stability of the allegiances that will eventually form the Humanx Commonwealth, an intergalactic political entity.

2. *Dirge* **(Del Rey, 2000)** The uneasy alliance between humans and Thranx is tested as they try to defeat a common enemy, the dread Pitar.

3. *Diuturnity's Dawn* **(Del Rey, 2002)** Idealists among the humans and Thranx are still dreaming of an alliance, but others are dead set against it.

V. The Spellsinger series is a mixture of light adventure with humor. Jonathan Thomas Meriweather (Jon-Tom) is whisked to another world by the turtle wizard Clothahump, where he joins Clothahump and his motley band of humans and animals in a battle against an ancient evil. Omnibus editions: *Season of the Spellsong* (Doubleday, 1984; numbers 1–3); *Spellsong's Scherzo* (Doubleday, 1987; numbers 4–6); and *Spellsinger at the Gate* (Phantasia, 1983; numbers 1–2).

1. *Spellsinger* **(Warner, 1983)** Graduate student and guitarist Jonathan Thomas Meriweather is magically transferred to another world by the turtle-wizard Clothahump, where he becomes Jon-Tom in the battle against some sinister enemies.

2. *Hour of the Gate, The* **(Warner, 1983)** Jon-Tom, Clothahump, Mudge the Otter, Talea and their associates embark on a suicide mission to the center of the earth.

3. *Day of the Dissonance, The* **(Phantasia, 1984)** Jon-Tom and his companions face a variety of enemies, including faeries and pirates, as he travels across the landscape trying to figure out his place in an alien world.

4. *Moment of the Magician, The* **(Phantasia, 1984)** A cunning new sorcerer poses danger to the Spellsinger and his allies.

5. *Paths of the Perambulator, The* **(Phantasia, 1985)** The Perambulator, a freak of supernature, enters Jon-Tom's world.

6. *Time of the Transference, The* **(Phantasia, 1986)** In the conclusion (for a while) to the Spellsinger series, Jon-Tom, his powerful "duar" broken, has his magical powers aborted, at least temporarily.

7. *Son of Spellsinger* **(Warner, 1993)** The Spellsinger saga is revived with the spellsinging group of Buncan Meriweather, Squill, and Neena, who rescue the merchant Gragelouth, who proposes a quest to find the Grand Veritable, the greatest threat to the world.

8. *Chorus Skating* **(Warner, 1994)** Jon-Tom and Mudge the Otter encounter a displaced "grunge band" who claim that someone named Hieronymus Mickel is stealing their music.

VI. The Chronicles of the Catechist is a trilogy wherein the herdsman Etjole Ehomba, because of a vow to a dying man, travels, with many vicissitudes, to rescue a captive princess in the kingdom ruled by Hymneth the Possessed. *Journey of the Catechist* (Warner, 2000) is an omnibus volume containing all three novels.

1. *Carnivores of Light and Darkness* **(Warner, 1998)** Herdsman Etjole Ehomba vows to a dying stranger that he will travel north to rescue a captive Visioness.

2. *Into the Thinking Kingdoms* **(Warner, 1998)** Etjole Ehomba and his motley group continue their quest to rescue the captive Visioness.

3. *Triumph of Souls, A* (**Warner, 2000**) Ignoring warnings that Ehomba will meet death at the hands of Hymneth the Possessed, the travelers reach the kingdom ruled by the evil wizard.

VII. In the military SF trilogy called the Damned, Earthlings are drawn into the fight between the Weave and their longtime enemies, the Amplitur.

1. *Call to Arms, A* (**Del Rey, 1991**) The Weave, seeking allies against their longtime foes the Amplitur, stumble across Earth and the composer Will Dulac. Although Will (rather disingenuously) says that Earth men dislike war, humanity is drawn into the struggle.
2. *False Mirror, The* (**Del Rey, 1992**) Ranji, discovering that he is of human ancestry, returns to his people and leads them in joining with other humans in the Weave.
3. *Spoils of War, The* (**Del Rey, 1993**) Weave expert on humans, Wais Scholar Historian Lalelang, travels among humans at the risk to her sanity.

VIII. In Foster's latest series, Taken, Chicago commodities trader Marcus Walker is abducted by aliens who plan to sell him as a "cute" pet in civilized regions of the galaxy. Marcus and the speech-enhanced dog, George, escape and try to find their way home through a series of mishaps and adventures.

1. *Lost and Found* (**Del Rey, 2004**) Marcus Walker is abducted by aliens and becomes part of a cargo of "primitive" and "cute" beings destined to be sold as pets to civilized regions of the galaxy.
2. *Light-Years beneath My Feet* (**Del Rey, 2005**) Marcus and the speech-enhanced dog, George, escape from their abductors but are still light years from Earth.
3. *Candle of Distant Earth, The* (**Del Rey, 2006**) Marcus and George land on the planet Hyff, where they help the Hyfft battle the invaders known as the Iollth.

Fowler, Christopher

Arthur Bryant and John May are elderly detectives in Scotland Yard's Peculiar Crimes Unit, which tries to solve locked-room murders and other untoward deaths. The series starts off, in odd fashion, with the death of the 80-year-old Bryant in an explosion, then flashes back to Bryant and May's first case, set in late 1940. Some reviewers feel that this series is a successful revival of the "impossible crimes" subgenre, and Fowler, who was best known for his horror fiction, is in the "first rank of contemporary mystery writers" (*Publishers Weekly*).

1. *Full Dark House* (**Bantam, 2004**) After 80-year-old police detective Arthur Bryant gets blown up in an explosion at the North London Peculiar Crimes Unit, John May, his longtime partner, investigates his death. A flashback takes the pair to their first case, during the London Blitz in 1940, when the footless body of a dancer is found.
2. *Water Room, The* (**Bantam, 2005**) A former colleague asks Bryant to investigate the death of his sister, who was found dead in her basement, apparently drowned, with no moisture on her body or her surroundings.
3. *Seventy-seven Clocks* (**Bantam, 2005**) Bryant and May investigate some Peculiar Crimes specialty cases: victims killed by snake bite, toxic makeup, and a starved tiger in rather strange places. These crimes all seem to have a connection with the strange Whitstable family, whose Victorian patriarch founded a group called the Alliance of Eternal Light.
4. *Ten Second Staircase* (**Bantam, 2006**) Bryant and May must resolve a cold case featuring the Leicester Square Vampire, whose victims included May's own daughter, and identify the Highwayman, whose specialty is locked-room murders of hated celebrities.
5. *White Corridor* (**Bantam, 2007**) Bryant and May find themselves trapped on the road near Dartmoor in a blizzard, with a possible multiple murderer in their midst.

Fowler, Earlene

Benni Harper, ex-cowgirl, quilter, and folk art expert, takes a job as curator of the San Celina, California (based on San Luis Obispo), folk-art museum after she is widowed and soon finds herself mixed up in a series of murder cases. Gabe Ortiz, chief of police in San Celina, objects to her involvement at first but eventually finds himself to be Benni's second husband. This is a breezy and humorous mystery series, all of whose titles are taken from quilting patterns. *The Saddlemaker's Wife* (Berkley, 2006) isn't a Benni Harper novel.

1. *Fool's Puzzle* (**Berkley, 1994**) Thirty-four-year-old recent widow Benni Harper takes a job as curator at the San Celina folk art museum. A local artist is murdered on the premises of the museum and, when Benni's cousin becomes a suspect, she gets involved in the case despite the objections of local police chief Gabe Ortiz.
2. *Irish Chain* (**Berkley, 1995**) Benni, again contrary to the objections of her now-boyfriend Gabe, investigates when the San Celina Senior Citizen Prom king is murdered, and turns up some dark secrets going back to World War II and the internment of Japanese Americans.
3. *Kansas Troubles* (**Berkley, 1996**) After marrying Gabe Ortiz, Benni accompanies him to his hometown in Kansas, only to find herself embroiled in another murder mystery.
4. *Goose in the Pond* (**Berkley, 1997**) The local library storyteller is found facedown in the lake, dressed in a Mother Goose costume.
5. *Dove in the Window* (**Berkley, 1998**) When photographer Shelby Johnson is murdered during the San Celina Heritage Days celebration, of course Benni has to become involved.
6. *Mariner's Compass* (**Berkley, 1999**) Jacob Chandler seemed to know everything about Benni Harper, but she had never even heard of Jacob Chandler. So, when Jacob dies, and leaves his house in Morro Bay and all its contents to Benni, with the stipulation that she has to stay in the house alone, for two weeks, before the inheritance is hers, she is somewhat nonplussed.
7. *Seven Sisters* (**Berkley, 2000**) When a member of the wealthy but feud-ridden Brown family is murdered, Benni uncovers some dark secrets.
8. *Arkansas Traveler* (**Berkley, 2001**) Benni, back in Sugartree, Arkansas, with her friend Elvira, discovers that racism is raising its ugly head again when two churches merge and a black woman runs for mayor.
9. *Steps to the Altar* (**Berkley, 2002**) Benni prepares for two upcoming weddings, digs up clues to a decades-old unsolved murder, and struggles with a personal crisis.
10. *Sunshine and Shadow* (**Berkley, 2003**) Benni's memories are brought back to 1978 and a closer look at her college days and her first husband, Jack, as she traces the connection between her favorite author, the murder of a family friend, and a crazy quilt.
11. *Broken Dishes* (**Berkley, 2004**) When her friends inherit the Broken DIS ranch and turn it into a dude ranch, Benni finds herself returning to her horseback days while helping them out. Then the remains of a long-dead murdered man are turned up from a shallow grave on the ranch.

12. *Delectable Mountains* (Berkley, 2005) Benni is volunteered to take over the musical direction of a children's play at her church. Then she finds the badly beaten body of the church handyman right in front of the altar.

13. *Tumbling Blocks* (Berkley, 2007) Was Arva "Pinky" Edmondson murdered by one of the local socialites vying for admittance to the exclusive 49 Club, as Benni's boss, Constance Sinclair, insists?

Francis, Dick

I. Though Francis has written many horsey puzzlers, only four of them are about Sid Halley, the ex-jockey whose detecting was featured on public television's *Mystery!* When an accident cripples one of his hands and ends his jockeying days. Halley finds work at the Radnor Agency as a specialist in their racing-investigation section. His first case offers action enough to take his mind off his ruined career and failed marriage. *Sid Halley Omnibus* (Pan [UK], 2002) contains numbers 1, 2, and 3.

1. *Odds Against* (Harper, 1965) Halley's first case involves stock manipulators who want to sell a racecourse.

2. *Whip Hand* (Harper, 1979) With his new battery-powered hand, Halley is hired to guard a friend's racehorse.

3. *Come to Grief* (Putnam, 1995) Thoroughbred racehorses are being savagely mutilated, and the trail seems to lead to Ellis Quint, respected ex-jockey and one of Sid's oldest friends.

4. *Under Orders* (Putnam, 2006) After an 11-year hiatus, Sid Halley returns to action, as he responds to the request of a mysterious government figure who asks him to assess the unintended consequences of Internet gambling.

II. Kit Fielding, "a knight in racing colors," practices Dick Francis's old profession of steeplechase jockeying. Kit also gets involved in detecting when necessary to help friends, relatives, and business associates.

1. *Break In* (Putnam, 1986) Kit comes to the aid of his twin sister, Holly, and her husband, horse trainer Bobby Allardeck, who are victims of a slander campaign.

2. *Bolt* (Putnam, 1987) Princess Casilia, Kit's employer, needs help when ruthless Henri Nanterre tries to turn her industrial empire into a munitions works.

Frankau, Pamela

The Clothes of a King's Son trilogy tells of the whole Weston family and their many friends and associates, but the central figure is the son Thomas. He is 10 as the story begins and spending the summer of 1926 with his father's theatrical troupe at the English seaside resort of Sawcombe. Thomas has psychic powers and, though all of his adventures are capable of rational explanation, they have an element of magic to them. Frankau shares the talent many English authors have for writing about families, and especially children, with humor and understanding.

1. *Sing for Your Summer* (Random House, 1963) Young Thomas, 14-year-old Sara, and 16-year-old Gerald are the children of widower Philip Weston, impecunious head of a theatrical troupe. Nanny Briggs looks after them all.

2. *Slaves of the Lamp* (Random House, 1965) Tom narrates this installment set against the background of the London theater and advertising worlds. Sara is now a writer, and Gerald is an actor.

3. *Over the Mountains* (Random House, 1967) Tom sees service in World War II and capture at Dunkirk, escapes, and meets his childhood sweetheart, Rob, again.

Franken, Rose

For a good, old-fashioned wallow in nostalgia, try reading or rereading the Claudia books that were so popular during the forties. No less a light than Diana Trilling admitted to enjoying Franken's unpretentious books more than many more serious novels. Though she criticized Claudia's "adorably feminine" ignorance of geography, insurance, and wartime politics (*Nation*, May 22, 1943), she also praised Franken's ability to fill every page with the "recognizable details of day-to-day living." *The Book of Claudia* (Farrar, 1950) contains numbers 1 and 2.

1. *Claudia: The Story of a Marriage* (Farrar, 1939) Claudia at 18 is the young wife of architect David Naughton. In this volume, David and Claudia weather in-law problems and budget problems, welcome their first child, and move to a farmhouse in Connecticut.

2. *Claudia and David* (Farrar, 1940) Claudia and David now have two boys. They decide to move back to New York for the sake of David's career, but Claudia continues to suppress her stage ambitions.

3. *Another Claudia* (Farrar, 1943) The war years bring Claudia a new maturity.

4. *Young Claudia* (Rinehart, 1946) Claudia keeps up the farm until David's return from the war.

5. *Marriage of Claudia, The* (Rinehart, 1948) The Connecticut farm is sold, the Naughtons move to New York, and David contracts tuberculosis.

6. *From Claudia to David* (Harper, 1960) David, recovering from TB, Claudia, their three children, and the maid Bertha rent a cottage in the Adirondacks.

7. *Fragile Years, The* (Doubleday, 1952) Claudia faces a series of tragedies including the death of her eldest son and David's illness. UK titles: *Those Fragile Years* and *The Return of Claudia*.

8. *Antic Years, The* (Doubleday, 1958) Beneficiaries of a legacy, Claudia, David, their two remaining children, and the faithful Bertha take a vacation to Europe.

Franklin, Miles

The success of the superb Australian film *My Brilliant Career* prompted the reissue of both of Miles Franklin's semi-autobiographical novels. Each novels has had a checkered career. *My Brilliant Career*, written in Australia, was published by Blackwood (Edinburgh & London) in 1901, won some acclaim in Australia as an example of a "real" Australian novel by an Australian, then was out of print for many years until Angus & Robertson reprinted it in 1965. In the wake of the film's success, Virago and St. Martin's published it in the United States in 1980, and it was touted by some critics as a "feminist classic." *The End of My Career* sat in a trunk for 40 years until it was published by Angus & Robertson in 1946 as *My Career Goes Bung*. Franklin's spunky young heroine, Sybylla, is an early feminist in Victorian Australia, where prim conventions contrast oddly with primitive conditions. In her determination to remain unhobbled by marriage, she must resist society's pressures and the temptations of her own weaker moments.

1. *My Brilliant Career* (St. Martin's, 1980) Country girl Sybylla, polished by her sophisticated city relatives, becomes a marriageable young lady, but her writing ambitions and her feminist conscience interfere. First published in 1901.

2. *End of My Career, The* (St. Martin's, 1981) The success of her book takes Sybylla from Possum Gully to Sydney and further trials and triumphs. First published in 1946. UK title: *My Career Goes Bung*.

Fraser, Anthea

I. English mystery writer Anthea Fraser, not to be confused with Antonia Fraser (q.v.) (no relation), is the author of a long-running puzzle mystery series featuring Detective Chief Inspector David Webb of Stillingham, England. Although Webb has a private life of sorts, in the form of his lady friend Hannah, most of the interest in these mysteries is in the puzzle plots and the delineation of a not-quite-rural England. Several of Anthea Frazer's nonseries mysteries have gothic overtones. She also publishes under the pseudonym of Vanessa Graham.

1. *Shroud for Delilah, A* (Doubleday, 1986) When recently separated Kate Romilly moves into a flat with her small son and begins a new job at Pennyfarthings, an antique shop, she is unaware that someone is killing divorcées nearby, leaving the name "Delilah" scrawled in lipstick on the victim's mirror. Originally published in the United Kingdom in 1984.

2. *Necessary End, A* (Walker, 1986) "Each member of Nancy Pendrick's family held one piece of the puzzle and it was Chief Inspector Webb's challenge to fit them together—for a picture of her killer" (publisher's blurb). Not to be confused with other books of the same title, such as Peter Robinson's (q.v.) Inspector Banks mystery.

3. *Pretty Maids All in a Row* (Doubleday, 1987) Actress Jessica Randal and her recently wed husband, Matthew Shelby, think that they will find tranquility in a cottage near the rustic English village of Westridge. However, there is a rapist and murderer at work. Nothing to do with the Roger Vadim movie of the same name (1971).

4. *Death Speaks Softly* (Doubleday, 1987) Inspector Webb repairs the rift in his relationship with Hannah, searches for a missing French girl, locates her broken-necked body, and traces the movements of her assumed killer.

5. *Nine Bright Shiners, The* (Doubleday, 1988) A rather complicated procedural reaching all the way to Peru, as recently separated Jan Coverdale is left in charge of her half brother's house in Broadminster as he and his wife take off for South America

6. *Six Proud Walkers* (Doubleday, 1989) The tranquil English village of Honeyford, home of the wealthy and prestigious Walker family, is also the location where more than one Walker is found murdered.

7. *April Rainers, The* (Doubleday, 1990) Who are the April Rainers? And why are they taking the law into their own hands?

8. *Symbols at Your Door* (Doubleday, 1991) Five houses in the remote village of Beckworth are defaced by graffiti featuring pictures of a leering gargoyle head. Then murder ensues.

9. *I'll Sing You Two-O* (St. Martin's, 2000) The bodies of two young men, twins, are found in an abandoned van outside the home of magistrate Monica Tovey. Originally published in the United Kingdom in 1991 as *The Lily-White Boys*.

10. *Three, Three, the Rivals* (St. Martin's, 1995) Old rivalries and mysteries are stirred up when Billy Makepeace is murdered in Inspector Webb's hometown. Originally published in the United Kingdom in 1991.

11. *Gospel Makers, The* (St. Martin's, 1996) Detective Inspector Nina Petrie, a psychologically frail single mother, is assigned by Webb to investigate a new religious cult, which may be involved in murder. Originally published in the United Kingdom in 1994.

12. *Seven Stars, The* (St. Martin's, 1997) Helen Campbell, staying at the Seven Stars Guest House, gets involved with the lives of the Seven Stars' proprietors and guests and gets enmeshed in a series of estate break-ins and murder that Inspector Webb is investigating. Originally published in the United Kingdom in 1995.

13. *One Is One and All Alone* (St. Martin's, 1998) Webb is seeking four young thieves whose violence seems to be escalating. Then his colleague DCI Bennett is found bludgeoned to death in his own home. Originally published in the United Kingdom in 1996.

14. *Ten Commandments, The* (St. Martin's, 2000) Elderly criminologist Frederick Mace becomes inadvertently involved while plugging his new book, as a man's body is discovered in a pub parking lot in a mystery with similarities to a six-year-old unsolved case.

15. *Eleven That Went to Heaven* (Severn House, 1999) "When Richard Vine, wealthy businessman and proprietor of Beckworth Grange, organizes a publicity event with 20 guests who all share his name, he little imagines that a few hours later nine of them would be dead" (publisher's blurb).

16. *Twelve Apostles, The* (Severn House, 2000) Verity Ryder is up to her neck when she witnesses the death of a clergyman who whispers, as his last words, "The Twelve Apostles."

II. David Webb has been abandoned, at least temporarily, for journalist, biographer, and amateur detective Rona Parish. Rona is married to an artist, Max Parish, and her mysteries take place mostly in the English countryside.

1. *Brought to Book* (Severn House, 2003) Best-selling author Theo Harvey, who led a colorful life and died in mysterious circumstances, seems like a good subject for successful biographer Rona Parish's next book.

2. *Jigsaw* (Severn House, 2004) Rona Parish, about to embark on a series of articles to coincide with the 500th anniversary of the local market town of Buckford, evokes some unanswered questions about a recent murder.

3. *Person or Persons Unknown* (Severn House, 2005) A young woman named Zara Crane approaches Rona with a request to help her trace her biological parents. Seems that Zara's birth mother was murdered in her bath 25 years earlier.

4. *Family Concern, A* (Severn House, 2006) Kate, an old friend, gets Rona involved in researching the histories of several established family firms in the town of Marsborough, including the Tarltons, a family Kate has married into.

5. *Rogue in Porcelain* (Severn House, 2007) While interviewing various Curzons, manufacturers of porcelain, for the celebration of their company's 150th anniversary and the unveiling of a new product line, Rona unearths a "skeleton" in the firm's archives and then stumbles upon the fresh corpse of a woman she knows.

Fraser, Antonia

British biographer and historian Antonia Fraser, author of *Marie Antoinette: The Journey* (Doubleday, 2001) and best-selling biographies of Tudor and Stuart figures, writes mystery stories as a change of pace. Her amateur sleuth, Londoner Jemima Shore, is the star of her own television program, *Jemima Shore—Investigator*. Jemima is intelligent, cool-headed, and stylish, living the life of a media celebrity with a married lover. The mysteries are brisk and satisfying, with just the right touch of satire. *Jemima Shore's First Case and Other Stories* (Norton,

1987) is a collection of 17 stories, 4 of which feature Jemima Shore. *Jemima Shore at the Sunny Grave and Other Stories* (Bantam, 1993) is a collection of 9 short stories, 4 of them featuring Jemima Shore. Two British omnibuses are *Three Great Novels* (Orion, 2005; numbers 1–3) and *Jemima Shore on the Case* (Orion, 2006; numbers 4–6).

1. *Quiet as a Nun* (Viking, **1977**) Jemima investigates the death of an old schoolmate at Blessed Eleanor's Convent in Sussex.
2. *Wild Island, The* (Norton, **1978**) On holiday in the Scottish Highlands, Jemima gets caught up in a family feud and a zany cabal of neo-Jacobites. Variant title: *Tartan Tragedy*.
3. *Splash of Red, A* (Norton, **1981**) Jemima agrees to "flat-and-cat sit" for author Chloe Fontaine, but Chloe doesn't leave her building alive.
4. *Cool Repentance* (Norton, **1982**) Actress Christabel Cartwright returns to her family after an affair with a young rock star and is scheduled to appear at a local drama festival that Jemima is televising.
5. *Oxford Blood* (Norton, **1985**) A nursemaid's deathbed confession concerning switched babies starts Jemima on a quest for an heir's true parentage.
6. *Your Royal Hostage* (Atheneum, **1988**) Jemima covers the impending royal wedding of Princess Amy of Cumberland, while a group of animal rights activists plot to kidnap Princess Amy.
7. *Cavalier Case, The* (Bantam, **1991**) The ghost of a 17th-century poet gets involved with an upscale tennis club and modern London society.
8. *Political Death* (Bantam, **1996**) Down on her luck former beauty Lady Imogen Swain offers to reveal to Jemima what happened to Franklyn Faber, who vanished during the middle of his 1964 trial for selling state secrets.

Fraser, George MacDonald

I. Harry Flashman, the cad who bullied the younger boys in Thomas Hughes's classic *Tom Brown's School Days* (1857), has been resurrected for these funny, sophisticated picaresque novels. Purporting to be Flashman's own memoirs (edited by Fraser), they relate his adventures in the most glowing terms and detail his many amorous conquests. Of course he is a thorough coward and bounder, perhaps the ultimate antihero, but that makes his adventures all the more interesting. Fraser provides vivid historical backgrounds without ever becoming dull, and his satire has the perfect light touch. One of the inspirations for Flashman was Conan Doyle's (q.v.) Brigadier Gerard. Fraser wrote the introduction for the republication of *The Exploits and Adventures of Brigadier Gerard* (New York Review, 2001). Two novels, though not part of the *Flashman Papers*, involve Harry peripherally. *Mr. American* (Simon & Schuster, 1980), which describes a mysterious American who invades Edwardian society, has the elderly Sir Harry in a cameo role (according to hints in the *Papers*, Flashman lives on to 1915). *Black Ajax* (Carroll & Graf, 1998) has Harry's father, General Flashman, describe his role in arranging the championship boxing match between American ex-slave Tom Molyneaux and English champion Tom Cribb. *Flashman's First Omnibus* (Barrie & Jenkins [UK], 1979) contains numbers 1, 2, and 5.

1. *Flashman: From the Flashman Papers, 1839–1842* (World, **1969**) This book gives a "true" account of Flashman's expulsion from school and of the beginning of his career in the 11th Light Dragoons under the Earl of Cardigan in India.
2. *Royal Flash: From the Flashman Papers, 1842–43 and 1847–48* (Knopf, **1970**) Flashman poses as Prince Carl Gustav and loses a fortune in jewels in this volume, which features Otto von Bismarck and Lola Montez and ties in with Anthony Hope's (q.v.) *Prisoner of Zenda*.
3. *Flashman's Lady: From the Flashman Papers, 1842–45* (Knopf, **1978**) Flashman's wife, the beautiful but dim-witted Elspeth, is kidnapped by a pirate. Extracts from Elspeth's diaries are a new treat.
4. *Flashman and the Mountain of Light: From the Flashman Papers, 1845–46* (Knopf, **1991**) Although he finds himself with the outnumbered British forces facing the Sikhs in the Punjab, Flashman survives again.
5. *Flash for Freedom! From the Flashman Papers, 1848–49* (Knopf, **1972**) At midcentury, Flashman becomes involved in the slave trade, comes to America, and runs into Abraham Lincoln, among others.
6. *Flashman and the Redskins: From the Flashman Papers, 1849–50 and 1875–76* (Knopf, **1982**) In New Orleans under an alias in 1849, Flashman marries a brothel-keeper, goes west as a wagon master, and eventually survives the Battle of Little Big Horn in 1876.
7. *Flashman at the Charge: From the Flashman Papers, 1854–55* (Knopf, **1973**) On the scene in the Crimea in 1854, Flashman naturally finds himself in the Charge of the Light Brigade.
8. *Flashman in the Great Game: From the Flashman Papers, 1856–58* (Knopf, **1975**) Flashman spies out the impending Indian Mutiny of 1857. His schoolmate East bites the dust in this installment.
9. *Flashman and the Angel of the Lord: From the Flashman Papers, 1858–59* (Knopf, **1995**) Nobody could resemble Flash less in character than fanatical abolitionist John Brown, but somehow they find themselves together at Harper's Ferry.
10. *Flashman and the Dragon: From the Flashman Papers, 1860* (Knopf, **1986**) Flashman is Britain's semi-official envoy to the rebels in China's Taiping Rebellion.
11. *Flashman on the March: From the Flashman Papers, 1867–8* (Knopf, **2005**) In a now-obscure incident in Victorian history, Flashman becomes the British envoy on a mission to rescue a couple of hundred European hostages held by Theodore, mad king of Abyssinia, who was miffed at not getting a response to a letter he wrote to Queen Victoria.
12. *Flashman and the Tiger: And Other Extracts from the Flashman Papers* (Knopf, **2000**) Contains three novellas. "The Road to Charing Cross" takes Flashman to the Congress of Berlin in 1878. "The Subtleties of Baccarat" involves Harry in the Tranby Croft Scandal of 1890. "Flashman and the Tiger" has him involved with the Zulu Uprising of 1879 and facing off against his nemesis "Tiger" Jack Moran in 1894.

II. In addition to the Flashman series, Fraser has written three books chronicling the wacky adventures of a certain very Scottish Highland Regiment from the end of World War II into peacetime. They might appeal to *M.A.S.H.* fans with a tolerance for Scottish dialect. *The Complete McAuslan*, published by HarperCollins (UK) in 2000, contains all three volumes.

Fraser also wrote *The Pyrates* (Knopf, 1984), a spoof, and *The Hollywood History of the World* (Beech Tree, 1988), which sardonically describes the history of Hollywood's encounters with history.

1. *General Danced at Dawn, The, and Other Stories* (Knopf, **1973**) The story begins as Dand MacNeill is commissioned; we meet the regimental characters, including Daft Bob, Sergeant Teller, and Private McAuslan, the dirtiest soldier in the world.
2. *McAuslan in the Rough and Other Stories* (Knopf, **1974**) The further adventures of McAuslan and other members of the Highland Regiment feature the top brass on the golf course and McAuslan in love.

3. *Sheikh and the Dustbin, The, and Other McAuslan Stories* (Collins Harvill [UK], 1988) Private McAuslan continues to lose, soil, or destroy all his equipment, whether map reading his way through the Sahara or confronting rioting Arabs. Apparently not published in the United States.

Frazer, Margaret

PSEUDONYM OF Gail Frazer

I. Sister Frevisse is a nun at St. Frideswide's Abbey in 15th-century England. The fictional Sister Frevisse, or "Dame" Frevisse, as she is sometimes called, is far from being a recluse. In fact, she is often away from the abbey on errands of mercy, or to investigate some murder. A granddaughter of Geoffrey Chaucer, she has connections with the nobility and even with royalty such as King Henry VI. Frevisse brings much compassion and strong powers of ratiocination to bear on her cases, which occur in a well-realized medieval English setting. "Margaret Frazer" was created when Gail Frazer and Mary Pulver Kuhfeld (aka Mary Monica Pulver [q.v.]) teamed up at a conference for the Society for Creative Anachronism to write a series of mysteries. After seven novels, Mary Monica Pulver pulled out, and Margaret Frazer has continued on her own.

1. *Novice's Tale, The* (Jove, 1992) Introduces Sister Frevisse. In 1431 the dowager Lady Ermentrude comes to St. Frideswide convent to remove her niece, the novice Thomasine. Ermentrude's death by poison brings the convent into conflict with a local family and a coroner.

2. *Servant's Tale, The* (Jove, 1993) Three murders occur between Christmas Epiphany, the first two murders, of villager Barnaby Shene and his son Sym, are blamed on a troupe of traveling players. Then the murder of Sister Fiacre, hot upon the revelation of a old feud between her brother and the players, throws Frevisse into despair.

3. *Outlaw's Tale, The* (Jove, 1994) Frevisse and her traveling companions are set upon by outlaws led by her cousin Nicholas, who asks Frevisse to speak to the king on his behalf.

4. *Bishop's Tale, The* (Berkley, 1994) In London to mourn the death of her uncle, Thomas Chaucer, Sister Frevisse is shocked at the funeral feast by the blasphemy of Sir Thomas Sharpe, who dares God to strike him down—then dies within the hour.

5. *Boy's Tale, The* (Berkley, 1995) Someone wants the young half brothers of King Henry VI dead. They seek sanctuary with Sister Frevisse, but apparently someone inside St. Frideswide's is in league with the assassins.

6. *Murderer's Tale, The* (Berkley, 1996) Frevisse leaves St. Frideswide to make what she anticipates to be a restful visit to the manor of Minster Lovell. Then a murder occurs, which is blamed on a man afflicted by epileptic fits.

7. *Prioress' Tale, The* (Berkley, 1997) The nuns at St. Frideswide's are getting increasingly impatient with their prioress, Alys, who is preoccupied with finding wealthy patrons who can bankroll her expansion plans. Then, some of Alys's relatives come to stay at the abbey, bringing a violent family complete with murder into the convent.

8. *Maiden's Tale, The* (Berkley, 1998) Frevisse is sent to escort a novice to London and to visit her wealthy cousin Alice, Countess of Suffolk. The Suffolks are involved in dangerous court intrigues concerning French hostage the Duc 'Orleans.

9. *Reeve's Tale, The* (Berkley, 1999) Sister Frevisse, representing St. Frideswide in a land dispute with Lord Lovell, walks into the middle of a controversy punctuated by murder, with Lord Lovell's reeve (agent) Simon Perryn the chief suspect.

10. *Squire's Tale, The* (Berkley, 2000) Dame Frevisse accompanies Dame Claire, who is asked to minister to Blaunche, pregnant wife of Squire Robert, and again gets involved in family feud over a manor claimed by Blaunche before she was wed.

11. *Clerk's Tale, The* (Berkley, 2002) Frevisse and the prioress of St. Frideswide travel to the town of Goring, where they learn that Master Montfort has been murdered in the cloister garden of St. Mary's.

12. *Bastard's Tale, The* (Berkley, 2003) In 1447 a session of Parliament is convened in the town of Bury St. Edmund's, and political chicanery is afoot. The Bishop of Winchester sends Frevisse to St. Edmund's to uncover a plot of treason and murder.

13. *Hunter's Tale, The* (Berkley, 2004) In the summer of 1448, Dame Frevisse accompanies 11-year-old Ursula, a student at St. Frideswide, to attend the funeral of Ursula's father, Sir Ralph Woderove, apparently murdered by a poacher.

14. *Widow's Tale, The* (Berkley, 2005) After landowner Edward Helyngton dies, his widow, Cristiana, is relegated to St. Frideswide's by his inheriting cousin Laurence to do penance for unspecified sins. Dame Frevisse, hearing Cristiana's tale of woe, gets involved.

15. *Sempster's Tale, The* (Berkley, 2006) Dame Frevisse has a twin errand: to procure some vestments from a sempster (seamstress) in London and to convey a secret stash of gold from the sempster to her cousin Lady Alice in a mystery involving a Jew who pretends to be Christian and accusations of a Jewish ritual killing.

16. *Traitor's Tale, The* (Berkley, 2007) Dame Frevisse, in London to attend the funeral of the late Duke of Suffolk, teams up with the wandering player Simon Joliffe (see series II) in a matter involving a conspiracy against the crown.

II. Simon Joliffe, traveling player, who appears in several Dame Frevisse mysteries (e.g., series I, number 16), has a series of his own. Simon and his troupe are as prone to get embroiled in mysteries, as is Dame Frevisse.

1. *Play of Isaac, A* (Berkley, 2004) In 1434, at the Corpus Christi Festival in Oxford, where Joliffe and company are performing, the body of the murdered Penteney is found outside the barn where the troupe is lodging.

2. *Play of Dux Moraud, The* (Berkley, 2005) Autumn 1434. The former fiancé of Sir Edmund Deneby's daughter met an untimely end, and so might the current bridegroom-to-be.

3. *Play of Knaves, A* (Berkley, 2006) Joliffe and his troupe are sent to the village Ashewell not only to stage plays but to uncover some dark secrets about the town's three wealthiest families.

Freed, Lynn

South African native Freed re-created part of her life in two autobiographical novels. Ruth Frank is the daughter of a Jewish theatrical family who grows up in Durban, South Africa, gradually learns the sordid reality of apartheid, and tries to escape her past in the United States. White South African family life and society is skewered in these savage comedies of manners.

1. *Home Ground* (Summit, 1986) Young Ruth Frank tries to perceive the reality behind the poses of her theatrical family.

2. *Bungalow, The* (Poseidon, 1993) After a failed marriage in America, Ruth returns to South Africa and an affair with reform-minded landowner Hugh Stillington.

Freedman, Nancy

Mrs. Mike, the fictionalized biography of Katherine Mary Flannigan, the wife of a Canadian Mountie stationed in the Canadian Northwest, was a best seller when it was first published in 1947. The novel was revised as *Mrs. Mike: The Story of Katherine Mary Flannigan* (Sun Dial, 1948) and was made into the popular movie of the same title, starring Evelyn Keyes and Dick Powell (1949). It took some 55 years for a sequel, featuring Katherine Mary's adopted Cree daughter, Kathy Forquet, to appear. Another sequel appeared two years later, this time the heroine is country singer Kathy Little Bird, Katherine Mary's granddaughter. Nancy Freedman's husband, mathematics professor Benedict Freedman, sometimes listed as the principal author, is the coauthor of all three novels. *Mrs. Mike* has been a fixture on secondary-school reading lists for more than 50 years, and its sequels may appeal to the same audience as well.

1. *Mrs. Mike* (Coward, 1947) A young Irish girl from Boston, Katherine Mary O'Fallon, marries Sergeant Mike Flannigan of the Royal Canadian Mounted Police, and shares his wilderness life in the Canadian Northwest with him. Revised edition published by Sun Dial (1948).
2. *Search for Joyful, The* (Berkley, 2002) The story of Mrs. Mike continues during World War II with one of her adopted children, Kathy Forquet. Kathy, who is of Cree heritage, sets out to learn more about her late biological mother, Oh-Be-Joyful, and to train as a nurse in the "sin city" of Montreal.
3. *Kathy Little Bird* (Berkley, 2004) Kathy Little Bird, who has heard stories from her Cree mother about her grandmother, Mrs. Mike, and having learned to sing in the Cree tradition, becomes a famous country-music singer in the 1970s.

Freeling, Nicolas

I. Inspector Van der Valk of the Amsterdam police is a kind of Dutch peasant Maigret, a large-hearted but pragmatic professional, impatient with paperwork and overfond of his French wife's gourmet cooking. Van der Valk plodded stubbornly through his cases before English writer Freeling felt that his character was going stale, so he killed him off. The Dutch setting gives the books a special interest, though Van der Valk usually pursues his investigations in the seamier neighborhoods and in towns where the annual rainfall must be a good deal higher than the average. Numbers 12 and 13 are unique addenda to the Van der Valk opus: they star Arlette, Van der Valk's widow, as their detective. Number 10, the latest published, resurrected Van der Valk for one more case. Arlette also teamed with Henri Castang in *Lady Macbeth* (see series II, number 10, below).

1. *Love in Amsterdam* (Harper, 1963) This account centers on the long interrogation of Martin, who is arrested when his ex-mistress is found shot to death. To write it, Freeling may have drawn on his own experience of having been arrested for a theft he did not commit. Variant title: *Death in Amsterdam*.
2. *Because of the Cats* (Harper, 1964) The affluent seaside town of Bloemendael is plagued by a juvenile gang whose activities take a nasty turn into vandalism, rape, and religious cults.
3. *Question of Loyalty, A* (Harper, 1964) A Dutch girl, Lucienne Englebert, gets mixed up with three Italian boys and lots of trouble. UK title: *Gun before Butter*.
4. *Double Barrel* (Harper, 1965) When poison-pen letters cause two suicides, Van der Valk goes to a dreary north Holland town to investigate.
5. *Criminal Conversation* (Harper, 1966) Inspector Van der Valk suspects a fashionable nerve specialist of murder.
6. *King of the Rainy Country, The* (Harper, 1966) Van der Valk uncovers some strange doings while tracking down two missing persons, a millionaire and a young girl.
7. *Strike Out Where Not Applicable* (Harper, 1968) Recovering from serious injuries, Van der Valk has been made *commissaire* of a small town in the tulip-growing country, where he investigates the suspicious death of a local café owner.
8. *Tsing-Boom!* (Harper, 1969) The trail of a woman's death leads back to Vietnam during the French's last stand in Southeast Asia. English title: *Tsing-Boum*.
9. *Lovely Ladies, The* (Harper, 1971) The strange death of an elderly gentleman in the marketplace in Amsterdam leads Van der Valk to Dublin to see the daughter of the deceased. UK title: *Over the High Side*.
10. *Sand Castles* (Mysterious, 1990) Inspector Van der Valk is resurrected by the author for this adventure in Groningen involving a child-pornography racket.
11. *Aupres de ma Blonde* (Harper, 1972) Van der Valk has been kicked upstairs to a desk job but can't resist the lure of this strange case brought to him by a young jeweler's assistant. UK title: *A Long Silence*.
12. *Widow, The* (Pantheon, 1979) Arlette, widowed, remarried, and running a counseling service, gets involved in a strange and dangerous affair.
13. *Arlette* (Pantheon, 1981) Arlette's second case involves a distraught widow and a young man in hiding from the Argentine police. UK title: *One Damn Thing After Another*.

II. Freeling's second detective is the Brussels police inspector Henri Castang. A member of a new young breed, Castang holds a university degree and has been known to paraphrase Goethe on the job. He has a gymnast's elasticity of frame and a tenacious and observant temperament. He is very much in love with his wife, Vera, a crippled former gymnast. The last book in the series found Castang retired and a grandfather. Nicolas Freeling wrote some nonseries novels, including *Some Day Tomorrow* (St. Martin's, 2000) before he died, in 2003.

1. *Dressing of Diamonds, A* (Harper, 1974) Castang investigates the kidnapping of the eight-year-old daughter of Colette Delavigne, judge in the juvenile courts.
2. *Bugles Blowing, The* (Harper, 1975) Three dead bodies—one of them the naked wife of a high government official—are found shot in the same bed. UK title: *What Are the Bugles Blowing For?*
3. *Sabine* (Harper, 1976) A frightened woman is convinced that her son and daughter-in-law are trying to murder her for her money. English title: *Lake Isle*.
4. *Night Lords, The* (Pantheon, 1978) The daughter of English high-court justice, vacationing in France, finds the corpse of a strange woman in the back seat of the family Rolls Royce.
5. *Castang's City* (Pantheon, 1980) When the deputy mayor is murdered in broad daylight, terrorism is suspected, but Castang has other ideas. Mrs. Castang has a baby in this installment.
6. *Wolfnight* (Pantheon, 1982) Politician Marc Vibert confesses to Castang that his car plunged off a mountain road with his secretary Viviane Kranitz trapped inside.
7. *Back of the North Wind, The* (Viking, 1983) Castang gets involved in two grotesque cases: the murder and cannibalization of a young woman, and some bludgeonings with an extremely heavy instrument.
8. *No Part in Your Death* (Viking, 1984) Three separate cases are investigated: a distraught woman in Munich, the disappearance

of an eccentric Englishwoman, and an apparent double suicide in Dorset.

9. *Cold Iron* (Viking, 1986) Newly posted to the provinces, Castang investigates the murder of an aristocratic lady with decidedly paranoid tendencies.

10. *Lady Macbeth* (Deutsch [UK], 1988) Arlette Van der Valk (see series I, above) teams up with Castang when her ex-neighbor, Sybille Lefevre, goes missing on a trip with her husband to the Vosges Mountains. Not published in the United States.

11. *Not as Far as Velma* (Mysterious, 1989) A missing person case and the bombing of a convent may both their roots back in a concentration camp in 1945.

12. *Those in Peril* (Mysterious, 1990) In an effort to keep him out of their hair, police brass have rusticated Castang to the Fine Arts Fraud Squad.

13. *Flanders Sky* (Mysterious, 1992) Rusticated again, this time to European Community headquarters, Castang gets back to sleuthing when his boss is accused of wife murder. UK title: *The Pretty How Town*.

14. *You Know Who* (Mysterious, 1994) Eamon Hickey, Irish bureaucrat with the European Community, is blown away by a shotgun blast.

15. *Seacoast of Bohemia, The* (Mysterious, 1995) Anita Rogier insists that she has talked by phone with her son, who had been kidnapped four years previously.

16. *Dwarf Kingdom, A* (Mysterious, 1996) Castang retires after the murder of old friends Gerald and Mathilde Gutierrez and the attempted rape of his wife, Vera. A trip to Biarritz brings him additional trouble, however.

Freemantle, Brian (Harry)

I. Charlie Muffin, once the leading British espionage operative, became an embarrassment to the leaders of British intelligence. Charlie is insubordinate, scruffy, drinks too much, has the wrong accent, and is not overly careful about finances. So, though Charlie is still the best spy in the business, his bosses try just about everything they can to get rid of him—rustication, assassination, dangerous missions, retirement— you name it. But the resilient Charlie always bounces back. Freemantle's Charlie M capers merge "the good humor of a Lawrence Block [q.v.] thriller, the seriousness of a le Carré [q.v.] spy novel and the slam-bang adventure of a popular espionage caper" (*Publishers Weekly*). *Charlie's Choice* (Do-Not, 1997) is an omnibus containing numbers 1, 2, and 3.

1. *Charlie Muffin* (Doubleday, 1977) Introduces Charlie Muffin who, despite the fact he is the best espionage agent in the business, has exhausted the patience of his superiors by his sloppiness, his "Non-U" accent, and his wayward ways. Variant title: *Charlie M*.

2. *Here Comes Charlie M* (Ballantine, 1980) Charlie is rich and free, ensconced in his Zurich hideaway. But his former bosses want him dead and send some international killers after him. Originally published in the United Kingdom in 1978 as *Clap Hands, Here Comes Charlie*.

3. *Inscrutable Charlie Muffin, The* (Doubleday, 1979) Charlie, on his own, no longer with British intelligence, investigates a fire in Hong Kong.

4. *Charlie Muffin U.S.A.* (Ballantine, 1982) Charlie, who has been hired to mastermind a multimillion dollar protection job for Tsar Nicholas II's priceless stamp collection, is unaware that he has become part of an FBI sting operation. Originally published in the United Kingdom in 1980 as *Charlie Muffin's Uncle Sam*.

5. *Madrigal for Charlie Muffin* (Hutchinson [UK], 1981) Charlie becomes a pawn in some tricky doings by British intelligence and the KGB concerning a mole in the British Embassy in Rome. Not published in the United States.

6. *Blind Run, The* (Bantam, 1986) The elusive KGB mole named Edwin Sampson is caught, sentenced and shipped to Wormword prison. Charlie is assigned to ferret out Sampson's secrets. UK title: *Charlie Muffin and Russian Rose*.

7. *See Charlie Run* (Bantam, 1987) Charlie is sent to Tokyo to share with the CIA in the reception of KGB defectors Yuri and Irene Kozlov, The CIA agents aren't very anxious to share. UK title: *Charlie Muffin San*.

8. *Run Around, The* (Bantam, 1989) Charlie is on the trail of a Russian sharpshooter whose target is a group of world leaders meeting in Geneva for a peace conference.

9. *Comrade Charlie* (St. Martin's, 1992) Charlie is beset by his own acting director general Richard Harkness, who is out to prove him a traitor, and by old KGB enemy Berenkov who uses his former lover Natalia as bait in a trap. Originally published in the United Kingdom in 1989.

10. *Charlie's Apprentice* (St. Martin's, 1994) Charlie is in semi-retirement training fledgling agents. Then one of his fledglings is captured in Beijing while trying to extract a British agent.

11. *Bomb Grade* (St. Martin's, 1997) Charlie is sent to Moscow as liaison to the Russian Interior Ministry in its attempt to control the theft and export of nuclear material and becomes involved with the Russian Mafia and his ex-lover Natalia. UK title: *Charlie's Chance*.

12. *Dead Men Living* (St. Martin's, 2000) Charlie is living in the "new" Russia with his lover, former KGB agent Natalia. Then three bodies turn up a Siberian thaw, and the cold war threatens to be resurrected.

13. *Kings of Many Castles* (St. Martin's, 2002) An assassination attempt upon the Russian and American presidents in Moscow leaves the Russian leader and the American First Lady mortally wounded. The gunman turns out to be the son of a British atomic physicist who defected to Russia nearly 30 years before.

II. Colonel Dimitri Danilov of the Moscow Militia and FBI Russian desk-head William Cowley are an odd couple thrown together by the investigation of the murder of an American girl in Moscow. The two become friends as each discovers that the other is battling some personal demons. The Russian Mafia figures heavily in these mixtures of procedural and thriller.

1. *Button Man, The* (St. Martin's, 1993) The murder, in Moscow, of a young American economist, who is the niece of a powerful American senator, elicits an uneasy collaboration between the Russian Dimitri Danilov and the American William Cowley. Variant title: *In the Name of a Killer*.

2. *No Time for Heroes* (St. Martin's, 1995) Dimitri, now an outcast in Moscow's Organized Crime Bureau, is called to Washington by Cowley to solve the murder of a Russian diplomat.

3. *Watchmen, The* (St. Martin's, 2002) Cowley and Danilov are reunited when a rocket containing anthrax and sarin, shot from a boat in New York Harbor, hits the United Nations Tower.

4. *Triple Cross* (St. Martin's, 2004) Igor Orlov, Russian mafioso, aims to take over as the boss of bosses of a global consortium for organized crime.

III. A pair of novels (so far) features Sebastian Holmes, estranged son of Sherlock, who gets involved in adventures shortly before World War I that put him into contact with many historical figures and characters from the Arthur Conan Doyle (q.v.) stories in a couple of ingenious Sherlock Holmes pastiches.

1. *Holmes Inheritance, The* **(Severn House, 2004)** Young Sebastian Holmes sails to America on the behest of his guardian, Uncle Mycroft, to investigate rumors of secret arms deals with the Germans just before World War I. Winston Churchill is among the historical characters who make an appearance.
2. *Holmes Factor, The* **(Severn House, 2005)** Sebastian travels to St. Petersburg to investigate rumors of German meddling in Russia's growing unrest in 1913. Josef Stalin, Alexander Kerensky, and Grand Duke Orlov are among the historical characters Sebastian meets along the way.

Freydont, Shelley

Linda Haggerty is a former dancer; "empty-nest" mother; rehearsal director for the Jeremy Ash Dance Company, a modern-dance outfit; and a sometime detective. These mysteries combines backstage dance knowledge, exotic locales, an interesting central character, and entertaining plots. Linda Haggerty is the alter ego of Shelley Freydont, former dancer (Twyla Tharp, etc.), choreographer, rehearsal director, dance teacher, consultant, and writer.

1. *Backstage Murder* **(Kensington, 1999)** Former dancer Lindy Haggerty is finding a need to do something now that her kids are grown and her husband is well embarked on his career. Then her former roommate Biddy McFee invites her to the opening performance of the Jeremy Ash Dance Company, where Lindy finds that all is not well.
2. *High Seas Murder* **(Kensington, 2000)** Lindy, now rehearsal director for the Jeremy Ash Dance Company, leads her troupe on a 10-day Caribbean luxury cruise aboard the *Maestro*.
3. *Midsummer Murder* **(Kensington, 2001)** Lindy accompanies the Jeremy Ash troupe to the Easton Arts Retreat in upstate New York, which is celebrating its 50th anniversary with a gala performance by its best-known alumni, including Jeremy Ash.
4. *Halloween Murder* **(Kensington, 2002)** Lindy returns from a long European business trip to find that the pranks based on the Seven Deadly Sins for the forthcoming Mischief Night Marathon have escalated into murder.
5. *Merry Little Murder, A* **(Kensington, 2003)** At Christmastime Lindy attends the glitzy International Ballroom Competition in Atlantic City, where, of course, murder happens.

Friedman, Bruce Jay

Bruce Jay Friedman, who is credited with coining the term *black humor*, is responsible for a series of short stories ("Change of Plan" was the basis for the movie *The Heartbreak Kid*), novels (*A Mother's Kisses*), plays (*Steambath*), and screenplays (*The Lonely Guy*) caricaturing the lives of neurotic, partially assimilated Jewish Americans. Harry Towns, who is dedicated to the writing craft but addicted to alcohol, cocaine, hookers, and other bad company, pours out his middle-aged angst in this pair of novels.

1. *About Harry Towns* **(Knopf, 1974)** Harry Towns, age 42, separated from his wife, and feeling that he is missing out on the fun in life, takes his son on a trip to Las Vegas.
2. *Current Climate, The* **(Little, Brown, 1989)** Harry, happily remarried and living on Long Island, but frustrated over a play he can't finish, yields to the temptations of controlled substances and seedy acquaintances on a trip to New York City.

Friedman, Kinky

Kinky Friedman's hero, sometime Texan and Greenwich Village denizen, country musician (Kinky Friedman and the Texas Jewboys), cigar-smoking, cat-loving friend of Ratso, Rambam, and McGovern, and sometime sleuth, goes by the name of . . . Kinky Friedman. The irreverent, mildly obscene, and very funny Kinkster, rather than the plots, is the real attraction of this mystery series. *Kill Two Birds and Get Stoned* (Morrow, 2003) and *The Christmas Pig* (Simon & Schuster, 2006) are not part of the series. *Kinky Friedman's Guide to Texas Etiquette; or, How to Get to Heaven or Hell without Going through Dallas-Fort Worth* (Morrow, 2001) is a nonfiction guide to Texas written in the Kinkster vein. Omnibus volumes: *Three Complete Mysteries* (Random House, 1993; numbers 1–3); *The Kinky Friedman Crime Club* (Faber [UK]; numbers 1–3); *More Kinky Friedman* (Faber [UK]; numbers 4–6); and *Even More Kinky Friedman* (Faber [UK]; numbers 7–9).

1. *Greenwich Killing Time* **(Beech Tree, 1986)** Kinky steps in to investigate when a friend is wrongfully accused of murder.
2. *Case of Lone Star, A* **(Beech Tree, 1987)** Country legend Larry Barkin is slain with a Gibson guitar.
3. *When the Cat's Away* **(Beech Tree, 1988)** A missing cat, a dead literary agent, painted paw prints, animal tranquilizers, and animal-worshipping Colombian drug dealers all play roles here.
4. *Frequent Flyer* **(Morrow, 1989)** Kinky attends the funeral of a Peace Corps buddy and discovers that a complete stranger is in the casket.
5. *Musical Chairs* **(Morrow, 1991)** Kinky brings the surviving Texas Jewboys to New York for a reunion tour after three members of the group die mysteriously.
6. *Elvis, Jesus and Coca-Cola* **(Simon & Schuster, 1993)** The Kinkster is looking for two missing items: a documentary film on Elvis impersonators and lover "Uptown Judy" (not to be confused with "Downtown Judy").
7. *Armadillos and Old Lace* **(Simon & Schuster, 1994)** Returning to his family home in Kerr County, Texas, Kinky is drafted to investigate the untimely demise of a series of little old ladies.
8. *God Bless John Wayne* **(Simon & Schuster, 1995)** Kinky's friend Ratso sets off on a quest to find his real parents but, rather understandably, turns up few claimants.
9. *Love Song of J. Edgar Hoover, The* **(Simon & Schuster, 1996)** Village Irregulars member Michael McGovern claims he is being tailed by government agents and receiving phone calls from Al Capone's former chef, the late Leaning Jesus.
10. *Road Kill* **(Simon & Schuster, 1997)** Legendary country singer Willie Nelson asks the depressed Kinkster to get involved in a case involving a deceased Native American medicine man.
11. *Blast from the Past* **(Simon & Schuster, 1998)** In what is essentially a prequel, Kinky harks back to the late 1970s when he is first assembling the Village Irregulars and thinking about becoming a detective. The late Abbie Hoffman plays a role here.
12. *Spanking Watson* **(Simon & Schuster, 1999)** Upstairs neighbor lesbian dance instructor Winnie Katz has done a number on the Kinkster's ceiling, so he calls on mobster Joey the Hyena for a favor.
13. *Mile High Club, The* **(Simon & Schuster, 2000)** Kinky is asked to keep an eye on the little pink suitcase of his airliner seatmate, Khadija Kejela, and then is left holding what may be a very dangerous bag.

14. *Steppin' on a Rainbow* (Simon & Schuster, 2001) Old friend McGovern is missing somewhere on the Hawaiian Islands, so the Kinkster and company travel there to look for him.

15. *Meanwhile, Back at the Ranch* (Simon & Schuster, 2002) Kinky has three cases, which he refers to as the Three Stooges. "Larry" involves a missing autistic boy, "Moe" a serial killer, and "Curly" a missing three-legged cat named Lucky.

16. *Prisoner of Vandorn Street, The* (Simon & Schuster, 2004) Kinky plays an unwonted passive role when he is assailed by malaria and happens to see a woman being physically assaulted in an adjacent apartment building.

17. *Ten Little New Yorkers* (Simon & Schuster, 2005) In what may be the last book in the series, Kinky, depressed by the disappearance of his cat, leaves New York for Texas, chased by his nemesis, NYPD Detective Sergeant Mort Cooperman.

Frommer, Sara Hoskinson

Joan Spencer, a fortyish widow with a teenage son and a grown daughter, moves to Oliver (aka Bloomington), Indiana, where she plays the viola for the city's symphony orchestra and, this being a series of cozies, gets involved in investigating murders. Author Sara Hoskinson Frommer has been an editor, an avid quilter, and a viola player for the Bloomington Symphony Orchestra.

1. *Murder in C Major* (St. Martin's, 1986) Joan Spencer moves to Oliver, Indiana, where she joins the local symphony orchestra as a violist. During her second rehearsal, the oboist drops dead, followed later by a flute player. Sara teams with local Detective Fred Lundquist to solve the crimes.

2. *Buried in Quilts* (St. Martin's, 1994) In a mystery involving the art of quilting, Joan and Fred Lundquist team up again to solve the murder of a woman whose corpse is found under a pile of quilts.

3. *Murder and Sullivan* (St. Martin's, 1997) The murder of judge David Putnam during a performance of Gilbert and Sullivan's rarely performed *Ruddigore* gets Joan Spencer on the case.

4. *Vanishing Violinist, The* (St. Martin's, 1999) Two weddings are anticipated: that of Joan and Fred and that of Joan's daughter. A Brazilian violinist's Stradivarius disappears, followed by the disappearance of the violinist.

5. *Witness in Bishop Hill* (St. Martin's, 2002) Joan and Fred travel to the small Swedish American community of Bishop Hill for a belated honeymoon. The only witness to the inevitable murder is Fred's Alzheimer's-afflicted mother.

6. *Death Climbs a Tree* (St. Martin's, 2005) Violinist Sylvia Purcell takes a deadly fall from a tree while protesting against the development of a wooded area for low-income housing. Joan's son, Andrew, becomes the prime suspect.

Fyfield, Frances

PSEUDONYM OF Frances Hegarty

I. English mystery writer Hegarty, who works as a criminal lawyer in London, writes novels under her real name and under the Fyfield pseudonym. Helen West, like her creator, is a Crown Prosecutor. Helen can't distance herself from her cases and so, with the sometime help of live-in lover Detective Superintendent Geoffrey Bailey, she does her own investigating to get to the bottom of them. Helen also has cameo roles in the Sarah Fortune novels (series II). Omnibus volumes: *A Helen West Omnibus* (Time Warner [UK]; numbers 3, 4, and 5) and *A Second Helen West Omnibus* (Time Warner [UK]; numbers 2 and 6).

1. *Question of Guilt, A* (Pocket, 1988) Stan Jaskowski, would-be private eye, is slated to be the fall guy when rich widow Eileen Cartwright arranges a hit on her solicitor's wife.

2. *Not That Kind of Place* (Pocket, 1990) A murder of passion in a village just outside London threatens the relationship of Helen West and Geoffrey Bailey. UK title: *Trial by Fire*.

3. *Deep Sleep* (Pocket, 1992) The cause of death of Margaret Carlton, wife of a pharmacist, is listed as an accidental overdose of chloroform.

4. *Shadow Play* (Pantheon, 1993) Road sweeper Mr. Logo is considered a harmless eccentric, but West is convinced that he is a sexual abuser and a possible murderer.

5. *Clear Conscience, A* (Pantheon, 1995) Helen is frustrated by battered women who won't testify against their abusers

6. *Without Consent* (Viking, 1997) Detective Sergeant Ryan, close friend of Geoffrey Bailey, is arrested for one of series of assaults on women.

II. Sarah Fortune is another lawyer creation of Fyfield's. Sarah is sexy and unconventional and gets involved in cases characterized by eccentric characters and improbable plots. Sarah makes cameo appearances in the Helen West novels (series I). *The Art of Drowning* (Little, Brown, 2006) is not a series novel.

1. *Shadows on the Mirror* (Pocket, 1991) The widowed Sarah is a free-spirited lawyer with a number of "kindly" male clients, one of whom is potentially dangerous.

2. *Perfectly Pure and Good* (Pantheon, 1994) Sarah is sent by her mentor Ernest Matthewson to the village of Merton-on-Sea to resolve some estate matters.

3. *Staring at the Light* (Viking, 2000) This case involves two brothers, misfit Cannon Smith and evil twin Johnny; Cannon's wife, Julie; and Fortune's dentist and hesitant lover, William.

4. *Looking Down* (Little, Brown, 2004) Richard Beaumont's obsession with the fatal fall of a young woman, which he witnessed, drives his wife, Lilian, to seek the aid of her neighbor Sarah Fortune.

5. *Safer Than Houses* (Little, Brown, 2005) Sara has inherited a flat from one of her many lovers. A son of the lover claims that the flat is his, morally, if not strictly legally, and he uses illegal means, including threatening letters, to persuade Sarah to give up the flat.

Gaan, Margaret

Margaret Gaan has written a historical trilogy about Shanghai that follows members of the Wei family as they fight against the British-imposed opium industry from the mid-19th century to 1927. Gaan was born in Shanghai, which she described in her recollections *Last Moment of a World* (Norton, 1978).

1. *Red Barbarian* (Dodd, 1984) Englishman Charles Tyson marries a daughter of the Wei family, but the eruption of the Opium War separates the "Red Barbarian" from his new in-laws.

2. *White Poppy* (Dodd, 1985) Donald Mathes, heir to his uncle Andrew's opium importing business, becomes disillusioned with the trade and is befriended by Wei Jin-see, who wants revenge for his father's murder.

3. *Blue Mountain* (Dodd, 1987) Wei Ta-yu, nicknamed Didi, tries to carry on his grandfather's mission of abolishing the opium trade.

Gabaldon, Diana

I. The huge success of the Outlander series represents a publishing Cinderella story. Gabaldon posted excerpts from her first novel (*Outlander*) on CompuServe. These excerpts attracted so much favorable attention that Gabaldon got an agent, who found a publisher (Delacorte) for what proved to be the first in a series of best sellers. The Outlander series, which Gabaldon calls "historical fantasy," features a 20th-century nurse, Claire Beauchamp Randall, married to historian Frank Randall, who travels back in time from 1945 to 1745; encounters Jack Randall, her husband's evil ancestor; and falls in love with the gallant Highlander James Fraser. This is a series full of action, passion, and historical detail in the best historical romance tradition. *The Outlandish Companion* (Delacorte, 1999; UK title: *Through the Stones*) is a reference book full of information about Gabaldon and her work. James Fraser appears as a subsidiary character in the Lord John series (series II, below).

1. *Outlander* **(Delacorte, 1991)** Claire Randall walks through a cleft stone in an ancient henge in the Scottish Highlands and travels back in time from 1945 to 1745. UK title: *Cross Stitch*.
2. *Dragonfly in Amber* **(Delacorte, 1992)** Knowing the disaster that awaits the Highlanders at Culloden, Claire and James Fraser travel to the court of Louis XV to sabotage Jacobite fund-raising efforts.
3. *Voyager* **(Delacorte, 1994)** Under the impression that Jamie had been killed at the Battle of Culloden, the pregnant Claire returns to the 20th century and her husband, Frank.
4. *Drums of Autumn* **(Delacorte, 1996)** Claire returns to the 18th century and Jamie, this time in colonial Charleston, South Carolina. Claire's daughter Brianna discovers that Jamie is her real father and journeys through time and space to confront her mother.
5. *Fiery Cross, The* **(Delacorte, 2001)** Claire, Jamie, Brianna, and Brianna's husband, Roger Wakefield, find themselves in the North Carolina mountains in 1771 and feel the first tremors of the American Revolution.
6. *Breath of Snow and Ashes, A* **(Delacorte, 2005)** In 1772, on the eve of the American Revolution, the governor of North Carolina calls upon Jamie Fraser to unite the backcountry and safeguard the colony for king and crown. But, of course, Claire knows what will happen a few years hence.

II. James Fraser is relegated to the sidelines in the new series featuring Lord John Grey, soldier, gentleman, and swordsman in the mid-18th-century Seven Years' War. The memory of the Duke of the Pardloe, John's father, a suicide and alleged Jacobite agent, hangs heavily over Lord Grey, who finds it difficult to expunge the blot on his family's escutcheon.

1. *Lord John and the Private Matter* **(Delacorte, 2003)** Lord John Grey is a mystery to the protagonists of the still-smouldering Jacobite Rebellion. Whose side is he on? Is French espionage responsible for the murder he is called upon to investigate?
2. *Lord John and the Brotherhood of the Blade* **(Delacorte, 2007)** In 1758, in the midst of the Seven Years' War, Lord John and his titled brother Hal fight by the side of Britain's Prussian allies. Then a page from their father's missing diary turns up, and the Grey family is resubjected to taunts of Jacobism.
3. *Lord John and the Hand of the Devils* **(Delacorte, 2007)** A trio of novellas spanning 1756–1758 sends Lord John off on mystery-adventures to investigate a deconsecrated abbey, a succubus bedeviling his Prussian encampment, and a cannon explosion in the English countryside.

Gainham, Sarah

The Julia Homberg trilogy follows the life of a beautiful leading lady of the Viennese theater from 1938 to the early 1950s. The first volume gives both a panoramic view of Austria during the war years and a close-up of the strain and terror of people living through that cataclysm. The second volume moves on to the fear and political intrigue of the cold war years. The third book movingly examines how survivors restore their shattered lives.

1. *Night Falls on the City* **(Holt, 1967)** Julia's Jewish husband, Franz, thought to have escaped abroad, is really hiding in their apartment.
2. *Place in the Country, A* **(Holt, 1969)** Young English officer Robert Inglis rescues Georg Kerenyi and falls in love with Julia's ward, Lali.
3. *Private Worlds* **(Holt, 1971)** Julia, now married to Georg Kerenyi, comes to term with tragedy and mystery echoing from the past.

Gallico, Paul (William)

Once Mrs. 'Arris, the plucky London charlady, got to Paris, there was no stopping her. Gallico followed that first success with three other adventures, all showing Ada Harris spreading her own inimitable brand of Cockney sweetness and light. "If you wants somefink bad enough, there's always ways" is the motto that buoys her through disappointments and temporary setbacks to the eventual accomplishment of her mission.

1. *Mrs. 'Arris Goes to Paris* **(Doubleday, 1958)** Ada Harris goes to Paris to pick out the Dior dress that she has skimped and saved for three years to buy. UK title: *Flowers for Mrs. Harris*.
2. *Mrs. 'Arris Goes to New York* **(Doubleday, 1960)** Mrs. 'Arris is off to the New World on a mission of mercy—Little 'Enry Gussett needs a father. UK title: *Mrs. Harris Goes to New York*.
3. *Mrs. 'Arris Goes to Parliament* **(Doubleday, 1965)** Mrs. 'Arris's slogan of Live and Let Live wins her a seat in Parliament and the loyal friendship of John Bayswater. UK title: *Mrs. Harris, M.P.*
4. *Mrs. 'Arris Goes to Moscow* **(Delacorte, 1974)** Accompanied this time by her friend Violet Butterfield, Mrs. Harris braves the Kremlin in her search for the lovely Lisabeta. UK title: *Mrs. Harris Goes to Moscow*.

Gallison, Kate (Katherine)

I. Lavinia Grey (Mother Vinnie), the vicar at St. Bede's Episcopal Church in Fishersville, New Jersey, gets involved in murder mysteries in this series of ecclesiastical detective novels. Mother Vinnie, with her assortment of oddball parishioners and eccentric Fishersville locals, is irrepressible and often acerbic. The novels cast a satirical eye on Church bureaucracy and politics, sometimes spoof the efforts of such detectives as Raymond Chandler's (q.v.) Philip Marlowe and Ross McDonald's (q.v.) Lew Archer and, at their best, can be quite funny.

1. *Bury the Bishop* **(Dell, 1995)** Introduces Mother Vinnie of St. Bede Episcopal Church in New Jersey. Mother Vinnie becomes prime suspect, in Detective Dogg's mind, anyway, when her bishop, with whom she has had many differences, is murdered.
2. *Devil's Workshop* **(Dell, 1996)** The disappearance of several cats and the discovery of a dead body are at issue here.

3. *Unholy Angels* **(Dell, 1996)** St. Bede's eccentric parishioners, Little League baseball, and the murders of two prominent citizens of Fishersville occupy Mother Vinnie here.

4. *Hasty Retreat* **(Delacorte, 1997)** Mother Vinnie sets off for a weekend retreat in upstate New York, where she runs into her ecclesiastical enemy, Father Rupert Bingley. Then an elderly monk is stabbed to death with a knitting needle. First appearance of Mother Lavinia Grey in hardcover.

5. *Grave Misgivings* **(Delacorte, 1998)** Memories of the flood that hit Fishersville in 1955 are stirred up when Mark Smith returns to place his mother's ashes with his father's remains. Seems nobody knows where Mark's father, James Smith, is buried.

II. An earlier trio of books features private eye Nick Magaracz of Trenton, New Jersey. Nick is, according to a *New York Times* reviewer, "a very poor man's Sam Spade." The hapless Nick is forced to take on other jobs, such as with the New Jersey Department of Tax Enforcement, to get such mundane things as dental benefits for his daughter. Some of Nick's adventures are quite farcical, and the characters he meets in Trenton's "mean streets" are, like Nick, stupid, incompetent, and funny.

1. *Unbalanced Accounts* **(Little, Brown, 1986)** Divorce-law reform in New Jersey has seriously cut into Nick Magaracz's investigatory business, so he takes a covert assignment with the New Jersey Department of Mental Rehabilitation to retrieve $9000 in stolen welfare checks.

2. *Death Tape, The* **(Little, Brown, 1987)** To pay the bills for his daughter's braces, Nick takes a job with New Jersey's Department of Tax Enforcement, where he uncovers the Posse Comitatus, a group of violent antitax, antigovernment survivalists.

3. *New Jersey Monkey, The* **(St. Martin's, 1992)** Nick is reduced to interrogating a monkey using sign language when he investigates the poisoning of two employees of a pharmaceutical company where a new AIDS drug is being developed.

Galsworthy, John

The Forsyte Saga was the first big American success of a literary work adapted for television—people canceled other engagements rather than miss an episode of the tortured affairs of Soames, Irene, and the other Forsytes. Of course the polished BBC production deserves some credit, but the main appeal was Galsworthy's compelling story, which, after all, was immensely popular when first published. Soames's death at the end of *Swan Song* was front-page material for London newspapers in 1928. As with most sagas, this one developed from a successful novel, *A Man of Property*, which featured characters and action that demanded a sequel. The first follow-up was "Indian Summer of a Forsyte": it is a story, or "interlude," as Galsworthy called it, connecting that first novel with its successor. Still more novels and interludes followed. The television version ended with Soames's death and did not include the last three volumes of the saga (numbers 7, 8, and 9 below), in which Fleur Forsyte plays only a minor role. The series is best grouped into three trilogies with connecting interludes, and the omnibus volumes are organized that way: *The Forsyte Saga* (Scribner, 1922) contains *A Man of Property*, *In Chancery*, and *To Let*; *A Modern Comedy* (Scribner, 1929) comprises *The White Monkey*, *The Silver Spoon*, and *Swan Song*; and *End of the Chapter* (Scribner, 1934) contains *Maid in Waiting*, *Flowering Wilderness*, and *Over the River*. For convenience, each book is listed here separately.

The Forsyte Saga was redone as an eight-part adaptation on PBS in 2002. Two volumes of stories by Galsworthy are concerned with the Forsytes, although they are not part of the saga. *On Forsyte Change* (Scribner, 1930) contains stories about various Forsytes from 1821 to 1918, and *Caravan* (Scribner, 1925), a collection of short stories, begins with a story about Swithin, "The Salvation of a Forsyte."

1. *Man of Property, A* **(Putnam, 1906)** The story begins in 1886 with the engagement of June Forsyte to Philip Bosinney. Soames's marriage to the beautiful Irene is proving disastrous. Young Jolyon ends his marriage and is cut off by Old Jolyon. The older Forsytes are prominent in this volume. "Indian Summer of a Forsyte," the interlude between Numbers 1 and 2, shows old Jolyon being charmed by Irene in the days just before his death.

2. *In Chancery* **(Scribner, 1920)** Freed by divorce, Irene marries young Jolyon and has a son, Jon. Soames marries Annette and has a daughter, Fleur. "Awakening," the interlude between numbers 2 and 3, is about little Jon's childhood.

3. *To Let* **(Scribner, 1921)** This volume begins in 1920 as Jon and Fleur meet, fall in love, and learn of the unbreakable rift that divides their families.

4. *White Monkey, The* **(Scribner, 1924)** Fleur's marriage to Michael Mont is threatened by an affair with an artist but strengthened by the birth of a son. "A Silent Wooing," the interlude connecting numbers 4 and 5, shows young Jon in America meeting the girl who will become his wife.

5. *Silver Spoon, The* **(Scribner, 1926)** Fleur gets involved in a nasty slander suit, and Soames comes to the rescue. "Passers By," the interlude between numbers 5 and 6, shows Soames and Irene crossing paths.

6. *Swan Song* **(Scribner, 1928)** In 1926 Jon Forsyte returns from America with his wife, Ann, and Fleur's revival of her affair with Jon ends in tragedy.

7. *Maid in Waiting* **(Scribner, 1931)** This episode features young Elizabeth Cherrell, known as Dinny, who is a cousin to Michael Mont. Fleur and Michael are expecting their second child.

8. *Flowering Wilderness* **(Scribner, 1932)** Dinny falls in love with the young poet Wilfred Desert, who is haunted by events surrounding his brush with Arab fanatics while traveling in the Middle East.

9. *Over the River* **(Scribner, 1937)** In 1932 Dinny worries over dwindling resources; her sister Clair, who has left her husband; and the newly elected MP Eustace Dornford.

Garcia-Aguilera, Carolina

Guadalupe "Lupe" Solano wasn't content to be a "Cuban-American princess," daughter of an elite Cuban American family in Miami. So she became a Mercedes-driving, Beretta-toting private investigator. Most of her cases take place in Miami's Cuban community. Carolina Garcia-Aguilera, born in Cuba, has firsthand knowledge of Cuba and Cubans. Garcia-Aguilera became a private investigator herself in Miami to gain the necessary experience to write her novels. Her latest novels, *One Hot Summer* (Rayo, 2002) and *Luck of the Draw* (Rayo, 2003), are stand-alones.

1. *Bloody Waters* **(Putnam, 1996)** The daughter Lucia and Jose Moreno adopted in a no-questions-asked transaction needs a bone-marrow transplant from her birth mother.

2. *Bloody Shame* **(Putnam, 1997)** Jeweler Alonso Arango Sr. claims self-defense in the shooting death of Gustavo Gaston, but Gaston's alleged knife has disappeared.

3. *Bloody Secrets* **(Putnam, 1998)** Cuban refugee Luis Delgado claims that the prominent philanthropic de la Torre family bilked his family out of $2 million before the Castro takeover.

4. *Miracle in Paradise, A* **(Putnam, 1999)** The Mother Superior of the Order of the Holy Rosary, where Lupe's sister Lourdes is a nun,

wants Lupe to look into claims that, on Cuban Independence Day (October 10), the holy statue of the Virgin de la Caritad del Cobre will shed tears over the separation of her people in Cuba and the United States.

5. *Havana Heat* (Morrow, 2000) The eighth tapestry of the Hunt of the Unicorn series in the Cloisters (New York City) is missing. While attending her niece's wedding, Lupe is given the chance of retrieving it from Havana.

6. *Bitter Sugar* (Morrow, 2001) Lupe is hired by her father's best friend to investigate a mysterious offer to buy property rights to his Cuban sugar mills, confiscated long ago by Castro.

Garcia-Roza, Luiz Alfredo

Inspector Espinosa, chief of the 12th (Copacabana) precinct in Rio de Janeiro, is middle-aged, unmarried, and frequents used-book stores when he is off duty, but he can navigate the streets of his native city and match wits with some clever murderers. Luiz Alfredo Garcia-Roza is a professor of philosophy at Rio University, and he evokes the atmosphere at Rio in this series of dark mysteries.

1. *Silence of the Rain, The* (Holt, 2002) Young corporate executive Ricardo Carvalho is found dead in a parking garage in downtown Rio de Janeiro. By the time the police arrive, all traces of the man's identity and the weapon have disappeared. Originally published as *O Silêncio da chuva* in 1997. Translated from the Portuguese by Benjamin Moser.

2. *December Heat* (Holt, 2003) When Viera, a retired policeman, wakes from an alcoholic evening with his prostitute girlfriend, he finds his girlfriend murdered, his wallet and car keys missing, and no memory of what happened the previous night. Originally published as *Achadas e perdidos* in 1998. Translated from the Portuguese by Benjamin Moser.

3. *Southwesterly Wind* (Holt, 2004) A frightened young man takes Inspector Espinosa from his paperwork with a bizarre story about how a psychic has predicted that he (the young man) will commit a murder, a murder that has become a fact in the young man's mind. Originally published as *Vento sudueste* in 1999. Translated from the Portuguese by Benjamin Moser.

4. *Window in Copacabana, A* (Holt, 2005) Three Rio policemen have been killed over the course of a few days by an assassin who fires at point-blank range and leaves no traces. Originally published as *Uma janela em Copacabana* in 2001. Translated from the Portuguese by Benjamin Moser.

5. *Pursuit* (Holt, 2006) The daughter of a hospital psychiatrist and one of his patients are missing. Then the patient turns up dead, the first of a chain of deaths. Originally published as *Persequido* in 2003. Translated from the Portuguese by Benjamin Moser.

Gardner, Craig Shaw

I. American writer Gardner is known for his movie novelizations and other tie-ins and for his comic fantasy. The Ebenezum-Wuntvor series is a pair of comic fantasy trilogies. The first trilogy features unfortunate wizard Ebenezum, who, having a curse put upon him by the demon Guxx Unfufadoo making him allergic to magic, is forced to wander through his world in search of a cure. The second trilogy relates the adventures of Ebenezum's apprentice, Wuntvor, as he travels to the Eastern Kingdoms to restore his master's powers and save their land. Perils such as tap-dancing dragons, enchanted chickens, monsters with an attitude, and death by custard await them. Omnibus vol-umes: *The Exploits of Ebenezum* (Doubleday, 1987; numbers 1–3) and *The Wanderings of Wuntvor* (Doubleday, 1989; numbers 4–6).

1. *Malady of Magicks, A* (Ace, 1986) Having failed to rid the Netherhells of the great wizard Ebenezum, the demon Guxx Unfufadoo curses the wizard, making him allergic to magic. Ebenezum and his apprentice Wuntvor embark upon a journey to the City of Forbidden Delights in search of a cure.

2. *Multitude of Monsters, A* (Ace, 1986) Still on their pilgrimage, Ebenezum and Wuntvor are sidetracked by the militant monsters of The Association for the Advancement of Mythical and Imaginary Beasts and Creatures.

3. *Night in the Netherhells, A* (Ace, 1987) The City of Delights having been dragged deep into the dire domain of Guxx, the rhyming demon, the hapless Wuntvor is volunteered to go deep into the Netherhells.

4. *Difficulty with Dwarves, A* (Ace, 1987) Wuntvor travels to the distant Eastern Kingdoms in search of a cure for his master Ebenezum.

5. *Excess of Enchantments, An* (Ace, 1988) Toxic fog and death by immersion in custard are among the perils that Wuntvor and his love, the witch Norei, must face.

6. *Disagreement with Death, A* (Ace, 1989) Death himself, desiring another recruit, casts a cold eye on Wuntvor.

II. With the aid of a Captain Crusader Decoder Ring, public relations man Roger Gordon enters the perilous world of B movies, where he encounters all the cliche perils of the westerns, thrillers, and romances of that fantasy world. Delores, Roger's love from another dimension, Menge the Merciless, Zabana the Jungle Prince, Dr. Dread, Big Bertha, and an amorous slime monster are among the denizens of the world of bad movies that Roger has to face. Omnibus volume: *The Cineverse Cycle* (Guild America, 1990; numbers 1–3).

1. *Slaves of the Volcano God* (Ace, 1989) Roger Gordon finds that his Captain Crusader Decoder Ring allows him to travel to, and return from, the Cineverse, a world of B-movie characters and cliches.

2. *Bride of the Slime Monster* (Ace, 1990) With Roger rendered helpless by the loss of his Decoder Ring, the Cineverse seems doomed to be taken over by the likes of Dr. Dread, Menge the Merciless, Big Bertha, and a slime monster who seems bent upon making Roger's love, Delores, his mate.

3. *Revenge of the Fluffy Bunnies* (Ace, 1990) Roger/Captain Crusader is up to his ears in trouble. The slime monster has his girl. His mother has become a whip-cracking archvillainess. His faithful sidekicks are entrapped in an Italian gladiator flick. The bad guys are on a roll.

III. In a takeoff on *The Arabian Nights*, Sinbad, Ali Baba, and Scheherazade are put through some comic paces.

1. *Other Sinbad, The* (Ace, 1991) Sinbad the Porter is inveigled into a perilous adventure by his more famous namesake, Sinbad the Sailor.

2. *Bad Day for Ali Baba, A* (Ace, 1992) The poor woodcutter Ali Baba, accompanied by his brother, who has been sliced into six pieces, is forced to join the Forty Thieves after he discovers their hidden lair.

3. *Last Arabian Night, The* (Ace, 1993) Forced to save her life by a series of long-winded tales, Scheherazade pulls out all the stops on her last night to thwart the homicidal king she has married. UK title: *Scheherazade's Night Out.*

IV. In the Dragon Circle trilogy, the suburban neighborhood of Chestnut Circle is transported by a bad storm into a netherworld of soldiers, wizards, and monsters where the suburbanites have to learn new skills to survive. A sleeping, malevolent dragon is a potential menace throughout and a teenager named Nick becomes a hero.

1. *Dragon Sleeping* (Ace, 1994) The suburban neighborhood of Chestnut Circle is blown by a great wind into the world of the Anno, the "brother wizards" Nunn and Obar and a sleeping dragon. UK title: *Raven Walking*. Variant title: *Dragon Circle: Dragon Sleeping*.

2. *Dragon Waking* (Ace, 1995) Death, resurrection, the discovery and allocation of dragons' eyes, and the development of characters such as Jason Dafoe and a creature combining the souls of men, wizards, and the creature Zachs all play a role. Variant title: *Dragon Circle: Dragon Waking*.

3. *Dragon Burning* (Ace, 1996) The neighbors of Chestnut Circle undergo some startling transformations into such things as nature spirits and lawn gods as they battle the Dragon that is about to destroy their world. Variant title: *Dragon Circle: Dragon Burning*.

Gardner, Erle Stanley

I. To everyone who remembers Perry Mason's long-running success on television, Raymond Burr will always be Erle Stanley Gardner's unflappable lawyer who saves clients with his courtroom wizardry. An earlier radio version was equally popular in the 1940s. Fans will also remember Paul Drake, Mason's fearless and resourceful investigator; Della Street, his faithful secretary; and Hamilton Burger, the Los Angeles DA who is Mason's most frequent adversary in court. The earliest Mason novels were crafted in the realistic hard-boiled manner, but by 1937 they had begun to soften som what to include more "love interest" for the growing *Saturday Evening Post* audience. Gardner maintained a remarkably consistent and professional standard in the production of all 85 of his fast-paced and complex Perry Mason criminal cases. Their colorful titles need no further annotation. See also the entry under Gardner's pseudonym, A. A. Fair (q.v.). *The Case of the Musical Cow* is not a Perry Mason mystery. For a book about Erle Stanley Gardner, see Dorothy B. Hughes: *Erle Stanley Gardner: The Case of the Real Perry Mason* (Morrow, 1978). Thomas Chastain wrote two novels based on the Perry Mason characters: *The Case of the Burning Bequest* (Morrow, 1989) and *The Case of Too Many Murders* (Morrow, 1990).

1. *Case of the Velvet Claws, The* (Morrow, 1933)
2. *Case of the Sulky Girl, The* (Morrow, 1933)
3. *Case of the Curious Bride, The* (Morrow, 1934)
4. *Case of the Howling Dog, The* (Morrow, 1934)
5. *Case of the Lucky Legs, The* (Morrow, 1934)
6. *Case of the Caretaker's Cat, The* (Morrow, 1935)
7. *Case of the Counterfeit Eye, The* (Morrow, 1935)
8. *Case of the Sleepwalker's Niece, The* (Morrow, 1936)
9. *Case of the Stuttering Bishop, The* (Morrow, 1936)
10. *Case of the Dangerous Dowager, The* (Morrow, 1937)
11. *Case of the Lame Canary, The* (Morrow, 1937)
12. *Case of the Shoplifter's Shoe, The* (Morrow, 1938)
13. *Case of the Substitute Face, The* (Morrow, 1938)
14. *Case of the Perjured Parrot, The* (Morrow, 1939)
15. *Case of the Rolling Bones, The* (Morrow, 1939)
16. *Case of the Baited Hook, The* (Morrow, 1940)
17. *Case of the Silent Partner, The* (Morrow, 1940)
18. *Case of the Empty Tin, The* (Morrow, 1941)
19. *Case of the Haunted Husband, The* (Morrow, 1941)
20. *Case of the Careless Kitten, The* (Morrow, 1942)
21. *Case of the Drowning Duck, The* (Morrow, 1942)
22. *Case of the Buried Clock, The* (Morrow, 1943)
23. *Case of the Drowsy Mosquito, The* (Morrow, 1943)
24. *Case of the Black-Eyed Blonde, The* (Morrow, 1944)
25. *Case of the Crooked Candle, The* (Morrow, 1944)
26. *Case of the Golddigger's Purse, The* (Morrow, 1945)
27. *Case of the Half-Wakened Wife, The* (Morrow, 1945)
28. *Case of the Borrowed Brunette, The* (Morrow, 1946)
29. *Case of the Fandancer's Horse, The* (Morrow, 1947)
30. *Case of the Lazy Lover, The* (Morrow, 1947)
31. *Case of the Lonely Heiress, The* (Morrow, 1948)
32. *Case of the Vagabond Virgin, The* (Morrow, 1948)
33. *Case of the Cautious Coquette, The* (Morrow, 1949)
34. *Case of the Dubious Bridegroom, The* (Morrow, 1949)
35. *Case of the Negligent Nymph, The* (Morrow, 1950)
36. *Case of the One-Eyed Witness, The* (Morrow, 1950)
37. *Case of the Fiery Fingers, The* (Morrow, 1951)
38. *Case of the Angry Mourner, The* (Morrow, 1951)
39. *Case of the Grinning Gorilla, The* (Morrow, 1952)
40. *Case of the Moth-Eaten Mink, The* (Morrow, 1952)
41. *Case of the Green-Eyed Sister, The* (Morrow, 1953)
42. *Case of the Hesitant Hostess, The* (Morrow, 1953)
43. *Case of the Fugitive Nurse, The* (Morrow, 1954)
44. *Case of the Restless Redhead, The* (Morrow, 1954)
45. *Case of the Runaway Corpse, The* (Morrow, 1954)
46. *Case of the Glamorous Ghost, The* (Morrow, 1955)
47. *Case of the Nervous Accomplice, The* (Morrow, 1955)
48. *Case of the Sun-Bather's Diary, The* (Morrow, 1955)
49. *Case of the Demure Defendant, The* (Morrow, 1956) Variant title: *The Case of the Missing Poison.*
50. *Case of the Gilded Lily, The* (Morrow, 1956)
51. *Case of the Terrified Typist, The* (Morrow, 1957)
52. *Case of the Daring Decoy, The* (Morrow, 1957)
53. *Case of the Lucky Loser, The* (Morrow, 1957)
54. *Case of the Screaming Woman, The* (Morrow, 1957)
55. *Case of the Calendar Girl, The* (Morrow, 1958)
56. *Case of the Foot-Loose Doll, The* (Morrow, 1958)
57. *Case of the Long-legged Models, The* (Morrow, 1958) Variant title: *The Case of the Dead Man's Daughters.*
58. *Case of the Deadly Toy, The* (Morrow, 1959) Variant title: *The Case of the Greedy Grandpa.*
59. *Case of the Mythical Monkeys, The* (Morrow, 1959)
60. *Case of the Singing Skirt, The* (Morrow, 1959)
61. *Case of the Waylaid Wolf, The* (Morrow, 1959)
62. *Case of the Duplicate Daughter, The* (Morrow, 1960)
63. *Case of the Shapely Shadow, The* (Morrow, 1960)
64. *Case of the Bigamous Spouse, The* (Morrow, 1961)
65. *Case of the Spurious Spinster, The* (Morrow, 1961)
66. *Case of the Blonde Bonanza, The* (Morrow, 1962)
67. *Case of the Ice-Cold Hands, The* (Morrow, 1962)
68. *Case of the Reluctant Model, The* (Morrow, 1962)
69. *Case of the Amorous Aunt, The* (Morrow, 1963)
70. *Case of the Mischievous Doll, The* (Morrow, 1963)
71. *Case of the Stepdaughter's Secret, The* (Morrow, 1963)
72. *Case of the Daring Divorcee, The* (Morrow, 1964)
73. *Case of the Horrified Heirs, The* (Morrow, 1964)
74. *Case of the Phantom Fortune, The* (Morrow, 1964)
75. *Case of the Beautiful Beggar, The* (Morrow, 1965)
76. *Case of the Troubled Trustee, The* (Morrow, 1965)
77. *Case of the Worried Waitress, The* (Morrow, 1966)
78. *Case of the Queenly Contestant, The* (Morrow, 1967)
79. *Case of the Careless Cupid, The* (Morrow, 1968)
80. *Case of the Fabulous Fake, The* (Morrow, 1969)

81. *Case of the Crimson Kiss, The* (Morrow, 1970) Subtitle: *A Perry Mason Novelette and Other Stories.*
82. *Case of the Crying-Swallow, The* (Morrow, 1971) Subtitle: *A Perry Mason Novelette and Other Stories.*
83. *Case of the Fenced-In Woman, The* (Morrow, 1972)
84. *Case of the Irate Witness, The* (Morrow, 1972) Subtitle: *A Perry Mason Mystery and Other Stories.*
85. *Case of the Postponed Murder, The* (Morrow, 1973)

II. Another series features small-town district attorney Doug Selby, who, in a switch, is the hero of the cases he argues against a slippery defense lawyer. The Selby novels are not annotated. A character named Terry Clane appears in two novels: *Murder Up My Sleeve* (Morrow, 1937) and *The Case of the Backward Mule* (Morrow, 1946). "Gramps" Wiggins is the protagonist of *The Case of the Turning Tide* (Morrow, 1941) and *The Case of the Smoking Chimney.*

1. *D.A. Calls It Murder, The* (Morrow, 1937)
2. *D.A. Holds a Candle, The* (Morrow, 1938)
3. *D.A. Draws a Circle, The* (Morrow, 1939)
4. *D.A. Goes to Trial, The* (Morrow, 1940)
5. *D.A. Cooks a Goose, The* (Morrow, 1942)
6. *D.A. Calls a Turn, The* (Morrow, 1944)
7. *D.A. Breaks a Seal, The* (Morrow, 1946)
8. *D.A. Takes a Chance, The* (Morrow, 1948)
9. *D.A. Breaks an Egg, The* (Morrow, 1949)

Gardner, John (Edmund)

I. The English John Gardner is the author of mysteries, World II suspense stories, and other entertaining volumes. He is perhaps best known for the Boysie Oakes series of comedy-mysteries, which parody the James Bond books. Boysie is luxury-loving, lecherous, and a mass of neuroses. He is afraid of flying and can't stand the sight of blood, and when Britain's Department of Special Security assigns him to "liquidate" anyone, he subcontracts the job to a Soho gangster. Rod Taylor played the Boysie role in the film version of *The Liquidator* (1966).

1. *Liquidator, The* (Viking, 1964) Boysie's first case shows his ingenious way of carrying out an assignment to liquidate some British Secret Service security risks.
2. *Understrike* (Viking, 1965) Boysie travels to San Diego, California, to watch some submarine tests, and the Russians send a carefully rehearsed double to take his place.
3. *Amber Nine* (Viking, 1966) Boysie's job this time is to liquidate a leftist MP.
4. *Madrigal* (Viking, 1968) Boysie learns about the Chinese the hard way.
5. *Founder Member* (Muller [UK], 1969) Now working with Griffin and Mostyn in the Grimobo security agency, Boysie gets involved in a rocket romp at Cape Kennedy. Not published in the United States.
6. *Air Apparent* (Putnam, 1971) Boysie is in charge of a charter airline, Air Apparent. UK title: *The Airline Pirates.*
7. *Traitor's Exit* (Muller [UK], 1970) Boysie helps a detective-story writer get a British defector out of Moscow.
8. *Killer for a Song, A* (Hodder [UK], 1975) This concerns a revenge plot for an old Secret Service killing in Mexico.

II. There is a touch of the old parodist in Gardner's revival of James Bond, but then Ian Fleming's (q.v.) later work had become almost self-parody in any case. Gardner's aging 007 now drives a fuel-efficient car

and smokes low-tar cigarettes (still specially made for him) but has lost little of his potency otherwise. Gardner eventually tired of Bond, and the franchise was continued by Raymond Benson (q.v.). Two omnibus volumes were published by Avenel: *Ian Fleming's James Bond: Three Complete Novels* (1987; numbers 1–3) and *Ian Fleming's James Bond: Back in Action* (1988; numbers 4–6). *License to Kill* (Armchair Detective, 1990) and *Goldeneye* (Berkley, 1995) are novelizations of screenplays.

1. *License Renewed* (Putnam, 1981) Bond tackles the megalomaniac nuclear physicist Anton Murik, who is up to nasty things in his Scottish castle.
2. *For Special Services* (Putnam, 1982) Bond is sent to the United States to infiltrate a SPECTRE stronghold and prevent their plot to control space satellites.
3. *Icebreaker* (Putnam, 1983) To thwart Count von Gloda's plan to create a Fourth Reich, Bond must travel to the Arctic Circle.
4. *Role of Honor* (Putnam, 1984) Dr. Jay Autem Holy has designed a computer system for waging war that Bond must destroy.
5. *Nobody Lives Forever* (Putnam, 1986) The entire criminal population of Europe is competing for the rich prize Tamil Rahani has offered for Bond's head on a silver platter.
6. *No Deals, Mr. Bond* (Putnam, 1987) Bond goes to East Germany to investigate a sexual-entrapment operation that has collapsed.
7. *Scorpius* (Putnam, 1988) Is Father Valentine a religious guru or the evil arms dealer Vladimir Scorpius in disguise?
8. *Win, Lose or Die* (Putnam, 1989) BAST (Brotherhood of Anarchy and Secret Terror) has sinister plans for the leaders of Britain, the Soviet Union, and the United States, who are meeting in secret.
9. *Brokenclaw* (Putnam, 1990) Bond returns from burnout recuperation to prevent submarine-detection documents from falling into the hands of the Chinese.
10. *Man from Barbarossa, The* (Putnam, 1991) A secret Soviet organization kidnaps a New Jersey man suspected of being involved in the Babi Yar massacre of 1941.
11. *Death Is Forever* (Putnam, 1992) Wolfgang Weisen, aka "the Poison Dwarf," is directing the assassination of members of the West's spy network in East Germany.
12. *Never Send Flowers* (Putnam, 1993) Bond and beautiful Swiss agent Flica von Grusse investigate the poison-pellet murder of a British agent.
13. *Seafire* (Putnam, 1994) Evil billionaire Maxwell Tarn has disappeared, and Bond and Flica have to find him.
14. *Cold Fall* (Putnam, 1996) Bond is assigned to find the persons behind the bombing of an airliner, which involves him with minor royalty, Italian mobsters, a power-crazed general in Idaho, and the neo-fascist terrorist organization, the Children of the Last Days.

III. In these two Sherlock Holmes spin-offs, Gardner has revived Holmes's archenemy, Moriarty, who, it seems, was not killed at Reichenbach Falls either but lived on to study London's criminal life in great detail. Gardner transforms the professor's notebooks into delightful period pieces.

1. *Return of Moriarty, The* (Putnam, 1974) A London gang led by a supercriminal has troubles with a rival mob. Variant title: *Moriarty.*
2. *Revenge of Moriarty, The* (Putnam, 1975) Following a trip to the United States, Moriarty lays an elaborate revenge plot for the destruction of his enemies.

IV. A pair of British procedurals with religious overtones features Scotland Yard Detective Inspector Derek Torry.

1. **Complete State of Death, A (Viking, 1969)** Introduces Detective Inspector Derek Torry, a Scotland Yard operative with religious problems. Variant title: *The Stone Killer*.
2. **Corner Men, The (Doubleday, 1974)** Seven gangland deaths in three days may portend open warfare in London's underworld.

V. The Secret Generations trilogy weds the genres of spy novel and family saga in rather complicated fashion. The English Railtons and the American Farthings are tied together by marriage and by commitment to the espionage trade. The action extends over several generations and decades of the 20th century.

1. **Secret Generations, The (Putnam, 1985)** Nearly everyone in three generations of the Railton family gets involved in espionage during the years 1909 to 1935.
2. **Secret Houses, The (Putnam, 1987)** The British investigation of a compromised French Resistance network involves both the Railtons and the Farthings in the late 1940s.
3. **Secret Families, The (Putnam, 1989)** Donald Railton and Arnold Farthing take part in an undercover operation inside Russia to clear the reputations of family members. Starts in 1964.

VI. Yet another espionage series by the prolific Gardner features the German-born British espionage agent "Big Herbie" Kruger. Herbie, whose avocations include drinking beer and listening to Mahler, appeared in a trilogy written in the late 1970s and early 1980s and reappeared in the 1990s in the Last Kruger trilogy, two volumes of which have appeared so far.

1. **Nostradamus Traitor, The (Doubleday, 1979)** NATO security agent Kruger is asked by a German woman to look for the site where her husband was executed in World War II.
2. **Garden of Weapons, The (McGraw-Hill, 1981)** Herbie's "Telegraph Boys," six British agents working in East Germany, have been infiltrated by a double agent.
3. **Quiet Dogs, The (Charter, 1982)** Herbie must rescue a double agent whom his own blunder has jeopardized from inside the Kremlin.
4. **Maestro (Penzler, 1993)** Kruger is brought out of retirement to debrief 90-year-old conductor Louis Passau.
5. **Confessor (Penzler, 1995)** Terrorists are bombing European and American sites as a prelude to a scheme called "Magic Lightning."

VII. Gardner's latest series is set in World War II London during the Blitz. Suzie Montford, a police officer, is featured in these procedurals with thriller overtones.

1. **Bottled Spider (Severn, 2002)** Because of a shortage of male police officers, Police Constable Suzie Montford is promoted to detective sergeant. She is paired with gentleman detective "Dandy Tom" Livermore in an investigation of a series of murders of young women.
2. **Streets of Town, The (Severn, 2003)** A pair of evil twins involved in black-market swindles and a necrophiliac serial killer, the Ghoul, engage Suzie's attention here.
3. **Angels Dining at the Ritz (Severn House, 2004)** August 17, 1942. Montford's investigation into the death of a barrister and his family in London leads the team to Norfolk and the US Air Force personnel stationed nearby.
4. **Troubled Midnight (St. Martin's, 2005)** Montford is drafted into British intelligence when her investigation of the torture-murder of a colonel reveals that the victim was part of the inner circle of military strategists.

Gash, Jonathan

PSEUDONYM OF John Grant

I. Lovejoy, an antiques dealer from East Anglia, is an eccentric amateur detective. He is bad-tempered and not overly scrupulous about how he acquires his antiques. But his expertise and ability to squeeze out of tough spots combine to make these books suspenseful, humorous, and instructive as well. John Grant, under his real name, is an English pathologist and microbiologist. The series has been made into a TV series that has been shown on cable in the United States. Lovejoy's madcap adventures and digressions about antiques will appeal to mystery lovers and fans of *Antiques Roadshow*.

1. **Judas Pair, The (Harper, 1977)** Lovejoy searches for the 13th, or "Judas," pair of dueling pistols made by Durs Egg.
2. **Gold by Gemini (Harper, 1979)** Lovejoy gets wind of a treasure trove of early Roman coins somewhere on the Isle of Man. UK title: *Gold from Gemini*.
3. **Grail Tree, The (Harper, 1980)** A quest for the Holy Grail turns into a quest for Lovejoy's own survival.
4. **Spend Game (Ticknor, 1981)** An old army friend and fellow antiques dealer is murdered after acquiring an item that some very nasty characters are after.
5. **Vatican Rip, The (Ticknor, 1982)** Lovejoy is forced into a plan to steal a Chippendale table from the Vatican.
6. **Firefly Gadroon (St. Martin's, 1984)** Lovejoy sets out to avenge the murder of an old silversmith and catch a ring of international antiques smugglers.
7. **Sleepers of Erin, The (Doubleday, 1983)** Mr. and Mrs. Hendricks want Lovejoy to find some "sleepers," valuable antiques that have been deliberately concealed.
8. **Gondola Scam, The (St. Martin's, 1984)** A quest to uncover an antiques manufacturing scam takes Lovejoy from an illegal auction in England to the canals of Venice.
9. **Pearlhanger (St. Martin's, 1985)** A colleague named Vernon has disappeared while hot on the trail of a fabulously rare piece of pearl jewelry.
10. **Tartan Sell, The (St. Martin's, 1986)** A missing bureau and a dead lorry driver bring Lovejoy to a crumbling manor house in the tiny Scottish town of Tachnadray. UK title: *The Tartan Ringers*.
11. **Moonspender (St. Martin's, 1987)** Lovejoy appears on a television game show and manages a big wedding in this caper.
12. **Jade Woman (St. Martin's, 1989)** Down and out in Hong Kong, Lovejoy gets involved with that city's criminal gangs and the beautiful but dangerous "jade woman."
13. **Very Last Gambado, The (St. Martin's, 1990)** Back in East Anglia, Lovejoy gets a job as technical advisor to a movie mogul making a film about a robbery at the British Museum.
14. **Great California Game, The (St. Martin's, 1991)** On the lam again, Lovejoy holes up as an illegal immigrant in Manhattan.
15. **Lies of Fair Ladies, The (St. Martin's, 1992)** Back again in East Anglia, Lovejoy gets wind of an enormous antiques scam.
16. **Paid and Loving Eyes (St. Martin's, 1993)** Lovejoy moonlights as a driver for Gaunt's Tryste Service, a sort of brothel on wheels
17. **Sin within Her Smile, The (Viking, 1994)** Purchased as "Slave for a Day" at a charity auction, Lovejoy finds himself in Wales driving a horse-drawn caravan full of mental patients.
18. **Grace in Older Women, The (Viking, 1995)** Tryer, proprietor of a mobile sex museum, is murdered, and Lovejoy gets stuck with a bunch of American tourists in the village of Fenstone.
19. **Possessions of a Lady (Viking, 1996)** Lovejoy's business is on the decline, perhaps because of competition, and he is forced to work for a chain dating service and be master of ceremonies at a combined fashion show and antique sale.

20. *Rich and the Profane, The* **(Viking, 1999)** Lovejoy's protégé, Irma Dominick, is arrested for attempted theft, and Lovejoy gets involved with Irma's aunt Jocina, a failing priory, a potentially adulterous prior with gambling debts, and a trip to the Channel Islands.

21. *Rag, a Bone and a Hank of Hair, A* **(Viking, 2000)** Dosh Callaghan, another shady operator, hires Lovejoy to figure out who tricked him in a matter involving some green gemstones.

22. *Every Last Cent* **(Macmillan [UK], 2001)** A local lad known as Mortimer, rumored to be Lovejoy's son, shares his extraordinary talent for distinguishing genuine antiques from fake. Unfortunately, Mortimer's honesty is ruining the local antiques trade.

23. *Ten Word Game, The* **(Thomas Dunne, 2004)** Lovejoy is on the run after stealing one of his own forgeries from the Marquis of Gotham. Bounty hunter David Buddy is hot on his trail.

II. A second series links an unlikely pair: naive physician Dr. Clare Burtonall and ex-seminarian and male prostitute Bonn. The smart but essentially conventional Clare and the nonchalantly immoral but somehow sympathetic Bonn have an odd relationship (she pays him for sex) that brings Clare into Bonn's violent and seamy world of drug addiction and sex-for-hire.

1. ***Different Women Dancing*** **(Viking, 1997)** Physician Clare Burtonall and male prostitute Bonn meet when they see a man get fatally hit by a taxi.

2. ***Prey Dancing*** **(Viking, 1998)** Clare becomes the target of a psychotic criminal after she comforts a young drug addict dying of AIDS and is thrust into Bonn's underworld.

3. ***Die Dancing*** **(Macmillan [UK], 2000)** Terence "Dulsie" Dulworth, who was a "fixer" for important businessmen, including Clare's ex-husband, dies, and somehow Clare, Bonn, and the escort agency he works for get involved.

4. ***Bone Dancing*** **(Allison & Busby [UK], 2003)** The death of one of the syndicate's street girls arouses Clare's suspicions.

Gaus, P(aul) L.

The Old Order Amish of Ohio's Holmes County are the subject of this series of mysteries. Although the Amish like to keep to themselves and be self-sufficient, they are occasionally forced to call upon the help of outsiders such as college professor Michael Branden and Sheriff Bruce Robinson when homicide strikes their community. The Amish way of life in rural Ohio is sensitively portrayed by P. L. Gaus, chair of the chemistry department at the College of Wooster in Ohio.

1. *Blood of the Prodigal* **(Ohio University, 1999)** Bishop Eli Miller of the Old Order Amish of Ohio's Holmes County goes for aid to college professor Michael Branden when his exiled son Jonah snatches Eli's grandson Jeremiah.

2. *Broken English* **(Ohio University, 2000)** Out of prison after 25 years, Jesse Sands breaks into the home of Janet Hawkins, whom he kills after a struggle. Then the victim's Amish father, David Hawkins, tries to kill Sands.

3. *Clouds without Rain* **(Ohio University, 2001)** Michael Branden goes undercover to investigate teenage buggy robbers on mountain bikes but soon becomes involved in something more sinister.

4. *Cast a Blue Shadow* **(Ohio University, 2003)** A blizzard devastates Millersburg College and the lives of many of the students and locals, including wealthy executive Juliet Favor, who is discovered dead in her bedroom.

5. *Prayer for the Night, A* **(Ohio University, 2006)** Eighteen-year-old Sara Yoder is torn between contemporary culture and her Amish community. Then two fellow teens fail to appear for a secret gathering.

Gear, W. Michael & Kathleen

I. Husband-and-wife team W. Michael and Kathleen O'Neal Gear are producing the long-running First North American series, which points up American prehistory by focusing on the personal stories of fictional Native Americans. The prehistorical period covered is from "ice-tunnel" migration to North America thousands of years ago to the 15th century CE, just before Europeans made their permanent settlements. The main themes of the series are the human response to environmental change and the conflict between "good" shamans and "bad" shamans or "true" dreamers and "false" dreamers. The novels are arranged below in rough chronological order rather than by date of publication. W. Michael Gear is listed as principal author in numbers 1 through 5, and Kathleen O'Neal Gear is listed as principal author for subsequent volumes. The Gears are professional archaeologists.

1. *People of the Wolf* **(Tor, 1990)** Wolf-Dreamer has a vision that makes him lead his people through the "ice tunnel" into new lands.

2. *People of the Nightland* **(Forge, 2007)** 1,000 years after Wolf Dreamer, the People of the Wolf have split into two clans: the People of the Nightland and the People of the Sunpath. The effects of global warming are being felt.

3. *People of the Fire* **(Tor, 1991)** Thousands of years after Wolf Dreamer's migration, game is dying out and the People have initiated agriculture. It is up to Little Dancer to recover the Wolf Bundle, a sacred fetish desecrated by Heavy Bear, and lead his people from their drought-stricken area.

4. *People of the Earth* **(Tor, 1992)** The Wolf Bundle continues to influence events as the clans migrate slowly southward along the Rocky Mountains. Brave Man, Bad Belly, and White Ash are the leading characters.

5. *People of the Sea* **(Forge, 1993)** In coastal California, 12,000 years ago, melting glaciers are causing the waters to rise. Sunchaser is unable to establish his link to the spirit world.

6. *People of the Raven* **(Forge, 2004)** Circa 7000–9000 BCE. "Caucasoids" have settled the Pacific Northwest. The North Wind People and the Raven People form two competing cultures.

7. *People of the Lightning* **(Forge, 1995)** Circa 6000 BCE, in what is now Florida, the Windover People, not closely related to other North Americans, have settled. Musselwhite, her husband, Diver, and Cottonmouth of the Standing Hollow Horn clan are the principal characters.

8. *People of the Owl* **(Forge, 2003)** Circa 2000 BCE, in what is now Louisiana. Mud Puppy, renamed Salamander, a 15-year-old seer, leads the Owl Clan.

9. *People of the Lakes* **(Forge, 1994)** Some 2,000 years ago, the Hopewell Culture. Star Shell hopes to save her people from the adverse effects of an evil totemic mask by destroying it at Niagara Falls.

10. *People of the River* **(Tor, 1992)** Circa 700–1500 CE. Depicts the culture of the "Mississippians" living in the area surrounding Chakokia, in what is now Illinois.

11. *People of the Moon* **(Forge, 2005)** In the Chimney Rock area of what is now New Mexico, the Chaco Anasazi have conquered the Moon People of the pueblos.

12. *People of the Masks* (Forge, 1998) Circa 1000 CE. Set in north-eastern North America. Rumbler, the dwarf seer of the Turtle Nation, is the hope of his people.

13. *People of the Silence* (Forge, 1996) An extended drought in the mid-12th century CE is driving the Anasazi civilization to "inevitable" decline and collapse. Cornsilk and Poor Singer are among the principal characters.

14. *People of the Weeping Eye* (Forge, 2008) Circa 13th century CE. Three wanderers with mysterious pasts—Old White the Seeker, Trader, and Two Petals—may hold the key to the fate of the warring Sky Hand and Chahta tribes.

15. *People of the Mist* (Forge, 1998) Circa 1400 CE. A murder mystery involving Flat Pearl and Copper Thunder of the Algonquins, who inhabit the Chesapeake Bay area.

II. The Gears collaborated on a trio of Anasazi mysteries with two story lines. The first story line, set in the present day, concerns archaeologist Dusty Stewart and anthropologist Maureen Cole, who are excavating a 13th-century Anasazi site, speculating on the fate of the people they are digging up. The second story takes place at the Anasazi site in the 13th century CE and relates how characters such as Browser, Catkin, and Stone Ghost cope with the disasters facing their people.

1. *Visitant, The* (Forge, 1999) Archaeologist Dusty Stewart, excavating an Anasazi site in the Sonoran Desert, uncovers mass graves containing the bodies of young Anasazi women with their skulls smashed. Back in the 13th century, the shaman Browser is trying to track down a serial killer.

2. *Summoning God, The* (Forge, 2000) Searching for answers to the fate of the Anasazi, Dusty Stewart and Maureen Cole continue with their excavation. Enemy attacks, attrition, and a serial killer bedevil Katsinas's People.

3. *Bone Walker* (Forge, 2001) Stewart and Cole are embroiled in a 20th-century mystery. Trying to end the blood strife that's tearing the Anasazi villages apart, Browser seeks to slay the evil Two Herons.

III. W. Michael Gear is also an SF writer. His Way of the Spider trilogy is set in a far-future universe in which the galaxy is run by the powerful few: genetically altered humans permanently linked with the Gi-net—a massive computer network containing everything there is to know about the planets and space stations claimed by mankind.

1. *Warriors of Spider, The* (DAW, 1988) Rebellion against the Directorate is stirring on the planet known only as "World," populated by the warrior descendants of survivors of a starship crash.

2. *Way of Spider, The* (DAW, 1989) The Directorate's only hope of defeating the Sirian rebels lies in three battle-damaged patrol ships, three backup warships, and a race of primitive, planet-bound warriors.

3. *Web of Spider, The* (DAW, 1989) Ngen Van Chow, leader of the failed Sirian rebellion, has fled to a distant world, establishing a base from which he plans to launch an interstellar holy war.

IV. Another SF trilogy written by W. Michael Gear alone is the Forbidden Borders space-opera series, set in the far future, in which the interplanetary empires of Rega and Sassa square off against each other.

1. *Requiem for the Conqueror* (DAW, 1991) Rega and Sassa, the only two significant space-empires remaining, must each turn to the man they fear more than each other, Staffa Kor Therma.

2. *Relic of Empire* (DAW, 1992) Skyla, Staffa's second-in-command and the woman he loves, has been kidnapped.

3. *Contermeasures* (DAW, 1993) Staffa is trying to break free of the alien-created Forbidden Borders, as the long-dreaded final war between Rega and Sassa looms.

V. Kathleen O'Neal Gear published an SF trilogy of her own under her maiden name: Kathleen O'Neal. The three novels—*Abyss of Light*, *Treasure of Light*, and *Redemption of Light*—were published by DAW in 1990–1991. She has also embarked, as Kathleen O'Neal Gear, upon a trilogy about matriarchal Native American life in which the High Chieftess of the Black Falcon nation struggles with her own physical problems, former lovers, and other enemies.

1. *It Sleeps in Me* (Forge, 2005) Sora, the High Chieftess of the Black Falcon nation, struggles with the spirit of her greatest lover, the murderously jealous Flint.

2. *It Wakes in Me* (Forge, 2006) The High Chieftess, subject to blackouts and fits, is haunted by two gleaming eyes—the Midnight Fox—and by accusations of seven murders.

3. *It Dreams in Me* (Forge, 2007) Sora has been banished by her own people until she can find healing for her broken spirit.

Gellis, Roberta (Leah Jacobs)

I. Roberta Gellis is a doyenne of the historical romance field. She has won a Lifetime Achievement Award for Historical Fiction and the Romantic Writers of America Lifetime Award. New York native Gellis began her professional career as a chemist but eventually got a master's degree in medieval literature from NYU and embarked upon a writing career. Most of her earlier books were set in medieval England, but she has branched out into the Regency period, Greek mythology, mysteries, and SF. One of her most popular series is the Roselynde Chronicles, sometimes called the Medieval Books, set in the reigns of Richard the Lionhearted and John in late-12th-century England. It follows the fortune of a noble family through its female members: Alinor (or Eleanor) and her daughter and granddaughter, all strong-willed women. The men aren't wimps, either. Number 2 is a spin-off from the series, published more than 20 years after the others.

1. *Roselynde* (Playboy, 1978) "As Richard the Lionheart's Crusade heads for Jerusalem, the lovely young Alinor of Roselynde Manor meets the man of her dreams" (cover description).

2. *Desiree* (Harlequin, 2005) Impecunious Sir Alexandre Beaudoin arrives at Roselynde and is smitten by the married Desiree of Exceat.

3. *Alinor* (Playboy, 1978) The widowed Lady Alinor, beset by King John, is strongly tempted by the marriage offer of Ian de Vipont.

4. *Joanna* (Playboy, 1979) Alinor's daughter, Joanna, a fiery redhead, her emotions "tragically frozen" by "the cold fear" of a man's love, comes face-to-face with the irresistible knight Geoffrey.

5. *Gilliane* (Playboy, 1980) Gilliane, unhappily married, comes into the power of her abhorred husband's most dangerous enemy, Adam Lemagne.

6. *Rhiannon* (Playboy, 1982) Rhiannon, raven-haired daughter of a Welsh prince, although irresistible to men, wants to keep her freedom until she meets the court's most eligible bachelor.

7. *Sybelle* (Jove, 1983) Sybelle, granddaughter to Alinor and heiress to the Roselynde dynasty, is bound by honor and passion to another free spirit, Walter de Clare.

II. The more recent Magdalen la Batarde novels are a mystery series set in King Stephen's chaotic 11th-century England. Magdalen la Batarde, the madam of the Old Priory "Guesthouse" in Southwark, is passionately attached to the women who work for her, and with the help of Sir Bellamy of Itchen (often called Bell), she embarks on murder cases that touch upon her beloved dependents.

1. *Mortal Bane, A* **(Forge, 1999)** When a messenger who has been partaking of the services offered by the Old Priory Guesthouse in 11th-century Southwark, England, is murdered on the steps of a nearby church, Magdalen de la Batarde, the madam of the Old Priory, finds herself and her women threatened, so she embarks upon an investigation aided by Sir Bellamy of Itchen.
2. *Personal Devil, A* **(Forge, 2001)** Blind Sabina, one of Magdalene's favorite workers, leaves the Old Priory to become the principal "leman" of Master Mainard. Then Mainard's wife dies in suspicious circumstances, and Mainard becomes prime suspect.
3. *Bone of Contention* **(Forge, 2002)** In June 1139, Magdalene's patron, William of Ypres, calls her to Oxford, where King Stephen is holding his great council. The obnoxious Aimery St. Cyr is stabbed to death, and one of Sir William's men, Niall Arvagh of Murcot, is the prime suspect.
4. *Chains of Folly* **(Five Stars, 2006)** When the Bishop of Winchester, brother of King Stephen, finds a dead whore in his bedchamber, he sends for Magdalen to investigate.

III. The Royal Dynasty series is a quartet of historical romances set in 13th-century France during the reign of Louis IX, later to become Saint Louis, and England during the reign of Henry III, a rather unsuccessful monarch. The beautiful, sensuous Fenice d'Aix, daughter of a noble father and a lowly mother, is one of the protagonists.

A pair of novels set in medieval Scotland: *A Tapestry of Dreams* (Jove, 1985) and *Fires of Winter* (Jove, 1987), called the Tales of Jernaeve, or the Jernaeve Chronicles, is sometimes linked with the Royal Dynasty series, as are such stand-alone medieval novels as *The Rope Dancer* (Jove, 1986) and *Masques of Gold* (Jove, 1988).

The Heiress novels are a loosely connected series of five books set during the late 18th and early 19th centuries published by Dell (1980–1984): *The English Heiress*; *The Cornish Heiress*; *The Kent Heiress*; *Fortune's Bride*; and *A Woman's Estate*.

1. *Siren Song* **(Playboy, 1981)** Lady Elizabeth was wrenched from her fiancé and thrust into the arms of a man she detested. Later, she meets her love again, when he is a knight with the courage to fight for her.
2. *Winter Song* **(Playboy, 1982)** The daughter of a humble knight married into the royal family and the nephew of the queen embark upon a passionate romance.
3. *Fire Song* **(Jove, 1984)** Fenice d'Aix, bearer of a noble name, is an outcast in French society due to her mother being a lowly serf.
4. *Silver Mirror, A* **(Jove/Berkley, 1989)** In 1264, during the reign of Henry III of England, Alphonse d'Aix, vassal of King Louis IX of France, and Barbara, illegitimate daughter of the Earl of Norfolk, try to rekindle their romance.

Gemmell, David

I. The late (d. 2006) British writer David Gemmell has been acknowledged as a master of heroic fantasy since his first novel, *Legend* (1984), introduced us to the world of Drenai. Drenai is a medieval-type world full of mighty axemen and swordsmasters, barbarian hordes, were-beasts, practical sorcerers, threatened kingdoms, and reincarnation. *Legend*, which made Gemmell a cult figure in the United Kingdom, was followed by several sequels, but the series has been slower to catch on in the United States. Chronology of the Drenai series is somewhat difficult to establish, because some of the major characters are reincarnated and some later titles are prequels to earlier novels. Three volumes of *Drenai Tales*, omnibus volumes containing all of the titles except numbers 1 and 11, have been published in the United Kingdom (Legend, 1991; Orbit, 2002; Bantam, 2002).

1. *White Wolf* **(Del Rey, 2003)** In this prequel, Skilgannon the swordmaster retires to a monastery to think things over after his troops sacked a city with such savagery that he received the cognomon "the Damned."
2. *First Chronicles of Druss the Legend, The* **(Del Rey, 1998)** Druss, Captain of the Axe, becomes a killing machine after his beloved wife, Rowena, is abducted by slavers. Originally published in the United Kingdom in 1993.
3. *Legend of Deathwalker, The* **(Del Rey, 1999)** Subtitle: *Chronicles of Druss the Axeman*. For centuries the Nadir, who have suffered under tyranny, have awaited a warlord who will unite them against their oppressors. Originally published in the United Kingdom in 1996. Variant title: *The Second Chronicles of Druss the Legend*.
4. *Against the Horde* **(New Infinities, 1988)** The novel that started it all. Druss, Captain of the Axe, had chosen to wait for death in a mountain hideaway, but Dros Delnoch, the last Drenai stronghold, is under threat from the Nadir hordes. Originally published in 1984 in the United Kingdom as *Legend*. Reprinted as *Legend* by Del Rey in 1994.
5. *Quest for Lost Heroes* **(Del Rey, 1995)** Dros Delnoch has fallen and Nadir hordes sweep across the land. When slavers kidnap a young girl from her village, a peasant boy sets off on a quest to free her. Originally published in the United Kingdom in 1990.
6. *King beyond the Gate, The* **(New Infinities, 1988)** A century after the last stand at Dros Delnoch, only one man, Tenaka Khan, the Prince of Shadows, stands against a mad emperor who is kept in power by the werebeast Joinings and the warlike Dark Templars. Originally published in the United Kingdom in 1985. Reprinted by Del Rey in 1995.
7. *Waylander* **(New Infinities, 1988)** Waylander must journey into the lands of the Nadir, find the legendary Armour of Bronze, and turn the tide against the enemies of the Drenai. Originally published in the United Kingdom in 1986. Reprinted by Del Rey in 1995.
8. *In the Realm of the Wolf* **(Del Rey, 1998)** Waylander the Slayer and his daughter, the Battle Queen of Kar Barzac, are beset at every turn by sorcerers, soldiers, and demons. Originally published in the United Kingdom in 1992 as *Waylander II: In the Realm of the Wolf*.
9. *Winter Warriors* **(Del Rey, 2000)** Waylander the Slayer has disappeared, but a secret society of trained assassins is on his trail. Originally published in the United Kingdom in 1993.
10. *Hero in the Shadows* **(Del Rey, 2000)** "An evil city, banished into limbo, starts to reappear after a thousand years when the once powerful spells that held it start to wane" (publisher's blurb).
11. *Swords of Night and Day, The* **(Del Rey, 2004)** Skilgannon the Slayer, Druss the Legend, and other Drenai characters have been reincarnated 1,000 years later by the priest Landis Khan, who has remastered ancient technology.

II. The Sipstrassi series consists of the Jon Shannow trilogy and the Stones of Power duet, seemingly unrelated but apparently linked in Gemmell's mind. Stones of Power is a retelling of the Arthur legend set in the Britain of the Dark Ages. The Jon Shannow trio is set in a world three years after the Earth has "toppled on its axis" and civilization has been destroyed. All the books have a mixture of fantasy and SF elements. The omnibus volume *Stones of Power* (Legend [UK], 1992) contains numbers 1 through 4. *The Complete Chronicles of the Jerusalem Man* (Legend [UK], 1995) contains numbers 3 through 5.

1. *Ghost King* (Del Rey, 1997) Britannia has been plunged into the Dark Ages by rebellion and invasion. The king has been slain, and the great Sword of Power has vanished beyond the Circle of Mist. Originally published in the United Kingdom in 1988.
2. *Last Sword of Power* (Del Rey, 1996) Only Uther Pendragon can save Britannia from the Goths and their bloodthirsty leader Wotan. But Uther is chained in hell, and all hope lies with the Warrior known as Revelation. Originally published in the United Kingdom in 1988.
3. *Jerusalem Man, The* (Baen, 1988) Three hundred years after the destruction of civilization, Jon Shannow, pursuing a dream to calm the violence in his soul, sees a fresh terror emerge from the Plague Lands. Originally published in the United Kingdom in 1987 as *Wolf in Shadow*. Reissued in the United States as *Wolf in Shadow* by Del Rey in 1996.
4. *Last Guardian, The* (Del Rey, 1997) It is up to Jon Shannow to retrieve the Sword of God from the clouds above the City of Beasts and close the gateway between past and present. Originally published in the United Kingdom in 1989.
5. *Bloodstone* (Del Rey, 1997) The Jerusalem Man is back, as the Deacon and his Jerusalem Riders have unleashed a sea of bigotry and hatred, killing Unbelievers and Mutants in the name of God and peace. Originally published in the United Kingdom in 1994.

III. The Rigante series, based, like most of Gemmell's fiction, on Celtic myth, is set in a world like medieval Scotland. Warriors with names like Connavar, Lonavar, Bane the Bastard, and Stormrider fight for the rights of the Rigante highlanders against the evil Varlish and a god who wishes to do away with the human race entirely.

1. *Sword in the Storm* (Del Rey, 2001) Connavar grows to manhood among the mist-covered mountains of Caer Druagh, where the Rigante tribe dwell in harmony with the land and its gods. Originally published in the United Kingdom in 1998.
2. *Midnight Falcon, The* (Del Rey, 2001) Bane the Bastard, illegitimate son of Connavar, rejected by his father and his fellow highlanders, becomes a gladiator harboring a desire for revenge. Originally published in the United Kingdom in 1999.
3. *Ravenheart* (Del Rey, 2001) The Varlish have subjugated the Rigante highlanders. A host of characters, including Jaim Grymauch, Lanovar, Kaelin Ring, and Gaise Macon, tries to deal with the Varlish and the local lord, the Moidart.
4. *Stormrider* (Del Rey, 2002) Stormrider is the Rigante "soul name" for Gaise Macon, a young nobleman, unloved from birth but determined to show his father his worth by becoming a general in the struggle against the king's enemies.

IV. Two novels known as the Hawk Queen are set in a vaguely Celtic realm in which the Highlanders live in subservience to the Outlanders after the battle of Colden Moor (Culloden?). The Hawk Queen is Sigarni, sole representative of a line of kings.

1. *Ironhand's Daughter* (Del Rey, 2004) After the disastrous battle of Colden Moor, the Highlanders live under the yoke of the Outlanders. Signari, last representative of a line of kings, is their last, best hope. Originally published in the United Kingdom in 1995.
2. *Hawk Eternal, The* (Del Rey, 2005) The story of the Hawk Queen, Sigarni, winner of many victories, including one against a demon from another universe, and of Caswallon, unwilling leader of the clans, and his foster son. Originally published in the United Kingdom in 1995.

V. *The Lion of Macedon* and its sequel, *The Dark Prince*, are historical fantasies set in ancient Greece. Parmenion, a Spartan of mixed ancestry, becomes a soldier-of-fortune, hiring on with the army of Philip of Macedonia, father of the Dark Prince, the future Alexander the Great.

1. *Lion of Macedon, The* (Del Rey, 1993) Describes three decades in the career of Parmenion, a Spartan of mixed ancestry, scorned as a half-breed by the Spartans, but shaped and monitored by an aging seeress. Originally published in the United Kingdom in 1990.
2. *Dark Prince* (Del Rey, 1993) "The Lion of Macedon" and "The Dark Prince," the future Alexander the Great, are forced into other dimensions and "enchanted worlds full of wonder." Originally published in the United Kingdom in 1991.

VI. A final trilogy by Gemmell, two of which have been published, present Gemmell's version of the Trojan War, in which a character variously called Helikaon, the Golden One, or Aeneas holds a central place. Many characters from Homer, including Odysseus, Hektor, Agamemnon, etc., appear along with characters invented by Gemmell.

1. *Lord of the Silver Bow* (Del Rey, 2005) Aeneas, who is blessed by luck, is the target of Agamemnon, king of Mykene, and his Greeks, who covet the riches of Troy. Variant title: *Troy: Lord of the Silver Bow*.
2. *Shield of Thunder, The* (Ballantine, 2007) The Greek invasion of Troy is planned, as Homeric characters like Andromache, Hektor, and Odysseus mix with Gemmell's creations, such as Piria, Kalliades, and Banokles. Variant title: *Troy: The Shield of Thunder*.

Gent, Pete(r)

Pete Gent, wide receiver for the Dallas Cowboys in the 1960s, wrote a very popular novel based on his experiences and the screenplay for the movie that followed. *North Dallas Forty* is the account of Phil Elliott, an injury-plagued fringe player for the Cowboys, who relates the sordid goings-on behind the scenes of a championship team. *North Dallas after Forty* reunites the team 20 years later.

1. *North Dallas Forty* (Morrow, 1973) Phil Elliott sourly observes the antics of his teammates and the racist, sexist, dictatorial organization that runs the team.
2. *North Dallas after Forty* (Morrow, 1989) The physically and psychologically battered Elliott gets a writing assignment covering the 20-year reunion of the champion Dallas team.

George, Anne

Tiny, quiet Patricia Anne Hollowell and her sister, large, flamboyant Mary Alice Craig, disagree on just about everything, but the sexagenarians from Birmingham, Alabama, form a competent amateur sleuthing team. The late Anne George (d. 2001) produced, in the Southern Sisters Mysteries, an entertaining, if uneven, series with sprightly dialogue and offbeat characters.

1. *Murder on a Girls' Night Out* (Avon, 2001) Retired Alabama schoolteacher Patricia Anne Hollowell becomes involved in a homicide investigation after her sister, Mary Alice, buys a country-western club, and the previous owner is found murdered.
2. *Murder on a Bad Hair Day* (Avon, 1996) Soon after the southern sisters observe and discuss a pair of well-coiffed heads at a gallery

opening, one of the ladies in question turns up dead, and the other shows up dazed on Patricia Anne's doorstep.

3. *Murder Runs in the Family* (**Avon, 1997**) Not long after the sisters befriend genealogist Meg Ryan at the wedding of Mary Alice's daughter, the seemingly sweet, elderly lady takes a fatal leap out of a courthouse window.

4. *Murder Makes Waves* (**Avon, 1997**) The sisters try to relax in a beachfront condo in Destin, Florida. But then a body washes up on the waves.

5. *Murder Gets a Life* (**Morrow, 1998**) Intent upon investigating the credentials of the intended of Patricia's son's, the sisters journey to the trailer of family matriarch Meemaw and find a corpse awaiting them.

6. *Murder Shoots the Bull* (**Morrow, 1999**) Arthur Phizer, Patricia Anne's next-door neighbor of 40 years standing, is accused of poisoning his ex-wife at a local restaurant.

7. *Murder Carries a Torch* (**Morrow, 2000**) The apparent elopement of cousin Luke's wife with a painter, a corpse in a "snake-handling" church, Mary Alice's flirtation with the investigating sheriff, and a rattlesnake in Mary Alice's car are among the events in this mystery.

8. *Murder Boogies with Elvis* (**Morrow, 2001**) The last of the **Southern Sisters Mysteries** features the death of an Elvis impersonator at a benefit attended by the sisters and of St. Clair County sheriff Virgil Stukey, prospective bridegroom of Mary Alice.

George, Elizabeth

Elizabeth George, like Martha Grimes (q.v.), is an American who writes mysteries set in England. Californian George, who maintains a flat in London, writes highly regarded, best-selling novels about the Scotland Yard partners aristocratic (eighth Earl of Asherton) Thomas Lynley and his proletarian assistant Sergeant Barbara Havers. They are a formidable team as they ferret out solutions in a series of complex puzzle mysteries.

1. *Great Deliverance, A* (**Bantam, 1988**) Lynley and Havers travel to Yorkshire where a girl has been found sitting by the headless corpse of her father.

2. *Payment in Blood* (**Bantam, 1989**) The author of a new play is found dead on the country estate in Scotland where a troupe of actors has gathered to read the drama.

3. *Well-Schooled in Murder* (**Bantam, 1990**) Lynley and Havers uncover the murderer of a young boy from an exclusive school near London.

4. *Suitable Vengeance, A* (**Bantam, 1991**) When Lynley brings his fiancée to Cornwall to meet his mother, they become embroiled in a series of murders.

5. *For the Sake of Elena* (**Bantam, 1992**) Cambridge student Elena Weaver jogs into a fatal ambush after crossing a bridge over the River Cam.

6. *Missing Joseph* (**Bantam, 1993**) Lynley and forensic analyst Simon St. James investigate the poisoning of the vicar of Winslough.

7. *Playing for the Ashes* (**Bantam, 1994**) Cricket star Kenneth Fleming is found dead in a burned cottage on the estate of his patron, Miriam Whitelaw.

8. *In the Presence of the Enemy* (**Bantam, 1996**) Lynley, Havers, and Simon St. James are drawn into a case involving the kidnapping of the daughter of Conservative MP Eve Bowen.

9. *Deception on His Mind* (**Bantam, 1997**) Lynley and his bride, Helen Clyde, are on their honeymoon. Sergeant Havers, recuperating from injuries suffered in number 8, goes to Balford-ne-Nez

on the Essex coast to help out her neighbors, microbiologist Taymullah Azhar and his daughter Hadiyyah.

10. *In Pursuit of the Proper Sinner* (**Bantam, 1999**) The suicide of musical writer–producer David King-Ryder may have a connection with a double homicide in Derbyshire, and the newlywed Lynley takes on the case.

11. *Traitor to Memory, A* (**Bantam, 2001**) When Eugenie Davies is struck, then backed over, by a hit-and-run driver, Lynley, Havers, and partner Winston Nkata unravel the mystery.

12. *Place of Hiding, A* (**Bantam, 2003**) Lynley has a cameo role, while forensic scientist Simon St. James and his photographer wife, Deborah, are featured in a case involving some architectural drawings, a trip to California, and a rich landowner from the island of Guernsey.

13. *With No One as Witness* (**HarperCollins, 2005**) Havers has been demoted from sergeant to constable. The linked murders of four youths, three of black or mixed parentage, are the prime issue here.

14. *What Came before He Shot Her* (**HarperCollins, 2006**) Why did a 12-year-old boy, Ness Campbell, fatally shoot Inspector Lynley's wife?

15. *Careless in Red* (**Harper, 2008**) Lynley, who has left Scotland Yard and is rusticating in Cornwall, stumbles on the body of teenager Santo Kerne, who fell from a cliff.

Germain, Sylvie

French author Sylvie Germain's family saga about the Peniels covers more than a hundred years of French history from the 1800s to the Paris of 1968. The Peniels are chronicled in a melange of realism, historical references, supernatural tales, grotesque images, and poetic passages, as the star-crossed family suffers more than its fair share of adversity. Reviewers found the narrations gripping but were less enthusiastic about the philosophical ruminations.

1. *Book of Nights, The* (**Godine, 1993**) A hundred years of French history, starting in the 1800s, are covered in the story of Victor-Flandrin Peniel, married five times and the father of 15 children, most of whom come to sticky ends. Originally published in 1985 as *Le livre des nuits*. Translated from the French by Christine Donougher.

2. *Night of Amber* (**Godine, 1999**) The death of Pauline Peniel, the torture of a young boy in the Algerian War, and the murder, by force-feeding, of a friend of Charles-Victor, "Night-of-Amber-Wind-of-Fire," the protagonist, spice up the history of the Peniel clan, which is continued to 1968. Originally published 1987 as *Nuit-d'ambre*. Translated from the French by Christine Donougher.

Gerritsen, Tess

Boston medical examiner Maura Isles and police detective Jane Rizzoli, a pair of complicated and complex characters, star in a series of medical suspense thrillers. Serial killers and other very nasty types populate these novels, reminiscent of the Kay Scarpetta mysteries by Patricia Cornwell (q.v.). Excellent medical details are mixed with plots that are just short of being superhero fantasies. Tess Gerritsen, California native, left her medical practice in Honolulu to raise her children and write medical thrillers.

1. *Surgeon, The* (**Ballantine, 2001**) A serial killer who rapes his victims and removes their wombs seems to have returned to bedevil Dr.

Catherine Cordell in Boston, two years after she thought she had shot and killed him.

2. *Apprentice, The* (Ballantine, 2002) Serial killer Warren Hoyt, whom Jane Rizzoli sent to prison in number 1, escapes and teams up with a second serial killer known as the Dominator.

3. *Sinner, The* (Ballantine, 2003) Medical Examiner Maura Isles joins Rizzoli in the investigation of the bludgeoning of two nuns in Boston's Graystones Abbey.

4. *Body Double* (Ballantine, 2004) Isles, an adopted child who never knew the identity of her birth parents, is confronted by the corpse of a murdered woman who appears to be her identical twin.

5. *Vanish* (Ballantine, 2005) Olena, thought to be dead, wakes up in Maura's morgue. Then, recovering in a hospital, Olena, with the help of a mysterious colleague, takes a group of hostages, including Jane, who is about to give birth.

6. *Mephisto Club, The* (Ballantine, 2006) Twenty-eight-year-old Lori-Ann Tucker is found dead Christmas morning in her apartment, lying amid a mess of severed limbs, black candles, and satanic symbols inscribed in blood.

Gerrold, David

I. The alien, wormlike Chtorr have infiltrated Earth after a series of devastating plagues. Their goal is to enslave and devour humanity. A few good men, such as James McCarthy, are determined to free Earth from the Chtorr. This is very popular military SF. *The War against the Chtorr: Invasion* (Doubleday, 1984) contains numbers 1 and 2. Three more novels were said to be in the offing but have not appeared.

1. *Matter for Men, A* (Timescape, 1983) The alien Chtorr arrive to begin the final phase of their invasion of a plague-devastated Earth. When the Chtorr take over, humans will be nothing but livestock.

2. *Day for Damnation, A* (Timescape, 1984) James McCarthy, drafted from his college biology studies to become a member of Special Forces, is given the opportunity to contact the Chtorr.

3. *Rage for Revenge, A* (Bantam, 1989) Lieutenant McCarthy, who has studied the Chtorr and had a violent first contact with them, must infiltrate a band of renegade humans who worship the Chtorr.

4. *Season for Slaughter, A* (Bantam, 1992) A Special Forces commando and a scientist lead a group of experts into the heart of the alien invasion in South America.

II. Tales of the Starwolf is another military-SF, alien-invasion series. Numbers 2, 3, and 4 are called a trilogy, while number 1 is now called a prequel. Jonathan Korie is the leading protagonist, first on the starship *Star Wolf* and then on the starship *Norway* pitted against the alien Morthan.

1. *Yesterday's Children* (Dell, 1972) First officer Jonathan Korie drives his captain and the crew of their obsolete starship on a search for an enemy that might be a phantom. Revised edition published as *Starhunt* (Popular Library, 1980).

2. *Voyage of the Star Wolf* (Bantam, 1990) Captain Jonathan Korie and the crew of the *Star Wolf* face the superhuman Morthans after most of the human fleet has been lost.

3. *Middle of Nowhere, The* (Bantam, 1995) Commander Jonathan Korie and his crew work to bring the *Star Wolf* to battle readiness, although the starship has been consigned to salvage and there is a deadly booby-trap on board.

4. *Blood and Fire* (Benbella, 2004) In the conclusion to the series, Executive Officer Korie and the crew of the starship *Norway* venture out on a far-from-routine rescue mission.

III. The Dingilliad, or Starsiders, trilogy features 13-year-old Charles "Chigger" Dingillian and the Beanstalk, an orbital elevator system designed to take humanity from the exhausted Earth to the moon, the planets, and the stars. The series, while apparently aimed at young adults, will also interest adult readers.

1. *Jumping Off the Planet* (Tor, 2000) "Chigger" Dingillian and his brothers, "Weird" and "Stinky," are placed aboard the Beanstalk, hoping to escape an Earth of crazies and plagues.

2. *Bouncing Off the Moon* (Tor, 2001) The Dingillian brothers move off Earth and discover that a robot monkey given to the youngest possesses a computer with a capacity far in excess of what is needed to power a toy.

3. *Leaping to the Stars* (Tor, 2002) Chigger's HARLIE unit, a AI unit packed into the body of a toy, is coveted by Lunar Authority and by anti-Authority revolutionaries. The family jumps from the frying pan of the moon into the fire of the colony ship *Cascade* en route to the Outbeyond, Earth's most distant colony.

IV. The Trackers is a pair of science-fiction novels, leavened with humor, featuring a galaxy dominated by the Regency, a government of vampires, dragons, mutant humans, the Phaestor, a race of genetically engineered killing machines, and the band of malcontents who oppose them.

1. *Under the Eye of God* (Bantam, 1993) On the planet Thoska-Roole, a loosely allied band of humans, androids, and bioforms makes one last stand against the Phaestors, a vampiric race of genetically engineered killing machines.

2. *Covenant of Justice, A* (Bantam, 1994) Mercenary tracker Finn Markham, infected with a vampiric blood disease, is near death. His brother Sawyer and his colleagues of the Alliance for Life must capture the sinister Lady Zillabar and defeat the Dragon Lord.

Ghose, Zulfikar

Ghose, born in Pakistan and raised and educated in India and England, is a resident of the United States. Ghose, who has experienced cultural alienation firsthand, uses South America as the locale for much of his fiction. A trio of novels examines the failures of the Brazilian economy and society through three centuries of the picaresque career of the oft-reincarnated Gregorio Peixoto da Silva Xavier.

1. *Incredible Brazilian, The* (Holt, 1972) The adventures of Gregorio, son a rich Brazilian plantation owner in the 17th century. UK title: *The Native*.

2. *Beautiful Empire, The* (Overlook, 1984) Reincarnated in the 19th century, Gregorio experiences the boom and bust of the rubber town of Manaos. Originally published in the United Kingdom in 1975.

3. *Different World, A* (Overlook, 1984) Gregorio, reincarnated again in the 20th century, gets involved with underground politics and becomes disgusted with both the Left and the Right.

Giardina, Denise

West Virginia native Giardina knows what she writes about in the two fact-based novels relating the tribulations of West Virginia mining town Blackberry Creek as its residents endure strikes, repression, and exploitation. The two books form a stark, compelling historical saga seen through the eyes of the coal miners and their families. Giardina, who ran for Governor of West Virginia on a third-party ticket, wrote a novelization of the life of Dietrich Bonhoefer (*Saints and Villains,* Norton, 1998) and a time-travel novel set in West Virginia (*Fallam's Secret,* Norton, 2003).

1. **Storming Heaven (Norton, 1987)** The story of the violent United Mine Workers strike of 1921 is told by several of the participants.
2. **Unquiet Earth, The (Norton, 1992)** The short-lived victories, overwhelming frustrations, and ultimate devastation of the mining town of Blackberry, West Virginia, from the 1930s to the present are related.

Gibbon, Lewis Grassic

PSEUDONYM OF James Leslie Mitchel

When *Sunset Song* was dramatized on public television's *Masterpiece Theatre,* Alastair Cooke called it *the* great Scottish novel. Two additional volumes complete the trilogy known as a Scots Quair, which tells the story of a Scottish woman, Chris Guthrie, from before the First World War to the Great Depression. Gibbon wrote from a Marxist point of view and described the harshness of peasant life in a poetic language rich in Scottish idiom and cadence. The trilogy is available in a one-volume edition, *A Scots Quair* (Schocken, 1977).

1. **Sunset Song (Century, 1932)** Young Chris at 15 had discovered books and longed to become a teacher. But the land and handsome Ewan Tavendale claim her.
2. **Cloud Howe (Doubleday, 1934)** Now Mrs. Colquohoun, wife of an idealistic minister, Chris is considered uppity by the local women.
3. **Grey Granite (Doubleday, 1935)** At age 38, Chris makes yet another new beginning. Her son Ewan, a Communist organizer, plays a large part in this volume.

Gibbons, Kaye

Ellen Foster, which Kaye Gibbons began as a poem while a student at the University of North Carolina, has become a classic for many and was recommended by Oprah. The 11-year-old narrator, Ellen Foster, who is bounced from relative to relative in the rural South after her mother commits suicide, somehow overcomes a horrific life to become a decent human being. Ellen's idiosyncratic worldview continues in its sequel, *The Life All around Me,* where she is hoping for early admission to Harvard on account of "all the surplus living that was jammed into the years." North Carolina author Kaye Gibbons has been cited by literary critics and has had some TV and film success with novels such as *A Virtuous Woman* (Algonquin, 1989) and *Charms for the Easy Life* (Putnam, 1993).

1. **Ellen Foster (Algonquin, 1987)** Eleven-year-old orphan Ellen Foster endures some nightmarish situations before she finds safe harbor in a good foster home.
2. **Life All around Me, The (Harcourt, 2005)** Subtitle: *By Ellen Foster.* Ellen writes and sells poetry, applies for early admission

to Harvard, negotiates a marriage proposal from her best friend, and learns that her aunt has cheated her out of her inheritance.

Gibbons, Stella

Cold Comfort Farm is a wickedly funny parody of the "rustic" novel as exemplified by Mary Webb's *Precious Bane* and other English novels of the 20s and 30s. The Starkadders of Cold Comfort Farm are knee-deep in mud and squalor when young Flora Poste comes to visit. In no time at all, their modern, no-nonsense city cousin has reformed their degenerate ways. Interestingly, this novel won Stella Gibbons the Femina Vie Heureuse, the same prize that had been awarded previously to Mary Webb. The recent movie version (1996) starring Kate Beckinsale, Ian McKellen, and Eileen Atkins wonderfully captured the comic spirt of the book.

1. **Cold Comfort Farm (Longmans, 1932)** Flora's sensible rearrangement of life on the farm brings happiness to the Starkadder family and Aunt Ada Doom.
2. **Christmas at Cold Comfort Farm (Longmans, 1940)** This is a volume of short stories.
3. **Conference at Cold Comfort Farm (Longmans, 1949)** Flora, now the mother of five, returns to Cold Comfort Farm for a postwar conference of the International Thinkers Group. This sequel, which pokes fun at modern artists and pretentious intellectuals, deserves to be better known.

Gibson, William

I. William Gibson, not to be confused with the dramatist (*The Miracle Worker*) or the late chairman of the NAACP, is credited with being the father of Cyberpunk, a style of science-fiction writing combining high-tech plots with unconventional social values. Gibson himself has mixed feelings about this attribution and the responses of some of the wilder fans of his books. In *Neuromancer* and its sequels (sometimes called the Matrix Trilogy), Gibson depicts a world of cultures and subcultures where governments don't matter much, and shadowy figures use technology to wield power over the rest of society. The novels, with their many subplots, different points of view, and "cyberpunk" language, are difficult to summarize adequately. The best thing a reader can do is to plunge right into Gibson's "farout," but frighteningly plausible, future.

1. **Neuromancer (Ace, 1984)** Computer cowboy Henry Case has overreached himself and has been given a large dose of a nerve poison that leaves him unable to plug into cyberspace.
2. **Count Zero (Arbor House, 1986)** Count Zero is Bobby Newmark, a teenage computer cowboy with grandiose visions.
3. **Mona Lisa Overdrive (Bantam, 1988)** Slick Henry is looking after the comatose Count Zero, while Sense/Net star Angie Mitchell leaves a drug rehabilitation center to resume her career.

II. Another cyberpunk trilogy is set in the near future (c. 2005). Ex-rent-a-cop Berry Rydell and media whiz Colin Laney are two of the main characters in fast-and-furious action that takes place in California, Japan, and virtual reality.

1. **Virtual Light (Bantam, 1993)** California, circa 2005. Things are worse for most people. Laid-off rent-a-cop Berry Rydell teams up with Lucius Warbaby to retrieve a pair of "virtual light" glasses that feeds images directly to the optic nerve.

2. *Idoru* (**Putnam, 1996**) Media whiz Colin Laney has taken a job in Japan. Chia Pet McKenzie, active in fan clubs for Lo/Rez, a Japanese rock duo, is used to smuggle illegal nanoware to the Russian Mafia. Rez, part of the Lo-Rez duo, wants to marry Rei Toei, an "idoru" who exists only in virtual reality.

3. *All Tomorrow's Parties* (**Putnam, 1999**) Colin Laney, disturbed by the world-shattering occurrences that he has anticipated, retreats to a cardboard box in a Tokyo subway station.

Gifford, Barry

Barry Gifford's tales set in New Orleans and Sailor are more of a series of interconnected novellas rather than true novels. They contain a host of weird characters who weave in and out of the action, such as the sociopathic lovers Sailor Ripley and Lula Fortune and other assorted "trash-Americans" who are depicted in surrealistic style. Great fun for lovers of strange characters and bizarre situations. David Lynch, of *Twin Peaks* fame, has directed an award-winning film version of *Wild at Heart*. Gifford's short stories have recently been collected as *American Falls: The Collected Short Stories* (Seven Stories, 2002).

1. *Wild at Heart* (**Grove, 1990**) Newly released ex-con Sailor and his girlfriend, Lula, flee from the scene of yet another one of Sailor's brushes with the law.

2. *Sailor's Holiday: The Wild Life of Sailor and Lula* (**Random, 1991**) Sailor emerges from prison once again, and the wild lovers go in search of their kidnapped son.

3. *Night People* (**Grove, 1992**) Lovers Big Betty Stalcup and Miss Cutie Early cut the throats of male chauvinists who come their way.

4. *Arise and Walk* (**Hyperion, 1994**) New Orleans characters such as Marble Lesson, Spit Spackle, Hipolyte Cortez, Roland Rocque, and Irma Soon carry on their bizarre lives.

5. *Baby Cat-Face* (**Harcourt, 1995**) Creole Esquerita "Baby Cat-Face" Reyna and Sailor and Lulu converge on the small town of Corinth, North Carolina.

Gifford, Thomas

I. *The Wind Chill Factor* and *The First Sacrifice* are regarded as two of the best "Fourth Reich" thrillers available. Set 20 years apart, the novels are connected by protagonist John Cooper and neo-Nazi takeover plots. They have plenty of action, intricate plots, interesting characters, and riveting suspense.

1. *Wind Chill Factor, The* (**Putnam, 1975**) John Cooper gets enmeshed in intrigue when his brother is murdered in the family mansion in Minnesota and secret Nazi documents are stolen.

2. *First Sacrifice, The* (**Bantam, 1994**) Twenty years later, Germany is unified. Cooper is running a movie house–bookstore in Boston. His sister Lee is married to Wolf Koller, secret sponsor of right-wing terrorist groups.

II. Another pair of thrillers features Ben Driskill, cynical ex-Catholic and former Jesuit seminarian. *The Assassini* is concerned with the actions of the Catholic Church in World War II and their aftermath. *Saints Rest* involves a near-future right-winger plot to remove the president of the United States.

1. *Assassini, The* (**Bantam, 1990**) Lawyer Ben Driskill's sister, a radical activist nun writing a book on the Catholic Church's role in

World War II, is killed hours after the murders of two prominent Catholics.

2. *Saints Rest* (**Bantam, 1996**) The town of Saints Rest, Iowa, seems to be connected to three murders and a right-wing conspiracy to sabotage the reelection campaign of President Charles Bonner.

Gilbert, Michael

I. Michael Gilbert, who died at the age of 93 in 2006, wrote more than 30 crime and adventure novels, many short stories, four successful plays, and numerous radio and television scripts, many of them while working as a solicitor. Most of his earlier fiction was in the classic English mystery tradition, including *Smallbone Deceased*, which makes many readers' top 10 lists of the best mysteries. Inspector Hazelrigg of Scotland Yard does the detecting in the mysteries listed below.

1. *Close Quarters* (**Walker, 1963**) Some unpleasantness in the insular world of Melchester Cathedral culminates in murder. Originally published in the United Kingdom in 1947.

2. *He Didn't Mind Danger* (**Harper, 1949**) A rash of well-planned London burglaries seems to be linked to recent army dischargees. UK title: *They Never Looked Inside*.

3. *Doors Open, The* (**Walker, 1962**) An accountant fired from his job for noticing a discrepancy in his firm's bookkeeping is an apparent suicide. Originally published in the United Kingdom in 1949.

4. *Smallbone Deceased* (**Harper, 1950**) A respected old law firm is disrupted by the death of its senior partner and the discovery of the corpse of a man the office had been seeking for several days.

5. *Death Has Deep Roots* (**Harper, 1951**) Mademoiselle Lamartine is arrested for the death of a Briton she had known during French Resistance days.

6. *Fear to Tread* (**Harper, 1953**) This novel deals with the headmaster of a boys' school in southwest London and his disadvantaged students and their families.

II. Patrick Petrella, who appeared in two novels and dozens of short stories over three decades, is one of Gilbert's best-liked characters. The sardonic, strongly moral Petrella rises to Detective Chief Inspector of the South London division, but knows he will never reach the top because he won't play the game of power politics.

1. *Blood and Judgment* (**Harper, 1959**) Sergeant Petrella investigates the murder of the wife of an escaped criminal.

2. *Petrella at Q* (**Harper, 1977**) A collection of short stories.

2. *Young Petrella* (**Harper, 1988**) More short stories.

4. *Roller-Coaster* (**Carroll & Graf, 1994**) Petrella runs afoul of child pornography, departmental politics, gang wars, and crime in high places when he tries to solve the murder of a police informer.

III. Something of a change of pace from his procedural novels, two espionage novels are set just before the outbreak of World War I. Luke Pagan and his assistant Joe Narrabone of the Metropolitan Police and M.O.5 match wits with German spy Erich Krieger.

1. *Ring of Terror* (**Carroll & Graf, 1995**) Luke Pagan and Joe Narrabone track three suspected Russian revolutionaries and run afoul of the Home Office (and its Home Secretary Winston Churchill) and the Czarist secret police. Originally published in the United Kingdom in 1957.

2. *Into Battle* (**Carroll & Graf, 1997**) Pagan and his cohorts in the fledgling intelligence agency M.O.5 match wits against German spy Erich Krieger. Originally published in the United Kingdom in 1957.

Giles, Janice Holt

I. The pioneers who carved out the first farms in the hills of Kentucky were brave and hardy folk. Giles's skillfully woven stories of their trials and hardships, their encounters with hostile Indians, their romances and growing families, and their push farther west have brought this period alive for many readers. Most of the novels concern members of the Cooper and Fowler families, and together they cover the years from 1769 to 1869. *Shady Grove* deals with the Fowler family in the 20th century.

1. *Kentuckians, The* (**Houghton Mifflin, 1963**) Young David Cooper sets out for the untouched beauty of the Kentucky frontier he'd heard Daniel Boone describe.
2. *Hannah Fowler* (**Houghton Mifflin, 1956**) Courageous pioneer Hannah Fowler braves the dangers of wilderness life, including blizzards, wolf attacks, and capture by Indians.
3. *Land beyond the Mountains, The* (**Houghton Mifflin, 1958**) The story of Cass Cartwright from 1783 to his death in 1825 tells of a Spanish conspiracy for control of Kentucky. Not one of the Cooper/Fowler stories.
4. *Believers, The* (**Houghton Mifflin, 1957**) Hannah Fowler's daughter Rebecca marries Richard Cooper and moves with him to a Shaker community during the early 1800s.
5. *Johnny Osage* (**Houghton Mifflin, 1960**) Hannah Fowler's son Johnny, an Oklahoma trader, is called Johnny Osage because of his friendship with that Indian tribe. The story is set in the 1820s.
6. *Voyage to Santa Fe* (**Houghton Mifflin, 1962**) Johnny Fowler and his new wife, Judith, set out on the three-month trip to Santa Fe in 1823.
7. *Savanna* (**Houghton Mifflin, 1961**) Hannah's granddaughter Savanna is the beautiful and willfully independent figure in this novel set on a frontier army post in the Arkansas Territory.
8. *Great Adventure, The* (**Houghton Mifflin, 1966**) Hannah's grandson Joe leads a group of mountain men on to Oregon.
9. *Six-Horse Hitch* (**Houghton Mifflin, 1969**) Joe Fowler's son Starr drives the Overland Stage west from Missouri.
10. *Shady Grove* (**Houghton Mifflin, 1968**) Broke Neck, Kentucky, is the scene of this chronicle of the Fowler Clan over the past 200 years.

II. Giles's first published work was a light romance with comic overtones partly set in the Kentucky hill country of the present. Two sequels followed to form the *Piney Ridge Trilogy* before the author turned to historical novels.

1. *Enduring Hills, The* (**Westminster, 1950**) The main character, Hod Pierce, is modeled somewhat on Giles's husband, Henry. It shows his youth, service in World War II, and return home with his new wife to Piney Ridge.
2. *Miss Willie* (**Westminster, 1951**) Miss Willie is the new school teacher who tries to reform the people of Piney Ridge with little success.
3. *Tata's Healing* (**Westminster, 1951**) A disillusioned doctor comes to Piney Ridge and learns the healing power of kindness.

Gill, Bartholomew

PSEUDONYM OF Mark McGarrity

Shrewd plotting, well-developed characters, and a charming Irish setting are the attractions of this mystery series. Chief Inspector of Detectives Peter McGarr of the Irish Police is a thoughtful, sensitive man with an uncanny ability to break seemingly insoluble cases. His pretty young wife, Noreen, lends a hand in some of them. Massachusetts-born, Trinity College (Dublin) graduate Mark McGarrity, who wrote newspaper columns under his birth name, and mystery novels under the pseudonym Bartholomew Gill, died in 2002.

1. *McGarr and the Politician's Wife* (**Scribner, 1977**) An attempted murder aboard an American schooner in Dublin leads McGarr into a case of political intrigue. Variant title: *The Death of an Irish Politician*.
2. *McGarr and the Sienese Conspiracy* (**Scribner, 1977**) Three high-ranking agents of the British Secret Service are murdered. Variant title: *The Death of an Irish Consul*.
3. *McGarr on the Cliffs of Moher* (**Scribner, 1978**) May Quick is found dead with $27,000 in American currency in her coat pocket. Variant title: *The Death of an Irish Lass*.
4. *McGarr at the Dublin Horse Show* (**Scribner, 1980**) A rigged riding accident and the strangling of an old woman blend in this unusual case. Variant title: *The Death of an Irish Tradition*.
5. *McGarr and the P.M. of Belgrave Square* (**Viking, 1983**) "The Prime Minister of Belgrave Square" is an old bomb-squad dog that helps McGarr investigate a murder and the theft of a French impressionist masterpiece.
6. *McGarr and the Method of Descartes* (**Viking, 1984**) McGarr traces an assassination plot back to its roots in the "troubles" in Northern Ireland.
7. *McGarr and the Legacy of a Woman Scorned* (**Viking, 1986**) When elderly spinster Fionnaula Watson is murdered, McGarr involves his wife, Noreen, in the investigation.
8. *Death of a Joyce Scholar, The* (**Morrow, 1989**) Kevin Coyle, English professor at Trinity College in Dublin, is murdered after leading the annual Bloomsday tour.
9. *Death of Love, The* (**Morrow, 1992**) The digitalis-induced death of banker, philanthropist, and political aspirant Paddy Power looks like murder.
10. *Death on a Cold, Wild River* (**Morrow, 1993**) Expert fisherwoman Nellie Millar drowns while salmon casting in Donegal's River Owenea.
11. *Death of an Ardent Bibliophile, The* (**Morrow, 1995**) Brian Herrick has a noted Jonathan Swift collection and an unnoted videotape collection recording orgies with himself as the star.
12. *Death of an Irish Sea Wolf, The* (**Morrow, 1996**) Clement Ford, World War Two era pirate, is confronted by someone from the bad old days who anchors off of Ford's remote Irish island.
13. *Death of an Irish Tinker, The* (**Morrow, 1997**) McGarr takes a back seat as tinker woman, street artist, and former heroin addict Biddy Nevins, on the run after witnessing a murder ordered by "the Toddler," Desmond Bacon, Dublin's biggest drug dealer, faces up to her nemesis. UK title: *Death of a Busker King*.
14. *Death of an Irish Lover, The* (**Avon, 2000**) Two "eel police" have been found dead in a compromising position in a guest room of Tim Tallon's inn in the Shannon River town to Leixleap.
15. *Death of an Irish Sinner, The* (**Morrow, 2001**) McGarr is pitted against the powerful, secretive Catholic organization Opus Dei when author Mary-Jo Stanton, a potential threat to their secrets, is murdered.
16. *Death in Dublin* (**Morrow, 2003**) In the last book of the series, McGarr tries to ferret out the thieves who have murdered a security guard and stolen the illuminated masterpiece the *Book of Kells* from Trinity College.

Gilman, Charlotte Perkins

Herland, when it was first published in the *Forerunner*, attracted little attention, although Charlotte Perkins Gilman was well known in the 1890s and early 1900s for nonfiction works such as *Women and Economics* (1898) and *Concerning Children* (1900). Gilman's reputation, possibly because of its combination of feminism and socialism, went into eclipse in the 1920s. Her utopian novel, which describes an all-female society (reproduction by parthenogenesis), in which peace, prosperity, and rational living flourish, languished until the Gilman revival in the 1960s, the republication of her famous autobiographical story, "The Yellow Wall-Paper" (originally published in 1892), and the first appearance in bookform of *Herland* in 1979. Since then Gilman has started to receive her due as a feminist (she preferred "humanist" to "feminist" as a description of her work) and classic American writer. As with most utopian novels, the plot in *Herland* is secondary to the ideas presented, which is even truer of *With Her in Ourland*, the sequel that followed in *The Forerunner* in 1916 and had to wait till 1997 for its publication in book form. Now *Herland* has taken its place beside Edward Bellamy's (q.v.) *Looking Backward* as a classic American utopian novel, while its sequel, like Bellamy's, still remains little known.

1. *Herland* (Pantheon, 1979) Three males have different reactions to the all-female utopia in Canada, where parthenogenesis has been practiced for 2,000 years. Originally published in 1915 in the *Forerunner* magazine, edited by Gilman.
2. *With Her in Ourland* (Praeger, 1997) *Herland*'s protagonists, Ellador and Van, resume their adventures in what is more a penetrating analysis of contemporary society than a utopian fantasy. Originally published in the *Forerunner* magazine in 1916.

Gilman, Dorothy

I. Rosalind Russell played Emily Pollifax in the movie made from Gilman's first novel. She is a widowed grandmother who resembles a cross between Agatha Christie's (q.v.) Miss Marple and Paul Gallico's (q.v.) Mrs. 'Arris. She ventures indomitably on mysterious missions to exotic lands and always emerges victorious. As there is no real sequence after the first, her adventures are listed here in order of their publication. *Three Complete Mrs. Pollifax Mysteries* (Barnes & Noble, 1993) contains numbers 1, 2, and 3.

1. *Unexpected Mrs. Pollifax, The* (Doubleday, 1966) At 63 Emily Pollifax is advised that a job would cure her depression, so she applies to the CIA for a position as spy and soon finds herself in Mexico as a courier. Variant title: *Mrs. Pollifax, Spy*.
2. *Amazing Mrs. Pollifax, The* (Doubleday, 1970) Emily is off to Istanbul to rescue a beautiful woman spy.
3. *Elusive Mrs. Pollifax, The* (Doubleday, 1971) Mrs. Pollifax carries forged passports to Bulgaria in her hat.
4. *Palm for Mrs. Pollifax, A* (Doubleday, 1973) Emily traces some stolen plutonium at a chic health spa in Switzerland.
5. *Mrs. Pollifax on Safari* (Doubleday, 1977) In Zambia to take photographs, Mrs. Pollifax falls for the dashing Cyrus Reed.
6. *Mrs. Pollifax on the China Station* (Doubleday, 1983) The CIA sends Mrs. Pollifax to China to find and rescue an engineer with secret information.
7. *Mrs. Pollifax and the Hong Kong Buddha* (Doubleday, 1985) The recently rewed Mrs. Reed-Pollifax goes to Hong Kong to find out why a CIA agent is sending worthless reports.

8. *Mrs. Pollifax and the Golden Triangle* (Doubleday, 1988) On vacation with her husband, Mrs. Pollifax seeks out some vital information about a ring of drug smugglers.
9. *Mrs. Pollifax and the Whirling Dervish* (Doubleday, 1990) Mrs. Pollifax poses as the aunt of a CIA agent on tour in Morocco.
10. *Mrs. Pollifax and the Second Thief* (Doubleday, 1993) John Sebastian Farrell, who has been sent to Sicily to authenticate a document signed by Julius Caesar, calls on Mrs. P when the going gets tough.
11. *Mrs. Pollifax Pursued* (Fawcett, 1995) Mrs. P goes underground as a carnival worker in an adventure involving the crowning of the ruler of the fictional African country of Ubangiba.
12. *Mrs. Pollifax and the Lion Killer* (Fawcett, 1996) Mrs. Pollifax and Kadi Hopkirk travel to Ubangiba for the crowning of Kadi's friend Sammat.
13. *Mrs. Pollifax, Innocent Tourist* (Fawcett, 1997) Mrs. P aids John Sebastian Farrell (see number 10) again, this time traveling to Jordan to receive a manuscript written by an executed dissident Iraqi novelist.
14. *Mrs. Pollifax Unveiled* (Ballantine, 2000) Mrs. P, again teamed up with John Sebastian Farrell, goes to Damascus to rescue Amanda Pym, a young American woman who has been kidnapped after thwarting a skyjacking attempt.

II. *The Clairvoyant Countess*, featuring the psychic Madame Karitska, was first published in 1975. It was followed by a sequel in 2002, *Kaleidoscope*. Perhaps we can expect more adventures of the "clairvoyant countess" and her friend Detective Lieutenant Pruden of the "Trafton" police force.

1. *Clairvoyant Countess, The* (Doubleday, 1975) A chance encounter with Detective-Lieutenant Pruden of the Trafton Police Department leads psychic-to-the-public Madame Karitska to some unforeseen adventures.
2. *Kaleidoscope* (Ballantine, 2002) The murderer of a young violinist, a deaf-mute, a spoiled heiress, an autistic boy, and a mad genius who is planning something terrible engage the attention of Madame Karitska and Detective Lieutenant Pruden.

Gingrich, Newt

Former Speaker of the House Newt Gingrich and veteran alternative history writer William Fortschen (q.v.) have combined to produce three alternative Civil War books based on the premise that the Confederates won at Gettysburg. The authors show a certain pro-Southern bias in their portrayal, but they are thoroughly familiar with their military history and can depict battle scenes authentically. Civil War buffs will love these books.

1. *Gettysburg* (St. Martin's, 2003) Robert E. Lee, not leaving matters to his subordinates, outmaneuvers Meade at Gettysburg, with disastrous consequences for the Union cause.
2. *Grant Comes East* (St. Martin's, 2004) The Confederates hope to capture Washington and President Lincoln, bring Maryland into the Confederacy, get recognition from European nations, and force the Union into peace negotiations.
3. *Never Call Retreat: Lee and Grant: The Final Victory* (St. Martin's, 2005) Lee fails to secure Washington although the Army of the Potomac is trapped and destroyed. The armies under Lee and Grant collide in central Maryland for a weeklong battle that will decide everything.

Girdner, Jacqueline

Kate Jasper is a real California type. She lives in Marin County, eats lots of vegetables, practices tai chi, collects old pinball machines, and owns Jest Gifts, a gag gift business. Kate gets divorced early in the series, and carries on an affair with bodyguard Wayne Caruso, whom she meets on her first "case" and eventually marries. This "karmic cozy series" (as the author calls it) is full of eccentric characters and far-out plots. Girdner closed this series with number 12 and is producing a new series, written as "Claire Daniels," about a clairvoyant named Cally Lazar.

1. *Adjusted to Death* (Diamond, 1991) On a visit to her chiropractor, mail-order novelty business owner Kate Jasper discovers a dead body and teams up with Wayne Caruso, the dead man's friend and bodyguard to investigate the crime.
2. *Last Resort, The* (Berkley, 1991) Kate's ex-husband Craig calls her with the news that he is the prime suspect in the murder of his new girlfriend, Suzanne Sorensen, at a health spa.
3. *Murder Most Mellow* (Berkley, 1992) After some personal problems, Kate decides to "mellow out" by hosting a support group in her hot tub. Then one of her New Age friend turns up murdered in the jacuzzi.
4. *Fat-Free and Fatal* (Berkley, 1993) One of the students at the vegetarian cooking class Kate is attending is choked to death, and Kate's friend Barbara is suspected.
5. *Tea-Totally Dead* (Berkley, 1994) Wayne Caruso's mother, recently released from a mental institution, threatens to expose a family secret, but is poisoned before she can reveal it.
6. *Stiff Critique, A* (Berkley, 1995) Slade Skinner, the only successfully published member of a rather contentious writers' group, is found beaten to death.
7. *Most Likely to Die* (Berkley, 1996) Kate's high school reunion, class of 1968, is sparked by the electrocution (via one of Kate's pinball machines) of a former classmate, practical joker Sid.
8. *Cry for Self-Help, A* (Berkley, 1997) Kate, perched on a seaside cliff observing an aquatic wedding, sees Marin County's top self-help guru, Sam Skyler, take a fatal plunge into the rocky surf below.
9. *Death Hits the Fan* (Berkley, 1998) One of three authors at a bookstore reading and signing attended by Kate and Wayne dies calling out Kate's name.
10. *Murder on the Astral Plane* (Berkley, 1999) Kate has to rely on her own perceptions when her psychic friend fails to turn up a murderer at a spiritual soiree.
11. *Murder, My Deer* (Berkley, 2000) When deer ruin newly married Kate and Wayne's garden, they join a support group, being good Californians. But Kate's presence proves to be fatal, yet again, when an antideer activist is killed.
12. *Sensitive Kind of Murder, A* (Berkley, 2002) Kate stumbles upon a body at a men's support group. And Wayne's car was the murder weapon!

Gironella, Jose Maria

This trilogy about the Alvear family shows how the Spanish Civil War affected the country and its people. The story begins in 1931 and continues through the postwar years. Using the middle-class Alvear family and their hometown of Gerona in Catalonia as a microcosm of Spanish society, Gironella vividly portrays the conflict and tragedy that seared through all facets of Spanish life. A traditionalist and conservative, Gironella's sympathies are with the Nationalist rebels (Franco's forces).

1. *Cypresses Believe in God, The* (Knopf, 1955) The years of political unrest from the beginning of the Republic to the war's outbreak are seen primarily through the eyes of Ignacio, the oldest Alvear son. Translated from the Spanish by Harriet de Onis. Original title: *Cipreses creen en Dios* (1953).
2. *One Million Dead* (Doubleday, 1963) During the Civil War years from July 1936 to April 1939, Ignacio is a Nationalist. Translated from the Spanish by Joan MacLean. Original title: *Un millón de muertos* (1955).
3. *Peace after War* (Knopf, 1969) This novel shows the peacetime problems of rebuilding and reconciliation amid food shortages and corruption. Translated from the Spanish by Joan MacLean. Original title: *Ha estallado la paz* (1966).

Giroux, E. X.

PSEUDONYM OF Doris Shannon

Young, urbane London barrister Robert Forsythe and his motherly secretary, Abigail "Sandy" Sanderson, play sleuth in this series of mysteries. Puzzle mysteries in the classic Agatha Christie tradition, the novels are often set in country homes full of eccentric characters. As the series has progressed, Sandy has taken an increasingly active role in detecting. Doris Shannon is a Canadian who started her writing career in her midforties.

1. *Death for Adonis, A* (St. Martin's, 1984) Forsythe is asked to clear the name of English sculptor Sebastian Calvert, who was convicted of the murder of his lover 25 years before.
2. *Death for a Darling, A* (St. Martin's, 1985) Forsythe and Sandy are guests in a country house along with the cast and crew of a company remaking the film *Wuthering Heights*.
3. *Death for a Dancer, A* (St. Martin's, 1985) A very dead blackmailer is found in a sarcophagus in the private mausoleum of eccentric Cheshire baronet Amyas Dancer.
4. *Death for a Doctor, A* (St. Martin's, 1986) Sandy gets directly involved in the investigation of the murders of country town physician Dr. Foster and his family.
5. *Death for a Dilettante, A* (St. Martin's, 1987) Someone is trying to prevent rich, elderly Winslow Maxwell Pendragon from becoming a centenarian.
6. *Death for a Dietician, A* (St. Martin's, 1988) Sandy plays sleuth on her own when a house party game of pretend murder mystery becomes real.
7. *Death for a Dreamer, A* (St. Martin's, 1989) The gift of four puppies to the Coralund Home for the elderly leads to murder.
8. *Death for a Double, A* (St. Martin's, 1990) Wealthy Italian American Anthony Funicelli summons Forsythe to his garishly modernized country house when he receives threatening letters.
9. *Death for a Dancing Doll, A* (St. Martin's, 1991) The accidental death of a seven-year-old girl at a Canadian waterfall may have led to the suicide of her aunt.
10. *Death for a Dodo, A* (St. Martin's, 1992) Convalescing from knee surgery at the Damien Day Health Home, Forsythe runs into an oddly assorted group of fellow patients.

Girzone, Joseph F(rancis)

Girzone, a retired Roman Catholic priest, states that he wished to write a novel conveying Christ's message in modern times unencumbered by the legalistic and divisive aspects of organized religion. To that end he has written a series of novels about Joshua, a mysterious, contemporary Christlike figure who travels the world preaching love, tolerance, and ecumenism. *Joshua*, the movie version of Girzone's novels, stars F. Murray Abraham, Giancarlo Giannini, and Tony Goldwyn, as Joshua. Besides the Joshua series, Girzone has written a number of popular religious books, including *A Portrait of Jesus* (Doubleday, 1998).

1. *Joshua's Family* (Doubleday, 2007) This prequel finds Joshua, 11 years old but wise beyond his years, moving into a ramshackle house in the town of Sharon with his father, Joseph, and mother, Miriam.
2. *Joshua* (Macmillan, 1983) Joshua, a simple woodcarver who has settled in a small upstate New York town, preaches the gospel of tolerance in churches of all denominations. Originally self-published (Richelieu Court). Variant titles: *Joshua: The Homecoming* and *Joshua: A Parable for Today*.
3. *Joshua and the Children* (Macmillan, 1989) Joshua reappears in a small town torn apart by the enmity between Catholics and Protestants.
4. *Joshua in the Holy Land* (Macmillan, 1992) Joshua wanders through the deserts of the Middle East uniting like-minded Jews, Muslims, and Christians as Children of Peace.
5. *Joshua and the City* (Doubleday, 1995) Joshua straightens out the confused denizens of an inner-city neighborhood in New York.
6. *Parables of Joshua* (Doubleday, 2001) This a reinvention of Jesus's New Testament parables rather than a story.
7. *Joshua in a Troubled World* (Doubleday, 2004) Joshua gets picked up by the FBI in Washington as an apparent drifter of Middle Eastern descent.

Glass, Leslie

According to Leslie Glass, her creator, April Woo is the "first Asian-American law enforcement officer in American crime fiction." The smart, funny NYPD detective with an old-fashioned Chinese mother is the leading character in a series of gory and suspenseful crime novels in which she teams up with New York psychoanalyst Dr. Jason Frank and Mexican American NYPD detective Mike Sanchez, her detecting partner and significant other. New York-based author Leslie Glass is also the author of several other novels, a play produced by the American Repertory Theater (*Strokes*, 1984) and two one-act plays.

1. *Burning Time* (Doubleday, 1993) April Woo, working on a missing persons report, learns that the missing girl has turned up dead and branded by fire near San Diego.
2. *Hanging Time* (Bantam, 1995) The body of a shop assistant at a Manhattan boutique is found hanging from a chandelier wearing an oversized dress and crudely applied makeup.
3. *Loving Time* (Bantam, 1996) Former psychiatric patient Raymond Cowles, who was "cured" of his homosexual fantasies 14 years earlier, is found with a plastic bag over his head.
4. *Judging Time* (Dutton, 1998) In an East Coast variation on the O. J. Simpson case, the wife of Rick Liberty, former football star who is now an investment banker, is stabbed to death along with a businessman friend.
5. *Stealing Time* (Dutton, 1999) Interracial marriage, illegal aliens, kidnapping, and illegal adoption are among the mix when Heather Rose Papescu, the Chinese American wife of an affluent lawyer, is beaten and her adopted baby vanishes.
6. *Tracking Time* (Dutton, 2000) Psychiatrist Maslow Atkins disappears while jogging in Central Park. Allegra Caldera, one of his patients who may have been stalking him, is the chief suspect.
7. *Silent Bride, The* (Onyx, 2002) A wealthy, young Orthodox Jewish bride is gunned down on her wedding day in what may possibly be a hate crime.

8. *Killing Gift, A* (Onyx, 2003) The victims of a serial killer with martial-arts expertise seem to share a connection with a local university.
9. *Clean Kill, A* (Onyx, 2005) Maddy Wilson, wife of a celebrity chef, is slashed to death in her fashionable townhouse on Manhattan's Upper East Side.

Godwin, Parke

I. Historical fantasist Godwin has written an interesting addition to the library of Robin Hood lore. His version of the legend places Robin in the England of William the Conqueror. Robin is Edward Aelredson, son of the thane of Denby, who encourages the downtrodden Anglo-Saxons in the series of exploits that made him a legend.

1. *Sherwood* (Morrow, 1991) A quarrel with the Sheriff of Nottingham results in the outlawry of young Edward Aelredson.
2. *Robin and the King* (Morrow, 1993) After living peacefully with his family for eight years, Robin is roused to action again when Ranulf of Bayeux, Keeper of the Seal, attempts to convert part of Sherwood Forest into a royal hunting preserve.

II. In the Firelord series, Godwin has also tried his hand at an Arthurian trilogy. This is a nonmystic or nonmagical retelling, where Godwin delves into the historical Arthur and his times (some historians believe Arthur really) existed), with rational explanations for some of the more difficult conceptions, such as Faeries.

1. *Firelord* (Doubleday, 1980) Tells the story of Artos, 5th-century-CE Celtic tribal leader fighting the Saxons.
2. *Beloved Exile* (Bantam, 1984) Guinevere's memoirs, which she started writing the day Arthur died.
3. *Last Rainbow, The* (Bantam, 1985) Concentrates on the Faerie: diminutive Stone Age nomads whose folkways were misunderstood by the Celts as sorcery. St. Patrick plays a prominent role.

III. The Snake Oil series is a pair of fantasy satires that lampoons many things, including human history, evolution, and Evangelicals. It all starts with two bored "energy beings."

Godwin has several other historical fantasy and SF novels to his credit as well as collaborating, with Marvin Kaye on two (a third was projected) novels set in a postapocalyptic future America: *The Masters of Solitude* (Doubleday, 1978) and *Wintermind* (Doubleday, 1982). Another collaboration with Kaye, *A Cold Blue Light* (Charter, 1983), was followed by a second novel written by Kaye alone.

1. *Waiting for the Galactic Bus* (Doubleday, 1988) Two bored alien schoolboys, Coyul and Barion, find themselves stranded on Earth after a spectacular drunk and decide to while away the time by tinkering with a couple of apes, enduing them with "minds," which leads to all kinds of trouble.
2. *Snake Oil Wars, The* (Doubleday, 1989) Subtitle: *Or, Scheherazade Ginsberg Strikes Again*. Preacher Lance Candor throws a bomb at Coyul, whom he supposes to be the devil, and a circus trial ensues, with celebrity walk-ons.

Gold, Herbert

The classic American generation clash between immigrant parents and Americanized children is the subject of Gold's two novels "in the form of a memoir." They are thought to be highly autobiographical. Gold captures his characters' colorful Yiddish-English speech and lovingly evokes their home life in a small town in Ohio. The author has also written *My Last Two Thousand Years* (Random House, 1972), which is an impressionistic exploration of Jewish history in relation to his personal history as a Jew.

1. *Fathers* **(Random House, 1967)** The story relates the life of Gold's father, who flees persecution in Russia and becomes a grocer in America.
2. *Family* **(Arbor House, 1981)** Gold's mother tries to impose her Old World standards of love on her American-born son.

Goldberg, Leonard S.

Forensic pathologist Joanna Blalock and her off-again, on-again lover Lieutenant Jake Sinclair of the Los Angeles Police Department are the leading protagonists in a series of medical thrillers, most of them involved with murders and in Los Angeles hospitals. Leonard Goldberg is a consulting physician in Los Angeles, clinical professor at UCLA Medical Center, and oft-called-upon expert witness in medical malpractice trials. Goldberg's medical knowledge the best thing in these thrillers whose plots and characters sometimes leave something to be desired.

1. *Deadly Medicine* **(Signet, 1992)** Introduces forensic pathologist Joanna Blalock and police detective Jake Sinclair, as they investigate a series of nurse killings at a Los Angeles hospital.
2. *Deadly Practice, A* **(Signet, 1993)** This time a serial killer has it in for doctors and has the expertise to imitate his victims' medical specialities.
3. *Deadly Care* **(Dutton, 1996)** Several fatalities, including a corpse with missing fingertips and every facial bone broken, seem to be connected to the same HMO. Joanna, suffering from amnesia after her car is forced off the road, is apparently the next designated victim.
4. *Deadly Harvest* **(Dutton, 1997)** Donors International, an organ-transplant service that also runs a reproductive clinic, is the target of a sniper. Joanna's sister Kate is stricken with an Ebola-like virus.
5. *Deadly Exposure* **(Dutton, 1998)** Joanna joins a world-class team of scientists on the *Global Explorer II*, a US Navy ship off the coast of Alaska, in an attempt to analyze a deadly extraterrestrial virus found in an iceberg.
6. *Lethal Measures* **(Dutton, 1999)** A series of terrorist bombings, including one that kills several dozen people in a quiet neighborhood, may have the US president as the ultimate target.
7. *Fatal Cure* **(Signet, 2001)** Bio-Med, a new bioengineering firm with a radical treatment for clogged arteries, is the connection between three seemly unrelated deaths.
8. *Brainwaves* **(Signet, 2002)** Noted neurologist Karen Crandell dies suspiciously, the latest in a string of tragedies at Los Angeles Memorial Medical Center.
9. *Fever Cell* **(Signet, 2003)** Joanna and Jake get involved in a plot to turn a viral medical nightmare into a terrifying reality.

Golding, William

The late Nobel Laureate William Golding (*Lord of the Flies*, etc.) published a trilogy describing a sea voyage in the Napoleonic Era (1814–1815). An aged ship of the line is carrying an assortment of passengers from England to Australia. Edmund Talbot, a young gentleman, provides a large part of the narrative thread of the novels in a journal he is keeping. Like most of Golding's fiction, these novels combine readability and authentic atmosphere with a deeper allegorical meaning and a pessimistic view of humanity. *To the Ends of the Earth* (Faber [UK], 1991) is an omnibus volume containing all three novels.

1. *Rites of Passage* **(Farrar, 1980)** Edmund Talbot records the events of the voyage and the fate of young Robert Colley, a clergyman who runs afoul of Captain Anderson.
2. *Close Quarters* **(Farrar, 1987)** The passengers learn of Napoléon's defeat and exile to Elba. Talbot falls in love, and the ship is dismasted in a storm.
3. *Fire Down Below* **(Farrar, 1989)** As the ship becomes increasingly unseaworthy, dissension among the passengers and crew reaches a dangerous level.

Goldman, William

Marathon Man is still Goldman's best-known novel. The movie version featured Dustin Hoffman as a brilliant but naive graduate student and aspiring marathon runner. Laurence Olivier's performance as Szell, the sadistic Nazi dentist, was unforgettable. Goldman is primarily a screen writer: he won Oscars for his scripts for *Butch Cassidy and the Sundance Kid* and *All the President's Men*. He has written amusing accounts of his life in Hollywood, including *Which Lie Did I Tell?* (Pantheon, 2000).

1. *Marathon Man* **(Delacorte, 1974)** Shocked by the murder of his brother, Babe Levy gets entangled in a plot involving Nazi war criminals. Hard to beat for nonstop action and suspense.
2. *Brothers* **(Warner, 1987)** Revived—somewhat incredibly—for this sequel set 10 years later, Scylla, Babe Levy's brother, attempts to alter the balance of world nuclear power.

Goldreich, Gloria

Leah's Journey and *Leah's Children* take artist and philanthropist Leah Goldfeder and her family through the significant historical events of the 1920s through the 1960s. *Leah's Journey* concentrates on Leah's life from postrevolution Russia to the formation of the state of Israel. *Leah's Children* brings the second generation to several trouble spots of the world in the 1950s and 1960s. This is an absorbing and often moving family saga with a strong sense of history.

1. *Leah's Journey* **(Harcourt, 1978)** Fleeing from a pogrom in Russia, Leah marries gentle David and emigrates with him to New York.
2. *Leah's Children* **(Macmillan, 1985)** Leah's children take on activist roles in Hungary, Mississippi, and Israel.

Goldsborough, Robert

The heirs of Rex Stout (q.v.) have given a "seal of approval" to Robert Goldsborough's re-creations of Nero Wolfe, Stout's orchid-growing, obese detective. Number 3 in the new series contains a memoir of Rex Stout by his daughter, Rebecca Stout Bradbury. Wolfe's faithful assistant, Archie Goodwin, continues to narrate the stories of Wolfe's sedentary detecting efforts from the brownstone on 35th Street.

1. *Murder in E Minor* **(Bantam, 1986)** Milan Stevens, controversial new director of the New York Symphony, has been receiving death threats.
2. *Death on Deadline* **(Bantam, 1987)** Wolfe disputes the verdict of suicide when elderly newspaper owner Harriet Haverhill dies.

3. *Bloodied Ivy, The* (Bantam, 1988) Wolfe leaves his Manhattan brownstone to investigate the fatal "accident" that befell conservative professor Hale Markham at an upstate New York university.

4. *Last Coincidence, The* (Bantam, 1989) Noreen James's brother Michael has confessed to the murder of Sparky Linville, Noreen's attacker, but Noreen doesn't believe he's guilty.

5. *Fade to Black* (Bantam, 1990) Nero is brought into a case of industrial espionage and murder at an advertising agency.

6. *Silver Spire* (Bantam, 1992) Scripture-quoting hate notes are turning up among the Sunday offerings at the Tabernacle of the Silver Spire.

7. *Missing Chapter, The* (Bantam, 1993) Charles Childress is chosen to continue the Orville Barnstable mystery series after the original author dies, but dies himself in mysterious circumstances.

Gooden, Philip

Nick Revill is a fledgling actor with William Shakespeare's newly formed Chamberlain's men at the turn of the 17th century and the end of Queen Elizabeth's reign. Like Edward Marston's (q.v.) Nicholas Bracewell, young Nick seems to get involved in a murder mystery on each outing, while hobnobbing with the likes of Shakespeare. Ben Jonson, and other Elizabethans of note. With the exception of number 6, the plot of each novel revolves around a Shakespearean play.

1. *Sleep of Death* (Carroll & Graf, 2000) Young actor Nick Revill, newly employed with the Chamberlain's men, finds some disturbing parallels between *Hamlet*, William Shakespeare's latest play, and events in the Thameside mansion where he is a lodger. UK title: *That Sleep of Death*.

2. *Death of Kings* (Carroll & Graf, 2001) London, 1601. Nick is drafted as a government spy when one of the Earl of Essex's men requests a repeat performance of *Richard II*.

3. *Pale Companion, The* (Carroll & Graf, 2002) A performance of *A Midsummer Night's Dream* turns into a nightmare for Nick as he is pursued by a "pale companion" during a walk in the woods.

4. *Alms for Oblivion* (Carroll & Graf, 2003) Nick becomes the chief suspect in the murder of his boyhood friend Peter Agate after Peter comes to London and competes with Nick for a part in the production of *Troilus and Cressida* to be performed at the Middle Temple.

5. *Mask of Night* (Carroll & Graf, 2004) In 1603, with Elizabeth's death imminent and the plague raging in London, the Chamberlain's company travels to Oxford to perform *Romeo and Juliet* for the benefit of two feud-prone families about to be united in marriage.

6. *Honorable Murder, An* (Carroll & Graf, 2005) Ben Jonson persuades Nick to act in a masque celebrating an impending peace treaty between England and Spain. Courtier Sir Philip Blake, portraying Truth, makes a deadly plunge during the final rehearsal of the drama.

Goodkind, Terry

Woodsman Richard Cypher eventually learns his heritage (he is the grandson of Zedd, the last true Wizard of the Lands and the son of the noble Darken Rahl), embarks upon a series of adventures in which he rescues and weds former Mother Confessor Kahlan Amnell, becomes the New World's Seeker of Truth, and, as Richard, Lord Rahl, becomes ruler of D'Hara and bearer of the Sword of Truth. Arrayed against Richard and his allies are the forces of the Imperial, or "Old" Order, under Jangang "the Just" and his minion Nicci, aka Death's

Mistress. This is epic sword-and-sorcery fantasy, more popular with Goodkind's legion of fans than with the critics. Number 1 is a prequel to the series.

1. *Debt of Bones* (Tor, 2004) This prequel involves Zedd, First Wizard in the time before the Boundaries are drawn, and poor peasant Abby, who has a claim upon him. Originally published in the United Kingdom in 2001.

2. *Wizard's First Rule* (Tor, 1994) Richard Cypher, unbeknownst to himself, is the Seeker, wielder of the Sword of Truth and the only possessor of the arcane knowledge contained in the *Book of Counted Shadows*.

3. *Stone of Tears* (Tor, 1995) Kahlan Amnell, Mother Confessor, to save her people, her world, and Richard from the Keeper of the Underworld, must sacrifice everything she holds dear,

4. *Blood of the Fold* (Tor, 1996) After unwittingly destroying the magical wards that had sealed off the Old World from the New for 3000 years, Richard Cypher has created a gate through which the evil Emperor Jagang and his minions can enter the Land.

5. *Temple of the Winds* (Tor, 1997) Emperor Jagang, not dead as supposed, lets loose a magical plague that brings horrible death, particularly to children. Richard and Kahlan must forswear their love for each other to find the long-lost Temple of the Winds.

6. *Soul of the Fire* (Tor, 1999) When Kahlan used a spell to save Richard from death in number 5, she inadvertently released the Chimes, deadly ancient beings who threaten to destroy the world by absorbing all its magic.

7. *Faith of the Fallen* (Tor, 2000) Kahlan takes command of the D'Haran army in a last-ditch attempt to ward off the forces of Jagang and his minion, Nicci, who has reduced Richard to slavery.

8. *Pillars of Creation, The* (Tor, 2001) After deposing his father, Lord Rahl, Richard lingers in the background at his fortress, as his half siblings, the oafish Oba and the vengeful Jennsen, battle for control of the realm.

9. *Naked Empire* (Tor, 2003) Richard and Kahlan continue the good fight against a host of adversaries, including giant, flesh-eating birds.

10. *Chainfire* (Tor, 2005) The sorely wounded Richard regains consciousness only to learn that Kahlan is missing, and nobody believes that she exists.

11. *Phantom* (Tor, 2006) The second volume of the Chainfire trilogy. Richard continues his search for the missing Kahlan and memorizes *The Book of Counted Shadows*, which will help open the three boxes of the Order.

12. *Confessor* (Tor, 2007) Richard and Kahlan face the coming dawn of a savage new world.

Goodman, Jo

I. Most of prolific and popular Jo Goodman's historical romances take place between the late 18th century and the turn of the 20th century. The McClellan Family trio is situated in England and America during the American Revolution. Each book features a member of the McClellan family and the man, or woman, who falls passionately in love with him or her.

1. *Crystal Passion* (Zebra, 1985) Ashley Lynne, ward of the cruel Duke of Linfield, resists being married to an elderly peer and winds up, drugged, in the bed of Captain Salem McClellan.

2. *Seaswept Abandon* (Zebra, 1986) "Green-eyed" Rae McClellan agrees to act as a courier for the Colonies and, after a wild night in a Redcoat tavern, finds herself aboard the private schooner of

a supposed British sympathizer and into the arms of "towering" Jericho Smith.

3. *Tempting Torment* **(Zebra, 1989)** Desperate to escape to America with her infant, Jessica Winter marries the supposedly mortally wounded Noah McClellan, not counting on Noah's will to live.

II. The Marshall brothers of New York indulge in the vicissitudes of the American Civil War and its aftermath and wild passions in a pair of novels.

1. *Midnight Princess* **(Zebra, 1989)** Jenny Holland arrives half-dead on the doorstep of the Fifth Avenue mansion of newspaper publisher and war hero Christian Marshall, who takes her in and takes on more than he bargained for.

2. *Passion's Sweet Revenge* **(Zebra, 1990)** When he spots Mary Catherine McCleary, aka Katy Dakota, on the stage of Wallock's Theatre, Logan Marshall vows revenge for her betrayal during the Civil War that sent him to the notorious Andersonville Prison.

III. Each of the five Dennehy sisters has her own novel, in which she braves the perils of the post–Civil War American West and the embraces of a handsome stud with a past.

1. *Wild Sweet Ecstasy* **(Zebra, 1992)** Newspaper Mary Dennehy is kidnapped from a Colorado-bound train by one of the train robbers, who is actually undercover detective Ethan Stone. Variant title: *More Than a Touch*

2. *Rogue's Mistress* **(Zebra, 1993)** Rennie Dennehy enlists the aid of bounty hunter Jarret Sullivan in searching for her lost father, but fears that their passion might be rekindled.

3. *Forever in My Heart* **(Zebra, 1994)** New York heiress Mary Margaret Dennehy and Colorado rancher Connor Holiday are brought together again in an arranged marriage, and memories of a "passion-filled night" in a bordello are rekindled.

4. *Always in My Dreams* **(Zebra, 1995)** Sent by her financier father to spy on a reclusive inventor, Skye Dennehy finds that Walker Caine has a past that he is keeping from her.

5. *Only in My Arms* **(Zebra, 1999)** Mary Dennehy shocks her family by leaving the convent and heading out West, where she runs into Apache-raised Ryder McKay, who is awaiting execution for a crime he didn't commit.

IV. The three Thorne brothers were separated in a London workhouse after their aristocratic parents were killed by highwaymen. Unbeknownst to the others, each brother claws his way to fortune, two as ship captains, and one as gambler. All three, of course, get involved with beautiful, passionate women.

1. *My Steadfast Heart* **(Zebra, 1997)** Colin Thorne and Mercedes Leydon are thrown together when the revengeful ship captain lays claim to Weybourne Park, the estate of Mercedes's uncle, the Earl of Weybourne.

2. *My Reckless Heart* **(Zebra, 1998)** Ship captain Decker Thorne and his employer, Jonna Remington, are drawn together when Jonna's life is threatened by an unseen enemy.

3. *With All My Heart* **(Zebra, 1999)** Psychic Berkeley Shaw, sent by Colin and Decker Thorne to San Francisco to search for their lost brother, runs into Grey Janeway, successful gambler and hotel owner without a past.

V. The Hamiltons are two members of an impoverished South Carolina family trying to rebuild their estates in Charleston and their lives after the Civil War. Each, of course, finds his or her significant other.

1. *More Than You Know* **(Zebra, 2000)** South Carolina plantation owner Rand Hamilton and London heiress Claire Bancroft are thrown together on a treasure-seeking voyage.

2. *More Than You Wished* **(Zebra, 2001)** Bria Hamilton needs the help of Northerner Lucas Kincaid to reclaim her family's South Carolina rice plantation from her ruthless stepfather, but Lucas has issues of his own.

VI. Four friends belonging to the Compass Club of Regency England separately engage in a series of adventures and passionate love affairs.

1. *Let Me Be the One* **(Zebra, 2002)** North, aka Brendan Hampton, Earl of Northam, meets the beautiful and mysterious Elizabeth Penrose while searching for the so-called Gentleman Thief, who steals jewels from members of the aristocracy.

2. *Everything I Ever Wanted* **(Zebra, 2003)** South, aka Matthew Forrester, Viscount Southerton, is sent to investigate actress India Parr's involvement in the murder of an intelligence agent.

3. *Everything I Ever Needed* **(Zebra, 2003)** East, aka Gabriel Whitney, Marquess of Eastlyn, hearing a false rumor that he and heiress Lady Sophia Colley are engaged, arrives at her home only to find that he wished the rumor to be true.

4. *Beyond a Wicked Kiss* **(Zebra, 2004)** West, aka Evan Marchman, Duke of Westphal, prefers the adventures and intrigues of the Compass Club to the responsibilities of an estate. Then Ria Ashby, headmistress of a ladies' academy, asks his help in finding a missing student.

Goonan, Kathleen Ann

Kathleen Ann Goonan's first novel, *Queen City Jazz*, which opened her Nanotech Quartet, immediately established her as an SF writer of note. The Nanotech Quartet explores the possibilities of nanotechnology in the near future, when information and technology have merged. The plots include hallucinogenic visions, the resurrection of historical characters such as Ernest Hemingway, the creation of a new nation, sentient cities, and other beings created by the microscopic machines. Goonan displays a great deal of knowledge of state-of-the-art technology and strong characters while exploring the meanings of being human, freedom and purpose, the nature of art, and the uses and abuses of power. Goonan has published two other SF novels: *The Bones of Time* (Tor, 1996) and *In War Times* (Tor, 2007).

1. *Queen City Jazz* **(Tor, 1994)** Sometime in the 22nd century, young Verity, raised by a Shaker group, discovers that she has strange powers and mysterious compulsions and travels to the "enlivened" city of Cincinnati, where she meets jazz musician Sphere and learns her true identity.

2. *Mississippi Blues* **(Tor, 1997)** Verity, Blaze, and other characters are driven down the Ohio and Mississippi rivers by the information-encoding Norleans Plague.

3. *Crescent City Rhapsody* **(Eos, 2000)** In 2012 a mysterious alien signal from space strikes Earth, sending the information age into a tailspin. In New Orleans resurrected Mob leader Marie Laveau sets out on a 20-year plan to save New Orleans and the world.

4. *Light Music* **(Eos, 2002)** In the 22nd century, young Angelina, a refugee from Argentina, embarks on a series of adventures on a robot ship and a one-way train to nano-ruled Paris, accompanied by Chester, a "sapient" doll.

Gordon, Alan

Alan Gordon's Medieval Mystery series takes the characters of Feste and Viola from Shakespeare's *Twelfth Night* and sets them down in the year 1201 for a series of adventures ranging from Italy to Constantinople to Austria to the Black Forest. The unifying thread is the Fool's Guild, to which Feste, Theophilus the jester, and Hamlet's "poor" Yorick (*Hamlet* comes in for a retelling in number 5) belong. This is an intriguing mixture of history and fiction that will appeal to fans of Tom Stoppard's *Rosencrantz and Guildenstern Are Dead* (Grove, 1967).

1. *Thirteenth Night* (St. Martin's, 1998) In 1201 the Fool's Guild receives word of the death of Duke Orsino of Illyria. Feste, the Fool in *Twelfth Night*, investigates, suspecting foul play at the hands of Malvolio, another prominent character in the play.
2. *Jester Leaps In, The* (St. Martin's, 2000) Feste the Fool and his wife, Viola (also from *Twelfth Night*), set off for Constantinople in 1202 in an attempt to make the Fourth Crusade stay on track to the Holy Land.
3. *Death in the Venetian Quarter, A* (St. Martin's, 2002) Feste and his wife, Aglaia (aka Viola), in Constantinople to keep an eye on events, are recruited by Philoxenites, the Byzantine emperor's spymaster, to make an unofficial investigation into the death of silk merchant and spy Bastiani in the Venetian Quarter.
4. *Widow of Jerusalem, The* (St. Martin's, 2003) In 1204 Theophilus the jester flees to Innsbruck, Austria, from the Fourth Crusade and from papal forces sent to destroy the Guild of Fools. In a story within a story, Theophilus relates how he and the Scarlet Dwarf got caught up in political intrigue in Tyre in 1191 during the Third Crusade.
5. *Antic Disposition, An* (St. Martin's, 2004) Members of the Fool's Guild are in hiding in the Black Forest. Father Gerald and Theophilus take turns in relating the tale of Amleth (Hamlet), Yorick, and the Danish throne.
6. *Lark's Lament, The* (St. Martin's, 2007) Theophilus and his wife, Claudia, both members of the Fool's Guild, visit Cistercian Abbot Folc, formerly a troubadour known as Folquet.

Gores, Joe (Joseph N.)

Dan Kearney Associates (DKA) is the name of a San Francisco–area based team of automobile repossessors. Somehow the proprietors of DKA, including Dan Kearney, Larry Ballard, Bart Heslip, Patrick O'Bannon, and Giselle Marc, often get involved in cases involving murder, mafiosos, blackmail, and other crimes seemingly unrelated to auto repossession in this series of procedurals that exposes the seamier side of life and delineates some very nasty characters.

Joe Gores, whose 12 years as a private investigator in San Francisco stand him in good stead, has written other mystery novels, such as *Hammett* (Putnam, 1975), in which a fictional Dashiell Hammett (q.v.) pursues his own investigation, and screenplays, some for his own novels, including *Hammett* (1982) and *32 Cadillacs* (1996).

1. *Dead Skip* (Random House, 1972) Dan Kearney and Larry Ballard of DKA try to track down the man who attempted to kill their colleague Bart Heslip and make it look like an accident.
2. *Final Notice* (Random House, 1973) The associates of DKA get drawn into an investigation that uncovers the attempted blackmail of a Mafia boss and get up to their necks in a mafioso power struggle, complete with two murders.
3. *Gone, No Forwarding* (Random House, 1978) Someone is trying very hard to get the State of California to revoke Kearney's license, apparently over a $200 snafu.

4. *32 Cadillacs* (Mysterious, 1992) First DKA novel after 14 years. The "king" of the Gypsies, dying in a small town in Iowa, wishes to be buried in a pink Cadillac.
5. *Contract Null and Void* (Mysterious, 1996) This novel has a melange of plots, including a near-dead cyclist, a labor dispute, a dead politician and a dead labor leader, a computer nerd who hits it big, and the usual repo work of seizing truck tires, band equipment, etc.
6. *Stakeout on Page Street: And Other DKA Files* (Crippen & Landru, 2000) Twelve shorter works about the DKA published between 1967 and 1989.
7. *Cons, Scams, and Grifts* (Mysterious, 2001) The associates of DKA face off again against the Gypsies they matched wits with in number 4. Con games galore, classic car rip-offs, a beautiful Gypsy witch, a millionaire's secret treasure, a cameo from Michael Connelly's (q.v.) Harry Bosch, and a nod to Donald E. Westlake (q.v.) are among the elements in this riotous affair.

Gorman, Ed(ward Joseph)

I. The Sam McCain series is probably the most popular that prolific mystery and western writer Ed Gorman has produced. Sam McCain is a young part-time lawyer and part-time private investigator in the town of Black River Falls, Iowa (pop. 27,300), in the late 1950s and early 1960s. Nostalgia buffs will enjoy Iowa denizen Gorman's evocation of those bygone days, which sound positively idyllic to readers in the 21st century. Sam McCain is a sympathetic character, and the delineation of his relatives, girlfriends, and fellow townspeople is sure-handed in these novels, each one titled with a refrain from a popular song of the era.

1. *Wake Up Little Susie* (Carroll & Graf, 1999) Black River Falls, Iowa, 1957. After Susan Squires's body is found in the trunk of a new Ford Edsel during a parade sponsored by the Ford Motor Company, Judge Esme Anne Whitney, not trusting the local sheriff, assigns young lawyer Sam McCain to investigate. Prequel to number 2.
2. *Day the Music Died, The* (Carroll & Graf, 1998) February 1958. The day after a long drive to what turned out to be Buddy Holly's last concert, Sam McCain discovers the body of the wife of Judge Whitney's nephew, Kenny.
3. *Will You Still Love Me Tomorrow?* (Carroll & Graf, 2000) The upcoming visit of Nikita Khruschev is at the center of a political storm in which Philip Mulchaey, outspoken advocate of leftist causes and the father of Sam's latest love, Lila Leigh Mulchaey, is murdered.
4. *Save the Last One for Me* (Carroll & Graf, 2002) Summer 1960. On the verge of the arrival of presidential candidate Richard Nixon to make a speech in Black River Falls, Sam is hired by Judge Whitney to investigate the murder of John Muldaur, a local fundamentalist preacher who used live rattlesnakes in his services.
5. *Everybody's Somebody's Fool* (Carroll & Graf, 2003) Summer 1961. A high school reunion results in the death of a girl and her drag-racing boyfriend, who crashes into a wall at 90 mph in a car with a severed brake line.
6. *Breaking Up Is Hard to Do* (Carroll & Graf, 2004) October 1962: Cuban missile crisis. When gubernatorial candidate Ross Murdoch pays McCain to look over his bomb shelter, Sam discovers the body of recently murdered Karen Hastings.
7. *Fools Rush In* (Pegasus, 2007) As thousands are gathering for Martin Luther King Jr.'s March on Washington, Sam seeks justice for a black college student found dead in a car trunk at the drive-in.

II. A somewhat darker series features Robert Payne, former FBI agent and psychological profiler who works out of author Gorman's hometown of Cedar Rapids, Iowa. Payne solves some gruesome crimes involving small-town Iowa denizens in this atmospheric series set in the present.

1. *Blood Moon* (St. Martin's, 1994) The suspect list in a series of child murders and mutilations has been whittled down to three men in New Hope, Iowa. Robert Payne, posing as a journalist, investigates at the behest of the mother of one of the victims.
2. *Hawk Moon* (St. Martin's, 1996) Payne assists Cindy Rhodes, a Native American policewoman, whose estranged husband, David, is suspected in the mutilation slayings of two Native American women. Interspersed with the present-day plot are flashbacks to an investigation of similar slayings in 1903.
3. *Harlot's Moon* (St. Martin's, 1998) Payne is asked by old school friend Monsignor Steven Gray to look into the murder of Father Daly, a fellow parish priest who had affairs with the women he counseled.
4. *Voodoo Moon* (St. Martin's, 2000) TV psychic Tandy West calls upon former lover Payne to help her in an investigation of a murder possibly committed by Paul Renard, rapist, murderer, and voodoo practitioner, who escaped from a mental hospital in the late 1960s.

III. The Cavalry Man series is set in the era after the American Civil War. The "Cavalry Man," Noah Ford, a military investigator and federal agent, is forced to deal with a series of villains, including his brother David, who are employing the latest in weapons technology to commit crimes.

1. *Killing Machine, The* (HarperTorch, 2005) The US Army's most lethal new weapon has disappeared. The theft may involve arms smuggler and former rebel David Ford, investigator Noah Ford's wayward brother. Variant title: *Cavalry Man: The Killing Machine*.
2. *Powder Keg* (HarperTorch, 2006) A Robin Hood–type bandit is using powerful explosives to knock off banks. Noah Ford, forced to work with two shady federal agents, finds himself in the middle of a fire that could destroy the town of Willow Bend. Variant title: *Cavalry Man: Powder Keg*.
3. *Doom Weapon* (HarperCollins, 2007) A rogue federal agent comes to Junction City, Colorado, to sell a "doomsday" weapon to men who are not reluctant to use it. Variant title: *Cavalry Man: Doom Weapon*.

IV. Jack Dwyer is an ex-cop turned actor who is forced to earn his living as a security guard. While his acting talents are rarely called for, his investigative talents are brought to the fore in this mystery series.

1. *New, Improved Murder* (St. Martin's, 1985) When Jane Branigan, Jack Dwyer's former lover, is found in a state of shock, holding a recently fired gun, actor and ex-cop Jack knows that his quiet days are numbered.
2. *Rough Cut* (St. Martin's, 1985) No annotation available.
3. *Murder Straight Up* (St. Martin's, 1986) A break-in at Channel 3 News costs Jack Dwyer his security job at the studio. Then anchorman David Curtis dies from poisoning just as the evening broadcast goes on the air.
4. *Murder in the Wings* (St. Martin's, 1984) Jack Dwyer is delighted to land a role in a production of O'Neill's *Long Day's Journey into Night*. But there will soon be a large fly in the ointment.
5. *Autumn Dead, The* (St. Martin's, 1987) Dwyer agrees to help Karen Lane, his high school love, to recover a lost suitcase. Then Karen dies suddenly.

6. *Cry of Shadows, A* (St. Martin's, 1990) Jack Dwyer is hired by Richard Coburn, one of the owners of Avanti, a chic restaurant/nightclub, to deal with "some problems" ostensibly caused by residents of a nearby homeless shelter.

V. Tobin, semipermanently drunk movie critic and ex-TV star, is the featured player in a pair of mysteries published in the 1980s.

1. *Murder on the Aisle* (St. Martin's, 1987) TV movie critics Tobin and Dunphy trade blows before a studio audience in Manhattan. Then Tobin is found removing a knife from Dunphy's back.
2. *Several Deaths Later* (St. Martin's, 1988) Tobin is guest panelist on *Celebrity Circle*, a TV game show being taped on a cruise to the Virgin Islands. The death of the show's host initiates a series of murders.

VI. Ed Gorman is also the author of several westerns, including a quartet about bounty hunter Leo Guild set sometime in the Old West.

1. *Guild* (Evans, 1987) Former lawman turned bounty hunter Leo Guild is interested in getting his prisoner to the Danton sheriff's office as soon as possible and collect his reward.
2. *Death Ground* (Evans, 1988) Suspicion falls on violent mountain man Kriker when Merle Rig, the man Guild is body-guarding, is killed along with Guild's teenage assistant.
3. *Blood Game* (Evans, 1989) Guild reluctantly agrees to retrieve a runaway boxer for promoter John T. Stoddard. The boxer is retrieved but then starts losing to his black opponent, which makes the crowd very unhappy.
4. *Dark Trail* (Evans, 1990) Leo Guild's runaway wife, Sarah, wants Leo to intervene in a gunfight involving her current lover, gunfighter Frank Evans.

Gosling, Paula

I. Lieutenant Jack Stryker is a midwestern police detective who appears in four books. Blackwater Bay, Michigan, a small resort town on the Great Lakes, whose sheriff Matt Gabriel is called upon to solve the occasional murder, appears in five books. Stryker is the protagonist in numbers 1 and 2. Stryker and Blackwater Bay intersect in number 3. Blackwater Bay is featured in numbers 4 through 7, while Stryker makes a return in number 8. This is a well-plotted, suspenseful series with some quirky characters. Midwest US native Paula Gosling has lived in the United Kingdom since the 1960s.

1. *Monkey Puzzle* (Doubleday, 1985) Jack Stryker is called upon to investigate the murder of Professor Aiken Adamson, whose body is found sans his malicious tongue.
2. *Backlash* (Doubleday, 1989) A sniper in the city of Grantham is killing police officers and getting away without a trace. Dana Marchant from the US Justice Department joins Jack Stryker and his colleagues when an undercover FBI agent is murdered.
3. *Body in Blackwater Bay* (Mysterious, 1992) Jack Stryker, recovering from a gunshot wound on tiny Paradise Island in the Great Lakes, gets involved in the intrigues surrounding the Mush, a seemingly undesirable bog on the island, and with Daria Gray, an artist on the run from her psychotic husband.
4. *Few Dying Words, A* (Mysterious, 1994) Just before the annual Howl, Blackwater Bay's traditional Halloween celebration, Sheriff Matt Gabriel agrees to meet with agitated retired pharmacist Tom Finnegan. Then Finnegan dies when he is run off the road, whispering the name "Jacky Morgan."

5. *Dead of Winter, The* (**Mysterious, 1996**) Home economics teacher Jess Gibbons and Sheriff Matt Gabriel get enmeshed in a murder mystery when an unidentified corpse is seen floating under the ice.

6. *Death and Shadows* (**Little, Brown, 1998**) Laura Brandon, niece of the owner of the Mountview Clinic in Blackwater Bay, gets involved when a young nurse at the clinic is murdered, supposedly by an itinerant.

7. *Underneath Every Stone* (**Little, Brown, 2000**) Frog Bartlett, ugliest man in Blackwater Bay, is the prime suspect when postman Moony Packard is murdered on his rounds.

8. *Ricochet* (**Little, Brown, 2002**) Jack Stryker comes to the fore again. The murder of Professor Mayhew in her own home may have a connection with the crank calls that Stryker's girlfriend, Kate Trevorne, is receiving.

II. Gosling has published several mysteries set in the United Kingdom, including a pair involving Detective Chief Inspector Luke Abbott.

1. *Wychford Murders, The* (**Doubleday, 1985**) Detective Chief Inspector Luke Abbott returns to his childhood home of Wychford when three women are found with their throats slit on the Wychford towpath.

2. *Death Penalties* (**Mysterious, 1991**) After Roger Leland dies in a car crash, his American interior-designer wife, Tess, is further troubled by a break-in at her home, a series of silent phone calls, and the siege of rheumatic fever her son Max undergoes.

Goudge, Elizabeth

Goudge wrote light fiction of the highest caliber. Her satisfying stories feature fully drawn characters, believable plots, beautiful settings, and highly polished prose. That they almost always have a happy ending requires no apology. Goudge's obvious love of gardening makes her descriptions of the flowering English countryside a real treat for the horticulturally inclined. These novels concern the Eliot family, especially grandmother Lucilla, and cover the years from 1938 to the early 1950s. All three novels were included in the omnibus volume *The Eliots of Damerosehay* (Hodder [UK], 1957).

Goudge wrote a trio of historical novels about English cathedral cities, variously known as the Cathedral Trilogy and the City of Bells series: *A City of Bells* (Coward-McCann, 1937); *Towers in the Mist* (Coward-McCann, 1938); and *The Dean's Watch* (Coward-McCann, 1960), as well as some well regarded stories for children.

1. *Bird in the Tree, The* (**Coward-McCann, 1940**) Seventy-eight-year-old Lucilla has made her home on the Hampshire coast a special haven for her children and grandchildren, but a romantic storm threatens.

2. *Pilgrim's Inn* (**Coward-McCann, 1948**) Lucilla, still charming and lively at 86, manipulates the family into becoming innkeepers. UK title: *The Herb of Grace*.

3. *Heart of the Family, The* (**Coward-McCann, 1953**) Lucilla, now 93, and the Eliot family help an Austrian refugee come to terms with his tragic past.

Goulart, Ron(ald Joseph)

Groucho Marx is the star of this mystery series set in the golden age of Hollywood (1930s–1940s). The novels are narrated by Groucho's (fictional?) sidekick, screenwriter Frank Denby. The dialogue is witty and laced with puns, as it should be, and many historical Hollywood figures play cameo roles. Fans of George Baxt's (q.v.) historical Hollywood mystery series titles (*The Dorothy Parker Murder Case*, etc.) will enjoy these entertaining confections.

Ron Goulart is a prolific writer. He has written other mysteries, including two featuring romance-novel-cover painter, H. J. Mavity, four novels published by Ace featuring a character named John Easy, and, as "Josephine Kains," six mystery novels published by Zebra.

Most of Goulart's fiction output is paperback SF, including several series: the Barnum System (at least a dozen novels set in the same fictional universe); Fragmented America (5 novels linked by their near-future setting); the Jack Conger trilogy; the Odd Jobs Inc. trilogy; and the Exchameleon trilogy.

Other series efforts include novel series based on comic-strip or comic-book characters, such as the *Phantom, Flash Gordon* (as "Con Steffanson"), *Vampirella*, the Star Hawks illustrated novel series, 10 novels in the Avenger series (as "Kenneth Robeson"), 3 Hardy Boys Casefiles (as "Franklin W. Dixon"), 4 western novels (as "Zeke Masters"), 3 novels based on the characters in the *Laverne and Shirley* television series (as "Con Steffanson"), a pair of adventure novels featuring a character named Harry Challenge, a collaboration with William Shatner (q.v.) on one of the Tek series, three collaborations on the Battlestar Galactica series (with Glen Larson), and several volumes in the Weird Heroes series.

Some of Goulart's best-known works are nonfiction volumes on the comics and pulp fiction, including *Cheap Thrills* (Arlington House, 1972).

1. *Groucho Marx, Master Detective* (**St. Martin's, 1998**) Feeling the need for a project between movies, Groucho Marx agrees to act in a radio serial. The death of a beautiful starlet before production begins sets Groucho off on a detective mission.

2. *Elementary, My Dear Groucho* (**St. Martin's, 1999**) Groucho and his writing partner, Frank Denby, stumble upon the body of German director Felix Denker on the 221b Baker Street set of a Sherlock Holmes (Arthur Conan Doyle [q.v.]) movie.

3. *Groucho Marx, Private Eye* (**St. Martin's, 1999**) 1938. Fading star Frances London is arrested for the murder of a leading plastic surgeon and drug supplier to the Hollywood elite, and her daughter, a singer on Groucho's show, asks for Groucho's assistance.

4. *Groucho Marx and the Broadway Murders* (**St. Martin's, 2001**) Groucho, who is going to perform in a Broadway play, agrees to join Frank and his wife, Jane, on the train trip to New York. A series of bizarre events occur, including murder.

5. *Groucho Marx, Secret Agent* (**St. Martin's, 2002**) 1939. The supposed suicide of British director Eric Olmstead may be tied to the Nazis and the war in Europe.

6. *Groucho Marx, King of the Jungle* (**St. Martin's, 2005**) Randy Spellman, who played the Tarzan-like Ty-Gor, had a rather energetic love life and a blackmail sideline, as the investigating Marx and Denby discover.

Grace, C. L.

PSEUDONYM OF P(aul) C. Doherty

Kathryn Swinbrooke is a "leech and physician" living in Canterbury, England in the 1460s and 1470s, during the off-again, on-again War of the Roses and the interrupted reign of King Edward IV. Kathryn's herbal remedies are successful more often than not, to the chagrin of the more traditional "physicians" of Canterbury. She is no slouch, either, at the murder investigations she takes on with the aid of her servant Thomasina and Irish mercenary Colum Murtagh, King's Commissioner in Canterbury. P. C. Doherty (q.v.), author of many historical mysteries, provides, in his series written as C. L. Grace, excellent mysteries flavored with authentic 15th-century background.

1. *Shrine of Murders, A* (St. Martin's, 1993) Canterbury's tourist trade is threatened by a spate of poisoned pilgrims. Kathryn suspects that the serial killer, who leaves a few lines of verse with each of his victims, is a physician.
2. *Eye of God, The* (St. Martin's, 1994) Before he is killed in battle, the Earl of Warwick gave the famed jewel, the Eye of God, to the keeping of his squire Robert Brandon, but no jewel is recorded among Brandon's possessions after he dies in captivity.
3. *Merchant of Death, The* (St. Martin's, 1995) Royal tax collector Sir Reginald Erpingham dies in a locked room at Canterbury's Wicker Man Inn, and King Edward is likely to be upset by the loss of the revenue he has collected.
4. *Book of Shadows, The* (St. Martin's, 1996) Is an apparently respectable guild of goldsmiths responsible for the death of evil warlock Tenebrae and the disappearance of *The Book of Shadows*, which holds damaging information invaluable to blackmailers?
5. *Saintly Murders* (St. Martin's, 2001) A plague of rats infesting Canterbury and the miracles attributed to the corpse of the recently deceased friar and confessor to the Queen Mother, Roger Atworth, engage Kathryn's investigative skills.
6. *Maze of Murders, A* (St. Martin's, 2003) The doughty Kathryn looks into the murder of Sir Walter Maltravers and the disappearance of the holy relic he owned, the Lacrima Christi.
7. *Feast of Poisons, A* (St. Martin's, 2004) England's Lord Henry is engaged in delicate negotiations with emissaries from France's Louis XI. Lord Henry's wife dies mysteriously, and a blacksmith and his wife are fatally poisoned.

Grafton, Sue

Produced conveniently in alphabetical order, this engaging detective series features Kinsey Millhone, a private investigator from the town of Santa Teresa, California. The tough but sensitive, shrewd, and funny Kinsey is wary of permanent relationships after losing her parents at an early age and going through two short marriages. The well-paced and suspenseful novels are filled with a cast of believably eccentric characters such as Kinsey's landlord Henry and Rosie, the owner of a tavern nearby. Kentucky native and California resident Sue Grafton, unlike her junk-food-eating, nature-hating creation, Kinsey, has a long-term marriage and likes cats, gardens, and good cuisine.

1. *A Is for Alibi* (Holt, 1982) Millhone is asked to solve the eight-year-old murder of divorce attorney Laurence Fife, for which his wife was wrongfully convicted.
2. *B Is for Burglar* (Holt, 1985) Wealthy Beverly Danziger asks Millhone to find her missing sister, Elaine Boldt, somewhere in Florida.
3. *C Is for Corpse* (Holt, 1986) Bobby Callahan, Millhone's gym acquaintance, is convinced that the car crash that injured him was really an attempt on his life.
4. *D Is for Deadbeat* (Holt, 1987) An alcoholic named Daggett gives Millhone $25,000 in stolen drug money to pass on to a third party.

5. *E Is for Evidence* (Holt, 1988) Someone tries to make it appear that Millhone is taking bribes while she is investigating a case of industrial arson.
6. *F Is for Fugitive* (Holt, 1989) Millhone goes to the town of Floral Beach to try to clear Bailey Fowler of a 17-year-old murder for which he was wrongfully convicted.
7. *G Is for Gumshoe* (Holt, 1990) Millhone is looking for an elderly woman who has disappeared from a nursing home while a contract killer is looking for Kinsey.
8. *H Is for Homicide* (Holt, 1991) Kinsey trails Bibianna Diaz from the Los Angeles barrio to Santa Teresa in search of answers to an insurance adjuster's murder.
9. *I Is for Innocent* (Holt, 1991) Architect David Barney, acquitted of murdering his estranged wife, Isabel, is charged with her "wrongful death" in civil court.
10. *J Is for Judgment* (Holt, 1993) Wendell Jaffe is spotted in Mexico just after his "widow" collects half a million dollars in insurance.
11. *K Is for Killer* (Holt, 1994) Janice Kepler, waitress in a 24-hour diner, asks Kinsey to investigate her daughter's death.
12. *L Is for Lawless* (Holt, 1995) Kinsey goes to Texas to investigate a case of missing loot from a decades-old bank robbery.
13. *M Is for Malice* (Holt, 1996) Bader Malek, recently deceased tycoon, left a considerable fortune to his four sons. However, one of them, Guy, has been missing since 1968.
14. *N Is for Noose* (Holt, 1998) Selma Newquist, of the small Sierra Mountains community of Nota Lake, hires Kinsey to find out what had been agitating her policeman husband before his recent death.
15. *O Is for Outlaw* (Holt, 1999) Kinsey uncovers evidence that her first ex-husband, former cop Mickey Magruder, contrary to her belief, had not been responsible for the beating death of Benny Quintero 14 years earlier.
16. *P Is for Peril* (Putnam, 2001) Dr. Dowan Purcell, an elderly physician who runs a nursing home that's being investigated for Medicare fraud, has disappeared.
17. *Q Is for Quarry* (Putnam, 2002) Kinsey joins Lieutenant Con Doyle and Stacey Oliphant in the investigation of an 18-year-old murder of a female adolescent who was never identified.
18. *R Is for Ricochet* (Putnam, 2004) Kinsey escorts newly paroled Reba Lafferty to her stately home, trying to keep Reba from liquor, gambling, and the charming and corrupt real-estate developer Alan Beckwith.
19. *S Is for Silence* (Putnam, 2005) Daisy, daughter of Violet Sullivan, who was 7 years old when her promiscuous mother disappeared 34 years ago, engages Kinsey to investigate her mother's true fate.
20. *T Is for Trespass* (Putnam, 2007) Millhone assumes responsibility for the well-being of old neighbor Gus Vronsky, injured in a fall. Then Vronsky's great-niece hires a home aide, Solana Rojas.

Graham, Caroline

Tim Barnaby, middle-aged policeman in the rural "Midsomer" area of England, is one the latest in a long line of low-key, sagacious, likable British police detectives. With his partner, the moody, snobbish, and sometimes bumbling Sergeant Troy, Barnaby solves a series of cases in these well-written procedurals. Barnaby's wife, Joyce, and his grown daughter Cully are prominent characters in the books and in the A&E television series (*Midsomer Murders*).

1. *Killings at Badger's Drift, The* (Adler, 1988) Barnaby and Troy investigate the poisoning of 80-year-old spinster Emily Simpson in picturesque Badger's Drift.

2. *Death of a Hollow Man, The* (Morrow, 1990) Acting out Salieri's attempted suicide in an amateur production of *Amadeus* proves fatal for Esslyn Carmichael.

3. *Murder at Madingley Grange* (Morrow, 1991) A mystery weekend hosted by a brother and sister in their aunt's Victorian mansion produces a real murder.

4. *Death in Disguise* (Morrow, 1993) The Lodge of the Golden Windhorse in the village of Compton Dando is the scene of a mystical cult and some suspicious deaths.

5. *Written in Blood* (Morrow, 1995) Gerald Hadleigh comes to a messy end after he objects to inviting Max Jennings to be guest speaker at the Midsomer Worthy Writers' Circle.

6. *Faithful unto Death* (St. Martin's, 1998) Three people disappear: housewife Simone Hollingsworth; her next-door neighbor, Brenda Brockley; and local artist Sarah Lawson. A ransom message for Simone and some exposed secrets eventually turn up.

7. *Place of Safety, A* (St. Martin's, 1999) In Ferne Basset a fight between Ann Lawrence, wife of the ex-vicar, and Carlotta, a young felon who Ann's husband has been sheltering, leads to a drowning, blackmail, and murder.

8. *Ghost in the Machine, A* (St. Martin's, 2004) After old Carey Lawson dies, Mallory, Kate, and Polly Lawson seem about to change their lives with her legacy. But further deaths occur.

Graham, Heather

PSEUDONYM OF Heather Pozzessere

I. Heather Graham Pozzessere is a prolific romance novelist under her married name of Pozzessere, as Shannon Drake (q.v.) and as Heather Graham (not to be confused with the actress of the same name). Most of the Florida-based Graham's novels are stand-alones, but she has published three historical series in which members of the same family are featured. The McKenzies, or Old Florida, series is set before and during the time of the American Civil War and delineates the adventures of various members of the part-Seminole Mackenzie family in Florida. Of course, the McKenzies are gorgeous, sexy, and supplied with raging hormones just waiting to bust out. A little American history is mentioned, by the way.

1. *Runaway* (Dell, 1994) Tara Brent and Jarrett McKenzie meet in a New Orleans tavern, Jarrett mourning his dead wife, and Tara trying to forget a past in which she was framed for a crime she didn't commit.

2. *Captive* (Topaz, 1996) Southern beauty Teela Warren and half-Seminole James McKenzie meet, but the Indian Wars intervene and threaten their romance.

3. *Rebel* (Topaz, 1997) Southern spy Alaina McCann, aka the Moccasin, is broken into the joys of marriage by Union army Major Ian McKenzie, aka the Panther, at the start of the Civil War.

4. *Surrender* (Topaz, 1998) Swashbuckling rebel captain Jerome McKenzie, skipper of the *Lady Varina*, and Union army general's daughter and nurse Risa Magee hate each other at first, but eventually they embark upon a tempestuous affair in the middle of the Civil War.

5. *Glory* (Topaz, 1999) Widow, healer, reputed witch, possessor of extrasensory powers, and Union sympathizer Rhiannon Tremaine betrays a Confederate platoon encamped at her plantation.

6. *Triumph* (Signet, 2000) Rebel Tia McKenzie, aka Godiva, who leads Union troops astray riding clad only in her long hair, and Union army Captain Taylor Douglas have a tumultuous affair.

II. The Civil War trilogy follows the fortunes of the Cameron clan, which is split by opposing Rebel and Union sympathies. Jesse Cameron fights for the Union; Daniel Cameron fights for the Confederacy; and sister Christa marries a Yankee Colonel and goes West. All three novels published in one volume by Rhapsody in 2004.

1. *One Wore Blue* (Dell, 1992) The story of Kiernan Miller's love for two brothers, Daniel and Jesse Cameron, who fight on opposite sides of the Civil War. Kiernan can't forgive Jesse for wearing the blue Union uniform, even though she loves him.

2. *And One Wore Gray* (Dell, 1992) Daniel Cameron wears Confederate gray and indulges in a obligatory tempestuous romance with Callie Michaelson.

3. *And One Rode West* (Dell, 1992) Christa Cameron, attempting to save her Virginia home, marries Yankee Colonel Jeremy McCauley, and the two go west and confront tarantulas, buffalo stampedes, hostile Comanches, and a marriage that seems to have nothing going for it except lust.

III. Another Civil War trilogy features the Slater brothers and the beautiful, hot-blooded women they fall in love with. *Summer Fires* (Topaz, 1998) is an omnibus volume containing all three novels.

1. *Dark Stranger* (Harlequin, 1988) Kristin McCahy is trying keep her family and ranch together during the Civil War, when Cole Slater rides into her life, guns and eyes ablaze.

2. *Rides a Hero* (Harlequin, 1989) Rebel on the run Malachi Slater and Yankee Shannon McCahy clash relentlessly on the Missouri border, but their developing passion engulfs them.

3. *Apache Summers* (Harlequin, 1989) Texan Tess Stuart needs a hired gun to avenge her uncle's murder. The only man willing to step in is the infuriating Jamie Slater.

Graham, Winston

Masterpiece Theatre viewers will remember the stark beauty of the Cornish coast that gives this historical-romance series its distinctive flavor. Ross Poldark must have been influenced by the Americans he fought against in the colonies, for his fiercely independent and egalitarian spirit is the vital force that sets this series moving. Blending humor, romance and its complications, and action that includes pirates and intrigue in France, the Poldark saga is hard to beat for pure entertainment. In *Poldark's Cornwall* (Bodley Head, 1985), Winston Graham depicts, in word and photograph, the real Cornish setting of the Poldark saga.

1. *Ross Poldark* (Doubleday, 1951) Ross comes home from the war in America to find that Elizabeth, the woman he loves, is engaged to another man. This action takes place during 1783–1787. Originally published in the United Kingdom in 1945.

2. *Demelza* (Doubleday, 1953) Ross weds the fiery and stubborn Demelza, his former kitchen maid. This volume covers the first years of their marriage, in 1788–1790. Originally published in the United Kingdom in 1946.

3. *Jeremy Poldark* (Doubleday, 1954) During 1790–1791, Ross faces imprisonment after being accused of leading a rebellion. Originally published in the United Kingdom in 1950.

4. *Warleggan* (Doubleday, 1955) In 1792–1793, Elizabeth is widowed, and Demelza fears for her marriage. Originally published in the United Kingdom in 1953 as *The Last Gamble*.

5. *Black Moon, The* (Doubleday, 1974) Amid the complications of love and war in 1794–1795, Elizabeth bears a son, who may be Ross's.

6. *Four Swans, The* (Doubleday, 1977) Ross wins a seat in Parliament and confronts his old attraction to Elizabeth. The time is 1795–1797.
7. *Angry Tide, The* (Doubleday, 1978) The shock of Elizabeth's death brings Ross to the realization of life's real importance in 1798–1799.
8. *Stranger from the Sea, The* (Doubleday, 1982) This episode begins in 1810, with Captain Poldark off fighting under Wellington and shows young Jeremy and Clowance Poldark growing up, getting into mischief, and falling in love.
9. *Miller's Dance, The* (Doubleday, 1983) This installment concentrates on the lives and loves of Jeremy and Clowance, the two elder Poldark children. It covers the years 1812–1813.
10. *Loving Cup, The* (Doubleday, 1985) As Napoléon meets his defeat, the Poldarks are engrossed in marriage settlements for Clowance and young Jeremy. Covers the years 1813–1815.
11. *Twisted Sword, The* (Carroll & Graf, 1991) Finds Ross and Demelza in France and young Jeremy and his bride in Brussels on the eve of the Battle of Waterloo. Covers 1815–1816.
12. *Bella Poldark* (Trafalgar Square, 2002) In the conclusion to the series, Bella Poldark takes center stage, moving between her home on the Cornish coast and the world of the theatre in London and the Continent. Takes place in 1818–1820.

Granger, Ann (Patricia Ann)

I. English mystery and historical romance (under the name of Ann Hulme) writer Granger authors a series of intricately plotted, atmospheric, well-characterized mysteries set in the Cotswolds. British consular officer Meredith Mitchell and Chief Inspector Markby of Bamford love one another, solve crimes together, but live separately.

1. *Say It with Poison* (St. Martin's, 1991) Mitchell and Markby solve two village murders working separately but along parallel lines.
2. *Season for Murder, A* (St. Martin's, 1992) Mitchell rents an isolated cottage in Pook's Common, renews her acquaintance with Markby, and helps him investigate the death of equestrienne Harriet Needham.
3. *Cold in the Earth* (St. Martin's, 1993) House-sitting for Markby's sister in Bamford, Mitchell joins him in investigating the death of a man buried alive at a development site.
4. *Murder among Us* (St. Martin's, 1993) The Society for the Preservation of Historic Bamford protests against turning Springwood Hall into a pricey country inn.
5. *Where Old Bones Lie* (St. Martin's, 1994) Several corpses of more recent vintage turn up when archaeologists conduct a dig at an old battlefield.
6. *Fine Place for Death, A* (St. Martin's, 1995) Mitchell becomes involved with the investigation of the murder of two young girls in Bamford against Markby's objections.
7. *Flowers for His Funeral* (St. Martin's, 1995) Mitchell runs into an old schoolmate, Rachel Hunter, at the Chelsea Flower Show and is somewhat upset to discover that Rachel was Markby's first wife.
8. *Candle for a Corpse* (St. Martin's, 1996) When grave diggers unearth the body of Kimberley Oates, who has been missing for 12 years, one question is answered, but more questions are raised.
9. *Touch of Mortality, A* (St. Martin's, 1997) Scientist Liam Caswell and his wife, Sally, friend of Meredith Mitchell, have settled in the village of Castle Derry in Oxfordshire near Mitchell. Then the Caswells receive a letter bomb.
10. *Word after Dying, A* (St. Martin's, 1998) Strange and sinister goings-on in village of Parsloe St. John: old recluse Olivia Smeaton

has fallen to her death; Olivia's horse Firefly has been poisoned; and the body of illiterate handyman Ernie has been found in one place, his head in another.
11. *Call the Dead Again* (St. Martin's, 1999) Who killed Markby's schoolmate Andrew Penhallow after he is confronted by Kate Drago, a beautiful but unwelcome visitor who had been given a lift to Bamford by Mitchell?
12. *Beneath These Stones* (St. Martin's, 2000) When the body of the wife of local farmer Hugh Franklin is discovered by Gypsy Danny Smith, Hugh and his 12-year-old daughter, Tammy, are both suspects.
13. *Shades of Murder* (St. Martin's, 2001) Jan Oakley, recent arrival from Poland, claims to be the great-grandson of William Oakley, acquitted of poisoning his wife in 1889. Jan, who has a will that entitles him to inherit part of the Oakley estate, is poisoned in his turn.
14. *Restless Evil, A* (St. Martin's, 2002) The house-hunting Mitchell and Markby look at a property in the village of Lower Stovey, the scene of an unsolved serial rape case that was Markby's first investigation.
15. *That Way Murder Lies* (St. Martin's, 2005) Alison Jenner was acquitted of murdering her aunt. Twenty-five years later, Alison is receiving poison-pen letters accusing her of the crime.

II. Granger has embarked on a second mystery series, which, so far, has been available in the United States only in large-print editions. Fran Varady, aspiring actress and sometime sleuth, is living by her wits in London after a childhood that featured her mother's desertion of her family.

1. *Asking for Trouble* (Headline [UK], 1997) Fran's former housemate Terry is found hanging from the ceiling of her room.
2. *Keeping Bad Company* (Headline [UK], 1997) An alcoholic who claims to be the only witness to the violent abduction of a young girl is found dead, and Fran is drawn into the case.
3. *Running Scared* (Headline [UK], 1998) Fran and her friend Ganesh aid a bleeding man in the shop where she works. The man leaves and then turns up stabbed to death outside her basement apartment.
4. *Risking It All* (Headline [UK], 2001) Private detective Clarence Duke reunites Fran with Eva, the mother who deserted her family when Fran was seven. Eva, who is dying, asks Fran to find her half sister, of whose existence Fran had been unaware.
5. *Watching Out* (Headline [UK], 2003) Fran seems to be back on track with a job at a trendy pizzeria and a role in a play. However, there is something not quite right about the pizzeria, and play rehearsals aren't going well.
6. *Mixing with Murder* (Headline [UK], 2005) Seedy club owner Mickey Allerton is holding Fran's dog, Bonnie, hostage, while Fran is tracking down Lisa, a dancer who has gone AWOL.

Granger, Bill

I. Devereaux, code-named "November," is a spy who works for the shadowy "R Section" set up by President Kennedy to "spy upon the spies." He is a loner so disenchanted with espionage that he has even tried arranging his own "official" death. His romance with reporter Rita Macklin gives a chronology of sorts to the series. Granger, an American author, captures that brooding atmosphere reminiscent of John le Carré (q.v.). His first book, *The November Man*, received a good deal of publicity for its prevision of the motives and methods used by the IRA in its assassination of Lord Mountbatten.

1. *November Man, The* (Fawcett, 1979) Devereaux investigates an IRA plot to kill Lord Slough, one of England's most important men.
2. *Schism* (Crown, 1981) Father Leo Tunney, missing and presumed dead after his capture by the Pathet Lao, turns up again after 20 years and is taken into CIA custody.
3. *Shattered Eye, The* (Crown, 1982) Inspired by their war game computer, the Russians plot to overthrow Mitterand's French government and replace it with a Communist one.
4. *British Cross, The* (Crown, 1983) Devereaux checks on a high KGB official who has offered to defect with a secret potent enough to topple governments.
5. *Zurich Numbers, The* (Crown, 1984) When his great aunt is threatened by two foreigners, Devereaux returns home to Chicago's South Side.
6. *Hemingway's Notebook* (Crown, 1986) Colonel Ready, Caribbean dictator and ex-CIA operative, brings Devereaux out of retirement to find a mysterious notebook.
7. *There Are No Spies* (Crown, 1986) Hanley, Devereaux's former boss, is committed to a mental hospital on the orders of his superiors.
8. *Infant of Prague, The* (Crown, 1987) An attempt to help deliver a Czech defector in Brussels runs into a snag when Anna Jelinak, Czech movie star touring the United States, carries out her own defection.
9. *Henry McGee Is Not Dead* (Warner, 1988) "Henry McGee," a defected Soviet scientist, disappears from a secret project in Alaska.
10. *Man Who Heard Too Much, The* (Warner, 1989) A secret tape that could cause a major international crisis is missing.
11. *League of Terror* (Warner, 1990) Henry McGee is working with the IRA in a scheme to extort $4 million from an airline with a nerve gas threat.
12. *Last Good German, The* (Warner, 1991) Devereaux is forced out of retirement to track down an elusive Japanese coding device.
13. *Burning the Apostle* (Warner, 1993) Rich, young ecoterrorist Britta Andrews is contemplating a Chernobyl-style nuclear disaster near Chicago.

II. Former Chicago sports reporter Jimmy Drover works now for a Las Vegas sports-betting oddsmaker. Drover is tough and not scrupulously moral, but he has his softer side.

1. *Drover* (Morrow, 1991) Mobster Tony Rolls wants Drover to check out what may be a rival betting pool operating out of the Chicago Commodities Exchange.
2. *Drover and the Zebras* (Morrow, 1992) The coach of the St. Mary's basketball team, which is headed for an NCAA tournament berth, is under investigation for recruiting and point-shaving violations.
3. *Drover and the Designated Hitter* (Morrow, 1994) Crusty Chicago Cubs veteran Homer White may be involved in clandestine and illegal betting.

III. Granger wrote a quartet of books in the 1980s about a Chicago Police Department team, Sergeant Terry Flynn and Detective Karen Kovac. Numbers 2 and 3 were published under the pseudonym of Joe Gash.

1. *Public Murders* (Jove, 1980) No annotation available.
2. *Priestly Murders* (Holt, 1984) Concerns the murder of a Chicago priest. Published under the pseudonym of Joe Gash.
3. *Newspaper Murders* (Holt, 1985) An alcoholic, bitter reporter is murdered. Published under the pseudonym of Joe Gash.
4. *El Murders, The* (Holt, 1987) Flynn and Kovac feel great frustration at the attitudes of their superiors and fellow cops when gay

businessman Lee Herran is murdered and Mary Ann Caldwell is raped on a Chicago El platform.

Granger, Pip

Queen Elizabeth's Coronation Summer of 1953 finds seven-year-old Rosa "Rosie" Featherby living in London's bohemian Soho district with "Aunt Maggie" and "Uncle Bert" above their Old Compton Street café. Rosie narrates her adventures among the pimps, prostitutes, con men, thieves, shady lawyers, and other lowlifes in this Dickensian milieu. English author Pip Granger draws upon her own experiences in 1950s Soho in the two Rosie novels and in two other novels: *Trouble in Paradise* (Poisoned Pen, 2005) and *No Peace for the Wicked* (Poisoned Pen, 2006). All of the novels are mysteries of sorts, but the real fun is in the loving evocation of a bygone working-class milieu.

1. *Not All Tarts Are Apple* (Poisoned Pen, 2002) During Queen Elizabeth's Coronation Summer, in 1953, seven-year-old Rosie Featherby, who lives with a couple she calls Auntie Maggie and Uncle Bert, enjoys the raffish life and characters of London's Soho district. The mysterious Perfumed Lady is the "tart" of the tale.
2. *Widow Ginger, The* (Poisoned Pen, 2003) An ex-GI known as the Widow Ginger, a wartime crony of Uncle Bert's, is a rather sinister presence in the continuation of Rosie's narrative.

Grant, Charles L(ewis)

I. The small Connecticut town of Oxrun Station would seem an idyllic place, at first glimpse. However, like Stephen King's (q.v.) and H. P. Lovecraft's bucolic burgs, it is home to horrific curses, sinister beings and nasty happenings, generally of a supernatural sort. The late (d. 2006) Charles L. Grant was a master of quiet horror, and the novels and stories in this series, tied more by location and theme than by characters, find him at his best.

Grant wrote many other novels and stories with horror themes, as well as fantasy and science fiction and juveniles. He used many pseudonyms, including Lionel Fenn (q.v.), Steven Charles, Simon Lake, Geoffrey March, Deborah Lewis, and Felicia Andrews. He was an editor of, and contributor to, many anthologies, including the *Shadows* and the *Chronicles of Greystone Bay*.

1. *Hour of the Oxrun Dead, The* (Doubleday, 1977) Natalie Windsor moves to Oxrun Station, Connecticut, and marries a local police officer. Then Natalie's husband is murdered and mutilated a year later by some cult that practices human sacrifice.
2. *Sound of Midnight, The* (Doubleday, 1978) A group of children play games that are re-creations of ancient rituals to a malevolent, still viable entity.
3. *Last Call of Mourning, The* (Doubleday, 1979) Cynthia Yarrow returns to her home in Oxrun Station after a long absence. Did she imagine that her father died and was resurrected?
4. *Grave, The* (Popular Library, 1981) Private investigator Josh Miller, searching for a missing body in Oxrun Station, finds that whatever he is hunting is hunting him.
5. *Bloodwind* (Popular Library, 1982) Artist and teacher Pat Shavers, trying to put her life together, feels an evil presence in the wind in Oxrun Station, which has marked her as its next victim.
6. *Nightmare Seasons* (Doubleday, 1982) Short stories.
7. *Soft Whisper of the Dead, The* (Grant, 1982) Although set in Oxrun Station, this vampire tale is a historical horror novel rather than a contemporary one. Count Braslov attempts to subject the population of Oxrun Station to his vampiric will.

8. *Dark Cry of the Moon, The* (Grant, 1986) This time a werewolf has gotten loose in the precincts of Oxrun Station.

9. *Long Night of the Grave, The* (Grant, 1986) A reactivated mummy, escaping from the artifacts of Isle Hall, is stalking the woods near Oxrun Station.

10. *Orchard, The* (Tor, 1986) A series of grotesque deaths and other bizarre phenomena spread out from an orchard and infect the town.

11. *Dialing the Wind* (Tor, 1988) Strange music is on the wind, heard only by those desperate for love.

12. *Black Carousel, The* (Tor, 1995) Whenever the Pilgrim's Travelers carnival comes to Oxrun Station, strange events occur: people disappear and ghosts seem to roam the streets.

II. The Millennium Quartet is a subtle, dark fantasy series set at the turn of the 21st century and based on the Book of Revelations. Episcopalian minister Casey Chisholm, who is one of the characters linking the four books, suddenly finds that he is endowed with miraculous powers and that he is the target of evil forces. The Four Horsemen of the Apocalypse are on the move: hunger, crime, war are on the increase. Can the final days be near?

1. *Symphony* (Forge, 1997) Casey Chisholm, who has rusticated himself in the sleepy town of Maple Landing, finds that he has suddenly gained miraculous powers, but evil, in the form of a carload of criminals, is speeding toward him.

2. *In the Mood* (Forge, 1998) In America's heartland, the crops have failed and the cattle are dying. Everywhere around the world, people are hungry and getting hungrier.

3. *Chariot* (Forge, 2000) *Plague* is the watchword here. Trey Falkirk cannot understand why he has a golden touch in gambling or why Las Vegas is the only part of America spared from a smallpox epidemic.

4. *Riders in the Sky* (Forge, 1999) War is breaking out around the world. Meanwhile, developer Norville Cutler, the puppet of evildoers on a large scale, is trying to acquire land on Georgia's Camoret Island, where Casey Chisholm is holed out, awaiting his destiny.

III. Black Oak Investigations, Ethan Proctor, proprietor, a firm that handles office fraud, missing persons, and a variety of white-collar crime, branches out when one of its agents runs afoul of a mysterious, homicidal creature. Then Black Oak gets involved with werewolves, satanic curses, vampires, and more.

1. *Genesis* (Roc, 1998) Ethan Proctor gets involved in an out-of-the-ordinary investigation when one of his operatives turns up dead in a town plagued by something homicidal roaming in the hills.

3. *Winter Knight* (Roc, 1999) Proctor's latest investigation takes place in a town whose inhabitants have become enslaved to an evil that grants them their heart's desire—in exchange for their souls.

3. *Hush of Dark Wings, The* (Roc, 1999) At the behest of a woman he once knew, Proctor, against his better judgment, gets involved in investigating strange happenings in her town.

4. *Hunting Ground* (Roc, 2000) Ethan Proctor, supposedly on vacation in Atlantic City, gets involved in lies, murders, and, possibly, vampires.

5. *When the Cold Wind Blows* (Roc, 2001) A series of disappearances and mutilations in the swampy woodlands of northwest Atlanta, which may be the work of a werewolf, bring Ethan onto the scene at the behest of an old friend of his father.

IV. Grant started his publishing career as a science-fiction writer. The Parric Family trilogy, set in the future, is about androids who run amok when a Plaguewind infests the Earth.

1. *Shadow of Alpha, The* (Berkley, 1976) Dorrin Parric is part of a experimental government project in which he lives secretly in a town entirely populated by androids. Then war and the Plaguewind break out.

2. *Ascension* (Berkley, 1977) Orion Parric has vowed to avenge his father, Dorrin, but he has to fend with human assassins, homicidal androids, paranoid dictators, and the Plaguewind.

3. *Legion* (Berkley, 1979) The dying Legion, the Rogues who rule the Earth, and the Plaguewind all seem to militate against the peaceful coexistence of humans and androids.

Grant, Linda

PSEUDONYM OF Linda V. Willliams

Catherine Sayler is a high-tech private investigator working out of San Francisco. Catherine, although single, is saddled with the care of her difficult teenage niece, Molly, who is rebelling against everything. Most of Catherine's jobs take place in corporate settings and involve computers. American author Linda Grant, not to be confused with the British columnist and author (*Sexing the Millennium*, etc.) of the same name, has published only the six Catherine Sayler mysteries, none since 1998.

1. *Random Access Murder* (Avon, 1988) When Catherine Sayler's lover is framed for the murder of a secretary, Catherine plunges into the case, determined to find the real killer amid a stew of corporate crime and greed.

2. *Blind Trust* (Scribner, 1990) After Catherine's biggest client goes broke, she accepts an offer from a First Central Bank executive to investigate a flawed computer system and the disappearance of one of the four men who know how it works.

3. *Love Nor Money* (Scribner, 1991) Catherine investigates, at the request of a friend, the death of his cousin, a recovering alcoholic who had threatened to expose the prominent judge who molested him as a child.

4. *Woman's Place, A* (Scribner, 1994) Systech, a software development company with sexual harassment problems, hires Catherine and her (male) partner Jesse to find "one guy" to make an example of.

5. *Lethal Genes* (Scribner, 1996) The "maize lab" at UC-Berkeley hires Catherine to root out sabotage and she finds herself investigating two suspicious deaths.

6. *Vampire Bytes* (Scribner, 1998) A new vampire game produced by a computer-gaming company seems to be behind the disappearance of its lead programmer and the discovery of the body of a young man drained of blood with two puncture wounds in his neck.

Grass, Günter

War and Nazism are the subjects of the grim allegories upon which Nobel Prize winner Grass's international reputation rests. *The Tin Drum*, still perhaps his best-known novel, was filmed in 1975 and won an Academy Award as the Best Foreign Film. Although most of Grass's work is connected by his political and historical preoccupations, the novels in the Danzig Trilogy (numbers 1–3; published as *The Danzig Trilogy*, Harcourt, 1987), set in Grass's native city of Danzig (now Gdańsk, in Poland), are linked together by their common setting. *The Rat* brings together the drum-playing dwarf of *The Tin Drum* and the magic fish of *The Flounder*. All five novels have been translated into English from the German by Ralph Manheim.

1. *Tin Drum, The* (Pantheon, 1963) Oskar Mazerath, who deliberately stopped growing when he was three years old and three feet tall, plays on a tin drum to stimulate his recall of the past. Originally published as *Die Blechtrommel* (1959).
2. *Cat and Mouse* (Harcourt, 1963) Mahlke, a teenager growing up in Danzig during the war, feels set apart by his huge Adam's apple. Originally published as *Katz und Maus* (1961).
3. *Dog Years* (Harcourt, 1965) The central relationship in this novel spanning the years from 1917 to 1957 is between athletic Walter Matern and his half-Jewish friend Eduard Amsel. Originally published as *Hundejahre* (1963).
4. *Flounder, The* (Harcourt, 1978) The magic fish from the fairy tale "The Fisherman and His Wife" is put on trial by a feminist group in a fable spanning centuries of history. Originally published as *Der Butt* (1977).
5. *Rat, The* (Harcourt, 1987) The narrator is troubled by apocalyptic dreams in which a talking rat documents humanity's demise through ecological and political ignorance. Originally published as *Die Rättin* (1986).

Graves, Robert

I. The stuttering, timid Claudius portrayed so brilliantly by Derek Jacobi in Masterpiece Theatre's dramatization of these books was a surprisingly admirable Roman in an age of sadistic tyrants. The "autobiography" that Graves has written for him is a fascinating reconstruction of the tumultuous years from 10 BCE to 54 CE, covering the reigns of Caesar Augustus, Tiberius, Caligula, and Claudius himself. Needless to say, this poisonous brew of murder and other assorted villainies won't be everybody's cup of tea.

Although he wrote several other historical fictions, Graves claimed that his novels were "the dogs I breed to feed my cat"—his "cat" being his poetry, which is what he wanted to be remembered for (*New Collected Poems*, Doubleday, 1977). He also wrote what many readers consider to be the best memoir of World War I, *Good-bye to All That* (Cape, 1930), and several volumes of essays and criticism (e.g., *The White Goddess*, Creative Age, 1948), which made him something of a cult figure.

1. *I, Claudius* (Smith & Haas, 1935) The machinations of Caesar Augustus and his sinister wife, Livia, seem mild compared to the cruelty of Tiberius and the outright insanity of Caligula.
2. *Claudius the God and His Wife Messalina* (Smith & Haas, 1935) Covers the reforms and the British conquest of Claudius's reign, as well as the debaucheries of the Empress Messalina. Three historical accounts of his death are appended.

II. Perhaps because they were published during the darkest days of World War II, Graves's pair of novels about the American Revolution never received the attention given to some of his other historical fiction. They are based on the memoirs of Roger Lamb, an Irishman who served with the British army against the American rebels in the Revolutionary War. In his foreword to *Sergeant Lamb's America*, Graves stated that he stuck to the historical facts as much as possible, and invented no main characters, yet he was not writing "straight history." The opinions, uncomplimentary for the most part, expressed about Americans are Lamb's, not necessarily Graves's.

Among other historical novels Graves published are *Count Belisarius* (Random House, 1938); *Homer's Daughter* (Doubleday, 1955); and *Wife to Mr. Milton* (Creative Age, 1944). He also wrote the enjoyable

fantasy *Watch the North Wind Rise* (Creative Age, 1949; UK title: *Seven Days in New Crete*).

1. *Sergeant Lamb's America* (Random House, 1940) Young Gerry Lamb enlists in King George's 9th Foot Regiment and, after several years of peacetime service, is shipped to Canada to fight the rebellious Americans. UK title: *Sergeant Lamb of the Ninth*.
2. *Proceed, Sergeant Lamb* (Random House, 1941) As part of Burgoyne's army defeated at Saratoga in 1777, Lamb becomes a prisoner of war, but escapes to fight again with the 23rd Foot, the Royal Welsh Fusiliers.

Graves, Sarah

Eastport, Maine, "the Easternmost city in the United States," is home to mystery writer Sarah Graves and her fictional character, amateur sleuth Jacobia "Jake" Tiptree. Like her creator, Jake lives in an 1823 Federal house that is constantly undergoing renovation. Unlike her creator, Jake is a single mother with a teenage son. As the series title, Home Repair Is Homicide, indicates, home repair is the shtick in this series of humorous, entertaining cozies full of home-repair tips and local Maine color.

1. *Dead Cat Bounce, The* (Crimeline, 1998) Jake Tiptree discovers the body of a man in her cellar with an ice pick stuck in his head. Then her neighbor Ellie White confesses to the crime.
2. *Triple Witch* (Crimeline, 1999) Jake has to deal with a crime wave in Eastport involving three murders and evidence of drug dealing while trying to prevent her philandering ex-husband Victor from moving in next door.
3. *Wicked Fix* (Crimeline, 2000) Nobody is very upset when Reuben Tate, Eastport's "bad boy," is found dead soon after his return, hanging from the cemetery gate and done in by a scalpel.
4. *Repair to Her Grave* (Bantam, 2001) Renovating her "stately" home is uppermost in Jake's mind until the charming and mysterious Jonathan Raines appears on her doorstep in quest of a "cursed" violin and then promptly disappears.
5. *Wreck the Halls* (Bantam, 2001) In her first hardcover appearance, Jake deals with the murder of wife-beating husband Merle Carmody.
6. *Unhinged* (Bantam, 2003) Jake and Ellie White investigate the disappearance and (so Jake thinks) murder of local busybody Harriet Hollingsworth.
7. *Mallets Aforethought* (Bantam, 2004) The renovation of the historic Harlequin House in Eastport turns up two corpses behind a hidden door: one the mummified body of a woman from the 1920s; the other that of historical society president and real-estate mogul Hector Gosling.
8. *Tool and Die* (Bantam, 2004) Bella, the housekeeper whose services Jake won as a prize, is driving everyone batty with her cleaning zeal. Then it turns out that Bella has been receiving death threats, apparently from her ex-con ex-husband.
9. *Nail Biter* (Bantam, 2005) Jake and Ellie invest in a rental property in upscale Quoddy Village. Unfortunately, the first renters are a coven of witches led by the charismatic Gregory Brand.
10. *Trap Door* (Bantam, 2006) Jake's dead ex-husband Victor is haunting her 1823 Federal-style house, and her friend Jemmy is on the run from hit men, including local resident Walter Henderson.
11. *Book of Old Houses, The* (Bantam, 2008) After Jake Tiptree uncovers a very old book while fixing up her 1823 house in Eastport, local antiquarian bookman, Horace Robotham, who offers to examine it, dies suspiciously.

Greeley, Andrew M(oran)

I. Father Andrew Greeley is recognized as one of America's leading authorities on the sociology of religion, a celibate expert on sex, a maverick priest who stays within the Catholic Church, and the author of more than 60 works on religion and sociology. While his nonfiction is highly regarded, if controversial, his fiction, despite (or because of) its popularity with the reading public, hasn't found much favor with critics. His Passover Trilogy (*Thy Brother's Wife*; *Ascent into Hell*; and *Lord of the Dance*) has no continuing characters, but the diverting mystery series featuring the Chicago-based Most Reverend John Blackwood "Blackie" Ryan, priest, church administrator (auxiliary bishop of Chicago), and amateur detective, does. Blackie is also featured in *White Smoke* (Forge, 1996), in which he accompanies his superior, Sean, Cardinal Cronin to the Vatican for the election of a new Pope. Blackie plays a peripheral role in the following novels: *Virgin and Martyr* (Warner, 1984); *Angels of September* (Warner, 1986); *God Game* (Forge, 1986); *Patience of a Saint* (Warner, 1987); *Saint Valentine's Night* (Warner, 1989); *Angel Fire* (Warner, 1990); and probably other novels.

1. *Happy Are the Meek* (Warner, 1985) Wolfe Tone Quinlan, wealthy industrialist and Satanist, is found crushed under a suit of armor in his home.
2. *Happy Are the Clean of Heart* (Warner, 1986) Lisa Malone, famous performer and Blackie's childhood sweetheart, is sadistically beaten in her hotel room.
3. *Happy Are Those Who Thirst for Justice* (Mysterious, 1987) Real-estate tycoon Violet Enright, matriarch of a rich but dysfunctional family, is found shot to death on her yacht.
4. *Happy Are the Merciful* (Warner, 1989) Bishop Ryan is called in to save the life of a woman on Death Row for the alleged murder of her adoptive parents.
5. *Happy Are the Peacemakers* (Jove, 1993) Former Chicago policeman Tim MacCarthy secures Blackie's help in solving a bombing murder in Dublin.
6. *Happy Are the Poor in Spirit* (Jove, 1995) Bart Cain's prom date, who disappeared more than 40 years ago, seems to be haunting him now.
7. *Happy Are Those Who Mourn* (Jove, 1995) The restless spirit of a recently deceased Monsignor and a conspiracy involving millions occupy Bishop Ryan in this volume.
8. *Happy Are the Oppressed* (Jove, 1996) Wealthy and elegant Catholic matron Chantal Cardin is afraid that the Cardin curse is about to strike her with fatal effect.
9. *Bishop at Sea, The* (Berkley, 1997) The *Langley*, a nuclear-powered US Navy aircraft carrier commanded by Cardinal Cronin's cousin, seems to be haunted.
10. *Bishop and the Three Kings, The* (Berkley, 1998) The remains of the Three Kings, an important Catholic relic, are stolen from the Cologne (Germany) Cathedral.
11. *Bishop and the Missing L Train, The* (Forge, 2000) A Chicago L train carrying the unpleasant and unpopular auxiliary bishop the Most Reverend Augustus "Gus" Quill disappears.
12. *Bishop and the Beggar Girl of St. Germain, The* (Forge, 2001) Charismatic young priest Father Jean-Claude has disappeared in Paris while escorting Cardinal Cronin's sister-in-law Nora Cronin.
13. *Bishop in the West Wing, The* (Forge, 2002) Blackie's old friend US president John Patrick McGurn has invited Blackie to the White House to smoke out a poltergeist that is roaming its corridors.
14. *Bishop Goes to the University, The* (Forge, 2003) An "extra" cardinal turns up in a sealed room at the University of Chicago Divinity School with his head blown off by a shotgun.
15. *Bishop in the Old Neighborhood, The* (Forge, 2005) Blackie starts digging into the past of Father Mikal Wolodyjowski, charismatic priest at St. Lucy's, a Chicago church where three corpses have turned up in the sanctuary.
16. *Bishop at the Lake, The* (Forge, 2007) When Malachi Howard-Nolan, an ambitious priest, is felled by a life-threatening attack of hornets, Blackie suspects that someone in Nolan's eccentric family wishes him ill.

II. *The Cardinal Sins*, one of Andrew Greeley's best sellers, had as one of its characters Laurence "Lar" McAuliffe, who becomes a priest. Father McAuliffe is the main character in an additional pair of novels involving Catholic doctrine.

1. *Cardinal Sins, The* (Warner, 1981) Two Irish boys on the West Side of Chicago discover themselves thanks to the help of the Catholic Church. One becomes a priest, the other a business man. Both are involved with the same girl.
2. *Cardinal Virtues, The* (Warner, 1990) Father McAuliffe comes to the aid of a young priest who has incurred the wrath of the leader of an ultra-right wing Catholic group.
3. *Occasion of Sin, An* (Putnam, 1991) Father Lar is enjoined to play's devil's advocate in the investigation of the canonization of Cardinal McGlynn.

III. Another mystery series features as its protagonists Dermot Coyne, young Chicago commodities trader and Nuala McGrail, beautiful Irish singer and actress, whom Dermot eventually marries. The foul-mouthed, feisty and fey (she has psychic powers) Nuala does most of the sleuthing, while Dermot does the Watson-like chronicling in these novels, which often get involved with historical people and events in Chicago and Ireland.

1. *Irish Gold* (Forge, 1994) Dermot Coyne hires Trinity College (Dublin) student Nuala McGrail to translate his grandmother's Irish diaries and runs into a lot of trouble involving a plot to reunite Ireland and the United Kingdom and links to the unsolved murder of Free Irish leader Michael Collins.
2. *Irish Lace* (Forge, 1996) Nuala joins Dermot, newly rich and now a writer, in Chicago, and the two get involved in a pair of mysteries: recent robberies in Chicago's art galleries linked to an IRA plot and the story of the US Civil War–era conspiracy to set Confederate prisoners at Camp Douglas free.
3. *Irish Whiskey* (Forge, 1997) Dermot is under investigation for the $3 million he made in commodities trading. Nuala "sees" an empty coffin in a cemetery plot, which leads to the investigation of the shooting death of onetime Al Capone rival Jimmy Sullivan.
4. *Irish Mist* (Forge, 1999) Nuala and Dermot, now married, go off to Dublin for her gig in Ireland's Irish Aid concert. On the plane from Chicago to Dublin, Nuala has a vision of the assassination of Kevin O'Higgins, successor to Michael Collins.
5. *Irish Eyes* (Forge, 2000) Nuala and Dermot's baby, Nelliecoyne, has inherited her mother's psychic powers: she senses the 1898 sinking of a passenger ship on Lake Michigan.
6. *Irish Love* (Forge, 2001) Nuala has abandoned her singing career and retreated to a country house on the West of Ireland with Nelliecoyne to sort herself out. It turns out that the site was the scene of a massacre in the 1880s.
7. *Irish Stew!* (Forge, 2002) Nuala gives premature birth to Socra Marie after psychically "sensing" that self-made Chicago lawyer Seamus Costelloe is doomed. Meanwhile Dermot involves himself in researching the historic (1880s) Haymarket Riot and the subsequent trial, which led to the controversial conviction of several anarchists.

8. *Irish Cream* (Forge, 2005) Mysteries past and present: the events chronicled in the diaries of 19th-century Donegal parish priest Father Richard Lonison, and current events involving Damian "Day" O'Sullivan, whom Nuala and Dermot hire to take care of their two Irish wolfhounds.

9. *Irish Crystal* (Forge, 2005) Nuala's fey abilities come into play again, as a car bombing strikes Chicago's powerful Curran family.

10. *Irish Linen* (Forge, 2007) When Desmond Doolin, a peacenik from her Chicago neighborhood, disappears in the Middle East, Nuala is convinced that he is still alive.

11. *Irish Tiger* (Forge, 2008) Nuala is asked to aid the marriage of wealthy widower Jack Patrick Donlan and his new wife, Maria Angelica Sabattini Connors, who has some shady brothers and is rumored to have slept around to aid her business.

IV. The prolific Greeley is embarked upon a series tracing the fortunes of Chicago's O'Malley family from the 1930s to the 1970s (so far). The O'Malleys are a boisterous group whose public and private fortunes are told in entertaining fashion.

1. *Midwinter's Tale, A* (Forge, 1998) Sergeant Charles "Chuck" O'Malley, after spending his youth as part of a large, close-knit family in Depression-era Chicago, finds himself in post–World War II Bamberg, Germany, helping an FBI agent locate a family of Nazis wanted by the Russians as war criminals.

2. *Younger Than Springtime* (Forge, 1999) Chuck O'Malley, returned from Germany in 1949, enrolls at Notre Dame, finds the curriculum intellectually stifling, and develops an interest in photography, which leads him to take a semi-risqué photo of Rosemarie Clancy, the daughter of a friend of the O'Malley family.

3. *Christmas Wedding, A* (Forge, 2000) Chuck and Rosemarie wed on Christmas in 1950. Chuck has some unresolved career and spiritual problems, while Rosemary has a troubled relationship with her father, doubts about the circumstances surrounding her mother's death, and an alcohol problem.

4. *September Song* (Forge, 2001) Covers the 1960s. Chuck hands in his resignation as ambassador to Germany to protest the Vietnam War and gets involved in the historic civil rights march in Selma, Alabama. Rosemarie, who has produced five children, does the narrating.

5. *Second Spring: A Love Story* (Forge, 2003) Chuck O'Malley, nearing 50 in the 1970s and stuck in a midlife and spiritual crisis, roams the Earth snapping historical photos and searching for his own happiness.

6. *Golden Years* (Forge, 2004) Chuck and Rosemarie enjoy their fifties in a still-passionate romance.

Green, Christine

I. Kate Kinsella is proprietor of Kinsella Medical and Nursing Investigators, located in an office room above the funeral home run by her landlord, friend, and sometime partner, the dour Hubert Humberstone. Kate, who supplements her PI income with temporary nursing jobs, is rather inefficient and gullible but makes up for those shortcomings by being spunky and determined.

1. *Deadly Errand* (Walker, 1992) Fledgling PI Kate Kinsella of Longborough, England, takes a nursing job at St. Dymphna's Hospital to investigate the stabbing death of Jacky Byfield, who was a nurse at the geriatric facility.

2. *Deadly Admirer* (Walker, 1993) Nurse Vanessa Wootten, who claims to being stalked, hires Kate. Is the reputedly neurotic, drug-taking Vanessa, who claims that she was raped by a former lover to be relied upon?

3. *Deadly Practice* (Walker, 1995) Hired by the mother of a young man suspected of murdering a nurse in a neighboring clinic, Kate takes the dead woman's job to find out who also might have been motivated to kill her.

4. *Deadly Partners* (Walker, 1997) Kate is hired by elderly Elizabeth Forrester to find her missing nephew Nigel, co-owner of a hotel on the Isle of Wight.

5. *Deadly Bond* (Severn House, 2002) Returning from a New Zealand sabbatical, Kate takes on the case of kleptomaniac Lorraine Farnworth, who seeks Kate's protection from an unknown man whom she saw shoot a woman.

6. *Deadly Echo* (Severn House, 2003) Kate and her terrier, Jasper, take home Megan Thomas, a disoriented young Welsh woman, who seems to be the target of a possible killer.

7. *Deadly Choice* (Severn House, 2004) Kate, Hubert Humberstone, old school friend Gill, and Jasper travel to Cornwall to visit Helen, another old school chum, who is planning to marry Paul Warriner, whose first wife supposedly killed herself and their two children.

8. *Deadly Night* (Severn House, 2005) Helping Hubert Humberstone prepare the body of an elderly woman for burial, Kate notices suspicious bruises on the woman's thighs that may indicate rape.

9. *Deadly Web* (Severn House, 2005) Although the police have declared her surgeon husband's death to be accidental, wealthy Victoria Decker-White asks Kate to investigate.

10. *Deadly Retreat* (Severn House, 2007) Mourning the death of her boyfriend, Kate goes to Peace Haven, a New Age therapy center in rural Wales, where she runs into Fran, who has been accused of murdering her baby son.

II. Three mystery novels feature Chief Inspector Connor O'Neill and Detective Sergeant Fran Watson. Widower Connor is overly fond of whiskey and women, while Fran has been ostracized by the rest of the police force after she turned in her former partner and lover for beating a suspect, but the odd couple finds that they work well together.

1. *Death in the Country* (Crimeline, 1995) The news of the discovery of a severed arm on the Harrington Farm creates consternation in the sleepy town of Fowchester. Then another arm is found.

2. *Die in My Dreams* (Crimeline, 1995) Fran Wilson and her new boss, Connor O'Neill, become involved in a murder case when a stabbed body is discovered, and the suspicion falls on Carol Ann Forbes, a newly released, self-confessed murderer.

3. *Fatal Cut* (Severn House, 2000) Well-hated Denise Parks is killed in a beauty salon, suffocated with hair mousse while trapped in a Turkish bath.

III. Green has written two procedural novels featuring Detective Inspector Rydell and Sergeant Denni Caldecote. They are a quite common British procedural pair: the tough and tight-lipped Rydell and the warm and intelligent Caldecote.

1. *Fire Angel* (Severn House, 2001) Rydell and Caldecote, aided by Sergeant Ramesh Patel, investigate some nasty murders and rapes.

2. *Vain Hope* (Severn House, 2002) Saul Ravenscroft, leading cosmetic surgeon at the Harmony Clinic, who had carried on an affair with the clinic's chief, Carla Robins, is murdered.

Green, Sharon

I. The Blending is an extremely popular series of fantasy novels. Every 25 years, the law calls for a new Blending: a combination of five high practitioners of the magic of Fire, Earth, Air, Water, and Spirit, to rule the land. In competition to be the new Blending are Tamrissa (Fire), Lorand (Earth), Clarion (Air), Vallant (Water), and Jovvi (Spirit). Unfortunately, this is the time foretold by the Prophets when the tyrannical Four would return to destroy the Land. A lively series leavened by humor by American fantasy, SF, and romance writer Green.

1. *Convergence* (Eos, 1996) The time has come for a new Blending to rule the Land. It is also the time foretold by the Prophecies, the time when the Four would return to bring destruction to Land.
2. *Competitions* (Eos, 1997) Lorand, Rion, Tamrissa, Jovvi, and Vallant compete in a series of deadly contests in order prove themselves to be the Chosen Five of the ancient Prophecies.
3. *Challenges* (Eos, 1998) Complications occur as the band of five enters the competition with dissension from within, competition from nobles, and judges determined to see the peasant mages lose.
4. *Betrayals* (Eos, 1999) Separated at the moment of their greatest triumph, the members of the Blending must travel across the empire to reunite and claim the throne.
5. *Prophecy* (Eos, 1999) The Chosen Five battle sinister usurpers, an invading army, and a peasant rebellion to finally gain their rightful throne.
6. *Intrigues* (Eos, 2000) The Chosen Five assume the leadership of a fledgling republic and face dark intrigues among their own people, plots by foreign powers, and an evil enemy with extraordinary power. Variant title: *The Blending Enthroned, Book 1.*
7. *Deceptions* (Eos, 2001) Now the Chosen Six, with the addition of Maran (Sight), the Blending have to defend their land against traitors and a terrible, massive army. Variant title: *The Blending Enthroned, Book 2.*
8. *Destiny* (Eos, 2002) The Chosen Six are hard-pressed to defend Gandistra against both its internal and external enemies. *The Blending Enthroned, Book 3.*

II. The Terrilian Saga tells the tale of Terril, "empath" and ambassador to distant planets, and of her submission to, and rebellion against, the huge barbarian, Tammad. This series, with its sadomasochistic scenes, has been compared to the Gor series of John Norman and the *Xena, Warrior-Princess* series on TV, although Green aficionados claim that it is superior to both in characterization and motivation.

1. *Warrior Within, The* (DAW, 1982) Terril, ambassador from an interstellar civilization, lands on Rimilia, a barbaric but strategically important planet, and falls into the hands of its ruler, the big blond barbarian Tammad.
2. *Warrior Enchained, The* (DAW, 1982) Dominated by and loving Tammad, Terril is kidnapped by the murderous Hamarda and manipulated by the duplicitous ruler Aesnil.
3. *Warrior Rearmed* (DAW, 1984) Terril has rescued a prince out of slavery. The prince wants to take her away from Tammad, but the barbarian owns her, body and soul.
4. *Warrior Challenged, The* (DAW, 1985) When Terril joins Tammad on a rescue expedition to the distant female-dominated city of Vediaster, neither one realizes that they are riding straight into a trap.
5. *Warrior Victorious, The* (DAW, 1988) The world of New Dawn, where the Primes, top agents of the interstellar government known as Central, have gathered, proves to be a prison for Terril.

III. Jalav, war leader of the Hosta clan of the Middana Amazons, in a world fallen into primitive barbarism, is enraged when thieves ransack the Tower of the Crystal of Mida and steal the holy Crystal. This series is somewhat reminiscent of series II, but Jalav is more domineering than dominated. Fans of the Jalav series claim that it is much more than a sex and bondage series.

1. *Crystals of Mida, The* (DAW, 1982) Jalav, war leader of the fearsome Hosta clan of the Midanni Amazons, swears that she will recover the stolen Crystal of Mida and revenge herself upon the thieves.
2. *Oath to Mida* (DAW, 1983) Jalav, wounded in battle, wants her spirit to fly to the bosom of Mida, but she has a journey into the glacial hell of Sigurr's Peak ahead of her.
3. *Chosen of Mida, The* (DAW, 1984) Jalav has pledged to Mida that she will forge an alliance with Mida's rival, the macho man-god Sigurr, against the invaders from the stars.
4. *Will of the Gods, The* (DAW, 1985) Jalav is ordered to go to the annual meeting of the Amazons and convince her fellow Amazons to return to the land of men and set their sisters free.
5. *To Battle the Gods* (DAW, 1985) Jalav, leader of all the tribes of the Amazons and the tribes of the "dark god," must be captured to free her people.

IV. Diana Santee, Spaceways Agent, is the heroine of a pair of novels set in star craft in the far future.

1. *Mind Guest* (DAW, 1984) Diana Santee is sent on what is meant to be a one-way trip to nowhere on a starship with all its controls destroyed.
2. *Gateway to Xanadu* (DAW, 1985) Special Agent Diana Santee, with her new partner, the alien Val, is a on voyage to the edges of space. Her mission: revenge against the slaver Radman.

V. The young sorceress Laciel is the heroine of a pair of fantasy novels involving quests: for a powerful jewel, and for her missing foster mother.

1. *Far Side of Forever, The* (DAW, 1987) Laciel the Sorceress and her five companions embark upon a quest to rescue the powerful gem, the Balance Stone, from a faraway land.
2. *Hellhound Magic* (DAW, 1989) Laciel, returned home after her quest for the Balance Stone, learns that Morgiana, her mentor and foster mother, is held captive on a terrible world.

VI. A trilogy pairs the shape-shifters Alexia and Tiran in adventures among evil kings, werewolves, ghouls, and other nasties.

1. *Silver Princess, Golden Knight* (Avon, 1993) Princess Alexia and the knight Tiran have been thrust through a secret portal into dangerous realms beyond the evil King Golran's magic powers.
2. *Dark Mirror, Dark Dreams* (Avon, 1994) Alexia and Tiran pool their occult powers with those of the magicians Chalaine and Bariden to liberate their empires from evil usurpers.
3. *Wind Whispers, Shadow Shouts* (Avon, 1995) Alexia and Tiran battle evil in the form of a mesmerizing voice that wants to devour their souls.

Green, Simon R(ichard)

I.   Husband-and-wife team Hawk and Fisher are the only honest cops in the magical city of Haven, where they deal with a melange of gods, vampires, sorcerers, and other fantastic beings in plots reminiscent of TV crime shows. The titles of most of the novels in this series are quite different in the United States and the United Kingdom. Omnibus volumes include *Swords of Haven* (Roc, 1982; numbers 1–3; UK title: *Haven of Lost Souls*) and *Guards of Haven* (Roc, 1999; numbers 4–6; UK title: *Fear and Loathing in Haven*).

1. *Hawk and Fisher* (Ace, 1990) Hawk and Fisher, assigned as bodyguards to a prominent Haven politician, find that even homes magically sealed from outside interference are not foolproof. UK title: *No Haven for the Guilty*.
2. *Winner Takes All* (Ace, 1991) Hawk and Fisher are hard-pressed to keep the "Reform" candidate alive in the last days before the Haven city elections. UK title: *Devil Take the Hindmost*.
3. *God Killer, The* (Ace, 1991) The Guard's God Squad have usually kept the rambunctious "Beings" and their religious followers more or less under control, but now someone, or something, is killing Gods.
4. *Wolf in the Fold* (Ace, 1991) A spy has eluded Hawk and Fisher and has slipped into the MacNeil family citadel, where the husband-and-wife team is ordered in after him. They will be hard-put to avoid being caught "impersonating Quality," a capital offense in Haven. UK title: *Vengeance for a Lonely Man*.
5. *Guard against Dishonor* (Ace, 1991) When Hawk and Fisher arrest the supplier of a street drug that causes users to tear themselves and anyone around them into pieces with their bare hands, they find that the course of justice in corrupt Haven doesn't always run smooth. UK title: *Guard against Dishonour*.
6. *Bones of Haven, The* (Ace, 1992) Hawk and Fisher join the SWAT (Special Wizardry and Tactics) team to stop a prison riot of sorcerers and worse; deal with a man who has escaped from a painting; and handle a hostage crisis involving terrorists and a pair of kings. UK title: *Two Kings in Haven*.
7. *Beyond the Blue Moon* (Roc, 2000) Hawk and Fisher mean to make the most of their last case as members of Haven's City Guard, trying to take down as many bad guys as possible. Meanwhile, in a prequel to series II, Prince Rupert and Princess of the Forest Kingdom return home to bring the murderer of King Harald to justice.

II.   The Forest Kingdom series is a rather loosely connected group of fantasy novels set in a quasi-medieval setting. Some traditional fantasy elements such as dragons and unicorns are mined, but English fantasist Green is an inveterate puller of switches and variations on traditional tropes. Number 7 in series I is partly set in the Forest Kingdom.

1. *Blue Moon Rising* (Roc, 1991) Prince Rupert "rescues" a damsel from a dragon only to find the damsel is perfectly capable of defending herself against the mild-mannered reptile.
2. *Blood and Honor* (Roc, 1992) Hired to pose as Prince Victor, the middle son of the recently assassinated King Malcolm, actor Jordan finds his "brothers" to be a treacherous bunch. UK title: *Blood and Honour*.
3. *Down among the Dead Men* (Roc, 1993) The Rangers, who have borne the brunt of the cleanup in the 10 years since the Demon Wars, are called upon to investigate a fort that no one who enters can leave. (Patricia Moyes [q.v.] uses the same book title in her Tibbett series.)

III.   Twilight of the Empire is an SF series with many of the trappings of the Hawk and Fisher and Forest Kingdom fantasy series, including a husband-and-wife investigative team. This series, set on the planets of Mistworld, Ghostworld, and Wolf IV, is a prelude to the Deathstalker and Deathstalker Legacy series (series IV and V). *Twilight of the Empire* (Roc, 1997; UK title: *Deathstalker Prelude*) is an omnibus volume containing numbers 1 through 3.

1. *Mistworld* (Ace, 1992) A "Typhoid Mary" carrying plague arrives on the planet of Mistworld, killing and "mindwiping" thousands of people.
2. *Ghostworld* (Ace, 1993) The ghosts of the rebels in a supposedly thwarted rebellion carry on fighting.
3. *Hellworld* (Ace, 1993) The indigenous life forms on the planet Wolf IV prove to be hostile and dangerous to the planetary survey team exploring its suitability for human colonization.

IV.   Owen Deathstalker, unwilling head of his clan, is a marked man despite his efforts to avoid involvement with the warring factions in the universe of Her Imperial Majesty Lionstone XIV. This is a sprawling "space opera," set in the universe of series III, with all the trappings of the subgenre, including an evil empire, aliens, space pirates, space battles, and plots, counterplots, and subplots. Series V is set in the same universe.

1. *Deathstalker* (Roc, 1994) Subtitle: *Being the First Part of the Life and Times of Owen Deathstalker*. Outlawed by Her Imperial Majesty Lionstone XIV, Owen Deathstalker, unwilling head of his clan, escapes to Mistworld with his companion Hazel d'Ark. Audio title: *The Man Who Had Everything*.
2. *Deathstalker Rebellion* (Roc, 1996) Subtitle: *Being the Second Part of the Life and Times of Owen Deathwalker*. On the planet of Mistworld, Deathstalker assembles a rather motley rebel crew and takes the first step on a journey to claim the role for which he, as a Deathstalker, had been destined since birth. Audio title: *Friends, Enemies and Allies*.
3. *Deathstalker War* (Roc, 1997) Lionstone XIV gives Captain John Silence the dubious honor of opening the Vaults of Sleepers on the ghost planet Grandel. Meanwhile, the Masked Gladiator reigns as undefeated champion of the Arena. Audio title: *Under the Ashes, the City*.
4. *Deathstalker Honor* (Roc, 1998) Subtitle: *Being the Fourth Part of the Life and Times of Owen Deathstalker*. Although Lionstone XIV is dead and her corrupt administration has been destroyed, Owen Deathstalker's work isn't finished. UK title: *Deathstalker Honour*.
5. *Deathstalker Destiny* (Roc, 1999) Subtitle: *Being the Fifth and Last Part of the Life and Times of Owen Deathstalker*. Owen's troubles aren't over: his greatest love has been abducted by a scientific cult, he is stranded with a leper colony, and he is called upon to fight in another intergalactic war.

V.   *Deathstalker Legacy* and its two sequels continue the saga of the Deathstalker clan of series IV in the person of Owen's descendant Lewis, who doesn't like trouble but finds plenty in wild and woolly adventures that include the resurrection, through time travel, of Owen Deathstalker himself.

1. *Deathstalker Legacy* (Roc, 2003) Lewis Deathstalker, descendant of the legendary Owen, falls in love with King Douglas's intended bride and is discredited by his rival, Finn Durandal.
2. *Deathstalker Return* (Roc, 2004) Lewis Deathstalker, dogged by his enemy, Finn Durandal, searches for Owen in a variety of locations, as the golden age that Owen had helped create 200 years earlier lies in disarray.

3. *Deathstalker Coda* (Roc, 2005) Lewis Deathstalker has brought his ancestor Owen back from the dead to battle the multidimensional Terror. Owen travels through time and Lewis travels through space in their efforts against the planet-devouring Terror and usurper Emperor Finn Durandal.

VI. John Taylor is a denizen of the Nightside, a city within the city of London, where it's always 3 a.m. and some very strange creatures and otherworldly gods rub shoulders together. Taylor isn't exactly a detective, but he has a knack for finding lost things. *A Walk on the Nightside* (Ace, 2006) is an omnibus volume containing numbers 1 through 3.

1. *Something from the Nightside* (Ace, 2003) John Taylor, who has a knack for finding lost things, is hired to return to his birthplace in the Nightside, a city within the city of London, where it is always 3 a.m. and the sun never shines.
2. *Agents of Light and Darkness* (Ace, 2003) John Taylor returns to the Nightside in a quest for the "Unholy Grail," the goblet from which Judas drank at the Last Supper.
3. *Nightingale's Lament* (Ace, 2004) The Nightingale is a singer whose voice has lured many a fan to suicide. John Taylor must find the elusive singer before the whole of Nightside falls under her spell.
4. *Hex and the City* (Ace, 2005) Hired by Lady Luck to investigate the origins of the Nightside, John Taylor starts to uncover some uncomfortable facts about his long-vanished mother.
5. *Paths Not Taken* (Ace, 2005) John Taylor discovers that his mother had created the Nightside and is poised to destroy it.
6. *Sharper Than a Serpent's Tooth* (Ace, 2006) John Taylor is the only thing standing between his "not-quite-human" mother and the destruction of Nightside.
7. *Hell to Pay* (Ace, 2006) A war has left the Nightside leaderless. Jeremiah Griffin, one of the last of immortal human families, plans to fill the power vacuum, but his granddaughter has disappeared, and he wants John Taylor to find her.
8. *Unnatural Inquirer, The* (Ace, 2008) Pen Donavon, who claims to have a DVD depicting footage of the afterlife, disappears shortly after signing an exclusive deal with the tabloid *Unnatural Inquirer*.

Green, Terence M(ichael)

I. Canadian writer Terence M. Green has written a trio of novels about the lives of three generations of Canadians of Irish descent. Leo Nolan and Martin John Radey relate the vicissitudes of their lives and times in poignant stories that contain dollops of the supernatural and SF (time travel).

1. *Witness to Life, A* (Forge, 1999) Martin John Radey, who has been dead for 34 years, visits, in spirit form, the deathbed of his daughter, Margaret, in 1984 and recalls his unsuccessful marriage and efforts at fatherhood, his retreat to a Trappist monastery after the disappearance of his son Jack, and events back to the great Toronto fire of 1904.
2. *Shadow of Ashland* (Forge, 1996) Days before she dies, Leo Nolan's mother shows her son a rose that she claims was just given to her by her brother Jack, who vanished 50 years ago.
3. *St. Patrick's Bed* (Forge, 2001) Leo Nolan comes to the aid of his stepson Adam, who wants to track down his absconding biological father.

II. Two semi-SF novels set in near-future Toronto feature Mitch Helwig, an honest cop who eventually becomes a rogue cop. This pair of vigilante novels features a few futuristic gimmicks.

1. *Barking Dogs* (St. Martin's, 1988) In 1999 the murder of his partner puts honest Toronto cop Mitch Helwig over the edge and, armed with a tiny lie detector and an illegal laser gun, he becomes a vigilante.
2. *Blue Limbo* (Tor, 1997) Blue Limbo is a technique for partially reviving the dead that is used on Mitch's boss, Captain Karoulis, after a murder attempt.

Greene, Bette

The NBC-TV dramatization of *Summer of My German Soldier*, starring Kristy McNichol, introduced many young readers to author Bette Greene. The poignant and suspenseful story of the friendship between a young Jewish girl and an escaped German prisoner of war may be enjoyed by older readers as well. Its appeal is similar to that of Harper Lee's *To Kill a Mockingbird*.

1. *Summer of My German Soldier* (Dial, 1973) Young Patty Bergen, living in Arkansas during World War II, befriends Anton Reiker, an escaped German prisoner of war.
2. *Morning Is a Long Time Coming* (Dial, 1978) Four years later, Patty finishes high school and sets out for Europe, where she falls in love and searches for Anton's parents.

Greenleaf, Stephen

Greenleaf, a lawyer turned mystery writer, writes novels about John Marshall Tanner, a lawyer turned private investigator. San Francisco-based Tanner is in the hard-boiled private-eye tradition of Dashiell Hammett's (q.v.) Sam Spade, Raymond Chandler's (q.v.) Philip Marlowe, and Ross MacDonald's (q.v.) Lew Archer. He hides his sensitive and ethical nature behind a cynical, wisecracking exterior. The complicated plots of the novels usually revolve around a missing person and dark family secrets.

1. *Grave Error* (Dial, 1979) The wife of consumer advocate Roland Nelson hires Tanner to see if her husband is being blackmailed.
2. *Death Bed* (Dial, 1980) Dying oil billionaire Max Kottle wants Tanner to find his estranged college activist son.
3. *State's Evidence* (Dial, 1982) Tanner is asked to find the missing eyewitness to a fatal hit-and-run accident in the corrupt town of El Gordo.
4. *Fatal Obsession* (Dial, 1983) The suicide of his Vietnam veteran nephew brings Tanner to a family reunion in the rural midwestern town of Chaldea.
5. *Beyond Blame* (Villard, 1986) Berkeley lawyer Lawrence Usser is trying to avoid conviction for his wife's murder by using the insanity plea he has successfully employed for his criminal clients.
6. *Toll Call* (Villard, 1987) Peggy Nettleton, Tanner's secretary, is being harassed by bizarre phone calls.
7. *Book Case* (Morrow, 1991) Tanner is engaged by the owner of a small San Francisco publishing firm to track down the author of a potentially best-selling manuscript.
8. *Blood Type* (Morrow, 1992) Although the death of Tanner's drinking buddy Tom Crandall looks like suicide, Marsh is suspicious of some of Tom's relationships.

9. *Southern Cross* (**Morrow, 1993**) Civil rights lawyer Seth Hartman of Charleston, South Carolina, has received death threats from a right-wing hate group.

10. *False Conception* (**Penzler, 1994**) Tanner investigates the potential surrogate mother of a child for the wealthy Stuart and Millicent Colbert.

11. *Flesh Wounds* (**Scribner, 1996**) Tanner goes to Seattle after receiving an urgent call from his former lover, Peggy Nettleton. Her planned marriage to wealthy businessman Ted Evans has been jeopardized by the disappearance of Evans's photographers' model daughter.

12. *Past Tense* (**Scribner, 1997**) San Francisco cop Charley Sleet, Tanner's best friend, guns down, in a crowded courtroom, the wealthy defendant in a recovered-memory child-abuse case.

13. *Strawberry Sunday* (**Scribner, 1999**) Tanner, recuperating from wounds suffered in the shoot-out at the end of *Past Tense*, is intrigued by Rita Lombardi, a young woman he meets on his walks in the hospital corridors.

14. *Ellipsis* (**Scribner, 2000**) Chandelier Wells, best-selling novelist with a flamboyant lifestyle, has been receiving death threats.

Greenwood, John

PSEUDONYM OF John Buxton Hilton

Detective Inspector Mosley is an elderly, old-fashioned rural policeman stationed in the north of England. He doesn't go by the book or move in straight lines to his conclusions, which sometimes disturbs his young assistant, Sergeant Beamish, but he always seems to wind up in the right place at the end. These mysteries are notable more for their local color and rural English characters than for the puzzles they present. John Buxton Hilton wrote other mystery series under his real name, but most of the titles in those series haven't been published in the United States.

1. *Murder, Mr. Mosley* (**Walker, 1983**) Mr. Mosley is confronted with his first murder case and with a new, scientific-minded, ambitious assistant.

2. *Mosley by Moonlight* (**Walker, 1985**) Mosley's investigation of the disappearance of Lottie Pearson, house-keeper and rumored mistress of Matthew Longden, is complicated by a television crew shooting a commercial.

3. *Missing Mr. Mosley, The* (**Walker, 1986**) Superintendent Grimstone sends Sergeant Beamish in search of the vacationing Mosley when villagers at Hempshaw End disappear, and a series of gallows turn up. UK title: *Mosley Went to Mow.*

4. *Mists over Mosley* (**Walker, 1986**) Nasty old Beatrice Cater is found hanged in her bedroom amid rumors of a coven of witches in Marldale.

5. *Mind of Mr. Mosley, The* (**Walker, 1987**) The village of Upper Crudshaw is rocked by the suicide of 74-year-old Reuben Tunicliffe.

6. *What Me, Mr. Mosley?* (**Walker, 1988**) Inspector Mosley identifies stolen property at a secondhand goods market stall in Bagshawe Brooke.

Greenwood, Kerry

Phryne (pronounced *Fry knee*) Fisher, Australia's inimitable flapper sleuth, has finally gotten a proper introduction to American fans since Poisoned Pen has been reprinting the cozy series in the United States. Phryne is a fabulously wealthy, single woman in the late 1920s. Although she has all the trappings of 1920s high life, Phryne, craving adventure, decides to leave London and work as a private investigator in Melbourne, Australia. Numbers 1 through 3 were first published in the United States in 1991–1993 as Fawcett Gold Medal paperbacks. Australian Kerry Greenwood, who worked at many jobs, is currently a solicitor married to a "registered wizard." She has also written the Delphic Women series and some loosely related young adult SF series, all published only in Australia. Poisoned Pen has published one novel in a contemporary series, featuring Corinna Chapman, a former accountant who runs a Melbourne bakery: *Earthly Delights* (2007).

1. *Cocaine Blues* (**Poisoned Pen, 2006**) The Honorable Phryne Fisher decides "it might be rather amusing" to try her hand at being a female private eye in Melbourne, Australia. Very soon after she gets Down Under, Phryne gets involved with poisoned wives, cocaine smuggling rings, corrupt cops, and Communism. Originally published in Australia in 1991. Published in paperback in the United States as *Death by Misadventure* (Fawcett, 1991).

2. *Flying Too High* (**Poisoned Pen, 2006**) Phryne, with time off for air walking and daredevil plane flying, tracks down the kidnappers of a young girl and identifies the murderer of a bully whose son has been charged with the offense. Originally published in Australia in 1992. Published in the United States in paperback by Fawcett in 1992.

3. *Murder on the Ballarat Train* (**Poisoned Pen, 2006**) What originally promised to be a sedate train ride and a restful country sojourn in Ballarat turns into chloroform poisoning, jewel robbery, and murder, with hints of black magic and white slavery. Originally published in Australia in 1992. Published in the United States in paperback by Fawcett in 1992.

4. *Death at Victoria Dock* (**Poisoned Pen, 2006**) After her windscreen is shot out, and she finds a handsome young man with an anarchist tattoo dying on the tarmac just outside Victoria Dock, Phryne gets involved in the world of Russian anarchists. Originally published in Australia in 1992.

5. *Green Mill Murder, The* (**Poisoned Pen, 2007**) After a man is murdered during a dance competition at Melbourne's Green Mill, Phryne gets involved with a family tragedy stemming from the Great War and winds up flying to the Australian Alps. Originally published in Australia in 1993.

6. *Blood and Circuses* (**Poisoned Pen, 2007**) At the request of her friends Samson the Strong Man, Alan the carousel operator, and Doreen the Snake Woman, Phryne goes undercover and takes a job as a trick horse rider in Farrell's Circus and Wild Beast Show. Originally published in Australia in 1994.

7. *Ruddy Gore* (**Poisoned Pen, 2005**) On the way to a gala performance of Gilbert and Sullivan's *Ruddigore*, Phryne disposes of some thugs in a dark alley and rescues the handsome Lin Chung and his grandmother. Originally published in Australia in 1995.

8. *Urn Burial* (**Poisoned Pen, 2005**) Lin Chung is still around, as Phryne tangles with some funerary urns, death threats, lethal traps, and murder while holidaying at Cave House, a Gothic mansion in Australia's Victorian mountain country. Originally published in Australia in 1996.

9. *Raisons and Almonds* (**Poisoned Pen, 2007**) Miss Fisher investigates the poisoning of a young man in a bookshop and the wrongful arrest of a young woman and gets involved with Jewish politics, alchemy, poison, and chicken soup. Originally published in Australia in 1997.

10. *Death before Wicket* (**Poisoned Pen, 2008**) Phryne goes to Sydney for a few days at the Test Cricket, a little sightseeing, and the Artist's Ball in the company of a young modernist. But then Phryne's maid discovers that her sister has gone "to the bad." Originally published in Australia in 1999.

11. *Away with the Fairies* (**Poisoned Pen, 2005**) Phryne goes undercover at a women's magazine while investigating the mysterious death of a famous author and illustrator of fairy stories. Originally published in Australia in 2001.
12. *Murder in Montparnasse* (**Poisoned Pen, 2004**) The first volume published in Poisoned Pen's American revival of Phryne Fisher. A young woman disappears, and two ex-soldiers die suspicious deaths that were officially declared accidental. Originally published in Australia in 2002.
13. *Castlemaine Murders, The* (**Poisoned Pen, 2004**) Phryne's household, which includes Lin Chung, is augmented by the arrival of her younger sister, the "Hon. Miss Eliza Fisher," apparently banished from England. A mystery dating back to 1857 may be connected to the discovery of a mummified corpse. Originally published in Australia in 2003.
14. *Queen of the Flowers* (**Poisoned Pen, 2008**) Phryne is chosen Queen of the Flowers for the St. Kilda's festival in 1928 but finds that she has more on her mind than a new dress and swimming costume, including a missing daughter, the return of an old lover, and a drowned young woman. Originally published in Australia in 2004.
15. *Death by Water* (**Allen & Unwin [Aus.], 2005**) The Mahrani, the Great Queen of Sapphires, is the bait as Phryne boards the SS *Hinemona* on a luxury cruise to New Zealand, determined to solve a series of jewelry thefts. Not yet published in the United States.
16. *Murder in the Dark* (**Allen & Unwin [Aus.], 2006**) Phryne decides to attend the best party of 1928, a four-day extravaganza being held at Werribee Manor House and grounds by the "golden twins," Isabella and Gerald Templar, when she receives anonymous threats warning her against going. Not yet published in the United States.

Gregory, Philippa

I. The Wideacre, or Lacey Family, trilogy, set in 18th-century Sussex, England, follows the Laceys through three generations of torrid romance, degeneracy, and gothic tribulations. Gregory, who has written other historical romances, writes a column for the *Manchester Guardian* under the pseudonym of Kate Wedd.

1. *Wideacre* (**Simon & Schuster, 1987**) Beatrice Lacey will stop at nothing, not even incest and murder, to gain possession of Wideacre, her family's ancestral estate.
2. *Favored Child, The* (**Pocket, 1989**) Cousins Richard and Julia learn the real reasons why their mansion was burned down and Richard's mother was killed.
3. *Meridon* (**Pocket, 1990**) Meridon, a young Gypsy, learns that she is the lost heiress of Wideacre.

II. A pair of novels featuring the Tradescants, father and son, royal gardeners to King James I, traces the history of 17th-century England and Virginia, supplying the reader with a great deal of historical and botanical knowledge in accessible form.

1. *Earthly Joys* (**St. Martin's, 1998**) Gardener John Tradescant, who works for Robert Cecil, King James's advisor, watches the transfer of power from the honest Cecil to the cynical Duke of Buckingham.
2. *Virgin Earth* (**St. Martin's, 1999**) John Tradescant the Younger, a royal gardener, flees to the Virginia colony, where he is aided in his plant collecting by Indian maiden Suckahanna.

Gregory, Susanna

PSEUDONYM OF Elizabeth Cruwys

Mid-14th-century Cambridge, England, is the stamping ground of Matthew Bartholomew. Matthew's more traditional and less-successful colleagues regard his Arab-based, unorthodox methods as heresy or witchcraft. Matthew also teaches at Michaelhouse, part of the fledgling University of Cambridge, and finds his skills on demand in investigations of the many unnatural deaths in this turbulent setting. The Black Death and its aftermath play large roles, as do the constant feuds among the Cambridge gentry and between town and gown. Fans of Ellis Peters's (q.v.) Brother Cadfael are likely to enjoy this series.

1. *Plague on Both Your Houses, A* (**Little, Brown, 1996**) In 1348 the Black Death is heading toward England. Cambridge physician Matthew Bartholomew will find his work cut out for him when this unprecedented pestilence arrives.
2. *Unholy Alliance, An* (**Little, Brown, 1996**) Three prostitutes have been murdered amid rumors of witchcraft, but after a Dominican friar meets his death while rifling the Cambridge University chest in the tower of St. Mary's Church, Matthew Bartholomew and Benedictine Brother Michael are called upon to investigate.
3. *Bone of Contention, A* (**Little, Brown, 1997**) In 1352, amid high tension between town and gown and rival colleges at the university, a young scholar, James Kenzie, is found dead in the King's Ditch, a sewage-filled channel.
4. *Deadly Brew, A* (**Little, Brown, 1998**) The opening of a new and very well endowed college creates the inevitable in-fighting among the academics vying for new appointments, while town–gown relations are worse than ever.
5. *Wicked Deed, A* (**Little, Brown, 1999**) Scholar Unwin is murdered as soon as he arrives at his new parish in Suffolk, the latest in a series of mishaps blamed on the curse of a village abandoned during the Plague.
6. *Masterly Murder, A* (**Little, Brown, 2000**) The new master of Michaelhouse, Runham, makes many enemies after he arranges his "election" to the position and starts to make life unpleasant for the scholars.
7. *Order for Death, An* (**Little, Brown, 2001**) Is a string of murders among the various religious orders in Cambridge based on theological differences, or are more mundane motives at work?
8. *Summer of Discontent, A* (**Little, Brown, 2002**) Matthew accompanies Brother Michael to Ely, where there is a library he wants to investigate. But when they arrive, they discover that the bishop of Ely has been accused of murder.
9. *Killer in Winter, A* (**Little, Brown, 2003**) During the approach of Christmas in 1354, Cambridge is gripped by the worst blizzard in living memory. Matthew's erstwhile love, Philippa, and her wealthy husband are among the travelers trapped by the snow.
10. *Hand of Justice, The* (**Little, Brown, 2004**) Two well-born murderers return to Cambridge in 1355 after receiving the King's Pardon, showing no remorse but ready to confront those who helped convict them.
11. *Mark of a Murderer, The* (**Little, Brown, 2005**) After one of the most serious riots in the history of the University of Oxford, many scholars flee the city, and some choose Cambridge as their refuge. But trouble follows them.
12. *Tarnished Chalice, The* (**Little, Brown, 2006**) The Hugh Chalice, a relic of the city of Lincoln, which Matthew and Brother Michael are visiting, has a bloody history, of which everyone is reminded when a guest at the local friary is murdered while holding it.

13. *To Kill or Cure* (**Little, Brown, 2007**) Matthew's professional reputation and his life are threatened by a charismatic physician whose methods rely more on magic than on medicine.

Griffin, W. E. B.

PSEUDONYM OF William E. Butterworth

I. William E. Butterworth, cited, among other things, as the "most prolific Alabama author of all time," has written more than 100 volumes of fiction and nonfiction under his own name and various pseudonyms. It is safe to say, however, that the series written under the W. E. B. Griffin nom de plume have been the most successful with the reading public. The Brotherhood of War series follows the military careers of several characters from World War II into the Vietnam era. The series displays army veteran (Korean War) Griffin's knowledge of military hardware and of the thoughts, feelings, and speech of the men who use the hardware. There is some shifting back and forth of the time frames of the novels, so they are listed in publication order. *Three Complete Novels: Brotherhood of War* (Putnam, 2001) is an omnibus containing numbers 1 through 3.

1. *Lieutenants, The* (**Jove, 1983**) Introduces many of the continuing characters as they receive their baptism of fire in World War II.
2. *Captains, The* (**Jove, 1983**) The army careers of many of the characters are continued or revived in the Korean War.
3. *Majors, The* (**Jove, 1984**) The American "secret war" in Indochina in the 1950s.
4. *Colonels, The* (**Jove, 1985**) American intervention in Vietnam and Cuba in the early 1960s.
5. *Berets, The* (**Jove, 1985**) The training, deployment, and battlefield actions of the Green Berets in Vietnam.
6. *Generals, The* (**Jove, 1986**) Many of the characters are embroiled in the Vietnam War, some of them at important decision-making levels.
7. *New Breed, The* (**Putnam, 1987**) The Congo rebellion of 1964 is the main focus here.
8. *Aviators, The* (**Putnam, 1988**) The escalation of the Vietnam War in the 1960s and the role of the US Army Air Assault Division.
9. *Special Ops* (**Putnam, 2000**) Che Guevara is going to the Congo to establish a Communist foothold in Africa. It is up to Top Secret Special Operations under Colonel Sanford T. Felter to stop him.

II. The Corps, another military history series, covers the US Marine Corps during World War II. The action is mostly in the Pacific, and historical characters such as Douglas MacArthur, Wild Bill Donovan of OSS, Admirals Nimitz and Leahy, and FDR play supporting roles. This series contains secret missions, coded messages, male bonding, and plenty of action. Numbers 9 and 10 move the corps into the Korean War.

1. *Semper Fi* (**Jove, 1986**) Finds US Marine PFC Kenneth J. McCoy at the US consulate in Shanghai in January 1941.
2. *Call to Arms* (**Jove, 1987**) Most of the action takes place on Wake Island shortly after the bombing of Pearl Harbor, in December 1941.
3. *Counterattack* (**Putnam, 1990**) Shows the transition of the US Marine Corps from peacetime duty to total war early in 1942.
4. *Battleground* (**Putnam, 1991**) Guadalcanal is one of the first big tests of the rejuvenated US Marine Corps in 1942.
5. *Line of Fire* (**Putnam, 1992**) The battle for Guadalcanal in August and September 1942 is viewed from various parts of the globe.
6. *Close Combat* (**Putnam, 1993**) While the Japanese attempt to recapture Guadalcanal, some of the US Marine heroes are sent on a war-bond tour back in the United States.
7. *Behind the Lines* (**Putnam, 1995**) A radio message from Wendell Fertig, who has established a guerrilla operation inside the Philippines, sets off a power struggle between Douglas MacArthur, Bill Donovan, and Fleming Pickering.
8. *In Danger's Path* (**Putnam, 1999**) Brigadier General Fleming Pickering, head of Pacific operations for the OSS during World War II, is the focus of attention here.
9. *Under Fire* (**Putnam, 2002**) When the North Koreans cross the 38th Parallel in 1950, it takes only a few weeks for Fleming Pickering and the old team to get back together again.
10. *Retreat, Hell!* (**Putnam, 2004**) Autumn 1950. The US Marines have made a crucial breakthrough at Inchon.

III. The Honor Bound trilogy describes the battle between Nazi and American operatives to secure Argentina for their side during World War II. OSS agent Cletus Frade, his father, Argentine politician Jorge Guillermo Frade, and Luftwaffe ace Peter von Wachtstein are among the protagonists.

1. *Honor Bound* (**Putnam, 1994**) US Marine fighter ace Clete Frade, army demolitions engineer Anthony Pelosi, and electronics wizard David Ettinger are sent by the OSS to neutral Argentina in 1942 on a secret mission.
2. *Blood and Honor* (**Putnam, 1997**) Clete Frade is set to Buenos Aires on an OSS mission to find out more about a suspected plot to overthrow the Argentine government.
3. *Secret Honor* (**Putnam, 2000**) A German general out to assassinate Hitler; the general's son in Argentina; and the loose cannon, Clete Frade, are all part of the mix here.

IV. Men at War, another series of novels about the OSS, was published in the 1980s under the pseudonym of "Alex Baldwin" and reprinted in the late 1990s by Putnam under Griffin's name. The main plot thread here is the ongoing American attempt to build an atomic bomb before the Germans do and the efforts to obtain uranium ore from diverse parts of the world. This series is somewhat less realistic than the others. Numbers 5 and 6 are coauthored by Griffin's son, William E. Butterworth IV.

1. *Last Heroes, The* (**Pocket, 1985**) In June 1941 Bill Donovan assembles a hand-picked group of agents for the OSS, among them fighter ace Dick Canidy and his friend Eric Fulmer, who are dispatched to secure a rare ore that will power a top-secret weapon. Reprinted in hardcover in 1997. UK title: *In the Line of Duty*.
2. *Secret Warriors, The* (**Pocket, 1985**) In December 1942 Canidy sets up an air maneuver that will drop agents into the Belgian Congo to smuggle out uranium ore. Reprinted in hardcover in 1998. UK title: *Covert Operations*.
3. *Soldier Spies, The* (**Pocket, 1986**) Caniday and Fulmer aim to smuggle out of Germany the scientist whose knowledge of metallurgy holds the key to the development of jet engines. Reprinted in hardcover in 1999. UK title: *Give Me Liberty*.
4. *Fighting Agents, The* (**Pocket, 1987**) In 1943 Dick Caniday, now the OSS's number-three man, goes behind enemy lines to aid Eric Fulmer. Meanwhile, a resistance group led by self-proclaimed Brigadier General Wendell Fertig (see series II, number 7) is fighting a guerilla war in the Philippines against the Japanese. Reprinted in hardcover in 2001. UK title: *Into Enemy Hands*.
5. *Saboteurs, The* (**Putnam, 2006**) In 1943 the United States' preparation for the Sicilian invasion and the fate of four German saboteurs

who landed in America are delineated. Coauthored with William E. Butterworth IV.

6. **Double Agents, The (Putnam, 2007)** David Niven, Peter Ustinov, and Ian Fleming (q.v.) put in appearances in 1943 as "Wild Bill" Donovan spearheads a disinformation campaign to trick the Axis into believing that the Western Allies won't invade Sicily. Coauthored by William E. Butterworth IV.

V. The Philadelphia Police Department is the hero of Badge of Honor, a series of procedurals chock-full of action and police lore. Matt Payne, something of a hotshot, has developed as one of the leading characters. Numbers 1 and 2 were written under the pseudonym "John Kevin Dugan."

1. **Men in Blue (Jove, 1988)** A Philadelphia policeman is killed in the line of duty. Written as "John Kevin Dugan."
2. **Special Operations (Jove, 1989)** A new task force under the command of Inspector Peter Wohl sets out after the perpetrator of a kidnapping and rape spree. Written as "John Kevin Dugan."
3. **Victim, The (Jove, 1991)** Drug dealer and mafioso Tony DeZego is killed by a professional hit man.
4. **Witness, The (Jove, 1991)** Eight men rob and shoot up the interior of a furniture store for no ostensible reason.
5. **Assassin, The (Jove, 1993)** Teamed with the Secret Service, Philadelphia's cops must prevent an assassination attempt on the vice president of the United States when he visits the city.
6. **Murderers, The (Putnam, 1995)** Centers around the murder of policeman Jerry Kellogg, who may have been killed by a fellow cop.
7. **Investigators, The (Putnam, 1998)** Philadelphia PD golden-boy Matt Payne gets involved in some shady doings in the narcotics unit and assists the FBI in pursuing an animal-rights terrorist group.
8. **Final Justice (Putnam, 2003)** Matt Payne has just been promoted and transferred to homicide, where he becomes involved in cases such as a shooting in a fast-food outlet, a rape and murder with political overtones, a fugitive murderer from France, and the supervision of a movie star who is looking for authenticity in his cop pictures.

VI. The Presidential Agent series is a contemporary, rather than historical, series. Major Carlos Guillermo Castillo, special assistant to the secretary of Homeland Security, deals with terrorism and international intrigue.

1. **By Order of the President (Putnam, 2004)** After a Boeing 727 is hijacked from an airport in Angola, the president uses the ensuing snafu to assign Charley Castillo to launch an investigation into the workings of government agencies and personnel charged with handling terrorist situations.
2. **Hostage, The (Putnam, 2006)** Charley Castillo and his team are charged with sorting out the murder of an American diplomat in Argentina, the kidnapping of his wife, and threats to murder her children unless she reveals the whereabouts of her brother, a UN diplomat involved in the food-for-Iraqi-oil scandal.
3. **Hunters, The (Putnam, 2007)** The mystery of the murder of American diplomat Jean-Paul Lorimer still engages Castillo and his team.
4. **Shooters, The (Putnam, 2008)** DEA Special Agent Byron J. Timmons is kidnapped in Paraguay, and Castillo is sent to rescue him.

Grimes, Martha

I. American writer Martha Grimes has taken Agatha Christie (q.v.) and Dorothy Sayers (q.v.) as models for this elegantly written series. Among the continuing characters are Richard Jury, a dedicated, sensitive Detective Inspector (later Superintendent) of Scotland Yard; Alfred Wiggins, his hypochondriacal professional assistant; Melrose Plant, his aristocratic, dilettantish, unofficial assistant; and Plant's officious American-born aunt Agatha. Like Elizabeth George (q.v.), another American who writes mysteries set in England, Grimes visits frequently to capture authentic atmosphere. Each book is named for the English pub that figures in the story.

1. **Man with a Load of Mischief, The (Little, Brown, 1981)** Five murder victims have been found in or near pubs in the village of Little Piddleton, Northamptonshire, including one corpse in a keg of ale.
2. **Old Fox Deceiv'd, The (Little, Brown, 1982)** A series of deaths and disappearances, including a corpse in Shakespearean costume, bedevil the Yorkshire fishing village of Rackmoor.
3. **Anodyne Necklace, The (Little, Brown, 1983)** Murders in London's East End and in the village of Littlebourne may be connected with a jewelry theft.
4. **Dirty Duck, The (Little, Brown, 1984)** Rich American tourists in Stratford are being kidnapped and murdered while a computer buff is trying to prove that Shakespeare killed Marlowe.
5. **Jerusalem Inn (Little, Brown, 1984)** The murder of Helen Minton, a chance acquaintance met during the Christmas holidays, brings Jury to a village near Newcastle.
6. **Help the Poor Struggler (Little, Brown, 1985)** A series of child murders in Devonshire may be linked with a 20-year-old homicide.
7. **Deer Leap, The (Little, Brown, 1985)** A series of suspicious accidents to people and pets brings Plant to an odd young girl who keeps a sanctuary for abused animals.
8. **I Am the Only Running Footman (Little, Brown, 1986)** The London strangling of Ivy Childess may be connected to a Devon homicide.
9. **Five Bells and Bladebone, The (Little, Brown, 1987)** The corpse of antique dealer Simon Lean is found in a desk at his shop in Plant's ancestral village.
10. **Old Silent, The (Little, Brown, 1989)** On vacation in Yorkshire, Jury sees Nell Healey shoot her husband and uncovers an old kidnapping.
11. **Old Contemptibles, The (Little, Brown, 1991)** Melrose Plant, posing as a seedy librarian, stakes out an inn in the Lake District while Jury is held as a suspect in the murder of a woman with whom he was involved.
12. **Horse You Came in On, The (Knopf, 1993)** Jury, Wiggins, and Plant turn up in Baltimore, Maryland, looking into the murder of a young American nephew of Jury's friend Lady Cray.
13. **Rainbow's End (Knopf, 1995)** Jury is in New Mexico investigating the murder of an American silversmith in Salisbury, England. There he meets teenage animal rights advocate Mary Dark Hope (who appears in a novel of her own: Biting the Moon, Holt, 1999).
14. **Case Has Altered, The (Holt, 1997)** In a case with a Lincolnshire setting, Jennifer Kennington, the woman whom Jury has loved, is accused of two murders.
15. **Stargazey, The (Holt, 1998)** Jury follows and loses a mysterious woman in a sable coat who has intrigued him by getting on and off a London bus in Fulham. The next day, she, or someone very like her, turns up murdered in a herb garden.

16. *Lamorna Wink, The* (Viking, 1999) Melrose Plant takes center stage as he leases an ocean-side house in Cornwall where, four years earlier, two children died from a fall down a flight of stone steps. Jury makes a late appearance in this one.

17. *Blue Last, The* (Viking, 2001) The skeletons of a woman and a child are found in Blackfriars Lane, London, apparently buried during the Blitz. They may be a clue to a contemporary fraud that Jury is investigating.

18. *Grave Maurice, The* (Viking, 2002) Jury, bedridden, is given a mystery to solve by Melrose Plant: the disappearance case of the daughter of Jury's surgeon.

19. *Winds of Change, The* (Viking, 2004) The fatal shooting of a five-year-old girl in a London street leads to a pedophile ring.

20. *Old Wine Shades, The* (Viking, 2006) While serving out a suspension, Jury gets involved in the saga of the disappearance of a mother, her autistic son, and their dog. The dog has turned up again, nine months later.

21. *Dust* (Viking, 2007) Jury goes to a shady London hotel to investigate the murder of wealthy bachelor Billy Maples.

II. Three "straight" novels with mystery overtones feature Emma Graham, a 12-year-old who lives in the Hotel Paradise, a run-down resort hotel managed by her family in a place called Cold Flat Junction, somewhere in America. Emma, who narrates, is a very inquisitive preteen who gets involved with some past murders, family skeletons, and other murky business.

1. *Hotel Paradise* (Knopf, 1996) Twelve-year-old Emma Graham, stuck with waiting on tables at her family's resort hotel, gets involved with investigating the 40-year-old drowning death of Mary-Evelyn Devereaux, another 12-year-old.

2. *Cold Flat Junction* (Viking, 2001) Emma Graham is back again, still puzzling over a local family that has produced three murders in 40 years, the latest being the shooting death of another young girl.

3. *Belle Ruin* (Viking, 2005) Emma, now a very young cub reporter, discovers the crumbling shell of a fabulous hotel hidden in the woods near the town of Spirit Lake.

III. Andi Oliver, a teenager with a mysterious past, is the leading character in two novels set in the American West. Andi's salient characteristic is a hatred of animal abuse. Mary Dark Hope, who appears in number 13 of series I, is a character in *Biting the Moon*.

1. *Biting the Moon* (Holt, 1999) Teenage Andi Oliver, who lives in a cabin in the mountains near Santa Fe and rescues animals caught in traps, decides to ferret out her real identity and that of the man called "Daddy," who left her in a motel without memory of her previous life.

2. *Dakota* (Viking, 2008) Andi, still unaware of her real name or her past, makes a temporary home for herself in the small town of Kingdom, in the Dakota Badlands, and takes a job at a pig farm to try to save the animals bred there.

Grippando, James

Miami-based criminal lawyer Jack Swyteck made his appearance in James Grippando's first novel. The next five novels were stand-alones, then Grippando returned to criminal defense attorney Jack in a series of suspenseful legal thrillers full of plot twists, some international intrigue, and some colorful characters. James Grippando is a Miami-based attorney himself.

1. *Pardon, The* (HarperCollins, 1994) Florida Governor Harold Swyteck has always been pro–death penalty, at least until his son, defense attorney Jack Swyteck, finds himself the chief suspect in the murder of admitted killer Eddie Goss.

2. *Beyond Suspicion* (HarperCollins, 2002) A complicated tale involving an old flame of Jack's who thinks she's dying of ALS, the Russian mobsters who bought up her insurance policy, a corpse in the Swyteck bathtub, a nasty prosecutor, and a vengeful young Cuban woman.

3. *Last to Die* (HarperCollins, 2003) In a version of the "last man" plot, wealthy divorcée Sally Fenning leaves an enormous estate to six heirs with the proviso that one of the heirs will collect everything only after all the others have died or renounced their share of the inheritance.

4. *Hear No Evil* (HarperCollins, 2004) Lindsey Hart, about to be charged with the murder of her husband, US Marine Captain Oscar Pintado, turns to Jack for the help, claiming that Jack is the biological father of her adopted 10-year-old son.

5. *Got the Look* (HarperCollins, 2006) Jack's girlfriend Mia Salazar is abducted by a sadistic murderer. Mia's husband isn't interested in paying ransom for the errant Mia, so it is up to Jack and FBI agent Andie Henning, a character from Grippando's nonseries novel *Under Cover of Darkness* (HarperCollins, 2000) to find her.

6. *When Darkness Falls* (HarperCollins, 2007) An armed homeless man known as Falcon takes, among his hostages in a seedy motel, Theo Knight, Jack's best friend.

Groom, Winston

Forrest Gump didn't make a particularly big splash when it was first published. In fact, critics rated the novel less highly than they did some of Winston Groom's previous works, such as the novels *Better Times Than These* (Summit, 1978) and *As Summers Die* (Summit, 1980) and the nonfiction book (written with Duncan Spencer) *Conversations with the Enemy* (Putnam, 1983). However, the movie (1994) with Tom Hanks's Oscar-winning performance made the simple, naive Gump almost into a household word. Basically a light, satiric novel about a Southern eccentric who, according to one reviewer, is "part Candide, part Huck Finn, and a whole lot of Andy Griffith," *Forrest Gump* brought its hero through football stardom for Bear Bryant's Alabama Crimson Tide, a tour in Vietnam, a space mission with an ape, a meeting with an educated cannibal in New Guinea, and scenes with the likes of Lyndon Johnson and Chairman Mao. Like most literary fools, Forrest is smarter than most of the people he encounters. In fact he is an "idiot-savant," a whiz with numbers. *Gumpisms: The Wit and Wisdom of Forrest Gump* (Pocket, 1994), which has copious quotes from the book and the movie, was brought out in anticipation of the movie. A sequel, *Gump & Co.*, which continues Forrest's saga through the 1980s, generally disappointed both readers and critics.

1. *Forrest Gump* (Doubleday, 1986) Idiot-savant (IQ of 75) Forrest Gump relates his experiences playing football for Bear Bryant, serving in Vietnam, working for NASA, and surviving the jungles of New Guinea and America in the 1970s and 1980s.

2. *Gump & Co.* (Simon & Schuster, 1995) Gump continues the story of his life through the 1980s and encounters with the likes of Oliver North and shows that he has learned a few things.

Gross, Joel

Two thousand years of Jewish history are related through a succession of heroines named Rachel, the name given to the first female child in each generation of the Cuhena, later called the Cohen, family. Each Rachel must pass a test, whether it be persecution, plague, or love for a Gentile. Readers of this pair of novels will learn much history and acquire a considerable knowledge of the diamond industry.

1. *Lives of Rachel, The* (New American Library, 1984) The crises of five early Rachels are related in a story spanning the time of the Maccabees to the Crusades.
2. *Books of Rachel, The* (Seaview, 1979) This continues the story of the family of diamond merchants through six centuries and many countries.

Guareschi, Giovanni

If Thurber had written about a little town in Italy's Po Valley, his stories might have been much like these. Don Camillo, the irascible parish priest, talks over all his problems with the Lord, who replies with calm good sense and sly humor. Don Camillo's chief antagonist is Mayor Peppone, leader of the local leftists and a prolific writer of party manifestoes distinguished by their bad spelling and numerous references to "a certain black-robed reactionary." The passage of time is only faintly discernible in these six episodes. Omnibus volumes: *Don Camillo: His Little World and His Dilemma* (Farrar, 1954; numbers 1 and 3) and *The Don Camillo Omnibus* (Gollancz [UK], 1974; numbers 1, 2, and 5).

1. *Little World of Don Camillo, The* (Pellegrini, 1950) Don Camillo, Peppone, and the other inhabitants of this wayward little parish are introduced. Translated from the Italian by Una V. Troubridge. Originally published as *Mondo piccolo "Don Camillo"* (1948).
2. *Don Camillo and His Flock* (Pellegrini, 1952) Temporary banishment for Don Camillo and a flood of the Po River are featured. UK title: *Don Camillo and the Prodigal Son*. Translated from the Italian by Frances Frenaye. Published in Italian as *Mondo piccolo "Don Camillo e il suo gregge"* (1953).
3. *Don Camillo's Dilemma* (Farrar, 1954) Neri the mason sells his soul, and a headless ghost wanders the village streets at night. Translated from the Italian by Frances Frenaye. Originally published as *Il dilemma di Don Camillo* (1953).
4. *Don Camillo Takes the Devil by the Tail* (Farrar, 1957) When Moscow orders the purging of Stalin's memory, Peppone must decide what to do about the enormous fresco at the People's Palace. UK title: *Don Camillo and the Devil*. Translated from the Italian by Frances Frenaye. Originally published as *Don Camillo prende il diavolo per la coda* (1956).
5. *Comrade Don Camillo* (Farrar, 1964) Peppone wins the soccer sweepstakes, and Don Camillo manipulates his way into an official delegation to Moscow. Translated from the Italian by Frances Frenaye. Originally published as *Mondo piccolo "Il compagno Don Camillo"* (1963).
6. *Don Camillo Meets the Flower Children* (Farrar, 1969) The flower child is Don Camillo's niece Flora, whose arrival with a troop of Hell's Angels brings the 1960s to Don Camillo's parish. UK title: *Don Camillo Meets Hell's Angels*. Translated from the Italian by L. K. Conrad. Originally published as *Don Camillo e i giovani d'oggi* (1969).

Guild, Nicholas

The Assyrians are usually portrayed as the bad guys in the Bible and most histories and historical fiction since then. Nicholas Guild's portrait of an Assyrian noble is a somewhat more sympathetic portrayal, although the plot has its share of treachery and violence. Tiglath Ashur is more believable than the average hero of a historical novel, and his adventures have considerable appeal.

1. *Assyrian, The* (Atheneum, 1987) Tiglath Ashur, one of the many sons of the Assyrian king, declines to be castrated, thus ensuring a succession fight with his brother Esarhaddon.
2. *Blood Star, The* (Atheneum, 1989) Fleeing Esarhaddon's assassins, Tiglath Ashur goes on an adventurous journey through the world of the Near East in the 7th century BCE.

Gulbranssen, Trygve

These two novels are set in the strange, primitive world of Bjoerndal in the far northern woods of Norway. The southern villagers fear their northern neighbors but eventually come to know them. The dominant figure is young Dag, who comes to the town of Broad Leas, wins the heart of Therese, and takes her back north to his prospering estate. The story begins around 1760. *The Bjoerndal Cycle* (Putnam, 1937) contains numbers 1 and 2.

1. *Beyond Sing the Woods* (Putnam, 1936) This book covers the period from Dag's arrival in Broad Leas to the engagement of his young son Dag to a village girl. Translated from the Norwegian by Naomi Walford. Originally published as *Og bakom synger skogene* (1933).
2. *Wind from the Mountains, The* (Putnam, 1937) This sequel continues from young Dag's marriage to Adelaide and old Dag's death. Translated from the Norwegian by Naomi Walford. Originally published as *Det blæser fra Dødningefjeld* (1934).

Gulley, Philip

Harmony, Indiana, is the home of Quaker pastor Sam Gardner and a host of other quirky but lovable characters. The Harmony series has won millions of readers with its Garrison Keillor (q.v.)–type wit, optimistic Christian message, and down-home mid-American types. Quaker pastor Philip Gulley, an Indiana native, gets just the right mixture of humor and pathos in this Christian fiction series. Gulley has also published *Front Porch Tales* (Multnomah, 1997) and *Home Town Tales* (Multnomah, 1998), collected in *A Philip Gulley Reader* (Multnomah, 2000), as well as coauthored (with James Mulholland) two nonfiction books: *If Grace Is True* (HarperSanFrancisco, 2003) and *If God Is Love* (HarperSanFrancisco, 2004), describing his optimistic view of God's love.

1. *Home to Harmony* (Multnomah, 2000) Introduces readers to the town of Harmony, Indiana, and its characters, including the Quaker pastor Sam Gardner, a childless couple who do everything they can to save their niece from her alcoholic parents, and church elder Dale Hinshaw, who "knew just enough Scripture to be annoying, but not enough to be transformed."
2. *Just Shy of Harmony* (HarperSanFrancisco, 2002) After reading an article in a Christian magazine, Sam Gardner discovers he has seven of "the ten warning signs of depression."
3. *Signs and Wonders* (HarperSanFrancisco, 2003) The plot revolves around Deena Morrison, the only single, attractive, well-educated

woman in town, and her attempts to find love. Dale Hinshaw launches "Salvation Balloons," another harebrained ministry scheme. Harvey Mulodock tries to store his beloved convertible in his garage attic, with disastrous results.

4. *Christmas in Harmony* (HarperSanFrancisco, 2002) A Christmas novella. Dale Hinshaw continues his crackpot schemes, which include a "progressive nativity scene" and a "Quaker militia" to fight terrorism.

5. *Life Goes On* (HarperSanFrancisco, 2004) When pastor Sam gets laryngitis, Dale Hinshaw takes the pulpit on Easter Sunday and delivers a 45-minute tirade that fails to mention the Resurrection. Deena Morrison finally meets her Prince Charming thanks to ringworm.

6. *Change of Heart, A* (HarperSanFrancisco, 2005) Sam Gardner celebrates five years at Harmony Friends Meeting. Deena Morrison marries the town's most eligible bachelor. Dale Hinshaw has a near-death experience. Amanda Hodges's prodigal biological parents return.

7. *Christmas Scrapbook, The* (HarperSanFrancisco, 2005) Another Christmas novella. Sam Gardner enrolls in a scrapbooking class to make a Christmas gift his wife will never forget.

8. *Almost Friends* (HarperSanFrancisco, 2006) While Sam Gardner is on sabbatical, his place is taken by seminary student Krista Riley, who is rumored to be gay, which arouses the prurient interest of church conservatives such as Dale Hinshaw and Fern Hampton.

Gunn, Elizabeth

Police detective Jake Hines is the protagonist in a series of procedurals set in Rutherford, a fictional city of 100,000 in southeast Minnesota. Trudy Hanson, a forensic scientist based in St. Paul and his eventual lover, sometimes assists Jake in investigating some nasty murders in this well-written series of thrillers with a believable and sympathetic main character. Author Elizabeth Gunn has plied many trades, including that of freelance travel writer.

1. *Triple Play* (Walker, 1997) Rutherford, Minnesota, police detective Jake Hines is convinced that the mutilation murders of two young men are the work of a serial killer.

2. *Par Four* (Walker, 1998) A spate of crimes, including the robbery and murder of Jake's old pal Babe Krueger, bedevil Jake, newly appointed chief of detectives in Rutherford.

3. *Five Card Stud* (Walker, 2000) The death of a half-naked man in a snowbank is determined to be the result of murder rather than hypothermia.

4. *Six-Pound Walleye* (Walker, 2001) The son of Rutherford chief of police McCafferty is the assailant in a brawl among members of the Rutherford High hockey team. Then a small boy waiting for the school bus is gunned down without anyone hearing a shot.

5. *Seventh Inning Stretch* (Walker, 2002) Jake and his lover, Trudy Hanson, are having problems with the farm they have bought midway between Rutherford and St. Paul. Two dead men turn up in a garbage barrel, one with a wad of cash stuck in his mouth.

6. *Crazy Eights* (Forge, 2005) Jake resolves to reinvestigate the case when Benny Niemeyer, implicated in the kidnapping and murder of IBM employee Shelley Gleason, is acquitted and Jake takes the blame for fouling up the case.

Gunning, Sally (Carlson)

Peter Bartholomew, owner of an odd-job company called Factotum, is a resident of the fictional island of Nashtoba, which is a mix of Cape Cod, Massachusetts, past and present. Nashtoba, like most quaint rural areas in mystery fiction, is a hotbed of crime, and Peter, his ex-wife Connie, whom he eventually remarries, and local police chief Will McOwat usually have their hands full of investigations. Sally Gunning, a resident of Cape Cod, recently published a historical novel, *The Widow's War* (Morrow, 2006).

1. *Hot Water* (Pocket, 1990) Introduces Nashtoba and Peter Bartholomew. Peter finds the body of Edna Hitchcock and is convinced that she was murdered although someone tried to make it look like suicide.

2. *Under Water* (Pocket, 1992) Peter finds a teenage girl's body floating in the sound, the only clues a class ring and the girl's pregnancy.

3. *Ice Water* (Pocket, 1993) A sniper has killed popular bait-shop owner Newby Dillingham and wounded another Nashtoban. Peter and local police chief Will McOwat try to piece together the identity of the murderer.

4. *Rough Water* (Pocket, 1994) Peter is asked by his sister Polly to go on a weekend whale watching cruise, so that he can meet her new fiancé, Jackson Beers. Jackson winds up with an antique harpoon sticking in him.

5. *Troubled Water* (Pocket, 1993) After Peter takes a job to clean up the house and garden of two elderly sisters, he arrives one morning to find them dead.

6. *Still Water* (Pocket, 1995) Peter, although he is trying to get back together with Connie, his ex-wife, finds himself drawn to a young bride, who has survived two almost fatal "accidents."

7. *Deep Water* (Pocket, 1996) Town drunk Cobie Small turns up at a local bar flashing a wad of cash, then turns up dead the next morning in a netful of mackerel.

8. *Muddy Water* (Pocket, 1997) Peter's friend's bride-to-be fails to turn up for her wedding and is found murdered.

9. *Dirty Water* (Pocket, 1998) Peter and Connie Bartholomew are determined to make their second try at marriage work. But their honeymoon is cut short when Peter's 88-year-old friend, Sarah Abrew, confesses to gunning down accountant Webster Sutton.

10. *Fire Water* (Pocket, 1999) Peter and Connie's ward, 5-year-old Lucy Suggs, finds a human skull while playing. What is more shocking is that the skull belongs to an old flame of Peter's who disappeared 15 years earlier.

Gur, Batya

The late Batya Gur (d. 2005), professor of literature in Jerusalem, created a classic detective in Michael Ohayon of the Jerusalem police. Moroccan-born Ohayon is a patient, shrewd investigator in a series of mysteries mixing detection with character studies and social history. Six novels of the 10 written by Gur have been translated into English.

1. *Saturday Morning Murder, The* (Harper, 1991) Psychoanalyst Eva Neidorf is shot dead shortly before her lecture on ethical and forensic problems in psychoanalysis. Translated from the Hebrew by Dalya Bilu. Originally published as *Resah be shabat baboker* (1988).

2. *Literary Murder* (Harper, 1993) Shaul Tirosh, head of Hebrew University's literature department and Israel's most prized poet, is found bludgeoned to death in his office. Translated from the

Hebrew by Dalya Bilu. Originally published as *Mavet bahug le-sifrut* (1989).

3. *Murder on a Kibbutz* (Harper, 1994) Beautiful, reform-minded kibbutz general secretary Osnat Harel is poisoned. Translated from the Hebrew by Dalya Bilu. Originally published as *Lihan meshutefet* (1991).

4. *Murder Duet* (HarperCollins, 1999) After a two-year study leave, Michael returns to work. Then an abandoned baby girl appears on his doorstep, and he turns for help to his upstairs neighbor, cellist Nita van Gelden. Translated from the Hebrew by Dalya Bilu. Originally published as *Marhak ha nakhon* (1996).

5. *Bethlehem Road Murder* (HarperCollins, 2004) Ohayon investigates the murder of a young woman whose bludgeoned corpse is found in the attic of a house undergoing renovation in Jerusalem's Baka neighborhood. Translated from the Hebrew by Vivian Eden. Originally published as *Retsan be-derek bet lehem* (2001).

6. *Murder in Jerusalem* (HarperCollins, 2006) The death of set designer Tirzah Rubin, found beneath a pillar on the set of a film adaptation of S. Y. Agnon's *Iddo and Eynam*, turns out to be murder. Translated from the Hebrew by Evan Fallenberg. Originally published as *Retsah metsalmim* (2003).

Guthrie, A(lfred) B(ertram), Jr.

I. Anyone who thinks westerns are all good-guy, bad-guy shoot-'em-ups should read A. B. Guthrie's intelligent novels, which combine action, authenticity, and fully realized characters. *The Way West* won the Pulitzer Prize for fiction in 1950. This loosely connected series of six novels covers the period from 1830 to the mid-1940s. Some characters appear in more than one book.

1. *Big Sky, The* (Houghton Mifflin, 1947) Boone Caudill, a violent man, leaves civilization behind for the life of a fur trapper in the remote Teton Mountains. His Indian wife, Teal Eye, and friends Jim Deakins and Dick Summers play supporting roles in this volume.

2. *Way West, The* (Houghton Mifflin, 1949) Dick Summers returns as the guide who leads a wagon train bound for Oregon. Young Brownie Evans meets the beautiful Mercy McBee in this volume.

3. *Fair Land, Fair Land* (Houghton Mifflin, 1982) The later life of Dick Summers is related as he observes the land being despoiled by miners and settlers. Covers 1845 to 1870.

4. *These Thousand Hills* (Houghton Mifflin, 1956) Lat Evans, Brownie's son, trails a herd of Durham cattle into Montana and stakes out a ranch.

5. *Arfive* (Houghton Mifflin, 1970) Benton Collingsworth, the new school principal, comes to the small town of Arfive, Montana, and is greeted by its leading citizen, rancher Mort Ewing.

6. *Last Valley, The* (Houghton Mifflin, 1975) Collingsworth and Ewing appear again in this volume, which begins in the mid-1920s when Ben Tate takes over the local newspaper.

II. Guthrie also wrote a series of mystery stories set in contemporary Midbury, Montana. They are narrated by young Jase Beard, deputy to Sheriff Chick Charleston. Viewed by Guthrie as "entertainments," they are readable portraits of the life and people of a small western town.

1. *Wild Pitch* (Houghton Mifflin, 1973) Buster Hogue is shot in the head at the town picnic, and his enemy Ben Day is killed soon after.

2. *Genuine Article, The* (Houghton Mifflin, 1977) Some cattle rustling is followed by the murder of irascible rancher F. Y. Grimsley.

3. *No Second Wind* (Houghton Mifflin, 1980) Mutilated cattle and murder may be linked to a feud between strip miners and locals opposed to strip mining.

4. *Playing Catch-Up* (Houghton Mifflin, 1985) A prostitute and a high school girl are strangled, and a sapphire brooch disappears.

5. *Murder in the Cotswolds* (Houghton Mifflin, 1989) While visiting England with his wife, Geeta, Chick Charleston assists in a murder investigation in the quaint village of Upper Beechwood.

Haddam, Jane

PSEUDONYM OF Orania Papazoglou

Philadelphia's Cavanaugh Street–based Armenian American Gregor Demarkian, retired head of the FBI's Behavioral Science Unit, is now a private investigator who, with the help of sidekick Father Tibor Kasparian and lover, science-fiction novelist Bennis Hannaford, solves crimes in a series of novels, many of which are based on holiday themes (numbers 1–13). Orania Papazoglou (q.v.), widow of the mystery writer William De Andrea (q.v.), also writes mysteries under her real name.

1. *Not a Creature Was Stirring* (Bantam, 1990) Gregor goes to dinner with wealthy eccentric Robert Hannaford on Christmas Eve.

2. *Precious Blood* (Bantam, 1991) Colchester, New York, at Easter is the scene for Demarkian's investigation of the murder of a young woman that was possibly committed by a Catholic priest.

3. *Act of Darkness* (Bantam, 1991) Election Day seems to be the focus, as a bill to benefit children with Down syndrome is discussed at a seminar at an estate on Long Island Sound.

4. *Quoth the Raven* (Bantam, 1991) The obnoxious Dr. Donegal Steele is missing from the Halloween festivities at Independence College.

5. *Great Day for the Deadly, A* (Bantam, 1991) Demarkian is summoned to Maryville, New York, where aspiring nun Brigit Ann Reilly has been found poisoned shortly before St. Patrick's Day.

6. *Feast of Murder, A* (Bantam, 1992) Jonathan Edgwick Baird, insider trader, is released from jail in time to celebrate Thanksgiving.

7. *Stillness in Bethlehem, A* (Bantam, 1992) In Bethlehem, Vermont, for the town's annual Nativity celebration, Gregor is asked by the local police chief for help with two unsolved crimes.

8. *Murder Superior* (Bantam, 1993) This is a Mother's Day mystery in which a nun ingests the poison intended for Mother Mary Bellarmine.

9. *Bleeding Hearts* (Bantam, 1994) Demarkian and friends are celebrating Valentine's Day when homely Hanna Krekorian turns up with the new man in her life.

10. *Dear Old Dead* (Bantam, 1994) In a case tangentially connected to Father's Day, the benefactor of a Harlem medical clinic is poisoned.

11. *Festival of Deaths* (Bantam, 1994) Hanukkah is being celebrated in Philadelphia when Lotte Goldman's sex-talk television show is hit by a series of murders.

12. *Fountain of Death* (Bantam, 1995) At the Fountain of Youth Work-Out Studio in New Haven, Connecticut, the naked and poisoned body of an aerobics instructor is found in the bushes behind the club, an ominous start to the New Year.

13. *And One to Die On* (Bantam, 1996) Silent screen star Tasheba Kent's 100th birthday celebration is marred by her death and that of a tabloid journalist on an island off the coast of Maine.

14. *Baptism in Blood* (Bantam, 1996) Bellerton, North Carolina, is the scene of a hurricane and the murder of an infant, whose body is

found on the grounds of Bonaventura, a controversial women's retreat.

15. *Deadly Beloved* (**Bantam, 1997**) Gregor, fleeing the perils of a Cavanaugh Street wedding, ventures out to the gated community of Fox Run Hill to investigate the death of Patty Willis's husband.

16. *Skeleton Key* (**St. Martin's, 2000**) Bennis Hannaford summons Gregor to the Anson estate in Connecticut after she finds the murdered body of debutante heiress Kayla Anson during a Halloween visit there.

17. *True Believers* (**St. Martin's, 2001**) The new cardinal archbishop of Philadelphia consults with Demarkian when the church, already reeling from a pedophilia scandal, has to deal with a suicide inside St. Anselm's.

18. *Somebody Else's Music* (**St. Martin's, 2002**) Author and TV panelist Liz Tolliver returns to a high school reunion in her hometown of Hollman, Pennsylvania, and her bullying classmates who, after 30 years, still hate and despise her.

19. *Conspiracy Theory* (**St. Martin's, 2003**) Is conspiracy group America on Alert behind the bombing of an Armenian church, which injures Father Tibor Kasparian, and the assassination of a prominent businessman on his front steps?

20. *Headmaster's Wife, The* (**St. Martin's, 2004**) The latest affair of Alice Makepeace, wife of the headmaster of Windsor Academy, near Boston, has resulted in the suicide of a 16-year-old.

21. *Hardscrabble Road* (**St. Martin's, 2006**) Right-wing Philadelphia radio host Drew Harrigan is in trouble. He has been arrested on drug charges. Then his alleged supplier, a homeless man named Sherman, is the victim of an apparent poisoning.

22. *Glass Houses* (**St. Martin's, 2007**) The Plate Glass Killer targets unattractive middle-aged women and leaves their mutilated bodies in alleys.

23. *Cheating at Solitaire* (**St. Martin's, 2008**) Wearied by the preparations for his wedding with Bennis Hannaford, Demarkian escapes to the island of Margaret's Harbor (i.e., Martha's Vineyard) to investigate the murder of pop-icon Arrow Normand's boyfriend.

Hagberg, David

Kirk McGarvey is a former CIA assassin who becomes a renegade, then makes it up with the CIA and gets what are supposed to be desk jobs. But the irrepressible McGarvey doesn't allow himself to get rusty with inaction, as he moves from doomsday plot to doomsday plot, mostly in the Middle East, and switches from KGB baddies to the likes of Saddam Hussein and Osama bin Laden. The series has elicited comparisons, not always favorable, to Tom Clancy (q.v.), Ian Fleming (q.v.), and John le Carré (q.v.). *Desert Fire* (Tor, 1993), about Saddam's attempts to obtain nukes, is sometimes included in the McGarvey series. David Hagberg has also written six volumes about the comic-strip character Flash Gordon (1980–1981); the four-volume Magic Man series (1983–1985), writing as "David Bannerman"; and four volumes featuring agent Bill Lane (writing as "Sean Flannery"), the last being *Eden's Gate* (Tor, 2001), which Hagberg published under his real name.

1. *Without Honor* (**Tor, 1989**) Subtitle: *When All Men Are Without Honor Which Man Do You Trust.* Introduces ex-CIA assassin Kirk McGarvey, who is called back to the Company after a fatal hijacking and intimations of a spy in the upper echelons of the US government.

2. *Countdown* (**St. Martin's, 1990**) KGB chief Valentin Baranov and his nasty field operative Arkady Kurshin hope to reactivate the cold war by destroying Israel's nuclear capacity and bringing down Gorbachev.

3. *Crossfire* (**Tor, 1991**) Kurshin and McGarvey are opposed again when the Paris CIA station is bombed, just as the United States returns 125 tons of frozen assets to Iran.

4. *Critical Mass* (**Tor, 1992**) An embittered Hiroshima survivor attempts to explode nuclear devices in San Francisco and Los Angeles on the anniversary of the atomic bomb attacks on Japan in 1945.

5. *High Flight* (**Forge, 1995**) McGarvey is up against a Japanese cabal seeking to destroy the US economy, a confrontation between Russian and Japanese ships, and an assassination team featuring a former East German operative, an ecoterrorist, and a computer whiz.

6. *Assassination* (**Forge, 1997**) Russian demagogue Trankov takes over the Yeltsin government and starts to engineer a reunion of the former members of the USSR.

7. *White House* (**Forge, 1999**) A terrorist bomb in a Georgetown restaurant fails to stop McGarvey from accepting a promotion in the CIA, as an underground nuclear explosion off the Korean Coast causes an East Asian confrontation.

8. *Joshua's Hammer* (**Forge, 2000**) Allen Trumble, CIA Chief of Station in Riyadh, Saudi Arabia, has a disturbing interview with Osama bin Laden, in which Osama claims to have a acquired a portable nuclear bomb from the Russian Mafia.

9. *Kill Zone, The* (**Forge, 2002**) Former KGB operatives want to reactivate cold war assassination plans that include McGarvey, who has been tapped to be interim CIA director, among their potential victims.

10. *Soldier of God* (**Forge, 2005**) After a terrorist attack upon an Alaskan cruise ship, McGarvey vows to track down the terrorist leader known as Khalil, who may be planning another 9/11 attack.

11. *Allah's Scorpion* (**Forge, 2007**) Al-Qaeda attacks Camp Echo, part of the US base at Guantánamo, as part of Osama bin Laden's plan to pull off an attack on America's West Coast that will make 9/11 seem like child's play.

12. *Dance with the Dragon* (**Forge, 2007**) McGarvey leaves retirement to look into Chinese superagent General Liu Hung and the shooting death of a CIA operative in Mexico.

Hager, Jean

I. Jean Hager has been compared to Tony Hillerman (q.v.) for her series of well-plotted mysteries with Native American detectives. Part-Cherokee Molly Bearpaw is an investigator for the Native American Advocacy League, situated on tribal lands in rural Oklahoma. Hager, part Cherokee herself, expertly depicts the interactions of the world of tribal myth and legend with contemporary Native American life.

1. *Ravenmocker* (**Mysterious, 1992**) Woodrow Mouse thinks that his father's death in a Tahlequah nursing home may have been caused by a Ravenmocker, a feared Cherokee witch.

2. *Redbird's Cry, The* (**Mysterious, 1994**) When storyteller Tom Battle collapses during a festival, suspicion falls on Wolf Kawaya, his political enemy and former husband of his lover.

3. *Seven Black Stones* (**Mysterious, 1995**) Zebediah Smoke's prophecy of death for all who promote bingo in the Cherokee Nation seems to be bearing fruit.

4. *Spirit Caller, The* (**Mysterious, 1997**) When self-appointed New Age shaman Talia Wind is found hanging from an old gallows, Molly finds several suspects.

II. Mitchell Bushyhead is another part-Cherokee Oklahoman who solves mysteries. Bushyhead is a professional, being police chief in the town of Buckskin. He and his full-blooded Cherokee deputy Virgil Rabbit are called upon to solve local crimes in a series of procedurals suffused with Cherokee culture.

1. *Grandfather Medicine, The* (St. Martin's, 1989) Local artist Joe Pigeon, who has a connection with the Nighthawk Keetowahs, a secret Cherokee society devoted to reviving old beliefs, is murdered.
2. *Night Walker* (St. Martin's, 1990) Graham Thornton, who built a resort lodge on an old Indian graveyard, has been felled by a Night Walker, a Cherokee witch, according to some of his employees.
3. *Ghost Land* (St. Martin's, 1992) The body of Tamara Birch, student at a Cherokee boarding school, is found in the woods on Cherokee Heritage Celebration Day.
4. *Fire Carrier, The* (Mysterious, 1996) Henderson Six-Killer, having escaped from jail to rescue his sister from her abusive husband, sees a moving light out in the wilds that suggests the evil spirit Fire Carrier.
5. *Masked Dancers* (Mysterious, 1998) Mitch's daughter Emily and her friends find the body of a murdered state wildlife officer in a cave. Could he have been done in by local high school principal Vian Brasfield, who has been killing eagles for their feathers?

III. The Iris House mystery series, which has been appearing in paperback originals, is a change of pace from Native American detective novels. Tess Darcy has transformed her aunt's old home in Victoria Springs, Missouri, into a bed-and-breakfast that would meet with Martha Stewart's approval. Unfortunately, Tess is sometimes distracted from her decorating schemes (and her upcoming marriage with longtime lover Luke Fredrik) by the murder of one of her guests, which she, because of the incompetence of local police chief Desmond Butts, has to solve herself.

1. *Blooming Murder* (Avon, 1994) Opening day for Iris House is marred by the discovery of the body of a guest planted in a bed of irises.
2. *Dead and Buried* (Avon, 1995) A notorious romance novelist, who is threatening to expose class secrets in a tell-all book, is among the attendees at the 20-year reunion of Victoria Springs High School.
3. *Death on the Drunkard's Path* (Avon, 1996) The annual Victoria Springs Quilt Show and Sale is a high-stakes affair. A blue ribbon for a quilt will translate into big dollars. Big enough to turn quilters into backstabbers—and perhaps murderers?
4. *Last Noel, The* (Avon, 1997) When drama professor Sherwood Draper becomes the director of the annual Christmas pageant, he succeeds in alienating not only the former director and the church organist but also a jealous husband.
5. *Sew Deadly* (Avon, 1998) The newly engaged Tess, planning her wedding to Luke Fredrik and volunteering her time at the local senior center, is an eyewitness to the death of elderly tyrant Edwina Riley.
6. *Weigh Dead* (Avon, 1999) Tess, refurbishing their living quarters at Iris House in anticipation of her wedding to Luke, runs into some snags when aerobics queen Lida Darnell checks in with a bunch of fitness aspirants.
7. *Bride and Doom* (Avon, 2000) Will Tess finally marry Luke? Aunt Dahlia and cousin Cinny are hosting a bridal shower for Tess at the Victoria Springs Country Club. But someone decides to do in Julian Walker, the talented but despised chef at the club.

Haggard, H(enry) Rider

I. *King Solomon's Mines*, which was consciously modeled after *Treasure Island*, was an immediate success with readers of all ages. Having spent his early adult years in Africa, Haggard could give an authentic ring to his books' settings, but his characters are flattened into stereotypes by a heavy romanticism and the racial and sexist prejudices of his day. Readers who can accept these genre conventions will find Haggard's tales quite entertaining. Allan Quatermain was so successful as the fictional hero of *King Solomon's Mines* that Haggard revived him again and again, even giving him adventures in previous incarnations, which makes a real chronology next to impossible. The books in which Quatermain appears are listed below in the order of their publication. Quatermain also appears in one She book (see series II) and in the Zikali trilogy (see series III). The early life of Umslopagaas, the Zulu warrior who plays a large part in *Allan Quatermain*, and who, like Allan, was resurrected for some of the later novels in the series, is told in the rousing *Nada the Lily* (Longmans, 1892). Recent additions include *Tales of Allan Quatermain and Others* (Burgo, 2002) and *Hunter Quatermain's Story: The Uncollected Adventures of Allan Quatermain* (Peter Owen [UK], 2004).

1. *King Solomon's Mines* (Harper, 1886) Allan Quatermain leads Sir Henry Curtis and Captain Good on a search for the fabulous lost diamonds of King Solomon. Quatermain is thought to have been based on the hunter F. C. Selous. Stewart Granger, among others, portrayed Allan in the movies.
2. *Allan Quatermain* (Harper, 1887) In this prototypical "lost city" romance, Quatermain follows a subterranean river to a hidden city in the African interior where Curtis finds romance, Allan meets his end, and the great Zulu warrior Umslopagaas fights a spectacular last stand.
3. *Maiwa's Revenge* (Harper, 1888) Allan does some fancy shooting and helps an African princess regain her heritage.
4. *Allan's Wife and Other Stories* (Munro, 1889) This book consists of four short stories, including "Tale of Three Lions" and "Long Odds."
5. *Holy Flower, The* (Ward & Lock, 1915) Allan searches for a fabled orchid in the heart of Africa. Variant title: *Allan and the Holy Flower*.
6. *Ivory Child, The* (Longmans, 1916) Quatermain leads an expedition to central Africa in search of a lady who has been spirited away.
7. *Ancient Allan, The* (Longmans, 1920) A drug throws Allan back into a previous existence in ancient Egypt.
8. *Heu-Heu* (Doubleday, 1924) Allan and Hans go in search of a lost race troubled by a monstrous, apelike "god."
9. *Treasure of the Lake, The* (Doubleday, 1926) Allan gets involved with yet another lost race and a white goddess.
10. *Allan and the Ice-Gods* (Doubleday, 1927) Features Allan in a previous existence as a prehistoric man.

II. "She" is Ayesha, a strange white goddess who rules a hidden city in deepest Africa. Haggard caught something of universal allure when he sat down to write his story of "an immortal woman inspired by an immortal love." *She* has been filmed several times. The 1935 film version inexplicably changed the setting from Africa to the Arctic. Allan Quatermain (series I) puts in an appearance in number 3.

1. *She* (Harper, 1886) Leo Vincey and Ludwig Holly search for the mysterious queen of a savage African tribe.
2. *Ayesha: The Return of She* (Doubleday, 1905) Leo Vincey, in pursuit of his love, Ayesha, is led to a monastery in the mountains of central Asia.

3. *She and Allan* **(Longmans, 1921)** Haggard's two leading characters meet, both a little past their prime.
4. *Wisdom's Daughter: The Life and Love Story of She-Who-Must-Be Obeyed* **(Doubleday, 1923)** Ayesha appears in one of her reincarnations as the daughter of an Arab chief during the 4th century BCE.

III. In the Zikali trilogy and in *Nada the Lily* (Longmans, 1892), Haggard documents the history of the Zulu people and culture. Allan Quatermain appears as a young man in this trilogy, his past somewhat altered from the one given him in series I. These books make superior reading to the later Allan Quatermain and She potboilers, in which Haggard recycled his most famous characters. Some readers feel that he has done for the Zulus what James Fenimore Cooper's (q.v.) Leatherstocking Tales did for the American Indian.

1. *Marie* **(Longmans, 1912)** Allan Quatermain is a young man in 1836, at the time of the Great Trek of the Boers into the African interior and their confrontation with the Zulus.
2. *Child of Storm* **(Longmans, 1913)** The beauty and ambition of Mameena, along with the plotting of the witch doctor Zikali, bring civil war to the Zulus. The story ends at the battle of Tugela in 1856.
3. *Finished* **(Longmans, 1917)** Zikali leads Cetewayo and the Zulus into their fatal clash with the British in the Zulu War of 1877–1884.

Hailey, J. P.

PSEUDONYM OF Parnell Hall

Parnell Hall (q.v) wrote, as J. P. Hailey, a series of five mysteries featuring shaggy-haired ex-actor Steve Winslow, who becomes a lawyer after getting hooked on Perry Mason and enduring a drought of acting jobs.

1. *Baxter Trust, The* **(Fine, 1988)** Steve Winslow is hired by a ditzy heiress to defend her in a murder case.
2. *Anonymous Client, The* **(Fine, 1989)** Winslow, scraping along with one client, receives a $10,000 check with an unsigned note requesting his help.
3. *Underground Man, The* **(Fine, 1990)** When eccentric businessman-turned-bum Jack Walsh is killed, Steve has to defend Walsh's loud-mouthed teenage nephew.
4. *Naked Typist, The* **(Fine, 1990)** A labor-management dispute escalates when a boss fires his secretary because she won't perform her clerical duties naked.
5. *Wrong Gun, The* **(Fine, 1992)** Gun collector Russ Timberlane discovers that one of his treasures, an 1862 Colt .45 once owned by a famous outlaw, has been stolen and replaced by a copy.

Haines, Carolyn

Sarah Booth Delaney, of Zinnia, Mississippi, is a southern belle of a different sort: she is a private investigator, a pursuit she embarks upon to save Dahlia House, the old family homestead. Encouraged by Jitty, the ghost of her great-great-grandmother's nanny, by Sheriff Coleman Peters, whom she hopes to make her lover, and friends such as Tinkie Richmond and Cece Dee (formerly Cecil) Falcon, the thirtysomething unwed Sarah solves a number of crimes in breezy fashion in this series of cozies. Alabama resident Carolyn Haines is also the author of a number of considerably darker novels, including two set in Jexville, Mississippi—*Touched* (Dutton, 1996) and *Judas Burning* (River City,

2005)—and several romance novels under the pseudonym of Caroline Burnes.

1. *Them Bones* **(Bantam, 1999)** Sarah Booth Delaney, of Zinnia, Sunflower County, Mississippi, is about to lose the family plantation until she is persuaded by Jitty, the ghost of her great-great-grandmother's nanny, to kidnap her friend's prize dog.
2. *Buried Bones* **(Bantam, 2000)** After Lawrence Ambrose, onetime famous man of southern letters, hosts a dinner at which he announces a tell-all biography exposing Zinnia's darkest secrets, someone offs Mr. Ambrose.
3. *Splintered Bones* **(Delacorte, 2002)** Sarah and her friends Tinkie Richmond and Cece Dee Falcon band together to save horse breeder Eulalee McBride from a murder rap.
4. *Crossed Bones* **(Delacorte, 2003)** Nightclub owner and black blues pianist Ivory Keys is stabbed to death at his club, and the prime suspect is Scott Hampton, a white blues guitarist with a history of racism.
5. *Hallowed Bones* **(Delacorte, 2004)** Doreen Mallory, tarot card reader, teacher, and leader of a devoted following, is in a New Orleans jail, accused of murdering her baby.
6. *Bones to Pick* **(Kensington, 2006)** Quentin McGee, local heiress and author of a memoir exposing her hometown, is found dead in a cotton field, and her lover is the prime suspect.
7. *Ham Bones* **(Kensington, 2007)** Sarah is arrested for killing obnoxious prima donna Renata Trovaioli when the New York cast of *Cat on a Hot Tin Roof* comes to Zinnia.

Haldeman, Joe (William)

I. *The Forever War* won Nebula and Hugo awards and is regarded as an SF classic. It describes the ordeal, partially based on Haldeman's Vietnam experience, of Private William Mandella who is drafted to fight in a distant thousand-year conflict. When Mandella survives the war he finds that, while he has aged only months, his home planet has aged centuries. The long-awaited sequel (25 years), *Forever Free*, finds humans a relict race, kept around to provide archaic genes in case they are ever needed by the newly evolved superhuman race of Man. *Forever Peace* (Ace, 1997), while on the same general theme, is not connected to *The Forever War* or *Forever Free*. The omnibus volume *Peace and War* (Gollancz [UK], 2006) contains all three *Forever* titles. The title story of *A Separate War and Other Stories* (Ace, 2006) returns to the conclusion of *The Forever War*, as seen through the eyes of another character.

1. *Forever War, The* **(St. Martin's, 1994)** Draftee William Mandella is sent as part of an elite force across light years of space to battle the alien Taurans in the initial stages of a war that will turn out to last "forever."
2. *Forever Free* **(Ace, 1999)** The newly evolved superhuman race of Man has exiled the remaining humans to the frozen planet Middle Finger, where they are kept around to provide, if needed, an "archaic gene" pool.

II. The Worlds, 41 orbiting satellites housing half a million people, seem to be humanity's only real hope late in the 21st century. When political-science student Marianne O'Hara comes from New New York to spend a postgraduate year on Earth, she has some really nasty surprises in store for her, including the end of Earth as they know it.

Multiple Nebula and Hugo awards winner Joe Haldeman, who has served twice as president of Science Fiction Writers of America (SFWA), has also penned, as "Robert Graham" a pair of SF adventure novels published by Pocket Books in 1975 featuring a character named Attar the Merman: *Attar's Revenge* and *War of Nerves*.

1. *Worlds* (**Viking, 1981**) Marianne O'Hara travels from the orbiting "World" of New New York in the 2080s to Earth, only to find herself in the middle of a bunch of fanatics who want to destroy Earth to save it.
2. *Worlds Apart* (**Viking, 1983**) In 2085 the one-day World War IV leaves Earth bereft of one-third of her population, and everyone left over the age of 18 is gripped by madness.
3. *Worlds Enough and Time* (**Morrow, 1992**) Marianne O'Hara, her spouses, and thousands of other colonists set out for an Earth-like planet in the Epsilon Eridani system. Then a rogue radio transmission scrambles their computer data.

Hall, Adam

PSEUDONYM OF Elleston Trevor

I. Like Sam Spade, Quiller refuses to carry a gun—he thinks they are for amateurs. And that is one thing nobody would ever consider British agent Quiller. His cold and cynical professionalism never shows a crack as he completes one hazardous mission after another for his Bureau, which handles even more sensitive operations than MI5. George Segal made a wonderful Quiller in the 1967 film of *The Quiller Memorandum*. English-born Trevor, a former RAF pilot, lived in the United States. As there is very little chronology to Quiller's cases, they are listed below in the order in which they were published. Numbers 11, 12, and 13 were published as paperbacks only.

1. *Quiller Memorandum, The* (**Simon &Schuster, 1965**) In West Berlin to help the Germans flush out dangerous ex-Nazis, Quiller proves his mettle. UK title: *The Berlin Memorandum*.
2. *Ninth Directive, The* (**Simon & Schuster, 1966**) In Bangkok, Quiller must protect a visiting English dignitary from assassination.
3. *Striker Portfolio, The* (**Simon & Schuster, 1969**) Thirty-six Striker planes have crashed, and Quiller must find out what happened.
4. *Warsaw Document, The* (**Doubleday, 1971**) To stop any disruption of important detente talks in Warsaw, Quiller infiltrates the Polish underground.
5. *Tango Briefing, The* (**Doubleday, 1973**) Control sends Quiller to the Sahara, where he must find a crashed and dangerous cargo plane.
6. *Mandarin Cypher, The* (**Doubleday, 1975**) Quiller is assigned to Hong Kong and a defecting British engineer.
7. *Kobra Manifesto, The* (**Doubleday, 1976**) Quiller follows five international terrorists, known as Kobra, to their unknown target.
8. *Sinkiang Executive, The* (**Doubleday, 1978**) After an inexcusable lapse, Quiller is sent on a suicide mission to Russia, but he proves indestructible.
9. *Scorpion Signal, The* (**Doubleday, 1980**) Quiller goes to Russia in search of his old colleague Shapiro and gets caught in a tangle of revenge.
10. *Peking Target, The* (**Playboy, 1982**) Dispatched to China as a bodyguard, Quiller soon finds himself pursuing the mysterious and deadly Mr. Tung to a monastery in the mountains. Variant title: *The Pekin Target*.
11. *Quiller* (**Jove, 1985**) When an American submarine spying on a Soviet base is torpedoed, Quiller must retrieve a secret tape of the incident. UK title: *Northlight: A Quiller Mission*.
12. *Quiller's Run* (**Jove, 1988**) Quiller leaves the "Bureau" and goes freelance to stop Cambodian arms and drug dealer Mariko Shoda.
13. *Quiller KGB* (**Berkley, 1989**) Quiller joins the KGB to foil an assassination plot aimed at Gorbachev.
14. *Quiller Barracuda* (**Morrow, 1990**) Quiller goes to Florida and gets involved with an American presidential election.
15. *Quiller Bamboo* (**Morrow, 1991**) Dr. Xingyu Baibing, astrophysicist and leader of the Chinese dissidents, needs safe passage out of China.
16. *Quiller Solitaire* (**Morrow, 1992**) Dieter Klaus, leader of a terrorist splinter group, may be linked to the murders of Quiller's fellow agent and a British attache in Berlin.
17. *Quiller Meridian* (**Morrow, 1993**) Quiller travels all the way from Rome to Vladivostok to salvage Operation Meridian.
18. *Quiller Salamander* (**Penzler, 1994**) It is up to Quiller to prevent a bloody Khmer Rouge takeover in Cambodia.
19. *Quiller Balalaika* (**Carroll & Graf, 2003**) To stop British-born head of the Russian Mafia Basil Seckes (aka Vasyl Sakkas), Quiller has to infiltrate a Siberian labor camp.

II. The late Elleston Trevor (d. 1995) had a nearly 50-year publishing career, publishing under his own name (e.g., *The Flight of the Phoenix*) and several pseudonyms. The first three Hugo Bishop mysteries were originally published under the pseudonym of "Simon Rattray." London-based Hugo Bishop was a sort of knight errant like the Saint (Leslie Charteris [q.v.]), a lone operator unconnected to any agency, who got himself involved in a series of cases featuring femme fatales. The Bishop books, all with titles evoking chess pieces, had a rather torturous publishing history: originally published in the 1950s; then reissued in paperback by Pyramid (1971–1972); and then again by Harper (1990–1991).

1. *Knight Sinister* (**Harper, 1951**) Nicole Pedley's husband is a famous London theatrical director. Her lover, a handsome young actor, has made a sudden exit. Enter Hugo Bishop.
2. *Queen in Danger* (**Harper, 1952**) Thelma, Queen Bee of the fashion world, is in danger, as two murderers are on the loose in London, including her husband.
3. *Bishop in Check* (**Harper, 1953**) Men who became involved with Melody Carr always seemed to die. Hugh Bishop allows himself to be lured into her arms to find out what dark secrets she is hiding.
4. *Pawn in Jeopardy* (**Harper, 1954**) Five scientists return from an Antarctic expedition with a dangerous secret. One scientist is murdered, and Hugo gets involved.
5. *Rook's Gambit* (**Harper, 1955**) A wild party including an Armenian race-driver, a dispossessed heir, four pot-smokers, a nymphomaniac, and gorgeous, coldhearted Georgina Hutton may be behind the suspicious deaths of four persons.

Hall, James W(ilson)

The Florida Keys are as much a part of James W. Hall's mystery series as is their protagonist, Thorn, a middle-aged recluse who lives in a shack on the Keys and makes a precarious living fishing, fashioning fishing lures and, eventually, as a private eye. Thorn has a series of girlfriends, most of whom come to bad ends, until he hooks up with crime-scene photographer Alexandra Rafferty. Alexandra gets a book of her own (number 7) before she and Thorn, who has affinities with John D. MacDonald's (q.v.) Travis McGee, get together and face a melange of South Florida psychopaths and bad guys reminiscent of the novels of Carl Hiaasen (q.v.). James W. Hall, literature and creative writing instructor at Florida International University, has published nonseries mystery novels, volumes of poetry and collections of Dave Barry–like essays.

1. *Under Cover of Daylight* (**Norton, 1987**) Introduces Thorn, a man with a past he is trying to live down. Thorn lives in a shack on Key Largo fishing and tying bonefish flies for a living until he meets

young prosecuting attorney Sarah Ryan, who draws him into a fight against greedy developers.

2. *Tropical Freeze* (Norton, 1989) When Thorn's boyhood friend, ex–FBI agent Gaeton Richards, disappears, Gaeton's sister Darcy enlists Thorn's help against Gaeton's boss, Benny Cousins, head of a multinational rent-a-cop business. UK title: *Squall Line*.

3. *Mean High Tide* (Delacorte, 1994) Darcy Richards, the love of Thorn's life and his assistant at buddy Sugarman's security agency, dies in a mysterious diving accident, which, of course, is no accident.

4. *Gone Wild* (Delacorte, 1995) Thorn's childhood friend Allison Farleigh, founder of the Wildlife Protection League, takes center stage when sociopathic animal collectors kill her eldest daughter in Borneo.

5. *Buzz Cut* (Delacorte, 1996) The usual psychopaths abound as Thorn and his buddy Sugarman get together again when Sugarman signs on as head of security for a billion-dollar Miami-based cruise line.

6. *Red Sky at Night* (Delacorte, 1997) A novel that starts with the decapitation of 11 dolphins and winds up with Thorn in a wheelchair after a confrontation with Keys VA Clinic director Bean Wilson Jr., a former friend turned mad doctor.

7. *Body Language* (St. Martin's, 1998) Thorn is left rusticating in a wheelchair as a new protagonist, crime photographer Alexandra Rafferty, has to deal with a senile father; her husband, Stan; an armored car driver planning the perfect robbery; and a serial killer.

8. *Blackwater Sound* (St. Martin's, 2002) Thorn and Alexandra join forces, uneasily at first, when Alexandra's dotty father wanders into the clutches of the Braswell family, which includes a boy genius, a psychopath, and the dangerously beautiful Morgan.

9. *Off the Chart* (St. Martin's, 2003) Thorn's long-ago fling with the beautiful Anne Joy comes back to haunt him when Anne's brother Vic, a modern-day pirate, covets Thorn's five-acre property.

10. *Magic City* (St. Martin's, 2007) Thorn follows Alexandra to Miami, where he is caught up in the violence swirling around a photograph taken during the 1964 championship fight between Cassius Clay and Sonny Liston.

11. *Hell's Bay* (St. Martin's, 2008) While helping old flame Rusty set up a houseboat for tourists deep in the Everglades, Thorn becomes entangled in the intrigue surrounding the murder of wealthy Abigail Bates.

Hall, Oakley (Maxwell)

Ambrose Bierce, at one time an American short story writer and essayist to be reckoned with (*In the Midst of Life*, *The Devil's Dictionary*, etc.), disappeared somewhere in Mexico in 1914. Ambrose has been revived, somewhat earlier in his career, by Oakley Hall in a series of historical mysteries. His young sidekick, Tom Redmond, acts as Watson to the curmudgeonly Bierce in mysteries set in the American West (mostly California) in the 1890s. Historical characters, such as William Randolph Hearst, sometimes play a role in these interesting mysteries with convincing period flavor.

Oakley Hall has written more than 20 novels, most of them set in the American West, including *Warlock* (Viking, 1958), which was nominated for a Pulitzer Prize, made into a film in 1959, reprinted by the presses of the University of Nebraska and the University of Nevada, and included in the *New York Review Books Classics* series (2005). *Warlock* is sometimes listed as the first part of a Legends West trio of novels that are linked only by theme.

1. *Ambrose Bierce and the Queen of Spades* (California, 1998) In 1880s San Francisco, the so-called Slasher has been leaving the corpses of his naked female victims in Union Square with a single spade playing card on their bodies.

2. *Ambrose Bierce and the Death of Kings* (Viking, 2001) Winter 1890–1891. As David Kalakaua (historical king of Hawaii) lies dying in a San Francisco hotel room, Bierce and Redmond are called upon to find a missing member of the royal entourage.

3. *Ambrose Bierce and the One-Eyed Jacks* (Viking, 2003) At the behest of millionaire publisher "Willie" Hearst, Bierce and Redmond investigate two murders and the theft of intimate photos of Hearst's mistress.

4. *Ambrose Bierce and the Trey of Pearls* (Viking, 2004) In 1892 Bierce and Redmond look into the shooting death of popular preacher and notorious ladies' man Henry Devine. Novelist Gertrude Atherton is among the historical characters who put in an appearance.

5. *Ambrose Bierce and the Ace of Shoots* (Viking, 2005) Train-robber Oz Bird has sworn vengeance on the Southern Pacific Railroad and Colonel Studely, owner of a Wild West show that employs Bird's ex-wife Dora Pratt.

Hall, Parnell

I. Stanley Hastings, aspiring actor, aspiring action-story writer, and licensed private investigator in New York, isn't very good at his paid vocation. In this series of one-word titles and with the begrudging help of his wife, Alice, Sergeant MacAuliff of the NYC police, and his lawyer and sometime-boss Richard Rosenberg, the whining, kvetching, self-deprecating Stanley stumbles into solutions in a series of tributes to the power of relentless mediocrity.

1. *Detective* (Fine, 1987) Stanley gets diverted from his ambulance-chasing work by the death of a man who has told him a tale of drugs, gambling, and murder.

2. *Murder* (Fine, 1988) Hastings becomes the prime suspect in the murder of a pimp who dabbled in blackmail.

3. *Favor* (Fine, 1988) Having gone to Atlantic City on a marriage-saving mission, Stanley is soon up to his neck in loan-sharking, casino gambling, and murder.

4. *Strangler* (Fine, 1989) Hastings keeps turning up at the residences of prospective clients only to find that a serial killer has been there ahead of him.

5. *Client* (Fine, 1990) Stanley becomes a prime suspect again when the woman he has been tailing turns up dead in a motel room near Poughkeepsie.

6. *Juror* (Fine, 1990) Stuck on a jury in "the most boring case in history," Stanley's interest is piqued when a fellow juror is murdered.

7. *Shot* (Fine, 1991) Wealthy Melissa Ford hires Hastings to find out the intentions of her boyfriend David Melrose.

8. *Actor* (Mysterious, 1993) Stanley's acting ambitions are revived when he is asked to step into a production of *Arms and the Man* in rural Connecticut.

9. *Blackmail* (Mysterious, 1994) Hastings's female client wants him to deliver a package of money to a man who has some photographs.

10. *Movie* (Mysterious, 1995) Producer Sidney Garfellow hires Stanley to write the screenplay for a karate movie.

11. *Trial* (Mysterious, 1996) Stanley's ambulance-chasing boss Richard Rosenberg is defending Anson Carbinder, who is accused of murdering his wife.

12. *Scam* (**Mysterious, 1997**) Stanley becomes the prime suspect again when Cranston Pritchert hires him to find information about a woman he met in a singles bar.

13. *Suspense* (**Mysterious, 1997**) The wife of best-selling thriller author Kenneth Winnington hires Stanley to find out who's making threatening calls on their unlisted phone.

14. *Cozy* (**Carroll & Graf, 2001**) Stanley finds himself on a busman's holiday as two guests are murdered at the Blue Frogs Inn in New Hampshire, where Stanley and his wife, Alice, are staying for a week.

15. *Manslaughter* (**Carroll & Graf, 2003**) Joe Balfour is arrested for the murder of Philip T. Grackle, who is blackmailing him for a barroom brawl manslaughter in his past.

16. *Hitman* (**Pegasus, 2007**) When hit man Martin Kessler retires before completing his final contract and hires Stanley to protect him from his irate employers, the bodies start piling up.

II. Cora Felton, nationally known to crossword puzzle buffs as "the Puzzle Lady," is an elderly, grandmotherly lady who solves crimes, like Agatha Christie's (q.v.) Miss Marple. The resemblance ends there, however. Cora is cigarette smoking, hard drinking, and oft-married. Actually Cora despises crossword puzzles: her niece, Sherry Carter, does all the work. Cora does love to solve mysteries, however, a task she is much better at than Dale Harper, the bumbling police chief of her hometown of Bakerhaven, Connecticut, who often seeks her help.

1. *Clue for the Puzzle Lady, A* (**Bantam, 1999**) "Puzzle Lady" Cora Felton and her niece, Sherry Carter, have moved to Bakerhaven, Connecticut, to avoid Sherry's abusive ex-husband. Then the body of a young girl turns up in Bakerhaven Cemetery, and perplexed Police Chief Dale Harper needs some assistance.

2. *Last Puzzle and Testament* (**Bantam, 2000**) Wealthy, eccentric Emma Hurley has died and left a will that requires her potential heirs to compete in a puzzle-solving contest and appointed Cora as final judge.

3. *Puzzled to Death* (**Bantam, 2001**) Cora is cohost of the Bakerhaven crossword puzzle contest when bodies accompanied by crossword puzzles or doodles begin turning up.

4. *Puzzle in a Pear Tree, A* (**Bantam, 2002**) Cora and Sherry both have roles in the annual Bakerhaven Christmas pageant. A threatening acrostic and the return of Jonathan Dodsworth, now a Scotland Yard operative, add to the festivities.

5. *With This Puzzle I Thee Kill* (**Bantam, 2003**) Distinguished widower Raymond Harstein III moves into town and makes a play for oft-wedded Cora Felton. But some cryptograms warn Cora off the match.

6. *And a Puzzle to Die On* (**Bantam, 2004**) Cora's birthday bash at the Bakerhaven Library is interrupted when a corpse thrown from the second floor stacks hits her birthday cake, decorated as a crossword puzzle, dead center.

7. *Stalking the Puzzle Lady* (**Bantam, 2005**) Despite extreme misgivings, Cora Felton and her long-suffering niece, Sherry Carter, take to the road on a bus tour of personal appearances at supermarkets to promote Granville Grains.

8. *You Have the Right to Remain Puzzled* (**Bantam, 2006**) When small-time hustler and crossword designer Benny Southstreet sues Cora for plagiarism, and then winds up dead, Cora is hard-put to protect her assumed identity as the Puzzle Lady.

9. *Sudoku Puzzle Murders, The* (**St. Martin's, 2008**) The body of a man found slain behind the abandoned Tastee Freez in Bakerhaven has a clipping from a New York City newspaper containing a sudoku and a crossword puzzle. Includes four sudokus contributed by *New York Times* puzzle expert Will Shortz.

Hall, Patricia

PSEUDONYM OF Maureen O'Connor

Laura Ackroyd, reporter for the *Bradfield Gazette,* and Detective Chief Inspector Michael Thackeray are still a couple after more than a dozen mysteries despite differences in temperament (she is lively; he is a brooder) and, quite often, disagreements about the guilt or innocence of the people under investigation. This series, by a native of Bradford (the original for Bradfield, presumably), set in Yorkshire, England, has the requisite North of England feeling. *The Masks of Darkness* (St. Martin's, 2004) is not an Ackroyd-Thackeray novel.

1. *Death by Election* (**St. Martin's, 1994**) Local reporter Laura Ackroyd and newly arrived DCI Michael Thackeray come together during a hotly contested local election in Bradfield, Yorkshire, England, as a student is murdered, a politician commits suicide, and Ackroyd's former professor is accused of homicide.

2. *Dying Fall* (**St. Martin's, 1995**) "The Heights," a grim Council housing estate in central Bradfield, was the scene of a murder 10 years ago.

3. *Dead of Winter* (**St. Martin's, 1997**) Development planners and New Agers clash as a sales agent for Cheetham and Moore Estate Agency dies in a truck crash. UK title: *In the Bleak Midwinter.*

4. *Perils of the Night* (**St. Martin's, 1998**) Ackroyd goes undercover as a hooker as Bradfield residents are running prostitutes off the streets and a student who was doing some hooking on the side is murdered.

5. *Italian Girl, The* (**St. Martin's, 2000**) Bones unearthed at a construction site may belong to a teenage girl missing since Coronation Day 1953.

6. *Dead on Arrival* (**St. Martin's, 2001**) Ackroyd goes on assignment to London to investigate the smuggling of illegal aliens, while Thackeray looks into the murder of a prominent Pakistani businessman in Bradfield.

7. *Skeleton at the Feast* (**St. Martin's, 2002**) Thackeray, exiled from Bradfield during the investigation into the shooting of one of his detectives, travels to his alma mater, Oxford University, where he is asked by a former tutor to look into the disappearance of an Oxford don named Mark Harrison.

8. *Deep Freeze* (**St. Martin's, 2003**) Abortion is an issue that divides many, including Ackroyd and Thackeray. When a young girl is shot dead as she walks out of the May Anderson Hospital, some think that the surgeon who runs the abortion unit may have been the real target.

9. *Death in Dark Waters* (**St. Martin's, 2004**) Ackroyd investigates the drug dealers controlling the Wuthering Heights estate and undermining any attempts to improve the area, while Thackeray looks into the case of the son of a wealthy businessman who is in a coma after being supplied with **Ecstasy**.

10. *Dead Reckoning* (**St. Martin's, 2005**) Simon Earnshaw, scion of the family that owns Earnshaw's Mill, is murdered; the mill is on the brink of bankruptcy; the mill's union is threatening strike action if the mill cuts staff; and racial tensions are heated by the far-right British Patriotic Party.

11. *False Witness* (**Allison & Busby [UK], 2004**) Although a black teenager has been arrested for the murder of unpopular teacher Peter Graves, a number of people, including Ackroyd, have doubts about the youth's guilt. Not yet published in the United States.

12. *Sins of the Fathers* (**Allison & Busby [UK], 2005**) This seems to be a family massacre, with the father missing. But who is Gordon Christie? Who is he hiding from? Who is looking for him besides the police? Not yet published in the United States.

13. *Death in a Far Country* (**Allison & Busby [UK], 2007**) The unidentified body of a young girl is found in a canal, while Ackroyd

gets involved in the brouhaha surrounding the appointment of a female chairman of the local football team. Not yet published in the United States.

14. *By Death Divided* (Allison & Busby [UK], 2008) Abused wife Jenny Holden finds refuge in a women's shelter, but her daughter Anna is missing. Not yet published in the United States.

Hall, Robert Lee

Given the proliferation of historical mystery novels, it was probably inevitable that the shrewd, multitalented, well-traveled, aphoristic Benjamin Franklin would get his own series. "Poor Richard" is found in London in the late 1750s acting as agent for Pennsylvania and solving crimes with the help of his assistant (and natural son), Nick Handy, in this entertaining series full of 18th-century-London ambience and historical tidbits.

1. *Benjamin Franklin Takes the Case* (St. Martin's, 1985) Ben's old printer friend, Eben Inch, is found dead and partially scalped in his own courtyard, mourned only by Nick Handy, his 11-year-old apprentice.
2. *Benjamin Franklin and a Case of Christmas Murder* (St. Martin's, 1991) Franklin suspects murder when a local merchant dies while presenting a Christmas Eve mummer's play.
3. *Murder at Drury Lane* (St. Martin's, 1992) Ben helps David Garrick's Drury Lane Theatre by devising improved stage lighting and investigating anonymous letters, attempted arson, and murder.
4. *Benjamin Franklin and a Case of Artful Murder* (St. Martin's, 1994) A missing gem, the Shenstone Diamond, is the subject of Franklin's investigations here.
5. *Murder by the Waters* (St. Martin's, 1995) Ben suspects that the attempted holdup of a stagecoach to Bath had been staged.
6. *London Blood* (St. Martin's, 1997) Magistrate John Fielding—who has his own series, by Bruce Alexander (q.v.)—seeks Franklin's aid when two unidentified women are found with their hearts cut out.

Hallinan, Timothy

Former college professor Simeon Grist, now a private investigator in Los Angeles, is another one of your tough but tender private eyes in this series of well-plotted, well-characterized mysteries with a good Southern California ambience. The marriage-shy Simeon has an off-again, on-again relationship with his Chinese American girlfriend Eleanor Chan.

1. *Four Last Things, The* (New American Library, 1989) The Church of the Eternal Moment has combined blackmail with New Age religion.
2. *Everything but the Squeal* (New American Library, 1990) Simeon is hired to find Aimee Sorrell, a 13-year-old runaway from Kansas City.
3. *Skin Deep* (Dutton, 1991) Grist is supposed to be keeping an eye on television series star Toby Vane, who has a secret history of abusing women.
4. *Incinerator* (Morrow, 1992) Simeon almost gets in over his head in a duel with the "Incinerator," a homicidal pyromaniac.
5. *Man with No Time, A* (Morrow, 1993) The children of Eleanor Chan's brother have been abducted and hidden somewhere in Chinatown.

6. *Bone Polisher, The* (Morrow, 1994) Grist is on the trail of a homophobe who kills gay men, then writes to their relatives exposing their sexual leanings.

Halter, Marek

The Book of Abraham has been called a Jewish *Roots*, because it is based on the author's research into the history of his own family. The Polish-born French human-activist writer dates the beginning of his narrative back to 70 CE and a scribe named Abraham, whose descendants are linked to Halter's ancestors, who were printers dating back to the days of Gutenberg. *The Book of Abraham* and its sequel form an interesting encapsulation of European history told through the story of one family.

1. *Book of Abraham, The* (Holt, 1986) A scribe named Abraham flees Jerusalem ahead of the Roman army, initiating a chronicle of births and deaths ending in the Warsaw ghetto in 1943. Translated from the French by Lowell Bair. Originally published as *Le memoire d'Abraham* in 1983.
2. *Children of Abraham, The* (Arcade, 1990) Opens with the unsolved murder of Hugo Halter on the outskirts of Jerusalem just prior to the Six Days' War, and follows the fortunes of the far-flung Halter cousins. Translated from the French by Lowell Bair. Originally published as *Fils d'Abraham* in 1989.

Hambly, Barbara (Joan)

I. Benjamin January, a "free man of color," is a multitalented person: musician, piano teacher, a Paris-trained physician, and a sometime detective in a series of historical whodunits. January, who has returned to New Orleans in 1833 after spending 16 years abroad, is acutely aware of the restrictions placed upon him by the mores of New Orleans, where degree of color (octoroon, quadroon, etc.) determines your place in the hierarchy. The evocation of antebellum New Orleans, with the exception of the modern-sounding dialogue, is very effective. Barbara Hambly, who made her reputation as a fantasy writer, has successfully branched into historical writing with novels like *The Emancipator's Wife* (Bantam, 2005).

1. *Free Man of Color, A* (Bantam, 1997) Benjamin January gets involved in investigating the murder of beautiful octoroon Angelique Crozat and becomes the scapegoat of the influential white suspects.
2. *Fever Season* (Bantam, 1998) During the cholera epidemic of 1834, January, mourning his recently deceased wife, becomes aware that free people of color are disappearing, perhaps into slavery.
3. *Graveyard Dust* (Bantam, 1999) Ben's own sister, voodoo priestess Olympe, has been accused of abetting the murder of Isaak Jumon by supplying a poison to Isaak's young wife.
4. *Sold Down the River* (Bantam, 2000) Ben goes undercover as a slave on the plantation of his former owner, the evil Simon Fourchet, to investigate possible sabotage, murder, and uprisings upstream from New Orleans.
5. *Die upon a Kiss* (Bantam, 2001) In 1835 January is in the orchestra of an Italian opera company in New Orleans when two members of the company are attacked, and a backer is murdered.
6. *Wet Grave* (Bantam, 2002) Benjamin becomes deeply involved in the investigation of the murder of a drunken prostitute and another murder much closer to home while trying to woo the mysterious Rose Vitrac.

7. *Days of the Dead* **(Bantam, 2003)** January and his recent bride, Rose, travel to Mexico at the behest of friend and fellow musician Hannibal Sefton (introduced in number 5), who is being held by a rich madman who believes that Sefton murdered his son.

8. *Dead Water* **(Bantam, 2004)** Benjamin and Rose have begun a school to educate young girls of color. But then the president of the bank where their money has been deposited tells them in confidence that an employee has cleaned out the bank.

II. The Darwath series began as a trilogy (boxed set: *The Darwath Trilogy*, Del Rey, 1989). Two Californians, Rudy Solis and Gil Patterson, have been transferred by the wizard Ingold Inglorion to his world of Dare, where the "Dark" have aroused themselves after thousands of years and threaten to take over. Punk and artist Rudy becomes a mage and academic. Gil becomes a warrior as Ingold desperately tries to keep the forces of the Dark at bay. Twelve years after Hambly concluded the trilogy, the world of the Keep of Dare faces a new menace: this time, a new global Ice Age, which threatens to make the world uninhabitable by humans.

1. *Time of the Dark, The* **(Del Rey, 1982)** The wizard Ingold recruits Californians Gil and Rudy to his threatened world where they become warrior and mage in an effort to stave off the encroaching Dark.

2. *Walls of Air, The* **(Del Rey, 1983)** Ingold and Rudy travel to the home of the wizards in Quo, seeking their help against the Dark, while Gil and Minalde, the Queen of Gae, seek knowledge of their own in the mysterious Keep.

3. *Armies of Daylight, The* **(Del Rey, 1983)** In the conclusion to the original trilogy, Rudy may have found a way to wipe out the Dark, but complications occur, and Rudy and Gil are forced to make a decision between returning to California or remaining on their adopted world.

4. *Mother of Winter* **(Del Rey, 1996)** Five years after the destruction of the Dark, a new menace, a crop-destroying "slunch," which portends a new Ice Age, makes itself known.

5. *Icefalcon's Quest* **(Del Rey, 1997)** Icefalcon, a minor character in earlier books, comes to the fore, as the inhabitants of the Keep of Dare struggle to rediscover 3,000-year-old lost technology.

III. Sun Wolf and Starhawk, another fantasy trilogy, features mercenary Captain Sun Wolf and his beloved Starhawk, who use white magic against black magic in the cities of Mandrigyn and Wenshar. Numbers 1 and 2 were published together as *The Unschooled Wizard* (Doubleday, 1987).

1. *Ladies of Mandrigyn, The* **(Del Rey, 1984)** The women of the City of Mandrigyn are quite insistent that Captain Sun Wolf and his mercenary army help them rescue their men from the mines of the evil Altiokis.

2. *Witches of Wenshar, The* **(Del Rey, 1987)** Although the witch Kaletha claimed to use the lost spells of the long dead witches of Wenshar only in the form of white magic, Sun Wolf has visions of evil magic and demon-controlling spells.

3. *Dark Hand of Magic, The* **(Del Rey, 1990)** Sun Wolf and his beloved Starhawk are still searching for a master wizard to teach him the skills needed to use the magic power he possesses.

IV. The four volumes of the Winterlands series are set in a world of wizards and dragons. The original novel, *Dragonsbane*, had to wait 14 years for a sequel, which was followed by two additional novels. Lord John Aversin and his lover, Jenny Waynest, have to battle some really evil demons before they can realize their destinies.

1. *Dragonsbane* **(Del Rey, 1985)** By slaying two dragons, Lord John Aversin earned himself the sobriquet "Dragonsbane." Young Gareth travels across the Winterland to persuade Lord John to rid the Deep of Ylferdun of the Black Dragon Morkeleb.

2. *Dragonshadow* **(Del Rey, 1999)** Lord John Aversin and mage-born Jenny Waynest, now husband and wife, return to the Winterlands to fight yet another dragon, but the real threat turns out to be demons from another plane of existence, who prey on both wizards and dragons.

3. *Knight of the Demon Queen* **(Del Rey, 2000)** In the winter following their summer ordeal against demons, John Aversin and Jenny Waynest find that their son Ian is haunted by demons, including archdemon Folcalor, who wishes no good to humanity.

4. *Dragonstar* **(Del Rey, 2002)** In the conclusion to the Winterlands series, Lord John Aversin sits in prison, condemned to die for consorting with demons, and a pitched battle rages between humans and the Hellspawn.

V. The Windrose Chronicles are another series involving a young lady, this time computer programmer Joanna, who is whisked from California to a universe next door, the Empire of Ferryth, where she teams up with Caris, a warrior of the Council of Wizards, and Antryg Windrose, a slightly crazy, imprisoned wizard in a series of adventures that takes them back and forth through the Gate in the Void into each other's worlds. Number 4 deals with the adventures of Kyra, a minor character from the earlier novels. *Darkmage* is an omnibus containing numbers 1 and 2 (Doubleday, 1988).

1. *Silent Tower, The* **(Del Rey, 1986)** Young computer programmer Joanna is kidnapped in California and whisked through the Gate in the Void to the world of the Empire of Ferryth, where she meets warrior Caris and slightly daffy wizard Antryg,

2. *Silicon Mage, The* **(Del Rey, 1988)** Back in California, Joanna rethinks her decision to betray Antryg and follows the new incarnation of Suraklin through the Void to rescue the wayward but basically good wizard.

3. *Dog Wizard* **(Del Rey, 1992)** Antryg Windrose and Joanna are living in California after they have been condemned to death in Ferryh. Then Joanna is kidnapped by someone in the robes of a mage.

4. *Stranger at the Wedding* **(Del Rey, 1994)** Kyra, a minor character in the previous novels, returns to her home in Angelshand determined to stop a wedding that portends the death of her sister Alix. UK title: *Sorcerer's Ward*.

VI. A pair of novels set in Edwardian England details the vampire subculture of early 20th-century Europe, as James Asher, his wife, Lydia, Charles Farren, the vampire Earl of Ernchester, and a host of other characters try to stop the destruction of vampires through exposure to sunlight. Fans of Anne Rice (q.v.) and Chelsea Quinn Yarbro (q.v.) will like these novels.

1. *Those Who Hunt the Night* **(Del Rey, 1988)** Oxford professor James Asher, at one time a British agent, is forced to help the vampires of Edwardian London, or his wife, biologist and female physician Lydia, will perish. UK title: *Immortal Blood*.

2. *Traveling with the Dead* **(Del Rey, 1995)** Lydia Asher is on the trail of her husband, James, who is on the trail of Charles Farren, the vampire Earl of Ernchester, and his mortal traveling companion, the mercenary Ignace Karolyi.

VII. Another pair of sword-and-sorcery novels set in another alternate world features the wizard Jaldis and his pupil Rhion, who discover a world on the side of the Dark Well in which magic doesn't exist. Published together as *Sun-Cross* (Guild America, 1992).

1. ***Rainbow Abyss, The*** (Del Rey, 1991) Blind, crippled, mute wizard Jaldis, who can see only by virtue of his magic, is horrified to discover a world on the other side of a Dark Well in which magic doesn't exist.
2. ***Magicians of Night, The*** (Del Rey, 1991) Rhion, apprentice of the wizard Jaldis, finds himself trapped in Nazi Germany with no certain way back to his own world.

VIII. *Sisters of the Raven* and *Circle of the Moon* are two novels in what may become parts of a longer feminist fantasy series inspired by Native American and ancient Egyptian lore. The women of Yellow City, where men have traditionally wielded the magic that has healed the sick and brought the rain, suddenly acquire magical powers.

1. ***Sisters of the Raven*** (Warner, 2002) The women of Yellow City have suddenly acquired magic powers, previously an all-male domain, with some mixed results.
2. ***Circle of the Moon*** (Aspect, 2005) Sun-mage-in-training Raeshaldis has received a psychic dream plea for help from a woman on a faraway island.

Hamilton, Laurell K.

I. Anita Blake, Vampire Hunter, is a federal marshal in an alternate world St. Louis, Missouri, where humans, the undead, and were-animals of various sorts coexist uneasily. Though mortal, Anita has some supernatural powers, including the ability to resurrect the dead. To keep her magical powers intact, and also to service the needs of her libido, Anita has recourse to six lovers, including a big-time vampire (Jean-Claude), a wereleopard (Micah), and a werewolf (Richard). This ribald, sexy, sometimes kinky series has built up a large following. Several omnibus volumes or sets have been published: *Club Vampyre* (Guild America, 1997; numbers 1–3); *The Midnight Cafe* (SFBC, 1997; numbers 4–6); *Black Moon Inn* (Berkley, 1998; numbers 7–8); *Anita Blake: Vampire Hunter Set* (four-volume boxed set, Jove, 2003; numbers 1–4); *Anita Blake, Vampire Hunter Omnibus* (Orbit [UK], 2005; numbers 1–3); and *Nightshade Tavern* (SFBC, 2005; numbers 9–10).

1. ***Guilty Pleasures*** (Ace, 1993) Vampire Hunter Anita Blake is forced by a 1,000-year-old master vampire to discover the identity of a serial murderer of vampires.
2. ***Laughing Corpse, The*** (Ace, 1994) The police enlist Anita's aid in stopping voodoo priestess Dominga Salvatore from creating zombies by reincorporating the souls of the deceased.
3. ***Circus of the Damned*** (Ace, 1995) Anita's services are fought over by Jean-Claude, reigning vampire master of alternate St. Louis, and Alejandro, an ambitious vampire who aspires to become the new master of the city.
4. ***Lunatic Cafe, The*** (Ace, 1996) As a member of the Regional Preternatural Investigation Team, Anita infiltrates the society of lycanthropes and shape-shifters to discover why lycanthropes are disappearing.
5. ***Bloody Bones*** (Ace, 1996) Anita is called upon to resurrect ancient dead from a cemetery to settle a property dispute between the family of the dead and a corporation that wants to develop the cemetery land.
6. ***Killing Dance, The*** (Ace, 1997) Anita's life is complicated enough, being courted by werewolf Richard and vampire Jean-Claude, but now someone has put a price on her head.

7. ***Burnt Offerings*** (Ace, 1998) Anita gets embroiled in a turf war between vampire and werewolf societies, as some firebug is torching vampire havens.
8. ***Blue Moon*** (Ace, 1998) When her werewolf lover, Richard, is accused of rape in rural Tennessee, Anita speeds to his defense.
9. ***Obsidian Butterfly*** (Ace, 2000) Anita is summoned to New Mexico by Edward (aka Death), a character from previous books, to investigate a series of nasty murders, mutilations, and flayings.
10. ***Narcissus in Chains*** (Berkley, 2001) Agonizing over making a decision between Richard the werewolf or Jean-Claude the vampire, Anita, further upset by the kidnapping of one of her were-leopards, wanders into kinky leather bar Narcissus in Chains.
11. ***Cerulean Sins*** (Berkley, 2003) Anita, Richard, and Jean-Claude are involved in some messy doings, as important vampiress Belle Morte demands that Jean-Claude return vampire Asher to her, a fate "worse than a stake through the heart."
12. ***Incubus Dreams*** (Berkley, 2004) As she gets her love life straightened out, Anita pursues a band of serial-killing vampires who preys on female strippers.
13. ***Micah*** (Jove, 2006) Anita travels to Philadelphia with Micah, her were-leopard lover, to reanimate a deceased federal witness.
14. ***Danse Macabre*** (Berkley, 2006) Anita discovers that she is pregnant. But who, or what, is the father? Meanwhile, she plays hostess to a gathering of North American vampire Masters of the City, ostensibly in St. Louis to witness a performance by a vampiric ballet troupe.
15. ***Harlequin, The*** (Berkley, 2007) Malcolm, the head of the vampire Church of the Eternal Life, is so desperate for help in dealing with the Harlequin that he turns to Anita and Jean-Claude.

II. Hamilton has started a new erotic fantasy series, involving faeries this time. The fey are not only terrific lovers, but members of the royal sidhe are addicted to sex. Real faeries seldom want to spend much time with humans, but Princess Meredith NicEssus, who has mixed faerie and human blood, has spent three years in Los Angeles as Merry Gentry, working in a detective agency that specializes in supernatural problems and magical solutions. This is another series of high imagination: sexy, funny, and full of memorable characters and situations.

1. ***Kiss of Shadows, A*** (Del Rey, 2000) Mixed faerie and human-blooded Merry Gentry (aka Princess Meredith NicEssus) has worked, disguised, for three years at a Los Angeles detective agency. Then her aunt, the Queen of Air and Darkness, causes Merry to be outed, to fulfill the queen's design for the faerie court.
2. ***Caress of Twilight, A*** (Ballantine, 2002) Still running her LA detective agency with the help of faery musclemen and a pet goblin, Merry takes on the case of film star Maeve Reed (actually a Seelie goddess), who needs her help in getting pregnant.
3. ***Seduced by Moonlight*** (Ballantine, 2004) Merry goes to St. Louis, the Unseelie court, and some really rough politics, while adding to her collection of sidhe lovers.
4. ***Stroke of Midnight, A*** (Ballantine, 2005) Merry intersperses wild sex with sidhe studs and a murder investigation, as a faery and a reporter get murdered inside the Unseelie headquarters.
5. ***Mistral's Kiss*** (Ballantine, 2006) Merry has given up detecting and has fully embraced her duties as Princess Meredith NicEssus, potential heir to the throne, including bedding her immortal sidhe guardsmen.
6. ***Lick of Frost, A*** (Ballantine, 2007) Meredith's bedding schedule is interrupted by Lady Caitrin of the Seelie court, who claims that she was raped by three of Meredith's guards.

Hamilton, Lyn

Toronto antiquities dealer Lara McClintoch is a globe-trotter who goes far afield—Mexico, Ireland, Thailand, Tunisia, Malta, and so forth—in her search for antiquities and to oblige her rich clients. This being a mystery series, she gets involved in homicide investigations wherever she goes. Author Lyn Hamilton is also a Toronto resident interested in antiquities.

1. *Xibalba Murders, The* (Berkley, 1997) The murder of an expert in Mayan history brings Lara McClintoch into the jungles surrounding Merida, Mexico, where she gets mixed up with the temples of the Mayan gods, modern-day Mayan rebels, and Xibalba, the Mayan underworld.
2. *Maltese Goddess, The* (Berkley, 1998) Lara flies to Malta to put the finishing touches on the interior of the new home of architect Martin Galea.
3. *Moche Warrior, The* (Berkley, 1999) Possession of authentic artifacts of the Moche, predecessors of the Inca, brings Lara into conflict with a black-market collector's chain and grave robbers in Peru.
4. *Celtic Riddle, The* (Berkley, 2000) Lara goes to County Kerry, Ireland, for the reading of Eamon Byrne's will, which presents his quarreling heirs with an exercise in puzzle solving.
5. *African Quest, The* (Berkley, 2001) While on a Tunisian tour, Lara gets sidetracked by the legend of a Carthaginian treasure ship at the bottom of the Gulf of Hammanet.
6. *Etruscan Chimera, The* (Berkley, 2002) In Rome Lara is hired by billionaire Crawford Lake to acquire the Bellerphon, a companion piece to the Chimera of Arezzo, one of the great Etruscan art treasures.
7. *Thai Amulet, The* (Berkley, 2003) Lara combines a buying trip to Thailand with a search for missing fellow-dealer William Beauchamp.
8. *Magyar Venus, The* (Berkley, 2004) Old flame Charlie Miller, aka Karoly Monar, unexpectedly turns up as curator of the Cottingham Museum and runs up a huge bill by purchasing the mysterious Magyar Venus.
9. *Moai Murders, The* (Berkley, 2005) While on vacation on Rapa Nui (aka Easter Island), Lara and her friend decide to register for the First Annual Rapa Nui Moai Congress, where they meet Jasper Robinson, who has his own theory about the Moai, the gigantic carved heads for which Easter Island is known.
10. *Orkney Scroll, The* (Berkley, 2006) After a supposedly authentic Charles Rennie Mackintosh writing cabinet turns out to be a fake, Lara ventures to Scotland's Orkney Islands to root out a network of art forgers and murderers.
11. *Chinese Alchemist, The* (Berkley, 2007) Lara is targeted by some ruthless criminals while trying to recover an 8th-century Tang Dynasty silver box with a formula for the elixir of immortality etched inside.

Hamilton, Steve

Steve Hamilton won both the Shamus and Edgar Awards for best first novel with *A Cold Day in Paradise*, and his subsequent novels have garnered critical praise and reader enthusiasm. The series concerns Alex McKnight, a Detroit cop who has retired to Paradise, on Michigan's Upper Peninsula, on disability with a bullet next to his heart. Somewhat reluctantly, Alex has taken out a private investigator's license, which leads him into a series of murder investigations on the US–Canada border.

1. *Cold Day in Paradise, A* (Thomas Dunne, 1998) Alex McKnight has retired to Michigan's Upper Peninsula on disability, but his past catches up with him after he takes out a private-detective license, and some local bookies are murdered.
2. *Winter of the Wolf Moon* (Thomas Dunne, 2000) Young Native American Dorothy Parrish disappears after approaching Alex with some unspecified problems. Drug-crazed hockey player Lonnie Bruckman seems to be at the center of Dorothy's problems.
3. *Hunting Wind, The* (Thomas Dunne, 2001) An old pal whom he hasn't seen in 30 years induces Alex to return to Detroit to help him find a former girlfriend he hasn't seen in decades.
4. *North of Nowhere* (St. Martin's, 2002) Alex has become so much of a recluse that friends in Paradise are concerned about him. Jackie Connery, proprietor of the bar where Alex sometimes hangs out, persuades Alex to join a poker session at the home of wealthy Win Vargas.
5. *Blood Is the Sky* (St. Martin's, 2003) Alex agrees to help Ojibway friend Vinnie Red Sky LeBlanc find his errant brother Tom, who hasn't returned from a job guiding a hunting party of wealthy Detroit men in the Canadian wilderness.
6. *Ice Run* (St. Martin's, 2004) Alex meets his new love, Constable Natalie Reynaud of the Ontario Provincial Police, at a hotel on the Canadian border, but matters don't prosper, as Natalie is shielding a Reynaud family secret.
7. *Stolen Season, A* (St. Martin's, 2006) On a frigid Fourth of July night, Alex and his sometime partner, Leon Prudell, save three men from a boating accident in Lake Superior's Waihkey Bay

Hammett, Dashiell

Dorothy Parker wrote that Hammett's detective was so hard-boiled "you could roll him on the White House lawn." Though Sam Spade, is without a doubt the most famous of the hard-boiled school of realistic private detectives, he actually figures in only one of Hammett's novels, *The Maltese Falcon*, and in some of the short stories. The unnamed "operative" who works for the San Francisco office of the Continental Agency stars in several earlier works. He differs from Sam Spade in one important respect: he carries a gun. Hammett based his Continental Op on the personality of a detective he met and admired during his service with the Pinkerton Agency. It is surprising to remember that Hammett also created the effervescent Nick and Nora Charles, the detective couple featured in *The Thin Man*. Though radio, television, and movie series eventually stretched these characters very thin indeed. Hammett only wrote one book about them. Just for the record, *The Glass Key* features Ned Beaumont as detective.

1. *Red Harvest* (Knopf, 1929) The Continental Op cleans up "Poisonville" by playing off the gangsters against each other.
2. *Dain Curse, The* (Knopf, 1929) Perhaps the Op's busiest case, this involves eight murders, one seduction, one jewel robbery, and a family curse. James Coburn played the Op in a made-for-TV movie.
3. *Blood Money* (World, 1943) Here are two linked adventures, "The Big Knockover" and "$106,000 Blood Money," previously published in *Black Mask* magazine.
4. *Continental Op, The* (Random House, 1974) A posthumous collection of stories is published here.

Hammond, Gerald

I. Keith Calder, ex-poacher, expert gunsmith, sports shop owner, partially unreconstructed rogue, and amateur sleuth, is the "hero" in these mysteries set in the town of Newton Lauder, Scotland. Keith's daughter Deborah sometimes does her own sleuthing in later books. Hunting and gun lore, Scottish local color, and quaint characters are featured in this long-running series.

1. *Dead Game* (Macmillan [UK], 1979) Keith Calder is a guest at a shoot on the Scottish Borders when one of the shooters is killed. Not published in the United States.
2. *Reward Game, The* (St. Martin's, 1980) A petty criminal has been shot-gunned to death in Keith's car, and naturally he is a suspect.
3. *Revenge Game, The* (St. Martin's, 1981) Calder is galvanized into action when an attempt to burn down his shop is followed by a nearly fatal attack on his wife.
4. *Fair Game* (St. Martin's, 1982) Ray Grass has left a strange will in which every bequest is bracketed with a grotesque request.
5. *Game, The* (St. Martin's, 1982) A high-class brothel on the outskirts of Edinburgh turns out to be a front for other high-priced businesses.
6. *Cousin Once Removed* (St. Martin's, 1984) When Keith refuses an offer from his local MP to buy a pair of dueling pistols, he is felled by a crossbow bolt.
7. *Sauce for the Pigeon* (St. Martin's, 1984) A charred Land Rover is found with a body in the driver's seat and over two dozen dead Wood Pigeons nearby.
8. *Pursuit of Arms* (St. Martin's, 1986) A shipment of guns for which Calder is responsible is hijacked, and two men are killed.
9. *Silver City Scandal* (St. Martin's, 1986) Keith testifies at the trial of Hugh Donald, who is accused of murdering Mary Spalding.
10. *Executor, The* (St. Martin's, 1987) After being named executor of Robin Winterton's estate, Calder learns that Winterton had been murdered and his valuable gun collection stolen.
11. *Worried Widow, The* (St. Martin's, 1987) The "worried widow" is Jenny Hendrickson, whose husband has been found fatally shot. Jenny doesn't believe that Sam committed suicide, as assumed, and asks Keith to look into the case.
12. *Adverse Report* (St. Martin's, 1989) Simon Parbitter, a struggling English writer, inherits a house in Scotland when his estranged uncle is killed in a shooting "accident."
13. *Stray Shot* (St. Martin's, 1989) Keith and Simon Parbitter team up again in the case of a missing dog and industrial espionage.
14. *Brace of Skeet, A* (St. Martin's, 1989) Keith's daughter Deborah takes charge of the investigation of a suspicious shooting accident at a local gun club.
15. *Let Us Prey* (St. Martin's, 1991) Calder and solicitor friend Ralph Enterkin investigate the poisoning death of a gamekeeper.
16. *Home to Roost* (St. Martin's, 1991) Local bobby Ian Fellowes narrates this tale of poaching and disappearance in which Deborah plays a large part.
17. *In Camera* (St. Martin's, 1992) Robert Hall quit his previous position after overhearing his employer contract to produce a rifle that could only be used for an assassination.
18. *Snatch Crop* (St. Martin's, 1993) Deborah Calder Fellowes investigates the kidnapping of 12-year-old Delia Thrower.
19. *Thin Air* (St. Martin's, 1994) There is no lack of suspects when foul-tempered tenant farmer Murdo Hemison is murdered.
20. *Hook or Crook* (St. Martin's, 1995) Calder's partner Wallace James takes inept fisherman Eric Bell on an angling trip in the Scottish Highlands.

21. *Carriage of Justice* (St. Martin's, 1996) Deborah and her uncle Ronnie think that they have unmasked a poacher, but the "poacher" may have a connection to a long unsolved murder.
22. *Sink or Swim* (St. Martin's, 1997) Ken Berry drowns while fishing. The official report claims that Colonel McInsch, his sworn enemy, tried valiantly to save him.
23. *Follow That Gun* (Macmillan [UK], 1997) Deborah is suspicious of Mr. Foster, agent for several major collectors, who always pays with large sums of cash and is known to another dealer under another name. Not published in the United States.

II. The Three Oaks series of novels, featuring retired British army officer John Cunningham, emphasizes dogs rather than guns. Cunningham is a gun-dog trainer, specializing in spaniels, in the Fife region of Scotland, who gets involved with mystery adventures rife with dog and hunting lore.

1. *Dog in the Dark* (St. Martin's, 1990) Invalided out of the army, John Cunningham sets up shop as a dog trainer, and soon inherits two loyal female helpers and some obnoxious neighbors.
2. *Whose Dog Are You?* (St. Martin's, 1991) While bird hunting on the Scottish coast with his wife, Cunningham turns up the floating corpse of an American financier.
3. *Doghouse* (St. Martin's, 1992) John's wife inherits a black Labrador and an oil painting from her uncle, who was the victim of a bizarre shooting accident. Originally published in the United Kingdom in 1989.
4. *Give a Dog a Name* (St. Martin's, 1993) A businessman in a hurry deposits a dog that has taken a double load of buckshot at Cunningham's kennel.
5. *Curse of the Cockers, The* (St. Martin's, 1994) A hit-and-run claiming the life of a petty thief leaves a spaniel pup and a complicated mystery on Cunningham's hands.
6. *Sting in the Tail* (St. Martin's, 1995) Somebody has cut the tail off of Clarence, a Springer Spaniel belonging to Cunningham's friend.
7. *Mad Dogs and Scotsmen* (St. Martin's, 1996) John's friend Noel Cochrane, boarding a black Lab named Jove with John, turns up unannounced to take Jove with him to America, and then a strange series of events occurs.
8. *Bloodlines* (St. Martin's, 1998) Cunningham becomes the prime suspect in the murder of oily neighbor Ben Garnet, who has tampered with John's champion spaniel.
9. *Twice Bitten* (St. Martin's, 1999) Cunningham's entire ménage comes under suspicion when young farm manager and part-time blackmailer Dougal Webb disappears.
10. *Dogsbody* (Macmillan [UK], 1999) Mrs. Hill's house has burned down, her housekeeper and her dead dog's body have disappeared, and a female corpse is found in the charred ruins. Not published in the United States.
11. *Shocking Affair, A* (Macmillan [UK], 1999) At Cunningham's behest, Henry Fitts takes a spaniel to his new owner, Sir Peter Hey. Sir Peter collapses and dies in sinister circumstances. Not published in the United States.
12. *Dead Weight* (Macmillan [UK], 2000) When lifetime busybody Jasmine Horner is found drowned, much to the satisfaction of many, Cunningham's friend Alastair Branch is arrested for murder. Not published in the United States.
13. *Illegal Tender* (St. Martin's, 2001) Cunningham's friend Henry Fitts gets involved in saving a local business and helping Elizabeth, his ward, after she has been robbed in an e-mail fraud.

III. The prolific Hammond, having abandoned Calder and Cunningham, is still publishing mysteries but with a host of different protagonists, many of them female. So far only nurse-physiotherapist Grace Gillespie has been featured in more than one book.

1. *Saving Grace* (Allison [UK], 2004) Nurse-physiotherapist Grace Gillespie decides that the supposed fall from a high school roof by her patient, Stuart Campbell, was no accident. Not published in the United States.
2. *Heirs and Graces* (Allison [UK], 2005) Stuart's uncle Duncan Cameron proves to be a burden for the newly married Grace and Stuart when he suffers a stroke, and even more so when he dies. Not published in the United States.

Hamner, Earl, Jr.

Hamner's warm and gently humorous stories of the mountain folk of Virginia during the Depression were the inspiration for the TV series *The Waltons*. These two books are companion pieces covering roughly the same time, 1933. While they focus on 15-year-old Clay-Boy, oldest of the eight Spencer children, the large circle of family and friends surrounding him at Spencer's Mountain is well drawn. TV script writer and producer Hamner also created *Falcon Crest*.

1. *Spencer's Mountain* (Dial, 1961) The action starts with Clay-Boy's first deer hunt at Thanksgiving and continues through the next summer's romance and preparation for departure to college.
2. *Homecoming, The* (Random House, 1970) This short novel covers the dramatic Christmas Eve when Clay fails to return home when expected and young Clay-Boy goes out in search of his father.

Handler, David

I. Stewart "Hoagy" Hoag produced a highly praised first novel, but can't seem to come up with a successor, so he is reduced to being a ghostwriter and a part-time sleuth. Hoagy isn't particularly troubled by his creative block or by personal angst, as he wisecracks his way through a series of amusing stories set in the publishing and entertainment worlds.

1. *Man Who Died Laughing, The* (Bantam, 1988) Hoag is hired to ghostwrite the memoirs of Sunny Day, part of the former smash-hit comedy team Knight and Day.
2. *Man Who Lived by Knight* (Bantam, 1989) Tristram Scarr, reclusive rock star for whom Hoagy is ghosting an autobiography, has the kind of lifestyle that embodies every negative feeling parents have about rock 'n' roll.
3. *Man Who Would Be F. Scott Fitzgerald, The* (Bantam, 1990) Hoagy is helping Sheffield Noyes to write his autobiography, which is an expose of the New York celebrity publishing scene.
4. *Woman Who Fell from Grace, The* (Doubleday, 1991) Hoag is writing the sequel to all-time best-seller *Oh, Shenandoah* 50 years after the accidental death of its author.
5. *Boy Who Never Grew Up, The* (Doubleday, 1992) Heading to Los Angeles to ghost-write a memoir for Hollywood director Matthew Wax, Hoagy finds himself in the middle of a divorce war.
6. *Man Who Cancelled Himself, The* (Doubleday, 1995) Hoagy is ghostwriting the autobiography of children's television star Lyle "Uncle Chubby" Hudnut, who is attempting his comeback after a morals rap.
7. *Girl Who Ran Off with Daddy, The* (Doubleday, 1996) Thor Gibbs, legendary author, turns up at Hoagy's Connecticut retreat with his stepdaughter, 18-year-old Clethra. Then Thor turns up dead in a pond.

8. *Man Who Loved Women to Death, The* (Doubleday, 1997) Hoagy, living in Manhattan with his ex-wife Merilee, his 18-month-old daughter, Tracy, and his exigent basset hound, Lulu, receives strange manuscripts from someone who calls himself the Answer Man.

II. New York film critic Mitch Berger and beautiful African American Connecticut state trooper Desiree Mitry make an intriguing pair of investigators. Mitch, author of film reference books and grieving widower, has retreated to Big Sister, a private island off Dorset, Connecticut, and Desiree, who is fond of stray cats and has a talent for drawing, which she is trying to foster in art classes at the famed Dorset Academy, meet when Mitch discovers the body of his landlady's husband in a garden plot. This odd couple develops a romance amid a crowd of interesting and believable small-town characters in a readable series embedded with film trivia.

1. *Cold Blue Blood, The* (St. Martin's, 2001) Echoes of the past surface on Big Sister Isle when Mitch Berger turns up the body of his landlady's second husband, and Connecticut state trooper Desiree Mitry leads the investigation of the crime.
2. *Hot Pink Farmhouse, The* (St. Martin's, 2002) Big Sister Isle residents are divided between pro-development locals and those who don't want their community to change. Eccentric sculptor Wendell "Hangtown" Frye and his two daughters play large roles here.
3. *Bright Silver Style, The* (St. Martin's, 2003) As if the arrival of Academy Award winner Esme Crockett and her husband, Tito Molina, aren't excitement enough for the denizens of Dorset, Tito proceeds to jump, fall, or be pushed off a cliff.
4. *Burnt Orange Sunrise, The* (St. Martin's, 2004) A "cut-off-from-civilization" caper set in Astrid's Castle, a snowbound inn in Connecticut, this one involves reclusive pioneer film director Ada Geiger and a series of unnatural deaths.
5. *Sweet Golden Parachute, The* (St. Martin's, 2006) A family feud in Dorset may be behind the murder of a homeless man known as Pete, found near the home of famed chef Poochie Vickers.

III. Handler has also written a pair of novels about Danny Levine, who struggles with his Jewish identity, his waistline, and relationships with the opposite sex.

1. *Kiddo* (Ballantine, 1987) In 1962, 13-year-old Danny Levine is going through the usual adolescent tribulations.
2. *Boss* (Ballantine, 1988) Danny's year in Europe helps him to prepare for marriage and work at his father's business.

Haney, Lauren

PSEUDONYM OF Betty J. Winkelman

This mystery series goes far back into history. Lieutenant Bak of the Medjay police is an operative during the reign of the redoubtable Queen Hatshepsut in 18th Dynasty Egypt (c. 1500 BCE). Exiled because of his overzealousness in raiding a brothel frequented by Egypt's high and mighty, Bak's investigatory abilities are such that he is still called upon to solve messy cases. These novels are nothing special in the way of mysteries, but the evocation of ancient Egypt makes them worth reading.

1. *Flesh of the God* (Avon, 2003) In this prequel, young Lieutenant Bak gets himself exiled to faraway Buhen in the Nile valley after leading his charioteers on a raid of a house of pleasure frequented by Egyptian VIPs.

2. *Right Hand of Amon, The* (**Avon, 1997**) While investigating the murder of a high-born army officer, Lieutenant Bak discovers a plot to assassinate the king.

3. *Face Turned Backward, A* (**Avon, 1999**) Lieutenant Bak and his Medjay police are called in to investigate the stabbing murder of the farmer Penhet. Then Commandant Thuty's office reports smuggling up the Nile.

4. *Vile Justice, A* (**Avon, 1999**) Are four odd murders the wrath of the gods or the work of human hands?

5. *Curse of Silence, A* (**Avon, 2000**) Queen Hatshepsut has sent her cousin Amonked to Lower Nubia to determine whether she should withdraw troops from the region. Then a local prince is murdered.

6. *Place of Darkness, A* (**Avon, 2001**) In transit from his exile in Buhen to a new posting, Bak stops at the capital in hopes of investigating a case of the plundering and smuggling of relics from ancient tombs. There is also trouble at the partially built temple dedicated to the divine Queen Hatshepsut.

7. *Cruel Deceit, A* (**Avon, 2002**) The Feast of Opet is the scene of the murder of a Hittite horse trader. Bak has no authority in this case, but then similar murders occur within the sacred precincts of the Lord Amon.

8. *Path of Shadows, A* (**Avon, 2003**) Lieutenant Bak is sent on what proves to be a bloody mission to find the missing explorer Minnakht.

Hansen, Joseph

I. Dave Brandstetter, Los Angeles insurance investigator, is true to the hard-boiled private-eye model of Dashiell Hammett (q.v.) and Raymond Chandler (q.v.), with one exception: he happens to be homosexual. Hansen's novels are distinguished by their matter-of-fact, nonapologetic presentation of a homosexual hero and the ambience in which he operates. They display strong characters, an authentic Southern California atmosphere, and an unblinking look at the underside of society. *Brandstetter and Others* (Countryman, 1984) contains two Brandstetter stories.

1. *Fadeout* (**Harper, 1970**) Fox Olsen's wrecked car is found, but his body is missing. Brandstetter, mourning his dead lover, is called in to investigate.

2. *Death Claims* (**Harper, 1973**) Rare book dealer John Oats is the victim of a suspicious drowning.

3. *Troublemaker* (**Harper, 1975**) A young homosexual is the prime suspect in the murder of the co-owner of a gay bar.

4. *Man Everybody Was Afraid Of, The* (**Holt, 1978**) When the despotic police chief of La Caleta is murdered, his colleagues instantly arrest a local gay activist leader.

5. *Skinflick* (**Holt, 1979**) Now an independently wealthy freelance investigator, Dave examines the murder of antipornography crusader Gerald Dawson.

6. *Gravedigger* (**Holt, 1982**) A young member of a strange desert cult, who is carrying a large insurance policy on her life, is missing.

7. *Nightwork* (**Holt, 1984**) Independent trucker Paul Myers is killed in a fiery crash shortly after he insured his life for $100,000.

8. *Little Dog Laughed, The* (**Holt, 1986**) Blind 17-year-old Chrissie finds the body of her father, prominent journalist Adam Streeter.

9. *Early Graves* (**Mysterious, 1987**) A serial killer is murdering young men dying of AIDS.

10. *Obedience* (**Mysterious, 1988**) After Brandstetter is interviewed by *Time* magazine, he is hired to investigate the murder of a prominent Vietnamese businessman.

11. *Boy Who Was Buried This Morning, The* (**Viking, 1990**) Although officially retired, Dave gets involved when a right-wing paramilitary group turns outdoor "war games" into a deadly affair.

12. *Country of Old Men, A* (**Viking, 1991**) In what the subtitle calls "the last Dave Brandstetter mystery," Dave comes out of retirement again to investigate an abused child's account of kidnapping and murder.

II. Having "finished off" Brandstetter, Hansen embarked upon a series of novels about struggling young gay writer Nathan Reed. Set in World War II Los Angeles, they are ostensibly mystery novels but are primarily pictures of life in the gay subculture of Southern California in the 1940s.

1. *Jack of Hearts* (**Dutton, 1995**) Seventeen-year-old Nathan Reed is struggling with his writing and self-doubt about his sexual identity, and getting involved with a theater group and an attempted murder.

2. *Living Upstairs* (**Dutton, 1993**) Nathan is working to finish his first novel, disturbed by the disappearance of his lover, painter Hoyt Stubblefield.

Harding, Paul

PSEUDONYM OF P. C. Doherty

Sir John Cranston, Falstaffian coroner of London, and his clerk Brother Athelstan, a priest with "a nose for mischief," are the protagonists in this mystery series set in late 14th-century England written by P. C. Doherty (q.v.) under the pseudonym of Paul Harding. As with all of Doherty's historical mysteries, the Sorrowful Mysteries of Brother Athelstan are characterized by intricate plots and interesting evocations of the times. Numbers 8 through 10 were published with "Paul Doherty" listed as author.

1. *Nightingale Gallery, The* (**Morrow, 1992**) Nobleman of the court, Sir Thomas Springall, has been poisoned, and the servant involved has apparently committed suicide. London coroner, Sir John Cranston, who makes Falstaff look like a pantywaist, and his clerk, the canny priest Brother Athelstan root out some intrigue in high places.

2. *Red Slayer, The* (**Morrow, 1994**) A locked-room mystery in which Sir Ralph Whitton, constable of the Tower of the London, is found with his throat slit in a locked and guarded room. UK title: *The House of the Red Slayer*.

3. *Murder Most Holy* (**Headline [UK], 1992**) Sir John Cranston has a murder case on his hands that he wants to solve within two weeks. However, his assistant, Brother Athelstan, has his own plate full, as renovation work at the sanctuary at St. Erconwald's has unearthed a skeleton. Not published in the United States.

4. *Anger of God, The* (**Headline [UK], 1993**) In 1379 John of Gaunt is Regent of England, but he has problems: the peasants are planning a revolt and a series of murders necessitates the intervention of Sir John Cranston and Brother Athelstan. Not published in the United States.

5. *By Murder's Bright Light* (**Headline [UK], 1994**) The warship *God's Bright Light* drops anchor in the Thames. Then an entire night watch of the ship disappears. Not published in the United States.

6. *House of Crows, The* (**Headline [UK], 1995**) 1380. John of Gaunt wants the murders of the representatives from Shrewsbury solved before Parliament suspects him. Not published in the United States.

7. *Assassin's Riddle, The* (Headline [UK], 1996) After the corpse of Edwin Chapler is pulled from the Thames, more clerks are murdered. Not published in the United States.

8. *Devil's Domain, The* (Headline [UK], 1998) One of five French prisoners held by John of Gaunt at Hawkmere Manor (aka the Devil's Domain) is poisoned, and French retaliation is feared. Not published in the United States. Author listed as Paul Doherty.

9. *Field of Blood, The* (Headline [UK], 1999) Can three recent murders be assigned to one of Brother Athelstan's parishioners, already accused of being a multiple murderer? Not published in the United States. Author listed as Paul Doherty.

10. *House of Shadows, The* (Headline [UK], 2003) Brother Athelstan's rehearsals for the annual Christmas mystery play are interrupted by a series of murders at a Southwark tavern, murders that may have their source in the Great Robbery of the Lombard Treasure, which occurred 20 years before. Not published in the United States. Author listed as Paul Doherty.

Hardwick, Mollie

I. Fans of Jonathan Gash's (q.v.) Lovejoy may be interested in another English antiques dealer who doubles in sleuthing. Doran Fairweather is a quite different character from the raffish Lovejoy. Early in the series she marries Rodney Chelmarsh, vicar in the village of Abbotsbourne, Kent.

1. *Malice Domestic* (St. Martin's, 1986) A wealthy bachelor takes over Abbotsbourne's "great house," precipitating a series of deadly events.

2. *Parson's Pleasure* (St. Martin's, 1987) Doran is in Warwickshire on a working holiday tracking down Lady Timberlake's stolen antiques.

3. *Uneaseful Death* (St. Martin's, 1988) Fairweather finds the first murder victim in the parking lot of an antiques exhibition where she has been performing as an expert appraiser.

4. *Bandersnatch, The* (St. Martin's, 1989) Now wife to Rodney and mother of Kit, Doran buys a carved wooden cherub that could be a portrait of Kit but has a deadly provenance.

5. *Perish in July* (St. Martin's, 1990) A church fund-raiser performance of *The Yeomen of the Guard* in the village of Elvesham is marred by the murder of its leading soprano.

6. *Dreaming Damozel, The* (St. Martin's, 1991) Feeling depressed because of a miscarriage and the loss of her business partner, Doran branches out into the Pre-Raphaelites, and acquires some rare Rossetti drawings.

7. *Come Away, Death* (Fawcett, 1997) Doran sublets a friend's London flat. She finds the flat depressing, especially when the friend is murdered beside the Thames. An oath of revenge sworn during the reign of Richard II may have a bearing on the case.

II. *The Duchess of Duke Street* was a BBC-TV success before it took book form. Mollie Hardwick skillfully adapted the story of peppery and indomitable Louisa Trotter. From the Cockney scullery maid who dreams of being the best cook in London, to the honorary "Duchess" of Duke Street where her famed Bentinck Hotel is located, Louisa's story is always engaging. Rosa Lewis, who was the real-life inspiration for the fictional character of Louisa, is the subject of two biographies that will interest fans of the series: *The Duchess of Jermyn Street*, by Daphne Fielding (Little, Brown, 1964), and *Rosa Lewis*, by Anthony Masters (St. Martin's, 1977). An American edition titled simply *The Duchess of Duke Street* (Holt, 1976) contains numbers 1 and 2 listed below. There are large-print editions of all three novels published by Ulverscroft (UK).

1. *Duchess of Duke Street, The: The Way Up* (Futura [UK], 1976) Louisa rises from apprentice cook in 1900 to proprietor of the Bentinck; she marries, has a liaison with the Prince of Wales, and bears a daughter.

2. *Duchess of Duke Street, The: The Golden Years* (Futura [UK], 1976) With Lord Haslemere in permanent residence and their child with foster parents in the country, propriety and prosperity reign.

3. *Duchess of Duke Street, The: The World Keeps Turning* (Hamish Hamilton [UK], 1977) This book begins in 1911, takes Louisa through the war years, and ends with her daughter Lottie's coming to stay at the Bentinck.

III. Hardwick also wrote two novelizations of the *Upstairs, Downstairs* television series, produced by John Hawkesworth (q.v.): *The Years of Change* (Dell, 1974) and *The War to End Wars* (Dell, 1975) as well as two novelizations of *Thomas and Sarah*, a spin-off from the *Upstairs, Downstairs* series that never had a network showing: *Thomas and Sarah* (Sphere, 1978) and *Thomas and Sarah: Two for a Spin* (Sphere, 1979); and two volumes in the *Upstairs Story* series: *Sarah's Story* (Michael Joseph [UK], 1973) and *Mrs. Bridges' Story* (Michael Joseph [UK], 1975), which novelized the earlier lives of the series characters.

1. *Years of Change, The* (Dell, 1974) War threatens and Lady Bellamy goes down on the *Titanic*. See entry under John Hawkesworth.

2. *War to End War, The* (Dell, 1975) Rose becomes a part-time bus conductor and Mr. Hudson is a special constable.

3. *Thomas and Sarah* (Sphere [UK], 1978) No annotation available.

4. *Thomas and Sarah: Two for a Spin* (Sphere [UK], 1978) No annotation available.

5. *Sarah's Story* (Michael Joseph [UK], 1973) No annotation available.

6. *Mrs. Bridges' Story* (Michael Joseph [UK], 1975) No annotation available.

IV. Hardwick provided the novelizations for another television series, *Juliet Bravo*, which focused on two female police inspectors, neither of whom was called Juliet Bravo, who worked in the fictional town of Hartley Lancashire.

1. *Juliet Bravo 1* (BBC Books [UK], 1980) No annotation available.

2. *Juliet Bravo 2* (BBC Books [UK], 1980) No annotation available.

3. *Calling Juliet Bravo: New Arrivals* (BBC Books [UK], 1981) No annotation available.

V. A trio of Regency romances focused on the three Atkinson brothers and their marriages. Francis betrayed his wife for the arms of an aspiring actress. Ephraim risked his career for an unpopular cause. John was a clergyman blind to evil. Published in paperback originals. Number 1 was coauthored with Michael Hardwick.

1. *Atkinson Heritage, The* (Bantam, 1979) Coauthored with Michael Hardwick. No annotation available.

2. *Sisters in Love* (Troubadour, 1979) No annotation available.

3. *Dove's Nest* (Futura [UK], 1980) No annotation available. Variant title: *The Atkinson Century*.

Hardy, James Earl

Mitchell "Little Bit" Crawford is young, black, educated, and gay. Mitchell has a lot going for him but feels there is something lacking until he meets the love of his life, Raheim "Pooquie" Rivers, a black male model with acting ambitions. The B-Boy Blues series is about the up-and-down, on-again, off-again relationship between Mitchell and

Raheim. This is a basically optimistic series, full of slangy vernacular and campy one-liners, but we are treated to many outspoken comments about politics, whites, the treatment of gays, and issues such as AIDS.

1. *B-Boy Blues* (**Alyson, 1994**) Mitchell Crawford, young, black, educated, and gay, finally finds the "B-boy" of his dreams in Raheim Rivers, and falls in love.
2. *2nd Time Around* (**Alyson, 1996**) The dialogues of Raheim Rivers, with himself or with the people in his life, as he tries to patch things up with Mitchell after a lovers' tiff and tries to be a better father to his son than his own father was to him.
3. *If Only for One Night* (**Alyson, 1998**) A novel, told mostly in flashbacks, about Mitchell Crawford's affair with his high school gymnastics coach.
4. *Day Eazy-E Died, The* (**Alyson, 2001**) Shaken by the news that his idol, rapper Eazy-E, has AIDS, Raheim reexamines his life and his relationships, especially with Mitchell and his six-year-old son.
5. *Love the One You're With* (**Amistad, 2002**) Raheim has gone to Hollywood to chase stardom, and Mitchell finds it difficult to remain faithful to him, especially with temptations like jazz singer "Montee" Sims.
6. *House Is Not a Home, A* (**Amistad, 2005**) In what is billed as the conclusion to the series, Raheim and Mitchell prepare for the birthday party of Errol, Raheim's 15-year-old son, and try to work out their midlife crises.

Harington, Donald

Arkansas novelist Donald Harington has created a Faulknerian (q.v.) world in his novels about the rural town of Stay More in the Ozarks. Stay More, which is based on the real Ozarks town of Drakes Creek, where Harington spent his boyhood summers, is the home of some real originals, such as Dawny, who is five-years-old when the series starts, Latha Bourne, the postmistress, and a host of others. Some of the novels, such as *The Choiring of the Trees* and *With* are based on real events. The "Staymorons" know that they are backward but are quite dubious about "progress," at least what they see of it. Harington, who acknowledges Styron, Nabokov, and García Márquez as influences, is something of a magical realist, and it isn't easy to establish a chronology, so the novels are listed in publication order. *The Cherry Pit* (Random House, 1965), Harington's first novel, isn't a Stay More book, although part of it is set in Arkansas, nor is *Some Other Place, The Right Place* (Little, Brown, 1972), although there are constant references to Harington's earlier novels. Some critics (such as Peter Straub) feel that Harington is grossly underrated, while others find his humor outlandish and his stories tediously self-referential, but readers will want to see for themselves what the fuss is about.

1. *Lightning Bug* (**Delacorte, 1970**) Introduces the village of Stay More, Arkansas, and characters such as the five-year-old Dawny and postmistress Latha Bourne. Set in the 1930s. UK title: *Sounds of a Summer Night*.
2. *Architecture of the Arkansas Ozarks, The* (**Little, Brown, 1975**) The history of Stay More is divulged as we follow the fortunes of the Ingledew brothers and their descendants for 150 years.
3. *Cockroaches of Stay More, The* (**Harcourt, 1989**) Harington returns to Stay More after a hiatus of 14 years, this time to chronicle the doings of Stay More's cockroach population in anthropomorphic fashion with love affairs, fundamentalist preachers, religious philosophizing and the works.

4. *Choiring of the Trees, The* (**Harcourt, 1991**) More serious in tone than earlier Stay More books, this novel, based on a real event, chronicles the tribulations of Nail Chism, a young shepherd and moonshiner falsely convicted of rape and sentenced to the electric chair.
5. *Ekaterina* (**Harcourt, 1993**) A sort of *Lolita* in reverse and a tribute to Vladimir Nabokov, this is about Soviet refugee Ekaterina, who has a passion for little boys. Ekaterina winds up in the town of Stick Around (which is really Stay More), Arkansas.
6. *Butterfly Weed* (**Harcourt, 1996**) Doc Swain, Stay More's physician, doesn't make much money despite his natural and supernatural (he treats patients through their dreams) skills, so he is forced to teach a high school hygiene class, where he runs into some witchcraft.
7. *When Angels Rest* (**Counterpoint, 1998**) World War II. Twelve-year-old Dawny—inspired by battle correspondent Ernie Pyle—keeps the townsfolk of Stay More informed by his weekly newspaper, the *Stay Morning Star*. Then real GIs arrive, in training for the invasion of Japan.
8. *Thirteen Albatrosses* (**Holt, 2002**) Subtitle: *Or, Falling Off the Mountain*. Vernon Ingledew, 48 years old and rich from his Ingledew Ham business, takes it into his head to run for governor despite "albatrosses" such as his atheism, a common-law-wife, and opposition to handguns.
9. *With* (**Toby, 2004**) Based on a real incident, this is about seven-year-old Robin Kerr, who is snatched from her mother by former state trooper Sog Alan and imprisoned on the remote pinnacle of Mt. Madewell, just outside Stay More.
10. *Pitcher Shower, The* (**Toby, 2005**) Landon "Hoppy" Boyd, Stay More native who travels the Arkansas countryside showing early western films from a trailer mounted on his truck, runs into the comely Sharline Whitlow and the annoying Emmett Binns, an antifilm preacher.

Harper, Karen

I. Given the number of mystery series featuring famous historical characters, it was almost inevitable that the wily, feisty Queen Elizabeth I would get her own series. The series starts before Elizabeth becomes queen, when she is simply Elizabeth Tudor, half sister of Queen Mary I. An entertaining and reasonably accurate portrayal of Tudor times, it may not be quite up to the historical series of Anne Perry (q.v.) and Ellis Peters (q.v.) but is worth perusal by historical-mystery fans.

1. *Poyson Garden, The* (**Delacorte, 1999**) In 1558 Elizabeth Tudor, half sister of, and probable successor to, Queen Mary I, is playing a waiting game but is threatened by a poisoner, possibly backed by Mary, who is killing members of the Boleyn family, Elizabeth's maternal relatives.
2. *Tidal Poole, The* (**Delacorte, 2000**) Elizabeth Tudor's triumphal procession to coronation at Westminster Abbey is spoiled by the murder of a young woman that casts suspicion on several of her trusted friends.
3. *Twylight Tower, The* (**Delacorte, 2001**) The historical (probable) murder of Amy Robsart Dudley, wife to Robert Dudley, with whom Elizabeth is besotted, threatens Elizabeth's hold on the throne.
4. *Queene's Cure, The* (**Delacorte, 2002**) Elizabeth's conflict with two physicians over the best way to treat disease is forced to take second place when a plot against her life surfaces.

5. *Thorne Maze, The* (St. Martin's, 2003) Was her assailant in the Hampton Court maze really after Elizabeth, or was someone else the target?

6. *Queene's Christmas, The* (St. Martin's, 2003) Murder threatens to spoil the Yule celebrations at Queen Elizabeth's court.

7. *Fyre Mirror, The* (St. Martin's, 2005) In 1565 portrait artist Gil Sharpe, protégé of Elizabeth, becomes a suspect when a fellow artist and his serving boy die in a mysterious fire.

8. *Fatal Fashione, The* (St. Martin's, 2005) Queen Elizabeth's herb mistress reports the discovery of the body of Her Majesty's favorite starcher in a vat of starch.

9. *Hooded Hawke, The* (St. Martin's, 2007) While Elizabeth is on a summer outing in 1569 with Sir Francis Drake, an arrow barely misses her, hitting her falconer instead.

II. Karen Harper is the author of many contemporary romantic suspense novels as well as historical ones. The Maplecreek Amish trilogy is set in a contemporary Amish community. The trilogy is linked primarily by its location. *Down to the Bone* (Mira [Can.], 2000) is also set in an Amish community.

1. *Dark Road Home* (Signet, 1996) Terrorized by a stalker, Columbus, Ohio, attorney Brooke Benton flees with her seven-year-old niece to the isolated Amish community of Maplecreek. Then a hit-and-run driver kills four Amish teenagers.

2. *Dark Harvest* (Mira (Canada), 2004) Policewoman Kat Lindley, a refugee from the big city, and Amish leader Luke Brand hook up together when Maplecreek's residents are under attack from unknown assailants.

3. *Dark Angel* (Mira (Canada), 2005) Young spinster schoolteacher Leach Kurtz agrees to adopt the infant daughter of a friend dying from one of the hereditary diseases plaguing the Amish.

Harris, Charlaine

I. When this series starts, Aurora "Roe" Teagarden is a 28-year-old "professional librarian" in the small community of Lawrenceton, Georgia. During the course of the series, Aurora inherits money, gets married, and solves a number of cases as an amateur sleuth in this cozy mix of murder and social satire. Mississippi native Charlaine Harris now lives in Arkansas.

1. *Real Murders* (Walker, 1990) The latest meeting of the Real Murders Club of Lawrenceton, Georgia, several enthusiasts who discuss famous unsolved crimes, becomes the scene of a "real murder" when librarian Aurora Teagarden finds the slain corpse of a member.

2. *Bone to Pick, A* (Walker, 1992) Aurora suddenly becomes rich when the late spinster Jane Engle leaves her a fortune, but when she arrives to take possession of Miss Engle's home, she turns up a bashed-in human skull.

3. *Three Bedrooms* (Scribner, 1994) After Aurora decides to help her mother, Aida, a real-estate agent in Lawrenceton, the naked corpse of a rival Realtor turns up in the master bedroom of a house she is showing.

4. *Julius House, The* (Scribner, 1995) Aurora returns to Lawrenceton, marries rich, secretive businessman Martin Bartell, and moves into the former home of the T. C. Julius family, who disappeared mysteriously six years earlier.

5. *Dead over Heels* (Scribner, 1996) The corpse of Detective Sergeant Jack Burns, Aurora's local law-enforcement nemesis, is dropped into her yard from an airplane.

6. *Fool and His Honey, A* (St. Martin's, 1999) Regina, niece of Aurora's husband, turns up on their doorstep with a new and unexpected baby. Then, several hours later, Regina's husband turns up dead, and Regina disappears.

7. *Last Scene Alive* (St. Martin's, 2002) Roe's once-significant other, true-crime writer Robin Crusoe, turns up again, having written a best-selling novel with TV movie rights about their experience in number 1.

8. *Poppy Done to Death* (St. Martin's, 2003) Uppity Women, Aurora's book discussion group, comes to the fore as she investigates the murder of her stepsister-in-law.

II. Although set in a town called Shakespeare and with a heroine whose last name is Bard, this series has nothing to do with the playwright. Like the Aurora Teagarden series, this is a small-town mystery series, albeit with a darker tone. Although well-educated, Lily Bard works as a cleaning lady in the Arkansas hamlet named Shakespeare and tries to forget the terrible events of her past. But, of course, like all small towns in mystery and suspense series, Shakespeare has more than its share of stalkers, murderers, and other malevolent types. Lily is a more serious character than the chatty Aurora, and the series gains in depth and suspense what it lacks in humor and quaint locals.

1. *Shakespeare's Landlord* (St. Martin's, 1996) Lily Bard, self-rusticated cleaning lady in tiny Shakespeare, Arkansas, has good reason to avoid questions about her past. Unfortunately, she is the one who discovers the body of her former landlord in a plastic bag dumped in the local park.

2. *Shakespeare's Champion* (St. Martin's, 1997) Lily discovers the body of Del Packard with a 290-pound barbell across his throat in the gym where she works out every day, the third Shakespeare murder in two months.

3. *Shakespeare's Christmas* (St. Martin's, 1998) Lily returns to her hometown of Bartley for her sister Varena's wedding and is plunged into the investigation of an unsolved eight-year-old kidnapping.

4. *Shakespeare's Trollop* (St. Martin's, 2000) One of Lily's employers, the promiscuous Deedra Dean, comes to a sticky end in her car on a deserted road.

5. *Shakespeare's Counselor* (St. Martin's, 2001) Lily joins a local support group headed by professional counselor Tamsin Lynd, who has her own problems: a stalker who has apparently followed her from Cleveland to Shakespeare.

III. The Sookie Stackhouse, or Southern Vampire, mystery series is something of a change of pace from series I and II. Sookie Stackhouse, cocktail waitress in small-town Louisiana, has telepathic powers, which she could do without. She also has a vampire for a boyfriend, a fellow named Bill, and a bad lack of self-confidence. Sookie's adventures are a fast-paced, sometimes funny, combination of the mystery and horror genres. Omnibus volumes: *Dead in Dixie* (SFBC, 2003; numbers 1–3) and *Dead by Day* (SFBC, 2005; numbers 4–5).

1. *Dead until Dark* (Ace, 2001) Sookie Stackhouse, cocktail waitress in Bon Temps, Louisiana, meets the man of her dreams, who unfortunately turns out to be Bill the vampire.

2. *Living Dead in Dallas* (Ace, 2002) One vampire asks Sookie to use her telepathic skills to turn up another missing vampire. But no one is supposed to get hurt.

3. *Club Dead* (Ace, 2003) Trying to locate Bill, Sookie travels to Mississippi to mingle with the vampire elite at Club Dead, but she has a nasty surprise in store.

4. *Dead to the World* (Ace, 2004) Bill the vampire goes off to Peru on a research mission, leaving Sookie with the odious Eric, Bill's boss and the district's top vampire honcho.

5. *Dead as a Doornail* (Ace, 2005) Vampires, were-creatures, shape-shifters, and a fairy godmother are all targets for a sniper, who seems to have a grudge against nonhumans.

6. *Definitely Dead* (Ace, 2006) Surprisingly, considering that she is one of the undead, Sookie's cousin Hadley dies, and Sookie is given the task of cleaning out her apartment in New Orleans.

7. *All Together Dead* (Ace, 2007) Sookie attends a vampire summit on the shoes of Lake Michigan to aid vampire queen of Louisiana, Sophie-Anne LeClerq, who will be tried for the murder of her king.

IV. The Grave series is Harris's latest. It features Harper Connelly, who, having survived a hit from a lightning bolt, finds that she has the ability to find dead people, a skill that she tries to put to good use, with mixed results, in this trio of suspenseful mysteries laced with deadpan humor.

1. *Grave Sight* (Berkley, 2005) Harper Connelly, with her lightning-bestowed gift of finding dead people, travels to the Ozark town of Sarne, Arkansas, to find a missing teenage girl's body.

2. *Grave Surprise* (Berkley, 2006) When sceptical anthropology professor Clyde Nunley tests Harper's gift of clairvoyance in a Memphis cemetery, she turns up the corpse of missing 12-year-old Tabitha Morgenstern, whom Harper failed to locate in Nashville two years earlier.

3. *Ice Cold Grave, An* (Berkley, 2007) Harper locates the bodies of eight "runaway" boys in Doraville, North Carolina, much to the surprise of sceptical sheriff Sandra Rockwell.

Harris, Lee

PSEUDONYM OF Syrell Rogovin Leahy

I. Author Syrell Rogovin Leahy (q.v.) is best known for the two series of mysteries she writes as Lee Harris. The first, longer-running series features ex-nun and amateur sleuth Christine Bennett. Most of the mysteries, each of which has a holiday title and theme, are set in New York City or upstate New York. Christine, who eventually marries NYPD Sergeant Jack Brooks, has a way of coming up with answers to puzzles of the past in this cozy series.

1. *Good Friday Murder, The* (Fawcett, 1992) Christine Bennett comes out of the convent to investigate a 40-year-old murder in which a pair of developmentally disabled savant twins, now senior citizens, were accused of killing their mother on Good Friday in 1950.

2. *Yom Kippur Murder, The* (Fawcett, 1992) Chris Bennett befriends three elderly tenants who are engaged in a bitter dispute with a landlord who wants to gut their building on Manhattan's Upper West Side. Then one of the tenants, Nathan Herskovitz, is found dead in his apartment on Yom Kippur.

3. *Christening Day Murder, The* (Fawcett, 1993) After 30 years of being under reservoir waters, the town of Studsburg, New York is temporarily uncovered during a drought. Visiting a childhood friend, Christine pokes around the town, and uncovers the remains of a young woman hidden in the Catholic church.

4. *St. Patrick's Day Murder, The* (Fawcett, 1994) An off-duty police officer is shot and killed, apparently for no motive.

5. *Christmas Night Murder, The* (Fawcett, 1994) Father Hudson McCormick, expected for a Christmas party after seven years' absence, never shows up.

6. *Thanksgiving Day Murder, The* (Fawcett, 1995) More than a year ago Natalie Gordon went to buy a balloon at the Thanksgiving Day Parade and disappeared. When Christine is persuaded to investigate by Natalie's husband, she discovers that Natalie's past as well as her present is shrouded in mystery.

7. *Passover Murder, The* (Fawcett, 1996) Christine, now married to NYPD detective Jack Brooks, looks into the 15-year-old mystery of Iris Grodnik's disappearance and murder during a Passover seder.

8. *Valentine's Day Murder, The* (Fawcett, 1996) Three old buddies disappeared during Valentine's night on Lake Erie. Two bodies turned up, one with a bullet in it. Was Val, whose body was never found, a murderer?

9. *New Year's Eve Murder, The* (Fawcett, 1997) Chris, who now has a six-week-old baby, and her husband, Jack, visit friends on New Year's Eve, where they learn about a young woman who's been missing for several days.

10. *Labor Day Murder, The* (Fawcett, 1998) The popular fire chief of the town of Blue Harbor is shot to death—then his house is torched. The residents of Blue Harbor are close-mouthed about possible reasons for the crimes.

11. *Father's Day Murder, The* (Fawcett, 1999) Novelist Arthur Wein, the most famous member of the Morris Avenue Boys, is stabbed with an ice pick during the group's Father's Day reunion dinner.

12. *Mother's Day Murder, The* (Fawcett, 2000) After a young woman who claims to the natural daughter of Sister Joseph, beloved Superior at St. Stephen's, is murdered, Sister Joseph is the prime suspect.

13. *April Fools' Day Murder, The* (Fawcett, 2001) Willard Platt fakes his own murder as an April Fools' Day stunt, but then he is really murdered, some say deservedly, several hours later.

14. *Happy Birthday Murder, The* (Fawcett, 2002) Christine's late aunt May treasured two mementos: a note mourning the death of a young man lost in a Connecticut wood and an obituary commemorating a wealthy local manufacturer who committed suicide just after his 50th birthday celebration.

15. *Bar Mitzvah Murder, The* (Fawcett, 2004) This one is set in Jerusalem, as Christine accompanies her best friend, Melanie Gross, to the Holy Land to help celebrate the belated bar mitzvah of Melanie's cousin Gabe.

16. *Silver Anniversary Murder, The* (Fawcett, 2005) Old secrets are revealed as Chris gets a phone call warning her that a body will turn up that will be traced to the apartment of a couple who are celebrating their 25th wedding anniversary.

17. *Cinco de Mayo Murder, The* (Fawcett, 2006) An invitation to a sightseeing trip to Arizona reminds Chris of the fate of former high school classmate Heinz Gruner, who died 20 years earlier on Cinco de Mayo while hiking near Tucson.

II. A second mystery series, variously titled the Manhattan, or the New York, series, features veteran NYPD detective Jane Bauer, whose plans for retiring to a cushy desk job are interrupted again and again.

1. *Murder in Hell's Kitchen* (Fawcett, 2003) Jane Bauer, approaching retirement, is working in a special unit that tackles unsolved crimes. The crime she is investigating is the death, four years earlier, of Arlen Quill, found dead in the entryway to his apartment building.

2. *Murder in Alphabet City* (Fawcett, 2005) Back to work after a nearly fatal encounter with a killer, and newly appointed to detective first-grade, Jane is investigating a recent death that may be connected to an eight-year-old suicide—which may not have been a suicide.

3. *Murder in Greenwich Village* **(Fawcett, 2006)** This time the 10-year-old murder of African American undercover cop Micah Anthony is reopened.

Harris, Marilyn

PSEUDONYM OF Marilyn Springer

The Eden saga won immediate acceptance among readers of historical romance. Harris blends an authentic 18th- and 19th-century English background into her fast-paced stories, which cover three generations of the stormy Eden family. The tangles begin with the seduction of young Marianne, a fisherman's daughter, have a bloody resolution with her grandson's return to Eden Castle many years later, and finally bring the family through World War I.

1. *This Other Eden* **(Putnam, 1977)** A beautiful young servant girl spurns the advances of lecherous Lord Thomas Eden.
2. *Prince of Eden, The* **(Putnam, 1978)** Illegitimate Edward inherits the Eden fortune, but not the title, and goes off to help the poor.
3. *Eden Passion, The* **(Putnam, 1979)** Young John, the illegitimate son of Edward Eden, works in the Eden Castle scullery until tragedy sends him off to foreign lands.
4. *Women of Eden, The* **(Putnam, 1980)** John Murrey Eden casts a blight on all five Eden women surrounding him, but especially on young Mary when she falls in love with Burke Stanhope. The action takes place in 1870–1871.
5. *Eden Rising* **(Putnam, 1982)** Bereft of his womenfolk, and haunted by the consequences of past financial dealings, John Murrey Eden is nursed back to health by virtuous Susan Mantle.
6. *American Eden* **(Doubleday, 1987)** Lady Mary Eden and her husband, Burke Stanhope, move to Alabama after the Civil War, where they run afoul of white supremacists.
7. *Eden and Honor* **(Doubleday, 1989)** John Murrey Eden disrupts a family reunion at Eden Castle at the turn of the century. This sees the Eden clan through the Boer War and World War I.

Harris, Mark

I.   Henry W. Wiggen, pitcher for the New York Mammoths baseball team, tells the story of his life and rise to fame in baseball. His semi-literate prose and exuberant vernacular give the tales a special humor as Wiggen grapples with universal concerns—the price of success, the death of a friend, aging gracefully, and so forth. Baseball adds flavor to the novels but is no barrier to readers not especially interested in the sport. Harris wrote the screenplay for *Bang the Drum Slowly*, a 1973 film starring Robert De Niro and Michael Moriarty.

1. *Southpaw, The* **(Bobbs-Merrill, 1953)** Pitcher Henry Wiggen moves up the baseball ladder from Perkinsville to the major leagues.
2. *Bang the Drum Slowly* **(Knopf, 1956)** His teammates gradually become aware that catcher Bruce Pearson is dying of Hodgkin's disease.
3. *Ticket for a Seamstitch, A* **(Knopf, 1957)** Catcher Piney Woods is being followed around the country by a devoted female fan.
4. *It Looked Like for Ever* **(McGraw-Hill, 1979)** Henry, now 39 and minus his fastball, is passed over for manager of the Mammoths and released.

II.   In this pair of wildly funny novels, college professor and novelist Lee Youngdahl tries to work his way through some personal crises. The stories are told through the letters and other documents written by and to Youngdahl.

1. *Wake Up, Stupid* **(Knopf, 1959)** Lee Youngdahl, professor of English at a San Francisco college, having just mailed a one-act play to his agent, is hit by an identity crisis.
2. *Lying in Bed* **(McGraw-Hill, 1984)** Now somewhat older, Youngdahl is smitten with a young student's physical charms and literary ability.

Harris, Thomas

With a big assist from Anthony Hopkins's Oscar-winning performance in the movie version of *The Silence of the Lambs* (1991), Hannibal "the Cannibal" Lecter has become an almost legendary fictional villain. The brilliant but insane psychologist and serial killer was first introduced in *Red Dragon*, but it was *The Silence of the Lambs,* in its book and movie versions, that really put him on the map. *Hannibal*, which is a sequel, and *Hannibal Rising*, which is a prequel that describes how Hannibal got that way, were generally regarded as disappointments. The reclusive Thomas Harris, a Mississippi native, has also written *Black Sunday* (Dutton, 1974), which describes an extremist Arab plot to bomb the Super Bowl.

1. *Hannibal Rising* **(Delacorte, 2006)** A prequel describing the earlier life of Hannibal Lecter, the murder of his younger sister, Mischa, and his love interest "Lady Mursasaki."
2. *Red Dragon* **(Putnam, 1981)** FBI agent and forensic expert Will Graham, the protagonist who tracks down a serial killer known as Red Dragon, has a traumatic experience with psychologist Hannibal Lecter along the way. Variant title: *Manhunter*, which was the title of the first movie version (1986). Another movie version of *Red Dragon* was made in 2002.
3. *Silence of the Lambs, The* **(St. Martin's, 1988)** FBI trainee Clarice Starling, in an attempt to track down a serial flayer-killer named Buffalo Bill, interviews criminally insane Hannibal Lecter in his jail cell. The movie version (1991) produced Oscars for Jodie Foster (Clarice) and Anthony Hopkins (Hannibal).
4. *Hannibal* **(Delacorte, 1999)** In a novel that delves into his past, Hannibal comes to the fore again as he tries to control the flow of time and bring his murdered sister, Mischa, back to life again. Movie version made in 2001.

Harrison, Harry

I.   Prolific science-fiction writer, editor, and critic Harry Harrison's most popular continuing character is undoubtedly "Slippery Jim" Di-Griz, aka "the Stainless Steel Rat," con man, thief, and antihero of a series of stories set in the high-tech (but recognizably hip) 25th century. Slippery Jim has his own code of morals and a satirical view of his (and our) society. This is lightweight entertainment full of fast action, humor, and lots of weird ideas. *The Adventures of the Stainless Steel Rat* (Berkley, 1978) contains numbers 2, 3, and 4. *A Stainless Steel Trio* (Tor, 2003) contains numbers 1, 8, and 9. *Stainless Steel Visions* (Tor, 1993), a collection of Harrison's short fiction, contains one Stainless Steel Rat story and "Roommates," the basis for the movie *Soylent Green.*

1. *Stainless Steel Rat Is Born, A* **(Bantam, 1985)** Jim narrates the story of his youth and early adult years when he was trained by The Bishop, an archcriminal.

2. *Stainless Steel Rat, The* (Pyramid, 1961) First published book in series. Supercriminal DiGriz is drafted into the ranks of the supersleuths to catch another supercriminal.

3. *Stainless Steel Rat's Revenge, The* (Walker, 1970) Slippery Jim is directed to find out why interstellar warfare, supposedly an impossibility, has become a going concern again.

4. *Stainless Steel Rat Saves the World, The* (Putnam, 1972) Someone back in 1984 is meddling with time, and the Stainless Steel Rat has to travel to that year to save the galaxy.

5. *Stainless Steel Rat Wants You!, The* (Doubleday, 1979) Slippery Jim saves the galaxy from some disgusting, lecherous, and somewhat simpleminded BEMs.

6. *Stainless Steel Rat for President, The* (Bantam, 1982) The Stainless Steel Rat investigates the dictatorship on Paraiso-Aqui, the tourist trap planet.

7. *Stainless Steel Rat Gets Drafted, The* (Bantam, 1987) Jim is looking to avenge the murder of his mentor-in-crime, the fabled Bishop.

8. *Stainless Steel Rat Sings the Blues, The* (Bantam, 1994) Caught red-handed, Slippery Jim is forced to infiltrate (as a rock band leader) a prison planet and recover an alien artifact.

9. *Stainless Steel Rat Goes to Hell, The* (Tor, 1996) Jim's beloved wife, Angelina, disappears in the Temple of Eternal Truth. Jim, getting to the bottom of things, turns up Justice Slakey, a mad scientist who is create a transuranic element that stops time and confers immortality.

10. *Stainless Steel Rat Joins the Circus, The* (Tor, 1999) The Stainless Steel Rat takes a job infiltrating a suspicious circus and finds himself and his family enmeshed in a planetwide swindle.

II. Another popular lightweight, humorous, satirical series features Bill the Galactic Hero. Bill is the perfect soldier: brave, strong, and dumb. Over the course of his adventures, Bill's body has become almost entirely rebuilt with spare (not always human) parts, but he retains his love of beer and girls. Originally a one-book hero, Bill was revived by Harrison in collaboration with other writers. *Galactic Dreams* (Tor, 1994), a Harrison short story collection, contains "Bill the Galactic Hero's Happy Holiday."

1. *Bill the Galactic Hero* (Doubleday, 1965) Country boy Bill gets press-ganged into the Empire Space Corps.

2. *Bill the Galactic Hero: On the Planet of Robot Slaves* (Avon, 1989) Bill is taken to a planet where robots, humans, and Chingers engage in constant warfare egged on by the god Mars.

3. *Bill the Galactic Hero: On the Planet of Bottled Brains* (Avon, 1990) Bill, somewhat concerned by the reptilian turn his new foot is taking, "volunteers" for a suicide mission to Tsuris, a planet nobody ever returns from, where most of the inhabitants reside in bottles. Coauthored with Robert Sheckley (q.v.).

4. *Bill the Galactic Hero: On the Planet of Tasteless Pleasure* (Avon, 1991) On the planet Colostomy IV for a spell of R & R, Bill finds himself in adventures on the fabled fields of Ozymandias and *The Starship Named Desire*. Coauthored with David Bischoff.

5. *Bill the Galactic Hero: On the Planet of Zombie Vampires* (Avon, 1991) Bill is a military policeman on a prison ship, all of whose officers seem to be bonkers. Coauthored with Jack C. Haldeman II.

6. *Bill the Galactic Hero: On the Planet of 10,000 Bars* (Avon, 1991) Bill is sent to Barworld, home planet of the finest beverages in the galaxy, to foil an evil conspiracy. Coauthored with David Bischoff. UK title: *Bill the Galactic Hero on the Planet of the Hippies from Hell*.

7. *Bill the Galactic Hero: The Final Incoherent Adventure!* (Avon, 1991) Bill is recruited by Captain Kadaffi, better known as Captain Cadaver, for a suicide mission on the planet Eyerack. Coauthored with David Harris.

III. Harrison has authored several alternative history sagas. Warriors of the Way is a trilogy set in the late 800s CE in an alternative Dark Age Europe. Shef Vigarthsson, a Viking with ambition, would like to establish the Way, an alternative to Christianity with Norse gods in the pantheon. Shef, an alternative Canute, eventually becomes king of England, Denmark, Norway, and Sweden, and his support for "new knowledge, or old knowledge recognized," produces technical developments such as paper, advanced armaments, and manned flight.

1. *Hammer and the Cross, The* (Tor, 1993) Shef Vigarthsson, bastard son of a Viking raider, enters the Viking camp in Northumbria to rescue his adopted sister Godive.

2. *One King's Way* (Tor, 1995) Shef, co-king of the English, flees north to the Way-College, an institution dedicated to technological innovation and the god Rig.

3. *King and Emperor* (Tor, 1996) Shef, ruler of England, Denmark, Sweden, and Norway, his thirst for power and the ascendancy of the Way still unslaked, plays power politics with the Byzantine emperor, the Holy Roman emperor, and the Caliph of Cordova.

IV. The Stars and Stripes trilogy postulates an alternative American Civil War in which the (historical) Trent Affair leads to open war between Great Britain and the North. British bungling leads to an alliance between North and South. Led by Robert E. Lee, William T. Sherman, U. S. Grant, and Stonewall Jackson, the united troops oust the British from North America and carry the war to Scotland. Some readers may find the depiction of Queen Victoria and the British ruling classes offensive, but Harrison does provide an interesting look at British–American relations in the 1860s and the development of modern warfare.

1. *Stars and Stripes Forever* (Del Rey, 1998) The Trent Affair (in which two Confederate diplomats were seized by forces of the North from a British ship on the open sea) leads to war between the North and Great Britain.

2. *Stars and Stripes in Peril* (Del Rey, 2001) Although the British have been beaten in America, Robert E. Lee, feeling that they still present a formidable danger, plans to attack Great Britain on its own soil.

3. *Stars and Stripes Triumphant* (Del Rey, 2003) The reunited North and South, under the leadership of Sherman, Lee, Jackson, and Grant, carry the war "across the pond."

V. Another alternative history series describes a world in which the dinosaurs survived the Cretaceous. Intelligent descendants of the dinosaurs vie with humans for the mastery of Earth. The dinosaur descendants, fearing extinction, escalate the war against the humans. A young hunter named Kerrick is humankind's best hope. The West of Eden trilogy is another intriguing look at what might have been.

1. *West of Eden* (Bantam, 1984) War between the dinosaur descendants and humankind becomes imminent. Kerrick, a young human hunter, who grew up among the dinosaurs, becomes their most feared enemy.

2. *Winter in Eden* (Bantam, 1986) A new ice age threatens Earth, as the dinosaurs reconquer human territory, and Kerrick goes on a quest to the land of the whale hunters.

3. *Return to Eden* (Bantam, 1988) Depicts the final decisive battle between humankind and the dinosaur descendants.

VI. To the Stars is a far-future trilogy in which engineer Jan Kulozik, one of Earth's privileged elite in an 23rd-century empire that has survived global collapse and colonized the stars, becomes a rebel to restore humanity's heritage of freedom. Omnibus volume: *To the Stars* (Doubleday, 1981).

1. *Homeworld* **(Bantam, 1980)** Jan Kulozik, engineer and one of Earth's privileged elite, meets Sara, member of a rebel underground, who encourages him to rebel against Earth's masters.
2. *Wheelworld* **(Bantam, 1981)** Battling heat, savage creatures, earthquakes, volcanoes, and the violence and treachery of the Families, Jan leads the people of Wheelworld to freedom.
3. *Starworld* **(Bantam, 1981)** Kulozik returns to Earth as a prisoner, but escapes to lead the forces of freedom with the aid of the lovely but lethal Dvora.

VII. The Deathworld trilogy, which has become a cult classic, postulates Pyrrus, a world in the far future that is inimical to human life. Everything on the planet (aka Felicity), animal, vegetable, and mineral, seems to have evolved just to thwart humankind. Enter one of Harrison's noble scoundrels, Jason dinAlt, tough guy, gambler, and survivor. Omnibus volume: *The Deathworld Trilogy* (Doubleday, 1968). Reissued as *The Deathworld Omnibus* (Orbit, 1999).

1. *Deathworld* **(Bantam, 1960)** The planet Pyrrus has developed an ecology whereby all beasts, plants, and natural elements seem designed to destroy its human settlers. The settlers, in their turn, have evolved into a race of lethal humans. Adventurer Jason dinAlt crash-lands into this dystopia. UK title: *Deathworld 1*.
2. *Deathworld 2* **(Bantam, 1964)** Jason dinAlt returns to Planet Pyrrus, which he finds to be a perfect hideout.
3. *Deathworld 3* **(Dell, 1968)** Jason and his companions set out to bring peace to "Felicity," but they find that the secret of the planet is beyond the wildest imaginations.

VIII. Brion Brandd, winner of the Twenties, a global competition that tests one's skills in 20 categories of human activities, is sent to other worlds in this pair of novels published 20 years apart.

1. *Planet of the Damned* **(Bantam, 1962)** Recent winner of the Twenties competition, Brion Brandd, is sent to the planet Dis, a horrible world dominated by the Magter, a once human race of homicidal maniacs.
2. *Planet of No Return* **(Tor, 1982)** The planet Selm, a shattered and mysterious world, seems to be programmed for destruction. Brion is sent by the Cultural Relationships Foundation to discover why.

IX. The two novels featuring FBI operative Tony Hawkin are something of an anomaly for Harry Harrison, dealing as they do with current international intrigue, rather than with alternative history or far-future adventures.

1. *Montezuma's Revenge* **(Doubleday, 1972)** Tony Hawkin is content to run the gift shop in the FBI building, but then he is called into a case that takes him to the middle of Mexico and pursuit by a ruthless killer.
2. *Queen Victoria's Revenge* **(Doubleday, 1974)** A skyjacking of an Arab airliner with supposed Muslims on board, supposedly by Cubans, finds Tony Hawkin handcuffed on the plane and with a lot of explaining to do.

Harrison, Janis

Bretta Solomon, relict of the late deputy sheriff Carl Solomon, owns a flower shop in River City, Missouri, and puts to good use the police skills she learned from her late husband in this series of cozies written by the owner and operator of a nursery in Windsor, Missouri.

1. *Roots of Murder* **(St. Martin's, 1999)** When local Amish flower grower Isaac Miller dies unexpectedly, his brother Evan asks flower-shop owner Bretta Solomon to look into the matter.
2. *Murder Sets Seed* **(St. Martin's, 2000)** After buying and partially restoring historic Beauchamp Mansion, Bretta puts on a preview dinner for a few of the town's more prominent citizens at the behest of former owner Cameo Beauchamp-Sinclair, a dinner that proves fatal for Cameo.
3. *Lilies That Fester* **(St. Martin's, 2001)** The first Show-Me Floral Designers' Competition and Conference at nearby Branson stirs up some ugly incidents and the disappearance of Vincent and Mabel McDuffy, friends of Bretta's late husband.
4. *Deadly Bouquet, A* **(St. Martin's, 2002)** Bretta looks into the suspicious deaths of a landscaper and a hair stylist shortly before an extravagant wedding celebration in River City.
5. *Reap a Wicked Harvest* **(St. Martin's, 2004)** Bretta once again turns amateur sleuth when her father, Albert McGinness, finds the body of lab assistant Marnie Frazier on the lawn of greenhouse owners Dan and Natalie Parker.
6. *Bindweed* **(St. Martin's, 2005)** When Bretta's slow-witted helper, Toby, is slain by a swarm of killer bees deliberately planted in his home, Bretta steps in once again.

Harrison, Jim

The Northridge family of Nebraska is the subject of two novels by novelist, poet, and nonfiction writer Jim Harrison. *Dalva* is the story of 45-year-old Dalva Northridge, who begins searching for the illegitimate son she bore 30 years earlier, while carrying on an affair with the self-destructive Michael. *The Road Home*, published 10 years later, is a family saga covering three generations, including patriarch, half-breed John Northridge. The two novels are epics of the American Great Plains, with much about the relationship between white and Native American cultures. Jim Harrison, who often writes about his native Upper Peninsula Michigan, is also the author of "Legends of the Fall," the title novella of *Legends of the Fall* (Delacorte, 1979), which was made into the movie of the same title starring Brad Pitt (1995). Harrison's last poetry collection is *Saving Daylight* (Copper Canyon, 2006).

1. *Dalva* **(Dutton, 1988)** Dalva Northridge recalls her teenage romance with the father of her illegitimate son, whom she gave up for adoption. The drunken history professor Michael is living at the Northridge family ranch while examining journals left by Dalva's great-grandfather. Made into a TV movie starring Farrah Fawcett (1995).
2. *Road Home, The* **(Atlantic Monthly, 1998)** Members of the Northridge family narrate the sagas of their lives on the Nebraskan plains from the late 1800s to 1987.

Harrison, Ray(mond Vincent)

Detective Sergeant Joseph Bragg and Constable James Morton are partners against crime in the London of the 1890s. Bragg is an old-style policeman, while Morton is from the upper classes, but they work well in this series noted for its attention to period detail. Numbers 11 through 16 have not been published in the United States.

1. *Why Kill Arthur Potter?* (Scribner, 1984) Bragg and Morton investigate the death of an insignificant little man who had a lowly job with a shipping company. UK title: *French Ordinary Murder.*
2. *Death of an Honourable Member* (Scribner, 1985) An anonymous call to police headquarters intimates that the fatal fall of Sir Walter Greville had been no accident.
3. *Deathwatch* (Scribner, 1986) The body of an undercover officer investigating union activity is found impaled on the spiked railing of Allhallows Church.
4. *Death of a Dancing Lady* (Scribner, 1986) While Morton is touring America with a cricket team, Bragg investigates a possible case of insurance fraud
5. *Counterfeit of Murder* (St. Martin's, 1987) Morton assumes the role of a dissolute New Zealander to infiltrate a gang of counterfeiters.
6. *Season for Death, A* (St. Martin's, 1988) A very tricky blackmailer, who has been plaguing some of Britain's "finest" citizens, turns his attentions to the Prince of Wales.
7. *Harvest of Death, A* (St. Martin's, 1988) Bragg, on leave from London, gets involved with murder in a Dorsetshire village.
8. *Tincture of Death* (St. Martin's, 1989) Bragg and Morton find themselves investigating the murder of the biggest opium dealer in the East.
9. *Sphere of Death* (St. Martin's, 1990) L. McCafferty, an American, has vanished after changing an unusually large sum of dollars into British sovereigns.
10. *Patently Murder* (St. Martin's, 1992) Morton's journalist friend Catherine Marsden finds the body of a murdered child prostitute.
11. *Akin to Murder* (Constable [UK], 1992) The body of a middle-aged man is found on his office floor, his throat cut.
12. *Murder in Petticoat Square* (Constable [UK], 1993) No annotation available.
13. *Hallmark of Murder* (Constable [UK], 1995) No annotation available.
14. *Murder by Design* (Constable [UK], 1996) Political tension in the higher ranks of the City of London Police forms the backdrop for a murder case.
15. *Facets of Murder* (Constable [UK], 1997) When Morton takes his fiancée to buy an engagement ring, he finds himself in the middle of a shop robbery, the murder of the shop owner, and the abduction of his fiancée.
16. *Draught of Death* (Constable [UK], 1998) The body of Edward Dawson, a professor at the university, is found in a vat in the brewery where he carried out his research. Although his death looks like an accident, the pathologist is convinced otherwise.

Harrison, Sue

I. The Ivory Carver trilogy follows the migration of a Native American tribe from the Aleutians seven thousand years BCE. Several generations of Aleuts live out their short, violent lives against an Arctic backdrop. This is a well-researched and well-written saga composed from re-created Native American legends, myths, and traditions.

1. *Mother Earth, Father Sky* (Doubleday, 1990) When her village is destroyed by another tribe, Chagak flees to her grandfather in the Whale Hunter tribe.
2. *My Sister the Moon* (Doubleday, 1992) Kiin, an unwanted girl, undergoes an early life of abuse, has an affair with the tall hunter Samiq, and is sold to the Walrus People by her brother.
3. *Brother Wind* (Morrow, 1994) Kiin's husband is killed by Raven of the Walrus People, and she is forced to return with him to his village as Samiq, her brother-in-law, seeks revenge.

II. The Storyteller trilogy is also set in prehistoric Alaska. As told by "storytellers," the trilogy relates sagas of harsh life in the frozen wastes, intertribal warfare, and passion among the Aleuts of some 8,000 years ago.

1. *Song of the River* (Avon, 1997) Chakluix, a club-footed Near River baby, abandoned by his parents and adopted by K'os, a Cousin River woman who is seeking revenge for her rape by Near River men, develops into a great storyteller.
2. *Cry of the Wind* (Avon, 1998) K'os is still pursuing revenge against Fox Barking, who had enslaved her after raping her. Chakliux the storyteller, her adopted son, is in love with the beautiful Aqamdax, who is trapped in a loveless marriage with Night Man.
3. *Call Down the Stars* (Morrow, 2001) Yikaas and Qumalix, two young storytellers, meet and relate the legends of their tribes, including the stories of K'os, Chakliux, and Aqamdax.

Harrod-Eagles, Cynthia

I. Cynthia Harrod-Eagles is a prolific author of genre fiction, including many romance and historical novels not published in the United States. The Morland Dynasty series is an example: numbers 1 through 6 only were published in paperback in the United States (Dell, 1980–1983) although the series has 29 titles so far, most of them published in both hardcover and paper in the United Kingdom. Many of the other titles, in their British paperback form, seem to be available in US bookstores. The Morland Dynasty series is "'history without tears': fictional characters in a real . . . historical background" (Harrod-Eagles website). It follows one family, the Morlands, through English history from the Wars of the Roses (15th century) to (so far) World War I, with plans to take them up to World War II. The events at Morland Place involve the family in constant romantic turmoils and, the Morlands being upper-class, constant embroilment in national and international affairs, sometimes rubbing elbows with historical figures. Nearly every novel in the series has characters continuing from the previous novels. Some characters appear in several novels. The women of the Morland family tend to have strong characters and the narratives are usually told from their points of view.

1. *Founding, The* (Dell, 1980) Begins in 1434. Ambitious Yorkshireman Edward Morland arranges a marriage between his son Robert and Eleanor, ward of the Beaufort family. Although Eleanor is secretly in love with Richard, Duke of York, the union proves to be the foundation of the Morland "dynasty."
2. *Dark Rose, The* (Dell, 1981) Starts in 1501. Bitter rivalry between the legitimate and the illegitimate sons of Paul, great grandson of Eleanor Morland, leads to tragedy. Paul's niece, Nanette, becomes maid-in-waiting to Anne Boleyn.
3. *Distant Wood, The* (Dell, 1981) Starts in 1558. John, heir to Morland Place, goes to the Borderlands to marry the daughter Black Will Percy, Northumberland cattle lord. Lettice, John's sister, marries Lord Robert Hamilton, and becomes involved in

the intrigues swirling around Mary, Queen of Scots. UK title: *The Princeling*.

4. *Crystal Crown, The* (Dell, 1982) Begins in 1630. His sons espousing rival sides in the English Civil War, Morland Place scion Edmund is hard put to steer a middle course. UK title: *The Oak Apple*.

5. *Black Pearl, The* (Macdonald [UK], 1983) Starts in 1659. Ralph, master of Morland Place, hopes to retrieve family fortunes with the accession of Charles II. Ralph's cousin Annunciata becomes part of the rakish Restoration court.

6. *Long Shadow, The* (Dell, 1983) Begins in 1670. Although Ralph and Annunciata seem to have flourished in their respective spheres, the accession of the Catholic James II threatens to open up religious rifts not completely healed since Henry VIII.

7. *Chevalier, The* (Macdonald [UK], 1984) Begins in 1689. Annunciata follows King James into exile, leaving her grandson Matt in charge of Morland Place. Matt unwisely marries heartless, beautiful India Neville.

8. *Maiden, The* (Macdonald [UK], 1985) Starts in 1720. Jemmy, heir to Morland Place, marries the chilly Lady Mary to secure Hanoverian protection and safeguard his inheritance.

9. *Flood-Tide, The* (Macdonald [UK], 1986) Starts in 1772. Morland Place is doing well under the stewardship of Jemima and her husband, Allen. Morland cousins find themselves involved in the American War for Independence, while by-blow Henri disports himself in Paris.

10. *Tangled Thread, The* (Macdonald [UK], 1987) Starts in 1788. Henri, trying to protect his family during the French Revolution, marries his daughter to a revolutionary and allies himself with Danton. Jemima's seven children cause constant anxiety, especially Lucy, who disguises herself as a boy and runs away to sea.

11. *Emperor, The* (Macdonald [UK], 1988) Starts in 1795. As the long shadow of Napoléon falls across Europe, the younger Morlands find themselves drawn into the events leading to war amid their tangled marriages and love affairs.

12. *Victory, The* (Macdonald [UK], 1989) Begins in 1803. Amid the events of the Regency, the Industrial Revolution, and the battle of Trafalgar, the Morlands find themselves, as usual, enmeshed in affairs of the heart. The ever-reckless Lucy, enjoying Regency London, neglects her husband, Chetwyn, while her lover, Weston, is off on naval blockade duty.

13. *Regency, The* (Macdonald [UK], 1990) Starts in 1807. Lucy, Captain Weston and Chetwyn having been removed from the scene, receives a marriage offer from an army officer. James and his second wife, Heloise, are happy at Morland Place except for the hostility of heiress Fanny toward her stepmother.

14. *Campaigners, The* (Macdonald [UK], 1991) Starts in 1815. The Battle of Waterloo is in the offing. Lucy and Heloise take their daughters to Brussels for a gala Season, while other Morlands such as Rosamund, Marcus, and Sophie engage in romantic entanglements.

15. *Reckoning, The* (Macdonald [UK], 1992) Starts in 1816. Postwar discontents and strife threaten Morland Place, where James and Heloise hold the fort. A trial in the House of Lords threatens to besmirch the Morland name.

16. *Devil's Horse, The* (Macdonald [UK], 1994) Starts in 1820. Sophie and Jasper try to ameliorate the lot of workers in Manchester. Lucy brings her sons home from their grand tour. At Morland Place, two very dissimilar brothers grow up.

17. *Poison Tree, The* (Macdonald [UK], 1995) Starts in 1831. Morland Place lacks the guiding hand of Heloise. Benedict leaves Morland Place to throw in his lot with the railway builders who are starting to transform Britain. Nicholas is left free to indulge the "dark side of his nature."

18. *Abyss, The* (Little, Brown [UK], 1996) Begins in 1833. The Stephensons are planning the railway line from Liverpool to London. Benedict returns to York as an engineer on the Leeds & Selby line, which reignites the conflict with Nicholas, and threatens the future of Morland Place.

19. *Hidden Shore, The* (Little, Brown [UK], 1997) Begins in 1843. A lawyer's letter reveals that Charlotte is part of the Morland family and wealthy and a countess in her own right. Charlotte and her vivacious cousin Fanny embark upon their first season.

20. *Winter Journey, The* (Little, Brown [UK], 1997) Starts in 1851. The Great Exhibition brings the Morlands to London. Charlotte defies convention by training a team of female nurses and embarking for the Crimea with her brother Cavendish.

21. *Outcast, The* (Little, Brown [UK], 1998) Begins in 1857. Benedict adopts a mysterious orphan, then takes him to America to join his daughter Mary, where he becomes enamored of the Southern way of life, just as the American Civil War is about to destroy it.

22. *Mirage, The* (Little, Brown [UK], 1999) Begins in 1870. George inherits Morland Place, then succumbs to the charms of the penniless but determined Miss Turlingham. Charlotte's daughter Venetia decides to become a doctor but has a tough row to hoe.

23. *Cause, The* (Little, Brown [UK], 2001) Starts in 1874. Venetia breaks off her engagement to Lord Hazlemere when she discovers that he is opposed to her training to be a doctor. George and Alfreda continue to spend money on grandiose building schemes at Morland Place.

24. *Homecoming, The* (Little, Brown [UK], 2002) Starts in 1885. After the death of her rector husband, Henrietta is free to marry her love, Jerome. His divorced status raises eyebrows, so the couple takes up an anonymous life in London. Venetia, now a doctor and married to Lord Hazlemere, finds herself drawn into the circle of Bertie, Prince of Wales.

25. *Question, The* (Little, Brown [UK], 2003) Starts in 1898. Teddy begins to restore Morland Place to its former glory, while Henrietta's family fills the house with life. Then nephew Bertie enlists for the Boer War.

26. *Dream Kingdom, The* (Little, Brown [UK], 2003) Begins in 1908. Teddy brings home a new wife to the now-thriving Morland Place, which gives sister Henrietta much anxiety as a threat to her role as mistress of the place. Jessie and Violet share a sparkling London debut.

27. *Restless Sea, The* (Little, Brown [UK], 2004) In 1912 the loss of the *Titanic* points up the deficits of engineering. Jessie and Violet cope with marriage and motherhood. Jack designs aircraft and trains airmen. Anne seeks comfort in her friendship with an unconventional young woman.

28. *White Road, The* (Little, Brown [UK], 2005) Unaware of the future, England greets the start of World War I in August 1914 with euphoria. Teddy Morland's nephews. Jack and Ned, volunteer.

29. *Burning Roses, The* (Little, Brown [UK], 2006) In 1915 the euphoria has worn off. Jessie is involved in various wartime charity works. Ned is going to the front ahead of his battalion.

II. The Kirov trilogy is readily available in the United States. It relates the adventures of the noble Russian Kirov family, which intermarries with the English in each generation from 1803 to 1917.

1. *Anna* (St. Martin's, 1991) Young English governess Anne Peters is hired by Count Nikolai Kirov to educate his daughters during the Napoleonic Wars.

2. *Fleur* (St. Martin's, 1993) A later Count Kirov is loved by Fleur, while Fleur's brother, member of the famous Light Brigade, is in love with Kirov's wife against the background of the Crimean War.

3. *Emily* (St. Martin's, 1993) Emily Paget, great-granddaughter of Count Peter Kirov, marries Prince Basil Narishkin but falls in love with his cousin Alexei as the Russian Revolution heats up.

III. Inspector Bill Slider is the protagonist of a series of British procedurals. Slider is a sensitive fellow who goes through some messy romantic complications while bringing his cases to a successful conclusion. Omnibus editions are available in the UK: *The Bill Slider Omnibus* (Time-Warner, 1998; numbers 1–3); *The Second Bill Slider Omnibus* (Time-Warner, 2005; numbers 4–6); and *The Third Bill Slider Omnibus* (Time-Warner, 2007; numbers 7–8).

1. *Orchestrated Death* (Scribner, 1992) Unhappily married Inspector Bill Slider becomes immersed in solving the murder of a beautiful young violin player, and finds his true love.
2. *Death Watch* (Scribner, 1993) Slider and his partner Sergeant Atherton investigate the arson murder of a womanizing salesman.
3. *Death to Go* (Scribner, 1994) A human finger found among the chips at a London fish-and-chips shop is only the first of a series of body parts to turn up. UK title: *Necrochip*.
4. *Grave Music* (Scribner, 1995) Sir Stefan Radek, conductor of the Royal London Philharmonic, is shot to death on the podium. UK title: *Dead End*.
5. *Blood Lines* (Scribner, 1996) A promiscuous and pompous music critic is found with his throat cut in the men's room at a TV studio where he is about to appear on a talk show.
6. *Killing Time* (Scribner, 1997) Someone has sent letters to gay erotic dancer Jay Paloma, threatening his life. A few days later, his battered body is found in the apartment he shared with barmaid and prostitute Busty Parnell.
7. *Shallow Grave* (Scribner, 1999) The body of a local woman is discovered in a trench dug during repairs to the home of a famous historian by the historian's daughter.
8. *Blood Sinister* (St. Martin's, 2001) Slider and his associates must discover who raped and murdered controversial journalist Phoebe Agnew.
9. *Gone Tomorrow* (St. Martin's, 2002) The body of Lenny, small-time dealer in drugs and stolen goods, turns up in a gated Shepherd's Bush playground.
10. *Dear Departed* (St. Martin's, 2004) It looks at first like another strike by the "Park Killer," but the murder of Chattie Cornfeld is different enough to arouse Slider's suspicions.

Hart, Carolyn G(impel)

I. Death on Demand is the name of the mystery bookshop run by Annie Laurance (later Darling) in the fictional town of Broward's Rock, South Carolina. The lively Annie sells mysteries herself, sometimes with the help of her husband, professional crime consultant Max Darling, in this series of Dixie cozies that pay ample tribute to Hart's great predecessor Agatha Christie (q.v.). Hart has served as president of Sisters in Crime, the female mystery writers' association, and has won such notable mystery book awards as the Agatha and the Anthony for her Death on Demand series. *Crime on Her Mind* (Five Star, 1999), a short story collection, contains two Death on Demand stories.

1. **Death on Demand** (Bantam, 1987) Author Elliot Morgan is killed during a weekly gathering of the Sunday Night Regulars, a group of famous mystery writers.

2. *Design for Murder* (Bantam, 1988) Annie is invited to stage a mystery night for the annual house tour of the Historical Preservation Society of Chastain, South Carolina.
3. *Something Wicked* (Bantam, 1988) A local summer stock production of *Arsenic and Old Lace* is scheduled to star Hollywood beach-blanket-hunk Shane Petrie.
4. *Honeymoon with Murder* (Bantam, 1989) While Annie and Max are away on their honeymoon, Annie's assistant disappears, leaving the body of a local Peeping Tom on her living room rug.
5. *Little Class on Murder, A* (Doubleday, 1989) Annie is teaching a course called "Three Great Ladies of Mystery" at Chastain Community College.
6. *Deadly Valentine* (Doubleday, 1990) Annie and Max's romantic Valentine's Day is spoiled by the arrest of Max's mother for murder.
7. *Christie Caper, The* (Bantam, 1991) Annie is cohosting the Christie Caper in honor of Agatha's centenary with reigning English crime queen Lady Gwendolyn Thompkins.
8. *Southern Ghost* (Bantam, 1992) Dark family memories surface when a young woman eager to find her birth parents reopens old wounds.
9. *Mint Julep Murder* (Bantam, 1995) Publisher Kenneth Hazlitt threatens to write an expose of several writers honored at the annual Dixie Book Festival on Hilton Head Island.
10. *Yankee Doodle Dead* (Avon, 1998) Retired Brigadier General Charlton "Bud" Hatch, newcomer to Broward's Rock, has offended many of the older residents by his arrogance and extreme right-wing views.
11. *White Elephant Dead* (Avon, 1999) Kathryn Girard, member of the local women's club, is slain, ostensibly while collecting donations for the annual white elephant sale.
12. *Sugar Plum Dead* (Morrow, 2000) The relatives of Marguerite Dumaney think that the retired movie star is overly fond of "psychic" charmer Emory Swanson, who has come to Broward's Rock to establish the Evermore Foundation, where rich old ladies can get in touch with their departed loved ones.
13. *April Fool Dead* (Morrow, 2002) Annie's book-signing gala for a local author is sabotaged by fake publicity flyers for the event. Then a high school teacher turns up dead.
14. *Engaged to Die* (Morrow, 2003) The gala opening of a new art collection at the Neville Gallery, owned by heiress Virginia Neville, is spoiled by the murder of Jake O'Neill, Virginia's intended.
15. *Murder Walks the Plank* (Morrow, 2004) The benefit cruise that Annie Darling has planned as a relief from the August heat of Broward's Rock is spoiled when the town's favorite volunteer, Pamela Potts, falls overboard.
16. *Death of the Party* (Morrow, 2005) Annie and Max investigate the death of media magnate Jeremiah Addison, who apparently fell by accident down a marble staircase in his home on a private South Carolina island.
17. *Dead Days of Summer* (Morrow, 2006) Max is in deep trouble after disappearing from his car on a remote road with a murder weapon in the trunk and a dead young woman nearby.
18. *Death Walked In* (Morrow, 2008) Gwen Jamison's son Robert is implicated in the death of his mother and the theft of eight gold coins worth nearly $2 million, but Max believes that he has been framed.

II. Hart has created her own Miss Marple in the person of Henrietta O'Dwyer Collins, retired investigative reporter. "Henrie O," whose investigative instincts haven't retired, is a redoubtable sleuth. Although Henrie O has a teaching gig at Thorndyke University in Missouri for a while, she moves around the country quite a bit. Eight of the 12 stories in *Crime on Her Mind* (Five Star, 1999) feature Henrie O.

1. *Dead Man's Island* (**Bantam, 1993**) Old flame Chase Prescott calls on Henrie O to help figure out who tried to kill him with poisoned candy.
2. *Scandal in Fair Haven* (**Bantam, 1994**) Henrie O is vacationing at a friend's cabin in the Tennessee mountains when the friend's nephew arrives covered with blood, telling a tale of finding his wife murdered.
3. *Death in Lover's Lane* (**Avon, 1996**) Maggie Winslow, Henrie O's journalism student at Thorndyke University in Missouri, is found dead in the lover's lane where two undergraduates were murdered 10 years earlier.
4. *Death in Paradise* (**Avon, 1998**) Henrie O gets an anonymous package in the mail that indicates that her husband Richard's death six years ago was murder, not an accident. Her investigations take her to Hawaii and Belle Ericsson, who was romantically involved with Richard.
5. *Death on the River Walk* (**Avon, 1999**) The disappearance of Iris Chavez, a friend's granddaughter, brings Henrie O to San Antonio, Texas, in a case involving Tesoros, a Mexican art gallery, and Maria Elena Garza, the formidable matriarch who runs it.
6. *Resort to Murder* (**Morrow, 2001**) The Bermuda wedding of Henrie O's son-in-law Lloyd Drake and wealthy widow Connor Bailey promises to be something of an ordeal, as Lloyd's daughter is strongly opposed to the wedding, and the bride-to-be has something of a roving eye.
7. *Set Sail for Murder* (**Morrow, 2007**) Henrie O's erstwhile lover, Jimmy, has married the dashing Sophia Montgomery, but he is afraid that one of Sophia's stepchildren from a previous marriage is trying to kill her.

Hart, Ellen

I. Jane Lawless is a Minneapolis restaurateur, a middle-aged lesbian mourning a lost lover, and an accomplished amateur sleuth. With her friend, but not lover, wisecracking theater director Cordelia Thorn, Lawless gets involved in a series of witty, complicated, well-told puzzle mysteries.

1. *Hallowed Murder* (**Seal, 1989**) Lawless and Thorne find the drowned body of a wealthy sorority member who fought with her lover the night she died.
2. *Vital Lies* (**Seal, 1991**) Fothergill Inn, an old Victorian structure, is the scene of a Christmas gathering and a series of bizarre events.
3. *Stage Fright* (**Seal, 1992**) Torald, son of famous dramatist Gaylord Werness, is found impaled on the stage set of the play he was to star in.
4. *Killing Cure, A* (**Seal, 1993**) Jane's father is hired to defend a young man accused of killing a prominent foundation head.
5. *Small Sacrifice, A* (**Seal, 1994**) Cordelia and five other former college chums take a trip to Wisconsin to persuade a former classmate, alcoholic actress Diana Stanwood, to enter a clinic.
6. *Faint Praise* (**Seal, 1995**) Local television personality Arno Heywood dons women's clothing before leaping to his death from the top of Foshay Tower in downtown Minneapolis.
7. *Robber's Wine* (**Seal, 1996**) Jane and Cordelia head north on vacation. Along with them is friend Anne Dumont, on her way to her mother Belle's. But when they arrive, Belle is missing and later found dead, and Jane and Cordelia begin to dig up some nasty family secrets.
8. *Wicked Games* (**St. Martin's, 1998**) Jane's new tenant, children's book author Elliot Beauman, and his sister Patricia, who have recently returned to their old neighborhood, seem to be harboring some dark family secrets.

9. *Hunting the Witch* (**St. Martin's, 1999**) Recuperating at her lover Julia's mountain cabin from wounds received in *Wicked Games*, Lawless finds herself enmeshed in the mystery of the murder of Jeffrey Chapel, who has opposed the conversion of the Winter Garden Hotel into an assisted-living community.
10. *Merchant of Venus, The* (**St. Martin's, 2001**) Jane accompanies Cordelia Thorne to an isolated mansion on the Connecticut coast to attend the marriage of Cordelia's sister Octavia to a reclusive movie director, octogenarian Roland Lester.
11. *Immaculate Midnight* (**St. Martin's, 2002**) Jane, still recovering from injuries and mourning the death of her dog and the end of the affair with Julia, receives a threatening communication, and then a stash of drugs is found in her office.
12. *Intimate Ghost, An* (**St. Martin's, 2004**) Someone spikes the eatables provided by Jane's catering staff, so that the entire wedding party of a school-teacher acquaintance of Jane's trips out, causing much embarrassment, litigation, and a serious injury when the groom leaps into an empty swimming pool.
13. *Iron Girl, The* (**St. Martin's, 2005**) Jane's father, Ray Lawless, unsuccessfully defends the accused serial murderer and arsonist "the Fireman." The Fireman kills himself in his cell, and someone is blaming Ray for failing to get him off.
14. *Night Vision* (**St. Martin's, 2006**) Movie star Joanna Kasimir, who returned home to Minnesota to perform in a production of *Who's Afraid of Virginia Woolf?* at Cordelia Thorn's St. Paul theater, asks Jane to tail her ex-husband Gordon.
15. *Mortal Groove, The* (**St. Martin's, 2007**) When Jane's father is drafted to run for governor of Minnesota, his chances look good until reporter Melanie Gunderson begins sniffing around a decades-old unsolved murder that might involve several of Ray's key staffers and financial backers.

II. Twin Cities (Minneapolis–St. Paul)–based food critic and amateur sleuth Sophie Greenway has a talk-show-host husband, Bram Baldric, and a tendency to get mixed up in mysteries. This is a paperback-only series.

1. *This Little Piggie Went to Murder* (**Ballantine, 1994**) Sophie and her husband, Bram, travel to Duluth, Minnesota, to cover the grand reopening of her friend's family restaurant.
2. *For Every Evil* (**Ballantine, 1995**) Sophie's son Rudy is a suspect when powerful critic Hale Mickenberg is shot at a stylish drawing exhibition.
3. *Oldest Sin, The* (**Ballantine, 1996**) Sophie, now owner of the Maxfield Plaza Hotel in St. Paul, is reunited with her college roommates while two conventions are going on: the Church of the Firstborn and Daughters of Sisyphus.
4. *Murder in the Air* (**Ballantine, 1997**) Sophie and Bram are mystified by the revival of a Twin Cities radio serial that deals with an unsolved 1950's murder, especially since the son of the radio station owner was a prime suspect in the case.
5. *Slice and Dice* (**Fawcett, 2000**) Famous doyenne of the food and hospitality industry and mother of Nathan, Sophie's former lover, Constance Buckridge is staying at the Maxfield Plaza Hotel. And so is Marie Damontraville, authoress of tell-all unauthorized biographies, who is researching her next subject: Constance.
6. *Dial M for Meatloaf* (**Fawcett, 2001**) A meat-loaf recipe contest is running in the *Times-Register*. The car bomb slaying of small-towner Kirby Runbeck engages Sophie's attention when friend of the family John Washburn confesses to the crime on his deathbed.
7. *Death on a Silver Platter* (**Fawcett, 2003**) When Sophie's friend Elaine Veelund announces her decision to sell Veelund Industries, she is beset by a series of misfortunes: her brother is shot at; her

suicidal daughter disappears; and her widowed mother dies of an insulin overdose.

8. *No Reservations Required* (Fawcett, 2005) A couple of murders down Ken Loy and the man who killed, in a car accident, Ken's wife, Bob Fabian. Sophie Greenway thinks that there is a connection.

Hart, Roy

Inspector Roper of the Bournemouth, England, CID is the protagonist of one of the more popular recent procedural series. Roper is dogged but compassionate. His investigations usually take place near the English seashore or in the countryside. No real surprises or outré characters here, just well-done classic puzzle mysteries.

1. *Seascape with Dead Figures* (St. Martin's, 1987) George Winterton, prominent citizen of a seaside town, had a blackmailing sideline that may have resulted in his death.
2. *Pretty Place for a Murder, A* (St. Martin's, 1987) Roper is called to the country village of Cort Abbas, where the body of a young woman has been found in a wayside ditch.
3. *Fox in the Night, A* (St. Martin's, 1988) Roper is on hand when a body is washed up at a local chandlery.
4. *Remains to Be Seen* (St. Martin's, 1989) Artist Cassandra Murcheson finds a corpse in the bricked-up cupboard of the cottage she is renting.
5. *Robbed Blind* (St. Martin's, 1990) Wealthy Stella Pumfrey is found dead at the foot of a staircase in the picturesque village of Little Crow.
6. *Breach of Promise* (St. Martin's, 1991) Zymunt Komarowski, former chemical engineer and RAF ace, is murdered in the village of Upper Groton.
7. *Blood Kin* (St. Martin's, 1992) A movie starlet of yesteryear disappears from her secluded cottage.
8. *Final Appointment* (St. Martin's, 1993) The decapitated motorcyclist found on the Appleford road turns out to be corrupt ex-policeman Gerry Pope.
9. *Deadly Schedule, A* (St. Martin's, 1994) Roper discovers the body of an Englishwoman at his hotel while vacationing in Crete.

Hartley, L(eslie) P(oles)

Those who enjoyed reading Hartley's *The Go-Between* or seeing the movie made of that novel will want to try other works by this English author. The Eustace and Hilda trilogy is a sensitive and beautifully written exploration of a brother-sister relationship. Some critics consider it Hartley's masterpiece. The omnibus volume *Eustace and Hilda: A Trilogy* (Putnam [UK], 1958) contains a short story entitled "Hilda's Letter," inserted between the first and second books listed below.

1. *West Window, The* (Doubleday, 1945) Eustace Cherrington is a gentle little boy with a weak heart who is dominated by his older sister Hilda. UK title: *The Shrimp and the Anemone*.
2. *Sixth Heaven, The* (Doubleday, 1947) Now an undergraduate at Oxford, Eustace hopes for a romance between Hilda and his aristocratic friend Dick Stavely.
3. *Eustace and Hilda* (Putnam [UK], 1947) After a holiday in Venice, Eustace attempts a drastic measure to help Hilda.

Hartog, Jan de

Dutch-born Jan de Hartog made himself a diverse literary reputation. His play *The Four-Poster* won Broadway's Tony Award for 1952 and is often revived by theater groups. *The Hospital* (1962), a nonfiction work describing conditions in a Texas charity hospital, attracted nationwide attention. An early novel, *Holland's Glory*, became a symbol of Dutch resistance against the Nazis. Hartog, who ran away to sea at the age of 10, was always on or near the water. The novels narrated by Martinus Harinxma, Dutch captain of oceangoing tugboats, display Hartog's extensive knowledge of the sea and his ability to write about it.

1. *Captain, The* (Atheneum, 1966) Captain Harinxma, who has escaped from the Nazis in the Netherlands, takes command of a Dutch tugboat slated for convoy duty on the Iceland-Murmansk run.
2. *Commodore, The* (Harper, 1986) Now 70 and retired, Harinxma agrees to act as a consultant on board an ultra-modern oceangoing tug that has been sold to a Taiwanese shipper.
3. *Centurion, The* (Harper, 1989) Harinxma takes up dowsing and gets involved with the life of a Roman centurion from the 4th century CE.
4. *Outer Buoy, The: A Story of the Ultimate Voyage* (Pantheon, 1994) The octogenarian Harinxma, recently widowed and suffering from cancer, experiences an out-of-body experience.

Hartzmark, Gini

Kate Millholland, Chicago heiress and socialite, is also a brilliant and ambitious corporate lawyer who works very hard and doesn't shun sticky cases even when they result in murder.

1. *Principal Defense* (Ivy, 1992) Kate Millholland tries to prevent the hostile takeover of a highly profitable pharmaceutical company owned by her former lover.
2. *Final Option* (Fawcett, 1994) The murder of futures trader Bart Hexter doesn't seem to overly disturb his family. Kate Millholland, who was hired to prepare a defense against charges of trading improprieties by Bart, aims to get to the bottom of his financial dealings and his murder.
3. *Bitter Business* (Ballantine, 1995) Kate is entrusted with the legal affairs of the wealthy but dysfunctional Cavanagh family, run by the obsessive Jack Cavanaugh, the founder and principal owner of Superior Plating and Specialty Chemicals. Only novel in the series to be published in hardcover.
4. *Fatal Reaction* (Ivy, 1998) Azor Pharmaceuticals, run by Kate's boyfriend and client, Stephen Azorini, is going broke with its search for the miracle drug ZK-501, and a deal with the Tokyo-baed Takisawa Corporation is its only hope to stay in business.
5. *Rough Trade* (Ivy, 1999) Kate's friend Jeff Rendell, general manager of the Milwaukee Monarchs professional football team, asks her help in bailing out the nearly bankrupt team.
6. *Dead Certain* (Fawcett, 2000) Prescott Memorial, a charitable hospital founded by Kate's family, is about to be taken over by the crooked Health Care Corporation (HCC), which has been buying up hospitals around the country.

Haruf, Kent

The bachelor McPheron brothers and their charges, the teenage Victoria and her daughter Katie, are the continuing characters in a pair of novels set in rural Holt, Colorado (near Denver). Not all that much happens in these books, which are portrayals of hard lives and strong, sympathetically drawn characters.

1. *Plainsong* (Knopf, 1999) High school teacher Tom Guthrie's wife moves out of their house, leaving him to care for their two young sons. Pregnant teenager Victoria Roubideaux, thrown out by her mother, moves in with the elderly, cattle-farming McPheron brothers.

2. *Eventide* (Knopf, 2004) Victoria goes off the college, while her daughter, Katie, remains with the McPheron brothers, one of whom is killed by an enraged bull. New characters are introduced, such as a disabled couple and their children and the Kepharts, where 11-year-old D. J. cares for his retired grandfather.

Harvey, John

I. Anglo-Polish, jazz-loving (especially Thelonius Monk) Inspector Charlie Resnick is the protagonist of one of the most engrossing of current procedural series. Set in Nottingham, a grimy English Midlands industrial city, this series combines the procedural detail of Ed McBain (q.v.), the atmosphere of James Lee Burke (q.v.), and the kitchen-sink realism of English authors like Alan Sillitoe (q.v.) and Keith Waterhouse. Readers can only hope that poet John Harvey's decision to leave Nottingham and Charlie Resnick behind after number 10 will be a temporary one.

1. *Lonely Hearts* (Holt, 1989) The Nottingham police track down child-molesting fathers and a lonely hearts serial killer.

2. *Rough Treatment* (Holt, 1990) Housebreakers who discovered and liberated a kilo of cocaine are offering it back, for a price.

3. *Cutting Edge* (Holt, 1991) Charlie investigates a series of brutal attacks on the medical personnel of a large Midlands hospital.

4. *Off Minor* (Holt, 1992) One of two missing six-year-old girls turns up dead.

5. *Wasted Years* (Holt, 1993) Two quite different criminal groups are committing their own series of violent armed robberies.

6. *Cold Light* (Holt, 1994) Charlie conducts a timid, desultory romance with the flatmate of a missing social worker.

7. *Living Proof* (Holt, 1995) Nottingham hosts a mystery writers' convention, and the authoress of American hard-boiled stories receives threatening letters in the mail.

8. *Easy Meat* (Holt, 1996) A 15-year-old, arrested for robbing and assaulting an elderly couple, hangs himself on his first night of juvenile detention.

9. *Still Waters* (Holt, 1997) A melange of events engage Resnick's attention: a case of art theft; a sting attempt on a crooked middleman; murdered young women found in a canal; the murder of Jane, a friend of Charlie's lover; the rise of an ambitious female colleague; and episodes involving a nun.

10. *Last Rites* (Holt, 1999) Michael Preston, who had gone willingly to jail for his father's murder, escapes while on an escorted visit to his mother's funeral. John Harvey stated that this would be his last Nottingham/Resnick book.

11. *Now's the Time: The Complete Resnick Stories* (Dufour, 2002) Twelve short stories about Resnick, including a new story written especially for this edition.

II. John Harvey has followed the Resnick series with another one: this time about Detective Inspector Frank Elder of the Nottingham Police, who retires to Cornwall after his wife betrays him and his teenage daughter is raped but still can't stay away from police work or Nottingham. So far, this series hasn't commanded the same loyalty as the Charley Resnick books.

1. *Flesh and Blood* (Carroll & Graf, 2004) Detective Inspector Frank Elder of Nottingham rusticates himself to Cornwall, but he is haunted by the past, particularly by the unsolved disappearance of 16-year-old Susan Blaylock.

2. *Ash and Bone* (Harcourt/Penzler, 2005) Frank joins his former lover, Detective Sergeant Maddy Birch, in London when her superior comes under scrutiny after having killed a much-wanted malefactor.

3. *Darkness and Light* (Harcourt/Penzler, 2006) Elder returns to Nottingham to search for the missing Claire Meecham, the older widowed sister of a friend of his ex-wife's.

Hasford, Gustav (Jerry Gustav)

The late Gustav Hasford had a checkered career. *The Short-Timers,* his first novel, which was based on his own experiences as a combat correspondent with US Marine Corps in Vietnam, was the basis for the Stanley Kubrick film *Full Metal Jacket.* Hasford was later convicted for possession of more than 700 books stolen from English and American libraries. *The Short-Timers* and its sequel are in Joseph Heller's [q.v.] *Catch-22* tradition of depicting warfare in surrealistic and black-humor terms.

1. *Short-Timers, The* (Harper, 1979) William "Joker" Doolittle is sent as a combat reporter to Vietnam, where he resists promotion and persists in wearing a peace button.

2. *Phantom Blooper, The* (Bantam, 1990) In pursuit of the legendary Phantom Blooper, allegedly a US Marine who joined the Vietcong, Joker is taken prisoner by the North Vietnamese.

Hassler, Jon

Jon Hassler, high school and college English instructor, has been producing a loosely connected series of novels based upon his experiences in the small Minnesota towns where he has lived most of his life. Among the continuing characters are elderly Catholic schoolteacher Agatha McGee. of the fictional town of Staggerford, who plays a major role in numbers 1, 4, 7, and 10, but the rural Minnesota setting is the primary link between the novels in this well-written, elegiac series. *My Staggerford Journal* (Ballantine, 1999) is the journal Hassler kept in 1975 when he took a sabbatical year from teaching and wrote *Staggerford.*

1. *Staggerford* (Atheneum, 1977) Miles Pruitt, a high school English teacher, spends his leisure time regretting old loves and lost opportunities.

2. *Simon's Night* (Atheneum, 1979) Retired professor Simon Peter Shea checks himself into a home for the aged after he accidentally sets his house on fire.

3. *Love Hunter, The* (Morrow, 1981) Two colleagues at a small Minnesota college go on a hunting trip to take one colleague's mind off his slow death from multiple sclerosis.

4. *Green Journey, A* (Morrow, 1985) Agatha McGee, her conservative Catholic beliefs challenged by a progressive bishop, goes on a church-sponsored trip to Ireland.

5. *Grand Opening* (Morrow, 1987) The Fosters and their family move to Plum, Minnesota, to open a new supermarket, and find it difficult to adjust to small-town life.

6. *North of Hope* (Ballantine, 1990) Father Frank Healy is reassigned to his hometown parish and the nearby Ojibway reservation church, and reencounters childhood love Libby Pearsall.

7. *Dear James* (Ballantine, 1993) Agatha McGee, forcibly retired from her teaching post, finds retirement life in Staggerford to be excruciating.

8. *Rookery Blues* (Ballantine, 1995) Several faculty members at Rookery State College start a blues music group called the Icejam Quintet.

9. *Dean's List, The* (Ballantine, 1997) Dean Leland Edwards of Rookery State College persuades elderly poet Richard Falcon to give a reading at Rookery.

10. *Staggerford Flood, The* (Viking, 2002) Agatha McGee is invigorated by the threat and onset of a flood as she provides shelter for several residents and holds the fort in her hilltop house during the deluge.

11. *Staggerford Murders, The, and The Life and Death of Nancy Clancy's Nephew* (Plume, 2004) Two unrelated novellas set in Staggerford.

12. *New Woman, The* (Viking, 2005) Agatha McGee, now 87, knows she is slowing down, but she isn't quite resigned to a schedule of Sunset Senior's arts-and-crafts classes.

Havill, Steven F.

Posadas County, New Mexico, is the scene of a long-running series of mystery novels featuring sexagenarian undersheriff Bill Gastner, his assistant, friend, and eventual successor Estelle Reyes-Guzman, and a host of other characters. Bill Gastner is overweight, eats way too much Mexican food and is laconic and curmudgeonly but lovable, honest and competent. Numbers 1 through 9 have a great deal to say about Gastner's uncertain health; he retires and is succeeded by the capable Reyes-Guzman in number 10 but is still ready to lend a hand. The ambience of a small Western town is important in making this series of procedurals work. Steven F. Havill wrote westerns (e.g., *The Killer*) before he turned his attention to mysteries.

1. *Heartshot* (St. Martin's, 1991) A complicated drug-smuggling operation is at the bottom of a series of suspicious deaths. Undersheriff Bill Gastner, sceptical of the benefits of modern life such as computers and of the skills of his newly elected boss, Martin Holman, manages, despite a heart attack, to bring the case to a satisfactory conclusion.

2. *Bitter Recoil* (St. Martin's, 1992) After bypass surgery, Bill Gastner won't settle down. Instead he drives across state to San Estevan to visit his former deputy, Estelle Guzman, and winds up helping her to investigate the case of a battered pregnant woman.

3. *Twice Buried* (St. Martin's, 1994) The "accidental" death of a retired school teacher, and the shooting of a real-estate mogul, ostensibly by old-timer Reuben Fuentes, granduncle of Estelle Reyes-Guzman, concern Bill here.

4. *Before She Dies* (St. Martin's, 1996) Sonny Trujillo dies in lockup and Bill may face charges of police brutality. The seemingly motiveless shootings of a Posadas County deputy and newspaper reporter Linda Real, who witnessed Trujillo's attack on Bill, complicate matters.

5. *Privileged to Kill* (St. Martin's, 1997) The mysterious death of 15-year-old Maria Ibarra, found under the high school field bleachers, occupies Bill Gastner here.

6. *Prolonged Exposure* (St. Martin's, 1998) While Gastner is recuperating from heart surgery at his daughter's Michigan home, his chief of detectives, Estelle Reyes-Guzman, calls to tell him that his home has been burglarized.

7. *Out of Season* (St. Martin's, 1999) Estelle is planning to move to Minnesota with her husband. Sheriff Holman, on his own investigation, dies in a suspicious small plane accident. It is up to Bill Gastner, retiring in a few months, to pull things together.

8. *Dead Weight* (St. Martin's, 2000) When a man is crushed to death by a backhoe, Gastner's instincts tell him that it was no accident. To add to his troubles, one of Bill's deputies is accused of harassing Mexicans. (*Dead Weight* is a very popular title, as novels under that name by John Francome, Brian Lecomber, J. R. Roberts, Gerald Hammond [q.v.], Diane Sherlock, Ruth Fenisong, and Theodore Magnuson indicate.)

9. *Bag Limit* (St. Martin's, 2001) Bill is days away from retirement when local teen Matt Baca drives drunkenly into the back of his police car.

10. *Scavengers* (St. Martin's, 2002) Bill has retired, only to become state livestock inspector, while Estelle has succeeded him as undersheriff of Posadas County. A couple of New Mexico murders may be connected to a murder south of the border.

11. *Discount for Death, A* (St. Martin's, 2003) Popular insurance salesman George Enriquez faces a grand jury indictment for fraud, a village patrolman gets involved in a messy domestic situation, and Estelle finds criminal activity striking close to her own family.

12. *Convenient Disposal* (St. Martin's, 2004) Do the savage beating and stabbing of middle-school tough girl Carmen Acosta and the disappearance of her neighbor Kevin Ziegler, the county manager, have any connection?

13. *Statute of Limitations* (St. Martin's, 2006) Estelle is swamped with medical reports, as the chief of police suffers a heart attack, Sheriff Robert Torrez has a pulmonary embolism, a deputy's fiancé is murdered, and former sheriff Bill Gastner is brutally attacked.

14. *Final Payment* (St. Martin's, 2007) Undersheriff Estelle Reyes-Guzman and her colleagues discover three Hispanics shot to death, execution-style, at a remote New Mexico airstrip.

Hawke, Simon

PSEUDONYM OF Nicholas Yermakov

I. William Shakespeare as a detective was bound to come sooner or later. This series presents young Will as an aspiring playwright with a Watson-like sidekick, Symington "Tuck" Smythe II, who would like to be an actor. The men go through a series of adventures, reminiscent of *Shakespeare in Love*, in Elizabethan England, many of which turn up, transmogrified, in Shakespeare's plays.

1. *Mystery of Errors, A* (Forge, 2000) Two stagestruck young men, William Shakespeare and Symington "Tuck" Smythe II, meet on the way to London and form a partnership that takes them through highwaymen, tavern brawls, and jobs as ostlers with the Queen's Men.

2. *Slaying of the Shrew, The* (Forge, 2001) The Queen's Men have been hired to perform during the wedding festivities for merchant Godfrey Middleton's shrewish daughter Catherine.

3. *Much Ado about Murder* (Forge, 2002) The plague has closed London theaters, but the murder of a London merchant with an enticing daughter, "the Dark Lady," occupies the time of Will and Tuck.

4. *Merchant of Vengeance, The* (Forge, 2003) Will wants to top Kit Marlowe's *Jew of Malta*, but he has never met a Jew. Then he discovers that a young tailor's marriage has been compromised by the discovery that his mother was Jewish.

II. Before he turned to historical mysteries, Simon Hawke was best known as an SF and fantasy writer. The Boomerang trilogy, written under his real name (Nicholas V. Yermakov), is sometimes rated more highly by critics than his later work. The trilogy, about an alien world whose inhabitants are able to absorb the personalities of dying humans, was published by Signet: *Last Communion* (1981); *Epiphany* (1982); and *Jehad* (1984). Hawke's longest series, known as Time Wars, is a time-travel and alternate Earth series in which various bands of time travelers try to change events in Earth's past, and other groups try to thwart them. Many of the books involve fictional characters, such as Ivanhoe, the Scarlet Pimpernel, and Dracula, who get mixed together with historical characters.

1. *Ivanhoe Gambit, The* **(Ace, 1984)** The world of Sir Walter Scott is invoked as Sergeant Major Lucas Priest of the US Army Temporal Corps and his men are called back into the past to impersonate characters like Ivanhoe and Robin Hood.
2. *Timekeeper Conspiracy, The* **(Ace, 1984)** Captain Lucas Priest has to infiltrate the terrorist underground called the Timekeepers in the 17th-century French world of Cardinal Richelieu and the Three Musketeers.
3. *Pimpernel Plot, The* **(Ace, 1985)** The world of revolutionary France and the Baroness Emmuska Orczy's (q.v.) Scarlet Pimpernel receive the attention of Lucas Priest and his Temporal Corps here.
4. *Zenda Vendetta, The* **(Ace, 1985)** The Timekeepers, the terrorist underground from the 27th century, go back to the 19th century and interfere with the kingdom of Ruritania and *The Prisoner of Zenda*.
5. *Nautilus Sanction* **(Ace, 1985)** A time traveler hijacks a 20th-century nuclear sub and time trips back to the era of the clipper ship and Jules Verne (q.v.).
6. *Khyber Connection, The* **(Ace, 1986)** The world of Kipling is invaded as the Corps goes back to 1897, the Khyber Pass, and Gunga Din.
7. *Argonaut Affair, The* **(Ace, 1987)** Preclassical Greece, the world of Jason, the Argonauts, and such mythical worthies as Hercules, Theseus, and Orpheus, is visited here.
8. *Dracula Caper, The* **(Ace, 1988)** It seems that the vampires and werewolves that plagued Victorian England were actually genetically engineered monsters from the far future.
9. *Lilliput Legion, The* **(Ace, 1989)** The Time Commandos fight bioengineered Lilliputian warriors out of the world of *Gulliver's Travels* and Jonathan Swift.
10. *Hellfire Rebellion, The* **(Ace, 1990)** Can the American Revolution be derailed? The Time Commandos travel to Boston in the 1760s to find out.
11. *Cleopatra Crisis, The* **(Ace, 1990)** Back to the time of the Ptolemies and Cleopatra, the "Serpent of the Nile." Will she and Antony win this time?
12. *Six-Gun Solution, The* **(Ace, 1991)** The Time Wars series is brought to a rousing conclusion in this Old West shoot-out.

III. The Wizard series combines elements of fantasy and SF. Wyrdrune is an incompetent student wizard in the 22nd century, a time when natural resources have run out and the great Merlin, who has been released from his imprisoning spell, has brought magic back into the world. Wyrdrune, the street-wise Kira, and evil-turned-good Modred use magical powers released by runestones to fight evil in a variety of settings.

1. *Wizard of 4th Street, The* **(Warner, 1987)** Incompetent student wizard Wyrdrune runs into street-wise cutie Kira at an auction for the mysterious and potent Euphrates rune stones, unaware that the stones have already chosen him for a great adventure.
2. *Wizard of Whitechapel, The* **(Warner, 1988)** Wyrdrune and Kira are called to England to save Modred, last survivor of Camelot. Teamed up with a French witch, a 300-pound faerie, and an English punk, they tackle an ancient power stalking London.
3. *Wizard of Sunset Strip, The* **(Warner, 1989)** Wyrdrune and his friends travel to the West Coast to stop the Dark Ones who are turning Hollywood into a fantasy land of eternal horror.
4. *Wizard of Rue Morgue, The* **(Warner, 1990)** The Dark Ones unleash a "Reign of Terror" from the sewers of Paris as a model is found murdered with runes carved all over her body.
5. *Samurai Wizard, The* **(Warner, 1991)** Japan is in danger of being turned into the "Land of the Setting Sun" by the Dark Ones.
6. *Wizard of Santa Fe, The* **(Warner, 1991)** Wyrdrune finds some strange new allies as the Dark Ones threaten New Mexico.
7. *Wizard of Camelot, The* **(Warner, 1993)** Merlin comes to the fore in a battle to save humanity.
8. *Wizard of Lovecraft's Cafe, The* **(Warner, 1993)** Wyrdrune, Billy Slade. King Gorlois, Modred, and Merlin are merged into one being to survive a necromantic ambush.
9. *Last Wizard, The* **(Warner, 1997)** Talon, most brilliant of the evil immortals, has captured all the surviving Dark Ones, and is using their life force to empower a cult of sorcerous assassins.

IV. Similar to the Wizard series is the trilogy featuring Dr. Marvin Brewster, a bumbling genius who is mistaken for a sorcerer and trapped in a parallel universe fighting the wizard Warrick in a series of humorous adventures.

1. *Reluctant Sorcerer, The* **(Warner, 1992)** Bumbling genius Marvin Brewster is accidentally transported to a parallel universe where magic really works and is mistaken for a sorcerer.
2. *Inadequate Adept, The* **(Warner, 1993)** Still trapped in a parallel universe, Dr. Brewster must stop an evil wizard who has captured a time machine.
3. *Ambivalent Magician, The* **(Warner, 1996)** Marvin assembles his motley crew to challenge the evil wizard Warrick, who is bent upon changing the rules of his universe.

V. The Psychodrome duo is a pair of SF novels about the settling by Earthlings of the planet Draconis and their encounters with the seemingly docile race of mammalian life-forms that inhabit the place.

1. *Psychodrome* **(Ace, 1987)** The humans who settled the planet Draconis, and started to feast on its tasty and seemingly docile inhabitants, have a nasty surprise in store for them.
2. *Shapechanger Scenario, The* **(Ace, 1988)** The mammalian beings on Draconis 9 prove to be shape-shifters who soon get the hang of taking human form, and preying on the predators.

VI. Sons of Glory is a pair of novels about the Gallios, race of men bound by honor and war from the founding of their clan in legendary Roman times to the Vietnam War.

1. *Sons of Glory* **(Jove, 1992)** Hanna the gladiator, Major A. W. Gallio in the American Civil War, and Tony Gallio, CIA agent and mercenary, are all part of the same family bound by honor and war.
2. *Call to Battle* **(Jove, 1993)** Continues the saga of the Gallios, who take pride in their military heritage, symbolized by the ring once worn by the legendary Roman founder of the family. Variant title: *Sons of Glory: Call to Battle.*

Hawkesworth, John

Upstairs, Downstairs had perhaps the widest appeal of any of PBS's Masterpiece Theatre series, drawing many viewers away from commercial television. The downstairs characters of Rose, Mrs. Bridges, and Mr. Hudson were the compelling figures; the upstairs Bellamy occupants paled by comparison. Fans will relish these competent novelizations almost as much as a summer rerun. Paperback originals, they are available in hardcover only in large-print editions (G. K. Hall, 1980). John Hawkesworth, the producer of *Upstairs, Downstairs* and other successful television series such as *The Duchess of Duke Street*, *The Flame Trees of Thika*, and Granada's *Sherlock Holmes* series, wrote numbers 1 and 2. Mollie Hardwick (q.v.) wrote numbers 3 and 4. Mollie's husband, Michael Hardwick, wrote numbers 5 and 6. Hawkesworth never got around to publishing his book on the making of *Upstairs, Downstairs*, but Richard Marson's *Inside Updown: The Story of Upstairs, Downstairs* (Kaleidoscope, 2002) fills the gap nicely.

1. *Upstairs Downstairs* (Dell, 1973) Sarah joins the Bellamy household as parlor maid, and young James takes too much of an interest in her.
2. *In My Lady's Chamber* (Dell, 1974) Scandals and indiscretions sweep the decks, and King Edward comes to dinner.
3. *Years of Change, The* (Dell, 1974) War threatens, and Lady Bellamy goes down on the *Titanic*. Written by Mollie Hardwick.
4. *War to End War, The* (Dell, 1975) Rose becomes a part-time bus conductor, and Mr. Hudson is a special constable as World War I envelops Europe. Written by Mollie Hardwick.
5. *On with the Dance* (Dell, 1975) James's mental scars from the War are slow to heal. Richard remarries. Mr. Hudson falls in love. Written by Michael Hardwick.
6. *Endings and Beginnings* (Dell, 1975) James sets out for the New World. Mr. Hudson has a heart attack. The household is finally dispersed. Written by Michael Hardwick.

Haydon, Elizabeth

Symphony of Ages has joined the ranks of best-selling adult epic fantasy series. Rhapsody the Singer, the Brother (aka Achmed the assassin-king), and Grunthor the giant sergeant-major are three of the main characters who must defeat the F'dor, the ancient demon who seeks to destroy the world. Numbers 1, 2, and 3 form a unit and were issued in a boxed set by Tor (2003), but many of Symphony's characters are carried into further volumes with new characters and events, and the adventures haven't stopped yet.

1. *Rhapsody: Child of Blood* (Tor, 1999) Rhapsody is abducted into an epic voyage across centuries and continents in a fantasy world, where she teams up with Achmed the assassin-king and giant Grunthor.
2. *Prophecy: Child of Earth* (Tor, 2000) Rhapsody seeks to save a religious leader, while Achmed and Grunthor go after the ancient demon, the F'dor, to fulfill the Prophecy of the Three.
3. *Destiny: Child of the Sky* (Tor, 2001) Time is running short before the Fellowship of Three have to face their final confrontation with the F'dor.
4. *Requiem for the Sun* (Tor, 2003) Rhapsody, her draconian husband, Ashe, Achmed, and Grunthor once more take on the demon F'dor and its human host, a man long believed dead.
5. *Elegy for a Lost Star* (Tor, 2004) The dragon Anwyn awakens after three years in a deathlike sleep and seeks revenge. Achmed has his own problems with a guild of assassins that is out to get him. A

horribly deformed but magical being may be the instrument by which a despot will conquer a continent.
6. *Assassin King, The* (Tor, 2006) A convocation of dragons meets to discuss ways and means of survival. A council of war is held between Ashe and Rhapsody, Gwydion, Anborn, Achmed, and Grunthor to prepare for a coming cataclysm.

Haymon, S(ylvia) T(heresa)

Haymon's darkly lyrical, emotionally intense style and her compassionate rendering of character reminds critics of P. D. James (q.v.). Haymon's hero, Inspector Ben Jurnet of the Angleby (England) CID is a fully realized character who, during the course of this disturbing, sometimes eerie procedural series, falls in love with and loses Miriam, a Jewish woman. The late Haymon (d. 1995) also wrote a pair of evocative memoirs subtitled *An East Anglian Childhood*: *Opposite the Cross Keys* (St. Martin's, 1988) and *The Quivering Tree* (St. Martin's, 1990).

1. *Death and the Pregnant Woman* (St. Martin's, 1980) The fifth anniversary of the rediscovery of an image from a medieval shrine in a Norfolk village is marked by murder.
2. *Ritual Murder* (St. Martin's, 1982) Choirboy Arthur Cossey is murdered and mutilated in a crime that seems to re-create an alleged ritual murder in 1144.
3. *Stately Homicide* (St. Martin's, 1985) Historic Bullen Hall is the scene of a bizarre series of events after a cache of love letters from Anne Bullen (Boleyn) to her brother is discovered.
4. *Death of a God* (St. Martin's, 1987) The concert of rock group the Second Coming is followed by the crucifixion of its lead singer.
5. *Very Particular Murder, A* (St. Martin's, 1989) Nobel laureate physicist Max Flaschner is poisoned with cyanide-laced orange juice.
6. *Death of a Warrior Queen* (St. Martin's, 1992) After giving security advice to a dig of Druid remains associated with Queen Boadicea, Jurnet, with Miriam, discovers the corpse of a small-town prostitute.
7. *Beautiful Death, A* (St. Martin's, 1994) Devastated when a car bomb intended for him kills his fiancée Miriam, Jurnet goes to Ireland in search of the terrorists who may have been responsible.
8. *Death of a Hero* (St. Martin's, 1996) After leading a staged happening of 10,000 unemployed men at a famous historical site, the charismatic Charlie Appleyard dies at the house of onetime college friend Jenny Nunn, who has somehow combined a History First with prostitution.

Haywood, Gar Anthony

I. Aaron Gunner is an African American private investigator working out of Los Angeles. Although he tries to avoid doing so, Aaron gets involved in some messy, contentious cases with large social and racial implications. Sharp dialogue, an interesting protagonist, and a gritty Los Angeles ambience mark this series.

1. *Fear of the Dark* (St. Martin's, 1988) When two innocent black men are killed by a white psychotic, Aaron reenters the private eye business at the urging of one of the victim's sisters
2. *Not Long for This World* (St. Martin's, 1990) Toby Mills, a member of the Imperial Blues gang, is a prime suspect when Darryl Lovejoy, who is trying to help gang members go straight, is murdered.
3. *You Can Die Trying* (St. Martin's, 1993) After brutal white cop Jack McGovern commits suicide over the fallout from his shooting

of an apparently unarmed black youth, a witness with a different story comes forward belatedly to Gunner.

4. *It's Not a Pretty Sight* (Putnam, 1996) Aaron, searching for the killer of former girlfriend Nina Pearson and a "skip" suspect for Best-Wily Electronics owner Roman Goody, runs into a raft of stories of abuse and mistreatment.

5. *When Last Seen Alive* (Putnam, 1997) Gunner is hired to take pictures of city councilman Gil Everson committing adultery and asked to look for the missing Elroy Covington, whom Gunner had met at the Million Man March in Washington, DC.

6. *All the Lucky Ones Are Dead* (Putnam, 2000) Aaron gets involved again with the racist Defenders of the Bloodline and the world of "gangsta rap" even though he has turned down assignments to guard African American talk-show host Sparkle Johnson and to investigate the death of rapper C. E. Digga Jones.

II. Retired policeman Joe Loudermilk and his wife, Dottie, are trying to take a relaxing cross-country trip in their Airstream trailer home, but they keep running into difficulties created by their sociopathic sons.

1. *Going Nowhere Fast* (Putnam, 1994) Stopping near the Grand Canyon, the Loudermilks are visited by their youngest son "Bad Dog," and a dead man turns up in the toilet of their trailer.

2. *Bad News Travels Fast* (Putnam, 1995) Joe and Dottie have dinner with their son Eddie in Washington, DC, and are somewhat disturbed by Eddie's virulent right-wing views.

Heald, Tim(othy Villiers)

I. British journalist and writer Heald's unlikely detective, Simon Bognor, is a pudgy, lazy fellow perfectly happy to drift between having meals at his London club and shuffling papers at his desk. But inevitably, his boss orders him off his "fat backside" to investigate some irregularity that has come to the Borard of Trade's attention. In the field, Bognor bungles each interview and follows false clues until the mystery seems to solve itself—allowing the reader a nice lead. A romance with girlfriend Monica, which ends in marriage, develops through the series.

1. *Unbecoming Habits* (Stein & Day, 1973) Are the friars at Beaubridge sending technological secrets to Russia in their jars of honey?

2. *Blue Blood Will Out* (Stein & Day, 1974) Simon investigates the murder of a flamboyant tycoon at a meeting of owners of England's stateliest homes.

3. *Deadline* (Stein & Day, 1975) To find the murderer of a gossip columnist, Bognor poses as a journalist.

4. *Let Sleeping Dogs Die* (Stein & Day, 1976) Sent to investigate a possible poisoning of a champion poodle, Simon uncovers dog smuggling, murder, and other hairy doings.

5. *Just Desserts* (Scribner, 1978) Bognor enters the international gourmet scene to investigate gourmet-cook Savarin Smith's strange death.

6. *Murder at Moose Jaw* (Doubleday, 1981) Finally wed to Monica-the-blase and fast approaching middle age, Bognor goes to Canada to investigate some LSD smuggling.

7. *Small Masterpiece, A* (Doubleday, 1982) Bognor's class reunion at Oxford is shaken up by the murder of Lord Beckenham, one of his former tutors. UK title: *Masterstroke*.

8. *Red Herrings* (Doubleday, 1986) The annual Popinjay Clout in the village of Herring St. George takes an unexpected turn when VAT inspector Brian Wilmslow is found shot full of arrows.

9. *Brought to Book* (Doubleday, 1988) Bognor becomes a suspect when Vernon Hemlock, publisher and erotica collector, is crushed between the shelves of his library stacks.

10. *Business Unusual* (Doubleday, 1989) Simon and Monica, in the town of Scarpington, find themselves involved with the local Rotary club and another club with a disturbingly sexual theme.

II. Tim Heald has started a new series featuring Doctor Tudor Cornwall, Reader in Criminal Studies at the University of Wessex. The only two titles published so far have appeared in the United States only in large-print editions.

1. *Death and the Visiting Fellow* (Hale [UK], 2004) When Dr. Tudor Cornwall arrives as a Visiting Fellow at an Australian university, he runs into a bevy of odd characters, including an ecologically correct axe man, a professor of wine, and the world's leading authority on the Australian hedgehog.

2. *Death and the D'Urbervilles* (Hale [UK], 2005) Doctor Cornwall decides to rewrite *Tess of the D'Urbervilles* in the style of Sir Arthur Conan Doyle (q.v.) to determine how Alec D'Urberville met his violent end.

Healy, Jeremiah F.

Like Robert B. Parker's (q.v.) Spenser, John Francis Cuddy is a Boston-based private eye created by a Boston-based college professor (New England School of Law). Like many fictional private eyes Cuddy is tough yet sensitive, attractive to women but reluctant to commit himself emotionally again, streetwise but too honest to get rich in his profession. What makes Cuddy a little different is that he still goes to his late wife's graveside to divulge his confidences.

1. *Blunt Darts* (Walker, 1984) John Cuddy, fired by his employer for inappropriate honesty, is hired to locate a wealthy woman's runaway grandson.

2. *Staked Goat, The* (Harper, 1986) Cuddy seeks to avenge the mutilation slaying of an old Vietnam buddy. UK title: *The Tethered Goat*.

3. *So Like Sleep* (Harper, 1987) Cuddy takes on the seemingly hopeless task of proving that young, black William Daniels is innocent of the murder of his white lover.

4. *Swan Dive* (Harper, 1988) Cuddy is a suspect in the murder of a sadistic philanderer who was vigorously opposing his wife's plea for a divorce.

5. *Yesterday's News* (Harper, 1989) A reporter who hires Cuddy to substantiate her theory that a murder is being covered up is herself murdered.

6. *Right to Die* (Pocket, 1991) Euthanasia advocate Maisy Andrus is receiving anonymous death threats.

7. *Shallow Graves* (Pocket, 1992) In what seems to be burglary gone wrong, Boston model Mau Tim Dani is strangled in her apartment.

8. *Foursome* (Pocket, 1993) When three members of a foursome vacationing in Maine are killed by crossbow bolts, the fourth is a prime suspect.

9. *Act of God* (Pocket, 1994) Furniture mogul Honest Abe Rivkind has been murdered, and his secretary Dabra Pfoft is missing from her New Jersey vacation.

10. *Rescue* (Pocket, 1995) Cuddy's search for a 10-year-old boy he had encountered on the road takes him from New Hampshire to Florida and the compound of the Church of the Lord Vigilant.

11. *Invasion of Privacy* (Pocket, 1996) Cuddy's client, banker Olga Evorova, is uneasy about the excessive secrecy of her lover,

businessman Andrew Dees. A beating by two hoods tells Cuddy that something isn't on the up-and-up.

12. *Concise Cuddy: A Collection of John Francis Cuddy Stories* (Crippen & Landru, 1998) A collection of 17 short stories.

13. *Only Good Lawyer, The* (Pocket, 1998) Reluctantly taking on the case of Alan Spaeth, a racist who is charged with killing his wife's African American divorce lawyer, Cuddy gradually begins to believe that his client is being framed.

14. *Spiral* (Pocket, 1999) Devastated by the death of his lover, Nancy Meagher, in an airline accident, Cuddy gets talked into investigating the murder of a 13-year-old girl in Florida.

15. *Cuddy Plus One* (Crippen & Landru, 2003) Thirteen previously unpublished Cuddy stories plus one about a character named Mairead Clare.

Heath, Roy A(ubrey) K(elvin)

I. British Guiana (now Guyana)-born Heath has lived in London since 1951, but his novels have helped put his homeland on the literary map. His Georgetown (capital of Guyana) trilogy, a panoramic depiction of the lives of the Armstrong family from the 1920s to the 1950s, is based in part on his own parents and siblings. *The Armstrong Trilogy* (Persea, 1994) is an omnibus volume containing all three novels.

1. *From the Heat of the Day* (Persea, 1992) Sonny Armstrong, postal worker and aspiring writer, woos Gladys Davis, youngest daughter of a family from the better part of town. Originally published in the United Kingdom in 1979.

2. *One Generation* (Allison & Busby [UK], 1980) The focus shifts to Rohan, son of Gladys and Sonny, as he seeks happiness in the Guyanese East Indian community by wooing the beautiful Indroni Mohammed.

3. *Genetha* (Allison & Busby [UK], 1981) Sexually dissatisfied Genetha runs from a boring relationship with the respectable Michael into a passionate affair with snooker ace Fingers.

II. A pair of novels follows the fortunes of Kwaku Cholmondeley as he tries to rise above his beginnings in a poor, backwater village. Kwaku sets up as a "healer," enjoys momentary success, but finally fetches up in Georgetown, where he falls under the sway of a shady civil servant nicknamed the Right Hand Man. Kwaku's struggles against his personal weaknesses, including his relationships with two women: his wife and the mother of his nine children, Miss Gwendoline, and childhood friend Blossom, who is married to another, are told in entertaining, comic fashion.

1. *Kwaku; or, The Man Who Could Not Keep His Mouth Shut* (Boyars, 1997) Kwaku Cholmondeley comes of age and tries to rise above his poor backwater village by becoming, among other things, a healer. Originally published in the United Kingdom in 1982.

2. *Ministry of Hope, The* (Boyars, 1996) Kwaku, starting over in Georgetown, comes under the patronage of the "Right Hand Man" and has trouble adjusting to city life.

Heaven, Constance

I. Ravensley, the home of the Aylsham family, is located in the Fen Country of England. It provides a picturesque setting for this pair of historical romances that chronicles two generations of Aylshams beginning in the early 1800s. Heaven, an English author, provides a lively mix of love affairs, scandals, natural disasters, and war scenes to keep readers of the genre glued to the page.

1. *Lord of Ravensley* (Coward, 1978) A plan to drain the fenlands brings conflict and heartbreak to members of the love-torn Aylsham family.

2. *Ravensley Touch, The* (Coward, 1982) The star-crossed love of Jethro Aylsham and Laurel Rutland, which begins in Rome, is carried to the battlegrounds of the Crimean War.

II. The Kuragin trilogy also takes place in the first half of the 19th century, but in Russia rather than England. Rebellions and revolutions, decadent aristocrats, and exotic scenery form the backdrop for this trio of historical romances.

1. *House of Kuragin, The* (Coward, 1972) Young Englishwoman Rilla Western travels to Russia to become governess to the aristocratic Kuragin family and falls into a love affair with Andrei, Count Kuragin's brother.

2. *Astrov Legacy, The* (Coward, 1973) Sophie Western, visiting her sister Rilla, meets Prince Leonid Astrov and observes the Decembrist Uprising of 1825. UK title: *The Astrov Inheritance*.

3. *Heir to Kuragin* (Coward, 1979) In 1846 Princess Gadiani, following her missing husband to his ancestral home in the Caucasus, is escorted through dangerous territory by Count Paul Kuragin.

Hebden, Juliet

PSEUDONYM OF Juliet Harris

Juliet Hebden, daughter of the late Mark Hebden (q.v.), continued his Pel series through several more titles, none of which were published in the United States.

1. *Pel Picks Up the Pieces* (Constable [UK], 1993) After Pel receives a letter from an old friend, two murders and a suspicious robbery at a nearby mansion are committed.

2. *Pel and the Perfect Partner* (Constable [UK], 1994) Pel is missing! And the notorious Poltergeist has escaped from a high-security prison.

3. *Pel and the Patriarch* (Constable [UK], 1996) Pel faces a mad rapist at Christmastime.

4. *Pel and the Precious Parcel* (Constable [UK], 1997) Masked men rob an airplane at gunpoint, stealing only a solitary package.

5. *Pel Is Provoked* (Constable [UK], 1998) Are vampires at work when the bodies of two girls, one in Spain, one in France, are found bearing bite wounds in the neck?

6. *Pel and the Death of the Detective* (Constable [UK], 2000) Pel, up against a group of violent terrorists, loses an associate.

7. *Pel and the Butchers' Blades* (Constable [UK], 2001) Pel faces a gruesome murder with no clue to the victim's identity and pressure from his new chief.

8. *Pel and the Nickname Game* (Constable [UK], 2002) A decomposing corpse in a locked room, a drowned nun, a knifer in a club, and an armed robbery that turns into tragedy are on Pel's plate this time.

Hebden, Mark

PSEUDONYM OF John Harris

Fans of Georges Simenon (q.v.) will enjoy this series starring Inspector Evariste Clovis Desire Pel of the French provincial police in Burgundy. Middle-aged and heavy-hearted, Pel often seems to brood his way to the core of each case. Continuing threads in the series include Pel's relationships with several young subordinates to whom he teaches the elements of detection, and his courtship of, and eventual marriage to, the widow Genevieve Faivre-Perret. The books are written in an oddly stilted English that reads like a translation. Englishman John Harris wrote several suspense novels as "Mark Hebden" in the 1960s and 1970s, three of which featured a character named Colonel Mostyn (*Mask of Violence*; *A Pride of Dolphins*; *The League of 89*), as well as three military series under the pseudonym of Max Hennessy (q.v.). After Mark Hebden's death in 1991, the Pel series was continued by his daughter Juliet Hebden (q.v.).

1. *Pel and the Faceless Corpse* (Walker, 1982) A corpse with its face shot away is found at the base of a monument to the French Resistance. Originally published in the United Kingdom in 1979. Variant title: *Pel and the Headless Corpse*.
2. *Death Set to Music* (Walker, 1983) Mme. Camille-Jeanne Chenandier is found bludgeoned to death in her living room. Originally published in the United Kingdom in 1979. Variant title: *Pel and the Parked Car*.
3. *Pel under Pressure* (Walker, 1983) Pel must deal with drug traffickers and a university prostitution ring. Originally published in the United Kingdom in 1980.
4. *Pel Is Puzzled* (Hamilton [UK], 1981) Spies, art theft, and a utilities swindle disturb Pel's peace of mind. Not published in the United States.
5. *Pel and the Staghound* (Walker, 1984) The disappearance of rich Francois Rensselaer causes more concern to his staghound Archer than to his wife and employees. Originally published in the United Kingdom in 1982.
6. *Pel and the Bombers* (Walker, 1985) Terrorists, murder, and a planned assassination get in the way of Pel's courtship of Madame Faivre-Perret. Originally published in the United Kingdom in 1983.
7. *Pel and the Pirates* (Walker, 1987) The honeymooning Pels find the corpse of a taxi driver on their doorstep on the Isle of St. Yves. Originally published in the United Kingdom in 1984.
8. *Pel and the Predators* (Walker, 1985) Pel must cope with a death threat and three cases of murder, one of them 40 years old.
9. *Pel and the Prowler* (Walker, 1986) A serial killer of young women leaves a cryptic message near each body and a mark on each victim's cheek.
10. *Pel and the Paris Mob* (Hamilton [UK], 1986) Gangs from Paris and Marseilles are invading Pel's home turf. Not published in the United States.
11. *Pel among the Pueblos* (Walker, 1988) The murder of a retired gangster leads Pel to Mexico.
12. *Pel and the Touch of Pitch* (Walker, 1988) Local deputy Claude Barclay is kidnapped on the eve of national elections.
13. *Pel and the Picture of Innocence* (St. Martin's, 1989) Pel gets depressed when Maurice Tagliatti and his gang return to town, but Maurice is soon murdered.
14. *Pel and the Party Spirit* (St. Martin's, 1991) A modern corpse is found when an old tower collapses. Murderous hitchhikers are thumbing their way on Route Nationale 6. The daughter of a wealthy family is kidnapped. And that isn't all. Originally published in the United Kingdom in 1989.
15. *Pel and the Missing Persons* (St. Martin's, 1991) Another crime wave hits Burgundy: a motorized holdup gang, a probable hit-and-run victim, and a rash of missing persons.
16. *Pel and the Promised Land* (St. Martin's, 1993) Welsh land speculators, a Spanish gangster, arson, and the murder of the wife of a local baron preoccupy Pel. Originally published in the United Kingdom in 1991.
17. *Pel and the Sepulchre Job* (St. Martin's, 1993) As Pel trains a new female member of his team, a body is pulled from a canal, two paintings are stolen, and a bank heist turns into a hostage situation.

Hebert, Ernest

Darby, New Hampshire, is a fictional town that has been compared to locations created by William Faulkner (q.v.) or Caroline Chute (q.v.). Ernest Hebert explores the class divisions in small-town America through trash collector Howie Elman and his son Frederick, hermit Cootie Patterson, the upper crust Salmons, and the tarpaper-shack-dwelling Jordan clan. Hebert's characters are treated with sympathy and understanding. Ernest Hebert has been a taxi driver, a gas station manager, editor and reporter for the *Keene (NH) Sentinel*, and professor of English at Dartmouth College. He is also the author of two other novels about New Hampshire: *Mad Boys* (University Press of New England, 1993) and *The Old American* (University Press of New England, 2000) and a book about picture post cards, *Greetings from New England* (Graphic Arts Center, 1988). Ernest Hebert is not to be confused with the French artist, Ernest Antoine Hebert. Numbers 2 and 4 were published together as *The Kinship: With a New Essay* (University Press of New England, 1993).

1. *Dogs of March, The* (Viking, 1979) Trash and junkyard man Howard Elman broods over life's unfairness, including the winter-weakened deer menaced by house pets in March and the class struggle between citified immigrants with "college degrees and big bank accounts" and the indigenous locals, who are scratching out a living.
2. *Little More Than Kin, A* (Viking, 1982) Focuses on the Jordans, a family in the rural "tar-paper-shack" underclass of New Hampshire, alcoholism, and retardation.
3. *Whisper My Name* (Viking, 1984) The proposal to build a giant shopping mall in Darby threatens to change the town's character, and produces some odd alliances among the townsfolk.
4. *Passion of Estelle Jordan, The* (Viking, 1987) Sixty-year-old prostitute Estelle Jordan is ready to take control of her own life, even if it means defying her kinfolk and townsfolk.
5. *Live Free or Die* (Viking, 1990) In what was originally to be the conclusion of the Darby cycle, Frederick Elman returns home to Darby and his father's trash-collection business and gets involved with Lilith, daughter of the late town "Squire" Reggie Salmon.
6. *Spoonwood* (University Press of New England, 2005) A sequel to *Live Free or Die* published 15 years after that novel. In the last book, Lilith Salmon died giving birth to Freddie Elman's son. Now Freddie, consumed by grief and anger and struggling with alcoholism, is ill-prepared to be a father to his son, Birch.

Heck, Peter J.

Mark Twain (q.v.) is a natural for a historical-mystery series, given that he wrote several "detection" stories himself, including *Tom Sawyer, Detective*. We find Samuel L. Clemens, already a world celebrity as "Mark Twain" but still unreluctant to poke his nose into things or pull a friend out of a jam. Other historical characters, including Rudyard Kipling and George Washington Cable, appear in these pages, as well as the occasional character out of someone else's writings, for example, Inspector Lestrade, Sherlock Holmes's foil. Peter J. Heck doesn't try to imitate the Twain style. Instead he provides Twain with Wentworth Cabot, ex-Yale man, as companion and narrator of his adventures. Peter J. Heck is also the coauthor of four of Robert Asprin's (q.v.) Phule novels.

1. *Death on the Mississippi* **(Berkley, 1995)** New York police discover a dead man who has Sam Clemens's address in his pocket, just before Sam and Wentworth Cabot leave for the West to retrieve some buried gold that Sam mentioned in *Life on the Mississippi*.
2. *Connecticut Yankee in Criminal Court, A* **(Berkley, 1996)** Author George Washington Cable is among several historical characters encountered by Mark and Wentworth on a lecture tour in New Orleans, where Mark is called upon to exonerate a black cook imprisoned for the poisoning of his employer.
3. *Prince and the Prosecutor, The* **(Berkley, 1997)** Twain and Cabot head for a lecture tour aboard the steamship *City of Baltimore*, where fellow passengers include a young Rudyard Kipling and his wife, a dubious German prince, and Robert Babson, a boorish young Philadelphian, who disappears one stormy night.
4. *Guilty Abroad, The* **(Berkley, 1999)** In London on a lecture tour, the boys encounter Slippery Ed McPhee, a con man dating back to Twain's riverboat days, and, after a murder occurs, Inspector G. Lestrade of Scotland Yard.
5. *Mysterious Strangler, The* **(Berkley, 2000)** Twain, his family, and Wentworth Cabot enjoy the weather in sunny Florence until a Raphael masterpiece and a beautiful young woman disappear at the same time.
6. *Tom's Lawyer* **(Berkley, 2001)** On a lecture tour out West, Sam is reunited with boyhood friend, and original of Huckleberry Finn, Tom Blankenship. Then it is up to Sam to get Tom out of a murder charge.

Heffernan, William

Paul Devlin is a former NYC police detective who rusticates himself to rural Vermont after he is forced to kill his partner, who was a serial murderer. However, the "sleepy" Vermont town turns out to be less bucolic than expected, and Devlin eventually winds up back in the New York police department in this suspenseful, action-filled series. William Heffernan, former award-winning reporter for the *New York Daily News*, has written other New York–based (e.g., *Ritual*) and Vermont-based (e.g., *Beulah Hill*) novels.

1. *Blood Rose* **(Dutton, 1991)** Haunted by bad memories, Paul Devlin has retreated to a rural Vermont town where he has become police chief. Devlin befriends Leslie Adams, who is fleeing her brutal husband. Meanwhile, a serial killer who leaves red roses as a signature is busy in Vermont.
2. *Scarred* **(Signet, 1993)** Another serial killer is on the loose in New York and Paul Devlin is asked by an old friend to look after his goddaughter, Adrianna Mendez, an old girlfriend of Paul's.
3. *Tarnished Blue* **(Onyx, 1995)** NYPD Captain Joe "Little Bat" Battaglia is murdered, and Paul Devlin, now inspector of detectives, is called in to cut through the corruption that has impeded the investigation.
4. *Winter's Gold* **(Onyx, 1997)** Natasha Winter, ex-wife of Donald Trump–type tycoon Roland Winter, is found dead in the bathtub of her suite in the Winter high-rise.
5. *Red Angel* **(Morrow, 2000)** Devlin accompanies lover Adrianna Menendez to Havana, where her aunt Maria, "the Red Angel," who was in a hospital, is dead and her body is missing.
6. *Unholy Order* **(Morrow, 2002)** A nun just back from Colombia is murdered and mutilated to retrieve the condoms filled with heroin she was forced to swallow, and higher-ups in her order, the Opus Christi, are reluctant to cooperate in the investigation.

Heinlein, Robert A(nson)

The late Nebula Grand Master Robert A. Heinlein included most of his earlier work in what he called a Future History series set in a not-too-distant future in which mankind had, largely through technology driven by private enterprise, managed to colonize the moon and other planets. Many of the stories were published in *Astounding Science Fiction* magazine in the 1940s and reprinted in book form in the 1950s and 1960s (numbers 1–5). After the 1950s, Heinlein more or less abandoned *Future History*, but did publish an occasional work related to the theme. Numbers 1, 6, and 8 have a somewhat closer relationship to each other, as do numbers 7 and 9. *The Past through Tomorrow* (Putnam, 1967) is an omnibus volume containing numbers 1 through 4 minus the story "There Be Light" and plus the stories "Searchlight" and "The Menace from Earth." Numbers 1 and 4 were published together in an omnibus volume: *Revolt in 2100/Methuselah's Children* (Baen, 1998). All of the titles in the series have been reprinted many times.

According to some critics, most of Heinlein's best work was done by the 1950s. *The Puppet Masters* (Doubleday, 1951) was called "paranoid" and "McCarthyite." *Starship Troopers* (Putnam, 1959) and *The Moon Is a Harsh Mistress* (Putnam, 1966) gave Heinlein a reputation as an extreme right-winger, although it would be fairer to label him as a libertarian rather than as a fascist. *Stranger in a Strange Land* (Putnam, 1961), however, became a cult classic, partly because of what was seen as its advocacy of free love.

1. *Methuselah's Children* **(Gnome, 1958)** The Howard Families, products of an interbreeding program that produced 100,000 people with an average life expectancy of 150 years, get into trouble, when their existence is finally revealed. The theme is developed further in numbers 6 and 8. Originally published in *Astounding Science Fiction* in 1941 and revised for book publication in 1958.
2. *Man Who Sold the Moon, The* **(Shasta, 1950)** Short stories, originally published in *Astounding Science Fiction* in the 1940s.
3. *Green Hills of Earth, The* **(Shasta, 1951)** Short stories, originally published in *Astounding Science Fiction* in the 1940s.
4. *Revolt in 2100* **(Shasta, 1953)** Collection of short stories published in *Astounding Science Fiction* in the 1940s.
5. *Orphans of the Sky* **(Putnam, 1964)** A ship drifting through space becomes a microcosm of society. Published in 1941 in *Astounding Science Fiction* as "Universe" and "Common Sense." *Universe* published separately (1951).
6. *Time Enough for Love* **(Putnam, 1973)** Subtitle: *The Lives of Lazarus Long*. Lazarus Long, two thousand years old in the year 4272, wishes to die, but he is rejuvenated because his memories are needed to reinvigorate a decaying society. Abridged version published as *The Notebooks of Lazarus Long* (Putnam, 1978).
7. *Moon Is a Harsh Mistress, The* **(Putnam, 1966)** Inmates of the Luna penal colony on the moon plan a revolt. Mike, a lonely computer who likes to make up jokes, is part of it. The story of Mike is continued in number 9.
8. *To Sail beyond the Sunset* **(Putnam, 1987)** Subtitle: *The Life and Loves of Maureen Johnson; Being the Memoirs of a Somewhat Irregular Lady*. Maureen Johnson lived on Earth from 1882 to 1982, when she moved to Tertius, was rejuvenated, and married into the Long family.
9. *Cat Who Walks through Walls, The* **(Putnam, 1985)** Richard Ames, a stand-in for Heinlein, marries Gwen Novak and escapes to the moon and then to the planet Tertius, headquarters of the Time Corps.

Hellenga, Robert

Three well-written novels tell the stories of Margot Harrington and her father, Rudy Harrington. The first novel takes place in Florence after the 1966 Arno flood, where book conservator Margot has journeyed as a "mud angel." The second novel concerns the efforts of the widowed Rudy to sell his Chicago home, buy an avocado ranch in Texas, and marry off his daughter Molly. Number 3 finds Margot still in Florence in 1990. The novels are full of charming characters and wise philosophical asides. Robert Hellenga, professor of English at Knox College in Illinois, is also the author of the novel *Blues Lessons* (Scribner, 2002).

1. *Sixteen Pleasures, The* (Warner, 1994) Margot Harrington arrives in Florence in the wake of the flood of 1966 to restore damaged volumes but gets involved in the sale of an erotic Renaissance manuscript owned by nuns at a Carmelite convent and a love affair with Dottor Alessandro "Sandro" Postiglione, married art restoration expert.
2. *Philosophy Made Simple* (Little, Brown, 2006) Widower Rudy Harrington decides to sell his home in Chicago, move to an avocado farm in Texas, and plan a big Indian-style wedding for his daughter Molly, who is marrying the nephew of Siva Singh, author of the college text *Philosophy Made Simple*.
3. *Italian Lover, The* (Little, Brown, 2007) In the fall of 1990, Margot is 53, living in her adopted Florence and awaiting the arrival of a film producer who wants to adapt her 1975 memoir for film.

Heller, Joseph

Catch-22 is a prime example of a novel that became a cult classic through word of mouth. It became a favorite counterculture text in the 1960s, was made into a hit movie, and eventually was accepted as a classic in the literary world. Reviewers who thought that all World War II novels were rip-offs of either *The Naked and the Dead* or *Mr. Roberts* didn't know what to make of the wild, surrealistic world of Yossarian and company. Although Joseph Heller published several quite good novels after *Catch-22*, none of them met with the same enthusiasm. Perhaps it was inevitable that Heller would be tempted into writing a sequel—and inevitable that nearly everyone would be disappointed by that sequel.

1. *Catch-22* (Simon & Schuster, 1961) John Yossarian, American bomber crew member stationed on the Mediterranean island of Planosa, is determined to survive World War II despite the best efforts of the American brass.
2. *Closing Time* (Simon & Schuster, 1994) Yossarian, Milo Minderbinder, Sammy Singer, and others have survived into the grotesque underground world of the 1980s and 1990s.

Henderson, Lauren

London-based sculptress Sam Jones is the heroine of a series of mysteries that author Lauren Henderson refers to as "tart noir." Sam is sexy, given to fetishism (she likes to wear rubber), politically incorrect (she takes hefty portions of tobacco and liquor along with her "coke"), full of acid commentary on the art and club scenes of London and New York (she never does get the hang of New York dating mores), and ready to take on the occasional murder mystery that comes her way.

1. *Dead White Female* (Hodder & Stoughton [UK], 1995) Sam Jones abandons the sculpture she is working on to investigate the suspicious death of her art tutor, Lee Jackson which, unlike the police, Sam believes is no accident. Not published in the United States.
2. *Too Many Blondes* (Hodder & Stoughton [UK], 1996) Sam is asked to investigate the death of a colleague at the gym. Not published in the United States.
3. *Black Rubber Dress, The* (Three Rivers, 1999) Sam finds herself in the midst of blackmail, drugs, anorexics, loud merchant bankers, and expensive dinners—and up to her ears in trouble. Originally published in the United Kingdom in 1997.
4. *Freeze My Margarita* (Three Rivers, 2000) Sam, undertaking a commission to create a series of mobiles for the latest production of an old friend from art school, runs into a series of enigmas. Is the acidly witty and very attractive actor Hugo gay? And what about the decaying corpse in the sump under the theater? Originally published in the United Kingdom in 1998.
5. *Strawberry Tattoo, The* (Three Rivers, 2000) Sam, exhibiting her massive sculptures at the cutting-edge Bergmann LaTouche Gallery in Soho, New York, gets involved in a melange of art desecration, messy relationships, and murder.
6. *Chained* (Three Rivers, 2002) Sam wakes up to find herself chained and handcuffed in a dank, roach-infested cellar, perhaps as a stand-in for a difficult and unpopular BBC TV actress named Sarah.
7. *Pretty Boy* (Three Rivers, 2002) With her actor boyfriend, Sam travels to the provinces, where she finds that bucolic villages in the English countryside are not immune to murder.

Hennessy, Max

PSEUDONYM OF John Harris

I. The Lion at Sea trilogy is a story of the British navy in World Wars I and II. The "Lion" is Kelly Maguire ("Ginger" to his shipmates), a young Anglo-Irishman with the courage and resourcefulness of a Hornblower (q.v.), destined to rise to a high rank. His sense of honor, sense of humor, and attractiveness to the ladies guarantee his fictional success. The late Englishman John Harris also wrote the Pel detective series under the pseudonym of Mark Hebden (q.v.).

1. *Lion at Sea, The* (Atheneum, 1978) The story begins in 1911, when Kelly rescues a drowning man and receives a medal even before taking his sublieutenant's exam. This volume introduces Kelly's childhood sweetheart, Charlotte (Charley) Upford, and continues to the Battle of Jutland, 1916.
2. *Dangerous Years, The* (Atheneum, 1979) After the war, Lieutenant Maguire rescues refugees in Yalta, is sent ashore to help some White Russians escape, and then is off to China.
3. *Back to Battle* (Atheneum, 1980) Beginning with some run-ins off the coast of Spain during that country's civil war and continuing through action in every major sea battle of World War II, Ginger Maguire remains indomitable.

II. This prolific British author also wrote a trio of British cavalry books featuring three generations of the Goff family of Yorkshire, who serve with the historic 19th Lancers.

1. *Soldier of the Queen* (Atheneum, 1980) Colby Goff joins the 19th Lancers just in time to see action with the Light Brigade at Balaclava in 1854. Over the next 25 years, he serves in India, America during the Civil War, and Africa during the Zulu wars.
2. *Blunted Lance* (Atheneum, 1981) Colby's son Dabney distinguishes himself in the Boer War and World War I.

3. *Iron Stallions, The* (Atheneum, 1982) Colby's grandson Joshua carries on the family cavalry tradition in the "iron stallions" (tanks) of World War II.

III. After trilogies about sea and land warfare, Hennessy took to the air in a trilogy that follows RAF pilot Dicken Quinney from teenage aerial derring-do in World War I to middle-aged heroics in World War II. Quinney does have a rather phlegmatic love life, and the novels are at their best when he is airborne.

1. *Bright Blue Sky, The* (Atheneum, 1983) Seventeen-year-old Dicken Quinney joins up as a flying wireless operator in 1914, but soon finds himself flying combat missions.
2. *Challenging Heights, The* (Atheneum, 1983) Quinney has trouble coping with postwar life in the 1920s and rejoins the RAF.
3. *Once More the Hawks* (Atheneum, 1984) Near retirement, Quinney is called back into action by the outbreak of World War II.

Henry, Sue

Sue Henry's mystery series makes the most of the rugged and beautiful Alaskan landscape as a setting. Alaskan state trooper Alex Jensen was the leading protagonist of the first four novels in the series, but eventually Jessie Arnold, "musher" (dogsled racer), his sometime girlfriend, introduced in number 1, took over the series, although recently (numbers 11, 13, and 14), 63-year-old widow and Winnebago driver, Maxine "Maxie" McNabb, a character introduced in number 8, and her mini-dachshund, Stretch, have come to the fore. But it is usually the Alaskan landscape that is the real star of this series written by longtime Alaska resident, and instructor at the University of Alaska, Sue Henry.

1. *Murder on the Iditarod Trail* (Atlantic Monthly, 1991) Alaskan state trooper Alex Jensen and "musher" Jessie Arnold have to get to the bottom of the killings on the famed dogsled race from Anchorage to Nome, the Iditarod. Made into a TV movie.
2. *Termination Dust* (Morrow, 1995) Jim Hampton discovers an old prospector's diary from the 1800s while on vacation in the Yukon. Then he becomes leading suspect in the murder of an ex-senator from Alaska.
3. *Sleeping Lady* (Morrow, 1996) Alex Jensen investigates a plane crash near the Sleeping Lady, Mt. Susitna, and discovers that the plane was shot down.
4. *Death Takes Passage* (Morrow, 1997) Alex Jensen and Jessie Arnold embark on a cruise celebrating the centennial of the Klondike gold rush. The cruise ship is carrying $1 million in gold.
5. *Deadfall* (Morrow, 1998) The target of an unknown stalker, Jessie rusticates herself on an almost uninhabited island in Kachemak Bay.
7. *Beneath the Ashes* (Morrow, 2000) A fatal fire destroys a local cabin, and Jessie is afraid that old friend Anne Holman may be an arsonist and murderer.
8. *Dead North* (Morrow, 2001) Her cabin burned up and her relationship with Jensen broken down, Jessie agrees to retrieve her contractor's Winnebago in Idaho.
9. *Cold Company* (Morrow, 2002) Rebuilding her home and reconstructing her life, Jessie turns up a skeleton that may have a connection with Robert Hansen, serial killer of decades ago.
10. *Death Trap* (Morrow, 2003) The Alaska State Fair is the scene of a murder, a kidnapping, and the dognapping of Tank, the lead dog of Jessie Arnold, who is recuperating from knee surgery.
11. *Serpents Tail, The* (New American Library, 2004) Sixty-three-year-old widow "Maxie" McNabb, introduced in number 8, goes to Grand Junction, Colorado, to visit an ailing friend and finds herself executor of the friend's will.
12. *Murder at Five Finger Light* (New American Library, 2005) Jessie's friends Laurie and Jim have acquired an old lighthouse on Alaska's Inland Passage and are throwing a big party to celebrate.
13. *Tooth of Time, The* (New American Library, 2006) Maxie McNabb and her mini-dachshund, Stretch, continue to explore the "lower 48" in her Winnebago, "Winnie Minnie." Her travels take her to Taos, New Mexico, where she meets an old friend from Alaska and runs into a deadly killer.
14. *Refuge, The* (New American Library, 2007) Maxie journeys to Hawaii to assist a widowed, injured acquaintance, Karen Parker Bailey, and gets involved with a prowler, a plumbing saboteur, a plumber's assistant, and a park called the Refuge, which turns out be anything but.

Hensley, Joe L. (Joseph Louis)

Donald Robak is a small-town Indiana defense attorney who becomes a circuit judge (number 13). Robak prefers sleuthing to civil cases, eschews courtroom pyrotechnics and, despite a penchant for defending outsiders, is a rather cautious fellow who generally picks the safer path, and doesn't like to rush into things. A well-realized rural Indiana and its characters are depicted in these mysteries, which emphasize character rather than action. Joe L. Hensley is a lawyer and former Indiana trial judge. His Bington, Indiana is modelled on his hometown of Madison. Most of his nonseries novels feature Robak-type characters. Hensley has also published some science fiction.

1. *Deliver Us to Evil* (Doubleday, 1971) Introduces Donald Robak, who is defending a husband on trial for murdering his wife.
2. *Legislative Body* (Doubleday, 1972) Concerns the mysterious death of an Indiana state senator who might have been helped in his fatal plunge from a window.
3. *Song of Corpus Juris* (Doubleday, 1974) Robak defends a beautiful young woman accused of murder.
4. *Rivertown Risk* (Doubleday, 1977) Rivertown political boss Amos Walker is on trial for murdering his wife. The presiding judge, Michael Tostini, is one of his protégés.
5. *Killing in Gold, A* (Doubleday, 1978) Numismatics, aka coin-collecting, is at the bottom of this case.
6. *Minor Murders* (Doubleday, 1979) A 15-year-old girl is accused of killing her foster parents.
7. *Outcasts* (Doubleday, 1981) Robak is defending his cousin, who is accused of murdering his girlfriend.
8. *Robak's Cross* (Doubleday, 1985) Robak defends a friend charged with murdering his promiscuous wife.
9. *Robak's Fire* (Doubleday, 1986) Robak is representing an insurance company that refuses to pay death benefits for one Avery Benjamin, who has reportedly been seen alive after his reported demise.
10. *Robak's Firm* (Doubleday, 1987) A collection of short stories.
11. *Robak's Run* (Doubleday, 1990) Another wife-murder case, this one involving Stanley "Stan the Man" Willetts. Donald also makes a trip to sin-ridden Capitol City in search of Judge Steinmetz's estranged daughter.
12. *Robak's Witch* (St. Martin's, 1997) Robak, recovering from a gunshot wound, defends herbalist Bertha Jones, who is accused of poisoning her nephew and niece.
13. *Robak in Black* (St. Martin's, 2001) Now a circuit judge in Bington, Robak worries that his wife might have been poisoned because of a decision he made concerning child rapist and murderer

Sweetboy Wolfer and an upcoming case involving the Macing Drug Company.

Herbert, Brian

I. Brian Herbert, son of the late Frank Herbert (q.v.), and prolific SF writer Kevin J. Anderson (q.v.) are continuing the legendary Dune series, to the delight of some readers and the criticism of others, who think that the original series should have been left alone. The Prelude to Dune (numbers 1–3) and Legends of Dune (numbers 4–6) trilogies are prequels. *Hunters of Dune* and *Sandworms of Dune* (numbers 7–8) continue the original Dune books. *Legends of Dune* has been reissued in a three-volume boxed set (Tor, 2006). Brian Herbert has written a biography of his father (*Dreamer of Dune*, Tor, 2003); edited *The Songs of Muad'dib: The Poetry of Frank Herbert* (Ace, 1992), *The Notebooks of Frank Herbert's Dune* (Perigee, 1988), and (with Kevin J. Anderson) *The Road to Dune* (Tor, 2005); coauthored, with his father, a non-Dune SF novel: *Man of Two Worlds* (Putnam, 1986); coauthored other novels with Kevin J. Anderson and Marie Landis; and written several books on his own, including the nonfiction *The Forgotten Heroes: The Heroic Story of the United States Merchant Marine* (Forge, 2004).

1. *House Atreides* **(Spectra, 1999)** In the first of a series of preludes to the original *Dune* and the first novel of the Prelude to Dune trilogy, Duke Atreides and his son Leto are faced with an attack by their ancient rival, House Harkonnen. Variant title: *Dune: House Atreides*. Coauthored with Kevin J. Anderson.
2. *House Harkonnen* **(Bantam, 2000)** In the second volume of the Prelude to Dune trilogy, the House Atreides, the House Harkonnen, the Bene Gesserit, and the enigmatic Bene Tleilax battle over the desert world Arrakis, or Dune, the key to the empire. Variant title: *Dune: House Harkonnen*. Coauthored with Kevin J. Anderson.
3. *House Corrino* **(Spectra, 2001)** In the conclusion to the Prelude to Dune trilogy, Emperor Shaddam Corrino seeks to grasp greater power than any of his predecessors and to rule the Million Worlds according to his whims. Variant title: *Dune: House Corrino*. Coauthored with Kevin J. Anderson.
4. *Butlerian Jihad, The* **(Tor, 2002)** The opening volume of Legends of Dune takes us to the beginnings of Arrakis and the boy Selim, who learns how to ride the giant sandworms. Coauthored with Kevin J. Anderson.
5. *Machine Crusade, The* **(Tor, 2003)** Twenty years after the events in *The Butlerian Jihad*, the crusade against the thinking robots has produced scant gains. The Cymeks, led by Agamemnon, hatch new plots to regain their lost power from Omnius. Coauthored with Kevin J. Anderson.
6. *Battle of Corrin, The* **(Tor, 2004)** In the conclusion to the Legends of Dune trilogy, a robot-engineered plague opens the Battle of Corrin, climaxing the century-long galactic war between humans and the robotic Synchronized Empire. Variant title: *Dune: The Battle of Corrin*. Coauthored with Kevin J. Anderson.
7. *Hunters of Dune* **(Tor, 2006)** This volume picks up where *Chapterhouse: Dune* left off (see Frank Herbert, series I, number 6). Duncan Idaho guides the refugee "no-ship" *Ithaca*, fleeing the Chapterhouse and the brutal Honored Matres, a corrupted faction of the Bene Gesserit. Coauthored with Kevin J. Anderson.
8. *Sandworms of Dune* **(Tor, 2007)** In the "wrap-up" of the original Dune cycle, Kwisatz Haderach is revealed in the ultimate face-off between humankind and the machine empire ruled by Omnius. Coauthored with Kevin J. Anderson.

II. Brian Herbert has embarked upon the Timeweb Chronicles, a new space-opera series set in the far future, where the far-flung Human race is pitted against an alien force "just beneath the surface of the galaxy."

1. *Timeweb* **(Five Star, 2006)** Galactic ecologist Noah Watanabe sets out upon an epic journey to restore the ancient balances of the crumbling galaxy, threatened by "another dominion" just below its surface.
2. *Web and the Stars, The* **(Five Star, 2007)** Subtitle: *Book 2 of the Timeweb Chronicles*. The alien Parvii derail a war between humankind and the shape-shifting Mutati, as guerrilla mystic Noah Watanabe and his nemesis, Doge Lorenzo, continue their rivalry.

Herbert, Frank

I. Even before *The Last Whole Earth Catalog* recommended *Dune* as an ecological primer, Herbert's novel showed signs of attracting a cult following, and his fans increased with each new sequel. The series combines the traditional science-fiction elements of heroism and peril in an alien world, overtones of religion, and an ecological message—on the desert planet Dune a drop of water is more precious than gold. The long-awaited movie version of *Dune* turned out to be a critical and financial disaster. *The Dune Encyclopedia*, edited by Willis McNelly (Putnam, 1984), is a compendious guide to the first four volumes of the series. The Dune series has been revived by Brian Herbert (q.v.), son of Frank, and Kevin J. Anderson (q.v.).

1. *Dune* **(Chilton, 1956)** Duke Leto Atreides and his family are exiled to the barren planet of Dune, which is inhabited by ferocious Fremen who ride giant sandworms.
2. *Dune Messiah* **(Putnam, 1969)** A mystical sisterhood plots to overthrow Dune's ruler Muad'Dib, who is really Paul Atreides, son of Duke Leto.
3. *Children of Dune* **(Berkley/Putnam, 1976)** As power struggles and ecological change rock Muad'Dib's crumbling empire, the twins Leto and Ghanima develop slowly.
4. *God Emperor of Dune* **(Berkley/Putnam, 1981)** On the now greening planet of Dune, specimen Fremen are museum attractions for tourists, and the God Emperor Leto Atreides (Paul's son) is turning into a sandworm.
5. *Heretics of Dune* **(Putnam, 1984)** The Bene Gesserit, a secret sisterhood, plans to mate Sheeana, who can talk to sandworms, with the latest incarnation of Duncan Idaho.
6. *Chapterhouse: Dune* **(Putnam, 1985)** The Bene Gesserit plans to use the sandworms to change Chapterhouse into another desert world.

II. Herbert has also written two books starring saboteur extraordinaire Jorj X. McKie of the Bureau of Sabotage in the Confederation of the Sentient Worlds.

1. *Whipping Star* **(Putnam, 1970)** On discovering that some stars are actually intelligent superpowerful beings, Jorj McKie makes a friend of one called Fannie May.
2. *Dosadi Experiment, The* **(Putnam, 1977)** Jorj McKie is assigned to investigate an experiment on extreme overcrowding in progress on the planet Dosadi.

III. *Destination: Void,* an early Herbert novel about a space colonization project and megalomaniac computer, was followed by a trilogy written in collaboration with Bill Ransom. The books continue the story of the transplanted human clone race as it copes with the harsh environment of the planet Pandora.

1. *Destination: Void* (Berkley, 1966) Scientists on a spaceship carrying human colonists to a supposedly idyllic planet are forced to create a new supercomputer.
2. *Jesus Incident, The* (Berkley, 1979) Humans deposited on the planet Pandora try to destroy its native life-forms, including a kind of sentient kelp, instead of trying to come to terms with them. Coauthored by Bill Ransom.
3. *Lazarus Effect, The* (Putnam, 1983) Centuries later, Pandoran humanity has split into high-tech Mermen living under the sea and mutant Islanders living on floating islands. Coauthored by Bill Ransom.
4. *Ascension Factor, The* (Putnam, 1988) The Pandoran humans have learned how to control the intelligent kelp beds that regulate the planet's water flow and are wreaking ecological havoc by creating land at an excessive rate. Coauthored by Bill Ransom.

Herndon, Nancy

Elena Jarvis is an officer with the Los Santos (i.e., El Paso), Texas, Department of Crimes against Persons. The wisecracking Elena has a "ruthless sense of justice," which she needs, since she is up against an ex-husband, a boss who treats her like a little girl, a partner who thinks women belong in the kitchen, and the usual bunch of weird killers. Nancy Herndon writes the Carolyn Blue mystery series as Nancy Fairbanks (q.v.) and romance novels as Elizabeth Chadwick.

1. *Acid Bath* (Berkley, 1995) A lecherous poet is found floating in his bathtub in an advanced state of decomposition.
2. *Widows' Walk* (Berkley, 1995) It seems that Boris Potemkin, struck down by a bullet, wasn't the first victim of a gang of female "widow-makers" in black.
3. *Lethal Statues* (Berkley, 1996) Someone tipped a heavy statue over on young student Annalee Ribbon, pinning her underneath and killing her.
4. *Hunting Game* (Berkley, 1996) Pansy, a heretofore gentle elephant at the Los Santos Zoo, has suddenly turned violent. Has Pansy been drugged?
5. *Time Bombs* (Berkley, 1997) The scarce water supply at Los Santos seems to be the subject of a series of bombings of trees and shrubs at the university graduation ceremony.
6. *C.O.P. Out* (Berkley, 1998) A Citizens on Patrol (C.O.P.) volunteer, the wife of a prominent mayoral candidate, is killed while accompanying a rookie officer on foot patrol.
7. *Casanova Crime* (Berkley, 1997) Someone has killed the campus Casanova, and that someone is after Elena now.

Hess, Joan

I. Arkansas native Joan Hess is a master of the humorous mystery. Maggody, Arkansas, is the home of a female police chief, Ariel "Arly" Hanks and as bizarre a collection of depraved locals as readers of Carolyn Chute (q.v.) or Stephen King (q.v.) could wish for. The whodunit plots are well-done, but it is the Ozark ambience and the humor that bring readers back for more.

1. *Malice in Maggody* (St. Martin's, 1987) Arly is frustrated in her search for a missing EPA bureaucrat by the lack of cooperation from the citizens of Maggody.

2. *Mischief in Maggody* (St. Martin's, 1988) Local moonshiner and prostitute Robin Buchanan has disappeared, leaving five hungry children behind.
3. *Much Ado in Maggody* (St. Martin's, 1990) A feminist rally over the demotion of a bank teller for taking maternity leaves leads to the burning of the offending bank.
4. *Madness in Maggody* (St. Martin's, 1991) The grand opening of a supermarket opposed by local merchants leads to murder.
5. *Mortal Remains in Maggody* (Dutton, 1991) A porno movie shot on location in Maggody leads to arson and murder.
6. *Maggody in Manhattan* (Dutton, 1992) Arly has to brave the urban horrors of New York when her mother, Ruby Bee, in the Big Apple for a baking contest, shoots a naked man in her bed.
7. *O Little Town of Maggody* (Dutton, 1993) Country-western singer Matt Montana hopes to rejuvenate his career with a Christmas visit to his natal town of Maggody.
8. *Martians in Maggody* (Dutton, 1994) The locals flock to Raz Buchanan's cornfield to speculate about the mysterious circles that have appeared there overnight.
9. *Miracles in Maggody* (Dutton, 1995) Televangelist Malachi Hope plans to build a huge theme park near Maggody.
10. *Maggody Militia, The* (Dutton, 1997) A recently arrived survivalist group led by "General" Sterling Pitts is conducting maneuvers on property recently purchased by newcomer Kayleen Smeltner.
11. *Misery Loves Maggody* (Simon & Schuster, 1998) Ruby Bee is hospitalized while on a four-day Elvis Presley Pilgrimage with her best friend, Estelle Oppers. Then one of the members of the group dies and one disappears, and Estelle starts investigating in her inimitable (and illegal) fashion.
12. *Murder@Maggody.Com* (Simon & Schuster, 1999) One of Maggody's high school teachers has obtained a grant to set up a computer lab for students and citizens. Some denizens of Maggody, including the mayor's wife, regard the Internet as an instrument of the devil.
13. *Maggody and the Moonbeams* (Simon & Schuster, 2001) Arly's chaperonage of a church youth group on a trip to Camp Pearly Gates is punctuated by the discovery of the body of one of the "moonbeams," an all-female cult group located near the camp.
14. *Muletrain to Maggody* (Simon & Schuster, 2004) As Maggody prepares for its documentary on the Civil War Skirmish at Cotter's Ridge of 1863, rumor has it that two saddlebags of Confederate gold were hidden in a local cave to keep them from the Yankees.
15. *Malpractice in Maggody* (Simon & Schuster, 2006) Maggody locals suspect that the new Stonebridge Foundation, a posh rehabilitation center surrounded by a brick wall and protected by a Spanish-speaking guard and a mean dog, is really a lunatic asylum.

II. Claire Malloy, proprietress of the Book Depot, a bookstore in the college town of Farberville, Arkansas (read Fayetteville, Arkansas, hometown of Hess and the University of Arkansas), can't seem to stay away from sleuthing. Claire is a middle-aged lady with a policeman lover and a teenage daughter "from Hell." Farberville isn't quite so zany a place as Maggody, but this series will also please readers of humorous mysteries.

1. *Strangled Prose* (St. Martin's, 1986) Claire is the reluctant hostess for romance writer Azalea Twilight's autograph party.
2. *Murder at the Mimosa Inn, The* (St. Martin's, 1986) Claire attends a mystery weekend with daughter Caron and policeman friend Peter Rosen.
3. *Dear Miss Demeanor* (St. Martin's, 1987) Claire becomes a substitute journalism teacher when Caron tries to clear up the case of the pilfered school paper funds.

4. *Really Cute Corpse, A* (St. Martin's, 1988) Malloy is the reluctant director of Farberville's Miss Thurberfest beauty pageant.

5. *Diet to Die For, A* (St. Martin's, 1989) Maribeth Galleston's diet and aerobic classes at the Ultima Diet Center seem to be working until she drives her car through the center's front door.

6. *Roll Over and Play Dead* (St. Martin's, 1991) When two basset hounds in Malloy's care disappear, they are traced to Newton Churls, who sells animals for medical research.

7. *Death by the Light of the Moon* (St. Martin's, 1992) Claire and Caron attend the birthday of Miss Justicia, mother of Claire's late husband, deep in the Louisiana bayous.

8. *Poisoned Pins* (Dutton, 1993) Claire finds herself embroiled in the affairs of Kappa Theta Eta, a sorority at Farber College.

9. *Tickled to Death* (Dutton, 1994) Claire's friend Luanne is having an affair with a local dentist who lost two wives under suspicious circumstances.

10. *Busy Bodies* (Dutton, 1995) Painter Zeno Gorgias is staging performance pieces on his front lawn starring a nearly nude young woman and a rubber snake.

11. *Closely Akin to Murder* (Dutton, 1996) Claire receives a call from Veronica Landonwood, a cousin she thought to have been dead for 30 years, asking for help against a blackmailer.

12. *Holly, Jolly Murder, A* (Dutton, 1997) Nicholas Chunder, wealthy physician, landlord, and founder of the Druids of the Saved Grove of Keltria, has been shot to death, and evidence points to several cult members

13. *Conventional Corpse* (St. Martin's, 2000) Claire has her hands full trying to manage a rather diverse group of mystery writers who have turned up at the first Farber College mystery convention.

14. *Out on a Limb* (St. Martin's, 2002) Miss Emily Parchester has chained herself to a platform in a tree to protest a new housing development. Claire's daughter Caron has brought home an infant whose mother is known only as Wal-Mart.

15. *Goodbye Body, The* (St. Martin's, 2005) Right after Claire, Caron, and friend Inez settle into Dolly Goforth's loaned palatial home, a body turns up behind the gazebo.

16. *Damsels in Distress* (St. Martin's, 2007) Claire, nervously looking toward her imminent marriage to Peter Rosen, finds some distraction when Edward Cobbin, a visiting member of a Renaissance fair group, confides that he is looking for his long-lost father.

17. *Mummy Dearest* (St. Martin's, 2008) Claire is on her honeymoon with her new husband, Peter Rosen, and her daughter Caron in Luxor (Egypt) and gets mixed up in a kidnapping and murders at an archaeological dig.

Heyer, Georgette

I. Georgette Heyer's admiration of Jane Austen is apparent in her numerous historical romances, which have entertained several generations of readers on both sides of the Atlantic. *Cotillion* (Putnam, 1953) and *Charity Girl* (Dutton, 1970) are among the best of her many novels set in Regency London. The first two titles listed below are uncharacteristic in that they are set in France and England during the reign of Louis XV.

1. *These Old Shades* (Small & Maynard, 1926) The Duke of Avon takes a Paris guttersnipe for a page—but Leon turns out to be a girl, the disinherited daughter of a French count.

2. *Devil's Cub* (Dutton, 1966) The handsome young son of the Duke of Avon flees to France after a duel in a London gambling house. Originally published in the United Kingdom in 1932.

3. *Infamous Army, An* (Dutton, 1965) The grandchildren of the "Devil's Cub" see action at the Battle of Waterloo. This book is also

a sort of sequel to *Regency Buck* (Dutton, 1966) in that a character named Judith Taverner Worth appears in both of them. Originally published in the United Kingdom in 1937.

II. Georgette Heyer published a classic mystery series featuring Superintendent Hannasyde and Sergeant Hemingway. Numbers 1 through 4 star the pair of police detectives. Numbers 5 through 8 are primarily about Hemingway.

1. *Merely Murder* (Doubleday, 1935) The corpse of a very unpopular man is found in evening clothes in the stocks on the village green. UK title: *Death in the Stocks*.

2. *Behold, Here's Poison!* (Doubleday, 1936) One of Gregory Matthews's eccentric relatives or friends, resenting his manner of offering charity, has murdered him.

3. *They Found Him Dead* (Doubleday, 1937) Elderly, crotchety Silas Kane is found dead at the bottom of a cliff the morning after his birthday party.

4. *Blunt Instrument, A* (Doubleday, 1938) Charming Ernest Fletcher has seemingly been murdered. But, after the police have pieced together all the evidence, they conclude that murder was impossible.

5. *No Wind of Blame* (Doubleday, 1939) Rich, good-hearted Ermyntrude Carter tries to entertain a bankrupt Russian prince amid snooty county society, a daughter "who switches stage roles every few hours," attempted blackmail, and a murder.

6. *Envious Casca* (Doubleday, 1941) Joseph Herriard attempts to have a good old-fashioned Christmas party with his relatives, but fractious guests, disapproving servants, and the stabbing death of Joseph's older, wealthy brother spoil the festivities.

7. *Duplicate Death* (Dutton, 1969) Despite her mother's best efforts, Mrs. Haddington's beautiful brainless daughter continues to consort with some dubious men friends. A murder at a bridge party brings in Inspector Hemingway and Tim Harte, a character from number 3. Originally published in the United Kingdom in 1951.

8. *Detection Unlimited* (Dutton, 1969) The shooting death of prominent lawyer Sampson Warrenby provides entertainment for the villagers of Thornden. Originally published in the United Kingdom in 1953.

Hiaasen, Carl

Carl Hiaasen has been called "a hybrid of Jonathan Swift, Randy Newman, and Elmore Leonard" (Jack Viertel, *Los Angeles Times Book Review*). Though none of Hiaasen's over-the-top satires set in southern Florida are, strictly speaking, sequels, several characters make multiple appearances, including Skink, the crazy, reclusive ex-governor of Florida; sometime investigator Mick Stranahan; and half-Seminole, half-white failed alligator-wrestler Sammy Tigertail. What remains constant are Hiaasen's bitter satires against developers, promoters of Florida tourism, and theme-park developers, especially Walt Disney and co. Hiaasen writes wildly funny, exciting novels full of crazy South Florida types, nasty villains, and sympathetic good guys and gals, who are sometimes naive and sometimes as zany as any of the villains.

A born and bred Floridian, Hiaasen has written, since 1965, a syndicated column for the *Miami Herald* that has been collected in two volumes: *Kick Ass* (University Press of Florida, 1999) and *Paradise Screwed* (Putnam, 2001) and a no-holds-barred attack on the Disney empire: *Team Rodent: How Disney Devours the World* (Ballantine, 1998); three juveniles also set in Florida: the Newbery Award–winning *Hoot* (Knopf, 2002; recently made into a movie), *Flush* (Knopf,

2005), and *Scat* (Knopf, 2009); three novels coauthored with William D. Montalbano and published by Vintage, two of which are set in Florida: *Powder Burn* (1981), *Trap Line* (1982), and *A Death in China* (1982); and a chapter in the multiauthor spoof *Naked Came the Manatee* (Putnam, 1996).

1. *Tourist Season* **(Putnam, 1986)** Ecoterrorists seem to be behind a series of bizarre murders in Miami and the Florida Keys. One victim, head of Miami's Chamber of Commerce, is found dead with a rubber alligator lodged in his throat.
2. *Double Whammy* **(Putnam, 1987)** Skink, ex-Florida governor turned crazy recluse, figures in this novel, which exposes skulduggery on the bass-fishing circuit.
3. *Skin Tight* **(Putnam, 1989)** Former Florida state investigator Mick Stranahan is the target of homicidal plastic surgeons, sensationalistic TV personalities, and moneygrubbing lawyers. Even the trained attack barracuda that Mick keeps under his stilt house may not be able to keep his opponents at bay forever.
4. *Native Tongue* **(Knopf, 1991)** Former investigative reporter Joe Winder now writes PR releases for the Amazing Kingdom of Thrills, a sleazy theme park owned by Francis X. Kingsbury, who hopes to engulf a nearby golf resort. Skink and the Mothers of Wilderness are among the dotty characters who inhabit this novel.
5. *Strip Tease* **(Knopf, 1993)** Former FBI clerk Erin Grant dances at the Eager Beaver, a topless bar in Fort Lauderdale, to pay the legal fees in her custody fight for her young daughter. Made into a motion picture starring Demi Moore (1996).
6. *Stormy Weather* **(Knopf, 1995)** New York ad executive Max Lamb decides to add excitement to his Orlando honeymoon by taking his bride and his camcorder into the teeth of Hurricane Andrew, exposing him to a series of crazy and corrupt individuals including Skink, grifter Edie March, and a bevy of escaped animals.
7. *Lucky You* **(Knopf, 1997)** JoLayne Lucks, of Grange, Florida, seems overly casual about a divided lottery ticket worth $14 million dollars and attracts unwanted attention from the promoters of Grange's Christian tourist trade, newspaper reporter Tom Krome, and poacher and counterfeiter Bodean Gazzer and his friend Chub, the only members of a white-supremacist, "anti-gummint," beer-drinking militia.
8. *Sick Puppy* **(Knopf, 2000)** Apprentice ecoterrorist Twilly Spree graduates from attacks on garbage trucks and dung beetles and kidnaps the dog and the wife of litterbug and political fixer Palmer Stoat. Ex-governor Clinton Tyree, aka Skink, and state trooper Jim Tile get into the action.
9. *Basket Case* **(Knopf, 2002)** Jack Tagger, relegated to the obit beat at a small-town Florida daily, stumbles into a real news story: the drowning death of has-been rocker Jimmy Stoma.
10. *Skinny Dip* **(Knopf, 2004)** Heiress Joey Perrone is tossed overboard from a cruise ship by her crooked, Everglades-polluting, pseudo–marine biologist husband, Chaz, and is rescued by Mick Stranahan.
11. *Nature Girl* **(Knopf, 2006)** Honey Santana, self-proclaimed "queen of lost causes," takes obnoxious telemarketer Boyd Shreave into the wilderness of Florida's Ten Thousand Islands to teach him a lesson, followed by her former employer, the digitally impaired Piejack, and her former husband, drug-runner Perry. When they pull up on Dismal Key, they run into half-Seminole, half-white failed alligator-wrestler Sammy Tigertail, who has decided to go the hermit route.

Higgins, George V(incent)

I. This quartet of novels is narrated by Jeremiah Francis Kennedy, a successful Boston criminal lawyer who defends clients of varying degrees of sleaziness. They show the pragmatic world of the criminal lawyer through a series of monologues and dialogues related in the inimitable Boston patois that Higgins made his own since *The Friends of Eddie Coyle* (Knopf, 1972) to his death, in 1999.

1. *Kennedy for the Defense* **(Knopf, 1990)** Jerry Kennedy tries to balance the demands of his clients against his desire to spend more time with his wife and teenage daughter.
2. *Penance for Jerry Kennedy* **(Knopf, 1985)** Jerry is in trouble with the IRS, a TV commentator, a judge, and his wife's real-estate partners.
3. *Defending Billy Ryan* **(Holt, 1992)** Kennedy is asked to defend Billy Ryan, longtime commissioner of the Department of Public Works, from corruption charges.
4. *Sandra Nichols Found Dead* **(Holt, 1996)** Kennedy is working for the three children of Sandra Nichols to prove that her most recent husband, Peter Wade, hired someone to kill her.

II. Politics and crime are the subjects of this pair of novels connected by Henry Briggs, ex–Boston Red Sox pitcher and aspiring Vermont politician.

1. *Trust* **(Holt, 1989)** Ex-con Earl Beale, now a car salesman in Rhode Island, is asked to get rid of a potentially hot Mercedes, but he has bigger ideas.
2. *Victories* **(Holt, 1990)** Henry Briggs has his past delved into when he becomes a candidate for US congressman from Vermont.

Higgins, Jack

PSEUDONYM OF Harry Patterson

I. Liam Devlin, former Irish freedom fighter, is the connecting link in this quartet of novels by best-selling suspense novelist Jack Higgins. Devlin hates the English but reluctantly finds himself working with them. Higgins's fans know to expect an intricate plot, realistic characters, and plenty of action and suspense. Michael Caine, Donald Sutherland, and Robert Duvall headed the star-studded cast in the 1976 movie version of *The Eagle Has Landed*. Belfast native Harry Patterson, veteran suspense novelist under his own name as well as under pseudonyms such as Jack Higgins, James Graham, and Martin Fallon, hit real pay dirt with *The Eagle Has Landed* and is now a multimillionaire in residence on one of the Channel Islands. Higgins's characters have a way of migrating from book to book. *Exocet* (New American Library, 1983) has, among its characters, British intelligence agent Tony Villiers, who also appears in *Confessional* (series I, number 4), and millionaire weapons dealer Max Donner, who also appears in *Midnight Never Comes* (series III, number 4). Liam Devlin, a character in series I, plays a major role in series II.

1. *Eagle Has Landed, The* **(Holt, 1975)** A small, elite force of German paratroopers lands secretly in wartime England to carry out a daring plan to capture Winston Churchill.
2. *Eagle Has Flown, The* **(Simon & Schuster, 1991)** Liam Devlin is called upon to rescue Kurt Steiner, the German officer who was captured in the foiled Churchill mission delineated in *The Eagle Has Landed*.
3. *Touch the Devil* **(Stein & Day, 1982)** Liam Devlin is recruited by British intelligence to stop Frank Barry, a former Irish colleague now working for the Soviet Union.

4. *Confessional* (New American Library, 1986) Tony Villiers of British intelligence reluctantly enlists the help of Liam Devlin to stop a crazed killer who is out to assassinate one of the world's most powerful and beloved men.

II. Liam Devlin plays a subsidiary role in this series of novels featuring IRA terrorist Sean Dillon, who works against the British and then for the elite British security force Group Four. Plenty of action, unrelenting suspense, and plots that sometimes call for the reader's suspension of disbelief are supplied.

1. *Eye of the Storm* (Putnam, 1992) Dillon is hired by operatives of Saddam Hussein, while the Gulf War is in full swing, with the mission of assassinating the British prime minister. Variant title: *Midnight Man.*

2. *Thunder Point* (Putnam, 1993) Dillon and the British government are working together to retrieve Martin Bormann's briefcase from a U-boat that sank in the West Indies nearly 50 years ago.

3. *On Dangerous Ground* (Putnam, 1994) Dillon is ordered to retrieve the Chungking Covenant, a document purportedly giving Britain an additional century of control over Hong Kong.

4. *Angel of Death* (Putnam, 1995) Grace Browning, Britain's greatest actress, moonlights as a black-leather-clad motorcyclist political assassin.

5. *Drink with the Devil* (Putnam, 1996) A hijacked cargo of gold bullion, sunk off Ireland in 1985, is the object of a search, 10 years later, by Sean Dillon, working for British intelligence, the Mafia, the IRA, and Irish Protestant terrorist Michael Ryan.

6. *President's Daughter, The* (Putnam, 1997) The illegitimate daughter of American president Jake Cazalet will be killed by a Jewish extremist who calls himself Judas Maccabeus if Cazalet doesn't bow to his demands for bombing Iraq, Iran, and Syria.

7. *White House Connection, The* (Putnam, 1999) American-born Lady Helen Lang, pledging herself to avenge the death of her son, Peter, at the hands of the fringe Irish nationalist group Sons of Erin, has managed to assassinate several persons with connections to the group and is now gunning for US Senator Cohan and somebody named the Connection, who is a mole at the White House.

8. *Day of Reckoning* (Putnam, 2000) When the journalist wife of Dillon's old comrade Blake Johnson is killed in Brooklyn on orders of Jack Fox of the Solazzo crime family, Blake and Sean set out to make life miserable for Jack.

9. *Edge of Danger* (Putnam, 2001) Paul Rashid, scion of a powerful English–Arab family, vows revenge on a Russian diplomat who killed his mother while driving drunk—a wide-ranging quest for vengeance that includes the American president.

10. *Midnight Runner* (Putnam, 2002) In a direct sequel to *Edge of Danger*, half-English Lady Kate Rashid, head of the Bedu tribe of Hazar, vows to continue her family's quest for revenge through acts of terrorism.

11. *Bad Company* (Putnam, 2003) The Rashid vendetta is continued by Baron Max von Berger, who escaped from Hitler's bunker to Switzerland during World War II. This time Sean Dillon and his boss, General Charles Ferguson, are the prime targets.

12. *Dark Justice* (Putnam, 2004) Sean Dillon and his boss, Charles Ferguson, are after Putin associate Joel Belov and a Russian oil billionaire bent on world domination

13. *Without Mercy* (Putnam, 2005) Some of the bad guys have survived the shoot-out in number 12 and are swearing revenge on Dillon and Ferguson. Vladimir Putin puts in several appearances.

14. *Killing Ground, The* (Putnam, 2008) Hussein Rashid, aka the Hammer of God, has his sights set on Charles Feguson, head of British intelligence.

III. Another foreign intrigue series, this one featuring a James Bond type of agent named Paul Chavasse, was originally published in the United Kingdom under another Patterson nom de plume, Martin Fallon. Some of them were republished in the United States in the 1970s and 1980s under the Jack Higgins pseudonym. In the 1990s, Berkley reprinted them again, including the rewritten numbers 2 and 3. The series is regarded as vintage Jack Higgins: plenty of suspense, action, and adventure.

1. *Testament of Caspar Shultz, The* (New American Library, 1985) Chavasse is wrenched from his holiday by British intelligence to retrieve a manuscript exposing the double life of an escaped Nazi. Originally published in 1962 under the name Martin Fallon. Variant title: *The Bormann Testament.*

2. *Year of the Tiger* (Berkeley, 1996) In 1962 Chavasse is sent to Tibet to smuggle out mathematician Karl Hoffner, who has a space travel plan that will enable the West to beat the Russians to the moon. Originally published by Abelard-Schuman in 1963 under the name Martin Fallon. Extensively rewritten for the Berkley edition.

3. *Keys of Hell, The* (Berkeley, 2001) Revised edition of a book originally published in 1965 under the name Martin Fallon. Opens in 2001 with an older Chavasse, now Belfast Bureau Chief, who recalls his earlier adventures in the 1960s in which he recovered a religious icon from Albania.

4. *Midnight Never Comes* (Fawcett, 1976) Recuperating from injuries, Chavasse is ready to take on weapons dealer Max Donner, who has a plan for stealing Britain's newest secret missile. Originally published in 1966 under the name Martin Fallon.

5. *Dark Side of the Street* (New American Library, 1984) The Baron is the code-name for someone who is breaking Britain's most notorious prisoners out of jail, and delivering convicted spies to the Communists. Paul Chavasse goes to prison as a decoy. Originally published in 1967 under the name Martin Fallon.

6. *Fine Night for Dying, A* (HarperCollins, 2003) The body of gangland boss Harvey Preston is found entangled in fishing nets in the English Channel. British intelligence suspects an international smuggling ring. Originally published in 1969 under the name Martin Fallon.

7. *Day of Judgement* (Holt, 1982) On the eve of President Kennedy's visit to Berlin in 1963, the East Germans plan a propaganda coup—a forced public confession from a concentration camp survivor and CIA operative.

IV. Martin Fallon is the protagonist of a pair of novels originally published in the 1960s under Harry Patterson's real name. Like several other Patterson/Higgins characters, Martin Fallon is a former IRA terrorist. *A Prayer for the Dying* was made into a movie with Mickey Rourke, Bob Hoskins, and Alan Bates (1987).

1. *Cry of the Hunter* (Long [UK], 1960) The head of IRA Ulster, Patrick Rogan, has been arrested, and IRA command fears that he will talk. Martin Fallon is assigned the task of "liberating" Rogan. Originally published under the name Harry Patterson.

2. *Prayer for the Dying, A* (Fawcett, 1975) Martin Fallon retires from the IRA and terrorism after he accidentally blows up a school bus full of children. Both the IRA and Scotland Yard want him badly, and Martin needs money and a passport to get out Ireland. Originally published in 1973 under the name Harry Patterson.

V. Also originally published under the name of Harry Patterson were three police thrillers featuring Detective Nick Miller. Miller, although an educated officer, is definitely a hard-boiled type who roughs suspects up and refers to women as "birds" and "tarts."

1. *Graveyard Shift, The* **(Signet, 1997)** Notorious thief Ben Garvald is getting out of prison, and several people are interested in him: his former wife and sister-in-law, who fear him, and Nick Miller and Miller's colleague Detective Constable Brady, who are interested in recovering the missing loot from his final crime. Originally published in 1965 under the name Harry Patterson.

2. *Brought in Dead* **(Signet, 1997)** Detective Sergeant Millets is out to discover who murdered a young girl whose body has just been dragged out of a canal. Originally published in 1967 under the name Harry Patterson.

3. *Hell Is Always Today* **(Berkley, 2005)** A serial killer is loose and terrorizing the city. Detectives Miller and Mallory have the unenviable job of finding him. Originally published in 1968 under the name Harry Patterson.

VI. Dougal Munro and Jack Carter are the British operatives in a trio of novels set in World War II. This series is sometimes given YA status. Characters named Kelso also appear in *East of Desolation* (Doubleday, 1989).

1. *Night of the Fox* **(Simon & Schuster, 1987)** The capture of Colonel Hugh Kelso off German-occupied Jersey threatens the Allies' secret invasion plan.

2. *Cold Harbour* **(Simon & Schuster, 1990)** The Allies are poised to play their dirtiest trick—a trained operative in a disguised E-boat with the name Lili Marlene on its bow.

3. *Flight of Eagles* **(Putnam, 1998)** Max and Harry Kelso, separated in youth, find themselves on opposite sides—Max flying for the Luftwaffe, Harry for the RAF.

Highsmith, Patricia

The Ripley novels are suspenseful black comedies starring American expatriate Tom Ripley, a charming psychopath who feels most at ease when he is doing something illegal or immoral. The five novels trace his development from callow youth to callous con man and killer. Ripley was played by Alain Delon in *Purple Noon* (the 1961 film version of *The Talented Mr. Ripley*), by Dennis Hopper in *The American Friend* (the 1978 film version of *Ripley's Game*), and by Matt Damon in *The Talented Mr. Ripley* (1999). Patricia Highsmith, who was born in Texas and died in Switzerland, also wrote *Strangers on a Train*, the basis for the classic Hitchcock film of that name (1951). Highsmith's books, which have never achieved in the United States the cult status they have in Europe (*Strangers on a Train* was out of print until it was reissued by Norton in 2001), may now be coming into their own here after the success of the Matt Damon movie; a new biography by Andrew Wilson, *Beautiful Shadow: A Life of Patricia Highsmith* (Bloomsbury, 2003); a memoir by her lesbian lover Marijane Meaker, *Highsmith: A Romance of the 1950s* (Cleis, 2003); and the inclusion of *The Talented Mr. Ripley* in the Library of America *Crime Noir: American Noir of the 1950s* (1997) and of *The Talented Mr. Ripley/Ripley under Ground/Ripley's Game* in one Everyman's Library volume (Knopf, 1996).

1. *Talented Mr. Ripley, The* **(Coward, 1955)** Tom Ripley goes to Italy at the request of Dickie Greenleaf's father to bring the young man home.

2. *Ripley Underground* **(Doubleday, 1970)** Now married to a wealthy woman and living on a French estate, Ripley is obliged to impersonate an artist whose works Ripley's associates have been forging.

3. *Ripley's Game* **(Knopf, 1974)** To avenge an insult, Ripley involves the offending Englishman in a plot to murder to Mafiosi.

4. *Boy Who Followed Ripley, The* **(Lippincott, 1980)** A 16-year-old American runaway chooses Ripley as his mentor.

5. *Ripley under Water* **(Knopf, 1992)** Ripley is annoyed and perplexed by obnoxious American neighbors in the French countryside who seem bent on exposing his past.

Hill, Reginald

I. Set in Yorkshire, this series features Superintendent Andy Dalziel and Sergeant (later Inspector) Peter Pascoe. Dalziel is intelligent but fat, boorish, and irascible; Pascoe is sensitive, introspective, and university educated. Despite their obvious incompatibility, each has developed a grudging respect for the other, and they work together as a surprisingly effective, if not always harmonious, team. *Pascoe's Ghost and Other Brief Chronicles* (New American Library, 1989; originally published in 1979) contains two Pascoe and Dalziel stories, both reprinted in *Asking for the Moon* (number 1).

1. *Asking for the Moon* **(Norton, 1996)** A collection of four Dalziel–Pascoe stories: "The National Service Man," which describes the first meeting of the two detectives; "One Small Step," a story set in the future, in which an older Dalziel takes a space flight (published separately as *One Small Step*, Collins [UK], 1990); and "Pascoe's Ghost" and "Dalziel's Ghost," which appeared in *Pascoe's Ghost and Other Brief Chronicles* (New American Library, 1989; originally published in the United Kingdom in 1979).

2. *Clubbable Woman, A* **(Countryman, 1984)** Former rugby star Sam Connan awakens to find that his wife, Mary, has been bludgeoned to death while watching television.

3. *Advancement of Learning, An* **(Countryman, 1983)** The corpse of the former head of Holm Coultram College is found under a statue on campus.

4. *Ruling Passion* **(Harper, 1977)** Pascoe and his girlfriend, Ellie Soper, find three friends shot to death at a weekend cottage.

5. *April Shroud, An* **(Countryman, 1986)** Pascoe is on his honeymoon when Dalziel gets caught up in a love affair of his own with a recently widowed woman whose husband met a strange end.

6. *Pinch of Snuff, A* **(Harper, 1978)** Pascoe gets involved in an investigation of pornographic films and murder.

7. *Killing Kindness, A* **(Pantheon, 1981)** The Yorkshire Choker, a serial killer who quotes Shakespeare, is pursued by Dalziel and Pascoe.

8. *Deadheads* **(Macmillan, 1984)** Patrick Aldermann, accountant and rose grower, is the beneficiary of a series of suspicious accidental deaths.

9. *Exit Lines* **(Macmillan, 1985)** Three old men die of unnatural causes on the same night, and Dalziel is suspected of having a hand in their demise.

10. *Child's Play* **(Macmillan, 1987)** A Yorkshire widow dies, willing money to a son reported missing in action in World War II.

11. *Under World* **(Scribner, 1988)** Young Colin Farr returns to a Yorkshire mining town where he hears disturbing rumors of child murder and suicide associated with his late father Billy.

12. *Bones and Silence* **(Delacorte, 1991)** A series of homicides and disappearances seems to be linked to a builder who is constructing garages for the police station.

13. *Recalled to Life* **(Delacorte, 1992)** New evidence crops up in the 30-year-old murder of Pamela Westropp for which a man was hanged and his alleged accomplice sentenced to life imprisonment.

14. *Pictures of Perfection* **(Delacorte, 1994)** The hamlet of Enscombe is the scene of the disappearance of a rookie constable and sightings of a naked man.

15. *Wood Beyond, The* (Delacorte, 1996) Animal rights activists blunder across old bones; a security guard at a research lab is killed; Dalziel falls for one of the activists; his grandfather's war diaries evoke World War I for Pascoe.

16. *On Beulah Height* (Delacorte, 1998) Fifteen years ago, the village of Dendale was flooded for the creation of a reservoir. Three young girls and loner Benny Lightfoot vanished at the same time. Now Benny seems to have returned, and another young girl disappears.

17. *Arms and the Women* (Delacorte, 1999) Pascoe's wife, Ellie, takes center stage, as she is almost abducted by a couple in an expensive car who claim to be from a local education authority.

18. *Dialogues of the Dead* (Delacorte, 2002) A killer describes the murders he has committed in a series of "short stories." Rookie constable "Hat" Bowler plays a leading role here.

19. *Death's Jest Book* (HarperCollins, 2003) Franny Roote, murderer and rising academic, writes a series of letters to Pascoe, which the latter finds unsettling despite their affectionate and forgiving tone.

20. *Good Morning, Midnight* (HarperCollins, 2004) Pat McIver is found dead in a locked room, an apparent suicide, his death echoing that of his father 10 years before.

21. *Death Comes for the Fat Man* (HarperCollins, 2007) Dalziel lies comatose in a hospital bed, the victim of a terrorist bombing, as Pascoe forces his way onto the team of antiterrorism specialists looking into the incident. UK title: *The Death of Dalziel.*

II. Joe Sixsmith, black, overweight, and balding, sets up as a private eye in Luton, Bedfordshire, after his lathe-operator job has been declared redundant. Although everything Joe knows about sleuthing has been learned from the movies, he has a kind heart, compassion, and the requisite amount of luck to succeed well enough to keep his cat, Whitey, in pork rinds and beer and indulge in his passion for choir singing.

1. *Blood Sympathy* (St. Martin's, 1994) Joe sets up his private investigating business and runs into a mass murder, a plane crash, dope smuggling, race wars, and voodoo.

2. *Born Guilty* (St. Martin's, 1995) Joe leaves choir practice and discovers the corpse of a young boy in a box among the monuments in the church graveyard.

3. *Killing the Lawyers* (St. Martin's, 1997) Joe consults a fancy lawyer in a suit against his insurance company; then the lawyer is killed, followed by the murder of another lawyer in the firm, which leads to the hiring of Joe by a remaining partner.

4. *Singing the Sadness* (St. Martin's, 1999) On a journey with the Boyling Corner Chapel choir to Wales, Joe rescues a nude woman from a burning cottage, which leads to some injuries and Joe's hiring for what turns out to be a rather complicated case.

Hillerman, Tony

Hillerman's mysteries are a unique blend of detective novel and contemporary western adventure. Lieutenant Joe Leaphorn and officer Jim Chee of the Navajo Tribal Police confront an extraordinary range of problems, from ancient witchcraft to modern-drug traffic. The novels present an authentic, uncondescending picture of the social life of the Navajo, Zuni, and Hopi cultures. Joe Leaphorn is the main protagonist in numbers 1, 2, and 3; Jim Chee in numbers 4, 5, and 6; and they work together in numbers 7 through 18. *The Joe Leaphorn Mysteries* (Harper, 1989) is an omnibus volume containing numbers 1, 2, and 3. *The Jim Chee Mysteries* (Harper, 1990) contains numbers 4, 5, and 6. Nonfiction books that will help readers get a feel for the mysteries are Tony Hillerman's *Hillerman Country: A Journey through the Southwest* (Harper, 1991); editor Martin H. Greenberg's *The Tony Hillerman Companion* (Harper, 1994); and Hillerman's autobiography, *Seldom Disappointed* (HarperCollins, 2001). *The Finding Moon* (Harper, 1995) isn't part of the series.

1. *Blessing Way, The* (Harper, 1970) Anthropologist Bergen McKee goes to the Navajo reservation to pursue his research on witchcraft and gets involved with murder.

2. *Dance Hall of the Dead* (Harper, 1973) When a Zuni youth is killed shortly before a Zuni religious ceremony, suspicion falls on his Navajo friend.

3. *Listening Woman, The* (Harper, 1978) Searching for the murderers of an old man and a missing helicopter, Leaphorn comes into conflict with the militant Buffalo Society.

4. *People of Darkness* (Harper, 1980) Jim Chee searches for a stolen box of keepsakes that may contain the key to a mysterious cult called the "People of Darkness."

5. *Dark Wind, The* (Harper, 1982) While searching for cocaine missing from a plane crash, Chee gets involved with a Hopi Kachina ceremony.

6. *Ghostway, The* (Harper, 1985) Chee pursues the men who killed three members of the Navajo Turkey Clan.

7. *Skinwalkers* (Harper, 1987) Three murders and an attempt on Chee's life may be the work of a "skinwalker," a Navajo witch.

8. *Thief of Time, A* (Harper, 1988) Leaphorn and Chee search for an archaeologist accused of stealing Anasazi cultural relics.

9. *Talking God* (Harper, 1989) The Smithsonian Institution in Washington, DC, and a Talking God ceremonial mask may hold the answer to two seemingly unrelated crimes.

10. *Coyote Waits* (Harper, 1990) Leaphorn and Chee are separately on the trail of the murderer of fellow policeman Delbert Nez.

11. *Sacred Clowns* (Harper, 1993) Leaphorn and Chee investigate several homicides, including the stabbing death of a "Koshare" (Sacred Clown).

12. *Fallen Man* (HarperCollins, 1996) The body of Hal Breedlove, scion of a local white family, is discovered on Shiprock 11 years after he had disappeared.

13. *First Eagle, The* (HarperCollins, 1998) Leaphorn, now retired, is hired by a Santa Fe woman to search for her granddaughter, biologist Catherine Pollard, who disappeared while doing field work collecting fleas carrying the bubonic plague.

14. *Hunting Badger* (HarperCollins, 1999) Chee, at the end of one romance and the beginning of another, is at risk from a sniper during the search for the men who robbed a casino owned by the Ute tribe. Contains an author's note by Hillerman referring to an actual 1998 case botched by the FBI.

15. *Wailing Wind, The* (HarperCollins, 2002) The finding of a dead white man in an abandoned pickup truck may have a connection with an earlier homicide and the disappearance of the killer's wife.

16. *Sinister Pig, The* (HarperCollins, 2003) The body of an undercover agent who's been looking for billions of dollars missing from the Tribal Trust Funds turns up on reservation property near Four Corners.

17. *Skeleton Man* (HarperCollins, 2004) Joe Leaphorn, with the assistance of Jim Chee, must connect an old robbery and a more recent crime and a security case full of diamonds missing from a 1956 plane crash.

18. *Shape Shifter, The* (HarperCollins, 2006) In a case starting with a picture of a Navajo rug from a glossy magazine, retired Lieutenant Joe Leaphorn enlists the aid of Sergeant Jim Chee and his bride, Bernadette Manuelito, as an old enemy resurfaces.

Himes, Chester

African American expatriate Chester Himes wrote his first detective novel in Paris for a popular French series of crime fiction. *For Love of Imabelle*, actually published first as a paperback original by Fawcett, became *La reine des pommes* and won the Grand Prix Policier for 1958.

Coffin Ed Johnson and Gravedigger Jones, who play subsidiary roles in *For Love of Imabelle*, are detectives in the American hard-boiled tradition except that they work for the New York Police Department and they are black. As a team they can be quite brutal as they dash about Harlem in their souped-up black VW. The series is full of violence, sex, absurdist humor, and grimly authentic portraits of life in Harlem in the 1950s and 1960s.

Although Himes felt ambivalent about his detective series, some critics think that it portrays black life in America more vividly than his early serious novels. Movies starring Raymond St. Jacques and Godfrey Cambridge have been made of two of the novels: *Cotton Comes to Harlem* and *Come Back, Charleston Blue*. For a critical study of this series and other works by Himes, see Stephen Milliken's *Chester Himes: A Critical Appraisal* (Univ. of Missouri, 1976). Numbers 1 through 5 were reprinted in hardcover by Chatham Booksellers in 1973. When Himes died, in 1984, he left an unfinished novel that has been edited by Michel Fabre and Robert Skinner. *Plan B* kills off Coffin Ed and Gravedigger in an apocalypse of racial violence.

1. *For Love of Imabelle* (Fawcett, 1957) An assortment of sinister characters are after the ore samples, supposedly gold, stolen by Imabelle from her con-man husband. Variant title: *A Rage in Harlem.*
2. *Crazy Kill, The* (Avon, 1959) A guest is killed at the riotous wake of Big Joe Pullen, a dining-car chef and gambler.
3. *Real Cool Killers, The* (Avon, 1959) Coffin Ed and Gravedigger have to find out which person out of a crowd of strongly motivated people murdered Ulysses Galen, a wealthy white pervert.
4. *All Shot Up* (Avon, 1960) An envelope filled with campaign funds disappears when a "robbery" arranged by crooked politician Casper Holmes gets out of hand.
5. *Big Gold Dream, The* (Avon, 1960) The search is on for the numbers winnings of a black maid who has apparently cached the money somewhere in the antique hand-me-down furniture that fills her apartment.
6. *Cotton Comes to Harlem* (Putnam, 1965) A fanatic white Alabama "colonel" has stuffed $87,000 stolen from the Back-to-Africa movement in a bale of cotton.
7. *Heat's On, The* (Putnam, 1966) Three million dollars worth of heroin in small plastic sacks has been stuffed into a string of five Hudson River eels. Variant title: *Come Back, Charleston Blue.*
8. *Blind Man with a Pistol* (Morrow, 1969) While Harlem is seething with racial unrest, Coffin Ed and Gravedigger are searching for a Gladstone bag containing an old man's life savings. Variant title: *Hot Day, Hot Night.*
9. *Plan B* (Univ. Press of Mississippi, 1993) The targeting of white policemen, rumors of caches of high-powered weapons among blacks, and random racial strife signal the beginnings of an armed uprising in Harlem.

Hodge, Jane Aiken

I. This serviceable saga of a family torn by divided loyalties during the American Revolution begins in Savannah in 1744. Hart Purchis, handsome 17-year-old heir to Winchelsea Plantation, rescues Mercy Phillips, a young English girl whose loyalist father has been murdered by an angry revolutionary mob. As they bravely weather the pain, danger, and personal loss of war, their commitment to each other grows.

1. *Judas Flowering* (Coward, 1976) Orphaned Mercy Phillips is welcomed into the Purchis family and her courage sustains them while young Hart is off fighting.
2. *Wide Is the Water* (Coward, 1981) The postwar story begins in 1780 as Hart is in London with his cousin Juliet and Mercy is in Philadelphia.
3. *Savannah Purchase* (Doubleday, 1971) Hyde Purchis's French wife, Josephine, meets her look-alike cousin, Juliette, in Savannah four years after they had been separated at the Battle of Waterloo.

II. Half-English, half-Portuguese Caterina Gomez is the heroine of a pair of novels set in the early 1800s. Oporto, Portugal is the main setting for the adventures, spanning some 20 years, of the brave and beautiful Caterina.

1. *Whispering* (St. Martin's, 1995) After being expelled from boarding school in England, Caterina Gomez returns to Oporto, Portugal, in the midst of the Napoleonic invasion. The (future) Duke of Wellington has a cameo here.
2. *Caterina* (St. Martin's, 1999) Twenty years later, in the 1830s, Caterina Fonsa copes with ossified social life in Oporto and the struggle between liberal Dom Pedro and autocratic Dom Miguel for control of Portugal.

Hodgins, Eric

Mr. Blandings's trials and tribulations are just as funny now as they were back in 1946. Hodgins's portrait of the city sophisticate helpless in the hands of the local craftsmen who are building his house in the country still delights readers—especially those who are home owners. Though Cary Grant seemed somewhat miscast as Mr. Blandings, the 1948 movie version was a great success.

1. *Mr. Blandings Builds His Dream House* (Simon & Schuster, 1946) When Mr. Blandings, an adman famous for his laxative slogans, is lured out of the city by a lilac-flanked farmhouse, the canny locals regard him as fair game.
2. *Blandings Way* (Simon & Schuster, 1950) The Blandings family leaves the countryside for the safety of the big city. Much of the humor of this volume is contributed by the two Blandings daughters.

Hoffman, Allen

Small Worlds was the first novel published by Abbeville Press, a noted art publisher. It was also the first of three volumes, with some continuing characters, about a group of Hasidic Jews, some of who emigrate from the Polish village of Krimsk to the St. Louis area in America, including Reb Yaakov Moshe Finebaum, baseball player Matti Stirnweiss, NKVD colonel Grisha Schwartzman, and Krimsk native Yechiel Katzman, in a saga that covers the years 1903 to 1942. The first two novels are a blend of comedy and tragedy. *The Two Devils* is grimmer. *Publishers Weekly* stated that Hoffman's work is "less folksy than Sholem Aleichem, and less obsessed with demons and sex than I. B. Singer [q.v.]."

1. *Small Worlds* (Abbeville, 1996) Begins in Krimsk, in Russian-controlled Poland, in 1903. Reb Yaakov Moshe Finebaum ends a self-imposed five-year silence, during which he struggled against

the forces of evil and impurity, and ushers in the Tisha B'Av holiday by dancing on a table with a developmentally disabled boy.

2. *Big League Dreams* **(Abbeville, 1997)** Matti Stirnweiss, starting catcher for the St. Louis Browns on a Saturday (Jewish Sabbath) in 1920, resists an impulse to throw the game.

3. *Two for the Devil* **(Abbeville, 1998)** The "devils" are Hitler and Stalin. In the first section, Grisha Shwartzman, NKVD colonel, finds himself brought to judgment for the crimes he has committed in Stalin's name. In the second part, Krimsk native Yechiel Katzman suffers a memory loss as he is being deported from the Warsaw Ghetto in 1942.

Hogan, Ray

I. If Hogan isn't as well known to the general reader as Louis L'Amour (q.v.), he does have a devoted following among readers of the classical western. Hogan, son of a lawman, and a New Mexico resident for many years, demonstrated that, while there are only a few basic formulas in genre fiction, a skilled writer can practice endless variations on them, as he did in more than 150 novels, published from 1956 to 1998, the year of his death at the age of 89. John Rye, the Doomsday Marshal, exemplifies everything a western hero should be: he has integrity, courage, tenacity, and he always gets his man.

1. *Doomsday Marshal, The* **(Doubleday, 1975)** John Rye takes on the task of delivering convicted killer Luke Braden to the hangman.

2. *Doomsday Posse, The* **(Doubleday, 1977)** Rye has been sent to dislodge an outlaw gang holed up in a canyon.

3. *Doomsday Trail, The* **(Doubleday, 1979)** The Doomsday Marshal has to track down the murderer of a Wyoming judge.

4. *Doomsday Bullet, The* **(Doubleday, 1981)** Rye's assignment is to regain control of a little town in the New Mexico panhandle called Crisscross for the forces of law and order.

5. *Doomsday Canyon, The* **(Doubleday, 1984)** Rye must stifle a desire for revenge while tracking down Jake Tolbert, the man who seduced his wife and drove her to suicide.

6. *Doomsday Marshal and the Hanging Judge, The* **(Doubleday, 1987)** The Doomsday Marshal has to escort "hanging judge" Asa Metzgar from Arizona to Nebraska in one piece.

7. *Doomsday Marshal and the Comancheros, The* **(Doubleday, 1990)** Will Dancy, a lawman Rye doesn't like, has been captured by the Comancheros.

8. *Doomsday Marshal and the Mountain Man, The* **(Doubleday, 1993)** The Marshal has to capture the accused murderer of a young Native American woman, then protect him from the incensed Kiowas.

II. Shawn Starbuck, another Hogan continuing character, is searching through the West for a lost brother. Like Rye, Starbuck has a strong sense of right and wrong and will act on behalf of justice when needed. The Starbuck novels, most of them published only in paperback, are listed without annotations.

1. *Rimrocker, The* **(New American Library, 1970)**
2. *Outlawed, The* **(New American Library, 1970)**
3. *Three Cross* **(New American Library, 1970)**
4. *Deputy of Violence* **(New American Library, 1971)**
5. *Bullet for Mister Texas, A* **(New American Library, 1971)**
6. *Marshal of Babylon, The* **(New American Library, 1971)**
7. *Brandon's Posse* **(New American Library, 1971)**
8. *Devil's Gunhand, The* **(New American Library, 1972)**
9. *Passage to Dodge City* **(New American Library, 1972)**
10. *Hell Merchant, The* **(New American Library, 1972)**
11. *Lawman for Slaughter Valley* **(New American Library, 1972)** Variant title: *Lawman for the Slaughter.*
12. *Guns of Stingaree, The* **(New American Library, 1973)**
13. *Highroller's Man* **(New American Library, 1973)**
14. *Skull Gold* **(New American Library, 1973)**
15. *Texas Brigade, The* **(New American Library, 1974)**
16. *Jenner Guns, The* **(New American Library, 1974)**
17. *Scorpion Killers, The* **(New American Library, 1974)**
18. *Tombstone Trail, The* **(New American Library, 1974)**
19. *Day of the Hangman* **(New American Library, 1975)**
20. *Last Comanchero, The* **(New American Library, 1975)**
21. *High Green Gun, The* **(New American Library, 1976)**
22. *Shotgun Rider, The* **(New American Library, 1976)**
23. *Bounty Hunter's Moon* **(New American Library, 1977)**
24. *Gun for Silver Rose, A* **(New American Library, 1977)**

Holdstock, Robert

I. Ryhope Wood is a small primeval forest in modern England. *Small* viewed from the outside, that is. Once an intrepid explorer manages to get inside the Wood's defenses, time and space have a different meaning. The Wood is teeming with Mythagos: embodiments of the human need for heroes, incarnations of the oldest human memories, and the place where the characters of myths and legends survive. *Mythago Wood*, first in the series, won the World Fantasy Award. *Ancient Echoes* (Roc, 1996), while dealing with the mythago theme, is not regarded as part of the series listed below. English writer Holdstock has also published series, most of them unavailable in the United States under pseudonyms such as Ken Blake (the Professionals), Chris Carlsen (Berserker series), Robert Faulcon (Night Hunter series), and Richard Kirk (Raven series).

1. *Mythago Wood* **(Arbor House, 1984)** Chris and Steve Huxley, entrapped by their father's obsession with the Rhyope Wood, enter the Wood separately and become mortal enemies.

2. *Lavondyss* **(Morrow, 1989)** Tallis Keeton, believing that her brother Harry (from *Mythago Wood*) is lost somewhere within Ryhope Wood, prepares herself for a quest into the Wood.

3. *Bone Forest, The* **(Avon, 1992)** Short stories.

4. *Hollowing, The* **(Roc, 1994)** Grieving father Richard Bradley becomes convinced that his son Alexander is still alive in another form in Ryhope Wood.

5. *Gate of Ivory, Gate of Horn* **(Roc, 1997)** Christian Huxley enters Ryhope Wood to find the secret behind his mother's suicide and his father's madness. He meets Celtic warrior-maiden Guiwenneth and Kylhuk's Legion, an army of Mythagos.

II. Holdstock has embarked upon a new series called the Merlin Codex, which is mingling Greek mythology and Arthurian legend together. Merlin, Jason, Medea, and the *Argo* (of Golden Fleece flame) come together in a new brew in which Merlin is responsible for the resurrection of *Argo* and Jason and the forming of a new crew (Celtic this time) of Argonauts, who go off in search of Jason's lost sons. *Merlin's Wood* (Collins [UK], 1994) is not part of this series or of the Mythago series.

1. *Celtika* **(Tor, 2003)** A young Antiokus (aka Merlin) is present at Medea's murder of her sons. Centuries later Merlin hears of a screaming ship in a frozen lake. Originally published in the United Kingdom in 2001.

2. *Iron Grail, The* **(Tor, 2004)** After helping Jason find his elder son, Merlin journeys back to Alba (the future England), but Jason,

believing that Merlin has betrayed him, and still searching for his second son, pursues him.

3. **Broken Kings, The** (Tor, 2007) Merlin and Jason journey to Alba to prevent Jason's two sons from usurping the throne in place of Pendragon (Arthur).

Holland, Cecelia

I. Californian Cecelia Holland has published more than 30 historical novels, but *Lily Nevada*, the follow-up to *Railroad Schemes*, was her first sequel. The two novels detail the life of Lily Viner in the late 19th century, as the orphaned Lily leaves the mining camps of Virginia City with outlaw King Callahan, moves to San Francisco and becomes an actress, and has to face her past. The battle against the ruthless railroad magnates of California forms the primary backdrop to Lily's life.

1. **Railroad Schemes** (Forge, 1997) After Lily Viner's father is killed in a shoot-out in a stagecoach robbery gone wrong, she is taken in hand by Irish outlaw King Callahan, who is on a vendetta against the Southern Pacific railroad.

2. **Lily Nevada** (Forge, 1999) After the demise of King Callahan, Lily goes to San Francisco and becomes the actress Lily Nevada. But her troubles with the past and the railroads are far from over.

II. Holland returned to her medieval stamping grounds for a series of novels about Irishman Corban Loosestrife, a Viking who doesn't fit the mold. The novels are a blend of history and fantasy, as Corban deals with Viking raiders, sorcery, ruthless kings, kidnapped relatives, romance, a settlement in Vinland, and many other adventures. The original trilogy has been followed by a sequel about the Corbansson cousins.

1. **Soul Thief, The** (Forge, 2002) Mav, twin sister of Corban Loosestrife, is abducted from a small Irish village by Eric Bloodaxe and taken to the Jorvik (now York, England) slave market, with Corban in pursuit.

2. **Witches' Kitchen, The** (Forge, 2004) Fifteen years after Corban escapes to Vinland from Jorvik with his love, Benna, and his sister Mav, he feels the need to make amends for the murder of Eric Bloodaxe.

3. **Serpent Dreamer, The** (Forge, 2005) After the death of Benna, his beloved wife, and the destruction of his new colony on Vinland, Corban takes refuge with the Wolf Clan.

4. **Varanger** (Forge, 2008) Cousins Conn and Raef Corbannsson escape the carnage at Hjorunga Bay and, finding themselves in Scandinavia, volunteer for an expedition to seize the Greek city of Chersonese.

Holmes, Marjorie

The late (d. 2002) Marjorie Holmes, writer of syndicated columns of inspiration such as "Love and Laughter" and "A Woman's Conversation with God" and books such as *I've Got to Talk to Somebody, God* (Doubleday, 1969), wrote a best-selling trilogy re-creating the life the life of Jesus, embellishing the biblical framework with a respectful, nondoctrinaire but inevitably controversial narrative that portrays Jesus as a human being.

1. **Two from Galilee** (Revell, 1972) The love story of Mary and Joseph, parents of Jesus.

2. **Three from Galilee: The Young Man from Nazareth** (Harper, 1985) Re-creates Jesus's "lost years" and his childhood and young manhood as part of a large extended family.

3. **Messiah, The** (Harper, 1987) Follows Jesus on his mission, leading to its well-known conclusion.

Holt, Hazel

Writer and amateur sleuth Sheila Malory is a middle-aged widow in the English village of Taviscombe. Mrs. Malory is something of a busybody, with a sharp eye and ear for detail and the ability to piece them together. The Malory books are pleasant, well-plotted English cozies with a likable heroine. Hazel Holt, mother of Tom Holt (q.v.) and literary executor and biographer of Barbara Pym (see *A Lot to Ask: A Life of Barbara Pym*, Dutton, 1993), published her first work of fiction at the age of 60 and has averaged one book a year since then.

1. **Mrs. Malory Investigates** (St. Martin's, 1990) Charles Richardson enlists the aid of Mrs. Malory when his fiancée Lee Montgomery disappears. UK title: *Gone Away*.

2. **Cruellest Month, The** (St. Martin's, 1991) Unpleasant librarian Gwen Richmond is found crushed under some collapsed bookshelves at the New Bodleian Library in Oxford.

3. **Shortest Journey, The** (St. Martin's, 1995) Edith Rossiter, gentle and timid resident of the West Lodge Nursing Home, vanishes during a routine shopping trip. Variant title: *Mrs. Malory's Shortest Journey*. Originally published in the United Kingdom in 1992.

4. **Mrs. Malory and the Festival Murder** (St. Martin's, 1993) Newcomer Adrian Palgrave has transformed the annual Taviscombe festival beyond recognition. UK title: *Uncertain Death*.

5. **Mrs. Malory: Detective in Residence** (Dutton, 1994) Mrs. Malory is invited to be a guest lecturer on Women's Studies at Wilmot College in Pennsylvania. UK title: *Murder on Campus*.

6. **Mrs. Malory Wonders Why** (Dutton, 1995) The elderly Miss Graham has been poisoned, and Dr. Cowley, her physician and landlord, is a prime suspect. UK title: *Superfluous Death*.

7. **Mrs. Malory: Death of a Dean** (Dutton, 1996) Actor David Beaumont becomes a prime suspect when his old nanny and his brother Francis, who stand in the way of his inheriting his ancestral home, die in suspicious circumstances. UK title: *Death of a Dean*.

8. **Mrs. Malory and the Only Good Lawyer** (Dutton, 1997) Attorney Graham Percy, irritating boyhood friend of the late Mr. Malory, is found stabbed to death on his annual visit to Taviscombe. UK title: *The Only Good Lawyer . . .*

9. **Mrs. Malory and Death among Friends** (Signet, 1999) The second attempt on the life of Frieda Spencer, chairwoman of the Taviscombe village fete, succeeds, and her lover is suspected. Mrs. Malory is convinced that the roots of the crime go back more than 50 years. UK title: *Dead and Buried*.

10. **Mrs. Malory and the Fatal Legacy** (Signet, 2000) When old college friend and best-selling author Beth dies of what seems to be an accidental drug overdose, Mrs. Malory is named literary executor of her work. UK title: *Fatal Legacy*.

11. **Mrs. Malory and the Lilies That Fester** (Signet, 2001) Mrs. Malory's son Michael announces his engagement to Thea Wyatt soon after Thea lands a position at a local law firm. Then a senior solicitor at Thea's firm dies suspiciously after an altercation with her. UK title: *Lilies That Fester*.

12. **Mrs. Mallory and the Delay of Execution** (Signet, 2002) Mrs. Malory is asked to help out at the prestigious Blakeney's School for Girls following the sudden death of a teacher. Then a second death occurs. UK title: *Delay of Execution*.

13. *Mrs. Malory and Death by Water* (Signet, 2003) When Leonora Staveley, reclusive former investigative journalist, dies from drinking contaminated water, most Taviscombe residents think that her death was a result of her peculiar lifestyle. UK title: *Leonora*.

14. *Mrs. Malory and Death in Practice* (Signet, 2003) The unpopular Malcolm Hardy, new partner at Taviscombe's veterinary practice, collapses and dies at the surgery, and the postmortem indicates foul play. UK title: *Death in Practice*.

15. *Mrs. Malory and the Silent Killer* (Signet, 2004) When widower Sidney Middleton dies in his cottage from carbon monoxide poisoning, Mrs. Malory is suspicious of the verdict of accidental death. UK title: *The Silent Killer*.

16. *Mrs. Malory and No Cure for Death* (Signet, 2005) The evidence points toward drug-addict Rhys Hampden when Dr. Morrison is found dead in his office, apparently murdered. UK title: *No Cure for Death*.

Holt, Tom (Thomas Charles Louis)

I. Until recently Eupolis, one of a trio of famous Athenian writers of Old Comedy, was known only through papyrus fragments, play titles, and some quotations in other classical writers. Now, thanks to English writer Tom Holt (son of Hazel Holt [q.v.]), we have access to Eupolis's memoirs. Through his eyes we get a vivid and sardonic view of 5th century BCE Athens. We hear Pericles orate. We rub shoulders with Socrates. We discuss farming with Euripides. We carry on a scurrilous rivalry with Aristophanes. And we have a front-row seat for the demise of Athenian democracy. The new edition of *The Walled Orchard* (Warner, 1997) contains numbers 1 and 2.

1. *Goatsong* (St. Martin's, 1990) Thanks to the divine intervention of Dionysus, Eupolis survives the plague, marries the beautiful termagant Phaedra, kills his first man, has his first play produced, and has his first run-in with Aristophanes.

2. *Walled Orchard, The* (St. Martin's, 1991) Eupolis survives the disastrous Sicilian campaign and a trial for treason and blasphemy, and eventually retires to his farm with the chastened Phaedra.

II. Holt revived the characters of E. F. Benson's (q.v.) much-loved Lucia series, and brought them, bloody but unbowed, through World War II. Holt gets Benson's gentle comic tone just right.

1. *Lucia in Wartime* (Macmillan, 1985) Lucia and Mapp compete for the dinner presence of the officers stationed near Tilling, and Georgie distinguishes himself as a radio chef.

2. *Lucia Triumphant* (Macmillan, 1986) Tilling is once again hurled into social warfare as Lucia contends with Mapp's latest ploy (*Monopoly*) for the hearts and minds of the town's social elite.

III. After Paul Carpenter starts work at the office of H. W. Wells & Co., he discovers that the apparently respectable establishment is a front for a deeply sinister organization that has a peculiar agenda, which includes consorting with goblins, dragons, werewolves, and other outré folk. Paul, partly because he has fallen in love with his peculiarly alluring colleague Sophie, hangs in there at the cost of the loss of his peace of mind, and perhaps of his life. More humorous fantasy by the author of *Expecting Someone Taller* (St. Martin's, 1988) and *Who's Afraid of Beowulf?* (St. Martin's, 1988). So far, no volumes in the series have been published in the United States.

1. *Portable Door, The* (Orbit [UK], 2003) Paul Carpenter, reluctantly taking on a job at H. W. Wells & Co., finds that the outwardly respectable company is a front for an organization with a peculiar clientele.

2. *In Your Dreams* (Orbit [UK], 2004) Paul, although promoted, still isn't sure he likes his job, which involves wrestling with goblins, traveling hundreds of miles in the blink of an eye, and dangerous office administration. Now he has been transferred to the pest-control department.

3. *Earth, Air, Fire and Custard* (Orbit [UK], 2005) Paul, still head over heels in love with Sophie, thought he was getting the hang of his clerical job at H. W. Wells & Co., but a fate worse than death or filing awaits him.

4. *You Don't Have to Be Evil to Work Here, but It Helps* (Orbit [UK], 2006) Colin Hollinghead, son of a widget manufacturer, is rather uneasy about the deal his father has made with someone who gives off a devilish aura. Perhaps his new friend from H. W. Wells & Co. will help.

Holton, Hugh

Larry Cole is a tall, black Chicago policeman who rises from rookie patrolman to become police commander. The Larry Cole novels are usually straight police stories but sometimes include elements of SF or fantasy. The plots of the novels are often unusual, sometimes verging on the unbelievable, not your usual police procedurals. The late Holton (d. 2001) was himself an African American policeman with the Chicago Police Department.

1. *Violent Crimes* (Forge, 1997) When a famous Chicago columnist is slain in ritualistic fashion, rookie patrolman Larry Cole and his older partner get on the trail of one Martin Zykus. Fourth Cole novel to be published.

2. *Presumed Dead* (Forge, 1994) Cole's investigation of a botched routine drug bust outside the National Science and Space Museum reveals that 188 people have disappeared from the museum over the years.

3. *Windy City* (Forge, 1995) While investigating the death of a fellow officer, Larry stumbles across a pattern of killings that leads him to ultrarich Margo and Neil DeWitt, who get their kicks by murdering people using methods from their favorite mystery stories.

4. *Chicago Blues* (Forge, 1996) The investigation of the murders of two hit men leads Cole to old colleague FBI Special Agent Reggie Stanton and a femme fatale nicknamed "Gunslinger."

5. *Red Lightning* (Forge, 1998) Investigative journalist Kate Ford enlists Larry's help in getting the goods on Jonathan Gault, who is installing lethal booby traps at the homes of the ultrarich.

6. *Left Hand of God, The* (Forge, 1999) Cole must foil a potential homicidal maniac, keep an eye on his teenage son, and prevent an international game-fixing scheme that could ruin the Olympic Games.

7. *Time of the Assassins* (Forge, 2000) Baron von Rianocek, hit man for drug lords allegedly financed by the CIA, has assassinated some high-profile individuals. Larry Cole is next on his list.

8. *Devil's Shadow, The* (Forge, 2001) Mob boss Jake Romano sponsors the heist of the North Michigan Avenue Bank by international thief Julianna Saint. Unfortunately someone gets killed.

9. *Criminal Element* (Forge, 2002) When Sophie Novak, sister of Cole's physician, goes missing, Larry gets involved in a nasty case involving crooked cop Joe Donegan and ambitious, corrupt Chicago alderman Skip Murphy.

Honig, Donald

I. Donald Honig is probably best known as the author of nonfiction books on baseball (e.g., *Baseball: An Illustrated History of America's Game*, Crown, 1990) and his interviews with old-time baseball players (e.g., *Baseball: When the Grass Was Real*, Coward, 1975). He has also written several novels about baseball, including two set in the 1940s featuring former marine and New York sportswriter Joe Tinker, a name that will resonate with old-time baseball fans. Although the books were generally well-received, and Tinker was regarded as an appealing character, there were no follow-ups.

1. *Last Man Out* (Dutton, 1993) 1946. Sportswriter Joe Tinker, just back from the Pacific, tackles the murder of a wealthy socialite and her maid in which the prime suspect is a member of the Brooklyn Dodgers. Prequel to number 2.
2. *Plot to Kill Jackie Robinson, The* (Dutton, 1992) Joe Tinker witnesses a murder with racial overtones, and is drawn into a complicated plot featuring a racist psychopath who is determined to prevent Jackie Robinson from playing for the Brooklyn Dodgers.

II. Honig has also written both fiction and nonfiction books about the American Civil War and its aftermath in the West of the 1870s. A pair of novels features US Army officer Thomas Maynard, who investigates murders in the Dakota and Montana Territories in the 1870s. Again, although the novels were praised for their evocation of time and place, there has been no follow-up to the first two.

1. *Ghost of Major Pryor, The* (Scribner, 1997) Subtitle: *A Novel of Murder in the Montana Territory, 1870*. In this prequel to number 2, US Army captain Thomas Maynard is called upon to investigate an alleged sighting of Major Andrew Pryor, who had supposedly been killed in the Civil War.
2. *Sword of General Englund, The* (Scribner, 1996) Subtitle: *A Novel of Murder in the Dakota Territory*. When General Alfred Englund is stabbed to death in his office and an enlisted man is found murdered nearby, the army sends Major Thomas Maynard to investigate.

Hooper, Kay

I. Prolific and popular romantic suspense author Kay Hooper has produced several series, most of them rather loosely connected. While the Once Upon a Time . . . novels are tied together only by theme (the modernizing of fairy tales), the Bishop Special Crime Unit series has FBI Agent Noah Bishop as coordinator, facilitator of investigations, and recruiter for the Special Crimes Unit of the FBI throughout. The series consists of four "trilogies": Shadows (numbers 1–3); Evil (numbers 4–6); and Fear (numbers 7–9) and the start of a new trilogy, Blood Trilogy (number 10). Each novel features different protagonists, usually endowed with psychic powers, and, in the later novels, members of the Special Crimes Unit. The crimes that they investigate have a paranormal or supernatural tinge and usually involve serial killers.

1. *Stealing Shadows* (Bantam, 2000) Psychic Cassie Neill flees to Ryan's Bluff, a small town in North Carolina, after a terrible mistake results in the death of an innocent child. Introduces FBI profiler Noah Bishop.
2. *Hiding in the Shadows* (Bantam, 2000) Accident victim Faith Parker has awakened from a weeks-long coma without memory of the crash, or her previous life, or of journalist Dinah Leighton, the steadfast friend who visited her in the hospital.

3. *Out of the Shadows* (Bantam, 2000) Noah Bishop has an important role as he helps former protégé Sheriff Miranda Knight, who has psychic abilities herself, solve some torture slayings in a small Tennessee town.
4. *Touching Evil* (Bantam, 2001) Seattle police artist Maggie Barnes has a special gift that allows her to work with crime victims and create perfect portraits of their attackers. Along comes an elusive predator who blinds his victims so that they can't identify him.
5. *Whisper of Evil* (Bantam, 2002) Psychic Nell Gallagher, haunted by memories, has returned home to the small town of Silence only to run into a serial killer.
6. *Sense of Evil* (Bantam, 2003) Special Agent Isabel Adams aids Police Chief Rafe Sullivan in apprehending the murderer of a series of beautiful, successful, and blond women.
7. *Hunting Fear* (Bantam, 2004) New Special Crimes Unit recruit Lucas Jordan, a specialist in finding missing people, is called in on what appears to be a series of ordinary kidnappings for ransom.
8. *Chill of Fear* (Bantam, 2005) Telepathic recruit Quentin Hayes and Noah Bishop, investigating a series of disappearances from an exclusive Tennessee resort, encounter guest Diana Brisco, who has psychic powers of which she wasn't aware.
9. *Sleeping with Fear* (Bantam, 2007) Psychic Agent Riley Crane, on assignment to Opal Island, off the South Carolina coast, wakes up one afternoon covered in blood and with no memory of the last three weeks.
10. *Blood Dreams* (Bantam, 2007) A serial killer murders the daughter of a powerful US senator.

II. The Men of Mysteries Past was a four-volume romantic suspense series published in 1993, followed by an additional two volumes published in 2002. Connecting links are Max Bannister, owner of a fabulous collection of jewelry, the mysterious master thief Quinn, and museum curator Morgan West.

1. *Touch of Max, The* (Bantam, 1993) Max Bannister agrees to provide the police with his family's jewelry collection as bait to catch a thief. Then beautiful Dinah Layton gets innocently entrapped. Variant title: *Men of Mysteries Past: The Touch of Max*.
2. *Hunting the Wolfe* (Bantam, 1993) Wolfe Nickerson, leader of the security team guarding the Bannister jewelry collection, gets entangled with the beautiful Storm Tremaine. Variant title: *Men of Mysteries Past: Hunting the Wolfe*.
3. *Trouble with Jared, The* (Bantam, 1993) Years after Jared Chavalier swept gemologist Danica Gray off her feet and forced her to choose between his love and her career, the two meet again. Variant title: *Men of Mysteries Past: The Trouble with Jared*.
4. *All for Quinn* (Bantam, 1993) Curator Morgan West knows she is taking a real chance when she spends an evening with the renowned and sensual cat burglar Quinn. Variant title: *Men of Mysteries Past: All for Quinn*.
5. *Once a Thief* (Bantam, 2002) In a revival and apparent rewrite of the Men of Mysteries Past quartet, Max Bannister once again risks his collection, and Morgan West and Quinn reappear.
6. *Always a Thief* (Bantam, 2002) The mysterious Quinn turns up in Morgan West's apartment one night to seek her aid in thwarting a deadly adversary.

III. The Hagen series, like the Bishop Special Crime Unit series (see series I), is connected by a facilitator. Hagen, a kind of gray eminence who always remains in the background, runs a group of undercover agents who get involved in one romantic adventure after another.

1. *In Serena's Web* (Bantam, 1987) Not technically one of the *Hagen* series, this novel introduces wealthy, powerful Josh Long, who is the main protagonist of number 2.
2. *Raven on the Wing* (Bantam, 1987) Woman of mystery Raven Anderson wins Josh Long's heart, but continues to elude him.
3. *Rafferty's Wife* (Bantam, 1987) Sarah Cavell is troubled when she meets tough and dangerous-looking Rafferty Lewis, the "husband" she has to work with on a secret mission.
4. *Zach's Law* (Bantam, 1987) When Teddy Tyler accidently threatens Zach Steele's stakeout, he makes her remain in his remote cabin until his mission is accomplished.
5. *Fall of Lucas Kendrick, The* (Bantam, 1988) Lucas Kendrick reenters Kyle Griffon's life 10 years after he left her and requests her help and understanding.
6. *Unmasking Kelsey* (Bantam, 1988) When Kelsey answers a mysterious call for help from a small southern town, he is prepared to charm or seduce Elizabeth Connor into telling him what he needs to know.
7. *Outlaw Derek* (Bantam, 1988) Derek Ross helps Shannon Brown to elude her life-threatening pursuers. But the ferocity of Derek's desire for Shannon stuns him, and mystifies her.
8. *Shades of Gray* (Bantam, 1988) Andres Sereno, charismatic ruler of the island of Kadeira, conducts a hot-and-heavy affair with Sara Marsh.
9. *Captain's Paradise* (Bantam, 1988) Robin Stuart is rescued from stormy seas by the mysterious and irresistible Michael Siran, who is on a dangerous mission.
10. *It Takes a Thief* (Bantam, 1989) A sophisticated lady sneak thief and a professional gambler share love and risk in a dangerous game. Not to be confused with the Grace Kelly movie of the same title
11. *Aces High* (Bantam, 1989) Tall, dark, and dangerous Skye Prescott has never forgotten how Katrina Keller had betrayed him years before.

IV. Lane Montana, finder of lost objects, and her lover, police lieutenant Trey Fortier, are the protagonists in a pair of relatively conventional mysteries.

1. *Crime of Passion* (Avon, 1991) Lane Montana, finder of lost objects, gets involved with murder and police lieutenant Trey Fortier.
2. *House of Cards* (Avon, 1991) Lane Montana's family reunion at her mother's estate is spoiled when cousin Lawrence drinks a cocktail laced with strychnine, possibly the innocent victim of a crime aimed at despised kinsman-by-marriage Innis Langdon.

Hope, Anthony

Hope's cape-and-sword romance, *The Prisoner of Zenda*, has been filmed four times, most successfully by David Selznick, whose 1937 version starred Ronald Colman and Douglas Fairbanks Jr. The story concerns Rudolf Rassendyll, a vacationing Englishman whose remarkable resemblance to the king of Ruritania enables him to rescue the king from Zenda Castle, where he is being held by his evil brother. Princess Flavia provides the love interest in these still very readable adventures. Rupert of Hentzau proved to be such an interesting villain that he was featured in a sequel. The two novels were reprinted as *Ruritania* (Dover, 2000).

1. *Prisoner of Zenda, The* (Holt, 1894) Rassendyll impersonates the king twice and falls in love with Princess Flavia, the king's betrothed.

2. *Rupert of Hentzau* (Holt, 1898) Rudolf returns to Ruritania to foil Rupert of Hentzau's evil plot.

Horgan, Paul

Horgan (d. 1995) was a seriously underrated author who was handicapped, like Wright Morris (q.v.), by the "regional" label. Despite his frequent use of the American Southwest as a setting for his historical and contemporary novels and as a source for his nonfiction, Horgan's themes are the universal ones of moral choice, personal temptation, charity and redemption, and the loss of innocence. His clear prose, expressive yet unmarred by excess, is a model most writers could profit from. The Richard trilogy, portraying a sensitive young boy growing up through childhood's customary traumas, is written with a grace and perception that are reminiscent of the English author L. P. Hartley (q.v.).

1. *Things as They Are* (Farrar, 1964) Richie, age five in 1908, learns about the world and its peculiar and sometimes cruel ways.
2. *Everything to Live For* (Farrar, 1968) Seventeen-year-old Richard tells the story of his cousin Max Chittenden, a Harvard student uneasy about his role as heir to the Chittenden fortune.
3. *Thin Mountain Air* (Farrar, 1977) When Richard's father contracts TB in the early 1920s, the family moves to Albuquerque, New Mexico, and Richie leaves college to "toughen up" at the WZL Ranch.

Hornsby, Wendy

I. Maggie McGowen, documentary filmmaker, mother of a teenager, and lover of Los Angeles homicide detective Mike Flint, is funny, clever, tough, idealistic, and quite believable in her various roles. Most of the crimes she solves come her way through her filming. *Nine Sons: Collected Mysteries* (Crippen, 2002), a collection of 11 short stories, contains "Essential Things," in which Mike Flint is featured.

1. *Telling Lies* (Dutton, 1992) Maggie's sister Dr. Emily Duschamps is assassinated, probably by someone in her activist past or present.
2. *Midnight Baby* (Dutton, 1993) Filming a documentary about children, Maggie runs into a 14-year-old prostitute named Pisces who seems unsuited for her role.
3. *Bad Intent* (Dutton, 1994) Making a film about growing in the projects, Maggie unintentionally interviews two women who witnessed a cop killing 14 years previously.
4. *77th Street Requiem* (Dutton, 1995) Maggie is producing a television documentary on the unsolved murder of Los Angeles policeman Ray Frady, an old buddy of Maggie's lover, Mike Flint.
5. *Hard Light, A* (Dutton, 1997) Maggie agrees to track down the Vietnamese man who attacked her old friend Khanh Nguyen.

II. Before the Maggie McGowen series, Wendy Hornsby wrote a pair of mystery novels featuring heiress Kate Teague and homicide detective Roger Tejeda.

1. *No Harm* (Dodd, Mead, 1987) The slaying of Kate Teague's mother by a common street mugger leaves Kate as sole beneficiary of a large inheritance.
2. *Half a Mind* (New American Library, 1990) Homicide detective Roger Tejeda, recovering from a fractured skull suffered on his

last case, is sent a human head, which sends him, with the help of his lover, Kate Teague, on a search for a sex killer.

Howard, Elizabeth Jane

English writer Howard has written many novels and television dramas (including scripts for *Upstairs, Downstairs*). The Cazalet Chronicle is a four-volume series about the numerous members of an upper-middle-class English family, their friends, and servants. Starting in 1937, the chronicle carried its characters through World War II. This is a detailed look at a particular time and place with well-conceived characters.

1. *Light Years, The* (Pocket, 1990) "Brig" and "Duchy" Cazalet, their three grown sons, and the son's wives and children are undertaking their summer relocation to the country house in Sussex in 1937.
2. *Marking Time* (Pocket, 1992) The nine young Cazalets are gathered for the duration of World War II in the Sussex country home of their grandparents.
3. *Confusion* (Pocket, 1994) Opens in the spring of 1942 and focuses on the eldest Cazalet cousins: Louise, Polly, and Clary.
4. *Casting Off* (Simon & Schuster, 1996) The Cazalets, having weathered World War II, now must face an England of shortages and a crumbling empire and a round of births, deaths, weddings, and divorces.

Howatch, Susan

I. Susan Howatch, English author of mysteries and best-selling gothics such as *Penmarric* (Simon & Schuster, 1971) and *Cashelmara* (Simon & Schuster, 1974), has written a two-volume family saga about the Van Zales, a predacious American banking clan full of odd characters and complicated relationships. According to Howatch (*Contemporary Authors, New Revision Series*, v. 24), the Van Zale saga is a modern-dress version of the story of Julius Caesar, Cleopatra, and the emperor Augustus.

1. *Rich Are Different, The* (Simon & Schuster, 1977) Dinah Slade, who needs money for the upkeep of her ancestral Norfolk manor, meets Paul Van Zale, a rich American banker looking for a mistress. Covers the years 1922 to 1940.
2. *Sins of the Fathers* (Simon & Schuster, 1980) In action spanning the years 1949 to 1967, Cornelius Van Zale, grandnephew and heir of Paul, wreaks havoc on friends and relations, especially his daughter Vicki.

II. With the publication of the first of the Starbridge Chronicles, Howatch's writing took a new turn. In a series chronicling the Church of England in the 20th century, Howatch delineates compelling stories about the sometimes tortured inner lives of the churchmen and gives readers an insiders look at English church politics and clerical life. Although the Starbridge Chronicles ended with number 6, some Starbridge characters reappear in numbers 7 and 8.

1. *Glittering Images* (Knopf, 1987) Canon Charles Ashworth suspects some highly irregular behavior in the domestic life of the charismatic Bishop of Starbridge. Father Jonathan Darrow helps Ashworth sort things out. Set in 1937.
2. *Glamorous Powers* (Knopf, 1988) Father Darrow takes center stage in this volume. After 17 years as an Anglican monk, he has a vision that leads him to leave the monastic life. Set in 1940.
3. *Ultimate Prizes* (Knopf, 1989) This novel focuses on Archdeacon Neville Aysgarth's crisis of faith following the death of his child. Set during World War II. Darrow appears briefly.
4. *Scandalous Risks* (Knopf, 1990) Explores the relationship between young Venetia Flaxton and 61-year-old Neville Aysgarth. Set in 1963.
5. *Mystical Paths* (Knopf, 1992) Nicholas, son of Jonathan Darrow, investigates the possible suicide of his friend Christian Aysgarth and uncovers some dark secrets.
6. *Absolute Truths* (Knopf, 1995) This novel focuses on the clash between middle-of-the-road Bishop Charles Ashworth and Dean of the Cathedral Neville Aysgarth, whom Ashworth feels is overly heterodox.
7. *Wonder Worker, The* (Knopf, 1997) Nicholas Darrow, who is a gifted healer, may be a victim of his own self-delusions and neuroses.
8. *High Flyer, The* (Knopf, 2000) Nicholas Darrow plays an important role when success-driven London lawyer Carter Graham is confronted by some nasty truths about her new husband Kim Betz's past and some paranormal phenomena for which she is unprepared.

Howells, William Dean

I. Henry Adams once said that if all reminders of the 1870s were lost, the age could be reconstructed from the novels of William Dean Howells. Though often overlooked by modern readers, Howells's novels were quite popular in his day, perhaps even more highly regarded than those of his contemporary Henry James. Perhaps it is time for a Howells revival. The married couple Basil and Isabel March were favorite characters with Howells. Basil is thought to be an autobiographical figure. They appear in all the books listed below, sometimes as main characters, sometimes as peripheral figures. Library of America has reprinted several of Howells's novels, including number 3.

1. *Their Wedding Journey* (Houghton, 1872) The young Bostonian couple Basil and Isabel March travel to Canada for their honeymoon.
2. *Chance Acquaintance, A* (Osgood, 1873) Kitty Ellison, who appears in *Their Wedding Journey*, has a shipboard romance with Miles Arbuton. The Marches are merely background.
3. *Hazard of New Fortunes, A* (Harper, 1890) In this novel, generally regarded as one of Howells's best, Basil March accepts the editorship of a literary magazine in New York.
4. *Shadow of a Dream, The* (Harper, 1890) Basil narrates and plays a small role in this sad tale of how a dying man's dream affects the romance that develops between his widow and his best friend.
5. *Open-Eyed Conspiracy, An* (Harper, 1897) At the resort of Saratoga, Mr. and Mrs. March are left in charge of a beautiful country girl and facilitate her getting engaged to a young author.
6. *Their Silver Wedding* (Harper, 1899) Now middle-aged, the Marches tour Germany and see the world in an "evening light."
7. *Pair of Patient Lovers, A* (Harper, 1901) The Marches play minor roles in two of the short stories in this collection.

II. Howells wrote two books about Altruria, a utopian society based on Christian principles of altruism. The first novel describes the reactions of Mr. Homos of Altruria as he visits the United States. The sequel is an epistolary novel containing the letters of the new American wife of Homos, who visits Altruria with him. Howells's Altruria novels have never had the impact of Edward Bellamy's (q.v.) *Looking Backward, 2000–1887*.

1. *Traveler from Altruria, A* **(Harper, 1894)** Mr. Homos, on vacation from the utopian republic of Altruria, pays a visit to the United States and finds that American democracy is not all it was cracked up to be.
2. *Through the Eye of the Needle* **(Harper, 1907)** Contains letters describing Altruria, written by Eveleth Strange, Mr. Homos's American wife, who has accompanied her husband to his homeland.

Hoyt, Richard

I. John Denson is a private eye based in Seattle who gets involved in some rather bawdy, funny, violent thrillers. With his partner, Native American shaman Willie Prettybird, Denison gets mixed up with journalists, ecologists, Chinese artwork, Elizabethan manuscripts, right-wing preachers, and the elements in a wild series of adventures. Hoyt, who was born and raised in Oregon, is familiar with the Pacific Northwest.

1. *Decoys* **(Evans, 1980)** Denson is hired by fellow private eye Pamela Yee, ostensibly to locate a pimp in San Francisco, but winds up getting involved with a valuable vase.
2. *30 for a Harry* **(Evans, 1981)** John is added to the reportorial staff of a Seattle newspaper when its owners get suspicious of an ace reporter who may be taking kickbacks.
3. *Siskiyou Two-Step, The* **(Morrow, 1983)** Denson competes with the FBI and British intelligence in locating an Elizabethan manuscript that purportedly proves that Shakespeare was the Earl of Oxford.
4. *Fish Story* **(Viking, 1985)** Willie Prettybird gets John involved with the suit of the Cowlitz Indians for fishing rights on the Columbia River.
5. *Whoo?* **(Tor, 1991)** The endangered spotted owl is the source of Denson's involvement with politics, murder, and an insane wildlife photographer.
6. *Bigfoot* **(Tor, 1993)** The elusive Sasquatch is the subject of a $100,000 reward from a local promoter and the spur to a frenzied search up the slopes of Mount St. Helen's.
7. *Snake Eyes* **(Forge, 1995)** Denson and Prettybird find themselves investigating an outbreak of anthrax in Enterprise, Oregon on the behest of the lawyer for anti-environmentalist rancher Monty Hook.
8. *Weatherman's Daughters, The* **(Forge, 2003)** The murder of two daughters of Portland's most popular weatherman leads John and Willie into the Oregon wilds and some really weird weather.
9. *Pony Girls* **(Forge, 2004)** Denson investigates the death of more than 20 Spanish mustangs.

II. Maverick CIA agent James Burlane (aka Sid Khartoum) is the protagonist in a series of over-the-top espionage adventures with plenty of satirical humor, sex, and convoluted plots. Richard Hoyt was a "counterintelligence operator" at one point in his career.

1. *Trotsky's Run* **(Morrow, 1982)** British turncoat Kim Philby has information that America's president-elect is really a Soviet mole.
2. *Head of State* **(Tor, 1985)** Refusenik poet Isaac Ginsburg plans to steal the head of Lenin to force the USSR to agree to one year of unrestricted emigration.
3. *Dragon Portfolio, The* **(Tor, 1986)** Beautiful agent Ella Nidech's purchase of secret Chinese documents is complicated by the antics of kung-fu movie stars and rich Texans.
4. *Siege* **(Tor, 1987)** Nidech and Burlane foil Palestinian terrorists occupying Gibraltar.

5. *Marimba* **(Tor, 1992)** Burlane becomes Sid Khartoum, swaggering cocaine cargo pilot, in an assignment to uncover corruption among American undercover forces in the drug war.
6. *Red Card* **(Tor, 1994)** Burlane, still in his Sid Khartoum role, is hired to stop the assassination of star soccer players as the United States is poised to host the World Cup.
7. *Japanese Game* **(Tor, 1995)** The daughter of the American vice president is kidnapped in the Philippines and sold to the Yakuza as a sex slave.
8. *Tyger! Tyger!* **(Forge, 1996)** Burlane is sent after the buyers of poached tigers while, at the same time, German detective Hermann Iversen is looking for a serial killer who paints his female victims with tiger stripes before killing them.
9. *Blood of Patriots* **(Forge, 1996)** Neil Abercrombie, US congressman from Hawaii, is the coauthor of this Burlane novel in which terrorists massacre more than 100 members of the House of Representatives with assault-weapons fire.

III. Hoyt has also written a widely separated, wildly plotted pair of novels in which Jim Quint, journalist, paperback novelist, and pothead, plays a leading role.

1. *Cool Runnings* **(Viking, 1984)** Jim Quint, sometime writer for *Rolling Stone*, on assignment in Europe, is enlisted by the CIA to help in the investigation of a stolen atomic bomb.
2. *Vivienne* **(Forge, 2000)** Quint, covering a speech by General Westmoreland, is invited by Colonel Del Lambert to inveigle from his Vietnamese wife, Vivienne, a missing film documenting a Vietcong massacre of a Vietnamese village.

Hughes, Richard

The years between the two wars are vividly pictured in these two novels that focus on a young upper-class Englishman named Augustine. Though part of the unfinished Human Predicament series, which Hughes conceived as a history of his own times up to the Second World War, these novels read well separately. They blend the story of Augustine's personal growth, travel, friendships, and romance with the larger events that swirl around him. Incidents of Hitler's rise, as reported through the eyes of Augustine's German relatives, give the novels their documentary quality.

1. *Fox in the Attic, The* **(Harper, 1961)** Augustine visits his Kessen relatives in Germany and falls in love with young Mitzi during the time of Hitler's ill-fated 1923 Munich putsch.
2. *Wooden Shepherdess, The* **(Harper, 1973)** Augustine travels in America, Bavaria, and Morocco as social unrest increases. The story ends in 1934 with the infamous "Night of the Long Knives."

Hughes, Thomas

Skimming quickly over the first three chapters will get the reader right into the action that was so splendidly dramatized on Masterpiece Theatre and in two previous movie versions. Young Tom is truthful, honest, and loyal—and courageous enough to defend his high principles. Though Hughes denied it, the story is probably autobiographical. The Rugby he depicts is the school as it was after the enlightened educator, Dr. Thomas Arnold, had instituted his reforms there. Hughes's sequel, *Tom Brown at Oxford,* never achieved the popularity or near-canonical status of *Tom Brown's School Days,* but George MacDonald Fraser's (q.v.) late 20th-century entertainments relating the later career of the ineffable Harry Flashman have proved to be quite popular.

1. *Tom Brown's School Days* (Houghton, 1857) Tom arrives at Rugby and meets his friend East; the two have schoolboy scrapes and a run-in with the bully Flashman.
2. *Tom Brown at Oxford* (Burt, 1861) Tom attends Oxford as the perfect athlete, scholar, and gentleman and finally is married.

Hunter, Evan

PSEUDONYM OF Salvatore A. Lombino

Last Summer is a chilling little tale of adolescent boredom erupting into violence. The peacefulness of the island resort where Sandy, Peter, and David spend their summer vacation provides an eerie contrast to the trio's sadistic bullying of poor Rhoda. Like William Golding's *Lord of the Flies*, which it resembles, *Last Summer* made a powerful film (1969). Both books listed below are narrated by young Peter, whose teenage slang rings true. Hunter (d. 2005), who also wrote police procedurals under the pseudonym of Ed McBain (q.v.), first made his mark with *The Blackboard Jungle* (Simon & Schuster, 1954).

1. *Last Summer* (Doubleday, 1968) Three teenage friends spending their summer at the shore befriend and then abuse the awkward and shy young Rhoda.
2. *Come Winter* (Doubleday, 1973) Five years later, on a pre-Christmas holiday, the three friends brave dangerous ski trails and deadly human passions.

Innes, Michael

PSEUDONYM OF J. I. M. Stewart

I. John Appleby's erudition and urbanity serve him well in the stately homes and academic settings where his cases usually take him; these qualities have, no doubt, contributed to his rapid rise from uniformed bobby through Scotland Yard to London police commissioner and ultimate knighthood. The late Oxford professor J. I. M. Stewart, who wrote novels, scholarly studies, and biographies under his real name, has endowed Appleby with a formidable command of literature and classics—though not with an Oxford education—and with useful social connections through his wife's family. Readers who like their mysteries spiced with quotations will enjoy these literate and witty entertainments.

1. *Seven Suspects* (Dodd, 1937) Young Inspector Appleby solves the locked-room murder of Dr. Umbleby, the president of one of Oxford's colleges. UK title: *Death at the President's Lodging*
2. *Hamlet, Revenge!* (Dodd, 1937) A murder is perpetrated onstage during an amateur production of *Hamlet* at the Duke of Horton's estate.
3. *Lament for a Murder* (Dodd, 1938) This case of death and mystery in remotest Scotland begins when a hated laird falls to his death from the top of his ancient, towered home.
4. *Spider Strikes, The* (Dodd, 1939) Richard Eliot, a mystery writer, is plagued by a series of practical jokes in which his character, "the Spider," seems to come alive. UK title: *Stop Press*.
5. *Comedy of Terrors, A* (Dodd, 1940) Death interrupts a Christmas family gathering when a stray bullet kills one of those present. UK title: *There Came Both Mist and Snow*.
6. *Secret Vanguard, The* (Dodd, 1941) Nazi spies in Scotland are the focus of this case, which involves some lively scenes of pursuit over the lonely Scottish heaths.
7. *Appleby on Ararat* (Dodd, 1941) When Appleby's ship is torpedoed in the South Seas, he drifts to an apparently uninhabited island, where he soon gets involved with murder and buried treasure.

8. *Daffodil Affair, The* (Dodd, 1942) Hannah Metcalfe, the descendant of a witch, leads Appleby on a lively search through a haunted Bloomsbury house amid London's air raids.
9. *Weight of the Evidence, The* (Dodd, 1943) Inspector Appleby goes to Nesfield University to investigate the mysterious death of Professor Pluckrose.
10. *Appleby's End* (Dodd, 1945) Sheltered by the unconventional Raven family during a winter storm in the country, Appleby solves some decidedly rustic mysteries and meets his future wife, sculptress Judith Raven.
11. *Night of Errors, A* (Dodd, 1947) Appleby is invited to sit in on the puzzling case of the murder of the last surviving member of a set of triplets.
12. *Paper Thunderbolt, The* (Dodd, 1951) Can the disappearance of a number of people from an English village be connected to the doings of a nasty gang of scientist-criminals? UK title: *Operation Pax*.
13. *One Man Show* (Dodd, 1952) Murder and a painting stolen from the Duke of Horton's mansion occupy Appleby in one of his best cases. UK title: *A Private View*. Variant title: *Murder Is an Art*.
14. *Dead Man's Shoes* (Dodd, 1954) Appleby stars in 23 short stories. UK title: *Appleby Talking*.
15. *Appleby Talks Again* (Dodd, 1957) This book has 18 more short stories about Appleby.
16. *Death on a Quiet Day* (Dodd, 1957) More thriller than mystery, this book concerns a young student who finds himself pursued by all sorts of villains. UK title: *Appleby Plays Chicken*.
17. *Long Farewell, The* (Dodd, 1958) This short case involves a dead man with two wives and a missing rare book from the Packford library.
18. *Hare Sitting Up* (Dodd, 1959) Sir John, in search of a bacteriologist missing from his lab, finds himself on a lonely island off the Scottish coast.
19. *Silence Observed* (Dodd, 1961) Art frauds and some particularly baffling murders occupy Commissioner Appleby's attention.
20. *Crabtree Affair, The* (Dodd, 1962) Sir John and his wife are on holiday when a murder draws them into an investigation in this exceptionally well-knit case. UK title: *A Connoisseur's Case*.
21. *Bloody Wood, The* (Dodd, 1966) Intrigue and murder by one of three possible heirs to a fortune keep Appleby guessing.
22. *Death by Water* (Dodd, 1968) While exploring a gazebo on a neighboring estate, Sir John discovers a dead body, still warm. UK title: *Appleby at Allington*.
23. *Picture of Guilt* (Dodd, 1969) This story of an art fraud is both mysterious and highly amusing. Appleby's young son Bobby helps in the detecting. UK title: *A Family Affair*.
24. *Death at the Chase* (Dodd, 1970) Young Bobby helps again as Appleby investigates the murder of an eccentric neighbor who believed his former Resistance comrades were trying to kill him.
25. *Awkward Lie, An* (Dodd, 1971) This complicated case involves a mentally straying old man, a large inheritance, and a suddenly illuminated stately home.
26. *Open House, The* (Dodd, 1972) Appleby's problem—an empty house all lit up with dinner waiting and pajamas laid out—has all the classic elements of a first-rate puzzler.
27. *Appleby's Answer* (Dodd, 1973) Sir John accidentally bumps into this case involving a lady author, a shady military man, and a goat.
28. *Appleby's Other Story* (Dodd, 1974) Maurice Tytherton, owner of the magnificent Elvedon Court, is murdered.
29. *Appleby File, The* (Dodd, 1976) Eighteen short stories continue Appleby's adventures.
30. *Gay Phoenix, The* (Dodd, 1977) Death aboard a yacht in the South Pacific is the central problem here.

31. *Ampersand Papers, The* (Dodd, 1979) Appleby is admiring an Old Cornish castle when Dr. Sutch, the archivist, plummets to his death from a collapsing staircase.
32. *Sheiks and Adders* (Dodd, 1982) Sir John investigates the murder of a pseudo-sheikh at a masquerade ball.
33. *Appleby and Honeybath* (Dodd, 1983) Sir John Appleby joins forces with Charles Honeybath, RA (see series II), to solve the mystery of the vanishing body in the library of Grinton Hall.
34. *Carson's Conspiracy* (Dodd, 1984) Appleby's neighbor Carl Carson must cover up his crazy wife and bankrupt business to pass himself off as a country squire.
35. *Appleby and the Ospreys* (Dodd, 1987) Sir John investigates the fatal stabbing of Lord Osprey and the disappearance of his coin collection.

II. Charles Honeybath, RA, is a successful portrait painter who doubles as an amateur detective. The Honeybath novels are much like the Appleby novels in structure, style, and ambience. Appleby (series I) and Honeybath collaborate in number 4.

1. *Mysterious Commission, The* (Dodd, 1975) Honeybath is offered a nice sum of money if he will agree to spend a fortnight at an unspecified country house painting the portrait of a client who must remain unidentified.
2. *Honeybath's Haven* (Dodd, 1978) Honeybath's attempt to aid old friend and fellow painter Edwin Lightfoot draws him into a dangerous mystery.
3. *Lord Mullion's Secret* (Dodd, 1978) Honeybath is commissioned to paint the portrait of Lady Mullion but is sidetracked by the theft of a valuable miniature.
4. *Appleby and Honeybath (2)* (Dodd, 1983) John Appleby (see series I) joins forces with Honeybath to solve the mystery of the vanishing body in the library of Grinton Hall.

Irvine, Robert R(alstone)

I. Former pro football player Moroni Traveler is no longer a Mormon, but he still lives and works in Salt Lake City, Utah, and many of the cases he takes on as a private investigator with his eccentric father-partner involve Mormon business, good plots and characterization, and Rocky Mountain ambience. *Barking Dogs* (St. Martin's, 1994) isn't part of the series.

1. *Baptism for the Dead* (Dodd, 1988) The black-sheep daughter of a powerful Mormon Elder hires Traveler to find her mother.
2. *Angels' Share, The* (St. Martin's, 1989) Moroni is hired by a Mormon bishop to find his daughter's missing fiancé, then fired because the authorities regard the affair as strictly church business.
3. *Gone to Glory* (St. Martin's, 1990) Minor league baseball manager Pepper Daulton is put in jail when his wealthy sister dies.
4. *Called Home* (St. Martin's, 1991) Moroni travels to rural Sanpete County to uncover the reason why Ellis Nibley's wife committed suicide.
5. *Spoken Word, The* (St. Martin's, 1992) The grandniece of the Mormon First Prophet has been kidnapped to force him to publish a revelation granting equal rights between the sexes in the church.
6. *Great Reminder, The* (St. Martin's, 1993) Traveler is hired by an elderly Utah farmer who wants to pay off a debt of nearly 50 years' standing to a former German POW.

7. *Hosanna Shout, The* (St. Martin's, 1994) Moroni is looking for a three-year-old boy, also called Moroni, whose mother had an affair with Traveler long before the child was conceived.
8. *Pillar of Fire* (St. Martin's, 1995) Traveler journeys to "cult country" in southwestern Utah to retrieve a Mormon official's daughter and grandson from a charismatic preacher.

II. Irvine wrote four novels, all except the last paperback only, about Bob Christopher, a TV cameraman who gets involved in mysteries. Listings are not annotated.

1. *Jump Cut* (Popular Library, 1974)
2. *Freeze Frame* (Popular Library, 1976)
3. *Horizontal Hold* (Popular Library, 1978)
4. *Ratings Are Murder* (Walker, 1985)

Irwin, Margaret

Anyone who enjoyed Glenda Jackson's portrayal of Queen Elizabeth I on the Masterpiece Theatre production of *Elizabeth R* will find Irwin's trilogy on Elizabeth's early years fascinating. Historical fiction at its best, these novels are lively, authentic, and gracefully written. Irwin's Elizabeth is a precocious, witty, cool-headed schemer who has only one aim in life—to become queen of England. Sixteenth-century English court life is vividly re-created. Jean Simmons played Elizabeth in the film version of *Young Bess* (1953), which also starred Stewart Granger and Charles Laughton. Irwin wrote many other historical novels, most them set in the 16th or 17th centuries, including a pair about James Graham, Marquis of Montrose: *The Proud Servant* (Harcourt, 1934) and *The Bride* (Harcourt, 1939).

1. *Young Bess* (Harcourt, 1945) This volume takes Elizabeth from the age of 12 to her stepbrother Edward VI's death in 1553.
2. *Elizabeth, Captive Princess* (Harcourt, 1948) Covers the period from the short reign of Lady Jane Grey to the marriage of Queen Mary.
3. *Elizabeth and the Prince of Spain* (Harcourt, 1953) Here we see Mary's relatively short reign, before her death and Elizabeth's coronation.

Isaacs, Susan

Susan Isaacs, not to be confused with the actress of the same name, writes novels featuring a distinctive type of heroine, a woman who seems quite ordinary but is in fact quite extraordinary when she is exposed to murder, political intrigue, or espionage. Two murder mysteries, published 23 years apart, feature Nassau County (Long Island, New York) housewife Judith Singer.

1. *Compromising Positions* (Times Books, 1978) Judith Singer is uprooted from her dull life by the murder of her periodontist, Dr. Bruce Fleckstein.
2. *Long Time No See* (HarperCollins, 2001) Two decades later, Judith is found widowed and still carrying the torch for Nassau County PD lieutenant Nelson Sharpe (introduced in number 1). Courtney Logan, wife, mother, collector of vintage needlepoint, ex-president of Citizens for a More Beautiful Shorehaven, and daughter-in-law of Long Island mobster "Fancy Phil" Lowenstein, vanishes.

Islas, Arturo

Islas, late professor of American and Chicano literatures at Stanford University, devoted his professional life to fighting for the recognition of Chicano literature. His planned trilogy (not completed due to his premature death) about the Mexican American Angel family of Del Sapo (read El Paso, Islas's birthplace), Texas, has autobiographical elements. The pair of published novels describes the lives of Mexican immigrants who settle on the US–Mexican border and endure racism and religious and ethnic identity problems.

1. *Rain God, The: A Desert Tale* **(Alexandrian, 1984)** The lives, deaths, and internal conflicts of a Mexican family that leaves Mexico as the result of the 1910 Revolution and settles in an American border city.
2. *Migrant Souls* **(Morrow, 1990)** Concentrates on a few members of the Angel family: religious zealot Jesus Maria, her willful niece Josie Salazar, and Miguel Chico Angel, who is coming to terms with his homosexuality.

Jack, Donald

These volumes, purporting to be the Bandy Papers, star the redoubtable World War I ace Bartholomew Bandy, a Canadian whose stentorian tones and brash disregard for bureaucratic detail invariably set his superior officers' teeth on edge. Donald Jack (d. 2003), a former RAF man, wrote lovingly of the early flying machines his pilot maneuvers through scene after scene of action. The wars Bandy engages in are backdrops, not realities that might impinge upon the hero's humorous and daring escapades.

1. *Three Cheers for Me* **(Doubleday, 1973)** Events on the western front get very lively indeed when Bartholomew Bandy arrives on the scene and begins to make his reputation in his Sopwith Camel.
2. *That's Me in the Middle* **(Doubleday, 1973)** Lieutenant-Colonel Bandy lands a liaison job in London, and further misadventures ensue.
3. *It's Me Again* **(Doubleday, 1975)** Bandy takes command of his own squadron of Sopwith Dolphins and gets to see a bit of action in Russia. Also published in two parts as *Me among the Ruins* and *It's Me, Again*.
4. *Me Bandy, You Cissie* **(Doubleday, 1979)** After the war, Bandy meets Cissie, a millionaire's daughter whom he eventually marries; crashes his first commercial airline flight; and gets into the movies.
5. *Me Too* **(Doubleday, 1983)** In the 1920s, Bandy smuggles whiskey, serves in Canada's Parliament, and is appointed to the cabinet by Prime Minister Mackenzie King.
6. *This One's on Me* **(Doubleday, 1988)** Bandy gets involved with Sigga, a beautiful Icelandic doctor, and tries his hand as a porter at St. Pancreas Hospital and as the leader of a maharajah's air force.
7. *Me So Far* **(Doubleday, 1989)** In what was purported to be the final volume of his memoirs, Bandy goes to India to organize the air force of the Indian state of Jhamjarh and immediately alienates the viceroy.
8. *Hitler vs. Me: The Return of Bartholomew Bandy* **(McClelland (Canada), 1996)** Bandy joins the Loyalist cause in the Spanish civil war, loses his beloved Sigga, gets sent to England by Mackenzie King, joins the RCAF with his hostile son, B. W., and gets shot down in Normandy in 1944.

Jackson, Jon A(nthony)

Detroit Detective Sergeant "Fang" Mulheisen usually seems to be only one step from total burnout. The soiled yet sensitive Fang sometimes plays only a supporting role in the Motown series, which features black humor, seamy settings, and violent action. Continuing characters such as Fang's mentor, Grootka, and incompetent hit-man Joe Service add spice to the mixture. An 11-year hiatus occurred between numbers 2 and 3. Jon Jackson was born in Royal Oak, a Detroit suburb, and currently resides in Montana, sometime scene of numbers 5 through 10. *Go by Go* (Dennis McMillan, 1993) is a historical mystery.

1. *Diehard, The* **(Random House, 1977)** The beautiful victim of a hired killer collapses nude on her neighbor's doorstep in an upper-class Detroit suburb.
2. *Blind Pig, The* **(Random House, 1979)** A shoot-out in a budding tycoon's garage leads Mulheisen to the Mafia, the Teamsters, and some "Blind Pigs" (illegal speakeasies).
3. *Grootka* **(Countryman, 1990)** Former cop Grootka is reminded of a 30-year-old murder case when he finds the corpse of a gang informer in the trunk of an abandoned car.
4. *Hit on the House* **(Atlantic, 1993)** Hit man Hal Good is picked up as a witness and taken to jail after he has rubbed out mobster Sid Sedlacek.
5. *Deadman* **(Atlantic, 1994)** Mulheisen is sent to Montana in search of the perpetrators of some Mob killings.
6. *Dead Folks* **(Atlantic, 1996)** Detroit hit-man Joe Service, recovering in Montana from a coma induced in *Deadman*, his memory still foggy, takes off for Salt Lake City with nurse Cathleen Yoder.
7. *Man with an Axe* **(Atlantic, 1998)** Begins on July 30, 1975, the day of Jimmy Hoffa's disappearance, then jumps ahead 20 years when Mulheisen finds Grootka's notebooks and reopens his late mentor's investigation.
8. *La Donna Detroit* **(Atlantic, 2000)** Characters from previous novels, such as mobster widow Helen Sedlacek (see number 4) and hit man Joe Service (see numbers 5 and 6), resurface in this story as we follow the less-than-honest career of mobster Humphrey DiEbola.
9. *Badger Games* **(Atlantic, 2002)** Joe Service and Helen Sedlacek, former Mob operatives, are now working for a vigilante group called the Lucani, who see their mission as ridding the world of international criminals.
10. *No Man's Dog* **(Atlantic, 2004)** The bombing of a municipal building that nearly kills his mother leads Fang to the backwoods of Michigan, where he tangles with extralegal militias.

Jaffe, Rona

Rona Jaffe's first book, *The Best of Everything* (1958), is still her best-known novel. *Class Reunion* and its sequel trace the fortunes of four Radcliffe graduates: golden girl Daphne, clever Chris, beautiful Annabel, and insecure Emily. The changing attitudes of the 1950s, 1960s and 1970s are chronicled through the lives and trials of the four women and the men with whom they become involved. The characters are recognizable types, even if they lead somewhat implausible lives. The novels are readable portraits of upper-middle-class American women.

1. *Class Reunion* **(Delacorte, 1979)** Four Radcliffe alumnae meet at their 20th class reunion in 1977 and review their lives from their entrance into college to the present.
2. *After the Reunion* **(Delacorte, 1985)** Their lives not, after all, dramatically improved since their 20th reunion, Chris, Annabel,

Daphne, and Emily face various sexual, family, and career problems.

Jahn, Michael (Joseph Michael)

Lieutenant (later Captain) Bill Donovan, head of the New York Police Department's Major Crime Unit, is high tech with his laptops, modems, and cellular phones, but he doesn't disdain ordinary gumshoeing. Donovan has a drinking problem and is involved in an interracial love affair, matters that he handles with varying degrees of success in these gritty procedurals. Michael Jahn is a prolific writer who has collaborated on such series as the *Rockford Files*, *Six Million Dollar Man*, and *Omega Sub*. As "Mike Jahn" he wrote a column for the *New York Times* about rock and roll and popular culture as well as several nonfiction books.

1. *Night Rituals* (Norton, 1982) Three young women are strangled in Central Park, and Donovan sets a trap for the killer with a young black female police officer.
2. *Death Games* (Norton, 1987) A lone female assassin is gunning down warring Mafia chieftains, making an organized-crime war seem imminent.
3. *City of God* (Norton, 1992) A killer named Marcus is trying to prevent New York's Cathedral of St. John the Divine from being used for secular affairs.
4. *Murder at the Museum of Natural History* (St. Martin's, 1994) The murder of explorer Paolo Lucci, who uncovered the Lost Treasures of the Silk Road, sets in motion a series of events that culminates in a shoot-out in the American Museum of Natural History.
5. *Murder on Theatre Row* (St. Martin's, 1997) The New Year's Eve premiere of *Casablanca: The Musical* is threatened by a water main break, followed by the discovery of the body of a murdered Asian man.
6. *Murder on Fifth Avenue* (St. Martin's, 1998) Donovan's wife is in the hospital, expecting their first child. Meanwhile, "Santa's Angel" is killing apparently random victims with a rare handgun.
7. *Murder in Central Park* (St. Martin's, 2000) After a night in a treehouse in Central Park monitoring crows, Captain Donovan discovers the corpse of computer wizard Harvey Cozzens floating in a pond.
8. *Murder on the Waterfront* (St. Martin's, 2001) When presidential candidate Pete Bennett's campaign manager is murdered, Donovan switches from reception host to investigator.
9. *Murder on Coney Island* (St. Martin's, 2003) The events of September 11 are in the background as Donovan investigates the murder of a Donald Trump–like developer whose body turns up in the basement of a candy store that has been threatened by the developer's plans.

Jakes, John

I. The Kent Family Chronicles, originally known as the American Bicentennial Series, was conceived as a series of historical novels in commemoration of the US bicentennial. With the appearance of each new volume, its readership increased, and the TV dramatization of part of the series created a second wave of popularity. Jakes attributed the series' success to his readers' need for solid stories about courageous and idealistic men and women who endure life's worst trials without losing faith in America. The Kent saga begins with Philip Kent in 1770 and continues to the 1880s. Originally published in paperback, the books were eventually issued in hardcover by Doubleday. In addition, Landfall Press published two omnibus volumes in 1976: *The Patriots* (numbers 1–2) and *The Pioneers* (numbers 3–4). Robert Hawkins has compiled *The Kent Family Chronicles Encyclopedia* (Bantam, 1979), which is a companion to the series and contains condensations of the first seven novels as well as historical essays, background materials, and "kitchen history" of interest.

1. *Bastard, The* (Pyramid, 1974) Philip Kent, the illegitimate son of an English duke, flees to America. The time is 1770–1775.
2. *Rebels, The* (Pyramid, 1975) In 1775–1781 Philip, now a patriot soldier, sees the horrors of battle and finds a new love.
3. *Seekers, The* (Pyramid, 1975) For 20 years after the war (1794–1814), two generations of Kents struggle to find their place in the new land. Philip's son Abraham falls in love with Amanda.
4. *Furies, The* (Pyramid, 1976) Amanda Kent progresses from the frontier to New York's high society during the period 1836–1852.
5. *Titans, The* (Pyramid, 1976) The Kent family is torn apart by hatred and greed as the Civil War turns brother against brother. The years are 1860–1862.
6. *Warriors, The* (Pyramid, 1978) The Kents set down new roots after a hard-won peace. In 1864–1868, Jeremiah goes west and Gideon moves north.
7. *Lawless, The* (Pyramid, 1978) Change sweeps the country in 1869–1877 as Gideon leads workers in New York and Jeremiah's love of violence leads him to his doom.
8. *Americans, The* (Jove, 1980) Will Kent, Gideon's youngest son, leaves Theodore Roosevelt's western ranch to practice medicine in the New York slums.

II. Jakes followed the Kent Family Chronicles with a Civil War trilogy covering American history from 1842 through 1876. It traces the fortunes of two families: the Hazards are industrialists; the Mains are slave-owning proprietors of a rice plantation. Many historical figures cross paths with the fictional Hazards and Mains. The trilogy is excellent popular history: authentic, dramatic, and entertaining. Numbers 1 and 2 have been made into a miniseries for television.

1. *North and South* (Harcourt, 1982) George Hazard and Orry Main, fellow students at West Point, become friends, and the fortunes of their families become intertwined. Covers 1842 to 1861.
2. *Love and War* (Harcourt, 1984) Orry Main and George Hazard fight on opposite sides in the Civil War. Covers 1861 to 1865.
3. *Heaven and Hell* (Harcourt, 1987) George Hazard goes into steelmaking, while his brother Stanley goes into politics. Madeleine Main runs the plantation despite threats from the Ku Klux Klan, while young Charles scouts for General Custer. Covers 1865 through 1876.

III. A pair of historical novels deals with the Kroner/Crowns, immigrants from Germany who prosper in America. The fictional Crowns interact with many historical figures such as Jane Addams, Theodore Roosevelt, Eugene Debs, Henry Ford, Thomas Edison, and Barney Oldfield. The period covered is 1890 to 1917.

1. *Homeland* (Doubleday, 1993) Orphaned Pauli Kroner travels by steerage from Germany to the United States to be reunited with his uncle, wealthy Chicago brewer Joseph Crown. Covers 1890 to 1900.
2. *American Dreams* (Dutton, 1998) Joe Crown's daughter Fritzi, hit by the acting bug, goes from Chicago to New York to Hollywood and some measure of film fame. Her brother Carl works for Henry Ford, drives race cars along with Barney

Oldfield and becomes an air ace in World War I. Covers 1906 to 1917.

IV. Before he made his mark as a historical novel writer, Jakes wrote a great deal of genre fiction, published mostly in paperback, including mysteries, westerns, science fiction, and fantasy. He continued William Ard's Lou Largo series as a ghostwriter after Ard's death with three novels, published by Monarch in 1961–1962: *Make Mine Mavis, And So to Bed*, and *Give Me This Woman*. Jakes created a paperback mystery series of his own featuring a diminutive (five foot, one inch) private eye named Johnny Havoc. The Havoc books were humorous and rather bawdy. *Johnny Havoc* was reprinted in hard cover by Armchair Detective in 1990. The series is listed below without annotations.

1. *Johnny Havoc* (Belmont, 1960)
2. *Johnny Havoc Meets Zelda* (Belmont, 1962) Variant title: *Havoc for Sale.*
3. *Johnny Havoc and the Doll Who Had It* (Belmont, 1963) Variant title: *Holiday for Havoc.*
4. *Making It Big* (Belmont, 1968) Variant title: *Johnny Havoc and Siren in Red.*

V. Among Jakes's science-fiction and fantasy work, there was a pair of fantasy novels featuring a character named Gavin Black: *Master of the Dark Gate* (Lancer, 1970) and *Witch of the Dark Gate* (Lancer, 1972), and a trio of SF novels set in II Galaxy: *When the Star Kings Die* (Ace, 1967); *The Planet Wizard* (Ace, 1969); and *Tonight We Steal the Stars* (Ace, 1969). Five volumes retailed the fantastic adventures of a muscle-man with a mission, Brak the Barbarian. The Brak the Barbarian series is listed below without annotations.

1. *Brak the Barbarian* (Avon, 1968)
2. *Brak versus the Mark of the Demons* (Paperback Library, 1969) UK title: *Brak the Barbarian—The Mark of the Demons.*
3. *Brak the Barbarian Versus the Sorceress* (Paperback Library, 1969) UK title: *Brak the Barbarian: The Sorceress.*
4. *Brak: When the Idols Walked* (Pocket Books, 1978) Variant title: *When the Idols Walked.*
5. *Fortunes of Brak, The* (Dell, 1980)

James, Bill

PSEUDONYM OF **James Tucker**

I. Detective Superintendent Colin Harpur isn't always the star of this series of procedurals set in an unnamed British city. Sometimes Desmond Iles, Colin's wily, borderline-paranoid boss, who usually gets the best lines, or sometimes ineffectual Chief Constable Mark Lane, or sometimes a villain with a name like "Panicking Ralph," or the potential victim takes center stage. A quite-fallible set of police populates these gripping mysteries, which teeter on the edge of black humor, and in which the "villains" sometimes come off as better human beings than the cops. Bill James, not to be confused with the baseball sabermetrician of the same name, is a pseudonym of British author James Tucker, who also writes under the name of David Craig.

1. *You'd Better Believe It* (St. Martin's, 1986) Colin Harpur comes perilously close to criminal involvement in his dealings with informants. Originally published in the United Kingdom in 1985.
2. *Lolita Man, The* (Foul Play, 1991) Harpur is after "the Lolita Man," a predator who rapes, tortures, and kills pubescent girls. Originally published in the United Kingdom in 1986.
3. *Halo Parade* (Foul Play, 1991) An undercover agent working under Harpur's supervision becomes too deeply involved in a drug

dealer's affairs. Originally published in the United Kingdom in 1987.

4. *Protection* (Foul Play, 1992) The gang feud between "Tenderness" Mellick and Ivor Wright has resulted in the kidnapping of Mellick's developmentally disabled 11-year-old son. Originally published in the United Kingdom in 1988.
5. *Come Clean* (Foul Play, 1993) Desmond Iles's promiscuous wife, Sarah, stumbles into the middle of a gang slaying while slumming with her slightly criminal lover. Originally published in the United Kingdom in 1989.
6. *Take* (Foul Play, 1994) A comedy (or tragedy) of errors as supercautious Ron "Planner" Preston throws caution to the winds in a payroll heist. Originally published in the United Kingdom in 1990.
7. *Club* (Foul Play, 1995) When Sarah Iles's lowlife lover, Ian Aston, is bumped off, Harpur replaces Ian in her affections, and "Panicking Ralph" Ember reluctantly replaces him in the gangland hierarchy. Originally published in the United Kingdom in 1991.
8. *Astride a Grave* (Foul Play, 1996) "Panicking Ralph" does "Caring Oliver" in and then has a rendezvous with the late Oliver's wife a few feet from his grave and right next to a car containing Harpur and Sarah, who are on a similar gambol. Originally published in the United Kingdom in 1991.
9. *Gospel* (Foul Play, 1997) When rich and corrupt art dealer Jack Lamb's information results in a police ambush of an armed robbery that results in the death of thief Martin Webb, his father, Doug Webb, vows revenge on Lamb and Harpur. Originally published in the United Kingdom in 1992.
10. *Roses, Roses* (Norton, 1998) Harpur's wife, Megan, tired of her husband's infidelities, embarks upon an affair of her own, then gets stabbed to death next to her lover. Originally published in the United Kingdom in 1993.
11. *In Good Hands* (Norton, 2000) Iles is suspected of carrying out revenge slayings of suspected cop killers. Harpur is caught in the middle between Iles and Chief Constable Mark Lane. Originally published in the United Kingdom in 1994.
12. *Detective Is Dead, The* (Norton, 2001) Illicit trade in narcotics is the focus here, where killers go free because no one, including the police, will testify against them, and drug kingpin Keith plays a double game as an informant. Originally published in the United Kingdom in 1995.
13. *Top Banana* (Norton, 1999) Another messy situation in which Iles is trying to undermine his superior, Mark Lane, and also to make a treaty with top drug dealers like Manse Shale. The inadvertent killing of a 13-year-old girl acting as a drug courier precipitates events, with Harpur stuck in the middle again. Originally published in the United Kingdom in 1996.
14. *Panicking Ralph* (Norton, 2001) "Panicking Ralph," owner of the Monty, a seedy local drinking club, comes to the fore again as a large player in the local drug trade. Harpur gets so enmeshed that his daughters and his young girlfriend begin to have doubts about him. Originally published in the United Kingdom in 1998.
15. *Lovely Mover* (Norton, 1998) While Harpur, unbeknownst to Iles and Lane, is playing an underground game with aspiring local drug lord Keith Vine, major players from London, including "Lovely Mover," are seeking to take over the local drug action.
16. *Eton Crop* (Norton, 1999) Iles is trying to push the honorable but ineffectual Lane into early retirement or an institution. Harpur inserts tough and ambitious undercover cop Naomi Anstruther into the local drug operation.
17. *Kill Me* (Norton, 2000) Naomi Anstruther, having survived a shoot-out in a London restaurant, forms an alliance with Esme, a young woman friend, to avenge the deaths of ex- and current boyfriends.

18. *Pay Days* (Norton, 2001) The murder of a small-time pusher and the disappearance of his body threatens to undermine the detente between "Panicking Ralph" Ember and Manse Slade and Harpur and Iles. Originally published in the United Kingdom in 2001.

19. *Naked at the Window* (Norton, 2002) The London drug mob is still trying to infiltrate the British midlands city where Harpur and Iles do their policing, and "Panicking Ralph," dreaming of turning the Monty into an upscale establishment, is trying to thwart them.

21. *Easy Streets* (Norton, 2005) The war between cops and local drug dealers escalates when someone firebombs the house of a small-time dealer.

21. *Girl with the Long Back, The* (Norton, 2004) Desmond Iles has problems: his ineffectual boss, Mark Lane, may be replaced by a tough new chief constable, and one of the city's top drug lords is rumored to want him dead.

22. *Wolves of Memory* (Norton, 2006) Harpur and Iles are deeply involved in the job of providing new lives for the family of a high-level informant hiding in their city after a big robbery goes bad.

23. *Sixth Man and Other Stories, The* (Severn House, 2006) A collection of short stories, three of them new Harpur and Iles tales.

24. *Girls* (Countryman, 2007) The peaceable arrangement between drug dealers Ember and Shale and Iles is threatened when foreign drug dealers move in and offer exploited girls from Eastern Europe as inducements.

II. Bill James has created a new series, not yet published in the United States, featuring Simon Abelard, black Cardiff native and Oxford graduate, who was recruited as a spy by British intelligence. After the fall of the Berlin Wall, Simon finds himself working as a glorified cop on a couple of messy assignments.

1. *Split* (Do-Not [UK], 2001) Agent Julian Bowling has taken advantage of his security service training to become a big-time crook. After he removes millions of dollars from the drug syndicate he helped to create, the drug dealers he robbed are out to get him.

2. *Man's Enemies, A* (Do-Not [UK], 2003) Olly Horton has left the service and threatens to write a book detailing his experiences, something his former chiefs want to squelch at all costs.

James, Henry

Christina Light, later the Princess Casamassima, is the one major character in the voluminous output of Henry James who appears in more than one novel. Daughter of an American expatriate, she is beautiful, intelligent, and charming but given to fads, and destructive to the men who become deeply involved with her. Both novels are available in the Library of America: *Roderick Hudson* in *Novels, 1871–1880* (1983); *The Princess Casamassima* in *Novels, 1886–1890* (1989).

1. *Roderick Hudson* (Osgood, 1876) Roderick Hudson's talent for sculpture attracts wealthy Roland Mallet, who takes him to Rome where he meets, among others, the fascinating Christina Light.

2. *Princess Casamassima, The* (Macmillan, 1886) Hyacinth Robinson, an orphan raised in London poverty, is attracted to revolutionary movements and to the Princess Casamassima, who shares his artistic temperament and sympathy for the downtrodden.

James, P. D.

PSEUDONYM OF Phyllis D. White

Though not as prolific as Agatha Christie (q.v.), P. D. James has the same mastery of pace, suspense, and polished characterization. Her detective, Chief Inspector, later Commander, Adam Dalgliesh, is Scotland Yard's star sleuth. He is tall and handsome, with a secret sorrow—his wife and baby died in childbirth. A skilled, no-nonsense interrogator who modifies his technique to suit the personality of each witness, Dalgliesh always draws out that last salient detail on which the whole case hinges. In some volumes of the series other characters come to the fore, in particular Cordelia Gray, who is the leading protagonist of numbers 5 and 8. Other possible romantic interests include Emma Lavenham, who appears in numbers 13 and 14, and Detective Inspector Kate Miskin, who appears in several of the later novels. *Crime Times Three* (Scribner, 1979) contains numbers 1, 2, and 4. *Murder in Triplicate* (Encore, 1980) contains numbers 3, 5, and 6. Several episodes have been televised on PBS's *Mystery!* P. D. James published her memoirs, *Time to Be in Earnest: A Fragment of Autobiography* (Knopf, 2000).

1. *Cover Her Face* (Scribner, 1962) Beautiful, scheming Sally Jupp comes to the Maxie house as a maid but plans to move up.

2. *Mind to Murder, A* (Scribner, 1963) The administrator of a London psychiatric clinic is murdered.

3. *Unnatural Causes* (Scribner, 1967) A corpse without hands drifts into Adam's vacation with his aunt in Suffolk.

4. *Shroud for a Nightingale* (Scribner, 1971) When two student nurses at Nightingale House are murdered, Adam Dalgliesh is called in.

5. *Unsuitable Job for a Woman, An* (Scribner, 1972) This book really stars Cordelia Gray, a young private eye investigating the death of a microbiologist's son. She and Adam cross paths and are mutually attracted.

6. *Black Tower, The* (Scribner, 1975) A minister friend of Adam's is the latest victim in a senseless series of murders that baffles the police.

7. *Death of an Expert Witness* (Scribner, 1977) Dalgliesh investigates the murder of Dr. Lorrimer, senior staff member of a forensic science lab.

8. *Skull beneath the Skin, The* (Scribner, 1982) Cordelia Gray is hired to protect actress Clarissa Lisle, who has been receiving threatening notes.

9. *Taste for Death, A* (Knopf, 1986) Sir Paul Perowne, former minister of the Crown and acquaintance of Dalgliesh, is found with his throat cut in a London church.

10. *Devices and Desires* (Knopf, 1990) Dalgliesh goes to the Norfolk town of Larksoken to settle the estate of a recently deceased aunt and becomes involved with antinuclear protestors and a serial killer called the "Whistler."

11. *Original Sin* (Knopf, 1995) A series of mishaps at venerable Peverell Press have culminated in the suspicious death of Gerard Etienne, its new director.

12. *Certain Justice, A* (Knopf, 1997) After successfully defending a young man named Ashe against murder charges, criminal lawyer Venetia Aldridge is found dead in her locked office. Dalgliesh, Kate Miskin, and Piers Tarrant investigate.

13. *Death in Holy Orders* (Knopf, 2001) Something is rotten at St. Anselm's, an Anglican theological college on the Suffolk coast. A young ordinant, a retired nurse, and an archdeacon all die under suspicious circumstances.

14. *Murder Room, The* (Knopf, 2003) After planning to vote for the closing of the Dupayne Museum, trustee Neville Dupayne is

murdered in a fashion reminiscent of a notorious historical murder exhibited in the museum's "Murder Room."

15. *Lighthouse, The* (Knopf, 2005) Acclaimed novelist Nathan Oliver, who has incurred the wrath of his fellow residents on Combe Island, a private retreat off the Cornish coast, is murdered.

Jameson, Storm

I. This prolific author (d. 1986 at the age of 95), a feminist and out-spoken liberal, had more than 45 novels to her credit. Her early trilogy was a Galsworthian (q.v.) saga following the life of Mary Hervey (née Hansyke) from her birth in 1841 to her death in 1923, tracing her family's shipbuilding business from sail to steam to turbine. Mary, a kind of "Woman of Property," has a stormy love life but a sure touch in business. The books are set in the Yorkshire seaport of Whitby, home of Jameson's own family, also shipbuilders. Omnibus volume, *The Triumph of Time* (Heinemann [UK], 1932).

1. *Lovely Ship, The* (Knopf, 1927) After two unsuccessful marriages, Mary, heir to the family shipbuilding business, meets the love of her life, Gerry.
2. *Voyage Home, The* (Knopf, 1930) At 40 Mary is the rich and successful head of the shipbuilding business, but family happiness eludes her.
3. *Richer Dust, A* (Knopf, 1931) Now an old woman living in a world gone slightly mad, Mary sells the business at the height of the war boom.

II. After the success of the Mary Hervey trilogy, Jameson's attention focused for a time on the figure of Hervey Russell, Mary's grand-daughter, most likely an autobiographical figure. She wrote several books about Hervey Russell and even planned a series of five novels on contemporary society around her, to be called the Mirror in Darkness, though that was never completed.

1. *Captain's Wife, The* (Macmillan, 1939) Hervey is just a child in this prequel, which is really the story of Sylvia, her mother, who rebels against her family and marries below her station. UK title: *Farewell, Night; Welcome, Day.*
2. *That Was Yesterday* (Knopf, 1932) Hervey survives unhappy early married years during World War I.
3. *Company Parade* (Knopf, 1934) Hervey struggles to make a living in postwar London. First novel in the *Mirror in Darkness* series. Reprinted by Virago (UK) in 1982.
4. *Love in Winter* (Knopf, 1935) In 1924–1925, her marriage a failure, Hervey meets and falls in love with Nicholas Roxby. Second in the *Mirror in Darkness* series. Reprinted by Virago (UK) in 1984.
5. *None Turn Back* (Cassell [UK], 1936) The General Strike and the reasons for its failure are at the center of this third installment of the *Mirror in Darkness* series. Reprinted by Virago (UK) in 1984.
6. *Journal of Mary Hervey Russell, The* (Macmillan, 1945) This last Hervey Russell book is a very thinly disguised autobiography. The journal shows a sensitive writer and how World War II affected her.

Jance, J(udith) A(nn)

I. Seattle police detective J. P. (for Jonas Piedmont) Beaumont is a grumpy fellow carrying a load of resentment about his name, his illegitimate birth, his divorce, and his relationships with women, among other things. Although he is supposed to be a team player, he is more like John D. MacDonald's (q.v.) Travis McGee than a member of Ed McBain's (q.v.) 87th Precinct squad, and his cases tend to take on the nature of private investigations rather than police procedurals. After he enters an alcohol rehabilitation facility in number 8, his attitude improves somewhat. Number 16 pairs Beaumont with Joanna Brady of series II. *Sentenced to Die* (Morrow, 2005) is an omnibus volume containing numbers 1, 2, and 3. Author J. A. Jance now resides in the state of Washington after a lengthy stay in Arizona.

1. *Until Proven Guilty* (Avon, 1985) Investigating the murder of a five-year-old girl, J. P. Beaumont of the Seattle Police Department thinks he has identified the killer until additional bodies turn up.
2. *Injustice for All* (Avon, 1986) Beaumont's vacation on the Washington coast is interrupted by the screaming of a beautiful blond who was discovered a dead man lying at her feet.
3. *Trial by Fury* (Avon, 1986) The naked body of a popular high school basketball coach is found in a dumpster.
4. *Taking the Fifth* (Avon, 1987) Unsavory union affairs may be behind a man's punctured corpse, a paycheck stub, a motel matchbook, and a woman's stiletto heel caked with blood.
5. *Improbable Cause* (Avon, 1988) Dr. Frederick Nielsen was a dentist who seemed to be fond of administering pain. No one is very sorry when he is murdered.
6. *More Perfect Union, A* (Avon, 1988) A woman plunges from an unfinished skyscraper. Accident, suicide, or murder? Maybe Iron Workers Local I has the answer.
7. *Dismissed with Prejudice* (Avon, 1989) Did software entrepreneur Tadeo Kurabani, who loved poetry and studied samurai history, commit hara-kiri with his samurai sword?
8. *Minor in Possession* (Avon, 1990) Beaumont checks into an alcohol and drug rehabilitation center in rural Arizona. Joey Rothman, his creepy roommate, winds up hanging from a tree.
9. *Payment in Kind* (Avon, 1991) Marcia Kelsey and Alvin Chambers are found dead at the public school district office partially naked with their legs entwined.
10. *Without Due Process* (Morrow, 1992) Seattle police officer Ben Weston and his family are murdered at a critical point in his undercover probe of young gangs.
11. *Failure to Appear* (Morrow, 1993) Beaumont is in Ashland, Oregon, during the Shakespeare festival with his lady friend, searching for her runaway daughter.
12. *Lying in Wait* (Morrow, 1994) Gunther Gebhardt, with his fingers and toes chopped off, is burned to death in a boat fire.
13. *Name Withheld* (Morrow, 1996) There are many suspects when the body of an executive from a biotechnology start-up company is found in Elliott Bay.
14. *Breach of Duty* (Avon, 1999) Beaumont has a new partner, Sue Danielson, as he investigates the arson death of Agnes Furman.
15. *Birds of Prey* (Morrow, 2001) Beaumont, now retired, joins a luxury cruise to Alaska at the request of his honeymooning grandmother.
16. *Partner in Crime* (Morrow, 2001) Now an investigator for the attorney general of Washington, Beaumont travels to Bisbee, Arizona, to investigate the murder of Rochelle Baxter, part of a witness-protection program. Here he hooks up with Joanna Brady of series II.
17. *Justice Denied* (Morrow, 2007) Beaumont works on the cases of a wrongly imprisoned ex-con, the disappearance of an electronics engineer in 1980, and the deaths of several former felons.

II. Joanna Brady becomes sheriff of Cochise County in Bisbee, Arizona, after her husband is gunned down while running for the office. Joanna, widowed with a child, has great outer strength and strong inner self-doubts. She interacts with J. P. Beaumont of series I in number 10.

1. *Desert Heat* (Avon, 1993) Joanna Brady finds her husband, Andy, fatally shot in the Arizona desert on the night of their 10th wedding anniversary.
2. *Tombstone Courage* (Morrow, 1994) Brady is running for election to the sheriff post in Bisbee in her own right.
3. *Shoot, Don't Shoot* (Morrow, 1995) Newly elected Cochise County sheriff, Joanna Brady, enrolled in a law-enforcement course in Tucson, is besieged by a number of domestic violence crimes and a serial murderer.
4. *Dead to Rights* (Avon, 1996) Veterinarian Amos Buckwallyn is murdered by arson after he kills Bonnie Morgan in a drunken-driving incident.
5. *Skeleton Canyon* (Avon, 1997) When high school valedictorian Bree O'Brien is found dead, suspicion falls on her boyfriend, Ignacio Ybarra.
6. *Rattlesnake Crossing* (Avon, 1998) Three young women are found shot and scalped. Then local gun dealer Clyde Philips turns up dead in an apparent suicide.
7. *Outlaw Mountain* (Avon, 1999) The mayor's mother has been murdered, Brady's chief deputy has resigned, and a mentally disabled man has been abandoned.
8. *Devil's Claw* (Morrow, 2000) Sandra Ridder is looking for an item she buried eight years ago, before going to prison for killing her husband.
9. *Paradise Lost* (Morrow, 2001) Joanna's daughter Jenny and a camping partner discover the corpse of a naked woman while Joanna and her new husband, Butch, are at a sheriffs' convention.
10. *Partner in Crime (2)* (Morrow, 2002) Joanna hooks up with J. P. Beaumont of series I when artist Rochelle Baxter, part of a witness-protection program, is murdered in Bisbee.
11. *Exit Wounds* (Morrow, 2003) Brady, pregnant again, and unofficially campaigning for reelection, learns that a woman has been found dead in a mobile home surrounded by 17 dead dogs.
12. *Dead Wrong* (Morrow, 2006) Brady, newly reelected, and expecting her second child, has to cope with the fingerless body of an unidentified man found in the desert and the seemingly senseless beating of animal control officer Jeannine Phillips.

III. A trio of novels featuring ex-sheriff Brandon Walker and his wife, writer Diana Ladd Walker, are also set in Arizona.

1. *Hour of the Hunter* (Morrow, 1991) Newly released rapist-murderer Andrew Carlisle goes on a rampage as he tracks down Diana Ladd, widow of his late accomplice.
2. *Kiss of the Bees* (Avon, 2000) Ex-con Mitch Johnson takes revenge on Diana and Brandon Walker by abducting their adopted Papago daughter.
3. *Day of the Dead* (Morrow, 2004) Emma Orizco, an old Tohono O'odham woman, asks Brandon Walker's help in solving the murder of her daughter Roseanne in 1970.

IV. A new series features laid-off (too old) high-profile broadcaster Alison "Ali" Reynolds, who is also getting a divorce from her philandering husband. Alison returns to her old home in Sedona, Arizona, but her troubles don't end with her move.

1. *Edge of Evil* (Avon, 2006) Alison Reynolds, who has returned home to Sedona after being fired and divorced, starts a personal blog on her computer only to have threatening posts appear.
2. *Web of Evil* (Touchstone, 2007) Ali becomes the chief suspect when her almost-ex-husband, Paul Grayson, is found dead in the trunk of a car hit by a train near Palm Springs, California.
3. *Hand of Evil* (Touchstone, 2007) Wealthy, reclusive Arabella Ashcroft has read Ali's blog, cutlooseblog.com, and asks Ali's help in writing an incest memoir.

Jeffries, Roderic (Graeme)

Prolific English mystery novelist Roderic Jeffries (pseudonyms include Peter Alding [q.v.], Jeffrey Ashford, Roderic Graeme, and Graham Hastings) moved to the Mediterranean island of Mallorca (Spain) in 1972 and began a detective series featuring Spanish policeman Enrique Alvarez. Alvarez is slow moving but not slow witted, overly fond of the pleasures of the table, and easygoing but tenacious in pursuit of solutions to crimes. Most of the skulduggery occurs among the tourists and English residents of Mallorca, and one of the continuous threads is the effect of tourism upon the natives of this once poor, backward island.

1. *Mistakenly in Mallorca* (Collins [UK], 1974) John Tatham conceals the ill-timed death of his great-aunt Elvina Woods.
2. *Two-Faced Death* (Severn, 2001) Con-man and womanizer John Calvin had good reason to commit suicide, but Alvarez suspects murder. Originally published in the United Kingdom in 1976.
3. *Troubled Deaths* (St. Martin's, 1978) An expatriate Englishman loathed by almost everyone dies of mushroom poisoning.
4. *Murder Begets Murder* (St. Martin's, 1979) Rich, sickly William Heron and his unfaithful mistress are found dead of suspected food poisoning.
5. *Just Deserts* (St. Martin's, 1981) Frank Finnister, failed novelist in need of money, woos plain, middle-aged Miriam Spiller, who takes a fatal spill from her balcony. "Jeffrey Ashford," one of Jeffries's pseudonyms, is listed as the author. Variant title: *Just Desserts*.
6. *Unseemly End* (St. Martin's, 1982) Polly Lund, wealthy, nasty, and unpopular, is murdered, and her young lover, Mark Erington, becomes her heir and the prime suspect.
7. *Deadly Petard* (St. Martin's, 1983) The apparent suicide of artist Gertrude Deen brings Alvarez together in a match of wits with English police officer Cullion.
8. *Three and One Make Five* (St. Martin's, 1984) Alvarez falls in love with young New Zealander Tracey Newcombe while investigating the suspicious death of her lover, Roger Clarke.
9. *Layers of Deceit* (St. Martin's, 1985) The murder of wealthy Steve Colum produces many suspects including Steve's half brother Alan.
10. *Almost Murder* (St. Martin's, 1986) After two Englishmen are blown up in a yacht explosion, an officious bureaucrat is sent from Madrid to bedevil Alvarez.
11. *Relatively Dangerous* (St. Martin's, 1987) A fatal car crash on a mountain road leads Alvarez to some complicated financial dealings among the British residents.
12. *Death Trick* (St. Martin's, 1988) There are numerous suspects when Pablo Roig, swindler and womanizer, is murdered.
13. *Dead Clever* (St. Martin's, 1989) Did heavily insured Englishman Henry Green really perish in a plane crash off Mallorca?
14. *Too Clever by Half* (St. Martin's, 1990) Art expert Justin Burnett appears to have committed suicide, but his sister insists that he was murdered.
15. *Murder's Long Memory* (St. Martin's, 1992) Alvarez suspects the motives of wealthy Giovanni Gasperi when the latter reports a burglary, then withdraws the complaint.

16. *Fatal Fleece, A* (**St. Martin's, 1992**) A poisonous love potion almost proves fatal to English businessman Walter Miller.

17. *Murder Confounded* (**St. Martin's, 1993**) When Englishman Franklin Gore is hospitalized with bruises and cigarette burns on his body, he insists that he received the injuries falling off a ladder.

18. *Death Takes Time* (**St. Martin's, 1994**) Alvarez takes an unauthorized trip to England in search of the link between seemingly unrelated deaths.

19. *Arcadian Death, An* (**St. Martin's, 1996**) An elderly peasant woman is found dead in her bedroom in a classic locked-room situation.

20. *Artistic Way to Go, An* (**St. Martin's, 1997**) A murdered British art dealer, his dealings with the Mafia, his unfaithful wife, her lover, and a struggling artist are the focus here.

21. *Maze of Murders, A* (**St. Martin's, 1998**) After young British tourist Neil Lewis disappears from a boat during the night, his three companions are very foggy about the details of the party that preceded the incident.

22. *Enigmatic Disappearance, An* (**St. Martin's, 2000**) Sabrina Ogden, the much younger wife of elderly Bevis Ogden, disappears. Alvarez suspects that it is a simple case of desertion, at first. Originally published in the United Kingdom in 1998.

23. *Ambiguity of Murder, The* (**St. Martin's, 2001**) Alvarez suspects foul play when the body of a retired Bolivian diplomat is found floating facedown in his swimming pool. Originally published in the United Kingdom in 1999.

24. *Artful Death, An* (**St. Martin's, 2002**) Alvarez enrages his superior when he questions a British cabinet minister after wealthy British émigré Keith Vickers disappears, then turns up dead in a local cove. Originally published in the United Kingdom in 2000.

25. *Definitely Deceased* (**Severn House, 2001**) Alvarez gets into all kinds of hot water when he agrees to help Munar, a distant relative who is being investigated for smuggling.

26. *Seeing Is Deceiving* (**Severn House, 2002**) All kinds of unsavory doings, including a window-scratching prowler, the murder of a bank executive, suspected incest, assault, and blackmail, engage Alvarez and his aide, Detective Fenton.

27. *Intriguing Murder, An* (**Severn House, 2003**) The murder of a wealthy, womanizing expatriate, who may have been responsible for the suicide of one woman, produces many suspects.

28. *Air of Murder, An* (**Severn House, 2004**) Alvarez looks into the suspicious drowning of an English tourist.

29. *Sunny Disappearance, A* (**Severn House, 2005**) Maurice Rook disappears after setting sail from Port Llueso in his luxury motor cruiser. English investigator Noyes thinks that an insurance scam is involved.

30. *Murder Delayed* (**Severn House, 2006**) A computer expert named Faber has absconded with half a million pounds from England and apparently blended in with the tourist population in the Llueso area.

31. *Murder Needs Imagination* (**Severn House, 2007**) Alvarez's investigation of the seemingly accidental death of Englishman Jasper Vickers turns out to be not so straightforward as it originally seemed.

Jenkins, Dan

Sportswriter Dan Jenkins has written a trio of novels set in the zany and vulgar worlds of professional football and television. The books are somewhat short on plot but full of hilarious commentary by and about a variety of colorful characters, including Billy Clyde Puckett, Giants fullback and television sports "color" man; Barbara Jane Bookman, heiress, model, and television sitcom starlet; her racist oilman father, Big Ed Bookman; and Shake Tiller, football player turned best-selling author. There is something to offend and amuse almost everyone. Burt Reynolds starred in the film version of *Semi-Tough* (1977). Kenny Puckett, Billy Clyde's uncle, is the protagonist in *Dead Solid Perfect* (Atheneum, 1974), a novel about professional golf.

1. *Semi-Tough* (**Atheneum, 1972**) The New York Giants are playing the despised Jets for the NFL championship, as Billy Clyde Puckett, the Giants' star fullback, tape-records his impression of Super Bowl week.

2. *Life Its Ownself* (**Simon & Schuster, 1984**) Billy Clyde, retired from football and working as a television sports commentator, observes the plot of the NFL players' union to deliberately play boring, bad football.

3. *Rude Behavior* (**Doubleday, 1998**) Billy Clyde is trying to use Big Ed Bookman's money to establish an NFL expansion team somewhere between Amarillo and Lubbock, Texas.

Jennings, Gary

I. *Aztec* is a historical novel about the great native civilization in Mexico, as told in the words of Dark Cloud, a traveler throughout his world. *Aztec Autumn*, published 17 years later, describes the Aztec world after the Conquistadors arrived. That novel was followed by two posthumous publications (Jennings died in 1999) cowritten by Robert Gleason and Junius Podrug. The Aztec Chronicles are well-written and evocative books about a lost world. Gary Jennings was an American historical novelist who also wrote SF stories.

1. *Aztec* (**Atheneum, 1980**) Preconquest Aztec Dark Cloud tells, in his own words, his rise from a lowly station through his adventures as a traveling merchant, exploring every part of what the Aztecs called the One World.

2. *Aztec Autumn* (**Forge, 1997**) Proud young Aztec Tenemaxtli dreams of leading a rebellion that will restore the Aztec Empire to its glory days before the Spanish conquest.

3. *Aztec Blood* (**Forge, 2001**) Mestizo (half-Aztec, half-Spanish) Cristo the Bastardo narrates his history while awaiting hanging in a 16th-century New Spain jail. Cowritten by Robert Gleason and Junius Podrug.

4. *Aztec Rage* (**Forge, 2006**) Don Juan de Zavala, the greatest warrior in New Spain, can't stay neutral as a warrior priest leads an Aztec revolt, while across the Atlantic, Spaniards are battling Napoléon's invading armies. Cowritten by Robert Gleason and Junius Podrug.

II. *Spangle* was intended by Jennings to be the definitive circus novel. If not quite that, it is a rousing well-researched yarn that begins just after the end of the Civil War when the stranded circus is joined by two ex-rebel soldiers in Virginia and ends with the circus, touring Europe, arriving in a France devastated by the Franco-Prussian War in 1870. Twelve years later, *Spangle* was reissued in three paperback parts by Forge (listed below).

1. *Road Show, The* (**Forge, 1999**) The Florilegium Circus, stranded in Virginia during the American Civil War, is joined, after Appomattox, by two ex-rebel soldiers.

2. *Center Ring, The* (**Forge, 1999**) The circus, returned to Europe, tours Europe through preunification Italy to Czarist Russia.

3. *Grand Promenade, The* (**Forge, 1999**) The grand tour of the circus ends in 1870, in a Paris besieged by the Prussians.

Jerome, Jerome K(lapka)

A topographical and historical account of the Thames River was what Jerome intended to write, but fortunately for generations of delighted readers, his sense of humor and knack for telling a good story got in the way. The resulting comic tale about the misadventures of three Englishmen and their dog, Montmorency, on a boat trip up the Thames was a best seller in its day, both in England and America, though the lack of transatlantic copyright laws lost Jerome any profit from his American sales. The digression that begins chapter 3 will be recognized as the story of Uncle Podger hanging the picture, adapted for children in *My Uncle Podger*, by Wallace Tripp (Little, Brown, 1975). The Everyman's Library edition (Dent/Dutton, 1957) contains number 1 and 2.

1. *Three Men in a Boat (To Say Nothing of the Dog)* (Holt, 1889) The characters of Harris and George were based on friends with whom Jerome often spent Sundays on the river. The dog, Montmorency, and many of the book's incidents are also based on fact.
2. *Three Men on Bicycles* (Holt, 1900) The same three men, somewhat older, and without the dog, take a leisurely cycling tour through Germany. The original English title, *Three Men on the Bummel*, puzzled readers unable to find the word "bummel" in the dictionary. Jerome defines the word, characteristically on the last page, as a rambling holiday without any definite object.

Johansen, Iris

I. Eve Duncan is an Atlanta-based forensic sculptor who can re-create the faces of the dead by reconstructing their skulls. Eve is especially interested in reconstructing the skulls of unidentified murdered children, since her seven-year-old daughter disappeared, presumably murdered by a serial killer. Eve hooks up with cop Joe Quinn and adopts troubled teenager Jane Maguire, who figures prominently in later novels in the series. Relatively little science but lots of action, suspense, and thrills are in this series.

1. *Face of Deception, The* (Bantam, 1998) A seemingly routine job turns complicated and nasty when the skull Eve Duncan reconstructs turns out to belong to a very important man who is supposed to be alive.
2. *Killing Game, The* (Bantam, 1999) Eve takes on the task of identifying nine skeletons found on a bluff near Georgia's Talladega Falls, hoping that one of the skulls might prove to be that of her missing daughter, Bonnie.
3. *Search, The* (Bantam, 2000) One of billionaire John Logan's search facilities is blown up, and a brilliant scientist is kidnapped.
4. *Body of Lies* (Bantam, 2002) A series of deaths and death threats ensue when Eve goes to Baton Rouge to identify a broken skull, which might be all that remains of former senatorial candidate Harold Bentley.
5. *No One to Trust* (Bantam, 2002) CIA operative Sean Galen, who made an appearance in number 4, comes to the aid of Elena Kyler and her son, who are being pursued by drug lord Rico Chavez.
6. *Blind Alley* (Bantam, 2004) Eve is shocked to discover that the young murder victim whose skull she has reconstructed bears an uncanny resemblance to Jane Maguire, the 17-year-old she and Joe Quinn have adopted.
7. *Countdown* (Bantam, 2005) Jane Maguire, already threatened by one serial killer in number 2 and another in number 6, may still be paying the price for her role in exposing the psychopath who was killing women who looked like the ancient actress Cira.
8. *Stalemate* (Bantam, 2006) Luis Montalvo, shady Colombian arms dealer, offers to solve the mystery of what happened to Eve's daughter, Bonnie, if she agrees to reconstruct a skull he believes to be his late wife's.
9. *Pandora's Daughter* (St. Martin's, 2007) Atlanta pediatrician Megan Blair discovers that the terrified voices she is hearing indicate that she has psychic powers.
10. *Quicksand* (St. Martin's, 2008) Megan Blair, protagonist of number 9, hooks up with Eve Duncan in a search for Bonnie's body in the Okefenokee Swamp, while Eve's lover, Joe Quinn, tracks down child predator Henry Kistle in a small town in Illinois.

II. Since 1983, Iris Johansen has been a prolific producer of romantic suspense stories, many of them published under the Loveswept imprint of Bantam. Some 13 novels in the Loveswept series are about two imaginary countries: the Middle Eastern kingdom of Sedikhan and the Balkan state of Tamrovia. Chronology is a bit difficult to determine, but Sedikhan sounds like something out of the Rudolph Valentino movie *The Sheik* (1921) and Tamrovia sounds like Anthony Hope's (q.v.) Zenda. Different characters wander in and out of the various novels. Titles are listed in Loveswept numerical order. Another loosely connected series is Clanad, which contains three to six novels, depending on who is counting, including *Across the River of Yesterday* (1987), *The Last Bridge Home* (1987), and *Magnificent Folly* (1989). Pairs of linked novels in the Loveswept series include *Return to Santa Flores* (1984) and *No Red Roses* (1984); *White Satin* (1985) and *Blue Velvet* (1985); *The Reluctant Lark* (1983) and *The Bronzed Hawk* (1990); and *Stormy Vows* (1986) and *Tempest at Sea* (1990). In addition, Johansen published at least eight more unlinked novels in the Loveswept series.

1. *Golden Valkyrie, The* (Bantam, 1984) Private detective Honey Winston, duped into invading Prince Rubinoff's hotel suite, discovers that, unlike the "Lusty Lance" depicted in the tabloids, the Prince is a sensitive artist, whose exquisite paintings the world will never see.
2. *Trustworthy Redhead, The* (Bantam, 1984) When Princess Rubinoff hired Sabrina Courtney to deliver special birthday wishes to Alex ben Rashid, she didn't warn her that Alex ben Rashid had a powerful weakness for red-haired ladies,
3. *Capture the Rainbow* (Bantam, 1984) Stuntwoman Kendra Michaels may have finally run into a situation that she couldn't handle.
4. *Touch the Horizon* (Bantam, 1984) Madcap adventuress Billie Callahan finds herself trapped in a sandstorm in the Sedikhan desert.
5. *Summer Smile, A* (Bantam, 1985) No annotation available.
6. *And the Desert Blooms* (Bantam, 1986) No annotation available.
7. *Always* (Bantam, 1986) The security chief of Sedikhan kidnaps an American singer to act as bait for a terrorist.
8. *Everlasting* (Bantam, 1986) No annotation available.
9. *Man from Half Moon Bay, The* (Bantam, 1988) No annotation available.
10. *Blue Skies and Shining Promises* (Bantam, 1988) Damita Shaughnessy slips into powerful executive Cameron Bandor's hotel suite disguised in veil and harem costume, determined to force him to help her find her mother Lola Torres.
11. *Strong, Hot Winds* (Bantam, 1988) Cory Brandel is furious when Sheikh Damon El Karim kidnaps her son Michael, product of a passionate tryst with Damon four years earlier.
12. *Notorious* (Bantam, 1990) Sabin Wyall becomes obsessed with actress Mallory Thane, even though she has been acquitted of his stepbrother's murder.
13. *Golden Barbarian, The* (Bantam, 1992) Tess, Princess Christina Rubinoff, fleeing from her oppressed status in Tamrovia, falls into the arms of desert warrior king Galen ben Raschid.

III. Wind Dancer, a trio of novels published in 1991, featured an exquisite golden statue of Pegasus, which wends its way from Renaissance Italy to current days. To complicate matters, another Wind Dancer novel was added in 2001.

1. *Wind Dancer, The* (Bantam, 1991) Lionello Andreas is bound by his vow to retrieve the Wind Dancer, a gold statue of Pegasus, in this novel set in Renaissance Florence.
2. *Storm Winds* (Bantam, 1991) Juliette de Clement, a confidante of the French royal family, could aid the search of Jean Marc Andreas for the Wind Dancer, in this novel set at the time of the French Revolution.
3. *Reap the Wind* (Bantam, 1991) In the conclusion of the trilogy, we move to contemporary times, where characters named Caitlin Vasaro and Alex Karazov vie over possession of the Wind Dancer, now owned by American politician Jonathan Andreas.
4. *Final Target* (Bantam, 2001) In a novel published 10 years after the end of the trilogy, the Wind Dancer becomes a pawn in the kidnapping plot aimed at Cassie, seven-year-old daughter of its owner, US president Jonathan Andreas.

Johnson, Pamela Hansford

I. Readers looking for a good, old-fashioned novel of manners should try anything by Pamela Hansford Johnson: they won't be disappointed. Her solid stories, perceptive characterizations, and satin-smooth prose won her a loyal public in the United States as well as in England. In private life she was Lady Snow, the wife of writer C. P. Snow (q.v.). The two books featuring Toby Roberts are good examples of her art. Toby is one of those attractive and intelligent young men who seem more comfortable observing life than taking part in it. His career languishes, and his love affairs prove almost tragic.

1. *Good Listener, The* (Scribner, 1975) Young Toby, the good listener, is detached and slow to commit himself as all his Cambridge friends rush madly into life's tangles.
2. *Good Husband, The* (Scribner, 1979) Toby, now 30, meets and marries widow Ann Thorold, a much older woman.

II. The Helena trilogy is an older series held together by the figure of Helena, who, even when not present, is a powerful influence on her friends and family. The trilogy was republished in three volumes by Scribner in the early 1970s.

1. *Too Dear for Possessing* (Macmillan, 1940) After childhood in Bruges with his author father and stepmother, Helena, Claud Pickering goes to England, but he cannot forget the city and Cecil, the English girl he met there.
2. *Avenue of Stone, An* (Macmillan, 1948) After the war, Helena, now widowed and afraid of her approaching old age, takes a young veteran under her wing.
3. *Summer to Decide, A* (Macmillan, 1948) Helena's daughter Charmian has a new baby and a rapidly deteriorating marriage.

Johnson, Uwe

Uwe Johnson, one of Germany's greatest postwar novelists, was an East German who emigrated to the West. The impact of the split between East and West, the "Free World," and the "People's Democracies" is the dominant theme of his fiction. In *Speculations about Jakob*, Johnson's characters speculated about the meaning of the life and enigmatic death of an East German railroad worker. Johnson eventually followed up this novel with the monumental *Anniversaries* (four volumes in German, two volumes in English), which describes one year in the life of Gesine Cresspahl, Jakob's lover and mother of his child, as she tries to come to terms with her memories of Germany. Johnson's work isn't easy or comforting reading, but it will reward the serious reader.

1. *Speculations about Jakob* (Grove, 1963) The mysterious death of Jakob Abs stirs up conflicting recollections of his life by those who knew him. Translation by Ursule Molinaro of *Mutmassungen über Jakob* (1959).
2. *Anniversaries: From the Life of Gesine Cresspahl, August 1967– February 1968* (Harcourt, 1975) Six months of the life and recollections of Gesine Cresspahl, who is living in New York with her daughter. Translation by Leila Vennewitz of volume 1 and part of volume 2 of *Jahrestage: Aus dem Leben von Gesine Cresspahl*, originally published in 1970 and 1972.
3. *Anniversaries II: From the Life of Gesine Cresspahl* (Harcourt, 1987) This continues the "journals" of Gesine Cresspahl from February 1968 to August 20, 1968, Translation by Leila Vennewitz and Walter Arndt of part of volume 2 and volumes 3 and 4 of *Jahrestage: Aus dem Leben von Gesine Cresspahl*. Originally published in 1972–1983.

Johnston, Terry C(onrad)

I. One-eyed trapper and mountain man Titus "Scratch" Bass has proved to be one of prolific frontier writer Terry Johnston's most popular characters. Bass and Josiah Paddock, the orphan he has befriended, are the central characters in a trilogy set in the American West in the 1830s (numbers 3–5). Numbers 1 and 2 recount the early years of Titus. The series, which was carried for a further four books, is best when the action is hot and heavy.

1. *Dance on the Wind* (Bantam, 1995) Kentucky farm boy Titus Bass joins the crew of a flatboat carrying cargo from Cincinnati to New Orleans.
2. *Buffalo Palace* (Bantam, 1996) In 1825, Titus heads west from St. Louis to become a trapper and a mountain man.
3. *Carry the Wind* (Delacorte, 1982) Josiah Paddock flees to the West after killing his lover's fiancé and hooks up with grizzled mountain man Titus Bass.
4. *BorderLords* (Caroline, 1984) Paddock and Bass have a misunderstanding over a Crow woman in a story that winds up with the famous Green River Rendezvous of 1833.
5. *One-Eyed Dream* (Jameson, 1988) Titus, Josiah, and their families move on to New Mexico, where Titus catches up with some ex-friends who betrayed him 10 years earlier.
6. *Crack in the Sky* (Bantam, 1997) Titus battles horse thieves, hostile Comanches, and bad terrain and carries the torch for an Indian woman.
7. *Ride the Moon Down* (Bantam, 1998) Now in his forties, the battle-scarred Titus roams across the West with his Crow Indian wife, Waits-by-Water, and two small children. Covers the years 1834–1840.
8. *Death Rattle* (Bantam, 1999) Titus embarks upon a horse raid in pre–Mexican War California, kills a bunch of evil Mexicans, and rescues some settlers caught in the Taos Rebellion of the Pueblo Indians.
9. *Wind Walker* (Bantam, 2001) In the final installment of his adventures, Titus and his family reunite with old friend Shadrach Sweete and run into Brigham Young and his fanatical Mormon brethren.

II. Jonah Hook, Confederate soldier turned Indian fighter, scout, and buffalo hunter, recalls the frontier days of the 1860s and 1870s in memoirs related to a journalist in 1908. A saga replete with a long quest, wicked Mormons and other outsized villains, friendly and not so friendly Indians, Chinese opium dens, and plenty of action.

1. *Cry of the Hawk* (Bantam, 1992) Jonah Hook volunteers to go west and fight Indians to get out of the Union Prison at Rock Island, Illinois.
2. *Winter Rain* (Bantam, 1993) Jonah sets out to find his wife and children after learning that they have been abducted by renegade Mormons.
3. *Dream Catcher* (Bantam, 1994) Jonah finally rescues his wife from Mormon zealot Jubilee Usher in Utah.

III. The Plainsmen is a historical series relating the "taming of the West" through battles from 1866 to 1877 (where Johnston left the series unfinished at his death in 2001). Scout Seamus Donegan is the primary continuing character in the series, which also includes historical personages such as Buffalo Bill, Wild Bill Hickok, Crazy Horse, and Red Cloud. The subtitles are more or less self-explanatory in this unannotated list.

1. *Sioux Dawn: The Fetterman Massacre, 1866* (St. Martin's, 1990)
2. *Red Cloud's Revenge: Showdown in the Northern Plains, 1867* (St. Martin's, 1990)
3. *Stalkers, The: The Battle of Beecher's Island, 1868* (St. Martin's, 1990)
4. *Black Sun: The Battle of Summit Springs, 1869* (St. Martin's, 1991)
5. *Devil's Backbone: The Modoc War, 1872–3* (St. Martin's, 1991)
6. *Shadow Riders: The Southern Plains Uprising, 1873* (St. Martin's, 1991)
7. *Dying Thunder: The Battle of Adobe Walls and Palo Canyon, 1874* (St. Martin's, 1992)
8. *Blood Song: The Battle of Powder River and the Beginning of the Great Sioux War, 1876* (St. Martin's, 1993)
9. *Reap the Whirlwind: The Battle of the Rosebud, June 1876* (St. Martin's, 1994)
10. *Trumpet on the Land: The Aftermath of Custer's Massacre, 1876* (Bantam, 1995)
11. *Cold Day in Hell, A: The Dull Knife Battle, 1876* (Bantam, 1996)
12. *Wolf Mountain Moon: The Battle of the Butte, 1877* (Bantam, 1997)
13. *Ashes of Heaven: The Lame Deer Fight on May 7, 1877 to the End of the Great Sioux War* (St. Martin's, 1998)
14. *Cries from the Earth: Outbreak of the Nez Perce War and the Battle of White Bird Canyon, June 17, 1877* (St. Martin's, 1999)
15. *Lay the Mountains Low: Flight of the Nez Perce from Idaho and the Battle of Big Hole, Aug. 9–10, 1877* (St. Martin's, 2000)
16. *Turn the Stars Upside Down: The Last Days and Tragic Death of Crazy Horse* (St. Martin's, 2001)

IV. Johnston also wrote Sons of the Plains, a trilogy about General George Armstrong Custer and his son by an Indian woman. The trilogy appeared only in paperback.

1. *Long Winter Gone* (Bantam, 1990) General Custer takes a lover captured in his winter campaign against the Cheyenne.
2. *Seize the Sky* (Bantam, 1991) General Custer, expecting glorious victory, meets catastrophic defeat at the Little Big Horn in June 1876.
3. *Whisper of the Wolf* (Bantam, 1991) The saga of General Custer's Cheyenne son and his fight to survive.

Jones, Douglas C.

I. Douglas C. Jones (d. 1998) was a highly regarded author of historical novels about the American West. *The Court-Martial of George Armstrong Custer* examines what might have happened if Custer had survived the battle of Little Big Horn. The other two novels in this trilogy deal with the history of the events leading up to, and including, the massacre at Wounded Knee. Jones's sympathies are with the Plains Indians. He blames an insensitive, inept government for their tragic defeat.

1. *Court-Martial of George Armstrong Custer, The* (Scribner, 1976) General Custer, one of the few white survivors of the Battle of Little Big Horn (1876), is put on military trial for insubordination.
2. *Arrest Sitting Bull* (Scribner, 1977) In December 1890 Sitting Bull is back on the reservation and in the middle of the Ghost Dance revolt of the Indians.
3. *Creek Called Wounded Knee, A* (Scribner, 1978) The story of the 1890 massacre at Wounded Knee, South Dakota, as seen through the eyes of the Indians, the federal troops, and the press.

II. Jones wrote a series of novels, the Hasford-Pay saga, set in his native Arkansas, that depicts the fortunes of two families from the Civil War to the present. The novels are partially based on Jones's own family history.

1. *Elkhorn Tavern* (Holt, 1980) Ora Hasford and her two teenage children are caught up in the Civil War when their farm becomes part of the battleground of the Battle of Pea Ridge.
2. *Roman* (Holt, 1986) In 1865 Roman Hasford leaves his parents and his childhood on an Arkansas farm to roam a while, make his fortune, and learn about life.
3. *Winding Stair* (Holt, 1979) Young Eben Pay is a lawyer temporarily assigned to the court of "hanging judge" Isaac C. Parker.
4. *Come Winter* (Holt, 1989) Roman Hasford, returned to his old home, tries to gain control of a bank and make his way politically.
5. *Search for Temperance Moon, The* (Holt, 1991) Takes place in Arkansas and the Indian Nations territory of the early 1890s. Jewel Moon hires former US deputy marshall Oscar Schiller to investigate the murder of her mother, celebrated madam Temperance Moon.
6. *Remember Santiago* (Holt, 1988) Eben Pay and his Osage friend Joe Mountain join up for the invasion of Cuba during the Spanish-American War of 1898.
7. *Spider for Loco Shoat, A* (Holt, 1997) In 1907, Oscar Schiller, now retired, becomes involved in the investigation into the murder of Gerald Wagstaff. Eben Pay and Joe Mountain make a return appearance.
8. *Weedy Rough* (Holt, 1981) Maudie Snowdon is the cause of the breakup of the friendship between Dune Gene Pay and Hoadie Renkin in the town of Weedy Rough, Arkansas, during the Great Depression.
9. *Hickory Cured* (Holt, 1987) Shanks Caulder reminisces about life in Weedy Rough from the early 1930s to the 1980s.

III. In Jones's second trilogy, it is the Comanche Indians of Texas who are forced to come to terms with the ascendancy of the white man.

1. *Season of Yellow Leaf* (Holt, 1983) In 1838 10-year-old Morfanna Perry is captured by Comanches and adopted by their chief under the name "Chosen."

2. *Barefoot Brigade, The* (Holt, 1984) This follows a group of Confederate army recruits from Arkansas through the Civil War.
3. *Gone the Dreams and Dancing* (Holt, 1984) In 1875 Comanche chief Kwahadi asks Liverpool Morgan, a survivor of the "Barefoot Brigade," to find out what happened to Chosen, his mother.

Jong, Erica

Fear of Flying was the funniest and most popular of the new wave of women's novels in the 1970s that portrayed modern women in the throes—usually graphic and hilarious—of liberation. Jong's heroine, Isadora Wing, is twice married, Barnard educated, under 30, and fiercely restless. Jong's crisp and pungent dialogue gives Isadora an edge among the newly liberated, and *Fear of Flying* will have a long life as a classic of the genre.

1. *Fear of Flying* (Holt, 1973) Isadora leaves her cool psychiatrist husband for a fling with a sexy English Laingian.
2. *How to Save Your Own Life* (Holt, 1977) Isadora, now a best-selling author, gets divorced and heads for other loves.
3. *Parachutes and Kisses* (New American Library, 1984) Isadora at 39, now a successful writer, wife, and mother, is jolted by the desertion of her third husband.

Jönsson, Reidar

Anyone who has seen the delightful film *My Life as a Dog* (1985) will be interested in these two books (a third is promised) about Ingemar Jönsson. Ingemar has the same name and nationality but little else in common with Sweden's only world heavyweight boxing champion. *My Life as a Dog* is a funny, tender picture of Ingemar's troubled 13th and 14th years in the 1950s. *My Father, His Son* picks up his life some 20 years later.

1. *My Life as a Dog* (Farrar, 1990) Ingemar's father is away at sea, his mother is dying of tuberculosis, and Ingemar is being shunted from relative to relative. Original title: *Mitt liv som hund*.
2. *My Father, His Son* (Arcade, 1991) Visiting his estranged wife in Algiers, Ingemar reminisces about his life at sea, his continued lack of rapport with his father, and his inability to "find himself." Translated from the Swedish by Marianne Ruuth. Originally published as *En hund begraven*.

Jordan, Robert

PSEUDONYM OF James Oliver Rigney

I. The popular Wheel of Time series will bear comparisons with any of the post-Tolkien worlds created by David Eddings (q.v.), Terry Brooks (q.v.), et al. Rand al-Thor, the Dragon Reborn, is the reluctant protagonist in a series of quests in the service of Light against Darkness. Each succeeding volume introduces new characters, and there is no end in sight. *New Spring*, the expansion of a short story that appeared in Robert Silverberg's anthology *Legends* (1998), is the first of three projected prequels to the series. Two three-volume boxed sets of the Wheel of Time have been issued by Tor (1993 and 1997). *The World of Robert Jordan's Wheel of Time* (Tor, 1997), cowritten with Teresa Patterson, contains short stories, literary sketches, legends about characters and events, and maps.

1. *New Spring* (Tor, 2004) In this prequel, during a three day battle around the city of Tar Valon, the Keeper of Amyrlin Seat foretells the rebirth of the Dragon. Answers many questions posed in the Wheel of Time series.
2. *Eye of the World, The* (Tor, 1989) Rand al-Thor and his companions flee from a magical terror. Reissued in two parts in 2002: *From the Two Rivers* and *To the Blight*.
3. *Great Hunt, The* (Tor, 1990) Rand al-Thor reluctantly faces the fact that is the Dragon Reborn, the champion of Light against Darkness. Reissued in two parts in 2004: *The Hunt Begins* and *New Threads in the Pattern*.
4. *Dragon Reborn, The* (Tor, 1991) Egwene, Nynaeve, and Elayne are deeply involved in the intrigues that are shaking the Aes Sedai, the nunlike order of female magic workers.
5. *Shadow Rising, The* (Tor, 1992) An unknown danger threatens the city of Tar Valon, home of the Aes Sedai.
6. *Fires of Heaven, The* (Tor, 1993) Rand al-Thor leads the clans of the Aiel in a war for unification.
7. *Lord of Chaos* (Tor, 1994) Rand al-Thor consolidates his power base and attempts to reach a rapprochement with the Aes Sedai.
8. *Crown of Swords, A* (Tor, 1996) Rand al-Thor is engaged in a fight for control of the weather and of the growing number of men and women who are magic-wielders.
9. *Path of Daggers, The* (Tor, 1998) The Seanchans, a race whose arsenal includes flying reptiles, enslaved female magic-workers, and powerful soldiers, have renewed their invasion.
10. *Winter's Heart* (Tor, 2000) The Seanchan are pouring into Ebou Dar. Perrian Aybara is pursuing the rebel Aiel who have kidnapped his wife. The Aes Sedai remain divided between Elaida and Egwene al'Vere.
11. *Crossroads of Twilight* (Tor, 2003) Rand al-Thor considers a truce with the Seanchan. The rebel Aes Sedai consider an alliance with the Asha'man. Caemlyn and Tar Valon are still being besieged.
12. *Knife of Dreams* (Tor, 2005) The climactic battle between the Dragon Reborn and the Dark One begins in earnest, while Faile, Mat, Elayne, and Egwene continue their adventures.

II. Jordan was one of many authors who continued Robert E. Howard's Conan series. Jordan wrote seven Conan pastiches in the 1980s. *The Conan Chronicles* (Tor, 1995) contains numbers 1, 2, and 3. *The Further Chronicles of Conan* (Tor, 1999) contains numbers 4, 5, and 6. Number 7 was designed as a tie-in to the film of the same name. Novels are listed without annotations.

1. *Conan the Invincible* (Tor, 1982)
2. *Conan the Defender* (Tor, 1983)
3. *Conan the Unconquered* (Tor, 1983)
4. *Conan the Triumphant* (Tor, 1983)
5. *Conan the Destroyer* (Tor, 1984)
6. *Conan the Magnificent* (Tor, 1984)
7. *Conan the Victorious* (Tor, 1984)

Joyce, James

The young life in Dublin in the 1880s and 1890s of Stephen Dedalus is depicted in James Joyce's autobiographical novel *A Portrait of the Artist as a Young Man*. Stephen Dedalus reappears as an adult in Joyce's *Ulysses*, where he is befriended by Leopold Bloom, who sees in Stephen a substitute for his lost son. *Portrait of the Artist as a Young Man* was serialized in the *Egoist* magazine before it was published in book form in 1916. It became a classic and has been reprinted many times, including a "definitive" edition, corrected by Chester G. Anderson and edited by Richard Ellman (Viking, 1964). The publishing history of *Ulysses* was even more torturous. Some of the chapters of *Ulysses* were serialized in the *Little Review* and the *Egoist*. Because of its alleged obscenity, *Ulysses* wasn't published in the United States or the United Kingdom. Instead it was published in Paris by Sylvia Beach's Shakespeare and Company. In the United States, in 1933, *Ulysses* was declared not pornographic, and Random House published it in 1934. *Ulysses* is now an acknowledged classic that, perhaps unfortunately, has become an academic industry. Its stream-of-consciousness mode has scared off many timid readers, but it is a comic classic and will reward the persevering reader.

1. *Portrait of the Artist as a Young Man, A* (Huebsch, 1916) In a story told in stream-of-consciousness style, Joyce's fictional counterpart, Stephen Dedalus, grows up in Ireland at the end of the 19th century, something of a loner, and is eventually convinced that he has a religious calling. Part of the first draft of *Portrait* was edited by Theodore Spencer and published as *Stephen Hero* (New Directions, 1944)
2. *Ulysses* (Random House, 1934) The events of one day in Dublin, June 16, 1904, now immortalized as "Bloomsday." Leopold Bloom, a Jewish advertisement canvasser, meets, among others, the would-be writer Stephen Dedalus. Originally published in Paris in 1922 by Shakespeare and Company.

Kahn, Sharon

Ruby Rothman, widow of the late rabbi of Eternal, Texas, computer expert, and amateur detective, finds life anything but dull in the small town where she has remained after her husband's death, as Eternal turns out to be one of those typical cozy towns, where murder occurs at least once a book. Ruby, the Rabbi's Wife is a very popular suspense series, leavened with humor ("chicken soup for the funnybone" according to *Publishers Weekly*) and information on Jewish food, fundraising, and the politics of choosing a rabbi. Kahn, herself the widow of a rabbi, started writing in the mid-1990s, in her sixties. She lives in Austin, Texas.

1. *Fax Me a Bagel* (Scribner, 1998) Ruby decides to investigate when the sister of Ruby's least favorite member of the congregation is felled, apparently by a poisoned bagel from Ruby's friend Milt's bagel shop.
2. *Never Nosh a Matzo Ball* (Scribner, 2000) Ruby, now running a bagel bakery and a software consulting business, and being pursued by the new rabbi, is inveigled by the owner of Eternal's only gym into selling frozen, reduced-fat matzo balls for a Temple Rita fund-raiser.
3. *Don't Cry for Me, Hot Pastrami* (Scribner, 2001) Willie Bob, lecturer on a ship taking Ruby and her cohorts on a Caribbean cruise, mysteriously collapses, forcing Ruby to endure inedible food, Elvis impersonators, and the amorous intentions of the ship's captain to solve the mystery.
4. *Hold the Cream Cheese, Kill the Lox* (Scribner, 2002) The murder of lox maven Herman Guenther wreaks havoc with a double bar mitzvah, and Ruby gets involved with a pair of 13-year-old twins, an investigation of the victim's past in Nazi-era Denmark, and a chase that takes her from Alaska to New Jersey.
5. *Which Big Giver Stole the Chopped Liver?* (Scribner, 2004) Essie Sue Margolis, "the terror of Temple Rita," decides it's time for a reunion fund-raiser to renovate the temple. Then an unknown man is found dead, keeled over in a platter of ice, where Essie Sue's chopped liver mold in the shape of the state of Texas once resided.
6. *Out of the Frying Pan, into the Choir* (Scribner, 2006) The Temple Rita Choir's upcoming excursion to Banff and Lake Louise is in jeopardy when latke sales fail to raise the needed money. Temple

Rita's star soprano, Serena Salit, collapses and dies, leaving some disturbing entries in her electronic diary.

Kallen, Lucille

The continuing subplot in this series of mysteries set in Sloan's Ford, Connecticut, was the relationship between C. B. Greenfield, newspaper editor and amateur detective, and Maggie Rome, reporter and reluctant participant in Greenfield's investigations. Greenfield is crotchety and conservative, a male chauvinist who thinks it is his natural right as the "boss" to order Maggie Rome around. Rome, happily married with grown children, gets involved in Greenfield's cases against her better judgment but gets a measure of revenge as narrator of the novels and acerbic commentator on Greenfield's foibles. Kallen (d. 1999), a former comedy writer for television, produced a series of witty and well-plotted mysteries.

1. *Introducing C. B. Greenfield* (Crown, 1979) The delivery boy for the *Sloan's Ford Reporter* is badly injured in a hit-and-run accident.
2. *Tanglewood Murder, The* (Wyndham, 1980) Noel Damaskin, violinist for the Boston Symphony Orchestra, is poisoned at a rehearsal during the Tanglewood Music festival.
3. *No Lady in the House* (Wyndham, 1982) Greenfield's stereo is stolen and his cleaning lady murdered.
4. *Piano Bird, The* (Random House, 1984) Maggie Rome is on Sanibel Island, Florida, nursing her invalid mother when thespian Thea Quinn is murdered.
5. *Little Madness, A* (Random House, 1985) After Maggie joins a women's peace group encamped outside a missile base, Alice Dakin, author of *Why God Gave Us the Bomb*, disappears.

Kaminsky, Stuart M.

I. Like Max Allan Collins (q.v.), Stuart M. Kaminsky is writing a series of detective novels set in the 1930s and 1940s that intermingle real and fictional characters. Toby Peters is a typical hard-boiled private eye of the era: tough and cynical but basically honest and good-hearted. His sidekicks include incompetent dentist and would-be inventor Sheldon Minck, multilingual Swiss midget Gunther Wherthman, and ex-wrestler-turned-poet Jeremy Butler. Peters works out of Los Angeles. His cases sooner or later involve him with celebrities of the past, many of them from the movie industry. Kaminsky is a film historian and critic. His blend of nostalgia, humor, mystery, and movie stars is a surefire mix.

1. *Bullet for a Star* (St. Martin's, 1977) Errol Flynn is Toby's client. The crimes are blackmail and murder. The scenic backdrop is the original set of *The Maltese Falcon*.
2. *Murder on the Yellow Brick Road* (St. Martin's, 1978) When a Munchkin from *The Wizard of Oz* is murdered on the MGM lot, Judy Garland and Louis B. Mayer call in Toby Peters.
3. *You Bet Your Life* (St. Martin's, 1979) Toby tries to clear Chico Marx of a fake gambling debt. Chicago is the scene of most of the action.
4. *Howard Hughes Affair, The* (St. Martin's, 1979) Howard Hughes thinks that someone is after the designs of his secret bomber.
5. *Never Cross a Vampire* (St. Martin's, 1980) Is the same person threatening Bela Lugosi and trying to frame William Faulkner for murder?

6. *High Midnight* (**St. Martin's, 1981**) Gary Cooper is being black-mailed into doing a grade "B" cowboy movie called *High Midnight*.

7. *Catch a Falling Clown* (**St. Martin's, 1982**) An elephant is electro-cuted at the Rose and Elder Circus, and famous clown Emmett Kelly suspects sabotage.

8. *He Done Her Wrong* (**St. Martin's, 1983**) Mae West's fictionalized autobiography is being held for ransom, while Toby runs into a slew of Mae West impersonators.

9. *Fala Factor, The* (**St. Martin's, 1984**) Eleanor Roosevelt suspects that an imposter has been substituted for FDR'S beloved Scottie, Fala.

10. *Down for the Count* (**St. Martin's, 1985**) Joe Louis has been set up to take the rap for the murder of Toby's ex-wife's second husband.

11. *Man Who Shot Lewis Vance, The* (**St. Martin's, 1986**) Someone wants to kill John Wayne, and a man named Lewis Vance does get killed after slipping Toby a drugged Pepsi.

12. *Smart Moves* (**St. Martin's, 1987**) Nazi fifth columnists are trying to discredit, and perhaps assassinate, Albert Einstein. Set mostly in New York.

13. *Think Fast, Mr. Peters* (**St. Martin's, 1988**) Mrs. Sheldon Minck, wife of Toby's dentist office mate, has run off with a Peter Lorre impersonator who is filming a B thriller on the roof of a hardware store.

14. *Buried Caesars* (**Mysterious, 1989**) Dashiell Hammett helps Toby look for some papers and money stolen from General Douglas MacArthur.

15. *Poor Butterfly* (**Mysterious, 1990**) Leopold Stokowski's perfor-mance of *Madame Butterfly* faces trouble from anti-Japanese "patriots" and San Francisco's own "Phantom of the Opera."

16. *Melting Clock, The* (**Mysterious, 1991**) Someone has stolen three paintings and three ornate Russian clocks from Salvador Dali's house in Carmel.

17. *Devil Met a Lady, The* (**Mysterious, 1993**) Nazi agents plan to kidnap Bette Davis to get access to plans for a new bombsight in the possession of her husband.

18. *Tomorrow Is Another Day* (**Mysterious, 1995**) Toby is hired by Clark Gable to find the killer of extras from the burning of Atlanta scene in *Gone with the Wind*.

19. *Dancing in the Dark* (**Mysterious, 1996**) Luna, mistress of Arthur Forbes (aka "Fingers" Intaglia), former Detroit mobster, wants Fred Astaire to give her dancing lessons.

20. *Fatal Glass of Beer, A* (**Mysterious, 1997**) Toby, W. C. Fields, and Toby's associate, midget Gunther Wherthman, are the trail of the person who has been emptying out Fields's bank accounts.

21. *Few Minutes past Midnight, A* (**Carroll & Graf, 2001**) Charlie Chaplin's movie project concerning a serial killer who seduces and murders older women has apparently offended a real-life counter-part.

22. *To Catch a Spy* (**Carroll & Graf, 2002**) Cary Grant hires Toby to deliver a satchel of money to a man who'll give him an envelope in return.

23. *Mildred Pierced* (**Carroll & Graf, 2003**) Sheldon Minck takes up with a survivalist group and, when his wife is slain with a crossbow bolt, becomes a prime murder suspect, with Joan Crawford as a witness.

24. *Now You See It* (**Carroll & Graf, 2004**) In 1945 Harry Blackstone approaches Toby after the magician has been challenged and threatened by a third-rate competitor.

II. Porfiry Petrovich Rostnikov, inspector in the Moscow Procu-rator's Office, is the hero of a series of police procedurals set in the (former) Soviet Union. Porfiry Petrovich is a good cop—dogged, stoic, honest—but his nonideological competence and his Jewish wife don't make him popular with his superiors or the KGB, who at one point succeed in having him demoted.

1. *Death of a Dissident* (**Ace, 1981**) Dissident Alexander Granovsky is murdered on the day before hie is due to be put on trial as an "enemy of the people." UK title: *Rostnikov's Corpse*.

2. *Black Knight in Red Square* (**Berkley, 1983**) Rostnikov and his associates uncover a plot to bomb Lenin's tomb at the Moscow Film Festival.

3. *Red Chameleon* (**Scribner, 1985**) A series of crimes such as the theft of the deputy procurator's automobile, the sniper killing of a policeman, and the death of an old man in his bathtub bedevil Rostnikov.

4. *Fine Red Rain, A* (**Scribner, 1987**) Rostnikov must find out who is killing trapeze artists at the Moscow Circus, while his colleague Karpo is trying to find a serial killer of prostitutes.

5. *Cold Red Sunrise, A* (**Scribner, 1988**) Rostnikov is assigned to the case of Commissar Illya Rutkin, killed in Siberia while investi-gating the death of a dissident's daughter.

6. *Man Who Walked Like a Bear, The* (**Scribner, 1990**) Porfiry has to deal with an assassination plot, skulduggery in a shoe factory, and a plot to destroy Lenin's tomb.

7. *Rostnikov's Vacation* (**Scribner, 1991**) On an enforced vacation in Yalta, Rostnikov stumbles upon a plot to assassinate Gorbachev and put the blame on the CIA.

8. *Death of a Russian Priest* (**Fawcett, 1992**) A prominent and outspoken priest has been dispatched with an ax, and a Syrian diplomat's daughter has been kidnapped.

9. *Hard Currency* (**Fawcett, 1995**) Porfiry is sent to Havana to help patch up Russian–Cuban relations, while Karpo tracks down a serial killer in Moscow.

10. *Blood and Rubles* (**Fawcett, 1996**) A gang of tattooed thugs kill a prostitute, three young boys are on a rampage on the streets, valu-able artifacts disappear, and there is an attempted kidnapping.

11. *Tarnished Icons* (**Ballantine, 1997**) In what appears to be an anti-Semitic attack, several people are gunned down in a local syna-gogue. Rostnikov suspects that this is more than a case of simple bigotry.

12. *Dog Who Bit a Policeman, The* (**Mysterious, 1998**) Now working in the Office of Special Investigation under Igor Yakovev, "the Yak," Rostnikov works with Karpo to head off a war between Mafia leaders.

13. *Fall of a Cosmonaut* (**Mysterious, 2000**) Porfiry and his son Iosef search for a missing cosmonaut; Karpo is looking for the murderer of a scientist at the Center for the Study of Technical Parapsychology; and someone has stolen an epic film on the life of Tolstoy.

14. *Murder on the Trans-Siberian Express* (**Mysterious, 2001**) Rost-nikov is assigned to take a ride on the Trans-Siberian Express to intercept a courier exchanging money for a package believed to contain an old secret document.

III. Chicago cop Abe Lieberman is smart, streetwise, and reason-ably conscientious, but he would rather be with his family or with his friends in the local deli than dealing with Chicago's mean streets or his drunken partner, Bill Hanrahan.

1. *Lieberman's Folly* (**St. Martin's, 1991**) Prostitute and informer Estralda Valdez is killed on Hanrahan's watch after she requests police protection.

2. *Lieberman's Choice* (**St. Martin's, 1993**) Fellow cop Bernie Shephard shoots his wife and her lover and then holes up on the roof of his apartment building.

3. *Lieberman's Day* (Holt, 1994) Lieberman's nephew is killed in a mugging, and his pregnant niece winds up in a hospital.

4. *Lieberman's Thief* (Holt, 1995) Professional burglar George Patniks is an unwilling spectator when Mr. Rozier kills Mrs. Rozier.

5. *Lieberman's Law* (Holt, 1996) Lieberman takes it personally when his synagogue is defaced and a priceless Torah is stolen.

6. *Big Silence, The* (Forge, 2001) Hanrahan goes on assignment to Cleveland to protect the wife and son of a Mob informant, while Lieberman deals with his rather unsatisfactory family and digestion.

7. *Not Quite Kosher* (Forge, 2002) Lieberman juggles personal problems, such as high cholesterol and financing his grandson's bar mitzvah, and professional problems, such as tracking down two inept stick-up men.

8. *Last Dark Place, The* (Forge, 2004) Abe is given the task of extraditing a professional assassin back to Chicago.

9. *Terror Town* (Forge, 2005) The crimes that bedevil Lieberman and Hanrahan are the murder of a young mother on the South Side, an assault by coke bottle on a former Cubs player, and the antics of a religious fanatic who dabbles in extortion.

10. *Dead Don't Lie, The* (Forge, 2007) Lieberman is drawn into a series of murders centered on the search for a long-lost journal rumored to "prove" that the Turks were *not* responsible for the massacre of Armenians in 1915.

IV. The prolific Kaminsky has also written a pair of novels about the popular television figure immortalized by James Garner, Jim Rockford. The low-rent California private investigator makes a fairly easy transition from the 1970s to the 1990s, as does his tricky ex-con buddy Angel Martinez.

1. *Rockford Files, The: The Green Bottle* (Forge, 1996) Jim Rockford recovers an antique bottle for a client, and then tracks down a missing girl.

2. *Rockford Files, The: Devil on My Doorstep* (Forge, 1998) A girl discovered sleeping on the deck of his trailer may be Rockford's daughter, and he feels obligated to track down the murderer of her mother, an old flame.

V. Not content with four detectives, Kaminsky has added a fifth to his stable. Lew Fonseca, Chicagoan moved to Sarasota, Florida, is a widowed former employee of the state attorney's office in Chicago. Now he works as process server, broods about his wife's hit-and-run death, and takes on the occasional case. Kaminsky melds sense of place and interesting characters into another winning series.

1. *Vengeance* (Forge, 1999) Lew tries to locate two missing persons, an abused teenage girl and a woman who has left her wealthy husband.

2. *Retribution* (Forge, 2001) Teenager Adele Hanford has gone missing again. Reclusive novelist Conrad Lonsberg and Adele's burger-flipping new boyfriend may know more than they are telling.

3. *Midnight Pass* (Forge, 2003) Lew is persuaded to look for a missing Sarasota city councilman on the eve of an important vote.

4. *Denial* (Forge, 2005) Octogenarian therapist Ann Horowitz tries to get to the bottom of what has been eating at Lew, who is investigating a hit-and-run case and the story of a nursing-home resident who is certain that she has witnessed a murder.

5. *Always Say Goodbye* (Forge, 2006) Lew emerges from his clinical depression and starts tracking down the hit-and-run driver who ran down his wife in Chicago four years earlier. Lew's investigation reactivates two warring assassins for hire.

Karon, Jan(ice Meredith Wilson)

The series set in the fictional North Carolina mountain town of Mitford (based on the real town of Blowing Rock, North Carolina, where Jan Karon resides) has been a publishing phenomenon. Readers have really taken to their hearts Episcopal priest Father Tim Kavanaugh and his neighbors. Mitford, unlike many fictional hamlets, has no violence or illicit sex. Its characters are slightly eccentric but nice, mainly concerned with their relationship with God and Jesus. The main story line concerns Father Tim's realization of his loneliness, his adoption of a stray dog, and his relationship with, and eventual marriage to, neighbor Cynthia Coppersmith. Several omnibus sets have been published, including *The Mitford Years* boxed sets (numbers 1–3 and 4–6; Penguin, 2002). Several "Mitford Gift Books" have been published, including *The Mitford Snowmen* (Viking, 2001); *Patches of Godlight: Father Tim's Favorite Quotes* (Viking, 2001); *Esther's Gift: A Mitford Christmas Story* (Viking, 2002); *The Trellis and the Seed: A Book of Encouragement for All Ages* (Viking, 2004); *Jan Karon's Mitford Cookbook and Kitchen Reader* (Viking, 2004); and *The Mitford Bedside Companion* (Viking, 2006).

1. *At Home in Mitford* (Viking, 1994) Father Tim Kavanaugh, Episcopal rector of the small mountain town of Mitford, North Carolina, is outwardly cheerful, but inwardly lonely. But then a stray dog, a seemingly stray boy, and his next-door neighbor Cynthia Coppersmith come into his life.

2. *Light in the Window, A* (Viking, 1995) Father Tim returns to Mitford after an extended journey to Ireland to be faced with parish problems as well as his own romantic problems with Cynthia.

3. *Common Life, A: The Wedding Story* (Viking, 2001) A prequel to numbers 4 through 6 describes the wedding of Father Tim Kavanagh and Cynthia Coppersmith.

4. *These High Green Hills* (Viking, 1995) The recently married Father Tim and his neighbors run into some real problems, such as a drunken, abusive father, and the loss of Father Tim's surrogate mother.

5. *Out to Canaan* (Viking, 1997) As Father Tim ponders retirement, Mitford is threatened by developers who want to build a health spa, and the Sweet Stuff Bakery may be closing.

6. *New Song, A* (Viking, 1999) Father Tim retires, but then agrees to serve as interim minister of a small church on Whitecap Island.

7. *In This Mountain* (Viking, 2002) Father Tim and Cynthia have returned to Mitford. Father Tim's adopted son, Dooley, looks forward to becoming a veterinarian; Joe Ivey and Fancy Skinner fight a no-holds-barred haircut-price war; and Percy steps out on a limb with a risky new menu item at the Grill.

8. *Shepherds Abiding* (Viking, 2003) Father Tim, who has never regarded himself as good with his hands, takes on the task of restoring a derelict nativity scene in need of repair.

9. *Light from Heaven* (Viking, 2005) In the ostensible conclusion to the Mitford novels, Father Tim takes on the seemingly impossible job of reviving Holy Trinity, a mountain church that's been closed for 40 years.

10. *Home to Holly Springs* (Viking, 2007) Father Tim returns to his childhood town of Holly Springs, Mississippi, where he reconnects with old friends and battles some old demons.

Katz, Jon

Christopher "Kit" Deeleuw, disgraced former Wall Streeter, has retired to the suburb of Rochambeau, New Jersey, where he has become a house-husband, devoted to raising his two children. Feeling the need for some outside activity, Kit opens an office in a mall, where he indulges in some part-time private sleuthing, taking on various cases, which usually end in murder and in exposing the scabrous side of suburbia. Jon Katz, formerly executive producer of *CBS Morning News* and media critic for journals such as *Rolling Stone*, *New York*, and *Wired*, has published several nonfiction books about the media and, recently books about dogs, such as *Katz on Dogs* (Villard, 2005).

1. *Death by Station Wagon* **(Doubleday, 1993)** Kit Deeleuw is hired by teenagers to investigate the alleged murder-suicide of their classmates Ken Dale and Carol Lombardo.
2. *Family Stalker, The* **(Doubleday, 1994)** Marianne Dow claims that another woman is trying to destroy her family. Kit thinks that she is overreacting, until Marianne disappears and her husband is found bludgeoned to death in the bathtub.
3. *Last Housewife, The* **(Doubleday, 1995)** A housewife is accused of murdering a feminist middle-school principal who was about to expel the housewife's son for sexual harassment.
4. *Fathers' Club, The* **(Doubleday, 1996)** Dale Lewis, ex-husband and normally dutiful father, has fallen behind in his child-support payments, and hasn't called or visited his children.
5. *Death Row* **(Doubleday, 1998)** Kit's friend Benchley, who has suffered a stroke and been incarcerated in a nursing home, dies of a drug overdose.

Kazan, Elia

Elia Kazan (d. 2003) was famous as the stage and screen director of *Death of a Salesman*, *On the Waterfront*, and many other notable successes. It's no accident that his first novel, *America, America*, has a certain cinematic quality. It tells the story of a young Greek man who is determined to leave his home in Anatolia (Turkey) and emigrate to America. The story is based on the experiences of Kazan's uncle. *America, America* was filmed in 1964 with Kazan as writer, director, and producer.

1. *America, America* **(Stein & Day, 1962)** Stavros Topouzoglou is entrusted with his family's wealth to establish himself in the rug business in Constantinople, but his deepest desire is to emigrate to America.
2. *Anatolian, The* **(Knopf, 1982)** In 1909 Stavros, known to his carpet-selling associates as Joe Arness, is living in New York and awaiting the arrival of his family from Anatolia.
3. *Beyond the Aegean* **(Knopf, 1994)** New York rug merchant Stavros returns to Greek Anatolia after World War I, as the Greeks and Turks engage in a bloody war.

Keating, H(enry) R(eymond) F(itzwalter)

I.   Inspector Ganesh Ghote (pronounced *Go'-tay*), who works in the crime branch of the Bombay Police Department, is a fellow who is pushed about by everyone—by his wife, Protima; by his superior officers; and by every sort of rascal and miscreant. But his persistence and wily intelligence enable him to bring all his varied assignments to successful conclusions. Keating's detective is very likable, and his unusual and colorful Indian setting will seem authentic to Western readers, though the English author admits to only one short visit to India. An additional attraction is that Keating wraps each of his books around a different philosophical theme. *The Inspector Ghote Mysteries: An Omnibus* (Macmillan [UK], 1996) contains numbers 1, 2 and 3. Keating's *Inspector Ghote, His Life and Crimes* (Hutchinson [UK], 1989) describes the series. *The Murder of the Maharajah* (Doubleday, 1980) is a non-Ghote novel set in the India of 1930.

1. *Perfect Murder, The* **(Dutton, 1965)** Naturally the newspapers labeled it the "perfect murder," but the victim, Mr. Perfect, wasn't dead, just bashed into a coma.
2. *Inspector Ghote's Good Crusade* **(Dutton, 1966)** When an American philanthropist and founder of the Masters Foundation for the Care of Juvenile Vagrants is poisoned with arsenic, Inspector Ghote investigates.
3. *Inspector Ghote Caught in Meshes* **(Dutton, 1968)** An American physicist is murdered by highway robbers, but there is more here than meets the eye.
4. *Inspector Ghote Hunts the Peacock* **(Dutton, 1968)** In London for a conference on drug smuggling, Inspector Ghote searches for his missing niece.
5. *Inspector Ghote Plays a Joker* **(Dutton, 1969)** On the trail of a practical joker, Inspector Ghote goes to the Victoria Gardens zoo to prevent the murder of a flamingo.
6. *Inspector Ghote Breaks an Egg* **(Doubleday, 1971)** Inspector Ghote, disguised as a chicken-feed salesman, investigates a murder that was committed 15 years earlier.
7. *Inspector Ghote Goes by Train* **(Doubleday, 1972)** Ghote journeys to Calcutta to pick up the con-man art forger Bhattacharya.
8. *Inspector Ghote Trusts the Heart* **(Doubleday, 1973)** This case involves a kidnapping that gets very mixed up.
9. *Bats Fly Up for Inspector Ghote* **(Doubleday, 1974)** After failing to make any arrests while assigned to the pickpocket squad, Ghote is transferred to the Black-Money and Allied Transactions squad to plug a leak.
10. *Filmi, Filmi, Inspector Ghote* **(Doubleday, 1976)** A film star is murdered during the production of a Bollywood version of *Macbeth*
11. *Inspector Ghote Draws a Line* **(Doubleday, 1979)** When anonymous letters threaten Judge Asif Ibrahim's life, Ghote is assigned to protect him.
12. *Go West, Inspector Ghote* **(Doubleday, 1981)** Inspector Ghote goes to Los Angeles to find Ranjee Shahani's daughter, a disciple of a slick swami in an American ashram.
13. *Sheriff of Bombay, The* **(Doubleday, 1984)** The popular sheriff of Bombay comes under suspicion for the "Ripper" murders of two women.
14. *Under a Monsoon Cloud* **(Viking, 1986)** When Inspector Ghote's longtime friend murders an insolent policeman, Ghote helps him to cover up the crime. But when the friend commits suicide, Ghote finds himself the object of an unfriendly investigation.
15. *Body in the Billiard Room, The* **(Viking, 1987)** The billiards marker at the Ooty Club in the hill station of Ootacacmund is murdered, and many of the club's silver trophies are missing.
16. *Dead on Time* **(Mysterious, 1989)** Murder is committed at the Tick Tock Watchworks, and a couple of watches, including Ghote's, are broken in this time-driven mystery.
17. *Iciest Sin, The* **(Mysterious, 1990)** The murder of blackmailer Dolly Durawala is witnessed by Ghote, who doesn't want to reveal the murderer.
18. *Cheating Death* **(Mysterious, 1994)** After a final exam paper is circulated throughout Oceanic College prior to the exam, the prime suspect winds up in a coma after a suicide or a murder attempt.

19. *Doing Wrong* **(Penzler, 1994)** Veteran politician Mrs. Shoba Popatkar is murdered after returning from a trip to the holy city of Banares.

20. *Asking Questions* **(St. Martin's, 1997)** An experimental drug made from snake venom has found its way to Bombay's film-celebrity community. Then a snake handler is found murdered in a locked room.

21. *Bribery, Corruption Also* **(St. Martin's, 1999)** Ganesh travels to Calcutta with his wife, Protima, to inspect the "mansion" that she has inherited.

22. *Breaking and Entering* **(St. Martin's, 2001)** As if domestic problems and his reassignment from a high-profile murder case to a low-profile cat burglar case weren't enough, Ghote is bedeviled by the return of Swede Axel Svensson (from number 1).

II. Closer to home than Inspector Ghote is Greater Birchester's (England) Detective Chief Inspector Harriet Martens. Martens is professionally tough and privately vulnerable. So far there have been six novels in this series. Neither *The Bad Detective* (St. Martin's, 1998) nor *The Soft Detective* (St. Martin's, 1998) nor *The Good Detective* (Scribner, 1991) are about Martens.

1. *Hard Detective, The* **(St. Martin's, 2000)** Detective Chief Inspector Harriet Martens's "Stop the Rot" campaign in Greater Birchester has stirred up a maniac who is killing police officers.

2. *Detective in Love, A* **(St. Martin's, 2002)** While investigating the murder of tennis star Bubbles Xingara, Harriet falls heavily for a fellow officer.

3. *Detective under Fire, A* **(St. Martin's, 2004)** Martens has to conduct a delicate probe into a possible scandal in the Maximum Crimes Squad.

4. *Dreaming Detective, The* **(St. Martin's, 2005)** DNA plays a role in solving the murder of Kumara Mangalam, the Boy Preacher, who was strangled 30 years earlier in a Birchester hotel ballroom.

5. *Detective at Death's Door, A* **(St. Martin's, 2005)** Harriet is slipped a near fatal dose of aconite into her Campari soda and winds up in a hospital.

6. *One Man and His Bomb* **(St. Martin's, 2006)** Harriet is devastated when one of her twin sons is killed, and the other gravely injured, by a terrorist bomb.

Keillor, Garrison

"News from Lake Wobegon" was, for many listeners, their favorite part of Garrison Keillor's radio show for Minnesota Public Radio, *A Prairie Home Companion*. Keillor's tales about the fictional town of Lake Wobegon, based on Anoka, Minnesota, his hometown, were suffused with his special brand of dry humor and also appealed to Americans who viewed small-town life of the past with nostalgia. Keillor quit *A Prairie Home Companion* to concentrate on writing. His first two Lake Wobegon books, *Lake Wobegon Days* and *Leaving Home*, are primarily collections of short stories and reworked radio sketches. *Wobegon Boy* and *Lake Wobegon Summer* are quasi-autobiographical novels. A third novel, *Pontoon*, was published in September 2007. *News from Lake Wobegon* (1982) and *More News from Lake Wobegon* (1988) are cassettes derived from the radio broadcasts by Minnesota Public Radio. *Love Me* (Viking, 2003) is an autobiographical novel not set in Lake Wobegon. *A Prairie Home Companion* (2005) is a fictional movie scripted by Keillor. *In Search of Lake Wobegon* (Viking, 2001) is a nonfiction book with photos.

1. *Lake Wobegon Days* **(Viking, 1985)** A collection of short stories relating the history of Lake Wobegon, Minnesota, from its beginnings to the present.

2. *Leaving Home* **(Viking, 1987)** More Lake Wobegon tales, edited versions of monologues from the last months of *A Prairie Home Companion*.

3. *Wobegon Boy* **(Viking, 1997)** John Tollefson, suffering from a midlife crisis, leaves Lake Wobegon, and takes a job at a radio station in a college town in upstate New York.

4. *Lake Wobegon Summer 1956* **(Viking, 2001)** Gary is a 14-year-old-boy trying to come to terms with coming-of-age and his life in rural Minnesota.

5. *Pontoon: A Lake Wobegon Novel* **(Viking, 2007)** After 82-year-old Evelyn Peterson dies, her secret life of romance and adventure is revealed. Her daughter, Barbara, plans to carry out her mother's wishes for a cremation ceremony involving a bowling ball filled with her ashes.

Kellerman, Faye

Faye Kellerman, wife of mystery writer Jonathan Kellerman (q.v.), is also the author of a successful mystery series. Homicide detective for the Los Angeles Police Department Peter Decker and Orthodox Jewish widow Rina Lazarus meet in the first novel, become a romantic and sleuthing pair, marry (after he has converted), and start a family. Full of Jewish lore, complicated plots, and sympathetic characters.

1. *Ritual Bath, The* **(Arbor House, 1986)** Rina Lazarus volunteers to help police in their investigation when a woman is raped at the ritual bath of the Orthodox Jewish community where she lives.

2. *Sacred and Profane* **(Arbor House, 1987)** Peter Decker uncovers a pornography ring that caters to the rich and powerful while investigating the murder of two girls.

3. *Milk and Honey* **(Morrow, 1990)** Decker finds a two-year-old girl in blood-soaked pajamas playing on a swing set in a housing development.

4. *Day of Atonement* **(Morrow, 1991)** Newlyweds Peter and Rina travel to the Brooklyn community in which the families of Rina and her late husband reside.

5. *False Prophet* **(Morrow, 1992)** Lilah Brecht, health-club owner and daughter of a movie starlet, is a probable rape victim.

6. *Grievous Sin* **(Morrow, 1993)** Complications in the delivery room lead to surgery for Rina, and a baby disappears from the hospital nursery.

7. *Sanctuary* **(Morrow, 1994)** Peter and his partner Marge Dunn investigate the disappearance of diamond dealer Arik Yalom and his family.

8. *Justice* **(Morrow, 1995)** High school senior Chris Whitman is implicated when his former girlfriend is found dead the morning after the prom.

9. *Prayers for the Dead* **(Morrow, 1996)** There are plenty of suspects when heart surgeon, researcher, and Fundamentalist Christian Azor Sparks is murdered and mutilated.

10. *Serpent's Tooth* **(Morrow, 1997)** Former bartender Harlan Manz kills and wounds dozens of diners at a Los Angeles restaurant. But was Manz acting alone?

11. *Jupiter's Bones* **(Morrow, 1999)** The religious cult called the Order of the Rings of God has a serial killer in their midst.

12. *Stalker* **(Morrow, 2000)** Cindy, Decker's daughter from his first marriage, is now a cop despite his disapproval. A series of carjackings and a stalker complicate the father-daughter relationship.

13. *Forgotten, The* **(Morrow, 2001)** After Ernesto Golding confesses to defacing a synagogue, he and his therapist are both murdered.

14. *Stone Kiss* (**Warner, 2002**) Ephraim Lieber, brother-in-law of Peter's half brother, has been murdered in a Manhattan hotel, and Ephraim's five-year-old niece is missing.

15. *Street Dreams* (**Warner, 2003**) Cindy Decker takes center stage again when she finds an abandoned baby in a dumpster and sets out to find the baby's developmentally disabled mother.

16. *Garden of Eden and Other Criminal Delights, The* (**Warner, 2006**) Collection of 17 short stories and essays, with two new Decker/Lazarus tales.

17. *Capital Crimes* (**Ballantine, 2006**) Two novellas, one an Alex Delaware tale by Jonathan Kellerman, the other Faye's *My Sister's Keeper*, in which Peter Decker has an extended cameo role in the investigation of the murder of Davida Grayson, an activist lesbian California state representative. Faye and Jonathan published a pair of nonseries novellas, *Double Homicide* (Warner, 2004).

18. *Burnt House, The* (**Morrow, 2007**) After a commuter airplane crashes into an apartment building shortly after takeoff from Burbank Airport, Decker and his team investigate what many fear was a terrorist attack.

Kellerman, Jonathan

Jonathan Kellerman, husband of mystery writer Faye Kellerman (q.v.), is also the author of a successful mystery series. Kellerman, a child psychologist and author of books on child psychology, writes a series about child psychologist Alex Delaware, who, encouraged by his gay friend Milo Sturgis from the Los Angeles Police Department, goes beyond counseling to ferreting out the crimes that may have caused the child's problems. An up-and-down relationship with sometime lover Robin Castagna adds to the interest. The series is popular with readers and critics alike for its psychological lore, interesting characters, and atmospheric plots. *The Conspiracy Club* (Ballantine, 2003), Kellerman's latest, is currently a stand-alone mystery but may be connected with the Delaware series in the future, as was *The Butcher's Theater*. Omnibuses include *The Jonathan Kellerman Omnibus* (Little, Brown, 1996; numbers 9 and 11); *The First Alex Delaware Omnibus* (Time-Warner, 2001; numbers 1 and 2); *Two Complete (Alex Delaware) Novels* (Wings, 2003; numbers 8 and 9); and *Blood Test/When the Bough Breaks/Over the Edge* (New American Library, 1990; numbers 1, 2, and 3).

1. *When the Bough Breaks* (**Atheneum, 1985**) Psychologist Alex Delaware turns detective when an interview with a young murder witness reveals a ring of child molesters. Variant title: *Shrunken Heads*.

2. *Blood Test* (**Atheneum, 1986**) Dr. Delaware is called in to evaluate the case of a young leukemia patient whose parents want to discontinue chemotherapy.

3. *Over the Edge* (**Atheneum, 1987**) Former patient Jamey Cadmus is accused of the "Lavender Slashings," a series of grisly homosexual murders.

4. *Butcher's Theater, The* (**Bantam, 1988**) Yemenite Israeli police inspector Daniel Sharavi is on the trail of a serial killer who is attracted to Arab women. Sharavi has an encore in number 13.

5. *Silent Partner* (**Bantam, 1989**) Alex suffers feelings of guilt when former lover Sharon Ranson commits suicide after he has decided against seeing her again.

6. *Time Bomb* (**Bantam, 1990**) Delaware is called upon to deal with the trauma of elementary school-children when a sniper is killed in their midst during lunch recess.

7. *Private Eyes* (**Bantam, 1992**) Former patient Melissa Dickinson tells Alex of her concerns about leaving her agoraphobic mother when the former lover who disfigured her is back in town.

8. *Devil's Waltz* (**Bantam, 1993**) Dr. Delaware is called in for consultation about the mysterious ailments afflicting 21-month-old Cassie Jones.

9. *Bad Love* (**Bantam, 1994**) Alex is the target of a series of ominous threats, including the tape of a child's voice repeating the phrase "bad love" over and over again.

10. *Self-Defense* (**Bantam, 1995**) Lucy Lowell is beset by a recurring nightmare in which she, as a youngster, watches three men bury a woman in the woods.

11. *Web, The* (**Bantam, 1995**) Alex, guitar-making lover Robin Castagna, and Spike, their French bulldog, leave for a four-month stay on the Pacific island of Aruk.

12. *Clinic, The* (**Bantam, 1996**) When best-selling psycho-pop author Hope Devane is murdered, the LAPD, after three months of frustration, hands the case over to Lieutenant Milo Sturgis who, in turn, calls upon his friend Alex Delaware.

13. *Survival of the Fittest* (**Bantam, 1997**) Milo seeks Alex's help in the murder case of Irit Carmeli, the deaf, slightly developmentally disabled teenage daughter of an Israeli diplomat. Daniel Sharavi, Israeli detective, and protagonist of the non-Delaware mystery *The Butcher's Theater* (Bantam, 1988) plays a key role in this story.

14. *Billy Straight* (**Random House, 1999**) Alex Delaware puts in only a brief appearance at the end of this mystery wherein 12-year-old homeless kid Billy Straight witnesses a murder in LA's Griffith Park. Homicide detectives Petra Connor (who appears in other Delaware mysteries) and Stu Bishop are the investigators here.

15. *Monster* (**Random House, 1999**) Alex and Milo work together again to untangle some grisly unsolved murders, including that of Claire Argent, a doctor at Starkweather Hospital for the Criminally Insane, and of an aspiring actor whose body has been sawn in half.

16. *Dr. Death* (**Random House, 2000**) Dr. Eldon Mate, a Dr. Kevorkian type, is himself found dead by two joggers and their dog on a high road above Los Angeles. Variant title: *Doctor Death*.

17. *Flesh and Blood* (**Random House, 2001**) Alex investigates the murder of Lauren Teague, a former patient whose checkered career has lead to her murder and disposal in a dumpster.

18. *Murder Book, The* (**Ballantine, 2002**) Milo accepts what seems to be an invitation to reopen the unsolved 20-year-old murder case of Janie Ingalls, a Hollywood High sophomore.

19. *Cold Heart, A* (**Ballantine, 2003**) Alex, Milo, and Petra Connor work together on a series of seemingly unconnected slayings of artists who were on the verge of breakthroughs in their careers.

20. *Therapy* (**Ballantine, 2004**) Alex and Milo are having dinner together when Milo is called to a nearby double homicide in a Mustang convertible.

21. *Twisted* (**Ballantine, 2004**) Petra Connor takes center stage as she investigates a seemingly random drive-by shooting that took the lives of four teenagers.

22. *Rage* (**Ballantine, 2005**) A shocking crime from the past is relived as Rand Duchay, survivor of a pair of teenagers who murdered a younger child, asks to talk again with Alex Delaware.

23. *Gone* (**Ballantine, 2006**) Aspiring actress Michaela Brand turns up dead after she and fellow acting student Dylan Meserve fake their abduction.

24. *Capital Crimes* (**Ballantine, 2006**) A pair of novellas, *My Sister's Keeper*, by Faye Kellerman (q.v.), and *Music City Breakdown*, in which Alex Delaware aids Nashville detectives probing the murder of recording artist Jack Jeffries. *Double Homicide* (Warner, 2004) is a pair of nonseries novellas by Faye and Jonathan.

25. *Obsession* (**Ballantine, 2007**) Teenager Tanya Bigelow, a former patient of Delaware, consults Alex because her late aunt Patty had conveyed a cryptic message to her, apparently confessing to a crime.

26. *Compulsion* (Ballantine, 2008) The perpetrator of several murders is using expensive black automobiles while committing his crimes.

Kelly, Susan

Susan Kelly, American author of the Liz Conners mystery series, is not to be confused with Susan Kelly (q.v.), British author of the Hope and Trevellyan and Summers mystery series. True-crime writer Liz Conners and her lover, Cambridge, Massachusetts, police detective Jack Lingemann, are partners in crime-solving in a gritty, suspenseful, violent series. Kelly, herself a true-crime writer, has authored *The Boston Stranglers* (Carol, 1995).

1. *Gemini Man, The* (Walker, 1985) Liz Conners sees a blood-soaked man flee the apartment of a slain female Harvard graduate student.
2. *Summertime Soldiers, The* (Walker, 1986) A group called the People's Revolutionary Cadre has resurfaced after 15 years and is killing people involved with the defense industry.
3. *Trail of the Dragon* (Walker, 1988) Liz is asked to look into the sudden disappearance of a woman requiring treatment for brain cancer.
4. *Until Proven Innocent* (Villard, 1990) Jack Lingemann, Liz's lover, is facing a battery of charges ranging from illegal wiretapping to rape and murder.
5. *And Soon I'll Come to Kill You* (Villard, 1991) After Liz gets a series of anonymous threats in the mail Jack convinces her to move in with him.
6. *Out of the Darkness* (Villard, 1992) Liz joins forces with author Griffin Marcus to research a book about the unsolved serial murders of seven young women found along the banks of the Merrimack River.

Kelly, Susan (2)

I. British author Susan Kelly is not to be confused with Susan Kelly (q.v.), American author of the Liz Conners mystery series. English computer expert and businesswoman Alison Hope and detective Nick Trevellyan are lovers and partners in sleuthing. Most of the action takes place in the village of Little Hopford in England's Hop Valley in this series blending mystery, romance, and humor.

1. *Hope against Hope* (Scribner, 1991) Alison Hope is the prime suspect in the murder of her business partner, but Detective Inspector Nick Trevellyan, who is smitten with her, looks for other suspects.
2. *Time of Hope* (Scribner, 1992) Promiscuous 19-year-old Frisco Carstairs is murdered, prompting suspicions against Dot Lawson, who strongly objected to her son's plan to marry Frisco.
3. *Hope Will Answer* (Scribner, 1993) Hope has gone incognito to London to unmask a malevolent computer hacker, while Nick searches for a rapist in the village of Hopbridge.
4. *Kid's Stuff* (Scribner, 1994) The relationship between Alison and Nick develops complications as Nick investigates the murder of child pornographer Arturo Bottone.
5. *Death Is Sweet* (Constable [UK], 1996) Nick Trevellyan investigates the suspicious drowning of a socialite and ex-tennis pro at a health club where friends of his are members. Not published in the United States.

II. Detective Superintendent Gregory Summers of the Newbury (England) police presents a rather bland exterior, but he is actually a complex fellow, and the cases he gets involved with can be quite tangled and nasty. Distributed in the United States by International Publishers Marketing.

1. *Lone Traveller, The* (Allison & Busby [UK], 2000) The annual summer solstice fair in Hungerford attracts many locals, Gypsies, and New Agers. Then a missing local child turns up dead, and a Gypsy youth is blamed.
2. *Killing the Fatted Calf* (Allison & Busby [UK], 2001) Summers is working with the National Crime Squad on Operation Cuckoo, which aims to break an immigrant smuggling ring. The main plot, however, concerns Elise Weissmann and Anthony, the son she abandoned 30 years before.
3. *Little Girl Lost* (Allison & Busby [UK], 2002) Summers and new chief inspector Megan Davies investigate the abduction of a child by her social worker.
4. *In Cold Blood* (Allison & Busby [UK], 2003) Eminent defense lawyer Sir John Hathaway has retired to the small village of Lambourn after successfully defending Graham Scobie on a murder charge. Now, inexplicably, Scobie seems to be harassing Hathaway.
5. *Death of a Ghost* (Allison & Busby [UK], 2005) Gillian Lestrange, who is ghostwriting the memoirs of retired spy Vinnie Latham, is found dead in a cottage owned by Vinnie.
6. *Disguise for Death, A* (Allison & Busby [UK], 2005) A complex case involving Liam Sullivan, former IRA terrorist. After finishing his term for his part in the Windsor bombing of 1981 (which killed six people), Liam has written a best-selling autobiography.
7. *Murder on the Dancefloor* (Allison & Busby [UK], 2007) Entrium Trilenium, aka Entry, a lethal new drug, is being hawked in the nightclubs around Newbury.

Kelton, Elmer

I. Texas native Elmer Kelton has won every important award to be given a writer of westerns, including the Western Heritage Award and the Spur Award of the Western Writers of America. Kelton has brought the genre into new territory, presenting a more realistic view of what people actually said and did. Many of Kelton's 40-plus novels are set in the present, but all of his series novels are set in the past. This pair is set in the period shortly after the American Civil War. The intertwining lives of several characters, including Confederate veteran Jeff Layne and Comanche warrior Crow Feather, are delineated as they try to make sense out of a changing world.

1. *Slaughter* (Doubleday, 1992) On the Great Plains shortly after the Civil War, Whites pursue buffalo for profit, while the Indians try to preserve their way of life.
2. *Far Canyon* (Doubleday, 1994) Jeff Layne's ranch has been given to his old enemy by the government, while Crow Feather finds life on the reservation degrading and demeaning.

II. The trio of novels featuring Hewey Calloway are a good-natured look at West Texas country life in the late 1800s and early 1900s. Hewey wants to be a cowboy wandering the open range, but the open range is slowly being eroded by "progress." Number 2 finds Hewey in 1910 older and sadder, mourning his lost love, his advancing age, and insisting that automobiles are a passing fad. The third novel is a prequel set in 1889. *The Good Old Boys* was the basis for a 1995 TV miniseries starring Tommy Lee Jones and Sissy Spacek.

1. *Six Bits a Day* (Forge, 2005) In a prequel set in 1889, Hewey and his younger brother, Walter, get mistaken for rustlers and almost

lynched and then hire on with C. C. Tarpley's cattle ranch for six bits (seventy-five cents) a day.

2. *Good Old Boys, The* (Doubleday, 1978) Hewey Calloway and his friends and neighbors try to resist the onset of progress and the erosion of the West Texas range around the turn of the 20th century.

3. *Smiling Country, The* (Forge, 1998) In 1910 Hewey is being increasingly beset by signs of "progress" and of his increasing age, mourning the old days and his lost love, Spring Renfro.

III. A third series is about the early days of the Texas Rangers, from the 1840s to the 1870s. The novels follow the fortunes of red-haired Rusty Shannon, former captive of the Comanches, as he grows up and observes the changing fortunes of the Texas Rangers before, during, and after the Civil War, when they represent just about the only "law" to be had in Texas. Master storyteller Kelton offers the right blend of action, romance, humor, suspense, and historical realism. If you haven't read westerns and would like to try them, this is a good place to begin. *Lone Star Rising* (Forge, 2003) is an omnibus volume containing numbers 1, 2, and 3. *Ranger's Law* (Forge, 2006) contains numbers 4, 5, and 6.

1. *Buckskin Line, The* (Forge, 1999) After his family is massacred by Indians, young Rusty is adopted by Comanches and subsequently by the Shannon family. Set in the 1840s.

2. *Badger Boy* (Forge, 2001) After leaving the Rangers in 1865 to return to his farm, Rusty finds his sweetheart married to someone else and his part of Texas in a state of near anarchy.

3. *Way of the Coyote, The* (Forge, 2001) Rusty and Andy Pickard, the Comanche captive whom Rusty has adopted, have to deal with carpetbaggers, Indian raids, old enemies, and corrupt lawmen.

4. *Ranger's Trail* (Forge, 2002) In 1874 Rusty hopes to settle down on his farm in South Texas and marry sweetheart Josie Monahan. The no-good, bank-robbing Bascom clan won't leave him in peace, however.

5. *Texas Vendetta* (Forge, 2003) Finds the Rangers in the middle of a bloody family feud between the Landon and Hopper clans.

6. *Jericho's Road* (Forge, 2004) Andy Pickard is assigned to an understaffed Ranger company along the Nueces Strip, a bit of desert fought over by Mexican rancher Guadalupe Chavez and Texas land baron Jericho Jackson.

7. *Hard Trail to Follow* (Forge, 2008) When the local sheriff, Tom Blessing, is murdered during a jailbreak, former Texas Ranger Andy Pickard drops his plow and picks up his guns again.

IV. The Sons of Texas trilogy, originally published under the pseudonym "Tom Early," is set in Mexican-ruled Texas from 1816 to 1836. The Lewis family from Tennessee provides the main characters in this series, in which fictional characters interact with historical people such as Stephen F. Austin, Sam Houston, and Davy Crockett.

1. *Sons of Texas* (Berkley, 1989) In 1816 the patriarch of the Lewis clan leaves his Tennessee farm to join a group planning to capture Texas wild horses. Reprinted by Forge in 2005.

2. *Raiders, The* (Berkley, 1989) In 1825–1826, Michael and Andrew Lewis, owning adjacent farms in Mexican territory, are trying to settle as legal immigrants, but a number of things interfere, including the farcical "Fredonian Rebellion." Reprinted by Forge in 2006.

3. *Rebels, The* (Berkley, 1989) The Lewis boys go off to fight in the battles at Velasco, the Alamo, and San Jacinto in the war for Texan independence, and some don't come home. Reprinted by Forge in 2007.

Kemal, Yaşar

I. Although Orhan Pamuk was awarded the Nobel Prize in 2006, Yaşar Kemal is still regarded by many critics as Turkey's greatest living writer. His novels and short stories about the harshness of Turkish peasant life are eloquent arguments for land reform and better treatment of the peasants. Kemal has been jailed often, and sometimes tortured, for his Socialist convictions. At the age of five he witnessed the murder of his father in a mosque. The Ince Memed series, which was published in four parts in Turkey, is represented by two novels translated into English. "Slim Memed" is a kind of Turkish Robin Hood who fights against the *aghas* (landowners) who exploit their peasants.

1. *Memed, My Hawk* (Pantheon, 1961) Young Memed flees his village and the cruel local *agha* who rules it for the freedom of the hills and life as a brigand. Translated from the Turkish by Edouard Roditi. Part 1 of *Ince Memed*, originally published in Turkey in 1955.

2. *They Burn the Thistles* (Morrow, 1977) Memed saves the village of Vavray from a greedy *agha*. Translated from the Turkish by Margaret Platon. Part 2 of *Ince Memed*, originally published in Turkey in 1955. English translation originally published in the United Kingdom in 1973.

II. *Dagin ote yuzu* ("Beyond the Mountain"), a three-part series featuring another peasant hero, "Long Ali," is more lyrical and less realistic than *Ince Memed*, but it also sympathetically delineates the harsh and exploited lives of the peasants. Life in the village is seen through the eyes of its residents, including the tyrant Muhatar Sefer and the activist and "saint" Tashbash.

1. *Wind from the Plain, The* (Dodd, 1969) Long Ali, his wife, and his mother make a hard journey through the mountains to a place where Ali hopes to find a job. Originally published in 1960 as *Ortadirek*. Translated from the Turkish by Thilda Kemal. English translation originally published in the United Kingdom in 1963.

2. *Iron Earth, Copper Sky* (Morrow, 1979) A small cotton harvest threatens the villagers of Yalak. Originally published in Turkey in 1963 as *Yer demir, gök bakir*. Translated from the Turkish by Thilda Kemal. English translation originally published in the United Kingdom in 1974.

3. *Undying Grass, The* (Morrow, 1978) The old woman Meryemdje is like "the undying grass" in her will to survive. Originally published in Turkey in 1968 as *Olmez ofu*. Translated from the Turkish by Thilda Kemal. English translation originally published in the United Kingdom in 1977.

Kemelman, Harry

Because Rabbi David Small used Talmudic logic to solve mysteries, his cases were simultaneously entertaining and instructive. In his hometown of Barnards Crossing, Massachusetts, Police Chief Lanigan often requested the rabbi's help, but even abroad in Israel, Small had a tendency to walk into situations that need his special brand of sorting out. Kemelman (d. 1996) aged his characters and showed the rabbi's family and congregation growing throughout the series.

Stuart Margolin played Rabbi Small and Art Carney played Police Chief Lanigan in *Lanigan's Rabbi*, the television version of *Friday the Rabbi Slept Late*, the pilot for a short-lived series. *Weekend with the Rabbi* is an omnibus volume containing numbers 1, 2, 3, and 4.

1. *Friday the Rabbi Slept Late* **(Crown, 1964)** When Rabbi Small is implicated in the murder of a young girl, he helps the town's Catholic police chief find the real murderer.
2. *Saturday the Rabbi Went Hungry* **(Crown, 1966)** A difficult congregational dilemma hangs on whether or not a death was suicide. The rabbi and his wife, Miriam, are expecting their first child.
3. *Sunday the Rabbi Stayed Home* **(Putnam, 1969)** During Passover, Rabbi Small finds himself deeply involved in the hang-ups of the younger generation who are home from college.
4. *Monday the Rabbi Took Off* **(Putnam, 1972)** In Jerusalem, Rabbi Small gets entangled in the mysterious doings of a TV commentator and some Arab militants.
5. *Tuesday the Rabbi Saw Red* **(Fields, 1973)** A bomb goes off in the dean's office at Windermere Christian College.
6. *Wednesday the Rabbi Got Wet* **(Morrow, 1976)** A young hippie is the suspect in this case of switched pills.
7. *Thursday the Rabbi Walked Out* **(Morrow, 1976)** There are too many suspects in the murder of nasty anti-Semite Ellsworth Jordan.
8. *Conversations with Rabbi Small* **(Morrow, 1981)** This book may disappoint mystery fans, but it offers plenty of Rabbi Small's theology as he counsels a young couple on marriage and conversion.
9. *Someday the Rabbi Will Leave* **(Morrow, 1985)** Rabbi Small is concerned about the arrest of a young neighbor for a hit-and-run killing.
10. *One Fine Day the Rabbi Bought a Cross* **(Morrow, 1987)** While on vacation in Jerusalem, Rabbi Small gets involved in a case concerning a Jewish fundamentalist charged with killing an Arab sympathizer.
11. *Day the Rabbi Resigned, The* **(Fawcett, 1992)** Rabbi Small is considering retirement, while Chief Lanigan is considering that the automobile death of a college professor was homicide.
12. *That Day the Rabbi Left Town* **(Fawcett, 1996)** Rabbi Small resigns from Barnard's Crossing Temple to start a Judaic studies department at Windermere College in Boston. Then his successor becomes a murder suspect.

Kemprecos, Paul

Aristotle "Soc" Socarides, commercial fisherman and off-season private investigator, practices both professions on Cape Cod, Massachusetts, in a series of well-plotted mysteries with a likable protagonist and nice regional ambience. Kemprecos is a veteran Cape Cod newspaperman.

1. *Cool Blue Tomb* **(Bantam, 1991)** Soc gets involved with a $50 million salvage operation and a woman with a black Porsche.
2. *Neptune's Eye* **(Bantam, 1991)** A sunken German sub, remote-controlled undersea vehicles, a missing girl, a sinister millionaire, and a caustic scientist are the ingredients in this mystery chowder.
3. *Death in Deep Water* **(Doubleday, 1992)** Soc goes underwater at Oceanus, the marine theme park, to find out whether or not killer whale Rocky is indeed a man killer.
4. *Feeding Frenzy* **(Doubleday, 1993)** Possible shark attacks, excessive official scrutiny of a summer camp, and a real-estate agent's interest in some valuable beachfront property may be connected.
5. *Mayflower Murder, The* **(St. Martin's, 1996)** Soc's Vietnam buddy, John Flagg, hires Soc to prove the innocence of Joe Quint, Narraganset advocate of Native American causes when a watchman is murdered at Plimoth Plantation.

6. *Bluefin Blues* **(St. Martin's, 1997)** Socarides is hired long-distance (from Japan) when a Japanese fish buyer is found fatally harpooned on a stolen tuna boat.

Kennealy, Jerry

I. The adventures of Nick Polo, San Francisco private eye, are based on Kennealy's 28 years of experience as a private investigator, but Nick isn't an autobiographical character. Nick, unlike his creator, isn't above bending the law with an occasional phone tap or jimmied lock, but he isn't really a hard-boiled type. These are fast-moving mysteries with a light tough and an interesting supporting cast. Kennealy has published several mystery novels since 1997, but none of them have featured Nick Polo.

1. *Polo Solo* **(St. Martin's, 1987)** Nick Polo is offered his freedom from prison and a private investigator's license if he tracks down the blackmailers who have embarrassing photos of San Francisco's mayor.
2. *Polo, Anyone?* **(St. Martin's, 1988)** Polo investigates a series of unfriendly card games conducted by deceitful bankers.
3. *Polo's Ponies* **(St. Martin's, 1988)** Nick confronts the masterminds of a racetrack scam and multiple murder.
4. *Polo in the Rough* **(St. Martin's, 1989)** Polo works as a bodyguard for an author who writes controversial exposes of government corruption.
5. *Polo's Wild Card* **(St. Martin's, 1990)** Nick's winning poker play at a swank charity bash is interrupted by the theft of some valuable paintings.
6. *Green with Envy* **(St. Martin's, 1991)** Polo is wrongfully accused of planting a bug on the telephone of a client of a fellow private eye.
7. *Special Delivery* **(St. Martin's, 1992)** Millionaire friend Raymond Singh's assignment takes Nick to London, a child prostitution ring, and a burning yacht.
8. *Vintage Polo* **(St. Martin's, 1993)** Somebody is sabotaging Angelo Baroni's vineyards, and it seems to be an inside job.
9. *Beggar's Choice* **(St. Martin's, 1994)** Asked by a street person to trace a license plate, Nick's interest is piqued when the street person is killed by a hit-and-run driver.
10. *All That Glitters* **(St. Martin's, 1997)** A Russian antiques dealer has hired Polo to locate Anna, the holder of a valuable Mongol bauble originally worn by Ogodai Khan.

II. A new series features Carroll Quint, entertainment critic for the *San Francisco Bulletin*. Quint, the son of a former Hollywood actress, figures in a series of suspenseful, but lighthearted plots.

1. *Jigsaw* **(St. Martin's, 2007)** A serial killer calling himself Thanatos, who e-mails Carroll Quint clues with an Alfred Hitchcock angle, is hitting Quint's acquaintances.
2. *Still Shot* **(St. Martin's, 2008)** Quint's editor, Katherine "the Great" Parkham, is concerned about the purchase of the *San Francisco Bulletin* by media magnate Sir Charles Talbot.

Kennealy (-Morrison), Patricia

Patricia Kennealy, who was married briefly to the late Jim Morrison (see *Strange Days: My Life with and without Jim Morrison*, Dutton, 1992), is the author of the Keltiad, a science-fiction and fantasy cycle based on Celtic myth and legend. The planet Keltia is the scene of most of the action, although there some earthly parallels, such as the Arthurian legend retold in numbers 5, 6, and 7. Aeron Aoibhell,

Princess of the Name, is featured in numbers 2 and 3, while number 1 is a prequel.

1. *Deer's Cry, The* (Harper, 1998) A rewriting of the Brendan legend as the Danaan flee Ireland and Christian oppression.
2. *Silver Branch, The* (New American Library, 1988) Aeron, Princess of the Name, undergoes the rigors of training to be ready to assume the role of High Queen.
3. *Copper Crown, The* (Bluejay, 1984) High Queen Aeron offers friendship to Federacy Captain Theo Haruko and proposes an alliance with the planet Earth.
4. *Throne of Scone, The* (Bluejay, 1986) A cryptic poem by the ancient bard Taliesin holds the key to the burial place of a legendary king.
5. *Hawk's Gray Feather, The* (New American Library, 1990) Arthur Pendriac, his cousin Gweniver, and the young bard Taliesin are the core of a resistance movement against a Druid theocracy.
6. *Oak above the Kings, The* (Roc, 1994) In volume 2 of the *Tales of Arthur*, Arthur, the heir to the last lawful king, triumphs over the tyranny of the Archdruid Ederyn.
7. *Hedge of Mist, The* (Harper, 1996) Volume 3 of the *Tales of Arthur*. A search for a magic grail, an internecine struggle for the crown, Gweniver's disgrace, and the death of Arthur are retold by Taliesin, chief bard of the realm.
8. *Blackmantle* (Harper, 1997) Athyn Cahanagh, known as Blackmantle because of the cloak she wears in battle, frees Keltia from the oppressive Firvolgi.

Kennedy, William

Albany, New York's state capital, has been put on the literary map by journalist, English professor, and novelist William Kennedy in his Albany cycle, a series of novels covering the history of Albany as told through the lives of the Phelan-Quinn family. The cycle is very well written, funny at times, moving at times, and full of Albany's crime and politics. *Ironweed* won both the Pulitzer Prize and the National Book Critics Circle Award for best novel and was made into a movie starring Jack Nicholson and Meryl Streep. Kennedy has also written a nonfiction delineation of Albany: *O, Albany! An Urban Tapestry* (Viking, 1983). *An Albany Trio* (Penguin, 1996) contains numbers 4, 5, and 6. *Albany Cycle, Book 1* (Scribner, 2002) contains numbers 5, 6, and 8. *Albany Cycle, Book 2* (Scribner, 2002) contains numbers 1, 2, and 4.

1. *Quinn's Book* (Viking, 1988) Daniel Quinn, America's foremost Civil War reporter, recalls his adolescent years and his 15-year pursuit of theater star Maud Fallon (1849–1864).
2. *Flaming Corsage, The* (Viking, 1996) Playwright Edward Daugherty rises above his Irish Catholic beginnings in North Albany, and marries patrician Katrina Taylor. Francis Phelan of *Ironweed* plays a role here.
3. *Ink Truck, The* (Dial, 1969) An Albany newspaper strike in the 1920s as seen through the eyes of a columnist named Bailey. Not always regarded as part of the Albany cycle.
4. *Legs* (Coward, 1975) The rise and fall of real-life gangster Jack "Legs" Diamond in the 1920s and 1930s.
5. *Billy Phelan's Greatest Game* (Viking, 1978) Small-time hustler Billy Phelan resists attempts to turn him into an informer. Takes place in 1938.
6. *Ironweed* (Viking, 1983) Francis Phelan, Billy's father, former major league baseball player, and current skid row bum, returns to Albany to exorcise his demons. Set around 1938.
7. *Roscoe* (Viking, 2001) Roscoe Owens Conway, Albany "fixer" for the New York State Democratic Party, is facing (on V-J Day,

1945) a threat from the New York's Republican governor (Thomas E. Dewey) and internal strife within the Democratic "machine." Not always regarded as part of the Albany cycle.
8. *Very Old Bones* (Viking, 1992) Elderly scapegrace artist Peter Phelan unveils a series of paintings based on a 19th-century family tragedy. Set in 1958.

Kenney, Susan

I. A pair of novels by Colby College (Maine) professor Susan Kenney relates stages in the life of Sara Boyd, a young Vermonter who is forced to face the death and insanity of loved ones more than once. Well-delineated portraits of marriage and family relationships.

1. *In Another Country* (Viking, 1984) Sara relates the story of her early life, her father's premature death, her mother's insanity, and her husband's battle with cancer.
2. *Sailing* (Viking, 1988) At Sara's insistence, her husband, Phil, buys a sailboat and becomes obsessed with sailing.

II. Kenney has also written a trio of novels about Roz Howard, a young English professor at Vassar, who gets involved in mysteries, which she solves with the aid of her Scottish lover, Alan Stewart.

1. *Garden of Malice* (Scribner, 1983) Roz Howard is hired by Giles Montfort-Snow to help edit the diaries and letters of his mother Viola, a famous poet, essayist, and gardener.
2. *Graves in Academe* (Viking, 1985) Roz Howard's English course syllabus is being used as a how-to-manual for murder at Canterbury College. Not to be confused with Richard Mitchell's nonfiction manifesto against American academic practices, *The Graves of Academe* (Little, Brown, 1981).
3. *One Fell Sloop* (Viking, 1990) While sailing the Maine coast Roz and Alan Stewart discover a corpse on an uninhabited island.

Kent, Alexander

PSEUDONYM OF Douglas Reeman

Just one year after C. S. Forester's (q.v.) last Hornblower story was published posthumously, Alexander Kent's Richard Bolitho made his debut in *To Glory We Steer* and was immediately accepted by readers of historical naval adventure as a worthy successor to Hornblower. Bolitho's service in the British navy begins earlier than Hornblower's—young Richard is only 12 years old when he goes to sea in 1768—and so he sees action in the American Revolution. Eventually he becomes an admiral and Sir Richard before he dies, and the naval torch is carried on by his nephew Adam Bolitho into the post-Napoleonic era. Kent served in the Royal Navy during World War II and is a self-taught naval historian. Under his real name, Douglas Reeman (q.v.), he has written many modern sea stories, usually with a World War II background, and a historical series about the Royal Marines. Various omnibuses have been published in the United Kingdom, including *The Bolitho Omnibus* (Hutchinson, 1991), containing numbers 3, 4, and 5; *Captain Richard Bolitho, R.N.* (Hutchinson, 1978), containing numbers 5, 6, and 7; and *Bolitho* (Heinemann, 1993), containing numbers 9, 18, and 19.

1. *Richard Bolitho—Midshipman* (Putnam, 1975) In 1772 16-year-old Cornish midshipman Bolitho joins the crew of the *Gorgon*, whose mission is to investigate the slave trade off Africa's west coast. Variant title: *Midshipman Bolitho*.

2. *Midshipman Bolitho and the Avenger* (Putnam, 1978) Home from sea and on leave in Cornwall in 1773, Bolitho gets involved with smugglers and murder.

3. *Stand into Danger* (Putnam, 1981) Promoted to third lieutenant in 1774, Bolitho boards the frigate *Destiny*, sails to the Caribbean in search of lost gold, and experiences his first love.

4. *In Gallant Company* (Putnam, 1977) In 1777 Bolitho's seamanship meets the test of war aboard the *Trojan* as she prevents supplies from reaching Washington's rebel army.

5. *Sloop of War* (Putnam, 1972) In 1778 Bolitho gets his first command, the sloop of war *Sparrow*, patrolling the busy American coast until Cornwallis's surrender.

6. *To Glory We Steer* (Putnam, 1968) In 1782 Bolitho is assigned to the near-mutinous frigate *Phalarope* in the Caribbean and redeems the ship's reputation in battle against pirates.

7. *Command a King's Ship* (Putnam, 1973) In 1784 Captain Bolitho protects British interests aboard the frigate *Undine* in the Indian Ocean.

8. *Passage to Mutiny* (Putnam, 1970) In 1789 stories of the *Bounty* mutiny reach Bolitho as he faces danger and death in the South Seas.

9. *With All Dispatch* (Putnam, 1988) It is spring 1792, and Britain is enjoying a troubled peace. Variant title: *With All Despatch*.

10. *Form Line of Battle!* (Putnam, 1969) Captain Bolitho, in command of the *Hyperion* in 1793, joins Lord Hood's operations against French revolutionary forces.

11. *Enemy in Sight!* (Putnam, 1970) In 1794, still aboard the *Hyperion* on blockade duty of France, Bolitho copes with a superior officer determined to avoid battle.

12. *Flag Captain, The* (Putnam, 1971) In 1795 Bolitho serves as flag captain to a stubborn admiral in a squadron attempting to penetrate the Mediterranean.

13. *Signal—Close Action!* (Putnam, 1974) Promoted to commodore in 1798, Bolitho is in charge of a squadron assigned to intercept supplies for Napoléon.

14. *Inshore Squadron, The* (Putnam, 1979) During the battle of Copenhagen in 1800, Lord Nelson leads the British to victory. Rear Admiral Bolitho's wounds send him ashore, where he meets and falls in love with a cousin of his late wife.

15. *Tradition of Victory, A* (Putnam, 1982) In 1801 Bolitho and Belinda are separated on the eve of their wedding, and Bolitho is captured by the French.

16. *Success to the Brave* (Putnam, 1983) In 1802 Vice Admiral Bolitho sails on the man-of-war *Achates* to the Caribbean to return the island of San Felipe to the French.

17. *Colors Aloft!* (Putnam, 1986) In September 1803, Vice Admiral Bolitho takes command of a squadron of ships bound for active duty in the Mediterranean. Variant title: *Colours Aloft!*

18. *Honor This Day* (Putnam, 1988) In 1804, aboard his beloved *Hyperion*, Vice Admiral Bolitho is on the trail of the bullion-heavy treasure fleet of the Spanish king. Variant title: *Honour This Day*.

19. *Only Victor, The* (McBooks, 2000) In February 1806 Vice Admiral Bolitho is off the coast of southern Africa, supporting an expeditionary force against Dutch-held Capetown. Originally published in 1990.

20. *Beyond the Reef* (McBooks, 2000) In March 1808, as Napoléon holds Portugal and threatens Spain, Sir Richard Bolitho is dispatched to the Cape of Good Hope to set up a permanent naval base. Originally published in 1993.

21. *Darkening Sea, The* (McBooks, 2000) Returning safely to Britain after the capture of Martinique in 1809, Vice Admiral Sir Richard Bolitho enjoys only a brief respite ashore before he is ordered to the Indian Ocean. Originally published in 1993.

22. *For My Country's Freedom* (McBooks, 2000) In March 1811, Admiral Sir Richard Bolitho is once again summoned to London as war looms in North America. Originally published in 1995.

23. *Cross of St. George* (McBooks, 2001) In February 1813, as convoys from Canada and the Caribbean fall victim to Yankee privateers, Sir Richard Bolitho returns. Originally published in 1996.

24. *Sword of Honor* (McBooks, 2001) In March 1814 Sir Richard returns from a wearing campaign in North America and takes up a new command in Malta. His nephew Adam remains behind on the American coast as captain of a frigate. Originally published in 1998. Variant title: *Sword of Honour*.

25. *Second to None* (McBooks, 2001) In the aftermath of the Battle of Waterloo (1815), Adam Bolitho, grieving for his uncle Richard, sails the Mediterranean against pirates and slavers. Originally published in 1999.

26. *Relentless Pursuit* (McBooks, 2003) In 1815 Adam Bolitho takes the frigate *Unrivalled* to Sierra Leone to battle slavers. Originally published in 2001.

27. *Man of War* (McBooks, 2003) In 1817 Adam Bolitho takes command of the 74-gun *Athena* and sails to the Caribbean as flag captain to Vice Admiral Sir Graham Bethune.

28. *Band of Brothers* (McBooks, 2005) Returns to the early years of Midshipman Bolitho.

29. *Heart of Oak* (McBooks, 2007) In February 1818, Adam Bolitho feels lucky to be offered HMS *Onward*, a new 38-gun Frigate, as consort to the French Frigate *Nautilus* in North African waters.

Kenyon, Michael

I. Chief Inspector Henry Peckover of Scotland Yard is a Cockney who likes to write verse (or doggerel, according to the unappreciative). The "Bard of the Yard" and his partner, Jason Twitty, who is a Harrow-educated son of Jamaican parents, have a rather wild series of adventures peopled with some rather improbable characters, all related in a quip-a-minute style.

1. *Molehill File, The* (Coward, 1978) Dawn de Nuit, slain girlfriend of an Arab sheikh, may hold the key to the Molehill File, a vast set of records on fraud and graft. English title: *Deep Pocket*.

2. *Elgar Variation, The* (Doubleday, 1981) Sent to Dublin after an erring stockbroker, Peckover gets involved with Superintendent O'Malley of the Garda (series II) in a crusade to keep pornography out of Ireland. UK title: *Zigzag*.

3. *Man at the Wheel, The* (Doubleday, 1982) From his hospital bed Henry narrates a story about a reporter following a hot tip and four Arabs with a link to a right-wing evangelist. English title: *The God Squad Bod*.

4. *Free-Range Wife, A* (Doubleday, 1983) While on holiday in France, Peckover is enlisted by the French to interview two English-speaking women in regards to a murder case.

5. *Healthy Way to Die, A* (Doubleday, 1986) Peckover and Twitty go to the sumptuous Simpson's SuperSpa where there has been a large turnover of pounds (monetary, as well as fleshy).

6. *Peckover Holds the Baby* (Doubleday, 1988) Henry is sent to Belize to extradite convicted drug smuggler Vivian White and return him to a British jail.

7. *Kill the Butler!* (St. Martin's, 1993) Peckover impersonates a butler in the American home of wealthy hit-and-run victim Lou Langley.

8. *Peckover Joins the Choir* (St. Martin's, 1994) Peckover and Twitty join the Sealeigh Choral Society to nab the individual who has been stealing relics from foreign churches.

9. *Peckover and the Bog Man* (**St. Martin's, 1995**) Scottish jokes abound as pompous archaeologist Sir Gilbert Potter is fatally stabbed at the traditional Robert Burns supper in Inverballoch.

II. An earlier series set in Ireland featured Garda (police) Superintendent O'Malley. Like Peckover (with whom he shares *Zigzag*) O'Malley covered a lot of territory inside and outside of his native country in a series of wild and woolly adventures.

1. *100,000 Welcomes, The* (**Coward, 1970**) No annotation available.
2. *Shooting of Dan McGrew, The* (**McKay, 1975**) Kate Kennedy and Henry Butt have an accident-prone courtship in and around the Kilkelly Castle Hotel. Originally published in 1972.
3. *Sorry State, A* (**McKay, 1974**) Superintendent O'Malley finds himself on a plane journey to the Philippines.
4. *Elgar Variation, The (2)* (**Doubleday, 1981**) O'Malley and Peckover (see series I, above) find themselves teamed up in an antipornography crusade in Ireland. UK title: *Zigzag*.

Kerr, Katherine

I. Deverry, a fantasy world built from Celtic myth and legend, is a very convincing piece of world building, richly detailed and with believable characters. Planned as a trilogy, the series has expanded into three "acts" or "quartets" of four novels each, with a final 13th volume added. Numbers 1 through 4 are the Deverry Books; numbers 5 through 8 are called the Westlands; numbers 9 through 12 are called the Dragon Mage. Katherine Kerr, not to be confused with dramatist E. Katherine Kerr (*Reuben, Reuben*, etc.), was born in Cleveland of British parents.

1. *Daggerspell* (**Doubleday, 1986**) Sorcerer Nevynn, who once wronged a woman, cannot die until he has righted that wrong through several incarnations.
2. *Darkspell* (**Ballantine, 1987**) Nevynn, Rhodry, and Jill join forces to combat the evil sorcerers of Annwn.
3. *Bristling Wood, The* (**Doubleday, 1989**) Rhodry is kidnapped and sold into slavery to lure Nevynn into a trap. UK title: *Dawnspell: The Bristling Wood*.
4. *Dragon Revenant, The* (**Doubleday, 1990**) Nevynn's vow is finally fulfilled as Jill travels across the ocean to rescue Rhodry. UK title: *Dragonspell: The Southern Sea*.
5. *Time of Exile, A* (**Doubleday, 1991**) Lord Rhodry Aberwyn's half-elven blood leads him on a quest to the elves' homeland.
6. *Time of Omens, A* (**Bantam, 1992**) Prince Rhodry and companions fight creatures of dark magic in action that takes place over three centuries.
7. *Days of Blood and Fire* (**Bantam, 1993**) A blind bard answers some of the questions of Jill and Rhodry, and Rhodry goes off on another perilous quest. UK title: *A Time of War*.
8. *Days of Air and Darkness* (**Bantam, 1994**) The city of Cenyan is under siege by a mixed army or humans and other beings under the spell of a dark goddess. UK title: *A Time of Justice*.
9. *Red Wyvern, The* (**Bantam, 1997**) Lilli, a young girl with potent if untrained magical powers, goes through coming-of-age, training, and survival in the midst of civil wars.
10. *Black Raven, The* (**Bantam, 1999**) Newly apprenticed Lilli fights with her untrained powers to save her beloved Prince Maryn from evil.
11. *Fire Dragon, The* (**Bantam, 2001**) A number of story lines in earlier novels in the series come to a climax. Raena's troublemaking in Cerr Cawnen comes to an end. Rhodry's strange "wyrd" is settled. Nevynn solves the riddle of the curse tablet.
12. *Gold Dragon, The* (**DAW, 2006**) Conclusion to the Dragon Mage series and book one of the Silver Wyrm. Neb, the scribe's son, and his brother Seth are sent to a desolate farm after a cholera epidemic has ravaged the city of TrevHael.
13. *Spirit Stone, The* (**DAW, 2007**) Book two of the Silver Wyrm. Horseskin raiders, inflamed by goddess Alshandra, are harrying the borders along the Westlands.

II. Kerr has also tried her hand at science fiction. A pair of science-fiction mystery novels is set in Polar City, the capital of Hagar, a small human-dominated republic uneasily situated between the giant alien consortia, the Interstellar Confederation and the Coreward Alliance.

1. *Polar City Blues* (**Bantam, 1990**) When an alien from the Interstellar Confederation is murdered, Polar City police chief Bates faces a very sticky situation.
2. *Polar City Nightmare* (**Millennium, 2000**) Coauthored with Kate Daniel. Blackmail and murder on two planets uncover an interstellar plot that threatens the precarious power balance between the Republic and the two alien confederations.

Keyes, Frances Parkinson

Mrs. Keyes's solid stories, frequently set against an interesting Louisiana background, had quite a large readership in the 1940s and 1950s. Today's readers will find themselves quickly absorbed in her felicitous blend of romance, history, and suspense. *Steamboat Gothic* (Messner, 1952) is perhaps her best-known novel. The pair of novels listed below tells of life in the fertile southwestern area of Louisiana where rice plantations flourished.

1. *Blue Camellia* (**Messner, 1957**) Brent Winslow and his wife and small daughter move from Illinois to Cajun country Louisiana in the 1880s.
2. *Victorine* (**Messner, 1958**) Brent's grandson Prosper is entangled in a murder that threatens his romance with the beautiful Victorine during the mid-1920s. UK title: *Gold Slippers*.

Kienzle, William X.

Father Robert Koesler is a priest in the Detroit archdiocese, editor of a Catholic weekly, reader of mysteries, and keen amateur sleuth. He bears some resemblance to his late creator, William X. Kienzle (d. 2001), onetime Detroit parish priest, former editor of a Catholic newspaper, and mystery writer. Unlike his creator, Father Bob remained as a priest until he retired near the end of the series. The Father Koesler stories are in the puzzle mystery tradition with an urban American setting and an undercurrent of social and religious commentary, as Catholics reacted to the changes and revelations of Vatican II. Donald Sutherland played Father Koesler in the 1987 movie version of *The Rosary Murders*. Other priest-detectives include Andrew Greeley's (q.v.) Blackie Ryan and Ralph McInerny's (q.v.) Father Dowling.

1. *Rosary Murders, The* (**Andrews, 1979**) Lieutenant Koznicki of the Detroit police enlists Father Koesler's aid in solving a series of murders of priests and nuns.
2. *Death Wears a Red Hat* (**Andrews, 1980**) A murderer is decapitating his victims and placing their heads on church statues.
3. *Mind over Murder* (**Andrews, 1981**) Tommy Thompson, head of the Roman Catholic matrimonial court in Detroit, is missing, but his revealing diary is published in the *Detroit News*.

4. *Assault with Intent* (Andrews, 1983) Father Koesler investigates an apparent plot to kill the priests in Detroit-area seminaries.
5. *Shadow of Death* (Andrews, 1983) An attempt is made on the life of Archbishop Boyle of Detroit, traveling to Rome for his investiture as Cardinal.
6. *Kill and Tell* (Andrews, 1984) Emma Hoffman drinks a poisoned Rob Roy cocktail intended for her husband, Frank, a Detroit automobile executive.
7. *Sudden Death* (Andrews, 1985) Hank "the Hun" Hunsinger, pro football star, is murdered and there is no lack of suspects.
8. *Deathbird* (Andrews, 1986) Father Koesler believes someone is trying to kill Sister Eileen, chief of a troubled inner-city Catholic hospital.
9. *Deadline for a Critic* (Andrews, 1987) Ridley Groendal, performing arts critic for the New York *Herald*, destroyed the careers of at least six people from the Detroit area.
10. *Marked for Murder* (Andrews, 1988) A man in clerical garb is ritually murdering prostitutes in Detroit's inner city.
11. *Eminence* (Andrews, 1989) A local monk is attracting media attention through his alleged miraculous cures.
12. *Masquerade* (Andrews, 1990) Televangelist Klaus Krieg is murdered at a mystery writers' conference, and several clergymen are among the suspects.
13. *Chameleon* (Andrews, 1991) Lieutenant Tully of the Detroit Police, a frequent associate, works with Father Koesler to unravel a series of murders in which clerics are targeted.
14. *Body Count* (Andrews, 1992) Hit-man Guido Vespa confesses to Father Koesler that he has murdered local priest Father Keating.
15. *Dead Wrong* (Andrews, 1992) Father Koesler gets involved in a 33-year-old murder case when millionaire Charles Nash asks him to intervene in his son's adulterous affair.
16. *Bishop as Pawn* (Andrews, 1994) When unpopular Auxiliary Bishop Ramon Diego is murdered, his aide, Father Don Carleson, is the prime suspect.
17. *Call No Man Father* (Andrews, 1995) The Pope's anticipated visit to Detroit sets in train elaborate security precautions and the murder of three priests.
18. *Requiem for Moses* (Andrews, 1996) Father Bob reluctantly agrees to hold a wake for nominal Jew Moe Green at the insistence of Moe's widow.
19. *Man Who Loved God, The* (Andrews, 1997) While Father Bob is on vacation, he is replaced by Father Zachary Tully (from Dallas), who is anxious to meet Detroit police lieutenant Alonzo Tully, a half brother he had never known.
20. *Greatest Evil, The* (Andrews, 1998) On the brink of retiring as pastor of St. Joseph's Parish, Father Bob attempts to explain the ultraconservative auxiliary bishop Vincent Delvecchio to Father Tully, his hand-picked replacement.
21. *No Greater Love* (Andrews, 1999) At the behest of Bishop McNiff, the retired Father Koesler takes up residence at the St. Joseph Major Seminary.
22. *Till Death* (Andrews, 2000) Lil Niedermier, lay principal of a parochial school, and Father Rick Casserly are carrying on a secret affair, which is complicated when former nun Dora Ricardo falls for Father Rick.
23. *Sacrifice, The* (Andrews, 2001) Prominent Episcopal priest Father George Wheatley is converting to Roman Catholicism, much to the dismay of his family and numerous Episcopalians and Roman Catholics.
24. *Gathering, The* (Andrews, 2002) The final book in the series follows six young people from Detroit, four boys intending to be priests, two girls intending to be nuns.

Kijewski, Karen

Kat Colorado, a Sacramento, California-based private investigator, has a lover, Hank Parker, who is a policeman in Las Vegas. Kat is a tough but vulnerable character with a social conscience in an award-winning (Shamus, Edgar, and Anthony) series that combines good plots with humor, pathos, suspense, and action.

1. *Katwalk* (St. Martin's, 1989) A routine divorce case takes Kat from Sacramento to some heavyweight crime circles in Las Vegas.
2. *Katapult* (St. Martin's, 1990) Kat's "adopted" grandmother has her life threatened after another "adopted" grandchild is stabbed to death in his car.
3. *Kat's Cradle* (Doubleday, 1992) Kat agrees to find Paige Morrell's birth parents after Paige's wealthy grandmother, who always refused to discuss them, has died.
4. *Copy Kat* (Doubleday, 1992) Kat goes undercover as Kate, a dyed-blond bartender in a California resort town, to discover who murdered a local bartender's wife.
5. *Wild Kat* (Doubleday, 1994) Amanda Hudson has discovered that her employer is covering up a product defect that could result in serious injury or death.
6. *Alley Kat Blues* (Doubleday, 1995) Kat is involved with a hit-and-run case that might be murder, while her boyfriend Hank appears to be having an affair with an exotic dancer in Las Vegas.
7. *Honky Tonk Cat* (Putnam, 1996) Kat gets involved with the country and western tour scene to discover why country star Dakota Jones is receiving threatening notes and bunches of dead roses.
8. *Kat Scratch Fever* (Putnam, 1997) Kat is brought on to investigate embezzlement, extortion, and suicide at Hope for Kids, a charity that aids crippled and disfigured children.
9. *Stray Kat Waltz* (Putnam, 1998) Kat reluctantly takes on the case of Sara Bernard, the abused wife of a popular local policeman.

King, Benjamin

A cold-blooded killer named Anderson is the connecting link between two Civil War–era historical novels that indulge some retro-conspiracy theories in well-plotted, historically plausible fashion. King is also the author of *The Loki Project* (Pelican, 2000), a novel about a scientist who tries to inveigle Hitler into making an atomic bomb.

1. *Bullet for Stonewall, A* (Pelican, 1990) Confederate general Stonewall Jackson wasn't killed accidentally by his own troops but was assassinated in a plot organized by Union forces.
2. *Bullet for Lincoln, A* (Pelican, 1993) John Wilkes Booth wasn't the actual killer of Lincoln but only the dupe of an assassin hired by financiers J. P. Morgan, Jim Fisk, and Jay Gould.

King, Laurie R.

I. Laurie R. King gives the Sherlock Holmes legend a decidedly feminist twist by inventing the character of Mary Russell, who matches Holmes's brilliant intellect, caustic wit, egotistical personality, and gift for detail. Mary and Holmes meet in Sussex during World War I. Mary is 15. Holmes is ostensibly retired. Holmes and Russell team up and eventually marry, belying Holmes's supposed misogyny, and experience a series of adventures narrated by Mary, who is more analytical and humorous than Watson. King created Mary Russell for those female readers who loved the Holmes mysteries but felt excluded by Holmes's supposed disdain for women. Baker Street purists may be offended, but King's novels are a loving, well-written addition to the Holmes mythology.

1. *Beekeeper's Apprentice, The* (St. Martin's, 1994) Subtitle: *On the Segregation of the Queen.* In 1914 Sherlock Holmes, retired on a Sussex farm, while walking on Sussex Downs, stumbles across 15-year-old Mary Russell.
2. *O Jerusalem* (Bantam, 1999) Follows number 1 chronologically. In 1918 Holmes and Mary Russell are sent on a mission to Palestine by Mycroft, Holmes's "smarter brother."
3. *Justice Hall* (Bantam, 2002) A British soldier in Palestine is executed for desertion. Ali Hazr and his brother Mahmoud, two characters from number 2, play roles.
4. *Monstrous Regiment of Women, A* (St. Martin's, 1995) In 1920 Mary is a week away from her 21st birthday, and has finished her studies at Oxford. She is introduced to Margery Childe, leader of the New Temple of God, a feminist theological and social activist institution.
5. *Letter of Mary, A* (St. Martin's, 1997) In 1923 Holmes and Russell, now married, investigate the suspicious death of amateur archaeologist Dorothy Ruskin, who gave Mary a letter written by "Mariam the Apostle," who died circa 70 CE. Dorothy L. Sayers's (q.v.) Lord Peter Wimsey appears in a cameo.
6. *Moor, The* (St. Martin's, 1998) Elderly and eccentric, the Reverend Sabine Baring-Gould asks his friend Holmes to investigate the Dartmoor death of a man beside "the footprints of a very large dog."
7. *Game, The* (Bantam, 2004) Holmes and Russell go to India on another mission from Mycroft.
8. *Locked Rooms* (Bantam, 2005) In 1924 Sherlock and Mary visit San Francisco, Mary's hometown, where Mary is troubled by memories of the 1906 earthquake.

II. Kate Martinelli is a tough female detective with the contemporary San Francisco Police Department. Kate and her embittered and tyrannical police partner, Al Hawken, investigate a series of crimes. Number 5 involves an Arthur Conan Doyle (q.v.) story.

1. *Grave Talent, A* (St. Martin's, 1993) The bodies of three children are found near a reclusive community of eccentrics not far from San Francisco.
2. *To Play the Fool* (St. Martin's, 1995) The murder and botched cremation of a homeless man in Golden Gate Park draws Kate into the world of the homeless.
3. *With Child* (St. Martin's, 1996) Kate's female lover, Lee, leaves to spend some time on an island off the Washington coast. Al Hawken is wooing a woman whose 12-year-old daughter asks Kate to help her find a missing homeless boy.
4. *Night Work* (Bantam, 2000) Kate and Al investigate the murder of a man who turns out to be a longtime wife abuser.
5. *Art of Detection, The* (Bantam, 2006) Kate investigates the death of obsessive Sherlock Holmes collector Philip Gilbert, who turned up a previously unpublished Arthur Conan Doyle (q.v.) story.

King, Stephen

Best-selling horror author King sets many of his stories in small-town Maine, but his only real series is something of a departure. It is an alternative world fantasy called the Dark Tower, which mixes elements of the western, Arthurian romance, science fiction, and horror into a rich stew redolent with spooky atmosphere. Roland the Gunslinger pursues his quest for the mysterious Dark Tower across a bleak landscape in a series initially inspired by Robert

Browning's poem "Childe Roland." Books in the Dark Tower series were published originally in limited hardcover editions by Grant, then in mass-market paperback by New American Library. Stephen King is the husband of novelist Tabitha King (q.v.). *The Complete Stephen King Universe: A Guide to the Worlds of Stephen King,* by Stanley Wiater, Christopher Golden, and Hank Wagner (St. Martin's, 2006), is an excellent guide to the thematic links in King's works. *The Dark Tower Boxed Set* (Plume, 2003) contains numbers 1 through 4.

1. *Gunslinger, The* (Grant, 1982) Roland the gunslinger, accompanied by a boy who seems to have lost his memory, chases a man in black through deserts and over mountains.
2. *Drawing of the Three, The* (Grant, 1987) Roland lives out the future predicted for him by the Dark Man's tarot cards by stepping through three doors into the minds of three 20th-century New Yorkers.
3. *Waste Lands, The* (Grant, 1991) Susannah Dean and Eddie Dean, from the New York of 1963 and 1987, respectively, accompany Roland on his quest for the Tower at the portal of all worlds.
4. *Wizard and Glass* (Grant, 1997) Roland and his band are held captive on a fast train run by a demented computer. There is a love story involving a witch, a crystal ball, an opening between worlds, and murder, among other things.
5. *Wolves of the Calla* (Grant, 2003) The band of five—Roland, Eddie, Susannah, Jake and the talking pet "Oy"—momentarily leaves the Path of the Beam to help the residents of a farm town, Calla Bryn Sturgis.
6. *Song of Susannah* (Grant, 2004) King weaves his own character into the narrative as Roland and Eddie travel to 1977 Maine. Susannah is transported to New York City in the summer of 1999, possessed by her "demon-mother," Mia.
7. *Dark Tower* (Grant, 2004) The final installment of the series is a philosophical exploration of free will and destiny.

King, Tabitha

Tabitha King, wife of Stephen King (q.v.), is no mean writer herself, but, although she started out in the 1980s with romantic-suspense novels, she writes more about normal human passions than about supernatural and psychological horror. The town of Nodd's Ridge, Maine, is the setting for the lives and loves of the blue-collar Styles family in the 1950s and 1960s in these sensitive depictions of small-town life.

1. *Book of Reuben, The* (Dutton, 1994) Teenager Reuben Styles has to support himself and his mother after the death of his abusive father.
2. *Pearl* (New American Library, 1988) Pearl Dickenson inherits a house in Maine and achieves financial success by running a local diner, but she is less successful with her romantic life.
3. *One on One* (Dutton, 1993) Sam Styles, Reuben's son, a clean-living high school basketball star, finds himself attracted to Deanie Gauthier, the not-so-clean-living captain of the girls' basketball team.

Kingsolver, Barbara

Barbara Kingsolver has built up a reputation as a superior novelist on the basis of novels that have been praised for their wonderful narrative voice, humor, moral vision, and empathy. Two of the novels follow Taylor Greer, a poor young white woman traveling cross-country, and Turtle, the little Cherokee girl she adopts.

1. *Bean Trees, The* (Harper, 1988) Taylor Greer, heading west from her Kentucky home, picks up a two-year-old Cherokee girl while passing through Oklahoma.
2. *Pigs in Heaven* (Harper, 1993) Taylor flees her Arizona home with the six-year-old Turtle when Native American lawyer Annawake Fourkiller insists that the child be returned to the Cherokee Nation.

Kirst, Hans Hellmut

Gunner Herbert Asch, the engaging hero of these satires on German life, can charm, bluff, and lie his way out of any scrape, while his guileless friend Vierbein gets caught in one snafu after another. *M.A.S.H.* fans and others will enjoy the ingenious way the young soldier subverts military discipline and makes fools of his commanding officers. The Nazi German setting seems oddly incongruous with Kirst's essentially comic view—his officers are inept buffoons rather than truly menacing. But the drudgery and mindless routine of military life are portrayed realistically enough, and Gunner Asch's rebellion is a heartening story. Numbers 1, 2, and 3 form a trilogy, *Null-acht fuenfzehn.* *Party Games* (Simon & Schuster, 1979), a novel that describes the Nazi takeover in Germany, was titled, in the original German, *Null-acht fuenfzehn in der Partei.*

1. *Revolt of Gunner Asch, The* (Little, Brown, 1955) Set in an army post in a small German town just before World War II, this story concerns Gunner Asch's revolt against the injustices of military life. Original German title: *In der Kaserne.* Translated by Robert Kee.
2. *Forward Gunner Asch!* (Little, Brown, 1956) The misadventures of Asch, Verbein, Schulz, and the others continue on the Russian front. Originally published in 1954 as *Null-acht fuenfzehn im Krieg.* Translated from the German by Robert Kee. UK title: *Gunner Asch Goes to War.*
3. *Return of Gunner Asch, The* (Little, Brown, 1957) Asch finishes a private war of his own, as he tracks down the two Nazi officers who ordered the troops on a last, doomed attack. Originally published in 1955 as *Null-acht fuenfzehn bis zum Ende.* Translated from the German by Robert Kee.
4. *What Became of Gunner Asch* (Little, Brown, 1964) The postwar years find Asch a hotel owner and mayor of a small West German town that is the seat of two rival garrisons. Originally published in 1963 as *Null-acht fuenfzehn heute.* Translated from the German by J. Maxwell Brownjohn.

Kita, Morio

PSEUDONYM OF Saito Sokichi

Since its publication in Japan in 1964, *The House of Nire* (*Nireke no hitobito*) has been regarded by Japanese critics as a comic masterpiece of Japanese society in the 20th century. Based to some extent on Morio Kita's own family history, it describes the rise and fall of the Nire family and the family-run Nire Mental Hospital in Tokyo. Both family and hospital were founded by the eccentric Kiichiro Nire, whose fondness for all things German inspired his unique approach to mental illness. The Nire Saga, from 1918 to 1946, is very funny, but it has its tragic aspects as well, particularly during World War II and its aftermath.

1. *House of Nire, The* (Kodansha, 1984) Kiichiro Nire changes his family name and founds the Nire Mental Hospital, which is really run by his tough-minded wife. Covers 1918 to 1941. Translation

from the Japanese by Dennis Keene of parts 1 and 2 of *Nireke no hitobito* (1964).
2. *Fall of the House of Nire, The* (Kodansha, 1985) Kiichiro's adopted son Tesukichi ineptly runs the hospital after Kiichiro's death, while Kiichiro's children and grandchildren are scattered by World War II. Covers 1941 to 1946. Translation from the Japanese by Dennis Keene of part 3 of *Nireke no hitobito* (1964).

Kittredge, Mary

I. Mary Kittredge's many nonfiction books on medical topics have prepared her well for her series featuring Edwina Crusoe, ex-nurse and private medical investigator in New Haven, Connecticut. Like many other fictional female sleuths, Edwina has a police detective as a significant other, in this case Martin MacIntyre, who marries her by the third volume in the series.

1. *Fatal Diagnosis* (St. Martin's, 1990) Edwina is urgently summoned back to Chelsea Memorial Hospital, where she worked, when a lab technician is shot dead and her protégé critically wounded.
2. *Rigor Mortis* (St. Martin's, 1991) Jillian Nash, nurse at Chelsea Memorial Hospital, has lost her third patient, and the niece of the latest dead person is accusing her of murder.
3. *Cadaver* (St. Martin's, 1992) Did medical journal editor Bennett Weissman commit suicide? Or was he murdered?
4. *Walking Dead Man* (St. Martin's, 1992) Dentist's wife Theresa Whitlock is murdered after telling Edwina a tale of ghosts and murder.
5. *Desperate Remedy* (St. Martin's, 1993) A murderous attack on Dr. Victor Clarke has left him unconscious and his wife and two of his nurses dead.
6. *Kill or Cure* (St. Martin's, 1995) Young Gerry Bailey's swollen ear is the result of a gunshot wound, not an allergic reaction.

II. Journalist Charlotte Kent is a poor, struggling writer battling her agent, her deadlines, and her moral scruples. Charlotte adopts a 12-year-old boy with physical and familial problems, and eventually moves to New Haven, Connecticut, where, someday, she may hook up with Edwina Crusoe on a case.

1. *Murder in Mendocino* (Walker, 1987) Charlotte is working on a biography of Dr. Stanley Hardwicke, local hero of Pelican Rock, California, when she discovers that someone else may have beaten her to the punch.
2. *Dead and Gone* (Walker, 1989) Young Joey is fighting for his life after a dangerous operation, and a prominent doctor is implicated in the poisoning death of a blackmailing medical writer.
3. *Poison Pen* (Walker, 1990) Wesley Bell, prominent novelist and most valuable contributor to Charlotte's journal *Pen and Pencil*, is found dead in her desk chair.

Klavan, Andrew

Scott Weiss is the head of Weiss Investigations in San Francisco, and Jim Bishop is one of his operatives. Weiss and Bishop are a study in contrasts: the former being a paunchy, moralistic, empathic ex-cop, while the latter is young, handsome, nihilistic, with a taste for violence, drugs, and loose women. Weiss has an unrequited passion for the prostitute Julie Wyant (aka Julie Angel), who is being chased by the elusive murderer the Shadowman. Sometimes the pair works together. Sometimes they conduct separate investigations. Readers love the gripping plots and engrossing Raymond Chandler–like (q.v.) characters, but some are put off by the author's interjection of himself as a character in the proceedings. At least two of Andrew Klavan's other novels have been produced as films: *True Crime* (1999; directed by Clint Eastwood) and *Don't Say a Word* (2001). As "Keith Peterson," Klavan authored six novels, five of which featured a character named John Wells, and coauthored a novel with his brother Laurence as "Margaret Tracy."

1. *Dynamite Road* (Forge, 2003) Scott Weiss, ex-cop and head of Weiss Investigations, dispatches operative Jim Bishop to get the goods on Bernie Hirschorn, co-owner of an aviation factory, who is up to his eyes in dirty doings.
2. *Shotgun Alley* (Forge, 2004) Jim Bishop is hired by a millionaire with political ambitions to retrieve his teenage daughter, Holly, who has run off with an outlaw biker gang. Scott Weiss takes on the case of a feminist professor at Berkeley who is being harassed by anonymous erotic e-mails.
3. *Damnation Street* (Harcourt/Penzler, 2006) Weiss is still searching for prostitute Julie Wyant (aka Julie Angel). "The Shadowman," a mysterious and relentless murderer, also seems to be on Julie's trail.

Knight, Damon

Damon Knight (d. 2002) was an all-around man in science fiction: author, editor, illustrator, translator, and critic. He won a Hugo Award for his criticism, and his collection of essays *In Search of Wonder: Essays on Modern Science Fiction* (2nd ed., Advent, 1967) is considered a classic. Knight has written many short stories and novels, but the Sea Venture (CV) trilogy, about an oceangoing city of the future, seems to be his only series venture. Knight was married to science-fiction and mystery writer Kate Wilhelm (q.v.).

1. *CV* (Tor, 1985) Sea Venture, an oceangoing city, is plagued by a mysterious parasite that is invading human bodies.
2. *Observers, The* (Tor, 1988) The citizens of Sea Venture seem to be cured of their alien infection, but have suffered a personality change.
3. *Reasonable World, A* (Tor, 1991) The intelligent alien virus seems to be taking over the entire planet while researchers on Sea Venture work to thwart it.

Knight, Kathryn Lasky

PSEUDONYM OF Kathryn Lasky

Kathryn Lasky Knight, who writes juveniles and collaborates on photo-essays with Christopher G. Knight as Kathryn Lasky, has created a mystery series with a children's book illustrator as protagonist. Calista Jacobs of Cambridge, Massachusetts, acclaimed illustrator and widowed mother of teenager Charley, is another amateur sleuth who gets drawn into criminal investigations while pursuing her primary profession. Knight provides many interesting vignettes of the art world in the course of her series.

1. *Trace Elements* (Norton, 1986) The murder of her scientist husband in the desert near Reno, Nevada, gets Calista involved in uncovering an archaeological scam and secret nuclear testing.
2. *Mortal Words* (Summit, 1990) Computer whiz Charley helps to ferret out a sinister plot involving creationists and racist scientists.
3. *Mumbo Jumbo* (Summit, 1991) Calista and Charley go on a dig to Arizona land owned by a cultist who claims to be the reincarnation of a 65,000-year-old Russian woman.

4. *Dark Swan* (St. Martin's, 1994) While drawing the bonsai trees tended by Beacon Hill matriarch Quintana Kingsley, Calista finds the elderly woman slain with her own pruning shears.

Koontz, Dean (Ray)

I. Dean Koontz, "America's most popular suspense novelist" (*Rolling Stone*), has written more than 80 novels under his own name and a dozen pseudonyms but very few sequels. The two novels featuring Christopher Snow of Moonlight Bay, California, are an exception. Chris has a rare genetic disease that renders him so light sensitive that he cannot leave his house in daylight or enter a normally lit room. Chris copes by doing his wandering and exploring at night.

1. *Fear Nothing* (Bantam, 1998) After his father's death, Christopher Snow finds that his parents, as well as many other residents of the supposedly idyllic town of Moonlight Bay, California, have been involved in some sinister goings-on.
2. *Seize the Night* (Bantam, 1998) Children are disappearing during the night at Moonlight Bay. There seems to be a connection with the secret research being carried on at the nearby military base, Fort Wyvern.

II. Odd Thomas, resident of St. Bartholomew's Abbey, a monastery in the Sierra Nevada Mountains, has the ability to see, feel, and talk to the dead (though the dead don't talk back). Odd's ability gets him into some strange and dangerous adventures in a trio of novels that will appeal to lovers of the supernatural.

1. *Odd Thomas* (HarperCollins, 2004) Odd Thomas, working as short-order cook at the Pico Mundo Grill in a small desert town, tries to do his best to help the souls that seek him out. Now Pico Mundo is threatened by a mysterious stranger, and Odd will try to avert catastrophe with the help of ghostly allies, including Elvis Presley.
2. *Forever Odd* (Bantam, 2005) Odd is summoned by the ghost of Dr. Wilbur Jessup, father of his best friend, Danny, to the Jessup home, the site of a gruesome murder.
3. *Brother Odd* (Bantam, 2006) Now a resident of St. Bartholomew's Abbey in the Sierra Nevada mountains, Odd is unsettled by visions of "bodachs," sinister ghostlike entities whose appearance foretells some dire tragedy.

Kraft, Eric

The Personal History, Adventures, Experiences and Observations of Peter Leroy is an ongoing series about the post–World War II boyhood of Peter Leroy (Kraft's alter ego) of Babbington, Long Island, New York ("Clam Capital of America"), by the adult Peter, now a hotel owner in his hometown. Peter often reads passages from his memoirs to the guests of the hotel after dinner. Kraft's funny, sentimental vignettes of growing up in the fifties have had a fairly complicated publishing history. Most of the novellas in number 2 were originally published as separate paperback volumes by Applewood Books (from 1982 to 1983). *Reservations Recommended* (Crown, 1990) isn't part of the series. *Flying Home*, the final installment in the trilogy, will be included with numbers 9 and 10 in *Flying*, to be published in 2009.

1. *Herb 'n' Lorna: A Love Story* (Crown, 1988) Peter Leroy writes the biographies of his grandparents Herb and Lorna Piper, who led interesting secret lives unbeknownst to each other.

2. *Little Follies* (**Crown, 1992**) Contains seven separately published novellas as well as the previously unpublished "The Young Tars": "My Mother Takes a Tumble," "Do Clams Bite?" "Life on the Bolotmy," "The Static of the Spheres," "The Fox and the Clam," "The Girl with the White Fur Muff," and "Take the Long Way Home." UK title: *Sweet Miseries*.

3. *Where Do You Stop?* (**Crown, 1992**) Peter is introduced into the treacherous waters of junior high school.

4. *What a Piece of Work I Am* (**Crown, 1994**) Peter's unrequited love for Ariane "Tootsie" Lodkochnikov is recounted in several different versions.

5. *At Home with the Glynns* (**Crown, 1995**) Peter's up-and-down relationship with the mischievous Glynn sisters is delineated here.

6. *Inflating a Dog* (**Picador USA, 2002**) Peter's mother, Ella, gets another one of her zany business visions. This time she decides to establish a cruise line for the bay near Babbington.

7. *Leaving Small's Hotel* (**Picador USA, 1998**) Peter is turning 50. The hotel he and his wife, Albertine, run on Small's Island is failing, and Peter is uneasily aware that Albertine is reaching the end of her tether.

8. *Passionate Spectator* (**St. Martin's, 2004**) Peter and Albertine are living in New York City. Albertine plays the piano, and Peter tries to set up a freelance business helping other people to write their memoirs.

9. *Taking Off* (**St. Martin's, 2006**) Upon hearing rumors that Babbington is to be turned into a theme park based on his childhood cross-country flight, Peter returns to his hometown "to set a few things straight." First volume of *Flying: A Trilogy*.

10. *On the Wing* (**St. Martin's, 2007**) Describes Peter's cross-country trip at age 14 on a homemade "aerocycle" and his return trip as an adult with Albertine. Volume 2 of *Flying: A Trilogy*.

Krantz, Judith

Best-selling novelist Krantz (*Princess Daisy*, etc.), who worked for fashion magazines for decades and is married to a television producer, knows something about the glamorous world she delineates, although her novels are basically fantasies about wealth, power, and forceful women. The Scruples trilogy is named after the chic store built by Billy Ikehorn on the choicest corner in Beverly Hills. Since Billy's husband, Vito Orsini, is a movie producer, we get a good peek at the film business as well. Gigi Orsini, Billy's glamorous stepdaughter, takes center stage in numbers 2 and 3. A wealth of information about the lives of the rich and famous, lots of conspicuous consumption, sex, and many subplots keep readers coming back for more.

1. *Scruples* (**Crown, 1979**) Wealthy, beautiful young widow Billy Ikehorn manages her boutique and a series of lovers.

2. *Scruples Two: Fifteen Years Later* (**Crown, 1992**) Gigi, heretofore unmentioned daughter of Billy's husband, Vito Orsini, turns up, and Billie is kept busy furnishing her with a new wardrobe and opening new branches of Scruples.

3. *Lovers* (**Crown, 1994**) In "Scruples Three" Billy's stepdaughter Gigi Orsini has torrid affairs with other rich and famous people and concocts clever marketing ideas for Victoria Frost, head of the advertising agency she joins.

Krentz, Jayne Ann

I. Jayne Ann Krentz is a highly successful writer, having published more than 120 books under her own name and least six pseudonyms, including Jayne Bentley, Jayne Castle, Amanda Glass, Stephanie James, Amanda Quick (q.v.), and Jayne Taylor. Most her books are romantic-suspense novels published in paperback-only editions by publishers such as Harlequin, Popular Library, Jove, and McFadden. Some of the "series" are quite loosely connected. Lost Colony (*Sweet Starfire, Crystal Flame, Shield's Lady*), is a romance trilogy with SF overtones (Popular Library, 1985–1989). *Dreams 1* and *Dreams 2* (both Harlequin, 1988) are a pair of novels about a curse, collected in *A Shared Dream* (Harlequin, 1992). The Ladies and Legends trilogy (*The Pirate, The Adventurer,* and *The Cowboy*) are linked stories about three friends who engage in some adventurous romances (all Harlequin, 1990). The three novels have been collected in one volume by Harlequin (2006).

The Eclipse Bay trilogy, collected in *Together in Eclipse Bay* (Berkley, 2003), set in the small town of that name on the coast of Oregon, is about two families, the Hartes and the Madisons, who have been feuding for generations.

1. *Eclipse Bay* (**Jove, 2000**) Rafe Madison is accused of murdering his girlfriend, and his only alibi is Hannah Harte, a member of a family that has been feuding with his family for generations.

2. *Dawn in Eclipse Bay* (**Jove, 2001**) Successful businessman Gabe Madison is distinctly dissatisfied with the computer matchmaking service run by Lilian Harte.

3. *Summer in Eclipse Bay* (**Jove, 2002**) Thriller writer Nick Harte and gallery owner Octavia Brightwell are brought together by a missing picture.

II. The Gift duo brings together Verity Ames and Jonas Quarrel.

1. *Gift of Gold* (**Popular Library, 1988**) Jonas Quarrel, the man who saved Verity Ames's life, appears at her restaurant.

2. *Gift of Fire* (**Popular Library, 1989**) Verity Ames and Jonas Quarrel are hired to find a lost medieval treasure.

III. A pair of novels set in Whispering Springs, Arizona, features interior decorator Zoe Luce, who can feel violence that has occurred in a room just by entering it and has nightmares about a place called Xanadu.

1. *Light in Shadow* (**Putnam, 2002**) Interior decorator Zoe Luce, who has psychic powers, works with investigator Ethan Truax to solve the murder of a local businessman.

2. *Truth or Dare* (**Putnam, 2003**) Zoe and Ethan are now married. Zoe is dealing with psychic "spider webs" that attach themselves to various places she has been.

Kuhlken, Ken(neth Wayne)

Tom Hickey, San Diego, California, jazz musician, nightclub owner, and sleuth and other members of the Hickey family, are the protagonists of a series of novels set during World War II and after. In the first three novels, Tom's basic decency gets him enmeshed in a series of brutal adventures with some weird characters. Numbers 4 and 5, published more than a decade later, involve other members of the Hickey family.

1. *Venus Deal, The* (**St. Martin's, 1993**) In 1942 San Diego nightclub owner Tom Hickey is searching for his missing headliner singer Cynthia Moon.
2. *Loud Adios, The* (**St. Martin's, 1991**) Tom Hickey, a military policeman stationed at the Mexican border, helps young soldier Clifford Rose rescue his beautiful but simpleminded sister, Wendy, from a Tijuana dive.
3. *Angel Gang, The* (**St. Martin's, 1994**) Old girlfriend Cynthia Tucker Jones is charged with murder, and Tom leaves his Lake Tahoe, Nevada, cabin and Wendy, now his pregnant wife, to help her out. Set in 1951.
4. *Do-Re-Mi, The* (**Poisoned Pen, 2006**) Twenty-two-year-old Clifford Hickey, son of Tom, takes one last stab at a folksinging career before heading to law school by performing at a jamboree at Evergreen, California.
5. *Vagabond Virgins* (**Poisoned Pen, 2008**) Young and beautiful Lourdes Shuler asks San Diego PI Alvaro Hickey to locate her missing twin sister, Lupe, on the eve of the 1979 Mexican election.

Kuniczak, W(iselaw) S(tanislaw)

W. S. Kuniczak, Polish American journalist and novelist, has written a trilogy about the tragedy of Poland in World War II, when it was invaded by the Germans and the Russians and millions of Poles were killed or forced into exile. The novels' epic sweep and large cast of both historical and fictional characters have led some critics to describe them as "Tolstoyan." Some of the characters appear in more than one of the novels; the heroic Polish general Janusaz Prus appears in all three. The saga is based on extensive research as well as the personal recollections of the author, who was born in Poland and lived through many of the events he describes. Kuniczak also retranslated Henryk Sienkiewicz' (q.v.) historical trilogy.

1. *Thousand Hour Day, The* (**Dial, 1967**) This covers the first thousand hours of World War II, when the German blitzkrieg invaded Poland in September 1939, and the Polish army fought a desperate holding action until their final surrender.
2. *March, The* (**Doubleday, 1979**) This volume describes what happened to the Poles when the Soviet Union "liberated" eastern Poland in 1939, massacred thousands, and sent thousands more into exile.
3. *Valedictory* (**Doubleday, 1983**) Polish pilots who escaped to England form the famed 303rd Squadron of the RAF, then shoot down hundreds of German planes during the war.

Kurland, Michael

I. Among the best of the Sherlock Holmes pastiches have been Michael Kurland's four Moriarty novels. According to Kurland, the brilliant Moriarty didn't always stay within the confines of the law but was not the amoral "Napoléon of Crime" Holmes made him out to be. Now the truth has been told. There was a nearly 20-year gap between numbers 2 and 3. *The Infernal Device and Others: A Professor Moriarty Omnibus* (St. Martin's, 2001) contains numbers 1 and 2 and a never-before-published short story "The Paradol Paradox." *My Sherlock Holmes: Untold Stories of the Great Detective* (St. Martin's, 2003), a collection containing stories by various authors told from the perspectives of characters in the Holmes canon excluding Watson and Holmes himself, contains Kurland's story "Years Ago and in a Different Place." *Sherlock Holmes: The Hidden Years* (St. Martin's, 2004),

another anthology edited by Kurland, contains the Kurland story "Reichenbach."

1. *Infernal Device, The* (**New American Library, 1979**) Moriarty is forced to collaborate with his nemesis, Sherlock Holmes, when a dangerous plot to overthrow the British monarchy unfolds.
2. *Death by Gaslight* (**New American Library, 1982**) A serial killer is stalking members of the British aristocracy, and the police and Holmes are baffled. Enter Professor Moriarty.
3. *Great Game, The* (**St. Martin's, 2001**) Moriarty suspects a vast conspiracy behind the cabal that seems to be using assassination to destabilize the rule of the crowned heads of Europe.
4. *Empress of India* (**St. Martin's, 2006**) Moriarty and his cohort Colonel Sebastian Moran try to abscond with the bejeweled statuette "Queen of Lamapoor" from the luxury liner *Empress of India.*

II. Syndicated columnist and sophisticate Alexander Brass is the voice of Manhattan high society and nightlife in the Depression year of 1935. Two novels and one short story, "He Couldn't Fly" (in *The Mammoth Book of Roaring Twenties Whodunnits*, edited by Mike Ashley; Carroll & Graf, 2004), describe Alexander's forays into detection.

Michael Kurland started out as an SF writer. The Mission or War, Incorporated books (*Third Force; Tank War;* and *Police Action*) were a trio of military SF novels published by Pyramid in 1967–1969. Two Lord Darcy novels are continuations of the character created by the late Randall Garrett: *Ten Little Wizards* (Ace, 1988) and *A Study in Sorcery* (Ace, 1989). *The Unicorn Girl* (Pyramid, 1969) is Kurland's contribution to the Greenwich Village trilogy, a linked series. The other authors were Chester Anderson and T. A. Waters. Kurland is the author of several nonfiction volumes, including reference books about espionage and crime, and at least three books in the Complete Idiot's Guide series.

1. *Too Soon Dead* (**St. Martin's, 1997**) In 1935 syndicated columnist Alexander Brass has brushes with historical characters such as Charles A. Lindbergh as he investigates what seems to be a simple case of compromising pictures and blackmail.
2. *Girls in the High-Heeled Shoes, The* (**St. Martin's, 1998**) Brass is asked to trace colorful Broadway character Two-Headed Mary.

Kurtz, Katherine

I. The world of the Eleven Kingdoms created by American fantasy writer Katherine Kurtz tells of the struggles between the two human races that inhabit the Kingdom of Gwynedd, a country that strongly resembles medieval Wales. The Deryni are mutants with magical abilities, who are distrusted and feared by the ordinary folk and their priests. Some Deryni uses their powers for the common good, while others are corrupt and seek only self-advancement. The Deryni novels are mostly a series of trilogies. Numbers 1, 2, and 3 are called the Legends of Camber of Culdi; numbers 4, 5, and 6 are called the Heirs of Saint Camber; numbers 7 and 8 are the first two volumes of a trilogy about Donal Haldane; numbers 9, 10, and 11 are called the Chronicles of the Deryni; numbers 12, 13, and 14 are called the Histories of King Kelson; number 15 is connected to the Histories of King Kelson trilogy. *Deryni Archives* (Ballantine, 1986) is a collection of short stories. There is also an irregularly issued fanzine of the same title. Kurtz's *Deryni Magic: A Grimoire* (Ballantine, 1990) is a (somewhat out of date) handbook to the series.

1. *Camber of Culdi* (**Ballantine, 1976**) Deryni Camber of Culdi helps to overthrow the evil Deryni King Imre and restore the rightful

heir, Cinhil Haldane, to the throne of Gwynedd. First of the Legends of Camber of Culdi.

2. *Saint Camber* (Ballantine, 1978) Ariella, sister of the deceased King Imre, plots war against King Cinhil, who is nursing a grudge against Camber for removing him from his quiet monastic life. Second of the Legends of Camber of Culdi.

3. *Camber the Heretic* (Ballantine, 1981) The period from the death of King Cinhil to Camber's death sees the start of open persecution of the Deryni. Third in the Legends of Camber of Culdi.

4. *Harrowing of Gwynedd, The* (Ballantine, 1989) The Cambrian Council must prevent the regents of young King Airoy from killing off all the Deryni leaders. First of the Heirs of Saint Camber.

5. *King Javan's Year* (Ballantine, 1992) Crippled Prince Javan, who has Deryni powers, succeeds King Airoy to the throne of Gwynedd. Second in the Heirs of King Camber.

6. *Bastard Prince, The* (Ballantine, 1994) The clash between King Rhys Michael and Marek of Festil, the bastard son of Gwynedd's last Deryni brings the Heirs of Saint Camber to a conclusion.

7. *In the King's Service* (Ace, 2003) King Donal Haldane sometimes uses his power to ensure his own dynastic needs. The Camberian Council have their own secret plans for Deryni and humans. Set in the time of the grandfather of King Kelson (see numbers 11–14).

8. *Childe Morgan* (Ace, 2006) King Donal Haldane is mourning the loss of his bastard son, Krispin, while Bishop Oliver de Nore escalates his campaign against the Deryni.

9. *Deryni Rising* (Ballantine, 1970) Evil Deryni sorceress Charissa assassinates King Brion and tries to take over the kingdom. 1st of the *Chronicles of the Deryni*. Newly revised edition: Ace, 2004.

10. *Deryni Checkmate* (Ballantine, 1972) The clergy of Gwynedd try to frame half-Deryni Alaric Morgan on treason charges. 2nd of the *Chronicles of the Deryni*. Newly revised edition: Ace, 2005.

11. *High Deryni* (Ballantine, 1973) Civil war almost breaks out before the clergy and the Deryni unite to resist the invasion of King Wencit of Torenth. Third in the Chronicles of the Deryni. Newly revised edition: Ace, 2007.

12. *Bishop's Heir, The* (Ballantine, 1984) King Kelson is challenged by anti-Deryni fanatic Archbishop Loris and a rival noble family. First of the Histories of King Kelson.

13. *King's Justice, The* (Ballantine, 1985) Kelson continues his war against the pretenders to the throne of Meara and anti-Deryni rebel Edmund Loris. Second of the Histories of King Kels.

14. *Quest for Saint Camber, The* (Ballantine, 1986) The Deryni attain high positions in court and church as King Kelson strives to restore Saint Camber to his rightful place in the Gwynedd pantheon. Third of the Histories of King Kelson.

15. *King Kelson's Bride* (Ace, 2000) King Kelson seeks a dynastic marriage with Araxie, daughter of the Hort of Orsil, another ruler from the Haldane line.

II. Kurtz has coauthored with Deborah Turner Harris a fantasy series set in contemporary Scotland in which Sir Adam Sinclair, reincarnated Adept with magical powers, and his ally, psychic painter Peregrine Lovat, do battle against assorted evil conspiracies.

1. *Adept, The* (Ace, 1991) Sir Adam Sinclair, the latest incarnation of the Adept, a spiritual force that battles evil, allies himself with Peregrine Lovat, a painter who is able to "see" the past and future of his subjects, when a wizard's sword is stolen from a Scottish museum.

2. *Lodge of the Lynx, The* (Ace, 1992) Investigating the assassination of Freemasons all over Scotland by means of magic, Sir Adam finds that the evil Lodge of the Lynx is back in business with a new headmaster, Rudolf Hess.

3. *Templar Treasure, The* (Ace, 1993) The theft of the ancient Seal of Solomon from York spells big trouble unless Adam can retrieve it.

4. *Dagger Magic* (Ace, 1995) The untimely arrival of a corpse, which upsets Peregrine Lovat's honeymoon, signals an ancient evil that is intimately connected with Nazi Germany, a demonic Aryan attempt at world conquest, and the evil mage Francis Raeburn.

5. *Death of an Adept* (Ace, 1996) Adam Sinclair returns from the United States engaged to be married, but he, Peregrine Lovat, and other mystically endowed members of the Hunting Lodge have to counter the resurgence of the evil Francis Raeburn (number 4) and the Lodge of the Lynx (number 2).

III. Kurtz and Deborah Turner Harris have embarked on a new series: a kind of alternate history of the medieval Knights Templar. French knight Arnault de Saint Claire and Scottish knight Torquil Lennox are members of "le Cercle," an initiated inner order of the Templars possessed of good magic with Hebrew, Christian, and Celtic sources.

1. *Temple and the Stone, The* (Warner, 1998) Members of the Knights Templar, protectors of the Temple of Jerusalem, are trying to establish a Fifth Temple in Scotland. They are opposed by the goddess Gruagah and her practitioners of blood magic.

2. *Temple and the Crown, The* (Warner, 2001) Begins in 1306 with the crowning of Robert Bruce in Scotland. The Templars' support of Bruce triggers a negative reaction in England, and greedy French King Philip the Fair tries to destroy the Templars with the aid of the Black Swan, a group of devil worshippers.

Lackey, Mercedes

I. Mercedes Lackey, former artist's model and computer programmer, has, since her first published novel in 1987 (*Arrows of the Queen*), been an extremely prolific fantasy writer, with many solo efforts and collaborations with other writers, including her husband, Larry Dixon, C. J. Cherryh (q.v.), Andre Norton (q.v.), Holly Lisle (q.v.), Piers Anthony (q.v.), Ellen Guon, Mark Shepherd, Rosemary Edghill, Josepha Sherman, James Mallory, Rue Emerson, and Marion Zimmer Bradley (q.v.), among others. The fantasy world of Valdemar is the scene of nearly 30 volumes of her works. Valdemar, like many fantasy worlds, is a world with many features like Medieval Europe, such as courts and kings or queens. Also like many fantasy worlds, it has lots of magic, intelligent nonhumans (the equinelike Companions of the Heralds), and coming-of-age and quest stories. The Valdemar stories are generally well characterized and fairly complex, although you can usually sort out the good characters from the evil characters. Most of the Valdemar novels are arranged in trilogies that are, for the most part, self-contained. The Valdemar stories are arranged here, as much as possible, chronologically rather than by order of publication. Readers wanting to know more about the plan, chronology, and geography of Valdemar are referred to *The Valdemar Companion* (DAW, 2001), edited by John Helfers and Denise Little, the "authorized" guide, which also contains "A Herald's Journey," an original novella by Lackey. Besides the books described in series I through VIII, there are three anthologies of Valdemar stories by Lackey and other writers: *Sword of Ice and Other Tales of Valdemar* (DAW, 1997); *Sun in Glory and Other Tales of Valdemar* (DAW, 2000); and *Crossroads and Other Tales of Valdemar* (DAW, 2005). The Mage Wars trilogy, relates the "prehistoric" events that shaped Valdemar. It describes the war between good Mage Urtho and evil mage Ma'ar and the war's aftermath. The trilogy was coauthored with Larry Dixon.

1. *Black Gryphon, The* (DAW, 1994) In the dark past of Valdemar, the most powerful mages in the world go to war. Good mage Urtho, with the aid of the intelligent creatures he has created, squares off against evil mage Ma'ar, who has his own constructs and allies. Cowritten by Larry Dixon.
2. *White Gryphon, The* (DAW, 1995) A decade after the end of the Mage Wars, the survivors establish a settlement within the boundaries of the Haighiel empire. Cowritten by Larry Dixon.
3. *Silver Gryphon, The* (DAW, 1996) Amberdrake, Skandranon, and others transport the magic Blade and other equipment to a remote and isolated guard post on their first solo assignment. Cowritten by Larry Dixon.

II. The Last Herald-Mage is a trilogy set more than a thousand years after I. It is about Vanyel, who can work both Herald and Mage magic, but who would rather be a bard. The trilogy was collected in an omnibus volume, *The Last Herald-Mage* (Guild America, 1990).

1. *Magic's Pawn* (DAW, 1989) Vanyel, born with the ability to work both Herald and Mage magic, would prefer to be a bard rather than a soldier or sorcerer.
2. *Magic's Promise* (DAW, 1990) Vanyel, now a Herald-Mage, is beset by a king, some evil Mages, and personal loneliness.
3. *Magic's Price* (DAW, 1990) King Randale is dying, and his heir, his cousin Treven, is being rushed through Herald's training as a result.

III. The Vows and Honor trilogy follows the fortunes of swordswoman Tarma and wizard Kethry, partners in an unending search for justice. Set about 500 years after the events in series II. Numbers 1 and 2 were published together as *Vows and Honor* (Guild America, 1994).

1. *Oathbound, The* (DAW, 1988) Bound by oaths to each other and to the Goddess, Tarma and Kethry begin careers as mercenaries.
2. *Oathbreakers* (DAW, 1989) Idra, leader of the Sunhawks, fails to return from a journey to her home kingdom of Rethwellan.
3. *Oathblood* (DAW, 1998) Contains 11 stories, including the novella "Oathblood."

IV. The Heralds of Valdemar trilogy, the first published Valdemar series, has as a protagonist Talia, a teenage misfit who trains for a position as Herald, one of the queen's elite bodyguards. Set about 100 years after series III. *Sun in Glory and Other Tales of Valdemar* (DAW, 2000) has a Lackey story about how Talia became a priestess of the Sun. *Queen's Own* (Guild America, 1987) is an omnibus volume containing numbers 1, 2 and 3.

1. *Arrows of the Queen* (DAW, 1987) Former runaway Talia is chosen by the mysterious telepathic horselike being Rulan to become a trainee Herald.
2. *Arrow's Flight* (DAW, 1987) Having finished her training, Talia sets out on her journeyman's circuit with a handsome, personable male Herald as mentor.
3. *Arrow's Fall* (DAW, 1988) Talia returns from her internship to find a court seething with intrigue because of an offer for the hand of the heir to the throne.

V. The Companions of the Heralds of Valdemar trilogy, which takes place at approximately the same time as series IV, has as a protagonist Alberich of Karse, who has a dangerously heretical gift of precognition. Number 3 has not yet been published.

1. *Exile's Honor* (DAW, 2002) Trained as a soldier from childhood, Alberich must tread a careful path between the priesthood Karse and the soldiers under his command because he has the dangerous gift of precognition.
2. *Exile's Valor* (DAW, 2003) Alberich, an exile from Karse and a Herald in Valdemar, trains young Heralds by day and chases down treasonous plots by night.

VI. The Mage Winds trilogy follows the adventures of the Herald Elspeth as she searches for an Adept who can teach her people both to use and to deflect the power of magic.

1. *Winds of Fate* (DAW, 1991) Young Elspeth starts out with equine companion Gwena to find an Adept and train as a Mage.
2. *Winds of Change* (DAW, 1992) Describes the adventures of Elspeth among the Hawkbrothers as she attempts to bring down the villain Falconsbane.
3. *Winds of Fury* (DAW, 1993) Elspeth returns with her Hawkbrother partner Darkwind to fight the peril threatened by Ancar of Harlorn.

VII. The Mage Storms trilogy picks up where Mage Winds left off, following the adventures of novice cleric Karal and the young Adept An'desha.

1. *Storm Warning* (DAW, 1994) An'desha must find the courage to sift through his memories to confront the waves of magic that are wrecking the kingdom.
2. *Storm Rising* (DAW, 1995) An'desha, Karal, and the neurotic Firesong are still trying to find themselves.
3. *Storm Breaking* (DAW, 1996) With help from Shin'a'in plainsmen, An'desha and Firesong excavate and unleash an ancient weapon that temporarily disrupts the magical vibrations that have emanated for two millennia.

VIII. In the Owl's Trilogy, or Darian's Tale, coauthored with Larry Dixon, Errold's Grove in the Pelagiris Forest is the setting for the coming-of-age of Darian and Keisha Alder.

1. *Owlflight* (DAW, 1997) When Darian's parents disappear form the Pelagiris Forest, he joins the magic-working Hawkbrothers. Coauthored with Larry Dixon.
2. *Owlsight* (DAW, 1998) As Errold's Grove recovers from a barbarian attack, Keisha Alder leaves her community to live study with the Hawkbrothers. Coauthored with Larry Dixon.
3. *Owlknight* (DAW, 1999) Mage and knight Darian hears that his parents may be alive after all, and sets off to the north with Keisha and others. Coauthored with Larry Dixon.

IX. The trilogy featuring Diana Tregarde, romance novelist, occult investigator, and practicing witch, is something of a departure from Valdemarian fantasy, being more in the mystery-horror line. The Tregarde series, the Bedlam Bard series (X), and the SERRated Edge series (XI) are all set "in the same universe" (i.e., contemporary America with an occult tinge).

1. *Burning Water* (Tor, 1989) Diana goes to Dallas to investigate something ancient and powerful that is killing cattle and people.
2. *Children of the Night* (Tor, 1990) The vampire Andre LeBrel is one of the good guys, but there are plenty of evil beings in New York that Diana has to cope with.
3. *Jinx High* (Tor, 1991) Tulsa, Oklahoma's Jenks High has some strange and sinister occult vibrations centering on young Deke Kestrel, son of an old ghost-hunting buddy of Tregarde.

X. Bedlam's Bard, part of the same "universe" as series IX and XI, is about Eric Banyon, a talented musician in Los Angeles, whose sad music frees Korendil, a young Elven noble, from the magical prison in which has been languishing. Eric discover that he is really a "Bard," and that he has magical powers that he and a few others can use to save the Elves of Southern California from such anti-Elven forces as Korendil's enemy, Perenor, Perenor's daughter Ria, and evil mages from Underhill such as Aerone, who want to destroy humanity as well. Number 1 was written solely by Ellen Guon. Numbers 2 and 3 were coauthored by Lackey and Guon. There was a hiatus of eight years; then the series was revived in 2001 with Rosemary Edghill as Lackey's coauthor. Numbers 2 and 3 were published together as *Bedlam's Bard* (Guild of America, 1992).

1. *Bedlam Boyz* (Baen, 1993) In this prequel, Kayla, a woman with miraculous healing powers, is sought not only by the Los Angeles gangs that need her power but by an ancient abomination and evil elves from another world. Written solely by Ellen Guon.

2. *Knights of Ghosts and Shadows* (Baen, 1990) When Eric Banyon frees the elf Korendil from his magic prison, Eric learns that he really is a Bard, that there are elves in Los Angeles, and that he, Korendil and Beth Konframe are the only ones who can save the elves of Southern California from destruction by the likes of Perenor and his daughter Ria. Cowritten with Ellen Guon.

3. *Summoned to Tourney* (Baen, 1992) Set in San Francisco. Evil researchers kidnap Beth for use in psychic experiments and other nastiness. Cowritten with Ellen Guon.

4. *Spirits White as Lightning* (Baen, 2001) Eric apprentices Hosea Song-Maker, a banjo-playing bard-to-be from Appalachia. Lord Aerone from Underhill appears, still determined to eradicate humanity. Cowritten with Rosemary Edghill.

5. *Beyond World's End* (Baen, 2002) T-Stroke, a drug with dangerous magical powers, is about to be let loose in New York. Lord Aerone and Ria Llewllyn reappear. Cowritten with Rosemary Edghill.

6. *Mad Maudlin* (Baen, 2003) In post 9/11 New York, Eric discovers that he has a 17-year-old brother who is now homeless in Manhattan. Cowritten with Rosemary Edghill.

7. *Music to My Sorrow* (Baen, 2005) Picks up where number 6 left off. Eric finishes the training of his bardic student, Hosea; seeks to adopt his brother, Magnus; and runs messages for his elf-lord.

XI. SERRated Edge is a fantasy series of rather loosely related novels that are tied together more by theme than by continuing characters. It ranges over Earth and Elfland and other places. Numbers 1 and 4 were coauthored with Larry Dixon and reprinted together as *The Chrome Borne* (Baen, 1999). Number 2, coauthored with Mark Shepherd, and number 3, coauthored with Holly Lisle, were reprinted together as *The Otherworld* (Baen, 2000). Numbers 5, 6, and 7 were written solely by Mark Shepherd. Number 8 was coauthored with Josepha Sherman.

1. *Born to Run* (Baen, 1992) Three runaway teenagers forced into child prostitution become unwitting pawns in an unearthly vendetta. Cowritten with Larry Dixon.

2. *Wheels of Fire* (Baen, 1992) Young Jamie is forced into a fanatical religious cult by his father. Jamie's mother enlists magical help in finding and retrieving him. Cowritten by Mark Shepherd.

3. *When the Bough Breaks* (Baen, 1993) Unless Amanda can be helped to control her life, her telekinetic abilities could destroy both Earth and Faerie. Cowritten with Holly Lisle.

4. *Chrome Circle* (Baen, 1994) Tannim has to muster all his defenses when the woman of his dreams appears as his challenger. Cowritten with Larry Dixon.

5. *Elvendude* (Baen, 1994) To preserve Aedhon from attack by evil devils, King Traighthren magically alters Aedhon's memory and hides him on Earth. Written solely by Mark Shepherd.

6. *Spiritride* (Baen, 1997) Petrus's reconnaissance mission to Earth gives evil Unseelie warriors an opportunity to ally themselves with devil worshippers and an ancient Egyptian Cat-Spirit. Written solely by Mark Shepherd.

7. *Lazerwarz* (Baen, 1999) Dobie's ambitions didn't extend much beyond working in a fast-food joint until he discovered the world of laser-tag and a warrior's persona he didn't know he possessed. Written solely by Mark Shepherd.

8. *Stoned Souls* (Baen, 2006) Conal, an elven car racer, goes on vacation with his human friend, ace auto mechanic Dottie, only to learn that the human world is about to be invaded by the evil elves of the Unselieghe Court.

XII. The Heirs of Alexandria series, coauthored with Eric Flint (q.v.) and Dave Freer, is (so far) a pair of hefty (800+ pages each) novels set in an alternative 16th-century Venice, where the world has taken a different path from ours since 349 CE, when Saint Hypatia saved the great library of Alexandria. The protagonists are two brothers, Marco and Benito Valdosta, who rise from being "water-rats" to being members of the Venetian nobility. *The Wizard of Karres* (Baen, 2004), also coauthored with Flint and Freer, is a stand-alone novel about an interstellar circus.

1. *Shadow of the Lion, The* (Baen, 2002) "Water-rats" Marco and Benito Valdosta are apprised of a higher destiny when the shadow of the Lion of St. Mark's falls upon Marco. Cowritten by Eric Flint and Dave Freer.

2. *This Rough Magic* (Baen, 2003) Marco and Benito are in the Venetian nobility, but Benito has been exiled to Corfu, and the Demon Chernebog has possessed the Grand Duke of Lithuania and formed an alliance with the witch-king Emeric of Hungary. Co-written by Eric Flint and Dave Freer. Not to be confused with other books with the same title: Mary Stewart's (q.v.) novel or Alexander Paul's biography of Sylvia Plath.

XIII. The Obsidian trilogy, coauthored with classical scholar James Mallory, concerns a world in which three kinds of magic are rivals for supremacy. Lackey and Mallory have created a new trilogy, Enduring Flame, set in the same universe (numbers 4 and 5 so far).

1. *Outstretched Shadow, The* (Tor, 2003) Kellen Tavadon, son of the Arch-Mage of Armethalion, raised to believe that High Magick is the only true magic, discovers a set of books about the heretical Wild Magic. Cowritten with James Mallory.

2. *To Light a Candle* (Tor, 2004) Elves of the House of Leaf and Star, with their allies, who include unicorns and centaurs, face some formidable foes: immortal demons, ice trolls, frost-giants, and goblins. Coauthored with James Mallory.

3. *When Darkness Falls* (Tor, 2006) Knight-Mage Kennen, leader of the alliance of humans and elves, teams with half-demon, half-human healer Vestakia against the forces of the demon queen Savilla. Coauthored with James Mallory.

4. *Phoenix Unchained, The* (Tor, 2007) A thousand years after the events in number 3, Harrier and Tiercel engage on a quest to rejuvenate the fading Magick of their world.

5. *Phoenix Endangered, The* (Tor, 2008) Not yet published.

XIV. The Bard's Tale, another series written with coauthors, is based on a computer series of that name. Again, we are in a fantasy universe in which Good and Evil are pitted against each other. Josepha Sherman coauthored number 1 and was the sole author of number

4. Ru Emerson coauthored number 2. Mark Shepherd coauthored number 3 and was the sole author of number 6. Aaron Allston and Holly Lisle coauthored number 5.

1. *Castle of Deception* (Baen, 1992) On a simple manuscript copying mission, Kevin loses the manuscript and meets Chrina, who is then kidnapped. Cowritten by Josepha Sherman.
2. *Fortress of Frost and Fire* (Baen, 1993) Rumors of a valley that remains snow covered even during summer provoke the trek of Yaitachal and Gawaine. Cowritten by Ru Emerson.
3. *Prison of Souls* (Baen, 1993) Alaire, the king's son, and his Dark Elf mentor are sent on a secret mission to Suonomen, a neighboring kingdom where magic is forbidden. Cowritten with Mark Shepherd.
4. *Chaos Gate* (Baen, 1994) Reformed Dark Elf Naitachal has become a bard, and his clan has disowned him. Written solely by Josepha Sherman.
5. *Wrath of the Princes* (Baen, 1997) Kin Underbridge and Halleyne der Dero have returned home to Feyndala, where certain forces are out to get them. Cowritten by Aaron Allston and Holly Lisle.
6. *Escape from Roksamur* (Baen, 1997) Bard Alaire has been made Ambassador to Suonomen, where he was once imprisoned for practicing magic. Written solely by Mark Shepherd.

XV. The Elemental Masters is a loosely connected fantasy series that is set in an alternate pre–World War I Earth, mainly in London. The Elemental Masters control the powers of Fire, Water, Air, and Earth. Some of the stories are the retelling of fairy tales.

1. *Fire Rose, The* (Baen, 1995) On the eve of the San Francisco earthquake (1906), recently orphaned Rose Hawkins travels there to work for Jason Cameron, who seeks a spell to free him from his half-man, half-wolf form.
2. *Serpent's Shadow, The* (DAW, 2002) Set in 1909. Maya Witherspoon exiles herself to India, where she spent the first 25 years of life, and she rediscovers the family's magical tradition spurned by her aristocratic mother, Surrya.
3. *Gates of Sleep, The* (DAW, 2002) In this retelling of "Sleeping Beauty" set in Devon, England, around 1912, Marina Rocswood has been trained as an Elemental Master by her foster parents. Now she has to reconnect with her birth parents.
4. *Phoenix and Ashes* (DAW, 2004) This Cinderella fairy tale is retold against the background of London in World War I.
5. *Wizard of London, The* (DAW, 2005) The story of Lord Alderscroft, Master of the British Elemental Masters Council, the most powerful Fire Master ever to lead the council. Loosely based on "The Snow Queen."
6. *Reserved for the Cat* (DAW, 2007) When Ninette Dupond is fired from the Paris Opera Ballet, her "elementally gifted" cat, Thomas, persuades her to immigrate to England and assume the identity of Russian prima donna Nina Tchereslavsky.

XVI. Lackey coauthored *Reaping the Whirlwind* (Baen, 1989) with C. J. Cherryh (q.v.). She coauthored *Wing Commander: Freedom Flight* (Baen, 1992) with Ellen Guon and the first of the Wing Commander series, which has been continued by William R. Fortschen (q.v.). She coauthored, with Piers Anthony (q.v.), *If I Pay Thee Not in Gold* (Baen, 1993). She coauthored one of the Darkover series (with Marion Zimmer Bradley [q.v.]): *Rediscovery* (Baen, 1993), and one of the Brain Ship series (with Anne McCaffrey [q.v.] and Margaret Ball): *The Ship Who Searched* (Baen, 1993; reissued in *Brain Ships* with McCaffrey's and Ball's *Partnership*, Baen, 2003). *Counting Crows* is a novella published with works by Catherine Asaro and Rachel Lee in *Charmed Destinies*

(Mills & Boon, Australia, 2005). *Moontide* is a novella published with works by Tanith Lee (q.v.) and C. E. Murphy in *Winter Moon* (Mills & Boon, Australia, 2005). *Tiger Burning Bright* (Morrow, 1995) is a stand-alone coauthored with Bradley and Andre Norton.

The Sword of Knowledge (Baen, 1995) is an omnibus volume containing three novels coauthored with Nancy Asire, C. J. Cherryh (q.v.), and Leslie Fish (*A Dirge for Sabis, Reap the Whirlwind*, and *Wizard Spawn* all Baen, 1989). Lackey also coauthored, with Andre Norton (q.v.), the Halfblood Chronicles, about which see under Norton. The Doubled Edge series, coauthored with Roberta Gellis, is set in an alternate-history 16th-century England, in which elves coexist with human beings, and take part in the struggle over the English throne in succession to Henry VIII.

1. *This Scepter'd Isle* (Baen, 2004) Rhoslyn and Pasgen Silverhair, elven twins kidnapped by Vidal Dhu and raised as Unseleighe Sidhe, receive alternate visions of the future succession to King Henry VIII of England.
2. *Ill Met by Moonlight* (Baen, 2005) The evil Unseleighe Sidhe are determined that the little red-haired girl Elizabeth will never grow up to become queen of England.
3. *By Slanderous Tongues* (Baen, 2007) The Dark Sidhe, or Unseleighe, play to destroy Lord Denoriel and his twin sister, Aleneil, the benevolent guardians of Princess Elizabeth.

XVII. The Dragon Jousters series, reminiscent of Anne McCaffrey's (q.v.) Dragon Riders of Pern series, is about warriors who ride flying dragons in a world inspired by the culture of ancient Egypt, the legends of Atlantis, and Lackey's knowledge of animal behavior and biology.

1. *Joust* (DAW, 2003) Vetch, a young serf, dreams of becoming a Dragon Jouster, one of the few warriors who can actually ride a flying dragon.
2. *Alta* (DAW, 2004) Vetch (aka Kiron) escapes to his homeland of Alta on the wings of a recently hatched dragon, with hopes of sharing his knowledge of dragon rearing and training with the Altan military.
3. *Sanctuary* (DAW, 2005) Wing-leader Kiron and a group of refugees from Alta and Tia flee to a hidden refuge in the desert that the gods uncovered and named Sanctuary.
4. *Aerie* (DAW, 2006) Kiron and his cohorts join other dragon riders in Sanctuary to rid their world of both war and magic domination. A new society is to be built in Aerie.

XVIII. The Five Hundred Kingdoms is a new Lackey series published by Luna, an imprint devoted to women and fantasy fiction. So far, it is a saga featuring a diverse cast of characters in romantic and fantastic situations.

1. *Fairy Godmother, The* (Luna, 2004) In this version of the Cinderella story, Elena Klovis, left holding the bag when her stepmother and stepsisters skip town to escape their debts, becomes an apprentice to a fairy godmother.
2. *One Good Knight* (Luna, 2006) Princess Andromeda offers herself as a virgin sacrifice to a dragon and is rescued, sort of, by Sir George.
3. *Fortune's Fool* (Luna, 2007) Princess Ekaterina, seventh daughter of the Sea King, is sent on a spying mission to the Drylands.

Lambdin, Dewey

Eighteenth-century Royal Navy officer Alan Lewrie is a cross between C. S. Forester's (q.v.) Horatio Hornblower and George MacDonald Fraser's (q.v.) Flashman. Unlike the relatively straitlaced Hornblower, Lewrie subscribes to the un-Victorian moral codes of his day and is, in fact, something of a scamp. Lewrie's military and amorous adventures feature historical accuracy, exciting battles, intriguing glimpses of 18th-century life on land and a likable rogue for a hero. *For King and Country* (Fine, 1994) is an omnibus volume containing numbers 3, 4, and 5.

1. *King's Coat, The* (Fine, 1989) In 1780 17-year-old Alan Lewrie is done out of his maternal inheritance and forced into the Royal Navy by his rake-hell father, Major General Sir Hugo St. George Willoughby.
2. *French Admiral, The* (Fine, 1990) In 1781 Midshipman Lewrie sails on the frigate *Desperate* for America to defend the Crown at Yorktown, Virginia.
3. *King's Commission, The* (Fine, 1991) In 1783 Alan has risen to First Lieutenant on the brig *Shrike* in the Caribbean under the command of ancient seaman Lieutenant Lilycrop.
4. *King's Privateer, The* (Fine, 1992) In 1783 Lewrie ships out to India, China, and the Spanish Pacific as Fourth Lieutenant on the trading ship *Telesco* to thwart Philippine pirates supported by the French.
5. *Gun Ketch, The* (Fine, 1993) In 1786 Alan marries Caroline, and the newlyweds head to the Bahamas, where he'll enforce the Navigation Acts aboard HMS *Alacrity*.
6. *H.M.S. Cockerel* (Fine, 1995) In 1792 Lewrie is recalled from his life as a gentleman farmer in Surrey. He becomes First Officer of the frigate *Cockerel*. He spices his service with the neurotic and overbearing Captain Braxton by a jaunt to Naples and an affair with Lady Emma Hamilton.
7. *King's Commander, A* (Fine, 1997) Now commander of HMS *Jester*, Lewrie is patrolling the Ligurian Sea and trying to catch and kill Guillaume Choudas ("Le Hideux"), a personal enemy whom he maimed several years before.
8. *Jester's Fortune* (Dutton, 1998) Still commander of the sloop *Jester*, Lewrie is in the Adriatic maintaining Britain's alliance with Venice. Then his squadron commander gets the bright idea of enlisting some Serbian pirates . . . Set in 1796.
9. *King's Captain* (St. Martin's, 2000) Begins with the British naval victory off Cape St. Vincent in 1797. Lewrie is made captain of the brand-new frigate *Proteus*, which proves to be a mixed blessing when British sailors mutiny at Spithead and the Nore.
10. *Sea of Grey* (St. Martin's, 2002) Lewrie sails to the Caribbean in command of the *Proteus*. The slaves of Santo Domingo (Haiti) have revolted under Toussaint L'Ouverture. The crew of the *Proteus* having been decimated by yellow fever, Lewrie enlists Blacks to keep afloat.
11. *Havoc's Sword* (St. Martin's, 2003) Lewrie is tasked with hounding his old nemesis, French commander Guillaume Choudas, who has been sent to sow discord on Hispaniola (Santo Domingo).
12. *Captain's Vengeance, The* (St. Martin's, 2004) 1799. Lewrie is in New Orleans in pursuit of pirates. Pirate leader Charite is plotting an anti-Spanish insurrection.
13. *King's Trade, A* (St. Martin's, 2006) Lewrie's slave-stealing escapade in number 10 comes back to haunt him two years later, as the Beaumann clan of Jamaica at last suspects him of the hanging offense.
14. *Troubled Waters* (St. Martin's, 2008) Captain Lewrie has been sentenced to death in absentia by a Jamaican court for stealing slaves and is pursued to England by enemies trying to carry out that sentence.

L'Amour, Louis

With over 120 books to his credit, Louis L'Amour surpassed even Zane Grey in popularity and sales. Though L'Amour preferred to call his novels "stories of the frontier" rather than westerns, they have all the traditional elements of the genre: lots of shoot-outs and hard riding and good solid storytelling. L'Amour took pride in giving his stories authentic settings and period detail, and his treatment of the American Indian avoided stereotype. Before his death in 1988, L'Amour wrote *The Sackett Companion* (Bantam, 1988), which helps sort out the various branches of the Sackett family tree as well as the two other families whose members intertwine with the Sacketts: the French Talon family and the Irish Chantry family. Media adaptations of L'Amour's works include an NBC-TV miniseries based on the Sackett series and the 1953 John Wayne movie *Hondo*, which is based on L'Amour's non-Sackett book of the same name. L'Amour also wrote the novelization of the movie *How the West Was Won*, and early in his career produced some of the Hopalong Cassidy series under the pseudonym Tex Burns. *Education of a Wandering Man* (Bantam, 1989) is an autobiography that fans will not want to miss. *The Sacketts: Beginning of a Dynasty* (Saturday Review, 1976) is an omnibus containing numbers 6, 7, and 8. Five volumes of posthumously collected short stories by L'Amour have been published by Bantam, the last in 2003.

1. *Sackett's Land* (Saturday Review, 1974) This starts in 1599 and shows Barnabas Sackett on the run in Elizabethan London pursued by the nasty Rupert Genester.
2. *To the Far Blue Mountains* (Saturday Review, 1976) Barnabas and Abigail settle on the James River in Virginia, fight off Indians, and raise a family.
3. *Warrior's Path, The* (Bantam, 1980) Kin-Ring Sackett and his brother Yance make a journey through treacherous territory to rescue a settler's beautiful daughter. Set in 1630 in what is now Boston.
4. *Jubal Sackett* (Bantam, 1985) Jubal Sackett, third son of Barnabas, moves west from the Carolinas to what is now New Mexico and wins a Natchez princess.
5. *Ride the River* (Bantam, 1983) This tells the story of Echo Sackett, youngest female descendant of Kin-Ring.
6. *Daybreakers, The* (Bantam, 1960) Tye Sackett tells the story of how he and his brother Orrin leave Tennessee for the Great Plains and beyond.
7. *Sackett* (Bantam, 1961) In this first published volume of the series, William Tell Sackett, brother of Orrin and Tye, meets the beautiful Ange in Colorado and brings her back to become his wife.
8. *Lando* (Bantam, 1962) In pursuit of buried gold in Mexico, Lando Sackett runs out of luck. Six years in a Mexican prison give him a thirst for revenge that nothing will quench.
9. *Mojave Crossing* (Bantam, 1964) Trouble, in the shape of a black-eyed woman, finds Tell Sackett as he crosses the Colorado River with his saddlebags full of gold.
10. *Sackett Brand, The* (Bantam, 1965) In 1877 Tell Sackett and his wife are shot, but his Sackett relatives from high and low come to his aid.
11. *Lonely Men, The* (Bantam, 1969) Tell Sackett is lured into Apache country by the icy beauty of his brother's wife.
12. *Treasure Mountain* (Bantam, 1972) Orrin Sackett runs into trouble in New Orleans when he tries to investigate his father's disappearance 20 years earlier.

13. *Mustang Man* **(Bantam, 1966)** Nolan Sackett, on the run from the law, is slowed down by women—first by the sly Sylvie who tries to poison him, then by Penelope.

14. *Galloway* **(Bantam, 1970)** Galloway Sackett goes searching for his brother Flagon, last seen naked and hand-tied by his Indian captors.

15. *Sky-Liners, The* **(Bantam, 1967)** Black Fletchen is coming for the Sackett boys—Galloway and Flagon—with the most expensive hired guns in the country.

16. *Man from Broken Hills, The* **(Bantam, 1975)** Milo Talon tracks a man through the post–Civil War West.

17. *Ride the Dark Trail* **(Bantam, 1972)** Old Emily Talon (née Sackett) of the MT Ranch needs help.

18. *Lonely on the Mountain* **(Bantam, 1980)** Tell, Tyrel, and Orrin Sackett herd cattle across the Dakota plains towards Canada through trails never crossed before.

Langton, Jane

Fans of Asey Mayo will enjoy meeting Homer Kelly, another Massachusetts sleuth, whose territory includes the affluent suburban towns northwest of Boston—Bedford, Concord, Lincoln, and the fictional "Nashoba." Homer is a "gentleman" detective, just as likely to quote Thoreau as to draw on his past experience as a detective in a district attorney's office. Now retired, Homer teaches an American literature class with his wife, Mary, at Harvard, and leisurely unravels the mysteries that come his way. Strong on character, local color, historical lore, and sly humor, the books are illustrated with wonderful line drawings by Langton. Langton is also the author of a series of juveniles set in Concord, Massachusetts.

1. *Transcendental Murder, The* **(Harper, 1964)** This first case shows Homer meeting his future wife, Mary, as he investigates the murders of some leading authorities on the Transcendentalists. Variant title: *The Minute Man Murder*.

2. *Dark Nantucket Moon* **(Harper, 1975)** A murder occurs on Nantucket during an eclipse of the sun, and Homer comes to the defense of the accused.

3. *Memorial Hall Murder* **(Harper, 1978)** An explosion in Harvard's Memorial Hall disturbs a rehearsal of Handel's *Messiah* and supplies a headless corpse for Homer to investigate.

4. *Natural Enemy* **(Ticknor, 1982)** Young John Hand is pursuing his study of spiders and working as a summer handyman when he finds a need for his uncle Homer's expert help.

5. *Emily Dickinson Is Dead* **(St. Martin's, 1984)** Arson and murder shock the academics assembled for an Emily Dickinson symposium in Amherst, but Homer is on hand to set things right.

6. *Good and Dead* **(St. Martin's, 1987)** Too many deaths among the parishioners of Old West Church in Nashoba give Homer an extraordinary case to ponder.

7. *Murder at the Gardner* **(St. Martin's, 1988)** Is the prankster haunting Boston's Isabella Stewart Gardner Museum out for profit or revenge?

8. *Dante Game, The* **(Viking, 1991)** Homer goes to teach in Florence, Italy, and gets involved in some Florentine scandals including murder.

9. *God in Concord* **(Viking, 1992)** Homer and a small band of Concord faithful try to fend off a rapacious Boston developer who wants to gets his clutches on Walden Pond.

10. *Divine Inspiration* **(Viking, 1993)** Inexplicable happenings occur when the First Church of the Commonwealth in Boston tries to install a new organ.

11. *Shortest Day, The* **(Viking, 1995)** In Cambridge the annual Christmas Revels is being rehearsed, the Harvard campus is home to a tent city, and Sarah Bailey's male colleagues are being killed off.

12. *Dead as a Dodo* **(Viking, 1996)** While Homer is a visiting lecturer at Oxford University in England, several mysteries crop up, some revolving around the long-lost zoological specimens from Darwin's voyage on the *Beagle*.

13. *Face on the Wall, The* **(Viking, 1998)** A mystery full of echoes of folk-tales and nursery rhymes that involves the disappearance of the much-abused wife of a greedy land developer and the violent death of Eddy, an eight-year-old Down syndrome child.

14. *Thief of Venice, The* **(Viking, 1999)** In Venice, Italy, for a scholarly conference on rare books, Homer and Mary get involved with expatriate English doctor Richard Henchard, who has stumbled upon a cache of golden artifacts and has already killed twice to preserve his secret.

15. *Murder at Monticello* **(Viking, 2001)** In Charlottesville, Virginia, for the bicentennial of Thomas Jefferson's presidential election, Homer comes to the aid of a researcher at Monticello, who is being stalked by a serial killer, and her boyfriend, who is being accused of murder.

16. *Escher Twist, The* **(Viking, 2002)** Homer and Mary assist crystallographer Leonard Sheldrake in his search for the elusive Frieda, who disappeared after they met at an exhibition of the illusory art of the Dutch printmaker M. C. Escher in Cambridge.

17. *Deserter, The* **(St. Martin's, 2003)** Subtitle: *Murder at Gettysburg*. In a tale that shifts between past and present, Homer and Mary try to exonerate Seth Morgan, Mary's ancestor, a Harvard man suspected of desertion at the Battle of Gettysburg (1863).

18. *Steeplechase* **(St. Martin's, 2005)** Homer and Mary decide to spice up *Steeplechase*, the book about Massachusetts churches that he is writing, by piecing together the conflict over an ancient chestnut tree between two 19th-century churchmen in Nashoba.

LaPierre, Janet

Port Sylva, a fictional small town on northern California's Mendocino coast, is the scene of a series of mysteries. The most prominent of a host of characters are Meg Halloran, widowed teacher, her daughter Katy, police chief Vince Gutierrez, whom Meg eventually marries, and the mother-and-daughter private investigator team, Patience and Verity McKellar. Some of the plots are fairly complicated, but characterization is the strongest point in these mystery novels.

1. *Unquiet Grave* **(St. Martin's, 1987)** Computer science professor Joe Mancuso is accused of murdering Ilona, a beautiful student found dead after leaving a party hosted by Mancuso.

2. *Children's Games* **(Scribner, 1989)** Widowed teacher Meg Halloran and her 10-year-old daughter Katy move from Arizona to Port Silva, where Meg becomes a suspect in the murder of a former student who had been harassing her.

3. *Cruel Mother, The* **(Scribner, 1990)** Meg Halloran, Vince Gutierrez and Vince's niece Cass, heading for a camping vacation in Idaho, get involved in an automobile accident.

4. *Grandmother's House* **(Scribner, 1991)** Piano teacher Charlotte Birdsong is being pressured by developers to sell the small house on a historic street that she has inherited.

5. *Old Enemies* **(Scribner, 1993)** Meg Halloran and Katy drive to Washington state to see a wolf reserve and a former student, and get caught up in a murderous battle over grazing rights.

6. *Baby Mine* (**Perseverance, 1999**) Meg and Vince are now married. Meg gets beaten up by a gang of local toughs, and there are some nasty incidents at a local fertility clinic.

7. *Keepers* (**Perseverance, 2001**) Introduces Patience and Verity McKellar, a mother-and-daughter private-eye team. A search for a lost child brings them to a reclusive religious community.

8. *Death Duties* (**Perseverance, 2004**) Verity and Patience are hired by Christina Larson to clear her grandfather's name of a pedophile accusation made 30 years earlier.

9. *Family Business* (**Perseverance, 2006**) A peaceful antiwar protest march turns into a riot, and one of the protestors disappears.

Lardo, Vincent

I. After the death of Lawrence Sanders (q.v.), Lardo took on the task of writing the Archy McNally series. The Palm Beach playboy-sleuth continues on his merry way in six new novels, for which Sanders is still listed as principal author. *McNally's Risk* and *McNally's Gamble*, which Vincent Lardo coauthored, are listed under Lawrence Sanders.

1. *McNally's Dilemma* (**Putnam, 1999**) Palm Beach socialite Melva Williams has just shot her husband, whom she caught in flagrante delicto with a younger woman, as she confesses to Archy.

2. *McNally's Folly* (**Putnam, 2000**) Archie takes on directing duties for the Palm Beach Community Theater's production of *Arsenic and Old Lace*, which is being graced by Hollywood legend Desdemona Darling. Then an actor takes a sip of prop wine and drops dead.

3. *McNally's Chance* (**Putnam, 2001**) Best-selling romance author Sabrina Wright asks Archy to find her missing husband and daughter.

4. *McNally's Alibi* (**Putnam, 2002**) Decimus Fortesque, wealthy collector of wives and manuscripts, hires Archy to locate the complete text of Truman Capote's *Answered Prayers*.

5. *McNally's Dare* (**Putnam, 2003**) A young waiter working Malcolm "Nifty" MacNiff's Tennis Everyone! annual benefit is found dead in Nifty's swimming pool, just after the arrival of Lance Talbot, putative heir to a Palm Beach fortune.

6. *McNally's Bluff* (**Putnam, 2004**) Marlena Marvel, wife of former carnival performer and impresario Matthew Hayes, is found dead in the garden hedge maze based on the one at Hampton Court.

II. Vincent Lardo has written a pair of mystery novels set in the posh Long Island, New York, enclave of East Hampton. Michael Reo, who has "wed it wealthfully," is one of the continuing characters in this pair of romps.

1. *Hampton Affair, The* (**Putnam, 2000**) Michael Reo is desperately trying to save his marriage, which is tied to his wife's money. Galen Miller is trying to save his stake in his suddenly valuable family farm. Detective Eddy Evans is caught in the middle.

2. *Hampton Connection, The* (**Putnam, 2001**) The corpse of a young lady is discovered, with a Freddy Parc jockstrap around her neck, by Paul Monroe, current poster boy for Freddy Parc briefs and Michael Reo's choice as leading man for his planned movie about the Hamptons's last big murder mystery.

Lashner, William

Victor Carl is a "Philadelphia Lawyer" in more ways than one: not only is he a defense attorney practicing in Philadelphia, Pennsylvania, but he is also shrewd and manipulative. Victor doesn't usually get the cases or the money that he feels he deserves, and he feels bitter about the prestige law firms and WASP blue bloods who have kept him down. Victor's character, however, ages well, and he becomes more philosophical and humorous, if not less venal and basically amoral. The mysteries Victor narrates are usually interesting, but it is the narration itself that is the real selling point of this series. William Lashner was once a Philadelphia lawyer himself, and still lives in the Philadelphia area.

1. *Hostile Witness* (**ReganBooks, 1995**) Down-at-the-heels Philadelphia defense attorney Victor Carl jumps at the chance to work with Talbott, Kittredge, and Chase, representing Chet Concannon, lieutenant of antidrug crusading councilman Jimmy Moore, under indictment for extortion, murder, and arson.

2. *Veritas* (**ReganBooks, 1997**) Victor's new client, Caroline Shaw, one of the filthy rich Reddmans, wants Victor to use his mob connections to get to the bottom of her sister Jacqueline's death. "Veritas" is the (inappropriate) name of the Reddman mansion. Variant title: *Bitter Truth*.

3. *Fatal Flaw* (**Morrow, 2003**) Victor receives a frantic call from his friend Guy Forest and finds Guy naked and sobbing on the steps of a suburban house, inside of which lies the corpse of Hailey Prouix, his lover.

4. *Past Due* (**Morrow, 2004**) Victor, while paying hospital visits to his dying father, gets involved in a complex case connecting a recent murder to one 20 years ago. A cheap thug named Joey Parma (aka Joey Cheaps) is at the bottom of both murders, one as a "perp," the other as the victim.

5. *Falls the Shadow* (**Morrow, 2005**) Victor is paid in advance to seek a new trial for French chef Francois Dub, who was convicted of murdering his beautiful wife.

6. *Marked Man* (**Morrow, 2006**) Victor wakes up after a bibulous evening with a terrible hangover and the name "Chantal Adair" tattooed on his chest.

7. *Killer's Kiss, A* (**Morrow, 2007**) Victor is a prime suspect in the murder of Dr. Wren Dienniston, husband of his former fiancée, Julia.

Lasswell, Mary

Three old girls who live in a southern California junkyard captured the affection of wartime readers all across America. Toothless Mrs. Feeley, the salty owner of the junkyard named "Noah's Ark," and her friends Mrs. Rasmussen, a marvelously resourceful cook, and Miss Tinkham, a retired music teacher, make the most of reduced circumstances and wartime shortages with high spirits and plenty of cold beer. Readers with a thirst for nostalgia will find the trio's high jinks still hit the spot; others will find pretzels more nutritious. George Price's cartoon illustrations add to the fun.

1. *Suds in Your Eye* (**Houghton Mifflin, 1942**) In their first adventure, the three ladies play cupid for their Spanish teacher, Miss Kate Logan.

2. *High Time* (**Houghton Mifflin, 1947**) Further high jinks as the ladies, determined to do their part in the war effort, donate blood, babysit, and take in hungry boarders.

3. *One on the House* (**Houghton Mifflin, 1949**) The merry trio visits New York and Newark, New Jersey, where they rescue a barroom from the jaws of bankruptcy while the owner is in the hospital.

4. *Wait for the Wagon* (**Houghton Mifflin, 1951**) This installment follows the ladies on their cross-country drive back to California in their 1926 Cadillac.

5. *Tooner Schooner* (**Houghton Mifflin, 1953**) While serving as crew of a chartered former tuna schooner, the ladies take time to straighten out the captain's love life.

6. *Lets Go for Broke* (Houghton Mifflin, 1962) The beer-loving ladies renovate a dilapidated Victorian house and find their little community much enlarged.

Lathen, Emma

PSEUDONYM OF Mary J. Latsis & Martha Hennissart

As everybody knows by now, "Emma Lathen" was really two Boston businesswomen, Mary J. Latsis and Martha Hennissart. Their entertaining mystery series mixes business, banking, and crime with style and wit. John Putnam Thatcher, who is senior vice president of New York's Sloan Guaranty Trust, the world's third largest bank, is their suave and perceptive amateur detective. They chose a banker because "there is nothing on God's earth a banker can't get into." Not incidentally, Lathen readers will pick up a lot of solid information about the various industries used as settings for each book. *Banking on Murder* (Macmillan, 1984) is an omnibus volume containing numbers 5, 6, and 7. Latsis and Hennissart also published mysteries under the name R. B. Dominic (q.v.).

1. *Banking on Death* (Macmillan, 1961) Thatcher's first case involves a missing heir, a murder and some funny business in industrial textiles.
2. *Place for Murder, A* (Macmillan, 1963) Thatcher solves a murder at a dog show in Connecticut.
3. *Accounting for Murder* (Macmillan, 1964) A murder at the National Calculating Corporation is Thatcher's next case.
4. *Murder Makes the Wheels Go Round* (Macmillan, 1966) In Detroit to investigate the auto industry as a potential investment for Sloan Guaranty Trust, Thatcher finds a corpse stashed in a bulletproof car.
5. *Death Shall Overcome* (Macmillan, 1966) Trouble on the New York Stock Exchange begins when black millionaire Edward Parry buys a seat.
6. *Murder against the Grain* (Macmillan, 1967) A phony wheat broker collects a check for $985,000, and all hell breaks loose on a big Russian wheat sale.
7. *Stitch in Time, A* (Macmillan, 1968) The medical industry comes in for some scrutiny in this case involving a possible suicide and $100,000 in insurance.
8. *Come to Dust* (Simon & Schuster, 1968) The peculiarities of fundraising by a small New Hampshire college become evident as Thatcher tries to find out who stole a $50,000 bearer bond intended for the college.
9. *When in Greece* (Simon & Schuster, 1969) The Greek colonels' revolution spells trouble for the Sloan's investment in a million dollar hydroelectric project.
10. *Murder to Go* (Simon & Schuster, 1969) Trouble in the fast-food industry starts with some very bad eating at a nationwide chain called Chicken Tonight.
11. *Pick Up Sticks* (Simon & Schuster, 1970) Hard-sell real estate in New Hampshire comes to grief.
12. *Ashes to Ashes* (Simon & Schuster, 1971) The funeral industry and a bankrupt parochial school share the spotlight in this case.
13. *Longer the Thread, The* (Simon & Schuster, 1971) This look at the ladies' garment industry in Puerto Rico focuses on some very suspicious accidents at Slax Unlimited.
14. *Murder without Icing* (Simon & Schuster, 1972) Multiple murder and professional ice hockey are the ingredients.
15. *Sweet and Low* (Simon & Schuster, 1974) The cocoa exchange and the candy industry are spotlighted when two high-ranking executives of the Dryer Chocolate Company are murdered.

16. *By Hook or by Crook* (Simon & Schuster, 1975) The Oriental rug business gives an exotic flavor to this case.
17. *Double, Double, Oil and Trouble* (Simon & Schuster, 1978) Murder and kidnapping trouble the North Sea offshore oil fields.
18. *Going for the Gold* (Simon & Schuster, 1981) Phony travelers checks and a murdered skier take Thatcher to the Winter Olympics at Lake Placid, New York.
19. *Green Grow the Dollars* (Simon & Schuster, 1982) The research and development of a new super tomato keep Thatcher and Miss Corso busy in this case of dirty dealings in the mail-order nursery business.
20. *Something in the Air* (Simon & Schuster, 1988) Sloan Guaranty Trust is concerned that Boston-based commuter airline Sparrow Flyways may be a fly-by-night operation.
21. *East Is East* (Simon & Schuster, 1991) Thatcher goes to Tokyo to witness the signing of an agreement between Lackawanna Electric Industries and Yonezawa Trading.
22. *Right on the Money* (Simon & Schuster, 1993) A merger between Sloan client Ecker and ASI, a water fixture manufacturer, is endangered by missing financial records, industrial sabotage, and murder.
23. *Brewing Up a Storm* (St. Martin's, 1996) Thatcher gets interested when anti-alcohol extremist Madeleine Underwood, head of NOBBY (No Beer Buying Youngsters), pickets Sloan client Rugby's, a chain of family restaurants, for carrying Quax, a nonalcoholic drink that she claims leads to alcoholism in the young.
24. *Shark out of Water, A* (St. Martin's, 1997) Polish police detective Oblonski enlists Thatcher's help in the murder of the chief of staff of BADA (Baltic Area Development Association) in Gdańsk as BADA acts as a clearing house for insurance claims related to a fog-induced disaster in Germany's Kiel Canal.

Laurence, Janet

I. British chef, caterer, and cookbook writer Darina Lisle is the heroine of a mystery series for gastronomes, full of loving descriptions of culinary fare seasoned with murders solved by Darina, sometimes with the aid of her lover (and eventual husband), Detective Sergeant William Pigram. English writer Janet Laurence (not to be confused with the Australian artist of the same name) has also written several cookbooks. *To Kill the Past* (St. Martin's, 1994) is not part of the series.

1. *Deepe Coffyn, A* (Doubleday, 1990) There are many suspects when the hateful president of the Society of Historical Gastronomes is killed in an old abbey after a weekend of gourmandizing.
2. *Tasty Way to Die, A* (Doubleday, 1991) Poisonings are disrupting business for Darina's former school chum, a London caterer.
3. *Hotel Morgue* (Doubleday, 1992) Darina tries to help the distraught owner of the Hotel Morgan to upgrade his declining country establishment.
4. *Recipe for Death* (Doubleday, 1993) After judging a cookery contest at London's Savoy Hotel, Darina visits winner Verity Fry's organic meat farm in Somerset.
5. *Death and the Epicure* (St. Martin's, 1994) Lisle is invited to write a cookbook with recipes using products packaged by importer Finer Foods, a family business that seems to be dysfunctional
6. *Death at the Table* (St. Martin's, 1997) Darina is invited to be part of a TV food show called Table for Four. The first broadcast seems to be a success until Australian wine expert Bruce Bennett drops dead on the air. Originally published in 1994.
7. *Death a la Provencale* (Macmillan [UK], 1995) Darina and her new husband, Detective Inspector William Pigram, are traveling in the South of France when one of their friends dies horribly.

8. *Diet for Death* (Macmillan [UK], 1996) Darina escorts her widowed mother to the Conifer Spa health farm, where Lady Barry's lifeless body is found in the spa pull and Pigram and his associate are called in to investigate.

9. *Appetite for Death* (Macmillan [UK], 1998) Darina's old school friend asks her to find the father of Rory Earlham, whose mother died in childbirth.

10. *Mermaid's Feast, The* (Macmillan [UK], 2000) Darina and William are on a cruise in the *Empress of India* when the ship's purser disappears overboard.

II. Laurence also authors a historical mystery series with the real-life Italian landscape painter Canaletto as the protagonist. The series takes place in the 1740s in England, where Canaletto has come seeking commissions.

1. *Canaletto and the Case of Westminster Bridge* (St. Martin's, 1998) Soon after Canaletto arrives in England, he is robbed and attacked twice. Both times he is rescued by Fanny Rooker, a young woman who aspires to be a painter.

2. *Canaletto and the Case of the Privy Garden* (Macmillan [UK], 1999) Set in 1747. One night Canaletto and his friend Owen McSwiney take refuge from a storm in an alley and stumble upon the stabbed body of a woman.

3. *Canaletto and the Case of Bonnie Prince Charlie* (Macmillan [UK], 2002) Only a few years after the Great Rebellion of 1745, English authorities are still nervous about Bonnie Prince Charlie. A rumor that he will be visiting London causes Canaletto to be enlisted as a spy at Badminton Park, which he has been commissioned to paint.

Law, Janice

PSEUDONYM OF Janice Law Trecka

Anna Peters is a private investigator and security specialist who moves around a lot. The latest title in her mystery series finds her in Orlando, Florida, but she was worked in Washington, DC; New York; Paris; Germany; Scotland; and elsewhere. Anna is a rather cool, cynical operative who sometimes gets involved with cases while accompanying her artist husband, Harry. Author Law gave strong hint in number 9 that she was retiring Anna Peters. At any rate, the three novels she has published since 1997 have all been stand-alones.

1. *Big Payoff, The* (Houghton Mifflin, 1976) Anna deals with oil financiers and international scoundrels in a case that winds up in Scotland.

2. *Gemini Trip* (Houghton Mifflin, 1977) Peters flies to Paris to find a brother and sister who are scheduled to inherit millions in oil money on their 21st birthdays.

3. *Under Orion* (Houghton Mifflin, 1978) Anna is in Germany with a fellow New World Oil employee on the trail of a new formula

4. *Shadow of the Palms, The* (Houghton Mifflin, 1980) Peters is persuaded by an old friend to investigate his nephew's sources of income, which may not be strictly on the up-and-up.

5. *Death under Par* (Houghton Mifflin, 1981) Anna accompanies her husband, Harry, to St. Andrews, Scotland for the British Open.

6. *Time Lapse* (Walker, 1992) Matinee idol and champion swimmer Henry Brook drowns while filming a movie on a estate in upstate New York.

7. *Safe Place to Die, A* (St. Martin's, 1993) Accompanying her husband to the opening of his show at a gallery in exclusive Branch Hill, Connecticut, Anna gets involved with suburban sin.

8. *Backfire* (St. Martin's, 1994) Peters is hired anonymously to prove the innocence of Maria Rivas, who is accused of setting the fire that killed her employer.

9. *Cross-Check* (St. Martin's, 1997) Alf Rene of the Orlando (Florida) Showmen hockey team has been murdered, and teammate Jorgen Parks is the prime suspect.

Lawhead, Stephen R.

I. Stephen R. Lawhead, popular Christian writer of fantasy, historical novels, science fiction, young adult fiction, and juveniles, is probably best-known for his Celtic and Arthurian cycles. His Song of Albion cycle features a Celtic "otherworld," Tuatha de Danaan, which can be entered can be entered through a stone cairn in Scotland. Oxford graduate student Lewis Gillies finds himself playing a major role in some important Celtic myths while fighting an ancient evil that threatens both worlds.

1. *Paradise War, The* (Lion, 1991) Lewis Gillies follows fellow Oxford graduate student Simon Rawnson through a hole in a Scottish cairn into the land of Tuatha de Danaan.

2. *Silver Hand, The* (Lion, 1992) After the assassination of Meldryn Mawr, King of the Llwyddi, the bard Tegid Tahal names Llew (Lewis) as king.

3. *Endless Knot, The* (Avon, 1993) Llew Silverhand, restored as king, fights the evil that threatens to take over Tuatha de Danaan.

II. The Pendragon cycle retells the story of King Arthur with some changes. The action shifts between a Roman-Celtic Britain and an "Atlantis" that is reminiscent of Minoan Crete. Arthur is a fairly orthodox Christian. Gwnewhyvar is faithful to Arthur. Mordred isn't Arthur's incestuous son. The climactic battle is fought against the Vandals and the Irish and isn't the end of Arthur, who has a final confrontation with the pagan Queen of Air and Darkness. *The Pendragon Cycle* (Crossway, 1989) is an omnibus volume containing numbers 1, 2, and 3.

1. *Taliesin* (Crossway, 1987) Tells the story of the love of the bard Taliesin and the Atlantean princess and bull dancer Charis.

2. *Merlin* (Crossway, 1988) Merlin's trials and tribulations before he becomes Arthur's mentor are told.

3. *Arthur* (Crossway, 1989) Arthur battles against the invading Saxons and treachery within his own ranks.

4. *Pendragon* (Morrow, 1994) Arthur fights his climactic battle against the combined forces of the Vandals and Irish.

5. *Grail* (Avon, 1997) Arthur's naive haste to establish the prophesied "Summer Kingdom" and to enshrine the Grail leads to much strife and a confrontation with the evil, pagan Queen of Air and Darkness.

III. The Celtic Crusades is a straight historical trilogy set in 11th- and 12th-century Europe. It follows the fortunes of four generations of one Orkneyan family through Medieval Europe as far afield as Constantinople and Spain. This is an action-packed trilogy full of historical detail.

1. *Iron Lance, The* (Harper, 1998) Lord Ranulf of Orkney sets off for the Crusades in 1095 with his two eldest sons. Youngest son Murdo is soon forced out of his family estate, and sets off on the Crusades himself.

2. *Black Rood, The* (Zondervan, 2000) In 1132, Duncan, son of Murdo, sets off on a perilous journey to find a remnant of the True Cross.

3. *Mystic Rose, The* **(Avon, 2001)** When Duncan is murdered in the Ayia Sophia in Constantinople, his daughter Caitrona, following a trail left by his murderer, the Templar Renaud de Bracineaux, sets sail for Spain in search of the Mystic Rose (Holy Grail).

IV. A pair of science-fiction novels, originally published in the 1980s and collected in one volume as *Empyrion* (Lion, 2002), also has a Christian theme. It is the saga of Orion Treet, writer of history books nobody buys, who becomes part of an expedition to an extraterrestrial colony where he finds two divergent human colonies.

1. *Search for Fierra, The* **(Crossway, 1985)** Orion Treet, invited to accompany a top-secret mission to observe and document the extraterrestrial colony of Dome, arrives and soon discovers that something has gone terribly wrong with Dome.
2. *Siege of Dome, The* **(Crossway, 1986)** Treet crosses the wasteland to the settlement of Fierra, a true utopia and a foretaste of heaven in this life. Unfortunately Dome has designs on Fierra.

V. The King Raven trilogy is a retelling of the Robin Hood saga, set in the reign of William Rufus (1087–1100). "Robin Hood" is Bran ap Brychan, son of a Welsh king.

1. *Hood* **(Nelson, 2006)** In 1093 CE, when his father's kingdom of Elfael is destroyed by the Normans, Bran ap Brychan takes to the woods. First volume of the King Raven trilogy.
2. *Scarlet* **(Nelson, 2007)** Will Scarlet is facing hanging. Bran makes a desperate voyage to France to thwart a plot against King William Rufus. Volume 2 of the King Raven trilogy.

Lawrence, D(avid) H(erbert)

The 1970 film *Women in Love*, starring Glenda Jackson, Alan Bates, and Oliver Reed, was as dense and dramatic as the novel it was based upon. Readers turning to the original for clarification found that the author's lush prose lapsed occasionally into impenetrability. But Lawrence's insistence on giving his characters a sexual dimension makes his books come alive for modern readers. What is shocking now is that *The Rainbow* could ever have been condemned as obscene, even in 1915. In 1989 *The Rainbow* was made into a film starring Sammi Davis and Glenda Jackson.

1. *Rainbow, The* **(Viking, 1915)** This covers three generations of the Brangwen family of farmers and craftsmen who live in the coal mining town of Nottinghamshire. Tom Brangwen marries Lydia, whose daughter Anna becomes the mother of Ursula and Gudrun.
2. *Women in Love* **(Viking, 1920)** Ursula and Gudrun, young women of the emancipated 20th century, seek love and meaning in life. Gudrun is said to have been based on Katherine Mansfield.

Le Carré, John

PSEUDONYM OF David Cornwall

Alec Guinness made a perfect George Smiley in the British production of *Tinker, Tailor, Soldier, Spy*, shown in the United States on PBS. Short, stodgy, and bespectacled, he is a man described by his frequently unfaithful wife, Ann, as "breathtakingly ordinary." But Smiley is such a master of espionage that he is always being dragged out of retirement and his study of obscure German poets for one last assignment. Some readers claim that they can actually follow all the convolutions of le Carré's corkscrew plots, but even readers who miss a turn

or two will feel the suspense and excitement le Carré spins out so exquisitely. Movie versions of le Carré's novels include the classic *The Spy Who Came in from the Cold* (1965), *The Deadly Affair* (1967; based on *Call for the Dead*), *The Tailor of Panama* (2001; nonseries novel, Knopf, 1996), and *The Looking Glass War* (1970). Numbers 1 and 2 are bound together as *The Incongruous Spy* (Walker, 1962). Since the cold war ended, le Carré, who spends most of his time in a remote corner of Cornwall, has found a new villain: multinational corporations. *Absolute Friends* (Little, Brown, 2004) is a scathing portrait of the events that led up to the latest American (and British) adventure in Iraq. *The Mission Song* (Little, Brown, 2006) is a look at the Congo and the botched efforts to bring democracy there.

1. *Call for the Dead* **(Walker, 1962)** Smiley solves a puzzle involving a twisted former hero of the German underground and a once-beautiful woman with a secret. Variant title: *The Deadly Affair*
2. *Murder of Quality, A* **(Walker, 1962)** The baffling, bloody murder of a teacher's wife brings Smiley to an ancient and renowned public school in Dorsetshire.
3. *Spy Who Came in from the Cold, A* **(Coward, 1964)** This story of Sean Leamas' last assignment is a classic of the genre. Smiley finds this operation distasteful and is only a shadowy figure throughout.
4. *Looking Glass War, The* **(Coward, 1965)** Spying seems an extraordinarily pedestrian and seedy business in this novel set in East Berlin. Smiley plays a very peripheral role.
5. *Tinker, Tailor, Soldier, Spy* **(Knopf, 1974)** Smiley is shown as a consummate spymaster as he flushes out the mole who has burrowed to the top of British intelligence.
6. *Honorable Schoolboy, The* **(Knopf, 1977)** As head of the circus, Smiley sends Jerry Westerby, the honorable schoolboy, on a mission to Hong Kong.
7. *Smiley's People* **(Knopf, 1979)** Smiley has a final confrontation with Karla, his mortal enemy and opposite number in the Soviet Union.
8. *Secret Pilgrim, The* **(Knopf, 1990)** Smiley's graduation remarks at Sarratt, the British intelligence school, trigger the memory of "Ned," the school's retiring head.

Le Guin, Ursula K(roeber)

The books in Le Guin's Ekumen, or Hainish, series are connected by their location in a future galactic federation of human-inhabited worlds. The novels are separated from each other by hundreds, or thousands, of years in the 3rd to the 5th millennia CE. Dozens of planets were populated millions of years ago by human beings from the original human world of Hain. Due to the lack of faster-than-light travel and communication, the Ekumen galaxy collapsed, and the colony planets (including Earth) lost touch with each other. Now there is instantaneous communication over the light-years and efforts to reestablish the galactic civilization. Ursula K. Le Guin is known as a soft science-fiction writer. She uses her settings primarily to exploit anthropological and sociological themes, including feminism, Taoism, and anarchism. Her universe is full of sympathetic beings, human and "semi-human." *Three Hainish Novels* (Doubleday, 1966), reprinted as *Worlds of Exile and Illusion* (Orb, 1996), is an omnibus volume containing numbers 3, 4, and 5. Books are arranged by the internal chronology of the series rather than by publication date.

Le Guin, daughter of anthropologist Alfred Kroeber and writer Theodora Kroeber (*Ishi in Two Worlds*), has written many other fiction and nonfiction works, including several series for juveniles, such as Earthsea, Adventures in Kroy, Catwings, and Chronicles of the Western Shore. The stand-alone SF novel *Lathe of Heaven* (Scribner,

1971) has been produced as a TV movie twice. Le Guin has published several short story collections, including *The Wind's Twelve Quarters* (Harper, 1975), which includes Hainish stories. Other story collections include *The Compass Rose* (HarperCollins, 1982); *A Fisherman of the Inland Sea* (HarperPrism, 1994); and *The Birthday of the World and Other Stories* (HarperCollins, 2002). The novel *Malafrena* (Putnam, 1979) and the short-story collection *Orsinian Tales* are set in imaginary countries.

Le Guin has explored her themes and ideas in essay collections such as *Dancing on the Edge of the World* (Grove, 1989) and *The Wave in the Mind* (Shambhala, 2994). Books about Le Guin include Donna R. White, *Dancing with Dragons* (Camden House, 1998).

1. **Dispossessed, The (Harper, 1974)** Shevek, a physicist trying to develop a General Temporal Theory, runs into opposition to his ideas from the power-structure on the moon Anarres and decides to journey to the planet Urras to open up a dialogue between the two worlds.

2. **Word for World Is Forest, The (Putnam, 1976)** Colonists from Earth have taken over the planet Athshe ("Forest"), enslaved its nonviolent inhabitants, and cut down trees to make room for farms and mines.

3. **Rocannon's World (Ace, 1966)** A young woman named Semley takes a space voyage from her unnamed, technologically primitive planet, not realizing that, while the trip will be of short duration for her, many years will elapse on her planet. First novel published by Le Guin.

4. **Planet of Exile (Ace, 1966)** The planet Werel, which has an orbital period of 60 years, is at the approach of its long winter. The humanoid tribe of the Tevarans and a dwindling colony of Earth humans are ill-at-ease with each other. Tevarans Wold and his daughter Rolery and human Jakob Agat are the main characters. Originally published together with Thomas M. Disch's *Mankind under the Leash*.

5. **City of Illusions (Ace, 1967)** A man from another planet arrives in a tiny village in eastern North America, naked, and amnesiac. Falk, as the villagers name him, comes into conflict with the ruling Shing, beings who said to be able to lie telepathically.

6. **Left Hand of Darkness, The (Ace, 1969)** In this classic of "feminist science fiction," which explores what remains basic to human nature when gender is no longer a factor, Gently Ai, representative of the Ekumen, travels to the totalitarian state of Orgoreyn on the planet Geth.

7. **Four Ways to Forgiveness (HarperCollins, 1995)** Four stories set on two planets named Werel and Yeowe, part of the Ekumen galaxy that explore the concepts of freedom and slavery, as the light-skinned Assets are in bondage to the blue-tinged Owners.

8. **Telling, The (Harcourt, 2000)** Sutty, an Earthling sent to be an Ekumen observer on the planet Aka, experiences the conflict between the Corporation, the capitalist government, and a resistance based on tradition.

Leahy, Syrell Rogovin

This is a family saga covering two generations of the Wolfe family, a rich, distinguished Jewish American clan that carries a curse: bad genes that sometimes produce defective children. Regina and Judy Wolfe, each in her generation, must come to terms with the "family secret," and eventually realize that family ties and love between family members are more important than individual happiness. Leahy has published no novels under her own name since 1989, but has been producing the Christine Bennett mystery series as "Lee Harris" (q.v.).

1. **Family Ties (Putnam, 1982)** Rich, well-bred Regina Wolfe cannot marry her cousin Jerrold because of the dark secret that haunts her family. Set in pre–World War I America.

2. **Family Truths (Putnam, 1984)** In 1959 Judy Wolfe drops her law school plans when she learns of her father's long-standing affair with her cousin Regina.

Lee, Gus (Augustus Samuel Mein-Sun)

A two-part fictional autobiography depicts the struggles of Kai Ting to reconcile his Chinese heritage with the bewildering worlds of American culture to which he is exposed. Kai, son of a Chinese couple fleeing Communism, endures a white stepmother, the mean streets of San Francisco's Panhandle district, and the flawed honor system at West Point. *Tiger's Tail* (Knopf, 1996) has a different autobiographical character.

1. **China Boy (Dutton, 1991)** Young Chinese immigrant Kai Ting is thrown upon his own resources in the tough streets of San Francisco.

2. **Honor and Duty (Knopf, 1994)** Kai Ting gets a West Point appointment but faces difficulties because of his lack of mathematical ability, his Asian heritage, and his sense of honor.

Lee, Tanith

I. British fantasist Tanith Lee is a World Fantasy Award–winning writer. One of her most highly regarded series is the Tales from the Flat Earth series, which depicts a far-distant past when the Earth was still flat, and Demons, the Lords of Darkness, still control the destinies of all creatures. Represents Lee's powerful, cruel, and erotic world creating at its best. *Tales from the Flat Earth: The Lords of Darkness* (Doubleday, 1987) contains numbers 1, 2, and 3. *Tales from the Flat Earth: Night's Daughter* (Doubleday, 1987) contains numbers 4 and 5.

1. **Night's Master (DAW, 1978)** Azhrarn, Night's Master, is supreme among the demons who trouble the Earth's surface.

2. **Death's Master (DAW, 1979)** Uhlume, Death's Master, challenges Azhrarn's supremacy.

3. **Delusion's Master (DAW, 1981)** Introduces Chuz, Delusion's Master, a new demigod, and pits him against Azhrarn, Night's Master.

4. **Delirium's Mistress (DAW, 1986)** Azhriaz, daughter of Night's Master, becomes the mistress of Delusion's Master.

5. **Night's Sorceries (DAW, 1987)** The further adventures of Chuz and Ashriaz, who are pursued by the Demon Lord of Night.

II. The Secret Books of Paradys is a tetralogy about a forgotten city where the lives once led by those who lie buried in its crypts and cemeteries are retold in a mix of horror, historical fantasy, poetic style, and eroticism. Omnibus volume: *The Secret Books of Paradys* (Overlook, 2007; numbers 1–4).

1. **Book of the Damned, The (Overlook, 1990)** Three linked novellas about vampires, vengeance, and murder.

2. **Book of the Beast, The (Overlook, 1991)** Involves demonic possession.

3. **Book of the Dead, The (Overlook, 1992)** Eight gothic tales of corruption and death.

4. **Book of the Mad, The (Overlook, 1993)** Three interconnected narratives about madness: modernistic, Victorian-style, and nightmarish.

III. The Wars of Vis series has the appearance of conventional sword and sorcery, but Lee's readers know that it will be anything but a conventional piece of fantasy world-building, as she infuses it with her original characterizations, sex, violence, and seemingly unlimited flow of ideas. *The Wars of Vis* (Doubleday, 1994) contains numbers 1 and 2.

1. *Storm Lord, The* (DAW, 1976) Rehdon, King of Dorthar, the Storm Lord, is king of kings, the de facto ruler of the continent of Vis.
2. *Anackire* (DAW, 1983) Young Prince Kearh, a lost son of the hero Raldnor, and of daughter of an incarnation of the goddess Anackire intrigue for power in the kingdom of Karmiss.
3. *White Serpent, The* (DAW, 1988) Focuses on the slave-gladiator Rehger and his dealings with the White Aztira and the gods themselves.

IV. The Blood Opera sequence is straight-forward gothic horror in present-day London, featuring the Scarabae, a concealed family of vampires who must interbreed to keep their bloodlines intact.

1. *Dark Dance* (Dell, 1992) Rachaela Day, London bookshop clerk, accepts a mysterious invitation to stay at the seaside house of Scarabae with her estranged father and his family.
2. *Personal Darkness* (Dell, 1994) Ruth, Rachaela's incestuous daughter, suffers from torment over her imminent destiny.
3. *Darkness, I* (St. Martin's, 1995) Several Scarabae roam the English countryside in the guise of bikers, while Rachaela lives in London with Althere Simon, and gives birth to their daughter, Anna.

V. The Secret Books of Venus series is set in an alternative 15th-century Venice. A large cast of characters deal with magical powers, curses, feuds, alchemy, a chronic shortage of burial space, and the encroaching sea.

1. *Faces under Water* (Overlook, 1998) Furian, scion of Venus (Venice), renounces his wealthy parents and goes to work for the alchemist Schaachen. Then he comes across an odd mask of Apollo.
2. *Saint Fire* (Overlook, 1999) Volpa, an innocent slave girl, has the ability to call deadly flame from her long, fox-red hair. When she incinerates her lecherous master, her adventures begin in earnest.
3. *Bed of Earth, A: The Gravedigger's Tale* (Overlook, 2002) The theme is the alchemical element of earth as a long-standing feud between two powerful families simmers over disputed burial grounds.
4. *Venus Preserved* (Overlook, 2003) The drowned city of Venus has been salvaged and rests under a dome beneath the sea. Those who can show descent from the historical inhabitants of the city are invited to live in the dome. Picaro, who has been haunted by a curse, accepts an invitation to live there.

VI. The Birthgrave trilogy was Lee's first effort for the adult market. It is a feminist fantasy featuring a strong heroine with awesome special powers and intense sexuality.

1. *Birthgrave, The* (DAW, 1975) A woman with magical powers awakens in the heart of a volcano without memory of her history, her race, or her name.
2. *Vazkor, Son of Vazkor* (DAW, 1978) Vazkor, son of the protagonist of *The Birthgrave*, embarks on his own series of adventures. UK title: *Shadowfire*.
3. *Quest for the White Witch* (DAW, 1978) Vazkor continues his journeys in search of the White Witch.

VII. The Four-BEE series is a pair of novels about a utopian city where you are taken care of by robots all your long life. "Jang" teenagers do anything they want, kill themselves, change bodies, change sex, and otherwise have a wild time. However, one person sets out to defy the system and the robots that run it.

1. *Don't Bite the Sun* (DAW, 1976) Finding that the controlling robots of the utopian city four-BEE have left him/her with nothing worthwhile to do, after all the pleasures of life and death, he/she finds it "jang" to rebel against the robots and start a new life, in exile.
2. *Drinking Sapphire Wine* (DAW, 1977) He/she finds it possible in exile to challenge the rules, declare independence, and set out to prove that a human was still smarter than the cleverest and most protective robot.

VIII. In *The Silver Metal Lover*, 16-year-old Jane defies tradition by falling in love with Silver, a robot who only looks human. In *Metallic Love*, a sequel published 24 years later, the legend of Jane and Silver lives on, as Loren, an orphan growing in the slums, becomes obsessed with the idea of humanlike robots.

1. *Silver Metal Lover, The* (Doubleday, 1981) The love of 16-year-old Jane's life, Silver, is a robot who only looks human, but is, according to those who created one of a race of gods whose very existence threatens human history.
2. *Metallic Love* (Spectra, 2005) Slum girl Loren, drawn by the clandestine legend of Jane and Silver, falls, in her turn, for the humanlike and more-than-human robot Verlis, created by the META Corporation.

IX. The Lionwolf trilogy is set in a world of eternal winter, with a shifting group of more-or-less civilized kingdoms who have only vague memories of warmer times. So far only two volumes of the trilogy have been published.

1. *Cast a Bright Shadow* (Tor, 2004) Saphay, daughter of a sub-king in the relatively civilized West of a winter world, is sent off to marry a leader of the barbaric Jafn.
2. *Here in Cold Hell* (Tor, 2005) Saphay is now a goddess. Lionwolf, killed by the power of the god Zezeth, his true father, is cast, with the other living dead, into a bleak and icy hell.

Lehane, Dennis

Private eyes Patrick Kenzie and Angela Gennaro work out of the Dorchester (Boston, Massachusetts) working-class neighborhood where Dennis Lehane grew up. Kenzie and Gennaro are an uneasy team. Both suffer losses during the series: Gennaro loses her husband, and Kenzie a former lover. They work together in a series characterized by sharp dialogue, gruesome violence, and dark humor. Eventually, the two are estranged personally and professionally, and Lehane dropped the series, at least temporarily, to write other books, including the best-selling *Mystic River* (Morrow, 2001), which was made into the Academy Award–winning movie of the same title made by Clint Eastwood.

1. *Drink before the War, A* (Harcourt, 1994) Patrick Kenzie and Angela Gennaro are hired by a trio of prominent politicians to find Jenna Angeline, a Massachusetts State House cleaning lady, who may have stolen some important "documents."
2. *Darkness, Take My Hand* (Morrow, 1996) Psychiatrist Diandra Warren's patient, "Moira Kenzie," said she was abused by Kevin Hurlihy, an Irish Mafia henchman who grew up in Angie and Patrick's Dorchester neighborhood.

3. *Sacred* **(Morrow, 1997)** Angela, recovering from the loss of her husband, and Patrick, recovering from facial injuries, are searching for Desiree Stone, missing daughter of dying billionaire Trevor Stone.

4. *Gone Baby, Gone* **(Morrow, 1998)** Patrick and Angela work with two cops from the Crimes Against Children Squad, searching for four-year-old Amanda McCready.

5. *Prayers for Rain* **(Morrow, 1999)** Kenzie and Gennaro, estranged personally and professionally, have gone their separate ways, at least temporarily. Karen Nichols, who is being stalked, dives to her death off the Custom House Tower.

Lehmann, Rosamond

These two novels about the Curtis sisters, Kate and Olivia, have the charm of elegant miniatures. In beautiful but spare prose, Lehmann shows the world unfolding for 17-year-old Olivia as she enters society. The coltish young girl is awkward and uncomfortable in the flame-colored dress that she chose especially for her first ball. At the evening's end, Kate has made a conquest, and Olivia has had a less conventional kind of success.

1. *Invitation to the Waltz* **(Holt, 1932)** In the winter of 1920 Olivia Curtis attends her first dress ball with her sister Kate; her young cousin Reggie is her escort.

2. *Weather in the Streets, The* **(Reynal, 1936)** Ten years later, Kate is a happy wife and mother. Olivia and Rollo, who have been less fortunate, meet again.

Lehrer, Jim (James Charles)

McNeil/Lehrer News Hour (PBS) coanchor (now anchor) Jim Lehrer's One-Eyed Mack novels are light spoofs of politics and good ol' boy novels. One-eyed Mack, whose early life is delineated in *Kick the Can*, is lieutenant governor of Oklahoma. Mack's relationship with his entrepreneurial wife and stepson Tommy, with his boss, the very political "Buffalo Joe" Hayman, and a bevy of American eccentrics, including some real people such as Stephen Dobyns (q.v.), is engagingly told in these genial satires.

1. *Kick the Can* **(Putnam, 1988)** After he loses his left eye in a bizarre kick-the-can mishap, Mack embarks on a tour of the Southwest.

2. *Crown Oklahoma* **(Putnam, 1989)** Lieutenant Governor Mack tries to get to the bottom of a supposed Mafia infiltration into Oklahoma.

3. *Sooner Spy, The* **(Putnam, 1990)** Mack's wife, Jackie, has cornered the drive-through grocery-store market, while stepson Tommy is trying to start a grease recycling business.

4. *Lost and Found* **(Putnam, 1991)** Mack goes to France to track down the missing Speaker of the Oklahoma House of Representatives who has left a note stating that he won't return until he is "good and ready."

5. *Short List* **(Putnam, 1992)** Mack's pinch-hit keynote speech at the 1976 Democratic National Convention gets him short-listed for the vice-presidential nomination.

6. *Fine Lines* **(Random House, 1994)** Four Democratic members of Oklahoma's House of Representatives die in suspiciously quick succession.

7. *Mack to the Rescue* **(University of Oklahoma, 2008)** In the first One-Eyed Mack book published in 14 years, Mack, recuperating from a heart-bypass operation intended for another patient, tries to save Oklahoma from Joe Hayman, its zany governor, who,

among other things, intends to privatize the entire state government.

Lem, Stanisław

Polish writer Lem is one of the giants of contemporary science fiction. He mixes brilliant speculations about our future with ingenious turns of language and satirical humor. His most prominent continuing character is Ijon Tichy, polymath, extraterrestrial cosmonaut, and hero of many universe-spanning misadventures. A good introduction to Stanisław Lem is *A Stanislaw Lem Reader* (Northwestern University, 1997), edited by Peter Swirski. Lem's autobiography *Highcastle: A Remembrance* (Harcourt, 1995) has been translated into English by Michael Kandel.

1. *Futurological Congress, The: From the Memoirs of Ijon Tichy* **(Seabury, 1974)** Cosmonaut Tichy attends a futurological congress back on Earth where he reacquaints himself with some odd Earthling customs. Originally published as "Ze wsomnien Ljona Tichego, Kongres Futurologiczny," collected in *Bezenosc* (1971). Translated from the Polish by Michael Kandel.

2. *Star Diaries, The* **(Seabury, 1976)** A collection of stories purportedly addressed to readers of the distant future. Originally published as *Dzienniki gwiazdowe* (1957). Translated from the Polish by Michael Kandel.

3. *Memoirs of a Space Traveler* **(Harcourt, 1982)** More reminiscences of Ijon Tichy. Stories included in the Polish but not the English-language edition of *The Star Diaries*. Originally published as *Dzienniki gwiazdowe* (1957). Translated from the Polish by Joel Stern and Maria Swieicka-Ziemianek.

4. *Peace on Earth* **(Harcourt, 1994)** Tichy travels to the Moon to uncover secret information about a new breed of intelligent, self-evolving war machines. Originally published as *Pokój na ziemi* (1987). Translated from the Polish by Michael Kandel and Elinor Ford.

Lemann, Nancy

Quirky, meandering, tragicomic musings about Louisiana's Collier clan told from the viewpoints of Louisianans who have traveled to New York for educational or professional reasons, but who can't get the South out of their minds. These two novels don't have much plot, but they have plenty of eccentric characters and some hilarious scenes.

1. *Lives of the Saints* **(Knopf, 1985)** Louise Brown, recent graduate of New York University, returns to Louisiana and renews her acquaintance with the eccentric Collier family.

2. *Sportsman's Paradise* **(Knopf, 1992)** Storey Collier, New York newspaper columnist, yearns for his home state of Louisiana, but makes do with visits to Long Island, seedy Times Square, and baseball.

Lemarchand, Elizabeth

New Scotland Yard detectives Tom Pollard and Gregory Toye are the protagonists of a long-running series of English procedurals. Pollard and Toye don't change much over the years, but there are humorous scenes, interesting minor characters, moorland settings, and intricate plots reminiscent of Agatha Christie (q.v.) or Dorothy Sayers (q.v.). Devonshire native Lemarchand (d. 2000) was headmistress of an English girls' school and started writing mysteries only after she retired.

1. *Death of an Old Girl* (Walker, 1985) Beatrice Baynes, vociferous leader of a clique of Old Girls from Old Meldon, turns up dead after she denounces an innovative art teacher. Originally published in 1967.
2. *Affacombe Affair, The* (Walker, 1985) A nurse at a local boys' school is found dead, leaving evidence that she was engaged in blackmail. Originally published in 1968.
3. *Alibi for a Corpse* (Walker, 1986) Pollard and Toye are summoned to the inbred village of Twiggadon to identify a skeleton found in a car trunk. Originally published in 1969.
4. *Death on Doomsday* (Walker, 1975) The stately home of the Earls of Seton is a popular tourist attraction until a body is discovered in a priest's hole. Originally published in 1971.
5. *Cyanide with Compliments* (Walker, 1973) Audrey Vickers eats from a box of poisoned chocolates just before she can cut her niece out of her will.
6. *No Vacation from Murder* (Walker, 1974) Quiet teenager Wendy Shaw disappears from the coastal village of Kittitoe. UK title: *Let or Hindrance*.
7. *Buried in the Past* (Walker, 1975) The death of the only person Bernard Lister remembered fondly from his unhappy childhood draws him back to the town of Corbury.
8. *Step in the Dark* (Walker, 1977) Employees of the Ramsden Literary and Scientific Society find a body on the library the morning after the Society's centenary celebration.
9. *Unhappy Returns* (Walker, 1978) Ethel Ridd, housekeeper to the late vicar of Ambercombe, is aware that a chalice used by the vicar is missing.
10. *Suddenly While Gardening* (Walker, 1978) A skeleton in a Bronze Age grave in the Cattesmoor turns out to be only a year old.
11. *Change for the Worse* (Walker, 1981) Just as Katherine Ridley had thought she had secured a sound future for Fairlynch Manor and her granddaughter, a figure from the past appeared.
12. *Nothing to Do with the Case* (Walker, 1981) Virginia Gould, niece by marriage to wealthy old Walter Kerslake, inherits his mansion and becomes subject to the rumor that she had hastened his death.
13. *Troubled Waters* (Walker, 1982) A young American in England to trace his ancestors dies in an apparent accident.
14. *Wheel Turns, The* (Walker, 1984) Aspiring politician Basil Railsdon accidently runs over a small child while driving.
15. *Light through Glass* (Walker, 1986) Dr. John Paterson's exterior as a charming, successful, and independently wealthy scientist-scholar hides a thoroughly despicable interior.
16. *Who Goes Home?* (Walker, 1987) The burned shell of Anstey Farm holds two surprises for the police: traces of heroin and a skeleton hidden behind a wall.
17. *Glade Manor Murder, The* (Walker, 1989) Nanky Glover, longtime nanny and housekeeper at Glade Manor, is found at the bottom of a quarry.

L'Engle, Madeleine

Madeleine L'Engle is best known for her award-winning science fiction and fantasy for children and young adults. *A Wrinkle in Time* won the 1963 Newbery Award, and is regarded as a classic. She has also written several books for adults, including this pair of novels about concert pianist Katherine (Katya) Forrester. The events of these novels are separated by some four decades, but with flashbacks they portray the transition of a lonely, artistic girl into an accomplished professional artist.

1. *Small Rain, The* (Vanguard, 1945) The lonely childhood and adolescence of pianist Katherine Forrester is split between Greenwich Village and a French boarding school. Reissued by Vanguard as *Prelude* in 1968. New edition under the original title published by Farrar in 1984.
2. *Severed Wasp, A* (Farrar, 1982) Decades later, Katherine Forrester Vigueras retires from the concert stage and returns to New York, where she agrees to play one last benefit recital for an old friend who has become an Episcopal priest.

Leon, Donna

Police Commissario Guido Brunetti of Venice is a stalwart and worldly policeman who must deal with corrupt officials, codes of silence, and distrust of the police in a series of well-written, complex, humorous procedurals set in the seedy ambience of the city of canals and gondolas. Venice itself is perhaps the leading character here, although the lives of Brunetti, his wife, Paola, his wealthy and somewhat sinister father-in-law, and his superior, the corrupt, sycophantic, and indolent Patti are well delineated. Donna Leon, a native of New Jersey, has lived in Venice since 1981. Like Patricia Highsmith (q.v.), Donna Leon's reputation and popularity have been higher in Europe than in the United States. No Brunetti novels were published in the United States for several years, but this situation has been somewhat remedied since the publication of number 12 and the reprinting of numbers 6 and 7 in the United States.

1. *Death at La Fenice* (Harper, 1992) Maestro Helmut Wellaver is poisoned at the intermission of a performance at the world-famed La Fenice theater.
2. *Death in a Strange Country* (Harper, 1993) An American soldier is found stabbed to death in a Venetian canal.
3. *Dressed for Death* (Harper, 1994) Brunetti isn't convinced that a transvestite who was murdered and had his face battered beyond recognition was the victim of a sex crime. UK title: *The Anonymous Venetian*.
4. *Death and Judgment* (Harper, 1995) A truck crash in the Dolomites that yields up the corpses of eight women and the murder of high-powered lawyer Carlo Trevisan on the Padua-Venice train may both be connected to a prostitution ring in Venice. UK title: *A Venetian Reckoning*.
5. *Acqua Alta* (HarperCollins, 1996) When a lesbian archaeologist, whose lover is an opera diva, is beaten up, she suspects that the beating has more to do with an exhibit of Chinese ceramics that is full of fakes than with gay bashing.
6. *Death of Faith, The* (HarperCollins, 1998) Maria Testa, a nun who once cared for Brunetti's ill mother, has left her convent after the unexpected deaths of five patients. Variant title: *Quietly in Their Sleep*.
7. *Noble Radiance, A* (Penguin, 2003) When the body of Robert Lorenzini, who was kidnapped two years earlier, is turned up by a rural landowner, Brunetti immediately suspects the victim's family. Originally published in the United Kingdom in 1998.
8. *Fatal Remedies* (Heinemann [UK], 1999) Brunetti's wife, Paola, is arrested for vandalism and malicious damage when she smashes the windows of a tourist agency specializing in "sex tourism." Not published in the United States.
9. *Friends in High Places* (Heinemann [UK], 2000) A young building inspector named Rossi tells Brunetti that his long-inhabited apartment doesn't exist, officially, at least. Then Rossi is murdered. Not published in the United States.
10. *Sea of Troubles, A* (Heinemann [UK], 2001) Brunetti is called to the poor fishing island of Pellestrina, where two fishermen, father and

son, have been killed. Once there he runs into a wall of silence put up by the distrustful locals. Not published in the United States.

11. *Wilful Behaviour* **(Heinemann [UK], 2002)** The death of an elderly Austrian woman, who had an extraordinary art collection in her apartment, turns up some old and unsavory secrets from World War II, such as collaboration and the exploitation of the Italian Jews. Not published in the United States.

12. *Uniform Justice* **(Grove/Atlantic, 2003)** The body of cadet Ernesto Moro has been found hanging in a lavatory at the exclusive San Martino Military Academy. Brunetti feels that his death is a homicide, not a suicide.

13. *Doctored Evidence* **(Atlantic Monthly, 2004)** After an anonymous Senegalese street vendor is murdered, uncut diamonds are found hidden in his room.

14. *Through a Glass Darkly* **(Atlantic Monthly, 2006)** Why has a glass worker on Murano, the glassmakers' island, been murdered? Family feud or the worker's environmental activism?

15. *Suffer the Little Children* **(Atlantic Monthly, 2007)** Both Brunetti and his colleagues and the Carabinieri are interested in a doctor who has illegally adopted an Albanian infant.

Leonard, Elmore

I. Elmore Leonard's best-selling crime novels relate the adventures of a host of sleazeballs, con artists, and psychopaths in a setting infused with black humor, moral ambivalence, and Leonard's unique prose style. Leonard started out writing westerns, but despite such hits as *Hombre* (Ballantine, 1961) and *Valdez Is Coming* (Gold Medal, 1970), he decided that the market for westerns was drying up and started writing his inimitable crime books ,which, over the years, have brought him a tremendous reader following and rave reviews from the critics. According to Bill Ott (*Booklist*), Leonard is "the only A-list crime fiction writer who doesn't rely on a series hero." However, at least four duos of novels can be called sequels, as they have continuing characters. Chili Palmer, Miami loan shark and would-be Hollywood entrepreneur, is the "hero" of two novels that send up the movie and music businesses in grand fashion, as he works with, and against, a host of characters as morally challenged as he is.

1. *Get Shorty* **(Delacorte, 1990)** In this send-up of the movie business, Miami loan-shark Chili Palmer pursues a man to California and gets involved with a host of dubious characters, including a third-rate producer, a washed-up actress, and several cocaine dealers. Made into a film (1995) with John Travolta, Gene Hackman, Danny DeVito, and a host of other Hollywood "names."

2. *Be Cool* **(Delacorte, 1999)** Chili Palmer redux. This time Chili decides to help a struggling young singer make it in the music industry (which is given a royal send-up) just to see whether her story would make a good movie.

II. Florida deputy US Marshal Raylan Givens and Miami Beach bookie Harry Arno are the main continuing characters in a pair of novels about the activities of a host of sleazy types.

1. *Pronto* **(Delacorte, 1993)** When a nasty FBI man spreads the story (which happens to be true) that elderly bookie Harry Arno has been skimming off the profits from his Mafia bosses for years, Harry splits to Rapallo, Italy, where he is joined by a host of characters, including US Marshal Raylan Givens.

2. *Riding the Rap* **(Delacorte, 1995)** When Harry Arno disappears while chasing down a tardy debtor named Chip Ganz, whose addled mind has hatched a complicated kidnapping scheme, Florida marshal Raylan Givens sets off in pursuit.

III. Two novels published in the 1970s are located in Detroit and feature a seedy type name Frank Ryan.

1. *Swag* **(Delacorte, 1976)** An armed robbery that will net its perps a tax-free hundred grand is in the offing in Detroit.

2. *Unknown Man No. 89* **(Delacorte, 1977)** Detroit process server and ex-thug Jack Ryan is being offered big bucks to locate a lost sleaze named Robert Leary, aka Bobby Lear.

IV. A pair of novels that hark back to Elmore Leonard's western writing days features gunslinging US Marshal Carlos "Carl" Leonard of Okmulgee, Oklahoma, in action that takes place in the 1930s and 1940s.

1. *Hot Kid, The* **(Morrow, 2005)** Young Carlos Webster has his first brush with crime at the age of 15, when bank robber Emmet Long robs an Okmulgee, Oklahoma, store; kills an Indian policeman; and snatches away Carlos's ice-cream cone. Seven years later, Carl, now a US deputy marshal, gets his revenge.

2. *Up in Honey's Room* **(Morrow, 2007)** Carl follows a pair of escaped German POWs from Okmulgee to Detroit, where he finds himself, though married, overcome by the charms of one Honey Deal.

Lescroart, John

I. Lawyer Dismas Hardy and San Francisco homicide cop Abe Glitsky are best friends, and alternate as the chief protagonist in this series of courtroom dramas with a San Francisco locale. Dismas has had his career ups and downs: cop, lawyer, bartender, Vietnam vet, alcoholic, prosecutor, defense attorney, and high-priced legal fixer, not necessarily in that order. Abe has had fewer career perturbations. He is the head of the SFPD's homicide detail, a job that he is eventually kicked upstairs from after a long absence due to a gunshot wound. Dismas and Abe are complex characters in this often gripping, thoughtful series, which usually ends up in a courtroom.

1. *Dead Irish* **(Fine, 1990)** Dismas Hardy, down-and-out former assistant DA, now tending bar and doing some heavy drinking, is galvanized into action by a friend's apparent suicide.

2. *Vig, The* **(Fine, 1991)** Hardy is warned that Louis Baker, one of the criminals he had put away in his former career, is out on bail and looking for revenge.

3. *Hard Evidence* **(Fine, 1993)** Returned to the DA's office, Dismas prosecutes the Japanese mistress of a murdered billionaire whose severed hand turned up in a shark's belly.

4. *13th Juror, The* **(Fine, 1994)** Now working as a defense attorney, Hardy lands the seemingly impossible case of defending Jennifer Witt, accused of murdering her husband and son.

5. *Certain Justice, A* **(Fine, 1995)** Only Abe Glitsky, head of San Francisco's homicide detail, seems to be able to be objective about Kevin Shea, accused of taking part in the lynching of an African American lawyer.

6. *Guilt* **(Delacorte, 1997)** Abe Glitsky finds enough odd clues to press for a murder charge against high-powered lawyer Mark Dooher, whose alcoholic wife was murdered in what seemed to be a burglary.

7. *Mercy Rule, The* **(Delacorte, 1998)** Graham Russo, accused of killing his ailing father Sal, wants Dismas to establish his complete innocence, rather than pursue a mercy killing defense.

8. *Nothing but the Truth* **(Delacorte, 2000)** Hardy's wife, Frannie, has been jailed for contempt by a grand jury investigating the murder

of Bree Beaumont after refusing to reveal a secret entrusted to her by the accused husband.

9. *Hearing, The* **(Dutton, 2001)** Dismas is defending heroin addict Cole Burgess, who is accused of murdering Assistant DA Elaine Wager, who, unbeknownst to everyone, was Abe Glitsky's daughter.

10. *Oath, The* **(Dutton, 2001)** In a case involving cost-cutting HMOs, Dismas finds himself representing Dr. Eric Kensing, accused of murdering his boss, Tim Markham, CEO of the Parnassus Medical Group.

11. *First Law, The* **(Dutton, 2003)** Abe returns to work after recuperating 13 months from a gunshot wound suffered in *The Oath*, only to find that he is no longer in charge of the homicide detail. This doesn't stop him from getting involved with a murder case that seems to be connected to a private security company.

12. *Second Chair, The* **(Dutton, 2004)** Dismas and Abe have climbed the career ladder only to find they miss the hands-on aspect of their work. Dismas's associate Amy Wu, defending Andrew North, a 17-year-old arrested for murdering his girlfriend and high-school drama coach, makes a serious error in judgment.

13. *Motive, The* **(Dutton, 2005)** When a politically connected socialite and his glamorous fiancé are murdered, the mayor of San Francisco demands a that a high-ranking detective be put on the case. That detective is Abe Glitsky.

14. *Suspect, The* **(Dutton, 2007)** Outdoor writer Stuart Gorman is the prime suspect in the murder of his wife, Caryn, whose nude body he discovers near their hot tub at their San Francisco home.

15. *Betrayal* **(Dutton, 2008)** Trying to wrap up the caseload of a Bay Area lawyer who disappeared, Hardy finds that an apparently straightforward murder case had its origins in Iraq.

II. Sherlock Holmes–inspired pastiches seem to have no end. This pair of re-creations features Auguste Lupa, chef and son of Sherlock Holmes, who solves a couple of cases during World War I with the partial assistance of Watson and Holmes himself.

1. *Son of Holmes* **(Fine, 1986)** Auguste Lupa, a 25-year-old chef, is put on the trail of a German saboteur by undercover spy Jules Giraud.

2. *Rasputin's Revenge* **(Fine, 1987)** Lupa and Giraud investigate the murders of men close to Czar Nicholas of Russia.

Lessing, Doris

I. Nobel Laureate (2007) Lessing is generally regarded as one of the major postwar women novelists, although it was only after the success of *The Golden Notebook* (Simon & Schuster, 1962) that her work caught on with American readers. The Children of Violence series attracted an immediate following when its first installments appeared in the United States in 1965. This five-volume series takes up the story of Martha Quest in 1938, when she is a rebellious 17-year-old living with her farming parents in "Zambesia" (Southern Rhodesia). Presumably autobiographical, the account shows the gradual development of Martha's feminist consciousness and leftist political convictions. Number 5, which is, in a way a warm-up for the Canopus in Argos series that followed, is disconcertingly hallucinatory and apocalyptic. The omnibus volume entitled *Children of Violence, Volume 1* (Simon & Schuster, 1965) contains numbers 1 and 2. *Children of Violence, Volume 2* (Simon & Schuster, 1966), contains numbers 3 and 4.

1. *Martha Quest* **(M. Joseph [UK], 1952)** Martha leaves her parents' farm in "Zambesia" for a job in the city, where she falls in with a fast crowd of politically active young people, and marries Douglas

Knowell. First published in the United States in *Children of Violence, Volume 1* (Simon & Schuster, 1965).

2. *Proper Marriage, A* **(M. Joseph [UK], 1954)** Martha has a short, unhappy marriage and bears a daughter, Caroline, as World War II begins. First published in the United States in *Children of Violence, Volume 1* (Simon & Schuster, 1965).

3. *Ripple from the Storm, A* **(M. Joseph [UK], 1958)** As a Communist Party member, Martha attends meetings and sells pamphlets while her marriage to Anton Hesse slowly dies. First published in the United States in *Children of Violence, Volume 2* (Simon & Schuster, 1966).

4. *Landlocked* **(MacGibbon & Kee, 1965)** As the war ends, Martha has an affair with Thomas Stern; she decides to leave Anton and make a new start in England. First published in the United States in *Children of Violence, Volume 2* (Simon & Schuster, 1966).

5. *Four-Gated City* **(Knopf, 1969)** In London, Martha sinks into madness in a commune of young people as Britain edges closer to an apocalyptic end.

II. Lessing's Canopus in Argos series is decidedly different from the Martha Quest books. Visionary parables rather than true science fiction, these books provide a forum for her provocative views of the future of Great Britain and civilization in general.

1. *Shikasta: Canopus in Argos—Archives* **(Knopf, 1979)** Initially successful but eventually doomed social experiments are performed by the benevolent Canopean Empire on the colonists of Planet 5, Shikasta (Earth).

2. *Marriages between Zones Three, Four and Five, The* **(Knopf, 1980)** Sexual politics in Lessing's Canopean world are illustrated by the story of the marriage of arrogant Ben Ata and the radiant queen of the Third Zone.

3. *Sirian Experiments, The: Report by Ambien II of the Five* **(Knopf, 1981)** The Sirians, rivals of the Canopeans, are the focus as narrator Ambien II tells of the dreadful experiments she leads and of her own eventual conversion.

4. *Making of the Representative for Planet 8, The* **(Knopf, 1982)** Doeg, a Representative on Planet 8, recalls the coming of the Ice Age, the people's hope for salvation, and their final destruction.

5. *Documents Relating to the Sentimental Agents in the Volyen Empire* **(Knopf, 1983)** The Canopean agent Klorathy reports to his superior Johor about the collapse of the five-world Volyen Empire.

III. The birth, growth, and eventual destruction of Ben Lovatt, a "monster child" or "throwback" born to middle-class British parents, is told in two widely separated (12 years), angry volumes.

1. *Fifth Child, The* **(Knopf, 1988)** Upper-middle-class British parents David and Harriet Lovatt have decided to exemplify "family values" by having four children in the first six years of their marriage. The four children are all blond and blue-eyed, but the fifth, unplanned child, Ben turns out quite differently.

2. *Ben, in the World* **(Knopf, 2000)** Ben Lovatt, a squat, hairy, fearsomely developed 18-year-old, runs away from his family. The terrifying Ben is terrified of society and, unable to read, handle money, or decipher even the simplest of social situations, is woefully unprepared to deal with it.

IV. A futuristic pair of novels relates the saga of Dann, the refugee boy prince of the Mahondi, who searches with his elder sister Mara for habitable land on a planet Earth beset by a new ice age.

1. *Mara and Dann: An Adventure* **(HarperCollins, 1999)** Seven-year-old Mara, accompanied by her brother Dann, encounters a

variety of strange peoples in her search for new habitable land and enlightenment in a distant future Earth.

2. **Story of General Dann and Mara's Daughter, Griot and the Snow Dog, The** (HarperCollins, 2006) Recycles a number of characters from *Mara and Dann*. Mara has died in childbirth. Dann, now General Dann, is too grief stricken to listen to the pleas of those who believe that he alone can save civilization from chaos.

Leverson, Ada

The Little Ottleys is the collective title for three novels that were believed to be a portrait of Ada Leverson's own failed marriage. The novels are exquisite comedies of manners among the upper middle classes of Edwardian England, and are still quite funny today. The autobiographical Edith Ottley's husband, the ineffable ass Bruce, is a great comic creation. Reprinted in one volume with an introduction by Colin MacInnes (Norton, 1962).

1. **Love's Shadow** (Richards [UK], 1908) Ostensibly about the courtship of Hyacinth Verney and Cecil Reeve. Edith Ottley is Hyacinth's confidante, while Bruce huffs and puffs about writing a hit play.
2. **Tenterhooks** (Richards [UK], 1912) Edith and Aylmer Ross fall deeply in love but are too honorable to act out their passion.
3. **Love at Second Sight** (Richards [UK], 1916) Bruce's hypochondria keeps him out of the war, and the Ottleys are saddled with Eglantine Frabelle, the English widow of a French wine merchant.

Levin, Ira

Rosemary's Baby, Ira Levin's novel about a young woman impregnated by the devil, was made into a popular film by Roman Polanski, starring Mia Farrow (1968), and was the inspiration for a whole slew of similar novels. Although Levin wrote more highly successful novels, such as *The Stepford Wives* (Random House, 1972), *The Boys from Brazil* (Random House, 1976), and *Deathtrap* (1979), "the longest running thriller in Broadway history," and all three titles became successful films, Levin fell upon relatively hard times, and publishing wisdom seemed to dictate that *Rosemary's Baby* should have a sequel. (In 1976 there was a made-for-TV sequel to the film: *Look What's Happened to Rosemary's Baby*, aka *Rosemary's Baby, II.*) Thirty years later, the printed sequel, *Son of Rosemary*, which finds Rosemary Reilly waking from a coma of 27 years, was published and, almost inevitably, proved to be a big disappointment.

1. **Rosemary's Baby** (Random House, 1967) Rosemary falls afoul of a witches' coven and becomes impregnated with what seems to be Satan's child.
2. **Son of Rosemary** (Dutton, 1997) Rosemary wakes from a coma after 27 years to find that Andy, the son born of her rape by Satan, has become a world-renowned spiritual teacher.

Levine, Paul

I. Jake Lassiter, former linebacker for the Miami Dolphins, is currently a lawyer with the Miami firm of Harmon and Fox. Jake is not averse to cutting corners in his professional and personal lives, but he is basically one of the good guys in a series of page-turners with a steamy Florida setting. *9 Scorpions* (Pocket, 1998) isn't a Lassiter novel.

1. **To Speak for the Dead** (Bantam, 1990) Jake takes on the case of a doctor accused of malpractice, or murder.
2. **Night Vision** (Bantam, 1991) Lassiter tracks down a serial killer whose first three victims were women who belonged to CompuMate, a sort of electronic sex network.
3. **False Dawn** (Bantam, 1993) Jake is asked to defend old friend Francesco Crespo, who falsely admits to killing a Russian coworker.
4. **Mortal Sin** (Morrow, 1994) Environmentalist Peter Tupton gets drunk at a party hosted by Nicky Florio, an unsavory developer, and dies in Florio's wine cellar.
5. **Slashback** (Morrow, 1995) Jake is involved with the theft of a million dollars in negotiable securities and with Lila Summers, best female windsurfer in the world.
6. **Fool Me Twice** (Morrow, 1995) Lassiter comes into the possession of 100 shares of stock in Rocky Mountain Treasures Inc., a buried treasure salvage firm in Colorado.
7. **Flesh and Bones** (Morrow, 1997) Fashion model Chrissy Bernhardt shoots her wealthy father because, she says, he raped her as a child, an event retrieved from her memory by Dr. Lawrence Schein.

II. Another Florida series features odd legal couple Steve Solomon and Victoria Lord. Steve, though smart, barely graduated from Key West School of Law, is inclined to cut legal corners, and dresses like a beach bum in his off-hours. Victoria is a Coral Gables blue blood, a Yale graduate, and a stickler for the law. Although they are often on opposite sides, somehow the two manage to work together while squabbling all the way in this series of funny, and accurate, courtroom dramas praised by the likes of Dave Barry and Carl Hiaasen (q.v.).

1. **Solomon vs. Lord** (Bantam, 2005) Steve Solomon and Victoria Lord make an unlikely team as they defend ex–figure skater Katrina Barksdale, who is charged with killing her rich, kinky husband.
2. **Deep Blue Alibi, The** (Bantam, 2006) Hal Griffin, onetime business partner of Victoria's late father, is accused of murdering an EPA official with a speargun.
3. **Kill All the Lawyers** (Bantam, 2006) Steve is bedeviled by local talk radio, a celebrity shrink, and an ex-client who wants him dead.
4. **Trial and Error** (Bantam, 2007) Solomon and Lord are on opposite sides in the case of an ecoterrorist who tried to liberate a pair of dolphins, and who is now facing a murder rap.

Levitsky, Ronald

Nate Rosen is a crusading civil rights lawyer with a rather messy personal life. He is unable to accept or completely reject his Orthodox Jewish upbringing, and her harbors guilt feelings over a daughter forsaken after his divorce and resentment over being disowned by his father. Nate is a complex character, and the cases he takes on usually have some social significance. Levitsky doesn't seem to have published anything since 1994.

1. **Love That Kills, The** (Scribner, 1991) Rosen despises his client Edison Basehart's neo-Nazi views, but believes him to be innocent of the murder of a young Vietnamese woman.
2. **Wisdom of Serpents** (Scribner, 1992) Nate travels to Tennessee to defend Gideon McCrae, pastor of a rattlesnake-handling fundamentalist church. Variant title: *The Truth That Kills*.
3. **Stone Boy** (Scribner, 1993) Native American Saul True Sky, who has been charged with murder, owns a strip of land highly desired by some South Dakotans as a gambling casino site. Variant title: *The Spirit That Kills*.

4. *Innocence That Kills, The* **(Scribner, 1994)** The trial of two young murderers brings Rosen back to Chicago, his childhood home and residence of his ex-wife and daughter.

Lewin, Michael Z.

I. Lewin wrote in *Murder Ink* (Workman, 1977) that his first detective story was begun as a takeoff to amuse his family. He chose Albert as a particularly un-detective-like first name and set him to work in his hometown of Indianapolis. Like many other fictional private eyes, Albert Samson is a seedy loner who hides his basic decency behind a wisecracking exterior. He is somewhat less inclined to violence than some of his predecessors, and his mid-American locale is a pleasant change from California. Albert has starred in eight books and appears as a minor character in the three books featuring Leroy Powder (series II).

1. *Ask the Right Question* **(Putnam, 1971)** The search for 16-year-old Eloise Crystal's biological father leads Samson into a closetful of family skeletons.
2. *Way We Die Now, The* **(Putnam, 1973)** Rosetta Tomrak comes to Samson for help when her Vietnam vet husband is charged with manslaughter.
3. *Enemies Within, The* **(Knopf, 1974)** Samson investigates another investigator who is harassing an antiques dealer in a case that involves some very ambiguous relationships.
4. *Silent Salesman, The* **(Knopf, 1978)** A frantic woman hires Samson to find out why she isn't allowed to visit her brother in the hospital. Samson's teenage daughter Sam appears in this volume.
5. *Missing Woman* **(Knopf, 1981)** The search for Priscilla Prynne is the thread that unravels a larger mystery.
6. *Out of Season* **(Morrow, 1984)** Paula Beller, wife of a bank executive, finds that her birth certificate is false, so Albert is called in to uncover the real facts of her birth.
7. *Called by a Panther* **(Mysterious, 1991)** Albert is hired by the Scum Front, a group of environmentalists accused of being ecoterrorists.
8. *Eye Opener* **(Five Star, 2004)** Albert's euphoria over getting his license back and hooking on to the best-paying job he has ever had begins to dissipate when he discovers that the job he has—working for lawyers defending a man accused of being a rapist and serial killer—is quite different from what it first appeared to be.

II. Leroy Powder is head of the Indianapolis Police Department's Missing Persons Bureau. Powder is more abrasive and confrontational than the introspective Samson, who appears in minor roles in this series, but he is honest and tenacious in his efforts to get to the bottom of his cases. Powder appears in *The Reluctant Detective and Other Stories* (Crippen & Landru, 2001), a collection of 21 stories.

1. *Night Cover* **(Knopf, 1976)** Leroy Powder stars in this case of unsolved murders and a bizarre school crime. He crosses Albert Samson's (Series I) path at times.
2. *Hard Line* **(Morrow, 1982)** Powder and his new sergeant, wheelchair-bound Caroline Fleetwood, work on cases involving a missing wife, an attempted suicide, some unidentified bodies, and the criminal activities of Leroy's son Ricky.
3. *Late Payments* **(Morrow, 1986)** A 12-year-old boy asks Powder to find his father. Powder is looking for his own son, who has broken parole.

III. Lewin moved to England in the 1990s and seems to have abandoned his Indianapolis setting, at least for now. His latest series

concerns three generations of the Italo-British clan of the Lunghis who, among other activities, run the Lunghi Detective Agency in Bath. Both novels published so far feature much interaction between work and personal interests. Wonderful food and copious infusions of tea are important elements in these light mysteries. The Lunghis have a part in Lewin's recent story collection *The Reluctant Detective and Other Stories* (Crippen & Landru, 2001).

1. *Family Business* **(Foul Play, 1995)** The Lunghi Detective Agency, founded by the Old Man, whose real-estate empire keeps the family afloat, handles the case of a model who has heard that one of the Lunghis has been making inquiries about her and a housewife who is concerned about a bottle of dish-washing liquid that was relocated.
2. *Family Planning* **(St. Martin's, 1999)** The Old Man's son Angelo and Angelo's wife, Gina, are looking into the case of woman who's been threatened by messages on her pager. The Old Man is asked to prove that client didn't murder his uncle 10 years ago.

Lewis, C(live) S(taples)

Not to be confused with Wyndham Lewis's (q.v.) allegorical series, this trilogy by the English literary scholar and Christian moralist is compulsively readable. Even readers not interested in theological speculation will find his stories inventive, funny, and satisfying adventures that blend fantasy, science fiction, and allegorical elements. C. S. Lewis was also of the author of the highly regarded *Narnia* series of children's books. Omnibus volumes containing all three novels: *Space Trilogy* (Collier, 1965) and *The Cosmic Trilogy* (Voyager [UK], 2002).

1. *Out of the Silent Planet* **(Macmillan, 1938)** Dr. Ransom, a Cambridge philologist, is transported to the planet Malacandra (Mars) and makes some surprising discoveries.
2. *Perelandra* **(Macmillan, 1944)** Dr. Ransom is ordered to Perelandra (Venus) to fight his old enemy Weston again, this time in a reenactment of the Adam and Eve story.
3. *That Hideous Strength* **(Macmillan, 1946)** Though the setting is an ordinary English village, some extraordinary beings visit, and the struggle between good and evil reaches a climax. Variant title: *The Tortured Planet*.

Lewis, Roy

I. Arnold Landon is a rather timid fellow, but his antiquarian passion for medieval archaeological sites keeps on landing him in the middle of battles with developers and with murder investigations in these mysteries set in the North of England (often around Newcastle-on-Tyne).

1. *Gathering of Ghosts, A* **(St. Martin's, 1983)** Landon suspects that an old Cumbrian farm, scheduled to be turned into an amusement center, holds invaluable medieval relics.
2. *Most Cunning Workmen* **(St. Martin's, 1985)** Arnold is studying historical documents at five-year-old Oakham Manor, which is about to be taken over by an American computer company.
3. *Trout in the Milk, A* **(St, Martin's, 1986)** The planning department that employs Landon is at the center of a fight over land that a consortium wants to develop into a retirement community.
4. *Men of Subtle Craft* **(St. Martin's, 1987)** Patrick Yates, a much disliked local magistrate, is felled by an arrow.

5. *Devil Is Dead, The* (St. Martin's, 1990) A university professor claims that a sinister cult with its roots in medieval times has revived its ancient rituals on the grounds of an abandoned church.

6. *Wisp of Smoke, A* (St. Martin's, 1992) Newcastle-on-Tyne is the scene of investigations by Arnold and his girlfriend, Jane Wilson, when the author of a book on which Arnold is doing research dies.

7. *Secret Dying, A* (St, Martin's, 1993) Landon gets a new job at the Department of Museums and Antiquities. His first assignment is to research a brochure on early British architecture.

8. *Bloodeagle* (St. Martin's, 1994) Arnold's boss sends him to a dig at Birley Thore, where what seems to be a reincarnated Viking "berserker" is on the loose.

9. *Cross Bearer, The* (St. Martin's, 1995) Long-hidden treasure left by the Knights Templar is the pretext for a dissertation on the evolution of secret societies.

10. *Short-Lived Ghost, A* (Collins [UK], 1995) The arrival of a new Deputy Director at the Department of Museums, the formidable Karen Stannard, disrupts Arnold's life.

11. *Angel of Death* (Collins [UK], 1996) A young woman is found murdered after what seems to have been a rape attempt at a Romano-Celtic burial site where Arnold is helping out.

12. *Suddenly as a Shadow* (Collins [UK], 1997) Developers want to turn an ancient Northumbrian burial site into a business and leisure complex. Then controversial pathologist Cate Nicholas is murdered.

13. *Shape-Shifter, The* (Collins [UK], 1998) Trouble is brewing at Haggburn Hall, where Arnold and Karen Stannard are on a dig to uncover evidence of an ancient cult devoted to the shape-shifter Morrigen.

14. *Ghost Dancers, The* (Collins [UK], 1999) The sudden death of the director of the Department of Museums leaves Landon, Stannard, and Steve O'Hara on a short list of possible successors. Then O'Hara has his skull bashed in.

15. *Assumption of Death, An* (Constable [UK], 2001) A missing heiress, the fatal fall of the chairman of the Archaeological Society, a headless corpse, illegal drugs, and a wealthy cult all figure in this episode.

16. *Dead Secret* (Carroll & Graf, 2001) A local developer may have something to do with the suspicious death of a young ecoprotester at the site of a peat bog in Northumberland.

17. *Ways of Death, The* (Constable [UK], 2002) A 30-year-old murder case resurfaces at the site of an ancient sea cave in Northumberland.

18. *Headhunter* (Carroll & Graf, 2004) When the headless body of a child is pulled out of the Tyne at North Shields, the police are unable to identify the corpse or discover a motive for the killing.

19. *Grave Error* (Carroll & Graf, 2006) Landon runs up against dashing local professor James MacLean, who seemingly refutes him on the authenticity of a Celtic cauldron that was stolen and sold on the international market.

20. *Dragon Head* (Carroll & Graf, 2007) An offer from a Chinese businessman leads Arnold into the world of a centuries-old criminal organization known as the Syndicate of the Ghost Shadow.

II. Eric Ward was released from the Newcastle-on-Tyne police force because of encroaching blindness due to chronic glaucoma. He eventually opens his own law practice, gets married, and seems to be forging a new life for himself, but complications involving skulduggery including murder, and his wife's seeming inconstancy don't allow him to settle down for long. Eric is a sensitively drawn character in a series of complex thrillers. Later titles (after number 7) were published in the United States only in large-print editions.

1. *Certain Blindness, A* (St. Martin's, 1981) Dismissed from the Newcastle Police force at the age of 40 because of chronic glaucoma, Eric Ward supports himself by working as an articled law clerk.

2. *Dwell in Danger* (St. Martin's, 1982) Ward becomes embroiled in a legal suit involving Northumberland farmer Amos Saxby's attempt to defraud his son Jack of his property.

3. *Limited Vision, A* (St. Martin's, 1984) Eric is offered a lucrative job as legal representative for entrepreneur Philip Scarn, who wants to get into the "entertainment industry."

4. *Once Dying, Twice Dead* (St. Martin's, 1984) Ward's glaucoma is in remission, he has married recently, and he's starting his own law practice when his case plunges him into a vicious gang world.

5. *Blurred Reality, A* (St. Martin's, 1985) Eric's investigation of a money-lender is complicated when a rich man's granddaughter is kidnapped.

6. *Premium on Death* (St. Martin's, 1987) Ward confronts a sophisticated financial cabal that threatens his wife's fortune and leads to murder on the Newcastle docks.

7. *Salamander Chill, The* (St. Martin's, 1989) Eric gets involved in some intricate financial maneuvering while fighting a hostile takeover bid and defending his wife's acquisitions advisor against murder charges.

8. *Necessary Dealing, A* (Collins [UK], 1991) Ward stirs up marital trouble when he agrees to advise a woman whose company is facing a leveraged buy-out, but refuses to advise his wife on her own business interests.

9. *Kind of Transaction, A* (Collins [UK], 1991) No annotation available.

10. *Form of Death, A* (Allison & Busby [UK], 2001) Eric suspects his wife, Anne, of having an affair on a business trip. He has a one-night stand himself and finds himself facing a murder charge when his paramour is found dead.

11. *Nightwalker, The* (Allison & Busby [UK], 2001) Ward agrees to represent a group protesting a local industrial-waste site. An explosion at the plant leaves a protestor dead.

12. *Phantom* (Allison & Busby [UK], 2002) Goldsteins, a local shipping firm, puts Eric on retainer when one of their ships, *Sierra Nova*, is held in port when one of the crew is caught smuggling drugs.

13. *Dead Man Running* (Allison & Busby [UK], 2004) Hill-farmer Paddy Fenton runs into a heap of trouble when agrees to lease one of his outbuildings for cash, then is charged as an accessory in an illegal meat-manufacturing racket.

14. *Embers of the Dead* (Allison & Busby [UK], 2005) Jason Sullivan QC, the reason behind Eric's marriage breakup, is involved in something big—illegal immigration? Prostitution? Drugs?—and it is up to Eric to find out what.

III. Only two of the eight novels in the early series featuring Inspector Crow of Scotland Yard were published in the United States. Crow, described as "skeletal" or "cadaverous," is a laconic but likable protagonist. Books in the series are listed without annotations.

1. *Lover Too Many, A* (World, 1971)

2. *Error of Judgement* (Collins [UK], 1971)

3. *Secret Singing, A* (Collins [UK], 1972)

4. *Blood Money* (Collins [UK], 1973)

5. *Question of Degree, A* (Collins [UK], 1974)

6. *Part of Virtue, A* (Collins [UK], 1975)

7. *Nothing but Foxes* (St. Martin's, 1979)

8. *Relative Distance, A* (Collins [UK], 1981)

Lewis, Wyndham

The Apes of God, a satire on dilettantism in art and literature in London in the 1920s, is the best-known work by the British writer and painter. Even his critics admit that Lewis was a keen satirist and a master of striking imagery. But few will agree with critic Walter Allen, who, in The Modern Novel (Dutton, 1964), calls the Human Age, Lewis's unfinished tetralogy, "the most remarkable piece of imaginative writing in English of the past two decades." Most will find the series unreadable or worse. Lewis's support of Fascism didn't help matters any. A projected last volume of the series, to be called The Trial of Man, was to have dealt with the final conflict between the human and the divine.

1. *Childermass, The* (Chatto [UK], 1928) This Judgment Day fantasy starring James Pullman includes parodies of Gertrude Stein and James Joyce.
2. *Monstre Gai* (Methuen [UK], 1955) Pullman and Sutters enter the Magnetic City and find that it is not heaven but a kind of purgatory. Published together with number 3 as *The Human Age, Volume 2.*
3. *Malign Fiesta* (Methuen [UK], 1955) This story is set in Matapolis, which is really hell; Lord Sammael is the devil. Published together with number 2 as *The Human Age, Volume 2.*

Limonov, Eduard

Russian émigré Limonov wrote a series of autobiographical novels recounting his experiences in the USSR and America. Eddie, Limonov's alter ego, is a self-confessed opportunist and con man who admits his own short-comings, but doubts that anyone else is really any better. Life at the bottom told in a style reminiscent of Henry Miller (q.v.) or Charles Bukowski. Numbers 1 and 3 were translated from the Russian by Judson Rosengrant; number 2 by S. L. Campbell. After a sojourn in Paris Limonov returned to Russia after Glasnost and became a leader of the radical National Bolshevik Party. He was recently released from prison after serving a term for buying weapons without a permit and illegally warehousing firearms and ammunition.

1. *Memoirs of a Russian Punk* (Grove, 1990) The misadventures of 15-year-old "Eddie-baby" in the city of Kharkov in Khrushchev's Soviet Union in 1958.
2. *It's Me, Eddie* (Random House, 1983) Eddie's existence as a Soviet émigré in New York City in the 1970s bereft of wife and visible means of support.
3. *His Butler's Story* (Grove, 1987) Eddie takes a job as a butler to a business tycoon and uses it as podium for cynical commentary on a wide range of subjects.

Lindsey, David

Mystery-thriller writer David Lindsey (not to be confused with David Lindsa, author of the science-fiction classic *A Voyage to Arcturus*) writes critically acclaimed novels set in an almost unremittingly dark and downbeat Houston, Texas. Houston homicide detective Stuart Haydon, a good man in a dirty business, is driven to examine the underbelly of American society in a series of suspenseful procedurals. While Lindsey continues to set his novels in Houston, none of the five published since 1992 features Stuart Haydon.

1. *Cold Mind, A* (Harper, 1983) When three high-priced call girls die in bizarre but seemingly unrelated incidents, Stuart Haydon suspects that there is a connection.
2. *Heat from Another Sun* (Harper, 1984) A Howard Hughes–type movie mogul may be making his own snuff films.
3. *Spiral* (Atheneum, 1986) Haydon investigates the torture-murder of a Mexican found dead just outside town with his forehead punctured by a nail.
4. *In the Lake of the Moon* (Atheneum, 1988) A series of provocative photographs invalidating what he thinks he knows about his deceased father lures Haydon to Mexico City.
5. *Body of Truth* (Doubleday, 1992) Haydon goes to Guatemala in search of a missing Houston girl and finds himself in the middle of flagrant human rights abuses.

Lindsey, Johanna

I. The Malorys, a family of English aristocrats, seem to produce more than their share of black sheep and rakehells, judging from Johanna Lindsey's novels. This romantic series is set some time in the 18th and 19th centuries, apparently during the Regency period. It is rather hard to establish a chronology or a family tree of the Malorys from just reading the cover blurbs, but Lindsey fans, of whom there are millions, can probably work those matters out by reading the novels. Suffice it to say that the heroines are all beautiful and passionate, the heroes are all handsome and lusty, and sparks fly when they get together.

1. *Love Only Once* (Avon, 1985) Nicholas Eden is intrigued by Regina Ashton, niece of Lord Edward and Lady Charlotte Malory.
2. *Tender Rebel* (Avon, 1988) Rosalyn, honoring her grandfather's deathbed request to hold onto her money, agrees to a marriage in name only with a fascinating rogue.
3. *Gentle Rogue* (Avon, 1990) Georgina Anderson boards the ship *Maiden Anne* disguised as a cabin boy, and is enslaved by ship's captain James Malory.
4. *Magic of You, The* (Avon, 1993) Amy Mallory sets her sights on Warren Anderson, ship's captain who had once almost had her uncle hanged for piracy.
5. *Say You Love Me* (Morrow, 1996) Penniless Kelsey Langton puts herself up for auction, and Lord Derek Malory is the highest bidder.
6. *Present, The* (Avon, 1998) Black sheep James Malory, his wife, Georgina, and a mysterious package figure largely in this holiday-themed offering. Reprinted, together with nonseries novel *Home for the Holidays*, as *The Holiday Present* (Avon, 2003).
7. *Loving Scoundrel, A* (Atria, 2004) In a story with a Pygmalion theme, Danny, a young woman of the streets, helps rakehell Jeremy Malory steal back the jewels his friend lost in a card game.
8. *Captive of My Desires* (Pocket, 2006) Eighteen-year-old Gabrielle Brooks sails to a Caribbean island in search of her estranged father, only to find that the former merchant captain has become a pirate.

II. At least eight other "series" of two or three novels by Lindsey, including Glorious Angel, Wyoming, Straton, Shefford, Warrior, Cardinian, and Sherring Cross, have been claimed, but only the Viking Family Tree trio seems to have any connection beyond that of theme or location. Three members of the Viking Haardrad family act as abductors or abductees and conduct passionate affairs in a vaguely medieval setting.

1. *Fires of Winter* (Avon, 1980) Lady Brenna vows vengeance on her abductor, Garrick Haardrad, son of a Viking chieftain.
2. *Hearts Aflame* (Avon, 1987) The Thane of Wyndhurst gets very interested in his captive, Kristen Haardrad.
3. *Surrender My Love* (Avon, 1994) Viking lord Selig Haardad, languishing in a prison because of a false spy charge, vows vengeance on his captor, Lady Erika of Gronwood.

Linington, Elizabeth

Elizabeth Linington's police procedurals under her own name haven't been as popular as those written under the pseudonyms of Dell Shannon (q.v.) and Lesley Egan (q.v.), although they are just as well written and involving. Sergeant Ivor Maddox of the Los Angeles Police Department (Hollywood branch) and detectives D'Arcy and Rodriguez are the main continuing characters. Love interest is provided by policewoman Sue Carstairs, who becomes Sue Maddox midway through the series. The first three volumes in the series were published in England under the pseudonym of Anne Blaisdell. No annotations are provided as each novel pursues several investigations, although it should be noted that Maddox uses an old Agatha Christie novel to solve the main mystery in *Greenmask!*

1. *Greenmask!* (Harper, 1964)
2. *No Evil Angel* (Harper, 1964)
3. *Date with Death* (Harper, 1966)
4. *Something Wrong* (Harper, 1967)
5. *Policeman's Lot* (Harper, 1968)
6. *Practice to Deceive* (Harper, 1971)
7. *Crime by Chance* (Lippincott, 1973)
8. *Perchance of Death* (Doubleday, 1977)
9. *No Villain Need Be* (Doubleday, 1979)
10. *Consequence of Crime* (Doubleday, 1980)
11. *Skeletons in the Closet* (Doubleday, 1982)
12. *Felony Report* (Doubleday, 1984)
13. *Strange Felony* (Doubleday, 1986)

Linscott, Gillian

I. Nell Bray, feminist, suffragette, and part-time sleuth, is a smart, feisty, and likable heroine. Nell gets herself involved in a number of the major issues facing England in the era just preceding and during World War I, especially votes for women. Some historical figures, such as Bernard Shaw, Lloyd George, and Emmeline Pankhurst make appearances in this series with vivid characters, excellent historical ambience, romance, and intrigue. Titles are arranged in approximate chronological order rather than by order of publication.

1. *Dead Man Riding* (St. Martin's, 2003) Nell and some Oxford friends spend a reading holiday at a farm in the Lake District. But it seems that the owner of the farm is engaged in a hot feud with his neighbors. Then he turns up dead in the saddle. Set in 1900.
2. *Sister beneath the Sheet* (St. Martin's, 1991) Nell is introduced in this novel. After a stay at Holloway Prison for heaving a brick through a window at 10 Downing Street, she is sent to Biarritz to retrieve a legacy left to the Women's Social and Political Union by celebrated courtesan Topaz Brown.
3. *Easy Day for a Lady, An* (St. Martin's, 1995) Nell vacations in the French Alps just as the body of Arthur Mordford is freed from the ice where it was frozen for 30 years. Variant title: *Widow's Peak*.

4. *Dead Man's Sweetheart* (St. Martin's, 1996) Nell is asked by the accused's sister and lawyer to intervene in the case of Davie Kendal, convicted of the murder of local mill owner Osbert Newbiggin. Variant title: *Dead Man's Music*.
5. *Dance on Blood* (St. Martin's, 1998) After Chancellor of the Exchequer Lloyd George's home is bombed, allegedly by suffragettes, Lloyd George prevails upon Nell to recover some comprising letters from an important government figure from an exotic dancer and her manager before they can pass them on to the Germans.
6. *Blood on the Wood* (St. Martin's, 2004) Nell is sent to the Venn estate in the Cotswolds to collect a valuable painting left to the suffragettes. When she discovers that she has been fobbed off with a copy, she determines to steal the original.
7. *Crown Witness* (St. Martin's, 1995) A precoronation parade for the new King George V is marred by violence culminating in murder. Nell is determined to get to the bottom of the murder.
8. *Stage Fright* (St. Martin's, 1993) Bray helps Bernard Shaw in his efforts to protect Isabella Flanagan, star of his latest play, from her estranged husband.
9. *Perfect Daughter, The* (St. Martin's, 2001) Nell finds the body of her cousin, Verona North, hanging in the family boathouse. Was it suicide? Was Verona the "perfect daughter" her parents imagined her to be? Set in 1914.
10. *Hanging on the Wire* (St. Martin's, 1993) World War I is raging. Nell is asked to help a hospital for shell-shock victims resist attacks by rabid war supporters who want it closed.
11. *Absent Friends* (St. Martin's, 1999) In 1918 Nell Bray is in Duxbury, near the Welsh border, standing as one of the candidates in the first British General Election in which women could vote. Her campaign is being funded by a widow who wants Nell to look into the suspicious death of her husband.

II. Former British policeman Birdie Linnet is well meaning but always seems to get the point later than anyone else in this lighthearted contemporary mystery series, which was abandoned for the Nell Bray mysteries.

1. *Healthy Body, A* (St. Martin's, 1984) Birdie follows his estranged wife and their daughter to a French seaside camp that turns out to be a naturist (nudist) resort.
2. *Murder Makes Tracks* (St. Martin's, 1985) Birdie and current girlfriend Nimue Hawthorne accompany a school group to the Alps and run into the crossbow murder of a tycoon.
3. *Knightfall* (Macmillan [UK], 1986) An old jam factory in Somerset where the court of King Arthur has been re-created, is the scene of a murder. Not published in the United States.
4. *Whiff of Sulphur, A* (St. Martin's, 1987) Birdie, working for Tooth and Claw Holidays, acts as leader to a bunch of clients taking a survival holiday on a small and unpleasant Caribbean island.

Lippman, Laura

Tess Monaghan is a reporter who was downsized out of job. To make ends meet, she works part-time at her aunt Kitty's bookstore and takes on cases as a private investigator. Tess is one of your hard-shelled types with a sweet center. Her cases take place in and around Baltimore, Maryland, which is the most compelling character in the books. Laura Lippman, former feature writer for the *Baltimore Sun*, has also written well-regarded stand-alone thrillers such as *What the Dead Know* (Morrow, 2007) and *Every Secret Thing* (Morrow, 2003).

1. *Baltimore Blues* (Avon, 1997) The fiancé that rowing buddy Rocky pays Tess to follow turns up dead.

2. *Charm City* (Avon, 1997) Tess poses as a reporter for the *Baltimore Beacon-Light* to look into the apparent suicide of hometown hero and tycoon "Wink" Wynkowski.

3. *Butchers Hill* (Avon, 1998) Tess, now a PI in Butchers Hill, a black section of Baltimore, takes on the case of the missing professional fund-raiser.

4. *In Big Trouble* (Avon, 1999) Tess ventures to Charlottesville, Texas, when she receives a photo of her former boyfriend "Crow" Ransome, with an indication that he is "in big trouble."

5. *Sugar House, The* (Morrow, 2000) Teen Henry Dombrow goes to prison after confessing to killing a young, unidentified girl. A month later, Henry is dead. First hardcover publication in the series.

6. *In a Strange City* (Morrow, 2001) Features an anonymous person who places a glass of brandy and a rose on Edgar Allan Poe's grave every January to honor his birthday.

7. *Last Place, The* (Morrow, 2002) Toll-facility cop Carl Dewitt finds a disembodied head on the roadway of a bridge.

8. *By a Spider's Thread* (Morrow, 2004) Tess agrees to help uptight Orthodox Jewish furrier Mark Ruben to find his missing Russian-born wife and children.

9. *No Good Deeds* (Morrow, 2006) Edgar "Crow" Ransome, sometime musician and Tess's boyfriend, brings home Lloyd, a homeless teenager who slashed Crow's tires.

10. *Another Thing to Fall* (Morrow, 2008) Tess is hired as a bodyguard for Selene Waites, star of *Man of Steel*, a TV miniseries being shot in Baltimore.

Livingston, Nancy

I.   Retired tax inspector G. D. H. Pringle and his companion, bar-maid Mavis Bignell, make an odd but effective mystery-solving couple. The quietly testy codger and the buxom friendly lady usually stumble into their cases while on holiday in this series with humor, engaging characters, and cozy atmosphere.

1. *Trouble at Aquitaine, The* (St. Martin's, 1986) A castle turned health clinic turns into a murder scene when a body turns up in the swimming pool.

2. *Fatality at Bath and Wells* (St. Martin's, 1987) Pringle and Mavis are vacationing in Bath when a murder is committed in the control room of the local television studio.

3. *Incident at Parga* (St. Martin's, 1988) Mr. Pringle's sail with his nephew in a small boat off Greece turns into a murder case when a fellow passenger is found dead.

4. *Death in a Distant Land* (St. Martin's, 1989) Mr. Pringle and Mavis travel to Australia to look for the grandson of Mavis's friend.

5. *Death in Closeup* (St. Martin's, 1989) Once-famous actress Margarite Pelouse is killed on the set of the soap opera "Doctors and Nurses."

6. *Mayhem in Parva* (St. Martin's, 1991) Mr. Pringle decides to visit Wuffinge Parva, the old English village where he lived as a child, and runs into a feud over the community fair.

7. *Unwillingly to Vegas* (St. Martin's, 1992) Pringle and Binell are lured to Las Vegas by a gang that plans a heist using Pringle as the fall guy.

8. *Quiet Murder* (St. Martin's, 1993) In their own London neighbor-hood for a change, G. D. H. and Mavis pursue the case of the murder of elderly Ernest Clare.

II.   Livingston (d. 1994) also proved to be an adept hand at the historical novel in this pair about the Scottish McKie family in the town of Darlington that follows two generations from the 1880s through World War I.

1. *Far Side of the Hill, The* (St. Martin's, 1988) Poor, rural Scots John and Davie McKie migrate to the town of Darlington and achieve success by opening its first department store.

2. *Land of Our Dreams, The* (St. Martin's, 1989) The McKie children are about to leave the parental nest when World War I breaks out.

Llewellyn, Richard

How Green Was My Valley, Richard Llewellyn's lyrical novel, won unanimous praise when it was published in 1940. In telling the story of the Morgan family, he gives a vivid picture of a Welsh coal-mining community from the first days of its new prosperity in the 19th century to the eventual desolation of both the countryside and its populace. Though their lives are hard and often tragic, Llewllyn shows their courage, independence and lusty humor. The 1941 film version, starring Walter Pidgeon and Maureen O'Hara, won the Academy Award for best picture.

1. *How Green Was My Valley* (Macmillan, 1940) Huw Morgan's reminiscences about his boyhood in a Welsh mining town include a loving portrait of his gentle tyrant of a father.

2. *Up, into the Singing Mountain* (Doubleday, 1960) Huw, now a skilled cabinetmaker, builds a life for himself in a Welsh community in Patagonia.

3. *Down Where the Moon Is Small* (Doubleday, 1966) Huw reminisces about the partnership with Moishe that brought him wealth and the tragic loss of his wife and son.

4. *Green, Green My Valley Now* (Doubleday, 1975) Huw, with his second wife, returns to Wales, renovates an ancient house, and finds himself involved with the IRA.

Lockridge, Frances & Richard

I.   The husband-and-wife team of Frances and Richard Lockridge wrote many mystery novels. Although their books can be regarded as one extended series, with characters who migrate from one series to another, the Mr. and Mrs. North books were the most popular, partly due to their movie and TV incarnations. *Mr. and Mrs. North*, a novel by Richard Lockridge alone, introduced the Norths in 1936. Four years later, the series began in earnest, with 25 books published over the space of 24 years. The series ended with the death of Frances Lockridge. Pam and Jerry North are amateur detectives who rely mostly on Pam's intuition. Subsidiary characters include Bill Wiegand, who features in a novel of his own, *The Tangled Cord* (Lippincott, 1957), and Nathan Shapiro (see series III), both of the New York City Police Department, and the Norths' cats. Each novels ends with a terror-filled chase in which the murderer is in hot pursuit of Pam. *Murder! Murder! Murder!* (Lippincott, 1956) is an omnibus volume containing numbers 2, 3, and 4. Readers don't have to read the Mr. and Mrs. North books in order, and probably will want to dip into the series rather than read all of the novels. Titles are listed below without annotations. Most of the information on the Lockridges and their work has been culled from Guy M. Townsend's article in *St. James Guide to Crime and Mystery Writers* (4th ed., St. James, 1996).

1. *Mr. and Mrs. North* (Stokes, 1936)
2. *Norths Meet Murder, The* (Stokes, 1940)
3. *Murder Out of Turn* (Stokes, 1941)

4. *Pinch of Poison, A* (Stokes, 1941)
5. *Death on the Aisle* (Lippincott, 1942)
6. *Hanged for a Sheep* (Lippincott, 1942)
7. *Death Takes a Bow* (Lippincott, 1943)
8. *Killing the Goose* (Lippincott, 1944)
9. *Payoff for the Banker* (Lippincott, 1945)
10. *Death of a Tall Man* (Lippincott, 1946)
11. *Murder within Murder* (Lippincott, 1946)
12. *Untidy Murder* (Lippincott, 1947)
13. *Murder Is Served* (Lippincott, 1948)
14. *Dishonest Murderer, The* (Lippincott, 1949)
15. *Murder in a Hurry* (Lippincott, 1950)
16. *Murder Comes First* (Lippincott, 1951)
17. *Dead as a Dinosaur* (Lippincott, 1952)
18. *Curtain for a Jester* (Lippincott, 1953)
19. *Key to Death, A* (Lippincott, 1954)
20. *Death of an Angel* (Lippincott, 1955) Variant title: *Mr. and Mrs. North and the Poisoned Playboy.*
21. *Voyage into Violence* (Lippincott, 1956)
22. *Long Skeleton, The* (Lippincott, 1958)
23. *Murder Is Suggested* (Lippincott, 1959)
24. *Judge Is Reversed, The* (Lippincott, 1960)
25. *Murder Has Its Points* (Lippincott, 1962)
26. *Murder by the Book* (Lippincott, 1963)

II. The series centered on Inspector Merton Heimrich of the New York State Police was regarded as more substantial in terms of plotting and characterization than the North series, but it was never as popular or well known. Heimrich was a developing character, who started off single but eventually acquired a wife, a son, and a home in the Putnam County, New York, hamlet of The Corners. Richard Lockridge continued the series alone after the death of Frances Lockridge in 1963 (numbers 17–24). Titles are listed below without annotations. For some reason, the UK editions of the novels published by Long (numbers 12–24) listed "Francis Richards" as the author.

1. *Think of Death* (Lippincott, 1947)
2. *I Want to Go Home* (Lippincott, 1948)
3. *Spin Your Web, Lady* (Lippincott, 1949)
4. *Foggy, Foggy Death* (Lippincott, 1950)
5. *Client Is Cancelled, A* (Lippincott, 1951)
6. *Death by Association* (Lippincott, 1952) Variant title: *Trial by Terror.*
7. *Stand Up and Die* (Lippincott, 1953)
8. *Death and the Gentle Bull* (Lippincott, 1954) Variant title: *Killer in the Straw.*
9. *Burnt Offering* (Lippincott, 1955)
10. *Let Dead Enough Alone* (Lippincott, 1956)
11. *Practice to Deceive* (Lippincott, 1957)
12. *Accent on Murder* (Lippincott, 1958)
13. *Show Red for Danger* (Lippincott, 1960)
14. *With One Stone* (Lippincott, 1961) UK title: *No Dignity in Death.*
15. *Distant Clue, The* (Lippincott, 1963)
16. *First Come, First Kill* (Lippincott, 1963)
17. *Murder Can't Wait* (Lippincott, 1964) Also features Nathan Shapiro (series III).
18. *Murder Roundabout* (Lippincott, 1966)
19. *With Option to Die* (Lippincott, 1967)
20. *Risky Way to Kill, A* (Lippincott, 1969)
21. *Inspector's Holiday* (Lippincott, 1971)
22. *Not I, Said the Sparrow* (Lippincott, 1973)
23. *Dead Run* (Lippincott, 1976)
24. *Tenth Life, The* (Lippincott, 1977)

III. Nathan Shapiro, a Jewish cop who works under Bill Wiegand in the NYPD (see series I), is the principal character in a series of 11 books. (He shares number 1 with Inspector Heimrich of series II). Although he is quite competent, Shapiro is full of self-doubts about his ability as a policeman. Numbers 4 through 11 were written by Richard Lockridge alone. Long (UK) editions (numbers 2–11) list "Francis Richards" as author. Titles are listed below without annotations.

1. *Faceless Adversary, The* (Lippincott, 1956) Variant title: *Case of the Missing Redhead.*
2. *Murder and Blueberry Pie* (Lippincott, 1959) UK title: *Call It Coincidence.*
3. *Drill Is Death, The* (Lippincott, 1961)
4. *Murder Can't Wait (2)* (Lippincott, 1964)
5. *Murder for Art's Sake* (Lippincott, 1967)
6. *Die Laughing* (Lippincott, 1969)
7. *Preach No More* (Lippincott, 1971)
8. *Write Murder Down* (Lippincott, 1972)
9. *Or Was He Pushed?* (Lippincott, 1975)
10. *Streak of Light, A* (Lippincott, 1978)
11. *Old Die Young, The* (Harper, 1980)

IV. A fourth series features assistant New York City DA Bernie Simmons. Retired professor Walter Brinkley, late of Dyckman University, and his majordomo Harry Washington play prominent roles in this series and make appearances in the other series, but have no series of their own. Richard Lockridge was the sole author for numbers 3 through 6. Numbers 2 through 7 were published by Long (UK) by "Francis Richards." Titles are listed without annotations.

1. *And Left for Dead* (Lippincott, 1962)
2. *Devious Ones, The* (Lippincott, 1964) UK title: *Four Hours to Fear.*
3. *Squire of Death* (Lippincott, 1965)
4. *Plate of Red Herrings, A* (Lippincott, 1968)
5. *Twice Retired* (Lippincott, 1970)
6. *Something Up a Sleeve* (Lippincott, 1972)
7. *Death on the Hour* (Lippincott, 1974)

Lodge, David

David Lodge's year as a visiting professor at the University of California, Berkeley, in 1969 must have been the inspiration for the hilarious Anglo-American relations depicted in this series of academic novels. Morris Zapp, a manic American superprofessor from California's Euphoria University, and Philip Sparrow, a mild-mannered English don from Rummidge University in the English Midlands, are the main characters in the first book, and make short appearances in the sequels. Lodge recently retired as professor of English literature at England's University of Birmingham, and is the author of many novels and critical works.

1. *Changing Places: A Tale of Two Campuses* (Penguin, 1979) Tells of the eventful year when American Morris Zapp and Britisher Philip Sparrow traded jobs. Originally published in hardcover in the United Kingdom (Secker & Warburg, 1975).
2. *Small World: An Academic Romance* (Macmillan, 1985) Young Irish professor Persse McGarrigle pursues the beautiful but elusive Angelica Pabst around the academic conference circuit.
3. *Nice Work* (Viking, 1989) Robin Penrose, youngest member of Rummidge University's English department, is drafted for an industrial exchange program and finds herself attracted to the factory manager with whom she must work one day a week.

Lodi, Maria

Paris in the 1860s is the dramatic setting for this readable three-volume romance. During the dictatorship of Napoléon III the city is a seething mixture of glittering salons and miserable slums. Charlotte Morel is a beautiful and headstrong provincial girl who comes to Paris as a young bride. The dashing journalist Thomas Becque, one of the fearless few who dare to criticize the government, meets Charlotte while protecting her from street rowdies and falls hopelessly in love with her. All three novels were translated from the French by Anne Carter.

1. *Charlotte Morel* (Putnam, 1969) From their meeting in the provinces to a final stormy scene Charlotte resists the passion that Thomas feels for her.
2. *Charlotte Morel: The Dream* (Putnam, 1970) In 1868 Thomas decides to marry Marie and relocate his press to Brussels, but he cannot tear himself away from Charlotte.
3. *Charlotte Morel: The Siege* (Putnam, 1970) The tragic last act of Thomas's love for Charlotte is set during the privations of the great siege of Paris in 1870.

Lofts, Norah

I. Norah Lofts's steady output of consistently interesting historical novels entertained readers for more than 30 years. Lofts could write convincingly of 15th-century England, Napoleonic France, or the colonial Dutch East Indies. Her books provide fascinating glimpses into domestic history and the lives of women, and they combine drama, romance, and suspense in just the right proportions. Her first trilogy follows the five-century history of a house in Suffolk, England, beginning with its original builder, Martin Reed, born a serf in 1381.

1. *Town House, The* (Doubleday, 1959) Martin Reed's rise from serf to prosperous merchant is told in five narrations-by himself, his servant, his daughter Ann, and his two grandchildren, Maude and Nicholas.
2. *House at Old Vine, The* (Doubleday, 1961) Seven more tales carry the history of the house from 1496 to the end of the 17th century.
3. *House at Sunset, The* (Doubleday, 1962) The story of the house's inhabitants is continued from the 18th century to the present.

II. The Godfrey Tallboys trilogy is set in 15th-century England. It stars Sir Godfrey, a feckless knight, his understanding wife, Sybilla, and their four children. Knight's Acre, the setting for all three novels, is the house Godfrey builds for his family in East Anglia. Numbers 1, 2, and 3 were published together in an omnibus volume, *The Suffolk Trilogy* (Coronet [UK], 1986).

1. *Knight's Acre* (Doubleday, 1975) Sir Godfrey leaves his family for a tourney in Spain and is detained for seven years before returning with the lovely young Moorish woman who helped him escape imprisonment.
2. *Homecoming, The* (Doubleday, 1976) An uneasy peace is established between Sybilla and the fiery young Tana, but Godfrey is soon off to serve in the War of the Roses.
3. *Lonely Furrow, The* (Doubleday, 1977) Henry, Godfrey's son, now plows the fields at Knight's Acre, and Joanna aims to make herself indispensable to him.

III. These two novels are about the mysteriously haunted English country house purchased by Bob and Jill Spender. What they learn about the 19th-century Thorley family and the tragic events that cause them to haunt Gad's Hall forms a story within a story.

1. *Gad's Hall* (Doubleday, 1978) When unwed Lavinia Thorley becomes pregnant, Mrs. Thorley keeps her hidden away in Gad's Hall.
2. *Haunting of Gad's Hall, The* (Doubleday, 1979) The Thorley children grow up, but the sealed room in the attic casts its spell. UK title: *Haunted House*.

Long, William Stuart

PSEUDONYM OF Vivian Stuart

The Australians is another of paperback series produced by book packer Lyle Kenyon Engel after the pattern of the Kent Family Chronicles by John Jakes (q.v.). Twelve volumes of this history of Australia were published covering from 1781 to the early 1900s. The reader-tested romance-adventure formula by veteran British author Vivian Stuart writing as "William Stuart Long," plus a renewed interest in things Australian (since Colleen McCullough's best seller, *The Thorn Birds*), guaranteed an audience for this series. Because Vivian Stuart died in 1986, numbers 9 or 10 through 12 were presumably written by some other author acting as "William Stuart Long." All of the titles were published as paperback originals: most of them have reprinted in hardcover by Gregg Press.

1. *Exiles, The* (Dell, 1979) This follows a group of convicts, including a young woman unjustly accused of theft, as they are shipped out from England in 1781.
2. *Settlers, The* (Dell, 1980) This focuses on fiery Jenny Taggart.
3. *Traitors, The* (Dell, 1981) This begins in 1807 as Abigail Tempest comes to Sydney and Jenny Broome struggles alone to raise her children in an alien land.
4. *Explorers, The* (Dell, 1981) In 1809 Highland lassie Jessica MacLaine travels to New South Wales as lady's maid to the wife of the new governor.
5. *Adventurers, The* (Dell, 1983) American beauty Katie O'Malley inspires the passion of George DeLancey as Napoleonic War veterans try to adjust to life "Down Under."
6. *Colonists, The* (Dell, 1984) Land speculators exploit exiled English convicts as the settlement of Australia continues in the 19th century.
7. *Goldseekers, The* (Dell, 1985) The fates of Elizabeth Tempest and Captain Red Broome become intertwined during the Australian gold rush of the 1850s.
8. *Gallant, The* (Dell, 1986) In 1856 heiress Kitty Cadogan travels from Ireland to the Outback.
9. *Empire Builders, The* (Dell, 1987) Lady Kitty is married to journalist Johnny Broome as the action shifts to New Zealand in 1859.
10. *Seafarers, The* (Dell, 1988) Jon Fisher, survivor of an 1879 Zulu massacre, and his friend Harry Ryan are both attracted to Jessica Broome, the "most beautiful girl in Sydney."
11. *Nationalists, The* (Dell, 1989) Java Gordon, daughter of Jessica Broome, gets involved with Slone Shannon, who gets involved with the Boer War.
12. *Imperialists, The* (Dell, 1990) Young Australian couples blaze new trials in unexplored New Guines.

Longstreet, Stephen

I. Stephen Longstreet (d. 2002) was an artist and screenwriter as well as a prolific writer of fiction and nonfiction books. The American Jewish Pedlock family has been the subject of some of his best-known novels. Peter Perry, the narrator of the Pedlock series, is assumed to be an autobiographical figure. He traces the family's colorful history from 1866 to the 1970s, beginning with Confederate army major Joseph Pedlock coming north, marrying Rebecca Mandersheid, and heading west to build a successful mining enterprise. The changing status of Jews in America is shown in the lives of his four children. Later volumes focus on the present-day doings of various branches of the large Pedlock family.

1. *Pedlocks, The: The Story of a Family* (Simon & Schuster, 1951) This book chronicles 80 years in the history of an American Jewish family from patriarch Joseph Pedlock to his young grandson Peter Perry.
2. *God and Sarah Pedlock* (McKay, 1976) Though written later than numbers 3 through 5, this volume is second chronologically. It shows Judith Pedlock, a rich and salty octogenarian, looking for a husband while her niece Sarah, a world-famous pianist, suffers a spiritual crisis.
3. *Pedlock and Sons* (Delacorte, 1966) Octogenarian Judith Pedlock decides to remarry, and the family takes steps to prevent her from selling her stock in the family department store.
4. *Pedlock Saint, Pedlock Sinner* (Delacorte, 1969) Turning to the West Coast branch of the family, this volume focuses on the conflict between two rabbis, the hypocritical Stephen Pedlock and his idealistic young nephew, David Mendoza.
5. *Pedlock Inheritance, The* (McKay, 1972) San Francisco judge Woodrow Pedlock's appointment to the US Supreme Court is jeopardized by his lawyer son Rufus's championing of unpopular causes.
6. *Pedlocks in Love, The* (Avon, 1978) At Woodrow's California ranch, two very different Pedlocks—comfortably married Angela and UC Berkeley professor David—are drawn to each other as a forest fire blazes toward them.

II. An Italian American banking family, the Fiores, is the subject of a trio of novels. The story begins with the founder of the clan, George Fiore, in the 1850s and takes us to the Vietnam War.

1. *All or Nothing* (Putnam, 1983) George Fiore, a poor Italian immigrant, goes into the moneylending business in San Francisco. Covers the 1850s to 1900.
2. *Our Father's House* (Putnam, 1985) In the 1920s, nonagenarian George Fiore and his family continue to expand their banking business and move into Texas oil and motion pictures.
3. *Sons and Daughters* (Putnam, 1987) Gregory Fiore continues the family banking business, but most of the younger Fiores are more interested in other pursuits. Covers from World War II to the Vietnam War.

III. The intertwined fortunes of George Washington and the fictional Cortlandt family are narrated in this trilogy of novels covering the period from the French and Indian War through the War of the American Revolution.

1. *War in the Golden Weather* (Doubleday, 1965) Itinerant painter and fugitive from the law meets Major George Washington and joins him in the French and Indian War campaign culminating in Braddock's defeat.
2. *Eagles Where I Walk* (Doubleday, 1961) In the 1770s young New York surgeon David Cortlandt serves in Washington's army during the Saratoga campaign.
3. *Few Painted Feathers, A* (Doubleday, 1963) David and his wife, Roxanne, follow Washington South for the climactic battles of the Revolutionary War.

Lorens, M. K.

PSEUDONYM OF Margaret Keilstrup

Portly septuagenarian professor of literature and Shakespearean scholar Winston Marlowe Sherman leads a double life. Under the pseudonym of Henrietta Slocum he writes a mystery series about a dashing Gilded Age sleuth named G. Winchester Hyde. Both the Sherman and the Slocum personas lead the curmudgeonly amateur sleuth into his own cases from time to time.

1. *Sweet Narcissus* (Bantam, 1990) An Elizabeth manuscript that disappeared during a 1953 party for Dylan Thomas turns up 30 years later.
2. *Ropedancer's Fall* (Bantam, 1990) Alcoholic author John Falkner and his son disappear at the same time, and Sherman goes in search of them.
3. *Deception Island* (Bantam, 1990) Reclusive artist Frances Woodville has shut out the press, the public, and her old friend Winston for 25 years.
4. *Dreamland* (Doubleday, 1992) When Winston attends an Edgar Awards banquet as a nominee, he finds himself a murder suspect when Imogen Vail, his former lover and his chief competitor, dies.
5. *Sorrowheart* (Doubleday, 1993) Serial murders and the arrival of a new chancellor at DeWitt Clinton College shake up things for Sherman and his colleagues.

Love, William F.

Former monk, priest, college professor, and banker Love has created a protagonist with some of the characteristics of Rex Stout's (q.v.) Nero Wolfe and Andrew Greeley's (q.v.) Blackie Ryan. Bishop Francis X. Regan of the Archdiocese of New York is a wheelchair-bound "frustrated cop." His Archie Goodwin is "atheistic Jew" private investigator David Goldman. The sarcastic but loyal Davey does the narrating and the legwork, while Bishop Regan gives his massive IQ a workout.

1. *Chartreuse Clue, The* (Fine, 1990) Regan and Goldman team up to protect a monk who wakes up in the apartment of a murdered woman.
2. *Fundamentals of Murder, The* (Fine, 1991) Young fundamentalist Oklahoman Jerry Fanning, sent by the Lord to convert sinners in New York City, is sent to jail for the alleged murders of three prostitutes and a model. Variant title: *The Ruby-Red Clue.*
3. *Bloody Ten* (Fine, 1992) Davey agrees to help Off-Off Broadway actor Jim Kearney check the background of long-lost half brother Nick, who has incurred debts to the mob.
4. *Bishop's Revenge* (Fine, 1993) Small-time punk Eddie Goode, who put Regan in his wheelchair eight years ago, is chief suspect in the robbery-murder of socialite Ladd Compton.
5. *Murder at St. Stephen's* (Fine, 1994) Regan's niece calls him for advice when she has doubts about the honesty of her fiancé's business practices. Then the fiancé is stabbed to death.

Lovell, Marc

PSEUDONYM OF Mark McShane

The Appleton Porter novels are entertaining spoofs of the spy genre. "Apple" is a linguist who speaks 6 or 7 languages fluently and 12 or 15 competently, a decided asset for a spy in British intelligence. Unfortunately, Apple is also awkwardly tall (6' 7")—a marvelous target for assassins—and a bit of a bumbler. He tries to be hard and ruthless like his cynical, nasty "control," Angus Watkin, but he is incurably gentle and idealistic. Native Australian Mark McShane has also written many mysteries under his real name, including *Seance on a Wet Afternoon* (Doubleday, 1962), which was made into a classic movie starring Richard Attenborough and Kim Stanley (1964). *Apple Spy in the Sky* was filmed as *Trouble with Spies* (1985).

1. *Spy Game, The* (Doubleday, 1980) Apple has to find out which members of visiting Russian ESP team can really read minds and which ones want to defect.

2. *Spy with His Head in the Clouds, The* (Doubleday, 1982) Apple goes to a circus in Somerset to discover why the Russians have planted the truth serum Soma-2 in British hands.

3. *Spy on the Run* (Doubleday, 1982) Because Russian Olympian Igor Kazov will pass on a secret formula for edible seaweed only on the run, Apple must enter a track meet.

4. *Apple Spy in the Sky* (Doubleday, 1983) A KGB plan to spread drugs on British army bases requires Apple's presence on the Spanish island of Ibiza. Filmed as *Trouble with Spies* (1985).

5. *Apple to the Core* (Doubleday, 1983) Apple has to arrange the defection of one of a famous quartet of Russian singers.

6. *How Green Was My Apple* (Doubleday, 1984) Apple teams up with a six-foot one-inch female agent to shadow a Russian in London, and loses "Ethel," his beloved converted taxicab.

7. *Only Good Apple in a Barrel of Spies, The* (Doubleday, 1984) The death of a Russian cultural attaché on a London train platform leads Apple to masquerade as a pickpocket.

8. *Spy Who Got His Feet Wet, The* (Doubleday, 1985) Apple joins the national basketball team at a tournament in Dublin to deal with a Russian player who has information to peddle.

9. *Spy Who Barked in the Night, The* (Doubleday, 1986) A film crew shooting a movie about Robert Burns in the Scottish Highlands is graced by the presence of Apple posing as an animal trainer.

10. *Good Spies Don't Grow on Trees* (Doubleday, 1986) Apple is assigned to the task of "compromising" Russian chess champion Alicia Suvov at a tournament in London.

11. *That Great Big Trenchcoat in the Sky* (Doubleday, 1988) Apple joins Blushers Anonymous, which may be a front for a Communist plot.

12. *Spy Who Fell off the Back of the Bus, The* (Doubleday, 1988) Apple is sent to Cannes disguised as a Canadian billionaire to buy a purported manuscript attack on Sherlock Holmes by his creator, Arthur Conan Doyle (q.v.).

13. *Ethel and the Naked Spy* (Doubleday, 1989) Ethel, Appleton's classic retired London taxicab, is entered in the British Old Vehicles Association's annual rally.

14. *Comfort Me with Spies* (Doubleday, 1990) Apple enters the ring himself as part of his mission to discredit "Bull" Massive, a wrestler who abets terrorists.

Lovesey, Peter

I. A 19th-century atmosphere, redolent of Holmes and Watson, gives these mysteries a special charm. Set in and around Victorian London, these cases star a crack team of detectives from Scotland Yard. The lean and irascible Detective Sergeant Cribb ferrets out the criminals, while stoutly patient Constable Thackeray performs the dirty jobs and gets no thanks for it. PBS's *Mystery!* aired the dramatizations imported from Britain, to the delight of many viewers.

1. *Wobble to Death* (Dodd, 1970) At a six-day walking race—or "wobble" as they were called—-first one-then another—participant is murdered.

2. *Detective Wore Silk Drawers, The* (Dodd, 1971) Clandestine boxing matches and headless corpses are the main ingredients in this spicy brew.

3. *Abracadaver* (Dodd, 1972) London's music hall performers are being sabotaged onstage, first by practical jokes, then by murder.

4. *Mad Hatter's Holiday* (Dodd, 1973) On vacation in Brighton, Albert Moscrop witnesses a gruesome murder through his telescope.

5. *Tick of Death, The* (Dodd, 1974) A London is plagued with bomb threats, Cribb and Thackeray find themselves the unwilling accomplices of a beautiful red-haired anarchist. UK title: *Invitation to a Dynamite Party.*

6. *Case of Spirits, A* (Dodd, 1975) When a medium is electrocuted during a seance, Cribb suspects that it was murder.

7. *Swing, Swing Together* (Dodd, 1976) On a secret midnight swim in the Thames, young Harriet gets separated from her schoolgirl companions and her clothes by three sinister men in a boat.

8. *Waxwork* (Pantheon, 1978) Miriam Cromer has confessed to poisoning her husband's assistant, but Sergeant Cribb smells something wrong.

II. Lovesey's second historical series has a Victorian ambience again, though set somewhat later in the era, and his detective is somewhat higher in rank, being none other than the Prince of Wales, Albert Edward ("Bertie"), the future King Edward VII. Bertie has his shortcomings, but he is a likable chap and astute enough when he wants to be in these good-natured ribbings of Victorian stuffiness. *Do Not Exceed the Stated Dose* (Little, Brown, 1998), a collection of short stories, includes one Bertie story.

1. *Bertie and the Tin Man* (Mysterious, 1987) Fred Archer, known as "the Tin Man," England's greatest jockey and a friend of Bertie's, is dead, an apparent suicide.

2. *Bertie and the Seven Bodies* (Mysterious, 1990) A shooting party at Desborough Hall incurs the usual slaughter of game and the unusual slaughter of some of the human guests.

3. *Bertie and the Crime of Passion* (Mysterious, 1995) Bertie is discreetly enjoying the pleasures of Paris and platonic meetings with Sarah Bernhardt when the prospective son-in-law of an old friend is shot dead at the Moulin Rouge.

III. Lovesey's third mystery series is set in contemporary Bath, England. It features Peter Diamond, chief superintendent of the Avon and Somerset Murder Squad. Peter is overweight, bald, unsocial, sensitive to slights, and old-fashioned in his methods, but he is basically decent, astute, and intrepid enough to get his man every time in this witty and urbane series, which features old style whodunits in modern dress. *Do Not Exceed the Stated Dose* (Little, Brown, 1998) and *The Sedgmoor Strangler: And Other Stories in Crime* (Crippen & Landru, 2001) are short story collections that include one Diamond story each.

1. *Last Detective, The* (**Doubleday, 1991**) The body of a naked woman, who turns out to be former soap-opera star Geraldine Snoo, is found floating in Chew Valley Lake.

2. *Diamond Solitaire* (**Mysterious, 1993**) Peter, stripped of his rank, is found working as a security guard in Harrod's of London when he finds a young Japanese girl hiding in the store.

3. *Summons, The* (**Mysterious, 1995**) John Mountjoy escape from prison and kidnaps the daughter of Bath's chief constable, forcing the Bath police to reopen his case and to reinstate Diamond.

4. *Bloodhounds* (**Mysterious, 1996**) One of the members of The Bloodhounds, a group of mystery fans, is the victim of a locked-room murder after he turns up a rare Penny Black stamp recently stolen from a nearby museum.

5. *Upon a Dark Night* (**Mysterious, 1998**) Two deaths—the apparent suicide of a lonely old farmer and the apparently accidental tumble from a roof during a wild party by a young girl—engage Diamond's suspicions.

6. *Vault, The* (**Soho, 2000**) A killer who fantasizes himself as Mary Shelley's Frankenstein monster threatens American literature professor Joe Dougan and his wife, Donna, after they arrive in Bath.

7. *Diamond Dust* (**Soho, 2002**) Stephanie, Diamond's wife of nearly 20 years, is murdered, and Diamond eventually becomes the prime suspect in the case.

8. *House Sitter, The* (**Soho, 2003**) Diamond is back at the helm of the Bath homicide squad when he hears about the discovery on a Sussex beach of the body of Emma Tysoe, reported missing from her teacher's position at the university in Bath.

9. *Secret Hangman, The* (**Soho, 2007**) Diamond doesn't share the belief of his superior, Assistant Chief Constable Georgina Dallymore, that the separate hangings of a woman and her onetime partner were murder-suicide.

IV. Henrietta "Hen" Mallin, Chichester CID inspector, who had a supporting role in *The House Sitter* (series III, number 8), now has a series of her own, which bears comparison with the Peter Diamond series.

1. *Circle, The* (**Soho, 2007**) The Chichester Writers' Circle, an eccentric writers' group, seems to be involved in arson and murder.

2. *Headhunters, The* (**Soho, 2008**) Mallin and her team have to identify the woman who washed up half naked on a beach and determine whether foul play was involved.

Ludlum, Robert

I. The late Robert Ludlum (d. 2001) was one of the most popular writers in the English language. His thrillers from *The Scarlatti Inheritance* (World, 1971) on have been automatic best sellers because of Ludlum's fast-paced, suspenseful delineations of conspiracies on a grand scale. One of Ludlum's relatively few series characters is Jason Bourne/David Webb, agent and assassin who suffers from amnesia and the attention of international terrorists in a trio of novels. *The Bourne Identity* was made into movies starring Richard Chamberlain (1988) and Matt Damon (2002). *The Bourne Supremacy* and *The Bourne Ultimatum* were made into Matt Damon movies (2004, 2007). Eric van Lustbader (q.v.) has continued the Bourne series. *The Bourne Trilogy* (Orion [UK], 2003) is an omnibus volume containing numbers 1 through 3.

1. *Bourne Identity, The* (**Marek, 1980**) Jason Bourne, shot, left for dead, and amnesiac, must retrace his past before he is hunted down by assassins sent by several governments, including his own.

2. *Bourne Supremacy, The* (**Random House, 1986**) David Webb, Bourne's alter ego, must return to his Bourne persona to track down an assassin in Hong Kong posing as Bourne.

3. *Bourne Ultimatum, The* (**Random House, 1990**) When Carlos the Jackal penetrates his civilian identity, Webb must again assume his Bourne persona to protect his family.

II. Ludlum has written a widely separated pair of novels that features the adventures of legal eagle Sam Deveraux and General MacKenzie Lochinvar Hawkins and are much lighter in tone than his usual fare.

1. *Road to Gandolfo, The* (**Dial, 1975**) General Hawkins and Deveraux get mixed up in a plot to kidnap the pope. Originally published under the pseudonym Michael Shepherd.

2. *Road to Omaha, The* (**Random House, 1992**) Hawkins uncovers loopholes in an old treaty that could lead to the Nebraska land containing Strategic Air Command Headquarters being returned to the Wopotami Indians.

III. The Matarese Circle was an international cabal of power brokers and assassins whose sole aim was to achieve worldwide. So sinister and dangerous was the Matarese dynasty that the CIA and KGB had to team up to destroy them. Twenty years later, the Materese form a new alliance.

1. *Matarese Circle, The* (**Putnam, 1979**) A former director of the KGB and the CIA's best assassin join forces to bring down the international cabal of power brokers and assassins known as the Matarese Circle.

2. *Matarese Countdown, The* (**Bantam, 1997**) Twenty years later, CIA case officer Cameron Pryce is following the trail of blood money and stone-cold killers to get to the heart of the new Matarese alliance.

Lumley, Brian

I. Brian Lumley started publishing in the 1970s while still a career soldier in the British army. Since the late 1980s, he has become a very popular writer in the horror genre. An avowed fan of H. P. Lovecraft, he originally wrote in the Lovecraft vein but eventually branched out to include other influences from the horror and fantasy ranks. Lumley's longest-running series has been the Necroscope vampire series. The basic theme of the series is that vampires are the descendants of alien beings who landed on Earth centuries ago and have been fighting each other and everyone else ever since. The hero of numbers 1 through 7 in this series is Britisher Harry Keogh, who has the ability to read the minds of the dead and speak with them. Harry is recruited by a paranormal branch of British intelligence and set to work battling with other intelligence agencies and the vampires, who are constantly stirring up trouble. Lumley's vampires are not the sympathetic vampires delineated by Anne Rice (q.v.) but are quite simply monsters, albeit clever ones. As the series progresses, Harry acquires new powers, such as teleportation. Eventually, his mind is transferred to the body of "total stranger" Alec Kyle. After his wife disappears with their son, Harry falls under the spell of Bonnie Jean Mirlu, a 200-year-old werewolf who masquerades as a young Edinburgh bartender. After Harry's death, his sons take center stage for awhile, and then the stalwarts of the ESP (or E-) Branch, led by Ben Trask and Jake Cutler, carry on the search-and-destroy mission against the vampires. Lumley is a horror traditionalist who eschews the "splatter-punk" tactics of some writers, and seeks to simply entertain his readers. The chronological listing below is somewhat different from the Necroscope Book numbering, which is by publication date. *Harry Keogh: Necroscope and Other*

Weird Heroes (Tor, 2003) is a short story collection that includes some Necroscope stories. A guide to Lumley's world is *The Brian Lumley Companion* (Tor, 2002), edited by Lumley and Stanley Winter.

1. *Necroscope* **(Tor, 1988)** Introduces Harry Keogh, only living "necroscope," who can communicate with the dead, his recruitment by the ESP wing of British intelligence, and his initial fights against Russian intelligence and the vampire menace.

2. *Necroscope II: Vamphyri!* **(Tor, 1989)** Fortified with new powers from the dead, Keogh continues the fight against the vampires and their allies in Russian intelligence. UK title: *Necroscope II: Whamphyri!*

3. *Necroscope: The Lost Years* **(Tor, 1995)** Book 9 of the Necroscope series and volume 1 of the Lost Years series. Harry has just vanquished Soviet vampire nemesis Boris Progosoni and has learned how to travel through space and time, but his wife and infant son disappear.

4. *Necroscope: Resurgence* **(Tor, 1996)** Book 10 of the Necroscope series; volume 2 of the Lost Years series. Edinburgh barmaid Bonnie Jean Mirlu, a werewolf working for Master Radu, tries to ensnare Keogh on his orders, but falls for Harry instead. Variant title: *Necroscope: The Lost Years, Volume 2.*

5. *Necroscope III: The Source* **(Tor, 1989)** Book 3 of the Necroscope series. This volume was originally planned to be the climax of a trilogy. Soviet scientists have inadvertently opened a gateway into a parallel world of Vampire lords, and Harry and a KGB agent are sent into this world.

6. *Necroscope IV: Deadspeak* **(Tor, 1990)** Book 4 of the Necroscope series. Harry and his colleagues use the latest technology to foil a master vampire's plans to move his nest and expand his troop of thralls.

7. *Necroscope V: Deadspawn* **(Tor, 1991)** Book 5 of the Necroscope series. Harry deals with a serial killer, and tries to uproot a vampire within himself. Last volume of the original Necroscope Series.

8. *Blood Brothers* **(Tor, 1992)** Book 6 of the Necroscope series; book 1 of the Vampire World series. The late Harry Keogh has passed the torch on to his unwitting sons, Nestor and Nathan. Variant title: *Vampire I: Blood Brothers.*

9. *Last Aeyrie, The* **(Tor, 1993)** Book 7 of the Necroscope series; book 2 of the Vampire World series. Nestor, now a vamphyri (vampirelord) of Starside, plots to kill his brother Nathan, who still lives on Sunside. Variant title: *Vampire World II: The Last Aerie.*

10. *Bloodwars* **(Tor, 1994)** Book 8 of the Necroscope series; book 3 of the Vampire World series. Nathan, cross-dimensional traveler and telepath, has been thrown to Earth through the Interworld Gate on orders of brother Nestor. Variant title: *Vampire World III: Bloodwars.*

11. *Necroscope: Invaders* **(Tor, 1999)** Book 11 of the Necroscope series; book 1 of the E-Branch series. ESP (E-) Branch discovers a nest of vampires in the Australian desert. Introduces Jake Cutler, who has been delivered to the unit by the deceased Harry Keogh. Variant title: *E-Branch: Invaders.*

12. *Necroscope: Defilers* **(Tor, 2001)** Book 12 of the Necroscope series; book 2 of the E-Branch series. Three other-dimensional Vamphyri are still at large, and Ben Trask is determined to stop them from spreading infectious vampire fungi. Variant title: *E-Branch: Defilers.*

13. *Necroscope: Avengers* **(Tor, 2001)** Book 13 of the Necroscope series; book 3 of the E-Branch series. Ben Trask, Jake Cutler, and their E-Branch colleagues chase the still-at-large Nephron Malinori, Lady Vavar, and Lord Szwirt from Greece into Turkey. Variant title: *E-Branch: Avengers.*

14. *Necroscope: The Touch* **(Tor, 2006)** Book 14 of the Necroscope series; book 4 of the E-Branch series. Scott St. John and his E-Branch

colleagues wind up on a mission to prevent the psychically gifted Shing't from destroying the Earth.

II. In an earlier series, Lumley, an H. P. Lovecraft acolyte, revived Lovecraft's sinister and baroque world of Cthulhu in a series of amalgams of gothic horror, space opera, and lost race fantasies evoking the Cthulhu Mythos. Titus Crow, his assistant Henri de Marigny, and Hank Silberhutte are investigators with a worldwide organization based at Miskatonic University (Lovecraft again) who battle a series of lost races and ancient horrors from the bowels of the earth. Tor (1996) published three *Titus Crow* omnibus volumes: volume 1 contains numbers 1 and 2; volume 2 contains numbers 3 and 4; and volume 3 contains numbers 5 and 6. HarperCollins (UK) published the series in two omnibus volumes entitled *Brian Lumley's Mythos Omnibus* (1997). *The Compleat Crow* (Ganley, 1987) contains short stories, some of them series related. *Harry Keogh: Necroscope and Other Weird Heroes* (Tor, 2003) contains three Titus Crow short stories.

1. *Burrowers Beneath, The* **(DAW, 1974)** Research into a series of underground explosions leads Titus Crow and Henri de Marigny into an encounter with the evil minions of Cthulhu.

2. *Transition of Titus Crow, The* **(DAW, 1975)** An old grandfather clock turns out to be a vehicle for traveling through space and time.

3. *Clock of Dreams, The* **(Jove, 1978)** Henri uses the magical grandfather clock to rescue Titus and his beloved Tiana from Cthulhu.

4. *Spawn of the Winds* **(Jove, 1978)** Hank Silberhutte is banished to the mystical land of Borea, where he woos the Woman of the Winds and encourages her to rebel against her father.

5. *In the Moons of Borea* **(Jove, 1979)** Henri de Marigny and Hank Silberhutte square off against Ithaqua the Wind-Walker in the Eskimo-like land of Borea.

6. *Elysia: The Coming of Cthulhu* **(Ganley, 1989)** The final confrontation (at least for now) with Cthulhu, the demigod who plots eternally to conquer the Earth involves Crow, de Marigny, Silberhutte, and characters from two other Cthulhu-based Lumley series: the Dreamland Series (see series III) and the Primal Land Series (see series IV).

III. Another Cthulhu-related series is the Dreamland Series, in which David Hero, mild-mannered wimp when awake, is a fierce dream warrior when asleep. David Hero, in his Dream-guise and with a little help, vanquishes zombies, witches, and other wicked beings in another dimension. The series was originally published by W. Paul Ganley Publisher of Buffalo, New York, and then reprinted by Tor in 1994. David Hero also appears in *Elysia*, the final volume of series II.

1. *Hero of Dreams* **(Ganley, 1986)** David Hero, unheroic when conscious but a fierce dream warrior when unconscious, is drawn into a world of other-dimensional evil that may prevent him from waking up.

2. *Ship of Dreams* **(Ganley, 1986)** David Hero faces an army of zombies threatening the Dreamlands. Wicked Queen Zura, who knows that she will be invincible if she can defeat David, makes him a target.

3. *Mad Moon of Dreams* **(Ganley, 1987)** David and his friends have to form an alliance with Queen Zura and her zombie armies to fight off the greatest threat that the Dreamlands have faced.

4. *Iced on Aran and Other Dream Quests* **(Ganley, 1992)** David Hero is invited to a mountain-top retreat where it is proposed that, like previous Dreamlands heros, he be sculpted in ice.

IV. A third Cthulhu series is the Primal Lands, which has appeared only as collections of short stories. Titles are listed below without annotations.

1. *House of Cthulhu and Other Tales of the Primal Land, The* **(Weirdbook, 1984)** Revised as *House of Cthulhu: Tales of the Primal Land, Volume One*: Headline (UK), 1991.
2. *Compleat Khash, The: Volume One; Never a Backward Glance* **(Ganley, 1991)** UK title: *Tarra Khash: Hrossak! Tales of the Primal Land, Volume Two*.
3. *Compleat Kash, The: Sorcery in Shad* **(Ganley, 1991)** UK title: *Sorcery in Shad: Tales of the Primal Land, Volume Three*. Reprinted in 2006 by Tor.

V. The Psychomech Trilogy concerns an alternate universe where inventor Richard Garrison's all-powerful machine, the Psychomech, can open up the Psychosphere, raise the dead, and seemingly bring peace to mankind.

1. *Psychomech* **(Tor, 1992)** Richard Garrison, British army corporal wounded by a terrorist bomb, makes the Psychomech, a mechanical psychiatrist begun by a German SS psychiatrist to help the Nazis build supermen. Richard revives old flame Vicki Maler from the cryogenic preservation tank in which she was placed. Originally published in 1984.
2. *Psychosphere* **(Tor, 1992)** Garrison's powers lead him into the Psychosphere, where he begins to purge and purify Earth of its evil humors. Originally published in 1984.
3. *Psychamok!* **(Tor, 1993)** Twenty years of peace on Earth are ended when Psychomech goes berserk and a million people feel the irreversible plague of insanity called the Gibbering. Originally published in 1985.

VI. A pair of related novels, more SF than horror, deals with alien invasions of Earth.

1. *House of Doors, The* **(Tor, 1998)** Aliens have landed on Earth, bringing with them the House of Doors, an enormous puzzle box. If Earth's best minds can't solve the puzzles, then all humanity is doomed.
2. *Maze of Worlds, A* **(Tor, 1998)** A renegade group of the Aliens have returned to Earth and have unleashed a sort of killer kudzu. UK title: *The House of Doors: Second Visit*.

Lupoff, Richard A(llen)

I. The off-and-on partnership between white, mild-mannered, middle-aged insurance claims adjustor Hobart Lindsey and black, tough, and street-smart Berkeley, California, homicide detective Marvia Plum, is one of the continuing attractions of this series mystery series along with tricky plots, subtle humor, and large doses of nostalgia. Lupoff is best known for his science-fiction stories, collected in such volumes as *Claremont Tales* (Golden Gryphon, 2001) and *Claremont Tales II* (Golden Gryphon, 2002).

1. *Comic Book Killer, The* **(Bantam, 1989)** A claim for a quarter of a million dollars is made against Lindsey's insurance firm when some rare comic books are stolen.
2. *Classic Car Killer, The* **(Bantam, 1992)** A 1928 SJ Duesenberg convertible Phaethon valued at $425,000 vanishes from the Kleiner mansion in Oakland during a "1929" gala.

3. *Bessie Blue Killer, The* **(St. Martin's, 1994)** A $100 million policy covers a film company producing a film about the Tuskegee Airmen, the all-black World War II flying corps.
4. *Sepia Siren Killer, The* **(St. Martin's, 1994)** The early days of black filmmaking in California are explored by Lindsey and Plum when an arson-caused fire kills a graduate student at the Pacific Film Archive.
5. *Cover Girl Killer, The* **(St. Martin's, 1995)** Rare pulp paperbacks enter the picture when Albert Vansittart's insurance policy names as its beneficiary "the girl on the cover of *Death in the Ditch*."
6. *Silver Chariot Killer, The* **(St. Martin's, 1996)** Marvia Plum has married someone else. Left on his own Hobart Lindsey leaves Denver, where he's deputy director of the Special Projects Unit for International Surety, for New York to investigate the murder his colleague Cletus Berry.
7. *Radio Red Killer, The* **(St. Martin's, 1997)** Marvia Plum, returned to the Berkeley Police Department, and living with her mother and rebellious teenage son, is the central character in this investigation of the suspicious on-air death of KRED radical radio commentator Bob Bjorner.
8. *One Murder at a Time: The Casebook of Lindsey and Plum* **(Cosmos, 2001)** A collection of short stories.

II. The Flat Earth, or Twin Planets, series is a broadly humorous, action-backed pair of novels about a doughnut-shaped alternate Earth, in which most of the familiar names of our own world exist.

1. *Circumpolar!* **(Timescape, 1984)** Amelia Earhart, Howard Hughes, and Charles Lindbergh are challenged by a team of evil Germans in a race to circumnavigate the Earth.
2. *Countersolar!* **(Arbor House, 1987)** A race through space between Albert Einstein and Eva Perón is set off by a message sent from Counter-Earth, another orbiting world.

III. Another pair of SF novels concerns a Japanese engineer who is resurrected in an artificial body after being "dead" for 80 years.

1. *Sun's End* **(Berkley, 1984)** A mortally injured Japanese engineer is awakened after 80 years of unconsciousness to find himself with an artificial body that possesses extraordinary and not entirely understood powers.
2. *Galaxy's End* **(Ace, 1988)** Finding that he cannot adjust to a Japan that has reverted to a lifestyle of centuries earlier, the engineer discovers that the solar system itself may be destroyed, a threat that only he can deal with.

Lurie, Alison

Alison Lurie's comedies-of-manners are usually about the marital travails of upper-middle-class characters situated in academia, or in the arts, who, although they are generally intelligent and rational beings, go off the rails more or less, and learn something about themselves. While they are not sequels in the usual sense, the novels are connected by characters who reappear, either as an onstage or as an off-stage presence. L(eonard) Zimmern, the acerbic literary critic, or members of his family turn up in many places. Zimmern appears as an adolescent in *Only Children*, the only Lurie novel that isn't set in contemporary times. He is present offstage as the critic who savages Vinnie Miner's book in *Foreign Affairs*. Roger Zimmern is the protagonist of *Imaginary Friends*. Lorin Jones, the deceased artist in *The Truth about Lorin Jones* started life as "Lolly" Zimmern. Corinth University, a stand-in for Cornell University, where Alison Lurie was a professor of children's literature, is where the action is in *The*

War between the Tates. The leading characters of *Foreign Affairs* are Corinth professors on sabbatical in London. The widow of Chuck Mumpson, a character in *Foreign Affairs* is represented by his widow, a strong off-stage presence in *The Last Resort*. *Foreign Affairs* won a Pulitzer Prize. *Imaginary Friends*, *The War between the Tates* and *Foreign Affairs* were filmed for TV. Alison Lurie is also the author of several nonfiction books, some about children's literature, such as *Don't Tell the Grown-Ups* (Little, Brown, 1990) and *Boys and Girls Forever* (Penguin, 2003).

1. *Only Children* (**Random House, 1979**) Two couples and their children spend a Depression-era Fourth of July on a farm owned by the headmistress of the progressive school that their daughters attend.

2. *Love and Friendship* (**Macmillan, 1962**) Emily Turner finds her new life as a collegiate wife at a rural college, and with her insensitive academic husband, stifling.

3. *Nowhere City, The* (**Coward, 1965**) Describes how California attitudes reshape the social presumptions of historian Paul Cattleman and his New England wife.

4. *Imaginary Friends* (**Coward, 1967**) Sociology professor Thomas McMann and his research assistant Roger Zimmern venture to upstate New York to do fieldwork among the Truth Seekers, an apocalyptic cult.

5. *Real People* (**Random House, 1970**) Janet Belle Smith, a successful novelist, goes to Illyria, a pastoral artists' retreat, and gets rather more than she bargained for.

6. *War between the Tates, The* (**Random House, 1974**) Brian Tate, professor of political science at Corinth University, has an affair with a student, much to the distress of his wife.

7. *Foreign Affairs* (**Random House, 1984**) Two academics from Corinth University: homely Vinnie Miner and handsome Fred Turner, learn a lot about love in London. Fred has an affair with an actress. Vinnie has an affair with Chuck Mumpson, a loud, retired waste disposal engineer from Tulsa.

8. *Truth about Lorin Jones, The* (**Little, Brown, 1988**) Biographer Polly Alter is forced into a considerable reassessment of the life and character of her subject, deceased abstract painter Lorin Jones.

9. *Last Resort, The* (**Holt, 1988**) Set in Key West. Jenny Walker reevaluates her idolization of her husband, eminent naturalist Wilkie Walker, who is under the impression he is suffering from terminal cancer.

10. *Truth and Consequences* (**Knopf, 2005**) Since he hurt his back, architectural historian Alan MacKenzie has become a royal pain to his faithful wife, Jane. Then flamboyant romance novelist Delia Delaney arrives on campus as a visiting scholar.

Lustbader, Eric (van)

I. Lustbader is one of the most popular practitioners of the samurai or ninja or kung-fu or martial arts novel. *The Ninja*, Lustbader's first novel about half-Asian, half-Caucasian fighting machine Nicholas Linnear, spawned several sequels and a movie and was an inspiration, along with the Bruce Lee movies, for the seemingly endless flow of Stallone/Norris/Van Damme, etc., films.

1. *Ninja, The* (**Evans, 1980**) Nicholas Linnear, son of a British father and a Japanese mother, uses martial arts skills learned from the Ninja, an ancient caste of warriors, to straighten out some matters of high finance.

2. *Miko, The* (**Random House, 1984**) Linnear encounters Akiko Ofuda, a beautiful, lethal sorceress, in a plot involving oil and a super-robot code-named Tenchi.

3. *White Ninja, The* (**Ballantine, 1990**) An "enemy" has seeped into Linnear's soul, leaving him helpless against marital problems, a computer virus, and pressure from a Japanese business cabal.

4. *Kaisho, The* (**Pocket, 1993**) Linnear finds himself allied with Mikio Okami, Kaisho, or Godfather, of the Yakuza, against a Vietnamese assassin.

5. *Floating City* (**Pocket, 1994**) Nicholas and private eye buddy Lew Croaker battle murderous drug lords in Washington, Tokyo, Vietnam, and other parts of the globe.

6. *Second Skin* (**Pocket, 1995**) Nicholas's computer firm is on the edge of a mega-breakthrough that is threatened by two crazed gangster brothers.

7. *Dark Homecoming* (**Pocket, 1997**) Lew Croaker, seen in numbers 5 and 6, takes center stage here. Lew, an ex–New York cop with a biomechanical hand, has retired to Florida, when he is notified that his niece needs a kidney replacement.

II. The Sunset Warrior series is sword-and-sorcery fantasy with a strong admixture of Eastern mythology. The far-future underground city of Kamada is threatened by mechanical failure and loss of moral fiber. To the rescue comes Ronin, strong of body, pure of heart, and seeker of esoteric knowledge.

1. *Sunset Warrior, The* (**Doubleday, 1977**) Ronin, refusing to pledge his loyalty to the warlords and priests of Kamada, seeks the truth on the Lower Levels and on the Surface.

2. *Shallows of Night* (**Doubleday, 1978**) Ronin hacks his way across the Continent of Man trying to warn mankind about the Makkon, dragonlike creatures who will destroy civilization if not stopped.

3. *Dai-san* (**Doubleday, 1979**) Ronin completes his quest by confronting the evil force of the Dolman.

4. *Beneath an Opal Moon* (**Doubleday, 1981**) A new hero, Moichi Annai-Nin, sails off on a quest to avenge a dead friend, rescue his abducted love, and battle an evil sorceress.

5. *Dragons on the Sea of Night* (**Voyager [UK], 1997**) Addition to the series after 16 years. Not published in the United States. Blurb reads: "He is Ronin no more. He is Dai-San, the Sunset Warrior, and terrible to behold. Neither man nor god, yet the power he wields is beyond description. However, the Dai-San is not invincible and he still has bitter lessons to learn."

III. Jake Maroc, Chinese American superspy, is the hero of a pair of novels that takes in a great deal of territory, involving international intrigue and a mystical plot to put China on the world economic map.

1. *Jian* (**Villard, 1985**) Jake Maroc and his cohorts in the Quarry, an American intelligence agency, match wits and muscle against the formidable KGB agent Nichiren.

2. *Shan* (**Random, 1987**) Jake becomes the "zhuan" to fulfill the Chinese dreams of his spiritual mentor Shi Zilin.

IV. Lustbader has embarked upon a planned multivolume epic fantasy, called the Pearl, which pits technology and spirituality against each other. The alien, technologically superior V'ornn have imposed rule upon the spiritually evolved people of Kundala, who wonder why their goddess Miina has abandoned them. The militaristic Gyrgon technomages of the V'ornn wish to learn the secrets of Kundalan magic, but their misuse of the lost Ring of Five Dragons, if they find it, could be disastrous. And so on. Two novels have been published so far, with of cast of more than 30 "major" characters. This series is for readers who like to sink deeply into a fantasy universe.

1. *Ring of the Five Dragons, The* (**Tor, 2001**) The spiritual Kundalans chafe under the tyranny of the alien V'ornn. The twin priestesses,

Giyan and Barrta, know they must locate and protect the prophesied savior, Dar Sala-at, "the Chosen One of Miina who would find The Pearl and use it to free the Kundala."

2. *Veil of a Thousand Tears, The* (Tor, 2002) Demons and archdemons arriving from the Abyss complicate the search for the Veil of a Thousand Tears and the Ring of Five Dragons.

3. *Cage of Nine Banestones, The* (Tor, 2004) Riane continues her search for the legendary Pearl. A resistance movement unites Kundalans with sympathetic V'ornns even as V'ornn scientists conduct experiments to master a rare radioactive substance.

V. The estate of Robert Ludlum (q.v.) has turned to Eric van Lustbader to continue Ludlum's popular Bourne series. So far Lustbader has produced two "Bourne" novels, continuing the adventures of international assassination Jason Bourne/David Webb.

1. *Bourne Legacy, The* (St. Martin's, 2004) David Webb, supposedly retired from the CIA and now a professor at Georgetown University, finds that he has become the target of an assassin and is framed for the murder of two associates. The Bourne identity asserts itself, leaving Jason Bourne in control. Variant title: *Robert Ludlum's The Bourne Legacy.*

2. *Bourne Betrayal, The* (Warner, 2007) Jason Bourne takes a mission to rescue his only friend in the CIA, Martin Lindros, who disappeared in Africa while tracking shipments of uranium. Variant title: *Robert Ludlum's The Bourne Betrayal.*

Lutz, John

I. Fred Carver is a middle-aged, limping private eye working out of Orlando, Florida. No, he doesn't spend his time in Disney World. The ex-cop, with his live-in black lover, Beth Jackson, has his time taken up by a series of cases with quirky characters and a Florida locale where "local criminals view tourists as game animals." Carver is one of the most complex and believable of the current crop of fictional private investigators.

1. *Tropical Heat* (Holt, 1986) When real-estate salesman Willis Davis disappears, his lover, Edwina Talbot, hires Carver.

2. *Scorcher* (Holt, 1987) A madman on the loose with a flamethrower kills Carver's eight-year-old son.

3. *Kiss* (Holt, 1988) A ruthless hit man is speeding up the inevitable for certain wealthy residents of Sunhaven retirement home.

4. *Flame* (Holt, 1989) A retiree who is offered a large sum of money to impersonate someone is killed in an explosion.

5. *Bloodfire* (Holt, 1991) Carver tracks down Robert Ghostly's heroin-addicted wife, but winds up protecting her when he discovers that Ghostly is a notorious drug dealer.

6. *Hot* (Holt, 1992) Fred is hired by ex-cop Henry Tiller to get the goods on suspected drug dealer Walter Rainer, Henry's neighbor on the Florida Keys.

7. *Spark* (Holt, 1993) An elderly schoolteacher is tormented by anonymous notes claiming that her deceased husband was murdered.

8. *Torch* (Holt, 1994) Wife and mother Donna Winship throws herself in front of a truck minutes after hiring Carver to follow her.

9. *Burn* (Holt, 1995) Successful building contractor Joel Brandt is accused of stalking a woman he claims he doesn't know.

10. *Lightning* (Holt, 1996) Carver's lover, Beth Jackson, stops by Women's Light Clinic to cancel her abortion appointment. Then an explosion rips the clinic just after she enters, killing a doctor and injuring Beth, who loses her baby.

II. Alo Nudger, like Fred Carver, is an ex-cop, an ex-husband, and a practicing private investigator, but the resemblance ends there. Alo, who works out of St. Louis, has a nagging conscience, a nervous stomach, and a distaste for violence.

1. *Buyer Beware* (Putnam, 1976) Private eye Aloysius "Alo" Nudger is hired to "kidnap" a seven-year-old girl by her father.

2. *Nightlines* (St. Martin's, 1985) Nudger is consulted by a woman whose twin sister was murdered, possibly by a serial killer who uses the service lines of the telephone company.

3. *Right to Sing the Blues, The* (St. Martin's, 1986) Jazz great "Fat Jack" McGee wants Nudger to come to New Orleans to run a check on his pianist Willy Hollister.

4. *Ride the Lightning* (St. Martin's, 1987) Alo is hired to interview eyewitnesses to a murder by the fiancée of the man who was convicted of the crime.

5. *Dancer's Debt* (St. Martin's, 1988) A well-built blond hires Nudger to keep tabs on her troubled boyfriend, Dancer, who suffers from gambling debts, alcoholism, nightmares, and long blackouts

6. *Time Exposure* (St. Martin's, 1989) Adelaide Lacy hires Alo to find her sister Mary and Mary's boss, Virgil Hiller, who are both missing along with half a million in public funds.

7. *Diamond Eyes* (St. Martin's, 1990) Nudger is at the airport when TWA Flight 243 explodes on the runway.

8. *Thicker Than Blood* (St. Martin's, 1993) Norvella Beane hires Alo to find junk-bond swindler Fred McMahon, who has absconded with her money.

9. *Death by Jury* (St. Martin's, 1995) Nudger is hired by defense attorney Martin Fleck to find evidence against his own client, who is accused of murdering his wife.

10. *Oops!* (St. Martin's, 1998) Nudger reluctantly agrees to help female colleague Lacy Tumulty investigate the case of a young woman dead from a fall down the stairs of her locked home.

11. *Nudger Dilemmas, The* (Five Star, 2003) A collection of 13 Nudger short stories.

Lyons, Arthur

Jacob Asch is a fairly typical Los Angeles–based hard-boiled private eye, except, perhaps, for the fact that he is half-Jewish. Asch started out as a Philip Marlowe clone, but with each novel in the series his character has shown more individuality and complexity. He gets involved with a wide variety of cases—Satanist cults, motorcycle gangs, boxing, movies, meatpacking, insurance, etc.—that tend to point up the seamy underside and lunatic fringe of southern California.

1. *Dead Are Discreet, The* (Mason, 1974) When Sheila Warren, the young disciple of a Satanist cult, is murdered, Asch investigates.

2. *All God's Children* (Mason, 1975) The search for 18-year-old Susan Gurney leads Asch to the Word of God commune and a motorcycle gang calling itself "Satan's Warriors."

3. *Killing Floor, The* (Mason, 1976) Asch goes looking for the missing partner of a meatpacking firm, a compulsive gambler.

4. *Dead Ringer* (Mason, 1977) Asch takes on the case of a heavyweight boxer and corruption in the fight game.

5. *Castles Burning* (Holt, 1980) A successful artist wants Asch to find the wife and son he had deserted in his less-successful past.

6. *Hard Trade* (Holt, 1982) Homely heiress Sylvia Calabrese hires Asch to find out if her fiancé truly loves her.

7. *At the Hands of Another* (Holt, 1983) Asch gets mixes up with doctors, lawyers, and the insurance business as he runs into a former lover for whom he had arranged an abortion.

8. *Three with a Bullet* (Holt, 1984) Rock concert promoter Freddie Segal hires Asch to find out who has been sabotaging his operation.

9. *Fast Fade* (Mysterious, 1987) Asch is hired to prove that movie director Walter Cairns is really William McVey, who deserted Asch's client 16 years ago.

10. *Other People's Money* (Mysterious, 1989) A Turk who wants his daughter tailed, a deep-sea diver involved with drug smuggling, and an attractive museum curator may be connected in some way.

11. *False Pretenses* (Mysterious, 1994) Asch finds himself a possible fall guy when his client Mark Jacobi turns up in his office with a bullet in his head.

MacAvoy, R(oberta) A(nn)

I. American writer R. A. MacAvoy's trilogy as been hailed as one of the best fantasy series of the nineties. The story of Nazhuret, the wandering lens maker, although it contains less action, has much better characterization and finer writing and involves the reader's emotions more than do most sword-and-sorcery epics.

1. *Lens of the World* (Morrow, 1990) Nazhuret, an orphan raised as a ward of the Sordaling Military Academy, is apprenticed to an optician.

2. *King of the Dead* (Morrow, 1991) Nazhuret travels from his native Velonya to the kingdom of Rezhmia to prevent a disastrous war.

3. *Belly of the Wolf, The* (Morrow, 1994) The aging, widowed, exiled Nazhuret feels compelled to return to Velonya to stop a civil war. UK title: *Winter of the Wolf*.

II. The Damiano trilogy is a fantasy series set in a Renaissance Italy. Young Damiano Delstrego, wizard's son heir to dark magics, is befriended by the Archangel Rafael, who instructs him in playing the lute. In the series' third book, the roles are reversed, as Rafael becomes a mere mortal, and Damiano provides spiritual guardianship. The sorceress Saara plays a major role in the trilogy. The trilogy was also published in an omnibus edition: *Trio for Lute* (Nelson Doubleday, 1985).

1. *Damiano* (Bantam, 1984) To save his beloved village from war, Damiano, accompanied by the Archangel Rafael, sets out on a pilgrimage, seeking the aid of the sorceress Saara.

2. *Damiano's Lute* (Bantam, 1984) Damiano, forsaking his magical heritage to live as a mortal man, travels through the plague-ridden French countryside accompanied by the guidance of Rafael and the memory of Saara.

3. *Raphael* (Bantam, 1984) Weakened by his contact with mortals, the Archangel Rafael is divested of his divinity by his brother Lucifer and is sold in the Moorish slave markets, sustained only by the spiritual guardianship of Damiano, while Saara embarks on a quest to rescue him.

III. *Tea with the Black Dragon*, MacAvoy's first novel, attracted much favorable critical attention. A contemporary fantasy set in San Francisco and Silicon Valley, it features two middle-aged protagonists: Mayland Long, who was once a Chinese dragon named Oolong; and Martha Macnamara, Celtic violinist and Zen master. *Twisting the Rope: Casadh an T'Sugain*, its sequel, continues the psychic saga.

1. *Tea with the Black Dragon* (Bantam, 1983) Violinist and Zen master Martha Macnamara is brought west to San Francisco by her daughter's request and subsequent disappearance. Martha is aided in her search by Mayland Long, former Chinese dragon.

2. *Twisting the Rope: Casadh an T'Sugain* (Bantam, 1986) Martha and Mayland (now manager of Martha's Celtic group) are pushed into another search when one of Martha's musicians is found hanging by a rope of twisted grass.

MacDonald, John D.

Not likely to be confused with Ross MacDonald's (q.v.) California detective, John D. MacDonald's flashy ladies' man Travis McGee lives on a houseboat, *The Busted Flush*, which he won in a poker game, in a Fort Lauderdale (Florida) marina. He drives a vintage Rolls Royce and makes a speciality of retrieving expensive lost articles, though he occasionally takes on less lucrative assignments for his friends. Though McGee is not licensed as a private eye, many of his adventures are essentially private eye–type stories. His pal Meyer, introduced in number 3, a retired economist, eventually becomes important to Travis as a confidant and assistant in salvage operations. The first 14 novels were originally published in paperback, then reprinted in hardcover. They are listed in order of original publication.

1. *Deep Blue Good-By, The* (Fawcett, 1964) This book concerns a stolen sapphire and a psycho lady-killer. Reprinted in hardcover by Lippincott (1975).

2. *Nightmare in Pink* (Fawcett, 1964) In New York to investigate the murder of a war buddy's sister, McGee gets slipped some LSD. Reprint in hardcover by Lippincott (1976).

3. *Purple Place for Dying, A* (Fawcett, 1964) Mona Yeoman, a potential client, is shot and her husband is poisoned. Reprinted in hardcover by Lippincott (1976)

4. *Quick Red Fox, The* (Fawcett, 1964) McGee investigates the blackmailing of movie star Lysa Dean. Published in hardcover by Lippincott (1974).

5. *Deadly Shade of Gold, A* (Fawcett, 1965) The death of an old friend and the loss of a priceless Aztec gold idol are the elements of this case. Reprinted in hardcover by Lippincott (1974).

6. *Bright Orange for the Shroud* (Fawcett, 1965) Poor Arthur Wilkinson is tricked into marrying a nasty woman. Reprinted in hardcover by Lippincott (1972).

7. *Darker Than Amber* (Fawcett, 1966) McGee gets involved when mobsters dump a corpse off a bridge. Reprinted in hardcover by Lippincott (1970).

8. *One Fearful Yellow Eye* (Fawcett, 1966) A widow finds that all her husband's money is gone and she is being accused of stealing it. Reprinted in hardcover by Lippincott (1977).

9. *Pale Gray for Guilt* (Fawcett, 1968) McGee encounters stock market speculators and a new love. Reprinted in hardcover by Lippincott (1971).

10. *Girl in the Plain Brown Wrapper, The* (Fawcett, 1968) The suicidal daughter of an old friend is McGee's concern. Reprinted in hardcover by Lippincott (1973).

11. *Dress Her in Indigo* (Fawcett, 1969) The investigation into the death of Bix Bowie takes McGee to a Mexican village and its sad and depraved inhabitants. Reprinted in hardcover by Lippincott (1971).

12. *Long Lavender Look, The* (Fawcett, 1970) When McGee swerves to avoid running his Rolls Royce into a young girl, he finds himself in big trouble. Reprinted in hardcover by Lippincott (1972).

13. *Tan and Sandy Silence, A* (Fawcett, 1972) Harry Brell, a land speculator of dubious reputation, accuses McGee of spiriting away his wife. Reprinted in hardcover by Lippincott (1979).

14. *Scarlet Ruse, The* (Fawcett, 1973) A Miami stamp dealer's assistant is murdered. Reprinted in hardcover by Lippincott (1980).

15. *Turquoise Lament, The* **(Lippincott, 1973)** A dead professor leaves McGee the problems of his lost notebook and his troubled daughter.

16. *Dreadful Lemon Sky, The* **(Lippincott, 1975)** A package entrusted to McGee by an old girlfriend leads him into a case of drug smuggling and murder.

17. *Empty Copper Sea, The* **(Lippincott, 1978)** A friend who has lost his skipper's license comes to McGee for help.

18. *Green Ripper, The* **(Lippincott, 1979)** When girlfriend Gretel is murdered, a stunned McGee investigates.

19. *Free Fall in Crimson* **(Harper, 1981)** This installment finds McGee in a small Iowa town exposing a pornography/drug ring and escaping by balloon.

20. *Cinnamon Skin* **(Harper, 1982)** When an explosion kills two people and destroys a friend's cruiser, McGee is called in to investigate.

21. *Lonely Silver Rain, The* **(Knopf, 1985)** McGee gets involved with drug dealers when he finds three mutilated corpses on board a luxury yacht stolen from financier Billy Ingraham.

Macdonald, Malcolm

PSEUDONYM OF M. Ross-Macdonald

Macdonald's smoothly crafted tale, with its lively characters and high drama, is an English family saga as easy to sink into as a comfortable old sofa. The story begins in 1839 when the young and ambitious railroad foreman John Stevenson gets his chance to make his fortune. The "canty wench" Nora joins him, and their story intertwines with that of Walter and Arabella Thornton, an unhappy upper-middle-class couple. The last volume centers on Abigail, John and Nora's daughter, and takes the family up to the 1890s. Ross Macdonald is a prolific writer of historical romances, nearly all of them published in the United States under the Macdonald pseudonym. In the United Kingdom he publishes fiction set in England as Malcolm Macdonald; fiction set in Cornwall as Malcolm Ross; and fiction set in Ireland as M. R. O'Donnell.

1. *World from Rough Stones, The* **(Knopf, 1975)** With Nora at his side, John Stevenson rises to a position of respect and influence as a railroad contractor.

2. *Rich Are with You Always, The* **(Knopf, 1976)** Turbulent years for the railroad industry bring financial crises to the Stevensons.

3. *Sons of Fortune* **(Knopf, 1978)** John is a rich man now and determined to be accepted into society. His sons, Caspar and Boy, play a larger part in this book.

4. *Abigail* **(Knopf, 1979)** Young Abigail is followed from the age of 17 through her career as a writer and feminist and her love for Victor.

Macdonald, Ross

PSEUDONYM OF Kenneth Millar

Ross Macdonald was a successor, probably the greatest, to the Dashiell Hammett (q.v.) and Raymond Chandler (q.v.) hardboiled tradition. His Lew Archer, a Los Angeles PI, is a loner who watches life from the shadows with compassion and an understanding of the tortured family tangles that his Los Angeles clients often bring him. Archer is an ex-policeman who was kicked out for being too honest, and an ex-husband whose wife divorced him because she couldn't stand his associates. William Goldman (q.v.), in a *New York Times* review, describes the Archer series as "the best detective stories ever written by an American." Omnibus volumes: *Archer in Hollywood* (Knopf, 1967), which contains numbers 1, 3,

and 7; *Archer at Large* (Knopf, 1970), which contains numbers 9, 12, 14; *Archer in Jeopardy* (Knopf, 1979), which contains numbers 8, 11, 15. There is an omnibus edition published in the United Kingdom called *The Lew Archer Omnibus*.

1. *Moving Target, The* **(Knopf, 1949)** A degenerate millionaire is kidnapped. The 1966 movie *Harper*, with Paul Newman, was based on this novel. Variant title: *Harper*.

2. *Drowning Pool, The* **(Knopf, 1950)** A woman is found drowned in a swimming pool. Paul Newman played Lew Archer in the film of the same name (1975).

3. *Way Some People Die, The* **(Knopf, 1951)** The heroin racket absorbs Archer's attention.

4. *Ivory Grin, The* **(Knopf, 1952)** Archer finds out what happened to the spoiled young Charles Singleton. Variant title: *Marked for Murder*.

5. *Find a Victim* **(Knopf, 1954)** A problem hitchhiker intrudes into Archer's drive to Sacramento.

6. *Name Is Archer, The* **(Bantam, 1955)** Seven stories about Archer are collected here.

7. *Barbarous Coast, The* **(Knopf, 1956)** The exclusive and fashionable Channel Club is at the center of this case of a missing woman.

8. *Doomsters, The* **(Knopf, 1958)** This case concerns an unscrupulous doctor.

9. *Galton Case, The* **(Knopf, 1959)** In search of a lost heir, Archer uncovers a 22-year-old murder.

10. *Wycherly Woman, The* **(Knopf, 1961)** Twenty-one-year-old Phoebe Wycherly is missing from her northern California college.

11. *Zebra-Striped Hearse, The* **(Knopf, 1962)** Archer investigates an ice-pick murder.

12. *Chill, The* **(Knopf, 1964)** Beautiful young Dolly Kincaid runs away from her new husband.

13. *Far Side of the Dollar, The* **(Knopf, 1965)** Archer must find a 17-year-old runaway from school.

14. *Black Money* **(Knopf, 1966)** The corruptions of the world intrude into a college campus.

15. *Instant Enemy, The* **(Knopf, 1968)** Archer tracks a high school runaway.

16. *Goodbye Look, The* **(Knopf, 1969)** A theft from the Chalmers family safe leads Archer into deeper problems.

17. *Underground Man, The* **(Knopf, 1971)** Set amid the drama of a California forest fire, this book concerns a missing little boy and pair of disturbed young people.

18. *Sleeping Beauty* **(Knopf, 1973)** This convoluted case centers around the kidnapped daughter of an oil millionaire.

19. *Blue Hammer, The* **(Knopf, 1976)** A painting is stolen and the daughter of a millionaire is missing.

20. *Lew Archer, Private Investigator* **(Mysterious, 1977)** Nine stories are collected here.

MacDougall, Ruth Doan

A trio of widely separated novels depict the life of Henrietta Snow from her sophomore year in a New Hampshire high school to late middle age as she goes through college, a career as a poet, marriage, motherhood, and widowhood. A sensitive portrait of a woman's development.

1. *Cheerleader, The* **(Putnam, 1973)** In 1955 Henrietta Snow achieves her goal of making the varsity cheerleading team at Gunthwaite High School in New Hampshire, attracting a boyfriend, and winning a college scholarship, but hopes for something more.

2. *Snowy* (St. Martin's, 1993) Henrietta concentrates on becoming a poet at Bennington College. She realizes some of her poetic ambitions, but is still troubled by the idea of unfulfilled potential.

3. *Henrietta Snow* (Frigate, 2004) Henrietta and her friends contemplate getting older as they move through their fifties to their sixties in the years 1987 to 2000.

MacGregor, T. J.

PSEUDONYM OF Patricia M. Janeschutz

I. Mike McCleary and Quin St. James are a Miami-based husband-and-wife private-eye team. Plenty of action, gripping plots, and the sometimes troubled relationship between Quin and "Mac" are the attractions in this series.

1. *Dark Fields* (Ballantine, 1986) After Quin St. James's lover is killed, she is left with some disturbing questions about his secret life. She hooks up with Mike McCleary, who is on the trail of a female serial killer.

2. *Kill Flash* (Ballantine, 1987) Hollywood producer Gill Kranish receives a videotape of the murder of one of his actors accompanied by a note saying that "this is the first!"

3. *Death Sweet* (Ballantine, 1988) Traces of sugar at the scene of the crime furnish the only clue in the mutilation and murder of Joyce Young.

4. *On Ice* (Ballantine, 1989) McCleary loses his memory and can't defend himself against a murder charge.

5. *Kin Dread* (Ballantine, 1990) A camping expedition to the Everglades to help patch up their relationship leads Quin and Mac to a band of contemporary savages.

6. *Death Flats* (Ballantine, 1991) John Bishop, psychiatrist specializing in near-death experiences, experiences his own death by an unknown hand.

7. *Spree* (Ballantine, 1992) Quin and Mac track down a psycho whose latest victim was Mac's sister.

8. *Storm Surge* (Hyperion, 1993) Just before retired professor of criminology Charlie Potemkin was shot to death, he mailed some mysterious photographs to Quin and Mac.

9. *Blue Pearl* (Hyperion, 1994) Mike is critically wounded while helping the police investigate the murder of a Miami socialite who was married to a Chilean faith healer.

10. *Mistress of the Bones* (Hyperion, 1995) A young car thief is the prime suspect when veteran bail bondsman Lou Hernando is knifed to death in his secluded, rundown homestead, a house rumored to be haunted.

II. MacGregor has dropped Quin and Mac, at least for the time being, to publish the Tango Key mysteries, novels with a strong paranormal flavor. The novels feature Mira Morales, Florida Keys New Age bookseller and psychic investigator. She is helped on her cases by Detective Wayne Sheppard.

1. *Hanged Man, The* (Kensington, 1998) After Mira Morales has a vision of a murder, Andrew Steele, a criminologist with ties to a top-secret government experiment that trains convicts to conduct psychic espionage, is killed, and his wife is kidnapped by a criminal psychic.

2. *Black Water* (Pinnacle, 2003) On a return journey to the Florida Keys on their motorboat, Mira is knocked unconscious, and her daughter Annie is kidnapped. Mira, her daughter, and her daughter's kidnapper enter the same "corridor" and are transported back in time to 1968.

3. *Total Silence* (Kensington, 2004) Mira, Annie, and "Shep" are spending Christmas at a friend's isolated country home in Asheville, North Carolina. The Mira gets kidnapped.

4. *Category Five* (Pinnacle, 2005) Mira and her family are being held hostage by three dangerous criminals during a Category Five hurricane.

5. *Cold as Death* (Pinnacle, 2006) Mira spies a ghostly woman running down the driveway of the burning house belonging to actress Suki Nichols.

Mackenzie, Compton

I. Mackenzie had to resist the pull of his theatrical family to become a writer. His early novels won him an immediate popular audience, and *Sinister Street* (Secker [UK], 1913) was a critical success as well. His novel *Monarch of the Glen* was made into a successful BBC/PBS television series (2000–). Another novel, *Whiskey Galore* (1947) was made into the movie *Tight Little Island* (1949), and published in the United States under that name (Houghton Mifflin, 1950). Edmund Wilson thought that Mackenzie was an underrated author and that the novel series *Four Winds of Love* had never been given the recognition it deserved as a serious defense of oppressed people and a plea for the rights of small nations.

1. *East Wind of Love, The* (Dodd, 1937) John Ogilvie is introduced as a 17-year-old Scottish boy at St. James School in 1900.

2. *South Wind of Love, The* (Dodd, 1937) Eleven years after the first volume, John has been to Oxford and is a successful playwright.

3. *West Wind of Love, The* (Dodd, 1940) John has a romance with a rich American, Athene Langridge.

4. *West to North* (Dodd, 1941) John is converted to Catholicism and becomes more political involved. Originally written as the second part of *The West Wind of Love*

5. *North Wind of Love, The* (Dodd, 1945) John's involvement with various Scottish nationalist groups are featured. US publication of part 1 only; part 2 published as *Again to the North* (number 6) in the United States.

6. *Again to the North* (Dodd, 1946) The deteriorating international scene in the Thirties, leading to World II is a major theme here. Published in the United Kingdom as part 2 of *The North Wind of Love*.

II. This early religious trilogy is of special interest because, like its protagonist, Mackenzie himself converted to Catholicism. Reviewers called these novels "beautifully serene."

1. *Altar Steps, The* (Doran, 1922) This book tells the story of Mark Lidderdale from his infancy, circa 1880, to his ordination as an Anglican priest.

2. *Parson's Progress, The* (Doran, 1923) Mark serves his first several curacies.

3. *Heavenly Ladder, The* (Doran, 1924) Mark ministers in a Cornish village, is expelled from the church, and converts to Roman Catholicism.

MacKenzie, Donald

The late Canadian-born Donald MacKenzie started his career in crime as a professional criminal. He was an international jewel thief and confidence man who began to write in jail, using his experiences in a long series of mystery novels. MacKenzie described his early life in his autobiography *Occupation Thief* (Bobbs, 1955). John Raven, Scotland

Yard detective turned private investigator, is the hero of MacKenzie's longest-running series. Raven lives on a converted Thames barge; has good taste in music, art, and whiskey; doesn't mesh well with bureaucracy; and gets involved in cases that sometimes take him far from London.

1. *Zaleski' s Percentage* (Houghton Mifflin, 1974) Zaleski, London restaurant owner, and two other Polish friends conspire to steal a jeweled relic belonging to the Italian government.
2. *Raven in Flight* (Houghton Mifflin, 1976) Vacationing in Spain after resigning from Scotland Yard, Raven is bored until he meets the alluring Giselle Dale.
3. *Raven and the Ratcatcher* (Houghton Mifflin, 1977) The Ratcatcher is an expert safecracker whom Raven suspects to be involved in a million dollar heist.
4. *Raven and the Kamikaze* (Houghton Mifflin, 1977) Casimir Zaleski returns, and Raven has to find him before he avenges his family by assassinating a top Soviet agent.
5. *Raven Settles a Score* (Houghton Mifflin, 1978) Raven thwarts a North Korean drug-smuggling ring and his old enemy, Superintendent Drake of Scotland Yard.
6. *Raven after Dark* (Houghton Mifflin, 1979) Kirstie Macfarlane pleads with Raven to exonerate her brother, who hanged himself in a jail cell after being convicted for stealing a Van Eyck painting. UK title: *Raven Feathers His Nest*.
7. *Raven and the Paperhangers* (Houghton Mifflin, 1980) Raven goes to Paris to protect girlfriend Kirstie, who has inadvertently photographed two forgers.
8. *Raven's Revenge* (Houghton Mifflin, 1982) Old enemy George Drake plots an elaborate heroin frame-up for Raven.
9. *Raven's Longest Night* (Doubleday, 1984) On a Portuguese vacation with his wife, Kirstie, Raven finds himself drawn into a situation involving $17 million worth of Hungarian money.
10. *Raven's Shadow* (Doubleday, 1985) Patrick O'Callaghan's client, a British Airways pilot, is murdered, but police don't seem to be very interested in solving the crime.
11. *Nobody Here by That Name* (Doubleday, 1986) The home of struggling used-car salesman and his lover, model Maggie Sanchez, is burglarized and George is the leading suspect.
12. *Savage State of Grace, A* (Doubleday, 1988) Jury member Raven firmly believes that German au pair girl Helga Heumann is innocent and that Piers Pelham, member of the British upper crust, is guilty of drug smuggling.
13. *By Any Illegal Means* (Doubleday, 1989) Involves an assassination attempt on Chilean dictator Pinochet, blackmail, and an artist friend of Kirstie Raven.
14. *Eyes of the Goat, The* (St. Martin's, 1993) Raven goes to Czechoslovakia on search for the codes needed to access computer disks that contain information collected before the collapse of Communism.
15. *Loose Cannon* (St. Martin's, 1993) Raven helps lawyer friend Patrick O'Callaghan who believes that he is the target of a financier recently extradited from California.

MacLean, Alistair

Gregory Peck, David Niven, and Anthony Quinn starred in the 1961 film *Guns of Navarone*, which is hard to beat for nonstop action and excitement. *Force 10 from Navarone*, its sequel, also received film treatment (1978). The most successful novels by this late, popular British author are still his World War II stories. His first, *H.M.S. Ulysses*, was a naval adventure; the two listed below feature Force 10, a special British army strike team. MacLean's deft character delineation, taut story line, and convincing atmosphere are uncluttered by romantic complications; his daring commandos need all their energy for the dangers that beset their every step.

1. *Guns of Navarone* (Doubleday, 1957) A five-man sabotage team is assigned to destroy two powerful guns off the Turkish coast in 1943.
2. *Force 10 from Navarone* (Doubleday, 1968) Mallory, Miller, and Stavros take on a second wartime assignment to blow up a bridge in the mountains of Yugoslavia.

MacLeod, Charlotte

I. Peter Shandy, a professor at the Balaclava Agricultural College in Massachusetts, is a mildly eccentric fellow on a campus full of odd fish. Peter and his wife, librarian Helen Marsh, whom meets and courts in number 1, usually get entangled in complicated situations quite innocently, and then must call upon their amateur sleuthing powers to sort things out. This entertaining series of cozies offers humor, clever plots, interesting characters, and happy endings. Canadian native, now US citizen Charlotte MacLeod worked for 30 years in a Boston advertising agency. MacLeod also writes mysteries under the pseudonym of Alisa Craig (q.v.). *It Was an Awful Shame: And Other Stories* (Five Star, 2002) contains some Shandy stories.

1. *Rest You Merry* (Doubleday, 1978) After temporarily abandoning his home because of its tacky Christmas decorations, Peter Shandy returns to find a corpse in his living room.
2. *Luck Runs Out, The* (Doubleday, 1979) Peter and Helen are held hostage at a local silversmith's; a prize pig is kidnapped; and the body of a lady farrier is found in a feed box.
3. *Wrack and Rune* (Doubleday, 1982) Shandy and Balaclava president Svenson deal with the death of a hired man and the discovery of a Norse rune store.
4. *Something the Cat Dragged In* (Doubleday, 1983) The secretive Balaclava Society gets some unwanted publicity when former Balaclava professor Ungley is found dead behind its clubhouse.
5. *Curse of the Giant Hogweed, The* (Doubleday, 1985) A consulting trip to Wales gets Shandy and two colleagues involved in the middle of a medieval Welsh legend complete with enchanted princes, griffins, and wyverns.
6. *Corpse in Oozak's Pond, The* (Mysterious, 1987) A frozen corpse attired in a suit from the 1800s, and eerily resembling Balaclava Buggins, founder of the college, is found floating in Oozak's Pond.
7. *Vane Pursuit* (Mysterious, 1989) Helen Shandy, who has been photographing antique weather vanes created by Praxiteles Lumpkin, discovers that many of the precious vanes have been stolen.
8. *Owl Too Many, An* (Mysterious, 1991) The annual owl count at Balaclava leads to a murder and two kidnappings, including that of millionairess Winifred Binks.
9. *Something in the Water* (Mysterious, 1994) The obnoxious Jasper Flodge, dinner guest at Bright's Inn on the Maine coast, eats a fatal plate of chicken potpie.
10. *Exit the Milkman* (Mysterious, 1996) James Feldster, Peter's neighbor, head of the Dairy Management department at Balaclava, and heir to a dairy fortune, disappears; then Feldster's wife is found dead.

II. Sarah Kelling, member of Boston's upper crust, finds her wealthy blue-blooded family of little help when she loses her first husband and most of her money. Sarah is the nicest, sanest member of a family that has more than its share of nasty, eccentric, or just plain ineffectual members. When Sarah gets mixed up with murder and other skulduggeries, she relies on Max Bittersohn, an art detective who eventually becomes her second husband. Like the Shandy novels, this series has a good deal of humor, some romance, slightly far-fetched plots, and odd characters with odd names who come to odd ends (one is soaked in honey and stung to death by bees). *It Was an Awful Shame: And Other Stories* (Five Star, 2002) contains some Kelling/Bittersohn stories.

1. *Family Vault, The* **(Doubleday, 1979)** When the family burial vault is open to receive another Kelling, it unexpectedly reveals the corpse of striptease artist Ruby Redd.

2. *Withdrawing Room, The* **(Doubleday, 1980)** Sarah Kelling, now widowed and forced to take in boarders at her heavily mortgaged Beacon Hill mansion, finds that the former "withdrawing room" is fatal to two of them.

3. *Palace Guard, The* **(Doubleday, 1981)** When Sarah's lodger Max Bittersohn takes her to the latest concert of impresario Nick Fieringer, guards at Madam Wilkins's palatial museum start dying of unnatural causes.

4. *Bilbao Looking Glass, The* **(Doubleday, 1983)** A series of off-season burglaries on Massachusetts's North Shore results in a valuable antique mirror turning up in the front hall of Sarah's summer home.

5. *Convivial Codfish, The* **(Doubleday, 1984)** Max Bittersohn investigates the Comrades of the Convivial Codfish when Sarah's uncle Jem, Grand Exalted Chowderhead, loses the silver codfish at the Scrooge Day Dinner.

6. *Plain Old Man, The* **(Doubleday, 1985)** When the performer playing the titular character in Sarah's Aunt Emma's production of *The Sorcerer* is found dead on his bathroom floor, Cousin Fred is hurled into the breach in more ways than one.

7. *Recycled Citizen, The* **(Mysterious, 1988)** Sarah's Uncle Adolphus is charged with drug smuggling and murder when heroin turns up in some soda cans at his recycling plant.

8. *Silver Ghost, The* **(Mysterious, 1988)** When Bill Billingsgate misses a 1927 New Phantom Rolls Royce from his collection of antique cars, Sarah and Max come to his annual Renaissance Revel to investigate.

9. *Gladstone Bag, The* **(Mysterious, 1990)** Sarah's aunt Emma plays hostess at a Maine vacation colony to a group of writers and artists who have treasure hunting on their agenda.

10. *Resurrection Man, The* **(Mysterious, 1992)** Bartolo Arbalest, the "resurrection man," does fine work in restoring furniture, but has some rather strange ways and dubious friends.

11. *Odd Job, The* **(Mysterious, 1995)** Sarah is left executrix of the will of Dolores Tawne, administrator of the Wilkins Museum, who was stabbed to death with an antique hairpin.

12. *Balloon Man, The* **(Mysterious, 1998)** The elegant North Shore wedding of Max Bittersohn's nephew, orchestrated by Sarah, is upset by some bizarre happenings: the Kelling Rubies turn up again; a burglar temporarily cripples Max; a hot-air balloon containing some long-lost neighbors crashes in the middle of the weeding tent; a smoke bomb is set off; and, of course, a dead body is found.

MacNeil, Duncan

PSEUDONYM OF Philip McCutchan

This series about the Royal British Army in India at the turn of the 20th century stars the dashing young James Ogilvie of the 114th Highlanders, the Queen's Own Royal Strathspeys. James's father, Sir Iain Ogilvie, is commander of the entire northern India army. Readers interested in the period and having a tolerance for a very British view of India will enjoy the fast-paced action and colorful setting. The series has been reprinted (2002–) by Severn House with new titles. Philip McCutchan (q.v.) has published several series under his own name.

1. *Drums along the Khyber* **(St. Martin's, 1972)** Young James is assigned to the 114th Highlanders; he meets and falls in love with Mrs. Archdale. Variant title: *The First Command*.

2. *Lieutenant of the Line* **(St. Martin's, 1972)** Ogilvie meets trouble on the Afghanistan border with a resourcefulness contrary to orders, and saves the day. Variant title: *Soldier of the Queen*.

3. *Sadhu on the Mountain Peak* **(St. Martin's, 1973)** Captain Ogilvie spies on a holy man to keep him from rousing rebel forces. Variant title: *Captain at Arms*.

4. *Gates of Kunarja, The* **(St. Martin's, 1974)** Ogilvie must cross through the Khyber Pass in winter to free the regimental commander, who is being held for ransom. Variant title: *Honour and Empire*.

5. *Red Daniel, The* **(St. Martin's, 1974)** Ogilvie and the 114th Highlanders see service in the Boer War at the Relief of Kimberley. Variant title: *Ogilvie at War*.

6. *Subaltern's Choice* **(St. Martin's, 1974)** Back in India, when a foolhardy young subaltern, Hamish Dewar, loses his whole patrol, Captain Ogilvie must take over. Variant title: *Ogilvie under Fire*.

7. *By Command of the Viceroy* **(St. Martin's, 1975)** Ogilvie escorts a Russian mission through the Indian frontier. Variant title: *Ogilvie's Royal Command*.

8. *Mullah from Kashmir, The* **(St. Martin's, 1976)** Captain Ogilvie infiltrates the Mullah's secret headquarters in an effort to prevent the assassination of a young maharajah. Variant title: *Ogilvie and the Mullah*.

9. *Wolf in the Fold* **(St. Martin's, 1977)** On leave in London, Captain Ogilvie takes on a special assignment to investigate a problem of security on the northwest frontier. Variant title: *Ogilvie and the Traitor*.

10. *Charge of Cowardice* **(St. Martin's, 1978)** Ogilvie is awaiting court-martial as invaders threaten from the north. Variant title: *Ogilvie's Act of Cowardice*.

11. *Restless Frontier, The* **(St. Martin's, 1980)** Rescuing beautiful Angela, Ogilvie is captured; the enemy suspends him over a pit of vipers in an effort to get him to talk. Variant title: *Ogilvie and the Mem'Sahib*.

12. *Cunningham's Revenge* **(Walker, 1985)** The Pathans stage an uprising, and Cunningham deserts after his wife is killed during an attack. Originally published in 1981. Variant title: *Ogilvie and the Uprising*.

13. *Train at Bundarbar, The* **(Walker, 1986)** Ogilvie deals with floods, mutinous Pathans, and a stranded train carrying a large sum in gold bullion and his beloved Fiona Elliott. Originally published in 1981. Variant title: *Ogilvie and the Gold of the Raj*.

14. *Matter for the Regiment, A* **(Hodder [UK], 1982)** Ogilvie is seconded to the Political Department to seek out the Pathan leader who calls himself the Star of Islam. Not published in the United States. Variant title: *Ogilvie's Dangerous Mission*.

Macomber, Debbie

I. Since she published her first novel in 1983, romance novelist Debbie Macomber has published more than 150 novels, many of them quite popular, and more than 50 in one series or another. Her most recent series is the Knitting Books series. Cancer survivor Lydia Goetz is the proprietor of knitting store in Seattle, Washington. When she decides to bring a group of friends together in a knitting club, they discuss their lives and get a chance to work out their problems and concerns. While Lydia acts as an anchor to the series, each book has a different set of club participants. Macomber, who says that knitting is her first love, has published a couple of *Knit Along with Debbie Macomber* nonfiction books with Leisure Arts.

1. *Shop on Blossom Street, The* (Mira, 2004) Lydia Goetz, knitting shop proprietor in Seattle, Washington, forms a knitting club with three other women. Their first project: a baby blanket (Macomber supplies the pattern in the book).
2. *Good Yarn, A* (Mira, 2005) The project is socks, as Lydia and three new club members tackle a different set of problems.
3. *Back on Blossom Street* (Mira, 2007) Colette Blake, grieving over her late husband, has concerns about her relationship with former boss and possible criminal Christian Dempsey. Alix Townsend, from a questionable family, wonders if she can be a good wife to the Reverend Jordan Turner. Lydia's niece Julia is the victim of a carjacking.
4. *Twenty Wishes* (Mira, 2008) Four widows meet at Anne Marie Roche's bookstore.

II. The fictional coastal town of Cedar Cove, Washington, is modeled after Macomber's hometown of Port Orchard, Washington. Most folks in Cedar Cove are good-hearted but somewhat inclined to gossip. Plenty of gossip material is provided by their fellow townsfolk and occasional visitors. Continuing characters include family court judge Olivia Lockhart, who makes some controversial decisions in a couple of novels, all for a good cause. Number 6 has a two-page list of the residents of Cedar Cove.

1. *16 Lighthouse Road* (Mira, 2001) Family court judge Olivia Lockhart makes a controversial decision: denying divorce to a couple she is convinced are still in love.
2. *204 Rosewood Lane* (Mira, 2002) Grace Sherman's husband, Dan, has disappeared, leaving Grace with two daughters.
3. *311 Pelican Court* (Mira, 2003) The split up of Rosie Cox and her husband, Zack, forces Olivia Lockhart to make a difficult decision about child custody.
4. *44 Cranberry Point* (Mira, 2004) A man named Max Russell dies, perhaps from poison, at Peggy Beldon's Thyme & Tide Bed-and-Breakfast.
5. *50 Harbor Street* (Mira, 2005) Carrie and Rog McAfee are receiving some mysterious and worrying postcards with the phrase "regret the past."
6. *6 Rainier Drive* (Mira, 2006) The Gundersons' Lighthouse Restaurant is burned down, perhaps by arson.
7. *74 Seaside Avenue* (Mira, 2007) Veiled threats from a Russian opponent have caused international chess champion Bobby Polgar to drop out of tournament play and keep a close watch over Teri, his hairdresser wife.

III. Another small town full of good people is Promise, Texas, a ranching town that, of course, has a few problems, although most of them seem to be brought in by people from California.

1. *Lonesome Cowboy* (Harlequin, 1998) Savannah Weston is an old-fashioned girl, with hopes along the matrimonial line.
2. *Texas Two-step* (Harlequin, 1998) Ellie Frasier and Chris Patterson are two people who probably should be together, but there are difficulties.
3. *Caroline's Child* (Harlequin, 1998) Who is the father of Caroline's child? Rancher Grady Weston would like to be.
4. *Dr. Texas* (Harlequin, 1998) "Dr. Texas" is Jane Dickinson, from California, who is working at the local clinic. Can she and "Mr. Grouch," Cal Patterson, hit it off?

5. *Nell's Cowboy* (Harlequin, 1998) "Easterner" Travis Grant, who writes books about the West, and dude-ranch owner Nell Bishop collide.
6. *Lone Star Baby* (Harlequin, 1998) Wade McMillan and Amy Thornton are the pair here.
7. *Promise, Texas* (Mira, 1999) Annie Applegate blows in from California and stirs things up.
8. *Return to Promise* (Mira, 2000) Cal Patterson and Dr. Texas return, only to have their marriage threatened by another woman.

IV. Buffalo Valley, North Dakota, is another town populated by the "salt of the earth." It was originally planned as a trilogy, though number 4 was added soon after.

1. *Dakota Born* (Mira, 2000) Lindsay Snyder returns to her vacation home in Buffalo Valley, North Dakota, and turns up some family secrets.
2. *Dakota Home* (Mira, 2000) Lindsay Snyder's closest friend, Maddy Washburn, and Jeb McKenna find that the "course of true love" isn't always smooth.
3. *Always Dakota* (Mira, 2001) Rancher Margaret Clemens and cowboy Matt Eillers are the romantic pair here.
4. *Buffalo Valley* (Mira, 2001) Vaughn Kyle reminds Hassie Knight of her dead son.

V. The Angels series mixes Macomber's usual Christian romance with a bit of humor. Shirley, Goodness, and Mercy are three angels with the best of intentions, but rather maladroit. The Archangel Gabriel, who likes them, sometimes gives them assignments to intervene, or interfere, with people who make Christmas wishes, and somehow they always bumble through to a satisfactory conclusion. *Angels Everywhere* (Avon, 2002) contains Numbers 1 and 3.

1. *Season of Angels, A* (HarperCollins, 1993) The three angels try to fulfill the wishes of Leah, who wants a baby, Timmy, who wants a father, and Monica, who wants true love.
2. *Trouble with Angels, The* (HarperCollins, 1994) Shirley, Goodness, and Mercy travel to the City of Angels, Los Angeles, to fulfill some wishes.
3. *Touched by Angels* (HarperCollins, 1995) The Archangel Gabriel sends the trio to the Big Apple, New York City, to fulfill some more Christmas wishes.
4. *Shirley, Goodness, and Mercy* (Harlequin/Mira, 1999) The heartfelt prayer of Greg Bennett, who has lived a selfish life of denial, is heard by Gabriel.
5. *Those Christmas Angels* (Silhouette, 2003) The angels are sent to Seattle to answer the Christmas prayers of a mother worried about her unhappy son and a couple of others.
6. *Where Angels Go* (Mira, 2007) Eighty-six-year-old Harry Alderwood prays that his increasingly forgetful wife, Rosalie, will agree to move into assisted living before he dies.

VI. The Orchard Valley trilogy features the Bloomfield sisters of Orchard Valley, Oregon, who return to Orchard Valley to keep vigil at the bedside of their father. Each sister has a romantic adventure in the novel that has her name in the title. Omnibuses that contain the trilogy: *Orchard Valley Weddings* (Harlequin [UK], 1997) and *Orchard Valley* (Mira, 1999). No annotations provided for the trio.

1. *Valerie* (Harlequin, 1992)
2. *Stephanie* (Harlequin, 1992)
3. *Norah* (Harlequin, 1992)

VII. The Manning series, set in Montana, is really a duo (the Manning Sisters, numbers 1–2) and a trio (Those Manning Men, numbers 3–5). Various members of the Manning family find romance when they reach Montana. *Montana* (Mira, 1997) and *Married in Montana* (Mira, 1998) are not part of the series. Titles are listed below without annotations.

1. *Sheriff Takes a Wife, The* (Silhouette, 1990)
2. *Cowboy's Lady, The* (Silhouette, 1990)
3. *Marriage of Inconvenience* (Silhouette, 1992)
4. *Stand-in Wife* (Silhouette, 1992)
5. *Bride on the Loose* (Silhouette, 1992)

VIII. The Navy series is a loosely connected bunch of six novels (number 6 was published after a gap of 14 years) concerning US Navy wives: they love their husbands, but their husbands are often at sea. Titles are listed below without annotations.

1. *Navy Wife* (Silhouette, 1988)
2. *Navy Blues* (Silhouette, 1989)
3. *Navy Brat* (Silhouette, 1991)
4. *Navy Woman* (Silhouette, 1991)
5. *Navy Baby* (Silhouette, 1991)
6. *Navy Husband* (Silhouette, 2005)

IX. The O'Halloran brothers run the Bush-Plane Charter Service out of the remote town of Hard Luck, Alaska (pop. 150, mostly male). Seeing a desperate need for marriageable women, they set up a mail-order bride scheme. The Midnight Sons series describes how this scheme works out. The six novels were reprinted in three volumes by Harlequin in 2000: *Mail-Order Marriages* (numbers 1 and 2); *Family Men* (numbers 3 and 4); *The Last Two Bachelors* (numbers 5 and 6). Titles are listed below without annotations.

1. *Brides for Brothers* (Harlequin, 1979)
2. *Marriage Risk, The* (Harlequin, 1995)
3. *Daddy's Little Helper* (Harlequin, 1995)
4. *Because of the Baby* (Harlequin, 1996)
5. *Falling for Him* (Harlequin, 1996)
6. *Ending in Marriage* (Harlequin, 1996)

Mahfouz, Naguib

The late (d. 2006) Nobel Prize winner Mahfouz is credited with popularizing the novel and short story as viable genres in the Arab literary world. His stories of urban Egypt have been compared with Dickens and Honoré de Balzac (q.v.). Like Salman Rushdie, Mahfouz ran afoul of Islamic fundamentalists. The Cairo trilogy follows the fortunes of three generations of a middle-class Egyptian family from the early part of the 20th century to the 1952 coup, which toppled the Egyptian monarchy. Omnibus volume containing the trilogy: *The Cairo Trilogy* (Everyman's, 2001).

1. *Palace Walk* (Doubleday, 1990) Al-Sayyid Ahmad tries to keep his wife and children in line as a good Egyptian patriarch should, but his own need for sexual and alcoholic diversions and his sons' growing independence interfere. Translated from the Arabic by William M. Hutchins and Olive E. Kenny. Originally published as *Bayn al-qasrayn* in 1956.
2. *Palace of Desire* (Doubleday, 1991) Five years later Mr. Ahmad is ending his self-imposed abstention from alcohol and women, while his children struggle with lives outside his domination. Translated from the Arabic by William M. Hutchins, Lorne M.

Kenny, and Olive E. Kenny. Originally published as *Qasr al-shawq* in 1957.
3. *Sugar Street* (Doubleday, 1992) By 1935 Mr. Ahmad has become a gaunt patriarch while his intellectual son Kamal has become a schoolteacher and philosopher who veers between debauchery and Spinoza. Translated from the Arabic by William M. Hutchins and Angele Botros Samaan. Originally published as *Al Sukkariya* in 1957.

Malcolm, John

PSEUDONYM OF John Malcolm Andrews

Tim Simpson is an investment advisor in art and antiques for a major London bank. Somehow Tim's investment tips lead him into cases of murder and other skulduggery, which the tough, hot-tempered former rugby player finds himself equal to. John Malcolm writes mystery plots with interesting sidelights on art, antiques, and the banking industry. Numbers 13 through 15 have not been published in the United States. Under his real name, John Malcolm Andrews, Malcolm has written nonfiction books about antiques.

1. *Back Room in Somers Town, A* (Scribner, 1985) An art-linked murder takes Simpson to a perfume factory in Brazil.
2. *Godwin Sideboard, The* (Scribner, 1985) The search for a rare sideboard made by E. W. Godwin leads to the murder of Simpson's friend, antiques dealer Peter Blackwell.
3. *Gwen John Sculpture, The* (Scribner, 1986) Elderly Frenchwoman Mme. Boiteau ask Tim to authenticate, and perhaps purchase, a Rodin work that is in her possession.
4. *Whistler in the Dark* (Scribner, 1987) Two obscure Whistler paintings lead to the beating and death of an old gentleman.
5. *Gothic Pursuit* (Scribner, 1987) Simpson once again becomes a target for murder in the course of his efforts to trace the whereabouts of an original Norman Richard Shaw bookcase.
6. *Mortal Ruin* (Scribner, 1988) Tim is in Chicago to trace the history of Winston Churchill's uncle Moreton Frewen, known as "Mortal Ruin" for his disastrous financial schemes.
7. *Wrong Impression, The* (Scribner, 1990) A connection between the London art and drug worlds may have led to the vicious attack on Tim's friend, Chief Inspector Nobby Roberts.
8. *Sheep, Goats and Soap* (Scribner, 1992) With Pre-Raphaelite paintings soaring in value, Tim agrees to search out a Holman Hunt or two on the Sussex seaside.
9. *Deceptive Appearance, A* (Scribner, 1992) Simpson is sent by White's Bank to help its French ally Maucourt Freres determine whether to buy Bellevie, a cosmetics firm in which it has a stake.
10. *Burning Ground, The* (Bloody Brits, 2007) Tim becomes involved in carpet firm mergers in Lancashire, Belgium, and Northern France against a background of World War I battlefields, the paintings of Christopher Nevinson, and the poetry of Robert Graves (q.v.). Originally published in the United Kingdom in 1993.
11. *Hung Over* (St. Martin's, 1995) Tim is outraged when White's Bank decides to buy a collection of mediocre horse paintings from an old client.
12. *Into the Vortex* (St. Martin's, 1997) The new director of Christerby's art auction house shows an unhealthy interest in a Wyndham Lewis (q.v.) painting and in Tim's wife, Sue.
13. *Simpson's Homer* (Allison & Busby [UK], 2002) Winslow Homer, that is. Jeremy White, Simpson's superior at White's Bank, sends Tim to Italy to see whether Jeremy's uncle, and Tim's mentor, Sir Richard White, has gone bonkers. The Protestant sect of the Waldensians also plays a role.

14. *Circles and Squares* (**Allison & Busby [UK], 2003**) The paintings of the Nicholsons, William the father and Ben the son, are involved here as well as the appearance of Tim Simpson's name in the diary of the murdered Moira Bassington.

15. *Rogues' Gallery* (**Allison & Busby [UK], 2004**) Tim Simpson reluctantly agrees to give a speech at a small art gallery in the tiny village of Highton. Then his bookseller, Mr. Goodston, is attacked by a pair of thugs.

Maling, Arthur

Chicago-based Arthur Maling worked for his family retail shoe store chain until he became a successful crime novel writer in his forties. Brock Potter, his continuing character, is a securities analyst in the Wall Street brokerage firm of Price, Potter and Petacque. Potter, like Emma Lathen's (q.v.) John Putnam Thatcher, is drawn into investigating crimes that come to light in the course of his business. Although he is financially a solid citizen, Potter is a loner who avoids close relationships. The Potter novels are well-plotted mix of business and crime. Maling doesn't seem to have published any new titles since 1988.

1. *Ripoff* (**Harper, 1976**) Potter investigates an insurance scandal involving $23 million worth of stolen securities.

2. *Schroeder's Game* (**Harper, 1977**) A scam involving a company handling the billing for hospital medical services leads to kidnap and murder.

3. *Lucky Devil* (**Harper, 1978**) Potter investigates the murder of an investor who has acquired some rather doubtful stocks.

4. *Koberg Link, The* (**Harper, 1979**) A paint company stock that suddenly rises, and the killing of the fiancé of Potter's secretary's niece, are the problems here.

5. *Taste of Treason, A* (**Harper, 1983**) Kevin Rand, Potter's close friend who was convicted of selling secret information to the East Germans, is murdered in prison.

Mankell, Henning

Swedish author Henning Mankell has written a series of international best sellers featuring Kurt Wallander, a middle-aged police officer of Ystad, near Malmo in the southern Swedish province of Skane. Wallander is one of your typical "dour Swedes." His personal life is a shambles: his wife has left him; his daughter isn't speaking to him; even his father barely tolerates him. Wallander works tirelessly, eats badly, and drinks the night away in a lonely, neglected flat. In other words, he is a provincial Martin Beck (Maj Sjöwall [q.v.] and Per Wahlöö [q.v.]). Most of the cases Kurt gets involved in have implications, some of them international, going beyond the nasty murders he investigates. The decline of Swedish civility is one of the underlying themes. In Number 10, the torch has been passed on to Wallander's daughter Linda, who joins the Ystad police force. The (Swedish) Yellow Bird Film series has filmed number 10 and 12 new stories by Mankell. "The Grave" (*Handelse om hosten*, 2004) is a 90-page novella published in Dutch only (so far) in which Wallander stumbles upon a human hand in the garden of a house he is considering buying. *The Pyramid* (*Pyramiden*, 1999), not translated into English so far, is a collection of five stories set chronologically in 1979–1989, before the series begins, and includes Wallander's first case. The novels are listed according to the dates of their original Swedish publications.

1. *Faceless Killers* (**New Press, 1996**) The Lovgrens, an elderly farm couple, are the victims of what seems to be senseless violence.

Maria, the wife, mutters the word "foreigners" before she dies, setting off racist vigilante attacks against a nearby refugee camp. Originally published in 1991 as *Mordre utan ansikte*. Translated from the Swedish by Steven T. Murray.

2. *Dogs of Riga, The* (**New Press, 2003**) Winter 1991. Corpses of two Eastern European criminals are washed ashore on a remote Swedish coastline. The ensuing investigation takes Wallander to Riga, Latvia, which is still under the Soviet yoke. Originally published in 1992 as *Hundarna Riga*. Translated from the Swedish by Laurie Thompson.

3. *White Lioness, The* (**New Press, 1998**) This novel links the murder of a real-estate agent in Ystad to events in South Africa, where the just-released Nelson Mandela is the object of a number of plots. Originally published in 1993 as *Den vita lejoninnah*. Translated from the Swedish by Laurie Thompson.

4. *Man Who Smiled, The* (**New Press, 2006**) "The Man Who Smiled" is a globe-trotting Swedish businessman who might be connected to the death of lawyer Gustav Tortensson, who was killed examining a seated "human-sized effigy" in the middle of a deserted highway. Originally published in 1994 as *Mannen somlog*. Translated from the Swedish by Laurie Thompson.

5. *Sidetracked* (**New Press, 1999**) A teenage girl douses herself with gasoline and sets herself on fire. The next day, Sweden's former minister of justice is axed and scalped: the first of a series of killings. Originally published in 1995 as *Villospar*. Translated from the Swedish by Steven T. Murray.

6. *Fifth Woman, The* (**New Press, 2000**) Holger Eriksson, an elderly bird-watcher, is found impaled in a trap with sharpened bamboo poles. Four nuns and an unidentified woman are found murdered in an Algerian convent. Originally published in 1996 as *Dem Femte Kvinnan*. Translated from the Swedish by Steven T. Murray.

7. *One Step Behind* (**New Press, 2002**) Three role-playing teenagers dressed in 18th-century garb are shot in a secluded meadow. Then Wallander's colleague Svedberg is found at home with most of her head blown away. Originally published in 1997 as *Steget efter*. Translated from the Swedish by Ebba Segerberg.

8. *Firewall* (**New Press, 2002**) A massive blackout, the death of man at an ATM, and the murder of a cab driver by two teenage girls could be connected in a complicated plot involving the world of computers and the Internet. Originally published in 1998 as *Brandvogg*. Translated from the Swedish by Ebba Segerberg.

9. *Before the Frost* (**New Press, 2005**) Wallander's daughter, Linda, joins him on the Ystad police force. A series of deliberate animal burnings is followed by the ritually mutilated corpse of Birgitta Medburg. The 1978 mass suicide in Jonestown, Guyana, has a follow-up here. Originally published in 2002 as *Innan frosten*. Translated from the Swedish by Ebba Segerberg. Stefan Lindman, the main character in the stand-alone novel *Return of the Dancing Master* (New Press, 2004) has a bit role here.

Mann, Thomas

Thomas Mann is generally regarded as the foremost German novelist of the 20th century. He had published *Buddenbrooks* and his masterpiece, *The Magic Mountain*, before beginning work on a novel with a biblical theme, which grew into a tetralogy. His winning the Nobel Prize in 1929 guaranteed the work an international audience, though he fled Germany in 1933 and his books were burned there. The four novels present a very detailed and leisurely recounting of the story of Joseph of the multihued coat. H. T. Lowe-Porter translated all four novels, which are available in an omnibus volume entitled *Joseph and His Brothers* (Knopf, 1948).

1. *Joseph and His Brothers* (**Knopf, 1934**) This book deals mostly with the story of Jacob, Joseph's father. Originally published as *Die Geschichten Jakobs* (1933). UK title: *The Tales of Jacob*.
2. *Young Joseph* (**Knopf, 1935**) As an adolescent, Joseph is the envy of his brothers, who sell him to an Ishmaelite trader. Originally published as *Der junge Joseph* (1934).
3. *Joseph in Egypt* (**Knopf, 1938**) Joseph becomes Potiphar's household steward, but is sent to jail after repelling the advances of Potiphar's wife. Original title: *Joseph in Aegypten* (1936).
4. *Joseph the Provider* (**Knopf, 1944**) Joseph is released from prison, rises to power in Pharaoh's court, and is reunited with his brothers. Original title: *Joseph, der Ernaehrer* (1944).

Manning, Olivia

The 1987 production of the PBS miniseries *Fortunes of War*, starring Kenneth Branagh and Emma Thompson, rekindled interest in English novelist Olivia Manning's Balkan trilogy and Levant trilogy, which form a six-part autobiographical novel set in Rumania, Greece, Egypt, Syria, and Palestine during World War II. Harriet and Guy Pringle, the two leading characters are somewhat mismatched: Harriet is a realist; Guy is an incurable idealist who selflessly devotes his time to everyone except his wife. How Harriet comes to terms with Guy's character and her own expectations is one of the continuing threads in the series, but there are many other characters who reappear from time to time, such as the ingratiating sponger Yakimov, the callow young officer Simon Boulderstone, and the poet Castlebar. More realistic and less exotic than Durrell's (q.v.) Alexandria Quartet, Fortunes of War is about ordinary people caught up in extraordinary events. Anthony Burgess called the Balkan trilogy "probably the most important long work of fiction written by a woman since the war" (*99 Novels*, Summit, 1984). The Balkan trilogy (numbers 1, 2, and 3) and the Levant trilogy (numbers 4, 5, and 6) have been published in single paperback volumes by Penguin.

1. *Great Fortune, The* (**Doubleday, 1961**) Guy Pringle, lecturer in English at the University of Bucharest, returns to Rumania with his bride Harriet just as the Germans invade Poland in September 1939.
2. *Spoilt City, The* (**Doubleday, 1962**) The German invasion and the collapse of Rumania are imminent, as the British residents of Bucharest form their various escape plans. Covers June-September 1940.
3. *Friends and Heroes* (**Doubleday, 1965**) The Pringles and other members of the British colony in Rumania have fled to Greece and set up temporary housekeeping in Athens, but it is only a matter of time before the invading Germans will force them to flee again.
4. *Danger Tree, The* (**Atheneum, 1977**) The Pringles have escaped to Egypt. Guy gets another position as an English instructor, while Harriet makes new friends with the poet Castlebar and a young officer, Simon Boulderstone.
5. *Battle Lost and Won, The* (**Atheneum, 1978**) Simon Boulderstone, mourning the loss of his brother, throws himself into the desert fighting just before the battle of El Alamein, as Harriet and Guy, often separated, go through a marital crisis.
6. *Sum of Things, The* (**Atheneum, 1981**) Simon is in a military hospital after being blown up by a land mine. Harriet, unbeknownst to Guy, has adventures in Syria and Palestine, while Guy, believing her to be dead, tries to carry on with his teaching.

Mapson, Jo-Ann

The Bad Girl Creek trilogy, set on a flower farm on California's Central Coast, features wheelchair-bound Phoebe DeThomas and her boarder-farmhands Ness, Nance, Beryl, and Maddy. The girls have all endured hard-luck and unsatisfactory relationships, but they settle down, get to know each other better, and form lasting friendships in these three feel-good novels with each chapter related by one of the girls. Jo-Ann Mapson, now resident in Alaska, is the author of five other novels, some of them best sellers, including *Hank and Chloe* (HarperCollins, 1993) and *Blue Rodeo* (HarperCollins, 1994).

1. *Bad Girl Creek* (**Simon & Schuster, 2001**) Thirty-eight-year-old wheelchair-bound (bad heart) Phoebe DeThomas inherits a flower farm on California's Central Coast and hires on three women as boarder-farmhands: Ness, a black cowgirl who fears that she has AIDS; Nance, a down-at-the-heels southern belle who has broken up with her boyfriend; and Beryl, a former kindergarten aide with a prison record.
2. *Along Came Mary* (**Simon & Schuster, 2003**) Rodeo performer Mary Madigan "Maddy" Caringella quits her job and hooks up with journalist Rick Heinrich. They run into Beryl, ex–Bad Girl, now touring the country with her guitarist beau, and eventually find their way to the flower farm on Bad Girl Creek.
3. *Goodbye, Earl* (**Simon & Schuster, 2004**) "Last episode" in the trilogy. Five years have passed. Beryl, Nance, and Ness have moved on but keep in touch. Phoebe is still at her flower farm, raising her five-year-old daughter Sally after the loss of Sally's father.

Maron, Margaret

I. *Bootlegger's Daughter* won every major mystery award for 1993: Edgar, Anthony, Agatha, and Macavity. Deborah Knott, lawyer, only daughter of a bootlegger with 11 sons, and candidate for District Court judge in the rural community of Cotton Grove, Colleton County, North Carolina, delighted readers and critics alike. Subsequent novels by native North Carolinian Maron have established Deborah as a superior series character in a well-realized small-town Carolina Piedmont setting whose inhabitants are being thrust into the contemporary world by the forces of integration and suburbanization. *Bloody Kin* (Doubleday, 1985), a mystery novel that shares the same setting and some of the same supporting characters, can be regarded as a prequel to the series. *Last Lessons of Summer* (Mysterious, 2003), also set in the Piedmont, is not part of the series. The short story collection *Shoveling Smoke* (Crippen & Landru, 1997) contains several Deborah Knott stories.

1. *Bootlegger's Daughter* (**Mysterious, 1992**) Just as Deborah Knott begins her campaign for the District Court judgeship, she is asked to investigate a murder case that has remained unsolved for 18 years.
2. *Southern Discomfort* (**Mysterious, 1993**) Sexual harassment, vanished pets, the theft of two boxes of deadly insect poison, the construction of a Women-Aid House, assault, and murder all disturb the tranquility of Colleton County and Judge Knott.
3. *Shooting at Loons* (**Mysterious, 1994**) Subbing for an ill colleague at the Harker's Island courthouse, Deborah stumbles across a corpse while clamming.
4. *Up Jumps the Devil* (**Mysterious, 1996**) There are several suspects, including one of Deborah's 11 brothers, when the Stancils, father and son, are murdered in a dispute over acreage to be sold to the developers of a superhighway from Raleigh.

5. *Killer Market* (**Mysterious, 1997**) Chan Nolan, furniture dealer in High Point, is felled by a penicillin-laced brownie during the Global Home Furnishings Market. Deborah, substituting for a vacationing colleague gets involved.

6. *Home Fires Burning* (**Mysterious, 1998**) Black cemeteries are being desecrated, and black churches are being torched. One of Deborah's nephews is suspected of being involved in both hate crimes.

7. *Storm Track* (**Mysterious, 2000**) As Hurricane Fran bears down on the Piedmont, promiscuous Lynn Bullock is found strangled in the Orchid Motel wearing black-lace underwear. There are plenty of suspects, including Lynn's husband.

8. *Uncommon Clay* (**Mysterious, 2001**) Deborah travels to Randolph County to settle the equitable distribution of the marital property of just-divorced potters Sandra Kay Nordon and James Lucas Nordan. Then James Lucas is found baked in a kiln.

9. *Slow Dollar* (**Mysterious, 2002**) Deborah is mourning the fate of her great-nephew, carnival worker Brazos Hartley, stomped to death, his mouth filled with quarters, at the Ames Amusement Corporation's show in Colleton County.

10. *High Country Fall* (**Mysterious, 2004**) Deborah fills in for a vacationing judge in the Blue Ridge high country. Before she arrives, there is a homicide at Cedar Gap.

11. *Rituals of the Season* (**Mysterious, 2005**) Assistant DA Tracy Johnston is shot to death while driving, and Deborah and her fiancé, Dwight Bryant, get involved in an investigation that will uncover a web of crime and corruption in Colleton County.

12. *Winter's Child* (**Mysterious, 2006**) Deborah and her new husband, Dwight Bryant, get involved in the investigation of the shooting of J. D. Rouse in his pickup truck. Then Dwight gets a call from his eight-year-old son, Cal, in Shaysville, Virginia, that Jonna—Cal's mother and Dwight's ex-wife— is missing.

13. *Hard Row* (**Grand Central, 2007**) Body parts that begin to appear in rural Colleton County turn out to belong to Buck Harris, a farmer known for his exploitation of immigrant labor and the missing plaintiff in a high-stakes divorce case.

II. Now apparently set aside for Deborah Knott, Sigrid Harald, homicide detective with the New York City Police Department, is another strong female character. The cool and determined professional isn't immune to the tender passion in her private life, as her affair with playboy artist Oscar Nauman attests. Several Harald stories appear in the collection *Shoveling Smoke* (Crippen & Landru, 1997).

1. *One Coffee With* (**Raven House, 1981**) A spoonful of poison in a professor's morning coffee was presumably doled out by one of the eight persons present in the Art Department office.

2. *Death of a Butterfly* (**Doubleday, 1984**) Many people had sufficient motive to kill beautiful but cold, self-centered, and demanding Julie Redmond.

3. *Death in Blue Folders* (**Doubleday, 1985**) A set of blue folders marked "personal" may shed light on the murder of attorney Clayton Gladwell and the looting of his office.

4. *Right Jack, The* (**Bantam, 1987**) An explosion at a cribbage tournament seriously injures Tilden, Sigrid's detective partner, but who was the real target?

5. *Baby Doll Games* (**Bantam, 1988**) A dancer in a small Greenwich Village theater is killed right before the eyes of an audience of horrified children.

6. *Corpus Christmas* (**Doubleday, 1989**) A major retrospective of Oscar Nauman's work at Erich Breul House is disrupted when one of the trustees of Breul House is pushed down a flight of stairs.

7. *Past Imperfect* (**Doubleday, 1991**) The fatal shooting of off-duty veteran detective Michael Cluett leads Harald to investigate the death of her policeman father in the line of duty many years before.

8. *Fugitive Colors* (**Mysterious, 1995**) Sigrid's lover, Oscar Nauman, is killed in an automobile crash, leaving his estate containing paintings said to be worth millions to her as both executor and legatee.

Marric, J. J.

PSEUDONYM OF John Creasey

John Creasey (q.v.) wrote the Gideon police procedurals under this pseudonym. Superintendent George Gideon of New Scotland Yard is a large, handsome man with steel-gray hair, whose customary quiet manner occasionally erupts into a towering rage. Gideon was pushing 50 when he made his fictional debut in *Gideon's Day*, and although his six children are glimpsed growing up through the years, Gideon himself, his wife, Kate, and his closest associate, Chief Inspector Lemaitre, never seem to grow older. The police procedural, by its nature, has too diffuse a plot to catch in a short annotation. The Gideon novels are considered by many to be Creasey's best work, and some regard them as the best British police procedurals. The last three titles in the list were written by William Vivian Butler after Creasey's death. *Gideon at Work* (Harper, 1957) is an omnibus containing numbers 1, 2, and 3.

1. *Gideon's Day* (**Harper, 1955**) Variant title: *Gideon of Scotland Yard*.
2. *Gideon's Week* (**Harper, 1956**) Variant title: *Gideon's Fear*.
3. *Gideon's Night* (**Harper, 1957**)
4. *Gideon's Month* (**Harper, 1958**)
5. *Gideon's Staff* (**Harper, 1959**)
6. *Gideon's Risk* (**Harper, 1960**)
7. *Gideon's Fire* (**Harper, 1961**) Edgar winner.
8. *Gideon's March* (**Harper, 1962**)
9. *Gideon's Ride* (**Harper, 1963**)
10. *Gideon's Vote* (**Harper, 1964**)
11. *Gideon's Lot* (**Harper, 1964**)
12. *Gideon's Badge* (**Harper, 1965**)
13. *Gideon's Wrath* (**Harper, 1967**)
14. *Gideon's River* (**Harper, 1968**)
15. *Gideon's Power* (**Harper, 1969**)
16. *Gideon's Sport* (**Harper, 1970**)
17. *Gideon's Art* (**Harper, 1971**)
18. *Gideon's Men* (**Harper, 1972**)
19. *Gideon's Press* (**Harper, 1973**)
20. *Gideon's Fog* (**Harper, 1974**)
21. *Gideon's Drive* (**Harper, 1976**)
22. *Gideon's Force* (**Stein & Day, 1985**) Written by William Vivian Butler. Originally published in 1978.
23. *Gideon's Law* (**Stein & Day, 1986**) Written by William Vivian Butler. Originally published in 1981.
24. *Gideon's Way* (**Stein & Day, 1986**) Written by William Vivian Butler. Originally published in 1983.

Marsh, Ngaio

Ngaio (pronounced *NY-o*) Marsh was born in New Zealand, and several of her mysteries are set there, but she wrote the classic Agatha Christie (q.v.) type of story, and her British detective Roderick Alleyn (pronounced *Allen*) rivals Dorothy Sayers's (q.v.) Peter Wimsey in his culture and connections. Unlike Wimsey, Alleyn is a professional Scotland Yard detective and is frequently assisted by the stolid Inspector

Fox. Marsh is vague about her detective's age but shows him first as a bachelor who meets and marries the young artist Agatha Troy; they have one son, who figures as an adult in one of the later books. *Three-Act Special* (Little, Brown, 1960) is an omnibus volume containing numbers 15, 16, and 17. *Another Three-Act Special* (Little, Brown, 1962) is an omnibus volume containing numbers 18, 20, and 21. *The Collected Short of Ngaio Marsh* (International Polygonics, 1989; UK title: *Death on the Air and Other Stories*) contains two Alleyn stories and a short essay by Marsh in which she analyzes Alleyn's character traits.

1. *Man Lay Dead, A* (Sheridan, 1942) Alleyn's first appearance is a classic case of murder during a parlor game at an English country-house weekend gathering. Originally published in the United Kingdom in 1934.
2. *Nursing-Home Murder, The* (Sheridan, 1941) When the British Home Secretary collapses in the House, he is rushed to a hospital where he soon dies. His wife claims he was murdered by anarchists. Written with Dr. Henry Jellett. Originally published in the United Kingdom in 1935.
3. *Enter a Murderer* (Pocket, 1941) Alleyn and his journalist friend Bathgate are in the audience when a stage gun shoots real bullets and an actor is wounded. Originally published in the United Kingdom in 1935.
4. *Death in Ecstasy* (Sheridan, 1941) Alleyn's friend Nigel Bathgate witnesses a religious cult murder. Originally published in the United Kingdom in 1936.
5. *Vintage Murder* (Sheridan, 1940) The earliest book with a New Zealand setting concerns the murder of a stage impresario. Originally published in the United Kingdom in 1937.
6. *Artists in Crime* (Furman, 1938) When an artist's model is murdered at Agatha Troy's art school, Alleyn investigates and falls in love with Agatha. First of series published in the United States.
7. *Death in a White Tie* (Furman, 1938) A case of high-society blackmail and murder draws Alleyn and Agatha together again, and they decide to tie the knot.
8. *Overture to Death* (Furman, 1939) Murder by a gun hidden in a very unlikely place disrupts life in the peaceful English village of Pen Cuckoo.
9. *Death at the Bar* (Little, Brown, 1940) Death is delivered by poison dart in the private taproom of the Plume and Feathers, Devon.
10. *Death of a Peer* (Little, Brown, 1940) Alleyn solves the murder of Uncle Gabriel, who held the purse strings of the delightfully irresponsible Lamprey family. UK title: *Surfeit of Lampreys*.
11. *Death and the Dancing Footman* (Little, Brown, 1941) The footman figures in the alibi upon which this case of murder and suicide hinges.
12. *Colour Scheme* (Little, Brown, 1943) When one of the guests is murdered in a boiling mud pool at a New Zealand spa, Alleyn gets involved in some international espionage.
13. *Died in the Wool* (Little, Brown, 1945) Alleyn spends the war years in New Zealand and is on hand to investigate the murder of Flossie Rubrick, an MP who is found in an odoriferous bale of wool.
14. *Final Curtain* (Little, Brown, 1947) Agatha Troy had finished Sir Henry Ancred's portrait just before his suspicious sudden death.
15. *Wreath for Rivera, A* (Little, Brown, 1949) Murder strikes the London jazz scene. Agatha is pregnant in this installment. UK title: *Swing, Brother, Swing*.
16. *Night at the Vulcan* (Little, Brown, 1951) Marsh, who wrote, acted in, and produced plays in London, uses her knowledge of the theater in this case of murder on opening night. UK title: *Opening Night*.

17. *Spinsters in Jeopardy* (Little, Brown, 1953) The strange doings in a chateau in the Alps include the kidnapping of Alleyn's little boy, Ricky. Variant title: *The Bride of Death*.
18. *Scales of Justice* (Little, Brown, 1955) Sir Harold Lacklander died peacefully in bed, but his memoirs in the hands of a neighbor promise trouble for a number of people.
19. *Death of a Fool* (Little, Brown, 1956) Murder at an annual folklorists' celebration of winter solstice. UK title: *Off with His Head*.
20. *Singing in the Shrouds* (Little, Brown, 1958) Investigating a case of murder at sea, Alleyn follows a suspect aboard ship and sets a trap to catch him.
21. *False Scent* (Little, Brown, 1959) The home of a flamboyant London is the scene of murder.
22. *Hand in Glove* (Little, Brown, 1962) Superintendent Alleyn investigates a murder at a posh country house in England.
23. *Dead Water* (Little, Brown, 1963) This case concerns the supposedly healing waters on a Cornish island owned by Alleyn's former French teacher.
24. *Killer Dolphin* (Little, Brown, 1966) Playwright and director Peregrine Jay saves an old theater from destruction and opens his new play before tragedy strikes. UK title: *Death at the Dolphin*.
25. *Clutch of Constables* (Little, Brown, 1969) Art forgery is featured in this case, as Alleyn investigates in America and his wife takes a riverboat trip through England.
26. *When in Rome* (Little, Brown, 1971) The Roman setting is a plus in this tale of blackmail and scandalous activities of a tour group.
27. *Tied Up in Tinsel* (Little, Brown, 1972) Christmas at Halberds Manor involves a missing man as well as plenty of mistletoe and holly. The Alleyns are guests.
28. *Black as He's Painted* (Little, Brown, 1974) A former classmate of Alleyn's, now president of an African nation, is in London on a state visit and is threatened by assassins.
29. *Last Ditch* (Little, Brown, 1977) Alleyn's son Ricky, now a young don spending the Easter holidays on the Channel Islands, falls in love and stumbles onto a drug-smuggling ring.
30. *Grave Mistake* (Little, Brown, 1978) An eccentric old lady in a nursing home dies suddenly, and Alleyn suspects murder.
31. *Photo-Finish* (Little, Brown, 1980) Alleyn visits a New Zealand paradise island estate to protect an opera star from an intrusive photographer.
32. *Light Thickens* (Little, Brown, 1982) A performance of *Macbeth* leads to a real severed head, instead of a prop, on MacDuff's spear as the climax to a series of odd incidents.

Marshall, William

I. Australian author William Marshall writes a kind of police procedural set in the Yellowthread Street Station in the fictional district of Hong Bay in Hong Kong. Chief Inspector Harry Feiffer and officers O'Yee, Auden, Spencer, and others deal with a variety of bizarre and often bloody crimes. The novels are a mixture of authentic Hong Kong ambience, screwball comedy, wild action, and slam-bang finales. Somehow Marshall makes this melange work in volume after volume to the delight of an increasing number of fans worldwide.

1. *Yellowthread Street* (Holt, 1976) A dismembered ear, a chopped-up wife, and a Mongolian giant with a knife are among the problems facing the Yellowthread Street force.
2. *Hatchet Man, The* (Holt, 1977) A deranged killer with a four-barrel pistol must be tracked down.
3. *Gelignite* (Holt, 1977) A madman is sending letter bombs through the mail.

4. *Thin Air* (Holt, 1978) Fifty-seven dead passengers on a chartered jet and six Chinese men machine-gunned in a sewer require police attention.

5. *Skulduggery* (Holt, 1980) The Yellowthread Street bunch deal with a two-decade-old murder, a series of muggings, a balky radiator, and a criminal gang of deaf-and-dumb persons.

6. *Sci Fi* (Holt, 1981) "The Spaceman," who cremates people with a ray gun, brings unanticipated excitement to the all-Asia Science Fiction and Horror Movie Congress.

7. *Perfect End* (Holt, 1983) Clawlike marks on the walls of an abandoned police station, the bodies of six policemen with strange chest wounds, and the reported sighting of a huge black cat give a sinister aura to this novel.

8. *War Machine* (Mysterious, 1988) Amid rumors of Japanese soldiers who never surrendered after World War II lurking in a tunnel waiting to attack Hong Kong, shots ring out all over Hong Bay.

9. *Far Away Man, The* (Holt, 1984) A pair of yellow vaccination certificates is found with each victim of a serial killer.

10. *Roadshow* (Holt, 1985) A series of explosions devastates Hong Kong while the police race to disarm the bombs and find the bomber's real target.

11. *Head First* (Holt, 1986) Corpses from mainland China with missing or rearranged body parts are turning up, and mail-carriers' bags are apparently combusting spontaneously.

12. *Frogmouth* (Mysterious, 1987) Every animal in the children's zoo is found mutilated and killed, while the walls at Yellowthread Street are producing mysterious voices and dripping slime.

13. *Out of Nowhere* (Mysterious, 1988) A van loaded with plate glass and four passengers crashes into a truck after speeding down the wrong side of a deserted freeway.

14. *Inches* (Mysterious, 1994) Nine employees of a branch bank have been poisoned by someone who took the trouble to wash out and put away the fatal teacups.

15. *Nightmare Syndrome* (Mysterious, 1997) O'Yee broods about the coming "Peaceful Transition of Authority" to China. Auden and Spencer, working to unstop the station's ancient plumbing, knock down a wall, revealing an unexploded 10-ton aerial bomb. Feiffer is hunting the person or "thing" that is scaring victims into clawing out their own eyes.

II. For a pair of novels, Marshall switched the location from Hong Kong to the Philippines. Manila Police Lieutenant Felix Elizalde and his bumbling cohorts try to deal with an assortment of crimes.

1. *Manila Bay* (Mysterious, 1986) The people around Battling Mendez, stellar fighting cock, are dying off, and it is up to Felix Elizalde to find out why.

2. *Whisper* (Mysterious, 1988) Several bizarre murders among the poor and homeless, a CIA-sponsored revolution, and the illegal skeleton trade are the issues here.

III. Detective Virgil Tillman and patrolman Ned Muldoon are two of New York's finest in this pair of novels set in the 1880s. Like the Yellowthread Street and Manila Bay novels, they feature humor, opulent prose, and a strong sense of locale.

1. *New York Detective, The* (Mysterious, 1989) Tillman and Muldoon investigate a murder in a New York playhouse that has links to a group associated with the Civil War.

2. *Faces in the Crowd* (Mysterious, 1991) Prostitute "Rosary Rosie" disappears, leaving behind 187 wedding rings, seven strangely marked telephones, and links to a secret society called the Custers.

Marston, Edward

PSEUDONYM OF Keith Miles

I. Nicholas Bracewell, stage manager of the Elizabethan theater troupe Lord Westerfield's Men, is a resourceful fellow whether called upon to find quarters during a plague outbreak, managing egotistical actors, or solving a murder. An exciting historical series, full of humor, suspense, and 16th-century atmosphere.

1. *Queen's Head, The* (St. Martin's, 1989) When one of his actors is murdered, Bracewell is determined to seek vengeance, but is temporarily sidetracked by more mishaps striking his troupe.

2. *Merry Devils, The* (St. Martin's, 1990) There is one "merry devil" too many prancing onstage during the premiere of a new play, but the extra "devil" is soon found dead.

3. *Trip to Jerusalem, The* (St. Martin's, 1990) Lord Westerfield's Men, driven from London by the plague, lose their costumes, have their best singer kidnapped, and attract the unwelcome attention of Walsingham's spies.

4. *Nine Giants, The* (St. Martin's, 1991) Bracewell has to deal with star actor Firethorn's ego, the lovesickness of playwright Edmund Hoode, the poetical pretensions of waterman Abel Strudwick, loss of quarters, and a corpse in the Thames.

5. *Mad Courtesan, The* (St. Martin's, 1992) The rivalry between actors Owen Elias and Sebastian Carrick may have led to Carrick's murder by an ax-wielder.

6. *Silent Woman, The* (St. Martin's, 1994) A fire at the Queen's Head sends the troupe on the road until repairs can bee made, and Bracewell returns to his North Devon home to sort out some memories.

7. *Roaring Boy, The* (St. Martin's, 1995) Lord Westerfield's Men find themselves in plenty of hot water when they stage *The Roaring Boy*, a play based on a recent murder.

8. *Laughing Hangman, The* (St. Martin's, 1996) As Lord Westerfield's men are about to perform the latest play by fat, egotistical, foul-mouthed, and controversial Jonas Applegarth, the choirmaster of a rival children's troupe is found hanging above his own stage.

9. *Fair Maid of Bohemia, The* (St. Martin's, 1997) Lord Westerfield's men travel to Prague to perform for the King of Bohemia. Someone kills one of the actors during the first performance there.

10. *Wanton Angel, The* (St. Martin's, 1999) When the Privy Council decrees that only two theatrical companies will be allowed to perform in London, Lord Westerfield's men feel at a disadvantage, because, as happens too often, they are without a theater.

11. *Devil's Apprentice, The* (St. Martin's, 2001) After a long, bitter winter, the company gets an opportunity to perform six plays at the Essex estate of Sir Michael Greenleaf. There is a catch, however: they have to perform a new play, called the *Witch of Rochester*, and take on an apprentice from hell.

12. *Bawdy Basket, The* (St. Martin's, 2002) Actor Frank Quilter is convinced that his father was framed for a murder. Meanwhile, big-time money lender Sir Eliard Slaney is having too much to say about the future of Lord Westerfield's Men.

13. *Vagabond Clown, The* (St. Martin's, 2003) A riot and a murder during a play performance deprive the company of a London venue and their chief "clown." Nicholas comes up with a new clown and a tour of Kent.

14. *Counterfeit Crank, The* (St. Martin's, 2004) Disasters aplenty afflict the Westerfields: thefts of their ticket money and costumes; the collapse of playwright Edmund Hoode; and the imprisonment in Bridewell Palace, now a brothel, of an actor and his love.

15. *Malevolent Comedy, The* (St. Martin's, 2005) The Westfield Players, losing their audience, hire difficult playwright Saul Hibbert, who raises everyone's hackles. When a young actor is poisoned on stage

on opening night of Hibbert's play, the players wonder if Hibbert's enemies are responsible.

16. *Princess of Denmark, The* (St. Martin's, 2006) The Westfield Men and their patron, Lord Westfield, wind up in remote Elsinore, Denmark, to which Lord Westfield is enticed by a miniature painting of Sigbrit Olsen, an alleged Danish beauty.

II. Marston's second historical mystery series is sent in the 11th-century England of William the Conqueror. Soldier Ralph Delchard and lawyer Gervase Bret make a good pair of detectives as they move across an England divided between Normans and Saxons, settling land disputes for the Domesday Book and solving murder cases.

1. *Wolves of Savernake, The* (St. Martin's, 1993) The investigation of Bedwyn Abbey's charter leads to a miller's death, apparently from a wolf attack, and the near lynching of an aged healer.

2. *Ravens of Blackwater, The* (St. Martin's, 1994) Ralph and Gervase are sent to the Essex town of Maldon to investigate charges of land-transfer irregularities against the powerful Hamo FitzCorbucion.

3. *Dragons of Archenfield, The* (St. Martin's, 1995) The detecting pair travel to the Welsh border to investigate three different claims to the same choice piece of property.

4. *Lions of the North, The* (St. Martin's, 1996) The pair travel to York to settle a series of tangled property disputes and run into some vicious trained lions.

5. *Serpents of Harbledown, The* (St. Martin's, 1998) The murder of the saintly Bertha (who ministered to lepers) and a mysterious, murdering, heretical monk absorb Delchard and Bret in Canterbury. Originally published in the United Kingdom in 1996.

6. *Stallions of Woodstock, The* (St. Martin's, 1999) In Oxford three Norman lords and a Saxon bet against each other on a horse race. Then a jockey is killed.

7. *Hawks of Delamere, The* (St. Martin's, 2000) The Earl of Chester executes two thralls when his prize hawk is killed by an arrow. Then one of his hunting companions is similarly felled. Set on the Welsh border. Originally published in the United Kingdom in 1998.

8. *Wildcats of Exeter, The* (St. Martin's, 2001) At Exeter in Devon, Nicolas Picard, involved in a property dispute, is supposedly killed by a wildcat, but a fatal wound could have been inflicted only by a human. Originally published in the United Kingdom in 1999.

9. *Foxes of Warwick, The* (St. Martin's, 2002) The crushed body of Martin Reynard, former reeve of Henry Beaumont, is found during a fox hunt. Originally published in the United Kingdom in 1999.

10. *Owls of Gloucester, The* (St. Martin's, 2003) The unpopular Brother Nicholas, missing for two days from Gloucester Abbey, is found dead in the abbey pantry. Originally published in the United Kingdom in 2003.

11. *Elephants of Norwich, The* (Headline [UK], 2000) Two golden elephants, being used by robber baron Richard de Fontenel to entice the beautiful Adelaide into marriage, have been stolen; and his steward is missing. Not yet published in the United States.

III. Marston has started a third series of historical mysteries, set in the Restoration England of Charles II in the 1660s. Christopher Redmayle, one of the architects working to restore London after the Great Fire and his friend, Puritan constable Jonathan Bale, are the detectives here. None of the series has been released in the United States.

1. *King's Evil, The* (Headline [UK], 2000) Architect Christopher Redmayle is a true "restoration man." He is one of the architects restoring London after the Great Fire of 1666.

2. *Amorous Nightingale, The* (Headline [UK], 2000) King Charles's favorite mistress, the acclaimed beauty and singer Harriet Gow, is kidnapped, and Charles calls on Redmayle for assistance.

3. *Repentant Rake, The* (Headline [UK], 2001) Repentant rake Niccolas Cheever is murdered.

4. *Frost Fair, The* (Allison & Busby [UK], 2003) A "frost fair" held on the iced-over Thames in December 1669 turns up the frozen body of a fencing master. Christopher and Jonathan Bale are on the case, but Christopher's brother turns out to be a prime suspect.

5. *Parliament House, The* (Allison & Busby [UK], 2006) London, 1670. Christopher's celebration of the completion of a new house for merchant Francis Polegate is marred when a guest is murdered upon leaving the house.

6. *Painted Lady, The* (Allison & Busby [UK], 2007) No annotation available.

IV. A fourth series, set in the England of the 1850s, features Robert Colbeck, a former attorney now serving as an inspector in the fledgling Scotland Yard. These mysteries, none of them published in the United States, are, so far, about crimes committed on British railways.

1. *Railway Detective, The* (Allison & Busby [UK], 2004) Questions arise after the London to Birmingham mail train is derailed and robbed, causing several injuries. Inspector Robert Colbeck of the fledgling Scotland Yard investigates.

2. *Excursion Train, The* (Allison & Busby [UK], 2005) Jake Bransby, former public executioner, is killed by a noose aboard the Great Railway excursion train embarked on a trip to an illegal prizefight in Berkshire.

3. *Railway Viaduct, The* (Allison & Busby [UK], 2006) When the dead body of Gaston Chabal, French engineer, is hurled into the canal below Sankey Viaduct, Colbeck and his assistant, Sergeant Victor Leeming, are presented with a very sticky case with international implications.

4. *Iron Horse, The* (Allison & Busby [UK], 2007) The discovery of a disembodied head on a passenger train at Crewe adds to the excitement of Derby Day at Epsom Downs.

Martin, James E.

Gil Disbro is a laid-off policeman who struggles to make ends meet as a private eye. Gil has a girlfriend who is an English professor (Hardy specialist) 10 years older than he is, a Chevy Caprice, and a Cleveland venue. A fast-paced, action-filled series of mysteries leavened by Gil's wisecracks.

1. *Mercy Trap, The* (Putnam, 1989) Disbro is hired to find the biological parents of a woman in need of a kidney transplant.

2. *Flip Side of Life, The* (Putnam, 1990) Hired to find a missing college professor and his son, Gil finds himself involved in blackmail and murder.

3. *And Then You Die* (Morrow, 1992) Wealthy Boyd Lassiter hires Disbro to find his wife, who is missing from a Nevada dude ranch where she was establishing residency prior to filing for divorce.

4. *Fine and Private Place, A* (Morrow, 1994) An elderly judge is being blackmailed because he allowed his nephew to bury a woman, supposedly dead from a drug overdose, on the grounds of his home.

Martin, Lee

PSEUDONYM OF Anne Wingate

Deb Ralston, member of the Fort Worth, Texas, police department, is long married, a recent mother, and a grandmother at 42, as well as being a stalwart cop. Deb isn't a superwoman, but as a person who has to hold down a tough job and keep her family together at the same, she is one of the most fully realized characters to appear in police procedurals. Former police officer and intelligence specialist Anne Wingate (q.v.) writes the Mark Shigata mystery novels under her own name as well.

1. *Too Sane a Murder* (St. Martin's, 1984) Former mental patient James Olead Baker is accused of killing his mother, stepfather, aunt, uncle, and sister.
2. *Conspiracy of Strangers, A* (St. Martin's, 1986) Deb exposes a ring that sells newborn babies for large sums after "disposing of" their mothers.
3. *Murder at the Blue Owl* (St. Martin's, 1988) Former movie star Margali Bowman Lang, now an aging drunk, is murdered at her own birthday party.
4. *Death Warmed Over* (St. Martin's, 1986) The murder of a part-time mailman and the torching of a classic 1957 Chevrolet are linked.
5. *Hal's Own Murder Case* (St. Martin's, 1989) On medical leave during the last month of her pregnancy, Deb learns that her adopted son is being held for murder in a New Mexico jail.
6. *Deficit Ending* (St. Martin's, 1990) While coping with her newborn son and her unemployed husband, Deb handles the case of an abducted and murdered bank teller.
7. *Mensa Murders, The* (St. Martin's, 1990) A serial killer who seems to have a profound hatred for intelligent women is terrorizing Fort Worth.
8. *Hacker* (St. Martin's, 1992) Ralston has several concerns, chief of which is a series of ax murders that may have been committed by a young man she has taken into her family.
9. *Day That Dusty Died, The* (St. Martin's, 1994) Why did 16-year-old Dusty Miller jump off the windowsill of a high-rise?
10. *Bird in a Cage* (St. Martin's, 1995) Deb and Harry's 25th-wedding-anniversary celebration at the Bird Cage restaurant is disrupted when a trapeze artist at the restaurant falls to her death.
11. *Inherited Murder* (St. Martin's, 1995) Deb gets involved in a murder case in Salt Lake City, where she has come to say good-bye to her adopted son, who is setting off on his Mormon mission.
12. *Genealogy of Murder* (St. Martin's, 1996) Deb's son-in-law, a medical intern, finds that he has an unaccounted for corpse on his hands. The corpse turns out to be that of a genealogist missing from a San Francisco mortuary.
13. *Thursday Club, The* (Bookcraft [Deseret], 1997) Deb, five years older and converted to Mormonism, is one of a group of three women who exercise together. Then, the husband of one of the women is found murdered. This is the latest Deb Ralston: is it the last?

Martin du Gard, Roger

Martin du Gard's reputation seems to be having something of a revival. Although he won the Nobel Prize for Literature in 1937, his reputation was in eclipse for decades, partly because of his personal elusiveness, but primarily because he was out of synch with the French literary establishment, which disdained the realistic tradition that he embodied in his novels. His *Correspondance generale* is being published in France (Gallimard, 1980-, eight volumes so far), and his unfinished novel *Le lieutenant-colonel de Maumort* was completed by Andre Daspre, published in 1983 (Gallimard), was translated into English by Luc Brebion and Timothy Crouse as *Lieutenant-Colonel de Maumort* (Knopf, 1999), and received some critical acclaim. Martin du Gard's major work is the Thibaults, a family saga published in France in eight parts and available in English translation (Stuart Gilbert) in two omnibus volumes: *The Thibaults* (Viking, 1939; numbers 1–6) and *Summer 1914* (Viking, 1941; numbers 7 and 8). The Catholic Thibault family is dominated by the father, an autocratic widower. Antoine, the older son, becomes a doctor, while his brother, the rebellious Jacques, is drawn into socialism and pacifism. The Protestant Fontanin family provides a counterpart throughout. The eight parts of the Thibaults are listed below in the order of their French publication.

1. *Cahier gris, Le* (Viking, 1939) In 1905 young Jacques and his friend Daniel Fontanin run away from home to Marseilles. First published in France in 1922.
2. *Penitencier, Le* (Viking, 1939) Jacques spend some time at a reform school as punishment for his escapade and is released through his brother's intercession. First published in France in 1922.
3. *Belle Saison, La* (Viking, 1939) Four interwoven love stories are set at the family's summer home. First published in France in 1923.
4. *Consultation, La* (Viking, 1939) The action takes place during a harrowing day in the life of the young doctor Antoine Thibault. First published in France in 1928.
5. *Sorellina, La* (Viking, 1939) Antoine reads a story that Jacques has written and goes to Lausanne to find him. First published in France in 1928.
6. *Mort du pere, La* (Viking, 1939) Antoine administers a deathbed dose of morphine to relieve his father's suffering. First published in France in 1929.
7. *Ete, L'* (Viking, 1941) Jacques becomes a confirmed pacifist and dies tragically. The events add up to powerful antiwar sentiment. First published in France in 1936.
8. *Epilogue* (Viking, 1941) Wounded and dying, Antoine returns home. First published in France in 1940.

Martini, Steve

California lawyer Paul Madriani is the hero of a series of gripping courtroom dramas. Whether he is representing the defense or the prosecution, Madriani gets involve in some very sticky cases that will keep readers glued to the pages of this mystery series. Author Martini is a lawyer who has been a state's attorney in California. *The Judge* has been made into a TV miniseries.

1. *Compelling Evidence* (Putnam, 1992) Madriani loses his law firm job when he is caught carrying on an affair with his boss's wife.
2. *Prime Witness* (Putnam, 1993) Paul comes to the aid of an ailing district attorney who is investigating six killings.
3. *Undue Influence* (Putnam, 1994) Madriani defends his deceased wife's sister in a vicious custody battle which turns into murder.
4. *Judge, The* (Putnam, 1996) Autocratic Judge Armando Acosta is arrested for soliciting an undercover vice operative: was he set up because he is currently in charge of a grand jury probing the police cover-up of a murder?
5. *Attorney, The* (Putnam, 2000) Madriani moves to San Diego to be closer to his lover, child advocate Susan McKay. One of his first cases in the new venue is that of Jonah Hale, whose granddaughter has been abducted by Vanishing Victims, which purports to be the rescuer of abused children.
6. *Jury, The* (Putnam, 2001) Paul, trying to get his San Diego law practice on track, defends genetic researcher Dr. David Crone, who is accused of murdering his colleague Kalista Jordan.

7. *Arraignment, The* (Putnam, 2003) Lawyer Nick Rush, Madriani's good friend, has been gunned down outside a courthouse. Paul has the job of defending Rush's trophy wife, Dana.

8. *Double Tap* (Putnam, 2004) Army veteran Emiliano Ruiz is accused of murdering Madelyn Chapman, the owner of a computer software company that sells a controversial security program to the US government.

Mason, F(rancis) Van Wyck

I. Yes, the Van Wyck Mason who wrote sea stories and the F(rancis) Van Wyck Mason who wrote spy stories are one and the same. The diversely talented Mason also wrote war stories, flying stories, children's books, and nonfiction. Mason claimed to have sold everything he'd ever written, with the exception of two short stories. Mason conceived of the four historical melodramas listed below as a tetralogy that would "depict the maritime peoples of the American colonies during the Revolution." They share the same theme but not the same characters or story lines.

1. *Three Harbors* (Lippincott, 1938) American merchant Rob Ashton stars in this romantic adventure set against the pre-Revolutionary turmoil in Boston, Norfolk, and Bermuda in 1774–1775.

2. *Stars on the Sea* (Lippincott, 1940) The story of young privateer Timothy Bennett and Lucy, the girl he loves. The action takes place in Rhode Island, South Carolina, and the Bahamas of 1775–1777.

3. *Rivers of Glory* (Lippincott, 1942) Andrew Warren takes his ship to Jamaica for supplies, but pirates and the beautiful but treacherous Minga delay his return to Boston. This book covers 1778–1779.

4. *Eagle in the Sky* (Lippincott, 1948) The central figures are three colonial doctors: Asa Peabody, Peter Burnham, and Lucius Devoe. The time is 1780–1781.

II. Captain, eventually Colonel, Hugh North undertook one sensitive and dangerous assignment after another in the service of G-2, US Army Intelligence. Though his six-foot frame was decorated with scars and his temples with gray, North remained invincible and attractive to the ladies throughout the series. Worlds away from the subtle international intrigue of le Carré's (q.v.) Smiley, North was a straight arrow who depended on quick thinking, eternal vigilance, and rugged, even merciless, methods. He never had an ambivalent moment and could always tell the good guys from the bad. The later stories were so similar in plot that the exotic locale in the title is sufficient annotation for most. *Captain North's Three Biggest Cases* (Grosset, 1932) is an omnibus volume containing numbers 3, 4, and 5 listed below; *Oriental Division G-2* (Reynal, 1933) contains numbers 2, 6, and 7; *Military Intelligence-8: Captain North's Most Celebrated Intrigues* (Stokes, 1941) includes numbers 9, 11, and 13; and *The Man from G-2* (Reynal, 1942) contains numbers 3, 12, and 15.

1. *Seeds of Murder* (Doubleday, 1930) Captain North's first perplexing case involves three seeds mysteriously placed under the bodies of two murdered men.

2. *Vesper Service Murders, The* (Doubleday, 1931) The small city of Deptford, Massachusetts, is the uncharacteristic setting for this study of corruption.

3. *Fort Terror Murders, The* (Doubleday, 1931) Murder and hidden treasure bring North to an old Spanish fort in the Philippines.

4. *Yellow Arrow Murders, The* (Doubleday, 1932) A laboratory in Cuba is the scene of an invention that will revolutionize naval warfare.

5. *Branded Spy Murders, The* (Doubleday, 1932) The action is set in Hawaii.

6. *Shanghai Bund Murders, The* (Doubleday, 1933) Revised edition: *The China Sea Murders* (Pocket, 1959).

7. *Sulu Sea Murders, The* (Doubleday, 1933) North returns to the Philippines.

8. *Budapest Parade Murders, The* (Doubleday, 1935)

9. *Washington Legation Murders, The* (Doubleday, 1935) Washington is overrun with spies.

10. *Seven Seas Murders, The* (Doubleday, 1936) This is a collection of four Captain North novellas: "Shanghai Sanctuary," "The Repeater," "Port of Intrigue," and "The Munitions Ship Murders."

11. *Castle Island Case, The* (Reynal, 1937) International intrigue in the Caribbean. Revised edition published as *The Multi-Million Dollar Murders* (Pocket, 1960).

12. *Hong Kong Airbase Murders, The* (Doubleday, 1937)

13. *Cairo Garter Murders, The* (Doubleday, 1939)

14. *Singapore Exile Murders, The* (Doubleday, 1939)

15. *Bucharest Ballerina Murders, The* (Stokes, 1940)

16. *Rio Casino Intrigue, The* (Reynal, 1941) A shipload of iron is headed for the Brazilian port.

17. *Saigon Singer* (Doubleday, 1946)

18. *Dardanelles Derelict* (Doubleday, 1949)

19. *Himalayan Assignment* (Doubleday, 1952)

20. *Two Tickets to Tangier* (Doubleday, 1955) The action concerns the formula for a lethal gas that can freeze victims to death in seconds.

21. *Gracious Lily Affair, The* (Doubleday, 1957) Colonel North investigates when a Portuguese plane off Bermuda is blown up.

22. *Secret Mission to Bangkok* (Doubleday, 1960) North is protecting Dr. Bracht, a top US scientist who is having marital problems.

23. *Trouble in Burma* (Doubleday, 1962)

24. *Zanzibar Intrigue* (Doubleday, 1963)

25. *Maracaibo Mission* (Doubleday, 1965)

26. *Deadly Orbit Mission, The* (Doubleday, 1968) A Russian satellite with a nuclear warhead is orbiting regularly over the United States.

Masters, John

I. John Masters planned a series of 35 novels depicting the history of the British presence in India. Before his death, in 1983, he had completed only 10 novels about India, 7 of which have one Anglo-Indian family, the Savages, as their connecting link. With the exception of *Coromandel*, which tells about Jason Savage, the first member of his family to go to India, and which is set in the 1600s, the novels deal with British India from the 1830s to the 1940s.

Masters, who was the fifth generation of an Anglo-Indian family, and who served as a professional soldier in the British Indian Army, knew India well, and his books capture the flavor of India with accurate historical detail, albeit from the British point of view. *Bhowani Junction* was made into a film starring Ava Gardner and Stewart Granger (1956). Masters published an autobiography: *Bugles and a Tiger* (Viking, 1956).

1. *Coromandel* (Viking, 1955) Jason Savage, illiterate son of an English tenant farmer, buys a map showing buried treasure in Coromandel, India, and goes treasure hunting. Set in the 1600s.

2. *Deceivers, The* (Viking, 1952) William Savage, English civil servant in India, sets out to infiltrate the Thugs and destroy their murderous cult. Set in the 1830s.

3. *Nightrunners of Bengal* (**Viking, 1950**) Captain Rodney Savage has to rescue himself and his son from the horrors of the Indian Mutiny of 1857.

4. *Lotus and the Wind, The* (**Viking, 1952**) Robin Savage, son of Rodney, trails Muralev, a Russian agent, through the Afghan wilderness in the late 1800s.

5. *Far, Far the Mountain Peak* (**Viking, 1957**) Peter Savage, grandson of General Rodney Savage, pursues his mountain-climbing obsession in Europe and India. Covers 1902 to 1922.

6. *Bhowani Junction* (**Viking, 1954**) Victoria Jones and Patrick Taylor, young Anglo-Indians unsure of their racial status, and Colonel Rodney Savage (Peter's son), who is in charge of guarding the trains at Bhowani Junction, are the main protagonists on the eve of India independence in 1946.

7. *To the Coral Strand* (**Harper, 1962**) Rodney Savage, who cannot come to terms with an independent India, goes through a series of positions from big-game hunter to diplomat.

II. Another pair of novels dealing with India describes the adventures of the Bateman family.

1. *Ravi Lancers, The* (**Doubleday, 1972**) Captain Warren Bateman commands an Indian regiment serving in the trenches of World War I.

2. *Himalayan Concerto, The* (**Doubleday, 1976**) Composer Rodney Bateman, vacationing in Kashmir, is recruited by Indian intelligence to monitor Chinese activities on India's northern border.

III. The Loss of Eden trilogy is a panoramic saga of World War I focusing on four families who are representative of British society: the Rowland family of auto manufacturers; the working-class Strattons; the Earl of Swanwick and his family; and Probyn Gorse, the crafty poacher and his brood. The war's effects on this large cast of characters make engrossing and moving novels that give a composite picture of the social and economic upheaval caused by the war's trauma.

1. *Now, God Be Thanked* (**McGraw-Hill, 1979**) This account begins on July 4, 1914, at the Henley Royal Regatta and continues to Christmas 1915 on the battlefield.

2. *Heart of War* (**McGraw-Hill, 1980**) Class distinctions begin to blur and a new society to emerge during 1916–1917.

3. *By the Green of the Spring* (**McGraw-Hill, 1981**) The war ends, and in its aftermath there emerge such new problems as union struggles and flu epidemics.

Matera, Lia

I. California lawyer Laura Di Palma has a tendency to get overly involved with her pro bono work, which eventually gets her laid off from her high-powered San Francisco law firm. The smart, feisty, engaging lawyer is sometimes aided in her investigations by her on-again, off-again private eye lover, Sandy Arklett. The title story of *Counsel for the Defense and Other Stories* (Five Star, 2000), a collection of nine Matera stories, is a Di Palma story.

1. *Smart Money, The* (**Bantam, 1988**) Although she has made it as defense attorney in a high-class law firm, Laura Di Palma still bears her ex-husband a grudge.

2. *Good Fight, The* (**Simon & Schuster, 1990**) Laura defends a radical activist against charges that he murdered an FBI agent.

3. *Hard Bargain, A* (**Simon & Schuster, 1992**) Former partner Sandy Arklett asks Di Palma to get involved with the case of a black paramedic who is accused of having driven his white wife to suicide.

4. *Face Value* (**Simon & Schuster, 1994**) New Age guru Brother Mike videotapes group sex sessions and, unbeknownst to his acolytes, sells the tapes to local video stores.

5. *Designer Crimes* (**Simon & Schuster, 1995**) Attorney Jocelyn Kinsley's last words before being killed by a masked intruder were "designer crimes."

II. Willa Jansson is another San Francisco–area lawyer who gets involved with murder and mayhem in a series of funny, offbeat mysteries. "Dream Lawyer," a Willa Jansson story, is included in the Matera collection: *Counsel for the Defense and Other Stories* (Five Star, 2000).

1. *Where Lawyers Fear to Tread* (**Bantam, 1987**) A series of untimely deaths at Malhousie Law School leaves the job of editor of the *Law Review* to Willa Jansson.

2. *Radical Departure, A* (**Bantam, 1988**) Radical lawyer Julian Warneke is poisoned by hemlock in front of the whole law firm.

3. *Hidden Agenda* (**Bantam, 1988**) Willa is concerned that her aging flower-child parents won't take kindly to her $90,000-a-year position at a prestigious law firm.

4. *Prior Convictions* (**Simon & Schuster, 1991**) After a miserable year at her Los Angeles law firm, Willa moves back to San Francisco and a clerkship with a liberal federal court judge.

5. *Last Chants* (**Simon & Schuster, 1996**) Willa spots elderly ethnobotanist and mythologist, Arthur Kenna, an old family friend, holding a man at gunpoint. To protect him from the police, she spirits Kenna off to a mountain cabin near Santa Cruz, where she gets involved with some odd characters with mind expansion on their agendas.

6. *Star Witness* (**Simon & Schuster, 1997**) Was Alan Miller actually in a UFO when his car fell on top of another car, killing the driver, as he claims in his recovered memory?

7. *Havana Twist* (**Simon & Schuster, 1998**) Willa goes to Havana to track down her social activist mother who has disappeared while on a golden-agers goodwill tour of Cuba.

Mathis, Edward

Dan Roman is a sort of Texan Travis McGee (John D. MacDonald [q.v.]). Ex-cop turned private eye, he is hard, flawed, tough but weak when it comes to matters like tequila, cigarettes, poker, and his ex-wife, Susie. Dan's stomping ground is the small towns and thickets of East Texas, and the series conveys a strong sense of Texas place, character, and speech. *Little Man Blues* (Tor, 1988) features Detective Sergeant Hamilton Pope.

1. *From a High Place* (**Scribner, 1985**) The strange death of a small-town librarian leads to Dan's reminiscences about his high school days.

2. *Dark Streaks and Empty Places* (**Scribner, 1986**) The thicket country of East Texas is the scene for Roman's hunt for a missing heiress.

3. *Natural Prey* (**Scribner, 1987**) Dan, unhappily married, helps Police Captain Sellers of Midway City, an old friend, solve some murders.

4. *Another Path, Another Dragon* (**Scribner, 1988**) A love affair between members of two leading families ends in the murder of two young lovers.

5. *Burned Woman, The* (**Scribner, 1989**) Roman's wife disappears after interviewing a rock star, and a high-rent call girl is killed in a car explosion.

6. *Out of the Shadows* (Scribner, 1990) Dan follows a 15-year-old trail from Los Angeles to Las Vegas to Tennessee while searching for Loretta Arganian.
7. *September Song* (Scribner, 1991) Still carrying the torch for his ex-wife Susie, Dan tries to protect her when she is followed, shot at, and threatened by the antisocial Wagermans.
8. *Fifth Level, The* (Scribner, 1992) Roman involves himself with the case of a cancer researcher who has been targeted for murder.

Matteson, Stefanie

Charlotte Graham is a seventyish actress and amateur sleuth described, by one reviewer, as "Miss Marple in fur and jewels." She does a great deal of traveling, often among the rich and famous. Her mysteries tend to be a pretext for the author to pass on knowledge about a diverse lot of subjects.

1. *Murder at the Spa* (Berkley, 1990) Charlotte's old friend Paulina Laugenberg asks Charlotte to investigate the sabotage that is threatening her luxurious health spa.
2. *Murder at Teatime* (Berkley, 1991) Graham's vacation on an island off the coast of Maine lands her in the middle of intrigue and murder.
3. *Murder on the Cliff* (Berkley, 1991) Japan's most famous geisha is the guest at a Newport, Rhode Island, celebration of the anniversary of Commodore Perry's "opening" of Japan.
4. *Murder on the Silk Road* (Berkley, 1992) Charlotte joins her stepdaughter Marsha Lundstrom on a study tour to an isolated oasis in northwestern China.
5. *Murder at the Falls* (Berkley, 1993) A trendy young artist takes a fatal plunge down Paterson, New Jersey's famous waterfalls as Charlotte and a friend enjoy dinner at the Falls View Diner.
6. *Murder on High* (Berkley, 1994) Charlotte helps Maine State Police Lieutenant Howard Tracey solve the murder of a woman shot by an arrow while climbing Mount Katahdin.
7. *Murder among the Angels* (Berkley, 1996) In search of a face-lift, Charlotte consults with cosmetic surgeon Dr. Victor Louria, who lives in the former home of the founder of Zion Hill, a Swedenborgian offshoot, and was married to the founder's granddaughter Lily, who drowned in Mexico a few years before.
8. *Murder under the Palms* (Berkely, 1997) While visiting Palm Beach, Florida, Charlotte gets reinvolved with her first love, piano-player Eddie Norwood, in a mystery tied to the sabotage of the luxury liner *Normandie* in 1942.

Matthews, Greg

I. Australian writer Greg Matthews displayed his deep interest in American culture with *The Further Adventures of Huckleberry Finn* (Crown, 1983), a continuation of Mark Twain's (q.v.) classic that captured Twain's sound and style. The pair of novels featuring 15-year-old Burris Weems of Indiana also reveals Matthews's command of the American idiom. Burris is intelligent and articulate, but is overwhelmed by his physical, psychological, and social problems and, like most teenagers, prone to self-pity. Burris speaks for himself in these funny, touching novels.

1. *Little Red Rooster* (NAL, 1987) Burris Weems uses a stolen tape recorder to relate his complaints about life, but finds that his life picks up somewhat when he gets a summer job stacking boxes.
2. *Gold Flake Hydrant, The* (NAL, 1988) Five months later, Burris has survived a suicide attempt, flunked out of high school, and lost

his girlfriend. He befriends town character "Lennie the Loop," which leads to more trouble.

II. Matthews has written a pair of rather wacky mystery novels set in the Hollywood of the 1940s. Keith Moody is a screenwriter of B westerns and aspiring novelist who manages to get into sticky situations while pursuing his writing career.

1. *Far from Heaven* (Walker, 1997) When long-lost cousin Russell Keys becomes a war-hero fighter pilot, and turns up on the cover of *Life*, Keith Moody figures that he might be able to cash in on Russell's fame, and write something better than B westerns.
2. *Come to Dust* (Walker, 1998) It's 1944, and Keith has published a novel to some critical acclaim but meager sales. When he offers to autograph a reader's copy of the book, the guy demands his wallet instead. Things get more complicated after that.

Matthiessen, Peter

Naturalist and novelist Peter Matthiessen has written a three-volume fictional recreation, based on a few facts and much local legend and conjecture, of the life and death of E.J. Watson, south Florida entrepreneur and outlaw, who was killed by his neighbors in 1910. *Killing Mr. Watson* relates, from a variety of points of view, the events leading up to the lynching. *Lost Man's River* details the efforts, some 40 years later, of E.J.'s son, Lucius Watson, to understand the circumstances of his father's death. *Bone by Bone* relates Watson's story in his own words. Matthiessen has brought to life an era of American history that standard history texts ignore or brush over.

1. *Killing Mr. Watson* (Random House, 1990) E.J. Watson, newcomer to the Everglades, starts a successful sugarcane plantation. But his neighbors become increasingly uneasy about the mystery that surrounds him. Did he really kill Belle Starr? Who else did he kill?
2. *Lost Man's River* (Random House, 1997) Four decades later, Lucius Watson attempts to understand the 1910 slaying, by his neighbors, of E.J. Watson.
3. *Bone by Bone* (Random House, 1999) E.J. Watson tells the story of his life (1860–1910) in his own words: his terrible childhood in South Carolina, his adventures in Indian Territory and elsewhere, his attempts to build a solid life for himself in south Florida, etc.

Maxwell, A. E.

PSEUDONYM OF Ann & Evan Maxwell

Fiddler is one of mysterydom's better-known one-name private investigators. Thanks to an inheritance and wise investments, Fiddler isn't one of your seedy private eyes. He could devote all his time to fast cars and beautiful women, but he likes action, particularly of the violent kind. With his ex-wife Flora, who often accompanies him, Fiddler gets involved in a series of action-packed mysteries with more than a dollop of wish-fulfillment flavor. Ann Maxwell of the husband-and-wife team of "A. E. Maxwell" writes science fiction under her own name and historical novels as Elizabeth Lowell. Evan Maxwell has published novels under his name: for example, *Season of the Swan* (HarperCollins, 1997).

1. *Just Another Day in Paradise* (Doubleday, 1985) Flora needs Fiddler's help when she is grilled by US Customs agents about the Silicon Valley export business owned by her twin brother.

2. *Frog and the Scorpion, The* (Doubleday, 1986) An Iranian Jew who is staying illegally in the United States needs Fiddler's help when he is blackmailed by an Arab terrorist.

3. *Gatsby's Vineyard* (Doubleday, 1987) Someone is trying to sabotage the prize vineyards owned by a beautiful woman in the Napa Valley.

4. *Just Enough Light to Kill* (Doubleday, 1988) Fiddler crosses paths with Volker, his Soviet nemesis, at the Mexican border.

5. *Art of Survival, The* (Doubleday, 1989) A previously unknown Georgia O'Keeffe painting that turns up in Santa Fe proves fatal to several persons.

6. *Money Burns* (Villard, 1991) Marianne Bradford Simms, board chairman of a bank, suspects that her son Brad, manager of a branch bank, is involved in some kind of shady business.

7. *King of Nothing, The* (Villard, 1992) Rory Cairns, Fiddler's mentor, was murdered a robbery in which his ceremonial Japanese sword was stolen.

8. *Murder Hurts* (Villard, 1993) After 20 years, Fiddler gets a chance to avenge the murder of his beloved uncle Jake.

May, Julian

I. Julian May's four-volume Saga of Pliocene Exile is an engrossing science-fiction epic spiced with plenty of action, frank sex, mythology, parapsychology, fantasy, and a host of other elements. The story begins when a group of dissidents, bored with life in the 22nd century, travels six million years back in time to the Pliocene epoch. There they encounter two warring groups of humanoids: the beautiful, arrogant Tanu and the ugly, outcast Firvulag. *The Pliocene Companion* (Houghton Mifflin, 1984), May's guide to the series, outlines her plans for a connected series, which would become the Galactic Milieu trilogy (see II, below). *Intervention* (Houghton Mifflin, 1987), which relates events from 1945 to 2113, is a "vinculum" between the Pliocene Exile series and the Galactic Milieu series. *Intervention* was reprinted in two parts by Ballantine: *The Surveillance* (1988) and *The Metaconcert* (1989).

1. *Many-Colored Land, The* (Houghton Mifflin, 1981) A group of dissatisfied inhabitants of the 22nd century take a one-way time trip to Pliocene Europe, where they find a world ruled by two warring groups of humanoids.

2. *Golden Torc, The* (Houghton Mifflin, 1981) The time-exiles work to overthrow the Tanu and close the time-gate.

3. *Nonborn King, The* (Houghton Mifflin, 1983) The balance of power between the time-exiles, the Tanu, and the Firvulag is upset by Aiken Drum and some new time-exiles from the Metapsychic Rebellion of 2083.

4. *Adversary, The* (Houghton Mifflin, 1984) King Aiken and the children of the time-exiles fight Marc Remillard and his Firvulag allies.

II. May returned to the near future in the Galactic Milieu trilogy, which relates the events of the period when Earth is awaiting acceptance into the Galactic Milieu, a political and telepathic alliance between alien races. Protagonists include the telepathic Remillard family and a demonic force calling itself the Fury.

1. *Jack the Bodiless* (Knopf, 1992) Teresa Remillard has conceived a child that who promises to be the most powerful mental talent ever, but who has serious genetic defects.

2. *Diamond Mask* (Knopf, 1994) Rogatien Remillard, writing his memoirs in 2113, recalls events back to 2040 and the conflict between young mutant Jon Remillard and the insane metapsychic Fury.

3. *Magnificat* (Knopf, 1996) Rogatien Remillard is still writing his memoirs. The marriage of Diamond Mask and Jack the Bodiless, the uncovering of the identity of the Fury, and the completion of Supermind, a project that will enable human minds to become the most powerful in the Galaxy, are related in this finale.

III. The Rampart World trilogy is a somewhat lighter science-fiction series than the Saga of Pliocene Exile or the Galactic Milieu trilogy. It is set 200 years in the future, when the galaxy is dominated by 100 great corporations. The relentless pursuit of wealth and power by the corporations has opened the door to the Haluk, a malevolent alien race, intent on engulfing the commonwealth of human worlds. The "hero" of the trilogy is the somewhat flawed Helmut Icycle, aka Asahel Frost, who is called upon to thwart the Haluk conspiracy. The trilogy was originally published in hardcover by Voyager (UK) and reprinted in paperback by Ballantine in the United States.

1. *Perseus Spur* (Ballantine, 1999) Helmut Icycle, leading a quiet life on the freesoil planet of Kedge-Lockaby, is plunged into turmoil when a Giant Sea-Toad eats his house, and he is unfairly exiled to a remote planet in the Perseus Spur where he is called upon to face a conspiracy against his family.

2. *Orion Arm* (Ballantine, 2000) After his brief heroic fling in *Perseus Spur*, Asahel Frost has returned to his ne'er-do-well Helmut Icycle persona and a riverboat life in a tiny galactic outpost. However, his sister Eve, genetically altered by the Haluk, begs Helly to expose their conspiracy.

3. *Sagittarius Whorl* (Ballantine, 2001) In the finale, Helly's distrust of the Haluk ambassador's declaration of peace and friendship, leads him on an investigation to the sleazy smuggler port of Phlegethon.

IV. May collaborated with Marion Zimmer Bradley (q.v.) and Andre Norton (q.v.) on the fantasy series Petals of the Living Trillium. All three authors collaborated on number 1; May was sole author of numbers 2 and 5; Norton was sole author of number 3; and Bradley and Elisabeth Waters coauthored number 4. Petals of the Living Trillium is set in a fantasy world where the kingdom of Ruwenda is attacked by neighboring Labernok and its rulers slain, and three sisters—Queen Anigel; Kadiya, Warrior Lady of the Eyes; and Haramis, Archimage of the Land—are given the task of forging a Sceptre of Power from the supernatural talismans that are the legacy of the Vanished Ones, who nearly destroyed the world.

1. *Black Trillium* (Bantam, 1990) Three daughters of the assassinated rulers of Ruwenda flee to the Archimage Binah, who directs them to the magic talismans that will help them to fulfill the prophesy of saving their country. Written by Marion Zimmer Bradley, Julian May, and Andre Norton.

2. *Blood Trillium* (Bantam, 1992) A dozen years later the World of Three Moons is endangered by another sorcerer, Portalagus, Master of Tuzamen, and the three sisters must resolve their differences to defeat him. Written by Julian May.

3. *Golden Trillium* (Bantam, 1993) Ruwenda is once again endangered by the legacy of the ancient Vanished Ones, and only Kadiya, Seeker-Warrior, one of the three daughters of the Black Trillium is in a position to act. Written by Andre Norton.

4. *Lady of the Trillium* (Bantam, 1995) Princess Haramis, archimage of Ruwenda, is aging and must find a successor. Written by Marion Zimmer Bradley and Elisabeth Waters.

5. *Sky Trillium* (Del Rey, 1997) The three sisters must battle the power-hungry Star Men to forge the Sceptre of Power. Haramis finds the third talisman, the Wand of the Wings.

V. May is engaged with a new fantasy series called the Boreal Moon, in which an island called High Blenholme is in perpetual political turmoil and is threatened by sea monsters and demonic woodland warriors called Green Men. Overhead looms a giant moon, which may contain otherworldly beings.

1. *Conqueror's Moon* (Ace, 2004) Bram, younger son of the sovereign king, invokes the aliens living on the moon, setting in train a disastrous series of events.
2. *Ironcrown Moon* (Ace, 2005) King Conrig has gained control of the entire island of High Blenholme, but he faces many challenges, including hiding his own illicit magical powers.
3. *Sorcerer's Moon* (Ace, 2006) As King Conrig readies for war with the tentacled Salka, his son and heir, Orrion, foolishly bargains with the magical Beaconfolk to gain the hand of his true love, Nyla.

Mayor, Archer

Brattleboro, Vermont, population 13,000, has a small but highly effective team of detectives led by Lieutenant Joe Gunther in this series by Vermont resident Mayor that demonstrates that small-town procedurals can be just as intricate and involving as big-city procedural. Gunther, who lives with his lover, prosecutor Gail Zigman, eventually becomes head of the (fictional) Vermont Bureau of Investigation (VBI), an elite group that coordinates crime investigations. At least one important social issue is dealt with in each book. A fine combination of cases, characters, and local color. Archer Mayor is an assistant medical examiner in Vermont.

1. *Open Season* (Putnam, 1988) A series of murders and assaults has been wreaked upon members of a jury who convicted a black Vietnam veteran of rape and murder three years ago.
2. *Borderlines* (Putnam, 1990) A cult that has upset the locals of Gannet, Vermont, is the victim of a fatal fire.
3. *Scent of Evil* (Mysterious, 1992) Police patrolman John Woll is the prime suspect when local stockbroker Charlie Jardine is found buried in an embankment near a busy street.
4. *Skeleton's Knee, The* (Mysterious, 1993) Recluse Abraham Fuller dies when a 25-year-old bullet shifts in his body, thus making the person who shot him guilty of homicide.
5. *Fruits of the Poisonous Tree* (Mysterious, 1994) Gunther's girlfriend Gail Zigman is raped, perhaps by a Brattleboro local who has been alleged to have committed rape before.
6. *Dark Root, The* (Mysterious, 1995) Rival Asian gangs from San Francisco battling over claims to the immigrant trade from Canada have set up shop in Vermont.
7. *Ragman's Memory, The* (Mysterious, 1996) Are the murders of troubled teenager Shawna Davis and a nursing-home patient, the mysterious death of a vagrant, the disappearance of local activist Mary Wallis, and the rather strenuous opposition to a police investigation by Selectman "NeverTom" Chambers connected?
8. *Bellows Falls* (Mysterious, 1997) Joe Gunther is loaned out to the police department in nearby Bellows Falls, another failed mill town in Vermont, to investigate officer Brian Badgett, who has been charged with sexual harassment by the troubled wife of a suspected drug dealer.
9. *Disposable Man, The* (Mysterious, 1998) Discovery of a corpse with Cyrillic tattoos on its toes throws Gunther into a murky confrontation that might be CIA versus KGB, a 40-year-old personal vendetta among now-aged cold warriors, a battle between rival Russian mafiosi, or something else entirely.
10. *Occam's Razor* (Mysterious, 1999) Toxic waste and the political infighting surrounding a plan to change the way Vermont's police agencies are run form the background to two murders and a series of phone calls implicating an ambitious politician in both crimes.
11. *Marble Mask, The* (Mysterious, 2000) Gunther has been appointed field commander of the newly created Vermont Bureau of Investigation. The VBI exists only on paper until the frozen body of Jean Deschamps, crime lord of Sherbrooke, Quebec, is found on Mount Mansfield, where it has lain since 1947.
12. *Tucker Peak* (Mysterious, 2001) The VBI looks into a string of condo burglaries at Tucker Peak, a local ski resort. Small-time thief Marty Gagnon is the prime suspect, but apparently a murderous someone else is looking for him also.
13. *Sniper's Wife, The* (Mysterious, 2002) Detective Willy Kunkle, Gunther's VBI colleague, returns to Manhattan and his troubled past when his former wife is found overdosed on heroin.
14. *Gatekeeper* (Mysterious, 2003) When a Rutland drug dealer is murdered, Vermont's governor pressures the VBI to join other police and antidrug agencies in an effort to eliminate the drug traffic in Vermont. Gunther's female colleague Sammie Martins goes undercover to ferret dealers out.
15. *Surrogate Thief, The* (Mysterious, 2004) When a woman shoots her ex-husband, the cops trace the gun to the murder of a shopkeeper 32 years ago, a murder not solved partly because Gunther was distracted by his wife dying of cancer.
16. *St. Albans Fire* (Mysterious, 2005) Gunther and sidekick Willy Kunkle travel to Newark, New Jersey, in search of answers to two barn burnings and deaths north of Burlington.
17. *Second Mouse, The* (Mysterious, 2006) When Joe Gunther tries to investigate an apparent suicide he is sceptical about, he finds himself hamstrung by his normally trustworthy medical examiner.
18. *Chat* (Grand Central, 2007) When Joe Gunther's mother and brother are almost killed in a suspicious car accident, he helps Deputy Sheriff Rob Barrows zero in on a local, lawless family with a grievance against the Gunthers.

McBain, Ed

PSEUDONYM OF Salvatore A. Lombino

I. Ed McBain (d. 2005) wrote the best US police procedurals. In *The Great Detectives* he explained that he conceived of the entire squad as the hero of its 87th Precinct series, but when he tried to kill off favorite Steve Carella in *The Pusher*, his editor wouldn't let him. So the staff of the 87th squadron of the "imaginary city" of Isola (recognized by everyone to be Manhattan with all of the place-names changed) Police Department changed very little over the years. Lieutenant Peter Byrnes leads the group, and Meyer Meyer is the senior detective. Next comes Steve Carella with his young pal Bert Kling. Other detectives include Bob O'Brien, Cotton Hawes, Hal Willis, Andy Parker, Arthur Brown, and "Fat Ollie" Weeks (numbers 52, 53, and 54 are known as Fat Ollie's Saga). There is even a series villain, "the Deaf Man," who has turned up in at least four novels: numbers 12, 22, 27, and 54. None of the characters has aged over the nearly 50 years the series has run. Because the multiple plots woven into police procedurals cannot be captured in a sentence or two, the books are listed without annotations in the order of their publication, which is also the correct chronological sequence. Excerpts from the 87th Precinct novels have been published in two volumes: *McBain's Ladies* (Mysterious, 1988) and *McBain's Ladies, Too* (Mysterious, 1989). *Fuzz* (1972), a movie based on the 87th Precinct series and scripted by "Evan Hunter" (real name, Salvatore A. Lombino), was a Burt Reynolds vehicle that featured Yul Brynner as the Deaf Man. Steve Carella also appears in *The Last Best Hope* in the

Matthew Hope series (see below). *Learning to Kill* (Harcourt, 2006) is a collection of stories written between 1952 and 1957, some of which, expanded, became 87th Precinct tales.

1. *Cop Hater* (Permabooks, 1956)
2. *Mugger, The* (Permabooks, 1956)
3. *Pusher, The* (Permabooks, 1956)
4. *Con Man, The* (Permabooks, 1957)
5. *Killer's Choice* (Simon & Schuster, 1957)
6. *Killer's Payoff* (Simon & Schuster, 1958)
7. *Lady Killer* (Simon & Schuster, 1958)
8. *Killer's Wedge* (Simon & Schuster, 1959)
9. *Til Death* (Simon & Schuster, 1959)
10. *King's Ransom* (Simon & Schuster, 1959)
11. *Give the Boys a Great Big Hand* (Simon & Schuster, 1960)
12. *Heckler, The* (Simon & Schuster, 1960)
13. *See Them Die* (Simon & Schuster, 1960)
14. *Lady, Lady, I Did It!* (Simon & Schuster, 1961)
15. *Like Love* (Simon & Schuster, 1962)
16. *Empty Hours, The* (Simon & Schuster, 1962) A collection of short stories.
17. *Ten Plus One* (Simon & Schuster, 1963)
18. *Ax* (Simon & Schuster, 1964)
19. *He Who Hesitates* (Delacorte, 1965)
20. *Doll* (Delacorte, 1965)
21. *Eighty Million Eyes* (Delacorte, 1965)
22. *Fuzz* (Doubleday, 1968)
23. *Shotgun* (Doubleday, 1969)
24. *Jigsaw* (Doubleday, 1970)
25. *Hail, Hail, the Gang's All Here!* (Doubleday, 1971)
26. *Sadie When She Died* (Doubleday, 1972)
27. *Let's Hear It for the Deaf Man* (Doubleday, 1973)
28. *Hail to the Chief* (Random House, 1973)
29. *Bread* (Random House, 1974)
30. *Blood Relatives* (Random House, 1975)
31. *So Long as You Both Shall Live* (Random House, 1976)
32. *Long Time No See* (Random House, 1977)
33. *Calypso* (Viking, 1979)
34. *Ghosts* (Viking, 1980)
35. *Heat* (Viking, 1981)
36. *Ice* (Arbor House, 1984)
37. *Lightning* (Arbor House, 1984)
38. *Eight Black Horses* (Arbor House, 1985)
39. *Poison* (Arbor House, 1986)
40. *Tricks* (Arbor House, 1987)
41. *Lullaby* (Morrow, 1989)
42. *Vespers* (Morrow, 1990)
43. *Widows* (Morrow, 1991)
44. *Kiss* (Morrow, 1992)
45. *Mischief* (Morrow, 1993)
46. *And All through the House* (Warner, 1994)
47. *Romance* (Warner, 1995)
48. *Nocturne* (Warner, 1997)
49. *Big Bad City, The* (Simon & Schuster, 1999)
50. *Last Dance, The* (Simon & Schuster, 1999)
51. *Money, Money, Money* (Simon & Schuster, 2001)
52. *Fat Ollie's Book* (Simon & Schuster, 2003)
53. *Frumious Bandersnatch, The* (Simon & Schuster, 2004)
54. *Hark!* (Simon & Schuster, 2004)
55. *Fiddlers* (Harcourt, 2005)

II. In addition to the 87th Precinct series, McBain added a Florida lawyer to the ranks of amateur private eyes. Matthew Hope lives in Calusa, Florida, and gets drawn into cases by his clients, often because of his weakness for beautiful women. The plots are usually macabre variations on the fairy tales that give most of the novels their titles. Some readers may find an excess of violence and gore in these well-plotted, fast-moving tales.

1. *Goldilocks* (Arbor House, 1978) Matthew Hope, who is conducting an adulterous affair, comes to the aid of a client who is suspected of massacring his wife and family.
2. *Rumpelstiltskin* (Viking, 1981) Newly divorced Matt Hope has a one-night stand with singer Vicky Miller, who is found murdered the next day.
3. *Beauty and the Beast* (Holt, 1983) The wife of George Harper, a gigantic black man, accuses him of spouse abuse, then is murdered.
4. *Jack and the Beanstalk* (Holt, 1984) Jack McKinney, Hope's client, is murdered after planning to invest in a snap bean farm.
5. *Snow White and Rose Red* (Holt, 1985) Matt falls for Sarah Whittaker, who is confined by her mother, perhaps illegally, in a mental institution.
6. *Cinderella* (Holt, 1986) A private eye pal of Hope's is killed while on assignment for him. "Cinderella" is a prostitute holding on to a fortune in stolen cocaine.
7. *Puss in Boots* (Holt, 1987) A recently completed porno film has disappeared along with its star actress, "Puss in Boots."
8. *House That Jack Built, The* (Holt, 1988) Midwesterner Ralph Parrish is charged with murdering his gay brother after a party in a beach house.
9. *Three Blind Mice* (Arcade, 1991) Did Stephen Leeds kill the three Vietnamese men who were acquitted of raping his wife?
10. *Mary, Mary* (Warner, 1992) Hope has to defend Mary Barton against murder charges after the bodies of three children are found in her backyard.
11. *There Was a Little Girl* (Warner, 1994) Hope is in a semicoma after being shot outside a seedy bar, so investigators Chambers, Kiley, and Berman have to reconstruct his sleuthing.
12. *Gladly the Cross-Eyed Bear* (Warner, 1996) Young toy designer Lainie Commins is suing her ex-boss, toy-manufacturer Brett Toland, for copyright and patent infringement, contending that his cross-eyed bear is a direct steal from hers.
13. *Last Best Hope, The* (Mysterious, 1998) Hope gets in touch with Steve Carella of the 87th Precinct (see series I) after a body carrying the ID papers of the missing husband of Matthew's client Jill Lawton turns out not to be that of Jack Lawton.

McCafferty, Megan

Readers are treated to the complaints and musings of Jessica Darling of Pineville, New Jersey, told in her inimitable style. We pick up Jessica as a 16-year-old high school student and follow her to Columbia University and beyond. Jessica has a hard life: her best friend moves out of town; she is unsure of her feelings about Marcus Flutie (and other boys and men); she feels estranged from her suburban family; she never has enough money, etc. These novels are funny, poignant, and will appeal to anyone who remembers what an ordeal being a teenager, or living with one, was.

1. *Sloppy Firsts* (Three Rivers, 2001) Sixteen-year-old Jessica Darling's best friend, Hope Weaver, the only person with whom Jessica could really communicate, has moved away from Pineville, and her unsympathetic parents have restricted her phone and e-mail privileges.
2. *Second Helpings* (Three Rivers, 2003) Jessica is spending the summer before her senior year of high school at SPECIAL, a New

Jersey academic enrichment camp, where she meets a handsome writing teacher, runs into a former crush, and broods about other men, including Marcus Flutie, who broke her heart last winter.

3. *Charmed Thirds* (Crown, 2006) Things are looking up for Jessica at Columbia University: she has picked a major (psychology), landed an internship with a hip Brooklyn magazine, and managed to stay together with Marcus Flutie for the entire school year. However, "the course of true love," etc., never runs smooth.

4. *Fourth Comings* (Crown, 2007) Jessica graduates from college, gets a low-paying job at a magazine, shares a tiny room in a basement sublet with her best friend, Hope, and decides to break it off with Marcus Flutie. But then Marcus confuses the issue by proposing marriage.

McCafferty, Taylor

I. Twin sisters Barbara Taylor McCafferty and Beverly Taylor Herald have written five mystery novels about identical twins Nan and Bert Tatum of Louisville, Kentucky. Bert is a housewife who has been dumped by her husband. Nan is a deejay for a country music station. Nan and Bert are often mistaken for one another, which leads to complications and mystery investigations. Alternate chapters are narrated by each sister, each of whom has a distinctly different take on things. This is a series of neatly plotted cozies punctuated by wisecracks.

1. *Double Murder* (Kensington, 1996) Bert is accosted by a stranger who later turns up on the TV news as a John Doe homicide victim. Then Nan's side of the duplex is ransacked and mysterious phone calls begin.

2. *Double Exposure* (Kensington, 1997) Bert is suspicious of Nan's love, Crane Morgan, whose identical twin brother killed his lover, then committed suicide.

3. *Double Cross* (Kensington, 1998) Bert's boss, attorney Stephanie Whitman, is murdered, and Nan runs into a man fleeing after he has apparently broken into the law office.

4. *Double Dealer* (Kensington, 2000) Is Bert's daughter, Ellie, covering up for someone when she confesses to shooting flea-market dealer Franklin Haggerty?

5. *Double Date* (Kensington, 2001) After Nan puts Bert's profile on the My Soul Mate website without her permission, Bert's date turns up murdered.

II. Barbara McCafferty has published four mysteries under the pseudonym Tierney McClellan and five comic mysteries as Taylor McCafferty about one Haskell Blevins, the only private investigator in the hamlet of Pigeon Fork, Kentucky. Blevins mysteries are listed below without annotations.

1. *Pet Peeves* (Pocket Books, 1990)
2. *Ruffled Feathers* (Pocket Books, 1992)
3. *Bed Bugs* (Pocket Books, 1993)
4. *Thin Skins* (Pocket Books, 1994)
5. *Funny Money* (Pocket Books, 2000)

McCaffrey, Anne

I. McCaffrey's Pern, or Dragonriders, series is a favorite of readers who like their science fiction with a touch of fantasy. Not that the dragons that inhabit Pern are anything but flesh and blood, or that the human denizens of Pern, who originally arrived by spaceship, employ magic instead of science and technology in their survival efforts on the watery planet, but somehow the idea of dragons and dragonriders who are the frontline in the struggle against the noxious "Thread," which appears from time to time in the history of Pern, has a touch of fantasy in it. Since *Dragonflight* and *Dragonquest* appeared as paperbound originals in 1968 and 1971, Pern has acquired a long history. The planet had been settled by humans long out of contact with Earth, who live in Holds, or population centers. The Weyrs are the homes of the fire-breathing, winged dragons and their noble riders, who protect Pern from the deadly Thread—spores that fall at certain times from the Red Star. Harper Hall, the center where young people are trained in the use of musical instruments used for long-distance communications on Pern; Aivas, an artificial intelligence; dolphins that can communicate with humans; and lot of derring-do by girls and women as well as by the usual men and boys, are also features of the series. Subsections include the Dragonriders trilogy (numbers 6, 7, and 10) and the Harper Hall trilogy aimed at younger readers (numbers 8, 9, and 11). Numbers 1 through 5 are prequels. *Dragon's Kin* (number 18) was coauthored by McCaffrey's son Todd. McCaffrey has collaborated with sometime coauthor Jody Lynn Nye (see series VII, VIII, and IX) on *The Dragonlover's Guide to Pern* (Ballantine, 1989), an illustrated handbook to the Planet of Pern. Pern stories have appeared in the McCaffrey collections *Get off the Unicorn*, Ballantine, 1977 ("The Smallest Dragonboy," which also appears in number 17); *The Girl Who Heard Dragons*, Tor, 1994 ("The Girl Who Heard Dragons," which also appears in number 17); and *The Dolphins' Bell*, Wildside, 1993 (a novella about the early days of Pern not listed by McCaffrey on her website). *Legends 2* (Tor, 1999), an anthology of three science-fiction writers (Terry Goodkind and George R. R. Martin are the others), edited by Robert Silverberg, contains "Runner of Pern," which also appears in number 17. Omnibuses include: *On Dragon Wings*, Del Rey, 2003 (numbers 1, 2, and 3); *The Dragonriders of Pern*, Doubleday, 1978 (numbers 6, 7, and 10); and *The Harper Hall of Pern*, Doubleday, 1984 (numbers 8, 9, and 11).

1. *Dragonsdawn* (Ballantine, 1988) Six thousand colonists escaping interstellar war and technocratic civilization settle on Pern. The colony thrives until the arrival of the Thread.

2. *Moreta: Dragon Lady of Pern* (Ballantine, 1983) The story of the great plague that nearly annihilated the population of Pern.

3. *Nerilka's Story* (Ballantine, 1986) Nerilka (a minor character in number 2), unhappy with life in the Hold after the death of her mother, goes out to combat the plague devastating Pern.

4. *Chronicles of Pern, The: First Fall* (Ballantine, 1993) Five short stories relate the beginnings of the human and dolphin colonies on Pern.

5. *Masterharper of Pern, The* (Ballantine, 1998) Set just before the opening of number 6. Hundreds of years after the last Threadfall, Robinton is born to musical parents. Animosity toward the Dragonriders is being orchestrated by the villainous Fax. The Weyrleader F'lon is murdered, but his son F'lar takes up his mission.

6. *Dragonflight* (Ballantine, 1968) The Dragon Weyrs have grown shabby, and the evil Lord Fax has grown very powerful, but proud young Lessa is determined to reclaim her birthright and save Pern from destruction. Reprinted in hardcover in 1978.

7. *Dragonquest* (Ballantine, 1971) Lessa mediates between the land-bound people and the Dragonriders as a new discovery threatens to change the planet radically. Reprinted in hardcover in 1979.

8. *Dragonsong* (Atheneum, 1976) Menolly runs away from her father, who has thwarted her love of music, and finds happiness among a group of fire lizards.

9. *Dragonsinger* (Atheneum, 1977) After coming to Harper Hall astride a bronze dragon, young Menolly is unhappy at first, but she soon finds her rightful place.

10. *White Dragon, The* (Ballantine, 1978) Young Lord Jaxon thwarts an attempt to steal a queen-dragon egg and makes a startling

discovery about Pern and its history. First two chapters predate number 11; remaining chapters take place after number 11.

11. *Dragondrums* (**Atheneum, 1979**) Piemur, Menolly's friend, comes of age, loses his singing voice, and must search for a new role at Harper Hall.

12. *Dragonseye* (**Del Rey, 1997**) Pern hasn't seen the Thread for more than 250 years, but ominous signs herald the approach of the Red Star, believed to be the source of Threadfall. UK title: *Red Star Rising*.

13. *Renegades of Pern, The* (**Ballantine, 1989**) The trader family of Jayge Lilcamp is menaced by the Thread and renegade leader Lady Thella, while Harper Piemur has exciting adventures in the South.

14. *All the Weyrs of Pern* (**Ballantine, 1991**) Aivas, an intelligent computer, may provide the means to finally control the Thread.

15. *Dolphins of Pern, The* (**Ballantine, 1994**) Humans and dolphins make contact again on Pern through the medium of a young boy who is rescued by dolphins and realizes that they can talk.

16. *Skies of Pern, The* (**Del Rey, 2001**) Neo-Luddite Abominators are bent on destroying all the gifts of artificial intelligence Aivas, returning Pern to its original state, as Dragonriders struggle to find a new purpose on a Threadless world.

17. *Gift of Dragons, A* (**Del Rey, 2002**) Contains the previously published "Runner of Pern," "The Smallest Dragonboy," and "The Girl Who Heard Dragons," as well as the newly published "Ever the Twain."

18. *Dragon's Kin* (**Del Rey, 2003**) Coauthored with Todd McCaffrey, Anne's son. The action centers on Camp Natalon, the site of a coal mine whose surface seams have run dry. Some of the miners employ Watch-whers, smaller cousins of the Dragons, to keep themselves safe in the mines.

19. *Dragon's Fire* (**Del Rey, 2006**) Pellar, a mute Apprentice Harper; Halla, a homeless girl; and Cristov, a miner's son, learn invaluable life lessons as Pern prepares for another onslaught of the Red Star and its Thread. Coauthored with Todd McCaffrey.

20. *Dragon Harper* (**Del Rey, 2008**) Kindan, a young Harpers' Guild apprentice, emerges as a hero when Pern is threatened with a plague. Coauthored with Todd McCaffrey.

II. The Pegasus trilogy describes how the Talented, humans who have exceptional "psionic" (telepathic and telekinetic) abilities, cope with "the untalented majority." *The Wings of Pegasus* (Guild America, 1991) is an omnibus volume containing all three novels. The history of The Talented is essentially carried on in series III.

1. *To Ride Pegasus* (**Ballantine, 1973**) Introduces the Talented and deals with the legal and ethical problems their gift creates and their dealings with "the untalented majority." Originally published in paperback. Hardcover reissue in 1990.

2. *Pegasus in Flight* (**Ballantine, 1990**) Rhysa Owen, director of the Jerhatten Center for Parapsychic Talents, tries to protect the Talented from the rest of humanity.

3. *Pegasus in Space* (**Ballantine, 2000**) Peter Reidinger, a quadriplegic with telekinetic abilities, helps other Talents to thwart a mutiny aboard a nearly finished space station.

III. This series, sometimes called the Tower and the Hive, and sometimes called the Rowan series, follows chronologically upon the previous series. The Talented, now called Primes, encounter two alien races, the Mrdini, and the insectoid Hivers, and eventually work out accommodations with them. The Raven family, especially Damia, are the leading human protagonists. Number 1 is an expansion of McCaffrey's first published story, "Lady in the Tower."

1. *Rowan, The* (**Putnam, 1990**) The Rowan, sole survivor of a mining disaster on a frontier planet, becomes one of the "Primes" who are responsible for telepathic communication and teleportation throughout the galaxy.

2. *Damia* (**Putnam, 1992**) Damia Raven, daughter of the Rowan, becomes the Prime in charge of the Federated Telepath and Teleport Network tower on the new colony of Iota Aurigae.

3. *Damia's Children* (**Putnam, 1993**) Damia's eight children have been raised with young Mrdinis, the only intelligent life that humans have encountered except for the malevolent Hiver culture.

4. *Lyon's Pride* (**Putnam, 1994**) Humans and Mrdinis continue to work together against the Hiver menace.

5. *Tower and the Hive, The* (**Ace, 1999**) Humans, Mrdini, and Hivers find ways to coexist.

IV. A pair of novels called the Ireta Adventure, or the Dinosaur Planet, relates the adventures of Kar and his beautiful coleader Varian, who accompany an expedition to an uninhabited planet to catalogue its flora and fauna and search for new energy sources, and unexpectedly discover dinosaur-like creatures. Published together in an omnibus volume, *The Mystery of Ireta* (Del Rey, 2003).

1. *Dinosaur Planet* (**Ballantine, 1978**) On a mission to catalogue life-forms on the planet Ireta for the Federated Sentient Planets, Kai and Varian encounter large, dinosaur-like creatures.

2. *Dinosaur Planet Survivors* (**Ballantine, 1984**) Awakening from their 40 years of cold-sleep, Kai and Varian discover that mutineers have taken over Ireta.

V. The Crystal Singer series follows the checkered career of Killashandra Ree, who has the rare gift of perfect pitch that can find and cut the Ballybran crystals on which the economy of the galaxy is based.

1. *Crystal Singer* (**Ballantine, 1982**) Killashandra travels to the planet of Ballybran to become a crystal miner.

2. *Killashandra* (**Ballantine, 1985**) Killashandra takes on the special assignment of replacing a shattered crystal on the planet Optheria and is kidnapped by handsome Lars Dahl.

3. *Crystal Line* (**Ballantine, 1992**) Lars Dahl becomes head of the Heptite Guild and tries to reorganize it, to the disenchantment of Killashandra.

VI. A series called Freedom or Catteni is about a planet called Botany, home of human exiles. The planet is dominated by a race called the Catteni, who in turn are dominated by a mysterious power. Escaped Human slave Kristin Bjornsen and Catteni rebel Zainal are the leading protagonists.

1. *Freedom's Landing* (**Ace, 1995**) Escaped human slave Kristin Bjornsen and Catteni renegade Zainal join the troublemakers exiled to the planet Freedom, aka Botany.

2. *Freedom's Choice* (**Ace, 1997**) Settlers on Botany are making plans to get even with the Catteni. Kris and Zinal learn the truth about the mysterious Farmers or Mech Makers.

3. *Freedom's Challenge* (**Ace, 1998**) The war of liberation is highlighted by the theft of Catteni ships, the liberation of cargoes of slave laborers, and an attack at the heart of the oppressors.

4. *Freedom's Ransom* (**Ace, 2002**) The gold standard has fallen on the planets Earth, Botany, and Borevi, and coffee, fresh bread, and meat have become more valuable than diamonds.

VII. McCaffrey has coauthored several series with other authors. The Doona trilogy, of which the first was solely written by McCaffrey, and numbers 2 and 3 coauthored with Jody Lynn Nye, is about the interaction between humans and the catlike Hrubans and, eventually, another alien race. Omnibus volume: *Doona* (Ace, 2004).

1. *Decision at Doona* (Ballantine, 1969) Unaware that Doona is inhabited by the sentient Hrubans, the Terran government sends colonists to the planet.
2. *Crisis on Doona* (Ace, 1992) After 25 years, the cohabitation contract between humans and Hrubans is up for renewal. Cowritten with Jody Lynn Nye.
3. *Treaty at Doona* (Ace, 1994) A third race arrives with promises of new technology and trade, but were they responsible for the destruction of life on another planet? UK title: *Treaty Planet*. Cowritten with Jody Lynn Nye.

VIII. The Planet Pirates trilogy, cowritten with Jody Lynn Nye (number 2) and Elizabeth Moon (numbers 1 and 3), is about Sassinak and her great-grandmother Lunzie and their battles against the Planet Pirates marauders. Omnibus volume containing all three novels: *The Planet Pirates* (Baen, 1993).

1. *Sassinak* (Baen, 1990) Sassinak's home is destroyed, and she is kidnapped by pirates. Eventually she joins the Fleet, seeking vengeance on her enemies. Written with Elizabeth Moon.
2. *Death of Sleep, The* (Baen, 1990) Lunzie Mespil receives a rude awakening and then a deep sleep when Planet Pirates attack the spaceship in which she is traveling. Eventually she is revived by Sassinak, her great-granddaughter after a sleep of nearly a century.
3. *Generation Warriors* (Baen, 1991) Lunzie discovers that the one good heavy-worlder she ever met isn't so good after all. Written with Elizabeth Moon.

IX. The Brainship series derived from one of McCaffrey's most famous stories, *The Ship Who Sang*. In the 1990s several more volumes were added in collaboration with different coauthors: Margaret Ball (number 2), Mercedes Lackey (q.v.) (number 3), S. M. Stirling (numbers 4 and 7), and Jody Lynn Nye (numbers 5 and 6). The novels describe the partnerships between the physically disadvantaged "Brains," or "Shell-persons," usually female, and the "brawn," usually male, who pilot the starships. Omnibuses: *Brain Ships*, Baen, 2003 (numbers 2 and 3); *The City and the Ship*, Baen, 2004 (numbers 4 and 7); and *The Ship Who Saved the Worlds*, Baen, 2003 (numbers 5 and 6).

1. *Ship Who Sang, The* (Walker, 1969) Helva was born human, but only her brain was spared and implanted into the body of an intergalactic scout ship. It is up to Helva to choose a human partner, or "brawn" to travel with her into space.
2. *Partnership* (Baen, 1992) Narnia, or NX-928, is the "brains" within one of the most advanced interstellar ships ever designed. Written with Margaret Ball.
3. *Ship Who Searched, The* (Baen, 1992) A precocious seven-year-old girl afflicted by a paralyzing alien virus "straps on" a spaceship, and sets out to find out what it was that laid her low.
4. *City Who Fought, The* (Baen, 1993) Simeon was bored, not with being a "shell-person," but with running the mining and processing station that made up his "body." Written with S. M. Stirling.
5. *Ship Who Won, The* (Baen, 1994) Physically disadvantaged Carracle decides to "become a space-ship." With her "brawn" Keffe she sets out in search of intelligent beings. Written with Jody Lynn Nye.
6. *Ship Errant, The* (Baen, 1996) Targeted by a humorless Inspector General who believes that she has been damaged by a past trauma, brain-ship Carracle finds support from her partner Keff and the

"globe-frog" race they discovered together. Written with Jody Lynn Nye.
7. *Ship Avenged, The* (Baen, 1997) Joat, one of the youngest commercial shipowners in space, is commissioned to transport a deadly "breakout disease" by Belazair of the Kolneri. Written with S. M. Stirling.

X. The Petaybee, or Power, trilogy was written in collaboration with Elizabeth Ann Scarborough. Petaybee is a sentient, or intelligent, planet, with whom its human settlers must come to terms if they wish to prosper. The series was revived in Twins of Petaybee, another trilogy, also coauthored by Scarborough.

1. *Powers That Be* (Ballantine, 1993) Major Yanaba Maddock, medically retired, is pressured into acting as a spy on the potentially rebellious inhabitants of Petaybee by Intergal Corporation, her employer. Written with Elizabeth Ann Scarborough.
2. *Power Lines* (Ballantine, 1994) Dr. Whittaker Fiske becomes convinced of the intelligence of the planet Petaybee and of the necessity of negotiating with it. Written with Elizabeth Ann Scarborough.
3. *Power Play* (Ballantine, 1995) The marriage of Yanaba Maddock, administrator of Petaybee, and selkie Sean Shongili is celebrated, while old enemy Torkel Fiske continues to cause trouble. Written with Elizabeth Ann Scarborough.
4. *Changelings* (Del Rey, 2005) Book one of the Twins of Petaybee. Murel and Ronan, twins born to Major Yanaba Maddock-Shongili, administrator of Petaybee, and geneticist-selkie Dr. Sean Shongili, lead an idyllic life on the icy planet for their first eight years. Written with Elizabeth Ann Scarborough.
5. *Maelstrom* (Del Rey, 2006) Book two of the Twins of Petaybee. Murel and Ronan Shongili, now 10 years old, rescue the inhabitants of the environmentally degraded planet Halau and bring them to Petaybee. Written with Elizabeth Ann Scarborough.
6. *Deluge* (Del Rey, 2008) In the concluding episode of the Twins of Petaybee trilogy, twin selkies Ronan and Muriel, with animal allies such as space-faring deep-sea otters and the telepathic cat Zuzu, endure a series of privations such as prison camp, a tsunami, and a volcanic eruption before they come through. Coauthored with Elizabeth Ann Scarborough.

XI. The Acorna series, McCaffrey's latest, has been written in collaboration with two other authors: Margaret Ball (numbers 1–2) and Elizabeth Ann Scarborough (numbers 3–9). It relates the adventures of Acorna, a young girl with a horn in her forehead and a mysterious provenance who is raised by a trio of asteroid prospectors. When she grows up, she goes in search of her ancestry, which she finds among the Linyaari, but she also finds love and the Khleevi, a nasty insectoid bunch. Two volumes of an additional trilogy, Acorna's Children, have been published.

1. *Acorna: The Unicorn Girl* (HarperCollins, 1997) A baby who has been put in a survival pod by her Linyaari parents to escape extermination by the Khlevii, is found by three asteroid miners who name her Acorna and raise her. Written with Margaret Ball.
2. *Acorna's Quest* (HarperCollins, 1998) Acorna sets off with her "Uncle" Calum to find "her own kind." Written with Margaret Ball.
3. *Acorna's People* (HarperCollins, 1999) After years of searching, Acorna finally returns to her home and her fellow Linyaari. Written with Elizabeth Ann Scarborough.
4. *Acorna's World* (Avon, 2000) Acorna answers a distress call that leads her to a planet of sentient vines that may hold the secret

to stopping the Khleevi and saving the Linyaari from extinction. Written with Elizabeth Ann Scarborough.

5. *Acorna's Search* (Eos, 2001) Acorna is attached to a Planet Survey whose teams are disappearing one by one, including the team containing her life mate, Aari. Written with Elizabeth Ann Scarborough.

6. *Acorna's Rebels* (Eos, 2003) Still searching for Aari, Acorna travels to the planet Makahomia, which she finds in the grip of a plague destroying its sacred Temple Cats. Written with Elizabeth Ann Scarborough.

7. *Acorna's Triumph* (Eos, 2004) Acorna finally locates her life mate, Aari, whose exile has resulted in a disturbing personality change. Written with Elizabeth Ann Scarborough.

8. *First Warning* (Eos, 2005) Book one of Acorna's Children. Khorii, the adolescent daughter of Acorna, has her share of problems while at school on an asteroid that serves as a refuge for war orphans. Coauthored with Elizabeth Ann Scarborough.

9. *Second Wave* (Eos, 2006) Book two of Acorna's Children. Khorii, her adopted android brother, Elviiz, and human survivors of the planet Paloduro struggle to devise a plague vaccine. Coauthored with Elizabeth Ann Scarborough.

10. *Third Watch* (Eos, 2007) Book three of Acorna's Children. Acorna's long-lost daughter, Korii, Korii's twin, Ariin, and their faithful cat, Khiindi, travel through time and space in search of the secret of the plague that's endangering galactic civilization.

McCaig, Donald

Dog lovers will appreciate Donald McCaig's pair of novels about Nop, "the finest sheep-dog in America," and his son Hope. They are heart-warming novels with well-realized human and dog characters (the dogs have their own language and culture) based on McCaig and his own border collies. McCaig also wrote *Eminent Dogs, Dangerous Men: Searching through Scotland for a Border Collie* (Harper, 1991). *Jacob's Ladder* (Norton, 1998) and *Canaan* (Norton, 2007), a pair of novels about the Civil War, seem to have no connecting fictional characters.

1. *Nop's Trials* (Crown, 1984) Nop, stock farmer Louis Burkholder's dog, is stolen from his Blue Ridge, Virginia, home and passes through various hands before he returns to his rightful owner.

2. *Nop's Hope* (Crown, 1994) Mourning her lost husband and daughter, Penny Burkholder sets off on a cross-country trip with Hope, son of Nop.

McCarry, Charles

Former CIA agent Charles McCarry writes novels about the worlds of intelligence and politics. He is sometimes compared with Richard Condon (q.v.) for his satirical wit, cynicism, and ability to tell a good story. The somewhat shadowy intelligence agent Paul Christopher is most prominent member of the cast of characters in a series of novels displaying imaginative but convincing plots and McCarry's insider knowledge of the espionage world. Although number 6 was billed as the last Christopher novel, but numbers 7 and 8 have Paul's daughter Zarah as a character. Number 1 is a prequel about Paul Christopher's life in 1939–1959. *Lucky Bastard* (Random House, 1998), a novel about the rise through politics of a lecherous draft dodger who is run by the KGB, doesn't seem to have any Christophers in it.

1. *Christopher's Ghosts* (Overlook, 2007) In 1939 Germany, 16-year-old Paul Christopher struggles, with his American novelist father and German aristocrat mother, against the Nazis.

2. *Miernik Dossier, The* (Saturday Review, 1973) Cold war espionage activities in the 1950s told in the form of a dossier on Miernik, a drunken Polish double or triple agent.

3. *Tears of Autumn, The* (Saturday Review, 1975) Paul Christopher follows his own ideas on the assassination of John F. Kennedy, and resigns from The Outfit.

4. *Secret Lovers, The* (Dutton, 1977) Christopher witnesses the murder of a Russian courier carrying a piece of literature potentially damaging to the Soviet regime.

5. *Last Supper, The* (Dutton, 1983) Christopher traces the history of his old organization The Outfit from Nazi Germany to the present.

6. *Second Sight* (Dutton, 1991) Brought out of retirement, Christopher foils the plans of a group that is kidnapping and drugging operatives of The Outfit.

7. *Old Boys* (Overlook, 2004) Paul Christopher has disappeared and has apparently died in a remote area of China, but former colleague Horace Hubbard and Paul's daughter Zarah cannot believe that he is dead.

8. *Shelley's Heart* (Random House, 1995) Zarah appears as a character in a novel set in the not-too-distant future about a disputed presidential election and computer tampering with the votes (!).

McCarthy, Cormac

The first two novels of the Border Trilogy detail, separately, the lives of two Texas teenagers, John Grady Cole and Billy Parham, who run away to Mexico and undergo a series of adventures. In Number 3, in 1952, the two come together as cowboys on a New Mexico ranch. With novels such as *Blood Meridian* (Random House, 1985), Cormac McCarthy is regarded by many critics as one of the greatest living American novelists, remarking upon McCarthy's "magisterial" prose, hypnotic evocation of barren landscapes, and western-gothic imagery, but the graphic violence depicted in his novels is not for the faint-hearted or the weak-stomached.

1. *All the Pretty Horses* (Knopf, 1992) Sixteen-year-old John Grady Cole, last of a long line of Texas ranchers, escapes to Mexico with friends.

2. *Crossing, The* (Knopf, 1994) Billy Parham, unwilling to shoot a wolf that he and his father have trapped, decides to take the animal to Mexico and let it loose down there.

3. *Cities of the Plain* (Knopf, 1998) In the fall of 1952, John Grady Cole and Billy Parham are cowboys on a New Mexico ranch. The two are bound by nature to horses and cattle and range but are still drawn to Mexico.

McClure, James

James McClure, who spent his later years in England, wrote an excellent series of police procedurals set in his native South Africa. His two police detectives from Trekkersburg (based on the real city of Pietermaritzburg) are Afrikaner Lieutenant Tromp Kramer and Bantu Sergeant Mickey Zondi. The pair work closely as a successful team, though their racist society inhibits any public display of the friendship and mutual respect they feel for each other. McClure deliberately chose the detective story format as means of reaching people who might not otherwise read much about the grim realities of apartheid. By simply portraying day-to-day life in South Africa with humor and without heavy-handed social comment, McClure helped to undermine apartheid without attracting the attention of the censors (except in *The Sunday Hangman*, which cut too close to the bone in depicting extralegal executions). *Four and Twenty Virgins* (Gollancz [UK], 1973), *Rogue Eagle*, and *Imago* (Mysterious, 1988) are not part of the series. For another view of Pietermaritzburg, see the Piemburg novels of Tom Sharpe (q.v.).

1. *Song Dog, The* (Mysterious, 1991) In a prequel set in 1962, Kramer and Zondi stumble over each other on the trails of separate murderers.
2. *Steam Pig, The* (Harper, 1972) A sharpened bicycle spoke, usually associated with "Kaffir" homicide, is used to murder a beautiful white girl.
3. *Caterpillar Cop, The* (Harper, 1973) A 12-year-old boy is mutilated and murdered in what appears to be a sex crime.
4. *Gooseberry Fool, The* (Harper, 1974) When a pious hypocrite is stabbed to death with a steak knife, Zondi pursues his own investigation.
5. *Snake* (Harper, 1976) A stripper with a snake act is found murdered with her pet wound around her neck.
6. *Sunday Hangman, The* (Harper, 1977) Afrikaner pathologist Dr. Strydom and Kramer suspect that some hanging suicides may actually be extralegal executions.
7. *Blood of an Englishman, The* (Harper, 1981) Apparently a giant has "ground the bones" of visiting former RAF airman Bonzo Hookham.
8. *Artful Egg, The* (Pantheon, 1985) Naomi Stride, world-famous author of novels banned in South Africa, is found naked, dead, and with the tip of a sword still in her body.

McCord, John S.

The Baynes Family westerns follow the fortunes of Darnell Baynes and his sons Luke, Milt, and Ward as they try to make their fortunes in the American West of the 1860s. McCord, a former US Air Force officer, produces well-written, action-filled westerns with believable characters. Numbers 1 through 3 are sometimes known as the Baynes Gang Trilogy. *Walking Hawk* (Doubleday, 1989), a novel set in the Montana of the 1880s, isn't part of the series. Numbers 4 through 6 were published as paperbound originals.

1. *Montana Horseman* (Doubleday, 1990) Louisiana farmer Darnell Baynes and his boys head west to avoid the Civil War and wind up in Montana territory.
2. *Texas Comebacker* (Doubleday, 1991) Milt Baynes hooks up with sharp-tongued redhead Cris Mills and her brother Win in the fight of Texas ranchers against outlaws and corrupt officials.
3. *Wyoming Giant* (Doubleday, 1992) After law-clerking in New York City, Luke Baynes accepts a federal judgeship in Wyoming Territory, where he uncovers a big land swindle.
4. *California Eagles* (Berkley, 1995) The outlaw clan of the Trampes plans to settle an old score by kidnapping Ward Baynes's son and charging a large ransom.
5. *Nevada Tough* (Berkley, 1996) When someone steals gold from the Baynes clan, Darnell Baynes gets on his horse and rides to Nevada to get to the bottom of things.
6. *Kansas Gambler* (Berkley, 1997) Rod Silvana, cousin to the Baynes clan, earns money by playing poker, falls under the spell of a seductive lady, and confronts a band of cattle rustlers.

McCrumb, Sharyn

I. The folk and folklore of Appalachia play a vital role in McCrumb's Ballad novels, which incorporate North Carolina native McCrumb's family history and memories in mystery settings. A connecting link in each novel of the series is the presence of a folk ballad that haunts the characters therein. Among the continuing characters in this atmospheric and spookily suspenseful series are Wake County, Tennessee, sheriff Spencer Arrowood (pronounced *Arwood*); clairvoyant Nora Bonesteel; the folks, past and present, of the village of Hamelin; and the hills of east Tennessee themselves. The Ballad novels are a constant reminder that there is, and was, a South beyond the South portrayed in plantation novels of Margaret Mitchell and others. *Once around the Track* (Kensington, 2007) is, like number 8, a novel about NASCAR but probably shouldn't be considered part of the Ballad series.

1. *If Ever I Return, Pretty Peggy-O* (Scribner, 1990) Hamelin, Tennessee, is stirred up by a high school reunion and the arrival of Peggy Muryan, famous folksinger from the sixties. UK title: *If Ever I Return*.
2. *Hangman's Beautiful Daughter, The* (Scribner, 1992) Sheriff Arrowood asks the wife of the local Baptist minister to comfort the survivors of a murder-suicide.
3. *She Walks These Hills* (Scribner, 1994) Ethno-historian Jeremy Cobb researches the 1779 journey of escaped Indian captive Katie Wyler, while convicted murderer Hiram "Harm" Sorley manages a contemporary escape.
4. *Rosewood Casket, The* (Dutton, 1996) Old clairvoyant Nora Bonesteel brings a small box containing a child's skeleton to place in the coffin that is being built for the dying Randall Stargill.
5. *Ballad of Frankie Silver, The* (Dutton, 1998) Recuperating from a gunshot wound, Sheriff Arrowood occupies himself by investigating the 1832 hanging, for her husband's murder, of 18-year-old Frankie Silver and finds disturbing parallels to a contemporary case.
6. *Songcatcher, The* (Dutton, 2001) The parallel stories of Malcolm McCourry, unwilling emigrant from Scotland in 1751, and his descendant, country-singer Lark McCourry, trapped in a small airplane while returning to see her estranged father, are related.
7. *Ghost Riders* (Dutton, 2003) The interwoven stories of historical characters Zebulon Vance, the unionist Civil War governor of North Carolina, and Malinda Blalock, who disguised herself as a boy to join her husband in the Confederate army, as well as ghosts of Confederate soldiers bedeviling a contemporary Civil War battle reenactment are related here.
8. *St. Dale* (Kensington, 2005) Novel based on the Dale Earnhardt Memorial Pilgrimage after the NASCAR legend's accidental death.

II. Elizabeth MacPherson is a forensic anthropologist with an interest in historical true-crime cases, the British Isles, and Scottish marine biologist Cameron Dawson, whom she marries, then loses. The settings of this mystery series are divided almost equally between the American South and Great Britain. For readers who like their mysteries spiced with wit, well-delineated setting, and large doses of true-crime lore. *Foggy Mountain Breakdown: And Other Stories* (Ballantine, 1997) contains "Love on First Bounce," a story written when McCrumb was in high school, which introduces Elizabeth MacPherson.

1. *Sick of Shadows* (Avon, 1984) Elizabeth MacPherson is invited to the wedding of cousin Eileen Chandler and Michael Savitsky, who, her family suspects, is after Eileen's money.

2. *Lovely in Her Bones* **(Avon, 1985)** Professor Lerch, leader of an archaeological dig to establish the claims of a North Carolina Indian tribe to the land they live on, is murdered in his tent.

3. *Highland Laddie Gone* **(Ballantine, 1986)** The annual Glencoe Mountain Games festival in Scotland is disrupted by the murder of the unpopular Colin Campbell.

4. *Paying the Piper* **(Ballantine, 1989)** A Murder Walk in Edinburgh, Cameron Dawson's seal research off the Scottish coast, an archaeological dig, and the sudden death of a London journalist all play roles.

5. *Windsor Knot, The* **(Ballantine, 1990)** The action shifts between Chandler Grove, Georgia and Edinburgh, Scotland, as Elizabeth and Cameron try to tie the knot on a rather tight schedule.

6. *Missing Susan* **(Ballantine, 1991)** Rowan Rover, tour guide to England's most notorious murder sites, has accepted a commission to commit a murder of his own.

7. *MacPherson's Lament* **(Ballantine, 1992)** Elizabeth's brother Bill sets up a law practice in Virginia in partnership with Amy Powell Hill, descendant of Confederate General A. P. Hill.

8. *If I'd Killed Him When I Met Him ...* **(Ballantine, 1995)** Contemporary and 19th-century murder cases involving wronged women figure in the plot when Elizabeth is hired as an investigator by brother Bill's law firm.

9. *PMS Outlaws, The* **(Ballantine, 2000)** Elizabeth has checked in a psychiatric hospital to deal with depression brought on by the death of her husband. Brother Bill has purchased an old mansion with an odd legacy for his law firm. Bill's partner A. P. Powell is chasing after the PMS Outlaws, who rob and humiliate men only.

III. A pair of wonderfully titled novels features MIT engineering professor and science-fiction author Jay Omega and his significant other, Marion Farley, professor of science fiction. While these two books are mystery novels, most of the fun comes from the satirical treatment of fantasy and science-fiction authors and their zany fans. *Bimbos and Zombies* (Mystery Guild, 1997) is an omnibus volume containing both novels.

1. *Bimbos of the Death Sun* **(TSR, 1987)** Obnoxious Appin Dungannon, creator of the Viking warrior Tratyn Runewind, is gunned down at a fantasy convention, and his killer is unmasked in a game of Dungeons and Dragons.

2. *Zombies of the Gene Pool* **(Simon & Schuster, 1992)** The surviving Lanthanides, a group of science-fiction writers, return to the Tennessee farm where they buried a time capsule 30 years ago.

McCullough, Colleen

Colleen McCullough, author of the best-selling *The Thorn Birds* (Harper, 1977), temporarily abandoned her native Australian setting to write Masters of Rome, an epic re-creation of the declining years of the Roman Republic in the 1st and 2nd centuries BCE. The principal characters in the series are such historical figures as Cicero, Marius, Sulla, Pompey, Octavian, Cleopatra, Cato, Mark Antony, Brutus, and Julius Caesar. A psychologically believable, historically accurate, and gripping saga chock full of historical detail. McCullough returned to Australia with *Morgan's Run* (Simon & Schuster, 2000) and *The Touch* (Simon & Schuster, 2003).

1. *First Man in Rome, The* **(Morrow, 1990)** Gaius Marius and Lucius Cornelius Sulla are rivals for recognition as the First Man in Rome between 110 and 100 BCE.

2. *Grass Crown, The* **(Morrow, 1991)** Sulla and Marius continue their rivalry during the period of the Social War between Rome and other Italian city-states (90-88 BCE).

3. *Fortune's Favorites* **(Morrow, 1993)** Sulla retires after a three-year reign of terror, setting the stage for the rivalry between Pompey and Julius Caesar (83–60 BCE).

4. *Caesar's Women* **(Morrow, 1995)** Caesar takes center stage as he maneuvers his way to control of the Roman world, opposed primarily by the vacillating Cicero.

5. *Caesar: Let the Dice Fly* **(Morrow, 1997)** Caesar is still at center stage as he conquers Gaul, crosses the Rubicon, and defeats Pompey at Pharsalus (48 BCE).

6. *October Horse, The* **(Simon & Schuster, 2002)** The conclusion to the Masters of Rome series begins with Caesar as dictator of Rome and ends with his nephew Octavian (the future Augustus) in pursuit of Caesar's assassins (44 BCE).

7. *Antony and Cleopatra* **(Simon & Schuster, 2007)** Antony and Cleopatra have their famous romance as Antony battles Octavian for control of Rome.

McCutchan, Philip

I. This series of naval adventures, set in the 1890s, shows the British navy a century after Hornblower's time, still the mightiest of the world's fleets. The "gunboat diplomacy" of the times offers enough action to give Lieutenant St. Vincent Halfhyde plenty of adventure. True to form, Halfhyde is a brave and resourceful sailor, perhaps a shade too independent for his superior officers. This series is a little more lighthearted and humorous than other naval adventures. McCutchan (d. 1996), a prolific British author, wrote several other series, including the Ogilvie series written under the pseudonym Duncan MacNeil (q.v.) and the Assignment series written as Robert Conington Galway.

1. *Beware the Bight of Benin* **(St. Martin's, 1974)** Halfhyde is sent to spy on the Russian navy off the coast of West Africa. UK title: *Beware, Beware the Bight of Benin*. Variant title: *Halfhyde at the Bight of Benin*.

2. *Halfhyde's Island* **(St. Martin's, 1975)** Halfhyde races to claim a Pacific island that the Russian and Japanese navies have also set their sights on.

3. *Halfhyde and the Guns of Arrest* **(St. Martin's, 1976)** Aboard the battleship *Prince Consort*, Halfhyde is assigned to find and capture Sir Russell Savory, who fled England with top-secret naval blueprints.

4. *Halfhyde to the Narrows* **(St. Martin's, 1977)** Halfhyde has his first command; his mission is to rescue a British merchant ship from her Russian captors in the Black Sea.

5. *Halfhyde for the Queen* **(St. Martin's, 1978)** Halfhyde's investigation into a Spanish plot to assassinate Queen Victoria ends at breakfast with Her Majesty in the royal railway car.

6. *Halfhyde Ordered South* **(St. Martin's, 1980)** Halfhyde confronts the German navy over South American trading interests.

7. *Halfhyde and the Flag Captain* **(St. Martin's, 1981)** Halfhyde must rescue the British ambassador who has been jailed during an Uruguayan revolution.

8. *Halfhyde on the Yangtze* **(Weidenfeld [UK], 1981)** Halfhyde's assignment takes him to China. Not published in the United States.

9. *Halfhyde on Zanatu* **(St. Martin's, 1982)** Halfhyde is sent to the Pacific to secure the rebellious island colony of Zanatu against possible Russian interference.

10. *Halfhyde Outward Bound* (St. Martin's, 1984) On the half-pay list and unhappily married, Halfhyde ships out as a seaman on a windjammer cruise to Chile and Australia.

11. *Halfhyde Line, The* (St. Martin's, 1985) Halfhyde has dreams of starting a merchant fleet of his own, but comes to grief when his first voyage is pirated by an Irish arms smuggler.

12. *Halfhyde and the Chain Gangs* (St. Martin's, 1985) Back in service in the Boer War, Halfhyde is put in command of a transport of convicts bound for South Africa.

13. *Halfhyde Goes to War* (St. Martin's, 1987) Halfhyde is supposed to be guarding a consignment of naval gunnery and a shipment of gold bullion on the way to South Africa.

14. *Halfhyde on the Amazon* (St. Martin's, 1988) Halfhyde—back on his own ship, the *Taronga Park*, with Victoria, his foul-mouthed Australian mistress—is sent to spy on a German outpost on the Amazon River.

15. *Halfhyde and the Admiral* (St. Martin's, 1990) Halfhyde's voyage to Valparaiso, Chile, is part of a mission to rescue Admiral Watkiss, commander of the Chilean navy, who was once a British naval officer.

16. *Halfhyde and the Fleet Review* (St. Martin's, 1992) Halfhyde's merchant freighter has been ordered to the fleet review for Victoria's Jubilee at Cowes.

II. This naval action series is set during World War II. Donald Cameron, who serves in various capacities during the war, is a rather phlegmatic type unlike the roguish Halfhyde, but this series is also full of naval detail, stirring action, a large cast of characters, and a little painless history. McCutchan, like Cameron, served in the Royal Naval Volunteer Reserve during the war.

1. *Cameron: Ordinary Seaman* (Barker [UK], 1980) Donald Cameron volunteers for the British navy and becomes an ordinary seaman on HMS *Carmarthen*. Not published in the United States.

2. *Cameron Comes Through* (St. Martin's, 1986) Brand-new Sub-Lieutenant Cameron is assigned to the destroyer *Wharfedale* supplying the besieged island of Malta in 1941. Originally published in 1980.

3. *Cameron of the Castle Bay* (Barker [UK], 1981) Cameron's knowledge of the Norwegian coastline is invaluable as the *Castle Bay* is sent to destroy a secret Nazi base. Not published in the United States.

4. *Lieutenant Cameron RNVR* (St. Martin's, 1985) Lieutenant Cameron is second officer under old-line Captain Lees-Remington on a cruiser fighting the Germans in the South Atlantic. Originally published in 1981.

5. *Cameron's Convoy* (Barker [UK], 1982) Shipping aboard the frigate *Sprinter*, Cameron is part of a convoy on the Archangel run. Not published in the United States.

6. *Cameron in the Gap* (St. Martin's, 1983) Cameron, serving aboard the destroyer *Burnside*, is part of the naval escort protecting a convoy to Malta.

7. *Orders for Cameron* (St. Martin's, 1983) Serving aboard the corvette *Oleander*, Cameron takes part in Operation Torch, the 1942 Allied invasion of North Africa.

8. *Cameron in Command* (St. Martin's, 1984) Given his first command, the corvette *Briar*, Lieutenant Commander Cameron is sent to protect the Falkland Islands from Japanese attack.

9. *Cameron and the Kaiserhof* (St. Martin's, 1984) Out of the water temporarily, Cameron is sent to neutral Spain to hijack the *Kaiserhof*, a liner being converted into a mother ship for mini-submarines.

10. *Cameron's Raid* (St. Martin's, 1985) Cameron is in command of one of three old P-class destroyers sent to destroy U-boat pens being built in Brest in occupied France.

11. *Cameron's Chase* (St. Martin's, 1986) Cameron, skipper of HMS *Glenshiel*, is part of a destroyer flotilla chasing *Attica*, the German navy's newest, most powerful battleship.

12. *Cameron's Troop Lift* (St. Martin's, 1987) Away from the Atlantic in the Bay of Bengal, Cameron decides to intercept a Japanese liner carrying British POWs.

13. *Cameron's Commitment* (St. Martin's, 1989) Cameron takes on a contingent of Royal Marines to carry out a secret mission: rescuing a British leader of a Resistance group from France.

14. *Cameron's Crossing* (St. Martin's, 1993) Commander Cameron takes passage on the escort carrier HMS *Charger* sailing from Belfast to Norfolk, Virginia.

III. Commander John Mason Kemp is the hero of another World War II British navy series. Kemp's cruise liner has been transformed into a troop carrier, and Kemp has become a commodore in the navy. A convoy vessel provides different problems than a combat vessel, but we still have plenty of action and a stiff-upper-lipped protagonist.

1. *Convoy Commodore, The* (St. Martin's, 1987) Kemp leads a nearly empty convoy to Halifax, Nova Scotia, and returns with ships filled with supplies and troops through U-boat-infested waters.

2. *Convoy North* (St. Martin's, 1988) Kemp is in charge of a troop convoy from Australia to America and a mysterious canvas bag holding intelligence for the American military.

3. *Convoy South* (St. Martin's, 1988) Involves a convoy carrying Australian soldiers to America, and a civilian official who is overly curious about Japanese activity in the Pacific.

4. *Convoy East* (St. Martin's, 1989) Kemp leads a convoy from Britain to Malta transporting British troops and supplies and a passel of WRENS (women sailors).

5. *Convoy of Fear* (St. Martin's, 1990) Kemp's convoy crosses the Mediterranean, sails through the Suez Canal, and on to Ceylon fighting the Axis, cholera, and typhoons.

6. *Convoy Homeward* (St. Martin's, 1992) On a convoy from India to Scotland, Kemp is burdened by German POWs, British expatriates, and a slightly demented brigadier.

IV. Tom Chatto, a 16-year-old from the West of Ireland, goes to England and becomes an apprentice seaman and eventually becomes an officer in the Royal Navy Volunteer Reserve in the first year of World War I. McCutchan's death limited this last series to three volumes.

1. *Apprentice to the Sea* (St. Martin's, 1995) In the 1890s young Tom Chatto travels from Ireland to England and is apprenticed to the commercial barque *Pass of Drumochter*, one of the few sailing ships left in the merchant marine. UK title: *Tom Chatto, Apprentice*.

2. *Second Mate, The* (St. Martin's, 1996) Armed with his Master's Certificate of Competency, Chatto becomes second officer on the newfangled steamship *Orvega*, which is making a voyage round Cape Horn. UK title: *Tom Chatto, Second Mate*.

3. *New Lieutenant, The* (St. Martin's, 1997) In the first year of World War I, Tom joins the Royal Navy Reserve and becomes navigator and third officer of an armed decoy battling U-boats in the Mediterranean. UK title: *Tom Chatto, RVR*.

V. McCutchan also authored a well-regarded espionage series set in the cold war featuring Commander Esmonde Shaw, initially of Naval Intelligence, but later of the semiofficial counterspy organization known as 6D2. Somewhat less flamboyant than, say, Ian Fleming's (q.v.) James Bond, Commander Shaw, a highly competent operative, gets involved with many a terrorist plot and much high-tech derring-do. Only the first half of the series was published in the United States. Many of the titles are listed without annotations.

1. *Gibraltar Road* (Berkley, 1965) Commander Shaw is sent to look for the physicist Ackroyd, who is the key to a nuclear sub network based on Gibraltar. Originally published in 1960.
2. *Redcap* (Berkley, 1965) Redcap is the code name for a nuclear project. Shaw is on the trail of Lubin, who is the crucial liaison to this apocalyptic project. Originally published in 1961.
3. *Bluebolt One* (Berkley, 1965) An African voodoo coven and a nuclear system controlled by an Anglo-American radio network in Nogalia, West Africa, are the keys to the action here. Originally published in 1962.
4. *Man from Moscow, The* (John Day, 1965) No annotation available. Originally published in 1963.
5. *Warmaster* (John Day, 1964) The liquidation of a US naval intelligence operative brings Commander Shaw to New York pursuing a lead linked to a Brooklyn-based packaging complex. Originally published in 1963.
6. *Moscow Coach* (John Day, 1966) A coach tour to Russia is the basis for this thriller. Originally published in 1964.
7. *Dead Line, The* (Berkley, 1966) No annotation available.
8. *Skyprobe* (John Day, 1967) Shaw scotches a threat to Skyprobe IV, a US spacecraft in his final mission for Special Services.
9. *Screaming Dead Balloons, The* (John Day, 1968) In his first mission for 6D2, Shaw is ordered to liquidate a megalomaniacal Maltese scientist who has developed a venomous fungus with lethal potential.
10. *Bright Red Businessmen, The* (John Day, 1969) No annotation available.
11. *All-Purpose Bodies, The* (John Day, 1969) Commander Shaw investigates the disappearance of Jake Dunwoodie, renowned Australian scientist.
12. *Hartinger's Mouse* (Harrap [UK], 1970) No annotation available.
13. *This Drakotny . . .* (Harrap [UK], 1971) No annotation available.
14. *Sunstrike* (Hodder [UK], 1979) No annotation available.
15. *Corpse* (Hodder [UK], 1980) No annotation available.
16. *Werewolf* (Hodder [UK], 1982) No annotation available.
17. *Rollerball* (Hodder [UK], 1984) No annotation available.
18. *Greenfly* (Hodder [UK], 1987) No annotation available.
19. *Boy Who Liked Monsters, The* (Hodder [UK], 1989) The grandson of a US arms-reduction negotiator has been kidnapped by the Soviet old guard who wish to thwart Glasnost.
20. *Spatchcock Plan, The* (Hodder [UK], 1990) Commander Shaw has to rescue his kidnapped colleague, Felicity Mandrake, from the friends of a Libyan terrorist in Pentonville.
21. *Polecat Brennan* (Hodder [UK], 1994) The French and British foreign ministers and hundreds of other people are targeted in a terrorist act in the Channel Tunnel.
22. *Burn Out* (Hodder [UK], 1995) The reappearance of notorious "Skin" Halloran in England alerts 6D2 to a conspiracy involving Arab terrorists and oil.

VI. Detective Chief Superintendent Simon Shard of Scotland Yard, seconded to the Foreign Office on special duty, is the hero of another espionage series. Like Commander Shaw, Shard travels a good deal, and often gets involved with terrorist plots. This series, which has not been published in the United States, is listed without annotations.

1. *Call for Simon Shard* (Harrap [UK], 1974)
2. *Very Big Bang, A* (Hodder [UK], 1975)
3. *Blood Run East* (Hodder [UK], 1976)
4. *Eros Affair, The* (Hodder [UK], 1977)
5. *Blackmail North* (Hodder [UK], 1978)
6. *Shard Calls the Tune* (Hodder [UK], 1981)
7. *Hoof, The* (Hodder [UK], 1983)
8. *Shard at Bay* (Hodder [UK], 1985)
9. *Executioners, The* (Hodder [UK], 1986)
10. *Overnight Express* (Hodder [UK], 1988)
11. *Logan File, The* (Hodder [UK], 1991)
12. *Abbot of Stockbridge, The* (Hodder [UK], 1992)
13. *Kidnap* (Hodder [UK], 1993)

McDermid, Val

I. Kate Brannigan is a hard-boiled PI working out of Manchester, England. Kate has been described as Sue Grafton's (q.v.) Kinsey Millhone with "a more demanding palate" (she likes Chinese food as well as the sport of kickboxing). The likable English Midlands detective has a rock journalist boyfriend named Richard (who is eventually killed off) and a specialty in ferreting out computer fraud. Scottish native McDermid, who was a journalist for 16 years before she became a full-time mystery writer, lives in South Manchester, England. She has also published *A Suitable Job for a Woman: Inside the World of Women Private Eyes* (Poisoned Pen, 1999; originally 1994), a collection of interviews with real female private investigators.

1. *Dead Beat* (St. Martin's, 1993) Kate is hired by rock legend Jett to locate his former partner and lover Moira.
2. *Kick Back* (St. Martin's, 1993) Conservatory builder Ted Barlow hires Kate to investigate the case of a disappearing greenhouse. Variant title: *Kickback*.
3. *Crack Down* (Scribner, 1994) Brannigan and Richard go undercover to investigate fraud in auto sales. Variant title: *Crackdown*.
4. *Clean Break* (Scribner, 1995) Kate's security system has been breached and a valuable Monet painting stolen.
5. *Blue Genes* (Scribner, 1996) Still mourning the loss of her lover, Richard, Kate is hired by two Glaswegian musicians to find out who is sending goons to break up their shows.
6. *Star Struck* (Bloody Brits, 2006) After Kate reluctantly takes on the job of bodyguarding a paranoid soap star, the self-styled "Seer to the Stars" is murdered. Originally published in the United Kingdom in 1998.

II. Lindsay Gordon is a Scottish lesbian, feminist, and socialist journalist. Lindsay has to balance journalism, amateur sleuthing and her personal relationships in this series of well-plotted mysteries. Only numbers 1 and 3 had been published in the United States before Spinsters Ink reprinted numbers 1 through 5, numbers 3 and 4 with new titles.

1. *Report for Murder* (St. Martin's, 1987) Cellist Lorna Smith-Couper, star attraction at a gala fund-raising concert at an English girls' school, is murdered moments before she is due onstage.
2. *Common Murder* (Spinsters Ink, 1995) Lindsay covers a women's peace group's protest at a missile base, and finds an ex-lover accused of murder and other crimes. Originally published in the United Kingdom in 1989.
3. *Open and Shut* (St. Martin's, 1991) Alison Maxwell is found strangled in Glasgow, and her ex-lover Jackie Mitchell is convicted of murder, but Jackie's and Lindsay's friends dispute the verdict. UK title: *Final Edition*. Reprinted in 1997 by Spinsters Ink as *Deadline for Murder*.
4. *Conferences Are Murder* (Spinsters Ink, 1999) Nine years after the events in number 3, Lindsay finds herself back in Britain and, reluctantly, in the nasty world of union politics. Lindsay is

the prime suspect when homophobic union boss Tom Jack falls out her hotel-room window. Originally published in 1993 in the United Kingdom as *Union Jack*.

5. *Booked for Murder* (**Spinsters Ink, 2000**) The death of best-selling author Penny Varnavides during a trip to London to see her publishers seems to be a freak accident until it is discovered that a character in her novel-in-progress was killed the same way. Originally published in the United Kingdom in 1996.

6. *Hostage to Murder* (**Bywater, 2005**) Jobless in Glasgow, Lindsay sprains her ankle, but the seeming misfortune leads to a new chapter in her life in the person of freelance journalist Rory McLaren. Originally published in the United Kingdom in 2003.

III. McDermid's third series, regarded by some critics as her breakthrough series, is darker, more complex, and more disturbing than her first two. Detective Chief Inspector Carol Jordan and psychological profiler Dr. Tony Hill of the fictional city of Bradfield in northern England, are the main characters. Tony, who has problems of sexual impotence, and Carol are brought together and separated more than once by cases involving serial murderers. *The Writing on the Wall and Other Stories* is a limited edition collection of short stories published by Revolver (UK), 1997. She has also published three stand-alone (so far) novels: *A Place of Execution* (St. Martin's, 2000); *Killing the Shadows* (St. Martin's, 2001); and *The Distant Echo* (St. Martin's, 2003).

1. *Mermaids Singing, The* (**St. Martin's, 1995**) When four men are killed and mutilated in Bradfield, seemingly by the same person, the police reluctantly call in Tony Hill, Home Office forensic psychologist who profiles criminals, and he forms a partnership with Detective Carol Jordan.

2. *Wire in the Blood, The* (**St. Martin's, 1997**) Now heading up the recently formed National Profiling Task Force, Dr. Hill sets his team an exercise in which they are given details about 30 missing teenagers and asked to see if they can find any links between the cases.

3. *Last Temptation, The* (**St. Martin's, 2002**) Jordan goes undercover to Germany as part of a dangerous operation to capture Tadeuz Radecki, international smuggler of narcotics and aliens.

4. *Torment of Others, The* (**St. Martin's, 2004**) Back in Bradfield, Carol is surprised to discover that Tony has taken a job at the local "secure" mental hospital. They are brought together when a prostitute is murdered in a manner reminiscent of the crimes for which Brock Tyler was convicted some years earlier.

McDonald, Gregory

I. Smart-mouthed reporter-adventurer Irwin Maurice Fletcher (Fletch to his friends) is a joy to read about. Though his heart is always in the right place, his methods frequently go beyond the strictly legal—he knows how to counterblackmail CIA agents, for instance, to his own advantage. He can tap his newspaper connections for information and is assured prominent press coverage when he wants it. Fletch likes liberated ladies and dislikes IRS agents curious about the source of his—largely undeclared—income in Swiss bank accounts, but he remains unflappable and witty no matter what. Chevy Chase has played Fletch in two movies, *Fletch* (1985) and *Fletch Lives* (1989), which is not based on any of the Fletch novels. A three-volume omnibus called *The Fletch Chronicles* was published by Hill in 1987–1988. Volume 1 contains numbers 1, 2, and 7. Volume 2 contains numbers 3, 4, and 5. Volume 3 contains numbers 6, 8, and 9. Numbers 1 and 2 are prequels. Numbers 10 and 11 are sometimes listed separately as the Son of Fletch series.

1. *Fletch Won* (**Warner, 1985**) When lawyer-philanthropist Donald Habek is killed, fledgling reporter Fletch sees a chance to beat out crime reporter Bill Wilson for front-page bylines.

2. *Fletch Too* (**Warner, 1986**) When Fletch marries Barbara, he receives an invitation from someone purporting to be his long-missing father to meet him in Kenya.

3. *Fletch* (**Bobbs-Merrill, 1974**) Introduces newspaperman Fletch, who investigates the California beach drug scene and is offered a job of murder.

4. *Carioca Fletch* (**Warner, 1984**) Holidaying in Rio de Janeiro, Fletch turns out to be a dead ringer for a Brazilian fisherman murdered 47 years ago.

5. *Confess, Fletch* (**Avon, 1976**) Fletch finds a naked dead woman in a friend's Boston apartment, where he is staying, and becomes the prime suspect of Inspector Flynn.

6. *Fletch's Fortune* (**Avon, 1978**) The CIA persuades Fletch to do a little bedroom bugging at a journalist's convention, and the case turns into the biggest murder story of the decade.

7. *Fletch and the Widow Bradley* (**Warner, 1981**) Fletch is in trouble with his newspaper for quoting the "recent" memos of a man who has been dead for two years—or has he?

8. *Fletch's Moxie* (**Warner, 1982**) "Moxie" is Moxie Mooney, a movie star who is the prime suspect in the talk-show murder of agent Steve Peterman.

9. *Fletch and the Man Who* (**Warner, 1983**) Fletch, working as press secretary for presidential candidate Caxton Wheeler, investigates the murder of three young women during the campaign.

10. *Son of Fletch* (**Putnam, 1993**) Fletch becomes abruptly aware of a hitherto unknown son, Jack, product of a one-night stand some 20 years ago.

11. *Fletch Reflected* (**Putnam, 1994**) Son Jack costars with Fletch in an adventure that takes place in the wilds of Wyoming and the Georgia estate of billionaire inventor Chester Radleigh.

II. Flynn, the Boston policeman, was such an engaging character in *Confess, Fletch* that McDonald has given him four books of his own to star in. As the series progresses, it is revealed that "Inspector Flynn" is really the cover name for superagent N.N.13. In *Flynn*, the Fletch connection is mentioned, though he never appears in the book.

1. *Flynn* (**Avon, 1977**) A Boeing 707 carrying some very important people explodes above Boston Harbor seconds before it was to land, and Inspector Flynn is showered with falling human debris.

2. *Buck Passes Flynn, The* (**Ballantine, 1981**) Flynn's Boston police job turns out to be just a cover for his more serious efforts as the superagent N.N.13 working for the mysterious "little man" on a case where sudden riches seem to be changing the lives of a lot of people.

3. *Flynn's In* (**Mysterious, 1984**) A murder at the elite Rod and Gun Club challenges Flynn to find the killer without publicizing the case.

4. *Flynn's World* (**Pantheon, 2003**) N.N.13 is believed dead by most players in the espionage game, but Inspector Flynn is still living in Boston with his poet wife and their five children and dealing with such puzzles as a human ear nailed to a tree, the harassment of a Harvard professor, and the politically incorrect arrest record of a rising police star.

III. A pair of novels deals with Skylar Whitfield, scion of a family from Greensdown County, Tennessee, who would prefer to be a farmer; who is supposedly "catnip" to women; and is supposedly masking his intelligence behind a cornpone exterior. Some readers feel that the cuteness and "aw-shucks" southern charm is overdone. Others are attracted by the smart dialogue and the contrast between the down-home Skylar and his effete Yankee relatives.

1. *Skylar* (Morrow, 1995) When Greensdown County beauty queen Mary Lou Simes is battered to death, Skylar becomes the prime suspect.
2. *Skylar in Yankeeland* (Morrow, 1996) Skylar goes north to Boston to study trumpet at a music school, and makes his wealthy Yankee kinsfolk wince at his uninhibited folksiness.

IV. McDonald also writes mainstream fiction, including these three books, which are part of a proposed Time-Savored Quartet about a group of people who come together in Paris during the 1950s. The main protagonist is David MacFarlane, a jazz pianist and composer. The fourth book, tentatively titled *Wise Saws*, hasn't been published.

1. *Merely Players* (Hill, 1988) David MacFarlane, Janet Twombly, and other characters come together in Paris during the 1950s.
2. *World Too Wide, A* (Hill, 1987) The upcoming marriage of children of old friends prompts David MacFarlane to propose a reunion of the group from the 1950s.
3. *Exits and Entrances* (Hill, 1988) Contains seven stories illustrating Shakespeare's Seven Ages of Man.

McDonald, Kay L.

Oregon native Kay L. McDonald has written a trilogy of historical novels about the first permanent white settlement in Oregon in the 1840s. The protagonist is Ross Chesnut, a white man raised by Indians, who becomes a guide for explorers and settlers. This is a good adventure series with some historical characters and events woven in.

1. *Vision of the Eagle* (Crowell, 1977) Abigail Whitteker, traveling west from New York to St. Louis in the early 1800s, is captured by Indians. Her son is raised by Sioux Indians under the name of White Eagle.
2. *Brightwood Expedition, The* (Liveright, 1976) In 1842 an Indian attack on an expedition exploring mountain trails to Oregon leaves two survivors, Marlette Brightwood and the guide, Ross Chesnut, aka White Eagle.
3. *Vision Is Fulfilled, The* (Walker, 1983) Ross Chesnut leads a wagon train over the Oregon Trail to Oregon and tragedy strikes in the form of a small-pox epidemic.

McGehee, Peter

The adventures of Zero MacNoo, Arkansan transplanted into Toronto's gay community, are alternately funny and sad. A clutch of vivid, zany characters living out their lives under the darkening shadow of AIDS is delineated with humor and sensitivity. Peter McGehee died of AIDS himself just before the publication of *Sweetheart*. Doug Wilson (Peter's lover who died of AIDS in 1992) continued his characters in *Labour of Love* (St. Martin's, 1993).

1. *Boys Like Us* (St. Martin's, 1991) When Zero MacNoo's best friend is diagnosed with AIDS, Zero belatedly realizes his true feelings for him but still can't stay faithful.
2. *Sweetheart* (St. Martin's, 1992) Zero meets Jeff at an AIDS research benefit and attends a riotous Arkansas wedding.

3. *Labour of Love* (St. Martin's, 1993) Zero is the central character and his lover, David, the narrator of this novel written by Doug Wilson. Although the subject, Zero's death from AIDS, is a grim one, there are many lighter touches and zany characters, such as the lesbian ménage-à-trois the Bermuda Triangle and a Socialist transvestite named Searcy.

McGown, Jill

Detective Chief Inspector Lloyd (he prefers not to use his first name) and his partner and lover, Sergeant (later Detective) Judy Hill, star in a series of intricately plotted procedurals by Scottish author McGown. Hill and Lloyd's sometimes tempestuous relationship (he is a husband and a father) is integrated with the action of this series of well-characterized mysteries set in the fictional English town of Stansfield.

1. *Perfect Match, A* (St. Martin's, 1983) A young woman is found murdered in a boathouse. The main suspect had spent the night drinking and is not being very cooperative or coherent.
2. *Murder at the Old Vicarage* (St. Martin's, 1989) The dysfunctional family of George Wheeler, vicar of Byford, provides the chief suspects when George's abusive son-in-law is murdered. UK title: *Redemption*.
3. *Gone to Her Death* (St. Martin's, 1990) The nymphomaniac wife of the deputy headmaster of an English school is found raped and murdered. UK title: *Death of a Dancer*.
4. *Murders of Mrs. Austin and Mrs. Beale, The* (St. Martin's, 1991) Lennie Austin, gifted, free-spirited artist, has her head bashed in, and her husband, a wealthy candidate for Parliament, may be implicated.
5. *Other Woman, The* (St. Martin's, 1993) Reporter Melissa Whitworth is working on a story about illicit love affairs when she realizes that she is interviewing her husband's mistress.
6. *Murder . . . Now and Then* (St. Martin's, 1993) The same circle of acquaintances is implicated in murders committed 13 years apart.
7. *Shred of Evidence, A* (Fawcett, 1996) After Natalie Ouspensky, a 15-year-old high school student, is found strangled near a public park, the rather lascivious goings-on among students and faculty at Oakland School are gradually uncovered.
8. *Verdict Unsafe* (Fawcett, 1996) Sexual predator Colin Drummond has been acquitted of several rape charges on technicalities. Now he is free to stalk his former victims and Judy Hill, who had arrested him.
9. *Picture of Innocence* (Fawcett, 1998) There are a number of suspects, including his battered second wife and grown daughter, when East Midlands farmer and landowner Bernard Bailey is murdered.
10. *Plots and Errors* (Ballantine, 1999) When Andrew Cope and his ex-policewoman wife, Kathy, are found dead in their exhaust-fume-filled car, Lloyd, who had worked with Kathy, doubts the verdict of suicide.
11. *Scene of Crime* (Ballantine, 2001) Lloyd and the pregnant Hill are attending a rehearsal of a local drama society's production of *Cinderella* when Lloyd is called away to investigate the suspicious death of the wife of one of the players.
12. *Death in the Family* (Ballantine, 2003) Hill and her fiancé, Lloyd, are enjoying their newborn daughter while she pursues a baby kidnapping case and he investigates a murder. UK title: *Births, Deaths, and Marriages*.

13. *Unlucky for Some* (Ballantine, 2005) Wilma Fenton, flush with her biggest-ever bingo win, dies at the hands of someone lurking in the dimly lit alleyway leading to her floor.

McIlvanney, William

"Black Jack Laidlaw, the mad detective," as his peers in the Glasgow, Scotland, police department dub him, is overcast with Calvinistic guilt feelings and existential angst over the loss of his idealism. Glasgow, home to author McIlvanney, is as much a protagonist as Jack Laidlaw in this thoughtful, melancholy series.

1. *Laidlaw* (Pantheon, 1977) Introduces Jack Laidlaw, who keeps Kierkegaard and Camus in his desk drawer and a bottle of whiskey handy nearby; his mistress, Jan; and his young colleague Harkness.
2. *Papers of Tony Veitch, The* (Pantheon, 1983) Alcoholic vagrant Eck Adamson, who had a message to deliver to Laidlaw, is killed before he can pass it on.
3. *Strange Loyalties* (Morrow, 1992) In despair at the death in traffic of his younger brother, Jack investigates and turns up some unpleasant revelations.

McInerny, Ralph

I. McInerny's Father Roger Dowling is a conservative (like his creator, he lacks enthusiasm for Vatican II) but compassionate Roman Catholic priest whose depressing early years serving on the archdiocesan marriage court led to a bout with alcoholism. Reformed and assigned to shepherd the sleepy little parish of St. Hilary's in Fox River, Illinois, his tolerant and slightly world-weary nature wins him a faithful following. His renewed acquaintance with Phil Keegan, now the town's chief of detectives, involves him in a series of mysteries. Catholic readers will find this modern successor to G. K. Chesterton's Father Brown a special treat. Father Dowling was featured in a network television series starring Tom Bosley that offended purists by giving Dowling a young nun assistant. McInerny also writes the popular Sister Mary Teresa novels under the pseudonym Monica Quill (q.v.).

1. *Her Death of Cold* (Vanguard, 1977) A rich, frightened widow phones Father Dowling in the middle of the night, then disappears and is feared murdered.
2. *Seventh Station, The* (Vanguard, 1977) Father Dowling goes on a retreat and finds a corpse stabbed with an ice pick on the lawn his first morning.
3. *Bishop as Pawn* (Vanguard, 1978) The return of a prodigal housekeeper and the kidnapping of a bishop are Father Dowling's concerns here.
4. *Lying Three* (Vanguard, 1979) A young Catholic woman is involved in the murder of a Jewish fund-raiser.
5. *Second Vespers* (Vanguard, 1980) Phyllis O'Rourke, heiress to her writer-brother's mansion and royalties, is found murdered in her swimming pool.
6. *Thicker Than Water* (Vanguard, 1981) A dead body is found in a truck parked in front of the rectory.
7. *Loss of Patients, A* (Vanguard, 1982) Four apparent suicides within a few weeks in Fox River arouse the suspicions of Father Dowling and Captain Keegan.
8. *Grass Widow, The* (Vanguard, 1983) Clare O'Leary tells Father Dowling that her radio-personality husband, Larry, plans to have her killed.

9. *Getting a Way with Murder* (Vanguard, 1984) Insurance executive Howard Downs, acquitted of his wife's murder, confesses to Father Dowling that he killed his defense attorney.
10. *Rest in Pieces* (Vanguard, 1985) Father Dowling is asked to give asylum to a member of a political family in Costa Verde, a Central American nation gripped by revolution.
11. *Basket Case, The* (St. Martin's, 1987) A baby is left in a basket at Father Dowling's church by a woman trying to accuse her ex-husband of plotting to kidnap it.
12. *Abracadaver* (St. Martin's, 1989) After a magician entertaining an elderly audience at the parish center borrows a ring from Aggie Miller for one of his tricks, Aggie is murdered. UK title: *Sleight of Body*.
13. *Four on the Floor* (St. Martin's, 1989) A collection of Dowling short stories.
14. *Judas Priest* (St. Martin's, 1991) Sonya, daughter of televangelist of sexual liberation Chris Bourke, is murdered before she can talk to Father Dowling.
15. *Desert Sinner* (St. Martin's, 1992) Dowling and Police Captain Phil Keegan disagree about the guilty verdict handed down to former showgirl Stacey Wilson for the murder of her wealthy husband.
16. *Seed of Doubt* (St. Martin's, 1993) When wealthy Margaret Sinclair dies unexpectedly, she leaves her fortune to set up a foundation and her diary to her great-granddaughter.
17. *Cardinal Offense, A* (St. Martin's, 1994) To attend the Notre Dame–USC football game, Dowling will also have to attend a meeting of the controversial Committee on Marriage and the Family.
18. *Tears of Things, The* (St. Martin's, 1996) Jerome Winegar returns to Fox River, still bitter about his experiences there 20 years ago. His reappearance sparks a chain of events culminating in the murder of pillar of the community Mitchell Striker.
19. *Grave Undertakings* (St. Martin's, 2000) Local mobster Vincent O'Toole is no sooner dead and buried than someone is trying to dig him up. His coffin is found empty.
20. *Triple Pursuit* (St. Martin's, 2001) Was it an accident when a young woman is struck down in traffic? A senior center with some amorous old men competing for the same woman also engages Father Dowling's attention.
21. *Prodigal Father* (St. Martin's, 2002) Father Dowling is on his annual retreat with the near-extinct Athanasian order when they are willed the rich estate of Marygrove together with the ill-will of the testator's surviving relatives.
22. *Last Things* (St. Martin's, 2003) The children of wealthy and fatally ill patriarch Fulvio Bernardo have been a grave disappointment to him, especially Raymond, the eldest, a priest who ran off to California with a nun. A tenure battle at St. Edmund's, the local college, leads to the murder of brilliant, arrogant Horst Cassirer.
23. *Requiem for a Realtor* (St. Martin's, 2004) After confiding to Father Dowling that his wife is having an affair with a dentist, Realtor Stanley Collins turns up dead in the parking lot of a popular nightspot.
24. *Blood Ties* (St. Martin's, 2005) Martha Lynch seeks to learn the identity of her birth mother on the eve of her engagement. Nathaniel Fleck is determined to learn the fate of his illegitimate child and make amends.
25. *Prudence of the Flesh, The* (St. Martin's, 2006) Popular NPR personality Gregory Barrett is accused of fathering a child with Madeline Murphy decades ago.
26. *Widow's Mate, The* (St. Martin's, 2007) Some years after he disappeared after receiving a large gift of money, Wallace Flanagan is found, his body mangled by a cement mixer belonging to the Flanagan family business.

II. Another mystery series is set at the University of Notre Dame, where McInerny has been a distinguished faculty member for many years. The brothers Knight, private investigator Philip and UND philosophy professor Roger, form a sort of Archie Godwin–Nero Wolfe team (Rex Stout [q.v.]) as they investigate a series of murders, some of them the result of the politicking and backbiting that seems to be endemic to academic institutions. The Notre Dame series, as indicated by the punning titles, are light and clever, on a par with the Father Dowling books. McInerny is known in philosophical circles for his books on St. Thomas Aquinas (e.g., *Ethica Thomistica: The Moral Philosophy of Thomas Aquinas*; rev. ed. Catholic University, 1997) and Jacques Maritain (*The Very Rich Hours of Jacques Maritain: A Spiritual Life*; Notre Dame, 2003) among others. He has also written a controversial defense of Pope Pius XII: *The Defamation of Pius XII* (St. Augustine's, 2001).

1. *On This Rockne* (St. Martin's, 1997) When billionaire alumnus Marcus Bramble offers the University of Notre Dame $10 million to erect a memorial to coaching great Knute Rockne, he arouses a great deal of controversy, which apparently leads to the murder of trustee Madeline Rune.
2. *Lack of the Irish* (St. Martin's, 1999) While Catholic power Notre Dame and Baptist power Baylor University square off on the football field for the first time, Hazel Noolin, a disliked bureaucrat at UND, is murdered.
3. *Irish Tenure* (St. Martin's, 1999) Two young philosophy professors, Amanda Pick and Hans Wiener, are vying for the single tenured position open in their department in this mystery, which has something to say about Catholic writer G. K. Chesterton, creator of the Father Brown mystery stories.
4. *Book of Kills, The* (St. Martin's, 2000) Are several pranks, including the kidnapping of the chancellor, connected to the Native American claim that the ground Notre Dame sits upon belongs to them?
5. *Emerald Aisle* (St. Martin's, 2001) Some rare literary documents are missing, and Dolores Torre and Larry Morton, now marrying other people, are vying for the reservation at the campus rectory made six years previously when they expected to marry each other.
6. *Celt and Pepper* (St. Martin's, 2002) A squabble over the proposed Malachy O'Neill Center of Catholic Literature turns sinister when Irish poet Martin Kilmartin, who had been proposed for the directorship, dies suspiciously.
7. *Irish Coffee* (St. Martin's, 2003) When assistant sports information director and aspiring writer Fred Neville dies mysteriously in bed, some odd secrets are turned up: not least that he was secretly engaged to at least two women.
8. *Green Thumb* (St. Martin's, 2004) The Knight brothers dig up dirt about the class of 1977 when a Notre Dame alumnus and benefactor drops dead on the golf course.
9. *Irish Gilt* (St. Martin's, 2005) Roger and Philip seek the missing diaries of Fr. John Zahn, an almost forgotten 19th-century theologian, which purport to shed light on the search for El Dorado.
10. *Letter Killeth, The* (St, Martin's, 2006) The football coach, an English professor, the provost, and the dean of arts and letters at Notre Dame all receive alarming bomb-threat letters.
11. *Irish Alibi* (St. Martin's, 2007) When Notre Dame faces Georgia Tech on the football field, two students seeking revenge for the South against Notre Dame's stand during the Civil War commit a prank that could lead to their expulsion, and their alibi makes them prime suspects when a woman is found murdered in a local motel.

III. Another trio of academic novels, not listed as a series, stars Matthew Rogerson, a customarily mild and genial humanities professor at Fort Elbow College in Ohio, whose rebellion causes a marvelous havoc on campus. Only the third Rogerson novel is a mystery, but McInerny has introduced Egidio Manfredi, detective near retirement, in charge of special projects at Fort Elbow, Ohio, and Noonan, his much younger partner, in a pair of novels.

1. *Jolly Rogerson* (Doubleday, 1967) After 20 years of teaching, Professor Rogerson decides that he is a failure, gives up being conventional and cooperative, and winds up winning the Teacher of the Year award.
2. *Rogerson at Bay* (Harper, 1976) Professor Rogerson negotiates various midlife crises with irreverence and contagious good humor.
3. *Search Committee, The* (Atheneum, 1991) Potential successors to disgraced Chancellor Laplace of the Fort Elbow campus are being poisoned.
4. *Still Life* (Five Star, 2001) Egidio Manfredi and his partner, Noonan, get involved in an unsolved missing-persons case when they are contacted by graduate student Virginia, who is working on papers left by the long-missing poet wife of emeritus professor Basil Bauer.
5. *Sub Rosa* (Five Star, 2001) Rosa Subiaco, unattractive, murdering romance-novel writer, has picked as her latest victim a rather sweet elderly man who has a winning $50 million lottery ticket in his pocket.

IV. Another mystery series features Andrew Broom, lawyer in the small city of Wyler, Indiana (based on South Bend). As with his other series, the novels are lively, touched with humor, and full of odd characters.

1. *Cause and Effect* (Atheneum, 1987) Love triangles are the basis for two nefarious plots, one of them designed to drive Andrew Broom to suicide.
2. *Body and Soil* (Atheneum, 1989) The family farm of Leo Barany holds a grisly secret, while Broom and his nephew Gerald Rowan are on opposite sides in a divorce case.
3. *Savings and Loam* (Atheneum, 1990) The abrupt departure of its German American owner in the early forties may have a connection with the murder of the new owner of a vacant farmhouse.
4. *Mom and Dead* (Atheneum, 1994) Wyler, Indiana, is the scene of a complicated mess of murder, drugs, politics, bingo, land deals, lust, and a human skull found buried on the riverbank.
5. *Law and Ardor* (Scribner, 1995) Wealthy investor Edgar Bissonet dies on an apparent heart attack on the seventh fairway of a local country club.
6. *Heirs and Parents* (St. Martin's, 2000) The murder of Helga Bjornson, college student and Broom's summer intern, may be connected with the appearance of her nude image on pornographic websites.

McMurtry, Larry

I. Although he no longer wears his "Minor Regional Novelist" sweatshirt and has written novels about other parts of the world, Larry McMurtry is indelibly associated with the state of Texas. His first six novels and many subsequent ones are set in primarily in Texas, as are the movies made from his novels such as *Hud* (1963), made from *Horseman, Pass By*.

Archer City, the north central Texas town where McMurtry grew up, and to which he has returned to establish a mammoth used-book store, is the model for Thalia, the fictional town that is the setting for a trio of widely spaced novels. *The Last Picture Show* is about growing up in a bleak small town where sports and sex are the only outlets for adolescent energies. *Texasville* returns to Thalia 30 years later when the town is demoralized by a sudden economic downturn. In *Duane's Depressed* the alienated protagonist more or less abandons his family and the town. The film version of *The Last Pic-+ture Show* (1971), which was shot in Archer City, won Academy awards for Cloris Leachman and Ben Johnson. The film version of *Texasville* (1990) was considerably less successful. Thalia plays a peripheral role in McMurtry's first two novels: *Horseman, Pass By* (Harper, 1961) and *Leaving Cheyenne* (Harper, 1963).

1. *Last Picture Show, The* (Dial, 1966) High school student Sonny Crawford, his best buddy, Duane Jackson, and Duane's girlfriend, Jacy Farrow, learn about life and love in 1950s Thalia, Texas.
2. *Texasville* (Simon & Schuster, 1987) Duane Jackson, onetime oil millionaire now on the verge of bankruptcy, is jolted when his high school sweetheart Jacy, now a movie actress, returns to Thalia.
3. *Duane's Depressed* (Simon & Schuster, 1999) Oil-rich leading citizen Duane Moore, depressed for no obvious reason, turns his business over to his recently detoxed eldest son, Archie, and does other eccentric things, such as walking instead of driving and consulting a psychoanalyst in Wichita Falls.
4. *When the Light Goes* (Simon & Schuster, 2007) Duane, now 64, returns from an impromptu trip to Egypt and is confronted by Anne Cameron, a young, flirtatious computer expert hired by Duane's son Dickie.

II. The novels in McMurtry's Urban series also have Texas settings, primarily Houston. Just as the Thalia novels show the bleakness of small-town life, the urban novels depict the rootlessness and anomie of modern urban life. The five books have a revolving cast of characters; supporting characters in one novel become the stars of another. *Terms of Endearment* is the best-known novel of series, partly because of the success of the movie version (1983), which won Academy Awards for Best Picture, Best Actress (Shirley MacLaine), and Best Supporting Actor (Jack Nicholson). The film version of *The Evening Star* (1996), in which Shirley MacLaine plays Aurora Greenway as a grandmother, was not so successful.

1. *Moving On* (Simon & Schuster, 1970) Patsy Carpenter and her husband, Jim, avoid facing up to a disintegrating marriage by having a series of affairs.
2. *All My Friends Are Going to Be Strangers* (Simon & Schuster, 1972) Young writer Danny Deck moves back and forth between Texas and California while trying to find himself.
3. *Terms of Endearment* (Simon & Schuster, 1975) Wealthy Houston widow Aurora Greenway deals with a series of suitors while trying to control the life of Emma, her married daughter.
4. *Some Can Whistle* (Simon & Schuster, 1989) Danny Deck, producer of a successful TV sitcom, rusticates himself to a remote Texas ranch, where he is found by T. R., the daughter he hasn't seen since her birth.
5. *Evening Star, The* (Simon & Schuster, 1992) Aurora Greenway, now in her seventies, has an affair with a much younger psychoanalyst while trying to deal with the neurotic behavior of her grandchildren.

III. Harmony, voluptuous but aging Las Vegas showgirl, is the protagonist in a pair of novels in which Harmony's naive optimism is put to the test in a series of raucous, picturesque adventures.

1. *Desert Rose, The* (Simon & Schuster, 1983) Harmony is a 38-year-old topless dancer in a Las Vegas casino who is facing rivalry from her teenage daughter Pepper.
2. *Late Child, The* (Simon & Schuster, 1995) Grief-stricken by news of Pepper's death in New York, Harmony packs all her possessions in a U-Haul and heads home to Tarwater, Oklahoma.

IV. *Lonesome Dove*, one of McMurtry's most popular and highly regarded novels (it won a Pulitzer Prize), is a historical novel, set in 19th-century Texas, of epic proportions, familiar but well-developed western characters, and authentic dialect and cowboy lore. The equally memorable *Streets of Laredo* picked up the life of Woodrow Call, one of the principal characters, some 20 years later, while *Dead Man's Walk* and *Comanche Moon* are prequels that take Call and McRae back to the time when they were Texas Rangers. *Lonesome Dove* and *Dead Man's Walk* have been filmed for TV.

1. *Dead Man's Walk* (Simon & Schuster, 1995) Gus McRae and Woodrow Call, teenage runaways, are recruited into the Rangers of the new Texas Republic.
2. *Comanche Moon* (Simon & Schuster, 1997) Harvard-educated Texas Ranger captain Inish Scull abandons his command and sets off on foot after Kicking Bird, the Indian who stole his horse. Buffalo Hump and his Comanches gather together for one final raid. Call and McRae are Ranger captains. Set in the 1850s and 1860s.
3. *Lonesome Dove* (Simon & Schuster, 1985) Former Texas Rangers Call and McRae give up their unsuccessful ranch and head for greater opportunities in the newly opened Montana Territory.
4. *Streets of Laredo* (Simon & Schuster, 1993) Twenty years after the death of McRae, Woodrow Call is hired by a railroad company to hunt down Joey Garza, young Mexican train robber and killer.

V. McMurtry's latest series is also set in the 19th-century American West but is considerably different in tone, more reminiscent of George MacDonald Fraser's (q.v.) Flashman series than of *Lonesome Dove*. The Berrybenders, a rich, obnoxious, aristocratic British family, travel through the American West in the 1830s and get involved in a series of melodramatically comic adventures. The Europeans are generally odious. The hairy, smelly mountain men and the Indians are generally honorable, if sometimes violent, characters. Historical characters such as Kit Carson put in appearances.

1. *Sin Killer* (Simon & Schuster, 2002) When the rich, inept, aristocratic Berrybenders journey up the Missouri River to cash in on the land boom of the 1830s, daughter Tamsin wanders off and is rescued by Jim Snow, "Sin Killer," a mountain man who has high moral standards for everyone except himself (he has two Indian wives).
2. *Wandering Hill, The* (Simon & Schuster, 2003) The Berrybenders, a bunch of hairy and smelly mountain men, marauding Sioux, and Kit Carson all play roles in this novel set in 1833 on the banks of the Yellowstone River.
3. *By Sorrow's River* (Simon & Schuster, 2003) The members of the hunting party travel slowly southward to Santa Fe from their winter camp.
4. *Folly and Glory* (Simon & Schuster, 2004) In the rather apocalyptic conclusion to the series, the Berrybenders are placed under house arrest in Santa Fe, then expelled to Vera Cruz. The last stand at the Alamo takes place, and Kit Carson reappears.

McNab, Andy

Nick Stone, former British soldier, quits the SAS (Special Air Service) and becomes a "deniable operator" for intelligence services such as the CIA, by whom he is sent on various secret missions, including assassination, around the world. Stone, who suffers some personal losses, tries to quit several times but is always drawn back into the covert world to act against al-Qaeda and other terrorist organizations. McNab's novels are gripping thrillers in the great British tradition of Alistair MacLean (q.v.). Andy McNab was a much-decorated soldier in the SAS himself. In the best-selling *Bravo Two Zero* (Bantam, 1993), McNab describes the patrol behind enemy lines that he commanded during the First Gulf War. *Immediate Action* (Bantam, 1995) relates his earlier life. McNab is also the coauthor, with Robert Rigby, of the YA series Boy Soldier.

1. *Remote Control* (Ballantine, 1999) Nick Stone, former Special Air Service soldier now working for British intelligence in "deniable operations," is tracking two IRA terrorists from London to Washington when he is alerted to the murder of a former SAS mate and his family.
2. *Crisis Four* (Ballantine, 2000) Nick is on the trail of Sarah Greenwood, who has disappeared from her counterterrorism job in Washington just before Arafat and Netanyahu are scheduled to meet with President Clinton.
3. *Firewall* (Atria, 2001) Stone's ward, Kelly, is catatonic with posttraumatic stress disorder stemming from her horrific experiences in number 1. Stone, looking for money for treatment, finds himself in the middle of a totally unprofessional kidnapping of a Russian Mafia kingpin in Helsinki.
4. *Last Light* (Atria, 2002) Nick orchestrates a precision team hit on a high-level target, only to have the team leader compromise the mission.
5. *Liberation Day* (Atria, 2003) Stone is working for a special antiterrorist US strike team in the south of France that is trying to choke off al-Qaeda's money line.
6. *Dark Winter* (Bantam, 2003) Stone, sent to Malaysia by the CIA to assassinate a biochemist, winds up facing a terrorist threat against New York, London, and Berlin.
7. *Deep Black* (Bantam, 2004) Stone feels bleak, having lost Kelly and being on the outs with everyone else, but he has a chance encounter with a man he saved 10 years ago.
8. *Aggressor* (Bantam, 2005) Vacationing in Australia, Nick feels blessedly out of things until he witnesses on TV the massacre of children in a terrorist siege.
9. *Recoil* (Bantam, 2006) Stone, recuperating in a Swiss hospital, asks his new girlfriend, Silky, to marry him. Then she disappears, and Nick winds up in the Democratic Republic of the Congo.
10. *Crossfire* (Bantam, 2007) Stone searches for a reporter who saved his life from a roadside bomb in Basra.

McNab, Claire

PSEUDONYM OF Claire Carmichael

I. Detective Inspector Carol Ashton is one of the stars of the Sydney, Australia police force. She always gets her man (or woman) despite bludgeonings, gunshot wounds, and other offenses to her person. Carol's private life is somewhat more complicated: she is a lesbian who is reluctant to come out because of career concerns. She has a tendency to get emotionally involved when an attractive woman enters the case. She has an on-again, off-again relationship with her lover, Sybil Quade, who sometimes removes herself from the scene altogether, as well as other affairs. The Australian ambience is a plus in this well-plotted series with an interesting protagonist. Claire McNab is a native Australian who now lives in Los Angeles.

1. *Lessons in Murder* (Naiad, 1988) Teacher Bill Pagett of Bellwether High School is left with a hole in his head, placed there by a Black & Decker drill.
2. *Fatal Reunion* (Naiad, 1989) When the husband of Carol's former lover Christine is murdered, Christine calls upon Carol for help in proving her innocence.
3. *Death Down Under* (Naiad, 1989) A strangler using an orange cord has dispatched four women and left their bodies ritually arranged.
4. *Cop Out* (Naiad, 1991) When Bruce Darcy is bludgeoned to death, his sister is found with his body, the murder weapon, and a case of amnesia.
5. *Dead Certain* (Naiad, 1993) Collie Raeburn, "Australia's Pavarotti," appears to have committed suicide in his Sydney hotel room.
6. *Body Guard* (Naiad, 1995) Carol has to guard a famous visiting American feminist from dangerous enemies.
7. *Double Bluff* (Naiad, 1996) After wealthy television star Tala Orlando is murdered or commits suicide, someone stalks her lover, Madeline Shipley.
8. *Inner Circle* (Naiad, 1996) While investigating a series of execution-style murders, Ashton encounters a deadly underground extremist group, putting her life in jeopardy.
9. *Chain Letter* (Naiad, 1997) An apparent serial murderer touches off an intense manhunt when well-loved Detective Sergeant Steve York is stabbed.
10. *Past Due* (Naiad, 1998) A scandal threatens to reveal leading fertility researcher Dr. Brian Halstead as a dangerous fanatic playing with his patient's lives.
11. *Set Up* (Naiad, 1999) Apparently unrelated but remarkably coincidental deaths of several major captains of industry may be linked to ecoterrorism.
12. *Under Suspicion* (Naiad, 2000) Ashton flies to Los Angeles for an international law-enforcement conference sponsored by the FBI. One of the FBI agents is Leona Woolfe, an attractive "woman of color." Then conference participants start dying off.
13. *Death Club* (Naiad, 2001) Fashion magnate Gussie Whitlew sponsors the Whitlew Challenge to lure the world's top woman golfers to her private clubhouse.
14. *Accidental Murder* (Bella, 2002) When people with no obvious connection to each other die in what appear to be accidents, no one suspects murder until an insurance investigator alerts Carol to the fact that all the victims were heavily insured.
15. *Blood Link* (Bella, 2003) A series of seemingly random deaths suddenly fall into a pattern when reclusive billionaire Thurmond Rule dies, leaving an immense estate, no valid will, and no close relatives.
16. *Fall Guy* (Bella, 2004) When practical joker Milton Royce is killed while skydiving, no one is particularly surprised to find that he was murdered.

II. A second series features Australian Security Intelligence Organization agent Denise Cleever, who made an appearance in the Carol Ashton series. Denise's specialty is undercover work, which exposes her to a series of dangerous situations.

1. *Murder Undercover* (Naiad, 2000) Undercover as a waitress in a posh resort near the Great Barrier Reef off the coast of Queensland, Denise runs into Roanna, the dangerously attractive daughter of the resort's owner, and a series of killings.
2. *Death Understood* (Naiad, 2000) Denise follows a bloody trail deep into the Outback when a murder threatens national security.

3. *Out of Sight* (Naiad, 2001) Denise infiltrates a terrorist training camp in the wilds of Australia, putting herself at grave risk.
4. *Recognition Factor* (Bella, 2003) As the only member of the intelligence community who has seen international terrorist Red Wolf face-to-face and lived, Cleever is sent to the United States to track him down.
5. *Death by Death* (Bella, 2004) Suicide bombers dispatched to Australia are killing high-profile Australian politicians and other public figures, and Denise is apparently on their hit list.
6. *Murder at Random* (Bella, 2006) A shadowy terrorist group is paying amateur contract killers a considerable bounty for every successful murder at random.

III. Kylie Kendall, managing a pub in the Outback town of Wollegudgerie, is lured to the United States by the bequest of 51 percent of a Los Angeles–based private investigation agency from a father she never knew. When she gets to LA, Kylie gets a chilly reception from Ariana Creeling, the surviving partner of the agency, but the Aussie "dyke" and the attractive Ariana find that they have to get along as partners.

1. *Wombat Strategy, The* (Bella, 2004) Kylie and Ariana handle their first case together when Dr. Dave Deer, "shrink to the stars," hires them to investigate the theft of records from and subsequent "suicide" of a successful but loathed film director.
2. *Kookaburra Gambit* (Alyson, 2005) Twins Alf and Chica Hartnidge, the hosts of Australia's hit children's television show *The Oz Mob*, hire Kylie to find out who's smuggling opals into the United States inside their Kelvin Kookaburra plush toys.
3. *Quokka Question, The* (Alyson, 2005) A dull stint at a routine security detail to prevent an academic rival from disrupting Dr. Oscar Braithwaite's keynote address at UCLA's Global Marsupial Symposium becomes more exciting when Dr. Braithwaite is murdered.
4. *Dingo Dilemma, The* (Alyson, 2006) Kylie's mother asks her to check in on distant relative Doug "Dingo" O'Rourke, who has a TV gig in Los Angeles, but Dingo wants nothing to do with Kylie.

McQuillan, Karin

Jazz Jasper, expatriate American owner of a safari-outfitting business in Kenya, gets involved with wildlife, poachers, and murderers in this series. The resourceful and courageous Jazz is an eloquent defender of endangered species in a well-realized contemporary African setting.

1. *Deadly Safari* (St. Martin's, 1990) Two members of Jasper's first tour group are murdered in a Kenyan luxury camp.
2. *Elephants' Graveyard* (Ballantine, 1993) Jazz is persuaded to investigate the shooting death of her friend Mikki's lover, Emmett Laird, head of the Save the Elephants Foundation.
3. *Cheetah Chase, The* (Ballantine, 1994) American investigative journalist Nick Hunter's interest in cheetahs may have brought about his fatal sting by a nonindigenous scorpion.

Medawar, Mardi Oakley

In four novels set in the 1860s and 1870s, the Kiowa healer, Tay-bodal, solves murder mysteries. The modest and humorous Tay-bodal is an agreeable narrator for a series replete with Native American lore. Indian activist Mardi Oakley Medawar lives on the Red Cliff Reservation in Wisconsin.

1. *Death at Rainy Mountain* (St. Martin's, 1996) A contender to succeed Little Mountain in the position of chieftain of the Kiowa nation is slain, and healer Tay-bodal is faced with the task of finding the murderer.
2. *Witch of the Palo Duro* (St. Martin's, 1997) In the winter of 1866, Tay-bodal is charged with finding a witch suspected of causing deaths and disappearances in the camp of the Rattle Band of the Kiowas, a witch many believe to be Tay-bodal's wife.
3. *Murder at Medicine Lodge* (St. Martin's, 1999) White Bear, the Kiowa representative at a peace conference with US officials at Medicine Lodge, Oklahoma Territory, is accused of murdering a US Army bugler.
4. *Ft. Larned Incident, The* (St. Martin's, 2000) Tay-bodal, having trouble with his feisty wife, Crying Wind, gets a temporary divorce. Then Three Elks has his throat slit, followed by the stabbing of womanizer Cheyenne Robber.

Meek, M(argaret) R(eid) D(uncan)

Lennox Kemp is a British lawyer and sometime detective with a checkered career. Originally a married solicitor who damaged his career and his marriage by a quixotic act, Kemp does time as an agent for McCready's Detective Agency of Walthamstow, before he is restored to respectability as solicitor in charge of the Newtown office of Gillorns, Solicitors and married to the Irish American Mary. Kemp is an intelligent and basically decent man who has an unfortunate habit of being attracted to women who spell trouble. Although he is sometimes compared to Ross MacDonald's (q.v.) Lew Archer or Raymond Chandler's (q.v.) Philip Marlowe by characters in the series, physically he is more like Hammett's (q.v.) Continental Op, stocky, balding, and fortyish. These are mysteries of the old school—well mannered, well thought out, relatively bloodless, crisp, amusing, entertaining, and extremely well written—by the Scottish-born Meek, who has been compared favorably to P. D. James (q.v.) and Ruth Rendell (q.v.).

1. *With Flowers That Fell* (Hale [UK], 1983) No annotation available.
2. *Sitting Ducks, The* (Collins [UK], 1984) The high suicide rate in a small Cornish town intrigues Kemp enough to make him delve into local family history for an explanation.
3. *Hang the Consequences* (Scribner, 1985) Kemp recalls his own past disgrace while probing the past of an architect who has disappeared twice.
4. *Split Second, The* (Scribner, 1987) Lennox is searching for a missing wealthy spinster and getting hoodwinked by a ruthless gang at every turn.
5. *In Remembrance of Rose* (Scribner, 1988) Kemp vows to find the person who killed elderly Rose Aumary, client and friend.
6. *Worm of Doubt, A* (Scribner, 1988) Frelis Lorimer attempts to blackmail Lennox into providing the name of a hit man who would get rid of her husband's lover.
7. *Mouthful of Sand, A* (Scribner, 1989) A decapitated head turns up in a fisherman's net at a resort on the Cornish coast.
8. *Loose Connection, A* (Scribner, 1989) Twenty years after her presumed death in a factory fire, Queenie Mangan returns rich, powerful, and married to the factory's ex-owner.
9. *This Blessed Plot* (Scribner, 1991) Kemp is seduced by the rich and enticing Courtenay twins into carrying out plans for Courtenay Manor that might not be strictly legal.
10. *Touch and Go* (Scribner, 1993) Muriel Probert's will left a suitcase full of rubies and shares in a Las Vegas casino to her first husband, but the rubies and original will are missing.

11. *Postscript to Murder* (St. Martin's, 1997) Kemp's recent bride, Irish American Mary, takes the lead in investigating a series of harassing incidents that culminate in the murder of one of Kemp's associates.

12. *House to Die For, A* (Severn, 2000) When a lodger at a place next door to their new house in Newtown dies suddenly, Lennox and Mary become involved in the defense of the prime suspect.

13. *If You Go Down to the Woods* (Severn, 2001) Is gang-leader and possible multiple-personality Lily Egerton the key to the murder of the 13-year-old daughter of Kemp's close friend?

14. *Vanishing Point, The* (Severn, 2003) Developer and chairman of the Newtown Council Mervyn Prentiss is about to marry the daughter of Lord Allen, and he wants Kemp to establish that his long-estranged wife, Linde, is dead, or to find her and procure him a divorce from her if she isn't dead.

15. *Kemp's Last Case* (Severn, 2004) Going through the affairs of the late Dr. Ayres, Lennox's curiosity is aroused by a cache of letters and diaries referring to a 20-year-old murder case that never came to trial because of the death of the chief suspect.

Meier, Leslie

Lucy Stone is a mother, part-time reporter and part-time amateur sleuth in these holiday-themed cozies set in the town of Tinker's Cove, Maine. The middle-aged Lucy likes to observe holidays by cooking and baking but, somehow, the holidays have a way of being fatal to one of the locals. Leslie Meier has been a reporter and editor for several Cape Cod, Massachusetts, newspapers.

1. *Mail-Order Murder* (Viking, 1991) While moonlighting during the Christmas rush for a trendy mail-order house, Lucy Stone stumbles upon the body of the company's founder. Variant title: *Mistletoe Murder.*

2. *Tippy-Toe Murder* (Viking, 1994) Lucy's neighbor, retired dance teacher Caro Binney, disappears, possibly because of the murder of Morrill Slack with a video camera.

3. *Trick or Treat Murder* (Kensington, 1996) Lucy has to take a break from baking Halloween cookies and rejuvenating old costumes for her children to hunt down an arsonist.

4. *Back to School Murder* (Kensington, 1997) Lucy investigates the bombing of the local elementary school.

5. *Christmas Cookie Murder* (Kensington, 1999) The annual Christmas Cookie Exchange is marred by the murder of Tucker Whitney, accused of stealing someone else's cookie recipe.

6. *Valentine Murder* (Kensington, 1999) New librarian Bitsy Howell has been murdered, and the killer is probably still in Tinker's Cove, according to Detective Horowitz.

7. *Turkey Day Murder* (Kensington, 2000) The annual Thanksgiving Day festivities are interrupted by the murder of Metinnicut Indian activist Curt Nolan.

8. *Wedding Day Murder* (Kensington, 2001) The daughter of a friend is supposed to married in Lucy's gazebo, but the groom is murdered on his wedding day.

9. *Birthday Party Murder* (Kensington, 2002) Lucy and some friends organize a 90th-birthday party for retired librarian Julia Ward Howe Tilley. Then respected lawyer Sherman Cobb is found dead in his office.

10. *Father's Day Murder* (Kensington, 2003) Lucy, attending a conference in Boston, gets involved with the murder, possibly by his children, of newspaper magnate Luther Read.

11. *Star Spangled Murder* (Kensington, 2004) Nudists swimming at the local pond, an endangered species of lichen, and the hit-and-run death of Lucy's neighbors get in the way of Fourth of July festivities.

12. *New Year's Eve Murder* (Kensington, 2005) Lucy and her oldest daughter, Elizabeth, travel to New York City after winning an all-expenses-paid mother-daughter makeover from *Jolie* magazine.

13. *Bake Sale Murder* (Kensington, 2006) Anonymous letters allege that Buck Burkhart, the new football coach, is condoning unsavory behavior by the high school's senior football players toward the junior players and the cheerleaders, one of whom is Lucy's daughter, Sara.

14. *St. Patrick's Day Murder* (Kensington, 2008) Lucy stumbles on a beheaded corpse at the end of the pier in Tinker's Cove.

Melville, Anne

PSEUDONYM OF Margaret Potter

I. This English romance and juvenile writer has produced a family saga that traces the fortunes of the Lorimer family of Bristol, England. The story begins in the 1870s when the family banking business fails because of the folly and chicanery of John Julius Lorimer, and continues into the 1970s showing how the second, third, and fourth generations of Lorimers deal with the problems of love, money, and vocation. This serviceable family chronicle is more realistic and less overheated than some of its kind.

1. *Lorimer Line, The* (Doubleday, 1977) The failure of the family bank, which brings hardship and lost love to Margaret Lorimer, also frees her from the restricted role of an upper-middle-class Victorian woman.

2. *Alexa* (Doubleday, 1979) Margaret Lorimer's half sister Alexa endures a series of calamities from unhappy love affairs to the San Francisco earthquake. Published in the United Kingdom as *The Lorimer Legacy.*

3. *Blaize* (Doubleday, 1981) The saga continues through both world wars chronicling the careers of the younger Lorimers. Blaize, the Lorimer country estate, becomes a field hospital in World War I. Published in the United Kingdom in two parts, as *Lorimers at War* and *Lorimers in Love.*

4. *Family Fortunes* (Doubleday, 1984) The lives of Lady Alexa Glanville and her relatives are traced from 1946 to 1977. Published in the United Kingdom in two parts, as *The Last of the Lorimers* and *Lorimer Loyalties.*

II. Another family saga, published only in the United Kingdom, deals with the Hardies, a Victorian family of tradespeople, whose younger members aspire to better things socially. The trilogy takes the reader through and beyond World War I.

1. *House of Hardie, The* (Grafton [UK], 1987) Set in Oxford, where the Hardies are successful wine merchants. The younger Hardies, Midge and Gordon, wish to be social equals with their aristocratic customers.

2. *Grace Hardie* (Grafton [UK], 1988) The earlier life of Grace Hardie, who struggles to find where her loyalties lie. The Great War and a case of assumed infanticide test her.

3. *Hardie Inheritance, The* (Grafton [UK], 1990) The later life of Grace Hardie at Greystones, the mansion that she owns but can't afford to maintain. Her life is transformed by four uninvited visitors.

Melville, Herman

These two novels by Melville are sometimes classed as nonfiction since they are based on his wanderings in the South Seas. They were his first published works and earned him an early reputation as a popular writer of adventure tales among readers who were dismayed at the turn that subsequent works, such as *Mardi* and *Moby Dick,* took. Although the pace of these tales slows occasionally for anthropological description, which is fascinating in itself, their main current sweeps along, as brisk and as exciting as any modern thriller. Like many romantics, Melville painted his "savages" as more noble than his corrupt white men. *Typee* and *Omoo* are published together with *Mardi* in a volume in the Library of America series (1982).

1. *Typee: A Peep at Polynesian Life* (Wiley & Putnam, 1846) The author and his friend Toby jump ship in the Marquesas and are eventually taken in by a cannibal tribe. The second edition, published in 1846, contained an addendum, "The Story of Toby," which is included in most later editions.

2. *Omoo: A Narrative of Adventures in the South Seas* (Harper, 1847) The author is taken aboard the Australian trader *Julia,* where he meets the learned and amiable Dr. Long Ghost. The ship's crew mutinies in Tahiti, and the author and Dr. Long Ghost have adventures in Tahiti and Imeeo.

Melville, James

PSEUDONYM OF Peter Martin

I. The Japanese city of Kobe is the setting for a series of police procedurals featuring Superintendent Tetsuo Otani and his lieutenants, the dapper Jiro Kimura and the sinister "Ninja" Noguchi. Superintendent Otani, although capable of instilling fear in the hearts of his nine-thousand-man police force, is basically a likable man with genial good manners, humor, and an endearing tenderness for his wife, Hanae. The well-plotted novels inform as well as entertain. English writer Melville, former head of the British Council in Tokyo, writes with accuracy and affection about daily life in contemporary Japan.

1. *Wages of Zen, The* (Fawcett, 1985) A Zen community composed of foreigners and led by a moneygrubbing priest gets involved in drugs and murder. Originally published in the United Kingdom in 1979.

2. *Chrysanthemum Chain, The* (St. Martin's, 1982) An English resident of Japan, an educator who has important political friends, is murdered.

3. *Sort of Samurai, A* (St. Martin's, 1982) A German businessman is found dead at his desk after an earthquake. Otani suspects foul play.

4. *Ninth Netsuke, The* (St. Martin's, 1982) Otani's wife finds a netsuke hidden in the drapes of a Kobe hotel room that may be a clue to a murder.

5. *Sayonara, Sweet Amaryllis* (St. Martin's, 1984) The poisoning of a prominent member of the expatriate community is linked to a drug-smuggling ring.

6. *Death of a Daimyo* (St. Martin's, 1985) While vacationing in England, Otani witnesses a murder that may be connected to an underworld power struggle in Japan.

7. *Death Ceremony, The* (St. Martin's, 1985) The hereditary grand master of the Southern School of the Tea Ceremony is shot through the head whiled ritually preparing the tea.

8. *Go Gently, Gaijin* (St. Martin's, 1986) Two foreigners (*gaijin*), Muslim members of KISS (Kinki International Students Society), die violently.

9. *Kimono for a Corpse* (St. Martin's, 1988) A gathering of international couturiers, invited to Japan by leading designer Madame Yashuda, is hit by murder.

10. *Reluctant Ronin, The* (Scribner, 1988) A Dutch woman linked to Otani's son-in-law dies under mysterious circumstances during a fire.

11. *Haiku for Hanae, A* (Scribner, 1989) Flashbacks relate Otani's 1968 involvement in the case of a young Mormon missionary who was found murdered near a Shinto shrine.

12. *Bogus Buddha, The* (Scribner, 1991) Otani investigates cases of murder at a meeting of academics and at a clandestine gathering of Japanese Mafia leaders.

13. *Body Wore Brocade, The* (Scribner, 1992) The attempted assassination of Otani may be linked with a wealthy computer software developer with amateur theater connections.

II. Melville followed the Otani series with a pair of novels about cultural attaché Ben Lazenby of the British Foreign Service. Lazenby, a likable bumbler, gets involved in a series of rather comic misadventures.

1. *Diplomatic Baggage* (Severn [UK], 1995) In the Spring of 1982 the newly divorced Lazenby is posted to Hungary, and given the assignment of escorting two truckloads of valuable British art from Budapest to Bucharest and back again.

2. *Reluctant Spy, The* (Severn [UK], 1995) Lazenby finds himself in Indonesia, ordered to penetrate a top secret microbiological research laboratory.

Melville, Jennie

PSEUDONYM OF Gwendoline Butler

Charmian Daniels, when we first meet her, is a sergeant in the Deerham Hills (England) police division. She eventually becomes Chief Superintendent in the supposedly bucolic town of Windsor. Charmian has her personal problems (she is widowed), but doesn't allow them to deter her from her investigations. This is a straightforward detective series, although the crimes investigated are often grisly murders with bizarre circumstances, and the "perps" are often women. Gwendoline Butler (q.v.) writes the Coffin series under her own name and romantic thrillers under the Melville pseudonym. Nearly half of the titles in the Daniels series have not been published in the United States.

1. *Come Home and Be Killed* (London House, 1964) No annotation available. Originally published in the United Kingdom in 1962.

2. *Burning Is a Substitute for Loving* (London House, 1964) No annotation available. Originally published in the United Kingdom in 1963.

3. *Murderers' Houses* (Joseph [UK], 1964) No annotation available. Not published in the United States.

4. *There Lies Your Love* (Joseph [UK], 1965) No annotation available. Not published in the United States.

5. *Different Kind of Summer, A* (Hodder [UK], 1967) No annotation available. Not published in the United States.

6. *New Kind of Killer, A* (McKay, 1971) No annotation available. UK title: *A New Kind of Killer, an Old Kind of Death.*

7. *Murder Has a Pretty Face* (St, Martin's, 1989) The recently widowed Charmian Daniels has to deal with the murder and sexual mutilation of a man carrying a card with her married surname. Originally published in the United Kingdom in 1981.

8. *Windsor Red* (St. Martin's, 1988) Daniels goes on sabbatical to research her thesis on the Gang of Girls, six female ex-cons.

9. *Making Good Blood* (St. Martin's, 1990) Daniels has to fight off an attack while returning home one night. Then two throat slittings surface: one of a horse, one of a woman. UK title: *A Cure for Dying*

10. *Footsteps in the Blood* (St. Martin's, 1993) Someone murdered Nella Fisher, who had connections with two friends of Charmian's. Originally published in the United Kingdom in 1990.

11. *Witching Murder* (St. Martin's, 1991) Vivien Charles, member of a witches' coven, is murdered.

12. *Dead Set* (St. Martin's, 1993) The suspect in a strangulation murder of a local school girl disappears.

13. *Whoever Has the Heart* (St. Martin's, 1994) On impulse, Daniels buys a weekend cottage in Brideswell, but doesn't succeed in getting away from it all.

14. *Death in the Family, A* (St, Martin's, 1995) The disappearance of eight-year-old Sarah Holt and the discovery of a baby's body are at issue here. Variant title: *Baby Drop*.

15. *Morbid Kitchen, The* (St. Martin's, 1995) After former schoolmistress Miss Bailey dies, her sister inherits her house and discovers a corpse that brings back memories of the scandal that closed Miss Bailey's School.

16. *Woman Who Was Not There, The* (Macmillan [UK], 1996) A London prostitute disappears, and a severed foot and some erotic, moveable wax models turn up in Windsor. Not published in the United States.

17. *Revengeful Death* (Macmillan [UK], 1998) Investigation of an abandoned house reveals a young boy cowering in a cupboard and a young man stabbed to death and his thymus removed. Not published in the United States.

18. *Stone Dead* (Macmillan [UK], 1998) The opening of a new bookshop owned by a friend of Charmian's is disrupted when a stone coffin containing the body of a woman is found in the garden. Not published in the United States.

19. *Dead Again* (Macmillan [UK], 2000) A spate of murders occurs as Joan Dingham awaits release from prison. Did Joan have anything to do with the murders, or are they copycat crimes? Not published in the United States.

Meredith, George

Meredith's reputation has already undergone several ups and downs. After an early success with *The Ordeal of Richard Feverel* in 1859, his subsequent novels, which were perhaps ahead of their time, failed to please either the public or the critics. By the 1880s his public had caught up with him, and his enlightened attitudes placed among the leaders of a modernism quickly displaced after World War I. Meredith will appeal to fans of Austen and Thackeray. The pleasures of his language, his droll humor, and his feminist sympathies are evident in this pair of novels about Emilia Alessandra Belloni.

1. *Sandra Belloni* (Roberts, 1887) Emilia's innocence and honesty contrast wittily with the hypocrisy of the three social-climbing Pole sisters, who take up the young Italian girl with the remarkable singing voice. Originally published by Chapman (UK) in 1864 as *Emilia in England*.

2. *Vittoria* (Roberts, 1888) Emilia, now the famous singer Vittoria Champa, travels to Italy. Less comic than the first novel, this book is more concerned with the Italian Revolution, which Vittoria symbolizes. Originally published by Chapman (UK) in 1866.

Merezhkovsky, D(mitri) S(ergeyivich)

Christ and Anti-Christ (*Khristos i Antikhrist*) is the series title of this trilogy of historical novels in which Russian author Merezhkovsky uses three vastly different epochs to illustrated his theme of the struggle between Christian and Pagan ideas. Though the "authorized" translation by Herbert Trench may seem a little wooden, the books' interesting story lines can still draw readers into richly woven portraits of the fascinating periods they depict. Merezhkovsky, who exiled himself from his native land in 1920, seems to be going through something of a revival in Russia, with many of his works being reprinted in the 1990s. He wrote two other trilogies, of which some volumes were translated into English (e.g., *December the Fourteenth*; *Jesus the Unknown*). *The Romance of Leonardo da Vinci*, which was published in a new translation by Bernard Guilbert Gurney in a Modern Library edition (1928), is the best-known book by Merezhkovsky to readers in English.

1. *Death of the Gods, The* (Putnam, 1901) The central theme is the life of the Roman emperor Julian from boyhood to his death (337–363 CE) and the wars and controversies of his times. Variant title: *Julian the Apostate*. Original title: *Smert bogov: Yulian Otstupnik*. Translated from the Russian by Herbert Trench.

2. *Romance of Leonardo da Vinci, The* (Putnam, 1902) The best-known of the trilogy, this volume gives special attention to Leonardo's scientific and medical researches during the period 1494–1519. Variant titles: *The Gods Reborn* and *The Forerunner*. Original title: *Voskresshiye bogi: Leonardo da Vinci*. Translated from the Russian by Herbert Trench and by Bernard Guilbert Guerney (Modern Library, 1928).

3. *Peter and Alexis* (Putnam, 1905) Peter the Great and his imbecile son Alexis are featured in this concluding volume, which covers the years 1715–1718 and gives a panoramic view of Russian society. Variant title: *Peter the Great*. Original Russian title: *Antikhrist: Pyotr i Aleksey*. Translated from the Russian by Herbert Trench.

Meyer, Nicholas

Screenwriter, film director, and novelist Meyer adroitly catches the Victorian atmosphere, language, and detail in these clever additions to the Holmes canon. *The Seven-Per-Cent Solution* was the subject of a successful 1976 movie, starring Nicol Williamson as Holmes, Robert Duvall as Watson, Alan Arkin as Freud, and Vanessa Redgrave as the mysterious lady who captures Holmes's heart.

1. *Seven-Per-Cent Solution, The* (Dutton, 1974) Dr. Watson relates how he spirited Holmes off to Vienna and turned him over to Dr. Sigmund Freud for treatment of his cocaine addiction.

2. *West End Horror, The* (Dutton, 1976) George Bernard Shaw and other historical characters are feature in Dr. Watson's "posthumous memoir" about Holmes's 1895 investigation of the murder of a theater critic.

3. *Canary Trainer, The* (Norton, 1993) Holmes takes on the identity of a Norwegian violinist with the Paris Opera, gets reinvolved with Irene Adler, and meets Gaston Leroux's "Phantom of the Opera."

Meyers, Annette

I. Smith and Wetzon, Wall Street headhunters and amateur detectives, are something of an odd couple. Xenia Smith is abrasive and opportunistic. Leslie Wetzon is a sensitive ex-dancer who has an off-again, on-again relationship with New York Police Department detective Silvestri. This set of mysteries displays considerable knowledge of both Wall Street and Broadway. Annette Meyers, who spent 16 years as executive assistant to Broadway producer Hal Prince, also collaborates on mysteries with her husband, Martin Meyers, as Maan Meyers (q.v.).

1. *Big Killing, The* (Bantam, 1989) Young stockbroker Barry Stark, who had expressed concerns to Wetzon about his firm's questionable business dealings, turns up murdered.
2. *Tender Death* (Bantam, 1990) Did Wetzon's rich old lady friend fall, or was she pushed from her 20th-floor apartment?
3. *Deadliest Option, The* (Bantam, 1991) Goldie Barnes, director of Wall Street firm Luwisher Brothers, drops dead just before making an announcement that will shake the financial community.
4. *Blood on the Street* (Doubleday, 1992) Stockbroker Brian Middleton is found dead in Central Park, leaving a 16-year-old mistress whose mother he once bilked.
5. *Murder: The Musical* (Doubleday, 1993) Wetzon becomes an associate producer for the forthcoming musical *Hotshot* after stage manager Dilla Crosby is murdered.
6. *These Bones Were Made for Dancin'* (Doubleday, 1995) A skeleton with a bullet in its skull turns up in a Greenwich Village brownstone.
7. *Groaning Board, The* (Doubleday, 1997) Is one of the co-owners of popular food store the Groaning Board connected with the mysterious poisoning (by cookie) of Silvestri's partner's sister-in-law?
8. *Hedging* (Five Star, 2005) Wetzon, who has lost her memory, is trying to escape the after-effects of the explosion of an executive jet at an airport in New Jersey.

II. Greenwich Village in 1920 is the scene of two mysteries involving Olivia Brown, hard-drinking, hard-smoking, and hard-loving poetess (who writes verse reminiscent of Edna St. Vincent Millay). Olivia is intimate with many of the leading literary and artistic lights of the Greenwich Village scene, both historical (e.g., Edmund Wilson) and fictional, but she turns to her downstairs tenant, the rather inarticulate private investigator Harry Melville, for assistance when the going gets rough. Read these novels for their historical ambience rather than their plots.

1. *Free Love* (Mysterious, 1999) Who is stalking Olivia, and did he (or she) murder the transvestite made up to resemble Olivia? Wary of the police, Olivia turns to PI Harry Melville for assistance.
2. *Murder Me Now* (Mysterious, 2000) The murder of a wealthy family's young nanny, who might have been a Pinkerton agent, is the focal point of the action here.

Meyers, Maan

PSEUDONYM OF Martin & Annette Meyers

Old New York in the 17th, 18th, and 19th centuries is the scene of these mysteries by husband-and-wife team Martin and Annette Meyers (q.v.). The main protagonists are members of the Tonneman family, from Pieter, sheriff and postmaster in Peter Stuvesant's New Amsterdam to John "Dutch" Tonneman, a detective in the New York of the 1890s. Many historical figures play cameo roles in these entertaining mysteries. Annette Meyers (q.v.) has also written the Smith and Wetzon and Olivia Brown mystery series. Martin Meyers authored the Patrick Hardy mystery series (1975–1976).

1. *Dutchman, The* (Doubleday, 1992) In 1664 New Amsterdam is facing an impending English invasion, and Schout (Sheriff) Peter Tonneman is investigating a friend's death.
2. *Dutchman's Dilemma, The* (Bantam, 1995) In the New York of 1675 Pieter is happily remarried but troubled by a maniac who is killing horses and strewing their entrails about the city.
3. *Kingsbridge Plot, The* (Doubleday, 1993) John Tonneman becomes New York City coroner on the eve of the American Revolution, and has to track down a killer who preys on redheads.
4. *High Constable, The* (Doubleday, 1994) The beginning of the 1800s finds the married and well-established John distracted by a live burial and a young woman's skull found nearby.
5. *Lucifer Contract, The* (Bantam, 1997) In 1864 young Peter Tonneman, a somewhat dissolute journalist, catches wind of a Southern plot to burn New York City to the ground.
6. *House on Mulberry Street, The* (Bantam, 1996) At 300 Mulberry Street is New York City police headquarters in 1895. Detective John "Dutch" Tonneman investigates the murder of a journalist.

Michael, Judith

PSEUDONYM OF Judith Barnard & Michael Fain

Wife-and-husband team Judith Barnard and Michael Fain write romance novels, including a pair about role-switching twin sisters. Of course, the concept isn't a new one, and readers must indulge in some suspension of disbelief, but *Deceptions* and *A Tangled Web* are quite enjoyable romantic fare.

1. *Deceptions* (Pocket, 1982) Rich aristocrat Lady Sabrina Longworth and suburban housewife Stephanie Anderson, identical twins, decide to exchange roles for a week.
2. *Tangled Web, A* (Simon & Schuster, 1994) Stephanie, plying her Sabrina role, has a survived a yacht explosion but is amnesiac, while Sabrina has settled into suburban life in Evanston, Illinois, with Stephanie's husband and children.

Michaels, Fern

PSEUDONYM OF Mary Ruth Kuczkir

I. "Fern Michaels" was the joint pseudonym for Mary Ruth Kuczkir and Roberta Anderson from 1974 to 1989. In 1989 Kuczkir acquired sole legal rights to "Fern Michaels." Fern Michaels has become a best-selling romance novelist, with several series to her credit. The Captives series concerns Sirena Cordez, who becomes the pirate, Sea Siren, after her sister is raped and murdered on a journey to Java. Various members of the Van der Rhys family, including Sirena's daughter, Fury Van der Rhys, get involved in these swashbuckling romances. *Captive Innocence* (Ballantine, 1981) is not part of the series.

1. *Captive Passions* (Ballantine, 1977) Sirena Cordez is on her way to Java with her betrothed sister when pirates attack, and her sister is raped and murdered.
2. *Captive Embraces* (Ballantine, 1979) Sirena, now the pirate leader Sea Siren, pursues her errant lover, Regan Van der Rhys.
3. *Captive Splendors* (Ballantine, 1980) After Wren tows away on the *Sea Siren*, she is captured by the pirate Caleb Van der Rhys.
4. *Captive Secrets* (Ballantine, 1991) Fury Van der Rhys, daughter of Sirena, the Sea Siren, goes into the family business.

II. Four generations of the Colemans have reigned over the Sunbridge, a 250,000-acre spread near Austin, Texas. The Coleman clan is also big in aeronautics and fashion, but of course, it has more than its share of deaths, divorces, tragic accidents, and outsized passions. Billie Ames, who marries into the clan in number 1, eventually becomes its matriarch. The Texas series (numbers 1–4) was followed by the Vegas series (numbers 5–7), which introduces the Thornton dynasty and revives the Coleman family. The Kentucky series (numbers 8–10) brings more Colemans and horse racing into the picture. *Texas Trilogy* (Ballantine, 1991) contains numbers 1 through 3. *Vegas Trilogy* (Kensington, 2001) contains numbers 5 through 7.

1. *Texas Rich* **(Ballantine, 1985)** Billie Ames meets Moss Coleman, scion of the Coleman family of Sunbridge Ranch, near Austin, Texas, at the Philadelphia Navy Yard during World War II.
2. *Texas Heat* **(Ballantine, 1986)** Sunbridge now belongs to Maggie, Moss's and Billie's daughter. A Fourth of July barbecue is the centerpiece of this book.
3. *Texas Fury* **(Ballantine, 1989)** The completion of Assante Towers is a dream come true for Cary Assante. This volume takes us from Texas to Hawaii to the Far East to Switzerland.
4. *Texas Sunrise* **(Ballantine, 1992)** Members of the Coleman family struggle to cope with Billie Coleman Kingsley's impending death.
5. *Vegas Rich* **(Kensington, 1996)** Introduces the Thornton dynasty and revives the Coleman dynasty. Begins in 1923 when Sallie Coleman, saloon singer and prostitute, inherits a fortune from an eccentric millionaire.
6. *Vegas Heat* **(Kensington, 1997)** Sallie Coleman Thornton bequeaths her fortune, including Babylon, the Thornton Las Vegas casino, to her daughter-in-law, Fannie, who has divorced the wheelchair-bound Ash Thornton
7. *Vegas Sunrise* **(Kensington, 1997)** Fannie Coleman Thornton Reed is now the family matriarch. Control of Babylon is to pass to Ash Thornton's illegitimate son, Jeff Lassiter.
8. *Kentucky Rich* **(Kensington, 2001)** Nealy Coleman Diamond returns to the deathbed of her father, Josh Coleman, in an attempt to find out what made him such a jerk.
9. *Kentucky Heat* **(Kensington, 2002)** Nealy Coleman Diamond Clay has dreams of winning horse-racing's Triple Crown. Nealy's screwed-up son and daughter and larger-than-life Native American Hatch Little-tree play important roles.
10. *Kentucky Sunrise* **(Kensington, 2002)** Nealy is still proprietor of Blue Diamond Farms, but her marriage to Hatch Little-tree has left daughter Emmie in charge.

III. According to *Booklist*, the Sisterhood series is "*Mission Impossible* meets Lorena Bobbitt." This series, which brings together seven women broken but not beaten by life and bent on revenge for crimes and indignities committed against them, is implausible in the extreme and gratuitously nasty at times but appeals to people who want to see evil-doers get what's coming to them.

1. *Weekend Warriors* **(Kensington, 2001)** A hit-and-run car driven by a Chinese diplomat immune from prosecution kills Nikki's best friend, Barbara.
2. *Payback* **(Kensington, 2004)** Julia Webster, a plastic surgeon married to a US senator, finds her own motive for revenge.
3. *Vendetta* **(Zebra, 2005)** Myra Rutledge, with help, sticks it to the Chinese diplomat who got away with the hit-and-run killing in number 1.
4. *Jury, The* **(Zebra, 2005)** Jack Emery, Nikki's former fiancé, tries to stop the Sisterhood from wreaking their just revenge.
5. *Sweet Revenge* **(Zebra, 2006)** Rosemary Hersley has done Isabelle Flanders wrong: stealing her man, her clients, and her reputation

and framing her for a drunk-driving incident in which three were killed.
6. *Lethal Justice* **(Zebra, 2006)** Successful stockbroker Alexis has been imprisoned for fraud, while the true criminals, Arden Gillespie and Roland Sullivan, have gotten away with it, for now.
7. *Free Fall* **(Zebra, 2007)** Yoko Akia, rich American movie star, seeks revenge against the people who sent her mother, whom she never saw, into a life of degradation in Japan.
8. *Hokus Pokus* **(Zebra, 2008)** The Sisterhood, living in exile in Barcelona, are informed by Pearl Barnes, chief justice of the US Supreme Court, that she will expose one of their contacts in the United States if they don't help her keep her own dark secret.

IV. A pair of novels describes the romantic lives of American buddies Reuben Tarz and Daniel Bishop from World War I to World War II.

1. *Sins of Omission* **(Ballantine, 1989)** American soldier Reuben Tarz, wounded near the end of World War I, is spirited by Marchioness Michele Fonsard to her lavish French chateau.
2. *Sins of the Flesh* **(Ballantine, 1990)** Lifelong friends Reuben Tarz and Daniel Bishop and their various women are brought together again in Occupied France as World War II begins.

V. In two novels (so far), the trials and tribulations of the Cisco triplets and their beloved Granny, of Larkspur, Pennsylvania, are depicted.

1. *No Place Like Home* **(Pocket Books, 2002)** The Cisco triplets, Sara, Hannah, and Sam, are incensed when their widowed father parks Granny Cisco in a nursing home.
2. *Family Blessings* **(Pocket Books, 2004)** Granny Cisco's home is destroyed by a tornado. The Cisco triplets are all married but having problems.

Michaels, Grant

Stan Kraychik is a gay therapist turned hairdresser ("shrink 'em at the sink"). He works at a tony Back Bay (Boston) salon, and gets involved in the occasional mystery while carrying on an affair with the ballet dancer Rafik and feeling unrequited passion for Boston police lieutenant Vito Branco. Michaels does a good job of mixing humor and intrigue in this series of mysteries.

1. *Body to Dye For, A* **(St. Martin's, 1990)** Stan is implicated in the murder of a handsome young visiting National Parks ranger.
2. *Love You to Death* **(St. Martin's, 1992)** A reception given by Godiva wannabe Le Jardin Chocolatier is broken up by death when someone "trifles with the truffles."
3. *Dead on Your Feet* **(St. Martin's, 1993)** The founder of Rafik's ballet company is the first in a series of murder victims.
4. *Mask for a Diva* **(St. Martin's, 1994)** Stan helps out with the wigs at an opera festival at the Sidney Blaustein Center for the Performing Arts.
5. *Time to Check Out* **(St. Martin's, 1996)** After receiving a large settlement from UPS related to Rafik's fatal encounter with a truck in Paris, Stan travels to Key West, Florida, where his homophobic landlady winds up dead, with an alarm clock stuffed into her mouth.
6. *Dead as a Doornail* **(St. Martin's, 1998)** Vito Branco advises Stan to keep a low profile after contractor Tim Shaugnessy, who could be Stan's double, is killed.

Miles, Keith

Although best known for the historical mysteries he writes as Edward Marston (q.v.), Keith Miles also writes contemporary mysteries under his real name. The larger Miles series concerns British pro golfer and amateur sleuth Alan Saxon, once a champion, still striving for a comeback and a way out of his financial and personal woes. Saxons gigs take him to many corners of the world. Miles has never really hit his stride with this series. Some readers complain that there isn't "enough golf" in it.

1. *Bullet Hole* (Harper, 1987) Former golf champion Alan Saxon hopes to get back in the money at the British Open on the historic Saint Andrews course in Scotland, but a series of misadventures, including a young female golf groupie who winds up naked and dead in his bed, cramps his style.
2. *Double Eagle* (HarperCollins, 1987) Saxon accompanies friend and fellow golf pro, Zuke Everett, to a tournament at the Golden Haze Golf Club in California.
3. *Green Murder* (Poisoned Pen, 2002) Saxon is in Australia competing with three other golfers for a 400,000 pound prize. Originally published in the United Kingdom in 1990.
4. *Flagstick* (Poisoned Pen, 2004) Alan is making an instructional video in Japan when one of his employees is blown to pieces. Originally published in the United Kingdom in 1991.
5. *Bermuda Grass* (Poisoned Pen, 2002) While helping to design a golf course at a new hotel in Bermuda, Alan is visited by his daughter Lynette and an obnoxious friend from Oxford.
6. *Honolulu Playoff* (Poisoned Pen, 2004) Saxon is in Hawaii, attending the wedding of a fellow golf pro.

Miller, Henry

I. Expatriate American author Henry Miller published his first novel, *Tropic of Cancer*, in France in 1934. It was promptly banned in all English-speaking countries until 1961, when Grove Press's American edition provoked a furor that eventually led to 60 lawsuits across the country. The book sold 2.5 million copies in two years, giving Miller a best seller in his native land after many years of poverty. Miller wrote a violent stream of consciousness in which lusty incident, virtuoso prose, and lyric reminiscence churn alternately crude and exuberant. Autobiographical, like most of Miller's work, these three novels cohere as a group. A chronology would be meaningless; they are perhaps best read in the order in which they were first published.

1. *Tropic of Cancer* (Grove, 1961) This is an account of an American in Paris in the 1930s wallowing in the lower depths. The narrator is named Henry Miller and is a writer. First published in France in 1934.
2. *Black Spring* (Grove, 1961) Dreams and nightmares of the artist's mind range from images of despair and horror to evocative memories of growing up in Brooklyn. First published in France in 1936.
3. *Tropic of Capricorn* (Grove, 1961) Before coming to Paris, the narrator, like Miller, worked as a personnel manager for a telegraph company—named the Cosmodemonic Company here. First published in France in 1939.

II. Although some critics have called the Rosy Crucifixion trilogy Miller's masterpieces, others have regarded it as a disaster: Miller's friend and admirer Lawrence Durrell (q.v.) urged him to withdraw it from publication. It, too, is a sexually explicit, highly autobiographical work. It describes life in New York and Paris from the 1920s to the 1940s.

1. *Sexus* (Grove, 1965) The author begins his recollections of his literary, intellectual, and amorous adventures in bohemian New York in the 1920s. First published in France in 1962.
2. *Plexus* (Grove, 1965) The author quits his job to write. His relationship with Mona, happy at first, becomes complicated. First published in France in 1949.
3. *Nexus* (Grove, 1965) Mona's crazy friend Stasia comes between her and Miller. First published in France in 1960.

Miller, Linda Lael

I. In recent years (mid-1990s on), best-selling romance author Linda Lael Miller has concentrated on the American West, both past and present. The McKettrick books, set mostly in Arizona from the early 20th century to the present day, are no exception. The McKettrick Cowboys (numbers 1–3) is a trilogy in which the three McKettrick brothers, Rafe, Kade, and Jeb, informed by their father that the first brother who marries and produces legitimate children will inherit his ranch in Arizona, the Triple M, set out to do just that. Number 4 in the series adds an older half brother, Holt McKettrick, and moves the scene to Texas. Number 5, the first in the subseries McKettrick Women, infusing a dab of supernaturalism, finds two female McKettricks leading parallel lives in two centuries. The McKettrick Men trilogy (numbers 6–8), features descendants of the original McKettricks. Of course, Rance, Rafe, Kade, Keegan, Jesse, and all the other male McKettricks are strong, handsome, and seething with passion beneath their gruff, taciturn exteriors. All the women are beautiful and generally brighter than the men. But they, too, are hiding volcanic passions beneath their sometimes prim outer coatings.

1. *High Country Bride* (Pocket Books, 2002) Rafe, who is the eldest McKettrick boy, to inherit his father's Triple M Ranch, marries Emmeline by mail order.
2. *Shotgun Bride* (Pocket Books, 2003) Kade McKettrick, faced with a choice between five potential mail-order brides, falls for Mandy Spearin, who is disguised as a nun.
3. *Secondhand Bride* (Pocket Books, 2004) Jeb, who is the youngest McKettrick brother, marries Chloe Wakefield in Tombstone. But it seems that she was already married to someone else.
4. *McKettrick's Choice* (HQN, 2005) In a sort of afterthought to the Cowboys trilogy, older half brother Holt McKettrick goes to Texas on a mission to save a buddy from hanging and falls in love with Lorelei Fellows, the daughter of the judge who sentenced Holt's friend to hang.
5. *Sierra's Homecoming* (Silhouette, 2006) In the only volume of the McKettrick Women subset, Sierra McKettrick and Hannah Mc-Kettrick seem to be leading parallel lives, one in the 21st century, the other in 1919.
6. *McKettrick's Luck* (HQN, 2007) Confirmed bachelor Jesse McKettrick refuses to sell land to Cheyenne Bridges's employer, not consciously aware of the feelings that Cheyenne stirs up him. First of the McKettrick Men trilogy.
7. *McKettrick's Pride* (HQN, 2007) Eccentric Chicagoan Echo Wells sparks interest, including that of widower Rance McKettrick, in the small ranching town of Indian Rock, Arizona, when she opens the hamlet's first bookstore
8. *McKettrick's Heart* (HQN, 2007) Keegan McKettrick has sworn off love following his divorce. But along comes saucy newcomer Molly Shields.

II. Another trilogy set in Arizona is a trio of mysteries featuring attorney Clare Westbrook of Phoenix and her once-and-future lover, homicide detective and FBI wannabe Tony Sonterra.

1. *Don't Look Now* **(Atria, 2003)** Defense lawyer Clare Westbrook, of Kredd & Associates, gets reinvolved with ex-flame homicide detective Tony Sonterra when her boss, Harvey Kredd, is murdered.
2. *Never Look Back* **(Atria, 2004)** A large inheritance out of the blue from her father allows Clare to set up her own practice. No sooner does she hang out her shingle than someone is shooting out the windows of her office.
3. *One Last Look* **(Pocket Books, 2006)** Clare is carrying Tony's child but isn't sure she wants to marry him because he is slated to be stationed in the nowhere town of Shelton.

III. The Women of Primrose Creek, set in 19th-century Nevada, is about the McQuarry women, who undergo various tribulations and romances before finding happiness and true love. *The Women of Primrose Creek* (Pocket, 2002) is an omnibus containing numbers 1 through 4.

1. *Bridget* **(Pocket, 2000)** Bridget McQuarry, widowed by the Civil War, loses the family farm to taxes. Will Trace Qualtrough come to the rescue?
2. *Christy* **(Pocket Books, 2000)** Christy McQuarry comes to settle in Primrose Creek with her sister Megan. Town Marshal Zachary Shaw will figure in this romance.
3. *Megan* **(Pocket Books, 2000)** Megan McQuarry, who attempted to be an actress, receives a shocking revelation. Webb Stratton, new owner of her land, will play a big role.
4. *Skye* **(Pocket Books, 2000)** Skye McQuarry loves lumber baron Jake Vigil, who has suffered heartbreak in the past.
5. *Last Chance Cafe, The* **(Pocket Book, 2002)** In what seems to be an add-on to the Primrose Creek series set later in time, Jace Stratton and Chance Qualtrough square off in a dispute over property lines.

IV. Springwater Seasons is a series set in the town of Springwater, Montana. The McCaffreys are among a range of characters who find romantic fruition in this series, which was originally supposed to conclude with number 5 but was continued for another couple of volumes. *Springwater Seasons* (Pocket Books, 2001) is an omnibus containing numbers 2 through 5.

1. *Springwater* **(Pocket Books, 1998)** Evangeline Keating goes to Montana Territory to make a new life for herself and her daughter, arrives in Springwater Station, and falls in love with Scully Wainwright, partner of the man she is to marry.
2. *Rachel* **(Pocket, 1999)** Rachel English, recent immigrant to Springwater, locks horns with Troy Hargreaves.
3. *Savannah* **(Pocket Books, 1999)** Savannah, a dance-hall girl who has maintained her virtue, finds friendship and love in Springwater.
4. *Miranda* **(Pocket Books, 1999)** Thrown out by her father, Miranda and her illegitimate child are looking for a new chance in Springwater.
5. *Jessica* **(Pocket Books, 1999)** Spinster Jessica lives in Springwater to help her ailing brother run the *Springwater Gazette*.
6. *Springwater Christmas, A* **(Pocket Books, 1999)** Jacob and June-bug McCaffrey get some startling new when a mysterious stranger returns to Springwater.
7. *Springwater Wedding* **(Pocket Books, 2001)** Maggie McCaffrey returns to Springwater to turn the old station into a modern inn and to reunite with old flame J. T. Wainwright.

V. The Corbin series is set in Oregon in the 1880s and 1890s. Various members of the Corbin family undergo romantic ups and downs. Number 4 seems to be an afterthought. Other "series," such as Valerian (which features vampires), Quade (romance set in Europe and Asia), and Beyond the Threshold (time travel), don't seem to have much except title and theme holding them together. *Two Brothers* (Pocket Books, 1998) included two novels, *The Lawman* and *The Gunslinger*, published together but published separately in large print (Wheeler) a year later.

1. *Banner O'Brien* **(Silhouette, 1984)** Oregon, 1886. Banner O'Brien, unable to overcome her nightmares, signs on with Dr. Adam Corbin, who is hiding a mysterious past himself.
2. *Corbin's Fancy* **(Silhouette, 1985)** Fancy Jordan falls in love with Jesse Corbin, who is still in love with his brother's wife.
3. *Memory's Embrace* **(Silhouette, 1986)** Tess Bishop decides to help stranger Keith Corbin.
4. *My Darling Melissa* **(Silhouette, 1990)** Melissa Corbin flees the altar on her wedding day when she discovers that her husband-to-be is plotting to take a second lover.

Millhiser, Marlys

Charlie Greene is a thirtysomething single mother of an ornery teenager, a literary agent, a bit of a psychic, and an amateur detective. Charlie works out of Hollywood but goes pretty far afield, to places like Oregon, Utah, Colorado, Nevada, and Iowa, in these mysteries full of eccentric characters and wacky situations, with a dollop of the supernatural thrown in. Marlys Millhiser also writes gothic suspense novels, such as *The Mirror* (Putnam, 1978) and *The Threshold* (Putnam, 1984).

1. *Murder at Moot Point* **(Doubleday, 1992)** Literary agent Charlie Greene drives from Beverly Hills to Moot Point, Oregon to meet client Jack Monroe, a New Age author who is experimenting with out-of-body experiences.
2. *Death of the Office Witch* **(Penzler, 1993)** Sharp-tongued office secretary Gloria Tuschman, found dead in some bushes, apparently manages to send a message from beyond the grave: "Charlie, I'm in the trash can. Help me."
3. *Murder in a Hot Flash* **(Penzler, 1995)** Charlie's biologist mother, Edwina, appalled by the cavalier attitude toward the ecosystem of horror film director Gordon Cabot, becomes the prime suspect when Cabot turns up dead on location in Utah.
4. *It's Murder Going Home* **(St. Martin's, 1996)** Charlie and her 16-year-old daughter, Libby, reluctantly return to Boulder, Colorado, to care for the ailing Edwina, who seems to have unleashed some murderous feelings in her neighbors by turning retired laboratory rats free in the neighborhood.
5. *Nobody Dies in a Casino* **(St. Martin's, 1999)** Charlie, on a working vacation in Las Vegas, sees two security guards shove a man in front of an oncoming car.
6. *Killer Commute* **(St. Martin's, 2000)** Charlie discovers the corpse of her gated-community neighbor Jeremy Fiedler and becomes the chief suspect in his murder.
7. *Rampant Reaper, The* **(St. Martin's, 2002)** Charlie agrees to accompany her biological (not *biologist* mother; that's Edwina) mother to Myrtle, Iowa, to attend the funeral of her great-great-aunt, and where Charlie goes, trouble follows.
8. *Voices in the Wardrobe* **(Severn House, 2005)** TV's "Doctor Judy" is found dead in the pool of a San Diego spa to which Charlie has accompanied her old friend Maggie.

Minahan, John

John Rawlings is a veteran New York City Police Department detective. "Little John" has seen it all, likes to wax avuncular about it, and employs a freewheeling approach to the mysteries that come the way of the 19th Precinct. Amusing characters such as Vadney, the publicity-mad chief of detectives, spice the action, and New York City is lovingly evoked in this entertaining procedural series.

1. *Great Hotel Robbery, The* (Norton, 1982) Three tuxedo-clad men and a uniformed chauffeur pull off the biggest hotel robbery in American history at New York's Hotel Champs-Élysées.
2. *Great Diamond Robbery, The* (Norton, 1984) Tara Alvarado tells Rawlings that she has been approached by three hoods who want her to be the "inside man" in a multimillion-dollar gem heist.
3. *Face behind the Mask, The* (Norton, 1986) The usually blase Rawlings is appalled by a series of rapes perpetrated by a handsome, smooth-talking rapist.
4. *Great Pyramid Robbery, The* (Norton, 1987) Eight million dollars in untraceable bills have been stolen from the allegedly impregnable warehouse of the New York Armored Car Courier Company.
5. *Great Harvard Robbery, The* (Norton, 1988) Strange pranks culminates in the theft of a Gutenberg Bible from Harvard University.
6. *Great Grave Robbery, The* (Norton, 1989) A robbery suspect believed to be 20 years dead turns up claiming to be a beneficiary of cryogenics.

Minichino, Camille

The Gloria Lamerino, or Periodic Table, series, features retired physicist Gloria Lamerino of Revere, Massachusetts, who gets mixed up in a series of murders connected with the chemical elements and environmental science. With her boyfriend, and eventual husband, homicide detective Matt Gennaro, Gloria manages to come up with the answers in this set of cozies.

Camille Minichino is a physicist with a long career in research, teaching, and writing. She is currently connected with Golden Gate University and the Lawrence Livermore National Laboratory.

1. *Hydrogen Murder, The* (Avalon, 1997) Gloria Lamerino, newly retired from a physics career in California, returns to her hometown of Revere, Massachusetts, to work with police on the case of Eric Bentsen, who was shot in his physics lab.
2. *Helium Murder, The* (Avalon, 1998) Congresswoman Margaret Hirley, member of the House Science and Technology Committee, is killed by a hit-and-run driver.
3. *Lithium Murder, The* (Morrow, 1999) Michael Deramo, janitor in the physics department of a local university, is strangled after overhearing a plot to conceal environmental hazards associated with the development of a new lithium battery.
4. *Beryllium Murder, The* (Morrow, 2000) The death, by beryllium poisoning, of former colleague Gary Larkin prompts Lamerino to visit old friends in Berkeley, California.
5. *Boric Acid Murder, The* (St. Martin's, 2002) John Galigani, son of Gloria's landlords, is accused of murdering Yolanda Fiore, a former girlfriend.
6. *Carbon Murder, The* (St. Martin's, 2004) The return to Revere of Mary Catherine Galigani, Gloria's goddaughter, is punctuated by two murders.
7. *Nitrogen Murder, The* (St. Martin's, 2005) A trip back to California for the wedding of a close friend involves Gloria in murder and secret government research on nitrogen.

8. *Oxygen Murder, The* (St. Martin's, 2006) Gloria and her new husband, Matt Gennaro, in New York City for a Christmas holiday, run into the murder of Amber Kennan, a camerawoman who had been working on a documentary film about the ozone layer.

Mishima, Yukio

PSEUDONYM OF Kimitake Hiraoka

Yukio Mishima's novels are quite unlike those of any Westerner. Born into a samurai family, Mishima mastered the traditional martial arts and became a charismatic rightist figure in Japan. He committed ritual suicide in 1970 at the age of 45 after completing the final volume of his masterpiece, the Sea of Fertility. This tetralogy begins in 1912 and examines the social, aesthetic, and moral life of Japan up to the 1960s. The character of Hondo is a continuing figure present in all four books of this sensual, violent, disturbing series. Omnibus edition, *The Sea of Fertility* (Secker [UK], 1985) contains all four titles.

1. *Spring Snow* (Knopf, 1972) Set in 1912, this narrative concerns the doomed affair between Ayakuras, son of a newly rich provincial family, and the beautiful Satoko, who is betrothed to a royal prince. Translated from the Japanese by Michael Gallagher. Originally published in 1968.
2. *Runaway Horses* (Knopf, 1973) A conspiracy during the 1930s by fanatical young patriot, Isao Iinuma, leads to his discovery, arrest, and trial. Translated from the Japanese by Michael Gallagher. Originally published in 1969.
3. *Temple of Dawn* (Knopf, 1973) Hondo journeys to Bangkok in 1940 and becomes obsessed with a Thai princess. The second half of the story skips to the 1950s. Translated from the Japanese by E. Dale Saunders and Cecilia Seigle. Originally published in 1970.
4. *Decay of the Angel, The* (Knopf, 1974) In the late 1960s Hondo, now old and rich, adopts a 16-year-old orphan boy as his heir. Translated from the Japanese by Edward Seidenstricker. Originally published in 1970.

Moberg, Vilhelm

Liv Ullmann and Max von Sydow starred in two riveting Swedish films—*The Emigrants* (1972) and *The New Land* (1973)—based on Moberg's tetralogy about a band of farmers from Smaland in southern Sweden, who emigrate to America. The story focuses on Oskar Nilsson, his wife, Kristina, their children, and his brother Robert as they leave their home in Ljuder Parish in 1850 and make the arduous Atlantic crossing. Confused but undaunted by the strangeness of the new world, they travel west and settle in the Minnesota wilderness. This is a vivid testament to the hardships of pioneer life and to the courage, fortitude, and humor of the Swedes who made the trip. Vilhelm Moberg (d. 1973) was a Swedish journalist, novelist, and dramatist who lived in various parts of the United States between 1949 and 1955. He also wrote an autobiographical series, the Knut Toring trilogy (1935–1939), apparently never translated into English, and nonfiction books such as *The Unknown Swedes: A Book about Swedes and America, Past and Present* (translated by Roger McKnight); Southern Illinois, 1988).

1. *Emigrants, The* (Simon & Schuster, 1951) The Nilssons leave Sweden and cross the Atlantic in a small, cramped boat carrying freight and 70 other passengers. Translated from the Swedish by Gustaf Lannestock. Originally published as *Utrandrarna* in 1949.
2. *Unto a Good Land* (Simon & Schuster, 1954) The family makes its way from the port of New York to its new home in Taylor Falls,

Minnesota, in June 1851. Translated from the Swedish by Gustaf Lannestock. Originally published as *Invandrarna* in 1952.

3. *Settlers, The* (Popular Library, 1978) The story from 1853 to 1860 as the Nilssons settle into their home in Minnesota fighting harsh conditions and Indian uprisings. Translated from the Swedish by Gustaf Lannestock. Originally published as *Nybyggarna* in 1956. First published in English with number 4 as *The Last Letter Home* (Simon & Schuster, 1961).

4. *Last Letter Home, The* (Popular Library, 1979) Takes the story through the Civil War until Karl's death in 1890. Translated from the Swedish by Gustav Lannestock. Originally published as *Sista Brevet till Sverige* in 1959. First published in English with number 3 as *The Last Letter Home* (Simon & Schuster, 1961).

Modesitt, L(eland) E(xton), Jr.

I. Modesitt has created a heroic fantasy planet in which the White forces of Chaos and the Black forces of Order are maintained in an uneasy equilibrium. He has created a complex world based on a plausible system of magic and peopled with realistic characters described in readable prose. The island continent Recluce is the scene of many of the novels, but other lands, such as Candor, Westwind, Wandernaught, and Sarronyn play roles as well. Overall chronology is a little difficult to establish, but numbers 1 and 2 describe the "founding" of Recluce by the engineer Nylan; numbers 4 and 5 chronicle the adventures of Lorn in the Empire of Cyador; numbers 6 and 7 feature Kharl the Cooper; numbers 8 and 9 feature Cerryl the White Mage of Fairhaven; and numbers 12 and 13 trace the career of the reluctant Mage Lerris.

1. *Fall of Angels* (Tor, 1996) Relates the prehistory of Recluce. The crew of the United Faith Forces' frigate *Winterlance* are stranded on a strange planet.

2. *Chaos Balance, The* (Tor, 1997) After engineer Nylan builds Tower Black and saves his shipmates, he is forced to leave his new home.

3. *Towers of the Sunset, The* (Tor, 1992) Chronicles the founding of the island nation of Recluce as young Creslin travels to Fairhaven, "city of wizards."

4. *Magi'i of Cyador* (Tor, 2000) Lorn, son of a high-ranking Magi'i, finds the magical order's rules too constricting and is sent off to join the Lancers.

5. *Scion of Cyador* (Tor, 2001) Lor has acquired a reputation as a survivor as well as a gifted, if unorthodox, officer. The death of the Emperor of Cyador leaves many claimants to his throne.

6. *Wellspring of Chaos* (Tor, 2004) Kharl, the Cooper of the city of Brysta, is forced to leave his city and prosperous business when he offends the local lord's son by a couple of good deeds.

7. *Ordermaster* (Tor, 2005) Kharl the Cooper, now lord of Cantyl, battles chaos-wielding white wizards, turns a mountain into glass, quashes a rebellion, and studies law.

8. *White Order, The* (Tor, 1998) Cerryl's father is killed by mages who disapproved of his studies. Despite his guardian's distrust of magic, books and mirrors attract Cerryl.

9. *Colors of Chaos* (Tor, 1999) Cerryl the White Mage has become a powerful wizard of Chaos, but he must face the unwanted attentions of seductive, sinister, redheaded mage Anya.

10. *Magic Engineer, The* (Tor, 1994) Dorrin, a young engineer, more interested in machinery than his family and government think appropriate, is sent into exile.

11. *Order War, The* (Tor, 1995) Order engineer Justen volunteers for a force sent by Recluce to aid the matriarchy of Sarronnyn under attack by the White Wizards of Fairhaven.

12. *Magic of Recluce, The* (Tor, 1991) In the first book published in the series, Young Lerris, who has the potential to become an Order-Master, but would rather be an artisan, is sent on a journey to find himself.

13. *Death of Chaos, The* (Tor, 1995) Lerris, now settled down as a carpenter with his warrior wife, Krystal, is called upon to battle the forces of the mad Emperor of Hamor.

14. *Natural Ordermage* (Tor, 2007) The impatient Rahl's short temper gets him into trouble again and again when he is banished to the distant continent of Hamor for dissing ordermages who are trying to teach him self-control.

II. The recently completed Spellsong cycle describes an alternate world where music literally creates magic. Anna Marshall, singing teacher from Ames, Iowa, discovers that her vocal talents and training on Earth have prepared her to wield great power in the kingdom of Defalk in the world of Erde, where female spellsongs contend against the magical drumming of male sorcerers.

1. *Soprano Sorceress, The* (Tor, 1997) Anna Marshall is transported from Iowa into the alternate world of Erde, where she finds that her vocal talents and training on Earth are potent magic.

2. *Spellsong War, The* (Tor, 1998) Anna, now regent of Defalk, finds the spellsong nation menaced once again by its warlike neighbors.

3. *Darksong Rising* (Tor, 2000) Anna finds no permanent peace in Defalk, being troubled by the adolescent silliness of its heir, the sexism of its nobility, a chronic shortage of money, new revelations about Defalk, and the temptation to abuse her powers.

4. *Shadow Sorceress, The* (Tor, 2001) Anna is dead, and the peace of the Liedwahr is threatened by the Order of Sea Priests, who assault Defalk's coast with a form of rhythmic magic based on drumming.

5. *Shadowsinger* (Tor, 2002) In the cycle's conclusion, Anna's successor, newlywed Secca, and her sorcerer husband, Alciren, attempt to end the military threat of the Sturrinese against Defalk.

III. The Ecolitan series is another "galactic empire" saga. The Ecolitan Institute is the leader in the planet Accord's efforts to break away from its Empire. Major Jimjoy Earle Wright, ace Imperial Special Operative, is disgraced and joins the Ecolitan Institute as Professor James Joyson Whaler against the Empire (numbers 1 and 2). Nathaniel Whaler, economist and commando leader, is the protagonist of numbers 3 and 4, as Accord secedes from the Empire and tries to steer a neutral course between the great powers of the galaxy. Omnibus editions: *Empire and Ecolitan* (Tor, 2001) contains numbers 1 and 2; *Ecolitan Prime* (Tor, 2003) contains numbers 3 and 4.

1. *Ecolitan Operation, The* (Tor, 1989) Major Jimjoy Earle Wright, ace Imperial Special Operative, succeeds all too well in overthrowing a planetary dictatorship, as the dictatorship is succeeded by a government that is strongly opposed to the Empire.

2. *Ecologic Succession, The* (Tor, 1990) Major Wright, now disgraced in the Empire, fakes his death and joins the Ecolitan Institute on Accord as Ecolitan Professor James Joyson Whaler.

3. *Ecologic Envoy, The* (Tor, 1986) After seceding from the Empire, Accord tries to sign a trade treaty on microchip exports. Nathaniel Whaler is sent to facilitate the operation. First novel in the series to be published.

4. *Ecolitan Enigma, The* (Tor, 1997) Sent ostensibly as economist to the backwater planet Artos, Nathaniel and his colleague Sylvia find themselves in the middle of a rivalry between two empires.

IV. The Ghost trilogy is somewhat of a change of pace, mixing fantasy and SF themes. It postulates an alternate history Earth in which the United States is divided into several different nations; Russia is still under the rule of the Romanovs; and the planet is shared by living people and the ghosts of the dead, who sometimes interact with the living. Protagonists are Johan Eschbach, retired spy for the nation of Columbia, who becomes a researcher in ghost control, and his opera singer wife, Llysette. *Ghosts of Columbia* (Tor, 2005) contains numbers 1 and 2.

1. *Of Tangible Ghosts* (Tor, 1994) Johan Eschbach retires as a spy for Columbia, returns to teach in the Northeast, still dominated by the Dutch, gets involved in ghost-control research, and finds himself marked for death.

2. *Ghost of the Revelator, The* (Tor, 1998) On a tour to the Mormon country of Deseret, Llysette, opera-singer wife of Johan, is kidnapped, and the kidnappers demand the resurrection of the ghost of Mormon founder Joseph Smith as ransom.

3. *Ghost of the White Nights* (Tor, 2001) Johan and Llysette travel on a cultural exchange to a Russia still ruled by the Romanovs. Meanwhile, the Russians are developing a rocket-delivered warhead that will turn humans into zombies.

V. The Corean Chronicles is a fantasy series in which humans and a variety of strange mutated animals share a world named Corus centuries after a great catastrophe. The humans are protected by a few people who (secretly) possess Magical Talent. Alucius, soldier, and secret Talent, is the leading protagonist of numbers 1, 2, and 3. Dainyl, an Alector, an eight-foot race with psychic powers, is the leading protagonist of numbers 4, 5, and 6.

1. *Legacies* (Tor, 2002) Alucius, raised on the family farm, is Talented but must keep it secret.

2. *Darknesses* (Tor, 2003) Alucius, now a soldier, is trying to keep himself and fellow members of the Iron Valley Militia alive until he's discharged and can return to his beloved wife, Wendra.

3. *Scepters* (Tor, 2004) Alucius is called back to duty as commander of the Northern and Southern Guard to quell rebels determined to reinitiate the old religion.

4. *Alector's Choice* (Tor, 2005) With the life force of the planet Ifryn almost exhausted, its population is about to migrate to Corus, where the Alectors, a giant race with psychic powers, are overseeing the biological preparation of this new world.

5. *Cadmian's Choice* (Tor, 2006) Dainyl, an Alector who's now a submarshal of the Myrmidons, and Mykel, a major commanding a rifle battalion who secretly possesses some of the psychic "Talent" of the Alectors, form an uneasy alliance.

6. *Soarer's Choice* (Tor, 2006) The conclusion of the Corean Chronicles, in which the High Alector Dainyl and the human major Mykel deal with the situation left by the Alector leaders' decision to move the bulk of their population to a planet other than Corus. The winged native Soarers, or Ancients, will ultimately determine the fate of Corus.

VI. The Forever Hero trio is an early SF series set in the distant future in which Earth is a desolate ruin inhabited by a few primitive remnants of humanity, one of whom is MacGregor Gerswin ("The Forever Hero"), of great intelligence, determination, almost immortal, and destined to restore Earth to its former glories. Omnibus volume: *The Forever Hero* (Tor, 1999) contains all three titles.

1. *Dawn for a Distant Earth* (Tor, 1986) The first human spaceship to return to Earth in millennia discovers some primitive remnants

of humanity, among whom is a boy of great native intelligence and determination.

2. *Silent Warrior, The* (Tor, 1987) MacGregor Gerswin, immortal soldier and schemer, wages an undeclared war to return Earth back to life.

3. *Endless Twilight, The* (Tor, 1988) The Forever Hero destroys the decayed, bureaucratic Empire, which is feeding off of humanity.

VII. Timediver's Dawn and the Timegod are a pair of loosely connected fantasy-sf novels set in the future and featuring a mixture of empires, magic, and creatures from Norse legend. Published together as *Timegods' World* (Tor, 2000).

1. *Timediver's Dawn* (Tor, 1992) The Empire of Westron faces an invasion by Frost Giants. Sammis, a descendant of the persecuted witches of Eastron finds himself on the run when Imperial troops destroy his home and country.

2. *Timegod, The* (Tor, 1993) Ingram Lovi, a young timediver who becomes a member of the Temporal Guard of the Planet Query, soon finds himself in rebellion against the powers-that-be. Expanded version of *The Fires of Paratime* (Pocket, 1982).

VIII. The Archform: Beauty series is a pair of novels (so far) about Earth in the 24th century, where nanomachines watch over the health of the elite and manufacture food and gadgets that take care of everyone's carnal needs but leave most people struggling to extract meaning from a life empty of commitment and human connection.

1. *Archform: Beauty* (Tor, 2002) The voices and experiences of five very different people on a 24th-century Earth dominated by nanotechnology are overlapped and combined.

2. *Flash* (Tor, 2004) Jonat de Vrai, rising star in the marines, starts his life over as the world's expert on the effectiveness of "prod"— product placement, a form of 24th-century advertising.

Monsarrat, Nicholas

I. These two books by the author of the World War II classic *The Cruel Sea* (Random House, 1951) still give a good picture of the conflicts and tensions found in developing African nations. Events as they unfold are seen mostly through the eyes of David Bracken, a novice British government official who feels a youthful rapport with Dinamaula, the young, Oxford-educated chief of the Maulas. The action is set on the fictional island of Pharamaul off the southwest coast of Africa.

1. *Tribe That Lost Its Head, The* (Sloane, 1956) A young African, who has been a student in England, is recalled to his native country when his father dies to take his place as chief.

2. *Richer Than All His Tribe* (Morrow, 1969) Bracken is disillusioned when sees Pharamaul's black leaders grow corrupt and tyrannical after independence.

II. The Master Mariner is the running title for a series of novels left unfinished at Monsarrat's death in 1979. His intent was to chronicle 400 years of British naval history through the eyes of a sailor condemned to roam the seas forever because of his cowardice while serving under Drake against the Spanish Armada. The chronicle was to have been continued past World War II, but it had gotten only as far as 1806 when Monsarrat died. What we have of the series are two rousing sea stories containing good, painless history. An omnibus volume containing both novels entitled *The Master Mariner* was published by Cassell (UK) in 1980.

1. *Running Proud* (Morrow, 1979) Matthew Lawe, doomed to wander the oceans forever, gets involved with several historical naval figures including Henry Hudson, Samuel Pepys, Captain Cook, and Lord Nelson.
3. *Darken Ship* (Morrow, 1981) In 1806 Lawe is the captain of an illegal slave trader. This novel, left unfinished at Monsarrat's death, concludes with his notes and sketches put together by his widow.

Montgomery, L(ucy) M(aud)

Mark Twain called Anne Shirley of Green Gables "the dearest and most lovable child in fiction since the immortal Alice." Certainly she has captured the hearts of millions of girls from 1905 onward, not only in English-speaking countries, but also in lands such as Japan. The 1980s television series on PBS starring Megan Follows as Anne and its 1999 sequel depicting a grown-up Anne introduced Green Gables to legions of new fans. *Anne of Green Gables* has attracted much scholarly attention as well, including a guide called *The Annotated Anne of Green Gables* (Oxford, 1997) and the controversial (and questionable) claim by a Canadian professor that Anne had strong lesbian leanings. Though the books are a trifle saccharine by today's standards, their underlying theme remains fresh and relevant, especially for young people: Anne struggles against conformity and demonstrates the possibility of winning acceptance as an individual on one's own merits. Montgomery's hometown of Cavendish, on Prince Edward Island in the Canadian Maritimes, provided the beautiful setting for the Anne books. Her house there has become a tourist attraction. L. M. Montgomery published other children's series such as the Emily series and a pair of novels about the King family, as well as adult novels including two about a character named Pat and an autobiography: *The Alpine Path: The Story of My Career* (1917). *The Selected Journals of L. M. Montgomery* have appeared in four volumes so far (1986–).

1. *Anne of Green Gables* (Page, 1908) Eleven-year-old Anne is sent from the orphanage to the home of an elderly brother and sister, Matthew and Marilla Cuthbert. They had requested a boy, but she soon wins their love.
2. *Anne of Avonlea* (Page, 1909) This account takes Anne from a winsome "half-past sixteen" to her departure for college.
3. *Chronicles of Avonlea* (Page, 1912) These are stories of Avonlea and Spencervale, only some of which include Anne.
4. *Anne of the Island* (Page, 1915) Anne is at Redmond College, studying to be a teacher; during her visits home, everything seems to be changing.
5. *Anne of Windy Poplars* (Stokes, 1936) During Anne's first three years of teaching at Summerside High School, she lives at a boardinghouse called Windy Poplars. UK title: *Anne of Windy Willows*.
6. *Anne's House of Dreams* (Stokes, 1917) At last Anne marries her old sweetheart, in the orchard at Green Gables.
7. *Anne of Ingleside* (Stokes, 1939) Fifteen years have passed, and Anne is the mother of a happy brood.
8. *Rainbow Valley* (Stokes, 1919) This book centers around Anne's young children and the romance of the widowed minister.
9. *Rilla of Ingleside* (Stokes, 1921) Anne's youngest daughter, Rilla, is the focus of this story that shows how World War I affected the family.
10. *Further Chronicles of Avonlea* (Page, 1920) These 15 short stories deal with Anne's friends and neighbors.

Moody, Bill

Jazz drummer Bill Moody has written a mystery series about jazz pianist, Evan Horne, who investigates cases involving the world of nightclubs, recording studios, and crooked agents. Three of the mysteries involve real-life jazz legends from the past. Moody is also the author of the nonfiction *The Jazz Exiles: American Musicians Abroad* (Nevada, 1993).

1. *Solo Hand* (Walker, 1994) Jazz pianist Evan Horne is in Los Angeles recovering from an auto accident that damaged his right hand when he learns that someone is blackmailing singer Lonnie Cole with some compromising photos.
2. *Death of a Tenor Man* (Walker, 1995) Evan is in Las Vegas helping a friend doing research into the death, back in 1955, from an alleged drug overdose, of real-life jazz saxophonist Ward Gray.
3. *Sound of the Trumpet, The* (Walker, 1996) Horne is in a studio helping a friend with tapes that may have been recorded by 1950s jazz trumpet legend Clifford Brown. Then the owner of the disputed tapes dies.
4. *Bird Lives!* (Walker, 1999) A serial killer is murdering jazz saxophonists and leaving behind references to jazz legend Charlie Parker in the form of bird feathers.
5. *Looking for Chet Baker* (Walker, 2002) Evan is doing a gig in Amsterdam when he gets interested in the mysterious death of real-life jazz trumpeter Chet Baker, found dead outside his Amsterdam hotel from what was either a fall, a jump, or a push.
6. *Shades of Blue* (Poisoned Pen, 2008) Horne's friend and mentor, pianist Calvin Hughes, dies and leaves everything to him. While sorting through Hughes's belongings in Los Angeles, Horne turns up some odd pieces of paper, including what might be the original, handwritten compositions of two famous Miles Davis recordings.

Moody, Skye Kathleen

The heroine of Skye Moody's mystery series is Venus Diamond, an under five-foot, sassy, leather-clad motorcycle riding US Fish and Wildlife Service Agent. Venus works out of Seattle in these novels characterized by a breezy style, humor, offbeat plots, and a modicum of environmental message. Skye Kathleen Moody is a writer, photographer, and former East Africa bush guide. She is also the author of the nonfiction *Washed Up: The Curious Journeys of Flotsam and Jetsam* (Sasquatch, 2006).

1. *Rain Dance* (St. Martin's, 1996) After surviving a near-fatal dose of malaria while tracking poachers in Southeast Asia, Venus Diamond is ordered to Seattle to work on what her boss calls "the Pelican Patrol." A bullet-riddled body has washed up on shores of Ozone Beach, a remote village that serves as both a Pelican sanctuary and home to 200 eccentrics.
2. *Blue Poppy* (St. Martin's, 1997) Venus is called in to investigate the murder of a biologist on government land leased to a perfumery that cultivates Tibetan Blue Poppies.
3. *Wildcrafters* (St. Martin's, 1998) When a baby disappears, Venus delays her honeymoon with Richard Winter to head the search in a wildlife preserve subject to elk poaching and the harvesting of environmentally protected plants.
4. *Habitat* (St. Martin's, 1999) Diamond is asked to investigate an arson case in a radical experimental genetics clinic.
5. *K Falls* (St. Martin's, 2001) Venus and a male colleague are on the trail of terrorists responsible for bombing dams along the Columbia River.

6. *Medusa* **(St. Martin's, 2003)** Diamond's teenage brother, Tim, is accused of murdering a friend while they were playing pirates on Tim's mother's yacht. A giant jellyfish plays a role here.

7. *Good Diamond, The* **(St. Martin's, 2004)** Venus is brought into the world of diamond smuggling when the prospector who found a 350-carat blue diamond in Canada's Northwest Territories is murdered and writes her name in blood at the scene.

Moody, Susan

I. Penny Wanawake (pronounced *Wa-na-wa-ke*), the daughter of Lady Helena Hurley and Dr. Benjamin Wanawake, Permanent Ambassador to the United Nations from the (fictional) republic of Senangaland, is a six-foot black female sleuth. Because of her connections, Penny leads a jet-set-style life, but she does have a social conscience, using her freelance photography to point up the plight of the Third World. Penny is not bound to conventional morality and not rigidly legalistic. Her lover, Barnaby Midas, is a con man and a jewel thief, and her "tenant-in-residence" in London, Antonia Ivory, runs a housekeeping service that specializes in placing women in wealthy homes they can rob, but Penny figures that they are just redistributing the wealth. However, she doesn't approve of murder, and devotes considerable effort to solving the homicide cases that come her way in this racy series told in wisecracking style. English author Susan Moody is also the author of the Cassie Swann series (series II, below), and of *Misselthwaite* (US title: *Return to the Secret Garden*, Signet, 1998), a sequel to the Frances Hodgson Burnett classic, *The Secret Garden* and of other novels, some of them written under the pseudonyms of Susannah James and Susan Madison.

1. *Penny Black* **(Fawcett, 1984)** Introduces Penny Wanawake. Blond model Marfa Lund, a friend of Penny's, is murdered.

2. *Penny Dreadful* **(Ballantine, 1986)** No annotation available. Originally published in the United Kingdom in 1984.

3. *Penny Post* **(Ballantine, 1986)** Wealthy Kendal Sartain asks old friend Penny to find out who is trying to kill him.

4. *Penny Royal* **(Ballantine, 1987)** An absent-minded archaeologist disappears, along with a few priceless gold statues.

5. *Penny Wise* **(Ballantine, 1989)** While on a yacht cruise in the Greek isles, Irene Lampeter drops dead of an apparent heart attack. However, Penny thinks there was something unnatural about her death.

6. *Penny Pinching* **(Ballantine, 1989)** While at her father's beach house, Penny and boyfriend Barnaby discover the body of a beautiful black woman who could have been Penny's twin.

7. *Penny Saving* **(Joseph [UK], 1990)** No annotation available. Not published in the United States.

II. Moody's second series heroine, Cassandra "Cassie" Swann, is, in some ways quite different from Penny Wanawake: she is white, heavyset, and lacking in Penny's self-confidence. Cassie Swann is a former biology teacher who has become a professional bridge player. The bridge world is cut-throat both figuratively and literally, and Cassie gets involved in several murder investigations.

1. *Death Takes a Hand* **(Penzler, 1994)** Three of Cassie's star bridge students are dead, which calls for an investigation in the tightly knit bridge circuit. UK title: *Takeout Double*.

2. *Grand Slam* **(Penzler, 1995)** Cassie stumbles over the body of Lady Portia Wickham.

3. *King of Hearts* **(Scribner, 1996)** While watching the Grand National Day Race on TV, Cassie spots Brigid Fraser, the mystery figure in the photo of Cassie's father, Handsome Harry, who was stabbed to death 20 years ago.

4. *Doubled in Spades* **(Scribner, 1997)** Why did Cassie's bridge partner, Naomi Harris, take a fatal overdose? And who is this young woman claiming to be Naomi's daughter.

5. *Sacrifice Bid* **(Headline [UK], 1997)** A village murder exposes a long-suppressed secret held by Lolly Haden White, one of Cassie's bridge group. Not published in the United States.

6. *Dummy Hand* **(Headline [UK], 1998)** While riding her bicycle, Cassie is clipped by a hit-and-run driver, who subsequently comes to the police station and confesses. Not published in the United States.

Moorcock, Michael

I. The prolific English writer Michael Moorcock has published more than 100 novels, more than 160 short stories, graphic novels, comic strips, a screenplay, songs, and nonfiction. Moorcock started out writing comics, then branched out as a songwriter and member of various rock bands. He is primarily a fantasy writer with some SF overtones, a great deal of humor, and much social commentary in between the lines. Some critics regard him as the godfather of the "cyberpunk" writers of the 1980s such as William Gibson (q.v.) and Neal Stephenson. Most of his fiction is in series, but the series are difficult to sort out and arrange because most of the stories are set in the "multiverse" in which time and place seem to have no real meaning, and characters wander from one time period (or even to the "end of time") to another or move from one parallel universe to another and one alternate "history" to another, and refuse to be restricted to one series. In addition, many of Moorcock's stories have been rewritten and revised, sometimes with new titles and new characters, and sometimes, without Moorcock's consent, by hamhanded editors and censors, especially in the United States. Millennium (UK) published a "uniform edition" of much of Moorcock's work in 1992–1993, and White Wolf published several omnibus volumes in the United States in 1996–1999. For the most part *Sequels* has chosen to arrange novels and story collections within each series by original publication date.

The Dancers at the End of Time trilogy is, according to Moorcock, his favorite "fantasy" effort. It still remains a favorite with many readers. It is set in the far future where time as we know it is about to end and the remaining humans have abandoned most of their goals and ideals as futile, and are engaging in the pursuit of pleasure. Jherek Carnelian (see also Jerry Cornelius in series II), bored with his decadent and hedonistic life, becomes obsessed with the "moral" 19th century and falls in love with a reluctant time traveler from Victorian London, Mrs. Amelia Underwood. Moorcock's satiric touch makes these imaginative stories sparkle. Two additional volumes (numbers 4 and 5) were added to the original trilogy and sort of muddied the waters by including characters from other series, such as Elric (see series III). Numbers 1 through 3 are available in an omnibus volume: *The Dancers at the End of Time* (White Wolf, 1998; originally United Kingdom, 1981), and numbers 4 and 5 are available together in *Tales from the End of Time* (Berkley, 1989).

1. *Alien Heat, An* **(Harper, 1972)** Jherek Carnelian follows Mrs. Amelia Underwood from the End of Time to the London of 1896 where he gets involved in a murder trial and sentenced to the gallows.

2. *Hollow Lands, The* **(Harper, 1974)** After escaping death in Victorian London, Jherek seesaws through time and space in search of his beloved Mrs. Underwood.

3. *End of All Songs, The* **(Harper, 1976)** Marooned by a faulty time-machine back in the Paleozoic, Jherek and Mrs. Underwood seem set at last to consummate their love.

4. *Legends from the End of Time* **(Harper, 1976)** Includes stories: "Pale Roses"; "White Stars"; and "Ancient Shadows," as well as the first chapter of "Constant Fire," which was expanded as "Elric at the End of Time" (included in White Wolf edition, 1999).

5. *Messiah at the End of Time, A* **(DAW, 1978)** The Fire Clown (see series XIII), a self-proclaimed savior, has arrived at the end of time and the impregnable spinster Miss Mavis Ming is more than a little charmed by his attention. UK title: *The Transformation of Miss Mavis Ming.*

II. Jerry Cornelius, a sort of ur-cyberpunk character and modern myth figure, is, like many of Moorcock's protagonists, engaged in an unrelenting search for his identity. Jerry has numerous professions (rock star, assassin, psychedelic guru, etc.), talents, and identities. The series starts in the swinging London of 1965, but before it is through (if it is "through"), it takes Jerry into a variety of times and places. The "core" Cornelius books are numbers 1, 2, 3, and 6. Numbers 4 and 8 feature Una Persson and her lover, Catherine Cornelius, with Jerry mostly on the sidelines. Numbers 5 and 9 are short story collections devoted mostly to Jerry. Omnibuses include *The Cornelius Chronicles* (Avon, 1977, in three volumes—numbers 1, 2, 3, and 6); *A Cornelius Calendar* (Phoenix House [UK], 1993—numbers 4, 7, and 8 and the short story "The Alchemist's Question"); and *The Cornelius Quartet* (Four Walls Eight Windows, 2001, originally published 1993; numbers 1, 2, 3, and 6). *The Nature of the Catastrophe* (Hutchinson [UK], 1971) and its much expanded (with some omissions) successor, *The New Nature of the Catastrophe* (Millennium [UK], 1993), edited by Moorcock and Langdon Jones, contain stories based on the Cornelius character by Moorcock and other authors. *Earl Aubec* (White Wolf, 1999; originally United Kingdom, 1993) contains 32 stories by Moorcock, stories and essays by other authors, the comic strip *The Adventures of Jerry Cornelius*, and "Jerry Cornelius: A Reader's Guide," by John Davey.

1. *Final Programme, The* **(Avon, 1968)** In the swinging London of 1965, Jerry Cornelius and Miss Brunner, a computer technician with enormous powers, embark upon an extraordinary joint venture. Revised edition: Fontana (UK), 1979. Made into a movie with the same title (1973) starring Jon Finch and Hugh Griffith. Truncated US version of movie called *The Last Days of Man on Earth.*

2. *Cure for Cancer, A* **(Holt, 1971)** Some years later Jerry reemerges as a black man with white hair; starts a strange transmogrification service; and visits "Amerika." Revised edition: Fontana (UK), 1979.

3. *English Assassin, The* **(Harper, 1972)** Jerry's foul-mouthed mother and the lovely Una Persson appear in this volume, set in the 1970s with Edwardian undertones. The destruction of the Earth is threatened.

4. *Adventures of Una Persson and Catherine Cornelius in the Twentieth Century* **(Quartet [UK], 1976)** Una Persson and Catherine Cornelius are lovers, revolutionaries, and time travelers. Jerry Cornelius is in the background. Not published in the United States.

5. *Lives and Times of Jerry Cornelius, The* **(Allison & Busby [UK], 1976)** A collection of 11 Cornelius short stories. An additional story ("The Dodgem Division") appeared in the Harrap (UK) edition (1987). Collection not published in the United States.

6. *Condition of Muzak, The* **(Gregg, 1977)** Jerry, as Pierrot the Weeper, confronts Death in Ladbroke Grove. Many of Moorcock's hobby-horses, such as Bob Dylan and the Arthurian legend appear here.

7. *Great Rock 'n' Roll Swindle, The* **(Virgin [UK], 1980)** The novelization of the screenplay for the Sex Pistols film of the same name (1975). Peripheral, but often listed in the Cornelius sequence. Revised as *Gold Diggers of 1977* in the collection *Casablanca* (Gollancz [UK], 1989).

8. *Entropy Tango, The* **(New English Library [UK], 1981)** An alternate history scenario involving Una and Catherine, the outbreak of the "second" World War, Bartok on the jukebox, the fall of Toronto, and many refugees from other books in the series. Not published in the United States.

9. *Opium General and Other Stories, The* **(Harrap [UK], 1984)** A short story collection including the "final" Cornelius story, "The Alchemist's Question," which features a nuclear winter in England, and the reappearance of all of the surviving characters from the sequence, including Miss Brunner, who has come to sound suspiciously like Margaret Thatcher.

10. *Firing the Cathedral* **(PS Publishing [UK], 2002)** Jerry Cornelius is resurrected to deal with 21st-century issues such as global terrorism and global warming. Not published in the United States.

III. Jerek Carnelian and Jerry Cornelius could be regarded as avatars of the Eternal Champion, a mortal endued with extraordinary powers and weaponry, usually cursed with some physical stigma (e.g., albinism, missing limbs or organs, a jewel embedded in his anatomy), doomed to a seemingly endless quest through time and space to find his identity or a lost love, or avenge a wrong done to him or his family or his people, or exorcise some curse or demon within him, or intervene in the struggle between Chaos and Order or Good and Evil, or to save the world or the multiverse, or several or all of above. The Eternal Champion appears, in one guise or another, almost throughout Moorcock's work. Ulrich von Bek (series IV), Corum (series V), Hawkmoon (series VI), Erekose (series VII), Oswald Bastable (series IX), Karl Glogauer (series XI), and the rascally Colonel Pyat (series VIII) can all be regarded as avatars of the Eternal Champion, but his best-known and most fully realized avatar is Elric of Melnibone. Elric, ruler of the diminished Elfen Empire of Melnibone, is an albino, Byronically moody, tormented by what he regards as the betrayal of his people, enmeshed in what seems to be an endless series of quests, in uneasy symbiosis with his sword Stormbringer, which has the power to feed on men's souls. *Stormbringer*, the first novel published in the series, actually brings the series to a conclusion, with later novels and short stories being essentially prequels that fill in Elric's earlier history. Some readers, while enjoying the stories, find Elric a tiresome character: indeed Moorcock himself may have grown somewhat tired of Elric, as indicated by the semifarcical "Elric at the End of Time" (1981—see series I). Elric turns up in several other series, either as himself, or as a thinly disguised avatar. The von Bek series (IV) has become inextricably embedded in the Elric series with the publication of a new Elric trilogy (numbers 9 and 10 and one more to come). *Elric: the Return to Melnibone* (Unicorn Book Shop [UK], 1973) is a graphic novel written by Moorcock and illustrated by Philippe Druillet. Omnibus volumes are *Elric of Melnibone* (Millennium [UK], 1993), which includes numbers 1, 2, and 3 and the stories "The Dreaming City," "While the Gods Laugh," and "The Singing Citadel"; *Stormbringer* (Millennium [UK], 1993), which includes numbers 5, 6, and 8 and the stories "The Stealer of Souls," "Kings in Darkness" and "The Caravan of Forgotten Dreams." *Elric of Melnibone* was reprinted by White Wolf (1997) as *Elric: Song of the Black Sword. Stormbringer* was reprinted by White Wolf (1998) as *Elric: The Stealer of Souls. The Jade Man's Eyes* (Unicorn [UK], 1973) is an Elric story published in a limited edition. *Elric: The Stealer of Souls* (Del Rey, 2008) is the first of six volumes collecting Moorcock's essays and stories about Elric.

1. *Dreaming City, The* (Lancer, 1972) Published in the United Kingdom as *Elric of Melnibone*. Title is confusing, as "The Dreaming City" was the title of an early Elric story, published in 1961. Regarded as the first in the series chronologically. Elric, emperor of a diminished empire, warrior, sorcerer, and melancholy philosopher at odds with his destiny, must cope with marauders attacking the Dragon Isle and his cruel and ambitious cousin Yyr Kocon.

2. *Fortress of the Pearl, The* (Ace, 1989) Tge Lord Gho Faazi, coveting the principal seat on the ruling council of the city of Quarzhasaat, lures Elric into a quest for the Pearl of the Heart of the World.

3. *Sailor on the Seas of Fate, The* (DAW, 1976) Considerably revised version of the short story "The Jade Man's Eyes," which was published separately as a chapbook by Unicorn Book Shop (UK) in 1973. Elric boards three mysterious ships for three mysterious quests through space and time along with other heroes.

4. *Weird of the White Wolf, The* (DAW, 1977) Originally four short stories published in magazines, collected together and called a novel. Elric and Stormbringer are more or less fused into a single being.

5. *Sleeping Sorceress, The* (Lancer, 1972) Elric wanders the lands of the young kingdoms in search of the evil sorcerer Theleb K'aana. Variant title: *The Vanishing Tower*.

6. *Revenge of the Rose, The* (Ace, 1991) Elric embarks on a quest across the multiverse for the rosewood box containing the soul of his father.

7. *Bane of the Black Sword, The* (DAW, 1977) Elric returns to Yishana and finds some peace, but meanwhile, at the world's rim, an unimaginable horde moves on Tanelorn (see series V).

8. *Stormbringer* (Lancer, 1967) The first novel published in the series, but he brings it to a (temporary?) conclusion. Evil supernatural beings have abducted Elric's wife, Zarozinra, and he has to renew his partnership with Stormbringer.

9. *Dreamthief's Daughter, The* (Warner, 2001) Count Ulrich von Bek (see series IV) returns home from World War I to find Germany overrun by proto-Nazi military bands. He delves into his family history and turns up the story of two pre-Teutonic swords: "Stormbringer" and "Traverklingge." His being starts to merge with Elric's. Number 1 in the new Elric trilogy.

10. *Skrayling Tree, The: The Albino in America* (Warner, 2003) Oona, the Dreamthief's (Elric's) daughter, and her husband, Ulrik von Bek, vacation in Nova Scotia where Ulrik is kidnapped by mysterious "Indian" warriors. Oona's search leads her to an America nearly 1000 years in the past. Number 2 in the new Elric trilogy.

11. *Stealer of Souls and Other Stories, The* (Lancer, 1967) Short stories: "The Dreaming City," "While the Gods Laugh," "The Stealer of Souls," "Kings in Darkness," and "The Flamebringers." Originally published in the United Kingdom in 1963.

12. *Singing Citadel, The* (Berkley, 1970) Short stories: "The Singing Citadel," "Master of Chaos," "The Greater Conqueror," "To Rescue Tanelorn."

IV. Graf Ulrich von Bek, a captain of mercenaries in the Thirty Years' War in Germany (1618–1648), becomes intimately involved with the devil and the quest for the Holy Grail. Ulrich (or Ulrik) and other members of the von Bek family continue the quest through time. The von Bek series is now closely intertwined with the Elric series (III). The latest volumes, *Dreamthief's Daughter* and *The Skrayling Tree*, are described under series III. There are also connections with the Hawkmoon (VI), Erekose (VII), and Second Ether (XIII) series. The omnibus volume *Von Bek* (White Wolf, 1996) contains numbers 1 and 2, the short story "The Pleasure Garden of Felipe Sagittarius," and the novel *The Dragon in the Sword*, which is described under the Erekose series (VII).

1. *War Hound and the World's Pain, The* (Timescape, 1981) Graf Ulrich von Bek, captain of mercenaries in the Thirty Years' War, deserts his soldiers after an outbreak of plague and takes refuge in Lucifer's castle.

2. *Brothel in Rosenstrasse, The* (Carroll & Graf, 1987) Mirenburg, 1900. The most famous brothel in Europe, Frau Schmetterling's in Rosenstrasse, receives a visit from famous roué Count von Bek, accompanied by his 16-year-old mistress, Alexandra. Originally published in 1982.

2. *City in the Autumn Stars, The* (Ace, 1987) In 1793 Ritter von Bek escapes the terrors of the French Revolution, goes hot-air ballooning, and fights men and demons to find his true love.

4. *Lunching with the Antichrist* (Ziesing, 1994) Seven stories about members of the von Bek family during the 20th and 21st centuries, as they each play the role of seeker.

V. The Corum Jhaelen Irsei series is more like standard sword-and-sorcery fare than most of Moorcock's output, but Corum is quite Elric-like: he is quest doomed, prince of a sadly diminished elfin race in a world dominated by humans, and marked by a missing hand and eye, which are replaced by magical equivalents. In the first Corum trilogy, he is pitted against the three Gods of Chaos (already encountered in *Stormbringer;* see series III). In the second trilogy, set in the future, Corum must battle a new batch of gods, the Eoi Myore, who hope to introduce a permanent "Fimbulwinter," as the best climate for their health. Corum's sidekick, Jary a-Conel, is a reminder of Jerry Cornelius (series II) and other characters related to the Eternal Champion. Omnibuses: *The Swords Trilogy* (Berkley, 1977; numbers 1–3), reprinted as *The Swords of Corum, Corum,* and *Corum: The Coming Chaos;* and *The Chronicles of Corum* (Berkley, 1978), numbers 4–6: reprinted as *The Prince with the Silver Hand* and *Corum: The Prince with the Silver Hand*.

1. *Knight of the Swords, The* (Berkley, 1971) No annotation available.

2. *Queen of the Swords, The* (Berkley, 1971) No annotation available.

3. *King of the Swords, The* (Berkley, 1971) Corum finds himself in love with a Mabden woman and caught in the cataclysmic war between Law and Chaos.

4. *Bull and the Spear, The* (Berkley, 1973) Corum is mourning his human wife, Rhaliza, and is haunted by strange voices in his dreams.

5. *Oak and the Ram, The* (Berkley, 1973) A victory has been won over the Ehoi Myore, the gods of the Cold Folk, but the Gods of Limbo are still a threat.

6. *Sword and the Stallion, The* (Berkley, 1974) Corum's quest takes him to Ynys Scarth, hazardous Isle of Shadows.

VI. Dorian Hawkmoon, Duke of Kolby, is another Eternal Champion, this time in a fairly conventional (for Moorcock) good-versus-evil saga. Dorian's particular quest is for the magical Runestaff; his particular cross to bear is a Black Jewel embedded in his skull—through which the forces of the Dark Empire can see everything that Hawkmoon can see—that has the potential for imploding in his brain. The seven novels are divided into two series. Numbers 1 through 4 are known as the History of the Runestaff, or the Runestaff Tetralogy. Numbers 5 through 7 are known as the Chronicles of Castle Brass, or Count Brass trilogy. A von Bek (series IV) puts in an appearance in number 6, and number 7 incorporates many characters from other series, including Elric (III), Corum (V), and Erekose (VII). Omnibuses include *Hawkmoon* (White Wolf, 1996; numbers 1–4), originally published as *The History of the Runestaff* (1979); and *Count Brass* (Millennium [UK], 1993; numbers 5–7), originally published as *The Chronicles of Count Brass* (1985). *The Crystal and the Amulet* (Savoy [UK], 1986) is a graphic novel illustrated by James Cawthorn.

1. *Jewel in the Skull, The* **(Lancer, 1967)** Dorian Hawkmoon, Duke of Kolby, Eternal Champion embarked upon a quest for the Runestaff, has a Black Jewel embedded in his skull by the Dark Empire that could spell his doom.
2. *Sorcerer's Amulet, The* **(Lancer, 1968)** Hawkmoon returns to his adopted homeland of Kamorg only to find Yisselda, his betrothed, abducted by the evil sorcerer, the Mad God. UK title: *The Mad God's Amulet.*
3. *Sword of the Dawn, The* **(Lancer, 1968)** Only the ancient Crystal Machine of the wraith folk can save the Kamorg people by thrusting them into another dimension.
4. *Secret of the Runestaff, The* **(Lancer, 1969)** Baron Melidolos of Kroiden, swearing an oath by the Runestaff, is determined that the fair Yisselda, Count Brass's daughter, will be his. UK title: *The Runestaff.*
5. *Count Brass* **(Dell, 1976)** The ancient Castle Brass, which dominates the marshes of Kamar, is the focus here, as Hawkmoon is forced to endure another series of quests. Originally published in 1973.
6. *Champion of Garathorm, The* **(Berkley, 1985)** Hawkmoon goes on a quest with Katinka von Bek, regent of Ukrania, to resurrect Yisselda, presumed dead. Originally published in 1973.
7. *Quest for Tanelorn, The* **(Dell, 1976)** Hawkmoon and Yisselda are reunited, but their children are lost somewhere in the stars. Hawkmoon begins a quest to Tanelorn, the eternal city and high seat of the holy.

VII. John Daker (or Erekose, or the Eternal Champion) is an eternal warrior, eternal lover, and eternal hero doomed to be forever reincarnated and fight against evil. John/Erekose gets his start on Earth in the 20th century, and in his peregrinations through time and space becomes involved with other Eternal Champions, especially Hawkmoon (series VI) and the von Beks (series IV). Omnibus: *The Eternal Champion* (Millennium [UK], 1992; numbers 1–3). Number 3 also appears in the omnibus volume *Von Bek* (White Wolf, 1996). *The Swords of Heaven, the Flowers of Hell* (HM, 1979) is a graphic novel illustrated by Howard V. Chaykin.

1. *Eternal Champion, The* **(Dell, 1970)** John Daker is pulled from the 20th century through time to a place where time doesn't exit. Novel expanded from the novella of the same name (1962).
2. *Silver Warriors, The* **(Dell, 1973)** Daker is transformed into Ulrik Skarsel, prince of the Southern Ice. His time of peace and happiness with the beautiful Ermizhad is shattered when the dreams begin again. Original title: *Phoenix in Obsidian* (1970).
3. *Dragon in the Sword, The* **(Ace, 1986)** Still searching for Ermizhad and for the key that will allow him to step off the wheel of infinite incarnations, the Eternal Champion embarks upon a dark ship piloted by a blind helmsman.

VIII. The unreliable memoirs of Maxim Arturovich Pyatnitski, aka Colonel Pyat, feature a somewhat different protagonist in this tetralogy. The roguish Pyat, who has more of George MacDonald Fraser's (q.v.) Flashman than Eternal Champion in his makeup, has epic, comic adventures taking him from his native Kiev to New York, Cairo, Marrakesh, Hollywood, and beyond. Pyat makes a brief appearance in *The Steel Tsar* (series IX). The Pyat series is sometimes known as the Between the Wars series.

1. *Byzantium Endures* **(Random House, 1981)** Born to Jewish parents in Kiev in 1900, Pyat is a student in St. Petersburg when the October Revolution breaks out.
2. *Laughter of Carthage, The* **(Random House, 1984)** Pyat escapes to America where he follows various professions, including being a

spokesman for the Ku Klux Klan and runs into his most enduring love, Mrs. Cornelius (see series II).
3. *Jerusalem Commands* **(Cape [UK], 1992)** Pyat schemes and fantasizes his way from New York to Casablanca to Marrakesh to Hollywood, where he finds cult success as a movie star.
4. *Vengeance of Rome, The* **(Cape [UK], 2006)** In the conclusion to the quartet, Pyat becomes intimate with top Fascists and Nazis, embracing their politics.

IX. Captain Oswald Bastable is a kind of Eternal Champion who goes through a series of alternate histories in this trilogy. He starts out in the North East Frontier of India in 1902, has adventures in alternate 1973 and with a different kind of African imperialist and in a Russia where the revolution never occurred. *The Nomad of Time* (Granada [UK], 1984) and *A Nomad of the Time Streams* (Millennium [UK], 1993) are omnibus volumes containing all three Bastable novels.

1. *Warlord of the Air, The* **(Ace, 1971)** Captain Oswald Bastable, leading a troop of soldiers to the ancient city of Teku Benga in 1902, suddenly finds himself in 1973 and a peaceful imperialist world ruled by Britain. Since the US edition was censored, readers may want to seek out the New English Library (UK, 1971) edition or one of the two omnibus volumes.
2. *Land Leviathan, The* **(Doubleday, 1974)** Oswald visits the Temple of the Future Buddha and is thrust to another 20th century, where he confronts Black Attila, his African hordes, and the juggernaut Land Leviathan.
3. *Steel Tsar, The* **(DAW, 1982)** Bastable finds himself in 1941 and a Russo-Japanese War involving Stalin and his cossacks and the League of Temporal Adventurers.

X. The Warrior of Mars, or Kane, Ta trilogy, written under the pseudonym of Edward P. Bradbury, and republished with new titles under Moorcock's real name, is a pastiche of the Edgar Rice Burroughs (q.v.) John Carter of Mars or Barsoomian series. Twentieth-century scientist Michael Kane finds himself transported to three very different Mars situations. Omnibuses containing all three novels: *Warrior of Mars* (New English Library [UK], 1981) and *Kane of Old Mars* (White Wolf, 1998).

1. *Warriors of Mars* **(Lancer, 1966)** Twentieth-century scientist Michael Kane finds himself transported to Mars. Originally published under the pseudonym "Edward P. Bradbury." Revised edition (Lancer, 1971) entitled *The City of the Beast* published under Moorcock's real name.
2. *Blades of Mars* **(Lancer, 1966)** Kane returns, via a matter transmitter, to a different Mars. Originally published under the pseudonym "Edward P. Bradbury." Revised edition (Lancer, 1971) published as *The Lord of Spiders* under Moorcock's real name.
3. *Barbarians of Mars* **(Lancer, 1966)** Kane travels, through time and space, to Mars for the last time, and finds a diseased, ravaged planet. Originally published under the pseudonym "Edward P. Bradbury." Revised edition (Lancer, 1971) published as *The Masters of the Pit* under Moorcock's real name.

XI. Karl Glogauer, another Eternal Champion, is the protagonist of a pair of novels referred to as "more psychology than physics." Glogauer travels through time and space in his search for Harmony and Freedom from Fear. The omnibus volume, *Behold the Man* (Phoenix House [UK], 1994), contains numbers 1 and 2 and the short story "Constant Fire."

1. *Behold the Man* **(Avon, 1970)** Time traveler Glogauer goes back to the time of Christ, where he discovers that the historical Jesus

didn't exist. Karl then steps into the role of savior and is judged and crucified. Original novella of the same title (1966) won a Nebula prize.

2. *Breakfast in the Ruins* **(Random House, 1974)** Karl continues his identity quest through time and space, searching for "Harmony" and "Freedom from Fear."

XII. The Nick Allard/Jerry Cornell espionage trio, presaging the Jerry Cornelius character (series II) were early novels. *The LSD Dossier* was an anonymously rewritten movie script ghosted for Roger Harris. Numbers 2 and 3 were originally published under the pseudonym "Bill Barclay," then completely rewritten with titles changed and the protagonist Nick Allard renamed Jerry Cornell, and published under Moorcock's real name.

1. *LSD Dossier, The* **(Compact [UK], 1966)** Anonymous novelization of script by Roger Harris, introducing the Nick Allard character.

2. *Chinese Agent, The* **(Macmillan, 1970)** When master jewel thief Arthur Hodgkins, alias Jewelry Jules, on a mission to steal the Crown Jewels, is mistaken for a Chinese agent, agent Jerry Cornell steps in. Originally published as *Somewhere in the Night* (Compact [UK], 1966) by Moorcock as Bill Barclay and Jerry Cornell as Nick Allard.

3. *Russian Intelligence, The* **(Savoy [UK], 1980)** Jerry finds a dying fellow agent clutching the comic strip, "The Devil Rider-Masked Fighter for Justice." Originally published by Moorcock as Bill Barclay (Compact [UK], 1966) under title *Printer's Devil* and Cornell as Nick Allard.

XIII. The Second Ether is a trio of volumes set in an alternate universe in the American Southern states, featuring characters Jack Karaquazian and Sam Oakenhurst, who go through a series of time and space adventures more reminiscent of Jherek Carnelian (series I) or Jerry Cornelius (series II) than of Elric (series III). The character Rose von Bek links this series to series IV.

1. *Blood: A Southern Fantasy* **(Millennium [UK], 1995)** Jack Karaquazian and his friend Sam Oakenhurst play out their days from New Orleans to Memphis to the Terminal Café, on the edge of the Biloxi Fault.

2. *Fabulous Harbors* **(Avon, 1997)** A collection of short stories featuring characters such as Rose von Bek and Captain Horatio Quelch.

3. *War amongst the Angels, The* **(Avon, 1998)** The adventures of Sam Oakenhurst, Rose von Bek, Captain Quelch, Pirate of the Singularity, and other characters take them to an alternate Texas.

XIV. The Roads between the Worlds is a loosely connected trilogy of straight science-fiction novels involving parallel earths. Published in the omnibus volume *The Road between the Worlds* (White Wolf, 1996).

1. *Winds of Limbo, The* **(Paperback Library, 1969)** A declining human civilization on Earth must face the challenge of the Fireclown, an enigmatic visitor who may be bringing either salvation or destruction. Originally published in a different version as *The Fireclown* (Compact [UK], 1965). The Fireclown was revived in series I (number 5).

2. *Rituals of Infinity, The* **(DAW, 1978)** A fairly straightforward space opera featuring parallel earths. Original version, *The Wrecks of Time,* published by Ace (1967) with *Tramontane* by Emil Pejata.

3. *Shores of Death, The* **(Berkley, 1970)** No annotation available. Original version: *The Twilight Man* (Compact [UK], 1966).

XV. Although most of Moorcock's output is series fiction, he published a number of novels and short story collections, some of which are listed here.

1. *Deep Fix, The* **(Compact [UK], 1966)** Short stories, including "The Pleasure Garden of Felipe Sagittarius" (see series IV) and "The Real Life Mr. Newman" (published separately in 1979).

2. *Ice Schooner, The* **(Berkley, 1969)** SF adventure set against the backdrop of a new ice age. Included in omnibus volume *Sailing to Utopia* (Millennium [UK], 1993).

3. *Time Dweller, The* **(Berkley, 1971)** A collection of short stories.

4. *Moorcock's Book of Martyrs* **(DAW, 1978)** A collection of short stories including "A Dead Singer" (series II); "The Greater Conqueror" (series V); "Behold the Man" (series XI); and "Flux" (series VII).

5. *Gloriana; or The Unfulfill'd Queen* **(Avon, 1979)** Fantasy set in an alternate Elizabethan London. Regarded by many readers as Moorcock's finest single fantasy performance.

6. *Golden Barge, The* **(DAW, 1980)** An allegory influenced by Mervyn Peake (q.v.). Actually Moorcock's first novel (1958). Reprinted in omnibus volume *Earl Aubec* (Millennium, 1993).

7. *My Experiences in the Third World War* **(Savoy [UK], 1980)** Collection including *The English Assassin* (see series II) and short story "The Dodgem Division" (see series II).

8. *Mother London* **(Harmony, 1989)** Three survivors of a German V-2 rocket bomb hear "voices" that bit by bit reveal the character of London itself. Moorcock's personal favorite among his novels.

9. *Casablanca* **(Gollancz [UK], 1989)** Short stories and essays.

10. *Sailing to Utopia* **(Millennium [UK], 1993)** An omnibus volume containing the novels *The Ice Schooner* (see number 2), *The Black Corridor* (Ace, 1969) and *The Distant Suns* (Unicorn Books [UK], 1973) and short stories.

11. *Tales from the Texas Woods* **(Mojo, 1997)** Short stories and essays with Texas themes.

12. *Silverheart* **(Simon & Schuster [UK], 2000)** Eternal Champion story coauthored with Storm Constantine featuring a character named Max Silverstein who has a mask on his chest known as the Silverheart.

13. *King of the City* **(Morrow, 2001)** Panoramic novel of London in the latter half of the 20th century.

14. *London Bone* **(Scribner [UK], 2001)** Collection of short stories.

Moore, George

At first influenced by the naturalism of Émile Zola (q.v.), George Moore's work later became more stylized, more elaborately textured, and symbolically weightier. These two books, characteristic of his mature style, were little appreciated at the time of their publication. Some modern critics have been more complimentary, but the works have never caught on, even to the limited extent that Moore's best-known novel, *Esther Waters,* has. However, these novels about the singer and eventual nun Evelyn Innes are well worth reading for their portrayal of the worlds of music and the Celtic Renaissance in the late 19th century.

1. *Evelyn Innes* **(Appleton, 1916)** The dashing Owen Asher takes Evelyn as protégée and mistress to the Continent, where she becomes a great singer but is torn between Asher and her love for the Irish poet and mystic Ulrick Dean. Originally published in the United Kingdom in 1898.

2. *Sister Teresa* **(Unwin [UK], 1901)** This novel of convent life shows Evelyn's search for a spiritual peace combining religion and music.

Morice, Anne

PSEUDONYM OF Felicity Shaw

Tessa Crichton is an actress married to Robin Price, a Scotland Yard detective. The impulsive, upbeat Tessa gets involved in more than her share of crimes, nearly two dozen in all, in this series combining ingenious puzzles, fine characterization, lively dialogue, and backstage lore reminiscent of Ngaio Marsh (q.v.). English author Felicity Shaw (d. 1989), who had theatrical connections of her own, also published two novels under her real name and two nonseries mysteries set in Sussex under her Morice pseudonym: *Design for Dying* (St. Martin's, 1988) and *Planning for Murder* (St. Martin's, 1991).

1. ***Death in the Grand Manor*** (Macmillan [UK], 1970) The Cornfords are alienating their neighbors in Roakes Common with a variety of cruel and petty tricks. Not published in the United States.
2. ***Death of a Gay Dog*** (Macmillan [UK], 1971) No annotation available. Not published in the United States.
3. ***Murder in Married Life*** (Macmillan [UK], 1971) Tessa is appalled by the meanness displayed in the unpublished diary of an old childhood acquaintance who is now the owner of a department store. Not published in the United States.
4. ***Murder on French Leave*** (Macmillan [UK], 1972) Tessa gets a part in a film to be made in Paris and enjoys the amenities there with her husband and cousin Ellen until murder intervenes. Not published in the United States.
5. ***Death and the Dutiful Daughter*** (St. Martin's, 1974) Opera singer Maud Stirling wrote a surprising new will hours before she died.
6. ***Death of a Heavenly Twin*** (St. Martin's, 1974) A garden fete given by a millionaire tycoon in aid of the local conservation society is the scene of a couple of murders.
7. ***Killing with Kindness*** (St. Martin's, 1975) After Mike Parsons disappears, his wife gradually learns about his hidden life.
8. ***Nursery Tea and Poison*** (St. Martin's, 1975) Serena Hargrave's cozy life in West Lodge may be at end when her brother-in-law turns up with a new young wife.
9. ***Death of a Wedding Guest*** (St. Martin's, 1976) A guest drops dead at the wedding of Tessa's cousin, Ellen Crichton.
10. ***Murder in Mimicry*** (St. Martin's, 1977) Tessa is in Washington, DC, for the American debut of the long-running British play, *Host of Pleasures*.
11. ***Scared to Death*** (St. Martin's, 1977) Edna Mortimer's health deteriorates rapidly after she "sees herself" in several different places.
12. ***Murder by Proxy*** (St. Martin's, 1978) Anne Monk, who lives with a married man with a nearby wife and daughter, thinks that someone is trying to kill her.
13. ***Murder in Outline*** (St. Martin's, 1979) Tessa is invited to serve as a judge for a competition at her alma mater, but isn't entirely pleased with the changes that have occurred at her old school.
14. ***Death in the Round*** (St. Martin's, 1980) When the teenage orphan whom she has befriended runs off with the petty cash, the patron of the Rotunda Theatre refuses to reach the seemingly obvious conclusion.
15. ***Men in Her Death, The*** (St. Martin's, 1981) Some time after a young American heiress disappears in London, a ransom note arrives from France.
16. ***Hollow Vengeance*** (St. Martin's, 1982) Mrs. Trelawney, a rich widow from Australia, is set on turning her estate into a ranch, much to the discomfort of her neighbors and tenants.
17. ***Sleep of Death*** (St. Martin's, 1983) The West End production of *Elders and Betters* is plagued with bad luck, culminating in disturbing anonymous letters sent to cast members.
18. ***Murder Post-Dated*** (St. Martin's, 1984) Visiting friends in Oxfordshire, Tessa meets James McGrath, who is rumored to have killed his wife.
19. ***Getting Away with Murder?*** (St. Martin's, 1984) Tessa's husband, Robin, obsessed by an unsolved murder, chooses a luxury hotel near the racecourse where the murder occurred for his and Tessa's vacation.
20. ***Dead on Cue*** (St. Martin's, 1985) Which wife of a recently deceased mystery writer actually wrote the script for the play Tessa is reading?
21. ***Publish and Be Killed*** (St. Martin's, 1987) The daughter of Edwardian dramatist Sheridan Seymour hints that she is engaged in writing a scandalous expose of her late father.
22. ***Treble Exposure*** (St. Martin's, 1988) Tessa, Robin, and cousin Toby get involved with a young American recovering from a nervous collapse.
23. ***Fatal Charm*** (St. Martin's, 1989) Tessa unravels some family entanglements when a member of a famous acting clan is murdered.

Morier, James

This comic masterpiece, modeled after LeSage's picaresque *Gil Blas*, has delighted generations of readers. Young Hajji Baba, the barber's son, starts off as a traveling secretary to a Baghdad merchant but is quickly involved in one harrowing adventure after another. Always living as the dervish advised, on men's weakness and credulity, the resourceful Hajji slips out of many tight spots with customary roguish charm. Morier, an Englishman, served at the British embassy in Tehran. His description of the life and manners of the Persia of his day is thought to be quite accurate. *The Adventures of Hajji Baba of Ispahan* has been reprinted numerous times, including by Random House (1937) and Hart (1976). Its sequel proved to be not nearly as successful, nor did his later novels attract much attention, although he did introduce the Turkish word *bosh* to the English language in one of them.

1. ***Adventures of Hajji Baba of Ispahan, The*** (Small, 1824) Before his triumphant return home, Hajji Baba does time as a Turcoman captive, a marriage broker, a physician, a poet's scribe, and an executioner. Variant title: *The Adventures of Hajji Baba, in Turkey, Persia and Russia*.
2. ***Hajji Baba in England*** (Harper, 1828) Hajji Baba accompanies the Persian ambassador to London, where he is amazed at the uncouthness of British manners and customs. UK title: *The Adventures of Hajji Baba of Ispahan in England*.

Morley, Christopher

Christopher Morley was an all-around man of letters—a poet and novelist; essayist for the *Saturday Review*, *New York Evening Post*, and other journals; an editor of anthologies and reference books including *Bartlett's Familiar Quotations*. He was a tireless promoter of literature for Doubleday, served as a judge of the Book-of-the-Month Club for more than 20 years, and found time to dabble in theater and to found the Baker Street Irregulars, the famous Sherlock Holmes fan club. Next to his popular hit *Kitty Foyle*, a novel about a young Irish American working girl, he is best remembered for these two books, which star Helen McGill and her mentor, Roger Mifflin, the lovably literate traveling bookseller.

1. ***Parnassus on Wheels*** (Doubleday, 1917) At 39 Helen McGill buys the horse-drawn van of itinerant bookseller Roger Mifflin, who shows her the ropes and wins her heart.

2. *Haunted Bookshop, The* (Doubleday, 1919) Mr. and Mrs. Roger Mifflin settle down permanently in a secondhand bookshop in Brooklyn called "Parnassus at Home." Set during World War I, this novel combines a spy plot and a romance.

Morris, Wright

I. Many of Wright Morris's books have a Nebraska setting, but to dismiss him as a regional writer would be to undervalue seriously this consistently original and rewarding author. His unsentimental studies of the American character often feature lonely and inarticulate people who are buffeted by circumstance in a disordered world. Morris catches their poignant and sometimes tragic moments of self-revelation in beautifully controlled prose, with the sympathy and respect that they deserve. This pair of haunting parables starring 84-year-old Nebraskan Floyd Warner is a good introduction to Morris's art.

1. *Fire Sermon* (Harper, 1971) Old Floyd takes his orphaned nephew to Nebraska and picks up two hippie hitchhikers on the way.
2. *Life, A* (Harper, 1973) After leaving his nephew in Nebraska, Floyd heads south to New Mexico, picking up a Native American Vietnam veteran as a passenger.

II. Morris wrote several other novels with Nebraska settings, including five novels about a town called Lone Tree, which is the fictional equivalent of Morris's birthplace, Central City. *The Home Place* and *The World in the Attic* are about Clyde Muncy revisiting his old haunts in Nebraska. *The Field of Vision* and *Ceremony in Lone Tree*, two of Morris's best novels, share several characters: lifelong failure Gordon Boy, his outwardly successful friend Walter McKee, and McKee's octogenarian father-in-law Tom Scanlon. All of these novels are strong on nostalgia and realistic dialogue.

1. *Man Who Was There, The* (Scribner, 1945) Agee Ward, missing in action in World War II, is remembered by his friends in Lone Tree.
2. *Home Place, The* (Scribner, 1948) Clyde Muncy revisits his uncle's Nebraska farm with his wife and children. Morris's photographs of Central City and Norfolk, Nebraska, give an added dimension to the fictional text.
3. *World in the Attic, The* (Scribner, 1949) Clyde Muncy and his family stop in Junction, Nebraska, on their way back east from Lone Tree.
4. *Field of Vision, The* (Harcourt, 1956) A group of Nebraskans including Gordon Boyd, Walter McKee, and Tom Scanlon spend an afternoon at a Mexican bullfight.
5. *Ceremony in Lone Tree* (Atheneum, 1960) Family and friends prepare to assemble in Lone Tree to celebrate the ninetieth birthday of its last inhabitant, Tom Scanlon.

Morrow, Honore

The last four years of Abraham Lincoln's life form the subject of this trilogy. The books satisfy as just plain good stories, but, in addition, they also give an accurate picture of the man and his times. Morrow claims to have used no fictitious characters and to have stepped outside of fact for conversation and thought processes only. Mrs. Lincoln (about whom Morrow wrote a biography) is pictured as a lovable if somewhat excitable helpmeet, not the deranged shrew that some have painted. Figures such as Clara Barton, the photographer Matthew Brady, and the war correspondent William Russell are memorably drawn. *Great Captain* (Morrow, 1935) is a three-in-one omnibus volume.

1. *Forever Free* (Morrow, 1927) The story begins in March 1861 as the Lincolns move into the White House and ends with the signing of the Emancipation Proclamation in January 1863.
2. *With Malice toward None* (Morrow, 1928) The Lincoln story is continued to the end of the Civil War.
3. *Last Full Measure, The* (Morrow, 1930) The last six months of Lincoln's life are described, ending with the gunshot in Ford's Theatre.

Mortimer, John

I. Barrister, novelist, dramatist, screen and television writer, and Commander of the British Empire, John Mortimer is probably best known for his television plays (shown on PBS's *Mystery!* and elsewhere) and short stories featuring Horace Rumpole, a portly and disheveled lawyer in his sixties (wonderfully portrayed by the late Leo McKern). The poetry-spouting, eloquent, and wily Rumpole—(almost) always for the defense—isn't overnice about legal boundaries and has a deplorable view of human nature, but he is a likable survivor. His life at home is dreary: his wife, Hilda ("She Who Must Be Obeyed"), compares him invidiously to her father; and his son Nicky is so ashamed of him that he has emigrated to America. It is the Old Bailey that is the scene for Rumpole's real life: rumors of his retirement or death have so far proved to be premature. Omnibus volumes include *The First Rumpole Omnibus* (Viking, 1983—numbers 1–3); *The Second Rumpole Omnibus* (Viking, 1988—numbers 4–6): and *The Third Rumpole Omnibus* (Viking, 1998—numbers 8–10). *The Best of Rumpole* (Viking, 1993) is a selection of stories from other volumes. Because the Rumpole series consists of short stories only, no annotations are provided.

1. *Rumpole of the Bailey* (Penguin, 1980) Originally published in the United Kingdom in 1978.
2. *Trials of Rumpole, The* (Penguin, 1981) Originally published in the United Kingdom in 1979.
3. *Rumpole's Return* (Penguin, 1982) Originally published in the United Kingdom in 1980.
4. *Rumpole for the Defence* (Penguin, 1982) Originally published in the United Kingdom as *Regina v. Rumpole* in 1981.
5. *Rumpole and the Golden Thread* (Penguin, 1983)
6. *Rumpole's Last Case* (Penguin, 1988)
7. *Rumpole and the Age of Miracles* (Penguin, 1988)
8. *Rumpole a la Carte* (Viking, 1990)
9. *Rumpole on Trial* (Viking, 1992)
10. *Rumpole and the Angel of Death* (Viking, 1995)
11. *Rumpole and the Younger Generation* (Viking, 1995)
12. *Rumpole Rests His Case* (Viking, 2001)
13. *Rumpole and the Primrose Path* (Viking, 2002)
14. *Rumpole and the Penge Bungalow Murders* (Viking, 2004)
15. *Rumpole and the Reign of Terror* (Viking, 2006)
16. *Rumpole Misbehaves* (Viking, 2007)

II. Rumpole is by no means Mortimer's only memorable creation: Leslie Titmuss, who rises from country boy to member of the Cabinet in Britain's Conservative government, is a distinctive creation in a trio of comedies of manners that reflect the history of postwar Britain. Although Mortimer is a Labour supporter, his satire is bipartisan. *The Rapstone Chronicles* (Viking [UK], 1992) contains numbers 1 and 2.

1. *Paradise Postponed* (Viking, 1986) The villagers of the London suburb of Rapstone Fanner, including the upwardly mobile politician Leslie Titmuss, are portrayed in the their postwar finery.

2. *Titmuss Regained* (Viking, 1990) Titmuss, now a Conservative minister, attempts to "go Green" when Mrs. Thatcher's privatization schemes threaten his newly purchased country manor.

3. *Sound of Trumpets, The* (Viking, 1999) Titmuss, retired from Whitehall and writing his dreaded tell-all memoirs, takes a keen interest in Terry Flitton, the Labour candidate for a seat in Parliament.

Morton, Anthony

PSEUDONYM OF John Creasey

Anthony Morton, one of the pseudonyms of the amazingly prolific John Creasey (q.v.) wrote 49 novels, all but two of which feature the Baron, John Mannering, prosperous London art connoisseur and proprietor of Quinn's Antique Shop. He has long since given up his early shady activities but uses his special knowledge of the art underworld and his mastery of disguise for occasional private detective jobs. Scotland Yard chief superintendent William Bristow has changed from adversary to friend and special employer through the years. Mannering's wife, Lorna, is a successful portrait artist. Curiously, the Baron was called the "Man in the Blue Mask" in the US editions of the early books. The Baron's adventures, too formulaic to annotate, are listed below in the order of first publication date.

1. *Man in the Blue Mask, The* (Lippincott, 1937) UK title: *Meet the Baron.*

2. *Return of Blue Mask, The* (Lippincott, 1937) UK title: *The Baron Returns.*

3. *Salute Blue Mask!* (Lippincott, 1938) UK title: *The Baron Again.*

4. *Blue Mask at Bay* (Lippincott, 1938) UK title: *The Baron at Bay.*

5. *Alias Blue Mask* (Lippincott, 1939) UK title: *Alias the Baron.*

6. *Challenge Blue Mask!* (Lippincott, 1939) UK title: *The Baron at Large.*

7. *Blue Mask Strikes Again* (Lippincott, 1939) UK title: *Versus the Baron.*

8. *Blue Mask Victorious* (Lippincott, 1940) UK title: *Call for the Baron.*

9. *Baron Comes Back, The* (Low [UK], 1943) Not published in the United States.

10. *Case for the Baron, A* (Duell, 1949) Originally published in the United Kingdom in 1945.

11. *Reward for the Baron* (Low [UK], 1945) Not published in the United States.

12. *Career for the Baron* (Duell, 1950) Originally published in the United Kingdom in 1946.

13. *Baron and the Beggar, The* (Duell, 1950) Originally published in the United Kingdom in 1947.

14. *Blame the Baron* (Duell, 1951) Originally published in the United Kingdom in 1948.

15. *Rope for the Baron, A* (Duell, 1949) Originally published in the United Kingdom in 1948.

16. *Books for the Baron* (Duell, 1952) Originally published in the United Kingdom in 1949.

17. *Cry for the Baron* (Walker, 1970) Originally published in the United Kingdom in 1950.

18. *Trap the Baron* (Walker, 1971) Originally published in the United Kingdom in 1950.

19. *Attack the Baron* (Low [UK], 1951) Not published in United States.

20. *Shadow the Baron* (Low [UK], 1951) Curley large print only US publication (1991).

21. *Warn the Baron* (Low [UK], 1952) Not published in the United States.

22. *Baron Goes East, The* (Low [UK], 1953) Not published in the United States.

23. *Baron in France, The* (Walker, 1976) Originally published in the United Kingdom in 1953.

24. *Danger for the Baron* (Walker, 1974) Originally published in the United Kingdom in 1953.

25. *Baron Goes Fast, The* (Walker, 1972) Originally published in the United Kingdom in 1954.

26. *Deaf, Dumb and Blonde* (Doubleday, 1961) Originally published in the United Kingdom in 1954 as *Nest Egg for the Baron.*

27. *Help from the Baron* (Walker, 1977) Originally published in the United Kingdom in 1955.

28. *Hide the Baron* (Walker, 1978) Originally published in the United Kingdom in 1956.

29. *Double Frame, The* (Doubleday, 1961) Originally published in the United Kingdom in 1957 as *Frame the Baron.*

30. *Blood Red* (Doubleday, 1960) Originally published in the United Kingdom in 1958 as *Red Eye for the Baron.*

31. *If Anything Happens to Hester* (Doubleday, 1962) Originally published in the United Kingdom in 1959 as *Black for the Baron.*

32. *Salute for the Baron* (Walker, 1973) Originally published in the United Kingdom in 1960.

33. *Baron Branches Out, The* (Scribner, 1967) Originally published in the United Kingdom in 1961 as *A Branch for the Baron.*

34. *Baron and the Stolen Legacy, The* (Scribner, 1967) Originally published in the United Kingdom in 1962 as *Bad for the Baron.*

35. *Baron and the Mogul Swords, The* (Scribner, 1966) Originally published in the United Kingdom in 1963 as *A Sword for the Baron.*

36. *Baron on Board, The* (Walker, 1968) Originally published in the United Kingdom in 1964.

37. *Baron and the Chinese Puzzle, The* (Scribner, 1966) Originally published in the United Kingdom in 1965.

38. *Sport for the Baron* (Walker, 1969) Originally published in the United Kingdom in 1966.

39. *Affair for the Baron* (Walker, 1968) Originally published in the United Kingdom in 1967.

40. *Baron and the Missing Old Masters, The* (Walker, 1969) Originally published in the United Kingdom in 1968.

41. *Baron and the Unfinished Portrait, The* (Walker, 1970) Originally published in the United Kingdom in 1969.

42. *Last Laugh for the Baron* (Walker, 1971) Originally published in the United Kingdom in 1970.

43. *Baron Goes A-Buying, The* (Walker, 1972) Originally published in the United Kingdom in 1971.

44. *Baron and the Arrogant Artist, The* (Walker, 1973) Originally published in the United Kingdom in 1972.

45. *Burgle the Baron* (Walker, 1974) Originally published in the United Kingdom in 1973.

46. *Baron, King-Maker, The* (Walker, 1975) Originally published in the United Kingdom in 1975.

47. *Love for the Baron* (Hodder [UK], 1979) Not published in the United States.

Mosley, Walter

I. The life of Ezekiel "Easy" Rawlins has never been "easy." The black veteran of World War II would settle for some respect and enough money to pay his mortgage, but even when he supplements his income acting as a "confidential agent," he has trouble making ends meet. Easy works out of Los Angeles, the Los Angeles of Watts, rather than the Los Angeles of Hollywood and Beverly Hills. Regarded as a successor to Chester Himes (q.v.) and Raymond Chandler (q.v.), Walter Mosley has created one of the most fully realized characters in fiction, a man who is painfully aware of the odds against him and others of his race, but who achieves a precarious respectability without forgetting his origins, and is warily optimistic about his ability to cope with a world he never made. The novels are indelible slices of American history as seen by the underdog. The earlier novels move forward with 5- to 10-year gaps in time: the later novels move more slowly through the sixties, a seminal time for African Americans. *Gone Fishin'* was actually Mosley's first novel, which he found to be unpublishable before the success of *Devil in a Blue Dress*. To encourage small African American presses, he gave the manuscript to Baltimore-based Black Classic Press. Mosley has created two other series characters (see series II and III) as well as science-fiction stories, a novel about the blues, *RL's Dream* (Norton, 1995) and works of nonfiction such as *Workin' on the Chain Gang* (Ballantine, 2000) and *What Next: A Memoir toward World Peace* (Black Classic, 2003), which urges blacks to use their unique experiences in helping to find solutions to the world's problems. *The Man in My Basement* (Little, Brown, 2004) is a nonseries novel about black-white relationships. *Walter Mosley Omnibus* (Picador [UK], 1995) contains numbers 1, 2, 3. Denzel Washington starred in the movie version of *Devil in a Blue Dress* (1995). Numbers 2 through 7 were repackaged and reissued (Washington Square, 2003), each with an original stand-alone story focusing on Easy's mentor and best friend, "Mouse" Alexander. The stories were collected, with one addition, in *Six Easy Pieces* (Atria, 2003).

1. *Gone Fishin'* **(Black Classic, 1997)** In this coming-of-age story set in 1939, 19-year-old Easy Rawlins and his friend "Mouse" Alexander leave Houston to seek out Mouse's hated stepfather in Pariah, Texas.
2. *Devil in a Blue Dress* **(Norton, 1990)** When Easy Rawlins is laid off from his factory job in 1948, he tries to make ends meet by doing errands for a white mobster who is looking for a blond, blue-eyed beauty.
3. *Red Death, A* **(Norton, 1991)** In the early 1950s, Easy is in trouble with the IRS, the FBI, the McCarthy Committee, and the Los Angeles police.
4. *White Butterfly* **(Norton, 1992)** Easy, married with children in 1958, gets entangled with a serial murderer and mutilator.
5. *Black Betty* **(Norton, 1994)** In 1960 Easy, broke and without family, takes on the search for Elizabeth Eady, "Black Betty," who had been a legend of the Houston streets he grew up on.
6. *Little Yellow Dog, A* **(Norton, 1996)** In the early 1960s, Easy, working as a school maintenance supervisor, and making a home for his two adopted kids, has again achieved a precarious respectability, but then bodies start turning up on the school grounds.
7. *Bad Boy Brawly Brown* **(Little, Brown, 2002)** In 1964, Easy, a home owner with a steady job and father to a teenage son and a daughter, is asked to track down Brawly Brown, son of a friend, who is apparently involved with a violent group calling itself the Urban Revolutionary Party.
8. *Six Easy Pieces* **(Atria, 2003)** Short stories, six republished from the Washington Square reissue of numbers 2 through 7, and one new, about Easy's friend and mentor, "Mouse" Alexander.
9. *Little Scarlet* **(Little, Brown, 2004)** In the last days of the Watts riots in 1966, a black woman, nicknamed "Little Scarlet," has been found murdered in her apartment, in the same building an unidentified white man appeared to enter, escaping from rioters.
10. *Cinnamon Kiss* **(Little, Brown, 2005)** At the height of the Vietnam War era, to earn money for medical treatment for his daughter, Easy travels to San Francisco on a missing-persons case.
11. *Blonde Faith* **(Little, Brown, 2007)** In 1967, Easy, dealing with the loss of Bonnie, the love of his life, and his decision to make her

leave him, is trying to find his friends "Mouse" Alexander and Christmas Black before those who want to destroy them do.

II. Another series character, represented by a pair of books, is Socrates Fortlow, an ex-con street philosopher in his sixties living in a shack in Watts. Socrates, is still trying to come to terms with the double murder he committed in his youth (for which he served 27 years in prison) and trying to make a decent life for himself, if only the LA police would get off his back.

1. *Always Outnumbered, Always Outgunned* **(Norton, 1997)** Sixty-year-old ex-con Socrates Fortlow lives in a makeshift shack in Watts with his two-legged dog, Killer. Looking for redemption for his past crimes, Socrates mentors a young boy, hoping that the lad will avoid the mistakes he made.
2. *Walkin' the Dog* **(Little, Brown, 1999)** Still living in his shack, but with a steady job, Socrates is still being harassed by the police. More a series of connected short stories than a novel.

III. Mosley's most recent serial characters are Paris Minton, a somewhat wimpy used-bookstore owner in Watts, and his friend, the dangerous but principled Fearless Jones. Set in 1950s Los Angeles, with Paris Minton as a narrator who is more educated but less street-smart than Easy Rawlins.

1. *Fearless Jones* **(Little, Brown, 2001)** When the beautiful Elana Love enters his bookstore, Paris Minton is embroiled in trouble, which he needs the efforts of Fearless Jones, ex-soldier and man of action, to get him out of.
2. *Fear Itself* **(Little, Brown, 2003)** Paris and Fearless, looking for Kit Mitchell (aka the Watermelon Man), get involved with millionaire black businesswoman Winifred L. Fine.
3. *Fear of the Dark* **(Little, Brown, 2006)** Paris's cousin, Ulysses "Useless" S. Grant IV, needs help after getting mixed up in a dubious scheme that has gotten totally out of hand.

Motley, Willard

Black novelist Willard Motley wrote two best-selling novels with Italian American protagonists. The novels are set mostly in the Chicago slums and depict the pervasive influence of a bad environment on its characters. *Knock on Any Door* is a grim naturalistic account of a young man's descent from altar boy to the electric chair. *Let No Man Write My Epitaph* is somewhat more optimistic. Both novels were made into Hollywood movies; *Knock on Any Door* starred John Derek and Humphrey Bogart (1949) and *Let No Man Write My Epitaph* starred Burl Ives, Shelley Winters, and James Darren (1960). A third novel was planned but never written.

1. *Knock on Any Door* **(Appleton, 1947)** Nick Romano starts off life in Denver as a good kid, but when his family loses its money during the Depression, he starts on the downward path to reform school, murder, and execution.
2. *Let No Man Write My Epitaph* **(Random House, 1958)** Young Nick Romano, illegitimate son of the executed murderer Nick Sr. and drug addict Nellie Watkins, struggles against drug addiction, while his uncle Louie sinks into the criminal underworld.

Moyes, Patricia

Inspector Henry Tibbett, of Scotland Yard, and his helpful wife, Emmy, are the protagonists in a long series of British procedurals that feature intricate plots and ingenious puzzle mysteries reminiscent of the golden age of whodunits. Several of the mysteries take place in the Caribbean, where the late Irish-born Moyes (d. 2000) resided for a number of years. *Murder by 3's* (Holt, 1965) contains numbers 1, 2, and 5.

1. *Dead Men Don't Ski* (**Rinehart, 1960**) Tibbett finds an Italian ski resort vacation a "busman's holiday" when he has to investigate murder and drug smuggling.
2. *Down among the Dead Men* (**Holt, 1961**) Another Tibbett vacation is spoiled by an "accidental" boating death that couldn't have been an accident. UK title: *The Sunken Sailor.*
3. *Death on the Agenda* (**Holt, 1962**) Henry is sent to Geneva, Switzerland, for a high-level conference on drug smuggling.
4. *Murder a la Mode* (**Holt, 1963**) The staff at *Style* magazine are in danger of missing their deadline for a special issue when one of their number is killed.
5. *Falling Star* (**Holt, 1964**) The leading man in a new movie, an aging British film star, falls under the wheels of a train.
6. *Johnny under Ground* (**Holt, 1966**) Emmy Tibbett attends a reunion of officers who had served at Dymfield in 1943 and agrees to write a history of the period.
7. *Murder Fantastical* (**Holt, 1967**) The brilliant eccentric Manciple family is shaken up when George Manciple is accused of shooting his neighbor Raymond Mason in his driveway.
8. *Death and the Dutch Uncle* (**Holt, 1968**) The murder of a small-time gambler in a seedy pub looks like the work of a professional hit man.
9. *Many Deadly Returns* (**Holt, 1970**) Lady Balaclava, who had expressed fear of being murdered, drops dead at a birthday party attended by Tibbett. UK title: *Who Saw Her Die?*
10. *Season of Snows and Sins* (**Holt, 1971**) A young couple living in a village near a Swiss ski resort gets caught up in a world of values they cannot comprehend, with tragic results.
11. *Curious Affair of the Third Dog, The* (**Holt, 1973**) A stay in the country with Emmy's sister Jane leads to an investigation of greyhound racing and a drunken driving conviction.
12. *Black Widower* (**Holt, 1975**) Mavis Ironmonger, wife of the ambassador from the new Caribbean nation of Tampica, is found dead during a reception in the new embassy in Washington.
13. *Coconut Killings, The* (**Holt, 1977**) A US senator is found dead on an exclusive golf course on a Caribbean island. UK title: *To Kill a Coconut.*
14. *Who Is Simon Warwick?* (**Holt, 1979**) When Lord Charlton dies just after changing his will to leave his fortune to a nephew he has never seen, two claimants turn up.
15. *Angel Death* (**Holt, 1981**) On a visit to the Caribbean, Miss Betsy Sprague spots a young woman who had been presumed lost at sea, then Miss Betsy herself disappears.
16. *Six-Letter Word for Death, A* (**Holt, 1983**) At first Tibbett is inclined to dismiss a homemade crossword puzzle received in the mail that has word clues referring to people who died mysteriously and hinting at murders to come.
17. *Night Ferry to Death* (**Holt, 1985**) Henry and Emmy are passengers on a ferry from the Netherlands to England when a corpse is discovered on board, and a fortune in stolen diamonds disappears.
18. *Black Girl, White Girl* (**Holt, 1989**) The Tibbetts pose as vacationers in the West Indies while investigating the local drug trade unofficially.
19. *Twice in a Blue Moon* (**Holt, 1993**) Londoner Susan Gardiner turns her unexpected inheritance, an old inn in Essex named the Blue Moon, into a fashionable restaurant.
20. *Who Killed Father Christmas? And Other Unseasonable Demises* (**Crippen & Landru, 1996**) Complete short mystery stories.

Mudrooroo (Narogin)

PSEUDONYM OF Colin Johnson

Mudrooroo has claim to being Australia's first published aboriginal poet, critic, and novelist, and has been a pioneer in establishing university courses in aboriginal literature and an activist in aboriginal cultural affairs. The Wildcat novels depict, with great wit and some cynicism, the trials of a young man of mixed aboriginal and white parentage who has difficulty in coming to terms with his heritage.

1. *Wildcat Falling* (**HarperCollins, 1993**) Young Wildcat, who is unable to follow his mothers advice on assimilating and "acting white," gets into a cycle of petty crime and incarceration. Originally published in Australia in 1965.
2. *Wildcat Screaming* (**HarperCollins, 1993**) Sent up for 10 years for shooting at a policeman, Wildcat is rescued from despair by his cell mate, Robbi Singh.
3. *Doin Wildcat: A Novel Kouri Script* (**Hyland (Australia), 1988**) Part novel, part script. Twenty-three years after he shot at a policeman, Wildcat has served his time and been released into a different world, where Aborigines and their cause have become hot media properties.

Muller, Marcia

I. Sharon McCone was the first, and is still one of the best, of the new breed of hard-boiled female investigators. The first McCone novel appeared in 1977. After a five-year hiatus, *Ask the Cards a Question* was published in 1982, the same year that Sara Paretsky's (q.v.) V.I. Warshawski and Sue Grafton's (q.v.) Kinsey Milhone first appeared between hard covers. McCone, until number 15, when she set up on her own, was an investigator for the All Souls Legal Cooperative in San Francisco. She is a young, intelligent, contemporary American woman who brings to her cases a calm, reasonable style of investigation and a knack for asking the right questions. Although she likes her independence she does get romantically involved at times: the latest and longest involvement has been with Hy Ripinsky, owner of a security firm. Sharon's character has developed over the years, sometimes as the result of new information she has discovered about her background. Marcia Muller has coauthored several books with her husband, Bill Pronzini (q.v.), and has edited many mystery anthologies. Besides two other series (see Series II and III), she has published three stand-alone mystery novels: *Point Deception* (Mysterious, 2001), *Cyanide Wells* (Mysterious, 2003), and *Cape Perdido* (Mysterious, 2005); and, with Pronzini, *The Lighthouse: A Novel of Terror* (St. Martin's, 1987); and two non-McCone series of short stories: *Deceptions* (Mystery Scene, 1991) and *Time of the Wolves: Western Stories* (Five Stars, 2003). *Duo* (Five Stars, 1998) is a collection of stories by Muller and Pronzini including one Sharon McCone tale.

1. *Edwin of the Iron Shoes* (**McKay, 1977**) An antique show owner, one of McCone's law cooperative's clients, is found murdered.
2. *Ask the Cards a Question* (**St. Martin's, 1982**) An old woman in McCone's building is strangled with a length of drapery cord taken from McCone's apartment.

3. *Cheshire Cat's Eye, The* (St. Martin's, 1983) McCone finds a friend murdered in one of the "Painted Ladies," a Victorian house being renovated.

4. *Games to Keep the Dark Away* (St. Martin's, 1984) Jane Anthony, roommate of famous photographer Abe Snelling is missing, and McCone is hired to find her.

5. *Leave a Message for Willie* (St. Martin's, 1984) Flea market king Willie Whelan is being tailed by a little man in a yarmulke.

6. *Double* (St. Martin's, 1984) Cowritten with Bill Pronzini (q.v.), this book features Sharon McCone and Pronzini's "Nameless Detective" meeting at a private eye convention in San Diego and teaming up to investigate the death of a hotel security officer.

7. *There's Nothing to Be Afraid Of* (St. Martin's, 1985) McCone investigates threats against Vietnamese refugees in San Francisco's Tenderloin.

8. *Eye of the Storm* (Mysterious, 1988) Sharon's sister Patsy asks her to come to Appleby Island, where a tycoon's decrepit Victorian mansion is being converted into a bed-and-breakfast. Cowritten with Bill Pronzini.

9. *There's Something in a Sunday* (Mysterious, 1989) Custom shirtmaker Rudy Goldring hires McCone to tail Frank Wilkonson, manager of the Burning Oak Ranch.

10. *Shape of Dread, The* (Mysterious, 1989) Bobby Fisher is scheduled to be executed for the murder of Tracy Kostakos, monologist at the Club Comedie.

11. *Trophies and Dead Things* (Mysterious, 1990) The second will of a murdered former anti–Vietnam War activist cuts off his family and leaves $1 million to four seemingly unrelated people.

12. *Where Echoes Live* (Mysterious, 1991) The prospector who sold the mineral rights for Tula Lake to the Transpacific Corporation has disappeared.

13. *Pennies on a Dead Woman's Eyes* (Mysterious, 1992) Jack Stuart, Sharon's colleague, hopes to clear Liz Bennett, who had been convicted of the murder of her husband's lover in 1956.

14. *Wolf in the Shadows* (Mysterious, 1993) McCone takes an unauthorized leave of absence to find her lover, Hy Ripinsky, who has disappeared while off on a dangerous assignment.

15. *Till the Butchers Cut Him Down* (Mysterious, 1994) Soon after McCone opens her own business, "Suitcase" Gordon, an eccentric friend from college days, asks her to investigate a case of industrial sabotage.

16. *Wild and Lonely Place, A* (Mysterious, 1995) "The Diplo-Bomber" has been blowing up embassies, consulates, and United Nations offices in the United States over the past five years.

17. *McCone Files, The: The Complete Sharon McCone Stories* (Crippen & Landru, 1995) Collection of McCone stories, including her introduction to All Souls at the age of about 30.

18. *Broken Promise Land, The* (Mysterious, 1996) Country music star Ricky Savage, who is Sharon's brother-in-law, has been receiving increasingly incoherent anonymous letters sent to his unlisted address, all with the same message: "Whatever happened to my song?"

19. *Both Ends of the Night* (Mysterious, 1997) Sharon's former flight instructor, Matty Wildress, dies in an acrobatics plane crash after she requested Sharon's help.

20. *While Other People Sleep* (Mysterious, 1998) Someone is impersonating McCone, wearing her name tag at parties, committing crimes of which Sharon can be accused, breaking into her apartment, using her credit cards, and more.

21. *Walk through the Fire, A* (Mysterious, 1999) McCone goes to Hawaii to sort out a series of accidents happening on the film set of office neighbor Glenna Stanleigh.

22. *McCone and Friends* (Crippen & Landru, 2000) Short stories.

23. *Listen to the Silence* (Mysterious, 2000) The death of Sharon's father brings the revelation that she was adopted. The search for her birth parents leads her to a Shoshone reservation in Idaho.

24. *Dead Midnight* (Mysterious, 2002) A pair of suicides, that of McCone's brother Joey and of Roger Nagasawa, scion of a wealthy Japanese American family, involve Sharo.

25. *Dangerous Hour, The* (Mysterious, 2004) Julia Rafael, one of Sharon's operatives, is arrested for credit-card theft, but what is the real motivation behind the accusation made by Hispanic politician Alex Aguilar?

26. *Vanishing Point* (Mysterious, 2006) Sharon finally weds Hy Ripinsky and gets involved with a case that takes her through the fishing villages of the California coast.

27. *Ever-Running Man, The* (Warner, 2007) Corporate security firm Renshaw & Kessell International hires McCone to look into a series of bombings at its facilities.

II. Elena Oliverez is an amateur who gets drawn into investigating crimes. She works as a curator (later director) at the Museum of Mexican Arts in Santa Barbara. In a volume coauthored with Bill Pronzini (q.v.), His character Quincannon plays a part.

1. *Tree of Death, The* (Walker, 1983) Oliverez has to clear herself of murder charges when her boss Frank De Palma is slain shortly after she yells at him: "Somebody ought to kill you!"

2. *Legend of the Slain Soldiers, The* (Walker, 1985) Oliverez's mother calls upon her to investigate the murder of Ciro Sisneros, who may have been killed to keep him from writing the truth about the slaying of Chicano workers in 1935.

3. *Beyond the Grave* (Walker, 1986) Using Quincannon's notes, Oliverez tries to solve a buried treasure mystery whose solution eluded Bill Pronzini's character in 1894. Cowritten with Bill Pronzini (q.v.).

III. A third female detective created by Marcia Muller was recently widowed Joanna Stark, San Francisco–based security consultant to art galleries. Somewhat older and wealthier than McCone and Oliverez, she is depressed by her husband's death and embittered by past betrayals.

1. *Cavalier in White, The* (St. Martin's, 1986) Stark has quit the security business and moved to the town of Sonoma, but is drawn back by the news of the theft of Frans Hals's painting *The Cavalier in White.*

2. *There Hangs the Knife* (St. Martin's, 1988) Art thief Tony Parducci is suspected of stealing several Brueghels. Joanna, who was deserted two decades earlier by Tony when she became pregnant, travels to London to trap him.

3. *Dark Star* (St. Martin's, 1989) When Joanna discovers a painting missing from her home, she realizes that Tony Parducci is still alive.

Munif, Abdelrahman

Munif's Cities of Salt trilogy brought him some critical and negative reactions. Saudi Arabia stripped Munif of his citizenship, and other countries banned his books because of his fictional portrayal of the history of the Sultanate of Mooran (a thinly disguised Saudi Arabia). The trilogy is far more than fictional history or satire, being a rumination on the poignancy of inevitable change and the sadness of the lives of men and women overwhelmed by the tides of history and by the juggernaut of big economics and politics over which they have no control. Peter Theroux was praised for his translation of the trilogy from the original Arabic. Munif shares, with Naguib Mahfouz (q.v.), the honor of transforming the novel in Arabic. Jordanian-born attorney Munif edited an oil industry journal in Baghdad, was active in Middle Eastern politics, and died recently (2004) in Damascus, Syria.

1. *Cities of Salt* **(Random House, 1987)** The actions of a team of American petroleum engineers at a desert oasis shortly after World War I baffles the Bedouin tribespeople, who cannot imagine what they are after. Originally published in 1984 as *Mudun al-milhal-tih: riwayan.* Translated from the Arabic by Petr Theroux.
2. *Trench, The* **(Random House, 1993)** Examines the sociopolitical strategies of the ruling clique in the Sultanate of Mooran as they deal with their newly found wealth. Originally published in 1985 as *Al-oukhdoud.* Translated from the Arabic by Peter Theroux.
3. *Variations on Night and Day* **(Pantheon, 1993)** Details, in a retrospective view, how Sultan Khureybit consolidated his power in Mooran and created a modern nation-state. Originally published in 1989 as *Taqasim al-layl wa-al enahar.* Translated from the Arabic by Peter Theroux.

Murakami, Haruki

Haruki Murakami (or Murakami Haruki) is one of Japan's most popular and critically controversial novelists. His books are usually characterized by restless characters, disturbing shifts into altered reality, roller-coaster plots, and cyberpunk style. The unnamed narrator of this linked pair of novels is a sort of Japanese Everyman, a freelance writer who muddles his way through absurd plots people with characters who are named by the roles they play or have no names at all.

1. *Wild Sheep Chase, A* **(Kodansha, 1989)** The unnamed narrator is coerced into searching for a phantom sheep who has plans for world domination. Originally published in 1982 as *Hitsuji o mega-ruboken.* Translated from the Japanese by Alfred Birnbaum.
2. *Dance Dance Dance* **(Kodansha, 1994)** Now 34 years old, divorced, bereaved, and abandoned by his various lovers, the unnamed narrator is drawn to the strange and lonely Dolphin Hotel. Originally published in 1988 as *Dansu dansu dansu.* Translated from the Japanese by Alfred Birnbaum.

Murphy, Haughton

PSEUDONYM OF James Henry Duffy

Reuben Frost is a septuagenarian, semiretired Wall Street lawyer who, with his wife, Cynthia, finds it difficult to keep his nose out of mysteries. The urbane Reuben is the creation of a former Wall Street lawyer who knows how to provide a realistic financial district background for his cases.

1. *Murder for Lunch* **(Simon & Schuster, 1986)** Former leader of the Wall street firm of Chase and Ward, Reuben Frost steps in when a senior partner is poisoned at a company lunch.
2. *Murder Takes a Partner* **(Simon & Schuster, 1987)** When Clifton Hoyt, artistic director and chief choreographer of New York's NatBallet, is stabbed to death, Reuben, as chair of the board of trustees, feels it is his duty to investigate.
3. *Murders and Acquisitions* **(Simon & Schuster, 1988)** A struggle for control over Anderson Foods Corporation culminates with the death of Chairman of the Board Flemming Anderson at a Connecticut estate.

4. *Murder Keeps a Secret* **(Simon & Schuster, 1989)** Frost's godson, Pulitzer Prize–winning historian David Rowan, is shoved from the window of his midtown Manhattan office.
5. *Murder Times Two* **(Simon & Schuster, 1990)** A book discussion of *Vanity Fair* is disrupted by the cyanide-induced death of Tobias Vandemeer, husband of the discussion leader.
6. *Murder Saves Face* **(Simon & Schuster, 1991)** Frost's old law firm Chase and Ward calls on him for help when associate Juliana Merriman is murdered at the firm's new Manhattan office.
7. *Very Venetian Murder, A* **(Simon & Schuster, 1992)** Reuben and his wife, Cynthia, on vacation in Venice, are invited to a dinner where fashion designer Gregg Baxter will introduce a colleague's new line of fabrics.

Murray, William

"Shifty Lou" Anderson is a member of IBM (the International Brotherhood of Magicians), a race-horse handicapper, and part-time sleuth in a series of thrillers set at racetracks in southern California. All Shifty Lou wants out of life is "a little magic, an occasional good woman and a few winning horses," but he doesn't find these goals easy to reach in these mysteries full of magic, horse-racing lore and Runyonesque characters. William Murray, longtime Rome correspondent for the *New Yorker* ("Letters from Italy"), is a race-horse owner himself and author of nonfiction books about racing (e.g., *The Right Horse: Winning More, Losing Less and Having a Great Time at the Racetrack*, Doubleday, 1997) and Italy (e.g., *City of the Soul: A Walk in Rome*, Crown Journeys, 2002). He has also published the autobiographical *Janet, My Mother and Me* (Simon & Schuster, 2000) about the relationship between Janet Flanner and his mother, Natalia Danesi Murray.

1. *Tip on a Dead Crab* **(Viking, 1984)** A horse-switching caper just before a big race engages Anderson and his pals Jay and Sam.
2. *Hard Knocker's Luck, The* **(Viking, 1985)** The art and racing worlds intersect in this mystery about forged masterpieces.
3. *When the Fat Man Sings* **(Bantam, 1987)** Shifty Lou is commandeered to serve as a sort of lucky charm for a world-famous tenor who is also a compulsive gambler.
4. *King of the Nightcap, The* **(Bantam, 1989)** Anderson has to retrieve a twice-stolen work of art and handle a wager on a horse with perhaps one good race left in him, or get his fingers broken by any one of a host of unsavory characters.
5. *Getaway Blues, The* **(Bantam, 1990)** In between magician gigs, Shifty Lou hires on as temporary chauffeur for a rich, elderly, horse-owning eccentric.
6. *I'm Getting Killed Right Here* **(Doubleday, 1991)** Anderson leaps into an affair with the wife of the new partner he had taken on to help support a potentially great horse he has inherited.
7. *We're Off to See the Killer* **(Doubleday, 1993)** Shifty Lou becomes assistant to an ailing horse-trainer, and soon becomes involved with a talent colt, a sexy female groom, a crooked jockey, and three nasty villains.
8. *Now You See Her, Now You Don't* **(Holt, 1994)** Statuesque redhead Megan Starbuck seems like the perfect match for Anderson, if only she wouldn't keep on disappearing.
9. *Fine Italian Hand, A* **(Evans, 1996)** At a magic conference in Italy, Shifty Lou meets a Bobby Jo Dawson, a young American fashion model, who soon turns up drugged, raped, and murdered near the villa of the son of a powerful Italian financier.

Myers, L(eopold) H(amilton)

British author L. H. Myers was preeminently a novelist of ideas. In the series entitled the Root and the Flower, he examined the illusions of the mind as they tempt a young prince in 16th-century India. Not historical in any documentary sense, Myers's books have a remote setting to lift their central philosophical concerns out of a contemporary context; yet they reflect pointedly on the London society of his day. Prince Jali's guru is clearly the author's spokesman, expressing Myers's own ethical preoccupations and his belief in the essential goodness of human nature. *Rajah Amar* (number 3) was never published separately. It first appeared in the omnibus edition of *The Root and the Flower* (Harcourt, 1935). The second edition of the omnibus (1940) contains all four books. *The Near and the Far* was the title of a British omnibus edition (Cape, 1943). Myers is in danger of being forgotten: perhaps the New York Review of Books omnibus edition (2001) will help keep his reputation alive.

1. *Near and the Far, The* (Harcourt, 1929) This volume introduces Hari Kahn, a tribal chieftain; Rajah Amar, a Buddhist; Sita, the Rajah's Christian wife; the Princess Lalita; and little Prince Jali, age 12.
2. *Prince Jali* (Harcourt, 1931) Now almost 15, Prince Jali falls in love with the low-caste beauty Gunevati.
3. *Rajah Amar* (Harcourt, 1935) Rajah Amar, Prince Jali's father, is the central character. Not published separately. Published in *The Root and the Flower* omnibus edition (Harcourt, 1935).
4. *Pool of Vishnu, The* (Harcourt, 1940) Jali learns from his guru how to be a good rajah of Vidyapur.

Myrdal, Jan

Jan Myrdal, son of Swedish icons Gunnar and Alva Myrdal, has been an outspoken critic of Western culture and society, particularly of the Swedish welfare state his father helped to establish (see *Confessions of a Dysloyal European*, Pantheon, 1968). Myrdal's thinly fictionalized autobiographical novels have created their own sensation with their portrayal of Gunnar and Alva Myrdal as abusive and unloving parents. Myrdal's sister Sissela Bok has published her own view of Myrdal family relations in *Alva Myrdal: A Daughter's Memoir* (Addison-Wesley, 1991).

1. *Childhood* (Ravenswood, 1991) Jan's life from ages 5 to 11 in the Sweden of the 1930s is depicted, his parents' lack of love being somewhat balanced by good times on his grandparents' farm. Translated from the Swedish by Christine Swanson. Original title: *Barndom* (1982).
2. *Another World* (Ravenswood, 1994) The Myrdals emigrate to New York in 1938, where the lonely, obese 11-year-old Jan endures his father's abuse and his mother's behavioral experiments. Translated from the Swedish by Alan Bernstein. Original title: *Annan varld* (1984).
3. *12 Going on 13* (Ravenswood, 1995) In 1940 the Myrdals return to Sweden, and Jan is left with his aunt and uncle while his parents travel and the Nazis take over Europe. Translated from the Swedish by Christine Swanson. Original title: *Tolv pa det trettonde* (1989).

Nabb, Magdalen

Marshal Salva Guarnaccia is a member of the Carabinieri, the Italian police force, assigned to the Palazzo Pitti area of Florence. Guarnaccia, a Sicilian, is a quiet, unassuming fellow who tends to be looked down upon by his superiors, but he is a tenacious detective who always gets to the bottom of each case. The mysteries are well plotted, with interesting characters, but the details of life in Florence and the surrounding countryside are what make them more interesting than the average whodunit. Magdalen Nabb, a native of Lancashire who has lived in Florence for more than 30 years, also writes children's books, some featuring series character Josie Smith.

1. *Death of an Englishman* (Scribner, 1982) The murder of an Englishman takes Marshal Guarnaccia out of his sickbed and keeps him away from a Christmas holiday trip to Sicily.
2. *Death of a Dutchman* (Scribner, 1983) Answering the summons of an elderly Florentine lady, Guarnaccia finds a Dutchman near death with slashed hands.
3. *Death in Springtime* (Scribner, 1984) Two teenage girls are kidnapped during a freak snowfall.
4. *Death in Autumn* (Scribner, 1985) German-born Hilde Vogel is found murdered in the river Arno.
5. *Marshal and the Murderer, The* (Scribner, 1988) Guarnaccia goes to a pottery factory outside of Florence to look for a missing Swiss student.
6. *Marshal and the Madwoman, The* (Scribner, 1988) Marshal Guarnaccia tries to find out why an impecunious former mental patient is killed and her death made to look like suicide.
7. *Marshal's Own Case, The* (Scribner, 1990) Lulu, a transsexual prostitute, has been murdered and dismembered.
8. *Marshal Makes His Report, The* (Harper, 1992) A marchesa tries to bully the marshal into filing an accidental death report in the suspicious shooting of the owner of the Palazzo Ulderighi.
9. *Marshal at the Villa Torrini, The* (Harper, 1994) The marshal is summoned to the Villa Torrini, where he finds the body of a well-known writer, and her husband in a drunken sleep nearby.
10. *Monster of Florence, The* (Harper, 1996) Investigating an art forgery, Guarnaccia is dragged into a final attempt to catch a serial killer who has been operating for 10 years.
11. *Property of Blood* (Soho, 1999) The kidnapping of Contessa Brunamonti by Sardinian-Tuscan bandits doesn't bring out the best in her son and daughter.
12. *Some Bitter Taste* (Soho, 2002) The break-in at Sara Hirsch's apartment, the robbery of some silver brushes from a wealthy English art collector, and the murder of an Albanian prostitute, seemingly unrelated crimes, may be connected.
13. *Innocent, The* (Soho, 2005) The woman's body found in a pond in the Boboli Gardens is that of Kiko, a young Japanese apprentice to the shoemaker Peruzzi.

Naipaul, V(idiahar) S(urajprasad)

Nobel laureate V. S. Naipaul, native of Trinidad, is the author of novels now regarded as classics, such as *A House for Mr. Biswas* (McGraw-Hill, 1962) and *A Bend in the River* (Knopf, 1979). His last two novels depict the life of Willie Chandran, son of a Hindu ascetic and an untouchable, as he travels from India to England to Africa to Germany and back to India. Willie is a rootless man, unable to feel empathy with anyone besides himself, and prone to despise the inhabitants of any country where he resides.

1. *Half a Life* (Knopf, 2002) Describes the first 40 years in the life of Willie Chandran, Indian expatriate who lives for a while in England, then follows his wife to a Portuguese-ruled African country.

2. *Magic Seeds* (Knopf, 2004) Willie is found 18 years later, living with his sister in Berlin. He subsequently joins a guerrilla group in India.

Narayan, R(asipuram) K(rishnaswami)

Like William Faulkner (q.v.), R. K. Narayan has created a detailed fictional world. All of his fiction is set in Malgudi, a contemporary South Indian town resembling Narayan's native Mysore. Malgudi's residents come brilliantly to life as they gossip and plot their enterprises, fall in love, win and lose fortunes, and worry over their children. Graham Greene, in his introduction to *The Bachelor of Arts,* called Narayan's novels "comedies of sadness" and compared them to the work of Chekhov. Narayan (d. 2001) wrote in English. *An Astrologer's Day*; *Cyclone*; *Lawley Road*; *Salt and Sawdust*; and *Old and New* are the titles of short story collections published in India or the United Kingdom but not in the United States. Most of the stories in these collections are collected in numbers 4, 12, and 15. Omnibus volumes including *A Malgudi Omnibus, Tales from Malgudi,* and *More Tales from Malgudi* have been published by Minerva in the United Kingdom. *Malgudi Landscapes*; *A Town Called Malgudi*; *Memories of Malgudi*; and *The Magic of Malgudi* have been published by Penguin India.

1. *Swami and Friends* (Michigan State, 1954) Humorous episodes in the life of 10-year-old Swami and his Malgudi school chums make up this novel. Bound with *The Bachelor of Arts.* Originally published in 1935.

2. *Bachelor of Arts, The* (Michigan State, 1954) Young Chandran graduates from college, has an unhappy love affair, travels for a while, and then returns home. Bound with *Swami and Friends.* Originally published in 1935.

3. *Dark Room, The* (University of Chicago, 1981) Mrs. Ramani leaves home when her husband falls for his secretary, but she returns because she misses her children. Originally published in 1938.

4. *Malgudi Days* (Viking, 1982) A collection of short stories. Originally published in 1943.

5. *Grateful to Life and Death* (Michigan State, 1953) Krishnan, a young schoolteacher, is consoled after his wife's death by his delightful infant daughter. Originally published in the United Kingdom in 1945 as *The English Teacher* and reprinted by the University of Chicago Press under that title (1980).

6. *Waiting for the Mahatma* (Michigan State, 1955) Sriram, a pampered young man, falls in love with a beautiful young woman who is a protégée of Gandhi. Though written later than numbers 7 and 8, this novel fits chronologically about here.

7. *Printer of Malgudi, The* (Michigan State, 1957) Srinivas, a young newspaper publisher, becomes involved in the zany Indian filmmaking business. Published in the United Kingdom in 1949 as *Mr. Sampath: The Printer of Malgudi* and reprinted under that title.

8. *Financial Expert, The* (Michigan State, 1953) Margayya, an entrepreneur who facilitates peasant loans, gets rich by publishing a pornographic book entitled *Domestic Harmony.*

9. *Guide, The* (Viking, 1958) Con man Raju finds himself thrust into the role of a saint.

10. *Man-Eater of Malgudi, The* (Viking, 1961) Vasu, a huge taxidermist, is somewhat mad.

11. *Vendor of Sweets, The* (Viking, 1967) Candy maker Jagan is troubled when his son Mali returns from America with a girlfriend and a story-writing machine he wants to mass produce. Variant title: *The Sweet-Vendor.*

12. *Horse and Two Goats, A* (Viking, 1970) Another collection of Malgudi stories including the priceless title story about mutual incomprehension between a poor Indian and an American tourist.

13. *Painter of Signs, The* (Viking, 1976) Raman, a college-educated sign painter, falls in love with Daisy, an itinerant family-planning advocate.

14. *Tiger for Malgudi, A* (Viking, 1983) Raj, an 11-foot-long tiger, relates his career as circus performer, film star, inadvertent man-eater, and disciple of a holy man.

15. *Under the Banyan Tree and Other Stories* (Viking, 1985) A collection of 28 short stories.

16. *Talkative Man* (Viking, 1987) Journalist T. M. narrates his encounter with the mysterious Dr. Rann, philanderer and "futurologist" who dresses in three-piece suits.

17. *World of Nagaraj, The* (Viking, 1990) Nagaraj dreams of writing the definitive treatise on the Sanskrit sage Narada, even though he has never gotten around to learning Sanskrit.

18. *Grandmother's Tale, The: And Selected Stories* (Viking, 1994) The title novella and 18 short stories, some previously unpublished.

Nathanson, E. M.

The extremely violent film version of *The Dirty Dozen* is probably more familiar to most people than the novel upon which it was based. Both of Nathanson's novels are set in World War II and concern difficult assignments carried out by OSS Major John Reisman. Both books are better-than-average war novels full of action, well-researched historical background, and insights into the relationships between war and politics, good and evil.

1. *Dirty Dozen, The* (Random House, 1965) OSS officer John Reisman is given the unpalatable assignment of training 12 vicious American soldier-prisoners for a mission behind German lines just before D-Day.

2. *Dirty Distant War, A* (Viking, 1987) Reisman parachutes into Burma to try to prevent a conflict between Kachin tribesmen and the Chinese Kuomintang, both allies against the Japanese.

Naylor, Gloria

The Women of Brewster Place was awarded the 1983 American Book Award for best first novel. This novel depicts the lives of seven black women who live in a dreary apartment complex that is isolated from the rest of New York City. *The Men of Brewster Place*, which depicts Brewster Place from the point of view of seven black men, is a direct sequel. *Linden Hills*, which resurrects one of the characters in *The Women of Brewster Place*, describes the materially prosperous but soulless lives of black suburbanites who try to imitate whites. *Mamma Day*, which is about a wise old woman with magical powers, gives book-length treatment to a walk-on character in *Linden Hills*. A sequel in progress to *Mama Day* seems to have been sidetracked, at least temporarily, by *1996* (Third World, 2005), a semi-fictionalized autobiographical narrative about Naylor's ordeal under surveillance by the FBI. *Bailey's Cafe* (Harcourt, 1992) is a stand-alone novel. *The Women of Brewster Place* was adapted as a miniseries, then as a weekly ABC series produced by Oprah Winfrey in 1989–1990.

1. *Women of Brewster Place, The* (Viking, 1982) Seven interconnected stories about seven black women living in a dreary, isolated

apartment complex in New York who form a support group against the racism and sexism that afflict them.

2. *Linden Hills* (**Ticknor, 1985**) Poets Willie Mason and Lester Tilson get jobs in Linden Hills, an exclusive black suburb dominated by Luther Nedeed, fifth-generation mortician and real-estate tycoon.

3. *Mama Day* (**Ticknor, 1988**) Cocoa, grandniece of Miranda "Mama" Day, a wise old woman with magical powers, brings George, her citified husband, to Willow Springs, an island off the Georgia and South Carolina coast that has been owned by blacks since before the Civil War

4. *Men of Brewster Place, The* (**Hyperion, 1998**) The "men" of Brewster Place had only a marginal, more-often-than-not harmful, role in number 1. This novel relates the interconnected stories of seven men, known as the "sons" of Brewster Place.

Neel, Janet

PSEUDONYM OF Janet Neel Cohen

When introduced, Francesca Wilson is a rising star at the Department of Trade and Industry who has four younger brothers, for whom she acts as surrogate mother. John McLeish is Detective Chief Inspector of the London Metropolitan Police. The two meet during number 1 and eventually marry and have a son. Both of them strong willed, the two find it necessary to work together on investigations that come their way. This is a series of civilized mysteries with good characterization and background. Janet Neel, who loosely bases the character of Francesca Wilson on herself, has also written the stand-alone *Ticket to Ride* (St. Martin's, 2005) and, writing under her married name of Janet Cohen, two other novels: *The Highest Bidder* (Joseph [UK], 1992) and *Children of a Harsh Winter* (Joseph [UK], 1994).

1. *Death's Bright Angel* (**St. Martin's, 1988**) Introduces Francesca Wilson, who gets involved in the investigation of a prominent businessman, and meets Detective Chief Inspector John McLeish of the London Metropolitan Police.

2. *Death on Site* (**St. Martin's, 1990**) On summer vacation in the Scottish Highlands, lovers Francesca and John rescue the victim of a near fatal fall. A later fall, in London, proves to be fatal.

3. *Death of a Partner* (**St. Martin's, 1991**) While Francesca is in America helping one of her brothers, John looks into the death of a cabinet minister's girlfriend.

4. *Death among the Dons* (**St. Martin's, 1994**) Francesca and John are now married and the parents of a son. Francesca hires a nanny, takes a part-time job at Gladstone College, and gets involved when a possible suicide and a knife attack on a professor hit the school.

5. *Timely Death, A* (**St. Martin's, 1997**) After her mother becomes too ill to handle the job, Francesca takes over a women's shelter, and takes on the case of a woman being abused by her live-in lover.

6. *To Die For* (**St. Martin's, 1999**) The Gemini Group wants to buy the Café de la Paix, a successful restaurant run by Selina March-Hayden and Judith Delves, who don't want to sell. Then Selina gets murdered.

7. *O Gentle Death* (**St. Martin's, 2000**) The "suicide" of troubled student Catriona Roberts turns out to be murder, and John McLeish finds at least three suspects.

Neely, Barbara

Blanche White is the first working-class African American woman to have her own mystery series. Blanche, despite her name, is quite dark, which exposes her to racial taunts from light-colored blacks as well as whites. Blanche is no pushover, she has an "attitude," and no one is going to shove her around. Blanche's job as a domestic worker doesn't always help her to make ends meet, especially with three teenagers to support, but does give her opportunities to indulge her penchant for eavesdropping and relentless prying. The novels are well written with nicely drawn black characters. The white characters don't fare so well.

1. *Blanche on the Lam* (**St. Martin's, 1992**) Blanche escapes from the Farleigh, North Carolina, jail after being imprisoned for writing a few bad checks, and winds up working for the wealthy Carter family in Boston.

2. *Blanche and the Talented Tenth* (**St. Martin's, 1994**) Blanche decides that even a resort of light-skinned blacks in Maine would be preferable to Boston—"the most racist city in which she'd ever lived."

3. *Blanche Cleans Up* (**Viking, 1998**) Blanche is hired as temporary cook for the Brindles, an aristocratic and politically ambitious family who have a few skeletons in their closet.

4. *Blanche Passes Go* (**Viking, 2000**) Blanche returns to Farleigh, where she confronts some old truths about the New South and the rapist, David Palmer, who drove her from her home eight years before.

Newman, Christopher

New York City is the stomping ground for Police Lieutenant Joe Dante and his cohorts in this series of action-filled, suspenseful procedural novels. Dante feels more comfortable with the rich and famous than he does with other cops, but he is smart and tough, and the series has a gritty, authentic feel.

1. *Midtown South* (**Ballantine, 1986**) Several look-alike prostitutes have been murdered in Dante's precinct bordering on Times Square.

2. *Sixth Precinct* (**Fawcett, 1987**) A millionaire art collector is killed in his Greenwich Village townhouse, and his paintings are slashed.

3. *Knock-Off* (**Fawcett, 1989**) The designer of a trend-setting new sportswear line for Close Apparel is bludgeoned to death.

4. *Midtown North* (**Fawcett, 1991**) Police Captain Warren Mott, a cop with enemies, is found dead in a drug- and prostitute-infested part of Manhattan.

5. *19th Precinct* (**Fawcett, 1992**) Dante goes undercover as a construction worker to locate IRA terrorist Billy Mannion.

6. *Precinct Command* (**Fawcett, 1993**) A conservative Tennessee Congresswoman is murdered in a New York City hotel room.

7. *Dead End Game* (**Putnam, 1994**) The rookie pitcher phenom for the Kansas City Royals is found dead of a heroin overdose on the morning of the final game of the playoff series with the Yankees.

8. *Killer* (**Dell, 1997**) Dante is shot by a sniper in the middle of the street, but recovers enough to chase after the Colombian drug dealers who ordered the hit.

9. *Hit and Run* (**Dell, 1997**) The victim of a hit-and-run accident turns out to be the brother of Dante's friend and neighbor, rock singer Diana Webster.

Nin, Anaïs

Fans of the seven-volume diary by the French American Nin (pronounced *Neen*) who want to sample her fiction should try this work, originally published as five separate novelettes. Their interwoven stories of several women explore the central theme, the quest for the self through the "intricate maze of modern confusion." Nin's poetic prose and her psychoanalytic view, emphasizing the importance of dreams and the interior life, and her almost exclusive focus on women have won her a devoted audience. Nin was born in France, moved to New York at the age of 11, then returned to France for a lengthy stay where she was associated with the American literary underground, including Henry Miller (q.v.) and Djuna Barnes. All five novelettes are collected in a one-volume omnibus, *Cities of the Interior* (Swallow, 1974).

1. *Ladders to Fire* (Self-published, 1946) This is the story of Lillian and Larry, an American couple living in Paris, and their friends, including Lillian's lover, Jay.
2. *Children of the Albatross* (Self-published, 1947) This focuses on Djuna, a free spirit, and her friendships with Lillian, Jay, and Sabina.
3. *Four-Chambered Heart, The* (Self-published, 1950) Djuna and her lover, Rango live on a houseboat on the Seine until Rango's deranged wife nearly wrecks their lives.
4. *Spy in the House of Love, A* (Self-published, 1954) The story of Sabina, now living in New York City, and her relationships with Philip, Mambo, and Jay.
5. *Seduction of the Minotaur* (Self-published, 1961) This expanded version of the fifth novelette, originally titled *Solar Barque*, focuses on Lillian's search for a new life in Mexico.

Niven, Larry (Laurence van Cott)

I. Niven, like Robert A. Heinlein (q.v.), has a master plan for his science-fiction universe, and his universe, like Heinlein's, is based upon a plausible scientific future. He believes that technology will bring about a more desirable universe in the ultimate future but that the wrong use of technology can be disastrous. Many of Niven's titles are assigned to what he calls Known Space, set in a time some 700 or 800 years in the future and a space some 60 or 70 light-years in diameter. Although some of the Known Space volumes are only loosely connected, the Ringworld series titles, set on an artificial planet created in the distant past, are definite sequels with a continuing protagonist named Louis Wu. The Hugo-winning *Ringworld* is regarded by many critics as Niven's best single work. See Larry Niven's and Kevin Stein's *Guide to Larry Niven's Ringworld* (Baen, 1994).

1. *Fleet of Worlds* (Tor, 2007) A prequel to *Ringworld* set in 2650, 500 years after the human colony ship *Long Pass* was captured by "Citizens" (aka "Puppeteers"), two-headed beings who have bred successive generations of human "Colonists" from the *Long Pass's* crew, while lying about their origins. Coauthored with Edward M. Lerner.
2. *Ringworld* (Ballantine, 1970) Ringworld is an artificial planet shaped like a vast hoop, created in the distant past and peopled by inhabitants who have forgotten technology.
3. *Ringworld Engineers, The* (Holt, 1980) Louis Wu and Speaker-to-Animals are returned to Ringworld by a mad Puppeteer so that they can steal a transmutation device.
4. *Ringworld Throne, The* (Ballantine, 1996) Louis Wu must find a solution to the many problems resulting from the interactions of the many races living on Ringworld: problems including a plethora

of vampires, attacks on incoming spaceships, and Protectors encroaching on species not in their care.

5. *Ringworld's Children* (St. Martin's, 2004) After a long sleep, Louis Wu reawakes to find himself held captive by the hyperintelligent alien Tunesmith. The decaying Ringworld is in urgent need of redesign.

II. Another pair of novels is set in the part of Known Space called the Smoke Ring: a strange star system with a neutron star surrounded by a ring of breathable atmosphere. The Smoke Ring is peopled by humans who have, over the period of 500 years, evolved into distinct species to meet the strange environmental conditions of their different colonies.

1. *Integral Trees, The* (Ballantine, 1984) A group of colonists in the Smoke Ring are forced to seek a new life beyond their own community.
2. *Smoke Ring, The* (Ballantine, 1987) The computer abandoned aboard the Earthship *Discipline* still tries to manipulate events in the Smoke Ring.

III. Another series set in Known Space has for a protagonist Gil "the Arm" Hamilton, who is a "psychic" detective whose "arm" can reach into men's brains. Set in a world where people are murdered by "organ-leggers" for body parts to be used in transplant surgery.

1. *Long Arm of Gil Hamilton, The* (Ballantine, 1976) Contains three novellas: "Death by Ecstasy," "The Defenseless Dead," and "Arm."
2. *Patchwork Girl, The* (Ace, 1980) Naomi Mitchison, the most beautiful woman on the moon, makes what looks like an assassination attempt on the Fourth Speaker of Asteroids, but Gil doesn't think that she is a murderer.
3. *Flatlander* (Ballantine, 1995) Subtitle: *The Collected Tales of Gil "The Arm" Hamilton*. Contains numbers 1 and 2 plus an original story, "The Woman in Del Rey Crater."

IV. Several other books are set in Known Space. Number 3 has connections with the Ringworld series (series I). Number 2 has the organ-transplant theme, which is dominant in the Gil Hamilton series (series III). Numbers 4, 5, and 6 are short story collections. *Three Books of Known Space* (Ballantine, 1989) contains numbers 1, 2, and 4. *A World out of Time* (Holt, 1976) and *Destiny's Road* are SF novels not associated with Known Space. General short story collections include *Inconstant Moon* (Gollancz [UK], 1973); *A Hole in Space* (Ballantine, 1974); *Limits* (Ballantine, 1985); *N-Space* (Tor, 1990); *Playgrounds of the Mind* (Tor, 1991); and *Scatterbrain* (Tor, 2003).

1. *World of Ptaavs* (Ballantine, 1966) The last survivor of the ancient Slaver Empire is awakened by unwitting earthfolk.
2. *Gift from Earth, A* (Ballantine, 1968) The Plateau on Mount Lookitthat is ruled by a hereditary "Crew" that uses the "Colonist" majority for organ transplants.
3. *Protector* (Ballantine, 1973) The Pak, builder of the Ringworld (see Series I) and ancestors of humanity, live in the center of the galaxy.
4. *Tales of Known Space* (Ballantine, 1975) Contains all Known Space short stories published until 1975. Earlier collections: *Neutron Star* (Ballantine, 1968) and *The Shape of Space* (Ballantine, 1969).
5. *Convergent Series* (Ballantine, 1979) Short story collection.
6. *Crashlander* (Ballantine, 1995) Contains all of the stories about Beowulf Schaeffner, one of the leading Known Space protagonists.

V. Although Niven has stated that he doesn't believe in the possibility of time travel, like most SF writers, he is intrigued by the concept. He has written a novel and several short stories about time traveler Hanville Svetz, who travels back in time from Year +1108 Atomic Era to collect now-extinct animals, such as a horse, for zoos.

1. *Flight of the Horse, The* (Ballantine, 1973) Short stories about Svetz's adventures in time.
2. *Rainbow Mars* (Tor, 2000) Hanville, on his way back from Year +390 with a snake he has collected, returns to Earth only to find that there has been a regime change and that he is to be sent back in time again, to Mars this time.

VI. With the exception of *Ringworld*, *The Mote in God's Eye*, written with Jerry Pournelle, is Niven's most famous single work. Set in the 31st century, *The Mote in God's Eye* and its sequel *The Gripping Hand* concern a highly intelligent species from a planet called the Mote in God's Eye that has the potential for explosive population growth and poses a real threat to the Empire of Man. See series VIII and X for other collaborative series with Jerry Pournelle. Niven and Pournelle have coauthored several stand-alone novels: *Inferno* (Pocket Books, 1976); *Lucifer's Hammer* (Playboy, 1977); *Oath of Fealty* (Phantasia, 1981); *Footfall* (Ballantine, 1985); and *Fallen Angels* (Easton, 1991; with Michael Flynn as coauthor).

1. *Mote in God's Eye, The* (Simon & Schuster, 1974) Humans make contact with an intelligent species in the Coal Sack Nebula. The "Moties" try to desperately to conceal their true nature. Written with Jerry Pournelle.
2. *Gripping Hand, The* (Pocket Books, 1993) Some quarter-century later, the "Moties" remain quarantined within their own star system, but the formation of a new star nearby gives them an opportunity to escape back into the galaxy. Written with Jerry Pournelle. Variant title: *The Moat Around Murcheson's Eye*.

VII. Steven Barnes (q.v.) is another one of Niven's collaborators. Niven and Barnes teamed up on the Dream Park trilogy, which is about a theme park with virtual fantasy role-playing games with interactive scenarios and a tendency to get all too real with fatal results for some of the participants. For another collaborative effort with Barnes, see series VIII. Stand-alone novels coauthored with Barnes include *The Descent of Anansi* (Tor, 1982); *Achilles' Choice* (Tor, 1991); and *Saturn's Race* (Tor, 2000).

1. *Dream Park* (Phantasia, 1981) Fifteen virtual-reality gamers embark upon a four-day quest against the simulated challenges of Dream Park, a computer fantasy world only to find that a murderer has added an element of real danger. Written with Steven Barnes.
2. *Barsoom Project, The* (Ace, 1989) Once again a group of computer gamers takes part in one of Dream Park's interactive scenarios and, of course, things go wrong. Written with Steven Barnes.
3. *California Voodoo Game, The* (Ballantine, 1992) Five teams of six players each will compete in the California Voodoo Game. One of the players may have committed murder to obtain information on the security systems. UK title: *The Voodoo Game*. Written with Steven Barnes.

VIII. Both Pournelle (see series VI and IX) and Barnes (see series VII) collaborated with Niven on the Heorot duo of novels, which features a future human colony in space pitted against a strange ecology and aliens known as "grendels."

1. *Legacy of Heorot, The* (Simon & Schuster, 1987) Human settlers start an agricultural colony on Avalon (Tau Ceti Four) but find themselves challenged by the planet's ecology and hostile aliens

they call grendels. Written with Jerry Pournelle and Steven Barnes.
2. *Beowulf's Children* (Tor, 1995) The seasons and the original ecology of Avalon start to come after the devastation by the grendels. UK title: *The Dragons of Heorot*. Written with Jerry Pournelle and Steven Barnes.

IX. Although many of his stories have fantasy elements in them, Niven has written relatively little "straight" fantasy. The Magic series is an exception. It is about a world in which magic was commonplace until selfish, short-sighted magicians used most of it up. Number 1 is a novel; numbers 2 and 3 are anthologies of short stories on the theme, edited by Niven. This series was followed by the Golden Road series (series X).

1. *Magic Goes Away, The* (Ace, 1978) Once there was magic in the world, but selfish, shortsighted magicians used up most of the mana that moved that world. Orolandes, the Sad Achaean, must take up his half a sword and try to right things.
2. *Magic May Return, The* (Berkley, 1981) Anthology of stories edited by Niven.
3. *More Magic* (Berkley, 1984) Another collection of stories edited by Niven.

X. Larry Niven, with the help of Jerry Pournelle, has revived the ancient world depicted in series IX. So far two novels (of a possible trilogy) have described the adventures of Whandall Placehold as he fights an evil god who possesses the "lordkins" of Whandall's city and turns them into pyromaniacs.

1. *Burning City, The* (Pocket Books, 2000) As Whandall Placehold comes of age, he fights to free his people from evil firegod, who possesses each lordkin in turn and makes him set fire to the city. Written with Jerry Pournelle.
2. *Burning Tower, The* (Orbit [UK], 2003) Whandall resists the firegod's command to burn his city and seeks to bend the firegod to his own will. Written with Jerry Pournelle. Not yet published in the United States.

XI. Niven created the series of collaborative anthologies called the Man-Kzin Wars in which humans fight against intelligent giant catlike beings. So far he has edited nine anthologies (Hal Colebatch has edited the tenth) to which he and other authors (e.g., Jerry Pournelle, Poul Anderson, Dean Ing, S. M. Stirling, Greg Bear) have contributed stories on the theme. *The Best of All Possible Wars* (Baen, 1998) contains selections from numbers 1 through 8. *Annals of the Man-Kzin Wars: An Unofficial Companion Guide* (Xlibris, 2001) has been written by Alan Michaud.

1. *Man-Kzin Wars, The* (Baen, 1988) Anthologies all published by Baen: I (1988); II (1989); III (1990); IV (1991); V (1992); VI (1994); VII (1995); VIII (1996; variant title: *Choosing Names*); IX (2002); X (2003; variant title: *The Wunder War*).

Nofziger, Lyn

The Tackett pentology is Republican political operative Nofziger's whimsical tribute to Louis L'Amour's (q.v.) Sackett saga. True to western tradition, Del Tackett is a loner and a drifter, quick with his gun and fists, but respectful to women. Del is constantly forced to remind people not to take him for that "two-bit gunslinger" Sackett. A series full of action and humor and characters with names like Algore, Wayne Johns, Twain Sawyer, the Smith twins (Lorrel and

Hardy), Orey O'Cooksie, and Hacken Sackett (of the New Jersey Sacketts).

1. *Tackett* (Regnery, 1993) Del take the job as foreman of the R Bar R Ranch, which is shorthanded and beset by rustlers.
2. *Tackett and the Teacher* (Regnery, 1994) Tackett rides into Abilene to find Liddy Doyle, daughter of his old saddle buddy Billy Bob Doyle.
3. *Tackett and the Saloon Keeper* (Tumbleweed, 1994) Drifting into Shalak Springs, Colorado, Del wins the local saloon, its book-keeper Annie Laurie Burns, and her mule Maxwelton in a poker game.
4. *Tackett and the Indian* (Jameson, 1999) Falsely accused of cattle-rustling upon his arrival in Montana, Tackett is rescued by a nubile Sioux maiden.
5. *Tacketts, The* (Jameson, 1999) Annie Laurie asks Del and Ben Bill for help in saving her saloon from an illegal takeover by Sam Websterby.

Nordhoff, Charles

Charles Nordhoff and James Norman Hall drew skillfully on the fascinating true story of the mutiny that took place aboard the British warship, *Bounty*, in the South Pacific in 1787. The first novel of the trilogy became an immediate best seller and was made into a classic movie starring Charles Laughton and Clark Gable (1935) and a not-so-good remake starring Trevor Howard and Marlon Brando (1962). *Men against the Sea* is, if anything, an even better read than *Mutiny on the Bounty*, and *Pitcairn's Island* is nearly as good. The trilogy's high drama, tense story, and compelling characters make it a classic of popular literature that no reader should miss. Omnibus volume: *The Bounty Trilogy* (Little, Brown, 1936). Nordhoff and Hall collaborated on several other books set in the South Seas, including *The Hurricane* (Little, Brown, 1936), which was made into a great "escape" film by John Ford (1937; starring Jon Hall and Dorothy Lamour) and *Botany Bay* (Little, Brown, 1941), which was also filmed (1953; Alan Ladd and James Mason).

1. *Mutiny on the Bounty* (Little, Brown, 1932) Mate Fletcher Christian and some of the *Bounty* crew rebel against tyrannous Captain Bligh in 1787.
2. *Men against the Sea* (Little, Brown, 1934) Relates the 3,600-mile voyage of the open boat to which Captain Bligh and members of the crew were consigned by the mutineers. Drawn from Bligh's own journal, in which he appears as a more sympathetic character than in *Mutiny on the Bounty*.
3. *Pitcairn's Island* (Little, Brown, 1934) What happened to the *Bounty* mutineers and the Polynesians who accompanied them, as they tried to make a home on remote Pitcairn's Island. This fact-based story is not for the squeamish.

Norris, Frank

An early admirer of Émile Zola (q.v.), Frank Norris was the first American novelist to incorporate the new naturalism into his work with any success. *McTeague* (1899), considered by some to be his masterpiece, is a grim tale of miserliness on which the classic Eric von Stroheim silent movie *Greed* (1925) was based. Norris conceived the Epic of Wheat as a trilogy of self-contained novels that would trace the story of a crop of wheat from the time of its sowing in California to the time of its consumption as bread in a European village. His early death at the age of 32 left unwritten the third volume, tentatively titled *The Wolf: A Story*

of Europe. *The Octopus* has been reprinted many times, including by the Library of America (1986).

1. *Octopus, The: A Story of California* (Doubleday, 1901) War breaks out between the railroads and the wheat growers, led by farmer Magnus Derrick.
2. *Pit, The: A Story of Chicago* (Doubleday, 1903) The story of the wheat's sale in the Chicago market, or wheat pit, features the ruthless stock speculator Curtis Jadwin and his unhappy wife.

Norton, Andre

PSEUDONYM OF Alice Mary Norton

I.   Andre Norton had a career as a children's librarian (Cleveland Public Library), editor (Gnome Press), and a prolific writer of fantasy and science fiction. Most of her earlier fiction was targeted for juvenile readers by her publishers, but for some time now she has been regarded as a classic adult fantasy writer. Although she wrote many stories that are classifiable as science fiction, she generally eschews the "hard" kind, not being comfortable with many aspects of technology. Since the 1950s she has been instrumental in introducing many younger readers to fantasy and science fiction, as well as attracting many adults. She is credited with inspiring such writers as Mary Zimmer Bradley (q.v.) and Anne McCaffrey (q.v.) and many others. Witch World, her longest and most popular series, defies summarization, but basically it is about an alternative world where a race of witches (Estcarpians) is beset by marauding savages (the people of Karsten and Alizon) and the Kolder, cruel alien invaders from another dimension. Continuing characters include Simon Tregarth and his lover, Jaelith (especially numbers 1, 2, 4, 5, and 6); Kerovan (especially numbers 8, 13, and 16); the Were-Riders (especially numbers 3 and 9); the Falconers, the Old Ones, Destree, Lady Frost, and the Keplian Mares. Although basically a sword-and-sorcery series, Witch World has always had strong female characters and generally avoids the hairy-chested "berserker" males often featured in the genre, especially in the early days. Norton's style, though sometimes defined by critics as "merely serviceable," is vigorous, and she is a great storyteller. Her stories are often coming-of-age tales with protagonists who achieve moral stature as well as power and are never excessively violent. Starting in the late 1980s, most of Norton's Witch World books have been collaborations with other authors or anthologies edited by Norton.

Subsets within the series include the Estcarp Cycle (numbers 1, 2, 4, 5, 6, 10, 15, 17, and 27); the High Halleck Cycle (numbers 3, 7, 8, 9, 11, 13, 14, 16, and 21); the Turning (numbers 20, 22, and 23); and Secrets of the Witch World (numbers 24, 25, and 26). *Witch World* is listed by publication date, but it should be noted that number 14 is really prehistory, and number 27 describes events simultaneous with numbers 1, 2, and 4.

The earlier novels were originally published in paperbound editions only. Gregg Press reprinted numbers 1 through 7 in hardcover. Omnibus editions include *Annals of the Witch World* (Guild America, 1994; numbers 1–3); *Chronicles of the Witch World* (Science Fiction Book Club, 1995; numbers 4–6); *The Gates of Witch World* (Tor, 2002; numbers 1–3); and *Lost Lands of Witch World* (Tor, 2004; numbers 4–6). *Ware-Wrath* was a limited edition publication (Cheap Street, 1984).

1. *Witch World* (Ace, 1963) Details Simon Tregarth's entry into the Witch World, the initial defeat of the Kolder, and the start of the love between Simon and Jaelithe.
2. *Web of the Witch World* (Ace, 1964) Describes the freeing of the Witch World from the Kolder's grip and the liberation of Jaelithe from her witch's training.

3. *Year of the Unicorn* (Ace, 1965) First in the High Halleck cycle. Gillan, ward of Norstead Abbey in High Hallack, is the protagonist.

4. *Three against the Witch World* (Ace, 1967) Kyllan, Kemoc, and Kaththea, Simon and Jaelithe's children, take center stage.

5. *Warlock of the Witch World* (Ace, 1967) Kemoth tells of his barely successful rescue of Kaththea from the seduction of the Dark Power.

6. *Sorceress of the Witch World* (Ace, 1968) Kaththea sets out to regain the magic she lost in her brush with the Dark Power.

7. *Spell of the Witch World* (DAW, 1972) About the twins Elys, the witch-sister, and Elyn, the warrior-brother, and the pact that draws them into unknown perils.

8. *Crystal Gryphon, The* (Atheneum, 1972) Kerovan, Lord-Heir in Ulmsdale, is born with amber eyes and cloven feet. Continued in number 13.

9. *Jargoon Pard, The* (Atheneum, 1974) Features the Were-riders from Number 3. Kethan, heir of the House of Car do Prawn, is traded at birth for the daughter of a power-hungry royal female.

10. *Trey of Swords* (Ace, 1977) Yonan finds a strange sword with mystic powers and uses it to free an ancient warrior.

11. *Zarsthor's Bane* (Ace, 1978) Brixia, formerly a lady of High Hallack, is now a wilderness wanderer, accompanied only by a hunting cat.

12. *Lore of the Witch World* (DAW, 1980) Collection of six previously published short stories about Witch World along with a new novella, "The Changeling."

13. *Gryphon in Glory* (Atheneum, 1981) Kerovan has renounced his wife, Joisan, to free her from their marriage bond and has left his kingdom to search for his destiny. Continues number 8; continued by number 16.

14. *Horn Crown* (DAW, 1981) The "prehistory" of Witch World. Relates the coming of the Dalesmen to what later becomes High Hallack.

15. *Ware Hawk* (Atheneum, 1983) Tirtha, last heir of the House of Hawkholme, is summoned by a recurring vision-dream to the ruins of the long-abandoned family holding.

16. *Gryphon's Eyrie* (Tor, 1984) Continues the adventures and love story of Kerovan and Joisan from number 13. Cowritten with A. C. Crispin.

17. *Gate of the Cat, The* (Ace, 1987) A stone ring in the Scottish Highlands becomes the gateway through which Kelsie McBlair enters a new world.

18. *Tales of the Witch World* (Tor, 1987) Three collections of short fiction about Witch World written by various authors and edited by Norton. Volume 1 published in 1987; volume 2 in 1988; volume 3 in 1990.

19. *Four from the Witch World* (Tor, 1989) A shared-world anthology edited by Norton containing the following stories: Elizabeth H. Boyer, "The Stillborn Heritage"; C. J. Cherryh (q.v.), "Stormbirds"; Meredith Ann Pierce, "Rampion"; Judith Tarr (q.v.), "Falcon Lore."

20. *Storms of Victory* (Tor, 1991) The Turning, book one. One novella by Norton: "Port of Dead Souls," in which Destree M'Regnant of the Sulcors saves a sea expedition from an ancient evil. One novella by P. M. Griffin: "Seakeep," in which Una of Seakeep hires the women-hating Falconers to defend her isolated hold from a wrecker.

21. *Songsmith* (Tor, 1992) Young songsmith Eydruth of Kar-Garudwyn ranges far from home seeking help for her brain-damaged father. Cowritten with A. C. Crispin

22. *Flight of Vengeance* (Tor, 1992) Book two of the Turning. Contains two novellas by Mary H. Schaub: "Exile," in which the inhabitants of Witch World continue to cope with the aftermath of the Turning. Nolar and Duratan are two leading characters; and "Falcon Hope," which takes up the tale of Holdlady Una of Sea Keep (see number 20) and the mercenary leader Tarlach the Falconer. Norton and P. M. Griffin wrote the introduction and the afterword.

23. *On Wings of Magic* (Tor, 1994) Book three of the Turning. Novellas set in Estcarp after the devastation of the Turning: "We, the Women," by Patricia Mathews, and "Falcon Magic," by Sasha Miller.

24. *Key of the Keplian, The* (Warner, 1995) A young girl of mixed Celtic and Native American ancestry passes into the Witch World and gets involved with the Keplian Mares, which are rather special horses. Coauthored with Lyn McConchie. Secrets of the Witch World, volume 1.

25. *Magestone, The* (Warner, 1996) Mereth and Kasarian, children of clans who have been at war for a thousand years, meet as strangers. Coauthored with Mary H. Schaub. Volume 2 of Secrets of the Witch World.

26. *Warding of the Witch World, The* (Warner, 1997) Alizondem nobles throw open the Gates to other worlds, allowing evil free access to Witch World, and Witch World's disparate forces of Light must combine to save its inhabitants. Many characters from earlier books, such as Simon Tregarth, Jaelinth, Destree, the Keplian Mares, the Falconers, and Lady Frost resurface in this novel, which is supposed to be the culmination of the Witch World series. Volume 3 of Secrets of the Witch World.

27. *Ciara's Song* (Warner, 1998) Events in the Witch World of numbers 1, 2, and 4 as seen through the eyes of Ciara, whose family in South Karsten is destroyed in the genocide committed against the Old Race. Coauthored with Lynn McConchie.

28. *Duke's Ballad, The* (Tor, 2005) Young half-breed witch Arsling must rid Karsten of the blight her brother's curse has spread. Coauthored with Lynn McConchie.

29. *Silver May Tarnish* (Tor, 2005) Lorcan, Keep Lord of Erondale, and beekeeper Meive of Landale, having lost their families to invaders and outlaws, work together to free the dalefolk from renegades and restore Landale as a haven. Written by Lyn McConchie with the "blessing" of Andre Norton.

II. Coauthored with Sasha Miller, the Book of the Oak, or the Oak, Yew, Ash, and Rowan Cycle, is a fantasy trilogy about the power struggle between royal houses. Yew Queen Ysa, her thuggish son, Florian, and an evil being called the Great One are among the protagonists in this series replete with swords, sorcery, and frosty, swampy, or invisible creatures.

1. *To the King a Daughter* (Tor, 2000) The Ash clan is facing annihilation as Yew Queen Ysa marshals the services of invisible beings to ensure her son Florian's royal seat. Cowritten with Sasha Miller.

2. *Knight or Knave* (Tor, 2001) Ysa has her hands full in trying to control her sadistic, vainglorious son, King Florian. Cowritten with Sasha Miller.

3. *Crown Disowned, A* (Tor, 2002) From the North, the evil Great One is threatening Rendel and all the lands of the South. Cowritten with Sasha Miller.

4. *Dragon Blade* (Tor, 2005) Although the Great Foulness has been defeated, and Earth has begun to heal, the Mother Ice Dragon has awakened to become a new menace, one that can be slain only with the Dragon Blade, which has been lost for ages. Written by Sasha Miller, with Andre Norton as coauthor.

III. Carolus Rex is a pair of alternate history novels written with Rosemary Edghill and set in an early 19th-century America that never went through an American Revolution. The Duke of Monmouth, rather than James II, had succeeded Charles II on the English throne and Henry IX now rules Britain. Thomas Jefferson is Lord Protector of America and the unsubjugated Native Americans are guided by their tribal deities. For another alternate 19th-century America, see Orson Scott Card's (q.v.) Tales of Alvin Maker.

1. *Shadow of Albion, The* (Tor, 1999) Napoléon and the Jacobite descendants of Charles II's uncrowned brother James plot against King Henry IX and an America governed by Lord Protector Thomas Jefferson. Cowritten with Rosemary Edghill.
2. *Leopard in Exile* (Tor, 2001) The Marquis de Sade, in charge at New Orleans, works with Napoléon to disrupt British North America, while the free Native Americans confer with their tribal deities. Cowritten with Rosemary Edghill.

IV. The Halfblood Chronicles, cowritten with Mercedes Lackey (q.v.), postulates a fantasy world where a decadent Elven society rules over the remnants of humanity, and wizards, intelligent dragons, Iron People, and other creatures and peoples abound.

1. *Elvenbane* (Tor, 1991) Shana, abandoned daughter of Elven Lord Dyran and a human concubine, is raised by the Dragon Alara, and becomes involved with her Dragon brother Keman in a revolt against the tyranny of the Elves. Cowritten with Mercedes Lackey.
2. *Elvenblood* (Tor, 1995) Sheyrene (Rena) and her brother Corryn, kept virtual prisoners by their father, escape and find their way to the Iron People, whose iron jewelry protects them from magic. Cowritten with Mercedes Lackey.
3. *Elvenborn* (Tor, 2002) An attempt by his rivals to discredit the young Elven Lord Kyrtian fails, and Kyrtian finds himself in command of the army sent against the revolutionaries. Cowritten by Mercedes Lackey.

V. Most of Norton's science fiction-fantasy tales are set in a different universe from that of Witch World. Although there are many designated series, characters can wander from series to series or even to stand-alone novels. Most of the ingenious, vigorously narrated plots have a space opera or a sword-and-sorcery component or both. Protagonists, often female, usually have to fight against great odds or struggle upward from lowly beginnings in what are, more often than not, coming-of-age sagas. Magic often plays a large role, though technology tends to take a backseat. Time travel, as well as space travel, is possible and sometimes engaged in. Animals, especially cats, play important roles, and may be more intelligent than the human characters.

One of the longest series set in this universe concerns the merchant spaceship *Solar Queen*, which, in its trading missions, brings its characters into high-adventure situations such as plots to take over the galaxy, criminal combines, plague, spaceship graveyards, poisonous planets and other cataclysms, hyperspace, wizards, and telepathy. Continuing characters, besides the *Solar Queen*, include cargo-master Dane Thorson, Captain Micael Jellico, and, later, Rael Cofort, who eventually marries Captain Jellico. This series is closely related to series VI (Free Traders). Numbers 1 through 3 were issued under the pseudonym Andrew North. Number 5 was coauthored with P. M. Griffin; numbers 6 and 7 with Sherwood Smith. Numbers 1 and 2, somewhat rewritten, have been reissued in the omnibus volume *The Solar Queen* (Tor, 2003).

1. *Sargasso of Space* (Gnome, 1955) Apprentice cargo-master Dane Thorson signs on for a voyage merchant spaceship *Solar Queen*. The "Queen" encounters many adventures, including a graveyard of lost spaceships. Written as Andrew North.

2. *Plague Ship* (Gnome, 1956) Although the *Solar Queen* is running out of supplies, she cannot land on any inhabited planet since there is plague on board. Also published with *Voodoo Planet* (number 3) in 1959. Written as Andrew North.
3. *Voodoo Planet* (Ace, 1959) Dane Thorson faces the mental wizards of the planet Khatka. Published together with *Plague Ship* (number 2) and later with *Star Hunter* (1983). Written as Andrew North.
4. *Postmarked the Stars* (Harcourt, 1969) The crew of the *Solar Queen* stumbles upon a criminal operation that involves the attempted conquest of the whole galaxy.
5. *Redline the Stars* (Tor, 1993) The crew of the *Solar Queen* has mixed reactions to new member Rael Cofort, who is the sister of rival Free Trader Teague Cofort. Cowritten with P. M. Griffin.
6. *Derelict for Trade* (Tor, 1997) The *Solar Queen* comes out of hyperspace and encounters a derelict spaceship inhabited only by two cats. Cowritten with Sherwood Smith.
7. *Mind for Trade, A* (Tor, 1997) Aboard the Queen's new sister ship *North Star*, Dane Thorson head toward Hesprid-IV, where a strange force is killing stranded miners. The *Solar Queen*'s new crew has formed a telepathic bond together.

VI. The Free Traders, or Moon Magic, series, related to the Solar Queen (series V) sequence, revolves around the Moon of Three Rings, where a good deal of magic and psychic goings-on take place. The continuing protagonist is Krip Vorlund. *Moonsinger* (Baen, 2006) is an omnibus volume containing numbers 1 and 2.

1. *Moon of Three Rings* (Viking, 1966) Krip the Free Trader is changed into an animal by the Moon Singer Marden in an effort to save him from an evil power.
2. *Exiles of the Stars* (Viking, 1971) A Free Trader's ship is forced down on a barren and seemingly uninhabited planet while on a mission for the Thorran priests.
3. *Flight in Yiktor* (Tor, 1986) In a novel in which most things seem to come in threes, a psychic sorceress, a telepath adventurer, and a deformed ex-slave use their extrasensory powers to stop a thieves' combine from looting the galaxy.
4. *Dare to Go A-Hunting* (Tor, 1990) Orphaned Farree embarks upon a quest to discover other winged, intelligent beings like himself.

VII. The Forerunners are a bygone race of beings whose legacy lives on in the minds of certain individuals who are the subject of intense study by "historians" trying to find the key to the beginning of civilization. This series, which has characters from other sequences such as the Dipple series (series IX). Shann Lantree, Jofre, mind-reader Ziatha, and beggar Simsa are some of the leading characters in a series featuring ancient wisdom, ESP, Wyverns, Throgs, magic stones, and out-of-body experiences.

1. *Storm over Warlock* (World, 1960) Thorval, Shann Lantee, and two wolverines, the only Terran survivors on the Planet Warlock, have to face an invasion of beetlelike Throgs, and deal with the local Wyverns (or witches).
2. *Ordeal in Otherwhere* (World, 1964) A young girl sold as a slave to a trader wishing to do business with the Wyverns of Warlock, finds herself in contact with these witch-beings.
3. *Forerunner Foray* (Viking, 1973) Mind-reader Ziatha is totally unprepared for contact with the strange green stone that takes her out-of-body and into the ancient Forerunner worlds. Also part of the Dipple series (series IX).
4. *Forerunner* (Tor, 1981) Historians wish to probe the mind of beggar-girl Simsa for the secrets of the ancient Forerunners, which might be the key to the future of the galaxy.

5. *Forerunner: The Second Venture* (**Tor, 1985**) Simsa escapes from the Burrows with the aid of the off-planet Rangers, but they want to return her to captivity for study by the Historians.

6. *Brother to Shadows* (**Morrow, 1973**) Jofre, expelled by the Brotherhood of Shadows (or Assassins) who raised him, rescues the reptilian alien Zurzal who engages him to help search for Forerunner ruins.

VIII. The two Janus novels concern a slave named Naill Renfro, a treasure that could spell trouble, creatures called Ifts, and a mysterious force that controls minds. Closely related to series VII and IX.

1. *Judgment on Janus* (**Harcourt, 1963**) Niall Renfro had been warned about the treasure sometimes found at the edge of the jungle, but he thought that one jewel surreptitiously picked up might earn his freedom.

2. *Victory on Janus* (**Harcourt, 1966**) Renfro and the Ifts are forced to battle an enemy that looks like themselves. Also in the Dipple series (series IX).

IX. Four books involve the Dipple, a sordid settlement where refugees from the interplanetary wars are consigned. Number 2 is also part of the Janus series (series VIII). Number 4 is also part of the Forerunner series (series VII). *Masks of the Outcasts* (Baen, 2005) is an omnibus volume containing numbers 1 and 3.

1. *Catseye* (**Harcourt, 1961**) Temporary work in a strange interplanetary petship led Troy Horan to the realization that he communicate wordlessly with certain animals.

2. *Judgment on Janus (Dipple)* (**Harcourt, 1963**) See series VIII, number 2.

3. *Night of Masks* (**Harcourt, 1964**) No price seemed too high for the cosmetic surgery that would restore Nik's hideously disfigured face and free him from the Dipple, a settlement of the dispossessed.

4. *Forerunner Foray (Dipple)* (**Viking, 1973**) See series VII, number 3.

X. Central Control, a pair of early novels, set 4,000 years apart, concerned the Star Rangers, an interplanetary police force. The two novels, somewhat revised, were reissued as *Star Soldiers* (Baen, 2001).

1. *Star Guard* (**Harcourt, 1955**) In circa 4000 CE, when humans are valued only as mercenaries, swordsman Kar Kair stumbles upon a conspiracy that threatens both Central Control and the human race.

2. *Star Rangers* (**Harcourt, 1953**) The patrol cruiser *Starfire* lands on an unknown but seemingly habitable planet. Although published first, this is set 4,000 years later than number 1.

XI. Another pair of early novels, the Pax or Astra series, is set in 2500 CE, where the Company of Pax has initiated a pogrom of scientists, who are blamed for all the galaxy's ills.

1. *Stars Are Ours!, The* (**World, 1954**) The Company of Pax, blaming science for all of Earth's miseries in 2500 CE, orders a holocaust of scientists. Dard Nordis escapes to the stars in the Free Scientists' secret spaceship.

2. *Star Born* (**World, 1957**) The Terran spaceship arrives at the distant planet of Astra, in which descendants of Terran emigrants and gray-furred mermen peacefully coexist.

XII. Time travel is the main theme of the Ross Murdock, or Time War, or Time Traders series. Young criminal Ross Murdock, because of his survival skills, is encouraged to volunteer for a secret research project that involves searching past time for the source of "illicit"

technological innovations. Ross and Apache Indian Travis Fox, Dr. Gordon Ashe, and Eveleen Riordan (who eventually marries Ross) take part in what was originally a tetralogy and, more than 30 years later, has expanded to seven volumes, the last three in collaboration with coauthors. *Time Traders I* (Baen, 2000; numbers 1–2) and *Time Traders II* (Baen 2001; numbers 3–4) are omnibus volumes.

1. *Time Traders, The* (**World, 1958**) Young criminal Ross Murdock is given the choice of "rehabilitation" or volunteering for a secret research project into the past.

2. *Galactic Derelict* (**World, 1959**) Apache Indian Travis Fox stumbles onto a time-travel project and is recruited for an involuntary trip aboard an alien starship that had crashed on a prehistoric Earth.

3. *Defiant Agents, The* (**World, 1962**) Travis Fox and some fellow Apaches volunteer for a mission colonizing the planet Topaz, and find themselves reverting to their ancient warrior roles.

4. *Key out of Time* (**World, 1963**) Murdock teams up with a Polynesian girl and telepathic dolphins to explore the sea-planet Hawaika.

5. *Firehand* (**Tor, 1994**) The Dominion of Virgin abruptly changed from a populous planet to a burnt cinder, apparently through the agency of the alien Baldies. Ross Murdock, Eveleen Riordan, and Gordon Ashe are sent to investigate. Cowritten with P. M. Griffin.

6. *Echoes in Time* (**Tor, 1999**) A group of scientists disappear from a remote planet where they were involved in a first-contact mission. Ross Murdock and Eveleen Riordan are sent to investigate. Cowritten with Sherwood Smith.

7. *Atlantis Endgame* (**Tor, 2002**) Did a natural disaster destroy the island of Thera (aka Atlantis)? Or was the blast engineered by the Baldies? Cowritten with Sherwood Smith.

XIII. The Murdoc Jern, or Zero Stone, duo is about a mysterious stone that is the key to unimaginable powers. Young trader Murdoc Jern and his mutant feline companion Eet travel to the edges of inhabited space to unravel the mystery of the stone. Related to the Forerunner series (series VII).

1. *Zero Stone, The* (**Viking, 1968**) Murdoc Jern and his catlike companion, Eet, are hunted through space when Murdoc comes into the possession of a mysterious gem.

2. *Uncharted Stars* (**Viking, 1969**) Murdoc and Eet are up against some unknown rivals as they search for Forerunner ruins on the fringes of inhabited space.

XIV. The Crosstime, or Blake Walker, series, another pair of early Norton novels, involves chases through alternate time and space.

1. *Crossroads of Time, The* (**Ace, 1956**) Blake Walker foils a murder attempt, then finds himself drafted into a chase through parallel universes for a dangerous criminal.

2. *Quest Crosstime* (**Viking, 1965**) Blake Walker continues his adventures on an Earth identical to ours geographically but in which historical events have taken sharply different turns. UK title: *Crosstime Agent*.

XV. The Beast Master, or Hosteen Storm, series is set on the refugee planet of Arzor after an interplanetary war has destroyed most of the planet Earth. In number 1 (said to be the first SF novel told from the viewpoint of a Native American) Native American Hosteen Storm, the Beast Master, one of the few Terran survivors, travels to Arzor in search of the man who killed his father. Arzor is no picnic, however: long dry seasons, unruly natives, and mysterious adversaries. Numbers 3 and 4, coauthored by Lyn McConchie and published 40 years after numbers 1 and 2, continue the adventures with other protagonists. Telepathic bonds with animals and alien creatures play a big role. *Beast Master* was made into a film of the same name (1982) followed by a film, then by a TV sequel. *Beast Master's Planet* (Tor, 2005) contains numbers 1 and 2. *Beast Master Team* (SFBC, 2004) contains numbers 3 and 4.

1. *Beast Master, The* (Harcourt, 1959) Hosteen Storm, one of the few survivors of a war-devastated Terra, emigrates to earthlike Arzor, revenge on his mind. Abridged version published together with stand-alone novel *Star Hunter* as an Ace Double (1961).
2. *Lord of Thunder* (Harcourt, 1962) The natives are restless on Azor. Hosteen Storm is sent to investigate on a dangerous mission to the Peaks.
3. *Beast Master's Ark* (Tor, 2002) Terrans and indigenous Arzorans face a common enemy, the mysterious Death by Night. Cowritten with Lyn McConchie.
4. *Beast Master's Circus* (Tor, 2004) Laris, a young animal trainer in thrall to a greedy Circus Master, develops a special telepathic bond with Prauo, a large alien catlike being.
5. *Beast Master's Quest* (Tor, 2006) Laris inherits a spaceship from a distant relative and goes off on voyage in search of Prauo's home planet. Written by Lyn McConchie, with Norton listed as coauthor.

XVI. Based on Karen Kuykendall's "Outer Regions" paintings, *The Mark of the Cat* and its sequel concentrate on several of Norton's favorite themes, including cats, telepathic bonds, and coming-of-age rites. Henkel, devastated by the loss of Mieu, his cat familiar, embarks upon a quest without the ceremonial support of his family. The sequel, *Year of the Rat*, was published together with *The Mark of the Cat* in one volume.

1. *Mark of the Cat, The* (Ace, 1992) Young Henkel, heartbroken by the loss of his cat familiar, travels into the unknown in the test of survival know as The Kotti.
2. *Year of the Rat* (Meisha Merlin, 2002) Involves the coronation of a new emperor and trade between five queendoms answering to the emperor. Published together with number 1 in one volume. Variant title: *The Mark of the Cat: Year of the Rat.*

O'Brian, Patrick

Patrick O'Brian's Aubrey/Maturin series is set in the period of the Napoleonic Wars (late 18th to early 19th centuries) like C. S. Forester's (q.v.) Hornblower and Dudley Pope's (q.v.) Ramage series. The novels are well written, full of action, and have well-defined main characters, but aficionados read them especially for the lavish and accurate historical and naval detail. The friendship between Captain Jack Aubrey, robust, perfectly at home on a ship but unsure of himself on land, and Stephen Maturin, doctor, intelligence agent, naturalist, philosopher, and sceptic who dislikes violence, has gone through many vicissitudes in the course of the series. O'Brian has written scholarly biographies of Joseph Banks and Picasso and the nonfiction *Men of War* (Norton, 1995), which describes the warships of the era. Readers who want more background on the novels can try Dean King's *A Sea of Words: A Lexicon and Companion for Patrick O'Brian's Seafaring Tales* (Holt, 1995) or *Patrick O'Brian: Critical Essays and a Bibliography* (ed. Arthur Cunningham, Norton, 1994). The novels *The Golden Ocean* (Day, 1957) and *The Unknown Shore* (Norton, 1995; original publication, 1959), about Commodore Anson's circumnavigation of the globe in 1740, are interesting prequels to the series. *Master and Commander*, first

in the series, has been made into a rousing movie starring Russell Crowe (2003). All 20 novels in the series as well as the first three chapters of the 21st novel left unfinished by O'Brian at his death in 2000 have been published in five volumes in *The Complete Aubrey/Maturin Novels* (Norton, 2004).

1. *Master and Commander* (Lippincott, 1969) Aubrey recruits Maturin as ship's doctor on his sloop, *Sophie,* after a chance encounter in Spain.
2. *Post Captain* (Lippincott, 1972) Aubrey and Maturin have a nearly fatal fallout over a woman.
3. *H.M.S. Surprise* (Lippincott, 1973) Aubrey is in charge of HMS *Surprise*, which is commissioned to deliver an English envoy to India.
4. *Mauritius Command, The* (Stein & Day, 1978) Maturin engineers a new mission for Aubrey off the coast of Madagascar after finding the captain ill-at-ease among his loved ones.
5. *Desolation Island* (Stein & Day, 1979) Aubrey is given the job of rescuing the infamous Bligh (see also the Bounty trilogy by Charles Nordhoff (q.v.) and James Norman Hall) from another mutiny in Australia.
6. *Fortune of War, The* (Norton, 1991) Aubrey and Maturin get involved in the American War of 1812, and are captured by the Yanks when the USS *Constitution* battles HMS *Java*. Originally published in 1979.
7. *Surgeon's Mate, The* (Norton, 1992) Aubrey, Maturin, and Maturin's enigmatic lover, Diana Villiers, sail from Nova Scotia to England, and then off to Paris to do some espionage. Originally published in 1980.
8. *Ionian Mission, The* (Norton, 1992) Aubrey gets a temporary command on the "rotten old *Worcester*," and sails to the Mediterranean for the Royal Navy's blockade of Toulon. Originally published in 1981.
9. *Treason's Harbour* (Norton, 1992) Maturin takes center stage for some complicated espionage work as Aubrey's ship is tied up in Malta for repairs. Originally published in 1983.
10. *Far Side of the World, The* (Norton, 1992) Aubrey sets course for Cape Horn to intercept an American frigate preying on the British whaling fleet. Originally published in 1984.
11. *Reverse of the Medal, The* (Norton, 1992) Ashore again, the naive Aubrey is persuaded to make some shaky investments and is caught up in the underworld and espionage. Originally published in 1986.
12. *Letter of Marque, The* (Norton, 1990) Aubrey, unfairly dismissed from the British navy, continues his sea career as a privateer. Originally published in 1988.
13. *Thirteen-Gun Salute, The* (Norton, 1991) Aubrey, newly rich and with his naval commission restored, is given command of the frigate *Diane*, which is being sent to Borneo.
14. *Nutmeg of Consolation, The* (Norton, 1991) Governor Raffles gives Aubrey the former Dutch ship *The Nutmeg of Consolation* to continue his circumnavigation of the globe.
15. *True-Love, The* (Norton, 1992) Aubrey and Maturin, assigned to help a Polynesian queen, are disrupted by a young convict woman smuggled aboard in Sydney. UK title: *Clarissa Oakes*.
16. *Wine-Dark Sea, The* (Norton, 1993) Aubrey and Maturin sail the frigate *Surprise* to South America and around Cape Horn, taking prizes, fighting battles, and getting involved in local politics.
17. *Commodore, The* (Norton, 1995) Aubrey and Maturin return to England, where Aubrey receives a promotion, but both suffer domestic troubles and are happy to go back to the wars.
18. *Yellow Admiral, The* (Norton, 1996) Aubrey, on blockade duty off Brittany, is fighting some expensive legal battles at home, while Maturin is making contact with Chilean independence fighters.

19. *Hundred Days, The* (Norton, 1998) When Napoléon escapes from Elba, Aubrey is given the task of stopping a Moorish galley loaded with gold for Napoléon's mercenaries from making its delivery.

20. *Blue at the Mizzen* (Norton, 2000) The *Surprise* sets sail for South America, ostensibly to do a survey but in reality to offer help to Chilean rebels against Spain.

21. *Final, Unfinished Voyage of Jack Aubrey, The* (Norton, 2004) The first three chapters of a work left unfinished by O'Brian at his death. Jack Aubrey, elevated to flag rank, Rear Admiral of the Blue Squadron, is ordered to sail from Chile to South Africa.

O'Brien, Edna

Edna O'Brien, an Irish writer living in England, established her reputation as a novelist with the Country Girls trilogy. The books feature intelligent, naive Caithleen (Kate) Brady and wisecracking, cynical Bridget (Baba) Brennan. The girls get expelled from their rural Irish convent school, have love affairs, go to Dublin, have more love affairs, go to London, get married, and have love affairs. The trilogy, though full of humor and sex, is about disillusionment with life and love, the repressiveness of Irish society, and the inadequacies of men in general and Irish men in particular. *The Lonely Girl* was filmed in 1964 as *Girl with Green Eyes*, with Rita Tushingham and Lynn Redgrave playing Kate and Baba. *The Country Girls Trilogy and Epilogue* (Farrar, 1986) is an omnibus volume containing all three novels.

1. *Country Girls, The* (Knopf, 1960) Country girls Kate and Baba go away to an Irish convent school and get expelled. Kate has an affair with rich Dublin solicitor Mr. Gentleman.

2. *Lonely Girl, The* (Random House, 1962) Kate and Baba live and work in Dublin. Kate has an affair with documentary filmmaker Eugene Gailliard before she discovers that he is married. Variant title: *Girl with Green Eyes*.

3. *Girls in Their Married Bliss* (Simon & Schuster, 1968) Living in London and unhappily married—Kate with Eugene and Baba with alcoholic Frank—the girls have more love affairs.

O'Callaghan, Maxine

I. Delilah West is the Orange County, California, counterpart of Sue Grafton's (q.v.) Kinsey Millhone. Actually she seems to have preceded Kinsey in publication, having made her debut in the story "A Change of Clients," which appeared in *Alfred Hitchcock's Mystery Magazine* in 1974. Delilah is another tough and determined but sensitive female sleuth. She is a widow (see number 1), is sceptical of, but not completely against further romance; and is sometimes forced to supplement her private eye income by working at other jobs such as waiting on tables.

1. *Death Is Forever* (Raven House, 1981) Delilah wakes up in a seedy hotel with the bloody corpse of the man who killed Jack West, her husband. Naturally the police don't bother to look for other suspects.

2. *Run from Nightmare* (Raven House, 1981) Still grieving for Jack, Delilah embarks upon a search for the missing Janet Valek. Two people who knew Janet have turned up dead.

3. *Hit and Run* (St. Martin's, 1989) After Delilah is nearly run down by a hit-and-run driver, she is reluctant to take on the case when requested by the driver's mother.

4. *Set-Up* (St. Martin's, 1991) Now owner of her own detective agency, Delilah takes on the case of political activist Bobbi Calder, accused of killing her young protégé.

5. *Trade-Off* (St. Martin's, 1994) West is hired by a wealthy lighting manufacturer to find his runaway daughter.

6. *Down for the Count* (St. Martin's, 1997) Trying to keep a low profile while having a high-profile affair with wealthy developer Erik Lundstrom, Delilah stops a gunman on a shooting spree at a mall, and then gets kidnapped along with Erik's hostile teenage daughter.

II. O'Callaghan also wrote a pair of paperback-only suspense novels featuring child psychologist Dr. Anne Menlo.

1. *Shadow of the Child* (Berkley, 1996) Three-year-old Danny has remained silent since he was found with his murdered nanny.

2. *Only in the Ashes* (Berkley, 1997) Dr. Menlo must build a psychological profile on a child who was already dead to get to the truth.

O'Donnell, Lillian

I. Norah Mulcahaney is the likable young New York policewoman who stars in this consistently interesting series. Her Irish father worries about the dangers his daughter faces but is understanding and supportive—though determined to find her a husband. Norah mixes professionalism and compassion, bravery, and prudence in just the right proportions. As the series progresses, she marries fellow policeman Joe Capretto, and then loses him, and is eventually promoted to sergeant and then lieutenant.

1. *Phone Calls, The* (Putnam, 1972) Norah's debut case involves an anonymous phone caller and the deaths of several lonely widows.

2. *Don't Wear Your Wedding Ring* (Putnam, 1973) Now promoted to detective, Norah investigates the messy death of a woman found beheaded in a hotel room.

3. *Dial 577 R-A-P-E* (Putnam, 1974) Detective Mulcahaney helps a young neighbor girl who has been raped.

4. *Baby Merchants, The* (Putnam, 1975) When Norah and her new husband, Lieutenant Joe Capretto, decide to adopt a baby, they get entangled in legal troubles, blackmail, and murder.

5. *Leisure Dying* (Putnam, 1976) Working with her husband on a special squad covering Central Park muggings causes Sergeant Mulcahaney some marital friction.

6. *No Business Being a Cop* (Putnam, 1979) A psychopath is murdering New York City policewomen.

7. *Children's Zoo, The* (Putnam, 1981) Some nasty kids are into thrill killing at Central Park Zoo.

8. *Cop without a Shield* (Putnam, 1983) After Joe is killed in the line of duty, Norah takes a leave of absence to a small Pennsylvania town, where she finds herself investigating a case of abduction and murder.

9. *Ladykiller* (Putnam, 1984) Back with the New York City Police Department, Norah investigates the murder of a young woman in Central Park.

10. *Casual Affairs* (Putnam, 1985) Is the drug-and-alcohol coma of a wealthy socialite attempted suicide or attempted murder?

11. *Other Side of the Door, The* (Putnam, 1988) Mulcahaney plays a small role, advising Gary Reissig, her partner from number 9, in a case involving attacks on young Alyssa Hanriot by an unknown assailant.

12. *Good Night to Kill, A* **(Putnam, 1989)** Norah's attention is divided between two homicide cases and the romantic attentions of a handsome television newsman.

13. *Private Crime, A* **(Putnam, 1991)** A teenage mother and a baby have been killed by a sniper firing into a crowded East Side flea market.

14. *Pushover* **(Putnam, 1992)** Norah, pushing 40, gets assigned to some frustrating cases, including one where a maniac is pushing young women off subway platforms.

15. *Lockout* **(Putnam, 1994)** Lieutenant Mulcahaney is applying to adopt a baby, investigating the murder of a rock star's brother, and facing accusations of shooting an unarmed mugger.

16. *Blue Death* **(Putnam, 1998)** After being left in the lurch by her nanny, Norah tries to balance the care of preschooler Patrick and an investigation into suicides at the NYPD from her living room.

II. O'Donnell's second engaging woman heroine is Mici Anhalt, a crusader for victim's rights. Her work for New York's Cime Victim's Compensation has involved in three cases so far.

1. *Aftershock* **(Putnam, 1977)** The wife of a murdered hairdresser is the police's top suspect, but Mici helps her.

2. *Falling Star* **(Putnam, 1979)** Julia Schuyler, a washed-up alcoholic actress, is murdered, and Mici was the last one to see her alive.

3. *Wicked Designs* **(Putnam, 1980)** When wealthy widow Blanch Landry is killed in a subway station, her nephew disputes the "accidental death" verdict.

III. O'Donnell's latest creation is Gwenn Ramadge, a private investigator working out of Brooklyn. Like O'Donnell's other series character she is tough but kind-hearted, resourceful, and has a private life.

1. *Wreath for the Bride, A* **(Putnam, 1990)** Gwenn suspects the groom of being responsible for a new bride's fatal plunge on a honeymoon cruise.

2. *Used to Kill* **(Putnam, 1993)** Dance teacher Emma Trent returns home to find her husband beaten to death with a baseball bat during an apparent burglary.

3. *Raggedy Man, The* **(Putnam, 1995)** Gwenn hires young narcotics cop Jayne Harrow after Jayne has been framed and suspended from the police force.

4. *Goddess Affair, The* **(Putnam, 1996)** Jewel theft and the body of a famous dress designer found floating in a swimming pool during a Caribbean cruise engage Gwenn and her significant other, NYPD Sergeant Ray Dixon.

O'Donnell, Peter

British writer Peter O'Donnell created Modesty Blaise, the woman's equivalent to James Bond, for the long-running comic strip (1963–2001), which he wrote, and a few years later fleshed out her adventures in book form. Modesty, orphaned by World War II at a tender age, became the tough and self-reliant leader of the "Network," whose lucrative smuggling and theft activities enabled her to "retire" a rich woman at 26. Retirement from crime didn't mean retirement from physical activity, however, she continued to take on dangerous missions until her last adventure at the age of 52, described in *Cobra Trap* (in number 13). Her missions, on which she was accompanied by Willy Garvin, with whom she had a close but platonic relationship, were sometimes undertaken at the behest of Sir Gerald Tarrant of the British Foreign Office but more often from a knight-errant's need to help a friend or right a wrong. For Modesty, although she had no use for conventional legality, had a very strong moral sense. Unlike Bond,

Modesty eschewed weapons gimmickry and always relied on her wits and physical prowess to get out of jams. Modesty has been a cult figure for many years, but her one movie, *Modesty Blaise* (1966), directed by Joseph Losey and starring Monica Vitti and Terence Stamp, was an artistic and financial disaster. From time to time, hopes have been raised for another film. Peter O'Donnell wrote also as Madeleine Brent.

1. *Modesty Blaise* **(Doubleday, 1965)** Modesty's first case for the British Foreign Office is to ensure the safe delivery of a crate of diamonds to an Arab sheikh.

2. *Sabre-Tooth* **(Doubleday, 1966)** Modesty and Willie fake a return to crime and infiltrate a plot to capture Kuwait.

3. *I, Lucifer* **(Doubleday, 1967)** Modesty and Willie are up against a fiendish group using a psychic's powers to predict death.

4. *Taste for Death, A* **(Doubleday, 1969)** Modesty and Willie set out to rescue an archaeological expedition in the Algerian desert from the clutches of an archvillain.

5. *Impossible Virgin, The* **(Doubleday, 1971)** Modesty must retrieve some stolen papers for Sir Gerald and keep a gifted and selfless African mission doctor from harm.

6. *Pieces of Modesty* **(Mysterious, 1986)** A collection of Modesty Blaise short stories. Originally published in the United Kingdom in 1972.

7. *Silver Mistress, The* **(Mysterious, 1986)** Modesty and Willie must rescue Sir Gerald from Colonel Jim, his criminal tycoon captor. Originally published in the United Kingdom in 1973.

8. *Last Day in Limbo* **(Mysterious, 1985)** An attempted kidnapping leads Modesty and Willie to Limbo, a slave-run coffee plantation in Central America. Originally published in the United Kingdom in 1976.

9. *Dragon's Claw* **(Mysterious, 1986)** A solo sail through the Tasman Sea leads Modesty to a kidnapped artist, murder in London, an attack in Malta, and criminal mastermind Beauregard Browne. Originally published in the United Kingdom in 1976.

10. *Xanadu Talisman, The* **(Mysterious, 1984)** A Frenchman mortally injured during an earthquake in Morocco gets Modesty involved in a search for a legendary "talisman." Originally published in the United Kingdom in 1981.

11. *Night of Morning Star, The* **(Mysterious, 1987)** A mysterious group called the Watchmen is making terrorist attacks on Eastern and Western governments. Originally published in the United Kingdom in 1982.

12. *Dead Man's Handle* **(Mysterious, 1986)** Willie is kidnapped and brainwashed by mad millionaire Thaddeus Pilgrim into attempting to kill Modesty. Originally published in the United Kingdom in 1985.

13. *Cobra Trap* **(Souvenir, 2001)** A collection of five Modesty Blaise short stories. In the title story, 52-year-old Modesty comes out of retirement to save some friends from a South American uprising. Originally published in the United Kingdom in 1996.

Ogilvie, Elisabeth

I. The Bennett Island series is composed of 11 novels set on a small lobstering island (based on the real Criehaven) set off the coast of Maine. Number 1 is a prequel set in 1820. The series proper begins with Joanna Bennett, daughter of the island's leading family, first met as a 15-year-old tomboy in the 1930s. The series follows her through adolescence, two marriages, and motherhood; through the World War II years; as the mother of some headstrong adolescents; and finally into the Vietnam era. Ogilvie's quiet, homespun charm and picturesque setting are enjoyed by young adult and adult readers. Down East publishers reprinted the entire series recently. Numbers 1 and 6 were reprinted in one volume (Down East, 2003). *A Mug Up with Elisabeth: A Companion for Readers of Elisabeth Ogilvie* (Down East, 2001), by Melissa Hayes and Marilyn Westervelt, is a guide to Ogilvie's works.

1. *Whistle for a Wind* (Scribner, 1954) A prequel set in 1820, the year Maine became a state, on the island of Brigport (Matinicus), where we are introduced to Jamie Bennett, the patriarch of the Bennett family, who is about to settle on the island that bears his name.
2. *High Tide at Noon* (Crowell, 1944) A slump in the lobster market causes the whole population of Bennett Island to move to the mainland, but Joanna returns to start a new life.
3. *Storm Tide* (Crowell, 1945) Joanna has high hopes and many plans for life on the island with her new husband, Nils Sorensen.
4. *Ebbing Tide* (Crowell, 1947) Nils see war duty in the Pacific and returns wounded.
5. *Dawning of the Day, The* (McGraw-Hill, 1954) The islanders are suspicious of Philipa Marshall's unorthodox teaching methods, but quiet Steve Bennett is supportive.
6. *How Wide the Heart* (McGraw-Hill, 1959) Ellen, Joanna's daughter, must choose between marrying her childhood sweetheart or going to art school in Boston.
7. *Seasons Hereafter, The* (McGraw-Hill, 1966) Vanessa Barton reluctantly follows her husband to Bennett Island.
8. *Strawberries in the Sea* (McGraw-Hill, 1973) Shy and quiet Rosa, who thinks herself plain and awkward, comes to Bennett Island to flee the memories of a painful divorce.
9. *Answer in the Tide, An* (McGraw-Hill, 1978) When Jamie Bennett sets up housekeeping with a married woman on the island, his parents, Joanna and Nils, disapprove.
10. *Summer of the Osprey, The* (McGraw-Hill, 1987) The arrival of rich Felix Drake with mysterious recluse Selina Bainbridge stirs up the inhabitants of Bennett Island.
11. *Day before Winter, The* (Down East, 1997) Brings Joanna Sorensen's family into the Vietnam era. Two young men descended from island families come to live on the island, hoping to shed memories of past mistakes.

II. Ogilvie has written a trilogy of historical romances set in early 19th-century Scotland and Maine. They tell the story of Jennie Hawthorne, later Glenroy, a headstrong but engaging young woman.

1. *Jennie about to Be* (McGraw-Hill, 1984) Set in the early 19th century, this tells of Jennie's arrival in Scotland.
2. *World of Jennie G., The* (McGraw-Hill, 1985) Tragic circumstances force Jennie to leave Scotland in 1809 and settle in Maine.
3. *Jennie Glenroy* (Down East, 1993) In 1826 Jennie and husband Alick Glenroy are found raising a rambunctious brood of five children on a Maine farm.

Oke, Janette

I. Canadian writer Janette Oke (pronounced "oak") became a word-of-mouth best seller when her first novel, *Love Comes Softly,* was published in 1979. Since then, her 70+ inspirational Christian novels, most of them set on the Canadian and US frontiers in the 19th century, have sold millions and been translated into 14 languages, although they were not noted, until recently, by mainstream reviewers, and were often not available in mainstream bookstores. *Love Comes Softly* was the first of 12 novels depicting the lives of Clark Davis, his wife, Marty, and their children and grandchildren in frontier Iowa in the 19th century. Three generations undergo stern testing on the harsh frontier and in relatively sophisticated places full of temptations, such as Boston,

but renewed faith in God and family always pulls them through. Numbers 9 through 12, a subset called Prairie Legacy, were published after an eight-year gap and are available in a boxed set (Bethany, 2000). Numbers 1 through 8 were sold in boxed sets as *Pioneer Love Stories* (Bethany, 1990, 1994).

1. *Love Comes Softly* (Bethany, 1979) Widower Clark Davis and 19-year-old Marty, widowed on the trek westward to Iowa, decide to face the hardships of frontier life together.
2. *Love's Enduring Promise* (Bethany, 1980) Clark and Marty struggle to raise their family and wonder if their new community can find a suitable teacher.
3. *Love's Long Journey* (Bethany, 1982) Clark and Marty's daughter, ready to start her own life, must rely on faith in the face of homesickness and hardship.
4. *Love's Abiding Joy* (Bethany, 1983) The new railroad enables Clark and Marty to see their grandchildren for the first time.
5. *Love's Unending Legacy* (Bethany, 1984) Marty and Clark return home, but worry about how the children will react to Clark's accidental loss of a foot.
6. *Love's Unfolding Dream* (Bethany, 1987) Belinda, Melissa, and Mary Jo find their friendship threatened when all three fall for the same boy.
7. *Love Takes a Wing* (Bethany, 1988) Belinda takes her nursing skills to Boston, but finds loneliness as well as opportunity there.
8. *Love Finds a Home* (Bethany, 1989) Belinda, torn between Boston and home, invites God back into her life.
9. *Tender Years, The* (Bethany, 1987) Takes place 20 years after number 8. In spite of the Christian faith she has learned from her grandparents, Clark and Marty, Virginia Stimpson finds the transition from childhood to adulthood difficult.
10. *Searching Heart, A* (Bethany, 1998) At the end of her time in college, Virginia finds her faith tested by the medical problems of her pregnant sister and a "Dear Jane" letter written to her by her boyfriend.
11. *Quiet Strength, A* (Bethany, 1999) Virginia endures additional hardships, as she and Jonathan, her new husband, try to build a new house and a new life on the Great Plains.
12. *Like Gold Refined* (Bethany, 2000) Living on the farm with Jonathan and their children, Virginia has to come to terms with the physical decline of her grandparents, Clark and Marty.

II. Seasons of the Heart is a quartet of novels about orphaned Josh Jones and his coming-of-age, as he questions life, love, and God, but eventually settles into family and farm. *Seasons of the Heart* (Bristol Park, 1993) contains numbers 1 through 4. *Father of My Heart* (Bethany, 1990) contains excerpts from the Seasons of the Heart series.

1. *Once upon a Summer* (Bethany, 1981) After orphan Josh Jones's aunt Mary marries and moves away, Josh has to learn to accept his pioneer family.
2. *Winds of Autumn* (Bethany, 1987) Josh struggles to grow up and understand the nature of love and life.
3. *Winter Is Not Forever* (Bethany, 1988) As high school graduation nears, Josh worries that he is the only member of his class who doesn't know what he wants to do with his life.
4. *Spring's Gentle Promise* (Bethany, 1989) Josh feels the added responsibility when his grandfather and uncle sign the family farm over to him.

III. The Canadian West series begins when Easterner Elizabeth Thatcher takes a position as a school teacher in rural Alberta, meets and marries Royal Canadian Mountie Wynn Delancy, and accompanies him to a frontier posting. Originally a quartet, Canadian West was augmented by two new novels, published 15 years later, wherein the vicissitudes of Elizabeth and Wynn's children, Henry and Christine, are addressed. *The Canadian West Saga* (Inspirational, 1995) contains numbers 1 through 4.

1. *When Calls the Heart* (Bethany, 1983) Lovely young school teacher, Elizabeth Thatcher travels from the East to remote Alberta, vowing never to marry a western rowdy.
2. *When Comes the Spring* (Bethany, 1985) Elizabeth plans her marriage to Wynn Delancy of the Royal Canadian Mounted Police.
3. *When Breaks the Dawn* (Bethany, 1986) Elizabeth and Wynn must rely on their faith to see them through when Wynn is posted to a more remote new location.
4. *When Hope Springs New* (Bethany, 1986) Elizabeth, now a real frontier woman, feels that she has triumphed over the worst life could offer. Or has she?
5. *Beyond the Gathering Storm* (Bethany, 2000) After following in his father Wynn's footsteps, Henry Delancy discovers that his RCMP career comes at a high emotional cost, while his sister, Christine, leaves home for the metropolis of Edmondton.
6. *When Tomorrow Comes* (Bethany, 2001) Christine, recovering from a broken heart, helps her brother Henry settle into married life.

IV. Song of Acadia, a quintet coauthored with T. Davis Bunn, is something of a change of pace, more of a historical romance series than the other series. Starting in 1753, it concerns two girls from different towns in the Acadia colony, one French and one English, who discover that they have the same father, and takes them through various vicissitudes in Britain and America and into the turbulent American Revolution.

1. *Meeting Place, The* (Bethany, 1999) A chance meeting between British Anne and French Nicole, from different towns in Acadia in 1753, opens up a secret fraught with meaning for the two of them. Coauthored with T. Davis Bunn.
2. *Sacred Shore, The* (Bethany, 2000) The French Acadians are banished from Canada. Andrew and Catherine Harrow endure separation as others are kindled with renewed hope. Coauthored with T. Davis Bunn.
3. *Birthright, The* (Bethany, 2001) Since their reunion at Uncle Charles's English estate, Anne and Nicole have become the best of friends, dedicated to preserving the secret of their birthright. Coauthored with T. Davis Bunn.
4. *Distant Beacon, The* (Bethany, 2002) Nicole returns to an America torn by revolution, encountering the gallant Captain Goodwind on the way. Coauthored with T. Davis Bunn.
5. *Beloved Land, The* (Bethany, 2002) Anne and Nicole brave the dangers of a revolution-torn America to reunite with their ailing father.

Okri, Ben

Nigerian-born poet and fiction writer Ben Okri is an African "magic realist." His novels use nightmarish imagery and surrealist contortions of reality to portray the bizarre social and political conditions inside his native Nigeria as seen from the African point of view. The dead aren't really dead, one's ancestors still have a role to play in the community, and there are innumerable gradations of reality. The Famished Road trilogy reflects life in an African village as seen by Azaro, a "spirit child" who maintains his ties with the supernatural. *The Famished Road* was awarded the 1991 Booker Prize for best novel.

1. *Famished Road, The* (Doubleday, 1992) Azaro chronicles the life of a village plagued by political thugs, grasping landlords, brutal bosses, demons, and witches.
2. *Songs of Enchantment* (Doubleday, 1993) Azaro's village is shattered by political factions, while his father shifts between cantankerous egotism and self-abasing sacrifice.
3. *Infinite Riches* (Weidenfeld [UK], 1999) Azaro's father, implicated in the murder of a neighbor, has been arrested and imprisoned. Not yet published in the United States.

Oldenbourg, Zoé

I. As a young Russian émigré, Oldenbourg began writing while supporting herself painting scarves in a Paris shop. Her fascination with the Middle Ages has led her to write several nonfiction works such as *The Crusades* (Pantheon, 1966) and *Massacre at Montsegur* (Pantheon, 1961) as well as the trio of novels listed below. Authentic, unsentimental, and solid with detail, her books have been compared to vast French tapestries showing the daily life of a castle in the 12th and 13th centuries. Oldenbourg has written other novels about the Crusades including *Cities of the Flesh* (Pantheon, 1963) and *The Heirs of the Kingdom* (Pantheon, 1971)

1. *World Is Not Enough, The* (Pantheon, 1948) The story of a petty French knight, Ansiau of Linnieres, and his wife, Lady Alis, covers the second and third crusades. Translated from the French by Willard Trask. Original title: *Argile et Cendres*.
2. *Cornerstone, The* (Pantheon, 1955) The story of Ansiau, Alis, and their descendants continues. Translated from the French by David Hyams. Original title: *La pierre angulaire*.
3. *Destiny of Fire* (Pantheon, 1961) Describes the fate and misfortune of the noble Seigneur of Montgeil and his family, victims of the Albigensian "crusade" in the early 13th century. Translated from the French by Peter Green. Original title: *Les brules*.

II. Presumably drawn somewhat from Oldenbourg's experiences as a Russian émigré in France, these two novels chronicle the growing romance of two young people, children of émigré families from Bolshevik Russia and Hitler's Germany amid the turbulence of the 1930s and 1940s in Paris.

1. *Awakened, The* (Pantheon, 1957) The story of young exiles Stephanie and Elie in Paris extends from the late 1930s to the German occupation. Translated from the French by Edward Hyams. Original title: *Reveiles de la vie*.
2. *Chains of Love* (Pantheon, 1959) Set in Paris between 1947 and 1951, this book shows the star-crossed lovers Stephanie and Elie reunited after seven years of separation during the war. Translated from the French by Michael Bullock. Original title: *Les irreductibles*.

Oleksiw, Susan

Mellingham, a small community north of Boston, is lucky to have former big-city cop Joe Silva as its chief of police. Joe is able to find solutions to the occasional violent crimes that hit Mellingham by ferreting out the family secrets and hidden motives behind the crimes. Susan Oleksiw, who has a PhD in Sanskrit from the University of

Pennsylvania, is editor of the *Larcom Review* and the author of *A Reader's Guide to the Classic British Mystery* (Mysterious, 1988).

1. *Murder in Mellingham* (**Scribner, 1993**) Beth O'Donnell travels from New York to Mellingham to visit her financier brother Howard, hoping to gain control of the trust fund he set up for her.
2. *Double Take* (**Scribner, 1994**) Hank Vinnio, work-study student at Massasoit College of Art, is found, his throat cut, beneath a toppled shelf of art supplies.
3. *Family Album* (**Scribner, 1995**) Chief Silva is asked to look into the security of the museum headquarters of the Arbella Historical Society because someone seems to be stealing valuable antiques.
4. *Friends and Enemies* (**Five Star, 2001**) The 25-year reunion of the class of 1969 of Mellingham High School brings some untoward events, such as the finding of Vic, whose wife, Mindy, has disappeared, comatose on his dining-room floor.

Oliphant, B. J.

PSEUDONYM OF Sheri S. Tepper

Science-fiction author Sheri S. Tepper (q.v.) writes mystery series under a pair of pseudonyms: A. J. Orde (q.v.) and B. J. Oliphant. The Oliphant series features Shirley McClintock, owner of a guest ranch in Santa Fe, New Mexico, an amateur detective who gets involved in a series of mysteries.

1. *Dead in the Shrub* (**Fawcett, 1990**) While seeking to put a wounded deer out of its misery, Santa Fe guest-ranch owner Shirley McClintock stumbles across a human skeleton half buried in the leaves.
2. *Unexpected Corpse, The* (**Fawcett, 1990**) When Alaris Bryan brings the ashes of her parents to a Colorado ranch for burial, she also brings along the ashes of "Cousin Willard."
3. *Deservedly Dead* (**Fawcett, 1992**) Shirley becomes prime suspect after the new greenhorn owner of Jewell Place, who has drained the wetlands, poisoned the scrub, and destroyed the wildlife, is murdered.
4. *Death and the Delinquent* (**Fawcett, 1992**) The young girl, found dead, was a liar and petty thief, but Shirley doesn't think that she deserved to be killed.
5. *Death Served Up Cold* (**Fawcett, 1994**) Her other guests seem unconcerned when a mysterious guest dies at McClintock's guest ranch.
6. *Ceremonial Death, A* (**Fawcett, 1996**) Shadow Dance, née Bridget McCree, a cosmic healer, is slain and mutilated as she prepares her hogan for a ceremony.
7. *Here's to the Newly Dead* (**Fawcett, 1997**) Two mysterious, free-spending newlyweds are found dead in a New Mexico canyon.

O'Marie, Carol Anne

Sister Carol Anne O'Marie, nun at the Sisters of St. Joseph of Carondelet in San Francisco, writes a series about an elderly (seventies and eighties) sleuthing nun, Sister Mary Helen. Sister Mary Helen, who is a combination of G. K. Chesterton's Father Brown and Agatha Christie's (q.v.) Miss Marple, begins the series as a teacher at Mount St. Francis College near San Francisco. She eventually retires from teaching and volunteers at a local women's refuge, where she continues her forays into crime investigation with the aid of fellow nuns such as Sister Eileen, and San Francisco cops such as Kate Murphy an Dan Gallagher. Sister Mary Helen is an appealing central character, the

convent background is authentic and interesting, and the plotting improves as the series progresses.

1. *Novena for Murder, A* (**Scribner, 1984**) At 75 Sister Mary Helen, not yet ready for retirement, starts teaching at Mount St. Francis College for Women, near San Francisco, where she is greeted by an earthquake, a hysterical secretary, and a history professor bludgeoned to death.
2. *Advent of Dying* (**Delacorte, 1986**) Sisters Mary Helen, Eileen, and Anne are invited by Mary Helen's secretary, Suzanne, to hear her blues-singing debut at the Sea Wench in Ghiradelli Square, a debut that turns out to be fatal.
3. *Missing Madonna, The* (**Delacorte, 1988**) Emma Duran, fellow OWL (Older Woman's League) member, has disappeared, and Sister Mary Helen suspects foul play.
4. *Murder in Ordinary Time* (**Dell, 1991**) As Sister Mary Helen appears on a local TV news show, investigative reporter Christina Kelly is felled by a poisoned cookie.
5. *Murder Makes a Pilgrimage* (**Delacorte, 1993**) One of the 10 winners of a free pilgrimage to Spain's famous shrine, Santiago de Compostela, is murdered, and one of the other pilgrims is surely the murderer.
6. *Death Goes on Retreat* (**Delacorte, 1995**) Sisters Mary Helen and Eileen arrive at St. Collette's Retreat House in Santa Cruz a week earlier than scheduled, and Mary Helen stumbles on the body of a former seminarian.
7. *Death of an Angel* (**St. Martin's, 1997**) The latest victim of a serial rapist-murderer is a wealthy benefactor of Mt. St. Francis College.
8. *Death Takes Up a Collection* (**St. Martin's, 1998**) Sisters Mary Helen and Eileen, delivering loaves of Irish soda bread to Mt. St. Francis benefactors, interrupt a meeting at St. Agatha's Church that includes Monsignor Joseph Higgins, who turns up dead the next day.
9. *Requiem at the Refuge* (**St. Martin's, 2000**) Mary Helen volunteers at the Refuge, a shelter for homeless women, and finds the battered corpse of a young prostitute.
10. *Corporal Works of Murder, The* (**St. Martin's, 2002**) An undercover police officer posing as a homeless woman is murdered at the Refuge.
11. *Murder at the Monks' Table* (**St. Martin's, 2005**) Mary Helen and Eileen travel to Ballyclarin, Ireland, "home of the Oyster Festival," and, of course, stumble on a body, this time of local reporter Willie Ward.

Onetti, Juan Carlos

Juan Carlos Onetti, one of Latin America's greatest novelists, isn't as well known in English-speaking countries as some of his contemporaries, but several works by the late Uruguayan-born writer have been translated into English in recent years. A pair of novels follows the affairs of Mr. Larsen (aka the Body Snatcher), a bookkeeper and pimp in the South American town of Santa Maria. Larsen's futile life is symbolic of the Latin American: an existence made up of talk and illusion.

1. *Body Snatcher* (**Pantheon, 1991**) The opening of a bordello in Santa Maria produces a "holy war" between "decent citizens" and prostitutes. Translated from the Spanish by Alfred MacAdam. Original title: *Junacadaveres* (1964).
2. *Shipyard, The* (**Scribner, 1968**) Mr. Larsen returns to Santa Maria and becomes manager of the local shipyard, still hoping to find some meaning to his life. Twice translated from the Spanish: by

Rachel Caffyn (Scribner, 1968) and by Nick Caistor (Serpent's Tail, 1993). Original title: *El astillero* (1961).

Orczy, Emmuska, Baroness

Emma Orczy (pronounced *ORT-zee*) was the daughter of a Hungarian baron who settled his family in London in 1880. After attending art school, marrying, and first trying her pen at writing children's books, Orczy turned to the spy story. *The Scarlet Pimpernel* was published as a novel after the play of the same title, coauthored with Montagu Barstow, became a hit (1903). Thereafter, Orczy's work was enormously popular, and 11 sequels followed. The seemingly foppish and indolent Sir Percy Blakeney is an early Clark Kent prototype and the literary ancestor of such (seemingly) foppish types as Ellery Queen (q.v.), Lord Peter Wimsey (q.v.), and Edmund Campion (q.v.). He is really the reckless and daring secret agent known as the Scarlet Pimpernel, who rescues innocent aristocrats from the guillotine in France during the Terror. The dashing master of disguise has been played in many stage versions, one of the latest (1997) being a musical version starring Douglas Sills and Christine Andreas, and in at least seven film versions, starring such notables as David Niven, James Mason, and Leslie Howard.

1. *Scarlet Pimpernel, The* (Putnam, 1905) Not even Lady Blakeney knows that her stupid husband is the famous Scarlet Pimpernel until she herself is rescued by him.
2. *I Will Repay* (Lippincott, 1906) Juliette Marny's stormy relationship with the man who killed her brother is at the center of the plot.
3. *Elusive Pimpernel, The* (Dodd, 1908) The daring Scarlet Pimpernel continues to rescue endangered members of the French nobility.
4. *League of the Scarlet Pimpernel, The* (Doran, 1919) The Scarlet Pimpernel continues his adventures, his real identity unbeknownst to anyone except his wife and his archenemy Citizen Chauvelin.
5. *Lord Tony's Wife* (Doran, 1917) When Mademoiselle Kernogan is lured back to France and almost certain death at the hands of revolutionaries, the Scarlet Pimpernel comes to her rescue.
6. *Triumph of the Scarlet Pimpernel, The* (Burt, 1922) Robespierre, at the height of his power, is determined to destroy the Scarlet Pimpernel.
7. *Eldorado* (Doran, 1913) The Scarlet Pimpernel rescues the French Dauphin.
8. *Sir Percy Leads the Band* (Hodder [UK], 1936) The members of the League of the Scarlet Pimpernel have disguised themselves as shabby, second-rate musicians.
9. *Sir Percy Hits Back* (Doran, 1927) The Scarlet Pimpernel rescues the daughter of his old enemy Chauvelin and engages in a final clash with him.
10. *Adventures of the Scarlet Pimpernel* (Doubleday, 1929) A collection of short stories continuing the Scarlet Pimpernel's exploits.
11. *Way of the Scarlet Pimpernel, The* (Putnam, 1934) The Scarlet Pimpernel outwits Chabot and saves Louise de Croissy and her little boy.
12. *Mam'zelle Guillotine* (Hodder [UK], 1940) Sir Percy saves one last victim from the guillotine.

Orde, A. J.

PSEUDONYM OF Sheri S. Tepper

Science-fiction writer Sheri S. Tepper (q.v.) writes mysteries under pseudonyms such as A. J. Orde and B. J. Oliphant (q.v.). The series under the Orde nom de plume features Jason Lynx, Denver antiques dealer, interior designer, amateur sleuth, and lover of policewoman Grace Willis.

1. *Little Neighborhood Murder, A* (Doubleday, 1989) The policeman in charge of the investigation into the murder of Jason Lynx's neighbors is convinced that Jason is the perpetrator.
2. *Death and the Dogwalker* (Doubleday, 1990) While walking his dog and a friend's cat, Jason comes across a corpse carefully laid out in a public park.
3. *Death for Old Times' Sake* (Doubleday, 1992) Grace Willis is assigned to protect an abortion clinic from right-to-lifers, one of whom is felled by an ice pick.
4. *Looking for the Aardvark* (Doubleday, 1993) Jason goes to pueblo lands near Santa Fe, New Mexico, after a friend's obnoxious evangelist brother has his throat cut. Variant title: *Death on Sunday*.
5. *Long Time Dead, A* (Fawcett, 1995) While Jason, Grace Willis, and her brother are exploring some property that is to be made into a research institute, the brother is killed by an explosive device. Paperback original.
6. *Death of Innocents, A* (Fawcett, 1997) Jason and his wife, Grace, want some answers when they find the remains of a young girl beneath their porch. Paperback original.

O'Shaughnessy, Perri

PSEUDONYM OF Pamela & Mary O'Shaughnessy

The O'Shaughnessy sisters, Pamela (a lawyer) and Mary (an editor), write a series of legal thrillers starring Nina Reilly, defense lawyer of South Lake Tahoe in the mountains of California. Nina, thirtysomething single mother, is tough, tenderhearted, unpredictable, and inclined to get in over her head in professional and personal matters. This is a series with well-rounded, likable characters, a colorful background, and plots that are sometimes not entirely believable. *Keeper of the Keys* (Delacorte, 2006) is a stand-alone novel. *Sinister Shorts* (Delacorte, 2006) is a collection of short stories.

1. *Motion to Suppress* (Delacorte, 1995) Having lost her job, her marriage, and her pride all in the same week, Nina Reilly leaves San Francisco for South Lake Tahoe in the California mountains, and sets up a one-woman defense attorney business. Her first case involves defending bartender Misty Patterson, accused of killing her abusive husband.
2. *Invasion of Privacy* (Delacorte, 1996) Nina defends a person who may be a serial murderer on the loose.
3. *Obstruction of Justice* (Delacorte, 1997) After one person is struck by lightning and another killed by a hit-and-run driver, Nina winds up defending Jason de Beers, accused of murdering his grandfather. Jason won't talk to anybody, including Nina.
4. *Breach of Promise* (Delacorte, 1998) Nina gets involved in a high-profile, high-stakes palimony suit that could make her or ruin her.
5. *Acts of Malice* (Delacorte, 1999) Jim Strong, member of a prominent Lake Tahoe family, is accused of killing his brother.
6. *Move to Strike* (Delacorte, 2000) In another make-or-break case for Nina, Nikki Zack is accused of murdering her uncle.
7. *Writ of Execution* (Delacorte, 2001) When a gambler is murdered, suspicion falls on Nina's client, a girl who won the biggest jackpot in Lake Tahoe history.
8. *Unfit to Practice* (Delacorte, 2002) After having her truck stolen along with her three most sensitive case files, Nina finds herself facing disbarment.

9. *Presumption of Death* **(Delacorte, 2003)** Nina is staying with her lover, ace PI Paul van Wagoner, when the Native American son of a former lover is accused of arson and murder.

10. *Unlucky in Law* **(Delacorte, 2004)** Nina's former boss and mentor begs Nina to take on the case of Stefan Wyatt, accused of grave-robbing and worse.

11. *Case of Lies* **(Delacorte, 2005)** Back in Lake Tahoe, Nina gets professionally involved with a masseuse whose aunt was killed during a motel robbery.

Padgett, Abigail

I. In Padgett's Bo Bradley series, the good guy, not the villain, has the psychiatric illness. Bo is a child abuse investigator for the San Diego, California, Child Protective Services and a manic-depressive who keeps her illness under control with medication. The plots of these mystery novels are grippingly suspenseful, and the workings of public child protection are convincingly delineated by Padgett, who was once a professional psychiatric social worker, but it is the portrayal of Bo Bradley and her efforts to live and work with her disability that sets this series apart. In the later novels in the series, Bo has a rather wary developing relationship with pediatrician Andrew La Marche.

1. *Child of Silence* **(Mysterious, 1993)** Bo is assigned the case of a four-year-old boy tied to a mattress in an abandoned house on an Indian reservation.

2. *Strawgirl* **(Mysterious, 1994)** When three-year-old Samantha Franer dies after being raped, her mother's boyfriend, the leading suspect, flees to an upstate New York location.

3. *Turtle Baby* **(Mysterious, 1995)** Eight-month-old Acito has been sickened by poison from a tropical plant.

4. *Moonbird Boy* **(Mysterious, 1996)** When Mort Wagman, single parent, is killed, Bo takes over the care of his six-year-old son at Ghost Flower Lodge, a psychiatric rehabilitation facility in the desert mountains of southern California.

5. *Dollmaker's Daughters, The* **(Mysterious, 1996)** Fifteen-year-old Janny Malcolm, who is in foster care, is found in a catatonic state at a popular vampire theme-club.

II. Bo Bradley has been put on hold in favor of another series with a social psychologist who is an amateur detective. Emily "Blue" Mc-Carren is first found living reclusively in an abandoned motel in the middle of a California desert with her Doberman Brontë, grieving over her lost lover. While she is investigating a murder, she develops a lesbian relationship with forensic psychologist Roxie Bouchie. This series is relatively lighthearted and far out compared to the Bo Bradley series.

1. *Blue* **(Mysterious, 1998)** Widow Muffin Crandall claims she killed an intruder in self-defense and left him in a freezer for five years, but Blue and Roxie are convinced that the story is a hoax.

2. *Last Blue Plate Special, The* **(Mysterious, 2001)** Some maniac is murdering prominent local female politicians and leaving a Blue Willow china plate as a memento for each crime.

Page, Jake (James Keena)

T. Moore "Mo" Bowdre took up sculpture after being blinded in a mining accident. With the help of his laconic Hopi lover, Connie Barnes, and the occasional assistance of Santa Fe, New Mexico, police sergeant Tony Ramirez, the burly but canny and sensitive Mo solves a series of mysteries full of lore about Native Americans and southwestern art. Jake Page, who was one of the founders of *Smithsonian* magazine, is also the author or coauthor of much well-regarded nonfiction, especially on Native Americans, such as *In the Hands of the Great Spirit: The 20,000-Year History of American Indians* (Free Press, 2003). He also wrote an alternate-history novel *Apacheria* (Del Rey, 1998), which postulates that the Apaches won the "Indian War" of 1890.

1. *Stolen Gods, The* **(Ballantine, 1993)** "Kachinas," representations of Hopi gods, are being stolen from their sacred cave and being sold on the art black market.

2. *Deadly Canyon, The* **(Ballantine, 1994)** Mo goes undercover for the FBI at a remote New Mexico research station to discover who is using it as a base for smuggling out Native American artifacts.

3. *Knotted Strings, The* **(Ballantine, 1995)** The Sweetwater Pictures production of a film about the 1680 Pueblo Rebellion is bedeviled by acts of sabotage including the murder of an actor and the bombing of the director's car.

4. *Lethal Partner, The* **(Ballantine, 1995)** The murders of two women and the discovery of seven paintings ascribed to Georgia O'Keeffe may be connected.

5. *Certain Malice, A* **(Ballantine, 1997)** The naked bodies of two teenagers, possible victims of ritual murder, are found side-by-side in a New Mexican desert arroyo, next to a mysterious symbol etched in stone.

Page, Katherine Hall

Native New Yorker Faith Fairchild finds bucolic Aleford, Massachusetts, to which she has moved with her minister husband, Tom, and infant son, a trifle boring after Manhattan until she reestablishes her catering business and starts involving herself in local affairs, including the occasional murder. Faith is an engaging heroine in a series of humorous and entertaining additions to the popular "murder-in-a-village" subgenre. Recipes are included in an appendix to each volume. Number 1 is a prequel set in New York City. Page also writes a YA series, *Christie and Company*.

1. *Body in the Big Apple, The* **(Morrow, 1999)** Faith, in her younger days as a Manhattanite wrapped up in starting her new catering business, is confided in by former schoolmate Emma Stanstead, now married to a budding politician, when Emma receives a threatening blackmail note.

2. *Body in the Belfrey, The* **(St. Martin's, 1990)** Faith discovers young Cindy Shepherd in Aleford's town watchtower with a knife in her chest.

3. *Body in the Kelp, The* **(St. Martin's, 1991)** Faith and her friend Pix discover a treasure map and two-year-old Ben discovers a man's body in a kelpy tidal pool during a vacation in coastal Maine.

4. *Body in the Bouillon, The* **(St. Martin's, 1991)** When asked to investigate a retirement retreat operated by the Hubbard family, Faith turns up blackmail, illicit sex, cocaine, and murder.

5. *Body in the Vestibule, The* **(St. Martin's, 1992)** The pregnant Faith, Tom, and three-year-old Ben are abroad in Lyons, France, when Faith discovers the body of a homeless man in a trash bin.

6. *Body in the Cast, The* **(St. Martin's, 1993)** Faith caters for a visiting movie team filming a new version of *The Scarlet Letter* and, of course, the shooting doesn't run smoothly.

7. *Body in the Basement, The* **(St. Martin's, 1994)** Faith's friend, Pix Miller, takes center stage when she discovers a quilt-wrapped body buried where the cement for the foundation of the Fairchild's summer cottage will soon be poured.

8. *Body in the Bog, The* (Morrow, 1996) When a local developer proposes building a housing subdivision on Aleford's bog, environmentalists are up in arms.

9. *Body in the Fjord, The* (Morrow, 1997) Pix Miller is featured again as she joins a tour group in Norway after learning that the granddaughter of an old family friend has disappeared after her fiancé died in a freak accident.

10. *Body in the Bookcase, The* (Morrow, 1998) Eighty-year-old Sarah Winslow is found dead after her house is burglarized. Faith takes a personal interest when her own home is broken into.

11. *Body in the Moonlight, The* (Morrow, 2001) When the Murder Mystery benefit she is catering is marred by a real murder, Faith finds herself suspected of the crime by some of the local busybodies.

12. *Body in the Bonfire, The* (Morrow, 2002) When the body of the alleged harasser of black student Daryl Martin is found in a bonfire set at Mansfield Academy, Daryl is accused of the crime.

13. *Body in the Lighthouse, The* (Morrow, 2003) Faith and Tom are fixing up their cottage on Maine's Sanpere Island when the body of developer Harold Hapswell is found wedged between two granite ledges at the base of the old lighthouse.

14. *Body in the Attic, The* (Morrow, 2004) When Tom takes a position at Harvard Divinity School for a semester, Faith, reluctantly taking up residence at a Brattle Street, Cambridge, house; turns up a diary in the attic; and is discomforted by the sudden reappearance, after 13 years, of an old boyfriend.

15. *Body in the Snowdrift, The* (Morrow, 2005) Faith and Tom join the extended Fairchild clan to celebrate the birthday of Tom's father, Dick, at the Vermont ski resort of Pine Slope.

16. *Body in the Ivy, The* (Morrow, 2006) Faith is invited to a remote New England island by reclusive best-selling author Barbara Bailey Bishop, along with several of the host's classmates from Pelham College in the 1970s. A northeaster cuts off the island, and the body count begins.

17. *Body in the Gallery, The* (Morrow, 2008) Sinister doings at the Ganley Museum of Art, and Faith's friend Patsy Avery asks her to investigate a potential forgery.

Paretsky, Sara

Paretsky has created one of the most believable female hard-boiled detectives. Her V(ictoria) I(phigenia) Warshawski is a Chicago-based lawyer-detective who specializes in corporate crime. Of Polish and Italian descent, Vic is attractive, tough, and independent. Her knowledge of Chicago's power structure and low opinion of businessmen and politicians usually sends her investigating in the right direction in cases, many of which involve matters of social concern. In a city whose real motto, according to the late Mike Royko, is "Ubi est Mea" ("Where's Mine"), Vic has plenty to work with. Paretsky's fans increase with each book as readers come to rely on her likable heroine for surefire action with a touch of bitter humor. Although Kathleen Turner made a convincing V. I. in the 1991 movie *V. I. Warshawski*, the film, perhaps because it was based on several of the novels, was not a success. *Ghost Country* (Delacorte, 1998) is not a Warshawski novel. Numbers 1, 2, and 3 were published together by Penguin (1993).

1. *Indemnity Only* (Dial, 1982) Warshawski's attempt to find a young woman leads her to murder, crooked unions, and an insurance scam.

2. *Deadlock* (Dial, 1984) When V. I.'s cousin, former hockey star Boom Boom Warshawski, is found broken to bits under a ship's propeller, she investigates the cargo shipping business.

3. *Killing Orders* (Morrow, 1985) V. I.'s aunt Rosa Vignelli asks her to investigate the theft of $5 million in stock certificates from a monastery.

4. *Bitter Medicine* (Morrow, 1987) The death in childbirth of young Consuelo Alvarado in a "model" suburban hospital leads V. I. into the world of hospital politics.

5. *Blood Shot* (Delacorte, 1988) A search for the father Caroline Dijak never knew brings Warshawski into contact with polluters and sleazy aldermen. UK title: *Toxic Shock*.

6. *Burn Marks* (Delacorte, 1990) Arson, homicide, corrupt cops and politicians, and construction executives take up V. I.'s time.

7. *Guardian Angel* (Delacorte, 1992) V. I. collaborates with some elderly neighbors in a case involving the manufacturing firm of Diamond Head Motors, some euthanized dogs, and a body in the Chicago Sanitary Canal.

8. *Tunnel Vision* (Delacorte, 1994) Warshawski's efforts to help a homeless family lead to murder and a gigantic financial scam involving some of Chicago's more prominent politicians.

9. *Windy City Blues* (Delacorte, 1995) A collection of nine V. I. Warshawski short stories. UK title: *V. I. for Short*.

10. *Hard Time* (Delacorte, 1999) The case of an escaped prisoner, whom she nearly runs over, leads to Vic's incarceration in Coolis, a privately operated prison in northwestern Illinois, in this exposé of for-profit prisons.

11. *Total Recall* (Delacorte, 2001) Two plots here: the life insurance policy of black factory worker Aaron Sommers, which Ajax Insurance Company reneges on; and the appearance of Paul Radbuka, who claims to be a Holocaust survivor and a kinsman of Vic's friend Max Loewenthal.

12. *Blacklist* (Putnam, 2003) While investigating reports about squatters in an empty mansion, Vic stumbles upon the corpse of a young African American journalist writing about the members of the 1930s Federal Negro Theater Project, some of whom ran afoul of the anti-Communist blacklists.

13. *Fire Sale* (Putnam, 2005) Vic gets involved in a missing-persons case and a factory explosion, among other things, when she volunteers to fill in for her old basketball coach on Chicago's South Side.

Pargeter, Edith

I. American readers of the Brother Cadfael novels by Ellis Peters (q.v.) may be excused for not being familiar with the late (d. 1995) Edith Pargeter's many excellent novels written under her own name, since they have, for the most part, been unavailable in the United States until recently. Pargeter wrote her World War II trilogy soon after that momentous event, in which she took part. (She received a British Empire Medal for her service in the WRENS.) Jim Benison, small-town boy from Morwen Hoe, joins up in 1939 and serves through the entire war with various Midshires regiments. The trilogy is an excellent picture of men and women at war and the awakening of a small-town boy to the great world. The three volumes were reprinted by Headline (UK) in 1990.

1. *Eighth Champion of Christendom, The* (Heinemann [UK], 1945) Jim Benison joins up with the 4th Midshires in 1939 and heads to France with his infantry unit.

2. *Reluctant Odyssey* (Heinemann [UK], 1946) The 4th Midshires fight the Italians, and then the Germans in Libya, then get transferred to Singapore on the eve of its fall to the Japanese.

3. *Warfare Accomplished* (Heinemann [UK], 1947) Benison becomes a sergeant in the 7th Midshires, trains men in England and leads them back to the Continent.

II. The Heaven Tree trilogy is set in 13th-century England and Wales, not too long after Brother Cadfael's heyday. The trilogy is a historically accurate portrayal of a family of master artisans, the Talvaces, who have a passion for stone carving. Pargeter knows the historical period, knows how to tell a tale, and knows how to bring a bygone era back to life. Published in one volume as *The Heaven Tree Trilogy* (Warner, 1993).

1. *Heaven Tree, The* (Doubleday, 1960) Harry Talvace designs a great church on the Welsh/English border for his imperious patron Ralf Isambard.
2. *Green Branch, The* (Heinemann [UK], 1962) Harry's son, also a stone carver, grows up vowing to slay Isambard, who had been responsible for Harry's murder.
3. *Scarlet Seed, The* (Heinemann [UK], 1963) Brings the action to a rousing conclusion with all kinds of revealed relationships and gothic surprises.

III. In the Brothers of Gwynedd quartet, Pargeter wrote the chronicle of Llewlyn, "first and only true Prince of Wales," who fought a losing battle for Welsh independence against the English King Edward I in the late 13th century. The novels are full of accurate historical detail and are hard to put down once the reader has gotten involved with the story. *The Brothers of Gwynedd* was published in one volume by Headline (UK) in 1990.

1. *Sunrise in the West* (Macmillan [UK], 1974) The already complicated political situation in Wales is further complicated by the struggle between David, a legitimate son, and the bastard Griffin, who, by Welsh law, is entitled to an equal share of the inheritance.
2. *Dragon at Noonday, The* (Macmillan [UK], 1975) Wales is brought into a fragile unity, while England is torn by civil war.
3. *Hounds of Sunset, The* (Macmillan [UK], 1976) Llewelyn's dreams of a free, united Wales are set back when the ruthless, able Edward I succeeds Henry III on the English throne.
4. *Afterglow and Nightfall* (Macmillan [UK], 1977) The fact, if not the dream, of Welsh independence dies with the death of Llewelyn in 1282.

Park, Paul

I. The Starbridge chronicles create a fascinating world somewhat reminiscent of Brian Aldiss's (q.v.) Helliconia in that each novel is set in a different season of the year that lasts for a lifetime. The chronicles create a complex, well-realized society on a distant planet (or perhaps on a far-future Earth) that seems to contain elements of the cultures of ancient India and Southeast Asia. *The Sugar Festival* (Guild America, 1989) contains numbers 1 and 2. More recently Park has been writing imaginative novels set in the time of Christ (*The Gospel of Corax*, Soho, 1996; and *Three Marys*, Wildside, 2003) and most recently has ventured into fantasy (see series II).

1. *Soldiers of Paradise* (Arbor House, 1987) The harsh, authoritarian Starbridge regime of Wintertime is delineated.
2. *Sugar Rain* (Arbor House, 1989) Two high-caste lovers try to avoid their predestined futures by wandering over the planet as Spring rains signify violent social change for the great city of Charn.
3. *Cult of Loving Kindness, The* (Morrow, 1991) A secular, populist government is in place in the prosperous Summertime, but remnants of the old ways remain in the more primitive rural areas.

II. Miranda Popescu, a 15-year-old living in a college town in Berkshire County, Massachusetts, finds that she is really from an alternate-reality "Roumania" in a land where alchemy really works. Miranda is a pawn in a complicated political game where the mad Baroness Ceausescu and the sinister alchemist the Elector of Ratisbon vie for political power. With the help of her friends Chevalier de Graz (aka Peter Gross) and the shape-shifting Lieutenant Prochenko (aka a girl named Andromeda), Miranda manages to survive in this imaginative, character-driven series.

1. *Princess of Roumania, A* (Tor, 2005) Teenager Miranda Popescu was hidden by her aunt in a quiet Massachusetts college town in "our world," but she is really a princess and at the fulcrum of a political battle between conjurers in an alternate world where Roumania is a leading European power.
2. *Tourmaline, The* (Tor, 2006) Five years later Miranda is at large in Roumania, where her true mother is imprisoned, while her two best friends, Peter and Andromeda, have been left behind in the forests of an alternate America.
3. *Whyte Tiger, The* (Tor, 2007) Miranda, with the help of her friends Chevalier de Graz and Lieutenant Prochenko, explores her new potential in the secret world of animal souls that underlies daily reality.
4. *Hidden World, The* (Tor, 2008) In the final volume, Miranda, now revealed as both a lost Roumanian princess and the shape-shifting White Tyger, is still opposed by Colonel Bocu and the ghost of Baroness Nicola Ceausescu.

Park, Ruth

Ruth Park, a native New Zealander living in Australia, wrote two novels in the 1940s about the Darcys, a poor family of Irish descent living in the slums of Sydney. Thirty-five years later, she published *Missus*, a prequel about the Darcy family at the turn of the century in the small Australian town of Trafalgar. The main characters in the trilogy are Hugh Darcy, irresponsible and irrepressible, seen in his youth in *Missus* and as "Dadda" in numbers 2 and 3; and the proud Margaret Kilker who becomes the "Missus," then mother of daughters of Roie and Dolour. The novels have their tragic moments but are full of gentle humor, realistic pictures of urban life in Australia, and well-realized characters. Park has written many children's books including The Muddle-Headed Wombat series.

1. *Missus* (St. Martin's, 1987) Young Hugh Darcy and his crippled brother, Jeremiah, run away from a brutal father and the town of Trafalgar at the turn of the 20th century.
2. *Harp in the South, The* (Houghton Mifflin, 1948) Roie Darcy, elder daughter of Hugh and Margaret, comes of age in the Sidney slums. Reissued by St. Martin's in 1987.
3. *12 1/2 Plymouth Street* (Houghton Mifflin, 1951) Sixteen-year-old Dolour Darcy must raise Roie's motherless children. Reissued as *Poorman's Orange* by St. Martin's in 1987.

Parker, Robert B.

I. Spenser, Boston's own private eye, seems a shade more literate than most of Sam Spade's descendants. He leavens his wise-cracking, tough-guy brand of detection with a smattering of culture and balances his weight-lifting machismo act with a tough-minded feminist philosophy and a sure hand in the kitchen. His girlfriend, psychologist Susan Silverman plays a large part in some of his cases, particularly in the mid-1980s, and not to everyone's liking. His black cohort Hawk also plays an important role, and well as a bunch of colorful mobsters. Spenser's Boston delights locals and will disabuse outsiders' notions of the city as a quaint Puritan town. For several years *Spenser: For Hire*, a network television series starring Robert Urich, was filmed on location in Boston. Robert B. Parker was a professor at a number of Boston area colleges, including Northeastern University.

1. *Godwulf Manuscript, The* (Houghton Mifflin, 1974) Spenser's debut case involves the theft of an illuminated 14th-century manuscript from a college library.
2. *God Save the Child* (Houghton Mifflin, 1974) An emotionally disturbed boy is kidnapped from a Boston suburban home.
3. *Mortal Stakes* (Houghton Mifflin, 1975) Is Boston Red Sox pitcher Marty Raab being blackmailed into throwing games?
4. *Promised Land* (Houghton Mifflin, 1976) Spenser must find Pam Shepard, wife of a shady real-estate dealer.
5. *Judas Goat, The* (Houghton Mifflin, 1978) Spenser gets to Europe to hunt down the terrorists whose bomb killed the family of a rich American.
6. *Looking for Rachel Wallace* (Delacorte, 1980) Spenser is hired as a bodyguard for a lesbian-feminist-radical author.
7. *Early Autumn* (Delacorte, 1981) While divorced parents feud over their 15-year-old son, Paul, Spenser gives a quick course in self-sufficiency in the wilds of Maine.
8. *Savage Place, A* (Delacorte, 1981) Spenser is looking after Candy Sloan, a TV news reporter investigating movie payoffs.
9. *Ceremony* (Delacorte, 1982) When young April Kyle drops out of her suburban high school and disappears, Spenser tracks her down in Boston's "Combat Zone."
10. *Widening Gyre, The* (Delacorte, 1983) Spenser acts as a security officer for Meade Alexander, candidate for the US Senate.
11. *Valediction* (Delacorte, 1984) Spenser takes on cult leader Reverend Bullard Winston, who is accused of abducting a young woman.
12. *Catskill Eagle, A* (Delacorte, 1985) Spenser and Hawk go to California to retrieve Susan Silverman from her lover, Russell Costigan, son of a wealthy dealer in illegal arms.
13. *Taming a Sea-Horse* (Delacorte, 1986) April Kyle, the young prostitute rescued by Spenser in number 9, disappears again when a young woman and her pimp are murdered.
14. *Pale Kings and Princes* (Delacorte, 1987) When newspaper reporter Eric Valdez is murdered while investigating a cocaine ring, Spenser journeys to Wheaton, Massachusetts, to expose the ringleaders.
15. *Crimson Joy* (Delacorte, 1988) A slasher who is victimizing middle-aged black women may be one of Susan Silverman's patients.
16. *Playmates* (Putnam, 1989) Dwayne Woodcock, all-American power forward, is suspected of point-shaving while playing for his nationally ranked basketball team.
17. *Stardust* (Putnam, 1990) Spenser is hired to protect Jilly Joyce, star of a top-ranked television show being shot on location in Boston Common.
18. *Pastime* (Putnam, 1991) Paul Giacomin, whom Spenser aided in number 7, wants him to find his missing mother.
19. *Double Deuce* (Putnam, 1992) Spenser's friend Hawk enlists him in defending the residents of Double Deuce, a gang-plagued Boston housing project.
20. *Paper Doll* (Putnam, 1993) Boston Brahmin Loudon Tripp hires Spenser to find the killer of his wife, Olivia.
21. *Walking Shadow* (Putnam, 1994) The artistic director of the Port City Theater Company hires Spenser to find out who is tailing him.
22. *Thin Air* (Putnam, 1995) Lisa St. Clair, radio disc jockey recently married to a Boston policeman, has been kidnapped and imprisoned in the depressed factory town of Proctor.

23. *Chance* (Putnam, 1996) When Boston mobster Julius Ventura approaches Spenser about finding his daughter's missing husband, it's clear that he isn't telling Spenser the whole truth.
24. *Small Vices* (Putnam, 1997) A kid with a long criminal record is the chief suspect in the murder of a student that Spenser is investigating.
25. *Sudden Mischief* (Putnam, 1998) Susan Silverman's ex-husband, fund-raiser Brad Sterling, appears after a long absence, nearly broke and facing a harassment suit.
26. *Hush Money* (Putnam, 1999) African American Robinson Nevins is denied tenure at the university, apparently because of an affair with a young gay activist.
27. *Hugger Mugger* (Putnam, 2000) Spenser travels to Georgia to protect promising two-year-old Hugger Mugger from being the next victim of an unknown person killing race horses.
28. *Potshot* (Putnam, 2001) Spenser heads west to Potshot, Arizona, to deal with the Dell, a local gang, led by someone called the Preacher, which is preying on the Los Angeles millionaires who thought they had found a nice hideaway.
29. *Widow's Walk* (Putnam, 2002) Fifty-one-year-old Nathan Smith is found in bed with a hole in his head, and his young bride, Mary, is the chief suspect.
30. *Back Story* (Putnam, 2003) Hired to dig into the 28-year-old murder of a woman during a bank robbery, Spenser teams up briefly with small-town police chief Jesse Stone (see series III).
31. *Bad Business* (Putnam, 2004) When Marlene Cowley hires Spenser to watch her husband, he runs into a second investigator hired by the husband to watch Marlene.
32. *Cold Service* (Putnam, 2005) Hawk is shot. Spenser helps Hawk to recover and then gets revenge on Boots Podolak and his Ukrainian mobsters, who run the Boston satellite city of "Marshport."
33. *School Days* (Putnam, 2005) Lily Ellsworth hires Spenser to prove the innocence of her grandson, Jared Clark, accused of a Columbine High School–style shooting that has left seven people dead.
34. *Hundred-Dollar Baby* (Putnam, 2006) April Kyle (see numbers 9 and 13) asks Spenser for help against the men trying to muscle in on the high-class whorehouse she is running.
35. *Now and Then* (Putnam, 2007) When a client who suspects his wife is cheating on him is murdered, Spenser, like Dashiell Hammett's (q.v.) Sam Spade, feels duty-bound to find the killer.

II. Parker, a great admirer of Raymond Chandler (q.v.), took on the job of finishing *Poodle Springs*, for which Chandler had written four chapters. A couple of years later, Parker published a sequel to Chandler's classic *The Big Sleep*. Both novels featured Chandler's famous private eye Philip Marlowe.

1. *Poodle Springs [Parker]* (Putnam, 1989) Married to true-love Linda Loring but ill-at-ease in posh Poodle (Palm) Springs, California, Marlowe takes on a missing persons case. Begun by Raymond Chandler; completed by Robert B. Parker.
2. *Perchance to Dream* (Putnam, 1991) In this sequel to Chandler's *The Big Sleep*, we return to the dysfunctional Sternwood family. The general is long dead, but daughter Vivian is dating a blackmailer, and psychotic daughter Carmen has escaped from the asylum where she was incarcerated.

III. Jesse Stone, discharged from the Los Angeles Police Department because of alcohol problems, finds a job as police chief in the small Massachusetts town of Paradise, a seeming sinecure that proves to be anything but, as Stone deals with a series of nasty cases, bouts with the bottle, and his inability to break free of his ex-wife, Jean. Stone appears as a character in number 30 of the Spenser series (series I), number 3

530 PARKINSON, C(YRIL) NORTHCOTE

of Stone's series. Stone teams up with Sunny Randall of series IV in numbers 6 and 7.

1. *Night Passage* (Putnam, 1997) Jesse Stone, after being kicked out of the LAPD, seems to have landed on his feet as chief of police in seemingly bucolic Paradise, Massachusetts, but he is up to his ears soon with homicides, militiamen, and psychopaths.
2. *Trouble in Paradise* (Putnam, 1998) A band of criminals led by James Macklin plans to invade the enclave of Stiles Island, destroy the bridge that connects it to the mainland, and loot the place.
3. *Death in Paradise* (Putnam, 2001) Jesse runs into Gino Fish and Vinnie Morris, characters from Spenser's world, as he investigates the murder of a troubled teenager.
4. *Stone Cold* (Putnam, 2003) Stone tries to come to terms with his alcoholism and his relationship with ex-wife Jean as he goes after a pair of serial killers and the three high-school students who gang-raped a younger schoolmate.
5. *Sea Change* (Putnam, 2006) Jesse has been off the bottle for a year and is tentatively reunited with his ex-wife, Jenn. After a woman is murdered aboard a sailboat, Jesse works with Fort Lauderdale, Florida, cop Kelly Cruz toward a solution.
6. *Blue Screen* (Putnam, 2006) Jesse Stone and Sunny Randall (see series IV) work together when the younger sister of actress and would-be major league baseball player Erin Flint is murdered in Paradise.
7. *High Profile* (Putnam, 2007) Stone and Randall work together again as right-wing radio commentator Walton Weeks is murdered, and Stone's ex-wife, Jean, is sexually assaulted.
8. *Stranger in Paradise* (Putnam, 2008) Ex-con Wilson "Crow" Cromartie, a character in number 2, shows up again and warns Stone not to interfere in his search for someone in Massachusetts.

IV. Sunny Randall, Parker's contribution to the female detective scene, was created at the behest of actress Helen Hunt, who wanted to play such a character in a film. Although the film still hasn't been made, Sunny's series has grown to four books. Sunny, a former cop turned private eye, paints on the side, can't cook, owns a miniature bull terrier, and has a complicated relationship with her ex-husband Richie. Her equivalent to Spenser's Hawk is gay waiter and karate expert Spike. Sunny gets professionally and romantically involved with Jesse Stone of series III in numbers 5 and 6. Susan Silverman, from the Spenser series (series I), makes an appearance in number 7.

1. *Family Honor* (Putnam, 1999) Sunny goes in search of wealthy Boston disappeared-runaway Millicent.
2. *Perish Twice* (Putnam, 2000) Randall is hired by prominent feminist Mary Lou Goddard to protect her from threatening phone calls and stalkers.
3. *Shrink Rap* (Putnam, 2002) Melanie Jean Hall needs a bodyguard-cum-escort to protect her ex-husband, psychopathic psychotherapist John Melvin.
4. *Melancholy Baby* (Putnam, 2004) College student Sarah Markham suspects that her mother and father have been lying about the identity of her true birth parents. Sunny goes to Chicago in search of Sarah's past.
5. *Blue Screen (2)* (Putnam, 2006) See series III, number 6.
6. *High Profile (2)* (Putnam, 2007) See series III, number 7.
7. *Spare Change* (Putnam, 2007) Sunny Randall helps her father, Phil, track down a serial killer who has reemerged after a 20-year hiatus.

Parkinson, C(yril) Northcote

After paying homage to C. S. Forester (q.v.) with a fictional biography of that author's famous hero, *The Life and Times of Horatio Hornblower*, Parkinson fashioned a series of naval adventures around a hero of his own creation—imitation being in this case not only the sincerest form of flattery but a boon to Forester fans and naval-adventure buffs. Parkinson's hero, Richard Delancey, a native of the island of Guernsey, is as brave and resourceful as his fictional forebear. The period covered is from the American Revolution (1776) to well into the Napoleonic Wars (1811). As to be expected from a naval historian, the historical details are very accurate.

1. *Guernseyman, The* (Houghton Mifflin, 1982) Sixteen-year-old Guernseyman Richard Delancey, inadvertently caught up in the Merseyside riots in Liverpool (1776), "volunteers" for the British navy, and sees service against the Americans.
2. *Devil to Pay* (Houghton Mifflin, 1973) Delancey's ability to speak French brings him a secret assignment and a chance to restore his tarnished reputation. The story begins in June 1794 and covers about two years.
3. *Fireship, The* (Houghton Mifflin, 1975) Posted to the *Glatton* in 1796, Delancey faces mutiny and destroys a French ship of the line by means of delicately maneuvered fire ship.
4. *Touch and Go* (Houghton Mifflin, 1977) In 1799 Delancey is posted to Gibraltar to command the sloop *Merlin*. He rescues a young slave girl in Africa and makes a desperate last effort to win a rich prize.
5. *So Near, So Far* (Houghton Mifflin, 1981) Ashore in London in 1802, Delancey falls in love with the beautiful actress Fiona Sinclair and learns about a new French underwater vessel called the *Nautilus*.
6. *Dead Reckoning* (Houghton Mifflin, 1978) In 1805 Delancey is promoted to post-captain and must leave his lovely young wife for the ancient frigate *Lydia*.

Patterson, James

I. Alex Cross is a black forensic psychologist in Washington, DC. Going from private practice to the Washington Police Department to the FBI, Alex employs his forensic skills mostly in investigating serial killers, one of whom murdered his wife, and several of whom are out to "get" Alex in return. James Patterson is an internationally popular writer, but not universally admired: Stephen King (q.v.) called his books "dopey" best sellers (*Entertainment Weekly*), but many other readers find themselves gripped by Patterson's nail-biting narratives and staccato prose in this series of nursery-rhyme murder cases.

1. *Along Came a Spider* (Little, Brown, 1992) Teacher Gary Soneji has kidnapped two rich kids from a DC-area school, and one of them has been found dead. Washington PD deputy chief of detectives Alex Cross and Secret Service agent Jezzie Flanagan are on the case.
2. *Kiss the Girls* (Little, Brown, 1995) Two serial killers, who seem to be in competition, are terrorizing different regions of America, and now copycats are horning in on the act.
3. *Jack and Jill* (Little, Brown, 1996) Two efficient killers are knocking off the "rich and famous" one by one.
4. *Cat and Mouse* (Little, Brown, 1997) Killer Gary Soneji (see number 1) is back, and he's after Alex Cross.
5. *Pop! Goes the Weasel* (Little, Brown, 1999) "The Weasel" is behind a series of Jane Doe murders in which bodies are dumped without clothes or IDs.

6. *Roses Are Red* (Little, Brown, 2000) A series of bank robberies, planned by "the Mastermind," turns nasty for Alex, who is investigating them.

7. *Violets Are Blue* (Little, Brown, 2001) Two joggers are murdered in San Francisco's Golden Gate Park. The killings are reminiscent of those committed in Washington, DC, and several other cities.

8. *Four Blind Mice* (Little, Brown, 2002) Alex Craig, the Mastermind, (see number 6) is in prison, but has he really been stopped? Alex Cross resigns from the DC police department, hoping to spend more time with Nana and the kids.

9. *Big Bad Wolf, The* (Little, Brown, 2003) Alex, now with the FBI, is investigating the disappearance of several women who seem to have been abducted by the Wolf, a former KGB agent and big-time Russian mobster.

10. *London Bridges* (Little, Brown, 2004) A series of bombings, signalized by anonymous calls, occur in various places in the United States.

11. *Mary, Mary* (Little, Brown, 2005) While Alex vacations in Disneyland with his family, "Mary Smith" is targeting prominent Hollywood stars.

12. *Cross* (Little, Brown, 2006) Alex Cross associates Michael Sullivan, aka the Butcher of Sligo, perpetrator of a series of rapes and killings, with the murder of his wife, Maria.

13. *Double Cross* (Little, Brown, 2007) Cross's former colleague in the FBI, the murderer called the Mastermind, has managed to escape from prison and is working his way through the list of those he holds responsible for his incarceration.

II. Two novels, published five years apart, which were followed by a trilogy called Maximum Ride, describe the adventures of six children (98 percent human, 2 percent bird) who are genetically engineered to fly. The first two novels describe the efforts of veterinarian Frannie O'Neill and FBI agent Kit Harrison to rescue the 11-year-olds from mad scientists and sinister school keepers. Numbers 3 through 5, which seem to be YA novels, show Max and her five siblings up against the half-human, half-wolf Erasers.

1. *When the Wind Blows* (Little, Brown, 1998) Vet Frannie O'Neill and FBI agent Kit Harrison investigate "the School," which seems to be harboring some genetically engineered children.

2. *Lake House, The* (Little, Brown, 2003) Max and her siblings are menaced by mad scientist Dr. Ethan Kane at his lab, "the Hospital."

2. *School's Out—Forever* (Little, Brown, 2006) On their way south to find their parents, the kids are forced to go to school by an FBI agent.

3. *Angel Experiment, The* (Little, Brown, 2005) The half-human, half-wolf Erasers kidnap Angel, and Max and her other four siblings are in pursuit.

5. *Saving the World: And Other Extreme Sports* (Little, Brown, 2007) The kids deal with a bunch of evil scientists who want to scientifically engineer the human race, so that a select population will rule the earth, and everyone else is exterminated.

III. The Women's Murder Club is a group of San Francisco professionals who take it upon themselves to investigate unsolved murders. The group consists of homicide detective Lindsay Boxer, coroner Claire Williams, reporter Cindy Thomas, and attorney Jill Bernhard (who is replaced by Yuki Castellano after number 4). Patterson wrote number 1 himself, but the other novels in the series have coauthors: Andrew Gross in numbers 2 and 3, and Maxine Paetro in numbers 4 through 7.

1. *1st to Die* (Little, Brown, 2001) The Women's Murder Club, led by homicide detective Lindsay Boxer, is formed to track down a maniac slaughtering newlywed couples.

2. *2nd Chance* (Little, Brown, 2002) When a little girl is shot is shot on the steps of a San Francisco church, the Women's Murder Club is reconvened. Coauthored with Andrew Gross.

3. *3rd Degree* (Little, Brown, 2004) The club watches as a San Francisco town house explodes in flames. Coauthored with Andrew Gross.

4. *4th of July* (Little, Brown, 2005) Lindsay finds herself on the spot when a young girl is killed in cross fire as a routine arrest goes wrong. Coauthored with Maxine Paetro.

5. *5th Horseman, The* (Little, Brown, 2006) The mother of Yuki Castellano, new member of the Women's Murder Club, is given the wrong medication at the San Francisco Medical Center. Coauthored with Maxine Paetro.

6. *6th Target, The* (Little, Brown, 2007) An attack leaves a WMC member struggling for life. Coauthored with Maxine Paetro.

7. *7th Heaven* (Little, Brown, 2008) Lindsay Boxer and her new partner, Rich Conklin, investigate the disappearance of Michael Campion, teenage son of a former California governor. Coauthored with Maxine Paetro.

Patterson, Richard North

Starting with the Edgar-winning *Lasko Tangent*, Richard North Patterson has written a series of courtroom and political thrillers. Numbers 1 through 3 and 8 feature lawyer Christopher Paget; number 4 stars attorney Caroline Masters, who eventually becomes a US Supreme Court nominee of President Kerry Kilcannon, who is at the center of numbers 5 through 7. Numbers 1 through 4 are fascinating courtroom dramas by lawyer Patterson; numbers 5 through 8 are adeptly written, suspenseful political and legal novels that explore explosive issues such as abortion, the Christian Right, campaign financing, gun control, and the death penalty. *Silent Witness* (Knopf, 1997) and *Dark Lady* (Knopf, 1999) are courtroom dramas that don't seem have any connection with the Paget/Masters/Kilcannon series.

1. *Lasko Tangent, The* (Norton, 1979) Christopher Paget, a lawyer in the Special Investigations Section of the Washington Economic Crimes Commission, investigates a possible stock scam involving a friend of the president.

2. *Degree of Guilt* (Knopf, 1993) When television journalist Mary Carelli shoots famous writer Mark Ransom in his hotel room, claiming that he tried to rape her, she hires former lover Paget as her defense attorney.

3. *Eyes of a Child* (Knopf, 1995) Christopher is the prime suspect when the husband of his aide and lover, young Latino lawyer Teresa Peralta, is killed in what looks like murder disguised as suicide.

4. *Final Judgment, The* (Knopf, 1995) Paget takes a backseat as Caroline Masters, candidate for the US Court of Appeals, becomes defense attorney for her niece, who is accused of murdering her slippery boyfriend.

5. *No Safe Place* (Knopf, 1998) Senator Kerry Kilcannon's campaign for president and his carefully weighed position on abortion could be torpedoed if his past affair with journalist Lara Costello is revealed.

6. *Protect and Defend* (Knopf, 2000) Appellate court judge Caroline Masters (protagonist of number 4) has been nominated for the US Supreme Court by President Kilcannon. The path to confirmation is strewn with obstacles, including a child she had out of wedlock and a sticky court case involving a pregnant 15-year-old.

7. *Balance of Power* (**Ballantine, 2003**) President Kerry Kilcannon is planning his marriage to old flame Lara Costello when Lara's sister Joan is brutally beaten by her husband, John Bowden, who subsequently runs amok in an airport. When Kilcannon goes after the manufacturer of the gun Bowden used, he arouses the ire of NRA types and Second Amendment fundamentalists.

8. *Convicting* (**Random House, 2005**) The death penalty is the issue when Christopher Paget and his wife, Terri, take on the case of a developmentally handicapped black man accused of a horrible sex crime.

Paul, Barbara

I. Marian Larch is a sergeant (later lieutenant) in the New York Police Department. She has the usual problems with chauvinistic partners, ambitious superiors, career burnout, and unsatisfactory personal relationships. A fast-paced, humorous, romantic, and well-plotted series with villains whom the reader isn't sure to hate or not. Barbara Paul is not to be confused with the "Barbara Paul" who writes gothic romances, a pseudonym used by Barbara Ovstedal, aka Rosalind Laker.

1. *Renewable Virgin, The* (**Scribner, 1984**) When friend Rudy Benedict is poisoned by cyanide-laced headache medicine, television actress Kelly Ingram realizes that the poison was intended for her.

2. *He Huffed and He Puffed* (**Scribner, 1989**) Financier A. J. Strode thinks he has the leverage to get the stocks he needs for a hostile takeover of House of Glass: three of the stockholders have committed murder and gotten away with it.

3. *Good King Sauerkraut* (**Scribner, 1990**) Robot-designer King "Good King Sauerkraut" Sarcowicz has caused the accidental deaths of two coworkers, but he wants the police to think that the deaths were homicides by an unknown hand.

4. *You Have the Right to Remain Silent* (**Scribner, 1992**) Four top-level employees of a laser-technology firm are found handcuffed together and shot through the eye.

5. *Apostrophe Thief, The* (**Scribner, 1993**) Marian is on the verge of resigning from the NYPD when friend Kelly gets her involved with finding the thief of a coat once owned by Sarah Bernhardt.

6. *Fare Play* (**Scribner, 1995**) Larch is hot on the trail of a contract killer whose most recent victims are an old man and a college student killed while riding on public transportation.

7. *Full Frontal Murder* (**Scribner, 1997**) The Galloways, Rita and Hugh, are in the middle of an acrimonious divorce and custody battle that leads to murder and other antisocial acts.

II. The New York Metropolitan Opera's golden age (the first decades of the 20th century) is the venue for a series of mysteries in which Enrico Caruso plays amateur detective. Caruso is joined by fellow opera stars Geraldine Farrar (who narrates numbers 2 and 3), Emmy Destinn, and others in these nicely detailed backstage period mysteries.

1. *Cadenza for Caruso, A* (**St. Martin's, 1984**) Composer Giacomo Puccini becomes the chief suspect when Caruso stumbles across a murdered impresario while rehearsing for the 1910 world premiere of *The Girl of the Golden West*.

2. *Prima Donna at Large* (**St. Martin's, 1985**) Met star soprano Geraldine Farrar and her favorite tenor Enrico Caruso team up to solve a murder when the replacement of a sick baritone in *Carmen* stirs up rivalries.

3. *Chorus of Detectives, A* (**St. Martin's, 1987**) A serial killer is murdering members of the Met chorus as Emmy Destinn, Rosa Ponselle, and Antonio Scotti join Caruso and Farrar as amateur sleuths.

Paulsen, Gary

Al Murphy is the protagonist in this series of westerns with elements of hard-boiled detective mysteries. Al is one of those tough, lonely romantics with a code of honor who tends to lose jobs and loved ones, gets on and off the wagon, and wanders from one small, mean western town to another in the 1880s. Gary Paulsen, who is also the author of numerous how-to books and juveniles (including the Brian, Francis Tucket, Duncan Culpepper series), won a Golden Spur for his western novels. Brian Burks is the coauthor of numbers 5 through 7.

1. *Murphy* (**Walker, 1987**) Sheriff Al Murphy searches for the rapist-murderer of a 12-year-old girl found in a livery stable in Clincherville, Colorado.

2. *Murphy's Gold* (**Walker, 1988**) Murphy and lover Midge plan to leave Clincherville as soon as they've amassed a grubstake, but first Al must investigate the disappearance of the town's Chinese laundryman.

3. *Murphy's Herd* (**Walker, 1989**) Al and Midge leave Clincherville for a homestead near Casper, Wyoming, but run smack into a feud.

4. *Murphy's War* (**Walker, 1991**) After his wife's death, Murphy takes to drink and wanders to the town of Fletcher, Wyoming, where a cowhand has been lynched by a mob led by a wealthy rancher.

5. *Murphy's Stand* (**Walker, 1993**) Saddle-bum Murphy stumbles onto some gunmen just after they have committed a murder, and barely escapes to the town of Turrett, Arizona. Cowritten with Brian Burks.

6. *Murphy's Ambush* (**Walker, 1995**) Dried out and a sheriff again, this time in New Mexico, Murphy investigates the murders of a rancher and his family and chases some renegade Apaches. Cowritten with Brian Burks.

7. *Murphy's Trail* (**Walker, 1996**) Rosa Villabisencio who, with her husband, Santiago, saved Murphy's life years before, asks for aid when Santiago is bushwhacked in Arizona Territory.

Paxson, Diana L.

I. California-based Paxson's longest fantasy series is about a kingdom called Westria, set in the far-future of what used to be the western United States. The basis for the Chronicles of Westria is a set of four magic jewels representing the elements of earth, water, air, and fire. The first two volumes are about Faris, a shy country girl who becomes the consort of King Jehan and set to, reluctantly, controlling the jewels. These two volumes are more easily available combined as *The Mistress of the Jewels* (Tor, 1991; UK title: *Lady of Light, Lady of Darkness*). Number 3 is an 18-year saga of the search of Farin for his twin sister, Faris. Numbers 4 through 7 describe the search, by Julian of Stanesvale, lost son of Jehan, for the four jewels. The wicked sorcerer, Caolin, is the main villain in the series.

1. *Lady of Light* (**Pocket Books, 1982**) Shy country girl Faris wishes to be Jehan's queen, but is reluctant to take up the duty of controlling the Jewels of Westria.

2. *Lady of Darkness* (**Pocket Books, 1983**) Faris and the evil sorcerer Caolin vie for control of the jewels.

3. *Silverhair the Wanderer* (**Tor, 1986**) Farin, twin brother of Faris, goes in search of his sister, who has disappeared, in an 18-year quest.

4. *Earthstone, The* **(Tor, 1987)** Julian of Stanesvale, lost son of Jehan and Faris, embarks upon a quest to recover the lost Jewels of Power that will prove him the rightful heir to the throne. The jewel in this volume represents the earth element.

5. *Sea Star, The* **(Tor, 1988)** The Sea Star, the jewel of water, lies hidden, waiting to be mastered.

6. *Wind Crystal, The* **(Tor, 1990)** The Wind Crystal, the jewel that is the key to the realm of air, is the talisman sought here.

7. *Jewel of Fire, The* **(Tor, 1992)** In the conclusion to the saga, Julian seeks the jewel of fire, which is hidden in a volcano.

8. *Golden Hills of Westria, The* **(Tor, 2006)** Set about 25 years after the action in number 7, this volume welcomes a new generation of Westrians: Prince Phoenix, who takes the name of Johan, and his lifelong female friend, Sombra, who assumes the name Luz.

II. Some of Paxson's readers feel that she is on stronger ground writing fantasy based on legendary material. The saga of Sigfrid and Brunahild, best known through Wagner's operatic version, is set in a 5th-century Rhineland full of migrant tribes and Teutonic gods and spirits and the legendary version of such historical characters as Attila the Hun. This series blends history, mythology, and fantasy in equal parts.

1. *Wolf and the Raven, The* **(Morrow, 1995)** While Sigfrid consorts with a wolf and studies shamanism, Brunahild trains as a Valkyrie and sorceress against a backdrop of stolen treasure and feuding Burgunds and Huns.

2. *Dragons of the Rhine, The* **(Avon, 1995)** Although Brunahild has secretly borne Sigfrid's child, she weds Gunodar and Sigfrid weds Gudrun while the Burgunds and the Huns continue their bloody feud.

3. *Lord of Horses, The* **(Avon, 1996)** Gudrun, the grieving widow of Sigfrid, agrees to wed Attila to save her people, but has revenge in mind.

III. Paxson collaborated with fellow fantasy writer Adrienne Martine-Barnes to write a trilogy about the legendary Irish hero Fionn mac Cumhal. The trilogy is a highly satisfying saga in which old Celtic legends come to life in a culture where the natural and the supernatural, the mythical and the mundane interact.

1. *Master of Earth and Water* **(Morrow, 1993)** Fionn mac Cumhal is raised in hiding by a wisewoman and a female warrior to save him from his murderous Druid grandfather.

2. *Shield between the Worlds, The* **(Morrow, 1994)** At the age of 24, Fionn is ready to assume leadership of his tribe against its enemies, which include a dragon and some goblin hordes.

3. *Sword of Fire and Shadow* **(Morrow, 1995)** Fionn and his Fianna serve the High King Cormac mac Airt while striving to keep their own country from being destroyed by blood feuds.

IV. The Hallowed Isle series is Paxson's contribution to the legend of King Arthur, or Artor, as he is called here. Each of the four volumes is told from the perspective of one of the prevalent tribal cultures of 6th-century Britain. Paxson also collaborated on the Avalon series with Marion Zimmer Bradley (q.v.) and wrote *The White Raven* (Morrow, 1988), a version of the Tristan and Iseult legend, and *The Serpent's Tooth* (Morrow, 1991), a version of the British legend of King Lear. *Hallowed Isle* (Avon, 2000) contains numbers 1 and 2. *The Book of the Cauldron and The Book of the Stone* (Eos, 2001) contains numbers 3 and 4.

1. *Book of the Sword, The* **(Avon, 1999)** The Druid priestess known as the Lady of the Lake calls upon the Spirit of War and Justice for a champion to unite Britain after the decampment of the Romans.

2. *Book of the Spear, The* **(Avon, 1999)** Oesca has fled the country to which he is heir to claim rich lands in Britain. He hopes to avenge his father's death through the old magic.

3. *Book of the Cauldron, The* **(Avon, 1999)** Wounded in body and spirit, King Artor summons his mother, the Lady of the Lake, to use the power of the cauldron to heal the land.

4. *Book of the Stone, The* **(Avon, 2000)** While Artor is fighting in Gallia, his illegitimate son, Medraut, plots to seize his crown and his queen, Guendivar.

V. Two novels set in contemporary Berkeley, California, are connected by Del Eden, who is knowledgeable about magic and the power of old legends.

1. *Bringsamen* **(Berkley, 1984)** Berkeley graduate student Karen Ingold finds the beads of a necklace at the bottom of an old chest. When she restrings the beads, she restores the spirit of the Norse goddess Freya.

2. *Paradise Tree, The* **(Berkley, 1987)** Through the medium of a hallucinogenic drug, Ruth Racusak and David Mason are brought into contact with demons, archangels, and other beings from the Judeo-Christian tradition.

Peake, Mervyn

Peake's massive incomplete fantasy, the Gormenghast Trilogy, has cult status among its admirers, and is given a place in the literary pantheon by some critics: Harold Bloom included it in his "Western Canon." However, it isn't for all tastes: the reader must have a liking for grotesque characters and settings. Titus, 77th Earl of Groan and heir to the castle of Gormenghast, is followed through birth, childhood, and youth. The action is set in some uncertain time (the present?) and country (Britain?) amid characters with names like Flay, Swelter, Rottcodd, and Sourdust (the librarian) and in a sprawling castle with baroque and medieval elements and a ritual-ridden routine, all of which give the trilogy a nightmarish quality. The first volume carries Titus only to the age of two. Action picks up in the second volume where Titus fights for his life and inheritance against the Iago-like Steerpike. The third volume, left unfinished by Peake, introduces Titus to the outside world. The trilogy was filmed for British TV in the 1990s. The first two volumes were reissued in 1967 by Weybright & Talley along with the first US printing of number 3. Published in an omnibus volume: *The Gormenghast Trilogy* (Viking, 1988; UK title: *The Titus Books*). Britisher (born of missionary parents in China) Peake was a true eccentric who also wrote poetry and children's books and achieved a reputation as an illustrator. He died in 1968 after a four-year bout with encephalitis.

1. *Titus Groan* **(Reynal, 1946)** Titus, 77th Earl of Groan, is born at Gormenghast, his family home. The austere Flay and the hedonistic cook Swelter vie for control over the household amid age-old ritual presided over by Master of Ritual Barquentine, while the evil scullion Steerpike bides his time.

2. *Gormenghast* **(British Book Center, 1950)** During Titus's childhood years, he becomes increasingly intolerant of the prescribed rituals that confine him, while Steerpike plots to marry Titus's sister Fuchsia and take control of the castle.

3. *Titus Alone* **(Weybright & Talley, 1967)** In this fragment of a novel, Titus is alone in the great world outside of Gormenghast. He has misgivings but continues to strive for understanding and maturity. First published in the United Kingdom in 1959.

Pearce, Mary E.

This lyrical family saga was published in five volumes in the United Kingdom and issued in three volumes in the United States. It focuses on three working-class families living in rural England from the 1880s to the 1940s. The Tewke family are a proud and headstrong lot, from old John (who was disowned by his father when he refused to follow him in the carpentry business) to young Beth (who refuses to marry the man her grandfather has picked out). The farmers who form the Izzard family are mild-mannered but no less staunch in their independence. The luckless Mercybright family rounds out the large cast of characters. Numbers 1 through 3 were published together in one volume as *Apple Tree Lean Down* (St. Martin's, 1976) and *Apple Tree Saga* (MacDonald [UK], 1977).

1. *Apple Tree Lean Down* (MacDonald [UK], 1976) The Tewke family is followed from Beth's girlhood in 1886 to her daughter Betony's 19th year in 1914.
2. *Jack Mercybright* (MacDonald [UK], 1974) Jack Mercybright comes to the Guff farm in 1891 and begins to reclaim the land.
3. *Sorrowing Wind, The* (MacDonald [UK], 1975) Betony Tewke becomes a nurse and falls in love with Michael Andrews. The story continues through World War I.
4. *Land Endures, The* (St. Martin's, 1978) The saga continues through the 1920s as Betony becomes the stern local schoolteacher and newcomers such as the Waymans try their luck at farming.
5. *Seedtime and Harvest* (St. Martin's, 1982) The deteriorating married life of Linn Mercybright and Charlie Truscott is the main theme of this story set in the years just before and during World War II.

Pearce, Michael

I. The Mamur Zapt is Captain Cadwallader Gareth Owen, head of the secret police in British-controlled Cairo, Egypt, circa 1908. Owen's politically sensitive job is more often dedicated to damage control than it is to justice per se. Owen must weave his way through thickets of politically sensitive cases, relations with foreigners, relations between Copts and Muslims, and relations between Egyptians and colonial authorities. The Mamur Zapt mystery series brilliantly evokes a past time and an exotic place. So far the series has carried us to 1914 and the start of World War I. *The Dragoman's Story* (Severn House [UK], 2000) is a nonseries story set in Egypt including historical characters like Florence Nightingale and Gustave Flaubert.

1. *Mamur Zapt and the Return of the Carpet, The* (Doubleday, 1990) A misfired assassination attempt leads to the discovery of a theft of grenades, grenades that will make an unwelcome appearance at the holiday of the Return of the Holy Carpet. Originally published in the United Kingdom in 1988. Variant title: *The Return of the Carpet*.
2. *Mamur Zapt and the Night of the Dog, The* (Doubleday, 1991) A dead dog left on a Coptic grave site leads to the murder of a Muslin dancer and to escalating violence in Cairo. Originally published in the United Kingdom in 1989. Variant title: *The Night of the Dog*.
3. *Mamur Zapt and the Donkey-Vous, The* (Mysterious, 1992) The Mamur Zapt must investigate the disappearances of European visitors from the terrace of Shepheard's Hotel. Originally published in the United Kingdom in 1990. Variant title: *The Donkey-Vous*.
4. *Mamur Zapt and the Men Behind, The* (Mysterious, 1993) After Egyptians and English visitors complain about being followed, a Customs official is shot at, and two students are killed by a café

bomb explosion. Originally published in the United Kingdom in 1991. Variant title: *The Men Behind*.
5. *Mamur Zapt and the Girl in the Nile, The* (Mysterious, 1994) The body of a young woman connected to the heir of Egypt's throne is found washed up on the banks of the Nile. Originally published in the United Kingdom in 1992. Variant title: *The Girl in the Nile*.
6. *Mamur Zapt and the Spoils of Egypt, The* (Mysterious, 1995) Miss Skinner, an influential young American woman, is asking embarrassing questions about the illegal trade in Egyptian antiquities. Originally published in the United Kingdom in 1993. Variant title: *The Spoils of Egypt*.
7. *Camel of Destruction, The* (Poisoned Pen, 2003) Owen becomes enmeshed in a homicide investigation when a Ministry of Agriculture employee is found dead at his desk. Originally published in the United Kingdom in 1993.
8. *Snake Catcher's Daughter, The* (Poisoned Pen, 2003) The Mamur Zapt finds a naked woman in his bed and a mysterious necklace in this girlfriend's boudoir, while the deputy commandant of police disappears after secretly attending a mysterious women-only exorcism rite Originally published in the United Kingdom in 1994.
9. *Mingrelian Conspiracy, The* (Poisoned Pen, 2003) Gangs of extortionists threatening the café owners of Cairo and the impending visit of a Russian grand duke engage the Mamur Zapt here. Originally published in the United Kingdom in 1995.
10. *Fig Tree Murder, The* (Poisoned Pen, 2003) A corpse is discovered on an unfinished piece of railroad track linking Cairo to a new city under development. Originally published in the United Kingdom in 1996.
11. *Last Cut, The* (Poisoned Pen, 2004) Owen is called in when one of Cairo's main dams is sabotaged by a bomb on the eve of the Cut, when the waters of the Nile are released to irrigate the crops. Originally published in the United Kingdom in 1998.
12. *Death of an Effendi* (Poisoned Pen, 2004) Owen is asked to guard Russian financier Tvardovsky during a shooting party for potential Egyptian investors. Originally published in the United Kingdom in 1999.
13. *Cold Touch of Ice, A* (Poisoned Pen, 2004) In 1912 a man named Morelli is murdered. Is this a case of ethnic cleansing? Originally published in the United Kingdom in 2000.
14. *Face in the Cemetery, The* (Poisoned Pen, 2006) The year is 1914. The World War has begun. The Mamur Zapt is given the complicated task of rounding up "enemy aliens." Originally published in the United Kingdom in 2001.
15. *Point in the Market, The* (Poisoned Pen, 2005) Owen, who has married his longtime lover, Zenaib, the pasha's daughter, is occupied with a spy providing intelligence to the Turks, several suspicious fires, and the murder of an informant.
16. *Mark of the Pasha, The* (Poisoned Pen, 2008) In 1918 Owen and his team begin an investigation to trace the bombers who tried to bomb a procession led by the Khedive.

II. Two novels, not published in the United States, are set in 1890s Russia. Their hero is Dmitri Kameron, of Scottish Russian descent, a lawyer who tries to take advantage of the fledgling reforms in the Czarist legal system.

1. *Dmitri and the Milk-Drinkers* (HarperCollins [UK], 1997) Russian courthouse officials have "lost" a beautiful young woman.
2. *Dmitri and the One-Legged Lady* (HarperCollins [UK], 1999) The "One-Legged Lady" is an important icon that has gone missing.

III. Seymour of Special Branch is a new series set in British embassies and consulates in the early 1900s.

1. *Dead Man in Trieste, A* **(Carroll & Graf, 2004)** In 1906 the British xonsul in Trieste, the Austro-Hungarian Empire's most important seaport, is missing.
2. *Dead Man in Istanbul, A* **(Carroll & Graf, 2005)** The second secretary of the embassy in 1908 Istanbul winds up with a bullet in his head when he attempts to swim the Dardanelles Straits.
3. *Dead Man in Tangier, A* **(Carroll & Graf, 2007)** Tangier, 1912. Seymour investigates a murder in the North African city.
4. *Dead Man in Athens, A* **(Carroll & Graf, 2006)** Athens, 1913. A cat belonging to the exiled former Ottoman sultan is poisoned. A tune-up for an attempt on the sultan?
4. *Dead Man in Barcelona, A* **(Soho, 2008)** Seymour goes to Barcelona to investigate a cold case—the death, while in a Spanish prison, of an English businessman.

Pears, Ian

Jonathan Argyll is a British art historian and art dealer in Rome. Jonathan is a rather diffident and incompetent fellow outside of his area of expertise, but fortunately the beautiful and resourceful Flavia di Stefano of the Italian National Art Theft Fund is usually on hand to bail him out of trouble. Pears, who has a doctorate in art history from Cambridge University, writes mysterious full of interesting characters, art lore, and playful satire on the art world. Pears has also published two historical mystery novels: the highly regarded *An Instance of the Fingerpost* (Riverhead, 1997), set in 17th-century Oxford, *The Dream of Scipio* (Riverhead, 2002), which covers 1500 years of history, and *The Portrait* (Riverhead, 2005), set in early 20th-century Brittany.

1. *Raphael Affair, The* **(Harcourt, 1992)** An unknown Raphael is smuggled out of Rome hidden under a painting by a second-rate artist.
2. *Titian Committee, The* **(Harcourt, 1993)** An American art historian, a British art collector, and a French art philosopher are murdered by different means and in different places, but there seems to be a connection.
3. *Bernini Bust, The* **(Harcourt, 1994)** Jonathan travels to Los Angeles to deliver a Titian to a private museum and gets involved with a Bernini bust of Pope Pius V and murder.
4. *Last Judgement, The* **(Scribner, 1996)** When Jonathan agrees to hand-deliver a small, undistinguished painting from a Paris art dealer to a Roman buyer, someone tries to steal the painting, two people are murdered, and the French authorities claim that the painting is stolen goods.
5. *Giotto's Hand* **(Scribner, 1997)** Argyll and Flavia di Stefano move through Italy and England on the trail of an art thief nicknamed "Giotto."
6. *Death and Restoration* **(Scribner, 1998)** Jonathan and Flavia investigate the theft of a seemingly worthless iconic painting of the Madonna from the monastery of San Giovanni and the apparently related attack on the head monk.
7. *Immaculate Deception, The* **(Scribner, 2000)** Flavia, now wed to Jonathan and acting head of the art-theft squad, is asked by the Italian prime minister to recover a Claude Lorraine landscape stolen from an Italian museum while on loan from the Louvre.

Pearson, Ridley

Sergeant (later Lieutenant) Lou Boldt and forensic pathologist Daphne Matthews are two of the leading lights of the Seattle Police Department in this series of thrillers by suspense novelist and screenplay writer (*Probable Cause*) Ridley Pearson. Pearson's investigators get mixed up in some messy cases and some messy personal relationships, but the medical detail is well done, the protagonists are sympathetic, and the plots are well-balanced cliff-hangers. Pearson is the coauthor, with Dave Barry, of two prequels to J. M. Barrie's (q.v.) *Peter Pan*.

1. *Undercurrents* **(St. Martin's, 1988)** The Cross Killer is supposed to be dead, but he still seems to be at work killing and mutilating new victims.
2. *Angel Maker, The* **(Delacorte, 1993)** Lou Boldt comes out of early retirement to help stop the "harvesting" of human organs from teenage runaways for sale on the black market.
3. *No Witnesses* **(Hyperion, 1994)** Someone is tampering with Adler Foods Corporation products, leaving a string of dead innocents paying for alleged wrongdoing by the company in the past.
4. *Beyond Recognition* **(Hyperion, 1996)** Boldt and Matthews have to profile a serial killer who uses rocket fuel to torch his female victims.
5. *Pied Piper, The* **(Hyperion, 1998)** When the serial kidnapper called the Pied Piper targets Seattle, Boldt's daughter becomes one of the victims.
6. *First Victim, The* **(Hyperion, 1999)** Lieutenant Boldt misses street work but gets involved when a gang smuggling illegal Chinese immigrant women into Seattle adds murder to their repertoire.
7. *Middle of Nowhere* **(Hyperion, 2000)** Lieutenant Boldt remains on the job when "blu flu" hits the Seattle PD. A strange series of burglaries, which have resulted in serious injuries to police personnel, may be connected with the police union or with career criminal Bryce Abbot Flek, who has a grudge against Boldt.
8. *Art of Deception, The* **(Hyperion, 2002)** Forensic pathologist Daphne Matthews and "stud" cop John La Moia investigate the murder of a woman who was pushed off a bridge, in a case that takes them through Seattle's strange "underground."
9. *Body of David Hayes, The* **(Hyperion, 2004)** Boldt has to protect his wife's reputation and save their marriage when her former coworker and lover, convicted embezzler David Hayes, gets out of jail, the $17 million he had stolen still unaccounted for.

Pearson, T(homas) R(eid)

I. The fictional town of Neely, North Carolina (near T. R. Pearson's hometown of Winston-Salem), has been recognized as a microcosm of the American South. The tales of the Pettigrews, Throckmortons, Eppersons, and Jetters, narrated by young Louis Benfield, are told in the tradition of southern storytelling. Pearson's prose, like William Faulkner's (q.v.), can be daunting to the timid or lazy reader, but there are comic riches and a subtle sadness lying within his meandering narratives. Pearson has been compared not only to Faulkner but also to Garrison Keillor (q.v.) and Dave Barry.

1. *Short History of a Small Place, A* **(Simon & Schuster, 1985)** The story of Miss Myra Angelique Pettigrew, of good family, beautiful, elegant, but quite insane.
2. *Off for the Sweet Hereafter* **(Simon & Schuster, 1986)** Concerning the death of the bald Mrs. Jeeter (not the fat Mrs. Jeeter), an expedition to rebury the local dead before a new dam dampens their eternal rest, and a passionate love affair.
3. *Last of How It Was, The* **(Simon & Schuster, 1987)** Louis Benfield traces his family back to the Civil War in this meandering chronicle of the pursuit of a stolen Chevrolet.
4. *Call and Response* **(Simon & Schuster, 1989)** Miss Mary Alice Celestine Lefler arrives from Berkeley Springs and captivates the imaginations of the male population of Neely.

5. *Glad News of the Natural World* **(Simon & Schuster, 2005)** Louis Benfield returns, after a publishing hiatus of 16 years, but to New York City rather than Neely. His first real job is at Meridian Life and Casualty, where he proceeds to work his way down.

II. Pearson has (for now) abandoned Neely, North Carolina, for the (greener?) pastures of Appalachian Virginia, where he now resides. *Gospel Hour* (Morrow, 1991) and *Cry Me a River* (Holt, 1993) are both located in Virginia but seem to be stand-alones. Pearson's latest three novels have as protagonists members of the Tatum family: deputy sheriff Ray Tatum of Hogarth, Virginia, and his cousin, actuary Paul Tatum of Roanoke, Virginia; Manhattan; and points beyond. Although each volume has a mystery embedded somewhere in the plot, the Virginia cycle is characterized by Pearson's idiosyncratic prose, digressions, and irreverent but insightful portrayals of the denizens of the small-town South.

1. *Blue Ridge* **(Viking, 2000)** Ray Tatum, new sheriff's deputy in Hogarth, Virginia, gets involved, along with Kit Carson, his African American park ranger girlfriend, in a murder investigation, while his cousin, actuary Paul Tatum, is called to Manhattan to identify the corpse of a son he never knew.
2. *Polar* **(Viking, 2001)** Ray Tatum and his off-again, on-again lover, Kit Carson, get involved in the case of a missing child and town recluse Clayton who becomes a "seer" named Titus after spending most of his time watching porno movies on this TV satellite dish.
3. *True Cross* **(Viking, 2003)** Paul Tatum, back in Virginia, is dating Mona, a predatory divorced single mother, while lusting after Maud Hooper, a local housewife married to a brutal Mafia-connected lawyer.

Pelecanos, George P.

I. Readers who like fiction with evil characters, graphic violence, lacerating views of urban angst colored with the noirest hues of crime fiction will love George Pelecanos's novels featuring Nick Stefanos, bartender, alcoholic, former sales manager, and sometime detective in the Washington, DC, that tourists never see. *Shoedog* (St. Martin's, 1994), *Drama City* (Little, Brown, 2005), and *The Night Gardener* (Little, Brown, 2006) have the same location and the same tone but different protagonists. Nick's father, also named Nick, appears as a character in series II, number 1, and Nick himself has a bit part in series II, number 4.

1. *Firing Offense, A* **(St. Martin's, 1992)** Jimmy Broda, stock boy at the electronics firm where Nick Stefanos works, is hanging out with skinheads, and Nick is asked by Jimmy's grandfather to find him.
2. *Nick's Trip* **(St. Martin's, 1993)** Nick is tending bar when a former buddy named Billy turns up and announces that his wife and $200,000 belonging to a numbers runner are missing.
3. *Down by the River Where the Dead Men Go* **(St. Martin's, 1995)** On a bender and nearly passed out, Nick overhears a murder being committed and sets out to find the killers.

II. All of Washington, DC, native Pelecanos's novels are set in or near the nation's capital, a Washington that, as portrayed by Pelecanos, has become more and more of an urban basket case since World War II. The DC Quartet features an interracial friendship, over a period of 50 years (1945–1995), between Dmitri "Pete" Karras and Marcus Clay. Pete, who starts the series as an enforcer, finds that he isn't hardhearted enough and drifts from job to job while supplementing his

income by dealing in pot. African American Marcus owns a series of slum record shops but isn't above a little dealing himself. Both characters are survivors who managed to preserve a certain personal decency in the middle of a blasted urban landscape. Nick Stephanos (series I) appears in number 4, which is a kind of summing-up of Pelecanos's fiction up to 2000. "Nick Stephanos," presumably his father, is a character in number 1.

1. *Big Blowdown, The* **(St. Martin's, 1996)** Washington 1945. Pete Karras and Joey Recedo both work for Mr. Burke's protection racket as enforcers, but Pete proves to be a little too soft-hearted. The pair confronts each other three years later.
2. *King Suckerman* **(Little, Brown, 1997)** Washington 1970s. *King Suckerman* is the blaxploitation film being shown at the drive-in where natural-born-killer Wilton Cooper meets up with his perfect partner. Meanwhile, Dmitri Karras and Vietnam vet Marcus Clay are trying to make a go of small-time business and drug dealing.
3. *Sweet Forever, The* **(Little, Brown, 1998)** Washington 1986. Clay and Karras witness a grisly car accident and the theft of drug money from the car by a suburbanite in town to purchase "supplies" from Dmitri.
4. *Shame the Devil* **(Little, Brown, 2000)** Washington 1995. Several people are killed in what should have been a routine pizza joint robbery. Dmitri's infant son is run over by the getaway car, and the driver of the car is killed by police. Three years later, gunman Frank Farrow, brother of the thug who was killed, is back in town and seeking revenge.

III. Pelecanos's latest series features another black-and-white team in Washington. African American Derek Strange and Irish Catholic Terry Quinn formed a partnership as private investigators after they confronted each other in a cop-killing case during the riots following the assassination of Martin Luther King Jr. in 1968. Derek Strange is the more fully realized character of the two, but, again, the crumbling city of Washington is the real protagonist.

1. *Hard Revolution* **(Little, Brown, 2004)** In this prequel, rookie policeman Derek Strange and Terry Quinn come together when Quinn is accused of killing a black cop during the 1968 riots in the aftermath of the Martin Luther King Jr. slaying.
2. *Right as Rain* **(Little, Brown, 2001)** When the nine-year-old quarterback of the peewee football team he coaches is shot and killed, Derek finds himself up against Washington's flourishing drug trade and the nation's most poorly trained and dangerous police force.
3. *Hell to Pay* **(Little, Brown, 2002)** A crooked cop, a missing 14-year-old girl from the suburbs turned hooker, and a victim mowed down by bullets intended for someone else engage Derek here.
3. *Soul Circus* **(Little, Brown, 2003)** Strange is hired by lawyers defending high-profile drug dealer Granvile Oliver, facing death row, and confronts the gun-dealer Ulysses Foreman, who is supplying the firearms Washington's ghetto kids are using against each other.

Pelletier, Cathie

Mattagash, Maine, sounds somewhat like Carolyn Chute's (q.v.) Egypt, Maine, and countless other fictional small towns. The people of Mattagash are generally "mean, undereducated, bored, gossipy, and oversexed," but they are entertaining to read about because of Cathie Pelletier's writing skills, her ear for dialogue, her humor, and her insider knowledge of her characters and settings. Pelletier, a native of

Allagash, Maine, went to Nashville to become a songwriter and has stayed there ever since. *The Bubble Reputation* (Crown, 1993) and *A Marriage Made at Woodstock* (Crown, 1994) are also set in Maine, but not in Mattagash.

1. *Funeral Makers, The* (Macmillan, 1986) In 1959 the McKinnon family is gathering to prepare for the death of Marge, whose 30-year diet of tea and rice has led to a terminal case of beriberi.
2. *Once upon a Time on the Banks* (Viking, 1989) Events taking place in 1969 center upon the impending marriage of Amy Joy Lawler and Jean-Claude Cloutier, a French-Canadian who has trouble with the English language.
3. *Weight of Winter, The* (Viking, 1991) Years later Amy is still single and faced with the problem of institutionalizing her mother, while 107-year-old Mathilda Fennelson reminisces about early settlers in Mattagash.
4. *Beaming Sonny Home* (Crown, 1996) Mattie Gifford's wayward son, Sonny, makes the national media when he takes two women and a dog hostage in his ex-wife's trailer.

Pence, Joanne

Angie Amalfi, food columnist and gourmet cook in San Francisco, has two major passions: a desire to come up with a scheme or job that will bring in money and her homicide detective boyfriend, Paavo Smith. Well, three, actually: she can't seem to keep her nose out of the murder investigations that all too often come her way in this series, which combines humor, romance, food, and recipes. San Francisco native and UC Berkeley grad Joanne Pence, who now lives north of Boise, Idaho, states that she is *not* a gourmet cook herself.

1. *Something's Cooking* (Avon, 1993) After a man who has been contributing recipes to her food column ends up dead, Angie Amalfi gets enmeshed with gun runners and food fanatics.
2. *Too Many Cooks* (Avon, 1994) As her romance with SF homicide detective, Paavo Smith, heats up, Angie talks her way into a job on a chef's radio call-in show.
3. *Cooking Up Trouble* (Avon, 1995) Angie receives some ominous threats at the new inn in northern California where she is working on the menu.
4. *Cooking Most Deadly* (Avon, 1996) Paavo is searching for the murderer of two San Francisco women. Doing a magazine survey, Angie finds a small restaurant with great food and three grumpy old men as proprietors.
5. *Cook's Night Out* (Avon, 1998) Angie, working on "angelinas," destined to be the perfect chocolate confection, donates the rejects to the Random Acts of Kindness Mission, which may be harboring someone more sinister than the usual poor souls.
6. *Cooks Overboard* (Avon, 1998) Angie and Paavo's cruise to Acapulco is fraught with incident: a cook tries to jump overboard, Paavo behaves oddly, the food is terrible, and murder is committed.
7. *Cook in Time, A* (Avon, 1999) Angie's first and only client for her "Fantasy Dinners" scheme is the Prometheus Group, a bunch of UFO-chasers and government conspiracy addicts.
8. *To Catch a Cook* (Avon, 2000) Angie is working on a video restaurant review scheme. Paavo starts brooding about the mother who abandoned him at four years of age when the one piece of jewelry she left behind disappears.
9. *Bell, Cook and Candle* (Avon, 2002) Angie, who seems to be having a success with her "comical cakes," delivers some to an after-hours goth club that might have a link with some ritual murders Paavo is investigating.

10. *If Cooks Could Kill* (Avon, 2003) Angie tries to pair up her best friend, Connie, with a handsome pro football player, who happens to be related to the owner of Angie's favorite Italian restaurant. But Connie is more interested in a sleazy boyfriend, who gets her into big trouble.
11. *Two Cooks A-Killing* (Avon, 2003) Angie is planning a banquet for a Christmas reunion special for the cast of the soap opera *Eagle Crest* when a corpse turns up at the mansion where the show was originally filmed.
12. *Courting Disaster* (Avon, 2004) Angie is disturbed by a few things: her control-freak mother is planning the party for her engagement to Paavo, and her neighbor Stan is infatuated with a very pregnant kitchen helper at a nearby Greek restaurant.
13. *Red Hot Murder* (Avon, 2006) Angie and Paavo are staying at the Ghost Hollow Guest Ranch in Jackpot, Arizona, when Angie's friend, Ned Paulson, manages to get himself bashed on the head.
14. *Da Vinci Cook, The* (Avon, 2007) Angie goes to Rome to help her sister clear her name in a complex murder case.

Pendleton, Don(ald Eugene)

I.   In Mack Bolan, "the Executioner," Pendleton created the quintessential vigilante hero. Mack, a guerilla warfare specialist who served in Vietnam, obsessively drives around the United States (and some places abroad) in his "war-wagon"—described in detail in the nonfiction *The Executioner's War Book* (Pinnacle, 1977)—looking for enemies of American society to mow down with his assortment of weapons (especially the AutoMag, a .44 Automatic Magnum, the world's most powerful handgun). The original target was the Mafia, who were responsible for killing most of Bolan's family and, from time to time, his girlfriends. After one final orgy of killing mafiosos described in "the last mile" (numbers 33–38), Mack accepts a position (and a full pardon for his extralegal activities) in a government counterterrorist unit. Many of the Executioner books published after 1980 have Don Pendleton's name attached to them, but Pendleton (d. 1995) had little or nothing to do with writing them. Appealing to what seems to be a basic instinct (blast your troubles away) in most red-blooded American males and many red-blooded American females, the Executioner series had great mass appeal, but because they were published in paperback-only editions, few of them turned up in libraries until libraries started carrying "mass-market" paperback books. William H. Young has written a book about the Executioner series: *A Study of Action-Adventure Fiction: The Executioner and Mack Bolan* (Mellen, 1996). Don Pendleton was a US Navy veteran and engineer who worked with NASA and was a senior editor and columnist for *Orion* magazine. As "Stephan Gregory" he wrote several Mickey Spillane–type novels and a series of sex self-help books in the 1960s. The Executioner novels, which are pretty much the same except for degrees of intensity, are listed without annotations. Bolan novels published after 1980 are not listed.

1. *War against the Mafia* (Pinnacle, 1969)
2. *Death Squad* (Pinnacle, 1969)
3. *Battle Mask* (Pinnacle, 1970)
4. *Miami Massacre* (Pinnacle, 1970)
5. *Continental Contract* (Pinnacle, 1971)
6. *Assault on Soho* (Pinnacle, 1971)
7. *Nightmare in New York* (Pinnacle, 1971)
8. *Chicago Wipe-Out* (Pinnacle, 1971)
9. *Vegas Vendetta* (Pinnacle, 1971)
10. *Caribbean Kill* (Pinnacle, 1972)
11. *California Hit* (Pinnacle, 1972)
12. *Boston Blitz* (Pinnacle, 1972)

13. *Washington IOU* (Pinnacle, 1972)
14. *San Diego Siege* (Pinnacle, 1972)
15. *Panic in Philly* (Pinnacle, 1973)
16. *Sicilian Slaughter* (Pinnacle, 1973) Written by William Crawford as "Jim Peterson."
17. *Jersey Guns* (Pinnacle, 1974)
18. *Texas Storm* (Pinnacle, 1974)
19. *Detroit Deathwatch* (Pinnacle, 1974)
20. *New Orleans Knockout* (Pinnacle, 1974)
21. *Firebase Seattle* (Pinnacle, 1975)
22. *Hawaiian Hellground* (Pinnacle, 1975)
23. *Canadian Crisis* (Pinnacle, 1975)
24. *St. Louis Showdown* (Pinnacle, 1975)
25. *Colorado Kill-Zone* (Pinnacle, 1976)
26. *Acapulco Rampage* (Pinnacle, 1976)
27. *Dixie Convoy* (Pinnacle, 1976)
28. *Savage Fire* (Pinnacle, 1977)
29. *Command Strike* (Pinnacle, 1977) Coauthored by Mike Newton and Stephen Mertz.
30. *Cleveland Pipeline* (Pinnacle, 1977) Coauthored with Mike Newton and Stephen Mertz.
31. *Arizona Ambush* (Pinnacle, 1977)
32. *Tennessee Smash* (Pinnacle, 1978) Cowritten with Mike Newton.
33. *Monday's Mob* (Pinnacle, 1978)
34. *Terrible Tuesday* (Pinnacle, 1979)
35. *Wednesday's Wrath* (Pinnacle, 1979)
36. *Thermal Thursday* (Pinnacle, 1979)
37. *Friday's Feast* (Pinnacle, 1979)
38. *Satan's Sabbath* (Pinnacle, 1980)

II. The Joe Copp adventures, about a Los Angeles private eye, written in neo–Mickey Spillane Mike Hammer mode, lacked the intensity of the Executioner series and were never as popular, but since they were published in hardcover, they are more likely to be found in public libraries. Not much angst but plenty of action, sex, and violence in these thrillers, which are to be taken about as seriously as Rambo movies.

1. *Copp for Hire* (Fine, 1987) Copp follows a string of corpses from LA to Honolulu, meeting up with a Chinese vice lord, a beautiful but dangerous woman, a kinky politician, and some nasty policemen.
2. *Copp on Fire* (Fine, 1988) Copp's new case takes him to the back lots of Hollywood, police stakeouts, the near death of a narcotics officer, and plenty of killing.
3. *Copp in Deep* (Fine, 1989) Old friend Tom Chase, security chief at a defense contractor, hires to Copp to check out an FBI sting operation aimed at the firm.
4. *Copp in the Dark* (Fine, 1990) Copp is shot at, stripped, and chained to a naked woman before he even agrees to take on the case of a murdered leading man!
5. *Copp on Ice* (Fine, 1991) Corpses pile up as Copp takes on the job of acting police chief in the town of Brighton, California.
6. *Copp in Shock* (Fine, 1992) Copp wakes up in a hospital suffering from amnesia and a gunshot wound.

III. A third series created by Pendleton featured Ashton Ford, an adventurer with psychic powers. The series never caught on and was dropped after six paperback originals, of which some were probably not written by Pendleton.

1. *Ashes to Ashes* (Warner, 1986)
2. *Eye to Eye* (Warner, 1986)
3. *Mind to Mind* (Warner, 1987)
4. *Life to Life* (Warner, 1987)
5. *Heart to Heart* (Warner, 1987)
6. *Time to Time* (Warner, 1987)

Penman, Sharon Kay

I. Historical novelist Penman's trilogy is set in 13th-century Wales and England, and features the clash of such historical characters as Llewelyn ap Gruffyd, Simon de Montfort, King John, Edward I and Henry III over the fate of Wales and the English throne. Penman writes well-researched, informative, and enjoyable historical fiction. Edith Pargeter (q.v.) covered much the same ground in her Brothers of Gwynedd quartet.

1. *Here Be Dragons* (Holt, 1985) Llewelyn, Prince of Wales, is King John of England's opponent, and Joanna, daughter of the former and wife of the latter is caught in the middle.
2. *Falls the Shadow* (Holt, 1988) The inept King Henry III is opposed by Llewelyn and Simon de Montfort, who are working toward different ends, but are united in their opposition to the English throne.
3. *Reckoning, The* (Holt, 1991) In 1272 the wily and determined Edward I succeeds Henry III, which spells trouble for the Welsh and Simon de Montfort's children.

II. A second trilogy, of which two novels have been published, is a historical prequel to series I. It takes place in the 12th century. The first volume covers the civil war between the Empress Maude and her cousin Stephen of Blois for the succession to the English throne held by Henry I. The second volume covers the reign of Henry II and Henry's ill-fated clash with Thomas Becket. Maude and Henry's Queen, Eleanor of Acquitaine are strong female characters, and there are a number of fictional characters, such as Maude's illegitimate half brother Ranulf. The third volume hasn't been published yet.

1. *When Christ and His Saints Slept* (Holt, 1995) "Christ and His Saints Slept" according to the Peterborough chronicler of the *Anglo-Saxon Chronicle*. The miseries of civil war are depicted in the struggle between Maude, Henry I's daughter and Stephen of Blois, who becomes King Stephen (1135–1154).
2. *Time and Chance* (Putnam, 2002) Henry II, with the help of Queen Eleanor and Thomas Becket, restores some stability to the English throne, but Henry falls out with both Eleanor and Thomas.

III. Penman's third series is a historical mystery series set in 12th-century England and Wales. Its protagonist is Justin de Quincy, illegitimate but educated son of a bishop, who becomes a special agent for Queen Eleanor of Acquitaine, acting as regent for the crusading Richard I (Lionheart), aiding her in her struggles against the machinations of Richard's ambitious brother John.

1. *Queen's Man, The* (Holt, 1986) In 1193 King Richard is missing on his way back from the Crusades. A goldsmith is murdered, but his letters intended for Queen Eleanor are located by Justin de Quincy, illegitimate son of a prelate.
2. *Cruel as the Grave* (Holt, 1998) Richard is a captive of the Holy Roman Emperor. Justin, special agent for Queen Eleanor, is asked to investigate the death of a young Welsh girl.
3. *Dragon's Lair* (Putnam, 2003) Eleanor sends Justin to Wales to recover a stolen treasure cache with which she hopes to ransom her son Richard before his brother John seizes the throne.
4. *Prince of Darkness* (Putnam, 2005) Prince John, scheming to replace his absent brother Richard on the throne, gets implicated in an obscure conspiracy aiming at assassination.

Percy, Walker

I. *The Moviegoer*, Walker Percy's first published novel, won the National Book Award in 1962. That book and all of his subsequent novels are set in the American South and take as their theme the moral and existential problems unique to modern times. His characters feel uncomfortable in a technological world devoid of spiritual values, and their search for meaning usually leads them to religion, particularly Roman Catholicism. Percy (d. 1990) had an ability to make philosophical questions take on flesh and become real and understandable to the average reader. His inventive plots, satirical eye for current mannerisms, and accessible prose add to his appeal. Williston Bibb Barrett, protagonist of two novels by Percy, is seen at two points in his life. He is deeply unhappy in the New South, an affluent society with no spiritual roots to which he can relate.

1. *Last Gentleman, The* (Farrar, 1966) At 25 young Will Barrett returns to the South suffering from amnesia and loss of identity.
2. *Second Coming, The* (Farrar, 1980) Will Barrett, now middle-aged, widowed, and wealthy, suffers from attacks of heightened memory that return him to his unhappy past.

II. Percy wrote two novels featuring Dr. Tom More, a descendant of the sainted Thomas. Dr. More is a psychiatrist and lapsed Catholic who fights social engineering in an America of the near future. Percy adds fantasy and suspense to his usual mix.

1. *Love in the Ruins* (Farrar, 1971) Subtitle: *The Adventures of a Bad Catholic at a Time near the End of the World*, this tells of Dr. Tom More's invention of a device that will measure "the perturbations of the soul."
2. *Thanatos Syndrome, The* (Farrar, 1987) Newly released from prison, Dr. Tom detects a scheme by a group of psychiatrists to eliminate antisocial behavior by putting tranquilizers in the local water supply.

Perry, Anne

I. The revelation that Anne Perry had been involved in a murder in her youth in New Zealand, unwelcome to the author as it may have been, didn't diminish interest in her crime fictions. Perry is a master at setting the scenes for her Victorian mysteries. Her longest-running series in set in late Victorian London and figures Inspector Thomas Pitt of Scotland Yard and his wife, Charlotte. The gentle-mannered but brilliant Pitt is complemented by the shrewd, intuitive Charlotte in a nicely evoked London in the 1880s. Series VI (below) is a spin-off in which characters from the Pitt novels, including Lady Vespasia Cumming-Gould, appear.

1. *Cater Street Hangman, The* (St. Martin's, 1979) The conventional upper-middle-class lives of young Charlotte and Emily Ellison are disrupted when one of their servant girls becomes a victim in a series of stranglings.
2. *Callander Square* (St. Martin's, 1980) Charlotte and Emily get involved with Inspector Pitt's investigation of infanticide in posh Callander Square.
3. *Paragon Walk* (St. Martin's, 1981) The fashionable London neighborhood of Paragon Walk is terrorized by a rapist-killer.
4. *Resurrection Row* (St. Martin's, 1981) Someone is digging up the corpses of recently deceased Londoners and depositing them in public places.
5. *Rutland Place* (St. Martin's, 1983) A lost trinket at the Rutland Place home of Charlotte's parents leads to an investigation of theft, blackmail, and murder.
6. *Bluegate Fields* (St. Martin's, 1984) A young tutor is the prime suspect in the bathtub murder of a teenager from a wealthy family.
7. *Death in the Devil's Acre* (St. Martin's, 1985) A slum neighborhood near Westminster Abbey is the scene of a series of murders and emasculations.
8. *Cardington Crescent* (St. Martin's, 1987) Emily Ashworth is suspected of poisoning her philandering husband, George.
9. *Silence in Hanover Close* (St. Martin's, 1988) Charlotte and Emily aid Inspector Pitt in the investigation of the murder of British diplomat Robert Yorke.
10. *Bethlehem Road* (St. Martin's, 1990) Three antisuffragist members of Parliament have had their throats cut while crossing Westminster Bridge.
11. *Highgate Rise* (Fawcett, 1991) The arson slaying of Clemency Shaw may be related to her exposes of slum housing owned by the rich and powerful.
12. *Belgrave Square* (Fawcett, 1992) When usurer William Weems is killed by one his gold coins fired from a gun, his blackmailing activities are exposed.
13. *Farriers' Lane* (Fawcett, 1993) When Appeals Court Justice Samuel Stafford tries to reopen the case of the young Jewish actor executed for a murder he may not have committed, he himself is murdered.
14. *Hyde Park Headsman, The* (Fawcett, 1994) The decapitated corpse of Oakley Winthrop, a naval captain from a titled family, is found in Hyde Park.
15. *Traitors Gate* (Fawcett, 1995) Pitt is inclined to agree with his friend Matthew Desmond that the death of the latter's father from a laudanum overdose was not suicide.
16. *Pentecost Alley* (Fawcett, 1996) A prostitute is found ritually murdered and a Hellfire Club badge is found underneath her body.
17. *Ashworth Hall* (Fawcett, 1997) In an effort to resolve the nettlesome issue of Irish Home Rule, a group of Irish Catholics and Protestants have gathered together at Ashworth Hall.
18. *Brunswick Gardens* (Fawcett, 1998) One of three devout men in a mansion in Brunswick Gardens is probably responsible for the death of beautiful, pregnant Darwinist Unity Bellwood.
19. *Bedford Square* (Ballantine, 1999) A man is found murdered on the doorstep of a house in Bedford Square.
20. *Half Moon Street* (Ballantine, 2000) A dead man in a green gown is found chained to a punt floating down the Thames.
21. *Whitechapel Conspiracy, The* (Ballantine, 2001) In the wake of the sentencing of a distinguished soldier for murder, Pitt is demoted and forced to work undercover in the dangerous East End section.
22. *Southampton Row* (Ballantine, 2002) Charles Voisy, member of the Inner Circle, is standing for election to Parliament, and it is up to Pitt to expose his corrupt activities.
23. *Seven Dials* (Ballantine, 2003) A murdered diplomat has been found in a wheelbarrow in a garden belonging to a beautiful and mysterious Egyptian woman.
24. *Long Spoon Lane* (Ballantine, 2005) Unknown anarchists are responsible for a bombing in protest of high-level police corruption.
25. *Africa Passage* (Headline [UK], 2007) A maid is murdered at Buckingham Palace, presumably by one of a group of houseguests discussing the funding of the Cape to Cairo railway.

26. **Buckingham Palace Gardens** (Ballantine, 2008) The Prince of Wales becomes a suspect when a prostitute's mutilated corpse is found in a Buckingham Palace cupboard.

II. Another mystery series is set in the London of the 1850s. The troubled, self-despising amnesiac William Monk is fired from the police because of his overly sensitive conscience, and sets up as a private "inquiry agent." He is aided by Hester Latterly, a nurse who served with Florence Nightingale in the Crimean War. Hester and William eventually marry. Justice Sir Oliver Rathbone sometimes engages Monk when he wants to get to the bottom of a case he feels uneasy about. *The William Monk Mysteries* (Ballantine, 2005) is an omnibus volume containing numbers 1 through 3.

1. **Face of a Stranger, The** (Fawcett, 1990) Inspector Monk, trying to conceal his case of amnesia, is assigned to investigate the murder of an aristocratic Crimean War veteran.

2. **Dangerous Mourning, A** (Fawcett, 1991) The murder of Octavia Haslett, found stabbed to death in her bedroom, was an inside job according to Monk.

3. **Defend and Betray** (Fawcett, 1992) Military hero Thaddeus Carlyon is pushed from the top of a staircase and impaled on a suit of armor.

4. **Sudden Fearful Death, A** (Fawcett, 1993) A London hospital nurse is strangled, and Monk is engaged by Lady Callandra Daviot to find the killer.

5. **Sins of the Wolf** (Fawcett, 1994) Hester Latterly faces murder charges when an elderly patient is given a fatal dose of digitalis and her pearl brooch finds its way into Hester's bag.

6. **Cain His Brother** (Fawcett, 1995) Monk is hired by Genevieve Stonefield, whose husband is missing, possibly murdered by his evil twin.

7. **Weighed in the Balance** (Fawcett, 1996) When Prince Friedrich is murdered, Countess Zorah Rostova blames his morganatic wife, Gisela, for the crime.

8. **Silent Cry, The** (Fawcett, 1997) Prominent solicitor Leigh Duff is found beaten to death in the unsavory Water Lane district. Duff's son Rhys is found dead beside him, but evidence seems to point toward Rhys guilt in his father's death.

9. **Breach of Promise, A** (Ballantine, 1998) The sensational breach-of-promise case brought by Zillah Lambert against William Melville leads to murder. UK title: *The Whited Sepulchres*.

10. **Twisted Root, The** (Ballantine, 1999) Miriam Gardiner makes a sudden exit from a party at the home of her fiancé and disappears.

11. **Slaves of Obsession** (Ballantine, 2000) A theft, a ritual murder, some disappearances, and a shady arms dealer are the subjects here.

12. **Funeral in Blue, A** (Ballantine, 2001) When two women are found strangled in the studio of a London artist, the artist's husband, Dr. Kristian Beck, is the chief suspect.

13. **Death of a Stranger** (Ballantine, 2002) Nolan Baltimore, head of the successful Baltimore & Sons railway company, is found dead in a brothel.

14. **Shifting Tide, The** (Ballantine, 2004) The docking in London of the ship *Maud Idris* after a voyage from Zanzibar is followed by the theft of ivory from its cargo and the murder of a seaman.

15. **Dark Assassin** (Ballantine, 2006) Newly appointed superintendent of the Thames River Police William Monk and his river patrol watch helplessly as two young lovers plunge to their deaths from a bridge.

III. A five-volume mystery series is set, one volume for each year (1914–1918), during World War II. The Reavley siblings of Cambridge, Joseph, Matthew, and Judith, are pitted against a "kill for peace"

antiwar group, led by the mysterious "Peacemaker," responsible for the deaths of their parents. Readers are advised to start with number 1.

1. **No Graves as Yet: 1914** (Ballantine, 2003) The deaths—by auto mishap, in June 1914—of the parents of Cambridge don Joseph Reavley lead him to the discovery of a mysterious document being carried by his father.

2. **Shoulder the Sky: 1915** (Ballantine, 2004) In 1915 members of the Reavley family are heavily involved in the war effort. Joseph is a military chaplain, while brother Matthew has the dangerous job of ferreting out the group of violent peace activists led by the mysterious Peacemaker.

3. **Angels in the Gloom: 1916** (Ballantine, 2005) March 1916. The wounded Protestant chaplain Joseph Reavley, set back to Cambridge to recuperate, gets involved in a Cambridgeshire murder case.

4. **At Some Disputed Barricade: 1917** (Ballantine, 2007) 1917. Matthew Reavley, British intelligence officer, continues his search for the Peacemaker, who is plotting to align Britain with Germany to end the war.

5. **We Shall Not Sleep: 1918** (Ballantine, 2007) 1918. In the conclusion to the series, the Reavley siblings—Joseph, Matthew, and Judith, find themselves together in the bloody trenches of Flanders.

IV. Two novels, which may have no real connection outside of time and place, are set in France in the years 1792 and 1793, when the French Revolution was getting untracked from its original idealistic goals.

1. **Dish Taken Cold, A** (Carroll & Graf, 2000) As the Terror goes into high gear, widowed servant Celie betrays the friend she held responsible for her baby's crib death.

2. **One Thing More, The** (Headline [UK], 2000) In 1793 a small group plots to rescue King Louis XVI from his impending execution. Not published in the United States.

V. A pair of fantasy novels represents a real change of pace for Anne Perry. They are basically an extended allegory of battle between good evil. Good is represented by Tathea, a former empress who is granted immortality; evil is represented by Asmodeus. The action in the two books is separated by a period of 500 years.

1. **Tathea** (Shadow Mount, 1999) Tathea, empress of Shinabar, flees her palace when her husband and son are murdered by evil forces.

2. **Come Armageddon** (Ace, 2003) Five hundred years later, Tathea, granted immortality, returns from exile with a talisman to prepare the warriors who will fight the battle of Armageddon against the forces of evil led by Asmodeus.

VI. The loosely connected Christmas Novellas series is a somewhat cozier spin-off from series I. Lady Vespasia Cumming-Gould, one of the most memorable characters in series I, appears as a young lady in number 1, and Charlotte Pitt's Grandmamma is the protagonist in number 3. Each novel is set in the Victorian countryside in Christmas season.

1. **Christmas Journey, A** (Ballantine, 2003) Vespasia Cumming-Gould, a lively young woman here, accompanies Gwendolen Kilmuir to the Scottish Highlands after a Christmas party in Berkshire that ended in tragedy. Variant title: *Journey toward Christmas*.

2. **Christmas Visitor, A** (Ballantine, 2004) Henry Rathbone, arriving to spend Christmas at the Dreghorn family manor, near Ullswater

in the Lake District, is greeted by the news that the master of the house, Judah Dreghorn, has drowned.

3. *Christmas Guest, A* **(Ballantine, 2005)** Charlotte Pitt's Grandmama (see series I) finds herself "banished" to the Romney Marshes home of her former daughter-in-law Caroline at Christmastime along with the obnoxious Maud Barrington, who soon turns up dead in her bedroom.

4. *Christmas Secret, A* **(Ballantine, 2006)** The Reverend Dominic Corde is invited to "fill the robe" as substitute vicar in the village of Cottisham while the Reverend Wynter is away, supposedly on a three-week Christmas holiday.

5. *Christmas Beginning, A* **(Ballantine, 2007)** Runcorn is sent to a remote Welsh island for Christmas, and he gets involved with the murder of Olivia Costain, the town vicar's single sister.

Perry, Thomas

I. Thomas Perry, not to be confused with the German musician of the same name, is a master at writing sophisticated, humorous crime thrillers featuring shrewd, unprincipled killers who somehow manage to be more sympathetic than the people and agencies who are after them. *The Butcher's Boy*, which won an Edgar for best first novel, features a protagonist on the lam from both the authorities and the mobsters who employed him in the first place. *Sleeping Dogs* resurrects "the butcher's boy" when a young mafioso recognizes him. Hit persons, con persons, gunrunners, or bounty hunters are the protagonists in several other Perry novels, including *Metzger's Dog* (Scribner, 1983), *Big Fish* (Scribner, 1985), and *Pursuit* (Random House, 2001).

1. *Butcher's Boy, The* **(Scribner, 1982)** "The Butcher's Boy" finds himself a liability to his Mafia employers after he gets himself distinctively scarred in a back-alley brawl. Now the hit man finds himself pursued by his former employers and a host of police operatives, including US Justice Department computer-analyst Elizabeth Waring.

2. *Sleeping Dogs* **(Random House, 1992)** When a young Mafia leader recognizes him, the Butcher's Boy is forced out of retirement.

II. Jane Whitefield is a Seneca Indian from upstate New York who helps people in jeopardy to "disappear." The wily, resourceful Jane, who is very much aware of her cultural heritage, tries to retire but keeps getting drawn back into her identity-changing business.

1. *Vanishing Act* **(Random House, 1995)** Jane Whitefield aids a woman fleeing her sadistic husband, then gets involved with a former policeman turned accountant who is on the run after being framed for embezzlement.

2. *Dance for the Dead* **(Random House, 1996)** Two clients for Jane: Timmy, young heir to a fortune, whose adoptive family has been slaughtered, and Mary Perkins, who is accused of stealing millions from savings-and-loans banks.

3. *Shadow Woman* **(Random House, 1997)** A Las Vegas casino executive who knows too much for his bosses' comfort is being pursued by a husband-and-wife hit team.

4. *Face-Changers, The* **(Random House, 1998)** Jane, who has promised her new husband that she would retire from her business, is lured out once again.

5. *Blood Money* **(Random House, 1999)** Bernie Lupus, accountant for the Mob, who fears being replaced by a computer, fakes his own death, and goes on the run with his teenage girlfriend.

Peters, Elizabeth

PSEUDONYM OF **Barbara Mertz**

I. American author Barbara Mertz, who holds a PhD in Egyptology, publishes popular works on the subject under her real name. As Barbara Michaels, she writes historical gothic romances. As Elizabeth Peters, she writes light mystery/suspense novels with interesting historical or archaeological slants. Peters has created three female sleuths: Amelia Peabody Emerson, Vicky Bliss, and Jacqueline Kirby. Since 1994 Peters has concentrated her efforts on Amelia, a late Victorian feminist who goes on digs in Egypt with her archaeologist husband, Radcliffe Emerson. The Emersons' excavations are usually bedeviled by some "curse," unexpected (and relatively recent) corpses turning up in tombs, and an assortment of evil, clever villains who are bent on tomb-robbery, illegal antiquities sales, a hatred of the Emersons, or all of the above. But the clever, managing, unsinkable Amelia is always more than a match for them. Other members of the Emerson clan play important roles, including their son Walter ("Ramses"), who develops from an exasperatingly precocious toddler into a resourceful young heartthrob during the course of the series; the beautiful and clever Egyptian girl Nefret, who becomes the Emersons' ward and, eventually, their daughter-in-law; and the Egyptian David, Ramses's friend and "cousin," who marries the Emersons' niece. Sethos, master of disguises, who has an unrequited passion for the happily married Amelia, is a "villain" who sometimes plays a benevolent role. The series, narrated by Amelia in a melodramatic period style laced with her sly wit, provides authentic historical background and suspenseful, enjoyable, if somewhat preposterous, plots. The redoubtable Amelia has attracted a large and loyal following among mystery readers. Readers new to the series should either start at the beginning or consult *Amelia Peabody's Egypt: A Compendium* (Morrow, 2003), edited by Elizabeth Peters and Kristen Whitbread.

1. *Crocodile on the Sandbank* **(Dodd, 1975)** Amelia Peabody and Evelyn Barton-Forbes take a break from their voyage on the Nile and get involved with the archaeologist Emerson brothers and a wandering mummy.

2. *Curse of the Pharaohs, The* **(Dodd, 1978)** Amelia and her husband, Radcliffe Emerson, take over the leadership of an archaeological expedition excavating a "cursed" tomb.

3. *Mummy Case, The* **(Congdon, 1985)** The Emersons' dig in Egypt is plagued by murder, theft, and the antics of four-year-old Ramses.

4. *Lion in the Valley* **(Atheneum, 1986)** On another Egyptian dig in 1896, Amelia has to be rescued from "a fate worse than death" by Radcliffe and eight-year-old Ramses.

5. *Deeds of the Disturber, The* **(Atheneum, 1988)** At home in England, the Emersons investigate strange goings-on at the British Museum supposedly perpetrated by a supernatural Egyptian priest.

6. *Last Camel Died at Noon, The* **(Warner, 1991)** Amelia and her family are in the Sudan searching for archaeologist Willoughby Forth, who disappeared 14 years previously.

7. *Snake, the Crocodile, and the Dog, The* **(Warner, 1992)** Amelia and Radcliffe battle the Master Criminal, kidnapping, superstition, and amnesia as they search for a lost city of gold.

8. *Hippopotamus Pool, The* **(Warner, 1996)** Returning to Egypt, Amelia, Radcliffe, and 13-year-old Ramses, shown a scarab ring by a mystery man, embark upon the excavation of the previously undisturbed tomb of Tetisteri.

9. *Seeing a Large Cat* **(Warner, 1997)** 1903. Ignoring the warning to "stay away from tomb Twenty-A," the Emersons find the mummified body of Coonle Bellington's missing wife. Ramses goes on adventures of his own with his adopted "cousin" David and "sister" Nefret.

10. *Ape Who Guards the Balance, The* **(Avon, 1998)** During the 1907 digging season, Ramses acquires, on the black market, an ancient papyrus, and another dead body turns up, this one ostensibly savaged by crocodiles.

11. *Guardian of the Horizon* **(Morrow, 2004)** Although published later, this title belongs here chronologically. As described in "the recently rediscovered journal of the 1907–1908 expedition," the Emersons return to the City of the Lost Oasis (introduced in number 7) in answer to a mysterious summons.

12. *Falcon at the Portal, The* **(Avon, 1999)** David, the Emersons' nephew by marriage, is accused of forging antiquities, while their obnoxious cousin Percy tries to come between Ramses and Nefret.

13. *He Shall Thunder in the Sky* **(Morrow, 2000)** In 1914 Ramses expresses pacifist sentiments, while a possible Turkish invasion of Egypt looms. Lawrence of Arabia has a bit part here. UK title: *Thunder in the Sky.*

14. *Lord of the Silent* **(Morrow, 2001)** Despite the fact "there's a war going on," the Emersons return in 1915 for another dig in Egypt. Amelia, concerned about Ramses and Nefret, sends them off to Luxor.

15. *Golden One, The* **(Morrow, 2002)** Two plots here. One concerns a comparatively fresh corpse found in a tomb. The other concerns Ramses's mission to Gaza for British intelligence. Sethos, master criminal and spy, is suspected of giving aid to the enemy.

16. *Children of the Storm* **(Morrow, 2003)** In 1919 the war is over, and Amelia is a grandmother. Ramses gets involved with a mysterious woman who claims to be the embodiment of the goddess Hathor.

17. *Serpent on the Crown, The* **(Morrow, 2005)** Magda Petherick, widow of archaeologist Pringle Petherick, wants Emerson to dispose of a golden statuette that she believes is carrying a curse.

18. *Tomb of the Golden Bird* **(Morrow, 2006)** Radcliffe Emerson gets mixed up in the (real-life) opening of King Tut's tomb in 1922. The arrival of Radcliffe's shady half brother Sethos helps to muddy the waters further.

II. Another series by Elizabeth Peters stars the thoroughly modern Victoria Bliss, a tall, blond art historian. Vicky is intelligent, strong-willed, and liberated; rather than get married, she has affairs with attractive men, including English con-man "Sir John Smythe," who has a habit of turning up now and again. Each of Vicky's cases naturally includes some element of art history or archaeology. Although Peters has been asked for "more Vicky," no novels in the series have been published since 1994. *The Camelot Caper* (Meredith, 1969), an otherwise stand-alone, introduces the character of John Smythe.

1. *Borrower of the Night* **(Dodd, 1973)** Vicky Bliss goes in search of a medieval treasure supposedly hidden in a German castle during the Peasants' Rebellion.

2. *Street of the Five Moons* **(Dodd, 1978)** Vicky gets involved with a forgery ring, fake antique jewelry, and handsome, dishonest "Sir John Smythe."

3. *Silhouette in Scarlet* **(Congdon, 1983)** After receiving an enigmatic message from "John Smythe," Vicky journeys to Stockholm in search of archaeological artifacts.

4. *Trojan Gold* **(Atheneum, 1987)** Trojan treasure buried by the Nazis after the fall of Berlin is the object of Vicky's search.

5. *Night Train to Memphis* **(Warner, 1994)** Vicky runs into "Sir John" again while on a cruise up the Nile to investigate a planned heist at the Cairo Museum.

III. Peters has also written four novels starring Jacqueline Kirby, a middle-aged librarian with a PhD in history and a dauntless sense of

adventure who eventually becomes a romance writer. *The Murders of Richard III*, which apparently offended the Ricardian Society, provides an interesting contrast with *The Daughter of Time* (1952), by Josephine Tey (q.v.).

1. *Seventh Sinner, The* **(Dodd, 1972)** Jacqueline Kirby and a Roman police official team up when someone is murdered in one of the underground passages of the Church of San Clemente.

2. *Murders of Richard III, The* **(Dodd, 1974)** Someone is overdoing the reenactment of the murders alleged to have been committed by Richard III.

3. *Die for Love* **(Congdon, 1984)** While attending the Historical Romance Writers of the World Conference in New York, Jacqueline gets involved with a murder mystery.

4. *Naked Once More* **(Warner, 1989)** Jacqueline Kirby goes to the Appalachians to write a sequel to vanished author Kathleen Darcy's best seller.

Peters, Ellis

PSEUDONYM OF Edith Pargeter

I. The late (d. 1995) English writer Edith Pargeter (q.v.) had a long and prolific career as a novelist and translator (from the Czech). She wrote more than two dozen historical novels under her real name. As Ellis Peters she wrote more than three dozen mystery novels. The Brother Cadfael novels brought Peters her widest reading audience and were instrumental in encouraging the current spate of historical detectives. The Chronicles of Brother Cadfael are set in England during the unsettled reign of King Stephen (1135–1154). Cadfael is a former Crusader turned monk and herbalist at the Benedictine Abbey of St. Peter and St. Paul in Shrewsbury. He has forsworn earthly vanities but can't resist involving himself in such profane pursuits as matchmaking and sleuthing. Brother Cadfael was brought to television screens on PBS with Derek Jacobi as a very convincing monk-sleuth. Ellis Peters collaborated with Roy Morgan on *Shropshire*, a nonfiction tour of Cadfael (and Pargeter) country, while Robin Whiteman has compiled *The Cadfael Companion* (rev. ed., Mysterious, 1995) for readers who want more background. All of the Cadfael books have been collected in seven omnibus volumes published by Time-Warner UK (1990–1997). *The Benediction of Brother Cadfael* (Mysterious, 1992) contains numbers 1 and 2.

1. *Rare Benedictine, A* **(Mysterious, 1989)** Subtitle: *The Advent of Brother Cadfael.* Three stories about Cadfael, including one that describes the origin of his connection with the Benedictines: "A Light on the Road to Woodstock," "The Price of Light," and "Eye Witness."

2. *Morbid Taste for Bones, A* **(Morrow, 1978)** Prior Robert's lust for the wonder-working relics of St. Winifred gets Brother Cadfael involved in a journey to Wales and a murder investigation.

3. *One Corpse Too Many* **(Morrow, 1980)** When Cadfael gives Christian burial to 94 victims of King Stephen's "justice," he finds one corpse too many.

4. *Monks-Hood* **(Morrow, 1981)** Wealthy Gervase Bonel, potential benefactor of Cadfael's monastery, is a victim of monks-hood poisoning.

5. *Saint Peter's Fair* **(Morrow, 1981)** Cadfael investigates some homicides that took place during the local St. Peter's Fair.

6. *Leper of Saint Giles, The* **(Morrow, 1982)** The love affair between squire Joscelin Lucy and Iveta de Massard runs a rough course when Joscelin is dismissed by his master, who wants Iveta for himself.

7. *Virgin in the Ice, The* (Morrow, 1983) When Brother Elyas is attacked while trying to deliver two orphans to their uncle Laurence d'Angers, Brother Cadfael intervenes.

8. *Sanctuary Sparrow, The* (Morrow, 1983) Juggler and acrobat Liliwin of Shrewsbury is accused of stealing valuables from the town's goldsmith.

9. *Devil's Novice, The* (Morrow, 1984) Nineteen-year-old aspirant to monkhood Meriet Aspley has such violent nightmares that he is dubbed "the devil's novice."

10. *Dead Man's Ransom* (Morrow, 1984) An exchange of prisoners between the Welsh and the English is thwarted by the mysterious death of the English captive Gilbert Prestcote, sheriff of Shropshire.

11. *Pilgrim of Hate, The* (Morrow, 1984) One of the pilgrims at the celebration for wonder-working St. Winifred may be responsible for the mysterious murder of a knight in Winchester.

12. *Excellent Mystery, An* (Morrow, 1986) The arrival in Shrewsbury of Brothers Humilis and Fidelis, refugees from the burned priory of Hyde Mead, may have some connection with a young girl named Julian Cruce.

13. *Raven in the Foregate, The* (Morrow, 1986) Ailnoth, unpopular priest of the parish of Holy Cross (known as Foregate), is found murdered in a frozen pond.

14. *Rose Rent, The* (Morrow, 1986) Brother Eluric is murdered while delivering Shrewsbury Abbey's annual rent (one rose) to the beautiful widow who owns the land the abbey is leasing.

15. *Hermit of Eyton Forest, The* (Mysterious, 1988) Ten-year-old heir Richard Ludel disappears from the abbey to whose care he was entrusted, and his grandmother, Dame Dionisia is suspected.

16. *Confession of Brother Haluin, The* (Mysterious, 1989) Believing that he is on his death-bed, Brother Haluin confesses to an affair he had 18 years ago, and the death of his lover from the abortive herbs he had supplied.

17. *Heretic's Apprentice, The* (Mysterious, 1990) Former clerk Elave returns from a pilgrimage to carry out his late master's behests, but falls prey to accusations of heresy and murder.

18. *Potter's Field, The* (Mysterious, 1990) The plowing of a field recently donated to the abbey turns up the corpse of a woman.

19. *Summer of the Danes, The* (Mysterious, 1991) Cadfael and two companions become pawns in the rivalry between two Welsh princes and the Danish mercenaries hired by one of the princes.

20. *Holy Thief, The* (Mysterious, 1993) The disappearance of the remains of St. Winifred from the abbey throws the monks into turmoil.

21. *Brother Cadfael's Penance* (Mysterious, 1994) Olivier de Bretagne, who, unknown to himself, is Cadfael's son, is taken prisoner by one of the factions during the ongoing civil wars, and Cadfael sets out to find him.

II. Although the Felse mysteries predated Cadfael by more than a quarter of a century, they never achieved the popularity of the historical mysteries, and many of the titles have been out of print until recently. George Felse started out in 1951 as an ordinary policeman walking a beat in the British town of Comerford, but eventually he was allowed to range as far as India. The stolid, intelligent George Felse and his son Dominic, who is the protagonist in several volumes are fully dimensional characters in this series of contemporary mysteries. Omnibus volumes: *The Dominic Felse Omnibus* (Headline [UK], 1991; numbers 5, 9, and 11); *The George Felse Omnibus* (Warner, 1994; numbers 1, 2, and 4); *The Second George Felse Omnibus* (Warner, 1995; numbers 6, 7, and 8).

1. *Fallen into the Pit* (Mysterious, 1994) Felse is found walking his beat in the Welsh town of Comerford shortly after World II, when an influx of refugees and a young Nazi stir things up. Originally published in the United Kingdom in 1951 under Edith Pargeter's own name.

2. *Death and the Joyful Woman* (Doubleday, 1962) Concerns the feud between brewery and pub owner Alfred Armiger and his rebellious son Leslie.

3. *Flight of a Witch* (Mysterious, 1991) Beautiful teenager Annet Beck takes a walk on the supposedly witch-infested Hallowmount, disappears for five days, then returns claiming to have been gone only a few hours. Originally published in the United Kingdom in 1964.

4. *Who Lies Here?* (Morrow, 1965) The Cornish coast is the scene for smugglers in the past and a recent corpse found in an old family tomb. UK title: *A Nice Derangement of Epitaphs*.

5. *Piper on the Mountain, The* (Morrow, 1966) Herbert Terrell, head of a security research institute, is killed in a mountain-climbing fall in Czechoslovakia.

6. *Black Is the Colour of My True-Love's Heart* (Morrow, 1967) A weekend seminar on folk music at Follymead College attracts a large audience and some well-known musicians who seem to be carrying on a feud.

7. *Grass-Widow's Tale, The* (Morrow, 1968) Inspector Felse's wife, Bunty, feeling depressed by her 41st birthday, accepts a ride from a sad young man who is carrying a corpse in his car trunk.

8. *House of Green Turf, The* (Morrow, 1969) An automobile accident brings back unpleasant memories to opera singer Maggie Tressider of a death in Austria 13 years earlier.

9. *Mourning Raga* (Morrow, 1970) Felse's son Dominic and his girlfriend Tossa Barber accompany 14-year-old Anjli Kumar back to her home in India, only to discover that Anjli's father has been missing for a year.

10. *Knocker on Death's Door, The* (Morrow, 1971) The return of an old church door to the church from which it had been removed during the time of Henry VIII doesn't render the monks' curse inoperative.

11. *Death to the Landlords* (Morrow, 1972) The Naxalites, an Indian antilandlord terrorist group, are responsible for the explosion of a boat on Periyar Lake.

12. *City of Gold and Shadows* (Morrow, 1974) Charlotte Rossignol, heiress to a missing archaeologist, examines a Roman ruin near the Welsh border that he had written about.

13. *Rainbow's End* (Morrow, 1979) Arthur Everard Rainbow, a self-proclaimed expert on antiques and music, raises hackles in the village of Middlehope when he tries to take over the local choir.

Petrakis, Harry Mark

Harry Mark Petrakis interprets the immigrant experience in America through novels—two of which were nominated for a National Book Award: *Pericles on 31st Street* (Quadrangle, 1965) and *A Dream of Kings*—and several volumes of short stories and memoirs based mostly on the people and events in Chicago's Greek community (largest in the world outside of Athens), where he grew up in the 1930s. Two widely separated novels relate the trials and tribulations of Leonidas Matsoukas, Greek American immigrant, in epic, impassioned terms. *A Dream of Kings* was filmed in 1969 with Anthony Quinn (who should have achieved honorary Greek status for his work here and in *Zorba the Greek*) as Leonidas.

1. *Dream of Kings, A* (McKay, 1966) Leonidas Matsoukas dreams of leaving his Chicago slum neighborhood and returning to his native Greece, where the healing sun may cure his dying son.

2. *Ghost of the Sun* (St. Martin's, 1990) Leonidas returns to Chicago after the death of his son and five years of torture and imprisonment in Greece, and he tries to readjust to life in his much changed family and neighborhood.

Phillips, Carly

I. Best-selling contemporary romance writer Carly Philips evokes adjectives such as *sizzling, steamy,* and *sexy.* Her stories are usually set in the romance-novelist's world of the rich and famous and are full of gorgeous, passionate career girls and gorgeous, hunky guys who are either athletes or detectives or playboys. Numbers 1 through 3 were originally supposed to be a trilogy about women with the surnames of Luck and Montgomery. Numbers 4 and 5, which have characters interlocking with those in numbers 1 through 3, bring in a brother and sister with the surname of Lowell.

1. *Simply Sinful* (Harlequin, 2000) Detective Kane McDermott is investigating Kayla Luck's etiquette school for awkward businessman to see if the school is really a front for some kind of escort service.
2. *Simply Sensual* (Harlequin, 2001) PI Ben Callahan, assigned to watch over spoiled heiress Grace Montgomery, hadn't figured on falling for Grace, who doesn't realize he is being paid to be with her.
3. *Simply Scandalous* (Harlequin, 2001) Matchmaker Emma Montgomery is determined to help her grandson, Logan, to wedded bliss, but his father wants him to run for public office. Caterer Catherine Luck might be the solution.
4. *Body Heat* (Harlequin, 2001) Injured detective Jake Lowell is in the hands of physical therapist Brianne Nelson, but maybe the "therapy" is getting out of hand.
5. *Simply Sexy* (Harlequin, 2002) Rina Lowell, wealthy, widowed sister of Jake Lowell, relocates to Ashford, Massachusetts; starts a column called "Hot Stuff" for the local newspaper; and gets involved with her new boss, sportswriter, Colin Lyons.

II. The three Chandler brothers of Yorkshire Falls, New York, are the town's most eligible bachelors, and hope to remain so. However, their desperately ill mother wants her sons to be married and provide her with grandchildren . . .

1. *Bachelor, The* (Warner, 2002) Foreign correspondent Roman Chandler has lost a coin toss. Now he is designated to be the brother who supplies his mother with grandchildren. Easy enough for him to do, but Roman has his heart set on heartbreaker and erotic lingerie entrepreneur Charlotte Bronson.
2. *Playboy, The* (Warner, 2003) Single cop Rick Chandler decides on a fake affair with Kendall Sutton, who seems to be equally reluctant to marry. But, of course, the charade is fated to turn into the real thing.
3. *Heartbreaker, The* (Warner, 2003) Sloane Carlisle, trying to recover from the shock of learning that she is not the biological daughter of Senator Michael Carlisle, runs into newsman Chase Chandler in a Washington, DC, bar.

III. The orphaned Jordan sisters—Annabelle, Michelle, and Sophie—are adopted by their uncle, Yank Morgan, who gives them a share in Hot Zone, his Manhattan sports agency. The girls thrive and are exposed to a series of sexy athletes in this light trilogy.

1. *Hot Stuff* (Harlequin, 2004) Annabelle Jordan, powerhouse PR person in her uncle's Manhattan sports agency, has a fatal attraction to egocentric bad boys. Then she meets her newest client, ex–football star Brandon Vaughn.
2. *Hot Number* (Harlequin, 2005) When Michelle "Miki" Jordan, publicist to the brightest stars in the sports world, decides to shuck off her tomboy ways, professional ballplayer and major league playboy Damian Fuller is a leading contender for her heart.
3. *Hot Item* (Harlequin, 2006) Big-time sports agent Spencer Atkins goes AWOL, just three weeks before the pro football draft, after a gossip columnist outs him as gay. Sophie Jordan, left in charge of the Hot Zone sports agency, and quarterback Riley Nash, Uncle Yank's client and Spencer's son from a failed marriage, try to track Spencer down.

IV. A pair of novels describes the adventures of sisters Ariana and Zoe Costas, twin sisters from a large Greek clan that operates an Atlantic City spa. Ariana is the quiet one, while Zoe is a true member of her wild and crazy family, but they both succumb to romance.

1. *Under the Boardwalk* (Warner, 2004) Ariana Costas, mistaken for her missing sister, Zoe, is rescued from a bullet intended for Zoe by handsome stranger Quinn Donovan.
2. *Summer Lovin'* (Harlequin, 2005) Security specialist Zoe Costas isn't about to be fooled by the charming and hunky Ryan Baldwin when he claims to be related to Sam, the little girl the Costas family is about to adopt.

Pickard, Nancy

I. Jennie Cain, head of the Port Frederick, Massachusetts, Civic Foundation, has a combination of can-do toughness and tender heart that always seems to get her into the middle of some kind of complicated skulduggery to the amusement, and occasional dismay, of her husband, Police Lieutenant Geof Bushfield. This is a series of nicely paced plots with Jenny's telling observations on small-town politics and life thrown in. Nancy Pickard, Kansas City, Missouri, native who now lives in Prairie Village, Kansas, a suburb of Kansas City, seem to have abandoned Jennie Cain for other series.

1. *Generous Death* (Avon, 1984) Several wealthy donors to the Port Frederick Civic Foundation have been murdered by a perpetrator who leaves nasty little poems with the bodies.
2. *Say No to Murder* (Pocket, 1985) A runaway truck slams into the Project Committee for the Liberty Harbor restoration.
3. *No Body* (Scribner, 1986) Some 133 bodies interred during the 19th century have disappeared from the old cemetery, while an extra corpse has been found in a casket slated to be buried in the new cemetery.
4. *Marriage Is Murder* (Scribner, 1987) Did three abused wives murder their abusive husbands, or did someone else do the job for them?
5. *Dead Crazy* (Scribner, 1988) Jenny's efforts to establish a shelter for the mentally ill run into community opposition and a couple of murders.
6. *Bum Steer* (Pocket, 1990) Jenny travels to Kansas City to find out why a dying millionaire has willed a vast cattle ranch to her little-known foundation. Published in the United Kingdom as *Crossbones.*
7. *I.O.U.* (Pocket, 1991) Cain probes the cause of her recently deceased mother's longtime mental illness and uncovers a lot of bad blood resulting from the bankruptcy of the Cain family business.

8. *But I Wouldn't Want to Die There* **(Pocket, 1993)** When a former New York colleague is killed, and the bereft foundation needs an interim director, Jenny travels to the Big Apple.

9. *Confession* **(Pocket, 1994)** Jenny and Geof are visited by 17-year-old David Mayer, who angrily announces that he is Geof's son by an old high school classmate.

10. *Twilight* **(Pocket, 1995)** The first ever Port Frederick Fall Festival is threatened by a dilatory insurance company, environmental activists, fundamentalists upset by the Festival's Halloween theme, and finally by arson.

II. Pickard has continued the late Virginia Rich's (q.v.) Eugenia Potter series. Number 1 was written by Pickard from notes left by Rich. Numbers 2 and 3 continue the adventures of the Arizona-based master chef and amateur sleuth, complete with mouth-watering recipes and discussions of cooking techniques.

1. *Twenty-seven Ingredient Chili Con Carne Murders, The* **(Delacorte, 1993)** Ricardo Ortega, manager of Eugenia's Arizona ranch, and his granddaughter have disappeared.

2. *Blue Corn Murders, The* **(Delacorte, 1998)** Genia visits the Medicine Wheel archaeological dig to see the ruins and taste the treats cooked by Bingo the cook, but then a busload full of Texas teenagers disappears.

3. *Secret Ingredient Murders, The* **(Delacorte, 2001)** On the Rhode Island coast supervising her teenage great-nephew and great-niece, Genia teams up with Stanley Parker, author of the forthcoming *Secret Ingredient Cook Book*, to prepare a gourmet meal for six select guests. And then . . .

III. Pickard has embarked upon a new series, which she says will only be a trilogy. Marie Lightfoot, of Bahia Beach, Florida, is a true-crime writer who gets really involved with the cases she is writing about and has a good instinct for when something is fishy. The Lightfoot stories skillfully mesh descriptions of the cases she is investigating with descriptions of her writing processes. Pickard has coauthored, with Lynn Lott, *Seven Steps on the Writer's Path* (Ballantine, 2004), a self-help book for writers.

1. *Whole Truth, The* **(Pocket, 2000)** Marie Lightfoot attends the trial of Raymond Raintree, about to be convicted of the abduction and murder of six-year-old Natalie McCullen. Lightfoot has reservations about certain aspects of the case, but then Raintree escapes from the courtroom.

2. *Ring of Truth* **(Pocket, 2001)** Lightfoot again has strong reservations, this time about the conviction for wife-murder of Bob Wing, a minister who has campaigned against the death penalty and who is now on death row next to Steve Orbach, the man he tried to free.

3. *Truth Hurts, The* **(Simon & Schuster, 2002)** Marie is working on a book about her parents, civil rights workers who disappeared in Alabama in 1963, when she was a small child. Then she is threatened by an e-mail stalker (who signs himself "Paulie Barnes") with the murders of her friends if she doesn't collaborate with him on a book about her own murder.

Piesman, Marissa

Piesman, coauthor (with Marilee Hartley) of *The Yuppie Handbook* (Pocket, 1984) and assistant New York State attorney general, has created a not so young, not so upwardly mobile professional, Nina Fischman, who is an attorney with Legal Services for the Elderly in New York, is on the wrong side of 40, has a mouthy Jewish mother,

lots of neuroses, and a history of rotten relationships with men. Nina is very funny in her frenetic, urban single woman, kvetching way, and New York City provides a good backdrop for her amateur sleuthing.

1. *Unorthodox Practices* **(Pocket, 1989)** Nina suspects foul play when two elderly clients die unexpectedly, leaving vacant, cockroach-free apartments, an unheard-of situation in Manhattan.

2. *Personal Effects* **(Pocket, 1991)** Nina's friend Susan Gold, who wanted to find a nice, stable husband in the "Personals," instead gets a man who strangles her during a trip to the Catskills.

3. *Heading Uptown* **(Delacorte, 1993)** Nina is named executor for the estate of her mother's late best friend, Helen, then turns detective when Helen's son Mark turns up dead.

4. *Close Quarters* **(Delacorte, 1994)** Sharing a house on Fire Island with 10 other romance-hungry New Yorkers proves to be no picnic when master seducer Barry Adleman is killed by a poisoned motion-sickness patch.

5. *Alternate Sides* **(Delacorte, 1995)** Jonathan, Nina's boyfriend, becomes a suspect when his doorman is murdered while moving Jonathan's car.

6. *Survival Instincts* **(Delacorte, 1997)** Andy Campbell, research scientist, is the victim of an apparent poisoning. Campbell's widow, Nina's brother-in-law Ken, and SPASM (Society for the Protection of All Small Mammals) are among the suspects.

Pike, Robert L.

PSEUDONYM OF Robert L. Fish

I. The prolific Robert L. Fish (q.v.) wrote two series of police procedurals under the pseudonym of Robert L. Pike. Lieutenant Clancy, of the Fifty-second Precinct in New York City, is a bit of a plodder, but his stories still make good reading, as none of Pike/Fish's characters are uninteresting. *Mute Witness* was the basis of the 1968 movie *Bullitt*, starring Steve McQueen and one of the greatest movie car chases.

1. *Mute Witness* **(Doubleday, 1963)** Clancy guards a West Coast mobster. The movie *Bullitt* shifted the scene to San Francisco. Variant title: *Bullitt*.

2. *Quarry, The* **(Doubleday, 1964)** Clancy must find an escapee from Sing Sing Prison.

3. *Police Blotter* **(Doubleday, 1965)** A murdered recluse, a theft of $16, and a threatened UN delegate make up this typical day for Lieutenant Clancy.

II. Lieutenant James Reardon is tough and aggressive, short tempered, and quick thinking, and his cases never fail to include at least one hair-raising car chase through scenic San Francisco. Reagan is ably assisted by Sergeant Dondero in all four of his cases.

1. *Reardon* **(Doubleday, 1970)** Reardon has a hunch there is something wrong with a seemingly open-and-shut case of accidental auto death.

2. *Gremlin's Grandpa, The* **(Doubleday, 1971)** A prominent gangster is murdered in a waterfront bar.

3. *Bank Job* **(Doubleday, 1974)** A shipyard payroll is taken from a bank by four masked men.

4. *Deadline: 2 A.M.* **(Doubleday, 1976)** "Pop" Holland, about to retire from the force, is kidnapped.

Plagemann, Bentz

These warm and humorous novels of the trials and tribulations of parenthood are obviously based on Plagemann's own experience. The books are narrated by Mr. Wallace, a writer who lives with his wife and son in Cliffside, a town very much like Plagemann's home, Palisades Park, New Jersey. The four books trace the development of young Cameron, nicknamed Goggle, from his early boyhood scrapes to his eventual marriage. Plagemann published an autobiography describing his bout with polio: *An American Past: An Early Autobiography* (Morrow, 1990).

1. *This Is Goggle* (McGraw-Hill, 1955) Subtitle: *The Education of a Father.* When Mr. Wallace returns home from five years in the navy, he must get reacquainted with his 10-year-old son.
2. *Father to the Man* (Morrow, 1964) Mr. and Mrs. Wallace do their best to steer their son through the treacherous waters of adolescence, a short and ignominious stay at Princeton University, and a tour of duty in the US Coast Guard.
3. *Best Is Yet to Be, The* (Morrow, 1966) Mr. and Mrs. Wallace sail for the Mediterranean, where they find themselves acting as surrogate parents to various hometown girls in need of help.
4. *World of Difference, A* (Morrow, 1969) The Wallaces are on the move, first to New York City where Bill writes a play, then on to the big time in Hollywood.

Plaidy, Jean

PSEUDONYM OF Eleanor Hibbert

I. Hibbert (d. 1993) wrote historical novels under the Plaidy pseudonym, costume gothics under the Philippa Carr (q.v.) pseudonym, and best-selling romantic suspense novels under the Victoria Holt pseudonym. (She also used the names Eleanor Burford, Elbur Ford, Katherine Kellow, and Ellalice Tate for her fiction.) The historical novels by "Jean Plaidy," with a few exceptions, can be arranged into series. Royal figures, for the most part, are the leading protagonists, and, very often, the leading protagonists are female. English royalty, from William the Conqueror through Victoria, predominates, but French, Spanish, and Scottish queens are also represented, as well as an Italian duchess, and some royal mistresses. The books are entertaining and solidly based on fact—each volume carries a brief bibliography. Most of the books where published in the United Kingdom (Hale was usually the publisher) before being published in the United States, sometimes with gaps of 20 or 30 years between publication. Several were never published in the United States. The series, except for series XII (the Queens of England), are arranged in chronological order as far as possible.

The Norman trilogy is the first set in Plaidy's chronicle of the English monarchy. It begins with William I, the Conqueror (1066–1087) and continues to the end of the turbulent reign of King Stephen in 1154.

1. *Bastard King, The* (Putnam, 1979) William's spectacular rise from bastard to king is described. Originally published in 1974.
2. *Lion of Justice, The* (Putnam, 1979) This book covers the long, successful reign of King Henry I, 1100–1135. Originally published in 1975.
3. *Passionate Enemies, The* (Putnam, 1979) Stephen and Malida are lovers and rivals in their ambition to succeed Henry I. Originally published in 1976.

II. The Plantagenet series begins with Eleanor of Acquitaine and Henry II, those colorful and contentious figures who have been the subject of much historical fiction and nonfiction, including James

Goldman's play and movie *The Lion in Winter.* The series ends with the triumph of the Tudors under Henry VII (number 15). Many of the Kings and Queens described here were also chronicled by Shakespeare in his "History" plays and by Christopher Marlowe in *Edward II.*

1. *Plantagenet Prelude, The* (Putnam, 1980) The story of Eleanor and Henry is carried up the death of Thomas a Becket. Eleanor is also the subject of *The Courts of Love* (series XII, number 1). Originally published in 1976.
2. *Revolt of the Eaglets, The* (Putnam, 1980) As Henry ages, his sons jockey for the succession to his throne. Originally published in 1977.
3. *Heart of the Lion, The* (Putnam, 1980) Richard I, the Lionhearted, reigns: 1189-1199. Originally published in 1977.
4. *Prince of Darkness, The* (Putnam, 1981) King John "Lackland" gets his usual bad press here; reigned: 1199–1216. Originally published in 1978.
5. *Battle of the Queens, The* (Putnam, 1981) The feuding queens are Isabella of Angouleme, King John's widow, and Blanche of Castile, widow of Louis VIII and mother of Louis IX of France. Originally published in 1978.
6. *Queen from Provence, The* (Putnam, 1981) Henry III marries Eleanor of Provence in 1236 and spends most of his long reign provoking his barons to rebellion.
7. *Hammer of the Scots* (Putnam, 1981) The long successful reign of Edward I is chronicled: 1272–1307. Original UK title: *Edward Longshanks* (1979).
8. *Follies of the King, The* (Putnam, 1982) The follies of Edward II and the intrigues of his unhappy Queen Isabella bring his reign to a disastrous close. Covers 1307–1327. Originally published in 1980.
9. *Vow on the Heron, The* (Putnam, 1982) This volume covers the long reign of Edward III and a long stretch of the Hundred Years' War in France. Originally published in 1980.
10. *Passage to Pontefract* (Putnam, 1982) The rivalry between Edward III's sons, Edward the Black Prince and John of Gaunt, is continued by their sons Richard II and Henry Bolingbroke (later Henry IV). Originally published in 1981.
11. *Star of Lancaster, The* (Putnam, 1982) This chronicles the lives and loves of Henry IV, his wife Mary of Bohun, and their son Henry V.
12. *Epitaph for Three Women* (Putnam, 1983) The story of three women who made an impact on 15th-century England and France: Henry V's queen Katherine of Valois, Joan of Arc, and Eleanor of Gloucester. Katherine of Valois is also the subject of Plaidy's *The Queen's Secret* (series XII, number 2). Originally published in 1981.
13. *Red Rose of Anjou* (Putnam, 1983) The dominant character is Margaret of Anjou, queen to the feeble Henry VI and the real leader of the Red Roses of Lancaster. Originally published in 1982.
14. *Sun in Splendour, The* (Putnam, 1983) The reign of Edward IV is troubled by the continuing rivalry between York and Lancaster. Originally published in 1982.
15. *Uneasy Lies the Head* (Putnam, 1984) Henry VII, victor over Richard III at the Battle of Bosworth Field, tries to shore up his shaky reign. This volume could also be listed as the first in the Tudor series (series V). Richard III's queen, Anne Neville, is profiled in *The Reluctant Queen* (series XII, number 3). Originally published in 1982.

III. Plaidy wrote two trilogies, the first never published in the United States, the second more than 30 years after first publication, about Ferdinand and Isabella of Spain and their daughter Katherine of Aragon, who became Henry VIII's first queen. Numbers 4, 5, and 6 have an obvious tie-in with the Tudor series (series V). *Isabella and Ferdinand* (Hale [UK], 1970) contains numbers 1, 2, and 3. *Katherine of Aragon* (Hale [UK], 1968) contains numbers 4, 5, and 6.

1. ***Castile for Isabella*** (Hale [UK], 1960) Isabella of Castile and Ferdinand of Aragon are united in marriage (1469), and eventually Spain is united under one rule.
2. ***Spain for the Sovereigns*** (Hale [UK], 1960) Isabella and Ferdinand drive the last remnant of the Moors out of Spain and finance the voyage of a Genoese adventurer named Cristoforo Colombo.
3. ***Daughters of Spain*** (Hale [UK], 1961) Ferdinand looks to his daughters to further his dynastic ambitions, while Isabella is more concerned about their well-being.
4. ***Katharine, the Virgin Widow*** (Putnam, 1993) Katharine, daughter of Ferdinand and Isabella, is sent to England to marry Arthur, Prince of Wales, heir to Henry VII. Arthur dies: was the marriage consummated? Originally published in 1961.
5. ***Shadow of the Pomegranate, The*** (Putnam, 1994) Katharine's inability to bear Henry VIII a son spells trouble for their marriage and the future of England. Originally published in 1961.
6. ***King's Secret Matter, The*** (Putnam, 1995) Henry's affair with Anne Boleyn and Katharine's failure to provide him with a male heir determine him to annul his marriage with Katharine. Originally published in 1962.

IV. Lucrezia Borgia (1480–1519) is a much-maligned figure, according to Plaidy, who sets out to clear her reputation in this pair of novels. Published together as *Lucrezia Borgia* (Hale [UK], 1976).

1. ***Madonna of the Seven Hills*** (Putnam, 1974) Lucrezia as a young girl is strongly influenced by her father, Pope Alexander VI, and her two brothers, Cesare and Giovanni. Originally published in 1958.
2. ***Light on Lucrezia*** (Putnam, 1976) With one marriage annulled and her second husband murdered, Lucrezia is used by her powerful family for their own ends. Originally published in 1958.

V. The novels in the Tudor series, published over a period of 15 years, don't have as tight a sequence as some of the other series. In fact, some sources don't list the Tudor books as a series at all. Series II, number 15, and series III, numbers 4, 5, and 6, are sometimes counted as part of the Tudor series, while series VI and VII describe events in Scotland and France during the part of the same period. Numbers 1 and 2 concentrate on two of Henry VIII's sisters; numbers 3, 4, and 5 on the events of Henry's reign; number 6 is about Mary I Tudor; and number 7 is set during the reign of Queen Elizabeth I.

1. ***Thistle and the Rose, The*** (Putnam, 1973) At 13, Margaret Tudor, older sister of the future Henry VIII, comes to Scotland to marry James IV. Originally published in 1963.
2. ***Mary, Queen of France*** (Three Rivers, 2003) Mary, Henry's younger sister, is yoked, against her will, with the elderly Louis XII of France. Originally published in 1964.
3. ***Murder Most Royal*** (Appleton, 1949) Anne Boleyn and Katherine Howard, two queens that Henry VIII had executed, are the central characters here. Originally published in the United Kingdom and reprinted in the United States as *The King's Pleasure*. Anne Boleyn is also featured in *The Lady in the Tower* and Katherine Howard in *The Rose without a Thorn*, both described in series XII.
4. ***St. Thomas's Eve*** (Putnam, 1970) Sir Thomas More puts service to his God before service to his king. Originally published in 1954.
5. ***Sixth Wife, The*** (Putnam, 1969) Henry VIII's sixth wife, Katherine Parr, manages to outlive him.

6. ***Spanish Bridegroom, The*** (MacRae Smith, 1956) Philip II of Spain marries Mary Tudor, who tries to restore Roman Catholicism to England. Originally published in 1954; reprinted by Putnam in 1971. Mary is also featured in *In the Shadow of the Crown*, described in series XII.
7. ***Gay Lord Robert*** (Putnam, 1971) The focus here is on the relationship between Queen Elizabeth and Robert Dudley, Earl of Leicester. Originally published in 1955. Elizabeth is also featured in *Queen of this Realm*, described in series XII.

VI. In what is sometimes called the Medici Trilogy, Plaidy moves to France for this series focusing on Catherine de Medici, daughter of Lorenzo the Magnificent, who married Henry of Orleans and became queen of France in 1547. Omnibus volume containing all three published by Hale (UK) in 1969.

1. ***Madame Serpent*** (Appleton, 1951) At 14 Catherine must leave her home and friends in Florence for the unfamiliar French court. Reprinted by Putnam in 1975.
2. ***Italian Woman, The*** (Putnam, 1975) Queen regent during her son Charles IX's minority (1560–1563), Catherine seeks revenge on those who slighted here. Originally published in 1952.
3. ***Queen Jezebel*** (Appleton, 1953) Catherine's last strife-ridden years last until 1589. Reprinted by Putnam in 1976.

VII. Mary, Queen of Scots is a magnetic figure for historical novelists. Plaidy has given her a two-volume series of her own. She sees the tragic queen in terms of her passionate nature, awakened partially by Darnley and then fully by Bothwell. Plaidy has also written the nonfiction *Mary Queen of Scots: The Fair Devil of Scotland* (Putnam, 1975).

1. ***Royal Road to Fotheringay*** (Putnam, 1968) This book takes Mary from the age of five to her death. Variant title: *Mary, Queen of Scotland, the Triumphant Years*. Originally published in 1955.
2. ***Captive Queen of Scots, The*** (Putnam, 1970) The story backs up to give more detail about Mary's years of captivity and escape attempts.

VIII. James I (VI of Scotland), son of Mary, Queen of Scots, was the first Stuart king of England and the first to rule a united England and Scotland. The seven-volume Stuart saga is set in 1603 to 1714 and covers all the Stuarts from James I to Queen Anne, although Charles I gets short shrift. Numbers 2, 3, and 4 are sometimes listed as the Charles II trilogy; numbers 5, 6, and 7 as the Last of the Stuarts trilogy. Numbers 5, 6, and 7 have been published in an omnibus volume: *The Last of the Stuarts* (Hale [UK], 1977). Three volumes in the Queens of England series are set in the Stuart period: *Myself My Enemy* (Charles I); *The Pleasures of Love* (Charles II); and *William's Wife* (William and Mary).

1. ***Murder in the Tower, The*** (Putnam, 1974) The poisoning of Sir Thomas Overbury in the Tower overshadows the relationship between King James and his favorite, Robert Carr. Originally published in 1964.
2. ***Wandering Prince, The*** (Putnam, 1971) This concerns Charles II's exile in France and Holland and the first years of his restoration as the English monarch. Originally published in 1956.
3. ***Health unto His Majesty, A*** (Putnam, 1972) Charles II's reign continues through the plague of 1665 and the Great Fire of London in 1666. Originally published in 1956.
4. ***Here Lies Our Sovereign Lord*** (Putnam, 1973) The last years of Charles II's reign include his liaison with Nell Gwynn. Originally published in 1957.

5. *Three Crowns, The* **(Putnam, 1977)** This book covers the childhood and youth of James II's daughter Mary, her marriage to William of Orange and her return to England after her father's exile. Originally published in 1965.

6. *Haunted Sisters, The* **(Putnam, 1977)** Anne and Mary are torn between allegiance to a Protestant England and love for their Catholic father, James, in exile in France. Originally published in 1966.

7. *Queen's Favorites, The* **(Putnam, 1978)** Queen Anne has two favorites, the vivacious and ambitious Sarah Churchill, Duchess of Marlborough, and Abigail Hill, a devoted poor relation. Originally published in 1966.

IX. The Georgian saga, published in the United Kingdom from 1967 to 1972, wasn't published in the United States until 1985 to 1990. It forms a link between Stuart saga (series VIII) and the Victorian quartet (series X), covering the reigns of the first four Georges of the House of Hanover and the fourth William, successors to the throne of Great Britain and Ireland in 1714.

1. *Princess of Celle, The* **(Putnam, 1985)** The intrigues of the House of Hanover eventually lead to George I's succession to the English throne with the death of Anne, who had no surviving children. Originally published in 1967.

2. *Queen in Waiting* **(Putnam, 1985)** Intelligent and cultured Caroline of Brandenburg-Anspach must put up with a dull-witted husband to become queen. Originally published in 1967.

3. *Caroline the Queen* **(Putnam, 1986)** Queen Caroline must deal with her loutish, unfaithful husband and his estrangement from his eldest son, Frederick Louis, Prince of Wales. Originally published in 1968.

4. *Prince and the Quakeress, The* **(Putnam, 1986)** George, Prince of Wales, the future George III, falls in love with Hannah Lightfoot, a young Quaker woman. Originally published in 1968.

5. *Third George, The* **(Putnam, 1987)** Beset by public disasters, including the loss of the American colonies, George III tries to console himself with his wife, Charlotte, and large brood of children. Originally published in 1969.

6. *Perdita's Prince* **(Putnam, 1987)** Another Prince of Wales, the future George IV, adds to his father's woes by having an affair with an actress at Drury Lane. Originally published in 1969.

7. *Sweet Lass of Richmond Hill* **(Putnam, 1988)** The liaison between George IV and Catholic commoner Mrs. Fitzherbert scandalizes his subjects. Originally published in 1970.

8. *Indiscretions of the Queen* **(Putnam, 1988)** George IV's Queen Caroline of Brunswick-Wolfenbuttel gets involved in a scandal of her own. Originally published in 1970.

9. *Regent's Daughter, The* **(Putnam, 1989)** Princess Charlotte, daughter of George IV and Queen Caroline, tries to live her own life, although "nobody ever had a stranger set of relations." Originally published in 1971.

10. *Goddess of the Green Room* **(Putnam, 1989)** William, Duke of Clarence, the future William IV, is smitten by Drury Land actress Dorothy Jordan. Originally published in 1971.

11. *Victoria in the Wings* **(Putnam, 1990)** With the death of Princess Charlotte, Victoria is left heir to the throne. Links Series IX and XI. Originally published in 1972.

X. The so-called French Revolution trilogy, never published in the United States, is really more about Louis XV and his mistresses than about the Revolution, which occurred in 1789, years after Louis died predicting a "deluge." Louis XV was a contemporary of the Hanover kings George I and George II. *Madame Du Barry* (Hale [UK], 1994) is a stand-alone about Louis's later mistress.

1. *Louis, the Well-Beloved* **(Hale [UK], 1959)** Louis fails to live up to the promise he showed in his early years as he dallies with mistresses, including the famed Madame de Pompadour.

2. *Road to Compiegne, The* **(Hale [UK], 1959)** After the Pompadour comes the Du Barry, as Louis XV passes on to his heir what prove to be insoluble problems.

3. *Flaunting, Extravagant Queen* **(Hale [UK], 1957)** Marie Antoinette leaves her home in Vienna to become queen to the well-meaning but hapless Louis XVI.

XI. Four volumes covering Queen Victoria's long reign bring Plaidy's chronicle up to the 20th century. Victoria is also the leading character in *Victoria in the Wings* (series IX) and in *Victoria Victorious*, a volume in the Queens of England series (series XII).

1. *Captive of Kensington Palace, The* **(Putnam, 1976)** Victoria's sheltered childhood is guarded by her mother and her faithful governess, Baroness Lehzen. Originally published in 1972.

2. *Queen and Lord M, The* **(Putnam, 1977)** A queen at 18, Victoria is still a rather silly, apolitical girl, madly in the love with the elderly Lord Melbourne. Originally published in 1973.

3. *Queen's Husband, The* **(Putnam, 1978)** Marriage to her adored Albert brings adjustments and the strain of childbearing to Victoria. Originally published in 1973.

4. *Widow of Windsor, The* **(Putnam, 1978)** Palmerston, Gladstone, and Disraeli figure prominently in Victoria's later years. Originally published in 1974.

XII. The Queens of England, Plaidy's last series, isn't really a series, just novels devoted to some of Britain's more interesting queens, some of whom were also covered in earlier series. The series is listed chronologically. With two exceptions, the books were published in the United States within a year of their British publication.

1. *Courts of Love, The* **(Putnam, 1988)** Eleanor of Aquitaine, Queen of King Henry II.

2. *Queen's Secret, The* **(Putnam, 1990)** Catherine of Valois, Queen of King Henry V.

3. *Reluctant Queen, The* **(Putnam, 1991)** Anne of York, Anne Neville, queen of King Richard III.

4. *Lady in the Tower, The* **(Putnam, 1986)** Anne Boleyn, second queen of Henry VIII.

5. *Rose without a Thorn, The* **(Putnam, 1994)** Katherine Howard, fifth queen of King Henry VIII. (Ford Madox Ford [q.v.] wrote the Fifth Queen trilogy.)

6. *In the Shadow of the Crown* **(Putnam, 1989)** Mary Tudor, Queen Mary I.

7. *Queen of This Realm* **(Putnam, 1985)** Queen Elizabeth I.

8. *Myself My Enemy* **(Putnam, 1984)** Henrietta Maria, queen of Charles I.

9. *Pleasures of Love, The* **(Putnam, 1992)** Catherine of Braganza, queen of Charles II.

10. *William's Wife* **(Putnam, 1993)** Queen Mary II, wife of King William III. Originally published in 1990.

11. *Victoria Victorious* **(Putnam, 1986)** Queen Victoria.

Plain, Belva

Evergreen, a first novel published with little fanfare in 1978, became a word-of-mouth best seller. The saga of Anna Friedman, which traces her life from a Polish village in the last century to affluence in 1970s New York, obviously struck a chord in millions of readers and viewers of the 1985 television miniseries based on the book. Two subsequent novels have dealt with the Werners and Roths, rich, aristocratic families living in New York, whose stories interconnect with Anna's. For the most part these novels have parallel story lines set in the early 1900s rather than succeeding each other chronologically. Belva Plain's novels are basically romantic family sagas told with restraint and without sensationalism.

1. *Evergreen* (Delacorte, 1978) Teenage Anna emigrates from Poland to New York where she falls in love with wealthy Paul Werner, but marries poor, ambitious David.
2. *Golden Cup, The* (Delacorte, 1986) This is the story of Henrietta De Rivera, who becomes Hennie Roth, suffragette, fighter for social justice, and Paul Werner's aunt.
3. *Tapestry* (Delacorte, 1988) Paul Werner, banker and philanthropist, unpassionately wedded, finds consolation for the loss of Anna, his first love, in an affair with his cousin Leah.
4. *Harvest* (Delacorte, 1990) Iris, daughter of Anna and Paul, is jealously married to wealthy, improvident Dr. Theo Stern while their four children grow up rather unsatisfactorily.

Plante, David

All of the novels in this series involve one or more members of the Francoeur family of Providence, Rhode Island. Jim and Reena Francoeur are a working-class couple of French-Canadian background. Their lives are observed and chronicled by Daniel, their next-to-youngest son, who becomes an expatriate writer. Daniel takes center stage in several of the novels. Since Plante is a Providence native who has lived in London since 1966, it is reasonable to assume that the Francoeurs are based on his own family and that Daniel is somewhat autobiographical. Although *The Woods* was published after *The Country*, Plante wrote it first and intended it to fit between *The Family* and *The Country*, as it does in the paperback omnibus *The Francoeur Novels* (Dutton, 1983). Establishing a chronology for the novels published after 1983 is trickier. All of the novels are slim volumes, well written and involving.

1. *Family, The* (Farrar, 1978) Adolescent Daniel Francoeur tries to come to terms with his feelings about sex, Catholicism, and his working-class parents.
2. *Woods, The* (Atheneum, 1982) During two years at a Boston college and a summer on a wooded island off the Rhode Island coast, Daniel tries to discover his role in life and succeed sexually with a young woman.
3. *Foreigner, The* (Atheneum, 1984) In 1959 Daniel, who has gone abroad to study, gets involved with Angela, a young black woman, and Vincent, her shady white boyfriend.
4. *Country, The* (Atheneum, 1981) Now resident in London, Daniel makes several trips back to Providence to visit his aging and failing parents.
5. *Catholic, The* (Atheneum, 1986) A one-night sexual relationship with a man named Henry takes on a great deal of significance for Daniel.
6. *Native, The* (Atheneum, 1988) Antoinette Francoeur, David's niece, is torn between the wider world of her college-educated father and the "Canuck" world of her Francoeur grandmother.

Plievier, Theodor

Plievier's work presents an interesting contrast to the World War II novels of Hans Helmut Kirst (q.v.) and to lighter historical novels with a wartime setting. His books give an unromanticized look at the horror and degradation of war from a soldier's point of view rather than a general's. Plievier's left-wing commitment and opposition to Nazism caused him to leave his native Germany in 1933. He settled in Russia but soon became disenchanted with that government, though not with communism per se. After the war he fled to American-occupied Bavaria and died in Switzerland in 1955.

1. *Stalingrad* (Appleton, 1948) A brutally realistic account of the siege of Stalingrad shows the German army's disintegration. Translated from the German by Richard and Clara Winston. Original title: *Stalingrad*.
2. *Moscow* (Doubleday, 1954) This grim story describes the eventually successful Russian attempts to halt Hitler's march on Moscow in 1941/42. The author's disillusionment with the Russians is evident. Translated from the German by Stuart Hood. Original title: *Moscow*.
3. *Berlin* (Doubleday, 1957) The German capital dies a slow death in 1945. Variant title: *Rape of a City*. Translated from the German by Louis Hagen and Vivian Milroy. Original title: *Berlin*.

Pohl, Frederik

I. Multi-Hugo and Nebula award-winning, Science Fiction Writers of America Grand Master Frederik Pohl has been publishing for more than 50 years. His best work combines plausible future technology, social commentary, and a sardonic style. Pohl's Heechee saga, which contains some of his best and most popular work, is set in the future and features a race of technically advanced, benevolent, but elusive beings called the Heechees, who frustrate the efforts of Earthlings to make contact with them.

1. *Gateway* (St. Martin's, 1977) Earthmen try to unlock the secret of the Heechee Gateway, as prospector Rob Brodhead narrates stories about his prospecting and psychoanalytic adventures.
2. *Beyond the Blue Event Horizon* (Ballantine, 1980) Brodhead, now a multimillionaire, backs an expedition to investigate one of the Heechees' "food factories" to relieve an Earth threatened by mass starvation.
3. *Heechee Rendezvous* (Ballantine, 1984) When the future of the universe is at stake, Rob faces another dangerous expedition, and the Heechees come out of hiding.
4. *Annals of the Heechee, The* (Ballantine, 1987) A century later, Brodhead, who has been transformed into a computer-stored intelligence, aids the Heechees against the Foe, a race of energy beings.
5. *Gateway Trip, The* (Ballantine, 1990) Ten stories about the Heechees, including the novella "Merchant of Venus."
6. *Boy Who Would Live Forever, The* (Tor, 2004) Set in a complicated universe in which humans have the option of having their personalities preserved forever.

II. *The Space Merchants*, written with frequent coauthor the late Cyril M. Kornbluth, is a classic of satirical science fiction. The novel is set in a near-future United States where monopoly capitalism rules and advertising agencies wield enormous power. *The Merchants' War*, a relatively disappointing sequel written by Pohl alone, followed 31 years later. Omnibus volume: *Venus, Inc.* (Doubleday, 1985).

1. *Space Merchants, The* (**Ballantine, 1953**) Star-Class copysmith Mitchell Courtenay is spearheading his firm's campaign to sell the colonization of the planet Venus to a gullible public.
2. *Merchants' War, The* (**St. Martin's, 1984**) Adman Tennison Tarb gets caught up in the struggle between the governments of Earth and Venus to subvert the beliefs and practices of each other's inhabitants.

III. Pohl has collaborated with fellow SFWA Grand Master Jack Williamson (q.v.) on several novels, including the Undersea Trilogy, for juveniles, and the Starchild Trilogy, another near-future saga in which Earth is governed by the Plan of Man, a worldwide computerized security network necessary for the Earth's survival, or so the plan's administrators say. Omnibus volume: *The Starchild Trilogy* (Doubleday, 1969).

1. *Reefs of Space, The* (**Ballantine, 1964**) A criminal who can't remember his crime is given the responsibility of developing a rocket propulsion system that will carry man into another solar system.
2. *Starchild* (**Ballantine, 1965**) Two generations after the events in *The Reefs of Space*, the rebellion against the Plan of Man is threatening the plan's very heart.
3. *Rogue Star* (**Ballantine, 1969**) A new star is formed, sentient in its fashion, needing companionship and other life to feed on.

IV. Another collaboration with Williamson is *The Saga of Cuckoo* (omnibus volume: Doubleday, 1983), a pair of novels about a mysterious body in space 20,000 light years away, advancing toward Earth, and with a potential for vast destruction.

1. *Farthest Star* (**Ballantine, 1975**) Object Lambda, nicknamed "Cuckoo," is a vast, light object discovered by a space probe and is heading toward Earth at one-sixth the speed of light.
2. *Wall around a Star* (**Ballantine, 1983**) If Jen Babylon could solve the mystery of Cuckoo's records, he might raise humanity's standing among the older races, and he might save the galaxy.

V. *Man Plus* and *Mars Plus* are two novels about the exploration and colonization of Mars. *Mars Plus* was coauthored by Thomas T. Thomas.

1. *Man Plus* (**Random House, 1976**) Plans are afoot for the exploration and colonization of Mars by humans surgically enhanced with cybernetic implants.
2. *Mars Plus* (**Baen, 1994**) Demeter Coughlan pays a visit to Mars both as a tourist and as an intelligence agent for her grandfather. Coauthored with Thomas T. Thomas.

VI. The Eschaton Sequence is a trilogy about alien contact. As usual, the contact has sinister implications. Federal agent Dan Dannerman is the leading protagonist in this space-opera saga as he battles the reptilian Horch and the mind-controlling Beloved Leaders. Omnibus volume: *The Eschaton Sequence* (SFBC, 1999).

1. *Other End of Time, The* (**Tor, 1996**) 2031: signals are received from an unusual radiation emanating from an abandoned Earth-orbiting observatory.
2. *Siege of Eternity, The* (**Tor, 1997**) Dan Dannerman and Pat Adcock return from the space station with no knowledge of the objects implanted in their brains.
3. *Far Shore of Time, The* (**Tor, 1999**) In the conclusion to the Eschaton Sequence, Dan Dannerman is cloned, imprisoned, and interrogated by the reptilian Horch. And there is an even bigger

threat to Earth: the mind-controlling, empire-building Beloved Leaders.

Pope, Dudley

I. Lieutenant Lord Nicholas Ramage was born to command ships for His Majesty's Royal Navy. Not only does he have the right combination of audacity, dry humor, and natural authority, but he is the son of "Old Blazeaway," an admiral before him. Ramage starts his career with an early disgrace: his leaving ship to rescue two Italian refugees—one of them a beautiful young woman—brings on court-martial proceedings. Ramage's service is roughly contemporary with that of C. S. Forester's (q.v.) Hornblower, and his adventures are written with the same dash. The Ramage novels have been reprinted in the United States by McBooks (2000–2002), including several that had no previous US publication. Pope (d. 1997) served in the merchant navy during World War II and his lifelong fascination with the British navy has resulted in several nonfiction volumes of maritime history as well as his Ramage novels.

1. *Ramage* (**Lippincott, 1965**) Off the coast of Italy, Ramage must take command of the ship after all the senior officers are killed in battle.
2. *Drumbeat* (**Doubleday, 1968**) The year 1796 is busy for Ramage as he captures a Spanish frigate, rescues a marchioness, and is taken prisoner. UK title: *Ramage and the Drumbeat*.
3. *Triton Brig, The* (**Doubleday, 1969**) In 1797 Ramage takes command of the mutinous crew of the *Triton* and sails on an urgent mission to the West Indies. UK title: *Ramage and the Freebooters*.
4. *Governor Ramage, R.N.* (**Doubleday, 1973**) Ramage's West Indian adventures include the discovery of buried treasure, but the vengeful Admiral Goddard raises storm clouds.
5. *Ramage's Prize* (**Simon & Schuster, 1974**) French privateers are interfering with the mail delivery to England from the West Indies, and Ramage goes to investigate.
6. *Ramage and the Guillotine* (**Simon & Schuster, 1975**) Ramage is sent to infiltrate the French High Command to gather information about the prospective French invasion of England.
7. *Ramage's Diamond* (**Avon, 1982**) In 1804 Captain Ramage rejuvenates the crew of the frigate *Juno* and ships out to the Caribbean for the decisive battle of Diamond Head. Originally published in 1976.
8. *Ramage's Mutiny* (**McBooks, 2001**) In Antigua to fit up a French frigate he captured, Ramage is called upon to sit on a court-martial trying a bloody mutiny. Originally published in 1977.
9. *Ramage and the Rebels* (**Walker, 1985**) While chasing French, Spanish, and Dutch privateers along the Spanish Main, Ramage and his men come upon a merchantman whose passengers and crew have been massacred by pirates. Originally published in 1978.
10. *Ramage Touch, The* (**Walker, 1984**) Captain Ramage, transferred from the West Indies to the Mediterranean, captures two French bomb ketches off Tuscany. Originally published in 1979.
11. *Ramage's Signal* (**Walker, 1984**) Ramage captures a French semaphore station and then takes off after a 15-member French merchant convoy. Originally published in 1980.
12. *Ramage and the Renegades* (**Avon, 1982**) Ramage, sent to claim the South Atlantic island of Trinidad for the Crown, finds a pirate ship and five captured merchantmen in its harbor.
13. *Ramage's Devil* (**McBooks, 2002**) During a temporary lull in the Napoleonic Wars, Ramage combines his honeymoon in Brittany with spying on French naval preparations. Originally published in 1982.

14. *Ramage's Trial* (McBooks, 2002) Thinks look bleak for Ramage when he faces a court-martial that could lead to his execution. Originally published in 1984.

15. *Ramage's Challenge* (McBooks, 2002) Ramage sail the *Calypso* to Italy on a secret mission to rescue British prisoners-of-war. Originally published in 1985.

16. *Ramage at Trafalgar* (McBooks, 2002) Lord Nelson orders Ramage back to his frigate, *Calypso*, and sends him to the fleet blockading the French and Spanish navies off Cadiz. Originally published in 1986.

17. *Ramage and the Saracens* (McBooks, 2002) Ramage and the *Calypso* are sent to Sicily to attack the Barbary pirates. Originally published in 1988.

18. *Ramage and the Dido* (McBooks, 2002) Ramage is appointed captain of the British "Seventy-Four" *Dido* and dispatched to the West Indies. Originally published in 1989.

II. The Ned Yorke series contains four books set in the 1650s in the West Indies. Ned Yorke, son of Royalist family, is forced to flee his Barbados plantation during the period of the rule of Oliver Cromwell, and becomes a buccaneer against the Spanish and the Roundheads. Yorke seems to be based loosely on the historical Sir Henry Morgan.

1. *Buccaneer* (Walker, 1984) In the 1650s Ned Yorke, scion of a Royalist family, is forced off his Barbados plantation and becomes a buccaneer, fighting and fleeing Spaniards and Roundheads alike. Originally published in 1981.

2. *Admiral* (Secker [UK], 1982) Yorke, following the death of Cromwell, returns to Jamaica, and is elected Admiral of the Brethren of the Coast in Tortuga.

3. *Galleon* (Wallker, 1987) The new, Royalist governor of Jamaica suspends the buccaneer's licenses. Yorke rescues his partner Sir Thomas Whetstone from the Spanish and assists the French of St. Martin's against a run-aground Spanish treasure galleon.

4. *Corsair* (Secker [UK], 1987) Ned uncovers evidence of Spanish plans to invade Jamaica but cannot convince Governor Luce of the threat until it is at hand.

III. A third series, containing two volumes, features Ned Yorke's descendant, another Ned Yorke, in naval action against the Germans in World War II.

1. *Convoy* (Walker, 1987) During World War II, the Germans are secretly attacking British convoys from inside of the convoys, and Ned Yorke is dispatched to find out how they are doing it. Originally published in 1979.

2. *Decoy* (Walker, 1984) York is ordered to capture a German U-boat with the new Enigma device, which enables the Germans to encode and decode ship-to-ship messages.

Porter, Joyce

I. Porter's (d. 1990) Inspector Wilfred Dover gives new meaning to the word *antihero*. The acknowledged "Shame of Scotland Yard" is enormously fat and pasty-faced, lazy, rude, and slovenly. He gobbles up everything on the tea table and then nods off while his competent assistant Sergeant MacGregor, handles the interrogations and sorts through the clues. Watching Dover being lured and prodded and falling for every red herring is part of the fun of these lighthearted mysteries. Porter's well-sketched characters tend to be as eccentric as her detective, and her puzzles are of the classic English variety.

1. *Dover One* (Scribner, 1964) Dover's first case involves the disappearance of Julia Rugg, an overweight 18-year-old housemaid.

2. *Dover Two* (Scribner, 1965) Dover must travel to the town of Curdley in northern England to investigate a strange case where a young girl is murdered twice.

3. *Dover Three* (Scribner, 1966) Dover tackles a case of poison-pen letters that have turned into murder.

4. *Dover and the Unkindest Cut of All* (Scribner, 1967) Dover sets up MacGregor as an absolute patsy in this murder case.

5. *Dover Goes to Pott* (Scribner, 1968) The daughter of the leading citizen of Pott Winckle is murdered one evening while watching television.

6. *Dover Strikes Again* (McKay, 1973) Dover must stay at a temperance hotel while he investigates a murder that was covered up in an earthquake. Originally published in 1970.

7. *It's Murder with Dover* (McKay, 1973) Dover hobnobs with some typically dotty and impoverished English aristocrats in this case of murder in a quiet village.

8. *Dover and the Claret Tappers* (Countryman, 1989) The Claret Tappers gang finds that kidnapping Dover doesn't pay. Originally published in 1977.

9. *Dead Easy for Dover* (St. Martin's, 1979) The residents of the posh suburban enclave in the village of Frenchy Botham are suspects in the murder of a young girl who is found among the well-kept shrubberies.

10. *Dover Beats the Band* (Countryman, 1991) An autopsy reveals that the stomach contents of an unidentified murdered man include a mysterious blue bead. Originally published in 1980.

11. *Dover: The Collected Short Stories* (Foul Play, 1995) Eleven Dover stories.

II. Eddie Brown is the inept and ineffective star of Porter's broadly humorous variation on the international espionage genre. Eddie would much rather crack jokes than spy rings, but he's not very good at anything but blundering into trouble.

1. *Sour Cream with Everything* (Scribner, 1966) Eddie's fluent Russian and resemblance to an undercover agent get him transferred from his provincial British teaching post to a rest home in the Soviet Union.

2. *Chinks in the Curtain, The* (Scribner, 1968) Eddie goes to Paris to uncover a plot to restore the Romanovs to the Russian throne.

3. *Neither a Candle nor a Pitchfork* (McCall, 1970) Eddie is parachuted back into the Soviet Union, where he finds that the Vavilov Collective Stud Farm has other interests besides horses.

4. *Only with a Bargepole* (McKay, 1974) When Miss Muriel Drom, daughter of Sir Maurice Drom, Eddie's boss at S.O.D. is kidnapped, Eddie somehow contrives to be a member of the kidnapper's gang.

III. Porter's spoof on the amateur detective genre features the Honourable Constance Ethel Morrison-Burke, an indomitable battleship of a woman who took up detecting as a hobby because she needed another outlet fro her tremendous energy. "The Hon. Con," as she is fondly known, blusters her way to, and sometimes right over, her quarry. Miss Jones is her long-suffering companion.

1. *Rather a Common Sort of Crime* (McCall, 1970) The first and only client of the Hon. Con's advice bureau is a distraught mother who is convinced that her son's "suicide" was really murder.

2. *Meddler and Her Murder, The* (McKay, 1973) The murder of an Irish au pair girl on Sneddon Avenue has the Hon. Con tearing up the town of Totterbridge.

3. *Package Included Murder, The* **(Bobbs-Merrill, 1976)** On a group tour to Russia, the Hon. Con and Miss Jones inevitably get involved when one of their fellow tourists suffers several violent attacks.

4. *Who the Heck Is Sylvia?* **(Weidenfeld [UK], 1977)** No annotation available.

5. *Cart before the Crime, The* **(Weidenfeld [UK], 1979)** To keep the Hon. Con from mucking up a royal visit, the townswomen of Totterbridge cook a mystery surrounding the sale of Totterford Manor.

Potok, Chaim

I. Potok (d. 2002), a rabbi and scholar, incorporated a good deal of Talmudic argument into his novels on contemporary Jewish life in America. His fully drawn characters and interesting situations make gratifying and thoughtful reading. The story of Danny and Reuven, the two main characters, begins in their teens in the 1940s and shows the conflict between secular and the mystical elements of the Jewish religion.

1. *Chosen, The* **(Simon & Schuster, 1967)** A friendship develops between young Danny and Reuven, who meet at a baseball game between their two very different schools in Brooklyn. The 1981 film starred Rod Steiger and Robby Benson.

2. *Promise, The* **(Knopf, 1969)** Now two young men entering different occupations—for Reuven the rabbinate, for Danny, clinical psychology—they offer different kinds of help to a troubled adolescent.

II. One of Potok's most popular novels was *My Name Is Asher Lev*, the story of an artist and his struggles with his intensely religious Jewish family to realize his goal. Eighteen years later *The Gift of Asher Lev* followed Asher into adulthood.

1. *My Name Is Asher Lev* **(Knopf, 1972)** Asher Lev, scion of Hasidic Jews in Brooklyn, realizes early in life that he has a compulsion to draw and paint.

2. *Gift of Asher Lev, The* **(Knopf, 1990)** Asher returns to Brooklyn from France with his wife and children and tries to reassimilate with his Hasidic community after 20 years' absence.

Powell, Anthony

Many readers of the individual volumes of Anthony Powell's (pronounced *Po-el*) 12-novel series A Dance to the Music of Time reread the whole series after the last volume was published. Narrated by Nicholas Jenkins, a stand-in for Powell, the books chronicle 50 years of English upper- and upper-middle-class life from 1921 to 1971 and encompass dozens of literary, political, and social figures, both fictional and historical. It is one of the most accomplished and absorbing works of modern literature. Hilary Spurling's companion to the series, *Invitation to the Dance* (Little, Brown, 1977), containing a complete character index as well as books, painting, and place indexes and synopses, is useful both for the novice and for the reader who has read the series more than once. Best read in sequence, the 12 individual volumes have been consolidated into four omnibus volumes under the title *A Dance to the Music of Time: First through Fourth Movements* (Little, Brown, 1962–1976). These four volumes were reissued in paperback by Popular Library in 1976 under the subtitles *Spring, Summer, Autumn* and *Winter*. Anthony Powell (d. 2000) published several other novels, a play, and four volumes of memoirs, *To Keep the Ball Rolling*, published together in one abridged and revised volume by Penguin (1983).

1. *Question of Upbringing, A* **(Scribner, 1951)** The story opens in 1921, introducing Nicholas Jenkins, the ineffable Widmerpool, and others at Eton. Nick goes to France for a year, then to Oxford.

2. *Buyer's Market, A* **(Scribner, 1953)** The characters participate in the social and intellectual life of London in the late 1920s.

3. *Acceptance World, The* **(Farrar, 1955)** The climax of this book, set in the early thirties, is a dinner party given by Nick and some other "old boys" for their Eton housemaster, Le Bas.

4. *At Lady Molly's* **(Little, Brown, 1957)** Lady Molly's 1934 New Year's Eve party begins events that lead to Nick's engagement to Isobel Tolland.

5. *Casanova's Chinese Restaurant* **(Little, Brown, 1960)** London's "smart" and "bohemian" sets contrast during 1936–1937.

6. *Kindly Ones, The* **(Little, Brown, 1962)** This account goes back in time to Nick's childhood in 1914, then progresses to the beginning of World War II.

7. *Valley of Bones, The* **(Little, Brown, 1964)** In 1940 Nick is a second lieutenant in a backwater post of the Welsh infantry, bored and distressed with the pettiness of civilian duty during war.

8. *Soldier's Art, The* **(Little, Brown, 1966)** Nick spends a dismal year at divisional headquarters under Widmerpool in 1941.

9. *Military Philosophers, The* **(Little, Brown, 1968)** This book covers from early in 1942, when Nick is assigned to intelligence, to his demobilization in 1945.

10. *Books Do Furnish a Room* **(Little, Brown, 1971)** Nick at 40 has two sons and several published novels, and his literary reputation is rising.

11. *Temporary Kings* **(Little, Brown, 1973)** Nick attends an international writers' conference in Venice in 1958 and meets old friends.

12. *Hearing Secret Harmonies* **(Little, Brown, 1975)** Now in his sixties, Nick reflects on his life and the follies of the younger generation. Widmerpool comes to an odd end.

Poyer, David

I. US Naval Academy graduate Poyer has reached a large audience with his naval technothrillers, which reveal an intimate knowledge of the workings of the modern US Navy. Dan Lenson is a career naval officer who goes through career and marital crises during the course of an ongoing series.

1. *Circle, The* **(St. Martin's, 1992)** Dan Lenson, fresh out of Annapolis, joins his first ship, the obsolete destroyer USS *Reynolds*, and tracks a renegade Soviet missile sub in the teeth of an Arctic storm. This is the first novel chronologically but the third published in the series.

2. *Med, The* **(St. Martin's, 1988)** "The Med" is the Mediterranean Sea, where Lieutenant Lenson is stationed when his wife, daughter, and other tourists are seized by Palestinian terrorists.

3. *Gulf, The* **(St. Martin's, 1990)** Lieutenant Commander Lenson is on duty in the Arabian Gulf with a captain who is bent on revenge and a beautiful defense expert.

4. *Passage, The* **(St. Martin's, 1995)** The newly commissioned USS *Barrett*, bound for Guantánamo Bay, is not a happy ship, what with a gay captain, a crewman who jumps overboard, and Lenson with his marriage and career on the rocks.

5. *Tomahawk* **(St. Martin's, 1998)** Lenson, holding a Pentagon position and involved in the trouble-plagued development of the

Tomahawk cruise missile, falls in love with peace activist Kerry Donovan.

6. **China Sea (St. Martin's, 2000)** Lenson takes command of the USS *Gaddis*, a vessel to be donated to the Pakistanis, a mission that somehow leads to a confrontation with Chinese pirates and a Chinese war vessel.

7. **Black Storm (St. Martin's, 2002)** Set in 1991, during the Persian Gulf War. Lenson, now a US Navy missile expert, and US Army major Maureen Maddox, a biological warfare specialist, trek across 500 miles of desert to stymie an unspecified weapon of mass destruction in Saddam Hussein's armory.

8. **Command, The (St. Martin's, 2004)** Lenson, promoted to commander and in charge of a helicopter-capable destroyer, the USS *Thomas Horner*, returns to the Persian Gulf.

9. **Threat, The (St. Martin's, 2006)** Lenson joins the National Security Council staff at the White House after the First Gulf War. He assumes a number of tasks, including performing antidrug duty and carrying the legendary briefcase with its nuclear launch codes.

10. **Korea Strait (St. Martin's, 2007)** Lenson is "put on the shelf" and ordered to oversee a small crew of civilians and retired military personnel on a training exercise off the Korean peninsula.

11. **Weapon, The (St. Martin's, 2008)** Lenson, failing to buy a powerful new rocket torpedo the Russians have developed, tries to "liberate" one and runs afoul of the Iranians.

II. Lyle "Tiller" Galloway is also attracted to the sea, but deepwater diver Tiller is considerable less "regular navy" than Lenson. Galloway has served a five-year term for cocaine smuggling and is trying to make ends meet with a debt-ridden recreational diving-salvage outfit operating out of Cape Hatteras, North Carolina.

1. **Hatteras Blue (St. Martin's, 1989)** Out of jail and on parole, Tiller accepts a commission to locate and salvage a World War II U-boat off Cape Hatteras.

2. **Bahamas Blue (St. Martin's, 1991)** Tiller and his friend Shad Aydlett agree to a 400-foot dive to recover 50 tons of cocaine believed to be lying off the coast of the Bahamas.

3. **Louisiana Blue (St. Martin's, 1994)** Tiller and Shad hook up with Deep Tech, a small company hired to perform underwater work on oil pipelines off the Louisiana coast.

4. **Down to a Sunless Sea (St. Martin's, 1996)** Galloway goes to Florida at the behest of the widow of an old friend, and learns the ropes of the scary art of cave diving.

III. Poyer's native Western Pennsylvania is scene for the Hemlock County series of novels, in which rural locals are beset by inclement weather and corrupt, polluting corporations. The leading continuing character in this series is W. T. "Racks" Halvorsen, former boxer and oil driller, who, despite, or because of, his personal integrity, gets enmeshed in prison, toxic waste, vigilante killers, winter storms, and other trials. *Winterlight* (Forge, 2001) contains numbers 3 and 4.

1. **Thunder on the Mountain (Forge, 1999)** Last published but first in chronology, this novel is set in 1936, in the throes of the Great Depression, when promising boxer Bill Halvorsen is hired as a driller by the Thunder Oil Company.

2. **Dead of Winter, The (Forge, 1988)** When Paul Michelson goes off a vigilante tear, shooting random hunters after his son is shot and left to die by a hunter, Halvorsen takes on the job of stopping him.

3. **Winter in the Heart (St. Martin's, 1993)** A corrupt oil-company CEO is at the bottom of the toxic waste spill that poisons the now-elderly Halvorsen and many other locals.

4. **As the Wolf Loves Winter (Forge, 1996)** After being jailed for blowing up a bridge in the battle against polluters, Halvorsen is released and returns to his beloved woods, only to get enmeshed again in murder and corporate corruption.

IV. Poyer is now engaged in writing a historical series, the Civil War at Sea, that describes the American Civil War from a naval aspect. Fictional characters mix with historical characters, such as *Monitor*-builder John Ericson, in this saga replete with authentic naval-action sequences.

1. **Fire on the Waters (Simon & Schuster, 2001)** In the wake of the fall of Fort Sumter, the USS *Owanee* is sent on a mysterious mission in Chesapeake Bay.

2. **Country of Our Own, A (Simon & Schuster, 2003)** Although not enamoured of slavery, US naval officer Ker Claiborne joins the Confederacy of his native Virginia and becomes commander of the raider CSS *Maryland*.

3. **That Anvil of Our Souls (Simon & Schuster, 2005)** Subtitle: *A Novel of the Monitor and the Merrimack*. Describes the preparations for the historic battle of the ironclads *Monitor* and *Merrimack* off Hampton Roads, Virginia, in March 1862.

Pratchett, Terry

Welcome to Discworld! Where fantasy archetypes are sent up with glee! English writer Pratchett approaches fantasy the same way that Douglas Adams (q.v.) approached science fiction. Discworld is a flat world riding on the backs of four giant elephants standing on an even bigger turtle and is inhabited by zany characters like the inept wizard Rincewind, the somewhat more ept witches Granny Weatherwax and Nanny Ogg, malevolent footlockers, Cohen the Barbarian, oversized dwarfs, Nazi-like elves, the Ankh-Morpork City Watch, a Grim Reaper who takes vacations, teenage gods, orangutan library directors, and a flying horse named Binky.

Although Discworld hasn't reaped comparable success in the United States, it has made Terry Pratchett the UK's best-selling author in the 1990s and beyond. There is also a Discworld series for children and numerous spin-offs such as annual Discworld calendars, *Nanny Ogg's Cookbook*, Discworld "Mapps," *The Discworld Companion*, and *The Science of Discworld* (flat-earth physics, naturally). Omnibus volumes include *Death Trilogy* (Orion [UK], 1998; numbers 4, 11, and 16); *City Watch Trilogy* (Orion [UK], 1999; numbers 8, 15, and 19); and *The Colour of Magic/The Light Fantastic* (Colin Smythe [UK], 1999; numbers 1 and 2).

1. **Colour of Magic, The (St. Martin's, 1983)** Inept wizard Rincewind unwillingly becomes a tour guide for Twoflowers, a wealthy, naive visitor.

2. **Light Fantastic, The (New American Library, 1986)** Rincewind, possessor of one of the Eight Great Spells, must be found before Great A'Tuin, the cosmic turtle, carries Discworld to almost certain destruction.

3. **Equal Rites (New American Library, 1987)** A dying wizard tries to pass on his powers to an eighth son of an eighth son being born in the town of Bad Ass, but "he" turns out to be a girl.

4. **Mort (New American Library, 1987)** Death decides to take a holiday, so he hires young Mort to look after things while he is away.

5. **Sourcery (New American Library, 1989)** Cain is the eighth son of a wizard, which means that he will become a *sorcerer* rather than an ordinary wizard. Originally published in 1987.

6. *Wyrd Sisters* **(Roc, 1989)** Granny Weatherwax and the Spell Sisters have their monthly cauldron stirring upset by regicide and the sudden arrival of a royal baby in the kingdom of Lancre.

7. *Pyramids* **(Roc, 1990)** Teenage god Teppic is taken away from his assassination training when his father, the pharaoh, is untimely mummified.

8. *Guards! Guards!* **(Roc, 1991)** The city of Ankh-Morpork gets along splendidly with its unionized criminals until an oversized dwarf gets the notion of cleaning up the place. Originally published in 1989.

9. *Eric* **(Roc, 1995)** Eric, Discworld's only demon hacker, calls up the wizard Rincewind and Rincewind's "Luggage," a sentient, malevolent footlocker, to have his three wishes granted. Originally published in 1989.

10. *Moving Pictures* **(Roc, 1992)** The death of an old cameraman sets the camera-box imps into a frenzy, which in turn sets Ankh-Morpork into a frenzy. Originally published in 1990.

11. *Reaper Man* **(Roc, 1992)** When Death starts having scruples about his job, he is retired, an act that upsets the Dead Rights activists.

12. *Witches Abroad* **(Roc, 1993)** Granny Weatherwax and the Spell Sisters try to keep fairy godmother Desiderata's appointment in Genua.

13. *Small Gods* **(HarperCollins, 1994)** Apprentice priest Brutha is suddenly privy to the thoughts of the turtle god Om, who is attempting to make a comeback. Originally published in 1992.

14. *Lords and Ladies* **(HarperCollins, 1994)** Granny Weatherwax and the Spell Sisters have to be called in when a bunch of smiling, sadistic elves tries to take over the human kingdom of Lancre.

15. *Men at Arms* **(HarperCollins, 1996)** Captain Sam Vimes of the Ankh-Morpork City Watch is planning to get married and retire, but something really nasty is afoot. Originally published in 1993.

16. *Soul Music* **(HarperCollins, 1995)** Susan, Death's granddaughter, is made aware of her inborn talent, which is making rock music with real rocks, by Death's servant, Albert. Originally published in 1994.

17. *Interesting Times* **(HarperCollins, 1997)** Rincewind, Cohen the Barbarian, Terrorand Panic, and a bunch of other characters are embroiled in the war and revolution resulting from a "What I Did on My Holidays" paper. Originally published in 1994.

18. *Maskerade* **(HarperCollins, 1997)** Granny Weatherwax and Nanny Ogg, spending a "night at the Opera," get embroiled in all kinds of mischief, including, of course, the opera house's resident phantom. Originally published in 1995.

19. *Feet of Clay* **(HarperCollins, 1996)** The golems are committing suicide, while the City Watch is trying to track down an unseen murderer and deal with a werewolf suffering from Pre-Lunar Tension.

20. *Hogfather* **(HarperCollins, 1998)** The fat man who delivers the presents is missing on the Night before Hogwatch. Susan the governess has to find him before morning or the sun won't rise.

21. *Jingo* **(HarperCollins, 1998)** War fever seizes Discworld, as armies of sardines, warriors, fishermen, and squid prepare for action, and Commander Vimes's Pocket Dis-organizer says "Die" under "Things to Do Today."

22. *Last Continent, The* **(HarperCollins, 1998)** The Last Continent is a separate creation, vaguely resembling Australia, where nearly everything that's not poisonous is venomous. Rincewind and Luggage are called upon to prevent the destruction of this idyllic world.

23. *Carpe Jugulum* **(HarperCollins, 1998)** Mightily Oats enters the mountain kingdom of Lancre, where dandified vampires and witches are at war.

24. *Fifth Elephant, The* **(HarperCollins, 2000)** Sam Vimes is racing through the forest with werewolves on his trail on a mission to stop war.

25. *Truth, The* **(HarperCollins, 2000)** Discworld's first newspaper editor just wants to get at the truth, but unfortunately, many people want him dead for a variety of reasons.

26. *Thief of Time* **(Harper Collins, 2001)** Time is managed by the Monks of History, who pump it up from underwater, where it is wasted, to the cities, where it is at a premium. A young horologist making the world's first truly accurate clock may bring Time to a stop.

27. *Last Hero, The* **(HarperCollins, 2001)** Cohen the Barbarian, all five feet of him, goes on one last quest to the highest mountain on Discworld. Coauthored with Paul Kidd.

28. *Night Watch* **(HarperCollins, 2002)** Sam Vimes, on a mission for the City Watch, is forced to live in the past to track down a murderer, teach his younger self the art of policing, and change the outcome of a bloody rebellion.

29. *Monstrous Regiment* **(HarperCollins, 2003)** Polly Perks, a Borogravian barmaid, decides to don a male disguise and infiltrate the Tenth Fool Light Infantry to find her missing brother, Paul.

30. *Going Postal* **(HarperCollins, 2004)** Moist von Lipwig (aka Alfred Spangler), who barely "scaped hanging," is offered the job of postmaster general of the Ankh-Morpork post office, which has been closed for 20 years.

31. *Thud!* **(HarperCollins, 2005)** Commander Sam Vimes is going to watch the rerun of the Kroom Valley Massacre, where the trolls ambushed the dwarves or, maybe, the dwarves ambushed the trolls

32. *Making Money* **(HarperCollins, 2007)** Moist von Lipwig, who reorganized the Ankh-Morpork post office in number 30, turns his attention to the Royal Mint.

Price, Eugenia

I. Eugenia Price's three novels set on St. Simon's Island, Georgia, are romantic, inspirational stories just right for readers looking for good, old-fashioned, and slightly prim stories. Her major characters are based on real people, and her scenery is painted with the appreciative eye of a loving resident. The novels are arranged chronologically below, which is the reserve order of their publication. Each novel can be enjoyed separately. Price (d. 1996) was also the author of much inspirational nonfiction and autobiographical works such as *St. Simon's Memoir: The Personal Story of Finding the Island and Writing the St. Simon's Trilogy of Novels* (Lippincott, 1978).

1. *Lighthouse* **(Lippincott, 1971)** Young James Gould leaves his New England home in 1791 and eventually settles with his wife and children on St. Simon's Island to build its lighthouse.

2. *New Moon Rising* **(Lippincott, 1969)** Horace Gould, James's son, is dismissed from Yale in 1830, then struggles to find himself and his place in the troubled times leading up to and through the Civil War.

3. *Beloved Invader, The* **(Lippincott, 1965)** Anson Dodge, a Northerner, comes to St. Simon's Island to rebuild a church destroyed during the Civil War.

II. Price published four novels in the Savannah Quartet, a series of historical romances set in antebellum Georgia. The fictional Brownings, Latimers, and Mackays interact with real people such as Robert E. Lee in a well-researched historical setting.

1. *Savannah* (**Doubleday, 1983**) Handsome Yankee Mark Browning comes to Savannah and joins Robert Mackay's mercantile firm, then finds himself falling in love with Mackay's wife.
2. *To See Your Face Again* (**Doubleday, 1985**) Romance blossoms when 16-year-old Natalie Browning and Burke Latimer survive the 1838 explosion of the steamship *Pulaski*.
3. *Before the Darkness Falls* (**Doubleday, 1987**) Natalie and Burke Latimer settle into married life together on the north Georgia frontier, while Natalie's brother Jonathan drops out of Yale to marry Indian Mary.
4. *Stranger in Savannah* (**Doubleday, 1989**) The Browning, Mackay, and Stiles families are all caught up in the Civil War in this volume covering 1864 to 1865 in Savannah.

III. Price published a third historical series, called the Georgia Trilogy, which, like series I, takes place on St. Simon's Island. It tells the life of Anne Fraser from the age of 18 in the War of 1812 through her courtship, marriage, widowhood, and subsequent life after the Civil War. As with the other series, the Georgia Trilogy has historical figures mixing with the fictional characters and lovingly lush descriptions of the Georgia landscape.

1. *Bright Captivity* (**Doubleday, 1991**) When the British capture St. Simon's Island during the War of 1812, young Anne Couper falls in love with Lieutenant John Fraser of the Royal Marines.
2. *Where Shadows Go* (**Doubleday, 1993**) Follows the happy couple from 1825, when they return to St. Simon's Island, to 1839, by which time John has become a successful planter.
3. *Beauty from Ashes* (**Doubleday, 1995**) In 1845 Anne is mourning her husband while living with their four children in their St. Simon home, which they are about to lose.

IV. The Florida Trilogy is a series connected by its historical setting rather than by its characters. It takes place in and around St. Augustine, Florida in a period from just after the American Revolution to beyond the Civil War, and is seen through the eyes of three different families who settle there.

1. *Don Juan McQueen* (**Lippincott, 1974**) John McQueen flees to Spanish-ruled Florida after the American Revolution. His wife joins him, and they settle in St. Augustine.
2. *Maria* (**Lippincott, 1977**) Maria Evans leaves Charles Town to come to St. Augustine, where her soldier husband is posted and proves her worth as a midwife. Set in the period after the relinquishment of Florida by the Spanish to the United States.
3. *Margaret's Story* (**Lippincott, 1980**) Margaret Seton helps her husband, Lewis, set up a plantation on the St. John's River in Florida in 1830; bears seven children; and survives the Seminole Wars, the Civil War, and Reconstruction.

Price, Reynolds

I. *A Long and Happy Life* was a highly praised first novel that won Price recognition as a talented young southern writer. Set in a small town in contemporary North Carolina, it tells the moving love story of Rosacoke Mustian, who gives herself too freely to an unworthy young man. The final scene, with Rosacoke playing Mary in a local Christmas pageant, gives the deceptively simple story symbolic overtones. A second novel starring Rosacoke's older brother Milo precedes the first chronologically. After a hiatus of more than 20 years, Price returned to Rosacoke and Wesley Beavers to see how they were faring after 30 years of marriage and to complete the Mustian trilogy.

Reynolds Price, like Larry McMurtry (q.v.), chafed under the designation of "regional writer." His books, although set in, and around, Price's native North Carolina, do not supply southern gothic themes, nor are they heavy on dialect. Price, who teaches English at Duke University, is a versatile writer who has written other novels (e.g., *Kate Vaiden*, Atheneum, 1986); many short stories (*The Collected Stories*, Atheneum, 1994); poetry (*The Collected Poems*, Scribner, 1997); plays; books about religion (he is a believing if unconventional Christian); and memoirs, including *A Whole New Life: An Illness and a Healing* (Atheneum, 1994), about his three-year bout with cancer of the spine, which left him wheelchair-bound.

1. *Generous Man, A* (**Atheneum, 1966**) The coming-of-age story of young Milo Mustian involves a python, a snake girl, and a desperate hunt through the woods for a possibly rabid dog.
2. *Long and Happy Life, A* (**Atheneum, 1962**) Milo's sister Rosacoke is in love with a young man who cares more about motorcycles than about the smitten young girl.
3. *Good Hearts* (**Atheneum, 1988**) Wesley Beavers, in the throes of a midlife crisis, begins an affair with a 26-year-old woman.

II. Price has also written a trilogy narrating the events of 90 years covering most of the 20th century in rural North Carolina and Virginia. The elopement of 30-year-old Forrest Mayfield and 16-year-old Eva Kendall sets in train a tormented family history. Price brings out his characters' harsh personalities and their North Carolina cadences in this passionate yet unsentimental family saga. Omnibus containing numbers 1 through 3: *A Great Circle* (Scribner, 2001).

1. *Surface of Earth, The* (**Atheneum, 1975**) Events spanning 40 years (1903–1944) in the Mayfield family are started by the elopement of Forrest Mayfield with Eva Kendall.
2. *Source of Light, The* (**Atheneum, 1981**) In 1955 Hutch Mayfield goes off to study at Oxford University, unaware that his father is dying of cancer.
3. *Promise of Rest, The* (**Scribner, 1995**) Wade Mayfield, great-grandson of Forrest and Eva, comes home to North Carolina to die of AIDS after the death of his black lover.

Pronzini, Bill (William John)

I. Bill Pronzini's Nameless Detective, who first appeared in a short story in 1969, has clearly modeled himself after the hard-boiled private eyes in the pulp magazines that he reads and collects. True to form, he hides his strong sense of justice and compassion under a tough, cynical exterior. Basically a loner, he does have a girlfriend (Kerry Wade, whom he eventually marries) and a male friend in the San Francisco Police Department who becomes his partner, breaks with him, and eventually commits suicide (Eb Eberhardt). Later novels give Nameless a home life and family, not to the liking of readers who feel that Nameless has developed a soft edge. Nameless is the hero of 31 novels, three collections of short stories, and two novelettes published in limited editions by Waves Press (*A Killing in Xanadu*, 1980, and *Catspaw*, 1983). Two of the novels in which Nameless appears were collaborations with other authors. Numbers 9 and 11, numbers 7 and 8, and numbers 6 and 15 were published together in three volumes by Knightsbridge in 1990. Pronzini's detective stories are reliably taut and satisfying. The San Francisco ambience is well done. Pronzini is married to Marcia Muller (q.v.), one of his coauthors.

1. *Snatch, The* (**Random House, 1971**) Wealthy Louis Martinetti calls in Nameless to deliver the ransom demanded for his nine-year-old son.

2. *Vanished, The* (**Random House, 1973**) Nameless is brought in the case of a missing soldier by the man's fiancée.

3. *Undercurrent* (**Random House, 1973**) Trailing a husband suspected of infidelity, Nameless finds the man murdered in a motel room.

4. *Blowback* (**Random House, 1977**) Nameless goes to a fishing camp in the Mother Lode country to help an old army buddy in trouble.

5. *Twospot* (**Putnam, 1978**) Nameless teams up with coauthor Collin Wilcox's (q.v.) Frank Hastings to investigate a case of murder and fraud at a California winery.

6. *Labyrinth* (**St. Martin's, 1980**) The seemingly unrelated deaths of two women, one by shooting, one by car accident, may be connected.

7. *Hoodwink* (**St. Martin's, 1981**) Six members of the Pulpeteers, a mystery writers' group, have received extortion threats.

8. *Scattershot* (**St. Martin's, 1982**) A philandering husband who disappears and a missing socialite who turns up dead are part of an intricate web of revenge.

9. *Dragonfire* (**St. Martin's, 1982**) Nameless, angry over the unjust revoking of his license, is further incensed when a Chinese gunman shoots him and Eberhardt.

10. *Bindlestiff* (**St. Martin's, 1983**) Charles Bradford, a government bureaucrat turned hobo, is being sought by one of his daughters.

11. *Casefile* (**St. Martin's, 1983**) Subtitle: *The Best of the "Nameless Detective" Stories*. A collection of short stories.

12. *Quicksilver* (**St. Martin's, 1984**) While investigating why someone is anonymously sending jewelry to a young Japanese American woman, Nameless runs into murder and the dread Yakuza.

13. *Nightshades* (**St. Martin's, 1984**) Nameless goes to an old ghost town in northern California to probe the fiery death of a real-estate developer.

14. *Double* (**St. Martin's, 1984**) Nameless and coauthor Marcia Muller's (q.v.) Sharon McCone meet at a private eye convention in San Diego and get involved in parallel investigations of the death of a hotel security officer.

15. *Bones* (**St. Martin's, 1985**) Asked to investigate the circumstances of the 1949 suicide of a pulp detective fiction writer, Nameless stirs up some long-buried scandals and corpses.

16. *Deadfall* (**St. Martin's, 1986**) After witnessing the shooting of prominent bisexual lawyer Leonard Purcell, Nameless is asked to investigate by Purcell's live-in lover.

17. *Shackles* (**St. Martin's, 1988**) A masked man leaves Nameless chained in a remote mountain cabin with only enough supplies to last three or four months.

18. *Jackpot* (**Delacorte, 1990**) Still recovering from his ordeal in number 17, Nameless investigates the suicide of a young man who has just won $200,000 gambling in Reno.

19. *Breakdown* (**Delacorte, 1991**) Nameless, undercover as "Art Canino," is watching a fellow drinker in the Hideaway, a seedy beach tavern near San Francisco, who may know something about a hit-and-run death.

20. *Quarry* (**Delacorte, 1992**) Grady Haas, daughter of rancher Arlo Haas, is being stalked by a brutal stranger who may have some connection with her job as an insurance adjuster.

21. *Epitaphs* (**Delacorte, 1992**) Nameless, pushing 60, is trying to locate the wandering granddaughter of an elderly North Beach resident.

22. *Demons* (**Delacorte, 1993**) Nameless is hired by Kay Runyon to exorcise her wandering husband's obsession with "man-killer" Nedra Merchant.

23. *Hardcase* (**Delacorte, 1995**) Nameless marries longtime girlfriend Kerry, and takes on the case of Melanie Ann Aldrich, who wants to find out who her birth parents were.

24. *Sentinels* (**Carroll & Graf, 1996**) Helen McDowell's daughter Allison and her black boyfriend have gone missing in the remote hamlet of Creekside, California, while on a auto trip from Oregon to San Francisco.

25. *Spadework* (**Crippen & Landru, 1996**) Subtitle: *A Collection of "Nameless Detective" Stories*. Fifteen previously uncollected short stories and two new ones.

26. *Illusions* (**Carrol & Graf, 1997**) Nameless, increasingly obsessed with his investigation into the suicide of estranged friend and former partner Eb Eberhardt, is hired to find a businessman's ex-wife.

27. *Boobytrap* (**Carroll & Graf, 1998**) David Michael Latner, a mad bomber out for revenge, is threatening some inhabitants of Deep Mountain Lake.

28. *Crazybone* (**Carroll & Graf, 2000**) A case of insurance fraud in the affluent community of Greenwood is the tip an iceberg of larceny, adultery, betrayal, and murder.

29. *Bleeders* (**Carroll & Graf, 2001**) Nameless exposes a scam that involves junior account executive Jay Cohalan, his wife, and his mistress.

30. *Spook* (**Carroll & Graf, 2002**) Nameless, still not retired, searches for the identity of a homeless man found shot in a doorway.

31. *Scenarios* (**Five Star, 2003**) Subtitle: *A "Nameless Detective" Casebook*. A collection of 14 stories.

32. *Nightcrawlers* (**Forge, 2005**) Nameless and his partners, Jake and Vanessa, intervene in some gay-bashing cases in San Francisco.

33. *Mourners* (**Forge, 2005**) Wealthy financial consultant James Troxell suddenly starts attending the funerals of women, all strangers who died violently.

34. *Savages* (**Forge, 2007**) Former client Celeste Ogden hires Nameless to prove that software mogul Brandon Mathias was responsible for her sister's fatal fall at her home.

II. Secret Service agent Quincannon of 1890s San Francisco stars in *Quincannon*; costars with his female partner in *Carpenter and Quincannon*, *Quincannon*, and *Quincannon's Game*; and appears posthumously in *Beyond the Grave*. The Quincannon books are entertaining combinations of western and mystery.

1. *Quincannon* (**Walker, 1985**) Quincannon is on the trail of a counterfeiting ring in San Francisco in 1893.

2. *Beyond the Grave* (**Walker, 1986**) In the 1980s, coauthor Marcia Muller's (q.v.) Elena Oliverez uses Quincannon's notes to find the solution to a mystery that eluded him in 1894.

3. *Carpenter and Quincannon: Professional Detective Services* (**Crippen & Landru, 1998**) A collection of nine short stories, one original, in which Quincannon teams up with the beautiful but physically unobtainable Sabina Carpenter.

4. *Quincannon's Game* (**Five Star, 2005**) Four new adventures, including "The Bughouse Caper," in which Quincannon matches wits with Sherlock Holmes (q.v.).

Proust, Marcel

In 2003 a new six-volume translation, *In Search of Lost Time*, of Marcel Proust's *A la recherche du temps perdu* was published by Penguin UK. This translation, edited by Christopher Prendergast, was produced by seven different translators, one for each volume of the original. This translation, based on the "definitive" 1987–1988 edition of the French text, is designed to be "more accessible" to English-speaking readers, and is closer to the original than previous efforts. Not surprisingly, given its multiple translators, this new version has received mixed reviews, some volumes being praised, others panned. So far only the first three volumes have been issued in the United States (Viking). Most readers have relied on the elegant translation by C. K. Scott Moncrieff (volume seven produced by Frederick Blossom after Scott Moncrieff's death, and retranslated by Andreas Mayor), entitled *Remembrance of Times Past* (published in two volumes by Random House in 1934) or the completely revised version by Terence Kilmartin, retitled *In Search of Lost Time* (three volumes, Random House, 1981), or the further revision by D. J. Enright (Modern Library, 1992).

Whatever the translation, *In Search of Times Past* has been enshrined in the critical pantheon for decades, being ranked as one of the greatest, if not *the* greatest, novels of the 20th century, and Proust, with his cork-lined bedroom, has become an almost legendary figure. Two massive new biographies have appeared in recent years, each entitled *Marcel Proust: A Life*, one by Jean-Yves Tadie (Viking, 2000) and one by William Carter (Yale, 2000). Many readers have found reading Proust's masterpiece a daunting experience and have given up somewhere not too far into *Swann's Way*, soon after Marcel has had his memories set in motion by the madeleine in the Paris café. Perseverance brings great rewards, however, as many readers who have stayed the course will attest: some recent examples include Phyllis Rose, *The Year of Reading Proust* (Scribner, 1997); Malcom Bowie, *Proust among the Stars* (Columbia, 1998); and Alain de Botton, *How Proust Can Change Your Life* (Pantheon, 1997). *In Search of Times Past* is a great comic (yes, comic) evocation of the social, literary, and artistic life of France before World War I. The narrator, Marcel, based on but not identical with Proust, and the other inhabitants of Proust's world, such as M. Swann, Baron de Charlus, Gilberte, the Duchesse de Guermantes, Albertine, and the Verdurins, were real people transmogrified by the author and are among the greatest creations in fiction.

The best "distillation" of *In Search of Times Past* is (film never produced) *The Proust Screenplay*, written by Harold Pinter (Grove, 1978). Film versions, not too successful, include *Swann in Love* (1984), starring Jeremy Irons and Ornella Muti, and *Time Regained* (1999), starring Marcello Mastroianni and Catherine Deneuve. Guides to the novel include Terence Kilmartin's *A Reader's Guide to Remembrance of Things Past* (Knopf, 1983) and Roger Shattuck's *Proust's Way* (Norton, 2000).

1. *Swann's Way* (Holt, 1922) This book covers Marcel's youth and the love story of M. Swann. Translated from the French by C. K. Scott Moncrieff, revised by Terence Kilmartin, and further revised by D. J. Enright. Retranslated by Lydia Davis as *The Way by Swann's* (Viking, 2003). First published in France in 1913 as *Du côté de chez Swann*.

2. *Within a Budding Grove* (Boni, 1924) Marcel's boyish affair with Gilberte comes to an end, and he goes off to the seaside for his health. Translated from the French by C. K. Scott Moncrieff. Translation revised by Terence Kilmartin and further revised by D. J. Enright. New translation by James Grieve entitled *In the Shadow of Young Girls in Flowers* (Viking, 2004). First published in France in 1918 as *A l'ombre des jeunes filles en fleurs*.

3. *Guermantes Way, The* (Seltzer, 1925) Marcel, now a young man of fashion, moves in the Duchess de Guermantes's exclusive social circle. Translated from the French by C. K. Scott Moncrieff. Revised translation by Terence Kilmartin; further revision by D. J. Enright. New translation by Mark Treharne (Viking, 2004). First published in France in 1920–1921 as *Le côté de Guermantes*.

4. *Cities of the Plain* (Boni, 1927) This volume concerns the homosexual Baron de Charlus and Marcel's growing attraction to Albertine. The Dreyfus Affair forms a background. Translated from the French by C. K. Scott Moncrieff. Revised translation by Terence Kilmartin; further revisions by D. J. Enright. Retranslated as *Sodom and Gomorrah*, by John Sturrock (Penguin [UK], 2003). First published in France in 1922 as *Sodom et Gomorrhe*.

5. *Captive, The* (Boni, 1929) Albertine now lives with Marcel, but he is tortured by jealousy of her lesbian friends. Translated from the French by C. K. Scott Moncrieff. Revised translation by Terence Kilmartin; further revision by D. J. Enright. Retranslated as *The Prisoner*, by Carol Clark (published together with number 6 by Penguin [UK], 2003). First published in France in 1923 as *La prisonniere*.

6. *Sweet Cheat Gone, The* (Boni, 1930) Albertine leaves Marcel and is killed in an accident. Translated from the French by C. K. Scott Moncrieff. Revised translation by Terence Kilmartin; further revision by D. J. Enright. Retranslated as *The Fugitive*, by Peter Collier (published together with number 5 by Penguin [UK], 2003). First published in France in 1925 as *La fugitive* (variant title: *Albertine disparue*).

7. *Past Recaptured, The* (Boni, 1932) This book, showing how World War I affected the lives of the surviving characters, concludes the series. Translated from the French by Frederick Blossom. Retranslated by Andreas Mayor (Random House, 1970). Revised translation by Terence Kilmartin; further revised by D. J. Enright. Retranslated as *Finding Time Again*, by Ian Patterson (Penguin [UK], 2003). Variant title: *Time Regained*. First published in France as *Le temps retrouvé*.

Pulver, Mary Monica

PSEUDONYM OF Mary Pulver Kuhfeld

Peter Brichter, sergeant in the Charter, Illinois, police department, is smart and determined but socially inept until he meets Kori, the emotionally troubled niece of a Chicago mobster. Their romance and subsequent marriage humanizes Peter to a certain degree in this series of small-town procedurals. More recently Kuhfeld has been producing the Betsy Devonshire mysteries as Monica Ferris (q.v.).

1. *Murder at the War* (St. Martin's, 1987) The Society for Creative Anachronism, an organization that re-creates medieval battles, has its annual event in Pennsylvania disrupted by a modern corpse. Brichter plays a minor role. Variant title: *Knight Fall*.

2. *Unforgiving Minutes, The* (St. Martin's, 1988) Brichter falls in love with Kori, niece of a reclusive Chicago mobster who may be at the center of a drug ring in Charter.

3. *Ashes to Ashes* (St. Martin's, 1988) Suspicious fires lead Peter to a renewed acquaintance with a local loan shark, an uneasy partnership with a cop rumored to be on the take, and an investigation of Charter's gangland ties.

4. *Original Sin* (Walker, 1990) The arrival of cousin Ellen Biggins at Kori and Peter's Christmas house party leads to murder and the uncovering of ancient scandals.

5. *Show Stopper* (Walker, 1992) Kori Brichter takes five horses to the Lafite, Illinois, All-Arab Show and runs into a corrupt trainer who soon comes to a bad end.

Puzo, Mario

After publishing two well-reviewed but poorly selling novels, *The Dark Arena* (Dell, 1955) and *The Fortunate Pilgrim* (Atheneum, 1964), Mario Puzo produced the potboiler novel *The Godfather* and was vaulted into commercial success and fame. The movie versions, directed by Francis Ford Coppola—*The Godfather* (1972); *The Godfather, Part II* (1974); and *The Godfather, Part III* (1990)—exponentially increased the success of the novel and made "the Godfather" recognizable worldwide. Both sequels were scripted by Puzo, but they have not appeared in novel form. The Godfather is Don Vito Corleone, Sicilian American patriarch of a Mafia family, determined to extend and consolidate his power in organized crime and to ensure the succession of his son Michael. *The Sicilian*, the book sequel, tells the story (based on fact) of Sicilian bandit and folk hero Salvatore Giuliani, with whom Michael Corleone becomes involved. *The Last Don* (Random House, 1996) and *Omerta* (Random House, 2000) are about the Mafia but not about the Corleone clan. *The Family* (ReganBooks, 2001), completed by Carol Gino after Puzo's death, in 1999, is about the Borgias, not the Corleones. Mark Winegardner (q.v.) has continued the series. Mario Puzo also wrote the nonfiction *The Godfather Papers: And Other Confessions* (Putnam, 1972).

1. *Godfather, The* (Putnam, 1969) "The Godfather" maintains order within his family while engaging in a bloody struggle for power.
2. *Sicilian, The* (Simon & Schuster, 1984) Michael Corleone, in exile in Sicily, is asked to help the Sicilian "Robin Hood," Salvatore Giuliani, escape to America.

Queen, Ellery

PSEUDONYM OF Frederic Dannay & Manfred Lee

Ellery Queen is both the pseudonymous author and the detective who stars in the mysteries by the famous team of writing cousins Frederic Dannay and Manfred Lee. Though Ellery didn't age much between 1929 and 1971, his style was changed to suit the times. In the early books, heavily influenced by S. S. Van Dine (q.v.), he is a supercilious young New Yorker given to tweeds and walking sticks and sporting a pince-nez. He gradually becomes less affected, develops a sense of humor, and acquires some sex appeal. The entree created by his father's police connections, and Ellery's own formidable deductive powers, are an unbeatable combination. As well as writing best-selling mystery novels, some of which are regarded as classics of the formal detective mystery genre, "Ellery Queen" had a profound influence on American mystery writing as an anthologist and editor of *Ellery Queen's Mystery Magazine*. "Ellery Queen" wrote most of the scripts for a long-running radio series (1939–1948). *The Adventure of the Murdered Moths and Other Radio Mysteries* (Crippen & Landru, 2005) is a collection of these radio scripts. There have been at least three television series (1950–1952, 1958–1959, 1975–1976) and numerous movies based on the character, five of the movies with Ralph Bellamy as Ellery. The Ellery Queen team also wrote the Drury Lane series under the name of Barnaby Ross (q.v.). At least three novels were ghosted by other authors: number 31 by Theodore Sturgeon; numbers 32 and 33 by Avram Davidson. More than two-dozen novels, most of them not containing the Queen characters, were written, with the blessing of Dannay and/ or Lee, by other authors calling themselves "Ellery Queen." *The Glass Village* (Little, Brown, 1954) and *Cop Out* (World, 1969) were written by Ellery Queen, but do not have either of the Queens as characters. Omnibus volumes include *Ellery Queen's Big Book* (Grosset, 1938; numbers 1 and 7); *Ellery Queen's Adventure Omnibus* (Grosset, 1940; numbers 9 and 16); *The Wrightsville Murders* (Little, Brown, 1956; numbers 17, 19, and 20); *The Hollywood Murders* (Lippincott, 1957; numbers 13, 14, and 23); and *The Bizarre Murders* (Lippincott, 1962; numbers 7, 8, and 10). *The Best of Ellery Queen* (Beaufort, 1985) is a collection of previously collected stories plus one new story.

1. *Greek Coffin Mystery, The* (Stokes, 1932) Though written later, this is book is first chronologically. It shows young Ellery, still in college, trying to solve a case involving three sudden deaths, a missing will, and a stolen painting.
2. *Roman Hat Mystery, The* (Stokes, 1929) A missing hat is the significant clue in this famous theater murder case that first introduced young Ellery and his police inspector father, Richard.

3. *French Powder Mystery, The* (Stokes, 1930) During a window demonstration at a Fifth Avenue department store, the dead body of the store owner's wife falls from an opening wall bed.
4. *Dutch Shoe Mystery, The* (Stokes, 1931) Two murders at the Dutch Memorial Hospital are the problem here.
5. *Egyptian Cross Mystery, The* (Stokes, 1932) This tale involves a series of bizarre murders where the victims are beheaded and fastened to crosses.
6. *American Gun Mystery, The* (Stokes, 1933) During a show with an audience of 20,000 watching, a rodeo rider is murdered at New York's latest sports palace. Variant title: *Death at the Rodeo*.
7. *Siamese Twin Mystery, The* (Stokes, 1933) The Queens escape from a forest fire to a lonely hilltop cabin and find the corpse of Dr. Xavier clutching a torn half of the six of spades.
8. *Chinese Orange Mystery, The* (Stokes, 1934) A murdered man with his clothes on backward is found in a locked room.
9. *Adventures of Ellery Queen, The* (Stokes, 1934) Eleven short stories. Later paperback editions have only six stories.
10. *Spanish Cape Mystery, The* (Lippincott, 1935) Handsome ladies' man John Marco is murdered.
11. *Halfway House* (Stokes, 1936) Queen deals with the murder of a man who has been leading a double life.
12. *Door Between, The* (Stokes, 1937) Ellery works to clear an innocent woman accused of murdering a prizewinning female novelist.
13. *Devil to Pay, The* (Stokes, 1938) The Hollywood murder of a crooked movie promoter is the focus here.
14. *Four of Hearts, The* (Stokes, 1938) Still in Hollywood, where he is an "idea man" for a movie company, Ellery looks into a feud between actors that has turned into murder.
15. *Dragon's Teeth, The* (Stokes, 1939) Queen and his partner, Beau Rummell, get involved in the death of eccentric millionaire Cadmus Cole. Variant title: *The Virgin Heiresses*.
16. *New Adventures of Ellery Queen, The* (Stokes, 1940) Nine short stories, including "The Lamp of God," which was published as a stand-alone paperback by Dell in 1951. *More Adventures of Ellery Queen* (Spivak, 1940) has slightly different contents.
17. *Calamity Town* (Little, Brown, 1942) Ellery witnesses a murder on Main Street in Wrightsville and does not solve the case until after the trial begins.
18. *There Was an Old Woman* (Little, Brown, 1943) A ruthless killer using Mother Goose rhymes as a pattern strikes the Potts household of New York's Riverside Drive. Variant title: *The Quick and the Dead*.
19. *Murderer Is a Fox, The* (Little, Brown, 1945) Ellery helps a friend, Dave Fox, absolve his father of guilt in the mysterious murder of his mother.
20. *Case Book of Ellery Queen, The* (Spivak, 1945) Eight stories and screenplays. Not to be confused with Gollancz (UK) omnibus of the same title published in 1949.
21. *Ten Days' Wonder* (Little, Brown, 1948) Queen unravels an anagram that solves a case of murder, blackmail, and theft.
22. *Cat of Many Tails* (Little, Brown, 1949) Ellery investigates a string of murders where all the corpses have a cord tied around their necks.
23. *Double, Double* (Little, Brown, 1950) Set in Wrightsville, scene of numbers 17 and 19, this story concerns a string of murders linked by a nursery rhyme. Variant title: *The Case of the Seven Murders*.
24. *Origin of Evil, The* (Little, Brown, 1951) Ellery is in Hollywood to work on a book, but two beautiful women with a mystery interrupt.
25. *King Is Dead, The* (Little, Brown, 1952) The locked-room murder of King Bendigo, a sinister munitions magnate, concerns Queen.
26. *Calendar of Crime* (Little, Brown, 1952) Seven short stories.

27. *Scarlet Letters, The* (**Little, Brown, 1953**) After a friend asks Ellery to decipher some strange letters, he fears that murder is imminent.

28. *Q.B.I: Queen's Bureau of Investigation* (**Little, Brown, 1954**) Nine short stories.

29. *Inspector Queen's Own Case* (**Simon & Schuster, 1956**) On vacation in Connecticut, retired Inspector Queen tests his detecting abilities on a case of the "accidental" death of a millionaire's adopted child.

30. *Finishing Stroke, The* (**Simon & Schuster, 1958**) Reminiscing on his first solo case, in which an unidentified stranger is murdered at a house party in 1929, Ellery finally solves the mystery in 1957.

31. *Player on the Other Side, The* (**Random House, 1963**) Someone is methodically killing off all the York family heirs. Ghostwritten by Theodore Sturgeon.

32. *And on the Eighth Day* (**Random House, 1964**) Ellery blunders into a secluded religious community unknown to the rest of the world. The story is uncharacteristic of Queen novels. Ghostwritten by Avrahm Davidson.

33. *Fourth Side of the Triangle, The* (**Random House, 1965**) A young man falls in love with his father's mistress and is trapped in her murder. Ghostwritten by Avram Davidson.

34. *Queens Full* (**Random House, 1965**) Three novelettes and two short-short stories.

35. *Study in Terror, A* (**Lancer, 1966**) Ellery reads a lost Watson manuscript and discovers a fresh solution to the Jack the Ripper case. This is the novelization of a screenplay. UK title: *Sherlock Holmes vs. Jack the Ripper.*

36. *Face to Face* (**New American Library, 1967**) The murder victim has scrawled the word *face*, the only clue Ellery has.

37. *House of Brass, The* (**New American Library, 1968**) Ellery solves the investigation started by his father of the murder of a very eccentric millionaire.

38. *Q.E.D: Queen's Experiments in Detection* (**New American Library, 1968**) Fifteen stories.

39. *Last Woman in His Life, The* (**World, 1970**) Ellery's old Wrightsville friend Johnny Benedict is murdered, and his three ex-wives are implicated.

40. *Fine and Private Place, A* (**World, 1971**) This bizarre and confusing case starts with embezzlement and blackmail in Nino Importuna's conglomerate.

41. *Tragedy of Errors and Others, The* (**Crippen & Landru, 1999**) Contains a detailed synopsis of Queen's last, unfinished novel, *A Tragedy of Errors*, six uncollected stories, and a raft of tributes to Ellery Queen by friends, relatives, and fans.

Quick, Amanda

PSEUDONYM OF Jayne Ann Krentz

Jayne Ann Krentz (q.v.) has written more than two-dozen historical romances under her Amanda Quick pseudonym. Three historical-romantic mysteries feature the Regency London team of Lavinia Lake and Tobias March. Lavinia is a successful business woman versed in the practice of mesmerism. Her professional and personal partner, Tobias, is a private investigator.

1. *Slightly Shady* (**Bantam, 2001**) Lavinia Lake returns to England after her antiques shop is destroyed by a stranger who claims to be on the trial of criminals. Eventually, after she becomes the target of a blackmailer, she finds out that the stranger is private investigator Tobias March.

2. *Don't Look Back* (**Bantam, 2002**) Celeste Hudson is murdered, and the Blue Medusa bracelet has disappeared from her wrist.

3. *Late for the Wedding* (**Bantam, 2003**) The Memento Mori Man, a hit man who operated decades ago, is resurrected by March's fellow spy Elland. After Elland commits suicide, a "memento mori" ring turns up on the doorstep of Elland's lover, Aspasia Gray.

Quill, Monica

PSEUDONYM OF Ralph McInerny

Ralph McInerny (q.v.), author of the Father Dowling mysteries, has created another clerical mystery series under the pseudonym of Monica Quill. Sister Mary Teresa, aka "Emtee" Dempsey, and her two companions, Sister Kim and Sister Joyce, are the last remnants of the Order of Martha and Mary. They live together in a wonderful Frank Lloyd Wright house on Walton Street in Chicago. Sister Mary Teresa is in her late seventies when the series begins; she is five feet two inches tall and weighs close to 200 pounds. Like Rex Stout's (q.v.) Nero Wolfe, she is a sedentary detective, solving mysteries while staying at home and working on her magnum opus about early monasticism in France. Siter Kim, who does the legwork, has a brother on the police force who is useful at times, but equal to Sister Mary Teresa. The Catholic Church ambience adds interest to these entertaining, well-written mysteries.

1. *Not a Blessed Thing!* (**Vanguard, 1981**) When socialite Cheryl Pitman's life is threatened, Detective Moriarity brings her to the sanctuary of the nuns's home.

2. *Let Us Prey* (**Vanguard, 1982**) Sister Joyce's willingness to babysit involves the nuns with the MOMSIEs, a group of divorced women, and with murder.

3. *And Then There Was None* (**Vanguard, 1984**) A visit from one of Sister Mary Teresa's former students is the prelude to the deaths of two people connected with a successful women's soccer team.

4. *Nun of the Above* (**Vanguard, 1985**) Sarah Pinking, former student of Mary Teresa and presumed lover of pornography king Ernesto Flavio, is murdered.

5. *Sine Qua Nun* (**Vanguard, 1986**) Geoffrey Chaser, novelist and fellow guest of Sister Mary Teresa on a television talk show, is strangled after insulting the show's host, Basil Murphy.

6. *Veil of Ignorance, The* (**St. Martin's, 1988**) Sister Mary Teresa believes that Lydia Hopkins, convicted of killing her husband and daughter, is really innocent.

7. *Sister Hood* (**St. Martin's, 1991**) Carmelite nun Mary Magdalene, the former Donna Moran, takes refuge with Sister Mary Teresa when she is subpoenaed to testify before a Chicago grand jury.

8. *Nun Plussed* (**St. Martin's, 1993**) A divorced former student has been stabbed to death in her home, and her ex-husband, an antiquarian book dealer, confesses to the crime.

9. *Half Past Nun* (**St. Martin's, 1997**) Sister Mary Teresa finds time to assist Lieutenant Richard Moriarity of the Chicago PD in solving a series of homicides perpetrated by a vicious stalker.

10. *Death Takes the Veil and Other Stories* (**Five Star, 2001**) Contains four novellas and three short-shorts.

Quinn, Sally

Sally Quinn, former CBS anchorwoman (see *We're Going to Make You a Star*, Simon & Schuster, 1975), *Washington Post* columnist, and Washington party giver (see *The Party: A Guide to Adventurous Entertaining*, Simon & Schuster, 1997), wrote a pair of contemporary romances set in Washington, DC. Leading roles in both novels are played by Allison Sterling, Washington journalist; Sadie Gray, wife of the US vice president; and media heavyweight Desmond Shaw, who is loved by both women. The novels are cozy variations on the life among the rich and famous theme.

1. *Regrets Only* (Simon & Schuster, 1986) Allison Sterling, reporter for the *Washington Daily*, and Second Lady Sadie Gray are both in love with Desmond Shaw.
2. *Happy Endings* (Simon & Schuster, 1991) Sadie and Allison have moved up even further in the world and still love Desmond, but Dr. Michael Lanzer of the National Cancer Institute complicates matters.

Radley, Sheila

PSEUDONYM OF Sheila Robinson

Detective Chief Inspector Doug Quantrill is the star of this pleasant detective series set in Breckham Market, a country village in Suffolk, England. Chief Inspector Quantrill dislikes his assistant, Sergeant Martin Tait, who is young, ambitious, and romantically involved with Quantrill's daughter Allison. When Sergeant Hilary Lloyd, a pretty young female assistant, joins the force, Quantrill loses his heart to her. Robinson is a British author who writes historical romances under the pseudonym of Hester Rowan. Her rural English village isn't a quaint and sleepy backwater but a contemporary town with contemporary problems. *New Blood from Old Bones* (Constable [UK], 1998) is a mystery set in the 1530s.

1. *Death in the Morning* (Scribner, 1979) Inspector Tait, newly graduated from police school, is convinced that 18-year-old Mary Gedge's death was not a suicide. UK title: *Death and the Maiden*.
2. *Chief Inspector's Daughter, The* (Scribner, 1980) Quantrill's daughter Allison, working as a secretary to a romance writer, finds her employer raped and murdered.
3. *Talent for Destruction, A* (Scribner, 1982) The unearthing of a skeleton on the grounds of the rectory in Breckham Market unnerves the rector and his wife.
4. *Quiet Road to Death, The* (Scribner, 1984) Quantrill and newcomer Hilary Lloyd investigate the case of a headless corpse found near a busy road. UK title: *Blood on the Happy Highway*.
5. *Fate Worse Than Death* (Scribner, 1986) Quantrill and Hilary Lloyd receive little cooperation from local villagers when they investigate the disappearance of a young woman on the eve of her wedding.
6. *Who Saw Him Die?* (Scribner, 1988) When John Goodrum, a newcomer to Breckham Market, runs over the town drunk, the coroner calls it an unavoidable accident, but the victim's sister disagrees.
7. *This Way Out* (Scribner, 1989) Hugh Packer engages Derek Cartwright in a plot to murder each other's elderly in-laws.
8. *Cross My Heart and Hope to Die* (Scribner, 1992) Elderly Ziggy and Gladys Zrzecszczuk disappear from their home in the Suffolk village of Byland, and Janet Thatcher, rural postmistress-author, becomes a suspect.
9. *Fair Game* (Constable [UK], 1994) Will Glaven's father arranges a pheasant hunt to introduce his prospective daughter-in-law, Hope Meynell, to country ways.

Rankin, Ian

Edinburgh's Detective Inspector John Rebus, number-one mystery best seller in Great Britain, deserves to be better known to American mystery readers, as comparisons to Colin Dexter's (q.v.) Inspector Morse and John Harvey's (q.v.) Charlie Resnick abound. Rebus, basically a decent human being, has trouble with alcohol and women, a bad temper, a tendency to place work before family and friends, and the Calvinistic demands of the "black comedy" of his life. Among the recurring characters in these procedurals are Rebus's estranged daughter, Samantha, his sometime police partner Siobhan Clarke, and "Big Ger" Cafferty, Edinburgh's leading gangster. Ian Rankin's view of Edinburgh is very different from that of outsiders, who rate it as the most beautiful and civilized city in northern Europe. He sees the Scottish capital as a mecca for racketeers, serial killers, drug dealers, and other antisocial types. Several omnibus volumes have been published by Orion (UK): *Rebus: The Early Years* (1999; numbers 1, 2, and 3); *Rebus: The St. Leonard's Years* (2001; numbers 5, 6, and 7); *Rebus: The Lost Years* (2003; numbers 8, 9, and 10); and *Capital Crimes* (2004; numbers 11, 13, and 14). *Beggars Banquet* (Orion [UK], 2002) contains 21 Rankin stories, 7 of them about Rebus. The Rebus mysteries are currently being filmed for Scottish television. *Rebus' Scotland: A Personal Journey* (Orion [UK], 2004) contains 120 photographs accompanied by passages from the novels.

1. *Knots and Crosses* (Doubleday, 1987) Solving the "Edinburgh Strangler" murders of four young girls has evolved into a hunt for an old friend turned vengeful enemy.
2. *Hide and Seek* (Penzler, 1994) The body of a young drug addict is found in the ritual posture of a sacrificial victim, his body full of tainted heroin. Originally published in 1991.
3. *Tooth and Nail* (St. Martin's, 1996) Rebus is sent to London to help track down the "Wolfman," a serial killer who takes a bite out of each victim. Originally published in the United Kingdom in 1992 as *Wolfman*.
4. *Good Hanging and Other Stories, A* (St. Martin's, 2002) Twelve Rebus short stories. Originally published in the United Kingdom in 1992.
5. *Strip Jack* (St. Martin's, 1994) Popular politician Gregor Jack is caught in a midnight raid on a brothel, and his wife is pulled from a river soon after.
6. *Black Book, The* (Penzler, 1994) Rebus's life takes a bad turn as his ex-con brother arrives in town, his lady friend rebuffs him, a local butcher is murdered, a convicted child molester returns to Edinburgh, etc., etc.
7. *Mortal Causes* (Simon & Schuster, 1995) Rebus's dislike of the annual Edinburgh Festival is exacerbated by the murder of Billy Cunningham, son of gangster Big Ger Cafferty.
8. *Let It Bleed* (Simon & Schuster, 1996) A trio of suicides may be connected to development plains for "Silicon Glen," home of Edinburgh's computer industry.
9. *Black and Blue* (St. Martin's, 1997) Rebus follows the trail of "Johnny Bible," a serial killer who seems to have taken over from "Bible John," a real-life killer, never caught, who terrorized Glasgow in the late 1960s.
10. *Hanging Garden, The* (St. Martin's, 1998) While Rebus's daughter Samantha lies in a coma after a hit-and-run accident, racketeer Ger Cafferty, languishing in jail while newcomer Tommy Telford is turning Edinburgh into the crime capital of the Western world, wants to make a deal with Rebus.
11. *Dead Souls* (St. Martin's, 1999) Rebus, hitting the bottle hard, is troubled by "visitations" from recently deceased comrade-in-arms Jack Martin, Samantha's paralysis, vigilantes after a child molester, a serial killer released in the United States, and the suicide of a colleague.
12. *Death Is Not the End* (St. Martin's, 2000) A novella published in a "limited edition," developing a subplot from number 11, in which Damon Mee, son of an old flame of Rebus, vanishes from a Kirkcaldy nightclub.
13. *Set in Darkness* (St. Martin's, 2000) Introducing new colleague Siobhan Clarke and involving the finding of a long-dead corpse

on the site of the new Scottish Parliament, followed by the homicide of a leading politician.

14. *Falls, The* (St. Martin's, 2001) Philippa Balfour, daughter of a prominent bank director, disappears, leaving two odd clues: an Internet role-playing game and a doll in a tiny wooden coffin.

15. *Resurrection Men* (Little, Brown, 2003) Rebus, after flinging a cup of coffee into the face of his superior, is sent back to police college for "retraining," which seems to involve infiltrating the ranks of fellow officers believed to be on the take.

16. *Question of Blood, A* (Little, Brown, 2004) Insane ex-soldier Lee Herdman, mirroring a real life incident in Dunblane, enters a school and shoots three students, two fatally, before killing himself.

17. *Fleshmarket Alley* (Little, Brown, 2005) A Kurdish refugee's death leads Rebus and Siobhan Clarke into a plot involving a modern-day version of the slave trade. UK title: *Fleshmarket Close*.

18. *Naming of the Dead, The* (Little, Brown, 2007) Two tenuously connected cases: the suspicious death of Ben Webster, Scottish delegate to the Group of Eight Summit, and the murder of sex offender and "muscle" for Big Ger Cafferty, Cyril Colliar.

Rawn, Melanie

I. The Dragon Prince (numbers 1–3) and Dragon Star (numbers 4–6) are large-scale fantasies in which men called Sunrunners, who wield power through sunlight, and dragons, who communicate in colors, share a world with several moons. Leading protagonists in this complex fantasy world with intricate plotting, a host of characters, intrigue, romance, and magic are Prince Rohan of Stronghold and his son Pol. *The Dragon Prince* (Penguin, 1990) is an omnibus volume containing numbers 1, 2, and 3.

1. *Dragon Prince* (DAW, 1988) An arranged marriage between Prince Rohan of Stronghold and the Sunrunner Sioned of Goddess Keep promises to bring peace until the self-serving High Prince plunges the world into war.

2. *Star Scroll, The* (DAW, 1989) The peaceful reign of Rohan and Sioned faces a serious challenge when the discovery of an ancient scroll and the machinations of Rohan's enemies threaten the life of their heir.

3. *Sunrunner's Fire* (DAW, 1994) The new Lord of Goddess Keep seeks the secret lore of the Star Scroll, while Rohan seeks to keep malevolent sorcerers from destroying his beleaguered lands.

4. *Stronghold* (DAW, 1990) Prince Rohan's dream of peace through law is put to the test when foreign invaders bring war to a land already strained by the tension between Rohan's heir, Pol, and the ambitious Lord of Goddess Keep.

5. *Dragon Token, The* (DAW, 1992) After Rohan dies, Prince Pol has to take over the war against an unknown army that seems bent upon annihilating him.

6. *Skybowl* (DAW, 1993) Pol must come to terms with his fanatical cousin Andry so that they can combine forces against a High Warlord who has sworn to destroy all the people of the Desert.

II. Exiles, an uncompleted trilogy, postulates Lenfell, refuge of the Mageborn, where women wield economic and social power through magic. Two sisters, Sarra and Cailet, Mage Guardians, are ranged against Glenin, the third sister, who has thrown in her lot with the Lords of Malleris, who practice a darker magic. The third volume of the trilogy, *The Captal's Tower*, hasn't been published yet.

1. *Ruins of Ambrai, The* (DAW, 1994) Torn apart in childhood by the rivalry between their elders, the Mageborn sisters—Glenin, Sarra, and Cailet—find themselves on opposing sides of the conflict between the Mage Guardians and the Lords of Malleris.

2. *Mageborn Traitor, The* (DAW, 1997) The Lords of Malleris, down but not out, abetted by Mageborn Glenin, haven't given up on their ambitions for world conquest. Meanwhile, Cailet, the new Mage Captal, and her sister Sarra, Councillor of Sheve, struggle to rebuild their war-torn society.

Ray, Robert J(oseph)

Matt Murdock is Orange County, California's entry in the hardboiled sweepstakes. Vietnam veteran, ex-cop, tough talker, loner with a select few friends, Matt bulls his way through a series of violent cases with a lot of firepower. Robert J. Ray has also written (with Jack Remick) two guides for aspiring fiction writers: *The Weekend Novelist* (Dell, 1994) and *The Weekend Novelist Writes a Mystery* (Dell, 1998).

1. *Bloody Murdock* (St. Martin's, 1986) Sexy, wild Gayla Jean is incinerated in movie star Jaime Modesto's Trans-Am on a lonely stretch of the Pacific Coast Highway.

2. *Murdock for Hire* (St. Martin's, 1987) Matt has an assignment to recover a fortune in gold coins and keep blackmailers away from the widow of California tycoon Eddie Hennessy.

3. *Dial M for Murdock* (St. Martin's, 1988) An old army pal hires Murdock to look into the case of a businessman who tripled the value of his life insurance four months before his death in a car crash.

4. *Merry Christmas, Murdock* (Delacorte, 1989) Murdock befriends a troubled kid who is hiding a dirty secret.

5. *Murdock Cracks Ice* (Delacorte, 1995) Chemistry student Rollie Nielsen, who was making good money selling a powerful kind of speed called "Ice," is bumped off by someone who doesn't like the competition.

Rayner, Claire

I. The Performer series tells of the intertwined fortunes of the Lackland and Lucas families, doctors and actors in London, from around 1800 to 1946. Rayner's characters thread their way through upper-class drawing rooms as well as the colorful theater world and the slums of the Seven Dials criminal section, and they even range out to the Crimea in wartime. The built-in drama of medicine and the fiery artistic temperaments of the stage actors keep the action moving along.

Claire Rayner, OBE, is the United Kingdom's best-known advice and medical columnist and broadcaster or "agony aunt." Among her more than 80 publications are more than 30 nonfiction works on nursing, health, child rearing, pop psychology and related works. Although she is a household word in Great Britain, she is virtually unknown in the United States. None of her more than 50 novels have been published here since the early 1980s.

1. *Gower Street* (Simon & Schuster, 1973) Around 1800 the young boy Abel Lackland is rescued from the slums and grows up to be an apothecary-surgeon.

2. *Haymarket, The* (Simon & Schuster, 1974) Jonah Lackland, Abel's son, rejects his family's plans for his medical career and follows the lure of the theater instead.

3. *Paddington Green* (Simon & Schuster, 1976) Abel is now the patriarch running St. Eleanor's Hospital. His four children take center stage in this volume.

4. *Soho Square* (Putnam, 1976) In the 1850s, young Freddie studies medicine at his grandfather's hospital, as his cousins Phoebe and Lydia force tragic choices upon him.

5. *Bedford Row* (Putnam, 1977) Spinster Martha Lackland leaves her father's London clinic to care for wounded soldiers during the Crimean War.

6. *Covent Garden* (Putnam, 1978) Brother and sister Amy and Fenton Lucas come to London to pursue stage careers and find themselves involved with the Lackland family. UK title: *Long Acre*.

7. *Charing Cross* (Putnam, 1979) Set in 1870, this is the story of Sophie, Abel Lackland's granddaughter, who becomes a pioneer doctor. Variant title: *Trafalgar Square*.

8. *Strand, The* (Putnam, 1981) London in 1892 is the setting for this story featuring Lewis, a young surgeon from Australia; Claudette, an aspiring actress; and Miriam, the beautiful and spoiled heiress of the Lackland family.

9. *Chelsea Reach* (Weidenfeld [UK], 1982) Medical student Letty Lackland meets Luke O'Hare, a young actor with plans to set up a theater for poor Londoners.

10. *Shaftesbury Avenue* (Weidenfeld [UK], 1983) Film producer Letty Lackland wants to make World War I hero Theo Caspar into her next star.

11. *Piccadilly* (Weidenfeld [UK], 1984) Leah, Harry, Kate, and Peter are among the Lacklands doing a 16-week Shakespearean tour of the Continent, including Hitler's Germany.

12. *Seven Dials* (Weidenfeld [UK], 1986) In October 1946, the Lackland and Lucas families help restore the battered St. Eleanor's hospital.

II. The Poppy Chronicles starts with the marriage between Mildred Amberly and Lizan "Kid" Harris, a Jewish boxer in the 1890s, and, following the life of their daughter Poppy, takes us into the 1960s. A chronicle taking the reader through a large chunk of British history as seen through the eyes of one character.

1. *Jubilee* (Weidenfeld [UK], 1987) Poppy's first memory is of Queen Victoria's Jubilee in 1897.

2. *Flanders* (Weidenfeld [UK], 1988) In 1911 Poppy is in love with Bobby, but the outbreak of war in 1914 changes everything. She becomes an ambulance driver in France and encounters Bobby again.

3. *Flapper* (Weidenfeld [UK], 1989) No annotation available.

4. *Blitz* (Weidenfeld [UK], 1990) Poppy and her family strive to lead normal lives during the Blitz of London in World War II.

5. *Festival* (Weidenfeld [UK], 1991) The 1951 Festival of Britain finds Poppy running her own business and being her family's anchor. Then she meets Peter Chantry.

6. *Sixties* (Weidenfeld [UK], 1992) The 1960s find Poppy coping with her mother's death and her teenage children and running her successful boutique.

III. Dr. George Barnabas is the first woman to hold the position of pathologist at London's Old East Hospital and the first to be a police surgeon. Her skills in forensic pathology and her curiosity lead her into a series of medical mysteries that she unravels with the help of her lover, Chief Inspector Gus Hathaway.

1. *First Blood* (Michael Joseph [UK], 1993) Dr. George Barnabas, newly appointed pathologist at Old East Hospital, performs her first postmortem, on a well-known author, and is unable to determine the cause of death.

2. *Second Opinion* (Michael Joseph [UK], 1994) The deaths of several babies at Old East appear to be crib deaths, but an anonymous hint dropped to Dr. Barnabas leads her to some sinister practices.

3. *Third Degree* (Michael Joseph [UK], 1995) Dr. George is unable to make her detective lover, Gus Hathaway, see the connections between several mysterious deaths.

4. *Fourth Attempt* (Michael Joseph [UK], 1996) Three deaths in as many days among staff at Old East: accidents or suicides? Then a fourth person nearly dies after an attempted murder.

5. *Fifth Member* (Michael Joseph [UK], 1997) The gruesome murder of a Conservative MP is followed by the killing of a Labour MP, both murders chillingly similar to the Jack the Ripper slayings.

IV. The Quentin Quartet is only a duet so far. It is a historical series following the fortunes of a hotel from its beginnings as a bed-and-breakfast run by an impoverished widow and her maid to a world-famous luxury palace.

1. *London Lodgings* (Michael Joseph [UK], 1994) Tilly Quentin (née Kingsley), after she is widowed by her husband's early death, turns her house into lodgings to avoid returning to her family.

2. *Paying Guests* (Michael Joseph [UK], 1995) Tilly and her maid, Dorcas, have turned Quentin's into a thriving guesthouse.

Read, Miss

PSEUDONYM OF Dora Saint

I. Dora Saint has taken her cue from Jane Austen, who wrote that "three or four families in a country village is the very thing to work on." The contemporary English village life Dora Saint writes about has a quaint appeal for American readers. "Miss Read," the pseudonymous author-narrator, wrote first about her own experiences as the schoolmistress in the little brick-and-thatch village of Fairacre. Saint, like her alter ego Miss Read, was a schoolteacher. She paints her south-of-England villagers with a kindly, pastoral eye just this side of sentimentality. Dora Saint has published two autobiographical volumes, *A Fortunate Grandchild* (Houghton Mifflin, 1983) and *Time Remembered* (Houghton Mifflin, 1987), which have been published together in the United Kingdom (Michael Joseph, 1995) as *Early Days*. The first three books in the series have been collected in the omnibus volume *Chronicles of Fairacre* (Houghton Mifflin, 1977). Several omnibus volumes have been published in the United Kingdom, including *The Last Chronicle of Fairacre* (Michael Joseph, 2001; numbers 18–20) and *Fairacre Affairs* (Michael Joseph, 1998; numbers 14–15).

1. *Village School* (Houghton Mifflin, 1956) One year in the life of Fairacre is seen through the eyes of Miss Read, the village schoolmistress.

2. *Village Diary* (Houghton Mifflin, 1957) Will romance blossom when a male schoolteacher retires to the village?

3. *Storm in the Village* (Houghton Mifflin, 1959) Fairacre unites in opposition to the building of a new housing development in the neighborhood.

4. *Miss Clare Remembers* (Houghton Mifflin, 1963) Another Fairacre schoolmistress, Dolly Clare, looks back over her career, which spanned six reigns and two world wars.

5. *Over the Gate* (Houghton Mifflin, 1964) These are episodes of Fairacre life that Miss Read has collected over the years.

6. *Village Christmas* (Houghton Mifflin, 1966) The young couple who live across the road from the Waters sisters in Fairacre have their new baby on Christmas. Republished together with *The Christmas Mouse* as *Miss Read's Christmas* (Academy Chicago, 1990).

7. *Fairacre Festival, The* (Houghton Mifflin, 1969) Fairacre's villagers must raise funds to repair the roof of St. Patrick's Church.

8. *Emily Davis* (Houghton Mifflin, 1971) Retired schoolteacher Emily Davis of Fairacre loses her friend and companion.

9. *Tyler's Row* (Houghton Mifflin, 1973) Newcomers Peter and Diana Hale take over Fairacre's ancient row house known as Tyler's Row.

10. *Farther Afield* (Houghton Mifflin, 1976) Miss Read, recovering from a fall in which she broke her arm, accompanies her friend Amy on a holiday trip to Crete.

11. *No Holly for Miss Quinn* (Houghton Mifflin, 1976) Miss Quinn, an efficient secretary who boards at Holly Lodge in Fairacre, must give up the quiet Christmas she had planned and, instead, tend her brother's noisy children.

12. *Village Affairs* (Houghton Mifflin, 1978) A rumor that Fairacre School is going to close upsets the town's residents.

13. *White Robin, The* (Houghton Mifflin, 1980) Is there such a thing as a white robin? Does one live in Fairacre?

14. *Village Centenary* (Houghton Mifflin, 1981) Fairacre has a busy year as everyone helps Miss Read celebrate the 100th anniversary of her school.

15. *Summer at Fairacre* (Houghton Mifflin, 1985) Miss Read worries about her missing friend Amy and nurses Mrs. Pringle, the school cleaning lady, invalided with a bad leg.

16. *Mrs. Pringle* (Houghton Mifflin, 1990) Mrs. Pringle, the prickly school custodian, takes center stage here. Variant title: *Mrs. Pringle of Fairacre.*

17. *Christmas at Fairacre* (Michael Joseph [UK], 1991) Collection of short stories.

18. *Changes at Fairacre* (Houghton Mifflin, 1992) Miss Read inherits Dolly Clare's cottage at Thrush Green, but enrollment at Fairacre is falling.

19. *Farewell to Fairacre* (Houghton Mifflin, 1994) Two minor strokes force Miss Read to retire from Fairacre School.

20. *Peaceful Retirement, A* (Houghton Mifflin, 1997) In the final novel in the Fairacre series, Miss Read settles into retirement and decides to write a book.

II. The warm reception of her Fairacre books encouraged "Miss Read" to go on to write about the neighboring Cotswold hamlet of Thrush Green, where the houses are built of stone, but the villagers are just as close-knit and amusing in their eccentricities. *The World of Thrush Green* (Houghton Mifflin, 1989) is a well-illustrated guide to 30 years of events in the fictional town. Several omnibus volumes containing two or three titles have been issued in the United Kingdom by Joseph (1987–2000).

1. *Thrush Green* (Houghton Mifflin, 1960) May Day brings Gypsy caravans to Thrush Green, and the whole town turns out for the fair.

2. *Winter in Thrush Green* (Houghton Mifflin, 1962) The arrival of elderly bachelor Harold Shoosmith brightens many an old maid's hopes.

3. *News from Thrush Green* (Houghton Mifflin, 1971) Thrush Green's newest resident, attractive young Phil, separated from her husband, gets the village's support and help with her son.

4. *Battles at Thrush Green* (Houghton Mifflin, 1976) The rector's innocent suggestion that the churchyard needs tidying up is the first of a series of tempests that roar through Thrush Green.

5. *Return to Thrush Green* (Houghton Mifflin, 1979) Joan Young's ailing father returns home, and the Curdles decide to settle in Thrush Green.

6. *Gossip from Thrush Green* (Houghton Mifflin, 1982) A fire at the rectory, a loud rock quartet, the closing of a tea shop, and a serious illness ruffle the calm of Thrush Green.

7. *Affairs at Thrush Green* (Houghton Mifflin, 1984) Runaway wife Nelly Piggott and long-absent Kit Armitage return, while the new vicar of Lully is having problems with the officious Mrs. Thurgood.

8. *At Home in Thrush Green* (Houghton Mifflin, 1985) Eight homes for the elderly are erected on the site of the old vicarage.

9. *School at Thrush Green, The* (Houghton Mifflin, 1988) Village primary schoolteachers Dorothy Watson and Agnes Fogerty decide to retire to Barton-on-Sea.

10. *Friends at Thrush Green* (Houghton Mifflin, 1991) New headmaster Alan Lester hesitates to move into the house vacated by Dorothy and Agnes.

11. *Celebrations at Thrush Green* (Houghton Mifflin, 1993) A newly discovered bundle of personal papers reveals how Thrush Green native Nathaniel Patten founded a mission school in Africa the same year that the Thrush Green School was founded.

12. *Year at Thrush Green, The* (Houghton Mifflin, 1996) Twelve chapters, one for each month. An abandoned dog in the church, a severely ill local, and a tall American blond are among the events chronicled.

III. Caxley, the neighboring market town, is the setting for two historical chronicles that trace the family history of the Norths and the Howards, two of Caxley's leading families, from 1901 to the 1950s. A third "Caxley" book, *The Christmas Mouse* (Houghton Mifflin, 1973), is a contemporary story about a mouse and a runaway boy. Numbers 1 and 2 were collected in *The Caxley Chronicles* (Houghton Mifflin, 2007); *The Christmas Mouse* was reissued, along with *Village Christmas* (series I, number 6) together as *Miss Read's Christmas Tales* (Houghton Mifflin, 1995).

1. *Market Square, The* (Houghton Mifflin, 1966) Set from 1901 to World War I, this book tells of the rise of Sep Howard's bakery and of Sep's friendship with Bender North.

2. *Howards of Caxley, The* (Houghton Mifflin, 1968) The Caxley chronicle continues from 1939 through the World War II years and up to the 1950s. The story focuses on Edward Howard, grandson of Sep and Bender.

Reaves, Sam

I. Cooper MacLeish is a Chicago cabdriver and amateur detective who does a little writing on the side to keep him sane. Cooper is a distinctly oddball type who gets himself involved in some very convoluted capers. The Chicago-based Reaves also writes suspense novels set in Europe under the pseudonym of Dominic Martell.

1. *Long Cold Fall, A* (Putnam, 1991) MacLeish is content with cabdriving and desultory attempts to write until an old friend becomes a police statistic.

2. *Fear Will Do It* (Putnam, 1992) Diana Froelich, Cooper's Puerto Rican girlfriend, is blackmailed into cooperating with a scheme to fleece porno publisher Moss Wetzel.

3. *Bury It Deep* (Putnam, 1993) MacLeish is called upon to provide some muscle for journalist pal Melvin Moreland, who is pursuing a story.

4. *Get What's Coming* (Putnam, 1995) Since Cooper is marrying Diana, he feels the need for more regular employment and takes on the job of chauffeur for real-estate tycoon Regis Swanson.

II. Reaves has started another Chicago-based series, about Frank Dooley, a Chicago cop who leaves the force after he takes care of his wife's killer—vigilante style. Eventually Dooley returns and runs up against some nasty mobsters in this series set in the 1960s.

1. *Dooley's Back* (Carroll & Graf, 2002) Former Chicago cop Frank Dooley is back after a sojourn in Mexico necessitated by his revenge killing of his wife's murderer. His former partner, Roy Ferguson, is in deep trouble, $15,000 in hock to the Mob, a sum that loan shark John Spanos plans to retrieve.
2. *Homicide 69* (Carroll & Graf, 2006) Summer 1969. Dooley is investigating the torture-murder of a former Playboy Bunny and mobster's girlfriend.

Redfield, James

The Celestine Prophecy, originally self-published, became a word-of-mouth best seller in the 1990s. *The Celestine Prophecy* is basically a vehicle for Redfield's New Age philosophy. Critics commented on *The Celestine Prophecy*'s bare-bones, *Raiders of the Lost Ark*–type plot, its simplistic writing style, and its antirational philosophy, but millions of readers responded favorably to Redfield's positive, spiritual message. A couple of sequels followed, taking the unnamed narrator from Peru to Appalachia to Tibet in search of manuscripts and "insights." *The Song of Celestine* (Little, Brown, 1998), coauthored with Dee Lillegard, and with paintings by Dean Morrissey, brought the Celestine message to juvenile readers. *The Celestine Vision: Living the New Spiritual Awareness* (Warner, 1997) "reveals the truth behind the fiction." Numbers 1 and 2 were published together in *The Celestine Insights* (Warner, 1997).

1. *Celestine Prophecy, The* (Warner, 1994) The unnamed, middle-aged male narrator drops everything to search out the Manuscript, an ancient Peruvian manuscript containing nine "Insights" that supposedly prophesy the modern emergence of New Age spirituality. Originally self-published.
2. *Tenth Insight, The* (Warner, 1996) Subtitle: *Holding the Vision*. Charlene, the friend who first brought word of the Manuscript, disappears somewhere in the Appalachian Mountains.
3. *Secret of Shambhala, The* (Warner, 1999) Subtitle: *The Search for the Tenth Insight*. The narrator makes an imaginary journey to Tibet in search of Shambhala (aka Shangri-la).

Reed, Ishmael

I. Ishmael Reed, American novelist, poet, essayist, editor, and critic, is a highly original satirist and writer of experimental fiction. Reed is trying to establish an alternative black aesthetic, which he terms "Neo-Hoo-Dooism," with which he hopes to purge African Americans and Third World peoples of what he calls Western conditioning. Papa LaBas, who represents the voodoo deity Legba, is the protagonist of two novels in which he attempts through voodoo to combat spells cast by the white establishment, which anesthetized the artistic and political black communities. The novels are parodies of the mystery genre in which Papa LaBas acts as a voodoo detective. Plot or theme summaries can't do justice to the mixture of "standard" English and language whose principal rules of discourse are taken from the streets, popular music, and television.

1. *Mumbo Jumbo* (Doubleday, 1972) A novel set in Harlem and New Orleans in the 1920s, depicting the battle between the ideologies

of Jes Grew, the instinctive black cultural impulse, and Atonism, the rationalist Judeo-Christian tradition.
2. *Last Days of Louisiana Red, The* (Random House, 1974) Set in Berkeley, California, in the 1970s, this novel revolves around Louisiana Red, a destructive mental state that afflicts certain black militants.

II. Another pair of novels satirizes the American political and economic systems of the Reagan years. There are continuing characters, such as detective Nance Saturday, Saint Nicholas, and Black Peter, but the real link between the novels is the bleak, caustic satire on American mores.

1. *Terrible Twos, The* (St. Martin's, 1982) The Reagan White House is alarmed by the number of "surplus people," while a conspiracy unfolds to nuke New York and Miami and blame it on Nigeria.
2. *Terrible Threes, The* (Atheneum, 1989) A neo-Nazi president discloses a White House plan to expel all minorities and poor, homeless people and to institute a fundamentalist Christian state.

Reeman, Douglas

Douglas Reeman, who writes the popular Richard Bolithos series under the pseudonym Alexander Kent (q.v.), has embarked upon another series of novels, which will cover the fortunes of the Blackwood family and 150 years of British Royal Marine history. The Blackwood tradition of serving in the Royal Marines is outlined in the first volume of the series. The Reeman novels, like the Kent novels, are full of stirring action scenes and easy-to-digest history.

1. *Badge of Glory* (Morrow, 1983) In 1850 26-year-old Royal Marine captain Philip Blackwood sails off to fight the West African slave trade, then sees action in the Crimean War.
2. *First to Land, The* (Morrow, 1985) In 1900 27-year-old Royal Marine captain David Blackwood, nephew of Philip, gets involved in the Boxer Rebellion in China.
3. *Horizon, The* (McBooks, 2002) Jonathan Blackwood carries on the family Royal Marine tradition in World War I at hot spots like Gallipoli and Flanders. Originally published in 1993.
4. *Dust on the Sea* (McBooks, 2002) In 1943—another war, another Blackwood serving in the Royal Marines. Captain Mike Blackwood leads his troops in the bloody Burmese campaign. Originally published in 1999.
5. *Knife Edge* (McBooks, 2005) Two more Blackwoods are engaged in battle, this time in Malaya and Singapore in the 1950s.

Reichs, Kathy (Kathleen J.)

Kathy Reichs, fiftysomething professor of anthropology at UNC Charlotte and forensic anthropologist for both the state of North Carolina and the province of Quebec, writes a series of novels about Temperance "Tempe" Brennan, fiftysomething professor of anthropology and forensic anthropologist who divides her time between North Carolina and Quebec. The novels, which have been compared favorably with Patricia Cornwell's (q.v.) Kay Scarpetta novels, feature cutting-edge forensic science and an interesting central character who battles male chauvinism and corrupt politicians to arrive at her conclusions. A love interest for the divorced Tempe is provided by off-again, on-again lover, Montreal detective Andrew Ryan. *Bones* (2006–), starring Emily Deschanel as Tempe, is a Fox TV series inspired by the real Kathy

Reichs. *Bones: Buried Deep* (Pocket Star, 2006) is a spin-off from the TV series coauthored by Max Allan Collins (q.v.) and Reichs.

1. **Deja Dead (Scribner, 1997)** Forensic anthropologist Temperance "Tempe" Brennan, a North Carolina transplant, has a tough time convincing the Canadian version of the old-boy network that the series of grisly murders and dismemberments of women in Montreal is the work of a single killer.
2. **Death du Jour (Scribner, 1999)** Tempe is exhuming the century-old remains of a nun in Montreal so that the church can declare her a saint, but the bones aren't where they are supposed to be
3. **Deadly Decisions (Scribner, 2000)** Tempe is called upon to examine the remains of two bikers blown up in a biker war raging in Quebec.
4. **Fatal Voyage (Scribner, 2001)** Brennan comes across a foot that doesn't appear to match any of the 88 dead in the remains of a passenger jet that crashed in the backwoods of North Carolina.
5. **Grave Secrets (Scribner, 2002)** Brennan finds herself in Guatemala, investigating a massacre site as a favor to a Guatemalan anthropology association.
6. **Bare Bones (Scribner, 2003)** Brennan, while awaiting the arrival of current flame Andrew Ryan, in Charlotte, North Carolina, is called in to investigate when the charred corpse of a local janitor's infant is found in an oven.
7. **Monday Mourning (Scribner, 2004)** Tempe is called in to examine three skeletons discovered in the basement of a pizza parlor in Montreal.
8. **Cross Bones (Scribner, 2005)** Brennan and boyfriend Andrew Ryan travel to Israel to uncover an old crime, which may be connected to the murder of illegal antiquities dealer Avram Ferris.
9. **Break No Bones (Scribner, 2006)** While supervising a dig of Native American burial grounds in Charleston, South Carolina, Temperance stumbles upon some more recent remains.
10. **Bones to Ashes (Scribner, 2007)** Brennan is convinced that the unidentified New Brunswick skeleton in Quebec's cold-case unit belongs to her childhood friend, Evangeline Landry, who disappeared at age 15.

Reiner, Carl

Carl Reiner—actor (*Ocean's Eleven*), director (*Oh, God*), creator and co-star of *The Dick Van Dyke Show*, "second banana" to Sid Caesar on *Your Show of Shows*, and father of actor-director Rob Reiner—has written a widely separated pair of semiautobiographical novels about a young man trying to break into showbiz in the 1940s. At their best, these coming-of-age tales are very funny and sometimes quite touching. Reiner is also the author of the memoir *My Anecdotal Life* (St. Martin's, 2003).

1. **Enter Laughing (Simon & Schuster, 1958)** David Kokolovitz wins an audition and begins his theatrical career with a local drama company, much to the chagrin of his parents in the Bronx, who think all actors are "bums."
2. **Continue Laughing (Birch Lane, 1995)** Nineteen-year-old aspiring actor David quits his job as a sewing-machine delivery boy, bids farewell to his Bronx girlfriend, and joins a Shakespeare repertory company touring the Deep South.

Remarque, Erich Maria

Since its publication in 1929, *All Quiet on the Western Front* has become one of the all-time international best sellers and, with the help of the classic film made of it (1930), *the* antiwar novel of the period between the two world wars—it was one of the first books burned by the Nazis when they came to power. This tale of endurance, based on Remarque's own experiences, follows young Paul Baumer from his enlistment in the German army to the armistice of November 1918. Although he wrote several subsequent best sellers, Remarque (d. 1970) never quite equaled the success of *All Quiet on the Western Front*. *The Road Back*, which contains several characters from *All Quiet on the Western Front*, and was also made into a film (1937), shows the difficulties faced by these disillusioned veterans of trench warfare when they return to civilian life in postwar Germany.

1. **All Quiet on the Western Front (Little, Brown, 1929)** Eighteen-year-old Paul Baumer enlists in the German army; undergoes a short, brutal basic training; and is sent to the trenches of the western front. Translated by A. W. Wheen. Original German title: *Im westen nichts neues*.
2. **Road Back, The (Little, Brown, 1931)** Ernest Birkholz and his fellow veterans of the trenches cope with civilian life after the 1918 armistice. Translated by A. W. Wheen. Original title: *Der Weg zurück*.

Renault, Mary

PSEUDONYM OF Eileen Mary Challans

I. Though her early works were contemporary romances—for example, *The Charioteer* (Pantheon, 1959)—Renault (d. 1983) was best known for her historical novels, which are masterful re-creations of life in ancient Greece. The saga of Alexander the Great begins in his early childhood and continues to the power struggles following his early death. Renault's treatment of the sexual freedom and homosexuality characteristic of the times is frank but unsensationalized. Fans will want to look for *The Nature of Alexander* (Pantheon, 1975), a beautifully illustrated nonfiction work by Renault. For a somewhat different fictional viewpoint of Alexander, see Tom Holt's (q.v.) *Alexander at the World's End* (Little, Brown [UK], 1999).

1. **Fire from Heaven, The (Pantheon, 1969)** Alexander's childhood, youth, and tutelage by Aristotle are traced up to the assassination of his father, Philip of Macedonia.
2. **Persian Boy, The (Pantheon, 1972)** Alexander's expedition into Asia is seen through the worshipful eyes of his young Persian servant-friend Bagoas.
3. **Funeral Games (Pantheon, 1981)** At Alexander's death, a murderous power struggle ensues as his mother and half brother vie with the regent for the throne and control of his empire.

II. In an earlier pair of novels based on the Theseus myth, Renault demythologizes her hero, showing Theseus as a vibrant young warrior in a brilliantly imagined portrait of Greek antiquity. She succeeds in making the preclassical mind, with its different worldview than that of contemporary Westerners or the "classical" Greeks, understandable to the modern reader.

1. **King Must Die, The (Pantheon, 1958)** At 17, Theseus is a wiry and quick-witted youth who volunteers to go to Crete for the bull dances, where he kills Minotaurus.
2. **Bull from the Sea, The (Pantheon, 1962)** Theseus is king of Athens, husband to Cretan princess Phaedra, and lover of the Amazon Hippolyta.

Rendell, Ruth

Inspector Reg Wexford gets little chance to enjoy the view of High Street that his police station office affords him. The town of Kingsmarkham and the surrounding mid-Sussex countryside provide enough crime to keep him and his handsome young assistant, Mike Burden, fully occupied. Wexford, at 55, is tall, heavyset, rather homely, and devoted to his wife, Dora, and their grown children; however, he is not immune to brief encounters with attractive ladies. Like June Thomson's (q.v.) Inspector Rudd and Catherine Aird's (q.v.) Inspector Sloan, Wexford solves cases cast in the classic English mold. Rendell has written numerous non-Wexford mysteries, some under the pseudonym of Barbara Vine. At least eight omnibuses, containing three or four Wexford novels each, have been published in the United Kingdom. *Collected Short Stories* (Pantheon, 1988); *Blood Lines: Long and Short Stories* (Crown, 1996); and *The Copper Peacock and Other Stories* (Mysterious, 1991) contain Wexford stories. Wexford has been on British TV.

1. *From Doon with Death* (Doubleday, 1965) Inspector Wexford can discover no motive for the murder of an unprepossessing housewife except for a possible connection to a mysterious correspondent named Doon, who sent books and letters.
2. *New Lease of Death, A* (Doubleday, 1967) Wexford gets involved when the Reverend Henry Archery tries to clear a young woman's father of an ax murder. Variant title: *Sins of the Fathers*.
3. *Wolf to the Slaughter* (Doubleday, 1967) Wexford investigates a case that looks like murder in a love nest except that the victim is missing.
4. *Best Man to Die, The* (Doubleday, 1969) A string of murders involving small-time gangsters, cheating husbands, and loose women puzzles Inspector Wexford.
5. *Guilty Thing Surprised, A* (Doubleday, 1970) Elizabeth Nightingale is murdered on one of her nocturnal walks through the grounds at her home, Myfleet Manor.
6. *No More Dying Then* (Doubleday, 1972) With one child dead and another missing, a young mother entangled in blackmail, scandal, and murder nears the brink of mental collapse.
7. *Murder Being Once Done* (Doubleday, 1972) A woman is strangled with her own silk scarf and left in a dusty moss-encrusted vault at a London cemetery.
8. *Some Lie and Some Die* (Doubleday, 1973) After a rock festival in Kingsmarkham, Wexford finds a girl dead and battered.
9. *Shake Hands Forever* (Doubleday, 1975) Inspector Wexford spends his vacation tracking down the murderer of Angela Hathall.
10. *Sleeping Life, A* (Doubleday, 1978) The murderer and the victim are inexplicably confused in this case that involves a woman who had been missing for 20 years.
11. *Means of Evil and Other Stories* (Doubleday, 1980) Five Wexford stories are collected here.
12. *Death Notes* (Pantheon, 1981) Rich old flutist Sir Manuel Camargue drowns in his own lake just days before marrying a young woman. UK title: *Put On by Cunning*.
13. *Speaker of Mandarin, The* (Pantheon, 1983) After a trip to China, Wexford is troubled by hallucinations and paranoid fantasies.
14. *Unkindness of Ravens, An* (Pantheon, 1985) Rodney Williams disappears, but his wife and daughter don't seem particularly disturbed.
15. *Veiled One, The* (Pantheon, 1988) Elderly Gwen Robson is murdered in a shopping-mall garage, and Wexford's home is bombed, possibly because of his antinuclear arms stand.
16. *Kissing the Gunner's Daughter* (Mysterious, 1992) Wexford, grieving over his estrangement from his daughter, takes an interest in teenage Daisy, only survivor of a massacre at the home of famous writer Davina Flory.
17. *Simisola* (Crown, 1995) Raymond Akande, black physician in the town of Kingsmarkham, asks for Wexford's help in finding his missing daughter.
18. *Road Rage* (Crown, 1997) Protests are expected at the planned bypass in Kingsmarkham, but the finding of the badly decomposed body of a young woman is not.
19. *Harm Done* (Crown, 1998) While his daughter Sylvia works in a refuge for battered women, Wexford runs into a messy situation: the disappearance of children, a released pedophile, and a stabbed kidnapping suspect.
20. *Babes in the Wood, The* (Crown, 2003) During a massive flood in Kingsmarkham, two young teenagers turn up missing, their "baby-sitter" is found dead, and a fundamentalist group called the Church of the Good Gospel comes under suspicion.
21. *End in Tears* (Crown, 2006) Teenage mother Amber Marshalson is found dead outside her home in Kingsmarkham, her skull crushed by a piece of brick. Then her pregnant friend, Megan Bartlow, also turns up murdered.
22. *Not in the Flesh* (Doubleday, 2007) A man and his dog unearth a human hand while searching for truffles in the woods.

Resnick, Laura

Laura Resnick, daughter of SF-fantasy writer Mike Resnick (q.v.), has made a real name for herself as a fantasy writer. Her first novel, *In Legend Born*, details how the fantasy island Sileria revolts against its foreign oppressors. Numbers 2 and 3 form *In Fire Forged*, a two-part saga that tells the history of Sileria after its successful revolution. Critics praised the Sileria books, finding them far superior to the general run of sword-and-sorcery fiction. Resnick writes romances as "Laura Leone."

1. *In Legend Born* (Tor, 1998) A peasant-turned-outlaw, a warrior, a beautiful aristocrat, a sorcerer, and a fiery Guardian reluctantly band together to free the island nation of Sileria from the Valdani, the latest in a series of foreign conquerors who have oppressed Sileria for a millennium.
2. *White Dragon, The* (Tor, 2003) Subtitle: *In Fire Forged, Part One*. Sileria, which has overthrown the Valdani, now faces civil war as the fire sorcerer Guardians of the Otherworld face off against the Honored Society and its water wizards.
3. *Destroyer Goddess, The* (Tor, 2003) Subtitle: *In Fire Forged, Part Two*. Tansen, Sileria's greatest warrior, and Mirabar, a prophetess and fire wizard, lead the rebellion against the Waterlords.

Resnick, Mike (Michael Diamond)

I. Science-fiction writer Mike Resnick's more recent novels are futuristic fables that chronicle the often disastrous consequences of mankind's attempt to colonize and annex alien worlds into its galaxywide Republic. This saga can be read as a thinly veiled critique of Western expansionism, particularly into Africa, represented here by the world of Faligor. That world is introduced to the dubious reversal of human "progress" in a tripartite reversal of the design of Dante's *Divine Comedy* in which a "Paradise" is transformed into an "Inferno." *Kirinyaga* (Ballantine, 1998), *A Miracle of Rare Design* (Tor, 1994), and *Bully!* (Tor, 1991) are variations on the same theme. Mike Resnick is the father of Laura Resnick (q.v.). *Mike Resnick's The Galactic Comedy* (Farthest Star, 2003) is an omnibus volume containing numbers 1 through 3.

1. *Paradise: A Chronicle of a Distant World* (Tor, 1991) The story of the settlement of the "primitive" world of Faligor by humans and the relations between humankind and Faligorians.
2. *Purgatory: A Chronicle of a Distant World* (Tor, 1993) The intelligent reptilian beings of Karimon find a brilliant chief who understands that the newly arrived humans are mortal beings rather than gods or demons.
3. *Inferno: A Chronicle of a Distant World* (Tor, 1993) Backed by the galaxywide resources of the Republic, Arthur Cartright launches a project to bestow the fruits of human progress on Faligor, with horrendous results.

II. Resnick, who started out doing a great deal of hack writing, has been a generally improving writer during his more than 30-year career. His latest books are his best, but some of his earlier paperback series are of interest. The Ganymede duo is a pair of pastiches of Edgar Rice Burroughs (q.v.) in his John Carter of Mars mode, featuring an American soldier-of-fortune against a horde of immortal monsters on a distant planet.

1. *Goddess of Ganymede* (Grant, 1967) American soldier-of-fortune Adam Thane must defeat a horde of nasty beings and an evil deathless race or the woman he loves, Princess Delisse, will be forced into marriage with the planet Ganymede's most evil god.
2. *Pursuit on Ganymede* (Paperback Library, 1968) Venturing into the Lands of the East, Adam Thane pits his sword against man-eating apes, giant carnivorous mutants, and ruthless cannibals.

III. Tales of the Galactic Midway are a quartet of light adventure novels describing what happens when a carny owner purchases a carnival sideshow, only to find out that what he thought were human freaks are actually aliens.

1. *Sideshow* (New American Library, 1982) Carny tycoon Thaddeus Flint gets more than he bargained for when he purchases a carnival sideshow.
2. *Three-Legged Hootch Dancer, The* (New American Library, 1983) More adventures, as the Galactic Midway goes out into the galaxy.
3. *Wild Alien Tamer, The* (New American Library, 1983) More comic adventures in space.
4. *Best Rootin' Tootin' Shootin' Gunslinger in the Whole Damn Galaxy, The* (New American Library, 1983) The final adventure of the Galactic Midway.

IV. Tales of the Velvet Comet, basically the history of a bordello in space, postulates an artificial world where everyone's fantasies come true but that becomes the secret battleground of a galactic power struggle. *Tales of the Velvet Comet* (Alexander, 2002) contains numbers 1 through 4.

1. *Eros Ascending* (Phantasia, 1984) The Velvet Comet, a giant orbiting bordello, one of the most popular pleasure palaces in space, is beset by internal power struggles and religious fanatics. Limited edition published by Phantasia, popular edition reprinted by New American Library.
2. *Eros at Zenith* (Phantasia, 1984) A murder mystery set in the Velvet Comet. Published in limited edition by Phantasia; popular edition by New American Library.
3. *Eros Descending* (New American Library, 1985) A religious leader becomes obsessed by the alien prostitutes aboard the Velvet Comet.

4. *Eros at Nadir* (New American Library, 1986) A hack writer is commissioned to create a totally false musical about the now decommissioned Velvet Comet.

V. The Oracle trilogy is about Penelope Bailey, a not especially nice little girl who has the power to foresee the future, and the efforts to control or destroy Penelope.

1. *Soothsayer* (Ace, 1991) After Mouse rescues little Penelope Bailey from an alien captor, she finds that she is being pursued by three governments and 200 bounty hunters who are after the child.
2. *Oracle* (Ace, 1992) Carlos "Iceman" Mendoza hires the Whistler to bring in Penelope, dead or alive.
3. *Prophet* (Ace, 1993) The Iceman continues to be obsessed with locating Penelope and destroying, or neutralizing, the threat she poses to human history by her prophetic powers.

VI. A pair of space westerns spotlights the legendary Santiago, a mysterious outlaw who may in truth be a kind of galactic freedom fighter. *The Return of Santiago* is set more than 100 years later. The Santiago books are sometimes regarded as part of a Far Future series including *Birthright: The Book of Man* (Signet, 1982), which is a blueprint for 18,000 years of human history, and *The Dark Lady: A Romance of the Far Future* (Tor, 1987), about an Ayesha-type figure (H. Rider Haggard [q.v.]) who remains forever young.

1. *Santiago: A Myth of the Far Future* (Tor, 1986) Bounty hunter Sebastian Nightingale Cain, reporter Virtue Mackenzie, and art thief Swagman are on the trail of the legendary and elusive outlaw Santiago to claim the largest reward in history for his capture.
2. *Return of Santiago, The* (Tor, 2003) More than a century later, small-time crook Danny Briggs stumbles upon an epic poem that chronicles the career of Santiago and decides to continue the poem, adopting the name of Dante Alighieri.

VII. Lucifer Jones is a parody of Indiana Jones, the peripatetic soldier of fortune, whose adventures were chronicled in print and on film (*Raiders of the Lost Ark*, etc.) Lucifer circles the globe, felling villains, tailing mythological creatures, and clobbering literary icons while searching for a place to build his tabernacle. Numbers 2 and 3 were published together as *Lucifer Jones* (Warner, 1992).

1. *Adventures* (New American Library, 1985) Lucifer Jones cons his way across Africa in search of misadventure.
2. *Exploits* (Wildside, 1992) Lucifer in Asia in the late 1920s.
3. *Encounters* (Wildside, 1994) Lucifer's adventures in Europe, including an encounter with the Loch Ness monster, in the 1930s.

VIII. The Widowmaker trio was about Jefferson Nighthawk, a galactic gun for hire in the far future, who is frozen cryogenically until a cure can be found for a loathsome disease, but he is thawed out prematurely a couple of times to embark upon assassination missions. A fourth volume was added in 2005. *Widowmakers* (SFBC, 1998) contains numbers 1 through 3.

1. *Widowmaker, The* (Bantam, 1996) Jefferson Nighthawk, created from the DNA of famed assassin Widowmaker, who is frozen until a cure is found for his disease, is given the assignment of killing the man who assassinated the dictator of Solio II.
2. *Widowmaker Reborn, The* (Bantam, 1997) Cloned again, Jefferson Nighthawk is given the assignment of rescuing the daughter of a politician and killing the rebel leader who holds her hostage.

3. *Widowmaker Unleashed, The* **(Bantam, 1998)** The Widowmaker, thawed out when a cure for his disease becomes available, wants to live a quiet life in retirement, but the enemies his previous clones have garnered are not about to let him rest.

4. *Gathering of Widowmakers, A* **(Meisha Merlin, 2005)** What Jefferson Nighthawk, the original Widowmaker, really wants to do is retire on a faraway planet and raise a garden; but he can't, because his two clones are feuding.

IX. Mike Resnick's approach to military SF is less about hardware and blood 'n' guts action than it is about strategy and leadership. So far he has published three novels of a projected five in the Starship series, about the starship *Theodore Roosevelt* and its maverick captain, Wilson Cole.

1. *Starship: Mutiny* **(Pyr, 2005)** First officer Wilson Cole stages a mutiny aboard the starship *Theodore Roosevelt*, wins a major galactic battle, and faces court-martial. Variant title: *Mutiny*.

2. *Starship: Pirate* **(Pyr, 2006)** The crew of the starship *Theodore Roosevelt* spring Wilson Cole from the brig, and Cole decides to set up as a pirate, albeit a moral pirate. Variant title: *Pirate*.

3. *Mercenary* **(Pyr, 2007)** Wilson Cole and the *Teddy R.* are pitted against Cole's former right-hand woman, the pirate queen known as the Valkyrie.

Resnicow, Herbert

I. Alexander and Norma Gold are 1980s Jewish American versions of Dashiell Hammett's (q.v.) Nick and Nora Charles. Alex, who is a detecting genius, starts solving crimes as a diversion while recovering from a heart attack. Eventually, he gives up his job as a consulting engineer, and he and Norma become full-time private investigators. Each one of the Gold mysteries involves someone in the arts: architecture, ballet, painting, opera, or a Broadway musical. These novels are a treat for readers who enjoy ingenious plots, witty banter, lots of New York ambience, a wealth of information about the arts, and a minimum of sex and violence.

1. *Gold Solution, The* **(St. Martin's, 1983)** Draftsman Jonathan Candell is arrested for murder after famous architect Roger Talbott is found with a knife in his back.

2. *Gold Deadline, The* **(St. Martin's, 1984)** Impresario Viktor Bogulslave is stabbed to death in his curtained box during a ballet gala.

3. *Gold Frame, The* **(St. Martin's, 1984)** The Golds are called in by Daniel Belmont, owner of the celebrated FAMONY Museum, to help authenticate a reputed Vermeer painting.

4. *Gold Curse, The* **(St. Martin's, 1986)** Opera singer Thea Malabar is stabbed (for real) while she is performing the role of Gilda in *Rigoletto*.

5. *Gold Gamble, The* **(St. Martin's, 1988)** After the Golds invest in a revival of *Guys and Dolls*, Carol Sands, Norma's choice for the role of Adelaide, becomes a prime murder suspect.

II. A pair of mystery novels showcases a father-and-son team: venture capitalist Ed Baer and his philosopher son, Warren. Ed's involvement with big money gives him entry into boardrooms and country clubs that the ordinary detective wouldn't have.

1. *Dead Room, The* **(Dodd, Mead, 1987)** Inventor Walter Kassel is stabbed to death while testing his secret HHF-10 sound system.

2. *Hot Place, The* **(St. Martin's, 1990)** Cordially disliked Bernie Brodsky, chairman of a country club on Long Island, is found suffocated in its steam room.

III. Crossword puzzles are the crucial element in the mysteries that retired lawyer Giles Sullivan and college administrator Isabel Macintosh solve in this puzzle mystery series, each of which features five crossword puzzles (with solutions) by Henry Hook. Published only in paperback.

1. *Murder Across and Down* **(Ballantine, 1985)** A despised member of the board of directors of the prestigious Cruciverbal Club drops dead over his dinner at the club's 50th-anniversary celebration.

2. *Seventh Crossword, The* **(Ballantine, 1985)** Dean of faculty Isabel Macintosh finds the answer to the murder of Fabian Humboldt in a crossword puzzle.

3. *Crossword Code, The* **(Ballantine, 1986)** FBI agent Burke is convinced that the innocent-appearing young Russian Valentin Zulkov must be a spy.

4. *Crossword Hunt, The* **(Ballantine, 1987)** Abraham Hardwick's bequest of millions to Windham University has a large catch: the money must be used to fund a new institute chaired by Hardwick's hand-picked appointee.

4. *Crossword Legacy, The* **(Ballantine, 1987)** "The ultimate challenge: solve the puzzle and learn the secret of a rich man's will" (blurb).

IV. Resnicow presumably did most of the writing, while his coauthors supplied the sports expertise in this trio of novels featuring the most prestigious events in sports. Sports reporter Marcus Aurelius Barr, former champion gymnast, is the linking character in these mysteries.

1. *Murder at the Superbowl* **(Morrow, 1986)** Former NFC quarterback Fran Tarkenton is the coauthor of this mystery set at the Super Bowl, the crown event of pro football.

2. *Beanball* **(Morrow, 1989)** Former pitching great Tom Seaver is the coauthor of this mystery set at baseball's World Series.

3. *World Cup Murder, The* **(Wynwood, 1989)** World soccer icon Pelé is the coauthor of this mystery set at the World Cup.

Reynolds, William J.

Nebraska (no first name) is a freelance writer and sometime sleuth who works out of Omaha, *Nebraska*. Although he works only part-time as a private eye, Nebraska is as hard-boiled and as wisecracking as they come. Sometimes Nebraska is an affectionate parody of the fictional detectives that he, being a "real" detective, likes to criticize. The Nebraska series is funny and full of strange characters, snappy dialogue, and a well-realized Heartland locale. Reynolds, an Omaha native, still lives in the Heartland (Sioux Falls, South Dakota).

1. *Nebraska Quotient, The* **(St. Martin's, 1984)** Would-be novelist Nebraska becomes his own main character when his fatally wounded former partner stumbles into his apartment one morning.

2. *Moving Targets* **(St. Martin's, 1986)** Nebraska investigates the murder of bank president Jack Castelar and the concomitant disappearance of Castelar's daughter.

3. *Money Trouble* **(Putnam, 1988)** A former high school sweetheart asks Nebraska to find out whether her late husband was really a bank robber.

4. *Things Invisible* **(Putnam, 1989)** A missing daughter, a worried mother who seems reluctant to involve the police, and a Mafia-connected father lead to a dark family secret and murder.

5. *Naked Eye, The* **(Putnam, 1990)** Nebraska goes to Minnesota to track down a young runaway and incurs the wrath of the boy's would-be abductor.

6. *Drive-By* **(Ex Machina, 1995)** Nebraska is appointed unofficial guardian angel of Darius Le Clerc, who is gunned down by what appears to be a juvenile gang.

Rice, Anne

I. The publication of *Interview with the Vampire* in 1976 was like a shot of adrenalin to the hoary. but somewhat somnolent, literary subgenre of vampire tales. After being galvanized by Bram Stoker's *Dracula* (1897), vampire tales had reached the point where they were primarily fodder for horror films and comic books. *Interview*, with its tale told from the vampire's point of view, and its successors by Rice and authors like Chelsea Quinn Yarbro (q.v.), Brian Lumley (q.v.), Tanith Lee (q.v.), and Poppy Z. Brite have provided readers with all the horror and passion of the traditional vampire tale but also the vampire as a complex, sympathetic character rather than the simple embodiment of evil. Rice's vampires are creatures who look exactly like the human beings they once were but are differentiated by their immortality and their need for human blood. Although most sensible vampires desire anonymity, a few individuals are so hungry for fame that they reveal themselves, much to the discomfort of their cohorts. The stories are told from the vampire's point of view in a wonderfully frenzied prose style. A great deal of arcane historical and religious lore is included along with the vampire's tortured philosophizing about the trials of immortality and their gradual loss of human feelings. The original Vampire Chronicles (numbers 1–3, 5, and 7) were gradually integrated with the Mayfair Witches, a series about a prominent and wealthy Louisiana family that has practiced witchcraft for five centuries with the aid of a supernatural entity who has brought them wealth intermingled with personal misery. The Mayfair Trilogy consists of numbers 4, 6, and 7. Another pair of books, initially separate from the Vampire Chronicles, is called New Tales of the Vampires (numbers 9 and 11). *The Complete Vampire Chronicles* (Ballantine, 1989) is an omnibus volume containing numbers 1, 2, and 3. After the death of her husband, in 2003, Anne Rice said that she would stop writing about vampires. Rice has written several nonseries novels including *Violin* (Knopf, 1997) and *The Servant of the Bones* (Knopf, 1996). Her son Christopher Rice and her sister Alice Borchardt are also writers. *Interview with the Vampire* was made into a motion picture starring Tom Cruise and Brad Pitt (1994). *Queen of the Damned* has also been filmed.

1. *Interview with the Vampire* **(Knopf, 1976)** Vampire Louis tells a reporter all about his death-in-life experience and his search for the meaning of his existence.

2. *Vampire Lestat, The* **(Knopf, 1985)** After centuries of wandering and uncovering lore about cults of the dead, vampire Lestat becomes a rock star in New Orleans.

3. *Queen of the Damned, The* **(Knopf, 1988)** Lestat awakens the evil and destructive Queen Akasha from her 6,000-year sleep.

4. *Witching Hour, The* **(Knopf, 1990)** Neurosurgeon Rowan Mayfair, who inherits the family fortune and the family curse, saves the life of Michael Curry, and together they try to exorcise the Mayfair demon. First of the Mayfair Witches trilogy.

5. *Tale of the Body Thief, The* **(Knopf, 1992)** Lestat is conned into switching bodies (temporarily, he thinks) with human psychic Raglan James.

6. *Lasher* **(Knopf, 1993)** Mayfair coven queen Rowan disappears after bearing Lasher, who has been jointly fathered by Michael Curry and the Mayfair family demon.

7. *Taltos* **(Knopf, 1994)** Another "Taltos," or superhuman offspring of two witches, has been fathered by Michael Curry, this time on 13-year-old Mona, the most powerful witch in the Mayfair clan.

8. *Memnoch the Devil* **(Knopf, 1995)** Lestat, restored to his immortal body, is recruited by Memnoch, the biblical devil, to help fight God, whom Memnoch paints as cruel and negligent. This was supposed to be the final volume in the chronicles.

9. *Pandora* **(Knopf, 1998)** Pandora, first introduced in number 3, sets the record straight (she was *not* a Greek courtesan) and journeys to Antioch for a reunion with Marius. First of the New Tales of the Vampires duo.

10. *Vampire Armand, The* **(Knopf, 1998)** Armand, leader of the Paris vampires, resurrected from his end in number 8, revisits his earthly existence, including medieval Russian beginnings and a stay in 16th-century Venice. Another Vampire Chronicle.

11. *Vittorio the Vampire* **(Knopf, 1999)** Vittorio di Riniari relates his life as a vampire and a Renaissance man who hobnobbed with the likes of Cosimo de Medici and Fra Filippo Lippi. Second of New Tales of the Vampire duo.

12. *Merrick* **(Knopf, 2000)** In the first volume to mix the Vampire Chronicles and the Mayfair Witches, the life of Merrick, octoroon ancestress of the Mayfair Witches, is related by David Talbot, formerly a psychic detective, now a vampire himself. Lestat puts in a cameo appearance.

13. *Blood and Gold* **(Knopf, 2001)** Marius, a character in several earlier chronicles, tells his story, which starts in Imperial Rome and includes a sojourn in Renaissance Venice and Florence, where he entertains an unrequited passion for Sandro Botticelli.

14. *Blackwood Farm* **(Knopf, 2002)** Quinn Blackwood, who is involved in a violent love-hate relationship with Goblin, his spirit-world doppelgänger, complicates matters by falling into a passionate relationship with 15-year-old nympho Mona Mayfair (see number 7).

15. *Blood Canticle* **(Knopf, 2003)** Lestat, obsessed with becoming a saint (at least in his actions), gets involved with Rowan Mayfair. Will Mona Mayfair become a vampire? May be the last in the series.

II. Anne Rice, returning to the Catholic faith and eschewing her vampire fiction, at least for now, has written *Christ the Lord*, two novels describing the early life of Yeshua (Jesus Christ). Although *Out of Egypt*, which describes the boyhood of Jesus, follows the Bible and biblical research closely, *The Road to Cana*, which describes his "lost" young adulthood, allows Rice to do some speculation.

1. *Christ the Lord: Out of Egypt* **(Knopf, 2005)** Seven-year-old Jesus, returning home to Nazareth from Egypt, describes his Torah education and immersion in the traditions of the Hebrew Bible and his gradual awareness of the miraculous birth his parents have never discussed.

2. *Christ the Lord: The Road to Cana* **(Knopf, 2008)** Jesus struggles with a sense of restlessness of purpose and a deep love for a kinswoman, as he comes to understand that serving the Lord's will takes precedence over the desires of his own heart.

Rich, Virginia

The late Virginia Rich, food writer and mystery author, wrote three novels featuring Eugenia Potter, master chef and amateur sleuth. Nancy Pickard (q.v.) wrote a fourth mystery using Rich's notes and recipes. The Eugenia Potter stories are enjoyable, chatty tales with vignettes of small-time life and discussions of recipes and cooking techniques.

1. *Cooking School Murders, The* **(Dutton, 1982)** The gourmet cooking class instructed by master chef James Redmond is reduced by three members in the course of one day.
2. *Baked Bean Supper Murders, The* **(Dutton, 1983)** Eugenia Potter arrives at her sometime home in Northcutt Harbor, Maine, just in time for the annual baked-bean dinner.
3. *Nantucket Diet Murders, The* **(Delacorte, 1985)** A charismatic diet doctor, the mysterious Count Tony Ferencz, has the well-to-do widows of Nantucket all in a flutter.
4. *Twenty-seven Ingredient Chili Con Carne Murders, The* **(Delacorte, 1993)** Ricardo Ortega, manager of Eugenia's Arizona ranch, and his granddaughter have disappeared. Written by Nancy Pickard (q.v.) from notes left by Virginia Rich.

Richardson, Dorothy

Dorothy Richardson was one of the first English novelists to employ stream of consciousness in her fiction. Her intimate, autobiographical portrayal of Miriam Henderson from youth to maturity is the subject of *Pilgrimage*, a novel in 13 sections published from 1915 to 1967. Miriam develops from a bright, sceptical, and socially uncertain young girl, through crises of faith and friendship, to maturity as an assured and independent thinker with mystical religious convictions. Richardson, like Virginia Woolf, had high regard for mystical and intuitive qualities, which both saw as essentially feminine. Richardson's style is perhaps less daunting than James Joyce's (q.v.) or Marcel Proust's (q.v.), but because critics haven't admitted her to the pantheon where they reside, *Pilgrimage* has apparently never been widely read, except, perhaps, by feminist intellectuals, and she remains in danger of being relegated to the literary sidelines as fodder for would-be PhDs. *Dimple Hill* (number 12) and *March Moonlight* were never published separately: the former was published in 1938 in the four-volume collected edition of *Pilgrimage* published by Dent (UK); the latter in the four-volume edition published by Knopf in 1967. Virago (UK) reissued the four-volume set in 1979.

1. *Pointed Roofs* **(Knopf, 1915)** Prompted by her father's financial collapse, Miriam Henderson at 17 decides to take a teaching position at a girls' school in Germany for a year.
2. *Backwater* **(Knopf, 1916)** Miriam returns home, then spends her 18th year as a resident teacher at a dreary north London school, Wordsworth House.
3. *Honeycomb* **(Knopf, 1917)** Miriam at 19 is a governess for the children of the wealthy Corrie family, who live at Newlands.
4. *Tunnel, The* **(Knopf, 1919)** Now living by herself at a rooming house and working as a dentist's assistant, Miriam discovers London's intellectual life.
5. *Interim* **(Knopf, 1919)** Miriam seems to come to terms with her feelings that religion and science include false male ideas, while she grows in intellectual sophistication.
6. *Deadlock* **(Knopf, 1921)** After several years during which she becomes increasingly self-assured and independent, Miriam meets Michael Shatov, a new boarder at her rooming house.
7. *Revolving Lights* **(Knopf, 1923)** Miriam is introduced to Quaker thought and appreciates its equal treatment of the sexes and its respect for silent meditation.
8. *Trap, The* **(Knopf, 1925)** Now 28, depressed and unsure of the writing career she had hoped for, Miriam debates the alternatives of marriage, celibacy, and free love.
9. *Oberland* **(Knopf, 1928)** Miriam, on holiday in the Swiss Alps, regains a sense of joy and is confirmed in her new mystical orientation.
10. *Dawn's Left Hand* **(Duckworth [UK], 1931)** Miriam has an affair with scientist Hypo Wilson, who is based on science-fiction writer, novelist, and science prophet H. G. Wells.
11. *Clear Horizon* **(Dent [UK], 1935)** Miriam and Hypo finally break off their unhappy love affair.
12. *Dimple Hill* **(Dent [UK], 1938)** Miriam takes a long prescribed rest with Quaker friends in Sussex, where her belief in Go is ecstatically affirmed. First published in the four-volume Dent (UK) collected edition of *Pilgrimage*.
13. *March Moonlight* **(Knopf, 1967)** Unfinished, posthumously published coda that attempted to round off the work. Published in the four-volume 1967 edition of *Pilgrimage* by Knopf.

Richardson, Henry Handel

PSEUDONYM OF Ethel Richardson

The Fortunes of Richard Mahoney is a trilogy that surveys Australian history from the 1850s onward. An Australian classic, it is a powerful and tragic work that has been compared to Thomas Mann's (q.v.) *Buddenbrooks* and Romain Rolland's (q.v.) *Jean-Christophe* and deserves to be better known elsewhere. The trilogy follows the life of Richard Mahoney from his arrival in Australia as a young Irish immigrant, through his medical progress, the acquiring and losing of wealth, his inability to settle down in England or Australia, and his final descent into madness and death. Richardson was born in Australia, the daughter of an Anglo-Irish physician. After moving to Europe and marrying professor of German literature J. G. Robertson, she devoted her life to writing. Other Richardson works (reprinted as Virago Modern Classics) include *Maurice Guest* and *The Getting of Wisdom*. Fortunes was published in three volumes (1917, 1925, and 1929). The first two volumes were reprinted in 1930. All three volumes were published together as *The Fortunes of Richard Mahoney* (Norton, 1931).

1. *Australia Felix* **(Norton, 1930)** This shows young Richard coming from Ireland to Australia during the gold rush, marrying and keeping store for a while, then returning to his profession of medicine and building up a successful practice. Published under the title *The Fortunes of Richard Mahoney* in a "small" edition by Holt in 1917.
2. *Way Home, The* **(Norton, 1930)** Richard is increasingly dissatisfied with life in both Australia and England, even though his mining shares have made him rich and his wife and children are devoted to him. Published in the United Kingdom in 1925.
3. *Ultima Thule* **(Norton, 1929)** Richard suffers a financial loss, tries to take up his medical practice again, but finally descends into madness and death.

Richter, Conrad

I. The Awakening Land is a trilogy of novels, also known as the American Pioneer trilogy, that begins in the 1790s as the Luckett family leaves home in Pennsylvania and crosses the Ohio River to uncharted wilderness. Sayward, the oldest and staunchest of the children, is 15 at the start, and the story, which continues to her death, is a notable portrait of an indomitable pioneer woman. Elizabeth Montgomery starred as Sayward in the television miniseries (1978) based on this trilogy. The trilogy is available in an omnibus edition, *The Awakening Land* (Knopf, 1966).

1. *Trees, The* **(Knopf, 1940)** After her mother's death, it falls to Sayward to keep the family together and safe from danger as they put down roots in the new land.

2. *Fields, The* **(Knopf, 1946)** Now married and with a growing family, Sayward makes a success of the farm and starts a school and church in the little community.
3. *Town, The* **(Knopf, 1950)** This concluding volume, which shows the thriving town and Sayward's move from the old cabin to a fancy new house, won a Pulitzer Prize.

II. Two more Richter novels are not really sequels, but they are companion volumes because they treat similar stories: young pioneer children are raised by Indians and then returned against their wills to white society. Both are justly popular with young adults. *The Light in the Forest* was made into movie starring James MacArthur (1958).

1. *Light in the Forest, The* **(Knopf, 1953)** At 15 True Son is returned from his adoptive Indian family to his parents, the Butlers.
2. *Country of Strangers, A* **(Knopf, 1966)** Stone Girl, at 15, is a squaw with a little boy when she is taken by Black Robe back to white society.

Riggs, Cynthia

Ninety-two-year-old Victoria Trumbull of Martha's Vineyard, Massachusetts, is a woman of many talents: poet, playwright, newspaper correspondent and editor, naturalist, deputy sheriff, and amateur sleuth. With the aid of a cutoff shoe (for her bunion) and a stout stick, she still perambulates the woods and fields of her native Vineyard and, this being a series of cozies, stumbles across the occasional corpse and applies her still-acute intelligence and intimate knowledge of the Vineyard's people and ways to solve the mystery attached to the corpse. Cynthia Riggs, a 13th-generation Islander, writes mysteries that give readers a great sense of Vineyard topography and characters and a worthy addition to the ranks of elderly lady detectives.

1. *Deadly Nightshade* **(St. Martin's, 2001)** Introduces Victoria Trumbull, 92-year-old native of Martha's Vineyard. While waiting on the dock one evening for her granddaughter to return with the harbormaster, Victoria hears a scream, followed by a splash, followed by the sound of tires skidding on sand.
2. *Cranefly Orchid Murders, The* **(St. Martin's, 2002)** Recluse Phoebe Eldredge decides to sell 200 acres of unspoiled Vineyard land to a developer rather than leave them to her descendants, in particular her obnoxious granddaughter. While searching the acreage of Phoebe's estate for rare plants to forestall the developers, Victoria stumbles across the corpse of sleazy lawyer Montgomery Mausz.
3. *Cemetery Yew, The* **(St. Martin's, 2003)** An empty grave, a misplaced coffin, and a missing hearse driver are the harbingers of a series of murders, all with a South American connection involving smuggling and an exotic bird.
4. *Jack in the Pulpit* **(St. Martin's, 2004)** The untimely death of four residents mars a beautiful September on Martha's Vineyard.
5. *Paperwhite Narcissus, The* **(St. Martin's, 2005)** Removed from her job as West Tisbury correspondent for the *Island Enquirer* by an editor looking for younger blood, the feisty Victoria turns her attention to making the two-page West Tisbury newsletter, *The Grackle,* into a competitor of the *Enquirer.*
6. *Indian Pipes* **(St. Martin's, 2006)** Victoria stumbles upon the body of reclusive engineer Jube Burkhardt, who appears to fallen to his death from a cliff.
7. *Shooting Star* **(St. Martin's, 2007)** Victoria becomes a playwright for a summer stage adaptation of *Frankenstein.* Then the production is beset by the disappearance of its star and the murder of an actress.

Riggs, John R(aymond)

Garth Ryland is editor and publisher of the *Oakalla Reporter,* a newspaper in a fictional small town in Wisconsin that is based on Riggs's hometown of Mulberry, Indiana. Garth is something of a dreamer, an unlucky lover, and a part-time sleuth. Oakalla, which seems more like *Wisconsin Death Trip* or *Twin Peaks* rather than an idyllic hamlet, is full of sinister folk, most of them more or less related.

1. *Last Laugh, The* **(Dembner, 1984)** A practical joker is buried on April Fool's Day, but his presence seems to live on, haunting the town and driving people to desperate measures.
2. *Let Sleeping Dogs Lie* **(Dembner, 1986)** After Garth brings a 1936 Cadillac convertible he found in a deserted barn to local handyman Woody Padgett for repair, Woody disappears, and a fire breaks out where the Caddy is housed.
3. *Glory Hound, The* **(Dembner, 1987)** After high school senior Frieda Whitlock has been missing for three days, Sheriff Roberts has Phillipee's Pond dredged and turns up a 20-year-old skull. Variant title: *Hunting Ground.*
4. *Haunt of the Nightingale* **(Dembner, 1988)** A young woman returns to her hometown of Oakalla after eight years, emotionally distraught, nearly mute, and on the run from a man who may still be living in the town.
5. *Wolf in Sheep's Clothing* **(Dembner, 1989)** Garth becomes involved with the disappearance of a former lover and her new boyfriend, who vanish somewhere in the Minnesota north woods.
6. *One Man's Poison* **(Dembner, 1991)** All kinds of weird things happen in Oakalla after an earthquake: a local boy and his father are missing, an enigmatic Indian is hanging out at the local diner, and the local water tastes bad.
7. *Dead Letter* **(Barricade, 1992)** Deaf dwarf Amel Pilkin, the local trash collector, is found dead in his truck after celebrating in the Corner Bar and Grill.
8. *Dragon Lives Forever, A* **(Barricade, 1992)** Two decades separate the still unresolved disappearance of a teenage boy and the recent death of a washed-up stock-car racer.
9. *Cold Hearts and Gentle People* **(Barricade, 1994)** Ryland investigates the death of antique collector Monroe Edmonds, whose 400-pound body was found in his home elevator.
10. *Killing Frost* **(Barricade, 1995)** Garth Ryland is one of the first to find the body with rubbery flesh and missing extremities near the pig farm.
11. *Snow on the Roses* **(Barricade, 1996)** It seems that 90-year-old Doc Airhart, who was about to have his memoirs published in the local paper, didn't die a natural death after all.
12. *He Who Waits* **(Barricade, 1997)** Nobody in town, except Garth, seems to be interested when a senator's gay lover turns up dead.
13. *Lost Scout, The* **(Barricade, 1998)** Concerns a right-wing militia and complications experienced by a veteran attempting to reenter everyday life.

Rikhoff, Jean

I. This popular author has two trilogies to her credit. The earlier one is a family saga concerning the Catholic Timble family of Springfield, Illinois. Beginning at the turn of the 20th century, the story focuses on the marriage of Frank and Lydia Timble and continues as their five daughters grow to maturity. These event-filled lives, realistically portrayed, are an engrossing study in love and duty.

1. *Dear Ones All* **(Viking, 1961)** Told mostly in flashbacks from a Thanksgiving Day family gathering in 1936, this account covers

the early years of Frank and Lydia's marriage and the growth of their family.

2. *Voyage In, Voyage Out* (Viking, 1963) In the 1950s, the Timble family gathers for a welcome-home party for prodigal Stu and visiting cousin Lois from New York, both with problems to sort out.

3. *Rites of Passage* (Viking, 1966) The children of the Timble sisters are now in their middle years.

II. Part family saga, part western, this series starts in 1807 as Odder Butte strikes out for the Adirondack Mountains of New York, and the narrative follows succeeding generations of the tough and isolated hardscrabble farmers as they prosper and move further west.

1. *Buttes Landing* (Dial, 1973) Three generations of the Butte family are followed, from old Odder's arrival in the Adirondacks up to the Civil War.

2. *One of the Raymonds* (Dial, 1974) The coming-of-age story of young Mason Raymond Butte is set in the Adirondacks and in rural North Carolina during Reconstruction.

3. *Sweetwater, The* (Dial, 1976) In 1876 young cousins Mason Raymond and John Butte travel west, braving the dangers of high rivers, prairie fires, dust storms, and Indian attack.

Riley, Judith Merkle

Margaret of Ashbery is a 14th-century Englishwoman who undergoes some picaresque and turbulent adventures in a trio of entertaining novels full of flying arrows, drunken noblemen, corrupt priests, defrocked monks, and truculent ghosts.

1. *Vision of Light, A* (Delacorte, 1989) Margaret relates how she married at 14, was left for dead in the plague, gained the healing art through apprenticeship to herbalist Mother Hilde, and endured accusations of witchcraft.

2. *In Pursuit of the Green Lion* (Delacorte, 1990) Margaret marries the unfrocked monk Gregory, who becomes a knight in France and has to be rescued from captivity under the sinister Count of St. Medard.

3. *Water Devil, The* (Three Rivers, 2007) Margaret's father-in-law has plans to use her daughter, Cecily, as a bargaining chip in a feud over riparian rights and borders. But the Water Devil, a creature who dwells in the spring at issue, has other plans.

Riordan, Rick

Tres Navarre is a former professor at UC Berkeley who tries to settle in as a private investigator in his native San Antonio, Texas. Tres is a self-deprecating, wisecracking type but a good investigator. Rick Riordan's authorial voice, according to a *Publishers Weekly* reviewer, is "hard-boiled Tex-Mex." Riordan, a teacher in San Antonio public and private middle and high schools and winner of Edgar, Anthony, and Shamus awards, also has written a trio of juveniles about Percy Jackson, a dyslexic 12-year-old who discovers that he is the modern-day son of a Greek god. *Cold Springs* (Bantam, 2003) is a nonseries adult suspense novel.

1. *Big Red Tequila* (Bantam, 1997) Tres Navarre returns to his native San Antonio to investigate and avenge an unsolved murder that he witnessed 10 years before.

2. *Widower's Two-Step, The* (Bantam, 1998) Navarre, just short of getting his PI license, witnesses the gunning down of musician Julie Kearnes and gets involved with singer Miranda Daniels.

3. *Last King of Texas, The* (Bantam, 2000) After the previous two tenants have met violent deaths, Tres accepts a chair in medieval studies at UT San Antonio and immediately finds himself a target.

4. *Devil Went Down to Austin, The* (Bantam, 2001) Navarre moves to Austin to teach at the flagship campus of the University of Texas and visit with his brother, software genius Garrett, whose startup business, Techsan, is the target of a truly hostile takeover.

5. *Southtown* (Bantam, 2004) Escaped convict Will Stirman is out to get Erainya Manos and her eight-year-old son, relicts of the late cop Fred Barrow, who got him sent to jail.

6. *Mission Road* (Bantam, 2006) Navarre's boyhood friend, reformed criminal Ralph Arguello, turns up on Tres's doorstep one step ahead of the San Antonio police and covered in blood.

7. *Rebel Island* (Bantam, 2007) Tres and his new wife, Maia, honeymoon on Rebel Island, where Tres and his older brother, Garret, spent vacations with their dysfunctional parents. Then US Marshal Jesse Longoria, a character from earlier books, is killed.

Ripley, Alexandra

Alexandra Ripley (d. 2004), whose best-known novel was *Scarlett* (Warner, 1991), the highly publicized "official" sequel to Margaret Mitchell's *Gone with the Wind*, wrote a pair of historical novels about her native Charleston, South Carolina. The novels follow the fortunes of two aristocratic Charleston families, the Tradds and the Ansons, from 1863 to 1935, as they slide from prominence into decadence and penury. Inbreeding, snobbery, and obstinacy are more responsible than bad economic times for the decline of these families. The history of the city of Charleston is lovingly delineated in these readable, historically accurate novels.

1. *Charleston* (Doubleday, 1981) Poor white Shad saves Pinckney Tradd's life in the Civil War, goes into partnership with him, but is forbidden to marry Pinckney's sister Lizzie. Covers 1863 to 1898.

2. *On Leaving Charleston* (Doubleday, 1984) Garden Tradd, Lizzie's niece, breaks away from her family's ruinous traditions. Covers 1900 to 1935.

Ripley, Ann

Gardener Louise Eldridge, wife of a foreign-service and CIA official, lives, gardens (organically), and solves mysteries in the Washington, DC, area. She eventually becomes host of the PBS show *Gardening with Nature*, which sometimes takes her to exotic places such as Hawaii, occasionally involves her with high-powered lobbyists and politicians, and allows her to investigate at least one murder per novel, in this entertaining series full of informative gardening tips. Ann Ripley, former newspaper person and organic gardener, lives in Colorado.

1. *Mulch* (St. Martin's, 1994) Foreign-service wife Louise Eldridge moves into a new home in northern Virginia, in the same neighborhood as Peter Hoffman, possible candidate for undersecretary of defense. Then Louise turns up a bag of leaves containing severed body parts.

2. *Death of a Garden Pest* (St. Martin's, 1996) Louise agrees to help host an organic gardening show for the northern Virginia public television station. When Madeleine Doering, whose place in the

series Louise has taken, winds up dead from an injection of pesticide, Louise becomes the prime suspect.

3. *Death of a Political Plant* (Bantam, 1998) Now cohost of Washington, DC, public television's *Gardening with Nature,* Louise finds herself embroiled in presidential politics and saddled with some unexpected houseguests, including one who winds up floating in a water garden.

4. *Garden Tour Affair, The* (Bantam, 1999) Louise and her family are spending the weekend at the Litchfield Falls Inn in Connecticut, when one of the inn's guests, a renowned professor of botany, tumbles, or is pushed, off a cliff.

5. *Perennial Killer, The* (Bantam, 2000) As soon as Eldridge arrives in Colorado to shoot her TV show, she finds herself embroiled in a struggle between environmentalists and developers over a 13,000-acre ranch.

6. *Harvest of Murder* (Kensington, 2002) After she discovers the slashed body of eccentric biologist Dr. Peter Whiting, with whom she shared dog walks, Louise is asked by Whiting's widow to help complete his plant experiments.

7. *Christmas Garden Affair, The* (Kensington, 2002) Bunny Banfield, whose program, *Bunny in the Garden,* is successfully competing with Eldridge's *Gardening with Nature,* imbibes a glass of poisoned wine at the First Lady–elect's Christmas conference held at an inn in Alexandria, Virginia.

8. *Death at the Spring Plant Sale* (Kensington, 2003) Louise had planned to cover the annual Bethesda Garden Club plant sale in Maryland for her TV show, but the club president, wife of a Washington VIP, is shot to death.

9. *Summer Garden Murder* (Kensington, 2005) Eldridge is shocked to see Peter Hoffman, a murderer she helped send to a mental prison five years earlier (see number 1), at a suburban party.

10. *Death in the Orchid Garden* (Kensington, 2006) Eldridge is hosting *Gardening with Nature* on the Hawaiian island of Kauai. Then one of her controversial guests turns up the victim of a homicide.

Robb, Candace

I. Owen Archer of York, former captain of bowmen, having lost an eye, is forced to look for other work. He hooks up with John Thoresby, Archbishop of York and sometime Lord Chancellor of England, a historical character, doing spying and detecting as needed. Set in the 1360s and 1370s, in the reign of King Edward III, these novels enable Owen to hobnob with historical characters such as Geoffrey Chaucer and Dame Alice Perrers and a host of interesting fictional characters such as Owen's wife, the apothecary Lucie Wilton. American writer Candace Robb is a member, among other organizations, of the Mystery Writers of America and the Medieval Academy of America.

1. *Apothecary Rose, The* (St. Martin's, 1993) Unemployed bowman Owen Archer accepts a position with John Thoresby, Archbishop of York and Lord Chancellor of England, to investigate the deaths, by poisoning, of Oswald Fitzwilliam and Sir Geoffrey Montaigne,

2. *Lady Chapel, The* (St. Martin's, 1994) Owen, now married to Master Apothecary Lucie Wilton, investigates the murder of Will Crounce, who played Jesus in the Mercers' Guild Corpus Christie play.

3. *Nun's Tale, The* (St. Martin's, 1995) Lucie is called into service to help cure and counsel the apparently insane Dame Joanna Calverly of Leeds, who claims that, while a novitiate at St. Clement's, she died and was resurrected.

4. *King's Bishop, The* (St. Martin's, 1996) While campaigning at two Cistercian abbeys for William Wykeham (a historical character),

King Edward's candidate for Bishop of Winchester, Owen gets entangled with the travails of his friend New Townley, who is accused of murdering a rival for the favors of a maid to Dame Alice Perrers, the king's mistress.

5. *Riddle of St. Leonard's, The* (St. Martin's, 1997) In 1369 Owen is called in to investigate the deaths of several "corridians," elderly pensioners at St. Leonard's Hospital, possibly due to aggressive health-care cost cutting.

6. *Gift of Sanctuary, A* (St. Martin's, 1998) Owen returns to his native Wales to recruit archers to ward off a prospective French invasion. He is occupied by civil servant and author Geoffrey Chaucer, who has been sent by John of Gaunt to inspect some fortifications.

7. *Spy for the Redeemer, A* (Mysterious, 2002) In 1371, still in Wales, Owen is looking for the killer of stonemason Cynog, who was working on Owen's father-in-law's tomb. Originally published in the United Kingdom in 1999.

8. *Cross-Legged Knight, The* (Mysterious, 2003) When William Wykeham, Bishop of Winchester, escorts the remains of Sir Ranulf Pagnall to York, he is shunned by the family of Sir Ranulf, who hold him responsible for failing to negotiate Sir Ranulf's ransom in France. Then Wykeham's townhouse is torched and the body of a midwife found within.

9. *Guilt of Innocents, The* (Heinemann [UK], 2007) In 1372 a river pilot is poisoned and drowned in the Ouse, and suspicion falls on Nicholas Ferriby, Vicar of Weston, master of a small grammar school and holder of unpopular beliefs. Not yet published in the United States.

10. *Vigil of Spies, A* (Century [UK], 2008) September 1373. The dying Archbishop Thoresby has agreed to a visit from Princess Joan, who wants advice from him about the royal succession. Not yet published in the United States.

II. Dame Margaret Kerr of Perth is the heroine of a trio of mysteries set in Scotland at the end of the 13th century. Margaret comes to Edinburgh in search of her missing husband, Roger, who is serving Robert the Bruce, and gets involved in Scotland's fight for independence against England and a series of murders.

1. *Trust Betrayed, A* (Warner, 2001) 1297. After Jack, cousin of her missing husband, Roger, is killed in a brawl in Edinburgh while searching for him, Margaret Kerr goes to Edinburgh with her priest brother to attempt to find out what is going on.

2. *Fire and the Flint, The* (Heinemann [UK], 2003) Raids and a murder on the Kerr property bring the wrath of the English down on the heads of Margaret and her uncle Murdoch during summer 1297. Then Roger, her missing husband, suddenly reappears, probably on a mission for Robert the Bruce. Not published in the United States.

3. *Cruel Courtship, A* (Heinemann [UK], 2004) Margaret, at the behest of James Comyn, kinsman of the deposed John Balliol, takes up residence in Stirling to discover why the informer who has been providing Wallace and Murray with details of the English plans has become unreliable. Not published in the United States.

Robb, J. D.

PSEUDONYM OF Nora Roberts

As J. D. Robb, prolific romance novelist Nora Roberts (q.v.) is churning out novels about Eve Dallas, lieutenant of the New York City Police and Safety Department. The series, which starts in 2058, is a combination of police drama, SF, and romance. Eve is everything a romance heroine should be: strong, determined, intelligent, and passionate. And—she has Roarke, hunky and fabulously rich, and a nasty childhood she prefers to forget. Guns have been outlawed and lasers are the street weapons of choice. Cloning plays a role in one novel and computers in a couple of others, but not much else has changed. Numbers 22, 24, and 25 are novella length (less than 100 pages). Number 24 is available in audio version only. Covers for the later novels in the series state that the author is "Nora Roberts writing as J. D. Robb."

1. *Naked in Death* (Berkley, 1995) In the year 2058, New York Police and Safety Department lieutenant Eve Dallas gets involved with Roarke, a suspect in her latest murder case.
2. *Glory in Death* (Berkley, 1995) Dallas sees a connection between the murders of two beautiful and highly successful women.
3. *Immortal in Death* (Berkley, 1996) The prime suspect in the murder of a top model is Eve's best friend.
4. *Rapture in Death* (Berkley, 1996) Dallas is drawn into the world of virtual reality.
5. *Ceremony in Death* (Berkley, 1997) Eve is conducting a top-secret investigation into the death of a fellow officer.
6. *Vengeance in Death* (Berkley, 1997) Two men have been murdered with lasers. They have links with each other and with Eve's new husband, Roarke.
7. *Holiday in Death* (Berkley, 1998) Lieutenant Dallas goes undercover to expose the ritualistic serial killer who is preying on the employees of an elite New York City escort service.
8. *Conspiracy in Death* (Berkley, 1999) Eve is after another serial killer. This killer has a surgeon's touch with lasers.
9. *Loyalty in Death* (Berkley, 1999) Dallas is out to get a bomber, and the bomber seems to be out to get her.
10. *Witness in Death* (Berkley, 2000) While watching Roarke's revival of Agatha Christie's (q.v.) *Witness for the Prosecution*, Eve is witness to the real stabbing death of actor Richard Draco on the stage. True to the Christie tradition, there is no lack of suspects.
11. *Judgment in Death* (Berkley, 2000) After a police officer is killed in an uptown strip joint, Dallas makes the acquaintance of a private club called Purgatory, where clients are given a chance to atone for their sins.
12. *Betrayal in Death* (Berkley, 2001) When a maid is murdered by a hit man at the Roarke Palace Hotel, Eve suspects that someone who wants Roarke dead is connected to the crime.
13. *Seduction in Death* (Berkley, 2001) A serial killer who lures his victims with poetry and brutal memories from her abused childhood bedevil Eve.
14. *Reunion in Death* (Berkley, 2002) Eve has an unsettling reunion at a birthday party with a killer from her past.
15. *Purity in Death* (Berkley, 2002) "Absolute Purity Achieved" is the message left on Louie Cogburn's computer screen just before Louie, overcome by rage, starts swinging his baseball bat at everyone in sight.
16. *Portrait in Death* (Berkley, 2003) A killer murders promising young people, photographs them after death, then taunts a top reporter and Eve Dallas with notes about his handiwork.
17. *Imitation in Death* (Berkley, 2003) A killer leaves a note signed "Jack" (after Jack the Ripper), taunting Eve by name on the body of a prostitute he has killed.
18. *Divided in Death* (Putnam, 2004) Reva Ewing, Roarke's security specialist, is accused of killing her adulterous husband and his lover.
19. *Visions in Death* (Putnam, 2004) Eve is aided by psychic Celina Sanchez after young mother Elisa Maplewood is raped and strangled.
20. *Survivor in Death* (Putnam, 2005) Dallas reluctantly provides a refuge for nine-year-old Nixie Swisher after her family is massacred in their beds.

21. *Origin in Death* (Putnam, 2005) Wilfred B. Icove, founder of the Wilfred B. Icove Center for Reconstructive and Cosmetic Surgery, is found with a scalpel in his heart.
22. *Midnight in Death* (Berkley, 2005) Eve is being stalked by an insane serial killer whom she had helped put behind bars. Novella length.
23. *Memory in Death* (Putnam, 2006) Trudy Lombard, Eve's former foster mom, wants Eve to pay $2 million to keep her past, which involved killing her abusive father at the age of nine, a secret.
24. *Haunted in Death* (Brilliance Audio, 2006) The murder of Radcliff Hopkins, new owner of Number Twelve, a former club of the 1960s, believed to be haunted, may be connected to the disappearance of a rock star some 85 years ago. Apparently available only in audio form.
25. *Interlude in Death* (Berkley, 2006) Novella-sized tale in which Eve is called "off planet" to give a seminar at a police conference held in a swanky resort owned by her husband, Roarke.
26. *Born in Death* (Putnam, 2006) As if Dallas didn't have enough on her plate with a double murder, Tandy Willis, one of the moms-to-be in the birthing class of Eve's buddy Mavis, seems to have disappeared.
27. *Innocent in Death* (Putnam, 2007) When private school history teacher Craig Fisher is killed by deadly ricin in the lunch packed by his young wife, Eve is initially hard-pressed to find a murder motive.
28. *Creation in Death* (Putnam, 2007) 2060. The serial killer nicknamed "the Groom" is back in town after an absence of nine years.
29. *Strangers in Death* (Putnam, 2008) Business tycoon Thomas Anders is apparently the victim of a kinky sex encounter gone bad.

Robbins, Harold

PSEUDONYM OF Harold Rubin

I. Although Harold Robbins wrote better novels (e.g., *A Stone for Danny Fisher*, Knopf, 1952) than *The Carpetbaggers*, he never wrote a more popular one. This novel, one of the all-time best sellers, spawned a successful movie starring George Peppard and Carroll Baker (1964) that spawned *Nevada Smith* (1966), a movie prequel. The tale of Jonas Cord (read Howard Hughes), who turned his father's company into a business empire and consorted with movie stars and moguls, finally spawned its own sequel, which carries Cord's life forward into the 1950s; revives characters from the earlier novel, such as Nevada Smith; and gives cameo appearances to such historical characters as the Kennedys, Jimmy Hoffa, and Jack Benny. Both novels are long, intricately plotted, and loaded with sex, violence, and power conflicts among the rich and famous.

1. *Carpetbaggers, The* (Trident, 1964) Jonas Cord inherits his father's business, his fortune, and his wife, movie sex-queen Rita Marlowe, and turns a fortune into a megafortune. Set in the 1920s and 1930s.
2. *Raiders, The* (Simon & Schuster, 1995) Cord buys a casino in Las Vegas, incurs the wrath of the Mob, flees to Mexico to avoid testifying in a Senate hearing, and discovers that he has fathered a son who is a chip off the old block.

II. *The Betsy*, another best seller, also engendered a movie of the same title (1978; starring Laurence Olivier and Robert Duvall) and its own sequel. Both novels feature the car-manufacturing Hardeman family of Bethlehem Motors and race-car driver Angelo Perino and lots of sex, violence, and power struggles.

1. *Betsy, The* (Simon & Schuster, 1971) The competition between, and among, the Hardeman family and racing-car driver and stud Angelo Perino comes to a head, as the Betsy, a new car model, is planned and produced.
2. *Stallion, The* (Simon & Schuster, 1995) Subtitle: *The Sequel to The Betsy*. After extensive plastic surgery for damage committed upon him in *The Betsy*, Angelo Perino returns to the fray to develop a new car called the Stallion and to bed all of the Hardeman women.

III. There is some question about how large a part Robbins played in producing the novels published under his name after a stroke in 1982 left him at least partially aphasic. After his death, in 1997, his name, like that of V. C. Andrews (q.v.), has lived on in the form of novels produced by anonymous ghostwriters. A pair of novels about a father-and-son duo, Jerry and Len Cooper, features the usual trademark Robbins steamy sex and empire building.

1. *Predators, The* (Forge, 1998) Eighteen-year-old Jerry Cooper goes to work for his sleazy uncle, numbers-runner Larry; then goes to France for World War II; makes money on the French black market; then makes more money marketing bottled water in the United States.
2. *Secret, The* (Forge, 2000) Len Cooper, Jerry's son, develops Cheeks, a successful lingerie empire (based on Victoria's Secret?) amid a slew of sexual encounters.

Roberson, Jennifer

I. The Cheysuli are a race of people in which each member has the power to communicate with a given animal through telepathy and the power to assume that animal's shape. Despite their powers, the Cheysuli are oppressed by the king of Homana. This is a saga, full of strong female characters, told over several generations, with love affairs, rivalries, sorcery, and supernatural beings driving the action. Four Cheysuli Omnibus Editions were published by DAW in 2001, containing the eight novels: *Shapechangers Song*; *Legacy of the Wolf*; *Children of the Lion*; and *The Lion Throne*. Jennifer Roberson is an Arizona-based writer, mostly of fantasy.

1. *Shapechangers* (DAW, 1984) The love affair between a princess of Homana and a Cheysuli warrior brings a war of annihilation upon the Cheysuli race by the jealous Homanan king.
2. *Song of Homana, The* (DAW, 1985) The time has come for Prince Carillon, Homana's rightful ruler, to free his land and restore the Cheysuli to their proper position.
3. *Legacy of the Sword* (DAW, 1986) Prince Donal is being groomed to be the first Cheysuli in generations to assume the throne.
4. *Track of the White Wolf* (DAW, 1987) Niall, heir to the crown, is forced to flee Homana.
5. *Pride of Princes, A* (DAW, 1988) The time has come for the three Cheysuli sons of Homana's current ruler to fulfill their destinies.
6. *Daughter of the Lion* (DAW, 1989) Keely, twin sister to Corin, and daughter of Niall, the ruler of Homana, can change her shape into any animal.
7. *Flight of the Raven* (DAW, 1990) Aidan, heir to the throne of Homana, is commanded by the Hunter to undertake a quest to claim a series of "god-given" golden links.
8. *Tapestry of Lions, A* (DAW, 1992) Kellin, heir to Homana's throne, turns away from the prophecy of his fate and his magical heritage, even as the Ihlini plot his death.

II. The Sword-Dancer saga relates the adventures of Tiger (Sandtiger), a male sword dancer, or soldier of fortune, and Del (Delilah), a female sword singer, on a desert world full of demonic dogs, powerful wizards, false messiahs, and other strange beings. *The Novels of Tiger and Del* (DAW, 2006), is a three-volume omnibus set containing all six novels.

1. *Sword-Dancer* (DAW, 1986) Exiles Tiger and Del go in search of Tiger's homeland.
2. *Sword-Singer* (DAW, 1988) Tiger and Del are reunited on a perilous journey to the North—the Place of Swords.
3. *Sword-Maker* (DAW, 1989) Tiger, on the trail of the Hounds of Hoolies, has to deal with the Dragon's Lair.
4. *Sword-Breaker* (DAW, 1991) Hunted by religious zealots and sword-dance assassins, Tiger and Del flee across the deadly Punja Desert.
5. *Sword-Born* (DAW, 1998) Tiger and Del travel to the land of Tiger's birth to uncover the mystery of his past.
6. *Sword-Sworn* (DAW, 1999) Tiger discovers that he is heir to a powerful magic that could hold the key to his fate.

III. A new fantasy saga is set on a world with Alisanos (a mobile and sentient forest), the war-torn land of Sancorra, the nasty Hecari (who have conquered Sancorra), "karavans," refugees Audrun and Davyd and their four children, diviners, prophecies, and other sword-and-sorcery paraphernalia.

1. *Karavans* (DAW, 2006) Alisanos, a sentient forest, is on the move after 40 years, as the pregnant Audrun, her husband, Davyd, and their four children seek to escape the war-torn land of Sancorra and the Hecari who have conquered it, by traveling on the last karavan of the season.
2. *Deepwood* (DAW, 2007) Alisanos surrounds the karavan, as Rhuan the demigod, disguised as a karavan guide who tries to protect Audrun's family, calls upon his semidivine cousin, Brodhi, for assistance.

Roberts, Gillian

PSEUDONYM OF Judith Greber

I. Amanda Pepper teaches English at Philly Prep in Philadelphia, Pennsylvania. The feisty Amanda can't seem to avoid getting involved with her students' problems to the extent of turning amateur sleuth on occasion. Sometimes she gets her live-in boyfriend, Philadelphia policeman C. K. Mackenzie, involved as well. The Amanda Pepper novels contain good characterization, humor, and a combination of big-city and cozy ambience. Gillian Roberts, who was born in Philadelphia and graduated from the University of Pennsylvania, knows the city well. She writes nonmystery novels under Judith Greber, her real name.

1. *Caught Dead in Philadelphia* (Scribner, 1987) Amanda is awakened on a Monday morning by part-time drama teacher Liza, who claims that her life is in danger.
2. *Philly Stakes* (Scribner, 1989) Sandy Chausen, prominent and unpleasant father of Amanda's most gifted pupil, is killed and his house torched.
3. *I'd Rather Be in Philadelphia* (Ballantine, 1992) At a used-book sale, Amanda runs into a book about battered women that contains a cry for help from a woman who fears that her husband plans to kill her.
4. *With Friends Like These . . .* (Ballantine, 1993) Insufferable television producer Lyle Zacharias is poisoned at the 50th birthday bash he was throwing for himself in his old neighborhood in South Philadelphia.

5. *How I Spent My Summer Vacation* (Ballantine, 1994) Amanda is sharing a hotel room in Atlantic City with Sasha Berg, a photographer friend, when a dead man turns up in their suite.

6. *In the Dead of Summer* (Ballantine, 1995) The tranquility of summer school at Philly Prep is broken by racist telephone calls, a drive-by shooting, and a kidnapping.

7. *Mummers' Curse, The* (Ballantine, 1996) The annual Philadelphia Mummers' Parade is taken very seriously by some of its participants, who vie for the Best Costume prize. This year's event is marred by the murder of one of the marchers, and a colleague of Amanda's is a leading suspect.

8. *Bluest Blood, The* (Ballantine, 1998) Two students at Philly Prep, the son of Main Liners Neddy and Tea Roederer and the stepson of Harry Spiers, head of the book-burning right-wing group Moral Ecology, are best friends. And then the Reverend Spiers is strangled and burned.

9. *Adam and Evil* (Ballantine, 1999) Adam, an intelligent but erratic student, has been giving Amanda a lot of trouble with his hostile, disturbing behavior. But did he commit murder?

10. *Helen Hath No Fury* (Ballantine, 2001) Amanda can't believe that fellow book-discussion group member Helen Coulter took her own life.

11. *Claire and Present Danger* (Ballantine, 2004) Amanda and C. K. Mackenzie, who is moonlighting as a private investigator while working on a PhD in criminology, are finally engaged. C. K. asks Amanda to interview Claire Fairchild, whose prospective daughter-in-law, Emmie Cade, has left a trail of dead lovers behind her.

12. *Till the End of Tom* (Ballantine, 2004) Absenting herself from the headmaster's annual address, Amanda steps onto the comatose of body of Tomas Severin, one of *the* Severins.

13. *Hole in Juan, A* (Ballantine, 2005) Newly married, Amanda and C. K. investigate a Halloween prank that took a deadly turn.

14. *All's Well That Ends Well* (Ballantine, 2007) In what is billed as the conclusion to the series, Amanda investigates an apparent suicide and the murder of a Realtor "stager" hired to get the deceased's house ready to sell.

II. Gillian Roberts, who now resides in California, has created a second series, about Emma Howe, middle-aged owner of a private investigator firm, and her assistant, young single-mom Billie August, who work out of Tiburon, California.

1. *Time and Trouble* (St. Martin's, 1998) After the inexperienced Billie August bungles her first assignment, she and Emma are hired by Sophia Richmond, subject of the assignment, to locate her missing teenage daughter Penny.

2. *Whatever Doesn't Kill You* (St. Martin's, 2001) A defense attorney hires Emma to look into the case of Gavin Riddock, a mentally handicapped young man who is accused of murdering his only friend.

Roberts, John Maddox

I. Fans of Lindsay Davis's (q.v.) Marcus Didius Falco and Steven Saylor's (q.v.) Gordianus the Finder will find much to like in the SPQR series of John Maddox Roberts. If Falco is a Roman Philip Marlowe, then playboy and sometime detective Decius Caecilius Metellus the Younger is a sort of classical Ellery Queen (q.v.), in these mysteries, narrated by Decius, set in the fading days of Republican Rome, circa 70-60 BCE. Historical characters such as Cicero, Catiline, Cato, Pompey, Crassus, and Julius Caesar (Decius's uncle by marriage) are all personally known to the patrician Decius, who,

despite his wild ways, has a certain civic conscience, as evidenced by his work as head of a civil detective-vigilante agency and his attempts at public office.

1. *SPQR* (Avon, 1990) In 70 BCE, playboy and amateur detective Decius Caecilius Metellus the Younger enlists the aid of a gangster and a detective in the guise of a Greek doctor when a freed gladiator and a foreign merchant are murdered. Variant title: *SPQR I: The King's Gambit.*

2. *Catiline Conspiracy, The* (Avon, 1991) *SPQR II.* In 63 BCE, a couple of seemingly unrelated murders may be connected to the vast conspiracy being hatched by Catiline.

3. *Sacrilege, The* (Avon, 1992) *SPQR III.* Big trouble ensues when a man in drag infiltrates some sacred rites reserved for women.

4. *Temple of the Muses, The* (Avon, 1992) *SPQR IV.* Decius goes to Alexandria with a diplomatic mission and gets called upon to exercise his detecting skills when a caustic philosopher is murdered.

5. *Saturnalia* (Avon, 1999) *SPQR V.* Decius is brought to Rome from Rhodes, where his family has rusticated him, to investigate the poisoning of Metellus Celer, possibly by his notorious wife, Clodia. *Saturnalia* is also a title in Lindsay Davis's (q.v.) Falco series.

6. *Nobody Loves a Centurion* (St. Martin's, 2001) *SPQR VI.* Julius Caesar finds some use for Decius in Gaul when the centurion Vinius is murdered.

7. *Tribune's Curse, The* (St. Martin's, 2003) *SPQR VII.* Decius is running for Aedile, the first step on the Roman political ladder. The Tribune Aetius is murdered after he curses multimillionaire and politician Crassus and his army.

8. *River God's Vengeance, The* (St. Martin's, 2004) *SPQR VIII.* Decius, who has been elected Aedile, stirs up a political storm when he investigates the fatal collapse of a Roman tenement building.

9. *Princess and the Pirates, The* (St. Martin's, 2005) *SPQR IX.* After Decius arrives in Cyprus to deal with some pirates, the governor of Cyprus is murdered.

10. *Point of Law, A* (St. Martin's, 2006) *SPQR X.* Decius seems to be a shoo-in in the election for Praetor, but then he is accused of corruption. And his accuser is promptly killed.

11. *Under Vesuvius* (St. Martin's, 2007) *SPQR XI.* Decius has been elected *praetor peregrinus*, traveling magistrate in charge of all cases involving foreigners. When Gorgo, the young daughter of the local priest of a town near Vesuvius, is murdered, her Numidian lover is suspected.

II. Gabe Treloar, Vietnam vet and burned-out and boozing Los Angeles cop, returns to his hometown of Monticello, Ohio, and sets up as a private investigator there, renewing some old acquaintances.

1. *Typical American Town, A* (St. Martin's, 1994) Gabe Treloar, burned-out Los Angeles cop, stops off in his hometown of Monticello, Ohio, to renew some old acquaintances. Returning from a date with old high school flame Lola, Gabe discovers that his landlord, Edna Tufts, has been murdered, and he is the prime suspect.

2. *Ghosts of Saigon* (St. Martin's, 1995) Gabe is urged to attend the reunion of his Vietnam War unit by movie producer Martin Starr, who is producing a movie about Vietnam.

3. *Desperate Highways* (St. Martin's, 1996) Gabe goes to Memphis in search of benefactor Kit Carson's daughter Sybil and her boyfriend, Nick Switzer.

III. The versatile Roberts also writes SF and fantasy. He has written a pair of alternate history, or "What if?" novels postulating that Hannibal did conquer Rome.

1. ***Hannibal's Children*** (Ace, 2000) Rome, which had fallen to Hannibal's Carthaginians, is on the rise again.
2. ***Seven Hills, The*** (Ace, 2005) Rome's victory over Carthage is complete. Now it is up to Marcus Scipio to unite the Romans.

IV. Stormlands is an SF series about a post-atomic-holocaust Earth, which has reverted to primitivism, its advanced technology forgotten, and steel being so rare that it is used as currency.

1. ***Islander, The*** (Tor, 1990) Young Hael, exiled from his tribe for killing a sacred animal, travels to distant lands and makes an exciting find.
2. ***Black Shields, The*** (Tor, 1991) Hael's discovery of a mountain of iron enables his tribe and others to make steel weapons.
3. ***Poisoned Lands, The*** (Tor, 1992) Ansa, son of Hael, takes center stage as war breaks out with Gronea over some ancient treasure.
4. ***Steel Kings, The*** (Tor, 1993) The land of Gozam craves Hael's priceless treasury of steel.
5. ***Queens of Land and Sea*** (Tor, 1994) Strange ships appear from the South, offering trade but harboring plague.

V. The Cingulum trio is about the spacecraft *Eurynome,* which wanders into a strange region of space, where the universe seems to be "turned inside out."

1. ***Cingulum, The*** (Tor, 1985) The spaceship *Eurynome,* with All Hakon and his friends, runs into a distinctly weird area of space.
2. ***Cloak of Illusion*** (Tor, 1985) Subtitle: *Cingulum II.* The adventures continue.
3. ***Sword, the Jewel, and the Mirror, The*** (Tor, 1988) The world of Meridian, the last bastion against the Bahadur Tyranny, is fought over by Pancho Villa, the emperor Montezuma, and the shogun of Japan.

VI. *Space Angel* and *Window of the Mind* are two comic space-opera novels about the space charter ship *Space Angel* and its ship's boy, Kelly.

1. ***Space Angel*** (Del Rey, 1979) Young street urchin Kelly signs on as a ship's boy on the charter spaceship, *Space Angel.*
2. ***Window of the Mind*** (Ace, 1988) Kelly's telepathic gift comes in handy when intergalactic war is threatened, and the crewmen of the *Space Angel* are the designated scapegoats. Variant title: *Spaces: Window of the Mind.*

Roberts, Kenneth

Roberts used his native town of Kennebunk (originally called Arundel), Maine, as the setting for four loosely connected historical novels, the Chronicles of Arundel. The Nason family and other characters from Arundel figure prominently in the dramatic stories of adventure and romance from Revolutionary times to the War of 1812. By championing Benedict Arnold in *Rabble in Arms* and a British loyalist in *Oliver Wiswell* (not one of the Arundel books), Roberts presented an unusual slant, corrective in its astringent, conservative viewpoint.

1. ***Arundel*** (Doubleday, 1930) Young Steven Nason accompanies his friend Benedict Arnold on a hazardous expedition to Quebec.
2. ***Rabble in Arms*** (Doubleday, 1933) A group of men from Arundel fights under Benedict Arnold's leadership. The story ends after the battle of Saratoga.
3. ***Lively Lady, The*** (Doubleday, 1931) Richard Nason, son of Steven, commands the armed sloop *Lively Lady* in the War of 1812.

4. ***Captain Caution*** (Doubleday, 1934) The crew of an Arundel merchant ship is captured and detained by the English during the War of 1812.

Roberts, Les

I. Les Roberts, television writer and producer (e.g., *The Hollywood Squares*), jazz pianist, and teacher, is writing two detective series, one set in Cleveland and featuring Slovenian American private eye Milan Jacovich. Jacovich is an ex-cop, ex–football player, ex-husband, tough but principled, and strongly attached to his hometown. *The Scent of Spiced Oranges and Other Stories* (Five Star, 2002), Roberts's first short-story collection, contains one Jacovich story.

1. ***Pepper Pike*** (St. Martin's, 1988) Judith Amber hires Milan to find her husband, advertising executive Richard Amber.
2. ***Full Cleveland*** (St. Martin's, 1989) A simple phony magazine ad scam gets complicated by Mob connections, blackmail, and murder.
3. ***Deep Shaker*** (St. Martin's, 1991) Jacovich becomes embroiled with the drug trade while trying to help childhood friend Matt Baznik, whose son seems to be dealing drugs.
4. ***Cleveland Connection, The*** (St. Martin's, 1993) Retired factory worker Bodan Zdrale is the victim of an execution-style killing in a plot that stretches back to World War II concentration camps.
5. ***Lake Effect, The*** (St. Martin's, 1994) Milan pays back a long-standing debt to Mob boss Victor Gaimari by going out to the posh suburb of Lake Erie Shores to make sure a mayoral election goes smoothly.
6. ***Duke of Cleveland, The*** (St. Martin's, 1995) Jacovich is hired by April Delavan to get back $18,000 from potter Jeff Feldman, whose wheeling and dealing skills exceed his talent with a potter's wheel.
7. ***Collision Bend*** (St. Martin's, 1996) Former lover Mary Soderberg gives Milan a call when Steve Cirini, his successor as her boyfriend, becomes the prime suspect in the strangulation death of TV newscaster Virginia Carville.
8. ***Cleveland Local, The*** (St. Martin's, 1997) Cleveland attorney Joel Kerner's homicide death while on vacation in the Caribbean island of San Carlos was *not* due to a botched robbery attempt, according to Joel's sister Patrice.
9. ***Shoot in Cleveland, A*** (St. Martin's, 1998) Milan agrees to try to keep Darren Anderson, star of a big-budget movie being shot in Cleveland, on the straight-and-narrow, but Darren's weakness for jailbait does him in.
10. ***Best-Kept Secret, The*** (St. Martin's, 1999) The "best-kept secret" is that Jason Crowell, ostracized on the Sherman College campus for the alleged rape of a girl, is really gay. But what about the heroin in Jason's bathroom and the sudden death of a college adviser?
11. ***Indian Sign, The*** (St. Martin's, 2000) Milan Jacovich snoops on a toy-company accountant with a secret agenda while also searching for a kidnapped Native American infant.
12. ***Dutch, The*** (St. Martin's, 2001) "Fat girl" chat rooms may lead to the killer of Ellen Carmine, website designer, who jumped, or fell, to her death off a bridge.
13. ***Irish Sports Pages, The*** (St. Martin's, 2002) "The Irish Sports Pages" are the obits in Cleveland newspapers. When Jacovich gets involved in exposing a two-bit scam, "Brian McFall," a small-time thug with a slew of aliases, winds up shot to death in a cheap motel.

II. Los Angeles–based private investigator and part-time actor Saxon is a wise guy, a health-food junkie, and an egotist who thinks he is

God's gift to women, but he is a pretty good detective when he has to be. This series started publication before the Cleveland series but seems to have been abandoned since 1994. *The Chinese Fire Drill* (Five Star, 2001) is an adventure set in Hong Kong featuring Anthony Holton, American expatriate novelist.

1. *Infinite Number of Monkeys, An* (St. Martin's, 1987) Pulp writer Buck Weldon's daughter hires Saxon to protect her father when a series of "accidents" threatens his life.
2. *Not Enough Horses* (St. Martin's, 1988) A bomb kills a young male prostitute in one car and injures a big-time television executive in another.
3. *Carrot for the Donkey, A* (St. Martin's, 1989) Saxon follows the trail of a sleazy producer's lost daughter from Hollywood to Tijuana.
4. *Snake Oil* (St. Martin's, 1990) An oil prospector is killed, and his girlfriend, a straying wife Saxon is being paid to tail, is the number-one suspect.
5. *Seeing the Elephant* (St. Martin's, 1992) Saxon flies to Chicago for the funeral of his erstwhile mentor, Gavin Cassidy.
6. *Lemon Chicken Jones, The* (St. Martin's, 1994) A washed-up comedy star hires Saxon to find his wife, a native of Hong Kong named Doll, whom he met through an organization called Asian Nights.

Roberts, Nora (Eleanor Marie)

I. Nora Roberts is an extremely prolific and popular romance novelist. Although most of her books are formulaic, thousands of readers find them to be page-turners, even though the endings are rarely in doubt. Outwardly cool but inwardly passionate women named Maggie, Serena, etc., find true love with passionate, brooding hunks named Seth, Caleb, Jared, etc. Most of the characters are Irish or Irish American, although a few passionate Ukrainians or WASPs are thrown in from time to time. Most of the series are contemporary romances relating the adventures of a pair, or trio, or quartet of brothers and sisters who find true love. Roberts occasionally writes a historical romance, or a romance with a supernatural dollop mixed in, or romantic mysteries; most of the novels in the last category are published under the pseudonym of J. D. Robb (q.v.). Most of Roberts's novels appeared in paperbacks published by Silhouette or Jove. Many of them have also appeared in hardcover editions, mostly for the library trade.

Irish Thoroughbred, Roberts's first published novel, is the first in a trio involving stable owners and stable workers in Ireland and America. Omnibus volumes include *Irish Hearts* (Silhouette, 2000; numbers 1–2) and *Irish Dreams* (Silhouette, 2007; number 3 and the nonseries *Sullivan's Woman*).

1. *Irish Thoroughbred* (Silhouette, 1981) Adelie Cunnane, who works at Royal Meadows stables in Ireland, is attracted to stable-owner Travis Grant.
2. *Irish Rose* (Silhouette, 1988) Adelie Cunnane's cousin, Erin McKinnon, meets Burke Logan, who won the farm next to Royal Meadows in a poker game.
3. *Irish Rebel* (Silhouette, 2000) Keeley Grant, heiress of an American horse-breeding dynasty, is attracted to Irishman Brian Donnelly, who comes to work on the Grant ranch.

II. Siblings Seth and Ruth Bannion search for true love and find it in the dance world. Omnibus volume: *Reflections and Dreams* (Silhouette, 2001).

1. *Reflections* (Silhouette, 1983) Architect Seth Bannion and dancer Lindsay Dunne hit it off, despite some initial reservations.

2. *Dance of Dreams* (Silhouette, 1983) Ballet dancer Ruth Bannion falls for difficult Russian choreographer Nickolai Davidov.

III. The MacGregor series is the longest Roberts romance series. Daniel MacGregor, a rich patriarch, delights in arranging romances leading to marriage for his children and grandchildren. Numbers 1 and 2 are historical prequels to the series, while number 3 describes how Daniel himself managed in the marriage. Omnibus volumes include *The MacGregors: Daniel-Ian* (Silhouette, 1999; numbers 2–3); *The MacGregors: Serena-Caine* (Silhouette, 1999; numbers 4–5); *The MacGregors: Alan-Grant* (Silhouette, 1999; numbers 6–7); *The MacGregors: Robert-Cybil* (Silhouette, 2007; numbers 9–11); and *All the Possibilities/One Man's Art* (Silhouette, 2006; numbers 6–7).

1. *Rebellion* (Harlequin, 1988) Proud Scottish woman Serena MacGregor is bent on revenging the rape of her mother by English soldiers in the 18th century.
2. *In from the Cold* (Harlequin, 1990) Originally published as a novella in *Historical Christmas Stories* (Harlequin, 1990). Injured Minuteman Ian MacGregor is cared for by Allanna Flynn.
3. *For Now, Forever* (Silhouette, 1987) Medical student Anna Whitfield finds it difficult to adjust to becoming Daniel MacGregor's submissive, heir-producing wife.
4. *Playing the Odds* (Silhouette, 1985) First novel published in series. Daniel MacGregor sends Justin Blade, part-Comanche gambler, to seduce his daughter, Serena MacGregor, who is working as a blackjack dealer on a luxury cruise ship.
5. *Tempting Fate* (Silhouette, 1985) Attorney Caine MacGregor, attempting to melt Diana Blade's icy wall, offers her a partnership.
6. *All the Possibilities* (Silhouette, 1985) Cynical senator Alan MacGregor falls for free-spirited beauty Shelby Campbell despite their long-standing family feud.
7. *One Man's Art* (Silhouette, 1985) When Genevieve Grandeau's car breaks down in coastal Maine, she makes the acquaintance of brooding satirist and political cartoonist Grant Campbell, who has ensconced himself in a lighthouse.
8. *MacGregor Brides, The* (Silhouette, 1997) In the MacGregor series revival after 10 years, old Daniel gets to work on his three granddaughters, who are career girls in the Boston area.
9. *Winning Hand, The* (Silhouette, 1998) Darcy Wallace, who has become a millionaire on one turn of a card, finds herself sharing candlelight dinners with Robert MacGregor Blade.
10. *MacGregor Grooms, The* (Silhouette, 1998) Old Daniel fixes up three grandsons with suitable brides.
11. *Perfect Neighbor, The* (Silhouette, 1999) Sunny Cybil Campbell and brooding lawyer Preston McQuinn are made for each other, although he doesn't know it at first.

IV. Night Tales is a series of romantic mysteries with some interlocking characters, including policeman Boyd Fletcher. Some of the novels have a touch of the gothic or supernatural. Omnibus volumes include *Night Tales* (Silhouette, 2000; numbers 1–4); *Night Shift/Night Shadow* (Silhouette, 2005; numbers 1–2); *Nightshade/Night Smoke* (Silhouette, 2005; numbers 3–4); and *Night Shield/Night Moves* (Silhouette, 2005; numbers 5–6).

1. *Night Shift* (Silhouette, 1990) Sultry-voiced Denver DJ Cilla O'Roarke, host of a late-night radio show, pursued by a stalker, enlists the help of policeman Boyd Fletcher.
2. *Night Shadow* (Silhouette, 1991) Cilla O'Roarke's younger sister, Deborah, falls in love with millionaire, Gage Guthrie, who has an alter ego: the costumed vigilante Nemesis.

3. *Nightshade* (Silhouette, 1993) Colt Nightshade is happy to have as a partner the ice goddess Althea Grayson in a search for a runaway girl.

4. *Night Smoke* (Silhouette, 1994) Natalie Fletcher, sister of Althea Grayson's former partner, Boyd Fletcher, needs the help of arson investigator Ryan Piasecki.

5. *Night Shield* (Silhouette, 2000) Allison Fletcher, Boyd's daughter, operating as an undercover cop, crosses paths with nightclub owner Jonah Blackhawk.

6. *Night Moves* (Silhouette, 2005) A short story added as a bonus to the reprinting of number 5: *Night Shield/Night Moves* (Silhouette, 2005). Maggie Fitzgerald and landscaper Cliff Delaney are the protagonists.

V. Members of the royal family of the Mediterranean island principality of Cordina find love and intrigue in four novels. Omnibus volumes: *Cordina's Royal Family* (Silhouette, 2002; numbers 1–3); *Cordina's Royal Family: Gabriella and Alexander* (Silhouette, 2006; numbers 1–2); and *Cordina's Royal Family: Bennett and Camilla* (Silhouette, 2006; numbers 3–4).

1. *Affaire Royale* (Silhouette, 1986) Prince Armand of Cortina calls in his friend, American detective Reeve MacGee, when Her Serene Highness Gabriella is abducted and loses her memory.

2. *Command Performance* (Silhouette, 1987) Prince Alexander de Cordina is happy to have Eve Hamilton and her theatrical troupe back in Cordina.

3. *Playboy Prince, The* (Silhouette, 1987) Playboy Prince Bennett and the mysterious Hannah Rothchild are an item here.

4. *Cordina's Crown Jewel* (Silhouette, 2002) Camilla de Cordina is escaping being Princess Camilla as she works for archaeologist Delaney Caine under the alias of Camilla MacGee.

VI. Two novels are tied together by characters working for *Celebrity Magazine*. Published together as *Summer Pleasures* (Silhouette, 1986).

1. *One Summer* (Silhouette, 1986) Celebrity photographer Bryan Michell and cynical, brooding photojournalist Shade Colby travel across America one summer on assignment.

2. *Second Nature* (Silhouette, 1985) *Celebrity Magazine* reporter Lee Radcliffe wangles an exclusive interview with reclusive writer Hunter Brown.

VII. Something of a change of pace are the two time-traveling novels featuring the brothers Hornblower from the 23rd century. Published together as *Time and Again* (Silhouette, 2001).

1. *Time Was* (Silhouette, 1989) Anthropologist Liberty Stone bumps into Caleb Hornblower, a time-traveling visitor from the 23rd century.

2. *Times Change* (Silhouette, 1989) Jacob Hornblower, searching for his brother, Caleb, arrives in the 20th century and runs into Sunny Stone, sister of Liberty.

VIII. A trio of novels revolves around romance writer Jackie MacNamara and her creations. Omnibus volume: *Love by Design* (Silhouette, 2003; numbers 1–2).

1. *Loving Jack* (Silhouette, 1989) Romance writer Jackie MacNamara falls for real-life brooding hero Nathan Powell.

2. *Best Laid Plans* (Silhouette, 1989) Architect Cody Johnson and structural engineer Abra Johnson are made for each other.

3. *Lawless* (Harlequin, 1989) Rugged Jake Redman falls in love with very proper Sarah Conway on the Arizona frontier in a book "written" by Jackie MacNamara.

IX. The O'Hurley triplets and a mysterious older brother are part of a charismatic family of Irish performers. Omnibus volumes: *Born O'Hurley* (Silhouette, 2002; numbers 1–2) and *O'Hurley's Return* (Silhouette, 2005; numbers 3–4).

1. *Last Honest Woman, The* (Silhouette, 1988) Abby O'Hurley Rockwell wants to keep family secrets from journalist Dylan Crosby, who is writing a book about her late, infamous husband.

2. *Dance to the Piper* (Silhouette, 1988) The relationship of Maddy O'Hurley and recording mogul Reed Valentine becomes more than a business one.

3. *Skin Deep* (Silhouette, 1988) PI Quinn Doran is hired to protect movie star Chantel O'Hurley, who is being stalked by a fanatical fan.

4. *Without a Trace* (Silhouette, 1990) When her brother disappears, Gillian Fitzpatrick finds that spy Trace O'Hurley may be her only hope in finding him and protecting herself.

X. "Those Wild Ukrainians" are the Stanislaskis, who have worked their way up from immigrant status in the land of opportunity. The dark and passionate Ukrainian Americans show a tendency to fall for passionate Irish Americans. Omnibus volumes: *The Stanislaski Sisters: Natasha and Rachel* (Silhouette, 1997; numbers 1 and 3) and *The Stanislaski Brothers: Mikhail and Alex* (Silhouette, 2000; numbers 2 and 4).

1. *Taming Natasha* (Silhouette, 1990) Toy-store owner Natasha Stanislaski finds romance in rural West Virginia.

2. *Luring a Lady* (Silhouette, 1991) Icy patrician Sydney Hayward locks horns with passionate plebeian Mikhail Stanislaski when she takes over the family corporation.

3. *Falling for Rachel* (Silhouette, 1993) Subtitle: *That Special Woman*. Public defender Rachel Stanislaski becomes involved with Zachary Muldoon, the older brother of one of her clients.

4. *Convincing Alex* (Silhouette, 1994) Detective Alex Stanislaski mistakenly arrests Bess McNee for soliciting.

5. *Waiting for Nick* (Silhouette, 1997) Frederica Kimball is waiting for Nicholas Lebeck (Stanislaski?).

6. *Considering Kate* (Silhouette, 2001) Natasha's daughter, Kate Stanislaski Kimball, after buying a run-down building for her dance school, encounters contractor Brady O'Connell.

XI. Four Calhoun sisters and a sister by marriage imbibe in a touch of gothic at Towers Retreat, the family mansion in Maine. The shtick is a generations-old mystery surrounding a priceless, hidden emerald necklace. There are several omnibus volumes: *Catherine and Amanda* (Silhouette, 1996; numbers 1–2); *Catherine, Amanda, and Lilah* (Silhouette, 2005; numbers 1–3); *Lilah and Suzanna* (Silhouette, 1998; numbers 3–4); *Susanna and Megan* (Silhouette, 2005; numbers 4–5); *The Calhoun Women* (Silhouette, 1996; numbers 1–4); and *The Calhouns* (Silhouette, 2006; numbers 1–5 in two volumes).

1. *Courting Catherine* (Silhouette, 1991) Mechanic Catherine "C. C." Calhoun attracts hotel magnate Trenton St. James.

2. *Man for Amanda, A* (Silhouette, 1991) Efficient Amanda Calhoun, planning her sister C. C.'s wedding, finds easygoing Sloan O'Riley insufferable and irresistible.

3. *For the Love of Lilah* (Silhouette, 1991) Sweet sister Lilah Calhoun saves mysterious stranger Max from drowning.

4. *Suzanna's Surrender* **(Silhouette, 1991)** Beautiful single-mom Suzanna is searching for the family emeralds with the help of ex-cop Holt Bradford.

5. *Megan's Mate* **(Silhouette, 1991)** Calhoun sister-in-law Megan O'Riley and boat captain Nate Fury find love and a possible solution to the emerald mystery.

XII. The Donovan cousins share a secret that's been handed down through generations. Omnibus volumes: *The Donovan Legacy* (Silhouette, 1999; numbers 1–3) and *Captivated and Entranced* (Silhouette, 2004; numbers 1–2).

1. *Captivated* **(Silhouette, 1992)** Nash Kirkland seeks out Morgana Donovan to help him research his latest screenplay.

2. *Entranced* **(Silhouette, 1992)** Mary Ellen Sutherland enlists Sebastian Donovan's help in finding a lost baby.

3. *Charmed* **(Silhouette, 1992)** Boone Sawyer and his daughter move next door to Anastasia Donovan.

4. *Enchanted* **(Silhouette, 1999)** Rowan and Liam are drawn to each other despite the frightening, magical secret of Liam's identity.

XIII. The three Concannon sisters of Ireland share a family secret and some painful memories, as do their lovers, but everything comes out okay in the end. Omnibus volumes: *Born in Fire/Born in Ice/Born in Shame* (Jove, 1996; numbers 1–3) and *Irish Born* (Berkley, 2003; numbers 1–3).

1. *Born in Fire* **(Jove, 1994)** Attempting to hide from her past, reclusive glassmaker Maggie Concannon devotes her life to her art until gallery owner Rogan Sweeney recognizes her talent.

2. *Born in Ice* **(Jove, 1995)** Brianna Concannon, owner of a bed-and-breakfast, awaits the arrival of Grayson Thane, American mystery writer with a painful past.

3. *Born in Shame* **(Jove, 1995)** Graphic artist Shannon Bodine, after learning the identity of her real father, Thomas Concannon, sets out to meet her family in County Clare.

XIV. The sinfully sexy MacKade Brothers meet their separate destinies somewhere out west. Omnibus volumes: *The MacKade Brothers: Rafe and Jared* (Silhouette, 2004; numbers 1–2) and *The MacKade Brothers: Devin and Shane* (Silhouette, 2004; numbers 3–4).

1. *Return of Rafe MacKade, The* **(Silhouette, 1995)** Black-sheep brother Rafe McKade returns home. Will his destiny be antiques dealer Regan Jones?

2. *Pride of Jared MacKade, The* **(Silhouette, 1995)** Attorney Jard MacKade tries to keep his dealings with Savannah Morningstar strictly business.

3. *Heart of Devin MacKade, The* **(Silhouette, 1996)** Sheriff Devin MacKade is awaiting the dissolution of Cassie Connor's marriage.

4. *Fall of Shane MacKade, The* **(Silhouette, 1996)** Shane MacKade, a man of the land, encounters Rebecca Knight.

XV. The Dream, or Templeton House, trilogy, set in San Francisco, deals with the romances of three friends—Margo, Kate, and Laura—who grew up together at the grandiose Templeton House. Omnibus volumes: *Three Complete Novels* (Putnam, 1999; numbers 1–3) and *Lovers and Dreamers* (Berkley, 2004; numbers 1–3). Also issued as a three-volume boxed set, *Roberts Dream Box Set* (Jove, 2002).

1. *Daring to Dream* **(Jove, 1996)** Margo, a housekeeper's daughter at Templeton House, dreams of being swept away.

2. *Holding the Dream* **(Jove, 1996)** Kate has a shrewd head for business, but faced with a professional impropriety, she is forced to look deep within herself.

3. *Finding the Dream* **(Jove, 1997)** Can beautiful, intelligent heiress Laura find true happiness with returned horse-breeder Michael Fury after her husband has betrayed her?

XVI. The Stars of Mithra are three big, blue diamonds that lead various characters into romantic adventures.

1. *Hidden Star* **(Silhouette, 1997)** PI Cade Parris, amnesiac client Bailey James, and a satchel full of diamonds are at issue here.

2. *Captive Star* **(Silhouette, 1997)** Bounty hunter Jack Dakota and M. J. O'Leary find themselves handcuffed together and on the run from hired killers.

3. *Secret Star* **(Silhouette, 1998)** Seth Buchanan meets up with Grace Fontaine, who is supposed to be dead.

XVII. The Quinn "brothers" are troubled young boys adopted by Raymond and Stella Quinn in the quiet Chesapeake Bay community of St. Christopher. Omnibus volumes: *Nora Roberts Boxed Set* (Jove, 2000; numbers 1–3); *The Quinn Brothers Trilogy* (Piatkus [UK], 2002; numbers 1–3); *The Chesapeake Series* (Jove, 2004; numbers 1–4); and *The Quinn Legacy* (Berkley, 2006; numbers 3 and 4).

1. *Sea Swept* **(Jove, 1997)** Oldest "brother" Cameron is called home to care for Seth, a young boy who is as troubled as he was. A tough but beautiful social worker adds love interest.

2. *Rising Tides* **(Jove, 1998)** Cameron, Ethan, and Philip Quinn care for 10-year-old Seth. Ethan, who shares the Quinn passion for the Maryland shore, goes into the family boat-building business.

3. *Inner Harbor* **(Jove, 1999)** Philip Quinn leaves his high-powered advertising job and gets involved with Dr. Sybill Griffin, who is doing research on the Quinn brothers.

4. *Chesapeake Blue* **(Putnam, 2002)** Youth Seth grows up and becomes involved with Drusilla Whitcomb Banks.

XVIII. Three Sisters Island, off the New England coast, houses three passionate, powerful women who seem to be mixed up with witchcraft.

1. *Dance upon the Air* **(Jove, 2001)** Nell Channing arrives on Three Sisters Island, with her abusive husband in pursuit.

2. *Heaven and Earth* **(Jove, 2001)** Ripley Todd, who has powers she can't control, and sheriff's deputy MacAllister Booke get involved in an investigation into witchcraft.

3. *Face the Fire* **(Jove, 2002)** Sam, hoping to win back Mia, returns as the new owner of the island's only hotel.

XIX. Three women, three keys. Each woman has 28 days to find her way through a dangerous quest. Omnibus volume: *The Key Trilogy Boxed Set* (Jove, 2004; numbers 1–3).

1. *Key of Light* **(Jove, 2003)** Malory, manager of a gallery in a small port town, receives the Key of Light at a reception attended by only three women.

2. *Key of Knowledge* **(Jove, 2003)** Bookish Dana receives the Key of Knowledge.

3. *Key of Valor* **(Jove, 2003)** Zoe, who has been handed the Key of Valor, discovers her true courageous spirit.

XX. The ghostly "Harper Bride" walks the halls of the Harper mansion near Memphis. Omnibus volume: *In the Garden Boxed Set* (Jove, 2006; numbers 1–3).

1. *Blue Dahlia* **(Jove, 2004)** Trying to escape the ghosts of the past, young widow Stella Rothchild moves back to her roots in southern Tennessee with her two little boys.
2. *Black Rose* **(Jove, 2005)** Roz Harper, owner of the Harper Mansion, unexpectedly finds love with a man researching her ancestors.
3. *Red Lily* **(Jove, 2005)** When Hayley Phillips finds love with Harper Ashby, the Harper Bride attempts to thwart the romance.

XXI. The Circle trilogy is Nora Roberts's venture into fantasy. A circle of six warriors, recruited by the goddess Morrigan, battles the evil vampire Lilith in the past and in the present.

1. *Morrigan's Cross* **(Jove, 2006)** The goddess Morrigan recruits wizard Hoyt, his vampire brother Cian, witch Glenna, Geallian princess Moira, shape-shifting Larkin, and demon hunter Blair for an all-or-nothing battle with the vampire Lilith and her minions.
2. *Dance of the Gods* **(Jove, 2006)** The Circle of Six prepares for a showdown with Lilith in modern Ireland.
3. *Valley of Silence* **(Jove, 2006)** Having traveled back through time to her ancient kingdom of Geall, Moira removes the fated sword from the fated stone and, with her companions, faces the fated showdown with Lilith.

Robertson, Don

These gently humorous and nostalgic novels star young Morris Bird III of Cleveland, Ohio, who is nine years old in 1944 when the first book takes place. Morris worries about love, bravery, and "self-respect" as he practices his famous dropkick, tries to be nice to his little sister, Sandra, and befriends the oafish Stanley Chaloupka. Adult and young adult readers alike will enjoy Morris's adventures. A television dramatization adapted the story of the third book for a black cast. Don Robertson, not to be confused with the songwriter or the test pilot or the baseball player or several other people with the same name, has written more than a dozen other novels, the most popular of which is probably the Ohio epic *Paradise Falls* (Putnam, 1968).

1. *Greatest Thing since Sliced Bread, The* **(Putnam, 1965)** Morris and Sandra use their red wagon to rescue two victims of a gas-tank explosion.
2. *Sum and Total of Now, The* **(Putnam, 1966)** Morris, now 13, wants to do something special for his dying grandmother.
3. *Greatest Thing That Almost Happened, The* **(Putnam, 1970)** Tragedy in the form of acute leukemia strikes Morris, who at 17 is in love and on the high school basketball team.

Robinson, Kevin

Nick "Stick" Foster is an Orlando, Florida, reporter, part-time amateur sleuth, and full-time paraplegic. Stick's wife, Samantha, is a paraplegic lawyer whom he married in a wheelchair. Foster is a determined fellow, and his author, himself a quadriplegic, gives graphic descriptions of what life in a wheelchair is like. Unfortunately, Robinson, freelance writer, photographer, and syndicated columnist, hasn't written any Stick mysteries since the original trio.

1. *Split Seconds* **(Walker, 1991)** Stick and his friend Phil Stilles discover the body of a NASA associate from the Kennedy Space Center while crabbing in the Intercoastal Waterway.

2. *Mall Rats* **(Walker, 1992)** Stick and Samantha's wheelchair wedding is upstaged when an elderly woman in the congregation imbibes punch laced with "crack, PCP, and amphetamine."
3. *Matter of Perspective, A* **(Walker, 1993)** The senior partner of Ketchum, Lathan and Bennett, Samantha's law firm, keels over at the firm's banquet, apparently the victim of a malfunctioning pacemaker.

Robinson, Kim Stanley

I. Kim Stanley Robinson, a California-based science-fiction writer, has won Nebulas and Hugos for his work and is regarded by many as the best current writer in the genre, a worthy heir to Philip K. Dick (q.v.) and Ursula K. Le Guin. His work, called "leftist," a somewhat meaningless term in the present level of discourse, by friend and foe alike, is distinguished by thoughtful analyses of civilization in the near future or in alternate futures. Robinson is, in the long run, an optimist: he feels that we can eventually develop a utopia run on ecological and economically democratic lines. In the short run, however, unless we wake up very soon to the dangers of global warming and "Götter-dämmerung capitalism," we are going to be in for a really rough time.

The novels in Robinson's Mars trilogy are regarded as among the best of the Mars fictions. The trilogy describes the settling of Mars by colonists from Earth in the near future and the various debates, punctuated by a couple of "revolutions," among the "Martians," about the direction their society society should be taking. *The Martians* (Bantam, 1999) is a coda to the trilogy, with several new short stories and the reprinting of "Green Mars," a novella originally published in the same volume with Arthur C. Clarke's (q.v.) "A Meeting with Medusa" (Tor, 1988), which is quite different from the *Green Mars* published as the second volume of the trilogy.

1. *Red Mars* **(Bantam, 1993)** The first permanent settlement on Mars is carried out in the 21st century by a multinational band of 100 hardy experts.
2. *Green Mars* **(Bantam, 1994)** Debate among the Mars settlers, including the surviving members of the "First Hundred," rages between those who love Mars the way it is and those who want to replicate Earth's environment.
3. *Blue Mars* **(Bantam, 1996)** After the second Martian revolution, a delegation visits Earth, while the many Martian groups try to agree upon a constitution they can all sign.

II. An earlier series by Robinson, sometimes called the Orange County trilogy, or Three Californias, postulates three alternate futures for Orange County, California. Another alternate history novel, *The Years of Rice and Salt* (Bantam, 2004), imagines an Earth dominated by China, Islam, and India after the Black Death wipes out 99 percent (instead of the actual 30 or 40 percent) of the European population in the 1300s.

1. *Wild Shore, The* **(Ace, 1984)** In the first alternate Orange County future, a simplified society is recovering from a nuclear holocaust.
2. *Gold Coast, The* **(Tor, 1988)** The second alternate Orange County future depicts a culture dominated by overpopulation, drugs, and economic exploitation.
3. *Pacific Edge* **(Tor, 1990)** A utopian, communal society rises from the ashes of the 20th century in Orange County.

III. Robinson's latest trilogy, set in the near future, convincingly delineates the efforts made by scientists, environmentalists, and such other ecological-minded types to ward off a worldwide catastrophe brought on by global warming and the indifference of the politicians and capitalists who run America.

1. *Forty Signs of Rain* **(Bantam, 2004)** While characters such as NSF official Anna Quibler and scientist Frank Vanderwal can see ecological disaster coming to the world, they are helpless before the indifference of America's power brokers to the impending crisis.
2. *Fifty Degrees Below* **(Bantam, 2005)** As global warming continues, the Antarctic ice mass crumbles, low-lying island nations are inundated with water, and the Gulf Stream stalls, bringing impossibly frigid winter temperatures to the Eastern Seaboard and Western Europe.
3. *Sixty Days and Counting* **(Bantam, 2007)** The Gulf Stream has been jump-started, and an ecologically minded Democrat from California, Phil Chase, has been elected president after a right-wing attempt to fix the election has been foiled, but the question remains whether the world has both the scientific know-how and the political will to reverse the rush toward an ecological precipice.

Robinson, Peter

Chief Inspector Alan Banks of the Eastvale (Yorkshire) regional police is revealed as a complicated character as this procedural series progresses. Hiding his basically civilized, gentle self behind a bluff exterior, Banks starts off as middle-aged family man, but eventually his wife, Sandra, leaves him, his children are estranged, and he shows a weakness for, and a tendency to get involved with, lively, intelligent women, including his police partners. Meanwhile, Banks becomes increasingly disenchanted with his obnoxious superior, Chief Constable Riddle, who finds Banks's procedures unorthodox, and, from time to time, considers leaving the force for some other agency. Intricate plots, strong characters, and a dense rural Yorkshire atmosphere combine to make this series one of the best going, *the best*, according to fans such as Stephen King (q.v.). Peter Robinson, who has a PhD in English literature, is a Yorkshire native who currently resides in Canada. *Not Safe after Dark and Other Stories* (Crippen & Landru, 1998) contains 13 short stories, including three Banks stories. *The First Cut* (Harper-Collins, 2004; UK title: *Caedmon's Song*; originally 1990) is a stand-alone novel.

1. *Gallows View* **(Scribner, 1990)** A series of burglaries, a rash of Peeping Tom incidents, and a murder hit Eastvale, a normally peaceful patch of Yorkshire countryside.
2. *Dedicated Man, A* **(Scribner, 1991)** Banks has trouble finding anyone with the motive and the opportunity to murder archaeologist Harry Steadman, whose body is found buried near a stone wall.
3. *Necessary End, A* **(Scribner, 1992)** What began as a peaceful anti-nuke demonstration in Eastvale ends as a riot, with one person dead.
4. *Hanging Valley, The* **(Scribner, 1992)** A rotting corpse found in the Yorkshire Dales turns out to be Bernard Allen, a local youth on a visit home from Canada.
5. *Past Reason Hated* **(Scribner, 1993)** Detective Constable Susan Gay, Banks's newest protégée, investigates the stabbing death of a beautiful lesbian actress.
6. *Wednesday's Child* **(Scribner, 1994)** Banks investigates the kidnapping of seven-year-old Gemma Scupham, who has been taken from her neglectful mum by two people posing as social workers.

7. *Final Account* **(Berkley, 1995)** A reclusive accountant is killed execution style while his wife and daughter are forced to watch. UK title: *Dry Bones That Dream*.
8. *Innocent Graves* **(Berkley, 1996)** Banks is in the background in this investigation of the strangulation murder of Deborah Harrison, daughter of a tycoon, found in a churchyard in Eastvale.
9. *Blood at the Root* **(Avon, 1997)** Teenager Jason Fox, member of the Albion League, a neo-Nazi white power organization, is found stomped to death after an altercation with three Pakistani youths. UK title: *Dead Right*.
10. *In a Dry Season* **(Avon, 1999)** Banks's wife, Sandra, has left him for another man. A young boy finds a human skeleton in the remains of a former village called Hobbs End, exposed by a drought that depletes Thornfield Reservoir.
11. *Cold Is the Grave* **(Morrow, 2000)** Chief Constable Riddle changes his mind about Banks's "unorthodox" methods after Riddle's 16-year-old daughter Emily runs away and turns up nude on a porno website.
12. *Aftermath* **(Morrow, 2001)** The identity of a serial killer called the Chameleon is revealed, but that proves to be only the start of a very messy investigation.
13. *Close to Home* **(Morrow, 2003)** A skeleton identified as that of Banks's 14-year-old friend Graham Marshall, who disappeared in 1965, is unearthed. UK title: *The Summer That Never Was*.
14. *Playing with Fire* **(Morrow, 2004)** An arson fire on two old canal boats reveals a body on each barge. Banks and partner and former lover Annie Cabot investigate.
15. *Strange Affair* **(Morrow, 2005)** After Banks receives an urgent phone message from his successful, slightly shady younger brother Roy, Roy disappears.
16. *Piece of My Heart* **(Morrow, 2006)** The murder of Nick Barber, rock journalist from London, and the fatal stabbing of a young woman at a local rock festival in 1969 may be connected.
17. *Friend of the Devil* **(Morrow, 2008)** Annie Cabbot, while on loan to a sister precinct, investigates the death of a paraplegic woman found with her throat slit on a desolate cliff. Meanwhile, back in Eastvale, Banks and his team discover the body of a young woman who has been raped and strangled.

Rock, Phillip

The Passing Bells trilogy has dozens of major characters and a host of minor ones in its panoramic view of English society from 1914 to the 1940s. The central focus of the trilogy is the aristocratic Greville family and their servants, each coping in their own ways with the horrors of the First World War and the cataclysmic social changes that took place in the postwar years. Phillip Rock is an American novelist and screenwriter.

1. *Passing Bells, The* **(Seaview, 1979)** Anthony Greville, ninth Earl of Stanmore, sees his idyllic country estate and its community of family and servants changed forever by the Great War and the years immediately following: 1914–1920.
2. *Circles of Time* **(Seaview, 1981)** Post–World War I England and Germany are the settings of this book and the Greville family among the protagonists observed by journalist Martin Rilke.
3. *Future Arrived, A* **(Seaview, 1985)** Colin Greville, Anthony's grandson, joins the Royal Air Force rather than attend Cambridge University as Britain lurches toward World War II.

Roe, Caroline

PSEUDONYM OF Medora Sale

Girona, Spain, is the site of one the best preserved medieval ghettos in Europe. It is also the site of a historical mystery series featuring the blind mid-14th-century Jewish physician, Isaac of Girona. Isaac's medical skills give him entrée into the highest ranks of an Aragonese society in which Muslims, Jews, and Christians form an uneasy alliance but are less effective against his bad-tempered wife. Medora Sale (q.v.) writes the Sanders/Jeffries mysteries, set in Toronto, under her own name.

1. *Remedy for Treason* (Berkley, 1998) 1353. The intensity of the Black Death has abated, but there is still plenty of work for the blind Jewish physician, Isaac of Girona. When an aristocratic young woman dies, possibly of poison, Isaac feels obliged to investigate.
2. *Cure for a Charlatan* (Berkley, 1999) Three young men die of a strange illness signaled by sleepwalking, delusions, and strange mutterings. Poison? Witchcraft?
3. *Antidote for Avarice, An* (Berkley, 1999) Isaac is summoned by Bishop Berenguer to accompany him to a bishop's council at Tarragona, as messengers from the pope come to bad ends.
4. *Solace for a Sinner* (Berkley, 2000) A respected merchant, who was preparing to purchase what he thought was the Holy Grail, is murdered.
5. *Potion for a Widow, A* (Berkley, 2001) Yusuf, Isaac's assistant, is sent off to Sardinia for his own safety, but then the seemingly innocuous clerk Pasqual Robert is attacked and killed outside the gates of Girona.
6. *Draught for a Dead Man, A* (Berkley, 2002) Isaac accompanies the beautiful Bonafilla and her family to Perpignan to attend her arranged wedding to David Bonhujes, the brother of Isaac's physician friend Jacob.
7. *Poultice for a Healer, A* (Berkley, 2003) While Isaac is treating Bishop Berenguer, a fatally poisoned man comes to warn the bishop of others' treachery. The marriage of Isaac's daughter, Racquel, is postponed while Daniel, the bridegroom, sails to Mallorca to investigate a supposed herbalist.
8. *Consolation for an Exile* (Berkley, 2004) Isaac's young Muslim apprentice, Yusuf Ibn Hasan, is summoned by his relative, the Emir of Granada, to return to Granada. Meanwhile, Isaac is treating a patient for insomnia and bad dreams.

Rogers, Rosemary

I. Rosemary Rogers, "Queen of Historical Romance," writes about heroines who travel, meet famous people, and have passionate romance infused with sizzling sex with intriguing men. Rogers's one real series, called the Steve and Ginny or the Morgan/Challenger series, has reached six volumes. *Sweet Savage Love*, *Dark Fires*, and *Lost Love, Last Love* originally formed a trilogy about the relationship, set in the 19th century and conducted in many points of the globe, between womanizing adventurer Steve Morgan and spirited heroine Virginia "Ginny" Brandon. *Wicked Loving Lies*, set earlier in the 19th century than the trilogy, matches up pirate Dominic Challenger with the passionate runaway Maris. *Savage Desire*, published 20 years after the last volume of the trilogy, reunites Steve and Ginny. *Bound by Desire* is about Laura, daughter of Ginny and Steve, and Trent Challenger, descendant of Dominic Challenger. Rogers, a native of Ceylon (now Sri Lanka), now a US citizen, enjoys playing the role of "romance writer."

1. *Wicked Loving Lies* (Avon, 1976) Wealthy, privileged, and beautiful Maris runs away from an arranged marriage and into the arms of roguish pirate Dominic Challenger.
2. *Sweet Savage Love* (Avon, 1974) The long, passionate, and occasionally violent relationship between womanizing soldier of fortune Stephen Morgan and spirited heroine Virginia "Ginny" Brandon shuttles and sizzles between Paris, New Orleans, and revolution-torn Mexico. This was the first novel published by Rosemary Rogers.
3. *Dark Fires* (Avon, 1975) The passion between Steve and Ginny takes them from Mexico to Russia and back to Paris.
4. *Lost Love, Last Love* (Avon, 1980) At opposite ends of the Earth, Steve and Ginny manage to keep their inner fires burning, despite revolutions and a stay in a sultan's harem.
5. *Savage Desire* (Mira, 2000) Steve and Ginny are reunited in London after many years apart.
6. *Bound by Desire* (Avon, 1988) Laura, daughter of Steve and Ginny, and Trent Challenger, pirate descendant of pirate Dominic Challenger, conduct a tempestuous affair throughout Europe.

II. A pair of novels, set in Mississippi just before and just after the Civil War, describes the off-again, on-again romance between Southern belle Cameron Campbell and blockade runner Jackson Logan.

1. *Honorable Man, An* (Mira, 2002) The Civil War is impending. Cameron Campbell, of Elmwood, Mississippi, daughter of a US senator, is still nursing a grudge against blockade runner Captain Jackson Logan.
2. *Return to Me* (Mira, 2003) After the Civil War, there is still some smoldering passion between Cameron and Jackson, despite four years' separation.

Rogow, Roberta

Roberta Rogow, New Jersey librarian, folk-song writer, and SF aficionado (see *Futurespeak: A Fan's Guide to the Language of Science Fiction*, Paragon, 1991), has brought together, in a series of mysteries, two Victorian authors who never met in real life: Sherlock Holmes creator Dr. Arthur Conan Doyle (q.v.), a recent medical school graduate, and the older Reverend Charles Dodgson, mathematician and curate of Christ Church, Oxford, aka Lewis Carroll (q.v.). Doyle plays the Watson role in this entertaining series that brings together many historical and fictional Victorian worthies.

1. *Problem of the Missing Miss, The* (St. Martin's, 1998) The Reverend Charles Dodgson and recent medical school graduate Arthur Conan Doyle meet accidentally in a Brighton train station in 1885. Soon they conduct a joint investigation into the kidnapping of Alicia Marbury, daughter of crusading politician Lord Richmond. UK title: *The Problem of the Missing Hoyden*.
2. *Problem of the Spiteful Spiritualist, The* (St. Martin's, 1999) Mrs. Cavanaugh, housekeeper of a late, retired sea captain who seems to have been involved with a missing treasure belonging to the Rajah of Rajitpoor, dies suddenly and suspiciously while conducting a séance. UK title: *The Problem of the Spurious Spiritualist*.
3. *Problem of the Evil Editor, The* (St. Martin's, 2000) Oscar Wilde is the chief suspect when loathsome children's magazine editor Samuel Bassett is murdered. Artists Whistler and Tenniel assist Doyle and Dodgson in their investigation.
4. *Problem of the Surly Servant, The* (St. Martin's, 2001) May 1886. The Reverend Charles Dodgson himself becomes a suspect when the murder of obnoxious Christchurch, Oxford, "scout" Ingram caps a series of untoward events.

Rohan, Michael Scott

I. Stephen Fisher is an inventor and businessman who periodically gets drawn into the Spiral Universe, a alternative world of inconstant time and space where he is the focal point in the struggle between order and chaos. Number 4 features a new protagonist. The Spiral Universe series is a cut above standard sword-and-sorcery fare, with colorful characters, atmospheric settings, and thoughtful political debate. Judging from the availability of his books, British fantasy writer Rohan is more popular in the United Kingdom than in the United States.

1. *Chase the Morning* (Morrow, 1990) Stephen Fisher enters a quaint gaslit pub while visiting the docksides of his youth and steps into another universe.
2. *Gates of Noon, The* (Morrow, 1993) Steve is baffled by the inexplicable setbacks his shipping company is experiencing until a bizarre supernatural experience in Bangkok reconnects him with the Spiral Universe.
3. *Cloud Castles* (Morrow, 1994) Fisher is inveigled into stealing the Spear of the Sangraal of Heilenburgh, primeval source of the goodness in the Spiral Universe.
4. *Maxie's Demon* (Orbit [UK], 1997) Maxie is introduced to the Spiral Universe when he runs off the highway going 120 mph. Soon he is consorting with Elizabethan alchemists and bands of pirates.

II. The Winter of the World series started out as a trilogy about a kind of alternate prehistoric northern European Ice Age whose human inhabitants match their magic skills against a series of dark and cold adversaries. The Ice Age itself is the ultimate enemy. The trilogy (numbers 4–6) ends with a final confrontation between the band of adventurers led by mastersmith Elof and the forces of ice and darkness. The Winter of the World series was revived 10 years later with *The Castle of the Winds*, which is really a prequel set 1,000 years before the action in the trilogy. *The Singer and the Sea* is a sequel set some 10 years later. *Shadow of the Seer*, although regarded as part of the series, is set in Asia rather than in northern Europe.

1. *Castle of the Winds, The* (Orbit [UK], 1998) When armorer Kunrad sets out to recover his life's work, which has been stolen, he stumbles upon a plot directed by the Powers of Ice, which may precipitate war between the lands of the North and the South.
2. *Singer and the Sea, The* (Orbit [UK], 1999) Ten years after the events in *The Castle of the Winds*, mastersmith and musician Gille Kilmarsson saves a Southern merchant ship from pirates and accepts as his only reward an old musical instrument that turns out to have magic powers.
3. *Shadow of the Seer* (Orbit [UK], 2001) Somewhere in prehistoric Asia, a lone boy is cast upon the icy wastes with only his latent powers as the son of a shaman to help him.
4. *Anvil of Ice, The* (Morrow, 1986) Elof Valantor and his band of adventurers fight the Mastersmith Mylio, who is backed by a far more sinister and powerful agency, the Ice itself.
5. *Forge in the Forest, The* (Morrow, 1987) Elof and his friends, vowing to protect the beloved city of Kerebryhane from the advances of ice and darkness, set off on a voyage of discovery to the mythical lands to the East.
6. *Hammer of the Sun, The* (Morrow, 1998) In the conclusion to the original trilogy, Elof and his friends face a final showdown with the power of the Ice.

Rolland, Romain

Jean-Christophe Krafft, Romain Rolland's larger-than-life hero, is a 19th-century musical genius obviously made from the same mold as Beethoven and resembling him in many of the details of his childhood. Krafft is just as obviously an alter ego for the sickly and neurotic Rolland, who confessed that Jean-Christophe was "the history of my soul transposed into one greater than I." In addition, Jean-Christophe symbolizes the regeneration of Europe, with the best forces of French nationalism leading the way toward defeat of the materialism and corruption rampant in pre–World War I society. It was this aspect of the work, no doubt, that won Rolland the Nobel Prize in 1915, and that, of course, makes the work seem very dated. Each book was originally published separately in France between 1904 and 1912; the English translation of the series, by Gilbert Cannan, was published in three volumes in 1910 to 1913. All 10 were collected in the Modern Library one-volume omnibus titled *Jean-Christophe* (Random House, 1938). An abridged edition was published by Dell in 1958. Recent reprints include Carroll & Graf (1996) and Kessinger (2004).

1. *Jean-Christophe: Dawn* (Holt, 1910) The story begins with Jean-Christophe in his cradle listening to the sounds of the river flowing through the small Rhineland town of his birth. Part 1 of *Jean-Christophe*. Originally published as *L'aube* (1904).
2. *Jean-Christophe: Morning* (Holt, 1910) Jean-Christophe, now almost 11 and well on his way as a prodigy, plays second violin in the local orchestra. Part 2 of *Jean-Christophe*. Originally published as *Le Matin* (1904).
3. *Jean-Christophe: Youth* (Holt, 1910) Jean-Christophe, now living alone with his widowed mother, has a stormy adolescence. Part 3 of *Jean-Christophe*. Originally published as *L'adolescent* (1905).
4. *Jean-Christophe: Revolt* (Holt, 1910) After a scuffle with some soldiers in an inn, Jean-Christophe leaves for Paris. Part 4 of *Jean-Christophe*. Originally published as *La revolte* (1906).
5. *Jean-Christophe in Paris: The Market Place* (Holt, 1911) The cultural life of Paris is a central subject here. Part 1 of *Jean-Christophe in Paris*. Originally published as *La foire sur la place* (1907).
6. *Jean-Christophe in Paris: Antoinette* (Holt, 1911) This volume backs up to trace the childhood of Jean-Christophe's friend Olivier Jeannin and his sister Antoinette Jeannin, who dies young. Part 2 of *Jean-Christophe in Paris*. Originally published as *Antoinette* (1908).
7. *Jean-Christophe in Paris: The House* (Holt, 1911) Jean-Christophe and Olivier take an apartment together in a middle-class house, where Jean-Christophe begins to find the real soul of France. Part 3 of *Jean-Christophe in Paris*. Originally published as *Dans le maison* (1909).
8. *Jean-Christophe Journey's End: Love and Friendship* (Holt, 1913) Olivier marries, and Jean-Christophe becomes famous. Part 1 of *Jean-Christophe Journey's End*. Originally published as *Les amies* (1910).
9. *Jean-Christophe Journey's End: The Burning Bush* (Holt, 1913) Olivier's marriage ends, and the two friends become close again until their involvement in the Paris May Day riots ends in tragedy. Part 2 of *Jean-Christophe Journey's End*. Originally published as *Le buisson ardent* (1911).
10. *Jean-Christophe Journey's End: The New Dawn* (Holt, 1913) The aged genius is surrounded by friends and success in Paris. Part 3 of *Jean-Christophe Journey's End*. Originally published as *La nouvelle aube* (1912).

Rølvaag, O(le) E(dvart)

Rølvaag emigrated from Norway in 1896 at the age of 20, earned his education as a farm and factory worker, and taught for many years at St. Olaf College in Minnesota. *Giants in the Earth* was first published in two volumes in Norway (1924–1925). Its US publication in English translation in 1927 was an immediate success. *Giants in the Earth* was followed by two more volumes about the Hansa family. The still very-readable account of the hardships and isolation braved by Per Hansa and his family as they settled in Spring Creek, Dakota Territory (now South Dakota), in 1873 was one of the first unromanticized views of the American immigrant experience. *Giants in the Earth* was on high school reading lists for decades (it still may be on some lists). All three novels were reprinted by the University of Nebraska Press in the 1980s.

1. *Giants in the Earth* **(Harper, 1927)** Per Hansa hopes to settle his family happily in Dakota Territory in 1873, but his wife, Beret, hates the hardships and the loneliness. Translated from the Norwegian by Lincoln Colcord and the author. Original title: *I de dage*.
2. *Peder Victorious* **(Harper, 1929)** Beret raises her family and manages the large and prosperous farm as her sons, especially Peder, the youngest, lose their Norwegian ways. Translated from the Norwegian by Norah O. Solon and the author. Original title: *Peder Seier*.
3. *Their Fathers' God* **(Harper, 1931)** Peder's 1894 marriage to Irish Catholic Susie Doheny turns out to be unhappy. Translated from the Norwegian by Trygve M. Ager. Original title: *Den signe de dag*.

Romains, Jules

PSEUDONYM OF Louis Farigoule

The 27-volume novel series Men of Good Will (*Les hommes de bonne volonte*) will stand as a monument to early 20th-century France when Romains's other novels, plays, and nonfiction are forgotten. Although his theories about "unanimism," a sort of secular religion having to do with universal human solidarity, may have been responsible for the broad sweep of the novel series, the work is essentially the story of particular individual destinies portrayed against a collective background. The novels cover events from October 6, 1908, to October 7, 1933, a span of 25 years, and encompass many characters and events, but the heart of the story concerns the lives of two young men from their student days through World War I and into the prime of their careers. Jallez is an introspective Parisian who becomes a famous writer; Jerphanion is a practical provincial who goes into politics and eventually becomes foreign minister. Priests and poets, murderers and millionaires, and occasional historical figures like Lenin appear in the 8,000-page work. Appended to the last book is an index to all the characters in the series. The 27 volumes were published in the United States as a 14-volume set called the Men of Good Will series. All of the novels were translated into English within a year or so of their original French publication. Numbers 1 through 6 were translated by W. B. Wells; numbers 7 through 27 by Gerard Hopkins.

1. *Men of Good Will: The Sixth of October* **(Knopf, 1933)** The events of this single day introduce most of the characters and anchor the reader firmly in the Paris of 1908. Original title: *Le 6 octobre*.
2. *Men of Good Will: Le crime de Quinette* **(Knopf, 1933)** Quinette, the bookbinder, gets involved with a murderer and plans to do him in. Original title: *Le crime de Quinette*.
3. *Passion's Pilgrims: Childhood's Loves* **(Knopf, 1934)** This novel covers two weeks in November 1908. The two friends Jallez and Jerphanion take the foreground. Original title: *Les amours enfantes*.
4. *Passion's Pilgrims: Eros in Paris* **(Knopf, 1934)** Jallez reviews his tortured romance with Juliette, while Jerphanion sets out straightforwardly to find a girl. Original title: *Eros de Paris*.
5. *Proud and the Meek, The: The Proud* **(Knopf, 1934)** Sammecaud has an affair with Marie, and Haverkamp develops a spa in Celle. Original title: *Les superbes*.
6. *Proud and the Meek, The: The Meek* **(Knopf, 1934)** The story of the poor Bastide family is told through the eyes of the young boy Louis, one of Clanricard's pupils. Original title: *Les humbles*.
7. *World from Below, The: The Lonely* **(Knopf, 1935)** Jerphanion, in search of something to believe in, meets the schoolteacher Clanricard. Both are attracted to Mathilde Cazalis. Original title: *Recherche d'un eglise*.
8. *World from Below, The: Provincial Interlude* **(Knopf, 1935)** The time is 1910, and the main focus is on the priest Mionnet, who is investigating a delicate case of mismanagement of funds by a provincial bishop. Original title: *Province*.
9. *Earth Trembles, The: Flood Warning* **(Knopf, 1936)** This novel is set in Paris during the General Strike of November 1910. Original title: *Montée des peris*.
10. *Earth Trembles, The: The Powers That Be* **(Knopf, 1936)** Gurau is prominent in this volume, which describes the Agadir incident of the summer of 1911. Original title: *Les pouvoirs*.
11. *Depths and the Heights, The: To the Gutter* **(Knopf, 1937)** This novel concentrates on Allory's sexual escapades. Jephanion is still in military service; Jallez is pursuing journalism and a literary career. Original title: *Recours à l'abîme*.
12. *Depths and the Heights, The: To the Stars* **(Knopf, 1937)** The question of creativity is examined as two previously unimportant characters take the foreground: Viaur, a doctor at Celle, and Strigelius, a poet. Original title: *Les createurs*.
13. *Death of a World: Mission to Rome* **(Knopf, 1938)** Poincare sends Mionnet on a delicate mission to the Vatican. Original title: *Mission a Rome*.
14. *Death of a World: Black Flag* **(Knopf, 1938)** Jerphanion marries Odette and settles in Paris; Jallez breaks up with Juliette and visits England. Original title: *Le drapeau noir*.
15. *Verdun: The Prelude* **(Knopf, 1939)** Jerphanion and Clanricard will see action with the infantry; Jallez, medically unfit, supervises boot repairs. Original title: *Prélude à Verdun*.
16. *Verdun: The Battle* **(Knopf, 1939)** The vast battle of Verdun is seen through some half-dozen different characters. Original title: *Verdun*.
17. *Aftermath: Vorge against Quinette* **(Knopf, 1941)** With armistice and demobilization, the story takes a rather sudden turn to focus on Vorge, a Dadaist poet who makes a cult figure of the murderer Quinette. Original title: *Vorge contre Quinette*.
18. *Aftermath: Sweets of Life* **(Knopf, 1941)** Jallez spends an idyllic winter (1919–1920) in Nice, has a romance, and renews acquaintance with some old friends. Original title: *La douceur de la vie*.
19. *New Day, The: Promise of Dawn* **(Knopf, 1942)** Jallez is doing League of Nations work; Jerphanion is secretary to a radical leader. Original title: *Cette grande lueur à l'est*.
20. *New Day, The: The World Is Your Adventure* **(Knopf, 1942)** Jallez and Jerphanion travel to Russia and return disillusioned. Original title: *Le monde est ton aventure*.
21. *Work and Play: Mountain Days* **(Knopf, 1944)** Jerphanion runs for election in 1924; Jallez is in Geneva; Doctor Viaur wins a Nobel Prize. Original title: *Journées dans la montagne*.

22. *Work and Play: Work and Play* (Knopf, 1944) Jerphanion is obsessed with the danger of a new war; Haverkamp, now very rich, tries to buy government influence. Original title: *Les travaux et les joies.*

23. *Wind Is Rising, The: The Gathering of the Gangs* (Knopf, 1945) In 1927 two Fascist movements develop. Original title: *Naissance de la bande.*

24. *Wind Is Rising, The: Offered in Evidence* (Knopf, 1945) Jallez feels there is something missing in his life; Jerphanion is totally pessimistic about the individual's ability to influence history. The time is February 1928. Original title: *Comparutions.*

25. *Escape in Passion: The Magic Carpet* (Knopf, 1946) This episode is mostly concerned with Jallez's amorous affairs. Original title: *Le tapis magique.*

26. *Escape in Passion: Françoise* (Knopf, 1946) Jallez meets his ideal love; Jerphanion resigns as foreign minister; Haverkamp loses all his money. Original title: *Françoise.*

27. *Seventh of October, The* (Knopf, 1946) The general despair is temporarily dispelled as old friends gather. The story concludes with a last look at all the characters. Original title: *Le 7 Octobre.*

Roosevelt, Elliott

I. Elliott Roosevelt, son of Eleanor and Franklin, stirred up a controversy when he revealed his father's extramarital affairs and portrayed Eisenhower, Joseph Kennedy, and others in a very unflattering light in *An Untold Story* (Putnam, 1973). But his detective novels starring Eleanor as an amateur investigator are generally applauded. They are pleasant and nostalgic diversions sure to please readers who remember the era (1933–1945). They feature classic mystery plots, lots of period flavor, and walk-ons by J. Edgar Hoover, Winston Churchill, and other luminaries. For other detective stories about this era, see Max Allan Collins (q.v.) and Stuart Kaminsky (q.v.). Roosevelt died in 1990 but supposedly left a large cache of unpublished mysteries that continue to appear at intervals. William Harrigan is credited with an assist for *Murder at the President's Door.* Novels are listed in chronological order (so far as possible) rather than publication order.

1. *Murder at the President's Door* (St. Martin's, 2001) During the first One Hundred Days, Douglas Douglas, a member of the White House police staff, is found stabbed to death at his customary station near the president's bedroom.

2. *Murder at Midnight* (St. Martin's, 1997) Judge Horace Blackwell, friend and adviser to FDR, is stabbed to death in his White House suite. Sarah Carter, the black maid who found the body, is arrested.

3. *Murder in the Oval Office* (St. Martin's, 1990) Alabama congressman Winstead Colmer, chairman of the House Banking Subcommittee, is found shot to death in the locked Oval Office.

4. *Murder in Georgetown* (St. Martin's, 1999) Sargent Peavy, member of the Board of Governors of the Federal Reserve, is found murdered in his Georgetown home, and Jessica Dee, Eleanor's friend and aide to Senator Huey Long, is the prime suspect. Not to be confused with Margaret Truman's novel of the same title (Arbor House, 1986).

5. *Murder and the First Lady* (St. Martin's, 1984) In the introductory volume of the series, Eleanor Roosevelt is the only person who believes in the innocence of her secretary when the secretary is arrested for the murder of her lover.

6. *Hyde Park Murder, The* (St. Martin's, 1985) A Dutchess County, New York, neighbor asks the First Lady to help clear her fiancé's father of an embezzlement charge.

7. *Murder in the West Wing* (St. Martin's, 1992) In March 1936 FDR's special assistant Paul Duroc is poisoned by cyanide, and there may be some connection with the late Huey Long.

8. *Murder in the Rose Garden* (St. Martin's, 1989) Washington hostess and secret blackmailer Vivian Talliafero is strangled in the Rose Garden of the White House.

9. *Murder in the Red Room* (St. Martin's, 1992) In action set in early 1937, small-time mobster "Shondor Jack" gets his throat cut in the Red Room as Franklin holds a dinner for Supreme Court justices.

10. *Murder at Hobcaw Barony* (St. Martin's, 1986) In autumn 1937, Eleanor and several Hollywood stars are fellow guests at Bernard Baruch's estate when an explosion kills a movie producer.

11. *Murder at the Palace* (St. Martin's, 1988) An equerry of King George VI is killed in Buckingham Palace during the First Lady's trip to England.

12. *First Class Murder, A* (St. Martin's, 1991) In 1938 a shady Russian envoy is murdered on board the luxury liner *Normandie.* Also on board are Charles Lindbergh, Jack Benny, a young JFK, and Eleanor.

13. *Murder in the Executive Mansion* (St. Martin's, 1995) On the brink of World War II and just after the departure of King George VI after a royal visit, Lucinda Robinson, Eleanor's missing social secretary is found dead in a third-floor closet.

14. *Murder in the East Room* (St. Martin's, 1993) Franklin is contemplating a third term in early 1940 when philandering senator Vance Gibson of Idaho meets a bloody end in the East Room.

15. *Royal Murder, A* (St. Martin's, 1994) Eleanor is sent to the Bahamas in September 1940 to deal with the new governor, the pro-German Duke of Windsor, and runs into a nest of Nazi spies.

16. *Murder in the Chateau* (St. Martin's, 1996) Just before Pearl Harbor, Eleanor is on a secret mission, representing FDR at a clandestine conference plotting the death of Hitler.

17. *White House Pantry Murder, The* (St. Martin's, 1987) A corpse is found in the White House refrigerator during the Christmas season of 1941, while FDR is plotting war strategy with the visiting Winston Churchill.

18. *Murder in the Blue Room* (St. Martin's, 1990) As Franklin tries to humor Molotov, who is demanding a "second front" in 1942, a White House secretary is killed by a blow from a candelabra.

19. *Murder in the Map Room* (St. Martin's, 1998) Eleanor discovers a murder in the White House during the state visit of Madame Chiang Kai-shek in 1943.

20. *Murder in the Lincoln Bedroom* (St. Martin's, 2000) While the secret Trident conference is going on, Special White House Counsel Paul Weyrich turns up dead in the Lincoln Bedroom with an unauthorized gun in his jacket.

II. Just before his death, Roosevelt completed a pair of novels about "Black Jack" Endicott, FDR's fictional friend and bodyguard. They also feature a blend of mystery fiction and historical events but are set in a time before Franklin became president.

1. *President's Man, The* (St. Martin's, 1991) Governor Roosevelt learns of a possible assassination attempt to be made on him on the eve of the 1932 Democratic Convention in Chicago.

2. *New Deal for Death* (St. Martin's, 1993) An unholy alliance of film producers and crooked union leaders is out to stop the newly nominated FDR from carrying out labor reform.

Roquelaure, A. N.

PSEUDONYM OF Anne Rice

Anne Rice (q.v.), writing as A. N. Roquelaure, wrote a trio of novels loosely based on the fairy tale "Sleeping Beauty." These riffs on the Sleeping Beauty theme explore the sexual undertones of the famous tale.

1. *Claiming of Sleepy Beauty, The* (Plume, 1983) Only the kiss of a prince can awaken Sleeping Beauty from the spell cast upon her.
2. *Beauty's Punishment* (Plume, 1984) Beauty, having indulged in a secret and forbidden affair with the rebellious slave Prince Tristan, is expelled from the erotic world of the castle.
3. *Beauty's Release* (Plume, 1985) Beauty finds herself captive in an eastern sultan's harem.

Rosen, Richard (Dean)

Harvey Blissberg, major league outfielder turned Cambridge, Massachusetts, private eye turned motivational speaker, is the protagonist in a series of mysteries in which the baseball ambience comes (numbers 2 and 5) and goes. Chicago native Richard Rosen has been a chef, a teacher, an editor, and the author of *Psychobabble* (Atheneum, 1977).

1. *Strike Three You're Dead* (Walker, 1984) Blissberg is having a pretty good year as center fielder for the Providence Jewels, an American League expansion team, until his roommate is fatally slugged with a baseball bat.
2. *Fadeaway* (Harper, 1986) Harvey, now in private-eye practice, is hired to find some professional basketball players who have vanished from Boston's Logan airport.
3. *Saturday Night Dead* (Viking, 1988) Murder disrupts a cast party for the late-night comedy show *Last Laughs.*
4. *World of Hurt* (Walker, 1994) Harvey is summoned to Chicago by his brother Norm to look into the murder of real-estate agent Larry Peplow.
5. *Dead Ball* (Walker, 2001) Black baseball player Moss Cooley, closing in on Joe DiMaggio's hitting streak record, is receiving his share of hate mail, but one of the hate mailers really seems to mean business.

Rosenbaum, Ray

Air force pilot Ross Colyer is the chief continuing character in Wings of War, a trio of novels set in World War II and shortly thereafter. Ray Rosenbaum, who based his novels on his own experiences as a bomber pilot during the war, gets high marks for historical accuracy conveyed through period detail and the feelings of his characters. Historical figures like General Chennault and Ben-Gurion sometimes turn up in this must-read series for World War II flying buffs.

1. *Falcons* (Presidio, 1993) The story of US heavy bombers at war from Pearl Harbor to the 1943 low-level raid on Ploesti, Romania.
2. *Hawks* (Presidio, 1994) Ross Colyer converts from B-24 bombers to P-51 Mustang fighters and transfers from the European theater to China.
3. *Condors* (Presidio, 1995) Shortly after the war, Colyer is running Allied Air, a small air-cargo operation that is hired by the Jewish Relief Foundation to transport Jewish immigrants to Palestine.

Rosenberg, Joel

I. Joel Rosenberg, not to be confused with Joel C. Rosenberg (q.v.), author of *The Last Jihad*, is a fantasy writer whose longest and most popular series is based on Dungeons and Dragons. The Guardians of the Flame series posits a group of seven Dungeons and Dragons players who are transferred to the world of their game, a magic-ridden medieval land, and assume their game identities there. This series of fast-moving fantasy adventures is somewhat above the sword-and-sorcery average. *Guardians of the Flame: The Warriors* (Doubleday, 1985) contains numbers 1, 2, and 3. *Guardians of the Flame: The Heroes* (Guild America, 1988) contains numbers 4 and 5. Numbers 8, 9, and 10 are set in the same universe but are a diversion, a sort of parody of *The Three Musketeers* and other cape-and-sword romances.

1. *Sleeping Dragon, The* (New American Library, 1983) Through the machinations of their game master, seven student Dungeons and Dragons players are transferred to their game world with only vague directions for getting home.
2. *Sword and the Chain, The* (New American Library, 1984) United by their vow to end slavery in their new home, Karl Cullinane and his companions find new purpose, and multiple threats, to their lives.
3. *Silver Crown, The* (New American Library, 1985) Karl and his comrades establish a haven for slaves, a stronghold called Home.
4. *Heir Apparent, The* (New American Library, 1987) Emperor Karl Cullinane's war with the Slaver's Guild continues 20 years after it began, as Jason, his son and heir, grows up.
5. *Warrior Lives, The* (New American Library, 1989) After Emperor Karl's apparent death, his untried son, Jason, strives to prove worthy of his father's crown.
6. *Road to Ehvenor, The* (Penguin, 1991) Jason and his companions take the road to Ehvenor to find out why the world of Faerie seems to be encroaching on Eren, the world of men.
7. *Road Home, The* (Penguin, 1995) The recent war with Faerie has left Eren devastated, the Slaver's Guild is making a comeback, and young Jason and veteran Walter Slovotsky have to keep things together.
8. *Not Exactly the Three Musketeers* (Tor, 1999) Apprentice soldiers Pirojil, Durine, and Kethol are ordered by the Dowager Empress to investigate whether an errant noblewoman is being coerced into an arranged marriage.
9. *Not Quite Scaramouche* (Tor, 2000) The "three musketeers" and fledgling wizard Erenor have sworn to protect Castle Cullinane and the somewhat erratic Jason Cullinane.
10. *Not Really the Prisoner of Zenda* (Tor, 2003) The trio of soldiers is down to one (Pirojil). Durine is dead, and Kethol has magically taken on the shape of Forinel to prevent Forinel's half brother from inheriting Barony Keranahan.
11. *Legacy* (Baen, 2004) Their earthly existence now a fading dream, the Dungeons and Dragons players have fought for power, justice for all, and the abolition of slavery, but they still have many powerful and dangerous enemies.
12. *To Home and Ehvenor* (Baen, 2004) Jason Cullinane has taken up his mysteriously vanished father's role when reports reach him of an attack on the realm by a rather extraordinary wolf pack.

II. The Thousand Worlds Contract Service, or Metzada Mercenary Corps, series is military SF combining martial arts and Sabra toughness. Numbers 1 and 2 are about an interplanetary mercenary service. Numbers 3 and 4, set on Metzada, a planet colonized by Israeli refugees, concentrates on one of the components of the first two books, the Metzadan Mercenary Corporation, famous throughout the galaxy for its soldiers.

1. *Ties of Blood and Silver* (New American Library, 1984) David is stolen as a baby and raised as a thief on the Planet Oroga, where power is concentrated in the hands of a privileged few.
2. *Emile and the Dutchman* (Roc, 1985) Rich boy Emile, the foul-mouthed Alonzo "the Dutchman" Norfeldt, and several others are forced into an uneasy alliance under the aegis of the Thousand Worlds Contract Service.
3. *Not for Glory* (New American Library, 1988) General Simon Bar El of Metzada, thought by some to be a traitor, gets involved in the machinations of his hit-man nephew, Tetsuo Hanavi.
4. *Hero* (Roc, 1990) Teenager Ari, descendant of the Hanavi warrior family, must convince himself that he isn't a coward.

III. The D'Shai duo is about Kami Khuzud (later Kami Dan'Shir), who works his way up through the planet's rigid caste system in a pair of more or less standard sword-and-sorcery books.

1. *D'Shai* (Ace, 1991) Kami Khuzud is a peasant whose only claim to fame is a (nonmagical) talent for acrobatics. Then he falls in love with an upper-class girl and is falsely accused of a nobleman's murder.
2. *Hour of the Octopus* (Ace, 1994) Kami Dan'Shir's recently recognized skill at detection is brought to the test when an attempt to foil a wedding leads to a murder accusation against the groom.

IV. The Keepers of the Hidden Ways trilogy is about the intersection of two worlds: Earth and Tor Na Nog. Martial-arts and fencing experts Ian Silverstein and Torrie Thorsen of North Dakota are thrust into an alternate world of Scandinavian myth when the latter learns that his father and uncle have come through the Hidden Ways from Tor Na Nog to Earth many years ago.

1. *Fire Duke, The* (Avon, 1995) While on vacation with friends at his parents' farm in North Dakota, Torrie Thorsen learns that his father and uncle Hosea, fleeing the Fire Duke of Tor Na Nog, had come through the Hidden Ways to this world.
2. *Silver Stone, The* (Avon, 1996) On a journey back to Tor Na Nog, Ian Silverstein finds himself a messenger for Odin himself, carrying the god's spar and a warning not to disturb his peace with plans of war.
3. *Crimson Sky, The* (Avon, 1998) A Son of Fenris, a fierce man-wolf shape changer, has been sent to Minneapolis to assassinate a member of the Thorsen family.

V. A pair of mysteries features copy editor Ernest "Sparky" Hemingway, who lives in the quaint North Dakota town of Hardwood among a host of queer characters.

1. *Home Front* (Forge, 2003) Sparky Hemingway gets an urgent call from his old buddy George Washington to come to Minneapolis from his home in Hardwoods, North Dakota.
2. *Family Matters* (Forge, 2004) Sparky, who has taken in a teenager from Minneapolis's inner city, is talked into becoming a deputy sheriff.

VI. *Paladins* and *Knight Moves* are set in the 17th century in an alternate universe where Modred defeated King Arthur, "the Tyrant," and founded the Pendragon Dynasty, which rules over an empire covering much of Europe, Asia, and the New World. The Order of Crown, Shield, and Dragon is a legion of special agents for the crown wielding white swords and red swords, which contain the souls of saints and sinners, respectively.

1. *Paladins* (Baen, 2004) Three knights of the Order of Crown, Shield, and Dragon have tracked down a previously unknown red sword that was found on a Grecian shore and that shows all signs having been recently forged.
2. *Knight Moves* (Baen, 2006) An ancient witch, long thought to be dead, has surfaced in Turkey; the deadly Darklings have started to appear throughout Europe; and Amadan Dubh, the Sidhe Fairy Fool, has appeared on the isle of Colonsay, maddening the inhabitants. Variant title: *Paladins II: Knight Moves*.

Rosenberg, Joel C.

An Evangelical Christian from an Orthodox Jewish heritage, Joel C. Rosenberg, not to be confused with fantasy author Joel Rosenberg (q.v.), has written a series of novels, mixing Tom Clancy (q.v.) with apocalyptic visions, about the Middle East in the near future. Wall Street strategist turned senior White House advisor Jon Bennett and his beautiful CIA partner, Erin McCoy, tackle a series of crises in an all-out effort to avoid Armageddon. *Epicenter: Why the Current Rumblings in the Middle East Will Change Your Future* (Tyndale House, 2006) is a nonfiction view of events in the Middle East.

1. *Last Jihad, The* (Forge, 2002) Saddam Hussein sends his top hit men to assassinate the US president, and Iraqi terrorists wreak havoc in London, Paris, and Riyadh. White House advisor Jon Bennett and his beautiful partner, Erin McCoy, are trying to negotiate a billion-dollar oil deal that could bring peace to the Middle East.
2. *Last Days, The* (Forge, 2003) Osama bin Laden and Saddam Hussein are dead. Baghdad is rubble. Bennett and McCoy are meeting with Yasser Arafat in an attempt to forge a historic Arab–Israeli peace treaty based on the discovery of huge oil and natural gas reserves under the Mediterranean Sea.
3. *Ezekiel Option, The* (Tyndale House, 2005) The Israelis and the Palestinians have signed a historic peace agreement, but Russia and Iran seem bent upon realizing the apocalypse prophesied more than 2,500 years ago.

Rosenberg, Nancy Taylor

I. Single mother, part-time law student, and overworked Ventura County, California, probation officer Carolyn Sullivan faces some nasty situations in this romantic suspense series by a former police and probation officer.

1. *Sullivan's Law* (Kensington, 2004) Brilliant schizophrenic Daniel Metroix, newly paroled, may not have committed the murder he was convicted of 23 years previously, but he has acquired some nasty enemies.
2. *Sullivan's Justice* (Kensington, 2005) Not only does he have to face Raphael Moreno, who beheaded his mom and killed his sister, but Sullivan's younger brother, meth addict Neil, has just discovered his girlfriend's body floating in his swimming pool.
3. *Sullivan's Evidence* (Kensington, 2006) Convicted murderer and rapist Carl Holden goes free when the head of the Ventura County forensic lab is found guilty of tampering with evidence, but Carolyn is not about to let him walk the streets.
4. *Revenge of Innocents* (Kensington, 2007) Sullivan's life is on an upturn: she's getting married and has been promoted. But the murder of her best childhood friend, Veronica Campbell, deflates her spirits.

II. Several of Rosenberg's novels are about women who face moral dilemmas involving victims of crime and vigilantism. In *Mitigating Circumstances*, Rosenberg's first published novel, California assistant DA Lily Forrester, chief of the sex-crimes unit has ethics problems in spades when she is forced to watch her daughter being raped, and then shoots the wrong man (who had it coming, anyway). Six years later, Lily faces some nasty decisions when the real rapist is paroled and takes up his old ways.

1. *Mitigating Circumstances* (**Dutton, 1993**) Lily Forrester, forced to watch her daughter being raped, goes on the vigilante trail.
2. *Buried Evidence* (**Hyperion, 2000**) Six years after the events in *Mitigating Circumstances*, Lily's ex-husband John Forester, faced with a vehicular manslaughter charge, blackmails Lily into bailing him out of jail. As if that weren't enough, the man who raped Lily's daughter, Shana, has been released on parole and is stalking them.

Rosenberg, Robert

Avram Cohen, Dachau survivor, is head of Jerusalem's Criminal Investigation Department in *Crimes of the City*, but he is forced into retirement by political enemies. But the stolid, crotchety, observant, and intelligent Cohen can't keep away from investigating crime, whether it is in Jerusalem, Los Angeles, or Germany. Boston native Robert Rosenberg, who has lived in Tel Aviv since 1973, provides a compelling portrait of a complex society poised on the edge of a political and religious precipice. Rosenberg is not to be confused with the Robert Rosenberg who wrote *This Is Not Civilization* (Houghton Mifflin, 2004).

1. *Crimes of the City* (**Simon & Schuster, 1991**) Two nuns, mother and daughter, are stabbed to death in the Red Russian Orthodox mission in Ein Kerem. Avram Cohen, head of Jerusalem's Criminal Investigation Department, battles the frustrations of Israeli politics to find a solution.
2. *Cutting Room, The* (**Simon & Schuster, 1993**) After being forcibly retired, for political reasons, Cohen accepts a long-standing invitation to visit fellow Dachau survivor and successful Hollywood director Max Broder, who is finishing a film about the Holocaust.
3. *House of Guilt* (**Scribner, 1996**) Israeli authorities believe that young Simon Levi-Tsur was murdered by Hamas, or some other Palestinian group. Avrahm Cohen isn't so sure.
4. *Accidental Murder, An* (**Scribner, 1998**) Staying at a German hotel while reluctantly touring to promote his new memoir, *Twentieth-Century Cop*, Avram's chambermaid is murdered, and a bomb is found under his bed.

Ross, Ann B.

Abbotsville, North Carolina, is the home of the redoubtable septuagenarian "Miss Julia," relict of the late, philandering Wesley Lloyd Springer. Staunch Presbyterian and decorous southern lady that she is, Miss Julia isn't afraid of challenge or change, or helping people in need of help, or taking in her late husband's mistress and illegitimate child. Local characters—such as Hazel Marie, Wesley Lloyd Springer's late mistress; Little Lloyd, Hazel Marie's son and Wesley's heir; Lillian, Miss Julia's faithful black housekeeper; and Sam Murdoch, a local lawyer who is courting Miss Julia—add to the fun. This is a series, reminiscent of Jan Karon's (q.v.) Mitford novels, full of humor, endearing local characters and soothing, but not syrupy, religious overlay.

1. *Miss Julia Speaks Her Mind* (**Morrow, 1999**) Miss Julia Springer faces down Abbotsville, North Carolina, small-town gossip and offers a home to her deceased husband's mistress, Hazel Marie Puckett, and nine-year-old son, Little Lloyd.
2. *Miss Julia Takes Over* (**Viking, 2001**) Protecting Hazel Marie from a slick church fund-raiser, Miss Julia hires private detective J. D. Pickens.
3. *Miss Julia Throws a Wedding* (**Viking, 2002**) Miss Julia takes charge when Deputy Sheriff Coleman Bates and attorney Binkie Enloe announce that they plan to get married.
4. *Miss Julia Hits the Road* (**Viking, 2003**) Miss Julia dashes to the rescue, with possible damage to her sense of propriety, when the Willow Lane neighborhood, which houses low-income blacks, including her housekeeper, Lillian, is threatened by a greedy developer.
5. *Miss Julia Meets Her Match* (**Viking, 2004**) Miss Julia is suspicious of the group who propose a Christian theme park on leased land.
6. *Miss Julia's School of Beauty* (**Viking, 2005**) Miss Julia and Sam Murdoch are finally married. Or are they? Something is not quite right about their spur-of-the moment nuptials at the Wedding Ring Chapel in Dollywood. Meanwhile, Hazel Marrie is organizing a beauty pageant to raise money for the sheriff departments canine unit.
7. *Miss Julia Stands Her Ground* (**Viking, 2006**) Miss Julia, facing a paternity dispute over her Little Lloyd, is forced to retrieve a specimen of the late Wesley Lloyd Springer's DNA.
8. *Miss Julia Strikes Back* (**Viking, 2007**) Miss Julia, deciding not to wait for police action after someone steals her rings and Hazel Marie's jewelry, drives off to Florida to recover the stolen items.
9. *Miss Julia Paints the Town* (**Viking, 2008**) Miss Julia deals with a New Jersey developer who plans to tear down the Abbotsville courthouse and replace it with condos and three friends whose husbands seem to have absconded, at least one with a great deal of money.

Ross, Barnaby

PSEUDONYM OF Frederic Dannay & Manfred Lee

Frederic Dannay and Manfred Lee, an uncle-nephew team, wrote published mysteries under the pseudonym of Ellery Queen (q.v.) and also produced, under the pseudonym of Barnaby Ross, four mysteries starring Drury Lane, a retired Shakespearean actor and connoisseur of crime who aided the New York police. Numbers 1, 2, and 3 are collected in an omnibus entitled *The XYZ Murders* (Lippincott, 1961).

1. *Tragedy of X, The* (**Viking, 1932**) A man is murdered on a crowded crosstown trolley in New York City and Drury Lane knows who did it but has trouble proving it.
2. *Tragedy of Y, The* (**Viking, 1932**) York Hatter is dead, and someone is trying to kill his blind and deaf stepdaughter.
3. *Tragedy of Z, The* (**Viking, 1933**) Drury advises Miss Patience Thumm in her investigation of a series of crimes.
4. *Drury Lane's Last Case* (**Viking, 1933**) Patience Thumm is again involved in this puzzling case involving the substitution of one rare book for another.

Ross, Dana Fuller

PSEUDONYM OF Noel B. Gerson

Wagons West was another series produced by Lyle Kenyon Engel, the book "packager" behind John Jakes's (q.v.) successful Kent Family Chronicles. The prolific fiction and nonfiction writer Noel

B. Gerson writes, as Dana Fuller Ross, a serviceable blend of romance and adventure in which the Holt family, the principal protagonists among a large cast of characters, "for freedom, fairness, and justice for all," are usually on the side of the angels as they settle the West. The original Wagons West series, 24 volumes in all (numbers 7–30), covers American frontier history from 1837 to 1876; the Holts: An American Dynasty series (numbers 31–40) brings the Holts and their descendants into the 20th century; the Empire (numbers 1–3) and Frontier trilogies (numbers 4–6) are prequel series with an earlier generation of Holts in the beginning of the 19th century. There are still some gaps in the Holt family saga, so there may be yarns to come.

1. *Honor!* (Bantam, 1998) President Thomas Jefferson asks the Holt brothers, Clay and Jeff, to investigate a murder that may masking a larger scheme. Number 1 in the Empire trilogy.

2. *Vengeance!* (Bantam, 1999) Clay Holt is steaming down the Mississippi River trying to stop a corrupt land deal, while his brother Jeff is on a sea journey to the Russian colony of Alaska. Number 2 in the Empire trilogy.

3. *Justice!* (Bantam, 1999) Clay Holt is on a government mission to track the Comte Jacques de la Carde, a French nobleman suspected of land-grabbing schemes and consorting with hostile Indians. Brother Jeff is returning from an Indian settlement in Russian Alaska. Number 3 in the Empire trilogy.

4. *Westward!* (Bantam, 1992) Clay and Jefferson Holt are involved in a blood feud with a murderous clan in the Ohio Valley, and light out for the Western frontier. Number 1 in the Frontier trilogy.

5. *Expedition!* (Bantam, 1993) Clay and his beautiful Sioux wife lead an expedition up the Yellowstone River; brother Jeff heads East on an equally perilous mission; while Sister Melissa tries to fend off an unscrupulous businessman who means to have her. Number 2 in the Frontier trilogy.

6. *Outpost!* (Bantam, 1993) Clay and Jeff are in the heart of the Western Territory in this conclusion to the Frontier trilogy.

7. *Independence!* (Bantam, 1979) In the first volume of the Wagons West series, Sam Brentwood takes a wagon train from Long Island to Independence (Missouri), meeting attractive widow Claudia Humphries along the way. The time is spring 1837.

8. *Nebraska!* (Bantam, 1979) In autumn 1837, frontiersman Mike "Whip" Holt takes the wagon train on from Independence, and Cathy van Ayl leaves her family behind in the hope of winning Whip's heart.

9. *Wyoming!* (Bantam, 1980) In 1838, with the Rockies looming ahead, Whip's Indian woman La-ena joins the wagon train.

10. *Oregon!* (Bantam, 1980) A band of Russian settlers and the English Royal Army complicate the wagon train's arrival and settlement. Cathy is now married to Lee Blake.

11. *Texas!* (Bantam, 1980) In 1843 some of the original wagon train members join the call to defend Texas against the Mexican army.

12. *California!* (Bantam, 1981) The discovery of gold in 1848 brings a new kind of lawlessness to the West. This novel features Whip Holt and many new characters.

13. *Colorado!* (Bantam, 1981) During the Civil War, General Lee Blake fights to keep Colorado in the Union, and Cathy is faced with a rival.

14. *Nevada!* (Bantam, 1981) This book covers events in Virginia City, Nevada, during the Civil War.

15. *Washington!* (Bantam, 1982) Two Civil War veterans fight a ruthless tycoon for timber rights in Washington Territory.

16. *Montana!* (Bantam, 1983) In 1866 young Toby Holt, Whip's son, faces the treacherous outlaw Sadie "Ma" Hastings and Thunder Cloud, chief of the mighty Sioux.

17. *Dakota!* (Bantam, 1983) Toby Holt leaves his wife, Clarissa, at home and sets out to make peace with the Indians in Dakota Territory.

18. *Utah!* (Bantam, 1984) In 1867 Toby and his friend Rob Martin bring peace and order to the lawless territory of Utah.

19. *Idaho!* (Bantam, 1984) Toby Holt, now governor of the Idaho Territory, must deal with the rowdy saloons and bordellos of Boise as well marauding Indian bands.

20. *Missouri!* (Bantam, 1985) Toby hunts down outlaws and renegade Indians with the aid of young army cadet Hank Blake and the loyal Chief Running Bear.

21. *Mississippi!* (Bantam, 1985) The Mississippi River is the scene of much of the action as Toby Holt and his ally Domino clash with wicked Karl Kellerman and Tong boss Kung Lee.

22. *Louisiana!* (Bantam, 1986) The exotic atmosphere of New Orleans with its Creole, Cajun, and Chinese population brings new challenges for Toby.

23. *Tennessee!* (Bantam, 1986) Toby is sent to quash a conspiracy of outlaws and backwoods misfits in the secluded hills of Tennessee.

24. *Illinois!* (Bantam, 1986) Set in the 1870s in Chicago at the time of the great fire. Toby has become prosperous and his daughter Janessa feels a calling to become a doctor.

25. *Wisconsin!* (Bantam, 1987) Toby, now widowed, watches romance bloom between his sister Cindy and friend Lieutenant Henry Blake.

26. *Kentucky!* (Bantam, 1987) Toby goes to Kentucky looking for an assassin plotting to kill President Grant. Set during the Great Panic of 1873.

27. *Arizona!* (Bantam, 1988) The new Winchester gun is used by Cindy Holt's husband to tame the sun-scorched frontier of Arizona.

28. *New Mexico!* (Bantam, 1988) Toby goes to New Mexico to infiltrate a band of desperadoes and bring justice to the land.

29. *Oklahoma!* (Bantam, 1989) Range wars threaten to erupt as Oklahoma's harsh open country beckons to farmers.

30. *Celebration!* (Bantam, 1989) A band of anarchists plans a bloody bomb to ruin the Centennial celebration of July 4, 1876.

31. *Oregon Legacy!* (Bantam, 1989) Catches up with Toby Holt and his family in 1887 as Toby loses his fortune in a Dakota blizzard and travels back to Oregon. Number 1 in the Holts: An American Dynasty series.

32. *Oklahoma Pride* (Bantam, 1990) Newspaperman Tim Holt heads to the heart of the Indian Territory in Oklahoma in an attempt to the print the truth in the name of justice. Number 2 in the Holts series.

33. *Carolina Courage!* (Bantam, 1990) Dr. Janessa Holt Lawrence comes to the Cherokee reservation to help a desperate people and learns the truth about her lost Indian past. Number 3 in the Holts series.

34. *California Glory!* (Bantam, 1991) Tim struggles to establish a newspaper in California printing the truth about the labor troubles of the 1890s. Number 4 in the Holts series.

35. *Hawaii Heritage!* (Bantam, 1991) Queen Liliuokalani is deposed from her throne by American settlers who wish to annex Hawaii to the United States. Number 5 in the Holts series.

36. *Sierra Triumph!* (Bantam, 1992) In 1895 the Holts remain embroiled in controversy: Frank Holt heads toward a bloody rendezvous; Tim Holt gets involved with a suffragette in Idaho. Number 6 in the Holts series.

37. *Yukon Justice!* (Bantam, 1992) In 1896 Frank Blake leaves Sierra, California for the untamed Yukon Territory. In New York Janessa runs full tilt into the establishment when she becomes an outspoken proponent of birth control. Number 7 in the Holts series.

38. *Pacific Destiny!* **(Bantam, 1994)** Jingoists use the explosion of the battleship *Maine* as a rallying cry for the Spanish-American War. Number 8 in the Holts series.
39. *Homecoming!* **(Bantam, 1994)** Frank Holt is again drawn westward, while Michael Holt is in New Mexico fighting for justice. Number 9 in the Holts series.
40. *Awakening!* **(Bantam, 1995)** Sally Holt and her friend India Blackstone move East to make new lives in New York City in the tenth and Holts series' last book, which takes them through World War I and the Jazz Age and into the Depression years.

Ross, JoAnn

I. Prolific American romance novelist JoAnn Ross is fond of trilogies, usually about members of the same family, who are, whether they are aware of it at first, driven by passion and have a tendency to wander in and out of each others' trilogies. For instance, Nate Callahan, one of the three brothers in the Callahan Brothers trilogy, also turns up in the novella, "Cajun Heat" (in the multiauthor *Bayou Bad Boys*, Kensington, 2005), while members of the Dupree family, also characters in the Callahan trilogy, turn up in "Cajun Heat" and in another novella, "Love Potion #9" (in the multiauthor *Bad Boys, Southern Style*, Kensington, 2006).

Blue Bayou, Louisiana, is home base for the Callahan brothers, Jack, Finn, and Nate, who wind up back there in the course of their peregrinations in search of true love. Omnibus volume: *The Callahan Brothers Trilogy* (Pocket Books, 2004).

1. *Blue Bayou* **(Pocket Books, 2002)** Danielle Dupree returns to Blue Bayou, Louisiana, after 13 years, to reunite with her ex-con father and rebuild her life after the death of her deceitful husband. Ex–DEA agent turned best-selling novelist Jack Callahan, her teenage heartthrob, is also back in Blue Bayou.
2. *River Road* **(Pocket Books, 2002)** FBI agent Finn Callahan returns to Blue Bayou, where Julia Summers, star of the soap *River Road*, which is filming in town, is in need of a bodyguard.
3. *Magnolia Moon* **(Pocket Books, 2003)** Nate Callahan, mayor of Blue Bayou, goes to Los Angeles to track down former Blue Bayou resident, Regan Hart, now a homicide detective, to tell her about a legacy.

II. The Scottish American Stewart sisters, Lily, Lark, and Laurel, have glamorous careers, a home base in a small community in western Tennessee, romantic futures, and share a family feud with the McDougalls of Scotland.

1. *Out of the Mist* **(Pocket Books, 2003)** Filmmaker Ian MacDougall is sent by Duncan, his Scottish grandfather, to America to reclaim the Brooch of Lorn from gallery owner Lily Stewart, who is ensconced in Tennessee.
2. *Out of the Blue* **(Pocket Books, 2004)** Famous country singer, Lark Stewart, beset by a stalker, returns to her home in the Smoky Mountains and her former boyfriend, Lucas McCloud.
3. *Out of the Storm* **(Pocket Books, 2004)** Washington political journalist, Laurel Stewart, wrongly fired for stealing secrets from the US vice president, goes to South Carolina, accompanied by detective Joe Gannon, in search of her missing roommate, Chloe Hollister.

III. Whiskey River is a quiet Arizona mountain town with its share of passionate people. Besides the official trilogy, two other novels have Whiskey River connections: *Confessions* (Mira, 1996), in which Clint Garvey, of number 1, makes an appearance; and *The Outlaw* (Harlequin, 1996), series IV, number 3, in which Whiskey River is visited by a member of the Montacroix "royal family" in 1896.

1. *Ambushed* **(Harlequin, 1996)** Sexy rancher Clint Garvey, although he has vowed not get in romantic entanglements again, takes on a beautiful, blond, green-eyed housekeeper.
2. *Wanted!* **(Harlequin, 1996)** Jessica rescues a wounded man who claims that he is on a mission to avenge a 100-year-old murder.
3. *Untamed* **(Harlequin, 1996)** What's bothering Tra Delaney when she faints in Gavin's arms?

IV. A historical trilogy features the Montacroix "royal family," a clan of aristocrats who undergo a series of romantic adventures in late-19th- and 20th-century Europe and America. The family also appears in *Angel of Desire* (Harlequin, 1994).

1. *Guarded Moments* **(Harlequin, 1990)** Princess Chantal Giraudeaux du Montacroix, expecting red carpet treatment on her American tour promoting a traveling art exhibit, is annoyed by the close attention that special agent Caine O'Bannion is paying to her.
2. *Prince and the Showgirl, The* **(Harlequin, 1993)** Sabrina Darling, daughter of a country and western superstar, is fixated on the idea of becoming a princess. Then she meets Prince Burke. No connection with the movie of the same title starring Laurence Olivier and Marilyn Monroe.
3. *Outlaw, The* **(Harlequin, 1996)** 1896. Princess Noel Giraudeaux finds herself in Whiskey River, Arizona Territory (see series III), saving Wolfe Longwalker from being hanged.

V. Castlelough, Ireland, is the quaint location for a trio of a novels featuring passionate Irish men and women (for a more jaundiced view of the romantic Irish, see Edna O'Brien's [q.v.] Country Girl trilogy). Several characters from this trilogy turn up elsewhere: Brendan O'Neill, from the local pub, appears in *Out of the Storm* (series II, number 2) and the nonseries *Blaze* (Pocket Books, 2005). Members of the O'Halloran family appear in the Coldwater Cove series (series VI), *Blaze*, and *The Return of Caine O'Halloran* (Harlequin, 1994).

1. *Woman's Heart, A* **(Mira, 1998)** Nora's story. Cynical, disillusioned novelist Quinn Gallagher had never met anyone like Nora Fitzgerald.
2. *Fair Haven* **(Pocket Books, 2000)** Michael's story. Erin O'Halloran travels to a western island and runs into photographer Michael Joyce.
3. *Legends Lake* **(Pocket Books, 2001)** Kate's story. Horse trainer Alex McKenna, trying to rebuild his shattered life by training troubled Thoroughbred Legends Lake, hooks up with horse-breeder Kate O'Sullivan.

VI. Coldwater Cove, in the state of Washington, is the setting for two novels in which two natives return from prosperous but unsatisfying lives elsewhere and find, or rekindle, romances with Jack and Daniel O'Halloran. Members of the O'Halloran clan also make appearances in *Fair Haven* (series V, number 2), *Blaze* (nonseries, Pocket Books, 2005), and *The Return of Caine O'Halloran* (nonseries, Harlequin, 1994).

1. *Homeplace* **(Pocket Books, 1999)** High-priced New York attorney Raine Cantrell returns to a family emergency in her hometown of Coldwater Cove, Washington, and falls for widowed sheriff Jack O'Halloran.
2. *Far Harbor* **(Pocket Books, 2000)** "After her seemingly idyllic marriage turns out to be a pretty illusion," Savannah Townsend returns to Coldwater Cove with plans for turning the old

lighthouse into an inn and runs into a man from her past, Daniel O'Halloran.

VII. The Knights of New Orleans are the three O'Malley brothers: Michael, Roarke, and Shayne. *Private Passions* (Harlequin, 1995) introduces Michael O'Malley as a character and also contains a member of the Dupree family (see series I).

1. *Roarke: The Adventurer* **(Harlequin, 1997)** Globe-trotting journalist Roarke O'Malley returns to New Orleans to recuperate after an attempt on his life.
2. *Shayne: The Pretender* **(Harlequin, 1997)** Suspected jewel thief and smuggler, Bliss Fortune, crosses the path of Shayne O'Malley.
3. *Michael: The Defender* **(Harlequin, 1997)** Someone wants to hurt movie star, Lorelei Longstreet. Michael O'Malley remembers their love affair.

Ross, Jonathan

PSEUDONYM OF John Rossiter

Devonshire native Rossiter, who served with the British police service in Wiltshire for over 30 years, can be counted upon to bring a solid knowledge of police procedures to this series about George Rogers, police detective in the provincial town of Abbotsburn. Rogers is highly intelligent, impatient, sometimes irascible, emotionally vulnerable, and highly susceptible to women but unable to maintain a relationship. His character has mellowed over the years, as his author's prose style: the later novels are generally better-written than the earlier ones. Fans of Colin Dexter's (q.v.) Inspector Morse might be interested in this series. Jonathan Ross is not to be confused with the British TV talk-show host and film critic of the same name. John Rossiter also wrote the Roger Tallis detective series under his own name.

1. *Blood Running Cold, The* **(Prescott, 1987)** Detective Inspector Rogers isn't very interested in searching for Mrs. Ewis's errant husband until his bloated corpse turns up in a river. Originally published in the United Kingdom in 1968.
2. *Diminished by Death* **(Bantam, 1984)** When a young couple returns their rented boat after a row on the river, the boat's owner finds a blood-stained knife. Originally published in the United Kingdom in 1968.
3. *Dead at First Hand* **(Cassell [UK], 1969)** No annotation available. Not published in the United States.
4. *Deadest Thing You Ever Saw, The* **(McCall, 1970)** Mrs. Bowker's attackers serve three years in prison for their fatal assault and rape, but someone feels that their debt isn't paid in full yet.
5. *Here Lies Nancy Frail* **(Saturday Review, 1972)** High-class prostitute Nancy Frail is found dead in a car crash, leaving behind seven cats, each named for a former lover.
6. *Burning of Billy Toober, The* **(Walker, 1976)** The police decide that a body found burned beyond recognition is that of local informer Billy Toober.
7. *I Know What It's Like to Die* **(Walker, 1978)** Four men are arrested and sentenced after a botched bank robbery, but the loot is never found.
8. *Rattling of Old Bones, A* **(Scribner, 1982)** The body of Judith Quint, five years dead, is found crammed in a cupboard. Originally published in 1979.
9. *Dark Blue and Dangerous* **(Scribner, 1981)** The career of up-and-coming police officer Christopher Proctor comes to an abrupt halt when he is drowned in a canal.

10. *Death's Head* **(St. Martin's, 1983)** The town drunk reports seeing a corpse on the church porch where he usually sleeps, but the police fail to find one when they arrive.
11. *Dead Eye* **(St. Martin's, 1984)** A private detective is stabbed through the eye; the weapon remains lodged in his head; then his head disappears.
12. *Dropped Dead* **(St. Martin's, 1985)** The body of a woman who was apparently killed by a fall is found by a gamekeeper in Sinderfell Wood.
13. *Burial Deferred* **(St. Martin's, 1986)** Rogers awakens from a near-fatal bludgeoning with retrograde amnesia.
14. *Fate Accomplished* **(St. Martin's, 1987)** After a train crashes into a car stalled at a railway crossing, an autopsy reveals that the man found in the car had been dead several hours before the train struck.
15. *Sudden Departures* **(St. Martin's, 1988)** A firebomb kills Andrew Lattimer, his wife disappears, and his wife's lover is found murdered.
16. *Time for Dying, A* **(St. Martin's, 1989)** A crossbow bolt kills Solon Stephanakis, drug dealer and pimp, and the woman he lived with is kidnapped.
17. *Daphne Dead and Done For* **(St. Martin's, 1991)** The editor of the Abbotsburn newspaper receives a classified ad seeking information on the whereabouts of Daphne Gosse and intimating foul play.
18. *Murder Be Hanged* **(St. Martin's, 1993)** Eighteen-year-old Willie Sloan tells Rogers that someone, probably his stepfather, is trying to kill his mother.
19. *None the Worse for Hanging* **(St. Martin's, 1995)** Philip Cruickshank's promiscuous common-in-law wife has vanished, while Philip is found hanged in his garage. UK title: *The Body of a Woman*.
20. *Murder! Murder! Burning Bright* **(St. Martin's, 1997)** Rogers works with Lesley Wing, the female chief security officer of a wildlife park, after a series of murders in the park.
21. *This Too, Too Sullied Flesh* **(Constable [UK], 1997)** The body of an unknown man with an arrow through his throat is found on the grounds of the exclusive Farquaharson Country Club. Published in the United States only in large print (G. K. Hall, 1998).

Roth, Henry

Mercy of a Rude Stream, Henry Roth's (d. 1995) autobiographical opus was completed in four volumes, two of them posthumous: *From Bondage* and *Requiem for Harlem*. Two more Roth works, apparently not part of the series, are still to be published. Roth's alter ego Ira Stigman is followed from his childhood in the immigrant slums of New York City in the first decades of the 20th century to 1927, when he is about to graduate from CCNY. The saga is seen both through the eyes of the youthful Ira and the musings, via desktop, of the octogenarian Ira, looking back on the agonies of his past life, and still not truly reconciled to what he regards as his personal failures and the betrayals of his friends and lovers. Roth's first novel, *Call It Sleep* (Ballou, 1934), was followed by an almost 60-year publishing silence. *Call It Sleep*, which was probably also autobiographical, was reprinted to acclaim in 1960 by Pageant.

1. *Star Shines over Mt. Morris Park, A* **(St. Martin's, 1994)** Young Ira Stigman's life in the slums of New York before and during World War I is related, sometimes through the now elderly Ira's word processor.

2. *Diving Rock on the Hudson, A* (St. Martin's, 1995) Ira recounts his incest with a younger sister and his behavior as a gauche outsider in high school and college.

3. *From Bondage* (St. Martin's, 1996) Ira's friend Larry Gordon and Larry's lover, poet and professor Edith Welles (in real life Eda Lou Walton), initiate Ira into the world of New York intellectuals and literati in the 1920s.

4. *Requiem for Harlem* (St. Martin's, 1998) In 1927 Ira, now a senior at CCNY, agonizes over his personal relationships, including the impregnation of his 16-year-old cousin Sheila, his mother's mental illness, and his perceived willingness to betray his best friend and family to get out of the Harlem slums.

Roth, Philip

I. Philip Roth is still probably best known among the reading public for his satires on American Jewish middle-class life such as *Portnoy's Complaint* (Random House, 1969) and *Goodbye, Columbus and Five Short Stories* (Houghton Mifflin, 1959), books that garnered him a large readership, a reputation among the literati, and the opprobrium of some Jewish Americans who branded Roth as an anti-Semite. Since then Roth has produced a large corpus of fiction that has attracted the attention and (largely) praise of readers and critics. In the eight books in which Nathan Zuckerman is a character, the literary life adds another dimension, as Roth examines the crises, responsibilities, sexual obsessions, pretensions, and anguished loves of a writer. Zuckerman strongly resembles his creator; he has even written a novel that, like *Portnoy's Complaint*, raised controversy in many quarters, including his own family. In numbers 6 and 7, Zuckerman is basically the ghostwriter, narrator, and mouthpiece for other characters. Number 8 is supposed to be the wrap-up of Zuckerman's career. In *My Life as a Man* (Holt, 1974) Zuckerman appears as a fictional character invented by that book's main character, Peter Tarnopol, an author who writes both his own story and that of his fictional alter ego. Philip Roth himself is the main character(s) in the hallucinatory *Operation Shylock* (Simon & Schuster, 1993). Roth has also written autobiographical nonfiction such as *The Facts* (Farrar, 1988) and *Patrimony* (Simon & Schuster, 1991). *The Plot against America* (Houghton Mifflin, 2004) depicts how an alternative-history family of Roths deals with the 1940 election, as US president, of anti-Semite Charles Lindbergh. *Zuckerman Bound* (Farrar, 1985) is an omnibus volume containing numbers 1 through 4.

1. *Ghost Writer, The* (Farrar, 1979) In the 1950s Zuckerman visits the famous author E. I. Lonoff at his house in the Berkshires and meets his beautiful protégée, who has curious Anne Frank fantasies.

2. *Zuckerman Unbound* (Farrar, 1981) Thirteen years later, Zuckerman, now reckoning with fame and the attacks of "crazies" that it brings him, attends his father's funeral and quarrels with his brother.

3. *Anatomy Lesson, The* (Farrar, 1983) Zuckerman, now a tormented 40-year-old, fights writer's block, baldness, and chest pains with drugs and drink until he collapses.

4. *Prague Orgy, The* (Vintage, 1996) Originally published as an epilogue to the Zuckerman saga in *Zuckerman Bound* (Farrar, 1985), this novella-length story takes Zuckerman to Prague in search of an unpublished manuscript.

5. *Counterlife, The* (Farrar, 1987) A collection of four episodes in which Zuckerman undergoes traumatic experiences in England, Israel, and New Jersey.

6. *American Pastoral* (Houghton Mifflin, 1997) Zuckerman tries to make sense of the life of high school hero Seymour "Swede" Levov, who has realized the American Dream with decidedly mixed results.

7. *Human Stain, The* (Houghton Mifflin, 2000) Zuckerman acts as confidant and ghostwriter for neighbor Coleman Silk, a professor at Athena College who has inadvertently fallen into the toils of the college's politically correct zealots for allegedly racist remarks, one of the ironies being that Silk is himself an African American who has passed as a white Jew for decades.

8. *Exit Ghost* (Houghton Mifflin, 2007) A 71-year-old Nathan Zuckerman returns to New York after a decade-long rustication in New England, ostensibly to see a doctor about a prostate condition that has left him incontinent and probably impotent.

II. In the rather bizarre satire *The Breast*, a character named David Kepesh becomes a giant female breast. Several years later, the character was revived in *The Professor of Desire*, in which Kepesh, somehow back in his original shape, has a series of sexual and intellectual adventures. *The Dying Animal*, published nearly a quarter of a century later, finds Kepesh in his seventies, still having sexual adventures.

1. *Breast, The* (Holt, 1972) Through a series of hormonal disasters, David Kepesh becomes physically a giant female breast, but he retains his human personality, his ability to talk, and his sex drive.

2. *Professor of Desire, The* (Farrar, 1977) David Kepesh, aspiring to become both a scholar and a rake, embarks upon a series of adventures from London to New York in pursuit of his sexual and intellectual goals.

3. *Dying Animal, The* (Houghton Mifflin, 2001) Now 70 years old, David Kepesh, TV culture critic and university lecturer, still sexually unsatiated, has an affair with another one of his female students, the beautiful daughter of Cuban émigrés.

Rouaud, Jean

Jean Rouaud, an unknown news vendor, won the Prix Goncourt for *Fields of Glory*, his first chronicle of French bourgeois life. Unlike Annie Ernaux's (q.v.) series, Rouaud's depiction of French provincial life is tender rather than bitter in this comedy of the daily lives of three generations of one family in the Loire Valley reaching back to the First World War.

1. *Fields of Glory* (Arcade, 1992) An unnamed and indeterminately aged narrator recalls the lives of his grandparents from the 1950s back to the carnage of World War I. Original title: *Champs d'honneur*. Translated from the French by Ralph Manheim.

2. *Of Illustrious Men* (Arcade, 1994) The narrator depicts the life of his father, Joseph, a porcelain and glassware salesman six days a week and a rock collector on Sundays. Original title: *Des hommes illustres*. Translated from the French by Barbara Wright.

3. *World More or Less, The* (Arcade, 1998) The coming-of-age of the narrator, as he endures eight years at a boarding school and further student years in the late 1960s as a myopic adolescent. Original title: *Monde à peu près*. Translated from the French by Barbara Wright.

Rowland, Laura Joh

Sano Ichiro, "Most Honorable Investigator of Events, Situations, and People," in late 17th-century Japan, is faithful to the *bushido*, or "way of the warrior," chivalrous tradition. As special investigator for the shogun, Sano Ichiro is called upon to investigate crimes with political implications, which gets him into some ticklish and volatile situations.

However, Sano perseveres, and by number 10, he has become chamberlain, second-in-command to the shogun, much to the chagrin of political rivals such as Yanagisawa. In number 4, Sano weds Lady Ueda Reiko, a feisty beauty who doesn't settle into the role of submissive Japanese consort. This is a very readable series of whodunits, although the plots are sometimes in danger of being submerged in the historical detail. Laura Joh Rowland, daughter of Chinese and Korean immigrants to the United States, was an engineer and writer at Martin Marietta in New Orleans before she started publishing the Sano Ichiro series.

1. *Shinju* (Random House, 1994) Beautiful, wealthy Ukiko and lowly artist Nuriyoshi are found drowned together in what looks like a case of *shinju*, or double suicide.
2. *Bundori* (Villard, 1996) Sano Ichiro, the shogun's special investigator, suspects that three of the most powerful men in the shogunate, including Chamberlain Yanagisawa, are behind a series of killings, with public displays of the severed heads of the victims in the manner of the custom known as *bundori*, or war trophy.
3. *Way of the Traitor, The* (Villard, 1997) 1690. Sano Ichiro thinks that he is being set up for a fall by an enemy when Jan Spaen, the trade director of the segregated Dutch enclave, disappears and is found murdered.
4. *Concubine's Tattoo, The* (St. Martin's, 1998) Sano's wedding to the beautiful Lady Ueda Reiko is interrupted when Hamune, one of the shogun's concubines, dies, the victim of poisoned ink that she used in giving herself a tattoo.
5. *Samurai's Wife, The* (St. Martin's, 2000) Sano is sent to the ancient court city of Miyako to investigate the martial art murder of Imperial Minister Konoe Bokuden, spy for the shogun, who may have discovered a secret plot against the shogun.
6. *Black Lotus* (St. Martin's, 2001) Sano and his wife, Reiko, disagree about the perpetrator of a case of murder and arson in the Black Lotus temple, the home of a mysterious sect and its charismatic leader.
7. *Pillow Book of Lady Wisteria, The* (St. Martin's, 2002) The shogun's cousin and probable heir has been slain in the bedchamber of Lady Wisteria, a high-priced courtesan, who has gone missing.
8. *Dragon King's Palace, The* (St. Martin's, 2003) The shogun's mother, Reiko (Sano's wife), the wife of Chamberlain Yanagisawa, and the pregnant wife of Sano's principal assistant have been kidnapped en route to Mount Fuji and their escort slaughtered.
9. *Perfumed Sleeve, The* (St. Martin's, 2004) Councilman Makino Narasida asks Sano to examine the circumstances of his own death.
10. *Assassin's Touch, The* (St. Martin's, 2005) Sano, now the shogun's chamberlain, returns to his role as criminal investigator after Japan's top spy, Ejima Senzaemon, drops dead on his mount during a horse race, the latest senior official to die without warning.
11. *Red Chrysanthemum* (St, Martin's, 2006) Sano's wife, Reiko, is discovered naked and blood covered next to the corpse of a nobleman suspected of treason.
12. *Snow Empress, The* (St. Martin's, 2007) Sano, in search of his kidnapped son, Masahiro, heads to the remote northern city of Ezogashima, where an insane local ruler is holding the entire community hostage as he searches for the murderer of the Snow Empress, his mistress.

Rowlands, Betty

I. Successful crime-novelist Melissa Craig lives in a cottage in the picturesque English Cotswolds after a London career (as does her creator, Betty Rowlands). Melissa is a somewhat younger and more modern Miss Marple who solves crimes in a series of cozies with nice English village (Upper Benbury) atmosphere and little overt bloodshed, sex, or profanity. Numbers 6 through 12 have not been published in the United States.

1. *Little Gentle Sleuthing, A* (Walker, 1991) Before she has time to unpack in her newly occupied cottage, Melissa receives a phone call for someone named Babs, who vanished a year earlier.
2. *Finishing Touch* (Walker, 1992) Melissa and her painter friend Iris Ash attend commencement ceremonies at Ravenswood College of Art and Design, where they witness an enraged artist slashing his fiancée's portrait.
3. *Over the Edge* (Walker, 1993) Melissa and Iris are on a working vacation near the Cevennes Mountains in the south of France when two bodies are found at the foot of a cliff.
4. *Exhaustive Enquiries* (Walker, 1994) An actor rehearsing a murder mystery Melissa has scripted is fatally injured in a fall down some cellar stairs.
5. *Malice Poetic* (Berkley, 1995) Disliked headmaster Stewart Haughn is murdered after receiving some mysterious and haunting poems in his mail.
6. *Smiling at Death* (Hodder [UK], 1995) Three murders within three months at the Cotswold village of Thanebury is followed by a fourth in Melissa's village of Upper Benbury.
7. *Deadly Legacy* (Hodder [UK], 1996) The town of Stowbridge has been plagued by a strangler and a series of burglaries. Then novelist Leonora Jewell dies, and Melissa is persuaded to complete her unfinished novel.
8. *Cherry Pickers, The* (Hodder [UK], 2000) Upper Benbury is shocked when the body of a Gypsy girl turns up in a freezer stolen from the Major's doorstep.
9. *Man at the Window, The* (Hodder [UK], 2000) Shortly after Graham Shipley arrives in Upper Benbury to take up a new teaching post and make a fresh start, the drowning of a young girl threatens to expose Graham's past life.
10. *Fourth Suspect, The* (Hodder [UK], 2001) Melissa's estranged father is found murdered in his shed.
11. *No Laughing Matter* (Hodder [UK], 2003) Two cases of fatal food poisoning at the smart residential home where she is staying provoke Melissa's mother, Sylvia, into an investigation of her own.
12. *Sweet Venom* (Hodder [UK], 2004) Apiarist Aidan Cresney is found dead of multiple bee stings. Then a second family member dies in similar circumstances.

II. A second series of mysteries, also set in the Cotswolds with a female protagonist, features Susan "Sukey" Reynolds, single mother of a teenage son, who is a Scene of Crimes Officer for Gloucester City. A Scene of Crimes Officer is only supposed to take photographs of the crime scene and look for physical evidence, but Sukey usually goes beyond her job description and gets further enmeshed in the investigation, much to the chagrin of her boyfriend, Detective Inspector Jim Castle. Some of the novels in this series, all published by Severn House (UK) have been distributed in the United States.

1. *Inconsiderate Death, An* (Severn House [UK], 1997) The wife of a wealthy businessman is found strangled in her home in the normally peaceful village of Marsden. Sukey is on the scene as police photographer.
2. *Death at Dearley Manor* (Severn House [UK], 1998) Paul Reynolds, Sukey's former husband, has married a second time, this time to a woman obsessed with money. He becomes one of the suspects when she is murdered.
3. *Copycat* (Severn House [UK], 1999) Art thief Miguel Rodriguez is quite angry to find that "Pepita," his newest girlfriend, is an

undercover policewoman. Which spells trouble for Sukey, since Pepita is her exact double.

4. *Touch Me Not* (Severn House [UK], 2001) The sudden deaths of two "initiates" at the Release Your Cosmic Energy (RYCE) Foundation seem suspicious to Sukey.

5. *Dirty Work* (Severn House [UK], 2003) The gory scene of Evita Stanton's murder gives Sukey nightmares, but doesn't dissuade her from further investigation, although she might be putting herself at risk.

6. *Deadly Obsession* (Severn House [UK], 2004) When Arthur Soames is found with a broken neck at the foot of an iron staircase in his back garden, everyone except Arthur's estranged daughter Sabrina thinks his death was accidental.

7. *Party to Murder* (Severn House [UK], 2005) Sir Digby Kirtling's estate manager, Una May, is found on the grounds, strangled with her own gold neck-chain.

8. *Alpha, Beta, Gamma . . . Dead* (Severn House [UK], 2007) Dr. Lamont is the prime suspect when ancient historian Dr. Whistler is found dead, and the letter he attributed to St. Paul is missing.

Rozan, S(hira) J.

Chinese American private investigator Lydia Chin and sometime partner and lover Bill Smith take turns in narrating this series of mysteries set in New York City: Chin narrates the odd volumes, Smith the even volumes. Some, but not all, of the investigations take place in New York's Chinatown. Several novels in this well-written, atmospheric series have received some of the highest awards for crime fiction: Shamus, Edgar, and Macavity. "A Tale about a Tiger" is a Chin short story that is part of the *Sounds like Murder* audiobook series (1998). S. J. Rozan (pronounced Rose *Anne*) is an architect for a New York firm and also runs an ongoing series of panels on "Crime Writing and the American Imagination" at the 92nd Street Y. *Absent Friends* (Delacorte, 2004) and *In This Rain* (Delacorte, 2006) are nonseries novels.

1. *China Trade* (St. Martin's, 1994) Readers are introduced to private investigator Lydia Chin, her sometime partner Bill Smith, her mother, who is obsessed with Lydia finding a Chinese husband, her brother Tim, who involves her in the robbery of a collection of porcelains, and other denizens of New York's Chinatown.

2. *Concourse* (St. Martin's, 1995) Bill Smith narrates this novel about a murder investigation at the Bronx Home for the Aged.

3. *Mandarin Plaid* (St. Martin's, 1996) Lydia is hired to deliver the ransom for a set of stolen sketches that comprise the inaugural collection of fashion designer Genna Jing and her new label, Mandarin Plaid.

4. *No Colder Place* (St. Martin's, 1997) Chin and Smith go undercover as a secretary and mason to investigate several thefts and murders at the construction site of a Manhattan apartment building.

5. *Bitter Feast, A* (St. Martin's, 1998) When the Chinese Restaurant Workers' Union tries to organize the restaurant workers in Chinatown, several workers, one of them a union organizer, disappear.

6. *Stone Quarry* (St. Martin's, 1999) Bill Smith is summoned from his hideaway in the woods in upstate New York by local farmer, Eva Colgate, who wants him to quietly recover some recently stolen possessions.

7. *Reflecting the Sky* (St. Martin's, 2001) When Chin and Smith are sent to Hong Kong to deliver the ashes of a family friend and a jade amulet to surviving relatives, they find themselves enmeshed in a kidnapping and the Chinese underworld of the triads.

8. *Winter and Night* (St. Martin's, 2002) Bill bails out his teenage nephew, Gary, who may have been involved in the murder of a young girl in his posh, high-school-football-obsessed New Jersey suburb.

Ruggero, Ed

US Army officer Mark Isen is the protagonist in a series of military techno-thrillers set in the near future. Although his prognostications, involving North Koreans and Neo-Nazi Germans but not Islamic terrorists, haven't quite panned out, Ruggero's novels are skillfully written and exciting. Former army infantry officer and English professor at West Point, Ruggero has apparently abandoned fiction and is currently promoting his version of "leadership" training. *The Academy* (Atri, 1997) is a nonseries novel about West Point.

1. *38 North Yankee* (Pocket, 1990) A second Korean War breaks out when Communist forces from North Korea launch a full-scale invasion of South Korea.

2. *Common Defense, The* (Pocket, 1992) Isen is assigned to the Mexican army as part of an antidrug campaign as neo-nationalist German infiltrators attack American targets in Mexico with bombs and nerve gas.

3. *Firefall* (Pocket, 1994) A fanatical German army reserve contingent has begun a military coup by attacking American Rangers on a multinational training exercise.

4. *Breaking Ranks* (Pocket, 1995) Isen is "driving a desk" in the Pentagon when he is asked to investigate the suicide of the nephew of his mentor, Major General Flynn.

Russo, Richard

Richard Russo's first two novels are set in the fictional upstate New York town of Mohawk, a place whose principal industry, leather tanning, has saddled it with unemployment and water polluted by chemical dumping. In *Mohawk*, we are introduced to the town and its denizens. In *Risk Pool*, we see Mohawk as depicted by Ned Hall, son of a unreliable father and a mentally ill mother, who escapes to tell his tale in college. Both novels are full of comical, pathetic, and, at the same time, sympathetic local characters, and the atmosphere of a blighted, hopeless town is delineated with a master touch.

Nobody's Fool (Random House, 1993), which was made into a movie starring Paul Newman, is set in another upstate New York town. *Straight Man* (Random House, 1997), one of the funniest academic novels ever, is set in Pennsylvania. The Pulitzer Prize–winning *Empire Falls* (Knopf, 2001) is set in Maine.

1. *Mohawk* (Random House, 1986) The wheelchair-bound Dan Wood; Anne, who is love with Dan; her father, Mather Grouse, guilt ridden over incidents in his past; and the unsavory Rory Gaffney are inhabitants of the depressed, polluted upstate New York town of Mohawk.

2. *Risk Pool, The* (Random House, 1988) Mowhawk native Ned Hall narrates his attempts to understand and to earn the love of his father, Sam, a carousing gambler and petty thief, who takes over his care when his mother suffers a mental breakdown.

Rybakov, Anatoli (Naumovich)

The late (d. 1999) best-selling Soviet author and Stalin Prize winner A. N. Rybakov's trilogy (tetralogy in Russian) about life under Stalin in the 1930s and 1940s was written in the 1960s but not published until the Glasnost years of the late 1980s and early 1990s. The trilogy of novels is a long but gripping saga of Soviet life during the Great Terror in the 1930s and World II in the 1940s as seen through the eyes of the semiautobiographical character and his friends from Moscow's Arbat District. Many historical characters appear in the trilogy, which features a chilling and believable portrait of the paranoid and megalomaniac Stalin.

1. *Children of the Arbat* (Little, Brown, 1988) Loyal student Sasha Pankratov is arrested, jailed, and exiled to Siberia for a satirical verse published in a student newspaper. Original title: *Deti Arbata*. Translated from the Russian by Harold Shukman.
2. *Fear* (Little, Brown, 1992) Forbidden to return to Moscow, Sasha migrates to a provincial town and finds work as a driver. Original title: *Tridtsat piatyi i drugie gody*. Translated from the Russian by Antonina W. Bouis.
3. *Dust and Ashes* (Little, Brown, 1996) Sasha leads an uneasy life as a political outcast, separated from his beloved Varya, until he "redeems" himself as a tank commander in the Russian army in the "War against the Germans." Original title: *Prakh i pepel*. Translated from the Russian by Antonina W. Bouis.

Sabatier, Robert

French poet, critic, and novelist Robert Sabatier has written many volumes that can be described as autobiographical, including most of his novels. *Le roman de Oliver* is a series of seven novels about Sabatier's early life. They follow the life of street urchin Olivier Chateauneuf, who is only nine years old when he is orphaned, leaving him the ward of some uncaring relatives. Armed with his ever-present box of safety matches—a talisman against fear—he wanders the colorful streets of Montmartre making friends with gangsters and prostitutes. Sabatier's spare, sensitive prose gives a vivid picture of Paris just before World War II. Only the first two novels in the series have been translated into English. The other five are listed in their French editions without annotations.

1. *Safety Matches, The* (Dutton, 1972) Befriended by some of Montmartre's most colorful citizens, young Olivier overcomes his grief and begins to leave childhood behind. Originally published in 1969 as *Les allumettes suedoises*. Translated from the French by Patsy Southgate. UK title: *The Match Boy*.
2. *Three Mint Lollipops* (Dutton, 1974) Olivier must adjust to life with his wealthy aunt and uncle and two cousins in their elegant Paris apartment. Originally published in 1971 as *Trois sucettes à la menthe*. Translated from the French by Patsy Southgate and Joan Wright Smith.
3. *Noisettes sauvages, Les* (Michel, 1974) No annotation available.
4. *Fillettes chantantes, Les* (Michel, 1980) No annotation available.
5. *David et Olivier* (Michel, 1986) No annotation available.
6. *Olivier et ses amis* (Michel, 1993) No annotation available.
7. *Olivier, 1940* (Michel, 2003) No annotation available.

Sabatini, Rafael

I. *Scaramouche* captured a big audience in the United States in 1921 as readers sought escape from the horrors of modern warfare in the romanticized high drama of French revolutionary times. The story features Andre-Louis Moreau, a brave, young strolling player who becomes known for his daring skirmishes in the revolutionary cause. Variously disguised as politician, lawyer, swordsman, and buffoon, the hero vanquishes his lady love with a flamboyance reminiscent of Baroness Emmuska Orczy's (q.v.) *Scarlet Pimpernel*. Stewart Granger starred in the rousing 1953 film *Scaramouche*. Sabatini, born in Italy of an Italian father and an English mother, settled in England and wrote his books in English.

1. *Scaramouche* (Houghton Mifflin, 1921) Sworn to avenge the death of his friend at the hands of a rich nobleman, Andre-Louis Moreau embarks on a series of exploits in the cause of the Revolution. Set in 1788–1792.
2. *Scaramouche the Kingmaker* (Houghton Mifflin, 1931) Scaramouche has further adventures in the days following the Revolution.

II. *Captain Blood*, the story of an English doctor forced into piracy, was an even bigger success than *Scaramouche*. The 1935 film version was Errol Flynn's first big swashbuckler. Basil Rathbone and Olivia de Havilland also starred.

1. *Captain Blood: His Odyssey* (Houghton Mifflin, 1922) This romance of the Spanish Main in the late 1600s stars Peter Blood, an English gentleman adventurer who can hold his own with bloodthirsty pirates and corrupt colonial governors alike.
2. *Captain Blood Returns* (Houghton Mifflin, 1931) Here the author relates 12 episodes in the adventures of Captain Blood that he omitted from his previous account. UK title: *Chronicles of Captain Blood*.
3. *Fortunes of Captain Blood, The* (Houghton Mifflin, 1936) Six further episodes are collected here.

Saberhagen, Fred

I. Fred Saberhagen writes popular fantasy, science fiction, and horror novels. His best-known fantasy series is classic swords and sorcery. Originally Saberhagen published the Book of Swords trilogy (numbers 1–3) about 12 swords forged by Vulcan, each with a separate magical power, so that the gods can play an elaborate game with the humans of a far-future world. The trilogy was continued by eight volumes of a saga called the Book of Lost Swords, in which a number of heroes continued the action by searching for the swords again. *The Complete Book of Swords* (Doubleday, 1985) contains numbers 1, 2, and 3. *The First Swords* (Tor, 1995) contains numbers 1, 2, and 3. *The Lost Swords: The First Triad* (Doubleday, 1988) contains numbers 4, 5, and 6, while *The Lost Swords: The Second Triad* (Guild America, 1991) contains numbers 7, 8, and 9. The Swords series was preceded by the Empire of the East trilogy, set in the same postholocaust universe (see series IV). *An Armory of Swords* (Tor, 1995) is a shared-universe book, edited by Saberhagen, with stories by Saberhagen and other authors.

1. *First Book of Swords, The* (Tor, 1983) Mark, son of the smith who helped Vulcan forge the swords, is driven from his native village by a duke who is ambitious to control as many of the swords as possible.

2. *Second Book of Swords, The* (Tor, 1983) Mark and his companions embark on a quest to aid Sir Andrew against human and magical foes and penetrate the treasury store of the Blue Temple.

3. *Third Book of Swords, The* (Tor, 1984) The war for possession of the swords has escalated to such an extent that the existence of the gods is in jeopardy.

4. *First Book of Lost Swords, The: Woundhealer's Story* (Tor, 1986) Hoping to find a cure for his son's illness, Prince Mark makes a pilgrimage to the shrine of the legendary sword, Woundhealer. Variant title: *Woundhealer's Story*.

5. *Second Book of Lost Swords, The: Sightblinder's Story* (Tor, 1987) Prince Mark is imprisoned in ice alongside the wizard Honan-fu by the usurper called the Ancient One. Variant title: *Sightblinder's Story*.

6. *Third Book of Lost Swords, The: Stonecutter's Story* (Tor, 1988) Prince al-Farabi and Magistrate Wen Chang search for the lost sword, Stonecutter. Variant title: *Stonecutter's Story*.

7. *Fourth Book of Lost Swords, The: Farslayer's Story* (Tor, 1989) Two rival families wage a war of attrition and vengeance for the possession of the sword, Farslayer. Variant title: *Farslayer's Story*.

8. *Fifth Book of Lost Swords, The: Coinspinner's Story* (Tor, 1989) The evil magician Wood tries to gain control of Coinspinner, the Sword of Chance, which can bring luck and take it away. Variant title: *Coinspinner's Story*.

9. *Sixth Book of Lost Swords, The: Mindsword's Story* (Tor, 1990) The Mindsword, which makes everyone within 100 yards fanatically loyal to the person who draws it, is planned as a gift for Prince Mark's wife, Kristen. Variant title: *Mindsword's Story*.

10. *Seventh Book of Lost Swords, The: Wayfinder's Story* (Tor, 1992) Wayfinder has the power to guide its possessor to whatever he is seeking. Variant title: *Wayfinder's Story*.

11. *Last Book of Swords, The: Shieldbreaker's Story* (Tor, 1994) Many of the swords play a role in this concluding volume as Prince Stephen, Mark's son, battles against Vikata the Dark Prince. Variant title: *Shieldbreaker's Story*.

II. The Berserker series is a military science-fiction saga that chronicles the ongoing conflict between space-faring humanity and the "Berserkers," war machines that are programmed to exterminate all life (reminiscent of the television series *Dr. Who and the Daleks*). Several of the Berserker volumes are short story collections, some of which were recycled into novels. *The Berserker Attack* (Waldenbooks, 1987) is a limited edition collection of some Berserker stories. *Berserker Base* is a shared-world anthology, edited by Saberhagen, with stories by Stephen R. Donaldson (q.v.), Larry Niven (q.v.), Roger Zelaszny (q.v.), and others, as well as by Saberhagen. *Berserkers: The Beginning* (Baen, 1998; numbers 1 and 5); *Berserker Man: Mega Book* (Baen, 2004; numbers 2, 3, 4, and 8); and *Berserker Death* (Baen, 2005; numbers 6, 9, and 11) are omnibuses. The Berserkers is a long-running series with some stark oppositions: man versus machine and life versus death.

1. *Berserker* (Ballantine, 1967) Short stories. Number 6 is an expanded version.

2. *Brother Assassin* (Ballantine, 1969) Short stories. UK title: *Brother Berserker*. Recycled as number 10.

3. *Berserker's Planet* (DAW, 1975) One of the Berserker's sets itself up as a planetary deity.

4. *Berserker Man* (Ace, 1979) One hundred years have passed with only an occasional Berserker sighting, but they have been regrouping and rebuilding until they are stronger than ever.

5. *Ultimate Enemy, The* (Ace, 1979) Short stories. Variant title: *Berserkers: The Ultimate Enemy*.

6. *Berserker Wars, The* (Tor, 1981) Short stories. Recycled from number 1.

7. *Earth Descended* (Tor, 1981) Short stories.

8. *Berserker Throne, The* (Simon & Schuster, 1985) A prince threatened by an assassin is presented with some serious ethical dilemmas.

9. *Berserker: Blue Death* (Tor, 1985) Niles Domingo seeks to destroy the Berserker known as Leviathan to avenge his daughter's death.

10. *Berserker Lies* (Tor, 1991) Short stories, some recycled from number 2.

11. *Berserker Kill* (Tor, 1993) A Berserker ship takes human prisoners, steals a research station, and heads back to its Mavronari hideout.

12. *Berserker Fury* (Tor, 1997) The Berserkers, preparing for a final attack on human-occupied space, are now able to construct units that look like human-created androids.

13. *Shiva in Steel* (Tor, 1998) The Berserkers, after a long stalemate, have developed a new tactical computer, nicknamed Shiva, that seems virtually unbeatable.

14. *Berserker's Star* (Tor, 2003) Gunrunner Harry Silver takes two businessmen-smugglers and a lady who is chasing her wayward husband to the planet Maracanda, where, because of its location, the normal laws of the universe are in abeyance.

15. *Berserker Prime* (Tor, 2003) The Berserkers invade the twin human worlds of Prairie and Timber, which are already facing war with the Huevans.

16. *Rogue Berserker* (Baen, 2005) Harry Silver is up against something even worse than an ordinary Berserker: a Rogue Berserker.

III. Saberhagen has also been active in the horror field, vampire subfield. His Dracula books form a loosely connected series in which Vlad Tepes, the Impaler, the legendary Dracula, did not die but became a Nosferatu. These literate, well-written additions to the Dracula canon employ other fictional characters, such as Arthur Conan Doyle's (q.v.) Sherlock Holmes, and downplay the horror, relying on fast pacing and vampire lore to keep the reader's interest. *The Vlad Tapes* (Baen, 2000) is an omnibus volume containing revised versions of numbers 1 and 2.

1. *Dracula Tape, The* (Warner, 1975) A revisionist view of Dracula that tells the count's side of the story through a tape sent to Mina Harker's grandson.

2. *Holmes-Dracula File, The* (Ace, 1978) Sherlock Holmes and Dracula, distantly related cousins, meet and form an alliance against a mad scientist who plans to loose bubonic plague on London.

3. *Old Friend of the Family, An* (Ace, 1979) Dracula comes to Chicago in the 1970s to protect Mina Harker's descendants and encounters a coven of evil vampires.

4. *Thorn* (Ace, 1980) Dracula travels to Arizona, where he clashes with the rich, decadent Seabright family amid flashbacks to the 15th century and Vlad's prevampire days.

5. *Dominion* (Tor, 1981) Dracula, living in Chicago under the name of Talisman, becomes involved in a clash between two ancient magicians.

6. *Matter of Taste, A* (Tor, 1990) Matthew Maule risks his un-life for the Sutherland family, and they have to return the favor when he is rendered comatose.

7. *Question of Time, A* (Tor, 1992) Nosferatu detective Mr. Strangeways, aka Drakuyla, helps Chicago-based private eye Joe Keogh find a teenager missing in the Grand Canyon.

8. *Seance for a Vampire* (Tor, 1994) Sherlock Holmes disappears during an investigation involving a fraudulent spiritualist, and Dr. Watson summons Holmes's cousin Count Dracula to save him.

9. *Sharpness on the Neck, A* (Tor, 1996) Two Philip Radcliffes, one in 1792 and one in the present, become involved with Vlad in his feud with his evil brother Radu.

10. *Coldness in the Blood, A* **(Tor, 2002)** Matthew Maule (see number 6) goes on a quest to find the ancient Egyptian statue that has a gem of unimaginable power in its center.

IV. The Empire of the East trilogy, set earlier in the same universe as the Swords series (series I) postulates a postnuclear holocaust Earth in which spirits usually associated with magic and primitive religion take over. More than 30 years later, Saberhagen added *Ardneh's Sword* to the series. An omnibus volume, *Empire of the East* (Ace, 1979), contains revised versions of numbers 1, 2, and 3.

1. *Broken Lands, The* **(Ace, 1968)** 50,000 years into the future a nuclear holocaust has changed Earth into a battlefield between Orcus, the holocaust itself in the form of a demon and Ardneh, the spiritual outgrowth of computer technology.
2. *Black Mountains, The* **(Ace, 1971)** In the conflict between "old" technology and "new" demonology, demon Lord Zapranoth, Lord Draffut, and the Bitch Goddess Charmain vie for power.
3. *Changeling Earth* **(DAW, 1973)** The spirits and demons dissipate and Earth returns to the realm of science once again. Variant title: *Ardneh's World*.
4. *Ardneh's Sword* **(Tor, 2006)** Chance Rolfson joins a forest expedition that seeks physical proof of Ardneh's existence.

V. A pair of science-fiction novels involves the mysterious space and time traveler Pilgrim, who is attempting to change history.

1. *Pyramids* **(Baen, 1987)** Tom Scheffler, whose great-uncle, Montgomery Chapel, had made a fortune in selling Egyptian artifacts, knows that Chapel fears a mysterious space and time traveler named Pilgrim.
2. *After the Fact* **(Baen, 1988)** Pilgrim, knowing that his only hope of returning home is to alter history, attempts to prevent the assassination of Abraham Lincoln.

VI. Saberhagen's latest series, the Books of the Gods, or the Faces of the Gods, retells mythology in the form of humans assuming the role of gods by putting on masks that imbue them with the power of the god they are impersonating. The first four books in the series deal primarily with Greek mythology, while the fifth moves the scene to Teutonic myth.

1. *Face of Apollo, The* **(Tor, 1998)** Rural youth Jeremy Redthorn puts on a mask that imbues him with the power and nature of the god Apollo, and finds himself being pursued by the avatars of Hades and Thamos.
2. *Ariadne's Web* **(Tor, 1999)** Another retelling of Greek myth in which Ariadne's thread is the magical ability to see connections; Theseus is an unscrupulous pirate; the mask of Dionysus is the source of a power struggle; and the Minotaur is the most sympathetic character.
3. *Arms of Hercules, The* **(Tor, 2001)** A retelling of the 12 labors of Hercules in which Hercules comes off as a rather modest fellow and mutant mastodons and "cameloids" roam the earth.
4. *God of the Golden Fleece* **(Tor, 2001)** Jason, the Argonauts, and the quest for the Golden Fleece, are recalled through the amnesiac memory of Proteus.
5. *Gods of Fire and Thunder* **(Tor, 2002)** Haraldur, or Hal, Argonaut survivor, shifts the scene to the North and a Wagnerian world including Baldur, Wodan, and Brunhilde.

Sale, Medora

PSEUDONYM OF Caroline Roe

Inspector John Sanders of the Toronto Police and photographer Harriet Jeffries have an off-again, on-again romantic and sleuthing relationship. Sometimes Sanders takes center stage, sometimes Jeffries is in the limelight, while a third character, Police Sergeant Rob Lucas, is the main protagonist of one novel in this well-done series of procedurals with in-depth characterization. Lately Canadian author Sale has been writing the Isaac of Girona series under her real name of Caroline Roe (q.v.).

1. *Murder on the Run* **(Scribner, 1986)** Inspector John Sanders of the Toronto Police Department is introduced in this tale of serial killers and copycat murders.
2. *Murder in Focus* **(Scribner, 1988)** Sanders, on a visit to Ottawa, stumbles onto architectural photographer Harriet Jeffries, who has taken a photograph that someone will stop at nothing to retrieve.
3. *Sleep of the Innocent* **(Scribner, 1991)** While John and Harriet vacation in the United States, Police Sergeant Rob Lucas is called upon to probe the shooting death of a corporate chairman.
3. *Murder in a Good Cause* **(Scribner, 1990)** A series of house burglaries is climaxed by the poisoning death of famous singer-actress Clara von Hohenkammer at her lavish Toronto home.
4. *Pursued by Shadows* **(Scribner, 1992)** Harriet's former lover, painter Guy Beaumont, returns to Toronto after two years in London, where he had lived with Jane Sinclair, Harriet's assistant.
6. *Short Cut to Santa Fe* **(Scribner, 1994)** On a New Mexico vacation, Sanders and Jeffries pick up 11-year-old twins at the Santa Fe airport, unaware that the bus the twins were trying to catch has been hijacked.

Sallis, James

I. Musicologist, poet, science-fiction writer, essayist, and biographer James Sallis has produced an interesting variation on the hard-boiled private eye theme. Lew Griffin is a black novelist, literature professor, and recovering alcoholic who views the world with genuine cynicism, not just the "trench coat deep" cynicism of your average literary shamus. Literary quotations and allusions and a New Orleans ambience are essential accompaniments to Lew's sleuthing. Chester Himes (q.v.), whose biography Sallis has written (*Chester Himes: A Life*; Walker, 2001) is the crime fiction writer with whom Sallis most identifies. The series should be read in publication order, or the reader may find himself lost as Griffin's musings range back and forth across time.

1. *Long-Legged Fly, The* **(Carroll & Graf, 1992)** Lew Griffin moves from his midtwenties to successful middle age as a writer burdened by some unpleasant memories and excessive alcohol and tobacco dependence.
2. *Moth* **(Carroll & Graf, 1993)** Griffin searches for Alouette, the runaway daughter of LaVerne Adams, his deceased former lover, amid many flashbacks and ruminations on loyalty and friendship.
3. *Black Hornet* **(Carroll & Graf, 1994)** Lew has a flashback to the late '60s and a long, hot summer in New Orleans, when a radically motivated sniper was shooting white people.
4. *Eye of the Cricket* **(Walker, 1997)** Lew is searching for missing children, including his long-lost son David.
5. *Bluebottle* **(Walker, 1999)** Griffin, recovering from gunshot wounds that have left him temporarily blind and semi-amnesiac, is searching for his assailant and carrying on a parallel search

for a missing writer who has been researching a group of white supremacists.

6. *Ghost of a Flea* (Walker, 2002) In the final volume of the series Griffin's son is once again missing, his latest romance has crumbled, a policeman friend has been shot, and the daughter of a friend has been receiving threatening notes.

II. Ex–Memphis police detective and ex-con Turner is working as a deputy sheriff in Cripple Creek, Tennessee. While serving nine years in prison for a couple of homicides, Turner earned a master's degree in psychology, and afterwards practiced as a therapist before returning to his native hills. Turner's attempt at small-town living isn't entirely successful, as painful memories, and big-city crimes intrude.

1. *Cypress Grove* (Walker, 2004) Turner's memories of his life as a big-city cop, a prison inmate, and a therapist, alternate with his investigation of the murder of an anonymous homeless man, who seems to be the victim of a ritual slaying.
2. *Cripple Creek* (Walker, 2006) After drunk driver Judd Kurtz is apprehended in Cripple Creek, $200,000 in a gym bag is found in the trunk of his car. Then Kurtz breaks out of jail, seriously wounding two officers, and deputy sheriff Turner is drawn into an investigation of organized crime in nearby Memphis.
3. *Salt River* (Walker, 2008) Turner, now the sheriff of a nameless rural community near Memphis, still grieving for his lover, Val, is galvanized into action when a speeding car driven by the former sheriff's son drives through the front wall of city hall.

Sams, Ferrol

Georgia farm boy Porter Osborne Jr. is the hero of an autobiographical trilogy by Georgia physician Ferrol Sams, who published his first novel at the age of 58. These coming-of-age novels are funny and moving and full of memorable characters and a rich Georgia ambience with much background material on rural manners and the storyteller tradition.

1. *Run with the Horsemen* (Peachtree, 1982) Porter Osborne Jr. is trying to make it through adolescence during the Depression years on a red-clay farm in rural Georgia.
2. *Whisper of the River, The* (Peachtree, 1985) Porter leaves his home in Peabody, Georgia, to enter the sophisticated world of Willingham University.
3. *When All the World Was Young* (Longstreet, 1991) Deliberately flunking out of medical school so that he can join the war effort, Porter is sent to Normandy as a medical assistant.

Sand, George

PSEUDONYM OF Amandine Aurore Lucie Dupin

George Sand is probably better known, in English-speaking countries at least, as a historical character in 19th-century France who dressed like a man and carried on scandalous love affairs with the likes of Chopin than as a enduring writer (see Judy Davis's wonderful portrayal in *Impromptu*, a 1990 film). A number of Sand's works have been translated (or retranslated) in recent years, including the novel *Indiana*, her correspondence with Flaubert, and her autobiography. Unfortunately the historical novels, *Consuelo* and *The Countess of Rudelstadt* haven't been retranslated into English since the 1840s (translator not identified). These novels, relating the story of the great singer Consuelo, reveal Sand's humanitarian

and socialist sympathies, and paint a vivid picture of European life and culture from 1740 to 1786. *Legends rustiques*, three stories of provincial French life (translated as *The Haunted Pool*, *The Country Waif*, and *Little Fadette*), are united by theme but not by plot or characters.

1. *Consuelo* (Ticknor, 1850) Consuelo is first seen as a child of the streets in Venice, where her striking voice brings her to the attention of a fine old maestro. First published as *Consuelo* in France in 1842.
2. *Countess of Rudelstadt, The* (Ticknor, 1847) Consuelo, now a great singer, performs for the kings and queens of Europe but remains unspoiled by her success. First published as *La comtesse de Rudolstadt* in France in 1843.

Sanders, Lawrence

I. Sanders's suspenseful storytelling, realistic New York setting, and believable characters have created a ready audience for his Delaney/Deadly Sin books. Edward X. Delaney is first met as a precinct captain, then as a retired chief detective on special cases for the New York Police Department. He is a dogged and sometimes unscrupulous investigator. Delaney first appeared as a character in Sanders's first success *The Anderson Tapes* (Putnam, 1970), which was made into a movie starring Sean Connery (1972). *The First Deadly Sin* was also made into a movie (1980), starring Frank Sinatra. *Three Complete Novels* (Putnam, 1993) contains numbers 1, 2, and 3.

Another series, the 10 Commandments, is a series in name only, featuring the adventures of various New York investigators such as Dora Conti, Joshua Bigg, and Samuel Todd.

1. *First Deadly Sin, The* (Putnam, 1973) The point of view in this novel alternates between that of Delaney, on the trail of the murderer, and that of a psychopathic killer sinking into total madness.
2. *Second Deadly Sin, The* (Putnam, 1977) New York's art world provides the colorful background for Delaney's investigation into the murder of painter Victor Maitland.
3. *Third Deadly Sin, The* (Putnam, 1981) Delaney is on the track of a psychopathic woman who is a mass murderer.
4. *Fourth Deadly Sin, The* (Putnam, 1985) Eminent psychiatrist Dr. Ellerbee has been murdered, perhaps by one of his patients.

II. Archy McNally, playboy and private investigator for his dad, Palm Beach attorney Prescott McNally, talks in a jargon that suggests Wodehouse's (q.v.) Bertie Wooster. Archy thoroughly enjoys the perks of upper-class life such as gourmet meals and a fire-engine red Miata automobile while solving the cases that come his way as manager of the "discreet inquiries" branch of his father's law firm. Since Sanders's death in 1998, the McNally series has been carried on by Vincent Lardo (q.v.). Three omnibus volumes have been published: *Three Complete Novels* (Putnam, 1997; numbers 1–3); *McNally's Files* (Berkley, 2006; numbers 1–3); and *Three Complete Novels* (Putnam, 1998; numbers 4–6).

1. *McNally's Secret* (Putnam, 1992) Archy has to find the thief who stole four "inverted Jennies" stamps from a wealthy matron in Palm Beach.
2. *McNally's Luck* (Putnam, 1992) The theft of an ill-tempered cat leads to a series of murders and an intricate plot.
3. *McNally's Risk* (Putnam, 1993) McNally is hired by Mrs. Smythe-Hersforth to check into the bona fides of Theodosia Johnson, beloved of Mrs. Smythe-Hersforth's airhead son Chauncey. Coauthored with Vincent Lardo.

4. *McNally's Caper* **(Putnam, 1994)** Gruswold Forsythe II, the dull patriarch of a prominent Palm Beach clan, engages Archy to find out which family member is stealing the Forsythe valuables.

5. *McNally's Trial* **(Putnam, 1995)** An executive at the exclusive Whitcomb Funeral Homes feels uneasy about the sudden upsurge in caskets being shipped north.

6. *McNally's Puzzle* **(Putnam, 1996)** Wealthy widower Hiram Gottschalk's fears for his life turn out to be justified.

7. *McNally's Gamble* **(Putnam, 1997)** Archy thinks, wrongly, that he has an easy job, when the children of wealthy widow Edythe Westman ask him to discourage her investment in a Faberge egg. Coauthored with Vincent Lardo.

III. Sanders wrote two books featuring Peter Tangent, an American oil company official who gets involved in some fast-moving and fairly grisly cases of skulduggery in Africa. *Three Complete Novels* (Putnam, 1994) contains numbers 1 and 2 plus the nonseries *The Tomorrow File*.

1. *Tangent Objective, The* **(Putnam, 1976)** Peter Tangent helps the ambitious, high-principled army captain Obiri Anokye plan a coup to overthrow the despotic ruler of Asante.

2. *Tangent Factor, The* **(Putnam, 1978)** Tangent helps Obiri Anokye, now leader of Asante, in his plan to unite Africa under his rule.

IV. Timothy Cone, New York City private investigator, was involved in several cases featuring corruption in big business and gang-land vendettas. Six novellas were published in the 1980s, collected in the two volumes listed below. *Three Complete Novels* (Putnam, 1999) contains numbers 1 and 2 and the nonseries *Sullivan's Story*.

Wolf Lannihan, insurance investigator, was featured in a number of stories published in *Swank* magazine in 1968–1969 and collected *Tales of the Wolf: The Cases of Wolf Lannihan* (Avon, 1986).

1. *Timothy Files, The* **(Putnam, 1987)** Contains three novellas: "The Wall Street Dick," "The Whirligig Action," and "A Covey of Cousins."

2. *Timothy's Game* **(Putnam, 1988)** Contains three novellas: "Run, Sally, Run," "A Case of the Shorts," and "One from Column A."

Sandford, John

PSEUDONYM OF John Camp

I. Minneapolis homicide policeman Lucas Davenport gets involved with some very nasty serial killers in this suspenseful, action-packed, violence-filled series. Davenport is a cool, cynical man of action who knows how to handle the media. Along the way in the Prey series, Lucas kills several people in the line of duty, invents a computer game that makes him rich, and has more than one torrid romance. *Three Complete Novels* (Putnam, 2000) is an omnibus volume containing numbers 7, 8, and 9. John Camp, a former Pulitzer Prize–winning journalist, lives in St. Paul, Minnesota. "John Sandford" is not to be confused with the children's book illustrator of the same name.

1. *Rules of Prey* **(Putnam, 1989)** A serial killer calling himself the "maddog" has been murdering women in Minneapolis and leaving a written message with each corpse.

2. *Shadow Prey* **(Putnam, 1990)** The killings of an Indian-gouging landlord and an Indian-hating parole officer are part of a conspiracy by Native American radicals leading all the way to New York.

3. *Eyes of Prey* **(Putnam, 1991)** A disfigured actor murders the wife of a forensic pathologist, and the drug-crazed doctor returns the

favor by dispatching a theater director who had intended to fire the actor.

4. *Silent Prey* **(Putnam, 1992)** "Dr. Death" escapes from his trial for crimes committed in *Eyes of Prey* and lands in New York where he plots vengeance on Lucas Davenport.

5. *Winter Prey* **(Putnam, 1993)** A family of three in rural Wisconsin is wiped out by the "Iceman," who then torches their home in pursuit of an incriminating photograph. UK title: *The Iceman*.

6. *Night Prey* **(Putnam, 1994)** Davenport is charged with finding a serial killer who disembowels his victims.

7. *Mind Prey* **(Putnam, 1995)** Psychiatrist Andi Manette and her two young daughters are kidnapped by former patient John Mail, who still harbors violent sex fantasies.

8. *Sudden Prey* **(Putnam, 1996)** Dick LaChaise and his two biker sidekicks are out get Davenport and his police team after the cops have stalked and killed a female bank robber who happened to be Dick's lover.

9. *Secret Prey* **(Putnam, 1998)** Lucas is sent to a hunting lodge north of Minneapolis to investigate the murder of banking executive Daniel Kresge.

10. *Certain Prey* **(Putnam, 1999)** Clara Rinker, Mob hit woman, is hired by the equally ruthless Minneapolis defense lawyer Carmel Loan to kill the wife of attorney Dale Allen, whom Carmel desires.

11. *Easy Prey* **(Putnam, 2000)** There are many suspects when fashion model Alie'e Marson is strangled, but most of them are killed in turn.

12. *Chosen Prey* **(Putnam, 2001)** James Qatar, professor of art history, has a passion for strangulation.

13. *Mortal Prey* **(Putnam, 2002)** Hit-woman Clara Rinker, who evaded Davenport in number 10, returns, looking for revenge against old enemies from Kansas City who killed her fiancé and her unborn baby.

14. *Naked Prey* **(Putnam, 2003)** Now married, a father, and a special agent for the Minnesota Bureau of Criminal Apprehension, Davenport trudges up to the northern tundra of Broderick, Minnesota to investigate the naked frozen corpses of a white woman and a black man.

15. *Hidden Prey* **(Putnam, 2004)** The members of a seemingly typical mid-American family have been working for the Soviet Union for 70 years. Then someone named Oleg Moshalov is murdered, and it is revealed that he is a KGB agent.

16. *Broken Prey* **(Putnam, 2005)** A psychopathic serial killer who mutilates his victims and taunts the police is bedeviling Davenport and his associate Sloan.

17. *Invisible Prey* **(Putnam, 2007)** A state senator accused of statutory rape and the beating death of wealthy widow Constance Bucher and her maid are on Davenport's plate here.

18. *Dark of the Moon* **(Putnam, 2007)** Virgil Flowers, who reports to Lucas Davenport, gets to operate pretty much on his own as he tackles a murder wave that hits the little town of Bluestem.

19. *Phantom Prey* **(Putnam, 2008)** A serial killer is targeting "goths" and anyone who gets in the way.

II. A lesser-known series, the first two of which were published under John Camp's real name, features St. Paul–based painter Kidd, computer whiz, tarot reader, and master criminal. The targets of Kidd and his part-time partner and lover, LuEllen, are corporations or rich people who don't deserve their money. There was a nine-year gap between numbers 2 and 3.

1. *Fool's Run, The* **(Holt, 1989)** When a rival defense industry corporation acquires plans for a targeting system stolen from Anhiser Aviation, Anhiser tries to get back by hiring Kidd.

2. *Empress File, The* (Holt, 1991) The target of this plot involving false identities, a houseboat, and a million dollar scam is the wealthy and corrupt mayor of a small Mississippi river town.
3. *Devil's Code, The* (Putnam, 2000) Kidd intervenes in a massive computer conspiracy masterminded by St. John Corbeil.
4. *Hanged Man's Song, The* (Putnam, 2003) Bobby, Kidd's genius hacker friend, is hammered to death by an intruder, and his laptop, which may contain several of Kidd's shadier deals, is stolen.

Sandstrom, Eve K.

I. Fourth generation Oklahoman and former reporter for the Lawton, Oklahoma, *Constitution*, Eve K. Sandstrom is uniquely qualified to write novels set in rural Oklahoma. Catlin County sheriff Sam Titus and his wife, Nicky, star in a series of tricky small-town mysteries full of "down home" country life and sympathetic humor.

1. *Death Down Home* (Scribner, 1990) Sam Titus, officer in the US Army's Criminal Investigation, and his new bride, Nicky, are called to Sam's hometown of Holton, Oklahoma, when his father becomes desperately ill.
2. *Devil Down Home, The* (Scribner, 1991) When a drifter is killed in a grisly ritualistic manner, Catlin County becomes a hotbed of speculation about Satanists and devil worshippers.
3. *Down Home Heifer Heist, The* (Scribner, 1993) Modern cattle rustlers are at the bottom of the death of rancher Joe Pilkington.

II. A second mystery series, set in rural Oklahoma, features Nell Matthews, reporter on the Violence Beat (police, sheriff, fire) of the Grantham *Gazette* and her policeman boyfriend Mike Svenson in a trio of books full of descriptions of newspaper making.

1. *Violence Beat, The* (Onyx, 1997) Nell gets involved in a hostage situation that turns into a possible murder and with hunky former big-city cop turned sheriff's deputy Mike Svenson.
2. *Homicide Report, The* (Onyx, 2000) Copy editor Martina Gilroy is found near death in the *Gazette* pressroom, muttering frantically about Nell's mysterious, long-absent father, Alan.
3. *Smoking Gun, The* (Signet, 2002) When Nell and Mike help out at a shelter for abused women, Mike is forced to shoot an intruder trying to stab the director of the shelter.

Saroyan, William

Saroyan, Thurber, and Gerald Durrell have lightened the burden of adolescence for many young readers with their humorous and high-spirited works, often told from the point of view of young narrators. Saroyan's offbeat and spontaneous characters the exhilarating way they create something quite magical out of the bare threads of their often sad lives are especially appealing to young adults. The first book listed below is unusual in having a young girl as narrator; most of Saroyan's narrators are boys.

1. *Mama, I Love You* (Little, Brown, 1956) Nine-year-old Twinkle, who lives with her divorced mother, wins a big part in a stage play, though she really wants to be a pitcher.
2. *Papa, You're Crazy* (Little, Brown, 1957) Twinkle's brother tells of his life with his father, an impecunious writer who lives in a beach house in Malibu.

Sartre, Jean-Paul

The Roads to Freedom (*Les chemins de la liberté*) is a trilogy of novels by this Nobel Prize–winning (prize refused by Sartre) French philosopher, political activist, and author of plays, novels, biography, and other nonfiction. *The Words* (*Les mots*, Braziller, 1964), his charming autobiography of childhood, is easily Sartre's most accessible work. Next, perhaps, is *The Age of Reason*, the first volume of this series, in which the main character faces an ethical dilemma and examines the existential issues of freedom and responsibility. The second and third volumes have a broader, more documentary interest but lack the first book's narrative tension. Two extracts from the unfinished fourth volume appeared in December 1949 in Sartre's review *Les tempes moderne* under the title "Drole d'amitie."

1. *Age of Reason, The* (Knopf, 1949) Philosophy teacher Mathieu Delarue faces the issues of maintaining his own personal freedom and behaving responsibly when his mistress, Marcelle, becomes pregnant. Originally published in 1945 as *L'âge de raison*. Translated from the French by Eric Sutton.
2. *Reprieve, The* (Knopf, 1947) Sartre shows Paris during the Munich crisis of 1938 with a Dos Passos–like (q.v.) sweep from character to character, including some of the principal characters from *The Age of Reason*. Originally published in 1945 as *Le sursis*. Translated from the French by Eric Sutton.
3. *Troubled Sleep* (Knopf, 1951) Familiar faces again reappear in this documentary look at World War II France after the fall of Paris. Variant title: *Iron in the Soul*. Originally published in 1949 as *La mort dans l'âme*. Translated from the French by Gerard Hopkins.

Saul, John (Woodruff)

John Saul, who has been called a poor man's Stephen King (q.v.), is extremely popular with readers, especially young adults, if not with critics. Since he published *Suffer the Children* (Dell, 1977), Saul has produced a nearly unbroken stream of best sellers. The plots are old-fashioned formulaic horror: an isolated small town, especially its young people, is threatened with some murderous evil. The Blackstone Chronicles is a serial novel, published in six parts, about Blackstone, a small town in New Hampshire, which is threatened by some monstrous emanating from a mysterious place called the Asylum. The evil takes the physical form of gifts sent to the town's prominent citizens. *The Blackstone Chronicles* (Fawcett, 1997) was immediately published as a single omnibus volume, and plans were hatched for a TV miniseries and a computer game.

1. *Eye for an Eye, An: The Doll* (Fawcett, 1997) Someone leaves a doll on the doorstep of the McGuire family of Blackstone, New Hampshire.
2. *Twist of Fate: The Locket* (Fawcett, 1997) The president of Blackstone's bank finds a silver heart-shaped locket in the seat of his wife's car.
3. *Ashes to Ashes: The Dragon's Flame* (Fawcett, 1997) Library assistant Rebecca Morrison comes across a beautifully ornate cigarette lighter in the shape of a fire-breathing dragon.
4. *In the Shadow of Evil: The Handkerchief* (Fawcett, 1997) An embroidered linen handkerchief isn't as innocent as it looks.
5. *Day of Reckoning: The Stereoscope* (Fawcett, 1997) A stereoscopic instrument presents horror in three dimensions.
6. *Asylum* (Fawcett, 1997) The ultimate key to the horrors of the Asylum lands on Harvey Connolly's front porch.

Saunders, Raymond M.

Fenwick Travers is America's answer to George MacDonald Fraser's (q.v.) Flashman. Fenwick, a turn-of-the-20th-century US Army officer, is a moneygrubbing, venal, cowardly rascal who lives by his wits and has never has done an honest day's work in his life. Historical figures make cameos in this satirical picture of an imperialist, racist era. Raymond M. Saunders, who has also written the mystery novel *Blood Tells* (Lyford, 1996) as Ray Saunders, is not to be confused with African American painter Raymond Saunders.

1. *Fenwick Travers and the Years of Empire* (Lyford, 1993) During the Spanish-American War, Travers acquires a completely fraudulent reputation for bravery under fire in Cuba.
2. *Fenwick Travers and the Forbidden Kingdom* (Lyford, 1994) After helping to put down the Boxer Rebellion in China, Fenwick makes use of his "anti-insurgency expertise" in the Philippines.
3. *Fenwick Travers and the Panama Canal* (Lyford, 1995) Captain Travers is sent to Panama to goad some rich Panamanians into revolting against Colombia so that Teddy Roosevelt can get his canal.

Sawyer, Corinne Holt

The energetic Angela Benbow and the dignified Caledonia Wingate, residents of Camden-sur-Mer Retirement Home near San Diego, California, are lovable senior sleuths in this humorous yet sympathetic look at retirement-home life and the social niceties and hazards of community living for seniors.

1. *J. Alfred Prufrock Murders, The* (Fine, 1988) When a fellow resident, a retired librarian from Duluth, is found murdered near the beach, recent retirement community arrival Angela Benbow gets involved.
2. *Murder in Gray and White* (Fine, 1989) The death of a none-too-popular resident at Camden-sur-Mer sets Angela and Caledonia off an investigation aided by Lieutenant Martinez of the San Diego Police.
3. *Murder by Owl Light* (Fine, 1992) Rollo the simple-minded gardener, a soft-drink machine attendant, and Mrs. Lena Gardner are all stabbed to death.
4. *Peanut Butter Murders, The* (Fine, 1993) Neighbor Alexander Lightfoot, who was engaged to a wealthy Camden-sur-Mer resident, is crushed by a train.
5. *Murder Has No Calories* (Fine, 1994) When a staff member is poached to death in the sauna, the owner of the Time-Out Inn, a fashionable fat farm, calls Angela in.
6. *Ho-Ho Homicide* (Fine, 1995) Retirement-home resident Birdy Benton is discovered dead under the Christmas tree in the lobby.
7. *Geezer Factory Murders, The* (Fine, 1996) After tenants of rival retirement home the Golden Years seem to be conducting an exodus to Camden-sur-Mer, one is found murdered.
8. *Murder Ole!* (Fine, 1997) When residents of Camden-sur-Mer embark upon a series of junkets to Baja California, deaths, including that of cranky Miss Braintree, start to occur.

Sayers, Dorothy L(eigh)

Ian Carmichael's portrayal of Lord Peter Wimsey on TV's *Masterpiece Theatre* won a whole new generation of fans for Dorothy Sayers's detective. In addition to being witty and well written, Sayers's books have the added attraction of some very engaging supporting characters including Bunter, the perfect gentleman's gentleman, and mystery writer Harriet Vane, the woman in Lord Peter's life. Lord Peter, although a World War I combat veteran, was originally a specimen of the monocled "silly-ass" type popular in mysteries of the 1920s. He matured in the later books, eventually marrying Harriet and becoming a family man. Dorothy Sayers, author of several books on religion and translator of Dante's *Divine Comedy* (Penguin Classics), has been the subject of at least four biographies, including Barbara Reynolds's *Dorothy L. Sayers: Her Life and Soul* (St. Martin's, 1993). After lying fallow for 60 years, an unfinished Wimsey manuscript was found among Sayers's papers. This was completed by Jill Paton Walsh as *Thrones, Dominations* (number 16) and published to mixed reviews. *Presumption of Death* (number 17), based on the Sayers characters, was also authored by Walsh. *The Documents in the Case* (Harper, 1987; originally 1930), coauthored with Robert Eustace, is a non–Lord Peter story. Real Wimsey fans will want to track down C. W. Scott-Giles's *The Wimsey Family* (Harper, 1977) and Stephan P. Clarke's *The Lord Peter Wimsey Companion* (2nd ed., 2002), published by the Dorothy L. Sayers Society, which is also the publisher of Sayers's letters.

1. *Whose Body?* (Boni, 1923) In his first appearance, Lord Peter conducts an unofficial inquiry into a strange case involving a nude corpse found in a bathtub. Note: The 1935 Harcourt reissue of this titles contains a droll biography of Lord Peter by "his uncle."
2. *Clouds of Witness* (Dial, 1927) When Lord Peter's brother, the Duke of Denver, is tried for murder before the House of Lords, Peter proves him innocent.
3. *Dawson Pedigree, The* (Dial, 1928) The "natural" death of an old lady turns out to be murder. Miss Climpson makes first appearance in this book. UK (and subsequent US) title: *Unnatural Death*.
4. *Lord Peter Views the Body* (Payson, 1929) This is a collection of short stories.
5. *Unpleasantness at the Bellona Club, The* (Payson, 1928) A curious will and suspicious timing raise questions when an elderly gentleman is found dead in his armchair at the club.
6. *Strong Poison* (Brewer, 1930) Lord Peter meets Harriet Vane in the Old Bailey, where she is on trial for poisoning her lover, and with Miss Climpson's help gets her off the hook. This escapade begins the six-year-old courtship of Harriet and Lord Peter.
7. *Five Red Herrings, The* (Brewer, 1931) Lord Peter's solution of this case involving the death of an artist in a Scottish village hinges on train timetables. Original UK title: *Suspicious Characters*.
8. *Have His Carcase* (Brewer, 1932) Harriet finds a body on the beach, and Lord Peter comes to investigate.
9. *Hangman's Holiday* (Harcourt, 1933) Four of these short stories feature Lord Peter, and the rest star Montague Egg, Sayers's lower-middle-class salesman-detective.
10. *Murder Must Advertise* (Harcourt, 1933) Lord Peter takes a job in an advertising agency to get to the bottom of some nasty drug-and-death business.
11. *Nine Tailors, The* (Harcourt, 1934) The art of church-bell ringing and a very ingenious murder figure prominently in this investigation of an anonymous corpse in a English village.
12. *Gaudy Night* (Harcourt, 1936) Poison-pen letters cause trouble at Oxford as Harriet returns for the Gaudy Dinner and Lord Peter comes to investigate. On the last page, Harriet accepts Peter's proposal of marriage.
13. *Busman's Honeymoon* (Harcourt, 1937) Subtitle: *A Love Story with Detective Interruptions*. Naturally Peter and Harriet encounter murder on their honeymoon.
14. *In the Teeth of the Evidence and Other Stories* (Harcourt, 1939) Of these short stories, only two feature Lord Peter.
15. *Lord Peter: A Collection of All the Lord Peter Wimsey Stories* (Harper, 1972) This collection includes "The Haunted Policeman,"

which mentions the birth of one Wimsey son, and "Talboys," in which two more have arrived.

16. *Thrones, Dominations* **(St. Martin's, 1998)** This mystery, finally completed by Jill Paton Walsh after 60 years, involves the murder, in a country cottage, of the beautiful Rosamund Harvell. Also includes a tour of the London sewers by Lord Peter.

17. *Presumption of Death, A* **(St, Martin's, 2003)** Written by Jill Paton Walsh. Peter is away during World War II, and Harriet takes on the task of solving the murder of a Land Girl. Features "The Wimsey Papers," a series of letters on home front conditions.

Sayers, Valerie

Due East, South Carolina, is the scene of Sayers's series of novels depicting the "New South" with affectionate but unrelenting satire. The family ties and frenzied struggles for sanity of several Due East families are treated with southern wit and forceful writing. Native South Carolinian Sayers graduated from Fordham University in New York, and is head of the creative writing department of Notre Dame University.

1. *Due East* **(Doubleday, 1987)** Jesse Rapple is sceptical of his daughter's claims of "virgin conception" when the 15-year-old becomes pregnant.

2. *How I Got Him Back* **(Doubleday, 1989)** Subtitle: *Under the Cold Moon's Shine.* Concerns the efforts of three Due East women to reclaim their wandering husbands.

3. *Who Do You Love?* **(Doubleday, 1991)** Focuses on the Irish Catholic Rooney family, outcasts in Due East because of their religion and Dolores Rooney's New York origins and outspoken support for integration.

4. *Distance between Us, The* **(Doubleday, 1993)** Starts off in Due East but ventures into strange geographical (New Orleans, Brooklyn, Dublin, Washington, DC) and emotional territories.

5. *Brain Fever* **(Doubleday, 1996)** Fiftyish and schizophrenic Tim Rooney (from number 3) panics when Mary Faith Rapple (from number 1) agrees to marry him, and he makes tracks for New York City with $15,000 in his shoes.

Saylor, Steven

Gordianus the Finder of Saylor's Roma sub Rosa series is a Roman gentleman finder, private investigator, and a protégé of the great orator Cicero, is known as the most honest man in Rome. His honesty and his detecting skills are put to the test in a series of murder mysterious set in the last, strife-ridden years of the Roman republic. Cicero himself receives a rather unflattering portrait. Gordianus bears comparison with Lindsey Davis's (q.v.) Marcus Didio Falco series, set in the next century, but Gordianus doesn't have Falco's wisecracking 20th-century private-eye sensibility. Saylor is also the author of other mysteries, including *A Twist at the End* (Simon & Schuster, 2000; UK title: *Honour the Dead*), a historical mystery about the writer O. Henry. *Roma* (St. Martin's, 2007) is not a Gordianus novel.

1. *Roman Blood* **(St. Martin's, 1991)** In 80 BCE, while fledgling orator Cicero is preparing his defense of accused parricide Sextus Roscius, Gordianus is given the task of finding the real truth of the matter.

2. *Arms of Nemesis* **(St. Martin's, 1992)** The cousin and factotum of Crassus, the wealthiest man in Rome, has been bludgeoned to death, ostensibly by two slaves. Set in 72 BCE during the slave revolt led by Spartacus.

3. *Catalina's Riddle* **(St. Martin's, 1993)** Gordianus becomes embroiled in the bitter political rivalry between his patron Cicero and clear up-and-comer Catilina. Set in 63 BCE.

4. *Venus Throw, The* **(St. Martin's, 1995)** In 56 BCE, Gordianus is visited by Dio, his old philosophy teacher, who fears the fate suffered by fellow Egyptian delegates in Rome.

5. *Murder on the Appian Way, A* **(St. Martin's, 1996)** When crowd-pleaser Clodius is killed in a brawl on the Appian Way, the patrician candidate Milo is accused of murder, Cicero sets out to defend Milo, and Gordianus is sent by Cicero to determine the real facts of the case.

6. *House of the Vestals, The* **(St. Martin's, 1997)** Subtitle: *The Investigations of Gordianus the Fixer.* Short stories featuring Gordianus.

7. *Rubicon* **(St. Martin's, 1998)** Civil war between Pompey and Julius Caesar has erupted. When a favorite of Pompey's is murdered at Gordianus's house, Pompey does some arm-twisting to force Gordianus to find the murderer.

8. *Last Seen in Massilia* **(St. Martin's, 2000)** At the siege of Massilia (now Marseilles) in 49 BCE, during the civil war between Pompey and Caesar, Gordianus finds himself trapped in the plague-ridden city, which he had entered in search of the fate of his son Meto.

9. *Mist of Prophecies, A* **(St. Martin's, 2000)** Set in 48 BCE. Prophetess Cassandra (not to be confused with the lady in Greek mythology) is seized by convulsive attacks of prophecy. When she dies in Gordianus's arms, apparently poisoned, Gordianus vows to find her killer.

10. *Judgement of Caesar, The* **(St. Martin's, 2004)** Alexandria, Egypt. Someone, apparently trying to poison Caesar and Cleopatra, has killed the Royal Taster. Gordianus is sent to find the killer and his possible connection with Cleopatra's brother and rival for the throne Ptolemy.

11. *Gladiator Dies Only Once, A* **(St. Martin's, 2005)** Subtitle: *The Further Investigations of Gordianus the Finder.* Nine more short stories.

Schine, Cathleen

In *Alice in Bed*, Alice Brody, college student from Connecticut, finds herself in a Manhattan teaching hospital after her legs suddenly cease to function. The tale of Alice's hospital stay, replete with medical tests, love affairs, and eventual rehabilitation is told with dry humor and considerable wit. *Alice in Bed* was followed seven years later by *To the Birdhouse*, which shows Alice gainfully employed and about to be married. Alice's mother, Brenda Brody, amateur child psychologist who takes on an unbalanced lover, takes center stage here. Cathleen Schine's subsequent comedies of manners include *Rameau's Niece* (Ticknor, 1993), which was filmed as *The Misadventures of Margaret* (2005); *The Love Letter* (Houghton Mifflin, 1995), which was made into a film in 1999; and, most recently, *The New Yorkers* (Farrar, 2007).

1. *Alice in Bed* **(Knopf, 1983)** College student Alice Brody, felled by a mysterious ailment that has denied her the use of her legs, finds herself a medical conundrum in a Manhattan teaching hospital.

2. *To the Birdhouse* **(Farrar, Straus, 1990)** Alice's postrecuperation life has been a success: she is gainfully employed and married. The same can't be said her eccentric relations: her father, who has run off to Vancouver and started a second family; her brother Willie, who is dating an assortment of women from other countries; and her naively optimistic mother, Brenda Brody, an amateur child psychologist who gets entangled with the unbalanced Louie Scifo.

Scholefield, Alan

I. George Macrae and Leo Silver are partners in the London Police who, despite their disparate personalities, work well together as a crime-solving team. Macrae is an oft-married Scottish veteran who hides his feelings behind a rough exterior. Silver is young, educated, but quite tough enough to handle police work. Alan Scholefield, author of these sparely written, well-nuanced procedurals, is a South African transplanted to England who also writes historical novels and suspense stories under his own name as well as the pseudonym Lee Jordan.

1. *Dirty Weekend* **(St. Martin's, 1991)** Several plotlines intertwine including Macrae and Silver's investigation of the murder of a journalist and talk-show host.
2. *Thief Taker* **(St. Martin's, 1992)** A nasty self-made shipping tycoon dies, leaving a high-priced prostitute as prime suspect, while Silver's girlfriend is harassed by a telephone caller who brags about a double murder he is planning.
3. *Never Die in January* **(St. Martin's, 1993)** A thug claiming to be the business manager for the widow of a bookie is demanding the return of a loan the bookie made to Macrae.
4. *Threats and Menaces* **(St. Martin's, 1994)** A rash of antique thefts, an injured and confused Philippine maid, the lonely daughter of a popular romance writer, and the murder of a rich Arab are all connected.
5. *Don't Be a Nice Girl* **(Macmillan [UK], 1994)** Macrae's girlfriend, ex-prostitute Frenchy, goes back to "work," unbeknownst to him, and stumbles upon the mutilated corpse of Julia Maddox. Not published in the United States.
6. *Night Moves* **(Macmillan [UK], 1996)** Four years ago, on the first case Macrae and Silver worked on together, Malcolm Underdown murdered his ex-girlfriend's fiancé and threatened to kill her. Now he's out of his minimum-security mental hospital and threatening revenge. Not published in the United States.

II. A second mystery series, strong on psychology and suspense, features Dr. Anne Vernon, the only woman in an all-male prison, who tends to the physical and mental well-being of the inmates, and sometimes gets a little too involved when she feels her patient has been wronged.

1. *Burn Out* **(St. Martin's, 1995)** Jason Newman, former international tennis star, is a suicide risk who has been charged with the attempted rape of a school girl and may be connected with the disappearance of two young girls.
2. *Buried Treasure* **(Headline [UK], 1995)** No annotation available. Not published in the United States.
3. *Bad Timing* **(Headline [UK], 1997)** Vernon realizes that a man serving time for assaulting his wife is in fact a battered husband. When he is released she asks him to do some work on her house while she is away. Then her daughter is kidnapped . . . Not published in the United States.

III. An earlier pair of books are historical novels about the Blacks, father and son, set in 19th-century South Africa.

1. *View of Vultures, A* **(Doubleday, 1966)** At the turn of the 19th century, Jamie Black escapes from incarceration in a South African prison colony, is adopted by a Dutch family, marries, and raises a family.
2. *Great Elephant* **(Morrow, 1968)** Follows the adventures of Jamie's son Robie, as the family flees Capetown for Zulu territory. "Great Elephant" is Chaka, founder of the Zulu empire in southern Africa.

Schutz, Benjamin M(errill)

Leo Haggerty is a private operating out of Washington, DC. Leo is a typical hard-boiled dick with a heart of gold, and he gets into some very violent, sexy, and kinky adventures on some very mean streets. Benjamin M. Schutz, a clinical (forensic) psychologist in the Washington, DC, area, ended a 10-year mystery-publishing silence with the nonseries *The Mongol Reply* (Five Star, 2004).

1. *Embrace the Wolf* **(Bluejay, 1985)** Leo is hired to find a man who has disappeared on a search for the psychopath who abducted his daughters five years earlier.
2. *All the Old Bargains* **(Bluejay, 1985)** Haggerty takes on the case of runaway teenager Miranda Benson, who has undergone an unfortunate personality change.
3. *Tax in Blood, A* **(Tor, 1987)** The widow of a South American diplomat hires Leo to prove that her late husband didn't commit suicide, so that she can collect his insurance.
4. *Things We Do for Love, The* **(Scribner, 1989)** Haggerty takes on the job of protecting rock singer Jane Doe (Savannah Jane Summers), who has received threatening letters.
5. *Fistful of Empty, A* **(Viking, 1991)** Samantha, Leo's girlfriend, gets raped while Leo is working late to help out a bounty hunter, and loses the child she is carrying.
6. *Mexico Is Forever* **(St. Martin's, 1994)** Haggerty investigates porn queen Sarabeth Timmons, who may be the heir to a sizable sum of money.

Scoppettone, Sandra

I. Lauren Laurano, former FBI agent, is a short, Italian, fortyish, quick-witted, feisty, feminist, chocoholic Manhattan private eye who has claims to being the first lesbian private eye in "mainstream" fiction. Lauren has a relationship with psychotherapist Kip Adams going back more than a decade and shares a Greenwich Village brownstone with her, but sometimes has trouble being a monogamist. Scoppettone, who has an intimate knowledge of the streets and shops of Manhattan's West Village, also writes young adult novels, picture books, plays, television and film scripts, and suspense novels under the pseudonym of Jack Early. Scoppettone says that *Everything You Have Is Mine* is the "first book I've ever written directly about myself."

1. *Everything You Have Is Mine* **(Little, Brown, 1991)** A complicated case that begins with the rape and subsequent murder of a young woman who runs a computer dating service.
2. *I'll Be Leaving You Always* **(Little, Brown, 1993)** When jewelry store owner Megan Harbruth, Lauren's childhood confidante and close friend, is shot, Lauren uncovers some disturbing secrets.
3. *My Sweet Untraceable You* **(Little, Brown, 1994)** Laurano is hired by ex-druggie "Boston Blackie" to investigate the death of his mother 38 years earlier.
4. *Let's Face the Music and Die* **(Little, Brown, 1996)** Lauren's friend Elissa is the prime suspect in the stabbing death of her widowed aunt. Lauren's investigation is complicated by her relationship with Kip and the recrudescence of Charlie West, who raped her and left her for dead years ago.
5. *Gonna Take a Homicidal Journey* **(Little, Brown, 1998)** Lauren and Kip's fence-mending vacation in the Long Island vacation town

of Seaview is interrupted by a wave of crime in the normally quiet town, including several murders.

II. In a series set in 1943 Manhattan, Faye Quick, secretary in a detective agency, takes up gumshoe work when her boss is drafted. Faye is tough and likable, and New York City in 1943 is lovingly re-created.

1. *This Dame for Hire* (**Ballantine, 2005**) Manhattan, 1943. Faye Turner, who has taken over her drafted employer's detective agency, looks for the killer of a young woman whose body she found on a snowy street.
2. *Too Darn Hot* (**Ballantine, 2006**) Wanamaker's salesgirl Claire Turner gets Faye to agree to look for her missing GI boyfriend, Charlie Ladd.

Scott, Justin

Wall Street trader Benjamin Abbott returns to his hometown of Newbury, Connecticut, and his family's real-estate business after serving a stint in prison. Ben becomes a private investigator on the side in this series in which developers are the villains, the victims, or both. Numbers 1 through 3 were originally published in the United Kingdom in the 1990s before being reissued in revised form by Poisoned Pen Press in the United States in 2003.

1. *HardScape* (**Poisoned Pen, 2003**) Back in his hometown of Newbury, Connecticut, after stints as a Wall Street trader and a jailbird, Benjamin Abbott finds himself hired by a New York City private eye to spy on the bedroom activities in the "castle" next door. Originally published in the United Kingdom in 1994.
2. *StoneDust* (**Poisoned Pen, 2003**) Ben takes up the case of old pal Reg Hopkins after Reg's body turns up after a notorious "sleepover" at the Fisks'. Originally published in the United Kingdom in 1995.
3. *FrostLine* (**Poisoned Pen, 2003**) Ben gets caught in a land battle between Vietnam veteran Richard Butler and former diplomat Harry King. Then the body of Dicky Butler, Richard's troubled son, turns up in pieces after an explosion at the dam that is enclosing the lake that King is creating. Originally published in the United Kingdom in 1997.
4. *McMansion* (**Poisoned Pen, 2007**) Young environmental activist Jeff Kimball is accused of running over sleazy developer Billy Tiller with a bulldozer.
5. *Mausoleum* (**Poisoned Pen, 2007**) After recorded classical music blasts from the large, ostentatious mausoleum nicknamed the "McTomb," the tomb is opened and its murdered owner, real-estate developer Brian Grose, is found inside.

Scott, Paul

The Raj Quartet is a sweeping epic covering the last turbulent years of British rule in India, from 1942 to 1948. Scott was a superb storyteller, well able to convey the ambiguous human relationships of his large cast of British and Indian characters. The violence of the times seems to emerge all the more effectively for Scott's restrained treatment of desperate events and situations in which various characters face their doom with varying degrees of stoicism. The four volumes do not carry the story forward sequentially but rather circle certain events and characters from various points of view. *Staying On* isn't part of the Raj Quartet but acts as a coda to it. The omnibus volume *The Raj Quartet* (Morrow, 1976) contains numbers 1 through 4. The

Raj Quartet was a very successful miniseries on PBS's *Masterpiece Theatre*.

1. *Jewel in the Crown, The* (**Morrow, 1966**) The central event in this volume, which gives a vivid picture of India before independence, concerns the rape of a young Englishwoman in the Bibighar Gardens in August 1942.
2. *Day of the Scorpion, The* (**Morrow, 1968**) Beginning with the arrest of ex–chief minister Kasim on August 9, 1942, this account shows India engulfed in violence following the Congress party's call for nationwide insurrection. The novel also includes the stories of Sarah and Susan Layton.
3. *Towers of Silence, The* (**Morrow, 1971**) From the Rose Cottage in Pankot, where Mabel Layton (stepmother of Susan and Sarah's father) lives with retired mission teacher Barbie Batchelor, the upheavals tearing through India seem remote, yet they eventually have their effect.
4. *Division of the Spoils, A* (**Morrow, 1975**) This concluding volume analyzes the transfer of power and the moral corruption during the pivotal years 1945–1947, just prior to independence. The story focuses on army intelligence officer Guy Perron and Susan Layton's husband, the cruel police colonel Ronald Merrick.
5. *Staying On* (**Morrow, 1977**) This graceful coda to the Raj Quartet shows Colonel Mrs. "Tusker" Smalley, minor characters in the Quartet, in 1972 and the life they have chosen by staying on in their Pankot home after Indian independence.

Scottoline, Lisa

Mary DiNunzio, Judy Carrier, and Benedetta "Bennie" Rosato are three smart, feisty female lawyers who band together as Rosato & Associates in Philadelphia and take on a series of engrossing cases in this courtroom series. Mary and Judy appear as characters in number 1. Bennie features in number 2. Rosato & Associates is formed in number 3. Former Philadelphia lawyer Lisa Scottoline has written 14 courtroom dramas starring Italian American heroines. *Final Appeal* (HarperCollins, 1994), *Running from the Law* (HarperCollins, 1995), *Devil's Corner* (HarperCollins, 2005), *Dirty Blonde* (HarperCollins, 2006), and *Daddy's Girl* (HarperCollins, 2007) feature Italian American female lawyers in Philadelphia, but they are not part of the Rosato & Associates series. *The First Two Novels* (HarperCollins, 2004) contains number 1 and *Final Appeal*.

1. *Everywhere That Mary Went* (**HarperCollins, 1993**) Fledgling lawyer Mary DiNunzio, who aspires to be a partner in her Philadelphia law firm, has been getting threatening phone calls.
2. *Legal Tender* (**HarperCollins, 1996**) After Bennie Rosato's former lover and current law partner, Mark Biscardi, announces that he is ousting her from the firm, Mark is murdered, and Bennie is the prime suspect.
3. *Rough Justice* (**HarperCollins, 1998**) Millionaire businessman Elliot Steere reveals to his lawyer, Marta Richter, that his self-defense claim in the murder of a homeless man is false.
4. *Mistaken Identity* (**HarperCollins, 1998**) Is the claim of accused murderess Alice Connolly to be the long-lost twin sister of Bennie Rosato really true?
5. *Moment of Truth* (**HarperCollins, 1999**) Jack Newlin, who thinks that his wife has been murdered by his daughter, tries to get himself framed and hires inexperienced lawyer Mary DiNunzio of Rosato & Associates to hammer the final nail in his coffin.
6. *Vendetta Defense, The* (**HarperCollins, 2001**) Judy Carrier takes on the Mob when she defends someone accused of murdering the head of a family of crooks.

7. *Courting Trouble* **(HarperCollins, 2002)** Anne Murphy, a dazzling redhead with a secret past, augments the firm of Rosato & Associates.

8. *Dead Ringer* **(HarperCollins, 2003)** Bennie Rosato fights to save financially troubled Rosato & Associates, tries to solve the murder of a valuable client, and battle Alice Connolly, her evil twin (see number 4).

9. *Killer Smile* **(HarperCollins, 2004)** Mary DiNunzio works for the heirs of Amadeo Brandolini, an Italian American who was interned as an enemy alien during World War II, and supposedly committed suicide in his internment camp.

10. *Lady Killer* **(Harper, 2008)** Trish Gambone, Mary DiNunzio's high school nemesis, begs Mary to help her escape from her abusive and possibly Mafia-connected boyfriend, Bobby Mancuso.

Seals, David

Powwow Highway was self-published by Seals, publisher of Sky and Sage Books of Rapid City, South Dakota, but achieved some popularity as a novel and was made into a cult film (1989), which Seals dislikes. The story of the wandering Cheyenne trio, Buddy Red Bird, his sister Bonnie, and her lover, Philibert Bono, has been followed by a sequel in which Seals continues their trek and does some editorializing about himself, his books, and the current state of Native Americans. Seals, who claims mixed Welsh and Huron ancestry (among other ethnic strains), also writes novels and poetry under the name of Davydd ap Saille. *Thunder Nation*, a four-volume saga, was published by Sky and Sage (1990). *Powwow Highway* was reprinted for the mass market by Plume in 1990.

1. *Powwow Highway* **(Sky & Sage, 1979)** Philibert Bono and Buddy Red Bird undertake an odyssey in an old Buick from Montana to New Mexico to bust Buddy's sister Bonnie out of jail.

2. *Sweet Medicine* **(Orion, 1992)** Buddy, Bonnie, and Philibert begin a winter trek from Santa Fe to the Black Hills, picking up other Native Americans as they go, and declaring their group a new nation.

Sedley, Kate

PSEUDONYM OF Brenda Clarke

Roger the Chapman is a strapping itinerant peddler in his twenties. The former monastic student travels from his home base of Bristol through the England of the 1470s, right in the middle of the War of the Roses. Roger has a flair for detection that comes to the attention of Edward IV's brother Richard, Duke of Gloucester (later Richard III of ill-fame but a relatively benign presence here). These are well-done mysteries and pictures of late medieval life that will interest historical mystery readers. Brenda Clarke also writes historical romances under her own name and the pseudonym Brenda Honeyman. *For King and Country* (Severn, 2006) is set in the 17th century.

1. *Death and the Chapman* **(St. Martin's, 1992)** A distraught Bristol alderman enlists Roger's aid in finding his missing son.

2. *Plymouth Cloak, The* **(St. Martin's, 1993)** Richard of Gloucester chooses Roger to guard Philip Underdown, who is carrying a message to Francis, Duke of Brittany, on behalf of King Edward IV.

3. *Weaver's Tale, The* **(St. Martin's, 1994)** As repayment for being nursed back to health by good-hearted widow Margaret Walker, Roger undertakes the investigation of the inexplicable disappearance and death of her elderly father. UK title: *The Hanged Man*.

4. *Holy Innocents, The* **(St. Martin's, 1995)** After his wife's untimely death, Roger entrusts their infant daughter to his mother-in-law and takes the road again only to run into suspected witchcraft and mysterious deaths.

5. *Eve of St. Hyacinth, The* **(St. Martin's, 1996)** It's 1475 and King Edward is about to invade France. However, Roger learns of a plot to kill Richard of Gloucester.

6. *Wicked Winter, The* **(St. Martin's, 1999)** Roger makes a winter sales journey to Cedarwell Manor only to find that his customer Lady Cedarwell has died suspiciously. Originally published in the United Kingdom in 1996.

7. *Brothers of Glastonbury, The* **(St. Martin's, 2001)** The bridegroom of a bride Roger was accompanying has vanished along with his brother. There may be a link to the discovery of an ancient manuscript that could lead to the Holy Grail. Originally published in the United Kingdom in 1997.

8. *Weaver's Inheritance, The* **(St. Martin's, 2001)** The long-lost son of a wealthy weaver, thought to be murdered six years before, turns up again, to the weaver's joy. However, Alison Burnett, the weaver's daughter refuses to believe that this stranger is her brother. Originally published in the United Kingdom in 1998.

9. *Saint John's Fern, The* **(St. Martin's, 2002)** Although he has remarried and fathered a second child, Roger succumbs to restlessness and sets off for Plymouth, where he learns of the murder of rich, elderly, reclusive Oliver Clapstick. Originally published in the United Kingdom in 1999.

10. *Goldsmith's Daughter, The* **(Severn, 2001)** Richard of Gloucester sets Roger to prove the innocence of Isolda Bonifant, cousin of Edward's chief mistress, when Isolda is accused of poisoning her husband.

11. *Lammas Feast, The* **(Severn, 2002)** Shady Bristol baker Jasper Fairbrother is stabbed to death after an argument with a mysterious Breton.

12. *Nine Men Dancing* **(Severn, 2003)** When Roger, on his way home to Bristol in the winter of 1478, stops at a small village, he is persuaded to investigate the disappearance of local belle Eris Lilywhite.

13. *Midsummer Rose, The* **(Severn, 2004)** The usually sceptical Roger decides that something strange is going on when he is attacked in the Bristol house where a woman murdered her violent husband 30 years earlier.

14. *Burgundian's Tale, The* **(Severn, 2005)** In 1480 Roger is planning a peddling excursion away from his troubled family in Bristol when he is summoned to London by the Duke of Gloucester's spymaster to look into the murder of Fulk Quantrell, son of a lady-in-waiting to the duke's sister.

15. *Prodigal Son, The* **(Severn, 2006)** Roger learns that he has a half brother who has just been accused of a murder committed six years before.

16. *Three Kings of Cologne, The* **(Severn, 2007)** John Foster, the mayor of Bristol, suspects foul play when the 20-year-old corpse of Isabella Linkinhorne is unearthed during the land clearing of a new chapel.

Segal, Erich

Love Story zoomed up the best-seller lists with amazing speed, and the movie starring Ryan O'Neal and Ali McGraw gave it indisputable status as a modern classic. The rich-boy-meets-poor-girl story against a Harvard-Radcliffe setting is capped with a tragic ending, but the witty dialogue, believable characters, and background leaven the schmaltz. Although Segal wrote a sequel to *Love Story*, which was also made into a film, and several other novels, he has never approached its success again. In recent years he has been concentrating on his academic career, and has recently published *The Death of Comedy* (Harvard, 2001), a study of classical drama he had been working on for 20 years.

1. *Love Story* **(Harper, 1970)** Oliver Barrett IV, a rich and popular Harvard senior, falls for scholarship student Jenny Cavilleri.
2. *Oliver's Story* **(Harper, 1977)** Two years after Jenny's death, Oliver, now a lawyer in New York, takes an interest in enigmatic Marcie Nash and finally begins to shake off the guilt and grief that haunt him.

Seranella, Barbara

Miranda "Munch" Mancini, who has seen a lot of hard times, including alcoholism, drug addiction, and prostitution, is trying to turn her life around by becoming an auto mechanic and attending a drug-rehab program. Munch's efforts at living normally are sidetracked often by the appearance of former acquaintances from her old life, but she perseveres, with the help of LAPD Detective Mace St. John, boyfriend-detective Rico Chacon, and adopted eight-year-old daughter Asia. Los Angeles in the 1970s and 1980s is the scene of these gritty mysteries. The late Barbara Seranella's (d. 2007) life had much in common with Munch Mancini's: she was a runaway at 14 and worked as an auto mechanic before she quit to become a full-time writer. Her last novel, *Deadman's Switch* (St. Martin's, 2007), featured a new heroine, Charlotte Lyon.

1. *No Human Involved* **(St. Martin's, 1997)** Miranda "Munch" Mancini, who wants to "leave the life," kick heroin, and sober up, talks herself into a mechanic's job at Happy Jack's Auto Repair. Meanwhile LAPD Detective Mace St. John wants to question Munch about murdered pimp Flower George.
2. *No Offense Intended* **(HarperCollins, 1999)** 1977. Munch Mancini is trying to live the regular life, working as a car mechanic, visiting her parole officer, and attending a drug rehab program. Then an acquaintance from the old days, Sleaze John, asks Munch to pick up his baby girl and drop her off at his sister's in Venice Beach.
3. *Unwanted Company* **(HarperCollins, 2000)** 1984. Munch Mancini is supplementing her auto mechanic income by running her own one-car limo service. Then she accepts unscrupulous federal agent Raleigh Ward, sleazy Romanian diplomat Victor Draicu, and two female friends as weeklong customers.
4. *Unfinished Business* **(Scribner, 2002)** Mace St. John and Munch Mancini join forces again when one of Munch's favorite customers, Diane Bergman, is found murdered, perhaps one of a series of rape victims.
5. *No Man Standing* **(Scribner, 2002)** The mother and stepfather of Munch's old buddy, jailbird Ellen Summers (who appeared in number 3), are murdered, and Ellen reappears to complicate Munch's rehabilitated life as auto mechanic, owner-operator of a limousine service, and single mother to an adopted eight-year-old daughter, Asia.
6. *Unpaid Dues* **(Scribner, 2003)** When homicide detective Mace St. John (see numbers 1 and 4) finds prints on a murdered woman, he finds Munch's photo in the arrest report, because 10 years earlier Munch used the dead woman's name in beating a DUI charge.
7. *Unwilling Accomplice* **(Scribner, 2004)** Lisa, sister of the late father of Munch's adopted daughter, Asia, and her two daughters have left a witness-protection program to see Asia.
8. *Unacceptable Death, An* **(St. Martin's, 2005)** Munch's fiancé, detective Rico Chacon, is shot dead by his fellow cops in a drug bust gone wrong. The Satan's Pride Motorcycle Gang has put a bounty on Munch's head because of her past efforts in taking them down.

Settle, Mary Lee

Mary Lee Settle attracted some notice when her *Blood Tie* (Houghton Mifflin, 1977) won the National Book Award for Fiction, but her Beulah quintet is likely to be her best claim to literary fame. The Beulah series begins in 17th-century England and traces the founding and development of the town of Beulah, Virginia (now West Virginia), through its frontier colonial days, Civil War strife, coal boom and labor confrontations, and finally, recent economic decline. While the Lacey family provides a focus throughout the series, Settle works many characters and viewpoints into her detailed tapestries. The Beulah quintet was reprinted with new introductions in 1996 by the University of South Carolina Press. Settle (d. 2005) remained active into her eighties, publishing the autobiographical *Addie: A Memoir* (South Carolina, 1998) and, posthumously, *Learning to Fly: A Writer's Memoir* (Norton, 2007).

1. *Prisons* **(Putnam, 1973)** Set in Cromwellian England, this story depicts the youth, army service, and dramatic rebellion of Jonathan Church, ancestor of the West Virginia settles whose stories are chronicled in later volumes. UK title: *The Long Road to Paradise*.
2. *O Beulah Land* **(Viking, 1956)** After the Battle of Little Meadows in 1775, young Jonathan Lacey sets with a group of settlers for the unclaimed land of Virginia's western frontier.
3. *Know Nothing* **(Viking, 1960)** The unhappy romance of Johnny Catlett and his orphaned cousin Melinda is set on a Beulah plantation just prior to the Civil War. Variant title: *Pride's Progress*.
4. *Scapegoat, The* **(Random House, 1980)** Young Lily Lacey, the Vassar-educated daughter of a mine owner, plays a fateful role in the 1912 strike that has paralyzed the coal mines of Beulah valley. An interesting portrait of radical leader Mother Jones is included.
5. *Killing Ground, The* **(Farrar, 1982)** This appears to be a reworking of an earlier novel, *Fight Night on a Sweet Saturday* (Viking, 1964). The story follows writer Hannah McKarkle as she returns to her West Virginia home and memories of the troubled and violent life of her wastrel brother Johnny. Two decades, 1960–1980, are covered.

Shankman, Sarah

Samantha "Sam" Adams is an investigative reporter and sometime sleuth. The smart-mouthed Sam works out of Atlanta, but her investigations take her to New Orleans, Atlantic City, and other hot spots. Sam has a series of unsatisfactory boyfriends and runs into a lot of strange characters in these entertaining mysteries. Numbers 1 and 2 were published under the pseudonym of Alice Storey. *Impersonal Attractions* (St. Martin's, 1985), an earlier novel, has as one of its two main characters a San Francisco crime reporter named Samantha, but is not regarded as part of the series. A possible future series character is country singer Shelby Kay Tate, who appears in one novel: *I Miss My Man But My Aim Is Getting Better* (Pocket, 1996).

1. *First Kill All the Lawyers* **(Pocket, 1988)** Sam comes home to Atlanta from the West Coast and runs into the suspicious death of a distinguished attorney.
2. *Then Hang All the Liars* **(Pocket, 1989)** The death of Mr. Randolph Percy, elderly gentleman con artist who preyed on old ladies, may uncover a 50-year-old secret.

3. *Now Let's Talk of Graves* (Pocket, 1990) Adams is in New Orleans attending a high-society Mardi Gras ball with her friend Kitty when Kitty's brother dies in an apparent hit-and-run accident.

4. *She Walks in Beauty* (Pocket, 1991) Sam plays sleuth again when she reluctantly covers the Miss America Pageant in Atlantic City and one of the judges disappears.

5. *King Is Dead, The* (Pocket, 1992) Adams attends the Third International Barbecue Cookoff in Tupelo, Mississippi with Harry Zack her restaurateur boyfriend and runs into some strange happenings in Elvis's birthplace.

6. *He Was Her Man* (Pocket, 1993) Fleeing from her unfaithful lover, Sam joins the guests at Jinx Watson's engagement celebration in Hot Springs, Arkansas, and, of course, someone disappears.

7. *Digging Up Mamma* (Pocket, 1998) Sam flies to Santa Fe and has a brief meeting with her mother that leaves her feeling that the older lady is afraid of something. Hours later, her mother is dead, an apparent suicide.

Shannon, Dell

PSEUDONYM OF Elizabeth Linington

Dell Shannon was the pseudonym Linington used for her Luis Mendoza books, the longest running and most popular of her police procedural series. This prolific California author earned the title "Queen of the Procedurals"; she also wrote them under the pseudonym Lesley Egan (q.v.) and her own name (q.v.). Each novel is complete in itself, but the character development and continuing relationships from book to book add an extra interest. Lieutenant Luis Mendoza is sophisticated, well read, and independently wealthy. His Mexican heritage serves him well in the Los Angeles Police Department. Since every novel concerns multiple cases under investigation, individual annotations are not supplied. Dell Shannon wrote several non-Mendoza titles.

1. *Case Pending* (Harper, 1960)
2. *Ace of Spades, The* (Harper, 1961)
3. *Extra Kill* (Morrow, 1962)
4. *Knave of Hearts* (Morrow, 1962)
5. *Death of a Busybody* (Morrow, 1963)
6. *Double Bluff* (Morrow, 1963)
7. *Mark of Murder* (Morrow, 1964)
8. *Root of All Evil* (Morrow, 1964)
9. *Death-Bringers, The* (Morrow, 1964)
10. *Death by Inches* (Morrow, 1965)
11. *Coffin Corner* (Morrow, 1966)
12. *With a Vengeance* (Morrow, 1966)
13. *Chance to Kill* (Morrow, 1967)
14. *Rain with Violence* (Morrow, 1967)
15. *Kill with Kindness* (Morrow, 1968)
16. *Schooled to Kill* (Morrow, 1969)
17. *Crime on Their Hands* (Morrow, 1969)
18. *Unexpected Death* (Morrow, 1970)
19. *Whim to Kill* (Morrow, 1971)
20. *Ringer, The* (Morrow, 1971)
21. *Murder with Love* (Morrow, 1972)
22. *With Intent to Kill* (Morrow, 1972)
23. *No Holiday for Crime* (Morrow, 1973)
24. *Spring of Violence* (Morrow, 1973)
25. *Crime File* (Morrow, 1974)
26. *Deuces Wild* (Morrow, 1975)
27. *Streets of Death* (Morrow, 1976)
28. *Appearances of Death* (Morrow, 1977)
29. *Cold Trail* (Morrow, 1978)
30. *Felony at Random* (Morrow, 1979)

31. *Felony File* (Morrow, 1980)
32. *Murder Most Strange* (Morrow, 1981)
33. *Motive on Record, The* (Morrow, 1982)
34. *Exploits of Death* (Morrow, 1983)
35. *Destiny of Death* (Morrow, 1984)
36. *Chaos of Crime* (Morrow, 1985)
37. *Blood Count* (Morrow, 1986)
38. *Murder by the Tale* (Morrow, 1987) A collection of short stories.

Shannon, John

Los Angeles–based Jack Liffey—who, in his fifties and a recovering alcoholic and drug abuser, has lost his wife and daughter to divorce and his aerospace job to downsizing—becomes a private investigator and seeker of lost children. The Marlowe-like (Raymond Chandler, q.v.) Liffey is a basically decent sort who never loses his steadfastness and wry sense of humor as he prowls the mean streets of LA in these novels with antiracist themes by unabashed leftist John Shannon.

1. *Concrete River, The* (John Brown, 1996) Jack Liffey, having lost his job and his family, becomes a private investigator specializing in finding lost children. Jack is asked by the mother of a recently murdered Latina activist to find the killer(s) of her daughter.

2. *Cracked Earth, The* (Berkley, 1999) Former actress Lori Bright pays Jack to find her missing daughter.

3. *Poison Sky, The* (Berkley, 2000) A runaway teen has hooked up with a sinister gang of spiritualists.

4. *Orange Curtain, The* (Carroll & Graf, 2001) Jack searches for missing Vietnamese American college student, Phuong Minh, in the Vietnamese community of Orange County and LA's Little Saigon.

5. *Streets on Fire* (Carroll & Graf, 2002) Young black student Amilcar Davis has disappeared with his white girlfriend after a nasty incident with a racist gang.

6. *City of Strangers* (Carroll & Graf, 2003) Dicky Auslander, old college buddy of Jack Liffey, and now a psychologist, won't hire Jack to look for his missing child unless Jack agrees to undergo therapy with him.

7. *Terminal Island* (Carroll & Graf, 2004) The internment of Japanese Americans in World War II is in the background of this case involving a missing child, a wrecked boat, and a destroyed manuscript.

8. *Dangerous Games* (Carroll & Graf, 2005) Jack figures that the bullet was meant for him when his daughter Maeve is shot in a drive-by shooting by someone in a car full of teenagers.

9. *Dark Streets* (Pegasus, 2006) Young female film student and activist, Soon-Lin Kim, goes missing in Koreatown while shooting a film about Korean "comfort women" in World War II.

10. *Devils of Bakersfield, The* (Pegasus, 2008) Jack's pregnant teenage daughter Maeve spends a short time in the Bakersfield (California) jail after being falsely arrested for drug possession, meets rebellious teen Toxie, and later returns to Bakersfield and a confrontation with Dennis Kohlmeyer, the paranoid pastor of the Olive Grove Evangelical Church. Readers get to vote on Shannon's website for one of two possible endings.

Sharp, Margery

This English author was the creator of a series of children's books starring the lovable mouse Miss Bianca, including *The Rescuers*, which was made into an animated feature film by Disney Productions. Sharp's adult books are deft and ironic sketches of slightly odd characters caught amusingly in predicaments of their own making. Readers who meet Martha, the fat and inarticulate but determined budding artist introduced in *The Eye of Love* (and who takes center stage in *Martha in Paris*), won't rest easy until they see how her story unfolds in *Martha, Eric and George*. Martha's single-minded pursuit of her artistic career results in some deliciously wicked role reversals.

1. *Eye of Love, The* (Little, Brown, 1957) Tells the story of the love affair of Martha's foster parents, the rather seedy Harry Gibson, and the ethereally thin Delores Diver. Martha is introduced as a chunky schoolgirl who can't stop drawing.
2. *Martha in Paris* (Little, Brown, 1962) At 18 an unprepossessing Martha is sent to Paris by her wealthy patron, and her artistic and sensual awakening has unexpected consequences.
3. *Martha, Eric and George* (Little, Brown, 1964) Now 28 and on the verge of international acclaim, Martha returns to Paris for her first successful show and comes to term with Eric and little George.

Sharpe, Tom (Thomas Ridley)

I. English writer Tom Sharpe writes bawdy, hilarious, vicious satires. Academics, the police, the military, the aristocracy, and political extremists right and left are all targets for his vitriolic pen. No single person or event in a Sharpe novel is impossible in real life, but his madcap plots are carried along by their own maniacal logic to a frenzied finish that may leave corpses and burned-out buildings in their wake. "Of the nasty Brits, probably the best," according to one American critic, Sharpe is very popular in the United Kingdom but not as popular as he should be in the United States.

Henry Wilt, one of Sharpe's relatively few likable characters and his most popular, teachers "liberal studies" to butcher's assistants, plasterer's helpers, and the other semiliterate students who attend the Fenland College of Arts and Technology, presumably based on the Cambridgeshire College of Arts and Technology where Sharpe taught before becoming a full-time writer. Wilt is a decent, unpretentious chap and a competent teacher. His buxom wife, Eva, is an amiably bovine woman who is given to enthusiasms, such as compost heaping, which sorely try Wilt's nerves. Wilt is also beset by precocious quadruplet daughters (numbers 2–3), incompetent superiors, paranoid security officers, terrorists, sexually voracious women, and police officials who are convinced that he is a diabolically clever criminal. Fortunately, Wilt always manages to triumph over adversity in the end. After a near 20-year hiatus, the fourth Wilt volume was published in the United Kingdom in September 2004. *Wilt in Triplicate* (Secker [UK], 1996) is an omnibus containing numbers 1, 2, and 3. *The Misadventures of Mr. Wilt* (1989) is an English film based on number 1.

1. *Wilt* (Vintage, 1984) Wilt acts out his wife-killing fantasies on a life-size plastic doll liberated from a kinky American couple, only to be arrested for murder when Eva disappears. Originally published in the United Kingdom in 1976.
2. *Wilt Alternative, The* (St. Martin's, 1980) Now on relatively good terms with Eva but saddled with quadruplets, Wilt has an unsettling encounter with a rosebush, and his house and children are held hostage by terrorists.
3. *Wilt on High* (Random House, 1985) Eva slips Wilt an aphrodisiac in his beer, producing alarming physical results, while an overzealous narcotics policeman bugs Wilt's car after one of his students ODs in the school basement.
4. *Wilt in Nowhere* (Hutchinson [UK], 2004) Wilt is back! Among the targets this time are rural life, both English and American, aristocratic perverts, politicians, and Britain's medical facilities. The quads play a role.

II. Sharpe spent 10 years in South Africa (1951–1961) before he was deported for a "seditious" play, and his first two novels are set there. Van Heerden, the Anglophile police chief of Piemburg (based on Pietermaritzburg, where Sharpe lived) is one of the protagonists of a pair of novels that satirize the racism, paranoia, and incompetence of South African officialdom. The detective novels of James McClure (q.v.), who lived in Pietermaritzburg during the same period as Sharpe, are also in a fictionalized version of that South African town and make an interesting contrast with Sharpe's novels.

1. *Riotous Assembly* (Atlantic Monthly, 1987) A member of the English Hazelstone family kills the transvestite Zulu cook with whom she has been having an affair. Van Heerden's efforts to cover up the crime lead to disastrous results. Originally published in the United Kingdom in 1971.
2. *Indecent Exposure* (Atlantic Monthly, 1987) Lieutenant Verkramp's aversion-therapy program, designed to discourage his men from having sexual relations with black women, produces 200 neurotically homosexual constables. Originally published in the United Kingdom in 1973.

III. Porterhouse College in Cambridge (based on Sharpe's alma mater, Pembroke) is the scene of a pair of novels in which British academia takes some hard hits. Porterhouse is noted for its gastronomic excellence, academic mediocrity, arrogant fellows, and the social cachet it confers on the athletic sons of county gentlemen. Published 20 years apart, both novels focus on the academic politics that surround the appointment and maintenance of the Master of Porterhouse. *Porterhouse Blue* was produced as a miniseries on ITV and shown on PBS (1987). *The Great Pursuit* (Harper, 1984) also lampoons certain aspects of Cambridge University.

1. *Porterhouse Blue* (Atlantic Monthly, 1989) Ex–cabinet minister Sir Godber Evans, abetted by his wife, Lady Mary, is determined to shake up Porterhouse College. The established order that he challenges, including the dean, the senior tutor, the bursar, and especially the head porter, Skullion, are determined to thwart Sir Godber.
2. *Grandchester United* (Secker [UK], 1995) Skullion, now the master, is partially disabled by a stroke, and questions of succession are awakened again. Complications include the perilous financial condition of Porterhouse, the attempts of American media mogul to make a documentary on-site, and Lady Mary, who is convinced that her late husband was murdered.

Shatner, William

I. William Shatner is identified with the role of Captain Kirk on the *Star Trek* television series (see *Star Trek Memories*, Harper, 1993), although he has played many other roles (e.g., "T. J. Hooker") and is still active in many entertainment areas. Since the late 1980s, Shatner has been writing SF novels, most of them space operas. The Tek series of hard-boiled or technothriller SF novels features Jake Cardigan, former cop turned private investigator in the 22nd century, who is matched up against killer robots, diabolic computers, and other nasty futuristic evils in the fight to control Tek, an addictive mind-controlling substance. Jake and his easygoing sidekick, Sid Gomez, represent the Forces of Good against the evil, almost omnipotent TekLords in a series of adventures with cardboardy characters and logical lapses, but with plenty of action. Although there are adult "Tekkies" as well as "Trekkies," the primary appeal of this series is for young adults. The Tek novels have spawned a comic-book series, trading cards, a cable TV series, and at least four TV movies.

1. *TekWar* **(Putnam, 1989)** Jack Cardigan fights the computerized drug barons in 22nd-century Los Angeles who are distributing the insidious Tek drug.
2. *TekLords* **(Putnam, 1991)** The TekLords are spreading an unknown virus that threatens the entire world while Jake battles programmed assassins and intransigent authorities.
3. *TekLab* **(Putnam, 1991)** A serial killer who calls himself the "Unknown Soldier" is stalking and executing people whom he perceives to be war criminals.
4. *Tek Vengeance* **(Putnam, 1993)** While Jake is on his way to Brazil, his girl Beth Kittridge is assassinated in Berlin by a TekLord conspiracy.
5. *Tek Secret* **(Putnam, 1993)** Cardigan and Gomez are investigating the disappearance of Alicia Bower, heiress to the Mechanix International Robotics fortune.
6. *Tek Power* **(Putnam, 1994)** Jake and Sid bump up against a plan to replace the president of the United States with an android while he is in rehab kicking his Tek addiction.
7. *Tek Money* **(Putnam, 1995)** Somebody is obtaining illegal weapons from a California research firm and disposing of people who know too much.
8. *Tek Kill* **(Putnam, 1996)** Walt Bascom, Jake's boss, is accused of murder in a frame-up involving a faked security camera tape.
9. *Tek Net* **(Ace, 1997)** Rumors of a simple nonchip alternative to Tek prove very worrisome to the TekLords.

II. A pair of novels features another macho guy, Benton Hawkes, who is a diplomat sent to Mars in the late 21st century. Benton is troubled by self-doubts occasionally, but basically he's a rock-'em, sock-'em type.

1. *Man O' War* **(Ace, 1996)** The human colonists on Mars are restive because of their near-slavelike status. Benton Hawkes is sent to Mars to defuse the situation because a Mars rebellion would threaten Earth's food supplies.
3. *Law of War, The* **(Ace, 1998)** Having joined the Mars freedom fighters, Hawkes is back on Earth trying to negotiate a peace settlement between Mars and their home planet.

III. Quest for Tomorrow, Shatner's latest series, is another space-opera set in the 22nd century. Its young hero, Jim Endicott, is another super-type guy, this time with DNA carrying information about a gigantic organic computer that is intended to help humanity against a bunch of superior aliens. Jim finds himself pitted not only against the aliens but against his own biological father, who is head of Delta, a mysterious organization on Earth that is into mind control. Plenty of action and a little sex and some implausible plot turns.

1. *Delta Search* **(HarperPrism, 1997)** Teenager Jim Endicott, who carries some supercharged genes, finds himself a fugitive in the 22nd century as he chases, and is chased by, Delta, his biological father, who has invented a group-mind technique that is causing mass psychosis on Earth.
2. *In Alien Hands* **(HarperPrism, 1997)** Lots of action as Jim acquires more powers, becomes a mercenary soldier and a space pilot, befriends the wolflike Albans, and fights the reptilian Hunzza.
3. *Step into Chaos* **(HarperPrism, 1999)** The superintelligence known as Outsider, the Albans, and the Hunzza are all taking an interest in Jim because of his altered genetic encoding, which could turn Earthlings into a race of godlike beings.
4. *Beyond the Stars* **(HarperCollins, 2000)** Set in an alternate universe in which Jim hasn't killed his father. Jim is sent off on the Outward Bound, a ship full of colonists headed for a distant galaxy; joins

the Stone Cowboys, a gang of space street thugs; enjoys some good sex; and invades an Ur-Barrba starship.
5. *Shadow Planet* **(HarperCollins, 2002)** In a follow-up to number 4, Jim and the Stone Cowboys have taken over the *Endeavour*, a renamed Kolumban spaceship, and discover that the gorilla-like Kolumbans are drug-peddling agents for another alien race, the Columbans.

Shaw, Irwin

PSEUDONYM OF Irwin Gilbert Shamforoff

ABC's dramatization of *Rich Man, Poor Man* was one of American television's most popular miniseries. Shaw's story of the three Jordache children has all the elements guaranteed to hold a wide audience. He chronicles the rise of Thomas, Rudolph, and Gretchen from their small hometown in New York in the 1940s and continues through their various struggles with love, ambition, courage, and corruption into the 1970s, with nary a dull moment. ABC commissioned the writing of a second series of *Rich Man, Poor Man* programs. Shaw, who was working on his own sequel at the time, disclaimed any responsibility for it. Shaw's best-known title was *The Young Lions* (Random House, 1948). His best claim to enduring literary fame may be his short stories, collected in *Short Stories: Five Decades* (Delacorte, 1978).

1. *Rich Man, Poor Man* **(Delacorte, 1970)** The three children of Axel Jordache, a baker, grow up: Thomas becomes a prizefighter, Rudolph a successful businessman, and Gretchen a successful actress.
2. *Beggarman, Thief* **(Delacorte, 1977)** The story continues into the next generation as Wesley, Tom's son, takes center stage.

Sheldon, Sidney

One of the all-time best-selling novels, *The Other Side of Midnight* was made into a movie and eventually inspired a sequel. *Memories of Midnight* carried over Onassis-type Greek tycoon Constantin Demiris and other characters in a sequel that was just as full of sex, violence, overwrought prose, and lifestyles of the rich as its predecessor. Sidney Sheldon (d. 2007), who was one of the world's most translated authors (more than 50 languages), was consistently on the best-seller lists for more than 30 years. *Are You Afraid of the Dark?* (Morrow, 2004) was his last published novel. *The Other Side of Me* (Warner, 2005) is his autobiography.

1. *Other Side of Midnight, The* **(Morrow, 1974)** After she is deserted by dashing American pilot Larry Douglas, French beauty Noelle Page becomes a great actress and marries Onassis-type tycoon Constantin Demeris.
2. *Memories of Midnight* **(Morrow, 1990)** Demeris orders the death of anyone who can prove that he engineered an unsuccessful plot to execute his unfaithful mistress, Catherine, and her lover.

Sherwood, John

I. English author John Sherwood writes a mystery series featuring diminutive, white-haired Celia Grant, horticulturist and amateur sleuth. Celia owns and operates the Archerscroft Nurseries in the village of Melbury, Sussex. Extensive botanical lore and gardening hints separate this series somewhat from the standard "murder in a village" formula.

1. *Green Trigger Fingers* (Scribner, 1984) Celia finds herself at the center of a brutal village killing: two weekenders are murdered for no apparent reason in Westfield.
2. *Botanist at Bay, A* (Scribner, 1985) Traveling to New Zealand for the birth of her grandchild, Grant finds herself in the thick of a controversy over a proposed dam.
3. *Mantrap Garden, The* (Scribner, 1986) Celia is elected to the board of trustees of a famous English garden designed by Gertrude Jekyll at Monk's Mede and finds the garden in disrepair.
4. *Flowers of Evil* (Scribner, 1987) Grant is asked to refurbish the neglected garden at a country house owned by a business family with strange personalities and bizarre behavior.
5. *Menacing Groves* (Scribner, 1989) Celia is on a tour of Italian gardens with a group that includes a South African couple whom she is sure that she remembers under a different guise.
6. *Bouquet of Thorns, A* (Scribner, 1989) Bill Watkins, Celia's assistant, is accused of killing the local ne'er-do-well in a drunken quarrel.
7. *Sunflower Plot, The* (Scribner, 1991) Celia takes on the task of creating a fake Elizabethan garden for Shakespeare enthusiast Victor Stratton.
8. *Hanging Garden, The* (Scribner, 1993) Grant reluctantly travels to the Portuguese island of Madeira to execute the will of her niece Antonia Hanbury.
9. *Creeping Jenny* (Scribner, 1993) Celia's recently hired assistant is involved in a "Green" plot to sabotage the Royal Horticultural Society's exhibition.
10. *Bones Gather No Moss* (Scribner, 1995) When English botanist Jane Greenwood disappears from the French chateau where she is editing a collection of wildflower drawings, Celia is obliged to intervene.
11. *Shady Borders* (Severn, 1996) Winthrop Court, where Celia has a commission to redesign the borders, is not a happy place. Then a nasty murder occurs.

II. John Sherwood's first mystery series featured an elderly and mild-mannered British treasury department bureaucrat in a series of rather whimsical international mysteries full of outlandish incidents in the world immediately after World War II.

1. *Dr. Bruderstein Vanishes* (Doubleday, 1949) No annotation available. UK title: *The Disappearance of Dr. Bruderstein*.
2. *Mr. Blessington's Imperialist Plot* (Doubleday, 1951) Mr. Blessington is kidnapped by Soviet agents in the Balkans. UK title: *Mr. Blessington's Plot*.
3. *Ambush for Anatole* (Doubleday, 1952) Mr. Blessington chases a blackmailer and currency exchange racketeer.
4. *Two Died in Singapore* (Hodder [UK], 1954) Mr. Blessington has to deal with two murders in Southeast Asia. Not published in the United States.
5. *Vote against Poison* (Hodder [UK], 1956) No annotation available. Not published in the United States.

Shoemaker, Bill (William Lee)

The late "Willie" Shoemaker, as he was known in his racing days, rode more than 8,000 winners, so he could be expected to know horses and horse racing. He could also write fast-paced thrillers, as the three novels featuring ex-jockey Coley Killebrew illustrate.

1. *Stalking Horse* (Ballantine, 1994) Coley is enlisted by billionaire Raymond Edgar Starbuck to help stop an underworld takeover of Louisiana's Magnolia Park, one of America's great racetracks.

2. *Fire Horse* (Ballantine, 1995) Killebrew is asked by restaurant partner Johnny Rousseau to shadow the daughter of right-wing rant-radio star Wilton Dresner.
3. *Dark Horse* (Fawcett, 1996) While covering the Triple Crown races for a cable network, Coley stumbles across the body of a PI working for Starbuck, his prospective father-in-law.

Sholokhov, Mikhail

Sholokhov was one of the few establishment Soviet writers with a reputation in the West. He was awarded the Nobel Prize in 1965. His books about the Don region of southern Russia chronicle the tumultuous years of revolution and collectivization in the arid steppe country and the feudal society of its Cossack inhabitants. Sholokhov, a native of the district himself, reveals the humanity behind the Cossack stereotype while still conveying the fierceness of the people and the primitive nature of their culture. All have been translated into English by Henry C. Stevens, who used the pseudonym Stephen Garry for the earlier books. Numbers 2 and 3 were originally published as *Tikhii Don* in four volumes from 1928 to 1940, and published in one volume as *The Silent Don* (Knopf, 1941). Numbers 4 and 5 were originally published as *Podnyataya tselina* (1932–1960).

1. *Tales of the Don* (Knopf, 1962) Short stories about the Don region during the Russian Revolution. Originally collected as *Donskie rasskazy* in 1926.
2. *And Quiet Flows the Don* (Knopf, 1934) The life, loves, and military adventures of a group of Cossacks living along the Don River are recounted. The story begins in 1914 and focuses on young Gregor Melekhov.
3. *Don Flows Home to the Sea, The* (Knopf, 1941) A group of Cossacks clashes with both Red and White forces during the civil war following the revolution, 1917–1921.
4. *Seeds of Tomorrow* (Knopf, 1959) The 1930 effort at total collectivization of farming in the Don region is directed by the gentle Davidov. UK title: *Virgin Soil Upturned*.
5. *Harvest on the Don* (Knopf, 1961) Davidov continues to meet obstacles as they arise and is increasingly drawn to Lushka. The story ends in the autumn of 1930.

Shreve, Anita

I. Three novels are set at different times in the same house in the small New Hampshire coastal town of Fortune's Rocks: *Fortune's Rocks*, at the turn of the 20th century; *Sea Glass*, in 1929; and *The Pilot's Wife*, in contemporary time (1990s). Anita Shreve writes popular novels about the psychology of marital and relationship problems, usually from the woman's point of view. They are, on the whole, well-written, subtle, romantic-suspense novels. Shreve has also published nonfiction books on women's issues, such as *Women Together, Women Alone: The Legacy of the Consciousness-Raising Movement* (Viking, 1989). *The Pilot's Wife* was adapted as a television movie starring Christine Lahti.

1. *Fortune's Rocks* (Little, Brown, 2000) In a novel set at the turn of the 20th century in the coastal town of Fortune's Rocks, New Hampshire, 15-year-old summer resident Olympia has an affair with the much older physician, John Haskell.
2. *Sea Glass* (Little, Brown, 2002) 1929. 20-year-old Honora marries the frequently dishonest traveling salesman, Sexton, just in time for the Crash to wipe them out financially.

3. *Pilot's Wife, The* (Little, Brown, 1998) After her husband, Jack, is killed in a plane crash, Kathryn Lyons uncovers the double life he was leading.

II. Another pair of novels is set partly off the New Hampshire shore. Photojournalist Jean is given the assignment to photograph the Isles of Shoals, where an infamous 19th-century double murder took place. *The Weight of Water* is about Jean's investigations of the historical truth behind the murders and the stresses that her marriage is undergoing. *The Last Time They Met* tells, through flashbacks, about the lifelong love affair Jean's husband, Thomas, has had with Linda Fallon.

1. *Weight of Water, The* (Little, Brown, 1997) Photojournalist Jean turns up some firsthand documents that seem to contradict the jury's decision in a famous 19th century murder case on the Isles of Shoals, off the New Hampshire coast.
2. *Last Time They Met, The* (Little, Brown, 2001) Jean's husband, Thomas, and fellow-poet Linda Fallon carry on a lifelong love affair, although they have met only three times.

Sibley, Celestine

Kate Mulcay, like Sarah Shankman's (q.v.) Sam Adams, is an Atlanta reporter and amateur sleuth. Kate is an intelligent, genteel, but plucky widow, and her work often takes her out of Atlanta into the southern countryside. Celestine Sibley (d. 1999) was for many years a columnist and reporter for the Atlanta *Constitution*. She published many nonfiction books including her memoir, *Turned Funny* (Harper, 1988).

1. *Ah, Sweet Mystery* (Harper, 1991) When someone murders a developer in northern Fulton County, police suspect a dear old lady neighbor of Kate's.
2. *Straight as an Arrow* (Harper, 1992) Nora Noble, Kate's friend, calls Kate to Ila Island off the Florida coast because she suspects that the deaths of island residents are really homicide.
3. *Dire Happenings at Scratch Ankle* (Harper, 1993) Kate travels to the town of Rising Fawn on the Georgia-Tennessee border to write up "Return" Pickett's campaign to reclaim Tennessee land stolen from his Cherokee Nation.
4. *Plague of Kinfolks, A* (Harper, 1995) Kate endures a visitation from her husband's kinfolks, an old man wandering in the woods, and a dead housewife the police suspect her of killing.
5. *Spider in the Sink* (Harper, 1997) When Kate arranges for two elderly street people, Shag and Warty, to spend Christmas with wealthy matron Iris Moon, Iris turns up murdered.

Sidhwa, Bapsi

Pakistani American Bapsi Sidhwa says that she desires to make statements about forgotten or misrepresented communities of India and Pakistan. Her pair of novels about two very different members of the Parsi Ginwalla family are good-humored chronicles about a pair of survivors in widely separated worlds.

1. *Crow Eaters, The* (St. Martin's, 1981) Faredoon "Fredy" Ginwilla (Junglewalla) is a beguiling rogue who cons his way through Lahore society, rising from bullock-cart driver to a position of power and influence.
2. *American Brat, An* (Milkweed, 1993) Sixteen-year-old Feroza Ginwalla's parents send her to the United States to escape an increasingly fundamentalist Pakistan, and Feroza learns to love America despite its flaws.

Siegel, Sheldon

Mike Daley—ex-priest, ex-public defender, and ex–corporate lawyer—and his former wife, Rosie Fernandez, have discovered, while running their San Francisco criminal defense firm, that they make a better legal team than a marital one. While most of their cases are routine and small-time, they do take on some sticky high-profile cases. Mike and Rosie are likable characters, and Siegel, a lawyer himself, writes intelligent and believable legal thrillers.

1. *Special Circumstances* (Bantam, 2000) Michael Daley, who has just been fired for failing to meet the stringent standards of productivity of high-pressure corporate law firm Simpson & Gates, comes to the defense of S&G associate attorney Joel Friedman when he is accused of a double murder.
2. *Incriminating Evidence* (Bantam, 2001) Mike's former boss, District Attorney Prentice Marshall Gates III, who got Mike fired from Simpson & Gates, needs Mike's help now: a short while ago he woke up in a chair in his hotel room and found the dead body of a young male prostitute in his bed.
3. *Criminal Intent* (Putnam, 2002) Rosie Fernandez's niece Angelina is accused of murdering movie director Richard "Big Dick" MacArthur. As if that weren't enough, Rosie's brother, Tony, may be on the wrong end of a strong-arm graft proposal; the son of one of the firm's lawyers has been busted on a drug charge; Mike is having a clandestine affair with a woman judge; and Rosie has a dark secret of her own.
4. *Final Verdict* (Putnam, 2003) Skid Row denizen Leon Walker, successfully represented by Mike and Rosie 10 years earlier, is charged with the murder of Tower Grayson, a Silicon Valley venture capitalist found stabbed to death in a dumpster behind a liquor store.
5. *Confession, The* (Putnam, 2004) Mike's old friend and colleague, Father Ramon Aguirre, is accused of murdering the lawyer of the plaintiff in a sexual-harassment suit filed against the San Francisco Catholic Archdiocese.

Sienkiewicz, Henryk

Sienkiewicz is best known in English-speaking countries for *Quo Vadis*, a novel about the persecution of early Christians during the reign of Emperor Nero. It was a best seller in its day (1896) and was made into a very successful movie in 1951, starring Robert Taylor, Deborah Kerr, and Peter Ustinov. Three earlier novels, Walter Scott–like historical romances based on Polish history, also enjoyed a huge international readership and secured Sienkiewicz's reputation as a leading Polish author. He was awarded the Nobel Prize in 1905. The trilogy, originally translated from the Polish by Jeremiah Curtin, was later (1991–1992) retranslated by W. S. Kuniczak (q.v.) for the Copernicus Society of America/Hippocrene.

1. *With Fire and Sword* (Little, Brown, 1890) This covers the events of 1648–1649 when the Ukrainian Cossacks revolted against Poland. Fiery heroism and epic battlefield scenes alternate with quieter domestic episodes. Originally published as *Ogniem i mieczem* in 1884.
2. *Deluge, The* (Little, Brown, 1893) Poland and Lithuania are invaded by Swedes under Charles Gustavus (1654–1655). Originally published as *Potop* in 1886.
3. *Pan Michael* (Little, Brown, 1893) In 1669–1673 the Poles war with the Tartars and the Turks. *Pan* is the term of address for a gentleman, like the English *Mr*. Originally published as *Pan Wolodyjowski* in 1887–1888. Variant title: *Fire in the Steppe*.

Sillitoe, Alan

I. English writer Alan Sillitoe made his reputation with the story "The Loneliness of the Long Distance Runner" (published in *The Loneliness of the Long Distance Runner*, Knopf, 1960) and *Saturday Night and Sunday Morning*, which introduced readers to his gritty Nottingham milieu as viewed through the eyes of working-class characters. Sometimes included with the "angry young men" of the 1950s and 1960s, and sometimes compared to the American proletarian fiction of the 1930s and D. H. Lawrence's (q.v.) works, Sillitoe's books bring a rare working-class perspective to English fiction. Both stories were made into popular films: *Saturday Night* (1960) starred a young Albert Finney, and *Loneliness* (1961) was directed by a young Tony Richardson. Although Sillitoe has written many novels and short stories, poetry, drama, screenplays, travel books, juveniles, and essays since then, *Saturday Night* and *Loneliness* remain his best-known and most popular works. Although much of his later work has been praised by critics, it remains less popular with readers, at least in the United States—few of Sillitoe's works published since the mid-1980s have been released in the United States.

Saturday Night and Sunday Morning—whose protagonist, factory worker Arthur Seaton, is fairly content with a decent-paying job and a good supply of beer, ale, and women—was followed by other books about the Seaton family. Numbers 2 and 3 relate the life of Arthur's brother, Brian, an autobiographical character who has a more intellectual take on things than Arthur. Number 4 brings an older Arthur and Brian together again.

1. *Saturday Night and Sunday Morning* (Knopf, 1959) Arthur Seaton, Nottingham factory worker, remembering how hard life had been for his father in the 1930s, lives for the moment, enjoying drink and women (including two married sisters).
2. *Key to the Door* (Knopf, 1962) Brian, Arthur's more thoughtful brother, who is based on the author, remembering the life "on the dole" of the elder Seatons, and reminiscing about his youthful days in Nottingham, searches for a more complete life.
3. *Open Door, The* (Grafton [UK], 1989) Brian's memories continue: an army tour in Malaya, a long bout with tuberculosis after he returns, and the beginnings of a writing career. Not published in the United States.
4. *Birthday* (Flamingo [UK], 2001) Brian and Arthur are on their way to the 70th birthday party of Brian's old sweetheart, Jenny. Not published in the United States.

II. In a trio of novels, Frank Dawley, another character from Nottingham's working-class, narrates his life in Nottingham and in Algeria supporting the liberation movement.

1. *Death of William Posters, The* (Knopf, 1965) Signs saying "Bill Posters will be Prosecuted" lead working class protagonist Frank Dawley of Nottingham to think about a character named "William Posters," the fictional image of the working class: defiant, hounded by society, but never caught.
2. *Tree on Fire, A* (Doubleday, 1968) Dawley decides that he would do more good raising money for the liberation cause in Algeria than in fighting for it, so he returns to England, following his lover, Myra, and their son.
3. *Flame of Life, The* (W. H. Allen [UK], 1974) Dawley and his friends and associates keep trying to disrupt English society, and establish a utopian community. Not published in the United States.

Silone, Ignazio

After devoting his youth to various Communist and anti-Fascist activities, Silone was forced to flee Italy in 1929. During his exile in Switzerland, he turned to writing fiction and produced his best-known novels, *Fontamara* (sometimes included with numbers 1 and 2 as part of an Abruzzi trilogy) and *Bread and Wine*. His novels cast a critical eye at contemporary Italian life and look with sympathy and respect at the endurance, pride, and basic goodness of the Italian peasant. Disillusioned with Communism, Silone broke with the party in 1930, but played an active role in the left wing of Italian democratic socialism from the time of his return to Italy after the war to 1950, when he retired from political life to devote more time to writing. After his death, in 1978, documents were found that seemed to implicate Silone as a double agent for the Italian police in the 1920s, starting a controversy that is still raging.

1. *Bread and Wine* (Harper, 1937) Pietro Spina, a young socialist disguised as a monk, tries to organize the peasants in his native village against the Fascists in 1935. Translated from the Italian by Gwen David and Eric Mosbacher. Not published in Italian (*Pane e vino*) until 1937 after the publication of the English translation. Revised edition published by Atheneum in 1962.
2. *Seed beneath the Snow, The* (Harper, 1942) Pietro Spina is now in hiding in the home of his grandmother, Donna Maria Vincenza. Translated from the Italian by Francis Frenaye. First published in a German translation in 1941. First published in Italian as *Il seme sotto la neve*. Revised edition published by Atheneum in 1965.

Silva, Daniel

I. Israeli Gabriel Allon's ostensible profession is restoring art, but he doubles as an Israeli agent and Mossad hit man. Several of Allon's assignments involve Islamic terrorists in Europe, but numbers 2 through 4 are dedicated to efforts against persons who will do anything, including murder, to cover up their country's or institution's collaboration in the Holocaust of World War II. Besides Allon, continuing characters include Israeli master spy Ari Shamron, Allon's mentally and physically damaged wife, Leah, and fellow agent Eli Lavon. Critics and readers rate Daniel Silva as one of the most suspenseful and intelligent thriller writers around.

1. *Kill Artist, The* (Random House, 2000) Art restorer and former Israeli agent, Gabriel Allon, whose family was killed by Palestinian assassin, Tariq al-Hourani, is brought back to the spy network by master spy Ari Shamron to thwart Tariq, who is devising a plan to kill Israel's primer minister.
2. *English Assassin, The* (Putnam, 2002) The so-called Council of Rutli, which is dedicated to eliminating anyone who threatens to expose Switzerland's collaboration with the Nazis in World War II, hires a hit man known as the Englishman to eliminate Allon.
3. *Confessor, The* (Putnam, 2003) A secret Vatican Society known as Crux Vera, composed of Roman Curia members and shady rich thugs, hires "the Leopard" to kill an academic working on an exposé of the Vatican's collaboration with the Nazis and plans to assassinate the current pope to keep him from exposing the Vatican's secret archives.
4. *Death in Vienna, A* (Putnam, 2004) Allon discovers that the man known as Ludwig Vogel—chairman of the Danube Valley Trade and Investment Corporation in Vienna, who may have been responsible for the bombing that left Eli Lavon, chief investigator of the Austrian Wartimes Claim and Inquiries office, near

death—was, in a previous incarnation, Sturmbannfuhrer Erich Radek, who nearly murdered Gabriel's mother.

5. *Prince of Fire* **(Putnam, 2005)** The mastermind behind the bombing of the Israeli embassy in Rome is French archaeologist Paul Martineau, aka Khaled, the adopted son of Yasir Arafat.

6. *Messenger, The* **(Putnam, 2006)** Ahmed bin Shafiq, former chief of a clandestine Saudi intelligence unit, has targeted the Vatican for attack, in particular Pope Paul VII [*sic*] and his top aide, Monsignor Luigi Donati.

7. *Secret Servant, The* **(Putnam, 2007)** When Solomon Rosner, professor in Amsterdam, is assassinated for his reports and articles detailing the dangers of militant Islam within the Netherlands, Allon is given the job of cleaning out Rosner's files.

II. Former CNN executive Daniel Silva's first novel, *The Unlikely Spy* (Villard, 1996), is set in World War II. He also wrote two novels about ex–CIA man Michael Osbourne, who interacts with various fictional and real-life characters to thwart plots by terrorist organizations.

1. *Mark of the Assassin, The* **(Villard, 1998)** An American arms manufacturer, concerned about the effect world peace might have on his profit margin, enlists in the Society, a secret organization designed to ensure wealth and power remain in the hands of its members.

2. *Marching Season, The* **(Random House, 1999)** Embittered ex–CIA agent Michael Osbourne is up against terrorists, assassins, and a worldwide conspiracy to keep the world safe for arms merchants in Belfast, Northern Ireland, and Washington, DC.

Silverberg, Robert

I. Like Isaac Asimov (q.v.), Robert Silverberg is a prolific writer and editor of fiction and nonfiction, with more than 100 books of his authoring published and more than 60 anthologies compiled. Although he has announced several times he is "quitting" science fiction, Silverberg is recognized as a master of SF, recently adding a SFWA Damon Knight Memorial Grand Master Award to his Nebulas and Hugos. Silverberg's Majipoor books are regarded as one the finest creations of an imaginary planet in science-fiction annals. Majipoor is a huge planet with 15 billion sentient beings of several species, including the humans who colonized it thousands of years in the past, ruled by two kings, the active Coronal and the more or less emeritus Pontifex. Numbers 1 through 4 are sometimes called the Majipoor quartet; numbers 5 through 7 the Prestimion trilogy.

1. *Lord Valentine's Castle* **(Harper, 1980)** Valentine, a young juggler suffering from amnesia, unaware of his true identity as rightful ruler of the planet of Majipoor, wanders into a festival celebrating the visit of the false Lord Valentine.

2. *Majipoor Chronicles* **(Arbor, 1982)** A young clerk in the Registry of Souls illegally calls up the records of the lives of famous and ordinary people from Majipoor's past.

3. *Valentine Pontifex* **(Arbor, 1983)** Lord Valentine, facing his elevation from Coronal to Pontifex, tries to find a way to communicate with the Metamorphs, who are destroying Majipoor's food crops.

4. *Mountains of Majipoor, The* **(Bantam, 1995)** Five hundred years after the events in number 3, Harpirias, a descendant of Valentine, is exiled from Castle Mount when he accidentally kills a rare and valuable animal belonging to another nobleman.

5. *Sorcerers of Majipoor, The* **(HarperPrism, 1997)** The aged Pontifex Pronkipan is near death and will be succeeded by Coronal Lord Confalume, but the succession to Coronal spells trouble as a civil war looms between Prince Pestimion of Muldemor and Korsibar, Confalume's son.

6. *Lord Prestimion* **(HarperPrism, 1999)** Having attained the rank of Coronal of Majipoor, Prestimion makes a bad mistake: he obliterates the recent civil war from the memory of Majipoor's inhabitants, causing a psychosis that sweeps the planet.

7. *King of Dreams, The* **(Eos, 2001)** Finally peace has been restored to Majipoor, and it is time for Pestimion to name Prince Dekkeret as his successor as Coronal and to descend to the Labyrinth as Pontifex.

II. Silverberg wrote a pair of fantasy novels about Gilgamesh, the Sumerian god-king of 5,000 years ago who is immortalized in the *Epic of Gilgamesh*. The novels are among Silverberg's most playful, bringing in many historical and mythical characters.

1. *Gilgamesh the King* **(Arbor, 1984)** Gilgamesh grows to maturity and reigns over an empire in the Middle East of circa 30 BCE.

2. *To the Land of the Living* **(Questar, 1990)** While trying to avoid the dangers of the Afterworld, Gilgamesh engages on a quest for his closest friend and interacts with various historical characters who, like himself, are caught up in the never-ending cycle of death and rebirth.

III. A pair of novels postulates a distant-future Earth in which a small group of humans emerges after 700 years of winter.

1. *At Winter's End* **(Warner, 1988)** After the Long Winter, which lasted 700 years, Koshmar and a small band of humans emerge from the underground cocoon where they have lived for centuries.

2. *New Springtime, The* **(Warner, 1990)** Begins 40 years after the end of *The Long Winter* as the humans clash with the People, an evolved race of apes, and the insectoid hijk for Earth's domination. UK title: *The Queen of Springtime*.

Simenon, Georges

The centenary of Simenon's birth (2003) was celebrated by a festival in his native city of Liege (Belgium) and the announcement that 21 of his books would be republished in Gallimard's celebrated Pleiades series. Simenon, who spent many years in Paris, Switzerland, and the United States, wrote some 200 pulp stories and novels including, apparently, several Maigret stories under a variety of pseudonyms before launching the Maigret mysteries (75 novels, 28 short stories) under his own name in 1931. The big, patient police inspector, who solved crimes by slowly coming to understand the criminal's mind and background, was an immediate hit in France and quickly caught on in England and America as well. When first introduced, Inspector Jules Maigret is about 45 years old. His quiet life with his wife in their Boulevard Richard-Lenoir apartment in Paris changes very little during the course of the series, though Maigret does travel—as far afield as Tucson, Arizona—and the novels continued to have a 1930s Paris ambience even though they were written during the course of more than four decades. All of the Maigret novels have been translated into English; all but number 75 have been published at some time in the United States.

Short story collections include *The Short Cases of Inspector Maigret* (Doubleday, 1959; partially based on *Les nouvelles enquêtes de Maigret*, 1947); *Maigret's Pipe* (Harcourt, 1978; translation by Jean Stewart of *La pipe de Maigret*, 1947); and *Maigret's Christmas* (translations by Jean Stewart; partially based on *Maigret et l'inspecteur malgracieux*, 1947).

Omnibuses include six published by Hamish Hamilton (UK, 1962– 1975) and 14 Simenon omnibuses, which include both Maigrets and non-Maigrets published by Penguin (1970–1979). Omnibuses published in the United States include *Five Times*

Maigret (Harcourt, 1964; numbers 36, 43, 44, 52, and 53); *Maigret cinq* (Harcourt, 1965; numbers 30, 33, 37, 45, and 50); and *A Maigret Trio* (Harcourt, 1973; numbers 49, 56, and 57).

Maigret has been brought to the large screen and the small screen many times in French and English (and in German, Dutch, etc.).

1. ***Strange Case of Peter the Lett, The* (Covici, 1933)** Maigret must identify the body of a man found in the lavatory of a Paris express train. This was the first Maigret published under Simenon's name. UK title: *The Case of Peter the Lett* published in *Inspector Maigret Investigates*. Originally translated by Anthony Abbot. Retranslated by Daphne Woodward as *Maigret and the Enigmatic Lett* (Penguin [UK], 1963). First published in France in 1931 as *Pietr-le-Letton*.

2. ***Crime at Lock 14, The* (Covici, 1934)** Bound with number 12 (below). As soon as the corpse of an elegantly dressed woman is identified, another dead body turns up to keep Maigret busy. Published in the United Kingdom in *The Triumph of Inspector Maigret*. Translated by Anthony Abbot. Retranslated by Robert Baldick as *Maigret Meets a Milord* (Penguin [UK], 1963). Variant title: *Lock 14*. First published in France in 1931 as *Le charretier de la Providence*.

3. ***Death of Monsieur Gallet, The* (Covici, 1933)** First Maigret case published in English. It concerns the corpse of M. Gallet, a commercial traveler, and the strange, sad tale that it has to tell. Published in the United Kingdom in *Introducing Inspector Maigret*. Translated by Anthony Abbot. Retranslated by Margaret Marshall as *Maigret Stonewalled* (Penguin [UK], 1963). First published in France in 1931 as *M. Gallet decede*.

4. ***Crime of Inspector Maigret, The* (Covici, 1932)** On a visit to Brussels, Maigret trails a down-at-the-heels man he had seen packing money into a suitcase. Published in the United Kingdom in *Introducing Inspector Maigret*. Translated by Anthony Abbot. Retranslated by Tony White as *Maigret and the Hundred Gibbets* (Penguin [UK], 1963). First published in France in 1931 as *Le pendu de Saint-Pholien*.

5. ***Battle of Nerves, A* (Harcourt, 1940)** Published in *The Patience of Maigret*. The Café Coupole in Montparnasse is the center of the action as Maigret, not convinced of the guilt of a condemned man, tries to find the true murderer of a rich old woman. Translated by Geoffrey Sainsbury. Variant titles: *A Man's Head*; *Maigret's War of Nerves*. First published in France in 1931 as *La tete d'un homme*. Republished as *L'homme de las Tour Eiffel*.

6. ***Face for a Clue, A* (Harcourt, 1940)** Published in *The Patience of Maigret*. The Breton fishing town of Concarneau is plagued by a series of murders and poisonings, a strange menacing giant who stalks at night, and a yellow dog that appears from nowhere. Translated by Geoffrey Sainsbury. Retranslated by Linda Asher as *Maigret and the Yellow Dog* (Harcourt, 1987). Variant titles: *Maigret and the Concarneau Murders*; *The Yellow Dog*. First published in France in 1931 as *Le chien jaune*.

7. ***Crossroad Murders, The* (Covici, 1933)** Maigret ferrets out the secrets of an eccentric brother and sister who live in an old country house. Published in the United Kingdom in *Inspector Maigret Investigates*. Translated by Anthony Abbot. Retranslated by Robert Baldick as *Maigret at the Crossroads* (Penguin [UK], 1963). First published in France in 1931 as *La nuit du carrefour*.

8. ***Crime in Holland, A* (Harcourt, 1940)** Published in *Maigret Abroad*. In Holland to investigate a murder in which a French citizen is involved, Maigret manages to stay one step ahead of the local police investigation, even though he speaks no Dutch. Translated by Geoffrey Sainsbury. Republished as *Maigret in Holland* (Harcourt, 1993). First published in France in 1931 as *Un crime en Hollande*.

9. ***Sailor's Rendezvous, The* (Harcourt, 1941)** Published in *Maigret Keeps a Rendezvous*. Captain Fallut, just back from three months's cod fishing in Newfoundland, is found strangled and floating near his trawler. Translated by Margaret Ludwig. Variant title: *Maigret Answers a Plea*. First published in France in 1931 as *Au rendez-vous des Terre-Neuvas*.

10. ***At the Gai-Moulin* (Harcourt, 1940)** Published in *Maigret Abroad*. A dancer named Adele, a spy ring, and a corpse found in a wicker basket are elements in this case. Translated by Geoffrey Sainsbury. Republished as *Maigret at the "Gai Moulin"* (Harcourt, 1991). First published in France in 1931 as *La danseuse du Gai-Moulin*.

11. ***Guinguette by the Seine* (Harcourt, 1941)** Published in *Maigret to the Rescue*. The setting is a weekend resort on the banks of the Seine. Translated by Geoffrey Sainsbury. Variant titles: *A Spot by the Seine*; *Maigret and the Tavern by the Seine*. Retranslated by David Watson as *The Bar on the Seine* (Penguin, 2003). First published in France in 1932 as *La guinguette a deux sous*.

12. ***Shadow in the Courtyard, The* (Covici, 1934)** Bound with number 2 (above). M. Couchet is found shot to death in his office with 300,000 francs missing from the sale of his pharmaceutical company. Published in the United Kingdom in *The Triumph of Inspector Maigret*. Translated by Anthony Abbot. Retranslated by Jean Stewart as *Maigret Mystified* (Penguin [UK], 1964). First published in France in 1932 as *L'ombre chinoise*.

13. ***Saint-Fiacre Affair, The* (Harcourt, 1941)** Published in *Maigret Keeps a Rendezvous*. Warned that a woman will be killed in his hometown of Saint-Fiacre, Maigret visits it for the first time in years. Translated by Margaret Ludwig. Variant titles: *Death of a Countess*; *Maigret and the Countess*. Retranslated by Robert Baldick as *Maigret Goes Home* (Viking, 1967). Variant title: *Maigret on Home Ground*. First published in France in 1932 as *L'affaire Saint-Fiacre*.

14. ***Flemish Shop, The* (Harcourt, 1941)** Published in *Maigret to the Rescue*. A little wineshop on the Franco-Belgian border is the setting for this case. Translated by Geoffrey Sainsbury. Variant title: *Maigret and the Flemish Shop*. First published in France in 1932 as *Chez les Flamands*.

15. ***Death of a Harbor Master* (Harcourt, 1942)** Published in *Maigret and M. Labbe*. Maigret escorts a mute and wounded man to his home in a little harbor town and identifies him as Captain Joris, the harbormaster. Translated by Stuart Gilbert. Variant titles: *Death of a Harbour Master*; *Death of a Harbormaster*; *Maigret and the Death of a Harbor Master*. First published in France in 1932 as *Le port des brumes*.

16. ***Madman of Bergerac, The* (Harcourt, 1940)** Published in *Maigret Travels South*. A psychopathic murderer has killed two women by plunging a long needle through their hearts. Translated by Geoffrey Sainsbury. First published in France in 1932 as *Le fou de Bergerac*.

17. ***Liberty Bar* (Harcourt, 1940)** Published in *Maigret Travels South*. Maigret is sent to the Rivera to investigate a murder that must be handled with the utmost tact. Translated by Geoffrey Sainsbury. Variant title; *Maigret on the Riviera*. First published in France in 1932 as *Liberty Bar*.

18. ***Lock at Charenton, The* (Harcourt, 1941)** Published in *Maigret Sits It Out*. Maigret returns to the world of the canal boats to investigate the attempted murder of Emile Ducrau. Translated by Margaret Ludwig. Variant titles: *Maigret Sits It Out*; *Lock No. 1*. First published in France in 1932 as *L'ecluse no. 1*.

19. ***Maigret Returns* (Harcourt, 1941)** Published in *Maigret Sits It Out*. Maigret's nephew, an inept detective, gets himself framed in a nightclub murder. Translated by Margaret Ludwig. First published in France in 1934 as *Maigret* (*Maigret revient*).

20. *Maigret and the Hotel Majestic* (Harcourt, 1978) Emilienne Clark is strangled, and all the residents and staff of the luxury Paris hotel *Majestic* are suspects. Translated by Caroline Hillier. UK title: *Maigret and the Ghost*. First published in France in 1942 as *Les caves du Majestic* (in *Maigret revient*). Variant title: *The Hotel Majestic*.

21. *Maigret in Exile* (Harcourt, 1979) Sent to the northern Provinces, Maigret is bored until a corpse is found in the home of a retired judge. Translated by Eileen Ellenbogen. First published in France in 1942 as *La maison du juge* (in *Maigret revient*).

22. *Maigret and the Spinster* (Harcourt, 1977) Maigret fails to follow up on the story of a pathetic old maid only to discover her strangled in a broom closet. Translated by Eileen Ellenbogen. First published in France in 1942 as *Cécile est morte* (in *Maigret revient*).

23. *Maigret and the Fortuneteller* (Harcourt, 1989) The story of the odious Madame Le Cloaquen is told. Translated by Geoffrey Sainsbury. Published in the United Kingdom in 1950 as *To Any Lengths* in *Maigret on Holiday*. First published in France in 1944 as *Signé Picpus*.

24. *Maigret and the Toy Village* (Harcourt, 1978) This concerns the murder of an old man in one of the new suburban housing developments, which remind Maigret of toy villages. Translated by Eileen Ellenbogen. First published in France in 1944 as *Felicie est la* (in *Signé Picpus*).

25. *Maigret's Rival* (Harcourt, 1980) Sent to a small French village to investigate the suspicious death of Genevieve Naud's secret lover, Maigret always seems to be one step behind the local policemen on the case. Translated by Helen Thomson. Variant title: *Inspector Cadaver*. First published in France in 1944 as *L'Inspecteur Cadavre* (in *Signé Picpus*).

26. *Maigret in Retirement* (Harcourt, 1976) Two years into his retirement at Meung-sur-Loire Maigret is virtually ordered by an old lady to look into a case in Orsennes where an 18-year-old-girl has been found dead in the Seine. Translated by Jean Stewart. Also in short collection *Maigret's Christmas* and in *Maigret among the Rich*. First published in France in 1947 as *Maigret se fâche*.

27. *Maigret in New York's Underworld* (Doubleday, 1955) A phone call across the Atlantic provides the surprising conclusion to this case, which is set in New York. Translated by Adrienne Foulke. Variant titles: *Maigret in New York*; *Inspector Maigret in New York's Underworld*. First published in France in 1947 as *Maigret a New York*.

28. *No Vacation for Maigret* (Doubleday, 1953) On vacation, Maigret's wife is hospitalized with an attack of appendicitis, and Maigret occupies himself by poking into the mysterious death of the girl in the next room. Translated by Geoffrey Sainsbury. UK title: *A Summer Holiday*. Retranslated by Jacqueline Baldick as *Maigret on Holiday* (Penguin [UK], 1970). First published in France in 1948 as *Les vacances de Maigret*.

29. *Maigret's Dead Man* (Doubleday, 1964) Maigret tracks down a particularly nasty and callous gang that killed a man who had asked Maigret for help. UK title: *Maigret's Special Murder*. Translated by Jean Stewart. First published in France in 1948 as *Maigret et son mort*.

30. *Maigret's First Case* (Harcourt, 1965) Published in *Maigret Cinq*. A prequel. In 1913, at the age of 26, Maigret tackles his first solo case, which concerns the complicated affairs of some coffee tycoons. Published in the United Kingdom in 1958. Translated by Robert Brain. First published in France in 1949 as *La premiere enquete de Maigret, 1913*.

31. *Methods of Maigret, The* (Doubleday, 1957) An inspector from Scotland Yard who is studying Maigret's methods accompanies him to the Mediterranean, where he investigates the murder of a tramp. Translated by Nigel Ryan. UK title: *My Friend Maigret*. First published in France in 1949 as *Mon ami Maigret*.

32. *Maigret at the Coroner's* (Harcourt, 1980) Maigret sits in on an inquest in Tucson, Arizona, and puzzles out how and why poor Bessie Mitchell had been left dead on the railroad tracks. Translated by Frances Keene. UK title: *Maigret and the Coroner*. First published in France in 1949 as *Maigret chez le coroner*.

33. *Maigret and the Old Lady* (Harcourt, 1965) Published in *Maigret Cinq*. Valentine Besson is the charming old lady whom Maigret tries to help. Published in the United Kingdom in 1958. Translated by Robert Brain. First published in France in 1949 as *Maigret et la vielle dame*.

34. *Madame Maigret's Own Case* (Doubleday, 1959) Madame Maigret must do a stint of babysitting to help her husband solve this case started by an anonymous tip. UK title: *Madame Maigret's Friend*. Translated by Helen Sebba. First published in France in 1950 as *L'amie de Mme Maigret*.

35. *Maigret's Memoirs* (Harcourt, 1985) Maigret reminisces about his early years: joining the Surete and working his way up to the elite homicide squad. Published in the United Kingdom in 1963. Translated by Jean Stewart. First published in France in 1951 as *Les memoires de Maigret*.

36. *Maigret and the Strangled Stripper* (Doubleday, 1954) A Montmartre striptease dancer is murdered when she overhears something she shouldn't have. Translated by Cornelia Schaeffer. Variant title: *Inspector Maigret and the Strangled Stripper*. Retranslated by Daphne Woodward as *Maigret in Montmartre* (Harcourt, 1989). First published in France in 1951 as *Maigret au "Picratt's."*

37. *Maigret Rents a Room* (Doubleday, 1961) Maigret moves into a rundown boardinghouse to keep a close watch on some suspects implicated in the shooting of his assistant, Janvier. UK title: *Maigret Takes a Room*. Translated by Robert Brain. First published in France in 1951 as *Maigret en meublé*.

38. *Inspector Maigret and the Burglar's Wife* (Doubleday, 1956) A burglar stumbles upon a murder, and his wife passes on the information to Maigret. Variant title: *Maigret and the Burglar's Wife*. Translated by J. Maclaren-Ross. First published in France in 1951 as *Maigret et la grande perche*.

39. *Inspector Maigret and the Killers* (Doubleday, 1954) American thugs and dead bodies dumped from cars figure in this case that Maigret helps a friend. UK title: *Maigret and the Gangsters*. Translated by Louise Varese. First published in France in 1952 as *Maigret, Lognon et les gangsters*.

40. *Maigret's Revolver* (Harcourt, 1984) While Maigret is visiting London, his revolver is stolen. Published in the United Kingdom in 1956. Translated by Nigel Ryan. First published in France in 1952 as *Le revolver de Maigret*.

41. *Maigret and the Man on the Bench* (Harcourt, 1975) A man is found dead in an alley, but Maigret does not believe that he died in a drunken brawl. UK title: *Maigret and the Man on the Boulevard*. Translated by Eileen Ellenbogen. First published in France in 1953 as *Maigret et l'homme du banc*.

42. *Maigret Afraid* (Harcourt, 1983) On a visit to an old school friend in a town near Poitiers, Maigret helps out on a murder case involving a grim domestic crisis complicated by class loyalties. Published in the United Kingdom in 1961. Translated by Margaret Duff. First published in France in 1953 as *Maigret a peur*.

43. *Maigret's Mistake* (Harcourt, 1988) The residents of a luxury apartment house becomes suspects when a woman is found murdered there. Published in the United Kingdom in 1954. Translated by Alan Hodge. First published in France in 1953 as *Maigret se trompe*.

44. *Maigret Goes to School* (Harcourt, 1964) Published in *Five Times Maigret*. Maigret goes to Saint-Andre-sur-mer to investigate the murder of the postmistress. Published in the United Kingdom in 1957. Translated by Daphne Woodward. First published in France in 1954 as *Maigret a l'ecole*.

45. *Inspector Maigret and the Dead Girl* (Doubleday, 1955) Maigret catches a young girl's murderer by getting to know the girl's personality. Variant title: *Maigret and the Young Girl*. Translated by Daphne Woodward. First published in France in 1954 as *Maigret et la jeune morte*.

46. *Maigret and the Calame Report* (Harcourt, 1969) Maigret reluctantly gets involved in the world of politics when he agrees to help Auguste Point, a cabinet minister, find some stolen papers. UK title: *Maigret and the Minister*. Translated by Moura Budberg. First published in France in 1954 as *Maigret chez le ministre*.

47. *Maigret and the Headless Corpse* (Harcourt, 1968) A man's body is fished out of a Paris canal limb by limb, but no head can be found. Translated by Eileen Ellenbogen. First published in France in 1955 as *Maigret et le corps sans tete*.

48. *Maigret Sets a Trap* (Harcourt, 1972) Five women have been stabbed to death on the streets of Montmartre. Published in the United Kingdom in 1965. Translated by Daphne Woodward. First published in France in 1955 as *Maigret tend un piege*.

49. *Maigret's Failure* (Harcourt, 1973) Published in *A Maigret Trio*. Maigret is reluctant to bring to justice the murderer of a thoroughly bad man, the "King of the Meat Trade." Published in the United Kingdom in 1962. Translated by Daphne Woodward. First published in France in 1956 as *Un echec de Maigret*.

50. *None of Maigret's Business* (Doubleday, 1958) Maigret is supposed to be on vacation at the seashore, but he prefers Paris and the problem of the murder of a doctor's wife. Variant title: *Maigret's Little Joke*. Translated by Richard Brain. First published in France in 1957 as *Maigret s'amuse*.

51. *Maigret and the Millionaires* (Harcourt, 1974) Maigret must transcend his dislike of the international set to investigate the death of Colonel David Ward, found drowned in his bath at the posh George V Hotel. Translated by Jean Stewart. First published in France in 1958 as *Maigret voyage*.

52. *Maigret Has Scruples* (Doubleday, 1960) Published in *Versus Inspector Maigret*. This case starts with a man's fears that his wife is trying to poison him. Translated by Robert Eglesfield. First published in France in 1958 as *Les scrupules de Maigret*.

53. *Maigret and the Reluctant Witnesses* (Doubleday, 1960) Published in *Versus Inspector Maigret*. Murder strikes a member of a family of biscuit makers. Translated by Daphne Woodward. First published in France in 1959 as *Maigret et les témoins récalcitrants*.

54. *Maigret Has Doubts* (Harcourt, 1982) Only Maigret doubts the guilt of a man condemned for poisoning his wife. Published in the United Kingdom in 1968. Translated by Lyn Moir. First published in France in 1959 as *Une confidence de Maigret*.

55. *Maigret in Court* (Harcourt, 1983) To save an innocent man on trial for murder, Maigret must reveal the infidelity of the man's wife. Published in the United Kingdom in 1961. Translated by Robert Brain. First published in France in 1960 as *Maigret aux assises*.

56. *Maigret in Society* (Harcourt, 1973) Published in *A Maigret Trio*. Maigret at first feels quite out of his depth in this case of a murderous ex-ambassador. Published in the United Kingdom in 1962. Translated by Robert Eglesfield. First published in France in 1960 as *Maigret et les vieillards*.

57. *Maigret and the Lazy Burglar* (Harcourt, 1973) Published in *A Maigret Trio*. Maigret recognizes the dead body found in the Bois de Boulogne as a small-time burglar he has known for years. Published in the United Kingdom in 1963. Translated by Daphne Woodward. First published in France in 1961 as *Maigret et le voleur paresseux*. Variant title: *Maigret and the Idle Burglar*.

58. *Maigret and the Black Sheep* (Harcourt, 1976) Maigret can discover no motive for the shooting of a retired carton manufacturer. Translated by Helen Thomson. First published in France in 1962 as *Maigret et les braves gens*.

59. *Maigret and the Saturday Caller* (Harcourt, 1991) A building contractor tells Maigret that he wants to kill his wife. Published in the United Kingdom in 1964. Translated by Tony White. First published in France in 1962 as *Maigret et le client du samedi*.

60. *Maigret and the Bum* (Harcourt, 1973) Maigret must discover the identity of the man who lived under a Paris bridge and why someone murdered him. UK title: *Maigret and the Dosser*. Translated by Jean Stewart. First published in France in 1963 as *Maigret et le clochard*.

61. *Maigret Loses His Temper* (Harcourt, 1974) This puzzling case concerns the murder of a hardworking family man who owns a nightclub in Montmartre. Published in the United Kingdom in 1965. Translated by Robert Eglesfield. First published in France in 1963 as *La colère de Maigret*.

62. *Maigret and the Apparition* (Harcourt, 1976) Maigret discovers that a badly wounded policeman was on the trail of a major international art conspiracy. UK title: *Maigret and the Ghost*. Translated by Eileen Ellenbogen. First published in France in 1964 as *Maigret et le fantôme*.

63. *Maigret on the Defensive* (Harcourt, 1981) A bizarre plot to discredit Maigret begins when a young girl accuses him of sexually abusing her. Published in the United Kingdom in 1966. Translated by Alastair Hamilton. First published in France in 1964 as *Maigret se defend*.

64. *Maigret Bides His Time* (Harcourt, 1966) After learning of the murder of a valued informant, Maigret painstakingly investigates all major suspects in the case. UK title: *The Patience of Maigret*. Translated by Alastair Hamilton. First published in France in 1965 as *La patience de Maigret*.

65. *Maigret and the Nahour Case* (Harcourt, 1982) A young woman turns up with her lover at a doctor's office for treatment of a bullet wound. Published in the United Kingdom in 1967. Translated by Alastair Hamilton. First published in France in 1966 as *Maigret et l'affaire Nahour*.

66. *Maigret's Pickpocket* (Harcourt, 1968) Maigret has his wallet lifted on a Paris bus. Variant title: *Maigret and the Pickpocket*. Translated by Nigel Ryan. First published in France in 1967 as *Le voleur de Maigret*.

67. *Maigret in Vichy* (Harcourt, 1969) The Maigrets are in Vichy taking the waters when a solitary spinster is murdered. UK title: *Maigret Takes the Waters*. Translated by Eileen Ellenbogen. First published in France in 1968 as *Maigret a Vichy*.

68. *Maigret Hesitates* (Harcourt, 1969) An anonymous letter warns Maigret of an imminent murder in the family of a famous Paris lawyer. Translated by Lyn Moir. First published in France in 1968 as *Maigret hesite*.

69. *Maigret's Boyhood Friend* (Harcourt, 1970) Leon Florentin, an old school friend of Maigret's, brings him a puzzling case of murder. Translated by Eileen Ellenbogen. First published in France in 1968 as *L'ami d'enfance de Maigret*.

70. *Maigret and the Killer* (Harcourt, 1971) A young man engaged in tape-recording voices of poor and working-class people is stabbed to death. Translated by Lyn Moir. First published in France in 1969 as *Maigret et le tueur*.

71. *Maigret and the Wine Merchant* (Harcourt, 1971) The shooting of a rich Paris wine merchant evokes strange reactions from his family and friends. Translated by Eileen Ellenbogen. First published in France in 1970 as *Maigret et le marchand de vin*.

72. *Maigret and the Madwoman* (Harcourt, 1972) An old woman comes to Maigret for protection when she notices little things out of place in her apartment. Translated by Eileen Ellenbogen. First published in France in 1970 as *La folle de Maigret*.

73. *Maigret and the Loner* (Harcourt, 1975) Maigret shaves the beard and mustache off a dead recluse and runs a photo of him in the newspaper hoping for clues to his identity. Translated by Eileen Ellenbogen. First published in France in 1971 as *Maigret et l'homme tout seul*.

74. *Maigret and the Informer* (Harcourt, 1973) Maigret rubs elbows with Parisian mobsters in this case of the murder of a well-known restaurateur with a beautiful wife. UK title: *Maigret and the Flea*. Translated by Lyn Moir. First published in France in 1971 as *Maigret et l'indicateur*.

75. *Maigret and Monsieur Charles* (Hamilton [UK], 1973) Madame Sabin-Levesque becomes concerned when her solicitor husband disappears for longer time than his usual week or two. Not published in the United States. Translated by Marianne Alexandre Sinclair. First published in France in 1972 as *Maigret et Monsieur Charles*.

Simmons, Dan

I. The Hyperion/Endymion series has been compared to Isaac Asimov's (q.v.) Foundation series for its world-building skill. The novels are set in a far future in which most of humanity have sold their souls to the machine-based "TechnoCore" in exchange for advanced cosmological knowledge. Only on the planet Hyperion, home of the Time Tombs, does humanity have a chance to redeem itself. Numbers 3 and 4 carry the story 300 years into the future, after the "fall" of Hyperion, where the Pax and a resurgent Catholic Church rule, and Raul Endymion describes his travels with Aenea, a genetically altered teenager who may be the new messiah. Number 4 left a number of unanswered questions, so a sequel may be coming. *Hyperion Cantos* (Guild America, 1990) contains numbers 1 and 2. *The Hyperion Omnibus* (Gollancz [UK], 2004) contains numbers 1 and 2, and *The Endymion Omnibus* (Gollancz [UK], 2005) contains numbers 3 and 4.

1. *Hyperion* (Doubleday, 1989) Seven pilgrims from the Hegemony of Man travel to Hyperion to reach the Time Tombs, which might have the answer to preventing war. The sinister Shrike hovers in the background.

2. *Fall of Hyperion, The* (Doubleday, 1990) The pilgrims reach the Time Tombs and the Shrike, achieving either transcendence or mere death. Joseph Severn, one of the pilgrims, a reincarnation of John Keats, plays a major role.

3. *Endymion* (Bantam, 1996) Three hundred years after the events in numbers 1 and 2, Raul Endymion is writing his memoirs while awaiting execution in the Schrodinger cat box. He recalls his travels with Aenea, a teenage girl with strange powers.

4. *Rise of Endymion, The* (Bantam, 1997) Endymion continues his memoirs in the Schrodinger cat box, describing his relationship and travels with Aenea, the One Who Teaches, who, glimpsing the future, realizes her destiny.

II. Simmons first made his reputation in the horror field. The Elm Haven series has a kind of Lovecraftian aura to it with terrible, devouring evils lurking in places like abandoned school houses. Number 1 tells the story of several schoolchildren in circa 1960 Elm Haven, Illinois, who are forced to confront an ancient evil. Number 3 is a direct sequel, bringing one of the children, Dale Stewart, back to Elm Haven some 40 years later. Number 2 is more loosely connected, concerning, among other things, the 1866 diary of Lorena Stewart, an ancestress of Dale. *Children of the Night* (Putnam, 1994), a vampire novel about the son of Dracula, is sometimes linked to this series.

1. *Summer of Night* (Putnam, 1991) A young boy disappears on the last day of classes at the Old Central school building, and his friends embark upon an investigation of the mystery.

2. *Fires of Eden* (Putnam, 1994) Shady real-estate mogul Byron Trumbo finds himself stuck with a luxury resort built on the slopes of an active Hawaiian volcano. Meanwhile, the gods, the ancient Hawaiian ones, that is, are angry about the pollution of their land. Eleanor Perry, vacationing in Hawaii, stumbles on to all this. Partially told in the 1866 diary of Lorena Stewart, Eleanor's aunt.

3. *Winter Haunting, A* (Morrow, 2002) Forty years after the events in number 1, Dale Stewart returns home to Elm Haven and moves into what was once the home of his late boyhood friend, Duane McBride.

III. Joe Kurtz, ex-PI, 11-year resident of Attica State Prison, New York, is consumed by the desire for vengeance against the killers of his beautiful partner, Samantha Fielding. In three novels so far, Kurtz has left bodies strewn left and right but still hasn't achieved catharsis. Kurtz is definitely a hard-boiled type and as amoral as any character in current crime fiction. The setting is in and around Buffalo, New York, which is grim enough without the drug-running mobsters and serial killers who come Kurtz's way.

1. *Hardcase* (St. Martin's, 2001) Ex-PI Joe Kurtz, after spending 11 years in Attica State Prison for killing the mobsters he believed to be responsible for the death of his partner, Samantha Fielding, returns to Buffalo, only to find his quest for revenge still unfulfilled.

2. *Hard Freeze* (St. Martin's, 2002) Mobster "Little Skag" Farino wants Kurtz dead and sends a whole slew of would-be assassins against him, including the Attica Three Stooges.

3. *Hard as Nails* (St. Martin's, 2003) A shooting leaves Kurtz with a terrific headache and his probation officer on life-support. Gay don Toma Gonzaga wants Kurtz dead, someone is killing heroin addicts, and a serial killer known as the Artful Dodger is on the loose.

IV. In a pair of works drawing upon Homer's *Iliad*, Shakespeare's *The Tempest*, and other poetical works, Simmons postulates posthumans, masquerading as the Greek gods and living on Mars, who travel back and forth through time and alternate universes to interfere with the real Trojan War, employing a resurrected late 20th-century classics professor, Thomas Hockenberry, as their tool.

1. *Ilium* (Eos, 2003) Travelers from 40,000 years in the future return to Homer's Greece and, acting in godlike fashion, rewrite the Trojan War.

2. *Olympos* (Eos, 2005) From the outer solar system, the Moravecs, an advanced race of semiorganic artificial intelligences, try to shift the balance of power before out-of-control quantum forces destroy everything.

Simon, Roger L(ichtenberg)

Moses Wine is cast in the Hammett/Chandler hard-boiled mold except that he is an ex-hippie who prefers marijuana to alcohol. Like most fictional private eyes, he is cynical, wisecracking, divorced, middle-aged, and impecunious. The plots of the Wine series aren't always completely convincing, but the novels are full of fast dialogue, ironic insights, sophisticated humor, and interesting West Coast backgrounds. Richard Dreyfuss played Moses Wine in the movie version of *The Big Fix* (1978), which Simon scripted. Simon has collaborated with Paul Mazursky on movie scripts such as *Enemies: A Love Story* (1989). *Heir* (Macmillan, 1968), reprinted as *Dead Meet*, Simon's first novel, is not part of the series.

1. *Big Fix, The* (Simon & Schuster, 1973) Moses Wine is asked by an ex-girlfriend to investigate the smear tactic sabotaging of a presidential primary campaign.
2. *Wild Turkey* (Simon & Schuster, 1975) A writer is suspected of the murder of a prominent television personality with whom he has been feuding.
3. *Peking Duck* (Simon & Schuster, 1979) Moses Wine, touring the People's Republic of China with Aunt Sonya and other wealthy leftist Americans, is called upon to solve the case of a missing gold duck.
4. *California Roll* (Villard, 1985) After Wine becomes head of security for Tulip Computer, the chief engineer is murdered, and the Black Widow computer program is stolen.
5. *Straight Man, The* (Villard, 1986) Wine takes on the investigation of the death of Mike Ptak, straight man for the black comic Otis King.
6. *Raising the Dead* (Villard, 1988) To clear the Arabs of suspicion in the murder of Jewish peacemaker Joseph Damoor, Wine flies to Israel.
7. *Lost Coast, The* (HarperCollins, 1997) Roger's radical environmentalist son Simon is missing and wanted by the FBI for his alleged role in killing a logger with a booby trap.
8. *Director's Cut* (Atria, 2003) Is an al-Qaeda cell or someone with a more personal motive behind the threats against a movie company shooting in Prague and the death of the Grand Rabbi of Prague?

Simpson, Dorothy

Detective Inspector Luke Thanet is one of those gentle English policemen who patiently untangles crimes by ferreting out subtle psychological clues and unraveling motives. Thanet is based in rural Sturrenden, a fictional Kentish town. He is a quiet and sensitive man, devoted to his children. His assistant, Sergeant Lineham, is dominated by his mother and his strong-minded wife. The novels are well crafted and the crimes unsensationalized. Welsh-born author Dorothy Simpson started writing in her forties. Her first novel, *Harbingers of Fear* (Macdonald [UK], 1977) isn't part of the series. For similar series, see Colin Dexter's (q.v.) Inspector Morse and Reginald Hill's (q.v.) Peter Pascoe.

1. *Night She Died, The* (Scribner, 1981) Inspector Thanet tries to discover what forgotten event in Julie Holmes's past led to her death.
2. *Six Feet Under* (Scribner, 1982) After middle-aged spinster Carrie Birch is murdered, Luke Thanet finds that she was the keeper of many of her village's darkest secrets.
3. *Puppet for a Corpse* (Scribner, 1983) Respected country physician Arnold Pettifer didn't seem to have a motive for suicide.
4. *Close Her Eyes* (Scribner, 1984) Fifteen-year-old Charity Pritchard is murdered after trying to break her ties with her father's fanatical religion.
5. *Last Seen Alive* (Scribner, 1985) The woman found murdered in the Black Swan Hotel turns out to be an old school friend Thanet hadn't seen in 20 years.

6. *Dead on Arrival* (Scribner, 1987) The investigation of Steven Long's murder turns up several persons who hated him, and only his twin brother, Geoffrey, has a kind word for him.
7. *Element of Doubt* (Scribner, 1988) There are many suspects when beautiful but unpleasant Nerine Tarrant is pushed over the balcony of her manor.
8. *Suspicious Death* (Scribner, 1988) The body of self-made businesswoman Marcia Salden is found in the River Sture.
9. *Dead by Morning* (Scribner, 1989) Leo Martindale returns to Longford Hall after more than 20 years only to be found dead in a ditch two days later.
10. *Doomed to Die* (Scribner, 1991) Artist Perdita Master is found dead with a plastic bag over her head after fleeing from her abusive husband to a nanny's job.
11. *Wake the Dead* (Scribner, 1992) Rich, ruthless, manipulative, old Isobel Fairleigh is smothered while half-conscious from a stroke.
12. *No Laughing Matter* (Scribner, 1993) After vintner Zak Randish takes a fatal fall through a window, Thanet investigates Zak's past, which includes womanizing and wife beating among a host of sins.
13. *Day for Dying, A* (Scribner, 1996) Playboy and travel writer Max Jeopard is found floating in the swimming pool at his own engagement party.
14. *Once Too Often* (Scribner, 1998) Newspaper reporter Jessica Dancer's husband, Desmond Manifest, is one of the leading suspects when she breaks her neck in an apparent fall.
15. *Dead and Gone* (Scribner, 2000) The wife of respected Kent legal figure Ralph Minter disappears during a dinner, and is found at the bottom of the garden well the next day.

Simpson, Mona (Elizabeth)

Wisconsin-born Simpson has written a pair of novels about the belated coming-of-age of a woman with a manipulative mother and an absent father. Ann Stevenson's search for her vanished father and the ideal home she has lost ends with her deciding that "maybe by the time you find somebody they are beside the point." A poignant story of a sympathetic character told with trenchant observations. *Anywhere but Here* was made into a film starring Susan Sarandon and Natalie Portman (1999). Two later novels: *A Regular Guy* (Knopf, 1996) and *Off Keck Road* (Knopf, 2000) are stand-alones.

1. *Anywhere but Here* (Knopf, 1987) Ann Stevenson and her mother, Adele, flee their Wisconsin home for a fresh start in California, where Ann becomes a child film star but longs for a rootedness her mother can't give her.
2. *Lost Father, The* (Knopf, 1992) Ann, now in her late twenties, has reassumed her birth name, Mayan Atassi, and is flunking out of medical school because she is obsessed with finding the father who deserted her when she was 12.

Sinclair, Upton

I. Sinclair was America's best-known muckraker. His zealous attack on social and economic injustice is still unequaled, and his following in his own day may well be envied by today's reformers. After a modest but commercially successful beginning writing boys' adventure stories, Sinclair produced *The Jungle* (Doubleday, 1906), a novel that shocked American readers by detailing the filth and corruption of Chicago's meat-packing industry. Actually, because of publishers' fear of libel suits, Sinclair was forced to excise several chapters to get *The Jungle* published in book form. The full version, which originally appeared in the Socialist journal *Appeal to Reason*, wasn't published by Doubleday until 1988. By the time of his death in 1968 at the age of 90, Sinclair had published close to 50 novels, more than 30 nonfiction works, and countless articles and editorials treating a wide variety of subjects from the horrors of venereal disease (see series II, below) and the exploitation of coal workers to the Sacco Vanzetti case (in *Boston*) and regrettably, various crank causes like fasting and extrasensory perception. Sinclair was nearly elected governor of California in 1934 before he was derailed by an early example of the cinematic "attack ad." The Lanny Budd series of 11 historical novels covers the history of the world from 1913 to 1949. Lanny is a rich, globe-trotting American whose presence on the scene at every significant event of those years provides a useful, though admittedly not too believable, narrative device and a unifying thread.

1. *World's End* (Viking, 1940) Lanny Budd is an idealistic youth of 13 when this story begins in 1913. World War I sends him home to America, but is back at the Versailles peace conference as a secretary to a Woodrow Wilson aide.
2. *Between Two Worlds* (Viking, 1941) The rise of Fascism is documented in this volume, which covers the 1920s.
3. *Dragon's Teeth* (Viking, 1942) This covers events in Germany from 1930 to 1934, ending with Hitler's Blood Purge.
4. *Wide Is the Gate* (Viking, 1943) This book covers the years 1935–1936 and the beginnings of the Spanish civil war.
5. *Presidential Agent* (Viking, 1945) Lanny serves as a special agent for President Roosevelt in Europe during 1937–1938.
6. *Dragon Harvest* (Viking, 1945) In 1939–1940 Franco wins in Spain, and France falls to Hitler.
7. *World to Win, A* (Viking, 1946) The events of 1940–1942 include America's entry into World War II.
8. *Presidential Mission* (Viking, 1947) The war continues in 1942–1943.
9. *One Clear Call* (Viking, 1948) Fears of Germany's possible nuclear capabilities mark 1943–1944.
10. *O Shepherd Speak* (Viking, 1949) Lanny uses his wealth to create the Peace Foundation in 1944–1946.
11. *Return of Lanny Budd, The* (Viking, 1953) The period is 1944–1949. The cold war begins, and Lanny turns in his half sister to the FBI as a Communist agent.

II. Two novels, somewhat reminiscent of Ibsen's play *Ghosts*, are about Virginia belle Sylvia, who schemes her way into an upper-class marriage only to discover that her husband has a venereal disease.

1. *Sylvia* (Winston, 1913) Young Virginia coquette Sylvia works her way up in society by marrying an upper-class man.
2. *Sylvia's Marriage* (Winston, 1914) The pregnant Sylvia discovers that her outwardly respectable husband has a venereal disease.

Singer, Isaac Bashevis

Isaac Bashevis Singer's centenary, in 2004, was celebrated by, among other things, the publication of three volumes of collected short stories in the Library of America. The works of Nobel laureate (1978) Singer were composed in Yiddish, then translated into English by Singer and other translators. Singer is best known for his supernaturally charged short stories and novels about Jewish life in the shtetls of Eastern Europe before the Holocaust (e.g., "Gimpel the Fool" and "The Spinoza of Market Street"), but he also published children's books, several volumes of memoirs, and family sagas that are reminiscent of his elder brother I. J. Singer, author of *The Brothers Ashkenazi*. *The Manor* and *The Estate* were originally a single novel, *Der*

hoyf, serialized in Yiddish in the *Jewish Daily Forward* (1953–1955), then translated into English, amplified, and published in two volumes. Later, the two volumes were combined into one: *The Manor* (Farrar, 1979). The novel is the saga of Calman Jacoby, a wealthy Jewish grain merchant who leases the Polish estate of Count Jampolski in 1863. The assimilation into Gentile society and the loss of Calman's family's religious and social heritage are chronicled to the end of the 19th century. Singer is a master storyteller who catches the passion and poignance of his characters' lives.

1. *Manor, The* (Farrar, 1967) Calman Jacoby becomes richer by selling the timber from the estate he has leased but loses his four daughters to assimilation and modernization. Translated from the Yiddish by Joseph Singer and Elaine Gottlieb.
2. *Estate, The* (Farrar, 1969) Sasha, the son of Calman's estranged wife, Clara, takes over management of the estate. Translated from the Yiddish by Joseph Singer and Elaine Gottlieb.

Singer, Shelley

PSEUDONYM OF Rochelle Singer

I. Jake Samson is an unlicensed private investigator living in Oakland, California. Like many of his ilk, he is a hard-boiled wisecracker who is basically sensitive and likable. What distinguishes him from his brethren is his sidekick, lesbian carpenter Rosie Vicente. The Samson novels are well-plotted, amusing entertainments with a San Francisco Bay ambience. Author Shelley Singer, who also lives in Oakland, worked at a variety of jobs including journalist, antique restorer, welfare worker, gardener, and carpenter before she started publishing the Jake Samson series. *The Demeter Flower* (St. Martin's, 1980) is not a series novel.

1. *Samson's Deal* (St. Martin's, 1983) Samson is asked to find the murderer of radical professor John Harley's wife by old friend Rebecca Lilly, who was having an affair with Harley.
2. *Free Draw* (St. Martin's, 1984) When Jake's friend Artie Perrine is charged with murder, Jake poses as a reporter for an investigatory magazine to find the real culprit.
3. *Full House* (St. Martin's, 1986) Samson is hired by a band of cultists building an ark in Oakland to find cult leader and health tycoon Noah, who has disappeared with a quarter of a million dollars.
4. *Spit in the Ocean* (St. Martin's, 1987) Someone has been taking the deposits from Nora Canfield's sperm bank and tossing them in the ocean.
5. *Suicide King* (St. Martin's, 1988) VIVO party gubernatorial candidate Joe Richmond is found hanging naked from a tree.
6. *Royal Flush* (Daniel, 1999) Although he is Jewish, Jake infiltrates the Aryan Command, a Marin County neo-Nazi group, to save a friend's goddaughter from a romantic entanglement with a member.

II. Singer's second mystery series has as a protagonist Barrett Lake, a history teacher who becomes a detective specializing in finding missing children. So far all of her cases have dealt with missing or murdered teenagers in the Berkeley–San Francisco area.

1. *Following Jane* (Signet, 1993) When student Jane Whalman runs away after the murder of a teacher, Berkeley Technical High instructor Barrett Lake asks private eye "Tito" Broz to train her as a private investigator.
2. *Picture of David* (Signet, 1993) Soon after 14-year-old David is kidnapped, his parents receive a partially burned photo of his upper torso and terrified face.

3. *Searching for Sara* (Signet, 1994) After finding 15-year-old runaway Sara at a shelter in San Francisco, Barrett becomes involved in a murder case.

4. *Interview with Mattie* (Signet, 1995) Missing teenager Mattie has been found dead, and Barrett finds herself involved with teenage gangs and a shadowy killer.

Sjöwall, Maj

The Swedish wife-and-husband team of Maj Sjöwall and Per Wahlöö quickly won an enthusiastic American audience with its fast-paced and chillingly suspenseful stories about Stockholm policeman Martin Beck. The books' gritty realism, interesting Swedish atmosphere, and strong socialist orientation make them unique. Walter Matthau was a surprisingly convincing Martin Beck in the 1974 American film *The Laughing Policeman*, but the substitution of San Francisco for Stockholm was a disappointment to fans. English translations of the novels appeared from one to three years after the Swedish originals. Another crime series was written by Wahlöö (q.v.) alone, whose death, in 1975, brought an end to the Beck series.

1. *Roseanna* (Pantheon, 1967) A naked woman is dredged up from the bottom of Sweden's Lake Vattern, and Martin Beck struggles to identify her and her murderer without any clues to go on. Translated from the original Swedish *Roseanna* by Lois Roth.

2. *Man on the Balcony, The* (Pantheon, 1968) Beck and the large special force assigned to him race against death in the pursuit of a child murderer in Stockholm. Translated from the Swedish *Mannen pa balkongen* by Alan Blair.

3. *Man Who Went Up in Smoke, The* (Pantheon, 1969) Beck is sent to Budapest on an exasperating search for the missing journalist Alf Matsson. Translated from the Swedish *Mannen som gick upp irök* by Joan Tate.

4. *Laughing Policeman, The* (Pantheon, 1970) When a young police colleague is one of the eight bus passengers killed by a mass murderer, Beck takes a special interest in bringing the criminal to justice. Translated from the Swedish *Den skrattende polisen* by Alan Blair.

5. *Fire Engine That Disappeared, The* (Pantheon, 1970) Elements in this baffling case include a cryptic suicide note and a bombed Stockholm apartment house. Translated from the Swedish *Brandbilen som försvann* by Joan Tate.

6. *Murder at the Savoy* (Pantheon, 1971) Victor Palmgren, a wealthy industrialist, is gunned down in the dining room of the posh Savoy Hotel in Malmo. Translated from the Swedish *Polis, polis, potatismos!* by Ann and Ken Knoespel.

7. *Abominable Man, The* (Pantheon, 1972) When a police colleague is murdered in his hospital bed, Beck must dig deep into the lives of Stockholm's police to solve the crime. Translated from the Swedish *Den veder vordige mannen fran Saffle* by Thomas Teal.

8. *Locked Room, The* (Pantheon, 1973) A decayed corpse with a bullet through its head is found inside a locked room, and the lack of a gun seems to eliminate suicide. Translated from the Swedish *Det slutna rummet* by Paul Britten Austin.

9. *Cop Killer* (Pantheon, 1975) Is the dead woman found by hikers in a small Swedish town related to the shoot-out that left one policeman dead and two others wounded? Translated from the Swedish *Polismordaren* by Thomas Teal.

10. *Terrorists, The* (Pantheon, 1976) Beck guards an American senator visiting Stockholm from attack by an international gang of terrorists. Translated from the Swedish *Terroristerna* by Joan Tate.

Skelton, C(lement) L(ister)

I. The three volumes of the Regimental "Quartet" (the fourth was apparently never published) are a cross between family saga and regimental history: they follow the fortunes of two Scottish families, the Maclarens and the Bruces, and the Highland regiment in which they served. Skelton gives the series numerous well-drawn characters and sweeps across class lines to show the crofters and merchants as well as the soldiers and aristocrats who inhabit the rugged Scottish hill country from the 1850s on.

1. *Maclarens, The* (Dial, 1978) Beginning with the July 1857 Indian Mutiny, this novel tells the story of Lieutenant Andrew Maclaren; his childhood friend, Sergeant Willie Bruce, and the beautiful woman they both love, Maud Westburn.

2. *Regiment, The* (Dial, 1979) In 1883 Andrew has retired, Willie has taken over the regiment, and their sons take center stage.

3. *Beloved Soldiers* (Crown, 1984) The men of the Maclaren and Bruce families fight the Germans in the first two years of World War I, as many of their women join up as nurses, ambulance drivers, or military recruiters.

II. A pair of novels, the second of which was never published in the United States, tells the rags-to-riches story of Yorkshireman Sam Hardacre from the 1880s until after World War II.

1. *Hardacre* (Dial, 1976) Sam Hardacre, a tough, colorful Yorkshire fish-gutter, rises in wealth and position, and his family rises with him. Starts in the 1880s.

2. *Hardacre's Luck* (HarperCollins [UK], 1985) The Hardacre saga continues into the 1950s and 1960s, as Sam Bisset Hardacre, formerly Brother Jude of the Order of St. Benedict, restores the family's fortunes. Not published in the United States.

Skvorecký, Josef

I. Josef Skvorecký, Czech native who emigrated to Canada, is a household name in the Czech Republic but little known in English-speaking countries. Many of Skvorecky's works are autobiographical or semiautobiographical, including such works as the memoir *Headed for the Blues* and the novella "The Bass Saxophone" (published in *The Bass Saxophone* Knopf, 1977). Four works are about a semiautobiographical character called Danny Smiricky. Danny is first picked up as a teenager in Nazi-occupied Czechoslovakia who finds an outlet in jazz. Jazz is a symbol for the individualism that authoritarian regimes cannot abide. Danny lives through decades of Communism in Czechoslovakia, then emigrates to Canada when he gets a chance.

1. *Cowards, The* (Grove, 1970) Twenty-year-old Danny Smiricky and his friends devote themselves to jazz and women as the Germans retreat and the Russians take over in a provincial Bohemian town in 1945. Translated from the Czech by Jeanne Nemcova. Originally published in 1958 as *Zbabelci*.

2. *Republic of Whores, The* (Ecco, 1994) Danny serves a stint in the Czech army during the 1950s and treats the whole experience as a bad joke. Translated from the Czech by Paul Wilson. Originally published in 1971 as *Tankový prator* (*The Tank Corps*).

3. *Miracle Game, The* (Knopf, 1991) Communist authorities try to discredit the Catholic church by perpetrating a hoax and blaming it on a priest. Danny fights venereal disease. Translated from the Czech by Paul Wilson. Originally published in 1972 as *Mirakl*.

4. *Engineer of Human Souls, The* (Knopf, 1984) Danny emigrates to Canada, accepts a position at the University of Toronto, observes

his fellow émigrés, and argues about politics and literature with his students and colleagues. Translated from the Czech by Paul Wilson. Originally published in 1977 as *Příběh inženýtra lidských doši*.

II. Skvorecký published two volumes of short stories and a novel about Lieutenant Josef Boruvka of the Prague police. Boruvka is a sensitive man whose humanism is a liability in a totalitarian regime. Eventually Boruvka is imprisoned for "political crimes" but escapes and emigrates to Canada, where he becomes a parking-lot attendant. The short story collection *Sins for Father Knox* (Norton, 1979) contains two Boruvka stories.

1. *Mournful Demeanor of Lieutenant Boruvka, The* (Norton, 1987) Short story collection. Translated from the Czech by Rosemary Kavan, Kaca Polackova, and George Trent. Originally published in 1966 as *Smutek porucika Boruvka*. English translation first published in Canada in 1973.
2. *End of Lieutenant Boruvka, The* (Norton, 1990) Short stories. Translated from the Czech by Paul Wilson. Originally published in 1975 as *Konec porucika Boruvka*.
3. *Return of Lieutenant Boruvka, The* (Norton, 1991) Boruvka, after escaping from a Czechoslovakian prison, emigrates to Canada, where an Canadian amateur detective enlists his help in a case of homicide among Czech émigrés. Translated from the Czech by Paul Wilson. Originally published in 1980 as *Návrat porucika Boruvka*.

Skye, Christina

I. Draycott Abbey in Scotland is overseen by a kindly ghost named Adrian; his gray cat, Gideon; and three ghostly sisters who appear from time to time. Passionate romance busts out every time a beautiful woman and a handsome guy get together in the medieval abbey. Christina Skye, expert on classical Chinese poetry and formerly an international consultant, has a large romance reader following. Although some critics have been enthusiastic about her books, others refer to them as "competent no-brainers" or worse. Number 6 originally appeared only as an audiobook, but now it has been combined with number 3 in an omnibus volume, *Bridge of Dreams/Enchantment* (Harlequin, 2007).

1. *Hour of the Rose* (Avon, 1994) When rugged ex–Royal Marine Michael Burke and beautiful archaeologist Kelly Hamilton arrive at Draycott Abbey, they are fated to repeat a tragic love affair from the abbey's medieval past.
2. *Bride of the Mist* (Avon, 1996) Bridal magazine editor Kara Fitzgerald is linked psychically by a necklace with the 19th century Arduaine of Draycotte, the beautiful, mute daughter of Lord Draycotte. Duncan MacKinnon, bad-tempered laird of Dunraven Castle, has an evil twin who is trying to blow up Kara and Duncan as their romantic attachment develops.
3. *Bridge of Dreams* (Avon, 1995) To inherit a fortune, Cathlin O'Neill must spend a week in Draycott Abbey, where her mother was murdered, with her co-inheritor, a former royal bodyguard.
4. *Key to Forever* (Avon, 1997) The priceless, but accursed, Cameron Claymore (a two-handed sword) is the McGuffin for antique-weapons expert Joanna Russell and Alexei Cameron, "the handsome, broad-shouldered, half-Gypsy, Earl of Greywood," who are fated to reenact their night of passion.
5. *Season of Wishes* (Avon, 1997) Concerned that their sister, fabric designer and heiress Jamee Night, might be kidnapped again,

Jamee's brothers secretly sign on kidnapping expert Ian McCall, the tenth laird of Glenlyle, to protect her.
6. *Enchantment* (Renaissance (audio), 1998) When Kacey Mallory arrives at Draycott Abbey, she is startled by an awareness that she doesn't understand, which Nicholas Draycott ascribes to the Draycott curse. Originally published in audio form. Published in book form, along with number 3, by Harlequin in 2007.
7. *Christmas Knight* (Avon, 1998) Is Ronan MacLeod, the mysterious stranger who has come riding into Hope O'Hara's life, really, as he claims, a medieval knight?
8. *Perfect Gift, The* (Avon, 1999) Maggie Kincade has won a stay in Draycott Abbey as a prize in an art competition. But who is Jared MacNeill, the mysterious, intriguing man who seems to shadow her around the place?

II. The Code Name series is populated by beautiful professional women and sexy, microchip-enhanced Navy SEALs, the reigning stars of contemporary romantic adventure. Continuing characters, such as the sexy, Denzel Washington–like Izzy Teague, a couple of pairs of twins, and the ostensibly villainous Gabriel Enrique Cruz wander in and out of this improbable, but readable, romantic action series.

1. *Code Name: Nanny* (Bantam, 2004) FBI agent Summer Mulcahey and Navy SEAL Gabe Morgan are working undercover to protect Cara O'Connor, soon to wed US Senator Tate Winslow.
2. *Code Name: Princess* (Bantam, 2004) Hotel evaluator Jess Mulcahey, twin sister of Summer Mulcahey of number 1, operating undercover as a minor European princess to do her job, and recuperating SEAL Hawk Mackenzie find themselves trapped together in an elevator.
3. *Code Name: Baby* (HQN, 2005) Navy SEAL Wolfe Houston arrives at the New Mexico ranch of gorgeous dog trainer Kit O'Halloran to protect her and the four genetically enhanced black Labradors that she is training.
4. *Code Name: Blondie* (HQN, 2006) When photographer Miki Fortune ends up on a remote island after a plane crash, she is rescued and taken captive by paranormally enhanced Navy SEAL Max Preston, who is convinced that she is working for the villain Gabriel Enrique Cruz (a character in number 3).
5. *Code Name: Bikini* (HQN, 2007) Microchip-enhanced Navy SEAL Trace O'Halloran, who has an assignment guarding valuable human tissue samples aboard a luxury cruise ship en route to Mexico, hooks up with pastry chef Gina Ryan.

III. A pair of Regency romances features members of the fabulously rich, aristocratic Delamere family.

1. *Come the Night* (Dell, 1994) Silver St. Clair, heir to a perfume business, is captured by the Black Lord, a highwayman who is really Lucien Delamere, heir to the richest title in Regency England.
2. *Come the Dawn* (Dell, 1995) Heiress India Delamere, daughter of the Duke of Devonham, secretly weds heartbreaker Devlyn Carlisle, 12th Earl of Thornwood, who disappears, for a while, at the ensuing battle of Waterloo.

Small, Bertrice

I. Best-selling historical romance writer Bertrice Small's favorite stamping ground is England in the Tudor and Stuart periods, although her characters have a way of turning up in more exotic climes such as the Ottoman Empire or India. Most of the Tudor/Stuart novels are connected by their main characters: Skye O'Malley and her descendants and Rosamond Bolton and her daughters. The series is divided into three subseries. Friarsgate Inheritance (numbers 1–4), set in the time of Henry VIII, featuring heiress Rosamund Bolton and her daughters, is first chronologically, but last in publishing order. It is connected with the other two subseries by the Leslies, Earls of Glenkirk, The Skye O'Malley series (numbers 5–10), set during the reigns of Elizabeth I and James I, features Irish spitfire Skye O'Malley and her children and grandchildren, and ranges from Ireland to England to Algiers to Constantinople to India. Skye's Legacy (numbers 11–16) continues the saga into the reigns of Charles I, Cromwell, and Charles II, and carries the "legacy" down to Skye's great-great-grandchildren.

1. *Rosamund* (New American Library, 2002) Rosamund Bolton, orphaned and widowed heiress to the Friarsgate fortune, serves Elizabeth of York and Katherine of Aragon in the court of Henry VIII.

2. *Until You* (New American Library, 2003) Now widowed thrice, Rosamund Bolton flees Friarsgate to escape yet another marriage and winds up in the court of Queen Margaret of Scotland, where she falls for Patrick Leslie, Earl of Glenkirk.

3. *Philippa* (New American Library, 2004) Philippa, Rosamund's eldest daughter, prefers serving Queen Katherine of Aragon in Henry VIII's court to marriage.

4. *Last Heiress, The* (New American Library, 2005) Concerns the romantic adventures of Elizabeth Meredith, Rosamund's youngest daughter.

5. *Skye O'Malley* (Ballantine, 1981) Fiery Skye O'Malley finds love with four different men in the time of Queen Elizabeth and romantic adventure in Ireland, England, and Algiers.

6. *All the Sweet Tomorrows* (Ballantine, 1984) Skye, believing her husband, Niall, to be dead, returns to Algiers.

7. *Love for All Time, A* (New American Library, 1986) Skye's brother, Conn O'Malley, marries heiress Aidan St. Michael and proceeds to fall in love with her.

8. *This Heart of Mine* (New American Library, 1985) Velvet de Marisco, Skye's youngest daughter, goes to India, and winds up as 40th wife of the Great Mogul Akbar.

9. *Lost Love Found* (Ballantine, 1989) Valentine St. Michell, daughter of Conn and Aidan, travels to India in the time of King James I.

10. *Wild Jasmine* (Ballantine, 1992) Jasmine, Velvet's daughter and Skye's granddaughter, endures a forced marriage.

11. *Darling Jasmine* (Kensington, 1997) Forced into marriage twice, Jasmine flees to France.

12. *Bedazzled* (Kensington, 1999) Lady India Lindley, bound for Italy, is captured by Barbary pirates.

13. *Besieged* (Kensington, 2000) Lady Fortune Lindley, slated to marry a Protestant aristocrat, falls in love, instead, with his disinherited Catholic brother.

14. *Intrigued* (Kensington, 2001) Lady Autumn Rose Lindley finds love in France, but is soon widowed.

15. *Just beyond Tomorrow* (Kensington, 2002) Patrick Leslie and Flann Brodie hit it off.

16. *Vixens* (Kensington, 2003) Three of Skye O'Malley's great-great granddaughters find romance in the reign of Charles II.

II. Lately Bertrice Small has branched out from historical romances into contemporary romance and fantasy. The Channel is a secret network that allows women to live out their wildest fantasies.

1. *Private Pleasures* (New American Library, 2004) Romance writer Emily Shann has her personal love upgraded by sexy editor Michael Devin and the Channel, a secret network that allows women to live out their wildest fantasies.

2. *Forbidden Pleasures* (New American Library, 2006) After Nora Buckley's husband leaves her for a younger woman, Nora is introduced to the delights of the Channel.

3. *Sudden Pleasures* (New American Library, 2007) Can the marriage of convenience of Ashley Kimbrough and millionaire Ryan Mulcahy have its passion level upgraded by the Channel?

III. The World of Hetar is a romantic fantasy series set in a kind of alternative England, a land of Forest Lords, Shadow Princes, Coastal Kings, and faeries. Lara, a beautiful half-faerie, is the leading character.

1. *Lara* (HQN, 2005) Lara, the beautiful half-faerie, embarks on a series of adventures in Hetar.

2. *Distant Tomorrow, A* (HQN, 2006) Five years after the Winter War between Hetar and the Outlands, Lara finds herself in the new world of Terah.

3. *Twilight Lord, The* (HQN, 2007) Lara, Domina of Terah, goes missing while visiting the New Outlands.

Smith, Alexander McCall

I. If the term *African cozies* seems like an oxymoron to you, try Alexander McCall Smith's delightful series set in Botswana. Mma "Precious" Ramotswe, "traditionally-built," divorced, and in her midthirties, sets up a storefront detective agency in the city of Gaborone, armed only with a detective manual, her readings of Agatha Christie (q.v.), and her instincts. With her assistant, Grace Makutsi, and J. L. B. Matekoni, the auto mechanic who becomes her fiancé and eventual husband, the redoubtable Mma Ramotswe serves as a family counselor, sometime investigator, and commentator on contemporary manners. Her primary concern is doing right by her clients. Plot is secondary here: Ramotswe, her cohorts, and her clients are likable characters, with all of their foibles, and the Botswana background is lovingly drawn.

Alexander McCall Smith, born in what is now called Zimbabwe, now a professor at Edinburgh (Scotland) University, has taught law at Botswana University. As well as writing mystery series, he is also the author or editor of several legal books, including *The Criminal Law of Botswana* (Juta, South Africa, 1992; coauthored with Kwame Frimpong) and *Errors, Medicine, and the Law* (Cambridge UP, 2001; coauthored with Alan Merry), as well as more than 50 juveniles, with continuing characters such as Harriet Bean, Akimbo, and Max and Maddy.

1. *No. 1 Ladies' Detective Agency, The* (Anchor, 2002) Introduces Mma "Precious" Ramotswe, who sets up the No. 1 Ladies' Detective Agency, a shoestring operation in the city of Gaborone, Botswana, Africa. Her earlier cases include women who suspect their cheating husbands, fathers who suspect their wandering daughters, an erratic doctor, and a missing child who may have been abducted by witch doctors. Originally published in South Africa in 1998.

2. *Tears of the Giraffe* (Anchor, 2002) Ramotswe tracks a missing American man at the request of his widowed mother, while dealing the resentful maid of her fiancé, auto mechanic J. L. B. Matekoni. Originally published in the United Kingdom in 2000.

3. *Morality for Beautiful Girls* (Anchor, 2002) An important government figure is poisoned just as Precious is trying to concentrate on the Miss Beauty and Integrity Contest—and on the odd doings of her fiancé, Mr. J. L. B. Matekoni.

4. *Kalahari Typing School for Men, The* (Pantheon, 2003) Ramotswe's assistant, Mma Grace Makutsi, opens a typing school for men,

while Precious is confronted with the arrival of a sexist rival detective who boasts of his New York City street smarts.

5. *Full Cupboard of Life, The* (Pantheon, 2004) A self-made founder of a chain of hairdressing salons wants to learn the real intentions of her four suitors. Precious's fiancé, J. L. B. Matekoni, has honorable intentions but is distracted by events.

6. *In the Company of Cheerful Ladies* (Pantheon, 2005) An intruder in her home (who has left behind a pair of trousers); a man from her past; Mr. Matekoni, now her husband, who has apprentice trouble; Mma Makutsi's new suitor; and a wrongfully imprisoned pharmacist engage Ramotswe in this episode.

7. *Blue Shoes and Happiness* (Pantheon, 2006) The search for the identity of a blackmailer and the source of malaise at a nearby game reserve are among the problems here.

8. *Good Husband of Zebra Drive, The* (Pantheon, 2007) Dr. Cronje, half-Xhosa and half-Afrikaner, consults Precious because patients at his hospital who have occupied a particular bed have been dying mysteriously at the same time of day.

9. *Miracle at Speedy Motors, The* (Pantheon, 2008) Precious Ramotswe deals with two problems: a series of threatening anonymous letters and the search for Manka Sebina's missing relatives.

II. Scottish American philosopher Isabel Dalhousie, single woman of independent means, edits the esteemed *Review of Applied Ethics* and presides over the Sunday Philosophy Club in Edinburgh (Scotland). The somewhat nosy Isabel, who, after all, is an expert on applied ethics, can't stop herself from getting involved in a series of puzzles that challenge or embody her principles. Plot is not of the essence in these well-characterized mysteries, which pose, and try to answer, some ethical conundrums.

1. *Sunday Philosophy Club, The* (Pantheon, 2004) When she witnesses the suspicious fall of fund manager Mark Fraser from a balcony at an Edinburgh concert hall, Isabel Dalhousie, editor of the *Review of Applied Ethics*, and presider over the Sunday Philosophy Club, feels conscience-bound to investigate.

2. *Friends, Lovers, Chocolate* (Pantheon, 2005) When she fills in at her niece Cat's gourmet shop–cum–delicatessen, Isabel meets Ian, who is haunted by visions of a man he believes to be the murdered donor of his transplanted heart.

3. *Right Attitude to Rain, The* (Pantheon, 2006) When Jamie, a classical musician 15 years her junior and former boyfriend of her niece Cat, begins to show interest in Isabel, she is thrown into an ethical crisis.

4. *Careful Use of Compliments, The* (Pantheon, 2007) Isabel, who has recently become a mother, has an ambiguous relationship with her son's father, Jamie, whom she is reluctant to marry. Isabel must also deal with the academic politics threatening to remove her from the editorship of the *Review of Applied Ethics* and investigate the mystery of a drowned Scottish painter.

III. In another series set in Edinburgh, the lives of residents of 44 Scotland Street, a Georgian townhouse turned into a home for boarders, are drolly and sympathetically chronicled.

1. *44 Scotland Street* (Anchor, 2005) Among the large cast of characters at 44 Scotland Street is Pat, aged 21, on her second "gap year" from her studies and working at a minor art gallery, who gets intrigued about a potentially valuable painting, which winds up in the possession of Ian Rankin (q.v.), real-life chronicler of Edinburgh mysteries.

2. *Espresso Tales* (Anchor, 2006) The lives of more Scotland Street residents are delineated: Bertie, gifted five-year-old boy who is taking yoga and Italian lessons in the "ungendered" life designed

by his mother, Irene; and Ramsey Dubarton, who puts his wife, Betty, to sleep by reading her installments of his memoirs.

3. *Love over Scotland* (Anchor, 2007) Anthropologist Domenica has flown off to the Straits of Malacca to study modern-day pirates, while back in Edinburgh, Pat develops a crush on fellow art student Wolf, child prodigy saxophonist Bertie becomes a member of the Edinburgh Teenage Orchestra at age six, and poet–portrait painter Angus's dog, Cyrus, is dognapped.

IV. Addled German philologist, Professor Dr. Moritz-Maria von Igelfeld, is the hero of three short, farcical, and broadly humorous novels, in which von Igelfeld, who yearns for respect, involves himself in some hilariously disastrous undertakings. Illustrated by Iain McIntosh.

1. *Portuguese Irregular Verbs* (Anchor, 2003) Philologist von Igelfeld takes a busman's holiday researching Old Irish obscenities, has a flirtation with a desirable lady dentist, and "volunteers" a friend for a duel.

2. *Finer Points of Sausage Dogs, The* (Anchor, 2005) Von Igelfeld performs surgery without a veterinary medicine license on an unfortunate dachshund, transports relics for a Coptic prelate, and is mobbed by marriage-minded widows on board a Mediterranean cruise ship.

3. *At the Villa of Reduced Circumstances* (Anchor, 2005) Von Igelfeld endures academic intrigue as a visiting fellow at Cambridge and, pursuing the person who has finally checked out of the library his tome on Portuguese irregular verbs, gets involved with Colombian revolutionaries.

Smith, Charles Merrill

Here is a Protestant clergyman–sleuth to keep the ranks ecumenical, along with Ralph McInerny's (q.v.) Father Dowling and Harry Kemelman's (q.v.) Rabbi Small. The Reverend Cesare Paul Randollph of Chicago's Episcopal Church of the Good Shepherd was the creation of clergyman (United Methodist) and author Smith, who injected interesting glimpses of ecclesiastical matters into his mysteries. The Reverend Randollph is a cheerfully red-blooded "muscular Christian," a former pro football player with a PhD. His investigative manner is thoughtful and suave but dogged. Charles Merrill Smith died in 1985. His son Terrence Lore Smith, a mystery writer in his own right (*The Thief Who Came to Dinner*, etc.), completed the sixth Reverend Randollph novel.

1. *Reverend Randollph and the Wages of Sin* (Putnam, 1974) Reverend C. P. Randollph arrives at the Church of the Good Shepherd just in time to investigate a murder and some funny financial business among the trustees.

2. *Reverend Randollph and the Avenging Angel* (Putnam, 1977) Just minutes after the wedding ceremony, the bride is bludgeoned to death, and Randollph, an old beau, is a suspect.

3. *Reverend Randollph and the Fall from Grace* (Putnam, 1978) Someone is trying to kill the TV evangelist Prince Hartman but keeps killing his aides by mistake.

4. *Reverend Randollph and the Holy Terror* (Putnam, 1980) Now married to the gorgeous TV star Samantha and ready to move to a posh new congregation, Reverend Randollph is threatened by a homicidal maniac who specializes in clergymen.

5. *Reverend Randollph and the Unholy Bible* (Putnam, 1983) A Mafia don is convinced that Randollph is a murderer and a thief when the Reverend's parishioner, Johannes Humbrecht, is killed, and his Gutenberg Bible disappears.

6. *Reverend Randollph and the Splendid Samaritan* (**Putnam, 1986**) Reverend Randollph suspects that murdered financier and philanthropist James Trent was hiding something unsavory.

Smith, Evelyn E.

Miss Susan Melville, former heiress, artist, and freelance assassin, was well into middle age (pushing 50) before she discovered her twin vocations, painting and shooting people. This is a frothy, funny, action-packed adventure series that pokes fun at fashionable New York society. Evelyn E. Smith (d. 2000) also wrote science fiction and gothics as Delphine C. Lyon.

1. *Miss Melville Regrets* (**Fine, 1986**) Down-at-the-heels heiress Susan Melville turns her talent for party crashing into the more lucrative, if more sinister, pursuit of political assassination.
2. *Miss Melville Returns* (**Fine, 1987**) Now a fashionable painter, Miss Melville feels her trigger finger itch when an artist and a gallery owner are murdered and the gallery is burned down.
3. *Miss Melville's Revenge* (**Fine, 1989**) Miss Melville decides to devote her life to rendering justice (i.e., death sentences) to individuals whose diplomatic immunity prevents their arrest and conviction for capital crimes.
4. *Miss Melville Rides a Tiger* (**Fine, 1991**) The international drug cartel is personified by the Begum of Gandistan, Miss Melville's old enemy, Berengaria Rundle.
5. *Miss Melville Runs for Cover* (**Fine, 1993**) No annotation available.

Smith, Julie

I. Skip Langdon is a smart and determined female New Orleans cop. Skip has a complicated personal and professional life, balancing a long-distance lover against one closer to hand. From number 6 on, a character named Errol Jacomine, preacher, talk-show host, politician, and psychopath has been Skip's leading nemesis. Talba Wallis, a character in number 8, now has a series of her one (see series II, below). Smith displays a good ear for New Orleans speech and a good feel for New Orleans ambience in this humorous, suspenseful mystery serials. *New Orleans Mourning* won the Edgar Award for Best Mystery Novel in 1991, the first time since 1956 an American woman won the award. *Mean Rooms* (Five Stars, 2000), a Julie Smith short story collection, contains several Skip Langdon stories.

1. *New Orleans Mourning* (**St. Martin's, 1990**) The King of Carnival at Mardi Gras is shot to death by a mysterious person decked out like Dolly Parton.
2. *Axeman's Jazz, The* (**St. Martin's, 1991**) "The Axeman," a serial killer modelling himself after a killer from 1919, is terrorizing contemporary New Orleans.
3. *Jazz Funeral* (**Fawcett, 1993**) Hamson Brocato, producer of the New Orleans Jazz and Heritage Festival, is stabbed to death in his kitchen on the night of the JazzFest party.
4. *New Orleans Beat* (**Fawcett, 1994**) Computer nerd Geoff Kavanagh's fatal fall off a ladder was no accident, according to his buddies in TOWN, a virtual online community.
5. *House of Blues* (**Fawcett, 1995**) Arthur Hebert, prominent restaurateur and domineering patriarch, is gunned down before the opening of his restaurant in New Orleans's first casino.
6. *Kindness of Strangers, The* (**Fawcett, 1996**) Skip, on a leave of absence from the New Orleans PD, is perturbed by the mayoral candidacy of charismatic preacher Errol Jacomine, whom she considers a manipulative psychopath.
7. *Crescent City Kill* (**Fawcett, 1997**) Errol Jacomine resurfaces, heading a group known as the Jury, whose intent is to rectify perceived failures of justice by assassination including that of New Orleans's newly appointed police chief.
8. *82 Desire* (**Fawcett, 1998**) Russell Fortier, executive at United Oil Company and husband of city councilwoman Bebe Fortier is missing. Introduces Talba Wallis (see series II, below).
9. *Mean Woman Blues* (**Forge, 2003**) Errol Jacomine is back: this time, with the help of plastic surgery, he has reinvented himself as a Texas talk-show host with presidential ambitions. UK title: *Boneyard Blues*.

II. Talba Wallis, aka the Baroness de Pontalba, is an African American performance poet, computer expert, and fledgling private eye. Talba lives with her mother, Miz Clara, and has a rather edgy relationship with her boss, 65-year-old private investigator Eddie Valentino. Her investigations, like Skip Langdon's, take her into a wide variety of New Orleans situations. Talba was introduced as a character in *82 Desire* (series I, number 8).

1. *Louisiana Hotshot* (**Forge, 2001**) Talba Wallis lands a job with crusty PI Eddie Valentino. Her first case involves a woman named Cassandra who is being plagued by a rap-star's hanger-on named "Toes."
2. *Louisiana Bigshot* (**Forge, 2002**) Talba is suspicious about the "suicide" verdict given for her friend Babalu's death. Then she finds out that Babalu had another identity.
3. *Louisiana Lament* (**Forge, 2004**) Talba's recently discovered half sister Janessa is accused of the murder of social climber and con artist Allyson Brower, who is found floating in her swimming pool.
4. *P.I. on a Hot Tin Roof* (**Forge, 2005**) Wallis goes undercover as a maid to investigate a shady New Orleans judge, Francis Champagne, aka "Daddy Buddy."

III. An earlier series, which seems to have been abandoned for the series set in New Orleans, featured Rebecca Schwartz, a San Francisco lawyer who acted as an amateur sleuth when one of her cases called for it. Rebecca Schwartz is represented by stories in Smith's short story collection *Mean Rooms* (Five Star, 2000).

1. *Death Turns a Trick* (**Walker, 1982**) Rebecca becomes the attorney for a group of San Francisco prostitutes who want to legalize the "oldest profession."
2. *Sourdough Wars, The* (**Walker, 1984**) Four rival bakers, two of them brothers, find themselves competing for a batch of sourdough starter.
3. *Tourist Trap* (**Ballantine, 1988**) An Easter morning sunrise service finds the body of a tourist nailed to a cross by the "Trapper," who is out to ruin the Bay Area tourist trade.
4. *Dead in the Water* (**Ballantine, 1991**) Rebecca's friend Mary Whitehead is the prime suspect when her boss, who is also her husband's lover, is found floating in the Kelp Forest in the Monterey Bay Aquarium.
5. *Other People's Skeletons* (**Ballantine, 1993**) Chris Nicholson, Schwartz's partner, becomes a prime suspect in the hit-and-run death of art critic Jason McKendrick.

IV. Another San Francisco series features Paul McDonald, a Bay Area would-be novelist and amateur sleuth in a pair of detective novels.

1. *True-Life Adventure* (**Mysterious, 1985**) After a private investigator drops dead in his living room, luckless, would-be, mystery novelist Paul McDonald would appear to be the murderer's next target.
2. *Huckleberry Fiend* (**Mysterious, 1987**) An original manuscript of *Huckleberry Finn*, written in Mark Twain's handwriting and long believed to be lost, leads McDonald on a tour of the world of rare book collecting.

Smith, Martin Cruz

I.   Martin Cruz Smith is America's preeminent writer of Russian-based thrillers. The first Arkady Renko novel, *Gorky Park*, was a best-selling book made into a movie (1983) starring William Hurt and Lee Marvin. Renko is a Moscow policeman who tries to do his job but finds himself hamstrung by the KGB and corruption in high places in a series of "Red-noir" mysteries rich in humor and generous in spirit. In six novels Renko has wended his weary and determined way to hot spots like Havana and Chernobyl and cold spots like the Bering Sea.

1. *Gorky Park* (**Random House, 1981**) With some help from New York policeman William Kirwan, brother of one of the victims, Renko tries to solve the mystery of three mutilated bodies found in Gorky Park.
2. *Polar Star* (**Random House, 1989**) In exile and toiling as a second-class seaman on a Russian factory ship in the Bering Sea, Renko gets involved in crime solving again when the body of a girl turns up in a fishing net.
3. *Red Square* (**Random House, 1992**) Arkady finds himself reestablished with the Moscow Police just prior to the attempted coup of 1991, struggling to contain the flourishing underworld in newly democratic Russia.
4. *Havana Bay* (**Random House, 1999**) Mourning his wife, Renko is summoned to Havana to identify the body of an old friend, Russian embassy attaché S. S. Pribulda, said to be dead of a heart attack.
5. *Wolves Eat Dogs* (**Simon & Schuster, 2004**) After he expresses scepticism about the "suicide" of a Russian millionaire, Renko is rusticated to the eerie Zone of Exclusion of postmeltdown Chernobyl.
6. *Stalin's Ghost* (**Simon & Schuster, 2007**) The ghost of Stalin has been reported on subway platforms. Renko suspects that two fellow police detectives, Nikolai Isakov and Marat Urman, both former members of the Black Berets, who served in Chechnya, are part of a murder-for-hire scheme.

II.   Martin Cruz Smith has written many other books under noms de plume such as Nick Carter, Simon Quinn (the Inquisitor series), Jake Logan, and Martin Smith. As Martin Smith, he produced a pair of novels about Roman Grey, a Gypsy art dealer in New York City who is also an amateur sleuth.

1. *Gypsy in Amber* (**Putnam, 1971**) When the New York police try to pin a murder on a member of New York's Gypsy community, Roman Grey sets out to find the real killer.
2. *Canto for a Gypsy* (**Putnam, 1972**) It seems unlikely that the heavily guarded Royal Crown of Hungary, on display in St. Patrick's Cathedral, could be the subject of a heist.

Smith, Robert Kimmel

Senior citizen (over 70) Sadie Shapiro, resident of Mount Eden Senior Citizens Hotel in Queens, New York, is the archetypal Jewish mother who offers sage advice in inimitable English. She is also a jogger, an irrepressible matchmaker and a champion knitter. Sadie catapults into sudden fame with her book on knitting, and she adapts quite nicely to the life of a television talk-show celebrity. The three Sadie Shapiro novels are funny, heart-warming and enjoyable reading. Robert Kimmel Smith has written other novels, television scripts, and juveniles, including the popular *Chocolate Fever* (Coward, 1972).

1. *Sadie Shapiro's Knitting Book* (**Simon & Schuster, 1973**) Sadie sends her knitting patterns to a third-rate publishing house and works with the firm's one female editor to produce a best-selling book.
2. *Sadie Shapiro in Miami* (**Simon & Schuster, 1975**) Sadie visits Florida to endorse a Disneyland for senior citizens and becomes involved with a scandal and a former boyfriend.
3. *Sadie Shapiro, Matchmaker* (**Simon & Schuster, 1977**) To fulfill the last request of a professional matchmaker friend, Sadie takes on the task of matching six singles into three happy couples.

Smith, Thorne

Thorne Smith wrote a number of amusing novels in the twenties and thirties, several of them with elements of fantasy or the supernatural. *Topper*, partly because of its film and television incarnations, is Smith's best-known novel. The plot concerns the trials and tribulations of one Cosmo Topper, respectable, repressed, middle-aged banker who is haunted by the ghosts of George and Marion Kerby, a Jazz Age couple who are to determined to show Topper how to have a good time whether he wants to or not. In 1937 *Topper* was made into a very successful motion picture starring Cary Grant. Two film sequels followed: *Topper Takes a Trip* (1939) and *Topper Returns* (1941). A network series starring Leo G. Carroll (1953–1955) and a made-for-TV movie starring Kate Jackson (1979) brought Topper to the small screen. Thorne Smith was a very funny writer. If you liked *Topper*, try *The Night Life of the Gods* (Doubleday, 1931).

1. *Topper: An Improbable Adventure* (**McBride, 1926**) George and Marion Kerby, killed in a drunken automobile crash, take on the mission of helping Cosmo Topper get more fun out of life. Variant title: *The Jovial Ghosts.*
2. *Topper Takes a Trip* (**Doubleday, 1932**) Cosmo Topper and his wife go off to the French Riviera to get away from things, but Marion Kerby (followed by George) turns up there.

Smith, Wilbur (Addison)

I.   Wilbur Smith was born in Northern Rhodesia (now Zambia) and now lives in South Africa. Most of his books are set in the Africa he knows so well. He has written four books that tell the story of the Ballantyne family from their departure from Scotland in the 1860s to the 1980s in Zimbabwe. Historical characters such as Cecil Rhodes and the African king Lobengula are woven into these fast-paced tales of adventure and cultural clash.

1. *Flight of the Falcon* (**Doubleday, 1982**) In 1860 idealistic Robyn and ambitious Zouga Ballantyne go to the African interior in search of their missing missionary-explorer father. Variant title: *A Falcon Flies.*

2. *Triumph of the Sun, The* (St. Martin's, 2005) The Ballantynes in the form of Captain Penrod Ballantyne of Her Majesty's 10th Hussars and the Courtneys in the form of cargo boat owner Ryder Courteney come together in this novel set at the Siege of Khartoum by the Mahdi in the 1885.

3. *Men of Men* (Doubleday, 1983) In the 1890s the Ballantynes, now settled in Rhodesia, are drawn into the imperialistic schemes of Cecil Rhodes and the subsequent bloody rebellion of the Matabeles.

4. *Angels Weep, The* (Doubleday, 1983) In the first part, set in 1895–1899, the Ballantynes amass wealth and face the Matabele rebellion. In the second part, set in 1977, the Ballantynes face terrorists in newly independent Zimbabwe.

5. *Leopard Hunts in Darkness, The* (Doubleday, 1984) Ballantyne descendant, writer and wildlife worker Craig Mellow, fights poachers in contemporary Zimbabwe and searches for a missing fortune in diamonds.

II. The Courtneys are the protagonists of another family saga, which reaches from the 1600s to contemporary Africa. The saga is full of action, passion, colorful African scenery, and feuds of brother against brother. The novels are listed in chronological order rather than publication order. *The Courtneys* is an omnibus volume containing numbers 4, 5, and 7.

1. *Birds of Prey* (St. Martin's, 1997) Young Hal Courtney learns seamanship from his father, Sir Francis Courtney, off the East African coast in the mid-1600s. The Dutch and the English are at war.

2. *Monsoon* (St. Martin's, 1999) Sir Hal Courtney combats Arab pirates in the Indian Ocean off the coast of East Africa during the late 17th and early 18th centuries.

3. *Blue Horizon* (St. Martin's, 2003) Set in the mid 1700s. Follows the adventures of Jim Courtney, seeking his fortune in the Cape of Good Hope Colony, administered by the Dutch.

4. *Triumph of the Sun (2), The* (St. Martin's, 2005) See series I, number 2.

5. *When the Lion Feeds* (Viking, 1964) First novel published in the series. Cattle rancher Sean Courtney is separated from his family, his girl, and his home during the Zulu campaigns of the 1890s.

6. *Roar of Thunder, The* (Simon & Schuster, 1966) Sean Courtney wins a fortune and loses it, and the bitter feud with his brother Garry continues through the Boer War. Variant title: *The Sound of Thunder*.

7. *Burning Shore, The* (Doubleday, 1985) Centaine, a young Frenchwoman, becomes engaged to a South African aviator during World War I, then migrates to South Africa after he is killed.

8. *Sparrow Falls, A* (Dutton, 1978) Mark Anders, returning World War I hero, is drawn into the business and family affairs of the Courtneys.

9. *Power of the Sword* (Little, Brown, 1986) Stepbrothers Manfred and Shasa, sons of Centaine Courtney, are destined to become enemies as they attach themselves to different sides of the Afrikaner-English controversy.

10. *Rage* (Little, Brown, 1987) The Courtneys remain at loggerheads in post–World War II South Africa, as their mother tries to mediate between them and Tara Courtney falls in love with a black activist.

11. *Time to Die, A* (Random House, 1990) Another Sean Courtney, a former Rhodesian officer turned big-game hunter, gets involved with Mozambican guerrillas and the beautiful daughter of a client.

12. *Golden Fox* (Random House, 1991) A disgraced Spanish aristocrat and KGB agent working with the Cuban guerrillas in Africa sets his sights on Isabella Courtney.

III. A quartet of novels ranges in time from the Egypt of circa 1780 BCE to the present. The connecting link is Taita the Eunuch, who leaves a scroll relating the events following his mistress's marriage to Pharaoh Mamose and the location of his treasure-filled tomb. Numbers 1 and 3 were published together in the *Wilbur Smith Omnibus* (Macmillan [UK], 2006).

1. *River God* (St. Martin's, 1994) Taita the Eunuch relates his part in the dramatic events occurring after the marriage of Pharoah Mamose in circa 1780 BCE.

2. *Seventh Scroll, The* (St. Martin's, 1995) "The Seventh Scroll," which was written by Taita, is the key to the location of the tomb of Pharoah Mamose, which is being sought after by an English adventurer, a half-Egyptian archaeologist, and a German collector.

3. *Warlock* (St. Martin's, 2001) The kingdoms of Upper Egypt and Lower Egypt have been warring for 60 years. Royal sorcerer Taita bends his efforts to helping Nefer, the rightful heir to the throne of Upper Egypt.

4. *Quest, The* (St. Martin's, 2007) Taita and his ally, Meren Cambyses, have returned to Egypt after many years to find that the country is beset by a series of plagues including giant flesh-eating toads and river water turned to blood.

Snow, C(harles) P(ercy)

C. P. Snow was trained as a physicist, taught at Cambridge, and was knighted for his government service during and after World War II. This diversity of experience gave his fiction remarkable authority and scope. In his ability to dramatize the power struggles that place among politicians, scientists, or academics, he was unrivaled in his day. Although popular with readers, Snow's novels were not generally admired by critics, who tended to dismiss him as a latter-day, inferior Trollope (q.v.). Readers who want to make up their own minds should start with *The Masters*. Strangers and Brothers, an 11-volume series, is the life story of narrator Lewis Eliot, a lawyer whose career follows Snow's in outline, covering the years from 1914 to the mid 1960s. Eliot is at the center of some novels and merely an observer in others. There is a three-volume omnibus edition entitled *Strangers and Brothers* (Scribner, 1972). Sir Charles Snow was the husband of novelist Pamela Hansford Johnson (q.v.).

1. *Time of Hope* (Macmillan, 1950) First chronologically but not in order of publication, this book shows Lewis Eliot's childhood in a poor provincial family from 1914 to his arrival in London as a young barrister in 1933.

2. *Strangers and Brothers* (Scribner, 1960) George Passant, a promising provincial lawyer, is much admired by Lewis Eliot and others, but his career ends in tragedy. The time period is 1925–1933. The title was changed to *George Passant* in the omnibus edition.

3. *Conscience of the Rich, The* (Scribner, 1958) Lewis Eliot's friend Charles March, the son of a wealthy and powerful Jewish family in London, struggles to reconcile independence and family loyalty. The account covers the years 1927–1936.

4. *Light and the Dark, The* (Scribner, 1948) Roy Calvert, a brilliant Cambridge scholar, suffers from, and is finally destroyed by, relentless personal despair. Covers 1935–1943.

5. *Masters, The* **(Macmillan, 1951)** This book centers on the suspenseful struggle among the fellows of a Cambridge College over who will succeed as the new Master. The time is 1937.

6. *New Men, The* **(Scribner, 1954)** The story of the wartime race to harness atomic fission and the moral issues involved is set in Cambridge and London from 1939 to 1946.

7. *Homecoming* **(Scribner, 1956)** Lewis Eliot takes center stage again in this volume, which shows his first wife's deepening mental illness and suicide and his happy second marriage. The period is 1939–1948. UK title: *Homecomings*.

8. *Affair, The* **(Scribner, 1960)** The story returns to the setting of *The Masters* to focus on a case of scientific fraud that Lewis Eliot must reopen in 1953–1954.

9. *Corridors of Power* **(Scribner, 1964)** In 1955–1958 politician Roger Quaife mounts a ruthless struggle for power but suffers eventual downfall.

10. *Sleep of Reason, The* **(Scribner, 1968)** Sir Lewis Eliot, now retired, is drawn into a nasty case of child murder (based on an actual case) in his native provincial town in 1963.

11. *Last Things* **(Scribner, 1970)** Lewis Eliot undergoes a harrowing eye operation, turns down a government appointment, and worries over his son, Charles. The time is the midsixties.

Solomita, Stephen

Stanley Moodrow is an old-timer, a longtime New York Police Department detective who retires midway in Solomita's series and becomes a portly and curmudgeonly private eye. A good, hard-boiled police fiction series, nicely evoking New York's meaner streets.

1. *Piece of the Action, A* **(Putnam, 1992)** In a prequel set in 1957, beat cop Moodrow is rewarded by promotion to the rank of detective for winning a boxing match.

2. *Twist of the Knife, A* **(Putnam, 1988)** Stanley tracks his girlfriend's killer through Manhattan, vowing revenge, while members of the terrorist group American Red Army carry out random attacks that leave the police baffled.

3. *Force of Nature* **(Putnam, 1989)** Moodrow, near retirement, "selects" Jim Tilley to succeed him and teachers Tilley the ropes as they search for a drug dealer and cop killer.

4. *Forced Entry* **(Putnam, 1990)** Now retired from the police, Moodrow intervenes in a scheme to force tenants out of rent-controlled apartments.

5. *Bad to the Bone* **(Putnam, 1991)** Private eye Moodrow and former partner Tilley try to crack down on a cult that is a front for producing and marketing a drug 30 times more addictive than heroin.

6. *Damaged Goods* **(Scribner, 1996)** Moodrow, turning 60 and suffering from prostate trouble, takes on young computer expert Guinevere Gadd as a partner, and they work together on the abduction of a four-year-old by her psychotic father.

Somers, Jane

PSEUDONYM OF Doris Lessing

The author Jane Somers and the character Janna Somers are creations of novelist Doris Lessing (q.v.), who wrote the two Somers novels under a pseudonym to draw attention to the plight of unknown writers and to receive unbiased criticism herself. After Lessing revealed her imposture, the novels were published together in paperback as *The Diaries of Jane Somers* (Vintage, 1984). Janna Somers is the widowed, middle-aged editor of a London fashion magazine. Her diary records her changing feelings about love, commitment, and the decline of civility in English society. It is a moving, sometimes funny, sometimes sad depiction of the life and feelings of an outwardly successful, inwardly troubled woman.

1. *Diary of a Good Neighbor, The* **(Knopf, 1983)** Fashion editor Janna Somers befriends smelly, fiercely independent nonagenarian Maude.

2. *If the Old Could . . .* **(Knopf, 1984)** When Janna's attractive niece Jill leaves her aunt's apartment, her unattractive sister Kate takes her place, while Janna gets involved in an affair with Richard, a married man.

Sorrentino, Gilbert

I. Gilbert Sorrentino (d. 2006) was a highly innovative writer of poetry and fiction. All of his novels are structured in different ways. According to Sorrentino: "form not only determines content, but form invents content." A good introduction to Sorrentino is the early novel, *The Imaginative Qualities of Actual Things*, which satirizes the New York avant-garde world of the 1950s and 1960s, of which Sorrentino was a part. This novel was followed by the Pack of Lies trilogy, which reconsiders and restructures *The Imaginative Qualities of Actual Things* in various ways: a series of questions asked of two character; a conversational account of events told in range of a narrative styles; an encyclopedic listing of all the people, places, and objects from the numbers 2 and 3. Omnibus volume containing numbers 2 through 4: *Pack of Lies: A Trilogy* (Dalkey Archive, 1997). Sorrentino obviously isn't an "easy" writer, but he can be bracing and funny.

1. *Imaginative Qualities of Actual Things, The* **(Pantheon, 1972)** Sorrentino was par of the avant-garde scene in the New York of the 1950s and 1960s, which he satirizes here.

2. *Odd Number* **(North Point, 1985)** A series of questions are asked, first of a reticent character, and then of an unreliable one, in an attempt to discover exactly what happened in number 1.

3. *Rose Theatre* **(Dalkey Archive, 1992)** A conversational account of the events in number 1 told in a range of narrative styles, in which female characters attempt to correct "misinformation" from that novel.

4. *Misterioso* **(Dalkey Archive, 1992)** Set in a supermarket among magazine racks and a cast of demons and flight attendants. Includes an encyclopedic, alphabetical listing of all the people, places, and objects in numbers 2 and 3.

II. *Steelwork* is a novel about the sites and characters of Sorrentino's Brooklyn childhood between 1935 and 1951. *Red the Fiend*, published a quarter of a century later, presents scenes from the childhood of Red Mulvaney, one of the characters in *Steelwork*.

2. *Red the Fiend* **(Fromm, 1995)** Scenes from an Irish American Roman Catholic boyhood in Brooklyn, 1940. Red Mulvaney, a boy of 12, son of an indifferent mother, and a drunken, estranged father, is constantly beaten by his sadistic grandmother.

2. *Steelwork* **(Pantheon, 1970)** A Brooklyn neighborhood is delineated from 1935 to 1951, showing a rise in material prosperity and a loss in spiritual hope among the inhabitants.

Sparks, Nicholas

I. Since the publication of *The Notebook*, his first novel, Nicholas Sparks has become an extremely popular author, his books at or near the top of best-seller lists. Three novels, *The Notebook*, *Message in a Bottle*, and *A Walk to Remember*, have been filmed, and *Nights in Rhodanthe* went into production in 2007. Sparks's romance-heavy novels are manipulative and very effective tear-jerkers that appeal to readers who like a good cry with their fiction. *The Notebook* relates the romance and long marriage of Allie and Noah Calhoun. *The Wedding*, its sequel, deals with Allie and Noah's children and grandchildren.

1. *Notebook, The* (Warner, 1996) A flashback from a present-day North Carolina nursing home reveals the off-again, on-again romance between Noah Calhoun and Allie, who broke up 1932 but get back together again in 1946.
2. *Wedding, The* (Warner, 2003) Attorney Wilson Lewis of New Bern, North Carolina, who has been married to Noah and Allie's daughter, Jane, for 30 years, feels that the passion and romance in their marriage needs a jump start.

II. Two novels, published within a few months of each other, also set in North Carolina, have a dollop of the paranormal in them. In *True Believer*, science journalist and debunker of the occult and paranormal, Jeremy Marsh, finds romance with Boone Creek, North Carolina, town librarian Lexie Darnell. In *At First Sight*, Jeremy and Lexie are planning to marry, and are discovering that the course of true love never runs smooth. Included among the many small-town characters is Lexie's psychic grandmother, Doris.

1. *True Believer* (Warner, 2005) New York–based science journalist, Jeremy Marsh, who enjoys debunking paranormal phenomena, goes to Boone Creek, North Carolina, where there is a mystery concerning lights in the local cemetery, and finds romance with Lexie Darnell, beautiful but unattached town librarian.
2. *At First Sight* (Warner, 2005) Jeremy moves to Boone Creek to marry the pregnant Lexie, but a number of glitches intervene, including e-mail-inspired doubts about the paternity of Lexie's child and the character of Lexie's psychic grandmother, Doris.

Speart, Jessica

Rachel Porter (a conflation of Rachel Carson and Eliot Porter) is a former actress who has joined the US Fish and Wildlife Service. Rachel hopes to put a dent in the lucrative animal poaching and smuggling trade, so the feisty agent fights chauvinistic superiors and people who are perfectly willing to kill humans as well as animals in their pursuit of illegal gain ($5 billion worldwide). Author Jessica Speart is herself a former actress (*One Life to Live*) and investigative journalist.

1. *Gator Aide* (Avon, 1997) US Fish and Wildlife Service agent Jessica Porter is put on the relatively unexciting "duck duty" in a Louisiana swamp until an alligator with a bullet in its head turns up in the apartment of a murdered prostitute in New Orleans's Latin Quarter.
2. *Tortoise Soup* (Avon, 1998) 350 endangered baby tortoises are stolen from a federally protected area in Nevada.
3. *Bird Brained* (Avon, 1999) An alleged smuggler of exotic birds is murdered.
4. *Border Prey* (Avon, 2000) Primates are being smuggled over the Mexican border and hidden on a hunting ranch.
5. *Black Delta Night* (Avon, 2001) Rachel poses as a corrupt agent to investigate the illegal poaching of Delta Gold—caviar from the endangered Mississippi River paddlefish.
6. *Killing Season, A* (Avon, 2002) Exiled to Montana, Rachel finds herself up against someone who is killing both grizzly bears and Blackfoot Indians.
7. *Coastal Disturbance* (Avon, 2003) An illegal manatee park is being maintained in the Georgia coastal swampland.
8. *Blue Twilight* (Avon, 2004) A biologist in search of a rare blue butterfly disappears in the northern wilds of California.
9. *Restless Waters* (Avon, 2005) Rachel is in Hawaii fighting illegal animal exports and a "shark-finning" scheme.
10. *Unsafe Harbor* (Avon, 2006) Back in her native New York, Rachel gets a job in Port Elizabeth, New Jersey, shifting papers until socialite Bitsy von Falken turns up murdered with an illegal shawl of Tibetan antelope fur around her neck.

Spencer, Sally

Inspector Woodend and his partner, Sergeant Rutter, of Scotland Yard, are the protagonists in a British procedural series, set in the 1960s, that has reached 18 volumes. Woodend sometimes ruffles the feathers of his superiors, which earns him a rustication or two, but he perseveres to the end in these gritty, realistic procedurals with good plots and believable characters. All of the novels have been published in the United Kingdom, but not all of them have been released in the United States yet. Sally Spencer is also the author of the Marston trilogy set in Victorian times (Orion [UK]), a pair of "London" books set in turn-of-the-20th-century Southwark, London (Orion [UK]), a four-volume series featuring Victorian detective, Sam Blackstone written by Spencer as Alan Rustage (Severn House [UK]), and a trio of novels starring an Inspector Ruiz written by Spencer as James Garcia Woods (Hale [UK]).

1. *Salton Killings, The* (Severn House [UK], 1998) A serial killer is on the loose in the English village of Salton.
2. *Murder at Swann's Lake* (Severn House [UK], 1999) An ex-criminal who became a club owner is murdered.
3. *Death of a Cave Dweller* (Severn House [UK], 2000) A guitarist in a new hit rock band in Liverpool is murdered.
4. *Dark Lady, The* (Severn House [UK], 2000) A German is murdered near an English manor for reasons that may have something to do with World War II.
5. *Golden Mile to Murder, The* (Severn House [UK], 2000) A local detective is murdered in the hinterlands after Woodend gets on the wrong side of his superiors and gets "sent down."
6. *Dead on Cue* (Severn House [UK], 2001) A television actor is murdered.
7. *Death of an Innocent* (Severn House [UK], 2002) Woodend is in trouble with his superiors again, and suspended for possible bribery.
8. *Red Herring, The* (Severn House [UK], 2002) A history teacher is murdered and a student is kidnapped.
9. *Enemy Within, The* (Severn House [UK], 2003) Woodend is on the trail of a murderer who stashes his victims in Guy Fawkes Night bonfires.
10. *Death Left Hanging, A* (Severn House [UK], 2003) Woodend tries to clear a woman hanged for murder 30 years ago.
11. *Witch Maker, The* (Severn House [UK], 2004) A person who makes witch effigies for burning as part of a historical reenactment is murdered.

12. *Butcher Beyond, The* (**Severn House [UK], 2004**) Woodend goes on vacation in Spain with his wife, and witnesses a man thrown off a balcony.

13. *Dying in the Dark* (**Severn House [UK], 2005**) While Woodend investigates the rape and murder of a secretary, Rutter is suspected of murdering his own wife.

14. *Stone Killer* (**Severn House [UK], 2005**) Ruth Maitland's husband threatens to kill the hostages he is holding if she is convicted of murder.

15. *Long Time Dead, A* (**Severn House [UK], 2006**) A body found on the near-derelict Haverton army base, turns out to be that of American captain Robert Kineally, who disappeared in 1944.

16. *Sins of the Fathers* (**Severn House [UK], 2006**) The partially disemboweled body of politician Bradley Pine is found by the side of a busy road.

17. *Dangerous Games* (**Severn House [UK], 2007**) Terry Pugh's headless body is found floating in a canal.

18. *Death Watch* (**Severn House [UK], 2007**) Woodend fears that Angela Jackson's kidnapper will torture and kill her before he can intervene.

Sprinkle, Patricia Houck

I. Sheila Beaufort Travis, an ambassador's widow and amateur sleuth, moves back to her hometown of Atlanta to manage a public relations firm in number 3 of these southern mysteries. Sheila is often aided by her deceptively naive aunt Mary in this mystery series that explores southern mores, particularly the preoccupation with family and social caste. Sprinkle, the daughter and the wife of Protestant ministers, has also written Christian fiction (see series II and III, below) and nonfiction self-help books such as *Women Who Do Too Much* (Zondervan, 1992) and *Children Who Do Too Little* (Zondervan, 1996).

1. *Murder at Markham* (**St. Martin's, 1988**) When Sheila finds employment at an exclusive diplomatic institute associated with the University of Chicago, she becomes embroiled in a series of homicides.

2. *Murder in the Charleston Manner* (**St. Martin's, 1990**) When she visits two elderly friends of Aunt Mary's in Charleston, South Carolina, Travis gets caught up in Charleston's slow ambience and robbery and murder.

3. *Murder on Peachtree Street* (**St. Martin's, 1991**) Sheila moves back to Atlanta to accept a position with Hosokawa International and gets involved in a murder investigation her first day on the job.

4. *Somebody's Dead in Snellville* (**St. Martin's, 1992**) Travis is drawn into the affairs of the extended Sims family when a developer offers $10 million for their farm, which is within commuting distance of Atlanta.

5. *Death of a Dunwoody Matron* (**Doubleday, 1993**) When old flame Walter Delacourt's wife, Yvonne, is murdered in the exclusive suburb of Dunwoody, Sheila steps in.

6. *Mystery Bred in Buckhead, A* (**Bantam, 1994**) A priceless manuscript that had been missing for many years turns up at Ripper Delacourt's annual Atlanta Christmas party.

7. *Deadly Secrets on the St. John's* (**Bantam, 1995**) Sheila travels to Jacksonville, Florida, as Daphne L'Arken dies at her own "do."

II. Sprinkle seems to have dropped Sheila Travis in favor of a series of Christian mysteries involving a character somewhat resembling Agatha Christie's (q.v.) Miss Marple. MacLaren "Mac" Yarbrough is a razor-sharp, witty, tenacious, and spunky sexagenarian who runs Yarbrough's Seed, Feed, and Nursery in the small town of Howell, Georgia (eventually becoming a magistrate when her husband, Joe Riddley, is struck down), and who is a redoubtable amateur sleuth. The Thoroughly Southern Mystery series has well-presented Christian values in a southern small-town setting.

1. *When Did We Lose Harriet?* (**Zondervan, 1997**) Visiting a sick brother in Montgomery, Alabama, MacLaren becomes involved in the missing person case of Harriet, a 15-year-old girl whose family seems to be indifferent to her disappearance.

2. *But Why Shoot the Magistrate?* (**Zondervan, 1998**) MacLaren, convinced of the innocence of popular youth pastor Luke Blessed, becomes involved in the murder case of young Amanda Kent. Then someone shoots magistrate Joe Riddley, MacLaren's husband.

3. *Who Invited the Dead Man?* (**Signet, 2002**) Harriet takes over her disabled husband's magistrate job. Then a local man is murdered at Joe Riddley's birthday gala.

4. *Who Left That Body in the Rain?* (**Signet, 2002**) Local civic leader Skye McDonald is found run over by his own car, and some dark secrets are uncovered.

5. *Who Let That Killer in the House?* (**Signet, 2003**) When a popular high school chemistry teacher and softball coach commits suicide, MacLaren isn't satisfied until she uncovers the reasons behind his act.

6. *When Will the Dead Lady Sing?* (**Signet, 2004**) When the body of a local vagrant is found dead, Mac's old college boyfriend is the prime suspect.

7. *Who Killed the Queen of Clubs?* (**Signet, 2005**) First state bridge champion and pecan grove owner's Edie Whelan Burkett's foreman dies, then she herself is taken off, not by natural causes.

8. *Did You Declare the Corpse?* (**Signet, 2006**) Yarbrough heads for Scotland with her friend Laura to explore her genealogical roots. Then two empty coffins mysteriously appear in the church in the small town where they are staying.

9. *Guess Who's Coming to Die?* (**Signet, 2007**) Willena Kenan, outgoing president of the Magnolia Ladies' Investment Club, is found dead on the bathroom floor with a corkscrew protruding from her neck.

10. *What Are You Wearing to Die?* (**Signet, 2008**) Despite her husband's strong disapproval, Mac Yarbrough plays sleuth again when two young mothers are murdered.

III. The Job's Corner Chronicles are a pair of novels about a small North Carolina town in 1949–1950 that is forced to deal with racial integration issues when Stephen Whitfield, the new Presbyterian minister, comes to town. The stories are seen in flashbacks through the eyes of Carley Marshall, Stephen's orphaned niece, who is 11–12 years old when the stories take place, and who is slowly introduced to the confusing world of adults.

1. *Remember Box, The* (**Zondervan, 2000**) When Uncle Stephen sends her Aunt Kate's Remember Box, Carley reflects on events in Job's Corner when, orphaned by mother's death by polio, she accompanies her aunt and uncle to the small town of Job's Corner as he takes up his position as pastor of the Presbyterian Bethel Church.

2. *Carley's Song* (**Zondervan, 2001**) In 1950 Carley is 12 years old and still living in Job's Corner, as three locals return home: Clay Lamont, who becomes Carley's first real crush; Maddie Raeburn, a divorcée who teaches seventh grade; and Jerry Donaldson, a former beau of Maddie's who becomes school principal.

Stabenow, Dana

I. Kate Shugak is a native Aleut who has been building up a solid reputation as a tough freelance investigator in Alaska. Shugak is tough, smart, feisty, funny, and compassionate, as a good private eye should be, and like many private investigators, she has had a checkered love life but she is fairly unusual in that her cases take her into real wilderness rather than urban wilderness. Stabenow has a gift for describing native cultures and contemporary life in the Alaska wilderness. Alaskan Dana Stabenow won an Edgar for *A Cold Day for Murder*.

1. *Cold Day for Murder, A* **(Berkley, 1992)** Retired to the wilderness after getting her throat cut while apprehending a child abuser, Shugak gets back into the detective business when a park ranger disappears.
2. *Fatal Thaw, A* **(Berkley, 1993)** Spring brings not only a thaw to the Alaskan wilderness but also a mass murderer who goes on a shooting spree.
3. *Dead in the Water* **(Berkley, 1993)** Kate is working on the crabbing ship *Avilda*, hoping to learn why two of its crew members disappeared during its previous trips.
4. *Cold-Blooded Business, A* **(Berkley, 1994)** Kate accepts a commission from Royal Petroleum Company to find out who is bringing drugs into the Prudhoe Bay work site.
5. *Play with Fire* **(Berkley, 1995)** Kate investigates the mysterious disappearance of Daniel Seabolt, son of a local born-again preacher who specializes in hellfire sermons.
6. *Blood Will Tell* **(Putnam, 1996)** Kate, at her grandmother's instigation, attends the annual Convention of the Alaskan Federation of Natives in Anchorage and investigates the suspicious deaths of antidevelopment members of the Nimiltha Tribal Council.
7. *Breakup* **(Putnam, 1997)** The "breakup" is that of Alaskan ice. Kate investigates the murders of a man found in the wreckage of a plane that crashed into her isolated cabin and that of a tourist ostensibly killed by a bear.
8. *Killing Grounds* **(Putnam, 1998)** An abusive salmon fisher in an Alaskan village is murdered, and Kate's aunts are among the numerous suspects.
9. *Hunter's Moon* **(Putnam, 1999)** Kate and her lover, Jack Morgan, agree to act as guides for a group of German computer company executives engaged in a big game hunt. The "game" turns out to be the Germans.
10. *Midnight Come Again* **(St. Martin's, 2000)** Kate, mourning the death of Jack Morgan under an assumed name in a western Alaskan fishing village, is sought out by state trooper "Chopper" Jim Chopin to help in a case involving what seems to be an international banking scandal.
11. *Singing of the Dead, The* **(St. Martin's, 2001)** Kate is hired as a security expert by Anne Gordaoff, Alaska state senate candidate, who has received threatening letters. Alaska's wild and woolly local politics and a century old scandal involving Angel Beecham, "Dawson Darling," are delineated.
12. *Fine and Bitter Snow, A* **(St. Martin's, 2002)** Parker ranger Dan O'Brien is about to lose his job, probably because he is against drilling for oil in the local wildlife preserve. Kate is trying to provide a stable environment for Johnny, the teenage son of her dead lover, Jack Morgan.
13. *Grave Denied, A* **(St. Martin's, 2003)** Local handyman Len Dreyer turns up dead at the mouth of a glacier. Investigation reveals him to have been a real mystery man.
14. *Taint in the Blood, A* **(St. Martin's, 2004)** Charlotte Moravieff, of an influential Alaskan family, hires Kate to prove that her imprisoned and terminally ill mother wasn't the perpetrator of a fire 30 years ago that killed her son.
15. *Deeper Sleep, A* **(St. Martin's, 2007)** After Louis Deem "gets away with murder" again, Kate determines that he won't "get away" with his next crime.

II. Another Alaskan protagonist is Liam Campbell, a state trooper and reformed drunk who is still suffering from the effects of a car crash that killed his son and left his wife in a coma. As with the Kate Shugak mysteries, the setting is a well-described rural and wilderness Alaska.

1. *Fire and Ice* **(Dutton, 1998)** Rusticated from his Anchorage job, state trooper Liam Campbell runs into the homicide of a bush pilot killed by his own propeller, the shooting up of a jukebox playing "Margaritaville," and a reunion with his first true love, Wy Chouinard.
2. *So Sure of Death* **(Dutton, 1999)** Liam, ferried about by Wy Chouinard in her air taxi, pursues two murderers: one wiped out an entire family on a fishing boat; the other killed an assistant on a archaeology dig.
3. *Nothing Gold Can Stay* **(Dutton, 2000)** The murders of a local postmistress and of a gold prospector reopen the case of a series of missing women for 20 years.
4. *Better to Rest* **(New American Library, 2002)** The discovery of a World War II–era US Army plane embedded in the face of a glacier and the murder of an elderly matriarch may have a connection.

III. Stabenow's earliest series is a trio of science-fiction novels set in the near future featuring space pioneer Star Svensdottir, the first of her strong female characters.

1. *Second Star* **(Berkley, 1991)** Star is in charge of building a space station in the face of such obstacles as terrorists, an attempted military takeover, and aliens.
2. *Handful of Stars, A* **(Berkley, 1991)** Svensdottir is involved in the colonization of an asteroid belt.
3. *Red Planet Run* **(Berkley, 1995)** Set partly on Mars, where Star is studying a new weapon.

Stableford, Brian M(ichael)

I. English author Brian Stableford has written a dark fantasy trilogy in which English physician David Lydyard becomes possessed by the Egyptian goddess Bast and encounters fallen angels, werewolves, and occultists over a period of more than 40 years. The series is as much given over to metaphysical speculation as it is to esoteric conspiracies and adventures.

1. *Werewolves of London, The* **(Carroll & Graf, 1992)** A near-death encounter in the Egyptian desert in 1873 leaves David Lydyard with a legacy of puzzling dreams and a sense that his consciousness is no longer entirely his own.
2. *Angel of Pain, The* **(Carroll & Graf, 1993)** Twenty years after being first possessed by Bast, Lydyard finds himself once again in thrall to this "fallen angel" and her alter ego, the Angel of Pain.
3. *Carnival of Destruction, The* **(Carroll & Graf, 1994)** The elderly and arthritic Lydyard thinks he is Satan until Anatole, a French atheist wounded in the World War and saved by Joan of Arc, delivers a message to him.

II. Stableford is a prolific writer of science fiction and the history and criticism of science fiction (e.g., *Historical Dictionary of Science Fiction Literature* Scarecrow, 2004), including eight SF series. Although Stableford, who is better known in the United Kingdom than in the

United States, tends to dismiss his earlier work, readers usually don't agree with him. Although the novels often have a space-opera format, they are full of ideas, well written, and very readable. Dies Irae (Day of Wrath), an early trilogy, is a retelling of the Iliad and the Odyssey in a world thousands of years in the future in which the Beast War, Mark Chaos, and Heljanita the Toymaker play the roles of the Trojan War, Odysseus, and the Greek Gods, respectively.

1. *Days of Glory, The* (Ace, 1971) Ten thousand years since the creation of the "Beasts," who are nearly identical to humans, Adam December's original plan has been forgotten, and the "Beast War" is raging.
2. *In the Kingdom of the Beasts* (Ace, 1971) Mark Chaos, after fighting for many years in the Beast War, goes on his wanderings.
3. *Day of Wrath* (Ace, 1971) The master plan of Heljanita the Toymaker is revealed as Mark Chaos reaches the Darkstar of Despair.

III. The Hooded Swan sextet is a series detailing the adventures of space pilot Grainger, a laconic and disillusioned antihero, who is forced to work out a debt to New Alexandria and its leader, Titus Charlot, by flying the starship *Hooded Swan* to various remote and unpleasant reaches of the galaxy. Although the Hooded Swan novels are in space-opera format, they have more the tone, according to one critic, of "space blues." The series has been reprinted in one large paperback omnibus volume as *Swan Songs* (Big Engine [UK], 2002).

1. *Halcyon Drift* (DAW, 1972) Grainger, in the first voyage of his indenture on the *Hooded Swan*, is sent to the Halcyon Drift, a dark nebula where the laws of physics are distorted, to answer the distress signal of a vessel lost many years before.
2. *Rhapsody in Black* (DAW, 1973) Grainger, whose brain had been invaded by some disembodied mentalism (the Wind) on Halcyon, goes to the planet Rhapsody, where the colonists of the Church of the Exclusive Reward, living out their lives in poverty and darkness, have made a potentially valuable discovery.
3. *Promised Land* (DAW, 1974) Grainger, on the trail of a kidnapped Anacaona maiden, goes to the Promised Land, a planet that is inhabited by the descendants of the starship *Zodiac* and a docile, indigenous humanoid race.
4. *Paradise Game, The* (DAW, 1974) The *Hooded Swan* lands on Pharos, which is sort of like Eden, with humanoid inhabitants and a Serpent of its own, where the Caradoc Company is giving New Alexandria some stiff competition.
5. *Fenris Device, The* (DAW, 1974) A Gallacellan warship abandoned on a giant gaseous planet contains a weapon known to legend as the Fenris Device.
6. *Swan Song* (DAW, 1975) The Wind, the alien intelligence that has taken up residence in Grainger's brain, senses that it is embarked upon its last voyage.

IV. The three-part Realms of Tartarus was published in the United States in one volume. The first volume, *The Face of Heaven*, was originally published separately in the United Kingdom. The trilogy describes an Earth in the far future in which a new world, 10,000 years in the making, was built on a platform covering the old, polluted world. While the Realms of Tartarus have been largely forgotten by the denizens of the platform, life goes on below, in grossly mutated form.

1. *Face of Heaven, The* (Quartet [UK], 1976) While most inhabitants of the upper Earth are happy in their Edenic existence, Carl Magner is tormented by dreams of the world below. Reprinted as part one of *The Realms of Tartarus* (DAW, 1977).

2. *Vision of Hell, A* (DAW, 1977) Randal Harkander leads Euchronia's first expedition into the wastes of the world below. Published as part 2 of *The Realms of Tartarus*.
3. *Glimpse of Infinity, A* (DAW, 1977) Hegemon Raphael Weres, obsessed by Carl Magner's ideas, declares an all-out war of obliteration against the People of the Darkness. Published as part 3 of *The Realms of Tartarus*.

V. The Daedalus Mission series is about a starship sent to find colonists on various planets who over a period of one or two centuries have not been in touch with their home planet. The *Daedalus* has a crew of seven, including commander Alexis Alexander and teenager Mariel, who has a special talent for assessing the emotional states of other beings. All of the colonies visited, whether they appear like paradise or like hell on the surface, turn out to have encountered problems in their adjustment to alien biospheres.

1. *Florians, The* (DAW, 1976) The first landfall of the *Daedalus* is on the planet Floria, whose surface masks a polis in trouble.
2. *Critical Threshold* (DAW, 1977) While the planet Dendra, a world with one vast forest, seemed to be an ideal place for human settlement, the colony is a disaster, reduced to a ragged band of illiterate degenerates.
3. *Wildebloode's Empire* (DAW, 1977) The colonists of what is now called Wildebloode are hardworking people who heed every wish of the descendants of founder James Wildebloode, biochemist and planetary leader.
4. *City of the Sun, The* (DAW, 1978) Arcadia is a city seemingly based on Tommasso Campanella's utopian vision *City of the Sun*. However, everyone carries a disfiguring parasite on his back.
5. *Balance of Power* (DAW, 1979) In a parallel to the European settlement of the Americas, the colonists of Attica have more or less enslaved or obliterated the Ore'l, the indigenous humanoids of the planet.
6. *Paradox of the Sets, The* (DAW, 1979) In a story with many overtones of Egyptian mythology, settlers of the Planet Geb have built their society upon the labor of semi-intelligent humanoids whose origins are a mystery.

VI. The Asgard trilogy is a relatively lighthearted space opera with overtones of Norse mythology. Asgard is an artificial world on the edge of the galaxy beneath whose surface lie many layers of Earth-like worlds with a great secret buried at the center. When the hidden worlds begin to be revealed, an interplanetary gold rush with many participants, including Earthling Mike Rousseau, ensues. The trilogy was reissued with different titles in 2004.

1. *Asgard's Secret* (Five Star, 2004) The race to explore the lower levels of Asgard is on, with Mike Rousseau among the leading contenders. Originally published by DAW as *Journey to the Center*. UK title: *Journey to the Centre* (1982).
2. *Asgard's Conquerors* (Five Star, 2004) The lower levels of Asgard are awakening. Mike Rousseau is sent back again at the behest of the Tetrax. Originally published by New English Library (UK) in 1990 as *Invaders from the Centre*.
3. *Asgard's Heart* (Five Star, 2004) The secret of the Centre and the machine intelligences who run it is about to be revealed, but the starlet at the Centre may go nova. Originally published by New English Library (UK) in 1990 as *The Centre Cannot Hold*.

VII. The Genesys trilogy contains more fantasy elements than science-fiction ones. It postulates a world where voracious molds rot everything, including mountains; where the human settlers have forgotten everything about their agreement with the indigenous

Serpents, Salamanders, and Chimeras; and soldier-of-fortune Prince Andris Myrasol, his lover, Princess Lucrezia, and a motley assortment of fellow voyagers struggle to expose the central mystery of the planet. The series hasn't been published in the United States.

1. *Serpent's Blood* (**Legend [UK], 1995**) Minor prince and soldier-of-fortune Andris Myrasol, imprisoned and facing a pair of unpalatable alternatives, breaks out of jail and joins an expedition to unknown parts.
2. *Salamander's Fire* (**Legend [UK], 1996**) Andris and Princess Lucrezia enter terra incognita in their search for the secret to their world.
3. *Chimera's Cradle* (**Legend [UK], 1997**) Andris, Lucrezia, and their companions spread far and wide in their continuing search for the center of their world's mystery.

VIII. The Emortals sextet is a series of riffs on the subject of immortality. By the 22nd century, biomedical nanotechnology has given all humans a life measured by centuries rather than by decades, and a chosen few are able to live 1,000 years, but the search for immortality goes on. The chronological order of the novels, which is somewhat different from their publication order, is observed here.

1. *Cassandra Complex, The* (**St. Martin's, 2001**) Set in the mid-21st century. Police forensic investigator Lisa Friemann has several mysteries to solve, including the disappearance of prominent scientist Morgan Maller.
2. *Inherit the Earth* (**Tor, 1998**) In a 22nd century world where longevity is a fact of life, Damon Hart, son of the scientist responsible for many of the benefits of longer life, runs into a shadowy terrorists who force him to reexamine his heritage.
3. *Dark Ararat* (**St. Martin's, 2002**) On Earth's first extrasolar colony, settled by the starship *Hope*, cultural and scientific conflicts arise when ecologist and televangelist Matthew Fleury is unfrozen from his state of suspended animation.
4. *Architects of Emortality* (**St. Martin's, 2000**) Hundreds of years in the future, on the cusp of radical change in longevity expectations, a series of inexplicable murders engage police officers Watson and Holmes and amateur detective Oscar Wilde.
5. *Fountains of Youth, The* (**St. Martin's, 2000**) Hundreds of years later, Mortimer Guy is born into a world where he can potentially live forever. But a terrible natural disaster that kills millions sets him on a 500-year investigation of death and its effects on human civilization.
6. *Omega Expedition, The* (**St. Martin's, 2002**) Adam Zimmerman awakens in the 35th century to find that his exotic hosts have recruited various immortals, including death historian Mortimer Gray, for a new project.

Stacey, Susannah

PSEUDONYM OF Jill Staynes & Margaret Storey

Superintendent Robert Bone is the protagonist of a series of British procedurals in the classic ratiocinative tradition. Bone is intelligent, civilized, and a sorrowing widower (until he marries again in number 6) with a feisty teenage daughter named Cha. This is a series of witty, soft-spoken, literate mysteries full of suspects, often in a country house setting. "Susannah Stacey" is the pseudonym for authors Margaret Storey and Jill Staynes. The pair also write the Sigismondo mysteries as Elizabeth Eyre (q.v.).

1. *Goodbye, Nanny Gray* (**Summit, 1988**) The discovery of retired governess Nanny Gray's body draws Detective Superintendent Bone's attention to a wide assortment of suspicious characters.
2. *Knife at the Opera, A* (**Summit, 1989**) Miss Fairlie, English teacher at Cha Bone's school, is found stabbed to death in a classroom during the performance of a school presentation of *The Beggar's Opera*.
3. *Body of Opinion* (**Summit, 1990**) Alix Hamilton, aka cross-dresser Alex Hervey, is shot to death at a rock-star's party.
4. *Grave Responsibility* (**Summit, 1991**) Dr. Lionel Clare is found with his throat slashed inside a car wash. Suicide or murder?
5. *Late Lady, The* (**Pocket, 1993**) The presumably accidental death of the Marsh's housekeeper in Adlingsden, Kent, is followed by some deaths that look like murder.
6. *Bone Idle* (**Pocket, 1995**) Superintendent Bone finds himself solving a murder on his honeymoon at Roke Castle where he is staying with his new bride Grizel.
7. *Dead Serious* (**Pocket, 1997**) A famous TV personality is found dead in Biddinghurst, reputedly the second most haunted village in Kent.
8. *Hunter's Quarry* (**Pocket, 1998**) The old secrets are uncovered as rock star and groom-to-be Ken Cryer wonders if he will live long enough to take the wedding vows. UK title: *Quarry*.

Standiford, Les

John Deal runs a small construction business in Miami, inherited from his father, who committed suicide after some questionable business deals. But, what with the construction business and Miami being the way they are, John often finds himself involved with some thoroughly nasty types, and is forced to take investigations, and the law, into his own hands in this very suspenseful and violent series. The plots are sometimes improbable, but readers are drawn into the action. *Spill* (Atlantic Monthly, 1991) and *Black Mountain* (Putnam, 2000) are stand-alones.

1. *Done Deal* (**HarperCollins, 1993**) John Deal, who runs the small construction business in Miami inherited from his father, who committed suicide under shadowy circumstances, thinks that things are going okay until his wife disappears after a highway crash.
2. *Raw Deal* (**HarperCollins, 1994**) After an arsonist destroys his house and almost kills his wife, Deal finds himself in mortal combat with a wealthy Cuban emigrant developer.
3. *Deal to Die For* (**HarperCollins, 1995**) After his best friend Barbara Cooper's alleged suicide, Deal investigates, bringing him in conflict with ruthless Chinese gangsters looking to get into the movie business.
4. *Deal on Ice* (**HarperCollins, 1997**) The murder of Arch Dolan the owner of a small Miami bookstore leads Deal into a clash with a millionaire preacher who is scheming to become the king of a vast media empire. Reissued as *Book Deal* by Poisoned Pen (2002).
5. *Presidential Deal* (**HarperCollins, 1998**) Deal and Linda Barnes Sheldon, wife of the US president, are taken captive by terrorists.
6. *Deal with the Dead* (**Putnam, 2001**) The shady past of John Deal's father comes back to haunt John in the form of a Miami mobster, his avenging son, and a hidden fortune.
7. *Bone Key* (**Putnam, 2002**) Two days after a hustler is beaten by a cop, the hustler is found murdered. Was he connected to a 70-year-old murder?
8. *Havana Run* (**Putnam, 2003**) Mysterious businessman Antonio Fuentes offers Deal a million dollar retainer, allegedly to oversee

a huge building project in Havana slated to begin once Castro is dead.

Stark, Richard

PSEUDONYM OF Donald E. Westlake

Donald E. Westlake (q.v.), author of the Dortmunder comic caper series, wrote, as Richard Stark, a long series of novels about another thief, one with the single name of "Parker." Parker is a cold-blooded professional thief who is very good at what he does, but, same as with Dortmunder, even the best-planned heist can unravel, and he finds himself on the run, often. Parker has only scorn for "amateurs" and law-enforcement officials. The Parker books are fairly grim, and Parker is not a comic character. Parker occasionally teams with Alan Grofield, a stage actor who robs banks and other institutions to support his not very scintillating career (numbers 5 and 20). Grofield has four novels of his own (numbers 10, 13, 15, and 18). After a 23-year hiatus, Parker was revived in 1997 with *Comeback*. Numbers 14 and 16 were published together as *The Sour Lemon Score/Deadly Edge* (Avon, 1985). Donald E. Westlake (d. 2008) was also the author of the Mitch Tobin PI series under the pseudonym of Tucker Coe (q.v.). The Parker/Grofield series is listed below, generally without annotations.

1. *Hunter, The* (Pocket Books, 1962) The first Parker novel. Freely adapted and filmed by John Boorman as *Point Blank* (also the UK title), which became a noir classic. Filmed again in 1997 as *Payback*, a Mel Gibson vehicle. Book was rereleased by Mysterious Press in 1999 under the *Payback* title.
2. *Man with the Getaway Face, The* (Pocket Books, 1963) UK title: *The Steel Hit*.
3. *Outfit, The* (Pocket Books, 1963)
4. *Mourner, The* (Pocket Books, 1963)
5. *Score, The* (Pocket Books, 1964) Alan Grofield has a role here. UK title: *Killtown*.
6. *Jugger, The* (Pocket Books, 1965)
7. *Seventh, The* (Pocket Books, 1966) UK title: *The Split*.
8. *Handle, The* (Pocket Books, 1966) UK title: *Run Lethal*.
9. *Rare Coin Score, The* (Fawcett, 1967)
10. *Damsel, The* (Macmillan, 1967) An Alan Grofield novel.
11. *Green Eagle Score, The* (Fawcett, 1967)
12. *Black Ice Score, The* (Fawcett, 1968)
13. *Dame, The* (Macmillan, 1969) An Alan Grofield novel.
14. *Sour Lemon Score, The* (Fawcett, 1969)
15. *Blackbird, The* (Macmillan, 1969) An Alan Grofield novel.
16. *Deadly Edge* (Random House, 1971)
17. *Slayground* (Random House, 1971)
18. *Lemons Never Lie* (World, 1971)
19. *Plunder Squad* (Random House, 1972)
20. *Butcher's Moon* (Random House, 1974) The last Parker novel for 23 years. Alan Grofield has a role.
21. *Comeback* (Mysterious, 1997) Parker is resurrected after a 23-year hiatus.
22. *Backflash* (Mysterious, 1998)
23. *Flashfire* (Mysterious, 2000)
24. *Firebreak* (Mysterious, 2001)
25. *Breakout* (Mysterious, 2002)
26. *Nobody Runs Forever* (Mysterious, 2004)
27. *Ask the Parrot* (Mysterious, 2006)
28. *Dirty Money* (Grand Central, 2008)

Stasheff, Christopher

I. *The Warlock in Spite of Himself* (1969) sparked a series, or combination of series. Earthling Rodney d'Armand, who soon renames himself Rod Gallowglass, lands on Gramarye, a planet where magic works, and witches, ghosts, goblins, elves, and humans live together in a feudal society. Rod falls in love with beautiful witch Gwen and takes it upon himself to introduce the democratic way of life to Gramarye. Eleven more adventures followed, including a prequel, until Stasheff decided to pass on the torch to a younger generation of Gallowglasses (see series II and III). In 2004 Stasheff added one last title to the original Warlock series. The Warlock is a lighthearted fantasy (although later volumes are less lighthearted) with elements of science fiction, which succeeds in entertaining the reader without making too many demands. Stasheff, who has a PhD in theater, is a college professor and writer for radio as well as a fantasy writer. Omnibus editions include: *To the Magic Born* (Doubleday, 1986; UK title: *Warlock to the Magic Born;* numbers 1–2); *The Warlock Enlarged* (Doubleday, 1986; numbers 3–5); *The Warlock's Night Out* (Guild America, 1988; numbers 6–7); and *Odd Warlock Out* (Guild America, 1989; numbers 8–10).

1. *Escape Velocity* (Ace, 1983) A prequel, taking place mostly on Earth, in which some questions about the origins of Gramarye are answered.
2. *Warlock in Spite of Himself, The* (Ace, 1969) Rodney d'Armand arrives on Gramarye, renames himself, falls in love, and saves the planet from a force from the future that is intent on preserving feudalism. First published in series and still the favorite with some readers.
3. *King Kobold Revived* (Ace, 1984) Rod Gallowglass has to save the planet Gramarye from an evil band of time-traveling Neanderthals. Revised version of title originally published as *King Kobold* (Ace, 1971).
4. *Warlock Unlocked, The* (Ace, 1982) Sinister time travelers cause a rift between church and state as Rod and his family are entrapped and sent to an alternate world.
5. *Warlock Enraged, The* (Ace, 1985) Rod's temper tantrums indicate he isn't completely in control of himself as a malignant magus encroaches on the North Country.
6. *Warlock Wandering, The* (Ace, 1986) Rod and Gwen are held captive on another world 500 years from their own time.
7. *Warlock Is Missing, The* (Ace, 1986) When Rod and Gwen spend a night away from home, the Gallowglass children go in search of them, being adopted by a unicorn along the way.
8. *Warlock Heretical, The* (Ace, 1987) The enemies of peace return, tempt the clergy with visions of power, and precipitate a revolt against the throne.
9. *Warlock's Companion, The* (Ace, 1988) The history of Fess, the Warlock's faithful cybernetic steed, as told to the Gallowglass children.
10. *Warlock Insane, The* (Ace, 1989) An evil sorcerer turns Rod's mind so that is fighting hallucinations and imaginary monsters.
11. *Warlock Rock, The* (Ace, 1990) Mysterious floating crystals have captured the eyes—and ears—of the good folk of Gramarye.
12. *Warlock and Son* (Ace, 1991) Magnus, the eldest Gallowglass son, goes off on adventures of his own, but Rod can't resist trailing him, in case he gets into trouble.
13. *Warlock's Last Ride, The* (Ace, 2004) Rod's last adventure, as grief-stricken by Gwen's sudden death, he rides off, abandoning his duties as Lord High Warlock of Gramarye.

II. Heirs to the Warlock continues the Gallowglass series in the persons of the children of Rod and Gwen: Magnus, Cordelia, Geoffrey, and Gregory. The eldest, Magnus, has a series of his own as well (see series III).

1. *Wizard in Absentia, A* (Ace, 1993) Magnus searches for his roots and identity on various worlds until he winds up engineering a rebellion of his own on a feudal planet. Sometimes regarded as first of the Rogue Wizard series (III).
2. *M'Lady Witch* (Ace, 1994) Cordelia Gallowglass, daughter of the family, can marry Prince Alain, heir-apparent to the throne, but would prefer not to.
3. *Quicksilver's Night* (Ace, 1995) Geoffrey, second son of Rod and Gwen, gets involved with the beautiful bandit Quicksilver and the sultry witch Moraga.
4. *Spell-Bound Scholar, The* (Ace, 1999) The witch Moraga sets out to destroy Gregory, the youngest son of Rod and Gwen.
5. *Here Be Monsters* (Ace, 2001) The wedding rites for Geoffrey, Cordelia, and Gregory are disrupted by the terrifying visions of Gregory's fiancée, Alouette.

III. Magnus d'Armand, aka Magnus Gallowglass, aka Gar Pike, Rod's eldest son, stars in his own series, the Rogue Wizard. Magnus finds himself rebelling against his father, whom he thinks too inclined to play by the rules, and tries to find his own way in life, traveling to other planets and righting wrongs with the aid of partners Dirk Dulaine and the formidable Alea (first met in number 6). Magnus also appears in *A Wizard in Absentia* (series II, number 1).

1. *Wizard in Mind, A* (Tor, 1995) Under the alias of "Gar Pike," Magnus travels to the island of Pirogia on the planet Petrarch, which he tries to convert to democracy.
2. *Wizard in Bedlam, A* (Doubleday, 1979) Originally a stand-alone volume, this title was reprinted as part of the Rogue Wizard series by Tor (1995). Gar Pike gets involved on the Melange where the Churl Pulain has started a rebellion against the heirs of the Wizard DeCade.
3. *Wizard in War, A* (Tor, 1995) Magnus and his partner Dirk Dulaine help to establish peace and impartial government on the planet Maltroit.
4. *Wizard in Peace, A* (Tor, 1996) Magnus and Dirk organize revolutionaries on a repressive and puritanical planet.
5. *Wizard in Chaos, A* (Tor, 1997) Gar Pike and Dirk Dulaine arrive on Duruc, which was settled by idealistic anarchists, but is now involved in constant warfare between rival strongholds.
6. *Wizard in Midgard, A* (Tor, 1998) The planet Siegfried, which has echoes of Norse mythology, is divided into three warring factions: giants, dwarfs, and "regular" humans. Gar teams up with Alea, who is not quite big enough to be a giantess.
7. *Wizard and a Warlord, A* (Tor, 2000) Accompanied by Alea, Gar Pike travels to a totally anarchic planet.
8. *Wizard in the Way, A* (Tor, 2000) Gar and Alea, on the planet Oldeira, try to persuade browbeaten serfs to rebel against the Wizard Lords who are oppressing them.
9. *Wizard in a Feud, A* (Tor, 2001) Gar and Alea try to make peace on a lost planetary colony apparently settled by Scots, where the humans are in conflict with the indigenous six-limbed elves and fairies.

IV. The Wizard in Rhyme series has no direct connection with the Warlock series, but can be regarded as a spin-off. Earthling Matt Mantrell is thrust onto the alternative world of Merovence, where words become truth and magic spells are created by verse, and becomes Lord Wizard.

1. *Her Majesty's Wizard* (Ballantine, 1986) When he reads a runic verse, Matt promptly finds himself enlisted in the cause of the young and beautiful Princess Alisande, rightful ruler of Merovence.
2. *Oathbound Wizard, The* (Ballantine, 1993) To prove himself worthy of Alisande's hand, Lord Wizard Matt rashly promises to dethrone Gordogrosso, evil sorcerer-king of neighboring Ibile.
3. *Witch Doctor, The* (Ballantine, 1994) Saul Bremener, Matt's friend from Earth, finds himself translated to Allustria, where he is enlisted in the rebellion against Queen Suettay.
4. *Secular Wizard, The* (Ballantine, 1995) Matt and Saul (now "Wizard of Sarcasm") are together again, until Prince Boncorro of Latruria decides to introduce supply-side economics to his kingdom.
5. *My Son, the Wizard* (Ballantine, 1997) Matt rescues his parents, both of whom prove to have magical powers, and, together with his father, confronts an evil sorcerer who wants to destroy two worlds.
6. *Haunted Wizard, The* (Ballantine, 2000) The murder of a hated prince could spell war between two kingdoms unless Matt can beat a powerful magician and an evil cult.
7. *Crusading Wizard, The* (Ballantine, 2000) Matt goes to Jerusalem to head off an approaching barbarian horde, but finds that the leader of the horde is in league with a powerful evil.
8. *Feline Wizard, The* (Ballantine, 2001) The feline sorceress Balkis has returned to Maracanda to claim her royal title.

V. The Star Stone series is a pair of novels featuring the wizard Ohaern who battles evil in the form of evil wizards and the nasty creatures they create. The Star Stone, which has magical powers, is the subject of a quest in number 2.

1. *Shaman, The* (Ballantine, 1995) Ohaern aids Lomallin as he battles Ulahane, who is campaigning against the humans with a host of nasty creatures that he has unleashed.
2. *Sage, The* (Ballantine, 1996) Five hundred years later, Ohaern must fight against the offspring of Ulahane. To do so he has to mold the ruffianly Culachra into a true warrior and forge Culachra's weapon from the Star Stone.

VI. Starship Troupers (not "Troopers") is a trio about a 23rd-century theatrical company that leaves a puritanical Earth on a tour of the inhabited planets. Two volumes, *The Crafter* (Ace, 1991; co-authored with Bill Fawcett) and *Blessings and Curses* (Ace, 1992) are sometimes linked together as "Crafters." *The Seaman* (Random House, 1997) and *Saint Vidicon to the Rescue* (Ace, 2005) are stand-alones (so far). *Mind Out of Time* (Five Stars, 2003) is a collection of stories.

1. *We Open on Venus* (Ballantine, 1884) The Star Company gets out of New York (barely) and journeys to New Venus where they will open with *Macbeth*, unaware of the draconian laws against starting fires on the petroleum-suffused planet.
1. *Company of Stars, A* (Ballantine, 1991) Ramon Lazarian, fleeing a forced marriage, comes to New York where he is mugged and then falls in with a company of actors who are planning a tour of the extraterrestrial colonies.
3. *Slight Detour, A* (Ballantine, 1994) The Star Company arrives on the prospector colony planet of Citadel.

Steed, Neville

PSEUDONYM OF **Norman Sharam**

I. Peter Marklin has a rather odd passion for an amateur sleuth, collecting antique toys. Peter runs the Toy Emporium in a surprisingly violent village in Dorset, England. With his live-in girlfriend Arabella, the beautiful and talented head writer of a local crime-new television show, and his friend Gus, a crusty retired fisherman, the truthful, kind, decent, if somewhat chatty Peter reluctantly handles the cases that fall his way.

1. *Tinplate* (St. Martin's, 1987) Macklin is hired to purchase several valuable tinplate models and deliver them to their wealthy buyer.
2. *Die-Cast* (St. Martin's, 1988) Peter is diverted from developing his new line of aircraft models to uncover both a kidnapper and a murderer.
3. *Chipped* (St. Martin's, 1988) While Arabella is off in San Francisco, Peter looks for a disappeared professional detective who last left behind three unfinished investigations.
4. *Clockwork* (St. Martin's, 1989) Martin gets involved when money for the local school is missing, and a teacher suspected of having AIDS is murdered.
5. *Wind-Up* (St. Martin's, 1991) Peter investigates the murder of a dour chap whose attic contained a half-million pounds' worth of vintage toys.
6. *Boxed-In* (St. Martin's, 1992) Peter finds the partially clothed, asphyxiated body of a teenage boy inside the trunk of a Packard at an antique fair.

II. Steed also wrote a pair of novels set in the 1930s featuring former pilot Johnny Black, a private investigator who gets involved in a couple of English country life murders.

1. *Black Eye* (St. Martin's, 1989) Diana Travis hires injured ex-pilot Johnny Black to investigate her brother-in-law Michael Seagrove, who she suspects of having arranged the "accident" that killed her sister.
2. *Black Mail* (Weidenfeld [UK], 1990) Not published in the United States. No annotation available.

Steen, Marguerite

The Sun Is My Undoing, by English author Steen, captured the same large popular audience that had just made *Gone with the Wind* a best seller. Readers looking for a long and lively action-romance won't be disappointed with the adventures of its dashing and impetuous hero, Matthew Flood, an 18th-century Englishman who gets involved in the slave trade. The book's central theme, the evils of slavery, is continued in two sequels that tell of Matthew's descendants and heirs to his shipping business. Steen (d. 1975) averaged nearly a novel a year between 1926 and the mid-1960s, including what is known as the Spanish Trilogy, a trio of novels whose connecting link is the Andalusia of the 1930s: *Matador* (Little, Brown, 1934); *The One-Eyed Moon* (Little, Brown, 1935); and *The Tavern* (Bobbs-Merrill, 1936).

1. *Sun Is My Undoing, The* (Viking, 1941) The beautiful English girl he loves is an ardent abolitionist, but Matthew Flood enters the slave trade, takes a black mistress, and has many adventures on the high seas, including capture by pirates.
2. *Twilight on the Flood* (Doubleday, 1949) John Flood, the thoughtful great-grandson of Matthew, stars in this sequel set in Bristol, England and Africa's Gold Coast.

3. *Jehovah's Blues* (Doubleday, 1952) In 1931 the beautiful, popular novelist Aldebaran Flood, the last of Matthew's descendants, comes to the United States in search of a lost love. UK title: *Phoenix Rising*.

Steinbeck, John

This Nobel Prize– and Pulitzer Prize–winning author once lived near Cannery Row, now a tourist attraction in Monterey, California. He first wrote about the seedy residents of the rundown neighborhood behind the waterfront sardine canneries in *Tortilla Flat* (Covici, 1935). Some of the same characters reappear in these two books, which focus on Doc and tell of the funny and bawdy doings of Dora, the orange-haired madam; Lee Chong and his "Old Tennis Shoe" whiskey; and the characters who frequent the Palace Flophouse and Grill. A relatively unsuccessful Rodgers and Hammerstein musical, *Pipe Dream* (1955), was based on the Cannery Row characters.

1. *Cannery Row* (Viking, 1945) The motley residents of Cannery Row work together to give Doc a birthday party he won't forget.
2. *Sweet Thursday* (Viking, 1954) World War II has brought change to Cannery Row, and Doc's spirits are running low, but Suzy arrives and livens things up considerably.

Stevenson, D(orothy) E(mily)

I. Popular Scottish novelist Dorothy Emily Stevenson was married to an officer in the Highland Infantry, and she used her own diaries as the basis of her Mrs. Tim books. These gently humorous and amiable volumes detail the life of an officer's wife in small English and Scottish garrison towns from the 1930s through the postwar period. Hester Christie records bits of regimental and neighborhood gossip, domestic crises, and the amusing doings of her two high-spirited children, Betty and Bryan. Stevenson, who produced light romances from the 1930s until shortly before her death in 1973, was a very reliable writer of engrossing and enjoyable fiction of the old-fashioned kind.

1. *Mrs. Tim Christie* (Farrar & Rinehart, 1940) Captain Christie and his family and friends in the town of Westburgh are introduced through the diary of his wife, Hester. Originally published in the United Kingdom in 1932 as *Mrs. Tim of the Regiment*.
2. *Mrs. Tim Carries On* (Farrar & Rinehart, 1941) Tim is posted to France in February 1940, and Hester stays on in the small garrison town of Danford through the difficult war years.
3. *Mrs. Tim Gets a Job* (Rinehart, 1947) Suffering postwar doldrums with Tim stationed in Egypt and the children away at school, Hester takes a job at Miss Clutterbuck's guesthouse.
4. *Mrs. Tim Flies Home* (Rinehart, 1952) Hester Christie leaves Kenya—where her husband, now a colonel, is stationed—to visit with her children in England.

II. Many readers have enjoyed escaping into the happier, simpler world of Stevenson's towns and farms, where problems always work out and the basic goodness of humanity is never in doubt. These loosely related books share some of the same characters but can be read as individual volumes.

1. *Vittoria Cottage* (Rinehart, 1949) Caroline Dering, widowed mother of three grown children, is attracted to the village of Ashbridge's newest resident, Robert Stepperton.

2. *Music in the Hills* (Rinehart, 1950) Caroline's son James goes to live with his aunt and uncle, Mamie and Jack Johnstone, on their farm on the Scottish border.

3. *Shoulder the Sky* (Rinehart, 1951) Rhoda, James's new bride, adjusts to life at Mureth Farm as a terrible winter storm hits their little community. UK title: *Winter and Rough Weather*.

III. These two books featuring Gerald Brown are pleasant adventure-romances set in London and Scotland.

1. *Gerald and Elizabeth* (Holt, 1969) When Gerald leaves South Africa under a cloud, he comes to stay with his beautiful half sister Elizabeth in London.

2. *House of the Deer* (Holt, 1971) Gerald goes deer stalking in the Scottish Highlands, where he makes friends, falls in love, and has a close scrape with tragedy.

IV. This pair of novels has as a connecting link a house in a small Scottish border town, where two generations of Melvilles enjoy life and love from 1905 to the 1940s.

1. *Celia's House* (Farrar, Rinehart, 1943) Celia Dunnian passes on her house to Humphrey Melville and his five children, who love life on the Scottish border.

2. *Listening Valley* (Farrar, Rinehart, 1944) About two sisters: the shy Antonia who marries an older man, and the younger, prettier sister who inherits "Celia's House" in 1952.

V. Another pair of novels relates the young life of David Kirk until he marries and of David and Jan's friend Barbie France and her rendezvous with a "tall stranger."

1. *Five Windows* (Rinehart, 1953) David Kirk grows up, goes to school, falls in love, and weds Jan.

2. *Tall Stranger, The* (Rinehart, 1957) When Barbie France falls ill, she leaves the flat she shares with her friend Nell and her secretarial job in London, and moves to her aunt's house in the country, where a fortune-teller tells her that she is fated to meet a tall stranger.

VI. In this trilogy, Miss Barbara Buncle writes a best seller, marries her publisher, settles down, and endures World War II with her husband's niece. Omnibus volume containing numbers 1, 2, and 3: *Miss Buncle* (Holt, 1964).

1. *Miss Buncle's Book* (Farrar, Rinehart, 1937) Barbara Buncle, not having much imagination, peoples her novel with characters based on her neighbors, much to their chagrin, especially when the novel becomes a best seller. Originally published in 1934.

2. *Miss Buncle Married* (Farrar, Rinehart, 1937) Miss Buncle marries her publisher, Mr. Abbott, moves to the country, and settles down to raise a family.

3. *Two Mrs. Abbotts, The* (Farrar, Rinehart, 1943) Barbara Abbott becomes friends with her husband's niece, and the two muddle through World War II together.

VII. Amberwell is the family estate of the Ayrtons on the west coast of Scotland. Its history is delineated in a pair of novels.

1. *Amberwell* (Rinehart, 1955) The five Ayrton children grow up on Ayrton, their Scottish family estate.

2. *Summerhills* (Rinehart, 1956) All the Ayrtons leave Amberwell except Nell, who holds the estate together so that her family will have a home after World War II.

Stevenson, Robert Louis

Kidnapped has all the strenuous adventure, thrilling encounters, and hairbreadth escapes of *Treasure Island*, combined with the romantic scenery of the Scottish Highlands and an underlying concern with the proud and noble Highlanders, now ravaged and forced to emigrate from their ancestral home after the defeat of the last Jacobite uprising at the Battle of Culloden in 1746. *Kidnapped* has long been a young adult favorite, but it has been underrated as an adult classic according to at least one of its editors, Barry Menikoff, who has prepared a new complete text with all of the excisions and deletions restored (Huntington Library Text, 1999). *Kidnapped* has been made into at least nine movie versions, none of them, unfortunately, particularly memorable. *David Balfour*, the sequel, has never been as popular as *Kidnapped*, but Stevenson was a master storyteller, and none of his works should be consigned to oblivion.

1. *Kidnapped* (Munro, 1886) Young David Balfour goes to the Highlands to claim his inheritance, but his evil uncle, Ebenezer, has him shanghaied aboard a ship headed for the Carolinas. There he befriends Highland rebel Alan Breck and begins an eventful homeward journey.

2. *David Balfour* (Scribner, 1895) This sequel continues David's story with his marriage to the loved and spirited Highland lass Catriona and recounts the story of the trial of James of the Glen. UK title: *Catriona*.

Stewart, Mary

Stewart's polished contemporary gothics set in picturesque European spots won her a huge audience before she turned to the legend of King Arthur for this tetralogy. Her skill in creating colorful characters, suspense, and a brooding atmosphere serves her well in portraying Britain's Dark Ages, where witches, sorcerers, and tragic kings moved heroically through an enchanted land. Though Arthur's rise to power is the subject, the true star and narrator of the tale is Merlin the magician. Among the other series based on the King Arthur legend are T. H. White's (q.v.) *Once and Future King* series and Henry Treece's (q.v.) *Great Captains* series. *Mary Stewart's Merlin Trilogy* (Morrow, 1980) is an omnibus containing numbers 1, 2, and 3.

1. *Crystal Cave, The* (Morrow, 1970) Merlin spends his youth in the court of his grandfather, the king of Wales.

2. *Hollow Hills, The* (Morrow, 1973) Merlin's story continues with the birth of Arthur, who has a secluded boyhood and then searches for the magical sword, Caliburn.

3. *Last Enchantment, The* (Morrow, 1979) After helping Arthur set up his kingdom, Merlin leaves the scene, while Arthur marries and fathers an illegitimate son, Modred.

4. *Wicked Day, The* (Morrow, 1983) Modred, incestuous son of Arthur and his half sister Morgause, is the unwilling agent who fulfills Merlin's prophecy of the "Wicked Day" when Arthur meets his end.

Stinson, Jim (James Emerson)

Stoney Winston is British, but he likes the atmosphere of southern California, where he pursues a not very successful living making low-budget films and solving a mystery or two. Stoney is self-deprecatory and laid-back but articulate, and his filming always seems to lead him into seamier things like drugs, pornography, bikers, and murder. Stinson, not to be confused with landscape photographer Jim

Sti*m*son, has also published a textbook: *Video: Communication and Production* (Goodheart, 2002).

1. *Double Exposure* (**Scribner, 1985**) Winston is asked to find the stepdaughter of the owner of a minor studio.
2. *Low Angles* (**Scribner, 1986**) An old friend and producer asks Stoney to help save a biker being filmed by a first-time female director in the hills outside of Los Angeles.
3. *Truck Shot* (**Scribner, 1989**) Stoney takes a part-time teaching job at Angeles Commercial Design College (ACDC), which has money problems, staff shortages, and a mysterious link to a rigged truck-designing contest.
4. *TV Safe* (**Scribner, 1991**) Winston is a junior writer on the *Oh-Pun Sesame* game show when he is given the assignment of stopping contestant Amber Sung Li from winning $1 million.

Stirling, Jessica

PSEUDONYM OF Mary M. Coghlan

I. "Jessica Stirling" is two writers: Mary M. Coghlan and Hugh C. Rae. According to Rae, Coghlan was the major partner until 1984, when she retired and Rae took over the nom de plume. "Jessica Stirling" has been producing novels for 30 years now. Most of them are set in Scotland in historic times, from the 18th century to World War II. While in some respects they are standard historical romance fare, they tend to deal with well-delineated working-class characters in realistic settings. The Stalker trilogy is set in and around the coal-mining town of Blacklaw, Scotland, in the late 19th century. In 1875 coal miner's daughter Mirrin Stalker is thrust rather hastily into the position of housekeeper at Strathmore, the mansion of mine owner Houston Lamont. Some fairly predictable complications develop. The sequels continue the story of the Stalker family, and Mirrin eventually winds up on a small farm.

1. *Strathmore* (**Delacorte, 1975**) Spirited young Mirrin comes to Strathmore with built-in prejudices against the Lamonts, but as she begins to understand them, her heart melts. The year is 1875. UK title: *The Spoiled Earth.*
2. *Call Home the Heart* (**St. Martin's, 1977**) The story of the Stalker family continues; Drew goes to law school in Edinburgh; Kate settles into the security of marriage; and Mirrin finds success on the music hall circuit as "The Songbird of the North." UK title: *The Hiring Fair.*
3. *Dark Pasture, The* (**St. Martin's, 1978**) 17 years after the events in number 2, Mirrin is married and living on a farm, but her husband Tom's eyesight is failing.

II. The Jewish Beckman family of London is the focus of three novels set in the 1920s to the 1940s. When young Holly inherits a share in an antique store, she is determined to make the most of the opportunity to pull herself out of the Lambeth slums and away from her drunkard father and crooked brother Ritchie. The vivid and convincing characters and interesting setting make for very enjoyable reading.

1. *Drums of Time, The* (**St. Martin's, 1980**) In 1918 young Holly Beckman becomes part owner of an antique shop when owner dies, and she is determined to make a success of it. UK title: *The Deep Well at Noon.*
2. *Blue Evening Gone, The* (**St. Martin's, 1981**) In 1933 love finds holly, Leo, Maury, and Ritchie as Holly investigates some art forgeries that threaten to ruin reputation as an art expert.
3. *Gates of Midnight, The* (**St. Martin's, 1983**) World War II finds widowed Holly Beckman Deems managing an antique business

and concerning herself about her son, her brothers, and her former lover, David Aspinwall.

III. Rural Scotland in the 18th and 19th centuries is the setting for the Patterson trilogy, which chronicles the hardships that Gaddy Cochran bears, first as a drover (a roaming cattle seller) and then as a farmer.

1. *Treasures on Earth* (**St. Martin's, 1985**) Gaddy Cochran adopts a newborn foundling and abandons her life as a drover's woman for the settled but harsh existence of tenant farmer.
2. *Creature Comforts* (**St. Martin's, 1986**) Gaddy's daughters, foundling Elspeth and Anna, are both disappointed in marriage.
3. *Hearts of Gold* (**St. Martin's, 1987**) Elspeth flees her sinister spouse for an anonymous life in the coalfields of Abbefield, while Anna is deserted by her husband.

IV. A historical quartet is set in the slums of Glasgow in the 19th century. The protagonists are Kirsty Barnes and her sweetheart and common-law husband, Craig Nicholson, who escape rural poverty only to land in urban poverty as they try to raise a family in a Glasgow tenement.

1. *Good Provider, The* (**St. Martin's, 1989**) Orphan Kirsty Barnes is rescued from the clutches of the lecherous old farmer to whom she is indentured by her sweetheart, Craig Nicholson.
2. *Asking Price, The* (**St. Martin's, 1990**) Kirsty, Craig, their son, Bobby, and several other family members are living cramped together in a small tenement apartment as Kirsty dreams of David Lockhart, a handsome upper-class minister.
3. *Wise Child, The* (**St. Martin's, 1990**) A series of melodramatic events almost cost Craig his job and Kirsty her husband as Craig's brother Gordon gets involved with a family with dark secrets.
4. *Welcome Light, The* (**St. Martin's, 1991**) Only love for their son, who is hit by a crippling disease, keeps Kirsty and Craig together in their tempestuous marriage.

V. Another pair of novels harks back to late 18th- and early 19th-century Scotland and follows the fortunes of Clare Kelso (later Quinn) through her life from prison on a charge of infanticide to prosperous widowhood.

1. *Lantern for the Dark* (**St. Martin's, 1992**) Cameron Adams, Clare Kelso's legal representative, is convinced that Clare is innocent of infanticide, but that she is holding back secrets that would save her from hanging.
2. *Shadows on the Shore* (**St. Martin's, 1994**) Now a prosperous salt dealer and a widow with an eight-year-old child, Clare Kelso Quinn faces the return of the charming but unscrupulous Frederick Stryker, who betrayed her in the past.

VI. The Great Depression of the 1930s in Glasgow is the scene of a pair of novels featuring young Alison Burnside, her struggles to obtain a medical degree, and her relationships with several men, especially one-armed World War I veteran Jim Abbott.

1. *Penny Wedding, The* (**St. Martin's, 1995**) Seventeen-year-old Alison Burnside is helped in her struggles to obtain a medical degree by teacher Jim Abbott and her four older brothers when her mother dies and her father loses his job during the Great Depression.
2. *Marrying Kind, The* (**St. Martin's, 1996**) Alison continues her medical education, but is torn between her commitment to Jim Abbott and affairs with poor, handsome Irishman Declan Slater and rich, dashing Howard McGrath.

VII. The Isle of Mull trilogy is set on an island off the west coast of Scotland between the years of 1878 and 1908. The Campbell family is at the center of the action, particularly two sisters, Biddy and Innis, daughters of the drunken Ronan and the capable Vassie. The lives and loves of a large cast of interesting characters are set against the rugged charm of the Isle of Mull.

1. *Island Wife, The* (St. Martin's, 1998) Ronan, the drunken black-sheep son of the hardworking Campbells of Mull, is fortunate in his competent wife, Vassie, and daughters Biddy, Innis, and Eileen. However, things change when the Baverstocks purchase the estate next door and hire a handsome young shepherd to tend their sheep. Starts in 1878.
2. *Wind from the Hills, The* (St. Martin's, 2000) Some years later, Biddy is a wealthy, childless, and promiscuous widow. Innis, converted to Catholicism, is married to the taciturn shepherd Michael Tarrant. Then widower schoolmaster Gillies Brown arrives on Mull and reopens the village school.
3. *Strawberry Season, The* (St. Martin's, 2000) By 1908 many of the younger natives of Mull have left the island for greener pastures. Fay Ludlow, the pregnant wife of Gavin, Innis's abusive son, throws herself on the mercy of her in-laws. A new arrival, the rascally Patrick Rattenbury, stirs things up among the womenfolk of Mull.

VIII. Another trilogy, set in Depression-era Glasgow again, features tenacious Lizzie Conway, who has fought her way out of the Gorbils slums, and her three daughters: Polly, Babs, and Rosie, who, in their various ways, seem determined to recapitulate Lizzie's unwise marriage.

1. *Prized Possessions* (St. Martin's, 2001) Lizzie Conway has, despite an unwise marriage, managed to claw her way out of Glasgow's Depression-era slums to provide for her daughters: Polly, Babs, and deaf Rosie. Originally published in 1998.
2. *Sisters Three* (St. Martin's, 2002) Polly is the well-provided-for but dissatisfied wife of mafioso Dominic Manone. Babs has her hands full managing her demanding brood and keeping her husband, Jackie, out of jail.
3. *Wives at War* (Hodder [UK], 2003) World War II. Babs, her husband in the army, sends three of her children to the country and goes back to work. Rosie takes a job as a factory worker. Polly, her husband in New York with their children, manages his shady empire in Glasgow. Not yet published in the United States.

IX. Another pair of novels is set in Edwardian Glasgow and Dublin. A large cast of characters includes 18-year-old Lindsay Franklin, who is given a share of her grandfather's shipbuilding business, her charming, conniving Irish cousin and eventual husband, Forbes McCulloch, and their Dublin relatives Sylvie, Gowry, and Maeve McCulloch, who get caught up in the fight for Irish freedom.

1. *Piper's Tune, The* (St. Martin's, 2002) Eighteen-year-old Lindsay Franklin is entrusted by her grandfather with a share of the family ship-building business, then makes a bad mistake by falling for her rascally cousin Forbes McCulloch.
2. *Shamrock Green* (St. Martin's, 2003) Sylvie and Gowry McCulloch and their daughter, Maeve, become involved in the fight for Irish freedom when Gowry's father and brothers acquire illegal weapons and Sylvie falls for Irish brotherhood leader Francis Hagarty.

Stockton, Frank (Francis R.)

This 19th-century American author wrote what have been called "grown-up juveniles"—that is, whimsical and paradoxical stories full of absurd characters and amusing incidents. Stockton's short fable "The Lady, or the Tiger?" won instant fame and is still anthologized and read today. Otherwise Stockton is almost totally forgotten, which is too bad, because his two books featuring the unlikely adventures of Mrs. Lecks and Mrs. Aleshine, two rather prosaic matrons, can still tickle the funny bone. They would make good hammock reading on a warm summer afternoon.

1. *Casting Away of Mrs. Lecks and Mrs. Aleshine, The* (Appleton, 1886) When their cruise ship sinks and they find themselves washed ashore on a desert island, these two unruffled matrons set up house as calmly as if they were at home in New England.
2. *Dusantes, The* (Century, 1888) The Crusoe ladies have further adventures as the Dusantes, owners of the desert island, follow them home to return the money they paid for the use of the property.

Storey, Gail Donohue

Houston librarian Colleen Sweeny, who suffers acutely from low self-esteem, goes through some problematic relationships before she finds some happiness with handsome doctor Gabriel Benedict in *The Lord's Motel*. The sequel, *God's Country Club*, finds Colleen and Gabriel working on their relationship while fretting about her unhappy childhood in Boston and impending job loss. This is a pair of humorous, insightful novels with send-ups of, among other things, of political correctness, self-improvement strategies, do-gooders, and networking. Cambridge, Massachusetts, native Gail Donohue Storey published a volume of poetry under her maiden name of Gail Donohue: *First Poems of Gail Donohue* (Pine Street, 1974) 18 years before *The Lord's Motel* came out.

1. *Lord's Motel, The* (Persea, 1992) Houston librarian Colleen, who runs the Service-to-the-Unserved library program, lives in the New Age–run Lord's Motel, and carries on a rather kinky relationship with cruise ship social director, Web Desiderio, becomes friends with Dolores, who is imprisoned for killing her abusive husband.
2. *God's Country Club* (Persea, 1996) Gail moves into Dr. Gabriel Benedict's condo at God's Country Club, but she still has doubts about her past: her terrible childhood in Boston, her "residentially challenged" father, her relationship with the cruise director, and her job, which is about to be downsized.

Stout, Rex

I. Created more than 70 years ago, Nero Wolfe, Rex Stout's obese, sedentary, Manhattan-dwelling, orchid-loving, brilliant detective, and Archie Goodwin, Nero's "legs," chronicler, and commentator, have proved to be enduring creations. The recent A&E television series starring Maury Chaikin and Timothy Hutton is the best effort yet to bring Wolfe to the screen. There also were a previous TV version starring William Conrad, two big screen versions in the 1930s (*Meet Nero Wolfe* and *The League of Frightened Men*, featuring Edward Arnold and Walter Connolly, respectively, as Wolfe), and a radio series with that quintessential stout actor Sydney Greenstreet doing the voice of Nero. Readers will find Rex Stout's plots even more clever and sophisticated in book form, where Archie's droll and witty comments add to the fun. Wolfe bears the mark of the 1930s golden age of mystery—he is one of those eccentric private detectives who solve relatively bloodless cases by ratiocination rather than rough stuff. Stout was one of the few Americans to master the genre. William Baring-Gould's lighthearted study, *Nero Wolfe of West 35th Street* (Viking, 1969), is very good but needs updating, as does John McAleer's *Rex Stout: A Biography* (Little, Brown, 1977), which gives an interesting picture of the author and a complete bibliography through 1975. Many of the Nero Wolfe books have also been published in omnibus volumes. *Full House* (Viking, 1955) contains numbers 2, 13, and 18. *All Aces* (Viking, 1958) comprises numbers 6, 12, and 15. *Five of a Kind* (Viking, 1961) includes numbers 3, 16, and 17. In *Royal Flush* (Viking, 1969) can be found numbers 1, 19, and 27. *Kings Full of Aces* (Viking, 1969) contains numbers 5, 21, and 32. *Three Aces* (Viking, 1971) contains numbers 26, 33, and 35. *Triple Zack* (Viking, 1974) has numbers 13, 14, and 16. Nero Wolfe has been resurrected by Ken Darby (in *The Brownstone House of Nero Wolfe*, Little, Brown, 1983) and Robert Goldsborough (q.v.).

1. *Fer-de-Lance* (Farrar & Rinehart, 1934) Nero Wolfe's first recorded case concerns university president Peter Oliver Barstow, who dies a strange, sudden death on the golf course. Stout teases his readers by having Wolfe and Archie refer to earlier cases. Variant title: *Meet Nero Wolfe*.

2. *League of Frightened Men, The* (Farrar & Rinehart, 1935) A group of old Harvard classmates is being murdered one by one.

3. *Rubber Band, The* (Farrar & Rinehart, 1936) Anthony Perry brings Wolfe a complicated mystery that involves blackmail, a lynching, and a final shoot-out in Wolfe's office. Variant title: *To Kill Again*.

4. *Red Box, The* (Farrar & Rinehart, 1937) Investigating a murder among the fashion models at Boyden McNair, Inc., proves very pleasant for Archie. Variant title: *Case of the Red Box*.

5. *Too Many Cooks* (Farrar & Rinehart, 1938) Wolfe and Archie go to a high-class cook's convention and find murder on the menu.

6. *Some Buried Caesar* (Farrar & Rinehart, 1939) Wolfe attends an agricultural exposition in upstate New York, where his orchids win all the prizes and he solves three murders—including one of a prizewinning bull. Variant title: *The Red Bull*.

7. *Over My Dead Body* (Farrar & Rinehart, 1940) The death of a fencing student, run through the heart with a strangely tipped foil, reunites Wolfe with his long lost adopted daughter, Anna.

8. *Where There's a Will* (Farrar & Rinehart, 1940) When eccentric millionaire Noel Hawthorne leaves a puzzling legacy to his three sisters, Wolfe must solve the riddle and investigate two murders.

9. *Black Orchids* (Farrar & Rinehart, 1942) This volume contains two novellas: "Black Orchids" and "Cordially Invited to Meet Death."

10. *Not Quite Dead Enough* (Farrar & Rinehart, 1944) Two novellas are included here: "Not Quite Dead Enough" and "Booby Trap."

11. *Silent Speaker, The* (Viking, 1946) Cheney Boone, director of the Bureau of Price Regulation, is killed backstage just before delivering a scheduled speech.

12. *Too Many Women* (Viking, 1947) Archie, in disguise as a personnel expert, delves into personalities and conflicts at an engineering supply company where a murder has occurred.

13. *And Be a Villain* (Viking, 1948) The mysterious X warns Wolfe off the investigation of horse tipster Cyril Orchad's murder. UK title: *More Deaths Than One*.

14. *Second Confession, The* (Viking, 1949) Archie goes off to Chappaqua to help the Sperling family solve a mystery—another case that X (Arnold Zack) doesn't like.

15. *Trouble in Triplicate* (Viking, 1949) Three novellas are included here: "Help Wanted, Male," "Instead of Evidence," and "Before I Die."

16. *In the Best Families* (Viking, 1950) The Rackham case brings about a showdown with evil Arnold Zack, but not before Wolfe goes into hiding and emerges 117 pounds lighter. UK title: *Even in the Best Families*.

17. *Three Doors to Death* (Viking, 1950) This book contains three novellas: "Man Alive," "Omit Flowers," and "Door to Death."

18. *Curtains for Three* (Viking, 1950) "Bullet for One," "The Gun with Wings," and "Disguise for Murder" are the three novellas that make up this book.

19. *Murder by the Book* (Viking, 1951) Wolfe investigates the seemingly unrelated murders of Joan Wellman and Leonard Dykes.

20. *Triple Jeopardy* (Viking, 1952) There are three more novellas here: "The Cop-Killer," "The Squirt and the Monkey," and "Home to Roost."

21. *Prisoner's Base* (Viking, 1952) Archie himself becomes one of Wolfe's clients in this search for a missing woman. UK title: *Out Goes She*.

22. *Golden Spiders, The* (Viking, 1953) The case involving golden spider earrings is brought to Wolfe by a neighborhood boy, who offers a retainer of $4.30.

23. *Three Men Out* (Viking, 1954) Three novellas form this book: "This Won't Kill You," "Invitation to Murder," and "The Zero Clue."

24. *Black Mountain, The* (Viking, 1954) Wolfe and Archie are off to Montenegro to investigate the apparent murder of Wolfe's oldest and best friend, Marko Vukcic.

25. *Before Midnight* (Viking, 1955) Louis Dahlman, the man who devised an ingenious contest, is murdered before revealing the current answers.

26. *Three Witnesses* (Viking, 1956) "When a Man Murders," "Die Like a Dog," and "The Next Witness" are the three novellas in this book.

27. *Might as Well Be Dead* (Viking, 1956) A search for a missing person leads Wolfe to the cell of an accused murderer in this surprising case.

28. *If Death Ever Slept* (Viking, 1957) The police suspect Archie of murder in this "distasteful" case.

29. *Three for the Chair* (Viking, 1957) This book contains three novellas: "Immune to Murder," "A Window for Death," and "Too Many Detectives."

30. *Champagne for One* (Viking, 1958) How does the one glass of poisoned champagne reach the right victim in a party full of people?

31. *And Four to Go* (Viking, 1958) Four stories are collected here: "Christmas Party," "Easter Parade," "Fourth of July Picnic," and "Murder Is No Joke." UK title: *Crime and Again*.

32. *Plot It Yourself* (Viking, 1959) Wolfe's investigation into burgeoning plagiarism in the book-publishing industry leads to murder. UK title: *Murder in Style*.

33. *Too Many Clients* (Viking, 1960) A murder occurs in the plush love nest of a corporation executive.

34. *Three at Wolfe's Door* (Viking, 1960) "Poison a la Carte," "Method Three for Murder," and "The Rodeo Murder" are the novellas collected here.

35. *Final Deduction, The* (Viking, 1961) Mrs. Jimmy Vail comes to Wolfe for help when her husband is being held for $500,000 ransom.

36. *Gambit* (Viking, 1962) A case of arsenic poisoning develops in a Manhattan chess club.

37. *Homicide Trinity* (Viking, 1962) Three novellas are collected here: "Death of a Demon," "Eeny Meeny Murder Mo," and "Counterfeit for Murder."

38. *Mother Hunt, The* (Viking, 1963) When a baby arrives on Lucy Valdon's doorstep, she turns to Wolfe for help in locating the mother.

39. *Right to Die, A* (Viking, 1964) Paul Whipple, a black assistant professor of anthropology at Columbia, comes to Wolfe for help with a personal problem.

40. *Trio for Blunt Instruments* (Viking, 1964) Three novellas make up this book: "Kill Now-Pay Later," "Murder Is Corny," and "Blood Will Tell."

41. *Doorbell Rang, The* (Viking, 1965) This very clever case involves the FBI's persecution of a woman out to cause them trouble.

42. *Death of a Doxy* (Viking, 1966) Wolfe's sometime assistant Orrie Cather is charged with murder, and Nero and Archie try to clear him.

43. *Father Hunt, The* (Viking, 1968) Wolfe and Archie try to find Amy Denovo's father without a clue to start with.

44. *Death of a Dude* (Viking, 1969) Wolfe actually travels to Montana to retrieve Archie from a dude ranch and helps clear his friend Harvey Greve of a murder charge.

45. *Please Pass the Guilt* (Viking, 1973) A potential candidate for the presidency of a large corporation is killed by a bomb explosion in New York.

46. *Family Affair, A* (Viking, 1975) Wolfe gives sanctuary to a frightened waiter and has a man killed on his doorstep in this mystifying case.

47. *Death Times Three* (Bantam, 1985) Three novellas published posthumously: "Bitter End," "Assault on a Brownstone," and "Frame-Up for Murder."

II. Yes, Rex Stout did write mysteries without Nero Wolfe in them: several stand-alones and this short series featuring Tecumseh Fox, who denies being part Indian, a first-rate private detective who works out of his farm in Westchester, New York.

1. *Double for Death* (Farrar & Rinehart, 1939) A laid-off copywriter is suspected of murdering rich, old Ridley Thorpe's double.

2. *Bad for Business* (Farrar & Rinehart, 1940) First published in *The Second Mystery Book* and omnibus volume published by Farrar & Rinehart. Uncle Arthur's horrible death and a nice lady sleuth occupy Tecumseh in this episode.

3. *Broken Vase, The* (Farrar & Rinehart, 1941) Tecumseh Fox investigates the murder of a musician at New York's finest concert auditorium.

Straight, Susan

Marietta Cook is a proud black woman who has made her own way through life in South Carolina and southern California from the 1950s to the 1980s. Marietta, who started out in rural poverty, has the satisfaction of seeing her twin sons become professional football players. The sequel, in which Marietta moves to Rio Seco, California, which is based on Riverside, Susan Straight's hometown. Straight, who is white, has the experience (Job Corps, teacher, counselor) and the ability to bring to poetic life Marietta, her friends and neighbors, and other black and Hispanic characters. Rio Seco is also the setting for *Aquaboogie: A Novel in Stories* (Milkweed, 1994); *The Gettin Place* (Hyperion, 1996); and *Highwire Moon* (Houghton Mifflin, 2001).

1. *I Been in Sorrow's Kitchen and Licked All the Pots* (Hyperion, 1992) The orphaned Marietta makes her way to Charleston at the age of 15, finds work, and raises a family.

2. *Blacker Than a Thousand Midnights* (Hyperion, 1994) Marietta moves to Rio Seco, a suburb of East Los Angeles, to be closer to her sons, where she and her friend Roscoe, a poetically minded gardener, are part of a racially mixed community.

Straley, John

The coastal town of Sitka, Alaska, is the setting for the efforts of Cecil Younger, reject from the law profession who has lost his wife and turned to alcohol for solace. Younger takes up the profession of private investigator, but he is "probably the least successful private eye in the world" (*Kirkus Reviews*). But Cecil soldiers on in this regional series set in a well-realized Alaskan frontier setting.

1. *Woman Who Married a Bear, The* (Soho, 1992) Louis Victor, prominent Alaskan businessman and big-game hunter, is murdered in a case fraught with state politics, family feuds, and Native American mythology.

2. *Curious Eat Themselves, The* (Soho, 1993) Louise Roots wants Cecil to break through corporate cover-ups and police apathy to find evidence against the man who raped her in an isolated mining camp.

3. *Music of What Happened, The* (Bantam, 1996) Younger finds himself at risk when a case of child custody turns into one of murder.

4. *Death and the Language of Happiness* (Bantam, 1997) Ninety-seven-year-old William Flynn wants Younger to find, and kill, Simon Delaney, husband of Angela Rameriez, whom he believes is responsible for Angela's murder.

5. *Angels Will Not Care, The* (Bantam, 1998) Cecil takes a break from surveilling a chicken coop being raided by a "fowl thief" by investigating a suspicious ship's doctor on the SS *Westward*, a luxurious cruise ship.

6. *Cold Water Burning* (Bantam, 2001) The three-year-old case of murder and arson aboard the scow *Mygirl* comes back to haunt Younger.

Straub, Peter

Peter Straub and Stephen King (q.v.), with whom he coauthored *The Talisman* (Viking, 1984) and *Black House* (Random House, 2001), are regarded as contemporary masters of the psychological suspense thriller and horror novel. The Blue Rose trilogy, followed 10 years later by another pair of novels, is a loosely connected series of psychological and supernatural thrillers linked by certain character such as novelist Tim Underhill and private investigator Tom Pasmore, the Vietnam War, and serial murders.

1. *Koko* (Dutton, 1988) Four Vietnam veterans recognize that a serial killer operating in Singapore must be a former member of their old platoon.

2. *Mystery* (Dutton, 1990) Tom Pasmore, having undergone a near-death experience, becomes obsessed with murder and detection, especially with a recent killing on Mill Walk, the Caribbean island where his family lives.

3. *Throat, The* (Dutton, 1993) The Blue Rose Killer, who terrorized Millhaven, Illinois, in the 1940s, seems to have risen again. John Ransom and Tom Pasmore join forces to solve both the earlier and the later murders.

4. *Lost Boy Lost Girl* (Random House, 2003) Novelist Tom Underhill returns to his home town when his sister-in-law commits suicide, and his teenage nephew Mark becomes involved with a mysterious house and a serial murderer.

5. *In the Night Room* (Random House, 2004) Willy Bryce Patrick, a character created by Tim Underhill, comes alive, and enmeshes Tim in a complicated plot of his own making and in a series of space-time variations.

Strieber, Whitley (Louis Whitley)

Whitley Strieber burst upon the publishing scene with *The Wolfen* (Morrow, 1978), a novel about werewolves, followed by *The Hunger* (Morrow, 1980). After several more novels, Strieber published *Communion: A True Story* (Morrow, 1987), which related the supposedly true tale of his abduction by aliens. Although branded as a liar by many critics, Strieber has stuck to his guns, publishing "factual" sequels such as *Transformation* (Avon, 1990) and *The Secret School* (HarperCollins, 1997), followed by avowedly fictional works about alien abduction, such as *The Grays* (Tor, 2006). Strieber has also been busy in the apocalyptic line of fiction and nonfiction, with disaster coming from such sources as nuclear war, global warming, and Earth's impending position in the "center of the galaxy" (*2012*, Tor, 2007).

If *Communion* and its sequels are considered to be nonfiction, then *The Hunger* and its two sequels are the only series fiction that Strieber has produced. These three novels relate the stories of the vampire, Miriam Blaylock, Paul Ward, the vampire-slaying Interpol agent, and Lilith, the "mother of all vampires."

1. *Hunter, The* (Morrow, 1980) This details the attempts of the vampire Miriam to find a human companion to share her immortality.
2. *Last Vampire, The* (Atria, 2001) Miriam Blaylock must use all of her seductive skills to evade destruction by Interpol agent Paul Ward, a man who is determined to rid the world of vampires.
3. *Lilith's Dream* (Atria, 2002) Subtitle: *A Tale of the Vampire Life.* Paul Ward, leader of a team of vampire hunters, confronts Lilith, the mother of all vampires, with the soul of his son Ian and the future of humanity at stake.

Strohmeyer, Sarah

Sarah Strohmeyer's Bubbles Yablonsky is Pennsylvania's answer to Janet Evanovich's (q.v.) Stephanie Plum. Bubbles comes on as your typical "dizzy blond" with her Barbie Doll looks, hot pants, and stiletto heels, but the "Polish/Lithuanian" blond has a certain "smarts" that she hopes to propel her from a career as a hairdresser into one as a journalist. She has a Mel Gibson look-alike boyfriend, photographer Steve Stiletto; a biker mother, Lulu; a way with one-liners; and an ability to bumble her way through a series of murder cases.

1. *Bubbles Unbound* (Dutton, 2001) Hairdresser with a yen for journalism Bubbles Yablonsky knows something about the death of Laura Buchman that could be the making of her, or the death of her.
2. *Bubbles in Trouble* (Dutton, 2002) Bubbles's friend Janice is missing on her bridal day, and Janice's uncle Elwood turns up dead.
3. *Bubbles Ablaze* (Dutton, 2002) Bubbles and boyfriend Steve Stiletto find themselves in an abandoned coal mine. Car-magnate Bud Price finds himself dead. Bubbles's cousin Karl "Stinky" Koolball finds himself in trouble.
4. *Bubbles a Broad* (Dutton, 2004) Bubbles's journalism career is at stake when she is assigned to find out who really murdered Carol Weaver's steel-executive husband with cyanide-tipped fingernails.
5. *Bubbles Betrothed* (Dutton, 2005) In her first day as a full-time reporter, Bubbles is granted an exclusive interview with a murder suspect named Crazy Popeye.
6. *Bubbles All the Way* (Onyx, 2006) Bubbles's friend Sandy, proprietor of the House of Beauty of Salon, gets the blame when

Debbie Shatsky dies from a reaction to the glue during her "hair extension."

Stubbs, Jean

I. Jean Stubbs has written a quartet of novels about the Lancashire-based Howarth family. The story begins in 1760 with Ned Howarth, the hardworking owner of Kit's Hill, a prosperous farm, and traces the family through succeeding generations to 1851. The series documents in fascinating incident and character the social history of Stubbs's native Lancashire country. Delderfield fans should enjoy these. Stubbs (b. 1926) is not to be confused with Jean Stubbs (b. 1946), professor of Caribbean studies and history, who has published several books on Cuba.

1. *By Our Beginnings* (St. Martin's, 1979) Ned Howarth woos and weds Dorcas Wilde, and educated woman from a nearby town, who has trouble adjusting to life on the farm. UK title: *Kit's Hill*.
2. *Imperfect Joy, An* (St. Martin's, 1981) The story of Ned's children continues from 1785 to 1812. Dick stays on the farm; William starts an ironworks that eventually dominates the valley; and Charlotte becomes a champion of social justice. UK title: *The Ironmaster*.
3. *Vivian Inheritance, The* (St. Martin's, 1982) Wealthy ironmaster William Howarth and his illegitimate son, Cornish engineer Hal Vivian, are the main characters as the railroad comes to the Valley of Wydendale.
4. *Northern Correspondent, The* (St. Martin's, 1984) Ambrose Longe, son of Charlotte Howarth Longe, joins forces with Naomi Blum to publish a newspaper, *The Northern Correspondent* from 1831 to 1851.

II. Stubbs wrote several historical mysteries before she abandoned the field for straight historical fiction, including three mysteries set around the turn of the 20th century featuring retired Scotland Yard inspector John Lintott.

1. *Dear Laura* (Stein & Day, 1973) It seems that Laura Crozier's unloving husband, Theodore, has died of lethal doses of morphine rather than from influenza. Set in late Victorian England. Based on a true case.
2. *Painted Face, The* (Stein & Day, 1974) The Edwardian age has begun. Lintott goes across the Channel to Paris on the trail of a child who allegedly died in a train wreck 20 years before.
3. *Golden Crucible, The* (Stein & Day, 1976) After an attack upon his wife, Lintott journeys to San Francisco on the trail of the perpetrator and arrives just in time for the 1906 earthquake.

Swanson, Denise

School psychologist Skye Denison returns to Scumble River (presumably based on Downer's Grove, Illinois, where Denise Swanson lives and works as a school psychologist) after fighting with her boyfriend and receiving a credit-card rejection. Of course, Scumble River is seething with scandalous secrets and is able to produce at least one murder per volume for Skye to investigate.

1. *Murder of a Small-Town Honey* (Signet, 2001) After school psychologist Skye Denison returns to her hometown of Scumble River, the elderly host of a beloved children's TV program is found dead at a festival.

2. *Murder of a Sweet Old Lady* (Signet, 2001) When the death of Skye's beloved grandmother is revealed by autopsy as murder, Skye realizes that the old lady was the keeper of some secrets, including those of her own family.

3. *Murder of a Sleeping Beauty* (Signet, 2002) A popular teenager who was cast as Sleeping Beauty in the school play is murdered.

4. *Murder of a Snake in the Grass* (Signet, 2003) Gabriel Scumble, the great-great grand nephew of Scumble River's founder and guest of honor at Scumble River's bicentennial, is found dead.

5. *Murder of a Barbie and Ken* (Signet, 2003) Barbie and Ken Addison, "the perfect couple," are found dead in their house.

6. *Murder of a Pink Elephant* (Signet, 2004) After Skye's brother forms a band called "Pink Elephant," a groupie seduces band members one-by-one, and one band member winds up dead.

7. *Murder of a Smart Cookie* (Signet, 2005) Skye organizes a "100-mile yard-sale." Then her former boss is murdered.

8. *Murder of a Real Bad Boy* (Signet, 2006) After Skye breaks up with her boyfriend, she tries to compensate with the sexy contractor who is renovating her home, but he turns out to be a roue, and a dead one, at that.

9. *Murder of a Botoxed Blonde* (Signet, 2007) Her best friend, Trixie, talks Skye into accepting a complimentary weekend at the new Scumble River spa.

Swinnerton, Frank

Swinnerton, who has been called one of England's most dependable storytellers, must surely rank among its most productive as well. In a literary career spanning more than 70 years (he died at the age of 98 in 1982), he wrote more than 40 novels in addition to numerous works of biography, criticism, and more. From his first best seller, *Nocturne* (Doran, 1917), to the tetralogy listed below, his fiction is distinguished by the solid craftsmanship with which he transforms the manners and morals of his contemporary characters into solid reading enjoyment. The books below treat four generations of the Grace family and delineate the changing relationships between men and women.

1. *Woman from Sicily, The* (Doubleday, 1957) A mystery of hate and revenge threatens the gentle and loving Jerome Grace and his family, who live in a quiet East Anglian country town.

2. *Tigress in the Village, A* (Doubleday, 1959) Set in 1921 in the village of Prothero, this story focuses on Mrs. Mary Grace, showing the activities of her four married children, her husband's business failures, and her attraction to her old friend Tom Tamplin. UK title: *A Tigress in Prothero*.

3. *Grace Divorce, The* (Doubleday, 1960) In 1937 Mary, now widowed, worries over her children's marriages, which seem doomed from the start.

4. *Quadrille* (Doubleday, 1965) In 1960 19-year-old Laura Grace, Philip's daughter, is caught in a desperate love triangle.

Sylvester, Martin

English wine merchant and amateur sleuth William Warner is charming, urbane, chauvinistic, and not overly burdened with moral or ethical scruples. He has a beautiful wife on his farm near Bordeaux and beautiful mistress willing to join him anywhere else at a moment's notice. For oenophiles and mystery readers who like their protagonists slightly caddish.

1. *Lethal Vintage, A* (Villard, 1988) Warner's close friend, whom he suspects of being his wife's lover, is blown away by a shotgun outside a fashionable restaurant in Chelsea.

2. *Dangerous Age, A* (Villard, 1988) Shot at and then disturbed by an intruder in his London home, Warner opts not to call the police but confides in his mistress instead.

3. *Rough Red* (Villard, 1990) Warner investigates the kidnapping of a teenage girl, which takes him to Barcelona and the sun-drenched villages of the Spanish Mediterranean coast.

4. *Sour Grapes* (Villard, 1992) William is called to Crete by a former lover to investigate the disappearance of con man Nick Cruickshank.

Taibo, Paco Ignatio, II

I. Mexican crime novelist Taibo, who is also a university professor and historian, writes brooding, anarchistic, surrealistic novels in which historical personages such as Leonardo da Vinci, Trotsky, and Laurel and Hardy weave in and out of wild plots. Many of Taibo's books haven't been translated into English, but five that have been translated feature one-eyed, half-Irish, half-Basque, Coca-Cola-swilling, limping private eye Hector Belascoaran Shayne. Shayne, who shares an office in Mexico City with a plumber, an upholsterer, and a sewer engineer, might have come from a collaboration between Gabriel García Márquez and Dashiell Hammett (q.v.). Novels are listed in order of publication in the original Spanish, which can be somewhat disconcerting, since Hector was killed off in number 2 only to be resurrected for number 3.

1. *Easy Thing, An* (Viking, 1990) Hector is confronted with three cases: a murder at a factory, threats against the daughter of a porn star, and an attempt to find Emiliano Zapata, the supposedly long-dead hero of the Mexican Revolution. Translated from the Spanish by William I. Neuman. Originally published in 1977 as *Cosa facil*.

2. *No Happy Ending* (Mysterious, 1993) A body dressed as a Roman soldier is found in the bathroom of Shayne's office, but Shayne is told "Don't get involved." Translated from the Spanish by William I. Neuman. Originally published in 1981 as *No habra final feliz*.

3. *Some Clouds* (Viking, 1992) Shayne rescues his sister's childhood friend after she is attacked and raped upon inheriting blood money from her murdered husband. Translated from the Spanish by William I. Neuman. Originally published in 1985 as *Algunas nubes*.

4. *Return to the Same City* (Mysterious, 1996) Hector is shadowing "Luke Estrella," a figure with many identities. A guns-for-drugs operation connected with the Contra War and an American reporter with ties to the CIA are involved. Translated from the Spanish by Laura Dail. Originally published in 1989 as *Regreso a la misma ciudad y bajo la lluvia*.

5. *Uncomfortable Dead, The* (Akashic, 2006) Subtitle: *What's Missing Is Missing; A Novel for Four Hands*. Coauthored with Subcomandante Marcos. Elias Contreras, a detective for the Zaptista National Liberation Army (and Marcos's creation), heads to Mexico City to investigate the case of a government-backed murderer named Morales. Hector Belascoaran Shayne becomes involved. Translated from the Spanish by Carlos Lopez. Originally published in 2004 as *Muertos incomodos*.

II. Jose Daniel Fierro is a crime novelist who is a mine of movie and crime-fiction lore. Although he has never fired a gun, and is a coward besides, Fierro keeps getting involved in mystery cases.

1. *Life Itself* (**Mysterious, 1994**) Fierro is tapped to be police chief in the Mexican–US border town of Santa Ana and is soon presented with the naked corpse of an American woman in a church. Translated from the Spanish by Beth Henson. Originally published in 1987 as *La vida misma*.

2. *Leonardo's Bicycle* (**Mysterious, 1995**) Fierro learns that Karen Turner, a blond University of Texas basketball player with whom he is obsessed, has been kidnapped in an attempt to steal one of her kidneys. Translated from the Spanish by Martin Michael Roberts. Originally published in 1994 as *Bicicleta de Leonardo*.

III. *The Shadow of the Shadow*, set in the 1922 Mexico of General Obregon, a curious mixture of fiction and history, describes the adventures of four friends who meet in Mexico City to play dominos. It was followed 15 years later by *Returning as Shadows*, which brings some of the characters 20 years into a World War II German plot in Mexico.

1. *Shadow of the Shadow, The* (**Viking, 1991**) Four domino-playing friends are drawn into a conspiracy to grab the oil fields and declare the area a republic independent of Mexico. Set in 1922. Translated from the Spanish by William I. Neuman. Originally published in 1986 as *Sombra de la sombra*.

2. *Returning as Shadows* (**St. Martin's, 2003**) In 1941–1942, government spy Fermin Valencia Taivo, a one-armed poet who has never written a poem, and his journalist friend Manterrla uncover a Nazi conspiracy to ally Mexico to Germany. Ernest Hemingway and Graham Greene make cameo appearances. Translated from the Spanish by Ezra R. Fitz. Originally published in 2001 as *Retornamos como sombras*.

Tanenbaum, Robert K.

New York Assistant District Attorney Butch Karp is the creation of former New York Assistant District Attorney Robert Tanenbaum. The somewhat autobiographical Butch and his colleague and eventual wife, Marlene Ciampi, have a tempestuous two-career Jewish Italian marriage and produce three children: the linguist, Lucy, and the twins, Giancarlo and Zak. No member of the family is left unscarred in this gritty, realistic series, which starts in the 1970s. The milieu of the New York City justice system is convincingly presented, warts and all. In 2004 Michael Gruber, Robert Tanenbaum's cousin, confessed that he was the ghostwriter for all of the Tanenbaum novels.

1. *No Lesser Plea* (**Watts, 1987**) Karp tries to keep multiple-killer Mandeville Lewis from getting off with an insanity plea through a bogus psychiatric report.

2. *Depraved Indifference* (**New American Library, 1989**) A group of Croatian nationalists hijacks a plane and gets involved with a bombing.

3. *Immoral Certainty* (**Dutton, 1991**) Several murders, including a gang slaying and the sex murder of a seven-year-old girl, are investigated by Butch and his associate and lover, Marlene Ciampi.

4. *Reversible Error* (**Dutton, 1991**) Butch is on the trail of a rogue cop who may be murdering drug dealers, while Marlene is after a serial rapist.

5. *Material Witness* (**Dutton, 1993**) Karp winds up as the 12th man on a professional basketball team when he becomes embroiled in the investigation of the murder of a basketball star.

6. *Justice Denied* (**Dutton, 1994**) The assassination of a Turkish diplomat may be Armenian revenge for past atrocities, or may revolve around a jewel-encrusted icon.

7. *Corruption of Blood* (**Dutton, 1995**) Karp, like his creator, is offered the position of chief investigator on the 1976 House Select Committee on the Assassination of John F. Kennedy.

8. *Falsely Accused* (**Dutton, 1996**) Butch and Marlene are both in private practice: Butch as a lawyer suing New York City over the summary firing of chief NYC medical examiner Murray Selig; Marlene as a private investigator handling abused-wife cases.

9. *Irresistible Impulse* (**Dutton, 1997**) Butch takes on his first case back at the DA's office, while Marlene finds herself protecting cello-player Edith Wooten from an obsessed fan.

10. *Reckless Endangerment* (**Dutton, 1998**) The murder of an elderly Jewish couple may be connected to a 16-year-old runaway Arab girl who has killed her pimp in self-defense.

11. *Act of Revenge* (**HarperCollins, 1999**) Marlene finds herself involved in an organized-crime plot, while Butch supervises the investigation into a mafioso's murder, and their daughter, Lucy, witnesses a murder.

12. *True Justice* (**Pocket Books, 2000**) After three infanticides, a 15-year-old unwedded mother is prosecuted. Marlene goes on a case to a small Delaware town.

13. *Enemy Within* (**Pocket Books, 2001**) Lucy volunteers at a homeless shelter where a serial killer is stalking the homeless.

14. *Absolute Rage* (**Pocket Books, 2002**) Marlene and Butch get involved with a family feud in a West Virginia coal town after their Long Island neighbors are massacred.

15. *Resolved* (**Atria, 2003**) Marlene tries to lead the quiet life, raising attack dogs. Butch gets involved in a fishy cop shooting and a strange sexual-assault case, while Feisal ibn-Salemeh and Felix Tighe, villains from previous books, plan a post-9/11 conspiracy.

16. *Hoax* (**Atria, 2004**) Butch is running for district attorney. Marlene and Lucy are attending an art-therapy school in Taos, New Mexico. Sociopath Andrew Kane is running for mayor of New York.

17. *Fury* (**Atria, 2005**) Karp is called in by the mayor to defend the city against a $250 million lawsuit filed by race-baiting lawyer Hugh Louis on behalf of a gang of convicted rapists known as the Coney Island Four.

18. *Counterplay* (**Atria, 2006**) Criminal mastermind Andrew Kane has escaped, is allied with al-Qaeda, and is planning a terrorist attack while getting revenge on Karp.

19. *Malice* (**Atria, 2007**) Is the supposedly dead Andrew Kane still at large and planning further terrorist outrages?

Tapply, William G(eorge)

I. Divorced, middle-aged Brady Coyne has a lucrative law practice among Boston's old rich, but his gilt-edged clients have a way of involving Brady in the seamier side of life and bringing out the amateur sleuth in him. The low-key Brady is an avid fly-fisherman, as is his creator, and has difficulty in maintaining relationships with women. Recently (numbers 19, 22, and 26), Tapply has collaborated with Philip R. Craig (q.v.), bringing Coyne and Craig's J. W. Jackson together in a trio of mysteries. *A Brady Coyne Omnibus* (St. Martin's, 2000) contains numbers 12, 13, and 14. William G. Tapply, former high school teacher and housemaster in Lexington, Massachusetts, is a contributing editor to *Field and Stream* magazine and the author of several nonfiction works on fishing, such as *Gone Fishin': Ruminations on Fly Fishing* (Lyons, 2004). *Thicker Than Water* (Signet, 1995), a suspense story coauthored with Linda Barlow, is not a Brady Coyne novel.

1. *Death at Charity's Point* (**Scribner, 1984**) George Gresham's mother is convinced that her son's plunge off a cliff was not a suicide.

2. *Dutch Blue Error, The* (**Scribner, 1985**) Oliver Hazard Perry Weston hires Coyne to meet a man who claims to have a duplicate of Perry's supposedly unique Dutch Blue Error postage stamp.

3. *Follow the Sharks* (**Scribner, 1985**) Ex–Boston Red Sox pitcher Eddie Donagan asks Red Sox fan Coyne to find his kidnapped 10-year-old son.

4. *Marine Corpse, The* (**Scribner, 1986**) Writer Stu Carver, doing research among Boston's homeless, is stabbed to death, and sections of his journals disappear. UK title: *A Rodent of Doubt.*

5. *Dead Meat* (**Scribner, 1987**) "Tiny" Wheeler turns down some interested buyers of his hunting lodge in Maine before he discovers that the resort may be on an ancient Indian burial ground.

6. *Vulgar Boatman, The* (**Scribner, 1988**) Brady's friend and client Tom Baron has his gubernatorial campaign rocked by the murder of a high school girl linked to Baron's ex-addict son.

7. *Void in Hearts, A* (**Scribner, 1988**) After private eye Les Katz sells some incriminating photographs to a philandering husband, he has some sobering second thoughts about his actions.

8. *Dead Winter* (**Delacorte, 1989**) Three murders engage Brady's attention: a friend's daughter-in-law killed on the family yacht, the murder of a mysterious bald man, and the death of a young waitress.

9. *Client Privilege* (**Delacorte, 1990**) The appointment of Brady's friend Judge Popowski to a federal court is threatened by a blackmailing television reporter.

10. *Spotted Cats, The* (**Delacorte, 1991**) Seven gold and emerald pre-Columbian jaguar statuettes are stolen from the Cape Cod house of Coyne client Jeff Newton.

11. *Tight Lines* (**Delacorte, 1992**) Dying widow Susan Ames wants Coyne to find the daughter she hasn't seen in 10 years.

12. *Snake Eater, The* (**Penzler, 1993**) Brady tries to help Daniel McCloud, a Vietnam veteran suffering from Agent Orange exposure, to defend himself against an arrest for cultivation and possession of marijuana.

13. *Seventh Enemy, The* (**Penzler, 1995**) Environmentalist and sportsman Walt Kinnick offends Gene McNiff, leader of Second Amendment for Ever (SAFE) by changing his mind on assault-weapon control.

14. *Close to the Bone* (**St. Martin's, 1996**) Paul Cizek, defense attorney and Brady's fishing buddy, increasingly depressed by his career and separation from his wife, disappears. Brady starts an affair with journalist Alexandra Shaw.

15. *Cutter's Run* (**St. Martin's, 1998**) On his way to rural Maine to visit Alex Shaw, Brady picks up Charlotte Gillispie, a black woman who seems to be the victim of some "hate" messages.

16. *Muscle Memory* (**St. Martin's, 1999**) Coyne's client and longtime drinking buddy Mick Fallon, a former pro basketball player, is lying to Brady and covering up his long-lying gambling problem.

17. *Scar Tissue* (**St. Martin's, 2000**) Brian, the 15-year-old son of Jake and Sharon Gold, is missing after what looks like a fatal accident leaving his girlfriend dead.

18. *Past Tense* (**St. Martin's, 2001**) Although he would rather sit at home listening to Red Sox games, Brady is persuaded to go to tourist-infested Cape Cod by his current girlfriend, Evie Banyon. Then, the corpse of a man who has been stalking Evie turns up right outside of their cottage.

19. *First Light* (**St. Martin's, 2001**) A fishing derby on Martha's Vineyard and a couple of disappearances bring Brady and Philip R. Craig's (q.v.) J. W. Jackson together. Coauthored with Philip R. Craig.

20. *Fine Line, A* (**St. Martin's, 2002**) Personal friend Walt Duffy, a recently paralyzed nature photographer, asks Coyne to carry a packet of letters purported to be written by Meriwether Lewis (of Lewis and Clark fame) to a noted book dealer for authentication.

21. *Shadow of Death* (**St. Martin's, 2003**) Brady is asked by a friend to look into the odd behavior of Albert Stoddard, the husband of a woman who hopes to become the first female US senator from Massachusetts.

22. *Second Sight* (**Scribner, 2005**) Brady and Philip R. Craig's (q.v.) J. W. Jackson are back together again as Coyne stays at Jackson's Martha's Vineyard cottage while searching for a runaway teenage girl. Coauthored with Philip R. Craig.

23. *Nervous Water* (**St. Martin's, 2005**) Coyne agrees to help his uncle Moze, a Maine lobsterman, locate Cassie, Moze's daughter, who hasn't been returning Moze's phone calls.

24. *Out Cold* (**St. Martin's, 2006**) Brady's dog uncovers a pregnant teenager dying in his snow-covered backyard.

25. *One-Way Ticket* (**St. Martin's, 2007**) Dalton Lancaster's son, Robert, who shares his father's gambling addiction, is kidnapped by "the mob."

26. *Third Strike* (**Scribner, 2007**) In the last book coauthored with the late Philip R. Craig (q.v.), Brady finds himself back on Martha's Vineyard at the behest of a call for help from an old client.

II. Stoney Calhoun, who is deaf in one ear and unable to drink alcohol and has a shaky remembrance of his past, knowing only that he was named after Stonewall Jackson and grew up in Beaumont, South Carolina, removes himself from a veterans' hospital, heads to Portland, Maine, and takes a job in Kate Balaban's bait-and-tackle shop. So far, Stoney has handled two mysteries in the outdoors that author Tapply knows and loves.

1. *Bitch Creek* (**Lyons, 2004**) Stoney Calhoun, who has settled down in Kate Balaban's Maine bait-and-tackle shop, feels impelled to investigate when obnoxious Floridian Fred Green and his guide, Lyle McMahan, disappear, and Lyle is found dead.

2. *Gray Ghost* (**St. Martin's, 2007**) Stoney struggles to find out why a burned corpse turns up on a small island and why the fishing client who was with him when they discovered the body is also killed. A "gray ghost" is an artificial fly used for salmon.

Tarr, Judith

I. Classical scholar, medievalist, teacher, and author of historical and science fiction, Judith Tarr is best known for her fantasy novels, which blend history and myth. The Avaryan series is an excellent piece of world building: well written, with realistic and appealing characters and full of convincing political and cultural detail. Numbers 1, 2, and 3 form a trilogy, while numbers 4, 5, and 6 relate events that take place nearly a century later. *Avaryan Rising* (Doubleday, 1988) is an omnibus volume containing numbers 1, 2, and 3. *Avaryan Resplendent* (Tor, 2003) contains numbers 4, 5, and 6. Judith Tarr, a Maine native now residing in Arizona, raises Lipizzaner horses.

1. *Hall of the Mountain King, The* (**Tor, 1986**) Mirain, heir to the realm of his father, the Sun God, defends his claim to the kingdom of Ianon against the treachery of his relatives.

2. *Lady of Han-Gilen, The* (**Tor, 1987**) Elian, the Lady of Han-Gilen, is so skilled at the martial and courtly arts that only two claimants to her hand, including her childhood companion Mirain, can compete with her.

3. *Fall of Princes, A* (**Tor, 1988**) Two princes of mutually hostile lands find themselves thrown together in a battle for survival that forges an unlikely bond between them.

4. *Arrows of the Sun* (**Tor, 1993**) The young emperor of the House of the Sunborn meets the last representative of the house that the Sunborn drove from the throne.

5. *Spear of Heaven* (Tor, 1994) Daruya, granddaughter of the emperor, and her daughter Kimeri go on a risky mission to resolve the crisis that occurs when one of Gates between the Worlds breaks.

6. *Tides of Darkness* (Tor, 2002) As punishment for illegally opening the Gates between the Worlds, Daros Kurleos, heir to the princedom of Han-Gilen, is exiled by Meiran, Lady of the Gates.

II. The Hound and the Falcon is a trilogy featuring an alternative universe set in the time of King Richard the Lionheart. Richard, Saladin, and other historical characters mix with elves and magic in an alternate Crusade that features half-elf characters as protagonists. *The Hound and the Falcon* (Doubleday, 1986) is an omnibus volume containing numbers 1, 2, and 3.

1. *Isle of Glass, The* (Bluejay, 1985) Alfred of St. Ruan's Abbey is content to live the life of a monk until the elf-king's ambassador send him into the world to carry a message to King Richard.

2. *Golden Horn, The* (Bluejay, 1985) During the Fourth Crusade, Alfred goes to Constantinople, where he is befriended by a Greek family, but he loses his friends when Crusaders sack the city.

3. *Hounds of God, The* (Bluejay, 1986) Ex-monk Alfred, now reconciled to his magic powers, is chancellor of the kingdom of Rhiyana when the kingdom is attacked by the Hounds of God.

III. The Alamut novels are something of a sequel to the Hound and the Falcon and are set in the same universe. The protagonist of this pair of novels is Aidan, half-elf son of the Rhiyanian king.

1. *Alamut* (Doubleday, 1990) Prince Aidan travels to the Holy Land in search of adventure only to find himself locked in a vendetta with the legendary Assassins.

2. *Dagger and the Cross, The* (Doubleday, 1991) Aidan is finally allowed to marry Morgiana, former Assassin and infidel, as Jerusalem falls to Saladin.

IV. Another series, perhaps more alternate history than alternative universe, relates the historical/mythical saga of King Richard the Lionheart, who conquers Jerusalem in this version of the Crusades but almost loses his soul in doing so.

1. *Pride of Kings* (Roc, 2001) When Richard the Lionheart goes on Crusade, he leaves England under the rule of his brother John.

2. *Devil's Bargain* (Roc, 2002) Richard's mother, Eleanor of Aquitaine, strikes a devil's bargain with the sorcerer Sihan, the Old Man of the Mountain: Richard's soul in exchange for Jerusalem.

3. *House of War* (Roc, 2003) Richard, crowned king of Jerusalem, hasn't extricated himself from the devil's bargain with Sihan and needs the help of his illegitimate half sister Siomed to save him.

V. Another two novels mixing history and myth have as their protagonist Alexander the Great of Macedon.

1. *Lord of the Two Lands* (Tor, 1993) The priests of Egypt, suffering under the yoke of Persia, believe that they have found a savior in the young king of Macedon, Alexander, but first Alexander has a lot of battles to fight.

2. *Queen of the Amazons* (Tor, 2004) Hippolyta, queen of the legendary Amazons, gives birth to Etta, a much-wanted daughter, but Etta has not yet received a soul. Then Alexander turns up.

VI. A quartet of novels, known as the Epona Sequence, set in Bronze Age Europe and Egypt, is loosely connected by the theme of a matriarchal Horse Goddess.

1. *White Mare's Daughter* (Forge, 1998) Tomboyish Serama of the nomadic White Horse Tribe, is the servant of the White Mare, the incarnation of the Horse Goddess. Set in eastern Europe circa 4500 BCE.

2. *Shepherd Kings, The* (Forge, 1999) The Pharaoh of Upper Egypt seeks to regain the Lower Kingdom from the Hyksos, the Shepherd Kings, by forging an alliance with the Horse Goddess and the maritime power of Minoan Crete.

3. *Lady of Horses* (Forge, 2000) Heroine Sparrow has to resist the patriarchal claims of the people of her nomadic society.

4. *Daughter of Lir* (Forge, 2001) The Priestess Mother of the matriarchal Bronze Age city of Lir rejects her baby daughter, Rhian, because of bad omens.

VII. A pair of novels presents an alternate-history view of William the Conqueror, who is here the bastard son of a magical woman of Druid descent. This is a world where magic plays a large role in William's rise to power and after.

1. *Rite of Conquest* (Roc, 2004) William, bastard son of a duke and a magical woman of Druid descent, resists the very idea of magic until beautiful French noblewoman Mathilda offers help—and her love.

2. *King's Blood* (Roc, 2005) William the Conqueror's heir, Red William, abjures all magic, so it is up to Edith, princess of Scotland, and Henry, the youngest of William's sons, to restore magic to England.

Tax, Meredith

Meredith Tax, who is a radical feminist and antiwar writer (e.g., *The Rising of the Women*, Monthly Review, 1980; reprint with new introduction, Illinois, 2001), writes fiction featuring strong immigrant women. A pair of novels describes the destinies of Russian-born immigrants who become workers and confirmed Marxists on New York's Lower East Side during the early 1900s. Women dominate these novels, in which historical events such as the Triangle Shirtwaist Factory fire play a large role.

1. *Rivington Street* (Morrow, 1982) Strong-willed Hannah Levy and her daughters struggle to survive the terrible working conditions and low pay of jobs in the garment industry.

2. *Union Square* (Morrow, 1988) Hannah's daughter Sarah marries Communist Avi Spector, and there is an ideological split between them when Avi becomes a Stalinist.

Taylor, Andrew (John Robert)

I. William Dougal, who starts the series as an English graduate student in medieval studies, is the amoral protagonist in a series of thrillers by Andrew Taylor, former London librarian. Dougal eventually acquires a girlfriend and an illegitimate daughter and goes into partnership with former rival James Hanbury in a private detective agency. More than with most series of this kind, the reader needs to read the initial volume to understand the subsequent volumes. The books are intricately plotted, suspenseful, leavened with humor, and filled with clever but rather nasty characters. Andrew Taylor, as well as being the author of three other series (see below), writes young adult novels as John Robert Taylor and the Bergerac series as Andrew Saville.

1. *Caroline Minuscule* (Dodd, 1983) The murder of William Dougal's professor, an expert on medieval scripts, leads Dougal into a search for a fortune in diamonds.
2. *Waiting for the End of the World* (Dodd, 1984) Dougal is forced into investigating the Sealed Serpents of the Apocalypse, a survivalist group.
3. *Our Fathers' Lies* (Dodd, 1985) When Richard Prentisse is drowned, his daughter seeks help from William Dougal and Dougal's father to unravel the mystery of his death.
4. *Old School Tie, An* (Dodd, 1986) Rosington school's old boy James Hanbury weds wealthfully, then is accused of murder when his bride is electrocuted by a faulty lamp fixture.
5. *Freelance Death* (Dodd, 1988) Rod Lorton is the beneficiary of some unpleasant facts about his recently deceased wife, Arabella, while Ivor Newley's rare coin collection comes under scrutiny.
6. *Blood Relation* (Doubleday, 1990) Dougal, now working with his old rival Hanbury in a private detection agency, becomes involved with the disappearance and suspected murder of publishing executive Oz Finwood.
7. *Sleeping Policeman, The* (Gollancz [UK], 1992) Young doctor Graham Hanslope asks Dougal to investigate a case of blackmail, which escalates into a hit-and-run incident, adultery, burglaries, and murder. Not published in the United States.
8. *Odd Man Out* (Gollancz [UK], 1993) Dougal, now the "responsible" father of an illegitimate daughter, and holding down a relatively respectable job, unfortunately kills a man during a quarrel. Not published in the United States.

II. Eric Blaines, a shadowy figure in the British espionage community, is the primary character in number 2 of the Blaines trilogy and a secondary character in numbers 1 and 3. He also appears in *Our Father's Lies* (see above, I, 3) and *The Suffering Night* (see below, III, 4). The Blaines trilogy has Blaines as a connecting link: otherwise, they are a loosely connected group of espionage novels in which the private lives of spies and their families receive more attention than their public affairs.

1. *Second Midnight, The* (Dodd, 1987) Hugh Kendall, son of a petty British spy, is cast adrift in World War II Czechoslovakia in a novel set in Prague and London from the 1930s to the 1956 Suez Crisis.
2. *Blacklist* (HarperCollins [UK], 1988) Set in the 1980s in the intelligence community, where someone is blackmailing victims of several nationalities and both sides of the cold war. Not published in the United States.
3. *Toyshop* (HarperCollins [UK], 1990) East German toy salesman Gerhard Herold comes to England ostensibly to sell toys but in reality to investigate the mysterious death of his beloved brother. Not published in the United States.

III. The Lydmouth novels form a detective series set in Wales in the early 1950s. Principal characters include the detecting pair of Detective Inspector Richard Thornhill and journalist Jill Francis. Although Thornhill is married to another woman, the pair grows closer as the series progresses amid some rather seamy small-town secrets. Numbers 4 through 8 were not published in the United States.

1. *Air That Kills, An* (St. Martin's, 1995) Jill Francis discovers a baby's skeleton inside a box. Although the skeleton originally seemed to date from the early 19th century, Jill and Richard Thornhill eventually conclude that the baby's death was much more recent.
2. *Mortal Sickness, The* (St. Martin's, 1996) Suspicion falls on the new vicar when a woman is found bludgeoned to death in St. John's and the Lydmouth Chalice, the church's most valuable possession, is missing.
3. *Lover of the Grave, The* (St. Martin's, 1997) Although the death of a sheep farmer found hanging from a tree at a crossroads is regarded as either suicide or a bizarre accident, Thornhill and Francis suspect foul play.
4. *Suffocating Night, The* (Hodder [UK], 1998) With echoes of the Korean War in the background, a reporter is murdered, squatters are evicted from a military camp, and there are new developments in the hunt for a missing teenager.
5. *Where Roses Fade* (Hodder [UK], 2000) When Mattie Harris's body is found in the river, one of Lydmouth's most prominent citizens is anxious to convince everyone that her death was an accident.
6. *Death's Own Door* (Hodder [UK], 2001) A widower with a distinguished war record is found dead in his summerhouse with a bottle of whiskey beside him. Jill and Richard reject the verdict of suicide.
7. *Call the Dying* (Hodder [UK], 2004) After Mr. Frederick, a television engineer, spends two nights in Lydmouth while selling and installing sets, the body of a local general practitioner is found.
8. *Naked to the Hangman* (Hodder [UK], 2006) When a retired police officer is found dead in the ruins of Lydmouth Castle, Thornhill becomes a suspect.

IV. The Roth trilogy is a series of interlocking suspense novels involving the Byfield and Appleyard families. Number 3 was published first, while numbers 1 and 2 are prequels delving into the past. *Requiem for an Angel* (HarperCollins [UK], 2002), variant title *Fallen Angel*, is an omnibus volume containing numbers 1, 2, and 3.

1. *Judgement of Strangers, The* (St. Martin's, 1998) Widowed Church of England parish priest David Byfield brings home a new wife. Then the murders and blasphemies begin.
2. *Office of the Dead, The* (St. Martin's, 2000) In 1988, penniless, jobless, and on the brink of divorce, Wendy Appleyard goes to live with a friend in the Cathedral Close of Rosington.
3. *Four Last Things, The* (St. Martin's, 1997) When Angel, a predator upon young children, steals Lucy Appleyard, she is overcome with an unwonted desire to tell about her life.

Taylor, Elizabeth Atwood

Elizabeth Atwood Taylor, who doesn't seem to be related to Phoebe Atwood Taylor (q.v.), is a Texas native who lives in Arizona, where she is an environmentalist and artist as well as a mystery writer. Taylor's protagonist, Maggie Elliott, is a professional private eye working out of San Francisco. Maggie, a Vassar graduate like her creator, is environmentally conscious, liberal, and politically correct but has to fight depression, alcoholism, and chronic fatigue syndrome. Apparently, Taylor has published nothing since 1992.

1. *Cable Car Murders, The* (St. Martin's, 1981) Maggie teams up with ex-policeman Richard Patrick O'Reagan, who was a witness to the suspicious cable car accident that killed her rich half sister.
2. *Murder at Vassar* (St. Martin's, 1987) When Maggie attends her 15th Vassar reunion, elderly alumna Chloe Warren and scholarship student Deborah Martin are murdered.
3. *Northwest Murders, The* (St. Martin's, 1992) Maggie, trying to recover from chronic fatigue syndrome, arrives at a cabin on the Oregon–California border two days after a young hiker is murdered and mutilated.

Taylor, Janelle (Diane Williams)

I. The Ecstasy, or Gray Eagle, saga remains Janelle Taylor's longest and most popular series. It relates the romance between Sioux warrior Gray Eagle and the beautiful white woman Alisha Williams and their descendants. Numbers 1 through 4 follow the passionate pair as they maintain their steadfast romance through ostracism, separation, and other impediments. Bright Arrow, the half-breed son of Gray Eagle and Alisha, gets romantically entangled with the white Rebecca Kerry in numbers 5 and 6, while granddaughters and great-granddaughters of the pair have their own interracial romances.

Taylor's western romances are notable for their sympathetic treatment of Native Americans and their mores. The three Lakota books—*Lakota Winds* (Kensington, 1998), *Lakota Dawn* (Kensington, 1999), and *Lakota Flower* (Kensington, 2003)—also portray the Sioux from their point of view. A pair of linked novels—*Sweet Savage Heart* (Zebra, 1986) and *Destiny Mine* (Zebra, 1995)—deal with white-Native American relationships. More than a dozen other Taylor romances are set in southern and western America in the 19th century.

1. *Savage Ecstasy* (**Zebra, 1981**) Beautiful pioneer woman Alisha Williams falls hard for the captive Oglala Sioux warrior Gray Eagle.
2. *Defiant Ecstasy* (**Zebra, 1982**) At Fort Pierre, Alisha, enduring the taunts and opprobrium of the white settlers, longs for Gray Eagle.
3. *Forbidden Ecstasy* (**Zebra, 1982**) Gray Eagle, seeking his destiny, has left Alisha behind.
4. *Brazen Ecstasy* (**Zebra, 1983**) For four years, Alisha has been princess Shalee, wife of Oglala chief Gray Eagle.
5. *Tender Ecstasy* (**Zebra, 1983**) Bright Arrow, the half-breed son of Gray Eagle and Alisha, slaughters the members of a wagon train but spares the beautiful Rebecca Kenny.
6. *Stolen Ecstasy* (**Zebra, 1985**) It has been seven years since Bright Arrow was banished by the Oglala for marrying Rebecca Kenny instead of keeping her as a slave.
7. *Bittersweet Ecstasy* (**Zebra, 1987**) No annotation available.
8. *Forever Ecstasy* (**Zebra, 1991**) Morning Star, granddaughter of Gray Eagle and Alisha, falls in love with a white man, Joseph Lawrence.
9. *Savage Conquest* (**Zebra, 1992**) Miranda Lawrence, daughter of Morning Star and Joseph, returns to the west and falls in love with Sioux warrior Blazing Star.

II. Three romances set in 5th-century Britain trace the romantic saga of Princess Alysa and Prince Gavin as they enjoy passionate love with each other and wage passionate war against marauding Norse Vikings.

1. *Wild Is My Love* (**Bantam, 1987**) A mysterious stranger rescues Princess Alysa from her father's beleaguered kingdom on the Isle of Britain.
2. *Wild, Sweet Promise* (**Bantam, 1989**) Continues the romantic saga of Princess Alysa and Prince Gavin, as Alysa takes up the sword against the Vikings.
3. *Last Viking Queen, The* (**Zebra, 1994**) Alysa and Gavin share a bond of power and passion as the Norsemen continue their incursions on the Isle of Britain.

III. Janelle Taylor ventured into science fiction, with not particularly happy results, in a quartet of novels describing the romantic throes of Commander Varian of the Starship *Wanderlust* and the lovely Jana Grayson.

1. *Moondust and Madness* (**Bantam, 1986**) Dr. Jana Grayson, abducted by Commander Varian Saar of the starship *Wanderlust*, finds herself a pawn in the intergalactic struggle.
2. *Stardust and Shadows* (**Pinnacle, 1992**) Jana awakens from a drugged sleep to find herself the captive bride of her beloved's evil half brother.
3. *Starlight and Splendor* (**Pinnacle, 1994**) Galen, son of Varian and Jana, seeks his destiny among the stars.
4. *Moonbeams and Magic* (**Pinnacle, 1995**) Starla and Dagan are star-crossed lovers in a magical universe.

IV. Three sisters, Amanda, Olivia, and Ivy Sedgwick, unexpectedly inherit a fortune and find themselves in harm's way in a trio of contemporary romantic suspense novels.

1. *Watching Amanda* (**Kensington, 2005**) Young mother Amanda Sedgwick inherits a fortune and becomes the target of a deadly obsession. Ethan Black is the man hired to protect her.
2. *Haunting Olivia* (**Zebra, 2006**) New York fashion editor Olivia Sedgwick, willed her wealthy, deceased father's college in Blueberry, Maine, returns to the hometown she fled 13 years before following a teenage pregnancy that supposedly ended in a stillbirth.
3. *Shadowing Ivy* (**Zebra, 2007**) After Declan McLean jilts police officer Ivy at the altar, she learns that he had murdered his other fiancée just hours earlier.

Taylor, Phoebe Atwood

Many readers will remember Asey Mayo, Cape Cod's famous fictional detective—he even had a large following in England. The modus operandi of the "Codfish Sherlock" is both salty and canny as he pokes into the various misdoings of the Cape's quaint locals and uppity summer people in the halcyon days before the post–World War II tourist and retirement boom. Most of his cases take place in the towns of Weesit and Pochet, which Taylor has adroitly tucked between the real towns of Wellfleet and Chatham. Taylor, a native of Boston, began producing these books after graduation and turned them out for 20 years with a casual facility until she fell silent for the last 25 years of her life. Her atmosphere never fails, and sometimes her mysteries are first-rate puzzlers. Taylor also wrote a mystery series under the pseudonym Alice Tilton (q.v.) and *Murder at the New York World's Fair* (Random House, 1938) under the pseudonym Freeman Dana.

1. *Cape Cod Mystery, The* (**Bobbs-Merrill, 1931**) After a famous but much disliked novelist is murdered during an unusually warm Cape Cod weekend, Asey tracks down the guilty person.
2. *Death Lights a Candle* (**Bobbs-Merrill, 1932**) Murder by poison at a house party leaves clues and suspects aplenty.
3. *Mystery of the Cape Cod Players, The* (**Norton, 1933**) Asey Mayo investigates the murder of Red Gilpin, a magician with an itinerant Punch and Judy troupe.
4. *Mystery of the Cape Cod Tavern, The* (**Norton, 1934**) Eve Prence, the proprietor of Prence's Tavern in Weesit, is murdered, and Asey tries to clear Anne Bradford of police suspicions.
5. *Sandbar Sinister* (**Norton, 1934**) Two people are murdered—one of whom claims to be a detective-story writer—one night in East Pochet after most of the local population had been drinking.
6. *Tinkling Symbol, The* (**Norton, 1935**) Was David Truman stabbed to death by someone who lost his savings when Truman's bank failed?
7. *Deathblow Hill* (**Norton, 1935**) This tricky case involves a family feud, a barbed-wire fence, and yellow handkerchiefs signaling trouble.

8. *Crimson Patch* (Norton, 1936) Rosalie Ray, the film star, is done in with a whale lance.

9. *Out of Order* (Norton, 1936) Neither bullets nor blizzards deter Asey's investigation of a puzzle that draws him away from his Cape Cod home.

10. *Figure Away* (Norton, 1937) A carnival of murder and mystery entangles Asey.

11. *Octagon House* (Norton, 1937) Murder, mayhem, and ambergris summon Asey Mayo to the mysterious Octagon House.

12. *Annulet of Guilt, The* (Norton, 1938) Asey spies on strange goings-on at Hector Colvin's house until murder gives him a more active role.

13. *Banbury Bog* (Norton, 1938) Asey clears a baker-benefactor at Weesit accused of distributing poisoned tarts.

14. *Spring Harrowing* (Norton, 1939) Murder and other strange doings—two bobcats set loose and a prisoner kept in a well—keep Asey busy.

15. *Criminal C.O.D., The* (Norton, 1940) Henry Slocum, an aspiring politician, seems to have vanished, but the corpse of his fiancée is left behind.

16. *Deadly Sunshade, The* (Norton, 1940) Asey's investigation into the Cape's latest murder is not helped by the Sketicket ladies' league to "Defend America at All Costs."

17. *Perennial Border, The* (Norton, 1941) Asey and his cousin Jennie find a corpse in a telephone booth in the Whale Inn, but it disappears mysteriously.

18. *Six Iron Spiders, The* (Norton, 1942) Asey helps in the war effort by becoming a tank expert at Bill Porter's factory, but on a weekend visit home, he gets involved in a case of a vanishing corpse.

19. *Three Plots for Asey Mayo* (Norton, 1942) Three short novels are collected here: "The Wander Bird Plot," "The Headacre Plot," and "The Swan-Boat Plot."

20. *Going, Going, Gone* (Norton, 1943) Asey's housekeeping cousin Jennie is sure there is hidden money somewhere in the Alden estate furnishings, which are being auctioned off.

21. *Proof of the Pudding* (Norton, 1945) A hurricane leaves Cape Cod in chaos and Asey Mayo with a compromising corpse on his hands.

22. *Asey Mayo Trio, The* (Messner, 1946) "The Third Murderer," "Murder Rides the Gale," and "The Stars Spell Death" are the three stories collected here.

23. *Punch with Care* (Farrar, 1946) Asey's new car figures in this case of a missing houseguest and a vanishing corpse.

24. *Diplomatic Corpse* (Little, Brown, 1951) The production of a patriotic historical pageant has fanned so many jealousies into flames that Asey is not surprised when murder results.

Tennant, Emma

Although there have been many sequels to individual Jane Austen novels over the past 150 years, Emma Tennant may be the first writer to publish a sequel to her own Austen sequel. *Pemberley*, which picks up Elizabeth Bennett of *Pride and Prejudice* soon after she becomes Mrs. Darcy, was followed by *An Unequal Marriage*, which takes the Darcys some 19 years into married life. Emma Tennant, author of satirical novels about contemporary English life, gets Austen's style quite well and uses Austen's characters to good effect. Tennant is the author of two other Jane Austen sequels, *Emma in Love* (Fourth Estate [UK], 1996) and *Eleanor and Marianne* (Simon & Schuster, 1996) as well as *Adele: Jane Eyre's Hidden Story* (Morrow, 2002); *Felony* (Cape [UK], 2002), an alternative version of Henry James's *The Aspern Papers*; and *Heathcliff's Tale*, a riff on *Wuthering Heights* (Tartarus [UK], 2005).

Tennant seems to be at least partly responsible for a spate of sequels to, and riffs on, *Pride and Prejudice* (with a bumper crop in 2007). They include Pamela Aidan's (q.v.) *Fitzwilliam Darcy: Gentleman* (Wytheringate, 2003–2006), a trilogy written from Darcy's point of view; Elizabeth Aston's (q.v.) sequels featuring the Darcy children (Touchstone, 2003–); Jane Dawkins's *Letters from Pemberley* (Chicken Soup, 1999) and *More Letters from Pemberley* (iUniverse, 2003); Carrie Bebris's mysteries, beginning with *Pride and Prescience* (Forge, 2004); and Linda Berdoll's *Mr. Darcy Takes a Wife* (Landmark, 2004) and *Darcy and Elizabeth* (Sourcebooks Landmark, 2006). In 2007 alone there have been Kathryn L. Nelson's *Pemberley Manor* (Egerton House [UK]), Kara Louise's *Pemberley's Promise* (Lulu), Abigail Reynolds's *Pemberley by the Sea* (Interdial), Amanda Grange's *Mr. Darcy's Diary* (Sourcebook [UK]), and Helen Halstead's *Mr. Darcy Presents His Bride* (Ulysses [UK]). *Pride and Prejudice* has been filmed yet again, with Keira Knightley as Elizabeth Bennett. Jane Austen herself is portrayed as a sleuth in Stephanie Barron's (q.v.) historical mystery series, and a recent movie, *Becoming Jane*, depicts Jane Austen's (alleged) only romance.

1. *Pemberley; or Pride and Prejudice Continued* (St. Martin's, 1993) Elizabeth Darcy is uneasily anticipating the arrival of her widowed mother and unmarried sisters at the Darcy estate of Pemberley.

2. *Unequal Marriage, An; or, Pride and Prejudice Twenty Years Later* (St. Martin's, 1994) Elizabeth and Darcy are still in love with each other after 19 years of marriage, but their teenage children are something of a trial.

Tepper, Sheri S(tewart)

I. Sheri S. Tepper, after holding down jobs in nonprofit organizations, published her first fantasy novels when she was in her fifties. What started as primarily entertainment developed, over the years, as Tepper honed her world-building and writing skills into science fiction with fantasy elements rather than fantasy with science-fiction elements. Her later novels, while retaining the complicated plots of the earlier ones, have increasingly become vehicles for Tepper's feminist, ecological, and antireligious ideas. Tepper's novels are often about the coming-of-age of strong female characters. Tepper is regarded by her fans and her peers—such as Ursula K. Le Guin (q.v.) and Roger Zelazny (q.v.)—as a writer and world builder of the first rank.

Much of Tepper's earlier fantasy work takes the form of three linked trilogies, the Books of the True Game, set in a universe far away in space and time in which an elite race uses magic for such activities as mind-reading, flying, and shape-shifting in an elaborate role-playing game called the True Game, which echoes, or anticipates, the Dungeons and Dragons craze of the 1980s and 1990s. The first trilogy (numbers 1–3), which was published together in an omnibus volume called *The True Game* (Doubleday, 1985), introduces the game and develops the character of Peter, shape-shifter and son of the legendary Mavin Manyshaped, whose own trilogy, *The Chronicles of Mavin Manyshaped* (numbers 4–6; omnibus volume, Ace, 1985), both predates and antedates the first trilogy. The third trilogy (numbers 7–9), published in an omnibus volume, *The End of the Game* (Doubleday, 1985), concentrates on the teenage years of Jinian Footseer, who eventually becomes Peter's partner as the True Game is brought to a rather sinister close. The trilogies should be read in publication order, as later volumes make references to previous characters and events.

Tepper also writes two series of detective stories: the Jason Lynx series, as A. J. Orde (q.v.), and the Shirley McClintock series, as B. J. Oliphant (q.v.). She has also used the pseudonym of E. E. Horlak.

1. *King's Blood Four* (Ace, 1983) Introduces readers to the True Game, in which, as you play it, your lifelong identity will emerge: Prince or Sorcerer, Armiger or Tragamor, Demon or Doyen.
2. *Necromancer Nine* (Ace, 1983) Peter, young son of legendary shape-shifter Mavin Manyshaped, can be any player he wishes to be, which threatens to destroy the True Game.
3. *Wizard's Eleven* (Ace, 1984) Peter, son of Mavin Manyshaped, is back; the giants are stalking; the Shadowpeople are gathering; and Wizard's Eleven are trapped in their domain.
4. *Song of Mavin Manyshaped, The* (Ace, 1985) The coming-of-age of Mavin Manyshaped, one of only two "she-shifters" in her tribe. Mavis has just discovered she can change the length of her toes. Will she be able to tame her headstrong nature as she develops her shape-shifting powers?
5. *Flight of Mavin Manyshaped, The* (Ace, 1985) Mavin develops wings and flies into the Chasm to lead the people in a dangerous quest.
6. *Search for Mavin Manyshaped, The* (Ace, 1985) Mavin, married and pregnant, her powers developed, has to track down an old friend.
7. *Jinian Footseer* (Tor, 1985) Fifteen-year-old Jinian of Stoneflight has no "talent," except the seemingly minor one of "footseer," which allows her feet to follow the Old Road as it winds through the Lands of the True Game.
8. *Dervish Daughter* (Tor, 1986) No annotation available.
9. *Jinian Star Eye* (Tor, 1986) Jinian Footseer and Peter are shape-shifters on a quest to control the powers of evil. The gaps in Lom's (Earth's) true nature are filled in.

II. The Marianne trilogy is a fantasy series set in our world, in which Marianne, native of the small principality of Alphenlicht, comes to the United States as a college student, discovers she has magical powers, and goes on a series of adventures involving such things as a magus, a manticore, the Madame, a matchbox, and a malachite mouse. Numbers 1, 2, and 3 were published in an omnibus volume as *The Marianne Trilogy* (Corgi [UK], 1990).

1. *Marianne, the Magus, and the Manticore* (Ace, 1985) Marianne, struggling college student, is visited by a magus, Makr Awehl Zahmen, the prime minister of her native Alphenlicht. She begins to understand her magic powers, not a minute too soon, as she is pursued by the Black Madame and the manticore.
2. *Marianne, the Madame, and the Momentary Gods* (Ace, 1988) Marianne learns how to alter time through the use of magic and tries to avert the death of her parents.
3. *Marianne, the Matchbox, and the Malachite Mouse* (Ace, 1989) Marianne becomes involved in a very odd board game as she tries to carry out her dying great-aunt's request to return a matchbox to its mysterious original owner.

III. The Awakeners is a diptych about the Awakeners, or keepers of the secrets of the dead, that combines fantasy and science-fiction elements, politics, religion, and a love story in a vividly created fantasy world. *The Awakeners* (Doubleday, 1987) contains both novels.

1. *Northshore* (Tor, 1987) Thrasne, boatman on the World River, and Awakener Pamra Don are brought together by a miracle and set out to discover the secrets of their world.
2. *Southshore* (Tor, 1987) Ex-Awakener Pamra Don leads a crusade against the evils done in the name of religion, while Thrasne embarks upon a voyage across the World River to the legendary "Southshore."

IV. A trio of loosely connected SF novels with fantasy overtones set in the far future explores ecological and religious questions when a series of disasters besets the human settlers of far-flung worlds. Number 3 is a sequel to number 2, while Lady "Jory" Westriding, a woman of many talents, is the connecting link between numbers 1 and 3.

1. *Grass* (Doubleday, 1989) A deadly plague spreads across inhabited space, sparing only one world, the planet Grass.
2. *Raising the Stones* (Doubleday, 1990) Hobbs Land is a quiet agricultural colony whose people work together to build a new society. Then they make the mistake of rebuilding the temple of the vanished Owlbrit race, and the old gods rush in.
3. *Sideshow* (Bantam, 1992) All humans remaining free of the gods of Hobbs Land are on Elsewhere, where diversity is practiced without interference or restraint within the borders of each community.

Tey, Josephine

PSEUDONYM OF Elizabeth MacKintosh

Tey ended her brief teaching career at the time of her mother's death and returned to her Inverness home to look after her father. She began writing stories and verse, and in 1929 her first mystery, *The Man in the Queue* (published under the name Gordon Daviot), was chosen as the winning entry in a publisher's contest. Inspector Alan Grant of Scotland Yard, her bachelor detective with a remarkable instinct for spotting criminals, stars in only six of her mysteries. He does not appear in two of her best known—*Miss Pym Disposes* (Macmillan, 1948) and *Brat Farrar* (Macmillan, 1950). Grant does appear in *The Daughter of Time*, which is recognized as a masterpiece of historical detection. Tey was a master of the classic British mystery. Many of her books are still in print. Elizabeth MacKintosh also wrote plays under the pseudonym Gordon Daviot.

1. *Man in the Queue, The* (Dutton, 1929) Someone is stabbed while standing in one of those patient English queues waiting to buy a theater ticket. Originally published under the pseudonym Gordon Daviot. Variant title: *Killer in the Crowd*.
2. *Shilling for Candles, A* (Macmillan, 1954) Inspired by a real crime, this book concerns the murder of Christine Clay, a famous British film star, near her seashore cottage. Originally published in the United Kingdom in 1936.
3. *Franchise Affair, The* (Macmillan, 1949) A mother and daughter are accused of imprisoning and mistreating a servant girl. The story is based on the real Elizabeth Canning–Mrs. Brownrigg case. Alan Grant has only a minor role in this one.
4. *To Love and Be Wise* (Macmillan, 1951) A handsome American photographer comes to an English artists' colony, launches a romance, then disappears and is feared murdered.
5. *Daughter of Time, The* (Macmillan, 1952) This is Tey's most famous book, in which Grant, laid up in a hospital, researches one of the oldest and most controversial unsolved murder cases in history—that of the two little princes in the Tower of London.
6. *Singing Sands, The* (Macmillan, 1953) The key to the solution of Bill Kendrick's murder is in a fragment of verse that Grant must puzzle out. This book was published posthumously.

Thackeray, William Makepeace

Vanity Fair, Thackeray's best-known novel, has received many film versions, most recently with Reese Witherspoon as Becky Sharp (2004), and *Barry Lyndon* was revived with Stanley Kubrick's 1975 film. But many critics, including Anthony Trollope (q.v.) and Thackeray himself, regarded *The History of Henry Esmond* as Thackeray's greatest work. Its amusing story of unhappy young love and hidden true identity is capped with a surprise ending. Set during the reign of Queen Anne (1702–1714), it is related in the first person in the language of that time by Esmond, writing from the gentleman's estate in Virginia where he settled. The sequel concerns his two grandsons. *The History of Pendennis* (Harper, 1850) contains some characters who are the descendants of characters in *The Virginians*.

1. *History of Henry Esmond, The* (Harper, 1879) The illegitimate son of the deceased old viscount, Henry Esmond, is brought up on the Castlewood estate and falls in love with the beautiful Beatrix, who rejects him for another. Set in the reign of Queen Anne (1702–1714). Some editions are titled simply *Henry Esmond*. Originally published in the United Kingdom in 1852.
2. *Virginians, The* (Fields, 1869) George and Harry Warrington of Virginia, the twin grandsons of Henry Esmond, fight on different sides during the American Revolution. Originally published in the United Kingdom in 1857.

Thane, Elswyth

Thane's Williamsburg novels chronicle American history from colonial times to World War II by focusing on various members of two Williamsburg, Virginia, families: the Days and the Spragues. Much of the action of the later volumes takes place in England, where the author spent part of each year and had a large readership. Thane was married to the famous naturalist-writer William Beebe and is perversely cataloged by some libraries under her married name.

1. *Dawn's Early Light* (Duell, 1943) Set in Williamsburg and the Carolinas from 1774 to 1781, this story describes schoolmaster Julian Day's arrival from London, his friendship with the aristocratic St. John Sprague, and his championing of the young girl Tibby Mawes.
2. *Yankee Stranger* (Duell, 1944) Cabot Murray, a handsome Yankee newspaper correspondent, comes to Williamsburg in 1860, and red-haired Eden Day (Julian's great-granddaughter) falls head over heels in love with him.
3. *Ever After* (Duell, 1945) The story continues into the next generation: young journalist Bracken Murray is in England for Queen Victoria's Jubilee (1897), while his cousin Fitz Sprague covers the Spanish-American War in Cuba.
4. *Light Heart, The* (Duell, 1947) Phoebe Sprague, newly engaged to marry cousin Miles, travels to London for Edward VII's coronation and falls in love with another man.
5. *Kissing Kin* (Duell, 1948) In 1917 the young twins Camilla and Calvert set out to help with the war effort—Calvert on a gun crew and Camilla as a nurse in England.
6. *This Was Tomorrow* (Duell, 1951) Two dancing cousins from Williamsburg take their show to London in 1934 and meet their English counterparts.
7. *Homing* (Duell, 1957) Set in England during World War II, this story focuses on young Jeff Day, a foreign correspondent in London, and his English distant cousin Mab.

Thayer, Nancy

The Hot Flash Club was formed by four ladies in their fifties and sixties—artist Faye, businesswoman Alice, academic Marilyn, and physical therapist Shirley—with the aim of helping each other and other women facing family, career, and emotional problems. They are joined by Polly (number 3). In this "chick lit for the AARP crowd" (*Publishers Weekly*), the ladies bond together and present a united front against the onset of the "golden years" by talking, shopping, eating, and laughing their way through their problems.

1. *Hot Flash Club, The* (Ballantine, 2003) Faye, Alice, Marilyn, and Shirley, meeting by chance at a Boston-area retirement party, decide to form the Hot Flash Club, in which women in, or approaching, their sixties can help each other.
2. *Hot Flash Club Strikes Again, The* (Ballantine, 2004) The Hot Flash Club members, meeting at Shirley's Hot Spot Spa, help four other women with in-law problems.
3. *Hot Flash Holidays* (Ballantine, 2005) The ladies of the Hot Flash Club, joined by newcomer Polly, try to weather the holidays through extensive planning, but mishaps occur.
4. *Hot Flash Club Chills Out, The* (Ballantine, 2006) The members of the Hot Flash Club are sharing an extended holiday on the island of Nantucket (author Nancy Thayer's home base).

Thirkell, Angela

Many contemporary readers will find Thirkell's very British charm hard to fathom, yet her books had a large American audience well into the 1950s. Part of the appeal, no doubt, was the fun of meeting old friends and catching up on the gossip offered by each new installment of her continuing chronicle of Barsetshire. Using Barset, the fictional town created by Anthony Trollope (q.v.), Thirkell follows its modern-day inhabitants, including the descendants of Trollopian characters, through the period of rapid social change after World War I into the post–World War II world of the 1950s. In her later novels, plots grow very thin, tea-table chat predominates, and her conservative characters ossify into the "tweeded dummies" who eventually alienated all but the most loyal fans. Amid all the engagements, marriages, and couplings, even the constant reader cannot keep abreast of all the characters in the series. Eventually, Angela Thirkell herself confessed to losing track of the ages and pairings of the third generation of her characters.

1. *High Rising* (Knopf, 1951) Introduces the autobiographical Mrs. Laura Morland, a widowed writer of very successful "good bad books." Laura is seen coping with her impossible young son, Tony, home on school holiday, and her publisher, Adrian Coates, who proposes marriage. Originally published in the United Kingdom in 1933.
2. *Demon in the House, The* (Smith & Haas, 1934) Continues the saga of the ineffable 13-year-old Tony Morland, his silent friend Donk, and other Barsetshire characters.
3. *Wild Strawberries* (Smith & Haas, 1934) Lady Emily Leslie and her family play the lead roles during the time that their home, Rushwater House, is used as a convalescent center for soldiers.
4. *August Folly* (Knopf, 1937) The village of Worsted is the scene of a performance of *Hippolytus* produced by the indefatigable Mrs. Palmer. Young Richard Tebbins falls in love with Mrs. Dean, mother of nine children.
5. *Summer Half* (Knopf, 1938) Philip Winters's engagement to the featherbrained Rose Birkett dismays both families. Tony Morland, now 17 and a "public" school student, shows signs of becoming a human being.

6. *Pomfret Towers* **(Knopf, 1938)** Lord and Lady Pomfret introduce cousin and heir, Gillie Foster, to the gentry and eligible young ladies of Barsetshire. Young Alice Barton breaks out of her shell of shyness.

7. *Before Lunch* **(Knopf, 1939)** John Middleton, architect and gentleman farmer, copes with the various romantic entanglements of his sister, Lilian, and her two stepchildren.

8. *Brandons, The* **(Knopf, 1939)** Mrs. Brandon, a middle-aged widow with two grown children, does her best not to be disinherited by her husband's rich old aunt.

9. *Cheerfulness Breaks In* **(Knopf, 1941)** During World War II, the headmaster of a state school and his wife evacuate their pupils to Barsetshire's Southbridge Public School.

10. *Northbridge Rectory* **(Knopf, 1941)** Northbridge Village during World War II is seen through the eyes of Mrs. Villars, the vicar's wife.

11. *Marling Hall* **(Knopf, 1942)** Lady Agnes Graham and other residents of Marling Hall cope with wartime shortages and dangers and Mrs. Smith's chickens.

12. *Growing Up* **(Knopf, 1943)** Sir Harry and Lady Waring have turned most of their mansion into a soldiers' convalescent home and make the best of their life in their servants' quarters.

13. *Headmistress, The* **(Knopf, 1944)** The Beltons of Harefield Park have leased their ancestral home to the Hosier's Girls School. Self-made industrialist Sam Adams and Heather, his gauche and homely daughter, are featured here.

14. *Miss Bunting* **(Knopf, 1945)** Miss Bunting, "governess to the county," plays a major role in this story about two middle-aged spinsters and the young girls they tutor.

15. *Peace Breaks Out* **(Knopf, 1946)** Sam Adams, the industrialist, defeats the incumbent Sir Robert Fielding in the postwar election, as the Labour Party—always referred to as "Them" by Thirkell's genteel characters—comes into power.

16. *Private Enterprise* **(Knopf, 1947)** Mrs. Arbuthnot, an attractive war widow, comes to Barsetshire hoping to find a new husband.

17. *Love among the Ruins* **(Knopf, 1948)** The romance of Susan Dean and Captain Belton is the main focus of this installment.

18. *Old Bank House, The* **(Knopf, 1949)** Sam Adams, MP, buys a period house, becomes engaged to the spinster daughter of Marling Hall, and is eventually accepted by the gentry.

19. *County Chronicle* **(Knopf, 1950)** The small market town of Edgewood is the focus here. Isabel Dale comes into money and marries Lord Silverbridge, a descendant of a character in Trollope's (q.v.) Palliser novels.

20. *Duke's Daughter, The* **(Knopf, 1951)** Three engagements in 24 hours take place, including that of Lady Cora Palliser, descendant of Trollope's (q.v.) Palliser family.

21. *Happy Returns* **(Knopf, 1952)** The return to power of the Conservative Party ("Us") makes the Barsetshire gentry much happier. Eric Swan, the master of Priory School, plays a leading role in this novel.

22. *Jutland Cottage* **(Knopf, 1953)** Glamorous Rose Fairweather takes poor Margot Phelps under her wing; gets her some fashionable new clothes, a new corset, and a new hairdo; and finds her a husband.

23. *What Did It Mean?* **(Knopf, 1954)** The Northbridge Coronation Pageant is among the events celebrating the coronation of Elizabeth II.

24. *Enter Sir Robert* **(Knopf, 1955)** Sir Robert Graham's return from London is anticipated throughout this novel, as Lady Graham plans to "settle things" with her husband.

25. *Never Too Late* **(Knopf, 1956)** Romances blossom between the vicar and Miss Merriman, and Lord Crosse and Mrs. Morland.

26. *Double Affair, A* **(Knopf, 1957)** Dean Crawley's granddaughters Grace and Jane have a double wedding.

27. *Close Quarters* **(Knopf, 1958)** Canon "Tubby" Fewling comes to the rescue of a bereaved Margot MacFayden.

28. *Love at All Ages* **(Knopf, 1959)** Many old friends reappear in this episode, which includes a birth, a baptism, a marriage, and a generous helping of young love.

29. *Three Score and Ten* **(Knopf, 1961)** Romance for both Dr. Ford and Lord Mellings provides the focus for this last novel, which acts as a reprise to the entire series. Completed from Thirkell's notes after her death by C. A. Lejeune.

Thomas, Craig (David)

I. *Firefox* and its successors are excellent examples of the thriller-espionage genre. They have plenty of action and suspense, excellent descriptions of aircraft and flying, and an interesting protagonist in Mitchell Gant, an American air ace damaged psychologically by his experiences in the Vietnam War. Part of the suspense is generated by the reader's knowledge that Gant is unstable and may crack under pressure during his missions. *Firefox* was a best seller as a novel and a successful film starring Clint Eastwood (1982).

1. *Firefox* **(Holt, 1977)** US Air Force major Mitchell Gant is sent by the CIA and Britain's SIS to steal the new Russian warplane, code-named *Firefox*, on its first test flight.

2. *Firefox Down!* **(Bantam, 1983)** Gant is forced to land the disabled *Firefox* on a frozen lake in Finnish Lapland, where it sinks through the ice, and Gant is captured by the Russians.

3. *Winter Hawk* **(Morrow, 1987)** Forty-eight hours is all the time Gant has to retrieve from the Soviet Union a spy who has information that could stop the signing of an arms-reduction treaty.

4. *Different War, A* **(Warner, 1998)** After a new American airliner crashes mysteriously in the Arizona desert on its last test flight, Gant is called upon to repeat the test flight in every detail.

II. Welsh writer Thomas has also been authoring a series of somewhat loosely connected novels featuring British intelligence chief Sir Kenneth Aubrey and his ace agent Patrick Hyde. Like the Firefox series and Thomas's other novels, the Aubrey-Hyde series is full of action, intrigue, exotic locales, and page-turning suspense. Thomas also writes thrillers under the pseudonym David Grant.

1. *Lion's Run* **(Bantam, 1985)** Sir Kenneth Aubrey, director-general of British intelligence, is besmirched by a Soviet plot to discredit and replace him with their own man.

2. *Wildcat* **(Putnam, 1989)** Nepal and Sir Kenneth's ward, ex-Gurkha Timothy Gardiner, are the targets of Brigitte Winterbach and Andrew Babbington, Aubrey's enemies.

3. *Last Raven, The* **(Harper, 1990)** Sir Kenneth's American-based niece gets involved in an Irangate-style situation, and an old friend is enmeshed in corporate espionage and possibly political assassination.

4. *Hooded Crow, A* **(Harper, 1992)** Nefarious South African businessman Paulus Malan and his brutal henchman Blantyre are behind the smuggling of Western high-tech military secrets to the Russians.

5. *Playing with Cobras* **(Harper, 1993)** Patrick Hyde is called out of retirement to handle a sticky problem involving operative Philip Cass, accused of murdering his lover, the wife of an Indian government minister.

Thomas, D(onald) M(ichael)

The Russian Nights quintet, which was originally planned as a trilogy, uses as its base an unfinished story by the great 19th-century Russian writer Alexander Pushkin, a story that author D. M. Thomas had translated into English. In *Ararat*, the Russian poet Rozanov improvises on the Pushkin story and creates three other improvisers attending a conference in Armenia. One of the improvisers improvises an Italian storyteller in St. Petersburg who does his own improvising, and so forth. The storytellers multiply within and around each other, and it becomes increasingly unclear as to who is the improviser and where the line is to be drawn between truth and fiction. *Swallow* and *Sphinx* provide further twists, while *Summit* provides a satirical commentary on big power diplomacy, and *Lying Together* introduces D. M. Thomas himself as a character. Each novel can stand alone. British (Cornish) novelist, poet, memoirist, biographer, and translator Thomas is probably best known in the United States for his novel *The White Hotel* (Viking, 1981).

1. *Ararat* (Viking, 1983) Russian poet Rozanov is asked to invent and tell a story by the blind woman in Gorki who is writing a thesis on his poetry.
2. *Swallow* (Viking, 1984) Rozanov becomes a fiction, the creation of the Italian storyteller Corinna, introduced in *Ararat,* who is improvising for an audience in St. Petersburg (Leningrad).
3. *Sphinx* (Viking, 1986) Brings back some of the earlier characters and introduces two new characters: Soviet Jewish storyteller Shimon Barash and Welsh journalist Lloyd George.
4. *Summit* (Viking, 1988) A farcical coda to the trilogy, in which superpower leaders "Grobichev" and "O'Reilly" (accompanied by vice-president "Shrub") meet in Geneva.
5. *Lying Together* (Viking, 1990) D. M. Thomas introduces himself as a character, attending a writers' conference in London, who gets together with some old friends from the Soviet Union.

Thompson, Flora

Critics have trouble deciding whether Thompson wrote fictionalized memoirs or autobiographical fiction, but few dispute the nostalgic appeal of Flora Thompson's picture of rural England during the 1880s and 1890s. Lark Rise and Candleford Green are tiny remote villages much like the Oxfordshire hamlet where Thompson (1876–1947) lived. She captures village life with fondness and humor but without sentimentality. The first three volumes were collected in one volume under the title *Lark Rise to Candleford* (Oxford, 1945). An abridged version, *The Illustrated Lark Rise to Candleford* (Crown, 1983), was a best seller in England.

1. *Lark Rise* (Oxford, 1939) Laura, daughter of the village stonemason, grows up in tiny remote Lark Rise in the 1880s.
2. *Over to Candleford* (Oxford, 1941) Miss Lane takes over her father's blacksmithing business and becomes the village postmistress.
3. *Candleford Green* (Oxford, 1943) Laura moves to the market town of Candleford Green as assistant to postmistress Miss Lane.
4. *Still Glides the Stream* (Oxford, 1948) This posthumously published volume tells of schoolmistress Charity Finch's return to the village of her birth.

Thomson, June

I.   Agatha Christie (q.v.) fans will enjoy this highly praised detective series by a British author who writes clever and bloodless mysteries in the traditional English manner. Her Inspector Rudd (Jack Finch in the English editions of this series) is a mellow, middle-aged, and middle-class chap who lives with his sister in Essex, where he is the local Criminal Investigation Department (CID) officer. His deliberately casual, gossipy method of interrogation and acute psychological assessments enable him to get to the bottom of each interesting case with a minimum of fuss but a full measure of reading pleasure. *Flowers for the Dead* (Constable [UK], 1992) is a collection of short stories, none of which seem to involve Rudd/Finch.

1. *Not One of Us* (Harper, 1971) When a small-town girl is murdered, a stranger is automatically suspected of the crime.
2. *Death Cap* (Doubleday, 1977) Somebody has slipped Rene King a batch of deadly poisonous mushrooms. Originally published in the United Kingdom in 1973.
3. *Long Revenge, The* (Doubleday, 1975) Rudd (Finch) takes on a special assignment to protect a retired British spy and finds himself in the strange, shadowy world of espionage.
4. *Case Closed* (Doubleday, 1977) Rudd (Finch) investigates the murder of a girl four years earlier after new evidence has reopened the case.
5. *Question of Identity, A* (Doubleday, 1977) When some archaeologists turn up a fresh corpse, Inspector Rudd (Finch) must investigate.
6. *Habit of Loving, The* (Doubleday, 1979) When a shy young man passes through a quiet village on a summer holiday, a puzzling murder results. UK title: *Deadly Relations*.
7. *Alibi in Time* (Doubleday, 1980) When the battered body of writer Patrick Vaughan is discovered by the roadside, Rudd (Finch) suspects murder.
8. *Shadow of a Doubt* (Doubleday, 1982) Claire Jordan, the victimized wife of London psychiatrist Howard Jordan, disappears from her husband's clinic.
9. *Portrait of Lilith* (Doubleday, 1983) Elderly, disabled artist Max Gifford has a fixation on portraits he made of a woman called Lilith. UK title: *To Make a Killing*.
10. *Sound Evidence* (Doubleday, 1985) An old chess player may have seen the killer of a young homosexual.
11. *Dying Fall, A* (Doubleday, 1986) The manipulative Rex Holt arranges a lunch at which his estranged son, his mistress, and an American scholar attempting blackmail will confront each other.
12. *Dark Stream, The* (Doubleday, 1986) The arrival of attractive, mysterious newcomer Alec Lawson brings events to a head in the village of Wynford.
13. *No Flowers, by Request* (Doubleday, 1987) David Hamilton's seemingly charmed life in the quaint village of Framden comes to a violent end.
14. *Rosemary for Remembrance* (Doubleday, 1988) The summer course in creative writing at the Morton Grange Girls' School is the scene of the murder of a director known for his womanizing.
15. *Spoils of Time, The* (Doubleday, 1989) The Aston family has gathered at Howlett Hall to await the imminent death of octogenarian Edgar Aston.
16. *Past Reckoning* (Doubleday, 1990) Imogen Kershaw, sister of forgotten writer William Kershaw and curator of the museum devoted to him, is murdered with his walking stick.
17. *Foul Play* (Constable [UK], 1991) Oliver Hampden is the central figure in a drama in which reality steals the show, providing Inspector Finch with a murder investigation.

18. *Burden of Innocence* (**Constable [UK], 1996**) When the beautiful, enigmatic Christa, with whom Alex Bennet has been obsessed, responds to her demand to see him, he finds her dead.

19. *Unquiet Grave, The* (**Constable [UK], 2000**) When a friend of Luke Gilchrist's recently deceased father presents Luke with some old letters, he discovers that his father had another family and may also have been a murderer.

20. *Going Home* (**Allison & Busby [UK], 2006**) DCI Rudd/Finch investigates the disappearance of Charlotte, the deaf daughter of widower Alex Lambert.

II. Thomson has published five collections of short stories featuring Sherlock Holmes that provide Holmes with new cases in authentic surroundings. She has also published a nonfiction book about Holmes: *Holmes and Watson: A Study in Friendship* (Carroll & Graf, 2001; originally 1995). The Holmes collections are listed below without annotations.

1. *Secret Files of Sherlock Holmes, The* (**Penzler, 1993**) Originally published in the United Kingdom in 1990.
2. *Secret Chronicles of Sherlock Holmes, The* (**Penzler, 1993**)
3. *Secret Journals of Sherlock Holmes, The* (**Constable [UK], 1993**)
4. *Secret Documents of Sherlock Holmes, The* (**Constable [UK], 1996**)
5. *Secret Notebooks of Sherlock Holmes, The* (**Allison & Busby [UK], 2004**)

Thurlo, Aimee & David

I. Navajo Ella Clah is a former FBI agent who has returned to her reservation to become a Navajo Tribal Police special investigator. The daughter of a Christian minister and a traditionalist mother, Ella has to deal with many conflicts both within and outside her family and the battles (which sometimes turn violent) between modernists—who try to accommodate to Euro-American society—and traditionalists, who prefer the old ways and try to preserve Navajo rituals and mores. Comparisons with Tony Hillerman (q.v.) may be invidious, but the series written by the Thurlos are quite readable and full of Navajo lore. Aimee and David Thurlo have been married for 37 years and have produced nearly 50 novels together. David was raised on a Navajo reservation, and the pair still lives in New Mexico.

1. *Blackening Song* (**Forge, 1995**) FBI agent Ella Clah returns to the Navajo reservation where she was born and raised after her father, a Christian minister, is murdered in a manner that suggests a ritual killing.
2. *Death Walker* (**Forge, 1996**) Ella, now back on the reservation as a sergeant and special investigator of the Navajo Tribal Police, is confronted with the serial killings of the reservation's elders.
3. *Bad Medicine* (**Forge, 1997**) Ella uncovers some suspicious links between racial tensions at a local mine and the allegedly accidental death of a powerful senator's daughter.
4. *Enemy Way* (**Forge, 1999**) A bungled assassination attempt and the murder of her friend's fiancé occupy Ella here.
5. *Shooting Chant* (**Forge, 2000**) Ella, being pregnant, is more than usually concerned about records of pregnant Navajo women being stolen from the clinic.
6. *Red Mesa* (**Forge, 2001**) Ella becomes the chief suspect when her troubled young cousin, Justine, is found dead on Red Mesa.
7. *Changing Woman* (**Forge, 2002**) Clah infiltrates a group of terrorists whose acts of vandalism may have something to do with the heated debate over a proposed gambling casino on the res.

8. *Plant Them Deep* (**Forge, 2003**) Ella's mother, Rose, is asked by the Navajo Tribal Council to investigate the disappearance of ritual and medicinal plants.
9. *Tracking Bear* (**Forge, 2003**) The murder of a Navajo policeman may be connected to a major supporter of a proposed nuclear power plant.
10. *Wind Spirit* (**Forge, 2004**) Arson and murder afflict the res.
11. *White Thunder* (**Forge, 2005**) An FBI area supervisor asks the Navajo Tribal Police to help locate Andrew Thomas, a federal agent who disappeared after interrupting a Navajo ritual ceremony.
12. *Mourning Dove* (**Forge, 2006**) A carjacking gone wrong kills Jimmy Blacksheep, a Navajo member of the New Mexico National Guard, who has just returned from a tour in Iraq.
13. *Turquoise Girl* (**Forge, 2007**) Young Navajo waitress Valerie So is murdered, and the vigilante group, the Fierce Ones, is competing with Clah in tracking down the killer.

II. Lee Nez is a Navajo vampire and police officer who teams up with FBI agent Diane Lopez, whose former partner was killed by a werewolf. Not bad for those who like this sort of thing.

1. *Second Sunrise* (**Forge, 2002**) The past comes back to haunt Navajo vampire and policeman Lee Nez when the German vampire he fought against 50 years ago returns to New Mexico on the hunt for lost plutonium.
2. *Blood Retribution* (**Forge, 2004**) Lee is investigating cop-killing smugglers bringing in jewels and silver from Mexico while, in turn, he is being stalked by a pair of vampire assassins who want revenge for the death of their leader.
3. *Pale Death* (**Forge, 2005**) Lee and FBI agent Diane Lopez are on the trail of a rogue vampire–serial killer who has murdered employees of a secret government laboratories.
4. *Surrogate Evil* (**Forge, 2006**) Clues link a missing child to gangster kingpin Newton Glover.

III. Sister Agatha of the Sisters of the Blessed Adoration in Our Lady of Hope Monastery in rural New Mexico has to deal with murder as well as with the chronic financial difficulties of her strapped retreat in this series of ecclesiastical cozies.

1. *Bad Faith* (**St. Martin's, 2002**) A chaplain is poisoned at Our Lady of Hope Monastery in the New Mexico desert.
2. *Thief in Retreat* (**St. Martin's, 2004**) Sister Agatha tries to uncover the truth about a closed monastery complete with a wandering ghost, thefts dating back 20 years, and local legends.
3. *Prey for a Miracle* (**St. Martin's, 2006**) A young girl, who according to her parents had received visions from the Virgin Mary, is kidnapped.
4. *False Witness* (**St. Martin's, 2007**) The crash of a stolen SUV into the monastery's outer wall being the final straw in Our Lady of Hope's financial miseries, Sister Agatha feels obliged to search for John Gutierrez's estranged niece in return for a large legacy to the monastery.

Tierney, Ronald

Dietrich "Deets" Shanahan is a 69-year-old former intelligence agent with a pension, a somewhat neglected private eye business, a marriage that has been over for 35 years, and a live-in 44-year-old girlfriend. Indianapolis-located Deets hasn't given up thinking for himself or seeing that justice is done. Ronald Tierney is an Indianapolis native himself and still lives there. *Eclipse of the Heart* (St. Martin's, 1993) is not a series novel.

1. *Stone Veil, The* (St. Martin's, 1990) When a wealthy Indianapolis socialite asks Deets to find her husband, he eventually takes on the case, mostly for lack of something better to do.
2. *Steel Web, The* (St. Martin's, 1991) Deets doesn't believe that two 16-year-old boys arrested for the murder of an undercover cop are guilty of the crime.
3. *Iron Glove, The* (St. Martin's, 1992) After the nude, strangely marked body of Senator Holland's wife is fished from a river, Deets investigates to help clear his friend Harry's prospective son-in-law.
4. *Concrete Pillow, The* (St. Martin's, 1995) Luke Lindstrom, one-fourth of the quadruplet brothers who won a high school basketball championship, hires Deets after two of his brothers have bad accidents.
5. *Nickel-Plated Soul* (Severn House, 2004) Deets gets involved in the case of Hugh Dart, who served 35 years in prison for murdering his wife, whom Hugh claims is still alive and stole millions of dollars that he accumulated through political bribes.
6. *Platinum Canary* (Severn House, 2005) Lianna, a young, attractive executive of one of the largest medical companies in the world, is pregnant and missing. The police suspect her fiancé, but Deets isn't so sure.
7. *Glass Chameleon* (Severn House, 2006) Deets is in New Orleans at the behest of an old enemy to investigate the murder of Michael LaSalle, who knew too many secrets.
8. *Asphalt Moon* (Severn House, 2007) A mysterious stalker is after Deets, but Deets is more concerned about his live-in girlfriend, Maureen.

Tilton, Alice

PSEUDONYM OF **Phoebe Atwood Taylor**

Under the pseudonym of Alice Tilton, Phoebe Atwood Taylor (q.v.) wrote the mysteries starring Leonidas Witherall, whose marked resemblance to Shakespeare earned him the nickname "Bill" during his teaching days at Meredith Academy. In his retirement, he fills his days with travel, amateur sleuthing, and writing his Lieutenant Hazeltine mysteries on the sly. He makes his home in Dalton, Massachusetts, which bears a distinct resemblance to Newton, Massachusetts, where Taylor lived. Mystery is secondary to comedy in these books, though some readers find them arch and dated.

1. *Beginning with a Bash* (Norton, 1937) Leonidas Witherall solves the murder of a professor in a bookstore and clears a former student of his.
2. *Cut Direct, The* (Norton, 1938) Witherall wakes up in a strange house to find himself confronted with a corpse. Witherall receives an inheritance in this book.
3. *Cold Steal* (Norton, 1939) Returning from abroad to his new house in Dalton, Witherall investigates some funny doings on the train, and the mystery follows him home.
4. *Left Leg, The* (Norton, 1940) This very funny case involves a corpse minus a left leg and a woman in a scarlet wimple, who becomes known, naturally, as the scarlet wimpernel.
5. *Hollow Chest, The* (Norton, 1941) A murdered VIP and a fickle kidnapper create havoc at Meredith Academy's Fifth Form Egg Day, when Witherall lends a hand.
6. *File for Record* (Norton, 1943) Witherall goes in search of a lost umbrella and finds himself mixed up in car theft and murder in wartime Dalton.
7. *Dead Ernest* (Norton, 1944) Two drunken truckers leave a freezer containing a leg of lamb, some fillets of haddock, and a human corpse in Witherall's kitchen.
8. *Iron Clew, The* (Farrar, 1947) An innocent-looking package that is wrapped in brown paper leads Witherall to Balderston Hall, a house that resembles a wedding cake. UK title: *The Iron Hand*.

Todd, Charles

PSEUDONYM OF **David Todd Watjen & Carolyn L. T. Watjen**

Ian Rutledge returns to Scotland Yard in 1919, shell-shocked and haunted by memories of the young Scottish soldier, Hamish, he had unwillingly executed during World War I. Because of the machinations of a jealous rival, Rutledge, who had a brilliant career in the Yard before the war, gets sent out to investigate a series of what seem to be hopeless cases in remote settings. Accompanied by his "demon," the memory of Hamish, Rutledge manages to find solutions in these atmospheric, well-plotted mysteries. "Charles Todd" is the pseudonym of a mother-son writing team. *The Murder Stone* (Bantam, 2003) is a stand-alone.

1. *Test of Wills, A* (St. Martin's, 1996) In 1919 Scotland Yard operative Rutledge, suffering from shell shock and bad memories of the war, is sent to a Warwickshire village where a popular retired military officer has been killed, and the chief suspect is a much-decorated war hero and a friend of the Prince of Wales.
2. *Wings of Fire* (St. Martin's, 1998) In a remote part of Cornwall, three members of the same family have died, including "Olivia," the reclusive writer whose war poetry gave Rutledge a handhold on sanity while he fought in France.
3. *Search the Dark* (St. Martin's, 1999) Rutledge is sent to a small Dorset town to locate two missing children. The body of a woman assumed to be their mother has been found. The leading suspect is a psychotic war veteran.
4. *Legacy of the Dead* (Bantam, 2000) The weathered remains found on a windswept Scottish mountainside may be those of the missing Eleanor Gray. The investigating Rutledge winds up in the village of Duncarrick, where a young mother is accused of murder.
5. *Watchers of Time* (Bantam, 2001) The town of Osterley, a marshy Norfolk backwater, holds some nasty secrets, including the murder of the town's Catholic priest.
6. *Fearsome Doubt, A* (Bantam, 2002) Seven years after Ben Shaw, alleged murderer of elderly woman, was hanged with the help of evidence gathered by Rutledge, he is confronted by Shaw's widow who has information she is convinced will prove her late husband's innocence.
7. *Cold Treachery, A* (Bantam, 2005) Gerald and Grace Elcott and three of their four children have been shot to death and the fourth is missing in the rustic Lake District town of Urksdale.
8. *Long Shadow, A* (Morrow, 2006) The town constable of the remote and desolate English village of Dudlington has been shot in the back with an arrow while exploring a forest shunned by the locals.
9. *False Mirror, A* (Morrow, 2007) Stephen Mallory, who served under Rutledge's command in the war, is holding hostages in the seaside village of Hampton and demanding Rutledge's presence.
10. *Pale Horse, A* (Morrow, 2007) The War Office wants Rutledge to locate a mysterious person of interest, connected with, and perhaps the same as, an unidentified corpse found at a Yorkshire abbey.

Toer, Pramoedya Ananta

The Buru Quartet has an interesting history. It was composed orally by Indonesian writer and political activist Toer while he was a political prisoner on Buru Island (1965–1979) and not allowed access to writing materials. Toer was subsequently placed on "City Arrest" in Jakarta, and his translator, Australian diplomat Max Lane, was expelled from Indonesia because of his English renditions of the Buru Quartet. The first three volumes are an extended autobiography of Madan Ras Minke, who is modeled on the early 20th-century Indonesian patriot-journalist Tirto Adi Soryo. The fourth novel is presented as a set of office notes made by Jacques Pangemanann, the first high-ranking native officer in the Dutch East Indies Colonial Service. The setting is late 19th- and early 20th-century Java under Dutch colonial rule. Minke's dream of a unified, free, multiethnic Indonesia is contrasted with the harsh realities of colonial occupation in these engrossing fictions that make Indonesian history come alive, spiced with the irony that the foreign oppressors were to be replaced by native ones. Max Lane translated all four novels from the Indonesian. The novels were reprinted in hardcover by Morrow (1991–1996) after softcover publication by Penguin.

1. *This Earth of Mankind* (Penguin, 1982) European-educated Javan Minke becomes involved, romantically and otherwise, with a wealthy family headed by a tough, self-education concubine. Originally published as *Bumi manusia* in 1980.
2. *Child of All Nations* (Penguin, 1982) Minke, in the process of recovering from the death of his Eurasian wife, has his eyes opened to colonial injustice. Originally published as *Anak semua bangsa* in 1980.
3. *Footsteps* (Penguin, 1990) Minke becomes a journalist, then a grass-roots political organizer, and eventually the crusading publisher of Indonesia's first native-owned daily newspaper. Originally published as *Jejak langkah* in 1985.
4. *House of Glass* (Penguin, 1992) Jacques Pangemanann, raised by Europeans, becomes the first high-ranking native officer in the Dutch Indies Colonial Service. Although he admires Minke, Pangemanann feels that it is his duty to arrest him.

Toland, John

The late (d. 2004) Pulitzer Prize–winning historian John Toland (e.g., *The Rising Sun*, Random House, 1970) had a special interest in Japan and World War II. This interest is expressed in his two volumes of fiction as well as in his nonfiction. This pair of novels tells about the fortunes of two families related by marriage, the American McGlynns and the Japanese Todas, from the period just before Pearl Harbor to the aftermath of World War II. The interest of the novels lies more with Toland's detailed and accurate rendering of historical events, especially from the Japanese point of view, rather than with the lives and loves of the fictional McGlynns and Todas.

1. *Gods of War* (Doubleday, 1985) Members of the McGlynn and Toda families see action of various kinds on their respective sides during World War II.
2. *Occupation* (Doubleday, 1987) The McGlynns and Todas continue their varying roles during the occupation of Japan and the war-crimes trials of Japanese leaders.

Tolkien, J(ohn) R(onald) R(euel)

I. The recent commercial and artistic success (*The Return of the King* netted 11 Oscars, including Best Picture) of the film trilogy of *The Lord of the Rings* has helped keep the Tolkien boom going. Tolkien studies are rife in universities and lobbying for academic respectability. Oxford professor J. R. R. Tolkien's interest in philology led him to devise an elaborate "Elvish" language and then to create the richly imagined world of Middle Earth, where his language could be spoken. *The Hobbit* (Houghton Mifflin, 1938), a fantasy for children, was the first book to be set in Middle Earth. Its story about Bilbo Baggins's adventures precedes the adult trilogy. Young Frodo Baggins, who inherits the magic ring from his uncle Bilbo, is the start of the Lord of the Rings trilogy. Frodo's struggle to prevent the powers of darkness from claiming the ring illustrates the works' central theme: the corruption of power. The posthumously published *Silmarillion* (Houghton Mifflin, 1977) contains stories of Middle-Earth's First Age and two stories set in the Third Age of the Lord of the Rings trilogy. Additional poems, songs, and tales related to the trilogy are contained in books such as *The Adventures of Tom Bombadil* (Houghton Mifflin, 1962). Tolkien's son Christopher has published a dozen additional books compiled from his father's manuscripts (see series II, below). Tolkien enthusiasts will want to check out guides to Middle Earth such as Robert Foster's *The Complete Guide to Middle Earth* (Ballantine, 2001); J. E. A. Tyler's *The Complete Tolkien Companion* (St. Martin's, 2004); or Wayne G. Hammond and Christina Scull's *The Lord of the Rings: A Reader's Companion* (Houghton Mifflin, 2005); as well as Humphrey Carpenter's authorized biography: *J. R. R. Tolkien: A Biography* (Houghton Mifflin, 1977).

1. *Fellowship of the Ring, The* (Houghton Mifflin, 1954) Frodo goes on the first leg of his journey and encounters elves, dwarves, men, and other strange beings.
2. *Two Towers, The* (Houghton Mifflin, 1954) The Companions of the Ring, separated, cross the Dead Marshes and prepare for the Great War.
3. *Return of the King, The* (Houghton Mifflin, 1956) The forces of evil are defeated in the War of the Rings, and Frodo and Sam bear the Ring to Mount Doom.

II. Christopher Tolkien, youngest son of J. R. R. Tolkien, published 12 books, compiled from his father's manuscripts, that contain stories, poems, and essays illuminating the earlier and later histories of Middle Earth. Numbers 1 through 5 are called the History of Middle-Earth series (a title sometimes given to all 12 volumes). Numbers 6 through 10 are called the History of *The Lord of the Rings* series. Numbers 10 and 11 are referred to as the Later Silmarillion series, while number 12 is a collection of essays about Middle-Earth. Christopher Tolkien has also compiled a *History of Middle-Earth Index* (HarperCollins [UK], 2002).

1. *Book of Lost Tales, The* (Houghton Mifflin, 1984) Short stories.
2. *Book of Lost Tales, Part Two* (Houghton Mifflin, 1984) Short stories.
3. *Lays of Beleriand, The* (Houghton Mifflin, 1985) The early years of Turin the Tall as he journeys through darkness on his quest to find his father.
4. *Shaping of Middle-Earth, The* (Houghton Mifflin, 1986) Short stories.
5. *Lost Road and Other Writings, The* (Houghton Mifflin, 1987) Shows how the Middle-Earth saga grew from an early idea of a new version of the Atlantis legend.

6. *Return of the Shadow, The* (**Houghton Mifflin, 1989**) Bilbo's "magic ring" evolves into the Ruling Ring of the Dark Lord, and a Black Rider first rides into the shire.

7. *Treason of Isengard, The* (**Houghton Mifflin, 1989**) Reaches the beginning of *The Lord of the Rings*, as the Company of the Ring, lacking Legolas and Gimli, stood before the tomb of Balin in the Mines of Moria.

8. *War of the Ring, The* (**Houghton Mifflin, 1990**) The Battle of Helm's Deep and the drowning of Isengard by the Ents.

9. *Sauron Defeated* (**Houghton Mifflin, 1992**) Begins with Sam's rescue of Frodo from the Tower of Cirith Ungol and ends with an epilogue, in which, years after the tale ends, Sam attempts to answer his children's questions. New edition published as *The End of the Third Age* (Houghton Mifflin, 2000).

10. *Morgoth's Ring: The Legends of Aman* (**Houghton Mifflin, 1993**) First of two volumes documenting the later writing of *The Silmarillion* (Houghton Mifflin, 1977).

11. *War of the Jewels: The Legends of Beleriad* (**Houghton Mifflin, 1994**) Second of two volumes documenting the later writing of *The Silmarillion*. Returns to Middle-Earth and the ruinous conflict of the High Elves and the Men.

12. *Peoples of Middle-Earth, The* (**Houghton Mifflin, 1996**) A collection of essays showing how J. R. R. Tolkien began the story of Middle-Earth's Second and Third Stages.

Tolkin, Michael

The Player, Michael Tolkin's satire about a power-hungry, paranoid Hollywood executive who will stop at nothing, including murder, to achieve riches and power, became a cult classic. *The Player* was made into a Robert Altman movie starring Tim Robbins (1992). *The Return of the Player* follows Griffin Mill as he continues his antiheroic career. Michael Tolkin, author of these noir satires on Hollywood, is a novelist, screenwriter, and film director.

1. *Player, The* (**Atlantic Monthly, 1988**) Power-hungry, aggressive, and increasingly paranoid upper-level film executive Griffin Mill takes the law into his own hands by killing an anonymous screenwriter who had been making harassing phone calls.

2. *Return of the Player, The* (**Grove, 2006**) Griffin Mill, his career stalled, bankruptcy looming (only $6 million in the bank), his family life a shambles, and suffering from erectile dysfunction, has a plan to regain control of everything.

Tolstoy, Leo

The 1853 publication of Tolstoy's first novel, the highly autobiographical *Childhood*, won him recognition as a promising young writer. Though he later claimed to dislike the book and its sequels, the trilogy ranks high as a sensitive portrayal of childhood and a vivid picture of Russian family life. The moral and egalitarian concerns characteristic of Tolstoy's later fiction are nascent in these early works. Tolstoy never wrote the fourth book he originally projected in this series, which he planned to entitle Four Epochs of Growth. The three existing books are available in an omnibus volume, *Childhood, Boyhood and Youth* (Dutton, 1912), which was translated from the Russian by Leo Wiener. Other translations were published, including one by Rosemary Edmonds: *Childhood, Boyhood, and Youth* (Penguin, 1964).

1. *Childhood* (**Crowell, 1886**) The young narrator, Nicholas Iretenyev, tells of his life from the age of 10, when he and his older brother leave the family's estate to reside with their father in Moscow. First published in Russia in 1852 as *Detstvo*.

2. *Boyhood* (**Crowell, 1886**) After their mother's death, Nikki's sisters join the boys in Moscow, and the family group is preoccupied with young love, school, and growing self-knowledge. First published in Russia in 1854 as *Otrochestvo*.

3. *Youth* (**Crowell, 1886**) Nikki's concerns from this 16th year to the end of his university days include his father's remarriage and his own friendships and romances. First published in Russia in 1857 as *Yunost*.

Tonkin, Peter (Francis)

I. Richard Mariner undergoes a series of melodramatic nautical adventures in which he is pitted against hurricanes and other natural disasters and international terrorists and other evildoers. Mariner's wife, Robin (née Heritage), daughter of the owner of Heritage-Mariner Shipping Company, often accompanies Richard in his adventures. The novels, written by Peter Tonkin, native of Northern Ireland, were originally published in the United Kingdom. Most of these "brisk, dashing, pleasantly brainless British adventure stories" (*Kirkus Reviews*) have been released in the United States by Trafalgar Square or Severn House. Tonkin is also the author of a series of Elizabethan mysteries (see series II, below), a horror novel—*The Journal of Edwin Underhill* (Hodder [UK], 1981)—and three stand-alone thrillers: *Killer* (Coward-McCann, 1978); *The Action* (Severn House, 1996); and *The Zero Option* (Severn House, 1997).

1. *Coffin Ship, The* (**Crown, 1989**) Captain Richard Mariner struggles against a faceless enemy and the elements aboard a seemingly doomed supertanker.

2. *Fire Ship, The* (**Crown, 1992**) Shipping magnates Richard and Robin Mariner take a break from their vacation to foil a high-seas hijacking and restore a steady supply of Persian Gulf oil. Originally published in the United Kingdom in 1990.

3. *Leper Ship, The* (**Thorndike, 1994**) The *Napoli* loses its captain while removing toxic waste. John Higgins to the rescue. Published only in large print in the United States. Originally published in the United Kingdom in 1992.

4. *Bomb Ship, The* (**Headline [UK], 1993**) One of the twin ships Mariner has commissioned to transport nuclear waste across the Atlantic is trapped behind ice. Distributed in the United States by Trafalgar, 1995.

5. *Iceberg* (**Headline [UK], 1994**) Mariner is commissioned to tow an iceberg to a drought-stricken nation, unaware that the iceberg is polluted with nuclear waste.

6. *Pirate Ship, The* (**Headline [UK], 1995**) The cargo ship *Sulu Queen* is drifting aimlessly in the South China Sea. Released in the United States by Trafalgar in 1997.

7. *Meltdown* (**Headline [UK], 1996**) Mariner delivers a giant iceberg, code-named Manhattan, to the drought-stricken West African country of Mau. Distributed in the United States by Trafalgar.

8. *Tiger Island* (**Headline [UK], 1997**) Mariner is marooned on Tiger Island during "the storm of the century."

9. *Hell Gate* (**Feature [UK], 1998**) A revolutionary jet-ship, preparing for her maiden voyage, is hijacked.

10. *Powerdown* (**Feature [UK], 1999**) Mariner, aboard HMS *Erebus*, which is delivering supplies to NASA's antarctic bases, becomes involved in an attempt to rescue a stranded astronaut.

11. *High Water* (**Feature [UK], 2000**) The battered World War II destroyer *Colorado*, awaiting decommissioning on the Colorado River, gets swept away with Robin on board.

12. *Thunder Bay* (**Severn House, 2001**) Richard and Robin, hoping to launch their Heritage-Mariner line of SuperCats, retrieve the frozen, mutilated body of a woman tossed from a Russian freighter and search for a kidnapped female Mountie.

13. *Titan 10* (**Severn House, 2004**) *Prometheus 4*, first of a new generation of tankers, is headed for a rendezvous in the Barents Sea with former nuclear submarine *Titan 10*.

14. *Wolf Rock* (**Severn House, 2005**) Richard saves most of the crew of a ship from the shoals of Wolf Rock only to find that he is cast as the villain in a subsequent inquiry.

15. *Resolution Burning* (**Severn House, 2006**) French supertanker *Lady Mary* is adrift in the Antarctic Ocean near the island of Kerguelen.

16. *Cape Farewell* (**Severn House, 2006**) While trying to aid the stricken submarine *Quebec*, the tug *Sisyphus* is hit by a huge wave off Cape Farewell on the Greenland coast.

17. *Ship Breakers, The* (**Severn House, 2007**) Richard and Robin are separated while supplying retired tankers to a Russian consortium.

18. *High Wind in Java* (**Severn House, 2007**) Mariner's attempt to buy the revolutionary vessel *Tai Fun* is hampered by multimillionaire "eco-warrior" Nic Greenbaum and a series of disasters at the island of Pulau Baya, the ship's last port of call.

II. Elizabethan sleuth Tom Musgrave is the hero of a series of mysteries set in London in the 1590s. Some of Shakespeare's plays, such as *Romeo and Juliet* and *A Midsummer Night's Dream*, play a role.

1. *Point of Death, The* (**Severn House, 2001**) London, 1594. The actor playing Mercutio is murdered on the opening night of *Romeo and Juliet*.

2. *One Head Too Many* (**Severn House, 2002**) The severed head rolling around a Southwark football field doesn't seem to be connected with the heads hanging from the Traitors' Gate.

3. *Hound of the Borders, The* (**Severn House, 2003**) During rehearsals for the debut of *A Midsummer Night's Dream*, Tom Musgrave's brother John is found clinging to the high branches of an ancient tree, transfixed by a sighting of the great mythical hound, the Borgan.

4. *Silent Woman, The* (**Severn House, 2003**) A young messenger bearing a coded message of distress from the mute Lady Margaret Outram is stabbed through the heart.

Tourney, Leonard (Don)

Matthew Stock, clothier and constable of Chelmsford, Essex, England, and his wife, Joan, are the heroes of a series of mysteries set in Elizabethan England. Good mystery plots with a nice evocation of England in the early 1600s. Tourney, who teaches at the University of California, Santa Barbara, has published a novel about Shakespeare: *Time's Fool: A Mystery of Shakespeare* (St. Martin's, 2004).

1. *Players' Boy Is Dead, The* (**Harper, 1980**) Richard Mull, the youngest actor in a group of players entertaining the household of Sir Henry Saltmarsh, is found disemboweled in the stable.

2. *Low Treason* (**Dutton, 1982**) When Thomas Ingram, apprentice to a London jeweler, tries to return home to Chelmsford, he is set upon by a group of men and left for dead.

3. *Familiar Spirits* (**St. Martin's, 1984**) Witchcraft is evoked as the cause of what is really just plain murder.

4. *Bartholomew Fair Murders, The* (**St. Martin's, 1986**) Matthew Stock is off to Bartholomew Fair, where he encounters murder in the bear-baiting pit.

5. *Old Saxon Blood* (**St. Martin's, 1988**) At the express wish of Queen Elizabeth, Matthew and Joan investigate the questionable drowning of the Lord of Thornecombe Castle.

6. *Knaves Templar* (**St. Martin's, 1991**) The Stocks are the guests of Londoner Thomas Cooke, member of the Inns of Court, when three sudden student deaths occur.

7. *Witness of Bones* (**St. Martin's, 1992**) Matthew and Joan are summoned to London by Elizabeth's chief minister, Robert Cecil, who wants them to investigate the seeming resurrection of a Catholic martyr.

8. *Frobisher's Savage* (**St. Martin's, 1994**) Matthew investigates the murder of a wealthy farm family, said to be committed by a deaf-mute and an Eskimo.

Townsend, Sue (Susan Lilian)

The Adrian Mole Diaries, which have amused readers on both sides of the Atlantic, are pictures of messy adolescence as recorded by the adolescent himself. Adrian Mole, 13¾ years old when first we first encounter him, relates his woes from zit-ridden adolescence to angst-ridden middle age as he struggles with his sexual yearnings, his dysfunctional family, his writing ambitions (among other things, he tried to write a vowel-free novel), and the absurdities of school and the adult world in general. Although he reaches adulthood (he is a good father, at least), he never really sheds his nerdiness, his yearnings for the sexy Pandora, or his naïveté (he believes everything Tony Blair says). The diaries have been adapted for stage, radio, TV, and computer games. Leicester (England) native Sue Townsend also wrote *The Queen and I* (Soho, 1993), a satirical picture of how the royal family would cope if Britain were declared a republic.

1. *Adrian Mole Diaries, The* (**Grove, 1986**) The messy and inconsistent world of adulthood seen through the critical eyes of Adrian Mole, aspiring intellectual and poet, 13 ¾ years old. A combined edition of *The Secret Diary of Adrian Mole, Aged 13 ¾* (Methuen [UK], 1982) and *The Growing Pains of Adrian Mole* (Methuen [UK], 1984).

2. *Adrian Mole: The Lost Years* (**Soho, 1994**) Adrian's outrageous clothes and strong views about nearly everything make him a royal pain, but there are hints that he may surmount his long adolescence and become some semblance of an adult human being. Includes *Adrian Mole: The Wilderness Years* (Methuen [UK], 1993) and material published in *The True Confessions of Adrian Albert Mole, Margaret Hilda Roberts and Susan Lilian Townsend* (Methuen [UK], 1989) and *Adrian Mole: From Minor to Major* (Methuen [UK], 1991).

3. *Adrian Mole: The Cappuccino Years* (**Soho, 1999**) In 1997 Adrian, now 30, has been ditched by his second wife (a beautiful Nigerian) and saddled with a 2-year-old boy (not to mention a 12-year-old boy from his first wife). He dreams of making it big as a TV writer.

4. *Adrian Mole and the Weapons of Mass Destruction* (**Soho, 2005**) At the age of 34¾, Adrian finds himself with a canceled trip to Cyprus (Tony Blair said that Cyprus was only 45 minutes away from an attack by Saddam Hussein), deeply in debt, in a dead-end job with an independent bookseller, and living in a canal-front conversion of an old battery factory in Leicester. Then his elder son is posted to Iraq.

Tranter, Nigel

I. The success of films like *Braveheart* and *Rob Roy* testifies to a continuing interest in Scottish history on both sides of the Atlantic. The late Scottish author Nigel Tranter (d. 2000) was one of the most prolific suppliers of readable fiction and nonfiction accounts of this history. As well as nonfiction histories, guidebooks, and children's books, Tranter wrote more than 90 novels about Scottish history of nearly every era up to the 19th century. There are only a few short breaks in Tranter's fictional history of Scotland from the reign of Alexander II (1214–1249) to that of George IV (1820–1830). Perhaps if Tranter had reached the century mark (he lived to be 90), he would have filled in those gaps. The basic formula of a Tranter novel is to add romantic fiction to historical facts, providing a "painless course" in Scottish history. While his fictional characters are sometimes two-dimensional, his historical characters are usually brought out in vivid detail. His history was accurate and his knowledge of Scottish scenery phenomenal. The biggest problem American readers will find with Tranter's novels is getting ahold of them: many were never released in the United States.

Tranter published several trilogies and a couple of duos among his fiction. They are listed below in historical order. The Robert the Bruce trilogy detailed the rise to power of Robert the Bruce, who became Scotland's Robert I and in 1314 won the decisive Battle of Bannockburn, which rid the Scots of English kings. Tranter re-creates this fascinating chapter in Scottish history with a full measure of realism—these were bloody and brutal times—but with some tender moments of romance and domesticity that usually focus on Robert's beautiful and spirited wife, Elizabeth de Burgh. *Robert the Bruce* (Hodder [UK], 1985) is an omnibus containing numbers 1, 2, and 3.

1. ***Robert the Bruce: The Steps to the Empty Throne*** **(St. Martin's, 1969)** This account begins in 1296, when Edward I of England removed John Balliol as Scotland's ruler, and ends in 1306, when Robert killed John Comyn at Dumfries Castle and claimed the throne. Variant title: *The Steps to the Empty Throne.*

2. ***Robert the Bruce: The Path of the Hero King*** **(St. Martin's, 1972)** In 1306 Robert is defeated in battle after claiming the Scottish throne but recoups in the Hebrides. The story is continued to his victory at Bannockburn in 1314. Variant title: *The Path of the Hero King.*

3. ***Robert the Bruce: The Price of the King's Peace*** **(St. Martin's, 1972)** The period covered here begins in 1314, when the captive queen returns, and ends in 1328, when the Treaty of Edinburgh is signed by a dying King Robert. Variant title: *The Price of the King's Peace.*

II. The Stuart trilogy is set during the reign of the weak king Robert III (1390–1406), in which "overmighty" nobles, especially the Douglas family, tried to dominate the rule of Scotland. Omnibus: *The Stuart Trilogy* (Coronet [UK], 1986). Not published in the United States.

1. ***Lords of Misrule*** **(Hodder [UK], 1976)** Foul play by the Stuarts is suspected when the second Earl of Douglas is killed at the Battle of Otterburn (1388).

2. ***Folly of Princes, A*** **(Hodder [UK], 1977)** Scotland is in a weak way when the lame Robert III clings to power but doesn't rule effectively.

3. ***Captive Crown, The*** **(Hodder [UK], 1977)** Under the weak rule of the sickly Robert III, two young men stand out: Alex Stewart and his cousin John of Coull.

III. Two novels about the 15th-century Scottish princess Mary Stewart (c. 1450–c. 1490), sister of King James III, were published together as *The Mary Stewart Omnibus* (Trafalgar Square, 1998).

1. ***Price of a Princess*** **(Hodder [UK], 1994)** Mary, eldest daughter of James II of Scotland, is married against her will to Thomas Boyd, future Earl of Arran.

2. ***Lord in Waiting*** **(Hodder [UK], 1994)** Mary Stewart's talent for diplomacy leads her to be compared favorably with her brother, King James III.

IV. The death of James IV at the disastrous battle of Flodden Field (1513) left Scotland with a baby as heir. James V was to spend most of his realm as the prisoner of various special interests. Published together as *The James V Trilogy* (Trafalgar Square, 1996).

1. ***Riven Realm, The*** **(Beaufort, 1984)** The overly gallant King James IV lies dead on Flodden's Field (1513), leaving his infant son entrusted to two loyal lairds.

2. ***James, by the Grace of God*** **(Hodder [UK], 1985)** James V at the age of 12 is fought over by warring nobility. Only David Lindsay remains faithful to the king.

3. ***Rough Wooing, The*** **(Hodder [UK], 1986)** After the Scots break off the betrothal of the future Mary Queen of Scots to the future Edward VI of England, the English try to bring about the marriage by force.

V. The Master of Gray trilogy depicts the life of Patrick, Master of Gray (c. 1558–1612), "the most handsome man in Europe" and an inveterate plotter during the reigns of King James (VI of Scotland and I of England). All three volumes were published together as *The Master of Gray Trilogy* (Coronet [UK], 1996). *Mail Royal* (Hodder [UK], 1994), not part of the trilogy, details the efforts of Gray's bastard son to find the hidden casket of letters that Gray used to blackmail King James.

1. ***Master of Gray, The*** **(Hodder [UK], 1961)** Patrick, Master of Gray, returns from many years in France to influence the young James VI and plot against James's mother, the imprisoned Mary Queen of Scots. Variant title: *Lord and Master.*

2. ***Courtesan, The*** **(Hodder [UK], 1963)** Mary, illegitimate daughter of Patrick, returns to Scotland determined to counter her father's plotting.

3. ***Past Master*** **(Hodder [UK], 1965)** Tells the story of the lovers Mary Gray and the Duke of Lennox. Mary is caught up in the plot by her father, Patrick, to ensure that James VI should succeed to the English throne.

VI. A pair of novels details the life of James Graham, Earl and Marquis of Montrose (1612–1650), who remained loyal to Charles I and the future Charles II during the English Civil War and was hanged for his pains. Both novels were published together as *The Montrose Omnibus* (Trafalgar Square, 1987).

1. ***Young Montrose, The*** **(Hodder [UK], 1972)** James Graham, Earl of Montrose, remains faithful to Charles I during the Civil War I but is betrayed by his king.

2. ***Montrose, the Captain General*** **(Hodder [UK], 1973)** In 1650 Montrose returns from exile to Scotland to fight for Prince Charles.

VII. Rob Roy MacGregor (1671–1734) has been depicted in a Walter Scott novel (*Rob Roy;* Ballantine, 1817) and at least two movies (1954, starring Richard Todd, and 1995, starring Liam Neeson). The historical Rob Roy, who started as a lowborn member of the MacGregor clan, was something of a slippery character, but he tends to be portrayed sympathetically in fictional accounts, and Tranter is no exception. *Children of the Mist* (Hodder [UK], 1992), not part of the

MacGregor trilogy, is a prequel that tells how the MacGregor clan ran afoul of the powerful Campbell family and was proscribed.

1. *MacGregor's Gathering* (Hodder [UK], 1957) Describes Rob Roy's rise and his attempt to get the proscription against the MacGregor clan lifted.
2. *Clansman, The* (Hodder [UK], 1959) Rob Roy's strange behavior in holding his clan back at the Battle of Sheriffmuir (1715) is explained by Tranter.
3. *Gold for Prince Charlie* (Hodder [UK], 1962) The fictional love story of Duncan MacGregor and Caroline Cameron is told against the background of Rob Roy's attempts to enlist French gold in the Jacobite Rebellion (1715).

Traven, B.

This novelist's best-known work, *The Treasure of the Sierra Madre* (Knopf, 1935), was memorably filmed in 1948, with Humphrey Bogart starring as one of three greedy prospectors in search of a lost Mexican gold mine. The six Jungle novels, sometimes called the Coaba or Mahogany Cycle, are also set in Mexico. They show how the Indians and the mahogany forests were exploited by capitalists and the inevitable rebellion such inhumanity and greed provoked. B. Traven was deliberately mysterious about his identity. For a good summary of the problem presented by this pseudonymous author who claimed to be American, wrote in German, and lived in Mexico, see Michael Baumann's *B. Traven: An Introduction* (Univ. of New Mexico Pr., 1976) or Will Wyatt's *The Secret of the Sierra Madre: The Man Who Was B. Traven* (Doubleday, 1980).

1. *Caretta, The* (Hill & Wang, 1970) Set in the Chiapas region of southern Mexico in the time of Porfirio Diaz's dictatorship (before 1910), this book shows the plight of the poor peon—more slave than peasant—through the story of Andreu Ugaldo, an oxcart driver. First published in Germany in 1931 as *Der Karren*. English translation by Basil Creighton first published in the United Kingdom in 1935. American edition "prepared by the author."
2. *Government* (Hill & Wang, 1971) The Mexican government, whose entrepreneurs like Don Gabriel Ordunez profit from mistreating poor workers, is contrasted with the more egalitarian government of an Indian tribe. First published in Germany in 1931 as *Regierung*. English translation by Basil Creighton.
3. *March to the Monteria* (Hill & Wang, 1971) Andreu Ugaldo journeys through the jungle to the labor camp on the mahogany plantation. First published in Germany in 1933 as *Der Marsch ins Reich der Caoba*. English translation first published in the United Kingdom in 1960 as *March to Caobaland* (perhaps translated by the author).
4. *Trozas* (Dee, 1994) This volume, only recently translated into English, shows life on the mahogany plantation and the grueling work of chopping down trees and cutting the mahogany logs to size. First published in Germany in 1936 as *Die Troza*. English translation by Hugh Young.
5. *Rebellion of the Hanged, The* (Hill & Wang, 1972) Violence breaks out among the Indian workers, and they learn to fight for their own interests, leaving the plantation. First published in Germany in 1936 as *Die Rebellion der Gehenkten*. English translation by Charles Duff first published in the United Kingdom in 1952.
6. *General from the Jungle* (Hill & Wang, 1972) The little army of rebels skirmishes with the government forces, bringing up the rear guard of the revolution. First published in Sweden in 1939 as *Djungelgeneralen*. Original German version published in 1940 as *Ein General kommt aus dem Dschungel*. English translation by Desmond Vesey first published in the United Kingdom in 1954.

Treece, Henry

I. Treece was an English poet and writer of historical novels for adults and young adults with a talent for reconstructing ancient Celtic Britain and an ability to draw readers into the plausible primitive psychology of his characters. The four loosely connected novels listed below range in time from the Bronze Age to the 6th century CE. Treece's unromanticized version of the King Arthur legend in *The Great Captains* makes an interesting contrast with the accounts of Mary Stewart (q.v.) and T. H. White (q.v.). In *The Green Man* (Putnam, 1966), the Hamlet legend is tracked back to its Dark Age origins. The Viking Saga trilogy (1956–1960) is a YA series.

1. *Golden Strangers, The* (Random House, 1957) Four thousand years ago, fair-haired "Aryan" people armed with metal tools triumph over the dark Neanderthal tribes who live in southern England. Variant title: *The Invaders*.
2. *Dark Island, The* (Random House, 1953) In the 1st century CE, Roman imperial forces with their invincible elephants conquer the Celtic tribe led by Caradoc. Variant title: *The Savage Warriors*.
3. *Red Queen, White Queen* (Random House, 1958) Boadicea's rebellion, around 60 CE, is seen through the eyes of the Roman soldier Gemellus, who has been dispatched with his Celtic half brother Duatha to kill the queen. Variant title: *The Pagan Queen*.
4. *Great Captains, The* (Random House, 1956) King Arthur appears as Artos the Bear, a rough figure in this history of 6th-century Britain.

II. A trilogy of loosely connected novels tracks some Greek myths—Jason, Electra, and Oedipus—back to their prehistoric Mediterranean origins.

1. *Jason* (Random House, 1961) The roots of the Minoan-Hellene conflict are explored in this novel about the mythical Jason, the Argonauts, the Golden Fleece, and the sinister priestess Medea.
2. *Amber Princess, The* (Random House, 1962) The Orestes legend is treated here as Electra, Orestes's sister, awaits the return of her brother to avenge the murder of Agamemnon, their father. UK title: *Electra*.
3. *Eagle King, The* (Random House, 1965) In a synthesis of myths, the club-footed Oedipus's long quest runs afoul of the priestess Jocasta and an evil destiny. UK title: *Oedipus*.

Tremayne, Peter

PSEUDONYM OF Peter Berresford Ellis

I. Sister Fidelma of Cashel, daughter and sister of 7th-century CE Irish "kings," is smart, highly educated, and outspoken, perhaps overbearing at times, but with the intelligence, sense of right, and energy to see that justice is done. Fidelma, usually accompanied by her friend, the Saxon Brother Eadulf, solves a series of mysteries set in a "golden age" of Irish gender equality, learning, and enlightenment. Readers find these books intellectually stimulating and enjoyable, although some complain about overmuch historical detail. *An Ensuing Evil and Others* (St. Martin's, 2006) is a collection of stories without Sister Fidelma. "Peter Tremayne" is the historian Peter Berresford Ellis, an authority on the ancient Celts.

1. *Absolution by Murder* (St. Martin's, 1996) During a conference held between the Irish Church and the Church of Rome in an attempt to iron out doctrinal differences, a Celtic spokesman is murdered. Originally published in the United Kingdom in 1994.

2. *Shroud for the Archbishop* (St. Martin's, 1995) Autumn 664. The Archbishop of Canterbury is found garroted in his chamber. The chief suspect is an Irish monk seen fleeing from the scene.

3. *Suffer Little Children* (St. Martin's, 1997) Sister Fidelma investigates the stabbing death of Venerable Dacan, an elder from the kingdom of Lagin. Originally published in the United Kingdom in 1995.

4. *Subtle Serpent, The* (St. Martin's, 1998) The murder and decapitation of a nun and a drifting, empty cargo ship may be connected. Originally published in the United Kingdom in 1996.

5. *Spider's Web, The* (St. Martin's, 1999) A deaf-mute is charged in the murder of a rural chieftain. Originally published in the United Kingdom in 1997.

6. *Valley of the Shadow* (St. Martin's, 2000) While negotiating with a Druid chieftain for the construction of a Christian church and school, Sister Fidelma and Brother Eadulf find the bodies of 36 young men covered with ritual scars. Originally published in the United Kingdom in 1998.

7. *Monk Who Vanished, The* (St. Martin's, 2001) Religious relics disappear from a monastery. Originally published in the United Kingdom in 1999.

8. *Act of Mercy* (St. Martin's, 2001) Sister Fidelma investigates the murder of a shipmate during a seagoing voyage off the Irish coast. Originally published in the United Kingdom in 1999.

9. *Hemlock at Vespers* (St. Martin's, 2000) Fifteen short stories about Sister Fidelma.

10. *Our Lady of Darkness* (St. Martin's, 2002) Brother Eadulf has been convicted of rape and murder and is about to be executed. Originally published in the United Kingdom in 2000.

11. *Smoke in the Wind* (St. Martin's, 2003) Sister Fidelma's ship is blown off course to Wales, where she finds that an entire community of monks has vanished. Originally published in the United Kingdom in 2001.

12. *Haunted Abbot, The* (St. Martin's, 2004) Sister Fidelma and Brother Eadulf travel to East Anglia to visit a childhood friend of Eadulf's only to find him murdered. Originally published in the United Kingdom in 2002.

13. *Badger's Moon* (St. Martin's, 2005) Murders are committed on the nights of three consecutive full moons. Originally published in the United Kingdom in 2003.

14. *Leper's Bell, The* (St. Martin's, 2006) Sister Fidelma returns home to her brother's castle only to discover that her son's nurse has been murdered and her son is missing. Originally published in the United Kingdom in 2004.

15. *Whispers of the Dead* (St. Martin's, 2004) Fifteen Sister Fidelma short stories.

16. *Master of Souls* (St. Martin's, 2006) Sister Fidelma investigates the murder of an abbess and the disappearance of six young female *religieuse*. Originally published in the United Kingdom in 2005.

17. *Prayer for the Damned, A* (St. Martin's, 2007) Fidelma and Eadulf are about to be married under old Irish custom, but Abbot Ultan, who was to perform the ceremony, is murdered. Originally published in the United Kingdom in 2006.

II. Before he published historical mysteries, Peter Tremayne was the author of several novels in the horror genre, including riffs on Frankenstein's monster, She/Ayesha, zombies, the Loch Ness Monster, and a Dracula trilogy that traces the history of the sanguinary count from the 15th century to the present. *Dracula Lives!* (Signet [UK], 1993) is an omnibus volume containing all three novels.

1. *Bloodright* (Walker, 1979) Subtitle: *Memoir of Mircea, Son of Vlad Tepes, Prince of Walachia, Also Known as Dracula . . .* A document written by Mircea, son of the 15th-century Count Dracula, is found in mysterious circumstances. Originally published in the United Kingdom in 1977 as *Dracula Unborn*.

2. *Revenge of Dracula, The* (Walker, 1979) An enigmatic jade figurine brings nightmares to its owner, and the woman he loves seems possessed. Originally published in the United Kingdom in 1978.

3. *Dracula, My Love* (Dell, 1983) Following the death of her lover, governess Morag MacLeod travels to Transylvania, where she is captivated by the evil count. Originally published in the United Kingdom in 1980.

III. The versatile Tremayne/Ellis also wrote a sword-and-sorcery Celtic fantasy trilogy about a land called Lan-Kern, which exists both before and after the 20th century.

1. *Fires of Lan-Kern, The* (St. Martin's, 1980) Twentieth-century botanist Frank Dryden is propelled into Lan-Kern, a land that exists both in the past and in the future. Originally published in the United Kingdom in 1978.

2. *Destroyers of Lan-Kern, The* (Methuen [UK], 1982) No annotation available. Not published in the United States.

3. *Buccaneers of Lan-Kern, The* (Methuen [UK], 1983) No annotation available. Not published in the United States.

Trenhaile, John (Stevens)

I. English lawyer and author Trenhaile is one of the leading writers of novels of international intrigue. Several of Trenhaile's books are told from the Russian viewpoint in an attempt to show that "Soviet man derives from the same stock of common humanity." Stepan Povin, protagonist of three suspenseful psychological thrillers, is a secret Christian (and homosexual) who is passing KGB secrets to British intelligence chief Sir Richard Bryant.

1. *Man Called Kyril, The* (Congdon, 1983) Kyril is told to defect to the West by Marshal Stanov, head of the KGB, to expose a mole planted by British intelligence. UK title: *Kyril*.

2. *View from the Square, A* (Congdon, 1984) Stepan Povin, double agent and secret Christian, is now head of the KGB, but he is about to be betrayed by a trusted assistant.

3. *Nocturne for the General* (Congdon, 1985) Former intelligence chief Povin, betrayed by his deputy and marked for death, languishes in an Arctic detention camp.

II. Simon Young, wealthy Hong Kong industrialist and Red Chinese agent, is the key to a trio of complex, suspenseful novels about politics and espionage in East Asia.

1. *Mah-Jongg Spies, The* (Dutton, 1986) Red Chinese agents approach Simon Young about helping them to sabotage a Soviet bank that is seeking a toehold in Hong Kong. UK title: *The Mahjong Spies*.

2. *Gates of Exquisite View, The* (Dutton, 1988) The Red Chinese contract with Young to develop a new computer-based defense system, then allow the work to be done in Taiwan.

3. *Scroll of Benevolence, The* (Collins [UK], 1988) The Scroll of Benevolence is the code name for the scheme of the Club of Twenty, the economic leaders of Hong Kong, to transfer their assets before the Chinese takeover.

Trevanian

PSEUDONYM OF Rod(ney) Whitaker

Trevanian is the pseudonym of a late professor of film and drama at the University of Texas who captured an immediate following with his two books about the homicidal and amorous adventures of Dr. Jonathan Hemlock, art professor and secret assassin. Hemlock was rescued from an underprivileged childhood by a wealthy spinster, and his innate discrimination has won him professional eminence but not the wealth to support his tastes. His other inborn trait, a shocking deficiency in conscience revealed by army testing, brings him lucrative freelance assignments from the mysterious albino Yurasis Dragon, head of CII, a counterespionage agency. A fair amount of grisly detail is sprinkled throughout these ironic and suspenseful entertainments. The film of *The Eiger Sanction* (1975) was a starring vehicle for Clint Eastwood.

1. *Eiger Sanction, The* (Crown, 1972) Revenge prompts Hemlock to accept a hazardous sanction (assassination) assignment, which tests his mountain-climbing skills and brings him the companionship of the tantalizing Jemima Brown.
2. *Loo Sanction, The* (Crown, 1973) Amazing Grace, a black bombshell, and the green-eyed Irish beauty Maggie aid and abet Hemlock as he wrests incriminating films of high-ranking British government officials from a perverse underworld figure.

Trocheck, Kathy Hogan

I. J. Callahan Garrity, former policewoman and failed private investigator, runs a cleaning service in Atlanta called "House Mouse" with Edna, her bossy, smart-mouthed mom. Although she is kept busy during the day by her cleaning schedule, Callahan has a live-in boyfriend named Mac McAuliffe, a past brush with breast cancer, and a jaundiced view of anyone who isn't a cleaning lady.

1. *Every Crooked Nanny* (HarperCollins, 1992) Society matron Lilah Rose Beemish hires Callahan to track down the family's Mormon nanny, who has absconded with some furs, jewels, and incriminating business secrets.
2. *To Live and Die in Dixie* (HarperCollins, 1993) While cleaning the mansion of racist Civil War buff Elliott Littlefield, Garrity's minions find the bloody corpse of a 17-year-old girl.
3. *Homemade Sin* (HarperCollins, 1994) Callahan won't believe that the shooting death of cousin Patti McNair was a random slaying.
4. *Happy Never After* (HarperCollins, 1995) Garrity is hired to find Delores Fontaine, a member of her favorite sixties singing group, the Velvet Teens.
5. *Heart Trouble* (Harper Collins, 1996) Bad racial feelings are stirred up when wealthy white woman Whitney Dobbs runs over a black child. Then Whitney is killed while doing her prescribed "community work."
6. *Strange Brew* (HarperCollins, 1997) Jackson Poole, microbrewery owner, is found dead after a tornado in a house he is renovating.
7. *Midnight Clear* (HarperCollins, 1998) Callahan's black-sheep brother, Brian, turns up after 10 years with the three-year-old daughter he has "liberated" from her unfit mother.
8. *Irish Eyes* (HarperCollins, 2000) On the way home from a St. Patrick's Day party, Garrity and former Atlanta PD partner Bucky Deavers stumble on a liquor store holdup. Bucky gets shot in the head, which is only the beginning of his troubles.

II. Truman Kicklighter, retired Associated Press writer living at the Fountain of Youth Residential Hotel in St. Petersburg, Florida, is the hero of a couple of mysteries. Truman, who has to devise ingenious means of keeping himself in funds, distracts himself with a little amateur sleuthing.

1. *Lickety Split* (HarperCollins, 1996) Truman's best pal, Mel Wisnewski, who recently arrived from Pennsylvania with symptoms of Alzheimer's disease, is found huddled by the corpse of race tout Rosie Figueroa at the local dog track.
2. *Crash Course* (HarperCollins, 1997) After Jackalleen Canaday, black waitress and pal of Truman's, goes back to a used-car dealership to complain about the lemon she bought, she finds the body of the person who sold her the car.

Trollope, Anthony

I. Trollope's popularity declined sharply after his death in 1882, partly because a posthumously published autobiography scandalized readers by revealing his frankly commercial attitude toward writing. Yet some of his books remained available and in high regard; in 1932 Virginia Woolf called *The Small House at Allington* one of the two perfect English novels (the other being *Pride and Prejudice*). Today, after a boost from the masterly BBC dramatization of the Pallisers (1974), Trollope is one of the most widely read Victorian novelists, and modern readers are discovering the joys of adjusting to the leisurely style and humor of his solidly satisfying characters and stories. Even occasional Trollope readers will want to browse through Michael Hardwick's informative and entertaining *Guide to Anthony Trollope* (Scribner, 1974).

Trollope's first and best-known series, the Chronicles of Barsetshire, grew out of its successful first novel and was written sporadically over a period of 14 years. As was customary with novels of the day, most of these were serialized before taking book form. Dates and publishers listed below are for the first English monographs. Trollope began appearing in the United States in the 1890s. The entry for Angela Thirkell (q.v.) offers stories about Barsetshire's 20th-century residents.

1. *Warden, The* (Longman [UK], 1855) This book concerns Eleanor Harding and her father, Septimus, a gentle and innocent old cleric who is accused of profiting unduly from his sinecure as the warden of an almshouse for 12 old men. The cathedral town of Salisbury is thought to have been the model for Barchester.
2. *Barchester Towers* (Longman [UK], 1857) Thomas Proudie, an insignificant man with a domineering wife, is appointed the new bishop, and Eleanor Harding, newly widowed, is courted by several suitors. Probably the most popular of Trollope's 47 novels.
3. *Dr. Thorne* (Chapman & Hall [UK], 1858) Dr. Thorne faces a series of moral dilemmas as his ward Mary's love for Frank Gresham grows.
4. *Framley Parsonage* (Smith & Elder [UK], 1861) Brother and sister Mark and Lucy Robarts both displease Lady Lufton of Framley Court but for different reasons. Dr. Thorne appears again in this volume, as do several characters from the Palliser books (see below), including the Duke of Omnium.
5. *Small House at Allington, The* (Smith & Elder [UK], 1864) Trollope did not consider this gem a part of the Barsetshire series, but it was included by his publishers in the 1879 omnibus edition and has been counted in the series ever since. It concerns a jilted maiden, Lily Dale, who lives with her widowed mother and sister at the Little House. Several characters from the Palliser novels make brief appearances in this volume too.
6. *Last Chronicle of Barset, The* (Chapman & Hall [UK], 1867) In what some critics consider to be Trollope's closest approach to tragedy and his best novel, the impecunious Reverend Josiah Crawley of Hogglestock is persecuted by Mrs. Proudie for an alleged theft.

II. The Palliser novels, also known as the Parliamentary novels, were conceived by Trollope as a series that would show the destinies of certain characters closely interwoven into a tapestry depicting the faults, frailties, and vices as well as the virtues, graces, and strengths of the upper classes. Considered by many to be the best 19th-century fictional portrait of English politics, the Palliser series influenced many later English "realists," including C. P. Snow (q.v.). A one-volume abridgement, *The Pallisers* (Coward, 1974), was issued in conjunction with Masterpiece Theatre's airing of the BBC dramatization of the series.

1. *Can You Forgive Her?* **(Chapman & Hall [UK], 1864)** Lady Glencora, a vivacious Scottish heiress married to dry and politically preoccupied Plantagenet Palliser, is tempted to run off with her first love.
2. *Phineas Finn* **(James Virtue [UK], 1869)** The leading characters of this story are Phineas Finn, a young Irishman entering English society, and the women in his life: his childhood sweetheart; his first advisor, Lady Laura Standish; and the rich widow Marie Goesler.
3. *Eustace Diamonds, The* **(Chapman & Hall [UK], 1872)** The pretty schemer, Lizzie Greystock, who is Sir Florian's widow, plays a part in the theft of the Eustace diamonds.
4. *Phineas Redux* **(Chapman & Hall [UK], 1873)** Phineas Finn, back from Ireland, raises Laura's hopes, gets entangled in a murder trial, and is saved by Marie Goesler.
5. *Prime Minister, The* **(Chapman & Hall [UK], 1876)** Glencora uses all her talents to help Plantagenet (now Duke of Omnium) become prime minister, but she finally goes too far.
6. *Duke's Children, The* **(Chapman & Hall [UK], 1880)** Plantagenet copes with Silverbridge and Gerald, who misbehave at school and run up debts, while Mary seems determined to marry unsuitably.

Troyat, Henri

PSEUDONYM OF Lev Tarassoff

I. Troyat's biographies, especially his masterful *Tolstoy* (Doubleday, 1967), have overshadowed his fiction, but this five-novel series, the Seed and the Fruit (*Les semailles et les moissons*), is a delightful family chronicle of French life not to be missed. Born in Russia, Troyat spent his youth in France. He has caught the special Gallic flavor, which pervades these books. The story begins with young Amelie's coming-of-age in 1912 and ends as her daughter Elizabeth sees France liberated in 1944.

1. *Amelie in Love* **(Simon & Schuster, 1956)** Shy and innocent at 17, young Amelie is courted by Jean, a local boy, until Pierre comes to capture her heart. Translated from the French by Lilly Duplaix. Originally published in 1953 as *Les semailleds et les moissons*.
2. *Amelie and Pierre* **(Simon & Schuster, 1957)** Amelie runs the café very successfully, while Pierre serves in the army and eventually returns home injured. Translated from the French by Mary V. Dodge. Originally published in 1955 as *Amelie*.
3. *Elizabeth* **(Simon & Schuster, 1959)** Elizabeth, the 10-year-old daughter of Amelie and Pierre, goes to convent school and stays with cousins in the country. Translated from the French by Nicholas Monjo. Originally published in 1956 as *La grive*.
4. *Tender and Violent Elizabeth* **(Simon & Schuster, 1960)** At 19 Elizabeth is torn between the sensual and violent Christian and the gentle and loving Patrice. Translated from the French by Mildred Marmur. Originally published in 1957 as *Tendre et violente Elizabeth*.

5. *Encounter, The* **(Simon & Schuster, 1962)** Elizabeth runs her shop alone in German-occupied Paris, and she meets the widowed Boris, a character who also appears in *Strangers on Earth* (see below). Translated from the French by Gerard Hopkins. Originally published in 1958 as *La rencontre*.

II. Troyat's understanding of Russian character is shown in the trilogy While the Earth Endures (*Tant que la terre durera*), which depicts the effect of the Russian Revolution on an upper-class family, presumably like his own, who became exiles in Paris. Troyat also wrote a five-volume series about Napoléon's rise to power, the Light of the Just (*La lumiere des justes*), only two volumes of which have been translated into English—*The Brotherhood of the Red Poppy* (Simon & Schuster, 1961) and *The Baroness* (Simon & Schuster, 1961)—as well as three trilogies that haven't been translated into English: *Les Eygletiere, Les Heritiers de l'avenor,* and *Le Moscovite*. Sylvie is a juvenile trilogy about a Parisian girl growing up.

1. *My Father's House* **(Duell, 1951)** The story of a love triangle between Tania and Michael Danov and their best friend, Volodia, covers the years from 1888 to 1914. Translated from the French by David Hapgood. Originally published in 1947 as *Tant que la terre durera*.
2. *Red and the White, The* **(Crowell, 1956)** The revolution affects the Danov family in various ways; their responses range from idealistic support to ardent czarist loyalties. UK title: *Sackcloth and Ashes*. Translated from the French by Anthony Hinton. Originally published in 1948 as *Le sac et la centre*.
3. *Strangers on Earth* **(Crowell, 1958)** The Danov family, exiled in Paris during the 1920s and 1930s, adjust and become reconciled to their new circumstances. Translated from the French by Anthony Hinton. Originally published in 1950 as *Étrangers sur la terre*.

Tryon, Thomas

The late movie actor (*The Cardinal*) and popular horror novelist—*The Other* (Knopf, 1971) and *Harvest House* (Knopf, 1973)—wrote a pair of historical novels set in pre–Civil War Connecticut. The feud between the abolitionist Talcotts and the pro-slavery Grimes family, the first families of Pequot Landing, is the main link between these two parts of an unfinished trilogy.

1. *Wings of Morning, The* **(Knopf, 1990)** Miller's daughter Georgie Ross, childhood friend of Sinjin Grimes and former servant and friend to the Talcotts, is the main protagonist of events set in the 1820s and 1830s.
2. *In the Fire of Spring* **(Knopf, 1992)** It's 1841 and the Talcott and Grimes families are still feuding. Fuel is added to the fire by the opening of a school for young black women.

Tucker, Kerry

Upper West Side Manhattanite and photojournalist Libby Kincaid is also a part-time amateur sleuth. Libby is a credible character in a series of fast, funny, action-filled mysteries.

1. *Still Waters* **(HarperCollins, 1991)** Libby reluctantly turns sleuth to investigate her brother Avery's alleged suicide in their Ohio hometown.
2. *Cold Feet* **(HarperCollins, 1992)** Libby is photographing the Non-Pareils, a veteran troupe of tap dancers, when the lead dancer is poisoned by a snakebite.

3. *Death Echo* (HarperCollins, 1993) Libby is visiting Ohio when old friend Pam Bates asks her to investigate the mysterious behavior of her foster mother, who seems to have turned into an agoraphobe.

4. *Drift Away* (HarperCollins, 1994) The press and police believe that the rapist she was defending killed lawyer Andrea Hales, but Libby has reason to believe that Andrea's husband is the culprit.

Turnbull, Peter

I. Glasgow, Scotland's largest city, is the scene for a procedural series featuring the policemen of "P Division." Glasgow and the men who police it are the protagonists rather than any individual in this gritty, intricately detailed series. Turnbull, a Yorkshire native, lives in Glasgow.

1. *Deep and Crisp and Even* (St. Martin's, 1982) Police find a couple of knifed corpses in the Glasgow snow, complete with notes from the killer.

2. *Dead Knock* (St. Martin's, 1983) Dominique Pahl comes into the police station to announce her own prospective murder.

3. *Fair Friday* (St. Martin's, 1983) Police investigate the alley murder of Bill McGarrigle, reporter for a Glasgow daily.

4. *Big Money* (St. Martin's, 1984) A post-office raid leaves a trail of murder and police corruption but few solid clues.

5. *Two Way Cut* (St. Martin's, 1985) A businessman unwilling to sell his land to an unscrupulous entrepreneur turns up as a headless corpse.

6. *Condition Purple* (St. Martin's, 1989) P Division investigates the death of a prostitute found with a knife wound in her neck, needle marks on her arms, and a tattoo with a man's name.

7. *And Did Murder Him* (St. Martin's, 1991) Petty drug pusher and addict Eddie Wroe is found stabbed to death in an alley.

8. *Long Day Monday* (St. Martin's, 1993) Twenty-five years separate the discoveries of two abandoned cars, each carefully parked near a stuffed toy rabbit.

9. *Killing Floor, The* (St. Martin's, 1995) The headless corpse of a social worker is found in the shrubbery near an empty house.

10. *Man with No Face, The* (St. Martin's, 1998) A small-time Glasgow thief is found with his face shot away just hours after he has been released from prison, where he had served time for arson.

II. Yorkshire native Turnbull has abandoned Glasgow for a series of procedurals set in the English city of York. Leading protagonists are Chief Inspector George Hennessey and Sergeant Yellich of the Yorkshire Constabulary, good family men and excellent detectives. Many of the crimes they investigate were committed in the past or have their roots in the past.

1. *Fear of Drowning* (St. Martin's, 2000) Hennessey and Yellich are called upon to solve the murder of a middle-aged husband and wife who, at first glimpse, seemed to have no enemies.

2. *Deathtrap* (Severn, 2000) The death of a local journalist turns out to have links to an unsolved murder case from years before.

3. *Perils and Dangers* (Severn, 2001) The murder of a professional blackmailer in his study leads to a difficult search.

4. *Return, The* (Severn, 2001) A skeleton with a broken skull discovered in a field turns out to be that of a law student missing for 20 years.

5. *After the Flood* (Severn, 2002) A Yorkshire farmer discovers the corpse of long-buried woman, but the head doesn't match the rest of the body.

6. *Dark Secrets* (Severn, 2003) An old drunk's confession that he had witnessed the murder of a young woman 20 years before leads to a weed-filled lot and four corpses.

7. *All Roads Leadeth* (Severn, 2003) Femme fatale Sandra Picardie seems to be the link between the murders of Muriel Bradbury and Jane Frost and the disappearance of Katie Ilford.

8. *Treasure Trove* (Severn, 2004) The bodies of four members of the aristocratic but eccentric Imgey family turn up in a deserted house in the village of Long Hundred.

9. *Dance Master, The* (Severn, 2004) A bag of bones containing the remains of 12 different women found by a homeless man points to a serial killer.

10. *Hopes and Fears* (Allison & Busby [UK], 2004) The frozen body of a young Russian student who had disappeared many years earlier is found in a wood in the Vale of York.

11. *Legacy, The* (Allison & Busby [UK], 2005) Musician Nigel Swannell discovers a headless, handless corpse in the undergrowth of gorse.

12. *Chill Factor, The* (Severn House, 2005) A man who has no record and has never been inside a police station may be behind a series of murders that look like professional hits.

13. *False Knight* (Severn House, 2006) Unhappily married Mary Golightly was looking happier lately, but then a garbageman finds her thigh in a refuse sack.

14. *Fire Burn* (Severn House, 2007) A trio of badly burned corpses turns up, one after another.

15. *Chelsea Smile* (Severn House, 2007) Duncan Percival, rendered a vegetable after a vicious attack, eventually dies.

16. *Once a Biker* (Severn House, 2007) The murder case of two members of the same bikers' gang is reopened 20 years after the crime after a deathbed confession.

Turow, Scott

Scott Turow is the author of a series of well-written, highly entertaining legal thrillers replete with well-delineated courtroom scenes. Cook County, Illinois, site of Chicago, Turow's home base, is the likely model for Turow's fictional Kindle County, where endemic municipal corruption and flaws in the criminal justice system engage a cast of characters such as deputy prosecutor Rusty Sabich (numbers 1 and 8), defense attorney and judge George Mason (numbers 5 and 8), and newspaperman Stewart Dubinsky (numbers 1 and 7). Scott Turow, who reached best-seller status with his first novel, *Presumed Innocent*, is a partner in a Chicago law firm and a former assistant US district attorney. His first publication was the nonfiction *One L: An Account of Life in the First Year at Harvard Law School* (Putnam, 1977), which has become required reading for law students. Another nonfiction book, *Ultimate Punishment: A Lawyer's Reflections on Dealing with the Death Penalty* (Farrar, 2003), is a detailed examination of capital punishment. *Presumed Innocent* was made into a film starring Harrison Ford (1990). *The Burden of Proof* was a TV film, and *Reversible Errors* was made into a TV miniseries.

1. *Presumed Innocent* (Farrar, Straus, 1987) Rusty Sabich, a big city deputy prosecutor, assigned to investigate the murder of a female colleague, finds himself on trial for the murder of a woman with whom he had an adulterous affair.

2. *Burden of Proof, The* (Farrar, Straus, 1990) Defense attorney Sandy Stern (who appeared in number 1) returns home to find his wife dead in an apparent suicide.

3. *Pleading Guilty* (Farrar, Straus, 1993) Former cop Mike Malloy is called upon to investigate the disappearance of a highly placed partner and $5.5 million from a prestigious law firm.

4. *Laws of Our Fathers, The* (Farrar, Straus, 1996) The shooting death of the wife of a state senator reunites a group of 1960s radicals who had drifted apart.

5. *Personal Injuries* (Farrar, Straus, 1999) In a story narrated by his defense attorney, George Mason, failed actor, womanizer, and corrupt personal injury lawyer Robbie Feaver turns FBI informer to avoid prosecution for various crimes and misdemeanors.

6. *Reversible Errors* (Farrar, Straus, 2002) Romeo Gandolph, who has confessed to a series of murders, recants his testimony while on death row, leaving his attorney, Martin Raven, looking at another person who has also confessed to the crimes.

7. *Ordinary Heroes* (Farrar, Straus, 2005) Retired newspaperman Stewart Dubinsky, a character in number 1, turns up a collection of letters dating from World II revealing the hidden past of his father, Captive David Dubin.

8. *Limitations* (Pinnacle, 2006) George Mason, a character in number 5, now an appellate judge, is faced with a tough decision in a high-profile sexual assault case.

Turtledove, Harry (Norman)

I. Harry Turtledove, American novelist and historian, is a master of the alternate-history subgenre. In his best-known series, he postulates about what would have happened if the South had won the Civil War at the battle of Antietam in 1862. The Confederate States would have become independent and there would have been a series of wars, including the "Mexican" war of 1881 and a World War I and World War II with a different configuration of allies and results. Number 1 is a prequel to the series, while numbers 2 through 4 form the Great War trilogy; numbers 5 through 7, the American Empire trilogy; and numbers 8 through 11, Settling Accounts. This is a vast series with many continuing characters, both historical and fictional. Of course, the historical characters play somewhat different roles from the ones they played in real life—Upton Sinclair becomes US president—and Turtledove has no compunction about killing off major characters in midstream. Turtledove returned to World War II in the Worldwar and Colonization series (see series II, below), in which science-fiction elements play a major role, and Days of Infamy, two novels in which the Japanese occupy Hawaii after Pearl Harbor (see series III, below). The Darkness series envisions a world war in a place where magic works (see series IV, below), while the War between the Provinces series restages the Civil War in another world, where magic plays a greater role than technology (see series V, below). Series 6 through 8 are not really connected. Series 6 is about an alternate Byzantine Empire. Series 7 is about a fantasy world in the Dark Ages. Series 8, Crosstime Traffic, is set in the late 21st century.

1. *How Few Remain* (Del Rey, 1997) The truncated United States wages war against the Confederate States of America in 1881.

2. *American Front* (Del Rey, 1998) The Great War, in which most of the action occurs in North America, finds the United States, allied with Germany, warring against the Confederate States, allied with the Canadians, the British, and the French. First novel in the Great War series.

3. *Walk in Hell* (Del Rey, 1999) The Great War continues, with Negroes revolting in the CSA and Mormons revolting in the USA. Second novel in the Great War series.

4. *Breakthroughs* (Del Rey, 2000) The Great War begins to tilt in favor of the USA. Book 3 in the Great War series.

5. *Blood and Iron* (Del Rey, 2001) In the pro-business USA, or American Empire, which includes a good bit of what was Canada, the Socialists oppose the Democrats. In the CSA, inflation and racism run rampant, as the Freedom Party, with Jake Featherston at its head, begins its rise. Part 1 of the American Empire series.

6. *Center Cannot Hold, The* (Del Rey, 2001) The Freedom Party is still on the rise in the CSA, as Wade Hampton IV is assassinated. President Upton Sinclair has his hands full in the USA.

7. *Victorious Opposition, The* (Del Rey, 2003) Jake Featherston is ruler of the CSA. The American Empire faces opposition in "Occupied Canada." Part 3 of the American Empire series.

8. *Return Engagement* (Del Rey, 2004) Jake Featherston orders a surprise attack on the USA. The Confederate blitzkrieg, which initiates "World War II," sends the forces of the American Empire reeling. Book 1 of Settling Accounts.

9. *Drive to the East* (Del Rey, 2005) The Confederates push eastward through Ohio and into Pennsylvania. US president Al Smith dies. Book 2 of Settling Accounts.

10. *Grapple, The* (Del Rey, 2006) The Confederate forces, reeling after a loss around Pittsburgh, are in danger of being forced out of Ohio by the US Army, led by General Irving Morrell, but a Mormon rebellion in the West complicates matters. Meanwhile, Jake Featherston is pursuing a "final solution" to the "Negro problem" in a death camp in Texas. Book 3 of Settling Accounts.

11. *In at the Death* (Del Rey, 2007) The closing months of the war and its aftermath are described. Book 4 of Settling Accounts.

II. "The Race," a small reptilian people, invade an Earth embroiled in World War II and find, to their surprise, that mankind has made large technological strides since the Middle Ages. The Worldwar (numbers 1–4) and Colonization (numbers 5–7) series depict how this war of alien invasion plays out in a series of shifting alliances both with and against the lizardlike invaders. Number 8 is a coda to the series. Numbers 1 and 2 were reissued together in *Aftershocks/Down to Earth* (Ballantine, 2002).

1. *In the Balance* (Ballantine, 1993) Planet Earth is invaded by the Race, a small reptilian people, in the midst of World War II. Alternate title: *Worldwar: In the Balance.*

2. *Tilting the Balance* (Ballantine, 1995) Takes place days after the events in number 1. The Race is waging victorious war against the Germans, Soviets, and Americans. Alternate title: *Worldwar: Tilting the Balance.*

3. *Upsetting the Balance* (Ballantine, 1996) The Race invades England only to be attacked by mustard gas. The Soviets and the Japanese work on their nuclear programs. Alternate title: *Worldwar: Upsetting the Balance.*

4. *Striking the Balance* (Ballantine, 1996) In the conclusion to the Worldwar subset, the Race is racked by dissension over strategic aims. Alternate title: *Worldwar: Striking the Balance.*

5. *Second Contact* (Ballantine, 1999) After what wound up as mostly a draw in number 4, the Race launches a second invasion in the 1960s with millions of aliens arriving to colonize the Earth. Alternate title: *Colonization: Second Contact.*

6. *Down to Earth* (Ballantine, 2000) The invading Race unites with Allied forces to destroy the Third Reich. Alternate title: *Colonization: Down to Earth.*

7. *Aftershocks* (Ballantine, 2001) Aliens and humans face a series of nuclear confrontations. Alternate title: *Colonization: Aftershocks.*

8. *Homeward Bound* (Ballantine, 2004) Earthlings develop faster-than-light space travel and cryonics, with the possibility of an invasion of the home planet of the Race in the future.

III. In the Pacific War, or Days of Infamy, series, the Japanese destroy the entire US fleet at Pearl Harbor and occupy Hawaii. Two novels have been published, with more likely to come.

1. *Days of Infamy* (Roc, 2004) The Japanese destroy the US fleet at Pearl Harbor and invade Hawaii.
2. *End of the Beginning* (Roc, 2005) The Japanese occupiers of Hawaii face an American counterattack.

IV. In the Darkness series, a world war rages on the planet of Derlavai. In a war in which World War I and World War II are conflated fantastically, trained flocks of dragons, sea leviathans, and magic are used as weapons, while the Algarvians (stand-ins for the Germans) strive for world domination over the Forthwegians, Valmierans, Jelgavans, Kaunians, and so forth.

1. *Into the Darkness* (Tor, 1999) A multitude of wars between the various kingdoms of Derlavai leads to one big war.
2. *Darkness Descending* (Tor, 2000) The nation of Algarve invades the nation of Unkerlant.
3. *Through the Darkness* (Tor, 2001) The Algarvians occupy the nations of Forthweg, Valmiera, and Jelgava.
4. *Rulers of the Darkness* (Tor, 2002) Advances are made on the front against the Algarvians. The Gyongyosians (i.e., Japanese) get involved.
5. *Jaws of Darkness* (Tor, 2003) The Kaunians (who are Jews cum descendants of the Romans) are massacred. Habakukkuk, a sorcery-made ship of ice, provides a turning-point in the war.
6. *Out of the Darkness* (Tor, 2004) The war winds down, and Derlavai faces a postwar world.

V. The War between the Provinces, or Fantastic Civil War, series describes, in a fantasy setting where magic supplements technology, a civil war between the northern and southern parts of the feudal kingdom of Detina. The roles of the North and South are reversed, as Grand Duke Geoffrey makes the northern provinces secede from Detina after King Avram announces plans to free the blond serfs. The later campaigns of the American Civil War are rehashed as troops led by generals, whose names are plays on the names of real Civil War generals, face off against each other.

1. *Sentry Peak* (Baen, 2000) General Guildenstern (i.e., Rosecrans) confronts General Joseph the Gamecock (i.e., Braxton Bragg) at the Detinan version of the Battle of Chickamauga.
2. *Marching through Peachtree* (Baen, 2001) Peachtree Province is defended by "loyalists" against the invading southern army.
3. *Advance and Retreat* (Baen, 2002) General Hood's Tennessee campaign is refought.

VI. Harry Turtledove, who is a historian with a specialty in Byzantine studies, has written three series, listed here as one, about Videssos, an alternate Byzantine Empire. The Videssos series (numbers 1–4) traces the history of the fantasy world of Videssos from the time when a Roman legion, commanded by Marcus Scaurus, is transported there. *Videssos Cycle* (Ballantine, 1988) is a boxed set containing numbers 1 through 4. The Krispos trilogy (numbers 5–7) is about a peasant named Krispos who rises through the ranks to become emperor. *The Tale of Krispos* (Ballantine, 2007) is an omnibus volume containing numbers 5 through 7. Numbers 8 through 11, called the Time of Troubles series, focus on the confrontation between Videssos and Makuran (i.e., the Persian Empire). *The Time of Troubles I* and *The Time of Troubles II* (both Baen, 2005) contain numbers 8 and 9 and numbers 10 and 11, respectively. Number 12 describes a civil war in Videssos.

1. *Misplaced Legion, The* (Ballantine, 1987) Part of a Roman legion in Gaul is transported to the fantasy world of Videssos, an alternate Byzantine Empire.

2. *Emperor for a Legion, An* (Ballantine, 1987) Tribune Marcus Scauros decides to challenge Ortaias Sphrantzes, who assumed the throne of Videssos.
3. *Legion of Videssos, The* (Ballantine, 1987) Marcus Scauros defeats an army of rebel mercenaries and returns to Videssos.
4. *Swords of the Legion* (Ballantine, 1987) Promised the hand of Alypia if he can reclaim a rebel province, Marcus Scauros faces some evil opposition.
5. *Krispos Rising* (Ballantine, 1991) Krispos rises from peasant to emperor in a Videssos beset by decadence at home and enemies without.
6. *Krispos of Videssos* (Ballantine, 1991) Krispos, who has attained the throne of Videssos, faces civil war.
7. *Krispos the Emperor* (Ballantine, 1994) After 22 years of comparative peace, Krispos and his sons face a rebellion of heretical farmers.
8. *Stolen Throne, The* (Ballantine, 1995) Abivard helps to place the Markuraner King of Kings Sharbaraz on the throne.
9. *Hammer and Anvil* (Ballantine, 1996) Maniakes the Elder is sent by the Autokrator Likinas to the island of Kalavria.
10. *Thousand Cities, The* (Ballantine, 1997) The Makuran satrap Abivard tries to invade Videssos.
11. *Videssos Besieged* (Ballantine, 1998) Focuses on Maniakes the Younger as he fights a joint Makuran and Kubrati attack on Videssos.
12. *Bridge of the Separator, The* (Baen, 2005) Rhavas, cousin of the Autokrator, faces a civil war and the invasion of Khormath barbarians.

VII. In a fantasy world somewhat similar to northern Europe in the Dark Ages, Gerin the Fox and his faithful companion Van struggle to make peace for their people in the hinterlands of a once-great Elabonian empire in a multideistic universe. Numbers 1 and 2, published in 1979, were published together 15 years later as *Wereknight* (Baen, 1994), and three more novels were added to the series. *Wisdom of the Fox* (Baen, 1999) is an omnibus volume containing numbers 1 through 3. *Tale of the Fox* (Baen, 2000) contains numbers 4 and 5. Numbers 1 and 2 were published under the pseudonym of Eric G. Iverson.

1. *Wereblood* (Belmont Tower, 1979) King Gerin quests south in search of a wizard to defeat the wizard who threatens his Northlands. Published under the pseudonym of Eric G. Iverson.
2. *Werenight* (Belmont Tower, 1979) Continues Gerin's adventures in the remnants of the Elabonian Empire. Published under the pseudonym of Eric G. Iverson.
3. *Prince of the North* (Baen, 1994) Gerin's wife, Elise, has absconded with a horse doctor; his four-year-old son, Auren, has been kidnapped; and the Northlands experience an incursion of "beastmen."
4. *King of the North* (Baen, 1996) Ten years later, Gerin faces an invasion of the Viking-like Gradi.
5. *Fox and Empire* (Baen, 1998) Twenty years later, Gerin faces war with Aragis the Archer and the Elabonian Empire.

VIII. The Crosstime Traffic series is generally considered a young adult series, partly because its protagonists are teenagers. In the late 21st century, the Crosstime Traffic organization has discovered that, though you can't travel backward or forward in time, you can visit alternate worlds in parallel time lines. In each novel in the series, characters are sent to a different alternate world.

1. *Gunpowder Empire* (Tor, 2003) In this time line, the Roman Empire has never ended.

2. *Curious Notions* (Tor, 2004) The United States has been under German hegemony since the 1950s.
3. *In High Places* (Tor, 2005) Muslims control most of Europe.
4. *Disunited States of America, The* (Tor, 2006) War between Ohio and Virginia in an America in which the Articles of Confederation were never succeeded by the Constitution.
5. *Gladiator, The* (Tor, 2007) The Soviet Union won the cold war.

Twain, Mark

PSEUDONYM OF Samuel L. Clemens

As Twain's preface to *The Adventures of Tom Sawyer* made clear, he intended the book for adult readers as well as for youngsters, in the hope that it would remind them of how they once felt and thought and of what "queer enterprises" they sometimes engaged in. The book's insight into the young mind is still as valid as its humor and adventure are fresh and exciting. *The Adventures of Huckleberry Finn*, in which Tom turns up late in the action, is Twain's and one of America's literary masterpieces, but the other two Tom Sawyer novels are disappointing addenda. *Tom Sawyer* and *Huckleberry Finn* have been reprinted countless times, including *Mark Twain: Mississippi Writings* (Library of America, 1982). *Tom Sawyer Abroad* and *Tom Sawyer, Detective* are also available from the Library of America (*The Gilded Age and Later Novels*, 2002).

1. *Adventures of Tom Sawyer, The* (American, 1876) The adventures of the two friends Tom Sawyer and Huck Finn begin when they witness a murder late one night in the cemetery, and the story concludes with their discovery of hidden treasure.
2. *Adventures of Huckleberry Finn, The* (Webster, 1885) Tom plays a role in this companion piece, in which Huck decides to run away from his drunken father, meets up with the runaway slave Jim, and embarks on his epochal raft voyage down the Mississippi.
3. *Tom Sawyer Abroad* (Webster, 1894) This short novel narrated by Huck shows Tom, Jim, and Huck traveling by balloon to Egypt and fantastical adventures.
4. *Tom Sawyer, Detective* (Harper, 1896) Another short sequel narrated by Huck has Tom solving a case of mixed-up brothers and diamond theft.
5. *Huck and Tom Sawyer among the Indians* (University of California, 1989) Subtitle: *And Other Unfinished Stories*. Eight stories and three autobiographical sketches, most of them never completed by Twain.

Uhnak, Dorothy

New York City police detective Christie Opara, a slender, 26-year-old blond, lives with her son, Mickey, and her mother-in-law in a quiet Queens neighborhood. Her husband, a policeman, was killed in the line of duty. The occasional hint of romance between Christie and her boss, Casey Reardon, has never developed into anything more. Uhnak was a policewoman with the New York City Transit Police for 14 years (see *Policewoman: A Young Woman's Initiation into the Realities of Justice* Simon & Schuster, 1964). She has not used Christie in her more recent novels.

1. *Bait, The* (Simon & Schuster, 1968) Christie plays a dangerous game when she sets herself up as the next victim to catch a mad killer who preys on young women.
2. *Witness, The* (Simon & Schuster, 1969) Christie is the only witness to the murder of a young, black civil rights leader, and only she can clear the policeman wrongly accused of the crime.

3. *Lodger, The* (Simon & Schuster, 1970) Christie must gain the confidence of the beautiful mistress of a drug-ring leader to locate his secret ledger.

Underwood, Michael

PSEUDONYM OF Michael Evelyn

I. Rosa Epton, a London solicitor (attorney) is the protagonist of a long-running series of British mysteries. Rosa has a tendency to get so involved in her cases that she acts as an amateur sleuth as well as an attorney for her clients. Michael Underwood's (d. 1992) career as a solicitor (30 years with the Department of Public Prosecutions) is put to good use in the authentic details he provides for legal goings-on and British courtroom scenes. Rosa Epton started her fictional life as a subsidiary character in mysteries featuring barrister Michael Ainsworth, but she had taken over the series by number 5.

1. *Unprofessional Spy, The* (Doubleday, 1964) For security reasons, Martin Ainsworth agrees to go to Berlin, where an old lover from the 1930s is an East German agent.
2. *Trout in the Milk, A* (Walker, 1972) Someone in the legal profession killed likable, competent barrister Robin Appleman.
3. *Reward for a Defector* (St. Martin's, 1973) Upper-class solicitor Charles Ashmore is uncomfortable defending a client's son, who is charged with espionage.
4. *Pinch of Snuff, A* (St. Martin's, 1974) Brian Tanner, new assistant wine steward at the Blackstone Club, is persuaded to take part in the burglary of the club's collection of snuff boxes.
5. *Crime upon Crime* (St. Martin's, 1981) Small-time crook Arthur Kedby tries a blackmail scheme that destroys two men before almost destroying Arthur himself.
6. *Double Jeopardy* (St. Martin's, 1981) Toby Nash's New Year's Eve date makes him wait outside in his car while she charges him with rape at a police station.
7. *Goddess of Death* (St. Martin's, 1982) Rosa defends the younger brother of a man she once knew, then discovers that the man is dead and someone is impersonating him on the telephone.
8. *Party to Murder, A* (St. Martin's, 1983) The Chief Prosecuting Solicitor's Office is rocked by the selection of a new chief, Murray Riston, a man universally despised.
9. *Death in Camera* (St. Martin's, 1984) At a photo session for the opening of a new courthouse, the unpopular senior judge falls out of a window into the Thames.
10. *Hidden Man, The* (St. Martin's, 1985) Jonathan Cool, idol of millions, is killed in a road accident, and the versions of the affair told by his girlfriend and the driver of the other car vary considerably.
11. *Death at Deepwood Grange* (St. Martin's, 1986) A corpse is found stuffed in the chimney of the one unoccupied apartment at Deepwood Grange.
12. *Uninvited Corpse, The* (St. Martin's, 1987) When Rosa appears on the television program *Legal Aid*, wealthy eccentric Vernon Gray decides to hire her to oversee the drafting of his will.
13. *Injudicious Judge, The* (St. Martin's, 1988) Notoriously abrasive Judge Celia Kilby receives a death threat and is subsequently stabbed to death.
14. *Dual Enigma* (St. Martin's, 1988) Former client Philip Atherly is found murdered on the grounds of East House School, where he once taught.
15. *Compelling Case, A* (St. Martin's, 1989) Rosa represents Stephen Lumley, who has been accused of participating in the robbery of his uncle's jewelry store.

16. *Rosa's Dilemma* (**St. Martin's, 1990**) An apparently straightforward brief leads to corpses on a park bench, a blasé park keeper, and persons anxious to confess to crimes.

17. *Dangerous Business, A* (**St. Martin's, 1991**) Rosa and her lover, Peter Chen, become involved with Britain's Security Service when Rosa sees former client Eddie Ruding in Amsterdam when he is supposed to be in an English prison.

18. *Seeds of Murder, The* (**St. Martin's, 1992**) Epton represents murder suspect Adrian Pickard, the new and much younger husband of her octogenarian godmother.

19. *Guilty Conscience* (**St. Martin's, 1993**) Evelyn Henshaw accuses her husband, Ralph, of murdering his first wife and targeting her as a second victim.

II. Underwood's earlier protagonists were usually police detectives. Inspector/Superintendent Simon Manton was the hero of a series of 13 mysteries, several of which were never published in the United States.

1. *Murder on Trial* (**Washburn, 1957**) William Edgar Tarrant, who has made a living charming money out of rich women, is on trial for shooting a policeman. Originally published in 1954.

2. *Murder Made Absolute* (**Washburn, 1957**) London barrister Christopher Henham finds himself in a ticklish situation when his wife is arrested for a hit-and-run accident involving her car but driven by him. Originally published in 1955.

3. *Death on Remand* (**Hammond [UK], 1956**) No annotation available.

4. *False Witness* (**Walker, 1961**) This is a case involving two rivals for the hand of Jennie Rawlins, barrister Jeremy Harper and cashier Derek Yates. Yates is attacked, and the company payroll he is carrying is stolen. Originally published in 1957.

5. *Lawful Pursuit* (**Doubleday, 1958**) A series of bail jumpers, followed by a Scotland Yard operative investigating them, seem to have resurfaced in Algeria.

6. *Arm of the Law* (**Hammond [UK], 1959**) No annotation available.

7. *Cause of Death* (**Hammond [UK], 1960**) Mrs. Sophie Easterberg is found dead, and the leading suspect is Dave Lucas, an ex-convict who had worked for—and been fired by—Mrs. Easterberg.

8. *Death by Misadventure* (**Hammond [UK], 1960**) No annotation available.

9. *Adam's Case* (**Doubleday, 1961**) Adam Cape fails to obtain the conviction of Carole Young's husband, accused of stabbing her during an argument.

10. *Case against Philip Quest, The* (**Macdonald [UK], 1962**) No annotation available.

11. *Girl Found Dead* (**Macdonald [UK], 1963**) No annotation available.

12. *Crime of Colin Wise, The* (**Doubleday, 1964**) Television repairman Colin Wise defrauds his boss's customers. Then he adds murder to his list of crime.

13. *Anxious Conspirator, The* (**Doubleday, 1965**) The police complicate matters when they arrest an informant along with four out of five counterfeiters during a raid.

III. Sergeant Nick Attwell, who is assisted by his wife, a former constable, is the protagonist of a later, shorter series.

1. *Crooked Wood, The* (**St. Martin's, 1978**) After leading police to the contract killer of the senior lawyer of a large law firm, an informant reports that there will be an attempt to tamper with the jury.

2. *Menaces, Menaces* (**St. Martin's, 1976**) Is someone using Herbert Sipson's blackmail modus operandi while he is in jail awaiting trail, or is he somehow behind the latest extortion?

3. *Juror, The* (**St. Martin's, 1975**) On trial for pornography and a host of other offenses, Bernie Mastyn and his colleagues carry jury tampering to extremes, including murder.

4. *Murder with Malice* (**St. Martin's, 1977**) A young gardener's father, a noted television personality, objects to the police's line of questioning when the son is a suspect in the murder of an old woman.

5. *Fatal Trip, The* (**St. Martin's, 1977**) Although Attwell has provided the court with enough evidence to convict Stephen Burley for burglary, he begins to have doubts about the verdict.

IV. Another pair of novels features a character named Richard Monk.

1. *Man Who Died on Friday, The* (**Macdonald [UK], 1967**) No annotation available.

2. *Man Who Killed Too Soon, The* (**Macdonald [UK], 1968**) No annotation available.

Undset, Sigrid

I. Winner of the Nobel Prize in 1928, Sigrid Undset produced epics of medieval Norway that show a primitive and feudal society only partially restrained by church and civil law. Her books offer an intimate picture of 14th-century family life and culture and breathtaking glimpses of Norway's natural beauty. Undset's strong Catholic and moral views are expressed through her characters' religious conflicts and the anguish they suffer for their sexual transgressions. The universality of her themes of loyalty, responsibility, and faith give her books a timeless quality and continuing appeal, especially for Catholic readers. Available in an omnibus volume, *Kristin Lavransdatter* (Knopf, 1929), the work was originally published in three separate volumes.

1. *Bridal Wreath, The* (**Knopf, 1923**) This introduces the headstrong young Kristin, oldest daughter of Lavrans Bjorgulfsson, a prosperous landowner of the Gudbrandsdal region. Kristin dishonors her family when she spurns her betrothed for her true love Erlend. UK title: *The Garland*. Translated from the Norwegian by Charles Archer and J. S. Scott. Retranslated by Tina Nunnally as *The Wreath* (Penguin, 1997). Originally published in 1920 as *Kronsen*.

2. *Mistress of Husaby, The* (**Knopf, 1925**) A repentant Kristin proves a good manager of Erlend's family estate at Husaby, and eventually they have seven sons, but Erlend gets involved in a treasonous plot. Translated from the Norwegian by Charles Archer. Retranslated by Tina Nunnally as *The Wife* (Penguin, 1999). Originally published in 1921 as *Husfrue*.

3. *Cross, The* (**Knopf, 1927**) With Erlend's lands forfeited, the family moves to the home Kristin inherited at her parents' death, but unhappiness and eventual tragedy follow them. Translated from the Norwegian by Charles Archer. Retranslated by Tina Nunnally as *The Cross* (Penguin, 2000). Originally published in 1922 as *Korset*.

II. Those who enjoyed *Kristin Lavransdatter* will want to go to read Undset's second medieval Norwegian saga about the ill-starred lovers Olav and Ingunn. Originally published in Norway in two volumes and in the United States in the four volumes listed below, the complete work is also available in an omnibus edition under the title *The Master of Hestviken* (Knopf, 1942).

1. *Axe, The* (Knopf, 1928) Olav and Ingunn, raised together as children, are torn apart by violent and tragic events. Translated from the Norwegian by Arthur G. Chater. Originally published in 1925 as the first part of *Olav Audunsson i Hestviken*.
2. *Snake Pit, The* (Knopf, 1929) The two are reunited at Olav's family estate in Hestviken, but true happiness still eludes them. Translated from the Norwegian by Arthur G. Chater. Originally published in 1925 as the second part of *Olav Audunsson i Hestviken*.
3. *In the Wilderness* (Knopf, 1929) After Ingunn's death, Olav raises little Eirik and Cecelia and travels to England. Translated from the Norwegian by Arthur G. Chater. Originally published in 1927 as the first part of *Olav Audonnson og hansborn*.
4. *Son Avenger, The* (Knopf, 1930) Cecelia marries, and Eirik seems destined for the church. Translated from the Norwegian by Arthur G. Chater. Originally published in 1927 as the second part of *Olav Audunsson og hansborn*.

III. Although Undset is best known for her historical novels, she also published novels set in the 20th century, such as the pair about Paul Selmer, his marriage, and his conversion to Catholicism, set in the World War I period.

1. *Wild Orchid, The* (Knopf, 1931) Paul Selmer discovers love after he grows up, in the person of the shallow and frivolous Bjorg. Translated from the Norwegian by Arthur G. Chater. Originally published in 1929 as *Gymnadenia*.
2. *Burning Bush, The* (Knopf, 1932) Paul and Bjorg are increasingly estranged as Paul converts to Catholicism. Translated from the Norwegian by Arthur G. Chater. Originally published in 1931 as *Den brennende busk*.

Updike, John

One of the most highly regarded contemporary American fiction writers, John Updike (d. 2009) attempted to catch the quintessential American male in his portrait of Harry "Rabbit" Angstrom. After the glory of his high school days as a basketball hero in a small town in Pennsylvania, Rabbit seems unable to find satisfaction in the responsibilities of the adult world. Lacking the self-knowledge to understand his feelings of meaninglessness, Rabbit's sporadic attempts to escape only make matters worse. In three sequels, Updike showed Rabbit growing older, if not wiser, until he is finally "at rest." Numbers 1, 2, and 3 were published together by Quality Paperback Book Club (1981). All four novels are included in the omnibus volumes *Rabbit Angstrom: The Four Novels* (Knopf, 1995) and *The Rabbit Novels* (Ballantine, 2003). "Rabbit Remembered," a coda, was published in *Licks of Love: Short Stories and a Sequel* (Knopf, 2000).

Henry Bech, Jewish American novelist, is the hero of three collections of short stories by Updike: *Bech: A Book* (Knopf, 1970); *Bech Is Back* (Knopf, 1982); and *Bech at Bay* (Knopf, 1998). These stories, with the addition of a new one, "His Oeuvre," were published in one volume as *The Complete Henry Bech: Twenty Stories* (Knopf/Everyman, 2001).

1. *Rabbit, Run* (Knopf, 1960) At 26 Rabbit leaves his pregnant wife, lives for a while with a prostitute, then returns after tragedy strikes.
2. *Rabbit Redux* (Knopf, 1971) Ten years later, Rabbit is a conservative suburbanite, abandoned by his wife and confronting drugs and black power in the radical sixties.
3. *Rabbit Is Rich* (Knopf, 1981) Rabbit, now 46 and paunchy, runs the Toyota dealership he inherited from his wife's family, engages in the wife-swapping games of the seventies, fights with his son Nelson, and searches for his illegitimate daughter.
4. *Rabbit at Rest* (Knopf, 1990) Rabbit is retired but restless. He shuttles between Pennsylvania and Florida, playing golf, eating junk food, and fretting about Nelson's incompetence and his wife Janice's growing independence.

Upfield, Arthur W(illiam)

The immense and primitive Australian outback pervades these detective stories starring Inspector Napoleon "Bony" Bonaparte of the Queensland Police. Rescued from the bush, where he lay beside his dead mother, Bony was raised at a mission school and went on to Brisbane University. His uncanny ability to track miscreants through the rough outback country may be attributed to his part-Aborigine heritage, but his ego and deductive powers come straight from Arthur Conan Doyle's (q.v.) Sherlock Holmes. Arthur W. Upfield was born in England but spent most of his adult life in Australia. Numbers 2 through 8 were originally published in Australia by Angus & Robertson.

1. *Lure of the Bush* (Doubleday, 1965) Trouble for prosperous New South Wales landowner John Thornton begins when King Henry, an Aborigine chief, is found murdered on his land. Originally published in the United Kingdom in 1929 as *The Barrakee Mystery*.
2. *Sands of Windee, The* (Aenonian, 1978) Bony proves that a murder took place at a bush station in New South Wales when others see no evidence of crime. This book became an exhibit and Upfield a witness in the trial of a man who patterned a real murder on it after reading Upfield's manuscript. Originally published in Australia in 1931.
3. *Wings above the Claypan* (Doubleday, 1943) Bony gets help from an ancient tribal chieftain to solve this case of a drugged and paralyzed young girl found in a stolen airplane. Originally published in Australia in 1936 as *Wings above the Diamantina*. Variant title: *The Winged Mystery*.
4. *Murder Down Under* (Doubleday, 1943) In this case, which introduced Upfield to US readers, Bony helps a policeman friend solve a missing-person case and runs across another mystery as well. Originally published in Australia in 1937 as *Mr. Jelly's Business*.
5. *Winds of Evil* (Doubleday, 1944) A sandstorm has obliterated all clues to the two murders Bony must solve. Originally published in Australia in 1937.
6. *Bone Is Pointed, The* (Doubleday, 1947) Black magic almost does Bony in as he investigates the disappearance and probable death of a white man hated by the local Aborigines. Originally published in Australia in 1938.
7. *Mystery of Swordfish Reef, The* (Doubleday, 1943) Bony learns the fine arts of sword fishing as he investigates the disappearance of a fishing party. Originally published in Australia in 1939.
8. *No Footprints in the Bush* (Doubleday, 1944) One policeman has already lost his life while investigating two murdered stockmen on Donald MacPherson's cattle station, and Bony himself narrowly escapes. Originally published in Australia in 1940 as *Bushranger of the Skies*.
9. *Death of a Swagman* (Doubleday, 1945) Bony reopens a two-year-old case of the murder of an itinerant worker, called a swagman in Australia.
10. *Devil's Steps, The* (Doubleday, 1946) An army intelligence assignment for Bony gets him involved in secret documents and sudden death in Melbourne.
11. *Author Bites the Dust, An* (Doubleday, 1948) Bony's jaundiced view of the Melbourne literary crowd shows as he investigates the death of writer Merwyn Blake.

12. *Mountains Have a Secret, The* (Doubleday, 1948) Two missing hitchhikers and a dead detective lead Bony to the closely guarded sheep ranch of Carl Benson.

13. *Widows of Broome, The* (Doubleday, 1950) Two rich widows are strangled in a lonely town on the tropical northwest coast of Australia.

14. *Bachelors of Broken Hill, The* (Doubleday, 1950) Someone has been dropping cyanide into the drinks of aging bachelors in the mining town of Broken Hill.

15. *New Shoe, The* (Doubleday, 1952) Bony investigates a corpse found entombed in the walls of a lighthouse. Variant title: *The Clue of the New Shoe.*

16. *Venom House* (Doubleday, 1952) The two hateful Ainsworth sisters and their lunatic brother are the central figures of this case.

17. *Murder Must Wait* (Doubleday, 1953) Bony helps the local police in Mitford, New South Wales, solve a puzzling case of the apparent theft of five babies.

18. *Death of a Lake* (Doubleday, 1954) As the water of Lake Otway recedes during a severe drought, tensions mount among the local residents, who expect a dead body to surface.

19. *Sinister Stones* (Doubleday, 1954) Aborigine justice clashes with the law in this case of the murder of Constable Stenhouse. UK title: *Cake in the Hatbox.*

20. *Battling Prophet, The* (American Reprint, 1980) Bony is called in to investigate the mysterious death of a weather prophet. Originally published in the United Kingdom in 1956.

21. *Man of Two Tribes, The* (Doubleday, 1956) A little dog and two wily camels help Bony search for an acquitted murderess involved in some atomic-secret business.

22. *Bushman Who Came Back, The* (Doubleday, 1957) Only Bony can save the kidnapped child of a murdered woman. UK title: *Bony Buys a Woman.*

23. *Bony and the Black Virgin* (Collier, 1965) Very similar in plot to *Lure of the Bush* (number 1), this novel has a theme of miscegenation and a setting in a remote outpost in New South Wales. Originally published in the United Kingdom in 1959. Variant title: *The Torn Branch.*

24. *Journey to the Hangman* (Doubleday, 1959) Three brutal murders in the remote West Australian village of Daybreak challenge Bony's detective skills as relations grow tense between the white and Aborigine populations. UK title: *Bony and the Mouse.*

25. *Valley of Smugglers* (Doubleday, 1960) Bony poses as a horse thief to investigate an Irish enclave in New South Wales. UK title: *Bony and the Kelly Gang.*

26. *White Savage, The* (Doubleday, 1961) Bony poses as stationmaster Nat Bonner as he patiently sniffs out a rapist-murderer being protected by his family. UK title: *Bony and the White Savage.*

27. *Will of the Tribe, The* (Doubleday, 1962) Inspector Bonaparte finds both whites and Aborigines strangely unhelpful while he investigates a body found in a desert meteor crater.

28. *Body at Madman's Bend, The* (Doubleday, 1963) Anybody might have murdered the drunk and violent William Lush, but suspicion falls on his pretty stepdaughter, Jill Madden. UK title: *Madman's Bend.*

29. *Lake Frome Monster, The* (American Reprint, 1976) This last episode was completed by J. L. Price and Dorothy Strange after the author's death. It concerns the sudden death of a roving photographer and something in the lake that frightens the natives. Originally published in the United Kingdom in 1966.

Uris, Leon

Best-selling author Leon Uris (*Exodus,* etc.) has written a two-volume fictional history of the Irish struggle against British rule that he traces through the history of three Irish clans: the Larkins, Catholic hill farmers of County Donegal; the Hubbles, English aristocrats and Irish landowners; and the MacLeods, Protestant shipyard workers in Belfast. The two volumes form a well-organized, multifaceted fictional history of Ireland during the "Troubles."

1. *Trinity* (Doubleday, 1976) The Larkins, the Hubbles, and the MacLeods work out their mutually exclusive destinies in Ireland between the 1840s and 1916.

2. *Redemption* (Harper, 1995) In action set during World War I the Larkins become, variously, New Zealand sheep farmers, Irish revolutionaries, and British war heroes, while the Hubbles try to keep their Irish tenants down.

Vachss, Andrew

Burke (no first name) is an ex-convict and an unlicensed private investigator who is a relentless crusader for abused children. Burke makes a living selling fake IDs and doing dirty work for wealthy clients, but the morose, paranoid private eye gets really involved only if a child is at risk. Burke generally works outside the legal system, which he feels is inept, unfair, and unworkable, in his passionate quest for justice and revenge against child abusers. Assisted by a continuing cast of characters including a 140-pound Mastiff named Pansy, transsexual hooker Michelle, computer wizard Mole, Strega the witch, the Prof, Pepper, Bruiser the rottweiler, Max the Silent, and others, Burke pursues his goal in novels full of violence and sordid ambience. Andrew Vachss is a New York lawyer, social worker, and child advocate. *A Bomb Built in Hell,* a novel written in 1973 but never published, is a prequel featuring Wesley, the Ice-Man, a character in the Burke novels. It was released online on Amazon.com in 2000.

1. *Flood* (Fine, 1985) A Miss Flood engages Burke to track down the man who raped and murdered her best friend's little girl.

2. *Strega* (Knopf, 1987) Hired by the beautiful and disturbing "Strega," Burke goes after a child-pornography racket.

3. *Blue Belle* (Knopf, 1988) Burke is hired by a local pimp to find out who is murdering young prostitutes and falls for Belle, a stripper with a victimized past.

4. *Hard Candy* (Knopf, 1989) A member of Burke's old gang, call girl and entrepreneur Candy, asks him to rescue her daughter from a cult in Brooklyn.

5. *Blossom* (Knopf, 1990) Burke is hired by a former cell mate whose nephew is the chief suspect in a serial murder case.

6. *Sacrifice* (Knopf, 1991) Burke works on both sides of the law to save Luke, an eight-year-old suspect in a series of baby murders.

7. *Down in the Zero* (Knopf, 1994) Burke journeys out of Manhattan to a Connecticut suburb shaken by a series of teen suicides to protect a young man whose mother did a favor for him years ago.

8. *Footsteps of the Hawk* (Knopf, 1995) Belinda, a policewoman, wants Burke to exonerate her lover, who is serving time as a serial killer.

9. *False Allegations* (Knopf, 1996) Burke comes up against Kite, an albino lawyer who specializes in debunking recovered memories of child sexual abuse. Dr. Bruce Perry, real-life head of the Civitas Child-Trauma programs in Houston, appears as a character.

10. *Safe House* (**Knopf, 1998**) Crystal Beth, operator of a Manhattan safe house, asks Burke to take the case of a mother being stalked by her estranged husband, the leader of a neo-Nazi cell.
11. *Choice of Evil* (**Knopf, 1999**) Burke is hired by gay activists to find a vigilante who is wiping out gay bashers around the city.
12. *Dead and Gone* (**Knopf, 2000**) Professional killers ambush Burke, shooting him in the head and killing his dog, Pansy.
13. *Pain Management* (**Knopf, 2001**) Burke, believed dead by some, has gone into hiding in Oregon but returns to New York to track down a runaway teenage girl, and he becomes involved with a clandestine society that illegally obtains prescription drugs for people suffering from extreme pain.
14. *Only Child* (**Knopf, 2002**) A New York Mafia boss hires Burke to solve the murder of his illegitimate teenage daughter, Vonni.
15. *Down Here* (**Knopf, 2004**) Beautiful crime fighter Wolfe is blamed for the attempted murder of John Anson Wychek, a convicted serial rapist she once put away.
16. *Mask Market* (**Pantheon, 2006**) Lying low after a gun wound, Burke is inveigled into meeting a client who is looking for a missing woman, Beryl Preston.
17. *Terminal* (**Pantheon, 2007**) Claw, boss of the local Aryan Brotherhood, gets Burke involved in a 30-year-old case of rape and child murder.

Vaite, Celestine (Hitiura)

We first catch up with Materena Mahi, the redoubtable Tahitian, when she is pregnant with her daughter, Leilani, and not yet married to the feckless Pito Tehana. Materena eventually becomes mother of three children and "champion professional cleaner" and, eventually, "champion professional listener," star of her own radio talk and advice show, and a grandmother-to-be. Materena is foremost among a host of agreeable characters and a mine of Tahitian folklore in these likable novels, which make Tahiti sound like the Botswana of Alexander McCall Smith's (q.v.) No. 1 Ladies' Detective Agency series. Not many mystery investigations here, except for Materena's search for her unknown French father, but lots of enjoyable reading by Tahitian-born Vaite.

1. *Breadfruit* (**Back Bay, 2006**) Pito Tehana, father of her children, proposes marriage to Materena Mahi, but he is drunk and forgets about it by morning. Undaunted, Materena makes wedding plans. Originally published in Australia in 2000.
2. *Frangipani* (**Back Bay, 2005**) Materena lovingly rears her daughter, Leilani, but fears that her daughter will fall in love too young and make her a grandmother before she is 40. Originally published in Australia in 2004.
3. *Tiare in Bloom* (**Back Bay, 2007**) Materena's call-in radio show seems to reach every woman in Tahiti. Pito and Materena squabble when Materena announces she is going to locate her unknown French father, but they get back together again when they become grandparents.

Valin, Jonathan

Harry Stoner is a decidedly hard-boiled private eye who practices in Cincinnati. His investigations take place among middle-class Americans rather than the upper and lower extremes of West Coast society. True to type, Stoner's compassion for the underdog sometimes gets him in trouble. The novels are fast paced and well plotted and, at times, very grim and violent. Valin, a native of Cincinnati, does his hometown justice.

1. *Lime Pit, The* (**Dodd, 1980**) Harry Stoner gets involved with the child-pornography racket when an old man asks him to find his "little girl."
2. *Final Notice* (**Dodd, 1980**) The vandal who is mutilating books in the Cincinnati library may also be murdering young women.
3. *Dead Letter* (**Dodd, 1981**) Physics professor Daryl Lovingwell suspects his radical daughter of stealing secret documents from him.
4. *Day of Wrath* (**Congdon, 1982**) A 14-year-old girl disappears, and her boyfriend is the victim of a torture slaying.
5. *Natural Causes* (**Congdon, 1983**) A writer for a daytime soap opera sponsored by a Cincinnati businessman's firm dies suddenly and suspiciously in Hollywood.
6. *Life's Work* (**Delacorte, 1986**) Bill Parks, player for the Cincinnati Cougars football team, disappears after signing a lucrative contract.
7. *Fire Lake* (**Delacorte, 1987**) Old friend Lonnie Jackowski signs into a Cincinnati motel under Harry Stoner's name and attempts suicide.
8. *Extenuating Circumstances* (**Delacorte, 1989**) Stoner is sceptical when teenager Terry Carnova confesses to the murder of businessman Ira Lessing.
9. *Second Chance* (**Delacorte, 1991**) Harry is hired to find psychiatrist Phil Pearson's daughter Kirsty, who is missing from the University of Chicago.
10. *Music Lovers, The* (**Delacorte, 1993**) Leon Tubin hires Harry to find some valuable missing long-playing records that he is convinced were stolen by the anti-Semitic Sherwood Loeffler.
11. *Missing* (**Delacorte, 1995**) Cindy Dorn hires Stoner to find her missing bisexual lover, Mason Greenleaf, who eventually turns up as an apparent suicide in a seedy hotel.

van de Wetering, Janwillem

Van de Wetering's Amsterdam police novels were based on first-hand knowledge—the author (d. 2008) had been a member of the Amsterdam Reserve Police since 1965. His cast included the stolid, henpecked Adjutant Grijpstra, the affable but dreamy and sensitive Sergeant de Gier, and the aged, arthritic, wise *commissaria*. One or more of the trio sometimes went as far afield as Maine or Japan pursuing their investigations, but the Amsterdam novels were generally regarded as the best. Van de Wetering's unique injection of Zen Buddhist ideas and perspective into his mysteries gave them a special distinction. Van de Wetering spent a year in a Japanese monastery and five years with a Buddhist group in Maine, experiences that he described in three autobiographical volumes: *The Empty Mirror* (Houghton Mifflin, 1974); *A Glimpse of Nothingness* (Houghton Mifflin, 1975); and *Afterzen* (St. Martin's, 1999). *The Sergeant's Cat and Other Stories* (Pantheon, 1987) contains eight Amsterdam cop stories; *Judge Dee Plays His Lute: A Play and Selected Mystery Stories* (Winderly, 1997) contains four stories. Police novels about Amsterdam from a different perspective can be found in Nicolas Freeling's Van der Valk series (q.v.). Van de Wetering was also the author of *Robert van Gulik: His Life and Work* (Soho, 1997).

1. *Outsider in Amsterdam* (**Houghton Mifflin, 1975**) The suspects include narcotics pushers, the victim's insane mother, and his exotic Papuan wife when the owner of a commune restaurant is left hanging.
2. *Tumbleweed* (**Houghton Mifflin, 1976**) Witchcraft may be involved in the murder of a young woman from Curaçao.

3. *Corpse on the Dike, The* (Houghton Mifflin, 1976) Their investigation of the murder of Tom Wernekink leads de Gier and Grijpstra to Cat in Boots, leader of a band of thieves.

4. *Death of a Hawker* (Houghton Mifflin, 1977) A street-market vendor is found murdered in a locked room while Amsterdam is being torn by riots.

5. *Japanese Corpse, The* (Houghton Mifflin, 1977) The Japanese criminal organization, the Yakuza, may be responsible for murder, art theft, and heroin smuggling into Amsterdam.

6. *Blond Baboon, The* (Houghton Mifflin, 1978) A fatal tumble by Elaine Carnet, retired cabaret singer, may have been no accident.

7. *Maine Massacre, The* (Houghton Mifflin, 1979) The *commissaria* and de Gier travel to Maine to help the former's sister, who has been widowed by a suspicious accident.

8. *Mind-Murders, The* (Houghton Mifflin, 1981) Grijpstra and de Gier have dark suspicions about a publisher's missing wife and a corpse that the coroner says died of natural causes.

9. *Streetbird, The* (Putnam, 1983) De Gier sees a vulture, an unusual sight in Amsterdam's red-light district, near the scene of a pimp's murder.

10. *Rattle-Rat, The* (Pantheon, 1985) The murder of a sheep farmer from Friesland brings Grijpstra and de Gier to that Dutch province.

11. *Hard Rain* (Putnam, 1986) The police trio suspect that the sniper killer of banker Martin Ijsbreker and the heroin overdose deaths of three drug addicts are linked.

12. *Just a Corpse at Twilight* (Soho, 1994) Grijpstra comes out of retirement to go to a small Maine island to help de Gier, who is in a mess of substance abuse, blackmail, and the suspicious death of his mistress.

13. *Hollow-Eyed Angel, The* (Soho, 1996) The *commissaria* and de Gier go to Manhattan when Bert Termeer, a Dutch national who operated a mail-order book business, is found dead in Central Park.

14. *Perfidious Parrot, The* (Soho, 1997) Grijpstra and de Gier, who have formed their own private agency in the wake of a windfall, get involved in the affair of a hijacked oil tanker.

15. *Amsterdam Cops, The: Collected Stories* (Soho, 1999) Collected short stories.

Van Dine, S. S.

PSEUDONYM OF Willard Huntington Wright

Like the early Ellery Queen (q.v.), Philo Vance is a rather insufferable young man whose languid erudition and aristocratic tastes make him a distant American cousin to Albert Campion (q.v.) and Lord Peter Wimsey. Dashiell Hammett (q.v.) dismissed Philo as having "the conversational manner of a high school girl who has been studying the foreign words and phrases at the back of the dictionary." Nevertheless, readers of the 1920s took to him immediately, and his successful translation into films starring William Powell and Basil Rathbone gave him enormous popularity. Willard Huntington Wright, an editor of *Smart Set* who unsuccessfully tried to interest Americans in modernism in art and realism in fiction, was something of a poseur himself. His theory that any detective writer had about "six good ideas in his system" was proved by his own work—the later volumes show a decided falling off. John Loughery's *Alias S. S. Van Dine* (Scribner, 1992) is an interesting biography of Willard Huntington Wright. Omnibus volumes include *A Philo Vance Weekend* (Grosset, 1928; numbers 1–3); *Philo Vance Murder Cases* (Scribner, 1936; numbers 5–7); and *Four Complete Novels* (Random House, 1984; numbers 1, 2, 4, and 5).

1. *Benson Murder Case, The* (Scribner, 1926) Vance spots the murderer of wealthy Wall Street broker Alvin Benson quickly, but the New York district attorney and police force flounder badly.

2. *Canary Murder Case, The* (Scribner, 1927) The "canary" is famous Broadway nightclub singer Margaret Odell, found strangled.

3. *Greene Family Murder Case, The* (Scribner, 1928) The Greene family is being murdered one by one, and Vance uses all his knowledge of criminal psychology to solve this sinister case.

4. *Bishop Murder Case, The* (Scribner, 1929) Mother Goose nursery rhymes seem to be inspiring a madman to murder.

5. *Scarab Murder Case, The* (Scribner, 1930) An ancient Egyptian mystery gives Vance a clue to the murder of philanthropist Benjamin Kyle.

6. *Kennel Murder Case, The* (Scribner, 1933) Archer Coe is found stabbed, shot, and battered, and Vance uses a scale model of his house to solve the crime.

7. *Dragon Murder Case, The* (Scribner, 1933) A man drowns in Mrs. Stamm's pond, called the Dragon Pool because of old Indian legends about lake monsters, and his body is never found.

8. *Casino Murder Case, The* (Scribner, 1934) This story, which begins and ends in a gambling casino, is about the poisoning of three members of the Llewllyn family.

9. *Garden Murder Case, The* (Scribner, 1935) The tension between Professor Garden and his nephew Woody, who bet the last of his fortune on a horse called Equanimity, turns into murder.

10. *Kidnap Murder Case, The* (Scribner, 1936) Vance gets a chance to show his sharpshooting skill in the case of the kidnap and murder of Kaspar Kenting.

11. *Gracie Allen Murder Case, The* (Scribner, 1938) Philo is assisted by George Burns's wife, the fey and funny radio comedienne Gracie Allen, in this case, which brings Philo and friends the acquaintance of a highly cultured underworld character. Variant title: *The Smell of Murder*.

12. *Winter Murder Case, The* (Scribner, 1939) This spare last case was left in draft form at the author's death; some critics think it shows Philo to his best advantage. The plot concerns a jewel theft at the Berkshire home of millionaire Tarrington Rexton.

Van Dyke, Henry

Not to be confused with the clergyman-author Henry Van Dyke (1852–1933), who wrote *The Story of the Other Wise Man* (Harper, 1896), which was a staple on secondary school reading lists, this Henry Van Dyke, born in Michigan in 1928, is a talented black writer whose books have been widely praised. The two novels listed below are narrated by Oliver, a young black boy who sees through the pretensions and defenses of the adults around him.

1. *Ladies of the Rachmaninoff Eyes* (Farrar, 1965) Etta Klein and her longtime black companion, Harriet Gibbs, bicker and fuss amusingly throughout the story, which focuses on Etta's attempts to contact her dead son through séances.

2. *Blood of Strawberries* (Farrar, 1969) Now a debonair college student, Oliver spends a summer in New York City with his well-heeled bohemian friends Max and Tanja Rhodes, who are producing a Gertrude Stein play.

Van Gieson, Judith

I. Neil Hamel is a fortyish female lawyer and amateur sleuth from Albuquerque, New Mexico. Neil is streetwise, smart, self-aware, and possessed of a sense of humor in this series with a well-realized Southwest atmosphere in which some basic issues facing the region are discussed.

1. *North of the Border* (HarperCollins, 1988) Neil, missing "the Kid," her part-time lover and auto mechanic, goes south to Mexico, where she finds a lawyer with his throat slit.
2. *Raptor* (HarperCollins, 1990) Neil goes to Montana go help look for the rarely seen "Arctic Falcon" in a tale involving murder and the rivalry between environmentalists and poachers.
3. *Other Side of Death, The* (HarperCollins, 1991) Neil and pal Lonnie find it hard give up sixties behavior, but then Lonnie turns up dead in some Indian ruins after a party.
4. *Wolf Path, The* (HarperCollins, 1992) Hamel heads for the southern part of New Mexico to help animal rights advocate Juan Sololobo as he tours the country with his licensed timber wolf, Sirius.
5. *Lies That Bind, The* (HarperCollins, 1993) The mother of childhood friend Cindy Reid is the chief suspect in a hit-and-run death.
6. *Parrot Blues* (HarperCollins, 1995) Rich Texan Terrance Lewellen hires Hamel to find his missing wife, anthropologist Deborah Dumaine, and Perigree, part of a pair of rare indigo macaws.
7. *Hotshots* (HarperCollins, 1996) The mother of Joni Baker, one of the nine "hotshots" (forest firefighters) who died battling a fire on federal land, wants Neil to represent them in a civil suit charging the government with negligence.
8. *Ditch Rider* (HarperCollins, 1998) Neil and her lover, The Kid, settled into a new house, have befriended troubled 13-year-old Cheyanne Moran, who claims to have killed a teenage boy.

II. Neil Hamel has been abandoned for another New Mexican, Claire Reynier, university archivist and rare-book librarian. Claire is in her fifties but just as feisty and clever as Neil. The University of New Mexico Press published the first four volumes in this series in hardcover, followed by paperback editions by Signet.

1. *Stolen Blue, The* (New Mexico, 2000) Claire retrieves a batch of particularly valuable Southwest books from a remote ranch. Then the books are stolen from her truck.
2. *Vanishing Point* (New Mexico, 2001) A graduate student unearths the 30-year-old journal of Jonathan Vail, sixties writer who vanished while hiking with his girlfriend.
3. *Confidence Woman* (New Mexico, 2002) Evelyn Martin, an old college friend, asks to stay at Claire's house while looking for a place to live. Then Evelyn is found dead with Claire's credit cards.
4. *Land of Burning Heat* (New Mexico, 2003) When Isabel Santos finds a document hidden in the basement of her adobe house, Claire thinks that it could contain the last words of a Jewish mystic condemned by the Spanish Inquisition of Mexico City hundreds of years before.
5. *Shadow of Venus, The* (Wheeler, 2004) A young woman with no identification is found dead in the basement of Zimmerman Library. Claire follows her trail into the slums of Albuquerque.

Van Vogt, A(lfred) E(lton)

I. Canadian-born California transplant A. E. Van Vogt was, along with Isaac Asimov (q.v.) and Robert A. Heinlein (q.v.), one of the giants of science fiction in the 1940s, whose stories explored ideas and themes that have since become staples of SF. Van Vogt's short stories and novels, published in the magazine *Astounding*, were characterized by frenetic action in space-opera plots; gripping suspense; intriguing situations involving matters such as telepathy, teleportation, mutant supermen, and technological wonders; and large doses of Van Vogt's philosophy. Many of his works were originally published in short form and stitched together later. They are not for readers who demand tight structure, careful characterization, or polished prose from their SF. Many readers felt that his later works were overfull of philosophy at the expense of plot, so his later works were less read, and his reputation declined.

Van Vogt's best works include *Slan* (Arkham, 1946; rev. ed., Simon & Schuster, 1951); *The Voyage of the Space Beagle* (Simon & Schuster, 1950); *The Weapon Shops of Isher* (see series II, below); and *The World of Null-A*. *The World of Null-A* and its two sequels feature Gilbert Gosseyn ("go-sane"), a superman with an extra brain who, despite his superpowers, which include immortality, instant teleportation, and telepathy, seems to be at the mercy of immense forces beyond his control. Null-A, which means "non-Aristotelian," is Van Vogt's version of general semantics, a philosophy that engaged many SF writers of the 1940s.

1. *World of Ā, The* (Simon & Schuster, 1948) In the universe of 2650 CE, Gilbert Gosseyn, a superman with an extra brain and the ability to move instantaneously through practically anywhere in space, finds himself beset by immense, inimical forces. Originally appeared in *Astounding* in 1945. Revised edition published by Berkley as *The World of Null-A* in 1970.
2. *Pawns of Null-A, The* (Ace, 1956) Gilbert Gosseyn continues his adventures, and Van Vogt continues his exposition of general semantics. Originally serialized as "The Players of Ā" in *Astounding* in 1948–1949. Revised edition published by Berkley (1966): *The Players of Null-A*.
3. *Null-A Three* (DAW, 1985) Continues the adventures of Gilbert Gosseyn. Regarded by critics as almost a "parody" of numbers 1 and 2. Variant title: *Null-A 3*.

II. *The Weapon Makers* and *The Weapon Shops of Isher* (published together as *The Empire of Isher*, Orb, 2000) are set in a National Rifle Association dream world, where authoritarian government is in a schizoid balance with galaxy-wide weapons "shops" whose slogan is "The right to buy weapons is the right to be free." The immortal Robert Hedrock has set up the weapons shops to balance the power of the Empire of Isher, which, so it turns out, he also created. The plot is concerned with Hedrock's struggle against the young and beautiful—but oppressive—Empress Innelda, who wants to shut down the shops.

1. *Weapon Makers, The* (Hadley, 1947) The corrupt Empire of Isher, ruled by the Empress Innelda, holds sway over the known universe, checked only by the Weapon Makers, a group of scientists who don't acknowledge the empire's authority. Originally published in *Astounding* in 1943. Revised edition published by Greenberg in 1952. Variant title: *One against Eternity*.
2. *Weapon Shops of Isher, The* (Greenberg, 1951) In some respects a prequel to number 2. Robert Hedrock, who has created both the Empire of Isher and the weapons shops, continues his adventures through time and space. Originally published as two stories in *Astounding* in 1941: "Seesaw" and "The Weapon Shop."

III. The Clane, or House of Linn, duo is set in a post–nuclear holocaust world where history and written records have been lost, and Lord Clane, the Wizard of Linn, is the only person who holds the key to preserving the Empire of Linn and keeping the human race from extinction.

1. *Empire of the Atom* **(Shasta, 1957)** In 12,000 CE, the remaining humans, having been reduced to barbarism by atomic wars, have formed the Empire of Linn. Novelization of five stories in the Gods series.
2. *Wizard of Linn, The* **(Ace, 1962)** Only the Wizard of Linn, Lord Clane, can hold off the invasion by the hostile alien Riss.

Van Wormer, Laura

TV reporter Sally Harrington is young, rich, beautiful, and talented, but her investigative work keeps on getting her involved in dangerous situations in places like Hollywood, and her romantic inclinations keep on getting her involved in affairs with a series of men. Characters from earlier novels have a way of turning up in later novels, so it may be a good idea to work your way through the series in publication order. If you are interested in the earlier doings of characters at DBE News, where Sally eventually works, try *Riverside Drive* (Doubleday, 1988), *West End* (Doubleday, 1989), *Any Given Moment* (Crown, 1995), or *Talk* (Mira, 1998). Connecticut resident Laura Van Wormer, regarded as a "master of romantic suspense," is currently working on a historical novel with "Fergie," aka the Duchess of York.

1. *Expose* **(Mira, 1999)** Sally Harrington returns home to Connecticut to be with her invalid mother, becomes a reporter for the local Castleford newspaper, and gets a freelance job profiling a TV executive for a slick national magazine.
2. *Last Lover, The* **(Mira, 2000)** Sally gets a job with a national TV network and becomes romantically involved with book editor Spencer Hawes. When Sally and Spencer travel to Los Angeles, they meet film star Lilliana Martin, who attempts to seduce Spencer. Then Lilliana and Spencer disappear.
3. *Trouble Becomes Her* **(Mira, 2001)** Sally, now working for DBS News in New York and rekindling a romance with Doug, an old beau, finds a dead body in the trunk of her rental car.
4. *Bad Witness, The* **(Mira, 2002)** Sally, key witness for the defense in the case of a mafioso who once tried to have her killed, is threatened again.
5. *Kill Fee, The* **(Mira, 2003)** Great-Uncle Percy gets in trouble with land speculators and has to be shipped off to Florida. Young LA policeman Paul McWilliams arrives in Connecticut.
6. *Mr. Murder* **(Mira, 2006)** A killer known as Mr. Murder targets a large number of antagonists from previous novels, including jealous ex-lovers and competitive coworkers, but his real target is Sally Harrington.

Vance, Jack (John Holbrook)

I. Veteran fantasy and science-fiction writer Jack Vance, a Nebula Grand Master, is known for his rich prose, bizarre and memorable characters, exotic settings, and ingenious plot devices. The Dying Earth series is a collection of rather loosely collected tales in which fantasy and science-fiction themes intermingle in adventures on a number of "Dying Earth" lands. Cugel the Clever is the picaresque hero of the middle two volumes in the series. *The Dying Earth* and *The Eyes of the Overworld*, especially, are regarded as classics of their genre. *Morreion*, *The Seventeen Virgins*, and *The Bagful of Dreams* (all Underwood/Miller, 1979) are "Dying Earth" stories published separately. A recent collection is *The Laughing Magician* (Underwood, 2007). Omnibus volume (numbers 1–4): *The Tales of Dying Earth* (Orb, 2000).

1. *Dying Earth, The* **(Hillman, 1950)** A dying far-future Earth, inhabited by incredible beings, in which magic has replaced science, is the eerie background for six somewhat-connected stories.
2. *Eyes of the Overworld, The* **(Ace, 1966)** Cugel the Clever, caught in the act of burglarizing the house of the "Laughing Magician," is sent on a series of adventures to recover the mate of a magic cusp owned by the latter.
3. *Cugel's Saga* **(Pocket Books, 1983)** Cugel the Clever must return to his home in Almery to find a means of taking revenge on Iucounu, the "Laughing Magician."
4. *Rhialto the Marvelous* **(Baen, 1984)** The magician Rhialto must deal with a time-traveling sorceress who has been turning his fellow magicians into women and causing various other complications.

II. The Lyonesse trilogy is a fantasy series set in the pre-Arthurian Celtic "Elder Isles" and full of intrigue, magic, gallant, deeds, and (unusually for Vance) strong female characters. Omnibus volume (numbers 1–3): *Lyonesse* (Book Club, 1990).

1. *Suldrun's Garden* **(Berkley, 1983)** Princess Suldrun is imprisoned by her ambitious father, King Casmir of Lyonesse, for her refusal to play any part in his schemes for uniting the Elder Isles under his rule. Variant title: *Lyonesse I: Suldrun's Garden*.
2. *Green Pearl, The* **(Underwood/Miller, 1985)** Aillas, young king of South Uliland and onetime lover of Suldrun, has their newborn son spirited away and replaced by a female changeling. Variant title: *Lyonesse II: The Green Pearl*.
3. *Madouc* **(Underwood/Miller, 1989)** Princess Madouc flees her father's court and lands in the middle of a mess of battles, magic, and court intrigues.

III. Vance has written more books that would be classified as science fiction rather than fantasy, although they contain little hard science fiction, and most of them have fantasy elements (especially magic) in them. The Cadwal Chronicles is a trilogy about a planet set up as the Conservancy, a natural preserve protected from settlement and development. Of course, the Conservancy is threatened from without by exploiters and from within by factional conflict.

1. *Araminta Station* **(Tor, 1988)** Two young people grow up in a tiny research station on Cadwal, a world set aside by the Conservancy and otherwise barred to human settlement.
2. *Ecce and Old Earth* **(Tor, 1991)** As powerful anticonservation factions try to open Cadwal to exploitation, the Conservators learn that the original charter guaranteeing Cadwal's status is missing.
3. *Throy* **(Tor, 1993)** Factional conflict erupts between the conservative Chartists and the radical Life, Peace and Freedom Party (LPF), which is championing the cause of the Yips, who are more or less illegal squatters on Cadwal.

IV. The Alastor Cluster is a sprawling system of 30,000 stars and 3,000 inhabited planets ruled over by the mysterious Connatic, who sees all and knows all. Omnibus containing numbers 1, 2, and 3: *Alastor* (Tor, 1995).

1. *Trullion: Alastor 2262* **(Ballantine, 1973)** On the seemingly idyllic planet of Trullion, the Trill, a once peaceful race populating the waters of the planet, are gambling their lives away on a planetwide game.
2. *Marune: Alastor 933* **(Ballantine, 1975)** Pardero is determined to find out who he is and what cruel enemy made him forget his

own life. But when he finally returns to World 933 (Marune), the mystery deepens.

3. *Wyst: Alastor 1716* (DAW, 1978) The Connatic has his suspicions about the planet Wyst, where, seemingly, millions of people live in harmony, work only a few hours a week, and divide their wealth equally.

V. The Big Planet is a huge world, 40,000 miles across, containing many different civilizations. *Showboat World* is a later sequel set on the Big Planet's River Vissel.

1. *Big Planet* (Avalon, 1957) An expedition sent from Earth to forestall the Big Planet's falling under the rule of the tyrant Lysander crashes, and the survivors face a 40,000-mile trek across the unknown surface of the planet.
2. *Showboat World* (Pyramid, 1975) Wily rogue Apollon Zamp plies his trade on the Big Planet's River Vissel. Variant title: *The Magnificent Showboat . . .*

VI. In what is essentially space opera with an admixture of magic, the Demon Princes are five evil beings who disguise themselves as human and delight in power and destruction. In this pentalogy, young Kirth Gerson resorts to vigilante justice to rid the universe, one by one, of these demons, who have destroyed not only his family but his entire world as well in the notorious Mount Pleasant Massacre. A two-volume omnibus, *The Demon Princes* (Tor, 1997), contains numbers 1, 2, and 3 and numbers 4 and 5, respectively.

1. *Star King, The* (Berkley, 1964) The first demon on Kirth Gerson's rub-out list is Attel Malagate, the Star King.
2. *Killing Machine, The* (Berkley, 1964) Kokor Hekkus, the Killing Machine, has been outlawed on every planet of the universe.
3. *Palace of Love, The* (Berkley, 1967) Viole Falushe hides monstrous beings in the so-called Palace of Love.
4. *Face, The* (DAW, 1979) Lens Larque, ugly on the outside, is still uglier in nature.
5. *Book of Dreams, The* (DAW, 1981) Last, but not least, of the Demon Princes, Howard Alan Treesong has poisoned his friends, tortured his colleagues, and written his own holy book, *The Book of Dreams*.

VII. Durdane is a world where men and women are marked for life with "torcs" around their necks and are bound to irrevocable destinies by the tenets of the Faceless Man. Then young Gastel Elzwak challenges the ruling order. Omnibus containing numbers 1, 2, and 3: *Durdane* (Gollancz [UK], 1989).

1. *Anome, The* (Dell, 1973) The supreme ruler of Durdane, the Faceless Man, is challenged by young Gastel Elzwak, who has sworn vengeance against the dreaded Rogushkei, who have killed his mother and sister. Variant title: *The Faceless Man.*
2. *Brave Free Men, The* (Dell, 1973) Gastel Elzwak has made the Faceless Man a prisoner in his own palace. The Brave Free Men are the elite corps of those who consider themselves liberated.
3. *Asutra, The* (Dell, 1974) The wild continent, Iay Coraz, is peopled by exiles, nomads, and slave traders.

VIII. The Tschai/Planet of Adventure series is more space opera about Tschai, a distant planet that is peopled by several alien races and the human slaves they have kidnapped early in Earth's history. It is up to young Adam Reith, sole survivor of a space mission to Tschai, to find a way to warn Earth of Tschai's deadly existence. Omnibus volume containing numbers 1, 2, 3, and 4: *Planet of Adventure* (Tor, 1993).

1. *City of the Chasch* (Ace, 1968) The Chasch are one of the three alien invaders of Tschai. Adam Reith, sole survivor of a mission from Earth to the planet, has to find a way to leave this hostile world.
2. *Servants of the Wankh* (Ace, 1969) The Wankh are another invader race, living far from the others. Variant title: *Wankh.*
3. *Dirdir, The* (Ace, 1969) The Dirdir are the third alien race to invade Tschai.
4. *Pnume, The* (Ace, 1970) The Pnume are an ancient race living underground with their human slaves. They are the "historians" of the planet.

IX. The escapades of Myron Tany, Captain Maloof, and their shipmates on the spaceship *Glica* are the subject of this rather lighthearted pair of novels.

1. *Ports of Call* (St. Martin's, 1998) When Myron Tany points out to his zany aunt that the captain of the space yacht that is taking them to alleged fountain of youth is a swindler, she throws him off the yacht. Myron signs on with a passing tramp cargo vessel.
2. *Lurulu* (St. Martin's, 2004) Captain Maloof, commander of the *Glica*, enlists Myron in a mission to track down a con artist on the captain's home planet of Fluter.

X. Vance has written a number of mystery novels, some as "Ellery Queen" (q.v.) but not containing the Ellery Queen character. A pair of novels features Sheriff Joe Bain of San Rodrigo County, California.

1. *Fox Valley Murders, The* (Bobbs-Merrill, 1966) No annotation available.
2. *Pleasant Grove Murders, The* (Bobbs-Merrill, 1967) No annotation available.

Varley, John

I. The Gaea trilogy is about mankind's first contact with intelligent extraterrestrial beings. Gaea, a wheel-shaped planetoid in orbit around Saturn, not only has sentient life-forms but it *is* a sentient life-form. The trilogy traces the changing relationship between Cirocco Jones, the earthwoman who commands the expedition to Gaea, and Gaea herself, an immense, fickle goddess. Varley's highly inventive plot and characters and his feminist point of view give the books a special slant. Varley is an American science-fiction writer who has won Nebula awards for his shorter fiction. Varley's shorter fiction is collected in *The John Varley Reader: Thirty Years of Short Fiction* (Ace, 2004).

1. *Titan* (Berkley, 1979) An expedition from Earth is stranded on a three-million-year-old world populated by singing centaurs and ruled by the goddess Gaea.
2. *Wizard* (Berkley, 1980) Twenty years later, two humans are sent on a quest through Gaea to receive the "miracles" promised by the goddess.
3. *Demon* (Putnam, 1984) Cirocco Jones and her human and nonhuman allies battle the insane goddess for control of Gaea.

II. Varley is highly regarded in the SF genre but relatively nonprolific. The Eight World series, consisting of two novels and two volumes of short stories, is about a future solar system in which Earth has been conquered by highly superior aliens and humankind is forced onto the moon and other bits of rock in space to survive.

1. *Ophiuchi Hotline, The* (Dial, 1977) Earthlings, forced off Earth by aliens, have managed to re-create a form of civilization on the

moon and other places with the help of a data stream from a star in the constellation Ophiucus, but after 400 years, the unknown helpers are sending for their services.

2. *Blue Champagne* (Berkley, 1977) Short stories.
3. *Persistence of Vision, The* (Dial, 1978) Short stories.
4. *Steel Beach* (Putnam, 1992) The Lunar Colony on the moon seems to be a virtual paradise, but its inhabitants, including the moon's central computer, are feeling suicidal. Reporter Hildy Johnson (think *Front Page*) sets out to get to the bottom of the problem.

III. Varley is working on a new series, full of his tub-thumping libertarian gospel, which details the American settlement of Mars in the near future.

1. *Red Thunder* (Ace, 2003) A manned mission to Mars becomes a personal mission for seven suburban misfits who have constructed Red Thunder, a spaceship built of old tanker cars.
2. *Red Lightning* (Ace, 2006) An object traveling at the speed of light slams into Earth, causing a massive tidal wave that swamps Atlantic islands and coasts, including the Florida home of the grandmother of Ray Garcia-Strickland, teenage son of two of the original Mars settlers.
3. *Rolling Thunder* (Ace, 2008) Podkayne, daughter of Ray Garcia-Strickland, after a visit to her stricken great-grandmother, heads to Europa, where she is exposed to 10 years of suspended animation.

Verne, Jules

I. Jules Verne is often called one of the fathers of science fiction, especially of the "nuts and bolts" variety, with its emphasis on the machinery of the future. *From the Earth to the Moon* and *All around the Moon*, an early pair of novels, sometimes published together in one volume, expressed Verne's optimistic 19th-century enthusiasm for technological progress and his faith in its benevolence (he was to have some reservations later in life). The two novels were followed some 20 years later by *The Purchase of the North Pole*, in which members of the Baltimore Gun Club, featuring the Baltimore Gun Club of the earlier books, embark upon a grandiose scheme of "global warming."

1. *From the Earth to the Moon* (Newark Printing, 1869) Michel Ardan, a Frenchman, joins two Americans on the first moon launch of a satellite named *Columbiad*, which is shot from a huge gun. Original translator not identified. First published in France in 1866 as *De la terre a la lune*. Variant titles: *The Baltimore Gun Club*, *The American Gun Club*, *The Moon Voyage*, and *A Voyage to the Moon*. Translation by Edward Roth published with number 2 (Dover, 1960). Translation by Lowell Bair (1967). Translation by Jacqueline Baldick and Robert Baldick (Dutton, 1970).
2. *All around the Moon* (Catholic Publication Society, 1876) The three astronauts, who were left stranded in moon orbit at the end of number 1, make a perilous return to Earth. Original translator not identified. First published in France in 1870 as *Autour de la lune*. Variant titles: *Round the Moon* and *Around the Moon*. Translation by Edward Roth published with number 1 (Dover, 1960). Translation by Jacqueline Baldick and Robert Baldick (*Around the Moon*, Dutton, 1970).
3. *Purchase of the North Pole, The* (Low, 1891) The Baltimore Gun Club, still undaunted, attempts to change Earth's climate: melting the poles and cooling the tropics. Original translator not identified. First published in France in 1889 as *Sans dessus dessous*. Variant title: *Topsy-Turvy*.

II. There is a good deal of Verne in the character of the megalomaniacal Captain Nemo, who steers his submarine *Nautilus* on its 20,000-league (about 60,000 miles) underwater journey. Partly because of the memorable 1954 Disney film starring Kirk Douglas, James Mason, and Peter Lorre, *Twenty Thousand Leagues under the Sea* shares honors with *Around the World in 80 Days* (which also benefited from a movie version) as the best-known Verne work. The presence of Captain Nemo links number 1 with the Crusoe-esque number 2.

1. *Twenty Thousand Leagues under the Sea* (Osgood, 1875) The inscrutable Captain Nemo battles monsters of the deep and braves other perils of the undersea world. Original translator not identified. First published in France in 1870. Recent translations: Mendor T. Brunetti (New American Library, 1981) and Anthony Bonner (Bantam, 1981); William Butcher (St. Martin's, 1991) and Emanuel J. Mickel (Indiana, 1991); and Walter James Miller and Frederick Paul Walker (Naval Institute, 1993).
2. *Mysterious Island, The* (Lovell, 1883) Captain Nemo reappears in this story, a new twist on the Crusoe theme in which five men and a dog land on a mysterious island. Original translator not identified. First published in France in three volumes in 1870 as *L'ile mysterieuse*. First published in four parts in the United States: *Abandoned* (Scribner, 1875); *Dropped from the Clouds* (Scribner, 1875); *The Secret of the Island* (Low, 1875); and *Wrecked in the Air* (Scribner, 1875). The 1986 New American Library edition doesn't identify the translator. Edition illustrated by N. C. Wyeth (Scribner, 1918).

Veryan, Patricia

PSEUDONYM OF Patricia V. Bannister

I. Acknowledging Jeffrey Farnol and Georgette Heyer as her models, Patricia Veryan has written a series of Georgian novels of consistently high quality. The years 1811–1820, when the future George IV was still Prince Regent, have been called the "Age of Elegance" and have attracted many chroniclers. While Veryan aims for historical accuracy and period ambience, it is her well-told love stories that carry readers through each installment. Many continuing characters are sprinkled throughout the series, including a villainous French family, the Sanaguinets, who plot to assassinate the Prince Regent and take over Britain. Some books in the series are only loosely connected: the core volumes are numbers 2, 5, 6, 7, 8, and 11.

1. *Some Brief Folly* (St. Martin's, 1981) During the period of the Napoleonic Wars, adventuress Euphonia has a coach wreck at the Garrick Estate, which has a rather sinister reputation.
2. *Feather Castles* (St. Martin's, 1982) After Waterloo, Rachel Strand helps a handsome amnesiac to escape to England.
3. *Lord and the Gypsy, The* (Walker, 1978) Lucian St. Clair is too enamored of a beautiful Gypsy to settle down in a prearranged marriage after he returns from the Napoleonic Wars. UK title: *Debt of Honour*.
4. *Love's Duet* (Walker, 1979) Young Sophia Drayton is surprised to find that Camille, Marquis of Damon, whom she blames for the loss of her brother's arm, is very handsome and seems to be hiding something behind his cold facade. UK title: *A Perfect Match*.
5. *Nanette* (Walker, 1981) Nanette escapes from her wealthy, wicked stepfather by disguising herself as her maid and meets aristocratic Harry Redmond.
6. *Noblest Frailty, The* (St. Martin's, 1983) Yolande Drummond has been promised to her handsome cousin Alain Devenish but is strongly attracted to Craig Tyndale, newly arrived from Canada.

7. *Married Past Redemption* (St. Martin's, 1983) Rachel Strand's brother Justin marries Lisette Van Lindsay, who really loves Rachel's husband, Tristram Leith.
8. *Sanguinet's Crown* (St. Martin's, 1985) Rakish Mitchell Redmond and his lover are the only ones who can save the Prince Regent from the poisoned crown that Claude Sanguinet has sent to him.
9. *Logic of the Heart* (St. Martin's, 1990) Susan Henley, who had inherited the Highperch legally, if not entirely ethically, is challenged by Valentine Montclair for the property.
10. *Lanterns* (St. Martin's, 1996) Since their father gambled away the family fortune, Marietta Warrington and her sister must make advantageous marriages.
11. *Give All to Love* (St. Martin's, 1987) Young Josie Storm tries to arouse the romantic interest of her guardian, Lain Devenish, as the Sanguinets plot to poison the Prince Regent.

II. The six Golden Chronicles are set in the period immediately following the Battle of Culloden (1746), when the forces of Bonnie Prince Charlie received a crushing defeat, and the Jacobite cause was lost. The plot of each novel revolves around a cipher that is the key to a treasure that the defeated Jacobites hope to smuggle to France. Each novel also contains a satisfying love story amid the intrigues of the Jacobites and their enemies. For the period immediately preceding these events, read Veryan's *Mistress of Willow Vale* (Walker, 1980) and *The Wagered Widow* (St. Martin's, 1984).

1. *Practice to Deceive* (St. Martin's, 1985) Penelope Montgomery joins the Jacobite cause of Quentin Chandler, a fugitive after the Battle of Culloden.
2. *Journey to Enchantment* (St. Martin's, 1986) Prudence MacTavish joins forces with the mysterious Ligun Doone to help the Jacobite cause.
3. *Tyrant, The* (St. Martin's, 1987) Wealthy bachelor Meredith Carruthers unwillingly aids his Jacobite friends by pretending to be betrothed to Phoebe Ramsay.
4. *Love Alters Not* (St. Martin's, 1988) Horatio Glendenning passes the treasure cipher to Miss Dimity Cranford, who gets involved in some adventures of her own.
5. *Cherished Enemy* (St. Martin's, 1988) Embittered against the Jacobites for her fiancé's death at Culloden, Rosamund joins forces with the mysterious Dr. Robert Victor.
6. *Dedicated Villain, The* (St. Martin's, 1989) Opportunistic Roland Mathieson loses his heart to Miss Fiona Bradford in the conclusion to the chronicles.

III. Tales of the Jewelled Men is another series set during the reign of George II (1727–1760), whose throne is threatened by a mysterious highly placed group of anti-Hanoverians called the League of Jewelled Men. The conspiracy is the connecting link between a series of novels about the love affairs of various members of the English aristocracy.

1. *Time's Fool* (St. Martin's, 1991) Captain Gideon Rossiter returns from the wars to find that his betrothed, Lady Naomi Lutonville, has cooled toward him and that his father is financially ruined.
2. *Had We Never Loved* (St. Martin's, 1992) Lord Horatio Glendenning's Jacobite activities and his stepbrother's gambling losses are being used by the Jewelled Men to steal the Glendenning estate.
3. *Ask Me No Questions* (St. Martin's, 1993) Aristocratic young widow Ruth Allington gets a job as a restorer with the Chandler family after the Jewelled Men have ruined her own family.
4. *Shadow's Bliss, A* (St. Martin's, 1994) Washed ashore in Cornwall, young aristocrat Jonathan is afflicted by an amnesia that leads the local visitors to call him "Crazy Jack."

5. *Never Doubt I Love* (St. Martin's, 1995) Wounded veteran Peregrine Cranford and beautiful Zoe Grainger meet under inauspicious circumstances and cordially dislike each other—at first.
6. *Mandarin of Mayfair, The* (St. Martin's, 1995) The pairing of Gwendolyn Rossiter, whose brother leads the fight to defend the Crown, and conspirator August Falcon, supposedly resistant to women, doesn't seem likely at first.

IV. The Riddles series is more Georgian romance, set during the Napoleonic Wars. Although all five novels are more or less connected, the first three form a trilogy featuring Captain John "Jack" Vespa.

1. *Riddle of Alabaster Royal, The* (St. Martin's, 1997) Captain John "Jack" Vespa, home from the Napoleonic Wars, returns to the reputedly haunted estate Alabaster Royal and becomes involved with Consuela Jones, granddaughter of an eccentric Italian duchess.
2. *Riddle of the Lost Lover, The* (St. Martin's, 1998) Jack Vespa discovers that he is not the son of the senior Vespa, but his search for his lost parentage may lose him Consuela's hand.
3. *Riddle of the Reluctant Rake, The* (St. Martin's, 1999) Lieutenant Colonel "Hasty" Adair finds himself in a compromising situation that may cost him his military career.
4. *Riddle of the Shipwrecked Spinster, The* (St. Martin's, 2001) Cordelia Stansbury runs away to seek romance on the high seas and becomes shipwrecked.
5. *Riddle of the Deplorable Dandy, The* (St. Martin's, 2002) Elspeth Clayton, whose brother Vance has become a soldier of fortune, and dandy Gervaise Valerian find a mutual antipathy.

Vidal, Gore

I. Vidal has woven American history, politics, and journalism into a rich and satisfying tapestry in the American Chronicle series. Both fictional and historical characters move convincingly through his books as he shows the human motives, maneuvers, and failings behind historical events. Vidal's wit, polished prose, and suspenseful plotting have made these books popular with a wide audience.

Gore Vidal has written several other novels, including the pair listed in series II (below); *The Smithsonian Institution* (Random House, 1998), a combination of American history and science fiction; and historical novels set in ancient times, such as *Julian* (Little, Brown, 1964) and *Creation* (Random House, 1981). He has also written plays (e.g., *Visit to a Small Planet* and *The Best Man*), many essays and other nonfiction on political and literary subjects (e.g., *United States: Essays, 1952–1992*, Random House, 1992), and has made many TV appearances. He enjoys the reputation of being the "American Empire's" most prominent political gadfly. He has also written detective stories under the pseudonym Edgar Box (q.v.).

1. *Burr* (Random House, 1973) Charles Schuyler, a young law clerk and aspiring journalist in the 1830s, tells of his friendship with the aging Aaron Burr. The account is interspersed with sections purporting to be Burr's own early journal, in which icons such as Thomas Jefferson are skewered.
2. *Lincoln* (Random House, 1984) The newly elected president Lincoln is held in light regard by Washington insiders, including William H. Seward, his secretary of state.
3. *1876* (Random House, 1976) Now a respected journalist in his sixties, Charlie Schuyler returns from Europe to America in its centennial year and is drawn into the politics of the notorious "stolen" presidential election of 1876.

4. *Empire* (**Random House, 1987**) Young Blaise Stanford learns about journalism from William Randolph Hearst during the presidencies of William McKinley and Theodore Roosevelt and the Spanish-American War.

5. *Hollywood* (**Random House, 1990**) In 1917 Caroline Stanford, Blaise's wife, travels to Hollywood to enlist the infant "photo play" industry in the war effort and is metamorphosed as film star Emma Traxler.

6. *Washington, D.C.* (**Random House, 1967**) Blaise Stanford, a ruthless newspaper tycoon, and his son Peter, a liberal editor, star in this volume set from the New Deal to the McCarthy years.

7. *Golden Age, The* (**Doubleday, 2000**) Covering much of the same historical ground as number 6 (1939–1950s), this novel concentrates on the fight to bring the United States into World War II (FDR at his most Machiavellian) and its aftermath. Gore Vidal allows himself several appearances as a character in the novel.

II. *Myra Breckenridge* and its sequel won a great deal of attention, if not critical appreciation, for their transsexual theme, questioning of sexual stereotypes, and satire on Hollywood and American mores in general. *Myra Breckenridge* was made into a well-publicized and critically panned movie starring Rex Reed, Racquel Welch, and Mae West. The novels were published together in a single volume by Random House (1986).

1. *Myra Breckenridge* (**Houghton Mifflin, 1968**) Myra, formerly Myron, Breckenridge rather effortlessly destroys movie mogul Buck Loner and conventional couple Rusty Godowsky and Mary-Ann Pringle before an accident changes her back into Myron.

2. *Myron* (**Random House, 1974**) Myron Breckenridge is sucked into his television screen and onto the set of *Siren of Babylon*, a 1948 film starring Maria Montex, as Myra tries to alter the male sex and save the world from overpopulation.

Viets, Elaine

I.   Former St. Louis businesswoman Helen Hawthorne is on the lam after trashing her philandering househusband's car, divorcing him, and being socked with alimony since *she* was the wage earner and he was the "dependent." The "dead-end" jobs Helen takes on in Fort Lauderdale, Florida, turn out to be potentially "dead-end" in a literal sense when she stumbles on murder, and her own life is jeopardized as she investigates. These novels are fast and funny, full of wry humor about the "nickel-and-dimed" world that many women are stuck in. Elaine Viets, St. Louis native and current Florida resident, has more than 25 years of journalism experience as a freelancer, fashion writer, editor, and columnist. The hands-on research she does on the various jobs she writes about have been something of a consciousness raiser for Viets: after *Murder with Reservations,* she always leaves a tip for the maid wherever she stays.

1. *Shop till You Drop* (**Signet, 2003**) On the lam from her alimony-demanding husband, Helen Hawthorne winds up in Fort Lauderdale, working as a sales clerk at Juliana's clothing boutique.

2. *Murder between the Covers* (**Signet, 2003**) Page Turner III, obnoxious owner of a bookstore in Fort Lauderdale, finds himself "off-the-books" when he is murdered.

3. *Dying to Call You* (**Signet, 2004**) Helen is a telemarketer for Girdner Surveys when she hears a murder at the other end of the telephone.

4. *Just Murdered* (**Signet, 2005**) Kiki, mother of the bride and one of the worst of an obnoxious series of customers at Millicent's upscale bridal salon, is murdered.

5. *Murder Unleashed* (**Signet, 2006**) While returning a Yorkie to Tammie Grimsbie, client of the exclusive Pampered Pet Boutique, Helen discovers Tammie naked by the pool with grooming shears stuck in her chest. As if that weren't enough, a Labradoodle puppy is missing.

6. *Murder with Reservations* (**Signet, 2007**) A bank robber has stashed away $100,000 in loot somewhere on the premises of the Full Moon Hotel, where Helen is working as a maid.

II.   Before she started the Dead-End Job series, Viets wrote four mysteries featuring Francesca Vierling, columnist for the *St. Louis City Gazette*. Viets says that the "evil" editors portrayed in these novels are a composite of editors she worked with during her journalism career.

1. *Backstab* (**Dell, 1997**) When her sources turn up dead, *St. Louis City Gazette* columnist Francesca Vierling searches for the killer in the seamy sidestreets of St. Louis.

2. *Rubout* (**Dell, 1998**) Who ruined a bikers' ball by killing a leather-clad but blue-blooded divorcée?

3. *Pink Flamingo Murders, The* (**Dell, 1999**) Rehabilitation at North Dakota Place has been punctuated by three murders: an old man painting his house purple, a drug dealer, and a socialite bludgeoned by a pink lawn flamingo.

4. *Doc in a Box* (**Dell, 2000**) While conveying her breast-cancer-stricken boss to therapy and searching for lost male stripper Leo D. Nardo, Francesca runs afoul of a killer who is eliminating the worst MDs in St. Louis.

III.   Viet's latest series, like her first, is set in St. Louis. "Mystery shopper" Josie Marcus, while conducting her anonymous investigations of various retail outlets, runs into murder.

1. *Dying in Style* (**Signet, 2005**) Danessa Celedine, owner of an exclusive store, is found strangled with one of her own $1,000 snakeskin belts.

2. *High Heels Are Murder* (**Signet, 2006**) While mystery shopping in a high-end shoe store, Josie Marcus decides that shoe salesman Mel Poulaine is overly fond of handling women's feet.

3. *Accessory to Murder* (**Signet, 2007**) Hot young designer Halley Hardwick has been killed in a parking lot.

Vinge, Joan D.

American writer Vinge came to science fiction via anthropology, and her novels and stories show a concern with the cultures, both human and nonhuman, of the worlds she has created. Two such worlds are Tiamat, where summer and winter alternate every 150 years, and World's End, a harsh frontier with a Fire Lake that seems to produce madness in those who approach it. A firm scientific basis underlies Vinge's worlds, but it is the characterization and portrayal of alien cultures that set her work apart. *The Snow Queen* won the 1981 Hugo Award, one of science fiction's highest honors. Vinge also wrote *Heaven Chronicles* (Warner, 1991), which contains the short story "Legacy" and the novel *The Outcasts of Heaven Belt* (Signet, 1978), which contains the same character, Wadie Abdhiamal. She also writes children's books, such as the Cat series.

1. *Snow Queen, The* (**Dial, 1980**) The reign of Arienrhod, the Snow Queen of Tiamat's 150-year winter, is nearing its end, but she hopes to extend her life through other winters by cloning.

2. *World's End* (**Blue Jay, 1984**) BZ Gundhalinu, having failed to win the love of Tiamat's prospective Summer Queen, finds himself on World's End, a harsh, barely inhabitable planet, searching for his treasure-hunting older brothers.

3. *Summer Queen, The* (**Warner, 1991**) Moon Dawntreader is the Summer Queen appointed to lead her people after more than a century of exploitation by the technologically advanced Hegemony.

4. *Tangled Up in Blue* (**Tor, 2000**) Hegemonic police officer Nyx Lais Tree loses his partner and his memory during a raid gone bad on a warehouse full of illegal tech the Snow Queen covets.

Vonnegut, Kurt, Jr.

The late Kurt Vonnegut Jr. (d. 2007) has been highly controversial at least since he graduated from being "just an SF writer" into the mainstream with *Slaughterhouse Five* in 1969. Some critics, including Gore Vidal (q.v.) (who called him America's worst writer) and Anthony Burgess (q.v.), have dismissed Vonnegut as a serious writer, but millions of readers, many of them quite intelligent and literate, rate him as one of their favorite authors. Vonnegut's pessimistic apocalypticism combined with a disjointed, often humorous style does turn off many readers, who feel that he shouldn't be taken seriously. Vonnegut, who had a life pocked with tragedy and breakdowns, wrote a series of "highly personal novels disguised as allegories disguised as science fiction," according to David Eggers in *The Salon.com Reader's Guide to Contemporary Authors* (Penguin, 2001). Many of Vonnegut's protagonists are autobiographical figures, including SF writer Kilgore Trout, one of many characters who appear in more than one of the Vonnegut novels. Most of the novels are apocalyptic in that they deal with a catastrophic event of some sort, often resulting in the end of the world, or of "civilization as we know it." Novels are listed in order of first publication. Among omnibus volumes published are *Three by Vonnegut* (Dial, 2007; numbers 4, 6, and 7) and *Kurt Vonnegut* (6) (Octopus, 1980; numbers 1–4 and 6–7).

Short story collections include *Canary in a Cat House* (Fawcett, 1961); *Welcome to the Monkey House* (Delacorte, 1968); and *Bagombo Snuff Box* (Putnam, 1999). Plays and TV dramas include *Happy Birthday, Wanda June* (Delacorte, 1970) and *Between Time and Timbuktu* (Delacorte, 1972). "Nonfiction" volumes include *Wampeters, Foma, and Granfalloons* (Delacorte, 1974); *Palm Sunday* (Delacorte, 1981); *Fates Worse Than Death* (Putnam, 1991); *God Bless You, Dr. Kevorkian* (Seven Stories, 2000); and *A Man without a Country* (Seven Stories, 2005).

1. *Player Piano* (**Scribner, 1952**) Engineer Paul Proteus, although one of the elite, joins the rebellion against a future world dominated by a supercomputer and run by machines, in which most people's lives have no real purpose.

2. *Sirens of Titan, The* (**Dell, 1959**) After crashing his spaceship, Winston Niles Rumfoord is transformed into a wave phenomenon who (that?) returns to Earth periodically and drafts Malachai Constant, "the Space Wanderer," as the prophet of a new religion. Earth's major events are controlled by robotic beings from Trafalmador. One of Vonnegut's funniest novels.

3. *Mother Night* (**Fawcett, 1962**) Howard W. Campell Jr., who was a double agent while "posing" as a Nazi propagandist during World II, is plucked from obscure exile in Greenwich Village and placed in a cell next to Adolf Eichmann. Perhaps Vonnegut's most realistic novel.

4. *Cat's Cradle* (**Holt, 1963**) A novel featuring a midget protagonist, a calypso singer who creates a complete and original theology, and Ice 9, which represents potential doom for the world.

5. *God Bless You, Mr. Rosewater* (**Holt, 1965**) Eliot Rosewater, firefighter, millionaire, and philanthropist, gives millions to poor and pathetic people. Kilgore Trout makes an appearance. Regarded as one of Vonnegut's weakest novels.

6. *Slaughterhouse-Five* (**Delacorte, 1969**) The novel that put Kurt Vonnegut on the mainstream literary map. Based on the author's experiences during World War II at the allied firebombing of the city of Dresden, which killed 130,000 people. Billy Pilgrim, American POW working in an underground slaughterhouse in Dresden in 1945, survives the bombing and is abducted by aliens.

7. *Breakfast of Champions* (**Delacorte, 1973**) Vonnegut's version of a writer writing about writing. Kilgore Trout, at a Festival of the Arts in the Midwest, runs into an insane Pontiac dealer who believes that Kilgore's SF writing is the gospel truth. Tiny aliens who communicate by tap-dancing and farting are part of one Vonnegut's funniest novels.

8. *Slapstick* (**Delacorte, 1976**) Wilbur Daffodil-II Swain, one of a pair of twins, last (and tallest) president of the United States, now "King" of Manhattan, celebrates his 100th birthday.

9. *Jailbird* (**Delacorte, 1979**) Walter J. Starbuck, member of the Nixon White House, is arrested for embezzlement. Kilgore Trout makes another appearance.

10. *Deadeye Dick* (**Delacorte, 1982**) Teenager Rudy Waltz, aka Deadeye Dick, inadvertently kills a pregnant woman while playing with one of his father's many gun.

11. *Galapagos* (**Delacorte, 1985**) A group of tourists, stranded on the Galapagos Islands by an apocalyptic event, become the progenitors of a new race of humans with small brains, flippers for hands, and no interest in sex. Leon Trout, son of Kilgore, plays a role here. One of Vonnegut's most pessimistic novels.

12. *Bluebeard* (**Delacorte, 1987**) Artist Rebo Karabekian, a character in *Breakfast of Champions*, wishes to be left alone on his Long Island estate with the secret he has locked in a potato barn. A send-up of modern art, especially abstract expressionism.

13. *Hocus Pocus* (**Putnam, 1990**) Protagonist Eugene Debs Hartke relates a biblical-scale apocalypse in 2001. Set in the same location as *Player Piano*.

14. *Timequake* (**Putnam, 1997**) Familiar anecdotes, complaints, and characters, such as Kilgore Trout, reappear in this autobiographical essay-cum-novel about not finishing a novel. Vonnegut called this his "last book" (it wasn't).

Wahlöö, Per

Per Wahlöö was half of the Swedish collaborative team that produced the Martin Beck series of detective stories, listed here under Maj Sjöwall (q.v.). Working independently, he wrote several suspense and detective novels including two starring Chief Inspector Peter Jensen. They are dark, symbol-laden explorations of society and the nature of crime.

1. *Thirty-first Floor, The* (**Knopf, 1966**) Though a bomb placed in the offices of a large publishing concern fails to go off, Chief Inspector Jensen is directed to catch the culprit in a week's time. Translated from the Swedish by Joan Tate. Originally published in Sweden in 1964 as *Mord paa 31: A vaaningen*. Variant title: *Murder on the 31st Floor.*

2. *Steel Spring, The* (**Delacorte, 1970**) In this futuristic novel, Peter Jensen, who left his country under the rule of benevolent despots, returns to find corpses littering the streets and all services and communications cut off. Translated from the Swedish by Joan Tate. Originally published in Sweden in 1968 as *Staalspraanget*.

Waldman, Ayelet

Juliet Applebaum, Los Angeles–based ex–public defender, "self-employed mother," and sometime private investigator, gets herself involved in the cases that interest her and don't seem to interest the LAPD very much. Funny, readable novels about "balancing home and career." Ayelet Waldman, herself a former public defender, also wrote the nonseries *Daughter's Keeper* (Sourcebooks, 2003) and *Love and Other Impossible Pursuits* (Doubleday, 2006).

1. *Nursery Crimes* (Berkley, 2000) Former public defender, stay-at-home mom Juliet Applebaum returns to law enforcement when her daughter's Hollywood preschool principal is killed by a hit-and-run driver.
2. *Big Nap, The* (Berkley, 2001) The suspicious disappearance of the Applebaum's babysitter gets Juliet involved.
3. *Playdate with Death, A* (Berkley, 2002) Juliet finds it hard to believe that her personal trainer at the local health club, Bobby Katz, would commit suicide.
4. *Death Gets a Time-Out* (Berkley, 2003) Juliet and her detecting partner, Al Hockey, take on the case of Jupiter Jones, stepbrother of her old pal, film star Lilly Green, who is accused of raping and murdering his new, very young stepmother.
5. *Murder Plays House* (Berkley, 2004) Pregnant with her third child, Juliet decides to hunt for a bigger house. She finds a nice place, perfect except for the corpse in the bathtub.
6. *Cradle Robbers, The* (Berkley, 2005) Sandra Lorgeree, an inmate of California's Dartmoor Prison, surrenders her baby to foster care only to discover that the baby and the foster parents have disappeared.
7. *Bye-Bye Black Sheep* (Berkley, 2006) At the behest of Heavenly, an African American transvestite, Juliet commits herself to tracking down the murderer of Heavenly's sister, Violetta, a drug addict and prostitute whose death has been ignored by the LAPD.

Walker, David (Harry)

The charming 1955 British movie *Wee Geordie* was based on Walker's first book about George MacTaggart of the Scottish village of Drumfechan. Embarrassed when his sweetheart, Jean, calls him "Wee Geordie," young George, at 14, embarks on a body-building program. After reaching a height of six feet, five inches and winning the shot-put event at the Boston Olympics, George returns to his Highland home to claim Jean's love. This is a good-humored *Rocky* story, set in a gentler time and place.

1. *Geordie* (Houghton Mifflin, 1950) Young Geordie MacTaggart is ashamed of being shorter than his girlfriend, Jean, and trains and exercises his way to success.
2. *Come Back, Geordie* (Houghton Mifflin, 1966) Geordie and his wife, Jean, worry about their son, Charlie, who seems to be turning into a discontented and aimless teenager.

Walker, Robert W(ayne)

I. Dr. Jessica Coran is an FBI medical examiner specializing in serial killers. The cases Jessica investigates involve clever, sadistic killers who kill for fun—they enjoy watching their victims die as painfully as possible—and they often double the fun by mutilating the bodies as well. These novels are more horror/suspense stories than mysteries and will appeal to readers who like their crime on the gruesome side.

1. *Killer Instinct* (Berkley, 1992) Wisconsin's Vampire-Killer doesn't kill vampires—he kills ordinary people by draining their blood. Now he is stalking FBI medical examiner Jessica Coran.
2. *Fatal Instinct* (Berkley, 1993) Jessica is in New York City, on the hunt for a modern-day Jack the Ripper.
3. *Primal Instinct* (Berkley, 1994) Dr. Coran cuts her Hawaiian vacation short to assist in the urgent investigation of a local serial killer called the Cane Cutter.
4. *Pure Instinct* (Berkley, 1995) The Queen of Hearts Killer, who removes hearts from young male victims, is on the loose in New Orleans. And the Vampire-Killer (see number 1) has escaped.
5. *Darkest Instinct* (Berkley, 1996) Human body parts are discovered in the bellies of sharks off the Florida Keys, but it seems that the bodies were already dead before they hit the water, thanks to a serial killer named the Night Crawler.
6. *Extreme Instinct* (Berkley, 1998) A serial killer operating from Arizona to Montana enjoys setting victims on fire and watching them die.
7. *Blind Instinct* (Berkley, 2000) London's elite New Scotland Yard calls upon Jessica to investigate a series of crucifixion murders.
8. *Bitter Instinct* (Berkley, 2001) The Poet's calling card is human skin engraved with toxic ink and verse.
9. *Unnatural Instinct* (Berkley, 2002) Jessica Coran's greatest adversary, practitioner of "revolving-door" justice, Judge Maureen DeCampe, has disappeared.
10. *Grave Instinct* (Berkley, 2003) Someone is drugging young women, cutting into their heads, making off with their brains, and leaving a sign carved into the back of each victim's skull. Daryl Thomas Cahil, who has just been released from a prison for the criminally insane, seems a likely suspect.
11. *Absolute Instinct* (Berkley, 2004) In a crime reminiscent of one for which a man already has been sentenced to death, a woman has been killed, and her spine has been removed from her body.

II. Native American ex-cop Lucas Stonecoat and police psychiatrist Meredyth Sanger of Houston investigate serial killings highly reminiscent of the murders and mutilations that Jessica Coran (see series I) is called upon to solve.

1. *Cutting Edge* (Jove, 1997) A popular computer game inspires a crime wave in Houston. Police psychiatrist Meredyth Sanger enlists the aid of Native American ex-cop Lucas Stonecoat.
2. *Double Edge* (Jove, 1998) The Snatcher preys on teens, outcasts whose sole reason for existence is satisfying his psychopathic needs.
3. *Cold Edge* (Jove, 2001) Native American Lucas Stonecoat has the unenviable task of tracking down the Scalper, a serial killer with a grisly calling card.
4. *Final Edge* (Jove, 2004) The bodies of young girls are turning up, piece by piece.

III. The novels featuring Dr. Dean Grant, head of Criminal Forensic Medicine for Chicago, are precursors to series I. Sadistic psychopaths prey on a series of victims.

1. *Dead Man's Float* (Pinnacle, 1988) Some psychopathic killer gets his kicks by watching his victims drown.
2. *Razor's Edge* (Pinnacle, 1989) Like the serial killers in *Grave Instinct* (series I, number 10) and *Cold Edge* (series II, number 3), this killer removes scalps. Set in Orlando rather than Chicago.
3. *Dying Breath* (Pinnacle, 1989) This killer likes to see his victims die by asphyxiation.

4. *Burning Obsession* (Pinnacle, 1989) Like the serial killer in *Extreme Instinct* (series I, number 6), this maniac gets a kick out of setting his victims on fire.

IV. Walker's latest series, starring Inspector Alastair Ransom and Dr. James Phineas Tewes, represents a change of pace, if only because it is set back in 1893, at Chicago's Columbian Exhibition, or World's Fair. We are dealing with serial killers again.

1. *City for Ransom* (Avon, 2006) The Phantom of the Fair is getting his own sort of fun out of the Worlds Fair in Chicago in 1893.
2. *Shadows in the White City* (Harper, 2007) Alastair Ransom decides to take the law into his own hands to rid the World's Fair of its "Phantom."
3. *City of the Absent* (Harper, 2007) In the final days of the Columbian Exposition, Ransom is hunting down the murderers who killed two of his acquaintances.

Wall, Kathryn R.

Lydia Baynard Simpson "Bay" Tanner had it all until her husband died. The high-powered financial consultant retired to her hideaway on Hilton Head, South Carolina, to lick her wounds. Eventually Bay formed, with her father, retired judge Talbot Simpson, and young computer wizard Erik Whiteside, Simpson & Tanner Inquiry Agents, a kind of quasi detective agency, and got involved in a series of mysteries, most of them featuring friends or relatives. This is a series with a regional "Low Country" South Carolina background. Kathryn R. Wall, Ohio native and retired accountant, has lived in Hilton Head for more than a decade now.

1. *In for a Penny* (iuniverse, 2000) Bay Tanner, in retreat on Hilton Head Island, South Carolina, after the murder of her husband, Rob, feels obliged to help out her "old money" friends and family when they unwittingly get involved in a shady land scheme that could lead them to financial disaster. Originally self-published. Reprinted by Coastal Villages Press in 2002.
2. *And Not a Penny More* (Coastal Villages, 2002) Bay's old school friend Jordan von Brandt is convinced that her mother, widowed socialite Leslie Herrington, found dead in a South American hotel room, was murdered.
3. *Perdition House* (St. Martin's, 2003) Bay has formed, with her father, retired judge Talbot Simpson, and young computer whiz Erik Whiteside, a sort of detective agency called Simpson & Tanner Inquiry Agents. Then Bay gets a phone call from the county jail where her "half fifth cousin" Mercer Mary Prescott is being charged with vagrancy.
4. *Judas Island* (St. Martin's, 2004) Eric Whiteside's old college friend, archaeologist Grey Palmer Jr., is murdered after he finds the remains of a recently killed man on the islands off of Beaufort, South Carolina.
5. *Resurrection Road* (St. Martin's, 2005) Bay and her lover, Alain Darnay, are the chief suspects when recently orphaned teenager Carl Anderson's empty car is found splattered with blood at an abandoned fort on St. Helena Island.
6. *Bishop's Reach* (St. Martin's, 2006) A two-year search by Erik Whiteside finally locates the black-sheep brother of Miss Addie, elderly lifelong friend of Bay's family, but the brother's return to Hilton Head ignites a series of criminal activities culminating in murder.
7. *Sanctuary Hill* (St. Martin's, 2007) Bay uncovers the body of an unidentified newborn baby girl who is wearing a strange charm around her neck.

8. *Mercy Oak, The* (St. Martin's, 2008) When Theresa Montalvo, sister of political activist Serena Montalvo, is killed in a hit-and-run, Bay gets involved in the murky world of illegal immigration.

Walpole, Hugh (Seymour)

I. Fans of Winston Graham's (q.v.) Poldark Saga should also enjoy Walpole's engaging adventures of the Herries family. Set in the picturesque lake country, these novels chronicle English history from Elizabethan times to the 1930s. *Rogue Herries*, the first of the series to be published, was a best seller on both sides of the Atlantic and shows Walpole at the peak of his storytelling powers.

Hugh Walpole was born in New Zealand and came to England at an early age. He wrote more than 40 novels, many of them best sellers. He was one of the most popular English writers between the world wars but was never a favorite of the literary critics. Somerset Maugham's nasty caricature of Walpole as Alroy Kear in *Cakes in Ale* (1930) hurt Walpole personally and may have seriously damaged his reputation. His popularity nose-dived, particularly after his death, in 1941, but several of his novels are still in print and will reward readers who seek them out.

The Herries books were originally intended to be a tetralogy and were published together in an omnibus edition: *The Herries Chronicles* (Macmillan [UK], 1939), but Walpole planned a second tetralogy set in time before the first. He died after completing one volume (number 1) and left an unfinished second volume (number 2).

1. *Bright Pavilions, The* (Doubleday, 1940) Set in Elizabethan England, this book tells the story of two Herries brothers: Robin, a dreamer, and Nicholas, a doer.
2. *Katherine Christian* (Doubleday, 1943) Intended as volume 2 of the second tetralogy, and continuing the family saga of *The Bright Pavilions*, this novel was left unfinished at Walpole's death.
3. *Rogue Herries* (Doubleday, 1930) The story of Francis "Rogue" Herries, an 18th-century gentleman, from his arrival in Cumberland in 1740 with wife, children, and mistress to his death in 1774 as his second Gypsy wife bears him a child.
4. *Judith Paris* (Doubleday, 1931) This book traces the turbulent life and loves of Judith, the daughter of Francis Herries and his Gypsy wife, from birth to death (1774–1820).
5. *Fortress, The* (Doubleday, 1932) Judith vies with Walter Herries, and young Adam reaches manhood during the period 1822–1874.
6. *Vanessa* (Doubleday, 1933) Vanessa, Judith's granddaughter, is a dreamer who makes a disastrous marriage. This account—and the first tetralogy—ends in 1932.

II. The Jeremy stories are a semiautobiographical look at an English childhood around the turn of the 20th century. They follow Jeremy from the age of 8 to the age of 15. Although often regarded as children's books, like Mark Twain's (q.v.) *The Adventures of Tom Sawyer*, they can be enjoyed by adults. Published together in an omnibus volume: *The Jeremy Stories* (Macmillan [UK], 1941).

1. *Jeremy* (Doran, 1919) Jeremy seen from ages eight to nine, along with his governess (whom he torments), his two older sisters, Reverend Cole, his aloof father, his placid mother, Aunt Amy, Uncle Samuel, and, not least, his dog, Hamlet.
2. *Jeremy and Hamlet* (Doran, 1923) Jeremy is sent off to school but comes home for Christmas, when his father almost ruins the festivities until Uncle Samuel intervenes.
3. *Jeremy at Crale* (Doran, 1927) Subtitle: *His Friends, His Ambitions, and His One Great Enemy*. Jeremy at age 15 has some problems at Crale School.

III. Four stories about different people are unified by their setting in the small seaside cathedral town of Polchester in "Glebeshire." *The Inquisitor,* published some years after the other three, is notable for its element of psychological horror, reminiscent of some of Walpole's horror fiction such as *The Killer and the Slain* (Doubleday, 1942) and the collection *All Soul's Night* (Doubleday, 1933).

1. *Cathedral, The* (Doran, 1922) Archdeacon Brandon does not find his lot an easy one, particularly since it includes the ambitious Canon Ronder.
2. *Old Ladies, The* (Doran, 1924) Three impecunious old women are drawn together by their longings for something.
3. *Harmer John* (Doran, 1926) Subtitle: *An Unworldly Story.* In the wake of a terrible storm, Swede Harmer John comes to town to open a gymnasium.
4. *Inquisitor, The* (Doubleday, 1935) A ghost seems to be walking the streets of Polchester as the townspeople and the cathedral folk continue their feuds.

IV. Young Englishman Henry Trenchard links this series, which is sometimes broken into two parts. The first part (numbers 1 and 2) relates Trenchard's story from childhood to youthful passion. Number 3, based on Walpole's own experiences, details events on the Russian front in the early going of World War I. Number 4 brings the two threads together in Russia at the time of the revolution.

1. *Green Mirror, The* (Doran, 1917) The childhood of Henry Trenchard, son of quintessential British parents.
2. *Young Enchanted, The* (Doran, 1921) Henry Trenchard falls in love.
3. *Dark Forest, The* (Doran, 1916) Henry Trenchard and the Russian Semyonov try, in their various ways, to survive the vicissitudes of World War I as the Russian front shifts back and forth in 1914–1915.
4. *Secret City, The* (Doran, 1919) Two Englishmen, Jerry Lawrence and Henry Bohun, travel together in Russia on separate errands for the British Foreign Office and get involved with the Semyonovs' niece Vera and the Markovitch family, as the Russian Revolution looms in 1917.

Walsh, Jill Paton

Imogen Quy (rhymes with *why*) is the quietly competent nurse at the fictional college of St. Agatha's at Cambridge University. The witty and inquisitive Quy gets herself involved in a series of academic mysteries in the classic English manner. If Imogene reminds readers of Dorothy Sayers's (q.v.) Harriet Vane, this is no accident since Walsh completed one Sayers novel—*Thrones, Dominations* (St. Martin's, 1998)—and wrote another novel—*A Presumption of Death* (St. Martin's, 2003)—using Sayers's beloved Wimsey character.

English author Jill Paton Walsh is the author of many novels for juveniles including *The Children of the Fox* (Farrar, 1978), a historical trilogy about ancient Greece. Walsh has also written several nonmystery novels for adults, including *Knowledge of Angels* (Houghton Mifflin, 1994), which was short-listed for the Booker Prize.

1. *Wyndham Case, The* (St. Martin's, 1993) A student is found dead in the Wyndham Case, an unrivaled collection of 17th-century volumes housed at St. Agatha's College. When another student is found dead in a fountain, the suspicions of college nurse Imogen Quy are aroused.
2. *Piece of Justice, A* (St. Martin's, 1995) Imogen's lodger, Fran Bullion, assigned to write a study of the late mathematician Gideon

Summerfield, discovers that three previous Summerfield biographers have died suspiciously.

3. *Debts of Dishonor* (St. Martin's, 2006) Imogen Quy is revived after more than a decade as billionaire St. Agatha's alumnus Sir Julius Farran, who has aroused hopes of a large donation to the financially straitened college, dies in questionable circumstances.
4. *Bad Quarto, The* (St. Martin's, 2007) The cutthroat world of modern Shakespearean scholarship is exposed as St. Agatha's College fellow John Talentire tumbles to his death while climbing a building and a stage production of a shorter version of *Hamlet* known as the *Bad Quarto* casts doubts upon the accidental nature of Talentire's death.

Waltari, Mika

Finnish author Mika Waltari wrote a number of epic historical novels that were translated into English, including *The Egyptian* (Putnam, 1949), an instant best seller that Hollywood made into a successful film spectacular in 1954 starring Victor Mature, Peter Ustinov, and a host of other big names. Waltari also published two picaresque novels about the adventures of a young Finn in 16th-century Europe.

1. *Adventurer, The* (Putnam, 1950) Michael the Finn is raised by a witch woman and educated by priests before he takes off for adventure in foreign lands. Translated from the Finnish by Naomi Walford. Originally published in Finland in 1948 as *Mikael Karvajalka.*
2. *Wanderer, The* (Putnam, 1951) Michael and his companion, Andy, are captured by Arab pirates and see North Africa and the Ottoman Empire in the days of Suleiman the Magnificent. Translated from the Finnish by Naomi Walford. Originally published in Finland in 1949 as *Mikael Hakin.*

Warner, Rex

These two volumes of Julius Caesar's fictional memoirs will interest readers who enjoyed Masterpiece Theatre's production of *I, Claudius,* which was based on Robert Graves's (q.v.) book. British author Rex Warner has combined his skill as a poet with his scholar's knowledge of classical history to produce these solid and authentic documentary fictions.

1. *Young Caesar, The* (Little, Brown, 1958) Caesar reminisces on his youth and rise to power.
2. *Imperial Caesar* (Little, Brown, 1960) Subjects covered include Caesar's military conquests, his affair with Cleopatra, and other activities of his last 15 years. UK title: *Julius Caesar.*

Watson, Larry

Montana 1948 was one of those sleepers that became a best seller mostly through word of mouth. The story of the scandals that wrecked a middle-class family in small-town Montana in 1948 was followed by a prequel that reaches back to 1924 and 1899 to give more detail on the Hayden family and show how it got the way it was in 1948. Honest writing about the Big Sky country and the people who settled it. Watson, who has been quoted as saying that he writes about "the dark side of Lake Wobegon," has published six novels, all set in small towns. *White Crosses* (Pocket, 1997) also has a Montana setting.

1. *Justice* (**Milkweed, 1995**) Starts in 1924 as Sheriff Julian Hayden's teenage sons get in trouble in North Dakota, then doubles back to 1899 to show Julian's frontier life as a struggling homesteader and rancher.
2. *Montana 1948* (**Milkweed, 1993**) David Hayden narrates the events when his uncle Frank is accused of molesting and raping Native American girls during routine medical examinations.

Waugh, Evelyn

I. Readers whose interest in Waugh was reawakened by the airing of *Brideshead Revisited* (Little, Brown; 1945) on Masterpiece Theatre will find his World War II trilogy similar in tone and appeal. Its central character is 35-year-old Guy Crouchback, an English Catholic of comfortable means whose wife's desertion and lack of strong family ties have left him a lonely and rather cold person. Stirred by patriotism and a desire to participate meaningfully in a worthy cause, Guy enlists and eventually sees action with the Halberdier Regiment abroad. Guy's experiences are based partly on Waugh's own World War II service. The one-volume omnibus edition entitled *Sword of Honor* (Little, Brown, 1966) incorporates some revisions.

1. *Men at Arms* (**Little, Brown, 1952**) After the boredom of training camp and duty in the English countryside, Guy's regiment is shipped to Dakar, where finds himself leading an unauthorized night raid.
2. *Officers and Gentlemen* (**Little, Brown, 1955**) Guy is in London during the worst of the German bombing, then sees action in Crete, where his disillusionment and feelings of betrayal are complete.
3. *End of the Battle, The* (**Little, Brown, 1961**) Amid the otherwise inane last years of Crouchback's military career, he aids a group of Jewish refugees and comes to his ex-wife's rescue. UK title: *Unconditional Surrender.*

II. Basil Seal, the "definitive cad," who messes up, with some help, the modernization of the African nation of Azania (Abyssinia, where Waugh spent some time as a correspondent) in *Black Mischief,* reappears in *Put Out More Flags* and in the short story "Basil Seal Rides Again." Basil, who is in some respects a survivor of the "Bright Young Things" of Waugh's earliest novels, *Decline and Fall* (Doran, 1925) and *Vile Bodies* (Cape, 1930), is in many respects the opposite of the basically decent Guy Crouchback.

1. *Black Mischief* (**Farrar, 1932**) The emperor Seth mistakenly enlists Englishman Basil Seal in an attempt to modernize his African nation, which winds up disastrously and with one of the more grotesque endings in modern fiction.
2. *Put Out More Flags* (**Little, Brown, 1942**) Basil Seal is one of several characters revived from earlier books in this depiction of the "Phoney War" of 1939–1940, the uneasy time after the German invasion of Poland.
3. *Basil Seal Rides Again* (**Little, Brown, 1963**) Subtitle: *The Rake's Regress.* A short story featuring Basil Seal in old age that appeared in limited editions on both sides of the Atlantic. Reprinted in *The Complete Stories of Evelyn Waugh* (Little, Brown, 1998).

Webster, Jan

Glasgow and the nearby mining towns provide a solid background to this three-volume saga that follows the Balfour, Kilgour, and Fleming families from 1840 to the present day. Star-crossed lovers, philandering mine owners, passionate union organizers, and some extraordinarily feisty women figure in the interrelated plots, which keep the reader moving right along.

1. *Colliers Row* (**Lippincott, 1977**) The story begins in 1840 as young Kate, pregnant and in disgrace, is dismissed from her job as housekeeper to the mine-owning Balfour family.
2. *Saturday City* (**St. Martin's, 1979**) This account follows the fortunes of Kate's children from 1880 to 1918 as Sandia opens a shop in Glasgow and Duncan fights to unionize the miners.
3. *Beggarman's Country* (**St. Martin's, 1980**) Wealthy Mairi Fleming marries a Communist while her brother Patie marries a beautiful aristocrat with Scots Nationalist sympathies.

Webster, Jean

PSEUDONYM OF Alice Jane Chandler

Jean Webster, an American author who died before the age of 40, is remembered today for two books—*Daddy-Long-Legs* and *Dear Enemy*—that are regarded as young adult classics, especially the former. Both are epistolary novels, linked by the John Grier Home, a home for orphans. *Daddy-Long-Legs* is told by Jerusha "Judy" Abbott, an orphan who writes about her college experiences to her mysterious benefactor. *Dear Enemy* describes the workings of the John Grier Home through letters written by its superintendent, Sally MacBride. At least four film versions have been made of *Daddy-Long-Legs*: a 1919 version starring Mary Pickford; a 1931 version starring Janet Gaynor; *Curly Top,* a 1935 adaptation starring Shirley Temple; and a musical version in 1955 starring Fred Astaire and Leslie Caron. Webster also wrote two volumes of humorous short stories about life at a woman's college: *When Patty Went to College* (Century, 1903; UK title: *Patty and Priscilla*) and *Just Patty* (Century, 1911).

1. *Daddy-Long-Legs* (**Century, 1912**) Judy Abbott, the oldest orphan at the John Grier Home, is sent to college by a mysterious benefactor to whom she writes entertainingly of her student days.
2. *Dear Enemy* (**Century, 1915**) Sallie MacBride, the new superintendent of the John Grier Home, writes of her work with the orphans to her friends, including Judy and Jervis Pendelton, and to the dour Scottish doctor who is the "Dear Enemy" of the title.

Weidman, Jerome

I. Although his Broadway musical *Fiorello* (1959) won a Pulitzer Prize, Jerome Weidman is probably best remembered for his acerbic early novel *I Can Get It for You Wholesale* (which was also made into a Broadway musical, in 1962) about the rise in the New York garment business in the 1930s of Harry Bogan, a prize heel. Harry gets his comeuppance in the sequel when he runs into a gold-digging starlet.

1. *I Can Get It for You Wholesale* (**Simon & Schuster, 1937**) Harry Bogan rises from shipping clerk in a New York garment factory to become a successful dress manufacturer, doubled-crossing everyone on the way up.
2. *What's in It for Me?* (**Simon & Schuster, 1938**) Harry meets his match in beautiful gold-digging starlet Martha Mills, who takes him for everything he has.

II. Less acerbic than his early works, the Benny Kramer books are warm and humorous recollections of growing up Jewish on the Lower East Side in the 1920s and of the Depression years spent "uptown" in the Bronx. These sharp and entertaining tales and portraits are thought to be highly autobiographical.

1. *Fourth Street East* (Random House, 1970) Young Benny, innocent of the dangerous lowlife all around him, wends his way through the neighborhood and meets success at school.
2. *Last Respects* (Random House, 1972) Benny at 14 helps in his mother's bootlegging business.
3. *Tiffany Street* (Random House, 1974) Benny, now a successful attorney, is plagued by feelings of inadequacy; his reaction to his son's decision to become a conscientious objector is a central concern.

Weir, Charlene

San Francisco cop Susan Wren moves to the small town of Hampstead, Kansas, when she marries Hampstead's police chief, Daniel Wren. Ten days later, she becomes a widow when Daniel is killed by a sniper's bullet. Undaunted, Susan takes over her husband's job and investigates his murder, the first of a series of cases she handles her in not-so-bucolic community.

1. *Winter Widow* (St. Martin's, 1992) Widowed 10 days after she arrives in Hampstead, Kansas, former San Francisco cop Susan Wren takes on her late husband's job as police chief and vows to find Daniel Wren's killer.
2. *Consider the Crows* (St. Martin's, 1993) The body of Lynnelle Hames, a quiet young woman recently arrived in Hampstead, is found near the isolated old house where she was living. Then Emerson College vice chancellor Hilary Kalazar disappears on her way to a convention in Dallas.
3. *Family Practice* (St. Martin's, 1995) Dr. Dorothy Barrington, eldest of five sibling doctors, is shot dead in her office, and 11-year-old Jen Bryant, whom Susan Wren was minding for the weekend, is critically wounded.
4. *Murder: Take Two* (St. Martin's, 1998) When a Hollywood film crew comes to Hampstead to shoot a film, stunt-double Kay Bender is killed in a fatal accident. Suspicions are that Kay may have been the innocent victim of a plot against look-alike screen star Laura Edwards.
5. *Cold Christmas, A* (St. Martin's, 2001) Recently arrived repairman and mystery man Tim Holiday is found dead in Caley James's basement.
6. *Up in Smoke* (St. Martin's, 2003) Jack Garrett, governor of Kansas and presidential candidate, is possibly implicated in the death of wheelchair-bound Wakely Fromm, his oldest and best friend.
7. *Edge of Midnight* (St. Martin's, 2007) Cary Black flees California to escape her abusive husband but finds that her contact in Kansas, Kelby Oliver, has vanished. Cary assumes Kelby's identity only to find that Kelby had enemies of her own.

Weld, William F(loyd)

Soon after he takes a job with a Boston law firm, Terrence Mullally becomes "the available man" to run against the incumbent district attorney. This is the beginning of a funny, suspenseful, cynical satire of American politics, where corruption is endemic. In *Big Ugly*, the sequel, Terrence, six months into his tenure as junior senator from Massachusetts, finds that politics in Washington is, if

anything, even rougher and sleazier than it is in Massachusetts.

William F. Weld knows something about politics, having been twice elected governor of Massachusetts. Looking for broader fields, as Massachusetts governors tend to do, Weld resigned in the middle of his second term to accept an appointment as ambassador to Mexico, only to find himself shot down by Senator Jesse Helms, an incident that provided fodder for the plot of *Big Ugly*.

1. *Mackerel by Moonlight* (Simon & Schuster, 1998) Terrence Mullally, recently arrived in Boston from a checkered past in Brooklyn, becomes the Democrats' "anti-corruption" nominee to run for district attorney. (John Randolph, of Roanoke, 1773–1833, said of a political opponent: "He shines and stinks like rotten mackerel by moonlight.")
2. *Big Ugly* (Simon & Schuster, 1999) Mullally, now a US senator, finds himself outmaneuvered and his political ambitions thwarted by a gaggle of Washingtonians, including the US vice president and the US senator from Big Ugly, West Virginia.

Wellman, Paul I(selin)

All the conflicts of passion and ambition that kept TV viewers watching *Dallas* are included in full measure in these readable novels set in Jericho, Kansas, in the 1880s and the early 1900s. The Wedge family, owner of Jericho's newspaper, the *Daily Clarion*, provides the unifying focus for the last three novels. Wellman drew effectively on his own experience as a midwestern newspaperman.

1. *Bowl of Brass, The* (Lippincott, 1944) Jericho eventually prevails in the Kansas county-seat wars in the 1880s.
2. *Walls of Jericho* (Doubleday, 1947) Tucker Wedge's new wife stirs up trouble when she comes to Jericho, and the friendship between Tucker and aspiring young politician Dave Constable is endangered.
3. *Chain, The* (Doubleday, 1949) The Reverend John Carlisle, a man of conscience, brings social reform and hope to Jericho and finds some bitter resistance.
4. *Jericho's Daughter* (Doubleday, 1956) Murder and blackmail are elements in this story about Mary Agnes Wedge and her unfaithful husband.

Wells, Rebecca

The first Ya-Ya book, *Little Altars Everywhere*, was published by a small press in Seattle and attracted relatively little attention, although it was awarded the Western States Book Award for Fiction. *Divine Secrets of the Ya-Ya Sisterhood* was published by a major publisher but with little fanfare. Word of mouth made *Divine Secrets* a best seller and something of a cult book, spawning "Ya-Ya Clubs" throughout the country. *Little Altars* and *Divine Secrets* were republished together as a boxed set (HarperCollins, 1999), and a hit movie, *Divine Secrets of the Ya-Ya Sisterhood*, made from material in the two books and featuring Sandra Bullock and a host of other Hollywood "names," was released in 2002. The third novel, *Ya Yas in Bloom*, was published and received favorably by critics and readers.

The Ya-Ya books are basically about four women friends and their families in a small town in Louisiana from the 1930s to the present. Through a series of flashbacks and reminiscences, we relive their adventures from the time when, as children in 1932, they disrupted a Shirley Temple look-alike contest. They are books about small-town life, family relationships, and female bonding through thick and thin. The books are irreverent, funny, sometimes poignant portraits of a group of women who face the vicissitudes of life with humor and style.

1. *Little Altars Everywhere* (**Broken Moon, 1992**) Introduces the Walkers, Shep, Vivi, Siddalee, Little Shep, Lulu, and Baylor, in the rural parish of Rapide, Louisiana, in the 1960s. Siddalee and her siblings reminiscence about their lives. Mom Vivi is one of the Ya-Ya Sisterhood, which is introduced here.
2. *Divine Secrets of the Ya-Ya Sisterhood* (**Harper Collins, 1996**) Vivi, one of the Ya-Yas, a sisterhood that dates back to 1932, gives her daughter Siddalee a scrapbook that evokes memories of the past and the enduring relationships among the four smart and sassy women.
3. *Ya-Yas in Bloom* (**HarperCollins, 2005**) More stories about the Ya-Yas, their children, and their grandchildren.

West, Rebecca

PSEUDONYM OF Cicily Isabel Fairfield

Rebecca West was best known as a literary critic and political journalist—see *Black Lamb and Grey Falcon* (Macmillan, 1937) and *The Meaning of Treason* (Viking, 1947)—and, in her early days, as an ardent feminist, but she also wrote fiction, including a three-volume family saga tracing the fortunes of the Aubrey family from Edwardian times to the years immediately following World War I. The Aubrey family is based on West's family. Rose Aubrey, the books' narrator and central character, is thought to be the autobiographical figure. The works are conventional in form, strong on characterization and period flavor. The last two volumes were published posthumously nearly 30 years after the appearance of *The Fountain Overflows*. *Cousin Rosamund* was not finished by West but was fully outlined in the manuscripts she left. Many of West's earlier works have been reprinted by Virago Press.

1. *Fountain Overflows, The* (**Viking, 1956**) The Aubrey family migrates from Edinburgh to London in the early 1900s and is kept together by their strong-minded mother, Clare.
2. *This Real Night* (**Viking, 1984**) The Aubrey family has been abandoned by their father, but the children reach adolescence strongly motivated to pursue musical careers.
3. *Cousin Rosamund* (**Viking, 1986**) The Aubrey children have reached adulthood after World War I. Rose pursues a career as a professional pianist and falls in love with a young composer.

Westlake, Donald E(dwin)

I. Westlake (d. 2008) was a master of the funny "big caper" novel. His effervescence, humor, and unflagging inventiveness have drawn comparison to P. G. Wodehouse (q.v.). John Dortmunder and his band of inept heist men, who often plan their ingenious but inevitably flawed capers at the O. J. Bar & Grill in New York City, are the comically hapless protagonists of a series of novels and short stories. Several novels have been made into films including *The Hot Rock* (1972, Robert Redford) and *Bank Shot* (1974, George C. Scott). Westlake was also an excellent noir-thriller writer (e.g., *The Ax*, Mysterious, 1997) and wrote mystery series novels under the pseudonyms of Tucker Coe (q.v.) and Richard Stark (q.v.).

1. *Hot Rock, The* (**Simon & Schuster, 1970**) The extraordinary John Dortmunder masterminds the theft of the Balambo emerald from an exhibit at New York's Coliseum.

2. *Bank Shot* (**Simon & Schuster, 1972**) Dortmunder returns with plans to steal a Long Island suburban bank—lock, stock, and barrel.
3. *Jimmy the Kid* (**Lippincott, 1974**) Using a tough, no-nonsense paperback thriller about a kidnapping as their guide, Dortmunder and his gang kidnap 12-year-old Jimmy Harrington, and the fun begins.
4. *Nobody's Perfect* (**Evans, 1977**) Stolen paintings, a missing old master, and a hired assassin on Dortmunder's trail keep this installment lively.
5. *Why Me?* (**Viking, 1983**) Dortmunder inadvertently comes into the possession of a ring with a very large ruby hotly desired by numerous law enforcement officials, criminals, and terrorists.
6. *Good Behavior* (**Mysterious, 1986**) Dortmunder drops in (through a skylight) on a group of nuns and finds that they regard him as a godsend.
7. *Drowned Hopes* (**Mysterious, 1990**) Dortmunder and his band attempt to recover $700,000 from an armored car buried under 50 feet of water in upstate New York.
8. *Don't Ask* (**Mysterious, 1993**) The possession of a 17th-century saint's relic will determine whether Tsergovia or Votskojek gets the available seat in the United Nations.
9. *What's the Worst That Could Happen?* (**Mysterious, 1996**) After billionaire Max Fairbanks catches Dortmunder burgling his Long Island estate, he falsely claims ownership of Dortmunder's good-luck ring.
10. *Bad News* (**Mysterious, 2001**) After a botched (what else?) burglary, Dortmunder is talked by his pal Andy Kelp into a grave robbery. Then the two get involved with an elaborate scheme engineered by self-styled master criminal Fitzroy Guilderpost.
11. *Road to Ruin, The* (**Mysterious, 2004**) Dortmunder and Co. get jobs on sleazy millionaire Monroe Hall's estate to hijack's Hall's valuable antique auto collection.
12. *Thieves' Dozen: The Dortmunder Stories* (**Mysterious, 2004**) Actually 11 stories, all featuring Dortmunder or a stand-in very much like him.
13. *Watch Your Back!* (**Mysterious, 2005**) Obnoxious fence Arnie Albright enlists Dortmunder and Co. for a hit on equally obnoxious millionaire Preston Fairweather's art collection.
14. *What's So Funny?* (**Warner, 2007**) Dortmunder gets blackmailed into trying to heist a gold chess set, originally intended as a gift for the czar of Russia, from a midtown Manhattan basement vault.

II. In a pair of novels, Westlake turned his comic attentions to the supermarket tabloids: the ones with screaming headlines about Elvis sightings, libidinous space aliens, and monstrous births. The *Weekly Galaxy* is right up there with the wildest of them as related in these satirical takes on contemporary journalism.

1. *Trust Me on This* (**Mysterious, 1988**) Sara Joslyn, en route to her new job at the *Galaxy*, finds a bloody corpse in a Buick Riviera, but her editor isn't interested in "nobodies who drive nothing cars."
2. *Baby, Would I Live* (**Mysterious, 1994**) Sara, now working for a trendy New York magazine called *Trend*, gets involved with the *Galaxy* again when *Trend*'s editor decides to expose their news-gathering practices.

Wharton, Edith

I. Edith Wharton's reputation has had its ups and downs. Recently, it seems to be in an upswing, what with the reopening of the Mount, her home in Lenox, Massachusetts, and film versions of two of her best novels: *The Age of Innocence* (1993) and *The House of Mirth* (2000). Old New York is a series of four vignettes of New York City set in four decades of the 19th century. Published in separate volumes in 1924, they were collected together in an omnibus, *Old New York,* by Scribner in 1952. They have also been published in the Library of America volume *Wharton: Novellas and Other Writings* (1990).

1. *False Dawn* (Appleton, 1924) In the 1840s, New York art collector Lewis Raycie buys Giottos and Mantegnas and other unfashionable Italian primitives on his visits abroad.
2. *Old Maid, The* (Appleton, 1924) The story of Charlotte Lovell, an old maid with a secret, is set in the "complacent '50s."
3. *Spark, The* (Appleton, 1924) The story of Hayley Delane, a young soldier wounded at the Civil War battle of Bull Run, has several ironic twists.
4. *New Year's Day* (Appleton, 1924) Hidden under the conventions of the 1870s lies the tragic heroism of Lizzie Hazeldean.

II. Reputed to be among Wharton's own favorites, these two later novels focus on Vance Weston, a young midwesterner who becomes a writer. Central to his artistic development is his relationship to young Halo Spears and the Willows, her family home. Vance expresses many of Wharton's ideas about the art of fiction.

1. *Hudson River Bracketed* (Appleton, 1929) New worlds of culture open to Vance when he visits his eastern relatives, meets Halo and Laura Lou, and marries the wrong girl.
2. *Gods Arrive, The* (Appleton, 1932) After his wife's death, Vance and Halo leave for Spain, where they both undergo artistic and emotional crises.

White, Antonia

Dial Press performed a service in republishing this brilliant quartet of autobiographical novels by an English author who deserves to be better known. After the publication of *Frost in May*, Antonia White worked in advertising, as a freelance journalist, and as a translator (of Colette, primarily), though plagued by bouts of mental illness. Then in 1950 she began writing fiction again, continuing the story of young Nanda—though changing her name—through a trilogy of novels. Together they form a vivid account of a young Catholic girl growing up amid complicated family relations.

1. *Frost in May* (Viking, 1934) In 1908, 9-year-old Nanda Grey's convert father takes her to the Lippington convent school. She stays until she is 13.
2. *Lost Traveller, The* (Viking, 1950) Clara Bachellor (the same character as Nanda in all respects except name) attends a London school in 1914 as this book begins. The story continues through her disastrous short stint as a governess.
3. *Sugar House, The* (Dial, 1981) Clara, now working as an actress in a small touring company, has her first love and a doomed first marriage. Originally published in the United Kingdom in 1952.
4. *Beyond the Glass* (Regnery, 1955) Clara has an intense new love affair, endures a harrowing descent into madness, and begins to recover.

White, Edmund

Edmund White's essays (e.g., *Arts and Letters,* Cleis, 2005), biographies (e.g., *Genet: A Biography,* Knopf, 1993), and novels have established him as perhaps the leading gay writer of his time, certainly one of the foremost writers in general. His autobiographical trilogy is a series of novels about an American boy growing up in the 1950s and 1960s and his adult life in the 1970s to the 1990s. Although the theme of these novels is the gradual awareness and acceptance of the narrator's homosexuality, they also deal movingly with the universal themes of growing up, dealing with adults, being loved, being popular, and finding one's way in the world.

1. *Boy's Own Story, A* (Dutton, 1982) The nameless narrator reminisces about his childhood and adolescence during the 1950s and his conflicting emotions about his homosexuality.
2. *Beautiful Room Is Empty, The* (Knopf, 1988) The narrator comes of age at the University of Michigan and in New York during the late 1950s and early 1960s.
3. *Farewell Symphony, The* (Knopf, 1997) Covers the 1970s to the 1990s, in which the narrator makes himself a career as a writer, mostly as an expatriate in Paris and Rome, and deals with the impact of AIDS on his friends, lovers, and colleagues.

White, Randy Wayne

Marion "Doc" Ford has retired from his dangerous secret operations in Latin America to savor life in Dinkin's Bay on Florida's west coat. He sells beer, operates a small biological supply business, fishes, researches local marine life, and hobnobs with the locals. However, Doc can't stay away from sleuthing when friends (or ex-lovers) call for help in these suspenseful "eco-adventure" tales with wild plots, quirky characters, wry wit, and a seedy Sunshine State ambience. Doc is a character reminiscent of John D. MacDonald's (q.v.) Travis McGee, and White's writing is reminiscent of Carl Hiaasen's (q.v.). White, who worked for many years as a fishing guide on Sanibel Island and knows his Florida well, also writes nonfiction books about fishing and adventure.

1. *Sanibel Flats* (St. Martin's, 1990) Doc is taking it easy on Sanibel Island until old soldiering buddy Raff Hollins turns up with a tale of his son being stolen by Latino thugs.
2. *Heat Islands, The* (St. Martin's, 1992) When the body of marina owner Marvin Rios is found in the Gulf after a storm, Doc's friend Jeth Nicholes is arrested.
3. *Man Who Invented Florida, The* (St. Martin's, 1993) Doc reluctantly gets involved with his uncle Tucker, who claims to have a well of healing water that will restore male potency.
4. *Captiva* (Putnam, 1996) A ban on net fishing and a fatal explosion on a jetty in a small Florida key dependent on subsistence fishing roil up the locals. Doc is called in by the explosion victim's widow, who practices voodoo.
5. *North of Havana* (Putnam, 1997) When Doc's Zen/druggy friend Tomlinson has his boat impounded in Havana, Doc and Dewey, Doc's sexually ambivalent golf-pro girlfriend, go to Cuba.
6. *Mangrove Coast, The* (Putnam, 1998) After real-estate baron Frank Calloway's body is found, Doc travels to the Canal Zone and matches wits with supervillain Jackie Merlot.
7. *Ten Thousand Islands* (Putnam, 2000) The grave of a 15-year-old girl who had an uncanny ability to find things is desecrated, and the search is on for a 400-year-old relic of the Calusa Indians, a gold medallion.

8. *Shark River* (Putnam, 2001) Doc accompanies Tomlinson to a workshop on Rinzai Zen on a posh island resort and runs into a mysterious Bahamian woman claiming to be his (Doc's) sister.

9. *Twelve Mile Limit* (Putnam, 2002) A boat with four female scuba divers sinks at a dive site off of Marco Island. One woman swims to shore, but the other three are picked by a ship reputedly involved in Colombian drug smuggling.

10. *Everglades* (Putnam, 2003) After Sally Minster, a former lover, asks Doc to determine whether her husband, real-estate developer Geoff, really drowned, Doc runs up against the International Church of Ashram Meditation Inc., run by phony guru Bagwan Shiva.

11. *Tampa Burn* (Putnam, 2004) Pilar, another former girlfriend, asks Doc to find their son Lake, who has been kidnapped in Central America by a carnival freak.

12. *Dead of Night* (Putnam, 2005) A madman plots to unleash guinea worms into Florida waterways and piranhas into Texas lakes to depress property values.

13. *Dark Light* (Putnam, 2006) In the aftermath of a hurricane, Ford and his salvage team discover Nazi artifacts on the wreck of a pleasure craft.

14. *Hunter's Moon* (Putnam, 2007) Former president Kal Wilson asks Ford's help in slipping his protective detail so that he can search for those he believes responsible for his wife's death in a mysterious plane crash.

15. *Black Widow* (Putnam, 2008) Doc, researching the potential use by terrorists of jellyfish and other venomous sea creatures, receives an appeal for help from old friend Shay Money, who is the subject of a sexually compromising videotape.

White, Stephen

Alan Gregory is a crime-solving psychologist based in Boulder, Colorado. Alan and deputy prosecutor Lauren Cowder, whom Alan eventually marries, get involved in a series of mysteries. Many of the plots revolve around Alan's patients and colleagues. Alan is a cerebral rather than a muscular detective, and Stephen White's mysteries have intricate plots, complex characters, and a good deal of suspense. Author White is himself a psychologist.

1. *Privileged Information* (Viking, 1991) Psychologist Alan Gregory becomes the object of suspicion after several of his patients die.

2. *Private Practices* (Viking, 1992) A husband shoots his estranged wife and her attorney before being killed by the police. What seemed to be a domestic tragedy may have deeper implications, as the wife was about to testify at a grand jury investigation.

3. *Higher Authority* (Viking, 1994) Alan Gregory helps his fiancé, Lauren Cowder, to track down her sister, who has vanished after filing a sexual harassment suit.

4. *Harm's Way* (Viking, 1996) Gregory investigates the death of a colleague whose corpse has been found in a theater.

5. *Remote Control* (Dutton, 1997) Lauren Cowder, now married to Alan Gregory and suffering from MS, fires at a figure threatening her friend Emma Spire in a case involving a missing computer program.

6. *Critical Conditions* (Dutton, 1998) Gregory is asked by police to work with a teenage girl suspected of killing the director of an insurance company that has refused authorize experimental treatment for her half sister.

7. *Manner of Death* (Dutton, 1999) Some of his former coworkers have been murdered, and Gregory himself is marked for death.

8. *Cold Case* (Dutton, 2000) Gregory is enlisted by an organization that helps families of murder victims to uncover the truth about

crimes against their beloveds to investigate an unsolved double murder.

9. *Program, The* (Doubleday, 2001) Gregory treats two members of the Witness Protection Program: a prosecutor who saw her husband executed and a hit man turned informant.

10. *Warning Signs* (Delacorte, 2001) Lauren is about to return to work after maternity leave when her boss, the district attorney, is found murdered in his living room.

11. *Best Revenge, The* (Delacorte, 2003) FBI agent Kelda James uncovers DNA evidence that overturns the murder conviction of former medical student Tom Clone after he spends 13 years in prison and winds up befriending him.

12. *Blinded* (Delacorte, 2004) One of Gregory's patients confides that her husband may be a serial killer.

13. *Missing Persons* (Dutton, 2005) Gregory goes to Las Vegas after his friend and fellow therapist, Hannah Grant, dies at her office, mysteriously and suddenly.

14. *Kill Me* (Dutton, 2006) A businessman has contracted with Death Angel, an organization whose purpose is to end the lives of their clients when they request it.

15. *Dry Ice* (Dutton, 2007) Michael McClelland, former meteorologist turned killer, has escaped from custody and has devised a complicated revenge scheme against everyone he holds responsible for his incarceration, including Alan and Lauren.

16. *Dead Time* (Dutton, 2008) Alan's ex-wife Meridith asks him to help her and her fiancé track down their surrogate, who disappeared soon after becoming pregnant with their child.

White, T(erence) H(anbury)

The Once and Future King, White's tetralogy of novels on the King Arthur legend, was the source for the musical play and movie *Camelot* (1960; 1967). Bending both legend and history to his needs, this English author fashioned a humorous, inventive, and compelling story that thoroughly debunks inflated chivalric myths and shows a fascinatingly detailed picture of medieval English life and manners. The one-volume omnibus, *The Once and Future King* (Putnam, 1958), shows considerable revision (not to everyone's taste), especially of *The Witch in the Wood*. *Horn Book* reviewer Jane Yolen (2000) declared that White's work would be the first Arthur volume she would give to children, but many adults have been charmed also. The Arthur legend, especially since Malory's 15th-century compilation *Le morte d'Arthur,* has been fascinating readers and nonreaders alike for centuries. Recent authors who have produced their own versions of King Arthur include Thomas Berger (q.v.), Marion Zimmer Bradley (q.v.), Stephen R. Lawhead (q.v.), Sharan Newman (q.v.), John Steinbeck (q.v.), and Mary Stewart (q.v.).

1. *Sword in the Stone, The* (Putnam, 1939) Two boys, Kay and Wart (who turns out to be King Arthur), learn the gentlemanly arts of jousting, hunting, hawking, and swordsmanship. A Disney film cartoon version of this book was made in 1963.

2. *Witch in the Wood, The* (Putnam, 1939) This volume tells the story of Queen Morgause (the witch in the wood) and her four sons. Arthur, now the young king, battles with other kings and debates might versus right with Merlin. The account, sadly truncated from the hard-to-find original version, is titled *The Queen of Air and Darkness* in the omnibus volume.

3. *Ill-Made Knight, The* (Putnam, 1940) The conflict between Lancelot, Guenevere, and Arthur forms this book's central focus. The musical *Camelot* was largely based on this volume.

4. *Candle in the Wind, The* (Putnam, 1958) Published only in *The Once and Future King* omnibus volume. The evil Modred brings disaster to Camelot as Arthur meets his end.

5. *Book of Merlin, The* (University of Texas, 1977) This posthumously published volume is made up of sections removed from earlier volumes and consists mostly of dialogue between Merlin and the defeated King Arthur and of animal fables illustrating an antiwar theme. Mostly written in the early 1940s, this volume reflects the gloomy and pessimistic view of White during this era.

Whittle, Tyler

PSEUDONYM OF Michael Sidney Tyler

Though this British author takes pains to stick to the known facts about Queen Victoria and the events of her long reign, his trilogy of novels shows the human and family side of the formidable monarch, making her seem much less stuffy and narrow-minded than she is usually portrayed. Those who enjoy this trilogy will want to read Whittle's equally interesting and well-written novel about Victoria's son and heir, *Bertie, Albert Edward, Prince of Wales* (St. Martin's, 1975). Whittle also wrote a nonfiction volume about Victoria entitled *Victoria and Albert at Home* (Routledge, 1980).

1. *Young Victoria, The* (St. Martin's, 1972) Victoria, portrayed from the age of seven until her marriage to Albert, is seen as a self-possessed and energetic young woman determined to have her own way.

2. *Albert's Victoria* (St. Martin's, 1973) Between their wedding and Albert's death 21 years later, the couple worked well together, complementing each other's talents, always with much affection.

3. *Widow of Windsor, The* (St. Martin's, 1974) Family and public service help Victoria conquer her grief in part, and Disraeli's help becomes indispensable.

Wibberley, Leonard

This prolific author of children's books and light adult fiction is best known for *The Mouse That Roared*, a delightful satire on cold war power struggles. Moviegoers will remember Peter Sellers's hilarious performance of multiple roles in the 1958 film of that book. Wibberley has set four equally amusing sequels in the Duchy of Grand Fenwick, the tiny European principality of 6,000 citizens whose leading product is the fine wine Pinot Grand Fenwick.

1. *Beware of the Mouse* (Putnam, 1958) Though written second, this book is first chronologically, as it concerns the great crisis of 1450 when Sir Roger Fenwick and an Irish knight, Sir Dermot of Ballycastle, unite and prove victorious over the new French invention, the cannon. Despite the chronology, this book is perhaps best read after *The Mouse That Roared*.

2. *Mouse That Roared, The* (Little, Brown, 1955) In 1956 Tully Bascomb leads the Duchy of Grand Fenwick's army of 23 longbowmen to war against the United States to win the generous economic aid usually allowed defeated enemies.

3. *Mouse on the Moon, The* (Morrow, 1962) After Duchess Gloriana buys her sable coat and has plumbing installed in the castle, there are still enough US dollars left over to allow Grand Fenwick to enter the space race.

4. *Mouse on Wall Street, The* (Morrow, 1969) Grand Fenwick invests its chewing-gum profit in the US stock market, expecting to lose it all and thus spare the country runaway affluence.

5. *Mouse That Saved the West, The* (Morrow, 1981) Grand Fenwick solves the world oil crisis by discovering "bird water," an alternative energy source.

Wilcox, Collin

I. Lieutenant Frank Hastings, homicide detective with the San Francisco Police Department, is the protagonist of a long-running series of procedurals that blend good plots and well-developed police characters with a noir San Francisco ambience reminiscent of Dashiell Hammett (q.v.). Lieutenant Hastings is a former pro football player, divorced, and a recovering alcoholic.

1. *Lonely Hunter, The* (Random House, 1969) Murder and drug dealing in the Haight-Ashbury hippie scene are made personal for Hastings by the fact that his runaway daughter is involved.

2. *Disappearance, The* (Random House, 1970) One night Carol Connoly walks off from husband, son, wealth, and assorted lovers.

3. *Dead Aim* (Random House, 1971) Among the cases to be solved is the double murder of a pair of upper-class San Franciscans found together in bed.

4. *Hiding Place* (Random House, 1973) Teenager June Towers is bludgeoned to death in Golden Gate Park, the first in a series of murders.

5. *Long Way Down* (Random House, 1974) Thomas King, owner of filmmaking company King Productions, is found murdered by a switchblade knife in the apartment of nude model Dianne Farley.

6. *Aftershock* (Random House, 1974) A sadistic youth wages a campaign of terror against Ann Haywood, Hastings's girlfriend.

7. *Doctor, Lawyer . . .* (Random House, 1977) The chief of police is the ultimate target of a killer and extortionist who signs notes as "The Masked Man."

8. *Watcher, The* (Random House, 1978) Hastings and his 15-year-old son go on a fishing trip and get trapped by one of Hastings's old adversaries.

9. *Twospot (2)* (Putnam, 1978) Hastings teams up with Bill Pronzini's (q.v.) Nameless Detective to investigate a murder and fraud at a California winery.

10. *Power Plays* (Random House, 1979) Former syndicated Washington columnist and television commentator Eliot Murdock is found murdered in the backseat of a car involved in a minor traffic accident.

11. *Mankiller* (Random House, 1980) The death of rock star Rebecca Carlton leaves thousands of fans bereft and Hastings with a murder case on his hands.

12. *Stalking Horse* (Random House, 1982) Hastings works with the FBI in trying to protect Senator Ryan as he attends the dedication of a federal office complex named in his honor.

13. *Victims* (Mysterious, 1985) Lawyer Alex Guest insists that former son-in-law Gordon Kramer killed his grandson's bodyguard.

14. *Night Games* (Mysterious, 1986) The murder victim in a posh residential district was wealthy and a pervert.

15. *Pariah, The* (Ballantine, 1988) A murdered prostitute is linked to powerful televangelist Austin Holloway.

16. *Death before Dying, A* (Holt, 1989) After confiding her fears to childhood friend Frank Hastings, Meredith Powell winds up dead in Golden Gate Park.

17. *Hire a Hangman* (Holt, 1991) Top transplant surgeon Brice Hanchett is shot and killed after leaving his mistress's apartment.

18. *Dead Center* (Holt, 1992) Members of the exclusive Rabelais Club are being knocked off one by one with a .22, a weapon favored by professional hit men.

19. *Switchback* (Holt, 1993) When beautiful young Lisa Franklin is killed, Hastings suspects that it wasn't a random killing.

20. *Calculated Risk* (Holt, 1995) The man blackmailing political figure Harold Best for a homosexual affair turns up dead.

II. Alan Bernhardt is a marginally successful actor, director, and playwright who supplements his income by working as a detective for Dancer Limited, a large investigative firm. Like Hastings, Bernhardt works in San Francisco, but the resemblance ends there, for Bernhardt would rather direct than detect any day.

1. *Bernhardt's Edge* (Tor, 1988) Bernhardt is assigned to find Betty Giles, a researcher for an investment company, in a case that involves stolen art.

2. *Silent Witness* (Tor, 1990) In the wine country near San Francisco, a wealthy woman is murdered late at night while her husband and son are sleeping.

3. *Except for the Bones* (Tor, 1991) Alan eventually winds up on Cape Cod, Massachusetts, investigating the suspicious death of the latest girlfriend of a New York real-estate tycoon.

4. *Find Her a Grave* (Tor, 1993) Bernhardt is hired to help the illegitimate daughter of a late Mafia chieftain collect her inheritance, which is buried by the headstone of her mother's grave.

5. *Full Circle* (Tor, 1994) The FBI is putting heat on Bernhardt to reveal the whereabouts of Betty Giles (see number 1) after he is hired by millionaire Raymond DuBois to return some stolen art.

III. The late Wilcox (d. 1996) also wrote a pair of somewhat different murder mysteries involving a San Francisco newspaper reporter who is blessed/cursed with ESP.

1. *Black Door, The* (Dodd, 1967) San Francisco reporter Stephen Drake uses his ESP abilities to solve a double murder connected with a right-wing political group.

2. *Third Figure, The* (Dodd, 1968) Drake gets involved with the murder of an underworld crime czar.

Wilcox, James

With one exception, James Wilcox's comic novels are set in the fictional town of Tula Springs, Louisiana, somewhere north of New Orleans, or involve people transplanted from Tula Springs. They are full of likably eccentric characters facing social change and a clash of cultures. While critics have generally praised Wilcox's novels, and *Modern Baptists* made it into Harold Bloom's "Western Canon," Wilcox's well-written stories, infused with gentle humor, have never been best sellers. *Guest of a Sinner* (Harper, 1993) contains no Tula Springs characters. Wilcox has returned to his native Louisiana after a stint in New York City and is now Robert Penn Warren Professor and director of creative writing at Louisiana State University.

1. *Modern Baptists* (Dial, 1983) Bobby Pickens, middle-aged assistant manager of Tula Springs's Sonny Boy Bargain Store, believing that he is terminally ill, has invited recently paroled half brother F. X. Pickens to live with him.

2. *North Gladiola* (Harper, 1985) Ethyl Mae Coco, 40-year resident of Tula Springs and mother of six grown children, dissatisfied with her life, attempts to bring culture to her adopted town.

3. *Miss Undine's Living Room* (Harper, 1987) The political aspirations of Olive Mackie, ex–city hall employee, are endangered by the suspicions of Tula Springs residents that her elderly great-stepuncle L. D. Loraine, has pushed his home attendant, Mr.

Versey, out of the second-floor window above the Sonny Boy Bargain Store.

4. *Sort of Rich* (Harper, 1989) Middle-aged native New Yorker Gretchen's hopes of finding a quiet place to finish writing her book are dashed by the strange members of the Tula Springs household of her recently married husband, Frank Dambar.

5. *Polite Sex* (Harper, 1991) Takes place in New York City but involves characters from Tula Springs. Emily Brix and Clara Edward Tilman (former girlfriend of F. X. Pickett of *Modern Baptists*), aspiring actresses from Tula Springs, meet rather different fates in New York.

6. *Plain and Normal* (Little, Brown, 1998) Lloyd Norris, always referred to as "Mr. Norris" by Wilcox, is a refugee from Tula Springs in Yonkers, New York, who, persuaded by his ex-wife Pearl Fay, has reluctantly and timidly come out of the closet but has yet to find a male lover.

7. *Heavenly Days* (Viking, 2003) Former college professor with a PhD in music, Lou Jones, who writes a column for the newsletter of the North American Bassoon Society but earns her living as a receptionist at WaistWatch, a fundamentalist-owned "makeover franchise," gets involved in a struggle over a handicap parking space.

8. *Hunk City* (Viking, 2007) Burma van Buren, richest woman in St. Jude Parish, thanks to an inheritance, is having trouble finding the right charity with which to share her fortune.

Wilcox, Stephen F.

I. Freelance crime writer T. S. W. "Timothy" Sheridan lives in upstate New York, and much of his amateur sleuthing takes place in the Finger Lakes District. Sheridan is a 1990s, sensitive variation on the hard-boiled private-eye theme. Author Stephen Wilcox is a native of Rochester, New York, and writes knowledgeably about upstate New York, its color, scenery, and "depraved locals."

1. *Dry White Tear, The* (St. Martin's, 1989) When his uncle Charlie is murdered, Manhattan journalist Timothy Sheridan inherits a rural upstate New York cottage, several acres of land, and an unsolved slaying.

2. *St. Lawrence Run, The* (St. Martin's, 1990) After a professor tells Sheridan about a 50-year-old murder that took place on the Thousand Islands, he dies in a suspicious mugging.

3. *All the Dead Heroes* (St. Martin's, 1992) Sheridan investigates the career and murder of Frank Wooley, controversial baseball Hall of Famer.

4. *Green Mosaic, The* (St. Martin's, 1994) Glenny Oldham, leader of a group called the Earth-Mothers, was killed by a suspicious fall near her Adirondack cabin three years ago.

II. Another upstate New York journalist and amateur sleuth is Elias Hackshaw, editor of a small-town weekly in western New York State. "Hack" likes card playing, drinking, scavenging old buildings, and pursuing women, not necessarily in that order.

1. *Twenty-Acre Plot, The* (St. Martin's, 1991) When an 80-year-old farmer with a plastic hip joint has a fatal fall from his hayloft, Hack's news nose twitches.

2. *Nimby Factor, The* (St. Martin's, 1992) A brouhaha over a proposed landfill results in the body of the anti-landfill leader turning up in the foyer of the Victorian mansion Hack is refurbishing.

3. *Painted Lady, The* (St. Martin's, 1994) Newcomer Hester DelGado wants to open a residence for "fallen" local girls, much to the displeasure of the nonfallen locals.

4. *Jericho Flower, The* **(Mystery & Suspense, 2002)** Policeman Mel Stoneman thinks that Hack is involved when con-man "Slow Eddie" Williamson is murdered and Gypsy princess Bimbo Wanka is kidnapped.

Wilhelm, Kate (Katie Gertrude)

I.   Kate Wilhelm is probably best known for her science-fiction work. *Where Late the Sweet Birds Sang* (Harper, 1976) was a Hugo Award winner, while *Juniper Time* (Harper, 1979) was nominated for an American Book Award, and several of her short stories have received Nebulas. However, Wilhelm's series work seems to be confined to the mystery genre. Her earlier series features retired arson investigator Charlie Meiklejohn and his psychologist wife, Constance Leidl, who live in upstate New York but move around quite a bit for the investigations they get involved in. Several of their cases involve psychological mysteries and occultism. Numbers 1 through 5 are included in the two-volume omnibus *The Casebook of Constance and Charlie* (St. Martin's, 1999–2000). Wilhelm was married to the late science-fiction and fantasy writer Damon Knight (q.v.).

1. *Hamlet Trap, The* **(St. Martin's, 1987)** Ashland, Oregon, home of the Oregon Shakespeare Festival, is stirred up when the new director of Harley Theatre selects a controversial winner in the playwright's contest.
2. *Dark Door, The* **(St. Martin's, 1988)** Constance and Charlie have to figure out who has been setting fire to abandoned hotels, restaurants, and schools around the country.
3. *Smart House* **(St. Martin's, 1989)** Gary Elringer is discovered floating facedown in the Jacuzzi of his automated dream house when shareholders in his computer firm gather for a birthday celebration.
4. *Sweet, Sweet Poison* **(St. Martin's, 1990)** When Bronx-bred Al and Sylvie win the lottery and resettle in an abandoned mill in upstate New York, all hell breaks loose.
5. *Seven Kinds of Death* **(St. Martin's, 1992)** Old friend "Tootles" Olson holds a party in her Maryland farmhouse that results in her sculptures being vandalized and the editor of an art magazine being strangled.
6. *Flush of Shadows, A* **(St. Martin's, 1995)** Five novellas about Constance and Charlie.

II.   Constance and Charlie seem to have been supplanted by attorney Barbara Holloway of Eugene, Oregon (where Kate Wilhelm lives), who does most of her business with pro bono work for the poor, taking on cases that nobody else wants. Barbara, who is in partnership with her father, Frank, is an attractive character in a series of well-written mysteries that usually feature vivid courtroom scenes. Wilhelm has written other mysteries set in Eugene but not featuring the Holloways: *The Deepest Water* (St. Martin's, 2000) and *Skeletons* (St. Martin's, 2002).

1. *Death Qualified* **(St. Martin's, 1991)** Nell Kendrick is charged with murdering her estranged husband, Lucas, who disappeared years ago while working on a top-secret experiment involving chaos theory.
2. *Best Defense, The* **(St. Martin's, 1994)** Barbara is asked to help Paul Kemmerman, dubbed the "Baby Killer" by the press, after her six-year-old daughter was burned to death.
3. *Malice Prepense* **(St. Martin's, 1996)** Barbara and her father, Frank, defend Teddy Wendover, a developmentally disabled man accused of killing a congressman. UK title: *For the Defence.*

4. *Defense for the Devil* **(St. Martin's, 1999)** Maggie Folsum's abusive ex-husband Mitch turns up again, then is murdered, perhaps by his brother Roy.
5. *No Defense* **(St. Martin's, 2000)** Lara Jessup is accused of the shooting death of her wealthy, older, terminally ill husband, Vinny, on an Oregon mountain road.
6. *Desperate Measures* **(St. Martin's, 2001)** Hideously deformed Alex Feldman is accused of killing his next-door neighbor, religious zealot Gus Marchand.
7. *Clear and Convincing Truth* **(Mira, 2003)** Neurosurgeon David McIvey is found shot to death after he threatens to shut down the Kelso-McIvey Rehabilitation Center.
8. *Unbidden Truth, The* **(Mira, 2004)** Holloway is asked to represent pianist Carol Fredricks, who is accused of murdering the manager of the bar where she plays. Carol's amnesiac past poses problems.
9. *Sleight of Hand* **(Mira, 2006)** Jay Wilkins, childhood friend of Las Vegas entertainer and reformed pickpocket Wally Lederer, accuses Wally of stealing a valuable artifact.
10. *Wrongful Death, A* **(Mira, 2007)** Barbara Holloway, heading to a remote California cabin for some time to herself, gets involved with Elizabeth and Jason Kurtz, on the run after discovering that the Diedricks Corporation, Elizabeth's ex-husband's family business, has been involved in illegal activities.

Willeford, Charles

Charles Willeford was finally receiving some mainstream attention just before he died, in 1988, after having a cult reputation as a writer of "crime-noir" mysteries. Hoke Moseley is a somewhat battered Miami policeman nearing retirement. He has dentures, bad eating habits, and a somewhat flexible moral code. These mysteries are a slice of the seamy side of Miami life but not as grim as some of Willeford's nonseries novels. Willeford retired as a US Army master sergeant before he launched his academic and writing career.

1. *Miami Blues* **(St. Martin's, 1984)** Hoke is attacked in his seedy room at the Eldorado Hotel and loses his gun, his badge, and his dentures.
2. *New Hope for the Dead* **(St. Martin's, 1985)** Moseley wants to solve the murder of a junkie but is distracted by two teenage daughters, his boss's insistence that he clean up a file of unsolved crimes, and the pregnancy of his partner.
3. *Sideswipe* **(St. Martin's, 1987)** Hoke is lying low at a beachfront condo managing his father's property while retired autoworker Stanley Sinkiewicz is being inveigled into a supermarket robbery.
4. *Way We Die Now, The* **(Random House, 1988)** Moseley is told to grow a beard in preparation for a dangerous mission south to the migrant farms, where rumors of slavery and murder have become persistent.

Williams, Ben Ames

House Divided, a best seller in its day, was frequently compared to *Gone with the Wind.* Its Civil War setting is quite authentic, though Williams never lets his thorough research intrude into the book's swing of action and romance. Though written from the aristocratic Currain family's Southern point of view, the series portrays historical figures realistically or with a slight revisionist touch—Jefferson Davis, for instance, is seen as a fool and a bit of a rogue.

1. *House Divided* (Houghton Mifflin, 1947) The Civil War is seen through the eyes of the Currain family of Virginia, loyal friends of James Longstreet and the Confederacy.
2. *Unconquered, The* (Houghton Mifflin, 1953) The narrative continues through the Reconstruction years of 1865–1874, focusing on the New Orleans branch of the Currain family.

Williams, David

I. Welsh author David Williams came to mystery writing in his fifties after a successful career in advertising. His novels are in the classic British mystery tradition: intricately plotted intellectual diversions starring an amateur sleuth. Mark Treasure is a British merchant banker and sometime detective. He is a civilized, unflappable fellow, fond of golf and old buildings. He and his actress wife, Molly, live at a fashionable London address. The Treasure novels are an urbane mix of comedy and detection, a delight for fans of the well-made mystery.

1. *Unholy Writ* (St. Martin's, 1977) The alleged discovery of the manuscript of Shakespeare's *As You Like It* involves a cast of characters including Mark Treasure and a vicar who knows karate.
2. *Treasure by Degrees* (St. Martin's, 1977) A nearly bankrupt British agricultural school must accept financial aid from Funny Farms Inc. of Pennsylvania.
3. *Treasure Up in Smoke* (St. Martin's, 1978) When the leading citizen of the West Indian island of King Charles is murdered, Treasure is on the spot to investigate.
4. *Murder for Treasure* (St. Martin's, 1981) A body located by a self-proclaimed psychic in a Welsh fishing village may have a connection with the competition between two foot-deodorant manufacturers.
5. *Copper, Gold, and Treasure* (St. Martin's, 1982) A schoolboy works with his elderly kidnappers to secure funds for a destitute old-age home, but things go awry.
6. *Treasure Preserved* (St. Martin's, 1983) Lady Louella Brasset dies in an explosion after she opposes a redevelopment scheme in the Sussex town of Tophaven.
7. *Advertise for Treasure* (St. Martin's, 1984) After Rorch, of the London advertising firm of Rorch, Timms and Bander, opposes its takeover by an American ad agency, he has a fatal "fall."
8. *Wedding Treasure* (St. Martin's, 1985) After Mark and Molly's journey to a wedding in a village near Wales, the father of the bride is killed by a golf ball.
9. *Murder in Advent* (St. Martin's, 1986) The argument over the disposition of a copy of the Magna Carta dating from 1225 may have led to arson and murder in Litchester Cathedral Close.
10. *Treasure in Roubles* (St. Martin's, 1987) When Mark joins Molly in a weekend tour of Leningrad, one of the tourist group is murdered at the Kirov Opera.
11. *Divided Treasure* (St. Martin's, 1988) Hundreds of workers may lose their jobs when a candy-manufacturing firm in North Wales is sold.
12. *Treasure in Oxford* (St. Martin's, 1989) The discovery of some rare architectural sketches leads to hot debate, behind-the-scenes maneuvering, and murder at the annual meeting of the Moneybuckle Architectural Endowment.
13. *Holy Treasure!* (St. Martin's, 1989) The campaign of Angela Culdlum, wife of the vicar of St. Martin's, to the save the church is ended by a suspicious fall of roof slates.
14. *Prescription for Murder* (St. Martin's, 1991) Closter Drug is well on its way to marketing a cure for migraine headaches when one of its board of directors is kidnapped by a group claiming to be animal-rights activists.
15. *Treasure by Post* (St. Martin's, 1992) All but one of the shareholders on the board of a West Country convent support dissolution of the assets of the convent until a series of events muddies the waters.
16. *Planning on Murder* (HarperCollins [UK], 1992) The sale of the grounds of a "stately home" to build a leisure complex arouses local passions. Published in the United States only in large print (Ulverscroft).
17. *Banking on Murder* (HarperCollins [UK], 1993) Sir Ray Burns is about to be charged as the principal in a Caribbean bank that's been laundering drug money. Not to be confused with the Emma Lathen (q.v.) mystery with the same title.

II. A second mystery series, published only in large print in the United States, features Chief Inspector Merlin Perry and Sergeant Gomer Lloyd.

1. *Last Seen Breathing* (HarperCollins [UK], 1994) The accidental death of ex-actress and rich widow Rhonwen Spencer, followed by the suspicious death of her son Elwyn, shakes up the Welsh market town of Tawrbach.
2. *Death of a Prodigal* (HarperCollins [UK], 1995) Merwyn Davies loses his head (literally) when he returns to Wales after 40 years to collect a vast inheritance from his friend Edwin.
3. *Dead in the Market* (HarperCollins [UK], 1996) The blackmailing of a housewife who had acquired a baby illegally is followed by a murder in Cardiff's covered Central Market in front of thousands of shoppers, but no witnesses.
4. *Terminal Case, A* (HarperCollins [UK], 1997) When the vicar of St. Samson's fiancée is murdered, there is no shortage of suspects, including the vicar's estranged wife, his student son, and a local spinster reputed to be enamoured of the vicar.
5. *Suicide Intended* (HarperCollins, 1998) When Freddy Gibbon's naked body is discovered in the basement of his college, there is more joy than sorrow amongst the pupils, teachers, and servants.
6. *Practise to Deceive* (Allison & Busby [UK], 2003) After well-regarded auxiliary nurse Kevin Reese of the Howell Clinic for stroke victims is murdered, some unsavory parts of his background are uncovered.

Williams, Jeanne

Although Jeanne Williams is best known for historical novels about the American West—she has won four Golden Spur Awards—her only series novels are two set in the 19th-century Scottish Hebrides that detail the struggles of the crofters of Clanna against rapacious landlords.

1. *Island Harp, The* (St. Martin's, 1991) When her grandfather is killed in a fire set by their landlord's factor, 17-year-old Mairi MacLeod has to lead her clan to a new home and a new livelihood.
2. *Daughter of the Storm* (St. Martin's, 1994) When Mairi loses her unborn child while trying to aid villagers who are being forcibly evicted, she is entrusted with an orphaned baby girl.

Williams, Tad (Robert Paul)

I. The Memory, Sorrow, and Thorn trilogy by American fantasy writer and radio- and television-show producer Tad Williams is an engrossing series about the quest for three magic swords set in a fantasy world inhabited by humans and the Sithi, an immortal elfin race.

1. *Dragonbone Chair, The* (DAW, **1988**) Young Simon, a scullion in the castle of evil King Elias, is taken under the wing of magician Morgenes and sets off on a quest for three magic swords.
2. *Stone of Farewell* (DAW, **1990**) Simon becomes the first mortal to enter the realm of the Sithi and enlists their aid against King Elias and the Storm King Ineluki.
3. *To Green Angel Tower* (DAW, **1993**) Prince Josua wins a first victory against the forces of his brother Elias, in preparation for the final confrontation between good and evil. Published in two parts in the United Kingdom: *Siege: To Green Angel Tower* and *Storm: To Green Angel Tower* (Legend, 1994).

II. The Otherland series is a gigantic (in terms of conception and actual pagination) tetralogy, a combination of fantasy and technological SF in which Otherland, a complete virtual-reality universe, exists alongside the "real" world. Chockfull of characters, including historical personages who can go on living in Otherworld after their demise. Unfortunately, Otherworld is controlled by the real world Grail Brotherhood, a group of rich men who want to prolong their lives, and they steal the minds of young people to achieve their aims. World I soldier Paul Jonas and South African teacher Renie Sulaweyo are the leading good guys, while the bad guys are typified by Brotherhead head Felix Jongfleur, pathological criminal John Dread, and a mysterious being called the Other. The tetralogy is for those readers who can't get enough of alternative fantasy worlds with a computer basis, the mixing of historical and mythological realms, and epic fights between good and evil.

1. *City of Golden Shadow* (DAW, **1996**) Infantryman Paul Jonas is snatched from a trench in World War I France and thrown into another time and space. South African teacher Renie Sulaweyo's brother is left comatose as his consciousness is stolen by the Grail Brotherhood.
2. *River of Blue Fire* (DAW, **1998**) Renie and Paul team up to try to save her brother's life and to thwart the Brotherhood in their efforts to depopulate the Earth.
3. *Mountain of Black Glass* (DAW, **1999**) Paul Jonas is trapped and hunted inside the Grail Project. Renie Sulaweyo is physically in the "real" world, but her consciousness is inside the virtual-reality network.
4. *Sea of Silver Light* (DAW, **2001**) In the conclusion, the pathological John Dread tries to take over the Grail network from Felix Jongfleur, and contact is made with the mysterious the Other.

III. The Shadowmarch trilogy, two volumes so far, envisions a very complicated fantasy world. The castle of Southmarch, which stood sentry along the border between the human kingdoms and the land of the immortal Qua, is threatened by an enfolding darkness and human usurpers.

1. *Shadowmarch* (DAW, **2004**) The Eddons, the royal family of Southmarch, which guards the border between humans and the immortal Qua, are beset by a series of catastrophes. Royal twins Barrick and Briony are separated.
2. *Shadowplay* (DAW, **2007**) Hendon Tolly has usurped the throne of Southmarch, while King Olin is held in captivity in Hierosol, and Princess Briony and Prince Barrick Eddon struggle to survive in separate exiles.

Williamson, Jack (John Stewart)

I. The Humanoids is a classic dystopia (the opposite of utopia) and one of the best "robot" novels outside of Isaac Asimov's (q.v.) Robot series. It is a parable of how mankind, in trying to create a universe without risk, produces a universe without freedom. *The Humanoid Touch*, written 30 years later, pursues the same theme.

Late (d. 2006) Nebula Grand Master Williamson celebrated 75 years of SF publication (see *Seventy-Five: The Diamond Anniversary of a Science Fiction Pioneer*, Haffner, 2004). His short stories have been collected in four volumes (Haffner, 2002). Born in Arizona when it was a territory, Williamson taught science fiction at Eastern New Mexico University for many years.

1. *Humanoids, The* (Simon & Schuster, **1949**) The Humanoids, robots designed to "serve and obey, and guard men from harm," have carried this injunction to its logical extreme of not allowing humans to do anything that might conceivably harm them. Original version: ". . . And Searching Mind," published in the SF magazine *Astounding* in 1948. Reissued in an expanded edition by Doubleday in 1980.
2. *Humanoid Touch, The* (Holt, **1980**) The Humanoids are only a legend to most of the inhabitants of a two-planet system populated by descendants of refugees from their benevolent despotism.

II. The Legion of Space is a classic of the space-opera subgenre of science fiction. It is about "a few good men" (in this case, four) in the 30th century who save the universe from doom. The most developed character is Giles Habibula, the shrewd, knavish, and greedy legionnaire who is a prototype for later SF antiheroes. The first three titles in the series were published in pulp-magazine form in the 1930s, republished in book form a number of years later, and combined in an omnibus volume: *Three from the Legion* (Doubleday, 1975). Number 4 is an add-on published many years later.

1. *Legion of Space, The* (Fantasy, **1947**) To prevent the destruction of the universe as they know it, the legionnaires have to protect the beautiful Aladoree, who held the key to the secrets of the most power weapon ever devised. Originally published in *Astounding* in 1934.
2. *Cometeers, The* (Fantasy, **1950**) The Cometeers, a fierce, inhuman, and apparently invincible race, is out to capture and control the universe. Originally published in *Astounding* in 1936.
3. *One against the Legion* (Fantasy, **1950**) The only clues to the identity of mankind's latest horrible enemy are a cryptic message and a serpentine trademark. Originally published in *Astounding* in 1939. Published together with Legion story "Nowhere Near" in 1950. Published separately by Pyramid in 1967.
4. *Queen of the Legion, The* (Simon & Schuster, **1983**) Jill Oyrel was a woman with a secret gift that would challenge the deadly secrets of the Great Hawkshead Nebula. A late add-on to the series.

III. The Legion of Time and After World's End are also pulp classics. They are about time travel and pioneering works in the alternative world subgenre. The plot, highly original in its day, is about the war between alternate futures to settle which of them will actually exist. Published together as *The Legion of Time* (Fantasy, 1952).

1. *Legion of Time, The* (Fantasy, **1952**) What a small boy picks up off the ground will determine the future of the denizens of two warring time lines. Published in *Astounding* in 1938. Published together with *After World's End* in 1952. Published separately by Galaxy in 1963.

2. *After World's End* (Fantasy, 1952) No annotation available. Published in *Astounding* in 1939. Published with *The Legion of Time* in 1952. Published separately by Galaxy in 1963.

IV. The Seekers/Eldren novels posit a hostile alien race: the Seekers, who are basically machines of destruction who have destroyed the technological civilization of Earth and have left only a few nomad hunter-gatherers in its stead; and the Eldren, who are potentially benevolent but don't want to get involved with primitives.

1. *Lifeburst* (Ballantine, 1984) When a Seeker Queen takes refuge in the asteroid belt, it spells the end for Earth's civilization. Only a few hunter-gatherers are left to face the ongoing scourge.
2. *Mazeway* (Ballantine, 1990) The Eldren of the Oort Cloud Council are reluctant to help the denizens of Earth, who they see as primitive and aggressive. It is up to three young Earthlings, including Benn Dain, son of the hero of *Lifeburst,* to solve the Mazeway, the testing ground of Eldren sons, and prove to the council that Earth is worthy of consideration.

V. Williamson, under the pseudonym of Will Stewart, wrote a pair of novels published in *Astounding* about asteroid miners and their troubles with antimatter. The novels were published in book form in reverse order of their magazine publication. These action novels, which were published together as *Seetee* (Jove, 1959), led to Williamson's 1950s comic strip *Beyond Mars.* Williamson collaborated with Frederik Pohl (q.v.) on three series; the Saga of Cuckoo, the Starchild trilogy, and the Undersea trilogy. For more information on these series, see the entry under Pohl.

1. *Seetee Ship* (Gnome, 1951) Rick Drake has to find a way to turn a potential energy source into useful rather than cataclysmic paths. Originally published in *Astounding* in 1942–1943.
2. *Seetee Shock* (Simon & Schuster, 1950) With only one week to live, Nick Jenkins has to harness the universe's greatest and deadliest source of energy. Originally published in *Astounding* in 1949.

Wilson, A(ndrew) N(orman)

A. N. Wilson is an English writer known for his farcical novels mocking contemporary Britain, more somber works delineating the shallowness of the British middle class, and a host of nonfiction works on history, religion, and literature. His Lampitt Papers quintet is the self-related story of Julian Ramsay's life from the 1950s to the year 2000. The novels are well-written evocations of an English childhood and coming-of-age in that period and ruminations on the relationship of fiction and biography by a practitioner of both literary forms.

1. *Incline Our Hearts* (Viking, 1989) The orphaned Julian Ramsay is brought up by his aunt and uncle in a Norfolk vicarage and endures a series of "English Gulags" such as National Service and the public school system.
2. *Bottle in the Smoke, A* (Viking, 1990) Having survived his youthful experiences, Julian is struggling to establish himself as a writer and actor in 1950s London.
3. *Daughters of Albion* (Viking, 1992) The "Daughters of Albion" are the numerous young women who come under the spell of a charismatic man named Rice Robey, who crosses Julian's path in the 1960s.
4. *Hearing Voices* (Norton, 1996) Julian, now 65 in the year 2000, is a radio performer, stage actor, and aspiring biographer of the belletrist James Petworth "Jimbo" Lampitt.

5. *Watch in the Night, A* (Norton, 1996) In the series conclusion, Julian broods about the true story behind the demises of Jimbo Lampitt and Virgil D. Everett, American collector of Lampitt's work. The talentless writer and opportunist Raphael Hunter, who may have had something to do with Lampitt's end, gets some heavy criticism here.

Wilson, F(rancis) Paul

I. Repairman Jack is a mercenary outlaw who solves a series of mysteries in this mystery-cum-SF-cum-horror series. First introduced in *The Tomb* (see series II, number 2), Repairman Jack, an extreme libertarian, is somewhat socialized in later novels by his girlfriend, Gia. An ongoing battle with the evil entity, the Otherness, whose tentacles spread everywhere, is a continuing theme in this suspenseful series, in which Repairman Jack battles demons, scientists gone wrong, and other sinister types. F. Paul Wilson has combined his writing career with an MD practice.

1. *Legacies* (Forge, 1998) Repairman Jack is revived, after a hiatus of several years (see series II), to team up with Alicia Clayton, the head of a pediatric AIDS clinic in New York, who is trying to sell a house with old memories of sexual child abuse, with fatal results for her collaborators. Published in the United Kingdom under the pseudonym of Colin Andrews.
2. *Conspiracies* (Forge, 1999) Repairman Jack is trying to hunt down the missing wife of a businessman. It seems that the wife was a leading conspiracy theorist about to announce her "unification" theory. Coauthored with Ed Gorman (q.v.).
3. *All the Rage* (Forge, 2000) Repairman Jack aids research chemist Nadia Razminsky in investigating Dr. Luc Monnet, who is involved with a Serbian gangster in trafficking steroids that induce bestial behavior in users.
4. *Hosts* (Forge, 2001) Jack's sister Kate asks to help her lover, Jeannette, who has been infected by a sentient virus that is organizing infected human hosts into "the Unity," a hive consciousness devoted to spreading itself throughout the world.
5. *Haunted Air, The* (Forge, 2002) Allied with a pair of sham spirit mediums, Jack is pitted against ghosts and the Circle, an association of ritual child murderers in a world under the spell of the Otherness.
6. *Gateways* (Forge, 2003) Visiting his comatose, estranged father in Florida, Jack has another confrontation with the Otherness. This time the Lovecraftian evil pervades a lagoon in the Everglades and a community of mutated rednecks.
7. *Crisscross* (Forge, 2004) Repairman Jack infiltrates the Dormentalists, a pseudoreligious organization with a maniacal leader.
8. *Last Rakosh, The* (Overlook Connection, 2005) In this novella, originally published online, Jack confronts a Rakosh, a being that Jack thought he had exterminated.
9. *Infernal* (Forge, 2005) Jack reconnects with his brother Tom, a corrupt Philadelphia judge, after their father is gunned down in a terrorist attack at LaGuardia Airport; gets talked into looking for the wreckage of a Spanish treasure ship; and engages in another bout with the Otherness.
10. *Harbingers* (Forge, 2006) Jack is approached by a regular at Julio's Bar to find his missing teenage niece and finds himself in conflict with the Adversary again.
11. *Bloodline* (Forge, 2007) Jack is up against a scheme to create an evil superman through gene manipulation when he agrees to help Christy Pickering break up a relationship between her daughter and violent criminal Jerry Bethlehem.

II. The six SF-horror novels beginning with *The Keep* are partly linked together by the presence of the evil Adversary, which reappears in the Repairman Jack series (see series I). Underground figure Repairman Jack makes his first appearance in number 2. As with series I, the occult and the paranormal play large roles.

1. *Keep, The* **(Morrow, 1981)** German soldiers occupying a remote fortress in the Transylvanian mountains in 1941 are being preyed upon by a mysterious, unseen force. Second edition published in 1982. Made into a film in 1983.
2. *Tomb, The* **(Whispers, 1984)** Introduces Repairman Jack, who tracks his former lover's missing aunts while simultaneously searching for another client's lost jewelry. Demons dominated by a vindictive Hindu play a big role here.
3. *Touch, The* **(Putnam, 1986)** A young physician finds himself capable of healing simply by touching people but at a physical cost to himself.
4. *Reborn* **(Dark Harvest, 1990)** Something of a sequel to number 1. The story of orphan Jim Hanley, who searches for his biological parents only to discover that he is actually the result of a cloning experiment conducted during World War II.
5. *Reprisal* **(Dark Harvest, 1991)** A sequel to number 4. Jim Hanley's son is a prodigy who manages the family finances and amasses millions of dollars. Posing as an adult named Rafe Losmara, he pursues an evil agenda.
6. *Nightworld* **(Dark Harvest, 1992)** A sequel to numbers 4 and 5, with tie-ins to numbers 2 and 3. The evil entity released in number 1 assaults humanity by wreaking havoc upon the laws of nature and plunging the world into darkness.

III. The earlier LaNague series is primarily science fiction, featuring cloning, aliens, and an evil from another galaxy that is bent upon undermining the intergalactic harmony enjoyed by various worlds belonging to the LaNague Federation. Numbers 1, 2, and 3 were revised and published together in the omnibus *The LaNague Chronicles* (Baen, 1992).

1. *Enemy of the State, An* **(Doubleday, 1980)** Although published third, this is the first novel chronologically. Heroic libertarian Peter LaNague leads the overthrow of statist forces by undermining their rule through the manipulation of economic inflation. Revised and republished in *The LaNague Chronicles* (Baen, 1992).
2. *Healer* **(Doubleday, 1976)** Wilson's first published novel. A hero who has extraordinary, alien-enhanced powers confronts the originators of a psychotic malady and returns the interworld harmony of the LaNague Federation. Revised edition included in *The LaNague Chronicles* (Baen, 1992).
3. *Wheels within Wheels* **(Doubleday, 1978)** An old man and a young woman team up to track the murderer of her father and uncover a sinister organization determined to undermine the LaNague Federation. Revised edition published in *The LaNague Chronicles* (Baen, 1992).
4. *Dydeetown World* **(Baen, 1989)** Sigmund Dreyer, a seedy detective hired by a Jean Harlow clone, uncovers a subterranean culture of murderers, prostitutes, and illegitimate children.
5. *Tery, The* **(Baen, 1989)** The Tery, a creature that is part monkey, part bear, bonds with a outcast teenager who lacks telepathic powers, and Tlad, a galaxy-roaming potter.

Wilson, John Morgan

I. Gay journalist and amateur sleuth Benjamin Justice hasn't had much to cheer about in recent years. His lover died from AIDS, and Benjamin has tested as HIV-positive. He lost his job at the *Los Angeles Times* after it was revealed that his Pulitzer Prize–winning story about a dying couple's struggle with AIDS was a fabrication. Now Benjamin takes on film writing, ghostwriting, and other gigs while fighting against alcoholism. His jobs often get him involved in investigations of murder. These Edgar and Lambda–winning novels, usually set in Los Angeles and environs, are noirish studies with a compelling, complicated, well-realized protagonist.

1. *Simple Justice* **(Doubleday, 1996)** Disgraced journalist Benjamin Justice is recruited by his former editor from the *Los Angeles Times* to do research on the murder of a gay man outside a Los Angeles bar, a murder to which a Hispanic gang member has, unconvincingly, confessed.
2. *Revision of Justice* **(Doubleday, 1997)** When a young Hollywood screenwriter is killed at a party, Justice investigates the lives of the party guests to determine who might have wanted him dead.
3. *Justice at Risk* **(Doubleday, 1999)** Political corruption and system-wide police brutality and prejudice against gays are outed when Tom Callahan, director of a documentary film about AIDS, disappears and is found murdered.
4. *Limits of Justice, The* **(Doubleday, 2000)** Justice is hired by Charlotte Preston, daughter of Hollywood star Rod Preston, to write a biography of her late father in response to a tell-all biography that accuses Rod of systematic predation of young boys.
5. *Blind Eye* **(St. Martin's, 2003)** Justice, the recipient of a large advance for his autobiography, goes in search of Father Blackley, the Catholic priest who debauched him when he was 12 years old.
6. *Moth and Flame* **(St. Martin's, 2004)** While finishing a book on West Hollywood that was begun by recently murdered actor-writer Bruce Bibby, Justice uncovers a shady real-estate development deal and the decades-old disappearance of a local handyman.
7. *Rhapsody in Blood* **(St. Martin's, 2006)** Benjamin accepts an offer from reporter friend Alexandra Templeton to spend time at a California desert resort, the Haunted Springs Hotel, the site, 50 years earlier, of the rape and murder of a movie star and the lynching of a black handyman accused of the crime.

II. Wilson has written a pair of music-themed mysteries set in the 1960s in collaboration with bandleader Peter Duchin. They feature sleuth and high-society bandleader Peter Damon. California-based journalist and freelancer Wilson is also the author of the stand-alone novel *Learning to Love* (Palgrave Macmillan, 2000) and the nonfiction *The Complete Guide to Magazine Article Writing* (Writer's Digest, 1993) and *Inside Hollywood: A Writer's Guide to the World of Movies and TV* (Writer's Digest, 1998).

1. *Blue Moon* **(Berkley, 2002)** Bandleader Peter Damon returns to the Venetian Room of the Fairmont Hotel in San Francisco, where he spots a woman who looks remarkably like his murdered wife. Co-written with Peter Duchin.
2. *Good Morning, Heartache* **(Berkley, 2003)** Working at the Cocoanut Grove, Damon reluctantly offers a fill-in gig to trumpeter, vocalist, drug-using Buddy Bixby. Then Bixby is murdered.

Wilson, Sloan

The Man in the Gray Flannel Suit added a phrase to the English language and, along with William H. Whyte's *The Organization Man* (Simon & Schuster, 1956), epitomized the American 1950s. It portrays the daily life of Tom Rath, middle-class, middle-aged corporate executive. Tom's ordinariness was well portrayed by Gregory Peck in the 1956 movie version. With the exception of *A Summer Place* (Simon & Schuster, 1958), *The Man in the Gray Flannel Suit* proved to be Sloan Wilson's only really popular book. Its sequel, *The Man in the Gray Flannel Suit II,* was not very popular with readers or critics, who preferred Wilson's autobiography: *What Shall We Wear to This Party? The Man in the Gray Flannel Suit Twenty Years Before and After* (Arbor House, 1976).

1. *Man in the Gray Flannel Suit, The* **(Simon & Schuster, 1955)** Thomas Rath works in a New York office, lives in Connecticut with his wife, Betsy, and their children, and has memories of the war and a romance in Italy.
2. *Man in the Gray Flannel Suit II, The* **(Arbor House, 1984)** The 1960s find Tom working for a broadcasting company, going to Washington to work for a Kennedy commission, and having an affair with his young assistant.

Wilson, T(imothy) R.

The Hardwick family of 18th-century England are the main protagonists of this historical trilogy. Lyrical prose, subtleties of language, and realistic characters lift this series above the general run of romantic fiction.

1. *Master of Morholm* **(St. Martin's, 1987)** Subtitle: *A Novel of the Fenland.* George Hardwick, reluctantly assuming his responsibilities as Squire of Morholm, must deal with freeloading relations, the problems of childhood friends, and his uncertain, unsettling feelings about his orphaned cousin.
2. *Ravished Earth, The* **(St. Martin's, 1990)** Joshua Walsoken, a pious, industrious, and ruthless merchant, gets into a bitter feud with the Hardwicks of Morholm.
3. *Straw Tower, The* **(St. Martin's, 1991)** Caroline Hardwick falls in love with a French prisoner of war during the Napoleonic Wars.

Wiltse, David

I. John Becker is the FBI's expert on serial killers. Becker's ability to plumb the minds of killers gets him involved in some very grisly and disturbing investigations in this series of nail-biters with gothic overtones, complex character development, and graphic violence.

1. *Close to the Bone* **(Putnam, 1992)** Prequel to number 2. Roger Bahoud, hired assassin for an Arab terrorist group, uses a sharp object in the ear as a preferred killing method.
2. *Prayer for the Dead* **(Putnam, 1991)** Serial killer Roger Dyce drains his victims' blood, so that the young men look prematurely old and resemble either his hated father or his beloved grandfather.
3. *Edge of Sleep, The* **(Putnam, 1993)** Becker is pressed back into service by Karen Crist, his former protégée, who is trying to track down a serial killer who leaves the bodies of young boys in trash bags on the side of highways.
4. *Into the Fire* **(Putnam, 1994)** Becker is drawn into the investigation of the torture-murder of two young girls in a Tennessee cave.

5. *Bone Deep* **(Putnam, 1995)** An elusive serial killer is preying on young women in the hamlet of Camden, Connecticut.
6. *Blown Away* **(Putnam, 1996)** Ex-professor Jason Cole is holding New York City hostage, blowing up routes in and out of Manhattan and demanding millions.

II. A pair of novels featuring ex–Secret Service agent turned rural deputy sheriff Billy Tree is set in Falls City in Wiltse's native Nebraska. The brooding Billy, who wanted to get away from it all, finds that Falls City isn't necessarily the answer to his prayers. David Wiltse is also the author of plays, including *Dance Lesson* (2004).

1. *Heartland* **(St. Martin's, 2001)** Ex-Secret Service agent Billy Tree exiles himself to his native town of Falls City, Nebraska, and becomes a deputy sheriff.
2. *Hangman's Knot, The* **(St. Martin's, 2002)** Falls City has had its share of crime, including a lynching in the past that involves Billy.

Winegardner, Mark

Random House tapped novelist Mark Winegardner—*The Veracruz Blues* (Viking, 1996) and *Crooked River Burning* (Harcourt, 2001)—to continue Mario Puzo's (q.v.) famed Godfather series. *The Godfather Returns,* which covers the years 1955–1962 in the lives of the Corleones, was an artistic and financial success, but the reception of its sequel, *The Godfather's Revenge,* which concentrates on Corleone rival, Nick Geraci, has been more problematic.

1. *Godfather Returns, The* **(Random House, 2004)** In 1955 Michael Corleone, winner of the war among New York's crime families, wants to consolidate his power, save his marriage, and take his family into legitimate businesses but finds himself confronted by former boxer and Corleone street enforcer Nick Geraci, who proves to be a dangerous adversary. UK titles: *The Godfather: The Lost Years* and *The Godfather Returns: The Lost Years.*
2. *Godfather's Revenge, The* **(Putnam, 2006)** Concentrates on Michael Corleone's main rival, Nick Geraci, who disappears and eludes capture by the authorities.

Wingate, Anne (Martha Anne Guice)

Mark Shigata, Japanese American police chief of Bayport, Texas, started off in this series as an FBI agent before he settled into Bayport. With his policeman sidekick, Al Quinn, Shigata deals with hurricanes, family problems, and the occasional murder in this Gulf Coast town. Anne Wingate is a former journalist and identification officer for police departments in Georgia and Texas who also writes under the names of Martha G. Webb and Lee Martin (q.v.; the Deb Ralston mysteries). She is also the author of two writers' guides to crime writing: *Scene of the Crime* (Writer's Digest, 1992) and (with Elaine Chase) *Amateur Detectives* (Writer's Digest, 1996).

1. *Death by Deception* **(Walker, 1988)** When FBI agent Mark Shigata's estranged wife is murdered and her daughter disappears, all the circumstances point to Mark as the perpetrator.
2. *Eye of Anna, The* **(Walker, 1990)** Bayport, Texas, police chief Mark Shigata has to fight Hurricane Anna and a serial killer.
3. *Buzzards Must Also Be Fed, The* **(Walker, 1990)** Former police sergeant Steve Hansen escapes from jail three years after he was framed for murder by Shigata's corrupt predecessor, Chief Dale Shipp.

4. *Exception to Murder* (**Walker, 1992**) Arkpark, combination zoo and religious theme park, is the scene for the murders of a Bayport city councilwoman and a nature activist.

5. *Yakuza, Go Home!* (**Walker, 1993**) Shigata's Japanese-born cousin and his wife are murdered in a Bayport motel, leaving Mark with a four-year-old nephew.

Wingrove, David

Wingrove's Chung Kuo series is a cross between Isaac Asimov's (q.v.) Foundation series and one of James Clavell's (q.v.) Asian epics. Earth in the 22nd and 23rd centuries is dominated by China, which has become a high-tech version of its ancestral, imperial self. Seven omnipotent but benevolent despots hold sway over 34 billion people at the top of a rigid hierarchy. Most of the tension comes between the T'angs, who enforce the status quo, and the European merchant class, which advocates change. Americans tend to play a sinister role in this series, which has apparently run its course after eight volumes. David Wingrove is the English coauthor, with Brian Aldiss (q.v.), of *Trillion-Year Spree: A History of Science Fiction* (2nd ed., Atheneum, 1986) and, with Rand and Robin Miller, of the book version of the best-selling *Myst* CD-ROM interactive game series.

1. *Middle Kingdom, The* (**Delacorte, 1990**) Introduces the world of Chung Kuo on the eve of the 23rd century and describes its hierarchical system of government.

2. *Broken Wheel, The* (**Delacorte, 1991**) Revolutionary terrorists plot to topple the Ruling Seven, who have been weakened by a five-year internal conflict.

3. *White Mountain, The* (**Delacorte, 1992**) The excesses committed by the ruling classes begin to haunt them as the hierarchy finds itself under attack by revolutionary groups while the poverty of the "Undesirables" worsens.

4. *Stone Within, The* (**Delacorte, 1993**) Intrigues among the Chinese elite, their servants, their own underclass, and various anti-Chinese forces, particularly in the former United States, abound.

5. *Beneath the Tree of Heaven* (**Dell, 1995**) In 2211 Mars revolts and loses much of its population. City North America is largely destroyed by a falling orbital settlement. The T'ang of City Africa becomes a homicidal maniac in his bid to become emperor.

6. *White Moon, Red Dragon* (**Dell, 1996**) Chung Kuo is in turmoil as its enemies marshal their armies against Li Yuan, the last emperor, and the rigid Chinese-ruled hierarchy.

7. *Days of Bitter Strength* (**Dell, 1997**) In the spring of 2232, things seem quiet on the surface; but DeVore, the master of an army of giant androids, plans a final holocaust.

8. *Marriage of the Living Dark, The* (**Hodder [UK], 1997**) In the conclusion to Chung Kuo, Kim Ward, the Star-Seeker who has left Earth to found a new world in space, has to choose whether he will return to fight a final battle against DeVore or leave Earth to its fate. Not published in the United States.

Winslow, Don

Neal Carey, private investigator, is part of a hush-hush investigative team attached to the ultraconservative Kittredge Banks. Neal, well educated and trained, thanks to his employers, is a specialist in finding missing persons. Neal is New York based but travels all over the world in this rather lighthearted series blending action, interesting characters, and humor. Neal Carey isn't a character in Winslow's last five novels. Don Winslow is not to be confused with the comic strip and movie serial character Don Winslow of the navy or (apparently) with the author of Victorian erotica, including the Ironwood series.

1. *Cool Breeze in the Underground, A* (**St. Martin's, 1991**) Neal flies to London to locate the missing teenage daughter of a candidate for vice president, erase all signs of her drug abuse, and deliver her in time for the political convention.

2. *Trail to Buddha's Mirror, The* (**St. Martin's, 1992**) Robert Pendleton, biochemist and fertilizer expert, is missing from a conference in San Francisco, where he reportedly became smitten with a beautiful Chinese woman.

3. *Way Down on the High Lonely* (**St. Martin's, 1993**) Two-year-old Cody McCall has been snatched by his divorced father and taken to a white supremacist redoubt in the wild backcountry of Nevada.

4. *Long Walk up the Water Side, A* (**St. Martin's, 1994**) Neal agrees to hide Polly Paget after she publicly accuses her former boss and lover, family television personality Jack Landis, of rape.

5. *While Drowning in the Desert* (**St. Martin's, 1996**) Neal has the task of driving aging comedian and nonstop talker Natty Silver from Las Vegas to California.

Wodehouse, P(elham) G(renville)

I. Even though the world it portrays went, along with many other things, down with World War I, P. G. Wodehouse's special brand of inspired zaniness and verbal sparkle has entertained generations of readers and kept the belly laugh in English humor for more than a century. Perhaps the best known of all Wodehouse's characters is Jeeves, the perfect gentleman's gentleman, who first appeared, briefly, in September 1915 in the short story "Extricating Young Gussie," published first on this side of the Atlantic in the *Saturday Evening Post* but not in book form until the short collection *The Man with Two Left Feet and Other Stories* (published in the United Kingdom by Methuen in 1917; in the United States by A. L. Burt in 1933). Jeeves's employer, the irresponsible and irrepressible young man-about-town Bertie Wooster, also made his debut in that story. The pair quickly became favorites, appearing in many more short stories and eventually in novels as well. They probably reached their peak in popularity in the 1930s, then took a nosedive during World War II, mainly because of Wodehouse's ill-judged (if essentially harmless) broadcast for the Germans, then made a postwar recovery that has continued to this day. More than half of Wodehouse's 90+ books are still in print. There are many audiobook presentations (sometimes several of the same title: the versions with Jonathan Cecil doing the voices are especially recommended). Edward Duke's one-man show *Jeeves Takes Charge* (1984) and *P. G. Wodehouse's Jeeves and Wooster* on Masterpiece Theatre, which featured Stephen Fry as Jeeves and Hugh Laurie as Bertie, have kept the ball rolling.

Bertie is the narrator of nearly all of the stories except for *The Return of Jeeves*, in which Bertie is offstage. Bertie's narration is a masterpiece of comic writing in its own right, seldom equaled and never surpassed. Bertie constantly gets into trouble, either getting engaged to unsuitable young ladies or running afoul of formidable aunts or becoming ensnared in some dubious activity, but the sagacious, unflappable, and amoral Jeeves always gets him out of it. The gallery of characters include Bertie's formidable aunts, Aunt Agatha and Aunt Dahlia, Gussie Fink-Nottle, Roderic Spode, Sir Watkyn and Madeline Bassett, Stiffy Byng, Bingo Little, Roderick Spode, and Honoria Glossop.

C. Northcote Parkinson's (q.v.) *Jeeves: A Gentleman's Personal Gentleman* (St. Martin's, 1981) is a "biography of Jeeves" that will delight fans. Other books of interest are David Jasen's *Bibliography and Reader's Guide to the First Editions of P. G. Wodehouse* (Archon, 1970); Richard Usborne's *The Penguin Wodehouse Companion* (Penguin,

1988); and Robert McGrath's *P. G. Wodehouse: A Life* (Norton, 2004).

Short story collections that are devoted to Jeeves and Bertie are described below. Other collections that have one or more Jeeves stories are *The Man with Two Left Feet and Other Stories* (Burt, 1933; originally United Kingdom, 1917); *A Few Quick Ones* (Simon & Schuster, 1959); and *Plum Pie* (Simon & Schuster, 1967). Omnibuses devoted to Jeeves include *Life with Jeeves* (Viking, 1983, numbers 2, 4, and 6); *The World of Jeeves* (HarperCollins, 1988); *The Jeeves Omnibus* (5 vols., Hutchinson [UK], 1989–1994); *Enter Jeeves: 15 Early Stories* (Dover, 1997); and *The Jeeves and Wooster Omnibus* (Penguin [UK], 2001).

1. *My Man Jeeves* (Newnes [UK], 1919) Four of the eight stories collected here are Jeeves/Bertie stories, revised editions of which appeared in number 3.

2. *Jeeves* (Doran, 1923) Ten short stories that could be said to form a loosely connected novel. UK title: *The Inimitable Jeeves*.

3. *Carry On, Jeeves* (Doran, 1926) Revised versions of the Jeeves short stories from number 1 are included with five new stories.

4. *Very Good, Jeeves* (Doubleday, 1930) A collection of 11 short stories.

5. *Thank You, Jeeves* (Little, Brown, 1934) In what could be said to be the first "proper" Jeeves novel, Bertie finds himself defenseless at a country house with Pauline Washburn, to whom he was once engaged, his hybrid musical instrument, the "banjolele," having alienated Jeeves.

6. *Brinkley Manor* (Little, Brown, 1934) Jeeves does his best to patch up two broken romances, but Bertie manages to get engaged accidentally to the soppy Madeline Bassett while trying to fix things up for the newt-loving Gussie Fink-Nottle. UK title: *Right-Ho, Jeeves*.

7. *Code of the Woosters, The* (Doubleday, 1938) Jeeves eventually sets things right in this sinister affair involving Madeline Bassett and her father, Sir Watkyn, an 18th-century cow creamer, and the formidable homegrown Nazi Roderick Spode.

8. *Joy in the Morning* (Doubleday, 1946) Bertie and Boko Fittleworth stage a fake burglary in the hope of winning over Uncle Perry and getting his consent for Boko's marriage to his young ward, Zenobia Hopwood. Variant title: *Jeeves in the Morning*.

9. *Mating Season, The* (Didier, 1949) The romantically inclined party at Deverill Hall includes Corky and Catsmeat Pirbright, Gussie Fink-Nottle, and Esmond Haddock and his five aunts.

10. *Return of Jeeves, The* (Simon & Schuster, 1954) In the only story that he doesn't narrate, Bertie is off at a school that teaches impoverished gentlemen how to take care of themselves. Jeeves aids his new employer, the ninth Earl of Rowcester, in his monetary and amorous pursuits by setting up a bookie operation. UK title: *Ring for Jeeves*.

11. *Bertie Wooster Sees It Through* (Simon & Schuster, 1955) Bertie's newly acquired mustache gets mixed reviews, but his attentions to Florence Craye bring him swift retribution from fiery-tempered ex-policeman Stilton Cheesewright. UK title: *Jeeves and the Feudal Spirit*.

12. *How Right You Are, Jeeves* (Simon & Schuster, 1960) While Jeeves is off on a holiday, Bertie gets himself into big trouble over some old silver at his aunt Dahlia's. UK title: *Jeeves in the Offing*.

13. *Stiff Upper Lip, Jeeves* (Simon & Schuster, 1963) Bertie, who has annoyed Jeeves by acquiring a Tyrolean hat, goes to Totleigh on a double mission, trying to heal the Gussie Fink-Nottle and Madeline Bassett rift and to steal a black amber statuette that Sir Watkyn had supposedly acquired unethically. Roderick Spode, now Lord Sidcup, is still a bullying menace.

14. *Jeeves and the Tie That Binds* (Simon & Schuster, 1971) Bertie's light fingers are exercised in aid of old pal Ginger Winship, who is standing for Parliament in Market Snodsbury. Madeline Basset

and Roderick Spode make return appearances, and we learn Jeeves's Christian name for the first time. UK title: *Much Obliged, Jeeves*.

15. *Cat-Nappers, The* (Simon & Schuster, 1974) Bertie, sent off to the country because of "spots on his chest," gets involved with a racehorse named Potato Chip that has fallen in love with a cat. UK title: *Aunts Aren't Gentlemen*.

II. Next to the Jeeves/Bertie series, the Blandings series has been the longest-running and most popular series. Blandings Castle in Shropshire is the stately home of Clarence, the ninth Earl of Emsworth, and his pride and joy, the prizewinning pig Empress of Blandings. Other Blandings residents include Beach, the butler, and Lord Emsworth's son, the Honorable Freddie Threepwood, a young chap made in the same mold as Bertie Wooster. The Honorable Galahad Threepwood, Lord Emsworth's younger brother, also makes occasional appearances, as do his formidable sisters, Dora, Constance, and Hermione. Psmith and Lord Ickenham ("Uncle Fred") are prominent characters who have their own series as well (see below). Rupert ("The Efficient") Baxter, Ronnie Fish, and the odious Percy Pilbeam wend their ways in and out of the series.

Single Blandings stories appeared in the collections *The Man Upstairs and Other Stories* (Methuen, 1914); *The Crime Wave at Blandings* (Doubleday, 1937; UK title: *Lord Emsworth and Others*; *Nothing Serious* (Doubleday, 1951); and *Plum Pie* (Simon & Schuster, 1967). *Life at Blandings* (Viking, 1988; numbers 1, 4, and 5) is an omnibus collection.

1. *Something New* (Appleton, 1915) A young American in London answers a newspaper ad for a young man to undertake "a delicate and dangerous enterprise," which takes him to Blandings Castle. UK title: *Something Fresh*.

2. *Leave It to Psmith (I)* (Doran, 1923) Lady Constance's necklace is stolen, and Freddie Threepwood loses his girl, Eve Halliday, to young man-about-town Psmith (see below).

3. *Blandings Castle* (Doubleday, 1935) Although published later than numbers 4 and 5, the Blandings stories in this collection belong here chronologically. UK title: *Blandings Castle and Elsewhere*.

4. *Fish Preferred* (Doubleday, 1929) Lady Constance objects to the weddings plans of both her niece Millicent and her nephew Ronnie Fish, but Blandings Castle has its usual effect. UK title: *Summer Lightning*.

5. *Heavy Weather* (Little, Brown, 1933) Ten days after the events in number 4, the saga continues: Ronnie Fish still determines to marry his chorus girl. Monty Bodkin, who has his own series (see below), makes an appearance.

6. *Uncle Fred in the Springtime (I)* (Doubleday, 1939) Uncle Fred, the fifth Earl of Ickenham, saves the Empress of Blandings from the clutches of the Duke of Dunstable and sets a romance to rights for Polly Potts. Uncle Fred, who will appear again in number 9, also has his own series (see below).

7. *Full Moon* (Doubleday, 1947) Colonel and Lady Hermione Wedge hope that a rich American bachelor will fall for their daughter Veronica.

8. *Pigs Have Wings* (Doubleday, 1952) The Empress of Blandings faces some stiff competition when Lord Emsworth's neighbor buys a new pig, the Queen of Matchingham.

9. *Service with a Smile* (Simon & Schuster, 1962) Some consider this novel about Uncle Fred's return visit to Blandings to be one of Wodehouse's masterpieces.

10. *Brinkmanship of Galahad Threepwood, The* (Simon & Schuster, 1965) Uncle Gally (Galahad) has his hands full as one Blandings romance after another seems to require his attention. UK title: *Galahad at Blandings*.

11. *No Nudes Is Good Nudes* **(Simon & Schuster, 1977)** A nude painting owned by the Duke of Dunstable is coveted by Lord Emsworth, who fancies that its subject resembles his empress. UK title: *A Pelican at Blandings*.

12. *Sunset at Blandings* **(Simon & Schuster, 1977)** Left unfinished at Wodehouse's death, at age 93, this novel concerns Galahad's efforts to straighten out his niece's love life. In a concluding note, Richard Usborne speculates how Wodehouse might have finished the book.

III. Wodehouse's earliest stories were "school stories." Two of his first three collections—*The Pothunters* (Black [UK], 1902) and *Tales of St. Austin's* (Black [UK], 1903) were set at a school called St. Austin's. St. Austin's was replaced by Wrykyn School as the school of choice. *The Gold Bat and Other School Stories* (Black [UK], 1904), *Love Among the Chickens* (Circle, 1909; Newnes [UK] 1906; featuring the first appearance of Uckridge—see series VI, below), and *The White Feather* (Black [UK], 1907) are all set at Wrykyn. *Sam in the Suburbs* (Doran, 1925; UK title: *Sam the Sudden*) features an old Wrkynite. Psmith makes his first appearance in the novel *Mike*, after Mike Jackson, the hero, is sent to Sedleigh to shape him up academically. In *Psmith in the City*, Psmith appears as Wodehouse's first adult, as opposed to schoolboy, "hero." According to Richard Usborne, "He leads us to the new world of the City, America, gangsters, crooks, Psocialism, and Blandings Castle." Psmith, who is a potential man of means, is disinclined to hard work but is clever enough to make his way when he needs to. His one real fear is of being bored. In *Leave It to Psmith*, he plays a central role at Blandings Castle (see series II, above), while in *Psmith in the City* and *Psmith, Journalist*, he continues his affiliation with Mike Jackson. Omnibus volume: *The World of Psmith* (Hutchinson [UK], 1974).

1. *Mike* **(Black [UK], 1909)** Mike Jackson, one of the cricketeering Jackson brothers, is transferred from Wrykyn to Sedleigh, another "public" school, where he is befriended by ex-Etonian Psmith. *Enter Psmith* (Macmillan, 1935) is basically the second half of *Mike*. *Mike* was republished in two parts by Jenkins (UK) in 1953 as *Mike at Wrykyn* and *Mike and Psmith*.

2. *Psmith in the City* **(Black [UK], 1910)** Psmith and Mike turn up working (sort of) at the New Asiatic Bank in the City, lodging at Clement's Inn, and enjoying all that London has to offer.

3. *Psmith Journalist* **(Black [UK], 1915)** Mike and Psmith head to America for awhile, where Psmith gets involved in journalism and with some rather thuggish characters. A revised version of *The Prince and Betty* (Watt, 1912).

4. *Leave It to Psmith* **(Doran, 1924)** See under *Blandings Castle* (series II, number 2).

IV. Frederick Altamont Cornwallis Twistleton, fifth Earl of Ickenham, known as "Uncle Fred," is a character in the Blandings Castle series (see *Uncle Fred in the Springtime* and *Service with a Smile*, series II, above), but he also appears in one story in *Young Men in Spats* (Doubleday, 1936) and in two novels of his own. Uncle Fred is a managing but benevolent character, one of whose chief aims is to put young love affairs to rights. *The World of Uncle Fred* (Hutchinson [UK], 1983) contains numbers 1, 2, and 3 and the story *Uncle Fred Flits By*.

1. *Uncle Fred in the Springtime* **(Doubleday, 1939)** See entry under Blandings Castle (series II, number 6).

2. *Uncle Dynamite* **(Dell, 1948)** Set in Hampshire. Uncle Fred wants Pongo Thistlewaite and American Sally Painter to make up. Other characters include Bill Oakeshott, Hermione Bostock, and Major Brabazon Plank (who also had a role in *Stiff Upper Lip, Jeeves*).

3. *Cocktail Time* **(Simon & Schuster, 1958)** Uncle Fred gets involved in several romances, including that of his brother-in-law, Sir Raymond "Beefy" Bastable. Starts off at the Drones Club, from whose window Lord Ickenham has knocked off the top hat of "Beefy" with a slingshot-fired Brazil nut. Pongo and Sally Painter are safely married. *Cocktail Time* is a scandalous best seller that Beefy has written but denies authorship of.

4. *Service with a Smile* **(Simon & Schuster, 1962)** See Blandings Castle series (series II, number 9).

V. Monty Bodkin is a character who made his first appearance in *Heavy Weather* (series II, number 5). Bodkin—who is another one of Wodehouse's young man-about-town, living by one's wits when one has to, characters—stars in two novels.

1. *Luck of the Bodkins, The* **(Little, Brown, 1936)** Monty Bodkin; his on-again, off-again fiancé, Gertrude Butterwick (center forward on an all-England ladies' field hockey team); Hollywood mogul Ivor Llewellyn—who appears also in nonseries novels *The Old Reliable* (Doubleday, 1951) and *Bachelors Anonymous* (Simon & Schuster, 1974); movie star Lottie Blossom; the Tennyson brothers, Reggie and Ambrose; and steward Albert Eustace Peasemarch (who appears again in *Cocktail Time*, series IV, number 3) are aboard the SS *Atlantic* headed for America.

2. *Plot That Thickened, The* **(Simon & Schuster, 1973)** Monty Bodkin is still indentured to Ivor Llewellyn, who has taken Mellingham Hall in Sussex for a season to gain the approval of Gertrude Butterwick's father. A valuable pearl necklace and the criminals Chimp Twist and Dolly and Soapy Malloy (who appear in other Wodehouse books) play a large role. UK title: *Pearls, Girls and Monty Bodkin*.

VI. Some of Wodehouse's major characters appear mainly in short stories. Mr. Mulliner, a raconteur with a stable of rather daffy relatives, has three volumes of short stories devoted to him and a number of stories in other collections. The stories have been collected in *The World of Mr. Mulliner* (Taplinger, 1972). Uckridge, who is something of a bounder, first appeared in *Love among the Chickens* (Black [UK], 1906), in several other collections, and in a collection of his own: *He Rather Enjoyed It* (Doran, 1925; UK title: *Uckridge*). *The World of Uckridge* (Hutchinson [UK], 1975) is an omnibus collection. Wodehouse wrote many stories about golf, most of which are related by the Oldest Member and collected in *The Golf Omnibus* (Outlet, 1991; originally United Kingdom, 1973). Separate volumes devoted to the Oldest Member are *Golf without Tears* (Doran, 1924; UK title: *The Clicking of Cuthbert*) and *Divots* (Doran, 1927; UK title: *The Heart of a Goof*). Modern Library published a volume of *Selected Stories* (1958). The Drones Club is populated by characters who appear in several Wodehouse series, including Blandings Castle and Uncle Fred. One of the zanier members, Freddie Wigeon, figures in *Ice in the Bedroom* (Simon & Schuster, 1961) and other books. Drones Club stories have been collected in *Tales from the Drones Club* (International Polygonics, 1991).

1. *Meet Mr. Mulliner* **(Doubleday, 1928)** Short stories.
2. *Mr. Mulliner Speaking* **(Doubleday, 1929)** Short stories.
3. *Mulliner Nights* **(Doubleday, 1933)** Short stories.

Woiwode, Larry

I. *Beyond the Bedroom Wall* was a popular and critical success, being nominated for the National Book Award and the National Book Critics Circle Award. It is a saga covering several generations of the Neumiller family of North Dakota and Illinois. Its sequel, *Born Brothers*, concentrates on two members of the younger generation of the Neumillers who appeared as characters in the earlier volume. Taken together, the two novels are a haunting portrait of the farms and small towns of America's heartland.

1. ***Beyond the Bedroom Wall*** (Farrar, 1975) The history of the Neumiller family is chronicled from the death of Otto, its patriarch, in 1935 to the late 1960s, when the younger generation is growing up and moving away.
2. ***Born Brothers*** (DiCapua, 1988) The stories of Jerome Neumiller, successful physician, and his brother Charles, who has failed in his career and is failing in life, are told by Charles.
3. ***Neumiller Stories, The*** (Farrar, 1989) Ten of the stories in this collection are the original versions of the stories reworked for *Beyond the Bedroom Wall*. Three new stories deal with Neumiller's son Charles, a struggling actor in New York.

II. *What I'm Going to Do, I Think* marked Woiwode's explosive entry on the American literary scene. It followed a young couple, Chris and Ellen, on an emotional roller coaster of a honeymoon in northern Michigan. *Indian Affairs* picks up the narrative seven years later, after the death of the child Ellen was carrying in *What I'm Going to Do, I Think*. Most of the action is seen through Chris's eyes.

1. ***What I'm Going to Do, I Think*** (Farrar, 1969) Chris and Ellen have gotten married after a year of estrangement and gone for a honeymoon in the Michigan woods, where they shoot a .22 rifle, make love, and quarrel.
2. ***Indian Affairs*** (Atheneum, 1992) Seven years later, Chris and Ellen return to the woods, where Chris broods over his Native American identity and what it means to his academic pursuits, and Ellen mourns her lost baby.

Wolfe, Gene

I. The Book of the New Sun is a science-fiction and fantasy classic by an author who was won Nebulas and the World Fantasy Award for Life Achievement. The series depicts an Earth (Urth) of the far future—a depleted planet revolving around a dying sun. Its humanity is so far past its great accomplishments that it has almost forgotten them. The protagonist of the series is Severian, who progresses from torturer's apprentice to potential savior of Urth over the course of five novels. Although there are elements of fantasy "quest" and Urth's civilization has medieval components, the Book of the New Sun is primarily science fiction. The technology, natural history, and anthropology of Wolfe's future world is painstakingly done, and his evocation of the far future is entirely convincing. *The Book of the New Sun* (Bantam, 1998) and *Shadow and Claw* (Orb, 1994) contain numbers 1 and 2. *Sword and Citadel* (Orb, 1994) contains numbers 3 and 4.

1. ***Shadow of the Torturer, The*** (Simon & Schuster, 1980) Severian, apprentice to the Seekers for Truth and Penitence, is expelled from the Citadel when he allows a "client" to commit suicide.
2. ***Claw of the Conciliator, The*** (Timescape, 1981) On his journey to distant Thrax to take up his new position of executioner, Severian inadvertently comes into possession of the Claw of the Conciliator, a gem with seemingly miraculous healing powers.
3. ***Sword of the Lictor, The*** (Timescape, 1982) Severian retreats to the mountains after failing as an executioner and encounters the Alzabo, a creature that can reproduce the voices of those whom it has eaten.
4. ***Citadel of the Autarch, The*** (Timescape, 1983) Arriving at the battlefield where his Commonwealth is fighting the Ascians,

Severian renews old acquaintances and realizes the destiny that had been awaiting him.
5. ***Urth of the New Sun, The*** (Tor, 1987) Autarch Severian embarks on a spaceship journey to a distant star in the hope of finding the "new sun" that will rejuvenate Urth.

II. Like the Book of the New Sun, the Book of the Long Sun combines science and medieval culture in a far future where humans, gods, and robots intermingle. Much of the action takes place on the Whorl, a massive space vehicle that is believed by most of its inhabitants to be a planet. The main protagonist is Patera Silk, a young cleric who, like Severian in New Sun, is fated to rise, unwittingly at first, to the heights. *Litany of the Long Sun* (Doubleday, 1994) contains numbers 1 and 2. *Epiphany of the Long Sun* (Doubleday, 1997) contains numbers 3 and 4.

1. ***Nightside the Long Sun*** (Tor, 1993) Patera Silk receives an enlightening mental message from one of his gods on the same day that he learns that his "manteion" (temple) has been sold to a wealthy crime lord for back taxes.
2. ***Lake of the Long Sun*** (Tor, 1994) Patera returns from underground with the knowledge that a vast conspiracy involving the government of Viron and even some of the "gods" is afoot.
3. ***Calde of the Long Sun*** (Tor, 1994) As "Calde" (leader) of the masses, Patera continues his quest to save the Holy City of Viron from the villainous Blood, while more information is revealed about his ultimate destiny.
4. ***Exodus from the Long Sun*** (Tor, 1995) Calde Silk fights a dirty and chaotic war with the city of Viron's corrupt former government.

III. The Book of the Short Sun series is a direct sequel to the Book of the Long Sun series and connects that series with the Book of the New Sun series as well. This series is narrated by Horn, the supposed author of the Book of the Long Sun, who is sent on a quest for the now legendary Calde Silk. The Whorl is still around, as are the planets Green and Blue. All three series have received extensive praise from SF and fantasy critics and have proved popular with readers, but Wolfe's complicated plots and rich but convoluted prose will scare off the semiliterate SF fan.

1. ***On Blue's Waters*** (Tor, 1999) Several decades after the action of *Exodus from the Long Sun*, on the Planet Blue, where civilization is slowly decaying, Horn is dispatched to find the long-missing Calde Silk.
2. ***In Green's Jungles*** (Tor, 2000) Horn, still on his quest for Calde Silk, the godlike ruler of the city of Viron, visits a world with a dying red sun that might be the long-lost Urth.
3. ***Return to the Whorl*** (Tor, 2001) Horn continues his search for Silk, which takes him to the aging spaceship Whorl.

IV. A trip of novels that could be categorized as historical sagas crossed with mythological allegory are set in the Greek world in the 5th century BCE. Latro, a Roman soldier who can communicate with the gods but can't remember who he is from one day to the next, wanders through the landscapes of preclassical Greece and Egypt. *Latro in the Mist* (Orb, 2003) contains numbers 1 and 2.

1. ***Soldier of the Mist*** (Tor, 1986) Latro wanders through Greece in the company of a slave, a necromancer, and other fictional and historical characters in search of a cure for his amnesia.
2. ***Soldier of Arete*** (Tor, 1989) Latro flees to Thessally, where he becomes involved with a band of centaurs, seeks the counsel of the Delphic oracle, and participates in the Pythian games.

3. *Soldier of Sidon* **(Tor, 2006)** Latro, still amnesiac, journeys to the Egypt described by Herodotus.

V. The Wizard Knight is a pair of fantasy novels where an American teenager sent into a multitiered fantasy universe of Frost Giants and other beings from Northern European heroic literature becomes a knight though he retains his teenage mentality. Somewhat more accessible to younger readers than Wolfe's previous efforts. *The Wizard Knight* (Gollancz [UK], 2005) contains both novels.

1. *Knight, The* **(Tor, 2003)** A contemporary American teenager is thrust into Mythgarthr, a multitiered fantasy universe, where he becomes Sir Able of the High Heart.
2. *Wizard, The* **(Tor, 2004)** When the king of the giants is slain, Sir Able is brought back after 20 years in limbo.

Wolfe, Thomas

I. Wolfe's lyrical novels memorializing his large and quarrelsome family and the provincial atmosphere of his hometown of Asheville, North Carolina, occupy a unique place in American letters. Criticized for their formlessness, the books are nonetheless a moving portrait of a sensitive young man's coming-of-age. The well-known editor Maxwell Perkins recognized genius in the manuscript Wolfe submitted to him at Scribner and helped the author fashion the first two books into their final form. The University of South Carolina Press issued the pre-edited form of *Look Homeward, Angel* in their centennial edition (*Lost: A Story of the Buried Life*, edited by Arlyn and Matthew J. Bruccoli, 2000). Wolfe's boyhood home in Asheville has been reopened to visitors after an arson attack in 1998.

1. *Look Homeward, Angel* **(Scribner, 1929)** Eugene, youngest son of the large and somewhat eccentric Gant family of Altamont (read Asheville), North Carolina, grows up, attends the local university, and leaves for Harvard.
2. *Of Time and the River* **(Scribner, 1935)** During Eugene's Harvard years, he strives for success as a playwright, accepts a teaching post at a New York university, and travels abroad.

II. When disagreements about his novel in progress caused Wolfe to break with Maxwell Perkins, he switched to Harper. But his untimely death from tuberculosis at the age of 38 prevented the completion of the sprawling manuscript on which he had been working. Perkins and Harper's Edward Aswell both worked to shape these books into their formal form.

1. *Web and the Rock, The* **(Harper, 1939)** George Webber is followed from his childhood in a small southern town through college and his early years in New York, including an affair with a married woman.
2. *You Can't Go Home Again* **(Harper, 1940)** George breaks with Esther, meets a helpful editor who shepherds his book to successful publication, and travels through Europe as Nazi power rises.

Wolitzer, Hilma

I. Brooklyn-born Wolitzer started writing as a 35-year-old suburban housewife. Called "a poet of domestic detail," her fiction is usually set in middle-class households where she weaves fascinating narratives out of unremarkable lives. Wolitzer, who also writes young adult novels, is the mother of novelist Meg Wolitzer (*Sleepwalking*, etc.). Two novels follow Linda Reismann, who finds herself widowed,

pregnant, and saddled with a sullen 13-year-old stepdaughter after six weeks of marriage. Linda is good-hearted, vulnerable, and easily overwhelmed.

1. *Hearts* **(Farrar, 1980)** Recently widowed Linda Reismann packs all her belongings in a car, drives west from New Jersey to get an abortion, drops off her stepdaughter in Iowa, and begins a new life in California.
2. *Tunnel of Love* **(Harper, 1994)** Linda bounces from job to job and boyfriend to boyfriend in Los Angeles, until she gets badly injured in a car wreck, while stepdaughter Robin moves in her own world with her own agenda.

II. Another pair of novels traces the up-and-down (mostly down) fortunes of the 25-year marriage of Paulette and Howard Flax.

1. *In the Flesh* **(Morrow, 1977)** Paulette married Howard because she was pregnant and desperate. Now she is stuck living in a Forest Hills apartment complex with two kids, getting fat, and losing her poetic impulse.
2. *Silver* **(Farrar, 1988)** Paulette is determined not to celebrate their silver wedding anniversary because she feels that Howard hasn't upheld his end of the marriage vows.

Womack, Steven

I. Former crime reporter turned private investigator Harry James Denton hasn't been put between hard covers so far. Although the plots aren't that great, the usually impecunious Denton is an appealing character, and Nashville, Tennessee, native Womack (no relation to SF writer Jack Womack) does a good job of describing the Nashville ambience in this series.

1. *Dead Folks' Blues* **(Ballantine, 1993)** Harry is hired by old flame Rachel Fletcher to help her settle her husband's gambling debts.
2. *Torch Town Boogie* **(Ballantine, 1993)** The East Nashville arsonist, who seems to disapprove of gentrification, has torched a mansion across the street from Denton's apartment.
3. *Way Past Dead* **(Ballantine, 1995)** Slim Gibson is in jail for murdering his singing partner, ex-wife Rebecca, shortly after a gig together.
4. *Chain of Fools* **(Ballantine, 1996)** Seventeen-year-old Stacy Jameson has run away from her rich, prominent Nashville family.
5. *Murder Manual* **(Ballantine, 1998)** Harry is asked to find Robert Jefferson Reid, philandering, best-selling author of *Life's Little Maintenance Manual*. He finds Reid strangled and drowned in a hot tub.
6. *Dirty Money* **(Fawcett, 2000)** Denton is working for the feds, secretly, at Nevada's Mustang Ranch, Reno's premier brothel, to ferret out a money-laundering operation.

II. Public relations expert Jack Lynch of New Orleans often has to get hip deep in the corrupt politics and deal making of Louisiana. Jack is a troubled soul with no love life to speak of, no steady source of income, and a drinking problem. New Orleans plays a major role in these mysteries but not a pretty one: it is full of gullible tourists, the people who fleece them, overrated restaurants, dirty streets, and seedy politicians.

1. *Murphy's Fault* **(St. Martin's, 1990)** Lynch's employer, a shady bank president, wants Jack to get the goods on greedy ward heeler Sheriff Murphy, who is about to sabotage a real-estate scheme the bank is interested in.

2. *Smash Cut* (**St. Martin's, 1992**) Film producer Andrew Kwang wants Lynch to help his bid to turn a failed nuclear plant into a major film studio.
3. *Software Bomb, The* (**St. Martin's, 1993**) A computer hacker demands $5 million before he will undo a virus infecting the computer file of a New Orleans bank just as the institution is poised to finance the city's new lottery.

Wood, Jane Roberts

The Lucy Richards trilogy is another example of a series whose first volume was published by a small press, while subsequent volumes were published by a large press and achieved best-seller status. The trilogy follows teacher Lucy Richards from 1911, when she arrives in Estelline, Texas, through several decades of marriage, motherhood, the Great Depression, a move to West Texas, and other events. Reviewers and other readers found the trilogy to be well written, with a simple story line and believable characters. All of Jane Roberts Wood's fiction is set in her native Texas, including the nonseries novels *Grace* (Thorndike, 2001) and *Roseborough* (Dutton, 2003) and the short story collection *Out of Dallas* (University of North Texas, 1989).

1. *Train to Estelline, The* (**Ellen C. Temple, 1987**) In 1911 young teacher Lucy Richards arrives by train in the east Texas community of Estelline.
2. *Place Called Sweet Shrub, A* (**Delacorte, 1990**) Follows Lucy through marriage, childbirth, the Great Depression, and some racial tensions.
3. *Dance a Little Longer* (**Delacorte, 1993**) Lucy, her husband, Josh, and her son move across the state from east to west Texas, where Josh is to be principal of the local school.

Wood, Ted (Edward John)

Reid Bennett, former Toronto policeman, is the one-man police department of Ontario resort town Murphy's Harbour. Reid, a strong, silent type, and his redoubtable German shepherd, Sam, are very good at police work in this action-filled procedural series. Ted Wood, not to be confused with the author of juveniles of the same name (*Iditarod Dream*, etc.), is a naturalized Canadian citizen who worked in the Toronto Police Department for three years. Wood also writes the John Locke mystery series as Jack Barnao.

1. *Dead in the Water* (**Scribner, 1983**) The serenity of Murphy's Harbour is disturbed when a high-powered drug network is uncovered and two murders hit the town.
2. *Murder on Ice* (**Scribner, 1984**) Agents of the feminist Canadian League of Angry Women (CLAW) kidnap the newly crowned queen of the Ice Festival. UK title: *The Killing Cold.*
3. *Live Bait* (**Scribner, 1985**) While on vacation, Bennett moonlights for a security firm whose guards are being assaulted on a Toronto construction site. UK title: *Dead Centre.*
4. *Fool's Gold* (**Scribner, 1986**) Reid investigates the death of a geologist who was apparently mauled by a bear in a mining camp.
5. *Corkscrew* (**Scribner, 1987**) A motorcycle gang establishes camp just outside Murphy's Harbour, and one of its members inveigles Bennett into a fight, which leads to his suspension from duty.
6. *When the Killing Starts* (**Scribner, 1989**) Reid accepts a private assignment from a rich woman who claims that her rebellious son has joined Freedom for Hire, a private band of mercenaries.
7. *On the Inside* (**Scribner, 1990**) Bennett takes a constable job in Elliot, a mining town in Ontario, to investigate allegations of police corruption there.
8. *Flashback* (**Scribner, 1992**) Reid faces imminent fatherhood and a local crime wave involving teenage vandalism, a car theft, a drug-running gang, a vengeful escaped felon, and a series of homicides.
9. *Snowjob* (**Scribner, 1993**) Bennett goes to Vermont to help an old Vietnam War buddy who is accused of killing a bookkeeper in a town where he is the only black officer on the police force.
10. *Clean Kill, A* (**HarperCollins [UK], 1995**) Reid and his dog, Sam, try to make a connection between the rape of a young woman and the murder of two men.

Woodhouse, Sarah

English historical novelist Woodhouse has produced three rather loosely connected novels set around the turn of the 19th century in Suffolk, England. Although there are continuing characters such as Dr. Alexander French and Ann Mathick Gerard, the rural English countryside is the real connecting link in these stories.

1. *Season of Mists, A* (**St. Martin's, 1984**) Ann Mathick inherits her uncle's dilapidated country estate in Suffolk and sets to work bringing it to rights.
2. *Peacock's Feather, The* (**St. Martin's, 1990**) A chance encounter on a coach brings adventurer Jardine Savage and retired army surgeon Alexander French together, as they struggle to save a fellow passenger, who dies in childbirth.
3. *Native Air, The* (**St. Martin's, 1991**) Dr. Alexander French returns briefly to Suffolk before leaving for India, still secretly in love with the widowed Lady Ann Gerard.

Woodiwiss, Kathleen

The late Kathleen Woodiwiss (d. 2007) was a pioneer of the "erotic historical romance" subgenre. Her first novel, *The Flame and the Flower*, which added detailed sexual descriptions to the romance mix, was the first of a series of heavily promoted best sellers such as *Shanna* (Avon, 1977) and *Ashes in the Wind. The Flame and the Flower*, set in the early 1800s in England and the Carolinas, follows the perils and passions of the beautiful and (seemingly) decorous Heather as she endures wardship by a cruel aunt and a forced marriage before her passions are aroused and she finds true love. Readers had to wait a quarter of a century for sequels to the saga of Heather and Brandon Birmingham. *The Elusive Flame* and *A Season beyond a Kiss* deal with two of the Birmingham sons.

1. *Flame and the Flower, The* (**Avon, 1972**) Circa 1800. Beautiful teenager Heather, the ward of a cruel aunt, moves from England to the Carolinas, where she unwillingly weds the attractive Yankee Brandon Birmingham.
2. *Elusive Flame, The* (**Avon, 1997**) Sea captain Beauregard Birmingham, son of Heather and Brandon, enters upon a stormy romance with the orphan Cerynise.
3. *Season beyond a Kiss, A* (**Avon, 2000**) The marriage of Brandon's younger brother, Jeffrey, and the beautiful Raelynn Barrett endures some stormy times when Jeffrey is accused of impregnating a young girl and subsequently murdering her.

Woodrell, Daniel

I. The fictional Louisiana bayou town of St. Bruno is the scene for three novels, the first two of which are mysteries featuring renegade cop Rene Shade and the third focusing on his dissolute father, John X. Shade. A series full of gritty detail and steamy Cajun bayou ambience.

1. *Under the Bright Lights* (Holt, 1986) Rene Shade pursues a small-time hood who has set off the murder of a local black politician in what originally appears to be a burglary gone wrong.
2. *Muscle for the Wing* (Holt, 1988) The Wing, a gang of prison inmates, attempts to muscle in on the local crime action in St. Bruno as an off-duty cop is killed while guarding an illegal card game.
3. *Ones You Do, The* (Holt, 1992) Aged rake and reprobate John X. Shade returns to his native bayou, followed by sociopath Lunch Pumphrey, who is bent on recovering $47,000 stored in John X.'s safe.

II. Ozarks native Woodrell, who is apparently something of a cult figure in Europe, has written two novels about the hardscrabble Ozarks town of West Table, Missouri. A bleak, rather nasty world is portrayed with great artistry. The plots are nothing special, but the ambience is, in this pair of realistic novels shot through with humor and rural wisdom.

1. *Tomato Red* (Holt, 1998) Sammy Barlach, employee of a dog-food firm, wants to branch out into burglary and hooks up with Jamalee and Jason Meridew, a rather weird brother and sister pair from Venus Hollow.
2. *Death of Sweet Mister, The* (Putnam, 2001) Fat, 13-year-old Shuggie Atkins lives rather uneasily with his drunken mother, Glenda, and his nasty stepfather, Red. Then Jimmy Vin Pearce turns up in his shiny T-bird and begins an affair with Glenda.

Woods, Sara

PSEUDONYM OF Sara Bowen-Judd

Sara Woods put her firsthand knowledge of law-office work to good use in this engaging series starring English barrister-detective Antony Maitland. With occasionally assists from his famous uncle, Sir Nicholas Harding, QC, and the loving support of his pretty young wife, Jenny Maitland, Tony sorts out one complicated puzzle after another. His solid deduction and skill at cross-examining witnesses enable him to prove his clients' innocence and reveal the real culprits with style and plenty of courtroom suspense. All Woods's titles are Shakespeare quotations. The late Sara Bowen-Judd also wrote mysteries under the pseudonyms of Anne Burton, Mary Challis, and Margaret Leek.

1. *They Love Not Poison* (Holt, 1972) In this prequel, set in 1947, Antony is just out of the service and taking up his law studies again when he and Jenny get caught up in a web of black magic and black marketers.
2. *Bloody Instructions* (Harper, 1961) After a long day interviewing clients in his law office, elderly senior partner James Winer is found stabbed to death.
3. *Malice Domestic* (Avon, 1986) William Castle returns home after 18 years to see his brother and other family members but is shot to death his first evening back. Published in the United Kingdom in 1962.
4. *Third Encounter, The* (Harper, 1963) Old grudges and betrayals of former members of the French Resistance figure in this case. UK title: *The Taste of Fears.*
5. *Error of the Moon* (Avon, 1986) Maitland and his uncle get mixed up in some secret missile research out in the moors. Published in the United Kingdom in 1963.
6. *Trusted like the Fox* (Harper, 1964) This treason case with several surprise twists shows Maitland at his finest.
7. *This Little Measure* (Avon, 1986) Roderick Gaskell has left his son Andrew the problem of a Velasquez that had been stolen from a museum in the 1940s. Published in the United Kingdom in 1964.
8. *Windy Side of the Law, The* (Harper, 1965) A boyhood friend of Antony's needs help with his amnesia and his apparent involvement in drugs and murder.
9. *Though I Know She Lies* (Holt, 1972) A young woman who admits to disliking her sister is accused of her murder. Published in the United Kingdom in 1965.
10. *Enter Certain Murderers* (Harper, 1966) Maitland defends a young man accused of murdering the blackmailer who drove his mother to suicide.
11. *Let's Choose Executors* (Harper, 1965) A young woman is accused of poisoning her godmother, wealthy old Mrs. Randall, to speed up her inheritance.
12. *Case Is Altered, The* (Harper, 1967) A young French girl forced into a loveless marriage starts the trouble here.
13. *And Shame the Devil* (Holt, 1972) When two Pakistanis sue the local Yorkshire police for false arrest, Maitland is retained to defend the police. Published in the United Kingdom in 1967.
14. *Knives Have Edges* (Holt, 1970) Tony risks disbarment and a murder charge in this case. Published in the United Kingdom in 1968.
15. *Past Praying For* (Harper, 1968) Camilla Barnard is twice tried for murder in this unusual case.
16. *Tarry and Be Hanged* (Holt, 1971) Dr. Henry Langton, family physician and avid gardener, who has just been cleared of his wife's murder, is accused of a second crime, and Tony's successful defense seems unlikely. Published in the United Kingdom in 1969.
17. *Improbable Fiction, An* (Holt, 1971) Tony defends Lynn Edison, a TV columnist, against charges of slander and murder in the death of her sister.
18. *Serpent's Tooth* (Holt, 1973) In a bleak industrial town in Yorkshire, Maitland defends a 17-year-old boy accused of murdering his foster father. Published in the United Kingdom in 1971.
19. *Knavish Crows, The* (Raven, 1981) While touring the United States by car, Tony and Jenny solve a mystery involving an inheritance. Published in the United Kingdom in 1971.
20. *Yet She Must Die* (Holt, 1974) Jeremy Skelton, a writer doing research on the famous Wallace murder, is accused of using the same modus operandi to kill his wife.
21. *Enter the Corpse* (Holt, 1974) Maitland helps his friends, Roger and Meg Farrell, whose ex-con uncle's arrival coincides with the mysterious appearance of a corpse.
22. *Done to Death* (Holt, 1975) Poison-pen letters in a peaceful English village touch off a lot of trouble for Jenny and Antony to solve.
23. *Show of Violence, A* (McKay, 1975) A Yorkshire boy of 13 who seems to have appeared from nowhere is charged with murder.
24. *My Life Is Done* (St. Martin's, 1976) Maitland and Jenny travel to the Northumbrian home of politician Graham Chadwick to investigate a blackmail attempt.
25. *Law's Delay, The* (St. Martin's, 1977) The outcome of Ellen Gray's murder trial hinges on a bizarre double murder that took place 20 years before.

26. *Thief or Two, A* (St. Martin's, 1977) Posh jeweler George DeLisle has been murdered, and the firm's costliest jewels have disappeared.

27. *Exit Murderer* (St. Martin's, 1978) Tony defends a policeman accused of wrongfully arresting some smugglers who hide their diamonds in pots of cheese.

28. *This Fatal Writ* (St. Martin's, 1979) Maitland's client is investigative reporter Harry Charlton, on trial for treason and suspected of murder.

29. *Proceed to Judgement* (St. Martin's, 1979) A diabetic receives a fatal dose of morphine with his insulin shot.

30. *They Stay for Death* (St. Martin's, 1980) Nasty gossip turns into a murder charge after four recent deaths at a nursing home.

31. *Weep for Her* (St. Martin's, 1981) Was Emily Walpole encouraged to commit suicide during the séances she was attending?

32. *Cry Guilty* (St. Martin's, 1981) A stolen Rubens painting leads to the murder of Maitland's client, young Alan Kirby.

33. *Dearest Enemy* (St. Martin's, 1981) When his wife is murdered on-stage, famous actor Leonard Buckley is charged with the crime.

34. *Enter a Gentlewoman* (St. Martin's, 1982) Maitland finds himself pitted against his uncle in this scandalous case of divorce and murder.

35. *Most Grievous Murder* (St. Martin's, 1982) While on holiday in New York, Maitland is asked by the British Ambassador to the United States to investigate the murder of a young African dignitary.

36. *Villains by Necessity* (St. Martin's, 1982) Jim Arnold, a supposedly reformed thief, is caught committing a burglary.

37. *Call Back Yesterday* (St. Martin's, 1983) Harriet Carr is convinced that Peter Wallace is her husband, although he is married to someone else.

38. *Lie Direct, The* (St. Martin's, 1983) Maitland defends John Ryder, on trial for treason after Soviet defector Boris Gollnow fingers him as a spy.

39. *Where Should He Die?* (St. Martin's, 1983) Two poisonings, a contested will, and beautiful twin sisters engage Maitland's attention.

40. *Bloody Book of Law, The* (St. Martin's, 1984) When he defends a young man accused of jewel theft, Maitland finds himself on the defensive.

41. *Murder's out of Tune* (St. Martin's, 1984) Actor Richard Willard is charged with hiring a hit man to kill his estranged wife.

42. *Defy the Devil* (St. Martin's, 1985) Simon Winthrop, accused of killing his grandfather, seems to have a split personality.

43. *Away with Them to Prison* (St. Martin's, 1985) Two policemen are suspected of involvement with a protection racket linked to organized crime.

44. *Obscure Grave, An* (St. Martin's, 1985) Oliver Linwood has been arrested for the murder of his two-week-old nephew.

45. *Put Out the Light* (St. Martin's, 1985) A dramatic production is plagued by what seems to be supernatural malevolence.

46. *Most Deadly Hate* (St. Martin's, 1986) A custody fight may have led to the strangulation murder of Philippa Osmond.

47. *Nor Live So Long* (St. Martin's, 1986) A Yorkshire village has been rocked by the murders of three young women.

48. *Naked Villainy* (St. Martin's, 1987) Was Emile Letendre's father murdered by his own son or by a coven of witches?

Woods, Stuart

I. Stone Barrington is an ex-policeman turned lawyer turned private investigator. He is New York City based, but his adventures take him far afield to places like London and Hollywood. During the series, Stone progresses from impecunious street operator to a jet-set favorite with an international clientele, with a series of romantic encounters along the way. Characters such as Dino Bacchetti, Stone's former NYPD partner, who often assists him with his cases, CIA agent Lance Cabot, and Orchid Beach, Florida, police chief Holly Barker, who has a series of her own (series II, below), make frequent appearances in this breezy and entertaining series. *Dead Paradise* (New American Library, 2006) contains numbers 6 and 7. Numbers 1 and 3 have been reprinted together in one volume (Avon, 2007). Stuart Woods, whose primary passion is yachting, divides his time between Atlanta, Georgia, and the Isle of Wight.

1. *New York Dead* (HarperCollins, 1991) While on disability from the New York City Police Department, Stone Barrington is a witness to the homicide of network news star Sasha Nijinsky, who is given a fatal push from her penthouse terrace.

2. *Dirt* (HarperCollins, 1996) Barrington is hired by dirt-dishing columnist Amanda Dart to find out who is faxing damaging information about her to influential people.

3. *Dead in the Water* (HarperCollins, 1998) Beautiful Alice Manning arrives in a yacht at the Caribbean island-nation of St. Mark's sans her wealthy, writer husband, who started the voyage with her.

4. *Swimming to Catalina* (HarperCollins, 1998) Stone is called in by Hollywood actor Vance Calder to investigate the disappearance of his wife, an ex-girlfriend of Barrington's.

5. *Worst Fears Realized* (HarperCollins, 1999) Stone enlists the aid of his former partner, NYPD lieutenant Dino Bacchetti, when his date, his neighbor, and his secretary all turn up dead.

6. *L.A. Dead* (Putnam, 2000) Barrington is back in film society when a celebrity murder threatens his former flame Arrington Calder.

7. *Cold Paradise* (Putnam, 2001) Barrington runs into Allison Manning, a woman he believed to be dead (see number 3), in a café in Palm Beach. Allison is now rich but is having problems with a charge of insurance fraud and a mysterious stalker.

8. *Short Forever, The* (Putnam, 2002) Barrington flies to London to see a client he's never met and becomes enmeshed with, among others, the CIA and British intelligence.

9. *Dirty Work* (Putnam, 2003) "Carpenter," the beautiful British intelligence agent first encountered in number 8, returns and inadvertently involves Stone in her deadly struggle with female assassin La Biche.

10. *Reckless Abandon* (Putnam, 2004) Barrington is joined in New York City by Holly Barker, the female police chief of Orchid Beach, Florida (see series II), in the search for a fugitive from her jurisdiction.

11. *Two-Dollar Bill* (Putnam, 2005) Stone and Dino are accosted by Billy Bob, a very successful con man from Texas, who is free with his collection of rare two-dollar bills.

12. *Dark Harbor* (Putnam, 2006) Stone goes to Maine with Dino, Holly, and CIA agent Lance Cabot to look into the deaths of his cousin Dick and his family.

13. *Fresh Disasters* (Putnam, 2007) Stone's bosses at the law firm of Woodman and Weld want him to sue Mafia don Carmine Dattila for beating up Herbie Fisher, a character from earlier novels.

14. *Shoot Him If He Runs* (Putnam, 2007) At the behest of US president Will Lee (see series III), Stone and Holly Barker (see series II) search for CIA agent turned assassin Teddy Fay on the island of St. Mark's (see number 3).

II. Holly Barker, a continuing character in series I, has her own series. Holly, a former US Army Military Police officer who was run out of the service after filing a sexual harassment suit against her superior, is now the chief of police in Orchid Beach, Florida, where she, with the help of her Doberman, Daisy, and her father, Ham, solves crimes. In number 4, Holly quits her police job to join the CIA.

1. *Orchid Beach* (HarperCollins, 1998) Ex–army major Holly Barker takes a job as deputy police chief in rural Orchid Beach, Florida.
2. *Orchid Blues* (Putnam, 2001) Holly's wedding to beau Jackson Oxenhandler is rudely interrupted when a bank in Orchid Beach is robbed by a highly disciplined team of men.
3. *Blood Orchid* (Putnam, 2002) Having lost her fiancé, Holly tries to settle back into her job again, when she and her father, Ham, meet developer Ed Shine, whose latest real-estate venture is called Blood Orchid after his favorite flower.
4. *Iron Orchid* (Putnam, 2005) After she joins the CIA, Holly, among others, is enlisted to track down killer, opera-buff, and former CIA agent Teddy Fay (first seen in *Capital Crimes*, series III, number 6, and making a reappearance in *Shoot Him if He Runs*, series I, number 14).

III. *Chiefs*, Woods's first novel, introduced the character Will Lee, who eventually becomes US president in this series of political thrillers. Along the way Will Lee becomes aide to a US senator, becomes a US senator from Georgia himself, and marries CIA operative Katherine Rule, who becomes director of the CIA. Will Lee appears as a character in series I, number 14.

1. *Chiefs* (Norton, 1981) Winter 1920. The naked body of an unidentified teenage boy, possibly the victim of a ritual crime, is discovered in the woods near a small Georgia town. Made into a TV drama starring Charlton Heston.
2. *Run before the Wind* (Norton, 1983) Young law student William Henry Lee IV, visiting his grandfather in Ireland, inadvertently becomes involved with the IRA.
3. *Deep Lie* (Norton, 1986) In 1982 Soviet submarines are detected in Swedish waters. CIA analyst Katharine Rule tries to thwart a Soviet plot involving a vanished KGB general and a Latvian military base.
4. *Grass Roots* (Simon & Schuster, 1989) Will Lee, now chief aide to US Senator Benjamin Carr and secretly engaged to Katherine Rule, gets involved with a Senate campaign, a murder trial, and a white-supremacist group.
5. *Run, The* (HarperCollins, 2000) US Senator Will Lee and his wife, Kate, are involved in a run for the presidency that is full of political scandal and intrigue, double-dealing advisors, obnoxious power brokers, and poisonous media moguls.
6. *Capital Crimes* (Putnam, 2003) Will Lee is now president. Rogue CIA agent Ted Fay (see also series II, number 4, and series I, number 14), on a vendetta against right-wingers, has eliminated the bigoted, hypocritical Republican senator Frederick Wallace, of South Carolina.

IV. Ace criminal defense lawyer Ed Eagle of Santa Fe, hero of 1992's *Santa Fe Rules*, makes a reappearance 14 years later in *Short Straw*.

1. *Santa Fe Rules* (HarperCollins, 1992) Learning that his wife and partner have died suspiciously while he was away, Hollywood producer Wolf Willett hires criminal defense lawyer Ed Eagle to clear his name of the murder charge.
2. *Short Straw* (Putnam, 2006) Ed Eagle awakens the morning after his 40th birthday to discover that his wife, Barbara, has vanished, and all his money has been wired to the Cayman Islands.

3. *Santa Fe Dead* (Putnam, 2008) Ed's ex-wife Barbara, who is still meditating mayhem upon him, escapes from custody while standing trial for arranging his murder.

V. Rick Barron, former detective on the Beverly Hills police force, works security for Centurion Pictures in the 1930s and 1940s, eventually becomes head of production at the studio, and gets involved in some mysteries and controversies along the way.

1. *Prince of Beverly Hills, The* (Putnam, 2004) Rick Barron, demoted from his job at the Beverly Hills police department, lands a job as security officer for big studio, Centurion Pictures, and finds himself involved with a couple of possible murders.
2. *Beverly Hills Dead* (Putnam, 2008) Rick Barron finds himself head of Centurion Studios production and runs into the Hollywood "blacklist" in the late 1940s.

Woolley, Persia

Woolley's Arthurian trilogy is more naturalistic than fantastic, with realistic portrayals of British life after the Roman occupation and historically plausible characters and events. The story is told from the point of view of Guinevere, who is portrayed as neither a scarlet woman nor an empty-headed twit.

1. *Child of the Northern Spring* (Poseidon, 1987) Gwen (Guinevere) rides with Sir Bedivere to become the bride of the High King, a man she has never seen.
2. *Queen of the Summer Stars* (Poseidon, 1990) Covers events of the early years of Arthur's reign and marriage to Guinevere and the beginnings of her love for Lancelot.
3. *Guinevere: The Legend in Autumn* (Poseidon, 1991) Guinevere adopts and raises Modred, the seed of Arthur's brief and unknowing coupling with his half sister Morgause.

Wouk, Herman

I. Wouk is best known for his Pulitzer Prize–winning novel, *The Caine Mutiny* (Doubleday, 1951), though most of his other novels have been popular successes as well. The two volumes listed below represent an ambitious attempt to capture an American era by examining the lives of Commander "Pug" Henry and his family. None of Wouk's readability has been sacrificed to the works' near monumental length and scope. Robert Mitchum played Pug in the television dramatizations of the two books (1983; 1988).

1. *Winds of War, The* (Little, Brown, 1971) In his prewar progress toward a command of his own, Pug Henry runs special missions for President Roosevelt, including one dramatic encounter with Hitler.
2. *War and Remembrance* (Little, Brown, 1978) This sequel describes Pug Henry's successful naval career in 1941–1945, the fortunes of his two sons, and his relationships with his two wives.

II. A pair of novels describes the creation and maintenance of the State of Israel from the 1940s to the early 1980s as seen through the eyes of several military men and their families. Zev Barak and Don Kishote are two of the leading fictional characters. They interact with many historical characters, such as Mickey Marcus, David Ben-Gurion, Moshe Dayan, Golda Meir, and Anwar Sadat in this very readable celebration of the Jewish State.

1. *Hope, The* (**Little, Brown, 1993**) The creation and early development from the end of World War II through the 1948 War of Independence, the 1956 Suez crisis, and the Six Days' War of 1967 is seen through the eyes of Zev Barak and others.
2. *Glory, The* (**Little, Brown, 1994**) The Barak family and the fortunes of Israel are followed from 1967 to 1981 (the bombing of Iraq's nuclear reactor).

Wren, P(ercival) C(hristopher)

I. P. C. Wren was an adventuresome, Oxford-educated Englishman who worked his way around the world as a schoolmaster, journalist, soldier, and so forth, serving in both the British army and the French foreign legion. He spent 10 years as a British government official in India and led Indian forces in East Africa during World War I. *Beau Geste,* the first of his romantic adventures about the French foreign legion, was a big success and was made into a silent film starring Ronald Colman and a talkie in 1939 starring Gary Cooper that is the classic foreign legion film. The Marty Feldman takeoff, *The Last Remake of Beau Geste* (1977), is one of many imitations and parodies. *Beau Geste* continues to be read: a Penguin reprint appeared as late as 1999.

1. *Beau Geste* (**Stokes, 1924**) The three valiant Geste brothers—Michael, aka "Beau"; Digby; and John—join the French foreign legion after Beau takes the blame for Lady Branden's stolen sapphire gem. Strange and desperate events take place at a Saharan outpost threatened by Arabs from without and mutiny from within.
2. *Beau Sabreur* (**Stokes, 1926**) Major Henri de Baujolais, the French soldier who played a significant minor role in *Beau Geste,* returns as the sword-wielding hero who aids a beautiful American girl.
3. *Beau Ideal* (**Stokes, 1928**) Otis Vanbrugh, an American, goes out to North Africa to search for John Geste, who is being held captive by an Arab tribe.
4. *Good Gestes* (**Stokes, 1929**) These stories detailing the early exploits of Beau Geste and his brothers and comrades in the French foreign legion are set chronologically before *Beau Geste,* but the latter is probably the best book to begin with.
5. *Desert Heritage* (**Houghton Mifflin, 1935**) This complicated tale of love and scandal features John Geste, the last of the famous brothers, and Consuelo Vanburgh, an American with a secret past. UK title: *Spanish Maine.*

II. Another action series, which never achieved the popularity of *Beau Geste,* featured Sinclair Noel Brody "Sinbad" Dysart, who has various adventures in North Africa, Arabia, and the Indian Ocean.

1. *Action and Passion* (**Stokes, 1933**) Sinclair "Sinbad" Dysart rises from naval apprentice to become captain of the *Valkyrie* while serving in the Royal Navy.
2. *Sinbad the Soldier* (**Houghton Mifflin, 1935**) Sinbad joins the Life Guards to acquire the requisite soldierly skills, has adventures in the Sahara Desert, and goes on a well-described hajj (pilgrimage) to Mecca.
3. *Fort in the Jungle* (**Houghton Mifflin, 1936**) Sinbad is sold into slavery and serves the white rajah Chandos in the jungles of Tonkin (Indochina).
4. *Disappearance of General Jason, The* (**Murray [UK], 1940**) Sinbad plays a peripheral role in this novel about the search for General Jason, who has been missing for a year after going to a small island in the Indian Ocean where some kind of genetic research is going on.

III. Wren wrote a pair of novels about Otto Belleme, boxer and soldier of fortune.

1. *Soldiers of Misfortune* (**Stokes, 1929**) Otto Belleme fights his way to the apex of the boxing world.
2. *Valiant Dust* (**Stokes, 1932**) The quixotic and romantic Otto, still in search of adventure, joins the French foreign legion.

Wright, Eric

I. Toronto police inspector Charlie Salter is a down-to-earth, happily married, middle-aged father of teenage sons. Charlie has a testy working-class father who sometimes plays a role in the stories. The Toronto setting is considerably less seedy and grim than ambience in comparable cities in the United States or the United Kingdom. Eric Wright, author of these low-key procedurals, is an Englishman who migrated to Canada many years ago. *A Charlie Salter Omnibus* (Castle Street, 2003) contains numbers 1, 2, and 3. *A Killing Climate: The Collected Mystery Stories* (Crippen & Landru, 2003) contains one newly published Salter novella.

1. *Night the Gods Smiled, The* (**Scribner, 1983**) Charlie Salter has to hobnob with members of the English department of Douglas College to find out who killed one of their number at a conference.
2. *Smoke Detector* (**Scribner, 1984**) Charlie is assigned to the arson-related death of a shady used-furniture dealer in a case that reaches back 40 years.
3. *Death in the Old Country* (**Scribner, 1985**) Charlie and his wife vacation in the English Midlands and get drawn into the investigation of the murder of an innkeeper.
4. *Man Who Changed His Name, The* (**Scribner, 1985**) Salter is asked to solve the murder of Nancy Cowell, a divorcée presumably killed by one of the men answering her newspaper ad for "companionship." UK title: *A Single Death.*
5. *Body Surrounded by Water, A* (**Scribner, 1987**) Vacationing with his wife and son on Prince Edward Island, Charlie is brought into the case of a murdered local historian.
6. *Question of Murder, A* (**Scribner, 1988**) A bombing attack within yards of a visiting English princess could have been the work of terrorists or drug dealers, or it could be a by-product of the feuding between peddlers and upscale shops.
7. *Sensitive Case, A* (**Scribner, 1990**) Older colleague Mel Pickett (see series II below) relieves Charlie of the anxiety of dealing with the murder of psychotherapist Linda Thomas.
8. *Final Cut* (**Scribner, 1991**) The Toronto movie set of a thriller about a Nazi concentration camp guard is troubled by acts of sabotage leading up to a murder.
9. *Fine Italian Hand, A* (**Scribner, 1992**) Actor Alec Hunter was stabbed and garroted in a sleazy lakefront hotel in what looks like a Mob-style murder.
10. *Death by Degrees* (**Scribner, 1993**) Salter's father is hospitalized after suffering a stroke, while Charlie tries to concentrate on the murder of a dean at Bathurst Community College.
11. *Last Hand, The* (**St. Martin's, 2002**) In what may be his last case, Charlie, facing mandatory retirement at age 60, investigates the murder of a prominent attorney.

II. Mel Pickett (see series I, number 7) is an older Toronto police colleague of Charlie Salter. Mel has retired and wants to enjoy the quiet in a rural retreat, but murder turns up twice in said retreat.

1. *Buried in Stone* (**Scribner, 1996**) Mel Pickett, retiring from the Toronto police force, has found an idyllic spot for building a weekend retreat in remote Larch River, but then a body turns up in the woods nearby.
2. *Death of a Hired Man* (**Dunne, 2001**) Newly retired and newly married, Charlie is disturbed to hear that local Larch River farmhand Norbert Thompson, who was staying in Charlie's cabin, has been murdered.

III. Lucy Brenner Trimble, a divorcée escaping from her philandering but possessive husband, starts a new life in Toronto as a librarian but then inherits a detective agency. Blessed, or cursed, with naïveté and a fertile imagination, Lucy blunders through a couple of cases.

1. *Death of a Sunday Writer* (**St. Martin's, 1998**) Lucy Trimble leaves her husband and moves to Toronto to become a librarian, but then her cousin leaves her in possession of an unfinished novel and a moribund detective agency.
2. *Death on the Rocks* (**St. Martin's, 1999**) Lucy is hired by Greta Golden to find out more about a man who is asking questions about her. The man turns out to be another detective.

IV. Yet another pair of Toronto-based detective novels features Joe Barley, lecturer on English literature and part-time security guard and private eye.

1. *Kidnapping of Rosie Dawn, The* (**Daniel, 2000**) Part-time lecturer in English literature and part-time security guard Joe Barley gets interested in the disappearance of Rosie Dawn, a student of classics who is working her way through school as an exotic dancer and the mistress of a fast-food proprietor.
2. *Hemingway Caper, The* (**Dundurn (Canada), 2003**) Now a full-time English professor and a part-time private eye, Barley gets involved with what seems to be a simple adultery case but that proves to concern a missing manuscript by a young Ernest Hemingway.

Wright, L(aurali) R.

Sergeant Karl Alberg of the Royal Canadian Mounted Police of Vancouver, British Columbia, is a worldly wise policeman who, unlike Sergeant Preston of the Yukon and radio fame, doesn't have much to do with sled dogs. Alberg, who has an off-again, on-again relationship with librarian Cassandra Mitchell (they finally get married in number 9), is in his fifties, an intelligent, complex, and interesting character in a series of mysteries which led critics to call L. R. Wright (d. 2001) a Canadian Ruth Rendell (q.v.) or P. D. James (q.v.).

1. *Suspect, The* (**Viking, 1985**) Eighty-five-year-old Carlyle Burke of Sechelt, British Columbia, is killed by his longtime friend George Wilcox.
2. *Sleep While I Sing* (**Viking, 1986**) Alberg is getting nowhere in his investigation of an unidentified murdered woman until he asks the school art teacher to draw the victim's portrait.
3. *Chill Rain in January, A* (**Viking, 1989**) Suspicion centers around the town recluse, an attractive, wealthy woman, who may have murdered her drifter brother after he disrupted her idyllic lifestyle.
4. *Fall from Grace* (**Viking, 1991**) Steven Grayson returns to Sechelt after a decade, harboring a dark secret, and then falls to his death from a cliff.
5. *Prized Possessions* (**Viking, 1993**) Alberg's neighbor Charlie O'Brea disappears, and simpleminded Eddie Addison's involvement with a college girl leads to tragic results.

6. *Touch of Panic, A* (**Scribner, 1994**) A highly skilled burglar with a peculiar taste in loot and a psychopath who is determined to find the "perfect mate" are among the idiosyncratic characters who make up this mystery.
7. *Mother Love* (**Scribner, 1995**) Maria Buscombe returns home seven years after abandoning her family only to be murdered a few hours after she sees her daughter.
8. *Strangers among Us* (**Doubleday, 1996**) A teenager kills his family and starts a chain reaction of violence in usually peaceful Vancouver.
9. *Acts of Murder* (**Doubleday, 1997**) The day of Alberg's marriage to Cassandra Mitchell is punctuated by another event: the first in a string of small-town murders.

Wright, Nina

I. Whiskey Mattimoe is a recently widowed thirtysomething real-estate broker in the "resort" town of Magnet Springs, Michigan. Whiskey's legacy from her late husband includes Abra, an Afghan hound, who has a "penchant for stealing purses and other forbidden treats." Abra's foibles get Whiskey enmeshed in a series of murder mysteries in this entertaining, whimsical series, which will appeal to dog lovers and cozy fans.

1. *Whiskey on the Rocks* (**Midnight Ink, 2005**) Introduces Whiskey Mattimoe and her Afghan, Abra. An out-of-towner drops dead at a local Magnet Springs massage parlor. Then the late out-of-towner's wife is bludgeoned to death in a house she has rented from Whiskey.
2. *Whiskey Straight Up* (**Midnight Ink, 2006**) Whiskey discovers that she may be ready for romance again as she gets enmeshed in another murder mystery.
3. *Whiskey and Tonic* (**Midnight Ink, 2007**) The "curse" of the Miss Blossom Pageant strikes again as Abra runs off with the Miss Blossom tiara, a former pageant winner dies, and the new Miss Blossom winds up in the hospital.
4. *Whiskey and Water* (**Midnight Ink, 2008**) The late former mayor Bill Gruen has been the subject of a couple of "sightings." Whiskey has acquired Velcro, a new "shitzapoo" pup; some hunky guys have Whiskey atwitter; and murder rears its ugly head again.

II. *Homefree,* the story of teenager Easter Hutton, who discovers that she has paranormal powers, has been followed by a sequel.

1. *Homefree* (**Llewellyn, 2006**) Sixteen-year-old Easter Hutton, miserable enough over her family situation, is dismayed to discover that she has paranormal powers: talents for time travel, astral projection, invisibility, and the ability to communicate with spirits.
2. *Sensitive* (**Flux, 2008**) Follows Easter Hutton through her first weeks at Fairless Grove Academy, headquarters of Homefree, an agency dedicated to helping teens with paranormal abilities learn how to use their talents.

Yarbro, Chelsea Quinn

I. Chelsea Quinn Yarbro's Saint-Germain novels are a solid entry in the vampire sweepstakes, although they are more historical fiction than horror stories, the vampirism of the main character being somewhat underplayed. Saint-Germain, who is loosely based on an 18th-century charlatan who claimed to possess the Philosopher's Stone, is a virtually immortal but sympathetic and tragic figure who suffers the agony of watching the mortals he loves age and die. The vampire characters in the series tend to be nicer than the human ones. The series can be read with interest by historical fiction fans, even those who aren't enamored of vampires. The novels have been arranged by the chronology of Saint-Germain's life rather than publishing order. *The Saint-Germain Chronicles* (Pocket, 1983) is a collection of short stories that carries Saint-Germain more forward in time (1981) than any of the novels. *Signs and Portents* (Dream, 1984) and *The Spider-Glass* (Pulphouse, 1991) also contain Saint-Germain stories.

1. *Blood Games* (St. Martin's, 1980) Saint-Germain becomes the lover of Olivia, whose husband enjoys seeing her sexually abused. Set in Nero's Rome (54–68 CE), this novel, which is first chronologically in the series, finds Saint-Germain already 3,000 years old. (Olivia, who turns up in other books in the series, is also featured in her own series: see series II, below.)

2. *Roman Dusk* (Tor, 2006) In the reign of the emperor Heliogabalus (218–222 CE), the vampire is threatened by minor but ambitious functionary Telemachus Batsho.

3. *Come Twilight* (Tor, 2000) In a plot beginning in 7th-century Spain but unfolding over a period of 500 years, the good vampire saves the life of Csimenae, at the cost of turning her into one of the few bad vampires in the series.

4. *Dark of the Sun* (Tor, 2004) Zangi-Ragozh (Saint-Germain) lands in 6th-century Yang-Chau (Shanghai), as an eruption by Krakatoa (not as well recorded as the 19th-century one) ushers in the Dark Ages.

5. *Night Blooming* (Warner, 2002) Begins in 796 CE. Hiernom Rakoczy (aka Saint-Germain) advises Charlemagne in Tours and Aachen. Atta Olivia Clemens (see number 1, above, and series II) turns up again, but Rakoczy falls in love with the pale Gynethe Mehaut.

6. *Better in the Dark* (Tor, 1993) The immortal vampire is shipwrecked and washed ashore in 10th-century Upper Saxony and held for ransom by Ranegonda, princess of the local castle.

7. *Path of the Eclipse* (St. Martin's, 1981) Ragoczy Saint-Germain gets involved in the defense of a Chinese fortress against the hordes of Genghis Khan (13th century).

8. *Blood Roses* (Tor, 1998) In 14th-century Orgon, France, the vampire falls in love again and comes under suspicion because of his culture and learning.

9. *Feast in Exile, A* (Tor, 2001) At the end of the 14th century in Delhi, India, Saint-Germain, living under the name of Samat Ji Mani, is captured by Timur-i-Lenhk (Tamburlaine), another world conqueror.

10. *Palace, The* (St. Martin's, 1979) Known as Francesco Ragoczy da San Germano in the Florence of the Medicis (late 15th century), the vampire befriends Lorenzo the Magnificent and Sandro Botticelli and becomes a target of the reforming monk Savonarola.

11. *States of Grace* (Tor, 2005) During the Reformation, Franzicco Ragoczy di Santo-Germano is a successful merchant based in Venice, but he is under scrutiny, as is his mistress, the beautiful musician Pier-Ariana Salier, and his publishing business in the Netherlands is being examined for the Spanish Inquisition.

12. *Mansions of Darkness* (Tor, 1996) Saint-Germain winds up in Peru shortly after the conquest of the Incas (16th century) and is accused of witchcraft by the local inquisition.

13. *Darker Jewels* (Tor, 1993) Ferenc Ragoczy visits Russia during the reign of Ivan the Terrible (1533–1584), is forced to marry a local girl, and suffers other indignities.

14. *Communion Blood* (Tor, 1999) The vampire runs afoul of the Inquisition again, this time in 17th-century Rome, as he tries to see that Olivia Atta Clemens's (see numbers 1 and 4, above, and series II) bequest goes to her loyal servant Niklos Aurilos.

15. *Hotel Transylvania* (St. Martin's, 1978) This is the novel that introduced Saint-Germain. In 18th-century Paris, Madelaine de Montalia (who also stars in numbers 17, 18, and 20) falls in love with a mysterious older man.

16. *Borne in Blood* (Tor, 2007) 1817. The Count Saint-Germain is living quietly in Switzerland with his paramour, Hero, whose husband died fighting Napoléon.

17. *Out of the House of Life* (Tor, 1990) Madelaine de Montalia (see numbers 15, 18, and 20) joins a French expedition excavating Egyptian ruins in 1825–1828 and receives letters from the count reminiscing about his 1,000-year stint in ancient Egypt.

18. *In the Face of Death* (Ben Bella, 2004) Madelaine de Montalia (see numbers 15, 17, and 20) goes off to the American Far West in the mid-19th century to study Indian tribes and has an encounter in San Francisco with the later-to-be-famous William Tecumseh Sherman.

19. *Writ in Blood* (Tor, 1997) On the eve of the First World War, Saint-Germain is working with Czar Nicholas II in a futile attempt to head off the impending cataclysm.

20. *Tempting Fate* (St. Martin's, 1982) Set in Russia and Germany in the 1920s. When his ward Laisha is killed by Brownshirts, the count swears revenge and turns to his former lover Madelaine de Montalia (see numbers 15, 17, and 18).

21. *Midnight Harvest* (Tor, 2003) Fleeing Spain during the Spanish civil war, the vampire winds up in San Francisco with an assassin in hot pursuit.

II. The trilogy about Atta Olivia Clemens is a spin-off from the Saint-Germain chronicles. Olivia is the count's lover in number 1 of that series and appears in other volumes as well. She embarks on a career of her own that ends some 1,600 years later in the France of the Three Musketeers.

1. *Flame in Byzantium, A* (Tor, 1987) In 545 CE the 500-year-old Olivia flees Rome for Constantinople, where she finds living more restricted than in Rome's relatively liberal society.

2. *Crusader's Torch* (Tor, 1988) Olivia's efforts to return to Rome from Tyre are complicated by the Third Crusade and the plague of the late 12th century.

3. *Candle for D'Artagnan, A* (Tor, 1989) Olivia arrives in 17th-century Paris in the suite of Cardinal Mazarin and meets the historical D'Artagnan, who becomes the love of her long life.

III. The Sisters of the Night, or Brides of Dracula, trilogy is somewhat more traditional vampire fare. It follows the fortunes of the three brides of Dracula who are mentioned in Bram Stoker's novel *Dracula*.

1. *Angry Angel, The* (Avon, 1998) Dracula prepares the young Greek damsel Kalene to be his consort. Variant title: *Kalene*.

2. *Soul of an Angel, The* (Avon, 1999) Beautiful Fenice Zucchi escapes Venice and an arranged marriage only to fall prey to Dracula. Variant title: *Fenice*.

3. *Angel of Death, The* (Avon, 2000) Zhameni becomes Dracula's third consort. Variant title: *Zhameni*.

IV. A humorous detective series written by Yarbro as C. Q. Yarbro features Native American lawyer Charlie Spotted Moon, who is an Ojibwa who sometimes uses his tribal knowledge when he acts as a "sleuth upon request." The prolific Yarbro also writes young adult fiction, the Mycroft Holmes and Mme. Victoire Vernet mysteries, in collaboration with Bill Fawcett, as "Quinn Fawcett" (q.v.); two volumes of the War and Honor series in collaboration with Gordon R. Dickson (q.v.); a volume in the Merchant Prince series in collaboration with Armin Shimerman; a volume in the multiauthor Star Trek series, and a "nonfiction" series in which the spiritual essence "Michael" hands out free advice (e.g., *Messages from Michael*, Putnam, 1979).

1. *Ogilvie, Tallant and Moon* **(Putnam, 1976)** Charlie solves a mystery with herbs, ritual, and a trance, putting himself in the dead man's shoes. Variant title: *Bad Medicine*.
2. *Music When Sweet Voices Die* **(Putnam, 1979)** French tenor Gui-Adam Feuier is murdered during the final act of *The Tales of Hoffmann* at the San Francisco Opera Company. Variant title: *False Notes*.
3. *Poison Fruit* **(Jove, 1991)** Five teenage girls have made some shocking suggestions about teacher Frank Girouard.
4. *Cat's Claw* **(Jove, 1992)** Did handsome, friendly Jared Eden leave the corpses of several women on San Francisco doorsteps?

Yglesias, Jose

Yglesias (d. 1995) was a longtime writer of nonfiction (*In the Fist of the Revolution,* Pantheon, 1968), novels, and short stories. The bilingual Yglesias, born in Tampa, Florida, of Cuban and Spanish parents, was also a film critic for the *Daily Worker,* an executive, and a translator. His wife, Helen Yglesias, and his son Rafael Jose Yglesias are also writers. Yglesias's pair of novels about the Granados family, once-famous left-wing writer Pinpin and his grandson Tristan, are funny and down-to-earth depictions of the clash between Hispanic and WASP mores.

1. *Home Again* **(Arbor House, 1987)** Pinpin Granados, 60-year-old left-wing novelist, returns to Tampa after many years in the North and gets reinvolved with his Hispanic relatives.
2. *Tristan and the Hispanics* **(Simon & Schuster, 1989)** When Pinpin dies, his grandson Tristan, a Waspy Yale student, is sent down to collect the old man's possessions but is thwarted by a mob of eccentric Hispanic relatives.

Zelazny, Roger

I. The versatile Zelazny (d. 1995) mastered several science-fiction subgenres. His award-winning early novels, *This Immortal* (Ace, 1966) and *The Dream Master* (Ace, 1966), are "new wave" psychological stories. His *Damnation Alley* (Putnam, 1969) is a post-Holocaust tour through a vicious America. And in the Amber series he created the imaginary world of Amber as the setting for his chronicle of fantasy and adventure starring Prince Corwin. Corwin, unbeknownst to himself, had been exiled for several hundred years on Earth, which he eventually discovered is but one of countless shadows of the one true world: Amber. The series is divided into two sequences of five novels each. Numbers 1 through 5, which concern Corwin, were collected in a two-volume omnibus set, *The Chronicles of Amber* (Doubleday, 1979). Numbers 6 through 10 follow the adventures of Corwin's son Merlin. *The Great Book of Amber* (Avon, 1999) is an omnibus volume containing all 10 novels. A limited-edition "chapbook" containing an Amber excerpt is *A Rhapsody in Amber* (Cheap Street, 1981). Zelazny was highly regarded as a stylist in the SF-fantasy ranks. The Amber series has remained popular and has many aficionados. Theodore Krulik's *The Complete Amber Sourcebook* (Avonva, 1996) is a relatively recent reference source.

1. *Nine Princes in Amber* **(Doubleday, 1970)** Corwin, in his earthly form, has an attack of amnesia and wakes up as a patient/prisoner in a hospital. He escapes and eventually realizes that he is one of nine competing princes of the alternate world of Amber.

2. *Guns of Avalon, The* **(Doubleday, 1972)** Corwin labors under an evil curse as dreadful forces impede his search for his stolen birthright.
3. *Sign of the Unicorn* **(Doubleday, 1975)** The princes and princesses of Amber unite temporarily to rescue one of their number held captive by evil beings.
4. *Hand of Oberon, The* **(Doubleday, 1976)** Corwin leads a group of his brothers in the search for the missing King Oberon but finds considerable opposition.
5. *Courts of Chaos, The* **(Doubleday, 1978)** The conclusion to the first Amber series explains many secrets of the world of Amber and clears up the mystery of Oberon's disappearance.
6. *Trumps of Doom* **(Arbor House, 1985)** The focus is on Merlin, son of Corwin of Amber and Dara of Chaos, who follows his father to Earth, actually only one of Amber's alternative worlds.
7. *Blood of Amber* **(Arbor House, 1986)** Merle Corey of San Francisco, aka Merlin, learns the identity of two would-be assassins.
8. *Sign of Chaos* **(Arbor House, 1987)** Merlin discovers that he has a guardian angel in the form of a noble lady.
9. *Knight of Shadows* **(Morrow, 1989)** When he escapes from the Citadel of the Four Worlds, Merlin becomes involved in a series of new adventures.
10. *Prince of Chaos* **(Morrow, 1991)** Merlin returns to the Courts of Chaos for a funeral and finds himself enmeshed in a deadly struggle for succession to the throne.

II. Zelazny teamed up with fellow SF-fantasy writer Robert Sheckley for a comic fantasy series. The Millennial Deeds Contests are held every 1,000 years to determine whether Good or Evil will dominate the next millennium of history. Good is represented by the naive Archangel Michael and evil by the urbane Mephistopheles, who enlists the resourceful fox-faced demon Azzie Elbub on his side.

1. *Bring Me the Head of Prince Charming* **(Bantam, 1991)** Azzie sets out to prove that fairy tales don't always have happy endings as Frankenstein meets Sleeping Beauty.
2. *If at Faust You Don't Succeed* **(Bantam, 1993)** Although Faust was supposed to be the pawn in the Millennial Deeds Contest, it is Mac, a failed monk-thief, who is inadvertently picked up and taken through his paces at the turning points in history.
3. *Farce to Be Reckoned With, A* **(Bantam, 1995)** Fresh from winning Hell's Evil Deed Award, Azzie decides to enlist Italian writer Pietro Aretino to stage an "immorality play" with Renaissance Europe as a backdrop.

III. A pair of novels set on Earth and the alternate world of Rondoval feature Pol Detson, changeling offspring of the Dragon Lord who is exiled from the land of magic to Earth but is called back home when he is needed. Omnibus volume containing both novels: *Wizard World* (Baen, 1989).

1. *Changeling* **(Ace, 1980)** Infant Pol Detson is taken to Earth by the good wizard Mor but is called back to Rondoval when his earthling substitute Chain threatens to enlist his magical powers in the forces of evil.
2. *Madwand* **(Phantasia, 1981)** Pol, who is a powerful but untrained sorcerer, a "Madwand," needs some rigorous magical training.

Zimmerman, Bruce

San Francisco phobia therapist Quinn Parker gets involved in more than his share of murder investigations in a literate series of puzzles. Parker is an "outdoor psychologist," who takes his clients on vacations designed to cure their phobias.

1. *Blood under the Bridge* (Harper, 1989) When Parker discovers the body of his former girlfriend, he also finds himself the chief suspect in a murder investigation.
2. *Thicker Than Water* (Harper, 1991) Quinn jets to Jamaica with his old friend, neophyte comedian and fearful flier Hank Wilkie, when Hank's son has been left an island estate.
3. *Full-Bodied Red* (Harper, 1993) Called to the Napa Valley mansion of his patient, Phillip Chesterton, Parker is attacked by Phil's step-father, who blames him for the young winery heir's disappear-ance.
4. *Crimson Green* (Harper, 1994) Quinn is caddying for high school friend Brad Helfan, who is three strokes away from winning the US Open, when Brad is shot to death on the 18th fairway.

Zola, Émile

I.   Although Émile Zola's realistic portraits of alcoholics and pros-titutes shocked the gentler sensibilities of the 1870s, modern readers will find his dark explorations on the themes of greed, obsession, and lust to be fascinating and powerful works. The 20-volume Rougon-Macquart series is an extended family chronicle tracing certain he-reditary traits through several generations. The series is also a detailed social history of France during the Second Empire (1852–1870). Early English translations, including those by E. A. Vizetelly, who trans-lated all titles in the series except *Nana* for the "official" Chatto & Windus edition, were much bowdlerized, but for some titles, there are no later translations available. J. G. Patterson's *A Zola Dictionary* (Dutton, 1912) is a helpful reader's companion to the series. *Therese Raquin* (originally 1867; Peterson, 1881; at least three translations in the last 50 years) is not part of the Rougon-Macquart series. F. W. J. Hemmings's *The Life and Times of Émile Zola* (Scribner, 1977) is the best biography of Zola in English. Titles are arranged according to first French publication dates.

1. *Rougon-Macquart Family, The* (Peterson, 1879) This volume intro-duces the widow Adelaide, who takes the drunken Macquart as her lover, then follows the stories of her children, Pierre Rougon and the illegitimate Antonie and Ursule Macquart. The narrative shows the effects of Louis Napoléon's coup d'état of 1851 on the small Provençal town of Plassons. Translated by "Stirling" (Mary Neal Sherwood). First published in France in 1871 as *La Fortune des Rougon-Macquart*. Variant title (Vizetelly translation): *The Fortune of the Rougons*.
2. *In the Whirlpool* (Peterson, 1879) Rich builder Aristide Saccard enters extravagant Parisian society. Translated by Stirling. First published in France in 1871 as *La Curee*. Variant titles: *The Rush for the Spoils* (translated by Vizetelly); *The Kill; Venus of the Counting House; In the Swim.*
3. *Markets of Paris, The* (Peterson, 1879) The great Paris market Les Halles and its contrasts between rich and poor are seen through the life of Lisa Macquart in 1857–1860. Translated by Stirling. First published in France in 1873 as *Le ventre de Paris*. Variant titles: *The Fat and the Thin* (translated by Vizetelly); *La belle Lisa; The Paris Market Girls; The Flower and Market Girls of Paris; The Belly of Paris;* and *Savage Paris* (translated by Marie-Jacqueline Mason and David Hughes, Elek, 1955).

4. *Conquest of Plassans, The* (Peterson, 1879) The story returns to the town of Plassans and focuses on the granddaughter of Adelaide, Marthe Mouret, a weak-willed heroine who destroys herself and her husband. Translated by Stirling. First published in France in 1874 as *La conquete de Plassans*. Variant titles: *A Mad Love* and *A Priest in the House* (translated by Brian Rhys, Citadel, 1957).
5. *Albine; or, The Abbe's Temptation* (Peterson, 1879) The evils of celibacy are the subject of this story, which focuses on Marthe Mouret's son, a village priest. Translated by Stirling. First published in France in 1875 as *La faute de L'Abbe Mouret*. Variant titles: *Abbe Mouret's Transgression* (translated by Vizetelly); *The Sin of the Abbe Mouret; The Sin of Father Mouret* (translated by Sandy Petrey, Nebraska, 1983); *The Abbe Mouret's Sin; The Sinful Priest;* and *Mouret's Transgression.*
6. *Clorinda* (Peterson, 1880) Eugene Rougon, a powerful and complex character, becomes prime minister under Napoléon III. Translated by Stirling. First published in France in 1876 as *Son Excellence Eugene Rougon*. Variant titles: *His Excellency, Eugene Rougon* (translated by Vizetelly); *His Excellence; His Excellency* (translated by Alec Brown, Elek, 1958); *The Mysteries of the Court of Louis Napoleon;* and *Zola's Count of Napoleon III.*
7. *L'Assommoir* (Peterson, 1879) This treatise on the evils of alcohol, focusing on the pathetic heroine Gervaise, was the book that brought Zola fame. Translated by Stirling. First published in France in 1877 as *L'Assommoir*. Latest translation by Leonard W. Tancock (Penguin, 1970). Variant titles: *The Dram Shop* (translated by Vizetelly); *Gervaise; The Gin Palace; Drink; Nana's Mother;* and *Drunkard.*
8. *Helene* (Peterson, 1880) This is a touching story about a Parisian widow, mother of a consumptive little girl, who falls in love with a doctor. Translated by Stirling. First published in France in 1878 as *Une page d'amour*. Variant titles: *A Love Episode; A Page of Love;* and *A Love Affair* (translated by Jean Stewart, Citadel, 1957).
9. *Nana* (Peterson, 1880) Nana, daughter of Gervaise, a beautiful Parisian actress and courtesan, brings ruin to her lover and dies a miserable death. This novel has probably been translated into English more often than anything else by Zola. Translated by Stirling. Some recent translations: Lowell Bair (Bantam, 1964) and Douglas Parmee (Oxford, 1992).
10. *Pot-Bouille* (Peterson, 1882) The home life of the French bour-geoisie is revealed to be a mass of obscene secrets and private vices. Translated by Stirling. First published in France in 1882 as *Pot-bouille*. Variant titles: *Piping Hot* (translated by Vizetelly); *Lesson in Love; Restless House;* and *Pot Luck* (translated by Brian Nelson, Oxford, 1999).
11. *Ladies' Paradise, The* (Peterson, 1883) This book deals with life in a big department store. Translated by Stirling. First published in France in 1883 as *Au bonheur des dames*. Recent translations: Bryan Nelson (Oxford, 1995) and Robin Buss (Penguin, 2000). Variant titles: *Ladies' Delight; The Bonheur des Dames;* and *Shop Girls of Paris.*
12. *Life's Joys* (Munro, 1884) Set in a seaside town in Normandy, this story contrasts the self-sacrificing Pauline and the miserable hypochondriac Lazare. Translated by "Philip." First published in France in 1884 as *La joie de vivre*. Variant titles: *How Jolly Life Is! The Joy of Life* (translated by Vizetelly); *Joys of Life;* and *Zest for Life* (translated by Jean Stewart, Elek, 1959).
13. *Germinal* (Belford, 1885) Étienne Lantier leads his fellow coal miners in a strike against a cruel and greedy capitalist. This book is regarded by most as Zola's masterpiece. Gerard Depardieu starred in the 1993 French movie version. First published in France in 1885 as *Germinal*. Translations by Havelock Ellis (originally Boni, 1924; latest Everyman, 1996); Peter Collier (Oxford, 1993); and

Stanley and Eleanor Hochman (New American Library, 1970), among others.

14. *His Masterpiece?* (Chatto [UK], 1886) Claude Lantier, an artist modeled after Manet and Cézanne, struggles to express his genius. Translated by Vizetelly. First published in France in 1886 as *L'oeuvre*. Variant title: *The Masterpiece* (translated by Thomas Walton, Macmillan, 1957; rev. ed. Oxford, 1993).

15. *Terre, La* (Laird & Lee, 1888) Zola's portrait of the French peasantry shows them to be a greedy and unprincipled lot who will do anything to acquire more land. Translated by "Chalmers." First published in France as *La terre*. Variant titles: *The Soil* (translated by Vizetelly) and *The Earth* (translated by Douglas Parmee, Penguin, 1980).

16. *Dream of Love, A* (Laird & Lee, 1890) Zola tells the idyllic story of Angelique, a foundling raised by an old married couple who tend a cathedral. Translated by Edgar de Vermont. First published in France in 1888 as *Le reve*. Variant title: *The Dream*.

17. *Human Brutes, The* (Laird & Lee, 1890) Jacques Lantier is a good train engineer but a pretty rotten human being otherwise. Translated by Edgar de Vermont. First published in France in 1890 as *Le bete humaine*. Variant titles: *The Monomaniac* (translated by Vizetelly); *The Beast in Man* (translated by P. J. R. Wright, New American Library, 1968); *La bete humaine* (translated by Leonard W. Tancock, Penguin, 1977; Roger Pearson, Oxford, 1996); and *The Human Beast*.

18. *Money* (Laird & Lee, 1891) The world of high finance and the evils of speculation are the subject here as Saccard again takes center stage. Translated by Max Maury. First published in France in 1891 as *L'argent*. Vizetelly 1894 translation reprinted by Sutton in 2000.

19. *Downfall, The* (Appleton, 1902) The brutality of modern warfare and the thunderous fall of the Second Empire as seen through the eyes of two young soldiers. Translated by Vizetelly (originally published in the United Kingdom in 1892). First published in France in 1892 as *La debacle*. Variant titles: *The Debacle* (translated by Leonard W. Tancock, Penguin, 1973) and *La debacle* (translated by Elinor Dorday, Oxford, 2000).

20. *Doctor Pascal* (Chatto [UK], 1893) In an apt conclusion to the series, Pascal, a student of heredity who is based on the real-life figure of Claude Bernard, draws up a Rougon-Macquart genealogy. Translated by Vizetelly. First published in France as *Le docteur Pascal*. Variant title: *Life and Heredity*.

II. The Three Cities trilogy follows Pierre Froment, a skeptical priest, as he seeks to regain his faith. The books are more successful as documentaries than as artistic works.

1. *Lourdes* (Chatto [UK], 1894) Pierre accompanies the cripple Marie de Guersaint, an old friend and sweetheart, to Lourdes, where she is cured. First published in France in 1894 as *Lourdes*. Translated by Vizetelly.

2. *Rome* (Chatto [UK], 1896) Pierre goes to Rome to protest papal condemnation of a book he has written. First published in France as *Rome*. Translated by Vizetelly.

3. *Paris* (Chatto [UK], 1898) Pierre leaves the church, falls in love, and marries. First published in France in 1898 as *Paris*. Translated by Vizetelly.

III. The Four Gospels series was left unfinished at Zola's death. A fourth book, entitled *Justice*, was to have completed the set, which aims to capture modern French life (at the turn of the 20th century) and to demonstrate Zola's standards of morality and social progress. Each book in the series concerns one of the sons of Pierre Froment, chief protagonist of the Three Cities series listed above.

1. *Fruitfulness* (Doubleday, 1900) Mathieu and Marianne are prolific parents in this anti-birth-control tract. First published in France in 1900 as *Féconditié*. Translated by Vizetelly.

2. *Work* (Harper, 1901) Luc Froment founds a utopian community. First published in France in 1901 as *Travail*. Translated by Vizetelly. Variant title: *Labor*.

3. *Truth* (Lane, 1903) Marc Froment defends a Jewish schoolteacher accused of murder. The story is modeled on the Dreyfus case. First published in France in 1903 as *Veritie*. Translated by Vizetelly.

■ TITLE INDEX

Titles are alphabetized letter-by-letter, ignoring punctuation. Numerals are alphabetized as if spelled out.

You may also be interested in

Virtual Reference Best Practices: When it comes to virtual reference, one size doesn't fit all. What works in one library won't necessarily work in another. How do you figure out what to do? The recently published Virtual Reference Service Guidelines from the Reference and User Services Association (RUSA) provide the starting point. Kern, a leading virtual reference expert, outlines the tools and decision-making processes that will help you and your library evaluate, tailor, and launch virtual reference services that are a perfect fit for your community and your library.

Magic Search: Grasping the importance and having command of LC subdivisions, now appearing in unexpected places beyond the library catalog, is key in this rapidly evolving, twenty-first-century information environment. No other work explores the LCSH subdivisions in such detail or with such commitment, making this book vital to every reference desk.

Reference Sources for Small and Medium-Sized Libraries, seventh edition: This book includes the best of the best and most affordable resources, websites, CD-ROMs, and electronic databases, as well as print. The contributors provide introductory overviews of the topics, then list their recommended selections with insightful annotations on each source. Specifications for each source (author/editor, publisher, format, price range, and Dewey and Library of Congress call numbers) make it easy to access the resources. Library patrons will find this an invaluable resource for current everyday topics, and librarians will appreciate it as a reference and collection development tool.

The Readers' Advisory Guide to Genre Fiction, second edition: This revised edition provides a way of understanding the vast universe of genre fiction in an easy-to-use format. Expert readers' advisor Joyce Saricks offers groundbreaking reconsideration of the connections between genres, providing key authors and themes within fifteen genres, an explanation of how the different genres overlap, the elements of fiction most likely to entice readers, and much more.

Check out these and other great titles at www.alastore.ala.org!